Chemistry for NEET

Volume 2

M P Sidana
Founder, Sidana Institutes, Rani ka Bagh, Amritsar

Universities Press

CHEMISTRY FOR NEET, VOLUME 2

UNIVERSITIES PRESS (INDIA) PRIVATE LIMITED

Registered Office
3-6-747/1/A & 3-6-754/1, Himayatnagar, Hyderabad 500 029, Telangana, India
info@universitiespress.com; www.universitiespress.com

Distributed by
Orient Blackswan Private Limited

Registered Office
3-6-752 Himayatnagar, Hyderabad 500 029, Telangana, India

Other Offices
Bengaluru / Chennai / Guwahati / Hyderabad
Kolkata / Mumbai / New Delhi / Noida / Patna

First published 2025

ISBN: 978-93-93330-72-7

Typeset in Times New Roman PS Std 10.5 *by*
SRS Publishing Services, Puducherry

Printed at
BB Press, Tronica city, Ghaziabad, UP

Published by
Universities Press (India) Private Limited
3-6-747/1/A & 3-6-754/1, Himayatnagar, Hyderabad 500 029, Telangana, India

Preface

I, Prof. M P Sidana, have dedicated over 35 years of my life to teaching chemistry to aspiring doctors and engineers. My passion for teaching chemistry and preparing students for competitive exams runs deep within me. My experience and expertise in simplifying complex concepts have enabled thousands of students to achieve prestigious positions both in India and abroad.

The inspiration to write these books (two volumes) stemmed from a desire to extend my reach beyond the classroom and assist thousands of students who may not have the opportunity to learn directly from me. This book is a manifestation of my lifelong commitment to education and my unwavering belief in the transformative power of clear, concise teaching.

These textbooks are designed to introduce students to the in-depth understanding required for competitive examinations, covering a wide range of objective-type questions aligned with current exam patterns. The solutions provided include detailed explanations. Well-illustrated with concise and easy-to-understand text, the books equip students with the skills needed to tackle challenging problems efficiently. They also help students test their analytical abilities, objective problem-solving approaches, and application of basic principles and concepts from Organic, Inorganic and Physical Chemistry within a limited time frame. The primary aim is to enable students to achieve high scores in competitive exams. The books employ a step-by-step approach and specialised techniques to master both the theoretical and numerical aspects of the subject, meeting all the core standards of competitive exams.

My goal is to enhance student achievement by making chemistry simple and comprehensible for all students. I hope these books serve as a valuable resource for students striving for excellence in their academic endeavours.

M P Sidana

Preface

Acknowledgements

‘Some are born great, some achieve greatness, and some have greatness thrust upon them’ is a profound saying. I consider the role of ‘Teacher’ to fall into the third category. I believe I am truly fortunate to be a teacher.

I am immensely grateful to all my alumni, whose success stories have motivated and inspired me to undertake this responsibility. Working on this project has been a privilege, and I feel genuinely lucky for this opportunity.

Furthermore, I owe a significant debt of gratitude to my wife, Jeewan Jyoti Sidana, my son, Rohan Sidana and my daughter, Ramina Sidana, and the staff members of my Institute, especially Ms Navneet Gill. Their unwavering support, inspiration, stimulating suggestions and encouragement have been crucial in enabling me to complete this work. They deserve special thanks for creating a conducive environment for this project.

Dr Gita S Dattatri, the editor of the book, was gracious in dedicating the time required to read the material multiple times and made numerous highly intelligent and useful suggestions. She consistently provided insightful feedback that helped me immensely in refining the content. Special thanks to her. The structure of the book has been shaped by the contributions of Mr Kallol Das and Mr Thomas Mathew Rajesh, who also deserve special thanks. Without the support of this team from Universities Press, this book would not exist.

Lastly, I wish to acknowledge the resources that have been invaluable in completing this book within a limited time frame. Libraries, online databases and books have been essential in gathering relevant information.

I consider myself fortunate to have had the opportunity to educate two generations of students, and my passion for teaching remains as strong as ever. I am deeply obliged to everyone for their love, respect and warmth which have enabled me to produce this book.

M P Sidana

Contents

Chapter 15: Principles Related to Practical Chemistry 808

Solid State

A solid is defined as that form of matter which possesses rigidity and hence possesses a definite shape and a definite volume. Whether a substance will exist as a solid, a liquid or a gas depends upon the net effect of the following two opposing forces.

(i) Intermolecular forces exist among the constituent particles which try to keep the constituent particles close together.

(ii) Thermal energy is possessed by the constituent particles due to temperature and tries to keep the constituent particles apart as it tends to make them move faster.

1.1 Classification of Solids

The solids are classified into crystalline and amorphous (Fig. 1.1).

- **Crystalline solids:** All solid elements (metals and non-metals) and compounds exist in this form.
- **Amorphous solids:** Examples are rubber, glass, pitch, tar, fused silica, plastics and polymers of high molecular mass.

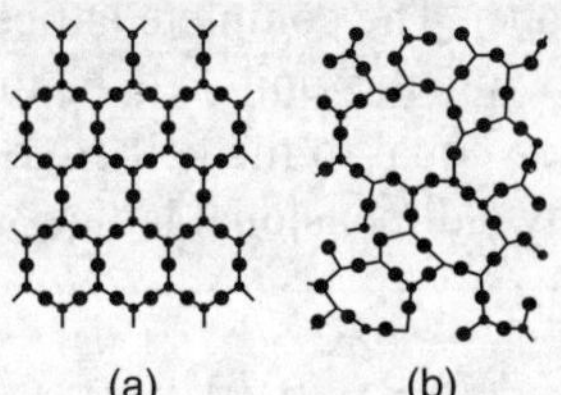

Fig. 1.1 Two dimensional structure of **(a)** quartz and **(b)** quartz glass

In the case of amorphous substances, properties like electrical conductivity, refractive index and thermal expansion are identical in all directions just as in the case of gases or liquids. This property is called *isotropy* and the substances showing this property are called *isotropic*. In the case of crystalline substances, the properties mentioned above have different values in different directions. This type of behaviour is called *anisotropy* and the substances exhibiting this type of behaviour are called *anisotropic*.

Table 1.1 Comparison of main characteristics of crystalline and amorphous solids

Crystalline solid	Amorphous solid
(i) The constituent particles are arranged in a regular fashion containing short-range as well as long-range order	(i) The constituent particles are not arranged in any regular fashion; there may be at the most some short-range order only
(ii) They have definite geometric shapes	(ii) They have irregular shapes
(iii) They have sharp melting points	(iii) They melt over a range of temperatures
(iv) They are anisotropic	(iv) They are isotropic
(v) They undergo a clean cleavage [Fig. 1.2(a)]	(v) They undergo an irregular cut [Fig. 1.2(b)]
(vi) They have definite heats of fusion	(vi) They do not have definite heats of fusion
(vii) They do not have smooth cooling curves [Fig. 1.3(b)]	(vii) They have smooth cooling curves [Fig. 1.3(a)]
(viii) They are true solids	(viii) They are pseudo solids or super-cooled liquids

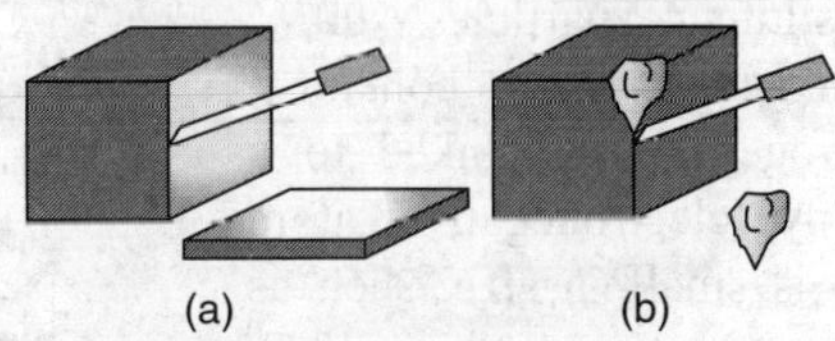

Fig. 1.2 **(a)** A crystalline solid undergoes a clean cleavage **(b)** An amorphous solid undergoes an irregular cut

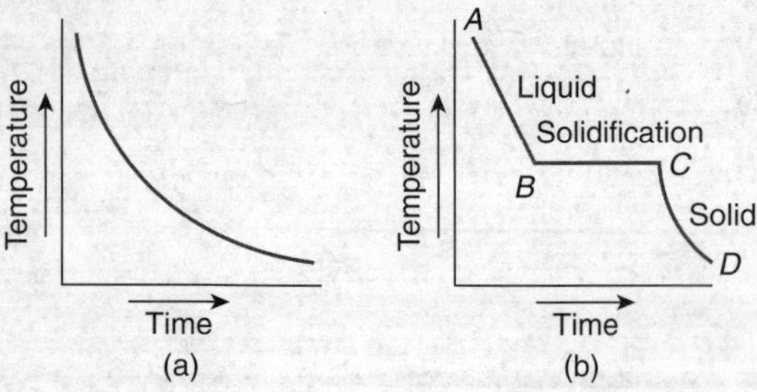

Fig. 1.3 **(a)** Cooling curve of amorphous solid; **(b)** Cooling curve of crystalline solid

1.2 Classification of Crystalline Solids

Based upon the nature of the constituent particles and the binding forces present between them, crystalline solids are further classified into the following four categories.

(i) Ionic solids: The constituent particles are positive and negative ions (cations and anions) held together by strong coulombic (electrostatic) forces of attraction. For example, Na^+ and Cl^- ions in the case of NaCl, arranged in three dimensional space.

(ii) Molecular solids: The constituent particles are molecules. Depending upon the nature of molecules, these are further sub-divided into three types.

- **Non-polar molecular solids:** The constituent particles are atoms of noble gases (helium, neon, argon) or non-polar molecules such as H_2, Cl_2, I_2 and CH_4 (Fig. 1.4).

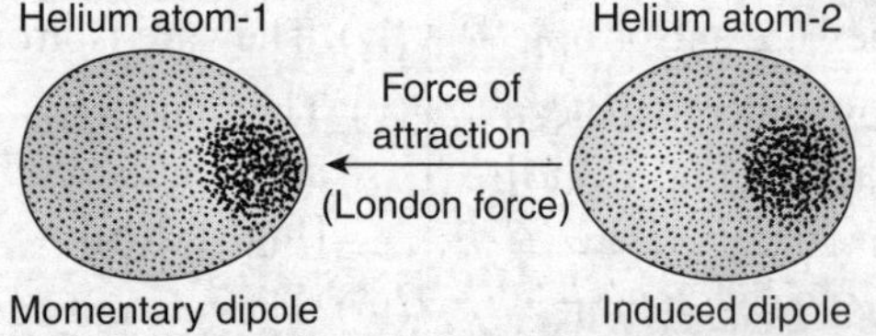

Fig. 1.4 Weak London dispersion forces

- **Polar molecular solids:** The constituent particles are polar molecules such as HCl and SO_2 (Fig. 1.5).

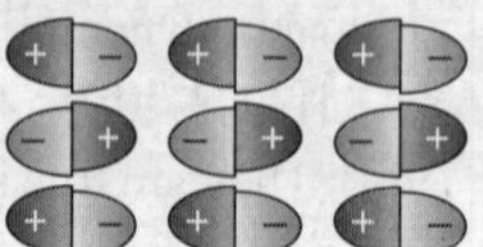

Fig. 1.5 Dipole–dipole forces of attraction

- **Hydrogen-bonded molecular solids:** The constituent particles are molecules that contain hydrogen atoms linked to a highly electronegative atom that is small in size, such as F, O or N. For example, H_2O, NH_3, and so on.

(iii) Covalent or network solids: The constituent particles are non-metal atoms linked to the adjacent atoms by covalent bonds throughout the crystal (Fig. 1.6).

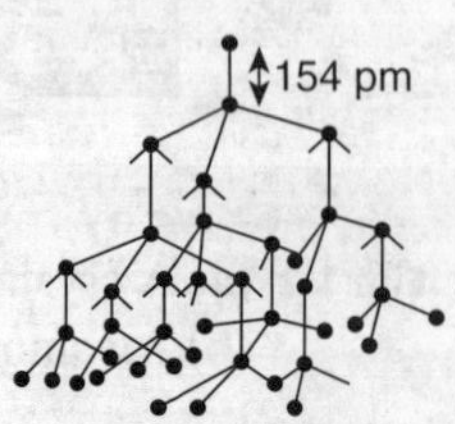

Fig. 1.6 Network structure of diamond

Exception: Graphite is also a covalent solid but it is soft and a good conductor of electricity due to its typical structure (Fig. 1.7). In this case, carbon atoms are arranged in layers with free electrons aiding conduction. The distance between the adjacent layers is greater than the carbon–carbon bond length. Hence, these layers are not bonded to each other and can easily slip over each other making graphite is soft and a good solid lubricant.

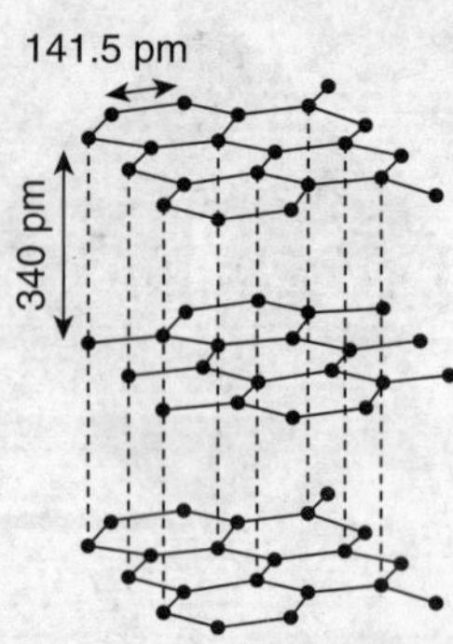

Fig. 1.7 Structure of graphite

(iv) Metallic solids: The constituent particles are positively charged metal ions and free electrons. These mobile electrons are attracted by the positive ions and hence hold these positive ions together (Fig. 1.8).

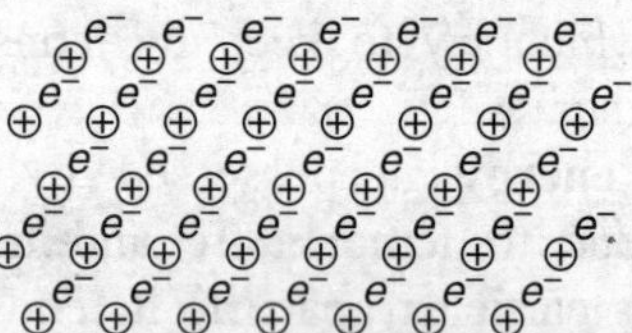

Fig. 1.8 Metallic solid-positive ions in a sea of mobile electrons (electron sea model)

1.3 Crystal Lattice (Space Lattices) and Unit Cells

A *space lattice* is a regular repeating arrangement of points in space. This small portion of the lattice is called a *unit cell*.

1.3.1 Two Dimensional Crystal Lattices

A two dimensional lattice is a regular arrangement of points in the plane of the paper. The complete lattice can be generated by repeatedly moving the unit cell in the direction of its edges by a distance equal to the cell edge [Fig. 1.9(b)]. The different types of two dimensional lattices are summarised in Table 1.2.

Table 1.2 Lattices and their unit cells, Fig. 1.9(a)

Lattice	Unit cell
(i) Square lattice	Square
(ii) Rectangular lattice	Rectangle
(iii) Parallelogram lattice	Parallelogram
(iv) Rhombic lattice	Rectangular with interior point
(v) Hexagonal lattice	Rhombus with an angle of 60°

1.3.2 Three Dimensional Crystal Lattices

The constituent particles are arranged in a definite fashion in three dimensional space. Such a regular arrangement of the

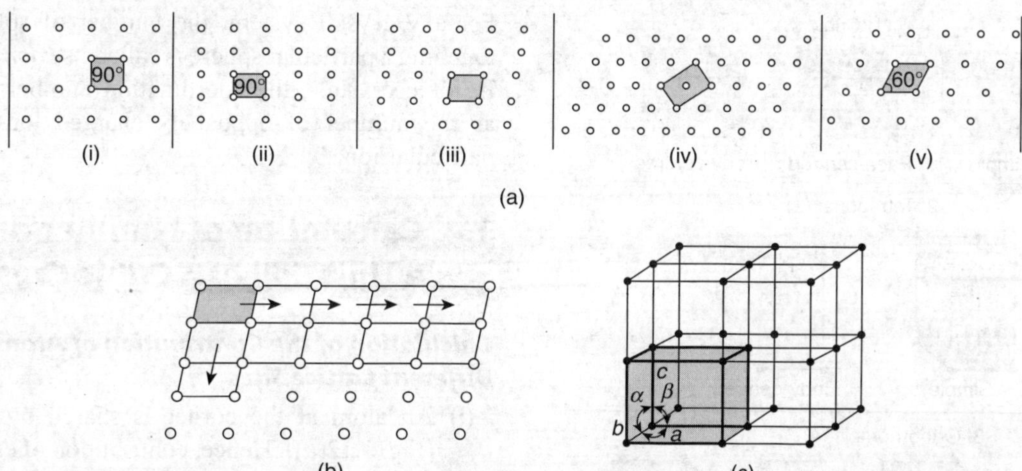

Fig. 1.9 **(a)** Five two dimensional with their unit cells as (i) square, (i) rectangular, (iii) parallelogram, (iv) rectangular with interior point and (v) rhombus; **(b)** Generating complete two dimensional lattice by repeatedly moving the unit cell in the direction of the cell edges by distance equal to cell edge; **(c)** Space lattice and unit cell

constituent particles (that is, atoms, ions or molecules) of a crystal in a three dimensional space is called a *crystal lattice* or a *space lattice* [Fig. 1.9(c)].

Unit cell: *The smallest three dimensional portion of a complete space lattice which when repeated over and again in different directions produces the complete space lattice is called the unit cell.* It is characterised by six parameters—axial lengths a, b, and c and axial angles α, β and γ.

1.3.3 Types of Unit Cells

Based upon the parameters of the unit cells (lengths a, b and c and the angles α, β and γ), there are seven types of unit cells (Table 1.3, Fig. 1.10). These are also called *crystal systems.*

1.3.4 Types of Lattices

Unit cells may be broadly divided into:

(a) Primitive unit cells: The unit cells in which the constituent particles are present only at the corners are called *simple unit cells* or *primitive unit cells* (Table 1.3).

(b) Non-primitive or centred unit cells: Those unit cells in which the constituent particles are present not only at the corners of the unit cells but also at some other positions are called *non-primitive unit cells* or *centred unit cells.* There are three types (Fig. 1.11).

- ***Face-centred:*** When the particles are present at the corners and at the centre of each face of the unit cell, it is called a face-centred unit cell.
- ***End-face centred:*** In addition to the particles at the corners, if there are particles at the centres of any two opposite faces, it is called end-face centred unit cell.
- ***Body-centred:*** In addition to the particles at the corners, if there is one particle present at the centre within the body of the unit cell, it is called a body-centred unit cell.

Table 1.3 Seven types of unit cells or crystal systems

System	Axial lengths	Axial angles	Examples
1. Cubic	$a = b = c$	$\alpha = \beta = \gamma = 90°$	Cu, NaCl, KCl, alums, zinc blende
2. Tetragonal	$a = b \neq c$	$\alpha = \beta = \gamma = 90°$	White tin (Sn), SnO_2, TiO_2, $CaSO_4$
3. Orthorhombic or rhombic	$a \neq b \neq c$	$\alpha = \beta = \gamma = 90°$	KNO_3, K_2SO_4, $BaSO_4$, $PbCO_3$, CaCO3, rhombic sulfur
4. Monoclinic	$a \neq b \neq c$	$\alpha = \gamma = 90° \neq \beta$	$Na_2SO_4.10H_2O$, $PbCrO_4$, monoclinic sulfur
5. Triclinic	$a \neq b \neq c$	$\alpha \neq \beta \neq \gamma \neq 90°$	$CuSO_4.5H_2O$, $K_2Cr_2O_7$, H_3BO_3
6. Rhombohedral or trigonal	$a = b = c$	$\alpha = \beta = \gamma \neq 90°$	$NaNO_3$, ICl, As, Sb, Bi, calcite ($CaCO_3$)
7. Hexagonal	$a = b \neq c$	$\alpha = \beta = 90°, \gamma = 120°$	Cinnabar (HgS), ice, graphite, Mg, Zn, Cd, ZnO, CdS, AgI, PbI_2

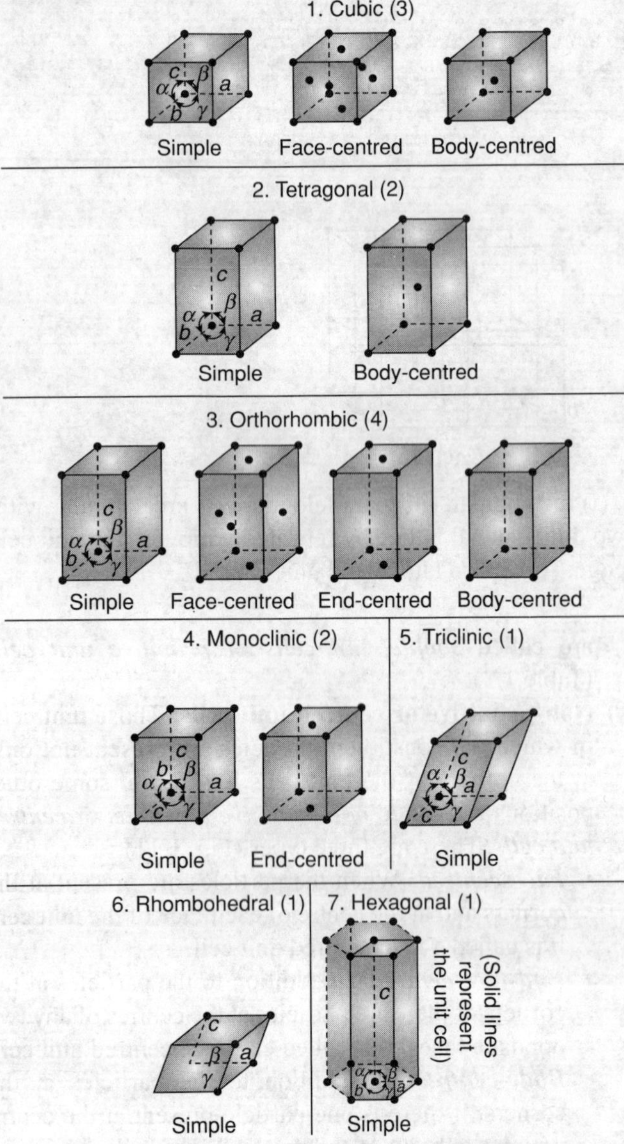

Fig. 1.10 Seven types of unit cells or crystal systems with 14 lattices called Bravais lattices (given in brackets)

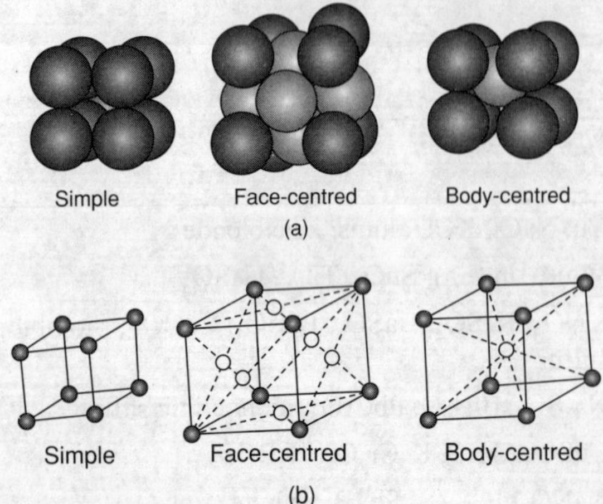

Fig. 1.11 **(a)** Space filling structures; **(b)** open structures of simple, face centered and body-centred cubic

For any crystal system, the number of spheres which are touching a particular sphere is called its *coordination number*. In ionic crystals, the coordination number may be defined as the number of oppositely charged ions surrounding a particular ion.

1.4 Calculation of Number of Atoms in a Unit Cell of a Cubic Crystal System

Calculation of the Contribution of Atoms Present at Different Lattice Sites

(i) An atom at the corner is shared by eight unit cells [Fig. 1.12(a)]. Hence, contribution of each atom present at the corner $= \frac{1}{8}$ [Fig. 1.12(b)].

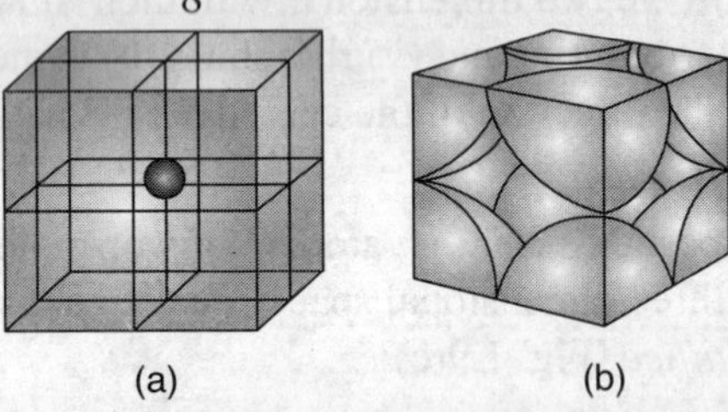

Fig. 1.12 An atom at the lattice point shared by 8 unit cells

(ii) An atom on the face is shared between two unit cells [Fig. 1.13(a)]. Hence, the contribution of each atom on the face $= \frac{1}{2}$ [Fig. 1.13(b)].

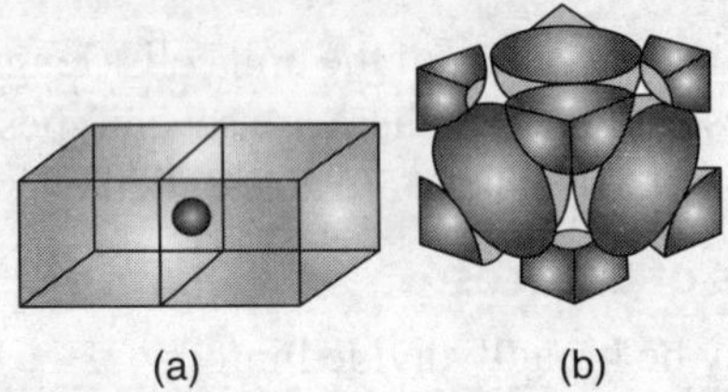

Fig. 1.13 An atom at the face centre shared by 2 unit cells

(iii) An atom present within the body of the unit cell is shared by no other unit cell [Fig. 1.14(a)]. Hence, the contribution of each atom within the body = 1 [Fig. 1.14(b)].

(iv) An atom present on the edge is shared by four unit cells [Fig. 1.15]. Hence, the contribution of each atom on the edge $= \frac{1}{4}$.

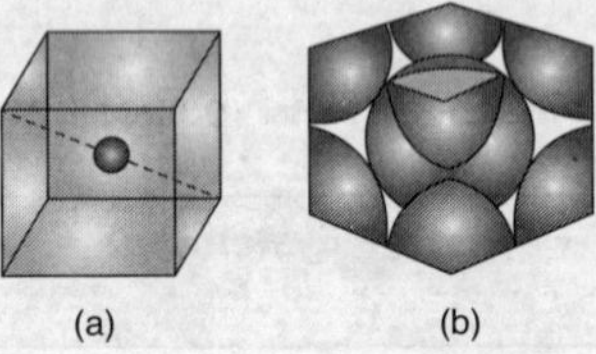

Fig. 1.14 An atom at the body centre not shared by any other unit cell

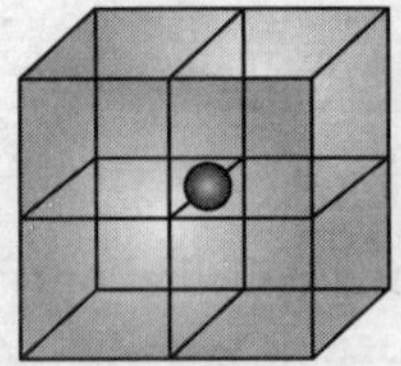

Fig. 1.15 An atom at the edge centre shared by 4 unit cells

Calculation of Number of Atoms Per Unit Cell

(i) Number of atoms in a unit cell of simple (primitive) cubic lattice: A simple cubic lattice has only eight atoms on the corners. As contribution by each = 1/8, therefore, number of atoms present in the unit cell $=\frac{1}{8}\times 8=1$.

(ii) Number of atoms in a unit cell of body centred cubic (BCC) lattice: This lattice has 8 atoms on the corners and one atom within the body.

∴ Contribution by 8 atoms present on the corners

$$=\frac{1}{8}\times 8=1$$

Contribution by the atom present within the body = 1

∴ Number of atoms present in the unit cell = 1 + 1 = 2

(iii) Number of atoms in a unit cell of the face centred cubic (FCC) lattice: This lattice has 8 atoms on the corners and 6 atoms on the faces (one on each face).

Contribution by atoms on the corners $=\frac{1}{2}\times 8=1$

Contribution by atoms on the faces $=\frac{1}{2}\times 6=3$

∴ Number of atoms present in the unit cell = 1 + 3 = 4

Volume of unit cell $=6\frac{\sqrt{3}}{4}a^2$

Worked Out Problem 1.1

An ionic compound made up of atoms A and B has a face-centred cubic arrangement in which atoms A are at the corners and atoms B are at the face-centres. If one of the atoms is missing from the corner, what is the simplest formula of the compound?

Solution

No. of atoms of A at the corners = 7 (because one A is missing)

∴ Contribution atoms of A towards unit cell $=7\times\frac{1}{8}=\frac{7}{8}$

No. of atoms B at face-centres = 6

∴ Contribution of atom B towards unit cell $=6\times\frac{1}{2}=3$

Ratio of A : B $=\frac{7}{8}:3=7:24$ ∴ Formula is A_7B_{24}

Worked Out Problem 1.2

Calculate the number of unit cells in 8.1 g of aluminium if it crystallises in a face-centred cubic (fcc) structure. (Atomic mass of Al = 27 g mol^{-1})

Solution

1 mole of Al = 27 g = 6.02×10^{23} atoms

∴ No. of Al atoms present in 8.1 g of

$$Al=\frac{6.02\times10^{23}}{27}\times 8.1=1.806\times 8.1=1.806\times10^{23}$$

As a face-centred cubic unit cell contains 4 atoms,

$$\text{Number of unit cells present}=\frac{1.806\times10^{23}}{4}=4.515\times10^{22}$$

1.5 Close Packing in Crystals (Close Packed Structures)

The packing of these spheres takes place in such a way that they occupy the maximum available space and there is minimum empty space and hence the crystal has maximum density. This type of packing is called *close packing*.

(i) Close packing in one dimension: The spheres touch each other in a row (Fig. 1.16). In this arrangement, each sphere is touching two neighbouring spheres. Hence, the coordination number is 2.

Fig. 1.16 Close packing of spheres in one dimension

(ii) Close packing in two dimensions: When the rows are stacked over each other, a two dimensional close packed structure (called *crystal plane*) is produced. This stacking can be done in two different ways. The spheres in the second row may be placed exactly above the spheres of the first row. If the first row is called an 'A' type row, the second row, being exactly same, will also be an A type row. Further rows may also be built up exactly in the same way. Hence, we call this arrangement as AAA type of arrangement [Fig. 1.17(a)]. In this arrangement, the coordination number is 4. This packing is called *square close packing in two dimensions.*

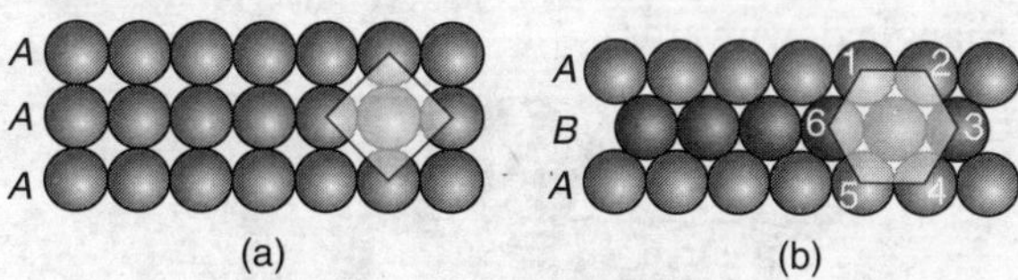

Fig. 1.17 Close packing of spheres in two dimensions **(a)** square close packing **(b)** hexagonal close packing

The spheres in the second row may be placed in the depressions of the first row [Fig. 1.17(b)]. This produces a row different from the first row; the second row may be called as B type. When the spheres in the third row are placed in the depressions of the second row, the third row formed is exactly similar to the first row, that is, A type. The fourth row formed will be again B type, and so on. Hence, this arrangement is called the ABAB type of arrangement. the coordination number is 6. Hence, this arrangement is called *two dimensional hexagonal close-packing.*

(iii) Close packing in three dimensions:

- *Three dimensional close packing from two dimensional square close packed layers:* Starting from the square close packed layer, all further layers will be built up such that they are horizontally as well as vertically aligned with each other. Hence, the lattice generated will be AAA...type. This will be a simple cubic lattice and its cell will be a primitive cubic unit cell [Fig.1.18(a)].

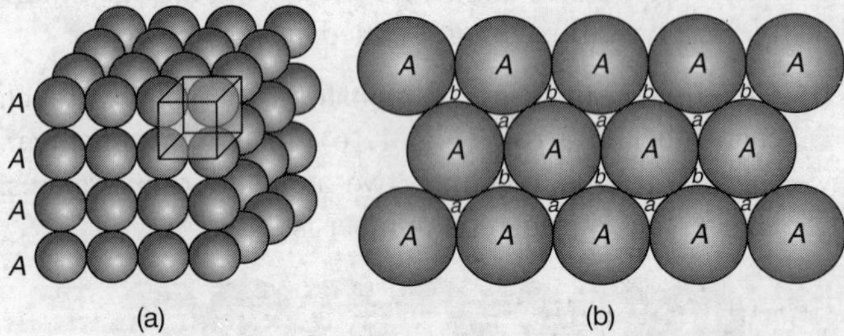

Fig. 1.18 **(a)** Three dimensional packing of square close packed layers forming simple cubit lattice with AAA-arrangement; **(b)** Representing the two types of triangular voids in hexagonal close packed layer

- *Three dimensional packing from two dimensional hexagonal close packed layers*: In the base layer [Fig. 1.18(b)], the spheres are marked as A and the voids between the spheres are marked as '*a*' and '*b*' alternately. Both *a* and *b* voids are triangular in shape. Now, there are two types of voids in the second layer. These are marked as voids *c* and voids *d* (Fig. 1.19). The *c* voids of the second layer are triangular. The *d* voids of the second layer are a combination of two triangular voids (on each of the first and second layers) with the vertex of one triangle upwards and the vertex of the other triangle downwards.

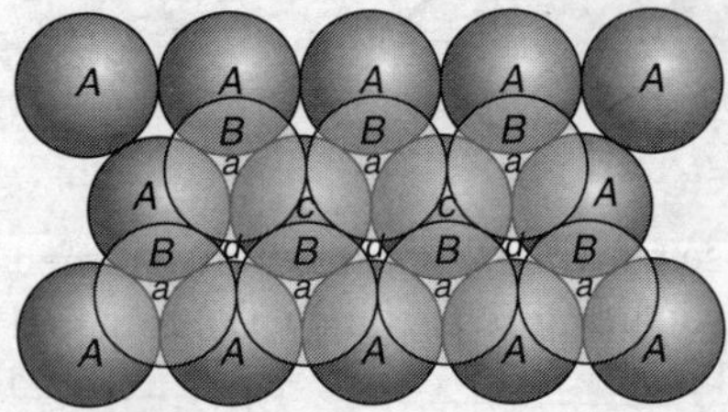

Fig. 1.19 Close packing of two layers with hexagonal close packed base layer

A simple triangular void like *c* in a crystal is surrounded by four spheres and is called a *tetrahedral void* [Fig. 1.20(a)]. A double triangular void like *d* is surrounded by six spheres and is called an *octahedral void* [Fig. 1.20(b)]. A tetrahedral void is surrounded by four spheres lying at the vertices of a regular tetrahedron and touching each other. An octahedral void is surrounded by six spheres lying at the vertices of a regular octahedron—four lying in one plane touching each other, one lying above the plane and one below the plane [Fig. 1.20(b)].

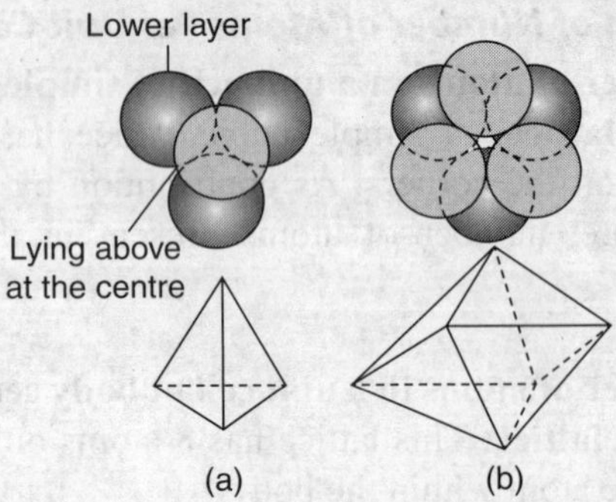

Fig. 1.20 Two types of voids in crystal **(a)** tetrahedral void **(b)** octahedral void

The voids or holes in crystals are also called *interstices*.

- When a third layer is placed over the second layer in such a way that the spheres cover the tetrahedral or *c* voids, a three dimensional closest packing is obtained where the spheres in every third or alternate layers are vertically aligned (that is, the third layer is directly above the first, the fourth above the second layer and so on). The arrangement is called an ABAB...pattern or *hexagonal close packing* (*hcp*) [Fig.1.21(a)(i) or (b)(i)]. Molybdenum, magnesium, zinc and beryllium crystallise in *hcp* (hexagonal close packing) structure.
- When the third layer is placed over the second layer in such a way that spheres cover the octahedral or *d* voids, a layer different from layers A and B is produced. This pattern of stacking spheres is called an ABCABC... pattern or cubic close packing (*ccp*). It is similar to face-centred cubic (*fcc*) packing [Fig. 1.21(a)(ii) or (b)(ii)]. Iron, nickel, copper, silver, gold and aluminium crystallise in *ccp* (cubic close packing) structures.

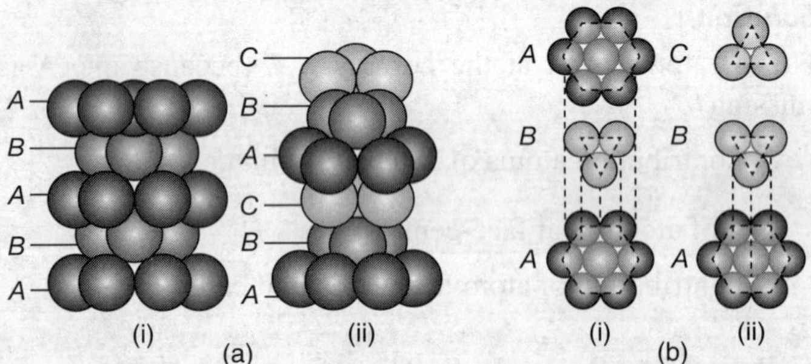

Fig. 1.21 **(a)** actual view of (i) hexagonal close packing (ii) cubic close packing; **(b)** A simplified view of (i) hexagonal close packing (AB AB .... pattern) (ii) cubic close packing (ABC ABC .... pattern)

Number of atoms per unit cell in hcp: Look at Fig. 1.22(a), a unit cell has 12 atoms at the corners, 2 atoms at the face-centres and 3 atoms within the body. Each atom at the corner is shared by 6 other unit cells, therefore, the contribution of an atom at the corner towards the unit cell is $\frac{1}{6}$. Similarly, an atom at the face centre makes a contribution of $\frac{1}{2}$ while an atom within the body is not shared by any other unit cell. Hence in hcp,

$$\text{No. of atoms per unit cell} = 12 \times \frac{1}{6} + 2 \times \frac{1}{2} + 3 = 6$$

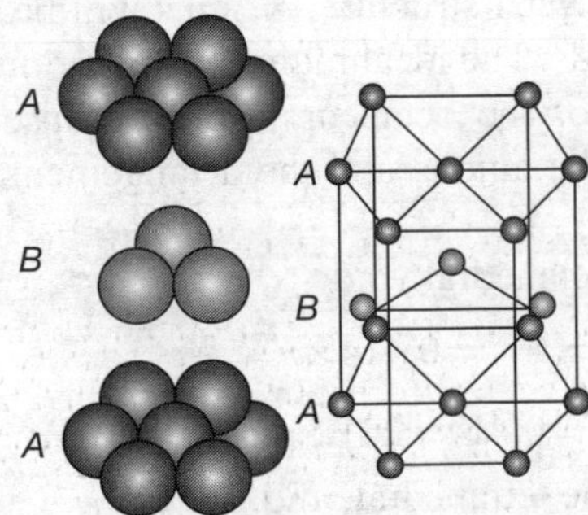

(a) Hexagonal close packing (HCP)

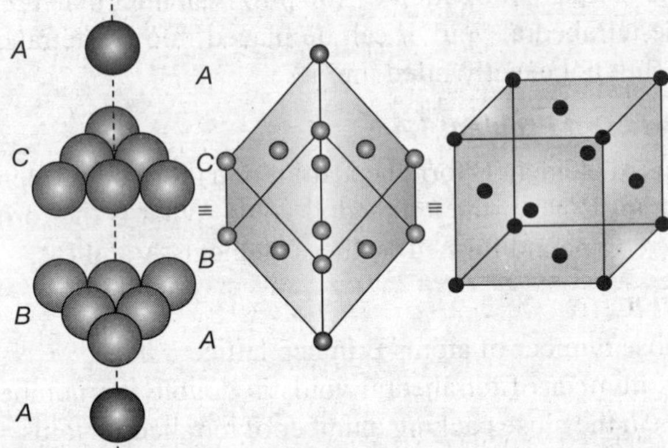

(b) Cubic close packing (CCP) ≡ Face-centred cubic (FCC)

Fig. 1.22 **(a)** ABAB.........type is hexagonal close packing **(b)** ABC ABC ....type is cubic close packing

1.6 Packing Efficiency/Packing Fractions

The percentage of the total space filled by the particles is called *packing efficiency*, or, the fraction of the total space filled is called *packing fraction*.

1.6.1 Packing Efficiency in a Simple Cubic Lattice

In Fig. 1.23(a), let the edge length of the unit cell $= a$ and radius of the sphere $= r$. As the spheres are touching each other, $a = 2r$ [Fig. 1.23(b)].

$$\text{No. of spheres per unit cell} = \frac{1}{8} \times 8 = 1$$

$$\text{Volume of the sphere} = \frac{4}{3}\pi r^3$$

$$\text{Volume of the cube} = a^3 = (2r)^3 = 8r^3$$

$$\therefore \text{Packing fraction} = \frac{\frac{4}{3}\pi r^3}{8r^3} = \frac{\pi}{6} = 0.524 \text{ or, \% occupied}$$

$$= 52.4\%$$

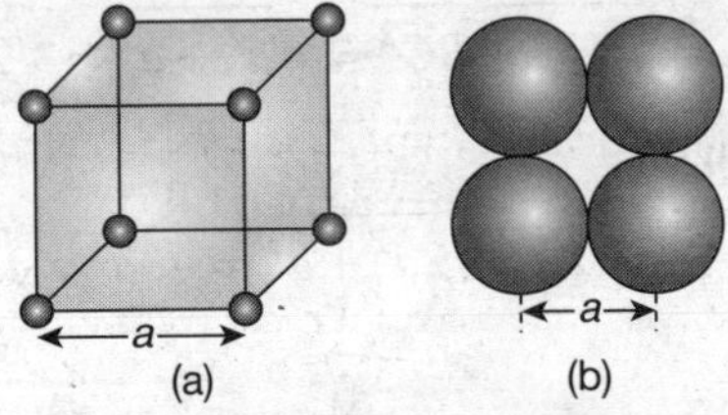

Fig. 1.23 **(a)** Simple cubit unit cell; **(b)** Top/bottom/side view of simple cubic unit cell

1.6.2 Packing Efficiency in Face-centred Cubic Structures (Cubic Close Packing)

See Fig. 1.24(a). As the sphere on the face centre is touching the spheres at the corners, $AC = 4r$ [Fig. 1.24(b)]. But from the right angled triangle ABC,

$$AC = \sqrt{AB^2 + BC^2} = \sqrt{a^2 + a^2} = \sqrt{2}a$$

$$\therefore \sqrt{2}a = 4r \text{ or } a = \frac{4}{\sqrt{2}}r$$

$$\therefore \quad \text{Volume of the unit cell} = a^3 = \left(\frac{4}{\sqrt{2}}r\right)^3 = \frac{32}{\sqrt{2}}r^3$$

$$\text{No. of spheres in the unit cell} = 8 \times \frac{1}{8} + 6 \times \frac{1}{2} = 4$$

$$\text{Volume of 4 spheres} = 4 \times \frac{4}{3}\pi r^3 = \frac{16}{3}\pi r^3$$

$$\therefore \quad \text{Packing fraction} = \frac{16\pi r^3/3}{32r^3/\sqrt{2}} = \frac{\pi\sqrt{2}}{6} = 0.74, \text{ or}$$

$$\text{\% occupied} = 74\%$$

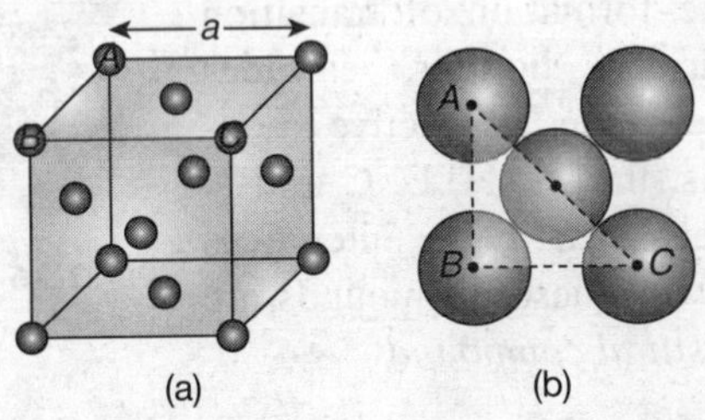

Fig. 1.24 **(a)** Face-centred cubic unit cell; **(b)** Top view of face-centred cubic unit cell

Packing efficiency of hcp and ccp structure. Cubic close packing (ccp) is the same as face-centred cubic packing. Hence, packing efficiency is 74%. Further, ccp and hcp are equally efficient. Hence, hcp also has a packing efficiency of 74%.

1.6.3 Packing Efficiency in Body Centred Cubic Structures

As the sphere at the body centre touches the spheres at the corners, the body diagonal, $AD = 4r$ (Fig. 1.25).

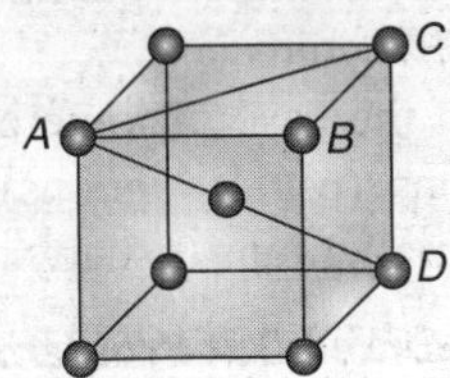

Fig. 1.25 Body-centred cubic unit cell

Further, face diagonal,

$$AC = \sqrt{AB^2 + BC^2} = \sqrt{a^2 + a^2} = \sqrt{2}a$$

and body diagonal,

$$AD = \sqrt{AC^2 + CD^2} = \sqrt{2a^2 + a^2} = \sqrt{3}a \therefore \sqrt{3}\,a = 4r \text{ or } a = \frac{4r}{\sqrt{3}}$$

$\therefore$ Volume of the unit cell $= a^3 = \left(\frac{4r}{\sqrt{3}}\right) = \frac{64r^3}{3\sqrt{3}}$

No. of spheres per unit cell $= 8 \times \frac{1}{8} + 1 = 2$

Volume of 2 spheres $= 2 \times \frac{4}{3}\pi r^3 = \frac{8}{3}\pi r^3$

$\therefore$ Fraction occupied, that is, packing fraction

$$= \frac{\frac{8}{3}\pi r^3}{\frac{64r^3}{3\sqrt{3}}} = \frac{\pi\sqrt{3}}{8} = 0.68, \text{ or \% occupied} = 68\%$$

1.7 Tetrahedral and Octahedral Voids

If R is the radius of the spheres in the close packed arrangement, then

Radius (r) of the tetrahedral void $= 0.225\ R$

Radius (r) of the octahedral void $= 0.414\ R$

In the case of ionic compounds, usually anions are present in the packing and cations occupy the voids. Thus, a tetrahedral void is much smaller than the octahedral void. In the formation of transition metal hydrides, borides, carbides and nitrides, the respective non-metal atoms, that is, H, B, C and N are accommodated in the interstices (Fig. 1.26). So, these compounds are called *interstitial compounds.*

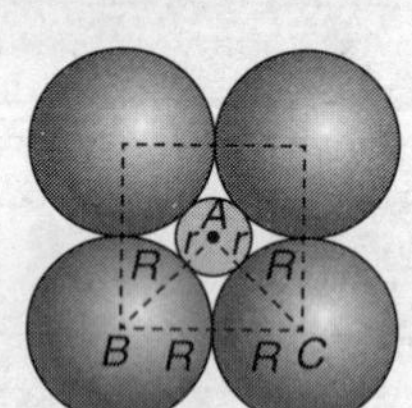

Fig. 1.26 Octahedral void

Formula of the Compound from Number of Voids Filled

In a close packed structure (hcp or ccp), there are two types of voids present in the lattice—tetrahedral and octahedral. It is found that

(i) Number of octahedral voids = Number of particles present in the close packing

(ii) Number of tetrahedral voids = 2 × Number of octahedral voids

In the case of ionic compounds, it is found that the bigger ions (usually anions) are present in the packing whereas smaller ions (usually cations) occupy the voids.

Worked Out Problem 1.3

A solid A^+B^- has NaCl type close packed structure. If the anion has a radius of 24.5 pm, what should be the ideal radius of the cation? Can a cation C^+ having a radius of 50 pm be fitted into the tetrahedral hole of the crystal A^+B^-?

Solution

As A^+B^- has NaCl structure, A^+ ions will be present in the octahedral voids. The ideal radius of the cation will be equal to the radius of the octahedral void because in that case, it will touch the anions and the arrangement will be close packed. Hence,

Radius of octahedral void

$$= r_{A^+} = 0.414 \times r_{B^-}$$
$$= 0.414 \times 241.5\ \text{pm} = 100.0\ \text{pm}$$

Radius of the tetrahedral void

$$= 0.225 \times r_{B^-} = 0.225 \times 241.5\ \text{pm} = 54.3\ \text{pm}$$

As the radius of the cation C^+ (50 pm) is smaller than the size of the tetrahedral void, it can be placed into the tetrahedral void (but not exactly fitted into it).

Worked Out Problem 1.4

Atoms of element B form hcp lattice and those of the element A occupy 2/3rd of the tetrahedral voids. What is the formula of the compound formed by these elements A and B?

Solution

Suppose number of atoms B in hcp lattice $= n$

As number of tetrahedral voids is double the number of atoms in the close packing, number of tetrahedral voids $= 2\,n$

A atoms occupy 2/3rd of the tetrahedral voids, therefore, number of atoms A in the lattice $= \frac{2}{3} \times 2n = \frac{4n}{3}$

$\therefore$ Ratio of A : B $= \frac{4n}{3} : n = \frac{4}{3} : 1 = 4 : 3$

Hence, the formula of the compound $\mathbf{A_4B_3}$.

1.7.1 Location of Tetrahedral and Octahedral Voids in a Crystal

(a) Octahedral voids: One octahedral void is present at the body centre of the cube and 12 octahedral voids are present on the centres of the 12 edges of the cube. But each void on the edge centre is shared by 4 unit cells [Figs 1.27(a)]. Hence, its contribution in the unit cell = 1/4. Therefore, the effective number of octahedral voids in the ccp structure $= 1 + 12 \times \frac{1}{4} = 1 + 3 = 4$.

(b) Tetrahedral voids: The 8 tetrahedral voids present in the ccp arises from the fact that there are 8 spheres at the corners of the unit cell and each sphere at the corner touches three spheres present on the face-centres of the three adjoining faces, each giving rise to one tetrahedral void [Fig. 1.27(b)]. These tetrahedral voids are found to be present on the body diagonals, two on each body diagonal at one-fourth of the distance from each end [Fig. 1.27(b)(ii)]. Thus, in ccp, the total number of voids per unit cell = 8 (tetrahedral) + 4 (octahedral) = 12.

Similarly, in hcp, the total number of voids per unit cell = 12 (tetrahedral) + 6 (octahedral) = 18

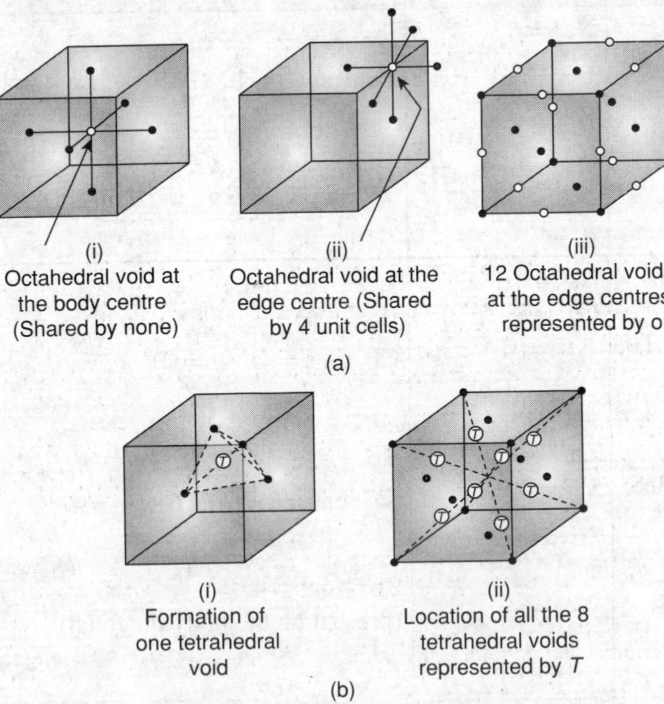

Fig. 1.27 **(a)** Representing (i) octaheeral void at the body-centred (ii) octaheeral void at the edge centre (iii) All the 12 octaheeral voids of CCP unit cell each shared by 4 other unit cells; **(b)** Representing the location of all the 8 tetrahedral voids on the body diagonals

Worked Out Problem 1.5

A compound forms a hexagonal close-packed structure. What is the total number of voids in 0.5 mol of the compound? How many of these are tetrahedral voids?

Solution:

No. of atoms in the close packing

$= 0.5 \text{ mol}$

$= 0.5 \times 6.022 \times 10^{23} = 3.011 \times 10^{23}$

No. of octahedral voids = No. of atoms in the packing

$= 3.011 \times 10^{23}$

No. of tetrahedral voids = 2 × No. of atoms in the packing

$= 2 \times 3.011 \times 10^{23} = 6.022 \times 10^{23}$

Total no. of voids

$= 3.011 \times 10 + 6.022 \times 10^{23} = 9.033 \times 10^{23}$

$\frac{1}{3}$ rd of the tetrahedral voids are occupied by M atoms, therefore, no. of M atoms $- \frac{2n}{3}$

1.8 Structure of Simple Ionic Compounds

(i) Rock salt (NaCl) type structure (Fig. 1.28), (ii) Sphalerite or zinc blende (ZnS) type structure (Fig. 1.29), (iii) Structure of CaF2 (Fig. 1.30). The features of the various structures are summarised in Table 1.4.

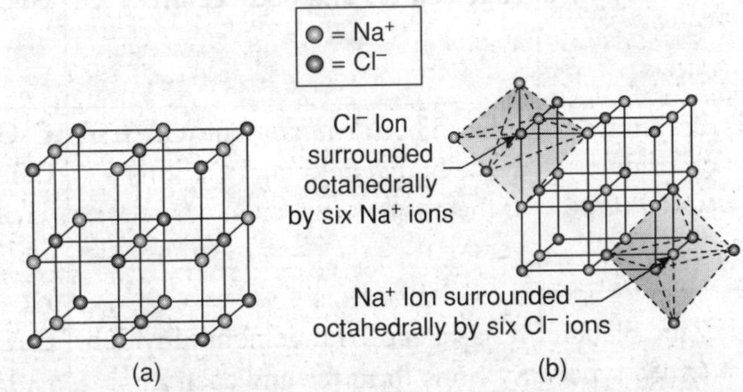

Fig. 1.28 **(a)** Structure of NaCl (Rock salt) **(b)** Showing coordination number of Na^+ and Cl^- ions

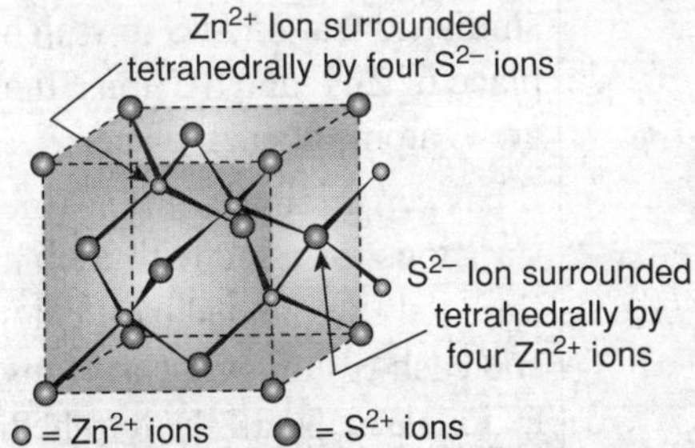

Fig. 1.29 Structure of ZnS (Zinc blende)

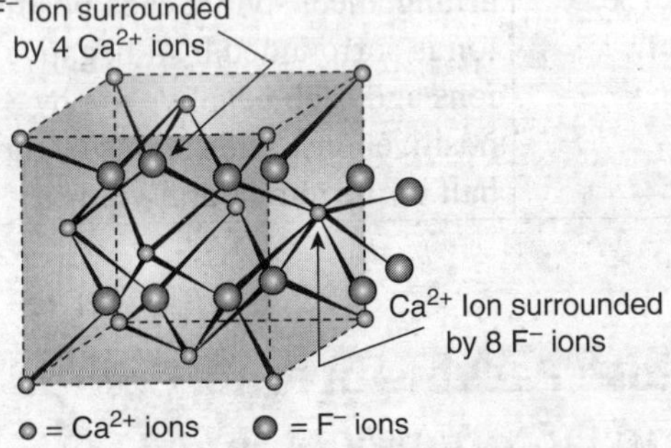

Fig. 1.30 Structure of CaF_2 (Fluorite)

1.8.1 Effect of Temperature and Pressure on Crystal Structure—Conversion of NaCl into CsCl Structure and Vice Versa

On applying high pressure, the NaCl structure with 6 : 6 coordination changes to the CsCl structure possessing 8 : 8 coordination. Similarly, CsCl with 8 : 8 coordination on heating to 760 K changes to the NaCl structure with 6 : 6 coordination. Thus, an increase in pressure increases the coordination number whereas an increase in temperature decreases the coordination number.

$$\underset{(6:6 \text{ coordination})}{\text{NaCl structure}} \underset{760 \text{ K}}{\overset{\text{Pressure}}{\rightleftharpoons}} \underset{(8:8 \text{ coordination})}{\text{CsCl structure}}$$

Table 1.4 Features of different arrangements

Crystal structure	Brief description	Examples	Coordination no.	Number of formula units per unit cell
Type AB (i) Rock salt ($NaCl$) type	It has an fcc arrangement in which Cl^- ions occupy the corners and face centres of a cube while Na^{a+} ions are present at the edge centres and body centres.	Halides of Li, Na, K, Rb, AgF, AgBr, NH_4Cl, NH_4Br, NH_4I	$Na^+ = 6$ $Cl^- = 6$	**4** (Na^+ ions = $\underbrace{12\times\frac{1}{4}}_{\text{edge centres}} + \underbrace{1}_{\text{body centre}} = 4$ Cl^- ions = $\underbrace{8\times\frac{1}{8}}_{\text{corners}} + \underbrace{6\times\frac{1}{2}}_{\text{body centre}} = 4$)
(ii) Cesium chloride ($CsCl$) type	It has a bcc arrangement with Cs^+ at the body centre and Cl^- ions at the corners of a cube or vice versa.	CsCl, CsBr, CsI, CsCN, TlCl, TlBr, TlI and TlCN	$Cs^+ = 8$ $Cl^- = 8$	**1** (Cs^+ ions = 1, at body centre Cl^- ions = $\underbrace{8\times\frac{1}{8}}_{\text{corners}} = 1$)
(iii) Zinc blende (ZnS) type	It has a ccp arrangement in which S^{2-} ions form fcc and each Zn^{2+} ion is surrounded tetrahedrally by four S^{2-} ions and vice versa. ***Note***: The structure of diamond is similar to that of ZnS in which in place of Zn^{2+} and S^{2-} ions, there are C atoms at each place.	CuCl, CuBr, CuI, AgI, BeS	$Zn^{2+} = 4$ $S^{2-} = 4$	**4** S^{2-} ions = $\underbrace{8\times\frac{1}{8}}_{\text{corners}} + \underbrace{6\times\frac{1}{2}}_{\text{face entres}} = 4$ Zn^{2+} ions = 4 (present on the body diagonal)
Type AB_2 (i) Fluorite (CaF_2) type	It has ccp arrangement in which Ca^{2+} ions form fcc with each Ca^{2+} ion surrounded by 8 F^- ions and each F^- ion by 4 Ca^{2+} ions. F^- ions occupy all the tetrahedral voids.	BaF_2, $BaCl_2$, SrF_2, $SrCl_2$, CdF_2, PbF_2	$Ca^{2+} = 8$ $F^- = 4$	**4** Ca^{2+} ions = $\underbrace{8\times\frac{1}{8}}_{\text{corners}} + \underbrace{6\times\frac{1}{2}}_{\text{face centres}} = 4$ F^- ions = 8 (present within the body)
(ii) Antifluorite type (A_2B type)	Here negative ions form the ccp arrangement so that each positive ion is surrounded by 4 negative ions and each negative ion by 8 positive ions. The cations occupy half of the tetrahedral voids.	Na_2O	$Na^+ = 4$ $O^{2-} = 8$	**4**

1.9 Close Packing in Ionic Compounds and Occupancy of Voids

Compound	**Ions forming the close-packed arrangement**	**Ions occupying the voids**
(i) NaCl	Cl^- ions (*fcc*)	Na^+ ions in all octahedral voids
(ii) ZnS	S^{2-} ions (*fcc*)	Zn^{2+} ions in alternate tetrahedral voids
(iii) CaF_2	Ca^{2+} ions (*fcc*)	F^- ions in all tetrahedral voids

(i) In NaCl, there are 4 octahedral voids, all of which are occupied by Na^+ ions. Hence, there are 4 NaCl units per unit cell.

(ii) In ZnS, there are 4 S^{2-} ions in the unit cell. Therefore, there are 8 tetrahedral voids, half of which are occupied by Zn^{2+} ions. Hence, again there 4 ZnS units per unit cell.

(iii) In CaF_2, there are 4 Ca^{2+} ions in the unit cell. Therefore, there are 8 tetrahedral voids all of which are occupied by F^- ions. Hence, there are 4 CaF_2 units per unit cell.

1.10 Radius Ratio Rules

$$\text{Radius ratio} = \frac{\text{Radius of the cation}(r_+)}{\text{Radius of the anion}(r_-)}$$

Evidently, greater the radius ratio, the larger is the size of the cation and hence greater is its coordination number (Table 1.5).

Table 1.5 Radius ratio rules for AB type structures

Radius ratio	Coordination no.	Structural arrangement	Structure type	Examples
0.155–0.225	3	Planar triangular	—	B_2O_3
0.225–0.414	4	Tetrahedral	Sphalerite, ZnS	CuCl, CuBr, CuI, BaS, HgS
0.414–0.732	6	Octahedral	Sodium chloride (rock salt)	NaBr, KBr, MgO, MnO, CaO, CaS NH_4Br*
0.732–1	8	Body-centred cubic	Cesium chloride	CsI, CsBr, TlBr, TlCl

1.11 Relationship Between Nearest Neighbour Distance (*d*), Edge of the Unit Cell (*a*) and Radius of the Atom (*r*) for Pure Elements

(i) Simple cubic unit cell: Distance between nearest neighbours $(d) = AB = a$. For pure elements, radius $r = \frac{d}{2}$ (because atoms are touching each other).

(ii) Face-centred cubic:

$$r = \frac{d}{2} = \frac{a}{2\sqrt{2}}$$

(iii) Body-centred cubic:

$$r = \frac{d}{2} = \frac{\sqrt{3}a}{4}$$

The structures of the unit cells are given in Fig. 1.31.

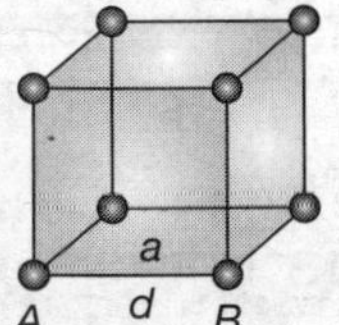

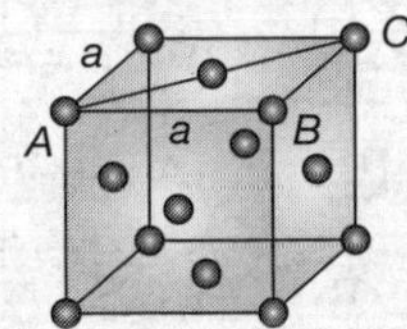

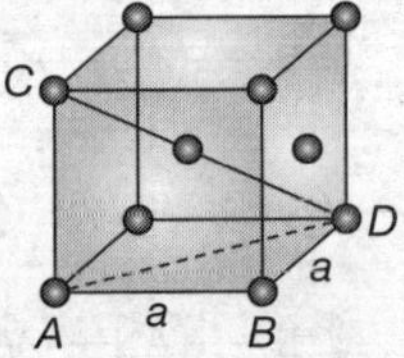

Fig. 1.31 **(a)** Simple cubic unit cell; **(b)** Face-centred cubic unit cell; **(c)** Body-centred cubic unit cell

Worked Out Problem 1.6

In a face-centred cubic (fcc) crystal lattice, the edge length is 400 pm. Find the diameter of the greatest sphere which can be fitted into the interstitial void without distortion of the lattice.

Solution:

For fcc, radius of atom $(R) = \frac{a}{2\sqrt{2}} = \frac{400}{2\sqrt{2}}$ pm $= 141.14$ pm

As the octahedral void is bigger than the tetrahedral void, the greatest sphere will fit into the octahedral void. Radius of octahedral void

$$(r) = 0.414\text{ R} = 0.414 \times 141.4\text{ pm} = 58.54\text{ pm}$$

∴ Diameter of the greatest sphere fitting into the void

$$= 2 \times 58.54\text{ pm} = 117.08\text{ pm}$$

1.12 Calculations Involving Unit Cell Dimensions

1.12.1 Calculation of Density of a Cubic Crystal from its Edge

Case I: Knowing the edge of a cubic crystal from X-ray studies and knowing the type of crystal structure possessed by it so that the number of particles per unit cell is known, the density of the crystal can be calculated.

where m = mass of each atom

$$= \frac{\text{Atomic mass}}{\text{Avogadro's number}} = \frac{M}{N_0}$$

Substituting this value, Density of the unit cell

$$= \frac{Z \times M / N_0}{a^3 \times 10^{-30}}, \text{ that is, } \rho = \frac{Z \times M}{a^3 \times N_0 \times 10^{-30}} \text{g/cm}^3$$

where the edge a is in pm and molar mass M is in g mol^{-1}. The density of the substance is the same as the density of the unit cell. The above equation involves five parameters. Knowing any four, the fifth can be calculated.

Case II: For cubic crystals of ionic compounds the formula is the same except that now Z is the number of formula units present in one unit the cell and M is the formula mass.

Worked Out Problem 1.7

Silver forms a ccp lattice and X-ray studies of its crystals show that the edge length of its unit cell is 408.6 pm. Calculate the density of silver (Atomic mass = 107.9u).

Solution:

$$\rho = \frac{Z \times M}{a^3 \times N_0}$$

For a ccp lattice (which is equivalent to fcc lattice), $Z = 4$ atoms/unit cell

Also, we are given that $M = 107.9$ g mol^{-1}

$$a = 408.6 \text{ pm}$$
$$= 408.6 \times 10^{-12} \text{ cml}$$

$$\therefore \quad \rho = \frac{4 \text{ atoms} \times 107.9 \text{ g mol}^{-1}}{(408.6 \times 10^{12} \text{ cm})^3 \left(6.022 \times 10^{23} \text{ atoms mol}^{-1}\right)}$$

$$= 105 \text{ g cm}^{-3}$$

1.13 Imperfections (Defects) in Solids

Any departure from a perfect arrangement of constituent particles in a crystal is called an *imperfection* or *defect*. Defects may also arise due to the heat absorbed by the crystals from the surroundings or due to the presence of impurities in the crystals. There are two types of defects—*point defects* and *line defects*. When the deviations or irregularities exist from the ideal arrangement around a point or an atom in a crystalline substance, the defect is called a *point defect*. However, when the deviation from the ideal arrangement exists in the entire row of lattice points, the defect is called a *line defect*.

1.13.1 Types of Point Defects

Point defects in a crystal may be classified into the following three types—(i) stoichiometric defects, (ii) non-stoichiometric defects and (iii) impurity defects.

(i) Stoichiometric defects: If imperfections in the crystal are such that the ratio between the cations and anions remains the same as represented by the molecular formula, the defects are called *stoichiometric defects.* These defects are of two types.

- **Vacancy defect:** In a crystalline substance, when some of the lattice sites are vacant, the crystal is said to have vacancy defect (Fig. 1.32). It results in the decrease in the density of the substance (because mass in the same volume of the crystal decreases).
- **Interstitial defect:** When some extra constituent particles are present in the interstitial sites, the crystal is said to have an *interstitial defect* (Fig. 1.33). This defect results in an increase in the density of the substance (because mass increases but volume remains the same).

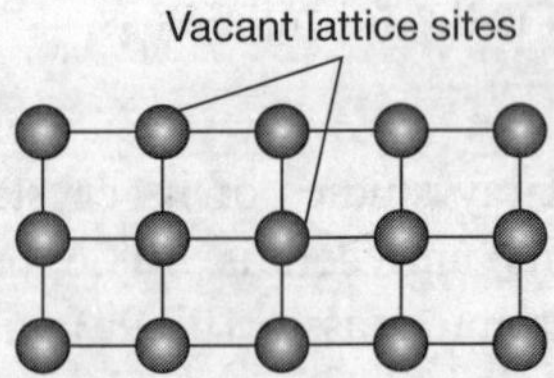

Fig. 1.32 Vacancy defect

Particles in the interstitial sites

Fig. 1.33 Interstitial defect

These two types of defects are generally shown by *non-ionic solids*. Ionic solids show Schottky and Frenkel defects.

- **Schottky defect:** In an ionic crystal of the type A^+B^-, if an equal number of cations and anions are missing from their lattice sites so that the electrical neutrality is maintained, it is called a *Schottky defect* (Fig. 1.34). This type of defect is shown by highly ionic compounds which have a high coordination number and a small difference in the size of cations and anions. A few examples are NaCl, KCl, KBr, AgBr and CsCl.
- **Frenkel defect:** If an ion is missing from its lattice site (causing a vacancy or a hole there) and it occupies an interstitial site, electrical neutrality as well as the stoichiometry of the compound are maintained. This type of defect is called a Frenkel defect (Fig. 1.35). This type of defect is present in those compounds which have a low coordination number and a large difference in the size of the cations and anions. Frenkel defects are found in silver halides (AgCl, AgBr and AgI), ZnS and so on. The density of the solid remains unchanged.

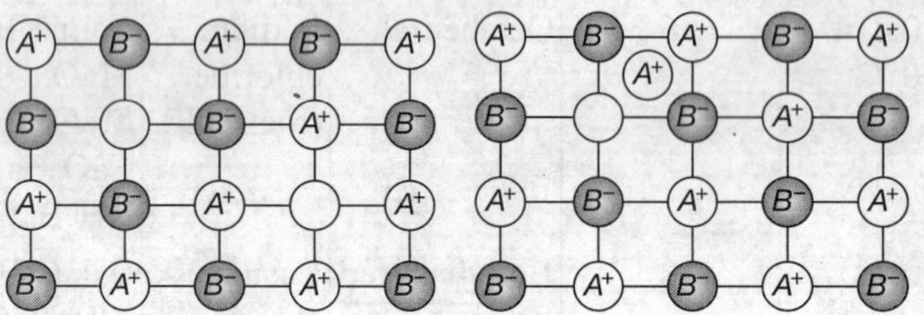

Fig. 1.34 Schottkty defect **Fig. 1.35** Frenkel defect

(ii) Non-stoichiometric defects: If, as a result of the imperfections in the crystal, the ratio of the cations to the anions becomes different from that the ideal chemical formula, the defects are called *non-stoichiometric defects.* These can occur as follows.

(a) Metal excess: This may occur in either of the following two ways.

- **Anion vacancies:** A negative ion may be missing from its lattice site, leaving a hole which is occupied by an electron, thereby maintaining the electrical balance (Fig. 1.36). The sites containing the electrons thus trapped in the anion vacancies are called *F-centres* because they are responsible for imparting colour to the crystals
- **Presence of extra cations in the interstitial sites:** Metal excess may also be caused by an extra cation occupying the interstitial sites (Fig. 1.37).

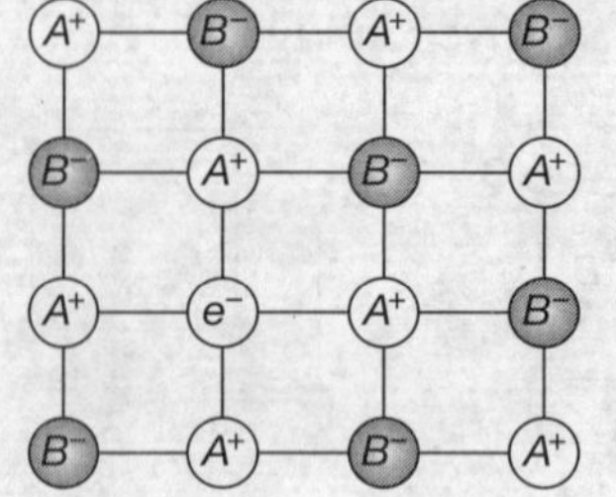

Fig. 1.36 Metal excess defect due to anion vacancy

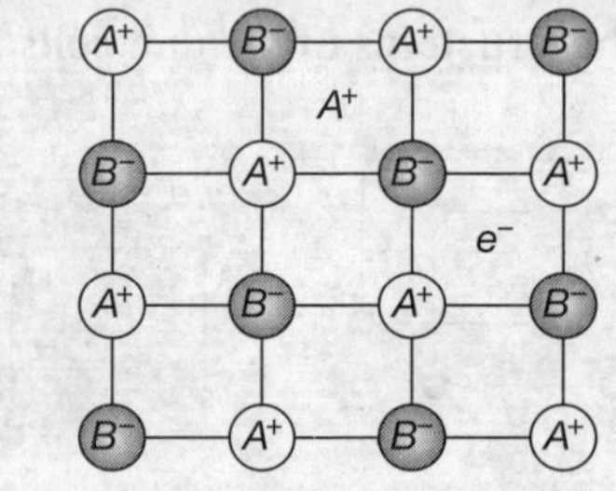

Fig. 1.37 Metal excess defect caused by extra cation in the interstitial site

For example, when ZnO is heated, it loses oxygen and turns yellow due to following reaction:

$$ZnO \rightarrow Zn^{2+} + \frac{1}{2}O_2 + 2e^-$$

(b) Metal deficiency: The defect usually occurs due to a cation missing from its lattice site and the presence of a cation having a higher charge (for example, +2 instead of +1) in the adjacent lattice site. Examples include FeO, FeS and NiO (Fig. 1.38).

(c) Impurity defects: These defects arise when foreign atoms are present at the lattice sites in the place of host atoms (Fig. 1.39). For example, in steel which is a carbide of iron, at the vacant interstitial sites, C atoms are present at the interstitial sites in the lattice of Fe atoms.

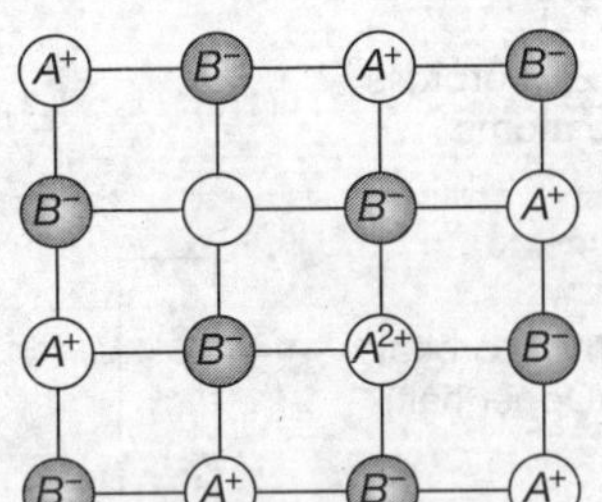

Fig. 1.38 Metal deficiency defect due to missing of a cation of a lower valency and another lattice site occupied by a cation of higher valency

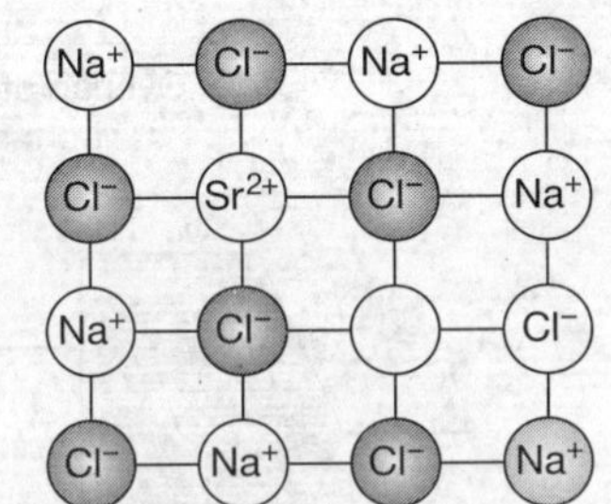

Fig. 1.39 Impurity defect introduced by substituting Na^+ ions Sr^{2+} ions

The process of adding impurities to a crystalline substance so as to change its properties is called *doping*.

1.13.2 Impurity Defects

(i) Introducing impurity defects in ionic solids: If the impurity ions are in a different valence state from that of the host ions, vacancies are created. For example, if molten NaCl, containing a little $SrCl_2$ as impurity is allowed to cool, in the crystals of NaCl, at some lattice sites, Na^+ ions are substituted by Sr^{2+} ions. For every Sr^{2+} ion thus introduced, two Na^+ ions are removed to maintain electrical neutrality. One of these lattice sites is occupied by the Sr^{2+} ion and the other remains vacant.

(ii) Introducing impurity defects in covalent solids: In the case *of covalent solids*, the impurities added may be elements which may be electron rich or electron deficient. The defects thus introduced in the crystals are called electronic defects.

- *Doping with electron rich impurities*: A group 14 element such as silicon or germanium has 4 electrons in the valence shell. Hence, it normally forms four covalent bonds with the neighbouring atoms [Fig.1.40(a)]. When it is doped with a group 15 element such as P or As, the silicon or germanium atoms at some lattice sites are substituted by atoms

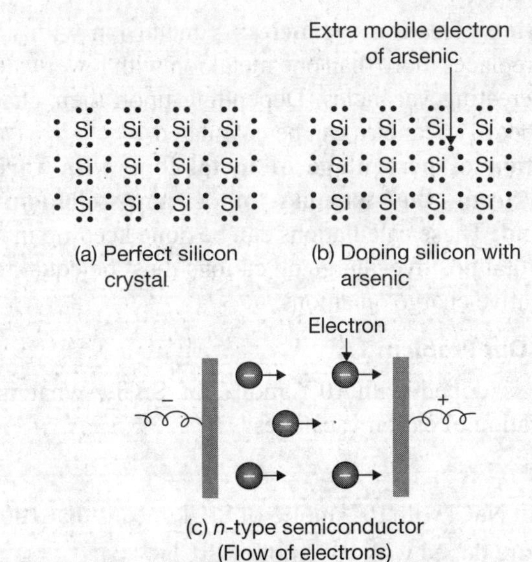

Fig. 1.40 Doping silicon with Group 15 elements to produce *n*-type semiconductors

of P or As. Now, as these atoms have 5 electrons in the valence shell, after forming four covalent bonds with the neighbouring silicon atoms, the fifth extra electron is free and gets delocalised [Fig.1.40(b)]. These delocalised electrons increase the conductivity of silicon or germanium [Fig. 1.40(c)]. These are called *n-type semiconductors*.

- *Doping with electron deficient impurities*: When a group 14 element like Si or Ge is doped with a group 13 element like B, Al or Ga, the Si or Ge atom at some lattice sites are substituted by those of B, Al or Ga. Now, as group 13 elements have only three valence electrons, they can form three covalent bonds with the neighbouring silicon atoms. Thus, a hole is created at the site where the fourth electron is missing [Fig. 1.41(b)]. This is called an *electron hole* or *electron vacancy*. These are called *p-type semiconductors*.

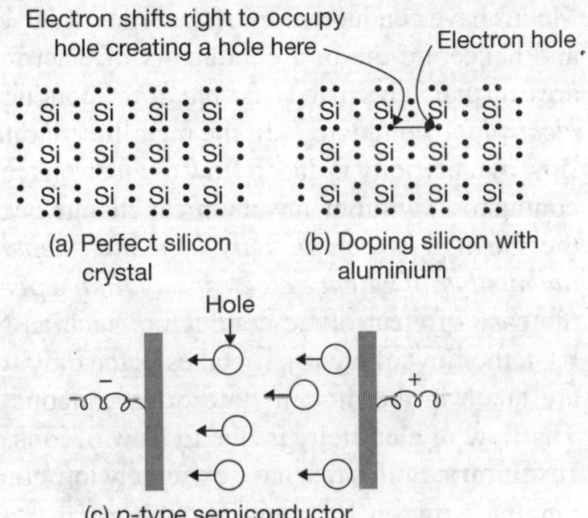

Fig. 1.41 Doping of silicon with group 13 elements to product *p*-type semiconductors with flow of holes like positive charge

Calculation of cation vacancies: A metal ion with higher valency replaces more than one metal ion with lower valency, thereby creating vacancies. Depending upon their charges, the number of vacancies can be calculated.

Calculation of percentage of metal ions with variable valency from the formula of a non-stoichiometric compound: These calculations can be done keeping in mind that the total positive charge on cations must be equal to the total negative charge on anions.

Worked Out Problem 1.8

If NaCl is doped with 10^{-3} mol% of $SrCl_2$, what is the concentration of cation vacancies?

Solution

Doping of NaCl with 10^{-3} mol% of $SrCl_2$ means that 100 mol of NaCl are doped with 10^{-3} mol of $SrCl_2$.

$$\therefore \text{1 mol of NaCl is doped with } SrCl_2 = \frac{10^{-3}}{100}\text{ mol} = 10^{-5}\text{ mol}$$

As each Sr^{2+} ion introduces one cation vacancy, the concentration of cation vacancies

$$= 10^{-5}\text{ mol / mol of NaCl}$$
$$= 10^{-5} \times 6.02 \times 10^{23}\text{ mol}^{-1}$$
$$= 6.02 \times 10^{18}\text{ mol}^{-1}$$

1.14 Electrical Properties of Solids

Classification of Solids on the Basis of Conductivity

Different types of solids show electrical conductivity which varies from as low as 10^{-20} ohm^{-1} m^{-1} to 10^7 ohm^{-1} m^{-1}. Depending upon the difference in electrical conductivities, solids are classified into the following three types.

(i) **Conductors:** Solids that have conductivities in the range 10^4 to 10^7 ohm^{-1} m^{-1} are called conductors. Metals have conductivities of the order of 10^7 ohm^{-1}m^{-1} and hence are the best conductors of electricity. They are further classified as *metallic* conductors and *electrolytic* conductors. In the metallic conductors, the flow of electricity is due to flow of electrons (electronic conductors) without any chemical change occurring in the metal. *The conductivity of metals depends upon the number of valence electrons available per atom.* In the case of electrolytic conductors such as NaCl and KCl, the flow of electricity takes place only when they are taken in the molten state or in aqueous solution. The flow of electricity is due to flow of ions.

(ii) **Insulators:** Solids that have extremely low conductivity ranging between 10^{-20} and 10^{-6} ohm^{-1} m^{-1} are called insulators. For example, plastics, wood, rubber, sulfur, phosphorus.

(iii) **Semiconductors:** Solids that have conductivity in between those of conductors and insulators (ranging from 10^{-6} to 10^4 ohm^{-1} m^{-1}) are called semiconductors.

1.14.1 Band Theory of Metals

In the case of a metal, the atomic orbitals of the metal atoms are so close in energy that they overlap to form a large number of molecular orbitals very close in energy. This set of molecular orbitals is called a *band*. For example, the formation of a band by overlap of the n $2s^1$ orbitals of n Li atoms is shown in Fig. 1.42. Just as two atomic orbitals combine to form two molecular orbitals, n atomic orbitals combine to form n molecular orbitals.

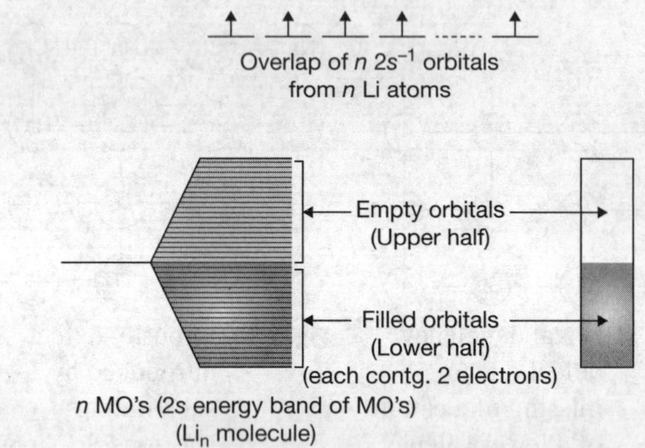

Fig. 1.42 2s orbitals of Li atoms combining to form molecular orbitals equal to the number of Li atoms (2s orbitals) combining together. (Li = $1s^1$, $2s^1$)

In the case of lithium, the lower half of the molecular orbitals are completely filled while the upper half is empty. On applying electric current, electrons can move into the vacant levels. Hence, electric current can flow. The band formed by the lower energy valence orbitals ($1s$) is called the *valence band* and the band formed by the slightly higher energy valence orbitals is called the *conduction band.* On applying electric current, electrons can flow from the valence band to the conduction band. The formation of the valence and conduction bands in the case of Be is shown in Fig. 1.43.

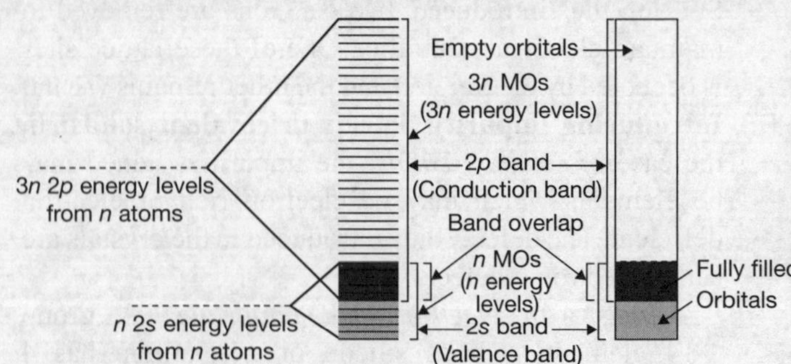

Fig. 1.43 Overlap of $2s$ energy band (valency band) and 2p energy band (conduction band) of beryllium (Be = $1s^2\ 2s^2\ 2p^0$)

1.14.2 Behaviour of Conductors, Insulators and Semiconductors on the Basis of Band Theory

If the valence band is partially filled (as in the case of lithium) or it overlaps with the higher energy or unoccupied conduction band (as in the case of beryllium), the electrons can easily flow under the influence of an applied electric field. Hence, the metal conducts electricity [Fig. 1.44(a)]. If the gap between the filled valence band and the unoccupied conduction band is large, electrons cannot jump from the valence band to the conduction band. Hence, the substance has extremely low conductivity and it behaves as an insulator [Fig. 1.44(b)].

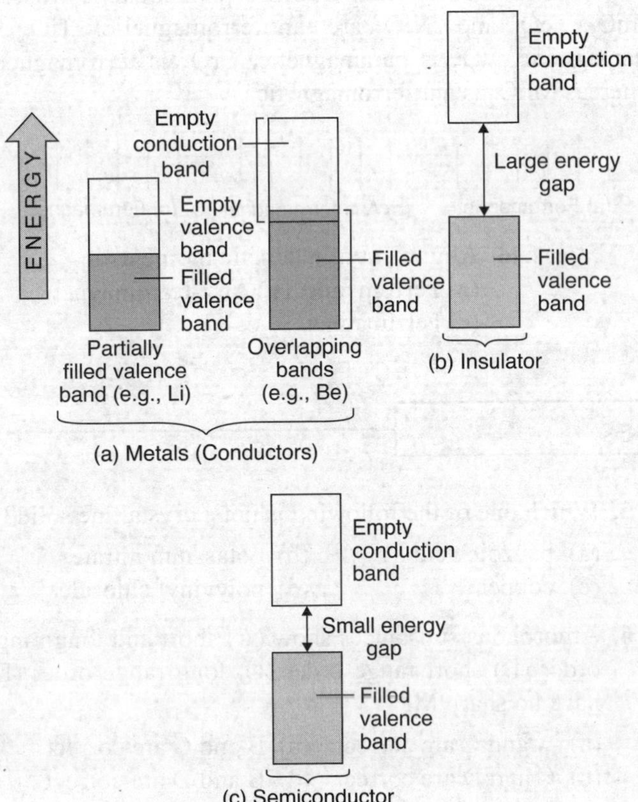

Fig. 1.44 Distinction between metals, insulators and semiconductors in terms of band theory

If the gap between the valence band and the conduction band is small, some electrons may jump from the valence band to the conduction band. Hence, the substance shows some conductivity and it acts as a semiconductor [Fig. 1.44(c)].

1.14.3 Effect of Temperature on Electrical Conductivity

Electrical conductivity of metals decreases with an increase in temperature. The electrical conductivity of semiconductors increases with an increase in temperature because more electrons can jump to the conduction band. Above 0 K, some covalent bonds break. As a result, some electrons are released and holes are created there. Due to free electrons and holes, Si and Ge show some electrical conductivity and hence become semiconductors. Substances like silicon and germanium which show this type of behaviour are called *intrinsic semiconductors*. The conductivity can be increased by either by adding *electron rich impurities* or *electron deficient impurities*. The semiconductors thus obtained are called *n*-type and *p*-type semiconductors. Collectively, they are called *extrinsic semiconductors*.

Applications of *n*-Type and *p*-Type Semiconductors

- A diode is a combination of *p*- and *n*-type semiconductors and is used as a *rectifier*.
- The solar cell is an efficient photodiode used for the conversion of light energy into electrical energy.
- *Transistors* are sandwich semiconductors of the type *pnp* or *npn* which are used to detect or amplify radio or audio signals.
- Gallium arsenide (GaAs) semiconductors have very fast response and have revolutionised the designs of semiconductor devices.

1.15 Magnetic Properties of Solids

Magnetic moments arise due to the orbital motion and spinning motion of the electrons (Fig. 1.45). Thus, each electron may be considered as a small magnet having a resultant permanent magnetic moment. Thus, a material may be considered to contain a number of *magnetic dipoles* (similar to a bar magnet with north and south poles). Based on the behaviour in the external magnetic field, the substances are divided into various categories.

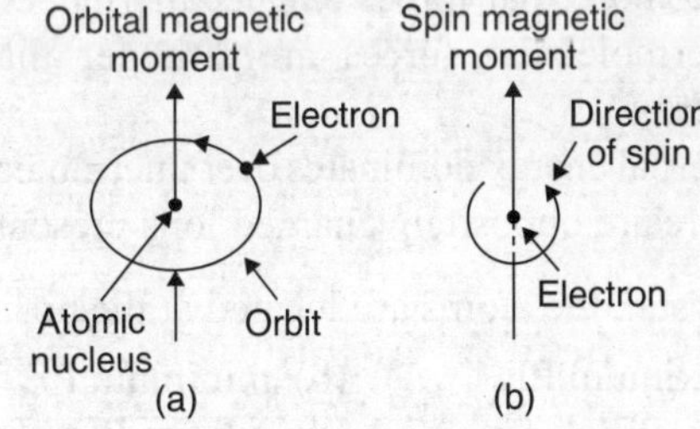

Fig. 1.45 **(a)** Magnetic moment of electron due to orbital motion; **(b)** magnetic moment of electron due to spin motion

(i) Diamagnetic substances: Substances which are weakly repelled by the external magnetic field are called *diamagnetic substances*. For example, TiO_2, H_2O, NaC, benzene. The property thus exhibited is called *diamagnetism*. This property is shown only by those substances in which no unpaired electron is present.

(ii) Paramagnetic substances: Substances which are attracted by the external magnetic field are called *paramagnetic substances*. The property thus exhibited is called *paramagnetism*. This property is shown substances which contain unpaired electrons as in O_2, Cu^{2+}, Fe^{3+} and Cr^{3+}. These substances, however, lose their magnetism in the absence of the magnetic field.

(iii) Ferromagnetic substances: Substances which show permanent magnetism even in the absence of a magnetic field are called *ferromagnetic substances*, such as, Fe, Ni, Co, Gd and CrO_2. Such substances remain permanently magnetised once they have been magnetised; the property is called *ferromagnetism*. In the solid state, the metal ions of these substances are grouped together into small regions called *domains*. Each domain acts as a tiny magnet having a definite magnetic moment. When the substance is placed in a magnetic field, all the domains get oriented in the direction of the magnetic field (Fig. 1.45) giving the substance a very high magnetic moment. This ordering of domains persists even when the external magnetic field is removed.

(iv) Anti-ferromagnetic substances: Substances which are expected to possess large magnetism on the basis of the magnetic moments of the domains but actually have a small net magnetic moment are called *ferrimagnetic substances*. For example, magnetite (Fe_3O_4), ferrites of the formula $M^{2+}Fe_2O_4$ where M = Mg, Cu, Zn, and so on. *Ferrimagnetism* arises due to the unequal number domains in opposite directions resulting in some net magnetic moment (Fig. 1.46).

Note that all magnetically ordered solids – ferromagnetic and anti-ferromagnetic – change into paramagnetic at high temperature. This is due to randomisation of domains (spins) on heating. Ferrimagnetic substances (Fe_3O_4) become paramagnetic at 580 K. Further, each ferromagnetic substance has a characteristic temperature above which no ferromagnetism is observed. This is known as the *curie temperature.* TiO, VO and CuO are paramagnetic whereas MnO, FeO and NiO are antiferromagnetic, TiO_2 is diamagnetic, VO_2 is paramagnetic, CrO_2 is ferromagnetic whereas MnO_2 is antiferromagnetic.

Fig. 1.46 Alignment of magnetic moments in **(a)** Ferromagnet **(b)** Anti-ferromagnet **(c)** Ferrimagnet

Exercises

OBJECTIVE QUESTIONS

General Characteristics of Solid State

1. A substance exists as solid only when
(a) intermolecular forces balance thermal energy
(b) intermolecular forces are stronger than thermal energy
(c) internal energy dominates over intermolecular forces
(d) there are oppositely charged ions present

2. In a crystal, the atoms are located at the position of
(a) maximum PE (b) minimum PE
(c) zero PE (d) infinite PE

3. The constituent particles of a solid have
(a) translatory motion only
(b) rotatory motion only
(c) vibratory motion only
(d) all the above types of motion

Amorphous and Crystalline Solids

4. Most crystals show good cleavage because their atoms, ions or molecules are
(a) weakly bonded together
(b) strongly bonded together
(c) spherically symmetrical
(d) arranged in planes

5. Which one of the following is not a crystalline solid?
(a) benzoic acid (b) potassium nitrate
(c) copper (d) polyvinyl chloride

6. Amorphous substances show (A) short and long range order (B) short range order (C) long range order (D) have no sharp MP
(a) A and C are correct (b) B and C are correct
(c) C and D are correct (d) B and D are correct

7. Which among the following will show anisotropy?
(a) glass (b) barium chloride
(c) wood (d) paper

8. A pseudo solid is
(a) glass (b) pitch
(c) KCl (d) glass and pitch both

9. Which one of the following is amorphous?
(a) polystyrene (b) table salt
(c) silica (d) diamond

10. The substance which does not show sharp melting point is
(a) KCl (b) glass (c) ice (d) diamond

11. Quartz is a crystalline variety of
(a) silica (b) sodium silicate
(c) silicon carbide (d) silicon

12. A crystalline solid
(a) changes abruptly from solid to liquid
(b) has no definite melting point
(c) undergoes deformation of its geometry easily
(d) has an irregular 3-dimensional arrangement
(e) softens slowly

13. Which of the following statements is correct about glass?
(a) It is an amorphous solid.
(b) It is considered as a supercooled liquid.
(c) It can be obtained from quartz by melting and then rapidly cooling the melt.
(d) All the above are correct.

14. A solid is found to have same refractive index in all directions. The nature of solid is
(a) ionic (b) covalent
(c) molecular (d) amorphous

Classification of Crystalline Solids

15. Graphite belongs to
(a) cubic system
(b) tetragonal system
(c) rhombohedral system
(d) hexagonal system

16. A solid A is very hard, electrical insulator in solid as well as molten state and melts at extremely high temperature. The type of solid is
(a) ionic (b) covalent network
(c) metallic (d) amorphous

17. Which of the following is not a molecular solid?
(a) urea (b) ice
(c) tin (d) graphite

18. Wax is an example of
(a) ionic crystal (b) covalent crystal
(c) molecular crystal (d) metallic crystal

19. Iodine crystals are
(a) metallic (b) ionic
(c) molecular (d) covalent

20. A molecular crystalline solid
(a) is very hard (b) is volatile
(c) has a high melting point
(d) is a good conductor

21. Among the following which crystal will be soft and have low melting point?
(a) covalent (b) ionic
(c) metallic (d) molecular

22. A solid X melts slightly above 273 K and is a poor conductor heat and electricity. To which of the following categories does it belong?
(a) ionic solid (b) covalent solid
(c) metallic (d) molecular

23. The major binding force of diamond, silicon and quartz is
(a) electrostatic force (b) electrical attraction
(c) covalent bond force (d) non-covalent bond force
(e) van der Waals force

24. Which of the following is an example of covalent solid?
(a) silicon carbide (b) $BaSO_4$
(c) solid CO_2 (d) iodine

25. Among solids, the highest melting point is exhibited by
(a) covalent solids (b) ionic solids
(c) pseudo solids (d) molecular solids

26. Which type of solid crystals will conduct heat and electricity?
(a) ionic (b) covalent
(c) metallic (d) molecular

27. An example of a covalent crystalline solid is
(a) Si (b) NaF (c) Ar (d) Al

28. In graphite, electrons are
(a) localised on each carbon atom
(b) spread out between the sheets
(c) localised on every third carbon atom
(d) present in antibonding orbital

29. The hardest substance among the following is
(a) Be_2C (b) titanium
(c) SiC (d) B_4C

30. A particular solid is very hard and has a very high melting point. In solid state, it is a non-conductor and its melt is a conductor of electricity. Classify the solid
(a) metallic (b) molecular
(c) network (d) ionic

31. Which one of the following is a molecular crystal?
(a) rock salt (b) quartz
(c) dry ice (d) diamond

Crystal Lattices and Unit Cells

32. Diamond belongs to the crystal system
(a) cubic (b) triclinic
(c) tetragonal (d) hexagonal

33. Which of the following are the correct axial distances and axial angles for rhombohedral system?
(a) $a = b = c, \alpha = \beta = \gamma \neq 90°$
(b) $a = b \neq c, \alpha = \beta = \gamma = 90°$

(c) $a \neq b = c, \alpha = \beta = \gamma = 90°$
(d) $a \neq b \neq c, \alpha \neq \beta \neq \gamma \neq 90°$

34. Copper belongs to
(a) cubic system (b) tetragonal system
(c) monoclinic system (d) triclinic system

35. TeO_2 is an example of
(a) monoclinic system (b) rhombic system
(c) tetragonal system (d) triclinic system

36. The unit cell with the structure given below represents ________ crystal system

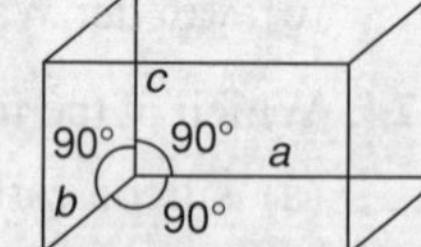

(a) cubic
(b) orthorhombic
(c) tetragonal (d) trigonal

37. The crystal systems having the highest and lowest symmetries are respectively
(a) cubic and monoclinic
(b) cubic and triclinic
(c) orthorhombic and monoclinic
(d) cubic and hexagonal

38. $\alpha \neq b \neq c, a \neq \beta \neq \gamma \neq 90°$
(a) tetragonal system (b) orthorhombic system
(c) monoclinic system (d) triclinic system

39. The crystal system of a compound with unit cell dimensions $a = 0.387$, $b = 0.387$ and $c = 0.504$ nm and $\alpha = \beta = 90°$ and $\gamma = 120°$ is
(a) cubic (b) hexagonal
(c) orthorhombic (d) rhomohedral

40. If $a = b \neq c$ and $\alpha = \beta = \gamma = 90°$, the crystal system is
(a) cubic (b) rhombic
(c) tetragonal (d) monoclinic

41. Which of the following are the correct axial lengths and axial angles of a monoclinic unit cell?
(a) $a = b \neq c, \alpha = \beta = \gamma = 90°$
(b) $a \neq b \neq c, \alpha = \beta = \gamma = 90°$
(c) $a \neq b \neq c, \alpha = \gamma = 90°$
(d) $a \neq b \neq c, \alpha = \beta = \gamma \neq 90°$

Number of Atoms in a Unit Cell

42. In metallic solids, the number of atoms for the face centred and the body centred cubic unit cells, are respectively
(a) 2, 4 (b) 2, 2 (c) 4, 2 (d) 4, 4

43. The coordination number for an atom in a primitive cubic unit cell is
(a) 6 (b) 8 (c) 10 (d) 12

44. Which of the following unit cell has maximum number of atoms?
(a) *bcc* (b) *hcp* (c) *fcc* (d) Cubic

45. How many atoms are there in a cube based unit cell having one atom on each corner and two atoms on each body diagonal of the cube?
(a) 8 (b) 6 (c) 4 (d) 9

46. An element has bcc structure having unit cells 12.08×10^{23}. The number of atoms in these cells is
(a) 12.08×10^{23} (b) 24.16×10^{23}
(c) 48.38×10^{23} (d) 12.08×10^{23}

47. Gold crystallises in the face centred cubic lattice. The number of unit cells in 1 g of gold (atomic mass = 197 u) will be
(a) 6.02×10^{23} (b) 7.64×10^{20}
(c) 3.82×10^{20} (d) 15.28×10^{20}

48. Number of unit cells in 4 g of X (atomic mass = 40) which crystallises in a *bcc* pattern is (N_A = Avogadro number)
(a) 0.1 N (b) $2 \times 0.1\ N_A$
(c) $\frac{0.1\ N_A}{2}$ (d) $2 \times N_A$

49. Three elements A, B and C crystallise into a cubic solid lattice. Atoms A occupy the corners, B atoms the cube centres and atoms C the edges. The formula of the compound is
(a) ABC (b) ABC_2 (c) ABC_3 (d) ABC_4

50. A compound formed from elements A and B has a cubic structure in which atoms A are present at the corners as well as face centres whereas atoms B are present on the edge centres as well as body centre. The formula of the compound will be
(a) A_2B (b) AB_2 (c) AB (d) A_2B_3

51. A compound M_pX_q has cubic close packing (ccp) arrangement of X. Its unit cell structure is shown below. The empirical formula of the compound is

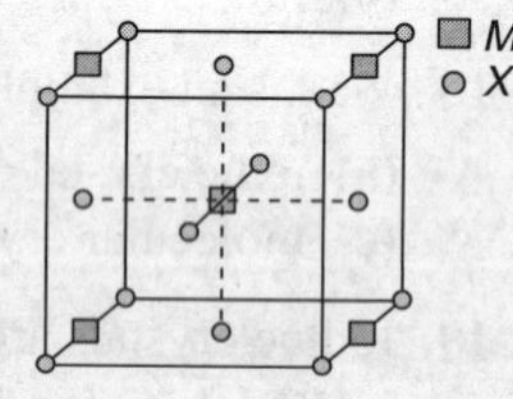

(a) MX (b) MX_2 (c) M_2X (d) M_2X_{14}

52. A substance A_xB_y crystallises in a face centred cubic (FCC) lattice in which A atoms occupy each corner of the cube and B atoms occupy the centres of each face of the cube. Identify the correct composition of the substance A_xB_y.
(a) AB_3 (b) A_4B_3
(c) A_3B
(d) composition cannot be specified

53. A cubic solid is made up of two elements P and Q. Atoms Q are present at the corners of the cube and atoms

P at the body-centre. The formula of the compound and coordination numbers of P and Q respectively are

(a) PQ, 8, 8 (b) P_2Q, 8, 4
(c) PQ_2, 4, 8 (d) PQ_3, 12, 4

54. In a face centred cubic arrangement of A and B atoms in which A atoms are at the corners of the unit cell and B atoms at the face centres, one of the A atom is missing from one corner in unit cell. The simplest formula of compound is

(a) A_7B_3 (b) AB_3 (c) A_7B_{24} (d) $A_{7/8}B_3$

55. Total volume of atoms present in a face centred cubic unit cell of a metal is (r is atomic radius)

(a) $\frac{12}{3}\pi r^3$ (b) $\frac{16}{3}\pi r^3$ (c) $\frac{20}{3}\pi r^3$ (d) $\frac{24}{3}\pi r^3$

56. In NaCl unit cell, all the ions lying along the axis as shown in the figure are removed. Then the number of Na^+ and Cl^{-1} ions remaining in the unit cell are

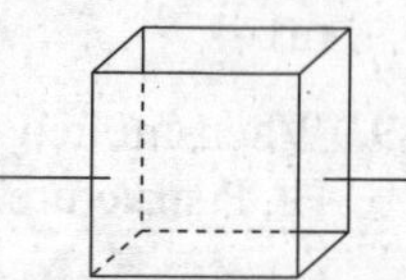

(a) 4 and 4 (b) 3 and 3 (c) 1 and 1 (d) 4 and 3

57. Na and Mg crystallise in *bcc* and *fcc* type crystals, then the number of Na and Mg atoms present in the unit cell of their respective crystals is

(a) 4 and 2 (b) 9 and 14
(c) 14 and 9 (d) 2 and 4

58. The number of lattice points in a unit cell of face centred cubic, face centred tetragonal and body centred cubic of an element respectively are

(a) 4, 4, 2 (b) 4, 2, 2
(c) 2, 4, 4 (d) 4, 2, 4

59. The edge atom of a cube provides how many atoms to the unit cell?

(a) 1/2 (b) 1/4 (c) 1/8 (d) 1

60. The number of atoms per unit cell is 2, the arrangement is

(a) octahedral (b) *fcc*
(c) *bcc* (d) none of these

Elements of Symmetry and Laws of Crystallography

61. Which has no rotational axis of symmetry?

(a) hexagonal (b) orthorhombic
(c) cubic (d) triclinic

62. The ability of a given substance to assume two or more crystalline structure is called

(a) amorphism (b) isomorphism
(c) polymorphism (d) isomerism

63. If (hkl) represent the Miller indices of a plane in a cubic crystal, its distance of separation from the adjacent parallel plane is

(a) $\frac{a}{h^2+k^2+l^2}$ (b) $\frac{h^2+k^2+l^2}{a}$

(c) $\frac{a}{\sqrt{h^2+k^2+l^2}}$ (d) $\frac{\sqrt{h^2+k^2+l^2}}{a}$

64. The interplanar spacing between the (221) planes of a cubic lattice of edge length 450 pm is

(a) 50 pm (b) 150 pm (c) 300 pm (d) 450 pm

65. A plane parallel to Z-axis cuts the X-axis and Y-axis at 2a and 3b respectively. The Miller indices of the plane are

(a) 230 (b) 238 (c) 320 (d) 032

66. Which of the following pairs is isomorphous?

(a) $FeSO_4.7H_2O$ and $CuSO_4.5H_2O$
(b) $FeSO_4.7H_2O$ and $MnSO_4.4H_2O$
(c) $FeSO_4.7H_2O$ and $ZnSO_4.7H_2O$
(d) $CuSO_4.5H_2O$ and $MnSO_4.4H_2O$

Close Packed Structures

67. The number of tetrahedral and octahedral voids in a *ccp* array of 100 atoms are respectively

(a) 200 and 100 (b) 100 and 200
(c) 200 and 200 (d) 100 and 100
(e) 50 and 50

68. In the cubic close packing, the unit cell has

(a) 4 tetrahedral voids each of which is shared by four adjacent unit cells
(b) 4 tetrahedral voids within the unit cell
(c) 8 tetrahedral voids each of which is shared by four adjacent unit cells
(d) 8 tetrahedral voids within the unit cell

69. A compound forms hexagonal close packed structure. The number of tetrahedral voids and total number of voids present in 0.5 mol of its respectively are

(a) 3.011×10^{23}, 6.022×10^{23}
(b) 6.022×10^{23}, 9.033×10^{23}
(c) 6.022×10^{23}, 9.033×10^{23}
(d) none of these

70. The size of an octahedral void formed in a closest packed lattice as compared to tetrahedral void is

(a) equal (b) smaller
(c) larger (d) not definite

71. Number of tetrahedral voids per atom in a crystal lattice is

(a) 1 (b) 2 (c) 4 (d) 8

72. The ratio of close-packed atoms to tetrahedral holes in cubic close packing is

(a) 1 : 1 (b) 1 : 2 (c) 1 : 3 (d) 2 : 1

73. The correct order of sizes of voids (holes) is

(a) trigonal > tetrahedral > octahedral
(b) tetrahedral > trigonal > octahedral
(c) octahedral > tetrahedral > trigonal
(d) octahedral = tetrahedral = trigonal

74. Which of the following crystallises in *ccp* structure?

(a) Ag (b) Be (c) Mg (d) Mo

75. All noble gases crystallise in the *ccp* structure except

(a) helium (b) neon (c) argon (d) krypton

76. Which of the following is an example of body centred cube?

(a) magnesium (b) zinc
(c) copper (d) sodium

77. An example for a face centred cubic lattice is

(a) zinc (b) sodium
(c) copper (d) cesium chloride

78. Potassium crystallises with a

(a) Face centred cubic lattice
(b) Body centred cubic lattice
(c) Simple cubic lattice
(d) Orthorhombic lattice

79. Silicon is found in nature in the form of

(a) body centred cubic structure
(b) hexagonal close-packed structure
(c) network solid
(d) face centred cubic structure

80. Which of the following describes the hexagonal close packed arrangement of spheres?

(a) ABCABA (b) ABCABC
(c) ABABAB (d) ABBABB

81. If the same type of atoms are packed in hexagonal close packing (*hcp*) and cubic close packing (*ccp*) separately, then

(a) density of *hcp* will be greater than *ccp*
(b) density of *hcp* will be less than *ccp*
(c) density of *hcp* will be equal to *hcp*
(d) density of *hcp* may be equal, greater or less depending upon temperature

82. The maximum proportion of available volume that can be filled by hard spheres in diamond is

(a) 0.52 (b) 0.34 (c) 0.42 (d) 0.68

83. Which one of the following is not a close packing?

(a) *hcp* (b) *ccp* (c) *hcp* (d) *fcc*

84. Close packing is maximum in the crystal lattice of

(a) simple cubic (b) face centred
(c) body centred (d) none

85. Which of the following patterns has void fraction of 0.26?

(a) AAAA.... (b) ABABAB....
(c) ABCABCABC.... (d) ABCCBAABC....

86. In a face centred cubic lattice, the number of nearest neighbours for a given lattice point is

(a) 6 (b) 8 (c) 12 (d) 14

87. If the coordination number of an element in its crystal lattice is 8, then packing is

(a) *fcc* (b) *hcp*
(c) *bcc* (d) none of the above

88. In a hexagonal closest packing in two layers one above the other, the coordination number of each sphere will be

(a) 4 (b) 6 (c) 8 (d) 9

89. When molten zinc is cooled to solid state, it assumes HCP structure. Then the number of nearest unit cells is

(a) 4 (b) 6 (c) 8 (d) 12

90. A binary solid $\left(A^+B^-\right)$ has a zinc blende structure with B^- ions constituting the lattice and A^+ ions occupying 25% tetrahedral holes. The formula of solids is

(a) AB (b) A_2B (c) AB_2 (d) AB_4

91. Atoms of element B form *hcp* lattice and those of element A occupy 2/3rd of tetrahedral voids. The formula of the compound formed between the elements A and B is

(a) A_2B_3 (b) A_3B_2 (c) A_3B_4 (d) A_4B_3

92. Iron oxide crystallises in a hexagonal close packed array of oxide ions with two out of every three octahedral holes occupied by ferric ions. The formula of the iron oxide is

(a) FeO (b) Fe_2O_3
(c) Fe_3O_4 (d) none of these

93. An alloy of copper, silver and gold is found to have copper forming the simple cubic close packed lattice. If silver atoms occupy the face centres and gold is present at the body centre, then the formula of the alloy will be

(a) Cu_4Ag_4Au (b) Cu_4Ag_2Au
(c) CuAgAu (d) $CuAg_3Au$

94. An ionic compound is formed between a metal M and a non-metal Y. If M occupies half of the tetrahedral voids in the cubic close, packed arrangement formed by Y, the chemical formula of the ionic compound is

(a) MY (b) MY_2 (c) M_2Y (d) MY_3

95. Aluminium crystallises in a cubic close packed structure. Its metallic radius is 125 pm. The number of unit cells present in 1.00 cm^3 of aluminium will be

(a) 2.25×10^{20} (b) 2.25×10^{21}
(c) 2.25×10^{22} (d) 2.25×10^{23}

96. If the radius of an atom of an element is 75 pm and the lattice is body centred cubic, the edge of the unit cell will be

(a) 32.475 pm (b) 173.2 pm
(c) 37.5 pm (d) 212.1 pm

97. Lithium metal crystallises in a body centred cubic crystal. If the length of the side of the unit cell of lithium is 351 pm, the atomic radius of the lithium will be

(a) 151.8 pm (b) 75.5 pm
(c) 300.5 pm (d) 240.8 pm

98. In face centred cubic unit cell, edge length is

(a) $\frac{4}{\sqrt{3}}r$ (b) $\frac{4}{\sqrt{2}}r$ (c) $2r$ (d) $\frac{\sqrt{3}}{2}r$

99. Copper crystallises in a face centred cubic lattice with a unit cell length of 361 pm. What the radius of copper atom in pm?

(a) 157 (b) 181 (c) 108 (d) 128

100. The radius of an atom is 300 pm. If it crystallises in a face centred cubic lattice, the length of the edge of the unit cell is

(a) 488.5 pm (b) 848.5 pm
(c) 884.5 pm (d) 484.5 pm

101. Sodium metal crystallises in a body centred cubic lattice with cell edge, 4.29 Å. What is the radius of sodium atom?

(a) 2.86 Å (b) 6.81 Å (c) 1.68 Å (d) 1.86 Å

102. Silicon and diamond have unit edge $a = 0.542$ nm. If both silicon and diamond have *fcc* structures then, the interatomic separation (neighbour distance) must be

(a) 0.191 nm (b) 0.234 nm
(c) 0.383 nm (d) 0.542 nm

103. A metal crystallises with a face centred cubic lattice. The edge of the unit cell is 408 pm. The diameter of the metal atom is

(a) 288 pm (b) 408 pm (c) 144 pm (d) 204 pm

104. The interionic distance for cesium chloride crystal will be

(a) a (b) $a/2$ (c) $\sqrt{3}a/2$ (d) $2a\sqrt{3}$

105. AB crystallises in a body centred cubic lattice with edge length 'a' equal to 387 pm. The distance between two oppositely charged ions in the lattice is

(a) 300 pm (b) 335 pm (c) 250 pm (d) 200 pm

106. A solid X^+Y^- has a *bcc* structure. If the distance of closest approach between the two atoms is 173 pm, the edge length of the cell is

(a) 200 pm (b) $\sqrt{3}/\sqrt{2}$ pm
(c) 142.2 pm (d) $\sqrt{2}$ pm

107. If 'Z' is the number of atoms in the unit cell that represents the closet packing sequence ....ABC ABC.... The number of tetrahedral voids in the unit cell is equal to

(a) Z (b) $2Z$ (c) $Z/2$ (d) $Z/4$

108. A crystalline solid XY_3 has *ccp* arrangement for its element Y, X occupies

(a) 66% of tetrahedral voids
(b) 33% of tetrahedral voids
(c) 66% of octahedral voids
(d) 33% of octahedral voids

Packing Efficiency

109. The available space filled in hexagonal close packing pattern in one layer is

(a) 40% (b) 42.4% (c) 60.4% (d) 70%

110. The packing efficiency of the face centred cubic (*fcc*), body centred cubic (*bcc*) and simple/primitive cube (*pc*) lattice follows the order

(a) *fcc* > *bcc* > *pc* (b) *bcc* > *fcc* > *pc*
(c) *pc* > *bcc* > *fcc* (d) *bcc* > *pc* > *fcc*

111. The percentages of void space for simple cubic, body centred cubic and hexagonal close packed arranged respectively are

(a) 48, 32, 26 (b) 48, 26, 32
(c) 26, 48, 32 (d) 32, 48, 26

112. Percentages of free space in cubic close packed structure and in body centred packed structure are respectively

(a) 32% and 48% (b) 48% and 26%
(c) 30% and 26% (d) 26% and 32%

113. Of the following crystal lattice, the one that has the largest packing fraction is

(a) body centred cubic (b) simple cubic
(c) simple tetragonal (d) face centred cubic

114. A metal crystallises into a lattice containing a sequence of layers of atoms of ABABAB.....What percentage by volume of this lattice has empty space?

(a) 74 (b) 26 (c) 20 (d) 16

115. The vacant space in bcc lattice unit cell is

(a) 23% (b) 32% (c) 26% (d) 48%

Structures of Simple Ionic Compounds

116. Sodium chloride, NaCl, usually crystallises in a face centred cubic lattice. How many ions are in contact with any single Na^+ ion?

(a) 4 (b) 6 (c) 8 (d) 1

117. Na^+ ions in NaCl structure are present at
(a) corners of the cube
(b) body centre of the cube
(c) edge centres of the cube
(d) both (b) and (c)

118. Which one of the following statements is incorrect about rock salt type?
(a) It has *fcc* arrangement of Na^+.
(b) Na^+ and Cl^- ions have a coordination number of 6 : 6.
(c) A unit cell of NaCl consists of four NaCl units.
(d) All halides of alkali metals have rock salt type structure.

119. The structure of sodium chloride is
(a) hexagonal (b) octahedral
(c) rhombohedral (d) tetrahedral

120. The structure of MgO is similar to NaCl. The coordination number of Mg is
(a) 2 (b) 6 (c) 4 (d) 8

121. The number of Na^+ ions filling all octahedral voids in NaCl structure are
(a) 6 (b) 12 (c) 13 (d) 14

122. The number of equidistant oppositely charged ions in a sodium chloride crystal is
(a) 8 (b) 6 (c) 4 (d) 2

123. What is the total number of ions present in one unit cell of sodium chloride lattice?
(a) 2 (b) 6 (c) 12 (d) 8

124. CsCl crystallises in a body centred cubic lattice. If '*a*' is the edge length then which of the following expressions is correct?
(a) $r_{Cs^+} + r_{Cs^-} = a\sqrt{3}$ (b) $r_{Cs^+} + r_{Cs^-} = 3a$
(c) $r_{Cs^+} + r_{Cs^-} = \frac{3a}{2}$ (d) $r_{Cs^+} + r_{Cs^-} = \frac{\sqrt{3}}{2}a$

125. The coordination number of Cs^+ and Cs^- ions in CsCl structure is
(a) 4 : 4 (b) 6 : 6 (c) 8 : 8 (d) 4 : 8

126. Which of the following contains zinc blende structure?
(a) CuCl (b) CuBr
(c) AgI (d) all the above

127. The coordination number of Zn^{2+} and S^{2-} ions in the zinc blende (ZnS) type structure is
(a) 4 : 4 (b) 6 : 6 (c) 8 : 8 (d) 4 : 8

128. If the structure of CuCl is similar to ZnS, the coordination number of Cu would be
(a) 2 (b) 4 (c) 8 (d) 12

129. If AgI crystallises in zinc blende structure with I^- ions at lattice points, what fraction of tetrahedral voids is occupied by Ag^+ ions?
(a) 25% (b) 50% (c) 100% (d) 75%

130. The Ca^+ and F^- ions are located in CaF_2 crystal, respectively at face centred cubic lattice points and in
(a) tetrahedral voids
(b) half of tetrahedral voids
(c) octahedral voids
(d) half of octahedral voids

131. Antifluorite structure is derived from fluorite structure by
(a) heating fluorite lattice
(b) subjecting fluorite structure to high pressure
(c) interchanging the position of positive and negative ions in the lattice
(d) none of these

132. A unit cell of calcium fluoride has four calcium ions. The number of fluoride ions in the unit cell is
(a) 2 (b) 4 (c) 6 (d) 8

133. Space lattice of CaF_2 is
(a) face centred cubic (b) body centred cubic
(c) simple cubic (d) hexagonal closed packing

134. In Na_2O having antifluorite structure
(a) oxide ions have a cubic close packed arrangement and Na^+ occupy all the eight tetrahedral voids
(b) oxide ions have a cubic close packed arrangement and Na^+ occupy all the octahedral voids
(c) Na^+ ions have a cubic close packed arrangement and O^{2-} occupy all the octahedral voids
(d) Na^+ ions have a cubic close arrangement and O^{2-} occupy all the tetrahedral voids

135. In calcium fluoride, having the fluorite structure, the coordination number for calcium ion (Ca^+) and fluoride ion (F^{-1}) are
(a) 4 and 2 (b) 6 and 6 (c) 8 and 4 (d) 4 and 8

136. In the crystal $A^{2+}B^{2-}$, having anions in the face centred cubic packing if the radius of the anion is 1.84 Å, ideal radius of the cation present in the tetrahedral hole will be
(a) 0.225 Å (b) 0.414 Å
(c) 0.732 Å (d) none of these

137. An ionic compound XY has a structure of ZnS type. If the radius of X^+ is 22.5 pm, the ideal radius of X^- will be
(a) 20 pm (b) 50 pm (c) 100 pm (d) 30 pm

138. The maximum radius of sphere that can be fitted in the tetrahedral hole of cubical closed packing of spheres of radius *r* is

(a) $0.732\,r$ (b) $0.414\,r$ (c) $0.225\,r$ (d) $0.155\,r$

139. The maximum radius of sphere that can be fitted in the octahedral hole of cubical closed packing of sphere of radius r is

(a) $0.732\,r$ (b) $0.414\,r$ (c) $0.225\,r$ (d) $0.155\,r$

140. The radius of Na^+ is 95 pm and that of Cl^- ion is 181 pm. Hence, the coordination number of Na^+ will be

(a) 4 (b) 6
(c) 8 (d) unpredictable

141. The radius ratio of the cation to the anion of an ionic compound is 0.4. Its structure arrangement is

(a) planar triangular (b) tetrahedral
(c) octahedral (d) body centred cubic

142. At the limiting value of radius ratio r_+ / r_-

(a) forces of attraction are larger than the forces of repulsion
(b) forces of attraction are smaller than the forces of repulsion
(c) forces of attraction and repulsion are just equal
(d) none of these

143. The radius radio $\left(\frac{r_+}{r_-}\right)$ of KF is 0.98. the structure of KF is of the type

(a) NaCl (b) ZnS (c) CsCl (d) graphite

144. In NaCl crystal r_+ / r_- ratio is

(a) 0.4 (b) 0.98 (c) 1.0 (d) 0.52

145. The range of radius ratio (cationic to anionic) for an octahedral arrangement of ions in an ionic solid is

(a) 0–0.155 (b) 0.155–0.225
(c) 0.225–0.414 (d) 0.414–0.732
(e) 0.732–1.000

146. An ionic compound is expected to have tetrahedral structure if r_+ / r_- lies in the range of

(a) 0.155 to 0.225 (b) 0.732 to 1
(c) 0.414 to 0.732 (d) 0.225 to 0.414

147. The radius ratio of a substance is 0.32. The coordination number of the substance is

(a) 8 (b) 3 (c) 6 (d) 4

148. Two ions A^+ and B^- have radii 104 and 200 pm respectively, in a cubic close packed crystal of compound AB. The coordination number of A is

(a) 4 (b) 8 (c) 6 (d) 3

149. AB is an ionic solid. If the ratio of ionic radius of A^+ and B^- is 0.52, what is the coordination number of B^-?

(a) 2 (b) 3 (c) 6 (d) 8

150. In A^+B^- ionic compound, radii of A^+ and B^- ions are 180 pm and 187 pm respectively. The crystal structure of this compound will be

(a) NaCl type (b) CsCl type
(c) ZnS type (d) similar to diamond

151. If we know the ionic radius ratio in a crystal of ionic solid, what can be known of the following?

(a) magnetic property
(b) nature of chemical bond
(c) type of defect
(d) geometrical shape of crystal

152. The ionic radii of A^+ and B^- ions are 0.98×10^{-10} m and 1.81×10^{-10} m. The coordination number of each ion in AB is

(a) 2 (b) 6 (c) 4 (d) 8

153. The ionic radii are in the order

(a) $Na^+ < Mg^{2+} < Al^{3+}$ (b) $Na^+ > Mg^{2+} > Al^{3+}$
(c) $Al^{3+}\left\langle Mg^{2+}\right\rangle Na^+$ (d) $Mg^{2+} < Na^+ < Al^{3+}$

154. A solid AB and NaCl type structure. If the radius of the cation A is 100 pm, then the radius of the anion B will be

(a) 241 pm (b) 414 pm (c) 225 pm (d) 44.4 pm

155. In the crystal of which of the following ionic compounds would you expect maximum distance between the centres of the cation and anions?

(a) LiF (b) CsF (c) CsI (d) LiI

156. The ionic radius of Cl^- ion is 1.81 Å. The interionic distances of NaCl and NaF are 2.79 Å and 2.31 Å respectively. The ionic radius of F^- ion will be

(a) 0.98 Å (b) 0.80 Å (c) 1.33 (d) 2.29 Å

157. The C–C and Si–C interatomic distances are 154 pm and 188 pm. The atomic radius of Si is

(a) 77 pm (b) 94 pm (c) 114 pm (d) 111 pm

158. Which one of the following is a ferrite?

(a) $Na_2Fe_2O_4$ (b) $MgFe_2O_4$
(c) $AlFe_4O_4$ (d) Zn_3FeO_4

159. The number of carbon atoms per unit cell of diamond unit cell is

(a) 4 (b) 8 (c) 6 (d) 1

160. Out of NaCl, ZnS, CaF_2 and CsCl, in which case do the cations form a *ccp* structure?

(a) NaCl (b) ZnS (c) CsCl (d) CaF_2

161. Which is not the correct statement for ionic solids in which positive and negative ions are held by strong electrostatic attractive forces?

(a) The radius ratio r_+ / r_- increases as coordination number increases.
(b) As the difference in size of ions increases, coordination number increases.
(c) When coordination number is eight, r_+ / r_- ratio lies between 0.225 or 0.414.
(d) In ionic solids of the type AX (ZnS, Wurtzite), the coordination number of Zn^{2+} and S^{2-} respectively are 4 and 4.

162. The structure of Na_2O crystal is
(a) CsCl type (b) NaCl type
(c) ZnS type (a) antifluorite

163. Which of the following adopts normal spinel structure?
(a) CsCl (b) $MgAl_2O_4$
(c) FeO (d) CaF_2

164. The compound in which the cations occupy alternate tetrahedral voids in cubic close packing (*ccp*) is
(a) NaCl (b) ZnS (c) Na_2O (d) CaF_2

165. Edge length of a cube is 400 pm, its body diagonal would be
(a) 566 pm (b) 600 pm (c) 500 pm (d) 693 pm

166. What type of lattice is found in potassium chloride crystal?
(a) face centred cubic (b) body centred cubic
(c) simple cubic (d) simple tetragonal

167. Body centred cubic lattice has a coordination number of
(a) 4 (b) 8 (c) 12 (d) 6

168. Select the incorrect statement.
(a) In CsCl unit cell, $r_{Cs^+} + r_{Cl^-} = \frac{\sqrt{3}}{2} l.$
(b) In NaCl unit cell, $r_{Na^+} + r_{Cl^-} = \frac{l}{2}.$
(c) In CsCl unit cell, 68% space is void.
(d) In NaCl unit cell, 26% space is void.

169. In crystal structure of sodium chloride, the arrangement of Cl^- ions is
(a) *fcc* (b) *bcc*
(c) both *fcc* and *bcc* (d) none of these

170. In sodium chloride, Cl^- ions form *ccp* arrangement. Which site will Na^+ ions occupy in this structure?
(a) cubic (b) tetragonal
(c) octahedral (d) trigonal bipyramidal

171. Which of the following does not have rock salt type structure?
(a) KBr (b) AgI (c) NH_4Cl (d) CaO

172. The number of Cl^- ions required to form *ccp* lattice of NaCl structure are
(a) 6 (b) 12 (c) 13 (d) 14

173. Each unit cell of NaCl consists of 13 Cl^- ions and
(a) 13 Na^+ (b) 14 Na^+
(c) 6 Na^+ (d) all are wrong

174. The tetrahedral voids formed by *ccp* arrangement of Cl^- ions in rock salt structure are
(a) all occupied by Na^+ ions
(b) 50% occupied by Na^+ ions
(c) occupied by either Na^+ or Cl^- ions
(d) vacant

Structure Determination by X-Ray Diffraction

175. To obtain a diffraction peak for a crystalline solid with interplanar distance equal to the wavelength of incident X-ray radiation, the angle of incidence should be
(a) 90° (b) 0° (c) 30° (d) 60°

176. The first order diffraction from a set of parallel planes of the crystal occurs at an angle of 30°. The interplanar distance (*d*) will be related to the wavelength (λ) of X-rays as
(a) $d = \frac{1}{2\lambda}$ (b) $d = 2\lambda$ (c) $d = \lambda$ (d) $d = 4\lambda$

177. The second order Bragg diffraction of X-rays with $\lambda = 1.00$ Å from a set of parallel in a metal occurs at an angle of 60°. The distance between the scattering planes in the crystal is
(a) 0.575 Å (b) 1.00 Å (c) 2.00 Å (d) 1.15 Å

178. X-rays of wavelength equal to 0.134 nm give a first order diffraction from the surface of a crystal when the value of θ is 10.5°. The distance between the planes in the crystal parallel to the surface is (sin 10.5° = 0.1822)
(a) 0.368 nm (b) 0.184 nm
(c) 0.726 nm (d) 0.92 nm

179. The wavelength of X-rays which gives a diffraction angle 2θ, equal to 16.80° for a first order diffraction for a crystal with interplanar distance 0.200 nm, is (given sin 8.4° and 0.146)
(a) 0.0584 nm (b) 0.1168 nm
(c) 0.0292 nm (d) 0.2336 nm

Calculations Involving Unit Cell Dimensions

180. CsBr crystallises in a body centred cubic lattice. The unit cell length is 436.6 pm. Given that the atomic mass of Cs = 133 and that of Br = 80 amu and Avogadro number being 6.02×10^{23} mol^{-1}, the density of CsBr is
(a) 8.25 g/cm^3 (b) 4.25 g/cm^3
(c) 42.5 g/cm^3 (d) 0.425 g/cm^3

181. A crystal of lead (II) sulfide has NaCl structure. In this crystal, the shortest distance between Pb^{2+} and S^{2-} ions is 297 pm. What is the volume of the unit cell of lead sulfide?

(a) 209.6×10^{-24} cm^3 (b) 26.2×10^{-24} cm^3
(c) 52.4×10^{-24} cm^3 (d) 104.8×10^{-24} cm^3

182. The radii of Na^+ and Cl^- ions are 95 pm and 181 pm respectively. the edge length of NaCl unit cell is

(a) 276 pm (b) 138 pm (c) 552 pm (d) 415 pm

183. The radius of K^+ is 133 pm and that of Cl^- is 181 pm. The volume of the unit cell of KCl is expressed in 10^{-22} cm^3 is

(a) 0.31 (b) 1.21 (c) 2.48 (d) 6.28

184. A metal has a *fcc* lattice. The edge length of the unit cell is 404 pm. The density of the metal is 2.72 g cm^{-3}. The molar mass of the metal is: (N_A Avogadro's constant = 6.02×10^{23} mol^{-1})

(a) 40 gmol^{-1} (b) 30 g mol^{-1}
(c) 27 g mol^{-1} (d) 20 g mol^{-1}

185. An element crystallising in body centred cubic lattice has an edge length of 500 pm. If its density is 4 g cm^{-3}, the atomic mass of the element (in g mol^{-1}) is (consider $N_A = 6 \times 10^{23}$)

(a) 100 (b) 250 (c) 125
(d) 150 (e) 50

186. The number of atoms in 100 g of an FCC crystal with density $d = 10$ g cm^{-3} and cell edge as 200 pm is equal to

(a) 3×10^{25} (b) 0.5×10^{25}
(c) 1×10^{25} (d) 2×10^{25}

187. The cubic unit cell of Al (molar mass 27 g mol^{-1}) has an edge length of 405 pm. Its density is 2.7 g cm^{-3}. The cubic unit cell is

(a) face centred (b) body centred (c) simple
(d) edge centred (e) simple

188. An element with molar mass 2.7×10^{-2} kg mol^{-1} forms a cubic unit cell with edge length 405 pm. If its density is 2.7×10^3 kg m^{-3}, the nature of its cubic unit cell is

(a) simple (b) body centred
(c) cubic closed packed (d) end face centred

189. In orthorhombic, the values of *a*, *b* and *c* are respectively 4.2 Å, 8.6 Å and 8.3 Å. Given molecular mass of the solid is 155 g mol^{-1} and density is 3.3 g/cc. The number of formula units per unit cell is

(a) 2 (b) 3 (c) 4 (d) 6

190. CsBr crystallises in a body centred cubic lattice. The unit cell length is 436.6 pm. Given that the atomic mas of Cs = 133 and that of Br = 80 amu and Avogadro number being 6.02×10^{23} mol^{-1}, the density of CsBr is

(a) 8.25 g/cm^3 (b) 4.25 g/cm^3
(c) 42.5 g/cm^3 (d) 0.425 g/cm^3

191. Copper (atomic mass = 63.5) crystallises a *fcc* lattice and has density 8.93 g cm^{-3}. The radius of copper atom is closest to

(a) 361.6 pm (b) 511.4 pm
(c) 127.8 pm (d) 102.8 pm

192. A metallic element has a cubic lattice. Each edge of the unit cell is 2 Å. The density of the metal is 2.5 g cm^{-3}. The unit cells in 200 g of metal are

(a) 1×10^{24} (b) 1×10^{20}
(c) 1×10^{22} (d) 1×10^{25}

193. Iron exhibits bcc structure at room temperature. Above 900°C, it transforms to fcc structure. The radio of the density of iron at room temperature to that 900°C (assuming molar mass and atomic radius of iron remain constant with temperature) is

(a) $\frac{\sqrt{3}}{\sqrt{2}}$ (b) $\frac{4\sqrt{3}}{3\sqrt{2}}$ (c) $\frac{3\sqrt{3}}{4\sqrt{2}}$ (d) $\frac{1}{2}$

194. Suppose the mass of a single Ag atom is '*m*' Ag metal crystallises in *fcc* lattice with unit cell length '*a*'. The density of Ag metal in terms of '*a*' and 'm' is

(a) $4m/a^3$ (b) $2m/a^3$
(c) m/a^3 (d) $m/4a^3$

195. A metal crystallises in a bcc lattice. Its unit edge length is about 300 pm and its molar mass is about 50 g mol^{-1}. What would be the density of the metal (in g cm^{-3})?

(a) 3.1 (b) 6.2 (c) 9.3 (d) 12.4

196. CsBr crystallises in a body centred cubic lattice. The unit cell length is 436.6 pm. Given that the atomic mass of Cs = 133 and that of Br = 80 amu and Avogadro number being 6.02×10^{23} mol^{-1}, the density of CsBr is

(a) 8.25 g/cm^3 (b) 4.25 g/cm^3
(c) 42.5 g/cm^3 (d) 0.425 g/cm^3

Imperfections in Solids

197. In AgBr, there can occur

(a) only Schottky defect (b) only Frenkel defect
(c) both (a) and (b) (d) none of these

198. Frenkel defect is found in crystals in which the radius ratio is

(a) low (b) 1.3
(c) 1.5 (d) slightly less than unity

199. In a solid lattice, the cation has left a lattice site and is located at an interstitial position. The lattice defect is

(a) an interstitial defect (b) a vacancy defect
(c) a Frenkel defect (d) a Schottky defect

200. In AgBr crystal, the ion size lies in the order $Ag^+ < Br^-$. The AgBr crystal should have the following characteristics
(a) defect-less (prefect) crystal
(b) Schottky defect only
(c) Frenkel defect only
(d) both Schottky and Frenkel defects

201. Which one of the following crystals does not exhibit Frenkel defects?
(a) AgBr (b) AgCl (c) KBr (d) ZnS

202. In the laboratory, sodium chloride is made by burning sodium in an atmosphere of chlorine. The salt obtained is yellow in colour, shows the
(a) presence of Na^+ ions in the crystal lattice
(b) presence of Cl^- ions in the crystal lattice
(c) presence of electrons in the crystal lattice
(d) presence of face centred cubic crystal lattice

203. The crystal with metal deficiency defect is
(a) NaCl (b) FeO (c) KCl
(d) ZnO (e) LiCl

204. Non-stoichlometric metal deficiency is shown in the salts of
(a) all metals
(b) alkali metals only
(c) alkaline earth metals only
(d) transition metals only

205. An example of a non-stoichiometric compound is
(a) Al_2O_3 (b) Fe_3O_4 (c) NiO_2 (d) PbO

206. The flame colours of metal ions are due to
(a) Frenkel defect (b) Schottky defect
(c) metal deficiency defect (d) excess defect

207. The compounds in which metal deficiency defects exist are
(a) FeS, FeO, CuO (b) FeS, FeO, KCl
(c) NaCl, ZnS, KCl (d) FeS, CuO KCl

208. With which one of the following elements should silicon be doped so as to get a *p*-type of semiconductor?
(a) germanium (b) arsenic
(c) selenium (d) boron

209. Which NaCl crystal is doped with $MgCl_2$, the nature of defect produced is
(a) interstitial defect (b) Schottky defect
(c) Frenkel defect (d) none of these

210. The addition of arsenic to germanium makes the latter a
(a) metallic conductor (b) intrinsic semiconductor
(c) mixed conductor (d) extrinsic semiconductor

211. On doping Ge metal with a little of In or Ga, one gets
(a) *p*-type semi conductor
(b) *n*-type semi conductor
(c) insulator
(d) rectifier

212. A *p*-type material is electrically
(a) positive (b) negative
(c) neutral
(d) dependent upon the concentration of *p* impurities

213. A semiconductor of Ge can be made *p* -type by adding
(a) trivalent impurity (b) tetravalent impurity
(c) pentavalent impurity (d) divalent impurity

214. 0.1 mol of $SrCl_2$ is added to 0.5 mol of NaCl. The number of cation vacancies created will be
(a) 0.1 mol (b) 0.05 mol
(c) 0.2 mol (d) 0.5 mol

215. If we mix a pentavalent impurity in a crystal lattice of germanium, what type of semiconductor formation will occur?
(a) *p*-type (b) *n*-type
(c) both (a) and (b) (d) none of the two

216. To get an *n*-type doped semiconductor, impurity to be added to silicon should have the following number of valence electrons
(a) 2 (b) 5 (c) 3 (d) 1

217. If indium is added in Ge metal we get
(a) an *n*-type semiconductor
(b) a *p*- type semiconductor
(c) a rectifier
(d) an insulator.

218. Doping silicon with boron produces a
(a) *n*-type semiconductor (b) metallic conductor
(c) *p*-type semiconductor (d) insulator

219. If NaCl is doped with 10^{-3} mol% $SrCl_2$ then the concentration of cation vacancies will be
(a) 1×10^{-3} mol% (b) 2×10^{-3} mol%
(c) 3×10^{-3} mol% (d) 4×10^{-3} mol%

220. A dipole used as a rectifier is
(a) *n*-type semiconductor
(b) *p*-type semiconductor
(c) a combination of the above two types
(d) none of the above

221. When *n*- and *p*-type semiconductor are allowed to come into contact
(a) some electrons will flow from *n* to *p*
(b) some electrons will flow from *p* to *n*

(c) the impurity element will flow from *n* to *p*
(d) the impurity element will flow from *p* to *n*

222. Mark the false statement.
(a) CsCl crystal shows Schottky defect.
(b) Crystals having F-centres are coloured and paramagnetic.
(c) Photosensitivity of AgBr is due to the presence of Frenkel defect in its crystals.
(d) None of these.

223. The defect that is likely to occur in almost all type of ionic compounds is
(a) non-stoichiometric defects
(b) Schottky defect
(c) Frenkel defect (d) all the above

224. Non-stoichiometric cuprous oxide (Cu_2O) can be prepared in the laboratory. In this oxide, copper to oxygen ratio is slightly less than 2 : 1. What type of semiconductor does it form?
(a) *n*-type (b) *p*-type
(c) *np*-type (d) any one of these

225. At zero kelvin, most of the ionic crystals possess
(a) Frenkel defect (b) Schottky defect
(c) metal excess defect (d) no defect

226. As a result of Schottky defect,
(a) there is no effect on the density
(b) density of the crystal increase
(c) density of the crystal decreases
(d) any of the above three can happen

227. Schottky defect is likely to be found in
(a) AgI (b) NaCl (c) ZnS (d) ZnO

228. Which of the following compounds shows both Frenkel and Schoottky defects?
(a) NaCl (b) AgCl (c) AgBr (d) KCl

229. Schottky defect occurs mainly in electrovalent compounds where
(a) positive ions and negative ions are of different sizes
(b) positive ions and negative ions are of the same size
(c) positive ions are small and negative ions are big
(d) positive ions are big and negative ions are small

230. Which one of the following is correct?
(a) Schottky defect lowers the density.
(b) Frenkel defect increases the dielectric constant of the crystals.
(c) Stoichiometric defects make the crystals good electrical conductors.
(d) All the three.

Electrical Properties of Solids and Superconductivity

231. An oxide of transition metal that has conductivity as well as appearance like that of copper is
(a) Ti_2O_3 (b) V_2O_3 (c) ReO_3 (d) Mn_2O_3

232. The oxide that is an insulator is
(a) VO (b) CoO (c) ReO_3 (d) Ti_2O_3

233. Superconductors are derived from compounds of
(a) *p*-block elements (b) lanthanides
(c) actinides (d) transition elements

234. Which one of the following is the best electrical conductor?
(a) $SiO_2(s)$ (b) $NaCl(s)$ (c) $Si(s)$ (d) $Br_2(l)$

235. Metals have conductivity of the order of ($ohm^{-1}m^{-1}$)
(a) $10^2 - 10^4$ (b) $10^4 - 10^7$
(c) $10^7 - 10^4$ (d) $>10^8$

236. Which substance acts as superconductor at 4 K?
(a) Hg (b) Cu (c) Na (d) Mg

237. A solid with high electrical and thermal conductivity from the following is
(a) Si (b) Li (c) NaCl (d) ICl

238. Which substance will conduct the current in the solid state?
(a) diamond (b) graphite
(c) iodine (d) sodium chloride

Magnetic Properties of Solids

239. Ferrimagnetic substances have
(a) zero magnetic moment
(b) small magnetic moment
(c) large magnetic moment
(d) any value of magnetic moment

240. Which of the following metal oxides is antiferromagnetic in nature?
(a) MnO_2 (b) TiO_2 (c) VO_2 (d) CrO_2

241. Which of the following is not ferromagnetic?
(a) cobalt (b) iron
(c) manganese (d) nickel

242. Which of the following is not an antiferromagnetic compound?
(a) V_2O_3 (b) MnO_2 (c) NiO (d) Fe_3O_4

243. Which of the following compound is metallic and ferromagnetic?
(a) CrO_2 (b) MnO_2 (c) MnO_2 (d) TiO_2

244. Which of the following is ferromagnetic?
(a) Ni (b) Co (c) Fe_3O_4 (d) all are correct

245. Which of the following shows ferrimagnetism?

(a) TiO_2 (b) CrO_2 (c) MnO (d) Fe_3O_4

246. Which one of the following arrangements shows schematic alignment of magnetic moments of antiferromagnetic substances?

(a) ↑ ↑ ↑ ↑ ↑ ↑

(b) ↓ ↓ ↓ ↓ ↓ ↓

(c) ↑ ↑ ↓ ↑ ↑ ↓

(d) ↑ ↓ ↑ ↓ ↑ ↓

Dielectric Properties of Solids

247. Crystals where dipoles may align themselves in an ordered manner so that there is a net dipole moment, exhibit

(a) pyroelectricity (b) piezoelectricity
(c) ferro-current (d) antiferro-electricity

248. Which one among the following is an example of a ferroelectric substance?

(a) quartz (b) lead chromate
(c) barium titanate (d) Rochelle salt

249. On heating some polar crystals, weak electric current is produced. It is termed as

(a) piezoelectricity (b) pyroelectricity
(c) photoelectric current (d) superconductivity

250. Which one of the following is used as a piezoelectric material?

(a) silicones (b) graphite (c) silica gel
(d) kieselghur (e) quartz

Miscellaneous

251. Malleability and ductility of metals can be accounted due to

(a) the capacity of layers of metal ions to slide over the other
(b) the interaction of electrons with metal ions in the other
(c) the presence of electrostatic force
(d) the crystalline structure in metal

252. The correct statement among the following is

(a) The ionic crystal of AgBr has Schottky defect only.
(b) The unit cell having crystal parameters, $a = b \neq c$, $\alpha = \beta = 90°$, $\gamma = 120°$ is hexagonal.
(c) In ionic compounds having Frenkel defect the ratio $\frac{r_+}{r_-}$ is high.
(d) The coordination number of Na^+ ion in NaCl is 4.

253. Which of the following is correct?

(a) Curie temperature is defined as the temperature above which no ferromagnetism is noticed.
(b) Transition temperature is defined as the temperature at which a substance starts behaving as a superconductor.
(c) Hexagonal close packing is denser than square close packing.
(d) All of these.

254. Which is the incorrect statement?

(a) $FeO_{0.98}$ has non-stoichiometric metal deficiency defect.
(b) Density decreases in the case of crystals with Schottky defects.
(c) NaCl(*s*) is insulator, silicon is semiconductor, silver is conductor, quartz is piezoelectric crystal.
(d) Frenkel defect is favoured in those ionic compounds in which the sizes of cations and anions are almost equal.

255. The liquefied metal expanding on solidification is

(a) Ga (b) Al (c) Zn (d) Cu

256. Metallic lustre is explained by

(a) diffusion of metal ions
(b) oscillation of loose electrons
(c) excitation of free protons
(d) existence of bcc lattice

Final Preparation

257. The pyknometric density of sodium chloride crystal is 2.165×10^3 kg m^{-3} while its X-ray density is 2.178×10^3 kg m^{-3}. The fraction of the unoccupied sites in sodium chloride crystal is

(a) 5.96 (b) 5.96×10^{-2}
(c) 5.96×10^{-1} (d) 5.96×10^{-3}

258. The packing efficiency of the two-dimensional square unit cell shown in the adjoining figure is

(a) 69.27% (b) 68.02%
(c) 74.05% (d) 78.54%

259. Which of the following compounds represents an inverse 2 : 3 spinel structure?

(a) $Fe^{III} [Fe^{II} Fe^{III}] O_4$ (b) PbO_2
(c) Al_2O_3 (d) Mn_3O_4

260. How many tetrahedral voids are occupied in diamond?

(a) 25% (b) 50% (c) 75% (d) 100%

261. AB crystallises in a body centred cubic lattice with edge length '*a*' equal to 387 pm. The distance between two oppositely charged ions in the lattice is

(a) 300 pm (b) 335 pm (c) 250 pm (d) 200 pm

262. Sodium metal crystalliss in a body centred cubic lattice with cell edge 4.29 Å. Length of the body diagonal will be

(a) 3.72 Å (b) 7.44 Å (c) 1.86 Å (d) 5.58 Å

263. In a face centred cubic (fcc) crystal lattice, edge length is 400 pm. The diameter of the greater sphere which can be fitted into the interstitial voids without distortion of the lattice is

(a) 117.08 pm (b) 58.54 pm
(c) 103.50 pm (d) 31.81 pm

264. How many effective Na^+ and Cl^- ions are present respectively in the rock salt (NaCl), if ions along the axis joining opposite faces are removed?

(a) $4, \frac{7}{2}$ (b) $\frac{7}{2}, \frac{7}{2}$ (c) $\frac{7}{2}, 4$ (d) 3, 3

265. The Ca^{+2} and F^- ions are located in CaF_2 crystal, respectively at face centred cubic lattice points and in

(a) tetrahedral voids (b) half of tetrahedral voids
(c) octahedral voids (d) half of octahedral voids

266. Which set of characteristics of ZnS crystal is correct?

(a) coordination number (4 : 4) ; *ccp*; Zn^{2+} ions in the alternate tetrahedral voids
(b) coordination number (6 : 6) ; *hcp*; Zn^{2+} ions in all tetrahedral voids
(c) coordination number (6 : 4); *hcp* ; Zn^{2+} ions in all octahedral voids
(d) coordination number (4 : 4); *ccp* ; Zn^{2+} ions in all tetrahedral voids

267. The ratio of Cs^+ to Cl^- is 0.90. If the radius of Cl^- ion is 1.80 Å, the false statement regarding CsCl structure is

(a) the nearest distance between the centres of two Cl^- ions is greater than 3.60 Å
(b) the nearest distance between the centres of two Cl^- ions is 3.60 Å
(c) the distance between Cs^+ ion and Cl^- ion is 3.42 Å
(d) the nearest distance between two Cs^+ ions is greater than 3.24 Å

268. KCl crystallises in the same type of lattice as does NaCl. Given that $r_{Na^+} / r_{Cl^-} = 0.55$ and $r_{K^+} / r_{Cl^-} = 0.74$. Calculate the ratio of the side of the unit cell of KCl to that of NaCl

(a) 1.123 (b) 0.891 (c) 1.414 (d) 0.414

269. Lithium iodide crystal has a face centred cubic unit cell. If the edge length of the unit cell is 620 pm, the ionic radius of I^- ion is

(a) 438.34 pm (b) 310 pm
(c) 219.17 pm (d) none of these is correct

270. For a cubic crystal, face diagonal is 3.50 Å. The face length is

(a) 1.750 Å (b) 2.475 Å (c) 2.021 Å (d) 3.50 Å

271. The limiting radius ratio of the complex $[Ni(CN)_4]^{2-}$ is

(a) 0.225–0.414 (b) 0.414–0.732
(c) 0.155–0.225 (d) none of these

272. The number of formula units in the crystals of NaCl, ZnS and MgO $\left(\frac{r_c}{r_a} = 0.5\right)$ will have the ratio

(a) 4 : 6 : 2 (b) 4 : 4 : 4
(c) 4 : 2 : 6 (d) 6 : 6 : 4

273. KCl has same structure as NaCl. If the volume of the unit cell is 247.7 cubic Angstroms, the distance between centres of K^+ and Cl^- ions is

(a) 1.24 Å (b) 2.48 Å (c) 3.14 Å (d) 6.28 Å

274. Sodium crystallies in bcc arrangement with the interfacial separation between the atoms at the edge as 53 pm. The density of the solid is

(a) 1.23 g/cc (b) 2.46 g/cc
(c) 4.92 g/cc (d) 9.87 g/cc

275. A metal crystalliises into cubic phases, face centred cubic (FCC) and body centred cubic (BCC) whose unit lengths are 3.5 and 3.0 Å respectively. The ratio of the densities of FCC and BCC is

(a) 2.0 (b) 1.5 (c) 1.75 (d) 1.25

276. AB crystallises in a rock salt structure with A : B : 1 : 1. The shortest distance between A and B is $Y^{1/3}$ nm. The formula mass of AB is 6.023 Y amu where Y is arbitrary constant. The theorctical dcnsity of the compound AB is

(a) 1.25 kg m^{-3} (b) 2.50 kg m^{-3}
(c) 5.0 kg m^{-3} (d) 7.50 kg m^{-3}

277. The edge length of the unit cell of a metal having molecular weight 75 g/mol is 5 Å which crystallises in cubic lattice. If the density is 2g/cc, the radius of the metal atom in picometer is

(a) 433.0 pm (b) 216.5 pm
(c) 108.25 pm (d) 54.125 pm

278. Element X crystallises in a 12 coordination *fcc* lattice. On applying high temperature, it changes to 8 coordination *bcc* lattice. The ratio of the density of the crystal lattice before and after applying high temperature will be

(a) 1 : 1 (b) 3 : 2
(c) $\sqrt{2} : \sqrt{3}$ (d) $2(\sqrt{2})^3 : (\sqrt{3})^3$

279. The density of KBr is 2.75 g cm^{-3}, length of the unit cell is 654 pm. (atomic mass: K = 39, Br = 80), then

what is true about the predicted nature of the solid if $r_{Br^-} = 400$ pm?
(a) solid has face centred cubic system with coordination number = 6
(b) solid has simple cubic system with coordination number = 4
(c) solid has face centred cubic system with coordination number = 1
(d) none of these

280. In an orthorhombic crystal, the value of *a*, *b* and *c* are respectively 4.2 Å, 8.6 Å and 8.3 Å. Given molecular mass of the solid is 155 g mol^{-1} and density is 3.3 g/cc. The number of formula units per unit cell is
(a) 2 (b) 3 (c) 4 (d) 6

281. The interplanar spacing between the (221) planes of a cubic lattice of wavelength 450 pm is
(a) 50 pm (b) 150 pm (c) 300 pm (d) 450 pm

282. If the angle of incidence of X-rays of wavelength 3 Å which produces a second order diffracted beam from the (100) planes in a simple cubic lattice with interlayer spacing *a* = 6 Å is 30°, the angle of incicence that produces a first order diffracted beam from the (200) planes is
(a) 15° (b) 45° (c) 30° (d) 160°

283. The density of KBr is 2.75 g cm^{-3}. The length of the unit cell is 654 pm. Atomic mass of K = 39. Br = 80. Then the solid is
(a) face centred cubic
(b) simple cubic system
(c) body centred cubic system
(d) none of these

284. Potassium has a *bcc* structure with nearest neighbour distance 4.52 Å. Its atomic weight is 39. Its density will be
(a) 454 km m^{-3} (b) 804 kg m^{-3}
(c) 852 kg m^{-3} (d) 908 kg m^{-3}

285. An element (with atomic mass = 250 g) crystallises in a simple cubic. If the density of the unit cell is 7.2 g cm^{-3}, what is the radius of the element?
(a) 1.93×10^{-6} cm (b) 1.93×10^{-8} cm
(c) 1.93×10^{-8} Å (d) 1.93×10^{-8} cm

286. The composition of a sample of wurtzite is $Fe_{0.93}O$. What percentage of iron is present in the form of Fe(III)?
(a) 5% (b) 7.08% (c) 15.05% (d) 23.6%

287. Doping of silicon with P or Al increases the conductivity. The difference in the two cases is
(a) P is a non-metal whereas Al is a metal
(b) P is a poor conductor while Al is a conductor
(c) P gives rise to extra electrons while Al gives rise to holes
(d) P gives rise to holes while Al gives rise to extra electrons

288. Which one of the following statements is wrong?
(a) The conductivity of metals decreases with increase in temperature.
(b) The conductivity of semiconductors increases with increase in temperature.
(c) There is no superconductor at room temperature.
(d) Ionic solids conduct electricity due to presence of ions.

289. The energy gas (E_g) between valence band and conduction band for diamond, silicon and germanium are in the order:
(a) E_g (diamond) > E_g (silicon) >E_g (germanium)
(b) E_g (diamond) < E_g (silicon) E_g (germanium)
(c) E_g (diamond) = E_g (germanium >E_g (silicon)
(d) E_g (diamond) > E_g (germanium) >E_g (silicon)

290. Which of the following statements is not correct?
(a) The fraction of the total volume unoccupied by the atoms in a primitive cell is 0.48..
(b) Molecular solids are generally volatile.
(c) The number of carbon atoms in a unit cell of diamond is 4.
(d) The number of Bravais lattices in which a crystal can be categorised is 14.

291. An alloy of iron (54%), nickel (45%) and manganese (1%) has a density of 8.17 g cm^{-3}. How many iron atoms are there in a block of alloy measuring 10 cm × 20 cm × 15 cm?
(a) 14.41×10^{26} (b) 14.23×10^{25}
(c) 14.69×10^{24} (d) 14.75×10^{23}

292. A sample of wurtzite contains one Fe (III) for every three Fe (II). The amount of oxygen atoms in moles is
(a) $\frac{9}{4}$ (b) $\frac{8}{9}$ (c) $\frac{4}{9}$ (d) $\frac{9}{8}$

293. Diamond is hard because
(a) all the four valence electrons are bonded to carbon atoms by covalent bonds
(b) it is a giant molecule
(c) it is made up of carbon atoms
(d) it cannot be burnt

294. A match box exhibits
(a) cubic geometry (b) monoclinic geometry
(c) tetragonal geometry (d) orthorhombic geometry

295. The total volume of atoms present in a face centred cubic unit cell of a metal is (*r* is atomic radius)

(a) $\frac{12}{3}\pi r^3$ (b) $\frac{16}{3}\pi r^3$ (c) $\frac{20}{3}\pi r^3$ (d) $\frac{24}{3}\pi r^3$

296. In a solid AB having the NaCl structure, 'A' atoms occupy the corners of the cubic unit cell. If all the face centred atoms along one of the axes are removed, then the resultant stoichiometry of the solid is

(a) AB_2 (b) A_2B (c) A_4B_3 (d) A_3B_4

297. In NaCl unit cell, all the ions lying along the axis as shown in the figure are removed. Then the number of Na^+ and Cl^- ions remaining in the unit cell are

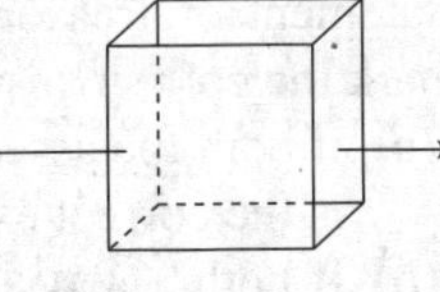

(a) 4 and 4 (b) 3 and 3
(c) 1 and 1 (d) 4 and 3

298. An alloy of copper, silver and gold is found to have copper constituting the *ccp* lattice. If silver atoms occupy the edge centres and gold is present at body centre, the alloy has a formula

(a) Cu_4Ag_2Au (b) Cu_4Ag_4Au
(c) Cu_4Ag_3Au (d) CuAgCu

299. How many unit cells are present in a cube-shaped ideal crystal of NaCl of mass 1.00 g? [Atomic masses: Na = 23, Cl = 35.5]

(a) 5.14×10^{21} (b) 1.28×10^{21}
(c) 1.71×10^{21} (d) 2.57×10^{21}

300. An ionic crystalline solid MX_2 has a cubic unit cell. Which of the following arrangement of ions is consistent with the stoichiometry of the compound?

(a) M^{2+} ions at each face-centre, 8X^- ions at the corners
(b) M^{2+} ions at the corners and at each face-centre, 8 X^- ions in the tetrahedral voids
(c) M^{2+} ions at the corners and X^- at each face-centre and 2 X^- ions on the body diagonals
(d) M^{2+} ions at the corners and at each face-centre, 4 X^- ions on the body diagonals

301. The coordinates of the corners of the shaded plane of a cubic unit cell are shown in the figure.

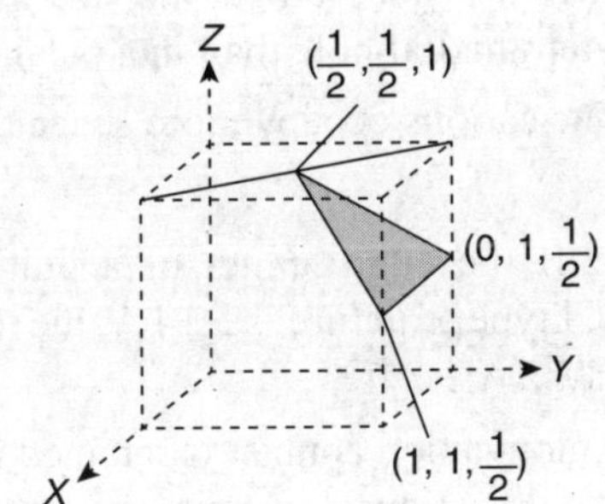

The Miller indices of the shaded plane will be

(a) (011) (b) (101) (c) (110) (d) (112)

302. Calculate the distance between 111 planes in a crystal of Ca. given that the edge length is 0.556 nm. The answer is

(a) 1.61 nm (b) 0.610 nm
(c) 0.321 nm (d) none of these

303. The number of octahedral sites per sphere in *fcc* structure is

(a) 8 (b) 4 (c) 2 (d) 1

304. Structure of a mixed oxide is cubic close-packed (ccp). The cubic unit cell of the mixed oxide is composed of oxide ions. One fourth of the tetrahedral voids are occupied by divalent metal A and the octahedral voids are occupied by a monovalent metal B. The formula of the oxide is:

(a) $A_2B_3O_4$ (b) AB_2O_2 (c) ABO_2 (d) A_2BO_2

305. The fraction of the total volume occupied by the atoms present in a simple cube is

(a) $\frac{\pi}{4}$ (b) $\frac{\pi}{6}$ (c) $\frac{\pi}{3\sqrt{2}}$ (d) $\frac{\pi}{4\sqrt{2}}$

306. If A is bivalent, B is trivalent cation, what is the formula of the oxide having spinal structure if 1/8th of tetrahedral voids and 1/2 of the octahedral voids are occupied?

(a) AB_2O_4 (b) A_2BO_4
(c) ABO_4 (d) $A_2B_2O_6$

MATCH THE FOLLOWING

307.

Column I (Cubic crystal)	Column II (Formula)
(A) Atom A at corners and B at face centres	(p) A_4B_3
(B) Atoms A at corners and face centres and atoms B at edge centres	(q) A_2B
(C) Anion (B) are arranged in ccp and cations (A) are equally distributed between tetrahedral and octahedral voids and all octahedral voids are occupied	(r) AB_3
(D) Cations (A) are arranged in fcc and anions (B) ocupy all the tetrahedral voids	(s) AB_2

308.

Column I	Column II
(A) Rock salt	(p) Anions have ccp arrangement, cations occupy alternate tetrahedral voids

Column I	Column II
(B) Zinc Blende	(q) Cations have fcc arrangement, anions occupy all tetrahedral voids
(C) Fluorite	(r) Anions have hcp arrangement, cations occupy alternate tetrahedral voids
(D) Wurtzite	(s) Anions have fcc arrangement, cations occupy all octahedral voids

(a) (A)—(r), (B)—(p), (C)—(q), (D)—(s)
(b) (A)—(s), (B)—(q), (C)—(p), (D)—(r)
(c) (A)—(s), (B)—(p), (C)—(q), (D)—(r)
(d) (A)—(p), (B)—(s), (C)—(q), (D)—(r)

309.

Column I (Compound)	Column II (Coordination No.)
(A) MgO	(p) 3
(B) B_2O_3	(q) 4
(C) MgS	(r) 6
(D) CsCl	(s) 8

(a) (A)—(p), (B)—(r), (C)—(q), (D)—(s)
(b) (A)—(r), (B)—(p), (C)—(q), (D)—(s)
(c) (A)—(r), (B)—(p), (C)—(s), (D)—(q)
(d) (A)—(r), (B)—(q), (C)—(p), (D)—(s)

310.

Column I	Column II
(A) Dry ice	(p) Ionic solid
(B) Silica	(q) Molecular solid
(C) Brass	(r) Network solid
(D) Wurtzite	(s) Metallic solid

(a) (A)—(q), (B)—(r), (C)—(s), (D)—(p)
(b) (A)—(p), (B)—(q), (C)—(s), (D)—(r)
(c) (A)—(r), (B)—(q), (C)—(s), (D)—(p)
(d) (A)—(p), (B)—(q), (C)—(r), (D)—(s)

311.

Column I (Axial Parameters)	Column II (Crystal System)
(A) $a = b = c$, $\alpha = \beta = \gamma \neq 90°$	(p) Orthorhombic
(B) $a \neq b \neq c$, $\alpha = \gamma = 90° \neq \beta$	(q) Triclinic
(C) $a \neq b \neq c$, $\alpha \neq \beta \neq \gamma \neq 90°$	(r) Monoclinic
(D) $a \neq b \neq c$, $\alpha = \beta = \gamma = 90°$	(s) Rhombohedral

(a) (A)—(p), (B)—(q), C—(r), D—(s)
(b) (A)—(s), (B)—(r), C—(q), D—(p)
(c) (A)—(r), (B)—(s), C—(q), D—(p)
(d) (A)—(s), (B)—(r), C—(p), D—(q)

ASSERTION REASON

Directions: In each of the following questions, a statement of Assertion (A) is given followed by a corresponding statement of Reason (R) just below it. Of the statements, mark the correct answer as

(a) if both the assertion and reason are true and the reason is the correct explanation of the assertion.
(b) if both assertion and reason are true but reason is not the correct explanation of assertion
(c) If assertion is true but reason is false
(d) If both assertion and reason are false

312. Assertion: Amorphous solids are isotropic.

Reason: Properties like refractive index and electrical conductance have different values in different directions for isotropic substances.

313. Assertion: Graphite is an example of a tetragonal crystal system.

Reason: For a tetragonal system, $a = b \neq c$, $\alpha = \beta = 90°$, $\gamma = 120°$.

314. Assertion: The number of tetrahedral voids is double the number of octahedral voids.

Reason: The size of the tetrahedral void is half of that of the octahedral void.

315. Assertion: In close packing of spheres, a tetrahedral void is surrounded by four spheres whereas an octahedral void is surrounded by six spheres.

Reason: A tetrahedral void has a tetrahedral shape whereas an octahedral void as an octahedral shape.

316. Assertion: Hexagonal close packing is more closely packed than cubic close packing.

Reason: Hexagonal close packing has a coordination number of 12 whereas cubic close packing has a coordination number of 8.

317. Assertion: In a crystal lattice, the size of the cation is larger in a tetrahedral hole than in a octahedral hole.

Reason: The cations occupy more space than in crystal packing.

318. Assertion: If the edge length of a unit cell of LiCl having NaCl type structure is 5.14 Å, the ionic radius of Cl^- ion is 1.82 Å.

Reason: Anion–anion contact is retained in LiCl structure because the anions constitute the lattice.

319. Assertion: In the NaCl crystal, each Na^+ ion is touching 6 Cl^- ions but these Cl^- ions do not touch each other.

Reason: The radius ratio $r_{Na^+} / r_{Cl} = 0.414$ is required for exact fitting.

320. Assertion: Zinc blende and wurtzite both have fcc arrangement of sulfide ions.

Reason: There are four formula units of ZnS in both.

321. Assertion: In any ionic solid (MX) with Schottky defects, the number of positive and negative ions is the same.

Reason: Equal number of cation and anion vacancies are present.

322. Assertion: No compound has both Schottky and Frenkel defects.

Reason: Both defects change the density of the solid.

323. Assertion: The presence of a large number of Schottky defects in NaCl lowers its density.

Reason: In NaCl, there are approximately 10^6 Schottky pairs per cm^3 at room temperature.

324. Assertion: Anion vacancies in alkali metals halides are produced by heating the alkali metal halides with alkali metal vapour.

Reason: Electrons trapped in anion vacancies are referred to as F-centres.

325. Assertion: When 1.0 mol of NaCl is doped with 10^{-3} mol $SrCl_2$, the number of cationic sites remaining vacant is 10^{-3}.

Reason: Each $SrCl_2$ unit produces two cation vacancies.

326. Assertion: The resistance of metals is zero at absolute zero.

Reason: The resistance of metals decreases with decrease in temperature.

327. Assertion: Anti-ferromagnetic substances can be made paramagnetic by heating.

Reason: On heating, some of the electrons change their direction of spin.

328. Assertion: Semiconductors are solids with conductivities in the intermediate range from $10^{-6} - 10^{4}\,ohm^{-1}cm^{-1}$

Reason: Intermediate conductivity in semiconductors is due to the partially filled valence band.

329. Assertion: Conductivity of silicon increases by doping it with group 15 elements.

Reason: Doping means introduction of small amount of impurities like, P, As or Bi into the pure crystal.

330. Assertion: Ferromagnetic property decreases as Fe > Co > Ni.

Reason: The number of unpaired electrons decreases as Fe > Co > Ni.

331. Assertion: There is no substance which is a perfect insulator.

Reason: The conductivity of insulators is equal to zero.

332. Assertion: Lead zirconate is a piezoelectric crystal.

Reason: Lead zirconate crystals have zero dipole moment.

333. Assertion: Crystalline solids are anisotropic.

Reason: The constituent particles are very closely packed.

334. Assertion: Amorphous solids are isotropic.

Reason: Amorphous solids do not possess rigidity.

335. Assertion: Molecular solids are characterised by low melting points.

Reason: Molecular solids are made up of covalent molecules.

336. Assertion: Diamond and graphite do not have the same crystal structure.

Reason: Diamond is crystalline while graphite is amorphous.

337. Assertion: Crystalline solids have short range order.

Reason: Amorphous solids have long range order.

Answer Key

1. (b)	2. (b)	3. (c)	4. (d)	5. (d)	6. (d)	7. (b)	8. (d)	9. (c)	10. (b)
11. (a)	12. (c)	13. (d)	14. (d)	15. (d)	16. (b)	17. (a)	18. (c)	19. (c)	20. (b)
21. (d)	22. (d)	23. (c)	24. (a)	25. (b)	26. (c)	27. (a)	28. (b)	29. (c)	30. (d)
31. (c)	32. (a)	33. (a)	34. (a)	35. (c)	36. (b)	37. (b)	38. (d)	39. (b)	40. (c)
41. (c)	42. (c)	43. (a)	44. (c)	45. (b)	46. (b)	47. (b)	48. (c)	49. (c)	50. (c)
51. (b)	52. (a)	53. (a)	54. (c)	55. (b)	56. (b)	57. (b)	58. (a)	59. (b)	60. (c)
61. (d)	62. (c)	63. (c)	64. (b)	65. (c)	66. (c)	67. (a)	68. (c)	69. (c)	70. (c)
71. (b)	72. (b)	73. (c)	74. (a)	75. (a)	76. (d)	77. (c)	78. (b)	79. (c)	80. (c)
81. (c)	82. (b)	83. (c)	84. (b)	85. (c)	86. (c)	87. (c)	88. (a)	89. (c)	90. (c)
91. (d)	92. (b)	93. (d)	94. (b)	95. (c)	96. (b)	97. (a)	98. (b)	99. (d)	100. (b)

101. (d)	102. (c)	103. (c)	104. (c)	105. (b)	106. (a)	107. (b)	108. (d)	109. (c)	110. (a)
111. (a)	112. (d)	113. (d)	114. (b)	115. (b)	116. (b)	117. (d)	118. (d)	119. (b)	120. (b)
121. (c)	122. (b)	123. (d)	124. (d)	125. (c)	126. (d)	127. (a)	128. (b)	129. (b)	130. (a)
131. (c)	132. (d)	133. (a)	134. (a)	135. (c)	136. (b)	137. (c)	138. (c)	139. (b)	140. (b)
141. (b)	142. (c)	143. (c)	144. (d)	145. (d)	146. (d)	147. (d)	148. (c)	149. (c)	150. (b)
151. (d)	152. (b)	153. (b)	154. (a)	155. (c)	156. (c)	157. (d)	158. (b)	159. (b)	160. (d)
161. (c)	162. (d)	163. (b)	164. (b)	165. (d)	166. (a)	167. (b)	168. (c)	169. (a)	170. (c)
171. (b)	172. (d)	173. (b)	174. (d)	175. (c)	176. (c)	177. (d)	178. (a)	179. (a)	180. (b)
181. (a)	182. (c)	183. (c)	184. (c)	185. (d)	186. (b)	187. (a)	188. (c)	189. (c)	190. (b)
191. (c)	192. (d)	193. (d)	194. (a)	195. (b)	196. (b)	197. (c)	198. (a)	199. (c)	200. (d)
201. (c)	202. (c)	203. (b)	204. (d)	205. (b)	206. (d)	207. (a)	208. (d)	209. (d)	210. (d)
211. (a)	212. (c)	213. (a)	214. (a)	215. (b)	216. (b)	217. (b)	218. (c)	219. (a)	220. (c)
221. (a)	222. (d)	223. (b)	224. (b)	225. (d)	226. (c)	227. (b)	228. (c)	229. (b)	230. (d)
231. (c)	232. (b)	233. (b)	234. (b)	235. (b)	236. (a)	237. (b)	238. (b)	239. (b)	240. (a)
241. (c)	242. (d)	243. (a)	244. (d)	245. (d)	246. (d)	247. (b)	248. (c)	249. (b)	250. (e)
251. (a)	252. (b)	253. (d)	254. (a,d)	255. (a)	256. (b)	257. (d)	258. (d)	259. (a)	260. (b)
261. (b)	262. (b)	263. (a)	264. (d)	265. (a)	266. (a)	267. (b)	268. (a)	269. (c)	270. (b)
271. (a)	272. (b)	273. (c)	274. (a)	275. (d)	276. (c)	277. (b)	278. (d)	279. (a)	280. (c)
281. (b)	282. (c)	283. (a)	284. (d)	285. (b)	286. (c)	287. (c)	288. (d)	289. (b)	290. (c)
291. (b)	292. (d)	293. (a)	294. (d)	295. (b)	296. (c)	297. (c)	298. (d)	299. (d)	300. (b)
301. (a)	302. (c)	303. (d)	304. (b)	305. (b)	306. (a)	307. (d)	308. (c)	309. (b)	310. (a)
311. (b)	312. (c)	313. (d)	314. (c)	315. (c)	316. (d)	317. (d)	318. (a)	319. (a)	320. (d)
321. (a)	322. (d)	323. (b)	324. (b)	325. (d)	326. (a)	327. (a)	328. (c)	329. (b)	330. (a)
331. (a)	332. (c)	333. (b)	334. (c)	335. (b)	336. (c)	337. (d)			

Hints and Solutions

OBJECTIVE QUESTIONS

General Characteristics of Solid State

1. **(b):** A substance exists as a solid when intermolecular forces are stronger than thermal energy.

2. **(b):** Minimum potential energy (PE) leads to maximum stability.

3. **(c):** Particles of a solid have vibratory motion only.

Amorphous and Crystalline Solids

4. **(d):** Crystals show good cleavage because their constituent particles are arranged in planes.

5. **(d):** Polyvinyl chloride is a polymer and an amorphous solid.

6. **(d):** Amorphous solids have short range order but no sharp MP.

7. **(b):** $BaCl_2$ is a crystalline solid and will show anisotropy.

8. **(d):** Glass and pitch are pseudo solids.

9. **(c):** Silica is amorphous. All other given substances are crystalline.

10. **(b):** Glass is an amorphous solid and hence does not have a sharp melting point.

11. **(a):** Quartz is a crystalline form of silica. It is a covalent crystal having a three dimensional network of SiO_4 tetrahedra.

12. **(c):** A crystalline solid undergoes deformation of its geometry by application of pressure or heat.

13. **(d):** All the given statements are correct about glass.

14. **(d):** Amorphous solids have same refractive index in all directions.

Classification of Crystalline Solids

15. **(d):** Graphite belongs to the hexagonal system.

16. **(b):** Covalent network solids (like SiO_2 or SiC or diamond) are very hard, electrical insulators in the solid as well as molten state and metal at extremely high temperatures.

17. **(a):** Graphite is a covalent network solid and not a molecular solid.

18. **(c):** Wax is a molecular crystal.

19. **(c):** Iodine crystals are molecular.

20. **(b):** Molecular crystalline solids are volatile.

21. **(d):** Molecular crystals are soft and have low MPs.

22. **(d):** Molecular solids have low MPs and are poor conductors of heat and electricity.

23. **(c):** The major binding force in diamond, silicon and quartz is covalent bond force.

24. **(a):** Silicon carbide is a covalent solid.

25. **(b):** Ionic solids have the highest melting point.

26. **(c):** Metallic solids conduct both heat and electricity.

27. **(a):** Silicon is a covalent crystalline solid.

28. (b): In graphite, the electrons are spread out between the sheets.

29. (c): SiC is the hardest substance out of the given substances.

30. (d): The given characteristics are for an ionic solid.

31. (c): Dry ice consists of H_2O molecules linked through hydrogen bonds. Hence, dry ice is a molecular crystal.

Crystal Lattices and Unit Cells

32. (a): Diamond belongs to the cubic system.

33. (a): For a rhombohedral system $a = b = c$, $\alpha = \beta = \gamma \neq 90°$.

34. (a): Copper belongs to the cubic system.

35. (c): TeO_2 belongs to the tetragonal system.

36. (b): Here $a \neq b \neq c$, $\alpha = \beta = \gamma = 90°$. It belongs to the orthorhombic system.

37. (b): Cubic a system is the most symmetrical ($a = b = c$, $\alpha = \beta = \gamma = 90°$).
Triclinic system is the least symmetrical ($a \neq b \neq c$, $\alpha \neq \beta \neq \gamma = 90°$).

38. (d): $a \neq b \neq c$, $\alpha \neq \beta \neq \gamma \neq 90°$ represents the triclinic system.

39. (b): $a = b \neq c$, $\alpha = \beta = 90°$, $\gamma = 120°$ means hexagonal system.

40. (c): $a = b \neq c$ and $\alpha = \beta = \gamma = 90°$ is for a tetragonal system.

41. (c): For a monocline unit cell, $a \neq b \neq c$, $\alpha = \gamma = 90° = 90° \neq \beta$.

Number of Atoms in a Unit Cell

42. (c): $FCC = 8 \times \frac{1}{8} + 6 \times \frac{1}{2} = 4$

$BCC = 8 \times \frac{1}{8} + 1 = 2$

43. (a): In a primitive cubic unit cell, each atom has 6 nearest neighbours (8 primitive unit cells are shown in the figure and arrows drawn to show the directions of nearest neighbours).

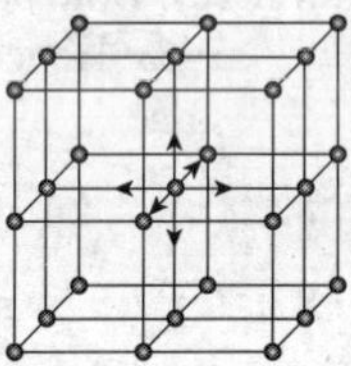

44. (c): $BCC = 8 \times \frac{1}{8} + 1 = 2$

$HCP = CCP = 8 \times \frac{1}{8} = 1$

$FCC = 8 \times \frac{1}{8} + 6 \times \frac{1}{2} = 4$

Hence, FCC has the maximum number of atoms per unit cell.

45. (b): There are four body diagonals. Atoms on the body diagonals are not shared by any other unit cell. Contribution by atoms on corners $= 8 \times \frac{1}{8} = 1$ and contribution by atoms on the body diagonal $= 2 \times 4 = 8$.

46. (b): One unit cell of *bcc* has atoms = 2. Hence, 12.08×10^{23} unit cells will have atoms $= 2 \times 10^{23} = 24.16 \times 10^{23}$.

47. (b): 1 mole of gold = 7 g = 6.02×10^{23} atoms

$\therefore$ 1 g gold $= \frac{6.02 \times 10^{23}}{197}$ atoms

As *fcc* contains 4 atoms per unit cell, therefore, number of unit cells $= \frac{6.02 \times 10^{23}}{197 \times 4} = 7.64 \times 10^{20}$

48. (c): 40 g of X contain 1 mole, that is, Avogardo's no. (N_A) of atoms

$\therefore$ 4 g of X will contain atoms $= \frac{N_A}{40} \times 4 = 0.1\, N_A$

No. of atoms in unit cell of *bcc* pattern = 2

$\therefore$ No. of unit cells is 4 g of X $= \frac{0.1\, N_A}{2}$

49. (c): Atoms A per unit cell $= 8 \times \frac{1}{8} = 1$

Atoms B per unit cell = 1

Atoms C per unit cell $= 12 \times \frac{1}{4} = 3$

Ratio A : B : C = 1 : 1 : 3.
Hence, the formula is ABC_3.

50. (c): Atoms A per unit cell

$= 8 \times \frac{1}{8} + 6 \times \frac{1}{2} = 1 + 3 = 4$

(corners) (face centres)

Atoms B per unit cell

$= 12 \times \frac{1}{4} + 1 = 3 + 1 = 4$

(edge centres) (body centre)

$\therefore$ Ratio A : B = 4 : 4.
Hence, the formula is AB.

51. (b): No. of M atoms

$= 4 \times \frac{1}{4} + 1 = 2$

(edge centres) (body-centre)

No. of X atoms $= 8 \times \frac{1}{8} + 6 \times \frac{1}{2} = 4$

(corners) (face-centres)

$\therefore$ Unit formula $= M_2X_4$ and empirical formula $= MX_2$.

52. (a): No. of atoms A per unit cell $= 8 \times \frac{1}{8} = 1$

No. of atoms B per unit cell $= 6 \times \frac{1}{2} = 3$

Hence, the composition is AB_3.

53. (a): Atoms Q present per unit cell $= 8 \times \frac{1}{8} = 1$ (from corners)

Atoms P present per unit cell = 1 (from body centre)
Ratio of P : Q = 1 : 1. Hence, formula = PQ.
P has 8 nearest neighbours and vice-versa. Hence, coordination number of each = 8.

54. (c): If one atom (A) is missing from one corner, no. of atoms A/unit cell $= 7 \times \frac{1}{8} = \frac{7}{8}$. No. of atoms B (Present at the face centres) $= 6 \times \frac{1}{2} = 3$. Thus, A : B $= \frac{7}{8} : 3$. Hence, the simplest formula is A_7B_{24}.

55. **(b):** The total number of atoms in the unit cell of FCC = 4

Volume of one atom $= \frac{4}{3}\pi r^3$

$\therefore$ Total volume of atoms in the unit cell

$= 4 \times \frac{4}{3}\pi r^3 = \frac{16}{3}\pi r^3$

56. **(b):** Cl^- ions are present at the corners and face centres and Na^+ ions at edge centres and one at body centre. The given axis is passing through two face centres and one body centre.

$\therefore$ No. of Na^+ ions $= 12 \times \frac{1}{4}$ (only from edge centres) = 3

No. of Cl^- ions $= 8 \times \frac{1}{8} + 4 \times \frac{1}{2} = 1 + 2 = 3$
(corners) (face centres)

57. **(b):** The number of atoms in a unit cell are: simple cubic lattice = 1, body centred = 2 face centred = 4.

58. **(a):** In a face centred cubic or tetragonal, number of lattice points unit cell

$= 8 \times \frac{1}{8} + 6 \times \frac{1}{2} = 1 + 3 = 4$
(corners) (face centres)

In a body centred cubic, number of lattice points per unit cell

$= 8 \times \frac{1}{8} + 1 = 1 + 1 = 2$
(corners) (body-centre)

59. **(b):** An atom on the edge is shared by 4 unit cells. Hence, its contribution to the cell $= \frac{1}{4}$

60. **(c):** The no. of atoms per unit cell is 2 for bcc.

Elements of Symmetry and Laws of Crystallography

61. **(d):** Triclinic system is the most unsymmetrical. Hence, it has no rotation of symmetry.

62. **(c):** The property of a substance to assume two or more crystalline structures is called polymorphism.

63. **(c):** The perpendicular distance of a plane (*hkl*) from the origin or distance of separation of parallel adjacent planes of a cubic crystal is given by $d = \frac{a}{\sqrt{h^2 + k^2 + l^2}}$.

64. **(b):** $d = \frac{a}{\sqrt{h^2 + k^2 + l^2}} = \frac{450}{\sqrt{2^2 + 2^2 + 1^2}} = \frac{450}{\sqrt{9}} = 150$ pm

65. **(c):** Reciprocals of coefficients $= \frac{1}{2}, \frac{1}{3}, \frac{1}{\infty} = \frac{1}{2}, \frac{1}{3}, 0$

Multiplying with LCM, that is 6, we get (320).

66. **(c):** Compounds having identical crystal structure and analogous chemical formula are called isomorphous.

Close Packed Structures

67. **(a):** If there are 100 atoms in the packing, octahedral voids = 100 and tetrahedral voids = 200.

68. **(c):** *ccp* (*fcc*) has 8 tetrahedral voids.

69. **(c):** Number of atoms in close packing

$= 0.5 \times 6.022 \times 10^{23} = 3.11 \times 10^{23}$

No. of octahedral voids = No. of atoms in packing

$= 3.11 \times 10^{23}$

No. of tetrahedral voids = 2 × No. of atoms in the packing

$= 2 \times 3.11 \times 10^{23} = 6.22 \times 10^{23}$

Total no. of voids $= (3.11 \times 10^{23}) + (6.022 \times 10^{23})$

$= 9.033 \times 10^{23}$

70. **(c):** Radius of tetrahedral voids = 0.225 R

Radius of octahedral voids = 0.414 R

$\therefore$ Octahedral void is larger than tetrahedral void.

71. **(b):** No. of tetrahedral voids = 2 × No. of atoms in the packing, that is, 2 per atom.

72. **(b):** If number of atoms in cubic close packing = *n*, the number of tetrahedral voids = 2*n*. Hence, ratio of number of atoms to tetrahedral holes = 1 : 2.

73. **(c):** Sizes of voids are: octahedral > tetrahedral > trigonal.

74. **(a):** As crystallises in *ccp* structure.

75. **(a):** All noble gases crystallise in the *ccp* structure except He which has *hcp* structure.

76. **(d):** Sodium is body centred cubic.

77. **(c):** Zinc = *hcp*, sodium = *bcc*, copper = *ccp* (*fcc*), CsCl = *bcc*.

78. **(b):** Potassium crystallises in a body centred cubic packing.

79. **(c):** Silicon is found in nature in the form of a network solid due to its property of catenation (self-linking of atoms).

80. **(c):** ABAB... is hexagonal close packing.

81. **(c):** Both *hcp* and *ccp* are equally efficient in packing, that is, 74%. Hence, for the same type of atoms, the density will be same.

82. **(b):** A known fact.

83. **(c):** *bcc* is not as closely packed as *hcp* and *ccp*.

84. **(b):** *fcc* = *ccp* and space occupied is 74%, that is, maximum.

85. **(c):** ABC ABC ... represents cubic close packing in which the space occupied by atoms = 74% = 0.74. Void space = 1 – 0.74 = 0.26.

86. **(c):** *fcc* = *ccp* has a coordination number = 12.

87. **(c):** *bcc* arrangement has a coordination number of 8.

88. **(a):** In *hcp*, for two layers only, the coordination number of each sphere will be 9 (6 in its own layer and 3 from the second layer).

89. **(c):** HCP has 12 nearest neighbours.

90. **(c):** Suppose no. of B^- ions constituting the lattice = 100

$\therefore$ No. of tetrahedral sites = 200

As 25% are occupied by A^+ ions, their number = 50

$\therefore$ Ratio of $A^+ : B^- = 50 : 100 = 1 : 2$, that is, the formula is AB_2.

91. **(d):** Suppose number of atoms B in the *hcp* lattice = *n*

As tetrahedral voids is double the number of atoms in the close packing, the number of tetrahedral voids = $2n$.
As atoms A occupy 2/3rd of the tetrahedral voids, the number of atoms A in the lattice $= \frac{2}{3} \times 2n = \frac{4n}{n}$

$\therefore$ Ratio of A : B $= \frac{4n}{3} : n = \frac{4}{3} : 1 = 4:3$

Hence, formula of the compound $= A_4B_3$

92. (b): Suppose no. of oxide ions (O^{2-}) in the packing = n
$\therefore$ No. of octahedral voids = n
As 2/3rd of the octahedral voids are occupied by ferric ions, the number of ferric ions (Fe^{3+}) present $= \frac{2}{3} \times n = \frac{2n}{3}$.

$\therefore$ Ratio of $Fe^{3+} : O^{2-} = \frac{2n}{3} : n = \frac{2}{3} : 1 = 2:3$

Hence, the formula of ferric oxide = Fe_2O_3.

93. (d): As Cu atoms are present at the corners, Cu atoms/unit cell $= 8 \times \frac{1}{8} = 1$

As Ag atoms occupy face centres, Ag atoms/unit cell $= 6 \times \frac{1}{2} = 3$

As Au atom is present at the body centre, Au atom/unit cell = 1
Hence, the formula is $CuAg_3Au$.

94. (b): Suppose atoms Y in the close packing = n
Then number of octahedral voids = n
As half of the octahedral voids are occupied by M, the number of atoms M present $= \frac{n}{2}$

$M : Y = \frac{n}{2} : n = \frac{1}{2} : 1 = 1:20$

Hence, the formula is MY_2.

95. (c): $ccp = fcc$. For fcc

$a = 2\sqrt{2}r = 2 \times 4.414 \times 125 \text{ pm} = 3.54 \text{ pm}$

Volume of the unit cell $= a^3 = (3.54 \times 10^{-10} \text{cm})^3$
$= 4.44 \times 10^{-23} \text{cm}^3$

$\therefore$ Unit cells in 1 cm^3 $= \frac{1}{4.44 \times 10^{-23}} = 2.25 \times 10^{22}$

96. (b): For bcc, $r = \frac{\sqrt{3}}{4}a$

or $a = \frac{4r}{\sqrt{3}} = \frac{4 \times 75}{1.732} = 173.2 \text{ pm}$

97. (a): For BCC, $r = \frac{\sqrt{3}}{4}a = 0.433a$
$= 0.433 \times 351 \text{ pm} = 151.98 \text{ pm}$

98. (b): In fcc structure, $r = \frac{a}{2\sqrt{2}}$

or $a = 2\sqrt{2}r = 2\sqrt{2}\,r \times \frac{\sqrt{2}}{\sqrt{2}} = \frac{4}{\sqrt{2}}r$

99. (d): For FCC, $r = \frac{1}{2\sqrt{2}} = 0.3535\,a$
$= 0.3535 \times 361 \text{ pm} = 127.6 \simeq 128 \text{ pm}.$

100. (b): For face centred cubic lattice, $r = \frac{a}{2\sqrt{2}} = 0.3535\,a$

or $a = \frac{r}{0.3535} = \frac{300}{0.3535} \text{ pm} = 848.6 \text{ pm}$

101. (d): For body centred cubic lattice, the radius of the atom is

$f = \frac{\sqrt{3}}{4}a = \frac{1.732 \times 4.29}{4} = 1.86 \text{ Å}$

102. (c): As silicon and diamond have fcc structure, in each case, the nearest neighbour distance, that is, the interatomic separation (d)

$= \frac{a}{\sqrt{2}} = \frac{0.542}{\sqrt{2}} = 0.383 \text{ nm}$

103. (c): For fcc lattice, $r = \frac{a}{2\sqrt{2}} = 0.3535\,a$
$= 0.3535 \times 408 \text{ pm} = 144 \text{ pm}$
$\therefore$ Diameter of metal atom $= 2\,r = 288$ pm.

104. (c): As CsCl is body centred, $d = \sqrt{3}a/2$

105. (b): For body centred cubic lattice,

$d = \frac{\sqrt{3}}{2}a = \frac{\sqrt{3}}{2} \times 387 \text{ pm} = 335 \text{ pm}$

106. (a): For bcc, $d = \frac{\sqrt{3}}{2}a$

or $a = \frac{2d}{\sqrt{3}} = \frac{2 \times 173}{1.732} = 200 \text{ pm}$

107. (b): No. of tetrahedral = 2 × No. of atoms in the packing = 2 × Z = 2Z

108. (d): According to the formula XY_3, if there are 3 Y atoms, there is one X atom. But if there are 3 Y atoms, in the packing there will be 3 octahedral voids and 6 tetrahedral voids. If X is in the octahedral void, voids occupied $= \frac{1}{3} = 33.3\%$

If X were in the tetrahedral void, voids occupied $= \frac{1}{6} = 16.25\%$

Hence, (d) is the correct option.

Packing Efficiency

109. (c): The space filled in one layer of hcp is 60.4% (by geometry).

110. (a): Packing efficiencies: fcc = 74%, bcc = 68%, pc = 52.4%
Hence, order is $fcc > bcc > pc$

111. (a): Void spaces are: simple cubic = 100 – 52 = 48%, body centred cubic = 100 – 68 = 32%, hexagonal close packing = 100 – 74 = 26%.

112. (d): Free space in ccp is 26% and that of bcc is 32 %

113. (d): fcc (= ccp) has maximum space occupied and hence the largest packing fraction.

114. (b): ABABAB... is hexagonal close packing (hcp) in which the space occupied s 74%. Hence, empty space = 26%

115. (b): Packing efficiency of bcc lattice = 68%
$\therefore$ Vacant space in bcc lattice = 100 – 68 = 32%

Structures of Simple Ionic Compounds

116. (b): As NaCl has *fcc* lattice, each Na^+ ion is surrounding by 6 Cl^- ions.

117. (d): Na^+ ions in NaCl are present at the edge centres and body centre.

118. (d): All halides of alkali metals do not have rock salt type structure.

119. (b): The structure of NaCl is octahedral (coordination number = 6).

120. (b): As the coordination number of $Na^+ = 6$, the coordination number of $Mg^{2+} = 6$.

121. (c): 12 Octahedral voids are present at the 12 edge centres and one at the body centre.

122. (b): In the NaCl crystal, each ion is surrounded by 6 oppositely charged ions at equal distance.

123. (d): One unit cell of NaCl has 4 Na^+ ions and 4 Cl^- ions. Hence, the total number of ions = 8.

124. (d): In *bcc* lattice, Cs^+ ion and Cl^- ions touch each other along the body diagonal.

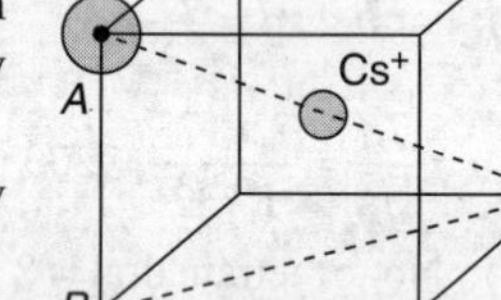

$2r_{Cs^+} + 2r_{Cs^-}$ = AD (body diagonal)

In right angled ΔBCD

$BD = \sqrt{BC^2 + CD^2} = \sqrt{a^2 + a^2} = \sqrt{2}a$

In right angled ΔABD,

$AD = \sqrt{AB^2 + BD^2} = \sqrt{a^2 + 2a^2} = \sqrt{3}a$

Thus, $2r_{Cs^+} + 2r_{Cs^-} = \sqrt{3}a$

or $r_{Cs^+} + r_{Cs^-} = \frac{\sqrt{3}}{2}a$

125. (c): The coordination number of Cs^+ and Cl^- ions in CsCl is 8 : 8.

126. (d): CuCl, CuBr, AgI all have zinc blende structure.

127. (a): In ZnS, the coordination number of Zn^{2+} and S^{2-} ions is 4 : 4.

128. (b): ZnS has coordination of 4 : 4. Hence, the coordination number of Cu in CuCl will be 4.

129. (b): AgI contains an equal number of Ag^+ and I^- ions. If the number of I^- ions in the packing is *n*, then the number of tetrahedral voids = 2*n*. But only *n* voids will be occupied by nAg^+ ions. Hence, the fraction of tetrahedral voids occupied = 50%.

130. (a): In CaF_2 crystal, Ca^{2+} ions are present at all corners and at the centre of each face of the cube and F^- ions occupy all the tetrahedral voids.

131. (c): Antiflourite structure is derived from fluorite structure by interchanging the positions of positive and negative ions.

132. (d): In CaF_2, F^- ions are double the number of Ca^{2+} ions. Hence, F^- ions in the unit cell = 8.

133. (a): Space lattice of CaF_2 is face centred cubic.

134. (a): In Na_2O having antifluorite structure, the O^{2-} ions have a cubic close packed (*fcc*) arrangement; O^{2-} ions per unit cell = 4. Hence, Na^+ ion per unit cell = 8. As the number of tetrahedral voids is 8, the Na^+ ions occupy all the eight tetrahedral voids.

135. (c): In CaF_2, having fluorite structure, the coordination of $Ca^{2+} = 8$ and that of $F^- = 4$.

136. (b): Radius of tetrahedral hole = $0.225 \times R = 0.225 \times 1.84$ Å = 0.414 Å.

137. (c): In ZnS, S^{2-} ions are in *ccp* and Zn^{2+} ions are in alternate tetrahedral voids. Hence, in XY, X^+ are in tetrahedral voids and Y^- ions are in *ccp*.

Radius of tetrahedral void = 0.225 of radius Y^- in the packing.

$\therefore$ Ideal radius of $Y^- = \frac{22.5}{0.225} = 100$ pm

138. (c): For tetrahedral structure arrangement, radius ratio (r_+/r_-) lies in the range 0.225–0.414. For exact fitting, radius of tetrahedral void = 0.225 × Radius of spheres in the packing.

139. (b): For tetrahedral arrangement, radius, ratio (r_+/r_-) lies in the range 0.414–0.732, Hence, for exact fitting, radius of octahedral void = 0.414 × Radius of sphere in the packing = $0.414 \times r$

140. (b): $r_{Na^+}/r_{Cl^-} = 95/181 = 0.52$ which lies in the range = 0.414–0.732. Hence, the coordination number of $Na^+ = 6$.

141. (b): As the radius ratio lies in the range 0.225–0.414, coordination number = 4. The arrangement is tetrahedral.

142. (c): At the limiting value of r_+/r_-, the forces of attraction and repulsion are equal.

143. (c): As r_+/r_- lies in the range 0.732–1.000, the coordination number = 8, that is, it is of CsCl type.

144. (d): Na^+ ions occupy octahedral voids $r_+/r_- = 0.414–0.732$ Actural $r_+/r_- = 0.52$.

145. (d): For an octahedral arrangement (coordination no. = 6), the radius ratio is in the range 0.414–0.732.

146. (d): For a tetrahedral structure, the coordination number is 4, $r_+/r_- = 0.225$ to 0.414.

147. (d): As the radius ratio lies in the range 0.225–0.414, the coordination number is 4 and the structure is tetrahedral.

148. (c): Radius ratio $(r_+/r_-) = 104/200 = 0.52$ which lies in the range 0.414–0.732. Hence, the coordination number is 6 and the structure is octahedral.

149. (c): r_+/r_- lies in the range 0.414–0.732.

150. (b): $r_+/r_- = 180/187 = 0.963$ which lies in the range 0.732–1.0. Hence, it has a body centred cubic structure, that is, CsCl type.

151. (d): Radius ratio, r_+ / r_- helps to know the geometrical shape of the crystal (0.155–0.225 = planar triangular, 0.225–0.414 = tetrahedral).

152. (b): Radius ratio, $\frac{r_+}{r_-} = \frac{0.98\times10^{-10}}{1.81\times10^{-10}} = 0.541$

It lies in the range 0.414–0.732. Hence, the coordination number of each ion will be 6, as in the case NaCl.

153. (b): For isoelectronic ions, greater the nuclear charge, smaller is the ionic radius.

154. (a): As in NaCl, Cl^- ions are arranged in *ccp* and Na^+ ions occupy octahedral voids and radius of octahedral void = 0.414 R, that is,

$r_{A^+} = 0.414\times r_{B^-}$ or $r_{B^-} = \frac{100}{0.414} = 241$ pm.

155. (c): Cs^+ and I^- ions have largest sizes.

156. (c): $d_{NaCl} = r_{Na^+} + r_{Cl^-}$; $2.79 = r_{Na^+} + 1.81$

or $r_{Na^+} = 2.79 - 1.81$ Å $= 0.98$ Å

$d_{NaF} = r_{Na^+} + r_{F^-}$, i.e., $2.31 = 0.98\ r_{F^-}$

or $r_{F^-} = 2.31 - 0.98 = 1.33$ Å

157. (d): Atomic radius of Si $= d_{Si-C} - \frac{1}{2} d_{C-C}$

158. (b): MgF_2O_4 is a ferrite.

159. (b): No. of C atoms per unit cell of diamond = 8

160. (d): In CaF_2, Ca^{2+} forms *ccp*(*fcc*) structure.

161. (c): When the coordination number is 8, r_+ / r_- ratio lies between 0.732 and 1.

162. (d): Na_2O has antifluorite structure.

163. (b): $MgAl_2O_4$ has a spinel structure.

164. (b): The compound in which the cations occupy alternate tetrahedral voids in a close packing (*ccp*) is ZnS.

165. (d): CE $= \sqrt{a^2 + a^2} = \sqrt{2}\,a$

AE $= \sqrt{(\sqrt{2}a)^2 + a^2} = \sqrt{3}a$

$= 1.732 \times 400$

$= 692.8$

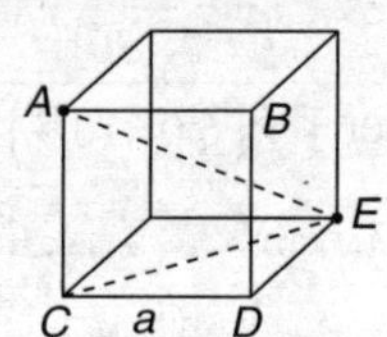

166. (a): KCl has a lattice similar to that of NaCl, that is, face centred cubic.

167. (b): Body centred cubic lattice has a coordination number of 8 (r_+ / r_- lies in the range 0.732–1.0).

168. (c): CsCl unit cell is body centred cubic in which the space occupied is 68% and 32% space is void.

169. (a): In NaCl, the arrangement of Cl^- ions is *fcc*.

170. (c): Na^+ ions in NaCl are present in octahedral voids.

171. (b): AgI does not have rock salt type structure.

172. (d): For forming *ccp* (*fcc*) lattice, Cl^- ions at the corners = 8, Cl^- ions at the face centres = 6. Hence, total = 14.

173. (b): 13 Cl^- ions means that they are present at the edge centres and the body centre. Hence, Na^+ ions are present at the corners and face centres. Total Na^+ ions = 8 + 6 = 14.

174. (d): Tetrahedral voids are vacant. All the octahedral voids are occupied by Na^+ ions.

Structure Determination by X-Ray Diffraction

175. (c): From Bragg's equation, $n = 2d \sin\theta 9$

Given $d =, n = 1$. Hence $1 \times = 2\times\times \sin\theta$

or $\sin\theta = \frac{1}{2}$ or $\theta = 30°$

176. (c): According to Bragg's equation, $2d \sin\theta = n$. When $n = 1$. $\theta = 30°$, $2d \sin 30° = \lambda$

or $2d \times \frac{1}{2}$ or $d = \lambda$

177. (d): $2d \sin\theta = n$

or $2 \times d \times \sin 60° = 2 \times 1$ Å

or $2 \times d \times 0.8660 = 2$ ($\sin 60° = \sqrt{3}/2$ or 0.8660).

or $d = 1.15$ Å

178. (a): $n = 2d \sin\theta$, that is,

$1 \times 0.134 = 2 \times d \times 0.1822$, or $d = 0.368$ nm.

179. (a): $n = 2\,d \sin\theta$, $1\,\lambda = 2 \times 0.200 \sin 8.4$ or λ

$= 2 \times 0.2 \times 0.146 = 0.0584$ nm

Calculations Involving Unit Cell Dimensions

180. (b): $\rho = \frac{Z \times M}{a^3 \times N_0 \times 10^{-30}}$

$= \frac{1\times(133+80)}{(436.6)^3 \times (6.02\times10^{23}) \times 10^{-30}}$

$= \frac{1\times(133+80)}{(436.6)^3 \times (6.02\times10^{23}) \times 10^{-30}}$

(CsBr contains one formula unit per unit cell) = 4.25 g/cm^3

181. (a): Edge, $a = 2(r_+ + r_-) = 2\times297\times10^{-10}$ cm $= 594\times10^{-10}$ cm

Volume $= a^3 = (594\times10^{-10}\text{ cm})^3 = 209.6\times10^{-24}\text{ cm}^3$

182. (c): As NaCl has *fcc* lattice, edge length

= 2 × distance between Na^+ and Cl^- ion

$= 2\,(r_{Na^+} + r_{Cl^-}) = 2\,(95 + 181)$ pm $= 552$ pm.

183. (c): KCl has NaCl type structure (FCC)

Edge (a) of KCl cubic unit cell $= 2\,(r_{K^+} + r_{Cl^-})$

$= 2\,(133 + 181)$ pm $= 628$ pm

Volume of unit cell $= a^3 = (628\text{ pm})^3$

$= (628 \times 10^{-10}\text{ cm})^3$

$= (6.28 \times 10^{-8}\text{ cm})^3$

$= 247.6 \times 10^{-24}\text{ cm}^3 = 2.48 \times 10^{-22}\text{ cm}^3$

184. (c): Density, $\rho = \frac{Z\times M}{a^3 \times N_A \times 10^{-30}}$

$\therefore 2.72 = \frac{4\times M}{(404)^3 \times (6.02\times10^{23}) \times 10^{-30}}$

or $M = \dfrac{2.72 \times (404)^3 \times 6.02 \times 10^{23} \times 10^{-30}}{4}$

$= 27 \text{ g mol}^{-1}$

185. (d): $\rho = \dfrac{Z \times M}{a^3 \times N_A}$

or $M = \dfrac{\rho \times a^3 \times N_A}{Z} = \dfrac{4 \times (500 \times 10^{-10})^3 \times 6 \times 10^{13}}{2}$

$= \dfrac{4 \times 125 \times 10^{-24} \times 6 \times 10^{13}}{2} = 150 \text{ g mol}^{-1}$

186. (b): $M = \dfrac{\rho \times a^3 \times N_0 \times 10^{-30}}{Z}$

$= \dfrac{10 \times 200)^3 \times \left(6.02 \times 10^{23}\right) \times 10^{-30}}{4} = 12.04$

No. of atoms in 100 g $= \dfrac{6.02 \times 10^{23}}{12.04} \times 100$

$= 0.5 \times 10^{25}$

187. (a): $\rho = \dfrac{Z \times M}{a^3 \times N_0 \times 10^{-30}}$

or $Z = \dfrac{\rho \times a^3 \times N_0 \times 10^{-30}}{M}$

$= \dfrac{2.7(405)^3 \times \left(6.02 \times 10^{23}\right) \times 10^{-30}}{27} = 4$

Hence, it is face centred cubic unit cell.

188. (c): $\rho = \dfrac{Z \times M}{a^3 \times N_A}$ or $Z = \dfrac{\rho \times a^3 \times N_A}{M}$

$= \dfrac{(2.7 \times 10^3 \text{ kg cm}^3)(4.05 \times 10^{-10} \text{m})^3 \left(6.022 \times 10^{23} \text{mol}^{-1}\right)}{2.7 \times 10^{-2} \text{kg mol}^{-1}}$

Thus, there are 4 atoms per unit cell. Hence, cubic unit cell must be face centred or cubic close packed.

189. (c): Volume of the unit cell

$= (4.2 \times 10^{-8} \text{ cm}) (8.6 \times 10^{-8} \text{ cm}) (8.4 \times 10^{-8} \text{ cm}$

$= 3.0 \times 10^{-22} \text{cm}^3$

$\rho = \dfrac{Z \times M}{a^3 \times N_0} = \dfrac{Z \times M}{V \times N_0}$ or $Z = \dfrac{\rho \times V \times N_0}{M}$

$= \dfrac{3.3 \times 3.0 \times 10^{-22} \times 6.0 \times 10^{23}}{155} = 3.83 = 4$

190. (b): $\rho = \dfrac{Z \times M}{a^3 \times N_0 \times 10^{-30}}$

$= \dfrac{1 \times (133 + 80)}{\left(436.6)^3\right) \times \left(6.02 \times 10^{23}\right) \times 10^{-30}} = 4.25 \text{ g/cm}^3$

(CsBr contains one formula unit per unit cell, that is, $Z = 1$.)

191. (c): $\rho = \dfrac{Z \times M}{a^3 \times N_0}$ or $a^3 \dfrac{Z \times M}{l \times N_0}$

$= \dfrac{4 \times 63.5}{8.93 \times 6.02 \times 10^{23}}$

$= 4.725 \times 10^{-23} = 47.25 \times 10^{-24}$

$a = (47.25)^{1/3} \times 10^{-8}$

Put $x 10^{-23} = 47.25 \times 10^{-24}$

$\log x = \dfrac{1}{3} \log 47.25 = \dfrac{1}{3}(1.6744)$

$x = \text{Antilog } (0.558) = 3.614$

$\therefore a = 3.614 \times 10^{-8} \text{ cm} = 7614 \times 10^{-10} \text{ cm} = 361.4$

For FCC, $r = \dfrac{a}{2\sqrt{2}} = 0.3535\, a$

$= 0.3535 \times 361.4 = 127.8 \text{ pm}$

192. (d): Edge of the unit cell (d)

$= 2 \text{ Å} = 2 \times 10^{-8} \text{ cm}$

Volume of the unit cell

$= (2 \times 10^{-8} \text{ cm})^3 = 8 \times 10^{-24} \text{ cm}^3$

Mass of one unit cell = Volume × Density

$= (8 \times 10^{-24}) \times (2.5) = 20 \times 10^{-24} \text{ g}$

$\therefore$ No. of unit cells in 200 g

$= \dfrac{1}{20 \times 10^{-24}} \times 200 = 10^{25}$

193. (d): Density $(\rho) = \dfrac{Z \times M}{a^3 \times N_0}$

As M and a remain constant and N_0 is also constant, $\rho \propto Z$

$\dfrac{A_{bcc}}{A_{fcc}} = \dfrac{Z_{bcc}}{Z_{fcc}} = \dfrac{2}{4} = \dfrac{1}{2}$

194. (a): Density $= \dfrac{\text{Mass of the unit cell}}{\text{Volume of the unit cell}}$

$= \dfrac{\text{No. of atoms per unit cell} \times \text{Mass of each atom}}{\text{Volume of unit cell}}$

$= \dfrac{4m}{a^3}$ ($\because$ in fcc, no. of atoms per unit (Z) = 4)

195. (b): $\rho = \dfrac{Z \times M}{a^3 \times N_0 \times 10^{-30}}$

$= \dfrac{2 \times 50}{(300)^3 \times \left(6.0 \times 10^{23}\right) \times 10^{-30}}$

$= 6.2 \text{ g cm}^{-3}$

196. (b): $\rho = \dfrac{Z \times M}{a^3 \times N_0 \times 10^{-30}}$

$= \dfrac{1 \times (133 + 80)}{(436.6)^3 \times \left(6.02 \times 10^{23}\right) \times 10^{-30}} = 4.25 \text{ g/cm}^3$

(CsBr contains one formula unit per unit cell.)

Imperfections in Solids

197. (c): AgBr has both Schottky and Frenkel defects.

198. (a): Frenkel defect is observed in crystals in which the radius ratio is low.

199. (c): When cation shifts from lattice to interstitial site, the defect is called Frenkel defect.

200. (d): AgBr shows Frenkel defect because Ag^+ ions are small in size. Also, the difference in the size of Ag^+ and Br^- ions is small, hence, it shows Schottky defect also.

201. (c): KBr exhibits Schottky defect and not Frenkel defect.

202. (c): Yellow colour on heating NaCl in presence of Na is due to the presence of electrons in anion vacancies (F-centres).

203. (b): Metal deficiency defect is observed in crystals in which metal shows variable valency, that is, Fe (II), Fe (III).

204. (d): Metal deficiency defect is shown by transition metal because they possess variable valency.

205. (b): Fe_3O_4 contains Fe as Fe(II) and Fe(III). The ratio of Fe and oxygen does not remain as represented by the ideal formula Fe_3O_4. Hence, it is a non-stoichiometric compound.

206. (d): In metal excess defect, some anions are missing and the vacant sites thus created are occupied by electrons. These centres are called F-centres. These are responsible for the colour.

207. (a): FeS, FeO and CuO have metal deficiency defect because they contain metal atoms with variable valency. For example, 3 Fe^{2+} may be replaced by 2 Fe^{3+}, and so on. ZnS, KCl and NaCl have metal excess defect because in these anions may leave lattice sites and holes created and occupied by electrons.

208. (d): *p* type of semiconductor is produced on doping with electron deficient impurities. Si belongs to Group 14 while B belongs to Group 13.

209. (d): NaCl doped with $MgCl_2$ is simply an impurity defect.

210. (d): As an external substance (As) is added to Ge, it is an extrinsic semiconductor.

211. (a): Ge belongs to Group 14 and In to Group 13. Hence, on doping, *p*-type semiconductor is obtained.

212. (c): A *p*-type material is electrically neutral as there are only holes and no extra electrons.

213. (a): Ge is a Group 14 element. Holes can be created by adding Group 13 elements, that is, trivalent impurities. These holes behave like positive charges.

214. (a): To maintain electrical neutrality, each Sr^{2+} ion replaces two Na^+ ions. One hole is occupied by Sr^{2+} ion while one hole remains vacant. Thus, each Sr^{2+} ion creates one cation vacancy. Hence, number of cation vacancies created by 0.1 mol of $SrCl_2 = 0.1$ mol.

215. (b): Pentavalent impurity mixed in germanium gives an *n*-type semiconductor.

216. (b): For an *n*-type, the impurity added to silicon should have more than 4 valence electrons.

217. (b): Indium is a group 13 element while Ge is a group 14 element. Hence, a *p*-type semiconductor is formed.

218. (c): Doping a Group 14 element (silicon) with trivalent impurity produces a *p*-type semiconductor.

219. (a): As each Sr^{2+} ion introduces one cation vacancy, the concentration of cation vacancies = mol% of $SrCl_2$ added.

220. (c): A diode is combination of *n* and *p*-type semiconductors.

221. (a): When *n* and *p*-type semiconductors come in contact, some electrons flow from *n* to *p*.

222. (d): None of the given statements is false.

223. (b): All highly ionic compounds like NaCl, KCl, KBr, AgBr, CsCl show Schottky defect.

224. (b): The ratio is less than 2 : 1 in Cu_2O shows that some cuprous (Cu^+) ions have been replaced by cupric (Cu^+) ions. To maintain electrical neutrality, every two Cu^+ ions will be replaced by one Cu^{2+} ion thereby creating a hole. As conduction will be due to presence of these positive holes, it is a *p*-type semiconductor.

225. (d): At 0 K, most of the ionic crystals possess no defects.

226. (c): As a result of Schottky defect, the density of the crystal decreases.

227. (b): Due to the small difference in size of Na^+ and Cl^- ions and high coordination number, NaCl has Schottky defect.

228. (c): AgBr shows both Frenkel and Schottky defects.

229. (b): Schottky defect is observed in electrovalent compounds in which there is a small difference in the size of cations and anions, that is, they are nearly of the same size.

230. (d): All the given statements are correct.

Electrical Properties of Solids and Superconductivity

231. (c): An oxide that has a conductivity and appearance like Cu is ReO_3.

232. (b): The oxide that is an insulator is CoO.

233. (b): Superconductors are derived from compounds of *p*-block elements.

234. (b): Si(*s*) is a semiconductor while all others are insulators.

235. (b): Metals have conductivity of the order of $10^4 - 10^7 \text{ohm}^{-1}\text{m}^{-1}$.

236. (a): Hg acts as a superconductor at 4 K.

237. (b): Out of the given substances, only Li has high electrical and thermal conductivity.

238. (b): Graphite conducts electricity in the solid state.

Magnetic Properties of Solids

239. (b): Ferrimagnetic substances have a small magnetic moment.

240. (a): MnO_2 = Antiferromagnetic, TiO_2 = Diamagnetic, VO_2 = Paramagnetic, CrO_2 = Ferromagnetic.

241. (c): Manganese is not ferromagnetic.

242. (d): Fe_3O_4 is ferromagnetic while V_2O_3, MnO_2 and NiO are antiferrmagnetic substances.

243. (a): CrO_2 is metallic and ferromagnetic.

244. (d): Ni, Co and Fe_3O_4 are all ferromagnetic.

245. (d): Fe_3O_4 shows ferrimagnetism.

246. (d): Alignment of magnetic moment of antiferromagnetic solids is such that the resultant dipole moment is zero.

Dielectric Properties of Solids

247. (b): Crystals having a net dipole moment show piezoelectricity.

248. (c): Barium titanate is an example of ferroelectric solid.

249. (b): Current produced on heating polar crystals is called piezoelectricity.

250. (e): Quartz is used as piezoelectric material.

Miscellaneous

251. (a): Malleability (beaten into sheets) and ductility (drawn into wires) of metals is due to the capacity of layers of metal ions to slide over the other.

252. (b): Only (b) is correct. For hexagonal system, $a, = b \neq c$, $\alpha = \beta = 90°$, $\gamma = 120°$.

253. (d): All the given statements are correct.

254. (a,d): Non-stoichiometric ferrous oxide is $Fe_{0.93-0.98}O_{1.00}$ (and not $FeO_{0.98}$) which is due to metal deficiency defect. Hence, (a) is incorrect. Frenkel defect is favoured in those ionic compounds in which sizes of cation and anion are largely different. Hence, (d) is incorrect.

255. (a): Gallium is a silvery white metal, liquid at room temperature. It expands by 3.1% on solidification. That is why it cannot be stored in glass vessels.

256. (b): Metallic lustre is due to oscillation of loose electrons.

Final Preparation

257. (d): Molar volume from pyknometric density $= \dfrac{M}{2.165 \times 10^3} m^3$

Molar volume from X-ray density $= \dfrac{M}{2.165 \times 10^3} m^3$

$\therefore$ Volume unoccupied $= \dfrac{M}{10^3}\left(\dfrac{1}{2.165} - \dfrac{1}{2.178}\right) m^3$

$\therefore$ Fraction unoccupied $= \left(\dfrac{0.013\, M \times 10^{-3}}{2.165 \times 2.178}\right) \Big/ \left(\dfrac{M \times 10^{-3}}{2.165}\right)$

$= 5.96 \times 10^{-3}$

258. (d):

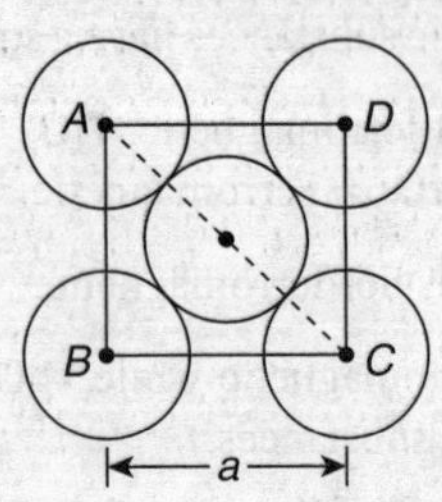

In the two-dimensional packing, Packing fraction

$= \dfrac{\text{Area occupied by circles within the square}}{\text{Area of the square}} = \dfrac{2 \times \pi r^2}{a^2}$

$AC = \sqrt{AB^2 + BC^2} = \sqrt{a^2 + a^2} = \sqrt{2}a$

But AC = $4r$ (r = radius of each sphere)

$\therefore \sqrt{2}\, a = 4r$ or $a = \dfrac{4}{\sqrt{2}} r = 2\sqrt{2}\, r$

$\therefore$ Packing fraction

$= \dfrac{2 \times \pi r^2}{(2\sqrt{2}r)^2} = \dfrac{\pi}{4} = \dfrac{3.143}{4} = 0.785$, i.e., 78.5%

259. (a): Fe^{III} $[Fe^{II}\ Fe^{III}]$ O_4 (magnetite) has inverse spinal structure.

260. (b): Diamond has *fcc* structure of C-atom and has one C-atom on each body diagonal. Hence, total number of C-atoms per unit cell of diamond = 4 (from *fcc*) + 4 (from body diagonal) = 8. The 4 C atoms on the body diagonals are present in the alternate tetrahedral voids (as total number are present in the packing = 4, therefore number of tetrahedral voids = 8). Thus, 50% of the tetrahedral voids are occupied.

261. (b): For body centred cubic lattice.

$d = \dfrac{\sqrt{3}}{2} a = \dfrac{\sqrt{3}}{2} \times 387 \text{ pm} = 335 \text{ pm}.$

262. (b): For a body centred cubic lattice, the relationship between the cell edge (α) and the atom is

$r = \dfrac{\sqrt{3}}{4} a = \dfrac{1.732}{4} \times 4.29 = 1.86$ Å

Length of the body diagonal

$= 4r = 4 \times 1.86$ Å $= 7.44$ Å

263. (a): For *fcc*, radius of atom (R)

$= \dfrac{a}{2\sqrt{2}} = \dfrac{400}{2\sqrt{2}}$ pm = 141.4 pm.

As an octahedral void is bigger in size than a tetrahedral void, the greater sphere will fit into the octahedral void.

Radius of octahedral void (r) = 0.414 R

= 0.414 × 141.4 pm = 58.54 R

$\therefore$ Diameter of the greatest sphere fitting into the void

$= 2 \times 58.54$ pm = 117.08 pm

264. (d): Ions along the axis joining opposite faces are two Cl^- ions at the face centres and one Na^+ ion at the body centre. Hence, now Na^+ ions per unit cell

$= 12 \times \dfrac{1}{4} + 0 = 3$

(edge centres) (body centre)

Cl^- ions per unit cell $= 8 \times \dfrac{1}{8} + 4 \times \dfrac{1}{2} = 1 + 2 = 3$

265. (a): In CaF_2 crystal, Ca^{2+} ions are present at all corners and at the centre of each face of the cube and F^- ions occupy all the tetrahedral voids.

266. (a): ZnS has *ccp* structure (*fcc*) in which S^{2-} ions occupy corners and face centres and Zn^{2+} ions are present in alternate tetrahedral voids. Further, each Zn^{2+} ion is surrounded tetrahedral by $4S^{2-}$ ions and vice versa.

267. (b): $r_{Cs^+}/r_{Cl^-} = 0.90$ or $r_{Cs^+} = 0.90 \times r_{Cl^-}$
$= 0.90 \times 1.80$ Å $= 1.62$ Å

For precise fitting of the cubic voids, r_{Cs^+}/r_{Cl^-} must be 0.732 which is smaller than the given value of 0.90. Hence, cubic packing of Cl^- ions is loose to some extent, that is, two Cl^- ions are not touching each other. Thus, the distance between two Cl^- ions will be greater than 3.60 Å (as radius of each Cl^- ion = 1.80 Å).

Cs^+ ion at the body centre touches the Cl^- ions at the opposite corners of the cube. Hence, distance between Cs^+ and Cl^- ions $= r_{Cs^+}/r_{Cl^-} = 1.62$ Å + 1.80 Å = 3.42 Å

As Cs^+ ions are not touching each other and radius of Cs^+ ion is 1.62 Å, the nearest distance between two Cs^+ ions in greater than 2×1.62 Å, that is, 3.24 Å.

268. (a): We aim at: $(r_{K^+} + r_{Cl^-})/(r_{Na^+} + r_{Cl^-})$

Given $\frac{r_{Na^+}}{r_{Cl^-}} = 0.55$ and $\frac{r_{K^+}}{r_{Cl^-}} = 0.74$

$\therefore \frac{r_{Na^+}}{r_{Cl^-}} + 1 = 1.55$ and $\frac{r_{K^+}}{r_{Cl^-}} + 1 = 1.74$

i.e., $\frac{r_{Na^+} + r_{Cl^-}}{r_{Cl^-}} = 1.55$ ...(i)

and $\frac{r_{K^+} + r_{Cl^-}}{r_{Cl^-}} = 1.74$ ...(ii)

Dividing (ii) by (i), $\frac{r_{K^+} + r_{Cl^-}}{r_{Na^+} + r_{Cl^-}} = \frac{1.74}{1.55} = 1.123$

269. (c): As LiI has *fcc* arrangement, I^- ions will occupy the corners and face-centres. These ions will touch each other along the face diagonal.

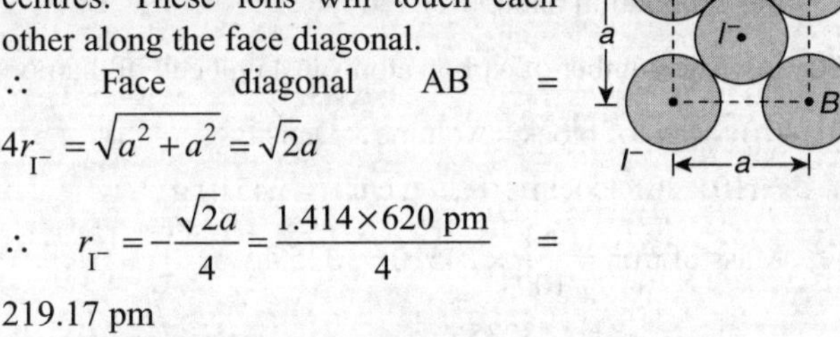

$\therefore$ Face diagonal AB =

$4r_{I^-} = \sqrt{a^2 + a^2} = \sqrt{2}a$

$\therefore r_{I^-} = \frac{\sqrt{2}a}{4} = \frac{1.414 \times 620 \text{ pm}}{4} =$ 219.17 pm

270. (b): Face diagonal $= \sqrt{a^2 + a^2} = \sqrt{2}a$,

Face length (a) $= \frac{\text{Face diagonal}}{\sqrt{2}} = \frac{3.50}{1.414} = 2.475$ Å

271. (a): The complex $[Ni(CN)_4]^{2-}$ has square planar geometry. Hence, its limiting, radius radius is the same as that of the octahedral structure, that is, 0.414–0.732.

272. (b): In NaCl, Cl^- ions are present at the corners and face centres whereas Na^+ ions are present at the edge centres and one at the body centre.

$\therefore$ In a unit cell, Na^+ ions $= \left(12 \times \frac{1}{4}\right) + 1 = 4$ and Cl^- ions $= \left(\frac{1}{8} \times 8\right) + \left(\frac{1}{2} \times 6\right) = 4$. Thus, formula units of NaCl/unit cell +4.

In ZnS, S^{2-} ions have *fcc* arrangement while Zn^{2+} ions are present at four tetrahedral sites. Hence, formula units of ZnS per unit cell = 4.

In MgO, $\frac{r_c}{r_z} = 0.5$ shows that it has NaCl type structure.

$\therefore$ Formula units of MgO per unit cell = 4

$\therefore$ Ratio is 4 : 4 : 4

273. (c): Volume of unit cell $= a^3$ (a = edge of the crystal)

$\therefore a^3 = 247.7$ Å

or 3 log a = log 247.7 = 2.3939 or log a = 0.7979

or a = antilog 0.7979 = 6.279 Å

But $a = 2(r_{K^+} + r_{Cl^-})$ or $r_{K^+} + r_{Cl^-} = 3.14$ Å

274. (a): For *bcc* lattice,

$r = \frac{\sqrt{3}}{4}a$ or $2r = \frac{\sqrt{3}}{2}a$

$\therefore a - \frac{\sqrt{3}}{2}a = 53$ or $a - 0.866a = 53$

or $0.134\,a = 53$

or $a = 395.5$ pm $= 3.955 \times 10^{-8}$ cm

$$\text{Density} = \frac{Z \times M}{a^3 \times N_0} = \frac{2 \times 23}{(3.955 \times 10^{-8}) \times 6.022 \times 10^{23}}$$

= 1.23 g/cc

275. (d): $\frac{\rho_{FCC}}{\rho_{BCC}} = \frac{Z_{FCC}}{(a^3)_{FCC}} \times \frac{(a^3)_{BCC}}{Z_{BCC}}$

$= \frac{4 \times (3.0)^3}{2 \times (3.5)^3} = 1.26$

276. (c): (i) Edge of the unit cell (a) $= 2 \times Y^{1/3}$ nm

Formula mass, $M = 6.023$ Y g mol^{-1} $= \frac{6.023 \text{ Y}}{1000}$ kg mol^{-1}

For rock salt type structure, $Z = 4$

$\therefore$ Density $(\rho) = \frac{Z \times M}{a^3 \times N_0}$

$$= \frac{4 \times (6.023 \times 10^{-3} \text{ Y kg mol}^{-1})}{\left(2 \times Y^{\frac{1}{3}} \times 10^{-9} \text{m}\right)^3 \times (6.023 \times 10^{23} \text{mol}^{-1})} = 5 \text{ kg m}^{-3}$$

277. (b): $\rho = \frac{Z \times M}{a^3 \times N_A}$ or $Z \frac{\rho \times a^3 \times N^A}{M}$

$$= \frac{(2\text{g cm}^{-3})(5 \times 10^{-8}\text{m})^3 \times (6 \times 10^{23}\text{mol}^{-1})}{75 \text{ mol}^{-1}} = 2$$

For a metal with $Z = 2$ means that it has body centred cubic (*bcc*) structure. For *bcc* structure,

Atomic radius $(r) = \frac{\sqrt{3}}{4}a = \frac{\sqrt{3}}{4} \times 5$ Å

$= 2.165 \text{ Å} = 216.5 \text{ pm}$

278. (d): For *fcc*, $d = \dfrac{Z \times M}{a^3 \times N_0}$ and $Z = 4, a = 2\sqrt{2}\,r$

For *bcc*, $d' = \dfrac{Z \times M}{a^3 \times N_0}$ and $Z = 2, a' = \dfrac{4}{\sqrt{3}} r$

$$\therefore \frac{d}{d'} = \frac{Z}{Z'} \times \frac{(a')^3}{(a)^3} = \frac{4}{2} \times \frac{(4r/\sqrt{3})^3}{(2\sqrt{2}r)^3}$$

$$= 2 \times (2)^3 \times \frac{1}{\left(\sqrt{2}\right)^3\left(\sqrt{3}\right)^3} = \frac{2\left(\sqrt{2}\right)^3}{\left(\sqrt{3}\right)^3}$$

$$= 2\left(\sqrt{2}\right)^3 : \left(\sqrt{3}\right)^3$$

279. (a): $Z = \dfrac{\rho \times a^3 \times N_0}{M}$

$$= \frac{(2.75)\left(654 \times 10^{-10}\right)\left(6.02 \times 20^{23}\right)}{39 + 80} = 3.9 = 4$$

Hence, it has an *fcc* structure with a coordination number = 6.

280. (c): Volume of the unit cell

$= (4.2 \times 10^{-8} \text{ cm})\left(8.6 \times 10^{-8} \text{ cm}\right)$

$(8.4 \times 10^{-8} \text{ cm}) = 3.0 \times 10^{-22} \text{cm}^3$

$$\rho = \frac{Z \times M}{a^3 \times N_0} = \frac{Z \times M}{V \times N_0}$$

$$\text{or } Z = \frac{\rho \times V \times N_0}{M}$$

$$= \frac{3.3 \times 3.0 \times 10^{-22} \times 6.0 \times 10^{23}}{15} = 3.83 \simeq 4$$

281. (b): $d = \dfrac{a}{\sqrt{h^2 + k^2 + l^2}} = \dfrac{450}{\sqrt{2^2 + 2^2 + 1^2}} = \dfrac{450}{\sqrt{9}} = 150 \text{ pm}$

282. (c): $d_{hkl} = \dfrac{a}{\sqrt{h^2 + k^2 + R^2}}$

$$d_{100} = \frac{a}{\sqrt{1^2 + 0^2 + 0^2}} = a,$$

$$d_{200} = \frac{a}{\sqrt{h^2 + 0^2 + 0^2}} = \frac{1}{2}$$

Thus, $d_{200} = \dfrac{1}{2} d_{100}$

From Bragg's equation, $n = 2d \sin \theta$

In 1st case, $2 \times 3 = 2 \times d_{100} \sin 30° = 2 \times d_{100} \times \dfrac{1}{2} = d_{100}$

$d_{100} = 6 \text{ Å} \therefore d_{200} = \dfrac{1}{2} \times 6 \text{ Å} = 3 \text{ Å}$

Again applying Bragg's equation for the second case, $n = 1$

$\therefore 1 \times 3 = 2 \times 3 \sin \theta$

or $\sin \theta = \dfrac{1}{2} \therefore \theta = 30°$

283. (a): $Z = \dfrac{\rho \times a^3 \times N_0 \times 10^{-30}}{M}$

$$= \frac{2.75 \times (654)^3 \times \left(6.02 \times 10^{23}\right) \times 10^{-30}}{39 + 80} = 3.9 = 4.$$

Hence, it is face centred.

284. (d): For *bcc*, $d = \dfrac{\sqrt{3}}{2} a$

or $a = \dfrac{2d}{\sqrt{3}} = \dfrac{2 \times 4.52}{1.732} = 5.219 \text{Å} = 522 \text{ pm}$

$$\rho = \frac{Z \times M}{a^3 \times N_0 \times 10^{-30}} = \frac{2 \times 39}{(522)^3 \times (6.02 \times 10^{23}) \times 10^{-30}}$$

$= 0.91 \text{ g/cm}^3 = 910 \text{ kg m}^{-3}$

285. (b): $\rho = \dfrac{Z \times M}{a^3 \times N_0} \therefore 7.2 = \dfrac{1 \times 250}{a^3 \times 6.02 \times 10^{23}}$

or $a^3 = 57.6 \times 10^{-24}$

or $a = 3.86 \times 10^{-8}$ cm

$\therefore$ Radius (r) of the atom $= \dfrac{a}{2} = 1.93 \times 10^{-8}$ cm.

286. (c): According to the composition $Fe_{0.93}O$, if there are 100 O atoms, then Fe atoms = 93. Suppose Fe as Fe(III) = x, then Fe as Fe(II) = $93 - x$

Total charge on 100 O^{2-} = 200

Total charge on Fe = $3 \times x + 2 \times (93 - x)$

As the compound a whole is electrically neutral.

$3x + 2(93 - x) = 200$ or $x = 14$

$\therefore$ % of Fe present as Fe (III) $= \dfrac{14}{93} \times 100 = 15.05\%$

287. (c): Doping of Si with P gives extra electrons while doping the Al gives rise to holes.

288. (d): Ionic solids conduct electricity not due to presence of ions but due to the presence of defects.

289. (b): Electrical conductivity of semiconductors increases with increase of temperature because more electrons can jump to the conduction band.

290. (c): The number of carbon atoms in a unit cell of diamond is 8.

291. (b): Mass of block = Volume × Density

$= (10 \times 20 \times 15)\text{cm}^3 \times 8.17 \text{ g cm}^{-3} = 24510 \text{ g}$

Mass of iron $= \dfrac{54}{100} \times 24510 = 1325.4\text{g}$

Moles of iron $= \dfrac{13235.4}{56} = 236.34$ moles

(At mass of Fe = 56)

No. of iron atoms $= 236.34 \times 6.022 \times 10^{23} = 14.23 \times 10^{25}$

292. (d): Suppose total Fe present = 1 mole, Then

Fe present as Fe (III) $= \dfrac{1}{4}$ mole

Fe present as Fe (II) $= \dfrac{3}{4}$ mole

Total moles of + ve charge $= 3 \times \dfrac{1}{4} + 2 \times \dfrac{3}{4} = \dfrac{3}{4} + \dfrac{6}{4} = \dfrac{9}{4}$ mole

Suppose oxygen present (O^{2-}) = x mole

Total mole of – ve charge on O = 2 x mole
As compound as a whole is electrically neutral.
Total + ve charge = Total – ve charge

$\frac{9}{4} = 2x$ or $x = \frac{9}{8}$ mole

293. (a): In diamond, each carbon atom is sp^3 hybridised and linked to four other carbon atoms tetrahedrally by covalent bonds. As the atoms are held firmly by covalent bonds, diamond is the hardest substance.

294. (d): A match box shows orthorhombic geometry ($a \neq b \neq c$, $\alpha = \beta = \gamma = 90°$).

295. (b): Total number. of atoms in the unit cell of FCC = 4

Volume of one atom $= \frac{4}{3}\pi r^3$

$\therefore$ Total volume of atoms in the unit cell $= 4 \times \frac{4}{3}\pi r^3 = \frac{16}{3}\pi r^3$

296. (c): Atoms A that occupy corners also occupy face centres. Removal of face centred atoms along one axis means removal of two atoms of A from the face centres. Hence, atoms A left per unit cell will be $= \frac{1}{8} \times 8 + \frac{1}{2} \times 4 = 3$. But atoms B (present at the edge centre and body centre) remain the same, that is, equal to $\frac{1}{4} \times 12 + 1 = 4$. Hence, ratio of A : B = 3 : 4, that is, the formula will be A_3B_4.

297. (c): Cl^- ions are present at the corners and centres and Na^+ ions at edge centres and one a body centre. The given axis is passing through two face centres and one body centre.

$\therefore$ No. of Na^+ ions $= 12 \times \frac{1}{4}$ (only from edge centres) = 3

No. of Cl^- ions $= 8 \times \frac{1}{8} + 4 \times \frac{1}{2} = 1 + 2 = 3$

(corners) (face centres)

298. (d): No. of Cu atoms in the unit cell (*fcc* / *ccp*)

$= 8 \times \frac{1}{8} + 6 \times \frac{1}{2} = 4$

Ag atoms occupying the edge centres $= 12 \times \frac{1}{4} = 4$

Au atoms present at the edge centre = 1.
Hence, the formula is Cu_4Ag_3Au.

299. (d): One unit cell of NaCl contains 4 NaCl units, that is, has mass

$= \frac{4 \times 58.5}{6.02 \times 10^{23}}$ g

$\therefore$ No. of unit cells in 1 g $= \frac{6.02 \times 10^{23}}{4 \times 58.5} = 2.57 \times 10^{21}$

300. (b): (a) No. of M^{2+} ions per unit cell $= 6 \times \frac{1}{2} = 3$

No. of X^- ions per unit cell $= \times \frac{1}{8} = 1$

$\therefore$ Formula = M_3X. It is not MX_2. Moreover, it is not neutral and hence wrong.

(b) No. of M^{2+} ions per unit cell $= 8 \times \frac{1}{8} + 6 \times \frac{1}{2} = +3 = 4$

(corners) (face centres)

As 8X^- ions are present in the tetrahedral voids, ratio of $M^{2+} : X^- = 4:8 = 1:2$, that is, formula = MX_2.

(c) M^{2+} ions = 4 (as above). As 2X^- ions are in the interior (not shared by any other unit cell), therefore ratio of $M^{2+} : X^-$ = 4:2 = 2:1, that is, the formula is M_2X. Moreover, it is not a neutral compound.

(d) M^{2+} ions = 4 (as above). As 4 X^- ions are in the interior, ratio of $M^{2+}; X^-$ = 4:4 = 1:1 which does not form a neutral compound.

301. (a): The shaded plane makes intercepts ∞, $2b$ and $2c$ on X-, Y- and Z-axis respectively. Their coefficients are ∞, 2, 2. Their reciprocals = 0, $\frac{1}{2}, \frac{1}{2}$. Clearing the fractions, Miller indices = (011).

302. (c): $d = \frac{a}{\sqrt{h^2 + k^2 + l^2}} \therefore d_{111} = \frac{0.556}{\sqrt{1^2 + 1^2 + 1^2}} = \frac{0.556}{\sqrt{3}}$

303. (d): No. of octahedral voids = No. of ions in the packing. Hence, octahedral voids per sphere = 1.

304. (b): Suppose number of O^{2-} ions in close packing = n
$\therefore$ No. of octahedral voids = n
No. of tetrahedral voids = 2 n

Divalent metal ions A present $= \frac{2n}{4} = \frac{n}{2}$

Monovalent metal ions B present = n

$\therefore$ Ratio A : B : O^{2-} $= \frac{n}{2} : n : n = \frac{1}{2} : 1 : 1 = 1 : 2 : 2$

Hence, the formula is AB_2O_2.

305. (b): In a simple cube, no. of atoms/unit cell $= 8 \times \frac{1}{8} = 1$

Volume of the atom $= \frac{4}{3}\pi r^3$

Volume of the cube $= a^3 = (2r)^3 = 8r^3$ ($\because a = 2r$)

$\therefore$ Fraction occupied $= \frac{\frac{4}{3}\pi r^3}{8r^3} = \frac{\pi}{6}$

306. (a): In spinel structure, oxide ions are arranged in *ccp* which means that there are 4 atoms per unit cell. Hence, there are 4 octahedral voids and 8 tetrahedral voids.
Divalent ions occupy tetrahedral voids and tripositive ions occupy octahedral voids.
$\therefore$ No. of divalent ions.

$A = 8 \times \frac{1}{8} = 1$

(as only $\frac{1}{8}$-th tetrahedral voids are occupied)

No. of trivalent ions, $B = \frac{1}{2} \times 4 = 2$

(as $\frac{1}{2}$ of octahedral voids are occupied)

Hence, formula of the oxide having spinel structure is AB_2O_4.

MATCH THE FOLLOWING

307. (d): (A) Atoms A/unit cell $= 8 \times \frac{1}{8} = 1$

Atoms B/unit cell $= 6 \times \frac{1}{2} = 3$. Formula $= AB_3$

(B) Atoms A/unit cell $= 8 \times \frac{1}{8} + 6 \times \frac{1}{2} = 4$

Atoms B/unit cell $= 12 \times \frac{1}{4} = 3$

Formula $= A_4B_3$

(C) Suppose anions B $= n$

Octahedral voids $= n$, Tetrahedral voids $= 2n$

Cations A$= n$ (in octahedral voids) $+ n$ (in tegrahedral voids) $= 2n$

$\therefore$ A : B $= 2n : n = 2 : 1$. Formula $= A_2B$

(D) Suppose cations A $= n$

Anions B $= 2n$

$\therefore$ A : B $= n : 2n = 1 : 2$

Formula $= AB_2$

308. (c): (A) Rock salt = Anions (Cl^-) have *fcc* arrangement; cations (Na^+) occupy all tetrahedral voids.

(B) Zinc blende = Anions (S^{2-}) have *ccp* arrangement; cations (Zn^{2+}) occupy alternate tetrahedral voids.

(C) Fluorite = Cations (Ca^{2+}) have *fcc* arrangement; anions (F^-) occupy all tetrahedral voids.

(D) Wurtzite = Anions (S^{2-}) have hcp arrangement; cations (Zn^{2+}) occupy alternate tetrahedral voids.

309. (b): (A) $r_{Mg^{2+}} / r_{O^{2-}} = 65/140 = 0.464$ (lies in the range 0.414 – 0.732) $\rightarrow$ Octahedral. Coord. no. = 6

(B) $r_{B^{3+}} / r_{O^{2-}} = 27/140 = 0.193$ (lies in the range 0.155–0.225) $\rightarrow$ Planar triangular. Coord. no. = 3

(C) $r_{Mg^{2+}} / r_{Cl^-} = 65/184 = 0.353$ (lies in the range 0.225–0.414) $\rightarrow$ Tetrahedral. Coord. no. = 4

(D) $r_{Cs^+} / r_{Cl^-} = 169/181 = 0.934$ (lies in the range 0.732–1) $\rightarrow$ BCC. Coord. no. = 8

310. (a): (A) Dry ice = Molecular solid (containing H_2O molecules held together) (B) Silica = Network solid (SiO_2 forming a network through covalent bonds)

(C) Brass = Metallic solid (Copper + Zinc)

2+ 2−

(D) Wurtzite = Ionic solid (ZnS)

311. (b): (A) a= b = c, $\alpha = \beta = \gamma \neq 90 \rightarrow$ Rhombohedral

(B) a $\neq$ b $\neq$ c, $\alpha = \gamma = 90° \neq \beta \rightarrow$ Monoclinic

(C) a $\neq$ b $\neq$ c, $\alpha \neq \beta \neq \gamma \neq 90° \rightarrow$ Triclinic

(D) a $\neq$ b$\neq$ c, $\alpha = \beta = \gamma = 90° \rightarrow$ Orthorhombic

ASSERTION REASON

312. (c): Correct R. Properties like refractive index AND electrical conductance have same values in different directions for isotropic substances

313. (d): Correct A. Graphite is an example of hexagonal crystal system (Each C atom is sp^2 hybridised and is linked to three other C atoms in a hexagonal planar structure).

Correct R. For a hexagonal system, $a = b \neq c$, $\alpha = \beta = 90°$, $\gamma = 120°$

314. (c): Correct R. The size of the tetrahedral voids is smaller than that of the octahedral voids.

315. (c): Correct R. A tetrahedral void is so called because it is surrounded tetrahedrally by four spheres whereas an octahedral void is so called because it is surrounded octahedrally by six spheres.

316. (d): Correct A. Hexagonal close packing and cubic close packing are equally closely packed.

Correct R. Both have a coordination number of 12.

317. (d): Correct A. Tetrahedral holes are smaller than octahedral holes.

Correct R. Cations are smaller in size than THE corresponding atoms.

318. (a): If anion–anion contact is retained, then, as in the figure,

Interionic distance of LiCl $= \frac{a}{2} = \frac{5.14 \text{ Å}}{2} = 2.57\text{Å}$

$BC = \sqrt{AB^2 + AC^2} = \sqrt{(2.57)^2 + (2.57)^2} = 3.63 \text{ Å}$

Radius of Cl^- ion $= \frac{1}{2} BC = \frac{1}{2} \times 3.63 = 1.81$ Å

Hence, **Reason** is the correct explanation of **Assertion.**

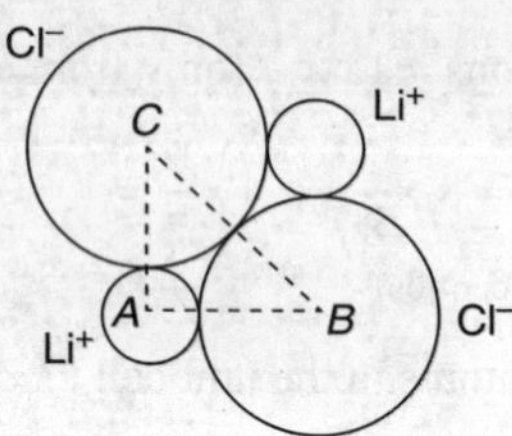

319. (a): R is the correct explanation of A.

320. (d): Correct A. Zinc blende has *ccp* or *fcc* arrangement of S^{2-} ions whereas wurtzite has *hcp* arrangement of S^{2-} ions.

Correct R. Wurtzite has six formula units of ZnS whereas zinc blende has four.

321. (a): R is the correct explanation of A.

322. (d): Correct A. Some compounds may have both Schottky and Frenkel defects (example, AgBr).

Correct R. Schottky defects lower the density because equal number of cations and anions are missing from lattice sites while Frenkel defect does not result in any change in the density because ions simply shift from lattice sites to interstitial sites.

323. (b): Both A and R are correct but R is not the correct explanation of A

324. (b): Correct explanation. Anion vacancies are produced because anions (like Cl^-) diffuse to the surface to combine with alkali metal atoms.

325. **(d): Correct A.** As each $SrCl_2$ unit creates one cation vacancy, the number of cation vacancies will be 10^{-3} mol = $10^{-3} \times (6.02 \times 10^{23}) = 6.02 \times 10^{20}$ unit produces one cation vacancy.

326. **(a):** R is the correct explanation of A.

327. **(a):** R is the correct explanation of A.

328. **(c): Correct R.** Intermediate conductivity is due to the small energy gap between filled valence band and empty conduction band.

329. **(b): Correct explanation.** Conductivity of Si increases because group 15 elements have an extra free electron.

330. **(a):** R is the correct explanation of A.

331. **(a):** R is the correct explanation of A.

332. **(c): Correct R**. In piezoelectric crystals, on applying an electric field, dipoles align themselves in such a manner that they have a net dipole moment.

333. **(b): Correct explanation.** Particles on the path in different directions are different.

334. **(c): Correct R.** Similar particles lie in the path in different directions of an amorphous solid (all solids possess rigidity).

335. **(b): Correct explanation.** Low melting point is due to weak intermolecular forces of attraction.

336. **(c): Correct R.** In diamond, C atoms are sp^3 hybridised while in graphite, they are sp^2 hybridised.

337. **(d): Correct A.** Crystalline solids have short range as well as long range order.
Correct R. Amorphous solids do not have long range order.

Solutions

2.1 Introduction

A *solution* is a homogeneous mixture of two or more substances whose composition can be varied within certain limits. A *homogeneous mixture* possesses uniform composition and properties throughout the solution. Depending upon the total number of components present in the solution, it is called a *binary solution* (two components), *ternary solution* (three components), *quaternary solution* (four components), and so on. The component which is present in the largest quantity is called the solvent while the component which is present in the lesser quantity is termed the solute.

2.2 Types of Solutions

2.2.1 Based on Physical State

On the basis of the physical state of the solute and the solvent, the following combinations are possible for a solution (Table 2.1).

Table 2.1 Different types of binary solutions

Solute	Solvent	Solution	Example
1. Solid	Solid	Solid	Certain alloys, brass (Cu + Zn), bronze (Cu + Sn), (Cu + Au)
2. Liquid	Solid	Solid } Solid solutions	Hg in Ag or Na (Amalgams)
3. Gas	Solid	Solid	Hydrated salts, dissolved gases in minerals, H_2 gas in Pd ($CO_2 + H_2O$)
4. Solid	Liquid	Liquid	Sugar in water, NaCl in water
5. Liquid	Liquid	Liquid } Liquid solutions	Benzene + toluene, $C_2H_5OH + H_2O$
6. Gas	Liquid	Liquid	O_2 in water, aerated drinks
7. Solid	Gas	Gas	Iodine vapours in air, camphor + N_2
8. Liquid	Gas	Gas } Gas solutions	Humidity (water vapours in air, $CHCl_3 + N_2$)
9. Gas	Gas	Gas	Air ($O_2 + N_2 + CO_2$)

Some solutions are not true solutions but are *colloidal solutions* due to the large size of the solute parties. Colloidal solutions are heterogeneous. For example, smoke, dust in air, starch solution.

Solid solutions: Solid solutions are formed when one component is distributed throughout another component in the solid state. They are of two types—substitutional solid solutions and interstitial solid solutions.

- **Substitutional solid solutions** are those in which atoms, molecules or ions of one substance take the place of the particles of another substance in a crystal lattice [Fig. 2.1(a)]. Brass is a common example of substitutional solid solution of copper and zinc.
- **Interstitial solid solutions** are those which are formed by placing atoms of one kind into the voids or interstices in the lattice of atoms of another substance. Fig. 2.1(b) shows solute particles in the interstices of the solvent lattice. A common example of an interstitial solid solution is tungsten carbide (WC).

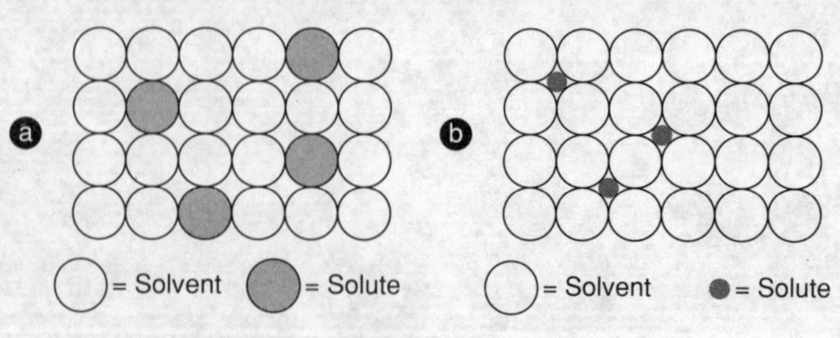

(a) Substitutional solid solution (b) Interstitial solid solution

Fig. 2.1 Solid solutions

2.3 Concentration of Solutions

Methods of expressing concentration are the following.

(i) Strength is the amount of solute (g) dissolved per litre of solution.

$$\text{Strength} = \frac{\text{Mass of solute in grams}}{\text{Volume of solution in litre (dm}^3)}$$

Units are gram per litre or gram per dm^3.

(ii) Molarity (M) is the number of moles of solute dissolved per litre of solution.

$$\text{Molarity} = \frac{\text{No. of moles of solute}}{\text{Volume of solution in litres}}$$

$$\text{Mole} = \frac{\text{Mass of solute}}{\text{Molecular mass of solute}}$$

$$M = \frac{\text{Weight of solute}}{\text{Molecular mass of solute}} \times \frac{1}{\text{Volume of solution (cc)}} \times 1000$$

Units are moles per litre (mole L^{-1}).

(iii) Normality (N) of a solution is the number of gram equivalents of the solute dissolved per litre of the solution.

$$\text{Normality } (N) = \frac{\text{Number of gram equivalents of solute}}{\text{Volume of solution in litres}}$$

$$\left(\text{Gram equivalent} = \frac{\text{Mass of solute}}{\text{Equivalent mass of solute}}\right)$$

$$N = \frac{\text{Mass of solute}}{\text{Equivalent mass of solute}} \times \frac{1}{\text{Volume of solution in litres}} \times 1000$$

Units are gm eq per litre (g eq L^{-1}).

Note: Strength = Molarity × Molecular weight of solute
Strength = Normality × Equivalent weight of solute

(iv) Molality (m) is number of moles of solute dissolved per kg of solvent.

$$\text{Molality} = \frac{\text{Number of moles of solute}}{\text{Mass of the solvent in kg}}$$

$$m = \frac{\text{Mass of solute}}{\text{Molecular mass of solute}} \times \frac{1}{\text{Mass of the solvent in grams}} \times 1000$$

Units are moles per kg (mol kg^{-1}).

- Hypophosphorous acid $H_3PO_2 \rightarrow$ Basicity = 1
- Phosphorous acid $H_3PO_2 \rightarrow$ Basicity = 2
- Orthophosphoric acid $H_3PO_4 \rightarrow$ Basicity = 3
- Orthoboric acid $H_3BO_3 \rightarrow$ Basicity = 1

(v) Percentage by weight (% w/W) is mass of solute dissolved per 100 grams of solution.

$$\text{Percentage by weight } (\% \ w/W) = \frac{\text{Mass of solute}}{\text{Mass of solution}}$$

20% w/W aq NaCl solution means that 20 g of NaCl is dissolved is 80 g H_2O. Total mass of solution is 100 g.

(vi) Percentage by volume: The volume percentage is defined as the volume of the component per 100 parts by volume of the solution. For example, if V_A and V_B are the volumes of two components A and B respectively in a solution, then

Volume percentage of A

$$= \frac{\text{Volume of A}}{\text{Volume of A + Volume of B}} \times 100$$

(vii) Percentage by weight–volume ($\%w/V$) is the mass of solute dissolved per 100 mL of solution.

$$\text{Percentage by weight–volume } (\% \ w/V) = \frac{\text{Mass of solute}}{\text{Total volume of solute}} \times 100$$

(viii) Mole fraction (x) of a component in the solution is the ratio of the number of moles of the component to the total number of moles of all the components of the solution. Suppose a solution contains two components A and B, n_A and n_B are the number of moles of the components.

$$\text{Mole fraction of component A } x_A = \frac{n_A}{n_A + n_B}$$

$$\text{Mole fraction of component B } x_A = \frac{n_A}{n_A + n_B}$$

$$x_A + x_B = 1$$

(x) Parts per million (ppm) is the mass (or volume) of solute dissolved per million parts (10^5) by mass (or volume) of solution.

$$\text{ppm} = \frac{\text{Mass of solute}}{\text{Total mass of solution}} \times 10^6$$

$$\text{ppm} = \frac{\text{Volume of solute}}{\text{Total volume of solution}} \times 10^6$$

(xi) Formality of solution (F)

$$\text{Formality } (F) = \frac{\text{Number of gram formula units of solute}}{\text{Volume of solution in litres}}$$

$$F = \frac{\text{Mass of solute}}{\text{Gram fomula unit mass of solute}} \times \frac{1}{\text{Volume of solution (mL)}} \times 1000$$

Molecular mass is called *formula unit mass*, mole is called *gram formula unit*.

Effect of Temperature on Concentration Terms

The concentration terms, molarity (m), mole fraction (x), mass fraction, percentage by weight, parts per million (ppm) do not change with change in temperature because these terms only depend on the mass of the solute and solvent, and do not depend on the volume of the solution. Temperature has no effect on mass, but volume of the solution changes with a change in temperature. Molarity (M), normality (N) and percentage by volume change with change in temperature because they depend on the volume of the solution.

∴ Molality (m) and mole fraction are preferred compared to molarity and normality.

2.4 Solubility

2.4.1 Solubility of a Solid in a Liquid

Dissolution process: In the dissolution process, solute particles are separated from each other in a process that absorbs energy, solvent particles are pushed apart, this also absorbs energy. Then, the solvent particles attract the solute particles and in the process, release energy. Overall, the formation of a solution can be exothermic or endothermic. The enthalpy of a solution is given by

$$\Delta H_{\text{solution}} = \underbrace{\Delta H_{\text{A-A}} + \Delta H_{\text{B-B}}}_{\text{Endothermic}} + \underbrace{(-\Delta H_{\text{A-B}})}_{\text{Exothermic}}$$

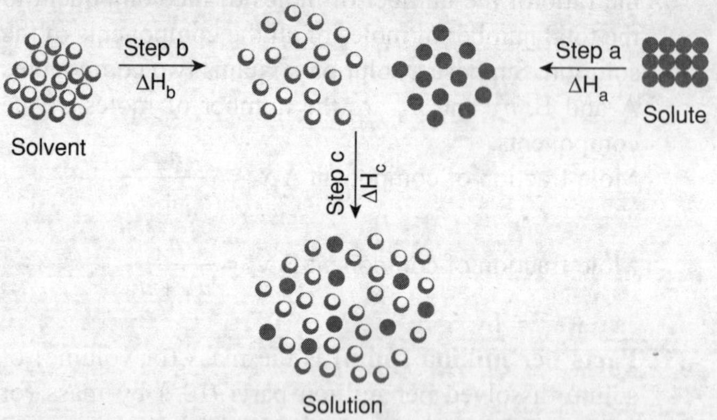

Solvent
Step b
ΔH$_b$
Step a
ΔH$_a$
Solute
Step c
ΔH$_c$
Solution

Fig. 2.2 A molecular view of the dissolution process

(i) In solute–solvent interactions, $\Delta H_{A-B} > [\Delta H_{A-A} + \Delta H_{B-B}]$, so the dissolution will be exothermic.

(ii) In solute–solvent interactions, they are weaker than solute–solute or solvent–solvent interactions. Then $\Delta H_{\text{A-B}} > [\Delta H_{\text{A-A}} + \Delta H_{\text{B-B}}]$ and the dissolution will be endothermic.

2.4.2 Factors Affecting the Solubility of a Solid in a Liquid

The important factors on which the solubility of a solid in a liquid depends are—nature of the solute, nature of the solvent and temperature.

(i) Nature of the solute and solvent: In general, a solid dissolves in a liquid (solvent) if the intermolecular interactions are similar in the solute and the solvent. Ionic (or polar) compounds dissolve more readily in polar solvents like water and are almost insoluble in non-polar solvents such as benzene, ether or carbon tetrachloride. Covalent compounds dissolve in non-polar solvents; the solubility is due to similar solute–solute, solute–solvent and solvent–solvent interactions.

(ii) Effect of temperature on solubility—solubility curves: On the basis of the effect of temperature on solubility in water, the various ionic substances are divided into three categories.

(a) *Those whose solubility increases continuously with increase in temperature*: Most of the substances such as $NaNO_3$, KNO_3, NaCl and KCl fall into this category. The reason for this behaviour is that the process of dissolution is *endothermic*.

(b) *Those whose solubility decreases continuously with increase in temperature*: In a few substances like cerium sulfate, lithium carbonate, sodium carbonate monohydrate ($Na_2CO_3.H_2O$), and so on, the process of dissolution is exothermic, due to the shifting of equilibrium in the backward direction.

(c) *Those substances whose solubility does not increase or decrease continuously*: There are some substances which on heating change at a particular temperature from one polymorphic form to another (such as α to β-form in the case of ammonium nitrate) or from one hydrated form to another (as in $CaCl_2.6H_2O \rightarrow CaCl_2.4H_2O \rightarrow CaCl_2.2H_2O$) or from a hydrated to an anhydrous form (as in $Na_2SO_4.10H_2O \rightarrow Na_2SO_4$). Such substances do not show a continuous increase or decrease in solubility. The temperature at which one form of the substance changes into another is called the *transition temperature.*

2.5 Solutions of Gases in Liquids

2.5.1 Solubility of a Gas in a Liquid

The solubility of any gas in a particular liquid is the volume of the gas in cc (converted to STP) that can dissolve in unit volume (1 cc) of the liquid to form the saturated solution at the temperature of the experiment and under a pressure of 1 atmosphere. This method of expressing the concentration is called the *absorption coefficient* of the gas and is usually represented by α.

The solubility of a gas in a liquid at a particular temperature is also expressed in terms of *molarity* (moles of the gas dissolved per litre of the solvent to form the saturated solution, that is, in terms of mol L^{-1}) or in terms of mole fraction (x_A) of the gas.

2.5.2 Factors on Which Solubility of a Gas in a Liquid Depends

(i) Effect of pressure (Henry's law): When the gas is dissolved in H_2O under pressure, the dissolved gas and undissolved gas come to equilibrium.

$$\underset{\text{Undissolved gas}}{CO_2(g)} + \text{aqueous} \underset{\text{Evaporation}}{\overset{\text{Dissolution}}{\rightleftharpoons}} \underset{\text{dissolved gas}}{CO_2(aq)}$$

When the pressure of the undissolved gas is increased, the equilibrium shifts in the forward direction (Le Chatelier principle). *Henry's law* states that the mass of a gas dissolved in a given volume of the liquid at constant temperature is directly proportional to the pressure of the undissolved gas present in equilibrium with the liquid.

Mathematically, $m \propto p$ or $m = Kp$ (2.1)

where m = mass of the gas dissolved in a unit volume of the solvent, p = pressure of the undissolved gas in equilibrium with the solvent, K = constant of proportionality whose value depends upon the nature of the gas, the nature of the solvent and the temperature.

Expressing solubility in terms of mole fraction of the gas in the solution, for a gas A, Henry's law can be written as

$$x_A = K'_{p_A} \quad (2.2)$$

where x_A is the mole fraction of the gas in the solution, p_A is the partial pressure of the gas above the solution and K' is the proportionality constant whose value depends upon the nature of the gas, nature of the solvent and the temperature.

From Eq. 2.2,

$$p_A = \frac{1}{K'} x_A \quad \text{or} \quad p_A = K_H\, x_A \quad (2.3)$$

where $K_H = \dfrac{1}{K'}$ is called Henry's constant.

- Greater the value of K_H, the lower is the solubility of the gas at the same partial pressure (according to Eq. 2.3) at a particular temperature.
- The value of K_H increases with an increase in temperature implying that the solubility decreases with an increase in temperature at the same pressure.

(ii) Limitations of Henry's law: Henry's law is applicable only if the following conditions are satisfied.

- The pressure should be low and the temperature should be high, that is, the gas should behave like an ideal gas.
- The gas should not undergo compound formation with the solvent. There should be no association or dissociation of solute (gas) in the solvent.

(iii) Effect of temperature: The dissolution of a gas in a liquid is an exothermic process.

$$\text{Gas} + \text{Solvent} \rightleftharpoons \text{Solution} + \text{Heat}$$

Applying Le Chatelier's principle, it is evident that an increase in temperature would shift the equilibrium in the backward direction, that is, the solubility would decrease.

(iv) Nature of the gas: Gases such as hydrogen, oxygen and nitrogen, dissolve in water only to a small extent whereas gases such as CO_2, HCl and NH_3, are highly soluble in water. The greater solubility of a gas in a solvent is again due to the chemical similarity between the gas and the solvent.

Worked Out Problem 2.1

If N_2 gas is bubbled through water at 293 K, how many mmol of N_2 gas would dissolve in 1 litre of water? Assume that N_2 exerts a partial pressure of 0.987 bar, given that Henry's law constant for N_2 at 293 K is 76.48 kbar.

Solution

According to Henry's law, $p_{N_2} = K_H \times x_{N_2}$

$$\therefore \quad x_{N_2} = \frac{p_{N_2}}{K_H} = \frac{0.987\text{ bar}}{76480\text{ bar}} = 1.29 \times 10^{-5}$$

If n moles of N_2 is present in 1 L of water (55.5 mol),

$$x_{N_2} = \frac{n}{n + 55.5} \simeq \frac{n}{55.5} \quad (\text{as } n \ll 55.5)$$

$$\therefore \quad \frac{n}{55.5} = 1.29 \times 10^{-5}$$

$$\text{or} \quad n = 1.29 \times 10^{-5} \times 55.5\text{ mol} = 71.595 \times 10^{-5}\text{ mol} = 0.716\text{ mmol}$$

2.6 Vapour Pressure of Pure Liquid

When a pure liquid is taken in an evacuated vessel (Fig. 2.3), the amount of the vapour in the space above the liquid keeps on increasing and ultimately becomes constant when an equilibrium is attained, that is, the rate of evaporation becomes equal to the rate of condensation. The pressure thus exerted by the vapour is called vapour pressure. Hence,

$$H_2O(l) \underset{\text{Condensation}}{\overset{\text{Evaporation}}{\rightleftharpoons}} H_2O(g)$$

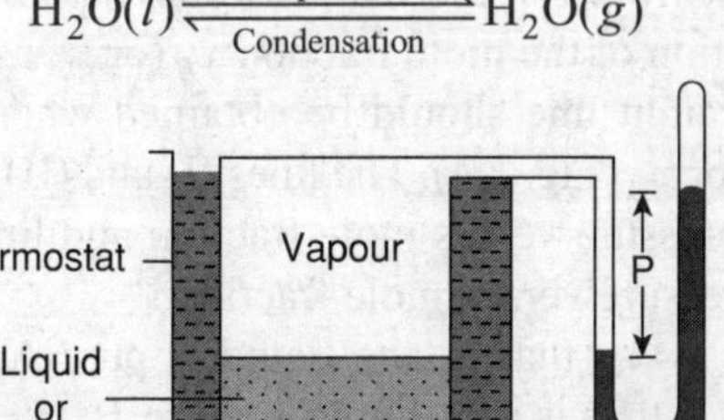

Fig. 2.3 Concept of measurement of vapour pressure of a liquid/solution at a particular temperature

Factors on which vapour pressure depends—(i) nature of liquid, (ii) temperature.

(i) Nature of liquid:

$$\text{Vapour pressure} \propto \frac{1}{\text{Boiling point of liquid}}$$

$$\text{Boiling point} \propto \text{Intermolecular forces}$$

$$\text{Vapour pressure} \propto \frac{1}{\text{Strength of intermolecular forces}}$$

Vapour pressure dimethyl ether > ethyl alcohol > water
BP = 52°C BP = 78°C BP = 100°C

Dimethyl ether does not form hydrogen bonds while ethyl alcohol and water form hydrogen bonds.

2.7 Vapour Pressure of Liquid Solution and Raoult's Law

2.7.1 Types of Solutions

Type I: Both solute and solvent are volatile and form vapour.

Type II: The solvent is volatile, the solute is non-volatile and does not form vapour.

Raoult's law: In a solution, the vapour pressure of a component at a given temperature is equal to the mole fraction of that component in the solution multiplied by the vapour pressure of that component in the pure state.

$$p \propto x \qquad p = p^\circ x$$

Consider a mixture of two completely miscible volatile liquids A and B, having mole fractions x_A and x_B. Suppose at a certain temperature, their partial vapour pressures are p_A and p_B and the vapour pressures in the pure state are $p^\circ{}_A$ and $p^\circ{}_B$, according to Raoult's law,

$$p_A = x_A\, p^\circ{}_A \quad \text{and} \quad p_B = x_B\, p^\circ{}_B \qquad (2.4)$$

If P is the total pressure of the system at the same temperature, then by applying Dalton's law of partial pressure,

$$P = p_A + p_B = x_A\, p^\circ{}_A + x_B\, p^\circ{}_B \qquad (2.5)$$

$$\text{or } P = (1 - x_B)p^\circ{}_A + x_B p^\circ{}_B = \left(p^\circ{}_B - p^\circ{}_A\right)x_B + p^\circ{}_A \qquad (2.6)$$

Since $p^\circ{}_A$ and $p^\circ{}_B$ are constant at a particular temperature, it is evident from Eq. 2.6 that the total vapour pressure is a linear function of the mole fraction x_B (or x_A as $x_A = 1 - x_B$). Thus, a straight line should be obtained when P is plotted against x_A or x_B (Fig. 2.4). The lines (I) and (II) give the plots of partial pressure versus mole fraction and line (III) that of the total pressure versus mole fraction.

When $x_A = 1$, that is, the liquid is pure A, $p = p^\circ{}_A$ and when $x_B = 1$, that is, the liquid is pure B, $p = p^\circ{}_B$. At any value of x_B (or x_A), the value of the total pressure is given by Eq. 2.6.

***Note*:** Raoult's law is not applicable if the two liquids are not completely miscible (not completely soluble).

If y_A and y_B represent the mole fractions of the components A and B respectively in the vapour phase, then

$y_A \propto n'_A$ $y_B \propto n'_B$ $n'_A \propto n'_B$ are moles of components in the vapour state

$$y_A = \frac{n'_A}{n'_A + n'_B} \qquad y_B = \frac{n'_B}{n'_A + n'_B}$$

Now, number and temperature are constant.

$$p_A \propto n'_A \quad p_B \propto n'_B$$

$$y_A = \frac{p_A}{p_A + p_B} = \frac{p_A}{P_{\text{Total}}}; \quad y_B = \frac{p_B}{p_A + p_B} = \frac{p_B}{P_{\text{Total}}}$$

The above results may also be written as

$$p_A = y_A \times P_{\text{Total}} \quad \text{and} \quad p_B = y_B \times P_{\text{Total}}$$

Worked Out Problem 2.2

The vapour pressure of chloroform ($CHCl_3$) and dichloromethane (CH_2Cl_2) at 298 K are 200 mm Hg and 415 mm Hg respectively. Calculate (i) the vapour pressure of the solution prepared by mixing 25.5 g of $CHCl_3$ and 40 g of CH_2Cl_2 at 298 K, and (ii) the mole fraction of each component in the vapour phase.

Solution

(i) Calculation of vapour pressure of the solution

Mass of $CHCl_3$ = 25.5 g

Mass of CH_2Cl_2 = 40 g

Molar mass of $CHCl_3$ = 12 + 1 + 3 × 35.5 = 119.5 g mol^{-1}

Molar mass of CH_2Cl_2 = 12 + 2 + 2 × 35.5 = 85 g mol^{-1}

$$\therefore \text{Moles of } CHCl_3 = \frac{25.5\text{ g}}{119.5\text{ g mol}^{-1}} = 0.213\text{ mol}$$

$$\text{Moles of } CH_2Cl_2 = \frac{40\text{ g}}{85\text{ g mol}^{-1}} = 0.470\text{ mol}$$

$$\text{Mole fraction of } CHCl_3\ (x_{CHCl_3}) = \frac{0.213}{0.213 + 0.470} = 0.312$$

$$\text{Mole fraction of } CH_2Cl_2\ (x_{CH_2Cl_2}) = 1 - 0.312 = 0.688$$

$$P_{\text{total}} = p_{CHCl_3} + p_{CH_2Cl_2}$$

$$= x_{CHCl_3} \times p^\circ{}_{CHCl_3} + x_{CH_2Cl_2} \times p^\circ{}_{CH_2Cl_2}$$

$$= 0.312 \times 200 + 0.688 \times 415 = 62.4 + 285.5 = 347.9\text{ mm}$$

(ii) Calculation of mole fraction of each component in the vapour phase

As calculated above, $p_{CHCl_3} = 62.4$ mm $p_{CH_2Cl_2} = 285.5$ mm $p_{\text{total}} = 347.9$ mm

Mole fraction of $CHCl_3$ in the vapour phase

$$\left(y_{CHCl_3}\right) = \frac{p_{CHCl_3}}{p_{\text{total}}} = \frac{62.4\text{ mm}}{347.9\text{ mm}} = 0.18$$

Mole fraction of CH_2Cl_2 in the vapour phase $(y_{CH_2Cl_2}) = -y_{CHCl_3} = 1 - 0.18 = 0.82$

2.8 Ideal Solution and Non-ideal Solution

On the basis of Raoult's law, liquid solutions can be classified into ideal and non-ideal solutions.

2.8.1 Ideal Solutions

An ideal solution is that in which the intermolecular interactions between the solvent and the solute (A–B) are of the same magnitude as the intermolecular interactions found in the pure solvent (A–A) and the pure solute (B–B).

Conditions for an Ideal Solution

(i) $\Delta H_{\text{mixing}} = 0$

(ii) $\Delta V_{\text{mixing}} = 0$

(iii) Solution obeys Raoult's law (Fig. 2.4) $p_A = p_A{}^\circ x_B$
$p_B = p_B{}^\circ x_B$

(iv) $\Delta S_{\text{mixing}} = +\text{ve}$

(v) $\Delta G_{\text{mixing}} = -\text{ve}$

$$-\Delta G_{\text{mixing}} = +T\Delta S_{\text{mixing}}$$

Very dilute solutions are nearly ideal. A few examples are given below:

(i) Benzene + Toluene
(ii) *n*-Hexane + *n*-Heptane
(iii) Ethyl bromide + Ethyl iodide
(iv) Chlorobenzene + Bromobenzene

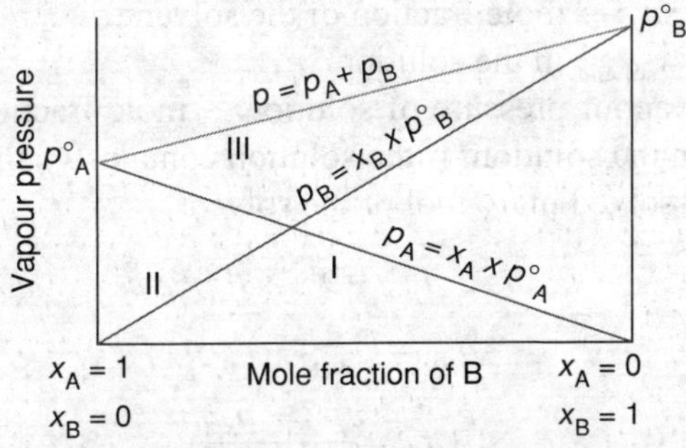

Fig. 2.4 The relationship between vapour pressure and mole fraction of an ideal solution at constant temeperature (*P*–*x* diagram)

2.8.2 Non-ideal Solution

A non-ideal solution is that solution where the intermolecular attraction between the solvent and solute (A–B) are not of the same magnitude as between the solvent and solvent (A–A) and the solute and solute (B–B).

Conditions for a Non-ideal Solution

(i) $\Delta H_{mixing} \neq$ zero.
(ii) $\Delta V_{mixing} \neq$ zero.
(iii) Solution does not obey Raoult's law.

$pA \neq pA^\circ x_A \qquad pB \neq pB^\circ x_B$

Types of non-ideal solutions

Non-ideal solutions showing positive deviation: This occurs when the solvent–solute (A–B) molecular interaction forces are weaker than the solvent–solvent (A–A) and the solute–solute (B–B) molecular interaction forces (Fig. 2.5). For example, when ethyl alcohol and cyclohexane are mixed, the force of attraction decreases.

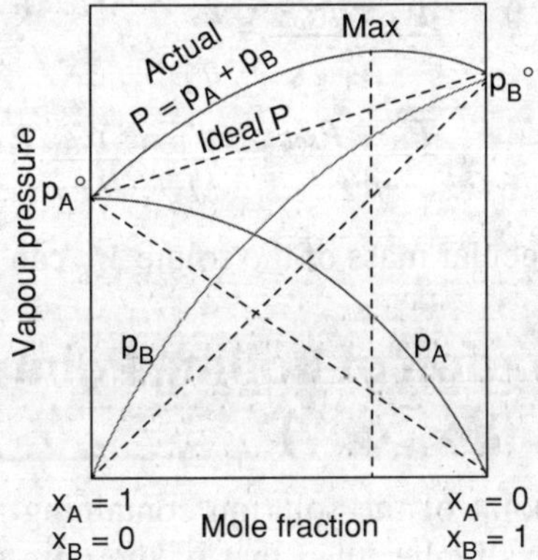

Fig. 2.5 A vapour pressure graph showing positive deviations (solid lines) from ideal behaviour (dotted lines)

For a non-ideal solution showing positive deviation,

(i) ΔH_{mixing} = +ve
(ii) ΔV_{mixing} = +ve
(iii) $p_A > x_A p_A^\circ$, $p_B > x_B p_B^\circ$, $p_{total} > x_A p_B^\circ + x_B p_B^\circ$

A few examples of non-ideal solutions showing positive deviations are—acetone + carbon disulfide, acetone + ethyl alcohol, acetone + benzene, methyl alcohol + water, ethyl alcohol + water, carbon tetrachloride + chloroform, carbon tetrachloride + benzene, carbon tetrachloride + toluene.

Non-ideal solutions showing negative deviation: When the forces of interaction between the solvent and solute (A–B) are stronger than the A–A and B–B forces of interaction, these solutions are said to show *negative* deviations (Fig. 2.6) from Raoult's law.

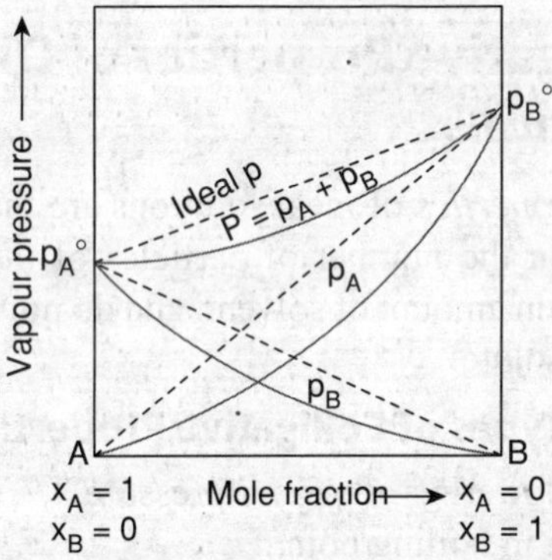

Fig. 2.6 Negative deviation from ideal behaviour [The dotted lines (----) represent ideal behaviour and solid lines (____) represent actual behaviour]

For a non-ideal solution showing negative deviation,

(i) ΔH_{mixing} = –ve
(ii) ΔV_{mixing} = –ve
(iii) $p_A < x_A p_A^\circ$, $p_B < x_B p_B^\circ$, $p_{total} < x_A p_A^\circ + x_B p_B^\circ$

A few examples of non-ideal solutions showing negative deviations are chloroform + benzene, chloroform + diethyl ether, acetone + aniline, HCl + water, HNO_3 + water, acetic acid + pyridine.

2.8.3 Azeotropic *Solution*

Minimum boiling point azeotrope: In the case of non-ideal solutions with positive deviations at one of the intermediate compositions, the vapour pressure of the solution is the highest and the boiling point is the lowest. This is called a *minimum boiling point azeotrope.* The mole fractions of compounds of the liquid and vapour phases is the same in an azeotrope, the liquid obtained by the condensation of the vapour also has same composition, that is, *the mixture distils over as if it were a pure liquid.* This type of liquid mixture, is called a *constant boiling mixture.*

In the case of minimum boiling azeotropes, the boiling point of the azeotrope is less than the boiling point of either of the pure components. For example, a mixture of ethanol

(BP 351.3 K) and water (BP 373 K) containing 95.4% of ethanol forms an azeotrope with a boiling point of 351.15 K.

Azeotropic mixtures cannot be separated into their constituents by fractional distillation.

Maximum boiling point azeotrope: A solution with intermediate composition which has the lowest vapour pressure and highest boiling point as compared to other solutions of same components is called a *maximum boiling point azeotrope*. The boiling point is constant, that is, it does not change when the azeotrope is boiled.

Similarly, in the case of maximum boiling azeotropes, the boiling point of the azeotrope is higher than that of either of the pure components. For example, a mixture of nitric acid (BP 359 K) and water (BP 373 K) containing 68% nitric acid forms an azeotrope with a boiling point of 393.5 K.

2.9 Colligative Properties of Dilute Solutions

Colligative properties of ideal solutions are those properties that depend on the number of particles of the non-volatile solute in a given amount of solvent, and do not depend on the nature of the solute.

2.9.1 Four Types of Colligative Properties

(i) Relative lowering of vapour pressure.
(ii) Elevation in boiling point.
(iii) Depression in freezing point.
(iv) Osmotic pressure.

2.10 Relative Lowering of Vapour Pressure and Its Measurement

When a non-volatile solute is added into the solvent, it reduces the escaping tendency of the solvent molecules into the vapour phase and thus lowers the vapour pressure of the solvent. It means that mole fraction of the solvent (Fig. 2.7) decreases in the solution, therefore, the vapour pressure of the solution decreases (Raoult's law).

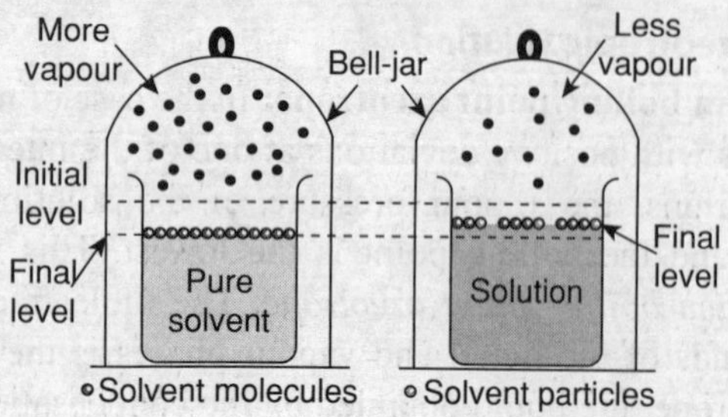

Fig. 2.7 Vapour pressure of (a) pure solvent (b) solution

2.10.1 Raoult's Law for Solutions Containing Non-volatile Solutes

Non-volatile solutes do not form vapour due to the strong force of attraction between molecules. Thus, the vapour pressure of the solution will be the vapour pressure due to the solvent in the solution only.

Vapour pressure of the solution =

$$\begin{bmatrix}\text{Mole fraction of the}\\ \text{solvent in solution}\end{bmatrix} \times \begin{bmatrix}\text{Vapour pressure of}\\ \text{the pure solvent}\end{bmatrix}$$

or in terms of symbols, we can write $p_{sol} = x_A \times p_A^\circ$

where, $x_A \rightarrow$ mole fraction of the solvent.

$p_{sol} \propto x_{solvent}$ in the solution

That is, vapour pressure of solution $\propto$ mole fraction of the solvent in the solution. If the solution contains n_B mol of the solute dissolved in n_A mol of the solvent,

$$p_{sol} = x_A \times p_A^\circ$$

$$p_{sol} = (1 - x_A)) \times p_A^\circ$$

$$x_B = \frac{p_A^\circ - p_{sol}}{p_A^\circ}$$

In this expression, $p_A^\circ - p_{sol}$ expresses the lowering of vapour pressure, $\frac{p_A^\circ - p_{sol}}{p_A^\circ}$ is called the relative lowering of the vapour pressure of the solution.

∴ According to Raoult's law, *the relative lowering of the vapour pressure of a solution containing a non-volatile solute is equal to the mole fraction of the solute in the solution.*

$$\frac{p_A^\circ - p_{sol}}{p_A^\circ} = x_B \quad (2.7)$$

Determination of molecular masses of solutes from lowering of vapour pressure

$$\frac{p_A^\circ - p_{sol}}{p_A^\circ} = \frac{\frac{w_B}{M_B}}{\frac{w_A}{M_A} + \frac{w_B}{M_B}}$$

For a dilute solution, n_A can be neglected in comparison with n_B, so Raoult's law equation becomes,

$$n_A \ggg n_B$$

or
$$\frac{p_A^\circ - p_{sol}}{p_A^\circ} \simeq \frac{n_B}{n_A}$$

or
$$\frac{p_A^\circ - p_{sol}}{p_A^\circ} = \frac{w_B}{M_B} \times \frac{w_A}{M_A} \quad (2.8)$$

Thus, the molecular mass of the solute M_B can be calculated.

2.11 Elevation of Boiling Point (Ebullioscopy)

The boiling point of the solution containing a non-volatile solute is always higher than that of the pure solvent as the vapour pressure of solution decreases due to a decrease in the mole fraction of the solvent. Therefore, more amount of heat is required to make the vapour pressure of the solution equal to the atmospheric pressure. The increase is called the elevation in boiling point.

The vapour pressure of the solvent increases with an increase in temperature, as shown by the curve AB (Fig. 2.8). At any temperature, the vapour pressure of the solution is less than that of the solvent, the curve for the solution lies below that of the solvent (curve CD). The temperatures at which the vapour pressure of the solvent and the solution become equal to the atmospheric pressure are T_b° and T_b respectively. The difference, called the elevation in boiling point, ΔT_b, is given by

$$\Delta T_b = T_b - T_b^{\circ}$$

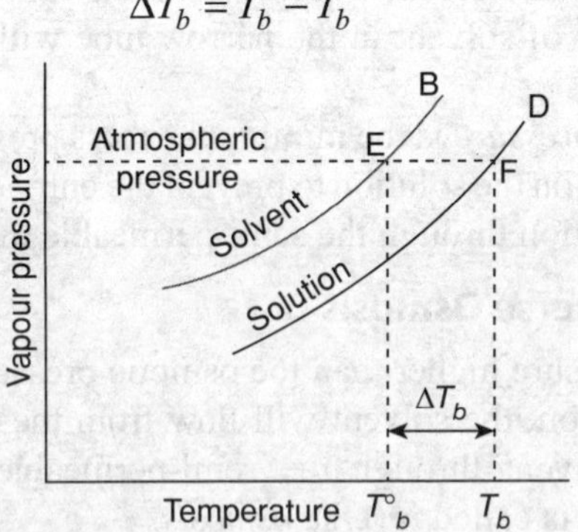

Fig. 2.8 Elevation in boiling point

Molal elevation constant of a solvent is the elevation in boiling point when the molality of the solution is unity. The units of K_b are, therefore, degree/molality, that is, K/m or °C/m or K kg mol^{-1}.

Mathematical equation for elevation in boiling point

$$x_B = \frac{n_B}{n_B + n_A} \simeq \frac{n_B}{n_A} \text{ if the solution is dilute.}$$

That is, $x_B = \dfrac{n_B}{w_B / M_B} \quad \therefore \Delta T_b = k\, M_A \dfrac{n_B}{w_A}$ (2.9)

If the mass of solvent, $w_A = 1$ kg, then evidently $\dfrac{n_B}{w_A} = m$, molality of the solution.

$$\Delta T_b = k \times M_A \times m$$

Also, for a given solvent, its molecular mass M_A is constant so that $kM_A = K_b$, another constant.

$$\Delta T_b = K_b\, m \qquad (2.10)$$

Calculation of molecular mass of the solute

$$\Delta T_b = K_b \times m$$

$$\Delta T_b = K_b \times \frac{w_B}{M_B} \times \frac{1000}{w_A}$$

Worked Out Problem 2.3

Calculate the molal elevation constant of water, given that its latent heat of vaporisation is 2.257 kJ/g.

Solution

$$K_b = \frac{RT_0^2}{1000 l_v} = \frac{8.314 \text{ J K}^{-1} \text{ mol}^{-1} \times (373 \text{ K})^2}{1000 \text{ g kg}^{-1} \times 2257 \text{ J g}^{-1}}$$
$$= 0.512 \text{ K kg mol}^{-1}$$

2.12 Depression in Freezing Point (Cryoscopy)

The freezing point of the solution containing a non-volatile solute is always lower than that of the pure solvent. This decrease is called the *depression in freezing point*.

On cooling, the vapour pressure of the liquid solvent decreases along the curve AB (Fig. 2.9). At B, the solid starts appearing and the vapour pressure decreases steeply along the path BC (because solids have a lower vapour pressure). At B, the liquid and the solid solvent are in equilibrium and have the same vapour pressure. Thus, B represents the freezing point T_f° of the pure solvent. At any temperature, the vapour pressure of the solution is less than that of the solvent, the curve for the solution lies below that of the solvent. On cooling, it will follow the path DE. At E, the solid appears. Hence, E represents the freezing point T_f of the solution. Obviously, T_f is less than T_f°. The difference, called the depression of freezing point, ΔT_f, is given by

$$\Delta T_f = T_f^{\circ} - T_f$$

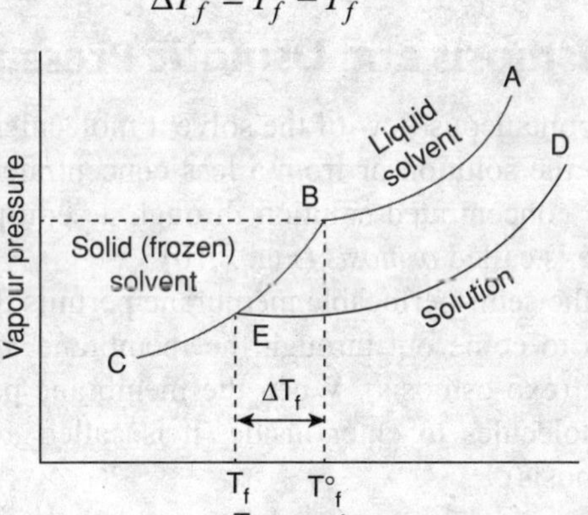

Fig. 2.9 Depression in freezing point

Equation for depression in freezing point

$$\Delta T_f = K_f \times m \qquad (2.11)$$

where K_f is a constant known as the *molal depression constant* or *cryoscopic constant* of the solvent and m is the molality of the solution.

If $\quad m = 1, \Delta T_f = K_f$

Hence, the molal depression constant may be defined as the depression in freezing point when the molality of the solution is unity.

Worked Out Problem 2.4

1.00 g of a non-electrolyte solute dissolved in 50 g of benzene lowered the freezing point of benzene by 0.40 K.

The freezing point depression constant of benzene is 5.12 K kg mol^{-1}. Find the molar mass of solute.

Solution

Here, we are given $w_2 = 1.00$ g, $w_1 = 50$ g, $\Delta T_f = 0.40$ K, $K_f = 5.12$ K kg mol^{-1}

Substituting these values in the formula $M_2 = \dfrac{1000\, K_f w_2}{w_1 \Delta T_f}$, we get

$$M_2 = \frac{1000\,\text{g kg}^{-1} \times 512\ \text{K kg mol}^{-1} \times 1.0\text{g}}{50\ \text{g} \times 0.40\ \text{K}} = 256\,\text{g mol}^{-1}$$

Worked Out Problem 2.5

Calculate the amount of ice that will separate out when a solution containing 50 of ethylene glycol in 200 of water is cooled to -9.3°C.(K_f for $H_2O = 1.86$ K kg mol^{-1})

Solution

$$\Delta T_f = \frac{1000\, K_f w_2}{w_1 M_2}$$

Let us calculate the amount of water (w_1) pressure when $\Delta T_f = 9.3°$

$$9.3 = \frac{1000 \times 1.86 \times 50}{w_1 \times 62} \quad [\text{Mol. mass of } (CH_2OH)_2 = 62]$$

or $$w_1 = 161.29\ \text{g}$$

∴ Water frozen to ice = 200 – 161.29 = 38.71 g

2.13 Osmosis and Osmotic Pressure

The net spontaneous flow of the solvent molecules from the solvent to the solution or from a less concentrated solution to a more concentrated solution through a semi-permeable membrane is called *osmosis* (Fig. 2.10).

When the semi-permeable membrane permits the solvent molecules to come out through the membrane, it is called *exosmosis* (exo-osmosis). When the membrane permits the solvent molecules to enter inside, it is called *endosmosis* (endo-osmosis).

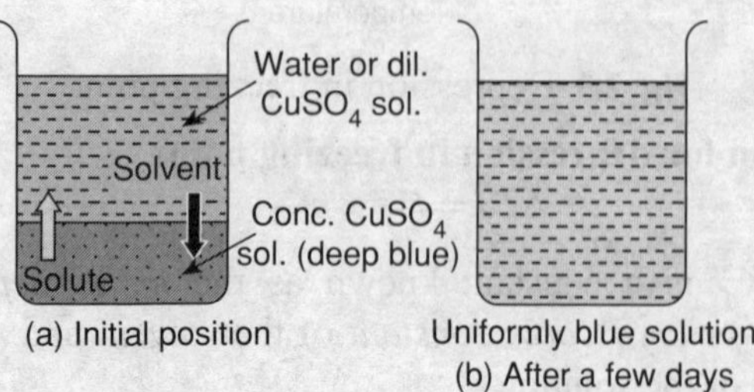

Fig. 2.10 Diffusion in solution

2.13.1 Measurement of Osmotic Pressure

Due to osmosis, there is a tendency for the net flow of solvent into the solution through the semi-permeable membrane, As a result, the piston will tend to move outwards and the level in the narrow tube will fall (Fig. 2.11).

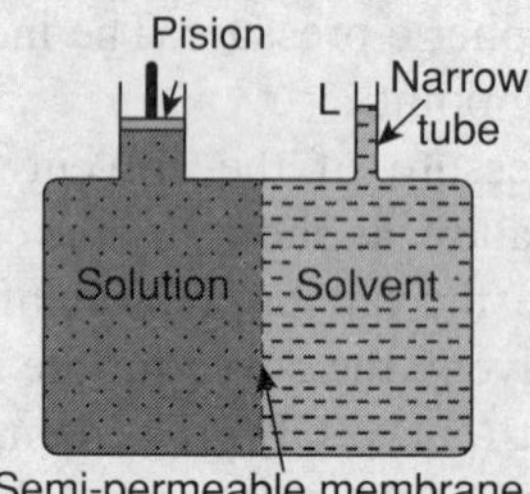

Fig. 2.11 Concept of osmotic pressure

However, if some suitable pressure is applied on the piston, the entry of the solvent into the solution can be prevented and the level of solvent in the narrow tube will then remain constant at L.

Osmotic pressure is the minimum excess pressure that has to be applied on the solution to prevent the entry of the solvent into the solution through the semi-permeable membrane.

2.13.2 Reverse Osmosis

When a pressure higher than the osmotic pressure is applied on the solution, the solvent will flow from the solution into the pure solvent through the semi-permeable membrane. This process is called *reverse osmosis.*

An important application of reverse osmosis is in the *desalination of sea water,* that is, removal of salts from sea water. On applying a pressure greater than the osmotic pressure, pure water can be made to flow through a semi-permeable membrane and this water can be used for drinking.

2.13.3 Mathematical Expression for the Osmotic Pressure

Osmotic pressure (π) of a solution is found to be directly proportional to the molar concentration (C) of the solution and its temperature (T). Mathematically,

$$\pi \propto C \quad \text{and} \quad \pi \propto T \quad \pi = R \times C \times T$$

where R is a constant (called solution constant) and its value is found to be the same as that of the *gas constant*.

But $$C = \frac{n_B}{V}$$

where C is concentration, that is, molarity, n is the number of moles of the solute and V is the volume of the solution in litres.

Hence, $$\pi = \frac{n_B}{V} RT \qquad (2.12)$$

This equation is called the *van't Hoff equation* for dilute solutions.

2.13.4 Isotonic Solutions

Solutions which have the same osmotic pressure at the same temperature are called *isotonic solutions*. Thus, two isotonic solutions are also *isosmotic*.

2.13.5 Biological Importance of Osmosis

- Plants absorb water from the soil through their roots due to osmosis because the concentration of cell sap inside the root hair cells is higher than that of the water present in the soil (Fig. 2.12).

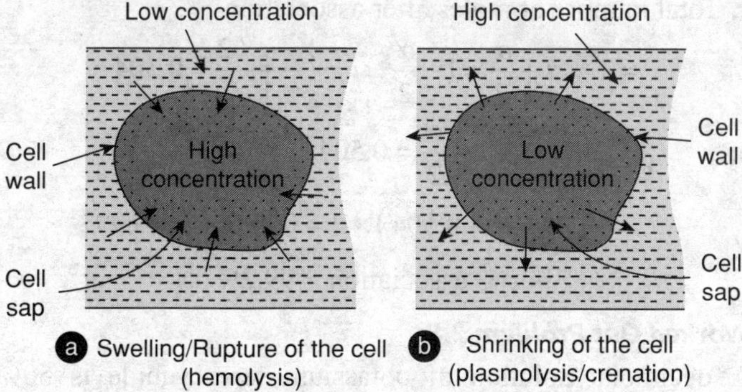

Fig. 2.12 Osmosis through the Semi-permeable membrane (cell walls)

- Stretching of leaves, flowers, germination of seeds, is controlled by osmosis.
- Bursting of red blood cells when placed in water is also due to osmosis. The salt concentration in blood plasma due to different species present in it is equivalent to 0.9% aqueous solution of NaCl (mass/volume).

A 0.9% solution of pure NaCl is isotonic with human red blood cells (RBC). Therefore, in this solution, RBCs neither swell nor undergo plasmolysis. A pure NaCl solution with a concentration less than 0.9% is a *hypotonic solution.* On placing RBCs in this solution, they will swell and even burst. A pure NaCl solution with a concentration more than 0.9% is called a *hypertonic solution.* On placing RBCs in this solution, they shrink due to plasmolysis.

Worked Out Problem 2.6

Calculate the osmotic pressure at 273 K of a 5% solution of urea (Mol. mass = 60, $R = 0.0821$ litre atm/degree/mol).

Solution

5% solution of urea means that it contains 5 g of urea per 100 cm^3 of the solution, that is,

$$w_2 = 5\text{ g}\quad V = 100\text{ cm}^3 = \frac{1}{10}\text{ litre} = 0.1\text{ litre}$$

$$M_2 = 60\text{ g mol}^{-1}, R = 0.0821\text{ L atm K}^{-1}\text{ mol}^{-1}, T = 237\text{ K}$$

$$\therefore\quad \pi = \frac{n}{V}RT = \frac{w_2}{M_2}\times\frac{1}{V}RT = \frac{w_2 RT}{M_2 V}$$

$$= \frac{(5\text{g})(0.0821\text{atm K}^{-1}\text{ mol}^{-1})(273\text{ K})}{(60\text{ g mol}^{-1})(0.1\text{ L})} = 18.68\text{ atm}$$

2.14 Abnormal Molar Masses

Molecular mass of a solute which undergoes association or dissociation is found to be different from the actual molecular mass as determined by colligative properties. For the solutes that dissociate completely or to a small extent in the solution, the number of particles increases. The experimentally observed value of the colligative property comes out to be higher than the theoretically expected value and the observed molecular mass comes out to be less than the theoretically expected value. Similarly, in some solutes, association takes place in the solution.

The number of particles in the solution decreases, the experimentally observed value of the colligative property decreases and the molecular mass is greater than the theoretical expected value. When the molecular mass of a substance determined by studying any of the colligative properties comes out to be different than the theoretically expected value, the substance is said to show *abnormal molecular mass.*

2.15 vant' Hoff Factor

To calculate the extent of association or dissociation, van't Hoff in 1880, introduced a factor *i*, called the *van't Hoff factor.*

The *van't Hoff factor* is defined as the ratio of the experimental value of the colligative property to the theoretical calculated value of the colligative property.

$$i = \frac{\text{Experimental observed value of the colligative property}}{\text{Theoretical calculated value of the colligative property}}$$

As the colligative property is inversely proportional to the molecular mass of the solute, van't Hoff factor can be

$$i = \frac{\text{Theoretical calculated molecular mass}}{\text{Experimental observed molecular mass}} = \frac{M_{\text{Normal}}}{M_{\text{Observed}}} \quad (2.13)$$

2.15.1 Modified Expressions of Colligative Properties for Substances Undergoing Association or Dissociation

For substances undergoing association or dissociation in the solution, the various expressions for the colligative properties are modified as follows.

(i) Relative lowering of vapour pressure, $\frac{p^\circ - p_s}{p^\circ} = x_2 \times i$

(ii) Elevation in boiling point, $\Delta T_b = K_b\,\text{m} \times i$

(iii) Depression in freezing point, $\Delta T_f = K_f\,\text{m} \times i$

(iv) Osmotic pressure, $\pi = \frac{n}{V}RT \times i$

Calculation of the degree of dissociation: The degree of dissociation is the fraction of the total no of molecules of solute that undergoes dissociation, Degree of dissociation

$$(\alpha) = \frac{\text{No. of moles of solute dissociated}}{\text{Total number of moles of solute}}$$

$$\therefore\quad \alpha = \frac{M_c - M_o}{M_o(n-1)}$$

Calculation of the degree of association: The degree of association is the fraction of the total no. of molecules of solute that undergoes association.

$$\alpha = \frac{M_o - M_c}{M_o}\cdot\frac{n}{(n-1)} \quad (2.14)$$

where M_c is the normal (calculated) molecular mass and M_o is the observed molecular mass.

Worked Out Problem 2.7

2.0 of benzoic acid dissolved in 25.0 g of benzene shows a depression in freezing point equal to 1.62 K. The molal depression constant (K_f) of benzene is 4.9 K kg mol^{-1}. What is the percentage association of the acid if it forms dimer in the solution?

Solution

Mass of solute (benzoic acid), $w_2 = 2.0$ g

Mass of solvent (benzene), $w_1 = 25.0$ g

Observed $\Delta T_f = 1.62\ K;\ K_f = 4.9$ K kg mol^{-1}

∴ Observed molar mass of benzoic acid

$$M_2 = \frac{1000 \times K_f \times w_2}{\Delta T_f \times w_1} = \frac{1000 \text{ g kg}^{-1} \times 4.9 \text{ K kg mol}^{-1} \times 2.0 \text{ g}}{1.62 \text{ K} \times 25.0 \text{ g}}$$

$$= 242 \text{ g mol}^{-1}$$

Calculated molal mass of benzoic acid (C_6H_5COOH) = 72 + 5 + 12 + 32 + 1 = 122 g mol^{-1}

$$\text{Van't Hoff factor, } \frac{\text{Calculted mol.mass}}{\text{Observed mol.mass}} = \frac{122}{242} = 0.504$$

If α is the degree of association of benzoic acid, then we have

$$2\,C_6H_5COOH \rightleftharpoons (C_6H_5COOH)_2$$

Initial moles	1	0
After association	$1-\alpha$	$\alpha/2$

∴ Total number of moles after association

$$= 1 - \alpha + \frac{\alpha}{2} = 1 - \frac{\alpha}{2}\ \therefore i = \frac{1-\alpha/2}{1} = 0.504$$

or $$1 - \frac{\alpha}{2} = 0.504$$

$$\alpha = (1 - 0.504) \times 2 = 0.496 \times 2 = 0.992$$

or % association = 99.2%

Worked Out Problem 2.8

A decimolar solution of potassium ferrocyanide is 50% dissociated at 300 K. Calculate the osmotic pressure of the solution. Given solution constant $R = 8.314$ J K^{-1} mol^{-1}.

Solution

Molar concentration = 0.1 mol L^{-1}

$$= \frac{0.1}{10^{-3}} \text{ mol m}^{-3} = 10^2 \text{ mol m}^{-3}$$

	$K_4[Fe(CN)_6]$ ⇌	$4K^+$ +	$[Fe(CN)_6]^{4-}$	
Initial	1 mole	0	0	
After 50% disso.	1–0.5 = 0.5	4 × 0.5 = 2	0.5	Total = 3

∴ $i = 3$

$$\pi = i\,CRT$$

$$= 3 \times 10^1 \times 8.314 \times 300 \text{ Nm}^{-2} = 7.483 \times 10^5 \text{ Nm}^{-2}$$

Exercises

OBJECTIVE QUESTIONS

Introduction

1. Which of the following statements is incorrect about a solution?
   (a) A solution is always a homogeneous mixture.
   (b) The size of the solute particles in a solution is less than 10 Å.
   (c) Brass cannot be called a solution.
   (d) An ionic compound dissolves in water if the hydration energy is greater than the lattice energy.

Types of Solutions

2. A solid solution formed between two substances, one whose particles are very large and the other whose particles are very small is known as a/an
   (a) heterogenous solution
   (b) homogeneous solution
   (c) substitutional solid solution
   (d) interstitial solid solution

3. Which one of the following is the most correct statement?
   (a) Brass is an interstitial alloy while steel is a substitutional alloy.
   (b) Brass is a substitutional alloy while steel is an interstitial alloy.
   (c) Brass and steel both are substitutional alloys.
   (d) Brass and steel are both interstitial alloys.

4. If a non-metal atom is added to the interstitial sites of a metal atom, then the metal becomes
   (a) softer (b) less tensile
   (c) less malleable (d) more ductile

5. $CuSO_4.5H_2O$ is a
   (a) solution of a solid in a liquid
   (b) solution of liquid in a solid
   (c) salt only and cannot be called a solution
   (d) coordination compound of copper with water molecules as the ligands

6. Which of the following statements is correct about steel (S) and tungsten chloride (WC)?
   (a) S is a substitutional solid while WC is an interstitial solid solution.
   (b) S is an interstitial solid while WC is a substitutional solid solution.
   (c) Both are interstitial solid solutions.
   (d) Both are substitutional solid solutions.

Expressing Concentration of Solutions

7. The number of moles of hydroxide (OH^-) ion in 0.3 litre of 0.005 M solution of $Ba(OH)_2$ is

(a) 0.0075 (b) 0.0015 (c) 0.0030 (d) 0.0050

8. 200 mL of $CaCl_2$ solution is found to contain 3.01×10^{22} chloride ions. The molarity of the solution is

(a) 0.250 M (b) 0.0625 M
(c) 0.125 M (d) 0.375 M

9. 25.3 g of sodium carbonate, Na_2CO_3 is dissolved in enough water to make 250 mL of solution. If sodium carbonate dissociates completely, the molar concentration of sodium ions, Na^+ and carbonate ions, CO_3^{2-} are respectively (molar mass of Na_2CO_3 = 106 g mol^{-1})

(a) 0.477 M and 0.477 M (b) 0.955 M and 1.910 M
(c) 1.910 M and 0.955 M (d) 1.90 M and 1.910 M

10. Concentrated nitric acid used in the laboratory is 68% nitric acid by mass in aqueous solution. If the density of the solution is 1.504 g mL^{-1}, the molarity of the solution will be

(a) 14.2 M (b) 15.2 M (c) 16.2 M (d) 17.2 M

11. The amount of benzoic acid (C_6H_5COOH) required for preparing 250 mL of 0.15 M solution in methanol is

(a) 5.625 g (b) 3.275 g (c) 4.575 g (d) 4.125 g

12. Calculate the molarity of a solution of 30 g of $Co(NO_3)_2.6H_2O$ in 4.3 L of solution. Consider atomic mass of Co = 59 u, N = 14 u, O = 16 u, H = 1 u.

(a) 0.023 M (b) 0.23 M (c) 0.046 M (d) 0.46 M

13. Volume of 0.2 M H_2SO_4 solution containing 20 mmol of the solute is

(a) 10 cm^3 (b) 100 cm^3 (c) 20 cm^3 (d) 200 cm^3

14. How many mmol are present in 250 mL solution of 0.1 M?

(a) 1000 (b) 100 (c) 50 (d) 25

15. The volume of ethyl alcohol (density 1.15 g/cc) that has to be added to prepare 100 cc of 0.5 M ethyl alcohol solution in water is

(a) 1.15 cc (b) 2 cc (c) 2.15 cc (d) 2.30 cc

16. Which statement is true for a solution of 0.020 M H_2SO_4?

(a) 2 litre of the solution contains 0.020 mol of SO_4^{2-}.
(b) 2 litre of the solution contains 0.080 mol H_3O^+.
(c) 1 litre of the solution contains 0.020 mol H_3O^+.
(d) None of these.

17. 0.115 g of pure sodium metal was dissolved in 500 mL distilled water. The normality of the above solution would be

(a) 0.010 N (b) 0.0115 N
(c) 0.023 N (d) 0.046 N

18. One litre of N/2 HCl solution is heated in a beaker. When the volume of the solution was reduced to 600 mL, 3.25 g of HCl was found to have been lost. The normality of the new solution is

(a) 0.585 N (b) 0.685 N
(c) 0.785 N (d) 0.885 N

19. Normality of a 2 M sulfuric acid is

(a) 2 N (b) 4 N (c) N/2 (d) N/4

20. Which amongst the following has the highest normality?

(a) 8.0 g of KOH/100 mL of solution
(b) 0.5 molar H_2SO_4
(c) 1 N H_3PO_4
(d) 6 g of NaOH/100 g of water

21. How much $CuSO_4.5H_2O$ (Eq. wt. = 249.5) is required to prepare 500 cc of 0.5 N solution?

(a) 249.5 (b) 249.5/2 (c) 249.5/4 (d) 249.5/5

22. To prepare 2 dm^3 of decinormal solution acid, the mass of oxalic acid required is

(a) 6.3 g (b) 0.63 g (c) 12.6 g (d) 1.26 g

23. Molarity of a given orthophosphoric acid solution is 3 M. Its normality is

(a) 9 N (b) 0.3 N (c) 3 N (d) 1 N

24. With 63 g of oxalic acid how many litres of $\frac{N}{10}$ solution can be prepared?

(a) 100 litre (b) 10 litre
(c) 1 litre (d) 1000 litre

25. How many grams of dibasic acid (mol. wt. 20) should be present in 100 mL of its aqueous solution to give decinormal strength?

(a) 1 g (b) 2 g (c) 10 g (d) 20 g

26. An aqueous solution of urea containing 18 g urea in 1500 cm^3 of the solution has a density equal to 1.052. If the molecular weight of urea is 60, then the molality of the solution is

(a) 0.200 (b) 0.192 (c) 0.100 (d) 1.200

27. If density of some lake water is 1.25 g mL^{-1} and contains 92 g of Na^+ ions per kg of water, the molality of Na^+ ions in the lake is

(a) 2 m (b) 4 m (c) 6 m (d) 8 m

28. Nalorphene ($C_{19}H_{22}NO_3$), similar to morphine, is used to combat withdrawal symptoms in narcotic users. Dose of nalorphene generally given is 1.5 mg. The mass of 1.5×10^{-3} m aqueous solution required for the above does is

(a) 2.15 g (b) 1.75 g (c) 2.97 g (d) 3.21 g

29. Calculate the molality of a solution that contains 51.2 g of naphthalene ($C_{10}H_8$) in 500 mL of carbon tetrachloride. The density of CCl_4 is 1.60 g/mL.

(a) 0.250 m (b) 0.500 m
(c) 0.750 m (d) 0.840 m

30. Calculate the mass of urea (NH_2CONH_2) required in making 2.5 kg 0.25 molal aqueous solution.
(a) 37.5 g (b) 73.5 g (c) 53.7 g (d) 75.3 g

31. The molality of 90% H_2SO_4 solution is [density = 1.8 g/mL]
(a) 1.8 (b) 48.4 (c) 91.83 (d) 94.6

32. A 5.2 molal aqueous solution of methyl alcohol, CH_3OH is supplied. What is the mole fraction of methyl alcohol in the solution?
(a) 0.190 (b) 0.086 (c) 0.050 (d) 0.100

33. Rectified spirit contains 95% ethanol by weight. The mole fraction of ethanol will be
(a) 0.881 (b) 0.99 (c) 0.118 (d) 0.81

34. The mole fraction of ethylene glycol ($C_2H_6O_2$) in a solution containing 20% of $C_2H_6O_2$ by mass is
(a) 0.322 (b) 0.034 (c) 0.068 (d) 0.932

35. The mole fraction of water in 20% aqueous solution (by weight) of H_2O_2 is
(a) $\frac{77}{68}$ (b) $\frac{68}{77}$ (c) $\frac{20}{80}$ (d) $\frac{80}{20}$

36. 5 litres of a solution contains 25 mg of $CaCO_3$. What is its concentration in ppm? [mol. wt. of $CaCO_3$ is 100]
(a) 25 (b) 1 (c) 5 (d) 2500

37. One kilogram of sea water contains 6 mg of dissolved oxygen. The concentration of O_2 in the sample in ppm is
(a) 0.6 (b) 6.0 (c) 60.0 (d) 16.0

38. 10 L of a sample of hard water contains 50 mg of $CaCO_3$. The concentration of the solution in terms of ppm will be
(a) 5 (b) 50 (c) 500 (d) 5000

39. The weight percent of sucrose (formula weight = 342 g mol^{-1}) in an aqueous solution is 3.42. The density of the solution is 1 g mL^{-1}. The concentration of sucrose in the solution in mol L^{-1} is
(a) 0.01 (b) 0.1 (c) 1.0 (d) 10

40. The solution of sulfuric acid contains 80% by weight H_2SO_4. Specific gravity of this solution is 1.71. Its normality is about
(a) 18.0 (b) 27.9 (c) 1.0 (d) 10.0

41. The molality of an aqueous solution in which the mole fraction of the solute is 0.018 will be
(a) 0.5 (b) 1.0 (c) 1.5 (d) 2.0

42. The mole fraction of the solute in one molal aqueous solution is
(a) 0.027 (b) 0.036 (c) 0.018 (d) 0.009

43. A sample of drinking water was found to be severely contaminated with chloroform, $CHCl_3$ (supposed to be a carcinogen). The level of contamination was 15 ppm (by mass). The molality of chloroform in water sample is
(a) 1.24×10^{-3} (b) 1.24×10^{-4}
(c) 1.24×10^{-5} (d) 1.24×10^{-6}

44. A molal solution of sodium chloride has a density of 1.21 g mL^{-1}. The molarity of this solution
(a) 4.15 (b) 1.143 (c) 2.95 (d) 3.15

45. The milli equivalents in 60 mL 4.0 M H_2SO_4 is
(a) 240 (b) 480 (c) 24 (d) 48

46. The molality of a sulfuric acid solution in which the mole fraction of water is 0.85 is
(a) 9.80 (b) 10.50 (c) 10.80 (d) 11.25

47. 2.52 g of oxalic acid dehydrate was dissolved in 100 mL of water. 10 mL of this solution was diluted to 50 mL. The normality of the final solution and the amount of oxalic acid (mg/mL) in the solution are respectively
(a) 0.16 N, 5.04 (b) 0.08 N, 3.60
(c) 0.04 N, 3.60 (d) 0.02 N, 10.08

48. The percentage (by weight) of sodium hydroxide in a 1.25 molal NaOH solution is
(a) 4.76% (b) 1.25% (c) 5% (d) 40%

49. Two bottles A and B contain 1 M and 1 m aqueous solution of sulfuric acid respectively.
(a) A is more concentrated than B
(b) B is more concentrated than A
(c) the concentration of A is equal to the concentration of B
(d) it is not possible to compare the concentrations

50. Molarity of H_2SO_4 is 18 M. Its density is 1.8 g/mL. Hence molality is
(a) 36 (b) 200 (c) 500 (d) 18

51. 100 mL of 0.1 M solution of solute A is mixed with 200 mL of 0.1 M solution of solute B. If A and B are non-reacting substances, the molarity of the final solution will be
(a) 0.3 M (b) 0.4 M (c) 0.1 M (d) 0.15 M

52. A solution is obtained by mixing 300 g of 25% and 400 g of 40% solution by mass. The mass percentage of the solute in the final solution will be
(a) 23.5% (b) 28.5% (c) 33.5% (d) 38.5%

53. 250 mL of 0.10 M K_2SO_4 solution is mixed with 250 mL of 0.20 M KCl solution. The concentration of K^+ ions in the resulting solution is
(a) 0.30 M (b) 0.15 M (c) 0.20 M (d) 0.40 M

54. 100 mL of 0.3 N HCl is mixed with 200 mL of 0.6 N H_2SO_4. The final normality of the resulting solution will be

(a) 0.1 N (b) 0.2 N (c) 0.3 N (d) 0.5 N

55. 2.5 litre of 1 M NaOH solution is mixed with another 3 litre of 0.5 M NaOH solution. Then the molarity of the resulting solution is

(a) 0.80 M (b) 1.0 M (c) 0.73 M (d) 0.50 M

56. 60 mL of $\frac{N}{5}$ H_2SO_4, 10 mL of $\frac{N}{2}$ HNO_3 and 30 mL of $\frac{N}{10}$ HCl are mixed together. The strength of the resulting mixture is

(a) 0.10 N (b) 0.2 N (c) 0.3 N (d) 0.4 N

57. In which ratio of volume 0.4 M HCl and 0.9 M HCl are to be mixed such that the concentration of the resultant solution becomes 0.7 M?

(a) 4 : 9 (b) 2 : 3 (c) 3 : 2 (d) 1 : 1

58. Concentrated sulfuric acid is approximately 18 molar. 5 cc of it is added to make 50 cc of the solution. The approximate normality of the solution will be

(a) 0.18 (b) 0.09 (c) 0.36 (d) 0.27

59. 2.5 cm^3 of 0.2 M H_2SO_4 solution is diluted to 0.5 dm^3. Find the normality of the diluted solution.

(a) 0.2 N (b) 0.02 N (c) 0.002 N (d) 0.04 N

60. The volume of water added to 100 cm^3 of 0.5 N H_2SO_4 to get decinormal concentration is

(a) 400 cm^3 (b) 450 cm^3 (c) 500 cm^3 (d) 100 cm^3

61. For converting a 100 mL KCl solution of 0.4 M concentration into a solution of KCl 0.05 M concentration, the quantity of water added is

(a) 900 mL (b) 700 mL (c) 500 mL (d) 300 mL

62. 10 mL of an aqueous solution containing 222 mg of calcium chloride (mol. wt. = 111) is diluted to 100 mL. The concentration of chloride ions in the resulting solution is

(a) 0.02 mol/L (b) 0.04 mol/L
(c) 0.01 mol/L (d) 2.0 mol/L

63. 35.4 mL of HCl is required for the neutralisation of a solution containing 0.275 g of sodium hydroxide. The normality of hydrochloric acid is

(a) 0.97 N (b) 0.142 N (c) 0.194 N (d) 0.244 N

64. 800 g of a 40% solution by weight was cooled. 100 g of solute precipitated out. The percentage composition of the remaining solution is

(a) 31.4% (b) 20.0% (c) 23.0% (d) 24.0%

65. Normal human blood sugar range is 65–105 mg/dL. Considering the density of human blood is 1.06 kg/L, if a patient's sugar level reads 720 ppm, his/her blood sugar at that time is

(a) normal (b) high
(c) low (d) cannot say

66. A solution of $CaCl_2$ is 0.5 mol/litre, then the moles of chloride ions in 500 mL will be

(a) 0.25 (b) 0.50 (c) 0.75 (d) 1.00

67. If Avogadro's number is A_0, the number of sulfur atoms present in 200 mL of 1 N H_2SO_2 is

(a) $A_0/5$ (b) $A_0/2$ (c) $A_0/10$ (d) A_0

68. Density of 3 M solution of NaCl is 1.25 g/mL. The mass of the solvent in the solution is

(a) 107.4 g (b) 10.745 g (c) 107.45 g (d) 1074.5 g

69. An aqueous solution of glucose is 10% in strength. The volume in which 1 g mole of it is dissolved will be

(a) 18 L (b) 9 L (c) 0.9 L (d) 1.8 L

70. Which of the following concentration terms is/are independent of temperature?

(a) molality only
(b) molality and mole fraction
(c) molarity and mole fraction
(d) molality and normality
(e) molarity only

71. Which of the following concentration terms is affected by change in temperature?

(a) molarity (b) molality
(c) mole fraction (d) weight fraction

72. How many grams of concentrated nitric acid solution should be used to prepare 250 mL of 2.0 M HNO_3? The concentrated acid is 7% HNO_3.

(a) 45.0 g conc. HNO_3 (b) 90.0 g conc. HNO_3
(c) 70.0 g conc. HNO_3 (d) 54.0 g conc. HNO_3

73. Molarity of HCl(l) if its density is 1.17 g/cc is

(a) 36.5 (b) 18.25 (c) 32.05 (d) 42.10

74. 6.02×10^{20} molecules of urea are present in 100 mL of its solution. the concentration of solution is:

(a) 0.02 M (b) 0.01 M (c) 0.001 M (d) 0.1 M

Solubility

75. The solubility of a gas in a liquid at any definite temperature depends upon

(a) pressure of the gas
(b) critical temperature of the gas
(c) both critical temperature and pressure
(d) neither pressure nor critical temperature but only on the nature of the solvent

76. Which of the following gases has the lowest value of Henry's constant?
(a) N_2 (b) He (c) H_2 (d) CO_2

77. The partial pressure of N_2 in the air is 0.76 atm and its Henry's law constant is 7.6×10^4 atm at 300 K. What is the mole fraction of N_2 in the solution obtained when air is bubbled through water at 300 K?
(a) 1×10^{-4} (b) 2×10^{-4}
(c) 1×10^{-5} (d) 2×10^{-5}

78. A bottle of cold drink contains 200 mL of liquid in which CO_2 is 0.1 M. Suppose CO_2 behaves like an ideal gas, the volume of dissolved oxygen at NTP is
(a) 0.224 L (b) 0.448 L (c) 22.4 L (d) 2.24 L

79. The K_H values for Ar(g), CO_2(g), HCHO(g) and CH_4(g) are 40.39, 1.67, 1.83×10^{-5} and 0.413 respectively. The correct order of their increasing solubility is
(a) HCHO < CH_4 < CO_2 < Ar
(b) HCHO < CO_2 < CH_4 < Ar
(c) Ar < CO_2 < CH_4 < HCHO
(d) Ar < CH_4 < CO_2 < HCHO

80. N_2 is bubbled through water at 293 K. The millimoles of N_2 gas that would dissolve in 1 litre of water will be (assume that N_2 exerts a partial pressure of 0.987 bar and Henry's law constant for N_2 at 293 K is 76.48 kbar)
(a) 0.716 (b) 7.16 (c) 71.6 (d) 0.0716

81. H_2S, a toxic gas with a rotten egg like smell is used for qualitative analysis. If the solubility of H_2S in water at STP is 0.195 m, Henry's law constant has the value
(a) 195 bar (b) 390 bar (c) 282 bar (d) 230 bar

82. Which of the following correctly represents Henry's law?
(a) $m = K_H P$ (b) $x_A = K_H P_A$
(c) $p_A = K_H x_A$ (d) all of these

83. Which of the following gases does not obey Henry's law?
(a) O_2 (b) N_2 (c) CO_2 (d) none of these

84. The variation of solubility of four different gases (G_1, G_2, ...) in a given solvent with pressure at a constant temperature is shown in the plot. The gas with the highest value of Henry's constant is

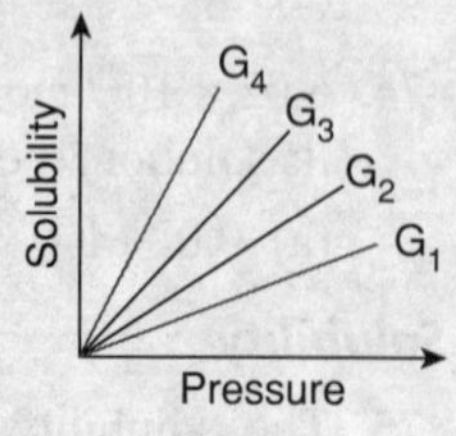

(a) G_4 (b) G_2 (c) G_3 (d) G_1

85. Henry's law constant for CO_2 in water is 1.67×10^8 Pa at 298 K. The quantity of CO_2 in 500 mL of soda water when packed under 2.5 atm CO_2 pressure at 298 K is
(a) 2.78 g (b) 1.83 g (c) 3.12 g (d) 0.12 g

86. Which of the following gas mixtures is used by the divers inside the sea?
(a) O_2 + He (b) O_2 + Xe (c) O_2 + Ar (d) O_2 + N_2

87. The statement 'If 0.003 mol of a gas is dissolved in 900 g of water under a pressure of 1 atmosphere, 0.006 mol will be dissolved under a pressure of 2 atmospheres', illustrates
(a) Dalton's law of partial pressure
(b) Graham's law
(c) Raoult's law (d) Henry's law

88. Which among the following gases will greatly deviate from Henry's law in water?
(a) H_2 (b) N_2 (c) CH_4 (d) CO_2 (e) Ar

89. A solid dissolves in water if
(a) lattice energy is greater than hydration energy
(b) lattice energy is less than hydration energy
(c) lattice energy is equal to hydration energy
(d) dissolution is exothermic

90. The solubility curve of $Na_2SO_4.10\ H_2O$ in water with temperature is given as

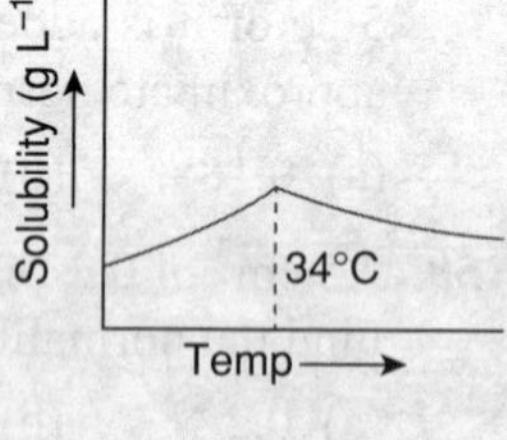

(a) solution process is exothermic
(b) solution process is exothermic till 34°C and endothermic after 34°C
(c) solution process is endothermic till 34°C and exothermic thereafter
(d) solution process is endothermic

91. In a pair of immiscible liquids, a common solute is dissolved and equilibrium is attained; then the concentration of the solution in the upper layer is
(a) in fixed ratio with that in the lower layer
(b) same as the lower layer
(c) lower than the lower layer
(d) higher than the lower layer

92. Iodine is more soluble in alcohol than in carbon tetrachloride because
(a) iodine and alcohol both are non-polar
(b) randomness factor is greater in alcohol than in CCl_4
(c) dissolution of iodine in alcohol is exothermic whereas it is endothermic in CCl_4
(d) dissolution of both is endothermic but heat of dissolution in alcohol is less than in CCl_4

93. From the diagram given below, which compound would be most apt to be easily purified by recrystallisation from water?

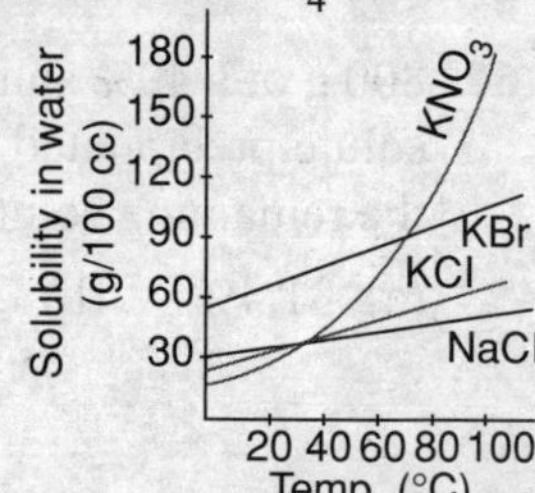

(a) NaCl (b) KCl (c) KBr (d) KNO_3

94. Which of the following represents a metastable system?

(a) a dilute solution
(b) an unsaturated solution
(c) a saturated solution
(d) a supersaturated solution

95. Sugar is soluble in water due to

(a) high solvation energy
(b) ionic character of sugar
(c) high dipole moment of water
(d) hydrogen bond formation with water

96. Given the solubility curves of KNO_3 and KCl, which of the following statements is not true?

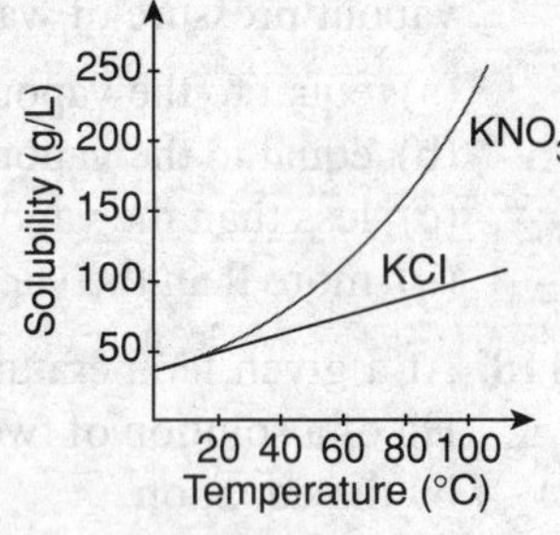

(a) At room temperature, the solubility of KNO_3 and KCl are not equal.
(b) The solubilities of KNO_3 and KCl increase with temperature.
(c) The solubility of KCl decreases with temperature.
(d) The solubility of KNO_3 increases much more compared to that of KCl with an increase in temperature.

97. The solubility curve of KNO_3 in water is given below:

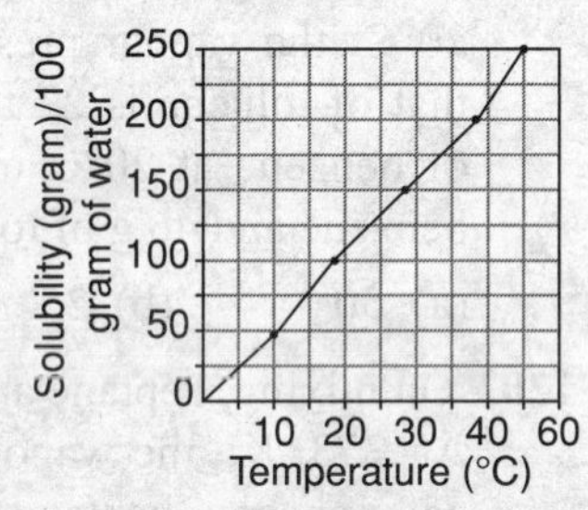

The amount of KNO_3 that dissolves in 50 g of water at 40°C is closest to

(a) 100 g (b) 150 g
(c) 200 g (d) 50 g

Vapour Pressure of Liquid Solutions and Raoult's Law

98. P_A and P_B are the vapour pressures of pure liquid components, A and B, respectively of an ideal binary solution. If X_A represents the mole fraction of component A, the total pressure of the solution will be

(a) $P_A + X_A(P_B - P_A)$ (b) $P_A + X_A(P_A - P_B)$
(c) $P_B + X_A(P_B - P_A)$ (d) $P_B + X_A(P_A - P_B)$

99. The vapour pressures of pure liquids A and B are 45 and 700 mm Hg at 350 K respectively. If their mixture has a total vapour pressure of 600 mm, the composition of the mixture in the vapour phase

(a) $x_A = 0.40, x_B = 0.60$ (b) $x_A = 0.60, x_B = 0.40$
(c) $x_A = 0.30, x_B = 0.70$ (d) $x_A = 0.70, x_B = 0.30$

100. 100 g of liquid A (molar mass 140 g mol^{-1}) was dissolved in 1000 g of liquid B (molar mass 180 g mol^{-1}). The vapour pressure of pure liquid B was found to be 500 torr. If the total vapour pressure of the solution is 475 torr, the vapour pressure of pure liquid A is

(a) 218.7 torr (b) 238.8 torr
(c) 258.2 torr (d) 280.7 torr

101. For an ideal solution with $p°_A > p°_B$, which of the following is true?

(a) $(x_A)_{liquid} = (x_A)_{vapour}$ (b) $(x_A)_{liquid} > (x_A)_{vapour}$
(c) $(x_A)_{liquid} < (x_A)_{vapour}$
(d) $(x_A)_{liquid}$ and $(x_A)_{vapour}$ do not bear any relationship with each other

102. Vapour pressure of a solution of a non-volatile solute is

(a) directly proportional to the mole fraction of the solvent
(b) inversely proportional to the mole fraction of the solute
(c) inversely proportional to the mole fraction of the solvent
(d) directly proportional to the mole fraction of the solute

103. Liquid A and B form an ideal solution. If the vapour pressure of pure A and B are 500 Nm^{-2} and 200 Nm^{-2} respectively, the vapour pressure of a solution of A in B containing 0.2 mole fraction of A would be

(a) 700 Nm^{-2} (b) 300 Nm^{-2} $\times 10^{-3}$
(c) 260 Nm^{-2} (d) 140 Nm^{-2}

104. At 300 K, the vapour pressures of two liquids A and B are 100 and 500 mm Hg respectively. If in a mixture of A and B, the vapour pressure is 300 mm Hg, the mole fractions of A in the liquid phase and in the vapour phase, respectively are

(a) $\frac{1}{2}$ and $\frac{1}{10}$ (b) $\frac{1}{4}$ and $\frac{1}{6}$
(c) $\frac{1}{4}$ and $\frac{1}{10}$ (d) $\frac{1}{2}$ and $\frac{1}{6}$

105. Which of the following statements about the composition of the vapour over an ideal 1 : 1 molar mixture of benzene and toluene is correct? Assume that the temperature is constant at 25°C (Given vapour pressure data at 25°C, benzene = 12.8 kPa, toluene = 3.85 kPa)

(a) The vapour will contain equal amounts of benzene and toluene.
(b) Not enough information is given to make a prediction.
(c) The vapour will contain a higher percentage of benzene.
(d) The vapour will contain a higher percentage of toluene.

106. At 300 K, the vapour pressure of an ideal solution containing 1 mol of liquid A and 2 mol of liquid B is

500 mm of Hg. The vapour pressure of the solution increases by 25 mm of Hg, if one more mol of B is added to the above ideal solution at 300 K, then the vapour pressure of A in its pure state is

(a) 300 mm of Hg (b) 400 mm of Hg
(c) 500 mm of Hg (d) 600 mm of Hg
(e) 200 mm of Hg

107. At 300 K two pure liquids A and B have vapour pressures respectively of 150 mm Hg and 100 mm Hg. In an equimolar liquid mixture of A and B, the mole fraction of B in the vapour mixture at the temperature is

(a) 0.6 (b) 0.5 (c) 0.8 (d) 0.4

108. An aqueous solution of methanol in water has vapour pressure

(a) equal to that of water
(b) equal to that of methanol
(c) more than that of water
(d) less than that of water

109. An ideal solution is obtained by mixing CH_3CHBr_2 and $CH_2Br—CH_2Br$ in the ratio 2 : 1, $\overset{\circ}{p}_{CH_2CHBr_2} = 173$, $\overset{\circ}{p}_{CH_2BrCH_2Br} = 127$. The vapour of the solution is

(a) 158 (b) 257 (c) 137 (d) 197

110. The mass of a non-volatile solute of molar mass 60 g mol^{-1} that should be dissolved in 126 g of water to reduce its vapour pressure to 99% will be

(a) 4 g (b) 8 g (c) 5.6 g (d) 3 g

111. Vapour pressure of water at 293 K is 17.535 mm Hg. The vapour pressure of water at 293 K containing 25 g of glucose dissolved in 450 g of water is

(a) 17.439 mm Hg (b) 17.535 mm Hg
(c) 0.097 mm Hg (d) 34.973 mm Hg

112. The lowering of vapour pressure of the solvent takes place

(a) only when the solute is non-volatile
(b) only when the solute is volatile
(c) only when the solute is a non-electrolyte
(d) in all the above three cases

113. Out of the compounds given below, the vapour pressure of B at a particular temperature is

(A): OH and NO_2 (para) substituted benzene ring; (B): OH and NO_2 (ortho) substituted benzene ring

(a) higher than that of A
(b) lower than that of A
(c) higher or lower than A, depending on the size of the vessel
(d) same as that of A

114. Which has maximum vapour pressure

(a) HI (b) HBr (c) HCl (d) HF

115. Vapour pressure increases with increase in

(a) concentration of solution containing a non-volatile solute
(b) temperature up to boiling point
(c) temperature up to triple point
(d) altitude of the concerned place of boiling

116. The relationship which describes the variation of vapour pressure with temperature is called

(a) Hess' law (b) Arrhenius equation
(c) Kirchhoff's law
(d) Clausius–Clapeyron equation

117. 5 mL of acetone is mixed with 100 mL of H_2O. The vapour pressure of water above the solution is

(a) equal to the vapour pressure of pure water
(b) equal to the vapour pressure of the solution
(c) less than the vapour pressure of pure water
(d) more than the vapour pressure of pure water

118. At a given temperature, the vapour pressure in mm of Hg of a solution of two volatile liquids A and B is given by the equation

$p = 120 - 80\, X_B (X_B =$ mole fraction of B)

Vapour pressure of pure A and B at the same temperature are respectively

(a) 120, 80 (b) 120, 200 (c) 120, 40 (d) 80, 40

119. Benzene and toluene form a nearly ideal solution. At 20°C, the vapour pressure of benzene is 75 torr and that of toluene is 22 torr. The partial vapour pressure of benzene at 20°C in a solution containing 78 g of benzene and 46 g of toluene in torr is

(a) 50 (b) 25 (c) 37.5 (d) 53.5

120. On mixing, heptane and octane form an ideal solution. At 373 K, the vapour pressure of the two liquid components (heptane and octane) are 105 kPa and 45 kPa respectively. Vapour pressure of the solution obtained by mixing 25.0 g of heptane and 35 g of octane will be (molar mass of heptane = 100 g mol^{-1} and of octane = 114 g mol^{-1})

(a) 96.2 kPa (b) 144.5 kPa
(c) 72.0 kPa (d) 36.1 kPa

Ideal and Non-ideal Solutions

121. Which of the following is correct for a solution showing positive deviation from Raoult's law?

(a) $\Delta V = +ve, \Delta H = +ve$
(b) $\Delta V = -ve, \Delta H = -ve$
(c) $\Delta V = +ve, \Delta H = -ve$
(d) $\Delta V = -ve, \Delta H = +ve$

122. Negative deviation from Raoult's law is observed in which one of the following binary liquid mixtures?

(a) ethanol and acetone (b) benzene and toluene

(c) acetone and chloroform
(d) chloroethane and bromoethane
(e) acetone and carbon disulfide

123. If ethanol dissolves in water, then which of the following would happen?
(a) absorption of heat and contraction of volume
(b) liberation of heat and contraction of volume
(c) absorption of heat and increase in volume
(d) liberation of heat and increase in volume

124. Which one of the following binary liquid systems shows a positive deviation from Raoult's law?
(a) benzene–toluene (b) carbon disulfide–acetone
(c) phenol–aniline (d) chloroform–acetone
(e) nitric acid–water

125. When ethyl alcohol and water are mixed, the solution will
(a) show positive deviations from Raoult's law
(b) have higher vapour pressure than that of water and alcohol
(c) have lowering boiling point than that of water and alcohol
(d) al the three above

126. The diagram given below is a vapour pressure–composition diagram for a binary solution of A and B.

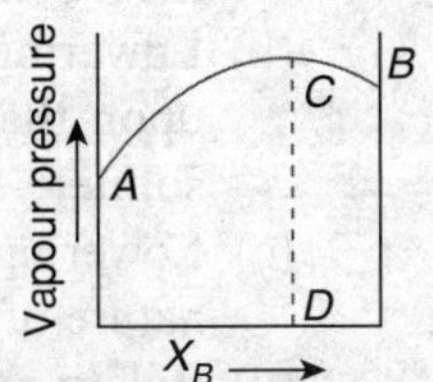

In the solution, A–B interactions are
(a) similar to A–A and B–B interactions
(b) greater than A–A and B–B interactions
(c) smaller than A–A and B–B interactions
(d) unpredictable

127. An aqueous solution of methanol has a vapour pressure
(a) equal to that of water
(b) equal to that of methanol
(c) more than that of water
(d) less than that of water

128. Which pair from the following will not form an ideal solution?
(a) $CCl_4 + SiCl_4$ (b) $H_2O + C_4H_9OH$
(c) $C_2H_5Br + C_2H_5I$ (d) $C_6H_{14} + C_7H_{16}$

129. All form ideal solutions except
(a) C_6H_6 and $C_6H_5CH_3$ (b) C_2H_5Br and C_2H_5I
(c) C_6H_5Cl and C_6H_5Br (d) C_2H_5I and C_2H_5OH

130. Which of the following liquid pairs shows a positive deviation from Raoult's law?
(a) water–hydrochloric acid
(b) water–nitric acid
(c) acetone–chloroform
(d) benzene–methanol

131. A solution of acetone in ethanol
(a) behaves like a near ideal solution
(b) obeys Raoult's law
(c) shows a negative deviation from Raoult's law
(d) shows a positive deviation from Raoult's law

132. Which of the following liquid pairs shows a positive deviation from Raoult's law?
(a) water–hydrochloric acid
(b) cyclohexane–ethanol
(c) chloroform–benzene (d) acetone–chloroform

133. The enthalpy change on mixing water and alcohol at room temperature is
(a) zero (b) positive
(c) negative
(d) depends on proportion of alcohol in mixture

134. Which of the following does not show a positive deviation from Raoult's law?
(a) benzene–chloroform
(b) benzene–acetone
(c) benzene–ethanol
(d) benzene–carbon tetrachloride

135. A solution of two liquids boils at a temperature more than the boiling point of either of them. Hence, the binary solution shows
(a) negative deviation from Raoult's law
(b) positive deviation from Raoult's law
(c) no deviation from Raoult's law
(d) positive or negative deviation from Raoult's law depending upon the composition

136. Which of the following azeotropic solutions has a boiling point less than boiling point of the constituents A and B?
(a) $CHCl_3$ and CH_3COCH_3
(b) CS_2 and CH_3COCH_3
(c) CH_3CH_2OH and CH_3COCH_3
(d) CH_3CHO and CS_2

137. The azeotropic mixture of water (BP 100°C) and HCl (BP 85°C) boils at 108.5°C. When this mixture is distilled it is possible to obtain
(a) pure HCl (b) pure water
(c) pure water as well as pure HCl
(d) neither HCl nor H_2O in their pure states

138. A non-ideal solution was prepared by mixing 30 mL chloroform and 50 mL acetone. The volume of the mixture will be
(a) > 80 mL (b) < 80 mL
(c) = 80 mL (d) ≥ 80 mL

139. In which case is Raoult's law not applicable?
(a) 1 M NaCl (b) 1 M urea
(c) 1 M glucose (d) 1 M sucrose

140. Which will form a maximum boiling azeotrope?
(a) $HNO_3 + H_2O$ solution
(b) $C_2H_5OH + H_2O$ solution
(c) $C_6H_6 + C_6H_5CH_3$ solution
(d) none of these

141. The boiling point of an azeotropic mixture of water and ethanol is less than that of water and ethanol. The mixture shows
(a) negative deviations from Raoult's law
(b) positive deviations from Raoult's law
(c) no deviation from Raoult's law
(d) deviations which cannot be predicted from the given information

142. The system that forms a maximum boiling azeotrope is
(a) carbon disulfide–acetone (b) benzene–toluene
(c) acetone–chloroform (d) *n*-hexane–acetone
(e) ethanol–acetone

143. Among the following, the azeotropic mixture is
(a) $CCl_4 + CHCl_3$ (b) $C_6H_{14} + C_7H_{16}$
(c) $C_2H_5Br + C_2H_5Cl$
(d) chlorobenzene + bromobenzene

144. An azeotropic mixture of HCl and water has
(a) 84% HCl (b) 22.2% HCl
(c) 63% HCl (d) 20.4% HCl

145. A solution of A and B with 0.2 mol fraction of A is found to have a total vapour pressure of 125 mm. Pure A and B have vapour pressures 100 mm and 150 mm respectively. Will it show
(a) +ve deviation (b) –ve deviation
(d) no deviation (d) anything can happen

146. Which one is not equal to zero for an ideal solution?
(a) ΔH_{mix} (b) ΔS_{mix}
(c) ΔV_{mix} (d) $\Delta P = P_{Observed} - P_{Raoults}$

147. A solution containing components A and B follows Raoult's law.
(a) A–B attractive force is greater than A–A and B–B
(b) A–B attraction force is less than A–A and B–B
(c) A–B attraction force remains the same as A–A and B–B
(d) volume of the solution is different from the sum of volumes of solute and solvent

148. The total vapour pressure of mixture of 1 mol A (p_B° = 240 torr) is 200 torr. In this case
(a) there is positive deviation from Raoult's law
(b) there is negative deviation from Raoult's law
(c) there is no deviation from Raoult's law
(d) molecular masses of A and B are also required for calculating the deviation

Colligative Properties

149. The vapour pressure of a solution of 5 g of non-electrolyte in 100 g of water at a particular temperature is 2985 N m^{-2}. The vapour pressure of pure water at that temperature is 3000 N m^{-2}. The molecular weight of the solute is
(a) 180 (b) 90 (c) 270 (d) 200

150. The vapour pressure of water is 12.3 kPa at 300 K. The vapour pressure of 1 molal solution of a solution in it is
(a) 10.8 kPa (b) 12.8 kPa
(c) 14.08 kPa (d) 16.08 kPa

151. For the determination of molecular weights, Raoult's law is applicable only to
(a) dilute solutions of electrolytes
(b) concentrated solutions of electrolytes
(c) dilute solutions of non-electrolytes
(d) concentrated solutions of non-electrolytes

152. Which of the following statements is correct?
(a) Lowering of vapour pressure takes place only in ideal solutions.
(b) Lowering of vapour pressure does not depend upon the solvent at a given concentration of the solute.
(c) Lowering of vapour pressure depends upon the nature of the solute.
(d) Relative lowering of vapour pressure does not depend upon the solvent at a given concentration of the solute.

153. If dry air is passed through two bulbs, one containing the solvent and the other containing the solution, the decrease in the weight will be
(a) more in the solvent bulbs
(b) more in the solution bulbs
(c) same in both the bulbs
(d) nil in both the bulbs

154. In 108 g of water, 18 g of non-volatile compound is dissolved. At 100°C the vapour pressure of the solution is 750 mm Hg. Assuming that the compound does not undergo association or dissociation, the molar mass of the compound in g mol^{-1} is
(a) 128 (b) 182 (c) 152 (d) 228

155. 4 g of a non-volatile solute dissolved in 36 g of water produces a relative lowering of vapour pressure of 0.1. The molecular mass of the solute is
(a) 40 (b) 20 (c) 80 (d) 100

156. The amount of solute (molar mass 60 g mol^{-1}) that must be added to 180 g of water so that vapour pressure of water is lowered by 10% is

(a) 30 g (b) 60 g (c) 24 g (d) 1 20 g

157. Two solutions A and B are separated by a semi-permeable membrane. As a result of osmosis, the level of solution A is found to rise. It implies that

(a) solution A is more concentrated than solution B
(b) solution B is more concentrated than solution A
(c) the solute molecules of A are smaller than those of B
(d) the solute molecules of B are smaller than those of A

158. The osmotic pressure of a solution of 0°C is 4 atm. What will be its osmotic pressure at 546 K under similar conditions?

(a) 4 atm. (b) 2 atm. (c) 8 atm. (d) 1 atm.

159. What is the volume of solution containing 1 g mol of sugar that will give rise to an osmotic pressure of 1 atm at STP?

(a) 224.0 litre (b) 22.0 litre
(c) 2.24 litre (d) none of the above

160. 0.6 g of a solute is dissolved in 0.1 litre of a solvent which develops an osmotic pressure of 1.23 atm. at 27°C. The molecular mass of the substance is

(a) 149.5 g mol^{-1} (b) 120 g mol^{-1}
(c) 430 g mol^{-1} (d) none of the above

161. A 1% aqueous solution (mass by volume) of a certain substance is isotonic with a 3% solution of dextrose, that is, glucose (molar mass 180) at a given temperature. The molar mass of the substance is

(a) 60 (b) 120 (c) 180 (d) 360

162. Which of the following acts as the best semi-permeable membrane?

(a) parchment paper (b) $Cu_2[Fe(CN)_6]$
(c) plant cell wall (d) cellophane

163. The osmotic pressure of a solution increases if

(a) temperature is decreased
(b) solution constant is increased
(c) number of solute particles is increased
(d) volume is increased

164. 100 cc of 1.5% solution of urea is found to have an osmotic pressure of 6.0 atm and 100 cc of 3.4% solution of cane sugar is found to have an osmotic pressure of 2.4 atm. If the two solutions are mixed, the osmotic pressure of the resulting solution will be

(a) 8.4 atm (b) 4.2 atm (c) 16.8 atm (d) 2.1 atm

165. 200 mL of an aqueous solution of a protein contains its 1.26 g. The osmotic pressure of this solution at 300 K is found to be 2.57×10^{-3} bar. The molar mass of the protein will be ($R = 0.083$ L bar mol^{-1} K^{-1})

(a) 51022 g mol^{-1} (b) 122044 g mol^{-1}
(c) 31011 g mol^{-1} (d) 61038 g mol^{-1}

166. Blood cells do not shrink in blood because blood is

(a) hypotonic (b) isotonic
(c) equimolar (d) hypertonic

167. At 300 K, 36 g of glucose present per litre in its solution has an osmotic pressure of 4.98 bar. If the osmotic pressure of the solution is 1.52 bar at the same temperature, what would be its concentration?

(a) 11 g L^{-1} (b) 22 g L^{-1} (c) 36 g L^{-1} (d) 42 g L^{-1}

168. At 300 K, 36 g of glucose present per litre in its solution has an osmotic pressure of 4.98 bar. If the osmotic pressure of a solution is 1.52 bar at the same temperature, its concentration would be

(a) 0.61 M (b) 0.061 M (c) 0.45 M (d) 0.045 M

169. Which one of the following statements is false about osmotic pressure?

(a) It is the pressure of the hydrostatic column set up due to osmosis.
(b) It is the pressure applied on the solution to prevent the entry of the solvent into it through the semi-permeable membrane.
(c) During osmosis, the flow of solvent is only from the dilute solution to the concentrated solution.
(d) Osmotic pressure is directly proportional to the temperature of the solution.

170. A plant cell shrinks when it is kept in

(a) a hypotonic solution
(b) a hypertonic solution
(c) a solution isotonic with cell sap
(d) water

171. At low concentrations, the statement that equimolal solutions under a given set of experimental conditions have equal osmotic pressures is true for

(a) all solutions
(b) solutions of non-electrolytes only
(c) solutions of electrolytes only
(d) none of these

172. The best and accurate method for determining osmotic pressure is

(a) calcium phosphate (b) nickel phosphate
(c) calcium sulfate (d) copper ferrocyanide

173. When a mango is placed in a dilute aqueous solution of hydrochloric acid, it

(a) shrinks (b) swells
(c) bursts (d) nothing happens

174. An aqueous solution of sucrose, $C_{12}H_{22}O_{11}$, containing 34.2 g/L has an osmotic pressure of 2.38 atm at 17°C. For an aqueous solution of glucose, $C_6H_{12}O_6$ to be isotonic with this solution, it would have

(a) 34.2 g/L (b) 17.1 g/L
(c) 18.0 g/L (d) 36.0 g/L of glucose

175. The osmotic pressure of 0.2 molar solution of urea at 27°C is ($R = 0.082$ litre atm mol^{-1} K^{-1}) is

(a) 4.92 atm (b) 1 atm (c) 0.2 atm (d) 27 atm

176. Osmotic pressure is 0.0821 atm at a temperature of 300 K. Find the concentration in mol/litre.

(a) 0.033 (b) 0.006 (c) 0.33×10^{-2} (d) 3

177. The osmotic pressure in atm of 10% solution of cane sugar at 69°C is

(a) 724 (b) 824 (c) 8.21 (d) 821

178. During osmosis, the flow of water through a semi-permeable membrane is

(a) from both sides of the semi-permeable membrane with unequal flow rates
(b) from solution having lower concentration only
(c) from solution having higher concentration only
(d) from both sides of the semi-permeable membrane with equal flow rates

179. A 5% solution of sugarcane (mol. wt. = 342) is isotonic with 1% solution of X under similar conditions. The mol. wt. of X is

(a) 136.2 (b) 68.4 (c) 34.2 (d) 171.2

180. The osmotic pressure of 0.4% urea solution is 1.64 atm and that of a solution of sugar of 3.42% is 2.46 atm. When equal volumes of both the solutions are mixed then the osmotic pressure of the resultant solution will be

(a) 1.64 atm (b) 2.46 atm
(c) 4.10 atm (d) 2.05 atm

181. What would happen if a thin slice of sugar beet is placed in concentrated solution of NaCl?

(a) the sugar beet will lose water from its cells
(b) the sugar beet will absorb water from solution
(c) the sugar beet will neither absorb nor lose water
(d) the sugar beet will dissolve in solution

182. At 298 K, the ratio of osmotic pressures of the solutions of s substance with concentrations of 0.01 M and 0.001 M respectively, is

(a) 1 (b) 100 (c) 10 (d) 1000

183. The osmotic pressure of 12% solution of cane sugar at 17°C is

(a) 2.42 atm (b) 4.33 atm
(c) 8.35 atm (d) 16.30 atm

184. The empirical formula of a non-electrolyte is CH_2O. A solution containing 3 g of the compound exerts the same osmotic pressure as that of 0.05 M glucose. The molecular formula of the compound is

(a) CH_2O (b) $C_2H_4O_2$ (c) $C_2H_8O_4$ (d) $C_3H_6O_3$

185. What happens when an egg is kept in a saturated solution of NaCl after removing its hard shell in dilute HCl?

(a) the egg will swell (b) the egg will shrink
(c) the egg will remain same
(d) the egg will first shrink and then swell

186. The osmotic pressure is expressed in the units of

(a) Me V (b) calorie (c) cm/s (d) atm

187. The temperature at which 10% aqueous solution (w/V) of glucose will exhibit the osmotic pressure of 16.4 atm, is ($R = 0.082$ dm^3 atm K^{-1} mol^{-1})

(a) 360° (b) 180 K (c) 90 K (d) 300 K

188. A solution containing 4 g polyvinyl chloride polymer in 1 L of dioxane was found to have an osmotic pressure of 4.1×10^{-4} atm at 27°C. The approximate molecular weight of the polymer is

(a) 1500 (b) 1000 (c) 2.4×10^5 (d) 2×10^{12}

189. A solution containing 10 g per dm^3 of urea (molecular mass = 60 g mol^{-1}) is isotonic with a 5% solution of a non-volatile solute. The molecular mass of the non-volatile solute is

(a) 250 g mol^{-1} (b) 300 g mol^{-1}
(c) 350 g mol^{-1} (d) 200 g mol^{-1}

190. The osmotic pressure of a 5% (wt/vol) solution of cane sugar at 150°C is

(a) 2.45 atm (b) 5.078 atm
(c) 3.4 atm (d) 4 atm

191. The relationship between osmotic pressure at 273 K when 10 g glucose (P_1), 10 g urea (P_2) and 10 g sucrose (P_3) are dissolved in 250 ml of water is

(a) $P_1 > P_2 > P_3$ (b) $P_3 > P_1 > P_2$
(c) $P_2 > P_1 > P_3$ (d) $P_2 > P_3 > P_1$

192. Two solutions A and B are separated by a semi-permeable membrane. If liquid flows from A to B then

(a) A is less concentrated than B
(b) A is more concentrated than B
(c) both have same concentration
(d) none of these

193. The solution in which the blood cells retain their normal form are with regard to the blood.

(a) isotonic (b) iso-osmotic
(c) hypertonic (d) equinormal

194. At a temperature of 327°C and a concentration of C, the osmotic pressure of a solution is P; the same solution at a concentration of C/2 and a temperature of 427°C shows an osmotic pressure of 2 atm. The value of P will

(a) $\frac{12}{7}$ (b) $\frac{24}{7}$ (c) $\frac{6}{5}$ (d) $\frac{5}{6}$

195. The phenomenon in which cells swell up and then burst if placed in hypotonic solutions is called
(a) plasmolysis (b) haemolysis
(c) exosmosis (d) none of these

196. A mixture containing 100 mL of 1 M urea solution and 300 mL of 1 M glucose solution at T K will have an osmotic pressure of
(a) $\frac{10RT}{4}$ (b) 3 RT (c) 4 RT (d) RT

197. The plant cells shrink when placed in
(a) water (b) a hypotonic solution
(d) a hypertonic solution (d) an isotonic solution

198. The molal BP constant for water is 0.513°C kg mol^{-1}. When 0.1 mol of sugar is dissolved in 200 g of water, the solution boils under a pressure of 1 atm at
(a) 100.513°C (b) 100.0513°C
(c) 100.256°C (d) 101.025°C

199. The rise in the boiling point of a solution containing 1.8 g of glucose in 100 g of solvent is 0.1°C. The molal elevation constant of the liquid is
(a) 0.01 K/m (b) 0.1 K/m
(c) 1 K/m (d) 10 K/m

200. 1.5 g of a non-volatile, non-electrolyte is dissolved in 50 g of benzene (K_b = 2.5 K kg mol^{-1}). The elevation of the boiling point of the solution is 0.75 K. The molecular weight of the solute in g mol^{-1} is
(a) 200 (b) 50 (c) 75 (d) 100

201. Boiling point of water at 750 mm Hg is 99.63°C. The amount of sucrose that should be added to 500 g of water such that it boils at 100°C is (molal elevation constant for water is 0.52 K kg mol^{-1})
(a) 111.7 g (b) 121.7 g (c) 131.7 g (d) 141.7 g

202. Molal depression constant is calculated from the enthalpy of fusion ($\Delta_f H$) and BP of solvent using the relation
(a) $K_f = \frac{M_1 RT_0^2}{1000\Delta_t H}$ (b) $K_f = \frac{1000 RT_0^2}{M_1 \Delta_f H}$
(c) $K_f = \frac{1000 M_1 T_0^2}{R\Delta_t H}$ (d) $K_f = \frac{\Delta_f H}{1000 M_1 RT_0^2}$

203. The molal elevation constant is the ratio of the elevation in BP to
(a) molarity (b) molality
(c) mole fraction of solute
(d) mole fraction of solvent

204. Which one of the following is not the correct unit of molal elevation constant?
(a) °C/m (b) K/m
(c) K kg mol^{-1} (d) K mol kg^{-1}

205. The molal elevation constant for water is 0.56°C per kg of water. The boiling point of a solution made by dissolving 6.0 g of urea (NH_2CONH_2) in 200 g of water is
(a) 10.028°C (b) 100.28°C
(c) 50.14°C (d) none of these

206. The boiling point of 0.1 molal aqueous solution of urea is 100.18°C at 1 atm. the molal elevation constant of water is
(a) 1.8 (b) 0.18 (c) 18 (d) 18.6

207. If the elevation in boiling point of a solution of 10 g of solute (mol. wt. = 100) in 100 g of water is ×10^{-3}, the ebullioscopic constant of water is
(a) 10 (b) 10ΔT_b (c) ΔT_b (d) ΔT_b/10

208. The ebullioscopic constant is the elevation of boiling point produced by
(a) 1 molar solution (b) 1 molal solution
(c) 1 N solution (d) 10% solution

209. Latent heat of vaporisation of water is 9.72 kcal mol^{-1} at 373.15 K. Calculate the molal boiling point elevation constant of water
(a) 5.2° (b) 0.052° (c) 52.2° (d) 0.52°

210. A pressure cooker reduces cooking time for food because
(a) the heat is more evenly distributed in the cooking space
(b) the boiling point of water involved in cooking is increased
(c) the higher pressure inside the cooker crushes the food material
(d) cooking involves chemical changes helped by a rise in temperature

211. Ebullioscopic constant represents
(a) boiling point of the solution when 1 mol of the solute is dissolved in 1 kg of the solvent
(b) elevation in boiling point of the solvent when one mol of the solute is dissolved in 1 L of the solution
(c) boiling point of the solution when 1 mol of solute is dissolved in 1 L of the solution
(d) elevation in boiling point of the solvent when 1 mol of the solute is dissolved in 1 kg of the solvent.

212. An aqueous solution containing 1 g of urea boils at 100.25°C. The aqueous solution containing 3 g of glucose in the same volume will boil at (molecular weight of urea and glucose are 60 and 180 respectively)

(a) 100.75°C (b) 100.5°C
(c) 100.25°C (d) 100°C

213. At higher altitudes the boiling point of water is lowered because

(a) atmospheric pressure is low
(b) temperature is low
(c) atmospheric pressure is high
(d) none of these

214. Normal boiling point of water is 373 K. Vapour pressure of water at 298 K is 23 mm and enthalpy of vaporisation is 40.656 kJ mol^{-1}. If the atmospheric pressure becomes 23 mm, the water will boil at

(a) 250 K (b) 298 K (c) 51.6 K (d) 12.5 K

215. A solution of 1 molal concentration of solute will have a maximum boiling point elevation when its solvent is

(a) ethyl alcohol (b) benzene
(c) acetone (d) chloroform

216. On freezing an aqueous solution of sugar, the solid that starts separating out is

(a) sugar (b) ice
(c) solution with the same composition
(d) solution with a different composition

217. In countries near the polar region, the roads are sprinkled with $CaCl_2$. This is

(a) to minimise the snow formation
(b) to minimise pollution
(c) to minimise the accumulation of dust on the road
(d) to minimise wear and tear of the roads

218. If all the following four compounds were sold at the same price, which would be cheapest for preparing an antifreeze solution for a car radiator?

(a) CH_3OH (b) C_2H_5OH
(c) $C_2H_4(OH)_2$ (d) $C_3H_5(OH)_3$

219. A solution containing 0.10 g of non-volatile solute X (molar mass: 100) in 200 g of benzene depresses the freezing of benzene by 0.25°C while 0.50 g of another non-volatile solute Y in 100 g of benzene also depresses the freezing point of benzene by 0.25°C. What is the molecular mass of Y?

(a) 50 (b) 100 (c) 150 (d) 1000

220. A solution containing 1.8 g of a compound (empirical formula CH_2O) in 40 g of water is observed to freeze at –0.645°C. The molecular formula of the compound is (K_f = 1.86 kg K mol^{-1}.

(a) $C_2H_4O_2$ (b) $C_4H_5O_4$
(c) $C_5H_{10}O_5$ (d) $C_6H_{12}O_6$

221. K_f for water is 1.86 K kg mol^{-1}. If your automobile radiator holds 1.0 kg of water, how many grams of ethylene glycol ($C_2H_6O_2$) must you add to get the freezing point of the solution lowered to –2.8°C?

(a) 27 g (b) 72 g (c) 93 g (d) 39 g

222. The greatest fall in freezing point is seen in

(a) camphor (b) naphthalene
(c) benzene (d) water

223. The molal depression constant depends upon the

(a) nature of the solute
(b) nature of the solvent
(c) heat of solution of the solute in the solvent
(d) vapour pressure of the solution

224. If molality of the dilute solution is doubled, the value of the molal depression constant (K_f) will be

(a) doubled (b) halved
(c) tripled (d) unchanged

225. A solution of 1.25 g of non-electrolyte in 20 g of water freezes at 271.94 K. If K_f = 1.86 K kg mol^{-1}, then the molecular weight of the solute will be

(a) 179.79 g mol^{-1} (b) 207.8 g mol^{-1}
(c) 209.6 g mol^{-1} (d) 109.6 g mol^{-1}

226. The amount of urea to be dissolved in 500 cc of water (K = 1.86) to produce a depression of 0.186°C in the freezing point is

(a) 0.3 g (b) 3 g (c) 6 g (d) 9 g

227. Pure benzene freezes at 5.45°C at a certain place but a 0.374 m solution of tetrachloroethane in benzene freezes at 3.55°C. The K_f for benzene is

(a) 5.08 K kg mol^{-1} (b) 508. K kg mol^{-1}
(c) 0.508 K kg mol^{-1} (d) 50.8°C kg mol^{-1}

228. A small amount of a solute in 100 g of water makes a solution that freezes at –1.0°C, then double the amount of the same solute in 100 g of water will make a solution that freezes at

(a) –0.5°C (b) –2.0°C (c) 0°C (d) 2.0°C

229. If an aqueous solution of glucose is allowed to freeze, then crystals of which will be separated out first?

(a) glucose (b) water
(c) both of these (d) none of these

230. A solution containing 8.0 g of nicotine in 92 g of water freezes 0.95 degree below the normal freezing point of water. If the molal freezing point depression constant K_f = 1.85°C mol^{-1}, then the molar mass of nicotine is

(a) 16 (b) 80 (c) 320 (d) 160

231. Cryoscopic constant is the depression in freezing point produced by

(a) 1% solution (b) 1 molar solution
(c) 1 molal solution (d) 1 N solution

232. A solution of sucrose (molar mass = 342 g mol^{-1}) has been prepared by dissolving 68.5 of sucrose in 1000 g of water. The freezing point of the solution obtained will be (K_f for water = 1.86 K kg mol^{-1})
(a) –0.570°C (b) –0.372°C
(c) –0.520°C (d) +0.372°C

233. A 5% solution (by mass) of cane sugar in water has freezing point of 272 K and freezing point of pure water is 273.15 K. The freezing point of a 5% solution (by mass) of glucose in water is
(a) 271 K (b) 273.15 K (c) 269.07 K (d) 277.23 K

234. An aqueous solution of the non-electrolyte solute boils at 100.52°C. The freezing point of the solution will be (K_f = 1.86 K kg mol^{-1}, K_b = 0.52 K kg mol^{-1})
(a) 0°C (b) –1.86°C
(c) 1.86°C (d) none of the above

235. Which one of the following statements is incorrect?
(a) Greater the lowering of vapour pressure, the greater is the boiling point of the solution.
(b) Greater the lowering of vapour pressure, the greater is the freezing point of the solution.
(c) At the freezing point, the solute and the solvent have same vapour pressure.
(d) The units of molal depression constant are K m^{-1}.

236. Camphor is often used in molecular mass determination because
(a) it is readily available
(b) it has a very high cryoscopic point
(c) it is volatile
(d) it is solvent for organic substances

237. When mercuric iodide is added to an aqueous solution of potassium iodide, the
(a) freezing point is raised
(b) freezing point is lowered
(c) freezing point does not change
(d) boiling point does not change

238. A solution of urea (mol mass 60 g mol^{-1}) boils at 100.18°C at the atmospheric pressure. If K_f and K_b for water are 1.86 and 0.512 K kg mol^{-1} respectively, the above solution will freeze at
(a) –6.54°C (b) –0.065°C (c) 6.54°C (d) 0.654°C

239. The order of boiling points of four equimolar aqueous solution is C < B < A < D. The correct order of their freezing points is
(a) D < C < B < A (b) D > C < B < A
(c) D < C < B < A (d) D > A > B > C

240. If the elevation in the boiling point of a solution of a non-volatile, non-electrolytic and non-associating solute in a solvent ($K_b = x\,K$ kg mol^{-1}) is y K, then the depression in freezing point of the solute point of the solute of the same concentration would be (K_f of the solvent = z K kg mol^{-1})
(a) $\frac{2xy}{y}$ (b) $\frac{yz}{x}$ (c) $\frac{xz}{y}$
(d) $\frac{yz}{2x}$ (e) $\frac{xz}{2y}$

241. When a substance is dissolved in a solvent, the vapour pressure of the solvent is decreased. This results in
(a) solvent is decreased
(b) a decrease in the BP of the solution
(c) the solution having a higher freezing point than the solvent
(d) the solution having a lower osmotic pressure than the solvent

242. At 100°C the vapour pressure of a solution of 6.5 g of a solute in 100 g water is 732 mm. If K_b = 0.52, the boiling point of this solution will be
(a) 102°C (b) 103°C (c) 101°C (d) 100°C

243. Choose the correct statement.
When the concentration of a salt solution is increased
(a) the boiling point increases while the vapour pressure decreases
(b) the boiling point decreases while the vapour pressure increases
(c) the freezing point decreases while the vapour pressure increases
(d) the freezing point increases while the vapour pressure decreases

244. Which of the following colligative properties can provide the molar mass of proteins (or polymers or colloids) with greater precision?
(a) relative lowering of vapour pressure
(b) elevation in boiling point
(c) depression in freezing point
(d) osmotic pressure

245. An aqueous solution of urea has a freezing point of –0.52°C. If molarity and molality are the same and K_f for H_2O = 1.86 K $molality^{-1}$, the osmotic pressure of solution at 37°C would be
(a) 6.886 atm (b) 68.86 atm
(c) 688.6 atm (d) 0.6886 atm

246. Which is not a colligative property?
(a) freezing point
(b) lowering of vapour pressure
(c) osmotic pressure
(d) elevation of boiling point

247. Which one of the statements given below concerning properties of solution, describes a colligative effect?
(a) boiling point of pure water deceases by the addition of ethanol
(b) vapour pressure of pure water decreases by the addition of nitric acid
(c) vapour pressure of pure benzene decreases by the addition of naphthalene
(d) boiling point of pure benzene increases by the addition of toluene

Colligative Properties of Solutes Which Dissociate (electrolytes) or Associate in Solution and Abnormal Molar Masses

248. Benzoic acid dissolved in benzene shows
(a) its normal molecular mass
(b) double of its normal molecular mass
(c) half of its normal molecular mass
(d) not definite

249. Which of the following compounds corresponds to the van't Hoff factor (*i*) to be equal to 2 for a dilute solution?
(a) K_2SO_4 (b) $NaHSO_4$ (c) sugar (d) $MgSO_4$

250. Acetic acid dissolved in benzene shows a molecular mass of
(a) 30 (b) 60 (c) 120 (d) 180

251. The experimental molecular weight of an electrolyte will always be less than its calculated value because the value of the van't Hoff factor *i* is
(a) less than 1 (b) greater than 1
(c) equivalent to 1 (d) zero

252. van't Hoff factor for a 0.1 M ideal solution is
(a) 0.1 (b) 1
(c) 0.01 (d) none of the three

253. Which one of the following salts will have the same value of van't Hoff factor (*i*) as that of $K_4[Fe(CN)_6]$
(a) $Al_2(SO_4)_3$ (b) NaCl (c) $Al(NO_3)_3$ (d) Na_2SO_4

254. The van't Hoff factor for a solute that associates in solution is
(a) zero (b) 1.0 (c) less than 1
(d) more than 1 (e) between 1 and 2

255. The van't Hoff factor (*i*) for a dilute aqueous solution of the strong electrolyte barium hydroxide is
(a) 0 (b) 1 (c) 2 (d) 3

256. A van't Hoff factor of more than unity indicates that the solute in solution is
(a) dissociated (b) associated
(c) both (a) and (b) (d) cannot say anything

257. Benzoic acid is dissolved in benzene, the van't Hoff factor will be
(a) 1 (b) 0.5 (c) 1.5 (d) 2

258. The correct equation for the degree of association α of an associating solute, *n* molecules of which undergo association in solution is
(a) $\alpha = \dfrac{n(i-1)}{1-n}$ (b) $\alpha = \dfrac{i(n-1)}{1+n}$
(c) $\alpha = \dfrac{1(n+1)}{1}$ (d) $\alpha = \dfrac{i(n+1)}{n-1}$
(e) $\alpha = \dfrac{n(1-i)}{1-n}$

259. The van't Hoff factor for $BaCl_2$ at 0.01 M concentration is 1.98. The percentage dissociation of $BaCl_2$ at this concentration is
(a) 49 (b) 69 (c) 89 (d) 98

260. If α is the degree of dissociation of Na_2SO_4 the van't Hoff factor (*i*) used for calculating the molecular mass is
(a) $1+\alpha$ (b) $1-\alpha$ (c) $1+2\alpha$ (d) $1-2\alpha$

261. A compound MX_2 has observed and normal and normal molar masses 65.6 and 164 respectively. Calculate the apparent degree of ionisation of MX_2
(a) 75% (b) 85% (c) 65% (d) 25%

262. The molar mass of the solute sodium hydroxide obtained from the measurement of the osmotic pressure of its aqueous solution at 27°C is 25 g mol^{-1}. Therefore, its ionisation percentage in this solution is
(a) 75 (b) 60 (c) 80 (d) 70

263. The vapour pressure of a solvent at 298 K is 100 mm Hg. Then the vapour pressure of a solution containing 1 mol of a strong electrolyte (AB_2) in 99 moles of the solvent at 293 K is (assume complete dissociation of the solute)
(a) 103 mm Hg (b) 99 mm Hg
(c) 97 mm Hg (d) 101 mm Hg
(e) 98 mm Hg

264. An aqueous solution is 1.00 molal in KI. Which change will cause the vapour pressure of the solution to increase?
(a) addition of water (b) addition of NaCl
(c) addition of Na_2SO_4 (d) addition of 1.00 molal KI

265. 0.1 M NaCl and 0.1 M CH_3COOH are found to have osmotic pressure of P_1 and P_2 respectively, then which is the correct statement?
(a) $P_1 > P_2$ (b) $P_1 = P_2$
(c) $P_1 < P_2$ (d) $P_1 = P_2 = 0$ atm

266. The correct order of osmotic pressure of 0.01 M aqueous solution of the following is:

(a) sucrose > CH_3COOH > KCl
(b) CH_3COOH > sucrose > KCl
(c) sucrose > KCl > CH_3COOH
(d) KCl > sucrose > CH_3COOH
(e) KCl > CH_3COOH > CH_3COOH

267. Which of the following solutions are isotonic with one another?

1. 0.15 M urea 2. 0.05 M $CaCl_2$
3. 0.1 M $MgSO_4$ 4. 0.15 M glucose

Select the correct answer using the codes given below:

(a) 1 and 4 (b) 2 and 3
(c) 1, 2 and 4 (d) 2, 3 and 4

268. If osmotic pressure of 1 M urea is π, what will be the osmotic pressure for 0.1 M NaCl?

(a) π (b) 0.1 π (c) 2 π (d) 0.2 π

269. 0.1 M NaCl and 0.05 M $BaCl_2$ solution are separated by a semi-permeable membrane in a container. For this system, choose the correct statement.

(a) There is no movement of any solution across the membrane.
(b) Water flows from $BaCl_2$ solution towards NaCl solution.
(c) Water flows from NaCl solution towards $BaCl_2$ solution.
(d) Osmotic pressure of 0.1 M NaCl is lower than the osmotic pressure of $BaCl_2$ (assume complete dissociation).

270. The average osmotic pressure of human blood is 7.8 bar at 37°C. What is the concentration of an aqueous NaCl solution that could be used in the blood steam?

(a) 0.15 mol/L (b) 0.30 mol/L
(c) 0.60 mol/L (d) 0.45 mol/L

271. An electrolyte (AB) is 100% ionised in 100% aqueous solution. What is the osmotic pressure (L atm) of a 10% solution of the electrolyte at 300 K, if the molecular weight of AB is 200 g mol^{-1}?
(R = 0.082 L atm K^{-1} mol^{-1})

(a) 200 (b) 100 (c) 246 (d) 24.6
(e) 2.46

272. The osmotic pressure of a solution prepared by dissolving 25 mg of K_2SO_4 in 2 litre of water at 25°C is (assuming that it is completely dissociated)

(a) 5.27×10^{-3} atm (b) 5.27×10^{-4} atm
(c) 5.27×10^{-5} atm (d) 5.27×10^{-6} atm

273. The molecular weight of sodium chloride determined by osmotic pressure method will be

(a) equal to 58.5 (b) greater than 58.5
(c) less than 58.5
(d) none of the above as this method cannot be used for molecular weight determination

274. Osmotic pressure observed when benzoic acid is dissolved in benzene is less than expected from theoretical considerations. This is because

(a) benzoic acid is an organic solute
(b) benzoic acid has higher molar mass than benzene
(c) benzoic acid gets associated in benzene
(d) benzoic acid gets dissociated in benzene

275. Which of the following aqueous solutions has the highest boiling point?

(a) 0.1 M KNO_3 (b) 0.1 M Na_3PO_4
(c) 0.1 M $BaCl_2$ (d) 0.1 M K_2SO_4

276. The boiling point of 0.2 mol kg^{-1} solution of X in water is greater than an equimolar solution of Y in water. Which one of the following statements is true in this case?

(a) X is undergoing dissociation in water.
(b) The molecular mass of X is greater than the molecular mass of Y.
(c) The molecular mass of X is less than the molecular mass of Y.
(d) Y undergoes dissociation in water while X undergoes no change.

277. The experimental and calculated elevation in boiling points of an electrolyte AB in its aqueous solution at a given concentration are 0.81 K and 0.54 K respectively. The percentage ionisation of the electrolyte at this concentration is

(a) 20 (b) 40 (c) 50 (d) 60

278. Pure benzene freezes at 5.3°C. A solution of 0.223 g of phenylacetic acid ($C_6H_5CH_2COOH$) in 4.4 g of benzene (K_f = 5.12 K kg mol^{-1}) freezes at 4.47°C. From this observation, one can conclude that

(a) phenylacetic acid exists as such in benzene
(b) phenylacetic acid undergoes partial ionisation in benzene
(c) phenylacetic acid undergoes complete ionisation in benzene
(d) phenylacetic acid dimerises in benzene

279. The freezing point of water is depressed by 0.37°C in a 0.01 molal NaCl solution. The freezing point of 0.02 molal solution of urea is depressed by

(a) 0.37°C (b) 0.74°C (c) 0.185°C (d) 0°C

280. The freezing point depression constant for water is –1.86 C m^{-1}. If 5.00 g of Na_2SO_4 is dissolved in 45.0 g of H_2O, the freezing point is found to be –3.82°C. Calculate the van't Hoff factor for Na_2SO_4.

(a) 0.381 (b) 2.05 (c) 2.63 (d) 3.11

281. 0.01 M solution of KCl and $BaCl_2$ are prepared in water. The freezing point of KCl solution is found to be –2°C. What is the freezing point of $BaCl_2$ solution, assuming complete ionisation?

(a) –3°C (b) +3°C (c) –2°C (d) 4°C

282. 0.5 molal aqueous solution of a weak acid (HX) is 20% ionised. If K_f for water is 1.86 K kg mol^{-1}, the lowering in freezing point of the solution is

(a) –0.56 K (b) –1.12 K (c) 0.56 K (d) 1.12 K

283. The degree of ionisation of HF in 0.100 M aqueous solution is (freezing point of the solution = –0.197°C and K_f of water = 1.86°C)

(a) 6% (b) 12% (c) 3 % (d) 9%

284. A solution of 1.25 g of P in 50 g of water lowers freezing point by 0.3°C. Molar mass of P is 94. $K_{f(\text{water})}$ = 1.86 K kg mol^{-1}. The degree of association of P in water is

(a) 80% (b) 60% (c) 65% (d) 75%

285. The van't Hof factor, (*i*), of a 0.5% (*w/W*) aqueous solution of KCl which freezes at –0.24°C is (K_f for water = 1.86 K kg mol^{-1}, molecular weight of KCl = 74.5)

(a) 1.52 (b) 2.32 (c) 1.92 (d) 1.32

286. For 1 molal aqueous solution of the following compounds, which one will show the highest freezing point?

(a) $[Co(H_2O)_6]Cl_3$ (b) $[Co(H_2O)_5Cl]Cl_2.H_2O$
(c) $[Co(H_2O)_4Cl_2]Cl.2H_2O$
(d) $[Co(H_2O)_3Cl_3].3H_2O$

287. The addition of common salt to a sample of water will

(a) increase its freezing point and decrease the boiling point
(b) decrease its freezing point and increase the boiling point
(c) increase both the boiling and the freezing point
(d) decrease both the boiling and the freezing point

288. A 0.6% solution of urea (molecular weight = 60) would be isotonic with

(a) 0.1 M glucose (b) 0.1 M KCl
(c) 0.6% glucose solution (d) 0.6% KCl solution

289. Which has the least freezing point?

(a) 1% sucrose (b) 1% NaCl
(c) 1% $CaCl_2$ (d) 1% glucose

290. The depression in freezing point of 0.1 M aqueous solutions of HCl, $CuSO_4$ and K_2SO_4 are in the ratio

(a) 1 : 1 : 1 (b) 1 : 2 : 3
(c) 1 : 1 : 1 : 5 (d) 2 : 4 : 3

291. Of the following 0.10 m aqueous solutions, which one will exhibit the largest freezing point depression?

(a) KCl (b) $C_6H_{12}O_6$
(c) $Al_2(SO_4)_3$ (d) K_2SO_4

292. Which of the following is incorrect?

(a) Molar weight of NaCl found by osmotic pressure measurements is half of the theoretical value.
(b) Molecular weight of CH_3COOH in benzene found by cryoscopic methods.
(c) Osmotic pressure of 0.1 M glucose solution is half of that of 0.1 M NaCl solution.
(d) Molecular weight of HCl found by colligative property will be same in the aqueous solution and benzene solution.

293. The freezing point of equimolal aqueous solutions will be highest for

(a) $C_6H_5NH_3Cl$ (anilinium chloride)
(b) $Ca(NO_3)_2$
(c) $La(NO_3)_2$
(d) $C_6H_{12}O_6$ (glucose)

294. Which one of the following statements is incorrect?

(a) A solution freezes at a lower temperature than the pure solvent.
(b) A solution boils at a higher temperature than the pure solvent.
(c) 0.1 M NaCl solution and 0.1 M sugar solution have the same boiling point.
(d) Osmosis cannot take place without a semi-permeable membrane.

295. Which of the following would exert maximum osmotic pressure?

(a) decinormal aluminium sulfate
(b) decinormal barium chloride
(c) decinormal sodium chloride
(d) a solution obtained by mixing equal volumes of (b) and (c) and filtering

296. Which of the following will have the highest FP at 1 atm?

(a) 0.1 M NaCl solution (b) 0.1 M sugar solution
(c) 0.1 M $BaCl_2$ solution (d) 0.1 M $FeCl_3$ solution

297. At the same temperature, which pair of the following solutions are isotonic?

(a) 0.2 M $BaCl_2$ and 0.2 M urea
(b) 0.1 M urea and 0.1 M NaCl
(c) 0.1 M NaCl and 0.1 M K_2SO_4
(d) 0.1 M $Ba(NO_3)_2$ and 0.1 M Na_2SO_4

298. The lowering in vapour pressure is maximum for

(a) 0.1 M urea solution (b) 0.1 M NaCl
(c) 0.1 M $MgCl_2$ (d) 0.1 M $K_4[FeCN)_6]$

299. The osmotic pressure of which solution is maximum (consider that deci-molar solution of each is 90% dissociated)

(a) aluminium sulfate (b) barium chloride
(c) sodium sulfate
(d) a mixture of equal volumes of (b) and (c)

300. Which of the following pairs of solutions is expected to be isotonic at the same temperature?
(a) 0.2 M urea and 0.2 M NaCl
(b) 0.1 M urea and 0.2 M $MgCl_2$
(c) 0.1 M NaCl and 0.1 M Na_2SO_4
(d) 0.1 M $Ca(NO_3)_2$ and 0.1 M Na_2SO_4

301. 58.5 of NaCl and 180 g of glucose were separately dissolved in 1000 mL of water. Identify the correct statement regarding the elevation of boiling point of the resulting solution.
(a) NaCl solution will show higher elevation of BP.
(b) Glucose solution will show higher elevation of BP.
(c) Both the solutions will show an equal elevation of BP.
(d) The BP elevation will be shown by neither of the solutions.

302. Assuming the salt to be ionised in solution, which of the following has highest the osmotic pressure?
(a) 1% CsCl (b) 1% RbCl
(c) 1% KCl (d) 1 NaCl

303. Four solutions of K_2SO_4 with the concentrations 0.1 m, 0.01 m, 0.001 m and 0.0001 m are available. The maximum value of the van't Hoff factor, *i*, corresponds to
(a) 0.0001 m solution (b) 0.001 m solution
(c) 0.01 m solution (d) 0.1 m solution

304. Which one of the following electrolytes has the same value of van't Hoff factor (*i*) as that of $Al_2(SO_4)_3$ (if all are 100%) ionised?
(a) K_2SO_4 (b) $K_3[Fe(CN)_6]$
(c) $Al(NO_3)_3$ (d) $K_4[Fe(CN)_6]$

Miscellaneous

305. Which one of the following statements is false?
(a) Raoult's law states that the vapour pressure of a component over a binary solution of volatile liquids is directly proportional to its mole fraction.
(b) Two sucrose solutions of the same molality prepared in different solvents will have the same depression in freezing point.
(c) The correct order of osmotic pressures of 0.01 M solution of each compound is $BaCl_2 > KCl > CH_3COOH >$ glucose.
(d) In the equation, osmotic pressure, $\pi = MRT$, M is the molarity of the solution.
(e) The molecular weight of NaCl determined by colligative property measurement is less than the theoretical molecular weight.

306. Based on solute–solvent interactions, the correct arrangement in order of increasing solubility in *n*-octane is
(a) cyclohexane < CH_3CN < CH_3OH < KCl
(b) KCl < CH_3OH < CH_3CN < cyclohexane
(c) CH_3OH < CH_3CN < KCl < cyclohexane
(d) CH_3CN < CH_3OH < CH_3CN < cyclohexane

Final Preparation

307. 250 mL of 6 M HCl and 650 mL of 3 M HCl were mixed together. The volume of water to be added so that the molarity of the final solution is 3 M will be
(a) 250 mL (b) 1150 mL (c) 500 mL (d) 575 mL

308. 5 g of NaOH is added to 250 mL of $\frac{M}{4}$ NaOH solution (density = 1.0 g/cm^3). The density of the new solution is found to be 1.08 g/cm^3. The molarity of the new solution will be
(a) 0.46 M (b) 0.56 M (c) 0.66 M (d) 0.76 M

309. Which of the following should be done in order to prepare 0.40 M NaCl starting with 100 mL of 0.30 M NaCl? (mol. wt. NaCl = 58.5)
(a) add 0.585 g NaCl (b) add 20 mL water
(c) add 0.010 mL/NaCl (d) evaporate 10 mL water

310. Hydrochloric acid solutions A and B have concentrations of 0.5 N and 0.1 N respectively. The volumes of solutions A and B required to make 2 litres of 0.2 N HCl are
(a) 0.5 L of A + 1.5 L of B
(b) 0.5 L of A + 0.5 L of B
(c) 1.0 L of A + 1.0 L of B
(d) 0.75 L of A + 1.25 L of B

311. The solubility of a gas in water at 300 K under a pressure of 100 atmosphere is 4×10^{-3} kg L^{-1}. Therefore, the mass of the gas in kg dissolved in 250 mL of water under a pressure of 250 atm at 300 K is
(a) 2.5×10^{-3} (b) 2.0×10^{-3}
(c) 1.25×10^{-3} (d) 5.0×10^{-3}

312. The millimoles of N_2 gas that will dissolve in 1 L of water at 298 K when it is bubbled through water and has a partial pressure of 0.96 bar will be (given that at 298 K K_H = 76.8 kbar)
(a) 0.59 (b) 0.69 (c) 0.79 (d) 0.89

313. When a gas is bubbled through water at 298 K, a very dilute solution of the gas is obtained. Henry's law constant for the gas at 298 K is 100 kbar. If the gas exerts a partial pressure of 1 bar, the number of millimoles of the gas dissolved in one litre of water is
(a) 0.555 (b) 5.55 (c) 00555 (d) 55.5
(e) 5.55×10^{-4}

314. A solution has 1 : 4 mole ratio of pentane to hexane. The vapour pressures of the pure hydrocarbons at 20°C are 440 mm Hg for pentane and 120 mm Hg for hexane. The mole fraction of pentane in the vapour phase is

(a) 0.200 (b) 0.478 (c) 0.549 (d) 0.786

315. If two substances A and B have $\overset{\circ}{p}_A : \overset{\circ}{p}_B = 1 : 2$ and have mole fraction in solution 1 : 2, then the mole fraction of A in the vapour is

(a) 0.33 (b) 0.25 (c) 0.52 (d) 0.2

316. Two liquids X and Y form an ideal solution. The mixture has a vapour pressure of 400 mm at 300 K when mixed in the molar ration of 1 : 1 and a vapour pressure of 350 mm when mixed in the molar ratio of 1 : 2 at the same temperature. The vapour pressures of the two pure liquids X and Y respectively are

(a) 250 mm, 550 mm (b) 350 mm, 450 mm
(c) 350 mm, 700 mm (d) 550 mm, 250 mm

317. Two liquids X and Y form in ideal solution. At 300 K, the vapour pressure of the solution containing 1 mol of X and 3 mol of Y is 550 mm Hg. At the same temperature if 1 mol of Y is further added to this solution, the vapour pressure of the solution increases by 10 mm Hg. Vapour pressure (in mm Hg) of X and Y in their pure states will be respectively:

(a) 200 and 300 (b) 300 and 400
(c) 400 and 600 (d) 500 and 600

318. For an ideal solution with $\overset{\circ}{p}_A > \overset{\circ}{p}_B$, which of the following is true?

(a) $(x_A)_{\text{liquid}} = (x_A)_{\text{vapour}}$

(b) $(x_A)_{\text{liquid}} > (x_A)_{\text{vapour}}$

(c) $(x_A)_{\text{liquid}}$ and $(x_A)_{\text{vapour}}$

(d) $(x_A)_{\text{liquid}}$ and $(x_A)_{\text{vapour}}$ do not bear any relationship with each other

319. An open beaker containing a pure solvent and a second beaker containing a solution in the same solvent with a non-volatile solute are sealed in a container. Over a period of time,

(a) the volumes of both the solution and solvent will decrease

(b) the volumes of both the solution and solvent will increase

(c) the volume of the solution will decrease while the volume of the solvent will increase

(d) the volume of the solution will increase and the volume of the solvent will decrease

320. The relative lowering of vapour pressure of an aqueous solution containing a non-volatile solute is 0.125. The molality of the solution

(a) 0.70 (b) 0.50 (c) 0.60 (d) 0.80

321. If at certain temperature, the vapour pressure of pure water is 25 mm Hg and that of a very dilute aqueous urea solution is 24.5 mm Hg, the molality of solution is

(a) 0.02 (b) 1.2 (c) 1.11
(d) 0.08 (e) 0.06

322. For an ideal binary liquid solution with $\overset{\circ}{p}_A > \overset{\circ}{p}_B$ which relation between X_A (mole fraction of A in liquid phase) and Y_A (mole fraction of A in vapour phase) is correct

(a) $X_A = Y_A$ (b) $X_A > Y_A$

(c) $X_A < Y_A$ (d) $\frac{X_A}{X_B} < \frac{Y_A}{Y_B}$

323. Formation of solution from two components can be considered as

(i) pure solvent → separated solvent molecules, ΔH_1
(ii) pure solute → separated solute molecules, ΔH_2
(iii) separated solvent and solute molecules → solution ΔH_3

The solution so formed will be ideal if

(a) $\Delta H_{\text{soln.}} = \Delta H_1 + \Delta H_2 + \Delta H_3$
(b) $\Delta H_{\text{soln.}} = \Delta H_1 + \Delta H_2 - \Delta H_3$
(c) $\Delta H_{\text{soln.}} = \Delta H_1 - \Delta H_2 - \Delta H_3$
(d) $\Delta H_{\text{soln.}} = \Delta H_3 - \Delta H_1 - \Delta H_2$

324. For an ideal binary liquid mixture

(a) $\Delta S_{(\text{mix})} = 0, \Delta G_{(\text{mix})} = 0$
(b) $\Delta H_{(\text{mix})} = 0, \Delta S_{(\text{mix})} < 0$
(c) $\Delta S_{(\text{mix})} = 0, \Delta G_{(\text{mix})} > 0$
(d) $\Delta S_{(\text{mix})} > 0, \Delta G_{(\text{mix})} < 0$

325. Which of the following plots correctly represents the behaviour of an ideal binary liquid solution?

(a) Plot of x_A (mole fraction of A in liquid phase) versus y_A (mole fraction of A in vapour phase) is linear.
(b) Plot of x_A versus y_B is linear.
(c) Plot $1/x_A$ versus $1/y_A$ is linear.
(d) Plot of $1/x_A$ versus $1/y_B$ is linear.

326. For an ideal binary solution of A and B, y_A is the mole fraction of A in the vapour phase. Then, which of the following plots should be linear?

(a) P_{Total} vs y_A (b) P_{Total} vs y_B
(c) $1/P_{\text{Total}}$ vs y_A (d) $1/P_{\text{Total}}$ vs $(y_B + y_A)$

327. Which of the following correctly represents the change in thermodynamic properties during the formation of 1 mol of an ideal binary solution?

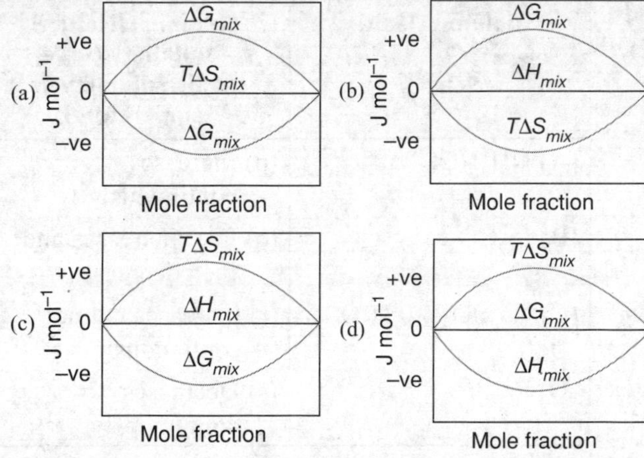

328. Dry air is passed through a solution containing 10 g of the solute in 90 g of water and then through pure water. The loss in weight of the solution is 2.5 g and that of the pure solvent is 0.05 g. Calculate the molecular weight of the solute.

(a) 50 (b) 180 (c) 100 (d) 25

329. The mass of glucose that should be dissolved in 50 g of water in order to produce the same lowering of vapour pressure as produced by dissolving 1 g of urea in same quantity of water is

(a) 1 g (b) 3 g (c) 6 g (d) 8 g

330. When 3 g of a non-volatile hydrocarbon containing 94.4% carbon is dissolved in 100 g benzene, the vapour pressure of benzene is lowered from 9.953 kPa to 9.823 kPa. The molecular formula of the hydrocarbon is

(a) C_7H_5 (b) $C_{14}H_{10}$ (c) C_5H_7 (d) $C_{10}H_{14}$

331. Two aqueous solutions S_1 and S_2 are separated by a semi-permeable membrane. S_2 has lower vapour pressure than S_1. Then

(a) more solvent will flow from S_1 to S_2
(b) more solvent will flow from S_2 to S_1
(c) solvent from S_1 and S_2 will flow at equal rates
(d) no flow will take place

332. Osmotic pressure of a urea solution at 10°C is 500 mm. Osmotic pressure of the solution becomes 105.3 mm when it is diluted and temperature raised to 25°C. The extent of dilution is

(a) 6 times (b) 5 times
(c) 7 times (d) 4 times

333. Two elements A and B form compounds having formulae AB_2 and AB_4. When dissolved in 20 g benzene, 1 g of AB_2 lowers the freezing point by 2.3° whereas 1.0 g of AB_4 lowers it by 1.3°C. K_f for benzene is 5.1 K mol^{-1} kg. The atomic masses of A and B are respectively

(a) 25.6, 42.6 (b) 42.6, 25.6
(c) 85.3, 25.6 (d) 25.6, 85.3

334. The freezing point of a 0.01 M aqueous glucose solution at 1 atm is –0.18°C. To it, an addition of equal volume of 0.002 M glucose solution will produce a solution with a freezing point of nearly

(a) –0.036°C (b) –0.108°C
(c) –0.216°C (d) –0.422°C

335. Increasing the temperature of an aqueous solution will cause a

(a) decrease in molality (b) decrease in molarity
(c) decrease in mole fraction
(d) decrease in % *w/w*

336. Normality of 0.3 M phosphorus acid (H_3PO_3) is

(a) 0.5 (b) 0.6 (c) 0.9 (d) 0.1

337. The mole fraction C_2H_5OH (Mol. wt. = 46) in 5 molal aqueous ethyl alcohol solution is

(a) 0.082 (b) 0.82 (c) 5 (d) $\frac{5}{55.55}$

338. The volume of 95% H_2SO_4 (density = 1.85 g cm^{-3}) needed to prepare 100 cm^3 of 15% solution of H_2SO_4 (density = 1.10 g cm^{-3}) will be

(a) 5 cc (b) 7.5 cc (c) 9.4 cc (d) 12.4 cc

339. The number of iodine atoms present in 1 cm^3 of its 0.1 M solution is

(a) 6.02×10^{23} (b) 6.02×10^{22}
(c) 6.02×10^{19} (d) 1.204×10^{20}

340. A sample of concentrated nitric acid is 63% *w/w*. If the density of the solution is 1.15 g mL^{-1}, the molarity of the acid solution is

(a) 12.6 M (b) 11.5 M (c) 6.3 M (d) 5.75 M

341. The normality of mixture obtained by mixing 100 mL of 0.2 M H_2SO_4 with 100 mL of 0.2 M NaOH is

(a) 0.2 (b) 0.01 (c) 0.1 (d) 0.3

342. Concentrated aqueous sulfric acid is 98% H_2SO_4 by mass and has a density of 1.80 g mL^{-1}. Volume of the acid required to make one litre of 0.1 M H_2SO_4 solution is

(a) 5.55 mL (b) 11.10 mL
(c) 16.65 mL (d) 22.20 mL

343. Equal volumes of 0.1 M $AgNO_3$ and 0.2 M NaCl solution are mixed. The concentrations of NO_3^- ions in the mixed solution will be

(a) 0.1 M (b) 0.05 M (c) 0.2 M (d) 0.15 M

344. The hardness of a water sample containing 0.002 mol of magnesium sulfate dissolved in a litre of water is expressed as

(a) 200 ppm (b) 120 ppm
(c) 20 ppm (d) 2000 ppm

345. Camphor is often used in molecular mass determination because

(a) it has a very high cryoscopic constant
(b) it is volatile
(c) it is a solvent for organic substances
(d) it is readily available

346. Which of the following colligative properties can provide the molar mass of proteins (or polymers or colloids) with greater precision?

(a) relative lowering of vapour pressure
(b) elevation of boiling point
(c) depression in freezing point
(d) osmotic pressure

MATCH THE FOLLOWING

347.

Column I	Column II
(A) Non-ideal solution showing positive deviation	(p) *n*-hexane + *n*-heptane
(B) Non-ideal solution showing negative deviation	(q) Carbon tetrachloride + benzene
(C) Solute showing abnormal molar mass	(r) Chloroform + benzene
(D) Ideal solution	(s) Acetic acid + benzene

(a) (A)—(p), (B)—(q), (C)—(r), (D)—(s)
(b) (A)—(q), (B)—(r), (C)—(s), (D)—(p)
(c) (A)—(p), (B)—(r), (C)—(s), (D)—(q)
(d) (A)—(q), (B)—(s), (C)—(r), (D)—(p)

348.

Column I	Column II
(A) 0.91% NaCl solution in contact with RBCs	(p) Hypertonic solution
(B) 1.25% NaCl solution in contact with RBC	(q) Hypotonic solution
(C) 0.75% NaCl solution in contact with RBCs	(r) Isotonic solution
(D) 5.85% NaCl solution in contact with a glass wall	(s) Normal solution

(a) (A)—(p), (B)—(q), (C)—(r), (D)—(s)
(b) (A)—(r), (B)—(p), (C)—(q), (D)—(s)
(c) (A)—(s), (B)—(p), (C)—(q), (D)—(r)
(d) (A)—(q), (B)—(p), (C)—(r), (D)—(s)

349.

Column I (Salt)	Column II (Nature of solubility curve, that is, solubility vs temperature)
(A) NH_4NO_3	(p) Increases continuously
(B) Li_2CO_3	(q) First increases and then decreases
(C) Na_2SO_4. 10 H_2O	(r) Increases but not continuously
(D) KCl	(s) Decreases continuously

(a) (A)—(r), (B)—(q), (C)—(s), (D)—(p)
(b) (A)—(p), (B)—(s), (C)—(q), (D)—(r)
(c) (A)—(s), (B)—(r), (C)—(q), (D)—(p)
(d) (A)—(r), (B)—(s), (C)—(q), (D)—(p)

350.

Column I (Term)	Column II (Meaning of the term)
(A) Plasmolysis	(p) Swelling and bursting of red blood cells when placed in hypotonic solution
(B) Hemolysis	(q) Shrinking of the red blood cells when placed in hypertonic solution
(C) Isohydric	(r) Solutions have same molar concentration
(D) Isoosmotic	(s) Solutions have the same $[H^+]$

(a) (A)—(q), (B)—(p), (C)—(s), (D)—(r)
(b) (A)—(p), (B)—(q), (C)—(s), (D)—(r)
(c) (A)—(q), (B)—(p), (C)—(r), (D)—(s)
(d) (A)—(r), (B)—(s), (C)—(p), (D)—(q)

351.

Column I	Column II
(A) 10.6 g Na_2CO_3 dissolved in 100 mL solution (density = 1.06 g mL^{-1})	(p) 0.1 M
(B) 34.2 g L^{-1} sucrose solution (density = 1.0342 g mL^{-1}	(q) 1 M
(C) 9.8% H_2SO_4 solution (density 1.25 g mL^{-1}	(r) 1.25 M
(D) 20% aqueous ethanol solution by volume (density = 0.938 g mL^{-1}	(s) 3.0 M

(a) (A)—(p), (B)—(q), (C)—(r), (D)—(s)
(b) (A)—(q), (B)—(p), (C)—(s), (D)—(r)
(c) (A)—(q), (B)—(r), (C)—(p), (D)—(s)
(d) (A)—(q), (B)—(p), (C)—(r), (D)—(s)

ASSERTION REASON

Directions: In each of the following questions, a statement of Assertion (A) is given followed by a corresponding statement of Reason (R) just below it. Of the statements, mark the correct answer as

(a) if both the assertion and reason are true and the reason is the correct explanation of the assertion.

(b) if both the assertion and reason are true but the reason is not the correct explanation of the assertion.

(c) if the assertion is true but the reason is false.

(d) if both the assertion and reason are false.

352. Assertion: Enthalpy changes are positive when $Na_2SO_4.10H_2O$, $CuSO_4.5H_2O$ and salts like NaCl, KCl and so on, which do not form hydrates are dissolved in water. But enthalpy changes are negative when anhydrous salts capable of forming hydrates are dissolved in water.

Reason: The difference in the behaviour is due to large differences in the molecular weights of the hydrated and anhydrous salts. The substances with larger molecular weight usually show positive enthalpy changes on dissolution.

353. Assertion: The dissolution of ammonia in water does not follow Henry's law.

Reason: Ammonia undergoes ionisation in water as $NH_3 + H_2O \rightleftharpoons NH_4^+ + OH^-$

354. Assertion: If a liquid solute more volatile than the solvent is added to the solvent, the vapour pressure of the solution may increase, that is, $p_s > p°$.

Reason: In the presence of a more volatile liquid solute, only the solute will form the vapours and the solvent will not.

355. Assertion: Lowering of vapour pressure of the solvent takes place only if the solute is non-volatile or less volatile than the solvent.

Reason: Glycerol added to water will raise the vapour pressure of water.

356. Assertion: The relative lowering of vapour pressure of a solution is equal to the mole fraction of the solute.

Reason: Raoult's law is applicable to all non-volatile electrolytes.

357. Assertion: On addition NaCl to water, its vapour pressure increases.

Reason: Addition of a non-volatile solute increases the vapour pressure.

358. Assertion: Azeotropic mixtures are formed only by non-ideal solutions.

Reason: Boiling point of an azeotrope is either higher than both the components or lower than both the components.

359. Assertion: The pressure of mixing of CH_3OH and CCl_4 is accompanied by an increase in enthalpy and is a spontaneous process.

Reason: When we mix CCl_4 and CH_3OH, we replace weaker forces of attraction by stronger forces of attraction.

360. Assertion: If red blood cells were removed from the body and placed in pure water, the pressure inside the cells increases.

Reason: The concentration of the salt content in the cells increases.

361. Assertion: Out of the various colligative properties, osmotic pressure is used for determination of molecular masses of polymers.

Reason: Polymer solutions do not possess a constant boiling point or freezing point.

362. Assertion: When a solution of a non-volatile solute in a volatile solvent is distilled, boiling point of the remaining solution keeps on increasing continuously.

Reason: Solutions do not have constant boiling points.

363. Assertion: When methanol is added to water, the boiling point of water increases.

Reason: When a volatile solute is added to a volatile solvent, elevation in boiling point is observed.

364. Assertion: Higher the molal depression constant of the solvent used, higher the freezing point of the solution.

Reason: Depression in freezing point does not depend on the nature of the solvent.

365. Assertion: Increasing pressure on pure water decreases its freezing point.

Reason: Density of water is maximum at 273 K.

366. Assertion: Camphor is used as a solvent in the determination of the molecular masses of naphthalene, anthracene, and so on.

Reason: Camphor has a high molal elevation constant.

367. Assertion: Larger the value of the cryoscopic constant of the solvent, lesser will be the freezing point of the solution.

Reason: Depression in freezing point depends upon the nature of the solvent.

368. Assertion: Molecular masses of polymers cannot be determined using the boiling point or freezing point method.

Reason: Polymer solutions do not possess constant boiling point or freezing points.

369. Assertion: The water pouch of an instant cold pack for treating athletic injury, breaks when squeezed and NH_4NO_4 dissolves lowering the temperature.

Reason: Addition of a non-volatile solute into a solvent, results in the depression of freezing point of the solvent.

370. Assertion: The vapour pressure of 0.1 M sugar solution is more than 0.1 M KCl solution.

Reason: Lowering of vapour pressure is directly proportional to the number of species present in the solution.

371. Assertion: The boiling point of 0.1 M KCl solution is greater than that 0.1 M urea solution.

Reason: KCl is an ionic compound with strong interionic forces whereas urea is a covalent compound.

372. Assertion: If 0.1 m NaCl solution boils at 101°C, then 0.1 m $BaCl_2$ solution will boil at approximately 101.5°C

Reason: $BaCl_2$ has a higher molecular mass than NaCl.

373. Assertion: The molecular weight of acetic acid by depression in freezing point method in benzene and water is found to be different.

Reason: Water is polar and benzene is non-polar.

374. Assertion: When methanol is added to water, the boiling point of water increases.

Reason: When a volatile solute is added to a volatile solvent, elevation in boiling point is observed.

375. Assertion: 1.575 g $H_2C_2O_4.2H_2O$ in 250 mL solution makes it 0.1 N.

Reason: $H_2C_2O_4.2H_2O$ is a dihydrate organic acid.

376. Assertion: One molar aqueous solution has always higher concentration than one molal.

Reason: The molality of a solution depends upon the density of the solution whereas molarity does not.

377. Assertion: If 100 cc of 0.10 HCl is mixed with 100 cc of 0.2 N HCl, the normality of the final solution will be 0.30.

Reason: Normalities of similar solution like HCl can be added.

378. Assertion: One molal aqueous solution of glucose contains 180 g of glucose in 1 kg water.

Reason: Solution containing one mole of solute in 1000 g of solvent is called one molal solution.

Answer Key

1. (c)	2. (d)	3. (c)	4. (b)	5. (b)	6. (a)	7. (a)	8. (c)	9. (c)	10. (c)
11. (c)	12. (a)	13. (b)	14. (d)	15. (b)	16. (b)	17. (a)	18. (b)	19. (b)	20. (d)
21. (c)	22. (c)	23. (a)	24. (b)	25. (a)	26. (b)	27. (b)	28. (b)	29. (b)	30. (a)
31. (c)	32. (b)	33. (a)	34. (c)	35. (b)	36. (c)	37. (b)	38. (a)	39. (b)	40. (b)
41. (b)	42. (c)	43. (b)	44. (b)	45. (b)	46. (a)	47. (None)	48. (a)	49. (a)	50. (c)
51. (c)	52. (c)	53. (c)	54. (d)	55. (c)	56. (b)	57. (b)	58. (c)	59. (c)	60. (a)
61. (b)	62. (a)	63. (c)	64. (a)	65. (a)	66. (b)	67. (c)	68. (d)	69. (d)	70. (b)
71. (a)	72. (a)	73. (c)	74. (c)	75. (c)	76. (d)	77. (c)	78. (b)	79. (c)	80. (a)
81. (c)	82. (d)	83. (c)	84. (d)	85. (b)	86. (a)	87. (d)	88. (d)	89. (b)	90. (c)
91. (a)	92. (d)	93. (d)	94. (d)	95. (d)	96. (c)	97. (d)	98. (d)	99. (c)	100. (d)
101. (a)	102. (a)	103. (c)	104. (d)	105. (c)	106. (a)	107. (d)	108. (c)	109. (a)	110. (a)
111. (a)	112. (d)	113. (a)	114. (c)	115. (b)	116. (d)	117. (c)	118. (c)	119. (a)	120. (c)
121. (a)	122. (c)	123. (c)	124. (b)	125. (d)	126. (c)	127. (c)	128. (b)	129. (d)	130. (d)
131. (d)	132. (b)	133. (b)	134. (a)	135. (a)	136. (c)	137. (d)	138. (b)	139. (a)	140. (a)
141. (b)	142. (c)	143. (a)	144. (d)	145. (b)	146. (b)	147. (c)	148. (b)	149. (a)	150. (b)
151. (c)	152. (d)	153. (a)	154. (d)	155. (b)	156. (b)	157. (c)	158. (c)	159. (b)	160. (b)
161. (a)	162. (b)	163. (c)	164. (b)	165. (d)	166. (b)	167. (a)	168. (b)	169. (c)	170. (b)
171. (b)	172. (d)	173. (b)	174. (c)	175. (a)	176. (c)	177. (c)	178. (a)	179. (b)	180. (d)
181. (a)	182. (c)	183. (c)	184. (c)	185. (b)	186. (d)	187. (e)	188. (c)	189. (b)	190. (b)
191. (c)	192. (a)	193. (a)	194. (b)	195. (b)	196. (d)	197. (c)	198. (c)	199. (c)	200. (d)
201. (b)	202. (a)	203. (b)	204. (d)	205. (b)	206. (a)	207. (c)	208. (b)	209. (d)	210. (b)
211. (d)	212. (c)	213. (a)	214. (b)	215. (d)	216. (b)	217. (d)	218. (a)	219. (d)	220. (d)
221. (c)	222. (a)	223. (b)	224. (d)	225. (d)	226. (b)	227. (a)	228. (b)	229. (b)	230. (d)
231. (c)	232. (b)	233. (c)	234. (b)	235. (b)	236. (b)	237. (a)	238. (b)	239. (c)	240. (b)
241. (a)	242. (c)	243. (a)	244. (d)	245. (a)	246. (a)	247. (c)	248. (b)	249. (d)	250. (c)
251. (b)	252. (b)	253. (a)	254. (c)	255. (d)	256. (a)	257. (b)	258. (a)	259. (a)	260. (c)
261. (a)	262. (b)	263. (c)	264. (a)	265. (a)	266. (e)	267. (c)	268. (d)	269. (b)	270. (a)
271. (d)	272. (a)	273. (c)	274. (c)	275. (b)	276. (a)	277. (c)	278. (d)	279. (a)	280. (c)

281. (a)	282. (d)	283. (a)	284. (a)	285. (c)	286. (d)	287. (b)	288. (a)	289. (b)	290. (c)
291. (c)	292. (d)	293. (d)	294. (c)	295. (a)	296. (b)	297. (d)	298. (d)	299. (a)	300. (d)
301. (a)	302. (d)	303. (a)	304. (d)	305. (b)	306. (b)	307. (a)	308. (d)	309. (a)	310. (a)
311. (a)	312. (b)	313. (a)	314. (b)	315. (d)	316. (d)	317. (c)	318. (c)	319. (d)	320. (a)
321. (c)	322. (d)	323. (a)	324. (d)	325. (c)	326. (c)	327. (c)	328. (c)	329. (b)	330. (b)
331. (a)	332. (b)	333. (a)	334. (b)	335. (b)	336. (b)	337. (a)	338. (c)	339. (d)	340. (b)
341. (c)	342. (a)	343. (b)	344. (a)	345. (a)	346. (d)	347. (b)	348. (b)	349. (d)	350. (a)
351. (d)	352. (a)	353. (a)	354. (c)	355. (c)	356. (c)	357. (c)	358. (b)	359. (c)	360. (c)
361. (c)	362. (c)	363. (d)	364. (d)	365. (c)	366. (c)	367. (a)	368. (c)	369. (a)	370. (a)
371. (b)	372. (b)	373. (b)	374. (d)	375. (b)	376. (b)	377. (d)	378. (a)		

Hints and Solutions

OBJECTIVE QUESTIONS

Introduction

1. **(c):** Brass is a solution of solid in solid (Cu + Zn).

Types of Solutions

2. **(d):** Smaller particles enter into interstitial sites. The solution formed is therefore called interstitial solid solution.

3. **(c):** Brass is a substitutional alloy (of Cu = 80%, Zn = 20%) because Cu and Zn atoms have similar size. Steel is an interstitial alloy in which small size C-atoms occupy interstitial sites of Fe lattice.

4. **(b):** On adding a non-metal atom to a metal, the metal becomes less tensible.

5. **(b):** Liquid H_2O is uniformly mixed into solid $CuSO_4$.

6. **(a):** In steel, some Fe atoms at the lattice sites are replaced by those of Cr or W or Ni or Mn. In WC, C atoms occupy interstitial sites in the lattice of tungsten (W) atoms.

Expressing Concentration of Solutions

7. **(a):** 0.3 L of 0.005 M $Ba(OH)_2$ solution
$= 0.005 \times 0.3$ mol $= 0.0015$ mol $Ba(OH)_2 = 0.003$ mol OH^-

8. **(c):** $CaCl_2 \rightarrow Ca^{2+} + 2Cl^-$
1 mole $\quad 2 \times 6.02 \times 10^{23}$ ions
$\therefore 3.01 \times 10^{22}$ Cl^- ions will be present in $CaCl_2$
$$= \frac{1}{2 \times 6.02 \times 10^{23}} \times 3.01 \times 10^{22} \text{ mole} = 0.025 \text{ mol}$$
$$\therefore \text{Molarity of solution} = \frac{0.025 \text{ mole}}{0.200 \text{ L}} = 0.125 \text{ M}$$

9. **(c):** Molarity of the solution $= \frac{25.3}{106} \times \frac{1000}{250} = 0.955$ M
$Na_2CO_3 \rightarrow 2\,Na^+ + CO_3^{2-}$
$\therefore [Na^+] = 2 \times 0.955$ M $= 1.910$ M; $[CO_3^{2-}] = 0.955$ M

10. **(c):** 68% nitric acid by mass means that
Mass of nitric acid = 68 g
Mass of solution = 100 g
Molar mass of $HNO_3 = 63$ g mol^{-1}
68 g of $HNO_3 = \frac{68}{63}$ mole $= 1.079$ mol
Density of solution = 1.504 g mL^{-1}
Volume of solution $= \frac{100}{1.504}$ mL $= 66.5$ mL $= 0.0665$ L
Molarity of the solution $= \frac{1.079}{0.0665}$ M $= 16.23$ M

11. **(c):** 0.15 M solution means that 0.15 mol of benzoic acid is present in 1 L, that is, 1000 mL of the solution
Molar mass of benzoic acid (C_6H_5COOH)
$= 72 + 5 + 12 + 32 + 1 = 122$ g mol^{-1}
$\therefore$ 0.15 mol of benzoic acid $= 0.15 \times 122$ g $= 18.3$ g
$\therefore$ 250 mL of the solution will contain benzoic acid
$= \frac{18.3}{1000} \times 250 = 4.575$ g

12. **(a):** Molar mass of $Co(NO_3)_2.6H_2O = 59 + 62 \times 2 + 18 \times 6 = 59 + 124 + 108 = 291$
Moles in 30 g $= \frac{30}{291}$
Molarity $= \frac{30}{291 \times 4.3} = 0.023$ M

13. **(b):** 0.2 mol, that is, 200 millimol is present in 1000 cc. Hence 20 millimol will be present in 100 cc.

14. **(d):** $\therefore$ 1000 mL of 0.1 M sol = 0.1 mol = 100 mmol
$\therefore$ 250 of sol. $= \frac{100}{1000} \times 250 = 25$ mmol

15. **(b):** 0.5 M ethyl alcohol solution means 0.5 mol of ethyl alcohol are present in 1000 cc of the solution
$\therefore$ 100 cc of the solution will contain ethyl alcohol = 0.05 mol
$= 0.05 \times 46$ g $(M_{C_2H_5OH} = 46)$
Volume of alcohol to be added $= \frac{\text{Mass}}{\text{Density}} = \frac{2.3 \text{ g}}{1.150 \text{g/cc}} = 2$ cc

16. (b): 0.02 M H_2SO_4 means 1 L solution contains 0.02 mol of H_2SO_4 or 0.04 mol of H^+ ions or $H_3O^+ \frac{\text{Mass}}{\text{Density}} = \frac{2.3\text{ g}}{1.150\text{g/cc}}$ = 2 ions

$\therefore$ 2 L solution will contain $H_3O^+ = 2 \times 0.04$ mol = 0.08 mol

17. (a): 0.115 g Na $= \frac{0.115}{23}$ g eq = 0.005 g eq

This amount is present in 500 mL

Hence, normality = 0.01 N

18. (b): 1 L of $\frac{N}{2}$ HCl contains HCl $= \frac{1}{2} \times 36.5$ g = 18.25 g

HCl now present = 18.25 – 3.25 g = 15 g

New volume = 600 mL = 0.600 L

Normality $\frac{15}{36.5}$ mol $\times \frac{1}{0.600\text{ L}} = 0.685$ N

19. (b): Normality of an acid = Basicity × Molarity

$\therefore$ Normality of 2 M $H_2SO_4 = 2 \times 2 = 4$ N

20. (d): 8 g KOH/100 cc $= \frac{8}{56} \times \frac{1000}{100} = \frac{10}{7}$ N = 1.4 N

0.5 M H_2SO_4 = 1 N H_2SO_4

6 g NaOH/100 cc $= \frac{6}{40} \times \frac{1000}{100} = 1.5$ N

21. (c): 1000 cc 1N $CuSO_4 . 5H_2O$ require = 249.5 g

$\therefore$ 500 cc 0.5 N will require $= \frac{249.5}{1000} \times 500 \times 0.5 = 249.5/4$g

22. (c): Molar mass of oxalic acid, $(COOH)_2.2H_2O$ = 126

Eq. mass of oxalic acid $= \frac{126}{2} = 63$

To prepare 1 dm^3 of 1 N solution, oxalic acid required = 63 g

$\therefore$ To prepare 2 dm^3 of 0.1 N solution, oxalic acid required = 63 ×2× 0.1 = 12.6g

23. (a): Orthophosphoric acid (H_3PO_4) is tribasic

Normality = Molarity × Basicity = 3 × 3 = 9N

24. (b): $\frac{N}{10}$ solution of oxalic acid means 0.1 g eq of oxalic acid in one litre of solution

0.1 g eq. of $(COOH)_2.2H_2O$ = 0.1 × 63 g = 6.3 g

(Eq. wt. of oxalic acid = 63)

With 6.3 g, 1 L of solution can be prepared

$\therefore$ 100 63 g, 10 L of solution can be prepared

25. (a): Eq. wt. of the acid $= \frac{200}{2} = 100$

0.1 N solution means 0.1 g eq. in 1000 mL of the solution

$\therefore$ 100 mL of the solution will contain 0.01 g eq. = 0.01 ×100 g = 1 g

26. (b): 1500 cc sol. = 1500 × 1.052 g = 1578 g

Solute = 18 g, solvent = 1560 g

Molarity $= \frac{18}{60} \times \frac{1000}{1560} = 0.192$

27. (b): No. of mol in 92 g of Na^+ ions $= \frac{92\text{ g}}{23\text{ g mol}^{-1}} = 4$ mol

(At. mass of Na = 23)

As these are present in 1 kg of water, by definition, molarity = 4 m

28. (b): 1.5 $\times 10^{-5}$ m solution means that 1.5 $\times 10^{-5}$ mol of nalorphene is dissolved in 1 kg of water

Molar mass of nalorphene ($C_{19}H_{21}NO_3$)

= 19 × 12 + 21 + 14 +48 = 311 g mol^{-1}

$\therefore$ 1.5 $\times 10^{-3}$ mol of $C_{19}H_{22}NO_3$

= 1.5 $\times 10^{-3}$ ×311 g = 0.467 g = 467 mg

$\therefore$ Mass of solution = 1000 g + 0.467 g = 1000.467 g

$\therefore$ 1.5 mg of nalorphene, solution required

$= \frac{1000.467}{467} \times 1.5 = 3.21$ g

29. (b): 500 mL of CCl_4 = 500 × 1.60 g = 800 g

51.2 g $C_{10}H_8 = \frac{51.2}{128}$ mol

$\therefore$ 1000 g of solvent (CCl_4) will contain naphthalene

$= \frac{51.2}{128} \times \frac{1}{800} \times 1000 = 0.50$ mol

$\therefore$ Molality = 0.50 m

30. (a): 0.25 molal aqueous solution of urea means 0.25 mol of urea are present in 1 kg of water

0.25 mol of urea (NH_2CONH_2) = 0.25 × 60 g

(Mol. mass of urea = 60)

$\therefore$ Mass of solution = 1000 g + 15 g = 1015 g

1015 g of solution contains urea = 15 g

$\therefore$ 2500 g of solution will contain urea

$= \frac{15}{1015} \times 2500$ g ≃ 37 g

31. (c): 90% H_2SO_4 means 90 g of H_2SO_4 100 g of solution, that is, water present = 10 g

90 g $H_2SO_4 = \frac{90}{98}$ mol

$\therefore$ Molality $= \frac{90/98}{10} \times 1000$ mol kg^{-1} = 91.83 m

32. (b): 5.2 molal solution means 5.2 mol of the solute (CH_3OH) are present in 1000 g of water, that is, 1000/18 mol = 55.55 moles of water

$\therefore$ Mole fraction of $CH_3OH = \frac{5.2}{5.2 + 55.55} = 0.086$

33. (a): 95% ethanol solution means 95 g ethanol in 100 g solvent, that is, 5 g water

$x_2 = \frac{95/46}{95/46 + 5/18} = \frac{2.065}{2.065 + 0.278} = \frac{2.065}{2.343} = 0.881$

34. (c): 20% of $C_2H_6O_2$ by mass means 20 g of $C_2H_6O_2$ is present in 100 g of the solution, that is,

Mass of solution ($C_2H_6O_2$) = 20 g

Mass of solvent (H_2O) = 100 – 20 = 80 g

Molar mass of $C_2H_6O_2$ = 62 g mol^{-1}

Molar mass of H_2O = 18 g mol^{-1}

No. of moles of $C_2H_6O_2 = \frac{20}{62} = 0.322$

No. of moles of $H_2O = \frac{80}{18} = 4.444$

Mole fraction of $C_2H_6O_2$ in the solution

$= \frac{0.322}{0.322+4.444} = 0.068$

35. (b): 20% aq. solution of H_2O_2 by weight means 20 g H_2O_2 in 100 g of solution

$\therefore$ H_2O present = 100 – 20 = 80 g

$H_2O_2 = 20\text{ g} = \frac{20}{34}\text{ mol} = \frac{10}{17}\text{ mol}$

$H_2O = 80\text{ g} = \frac{80}{18}\text{ mol} = \frac{40}{9}\text{ mol}$

$\therefore$ Mole fraction of H_2O

$= \frac{40/9}{40/9+10/17} = 40/9 \times \frac{9\times17}{680+90} = \frac{680}{770} = \frac{68}{77}$

36. (c): 5 L dilute solution = 5000 mL = 5000 g = 5×10^6 mg

ppm of $CaCO_3$ in solution $= \frac{25}{5\times10^6}\times10^6 = 5$ ppm

37. (b): ppm $= \frac{\text{Mass of solute in g}}{\text{Mass of solution in g}}\times10^6$

$= \frac{6\times10^{-3}}{1000}\times10^6 = 6$

38. (a): 10 L water = 10^4 mL = 10^4 g (as solution is very dilute and density can be taken as 1 g mL^{-1})

50 mg $CaCO_3$ in the solution $= \frac{50\times10^{-3}}{10^4}\times10^6 = 5$

39. (b): 3.42 g of sucrose in present in 100 g of the solution = 100 mL of the solution because density = 1 g mL^{-1}

3.42 g of sucrose ($C_{12}H_{22}O_{11}$) $= \frac{3.42}{342}$ mol = 0.01 mol

(Molecular mass of sucrose = 342)

Thus, 100 mL of the solution contains 0.01 mol of sucrose.

$\therefore$ Concentration in mol $L^{-1} = \frac{0.01}{100}\times1000 = 0.1$

40. (b): 80 g H_2SO_4 is present in 100 g of the solution = 100/1.71 cc = 58.5 cc

Normality $= \frac{80}{49}\times\frac{1000}{58.5} = 27.9$

$\left(\text{Eq. wt. of } H_2SO_4 = \frac{98}{2} = 49\right)$

41. (b): Mole fraction of solute in solution $= \frac{n_{solute}}{n_{solute}+n_{solvent}}$

Molality of a solution means number of moles of the solute in 1000 g of the solvent, that is, when $n_{solvent}$ $(n_{H_2O}) = \frac{1000}{18}$ moles = 55.55 moles

$\therefore 0.018 = \frac{n_{solute}}{n_{solute}+55.55}$

or $0.018\, n_{solute} + 55.55\times0.018 = n_{solute}$

or $0.982\, n_{solute} = 55.55\times0.018$ or $n_{solute} = 1.0$

Hence, molality = 1.0 m

42. (c): 1 molal aqueous solution means 1 mol of the solute in 1000 g of solvent (water), that is, 1000/18 mol = 55.55 mol

$\therefore$ Mole fraction of solute $= \frac{1}{1+55.55} = 0.018$

43. (b): 15 ppm means 15 parts in million (10^6) parts by mass in the solution. Taking 15 g chloroform in 10^6 g of the solution, mass of solvent $\simeq 10^6$g

Molar mass of chloroform ($CHCl_3$)

= 12 + 1 + 3 ×35.5 = 119.5 g mol^{-1}

Molality $= \frac{15/119.5}{10^6}\times1000 = 1.25\times10^{-4}$m

44. (b): 1 m NaCl solution = 1 mol NaCl in 1000 g water = 58.5 + 1000 g solution = 1058 g solution = 1058.5/1.21 mL = 875 mL

Molarity $= \frac{1}{875}\times1000 = 1.143$ M

45. (b): 60 mL of 4 M $H_2SO_4 = \frac{4}{1000}\times60$ mol

= 0.24 mol = 0.24 ×2 g eq.

= 0.48 g eq. = 480 milli equivalents

46. (a): $x_{H_2O} = 0.85 \therefore x_{H_2SO_4} = 0.15$

i.e., $\frac{n_1}{n_1+n_2} = 0.85$ and $\frac{n_2}{n_1+n_2} = 0.15$

Dividing $\frac{n_2}{n_1} = \frac{0.15}{0.85}$

Taking n_1 = 1000/18 mol

$n_2 = \frac{0.15}{0.85}\times\frac{1000}{18} = 9.80$

47. (None): 100 mL of the solution contains $(COOH)_2.2H_2O$ = 2.52 g

10 mL of the solution will contain $(COOH)_2.2H_2O$ = 0.252 g

Now, 500 mL of the solution contains $(COOH)_2.2\ H_2O$ =0.252 g = 252 mg

$\therefore$ 1 mL of the solution will contain $(COOH)_2.2H_2O$

$= \frac{252}{500} = 0.504$ mg/mL

Equivalent mass of $(COOH)_2.2H_2O = \frac{126}{2} = 63$

Normality $= \frac{0.252}{63}\times\frac{1}{500}\times1000 = 0.008$ N

Out of the given answers, none is correct.

48. (a): 1.25 molal NaOH means 1.25 mol of NaOH is present in 1000 g of the solution

1.25 mol of NaOH = 1.25 ×40 g = 50 g

$\therefore$ Mass of the solution = 1000 + 50 g = 1050 g

Thus 1050 g of solution contains NaOH = 50 g

$\therefore$ % by mass of NaOH $= \frac{50}{1050}\times100 = 4.76\%$

49. (a): 1 M solution means 1 mol of the solute in 1000 cc of the solution whereas 1 m solution means 1 mol of the solute in 1000 g of water (= 1000 cc of water)

$\therefore$ total volume of 1 m solution > 1000 cc due to the presence of an extra 1 mol of the solute. Hence, concentration in mol/cc of 1 m solution is less than that of 1 M. In other words, 1 M is more concentrated than 1 m.

50. (c): 18 M H_2SO_4 means 18 mol of H_2SO_4 in 1 L of the solution 1 L solution = 1000 ×1.8 g = 1800 g
∴ 18 mol H_2SO_4 = 18 ×98 g = 1764 g
∴ H_2O present = 1800 – 1764 = 36 g

$$\text{Molality} = \frac{18}{36} \times 1000 \text{ mol kg}^{-1} = 500 \text{ m}$$

51. (c): $M_1V_1 + M_2V_2 = M_3V_2$
∴ 100 ×0.1 + 200 ×0.1 = 300 × M_3 or M_3 = 0.1

52. (c): 300 g of 25% solution contains solute = 75 g
400 g of 40% solution contains solute = 160 g
Total solute = 75 + 160 = 235g
Total solution = 300 + 400 = 700 g

$$\text{Mass \% of solute in final solution} = \frac{235}{700} \times 100 = 33.5\%$$

53. (c): No. of mol of K^+ in 250 mL of 0.1 M K_2SO_4

$$= \frac{0.1 \times 2}{1000} \times 250 = 0.05 \text{ mol}$$

No. of mol of K^+ in 250 mL of 0.2 M KCl

$$= \frac{0.2}{1000} \times 250 = 0.05 \text{ mol}$$

Total volume of the solution after making = 500 mL = 0.500 L
Total no. of mol of K^+ present = 0.05 + 0.05 = 0.1

$$\therefore \text{Molar conc. of K}^+ \text{ in the final solution} = \frac{0.1 \text{ mole}}{0.500 \text{ L}} = 0.2 \text{ M}$$

54. (d): 100 mL of 0.3 N HCl contains HCl = 100 × 0.3 meq = 30 meq
200 mL of 0.6 N H_2SO_4 contains H_2SO_4 = 200 × 0.6 meq = 120 meq
Total acid = 150 meq
Total volume = 300 mL

$$\text{Final normality} = \frac{150}{300} = 0.5$$

Alternatively, $N_1V_1 + N_2V_2 = N_3V_3$, that is,
0.3 × 100 + 0.6 × 200 = N_3 × 300
or 0.3 + 1.2 = 3 N_3 or N_3 = 1.5/3 = 0.5

55. (c): $M_1V_1 + M_2V_2 = M_3(V_1 + V_2)$
2.5 × 1 + 3 × 0.5 = M_3 × 5.5
or 2.5 + 1.5 = M_3 × 5.5
M_3 = 0.7272

56. (b): $N_1V_1 + N_2V_2 + N_3V_3 = M_4(V_1 + V_2 + V_3)$

$$\frac{1}{5} \times 60 + \frac{1}{2} \times 10 + \frac{1}{10} \times 30 = N_2(60 + 10 + 30)$$

$$12 + 5 + 3 = N_4(100) \text{ or } N_4 = \frac{20}{100} = 0.2 \text{ N}$$

57. (b): $M_1V_1 + M_2V_2 = M_3(V_1 + V_2)$
0.4 V_1 + 0.9 V_2 = 0.7 = 0.7 (V_1 + V_2)

$$\text{or } 0.3\,V_1 = 0.2\,V_2 \text{ or } \frac{V_1}{V_2} = \frac{2}{3} = 2:3$$

58. (c): 18 M H_2SO_4 ≡ 36 N H_2SO_4
Applying $N_1 \times V_1 = N_2 \times V_2$
5 × 36 = 500 × N_2 or N_2 = 0.36

59. (c): 0.2 M H_2SO_4 = 0.4 N H_2SO_4,
0.5 dm^3 = 0.5×1000 cm^3 = 500 cm^3

$N_1 \times V_1$ = $N_2 \times V_2$
(Before dilution) (After dilution)
0.4 × 2.5 = N_2 × 500 or N_2 = 0.002 N

60. (a): N_1V_1 = N_2V_2
(Before dilution) (After dilution)
0.5 × 100 = 0.1× V_2 = 500 mL
V_2 is the final volume of the solution after dilution
∴ Volume of water to be added = 500 – 100 = 400 mL

61. (b): $M_1V_1 = V_2V_2$
0.4 × 100 = 0.05 × V_2 or V_2 = 800 mL
∴ Water to be added = 800 – 100 = 700 mL

62. (a): 222 mg of $CaCl_2$ = 0.222 g = $\frac{0.222}{111} = 2\times10^{-3}$ mol

100 mL of the solution contains $CaCl_2$ = 2×10^{-3} mol
∴ 1000 mL of the solution will contain $CaCl_2$

$$= \frac{2\times10^{-3}}{100} \times 1000 = 2\times10^{-2} = 0.02 \text{ mol/lit}$$

63. (c): NaOH + HCl → NaCl + H_2O
40 g 36.5 g
0.275 g NaOH will be neutralised by HCl

$$= \frac{36.5}{40} \times 0.275 \text{ g} = 0.251 \text{ g}$$

Thus, 35.4 mL of HCl contains HCl = 0.251 g
∴ Normality of HCl solution

$$= \frac{0.251}{36.5} \times \frac{1}{35.4} \times 1000 = 0.194 \text{ N}$$

64. (a): 40% solution by weight means 40 g of solute are present in 100 g of the solution
∴ 800 g of the solution will contain solute

$$= \frac{40}{100} \times 800 = 320 \text{ g}$$

Solute precipitated = 100 g
∴ Solute left in the solution = 320 – 100 = 220 g
Solution left = 800 – 100 = 700 g

$$\therefore \text{ \% of solute in the solution left} = \frac{220}{700} \times 100 = 31.43\%$$

65. (a): 720 ppm means 720 mg of sugar is present in 10^6 mg of blood

$$10^6 \text{ mg} = 10^3 \text{ g} = 1 \text{ kg} = \frac{1}{1.06} \text{ L} = \frac{10}{1.06} \text{ dL} = 9.43 \text{ dL}$$

∴ Sugar in mg/dL = $\frac{720}{9.43}$ = 76.4 which lies in the normal range

66. (b): 500 cc sol ≡ 0.25 mol $CaCl_2$ = 0.5 mol Cl^- ions

67. (c): 1 N $H_2SO_4 = \frac{N}{2}$ M

1000 mL of H_2SO_4 contains $\frac{1}{2}$ mol of H_2SO_4

200 mL of H_2SO_4 will contain H_2SO_4

$$= \frac{1}{2} \times \frac{1}{1000} \times 200 = \frac{1}{10} \text{ mol}$$

1 mol of H_2SO_4 contains 1 g atoms (A_0 atoms) of sulfur

$\therefore \frac{1}{10}$ mol of H_2SO_4 will contain $= \frac{1}{10} \times A_0$ atoms of S $= \frac{A_0}{10}$

68. (d): 3 M solution means 3 mol of solute (NaCl) in 1 L of solution, that is,
1000×1.25 g of the solution = 1250 g of the solution
1000×1.25 g of the solution = 1250 g of the solution
3 mol of NaCl = 3×58.5 g = 175.5 g
$\therefore$ Mass of solvent = 1250 – 175 – 5 = 1074.5 g

69. (d): 10% strength means 10 g of the solute (glucose) is present in 100 mL of the solution
1 g mol of glucose ($C_6H_{12}O_6$) = 180 g
10 g of glucose is dissolved in 100 mL of solution
$\therefore$ 180 g of glucose will be dissolved in solution

$= \frac{100}{10} \times 180 \, p_A^\circ + \frac{2}{3}$ mL = 1800 mL = 1.8 L

70. (b): Molality and mole fraction involve only masses of the solute and solvent which do not change with temperature.

71. (a): Molarity of the solution involves volume of the solution which changes with a change in temperature.

72. (a): 250 mL of 2.0 M HNO_3 will contain HNO_3

$= \frac{2}{1000} \times 250 = 0.5$ mol $= 0.5 \times 63$ g = 31.5 g

As concentrated HNO_3 is 70%, therefore, concentrated HNO_3 required $= \frac{100}{70} \times 31.5 = 45$ g

73. (c): Suppose molarity = x
$\therefore$ x mol of HCl is present in 1000 cc of the solution or $x \times 36.5$ g of HCl is present in 1000 cc of the solution

Density $= \frac{36.5\,x}{1000} = 1.17$ g/cc (given)

$\therefore x = 32.05$

74. (c): No. of mol of urea present in 100 mL of solution
$\therefore$ Molar concentration of urea in the solution

$\frac{10^{-3}}{100} \times 1000 = 10^{-2}$ M = 0.01 M

Solubility

75. (c): Solubility of a gas in a liquid depends both upon pressure of the gas and critical temperature of the gas (nature of the gas).

76. (d): Higher the solubility, lower is the value of Henry's constant. As CO_2 has highest solubility of the given gases, it will have the lowest value of Henry's constant.

77. (c): $p_{N_2} = K_H . x_{N_2} = \frac{p_{N_2}}{K_H} = \frac{0.76}{7.6 \times 10^4} = 1 \times 10^{-5}$

78. (b): 0.1 M CO_2 means 0.1 mol of CO_2 is present in 1000 mL of the liquid
$\therefore$ 200 mL of the liquid will contain CO_2

$= \frac{0.1}{1000} \times 200 = 0.02$ mol

$= 0.02 \times 22.4$ L at NTP = 0.448 L

79. (c): Greater the value of K_H, lower is the solubility at the same pressure and temperature.
Solubility $\propto 1/K_H$
Solubility: Ar < CO_2 < CH_4 < HCHO
(K_H) (40.39) (1.67) (0.413) (1.83×10^{-5})

80. (a): According to Henry's law,
$p_{N_2} = K_H \times x_{N_2}$

$x_{N_2} = \frac{p_{N_2}}{K_H} = \frac{0.987 \text{ bar}}{76480 \text{ bar}} = 1.29 \times 10^{-5}$

if n mol of N_2 is present in 1 L of water (55.55 moles)

$x_{N_2} = \frac{n}{n + 55.5} = \frac{n}{55.5}$ (as $n << 55.5$)

$\therefore \frac{n}{55.5} = 1.29 \times 10^{-5}$ or $n = (1.29 \times 10^{-5}) \times 55.5$

$= 71.595 \times 10^{-5}$ mol = 0.716 mmol

81. (c): Solubility of H_2O = 0.195 m
= 0.195 mol in 1 kg of solvent (water)
1 kg of solvent (water) = 1000 g

$= \frac{1000 \text{ g}}{18 \text{ g mol}^{-1}} = 55.55$ mol

Mole fraction of H_2S gas in the solution (x)

$= \frac{0.195}{0.195 + 55.55} = \frac{0.195}{55.745} = 0.0035$

Pressure at STP = 0.987 bar
Applying Henry's law, $p_{H_2O} = K_H \times x_{H_2O}$

or $K_H = \frac{p_{H_2O}}{p_{H_2O}} = \frac{0.987 \text{ bar}}{0.0035} = 282$ bar

82. (d): All the given expressions represent Henry's law.

83. (c): CO_2 reacts with H_2O to form H_2CO_3. Hence, it does not obey Henry's law.

84. (d): $p_A = K_H \times x_A$ or $x_A = \frac{p_A}{K_H}$

Thus, plot of x_A vs p_A is linear with slope $= \frac{1}{K_H}$

G_1 has the least slope and hence highest value of K_H

85. (b): By Henry's law, $p_{CO_2} = K_H \times x_{CO_2}$

or $x_{CO_2} = \frac{p_{CO_2}}{K_H} = \frac{2.5 \times 10^5 \text{ Pa}}{1.67 \times 10^8 \text{ Pa}}$ (1 atm $\simeq 10^5$ Pa)

$= 1.50 \times 10^{-3}$
If n mol of CO_2 is present in 500 mL (500 g) of water, then

$x_{CO_2} = \frac{n}{n + 500/18} = \frac{n}{n + 27.7} \approx \frac{n}{27.7}$ ($\because n << 27.7$)

$\therefore \frac{n}{27.7} = 1.50 \times 10^{-3}$

or $n = 0.04155$ mol $= 0.04155 \times 44$g = 1.83 g

86. (a): Helium–oxygen mixture is used by deep sea divers because of its very low solubility in blood.

87. (d): Solubility α pressure of the gas is given by Henry's law.

88. (d): Henry's law is applicable only if the gas is not highly soluble. CO_2 is highly soluble in water.

89. (b): A solid dissolves in water if lattice energy is less than hydration energy.

90. (c): Solubility increases with temperature up to 34°C and then decreases. So, the process is endothermic up to 34°C and exothermic thereafter.

91. (a): By definition of Nernst distribution law.

92. (d): In an endothermic process of dissolution, the energy factor opposes the dissolution. Lesser the heat of dissolution, that is, lesser the opposing factor, greater is the solubility.

93. (d): The substance which dissolves more on heating throws out more on cooling. Hence, KNO_3 is the correct option.

94. (d): A supersaturated solution is metastable because on slight disturbance, solid separates out.

95. (d): –OH groups present in sugars form hydrogen bonds with H_2O.

96. (c): The solubility of KCl also increases with an increase in temperature, but slowly.

97. (d): At 40°C, the solubility is 200 g per 100 g of water (approx.).

$\therefore$ 50 g of water at 40°C will dissolve KNO_3 = 100 g (approx.)

Vapour Pressure of Liquid Solutions and Raoult's Law

98. (d): $P_{total} = X_A P_A + X_B P_B$

$= X_A P_A + (1 - X_A) P_B = P_B + X_A(P_A - P_B)$

99. (c): $p_A^\circ = 450$ mm, $p_B^\circ = 700$ mm,

$P_{total} = 600$ mm

Applying Raoult's law, $p_A = x_A \times p_B^\circ$

$p_B = x_B \times p_B^\circ = (1 - x_A)\, p_B^\circ$

$\therefore P_{total} = p_A + p_B = x_A\, p_A^\circ + (1 - x_A)\, p_B^\circ$

$= p_B^\circ + (p_A^\circ - p_B^\circ) x_A$

Substituting the given values

$600 = 700 + (450 - 700)\, x_A$

or $250\, x_A = 100$ or $x_A = 0.40$

Hence $x_B = 1 - 0.40 = 0.60$

100. (d): No. of mol of liquid A (solute) $= \frac{100}{140} = \frac{5}{7}$ mol

No. of mol of liquid B (solvent) $= \frac{1000}{180} = \frac{50}{9}$ mol

$\therefore$ Mole fraction of A in the solution (x_A)

$$= \frac{\frac{5}{7}}{\frac{5}{7} + \frac{50}{9}} = \frac{\frac{5}{7}}{\frac{395}{63}} = \frac{5}{7} \times \frac{63}{395} = \frac{45}{395} = 0.114$$

Mole fraction of B in the solution $(x_B) = 1 - 0.114 = 0.886$

Also, given $p_B^\circ = 500$ torr

Applying Raoult's law,

$p_B \times x_B\, p_B^\circ = 0.886 \times 500 = 443$ torr

$P_{total} = p_A + p_B$

$475 = 0.114\, p_A^\circ + 443$ or $p_A^\circ = \frac{475 - 443}{0.114} = 280.7$ torr

101. (a): $(x_A)_{vapour} = \frac{p_A}{P_{total}} = \frac{(x_A)_{vapour}\, p_A^\circ}{P_{total}}$ or $\frac{(x_A)_{vap}}{(x_A)_{liq}} = \frac{p_A^\circ}{P_{total}}$

As B is less volatile, $P_{total} < p_A^\circ$

$\therefore \frac{(x_A)_{vap}}{(x_A)_{liq}} > 1$ or $(x_A)_{vapour} > (x_A)_{liquid}$

102. (a): VP of solution of non-volatile solute = VP of solvent in the solution which is directly proportional to mole fraction of solvent in the solution.

103. (c): $p_A = x_A\, p_A^\circ (x_A)_{vapour} = 0.2 \times 500 = 100$ N m^{-2}

$p_B = x_B p_B^\circ = 0.8 \times 200 = 160$ N m^{-2}

Total VP of the solution = 100 + 160 = 260 N m^{-2}

104. (d): $p_A^\circ = 100$ mm

$p_A^\circ = 500$ mm $P_{total} = 300$ mm

$P_{total} = x_A \times p_A^\circ + x_B \times p_B^\circ = x_A\, p_A^\circ + (1 - x_A)\, p_B^\circ$

$\therefore 300 = x_A (100) + (1 - x_A)(500) = 500 - 400\, x_A$

or $400\, x_A = 200$ or $x_A = 0.5 = \frac{1}{2}$

$\therefore p_A = x_A \times p_A^\circ = \frac{1}{2} \times 100 = 50$ mm

Mole fraction of A in vapour phase

$= \frac{\text{Partial pressure of A}}{P_{total}} = \frac{50}{300} = \frac{1}{6}$

105. (c): $P_{Benzene} = x_{Benzene} P^\circ_{Benzene}$

$P_{Toluene} = x_{Toluene} \times P^\circ_{Toluene}$

For an ideal 1 : 1 mixture of benzene and toluene

$x_{Benzene} = \frac{1}{2}, x_{Toluene} = \frac{1}{2}$

$P_{Benzene} = \frac{1}{2} \times P^\circ_{Benzene} = \frac{1}{2} \times 128.8$ kPa = 6.4 kPa

$P_{Toluene} = \frac{1}{2} \times P^\circ_{Toluene} = \frac{1}{2} \times 3.85$ kPa = 1.925 kPa

Thus, the vapour will contain a higher percentage of benzene as the partial vapour pressure of benzene is higher than that of toluene.

106. (a): In the 1st case, $p_t = x_A\, p_A^\circ + x_B\, p_B^\circ$

$500 = \frac{1}{3}\, p_A^\circ + \frac{2}{3}\, p_B^\circ$

or $p_A^\circ + 2\, p_B^\circ = 1500$ (i)

In the 2nd case, $(500 + 25) = \frac{1}{4}\, p_A^\circ + \frac{3}{4} p_B^\circ$ (ii)

or $p_A^\circ + 3 p_B^\circ = 2100$

Subtracting Eq. (i) from Eq. (ii),

$p_B^\circ = 600$ mm

Substituting in Eq. (i), $p_A^\circ = 1500 - 2\,p_B^\circ = 1500 - 1200$
$= 300$ mm

107. (d): In an equimolar mixture of A and B, $x_A = x_B = 0.5$
$p_A = x_A\, p_A^\circ = 0.5 \times 150\text{ mm} = 75\text{ mm}$
$p_B = 0.5 \times 100\text{ mm} = 50\text{ mm}$
Mole fraction of B in vapour phase (y_B)
$$= \frac{p_B}{p_A + p_A} = \frac{50}{75+50} = 0.4$$

108. (c): As methanol is more volatile than water, addition of methanol to water will result in an increase in the vapour pressure of water.

109. (a): $CH_3CHBr_2 : CH_2Br\text{–}CH_2Br = 2 : 1$
$$x(CH_3CHBr_2) = \frac{2}{3},\ x\,(CH_2Br - CH_2Br) = \frac{1}{3}$$
$p_{\text{total}} = x \times p^\circ c_2\,(CH_3CHBr_2) + x \times p^\circ$
$(CH_2Br\text{–}CH_2Br)$
$$= \frac{2}{3} \times 173 + \frac{1}{3} \times 127\text{ mm}$$
$= 115.3 + 42.3 = 157.6 \simeq 158$ mm

110. (a): If vapour pressure of pure water = 100 mm, then vapour pressure of solution = 99 mm
$$\frac{p^\circ - p_s}{p^\circ} = \frac{w_2 / M_2}{w_1 / M_1} \therefore \frac{100-99}{100} = \frac{w_2/60}{126/18}$$
$$\text{or } \frac{1}{100} = \frac{w_2}{60} \times \frac{18}{126} = \frac{w_2}{420} \text{ or } w_2 = 4.2\text{ g}$$

111. (a): $\dfrac{p^\circ - p_s}{p^\circ} = \dfrac{w_2/M_2}{w_1/M_1}$ or $\dfrac{1-p_s}{p^\circ}$
$$= \frac{25/180}{450/18} = \frac{25}{80} \times \frac{18}{450} \qquad (\text{Mol. mass of } C_6H_{12}O_6 = 180)$$
$$\text{or } 1 - \frac{p_s}{p^\circ} = \frac{25}{4500} \text{ or } \frac{p_s}{p^\circ} = 1 - \frac{25}{4500} = \frac{4475}{4500}$$
$$\text{or } p_s = \frac{4475}{4500} \times 17.535 = 17.438\text{ mm Hg}$$

112. (d): Lowering of VP of solvent takes place—the solute may be volatile, non-volatile, electrolyte or non-electrolyte.

113. (a): Compound A involves intermolecular hydrogen bonding whereas compound B involves intramolecular hydrogen bonding. As a result, boiling point of B is lower than that of A and hence B has a higher vapour pressure than A.

114. (c): Lower the boiling point, greater is the vapour pressure. Boiling points are in the order HCl < HBr < HI < HF. Thus, HCl has lowest boiling point and hence maximum vapour pressure.

115. (b): Vapour pressure increases with an increase in temperature up to the boiling point. At the boiling point, the vapour pressure becomes equal to the atmospheric pressure. Further heating results only in evaporation of the liquid.

116. (d): The variation in vapour pressure with temperature is given by Clausius–Clapeyron equation,
$$\log \frac{P_2}{P_1} = \frac{\Delta H_v}{2.303\,R} = \left(\frac{1}{T_1} - \frac{1}{T_2}\right)$$

117. (c): VP of any component in the solution = mole fraction of the component × VP of that component in the pure state. Mole fraction is always < 1.

118. (c): When $X_B = 0$, we have pure A
$\therefore p_A^\circ = 120 - 80 \times 0 = 120$ mm
The given expression can be rewritten as
$p = 120 - 80(1 - X_A)$
When $X_A = 0$, we have pure B
$\therefore p_B^\circ = 120 - 80\,(1 - 0) = 120 - 80 = 40$ mm

119. (a): $n_B = \dfrac{78}{78} = 1$ mol
$$n_T = \frac{46}{92} = 0.5\text{ mol},\ x_B = \frac{1}{1.5}$$
$$\therefore p_B = x_B \times p_B = \frac{1}{1.5} \times 75 = 50\text{ torr}$$

120. (c): $P_{\text{total}} = x_{hep} \times p_{hep}^\circ + x_{oct} \times p_{oct}^\circ$
$$n_{hep} = \frac{25}{100} = 0.25,\ n_{oct} = \frac{35}{114} = 0.307$$
$$x_{hep} = \frac{0.25}{0.25 + 0.307} = 0.45$$
$\therefore x_{oct} = 1 - 0.45 = 0.55$
$P_{\text{total}} = 0.45 \times 105 + 0.55 \times 45\text{ kPa} = 47.25 + 24.75 = 72\text{ kPa}$

Ideal and Non-ideal Solutions

121. (a): For a non-ideal solution showing positive deviation, $\Delta V = +\text{ve}\ \Delta H = +\text{ve}$.

122. (c): On mixing acetone and chloroform, dipole–dipole interactions take place. Hence, negative deviation from Raoult's law is observed.

123. (c): Ethanol + water form a non-ideal solution showing +ve deviation from Raoult's law. Hence, $\Delta H = +\text{ve}$, that is, there is absorption of heat and $\Delta V = +\text{ve}$, that is, there is an increase in volume.

124. (b): In CS_2–acetone, A–B interactions are weaker than A–A, B–B interactions.

125. (d): There is strong hydrogen bonding in alcohol molecules as well as water molecules. On mixing, the molecular interactions are weakened. Hence, their solution will show a positive deviation from ideal behaviour. As a result, the solution will have higher vapour pressure and lower boiling point than that of water and alcohol.

126. (c): As solution shows positive deviations, A–B interactions are smaller.

127. (c): Methanol–water system shows positive deviations from Raoult's law. Hence, vapour pressure of the solution is more than that of water.

128. (b): There is H-bonding between H_2O and C_4H_9OH.

129. (d): C_2H_5I and C_2H_5OH are dissimilar liquids.

130. (d): Methanol has H-bonding. When benzene is added, H-bonds are broken.

131. (d): A solution of acetone in ethanol shows a positive deviation from Raoult's law.

132. (b): Cyclohexane molecules cut off the hydrogen boding present in ethanol molecules.

133. (b): It is a solution with positive deviation for which ΔH is positive.

134. (a): Benzene + chloroform show negative deviation from Raoult's law.

135. (a): When a solution of two liquids boils at a higher temperature than either of them, it is so when vapour pressure is less than expected from Raoult's law, that is, it shows a negative deviation from Raoult's law.

136. (c): Boiling point is less than that of either of the pure components when vapour pressure is higher than expected from Raoult's law, that is, when it shows positive deviation ($CH_3CH_2OH + CH_3COCH_3$).

137. (d): In an azeotropic mixture, pure components cannot be separated by distillation.

138. (b): Chloroform and acetone form a non-ideal solution with negative deviation from Raoult's law. For such a solution, ΔV_{mixing} is –ve, that is, new volume after mixing < (30 + 50), that is, 80 mL.

139. (a): Raoult's law is applicable to non-electrolytes. NaCl is an electrolyte which dissociates in the solution.

140. (a): $HNO_3 + H_2O$ solution shows negative deviation from ideal behaviour. Hence, it forms an azeotrope with maximum boiling point.

141. (b): Boiling point of azeotropic mixture is less when it shows positive deviations.

142. (c): Maximum boiling azeotropes are formed by non-ideal solutions which show negative deviation from Raoult's law, that is, acetone + chloroform.

143. (a): $CCl_4 + CHCl_3$ form a non-ideal solution. Hence, it will form an azetropic mixture.

144. (d): Azeotropic mixture of HCl and water contains 20.4% HCl.

145. (b): From Raoult's law,

$P_A = x_A \times p_A^\circ = 0.2 \times 100 = 50$ mm

$P_A = x_A \times p_B^\circ = 0.8 \times 150 = 120$ mm

$P_{total} = 50 + 120 = 170$ mm

As the actual vapour pressure is less than the expected value, it shows a –ve deviation.

146. (b): For an ideal solution,

$\Delta H_{mix} = 0, \Delta V_{mix} = 0, \Delta P = 0 \quad (\because P_{Observed} = P_{Raoults})$

but $\Delta S_{mix} \neq 0$ because on mixing, entropy always increases.

147. (c): A solution of A and B follows Raoult's law when new interactions (A–B) are the same as in the pure component (A–A, B–B).

148. (b): P_{total} (expected from Raoult's law) $= x_A p_A^\circ + x_B p_B^\circ$

$= \frac{1}{3} \times 150 + \frac{2}{3} \times 240 = 50 + 160 = 210$ torr which is greater than the experimental value of 200 torr. As observed, vapour pressure is less than that expected from Raoult's law, it shows –ve deviation from Raoult's law.

Colligative Properties

149. (a): $\frac{p^\circ - p_s}{p^\circ} = \frac{n_2}{n_1} = \frac{w_2 / M_2}{w_1 / M_1}$

That is, $\frac{3000 - 2985}{3000} = \frac{5 / M_2}{100/18}$ or $M_2 = 180$

150. (b): 1 molal solution means 1 mol of the solution in 1 kg of the solvent (water).

$\therefore$ Mole fraction of solute $= \frac{1}{1 + 55.5} = 0.0177$

Now $\frac{p^\circ - p_s}{p^\circ} = x_2$

$\therefore \frac{12.3 - p_s}{12.3} = 0.0177$ or $p_s = 12.08$ kPa

151. (c): Molecular weight determination by Raoult's law is for dilute solutions of non-electrolytes.

152. (d): Relative lowering of VP = mole fraction (conc.) of solute only

153. (a): VP in the solvent bulb is greater. So, loss in weight will be more.

154. (d): $\frac{p^\circ - p_s}{p^\circ} = \frac{n_2}{n_1} = \frac{w_2 / M_2}{w_1 / M_1}$

$\frac{760 - 750}{760} = \frac{18 / M_2}{108/18} = \frac{3}{M_2}$ or $M_2 = \frac{3 \times 760}{10} = 228 \text{ g mol}^{-1}$

155. (b): $\frac{p^\circ - p_s}{p^\circ} = \frac{n_2}{n_1} = \frac{w_2 / M_2}{w_1 / M_1}$

$\therefore 0.1 = \frac{4 / M_2}{36/18} = \frac{4}{M_2} \times \frac{1}{2} = \frac{2}{M_2}$

$\therefore M_2 = 20$

156. (b): If $p^\circ = 100$, $p_s = 100 - 10 = 90$ mm

$\frac{p^\circ - p_s}{p^\circ} = \frac{w_2 / M_2}{w_1 / M_1} = \frac{w_2}{M_2} \times \frac{w_1}{M_1}$

$\frac{100 - 90}{100} = \frac{w_2}{60} \times 18/180$ or $w_2 = \frac{10}{100} \times 60 \times 10 = 60$ g

157. (c): The net flow of the solvent is from dilute solution to concentrated solution.

158. (c): $\pi \propto T$. If T is doubled, π is also doubled.

159. (b): $\pi = \frac{n}{V} RT$ or $V = \frac{nRT}{\pi} = \frac{1 \times 0.0821 \times 273}{1} = 22.4$ L

160. (b): $M = \frac{wRT}{\pi V} = \frac{0.6 \times 0.082 \times 300}{1.23 \times 0.1} = 120$

161. (a): Isotonic solutions have the same molar concentrations.

Hence, $\frac{30}{180} = \frac{10}{M_2}$ or $M_2 = 60$

162. (b): $Cu_2[Fe(CN)_6]$ ppt supported on a porous pot acts as the best semi-permeable membrane. (Plant cell wall is permeable as both salt and water can diffuse through it.)

163. (c): Osmotic pressure is a colligative property, that is, it depends upon the number of particles of the solute.

164. (b): On mixing, the concentrations are reduced to half of the original values. So, osmotic pressures also become half.
$P_{urea} = 3.0$ atm, $P_{cane\ sugar} = 1.2$ atm
Total = 4.2 atm

165. (d): $\pi = CRT\left(\frac{w_2}{M_2}\times\frac{1}{V}\right)RT$

or $M_2 = \frac{w_2RT}{\pi V} P_{cane\ sugar} = 1.2p°$

$= \frac{1.26\text{ g}\times 0.083\text{ L bar mol}^{-1}\text{ K}^{-1}\times 300\text{ K}}{2.57\times 10^{-3}\text{ bar}\times 0.200\text{ L}} = 61038\text{ g mol}^{-1}$

166. (b): Blood cells do not shrink because they are isotonic with the solution present outside.

167. (a): $\pi_1 = c_1 RT, \pi_2 = c_2RT$

$\therefore \frac{\pi_1}{\pi_2} = \frac{c_1}{c_2}$

$c_1 = 36\text{ g L}^{-1} = \frac{36}{180}\text{ mol L}^{-1}$

$\pi_1 = 4.98$ bar, $\pi_2 = 1.52$ bar, $c_2 = ?$

$\therefore \frac{4.98}{1.52} = \frac{36/180}{c_2}$ or $c_2 = \frac{36}{180}\times\frac{1.52}{4.98}\text{ mol L}^{-1}$

$= \frac{36\times 1.52}{4.98}\text{ g L}^{-1} \simeq 11\text{ g L}^{-1}$

168. (b): $\pi = CRT$

In the 1st case, $4.98 = \frac{36}{180}\times R\times 300 = 60R$ (i)

In the 2nd case, $1.52 = C\times R\times 300$ (ii)

Dividing (ii) by (i), we get $C = 0.061$ M

169. (c): During osmosis, the flow of solvent is from both sides (net flow is from dilute solution to concentrated solution).

170. (b): A hypertonic solution has higher concentration.

171. (b): Non-electrolytes do not undergo dissociation.

172. (d): Copper ferrocyanide precipitate acts as a semi-permeable membrane.

173. (b): Due to osmosis.

174. (c): 34.2 g L^{-1} sucrose = 0.1 M,
18 g L^{-1} glucose = 0.1 M

175. (a): $\pi = CRT = 0.2\times 0.082\times 300 = 4.92$ atm

176. (c): $C = \frac{\pi}{RT} = \frac{0.0821}{0.0821\times 300} = \frac{1}{300} = 0.33\times 10^{-2}$ M

177. (c): $\pi = \left(\frac{10}{342}\times\frac{1000}{100}\right)\times 0.0821\times(273+69) = 821$ atm

178. (a): In osmosis, flow of water is from both sides of the semi-permeable membrane with unequal flow rates.

179. (b): Molar conc. of sugar solution

$= \frac{50\text{ g L}^{-1}}{342\text{ g mol}^{-1}} = \frac{50}{342}\text{ mol L}^{-1}$

Molar conc. of solution X $= \frac{10\text{ g L}^{-1}}{M_X\text{ g mol}^{-1}} = \frac{10}{M_X}\text{ mol L}^{-1}$

For solutions to be isotonic,

$\frac{10}{M_X} = \frac{50}{342}$ or $M_X = 68.4$

180. (d): On mixing equal volumes, concentrations are halved and so are the osmotic pressures. Hence, total osmotic pressure

$= \frac{1.64+2.46}{2} = 2.04$

181. (a): Solvent flows from lower concentration to higher concentration.

182. (c): Osmotic pressure, $\pi = CRT$

$\therefore \frac{\pi_1}{\pi_2} = \frac{C_1}{C_2} = \frac{0.01}{0.001} = 10$

183. (c): 12% solution of cane sugar in water means 12 g of cane sugar in 100 mL of the solution, that is, $w_2 = 12$ g, $V = 100$ mL = 0.1 L.

Osmotic pressure,

$\pi = CRT = \frac{n}{V}RT = \frac{w_2}{M}\frac{RT}{V} = \frac{12\times 0.0821\times 290}{342\times 0.1} = 8.35$ atm

(Mol. mass of $C_{12}H_{22}O_{11} = 342$)

184. (c): As the two solutions are isotonic, $C_1 = C_2$

$\frac{6}{M_2} = 0.05$ or $M_2 = 120$

EF mass $CH_2O = 30$

$\therefore n = \frac{\text{Molar mass}}{\text{EF mass}} = \frac{120}{30} = 40$

$\therefore$ Molecular formula = $C_4H_8O_4$

185. (b): After removing the hard shell of the egg, a semi-permeable membrane is present on its surface. By osmosis, the solvent flows from the less concentrated to the more concentrated solution. As the outside concentration is high, the solvent will flow out from inside the egg. Hence, it will shrink.

186. (d): Osmotic pressure is expressed in atmospheres.

187. (e): $\pi = CRT = \frac{n}{V}RT = \frac{w}{M_2}\times\frac{RT}{V}$

$T = \frac{n\times M_2\times V}{w\times R} = \frac{16.4\times 180\times 0.1}{10\times 0.0821}\text{ K} = 360\text{ K}$

188. (c): $M_2 = \frac{w\,RT}{\pi V} = \frac{4\times 180\times 300}{4.1\times 10^{-4}\times 1} = 2.4\times 10^5$

189. (b): Molar concentration of urea $= \frac{10}{60}\text{ mol L}^{-1} = \frac{1}{6}\text{ mol L}^{-1}$

Molar concentration of 5% solution of unknown solute

$= \frac{5}{M} \times \frac{1}{100} \times 1000 = \frac{50}{M}$ mol L^{-1}

Isotonic solutions have the same molar concentrations. Hence,

$\frac{50}{M} = \frac{1}{6}$ or $M = 300$ g mol^{-1}

190. (b): $\pi = \frac{wRT}{M_2 V} = \frac{5 \times 0.0821 \times 423}{342 \times 0.1} = 5.077$ atm

191. (c): $P = \frac{wRT}{MV}$ As w, R, T and V are the same for each solution.

$P \propto \frac{1}{M}$

Molecular masses: glucose ($C_6H_{12}O_6$) = 180, urea (NH_2CONH_2) = 60, sucrose ($C_4H_{12}O_{11}$) = 342

∴ Molecular masses are urea < glucose < sucrose. Hence $P_2 > P_1 > P_3$.

192. (a): Due to osmosis, the liquid flows from a less concentrated to a more concentrated solution through the semi-permeable membrane. As liquid flows from A to B, A is less concentrated than B.

193. (a): Blood cells will remain in normal form, that is, neither shrink nor swell in a solution which is isotonic with cell sap.

194. (b): $\pi = CRT$

$\frac{\pi_1}{\pi_2} = \frac{C_1RT_1}{C_2RT_2} = \frac{C_1T_1}{C_2T_2}$

$\therefore \frac{P}{2} = \frac{C \times 600}{(C/2) \times 700}$ or $P = \frac{1200}{700} \times 2 = \frac{24}{7}$ atm

195. (b): The bursting of cells after swelling in a hypotonic solution is called hemolysis.

196. (d): After mixing, the total volume of solution = 100 + 300 = 400 mL. In the final solution,

Concentration of urea $= \frac{100}{400} \times M = 0.25$ M

Concentration of glucose $= \frac{300}{400} \times 1\text{M} = 0.75$ M

$\pi_{\text{urea}} = CRT = 0.25\ RT$

$\pi_{\text{glucose}} = 0.75\ RT$

Total $\pi = 0.25\ RT + 0.75\ RT = RT$

197. (c): Hypertonic solution has a higher osmotic pressure than that of plant cell sap, that is, higher concentration than cell sap. Hence, water will flow from the cell sap to the hypertonic solution and, therefore, the plant cell will shrink.

198. (c): $\Delta T_b = K_b \times m = 0.513 \times \left(\frac{0.1}{200} \times 1000\right) = 0.265°$

$T_b = 100.2565°\text{C}$

199. (c): Molality $= \frac{1.8/180}{100} \times 1000 = 0.1$

$\Delta T_b = K_b m$ or $K_b = \Delta T_b / m = 0.1/0.1 = \text{K/m}$

200. (d): $M_2 = \frac{1000 K_b w_2}{w_1 \Delta T_b} = \frac{1000 \times 2.5 \times 1.5}{50 \times 0.75} = 100$

201. (b): Elevation in boiling point required (ΔT_b) = 100 – 99.63° = 0.37°

Mass of solvent (water), $w_1 = 500$ g

Molar mass of solvent, $M_1 = 18$ g mol^{-1}

Molar mass of solute, $C_{12}H_{22}O_{11} = 342$ g mol^{-1}

$M_2 = \frac{1000 k_b w_2}{w_1 \Delta T_b}$ or $w_2 = \frac{M_2 \times w_1 \times \Delta T_b}{1000 \times \Delta T_b}$

$= \frac{342 \times 500 \times 0.37}{1000 \times 0.52} = 121.7$ g

202. (a): $K_f = \frac{M_1 RT_0^2}{1000 \Delta_f H}$

203. (b): $\Delta T_2 = k_b \times m$ or $k_b = \Delta T_b / m$

204. (d): (d) is not the correct unit of K_b

205. (b): $\Delta T_b = \frac{1000 \times K_b \times w_2}{w_1 M_2} = \frac{1000 \times 0.56 \times 6.0}{200 \times 60}$

$= 0.28°,\ T_b = 100.28°\text{C}$

206. (a): $K_b = \frac{0.18}{0.1} = 1.8°$

207. (c): $\Delta T_b = K_b \times m = K_b \times \left(\frac{10}{100} \times \frac{1}{100} \times 1000\right) = K_b$

208. (b): $\Delta T_b = K_b \times m$. $\Delta T_b = K_b$ when molality, m = 1 mol kg^{-1}

209. (d): $K_b = \frac{RT_0^2}{1000 l_v}$ (l_v = latent heat of vaporisation per g of the solvent)

$\frac{M_1 RT_0^2}{1000\ \Delta H_v}$ (ΔH_v = latent heat of vaporisation per mol of solvent)

$= \frac{18 \times 0.002 \times (375.15)^2}{1000 \times 9.72} = 0.52°\text{C kg mol}^{-1}$

210. (b): Due to high pressure inside the cooker, the boiling point is increased.

211. (d): Ebullioscopic constant represents the elevation in boiling point when 1 mol of the solute is dissolved in 1 kg of the solvent.

212. (c): 1 g urea $= \frac{1}{60}$ mol, 3 g glucose $= \frac{3}{100} = \frac{1}{60}$ mol

As the two solutions have the same molar concentration, the elevation in boiling point will be the same and hence the boiling point will be the same.

213. (a): At high altitudes, atmospheric pressure is low and hence the boiling point is lowered.

214. (b): Vapour pressure of water at 298 K is 23 mm. A liquid boils when the vapour pressure becomes equal to the atmospheric pressure. Hence, when the atmospheric pressure is 23 mm, the liquid will boil at 298 K.

215. (d): Out of the given solvents, chloroform has the maximum boiling point elevation constant. As $\Delta T_b = K_b \times m$, for the same value of m, ΔT_b is maximum of which K_b is maximum.

216. (b): When a solid is the solute, it is the solvent that freezes.

217. (d): $CaCl_2$ lowers the freezing point of water. Hence, the formation of snow is reduced.

218. (a): $\Delta T_f = \dfrac{100 K_f w_2}{w_1 M_2}$. For getting the same ΔT_f, less is the molecular weight M_2 of the solute to be added, less will be the weight w_2 of the solute required.

219. (d): $\Delta T_f = \dfrac{1000 K_f w_2}{w_1 \times M_2} = \dfrac{1000 K_f w_2'}{w_1' \times M_2'}$

or $M_2' = \dfrac{w_2'}{w_1'} \times \dfrac{w_1}{w_2} \times M_2 = \dfrac{0.50}{100} \times \dfrac{200}{0.10} \times 100 = 1000$

220. (d): $M_2 = \dfrac{1000 K_f w_2}{w_1 \times \Delta T_f} = \dfrac{1000 \times 1.86 \times 1.8}{40 \times 0.465} = 180$

EF mass of $CH_2O = 30$

$\therefore n = \dfrac{180}{30} = 6$

$\therefore$ Molecular formula $= 6 \times CH_2O = C_6H_{12}O_6$

221. (c): $\Delta T_f = \dfrac{1000 K_f w_2}{w_1 \times M_2}$

$\therefore 2.8 = \dfrac{1000 \times 1.86 \times w_2}{1000 \times 60}$ or $w_2 = 93$ g

222. (a): Camphor has the maximum value of K_f (= 39.7°).

223. (b): Molal depression constant depends only on the nature of solvent.

224. (d): Molal depression constant (K_f) depends only on the solvent and is independent of the molality of the solution.

225. (d): $M_2 = \dfrac{1000 K_f w_2}{w_1 \times \Delta T_f} = \dfrac{1000 \times 1.86 \times 1.25}{20 \times (273 - 271.94)} = 109.6$

226. (b): $60 = \dfrac{1000 \times 1.86 \times w_2}{500 \times 0.186}$ or $w_2 = 3$ g

227. (a): $K_f = \Delta T_f / m$ =(5.45 – 355)/0.374 = 5.08 K kg mol^{-1}

228. (b): As the amount of the solute is doubled, ΔT_f will also be doubled.

229. (b): As the solute is solid, the solvent, that is water, will freeze out.

230. (d): $M_2 = \dfrac{1000 K_f w_2}{w_1 \times \Delta T_f} = \dfrac{1000 \times 1.85 \times \times 8.0}{92 \times 0.925} \simeq 174$

(close to 160)

231. (c): $\Delta T_f = K_f \times m$. $\Delta T_f = K_f$ when molality, $m = 1$ mol kg^{-1}

232. (b): $\Delta T_f = \dfrac{1000 K_f w_2}{w_1 \times M_2} = \dfrac{1000 \times 1.86 \times 68.5}{1000 \times 342} = 0.372°$

$T_f = T_f^0 - \Delta T_f = 0 - 0.372 = -0.372°C$

233. (c): $\Delta T_f = \dfrac{1000 K_f w_2}{w_1 \times M_2}$

$\dfrac{(\Delta T_f)_{canesugar}}{(\Delta T_f)_{glucose}} = \dfrac{(M_2)_{glucose}}{(M_2)_{canesugar}}$

(w_2, w_1 are same as both solutions are 5% of mass)

$\dfrac{273.15 - 271}{(\Delta T_f)_{glucose}} = \dfrac{180}{342} (\Delta T_f)_{glucose} = 4.085$

$(\Delta T_f)_{glucose}$ =273.15 – 4.085 = 269.07

234. (b): $\Delta T_b = K_b \times m$, that is,

$0.52 = 0.52 \times m$ or $m = 1$

$\Delta T_f = K_f \times m = 1.86 \times 1 = 1.86°$, that is, $T_f = -1.86°C$

235. (b): Greater the lowering of VP, greater is the depression in FP, that is, lower is the actual FP.

236. (b): Camphor has a very high cryoscopic constant (= 39.7°). Hence, it gives a larger depression in melting point when an organic solute is dissolved in it.

237. (a): $2\ KI + HgI_2 \rightarrow K_2HgI_4$. As a result of this reaction, the number of ions decreases. So, the lowering in FP is less or the actual FP is more.

238. (b): $\Delta T_b = K_b \times m$

$\therefore m = \dfrac{\Delta T_b}{K_b} = \dfrac{0.18}{0.512}$

$\Delta T_f = K_f \times m = 1.86 \times \dfrac{0.18}{0.512} = 0.654°C$

$\therefore T_f = 0° - 0.6540° = -0.654°C$

239. (c): Higher the boiling point, greater is the elevation in boiling point. Hence, elevations in boiling points are in the order: C < B < A < D.

Greater is the elevation in boiling point, greater is the depression in freezing point. Hence, depressions in freezing point are in the order: C < B < A < D.

Greater the depression in freezing point, lower is the actual freezing point. Hence, freezing points will be in the opposite order, that is, D < A < B < C or D < B > A < C.

240. (b): $\Delta T_b = K_b \times m \;\therefore y = x \times m$ or $m = \dfrac{y}{x}$

$\Delta T_f = K_f \times m = z \times m = z \times \dfrac{y}{x} = \dfrac{yz}{x}$

241. (a): Greater the lowering in VP, higher is the BP.

242. (c): $\dfrac{p^\circ - p_s}{p^\circ} = \dfrac{n_2}{n_1} = \dfrac{n_2}{w_1 / M_1}$

$\therefore \dfrac{760 - 732}{760} = \dfrac{n_2}{100/18}$ or $n_2 = \dfrac{28}{760} \times \dfrac{100}{18} = 0.2046$ mol

Molality of the solution

$= \dfrac{0.2046 \text{ mol}}{100/1000 \text{ kg}} = 2.046$ mol kg^{-1}

$\Delta T_b = K_b \times$ molality $= 0.52 \times 2.046 = 1.06°$

That is, $T_b - T_b^\circ = 1.06°$

or $T_b - T_b^\circ + 1.06 = 100 + 1.06°C = 101.06°C$

243. (a): When the concentration is increased, the boiling point increases (because $\Delta T_f \times \alpha$ concentration). Increase of concentration lowers the vapour pressure.

244. (d): Osmotic pressure measurement is the most suitable for polymers because other properties like ΔT_f or ΔT_b are too low to be measured accurately but osmotic pressure is measureable in mm.

245. (a): $\Delta T_f = K_f \times m \therefore 0.52 = 1.86 \times m$ or $m = 0.28$
$\pi = CRT = 0.28 \times 0.0821 \times 300 = 6.89$ atm ($C = m$, given)

246. (a): Depression in freezing point (and not the freezing point) is a colligative property.

247. (c): The addition of a non-volatile solute to the solvent lowers the vapour pressure of the solvent.

Colligative Properties of Solute Which Dissociate (electrolytes) or Associate in Solution and Abnormal Molar Masses

248. (b): Benzoic acid dimerises in benzene.

249. (d): $MgSO_4$ dissociates to give 2 ions.

250. (c): Acetic acid in benzene dimerises to form $(CH_3COOH)_2$.

251. (b): Electrolyte dissociates. Hence, $i > 1$.

252. (b): For any ideal solution, $i = 1$.

253. (a): $K_4[Fe(CN)_6]$ and $Al_2(SO_4)_3$ each dissociates to give 5 ions.

254. (c): $i < 1$ means association.

255. (d): As $Ba(OH)_2$ is a strong electrolyte, it is dissociated completely as
$Ba(OH)_2 \rightarrow Ba^{2+} + 2\,OH^-$
Ions produced = 3. Hence, van't Hoff factor = 3.

256. (a): $i > 1$ shows that the solute is dissociated in the solution.

257. (b): Benzoic acid is associated in benzene as
$2\,C_6H_5COOH \rightleftharpoons (C_6H_5COOH)_2$

$$i = \frac{\text{No. of particles after asociation or dissociation}}{\text{No. of particles before association or disociation}}$$

$$= \frac{1}{2} = 0.5$$

258. (a): See text

259. (a): $BaCl_2 \rightleftharpoons Ba^{2+} + 2Cl^-$

Initial c

After disso. $c - c\,\alpha$ $\quad c\alpha$ $\quad 2c\alpha$

Total $= c + 2c\,\alpha = c\,(1 + 2\alpha)$

$$i = \frac{c(1+2)}{c} = 1 + 2 \text{ (Note that } c \text{ cancels out)}$$

$$\text{or } \alpha = \frac{i-1}{2} = \frac{1.98-1}{2} = 0.49 = 49\%$$

Alternatively,

$BaCl_2 \rightleftharpoons Ba^{2+} + 2Cl^-$

Initial 1 mol

After disso. $1 - \alpha$ $\quad \alpha$ $\quad 2\alpha$

Total $= 1 + 2\,\alpha$

$$i = 1 + 2\,\alpha \text{ or } \alpha = \frac{i+1}{2}$$

which is the same as above.

260. (c): $Na_2SO_4 \rightarrow 2\,Na^+ + SO_4^{2-}$

Total $= 1 + 2\,\alpha$

$1 - \alpha$ $\quad 2\alpha$ $\quad \alpha$

$\therefore i = 1 + 2\,\alpha$

261. (a): $$i = \frac{\text{Normal molecular mass}}{\text{Observed molecular mass}} = \frac{164}{65.6} = 2.5$$

$MX_2 \rightleftharpoons M^{2+} + 2X^-$

Initial 1 mol $\quad 0 \quad 0$

After disso. $1 - \alpha$ $\quad \alpha$ $\quad 2\alpha$

Total $= 1 + 2\,\alpha$

$\therefore i = 1 + 2\,\alpha = 2.5$ or $2\,\alpha = 1.5$

or $= 0.75$ or 75%

262. (b): Observed molar mass of NaOH = 25 g mol^{-1}
Calculated molar mass of NaOH = 40 g mol^{-1}

$$\therefore i = \frac{\text{Calculated molar mass}}{\text{Observed molar mass}} = \frac{40}{25} = 1.6$$

$\therefore$ $NaOH \rightleftharpoons Na^+ + OH^-$

Initial 1 mol $\quad 0 \quad 0$

After ionisation $1 - \alpha$ $\quad \alpha$ $\quad \alpha$

Total $= 1 + \alpha$

$i = 1 + \alpha$ or $\alpha = i = 1 = 1.6 - 1 = 0.6$ or 60%

263. (c): $$\frac{p^\circ - p_s}{p^\circ} = i \times \frac{n_2}{n_1 + n_2}$$

$$\therefore \frac{100 - p_s}{100} = 3 \times \frac{1}{99+1} = \frac{3}{100}$$

or $100 - p_s = 3$ or $p_s = 97$ mm

264. (a): Actual vapour pressure will increase when the lowering of vapour pressure is decreased. On adding water, concentration of the solution will decrease and so lowering will be less. In all other cases, electrolytes are being added which will increase the number of particles and hence increase the lowering of vapour pressure, tht is, the actual vapour pressure will decrease.

265. (a): NaCl dissociates completely while CH_3COOH dissociates to a small extent. Hence, $P_1 > P_2$.

266. (e): $\pi = i\,CRT$
As C is same and R and T are constant,
$\pi \propto i$
Hence, KCl (Strong electrolyte) > CH_3COOH (weak electrolyte) > Sucrose (Non-electrolyte)

267. (c): Isotonic solutions have the same molar concentration of particles.
1. 0.15 M urea solution = 0.15 M
2. 0.05 M $CaCl_2$ solution = 0.05×3, that is, 0.15 M particles
3. 0.15 M $MgSO_4$ = 0.1×2 M, that is, 0.2 M
4. 0.15 M glucose = 0.15 M

268. (d): $\pi_1 = C_1\,RT$, $\pi_2 = C_2\,RT$

$$\alpha \frac{\pi_1}{\pi_2} = \frac{C_1}{C_2}$$

or $\frac{\pi}{\pi_2} = \frac{1}{0.2}$ (C_2 for 0.1 M NaCl = 0.2 M) or $\pi_2 = 0.2\,\pi$

269. (b): Conc. of ions in 0.1 M NaCl solution = 0.2 M
Conc. of ions in 0.05 M $BaCl_2$ solution = $3 \times 0.05 = 0.15$ M
Net flow of solvent is from the less concentrated solution to the more concentrated solution.

270. (a): NaCl solution used should be isotonic with the blood stream.
For NaCl, $i = 2$

$$\pi = iCRT \text{ or } C = \frac{\pi}{iRT}$$

$$= \frac{7.8 \text{ bar}}{2 \times 0.083 \times \text{bar LK}^{-1}\text{ mol}^{-1} \times 310 \text{ K}} = 0.15 \text{ mol L}^{-1}$$

271. (d): $AB \rightarrow A^+ + B^-$
As AB is 100% ionised, $i = 2$

$$\pi = iCRT = i\frac{w}{M_2} = \frac{1}{V} \times R \times T = i\frac{wRT}{M_2 V}$$

$$= 2 \times \frac{10 \times 0.082 \times 300}{200 \times 0.1 \text{ L}} \quad \text{(10\% means 10 g in 100 mL)}$$

= 24.6 L atm

272. (a): K_2SO_4 dissolved = 25 mg = 0.025 g
Volume of solution = 2 L, T = 25°C = 298 K
Molar mass of $K_2SO_4 = 2\times39 + 32 + 4\times16 = 174$ g mol^{-1}
As K_2SO_4 dissociates completely,
$K_2SO_4 \rightarrow 2K^+ + SO_4^{2-}$, that is,
ions produced = 3
$\therefore i = 3$

$$\pi = iCRT = -\frac{n}{V}RT = \frac{1}{M} \times \frac{1}{V}RT$$

$$= 3 \times \frac{0.025}{174} \times \frac{1}{2} \times 0.0821 \times 298 = 5.27 \times 10^{-3} \text{ atm}$$

273. (c): NaCl dissociates into ions. As the number of particles increases, the value of the colligative property is more and so molecular mass is less

274. (c): $i = \frac{\text{Observed osmotic pressure}}{\text{Theoretical osmotic pressure}}$

As $\pi_{\text{obs.}} < \pi_{\text{calc.}}$, $i < 1$ which is so when the solute is associated in the solvent.

275. (b): Higher the concentration of ions in the solution, greater is the elevation in boiling point. As 0.1 M Na_3PO_4 has the highest concentration of ions, elevation in boiling point is the highest for 0.1 M Na_3PO_4 and so is the boiling point. Alternatively, $\Delta T_b = iK_b m$. For the same value of m, higher the value of i, higher is the elevation in boiling point

276. (a): For equimolal solutions of two substances, the one that undergoes dissociation produces a greater number of particles (ions) in the solution and hence has a greater boiling point.

277. (c): $i = \frac{\text{Observed } \Delta T_b}{\text{Calculated } \Delta T_b} = \frac{0.81}{0.54} = 1.5$

$AB \rightleftharpoons A^+ + B^-$

$1-\alpha \quad \alpha \quad \alpha$ Total = $1 + \alpha$

$i = 1 + \alpha$ or $\alpha = i - 1 = 1.5 - 1 = 0.5 = 50\%$

278. (d): Observed molecular mass of phenylacetic acid

$$= \frac{1000 \times 5.12 \times 0.223}{(5.3 - 4.47) \times 4.4} = 312.6$$

Calculated molecular mass of $C_6H_5CH_2COOH$
$= 72 + 5 + 12 + 2 + 12 + 32 + 1 = 136$
As observed molecular mass is nearly double of the theoretical value, it dimerises in benzene.

279. (a): $(\Delta T_b)_{\text{NaCl}} = iK_f m$

$\therefore 0.37 = 2 \times K_f \times 0.01$ (For NaCl), $i = 2$)

$(\Delta T_f)_{\text{urea}} = K_f m = K_f \times 0.02$

Dividing (ii) by (i), we get

$$\frac{(\Delta T_f)_{\text{urea}}}{0.37} = \frac{2 \times 0.01}{0.02} = 1 \text{ or } (\Delta T_f)_{\text{urea}} = 0.37°\text{C}$$

280. (c): $\Delta T_f = i \times K_f \times m = i \times K_f \times \frac{w_2}{M_2} \times \frac{1}{w_1} \times 1000$

$$\therefore 3.82 = i \times 1.86 \times \frac{1}{142} \times \frac{1}{45} \times 1000$$

(Molar mass of Na_2SO_4 = 142) or $i = 2.62$

281. (a): i for KCl = 2, i for $BaCl_2$ = 3

ΔT_f (KCl) $= iK_f m = 2 \times K_f \times 0.1$

$$\Delta T_f(BaCl_2) i K_f m = iK_f m = 3 \times K_f \times \frac{1}{111} \times \frac{1}{100} \times 1000$$

$$\therefore \frac{\Delta T_{f(BaCl_2)}}{\Delta T_{f(KCl)}} = \frac{3}{2}$$

$\therefore \Delta T_f(BaCl_2) = \frac{3}{2} \times 2 = 3°$

$\therefore T_{f(BaCl_2)} = 0 - 3°C = -3°C$

282. (d): $HX \rightleftharpoons H^+ + X^-$

Initial 1 mol

After ionisation $1 - \alpha \quad \alpha \quad \alpha$

Total = $1 + \alpha$

$i = 1 + \alpha = 1 + 0.20 = 1.20$

$\Delta T_f = iK_f m = 1.20 \times 1.86 \times 0.5 = 1.12$ K

283. (a): Observed $\Delta T_f = 0.19°C$

Calculated $\Delta T_f = K_f \times m = 1.86 \times 0.1 = 186°C$

$$i = \frac{\text{Observed } \Delta T_f}{\text{Calculated } \Delta T_f} = \frac{0.197}{0.186} = 1.06$$

$HF \rightleftharpoons H^+ + F^-$

Initial mol $1 \quad 0 \quad 0$

After disso. $1 - \alpha \quad \alpha \quad \alpha$

Total = $1 + \alpha$

$i - 1 + \alpha$ or $\alpha = i - 1 = 1.06 - 1$
$= 0.06 = 6\%$

284. (a): As P undergoes association,

$2P \rightarrow P_2$

Initial mol $1 \quad 0$

After assoc. $1 - \alpha \quad \frac{\alpha}{2}$ (α = degree of association)

Total moles $= 1-\alpha+\frac{\alpha}{2}=1-\frac{\alpha}{2}$

$\therefore i=1-\frac{\alpha}{2}$ or $\alpha=(1-i)\times 2$

$\left(\Delta T_f\right)_{\text{observed}}=0.3°\text{C}$

$\left(\Delta T_f\right)_{\text{calculated}}=\frac{1000\,K_f\,w_2}{w_1\times M_2}=\frac{1000\times 1.86\times 1.25}{50\times 94}=0.5°$

$i=\frac{\left(\Delta T_f\right)_{\text{obs}}}{\left(\Delta T_f\right)_{\text{cal}}}=\frac{0.3}{0.5}=0.6$

$\therefore \alpha=(1-0.6)\times 2=0.80=80\%$

285. (c): 0.5% (*w/W*) aqueous KCl solution means 0.5 g KCl are present in 100 g of the solution. Mass of solvent $(H_2O)=99.5$ g

Molality of the solution $=\frac{0.5}{74.5}\times\frac{1}{99.5}\times 1000=0.067$

$\Delta T_f=i\,K_f m$

$0.24=i\,(1.86)\,(0.067)\;\therefore i=1.92$

286. (d): Maximum freezing point means minimum depression in freezing point. Less the number of particles produced, less is the depression in freezing point. We have:

(a) $[Co(H_2O)_6]Cl_3 \rightarrow [Co(H_2O)_6]^{3+}+3\,Cl^-, i=4$

(b) $[Co(H_2O)_5Cl]Cl_2.H_2O \rightarrow [Co(H_2O)_5Cl]^{2+}+2\,Cl^-, i=3$

(c) $[Co(H_2O)_4Cl_2]Cl.2H_2O \rightarrow [Co(H_2O)_4Cl_2]^{+}+Cl^-, i=2$

(d) $[Co(H_2O)_3Cl_3].3H_2O \rightarrow$ No ionisation, $i=1$

Thus $[Co(H_2O)_3Cl_3].3H_2O$ produces the minimum number of particles. Hence, it has the highest freezing point.

287. (b): Addition of solute decreases the freezing point and increases the boiling point.

288. (a): 0.6% urea solution $=\frac{0.6}{60}\times\frac{1}{100}\times 1000=0.1$ M

Hence, it will be isotonic with 0.1 M glucose solution.

289. (b): Molar concentration will be

Sucrose $=\frac{1}{342}\times\frac{1}{100}\times 1000=\frac{10}{342}\,\text{M}=0.029$

NaCl $=\frac{1}{58.5}\times\frac{1}{100}\times 1000=\frac{10}{58.5}$ M

$=\frac{20}{58.5}\,Na^+$ and Cl^- ions $=0.34$

$CaCl_2=\frac{1}{111}\times\frac{1}{100}\times 1000=\frac{10}{111}=\frac{30}{111}$

Ca^+ and Cl^- ions 0.27

Glucose $=\frac{1}{180}\times\times\frac{1}{100}\times 1000=\frac{1}{18}\,\text{M}=0.056$

Particle concentrations are Sucrose < Glucose < $CaCl_2$ < NaCl. Thus, ΔT_f will be maximum in NaCl and freezing point will be least.

290. (c): Ratio of concentrations of particles $=0.2:0.2:0.3=1:1:1.5$

291. (c): $\Delta T_f=i\,K_f m$, Thus $\Delta T_f \propto i$ (van't Hoff factor)

Value of i will be KCl = 2, $C_6H_{12}O_6=1$, $Al_2(SO_4)_3=5$, $K_2SO_4=3$

Thus, i is maximum for $Al_2(SO_4)_3$.

292. (d): In aq. solution, HCl dissociates but in benzene it does not.

293. (d): Out of the given compounds, glucose does not undergo dissociation. Depression in freezing point will be minimum and hence actual freezing point will be highest.

294. (c): NaCl dissociates. Hence, conc. of particles is greater.

295. (a): $Al_2(SO_4)_3$ gives maximum number of ions. Hence, its osmotic pressure is maximum.

296. (b): All others dissociate except sugar. Sugar solution will have minimum depression in FP and hence maximum FP.

297. (d): Two solutions are isotonic if they have the same molar concentration of particles. In (d),

0.1 M $Ba(NO_3)_2=0.3$ M ion conc.

0.1 M $Na_2SO_4=0.3$ ion conc.

298. (d): $K_4[Fe(CN)_6] \rightarrow 4\,K^+ + [Fe(CN)_6]^{4-}$. It produces maximum number of particles in the solution. Hence, it will show maximum lowering of vapour pressure.

299. (a): $Al_2\,(SO_4)_3$ will produce maximum particles in the solution and hence will have maximum osmotic pressure.

300. (d): Isotonic solutions have the same concentration of particles in solution.

0.2 M urea = 0.2 M

0.2 M NaCl = 0.4 Na^+ and Cl^- ions

0.1 M urea = 0.1 M

0.2 M $MgCl_2=0.6$ M Mg^{2+} and Cl^- ions

0.1 M NaCl = 0.2 M Na^+ and Cl^- ions

0.1 M $Na_2SO_4=0.3$ M Na^+ and SO_4^{2-} ions

0.1 M $Ca(NO_3)_2=0.3$ M Ca^{2+} and NO_3^- ions

0.1 M $Na_2SO_4=0.3$ Na^+ and SO_4^{2-} ions

Hence, 0.14 $Ca(NO_3)_2$ and 0.1 Na_2SO_4 are isotonic.

301. (a): 58.5 g NaCl $=\frac{58.5}{58.5}$ mol = 1 mol

180 g glucose $(C_6H_{12}O_6)=\frac{180}{180}$ mol = 1 mol

Thus, we have 1 M NaCl and 1 M glucose solution. But NaCl dissociates in the solution while glucose does not. Thus, particle concentration is more in NaCl. Hence, NaCl will have higher elevation in boiling point.

302. (d): 1% concentration means molar concentration

$=\frac{1}{\text{Molar mass}}\times\frac{1}{100}\times 1000$

Thus, molar conc. $\propto \frac{1}{\text{Molar mass}}\frac{0.18}{\left(\Delta T_f\right)_2}=0.01/0.006$

As NaCl has least molar mass, its molar concentration will be highest and hence the osmotic pressure will be highest.

303. (a): Greater the dilution, greater is the dissociation into ions and hence greater is the van't Hoff factor.

304. (d): $Al_2(SO_4)_3$ and $K_4[Fe(CN)_6)]$ produce the same number of ions in the solution (5). Hence, they have the same value of van't Hoff factor.

Miscellaneous

305. (b): $\Delta T_f=K_f\times m$. As K_f for different solvents is different, ΔT_f will be different for the same value of m.

306. (b): (i) Cyclohexane and *n*-octane are both non-polar. Hence, they mix completely in all proportions.
(ii) KCl is an ionic compound while *n*-octane is non-polar. Hence, KCl will not dissolve at all in *n*-octane.
(iii) CH_3OH and CH_3CN are both polar but CH_3CN is less polar than CH_3OH. As the solvent (*n*-octane) is non-polar, CH_3CN will dissolve more than CH_3OH in *n*-octane.
Thus, the order of solubility will be
$KCl < CH_3OH < CH_3CN <$ Cyclohexane

Final Preparation

307. (a): $M_1V_1 + M_2V_2 = M_3(V_1 + V_2)$
$6 \times 250 + 3 \times 650 = M_3(250 + 650)$
or $1500 + 1950 = 900\ M_3$
or $M_3 = 3450/900$ M
That is, molarity of solution after mixing = 3450/900 M
Again applying
$M_1' V_1' = M_2' V_2'$
(Before dilution) (After dilution)
$\frac{3450}{900} \times 900 = 3 \times V_2'$ or $V_2' = 1150$ mL
$\therefore$ Volume of water to be added = 1150 – 900 = 250 mL

308. (d): 250 mL of $\frac{M}{4}$ NaOH contains
$= \frac{40}{4} \times \frac{250}{1000}$ g = 2.5 g NaOH
250 mL of NaOH sol = 250 × 1.05 g = 262.5 g
After adding 5g NaOH, now solute = 7.5 g and solution = 267.5 g
Volume of new solution $= \frac{267.5}{1.08} = 247.7$ mL = 0.2477 L
Molarity $= \frac{7.5}{40}$ mol $\times \frac{1}{0.2477\ L} = 0.76$ M

309. (a): 100 mL of 0.30 M NaCl = ? mL of 0.40 NaCl
$M_1 \times V_1 = M_2 \times V_2$
$0.3 \times 100 = 0.40 \times V_2$
or $V_2 = 75$ mL
That is, one way is to evaporate off 25 mL of water.
Another way is to add more of NaCl (as 0.4 M is more concentrated than 0.3 M).
100 mL of 0.30 M NaCl contains 0.03 mol of NaCl
100 mL of 0.40 M NaCl contains 0.04 mol NaCl
Thus 0.01 mol NaCl should be added which is equal to 0.01 × 58.5 g = 0.585 g

310. (a): Total volume of solution to be made = 2 L
Suppose solution A (0.5 N HCl) taken = *x* L
Then solution B (0.1 N HCl) to be taken = (2 – *x*) L
$N_1V_1 + N_2V_2 = N_3(V_1 + V_2)$
$0.5 \times x + 0.1(2 - x) = 0.2 \times 2$
or $0.4\,x = 0.4 - 0.2 = 0.2$ or $x = \frac{0.2}{0.4} = 0.5$ L
Hence, solution A = 0.5 L
solution B = 2 – 0.5 = 1.5 L

311. (a): By Henry's law, $m = K_H p$
At constant temperature, K_H is constant
$\therefore$ At two different pressures,
$\frac{m}{m'} = \frac{p}{p'} \therefore \frac{4 \times 10^{-3} L^{-1}}{m'} = \frac{100}{250}$ or $m' = \frac{250}{100} \times 4 \times 10^{-3}\,kg\,L^{-1}$
$= 10^{-2}\,kg\,L^{-1} = \frac{10^{-2}}{4}$ kg in 250 mL $= 2.5 \times 10^{-3}$ kg

312. (b): $p_{N_2} = K_H \times x_{N_2}$ or $x_{N_2} = \frac{p_{N_2}}{K_H} = \frac{0.96\ bar}{76800\ bar} = 1.25 \times 10^{-5}$
If *n* mol of N_2 are present in 1 L of water (55.5 mol)
$x_{N_2} = \frac{n}{n + 55.5} = \frac{n}{55.5}$
or $n = x_{N_2} \times 55.5 = 1.25 \times 10^{-5} \times 55.5$ mol
$= 69.3 \times 10^{-5}$ mol = 0.693 mmol

313. (a): $p_A = K_H \times x_A\ (A = O_2)$
$\therefore x_{O_2} = \frac{p_2}{K_H} = \frac{1\ bar}{100 \times 10^3\ bar} = 10^{-5}$
Suppose millimoles of O_2 dissolved = *x*
1 L of water = 1000 mL = 1000 g
$\frac{1000}{18}$ mol = 55.55 mol = 55.55×10^3 mmol
$\therefore x_{N_2} = \frac{x}{x + 55.55 \times 10^3} = 10^{-5}$ (calculated above)
But $x <<< 55.55 \times 10^3$, hence
$\frac{x}{55.55 \times 10^3} = 10^{-5}$ or $x = 55.55 \times 10^{-2} = 0.555$ mmol

314. (b): $x_{C_5H_{12}} = \frac{1}{5} = 0.2; x_{C_6H_{14}} = 1 - 0.2 = 0.8$
$p_{C_5H_{12}} = x_{C_5H_{12}} \times p^\circ_{C_5H_{12}} = 0.2 \times 440$ mm
$p_{C_5H_{12}} = 88$ mm
$p_{C_6H_{14}} = x_{C_6H_{14}} \times p^\circ_{C_6H_{14}} = 0.8 \times 120$ mm = 96 mm
$p_{Total} = 88 + 96 = 184$ mm
Mole fraction of pentane in the vapour phase
$= \frac{p_{C_5H_{12}}}{p_{total}} = \frac{88}{184} = 0.478$

315. (d): In solution if $x_A = x$, $x_B = 2x$ and if $p_A^\circ = p$, $p_B^\circ = 2p$
$\therefore p_A = x \times p$, $p_B = 2x \times 2p = 4\,x \times p \therefore p_{total} = 5xp$
Mole fraction in vapour phase
$(y_A) = \frac{p_A}{p_{Total}} = \frac{xp}{5xp} = \frac{1}{5} = 0.2$

316. (d): Molar ratio of 1 : 1 means $x_X = x_Y = 0.5$
$p_{total} = x_X\,p_X^\circ + x_Y\,p_Y^\circ$
$\therefore 400 = 0.5\ p_X^\circ + 0.5\ p_Y^\circ$
or $p_X^\circ + p_Y^\circ = 800$ (i)
Molar ratio of 1 : 2 means, $x_X = \frac{1}{3}, x_y = \frac{2}{3}$
$\therefore 350 = \frac{1}{3}\,p_X^\circ + \frac{1}{3}\,p_Y^\circ$ or $p_X^\circ + 2\,p_Y^\circ = 1050$ (ii)
Eq. (ii) – Eq. (i) gives $p_Y^\circ = 250$ mm
Putting in (i), we get $p_X^\circ = 550$ mm

317. (c): $x_A = \frac{1}{4} = 0.25$, $x_Y = 0.75$

$p_{\text{total}} = x_X \times p_X^\circ + x_Y \times p_Y^\circ$

That is, 550 = 0.25

$p_X^\circ + 0.75 p_Y^\circ$ (i)

After adding 1 mol of Y, $x_X = \frac{1}{5} = 0.20$,

$x_Y = 0.80$

$\therefore$ $560 = 0.20\ p_X^\circ + 0.80\ p_Y^\circ$

or $2800 = p_X^\circ + 4 p_Y^\circ$ (ii)

Solving the two equations, $p_Y^\circ = 600$ mm, $p_X^\circ = 400$ mm

318. (c): $(x_A)_{\text{vapour}} = \frac{p_A}{P_{\text{total}}} = \frac{(x_A)_{\text{vapour}}\, p_A^\circ}{P_{\text{total}}}$ or $\frac{(x_A)_{\text{vap}}}{(x_A)_{\text{liq}}} = \frac{p_A^\circ}{P_{\text{total}}}$

As B is less volatile, $P_{\text{total}} < p_A^\circ$

$\therefore \frac{(x_A)_{\text{vap}}}{(x_A)_{\text{liq}}} > 1$ or $(x_A)_{\text{vapour}} > (x_A)_{\text{liquid}}$

319. (d): Pure solvent will form more vapour than the solution. Hence some vapour will condense into the solution. As a result, the volume of solution will increase but that of the pure solvent will decrease.

320. (a): Relative lowering of vapour pressure = mole fraction of the solute in the solution

$\frac{n_2}{n_1 + n_2} = 0.0125$ (given)

Molality = n_2

when n_1 100/18 mol = 55.55 mol)

$\frac{n_2}{n_1 + n_2} = \frac{1}{0.0125} = 80$ or $\frac{n_1}{n_2} + 1 = 80$

or $\frac{n_1}{n_2} = 79$ or $n_2 = \frac{n_1}{79} = \frac{55.55}{79} = 0.70$

321. (c): $\frac{p^\circ - p_s}{p^\circ} = \frac{n_2}{n_1}$ $\therefore$ $\frac{25 - 24.5}{25} = \frac{n_2}{n_1}$ or $\frac{n_2}{n_1} = \frac{0.5}{25} = \frac{1}{50}$

Molality is number of mol in 1000 g of the solvent (H_2O)

$\therefore$ Putting n_1 = 1000/18 mol = 55.5 mol, n_2 becomes molality.

$\therefore \frac{n_2}{55.5} = \frac{1}{50}$ or $n_2 = \frac{55.5}{50} = 1.11$

322. (d): $p_A = X_A p_A^\circ$ $\quad X_B p_B^\circ$

$Y_A = \frac{p_A}{p_A + p_B}$ $\quad Y_B = \frac{p_B}{p_A + p_B}$

$\therefore \frac{Y_A}{Y_B} = \frac{p_A}{p_B} = \frac{X_A p_A^\circ}{X_B p_B^\circ}$ $\therefore \frac{Y_A}{Y_B} = \frac{Y_A}{Y_B} = \frac{p_B^\circ}{p_A^\circ}$

As $p_A^\circ > p_B^\circ$, $\frac{p_B^\circ}{p_A^\circ} < 1$. Hence, $\frac{X_A}{X_B} < \frac{Y_A}{Y_B}$

323. (a): If net ΔH_{soln} is the sum of three steps, this means that the solute–solvent interactions are similar to solvent–solvent and solute–solute interactions.

324. (d): For an ideal solution, $(\Delta H)_{\text{mix}} = 0, (\Delta V)_{\text{mix}} = 0$

As formation of an ideal solution is a spontaneous process, $(\Delta G)_{\text{mix}}$ < (ΔG = –ve). As $\Delta G = \Delta H - T\Delta S$ and $\Delta H = 0$, $\Delta G = -T\Delta S$. As ΔG = –ve, ΔS must be +ve, that is, $(\Delta G)_{\text{mix}} > 0$

325. (c): Plot of $1/x_A$ vs $1/y_A$ is linear.

326. (c): According to Raoult's law, vapour pressure of A is $P_A = y_A P_{\text{total}}$

$y_A = P_A \times P_{\text{total}} 1$

$\therefore y_A$ vs $P_{\text{total}} 1$ is a straight line.

327. (c): For an ideal solution, $\Delta H_{\text{mixing}} = 0$. As process is spontaneous $\Delta G_{\text{mixing}} = \Delta H_{\text{mixing}} - T\Delta S_{\text{mixing}}$ and $\Delta H_{\text{mixing}} = 0$.

$\therefore \Delta H_{\text{mixing}} = -T\Delta S_{\text{mixing}}$. Hence, ΔG_{mixing} can be +ve only if $T\Delta S_{\text{mixing}}$ is +ve.

328. (c): Loss in weight of solution ∝ VP of solution (p_s)

Loss in weight of solvent ∝ $p^\circ - p_s$

$\therefore \frac{p^\circ - p_s}{p_s} = \frac{\text{Loss in weight of solvent}}{\text{Loss in weight of solution}} = \frac{w_2/M_2}{w_1/M_1}$

$\frac{0.05}{2.5} = \frac{10/M_2}{90/18} = \frac{2}{M_2}$ or $M_2 = 100$

329. (b): $\frac{p^\circ - p_s}{p^\circ} = \frac{n_2}{n_1} = \frac{w_2 M_1}{w_1 M_2}$

As $(p^\circ - p_s)/p^\circ$ is the same in the two cases

$\left(\frac{w_2 M_1}{w_1 M_2}\right)_{\text{glucose}} = \left(\frac{w_2 M_1}{w_1 M_2}\right)_{\text{urea}}$

$\frac{w_2 \times 18}{50 \times 180} = \frac{1 \times 18}{50 \times 60}$ or $w_2 = 3$ g

330. (b): Calculation of molecular mass of the hydrocarbon

$\frac{p^\circ - p_s}{p^\circ} = \frac{n_2}{n_1} = \frac{w_2 M_2}{w_1 M_1}$; $\frac{9.953 - 9.823}{9.953} = \frac{3/M_2}{100/78}$

or $\frac{0.130}{9.953} = \frac{3}{M_2} \times \frac{78}{100}$ or $M_2 = 179.1$ u

Calculation of empirical formula

Element	C	H
%	94.4	5.6
At. mass	12	1
Atomic ratio	94.4/12 = 7.87	5.6/1 = 5.6
Simplest ratio	$\frac{7.87}{5.6} = 1.4$	1.0
Simplest whole no. ratio	7	5

$\therefore$ Empirical formula = C_7H_5

Empirical formula mass = 7 × 12 + 5 × 1 = 89

$\therefore n = \frac{\text{Molecular mass}}{\text{E.F. mass}} = \frac{179.1}{89} = 2$

Hence, molecular formula = 2 × (C_7H_5) = $C_{14}H_{10}$

331. (a): Higher the concentration, lower is the vapour pressure. Thus, S_1 has lower conc than S_2. More solvent will flow from S_1 to S_2.

332. (b): $\pi V = nRT$ or $\frac{\pi_1 V_1}{\pi_2 V_2} = \frac{nRT_1}{nRT_2} = \frac{T_1}{T_2}$.

$\frac{500 \times V_1}{105.3 \times V_2} = \frac{273 + 10}{273 + 25} = \frac{283}{298}$

$\therefore \frac{V_1}{V_2} = \frac{1}{5}$ or $V_2 = 5V_1$

333. (a): $\Delta T_f = \dfrac{1000 K_f w_2}{w_1 M_2}$

For AB_2, $2.3 = \dfrac{1000 \times \times 5.1 \times 1}{20 \times M_{AB_2}}$ or $M_{AB_2} = 11087$

For AB_4, $1.3 = \dfrac{1000 \times \times 5.1 \times 1}{20 \times M_{AB_4}}$ or $M_{AB_4} = 196.15$

Suppose atomic mass of A = a and that of B = b, then $a + 2b = 110.87$ and $a + 4b = 196.15$.

On solving, we get

$a = 25.59 \simeq 25.6$ and $b = 42.64 \simeq 42.6$

334. (b): All other factors remaining the same, $\Delta T_f \propto$ molar concentration

$\dfrac{(\Delta T_f)_1}{(\Delta T_f)_2} = \dfrac{C_1}{C_2}$

Molar concentration after mixing can be calculated as

$M_1 V_1 + M_2 V_2 = M_3 (V_1 + V_2)$

$0.01 \times V + 0.002 V = M_3 (2V)$ or $M_3 = \dfrac{0.012}{2} = 0.006$

$\dfrac{0.18}{(\Delta T_f)_2} = 0.01/0.006$ or $(\Delta T_f)_2 = 0.108$

$\therefore T_f$ of solution after mixing = 0 – 0.108 = –0.108°C

335. (b): On increasing the temperature, volume of the solution increases. Hence, molarity decreases.

336. (b): Basicity of H_3PO_3 is 2. Hence,

0.3 M H_3PO_3 = 0.6 N H_3PO_3

337. (a): 5 molal aqueous ethyl alcohol solution means 5 mol of ethyl alcohol in 1000 g of water = 1000/18 mol = 55.5 mol

$x_2 = \dfrac{5}{5 + 55.5} = \dfrac{5}{60.5} = 0.082$

338. (c): Molarity of 95% H_2SO_4

$= \dfrac{95}{98} \times \dfrac{1}{100/1.85} \times 1000 = 17.93$ M

Molarity of 15% $H_2SO_4 = \dfrac{15}{98} \times \dfrac{1}{100/1.10} \times 1000$

= 1.68 M

$M_1 V_1 = M_2 V_2$

(95% H_2SO_4) (15% H_2SO_4)

$17.93 \times V_1 = 1.68 \times 100$ or $V_1 = 9.4\ cm^3$

339. (d): 1 cc of 0.1 M I_2 sol. $\dfrac{0.1}{1000}$

$= 10^{-4}$ mol $= 10^{-4} \times 6.02 \times 10^{23}$ molecules

$= 6.02 \times 10^{19}$ molecules $= 2 \times 6.02 \times 10^{19}$ atoms

$= 1.204 \times 10^{20}$ atoms

340. (b): 63% *w/w* means 63 g of HNO_3 are present in 100 g of the solution.

Volume of 100 g of solution $= \dfrac{100}{1.15} = 86.96$ mL

Mol of $HNO_3 = \dfrac{63}{63} = 1$ mol

Molarity of solution $= \dfrac{1}{86.96} \times 1000 = 11.5$ M

341. (c): 100 mL of 0.2 M $H_2SO_4 = 100 \times 0.2$ mmol

= 20 mmol = 40 milli eq

100 mL of 0.2 M NaOH = 100×0.2 mmol

= 20 mmol = 20 milli eq

20 milli eq. NaOH neutralise 20 milli eq of H_2SO_4

$\therefore$ Normality $= \dfrac{20}{200} = 0.1$ N

342. (a): 98% H_2SO_4 by mass means 98 g H_2SO_4 present in 100 g of the solution, that is, 100/1.80 mL = 55.5 mL

Also 98 g H_2SO_4 = 1 mol H_2SO_4

$\therefore$ Molarity of 98% H_2SO_4 solution $= \dfrac{1}{55.5} \times 1000$ mol L^{-1}

Now, $M_1 V_1 = M_2 V_2$

Hence, $\dfrac{1000}{55.5} M \times V_1 = 1000$ mL $\times$ 0.1 M or $V_1 = 5.55$ mL

343. (b): Suppose 1 L of 0.1 M $AgNO_3$ is mixed with 1 L of 0.2 M NaCl solution, then, 0.1 mol of $AgNO_3$ will react with 0.1 mol of NaCl to form 0.1 mol of $NaNO_3$ in the solution which will ionise to produce 0.1 mol NO_3^- ions. But now volume after mixing = 2 L. Hence, concentration of NO_3^- ions in the mixed solution = 0.1/2 = 0.05 M.

344. (a): Amount of $MgSO_4 = 0.02 \times 120 \times 1000$ mg = 240 mg

Now 120 mg $MgSO_4$ = 100 mg $CaCO_3$

$\therefore$ 240 mg $MgSO_4$ = 200 mg $CaCO_3$

Thus, 1 L (10^3 mL = 10^3 g = 10^6 mg) of water contains

= 200 mg of $CaCO_3$

Degree of hardness = 200 ppm

345. (a): Camphor has a very high cryoscopic constant (39.7°) and hence it gives a large depression in freezing point when an organic solute is dissolved in it.

346. (d): Molar mass of macromolecules (proteins, colloids) can be determined with greater accuracy by finding osmotic pressure because the magnitude of this colligative property is comparatively large even in dilute solutions.

MATCH THE FOLLOWING

347. (b): In an ideal solution, the intermolecular interactions between solute-solute (A–A) and solvent-solvent (B–B) are similar to the interaction between solute-solvent (A–B). The interaction between solute-solvent (A–B) is weaker than those of pure components (A–A or B–B) in solutions showing a positive deviation. The interaction between solute-solvent (A–B) is stronger than those of pure components (A–A or B–B) in solutions showing negative deviation.

348. (b): 0.91% NaCl solution is isotonic with RBCs > 0.91% is hypertonic < 0.91% is hypotonic, 5.85% NaCl solution means 1 N solution.

349. (d): Solubility of NH_4NO_3 increases with temperature but not continuously. Hence, (A) $\rightarrow$ (r)

Solubility of Li_2CO_3 decreases continuously with temperature. Hence, (B) $\rightarrow$ (s)

Solubility of $Na_2SO_4.10H_2O$ first increases up to 32.4°C and then decreases. Hence, (C) $\rightarrow$ (q)

Solubility of KCl increases continuously with temperature. Hence, (D) $\rightarrow$ (p)

350. (a): Shrinking of red blood cells is called plasmolysis. Swelling and bursting of red blood cells is called hemolysis. Solutions having same $[H^+]$ are called isohydric.

Solutions having the same molar concentration of particles in the solution have the same osmotic pressure and hence are iso-osmotic.

351. (d): (A) Molarity $= \frac{10.6}{106} \times \frac{1000}{100} = 1$ M

(B) Molarity $= \frac{34.2 \text{ g L}^{-1}}{342 \text{ g mol}^{-1}} = 0.1$ M

(C) 9.8% H_2SO_4 means 9.8 g in 100 g of solution. Volume of solution = 100/1.25 = 80 mL

Molarity $= \frac{9.8}{98} \times \frac{1}{80} \times 1000 = 1.25$ M

(D) 20% of ethanol solution means 20 cc ethanol in 100 cc of solution

Mass of solution = 100 × 0.938 = 93.8 g
Volume of water = 80 cc
Mass of water = 80 g
Mass of 20 cc ethanol = 93.8 – 80 = 13.8 g

Molarity $= \frac{13.8}{46} \times \frac{1}{100} \times 1000 = 3.0$ M

ASSERTION REASON

352. (a): R is the correct explanation of A.

353. (a): R is the correct explanation of A because Henry's law is applicable only when the solute does not undergo association or dissociation in the solution.

354. (c): Correct R. Both the solute and solvent will form the vapour but the vapour phase will be richer in the more volatile component.

355. (c): Correct R. Glycerol added to water will lower the vapour pressure of water.

356. (c): Correct R. Raoult's law is not applicable to those electrolytes which produce a non-ideal solution.

357. (c): Correct A. On adding NaCl to water, its vapour pressure decreases.
Correct R. Addition of a non-volatile solute lowers the vapour pressure.

358. (b): Correct explanation. Non-ideal solutions show positive or negative deviations.

359. (c): Correct R. CCl_4 breaks the H-bonding of CH_3OH molecules. Thus, stronger forces are replaced by weaker forces, that is, the solution shows positive deviation from Raoult's law (ΔH = +ve).

360. (c): Correct R. Water enters into the cells.

361. (c): Correct R. Polymer solutions possess very little elevation in boiling point or depression in freezing point.

362. (c): Correct R. As the solvent from the solution keeps on distilling over, the molality of the remaining solution keeps on increasing (otherwise, a solution of a particular concentration has a constant boiling point).

363. (d): Correct A. The freezing point keeps on becoming lower and lower.
Correct R. Depression in freezing point is a colligative property.

364. (d): Correct A. Higher the molal depression constant of the solvent used, higher is the depression in freezing point.
Correct R. Depression in freezing point depends upon the nature of the solvent.

365. (c): Correct R. Density of water is maximum at 277 K.

366. (c): Correct R. Camphor has a higher molal depression constant.

367. (a): R is the correct explanation of A.

368. (c): Correct R. Polymer solutions give an extremely small value of elevation in boiling point or depression in freezing point.

369. (a): R is the correct explanation of A.

370. (a): R is the correct explanation of A.

371. (b): Correct explanation. KCl is an electrolyte which dissociates whereas urea is a non-electrolyte which does not dissociate or associate in the aqueous solution.

372. (b): Correct explanation. 0.1 m NaCl = 0.2 m Na^+ and Cl^- ions; 0.1 m $BaCl_2$ = 0.3 m Ba^+ and Cl^- ions. Thus, concentration is 1.5 times. Hence, elevation in boiling point will be 1.5 times.

373. (b): Correct explanation. In water, acetic acid undergoes dissociation while in benzene, it undergoes association.

374. (d): Correct A. When methanol is added to water, the boiling point of water decreases.
Correct R. When a more volatile solute is added to a volatile solvent, vapour pressure of the solvent increases.

375. (b): Eq. wt. of $H_2C_2O_4.2H_2O = \frac{\text{Mol.mass}}{\text{Basicity}} = \frac{126}{2} = 63$

$\therefore$ Normality of the solution $= \frac{1.575}{6.3} \times \frac{1}{250} \times 1000 = 0.1$ N

Hence, Assertion is true.
Correct explanation. $H_2C_2O_4.2H_2O$ is a dibasic acid.

376. (b): Correct explanation. One molar aqueous solution has 1 mol in less than 1000 g of water while 1 molal has 1 mol in 1000 g of water.

377. (d): Correct A. $N_1V_1 + N_2V_2 = N_3(V_1 + V_3)$
$\therefore$ 100 ×0.1 + 100 × ×0.2 = N_3 (100 + 100)

or $N_3 = \frac{30}{200} = 0.15$ N

Reason R. Normalities of even similar solutions cannot be added.

378. (a): R is the correct explanation of A.

Electrochemistry

3.1 Redox Reactions

The reactions which involve both oxidation and reduction are called *redox reactions*. In these reactions, electrons are transferred from one reactant to another. A substance that can lose one or more electrons (gets oxidised) is called a *reducing agent* or *reductant* while a substance that can gain one or more electrons (gets reduced) is called an *oxidising agent* or *oxidant*. In this reaction, zinc loses electrons and gets oxidised whereas Cu^{2+} ions gain electrons and get reduced.

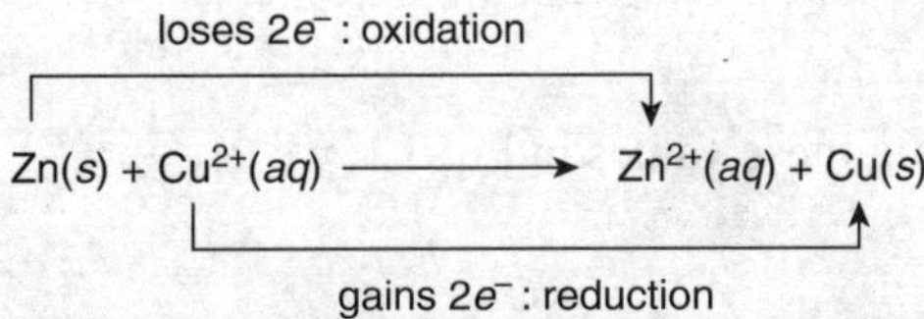

3.2 Metallic and Electrolytic Conductance

Conductors are divided into two classes.

(i) Those that conduct electricity *without undergoing any decomposition*. These are called *electronic conductors*. For example, metals, graphite and certain minerals. The conduction in this case is due the *flow of electrons*.

(ii) Those that undergo decomposition when current is passed through them. These are known as *electrolytic conductors* or *electrolytes*. For example, solutions of acids, bases and salts in water, fused salts, and so on.

In this case, the flow of electricity is due to the movement of ions. Hence, electrolytic conductance is also called *ionic conductance*.

3.2.1 Metallic Conductance

Electrical conductance through metals is called metallic conductance or electronic conductance. The electronic conductance depends on

- the nature and structure of the metal,
- the number of valence electrons per atom,
- the density of metal, and
- temperature (it decreases with an increase in temperature).

3.2.2 Electrolytes or Electrolytic Conductors

The flow of electric current through an electrolytic solution is called *electrolytic conduction*. In this type of conduction, charge is carried by ions. Therefore, it is also called ionic conductance. These substances do not conduct electricity in the solid state but conduct electricity in the molten state or in their aqueous solutions due to the movement of ions.

Non–electrolytes

The substances which do not conduct electricity either in their molten state or through their aqueous solutions are called non-electrolytes. For example, sugar, glucose, ethyl alcohol and urea.

3.3 Classification of Electrolytes

Electrolytes are classified into two main categories—strong electrolytes and weak electrolytes.

Strong electrolytes

The electrolytes that are almost completely dissociated into ions in solution and conduct electricity to a large extent are called *strong electrolytes*. For example, strong acids (HCl, HNO_3, H_2SO_4), strong bases (NaOH and KOH), and most of the inorganic salts.

Weak electrolytes

The electrolytes that dissociate to a small extent and hence conduct electricity to a small extent are called *weak electrolytes*. For example, weak acids (CH_3COOH, HCN, H_2CO_3, H_3PO_4) and weak bases [NH_4OH, $Ca(OH)_2$, $Al(OH)_3$].

The fraction of the total number of molecules of the electrolyte which ionises in the solution is called *degree of ionisation*. It is usually represented by α. For strong electrolytes, it is almost equal to 1 and for weak electrolytes, it is always less than 1.

3.3.1 Factors Affecting Electrolytic Conduction

The conductance of the solution of an electrolyte depends upon the following factors.

(i) *Nature of the electrolyte*: Strong electrolytes ionise almost completely in the solution and hence conduct electricity to a large extent whereas weak electrolytes ionise to a small extent and hence conduct electricity also to a small extent.

(ii) *Size of the ions produced and their solvation*: Greater the size of the ions or greater the solvation of the ions (that is, combination of the ions with the solvent), less is the conductance.

(iii) *Nature of the solvent and its viscosity*: Electrolytes ionise more in a polar solvent. Thus, greater the polarity of the solvent, greater is the ionisation and hence greater is the conductance. Similarly, greater the viscosity of a solvent, less is the conductance.

(iv) *Concentration of the solution*: Higher the concentration of the solution, less is the conduction. In a weak electrolyte, the ionisation is less whereas in a strong electrolyte, the *interionic attractions* are high at higher concentrations. With dilution, in the case of weak electrolytes, the ionisation increases and in the case of strong electrolytes, interionic attractions decrease and hence conduction increases.

(v) *Temperature*: On increasing the temperature, the dissociation increases and hence the conduction increases.

3.4 Electrical Resistance and Conductance

The law that gives the exact value of the resistance is known as *Ohm's law*. It states that, if to the ends of a conductor is applied a voltage 'E' and a current 'I' flows through it, then the resistance 'R' of the conductor is E/I. If one ampere of current flows through a conductor when a voltage of one volt is applied to it, the resistance of the conductor is taken as 1 ohm (written) as 1 Ω. Thus, according to Ohm's law,

$$R = \frac{E}{I} \quad \text{or} \quad \text{Ohms} = \frac{\text{Volts}}{\text{Amperes}}$$

In terms of SI base units, $\Omega = (\text{kg m}^2)/(\text{s}^3\text{A}^2)$. This is explained below:

$$\Omega = \frac{V}{A} = \frac{\text{Work per unit charge}}{A} = \frac{\text{Work}}{\text{Charge}} \times \frac{1}{A} = \frac{F \times l}{A \times s} \times \frac{1}{A}$$

$$= \frac{\text{m} \times a \times l}{A^2 s} = \frac{\text{kg} \times \text{m s}^{-2}}{A^2 s} = \frac{\text{kg m}^2}{s^3 A^2}$$

It is seen that, like metallic conductors, solutions of all electrolytes also obey Ohm's law. This result also follows from Ohm's law according to which $I \propto \frac{1}{R}$.

The reciprocal of the electrical resistance is called the *conductance*. It is usually represented by G. Thus, $G = \frac{1}{R}$.

Units: The units of conductance are: ohm^{-1} or mhos or siemens (S).

3.5 Specific, Equivalent and Molar Conductivities

Specific Conductivity (or simply, conductivity)

It is observed that the resistance R of a conductor is (i) directly proportional to its length (l) and (ii) inversely proportional to its area of cross section (a). That is,

$$R \propto \frac{l}{a} \quad \text{or} \quad R = \rho \frac{l}{a} \tag{3.1}$$

where ρ is a constant of proportionality, called the *specific resistance* or *resistivity*. Its value depends upon the material of the conductor. *Resistivity* is defined as the resistance of a conductor whose length is 1 cm and area of cross section is 1 cm^2. The reciprocal of resistivity is known as *specific conductance* or simply *conductivity*, κ (kappa). If κ is the conductivity and G is the conductance of the solution, then

$$R = \frac{1}{G} \quad \text{and} \quad \rho = \frac{1}{\kappa}$$

Substituting these values in Eq. 3.1, we get $\frac{1}{G} = \frac{1}{\kappa} \times \frac{l}{a}$

Or,

$$\kappa = G \times \frac{l}{a} \tag{3.2}$$

The *conductivity* of a solution is defined as the conductance of a solution of 1 cm length and having 1 sq. cm as the area of cross section.

Units: Resistivity $(\rho) = R = \frac{a}{l} = \text{ohm}\frac{(\text{cm}^2)}{\text{cm}} = \text{ohm cm}$ or Ω cm or Ω m in SI units

$$1\ \Omega\ \text{m} = 100\ \Omega\ \text{cm}$$

Specific conductivity (κ) $= \frac{1}{\rho} = \frac{1}{\text{ohm cm}} = \text{ohm}^{-1}\ \text{cm}^{-1}$ or $\Omega^{-1}\ \text{cm}^{-1}$ or S cm^{-1} or S m^{-1} in SI units

$$1\ \text{S cm}^{-1} = 100\ \text{S m}^{-1}$$

Substances having zero resistivity or infinite conductivity are known as superconductors.

3.5.1 Equivalent Conductivity

Equivalent conductivity of a solution at a dilution V is defined as the conductance of all the ions produced from one gram equivalent of the electrolyte dissolved in V cm^3 of the solution when the distance between the electrodes is one cm and the area of the electrodes is so large that the whole of the solution is contained between them. It is represented by Λ_{eq} (lambda).

Relationship Between Equivalent Conductivity and Specific Conductivity

When 1 cm^3 of the solution containing one gram equivalent of the electrolyte is considered, *the equivalent conductivity is equal to its specific conductivity.* In general, if the volume of the solution containing one gram equivalent of the electrolyte is V cm^3, we have, Equivalent conductivity = Specific conductivity × V

$$\Lambda_{eq} = \kappa_c \times V$$

In terms of concentration, if c gram equivalents are present in 1000 cm^3 of the solution, then the volume of the solution containing one gram equivalent will be $\frac{1000}{c}$, that is, $V = \frac{1000}{c}$. Hence, the above expression may be written as

$$\Lambda_{eq} = \kappa_c \times \frac{1000}{c_{eq}} = \kappa_c \times \frac{1000}{\text{Normality}}$$

Units: $\Lambda_{eq} = \kappa \times V = \text{ohms}^{-1}\text{cm}^{-1} \times \frac{\text{cm}^3}{\text{gram eq.}} = \text{ohms}^{-1}\text{cm}^{-2}$ (g eq)$^{-1}$

or Ω^{-1} cm^{2}eq^{-1} or S cm^2 eq^{-1} or m^2 eq^{-1} in SI units

$$1 \text{ S m}^2\text{eq}^{-1} = 10^4 \text{ S cm}^2\text{eq}^{-1}$$

3.5.2 Molar Conductivity

Molar conductivity of a solution at a dilution V is the conductance of all the ions produced from one mole of the electrolyte dissolved in V cm^3 of the solution when the electrodes are one cm apart and the area of the electrodes is so large that the whole of the solution is contained between them. It is usually represented by Λ_m.

Relationship Between Molar Conductivity and Specific Conductivity

As in the case of equivalent conductivity, the molar conductivity is related to the specific conductivity:

$$\Lambda_m = k_v \times V \quad \text{or} \quad \Lambda_m = k_c \times \frac{1000}{c} = k_c \times \frac{1000}{\text{Molarity}}$$

where κ is the specific conductivity, V is the volume of the solution containing *one mole of the electrolyte* and c is the *molar concentration,* that is, mol L^{-1} (or mol dm^{-3}).

Units: The units of Λ_m will be ohms^{-1}cm^{-2} mol^{-1} or S cm^{2}mol^{-1} or cm^{2}mol^{-1} in SI units

$$1 \text{ S m}^2 \text{ mol}^{-1} = 10^4 \text{ S cm}^2 \text{ mol}^{-1} \text{ or } 1 \text{ S cm}^2 \text{ mol}^{-1} = 10^4 \text{ S m}^2\text{mol}^{-1}$$

3.5.3 Specific Conductivity

Specific conductivity or *conductivity* (κ) is related to the conductance (G) according to the expression:

$$\kappa = G \times \frac{l}{a}$$

Thus, the conductivity of a solution can be determined by measuring its conductance and the distance (l) between the electrodes and the area of cross section (a) of each of the electrodes. For a particular cell, l/a is constant and this constant is called the *cell constant*. It is usually represented by G. Thus, $G = \frac{l}{a}$ = cell constant.

∴ Conductivity (κ) = Conductance (G) × Cell constant (G).

Units of cell constant,

$$G = \frac{l}{a} = \frac{\text{cm}}{\text{cm}^2} = \text{cm}^{-1} \left(\text{or m}^{-1} \text{ in SI units}\right) \tag{3.3}$$

3.5.4 Equivalent Conductivity

Equivalent conductivity (Λ_{eq}) is related to the specific conductivity (κ) according to the equation:

$$\kappa \times \frac{1000}{c_{eg}} = \frac{\kappa \times 1000}{\text{Molarity(M)}} \tag{3.4}$$

where c_{eg} is the concentration of the solution in gram equivalents per litre.

3.5.5 Molar Conductivity

The molar conductivity is related to the specific conductivity according to the relation:

$$\Lambda_m = \kappa \times \frac{1000}{c} = \frac{\kappa \times 1000}{\text{Molarity (M)}}$$

where c is the molar concentration. Thus, knowing molar concentration c and the specific conductivity κ, Λ_m can be calculated.

Worked Out Problem 3.1

0.5 Normal solution of a salt placed between two platinum electrodes 2.0 cm apart and of area of cross section 4.0 sq. cm has a resistance of 25 ohms. Calculate the equivalent conductivity of the solution.

Solution

Step 1: Calculation of specific conductivity.

Here, $l = 2.0$ cm, $a = 4.0$ cm^2

$$R = 25 \text{ ohms}$$

$$\therefore \quad \text{Conductance } G = \frac{1}{R} = \frac{1}{25} \text{ ohm}^{-1}$$

$$\text{Cell constant} = \frac{l}{a} = \frac{2 \text{ cm}}{4 \text{ cm}^2} = \frac{1}{2} \text{ cm}^{-1}$$

∴ Sp. conductivity (κ) = Observed conductance × Cell constant

$$= \frac{1}{25} \Omega^{-1} \times \frac{1}{2} \text{cm}^{-1} = 0.02 \, \Omega^{-1}\text{cm}^{-1}$$

Step 2: Calculation of equivalent conductivity.

$$\Lambda_{eq} = \kappa \times \frac{1000}{c_{eq}}$$

Here, $c = 0.5$ N, $\kappa = 0.02$ ohm^{-1} cm^{-1} (calculated above)

$$\therefore \quad \Lambda_{eq} = \frac{\left(0.02\ \Omega^{-1}\text{cm}^{-1}\right)\times\left(1000\ \text{cm}^3\ \text{L}^{-1}\right)}{\left(0.5\ \text{g eq L}^{-1}\right)} = 40\ \Omega^{-1}\ \text{cm}^2$$

eq^1 or 40 S cm^2 eq^1

Worked Out Problem 3.2

Resistance of a conductivity cell filled with 0.1 mol L^{-1} KCl solution is 100 Ω. If the resistance of the same cell when filled with 0.02 mol L^{-1} KCl solution is 520 Ω, calculate the conductivity and molar conductivity of 0.02 M KCl solution. The conductivity of 0.1 M KCl solution is 1.29 S/m.

Solution

(i) For 0.1 M KCl solution, $R = 100\ \Omega$, $\kappa = 1.29$ S m^{-1}
Cell constant = Conductivity × Resistance = 1.29 S m^{-1} × 100 Ω
= 129 m^{-1} (S = Ω^{-1}) = 1.29 cm^{-1}

(ii) Conductivity of 0.02 M KCl solution (κ) = $\frac{\text{Cell constant}}{\text{Resistance}} = \frac{129\ \text{m}^{-1}}{520\ \Omega}$
= 0.248 Ω^{-1} m^{-1} or 0.248 S m^{-1}
Concentration of the solution = 0.02 M mol L^{-1} = 0.02 ×10^3 mol m^{-3} = 20 mol m^{-3}

$$\Lambda_m = \frac{\kappa}{c_m} = \frac{0.00248\ \text{S cm}^{-1} \times 1000\ \text{cm}^3\ \text{L}^{-1}}{0.02\ \text{mol L}^{-1}} = 124\ \text{S m}^2\ \text{mol}^{-1}$$

3.6 Behaviour of Electrolytes

3.6.1 Variation of Conductance, Specific Conductivity, Equivalent Conductivity and Molar Conductivity with Concentration or Dilution

The conductance of a solution is due to the presence of ions in the solution. The greater the number of ions, the greater is the conductance. On dilution, more ions are produced in solution, so the conductance should also increase on dilution.

The specific conductivity of an electrolyte falls with dilution because the number of current-carrying particles, that is, the ions present per centimetre cube of the solution, becomes less and less on dilution.

3.6.2 Conductance Behaviour of Strong Electrolytes

The molar conductivity of strong electrolytes is found to vary with concentration according to the equation:

$$\Lambda^\circ_m = \Lambda^\circ_m - A\sqrt{c}$$

where A is a constant depending upon the type of the electrolyte, the nature of the solvent and the temperature, and Λ°_m is the molar conductivity at infinite dilution, called *limiting molar conductivity.* At higher concentrations, the *greater interionic attractions* retard the motion of ions and, therefore, the conductance falls with increasing concentrations. With a decrease in concentration (with dilution), the ions are far apart and, therefore, the interionic attractions decrease due to which the conductance increases with dilution and approaches a maximum limiting value at finite dilution, designated as Λ°_m or Λ^∞_m.

3.6.3 Conductance Behaviour of Weak Electrolytes

A weak electrolyte dissociates to a much lesser extent compared to a strong electrolyte, therefore, the conductance of a weak electrolyte is much lower than that of a strong electrolyte at the same concentration. There is *a very large increase in conductance with dilution especially near infinite dilution.* This is because *as the concentration of the weak electrolyte is reduced, more of it ionises.*

Figure 3.1 shows nearly a straight line. From the intercept (when $c^{1/2} = 0$), we find that

$$\Lambda^\circ_m = 150.0\ \text{S cm}^2\text{mol}^{-1}$$

and $A = -\text{slope} = \frac{\Delta y}{\Delta x} = \frac{150.0 - 147.0}{0.034} = 88.23$ S cm^{2}mol^{-1}/(mol L^{-1})$^{1/2}$

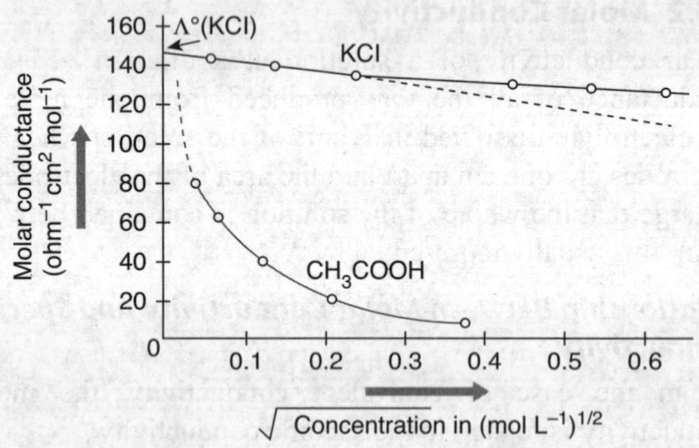

Fig. 3.1 Variation of molar conductivity of a strong electrolyte (KCl) and weak electrolyte (CH_3COOH) with concentration

3.7 Kohlrausch's Law

Kohlrausch said that *each ion makes a definite contribution to the total molar conductivity of an electrolyte at infinite dilution, irrespective of the nature of the other ion of the electrolyte.* It states that *the limiting molar conductivity of an electrolyte (molar conductivity at infinite dilution) is the sum of the limiting ionic conductivities of the cation and the anion each multiplied with the number of ions present in one formula unit of the electrolyte.*

Mathematically, Λ_m° for $A_xB_y = x\lambda_+^{\circ} + y\lambda_-^{\circ}$

where Λ_m° is the limiting molar conductivity of the electrolyte, λ_+° and λ_-° are the limiting molar conductivities of the cation (A^{y+}) and the anion (B^{x-}) respectively.

For example, Λ_m° for NaCl $= \lambda^{\circ}_{Na^+} + \lambda^{\circ}_{Cl^-}$, Λ_m° for $BaCl_2$ $= \lambda^{\circ}_{Ba^{2+}} + 2\lambda^{\circ}_{Cl^-}$,

$$\Lambda_m^{\circ} \text{ for } Al_2(SO_4)_3 = 2\lambda^{\circ}_{Al^{3+}} + 3\lambda^{\circ}_{SO_4^{2-}}$$

3.7.1 Applications of Kohlarausch's Law

(i) Calculation of molar conductivity at infinite dilution (Λ°) for weak electrolytes: The molar conductivity of a weak electrolyte at infinite dilution cannot be determined experimentally; firstly because the conductance of such a solution is low and secondly because the dissociation of such an electrolyte is not complete even at very high dilutions. The molar conductivity of such an electrolyte at infinite dilution can be calculated using Kohlrausch's law.

Worked Out Problem 3.3

If the molar conductivities at infinite dilution of NaCl, HCl and CH_3COONa (NaAc) are 126.4, 425.9 and 91.0 S $cm^2 mol^{-1}$ respectively, what will be that of acetic acid (HAc)? **(NCERT)**

Solution

According to Kohrausch's law Λ° for CH_3COOH = $\left(\lambda^{\circ}_{CH_3COO^-}\right) + \lambda^{\circ}_{H^+}$

$$\Lambda^{\circ} \text{ for NaCl} = \lambda^{\circ}_{Na^+} + \lambda^{\circ}_{Cl^-} = 126.4 \text{ S cm}^2 \text{ mol}^{-1} \quad \text{(i)}$$

$$\Lambda^{\circ} \text{ for HCl} = \lambda^{\circ}_{H^+} + \lambda^{\circ}_{Cl^-} = 425.9 \text{ S cm}^2\text{mol}^{-1} \quad \text{(ii)}$$

$$\Lambda^{\circ} \text{ for } CH_3COONa = \lambda^{\circ}_{CH_3COO^-} + \lambda^{\circ}_{Na^+}$$

$$= 91.0 \text{ S cm}^2\text{mol}^{-1} \quad \text{(iii)}$$

Adding Eqs (ii) and (iii) and subtracting (i), we get,

$$\lambda^{\circ}_{H^+} + \lambda^{\circ}_{Cl^-} + \lambda^{\circ}_{CH_3COO^-} + \lambda^{\circ}_{Na^+} - \lambda^{\circ}_{Na^+} - \lambda^{\circ}_{Cl^-}$$

$$= 425.9 + 91.0 - 126.4 \text{ S cm}^2\text{mol}^{-1}$$

or $\lambda^{\circ}_{CH_3COO^-} + \lambda^{\circ}_{H^+} = 390.5 \text{ S cm}^2 \text{ mol}^{-1}$, that is,

$$\Lambda^{\circ} \text{ for } CH_3COOH = 390.5 \text{ S cm}^2 \text{ mol}^{-1}$$

(ii) Calculation of the degree of dissociation:

$$\text{Degree of dissociation } (\alpha) = \frac{\Lambda_m^c}{\Lambda_m^{\circ}}$$

However, this relationship is found to hold good only for *weak electrolytes*.

(iii) Calculation of dissociation constant of a weak electrolyte: Knowing the degree of dissociation α (as calculated above), the dissociation constant (K) of a weak electrolyte like CH_3COOH or NH_4OH at a concentration c of the solution can be calculated using the formula,

$$K_c = \frac{c\alpha^2}{1-\alpha} \quad (3.5)$$

(iv) Calculation of solubility of a sparingly soluble salt: Salts such as AgCl, $BaSO_4$ and $PbSO_4$ which dissolve to a very small extent in water As their solutions are saturated, their concentration is equal to their solubility. Thus, by determining the specific conductivity (κ) and the molar conductivity, we can calculate their solubility.

(v) Calculation of ionic product of water: It is found that the ionic conductances of H^+ and OH^- at infinite dilution are $\lambda^{\circ}_{H^+} = 349.8 \text{ S cm}^2 \text{ mol}^{-1}$ and $\lambda^{\circ}_{OH^-} = 198.5$ S $cm^2 mol^{-1}$. By Kohlraushch's law, $\lambda^{\circ}_{H_2O} = \lambda^{\circ}_{H^+} + \lambda^{\circ}_{OH^-} = 349.8 + 198.5 = 548.7 \text{ S cm}^2\text{mol}^{-1}$.

Specific conductance of pure water at 298 K is found to be: $\kappa = 5.54\times10^{-8} \text{ S cm}^{-1}$

$$\text{Applying the formula, } \Lambda_m^{\circ} = \kappa \times \frac{1000}{\text{Molarity}}$$

$$\text{Molarity, that is, } [H^+] \text{ or } [OH^-] = \frac{\kappa \times 1000}{\Lambda_m^{\circ}}$$

$$= \frac{5.54\times10^{-8}\times1000}{548.3} = 1.01\times10^{-7} \text{ g ions L}^{-1}$$

$$\therefore K_w = [H^+] \text{ or } [OH^-] = (1.01\times10^{-7})\times\left(1.01\times10^{-7}\right)$$

$$= 1.02\times10^{-14}$$

Worked Out Problem 3.4

The conductivity of a 0.01 M solution of acetic acid at 298 K is 1.65×10^{-4} S cm^{-1}. Calculate

(i) molar conductivity of the solution
(ii) degree of dissociation of CH_3COOH
(iii) dissociation constant for acetic acid

given that $\lambda^{\circ}(H^+) = 349.1$ S $cm^2 mol^{-1}$ and $\lambda^{\circ}(CH_3COO^-) = 40.9$ S $cm^2 mol^{-1}$.

Solution

(i) Calculation of molar conductivity of solution

$$\Lambda = \frac{\kappa\times1000}{C}$$

$$\kappa = 1.65\times10^{-4} \text{ S cm}^{-1}, C = 0.01 \text{ M}$$

$$\Lambda = \frac{1.65\times10^{-4}\times1000}{0.01} = 16.5 \text{ S cm}^2 \text{ mol}^{-1}$$

(ii) Calculation of degree of dissociation of acetic acid.

$$\alpha = \frac{\Lambda^c}{\Lambda^{\circ}}$$

$$\Lambda^{\circ}(CH_3COOH) = \lambda^{\circ}(H^+) + \lambda^{\circ}(CH_3COO^-)$$
$$= 349.1 + 40.9 = 390\ S\ cm^2\ mol^{-1}$$
$$\therefore \alpha = \frac{16.5}{390} = 0.0423$$

(iii) Calculation of dissociation constant, K
Acetic acid dissociaties as:

$$CH_3COOH \rightleftharpoons CH_3COO^- + H^+$$

Initial conc.	c	0	0
Equilibrium conc.	$c(1-\alpha)$	$c\alpha$	$c\alpha$

$$\text{Dissociation constant, } K = \frac{[CH_3COO^-][H^+]}{CH_3COOH}$$
$$= \frac{c \times c}{c(1-a)} = \frac{c^2}{1-a}$$

Substituting the values,

$$K = \frac{0.01 \times (0.0423)^2}{1 - 0.0423} = 1.87 \times 10^{-5}$$

3.8 Galvanic Cells

When a zinc rod is placed in copper sulfate solution (Fig. 3.2), the solution is found to be warmer as the reaction proceeds according to the equation.

$$Zn(s) + CuSO_4(aq) \rightarrow ZnSO_4(aq) + Cu(s)$$

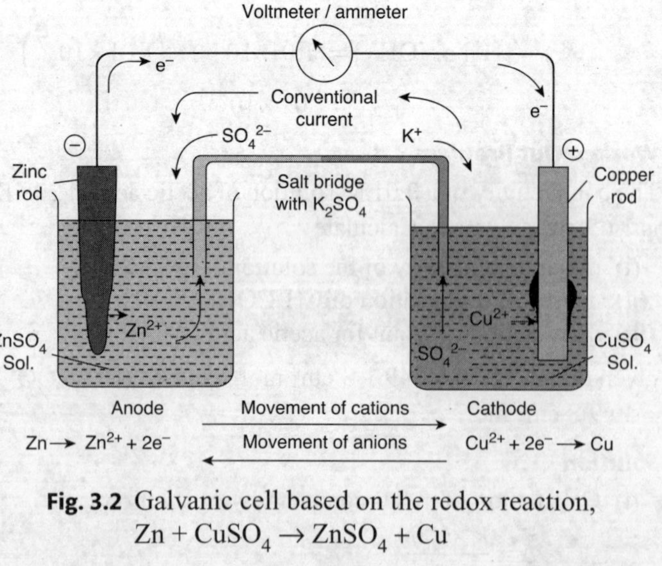

Fig. 3.2 Galvanic cell based on the redox reaction, $Zn + CuSO_4 \rightarrow ZnSO_4 + Cu$

A device used to convert chemical energy produced in a redox reaction into electrical energy is called a *galvanic cell* or *voltaic cell*.

During the reaction, zinc is oxidised to Zn^{2+} ions which go into the solution. Therefore,

$$Zn \rightarrow Zn^{2+} + 2e^- \quad \text{(Oxidation half reaction)}$$

The zinc rod gradually loses weight. The electrons released at the zinc electrode move towards the other electrode through the outer circuit. Here, these are accepted by Cu^{2+} ions of $CuSO_4$ solution which are reduced to copper. The metal gets deposited on the copper electrode.

$$Cu^{2+} + 2e^- \rightarrow Cu \quad \text{(Reduction half reaction)}$$

The first reaction is called the *oxidation half reaction* and the second is called the *reduction half reaction.*

3.8.1 Salt Bridge and its Function

A salt bridge is a U-shaped tube containing a concentrated solution of an inert electrolyte such as KCl, KNO_3, K_2SO_4 or a solidified solution of such an electrolyte in agar agar and gelatine. Its function is to allow the movement of ions from one solution to the other without mixing of the two solutions. Thus, whereas electrons flow in the outer circuit in the wire, the inner circuit is completed by the flow of ions from one solution to the other through the salt bridge. Moreover, it helps to maintain the electrical neutrality of the solution in the two half cells.

- The zinc electrode at which *oxidation* takes place is called the *anode*. The copper electrode at which reduction takes place is called the cathode.
- Since electrons are produced at the zinc electrode, this electrode is *rich* in electrons and *pushes* the electrons into the external circuit and hence it is designated as the *negative pole*. The other electrode, that is the copper electrode, is in need of electrons for the reduction of Cu^{2+} ions to Cu. This electrode is *deficient* in electrons and *pulls* the electrons from the external circuit, therefore it acts as the *positive pole.*

The cell now acts like an electrolytic cell called the *Daniell cell* (Fig. 3.3). It has an electrical potential of 1.1 V when the concentration of Zn^{2+} and Cu^{2+} ions is unity (1 mol dm^{-3}).

A popular form of this cell is shown in Fig. 3.4.

Redox Reaction between Copper and Silver Nitrate Solution

The reaction is

$$Cu + 2AgNO_3 \rightarrow Cu(NO_3)_2 + 2Ag$$

Or, it may be written as:

$$Cu + 2Ag^+ \rightarrow Cu^{2+} + 2Ag$$

The two half reactions will be:

$$Cu \rightarrow Cu^{2+} + 2e^- \quad \text{(Oxidation half reaction)}$$
$$2Ag^+ + 2e^- \rightarrow 2Ag \quad \text{(Reduction half reaction)}$$

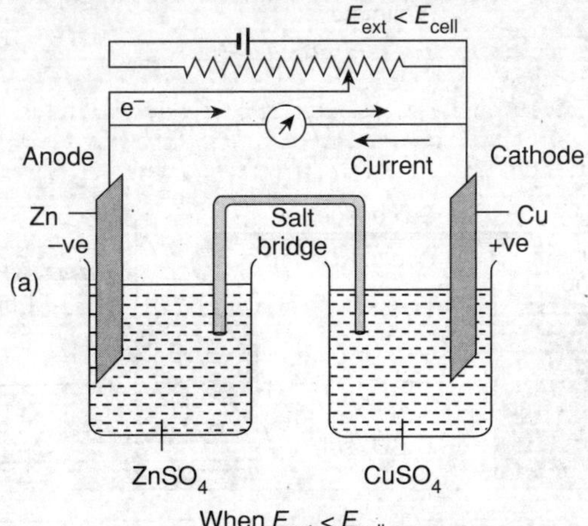

When $E_{ext} < E_{cell}$

(i) Electrons flow from Zn rod to Cu rod. Hence, current flows from Cu to Zn.

(ii) Zn dissolves at anode and Cu deposits at cathode.

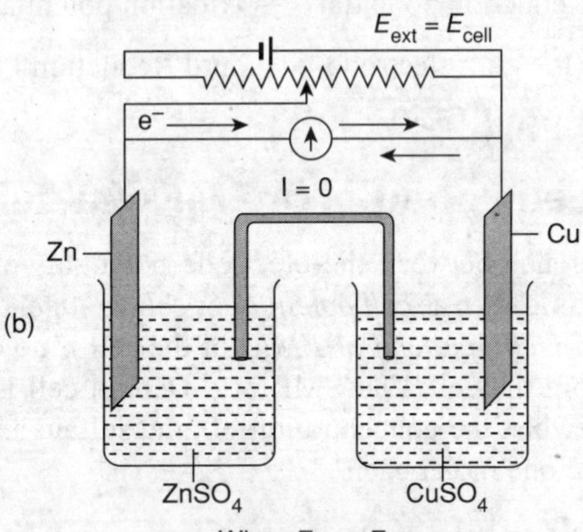

When $E_{ext} = E_{cell}$

(i) No flow of electrons or current.

(ii) No chemical reaction.

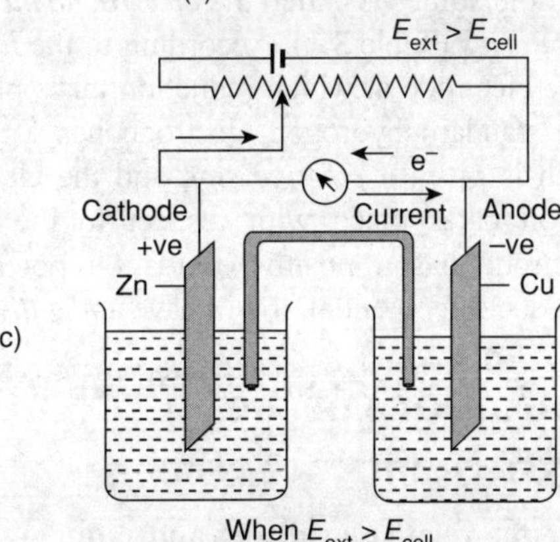

When $E_{ext} > E_{cell}$

(i) Electrons flow from Cu to Zn. Current flows from Zn to Cu.

(ii) Zn is deposited at Zn electrode and Cu dissolves at Cu electrode.

Fig. 3.3 Direction of flow of current on applying external opposing potential when **(a)** $E_{external} < E_{cell}$ **(b)** $E_{external} = E_{cell}$ **(c)** $E_{external} > E_{cell}$

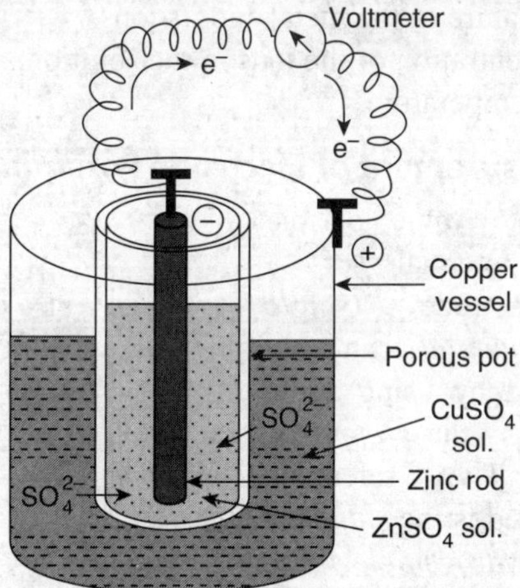

Fig. 3.4 Daniell cell

3.8.2 Representation of Galvanic Cell

The galvanic cell is represented in a manner as illustrated below for the Daniell cell.

$$Zn \mid Zn^{2+}(c_1) \parallel Cu^{2+}(c_2) \mid Cu$$

The electrode on the left hand side is written by writing the symbol of the metal (or the gas) first, followed by the symbol of the ion with its concentration in brackets. The electrode on the right hand side is written by first writing the ions along with its concentration in brackets followed by the symbol of the metal (or the gas). Single vertical lines represent the phase boundaries of the electrodes and the double line represents the salt bridge, c_1 and c_2 represent the concentrations of Zn^{2+} ions and Cu^{2+} ions respectively.

3.9 Electrode Potential and EMF of Galvanic Cell

Electrode Potential

The flow of electric current in an electrochemical cell indicates that a potential difference exists between two electrodes. The *electrical potential difference* set up between the metal and its ions in the solution is called *electrode potential*. Or, the electrode potential may be simply defined as, the tendency of an electrode to lose or gain electrons when it is in contact with solution of its own ions. Electrode potential may be of two types.

(i) Oxidation potential: The tendency of an electrode to lose electrons or to get oxidised is called its *oxidation potential.*

(ii) Reduction potential: The tendency of an electrode to gain electrons or to get reduced is called its *reduction potential.*

The oxidation potential is the reverse of the reduction potential. For example, if the reduction potential of Zn is –0.76 volts, its oxidation potential is +0.76 volts. The electrode potential depends upon:

- the nature of the metal and its ions,
- concentration of the ions in the solution, and
- the temperature.

3.9.1 Measurement of Electrode Potential

The absolute value of the electrode potential of a single electrode (*single electrode potential*) can only be measured by using some electrode as the *reference electrode.* The reference electrode used is the *standard* or *normal hydrogen electrode* (*SHE* or *NHE*). In the standard hydrogen gas electrode, hydrogen gas at 1 bar pressure is passed into 1 M HCl at 298 K in which a foil of platinum coated with platinum black (finely divided platinum) remains immersed. It simply acts as an inert electrode through which inflow or outflow of electrons takes place (Fig. 3.5).

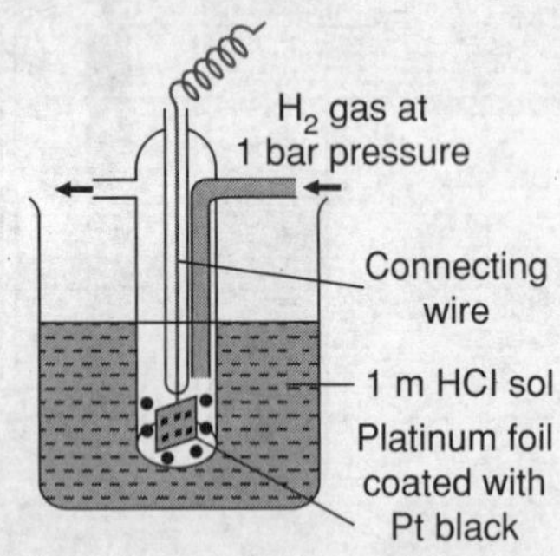

Fig. 3.5 Hydrogen electrode

When in a cell, if this electrode acts as the anode (oxidation takes place), the following reaction takes place.

$$H_2 \rightarrow 2H^+ + 2e^-$$

That is, some hydrogen gas changes into H^+ ions which go into the solution. When this electrode acts as the cathode (reduction takes place), the following reaction occurs.

$$2H^+ + 2e^- \rightarrow H_2$$

That is, some H^+ ions from the solution change into H_2 gas. Thus, the electrode is reversible with respect to H^+ ions. This electrode is usually represented as: Pt, $H_2(g)$ | H^+ (Conc = *c*). The electrode potential of the standard hydrogen electrode is taken as 0.000 at 298 K.

To determine the electrode potential of any electrode, a cell is set up using this electrode as one of the electrodes and the second electrode is the standard hydrogen electrode. The EMF of the cell is measured.

emf = Reduction potential of cathode – Reduction potential of anode

or, $E_{cell} = E(\text{cathode}) - E(\text{anode})$

Determination of standard electrode potential of Zn/Zn^{2+} electrode: A cell comprising a zinc electrode immersed in 1 M $ZnSO_4$ solution and a standard hydrogen electrode is set up (Fig. 3.16). The EMF of the above cell comes out to be 0.76 volt. Hence, the standard electrode potential of the Zn/Zn^{2+} electrode = 0.76 volt. Further, the direction of flow of current indicates that oxidation takes place at the zinc electrode. Hence, 0.76 volt is the *standard oxidation potential* of the Zn/Zn^{2+} electrode.

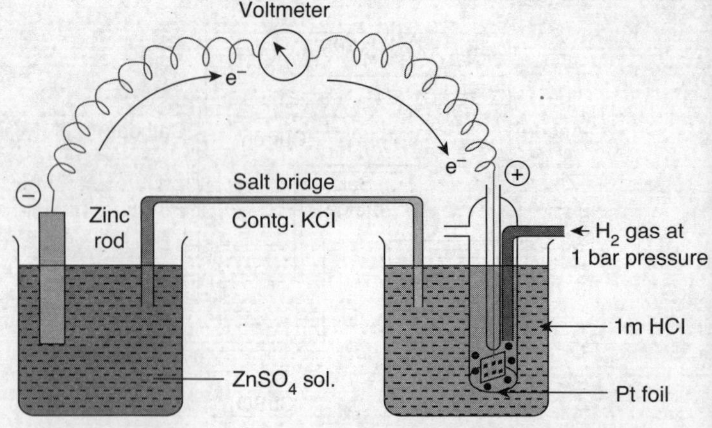

Fig. 3.6 Measurement of standard potential of Zn/Zn^{2+} elctrode using standard hydrogen electrode as the reference electrode

Reduction potential = –Oxidation potential

Thus, for the zinc electrode, Standard Reduction Potential = –0.76 V.

3.10 Cell Potential or EMF of a Cell

The difference between the electrode potentials of the two half cells is known as *cell potential* or *cell voltage.* It is called *electromotive force (emf or EMF)* of the cell if no current is drawn from the cell. The EMF of a Daniell cell is 1.1 volt at 298 K when the concentration of zinc sulfate and copper sulfate are one molar each.

3.11 Electrochemical Series

The arrangement of elements in the order of increasing electrode potential values is called the *electrochemical series* or the *activity series* (Table 3.1). According to the *latest sign convention*, the electrode at which reduction takes place with respect to the standard hydrogen electrode has a reduction potential which is given a *positive sign* and the electrode at which oxidation takes place with respect to the standard hydrogen electrode has a positive oxidation potential (or, expressed as reduction potential, it will have a *negative sign*).

3.12 Applications of the Electrochemical Series

(i) Compare the relative oxidising and reducing powers: F_2 has the highest reduction potential and Li^+ ion has the lowest reduction potential, F_2 is reduced most easily whereas Li^+ ions are reduced with the greatest difficulty. Therefore, F_2 is the strongest oxidising agent whereas the Li^+ ion is the weakest oxidising agent.

(ii) Compare the relative activities of metals: A metal with greater oxidation potential can displace metals with lower oxidation potentials from their salt solutions.

Table 3.1 Standard reduction potentials at 298 K (Electrochemical series)

Electrode	Electrode reaction (Oxidised form + ne^- Reduced form)	$E^\ominus$ (V)
$F_2 \mid F^-$	$F_2(g) + 2e^- \rightarrow 2F^-(aq)$	2.87
$Co^{3+} \mid Co^{2+}$	$Co^{3+} + e^- \rightarrow Co^{2+}$	1.81
$H_2O_2 \mid H_2O$	$H_2O_2 + 2H^+ + 2e^- \rightarrow 2H_2O$	1.78
$MnO_2, H^+ 1 Mn^{2+}$	$MnO_2(s) + 4H^+ + 2e^- \rightarrow Mn^{2+} + 2H_2O$	1.61
$Au^{3+} \mid Au$	$Au^{3+} + 3e^- \rightarrow Au(s)$	1.50
$MnO_4^- \mid Mn^{2+}$	$MnO_4^- + 8H^+ + 5e^- \rightarrow Mn^{2+} + 4H_2O$	1.49
$Cl_2 \mid Cl^-$	$Cl_2(g) + 2e^- \rightarrow 2Cl^-$	1.36
$Cr_2O_7^{2-}, H^+ \mid Cr^{3+}$	$Cr_2O_7^{2-} + 4H^+ + 6e^- \rightarrow 2Cr^{3+} + 7H_2O$	1.33
$O_2, H^+ \mid H_2O$	$O_2 + 4H^+ + 4e^- \rightarrow 2H_2O$	1.23
$Br_2 \mid Br^-$	$Br_2(l) + 2e^- \rightarrow 2Br^-$	1.09
$NO_3^-, H^+ \mid NO$	$NO_3^- + 4H^+ + 3e^- \rightarrow NO(g) + 2H_2O$	0.97
$Hg^{2+} \mid Hg_2^{2+}$	$2Hg^{2+} + 2e^- \rightarrow Hg_2^{2+}$	0.92
$ClO^- \mid Cl^-$	$ClO^- + H_2O + 2e^- \rightarrow Cl^- + 2OH^-$	0.89
$Hg^{2+} \mid Hg$	$Hg^{2+} + 2e^- \rightarrow Hg$	0.85
$Ag^+ \mid Ag$	$Ag^+ + e^- \rightarrow Ag$	0.80
$Hg_2^{2+} \mid Hg$	$Hg_2^{2+} + e^- \rightarrow 2Hg$	0.79
$Fe^3 \mid Fe^{2+}$	$Fe^{3+} + e^- \rightarrow Fe^{2+}$	0.78
$MnO_4^- \mid MnO_4^{2-}$	$MnO_4^- + e^- \rightarrow MnO_4^{2-}$	0.56
$1_2 \mid I^-$	$I_2 + 2e^- \rightarrow 2I^-$	0.54
$Cu^+ \mid Cu$	$Cu^+ + e^- \rightarrow Cu$	0.52
$Cu^{2+} \mid Cu$	$Cu^{2+} + 2e^- \rightarrow Cu$	0.34
$AgCl \mid Ag$	$AgCl + e^- \rightarrow Ag + Cl^-$	0.22
$Cu^{2+} \mid Cu$	$Cu^{2+} + e^- \rightarrow Cu^+$	0.15
$AgBr \mid Ag$	$AgBr + e^- \rightarrow Ag + Br$	0.10
$H^+ \mid H_2$	**$2H^+ + \mid 2e \rightarrow H_2$**	**0.00**
$Fe^{3+} \mid Fe$	$Fe^{3+} + 3e^- \rightarrow Fe$	−0.04
$Pb^{2+} \mid Pb$	$Pb^{2+} + 2e^- \rightarrow Pb$	−0.13
$Sn^{2+} \mid Sn$	$Sn^{2+} + 2e^- \rightarrow Sn$	−0.16
$Ni^{2+} \mid Ni$	$Ni^{2+} + 2e^- \rightarrow Ni$	−0.25
$Co^{2+} \mid Co$	$Co^{2+} + 2e^- \rightarrow Co$	− 0.28
$Cd^{2+} \mid Cd$	$Cd^{2+} + 2e^- \rightarrow Cd$	−0.40
$Fe^{2+} \mid Fe$	$Fe^{2+} + 2e^- \rightarrow Fe$	− 0.44
$Cr^{3+} \mid Cr$	$Cr^+ + 3e^- \rightarrow Cr$	−0.74
$Zn^{2+} \mid Zn$	$Zn^{2+} + 2e^- \rightarrow Zn$	− 0.7
$Mn^{2+} \mid Mn$	$Mn^{2+} + 2e^{-+} \rightarrow Mn$	− 1.18
$Al^{3+} \mid Al$	$Al^{3+} + 3e^- \rightarrow Al$	−1.66
$Mg^{2+} \mid Mg$	$Mg^{2+} + 2e^- \rightarrow Mg$	−2.36
$Ce^{3+} \mid Ce$	$Ce^{3+} + 3e^- \rightarrow Ce$	− 2.48
$Na^+ \mid Na$	$Na^+ + e^- \rightarrow Na$	−2.71
$Ca^{2+} \mid Ca$	$Ca^{2+} + 2e^- \rightarrow Ca$	−2.87
$Ba^{2+} \mid Ba$	$Ba^{2+} + 2e^- \rightarrow Ba$	−2.91
$Cs^+ \mid Cs$	$Cs^+ + e^- \rightarrow Cs$	−2.92
$K^\mid \mid K$	$K^+ + e^- \rightarrow K$	− 2.93
$Li^+ \mid Li$	$Li^+ + e^- \rightarrow Li$	−3.05

Strongest reducing agent (top, left) — Weakest oxidising agent (top, right)

INCREASING STRENGTH OF OXIDISING AGENT (arrow pointing upward) — INCREASING STRENGTH OF REDUCING AGENT (arrow pointing downward)

Weakest oxidising agent (bottom, left) — Strongest reducing agent (bottom, right)

(iii) Calculate the standard EMF of any galvanic cell (E_{cell}):
Standard EMF of the cell

$$= \begin{bmatrix} \text{Standard reduction potential} \\ \text{of the reduction half reaction} \end{bmatrix} - \begin{bmatrix} \text{Standard reduction potential} \\ \text{of the oxidation half reaction} \end{bmatrix}$$

Worked Out Problem 3.5

Calculate the standard EMF of a cell which involves the cell reaction: $Zn + 2\,Ag^+ \rightarrow Zn^{2+} + 2\,Ag$, given that $E^\circ_{Zn,Zn^{2+}} = 0.76$ volt and $E^\circ_{Ag,Ag^+} = -0.80$ volts.

Solution

The cell reaction may be split into two half reactions:

$$Zn \rightarrow Zn^{2+} + 2Ag \quad \text{(Oxidation half reaction)}$$
$$2Ag^+ + 2e^- \rightarrow 2Ag \quad \text{(Reduction half reaction)}$$

Here, we are given the standard oxidation potentials as $E^\circ_{Zn,\,Zn^{2+}} = 0.76$ volt and $E^\circ_{Ag,\,Ag^+} = -0.80$ volt

We need the oxidation potential of the zinc electrode but the reduction potential of the silver electrode.

Reduction potential of Ag electrode = –Oxidation potential of Ag electrode

$$0 - (0.80 \text{ volt}) = +0.80 \text{ volt}$$

Std. EMF of the cell = Std. oxidation potential of zinc electrode + Std. reduction potential of Ag electrode

$$+0.76 + 0.80 \text{ volt} = 1.56 \text{ volts}$$

Alternatively, as oxidation takes place at the zinc electrode and reduction at the silver electrode, by convention, the cell may be represented as:

$$Zn \,|\, Zn^{2+} \,||\, Ag^+ \,|\, Ag$$

E°_{cell} = Standard reduction potential of RHS electrode ($E^\circ_{cathode}$) – Standard reduction potential of LHS electrode (E°_{anode}).

As the standard oxidation potential of the zinc electrode and silver electrode are given as 0.76 volt and –0.80 volt, their standard reduction potentials will be –0.76 volt and +0.80 volt respectively. Hence,

$$E^\circ_{cell} = 0.80 - (-0.76) = 1.56 \text{ volt}$$

(iv) Predict whether a metal reacts with acid to give hydrogen gas:
All metals lying above hydrogen in the electrochemical series react with the acid to give hydrogen gas. Further, evidently, lower the reduction potential (more negative the reduction potential) higher is the reactivity.

(v) Predict the spontaneity of a redox reaction: For a redox reaction to be spontaneous, the EMF of the cell must be positive. If the EMF comes out to be negative, the direct reaction, as given, cannot take place; the reverse reaction may take place.

Worked Out Problem 3.6

Predict whether zinc and silver react with 1 M sulfuric acid to give out hydrogen gas or not, given that the standard reduction potential of zinc and silver are –0.76 volt and 0.80 volt respectively.

Solution

(a) To predict reaction of zinc with sulfuric acid: If it reacts, the following reaction should take place:

$$Zn + H_2SO_4 \rightarrow ZnSO_4 + H_2, \text{ that is,}$$
$$Zn + 2H^+ \rightarrow Zn^{2+} + H_2$$

By convention, the cell will be represented as:
$Zn \,|\, Zn^{2+} \,||\, H^+ \,|\, H_2$

Std. EMF of the cell (E°_{cell})

$$= \begin{bmatrix} \text{Std redn pot. of} \\ \text{RHS electrode} \end{bmatrix} - \begin{bmatrix} \text{Std redn pot. of} \\ \text{LHS electrode} \end{bmatrix}$$
$$= 0 - (-0.76) = +0.76 \text{ volt}$$

Thus, the EMF of the cell comes out to be positive. Hence, the reaction takes place.

(b) To predict the reaction of silver with sulfuric acid: If it reacts, the following reaction should take place:

$$2Ag + H_2SO_4 \rightarrow Ag_2SO_4 + H_2, \text{ that is,}$$
$$2Ag + 2H^+ \rightarrow 2Ag^+ + H_2$$

By convention, the cell may be represented as:
$Ag \,|\, Ag^+ \,||\, H^+ \,|\, H_2$

$$E^\circ_{cell} = E^\circ_{H^+,H_2} - E^\circ_{Ag^+,\,Ag} = 0 - 0.80 = -0.80 \text{ volt}$$

Thus, the EMF of the supposed cell comes out to be negative. Hence, this reaction does not take place.

3.12.1 Effect of Electrolyte Concentration and Temperature on the Electrode Potential (Nernst Equation for Electrode Potential)

The electrode potential of an electrode is said to be the *standard electrode potential* if it is measured under standard conditions, that is, electrolyte concentration is 1 M and the temperature is 298 K. However, if the electrolyte concentration is different from 1 M and/or the temperature is different from 298 K, the electrode potential has a different value. This value is obtained using the Nernst equation. In general,

$$M^{n+} + ne^- \rightarrow M \qquad (\text{for example, } Zn^{2+} + 2e^- \rightarrow Zn)$$

The Nernst equation is

$$E\,(M^{n+} \,|\, M) = E^\circ\,(M^{n+} \,|M) - \frac{RT}{nF}\ln\frac{[M(s)]}{[M^{n+}(aq)]}$$

or $E\,(M^{n+} \mid M) = E^\circ\,(M^{n+} \mid M) - \frac{2.303\,RT}{nF}\log\frac{[M(s)]}{[M^{n+}(aq)]}$

$(\because \ln x = 2.303 \log x)$

where $E\,(M^{n+} \mid M)$ = Electrode potential.

$E^\circ(M^{n+} \mid M)$ = Standard electrode potential [for a 1 M solution of metal ions, M^{n+} (aq)], R = gas constant, T = temperature, F = faraday of electricity, n = number of electrons gained during the electrode reaction, $[M^{n+}(aq)]$ = molar concentration of ions, [M] = molar concentration of metal.

or $E\,(M^{n+} \mid M) = E^\circ\,(M^{n+} \mid M) - \frac{0.059}{n}\log\frac{1}{[M^{n+}(aq)]}$

It may be noted that the concentration of the solid phase, $[M(s)]$ is taken to be unity.

3.12.2 Effect of Electrolyte Concentration and Temperature on the EMF of a Cell (Nernst Equation for the EMF of a Cell)

In general, if the cell reaction is

$$aA + bB \xrightarrow{ne^-} xX + yY$$

Applying Nernst equation, we have E_{cell} =

$$E^\circ_{cell} - \frac{RT}{2F}\ln\frac{[X]^x.[Y]^y}{[A]^a.[B]^b}$$

At 25°C (298 K),

$$E_{cell} = E^\circ_{cell} - \frac{0.0591}{n}\log\frac{[X]^x.[Y]^y}{[A]^a.[B]^b} \quad (3.6)$$

where n is the number of electrons involved in the cell reaction.

3.13 Concentration Cells

Concentration cells are the cells in which either the two electrodes are of the same material and the concentration of the electrolyte in them is different, or the two electrodes have different concentration but they are immersed in the same solution of the electrolyte. The former are called *electrolyte concentration cells* while the latter are called *electrode concentration cells*. The most common concentration cell is the electrolyte concentration cells. For example,

$$H_2 \mid H^+ (C_1) \parallel H^+ (C_2) \mid H_2$$

and $$Zn \mid Zn^{2+} (C_1) \parallel Zn^{2+} (C_2) \mid Zn$$

One such cell consisting of zinc electrodes is shown in Fig. 3.7. The EMF of a concentration cell at 298 K is given by

$$E_{cell} = \frac{0.0591}{n}\log\frac{C_2}{C_1}$$

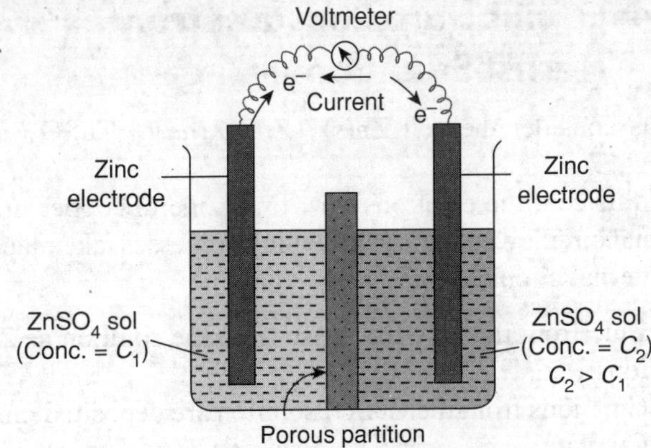

Fig. 3.7 Concentration cell consisting of zinc electrodes

Obviously, the EMF of the cell will be positive only if $C_2 > C_1$. In such a cell, *oxidation* takes place on the electrode *with lower concentration*. Hence, it acts as the anode (or –ve pole). The *reduction* takes place on the electrode *with higher concentration* which, therefore, acts as the cathode (or +ve pole).

Thus, there is *no net chemical reaction*. It simply involves the transfer of electrolyte from one concentration to the other.

Applying Nernst equation at 298 K,

$$E_{cell} = -\frac{0.0591}{n}\log\frac{C_1}{C_2} = \frac{0.0591}{n}\log\frac{C_2}{C_1} \quad (3.7)$$

Further, as the cell reaction proceeds, C_2 decreases whereas C_1 increases till the two become equal, that is, $C_1 = C_2$. At this stage, $E_{cell} = 0$ and hence the cell stops working.

Similarly, in a concentration cell of the type, Pt, H_2 (P_1 atm) | H^+ (conc. = C) | $H_2(P_2$ atm), Pt (called an electrode concentration cell) in which the two electrodes are immersed in the same solution but have different pressure or concentrations,

$$E_{cell} = \frac{0.0591}{n}\log\frac{P_1}{P_2}\ (P_1 > P_2) \quad (3.8)$$

Worked Out Problem 3.7

A cell consists of two hydrogen electrodes. The negative electrode is in contact with a solution having 10^{-6} M H^+ ion concentration. Calculate the concentration of H^+ ions at the positive electrode, if the cell is found to be 0.118 V at 298 K.

Solution

Here, $C_1 = 10^{-6}$ M, C_2 = to be calculated.

For the given concentration cell, $E_{cell} = \frac{0.0591}{n}\log\frac{C_2}{C_1}$

$$0.118 = \frac{0.0591}{1}\log\frac{C_2}{10^{-6}} \text{ or } \log\frac{C_2}{10^{-6}} = 2$$

or $$\frac{C_2}{10^{-6}} = \text{Antilog } 2 = 10^2$$

$$\therefore\ C_2 = 10^2 \times 10^{-6} = 10^{-4}\text{ M}$$

3.14 Equilibrium Constant from Nernst Equation

Let us consider the cell Zn(s) | $ZnSO_4$(aq) || $CuSO_4$(aq) | Cu(s)

In this cell, the electrons flow from zinc to copper in the external circuit whereas the following processes take place in the internal circuit.

- Zinc from the zinc rod passes into the solution as Zn^{2+} ions.
- Cu^{2+} ions from the $CuSO_4$ solution are deposited on the Cu plate.
- SO_4^{2-} ions from the $CuSO_4$ solution flow to the $ZnSO_4$ solution through the salt bridge

As a result, the concentration of $CuSO_4$ solution decreases whereas that of the $ZnSO_4$ solution increases. The electrode potentials of the two electrodes involved, keep on changing. Ultimately, a stage comes when the electrode potentials of the two electrodes becomes equal and the current stops flowing in the circuit, the cell reaction is said to have attained equilibrium (Fig. 3.8). That is,

$$\text{Zn}(s) + \text{Cu}^{2+}(aq) \rightleftharpoons \text{Zn}^{2+}(aq) + \text{Cu}(s)$$

Fig. 3.8 Representing how the cell stops working or cell reation reaches equilibrium

$$\frac{\left[\text{Zn}^{2+}(aq)\right]_{eqm}}{\left[\text{Cu}^{2+}(aq)\right]_{eqm}} = K_c,$$

where K_c represents the equilibrium constant when $E°_{\text{cell}} = 0$. Putting these values in the Nernst equation, we get

$$0 = E°_{\text{cell}} - \frac{RT}{nF}\ln\frac{\left[\text{Zn}^{2+}(aq)\right]_{eqm}}{\left[\text{Cu}^{2+}(aq)\right]_{eqm}} = E°_{\text{cell}} - \frac{RT}{nF}\ln K_c$$

or $$E°_{\text{cell}} = \frac{RT}{nF}\ln K_c = \frac{2.303\,RT}{nF}\log K_c$$

or $$E°_{\text{cell}} = \frac{0.0591}{n}\log K_c \text{ at 298 K} \quad (3.9)$$

Worked Out Problem 3.8

Calculate the equilibrium constant for the reaction

$$\text{Cu}(s) + 2\text{Ag}^+(aq) \rightleftharpoons \text{Cu}^{2+}(aq) + 2\text{Ag}(s)$$

given that $E°_{\text{Ag}^+/\text{Ag}} = 0.80$ and $E°_{\text{Cu}^{2+}/\text{Cu}} = 0.34$ V.

Solution

The cell may be represented as: Cu | Cu^{2+}(aq) || Ag^+(aq) | Ag

$$E°_{\text{cell}} = E°_{\text{RHS}} - E°_{\text{LHS}} = 0.80\text{ V} - (0.34\text{ V}) = 0.46\text{ V}$$

$$E°_{\text{cell}} = \frac{0.0591}{n}\log K_c$$

For the given reaction, $n = 2$, $E°_{\text{cell}} = 0.46$ V

$$\therefore\ 0.46 = \frac{0.0591}{2}\log K_c \quad \text{or} \quad \log K_c = \frac{0.46\times 2}{0.0591} = 15.5668$$

$$\therefore\ K_c = \text{antilog } 15.5668 = 3.6\times 10^{15}$$

Relation between $\Delta G°$ and $E°_{\text{cell}}$

Electrical work done = Electrical energy produced = Quantity of electricity flowing × EMF

If n moles of electrons are transferred in any cell reaction, the quantity of electricity flowing = n F faradays. If E_{cell} represents the EMF of the cell, then

$$\text{Electrical work done} = nFE_{\text{cell}}$$

Hence, $$-\Delta_r G = nFE_{\text{cell}}$$

$$-\Delta_r G° = n\text{F}.\frac{RT}{nF}\ln K_c \quad \text{or} \quad \Delta_r G° = -RT\ln K_c$$

or $$\Delta_r G° = -2.303\,RT\log K_c \quad (3.10)$$

Hence, the decrease in free energy is equal to the maximum work that can be obtained from the cell.

3.15 Products of Electrolysis from Electrode Potentials

The products of electrolysis mainly depend on the different oxidising and reducing species present in the electrolytic cell and their standard electrode potentials.

(i) Electrolysis of melt/aqueous solution of NaCl: Electrolysis of molten NaCl gives sodium metal at the cathode and chlorine gas at the anode.

$$\text{NaCl}(s) \xrightarrow{\text{Melting}} \text{Na}^+(l) + \text{Cl}^-(l)$$

At cathode: $\text{Na}^+(l) + e^- \rightarrow \text{Na}(l)$ (Reduction)

At anode: $\text{Cl}^-(l) \rightarrow \text{Cl}(g) + e^-$ (Oxidation)

$$\text{Cl}(g) + \text{Cl}(g) \rightarrow \text{Cl}_2(g)$$

The overall reaction is

$$\underset{\text{(molten)}}{2\text{NaCl}} \xrightarrow{\text{Electrolysis}} \underset{\text{(at cathode)}}{2\text{Na}} + \underset{\text{(at anode)}}{\text{Cl}_2(g)}$$

(ii) Electrolysis of aqueous sodium chloride:

The products of electrolysis of aqueous NaCl solution are chlorine at the anode and hydrogen (and not sodium) at the cathode.

Since the standard reduction potential of water (–0.83 volt) is greater than the standard reduction potential of sodium (–2.71 volt), therefore, reduction of water takes place easily.

(iii) Electrolysis of an aqueous solution of $CuBr_2$: The products of electrolysis are copper at the cathode and bromine at the anode.

In general, if more than one substance is present in the electrolytic cell, the substance liberated at the cathode is one which has the highest reduction potential and that liberated at the anode is the one which has the highest oxidation potential. In view of these conclusions, some more results are given below.

- Na^+, Ca^{2+}, Mg^{2+} and Al^{3+} have much lower reduction potentials than that of water. Hence, these ions are not reduced in the aqueous solution. Instead, reduction of water occurs, evolving H_2 gas at the cathode.
- Cu^{2+} and Ag^+ ions have a much higher reduction potential than that of water. Hence, these ions are easily reduced and deposited as Cu and Ag at the cathode.
- Br^- and I^- ions have a much higher oxidation potential than that of water. Hence, they are more easily oxidised in the aqueous solution giving Br_2 and I_2 respectively at the anode. On the other hand, F^- ions have a much lower oxidation potential than that of water. Hence, F^- ions are not oxidised in the aqueous solution to give F_2. Instead, H_2O gets oxidised to give O_2 gas.

3.16 Batteries (Commercial Cells)

A battery is an arrangement of electrochemical cells that can be used as a source of direct electric current at a constant voltage. The batteries (or cells) are classified into two types. ***Primary cells*** are those in which the redox reaction occurs only once and the cell becomes dead after some time, and cannot be used again. For example, dry cell and mercury cell. ***Secondary cells*** are those that can be recharged by passing an electric current through them and hence can be used over and again. For example, lead storage battery and nickel–cadmium storage cell.

3.16.1 Primary Batteries or Cells

(i) Dry cell: It consists of a cylindrical zinc container which acts as the anode. A graphite rod placed in the centre (but not touching the base) acts as the cathode. The space between the anode and the cathode is so packed that the zinc container is in touch with the paste of NH_4Cl and $ZnCl_2$ and the graphite rod is surrounded by powdered MnO_2 and carbon (Fig. 3.9). The graphite rod is fitted with a metal cap and the cylinder is sealed at the top with pitch. The reactions taking place at the electrodes are given below:

At anode: $Zn(s) \rightarrow Zn^{2+}(aq) + 2e^-$

At cathode: $2MnO_2(s) + 2NH_4^+(aq) + 2e^- \rightarrow Mn_2O_3(s) + 2NH_3(g) + H_2O$

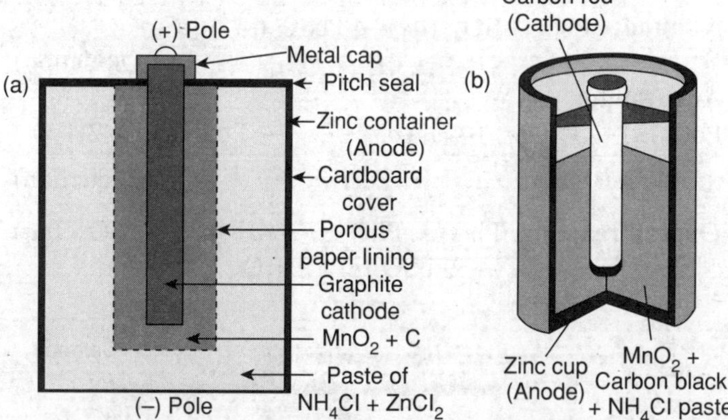

Fig. 3.9 The dry cell **(a)** Descriptive diagram **(b)** A section of the three dimensional actual look

(ii) Mercury cell: It consists of a zinc container as the anode, a carbon rod as the cathode and a paste of mercuric oxide mixed with KOH as the electrolyte. A lining of porous paper keeps the electrolyte separated from the zinc anode (Fig. 3.10).

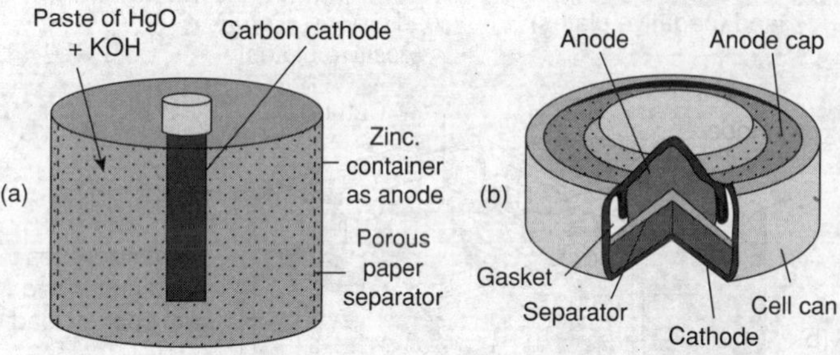

Fig. 3.10 Mercury cell **(a)** Descripitive diagram **(b)** A section of the three dimensional actual look

The cell produces electrical energy by the following reactions:

At anode: $Zn(s) + 2OH^- \rightarrow ZnO(s) + H_2O(l) + 2e^-$

At cathode:

$$HgO(s) + H_2O(l) + 2e^- \rightarrow Hg(l) + 2OH^-$$

Overall reaction: $Zn(s) + HgO(s) \rightarrow ZnO(s) + Hg(l)$

3.16.2 Secondary Batteries or Cells

Lead Storage Cell

A 12 V lead storage battery is generally used which consists of 6 cells each producing 2 V. Each cell consists of a lead anode (or a grid of lead filled with finely divided spongy lead as the anode) and a grid of lead packed with lead dioxide as the cathode. These electrodes are arranged alternately, separated by thin wooden or fibre glass sheets and suspended in dilute sulfuric acid (38% by mass or having a density of 1.30 g cm^{-3}) which acts as the electrolyte.

Reactions Occurring During Discharge and Recharging

The electrode reactions that occur *during discharge*, that is, when the battery is in use (Fig. 3.11) are as follows.

At anode: $Pb(s) + SO_4^{2-}(aq) \rightarrow PbSO_4(s) + 2e^-$ (Oxidation)

At cathode:
$PbO_2(s) + O_4^{2-}(aq) + 4H^+(aq) + 2e^- \rightarrow PbSO_4(s) + 2H_2O$ (Reduction)

Overall reaction: $Pb(s) + PbO_2(s) + 4H^+(aq) + 2SO_4^{2-}(aq) \rightarrow 2PbSO_4(s) + 2H_2O$

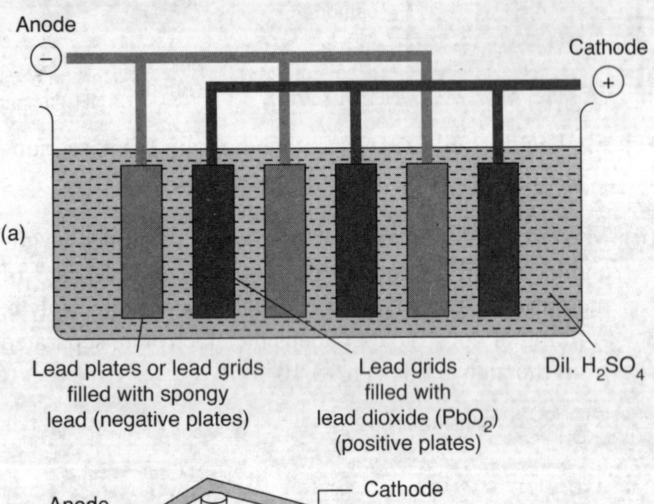

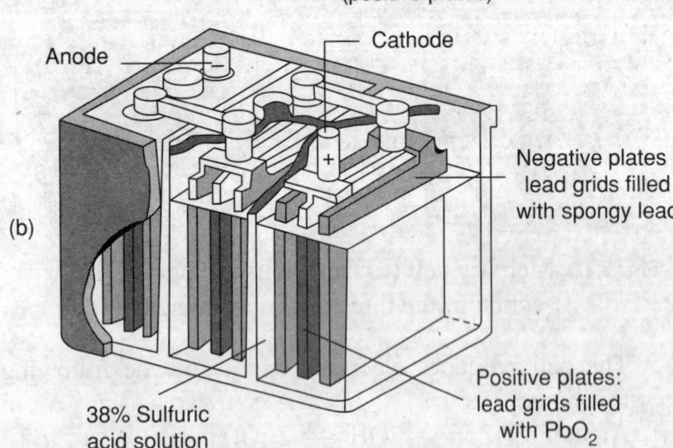

Fig. 3.11 Lead storage battery of 6 volts **(a)** Descriptive diagram **(b)** A section of the three dimensional actual look

The density of H_2SO_4 falls. When it falls below 1.20 g cm^{-3}, the battery needs recharging.

Recharging the Battery

The cell can be recharged by passing electric current of a suitable voltage in the opposite direction. Now the PbO_2 electrode is anode (+ve) and Pb is cathode (–ve) (Fig. 3.12).

At cathode: $PbSO_4(s) + 2e^- \rightarrow Pb(s) + SO_4^{2-}(aq)$ (Reduction)

At anode:
$PbSO_4(s) + 2H_2O \rightarrow PbO_2(s) + SO_4^{2-}(aq) + 4H^+(aq) + 2e^-$ (Oxidation)

Overall reaction: $2PbSO_4(s) + 2H_2O \rightarrow Pb(s) + PbO_2(s) + 4H^+(aq) + 2SO_4^{2-}(aq)$

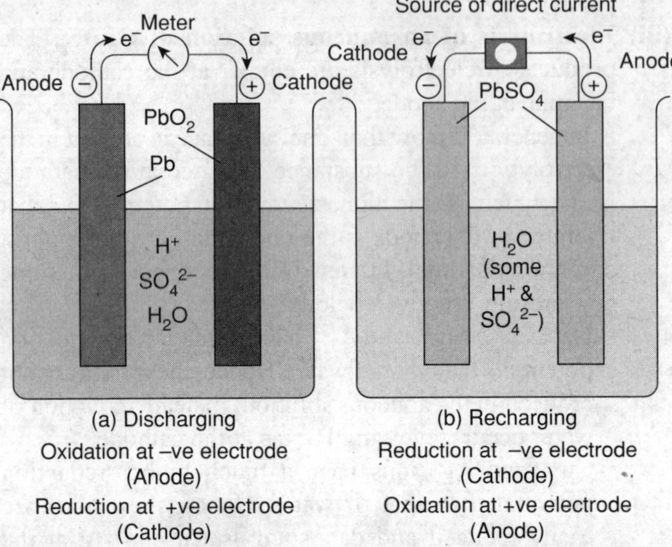

Fig. 3.12 Discharging and recharging of a lead storage cell

Nickel-Cadmium Storage Cell

It consists of a cadmium electrode (as anode) and a metal grid containing nickel (IV) oxide (as cathode) immersed in KOH solution. The electrode reactions occurring during discharge are as follows.

At anode: $Cd(s) + 2OH^-(aq) \rightarrow Cd(OH)_2(s) + 2e^-$

At cathode: $NiO_2(s) + 2H_2O + 2e^- \rightarrow Ni(OH)_2(s) + 2OH^-(aq)$

The potential of each Ni–Cd cell is approximately 1.4 V.

3.17 Fuel Cells

Fuel cells are the devices which convert the energy produced during the combustion of fuels such as hydrogen, methane, methanol and so on, directly into electrical energy. The H_2–O_2 fuel cells (Fig. 3.13) consist of porous carbon electrodes containing suitable catalysts (generally finely divided platinum and palladium) incorporated in them. Concentrated KOH or NaOH solution is placed between the electrodes to act as the electrolyte. Hydrogen and oxygen gases are bubbled through the porous electrodes into the KOH/NaOH solution. The following electrode reactions take place.

At anode: $2H_2(g) + 4OH^-(aq) \rightarrow 4H_2O(l) + 4e^-$

At cathode: $O_2(g) + 2H_2O(l) + 4e^- \rightarrow 4OH^-(aq)$

Overall reaction: $2H_2(g) + O_2(g) \rightarrow 2H_2O(l)$

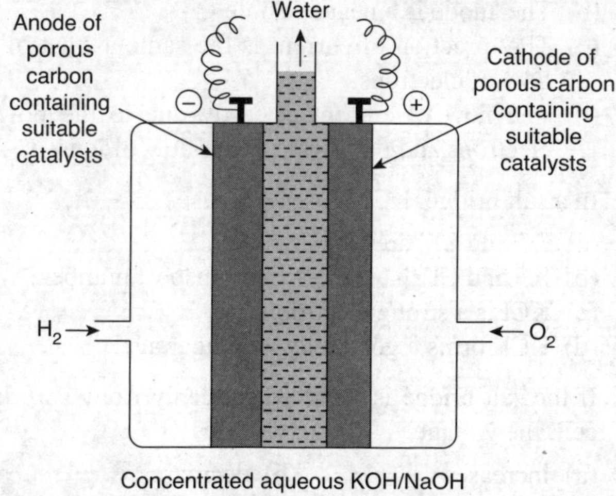

Fig. 3.13 H_2–O_2 fuel cell

Advantages of Fuel Cells

The fuel cells have three main advantages.

- Because of the continuous supply, such cells never become dead. Such a cell is usually operated at a temperature of 70–140°C and gives a potential of about 0.9 V.
- In practice they give an efficiency of 60%–70%.
- They do not cause any pollution problems.

Efficiency of the Fuel Cell

As ΔH is the heat of combustion and ΔG is the useful work done (electrical energy produced), the *thermodynamic efficiency* (η) of a fuel cell $= \frac{\Delta G}{\Delta H} \times 100$.

Exercises

OBJECTIVE QUESTIONS

Electrochemical Cells

1. When a zinc rod is suspended in copper sulfate solution
(a) the temperature of the solution rises
(b) the temperature of the solution falls
(c) the temperature of the solution remains unchanged
(d) copper is deposited on zinc rod thereby increasing its weight

2. Which of the following reactions cannot be a basis for electrochemical cell
(a) $H_2 + O_2 \rightarrow H_2O$
(b) $AgNO_3 + Zn \rightarrow Zn(NO_3)_2 + Ag$
(c) $AgNO_3 + NaCl \rightarrow AgCl \downarrow NaNO_3$
(d) $KMnO_4 + FeSO_4 + H_2SO_4 \rightarrow K_2SO_4 + Fe_2(SO_4)_3 + MnSO_4 + H_2O$

3. A galvanic cell functions as an electrolytic cell when
(a) External voltage applied (E_{ext}) is less than EMF of the cell (E_{cell})
(b) $E_{ext} = E_{cell}$
(c) $E_{ext} = E_{cell}$
(d) a galvanic cell can never act as an electrolytic cell

4. Which of the following involves an electrochemical phenomenon?
(a) manufacture of aluminium from bauxite
(b) manufacture of caustic soda by Castner–Kellner method
(c) sensory signals sent to the brain through cells
(d) all the three above

Galvanic cells

5. The galvanic cell
$Zn(s) + 2\,Ag^+(aq) \rightarrow Zn^{2+}(aq) + 2Ag(s)$
is correctly represented as
(a) $Ag(s) \mid Ag^+(aq) \parallel Zn^{2+}(aq) \mid Zn(s)$
(b) $Zn(s) \mid Zn^{2+}(aq) \parallel Ag^+(aq) \mid Ag(s)$
(c) $Ag^+(aq) \mid Ag(s) \parallel Zn(s) \mid Zn^{2+}(aq)$
(d) $Zn^{2+}(aq) \mid Zn(s) \parallel Ag^+(aq) \mid Ag(s)$

6. Which of the following statements is correct for a galvanic cell?
(a) reduction occurs at the cathode
(b) oxidation occurs at the anode
(c) electrons flow from the anode to the cathode
(d) all the statements are correct

7. Which of the following statements is correct about the Zn–$CuSO_4$ cell?
(a) The flow of electrons occurs from copper to zinc.
(b) The value of E°_{cell} of copper electrode is less than that of zinc electrode.
(c) Zinc is the anode while Cu is the cathode
(d) All the statements are correct.

8. In the Cu–Ag cell
(a) electrons flow from Cu to Ag
(b) Cu acts as the anode
(c) Ag acts as the positive pole
(d) all the above are correct

9. Which one of the following is not a function of the salt bridge?

(a) To allow the flow of cations from one solution to the other.
(b) To allow the flow of anions from one solution to the other.
(c) To allow the electrons to flow from one solution to the other.
(d) To maintain electrical neutrality of the two solutions.

10. KCl cannot be used as a salt bridge for the cell
$Cu(s) \mid CuSO_4(aq) \parallel AgNO_3(aq) \mid Ag(s)$
because
(a) $CuCl_2$ gets precipitated
(b) Cl_2 gas is evolved
(c) AgCl gets precipitated
(d) none of the above

11. The cell reaction of the galvanic cell
$Cu(s) \mid Cu^{2+}(aq) \parallel Hg^{2+}(aq) \mid Hg(l)$ is
(a) $Hg + Cu^{2+} \rightarrow Hg^{2+} + Cu$
(b) $Hg + Cu^{2+} \rightarrow Hg^{+} + Cu^{+}$
(c) $Cu + Hg \rightarrow CuHg$
(d) $Cu + Hg^{2+} \rightarrow Cu^{2+} + Hg$

12. Saturated solution of KNO_3 is used to make a salt bridge because
(a) velocity of K^+ is greater than that of NO_3^-
(b) velocity of NO_3^- is greater than that of K^+
(c) velocity of both K^+ and NO_3^- are nearly the same
(d) KNO_3 is soluble in water

13. Anode in the galvanic cell, is the
(a) negative electrode (b) positive electrode
(c) neutral electrode (d) none of these

14. The electrochemical cell stops working after sometime because
(a) electrode potential of both the electrodes becomes zero
(b) electrode potential of both the electrodes become equal
(c) one of the electrodes is eaten away
(d) the cell reaction gets reversed

15. The passage of electricity in the Daniell cell when Zn and Cu electrodes are connected is from
(a) Cu to Zn in the cell
(b) Cu to Zn outside the cell
(c) Zn to Cu outside the cell
(d) Zn to Cu in the cell

16. Which one of the following statements is incorrect regarding a galvanic cell?
(a) The electrode on which oxidation takes place is called the anode.
(b) The anode is a negative pole.
(c) The direction of current is the same as that of the flow of electrons.
(d) The flow of current is partly due to the flow of electrons and partly due to the flow of ions.

17. In a salt bridge, KCl is used because
(a) K^+ and Cl^- are isoelectronic
(b) K^+ and Cl^- have the same transport number
(c) KCl is a strong electrolyte
(d) KCl forms a good jelly with agar agar

18. If the salt bridge is removed suddenly from a working cell, the voltage
(a) increases (b) decreases
(c) drops to zero
(d) may increase or decrease depending upon the cell reaction

Electrode Potential, EMF of a Cell and Electrochemical Series

19. The reference calomel electrode is made from which of the following?
(a) $ZnCl_2$ (b) $CuSO_4$ (c) Hg_2Cl_2 (d) $HgCl_2$

20. Oxidation potential of calomel is
(a) +0.2 V (b) 0.00 V (c) +0.287 V (d) –0.287 V

21. The correct order of chemical reactivity with water according to the electrochemical series is
(a) K > Mg > Zn > Cu (b) Mg > Zn > Cu > K
(c) K > Zn > Mg > Cu (d) Cu > Zn > Mg > K

22. Li occupies a higher position in the electrochemical series of metals as compared to Cu since
(a) the standard reduction potential of Li^+/Li is lower than that of Cu^{2+}/Cu
(b) the standard reduction of Cu^{2+}/Cu is lower than that of Li^+/Li
(c) the standard oxidation potential of Li/Li^+ is lower than that of Cu/Cu^{2+}
(d) Li is smaller in size compound to Cu

23. Which one is the wrong statement about the electrochemical series?
(a) Active metals have negative reduction potentials.
(b) Active non-metals have positive reduction potentials.
(c) Metals above hydrogen liberate hydrogen from acids.
(d) Metals below hydrogen are strong reducing agents.

24. A button cell used in watches functions as follows:
$Zn(s) + Ag_2O(s) + H_2O(l) \rightleftharpoons 2Ag(s) + Zn^{2+}(aq) + 2\,OH^-(aq)$
The half cell potentials are

$Zn^{2+}(aq) + 2e^- \rightarrow Zn(s)$, $E° = -0.76$ V
$Ag_2O(s) + H_2O(l) + 2e^- \rightarrow 2Ag(s) + 2OH^-(aq)$,
$E° = 0.34$ V
The cell potential will be:
(a) 1.10 V (b) 0.42 V (c) 0.84 V (d) 1.34 V

25. If $E°_{Fe^{2+}/Fe} = -0.441$ V and $E°_{Fe^{3+}/Fe^{2+}} = 0.771$ V the standard emf of the reaction $Fe + Fe^{3+} \rightarrow 3\,Fe^{2+}$ will be
(a) 1.212 V (b) 0.111 V (c) 0.330 V (d) 1.653 V

26. Consider the following relations for the emf of an electrochemical cell
(i) emf of cell = (Oxidation potential of anode) – (Reduction potential of cathode)
(ii) emf of cell = Oxidation potential of anode) + (Reduction potential of cathode)
(iii) emf of cell = (Reduction potential of anode + (Reduction potential of cathode)
(iv) emf of cell = (Oxidation potential of anode) – (Oxidation potential of cathode)

Which of the above relations are correct?
(a) (iii) and (i) (b) (i) and (ii)
(c) (iii) and (iv) (d) (ii) and (iv)

27. If the half cell reactions are givens as
(i) $Fe^{2+}(aq) + 2e^- \rightarrow Fe(s)$, $E° = -0.44$ V
(ii) $2\,H^+(aq) + \frac{1}{2}O_2(g) + 2e^- \rightarrow H_2O(l)$, $E° = +1.23$ V

The $E°$ for the reaction
$Fe(s) + 2\,H^+ + \frac{1}{2}O_2(g) \rightarrow Fe^{2+}(aq) + H_2O(l)$ is
(a) +1.67 V (b) –1.67 V (c) +0.79 V (d) –0.79 V

28. Normal aluminium electrode coupled with normal hydrogen electrode gives an emf of 1.66 volts. So, the standard electrode potential of aluminium is
(a) –1.66 V (b) +1.66 V (c) –0.55 (d) +0.55

29. Which one of the following will provide maximum voltage? Given that
$Co^{2+}/Co = -0.28$ V $Zn^{2+}/Zn = -0.76$V
$Ag^+/Ag = 0.80$ V $Cu^{2+}/Cu = +0.34$

(a) $Co(s) + 2\,H^+(aq) \rightarrow Co^{++}(aq) + H_2(g)$
(b) $Zn + 2Ag^+ \rightarrow Zn^2 + 2\,Ag$
(c) $H_2(g) + Cu^{2+}(aq) \rightarrow Zn^{++}(aq) + Cu(s)$
(d) $Zn(s) + Cu^{2+}(aq) \rightarrow Zn^{++}(aq) + Cu(s)$

30. Two electrochemical cells, $Zn\,|\,Zn^{2+}\,||\,Cu^{2+}\,|\,Cu$ and $Fe\,|\,Fe^{2+}\,||\,Cu^{2+}\,|\,Cu$ are connected in series. What will be the net emf of the cell at 25°C? Given: $E°$ of $Zn^{2+} + Zn = -0.76$ V, $Cu^{2+}\,|\,Cu + 80.34$ V, $Fe^{2+}\,|\,Fe = -0.76$ V
(a) +1.85 V (b) –1.85 V (c) +0.83 V (d) –0.83 V

31. For some reactions, the standard reduction potentials are given below.
$Zn^{2+} + 2e^- \rightarrow Zn$, $E° = -0.762$ V
$Fe^{2+} + 2e^- \rightarrow Fe$, $E° = -0.440$ V
$Cu^{2+} + 2e^- \rightarrow Cu$, $E° = -0.345$ V
$Ag^+ + e^- \rightarrow Ag$, $E° = +0.800$ V
Which one of the following is most easily oxidised?
(a) Zn (b) Cu (c) Fe (d) Ag

32. Select the strongest reducing agent from amongst the substances involved in the following half-reactions.
$Cl_2(g) + 2e^- \rightarrow 2\,Cl^-(aq)$ +1.36 V
$Br_2(g) + 2e^- \rightarrow 2\,Br^-(aq)$ +1.09 V
$Sn^{2+} + 2e^- \rightarrow Sn$ –0.14 V
(a) Cl^- (b) Br^- (c) Sn (d) Sn^{2+}

33. If the half cell reaction $A + e^- \rightarrow A^-$ has a large negative reduction potential, it follows that
(a) A is readily reduced (b) A is readily oxidised
(c) A^- is readily reduced (d) A^- is readily oxidised

34. Standard potentials ($E°$) for some half reactions are given below:
$Sn^{4+} + 2e^- \rightarrow Sn^{2+}$; $E° = +0.15$ V
$2\,Hg^{2+} + 2e^- \rightarrow Hg_2^{2+}$; $E° = 0.92$ V
$PbO_2 + 4\,H^+ + 2e^- \rightarrow Pb^{2+} + 2H_2O$; $E° = +1.45$ F
Based on the above, which one of the following statements is correct?
(a) Sn^{4+} is a stronger oxidising agent than Pb^{4+}.
(b) Sn^{2+} is a stronger reducing agent than Hg_2^{2+}.
(c) Pb^{2+} is a stronger oxidising agent than Pb^{4+}.
(d) Pb^{2+} is a stronger reducing agent than Sn^{2+}.

35. The standard reduction potential values of the three metallic cation X, Y and Z are 0.52, –3.03 and –1.18 V respectively. The order of reducing power of the corresponding metals is
(a) Y > Z > X (b) X > Y > Z
(c) Z > Y > X (d) Z > X > Y

36. Standard reduction potentials of the half reactions are given below:
$F_2(g) + 2e^- \rightarrow 2\,F^-(aq)$; $E° = +2.85$ V
$Cl_2(g) + 2e^- \rightarrow 2\,Cl^-(aq)$; $E° = +1.36$
$Br_2(l) + 2e^- \rightarrow 2\,Br^-(aq)$; $E° = +1.06$ V
$I_2(s) + 2e^- \rightarrow 2\,I^-(aq)$; $E° = +0.53$ V
The strongest oxidising and reducing agents respectively are:
(a) Cl_2 and Br^- (b) Cl_2 and I_2
(c) F_2 and I^- (d) Br_2 and Cl^-

37. Using the data given below, find out the strongest reducing agent

$E^\circ_{Cr_2O_4/Cr^{3+}} = 1.33$ V $\quad E^\circ_{Cl_2/Cl^-} = 1.36$ V

$E^\circ_{MnO_4^-/Mn^{2+}} = 1.51$, $\quad E^\circ_{Cr^{3+}/Cr} = -0.74$ V

(a) Cl^- (b) Mn^{2+} (c) Cr (d) Cr^{2+}

38. The standard reducing potentials at 25°C of L^+/Li, Ba^{2+}/Ba, Na^+/Na and Mg^{2+}/Mg are –3.03, –2.73, 2.71, and –2.37 V respectively. Which one of the following is the strongest oxidising agent?

(a) Na^+ (b) Li^+ (c) Ba^{2+} (d) Mg^{2+}

39. Among the following, which is the strongest oxidising agent?

(a) Br_2 (b) I_2 (c) Cl_2 (d) F_2

40. E° for Mg^{2+}/Mg = –2.37 V, Zn^{2+}/Zn = –0.76 V and Fe^{2+}/Fe = –0.44 V. Which statement is correct?

(a) Zn reduces Fe^{2+} (b) Zn reduces Mg^{2+}
(c) Mg oxidises Fe (d) Zn oxidises Fe

41. (i) Copper metal dissolves in 1 M silver nitrate solution and crystals of silver metal get deposited.
(ii) Silver metal does not react with 1 M zinc nitrate solution.
(iii) Zinc metal dissolves in 1 M copper sulfate solution and copper metal gets deposited.

Hence the order of decreasing strength of the three metals as reducing agents will be

(a) Cu > Ag > Zn (b) Ag < Cu > Zn
(c) Zn > Cu > Ag (d) Cu > Zn > Ag

42. Zn gives H_2 gas with H_2SO_4 and HCl but not with HNO_3 because

(a) Zn acts as an oxidising agent when it reacts with HNO_3.
(b) HNO_3 is a weaker acid H_2SO_4 than HCl
(c) in the electrochemical series, Zn is above hydrogen
(d) NO_3^- is reduced in preference to the hydronium ion

43. To a mixture containing pieces of zinc, copper and silver, 1 M H_2SO_4 was added. H_2 gas was found to be evolved. Which of the metal/metals do you think has/have reacted? Given

$E^\circ_{Zn/Zn^{2+}} = +0.76$ V, $E^\circ_{Cu^{2+}/Cu} = +0.3$ V,

$E^\circ_{Ag^+/Ag} = +0.80$ V

(a) all the metals (b) only Zn
(c) both Zn and Cu (d) only Ag

44. Which of the following solutions can be safely stored in a copper vessel?

(a) $ZnSO_4$ (b) $AgNO_3$
(c) $AuCl_3$ (d) all of them

45. Electrode potentials (E°_{red}) of 4 elements A, B C, D are –1.36, –0.32, 0, –1.26 V respectively. The decreasing reactivity order of these elements is

(a) A, D, B and C (b) C, B, D and A
(c) B, D, C and A (d) C, A, D and B

46. A smuggler could not carry gold by depositing iron on the gold surface since

(a) gold is denser (b) iron rusts
(c) gold has a higher reduction potential than iron
(d) gold has lower reduction potential than iron

47. The standard reduction potentials of three electrodes P, Q and R are respectively –1.76 V, 0.34 V and 0.8 V. Then,

(a) metal Q will displace the cation of P from its aqueous solution and deposit the metal P
(b) both metals Q and R will displace the cation of P from its aqueous solution and deposit the metal P
(c) metal P will displace the cation of R from its aqueous solution and deposit the metal R
(d) metal R will displace the cation of Q and deposit the metal Q

48. Which of the following cannot be stored?

(a) $ZnSO_4$ solution in an iron vessel
(b) $FeSO_4$ solution in a nickel vessel
(c) $MgSO_4$ solution in an aluminium vessel
(d) $CuSO_4$ solution in a zinc vessel

49. If a strip of copper metal is placed in a solution of ferrous sulfate

(a) copper will precipitate out
(b) iron will precipitate out
(c) copper and iron both will be dissolved
(d) no reaction will take place

50. A concentrated solution of lead nitrate can be stored in

(a) an iron vessel (b) a zinc vessel
(c) a copper vessel (d) a magnesium vessel

51. Which of the following reactions is correct for a given electrochemical cell at 25°C?

Pt | $Br_2(g)$ | $Br^-(aq)$ || $Cl^-(aq)$ | $Cl_2(g)$ | Pt

(a) $2Br^-(aq) + Cl_2(g) \rightarrow 2Cl^-(aq) + Br_2(g)$
(b) $Br_2(g) + 2Cl^-(aq) \rightarrow 2Br^-(aq) + Cl_2(g)$
(c) $Br_2(g) + Cl_2(g) \rightarrow 2Br^-(aq) + 2\,Cl^-(aq)$
(d) $2Br^-(aq) + 2Cl^-(aq) \rightarrow Br_2(g) + Cl_2(g)$

52. The following facts are available:

$2\,A^- + B_2 \rightarrow 2\,B^- + A_2$
$2\,C^- + B_2 \rightarrow$ No reaction
$2\,D^- + A_2 \rightarrow 2\,A^- + D_2$

Which of the following statements is correct?

(a) $E^\circ_{C^-|C_2} > E^\circ_{B^-|B_2} > E^\circ_{A^-|A_2} > E^\circ_{D^-|D_2}$
(b) $E^\circ_{C^-|C_2} < E^\circ_{B^-|B_2} < E^\circ_{A^-|A_2} < E^\circ_{D^-|D_2}$
(c) $E^\circ_{C^-|C_2} < E^\circ_{B^-|B_2} > E^\circ_{A^-|A_2} > E^\circ_{D^-|D_2}$
(d) $E^\circ_{C^-|C_2} > E^\circ_{B^-|B_2} < E^\circ_{A^-|A_2} < E^\circ_{D^-|D_2}$

53. Red hot carbon will remove oxygen from the oxide XO and YO but not from ZO. Y will remove oxygen from XO. Use this evidence to deduce the order of activity of the three metals X, Y and Z putting the most active first

(a) XYZ (b) ZYX (c) YXZ (d) ZXY

54. What takes place when zinc metal is added to an aqueous solution containing magnesium nitrate and silver nitrate?

1. Zn is oxidised 2. Mg^{2+} is reduced
3. Ag^{2+} is reduced 4. no reaction takes place

(a) 1 and 2 only (b) 1 and 3 only
(c) 1, 2 and 3 only (d) 4 only

55. A hypothetical electrochemical cell is shown below

$A | A^+ (x\,M) || B^+ (y\,M) | B$

The emf measured is +0.20 V. The cell reaction is

(a) the cell reaction cannot be predicted
(b) $A + B^+ \rightarrow A^+ + B$
(c) $A^+ + B \rightarrow A + B^+$
(d) $A^+ + e^- \rightarrow A$; $B^+ + e^- \rightarrow B$

56. In a simple electrochemical cell, which is in the standard state, half cell reactions with their appropriate oxidation potentials are

$Pb(s) - 2e^- \rightarrow Pb^{2+}(aq)$, $E° = +0.13$ volt
$Ag(s) - 2e^- \rightarrow Ag^+(aq)$, $E = -0.80$ volt

Which of the following reactions takes place?

(a) $Pb^{2+}(aq) + 2Ag(s) \rightarrow 2\,Ag^+(aq) + Pb(s)$
(b) $Pb^{2+}(aq) + Ag(s) \rightarrow Ag^+(aq) + Pb(s)$
(c) $Ag^+(aq) + Pb(s) \rightarrow Ag(s) + Pb^{2+}(aq)$
(d) $2\,Ag^+(aq) + Pb(s) \rightarrow 2Ag(s) + Pb^{2+}(aq)$

57. Which reaction is not feasible?

(a) $2KI + Br_2 \rightarrow 2KBr + I_2$
(b) $2KBr + I_2 \rightarrow 2KI + Br_2$
(c) $2KBr + Cl_2 \rightarrow 2KCl + Br_2$
(d) $2H_2O + 2F_2 \rightarrow 4Hf + O_2$

58. A solution is one molar in each of NaCl, $CdCl_2$, $ZnCl_2$ and $PbCl_2$. To this, tin metal is added. Which of the following is true? Given:

$E°_{Pb^{2+}/Pb} = -0.216$ V
$E°_{Sn^{2+}/Sn} = -0.136$ V
$E°_{Cd^{2+}/Cd} = -0.40$ V
$E°_{Zn^{2+}/Zn} = -0.763$ V
$E°_{Na^+/Na} = -2.71$ V

(a) Sn can reduce Na^+ to Na
(b) Sn can reduce Zn^{2+} to Zn
(c) Sn can reduce Cd^{2+} to Cd
(d) Sn can reduce Pb^{2+} to Pb

59. For the electrochemical cell, $M | M^+ || X^- | X$, $E°_{(M^+/M)} = 0.44$ V and $E°_{(X/X^-)} = 0.33$. From this, one can deduce that

(a) $M + X \rightarrow M^+ + X^-$ is a spontaneous reaction
(b) $M^+ + X^- \rightarrow M + X$ is a spontaneous reaction
(c) $E_{cell} = 0.77$ V
(d) $E_{cell} = -0.77$ V

60. For $I_2 + 2e \rightarrow 2I^-$, standard reduction potential = +0.54 volt. For $2Br^- \rightarrow Br_2 + 2$, standard oxidation = –1.09 volt. For $Fe \rightarrow Fe^{2+} + 2e^-$, standard oxidation potential = +0.44 volt. Which of the following reactions is non‾spontaneous?

(a) $Br_2 + 2\,I^- \rightarrow 2\,Br^- + I_2$
(b) $Fe + Br_2 \rightarrow Fe^{2+} + 2\,Br^-$
(c) $Fe + I_2 \rightarrow Fe^{2+} + 2\,I^-$
(d) $I_2 + 2Br^- \rightarrow 2\,I^- + Br_2$

61. The metal oxide which decomposes on heating is

(a) ZnO (b) HgO (c) Al_2O_3 (d) CuO

62. For the reaction Pt | H_2 (1 atm) | H^+ (aq) || Cl^- (aq) | AgCl | Ag, K_c (equilibrium constant) is represented as

(a) $K_c = \frac{[Cl^-][AgCl]}{[H^+][H_2]}$ (b) $K_c = [H^+][Cl^-]$

(c) $K_c = \frac{[H^+][H_2]}{[Cl^-][AgCl]}$ (d) $K_c = \frac{[H_2]}{[Ag]}$

63. The $E°_{M^{3+}/M^{2+}}$ values for Cr, Mn, Fe and Co are –0.41, +1.57, +0.77 and +1.97 V respectively. For which one of these metals, is the change in oxidation state from +2 to +3 easiest?

(a) Cr (b) Mn (c) Fe (d) Co

64. The electrode potential for $Cu^{2+}(aq) + e^- \rightarrow Cu^+(aq)$ and $Cu^+(aq) + e^- \rightarrow Cu(s)$ are +0.15 V and +0.50 V respectively.

The value of $E°_{Cu^{2+}/Cu}$ will be

(a) 0.15 V (b) 0.500 V (c) 0.325 V (d) 0.650 V

65. The standard hydrogen electrode potential is zero, because

(a) there is no potential difference between the electrode and the solution
(b) hydrogen ions acquire electrons from a platinum electrode
(c) it has been measured accurately
(d) it has been defined that way

66. The correct electrochemical series can be obtained from K, Na, Ca, Al, Mg, Zn, Fe, Pb, H, Cu, Hg, Ag and Au by interchanging

(a) only Al and Mg (b) only Na and Ca
(c) both (d) none

67. Which one of the following statements is incorrect?
(a) The tendency of an electrode to lose electrons with respect to the Normal Hydrogen Electrode is called its oxidation potential.
(b) The standard oxidation potentials are taken as positive whereas standard reduction potentials are taken as negative.
(c) Oxidation potential and reduction potential of an electrode are equal in magnitude.
(d) The absolute value of the electrode potential cannot be determined.

68. Which one of the following statements is wrong?
(a) The electrode potential is called standard electrode potential if the electrode is set up in 1 M solution at 298 K.
(b) The electrode potential of Pt, H_2(1 atm) | H^+(1 M) is taken as zero.
(c) Metals which have higher standard electrode potential than the NHE react with 1 M H_2SO_4 to give H_2 gas.
(d) Greater the oxidation potential of a metal, more active is the metal.

Nernst Equation

69. Consider the following four electrodes
P = Cu^{2+} (0.0001 M) | Cu(*s*)
Q = Cu^{2+} (0.1 M) | Cu(*s*)
R = Cu^{2+} (0.01 M) | Cu(*s*)
S = Cu^{2+} (0.001 M) | Cu(*s*)
If the electrode potential of Cu^{2+}/Cu is +0.34 V, the reduction potential in volts of the above electrodes follow the order
(a) P > S > R > Q (b) S > R > Q > P
(c) R > S > Q > P (d) P > Q > R > S
(e) Q > R > S > P

70. The electrode potential of a half cell depends upon
(a) the nature of the metal
(b) the concentration of metal ions in solution
(c) the temperature
(d) all

71. The reduction potential of an electrode
(a) increases with an increase in the concentration of ions
(b) decreases with an increase in the concentration of ions
(c) remains unaffected with an increase in the concentration of ions
(d) increase with an increase in temperature

72. The standard reduction potential for Cu^{2+}/Cu is +0.34 V. The reduction potential at pH = 14 for the above couple is ([Cu^{2+}] at pH 14 is 10^{-19})
(a) –0.22 V (b) +0.22 V (c) –0.34 V (d) +0.34 V

73. The reduction potential of the hydrogen half cell will be negative if
(a) $p\,(H_2) = 1$ atm and $\left[H^+\right] = 1$ M
(b) $p\,(H_2) = 1$ atm and $\left[H^+\right] = 2$ M
(c) $p\,(H_2) = 2$ atm and $\left[H^+\right] = 1$ M
(d) $p\,(H_2) = 2$ atm and $\left[H^+\right] = 2$ M

74. If the standard electrode potential of the Cu^{2+}/Cu electrode is 0.34 V, what is the electrode potential of 0.01 M concentration of Cu^{2+}? ($T = 298$ K)
(a) 0.399 V (b) 0.281 V (c) 0.222 V (d) 0.176 V

75. The pressure of H_2 required to make the potential of the H_2 electrode zero in pure water at 298 K is
(a) 10^{-10} atm (b) 10^{-4} atm
(c) 10^{-14} atm (d) 10^{-12} atm

76. Which is the potential of platinum wire dipped into a solution of 0.1 M in Sn^{2+} and 0.01 M in Sn^{4+}?
(a) $E°$ (b) $E° + 0.059$
(c) $E° + \frac{0.059}{2}$ (d) $E° - \frac{0.059}{2}$

77. The formal potential of Fe^{3+} / Fe^{2+} in a sulfuric acid and phosphoric acid mixture ($E°$ = +0.16 V) is much lower than the standard potential ($E°$ = +0.77 V). This is due to
(a) formation of the species $[FeHPO_4]^+$
(b) lowering of potential upon complexation
(c) formation of the species $[FeSO_4]^+$
(d) high acidity of the medium

78. The emf of the cell
Tl | Tl^+(0.001 M) || Cu^{2+}(0.01 M) | Cu is 0.3 V. The emf of this cell could be increased by
(a) increasing the concentration of Tl^+ ions
(b) increasing the concentration of Cu^{2+} ions
(c) increasing the concentration of both
(d) none of the above

79. The EMF of the cell Mg | Mg^{2+}(0.01 M) || Sn^{2+}(0.1 M) | Sn at 298 K is (given $E°_{Mg^{2+}, Mg} = -2.34$ V, $E°_{Sn^{2+}, Sn} = -0.14$ V)
(a) 2.17 V (b) 2.23 V (c) 2.51 V (d) 2.45 V

80. The emf of the following Daniell cell at 298 K is E_1
Zn | $ZnSO_4$(0.01 M) || $CuSO_4$(1.0 M) | Cu
When the concentration of $ZnSO_4$ is 1.0 M and that of $CuSO_4$ is 0.01 M, the emf changed to E_2. What is the relationship between E_1 and E_2?
(a) $E_1 > E_2$ (b) $E_1 < E_2$
(c) $E_1 = E_2$ (d) $E_2 = 0 \neq E_1$

81. For $Cr_2O_7^{2-} + 14H^+ + 6e^- \rightarrow 2Cr^{3+} + 7H_2O, E° = 1.33$ V. At $[Cr_2O_7^{2-}] = 4.5$ mmol, $[Cr^{3+}] = 15$ mmol, E is 1.067 V. The pH of the solution is nearly equal to
(a) 2 (b) 3 (c) 5 (d) 4

82. What will be the emf of the following cell, given that $E°_{cell} = 1.05$ V?
$Ni(s) + 2Ag^+(0.002)\,M \rightarrow Ni^{2+}(0.160\,M) + 2Ag(s)$
(a) 0.994 V (b) 1.06 V (c) 0.91 V (d) 1.19 V

83. Two Daniell cells were set up; one with 1 M $ZnSO_4$ and 1 M $CuSO_4$, the other with 2 M $ZnSO_4$ and 2 M $CuSO_4$. Their emfs are E_1 and E_2 respectively. Then
(a) $E_1 = 2E_2$ (b) $E_1 = 2E_1$ (c) $E_2 = 4E_1$ (d) $E_1 = E_2$

84. Nernst equation gives the effect of
(a) temperature on EMF
(b) concentration on EMF
(c) pressure of the gas (if any) on EMF
(d) all the three

85. Which one of the following will increase the voltage of the cell
$Sn(s) + 2Ag^+(aq) \rightarrow Sn^{2+}(aq) + 2Ag(s)$?
(a) increase in the size of the silver rod
(b) increase in the concentration of Sn^{2+} ions
(c) increase in the concentration of Ag^+ ions
(d) none of the above

86. $Zn(s) + Cl_2(1\text{ atm}) \rightarrow Zn^{2+} + 2Cl^-$
The $E°$ of the cell is 2.12 V. To increase E,
(a) Zn^{2+} concentration should be increased
(b) Zn^{2+} concentration should be decreased
(c) Cl^- concentration should be increased
(d) partial pressure of Cl_2 should be decreased

87. Which of the following will form a cell with the highest voltage?
($E°_{Co^{2+}/Co} = -0.28$ V, $E°_{Ag^+/Ag} = 0.80$ V)
(a) 1 M Ag^+, 1 M Co^{2+} (b) 2 M Ag^+, 2 M Co^{2+}
(c) 0.1 M Ag^+, 2 M Co^{2+} (d) 2 M Ag^+, 0.1 M Co^{2+}

88. In the cell reaction,
$Cu(s) + 2Ag^+(aq) \rightarrow Cu^{2+}(aq) + 2Ag(s)$
$E°_{cell} = 0.46$ V. By doubling the concentration of Cu^{2+}, $E°_{cell}$ is:
(a) doubled
(b) halved
(c) increased but less than double
(d) decreased by a small fraction

89. In which of the following cells will the emf be independent of the activity of the chloride ions?
(a) $Zn \mid ZnCl_2(aq) \parallel Pt\,(Cl)_2$
(b) $Zn \mid ZnCl_2(aq) \parallel KCl(aq) \mid AgCl(s), Ag(s)$
(c) $Ag, AgCl(s) \parallel KCl(aq) \mid Pt(Cl_2)$
(d) $Hg, Hg_2Cl_2(s) \mid KCl(aq) \parallel AgNO_3(aq) \mid Ag(s)$

90. The standard cell potential for $Zn \mid Zn^{2+} \parallel Cu^{2+} \mid Cu$ is 1.10 V. When the cell is completely discharged, $\log \frac{[Zn^{2+}]}{[Cu^{2+}]}$ is close to
(a) 37.3 (b) 0.026 (c) 18.7 (d) 0.052

91. For the half cell

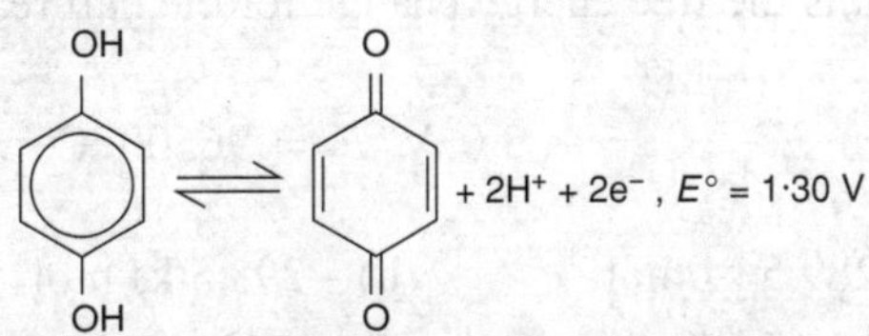

At pH = 2, electrode potential
(a) 1.36 V (b) 1.30 V (c) 1.42 V (d) 1.20 V

92. If the pressure of hydrogen gas is increased from 1 atm to 100 atm, keeping the hydrogen ion concentration constant at 1 M, the voltage of the hydrogen half cell is at 25°C will be
(a) 0.059 V (b) –0.059 V (c) 0.295 V (d) 0.118 V

93. The oxidation potential of 0.05 H_2SO_4 is
(a) -2×0.0591 (b) -0.01×0.0591
(c) -2.321×0.0591 (d) $+1 \times 0.0591$

94. A hydrogen gas electrode is made by dipping platinum wire in a solution of HCl of pH = 10 and by passing hydrogen gas around the platinum wire at one atm pressure. The oxidation potential of the electrode would be
(a) 0.059 V (b) 0.59 V (c) 0.118 V (d) 1.18 V

Equilibrium Constant from Nernst Equation

95. $2Hg \rightarrow Hg_2^{2+}, E° = -0.799$ V; $Hg \rightarrow Hg^{2+}, E° = 0.855$ V
Equilibrium constant for the reaction
$Hg + Hg^{2+} \rightarrow Hg_2^{2+}$ at 27°C is
(a) 89 (b) 82.3 (c) 79 (d) none of these

96. The standard reduction potentials in acidic conditions are 0.7 V and 0.54 V respectively for the Fe^{3+}/Fe^{2+} and I_3^-/I^- couple
$2Fe^{3+} + 3I^- \rightleftharpoons 2Fe^{2+} + I_3^-$
What will be the equilibrium constant for the reaction?
(a) 7.07×10^8 (b) 7.07×10^3
(c) 6.07×10^9 (d) 6.07×10^7

97. The value of equilibrium constant for a feasible cell reaction is
(a) < 1 (b) = 1 (c) > 1 (d) zero

98. The equilibrium constant of the reaction,
$Cu(s) + 2Ag^+(aq) \rightarrow Cu^{2+}(aq) + 2Ag(s)$

$E° = 0.46$ V at 298 K is

(a) 2.4×10^{10} (b) 2.0×10^{10}
(c) 4.0×10^{10} (d) 4.0×10^{15}

99. For a reaction $A(s) + 2B^+ \rightarrow A^{2+} + 2B$, K_c has been found to be 10^{12}. The $E°_{cell}$ is:
(a) 0.354 V (b) 0.708 V (c) 0.0098 V (d) 1.36 V

Electrochemical Cell and Gibbs Free Energy Change of the Reaction

100. What is the free energy change for the half reaction $Li^+ + e^- \rightarrow Li$?
Given $E°_{Li^+/Li} = -3.0$ V, $F = 96500$ C mol^{-1} and $T = 298$ K.
(a) 289.5 kJ mol^{-1} (b) –298.5 kJ mol^{-1}
(c) 32.166 C V^{-1} mol^{-1} (d) – 289500 C V mol^{-1}

101. The standard Gibbs free energy change ($\Delta G°$ in kJ mol^{-1}) in a Daniell cell ($E°_{cell} = 1.1$ V), when 2 mol of Zn(*s*) is oxidised at 298 K, is closest to
(a) –212.3 (b) –106.2 (c) –424.6 (d) –53.1

102. The standard free energy change (in J mol^{-1}) for the reaction $3Fe^{2+}(aq) + 2Cr(s) \rightarrow 2Cr^{3+}(aq) + 3Fe(s)$ is (given $E°_{Fe^{2+}/Fe} = -0.44$ V, $E°_{Cr^{3+}/Cr} = -0.74$ V, $F = 96500$ C)
(a) 57900 (b) –57900 (c) –173700 (d) 173700

103. Calculate standard free energy change for the reaction $\frac{1}{2}Cu(s) + \frac{1}{2}Cl_2(g) \rightleftharpoons \frac{1}{2}Cu^{2+} + Cl^-$ taking place at 25°C in a cell whose standard emf is 1.02 volts.
(a) –98430 J (b) 98430 J (c) 96500 J (d) –49215 J

104. The Gibbs energy for the decomposition of Al_2O_3 at 500°C is as follows:
$\frac{2}{3}Al_2O_3 \rightarrow \frac{4}{3}Al + O_2$; $\Delta_r G = +960$ kJ mol^{-1}
The potential difference needed for the electrolytic reduction of aluminium oxide (Al_2O_3) at 500°C is at least:
(a) 2.5 V (b) 5.0 V (c) 4.5 V (d) 3.0 V

105. The cell in which the following reaction occurs $2Fe^{3+}(aq) + 2I^-(aq) \rightarrow 2Fe^{3+}(aq) + I_2(s)$ has $E°_{cell} = 0.2360$ at 298 K. The standard free energy and equilibrium constant of the cell reaction will be respectively
(a) –45.55 kJ mol^{-1}, 9.62×10^7
(b) –22.77 kJ mol^{-1}, 4.81×10^7
(c) –91.10 mol^{-1}, 19.24×10^7
(d) none of these

106. For the cell reaction, $Cu^{2+}[C_1(aq)] + Zn(s) \rightarrow Zn^{2+}[C_2(aq)] + Cu(s)$ of an electrochemical cell, the change in free energy ΔG at a given temperature is a function of
(a) $\ln(C_1)$ (b) $\ln(C_2/C_1)$
(c) $\ln(C_1 + C_2)$ (d) $\ln(C_2)$

107. If the $E°_{cell}$ for a given reaction has a negative value, which of the following gives the correct relationship for the values of $\Delta G°$ and K_{eq}?
(a) $\Delta G° > 0, K_{eq} < 1$ (b) $\Delta G° > 0, K_{eq} > 1$
(c) $\Delta G° < 0, K_{eq} > 1$ (d) $\Delta G° < 0, K_{eq} < 1$

108. For the following cell reaction
$Ag \mid Ag^+ \mid AgCl \parallel Cl^- \mid Cl_2, Pt$
$\Delta G_f^\circ(AgCl) = -109$ kJ/mol
$\Delta G_f^\circ(Cl^-) = -129$ kJ/mol
$\Delta G_f^\circ(Ag^+) = 78$ kJ/mol
$E°$ of the cell is
(a) –0.60 V (b) 0.60 V
(c) 6.0 V (d) none of these

109. The standard emf of a Daniell cell is 1.0 volt. The maximum electrical work obtained from the Daniell cell is
(a) 212.3 kJ (b) 175.4 kJ (c) 106.15 kJ (d) 53.07 kJ

110. Calculate the standard free energy change for the reaction,
$2Ag + 2H^+ \rightarrow H_2 + 2Ag^+$
$E°$ for $Ag^+ + e^- \rightarrow Ag$ is 0.80 V
(a) +154.4 kJ (b) +308.8 kJ
(c) –154.4 kJ (d) –308.8 kJ

Concentration Cells and Liquid Junction Potential

111. Two concentration cells have Ag with Ag electrodes in $AgNO_3$. In the first cell, the concentration of one electrode is 1 M and the other electrode is 0.1 M; the emf is 0.06 V. In the second cell, the concentration of one electrode is 1 M and the other electrode is 0.01 M. Calculate the emf of the second cell.
(a) 0.12 V (b) 0.06 V (c) 0.09 V (d) 0.16 V

112. If hydrogen electrodes dipped in two solutions of pH = 3 and pH = 6 are connected via a salt bridge, the emf of the resulting cell is
(a) 0.177 V (b) 0.3 V (c) 0.052 V (d) 0.104 V

113. What will be the emf for the given cell
$Pt \mid H_2(P_1) \mid H^+(aq) \parallel H_2(P_2) \mid Pt$
(a) $\frac{RT}{f}\ln\frac{P_1}{P_2}$ (b) $\frac{RT}{2f}\ln\frac{P_1}{P_2}$

(c) $\frac{RT}{f}\ln\frac{P_2}{P_1}$ (d) none of these

114. [Pt (H_2) | H^+(1 M) || H^+(1 M) | Pt (H_2)]
P_1 P_2
P_1 and P_2 are the pressures. The cell reaction will be spontaneous if
(a) $P_1 = P_2$ (b) $P_1 > P_2$ (c) $P_2 > P_1$ (d) $P_1 = 1$ atm

115. The potential of the cell containing two hydrogen electrodes is as represented below.
Pt, $H_2(g)$ | $H^+(10^{-6}$ M) || $H^+(10^{-4}$ M) | $H_2(g)$, Pt at 298 K is
(a) –0.118 V (b) –0.0591 V
(c) 0.118 V (d) 0.0591 V

116. The emf of the cell
Pt, $Cl_2(g)$, P_1 atm | $Cl^-(aq)$(1 M) | $Cl_2(g)$, Pt, P_2 atm will be positive if
(a) $P_1 = P_2$ (b) $P_1 < P_2$
(c) $P_1 > P_2$
(d) the given cell cannot have a positive emf

117. An electrochemical cell is set up as follows:
Pt (H_2, 1 atm)/0.1 M H^+C_l/0.1 M acetic acid/(H_2, 1 atm) Pt. The emf of this cell will not be zero because
(a) the temperature is constant
(b) the pH of 0.1 M HCl and 0.1 M acetic acid is not the same
(c) acids used in the two compartments are different
(d) the emf of the cell depends on molarities of the acids used

118. Zn | $Zn^{2+}(C_1)$ || $Zn^{2+}(C_2)$ | Zn
For this cell, ΔG is negative if
(a) $C_1 = C_2$ (b) $C_1 > C_2$
(c) $C_2 > C_1$ (d) none of these

Conductance of Electrolytic Solutions

119. Electrolytic conduction differs from metallic conduction in the fact in the case of electrolytic conduction
(a) the resistance increases with increasing temperature
(b) the resistance decreases with increasing temperature
(c) the flow of current does not generate heat
(d) the resistance is independent of the length of the conductor

120. Which of the following is an insulator?
(a) graphite (b) aluminium
(c) diamond (d) silicon

121. The effect of temperature increase on conduction is as follows:
(a) metallic conduction increases, electrolytic conduction decreases
(b) electrolytic conduction increases, metallic conduction decreases
(c) both metallic and electrolytic conduction decrease
(d) both metallic and electrolytic conduction decrease

122. In terms of SI base units, ohm stands for
(a) (kg m^2)/(As) (b) (kg m^2)/(A^2s^2)
(c) (kg m^2)/(A^2s^2) (d) (kg m^2)/(A^2s^3)

123. The unit of conductivity is
(a) ohm^{-1} (b) ohm^{-1} cm^{-1}
(c) ohm^{-2} cm^{-2} $equivalent^{-1}$ (d) ohm^{-1} cm^2

124. The correct expression in the SI system relating the equivalent conductance (λ_C), specific conductance (κ) and equivalent concentration (C) is
(a) $A_C = \frac{\kappa}{C}$ (b) $A_C = \kappa \times \frac{1000}{C}$
(c) $A_C = \frac{\kappa \times 10^{-3}}{C}$ (d) $A_C = \frac{\kappa \times 10^{-6}}{C}$
where C is the number of g eq in one litre of the solution.

125. If the specific resistance of a solution of concentration C g eq L^{-1} R, then its equivalent conductance is
(a) $\frac{100\,R}{C}$ (b) $\frac{RC}{1000}$ (c) $\frac{100\,R}{RC}$ (d) $\frac{C}{1000\,R}$

126. A conductivity cell having a cell constant of 8.76 cm^{-1} placed in a 0.01 M solution of an electrolyte offered a resistance of 10000 ohms. What is the specific conductance of the electrolyte?
(a) 8.76×10^4 ohm^{-1} cm^{-1}
(b) 8.76×10^{-4} ohm^{-1} cm^{-1}
(c) 8.76×10^{-2} ohm^{-1} cm^{-1}
(d) 8.76×10^{-3} ohm^{-1} cm^{-1}

127. The cell constant of a given cell is 0.47 cm^{-1}. The resistance of a solution placed in this cell is measured to be 31.6 ohm. The conductivity of the solution (in S cm^{-1} where S has usual meaning) is
(a) 0.15 (b) 1.5 (c) 0.015 (d) 150

128. The resistance of a 0.1 N solution of a salt is found to be 2.5 $\times 10^3$ ohms. The equivalent conductance of the solution is (cell constant = 1.15 cm^{-1})
(a) 4.6 (b) 5.6 (c) 6.6 (d) 7.6

129. The equivalent conductivity of 0.1 M H_2SO_4 whose specific conductivity is 2.6 $\times 10^{-2}$ ohm^{-1} cm^{-1} will be
(a) 260 (b) 130 (c) 65 (d) 200

130. Molar conductivity of a solution of an electrolyte AB_2 is 150 ohm^{-1} cm^2 mol^{-1}. If it ionises as $AB_2 \rightarrow A^{+2} + 2\,B^{-1}$. Its equivalent conductivity will be
(a) 50 ohm^{-1} cm^{-1} mol^{-1} (b) 75 ohm^{-1} cm^{-1} mol^{-1}

(c) 150 $ohm^{-1} cm^{-1} mol^{-1}$ (d) all of these

131. The electrical resistance of a column of 0.05 mol L^{-1} NaOH solution of diameter 1 cm and length 50 cm is 5.55×10^3 ohm. Its molar conductivity is

(a) 229.6 S cm^2 mol^{-1} (b) 22.96 S cm^2 mol^{-1}
(c) 2296 S cm^2 mol^{-1} (d) 55.9 S cm^2 mol^{-1}

132. A 0.05 M NaOH solution offered a resistance of 31.6 ohm in a conductivity cell at 298 K. If the cell constant of the conductivity cell is 0.367 cm^{-1}, the molar conductance of the sodium hydroxide solution is

(a) 232 S cm^2 mol^{-1} (b) 116 S cm^2 mol^{-1}
(c) 58 S cm^2 mol^{-1} (d) 105 S cm^2 mol^{-1}

133. The molar conductivity of 0.5 mol/dm^2 solution of $AgNO_3$ with electrolyte conductivity of 5.76×10^{-3} S cm^{-1} at 298 K is

(a) 2.88 S cm^2/mol (b) 11.52 S cm^2/mol
(c) 0.086 S cm^2/mol (d) 28.8 S cm^2/mol

134. The specific conductivity of *N*/10 KCl solution at 20°C is 0.0212 $ohm^{-1} cm^{-1}$ and the resistance of the cell containing this solution at 20°C is 55 ohm. The cell constant is

(a) 4.616 cm^{-1} (b) 1.166 cm^{-1}
(c) 2.173 cm^{-1} (d) 3.324 cm^{-1}

135. The conductance of a solution of an electrolyte is equal to that of its specific conductance. The cell constant of the conductivity cell is equal to

(a) resistance (b) faraday
(c) zero (d) unity

136. Which one of the following statements is incorrect?

(a) Specific conductivity decreases with dilution.
(b) Equivalent and molar conductivities increase with dilution
(c) Λ_∞ for a weak electrolyte cannot be found by extrapolation of the graph between Λ and concentration to zero concentration.
(d) Molar conductivity of a strong electrolyte increases with dilution because ionisation increases with dilution.

137. The variation of Λ_m of acetic acid with concentration is correctly represented by

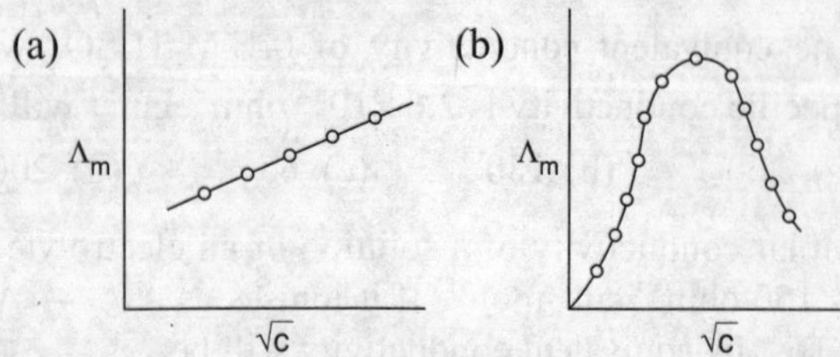

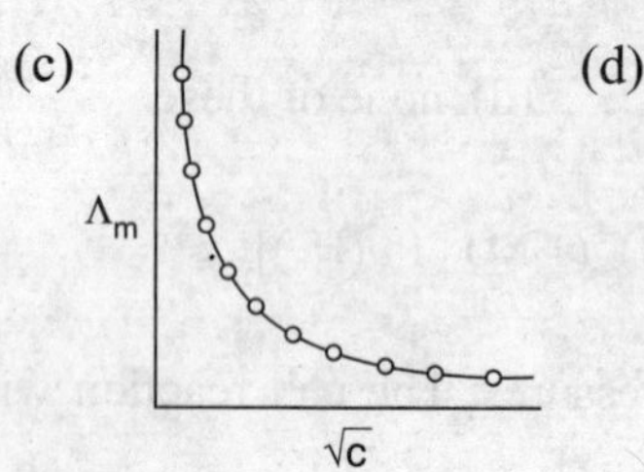

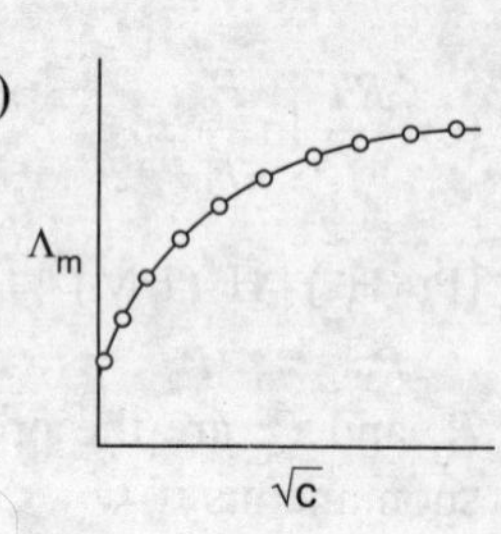

138. An increase in the equivalent conductance of a strong electrolyte with dilution is mainly due to

(a) an increase in the number of ions
(b) an increase in the ionic mobility of ions
(c) an increase in both, that is, number of ions and ionic mobility of ions
(d) 100% ionisation of the electrolyte at normal dilution

139. The increase in the molar conductivity of HCl with dilution is due to

(a) an increase in the self-ionisation of water
(b) hydrolysis of HCl
(c) decrease in the self-ionisation of water
(d) decrease in the interionic forces

140. The increase in the value of molar conductivity of acetic acid with dilution is due to

(a) a decrease in interionic forces
(b) an increase in degree of ionisation
(c) an increase in self- ionisation of water
(d) none of these

141. The molar conductivity of a strong electrolyte

(a) increases linearly with concentration
(b) increases with square root of concentration in a linear fashion
(c) decreases linearly with concentration
(d) decreases with square root of concentration in a linear fashion

142. With dilution

(a) specific conductivity increases, equivalent conductivity decreases
(b) specific conductivity decreases, equivalent conductivity increases
(c) both decrease with dilution
(d) both increase with dilution

143. Highest molar conductivity is given by

(a) 0.005 M NaCl (b) 0.1 M NaCl
(c) 0.5 M NaCl (d) 0.01 M NaCl

144. Which solution will show the highest resistance during the passage of current?

(a) 0.005 N NaCl (b) 2 N NaCl
(c) 0.1 N NaCl (d) 1 N NaCl

145. The compound exhibiting a maximum value of equivalent conductance in the fused state is

(a) $SrCl_2$ (b) $CaCl_2$ (c) $MgCl_2$ (d) $BeCl_2$

146. The molar conductivities of HCl, NaCl, CH_3COOH and CH_3COONa at infinite dilution follow the order

(a) $HCl > CH_3COOH > NaCl > CH_3COONa$
(b) $CH_3COONa > HCl > NaCl > CH_3COOH$
(c) $HCl > NaCl > CH_3COOH > CH_3COONa$
(d) $CH_3COOH > CH_3COONa > HCl > NaCl$

147. The order of equivalent conductance at infinite dilution for LiCl, NaCl, and KCl is

(a) LiCl > NaCl > KCl (b) KCl > NaCl > LiCl
(c) NaCl > KCl > LiCl (d) LiCl > KCl > NaCl

148. Which one of the following solutions will have the highest conductivity?

(a) 0.1 M CH_3COOH (b) 0.1 M NaCl
(c) 0.1 M KNO_3 (d) 0.1 M HCl

149. The equivalent conductance is the conductance of a solution provided the following conditions are satisfied. Which one of the following is wrong?

(a) The solution should contain 1 g equivalent of the electrolyte.
(b) The distance between the electrodes should be about 1 cm.
(c) The area of the electrodes should be so large that the solution should touch them completely.
(d) The volume of the solution should be very small.

150. Which of the following is wrong about molar conductivity?

(a) The solution contains Avogadro's number of molecules of the electrolyte.
(b) It is the product of specific conductivity and volume of solution in cc containing 1 mol of the electrolyte.
(c) Its units are $ohm^{-1}\ cm^2\ mol^{-1}$.
(d) Its value for 1 M NaCl solution is same as that of 1 M glucose solution.

151. A conductivity cell is platinised

(a) to prolong its life
(b) to avoid polarisation effect
(c) to avoid capacitance of the cell
(d) to avoid temperature effects

Kohlrausch's Law and its Applications

152. The molar conductances of $BaCl_2.H_2SO_4$ and HCl at infinite dilutions are x_1, x_2 and x_3 respectively. The equivalent conductance of $BaSO_4$ at infinite dilution will be

(a) $\frac{(x_1 + x_2 - x_3)}{2}$ (b) $\frac{(x_1 - x_2 - x_3)}{2}$
(c) $2(x_1 + x_2 - 2x_3)$ (d) $\frac{x_1 + x_2 - 2x_3}{2}$

153. Which of the following is correct for calculating Λ_m° for water?

(a) $\lambda_m^\circ(H_2O) = \lambda_m^\circ(HCl) + \lambda_m^\circ(NaCl) - \lambda_m^\circ(NaOH)$
(b) $\lambda_m^\circ(H_2O) = \lambda_m^\circ(HCl) - \lambda_m^\circ(NaCl) + \lambda_m^\circ(NaOH)$
(c) $\lambda_m^\circ(H_2O) = \lambda_m^\circ(NaCl) - \lambda_m^\circ(HCl) - \lambda_m^\circ(NaOH)$
(d) $\lambda_m^\circ(H_2O) = \lambda_m^\circ(BaCl_2) + \lambda_m^\circ(NaOH) - \lambda_m^\circ(Ba(OH)_2)$

154. According to Kohlrausch's law, the limiting value of molar conductivity of an electrolyte, A_2B is

(a) $\lambda^\infty_{(A^+)} = \lambda^\infty_{(B^-)}$ (b) $\lambda^\infty_{(A^+)} - \lambda^\infty_{(B^-)}$
(c) $2\lambda^\infty_{(A^+)} + \lambda\frac{1}{2}^\infty_{(B^-)}$ (d) $2\lambda^\infty_{(A^+)} + \lambda^\infty_{(B^-)}$

155. The equivalent conductance at infinite dilution of a weak acid such as HF

(a) can be determined by extrapolation of measurements on dilute solutions of HCl, HBr and HI
(b) can be determined by measurement on very dilute HF solution
(c) can best be determined from measurements on dilute solutions of NaF, NaCl and HCl
(d) is an undefined quantity

156. Molar ionic conductivities of a bi-bivalent electrolyte are 57 and 73. The molar conductivity of the solution will be

(a) $130\ S\ cm^2\ mol^{-1}$ (b) $65\ S\ cm^2\ mol^{-1}$
(c) $260\ S\ cm^2\ mol^{-1}$ (d) $187\ S\ cm^2\ mol^{-1}$

157. If the molar conductance values of Ca^{2+} and Cl^- at infinite dilution are respectively $118.88 \times 10^{-4}\ m^2$ mho mol^{-1} and $77.33 \times 10^{-4}\ m^2$ mho mol^{-1} then that of $CaCl_2$ in (in m^2 mho mol^{-1})

(a) 118.88×10^{-4} (b) 154.66×10^{-4}
(c) 273.54×10^{-4} (d) 196.21×10^{-4}

158. If the molar conductivities (in $S\ cm^2\ mol^{-1}$) of NaCl, KCl and NaOH at infinite dilution are 126, 150 and 250 respectively, the molar conductivity of KOH (in $S\ cm^2\ mol^{-1}$)is

(a) 526 (b) 226 (c) 26 (d) 274

159. The molar conductivities of NaOH, NaCl and $BaCl_2$ at infinite dilution are $2.481 \times 10^{-2}\ S\ m^2\ mol^{-1}$, $1.265 \times 10^{-2}\ S\ m^2\ mol^{-1}$ and $2.800 \times 10^{-2}\ S\ m^2\ mol^{-1}$ respectively. The molar conductivity of $Ba(OH)_2$ at infinite dilution will be

(a) $5.232 \times 10^{-2}\ S\ m^2\ mol^{-1}$
(b) $9.654 \times 10^{-2}\ S\ m^2\ mol^{-1}$
(c) $4.016 \times 10^{-2}\ S\ m^2\ mol^{-1}$
(d) $1.145 \times 10^{-2}\ S\ m^2\ mol^{-1}$

160. The ionic conductance of Ba^{2+} and Cl^- are respectively 127 and 76 Ω^{-1} cm^2 at infinite dilution. The equivalent conductance (in Ω^{-1} cm^2) of $BaCl_2$ at infinite dilution will be

(a) 139.5 (b) 203 (c) 279 (d) 101.5

161. The equivalent conductances at infinite dilution (Λ_0) for electrolytes BA and CA re 140 and 120 S cm^2 eq^{-1}. The Λ_0 (in S cm^2 eq^{-1}) of CS is

(a) 178 (b) 198 (c) 218 (d) 130

162. Given that the limiting molar conductances of $Ba(OH)_2$, $BaCl_2$ and NH_4Cl are 523.28, 280.0 and 129.8 Scm^2 mol^{-1} respectively, the limiting molar conductance of NH_4OH (in S cm^2 mol^{-1}) will be

(a) 251.44 (b) 373.80 (c) 543.68 (d) 673.48

163. Equivalent conductivity at infinite dilution for sodium potassium oxalate, $(COO^-)_2$ Na^2 K^+, will be (given, molar conductivities of oxalate K^+ and Na^+ ions at infinite dilution are 148.2, 50.1, 73.5 S cm^2 mol^{-1} respectively)

(a) 271.8 S cm^2 eq^{-1} (b) 67.95 S cm^2 eq^{-1}
(c) 543.6 S cm^2 eq^{-1} (d) 135.9 S cm^2 eq^{-1}

164. The molar conductivity of 0.025 mol L^{-1} methanoic acid is 46.1 S cm^2 mol^{-1}. Its dissociation constant will be (given, $\lambda^\circ_{H^+}$ = 349.6 S cm^2 mol^{-1} and $\lambda^\circ_{HCOO^-}$ = 54.6 S cm^2 mol^{-1})

(a) 3.67×10^{-4} (b) 3.22×10^{-3}
(c) 6.67×10^{-5} (d) 3.22×10^{-4}

165. The degree of ionisation increases

(a) with an increase in the concentration of the solution
(b) on addition of excess of water to the solution
(c) on decreasing the temperature of the solution
(d) on stirring the solution vigorously

166. The molar ionic conductivities of NH_4^+ and OH^- at infinite dilution are 72 and 198 ohm^{-1} cm^2 respectively. The molar conductivity of a centinormal NH_4OH solution at the same temperature is found to be 9 ohm^{-1} cm^2. The percentage dissociation of NH_4OH at this concentration will be

(a) 3.33% (b) 7.14 % (c) 12.5% (d) 4.54 %

167. If the equivalent conductance of 1 M benzoic acid is 12.8 ohm^{-1} cm^2 and if the conductances of benzoate ion and H^+ ion are 42 and 288.42 ohm^{-1} cm^2 respectively, its degree of dissociation is

(a) 39% (b) 3.9% (c) 0.35% (d) 0.039%

168. The equivalent conductance of $\frac{M}{32}$ solution of a weak monobasic acid is 8.0 mho cm^2 and at infinite dilution is 400 mho cm^2. The dissociation constant of the acid is

(a) 1.25×10^{-6} (b) 6.25×10^{-4}
(c) 1.25×10^{-4} (d) 1.25×10^{-5}

169. The specific conductance (κ) of 0.02 M aqueous acetic acid solution at 298 K is 1.65×10^{-4} S cm^{-1}. The degree of dissociation of acetic acid is (given: equivalent conductance at infinite dilution of H^+ = 349.1 S cm^2 mol^{-1} and CH_3COO^- = 40.9 S cm^2 mol^{-1})

(a) 0.021 (b) 0.21 (c) 0.012 (d) 0.12

170. The solubility of a sparingly soluble salt *S*, specific conductance κ and the equivalent conductance Λ_0 are related as

(a) $S = \frac{1000\Lambda_c}{\kappa}$ (b) $S = \kappa\Lambda_0$
(c) $S = \frac{\kappa}{1000\Lambda_c}$ (d) $S = \frac{1000}{\Lambda_0}$

171. The specific conductance of saturated solution of AgCl is found to be 1.86×10^{-6} ohm^{-1} cm^{-1} and that of water is 6×10^{-8} ohm^{-1} cm^{-1}. The solubility of AgCl is (Given Λ°_{AgCl} = 137.2 ohm^{-1} cm^2 eq^{-1})

(a) 1.7×10^{-3} M (b) 1.3×10^{-5} M
(c) 1.3×10^{-4} M (d) 1.3×10^{-6} M

172. Unit of ionic mobility is

(a) m^2 s^{-1} V^{-1} (b) ms^{-1} (c) ms^{-1} V (d) ms^{-1} V^{-1}

173. The correct order of the mobility of the alkali metal ions in aqueous solution is

(a) $K^+ > Rb^+ > Na^+ > Li^+$
(b) $Rb^+ > K^+ > Na^+ > Li^+$
(c) $Li^+ > Na^+ > K^+ > Rb^+$
(d) $Na^+ > K^+ > Rb^+ > Li^+$

174. Which one of the following ions has the highest limiting molar conductivity?

(a) Na^+ (b) Mg^{2+} (c) K^+ (d) Ca^{2+}

175. Which one of the following statements is wrong?

(a) K^+ has different molar ionic conductivity at infinite dilution in KCl and KBr.
(b) Λ°_m for $BaCl_2 = \Lambda^\circ_m(Ba^{2+}) + 2\Lambda^\circ_m(Cl^-)$.
(c) Degree of dissociation, $\alpha = \frac{\Lambda_c}{\Lambda_0}$.
(d) Kohlrausch's law can be used for finding Λ_0 for weak electrolytes.

176. Ionic mobility of which of the following alkali metal ions is the lowest when aqueous solutions of their salts are put under an electric field?

(a) Na (b) K (c) Rb (d) Li

177. Given the limiting molar conductivity as

$\overset{\circ}{\Lambda}_m$ (HCl) = 425.9 Ω^{-1} cm^{-2} mol^{-1}

$\overset{\circ}{\Lambda}_m$ (NaCl) = 126.4 Ω^{-1} cm^2 mol^{-1}

$\overset{\circ}{\Lambda}_m$ (CH_3COONa) = 91 Ω^{-1} cm^2 mol^{-1}

The molar conductivity at infinite dilution of acetic acid (in Ω^{-1} cm^2 mol^{-1}) will be

(a) 481.5 (b) 390.5 (c) 299.5 (d) 516.9

178.

Electrolyte	KCl	KNO_3	HCl	NaOAc	NaCl
Λ_∞ (S cm^2 mol^{-1})	149.9	145.9	426.2	91.0	126.5

Calculate Λ^∞_{HOAc} using appropriate molar conductances of the electrolytes listed above at infinite dilution in H_2O at 25 °C.

(a) 517.2 (b) 552.7 (c) 390.7 (d) 217.5

179. Which of the following expressions correctly represents the equivalent conductance at infinite dilution of $Al_2(SO_4)_3$, given that $\overset{\circ}{\lambda}_{Al^{3+}}$ and $\overset{\circ}{\lambda}_{SO_4^{2-}}$ are the equivalent conductances at infinite dilution of the respective ions?

(a) $2\overset{\circ}{\lambda}_{Al^{3+}} + 3\overset{\circ}{\lambda}_{SO_4^{2-}}$ (b) $\overset{\circ}{\lambda}_{Al^{3+}} + \overset{\circ}{\lambda}_{SO_4^{2-}}$

(c) $(\overset{\circ}{\lambda}_{Al^{3+}} + \overset{\circ}{\lambda}_{SO_4^{2-}}) \times 6$ (d) $\frac{1}{3}\overset{\circ}{\lambda}_{Al^{3+}} + \frac{1}{2}\overset{\circ}{\lambda}_{SO_4^{2-}}$

Electrolytic Cells and Electrolysis

180. On electrolysing a solution of dilute H_2SO_4 between platinum electrodes, the gas evolved at the anode is

(a) SO_2 (b) SO_3 (c) O_2 (d) H_2

181. On electrolysis, which of the following does not give out oxygen?

(a) acidic water using Pt electrodes
(b) fused NaOH using Pt electrodes
(c) dilute H_2SO_4 using Pt electrodes
(d) dilute H_2SO_4 using Cu electrodes

182. Which one of the following reactions occurs at the anode on electrolysis of an aqueous solution of $CuCl_2$?

(a) $Cu \rightarrow Cu^{2+} + 2e^-$
(b) $2Cl^- \rightarrow Cl_2 + 2e^-$
(c) $2H_2O \rightarrow O_2 + 4H^+ + 4e^-$
(d) $4Cl^- + 2H_2O \rightarrow 4HCl + O_2 + 4e^-$

183. In the electrolysis of which solution, are OH^- ions discharged in preference to Cl^- ions?

(a) dilute NaCl (b) very dilute NaCl
(c) fused NaCl (d) solid NaCl

184. Which pair of electrolytes cannot be distinguished by the products of electrolysis using inert electrodes?

(a) 1 M $CuSO_4$ solution, 1 M $CuCl_2$ solution
(b) 1 M KCl solution, 1 M KI solution
(c) 1 M $AgNO_3$ solution, 1 M $Cu(NO_3)_2$ solution
(d) 1 M KCl solution, 1 M NaCl solution
(e) I M $CuBr_2$ solution, 1 M $CuSO_4$ solution

185. In the electrolysis of an aqueous solution of NaF, the product obtained at the cathode and anode respectively are

(a) Na, F_2 (b) Na, O_2 (c) H_2, O_2 (d) H_2, F_2

186. The products formed when an aqueous solution of NaBr is electrolysed in a cell having inert electrodes, are

(a) Na and Br_2 (b) Na and O_2
(c) H_2, Br_2 and NaOH (d) H_2 and O_2

187. Products of electrolysis of an aqueous solution of $AgNO_3$ using silver electrodes will be (given $\overset{\circ}{E}_{Ag^+/Ag}$ = +0.80 V)

(a) Ag at cathode, O_2 at anode
(b) H_2 at cathode, O_2 at anode
(c) Ag at cathode, dissolution of Ag from anode
(d) H_2 at cathode, dissolution of Ag from anode

188. During the electrolysis of aqueous sodium chloride, the cathodic reaction is

(a) oxidation of Cl^- ions (b) reduction of Na^+ ions
(c) reduction of H_2O (d) oxidation of H_2O

189. Which one of the following takes place at the anode when an aqueous solution of $CuSO_4$ is electrolysed using copper electrodes?

(a) $Cu \rightarrow Cu^{2+} + 2e^-$
(b) $SO_4^{2-} \rightarrow SO_2 + O_2 + 2e^-$
(c) $2SO_4^{2-} + 2H_2O \rightarrow 2H_2SO_4 + O_2 + 4e^-$
(d) $2H_2O \rightarrow O_2 + 4H^+ + 4e^-$

190. Of the following, metals that cannot be obtained by electrolysis of the aqueous solution of their salts are

(a) Ag and Mg (b) Ag and Al
(c) Mg and Al (d) Cu and Cr

191. The metal that cannot be obtained by electrolysis of an aqueous solution of its salt is

(a) Cr (b) Ag (c) Ca (d) Cu

192. Give the products available on the cathode and the anode respectively during the electrolysis of an aqueous solution of $MgSO_4$ between inert electrodes.

(a) $H_2(g)$ and $O_2(g)$ (b) $O_2(g)$ and $H_2(g)$
(c) $O_2(g)$ and $Mg(g)$ (d) $O_2(g)$ and $SO_2(g)$

193. On passing C ampere of electricity through an electrolyte solution for t seconds, m gram metal deposits on the cathode. The eq. wt. of metal is

(a) $E = \frac{Ct}{m \times 96500}$ (b) $E = \frac{C \times m}{t \times 96500}$

(c) $E = \frac{96500 \times m}{C \times t}$ (d) $E = \frac{C \times t \times 96500}{m}$

194. A certain quantity of electricity is passed through an aqueous solution of $AgNO_3$ and cupric salt solution connected in series. If the amount of Ag deposited is 1.08 g, then the amount of copper deposited is (At. wt. Cu = 63.5; Ag = 108).

(a) 0.6454 g (b) 6.354 g (c) 0.3177 g (d) 3.177 g

195. What current is to be passed for 0.25 s for deposition of a certain weight of metal which is equal to its electrochemical equivalent?

(a) 4 A (b) 100 A (c) 200 A (d) 2 A

196. An electric current is passed through a silver voltameter connected to a water voltameter. The cathode of the silver voltameter weighed 0.108 g more at the end of the electrolysis. The volume of the oxygen evolved at STP is

(a) 56 cm^3 (b) 560 cm^3 (c) 5.6 cm^3 (d) 11.2 cm^3

197. Three electrolytic cells A, B and C containing electrolytes $ZnSO_4$, $AgNO_3$ and $CuSO_4$ respectively are connected in series. A steady current of 1.50 ampere was passed through them until 1.45 g of Ag was deposited at the cathode of cell B. The mass of Cu and Zn deposited will be respectively (At. wt: Cu = 63.5, Zn = 65.3, Ag = 108)

(a) 0.426 g, 0.438 g (b) 0.852 g, 0.876 g
(c) 0.852 g, 0.438 g (d) 0.426 g, 0.876 g

198. A current is passed through two cells connected in series. The first cell contains $X(NO_3)_3(aq)$ and the second cell contains $Y(NO_3)_2(aq)$. The relative atomic masses of X and Y are in the ratio 1 : 2. What is the ratio of the liberated mass of X to that of Y?

(a) 3 : 2 (b) 1 : 2 (c) 1 : 3 (d) 3 : 1

199. Equal quantities of electricity are passed through three voltameters containing $FeSO_4$, $Fe_2(SO_4)_2$ and $Fe(NO_3)_3$ Consider the following statements in the regard:

1. The amount of iron deposited in $FeSO_4$ and $Fe_2(SO_4)_3$ are equal.
2. The amount of iron deposited in $Fe(NO_3)_3$ is two-thirds of the amount of iron deposited in $FeSO_4$.
3. The amount of iron deposited in $Fe_2(SO_4)_3$ and $Fe(NO_3)_3$ is equal.

Of these statements

(a) 1 alone is correct (b) 1 and 2 are correct
(c) 2 and 3 are correct (d) 3 alone is correct

200. The weight of silver (at. wt. = 108) displaced by a quantity of electricity which displaces 5600 mL of O_2 at STP will be

(a) 5.4 g (b) 10.8 g (c) 54.0 g (d) 108.0 g

201. The number of faradays needed to reduce 4 g eq of Cu^{2+} to Cu metal will be

(a) 1 (b) 2 (c) 1/2 (d) 4

202. The electrochemical equivalent of silver is 0.001118 g. When an electric current of 0.5 ampere is passed through an aqueous silver nitrate solution for 200 seconds, the amount of silver deposited is

(a) 1.118 g (b) 0.1118 g (c) 5.590 g (d) 0.5590 g

203. The same amount of electricity was passed through two separate electrolytic cells containing solutions of nickel nitrate and chromium nitrate respectively. If 0.3 g of nickel was deposited in the first cell, the amount of chromium deposited is (At. wt. of Ni = 59, Cr = 52)

(a) 0.1 g (b) 0.17 g (c) 0.3 g (d) 0.6 g

204. From the solution of an electrolyte, one mol of electrons will deposit at cathode

(a) 63.5 g of Cu (b) 24 g of Mg
(c) 1.5 g of Na (d) 9.0 g of Al

205. When an electric current is passed through acidulated water, 112 mL of hydrogen gas at NTP is collected at the cathode in 965 seconds. The current passed in amperes, is

(a) 1.0 (b) 0.5 (c) 0.1 (d) 2.0

206. When one faraday of electric current is passed, the mass deposited is equal to

(a) equivalent weight (b) molecular weight
(c) electrochemical equivalent
(d) one gram

207. On passing 3 A of electricity for 50 min, 1.8 g metal deposits. The equivalent mass of metal is

(a) 9.3 (b) 19.3 (c) 38.3 (d) 39.9

208. 1 C electricity deposits

(a) 10.8 g of Ag
(b) 96500 g of Ag
(c) electrochemical equivalent of Ag
(d) half of electrochemical equivalent of Ag

209. 4.5 g of aluminium (atomic mass 27 is deposited at the cathode from a molten electrolyte containing Al^{3+} ions by a certain quantity of electric charge. The volume of hydrogen produced at STP from H^+ ions in a solution by the same quantity of electric charge will be

(a) 44.8 L (b) 11.2 L (c) 22.4 L (d) 5.6 L

210. During the electrolysis of an electrolyte, the number of ions produced, is directly proportional to the

(a) time consumed
(b) electrochemical equivalent of electrolysis
(c) quantity of electricity passed
(d) mass of electrons

211. Two electrolytic cells, one containing acidified ferrous chloride and another acidified ferric chloride are connected in series. The ratio of iron deposited at the cathodes in the two cells when electricity is passed through the cells will be

(a) 3 : 1 (b) 2 : 1 (c) 1 : 1 (d) 3 : 2

212. 2.5 F of electricity is passed through a $CuSO_4$ solution. The number of g eq of Cu deposited on the cathode is

(a) zero (b) 1.25 (c) 2.5 (d) 5.0

213. Copper can be deposited from acidified copper sulfate and alkaline cuprous cyanide. If the same current is passed for a definite time

(a) the amount of copper deposited from acidic copper sulfate will be higher
(b) the amount of copper deposited from alkaline cuprous cyanide will be higher
(c) the same amount of copper will be deposited
(d) none of these

214. If same amount of electricity is passed through aqueous solutions of $AgNO_3$ and $CuSO_4$ and the number of Ag and Cu atoms deposited are x and y respectively, then

(a) $x = y$ (b) $x < y$ (c) $y = 2x$ (d) $x = 2y$

215. How many cc of oxygen will be liberated by 2 ampere current flowing for 3 minutes and 13 seconds through acidulated water?

(a) 11.2 cc (b) 33.6 cc (c) 44.8 cc (d) 22.4 cc

216. A current of strength 2.5 ampere was passed through $CuSO_4$ solution for 6 minutes 26 seconds. The amount of copper deposited is (At. wt of Cu = 63.5; faraday = 96500 coulombs)

(a) 0.3175 g (b) 3.175 g (c) 0.635 g (d) 6.35 g

217. The number of coulombs required for oxidation of 1 mol of H_2O to O_2 is

(a) 9.65×10^4 (b) 1.93×10^5
(c) 1.93×10^4 (d) 1.93×10^2

218. At STP 1.2 litre of H_2 is obtained on flowing a current for 96.5 s in a solution. The value of current in amperes is

(a) 10 (b) 1.0 (c) 1.5 (d) 2.0

219. Aluminium oxide may be electrolysed at 1000°C to furnish aluminium metal (atomic mass = 27 amu, 1 faraday = 96500 coulombs). The cathode reaction is

$Al^{3+} + 3e^- \rightarrow Al^0$

To prepare 5.12 kg of aluminium metal by this method would require

(a) 5.49×10^7 C of electricity
(b) 1.83×10^7 C of electricity
(c) 5.59×10^4 C of electricity
(d) 5.49×10^1 C of electricity

220. The quantity of electricity required for the oxidation of 1 mol of FeO to Fe_2O_3 is

(a) 1 F (b) 2 F (c) 4 F (d) 0.5 F

221. How many coulombs of electricity are required for the reduction of 1 mol of MnO_4^- to Mn^{2+}

(a) 96500 C (b) 1.93×10^5 C
(c) 4.83×10^5 C (d) 9.65×10^6 C

222. How many coulombs are required for the oxidation of 1 mol of H_2O_2 to O_2?

(a) 93000 C (b) 1.93×10^5 C
(c) 9.65×10^4 C (d) 19.3×10^3 C

223. How much quantity of electricity has to be passed through 200 mL of 0.5 M $CuSO_4$ solution to completely deposit copper?

(a) 96500 C (b) 2×9650 C
(c) 2×96500 C (d) 4×96500 C

224. If three faradays of electricity is passed through the solutions of $AgNO_3$, $CuSO_4$ and $AuCl_3$, the molar ratio of the cations deposited at the cathodes will be

(a) 1 : 1 : 1 (b) 1 : 2 : 3 (c) 3 : 2 : 1 (d) 6 : 3 : 2

225. Al_2O_3 is reduced by electrolysis at low potentials and high currents. If 4.0×10^4 amperes of current is passed through molten Al_2O_3 for 6 hours, what mass of aluminium is produced? (Assume 100% current efficiency. At mass of Al = 27 g mol^{-1})

(a) 8.1×10^4 g (b) 2.4×10^5 g
(c) 1.3×10^4 g (d) 9.0×10^3 g

226. The number of chlorine molecules deposited from molten sodium chloride in one minute by current of 300 milliamperes is

(a) 5.616×10^{18} (b) 5.616×10^{19}
(c) 5.616×10^{20} (d) 5.616×10^{21}

227. How many atoms of calcium will be deposited from a solution of $CaCl_2$ by a current of 5 mA flowing for 60 s?

(a) 4.68×10^{18} (b) 4.68×10^{15}
(c) 4.68×10^{12} (d) 4.68×10^9

228. When 0.1 mol MnO_4^{2-} is oxidised, the quantity of electricity required to completely oxidise MnO_4^{2-} to MnO_4^- is

(a) 96500 C (b) 2×96500 C
(c) 9650 C (d) 96.50 C

229. One faraday of electricity is passed through an aqueous solution of sodium chloride. It produces

(a) one mol of oxygen at the anode
(b) 1 g of hydrogen at the cathode
(c) neither hydrogen nor oxygen is produced
(d) sodium is deposited at the cathode in equivalent proportion

230. At STP, 1.12 litre of H_2 is obtained on flowing a current for 965 seconds in a solution. The value of current in amperes is

(a) 10 (b) 1.0 (c) 1.5 (d) 2.0

231. The time required to deposit one mmol of aluminium metal by the passage of 9.65 amperes through an aqueous solution of aluminium ions is

(a) 30 s (b) 10 s
(c) 30000 s (d) 10000 s

232. On the basis of information available from the reaction

$$\frac{4}{3}\text{Al} + O_2 \rightarrow \frac{2}{3}\text{Al}_2O_3,\ \Delta G = -8.27\ \text{kJ mol}^{-1}$$

(a) 2.14 V (b) 4.28 V (c) 6.42 V (d) 8.56 V

233. The change required for the reduction of 1 mol of MnO_4^- to MnO_2 is

(a) 1 F (b) 3 F (c) 5 F (d) 7 F

234. A current of 9.65 A is drawn from a Daniell cell for exactly one hour. Given the weights of Cu and Zn are 63.5 g mol^{-1} and 65.4 g mol^{-1} respectively, the decrease in mass of anode and increase in the mass of cathode will be respectively

(a) 11.43 g, 11.77 g (b) 11.77 g, 11.43 g
(c) 22.86 g, 23.54 g (d) 23.54 g, 22.86 g

235. The quantity of electricity required to liberate 112 cc of hydrogen at STP from acidified water is

(a) 965 C (b) 9650 C (c) 96500 C (d) 4825 C

236. The volume of H_2 obtained at STP when Mg is obtained by passing a current of 0.5 amp through molten $MgCl_2$ for 32.2 minutes is treated with excess dilute HCl is approximately (Eq. mass of Mg = 12)

(a) 56 cm^3 (b) 28 cm^3 (c) 5.6 cm^3 (d) 112 cm^3

237. What is the time required (in s) for depositing all the silver present in 125 of 1 M $AgNO_3$ solution by passing a current of 241.25 A? (1 F = 96500 C)

(a) 10 (b) 50 (c) 1000 (d) 100

238. How many coulombs are required to deposit 50 g of aluminium when the electrode reaction is

$Al^{3+} + 3e^- \rightarrow Al$

(a) 536111 C (b) 536.111 C
(c) 96500 C (d) 38600 C

239. The number of electrons involved in redox reactions when a faraday of electricity is passed through an electrolyte in solution is

(a) 6×10^{23} (b) 6×10^{22} (c) 96500 (d) 8×10^{19}

240. The number of electrons required to deposit 1 g atom of aluminium (at. wt. = 27) from a solution of aluminium chloride will be (where *N* is the Avogadro's number)

(a) 1 N (b) 2 N (c) 3 N (d) 4 N

241. The amount of copper deposited by one faraday current will be maximum in an acidic solution of one litre of

(a) 1 M Cu_2Cl_2 (b) 2 M $Cu(NO_3)_2$ (c) 5 M $CuSO_4$
(d) 5 M $Cu_3(PO_4)_2$ (e) 10 M CuF_2

242. From the solution of which of the following, will one faraday of electricity liberate one gram atom of metal?

(a) NaCl (b) $BaCl_2$ (c) $CuSO_4$ (d) $AlCl_3$

243. Silver is removed electrically from 200 mL of a 0.1 N solution of $AgNO_3$ by a current of 10 ampere. How long will it take to remove half of the silver from the solution

(a) 16 s (b) 96.5 s (c) 100 s (d) 10 s

244. In order to separate oxygen from one mol of H_2O, the required quantity of coulombs would be

(a) 1.93×10^5 (b) 9.6×10^4 (c) 1.8 (d) 3.2

245. The number of coulombs required to reduce 12.3 g of nitrobenzene to aniline

(a) 115800 C (b) 5790 C
(c) 28950 C (d) 57900 C

246. On passing electric current through molten aluminium chloride, 11.2 litre of Cl_2 is liberated at NTP at the anode. The quantity of aluminium deposited at the cathode is (at. wt. of Al = 27)

(a) 9 g (b) 18 g (c) 27 g (d) 36 g

247. In the electrolysis of an aqueous solution of NaOH, 2.8 litre of oxygen gas at NTP was liberated at the anode. How much of hydrogen gas was liberated at the cathode?

(a) 2.8 litre (b) 5.6 litre
(c) 11.2 litre (d) 22.4 litre

248. Which one of following statements is wrong about a galvanic cell (GC) and an electrolytic cell (EC)?

(a) GC produces electricity, EC consumes electricity.
(b) GC uses a salt bridge/porous pot, EC does not.
(c) Anode of GC is negative while anode of EC is positive.
(d) In both GC and EC, the redox reaction is spontaneous.

249. The cathode in a galvanic cell and electrolytic cell is

(a) negatively charged in both cases
(b) positively charged in both cases
(c) positively charged in galvanic cell but negatively charged in an electrolytic cell
(d) negatively charged in a galvanic cell but positively charged in an electrolytic cell

250. Which one of the following statements is correct?

(a) In a galvanic cell, the free energy of the system decreases while in an electrolytic cell, it increases.
(b) In an electrolytic cell, the free energy of the system decreases while in a galvanic cell it increases.
(c) Free energy increases in both.
(d) Free energy decreases in both.

251. Charge on one monovalent ion is
(a) 96500 faraday (b) 1 faraday
(c) 1.60×10^{19} coulomb (d) 1 coulomb

252. Four mol of electrons were transferred from the anode to the cathode in an experiment on electrolysis of water. The total volume of the two gases (dry and at STP) produced will be approximately (in litres)
(a) 22.4 (b) 44.8 (c) 67.2 (d) 89.4

253. If a current of 0.5 ampere flows through a metallic wire for 2 h, the number of electrons flowing through the wire is
(a) 2.246×10^{20} (b) 2.246×10^{21}
(c) 2.246×10^{22} (d) 2.246×10^{23}

254. A current of 2.0 A passed for 5 h through a molten metal salt deposits 22.2 g of metal (At wt. = 177). The oxidation state of the metal in the metal salt is
(a) +1 (b) +2 (c) +3 (d) +4

255. In the electrolysis of alkaline water, a total of 1 mol of gases is evolved. The amount of water decomposed is
(a) 1 mol (b) 2 mol (c) 1/3 mol (d) 2/3 mol

256. Time required to deposit one mmol of aluminium metal by the passage of 9.65 amperes through an aqueous solution of aluminium ions is
(a) 30 s (b) 10 s (c) 30000 s (d) 10000 s

257. In the electrolysis of NaCl when a Pt electrode is taken, H_2 is liberated at the cathode. While with a Hg cathode, it forms sodium amalgam. This is because
(a) Hg is more inert than Pt
(b) more voltage is required to reduce H^+ at Hg than at Pt
(c) Na is dissolved in Hg while it does not dissolve in Pt
(d) concentration of H^+ ions is larger when Pt electrode is taken

258. In electroplating, the article to be electroplated is made
(a) the cathode (b) the anode
(c) either the cathode or anode
(d) simply suspended in the electrolytic bath

259. In the electroplating of silver over an article made of iron, the electrolyte generally used is
(a) $AgNO_3$ (b) AgCl
(c) Ag_2SO_4 (d) $Na[Ag(CN)_2]$

260. How many coulombs of electricity are consumed when 100 mA current is passed through a solution of $AgNO_3$ for half an hour during an electrolysis experiment?
(a) 108 (b) 180 (c) 1800 (d) 18000

261. 10800 C of electricity passed through an electrolyte solution deposited 2.977 g of a metal with atomic mass 106.4 g mol^{-1}. The charge on the metal cation is
(a) +4 (b) +3 (c) +2 (d) +1

262. The density and eq. wt of a metal are 10.5 g cm^{-3} and 100 respectively. The time required for a current of 3 amp to deposit a 0.005 mm thick layer of the same metal on an area of 80 cm^2 is closest to
(a) 120 s (b) 135 s (c) 67.5 s (d) 270 s

263. For electroplating, 1.5 amp current is passed for 250 s through 250 mL of 0.05 M solution of MSO_4. Only 85% of the current was utilised for electrolysis. The molarity of MSO_4 solution after electrolysis is closest to (assume that the volume of the solution remains constant)
(a) 0.14 (b) 0.014 (c) 0.07 (d) 0.035

264. The number of electrons delivered at the cathode during electrolysis by a current of 1 amp in 60 s is (change on the electron = 1.60×10^{-19} C)
(a) 6×10^{23} (b) 6×10^{20}
(c) 3.75×10^{20} (d) 7.48×10^{23}

265. One litre of 1 M $CuSO_4$ solution is electrolysed. After the passage of 2 F charge, the molarity of $CuSO_4$ solution will be
(a) M/2 (b) M/4 (c) M (d) zero

266. Platinum electrodes were immersed in a solution of cupric sulfate and electric current passed through the solution. After some time, it was found that the colour of copper sulfate disappeared with the evolution of a gas at the electrode. The colourless solution contains
(a) platinum sulfate (b) copper hydroxide
(c) copper sulfate (d) sulfuric acid

267. Total charge on 1 mol of a monovalent metal ion is equal to
(a) 9.65×10^4 coulomb (b) 6.28×10^{18} coulomb
(c) 1.6×10^{-19} coulomb (d) none of these

268. In the electrolytic cell, flow of electrons is from
(a) cathode to anode in the solution
(b) cathode to anode through the external supply
(c) cathode to anode through the internal supply
(d) anode to cathode through internal supply

269. When electric current is passed through a cell having an electrolyte, the positive ions move towards the cathode and the negative ions towards the anode. If the cathode is pulled out of the solution
(a) the positive and negative ions will move towards the anode
(b) the positive ions will start moving towards the anode; the negative ions will stop moving
(c) the negative ions will continue to move towards the anode; the positive ions will stop moving
(d) the positive and negative ions will start moving randomly

270. In an electrolytic cell, the cathode acts as an/a
(a) oxidising agent (b) reducing agent
(c) either of the two (d) neither (a) nor (b)

271. In electrolysis of a fused salt, the weight of the deposit on an electrode will not depend on the
(a) temperature of the bath
(b) current intensity
(c) electrochemical equivalent of ions
(d) time for electrolysis

Batteries/Commercial Cells

272. Which of the following materials is not present in a dry cell?
(a) MnO_2 (b) NH_4Cl (c) $ZnCl_2$ (d) KCl

273. The cathode reaction in the dry cell is
(a) $Zn(s) \rightarrow Zn^{2+} + 2e^-$
(b) $MnO_2 + NH_4^+ + e^- \rightarrow MnO(OH) + NH_3$
(c) $Zn(g) + 2\,OH^- \rightarrow ZnO(s) + H_2O + 2e^-$
(d) $MnO\,(OH) + NH_3 \rightarrow MnO_2 + NH_4^+ + 2e^-$

274. A depolariser used in a dry cell battery is
(a) ammonium chloride (b) manganese dioxide
(c) potassium hydroxide (d) sodium phosphate

275. The space in the dry cell is filled with
(a) paste of KOH and ZnO
(b) MnO_2, $ZnCl_2$, a filter
(c) MnO_2, $ZnCl_2$, NH_4Cl and a filter
(d) $MnCl_2$, $ZnCl_2$, NH_4Cl and a filter

276. The reaction occurring at the anode during the discharge of a lead storage battery is
(a) $Pb + SO_4^{2-} \rightarrow PbSO_4 + 2e^-$
(b) $PbSO_4 + 2e^- \rightarrow Pb + SO_4^{2-}$
(c) $PbSO_4 + 2H_2O \rightarrow PbO_2 + SO_4^{2-} + 4H^+ + 2e^-$
(d) $Pb^{2+} + SO_4^{2-} \rightarrow PbSO_4$

277. Which of the following is widely used in the manufacture of lead storage batteries?
(a) arsenic (b) lithium
(c) bismuth (d) antimony

278. The reaction occurring at the cathode during recharging of the lead storage battery is
(a) $PbSO_4(s) + 2\,H_2O(l) \rightarrow PbO_2(s) + SO_4^{2-}(aq) + 4\,H^+ + 2e^-$
(b) $PbSO_4(s) + 2e^- \rightarrow Pb(s) + SO_4^{2-}(aq)$
(c) $PbO_2(s) + SO_4(aq) + 4\,H^+(aq) + 2e^- \rightarrow PbSO_4(s) + 2\,H_2O(l)$
(d) $Pb(s) + SO_4^{2-}(aq) \rightarrow PbSO_4(s) + 2e^-$

279. When a lead storage battery discharges
(a) SO_2 is evolved (b) $PbSO_4$ is consumed
(c) lead is formed (d) H_2SO_4 is consumed

280. In charging the lead accumulator battery
(a) PbO_2 dissolves
(b) H_2SO_4 is reproduced
(c) $PbSO_4$ deposits on the lead electrode
(d) Pb deposits on the lead electrode

281. When the lead accumulator is charged, it is
(a) an electrolytic cell (b) a galvanic cell
(c) a Daniell cell (d) none of these

282. Which cell has a constant voltage throughout its life?
(a) Leclanche cell (b) electrolytic cell
(c) mercury cell (d) Daniell cell

Fuel Cells

283. In which cell is the free energy of a chemical reaction directly converted into electricity?
(a) Leclanche cell (b) concentration cell
(c) fuel cell (d) lead storage battery

284. A device that converts the energy of combustion of fuels such as hydrogen and methane, directly into electrical energy is known as
(a) fuel cell (b) electrolytic cell
(c) dynamo (d) Ni–Cd cell

285. In the H_2–O_2 fuel cell, the reaction occurring at the cathode is
(a) $4\,H^+ + O_2 + 4e^- \rightarrow 2H_2O\,(l)$
(b) $H^+ + OH^- \rightarrow H_2O$
(c) $O_2 + 2H_2O + 4e^- \rightarrow 4\,OH^-$
(d) $H^+ + e^- \rightarrow \frac{1}{2}H_2$

286. The efficiency of a fuel cell is given by
(a) $\frac{\Delta S}{\Delta G}$ (b) $\frac{\Delta H}{\Delta G}$ (c) $\frac{\Delta G}{\Delta S}$ (d) $\frac{\Delta G}{\Delta H}$

287. Consider the following statements pertaining to fuel cells:
1. Hydrogen–oxygen fuel cell makes use of conc. KOH solution as electrolyte and porous graphite impregnated with platinum as electrodes.
2. The efficiency of the fuel cell is less than unity due to polarisation at the electrodes and the resistance offered by the electrode and the electrolyte.
3. The electrical work, assuming that the cell is working reversibly, may be represented as $-\Delta G = W_{elec} = -\Delta H + T\Delta S$.

Which of the above statements are correct?
(a) 1 and 2 (b) 1 and 3
(c) 2 and 3 (d) 1, 2 and 3

288. In the H_2–O_2 fuel cell, the reaction occurring at the anode is

(a) $2H_2 + O_2 \rightarrow 2\,H_2O(l)$
(b) $H^+ + OH^- \rightarrow H_2O$
(c) $2H_2 + 4\,OH^- \rightarrow 4H_2O + 4\,e^-$
(d) $4\,OH^- \rightarrow 2H_2O + O_2 + 4\,e^-$

289. Which of the following statements is true for fuel cells?
(a) They are more efficient.
(b) They are free from pollution.
(c) They run till reactants are active.
(d) All of these.

290. The efficiency of the following cell is 84%.
$A(s) + B^{2+}(aq) \rightleftharpoons A^{2+}(aq) + B(s);\ \Delta H = -285$ kJ
Then the standard electrode potential of the cell will be
(a) 1.20 V (b) 2.40 V (c) 1.10 V (d) 1.24 V

291. Among the Leclanche cell (I), Nickel–cadmium cell (II), lead storage battery (III), mercury cell (IV), the primary cells are
(a) I and II (b) I and III
(c) II and III (d) I and IV

292. Which of the following cells is a secondary cell?
(a) mercury cell (b) Ni cell
(c) dry cell (d) fuel cell

293. A secondary cell is one which
(a) can be recharged
(b) can be recharged by passing current through it in the same direction
(c) can be recharged by passing current through it in the opposite direction
(d) cannot be recharged

294. The electrolyte used in the leclanche cell is
(a) paste of KOH and ZnO
(b) 38% solution of H_2SO_4
(c) moist paste of NH_4Cl and $ZnCl_2$
(d) moist sodium hydroxide
(e) moist potassium hydroxide

Corrosion

295. The green layer of basic carbonates formed by the action of CO_2 is
(a) $Cu(CO_3)_2OH$ (b) $Cu(OH)_2.CuCO_3$
(c) Cu_2CO_3 (d) $Cu_2CO_3(OH)_2$

296. Rust is
(a) ferric oxide (b) ferrous oxide
(c) hydrated ferric oxide (d) ferric hydroxide

297. Zinc can be coated on iron to produce galvanised iron but the reverse is not possible. This is because
(a) zinc is lighter than iron
(b) zinc has a lower melting point than iron
(c) zinc has a higher negative electrode potential than iron
(d) none of the above

298. On the basis of electrochemical theory of aqueous corrosion, the reaction occurring at the cathode is
(a) $O_2(g) + 4\,H^+(aq) + 4\,e^- \rightarrow 2H_2O(l)$
(b) $Fe(s) \rightarrow Fe^{2+}(aq) + 2\,e^-$
(c) $Fe^{2+}(aq) \rightarrow Fe^{3+}(aq) + 2\,e^-$
(d) $H_2(g) + 2\,OH^-(aq) \rightarrow 2H_2O(l) + 2\,e^-$

299. When iron is rusted, it is
(a) reduced (b) decomposed
(c) oxidised (d) changed into fine powder

300. The rusting of iron is catalysed by
(a) Fe (b) O_2 (c) H^+ (d) Zn

301. The metal that forms a self-protecting film of oxide to prevent corrosion, is
(a) Cu (b) Al (c) Na (d) Au

302. Which of the following solutions is used as an anti-rusting solution?
(a) Na_2SO_4 (b) Na_3PO_4 (c) Na_3BO_3 (d) Na_2S

303. Dipping an iron article into a strongly alkaline solution of sodium phosphate
(a) does not affect the article
(b) forms $Fe_2O_3.xH_2O$ on the surface
(c) forms iron phosphate film
(d) forms ferric hydroxide

304. Which of the following metals is most readily corroded in moist air?
(a) copper (b) iron (c) silver (d) nickel

305. Zinc is used to protect iron from rusting. This is because
(a) E°_{red} of zinc is greater than that of Fe
(b) E°_{ox} of Zn is greater than that of Fe
(c) E°_{red} of Zn is nearly equal to that of Fe
(d) Zn is cheap

306. According to the electrochemical theory of corrosion, the metal undergoing corrosion acts as
(a) the anode
(b) the cathode
(c) neither the anode nor cathode
(d) either the anode or cathode depending upon its standard reduction potential

307. Iron can be protected by coating with zinc or tin. If the coating is broken
(a) iron will corrode faster if coated with zinc
(b) iron will corrode faster if coated with tin
(c) iron will corrode faster in both cases
(d) iron will not undergo any corrosion in both cases

308. The overall reaction of the miniature cell occurring during rusting of iron is

(a) $2\,Fe^{2+}(aq) + 2H_2O(l) \rightarrow 2Fe(s) + O_2(g) + 4\,H^+(aq)$
(b) $2Fe(s) + O_2(g) + 4\,H^+(aq) \rightarrow 2\,Fe^{2+} + 2\,H_2O(l)$
(c) $2Fe + 3H_2O \rightarrow Fe_2O_3 + 3H_2$
(d) $2Fe + O_2 + H_2O \rightarrow Fe_2O_3 + 2\,H^+$

309. A metal is left exposed to the atmosphere for some time. It gets coated with green carbonate. The metal must be

(a) silver (b) copper (c) iron (d) zinc

Miscellaneous

310. Mark the false statement.

(a) A salt bridge is used to eliminate liquid junction potential.
(b) The Gibbs free energy change, ΔG is related to electromotive force as $\Delta G = -nFE$.
(c) Nernst equation for single electrode potential is $E = E° - \dfrac{RT}{nF}\log a_{M^{n+}}$.
(d) The efficiency of a hydrogen–oxygen fuel cell is 60%–70%.

311. Identify the wrong statement.

(a) The oxidation potential for $E°_{25°C, F_2/2F^-}$ being the highest, +2.85 V, makes the halogen the strongest oxidising agent.
(b) $LiAlH_4$ is the best reducing agent in organic synthesis; $E°_{25°C, Li^+/Li}$ is –3.05 V.
(c) $HClO_4$ is a powerful reducing agent because the oxidation state of chlorine atom is as high as +7.
(d) A cotton piece dipped in spirit caught fire in Mn_2O_7 due to the highest oxidation state of the metal.
(e) Manganese atom in MnO_4^- has a high +ve oxidation state that allows charge transfer transition, imparting a dark violet colour.

312. $Cu^+ + e \rightarrow Cu$, $E° = X_1$ volt
$Cu^{2+} + 2\,e \rightarrow Cu$, $E° = X_2$ volt
For $Cu^{2+} + e \rightarrow Cu^+$, $E°$ will be

(a) $X_1 - 2X_2$ (b) $X_1 + 2X_2$
(c) $X_1 - X_2$ (d) $2X_2 - X_1$

313. Calculate the molarity of a solution containing 5 g of NaOH dissolved in the product of a H_2–O_2 fuel cell operated at 1 A current for 595.1 hours. (Assume $F = 96500$ C/mol of electrons and molecular weight of NaOH as 40 g mol^{-1})

(a) 0.05 M (b) 0.625 M (c) 0.1 M
(d) 0.075 M (e) 1 M

314. Consider the galvanic cell

$Pt(s)\,|\,H_2(1\ bar)\,|\,HCl(aq)(1\ M)\,|\,Cl_2(1\ bar)\,|\,Pt(s)\,|$

After running the cell for some time, the concentration of the electrolyte is automatically raised to 3 M HCl. Molar conductivity of the 3 M HCl is about 240 S cm^2 mol^{-1} and the limiting molar conductivity of HCl is about 420 S cm^2 mol^{-1}. If K_b of water is 0.52 K g mol^{-1}, calculate the boiling point of the electrolyte at the end of the experiment

(a) 375.6 K (b) 376.3 K (c) 378.1 K
(d) 380.3 K (e) 381.6 K

315. Consider the change in oxidation state of bromine corresponding to different emf values as shown in the diagram below:

$BrO_4^- \xrightarrow{1.82\ V} BrO_3^- \xrightarrow{1.5\ V} HBrO \xrightarrow{1.595\ V} Br_2 \xrightarrow{1.0652\ V} Br^-$

Then the species under disproportionation is

(a) Br (b) BrO_4^- (c) BrO_3^- (d) HBrO

316. How long (approximate) should water be electrolysed by passing through 100 amperes current so that the oxygen released can completely burn 27.66 g of diborane?

(Atomic weight of B = 10.8 u)

(a) 6.4 h (b) 0.8 h (c) 3.2 h (d) 1.6 h

317. If HCl is titrated with NaOH, variation of conductance (x-axis) will be

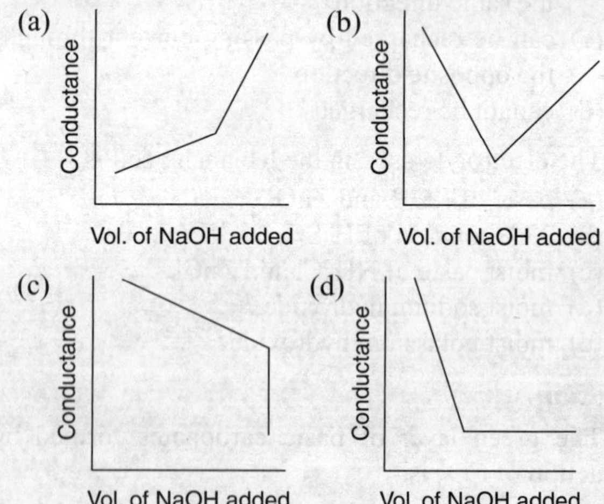

Final Preparation

318. Standard electrode potentials for Fe electrodes are given as

$Fe^{2+} + 2\,e^- \rightarrow Fe$, $E° = -0.44$ V
$Fe^{3+} + e^- \rightarrow Fe^{3+}$, $E° = +0.77$ V

(a) $[Fe^{3+}]$ decreases
(b) $[Fe^{3+}]$ increases
(c) $[Fe^{2+} / Fe^{3+}]$ remains unchanged
(d) $[Fe^{2+}]$ decreases

319. If Zn^{2+}/Zn electrode is diluted 100 times, then the change in emf is

(a) increase of 59 mV (b) decrease of 59 mV
(c) increase of 29.5 mV (d) decrease of 29.5 mV

320. Given that $E^{\circ}_{Zn^{2+}/Zn} = -0.764$ V and $E^{\circ}_{Cd^{2+}/Cd} = -0.403$ V, the emf of the cell $Zn \mid Zn^{2+} \mid\mid Cd^{2+} \mid Cd$ will be given by

(a) $E = -0.36 + (0.059/2) \log (0.004/2)$
(b) $E = +0.36 + (0.059/2) \log (0.004/2)$
(c) $E = -0.36 + (0.059/2) \log (0.2/0.004)$
(d) $E = +0.36 + (0.059/2) \log (0.2/0.004)$

321. The standard reduction potential for two reactions are given below:

$AgCl(s) + e^- \rightarrow Ag(s) + Cl^-(aq)$; $E° = 0.22$ V
$Ag^+(aq) + e^- \rightarrow Ag(s)$, $E° = 0.80$ V

The solubility product of AgCl under standard conditions of temperature (298 K) is given by

(a) 1.6×10^{-5} (b) 1.5×10^{-8} (c) 3.2×10^{-10}
(d) 1.5×10^{-10} (e) 3.2×10^{-8}

322. In a cell that utilises the reaction

$Zn(s) + 2H^+(aq) \rightarrow Zn^{2+}(aq) + H_2(g)$

addition of H_2SO_4 to the cathode compartment will

(a) lower the E and shift equilibrium to the left
(b) lower the E and shift equilibrium to the right
(c) increase the E and shift equilibrium to the right
(d) increase the E and shift equilibrium to the left

323. The cell, $Zn \mid Zn^{2+}(1\text{ M}) \mid\mid Cu^{2+}(1\text{ M}) \mid Cu$, ($E_{cell} = 1.10$ V), was allowed to be completely discharged at 298 K. The relative concentration of Zn^{2+} to Cu^{2+}, $\left(\frac{[Zn^{2+}]}{[Cu^{2+}]}\right)$ is

(a) 9.65×10^4 (b) antilog 24.08
(c) 37.3 (d) $10^{37.3}$

324. Consider the electrochemical reaction between Ag(*s*) and $Cl_2(g)$ electrodes in 1 litre of 0.1 M KCl aqueous solution. Solubility product of AgCl is 1.8×10^{-10} and $F = 96500$ C/mol. At 1 μA current, calculate the time required to start observing the AgCl precipitation in the galvanic cell

(a) 173 s (b) 346 s
(c) 1.25×10^6 s (d) 1.25×10^5 s

325. The emf of a Daniell cell was found using different concentrations of Zn^{2+} ion and Cu^{2+} ion. A graph was plotted between E_{cell} and $\log \frac{[Zn^{2+}]}{[Cu^{2+}]}$. The plot was found to be linear with the intercept on E_{cell} axis for $Zn \mid Zn^{2+}(0.1\text{ M}) \mid\mid Cu^{2+}(0.01\text{ M}) \mid Cu$ will be

(a) 1.10 V (b) 1.0705 V
(c) 0.93 V (d) 0.078 V

326. Consider the cell

$Pt \mid H_2(g), (\text{atm}) \mid H^+(aq, 1\text{ M}) \mid\mid Fe^{3+}(aq) \mid Pt(s)$

Given that $E^{\circ}_{Fe^{3+}/Fe^{2+}} = 0.771$ V, the ratio of conc. of $Fe^{2+}(aq)$ to $Fe^{3+}(aq)$ is, when the cell potential is 0.830 V

(a) 0.101 (b) 0.924
(c) 0.120 (d) none of these

327. The reduction potential at pH = 14 for the Cu^{2+}/Cu couple is [given $E^{\circ}_{Cu^{2+}/Cu} = 0.34$ V, K_{sp} $[Cu(OH)_2] = 1 \times 10^{-19}$]

(a) 0.34 V (b) –0.34 V (c) 0.22 V (d) –0.22 V

328. $Cu^{2+} + 2e \rightarrow Cu$; $\log [Cu^{2+}]$ vs E_{red} graph is of the type shown in the figure where OA = 0.34 V. Then the electrode potential of the half cell of $Cu \mid Cu^{2+}$ (0.1 M) will be

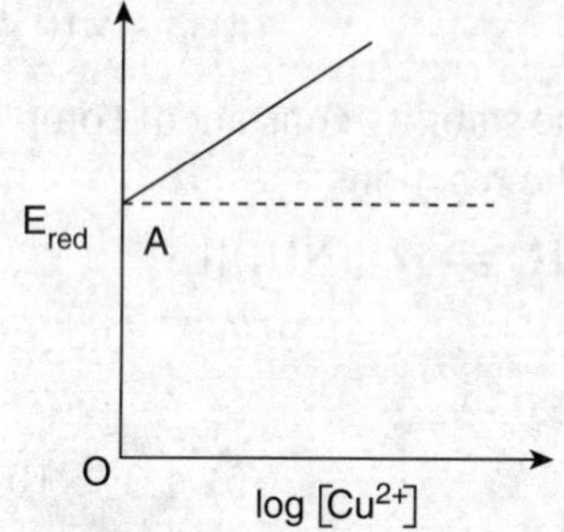

(a) $-0.34 + \frac{0.0591}{2}$ V (b) 0.34 + 0.0591 V
(c) 0.34 V (d) none of these

329. For the redox process,

$Zn(s) + Cu^{2+} \rightleftharpoons Zn^{2+} + Cu(s)$; $E°_{cell} = +1.10$ V, which graph correctly represents E_{cell} (Y-axis) as a function $\log \frac{[Zn^{2+}]}{[Cu^{2+}]}$ (X-axis)?

(a)
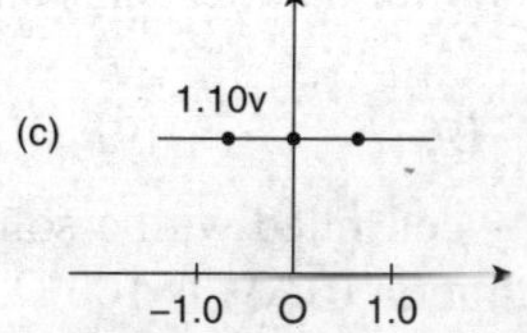

(b)
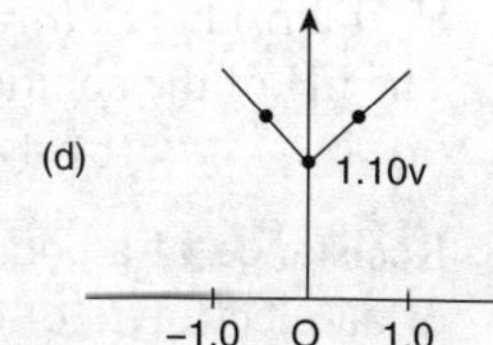

(c)

(d)

330. How much will the reduction potential of a hydrogen electrode change when its solution initially at pH = 0 is neutralised to pH = 7?

(a) increases by 0.059 V (b) decreases by 0.059 V
(c) increases by 0.41 V (d) decreases by 0.41 V

331. Consider the reaction,

$Cl_2(g) + 2\,Br^-(aq) \rightarrow 2\,Cl^-(aq) + Br_2$

The emf of the cell, when $[Cl^-] = [Br_2] = [Br^-] = 0.01$ and Cl_2 gas is at 1 atm pressure, will be ($E°$ for the reaction is 0.29 volt)

(a) 0.54 volt (b) 0.35 volt
(c) 0.24 volt (d) – 0.29 volt

332. The emf of the cell Zn | Zn^{2+} (0.01 M) | | Fe^{2+} (0.01 M) | Fe at 298 K is 0.2905 volt. Then the value of equilibrium constant for the cell reaction is

(a) $\dfrac{0.32}{e^{0.0295}}$ (b) $\dfrac{0.32}{10^{0.0295}}$ (c) $\dfrac{0.26}{10^{0.0295}}$ (d) $\dfrac{0.32}{10^{0.0591}}$

333. $E°_{cell}$ for the reaction, Fe + $Zn^{2+} \rightleftharpoons Fe^{2+}$ when a piece of iron is placed in 1 M Zn^{2+} solution is

(a) 1.4×10^{-11} M (b) 1.5×10^{-10} M
(c) 3.5×10^{-11} M (d) 3.5×10^{-10} M

334. Calculate the stability constant of complex $[Zn(NH_3)_4]^{2+}$ formed in the reaction

$Zn^{2+} + 4\,NH_3 \rightleftharpoons [Zn(NH_3)_4]^{2+}$

given that $E^{\circ}_{Zn^{2+}/Zn} = -0.76$ V and $E°_{[Zn(NH_3)_4]^{2+}}$/Zn, 4 $NH_3 = -1.03$ V.

(a) 2.37×10^{9} (b) 1.37×10^{9}
(c) 2.37×10^{10} (d) 1.37×10^{10}

335. For the reaction Pt | H_2(1 atm) | $H^+(aq)$ | | $Cl^-(aq)$ | AgCl | Ag; K_c (equilibrium constant) is represented as

(a) $K_c = \dfrac{[Cl^-][AgCl]}{[H^+][H_2]}$ (b) $K_c = [H^+][H_2]$

(c) $K_c = \dfrac{[H^+][H_2]}{[Cl^-][AgCl]}$ (d) $K_c = \dfrac{[H_2]}{[Ag]}$

336. The value of reaction quotient Q, for the cell

Zn(*s*) | Zn^{2+}(0.01 M) | | Ag^+(1.25 M) | Ag(*s*) is

(a) 1.56 (b) 125
(c) 1.25×10^{-2} (d) 6.4×10^{-3}

337. The emf of the cell

H_2(1 atm) Pt | $H^+(a = 1)$ | H_2(1 atm) Pt at 25 °C is 0.59 V. The pH of the solution is

(a) 1 (b) 4 (c) 7 (d) 10

338. Resistance of a conductivity cell filled with a solution of an electrolyte of concentration 0.1 M is 100 Ω. The conductivity of this solution is 1.29 S m^{-1}. Resistance of the same cell when filled with 0.2 M of the same solution is 250 Ω. The molar conductivity of 0.02 M solution of the electrolyte will be

(a) 1.24×10^{-4} S m^2 mol^{-1}
(b) 12.4×10^{-4} S m^2 mol^{-1}
(c) 124×10^{-4} S m^2 mol^{-1}
(d) 1240×10^{-4} S m^2 mol^{-1}

339. The ionisation constant of a weak electrolyte is 25×10^{-6} while the equivalent conductance of its 0.01 M solution is 19.6 S cm^2 eq^{-1}. The equivalent conductance of the electrolyte at infinite dilution (in S cm^2 eq^{-1}) will be

(a) 250 (b) 196 (c) 392 (d) 384

340. Given $\Lambda^{\circ}\left(\frac{1}{3}Al^{3+}\right) = 63\ \Omega^{-1}\ cm^2\ mol^{-1}$ and $\Lambda^{\circ}\left(\frac{1}{3}SO_4^{2-}\right) = 80\ \Omega^{-1}\ cm^2\ mol^{-1}$

The value of Λ^{∞} $Al_2(SO_4)_3$ would be

(a) 143 Ω^{-1} cm^2 mol^{-1} (b) 206 Ω^{-1} cm^2 mol^{-1}
(c) 286 Ω^{-1} cm^2 mol^{-1} (d) 858 Ω^{-1} cm^2 mol^{-1}

341. The conductivity of a saturated solution of $BaSO_4$ is 3.06×10^{-6} ohm^{-1} cm^{-1} and its equivalent conductance is 1.53 ohm^{-1} cm^2 eq^{-1}. The K_{sp} for $BaSO_4$ will be

(a) 4×10^{-12} (b) 2.5×10^{-9}
(c) 2.5×10^{-13} (d) 4×10^{-6}

342. Given that the dissociation constant of acetic acid is 1.8×10^{-5} and its molar conductivity at infinite dilution is 390.7 Ω^{-1} cm^2 mol^{-1}, the molar conductivity of 0.01 M acetic acid solution will be

(a) 1.657 Ω^{-1} cm^2 (b) 16.57 Ω^{-1} cm^2
(c) 165.7 Ω^{-1} cm^2 (d) 33.04 Ω^{-1} cm^2

343. A weak electrolyte having a limiting equivalent conductance of 400 S cm^2 g eq^{-1} at 298 K is 2% ionised in its 0.1 N solution. The resistance of this solution (in ohms) in an electrolytic cell of cell constant 0.4 cm^{-1} at this temperature is

(a) 200 (b) 300 (c) 400
(d) 500 (e) 600

344. Which of the following is incorrect about transport number?

(a) it decreases with increase in concentration
(b) it may increase or decrease with increase in temperature
(c) it is never zero
(d) it is different for Cl^- ion in 0.1 M HCl 0.1 M NaCl solution

345. The conductivity of a saturated solution of $BaSO_4$ is 3.06×10^{-6} mho cm^{-1} and its equivalent conductance is 1.53 mho cm^2 eq^{-1}. The K_{sp} for $BaSO_4$ will be

(a) 4×10^{-12} M (b) 6×10^{-6} M
(c) 2.5×10^{-12} M (d) 4×10^{-6} M^2

346. The time required to coat a metal surface of 800 cm^2 with 5×10^{-3} mm thick layer of silver (density = 10.5 g cm^{-3}) with the passage of 3 A current through a silver nitrate solution is nearly

(a) 1150 s (b) 1250 s (c) 1350 s (d) 1450 s

347. In an electroplating experiment, m g of silver is deposited when 4 amperes of current flows for 2 minutes. The amount (in g) of silver deposited by 6 amperes of current flowing for 40 seconds will be
(a) $4m$ (b) $m/2$ (c) $m/4$ (d) $2\,m$

348. How long will it take for a current of 3 amperes to decompose 36 g of water? (Eq. wt of hydrogen is 1 and that of oxygen 8)
(a) 36 hours (b) 18 hours
(c) 9 hours (d) 4.5 hours

349. Calculate the weight of copper that will be deposited at the cathode in the electrolysis of a 0.2 M solution of copper sulfate when a quantity of electricity equal to that required to liberate 2.24 *l* of hydrogen at NTP from a 0.1 M aqueous sulfuric acid, is passed, (atomic mass of Cu = 63.5)
(a) 1.59 g (b) 6.35 g (c) 3.18 g (d) 12.70 g

350. On passing a current of 1.0 ampere for 16 min and 5 s through a one litre solution of $CuCl_2$, all copper of the solution was deposited at the cathode. The strength of the $CuCl_2$ solution was (Molar mass of Cu = 63.5, Faraday constant = 96500 C mol^{-1}).
(a) 0.07 M (b) 0.2 N (c) 0.005 M (d) 0.02 N

351. The pH of 0.5 L of 1.0 M NaCl solution after electrolysis for 965 s using 5.0 A current, is
(a) 10 (b) 12.7 (c) 13.0 (d) 1.30

352. 9.65 C electric current is passed through fused anhydrous magnesium chloride. The magnesium metal thus obtained is completely converted into a Grignard reagent. The number of moles of the Grignard reagent obtained is
(a) 5×10^{-4} (b) 1×10^{-4} (c) 5×10^{-5} (d) 1×10^{-5}

353. When same quantity of electricity is passed for half an hour, the amount of Cu and Cr deposited are respectively 0.375 g and 0.30 g. The ratio of electrochemical equivalents of Cu and Cr is
(a) 0.8 (b) 1.25 (c) 2.5 (d) 1.62

354. A galvanic cell is set up from a zinc bar weighing 100 g and 1.0 litre of 1.0 M $CuSO_4$ solution. How long would the cell run if it is assumed to deliver a steady current of 1.0 amp? (Atomic mass of Zn = 65)
(a) 1.1 h (b) 46 h (c) 53.6 h (d) 24.00 h

355. A current of 9.65 A is passed for 3 hours between nickel electrodes is 0.55 L of a 2 M solution of $Ni(NO_3)_2$. The molarity of the solution after electrolysis would be
(a) 0.46 M (b) 0.625 M (c) 0.92 M (d) 1.25 M

356. A current of 12 ampere is passed through an electrolysis cell containing aq. $NiSO_4$ solution. Both Ni and H_2 gas are formed at the cathode. The current efficiency is 60%. What is the mass of nickel deposited on the cathode per hour? (At. wt of Ni = 98.7)
(a) 7.883 g (b) 3.941 g (c) 5.91 g (d) 2.645 g

357. Salts of metals A, B and C are electrolysed under identical conditions using a certain quantity of electricity. It was observed that 4.2 g of A, 5.4 g of B and 19.2 g of C were deposited at the respective cathodes. If the atomic weight of A, B and C are 7, 27 and 64 respectively, then the ratio of their valencies is
(a) 1 : 2 : 3 (b) 1 : 3 : 2 (c) 2 : 3 : 1 (d) 3 : 2 : 1

358. In an experiment, 0.40 F was passed through 400 mL of 1 M solution of NaCl. What would be the pH of the solution after the electrolysis?
(a) 8 (b) 10 (c) 13 (d) 6
(e) 9

359. In a H_2–O_2 fuel cell, 67.3 litre of H_2 at STP reacts in 10 minutes as per following reaction
Anode: $H_2 + 2OH \rightarrow H_2O + 2\,e^-$
Cathode: $O_2 + 2H_2O + 2\,e^- \rightarrow 4\,OH^-$
The average current produced by the fuel cell will be
(a) 482.7 ampere (b) 10 milliampere
(c) 5 milliampere (d) 966.4 ampere

360. In the electrolysis of $CuCl_2$ solution, the mass of the cathode increased by 6.4 g. What occurred at the copper anode?
(a) 0.224 litre of Cl_2 was liberated
(b) 1.12 litre of oxygen was liberated
(c) 0.05 mol of Cu^{2+} passed into the solution
(d) 0.1 mol of Cu^{2+} passed into the solution

361. A solution containing one mol per litre of each $Cu(NO_3)_2$, $AgNO_3$, $Hg_2(NO_3)_2$ and $Mg(NO_3)_2$ is being electrolysed by using inert electrodes. The values of standard electrode potentials in volts (reduction potentials) are:
$Ag/Ag^+ = 0.80$, $2\,Hg/Hg_2^{++} = 0.79$
$Cu/Cu^{++} = 0.34$, $Mg/Mg^{++} = -2.37$
With increasing voltage, the sequence of deposition of metals on the cathode will be
(a) Ag, Hg, Cu, Mg (b) Mg, Cu, Hg, Ag
(c) Ag, Hg, Cu (d) Cu, Hg, Ag

362. Given the following standard reduction potentials:
$Mn^{2+}(aq) + 2\,e^- \rightarrow Mn(s)$, $E^\circ = -1.18$ V
$2H_2O + 2\,e^- \rightarrow H_2(g) + 2\,OH^-(aq)$, $E^\circ = -0.83$ V
$I_2 + 2\,e^- \rightarrow 2\,I^-(aq)$, $E^\circ = +1.23$ V
$O_2(g) + 4\,H^+(aq) + 4\,e^- \rightarrow 2H_2O$, $E^\circ = +1.23$ V
Electrolysis of an aqueous solution of MnI_2 would give
(a) H_2, I_2 (b) H_2, O_2 (c) Mn, O_2 (d) Mn, I_2

363. The following reaction takes place during the discharge of a lead storage acid battery:
$Pb(s) + PbO_2(s) + 2H_2SO_4(aq) \rightarrow 2PbSO_4(s) + 2H_2O(l)$

If 2.5 ampere of current is drawn for 965 minutes, H_2SO_4 consumed is
(a) 0.75 mol (b) 2.00 mol
(c) 1.50 mol (d) 3.50 mol

364. Standard free energies of formation (in kJ/mol) at 298 K are –237.2, –39.4 and –8.2 for $H_2O(l)$, $CO_2(g)$ and pentane(*g*) respectively. The value of $E°_{cell}$ for the pentane–oxygen fuel cell is
(a) 1.968 V (b) 2.0968 V
(c) 1.0968 V (d) 0.0968 V

365. Corrosion of iron is essentially an electrochemical phenomenon where the cell reactions are
(a) Fe is oxidised to Fe^{2+} and dissolved oxygen in water is reduced to OH^-
(b) Fe is oxidised to Fe^{2+} and H_2O is reduced to O_2^{2-}
(c) Fe is oxidised to Fe^{2+} and H_2O is reduced to O_2^-
(d) Fe is oxidised to Fe^{2+} and H_2O is reduced to O_2

366. The amount of energy used in the passage of 1 amp current for 100 s under a potential of 115 V is
(a) 20 kJ (b) 11.5 kJ (c) 115 kJ (d) 0.115 kJ

367. The reaction
$\frac{1}{2}H_2(g) + AgCl(s) \rightarrow H^+(aq) + Cl^-(aq) + Ag(s)$
Occurs in the galvanic cell
(a) Ag | AgCl(*s*) | KCl(*aq*) || $AgNO_3(aq)$ | Ag
(b) Pt | $H_2(g)$ | HCl(*aq*) || $AgNO_3(aq)$ | Ag
(c) Pt | $H_2(g)$ | HCl(*aq*) || AgCl(*s*) | Ag
(d) Pt | $H_2(g)$ | KCl(*aq*) || AgCl(*s*) | Ag

368. Which of the following statements is true for the electrochemical Daniell cell?
(a) Electrons flow from the copper electrode to the zinc electrode.
(b) Current flows from the zinc electrode to the copper electrode.
(c) Cations move towards the copper electrode.
(d) Cations move towards the zinc electrode.

369. I_2 and Br_2 are added to a solution containing 1 M each of I^- and Br^- ions. Which of the following reactions will take place? (Given: standard reduction potentials of I_2 and Br_2 are 0.53 and 1.09 volts respectively)
(a) iodine will reduce bromide ions
(b) bromine will reduce iodide ions
(c) iodide ions will reduce bromine
(d) bromide ions will reduce iodine

370. An unknown metal M displaces nickel from nickel (II) sulfate solution but does not displace manganese from manganese sulfate solution. Which order represents the correct order of reducing power?
(a) Mn > Ni > M (b) Ni > Mn > M
(c) Mn > M > Ni (d) M > Ni > Mn

371. The emfs of the following cells are
Cu | Cu^{2+} (1 M) || Ag^+ (1 M) | Ag, $E° = 0.46$ V
Zn | Zn^{2+} (1 M) || Cu^{2+} (1 M) | Cu, $E° = 1.10$ V
The emf of the cell Zn | Zn^{2+} || Ag^+ (1 M) | Ag will be
(a) 1.56 V (b) 0.64 V (c) –1.56 V (d) 2.02 V

372. The standard electrode potential ($E°$) for OCl^-/Cl^- $Cl^-/\frac{1}{2}Cl_2$ respectively are 0.94 V and – 1.36 V. The $E°$ value for $OCl^-/\frac{1}{2}Cl_2$ will be
(a) –0.42 V (b) –2.20 V (c) 0.52 V (d) 1.04 V

373. $Cr_2O_7^{2-} + I^- \rightarrow I_2 + Cr^{3+}$
$E°_{cell} = 0.79$ V, $E°_{Cr_2O_7^{2-}} = 1.33$ V, $E°_{I_2} = ?$
(a) 0.54 V (b) –0.54 V (c) +0.18 V (d) –0.18 V

374. On the basis of the following $E°$ values, the strongest oxidising agent is
$[Fe(CN)_6]^{4-} \rightarrow [Fe(CN)_6]^{3-} + e^-$; $E° = -0.35$ V
$Fe^{2+} \rightarrow Fe^{3+} + e^{-1}$; $E° = -0.77$V
(a) $[Fe(CN)_6]^{4-}$ (b) Fe^{2+}
(c) Fe^{3+} (d) $[Fe(CN)_6]^{3-}$

375. A gas X at 1 atm is bubbled through a solution containing a mixture of a M Y^- and 1 M Z^- ions at 25°C. If the reduction potential of Z > Y > X, then
(a) Y will oxidise X but not Z
(b) Y will oxidise both X and Z
(c) Y will oxidise Z but not X
(d) Y will reduce both X and Z

376. A solution contains Fe^{2+}, Fe^{3+} and I^- ions. This solution was treated with iodine at 25°C. $E°$ for Fe^{3+}/Fe^{2+} is +0.77 V and $E°$ for $I_2/2\,I^-$ is 0.5336 V. The favourable redox reaction is
(a) I_2 will be reduced to I^-
(b) there will be no redox reaction
(c) I^- will be oxidised to I_2
(d) Fe^{2+} will be oxidised to Fe^{3+}

MATCH THE FOLLOWING

377.

Column I	Column II
(A) Oxidation potential of hydrogen electrode set up in a solution with pH = 2	(p) 0.018 V
(B) Oxidation potential of hydrogen electrode set up in 0.5 M HCl solution	(q) 0.059 V
(C) emf of concentration cell with hydrogen electrodes set up in 0.1 M and 0.01 M HCl solution	(r) 0.035 V

Column I	Column II
(D) emf of concentration cell with hydrogen electrodes set up in 0.1 M and 0.4 M HCl solution	(s) 0.118 V

(a) (A)—(p), (B)—(s), (C)—(q), (D)—(r)
(b) (A)—(r), (B)—(p), (C)—(q), (D)—(s)
(c) (A)—(q), (B)—(p), (C)—(s), (D)—(r)
(d) (A)—(s), (B)—(p), (C)—(q), (D)—(r)

378.

Column I	Column II
(A) Reference electrode	(p) Pt | $Fe^{2+}(aq)$, $Fe^{3+}(aq)$
(B) Redox electrode	(q) Hg(l) | $HgCl_2(s)$ | KCl (1 M)
(C) Electrode reversible with respect to cation	(r) Ag | AgCl(s), KCl(aq)
(D) Electrode reversible with respect to anion	(s) Zn(Hg) | $ZnSO_4(aq)$

(a) (A)—(r), (B)—(q), (C)—(r), (D)—(p)
(b) (A)—(p), (B)—(q), (C)—(r), (D)—(s)
(c) (A)—(r), (B)—(s), (C)—(p), (D)—(q)
(d) (A)—(q), (B)—(p), (C)—(s), (D)—(r)

ASSERTION REASON

Directions: In each of the following questions, a statement of Assertion (A) is given followed by a corresponding statement of Reason (R) just below it. Of the statements, mark the correct answer as

(a) if both assertion and reason are true and reason is the correct explanation of assertion.
(b) if both assertion and reason are true but reason is not the correct explanation of assertion.
(c) if assertion is true but reason is false.
(d) if both assertion and reason are false.

379. Assertion: For the Daniel cell Zn | Zn^{2+} || Cu^{2+} | Cu with $E_{cell} = 1.1$ V, the application of opposite potential greater than 1.1 V results in the flow of electrons from the cathode to the anode.

Reason: Zinc is deposited at the anode and Cu is dissolved at the cathode.

380. Assertion: An electrochemical cell can be set up only if the redox reaction is spontaneous.

Reason: A reaction is spontaneous if the free energy change is negative.

381. Assertion: The Daniell cell becomes dead after some time.

Reason: Oxidation potential of the zinc anode decreases and that of copper increases.

382. Assertion: In an electrochemical cell, the anode is the negative electrode whereas the cathode is a positive electrode.

Reason: Reduction takes place at the negative electrode whereas oxidation takes place at the positive electrode.

383. Assertion: Fluorine is a stronger oxidising agent that I_2.

Reason: Fluorine has greater electronegativity than iodine.

384. Assertion: Zinc reacts with H_2SO_4 to give H_2 gas but copper does not.

Reason: Zinc has a higher reduction potential than copper.

385. Assertion: Fe filings added to copper sulfate solution make it colourless but Cu filings added to $AgNO_3$ solution give it a blue colour.

Reason: The standard reduction potentials are in the order Fe > Cu > Ag.

386. Assertion: If the standard reduction potential for the reaction

$Ag^+ + e^- \rightarrow Ag$ is 0.80 volt, then for the reaction
$2\,Ag^+ + 2\,e^- \rightarrow 2Ag$, it will be 1.60 volt.

Reason: If the concentration of Ag^+ ions is doubled, its standard electrode potential is also doubled.

387. Assertion: Auric chloride ($AuCl_3$) cannot be stored in vessels made of copper, iron, nickel, chromium, zinc or tin.

Reason: $AuCl_3$ is a salt of a very precious metal, namely, gold.

388. Assertion: emf and potential difference are the same for a cell.

Reason: Both give the difference in electrode potentials under any condition.

389. Assertion: In a galvanic cell Zn | Zn^{2+} || Cu^{2+} | Cu after complete discharging, the equilibrium gets established.

Reason: In a galvanic cell, Zn | Zn^{2+} || Cu^{2+} | Cu, after complete discharging, [Zn^{2+}] becomes equal to Zn^{2+} [Cu^{2+}].

390. Assertion: To obtain maximum work from a galvanic cell, the cell must function reversibly.

Reason: The reversible work done by a galvanic cell is equal to the decrease in Gibbs energy.

391. Assertion: When acidified zinc sulfate solution is electrolysed between zinc electrodes, zinc is deposited at the cathode and hydrogen evolution does not take place.

Reason: The electrode potential of zinc is more negative than hydrogen as the overvoltage for the hydrogen evolution on zinc is quite large.

392. Assertion: Electrolysis of an aqueous solution of a bromide or iodide gives Br_2 or I_2 at the anode whereas that of NaF gives O_2 and not F_2.

Reason: F_2 is highly reactive whereas Br_2 and I_2 are less reactive gases.

393. Assertion: If an aqueous solution of NaCl is electrolysed, the product obtained at the cathode is H_2 gas and not Na.

Reason: Gases are liberated faster than the metals.

394. Assertion: In the electrolysis of aqueous NaCl, Na is preferentially discharged at the mercury cathode forming sodium amalgam.

Reason: It is due to the fact that hydrogen has high overvoltage at the mercury cathode.

395. Assertion: The cell potential of the mercury cell is 1.35 which remains constant.

Reason: In a mercury cell, the electrolyte is a paste of KOH and HgO.

396. Assertion: As a lead storage battery gets discharged, the density of the electrolyte present in it decreases.

Reason: Lead and lead dioxide both react with sulfuric acid to form lead sulfate.

397. Assertion: Copper gets readily corroded in acidic or aqueous solutions.

Reason: The free energy for this process is positive.

398. Assertion: Galvanised iron does not rust.

Reason: Zinc has a more negative electrode potential than iron.

399. Assertion: Electrolysis of molten CaH_2 produces hydrogen gas at the anode.

Reason: In CaH_2, hydrogen is present in the form of H^-.

400. Assertion: At the end of electrolysis using platinum electrodes, an aqueous solution of copper sulfate turns colourless.

Reason: Copper in copper sulfate is converted to copper hydroxide during the electrolysis.

401. Assertion: Electrical conduction by metals and by electrolytic solution increases with an increase in temperature.

Reason: In metals, with an increase in temperature, the flow of electrons becomes faster whereas in an electrolytic solution, the number of ions increases.

402. Assertion: In electrolysis, the quantity of electricity needed for depositing 1 mol of silver is different from that required for 1 mol of copper.

Reason: The atomic weights of silver and copper are different.

403. Assertion: A small amount of acid or alkali is added before electrolysis of water.

Reason: Pure water is a weak electrolyte.

404. Assertion: One coulomb of electric charge deposits weight equal to the electrochemical equivalent of the substance.

Reason: One faraday deposits one mol of the substance.

405. Assertion: On dilution, the equivalent as well as molar conductivity of a solution increases.

Reason: With dilution, the number of current carrying particles per cm^3 increases.

406. Assertion: Equivalent conductivity of a weak electrolyte at infinite dilution can be found by Kohlrausch's law.

Reason: Kohlrausch's law is applicable only to weak electrolytes.

407. Assertion: The transport number of Cl^- in HCl is less than that in NaCl solution.

Reason: Velocity of H^+ ions in solution is less than the velocity of Na^+ ions.

408. Assertion: According to Kohlrausch's law, the molar conductivity of a strong electrolyte at infinite dilution is sum of the molar conductivities of its ions.

Reason: The current carried by the cation and the anion is always equal.

409. Assertion: The mobility of sodium ion is lower than that of potassium ion.

Reason: The ionic mobilities depend upon the effective radius of the ion.

Answer Key

1. (a)	2. (c)	3. (c)	4. (d)	5. (b)	6. (d)	7. (c)	8. (d)	9. (c)	10. (c)
11. (d)	12. (c)	13. (a)	14. (b)	15. (b)	16. (c)	17. (b)	18. (c)	19. (c)	20. (d)
21. (a)	22. (a)	23. (d)	24. (a)	25. (a)	26. (d)	27. (a)	28. (a)	29. (b)	30. (a)
31. (a)	32. (c)	33. (d)	34. (b)	35. (a)	36. (c)	37. (d)	38. (c)	39. (d)	40. (a)
41. (c)	42. (d)	43. (a)	44. (a)	45. (a)	46. (c)	47. (c)	48. (d)	49. (d)	50. (c)

51. (a) 52. (b) 53. (b) 54. (b) 55. (b) 56. (d) 57. (b) 58. (d) 59. (b) 60. (d)
61. (b) 62. (b) 63. (a) 64. (c) 65. (d) 66. (c) 67. (b) 68. (c) 69. (e) 70. (d)
71. (a) 72. (a) 73. (c) 74. (b) 75. (c) 76. (d) 77. (a) 78. (b) 79. (b) 80. (a)
81. (a) 82. (c) 83. (d) 84. (d) 85. (c) 86. (b) 87. (d) 88. (d) 89. (c) 90. (a)
91. (c) 92. (b) 93. (d) 94. (b) 95. (c) 96. (d) 97. (c) 98. (d) 99. (a) 100. (a)
101. (c) 102. (c) 103. (a) 104. (a) 105. (a) 106. (b) 107. (a) 108. (a) 109. (a) 110. (a)
111. (a) 112. (a) 113. (b) 114. (b) 115. (c) 116. (c) 117. (b) 118. (c) 119. (b) 120. (c)
121. (b) 122. (d) 123. (b) 124. (b) 125. (c) 126. (b) 127. (c) 128. (a) 129. (b) 130. (b)
131. (a) 132. (a) 133. (b) 134. (b) 135. (d) 136. (d) 137. (c) 138. (b) 139. (d) 140. (b)
141. (d) 142. (b) 143. (a) 144. (b) 145. (a) 146. (a) 147. (b) 148. (b) 149. (d) 150. (d)
151. (b) 152. (d) 153. (b) 154. (d) 155. (c) 156. (a) 157. (c) 158. (d) 159. (a) 160. (a)
161. (a) 162. (a) 163. (d) 164. (a) 165. (b) 166. (a) 167. (b) 168. (d) 169. (a) 170. (d)
171. (b) 172. (a) 173. (b) 174. (d) 175. (a) 176. (d) 177. (b) 178. (c) 179. (b) 180. (c)
181. (d) 182. (b) 183. (b) 184. (d) 185. (c) 186. (c) 187. (c) 188. (c) 189. (a) 190. (c)
191. (c) 192. (a) 193. (c) 194. (c) 195. (a) 196. (c) 197. (a) 198. (c) 199. (c) 200. (d)
201. (d) 202. (b) 203. (b) 204. (d) 205. (a) 206. (a) 207. (b) 208. (c) 209. (d) 210. (c)
211. (d) 212. (c) 213. (b) 214. (d) 215. (d) 216. (a) 217. (b) 218. (a) 219. (a) 220. (a)
221. (c) 222. (b) 223. (b) 224. (d) 225. (a) 226. (b) 227. (a) 228. (c) 229. (b) 230. (a)
231. (a) 232. (a) 233. (b) 234. (b) 235. (a) 236. (d) 237. (b) 238. (a) 239. (a) 240. (c)
241. (a) 242. (a) 243. (b) 244. (a) 245. (d) 246. (a) 247. (b) 248. (d) 249. (c) 250. (a)
251. (c) 252. (c) 253. (c) 254. (c) 255. (d) 256. (a) 257. (b) 258. (a) 259. (d) 260. (b)
261. (a) 262. (b) 263. (a) 264. (c) 265. (d) 266. (d) 267. (a) 268. (b) 269. (d) 270. (b)
271. (a) 272. (d) 273. (b) 274. (b) 275. (c) 276. (a) 277. (d) 278. (b) 279. (d) 280. (b)
281. (a) 282. (c) 283. (c) 284. (a) 285. (c) 286. (d) 287. (d) 288. (c) 289. (d) 290. (d)
291. (d) 292. (b) 293. (c) 294. (c) 295. (b) 296. (c) 297. (d) 298. (a) 299. (c) 300. (c)
301. (b) 302. (b) 303. (c) 304. (b) 305. (b) 306. (a) 307. (b) 308. (b) 309. (b) 310. (c)
311. (c) 312. (d) 313. (b) 314. (a) 315. (d) 316. (c) 317. (b) 318. (a) 319. (b) 320. (d)
321. (d) 322. (c) 323. (d) 324. (a) 325. (b) 326. (a) 327. (d) 328. (a) 329. (b) 330. (d)
331. (b) 332. (b) 333. (a) 334. (b) 335. (b) 336. (d) 337. (d) 338. (c) 339. (c) 340. (d)
341. (d) 342. (b) 343. (d) 344. (c) 345. (d) 346. (b) 347. (b) 348. (a) 349. (b) 350. (c)
351. (c) 352. (c) 353. (b) 354. (c) 355. (c) 356. (a) 357. (b) 358. (c) 359. (d) 360. (d)
361. (c) 362. (a) 363. (c) 364. (c) 365. (a) 366. (b) 367. (c) 368. (c) 369. (c) 370. (c)
371. (a) 372. (c) 373. (a) 374. (c) 375. (a) 376. (c) 377. (d) 378. (d) 379. (c) 380. (b)
381. (a) 382. (c) 383. (b) 384. (c) 385. (c) 386. (d) 387. (b) 388. (d) 389. (c) 390. (a)
391. (a) 392. (b) 393. (c) 394. (a) 395. (b) 396. (a) 397. (d) 398. (a) 399. (a) 400. (c)
401. (d) 402. (b) 403. (a) 404. (c) 405. (c) 406. (c) 407. (a) 408. (c) 409. (a)

Hints and Solutions

Electrochemical Cells

1. (a): A redox reaction is exothermic.

2. (c): An electrochemical cell is based on a redox reaction. All except (c) are redox reactions.

3. (c): When the external voltage applied is greater than the cell voltage, the reverse of the cell reaction occurs, that is, a reaction which is otherwise non-spontaneous. Hence, it functions as an electrolytic cell.

4. (d): All the given processes involve electrochemical phenomena.

Galvanic Cells

5. (b): By convention, the cell is represented by (b).

6. (d): The first three statements are correct.

7. (c): In the Zn–$CuSO_4$ cell, zinc is the anode while copper is the cathode.

8. (d): All the given statements are correct.

9. (c): Salt bridge allows ions to flow through it.

10. (c): KCl reacts with $AgNO_3$ to form a precipitate of AgCl.

11. **(d):** $Cu \rightarrow Cu^{2+} + 2e^-$ (Oxidation)
$Hg^{2+} + 2e^- \rightarrow Hg$ (Reduction)
$Cu + Hg^{2+} \rightarrow Cu^{2+} + Hg$

12. **(c):** KNO_3 is used in the salt bridge because K^+ and NO_3^- ions have the nearly same velocity (or transport number).

13. **(a):** The anode in a galvanic cell is the negative electrode.

14. **(b):** An electrochemical cell stops working after some time because the electrode potentials of both the electrodes become equal.

15. **(b):** In the Daniell cell, electrons from flow from Zn to Cu but conventional electricity flows in the opposite direction, that is, from Cu to Zn, outside the cell.

16. **(c):** The direction of conventional current is opposite to that of the flow of electrons.

17. **(b):** KCl is preferred in a salt bridge because K^+ and Cl^- ions have the same transport number.

18. **(c):** If the salt bridge is removed, the current stops flowing.

Electrode Potential, EMF of a Cell, Electrochemical Series

19. **(c):** Hg_2Cl_2 is used in the calomel electrode.

20. **(d):** As Hg is less reactive than hydrogen, the standard reduction potential of calomel is positive. Hence, its standard oxidation potential must be negative.

21. **(a):** The correct order of reactivity according to the electrochemical series is K > Mg > Zn > Cu.

22. **(a):** In the electrochemical series, metals are arranged in the order of increasing standard reduction potentials from top to bottom.

23. **(d):** Metals below hydrogen have higher reduction potential and are hence strong oxidising agents.

24. **(a):** $E^\circ_{Cell} = E^\circ_{Cathode} - E^\circ_{Anode} = 0.34 - (-0.76) = 1.10$ V.

25. **(a):** The cell corresponding to the given reaction is
$Fe \mid Fe^{2+} \mid\mid Fe^{3+} \mid Fe^{2+}$
$E^\circ_{Cell} = E^\circ_{Fe^{3+}/Fe^{2+}} - E^\circ_{Fe^{2+}/Fe}$
$= 0.771\text{ V} - (-0.441\text{ V}) = 1.212$ V

26. **(d):** emf of a cell = Oxidation potential of electrode on which oxidation occurs + Reduction potential of electrode on which reduction occurs
= Oxidation potential of anode + Reduction potential of cathode = (ii)
= Oxidation potential of anode – Oxidation potential of cathode = (iv)

27. **(a):** Eq. (ii) – Eq. (i) gives the required cell with
$E^\circ = 1.23 - (-0.44) = 1.67$ V.

28. **(a):** Al undergoes oxidation with respect to the NHE. Hence, its standard electrode potential must be negative and equal to the emf because $E^\circ_{H^+/H_2} = 0$.

29. **(b):** Voltage of (a) = 0.28 V, (b) = 1.56 V
(c) = 0.34 V (d) = 1.10 V

30. **(a):** EMF of the cell $Zn \mid Zn^{2+} \mid\mid Cu^{2+} \mid Cu$
$= E^\circ_{Cu^{2+}/Cu} - E^\circ_{Zn^{2+}/Zn} = +0.34 - (-0.76) = 1.10$ V
emf of the cell $Fe \mid Fe^{2+} \mid\mid Cu^{2+} \mid Cu$
$= E^\circ_{Cu^{2+}/Cu} - E^\circ_{Fe^{2+}/Fe} = +0.34 - (-0.41)\text{ V} = 0.75$ V
As the two cells are connected in series, the net EMF of the two cells = 1.10 + 0.75 = 1.85 V.

31. **(a):** Lesser the reduction potential or greater the oxidation potential, more easily the substance is oxidised.

32. **(c):** Higher the oxidation potential, stronger is the reducing agent.

33. **(d):** A large negative reduction potential implies a high oxidation potential; so, A^- is easily oxidised.

34. **(b):** Greater the reduction potential, stronger is the oxidising agent or weaker is the reducing agent.

35. **(a):** Greater the reduction potential, lesser is the reducing power.

36. **(c):** Higher the reduction potential, the more easily it is reduced and hence stronger is the oxidising agent. F_2 has the highest reduction potential. Hence F_2 is the strongest oxidising agent. Considering the reverse reactions (oxidation reactions), higher the oxidation potential, more easily it is oxidised and hence stronger is the reducing agent. The oxidation potential of I^- ion (–0.53 V) is the highest out of –2.85, –1.36, –1.06, –0.53 V. Hence, I^- is the strongest reducing agent.

37. **(d):** Lesser the reduction potential, higher is the reducing capacity.

38. **(c):** Lesser the reduction potential, stronger is the reducing agent.

39. **(d):** F_2 has the highest standard reduction potential. Hence, it is reduced most easily and, therefore, is the strongest oxidising agent.

40. **(a):** Reduction potentials are in the order:
$Mg^{2+}/Mg < Zn^{2+}/Zn < Fe^{2+}/Fe$
Oxidation potentials are in the order:
$Mg/Mg^{2+} > Zn/Zn^{2+} > Fe/Fe^{2+}$
Greater the reducing potential, stronger is the oxidising agent. Greater the oxidation potential, stronger is the reducing agent. Thus, Fe can oxidise Mg and Zn whereas Mg can reduce Zn^{2+} and Zn can reduce Fe^{2+}.

41. **(c):** $Cu + Pb(NO_3)_2 \rightarrow$ No reaction.
Pb is a stronger reducing agent than Cu.
$Pb + 2AgNO_3 \rightarrow Pb(NO_3)_2 + 2Ag$
Pb is a stronger reducing than Ag.
$Ag + Cu(NO_3)_2 \rightarrow$ No reaction.
Cu is a stronger reducing agent than Ag.
Combining these, reducing character is Pb > Cu > Ag.

42. **(d):** NO_3^- is reduced in preference to the hydronium ion.

43. **(a):** Ag has lower oxidation potential than hydrogen.

44. (a): Cu does not react with $ZnSO_4$ solution.

45. (a): Greater the oxidation potential, greater is the reactivity.

46. (c): Gold has a higher reduction potential than iron. Hence, Fe is easily oxidised to Fe^{2+}.

47. (c): A metal with a lower reduction potential displaces a metal with a higher reduction potential from its aqueous solution.

48. (d): Zn is more reactive than Cu. Hence, Zn can displace Cu from $CuSO_4$ solution, that is, the reaction occurs. Hence, $CuSO_4$ solution cannot be stored in a zinc vessel. This is not so in the first three cases.

49. (d): Cu is less reactive than Fe.

50. (c): Copper lies below lead in the electrochemical series. Hence, copper is less reactive than lead. Hence, $Pb(NO_3)_2$ can be stored in a Cu vessel.

51. (a): Cl_2 is more reactive than Br_2. Hence, Cl_2 can displace Br^- ions from its solution, that is,
$2\,Br^-\,(aq) + Cl_2 \rightarrow Br_2(g) + 2\,Cl^-$.

52. (b): This is similar to the halogens (F_2, Cl_2, Br_2, I_2).
From (i) Br_2 is more reactive than A_2. From (ii) Br is less reactive than C_2, that is, C_2 is more reactive than B_2. From (iii) A_2 is more reactive than D_2.
Combining these, the order of reactivity is $C_2 > B_2 > A_2 > D_2$. As these are non-metals, lesser the oxidation potential, greater is the reactivity, therefore oxidation will be the order
$E^\circ_{C^-/C_2} < E^\circ_{B^-/B_2} < E^\circ_{A^-/A_2} < E^\circ_{D^-/D_2}$

53. (b): The given data show that C is more active than X and Y but less active than Z, and Y is more active than X. Thus, Z is more active than X and Y, and Y is more active than X. Hence Z > Y > X.

54. (b): Zn is more active than Ag. Hence Ag^+ ions will be reduced to Ag, and Zn will be oxidised to Zn^{2+} ions ($Zn + 2\,Ag^+ \rightarrow Zn^{2+} + 2Ag$). Zn is less active than Mg. The reaction $Zn + Mg^{2+} \rightarrow Zn^{2+} + Mg$ cannot occur.

55. (b): $\bar{A}/A^+\ (xM)$ represents a –ve pole (anode) on which oxidation occurs. $B^+\ (yM)/B$ represents a +ve pole (cathode) on which reduction occurs. Hence, the cell reaction is
$A + B^+ \rightarrow A^+ + B$

56. (d): Check the spontaneity of each reaction by finding the emf. For a spontaneous reaction, the emf should be +ve.

57. (b): I_2 is less reactive than Br_2. Hence I_2 cannot displace Br_2 from KBr.

58. (d): Oxidation potential of Sn ($E^\circ_{Sn/Sn^{2+}}$) = +0.136 V. It can reduce the substance having a lower oxidation potential, Pb.

59. (b): $M + X \rightarrow M^+ + X^-$
$E^\circ_{cell} = E^\circ_{M/M^+} + E^\circ_{X/X^-} = -0.44 + 0.33 = -0.11\ V$
As E_{cell} is –ve, this reaction is not spontaneous. For the reverse reaction $M^+ + X^- \rightarrow M + X$, $E^\circ_{cell} = +0.11$ V. Hence, this reaction will be spontaneous.

60. (d): I_2 is less reactive than Br_2. I_2 cannot displace Br^- ions from its solution. Hence, (d) is non-spontaneous.

61. (b): Greater the oxidation potential of a metal (or lesser is the reduction potential, the more easily it can lose electrons, that is, greater is its electropositive character and hence more stable is its oxide. Hg is the least electropositive. Hence, its oxide can decompose on heating.

62. (b): Left electrode: $H_2(g) \rightarrow 2\,H^+\,(aq) + 2\,e^-$
Right electrode: $2AgCl(s) + 2\,e^- \rightarrow 2Ag(s) + 2\,Cl^-\,(aq)$
Cell reaction: $2AgCl(s) + H_2(g) \rightarrow 2Ag(s) + 2\,H^+\,(aq) + 2\,Cl^-\,(aq)$

$K_c = [H^+]^2\,[Cl^-]^2$ or $K_c'\,[H^+]\,[Cl^-]$

63. (a): Change of oxidation state from +2 to +3 indicates oxidation. Oxidation will be the easiest where the oxidation potential is highest, which is for Cr ($E_{Cr^{2+}/Cr^{3+}}$ = + 0.41 V).

64. (c):
(i) $Cu^{2+} + e^- \rightarrow Cu^+$

$$\Delta G_1 = -n\,FE^\circ$$
$$= -1 \times F \times 0.15 = -\ 0.15\ F$$

(ii) $Cu^+ + e^- \rightarrow Cu$

$$\Delta G_2 = -n\,FE^\circ$$
$$= -1 \times F \times 0.50 = -\ 0.50\ F$$

Aim: $Cu^+ + 2\,e^- \rightarrow Cu$

$$\Delta G_3 = -\ 2 \times F \times E^\circ_{Cu^{2+}/Cu}$$

Eq. (i) + Eq. (ii) gives the required equation.

$$\therefore\ -2FE^\circ_{Cu^{2+}/Cu} = -\ 0.15 + (-0.50\ F)$$

$$2\,E^\circ_{Cu^{2+}/Cu} = 0.65$$

or $E^\circ_{Cu^{2+}/Cu} = 0.325$ V

65. (d): The electrode potential of the standard hydrogen electrode has been arbitrarily fixed as zero.

66. (c): Refer to the electrochemical series.

67. (b): Standard reduction potentials are taken as positive.

68. (c): Metals with a higher oxidation potential (lower reduction potentials) react with acids to give H_2 gas.

Nernst Equation for Electrode Potential and EMF of a Cell

69. (e): $E^\circ_{Cu^{2+}/Cu} = E^\circ_{Cu^{2+}/Cu} - \dfrac{0.0591}{2}\log\dfrac{1}{\left[Cu^{2+}\right]}$

$$= E^\circ_{Cu^{2+}/Cu} + \frac{0.0591}{2}\log\left[Cu^{2+}\right]$$

Lower the value of $\left[Cu^{2+}\right]$, lower is $E^\circ_{Cu^{2+}/Cu}$.

70. (d): Electrode potential of the half cell depends on (a), (b) and (c).

71. (a): $Mn^{n+} + ne^- \rightarrow M$

$$E = E^\circ - \frac{RT}{nF}\ln\frac{1}{\left[Mn^{n+}\right]}$$

As $[Mn^{n+}]$ increases, E will increase.

72. (a): $Cu^{2+} + 2e^- \rightarrow Cu$,

$$E = E^\circ - \frac{0.059}{1}\log\frac{1}{[Cu^{2+}]}$$

$$= 0.34 - \frac{0.059}{1}\log\frac{1}{10^{-19}} = -0.22\text{ V}$$

73. (c): $H^+ + e^- \rightarrow \frac{1}{2}H_2$

$$E = E^\circ - \frac{0.059}{1}\log\frac{p_{H_2}^{1/2}}{[H^+]} = -0.059\log\frac{p_{H_2}^{1/2}}{[H^+]}$$

E will be negative when $p_{H_2}^{1/2}/[H^+]$ is greater than 1.

That is, when $p_{H_2} = 2$ atm and $[H^+] = 1$ M.

74. (b): $Cu^{2+} + 2e^- \rightarrow Cu$,

$$E = E^\circ - \frac{0.0591}{n}\log\frac{1}{[Cu^{2+}]}$$

$$= 0.34 - \frac{0.0591}{1}\log\frac{1}{0.01}$$

$$= 0.2809 = 0.281\text{ V}$$

75. (c): The reduction reaction for the H_2 electrode is $2H^+(aq) + 2e^- \rightarrow H_2(g)$

$$E_{H^+/H_2} = E^\circ_{H^+/H_2} - \frac{0.0591}{2}\log\frac{p_{H_2}}{[H^+]^2}$$

In pure water at 298 K; $[H^+] = 10^{-7}$ M

$$\therefore 0 = 0 - \frac{0.0591}{2}\log\frac{p_{H_2}}{(10^{-7})^2}$$

or $\log\frac{p_{H_2}}{10^{-7}} = 0$ or $\frac{p_{H_2}}{10^{-14}} = 1$ ($\because \log 1 = 0$)

or $p_{H_2} = 10^{-14}$ atm

76. (d): It is a redox electrode. The reduction reaction is $Sn^{4+} + 2e^- \rightarrow Sn^{2+}, n = 2$

$$E^\circ_{Sn^{4+}/Sn^{2+}} = E^\circ - \frac{0.0591}{2}\log\frac{[Sn^{2+}]}{[Sn^{4+}]}$$

$$= E^\circ - \frac{0.0591}{2}\log\frac{0.1}{0.01} = E^\circ - \frac{0.059}{2}$$

77. (a): In a mixture of H_2SO_4 and H_3PO_4, Fe^{3+} ion forms the complex $[FeHPO_4]^+$. As a result, the concentration of Fe^{3+} ions is reduced, which results in the lowering of reduction potential.

78. (b): Cell reaction is $2Tl + Cu^{2+} \rightarrow 2Tl^+ + Cu$

$$E_{cell} = E^\circ_{cell} - \frac{2.303}{nF}\log\frac{[Tl^+]}{[Cu^{2+}]}$$

E_{cell} can be increased by increasing the concentration of Cu^{2+} ions.

79. (b): Cell reaction is $Mg + Sn^{2+} \rightarrow Mg^{2+} + Sn$

$$E_{cell} = E^\circ_{cell} - \frac{0.0591}{2}\log\frac{[Mg^{2+}]}{[Sn^{2+}]}$$

$$= (2.34 - 0.14) - \frac{0.0591}{2}\log\frac{10^{-2}}{10^{-1}} \simeq 2.23\text{ V}$$

80. (a): For the given cell, $Zn + Cu^{2+} \rightarrow Zn^{2+} + Cu$

$$E = E^\circ - \frac{0.0591}{2}\log\frac{[Zn^{2+}]}{[Cu^{2+}]}$$

$$\therefore E_1 = E^\circ - \frac{0.0591}{2}\log\frac{0.01}{1.0}$$

$$E_2 = E^\circ - \frac{0.0591}{2}\log\frac{0.1}{0.01}$$

Thus, $E_1 > E_2$.

81. (a): For the given reaction,

$Cr_2O_7^{2-} + 14H^+ + 6e^- \rightarrow 2Cr^{3+} + 7H_2O$

$$E = E^\circ - \frac{0.0591}{2}\log\frac{[Cr^{3+}][H_2O]^7}{[Cr_2O_7^{2-}][H^+]^{14}}$$

$$1.067 = 1.33 - 9.85 \times 10^{-3}$$

$$\log\frac{[15\times10^{-3}]^2[1]^7}{[4.5\times10^{-3}][H^+]^{14}}$$

$$\frac{-0.263}{-9.85\times10^{-3}} = 2\log(15\times10^{-3}) - \log(4.5\times10^{-3}) - 14\log$$

(H^+) $26.7 = 2(-1.82) + 2.34 + 14$ pH

or pH $= \frac{28}{14} = 2$

82. (c): Applying Nernst equation to the given cell reaction,

$$E_{cell} = E^\circ_{cell} - \frac{0.0591}{n}\log\frac{[Ni^{2+}]}{[Ag^+]^2}$$

$$= 1.05\text{ V} - \frac{0.0591}{2}\log\frac{0.160}{(0.002)^2}$$

$$= 1.05 - \frac{0.0591}{2}\log(4\times10^{-4})$$

$$= 1.05 - \frac{0.0591}{2}(4.6021)$$

$$= 1.05 - 0.14\text{ V} = 0.91\text{ V}$$

83. (d): The cell reaction is

$Zn + Cu^{2+} \rightarrow Zn^{2+} + Cu$

$$E_{cell} = E^\circ_{cell} - \frac{RT}{nF}\ln\frac{[Zn^{2+}]}{[Cu^{2+}]}$$

As the factor $[Zn^{2+}]/[Cu^{2+}]$ remains the same, $E_1 = E_2$.

84. (d): The Nernst equation gives the effect of temperature, concentration and pressure of the gas (if any).

85. (c): $E_{cell} = E°_{cell} - \frac{RT}{nF}\ln\frac{[Sn^{2+}]}{[Ag^+]^2}$

86. (b): $E_{cell} = E°_{cell} - \frac{RT}{nF}\ln\frac{[Zn^{2+}][Cl^-]^2}{P_{Cl_2}}$

87. (d): $E^\circ_{Co^{2+}/Co} = -\ 0.28\text{ V}$

$E^\circ_{Ag^+/Ag} = 0.80\text{ V}$

Hence cobalt is the anode, that is, oxidation takes place on the cobalt electrode. The cell reaction is $Co + 2\ Ag^+ \rightarrow Co^{2+} + 2Ag$

$\therefore\ E_{cell} = E°_{cell} - \frac{RT}{nF}\ \ln\frac{[Co^{2+}]}{[Ag^+]^2}$

Lesser the factor $[Co^{2+}]/[Ag^+]$, greater is the E_{cell}.

88. (d): $E_{cell} = E°_{cell} - \frac{0.0591}{2}\log\frac{[Cu^{2+}]}{[Ag^+]^2}$

Thus, if $[Cu^{2+}]$ is doubled, E_{cell} will decrease only by a small fraction.

89. (c): When Ag changes into Ag^+ ions, these ions combine with Cl^- ions of KCl and the concentration of AgCl remains constant.

90. (a): $Zn + Cu^{2+} \rightarrow Zn^{2+} + Cu$

$$E_{cell} = E°_{cell} - \frac{0.0591}{n}\log\frac{[Zn^{2+}]}{[Cu^{2+}]}$$

When the cell is completely discharged, $E_{cell} = 0$.

$$\therefore\ 0 = 1.10 - \frac{0.0591}{n}\log\frac{[Zn^{2+}]}{[Cu^{2+}]}$$

$$\text{or}\ \log\frac{[Zn^{2+}]}{[Cu^{2+}]} = 1.10 \times \frac{2}{0.0591} = 37.2$$

91. (c): Applying Nernst equation to the given half reaction

$$E = E° - \frac{0.0591}{2}\ \log[H^+]^2$$

$$= 1.30 - \frac{0.0591}{2}\log(10^{-2})^2$$

$$= 1.30 + 4 \times \frac{0.0591}{2} = 1.30 + 0.1182 = 1.42\text{ V}$$

92. (b): $H^+ + e^- \rightarrow \frac{1}{2}\ H_2$

$$E = E° \ \frac{0.059}{n}\ \log\frac{p_{H_2}^{1/2}}{[H^+]}$$

$$= 0 - \frac{0.059}{1}\log\frac{(100)^{1/3}}{1} = -0.059\text{ V}$$

93. (d): $[H^+] = 0.1\text{ M}$

$H^+ + e^- \rightarrow \frac{1}{2}\ H_2$

Applying Nernst equation,

$$E_{Red} = E°_{Red}\ \frac{0.0591}{n}\log\frac{1}{[H^+]}$$

$$= 0 + \frac{0.0591}{1}\ \log(0.1) = -\ 0.0591\text{ V}$$

$E_{ox} = 0.0591\text{ V}$

94. (b): For the hydrogen electrode, reduction reaction is

$H^+ + e^- \rightarrow \frac{1}{2}\ H_2$

$$E^\circ_{H^+/H_2} = E^\circ_{H^+/H_2} - \frac{0.0591}{n}\log\frac{p_{H_2}^{1/2}}{[H^+]}$$

$$= 0 - \frac{0.0591}{1}\log\frac{1}{10^{-10}} = -\ 0.591\text{ V}$$

(pH = 10 means $[H^+] = 10^{-10}$ M)

$\therefore$ Oxidation potential = 0.591 V

Equilibrium Constant from Nernst Equation

95. (c): $E°$ for the given reaction = 0.855 – 0.799 = 0.056 V

$$E_{cell} = \frac{0.0591}{2}\ \log K_c$$

$$\text{or}\ \log K_c = \frac{0.056 \times 2}{0.059} = 1.8983$$

K_c = Antilog 1.8983 = 79.12 = 79

96. (d): $E°_{cell} = E°_{Cathode} - E°_{Anode}$

$= 0.77 - 0.54 = 0.23\text{ V}$

$$E°_{cell} = \frac{0.0591}{n}\ \log K$$

$$\text{or}\quad \log K = \frac{E°_{cell} \times n}{0.0591} = \frac{0.23 \times 2}{0.0591} = 7.783$$

K = Antilog (7.783) = 6.07×10^7

($n = 2$ for the given reaction)

97. (c): $E°_{cell} = \frac{0.0591}{n}\log K$

or $\log K = \frac{nE°_{cell}}{0.0591}$. For a feasible reaction $E°_{cell}$ is +ve.

Hence, log K should be +ve, that is, $K > 1$.

98. (d): $E°_{cell} = \frac{0.059}{n}\log K$

$$\text{Or,}\quad \log K = \frac{nE°_{cell}}{0.059} = \frac{2 \times 0.46}{0.059} = 15.59$$

K = Antilog (15.59) = $3.89 \times 10^{15} \simeq 4 \times 10^{15}$

99. (a): $E°_{cell} = \frac{0.059}{2}\log 10^{12} = 0.354\ \text{V}$

Electrochemical Cell and Gibbs Free Energy Change of the Reaction

100. (a): $\Delta G^\circ = -nFE = -1 \times 96500 \times (-3.0)\ J = 289.5\ kJ$

101. (c): $Zn + Cu^{2+} \rightarrow Zn^{2+} + Cu$ for 1 mol of Zn

For 2 mol of Zn,

$2Zn + 2\ Cu^{2+} \rightarrow 2\ Zn^{2+} + 2Cu,\ n = 4$

$$\Delta G^\circ = -nFE^\circ_{cell}$$

$= -4 \times 96500 \times 1.1 = -424600\ J = -424.6\ kJ$

102. (c): $E^\circ_{cell} = E^\circ_{Cathode} - E^\circ_{Anode}$

$= -0.44 - (-0.74) = 0.30\ V$

$\Delta G^\circ = -nFE^\circ_{cell}$

$= -6 \times 96500 \times 0.30\ J$

$= -173700 (n = 6)$

103. (a): $\Delta G^\circ = -nFE^\circ_{cell}$

$= -1 \times 96500 \times 1.02 = -98430\ J$

104. (a): $\Delta_r G = +960\ kJ\ mol^{-1}$

$= 960{,}000\ J\ mol^{-1}$

Applying $\Delta G = -nFE^\circ$, for the given reaction,

$n = 4\left[\frac{2}{3}(2Al^{3+}) + 4e^- \rightarrow \frac{4}{5}Al\right]$

Hence, $960{,}000 = 4 \times 96500 \times E^\circ$

$\therefore E^\circ = 2.5\ V$

105. (a): $2\ Fe^{3+} + 2e^- \rightarrow 2\ Fe^{3+}$

or $2I^- \rightarrow I_2 + 2e^-$

Hence, for the given cell reaction, $n = 2$

$\Delta G^\circ = -nFE^\circ_{cell}$

$= -2 \times 96500 \times 0.36\ J$

$= -45.55\ kJ\ mol^{-1}$

$\Delta G^\circ = -2.303\ RT \log K$ or $\log K$

$= \frac{\Delta G^\circ}{2.303 RT}$

$= -\frac{-45.55\ kJ\ mol^{-1}}{2.303 \times 8.314 \times 10^{-3} kJ\ K^{-1}\ mol^{-1} \times 298\ K}$

$= 7.983$

$K = \text{Antilog}\ (7.983) = 9.616 \times 10^7$

106. (b): $E_{cell} = E^\circ_{cell} - \frac{RT}{nF}\ln\frac{C_2}{C_1}$ and $\Delta G = -nFE_{cell}$

Hence, ΔG is a function of $\ln (C_2/C_1)$

107. (a): $\Delta G^\circ = -nFE^\circ_{cell}$

If E°_{cell} is –ve, ΔG° = +ve, that is, $\Delta G^\circ > 0$

Also $\Delta G^\circ = -\ 2.303\ RT \log\ K_{eq}$

As ΔG° = +ve, $\log\ K_{eq}$ = – ve

Hence, $K_{eq} < 1$.

108. (a): For the given cell, cell reactions are

At anode: $Ag \rightarrow Ag^+ + e^-$

At cathode: $AgCl + e^- \rightarrow Ag(s) + Cl^-$

Net cell reaction $AgCl \rightarrow Ag^+ + Cl^-,\ n = 1$

$\Delta G^\circ_r = \Sigma \Delta G^\circ_P \rightarrow \Sigma\ \Delta G^\circ_R$

$= (78 - 129) - (-109) = +58\ kJ\ mol^{-1}$

$\Delta G^\circ = -nFE^\circ_{cell}$

$\therefore 58 \times 10^3 = -1 \times 96500 \times E^\circ_{cell}$

or $E^\circ_{cell} = \frac{-58 \times 1000}{96500} = -0.60\ V$

109. (a): Maximum work obtained $= nFE^\circ_{cell}$

$= 2 \times 96500 \times 1.1\ J = 212.3\ kJ$

110. (a): For the given reaction $E^\circ_{cell} = -\ 0.80\ V$

$\Delta G = -\ nFE^\circ_{cell} = -2 \times 96500 \times (-0.80)\ J = 154.4\ kJ$

Concentration Cells and Liquid Junction Potential

111. (a): The emf of a concentration cell, $E_{cell} = \frac{0.0591}{n}\log\frac{C_2}{C_1}$ $(C_2 > C_1)$

$\therefore (E_{cell})_1 = \frac{0.0591}{1}\log\frac{1}{0.1} = 0.0591$

$(E_{cell})_2 = \frac{0.591}{1}\log\frac{1}{0.01} = 0.0591 \times 2$

$\therefore \frac{(E_{cell})_2}{(E_{cell})_1} = 2$ or $(E_{cell})_2 = 2 \times (E_{cell})_1$

$= 2 \times 0.06 = 0.12\ V$

112. (a): pH = means $[H^+] = 10^{-3}$ M and pH = 6 $[H^+] = 10^{-6}$ H

For concentration cell, $E_{cell} = \frac{0.0591}{n}\log\frac{c_2}{c_1}\ (c_2 > c_1)$

$= \frac{0.0591}{1}\log\frac{10^{-3}}{10^{-6}} = 0.0591 \times 3 = 0.1773\ V$

113. (b): For the cell Pt | $H_2(P_1)$ | $H^+ (aq)$ | $H_2(P_2)$ | Pt

At anode: $H_2(P_1) \rightarrow 2\ H^+ + 2\ e^- (n = 2)$

At cathode: $2\ H^+ + 2\ e^- \rightarrow H_2(P_2)(n = 2)$

Overall reaction: $H_2(P_1) \rightarrow H_2(P_2)$

$$E_{cell} = E^\circ - \frac{RT}{F}\ln\frac{P_2}{P_1} = \frac{RT}{2F}\ln\frac{P_1}{P_2}$$

114. (b): For a concentration cell, E_{cell}

$= \frac{0.0591}{n}\log\frac{P_1}{P_2}$

The emf will be +ve, if $P_1 > P_2$.

115. (c): This is a concentration cell.

$$E_{cell} = \frac{0.059}{n}\log\frac{C_2}{C_1} = \frac{0.059}{1}\log\frac{10^{-4}}{10^{-6}} = 0.059 \times 2 = 0.118\ V$$

116. (c): The given cell is a concentration cell.

$$E_{cell} = \frac{0.059}{n} \log \frac{P_1}{P_2}$$

E_{cell} will be +ve if $P_1 > P_2$.

117. (b): It is a concentration cell. EMF ≠ 0 because 0.1 M HCl and 0.1 M CH_3COOH have different $[H^+]$, that is, their pH values are not equal (because HCl is strong while CH_3COOH is a weak acid).

118. (c): The cell reaction is

$$Zn \rightarrow Zn^{2+}(C_1) + 2e^-$$
$$Zn^{2+}(C_1) + 2e^- \rightarrow Zn$$
$$Zn^{2+}(C_2) \rightarrow Zn^{2+}(C_1)$$

$$E^\circ_{cell} = \frac{0.0591}{2} \log \frac{[Zn^{2+}(C_2)]}{[Zn^{2+}(C_1)]}$$

$\Delta G - nFE^\circ_{cell}$. ΔG will be –ve only if E°_{cell} is +ve which can be so only if $C_2 > C_1$.

Conductance of Electrolytic Solution

119. (b): Electrolytic conduction increases. Or, resistance decreases with an increase in temperature.

120. (c): Diamond is an insulator.

121. (b): With an increase in temperature, electrolytic conduction increases because dissociation increases. Metallic conduction decreases because kernels start vibrating and hinder the flow of electrons.

122. (d): In SI units, $\Omega = (kg\ m^2)/(A^2s^3)$.

123. (b): The unit of conductivity (specific conductance) is $ohm^{-1}\ cm^{-1}$.

124. (b): $\Lambda_c = \kappa \times \frac{1000}{C}$

125. (c): Specific resistance = R

$\therefore$ Specific conductance $(\kappa) = \frac{1}{R}$

$$\Lambda_{eq} = \frac{1000\times}{C_{eq}} 1000 \times \frac{1}{R} \times \frac{1}{C} = \frac{1000}{RC}$$

126. (b): $\kappa = \frac{1}{R} \times$ cell const $= \frac{1}{10000} \times 8.76$

$= 8.76 \times 10^{-4}\ \Omega^{-1}\ cm^{-1}$

127. (c): $\kappa = \frac{1}{R} \times$ cell const. $= \frac{1}{31.6} \times 0.47$

$= 0.015\ S\ cm^{-1}$

128. (a): Sp. cond. = Obs. cond. × Cell constant

$$= \frac{1}{2.5 \times 10^3} \times 1.15 = 4.6 \times 10^{-4}$$

$$\Lambda_{eq} = \frac{\kappa \times 1000}{Normality} = \frac{4.6 \times 10^{-4} \times 1000}{0.1}$$

$= 4.6\ \Omega^{-1}\ cm^2\ eq^{-1}$

129. (b): 0.1 M = 0.2 N H_2SO_4

$$\Lambda_{eq} = k \times \frac{1000}{Normality}$$

$$= \frac{2.6 \times 10^{-2} \times 1000}{0.2} = 130\ \Omega^{-1}\ cm^2$$

130. (b): $\Lambda_{eq} = \frac{\Lambda_m}{\text{Total charge on cations / anions}}$

$= \frac{150}{2}\ ohm^{-1}\ cm^2\ mol^{-1}$

$= 75\ ohm^{-1}\ cm^2\ mol^{-1}$

131. (a): $R = \rho \frac{l}{a} = \frac{1}{R}\frac{l}{a}$

(ρ = sp. resistance, κ = sp. conductivity)

or $\kappa = \frac{1}{R}\frac{l}{a} = \frac{1}{5.55 \times 10^3\ \Omega 3.14 \times (0.5\ cm)^2}$

$(a = \pi r^2)$

$= 0.01148\ \Omega^{-1}\ cm^{-1}$ or $S\ cm^{-1}$

$$\Lambda_m = \frac{\kappa \times 1000}{Molarity}$$

$$= \frac{(0.01148\ S\ cm^{-1}) \times 1000\ cm^3\ L^{-1}}{(0.05\ mol\ L^{-1})} = 229.6\ S\ cm^2\ mol^{-1}$$

132. (a): Specific cond. (κ) = Observed cond. × Cell const.

$= \frac{1}{31.6} \times 0.367$

Molar cond. $(\propto) = \frac{1000 \times \kappa}{Molarity} = \frac{1000 \times 0.367}{31.6 \times 0.05}$

$= 232\ S\ cm^2\ mol^{-1}$

133. (b): $\Lambda_m = \frac{\kappa \times 1000}{Molarity}$

$$= \frac{(5.76 \times 10^{-3}\ S\ cm^{-1}) \times 1000\ cm^3\ L^{-1}}{(0.5\ mol\ L^{-1})}$$

$$= \frac{5.76}{0.5} = 11.52\ S\ cm^2/mol$$

134. (b): $\kappa = \frac{1}{R} \times$ cell const

or cell const = $\kappa \times R = 0.0212 \times 55 = 1.166\ cm^{-1}$

135. (d): Specific conductance (κ) = Conductance (C_1) × Cell constant

When $\kappa = G$, Cell constant = 1

136. (d): The increase in molar conductivity of any strong electrolyte with dilution is due to a decrease in the interionic forces.

137. (c): For a weak electrolyte, Λ_m first increases slowly and then rapidly with dilution but does not become constant.

138. (b): In a strong electrolyte, on dilution, the number of ions remains the same but ionic mobility of the ions increases and hence the equivalent conductance increases.

139. (d): The increase in molar conductivity of any strong electrolyte with dilution is due to a decrease in the interionic forces.

140. (b): In a weak electrolyte like acetic acid, the degree of ionisation increases with dilution.

141. (d): $\Lambda_m^c = \Lambda_m^\circ - A\sqrt{c}$

142. (b): Specific conductance decreases because the number of ions per cc decreases on dilution. Equivalent conductivity increases because $\Lambda_{eq} = \kappa \times V$ and the increase in V is much more than the decrease in κ.

143. (a): $\Lambda_m = \kappa \times V$ where V is the volume of the solution containing 1 mol of the solute. The specific conductivity (κ) decreases with dilution but volume V increases much more on dilution. Hence, Λ_m increases with dilution. As the volume containing 1 mol of NaCl will be the highest for 0.005 M NaCl solution, the product $\kappa \times V$ will be highest and hence its molar conductivity will be the highest.

144. (b): The more concentrated the solution, the lesser is the conductance and greater is the resistance.

145. (a): Sr^{2+} ion being the largest in size will be the least hydrated. Hence, it will show maximum conductivity.

146. (a): Two deciding factors are, degree of ionisation and size of the ions.

147. (b): In the gaseous state, size of $Li^+ < Na^+ < K^+$. Smaller the ion, greater is the charge density, hence greater is the hydration. Hence, the size of hydrated ions is $Li^+ > Na^+ > K^+$. Greater the size, less is the mobility and hence lesser is the conductance. Thus, conductance will be in the order KCl > NaCl > LiCl.

148. (b): The conductance of an electrolyte depends upon the nature of the electrolyte. NaCl and KNO_3 are stronger electrolytes than CH_3COOH and HCl, NaCl is stronger than KNO_3 because the size of ions is smaller. Hence, 0.1 M NaCl solution will have the highest conductance.

149. (d): By definition of equivalent conductance.

150. (d): Glucose is a non-electrolyte and hence a non-conductor.

151. (b): Conductivity cell is platinised to avoid polarisation effects.

Kohlrausch's Law and its Applications

152. (d): $\Lambda_m^\infty (BaSO_4) = \lambda^\circ_{Ba^{2+}} + \lambda^\circ_{SO_4^{2-}}$

$= \Lambda_m^\circ (BaCl_2) + \Lambda_m^\circ (H_2SO_4) - 2\Lambda_m^\circ (HCl)$

$= x_1 + x_2 - 2x_3$

$\Lambda_{eq} (BaSO_4) = \dfrac{\Lambda_m^\circ}{4}\ \dfrac{(x_1 + x_2 - 2x_3)}{2}$

153. (b): $\Lambda_m^\circ (H_2O) = \lambda_m^\circ (H^+) + \lambda_m^\circ (OH^-)$

$= \Lambda_m^\circ (HCl) + \lambda_m^\circ (NaOH) - \lambda_m^\circ (NaCl)$

154. (d): By the definition of Kohlrausch's law in terms of molar conductivities.

155. (c): By Kohlrausch's law.

156. (a): $\Lambda_m^\circ = 57 + 73 = 130$ S cm^2 mol^{-1}

(Salt is $A^{2+}B^{2-}$)

157. (c): $\Lambda_m^\circ (CaCl_2) = \lambda_m^\circ (Ca^{2+}) + 2\lambda_m^\circ (Cl^-)$

$= 118.88 \times 10^{-4} + 2\,(77.33 \times 10^{-4})$

$= 273.54 \times 10^{-4}$ m^2 mho mol^{-1}

158. (d): $\Lambda^\circ_{KOH} = \Lambda^\circ_{KCl} + \Lambda^\circ_{NaOH} - \Lambda^\circ_{NaCl}$

$= 150 + 250 - 126 = 274$

159. (a): $\Lambda_m^\circ (BaOH)_2 = \Lambda_m^\circ (BaCl_2) + 2\ \Lambda_m^\circ (NaOH) - 2\ \Lambda_m^\circ (NaCl)$

$= 2.800 \times 10^{-2}) + 2\,(2.481 \times 10^{-2})$

$- 2(1.265 \times 10^{-2})$ S m^2 mol^{-1}

$= (2.800 + 4.962 - 2.530) \times 10^{-2}$ S m^2 mol^{-1}

$= 5.232 \times 10^{-2}$ S m^2 mol^{-1}

160. (a): $\Lambda_{eq}^\circ = \lambda_+^\circ + \lambda_{Cl^-}^\circ$

$\therefore \Lambda^\circ_{BaCl_2} = \frac{1}{2}\lambda^\circ_{Ba^{2+}} + \lambda^\circ_{Cl^-}$

$= 63.5 + 76 = 139.5\ \Omega^{-1}$ cm^2

$\left(\lambda_{eq}^\circ (Ba^{2+}) = \dfrac{\lambda_m^\circ (Ba^{2+})}{2}\right)$

161. (a): $\Lambda^\circ (CX) = \lambda_C^\circ + \lambda_X^\circ$

$= \Lambda^\circ (BX) + \Lambda^\circ (CA) - \Lambda^\circ (BA)$

$= 198 + 120 - 140 = 178$ S cm^2 eq^{-1}

162. (a): $\Lambda_m^\circ (NH_4OH)$

$= \Lambda_m^\circ (NH_4Cl) + \frac{1}{2}\ \Lambda_m^\circ [Ba(OH)_2] - \frac{1}{2}\Lambda_m^\circ (BaCl_2)$

$= 129.8 + \frac{1}{2}(523.28) - \frac{1}{2}(280.0)$ S cm^2 mol^{-1}

$= 129.8 + 261.64 - 140.0$ S cm^2 mol^{-1}

$= 251.44$ S cm^2 mol^{-1}

163. (d): Λ_m° (Sod. pot oxalate) $= \lambda_m^\circ (Na^+) + \Lambda_m^\circ (K^+) + \lambda^\circ_{(oxalate)}$

$= (150.1 + 73.5 + 148.2)$ S cm^2 mol^{-1}

$= 271.8$ S cm^2 mol^{-1}

$\Lambda_{eq}^\circ = \dfrac{\Lambda_m^\circ}{\text{Total charge on cations or anion } (n \text{ factor})}$

$= \dfrac{271.8}{2} = 135.9$ S cm^2 eq^{-1}

164. (a): $\Lambda_m^\circ (HCOOH) = \lambda^\circ_{HCOO^-} + \lambda^\circ_{H^+}$

$= 54.6 + 349.6 = 404.2$ S cm^2 mol^{-1}

$$\alpha = \frac{\Lambda_m^\circ}{\Lambda_m^\circ} = \frac{46.1}{404.2} = 0.114$$

$HCOOH \rightleftharpoons HCOO^- + H^+$

Initial conc. c mol L^{-1} 0 0

Conc. at eqm $c(1-\alpha)$ $c\alpha$ $c\alpha$

$$K_a = \frac{c.c}{c(1-\alpha)} = \frac{c}{1-\alpha} = \frac{0.025\times(0.114)^2}{1-0.114} = 3.67\times10^{-4}$$

165. (b): Degree of ionisation increases with dilution.

166. (a): $\Lambda_m^\circ(NH_4OH) = \lambda^\circ_{NH_4^+} + \lambda^\circ_{OH^-}$

$= 72 + 198 = 270$ ohm^{-1} cm^2

$\alpha = \Lambda_m^\circ / \Lambda_m^\circ = 9/270 = 1/30 = 3.33\%$

167. (b): $\Lambda^\circ_{C_6H_5COOH} = \Lambda^\circ_{C_6H_5COO^-} + \lambda^\circ_{H^+}$

$= 42 + 288.42 = 330.42$

$$\alpha = \frac{\Lambda_m^c}{\Lambda_m^\circ} = \frac{12.8}{330.42} = 0.039 = 3.9\%$$

168. (d): $\alpha = \frac{\Lambda_{eq}^c}{\Lambda_{eq}^\circ} = \frac{80}{400} = 2\times10^{-2}$

$$K_a = \frac{C^2}{1-\alpha} \simeq C^2 = \frac{1}{32}\times(2\times10^{-2})^2$$

$= 1.25\times10^{-5}$

169. (a): $\Lambda^\circ_{CH_3COOH} = \lambda^\circ_{CH_3COO^-} + \lambda^\circ_{H^+}$

$= 40.9 + 349.1 = 390.0$ S cm^2 mol^{-1}

$$\Lambda^c_{CH_3COOH} = \frac{\kappa\times1000}{\text{Normality}} = \frac{1.65\times10^{-4}\times1000}{0.02}$$

$= 8.25$ S cm^2 mol^{-1}

$$\alpha = \frac{\Lambda^c_{CH_3COOH}}{\Lambda^\circ_{CH_3COOH}} = \frac{8.25}{390} = 0.021$$

170. (d): $\Lambda = \frac{\kappa\times1000}{\text{Normality}}$

For a sparingly soluble salt,

$\Lambda = \Lambda_0$ and Molarity = Solubility (S)

Hence $S = \kappa\times1000/\Lambda_0$

171. (b): $\kappa(AgCl) = \kappa(\text{Solubility}) - \kappa(H_2O)$

$= 1.86\times10^{-6} - 6\times10^{-8}$

$= 1.80\times10^{-6}$ ohm^{-1} cm^{-1}

$$\Lambda^\circ_{AgCl} = \frac{\kappa\times1000}{S}$$

(For AgCl solution, C_m = solubility as the solution is saturated)

$$\text{or } S = \frac{\times1000}{\Lambda^\circ_{AgCl}} = \frac{1.8\times10^{-6}\times1000}{137.2} = 1.31\times10^{-5}\text{ M}$$

172. (a): Ionic mobility is the speed of the ion in ms^{-1} under a potential gradient of 1 V m^{-1}.

$$\text{Ionic mobility, } \frac{v}{\text{V m}^{-1}} = \frac{\text{m s}^{-1}}{\text{V m}^{-1}} = \text{m}^2\ \text{s}^{-1}\ \text{V}^{-1}$$

173. (b): The smaller the size of the ion in the gaseous state, the larger is its hydration in aqueous solution and hence larger is the size of the hydrated ion and so less is its mobility. Thus, the correct order of mobility in aqueous solution will be $Rb^+ > K^+ > Na^+ > Li^+$.

174. (d):

Ion	Na^+	K^+	Mg^{2+}	Ca^{2+}
Limiting ionic conductivity in water at 298 K (S cm^2 mol^{-1})	50.10	73.50	106.0	119.0

The size of the hydrated Na^+ ion is largest and that of Ca^{2+} ion is the smallest. Hence, they follow the above order.

175. (a): A particular ion has a definite value of Λ_m° irrespective of the electrolyte.

176. (d): Li^+ ion is the smallest and has maximum charge density. As a result, in the aqueous solution, it is most heavily hydrated out of all the alkali metal ions. Thus, hydrated Li^+ has the largest size. Hence, its mobility is slowest under the electric field.

177. (b): $\Lambda_m^\circ(CH_3COOH)$

$= \Lambda_m^\circ(CH_3COONa) + \Lambda_m^\circ(HCl) - \Lambda_m^\circ(NaCl)$

$= 91 + 425.9 - 126.4$

$= 390.5\ \Omega^{-1}$ cm^2 mol^{-1}

178. (c): $\Lambda^\infty_{HOAc} = \Lambda^\infty_{NaOAc} + \Lambda^\infty_{HCl} - \Lambda^\infty_{NaCl}$

$= 91.0 + 426.2 - 126.5$ S cm^2 mol^{-1}

$= 390.7$ S cm^2 mol^{-1} $= 258.7\ \Omega^{-1}$ cm^2 mol^{-1}

179. (b): $\Lambda^\infty_{eq}[Al_2(SO_4)_3] = \lambda^\circ_{Al^{3+}} + \lambda^\circ_{SO_4^{2-}}$

Electrolytic Cells and Electrolysis

180. (c): At anode $OH^- \rightarrow OH + e^-$

$2OH \rightarrow H_2O + O_2$

181. (d): Electrolysis of dil. H_2SO_4 using Pt electrodes gives O_2.

182. (b): Cl^- ions are oxidised more easily than H_2O.

183. (b): In very dilute NaCl solution, the following changes occur:

Anode: $2\ OH^- \rightarrow H_2O + \frac{1}{2}O_2 + 2e^-$

Cathode: $2H^+ + 2e^- \rightarrow H_2$

184. (d): Electrolysis of both KCl and NaCl solutions liberates H_2 at the cathode and Cl_2 at the anode (of course, resulting solutions will be different).

185. (c): At the cathode, H_2O is more easily reduced than Na^+ to give H_2.

At the anode, H_2O is more easily oxidised than F^- to give O_2.

186. (c): $NaBr \xrightarrow{+aq} Na^+ + Br^-$

$H_2O \rightleftharpoons H^+ + Br^-$

H^+ ions have a lower discharge potential than Na^+ ions, therefore, at the cathode,

$2\ H^+ + 2\ e^- \rightarrow H_2$

Br^- ions have a lower discharge potential than OH^- ions, therefore, at the anode,

$2\ Br^- \rightarrow Br_2 + 2\ e^-$

In the solution,

$Na^+ + OH^- \rightarrow NaOH$

187. (c): Probable reactions at the cathode (reduction)

$Ag^+ + e^- \rightarrow Ag,\ E^\circ_{red} = 0.80\ V$

$2H_2O + 2\ e^- \rightarrow H_2 + 2\ OH^-,\ E^\circ_{red} = -0.83\ V$

Ag^+ ion has a higher reduction potential than H_2O. Hence, Ag^+ ions are reduced more easily and deposited as Ag.

Probable reactions at anode (oxidation)

Ag (from anode) $\rightarrow Ag^+ (aq) + e^-, E^\circ_{ox} = -\ 0.80\ V$

$H_2O(l) \rightarrow \frac{1}{2}\ O_2(g) + 2\ H^+(aq),\ E^\circ_{ox} = -1.23\ V$

The first reaction has a higher oxidation potential. Hence, Ag from the anode dissolves to form Ag^+ ions in the solution.

188. (c): At the cathode, H_2O is reduced more easily than Na^+ ions.

189. (a): With the attackable Cu electrode, the reaction taking place is

$Cu \rightarrow Cu^{2+} + 2\ e^-$

190. (c): Mg and Al have lower reduction potentials than H_2O. Hence, H_2O is reduced more easily to give H_2 gas at the cathode.

191. (c): Ca^{2+} ions have a much lower reduction potential than that of H_2O. Hence, it is not reduced in aqueous solution. Instead, H_2O is reduced to H_2.

192. (a) An aqueous solution of $MgSO_4$ contains Mg^{2+}, SO_4^{2-}, H^+, and OH^- ions. On the basis of their relative discharge potentials, the following reactions occur at the anode and cathode.

At the cathode, H^+ ions are discharged in preference to Mg^{2+} ions. Hence,

$2\ H^+ + 2\ e^- \rightarrow H_2(g)$

At the anode, OH^- ions are discharged in preference to SO_4^{2-} ions. Hence,

$4\ OH^- \rightarrow 2H_2O + O_2 + 4\ e^-$

193. (c): 1 F (96500 C) deposits 1 g eq., that is, $E = \frac{m}{C \times t} \times 96500$

194. (c): $\frac{\text{Wt. of Cu}}{\text{Wt. of Ag}} = \frac{\text{Eq. wt. of Cu}}{\text{Eq. wt. of Ag}^+}, \frac{\text{Wt. of Cu}}{1.08}$

$= \frac{63.5/2}{108}$

or Wt. of Cu = 0.3177 g

195. (a): Electrochemical equivalent is the weight deposited by 1 coulomb

$Q = 1 \times 1$

$\therefore 1 = I \times 0.25$ or $I = 4$ A

196. (c): $\frac{\text{Wt. of silver deposited}}{\text{Wt. of } O_2 \text{ produced}}$

$= \frac{\text{Eq. wt. of Ag}}{\text{Eq. wt. of oxygen}} \frac{0.108}{\text{Wt. of } O_2} = \frac{108}{8}$

or Wt. of O_2 produced $= 0.108 \times \frac{8}{108}$

$= 8 \times 10^{-3}$ g

$= \frac{22400}{32} \times 8 \times 10^{-3}\ cm^3 = 5.6\ cm^3$

197. (a): For the same quantity of electricity flowing through different cells,

$\frac{\text{Mass of Ag}}{\text{Mass of Cu}} = \frac{\text{Eq. mass of Ag}}{\text{Eq. mass of Cu}}$

$\frac{1.45}{\text{Mass of Cu}} = \frac{108}{65.3/2}$

or Mass of Cu $= \frac{1.45}{108} \times \frac{63.5}{2} = 0.426$ g

$\frac{\text{Mass of Ag}}{\text{Mass of Zn}} = \frac{\text{Eq. mass of Ag}}{\text{Eq. mass of Zn}}$

$\frac{1.45}{\text{Mass of Zn}} = \frac{108}{65.3/2}$

or Mass of Zn $= \frac{1.45}{108} \times \frac{65.3}{2} = 0.438$ g

198. (c): If the atomic mass of X = a, then that of Y = 2 a

Eq. wt = Atomic mass/Valency

Eq. wt of X = $a/3$, Eq. wt of Y = $2a/2 = a$

$\frac{\text{Mass of X}}{\text{Mass of Y}} = \frac{\text{Eq. wt. of X}}{\text{Eq. wt. of Y}} = \frac{a/3}{a} = \frac{1}{3} = 1:3$

199. (c): $Fe^{2+} + 2\ e^- \rightarrow Fe$

$Fe^{3+} + 3\ e^- \rightarrow Fe$

Weights deposited are in the ratio of their eq. wt. Hence, (2) and (3) are correct

200. (d): According to Faraday's second law,

$\frac{W_{Ag}}{W_{O_2}} = \frac{E_{Ag}}{E_{O_2}}$

Wt. of 5600 mL of O_2 at STP $= \frac{32}{22400} \times 5600 = 8$ g

$\therefore \frac{W_{Ag}}{8} = \frac{108}{8}$ or $W_{Ag} = 108$ g

201. (d): 1 g eq. requires 1 F.

202. (b): $W = Z \times C \times t$

$= 0.001118 \times 0.5 \times 200 = 0.1118$ g

203. (b): $\frac{\text{Wt. of Ni}}{\text{Wt. of Cr}} = \frac{\text{Eq. wt. of Ni}}{\text{Eq. wt. of Cr}}$

$\frac{0.3}{\text{Wt. of Cr}} = \frac{59/2}{52/3}$ or Wt. of Cr = 0.17 g

204. (d): One mol of electrons (that is, 1 F) will deposit 1 g eq. Eq. wt of Al = 27/3 = 9.

205. (a): 1 g eq. of H_2, that is, 1 g or 11200 cc is obtained from 96500 C

∴ 112 mL will be obtained from 965 C.

$I(A) = \frac{Q}{t} = \frac{965}{965} = 1$ A

206. (a): One faraday deposits one gram equivalent of the substance.

207. (b): Quantity of electricity passed (Q) = $I \times t = 3 \times (50 \times 60)$ = 9000 C

9000 C deposit metal = 1.8 g

∴ 96500 C will deposit metal

$= \frac{1.8}{9000} \times 96500 = 19.3$ g

But 96500 C deposits one gram equivalent of the metal. Hence, equivalent mass of the metal = 19.3

208. (c): From Faraday's first law, mass deposited $(W) = Z \times Q$ When $Q = 1$ coulomb, $W = Z$ (electrochemical equivalent).

209. (d): $\frac{\text{Weight of Al deposited}}{\text{Weight of } H_2 \text{ gas liberated}}$

$= \frac{\text{Eq. wt. of Al}}{\text{Eq. wt. of H}}$

$\frac{4.5}{m_{H_2}} = \frac{27/3}{1}$

$\therefore m_{H_2} = \frac{4.5}{9} = 0.5$ g

2 g H_2 at STP have volume = 22.4 L

∴ 0.5 g of H_2 at STP will have volume

$= \frac{22.4}{2} \times 0.5 = 5.6$ L

210. (c): Mass of ions or number of ions produced ∝ quantity of electricity passed (by Faraday's first law)

211. (d): Eq. wt. of Fe^{2+} = At. wt/2 = 56/2

Eq. wt. of Fe^{3+} = At. wt/2 = 56/2

Weights deposited are in the ratio of their equivalent weights.

∴ Ratio of weights deposited is

$Fe^{2+} : Fe^{3+} = \frac{56}{2} : \frac{56}{3} = \frac{1}{2} : \frac{1}{3} = 3:2$

212. (c): 1 F deposits 1 g equivalent. Hence, 2.5 F will deposit 2.5 g equivalents.

213. (b): In $CuSO_4$ solution, eq. mass of Cu $= \frac{M}{2}$

In CuCN solution, eq. mass of Cu = M

When the same quantity of electricity is passed, masses deposited are in the ratio of their equivalent masses. As equivalent mass of Cu in CuCN is higher, mass deposited will be higher.

214. (d): $Ag^+ + e^- \rightarrow Ag$, $Cu^{2+} + 2e^- \rightarrow Cu$. Thus, same quantity of electricity will deposit double the number of Ag atoms than Cu, that is, $x = 2y$.

215. (d): $Q = 2 \times 193$ C = 386 C

$H_2O \rightarrow H_2 + \frac{1}{2} O_2$, that is,

$O^{2-} \rightarrow \frac{1}{2} O_2 + 2e^-$

That is, 2 F = 2 × 96500 C give $O_2 = \frac{1}{2}$ mol = 11200 cc

∴ 386 C will give $O_2 = \frac{11200}{2 \times 96500} \times 386 = 22.4$ cc

216. (a): $Q = 2.5 \times 386 = 96500$ C

2 F (2 × 96500 C) deposit Cu = 63.5 g

Hence, 965 C will deposit Cu = 0.3175 g

217. (b): $H_2O \rightarrow H_2 + \frac{1}{2} O_2$ that is,

$O^{2-} \rightarrow \frac{1}{2} O_2 + 2e^-$

That is, 1 mol of H_2O requires = 2 × 96500 C = 1.93×10^5 C

218. (a): 1.12 L H_2 = 0.1 g eq. of H_2

$Q = 0.1$ F = 9650 C

Hence, $I = \frac{Q}{t} = \frac{9650}{965} = 10$ A

219. (a): $Al^{3+} + 3e \rightarrow Al$

3 F   1 mol

= 3 × 96500 C = 27 g

Thus, 27 g of Al require electricity = 3 × 96500 C

∴ 5.12 kg = 5120 g will require electricity

$= \frac{3 \times 96500}{27} \times 5120$ C $= 5.49 \times 10^7$ C

220. (a): $FeO \rightarrow \frac{1}{2} Fe_2O_3$, that is,

$Fe^{2+} \rightarrow Fe^{3+} + e^-$

Thus, oxidation of 1 mol of Fe^{2+} will require 1 F.

221. (c): $(MnO_4)^{-1} \rightarrow Mn^{2+}$

That is, $Mn^{7+} + 5e^- \rightarrow Mn^{2+}$

Thus, 1 mol of MnO_4^- requires 5 F

$= 5 \times 96500$ C = 482500 ≃ 4.83×10^5 C

222. (b): $H_2O_2 \rightarrow H_2O + \frac{1}{2} O_2$

Oxidation of 1 mol of H_2O_2 means both O^{-1} ions should change to O_2,

That is, $2\ O^{-1} \rightarrow O_2 + 2\ e^-$

Thus, 1 mol of H_2O_2 require = 2 F

$= 2 \times 96500\ C = 1.93 \times 10^5\ C$

[**Remember** that the given reaction is a disproportionation reaction.

$2H_2O_2 \rightarrow 2H_2O + O_2$ in which 1 mol is reduced, $H_2O_2 \rightarrow H_2O + (O)$ and 1 mol is oxidised, $H_2O_2 + O \rightarrow H_2O + O_2$]

223. (b): 200 mL of 0.5 M $CuSO_4$ contains $CuSO_4$ = 0.1 mol

$Cu^{2+} + 2\ e^- \rightarrow Cu$

To deposit 0.1 mol of Cu^{2+}, electricity required

$= 0.2\ F = 0.2 \times 96500\ C = 2 \times 9650\ C$

224. (d): $Ag^+ + e^- \rightarrow Ag$,

$Cu^{2+} + 2\ e^- \rightarrow Cu$

$Au^{3+} + 3\ e^- \rightarrow Au$

3 F will deposit 3 mol of Ag, $\frac{3}{2}$ mol of Cu and 1 mol of Au.

$\therefore$ Molar ratio $= 3 : \frac{3}{2} : 1 = 6 : 3 : 2$

225. (a): $Al^{3+} + 3\ e^- \rightarrow Al$

Quantity of electricity passed

$= (4.0 \times 10^4\ A) \times (6 \times 60 \times s) = 864 \times 10^6$ coulombs

3 F, that is, 3×96500 C produce Al = 1 mol, that is, 27 g

$\therefore 864 \times 10^6$ C will produce Al

$= \frac{27}{3 \times 96500} \times 864 \times 10^6\ g = 8.058 \times 10^4\ g = 8.1 \times 10^4\ g$

226. (b): Quantity of electricity passed

$= \frac{300}{1000} \times 60 = 18$ coulombs

$2\ Cl^- \rightarrow Cl_2 + 2\ e^-$

$2\ F = 2 \times 96500$ coulombs deposit Cl_2 = 1 mol

$\therefore$ 18 coulombs will deposit Cl_2

$= \frac{1}{2 \times 96500} \times 18$ mol

$= \frac{1}{2 \times 96500} \times 18 \times 6.022 \times 10^{23}$ molecules

$= 5.616 \times 10^{19}$ molecules

227. (a): $CaCl_2 \rightarrow Ca^{2+} + 2\ Cl^-$

Quantity of electricity passed $= 0.0025 \times 60 = 1.5$ C

(25 mA = 0.0025 A)

2×96500 C deposit Ca = 1 mol

$\therefore$ 1.5 C will deposit Ca $= \frac{1}{2 \times 96500} \times 1.5$ mol

$= \frac{1.5}{2 \times 96500} \times 6.02 \times 10^{23}$ atoms

$= 4.68 \times 10^{18}$ atoms

228. (c): The oxidation reaction is:

$MnO_4^{2-} \rightarrow MnO_4^- + e^-$

1 mol of MnO_4^{2-} requires electricity = 1 F = 96500 C

$\therefore$ 0.1 mol of MnO_4^{2-} will require electricity = 9650 C

229. (b): $NaCl + aq \rightarrow Na^+ (aq) + Cl^- (aq)$

$H_2O \rightarrow H^+ + OH^-$

At cathode: $H^+ + e^- \rightarrow \frac{1}{2} H_2$

1 F liberates 1 g eq. of H_2 gas, that is, 1 g of H_2 at the cathode.

230. (a): 1.12 L H_2 = 0.1 g eq. of H_2

$Q = 0.1\ F = 9650\ C$

Hence, $I = \frac{Q}{t} = \frac{9650}{965} = 10\ A$

231. (a): $Al^{3+} + 3e^- \rightarrow Al$

One mol requires 3×96500 C

$\therefore$ One mmol requires $= 3 \times 96.5\ C = 9.65\ A \times$ time in s

$\therefore$ Time $= \frac{3 \times 96.5}{9.65} = 30$ s

232. (a): For 1 mol of O_2, $O_2 \rightarrow 2\ O^{2-}$ $\left(\text{that is, } \frac{2}{3} \times 3O^{2-}\right)$

or $\frac{4}{3}$ mol of Al to change into Al^{3+} ions, $n = 4$. Hence,

$\Delta G = -nFE$ gives $E = \frac{\Delta G}{-nF}$

$= \frac{-827000}{-4 \times 96500} = 2.14$ volt

233. (b): $\overset{+7}{MnO_4^-} + 3\ e^- \rightarrow \overset{+4}{MnO_2}$

Thus, 3 F charge will be required to reduce 1 mol of MnO_4^- to MnO_2

234. (b): Quantity of electricity passed $= 9.65 \times 60 \times 60$ C

As $Zn \rightarrow Zn^{2+} + 2e^-$

2×96500 coulombs result in the loss of Zn = 1 mol, that is, 65.4 g

$\therefore 9.65 \times 60 \times 60$ C result in the loss of Zn

$= \frac{65.4}{2 \times 96500} \times 9.65 \times 60 \times 60\ g = 11.7\ g$

As $Cu^{2+} + 2e^- \rightarrow Cu$, as in the above case, gain in the mass of Cu cathode

$= \frac{63.5}{2 \times 96500} \times 9.65 \times 60 \times 60\ g = 11.43\ g$

235. (a): $2\ H^+ + 2\ e^- \rightarrow H_2$

2 F or 2×96500 C liberates H_2 gas = 1 mol = 22400 cc at STP

$\therefore$ 112 cc H_2 at STP will be liberated by electricity

$= \frac{2 \times 96500}{22400} \times 112\ C = 965\ C$

236. (d): ∵ Quantity of electricity passed $(Q) = I \times t$
$= 0.5 \times 32.2 \times 60$ C = 966 C
1 F, that is, 96500 C deposits Mg = 1 g eq = 12 g

$\therefore$ 966 C will deposit Mg $= \dfrac{12}{96500} \times 966 = 0.12$ g

$Mg + 2HCl \rightarrow MgCl_2 + H_2$
24 g 22400 cc
24 g Mg produce H_2 = 22400 cc at STP
$\therefore$ 0.12 g Mg will produce H_2

$= \dfrac{22400}{24} \times 0.12$ cc = 112 cc

237. (b): 1000 mL of 1 M $AgNO_3$ solution contains Ag = 108 g
$\therefore$ 125 mL of 1 M $AgNO_3$ solution will contain Ag

$= \dfrac{108}{100} \times 125 = 13.5$ g

$Ag^+ + e^- \rightarrow Ag$
108 g is deposited by 96500 coulomb
$\therefore$ 13.5 g Ag will be deposited by charge

$= \dfrac{96500}{108} \times 13.5$ coulombs = 12062.5 C

$Q = I \times t$

$t = \dfrac{Q}{I} = \dfrac{12062.5}{241.25}$ s = 50 s

238. (a): $Al^{3+} + 3e^- \rightarrow Al$
27 g of Al requires charge = 3 × 96500 C
$\therefore$ 50 g of Al will require charge

$= \dfrac{3 \times 96500}{27} \times$ C = 536111 C

239. (a): 1 F of electricity is the charge on one mol of electrons. Thus, the number of electrons involved = one mol $= 6.02 \times 10^{23}$.

240. (c): $Al^{3+} + 3e^- \rightarrow Al$
Thus, to deposit one gram atom of Al, 3 F or 3 mol of electrons, that is, 3 *N* electrons will be required.

241. (a): $Cu_2Cl_2 \rightarrow 2\ Cu^{2+} + 2Cl^-$
$Cu^{2+} + e^- \rightarrow Cu$, 1 F will deposit 1 mol of Cu.
$Cu(NO_3)_2 \rightarrow Cu^{2+} + 2\ NO_3^-$
$Cu^{2+} + 2e^- \rightarrow Cu$, 1 F will deposit 0.5 mol of Cu.
$CuSO_4 \rightarrow Cu^{2+} + SO_4^{2-}$
$Cu^{2+} + 2e^- \rightarrow Cu$, 1 F will deposit 0.5 mol of Cu.
$Cu_3(PO_4)_2 \rightarrow 3\ Cu^{2+} + 2\ PO_4^3$
$Cu^{2+} + 2e \rightarrow Cu$, 1 F will deposit 0.5 mol.
$CuF_2 \rightarrow Cu^{2+} + 2\ F^-$
$Cu^{2+} + 2e^- \rightarrow Cu$, 1 F will deposit 0.5 mol.
Thus, the amount deposited will be maximum from 1 M Cu_2Cl_2 solution.

242. (a): $Na^+ + e^- \rightarrow Na$,
$Ba^{2+} + 2e^- \rightarrow Ba$,
$Cu^{2+} + 2e^- \rightarrow Cu$,
$Ag^{3+} + 3e^- \rightarrow Al$
Hence, only in the case of NaCl, 1 F will liberate 1 g atom of the metal (Na).

243. (b): 200 mL of 0.1 N $AgNO_3$ solution contains Ag

$= \dfrac{0.1}{1000} \times 200$ g eq. = 0.02 g eq
= 0.02 × 108 g = 2.16 g

Ag to be removed $= \dfrac{1}{2} \times 2.16 = 1.08$ g

$Ag^+ + e^- \rightarrow Ag$
108 g of Ag is removed by 96500 C
$\therefore$ 108 g Ag will be removed by electric charge

$= \dfrac{96500}{108} \times 1.08$ C = 965 C

Current = 10 ampere
$Q = I \times t$

$t = \dfrac{Q}{I} = \dfrac{965}{10} = 96.5$ s

244. (a): 1 mol H_2O = 1 mol of O^{2-},

$O^{2-} \rightarrow \dfrac{1}{2}\ O_2 + 2e^-$

Thus, to separate out oxygen from 1 mol of H_2O, charge required = 2 F = 2 × 96500 C = 1.93×10^5 C.

245. (d): $C_6H_5NO_2 + 6H^+ + 6e^- \rightarrow C_6H_5NH_2 + 2H_2O$
1 mol of $C_6H_5NO_2$, that is, (72 + 5 + 14 + 32) = 123 g require 6 F or 6 × 96500 C
12.3 g of $C_6H_5NO_2$ will require charge

$= \dfrac{6 \times 96500}{123} \times 12.3$ C = 57900 C

246. (a): $2AlCl_3 \rightarrow 2Al + 3Cl_2$
When 3 × 22.4 L of Cl_2 is liberated,
Al liberated = 2 × 27 g = 54 g
When 11.2 L of Cl_2 is liberated,

Al liberated $= \dfrac{54}{3 \times 22.4} \times 11.2$ g = 9 g

247. (b): NaOH makes water a good conductor. Net reaction on electrolysis is

$H_2O \rightarrow H_2 + \dfrac{1}{2}\ O_2$

Thus, if 2.8 L O_2 gas is liberated,
H_2 liberated = 2 × 2.8 L = 5.6 L

248. (d): Only in a galvanic cell (GC), the redox reaction is spontaneous.

249. (c): In a galvanic cell, the cathode is positive but in an electrolytic cell, the cathode is negative.

250. (a): In an electrochemical cell, electrical energy produced = decrease in free energy. In an electrolytic cell, electrical energy supplied = increase in free energy.

251. (c): Charge on one monovalent ion = electronic charge = 1.60×10^{-19} coulomb.

252. (c): $H_2O \rightarrow H_2 + \frac{1}{2} O_2$

or $2 H^+ + 2e^- \rightarrow H_2$

That is, 2 mol e^- produce 1 mol of H_2, that is, 22.4 L. Hence, 4 mol of e^- will give $H_2 = 44.8$ L.

O_2 produced $= \frac{1}{2}$ of $H_2 = 22.4$ L

Total volume = 44.8 + 22.4 = 67.2 L

253. (c): Q (coulombs) I (ampere) $\times t$ (s) $= 0.5 \text{ A} \times (2\times 60 \times 60 \text{ s}) = 3600$ C

A flow of 1 F, that is, 96500 C is equivalent to flow of 1 mol of electrons, that is, 6.02×10^{23} electrons.

∴ 3600 C is equivalent to flow of electrons

$$= \frac{6.02\times10^{23}}{96500} \times 3600 = 2.246 \times 10^{22} \text{ electrons}$$

254. (c): $E = \frac{m}{Q}\times 96500 = \frac{22.2}{2\times5\times60\times60}\times 96500 = 59.5$

$$\text{Ox. state} = \frac{\text{At. wt.}}{\text{Eq. wt.}} = \frac{177}{59.5} = 3$$

255. (d): $H_2O \rightarrow H_2 + \frac{1}{2} O_2$

Suppose H_2O decomposed = x mol, then

$H_2 = x$, $O_2 = \frac{1}{2}x$, that is, $x + \frac{1}{2}x = 1$

or $\frac{3}{2}x = 1$ or $x = \frac{2}{3}$

256. (a): $Al^{3+} + 3e^- \rightarrow Al$

One mol of Al requires 3 × 96500 C

∴ One mmol will require = 3 × 96.5 C = 9.65 A × time in s

$$\therefore \text{Time} = \frac{3\times96.5}{9.65} = 30 \text{ s}$$

257. (b): More voltage is required to reduce H^+ at Hg than at Pt.

258. (a): The article to be electroplated is made the cathode.

259. (d): Complexes are preferred.

260. (b): $Q = C \times t = \left(\frac{10}{1000} A\right)\times\left(\frac{1}{2}\times60\times60\text{s}\right) = 180$ coulombs

261. (a): Weight deposited by 1 F (96,500 C)

$$= \frac{2.977}{10800}\times96500 = 26.6 \text{ g}$$

$$\text{Valency} = \frac{\text{At. wt}}{\text{Eq. wt}} = \frac{106.4}{26.4} = 4$$

262. (b): Volume of metal to be deposited = Area × Thickness

$= 80 \text{ cm}^2 \times \frac{0.05}{10} \text{ cm} = 0.04 \text{ cm}^3$

Mass to be deposited = volume × density

= 0.04 × 10.5 = 0.42 g

1 Faraday (96500 C) deposited metal = 1 g eq = 100 g

or 100 g is deposited by charge = 96500 C

∴ 0.42 g will be deposited by $\frac{96500}{100}\times 0.42 \text{ C} = 405.3$ C

$Q = I \times t$

$t = \frac{Q}{I} = \frac{405.3}{3} = 135$ s

263. (a): Charge passed = $I \times t$

= 1.5× 250 coulombs = 375 coulombs

Charge utilised $= \frac{85}{100}\times 375 = 318.75$ coulombs

$Mn^{2+} + 2e^- \rightarrow M$

2 × 96500 coulombs decompose MSO_4 = mol

318.75 coulombs will decompose MSO_4

$$= \frac{1}{2\times96500}\times 318.75$$

No. of mol = 0.00165 mol

Mol of MSO_4 originally present in 250 mL of 0.15 M solution

$$= \frac{0.15}{1000}\times 250 = 0.0375$$

Mol now left = 0.0375 – 0.00165 = 0.03585 mol

∴ Now, molarity $= \frac{0.03585}{250}\times 1000$

$= 0.1434 \text{ M} \simeq 0.14$ M

264. (c): Charge flowing during electrolysis = $I \times t = 1 \times 60 = 60$ coulombs

But charge flowing = number of electrons flowing × charge on each electron

∴ $60 = n\times1.60\times10^{-19}$

or $n = \frac{60}{1.60\times10^{-19}} = 37.5 \times 10^{19} = 3.75 \times 10^{20}$

265. (d): 1 L of 1 M $CuSO_4$ solution contains 1 mol of $CuSO_4$

$Cu^{2+} + 2e^- \rightarrow Cu$

Thus, 2 F will deposit 1 mol of $CuSO_4$. Hence, molarity of the solution will become zero.

266. (d): $CuSO_4$ solution contains Cu^{2+}, SO_4^{2-}, H^+ and OH^- ions. As after some time, the colour of the solution disappears, this means Cu^{2+} has been deposited at the cathode in preference to H^+ ions. Similarly, at the anode, OH^- ions are discharged in preference to SO_4^{2-} ions to give O_2. Solution now contains H^+ ions and SO_4^{2-} ions, that is, H_2SO_4.

267. (a): Charge on 1 mol of monovalent ions = charge on 1 mol of electrons = $(1.6021 \times 10^{-19}$ C$)(6.022 \times 10^{-23})$

$\simeq 964500 \text{ C} = 9.54 \times 10^4$ coulombs

268. (b): Electrons flow from the cathode to the anode through the external supply. In solution, ions flow and not the electrons.

269. (d): If the cathode or anode is pulled out, no electrolysis will take place. The ions will start moving randomly.

270. (b): At the cathode, reduction takes place, that is, the cathode helps in bringing about reduction. Hence, it acts as a reducing agent.

271. (a): In the electrolysis of a fused salt, the weight of the deposit does not depend upon the temperature of the bath.

Batteries/Commercial Cells

272. (d): KCl is not used in a dry cell.

273. (b): The reaction occurring at the cathode is the reduction reaction.

$MnO_2 + NH_4^+ + e^- \rightarrow MnO(OH) + NH_3$

274. (b): MnO_2 is used as a depolariser in dry cell batteries.

275. (c): The space in a dry cell is filled with MnO_2, $ZnCl_2$, NH_4Cl and a filter.

276. (a): During discharge, the reaction at the anode is the oxidation reaction.

$Pb + SO_4^{2-} \rightarrow PbSO_4 + 2e^-$

277. (d): Antimony is used in making lead storage batteries because lead containing antimony is harder and more resistant to the action of acids than ordinary lead.

278. (b): When the battery is in use (discharging), the following reactions take place.

At anode: $Pb(s) + SO_4^{2-}(aq) \rightarrow PbSO_4(s) + 2e^-$ (i)

At cathode: $PbO_2(s) + SO_4^{2-}(aq) + 4H^+(aq) + 2e^- \rightarrow PbSO_4(s) + 2H_2O(l)$ (ii)

On charging the battery, the reverse reactions occur. The reverse of reaction (i) will be reduction and hence will take place at the cathode.

279. (d): The overall reaction occurring in the lead storage battery during discharge is

$Pb(s) + PbO_2(s) + 2H_2SO_4(aq) \rightarrow 2PbSO_4(s) + 2H_2O(l)$

Hence, H_2SO_4 is consumed when the lead storage battery is used (discharged).

280. (b): The reaction occurring during charging of the lead accumulator battery is

$2PbSO_4(s) + 2H_2O(l) \rightarrow Pb(s) + PbO_2(s) + 4H^+(aq) + 2SO_4^{2-}$

Thus, H_2SO_4 is reproduced.

281. (a): When a lead accumulator is charged, it acts as an electrolytic cell, that is, now electrical energy is supplied to it from an external source.

282. (c): Mercury cell has a constant voltage throughout its life.

Fuel Cells

283. (c): A fuel cell converts the free energy of a chemical reaction.

284. (a): Fuel cell.

285. (c): In the H_2–O_2 fuel cell, the reaction at the cathode is

$O_2 + 2H_2O + 4e^- \rightarrow 4OH^-$

286. (d): Efficiency of a fuel cell $= \dfrac{\Delta G}{\Delta H}$.

287. (d): All the given statements about the fuel cells are correct.

288. (c): In the H_2–O_2 cell, at the anode

$2H_2 + OH^- \rightarrow 4H_2O + 4e^-$

289. (d): Fuel cells are more efficient, free from pollution and run till the reactants are active.

290. (d): Efficiency $= \dfrac{\Delta G^\circ}{\Delta H^\circ} = \dfrac{-nFE^\circ}{\Delta H^\circ}$

$\therefore 0.84 = \dfrac{-2 \times 6500 \times E^\circ}{-285 \times 1000}$ or $E^\circ = +1.24$ V

291. (d): Leclanche cell and mercury cell are primary cells.

292. (b): Ni–Cd cell is rechargeable (it is a secondary cell).

293. (c): A secondary cell can be recharged by passing current through it in the opposite direction.

294. (c): A moist paste of NH_4Cl and $ZnCl_2$ is used.

Corrosion

295. (b): The green layer is $Cu(OH)_2.CuCO_3$.

296. (c): Rust is hydrated ferric oxide, $Fe_2O_3 \cdot x\ H_2O$.

297. (d): Zinc has a higher negative electrode potential than iron, so iron cannot be coated on zinc.

298. (a): According to electrochemical theory of corrosion, the reactions occurring are

At anode: $Fe \rightarrow Fe^{2+}(aq) + 2e^-$

At cathode: $O_2 + 4H^+ + 4e^- \rightarrow 2H_2O(l)$

(H^+ ions from $H_2CO_3 \rightleftharpoons 2H^+ + CO_3^{2-}$)

Adding the above equations, the overall reaction of the miniature cell is

$2Fe(s) + O_2(g) + 4H^+(aq) \rightarrow 2Fe^{2+}(aq) + 2H_2O(l)$

299. (c): When iron is rusted, it is oxidised $Fe \rightarrow Fe^{2+} + 2e^-$ and further $Fe^{2+} \rightarrow Fe^{3+} + e^-$.

300. (c): During rusting, the Fe^{2+} ions first formed react with dissolved oxygen to form ferric oxide and H^+ ions.

$4Fe^{2+} + O_2 + 4H_2O \rightarrow 2Fe_2O_3 + 8H^+(aq)$

The H^+ ions thus produced further catalyse the reaction.

301. (b): Al forms a self-protecting film of oxide to prevent corrosion.

302. (b): Na_3PO_4 is used as an anti-rusting solution.

303. (c): Dipping an iron article into a strongly alkaline solution of Na_3PO_4 forms an iron phosphate film.

304. (b): Fe is corroded more readily than Cu, Ag and Ni

305. (b): Zn is oxidised more easily than Fe and hence prevents rusting of iron. This is because E°_{OP} of Zn > E°_{OP} of Fe. It is called sacrificial protection.

306. (a): Metal undergoing corrosion acts as anode.

307. (b): If coating is broken, iron will corrode faster if coated with tin. This is because their standard oxidation potentials are:

$$E^\circ_{Zn,Zn^{2+}} = +0.76 \text{ V}; \ E^\circ_{Fe,Fe^{2+}} = +0.44 \text{ V}; \ E^\circ_{Sn,Sn^{2+}} = +0.14 \text{ V}$$

308. (b): In the presence of H^+ ions (from $H_2O + CO_2 \rightarrow H_2CO_3 \rightleftharpoons 2H^+ + CO_3^{2-}$)

At anode: $Fe(s) \rightarrow Fe^{2+}(aq) + 2e^-$

At cathode: $O_2 \text{ (dissolved)} + 4H^+(aq) + 4e^- + 2H_2O(l)$

Overall reaction : $2Fe(s) + O_2(g) + 4H^+(aq) \rightarrow 2Fe^{2+}(aq) + 2H_2O(l)$

309. (b): $CuCO_3$ is green.

Miscellaneous

310. (c): Correct (c) is $E = E^\circ + \frac{RT}{nF} \ln a_{M^{n+}}$

311. (c): $HClO_4$ is a powerful oxidising agent because Cl is in the highest oxidation state of +7.

312. (d): (i) $Cu^+ + e^- \rightarrow Cu, \ \Delta G_1 = -nFE$

$= -1 \times F \times X_1 = -FX_1$

(ii) $Cu^{2+} + 2e^- \rightarrow Cu, \ \Delta G_2$

$= -2 \times F \times X_2 = -2FX_2$

(iii) $Cu^{2+} + e^- \rightarrow Cu^+, \ \Delta G_3$

$= -1 \times F \times X_3 = -FX_3$

Eq. (iii) = Eq. (ii) – Eq. (i)

Hence $-FX_3 = -2FX_2 - (-FX_1)$

or $X_3 = 2X_2 - X_1$

313. (b): The net reaction of the H_2–O_2 fuel cell is

$2H_2 + O_2 \rightarrow 2H_2O$

Thus, 4 F = 4 × 96500 C produces water = 2 mol = 36 g

Charge actually passed = $I \times t$ = 1 × 595.1 × 60 × 60 C

= 2,142,360 C

∴ Water produced

$$= \frac{36}{4 \times 96500} \times 2{,}142{,}360 \text{ g} \simeq 200 \text{ g} = 200 \text{ mL}$$

∴ Molarity of NaOH solution = $\frac{5}{40} \times \frac{1}{200} \times 1000 = 0.625$ M

314. (a): For 3 M HCl solution, $\Lambda_m = 240 \text{ S cm}^2 \text{ mol}^{-1}$ and $\Lambda^\circ_m = 420 \text{ S cm}^2 \text{ mol}^{-1}$

$$\alpha = \frac{\Lambda_m}{\Lambda^\circ_m} = \frac{240}{420} = \frac{12}{21}$$

For HCl, $HCl \rightleftharpoons H^+ + Cl^-$

1 M		
$1-\alpha$	α	α

Total = $1 + \alpha$

$$i = 1 + \alpha = 1 + \frac{12}{21} = \frac{33}{21}$$

$$\Delta T_b = iK_b m = \frac{33}{21} \times 0.52 \times 3 = 2.45 \text{ K}$$

$$T_b = T_b^\circ + \Delta T_b = 373.15 + 2.45 \text{ K} = 375.6 \text{ K}$$

315. (d): $\overset{+1}{HBrO} \xrightarrow{Red} \overset{0}{Br_2}$

$E^\circ_{HBrO/Br_2} = 1.595$ V

$\overset{+1}{HBrO} \xrightarrow{Ox.} \overset{+5}{BrO_3^-}$

$E^\circ_{BrO_3^-/HBrO} = 1.595 - 1.5 = 0.095 \text{ V} = +ve$

Hence, option (d) is correct.

316. (c): $B_2H_6 + 3O_2 \rightarrow B_2O_3 + 3H_2O$

27.66 g of B_2H_6 = 1 mol of B_2H_6

It requires 3 mol of O_2 for complete burning

$H_2O \rightarrow H_2 + \frac{1}{2}O_2$

$\frac{1}{2}$ mol of O_2 requires 2 faradays

∴ 3 mol of O_2 will require = 12 faradays

$12 \times 96500 = i \times t = 100 \times t$

or $t = \frac{12 \times 9600}{100} \text{ s} = \frac{12 \times 96500}{100 \times 3600} \text{ h} = 3.2 \text{ h}$

317. (b): $NaOH + HCl \rightarrow NaCl + H_2O$

or $Na^+ + OH^- + H^+ + Cl^- \rightarrow Na^+ + Cl^- + H_2O$

HCl has a large conductance. When NaOH is added to it, small H^+ ions are replaced by large Na^+ ions. Hence, the conductance decreases. This continues up to the end point. Now, if further HCl is added, the H^+ ions remain in the solution and conductance begins to increase. Hence, the correct plot is (b).

Final Preparation

318. (a): E_{cell} will be +ve only if the following half reactions occur.

$Fe \rightarrow Fe^{2+} + 2e^-, \ E^\circ = +0.44$ V

$Fe^{3+} + e^- \rightarrow Fe^{2+}, \quad E^\circ = +0.77$ V

Thus, $[Fe^{3+}]$ decreases as Fe^{3+} is reduced to Fe^{2+}.

319. (b): $E_{cell} = E^\circ_{cell} - \frac{0.0591}{2} \log \frac{1}{[Zn^{2+}]}$

$= E^\circ_{cell} + 0.02955 \log C$

$E'_{cell} = E^\circ_{cell} + 0.02955 \log \frac{C}{100}$

$= E^\circ_{cell} + 0.02955 \log C + 0.02955(-2)$

∴ E°_{cell} will decrease by 0.02955 × 2 V

= 0.059 V = 59 m V

320. (d): $Zn + Cd^{2+} \rightarrow Zn^{2+} + Cd$

$$E_{cell} = E^\circ_{cell} - \frac{0.059}{2} \log \frac{a_{Zn^{2+}}}{a_{Cd^{2+}}}$$

$$= \left[(-0.403)-(-0.763)-\frac{0.059}{2}\log\frac{0.04}{0.2}\right]$$

$$= 0.36 + \frac{0.059}{2}\log\frac{0.2}{0.004}$$

321. (d): Subtracting the second equation from the first equation, we get,

$AgCl(s) \rightleftharpoons Ag^+(aq) + Cl^-(aq), E° = -0.50$ V

Applying Nernst equation,

$$E = E° - \frac{0.0591}{2}\log\frac{[Ag^+][Cl^-]}{[AgCl(s)]}$$

Putting $[AgCl(s)] = 1$ and at equilibrium $E = 0$.

$E° = 0.0591 \log [Ag^+][Cl^-]$

$= 0.0591 \log K_p$

or $-0.5 = 0.0591 \log K_{sp}$

or $\log K_{sp} = -9.8139 = \overline{10}.1861$

or $K_{sp} = 1.535 \times 10^{-10}$

322. (c): $E_{cell} = E^{\circ}_{cell} - \frac{0.0595}{2}\log\frac{[Zn^{2+}]\times p_{H_2}}{[H^+]^2}$

On adding H_2SO_4, $[H^+]$ will increase, therefore E_{cell} will increase. The equilibrium $Zn + 2H^+ \rightleftharpoons Zn^{2+} + H_2$ will shift towards the right on increasing the concentration of H^+ ions.

323. (d): The cell reaction is: $Zn + Cu^{2+} \rightarrow Zn^{2+} + Cu$

When the cell is completely discharged, $E_{cell} = 0$.

$$\text{Hence, } E^{\circ}_{cell} - \frac{0.0591}{2}\log\frac{[Zn^{2+}]}{[Cu^{2+}]}$$

$$\text{That is, } 1.10 = \frac{0.0591}{2}\log\frac{[Zn^{2+}]}{[Cu^{2+}]}$$

$$\text{or } \log\frac{[Zn^{2+}]}{[Cu^{2+}]} = 37.3 \text{ or } \frac{[Zn^{2+}]}{[Cu^{2+}]} = 10^{37.3}$$

324. (a): The product formed in the electrochemical reaction will be AgCl(*s*). Suppose its solubility in 0.1 M KCl solution is x, then,

$AgCl(s) \rightleftharpoons Ag^+(aq) + Cl^-(aq)$

$\quad\quad\quad\quad x \quad\quad x + 0.1 = 0.1$

$K_{sp} = [Ag^+][Cl^-]$ (just to start precipitation)

That is, $1.8 \times 10^{-10} = x(0.1)$

or $x = 1.8 \times 10^{-9}$ M $= 1.8 \times 10^{-9} \times 108.5$ g

108 g of Ag^+ is deposited by charge = 1 F = 96,500 C

$\therefore 1.8 \times 10^{-9} \times 108$ g Ag^+ will be deposited by charge

$$= \frac{96500}{108}\times 1.8\times 10^{-9} \times 108 = 96500 \times 1.8\times 10^{-9}\text{ C}$$

$Q = I \times t$

$$t = \frac{Q}{I} = \frac{96500\times 1.8\times 10^{-9}}{10^{-6}} = 173.7\text{ s } (1 \propto A = 10^{-6}\text{ A})$$

325. (b): For a Daniell cell,

$Zn + Cu^{2+} \rightarrow Zn^{2+} + Cu, n = 2$

$$E_{cell} = E^{\circ}_{cell} - \frac{0.059}{2}\log\frac{[Zn^{2+}]}{[Cu^{2+}]}$$

When E_{cell} is plotted against $\log\frac{[Zn^{2+}]}{[Cu^{2+}]}$,

intercept $= E^{\circ}_{cell} = 1.10$ V.

$$\therefore E^{\circ}_{cell} = 1.10 - \frac{0.0591}{2}\log\frac{0.1}{0.01} = 1.10 - 0.0295 = 1.0705\text{ V}$$

326. (a): The RHS electrode is a redox electrode on which reduction occurs. The LHS electrode is the standard hydrogen electrode. Hence,

$E_{cell} = E^{\circ}_{Fe^{3+}/Fe^{2+}} = 0.771$ V (Given)

Writing the RHS electrode reaction as a reduction reaction,

$Fe^{3+} + e^- \rightarrow Fe^{2+}$

$$\therefore E_{Fe^{3+}/Fe^{2+}} = E^{\circ}_{Fe^{3+}/Fe^{2+}} - \frac{0.0591}{3}\log\frac{[Fe^{2+}]}{[Fe^{3+}]}$$

$$0.830 = 0.771 - 0.0591\log\frac{[Fe^{2+}]}{[Fe^{3+}]}$$

$$\text{or } \log\frac{[Fe^{2+}]}{[Fe^{3+}]} = \frac{0.771-0.830}{0.0591} = -0.9983 = \bar{1}.0017$$

$\therefore [Fe^{2+}]/[Fe^{3+}] = \text{Antilog}(\bar{1}.0017) = 0.1004$

327. (d): $pH = 14$ means $pOH = 0$, that is, $[OH^-] = 1$ M

$pOH = -\log[OH^-]$

$Cu(OH)_2 \rightleftharpoons Cu^{2+} + 2OH^-$

$K_{sp} = [Cu^{2+}][OH^-]^2$

$10^{-19} = [Cu^{2+}](1)^2$, that is, $[Cu^{2+}]$

$= 10^{-19}$ M

For the half cell reaction,

$Cu^{2+} + 2e^- \rightarrow Cu, n = 2$

$$E_{Cu^{2+}/Cu} = E^{\circ}_{Cu^{2+}/Cu} - \frac{0.0591}{2}\log\frac{1}{[Cu^{2+}]}$$

$$= 0.34 - \frac{0.0591}{2}\log\frac{1}{10^{-19}} = 0.34 - \frac{0.0591}{2}\times 19 = -0.22\text{ V}$$

328. (a): $E_{Cu^{2+}/Cu} = E^{\circ}_{Cu^{2+}/Cu}$

$$-\frac{0.0591}{2}\log\frac{1}{[Cu^{2+}]}$$

or $E_{cell} = E^\circ_{cell} - \frac{0.0591}{2}\log\frac{1}{0.1} = E^\circ_{red} - \frac{0.0591}{2}$

It is the equation of a straight line ($y = mx + c$) where the intercept is c,

A or $E^\circ_{red} = 0.34$ V

Hence, $E^\circ_{red} = 0.34 - \frac{0.0591}{2}$

or E°_{ox}, that is, $E_{Cu/Cu^{2+}}$

$= -0.34 + \frac{0.0591}{2}$ V

329. (b): $E_{cell} = E^\circ_{cell} - \frac{0.0591}{2}\log\frac{[Zn^{2+}]}{[Cu^{2+}]}$

Hence, plot of E_{cell} vs $\log\frac{[Zn^{2+}]}{[Cu^{2+}]}$ will be linear with a –ve slope and when $\log\frac{[Zn^{2+}]}{[Cu^{2+}]} = 0$, $E_{cell} = E^\circ_{cell} = 1.10$ V, that is, the line should intersect the Y axis at 1.10 V. These conditions are satisfied in (b).

330. (d): When $pH = 0, [H^+] = 10^0 = 1$ M, electrode potential $= 0$.

When pH = 7, $[H^+] = 10^{-7}$ M.

$$H^+ + e^- \rightarrow \frac{1}{2}H_2$$

$$E_{H^+/H_2} = E^\circ_{H^+/H_2} - \frac{0.0591}{1}\log\frac{1}{[H^+]}$$

$$= 0 - 0.0591\log\frac{1}{10^{-7}} = -0.4137 \text{ V}$$

Thus, it will decrease by 0.41 V.

331. (b): For the given cell reaction,

$$E_{cell} = E^\circ_{cell} - \frac{0.0591}{2}\log\frac{[Cl^-][Br_2]}{[Cl_2][Br^-]^2}$$

$$= 0.29 - \frac{0.0591}{2}\log\frac{(0.01)(0.01)}{(0.01)}$$

$$= 0.29 - \frac{0.0591}{2}\log 10^{-2} \simeq 0.35 \text{ V}$$

332. (b): $Zn + Fe^{2+} \rightarrow Zn^{2+} + Fe$ ($n = 2$)

$$E = E^\circ - \frac{0.0591}{n}\log K_e$$

$$\therefore 0.2905 = E^\circ = \frac{0.0591}{2}\log\frac{0.01}{0.001}$$

or $E^\circ = 0.2905 + 0.0295 = 0.32$ volt

$$E^\circ = \frac{0.0591}{2}\log K_{eg}$$

$$\therefore 0.32 = \frac{0.0591}{2}\log K_{eg} = 0.0295\log K_{eg}$$

or $\log K_{eg} = \frac{0.32}{0.0295}$ or $K_{eg} = 0.32/10^{0.0295}$

333. (a): As E° for the given reaction is –ve, only the reverse reaction will be spontaneous, that is,

$Fe^{2+} + Zn \rightleftharpoons Fe + Zn^{2+}$

$E^\circ_{cell} = +0.32$ V

At equilibrium, $E_{cell} = 0$

$$E^\circ_{cell} = \frac{0.0591}{n}\log\frac{1}{[Fe^{2+}]}$$

$$\text{or } 0.32 = \frac{0.0591}{2}\log\frac{1}{[Fe^{2+}]}$$

or $\log[Fe^{2+}] = -[0.89] = \overline{11}.153$

or $[Fe^{2+}] = 1.422 \times 10^{-11}$ mol L^{-1}

334. (b): We are given

$Zn^{2+}(aq) + 2e^- \rightleftharpoons Zn(s)$

$E^\circ = -0.76$ V

$[Zn(NH_3)_4]^{2+} + 2e^- \rightleftharpoons Zn(s) + 4NH_3$, $E^\circ = -1.03$ V

To get the overall reaction, we should write

$Zn^{2+}(aq) + 2e^- \rightleftharpoons Zn(s)$

$E^\circ = -0.76$ V

$Zn(s) + 4NH_3 \rightleftharpoons [Zn(NH_3)_4]^{2+} + 2e^-$, $E^\circ = 1.03$ V

Adding, we get

$E^\circ_{cell} = 1.03 - 0.76 = 0.27$ V

$E^\circ_{cell} = \frac{0.0591}{n}\log K$ or $\log K = \frac{0.27 \times 2}{0.0591} = 9.1371$

or $K = $ Antilog $9.1371 = 1.371 \times 10^9$

335. (b): Left electrode: $H_2(g) \rightarrow 2H^+(aq) + 2e^-$

Right electrode: $2AgCl(s) + 2e^- \rightarrow 2Ag(s) + 2Cl^-(aq)$

Cell reaction: $2AgCl(s) + H_2(g) \rightarrow 2Ag(s) + 2H^+(aq) + 2Cl^-(aq)$

$K_c = [H^+]^2[Cl^-]^2$ or $K'_c = [H^+][Cl^-]$

336. (d): The cell reaction is $Zn + 2Ag^+ \rightarrow Zn^{2+} + 2Ag$

Reaction quotient, $Q = \frac{[Zn^{2+}]}{[Ag^+]^2} = \frac{(0.01)}{(1.25)^2} = 6.4 \times 10^{-3}$

337. (d): It is a concentration cell, whose

$$\therefore E_{cell} = \frac{0.0591}{n}\log\frac{c_2}{c_1}$$

$E_{cell} = \frac{0.059}{1}\log\frac{1}{[H^+]}$ or $0.59 = 0.059$ pH or pH $= 10$

338. (c): Cell constant = $\kappa \times R$

$= 1.29\ \text{S m}^{-1} \times 100\ \Omega = 129\ \text{m}^{-1}$

In the second case,

$$\kappa = \frac{\text{Cell constant}}{\text{Resistant}} = \frac{129\ \text{m}^{-1}}{520\ \Omega}$$

$$= 0.248\ \Omega^{-1}\ \text{m}^{-1}$$

$$\Lambda_m = \frac{\kappa}{\text{Molarity}} = \frac{0.248\ \Omega^{-1}\ \text{m}^{-1}}{0.02 \times 10^3\ \text{mol m}^{-3}}$$

$$= 124 \times 10^{-4}\ \text{S m}^2\ \text{mol}^{-1}$$

339. (c): $HA \rightleftharpoons H^+ + A^-$

$C \quad 0 \quad 0$

$C(1-\alpha) \quad C\alpha \quad C\alpha$

$$K = \frac{C.C}{C(1-\alpha)} = \frac{C}{1} = C$$

$$25 \times 10^{-6} = 10^{-2} \times (1-\alpha)^2 \text{ or } \alpha = 5 \times 10^{-2}$$

$$\alpha = \frac{\Lambda°}{\Lambda°} \text{ or } \Lambda° = \frac{\Lambda^c}{\alpha} = \frac{19.6}{5 \times 10^{-2}} = 392\ \Omega^{-1}\ \text{cm}^2$$

340. (d): $\Lambda°(Al^{3+}) = 3\ \Lambda°\left(\frac{1}{3}Al^{3+}\right)$

$$= 3 \times 63 = 189\ \Omega^{-1}\text{cm}^2\ \text{mol}^{-1}$$

$$\Lambda°\ (SO_4^{2-}) = 2\Lambda°\left(\frac{1}{2}SO_4^{2-}\right)$$

$$= 2 \times 80 = 160\ \Omega^{-1}\text{cm}^2\ \text{mol}^{-1}$$

$$\Lambda°\ (Al_2SO_4)_3 = 2\ \Lambda°(Al^{3+}) + 3\ \Lambda°\ (SO_4^{2-})$$

$$= 2 \times 189 + 3 \times 160 = 858\ \Omega^{-1}\text{cm}^2\ \text{mol}^{-1}$$

341. (d): Solubility, $S = \frac{\times 1000}{\Lambda_0}$

$$= \frac{3.06 \times 10^{-6} \times 1000}{1.53} = 2 \times 10^{-3}\ \text{mol L}^{-1}$$

$$K_{sp} = S^2 = 4 \times 10^{-6}$$

342. (b): $CH_3COOH \rightleftharpoons CH_3COO^- + H^+$

$$K_{eq} = c^2$$

$$\text{or } \alpha = \sqrt{K_{eq}/c} = \frac{\Lambda_m^c}{\Lambda_m^\infty}$$

$$\therefore \frac{\Lambda_m^c}{390.7} = \sqrt{\frac{1.8 \times 10^{-5}}{0.01}} = \sqrt{18 \times 10^{-4}} = 4.243 \times 10^{-2}$$

$$\text{or } \Lambda_m^c = 16.57\ \Omega^{-1}\ \text{cm}^2$$

343. (d): $\alpha = \frac{\Lambda_m}{\Lambda_\infty}$ or $\Lambda_m = \Lambda_\infty \times \alpha = 400 \times \frac{2}{100}$

$$= 8\ \text{ohm}^{-1}\ \Omega^{-1}\text{cm}^2\ \text{mol}^{-1}$$

$$\Lambda_m = \frac{\kappa \times 1000}{C} \text{ and } \kappa = \frac{1}{R} \times \text{Cell constant}$$

$$\therefore \Lambda_m = \frac{1}{R} \times \text{Cell constant} \times \frac{1000}{C}$$

$$\text{or } R = \frac{\text{Cell constant}}{\Lambda_m \times C} \times 1000 = \frac{0.4 \times 1000}{8 \times 0.1} = 500\ \text{ohm}$$

344. (c): Transport number can be zero (for example, at high concentration of CdI_2 solution, Cd^{2+} may have zero or even negative transport number due to the formation of the complex ion, CdI_4^{2-}).

345. (d): For a sparingly soluble salt, $BaSO_4$, if S is the solubility

$$\Lambda_{eq} = \frac{1000 \times k}{S}$$

$$\text{or } S = \frac{1000 \times k}{\Lambda_{eq}} = \frac{1000 \times 3.06 \times 10^{-6}}{1.53} = 2.0 \times 10^{-3}\ \text{mol L}^{-1}$$

$$BaSO_4 \rightarrow Ba^{2+} + SO_4^{2-}$$

$$K_{sp} = [Ba^{2+}][SO_4^{2-}]$$

$$= (2 \times 10^{-3})(2 \times 10^{-3}) = 4 \times 10^{-6}$$

346. (b): Vol. of Ag = $800 \times 5 \times 10^{-4}\ \text{cm}^3$

Mass of Ag = $V \times d = 0.4 \times 10.5 = 4.2$ g

$Ag^+ + e^- \rightarrow Ag$

108 g Ag requires 96500 C

$$\therefore 4.2 \text{ g requires} = \frac{96500}{108} \times 4.2 = 3753\ \text{C}$$

$$\text{Hence, } t = \frac{Q}{I} = \frac{3753}{3} = 1251\ \text{s}$$

347. (b): $m = Z \times 4 \times 120$ $m' = Z \times 6 \times 40$

$$\therefore \frac{m'}{m} = \frac{6 \times 40}{4 \times 120} = \frac{1}{2} \text{ or } m' = m/2$$

348. (a): Eq. wt of $H_2O = 1 + 8 = 9$. Hence, 9 g is decomposed by 96500 C. So, 36 g will be decomposed by $Q = 96500 \times$ C.

$$\text{Hence, } t = \frac{Q}{I} = \frac{96500 \times 4}{3} s = 35.7\ \text{h} \simeq 36\ \text{h}$$

349. (b): 2.24 L of H_2 at NTP = 0.2 g of H_2

$$\frac{\text{Wt of Cu}}{\text{Wt of } H_2} = \frac{\text{Eq. wt of Cu}}{\text{Eq. wt of } H_2}$$

$$\therefore \frac{\text{Wt of Cu}}{0.2} = \frac{63.5/2}{1}$$

or Wt of Cu = 6.35 g

350. (c): $Q = 1 \times 965 = 965$ C

$Cu^{2+} + 2e^- \rightarrow Cu$

2×96500 C decompose $CuCl_2$ = 1 mol

$\therefore$ 965 C dcompose $CuCl_2 = \frac{1}{200}$ mol = 0.05 mol

This was present in one litre of $CuCl_2$ solution. Hence, strength = 0.005 M.

351. (c): $NaCl + H_2O \xrightarrow{\text{Electrolysis}} \frac{1}{2}H_2 + Cl_2 + NaOH$

Amount of NaCl present in 0.5 L of 1.0 M, NaCl = 0.5 mol

Quantity of electricity passed = 965×5 coulombs

1 mol of NaCl is decomposed by 96500 coulombs

$\therefore$ 4825 coulombs will decompose NaCl

$= \frac{4825}{96500}$ mol = 0.05 mol

NaOH formed in the solution will also be 0.05 mol

Volume of solution = 0.5 L

∴ Molarity of NaOH in the solution

$= \frac{0.05}{0.5} = 0.1\,M = 10^{-1}\ M$

∴ pOH = 1 Or pH = 14 – 1 = 13

352. (c): $Mg^{2+} + 2e^- \rightarrow Mg$

2 F, that is, 2 × 96500 C deposit Mg = 1 mol

∴ 9.65 C will deposit Mg $= \frac{1}{2 \times 96500} \times 9.65 = 5 \times 10^{-5}$ mol

RX × Mg → RMgX

1 mol of Mg form GR = 1 mol

∴ 5×10^{-5}

Mol of Mg that will form GR = 5×10^{-5} mol

353. (b): Weights deposited are in the ratio of their eq. wts ($W_1/W_2 = E_1/E_2$)

Further $Z = E/96500$, that is, $Z \propto E$.

Hence, $\frac{W_1}{W_2} = \frac{Z_1}{Z_2}$

$\therefore \frac{Z_1}{Z_2} = \frac{0.375}{0.300} = 1.25$

354. (c): 100 g Zn $= \frac{100}{65}$ mol = 1.53 mol

1 L of 1 M $CuSO_4$ contains 1 mol of $CuSO_4$

∴ In the reaction Zn + $CuSO_4$ → $ZnSO_4$ + Cu, $CuSO_4$ is the limiting reagent. To deposit completely 1 mol of Cu, electricity required = 2×96500 C

$t = \frac{Q}{I} = \frac{2 \times 96500}{1}\ s = \frac{2 \times 96500}{3600}\ h = 53.6\ h$

355. (c): $Q = 9.65 \times 3 \times 60 \times 60 = 104220$ C

$Ni^{2+} + 2\,e^- \rightarrow Ni$

2 × 96500 C deposits 1 mol of Ni^{2+}

∴ 104220 C will deposit Ni^{2+}

$= \frac{1}{2 \times 96500} \times 104220 = 0.54$ mol

Originally 0.5 L of 2 M solution contained Ni^{2+} = 1 mol. Now 0.5 L will contain Ni^{2+} = 1 – 0.54 = 0.46 mol. Hence, molarity = 0.92 mol L^{-1}.

356. (a): $Q = 12 \times 60 \times 60 = 43200$ C

$Ni^{2+} + 2\,e^- \rightarrow Ni$. Theoretically 2×96500 C will deposit Ni = 58.7 g. Hence, 43200 C will deposit Ni = 13.137 g. As current efficiency is 60%, mass actually deposited

$= \frac{60}{100} \times 13.137 = 7.88$ g.

357. (b): As the weights deposited by the same quantity of electricity are in the ratio of their equivalent weights,

Ratio of equivalent wts: A : B : C = 4.2 : 5.4 : 192

As valency = At. wt/Eq. wt,

∴ Ratio of valencies:

$A : B : C = \frac{7}{4.2} : \frac{27}{5.4} : \frac{69}{19.2} = \frac{1}{0.6} : \frac{1}{0.2} : \frac{1}{0.3}$

$= \frac{1}{6} : \frac{1}{2} : \frac{1}{3} = 1 : 3 : 2$

358. (c): $\overset{(+5)}{NaCl} + \overset{(-3)}{H_2O} \xrightarrow{\text{Electrolysis}} NaOH + \frac{1}{2} H_2 + \frac{1}{2} Cl_2$

At anode At cathode

400 mL of 1 M NaCl solution contains NaCl

$= \frac{1}{1000} \times 400$ mol = 0.4 mol

As $Na^+ e^- \rightarrow Na \xrightarrow{H_2O} NaOH + \frac{1}{2} H_2$

1 F produces 1 mol of NaOH

∴ 0.04 F produces NaOH = 0.04 mol

Thus, 400 mL of the solution now contains 0.04 mol of NaOH.

∴ Molar concentration of NaOH sol.

$\frac{0.04}{400} \times 1000 = 0.1$ M

$[OH^-] = 0.1$ M, $[H^+] = 10^{-13}$ M

pH = 13

359. (d): According to the given reaction, when 22.4 L of H_2 reacts, charge produced = 2 F = 2 × 96500 C

∴ When 67.3 L of H_2 reacts, charge produced

$= \frac{2 \times 96500}{22.4} \times 67.3\ C = 579861.6$ C

This is the charge produced in 10 minutes, that is, 600 s

∴ Current, $I = \frac{Q}{t} = \frac{579861.6}{600} = 966.4$ ampere

360. (d): $Cu^{2+} + 2\,e^- \rightarrow Cu$

Cu is deposited on the cathode. If the mass of the cathode increases by 64 g (atomic mass of Cu), 1 mol of Cu^{2+} ions would pass into the solution. As mass has increased by 6.4 g, 0.1 mol of Cu^{2+} passed into the solution.

361. (c): Higher the reduction potential more easily is the metal deposited. ($M^{n+} + ne^- \rightarrow M$). Mg^{2+} ions will not be deposited because H_2O is reduced more easily than Mg^{2+} ions.

362. (a): In an aqueous solution of MnI_2, either Mn^{2+} will be reduced or H_2O will be reduced and either I^- will be oxidised or H_2O will be oxidised. Comparing the standard reduction potentials of Mn^{2+} and H_2O, H_2O has a higher reduction potential and hence is more easily reduced to give H_2. Comparing oxidation potentials of I^- and H_2O (sign reversed), I^- has a higher oxidation potential and is hence more easily oxidised to I_2.

363. (c): Oxidation: $Pb(s) + SO_4^{2-}(aq) \rightarrow PbSO_4(s) + 2\ e^-$

Reduction: $PbO_2(s) + 4\ H^+(aq) + SO_4^{2-}(aq) + 2\ e^- \rightarrow PbSO_4(s) + H_2O(l)$

Overall reaction: $Pb(aq) + PbO_2(s) + 2H_2SO_4(aq) \rightarrow 2PbSO_4(s) + 2H_2O(l)$

Thus, for drawing 2 F of electricity, H_2SO_4 consumed = 2 mol

Actual quantity of electricity drawn = $C \times t$

$= 2.5 \times 965 \times 60\ C = \dfrac{2.5 \times 965 \times 60}{96500}\ F = 1.5\ F$

$\therefore H_2SO_4$ consumed = 1.5 mol

364. (c): The balanced equation for pentane–oxygen cell reaction will be

$C_5H_{12} + 8O_2 \rightarrow 5CO_2 + 6H_2O,\ n = 32$

$[\because 16\ (O) + 32\ e^- \rightarrow 16\ O^{2-}]$

$\Delta_r G° = [5 \times \Delta_r G°\ (CO_2) + 6\ \Delta_f G°\ (H_2O)]$

$-[\Delta_f G°\ (C_5H_{12}) + 8\ \Delta_f G°\ (O_2)]$

$= [5\ (-394.5) + 6\ (-237.2)] - [(-8.2) + 0]$

$= -1972 - 1423.2 + 8.2$

$= -3387\ kJ\ mol^{-1}$

$\Delta_f G° = -nFE°_{cell}$

$\therefore -3387000 = -32 \times 96500 \times E°_{cell}$ or $E°_{cell} = 1.0968\ V$

365. (a): At anode: $Fe \rightarrow Fe^{2+} + 2e^-$

At cathode: $O_2 + 2H_2O + 4\ e^- \rightarrow 4\ OH^-$

366. (b): $Q = I \times t = 1 \times 100 = 100\ C$

Energy = Charge × Potential

$= 100 \times 115 = 11500\ J = 11.5\ kJ$

367. (c): H_2 undergoes oxidation and AgCl (Ag^+) undergoes reduction.

368. (c): Cu^{2+} ions gain electrons and are deposited on copper.

369. (c): Check the spontaneity of each reaction by finding the emf. For a spontaneous reaction, the EMF should be +ve.

370. (c): M has a higher oxidation potential than Ni but lower oxidation potential than Mn. That is, the oxidation potentials are Mn > M > Ni. Greater the oxidation potential, greater is the reducing power.

371. (a): (i) $E°_{Ag^+/Ag} - E°_{Cu^{2+}/Cu} = 0.46$

(ii) $E°_{Cu^{2+}/Cu} - E°_{Zn^{2+}/Zn} = 1.10$

Aim: $E°_{Ag^+/Ag} - E°_{Zn^{2+}/Zn} = ?$

Eq. (i) + Eq. (ii) gives the required result.

372. (c): The given half cell reactions may be written as

(i) $OCl^- + H_2O + 2\ e^- \rightarrow Cl^- + 2\ OH^-,\ E°_1 = -0.94\ V$

(ii) $Cl^- \rightarrow \frac{1}{2}\ Cl_2 + e^-,\ E°_2 = -1.36\ V$

(iii) $OCl^- + H_2O + e^- \rightarrow \frac{1}{2}\ Cl_2 + 2\ OH^-,\ E°_3 = ?$

Eq. (iii) can be obtained by adding Eqs (i) and (ii). Hence, in terms of their free energies, ($\Delta G° = -nFE°$)

$\Delta G°_3 = \Delta G°_1 + \Delta G°_2$

$-1 \times F \times E°_3 = -2 \times n \times F \times (0.94) - 1F(-1.36)$

or $E°_3 = 2 \times 0.94 = 1.36 = 0.52\ V$

373. (a): In the given reaction, I^- has been oxidised to I_2 and $Cr_2O_7^{2-}$ has been reduced to Cr^{3+}.

$\therefore E°_{cell} = E°_{Cr_2O_7^{2-}} - E°_{I_2}$

$0.79 = 1.33 - E°_{I_2}$ or $E°_{I_2} = 0.54\ V$

374. (c): The strongest oxidising agent is the substance which is reduced most easily, that is, has the highest reduction potential. Reduction potential of $[Fe(CN)_6]^{3-}$], and Fe^{3+} are +0.35 V and +0.77 V. Thus, Fe^{3+} is reduced most easily and hence is the strongest oxidising agent.

375. (a): Reduction potentials in the order Z > Y > X, means that Z can be reduced most easily and X least easily, that is, their oxidising powers are Z > Y > X.
Thus, Y will oxidise X but not Z.

376. (c): The reaction will take place for which $E°_{cell}$ is +ve.

(a) $I_2 + 2\ e^- \rightarrow 2\ I^-,\ E°_{red} = 0.536\ V$

$Fe^{2+} \rightarrow Fe^{3+} + e^-,\ E°_{ox} = -0.770\ V$

$\therefore E°_{cell}$ will be –ve.

(b) Redox reaction will occur

(c) $2\ I^- \rightarrow I_2 + 2\ e^-,\ E°_{ox} = -0.536\ V$

$Fe^{3+} + e^- \rightarrow Fe^{2+},\ E°_{red} = +0.770\ V$

$2Fe^{3+} + 2I^- \rightarrow 2Fe^{2+} + I_2, E°_{cell} = +0.164\ V$

Thus, $E°_{cell}$ is +ve. Hence, this reaction will occur.
(a) also will not occur.

MATCH THE FOLLOWING

377. (d): (A) $H^+ + e^- \rightarrow \frac{1}{2}\ H_2$

$E_{H^+/\frac{1}{2}H_2} = E° - \dfrac{0.059}{1} \log \dfrac{1}{[H^+]}$

$\therefore$ Ox. potential = 0.018 V

(C) $E_{cell} = \dfrac{0.059}{1}\ \log \dfrac{c_2}{c_1} = 0.059$

$\log \dfrac{0.1}{0.01} = 0.059\ V$

(D) $E_{cell} = \dfrac{0.059}{1}\ \log \dfrac{0.4}{0.1} = 0.0591\ \log 4 = 0.035\ V$

378. (d): (q) represents the calomel electrode used as a reference electrode.

(p) represents the redox electrode.

(s) represents the electrode reversible with respect to Zn^{2+} ion.

(q) and (r) represent electrodes reversible with respect to the Cl^- ion.

ASSERTION REASON

379. (c): Correct explanation: On applying external voltage greater than 1.1 V in the Daniell cell, current flows in the reverse direction, that is, electrons flow from cathode (Cu^{2+}/Cu) to anode (Zn/Zn^{2+}). The reverse reaction takes place, namely,
$Zn^{2+} + Cu \rightarrow Zn + Cu^{2+}$

380. (b): Correct explanation. If redox reaction is spontaneous, ΔG is –ve and hence, E°_{cell} is +ve ($-\Delta G^\circ = nFE^\circ_{cell}$).

381. (a): R is the correct explanation of A.

382. (c): Correct R. Oxidation takes place at the anode (negative electrode) whereas reduction takes place at the cathode (positive electrode).

383. (b): Correct explanation. Fluorine has a higher standard electrode potential (reduction potential) than iodine.

384. (c): Correct R. Zinc has a lower reduction potential whereas copper has a higher reduction potential than hydrogen.

385. (c): Correct R. The standard reduction potentials are in the order Fe < Cu < Ag.

386. (d): Correct A. Standard reduction potential of an electrode has a fixed value.
Correct R. Effect of concentration is studied by Nernst equation.
Correct R. Copper lies below hydrogen in the electrochemical series.

387. (b): Correct explanation. Gold has a higher reduction potential than the given metals. Hence, $AuCl_3$ will react with these metals.

388. (d): Both A and R are false. Potential difference is the difference between the electrode potentials when the cell is working, that is, we are drawing current from the cell whereas emf is the potential difference when we are not drawing any current from the cell.

389. (c): Correct R. When the cell is completely discharged, electrode potentials of the anode and cathode become equal.

390. (a): R is the correct explanation of A.

391. (a): R is the correct explanation of A.

392. (b): Correct explanation. Br^- and I^- have much higher oxidation potential than water whereas F^- ions have lower oxidation potential than water. Hence, H_2O is oxidised to give O_2.

393. (c): Correct R. H_2O has a higher reduction potential than sodium.

394. (a): R is the correct explanation of A.

395. (b): Correct explanation. The cell reaction, $Zn + HgO \rightarrow ZnO + Hg$ does not involve any ion whose concentration may change (OH^- ions consumed in one half reaction are produced in the second half-reaction).

396. (a): R is the correct explanation of A because sulfuric acid is consumed due to the formation of lead sulfate and hence the density decreases.

397. (d): Correct A. Pure copper does not corrode even in the most corrosive environments.
Correct R. Corrosion is a spontaneous process for which ΔG is –ve.

398. (a): R is the correct explanation of A. (More negative electrode potential of zinc means higher oxidation potential. Hence, zinc is more easily oxidised than iron).

399. (a): $CaH_2 \xrightarrow{\text{Melt}} Ca^{2+} + 2\,H^-$
At anode: $H^- \rightarrow H + e^-$; $H + H \rightarrow H_2$
Hence, R is the correct explanation of A.

400. (c): Correct R. Cu^{2+} is deposited as Cu.

401. (d): Correct A. Electrical conduction by metals decreases and by electrolytic solution it increases with an increase in temperature.
Correct R. In metals, with an increase of temperature, the flow of electrons is hindered by the vibrating kernels.

402. (b): Correct explanation. 1 mol of Ag = 1 g equivalent of Ag but 1 mol of Cu = 2 g equivalents of copper.

403. (a): A small amount of acid or alkali increases the conductivity of water by increasing ionisation.

404. (c): Correct R. One faraday deposits one gram equivalent of the substance.

405. (c): Correct R. On dilution, the number of current-carrying particles per cm^3 decreases (and hence specific conductivity decreases). Λ_{eq} and Λ_m increase because an increase in volume of the solution is much more than the decrease in specific conductivity. Λ_{eq} = sp. conductivity × volume of solution containing 1 g eq. of the electrolyte. Λ_m = sp. Conductivity × volume of solution containing 1 mol of the electrolyte.

406. (c): Correct R. Kohlrausch's law is applicable to weak as well as strong electrolytes.

407. (a): R is the correct explanation of A.

408. (c): Correct R. The current carried by the cation and the anion is not equal but depends upon their transport numbers.

409. (a): Na^+ ion is smaller in size than K^+ ion. Hence, it gets more hydrated so that size of the hydrated Na^+ ion is greater. Therefore, the ionic mobility of the Na^+ ion is lower than that of the K^+ ion.

Chemical Kinetics

4.1 Classification of Reactions on the Basis of Rates

Based upon their rates, the various chemical reactions are classified into three types.

(i) *Very fast reactions*, that is, those that take place instantaneously (time taken is generally 10^{-12} to 10^{-16} s). For example, ionic reactions such as,

$$AgNO_3(aq) + NaCl(aq) \rightarrow AgCl(s) + NaNO_3(aq)$$
$$BaCl_2(aq) + H_2SO_4(aq) \rightarrow BaSO_4(s) + 2HCl(aq)$$
$$NaOH(aq) + HCl(aq) \rightarrow Na^+Cl^-(aq) + H_2O(l)$$

(ii) *Very slow reactions*, that is, those that may take days or months. For example, rusting of iron.

(iii) *Reactions which are neither very slow not very fast but take place at moderate speeds.* A few examples are:

- Hydrolysis of ethyl acetate:

$$\underset{\text{Ethyl acetate}}{CH_3COOC_2H_5} + H_2O \xrightarrow{H^+} \underset{\text{Acetic acid}}{CH_3COOH} + \underset{\text{Ethyl alcohol}}{C_2H_5OH}$$

- Hydrolysis of sucrose:

$$\underset{\text{Sucrose}}{C_{12}H_{22}O_{11}} + H_2O \xrightarrow{H^+} \underset{\text{Glucose}}{C_6H_{12}O_6} + \underset{\text{Fructose}}{C_6H_{12}O_6}$$

Reasons for the Difference in Rates

Since different bonds require different amounts of energy for breaking, and different amounts of energies are evolved when different kinds of new bonds are formed, the rates of different reactions are different.

4.2 Rate of Reaction, Its Measurement and Dependence on Various Factors

4.2.1 Rate of Reaction

For a hypothetical reaction $R \rightarrow P$,

$$\text{Rate of reaction} = \frac{\text{Decrease in the concentration of a reactant R}}{\text{Time interval}}$$

or

$$= \frac{\text{Increase in the concentration of a product P}}{\text{Time interval}}$$

If $[R_1]$ and $[P_1]$ are the molar concentrations of the reactant and the product respectively at time t_1 and $[R_2]$ and $[P_2]$ are their respective concentrations at time t_2, then the changes in the concentrations of the reactant and product will be: $\Delta[R] = R_2 - R_1$, $\Delta [P] = P_2 - P_1$ and the time interval is $\Delta t = t_2 - t_1$.

$$\text{Rate of reaction} = -\frac{\Delta[R]}{\Delta t} = +\frac{\Delta[P]}{\Delta t}$$

Significance of negative and positive sign

It may be noted that the rate of a reaction is always positive. The minus sign along with the first term is used simply to show that the concentration of the reactant is decreasing.

In general, for any reaction of the type: $A + B \rightarrow C + D$,

$$\text{Rate of reaction} = -\frac{\Delta[A]}{\Delta t} = -\frac{\Delta[B]}{\Delta t} = +\frac{\Delta[C]}{\Delta t} = +\frac{\Delta[D]}{\Delta t}$$

4.2.2 Reactions involving Different Stoichiometric Coefficients of Reactants and Products

Consider the reaction $A + B \rightarrow 2C$

$2 \times$ Rate of disappearance of A = $2 \times$ Rate of disappearance of B = Rate of appearance of C

Thus, for the above reaction,

$$\text{Rate of reaction} = -\frac{\Delta[A]}{\Delta t} = -\frac{\Delta[B]}{\Delta t} = \frac{1}{2}\frac{\Delta[C]}{\Delta t}$$

For example, for the decomposition of gaseous nitrogen pentoxide (N_2O_5) as:

$$2N_2O_5(g) \rightarrow 4NO_2(g) + O_2(g)$$

$$\text{Rate of reaction} = -\frac{1}{2}\frac{[N_2O_5]}{\Delta t} = \frac{1}{4}\frac{\Delta[NO_2]}{\Delta t} = \frac{\Delta[O_2]}{\Delta t}$$

4.2.3 Units of the Rate of Reaction

The unit of the rate of reaction is mol litre^{-1} s^{-1} (mol L^{-1}s^{-1}) or mol litre^{-1}min^{-1} (mol L^{-1}min^{-1}). In the case of gaseous reactions, pressures are used in place of molar concentrations. The units of the rate of reaction are atm min^{-1} or atm s^{-1}.

4.3 Average Rate and Instantaneous Rate of Reaction

$$\text{Rate} = \frac{\text{Change in concentration}}{\text{Time interval}} = \frac{\Delta x}{\Delta t}$$

$$\text{Average rate of reaction } (r_{av}) = -\frac{\Delta[\text{R}]}{\Delta t} = +\frac{\Delta[\text{P}]}{\Delta t}$$

The instantaneous rate of a reaction may be defined as the *rate of reaction at any instant of time* is the rate of change of concentration (that is, change of concentration per unit time) of any one of the reactants or products at that particular instant of time. Suppose the small change in concentration is dx in the small interval of time dt. Instantaneous rate $(r_{\text{inst}}) = \frac{dx}{dt}$

For a general reaction,

$$aA + bB \rightleftharpoons cC + dD$$

the rate of the reaction is defined as:

$$\text{Rate of reaction} = -\frac{1}{a}\frac{d[\text{A}]}{dt} = -\frac{1}{b}\frac{d[\text{B}]}{dt}$$

$$= -\frac{1}{c}\frac{d[\text{C}]}{dt} = -\frac{1}{b}\frac{d[\text{D}]}{dt}$$

4.3.1 Calculation of Instantaneous Rate of a Reaction

To know the rate of the reaction at any time t, a tangent is drawn to the curve at the point corresponding to that time [Fig. 4.1(a)].

$$\text{Rate of reaction} = \frac{\text{Change in the concentration}}{\text{Time}}$$

$$= \frac{\Delta x}{\Delta t} = \frac{\text{OA}}{\text{OB}} = \text{Slope of the tangent}$$

4.3.2 Expressing Rate of Reaction in Terms of Different Reactants and Products

Consider the reaction, $2N_2O_5 \rightarrow 4NO_2 + O_2$.

For this reaction, Rate of decomposition (disappearance) of $N_2O_5 = -\frac{d[N_2O_5]}{dt}$

$$\text{Rate of formation of } NO_2 = +\frac{d[NO_2]}{dt}$$

$$\text{Rate of formation of } O_2 = +\frac{d[O_2]}{dt}$$

However, the rates as expressed above are not equal. This is because, when 2 mol of N_2O_5 decomposes, 4 mol of NO_2 and 1 mol of O_2 are produced in the same time. Thus, the rate of decomposition of N_2O_5 is twice as fast as that of formation of O_2 and the rate of formation of NO_2 is four times as fast as that of O_2. Thus, for the above reaction,

$$\text{Rate of reaction} = -\frac{1}{2}\frac{d[N_2O_5]}{dt} = +\frac{1}{4}\frac{d[NO_2]}{dt} = +\frac{[O_2]}{dt}$$

For the reaction $5\,Br^-(aq) + BrO_3^-(aq) + 6H^+(aq) \rightarrow 3Br_2(aq) + 3H_2O(l)$

$$\text{Rate} = -\frac{1}{5}\frac{d[Br^-]}{dt} = -\frac{d[BrO_3^-]}{dt}$$

$$= -\frac{1}{6}\frac{d[H^+]}{dt} = +\frac{1}{3}\frac{d[Br_2]}{dt}$$

Note: In aqueous solutions, the rate of reaction is not expressed in terms of change of concentration of water because the change is very small.

Worked Out Problem 4.1

For the decomposition of dinitrogen pentoxide at 200°C,

$$N_2O_5(g) \rightarrow N_2O_4(g) + \frac{1}{2}O_2(g)$$

If the initial pressure is 114 mm and after 25 minutes of the reaction, the total pressure of the gaseous mixture is 133 mm,

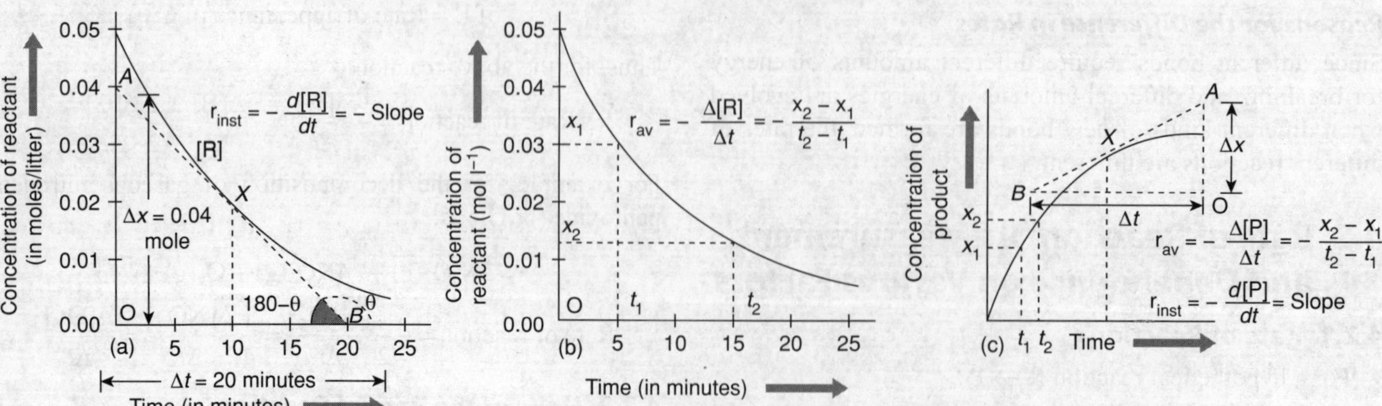

Fig. 4.1 (a) Calculation of the instantaneous rate of a reaction from plot of concentration of a reactant vs time **(b)** Calculation of the average rate of reaction **(c)** Calculation of instantaneous rate and average rate of a reaction from a plot of concentration of a product vs time

calculate the average rate of reaction in (i) atm mol^{-1} (ii) mol $L^{-1}s^{-1}$.

Solution

(i) If p is the decrease in pressure of N_2O_5 in 25 min, then

$$N_2O_5(g) \rightarrow N_2O_4(g) + \frac{1}{2}O_2(g)$$

Initial pressure	114 mm	0	0
After 25 min	$114-p$	p	$\frac{1}{2}p$

Total pressure =

$$114 - p + p + \frac{1}{2}p = 114 + \frac{1}{2}p = 133 \text{ mm} \quad \text{(Given)}$$

$$\therefore \quad p = 2 \times (133 - 144) = 38 \text{ mm}$$

Decrease in pressure in 25 min = 38 mm = $\frac{38}{760}$ atm

$$\therefore \text{ Average rate of reaction} = \frac{\frac{38}{760}\text{atm}}{25\,\text{min}} = 0.002\,\text{atm min}^{-1}$$

(ii) Applying $pV = nRT$, $\quad \frac{n}{V} = \frac{p}{RT}$

Decrease in molar concentration =

$$\frac{38/760 \text{ atm}}{0.0821 \text{ L atm K}^{-1}\text{ mol}^{-1} \times 473 \text{ K}} = 0.0012875 \text{ mol L}^{-1}$$

$\therefore$ Average rate of reaction =

$$\frac{0.0012875 \text{ mol L}^{-1}}{25 \times 60\text{s}} = 8.58 \times 10^{-7} \text{ mol L}^{-1}\text{ s}^{-1}$$

4.4 Factors Influencing Rate of a Reaction

There are a number of important factors that influence the rate of a reaction.

(i) *Nature of the reactants:* The reactivity of a substance is related to the ease with which the specific bonds are broken or formed and the number of such bonds involved. Consider the following two reactions.

$$2NO(g) + O_2(g) \rightarrow 2NO_2(g) \quad \text{fast}$$
$$2CO(g) + O_2(g) \rightarrow 2CO_2(g) \quad \text{slow}$$

These reactions appear to be similar but the first is fast while the second is slow.

(ii) *Concentration of the reactants:* Greater the concentrations of the reactants, faster is the reaction.

(iii) *Temperature:* The rate of reaction increases with an increase in temperature.

(iv) *Presence of catalyst:* In the case of reversible reactions, a catalyst helps to attain the equilibrium quickly without disturbing the state of equilibrium.

(v) *Surface area of the reactants:* Greater the surface area, the faster is the reaction. Finely divided solids react faster than a large lump of the substance.

(vi) *Presence of radiation:* The absorption of quantum energy of light facilitates the breaking of bonds of the reactants. The photons of these radiations having frequencies (ν) possess sufficient energies ($E = h\nu$) to break certain bonds in reactants. Further, the rate increases with an increase in the intensity of light.

4.5 Dependence of Rate on Concentration of Reactants

When a chemical reaction proceeds, the concentrations of the reactants keep on decreasing while those of the products keep on increasing (Fig. 4.2). However, the rate of reaction is also found to decrease. This shows that the rate of reaction is directly related to the concentration of reactants. Figure 4.2 shows that the rate of a reaction is directly proportional to the concentration of the reactants. In the gas phase reaction, an increase in the pressure of the reactant gases increases the rate of the reaction. With an increase in pressure, the number of molecules per unit volume increases and, therefore, the rate of reaction increases.

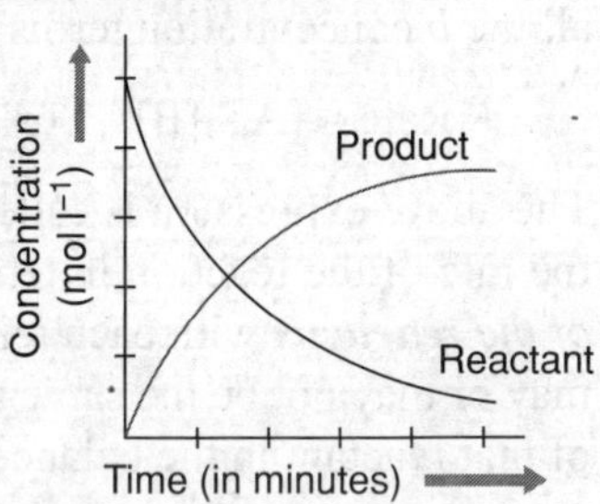

Fig. 4.2 Variation of concentration of reactants and products with time

4.5.1 Law of Mass Action

Let us consider a simple reaction of the type,

$$aA + bB \rightarrow \text{Products}$$

According to law of mass action, the rate of the reaction may be written as:

$$\text{Rate} \propto [A]^a\,[B]^b \quad \text{or} \quad \text{Rate} = k[A]^a\,[B]^b$$

where [A] and [B] are the molar concentrations of reactants, k is constant of proportionality and is called the rate constant. The rate constant is also called the velocity constant and is a measure of the rate of the reaction.

If [A] = [B] = 1, then we get

$$\text{Rate of reaction} = k \times 1 \times 1 = k$$

Thus, the *rate constant* of a reaction at a given temperature may be defined as the rate of the reaction when the molar concentration of each of the reactants is unity.

Characteristics of rate constant

- The rate constant is a measure of the rate of reaction. Greater the value of the rate constant, the faster is the reaction.
- Each reaction has a definite value of the rate constant at a particular temperature.

- The value of the rate constant for the same reaction changes with temperature.
- The value of the rate constant of a reaction does not depend upon the concentrations of the reactions.
- The units of the rate constant depend upon the order of reaction (as will be discussed later).

4.5.2 Rate Law Expression

Experimentally, it is observed that the rate of the reaction may not depend upon all the *a* concentration terms of A and all the *b* concentration terms of B.

$$\text{Rate} \propto [A]^{\alpha}[B]^{\beta} \quad \text{or} \quad \text{Rate} = k[A]^{\alpha}[B]^{\beta} \qquad (4.1)$$

The above expression is called the *rate law*. which expresses the rate of the reaction in terms of the *molar concentrations of the reactants* with each term raised to some power, which may or may not be the same as the stoichiometric coefficient of that reactant in the balanced chemical equation.

4.6 Order of Reaction

The *order of a reaction* is defined as the sum of the exponents (powers) to which the molar concentrations in the rate law equation are raised to express the observed rate of the reaction.

Thus, if the rate of a reaction

$$aA + bB + \rightarrow \text{Products}$$

in the above case, the order of the reaction = $\alpha + \beta$, where α, β are the orders with respect to individual reactants.

4.6.1 Common Examples of Reactions of Different Orders

(i) $H_2(g) + Cl_2(g) \xrightarrow{hv} 2HCl$

This is a reaction of zero order. Evidently, for such reactions, Rate = k.

(ii) $2N_2O_5 \rightarrow 4NO_2 + O_2$

Rate of reaction $\propto [N_2O_5]$

Hence, the reaction is said to be of the *first order*.

(iii) $2NO_2(g) + F_2(g) \rightarrow 2NO_2F(g)$

Rate of reaction $\propto$ $[NO_2]$ $[F_2]$. Hence, the order of reaction is 2, that is, it is a reaction of the *second order*.

Further, *the order of a reaction may not always be a whole number*. For example, at 723 K, acetaldehyde decomposes as:

$$CH_3CHO \xrightarrow{723K} CH_4 + CO$$

Experimentally, it is found that, Rate of reaction $\propto [CH_3CHO]^{1.5}$. Hence, the order of the reaction is 1.5.

4.6.2 Units of Reaction Rate Constant

Unit of rate

$$\text{Rate} = \frac{\text{Concentration}}{\text{Time}} = \frac{\text{mol L}^{-1}}{\text{s}} = \text{mol L}^{-1}\text{s}^{-1}$$

Units of rate constant

(i) *Zero order reaction:*

$$\text{Rate} = k[A]^0 \quad \text{or} = k$$

$$\frac{\text{mol L}^{-1}}{\text{s}} = k \quad \text{or} \quad k = \text{mol L}^{-1}\text{s}^{-1}$$

$\therefore$ The units of the rate constant of a zero order reaction are mol $L^{-1}s^{-1}$.

(ii) *First order reaction:*

$$\text{Rate} = k[A]$$

$$\frac{\text{mol L}^{-1}}{\text{s}} = k\,(\text{mol L}^{-1}) \quad \text{or} \quad k = \text{s}^{-1}$$

$\therefore$ The units of the rate constant of a first order reaction are s^{-1}.

(iii) *Second order reaction:*

$$\text{Rate} = k[A]^2$$

$$\frac{\text{mol L}^{-1}}{\text{s}} = k(\text{mol L}^{-1})^2 \quad \text{or} \quad k = \frac{1}{\text{mol L}^{-1}\text{ s}} = \text{L mol}^{-1}\text{ s}^{-1}$$

$\therefore$ The units of the rate constant for a second order reaction are L $mol^{-1}s^{-1}$.

(iv) *Third order reaction:*

$$\text{Rate} = k[A]^3$$

$$\frac{\text{mol L}^{-1}}{\text{s}} = k(\text{mol L}^{-1})^3 \text{ or } k = \frac{1}{\text{mol}^2\text{ L}^{-2}\text{s}} = \text{L}^2\text{ mol}^{-2}\text{s}^{-1}$$

The units of the rate constant for a third order reaction are L^2 $mol^{-2}s^{-1}$.

Units of Rate Constants for a Gaseous Reaction

In the case of gaseous reactions, the concentrations are expressed in terms of pressure in units of atmospheres.

(i) Zero order reaction : atm s^{-1}
(ii) First order reaction : s^{-1}
(iii) Second order reaction : atm^{-1} s^{-1}
(iv) Third order reaction : atm^{-2} s^{-1} and so on

4.7 Molecularity of a Reaction

The number of reactants (atoms, ions or molecules) that must collide with one another simultaneously for a reaction to take place is called the *molecularity of the reaction.* If a reaction involves the decomposition of only a single species, the molecularity is one; it is called a *unimolecular reaction*. For example,

$$H_2O_2 \rightarrow H_2O + \frac{1}{2}O_2$$

Similarly, if the reaction involves the collision of two species, it is *bimolecular* and if three species take part in a collision leading to the formation of the products, it is called *termolecular*, and so on.

$$2NO + O_2 \rightarrow 2NO_2$$

The different elementary reactions of a complex reaction have different rates. *The overall rate of the reaction depends upon the slowest step.* Hence, the slowest step is called the *rate determining step.* For example,

$$2NO_2 + F_2 \rightarrow 2NO_2F \text{ (termolecular)}$$

Experimentally, rate of reaction = $k\,[NO_2]\,[F_2]$

That is, the rate law equation involves only one molecule of NO_2 and one molecule of F_2.

Step 1: $NO_2 + F_2 \xrightarrow{\text{Slow}} NO_2F + F$

Step 2: $NO_2 + F \xrightarrow{\text{Fast}} NO_2F$

Here, the slow step is bimolecular. Hence, the above reaction is a bimolecular reaction, and the molecularity of the slowest step is two.

4.8 Experimental Measurement of Order of Reaction

Integrated Rate Equations for Different Orders

For a general reaction, $a\text{A} + b\text{B} \rightarrow c\text{C} + d\text{D}$,

$$\text{Rate} = -\frac{d[R]}{dt} = k[\text{A}]^{\alpha}[\text{B}]^{\beta}$$

This equation is called a *differential rate equation.* The *integrated rate equations* are different for reactions of different orders.

Consider the general reaction R → Products
Initial concentration of reactant
At zero time $a = [R]_0$
After a time t, the amount reacted = $x = [R]_0 - [R]$
Final concentration of reactant after time $t = a - x = [R]$
is the integrated equation for a zero order reaction.

Important Characteristics of Reactions of Zero Order

(i) **Half-life period:** *Half-life period* ($t_{1/2}$) is the time in which half of the reactants are converted into products. When $t = t_{1/2}$,
The half-life period of a zero order reaction is directly proportional to the initial concentration, that is, $t_{1/2} \propto [R]_0$. Hence, a plot of $t_{1/2}$ versus $[R]_0$ or a will be a straight line passing through the origin with a slope = $\frac{1}{2k}$ (Fig. 4.3).

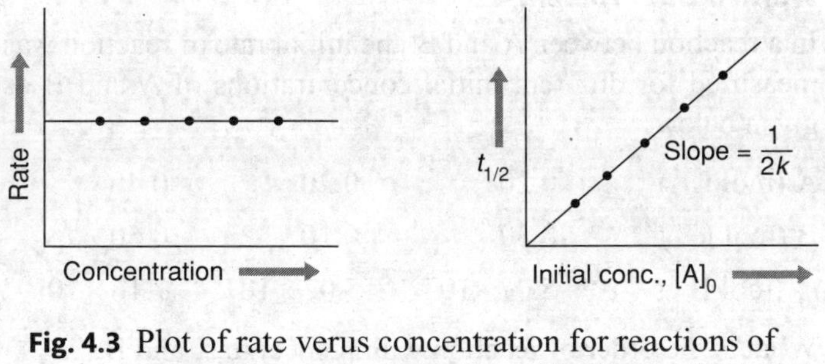

Fig. 4.3 Plot of rate verus concentration for reactions of zero order Plot of hafe-life ($t_{1/2}$) versus initial concentration for a zero order reaction

Worked Out Problem 4.2

The rate constant of a reaction of zero order in A is 0.0030 mol $L^{-1}s^{-1}$. How long will it take for the initial concentration of A to fall from 0.10 M to 0.075 M?

Solution

For a zero order reaction,

$$t = \frac{1}{k}\,[[R]_0 - [R]] = \frac{1}{0.003\text{M s}^{-1}}(0.10 - 0.075)\text{M} = 8.3\text{s}$$

Integrated Rate Equation for First Order Reactions

In a first order reaction the rate of the reaction depends upon only one power of concentration of reactant. For the reaction:

$$R \rightarrow \text{Products}, \quad \frac{dx}{dt} \propto [R] \quad \frac{dx}{dt} = k[R]$$

where k is the first order rate constant or specific reaction rate (Fig. 4.4). Suppose the initial concentration of reactant = $[R]_0 = a$ mol per litre, after a time t, x mol per litre of reactant have reacted. The concentration of reactant after time $t = (a - x)$ mol per litre = [R]

$$\therefore \quad k = \frac{2.303}{t}\log\frac{a}{a-x} \quad (4.2)$$

$$k = \frac{2.303}{t}\log\frac{[R_0]}{[R]}$$

Expression for the rate constant for a first order reaction from concentrations of the reactant at two different times:

$$k = \frac{2.303}{(t_2 - t_1)}\log\frac{[R]_1}{[R]_2}$$

When half the reaction is complete, $x = a/2$, $t = t_{\frac{1}{2}}$

$$t_{1/2} = \frac{2.303}{k}\log\frac{a}{a - \frac{a}{2}} = \frac{2.303}{k}\log 2 = \frac{0.693}{k},\; t_{1/2} = \frac{0.693}{k}$$

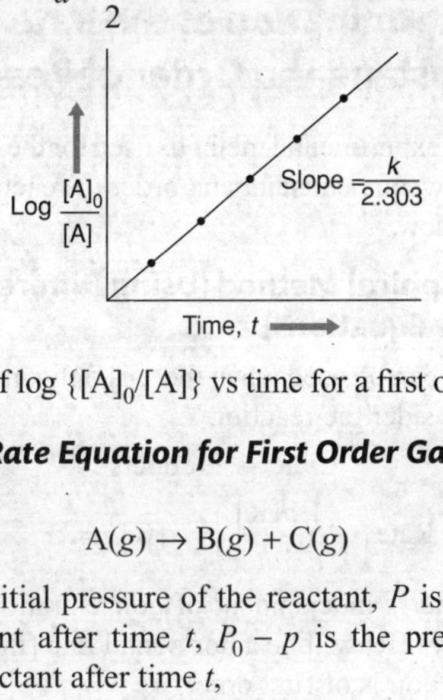

Fig. 4.4 Plot of log $\{[A]_0/[A]\}$ vs time for a first order reaction

Integrated Rate Equation for First Order Gas Phase Reactions

$$A(g) \rightarrow B(g) + C(g)$$

If P_0 is the initial pressure of the reactant, P is the pressure of the reactant after time t, $P_0 - p$ is the pressure of the unreacted reactant after time t,

	A(g)	→	B(g) +	C(g)
Initial pressure of reactant	P_0 atm		0	0
Pressure of reactant after time t:	$(P_0 - p)$		p atm	p atm

Total pressure of the reaction mixture after time t,

$$P_t = (P_0 - p) + p + p = P_0 + p \text{ atm}$$

$$\therefore \quad p = P_t - P_0$$

$\therefore$ Pressure of A after time

$$t = P_0 - p = P_0 - (P_t - P_0) = 2P_0 - P_t$$

Initial pressure of reactant $(P_0) \propto$ initial conc. $[A]_0$
Final pressure of reactant after time t $\propto$ conc. of reactant [A] after time t

Substituting these values in the first order rate equation,

$$k = \frac{2.303}{t}\log\frac{[R]_0}{[R]}$$

$$k = \frac{2.303}{t}\log\frac{P_0}{2P_0 - P_t} \qquad (4.3)$$

4.9 Half-Life Period of a Reaction

The time taken for half the reaction to complete, that is, the time in which the concentration of a reactant is reduced to half of its original value is called the *half-life period* of the reaction.

General expression for half-life period of a reaction of nth order: As already discussed, for zero order, $t_{1/2} \propto [R_0]$ for 1st order, $t_{1/2} \propto [R_0]^0$

Similarly for 2nd order, $t_{1/2} \propto [R_0]^{-1}$, and so on.

In general, for a reaction of the nth order,

$$t_{1/2} \propto [R_0]^{1-n} \quad \text{or} \quad t_{1/2} \propto \frac{1}{[R_0]^{1-n}} \qquad (4.4)$$

4.10 Determination of the Rate Law, Rate Constant and Order of Reaction

The different experimental methods used for the determination of the rate law, rate constant and order of reaction are briefly described below.

4.10.1 Graphical Method (Using Differential Rate Law Equations)

This method can be used when there is only one reactant. For example, consider the reaction

$$n\,R \rightarrow \text{Products}$$

$$\text{Rate}\left(-\frac{1}{n}\frac{d[R]}{dt}\right) = k[R]^0 = k \qquad (4.5)$$

Thus, the rate is independent of concentration. Hence, the plot of Rate vs [R] will be a horizontal line [Fig. 4.5(a)].

It the reaction is of first order,

$$\text{Rate} \propto [R] \quad \text{or} \quad \text{Rate} = k[R] \qquad (4.6)$$

Thus, the plot of rate vs molar concentration of the reactant would be linear [Fig. 4.5(b)] and Eq. 4.6 will be the *rate law*.

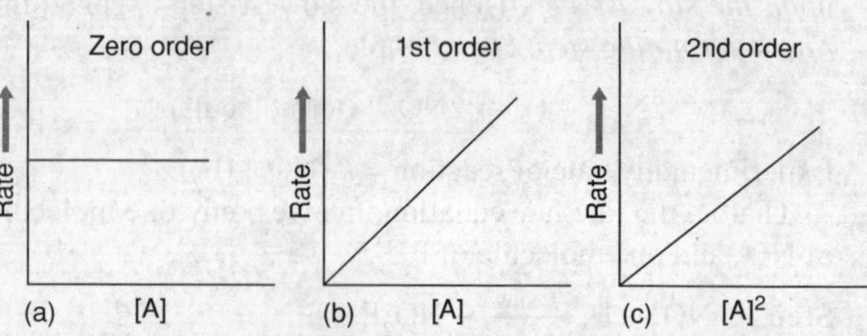

Fig. 4.5 Differential rate law method for testing the order of a reaction graphically

If the above reaction is second order,

$$\text{Rate} \propto [R]^2 \quad \text{or} \quad \text{Rate} = k[R]^2 \qquad (4.7)$$

Thus, the plot of rate vs $[R]^2$ would be linear [Fig. 4.5(c)].

4.10.2 Initial Rate Method

This method can be used irrespective of the number of reactants involved. For example, consider the reaction,

$$n_1\,A + n_2\,B + n_3\,C \rightarrow \text{Products}$$

- Keeping the concentrations of B and C constant, if the concentration of A is doubled, the rate of reaction becomes four times.
  Rate $\propto [A]^2$, that is, the order with respect to A is 2
- Keeping the concentrations of A and C constant, if the concentration of B is doubled, the rate of reaction is also doubled. This means that
  Rate $\propto$ [B], that is, the order with respect to B is 1
- Keeping the concentrations of A and B constant, if the concentration of C is doubled, the rate of the reaction remains unaffected. This means that the rate is independent of the concentration of C, that is, the order with respect to C is zero.

Hence, the overall rate law expression will be

$$\text{Rate} = k[A]^2[B][C]^0$$

$\therefore$ Overall order of reaction = 2 + 1 + 0 = 3

Alternatively, if the orders with respect to A, B and C are α, β and γ, then we have:

$$\text{Rate} = k[A]^\alpha[B]^\beta[C]^\gamma$$

Worked Out Problem 4.3

In a reaction between A and B, the initial rate of reaction was measured for different initial concentrations of A and B as given below:

A (mol L^{-1})	0.20	0.20	0.40
B (mol L^{-1})	0.30	0.10	0.50
r_0 (mol L^{-1} s^{-1})	5.07×10^{-5}	5.07×10^{-5}	7.16×10^{-5}

What is the order of reaction with respect to A and B?

Solution

$$r_0 = [A]^\alpha [B]^\beta$$

$$(r_0)_1 = 5.07 \times 10^{-5} = (0.20)^\alpha (0.30)^\beta \quad \text{(i)}$$

$$(r_0)_1 = 5.07 \times 10^{-5} = (0.20)^\alpha (0.10)^\beta \quad \text{(ii)}$$

$$(r_0)_3 = 7.16 \times 10^{-5} = (0.40)^\alpha (0.05)^\beta \quad \text{(iii)}$$

$$\frac{(r_0)_1}{(r_0)_2} = 1 = \left(\frac{0.30}{0.10}\right)^\beta = (3)^\beta$$

$$\therefore \quad \beta = 0$$

$$\frac{(r_0)_3}{(r_0)_2} = \frac{7.16}{5.07} = \left(\frac{0.40}{0.20}\right)^\alpha \left(\frac{0.05}{0.10}\right)^\beta$$

or $$1.412 = 2^\alpha \left(\frac{1}{2}\right)^\beta = 2^\alpha (\because \beta = 0)$$

$$\log 1.412 = \alpha \log 2 \quad \text{or} \quad \alpha = 0.1523/0.3010 = 0.5$$

(or directly $1.412 = \sqrt{2} = 2^{1/2} \therefore 2^\alpha = 2^{1/2}$ or $\alpha \tfrac{1}{2}$)

Thus, the order with respect to A = 0.5, and the order with respect to B = 0.

4.10.3 Integrated Rate Law Method

For zero order, $k = \frac{1}{t}\{[R_0] - [R]\}$

For 1st order, $k = \frac{2.303}{t} \log \frac{[R_0]}{[R]}$

For 2nd order, $k = \frac{1}{t}\left\{\frac{1}{[R]} - \frac{1}{[R_0]}\right\}$

The above expressions can be used to test the order of reaction by either of the following two methods:

(i) Substitution method: The results of the experiment are substituted in the expressions for the rate constant of different orders one by one. The expression which gives a constant value of the rate constant k decides the order of the reaction.

(ii) Graphical method: The above expressions can also be tested graphically by rearranging them in suitable forms (Fig. 4.6).

For zero order, $[R] = -kt + [R]_0$, so that the plot of [R] vs t will be linear with a slope $= -k$ and intercept $= [R]_0$.

For 1st order, $\log [R] = -\frac{k}{2.303} + \log [R]_0$, so that the plot of log [R] vs t will be linear with a slope $= -\frac{k}{2.303}$ and intercept $= \log [R]_0$.

For 2nd order, $\frac{1}{[R]} = kt + \frac{1}{[R]_0}$, so that the plot of $\frac{1}{[R]}$ vs t will be linear with a slope $= k$ and intercept $= \frac{1}{[R]_0}$.

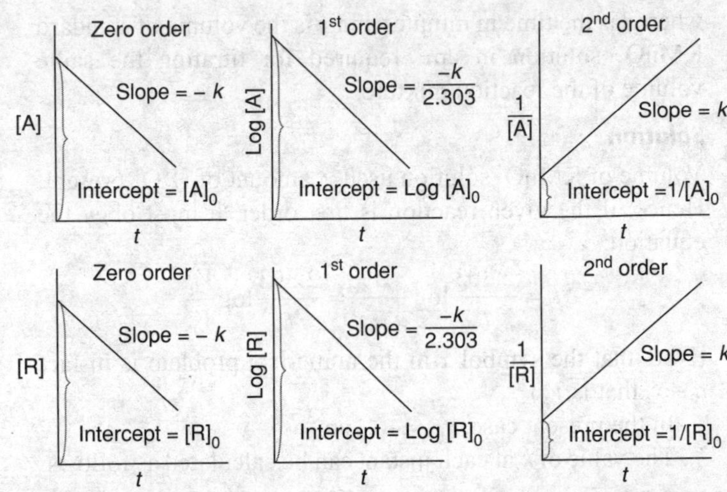

Fig. 4.6 Graphical method for testing order of reaction using integrated equations

4.10.4 Half-life Method

The half-life period of a reaction of the nth order is related to the initial concentration of the reactant as: $t_{1/2} \propto \frac{1}{[R_0]^{n-1}}$.

The order 'n' can be found by either of the following two methods.

4.10.5 Ostwald's Isolation Method

This method is used when there are a number of reactants. All reactants except one are taken in a large excess so that the change in their concentrations is negligible and the rate of reaction depends only on the reactant (which is taken in a smaller amount). Thus, for the reaction,

$$aA + bB + cC \rightarrow \text{Products},$$

if the order with respect to A, B and C are α, β and γ respectively, then according to the rate law,

$$\text{Rate} = k\,[A]^\alpha [B]^\beta [C]^\gamma$$

If B and C are in a large excess, their concentrations remain almost constant. These can be included in the rate constant. Hence, we can write,

$$\text{Rate} = k_0 = [A]^\alpha$$

Thus, the order with respect to A is found out. Similarly, the orders with respect to B and C can be determined and hence the overall order of the reaction can be determined.

Worked Out Problem 4.4

From the following data, show that the decomposition of hydrogen peroxide is a reaction of the first order:

t	0	10	20
x	46.1	29.8	19.3

where t is the time in minutes and x is the volume of standard $KMnO_4$ solution in cm^3 required for titrating the same volume of the reaction mixture.

Solution

Volume of $KMnO_4$ solution used ∝ amount of H_2O_2 present. Hence, if the given reaction is first order, it must obey the equation:

$$k = \frac{2.303}{t}\log\frac{a}{a-x} = \frac{2.303}{t}\log\frac{V_0}{V_t}$$

(Note that the symbol x in the numerical problem is in fact $a-x$, that is, V_t)

In the present case, $V_0 = 46.1\ cm^3$

The value of k at each instant can be calculated as follows:

t(min)	V_t	$k = \frac{2.303}{t}\log\frac{V_0}{V_t}$
10	29.8	$k = \frac{2.303}{10\ min}\log\frac{46.1}{29.8} = 0.0436\ min^{-1}$
20	19.3	$k = \frac{2.303}{20\ min}\log\frac{46.1}{19.3} = 0.0435\ min^{-1}$

Thus, the calculated value of k is nearly constant. Hence, it is a first order reaction.

4.11 Pseudo First Order Reactions

Some reactions are first order each with respect to two different reactants, that is,

$$A + B \rightarrow Products$$

$$Rate = k\ [A]\ [B]$$

However, if one of the reactants is present in high concentration (solvent) then there is very little change in its concentration. For example, if [A] = 0.01 M and that of the solvent, water [B] = 55.5 M, the concentration of B changes only from 55.50 M to 55.49 M even after the completion of the reaction. Under such conditions, we may write,

$$Rate = k_0\ [A] \text{ where } k_0 = k\ [B]$$

The reaction, therefore, behaves as a first order reaction in A.

Such reactions which are not truly first order but under certain conditions become first order reactions are called *pseudo-first order reactions*. Acid-catalysed hydrolysis of ethyl acetate.

$$\underset{\text{Ethyl acetate}}{CH_3COOC_2H_5} + H_2O \xrightarrow{H^+} \underset{\text{Acetic acid}}{CH_3COOH} + \underset{\text{Ethyl alcohol}}{C_2H_5OH}$$

The molecularity of the reaction is two because it involves two reacting species—ethyl acetate and water. Water is present in such a large excess that its concentration remains practically unchanged. Therefore, the rate of the reaction depends only on the concentration of ethyl acetate and hence the order of the reaction is one.

$$Rate = k'\ [CH_3COOC_2H_5]\ [H_2O]$$

$[H_2O]$ can be takes as constant. Therefore,

$$Rate = k\ [CH_3COOC_2H_5]$$

where $k = k'\ [H_2O]$. Thus, the reaction appears to be second order but follows first order kinetics.

Worked Out Problem 4.5

1.0 mL of ethyl acetate was added to 25 mL of N/2 HCl. 2 mL of the mixture was withdrawn from time to time during the progress of the hydrolysis of the ester and titrated against standard NaOH solution. The amount of NaOH required for titration at various intervals is given below.

Time (min):	0	20	75	119	183	∞
NaOH used (mL):	20.24	21.73	25.20	27.60	30.22	43.95

The value at ∞ time was obtained by completing the hydrolysis on boiling. Show that it is a reaction of the first order and find the average value of the velocity constant.

Solution

As explained above, if the given reaction is first order, it must obey the equation

t (min)	V_t	$V_\infty - V_t$	$k = \frac{2.303}{t}\log\frac{V_\infty - V_0}{V_\infty - V_t}$
20	21.73	43.95 – 21.73 = 22.22	$k = \frac{2.303}{20\ min}\log\frac{23.72}{22.22} = 0.00324\ min^{-1}$
75	25.20	43.95 – 25.20 = 18.75	$k = \frac{2.303}{75\ min}\log\frac{23.71}{18.75} = 0.00313\ min^{-1}$
119	27.60	43.95 – 27.60 = 16.35	$k = \frac{2.303}{119\ min}\log\frac{23.71}{16.35} = 0.00312\ min^{-1}$
183	30.22	43.95 – 30.22 = 13.73	$k = \frac{2.303}{183\ min}\log\frac{23.71}{13.73} = 0.00299\ min^{-1}$

$$k = \frac{2.303}{t}\log\frac{a}{a-x} = \frac{2.303}{t}\log\frac{V_\infty - V_0}{V_\infty - V_t}$$

In the present case, $V_0 = 20.24$ mL and $V_\infty = 43.95$ mL

$\therefore \quad V_\infty - V_0 = 43.95 - 20.24 = 23.71$ mL

The values of k at different instants can be calculated. Since the calculated value of k is nearly constant, it is a first order reaction. The mean value of $k = 0.00312 \text{ min}^{-1}$.

Worked Out Problem 4.6

A first order reaction is 40% complete in 50 minutes. Calculate the value of the rate constant. In what time will the reaction be 80% complete?

Solution

(i) For a first order reaction $k = \dfrac{2.303}{t}\log\dfrac{a}{a-x}$

When $x = \dfrac{40}{100}a = 0.4a, \quad t = 50$ minutes (given)

$$\therefore \quad k = \frac{2.303}{50}\log\frac{a}{a-0.4a} \quad \text{or} \quad k = \frac{2.303}{50\text{min}}\log\frac{a}{0.6}$$

$$= 0.010216 \text{ min}^{-1}$$

(ii) $t = ?$, when reaction is 80% complete,

$x = 0.8a$; $k = 0.010216 \text{ min}^{-1}$ (calculated above)

$$\therefore \quad t = \frac{2.303}{k}\log\frac{a}{a-x} = \frac{2.303}{0.010216 \text{ min}^{-1}}\log\frac{a}{a-0.8a}$$

$$= \frac{2.303}{0.010216 \text{ min}^{-1}}\log\frac{1}{0.2} = 157.58 \text{ min}$$

4.12 Collision Theory

The number of collisions that take place per second per unit volume of the reaction mixture is known as the *collision frequency Z*. Under ordinary conditions of temperature and pressure in a gaseous system, the collision frequency of binary collisions is of the order of 10^{25} to 10^{28}. The collisions which actually produce the products and therefore result in the chemical reactions are called *effective collisions*. The conditions for effective collisions are,

- threshold energy, and
- orientation barrier.

4.12.1 Threshold Energy

For the reacting species to make effective collisions, they should have sufficient energy to break the chemical bonds in the reacting molecules. This means that only those collisions of reactants will give products which possess energies greater than the threshold energy.

4.12.2 Orientation Factor

$$NO_2(g) + NO_2(g) \rightarrow N_2O_4(g)$$

During this reaction, the products are formed only when the colliding molecules have a proper orientation at the time of collisions. These are called effective collisions. The fraction of effective collisions, under ordinary conditions may vary from nearly zero to about one for ordinary reactions. Thus, the rate of reaction is proportional to

- the number of collisions per unit volume per second (collision frequency, Z) between the reacting species, and
- the fraction of effective collisions (properly oriented and possessing sufficient energy), f:

$$\text{Rate} = -\frac{dx}{dt} = f \times Z$$

4.13 Concept of Activation Energy

The minimum extra amount of energy above the average energy of reactants which is absorbed energy of reactant molecule becomes equal to threshold value and collision becomes effective is called *activation energy*.

Activation energy = Threshold energy—Average kinetic energy of the reactants

Each reaction has a definite value of activation energy. *Lower the activation energy, greater is the rate of reaction.* For example,

$2NO + O_2 \rightarrow 2NO_2$ is a *fast reaction* because of *smaller activation energy*.

$2CO + O_2 \rightarrow 2CO_2$ is a *slow reaction* because *of high activation energy*.

When the reactant molecules absorb energy, their bonds are loosened and new loose bonds are formed. The intermediate thus formed is called an *activated complex* or *transition state complex*. It is unstable and immediately dissociates to form the stable products.

A—A + B—B ⟶ (Reactants) A-------A / B-------B (Activated complex) ⟶ 2 AB (Products)

e.g., H—H (0·74 Å), I—I (2·66 Å) ⟶ H-------H (0·77 Å), I-------I (2·95 Å) ⟶ H—I + H—I (1·06 Å)

Reactant molecules — Activated complex — Product molecules

Transition state

It may be noted that when the activated complex dissociates to form the products, it is accompanied by a release of energy. But the enthalpy change (ΔH) during the reaction at a particular temperature remains constant because it depends only on the nature of the reactants and the products (Fig. 4.7).

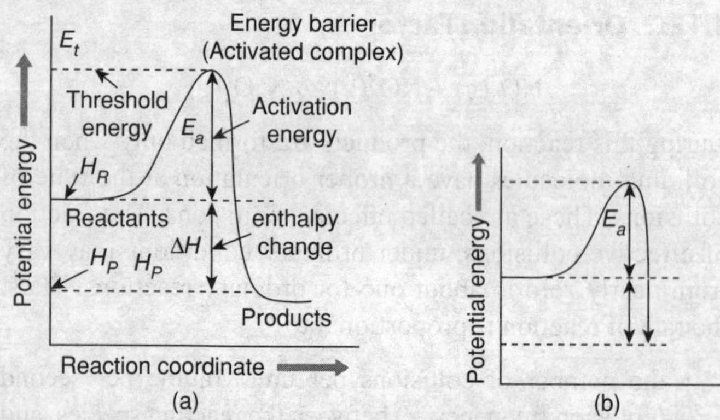

Fig. 4.7 Activation energy diagram for an **(a)** exothermic reaction **(b)** endothermic reaction

4.13.1 Activation Energies and Reversible Reactions

Consider a reversible reaction:

$$A + B \rightleftharpoons C + D$$

Just as activation energy is required for the forward reaction, activation energy is also required for the backward reaction. During the progress of the reaction, the reactant molecules in the forward reaction and the product molecules in the backward reaction follow the same path and form the same activated complex. However, the activation energies of the two are different (Fig. 4.8).

$$\Delta H = E_a \text{ (forward)} - E_a \text{ (backward)}$$

As evident from Fig. 4.8(a), for the exothermic reaction

$$\begin{bmatrix}\text{Activation energy for} \\ \text{the forward reaction}\end{bmatrix} < \begin{bmatrix}\text{Activation energy for} \\ \text{the backward reaction}\end{bmatrix}$$

$$E_a \text{ (forward)} < E_a \text{ (backward)}$$

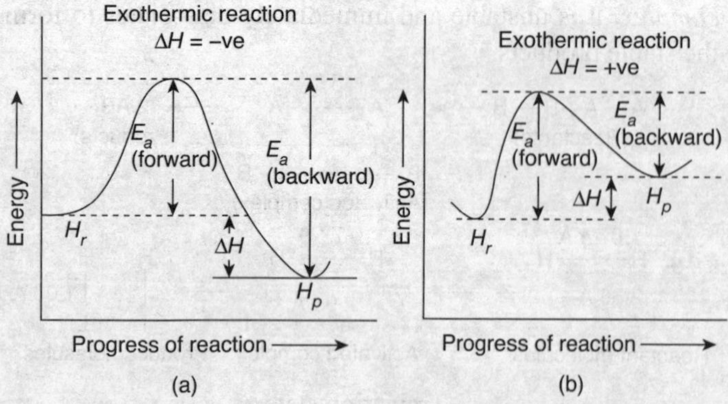

Fig. 4.8 Activation energies for the forward and backward reactions in case of **(a)** exothermic and **(b)** endothermic reactions

Thus, $\Delta H = E_a$ (forward) $- E_a$ (backward)$= -$ve

On the other hand, for the endothermic reaction

$$\begin{bmatrix}\text{Activation energy for} \\ \text{the forward reaction}\end{bmatrix} < \begin{bmatrix}\text{Activation energy for} \\ \text{the backward reaction}\end{bmatrix}$$

$$E_a \text{ (forward)} < E_a \text{ (backward)}$$

Thus, $\Delta H = E_a$ (forward) $- E_a$ (backward) $= +$ve

4.14 Effect of Catalyst on Rate of Reaction

The phenomenon of increasing the rate of a reaction by the use of a catalyst is called *catalysis*. It is observed that a catalyst is not consumed in the reaction; it is used in one step and is regenerated in a subsequent step and therefore, it is used again and again without undergoing any permanent change.

The effect of a catalyst can be explained on the basis of *intermediate complex formation theory*; it is believed that the reactants first combine with the catalyst to form an intermediate complex which is short-lived and then decomposes to form the products and the catalyst. Consider a hypothetical reaction,

$$A + B \rightarrow AB$$

The reaction proceeds through the formation of an activated complex (Fig. 4.9).

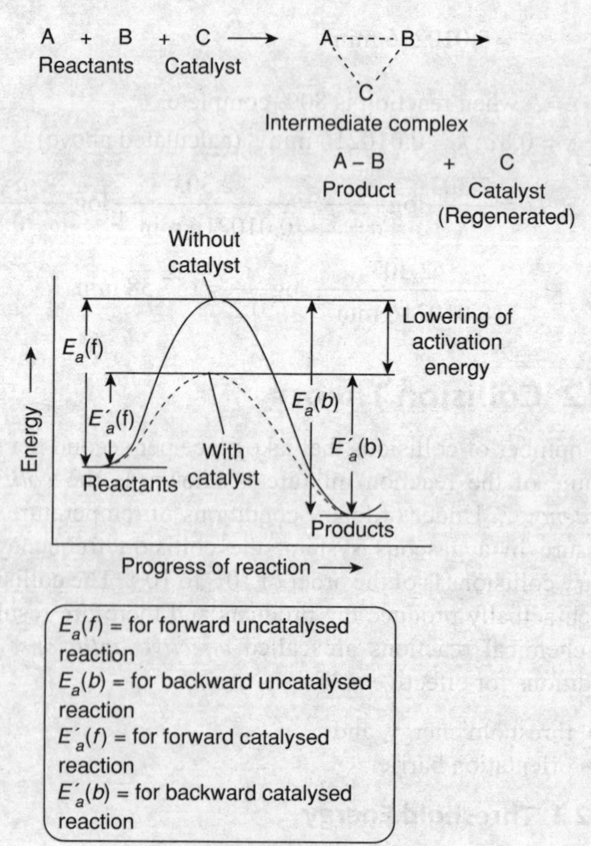

Fig. 4.9 Effect of catalyst

A + B	→	[A……B]	→	AB
Reactants		Activated complex		Product

The addition of a catalyst C results in the formation of a new activated complex of lower activation energy. Thus, a catalyst provides a new pathway for the reaction with a lower activation energy; so, the reaction becomes fast and the reactants are converted to products quickly. The intermediate complex formed has much lower potential energy than the intermediate complex formed between the reactants in the absence of the catalyst (Fig. 4.10).

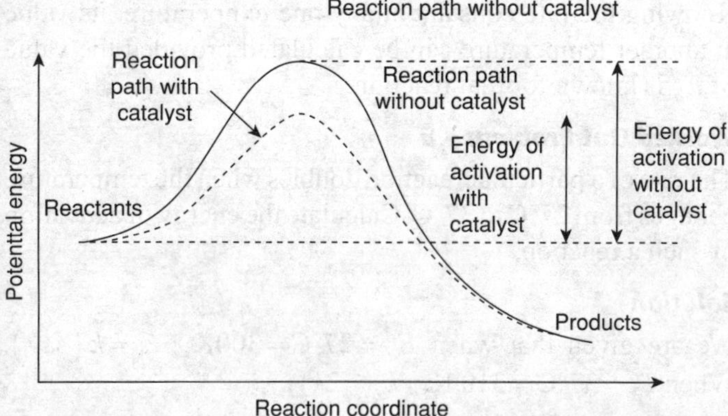

Fig. 4.10 Change in activation energy with catalyst

The catalyst decreases activation energy by changing the mechanism of the reaction without shifting the equilibrium position. Lesser the activation energy, faster is the rate of reaction because more reactant molecules acquire activation energy and change into products.

The lowering in activation energy is to the same extent for the forward as well as for the backward reaction (Fig. 4.10). As both the rates are increased, equilibrium is attained earlier.

Worked Out Problem 4.7

Consider the diagram below, for the reaction $A_2 + B_2 \rightleftharpoons 2AB$.

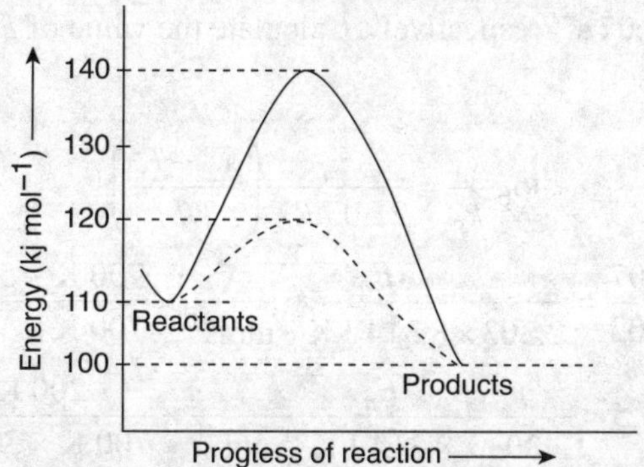

(i) Calculate ΔE for the reaction.

(ii) Calculate the energy of activation for the forward and the backward reactions.

(iii) The dotted curve is the reaction path in the presence of the catalyst. What is the energy of activation for the forward and backward reactions in the presence of the catalyst? What is the lowering in activation energy in the presence of the catalyst?

(iv) Will the catalyst change the extent of the reaction?

Solution

(i) It is clear from the figure that
Energy of reactants (A_2 and B_2) = 110 kJ mol^{-1}
Energy of products (2AB) = 100 kJ mol^{-1}
$\therefore \Delta E = E_p - E_r = 100 - 110 = -10$ kJ mol^{-1}
$\therefore$ The reaction is exothermic.

(ii) Threshold energy = 140 kJ mol^{-1}
Energy of reactants = 110 kJ mol^{-1}
E_a (forward) = $E_t - E_r = 140 - 110 = 30$ kJ mol^{-1}
Energy of products, E_p = 100 kJ mol^{-1}
E_a (backward) = $E_t - E_r = 140 - 100 = 40$ kJ mol^{-1}

(iii) In the presence of the catalyst, the threshold energy becomes 120 kJ
E'_a (forward) = 120 – 110 = 10 kJ mol^{-1}
E'_a (backward) = 120 – 100 = 20 kJ mol^{-1}
Lowering in activation energy
= E_t (without catalyst) – E_t (with catalyst)
= 140 – 120 = 20 kJ mol^{-1}

(iv) There will be no change in the extent of the reaction because the activation energy for the forward reaction and the backward reaction have decreased equally.

4.15 Effect of Temperature of the Rate of Reaction (Effect of Temperature on Rate Constant), Arrhenius Equation

A general approximate rule for the effect of temperature on reaction rates is that the rate of a reaction or rate constant doubles for every 10° rise in temperature. This is also called the *temperature coefficient*. It is the ratio of rate constants of the reaction at two temperatures differing by 10°.

$$\text{Temperature coefficient } (n) = \frac{\text{Rate constant at } T + 10°(308\text{ K})}{\text{Rate constant at } T° \text{ (298 K)}}$$

Explanation: According to the collision theory of chemical reactions, the rate of a reaction depends upon the collision frequency (Z) and the fraction of the effective collisions. The increase in the rate of a reaction with temperature is brought about by either of the two or a combination of both factors.

(i) Increase in collision frequency: With an increase in temperature, the average kinetic energy of the molecules increases and this leads to an increase in number of collisions per unit time (Z).

(ii) Effective collisions: All the molecules in a substance do not possess the same kinetic energy. This is due to collisions between the moving molecules so that their energies are transferred from one molecule to another. Thus, there is a distribution of kinetic energies among reacting molecules (Fig. 4.11).

According to Maxwell's distribution of energies, at a particular temperature T, all the reacting molecules do not have the same kinetic energy (Fig. 4.11). The fraction of molecules having a particular kinetic energy at a particular temperature remains constant. If the point a represents the threshold energy, the shaded area *abcd* represents the fraction of molecules having an energy greater than the threshold value.

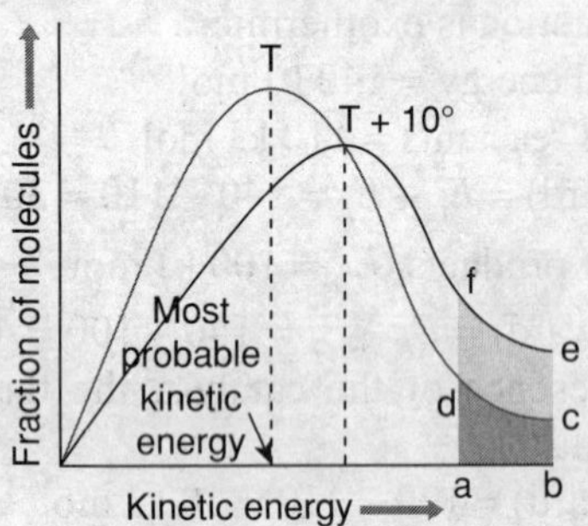

Fig. 4.11 Distribution of energy at temperatures T and $T + 10$°K

When the temperature is increased to $T + 10°$, the curve shifts as seen in Fig. 4.11. The area *abcd* represents the fraction of molecules having a kinetic energy greater than the threshold value and the area becomes nearly. Thus, the increase in the rate of reaction with an increase in temperature is mainly due to an increase in the number of *effective collisions*.

4.15.1 Arrhenius Equation

Arrhenius equation, is usually written in the form

$$k = Ae^{-E_a/RT} \tag{4.8}$$

where the *pre-exponential factor A* is a constant and is called the *frequency factor* (because it gives the frequency of binary collisions of the reacting molecules per second per litre), E_a is the *energy of activation*, R is the gas constant and T is the absolute temperature. The two quantities A and E_a are collectively called the *Arrhenius parameters*.

$$\log k = \log A - \frac{E_a}{2.303\ RT} \tag{4.9}$$

Increasing the temperature or decreasing the activation energy will result in an increase in the rate of reaction.

4.15.2 Calculation of Activation Energy

When $\log k$ is plotted against $\frac{1}{T}$, we get a straight line (Fig. 4.12). The intercept of this line is equal to $\log A$ and the slope is equal to $\frac{E_a}{2.030\ R}$.

Therefore, Slope $= -\frac{E_a}{2.030\ R}$

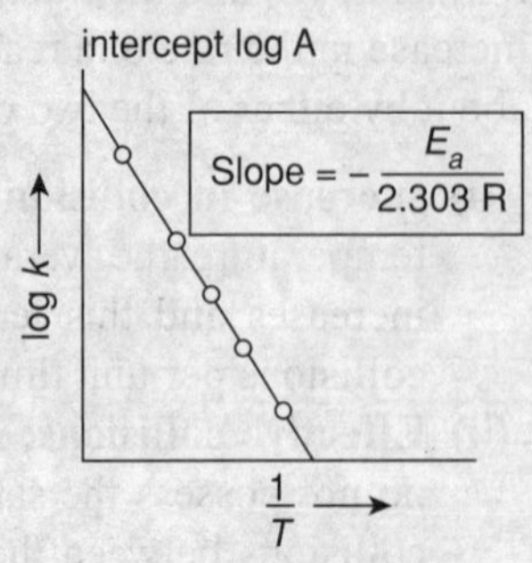

Fig. 4.12 Plot of log k versus $1/T$ to calculate activation energy

Knowing the value of the slope and the gas constant R, the activation energy can be calculated as

$$E_a = -2.303\ R \times \text{Slope}$$

If the value of the rate constant at temperature T_1 and T_2 are k_1 and k_2 respectively, then we have

or $$\log \frac{k_2}{k_1} = \frac{E_a}{2.303\ R}\left[\frac{T_2 - T_1}{T_1 T_2}\right] \tag{4.10}$$

Knowing the rate constant at any one temperature, its value at another temperature can be calculated provided the value of E_a is known for that reaction.

Worked Out Problem 4.8

The rate of a particular reaction doubles when the temperature changes from 27°C to 37°C. Calculate the energy of activation of such a reaction.

Solution

We are given that when $E_a = 27°\text{C} = 300\text{K},\ k_1 = k\,(\text{say})$.
When $T_2 = 37°\text{C} = 310\ \text{K},\ k_2 = 2k$

Substituting these values in the equation:

$$\log \frac{k_1}{k_2} = \frac{E_a}{2.303\ R}\left(\frac{T_2 - T_1}{T_1 T_2}\right)$$

we get, $$\frac{2k}{k} = \frac{E_a}{2.303 \times 8.314\ \text{J K}^{-1}\ \text{mol}^{-1}} \times \frac{310\ \text{K} - 300\ \text{K}}{300\ \text{K} \times 310\ \text{K}}$$

or $$\log 2 = \frac{E_a}{2.303 \times 8.314} \times \frac{10}{300 \times 310 (\text{J mol}^{-1})}$$

or $$\log 2 = \frac{E_a}{2.303 \times 8.314} \times \frac{10}{300 \times 310 (\text{J mol}^{-1})}$$

This on solving gives $E_a = 53598.6\ \text{J mol}^{-1} = 53.6\ \text{kJ mol}^{-1}$

Worked Out Problem 4.9

The rate constants of a reaction at 500 K and 700 K are 0.02 s^{-1} and 0.07 s^{-1} respectively. Calculate the value of E_a and A.

Solution

$$\log \frac{k_2}{k_1} = \frac{E_a}{2.303\ RT}\left(\frac{T_2 - T_1}{T_1 T_2}\right)$$

$$\log \frac{0.07}{0.02} = \frac{E_a}{2.303 \times 8.314\ \text{J K}^{-1}\text{mol}^{-1}} \times \frac{700\ \text{K} - 500\ \text{K}}{700\ \text{K} \times 500\ \text{K}}$$

$$\log 3.5 = \frac{E_a}{2.303 \times 8.314\ \text{J K}^{-1}\text{mol}^{-1}} \times \frac{200\ \text{K}}{700\ \text{K} \times 500\ \text{K}}$$

or $$E_a = \frac{0.5441 \times 2.303 \times 8.314 \times 700 \times 500}{200}\ \text{J mol}^{-1}$$

$$= 18231.4\ \text{J mol}^{-1} = 18.23\ \text{kJ mol}^{-1}$$

Further, $$\log k = -\frac{E_a}{2.303\ R} + \log A$$

or $$\log A - \log k = \frac{E_a}{2.303\ RT}$$

Substituting $T = 500$ K, $k = 0.02\ s^{-1}$, we get

$$\log A = \log 0.02 + \frac{18231.4\ J\ mol^{-1}}{2.303 \times 8.314\ J\ K^{-1}\ mol^{-1} \times 500\ K}$$

$$= -\log 50 + 12.4095 = -1.699 + 1.904 = 0.205$$

$$A = \text{Antilog}\ (0.205) = 1.603$$

Exercises

OBJECTIVE QUESTIONS

Rate of a Chemical Reaction

1. In the reaction, $A + 2B \rightarrow C + 2D$, the initial rate $d[A]dt$ at $t = 0$ was found to be $2.6 \times 10^{-2}\ M\ s^{-1}$. What is the value of $-d[B]/dt$ at $t = 0$ in $M\ s^{-1}$?

(a) 2.6×10^{-2} (b) 5.2×10^{-2}
(c) 1.0×10^{-1} (d) 6.5×10^{-3}

2. $3A \rightarrow 2B$, rate of reaction $+\frac{d[B]}{dt}$ is equal to

(a) $-\frac{3}{2}\frac{d[A]}{dt}$ (b) $-\frac{2}{3}\frac{d[A]}{dt}$
(c) $-\frac{1}{3}\frac{d[A]}{dt}$ (d) $+2\frac{d[A]}{dt}$

3. For the reaction $2A + B \rightarrow 3C + D$

Which of the following does not express the reaction rate?

(a) $\frac{d[D]}{dt}$ (b) $-\frac{d[A]}{2dt}$ (c) $-\frac{d[C]}{3dt}$ (d) $-\frac{d[B]}{dt}$

4. Consider the reaction

$N_2(g) + 3H_2(g) \rightarrow 2NH_3(g)$

The equality relationship between $\frac{d[NH_3]}{dt}$ and $\frac{d[H_2]}{dt}$ is

(a) $+\frac{d[NH_3]}{dt} = -\frac{3}{2}\frac{d[H_2]}{dt}$

(b) $\frac{d[NH_3]}{dt} = -\frac{d[H_2]}{dt}$

(c) $\frac{d[NH_3]}{dt} = -\frac{1}{3}\frac{d[H_2]}{dt}$

(d) $+\frac{d[NH_3]}{dt} = -\frac{2}{3}\frac{d[H_2]}{dt}$

5. For the reaction, $2N_2O_5 \rightarrow 4NO_2 + O_2$, the rate of the reaction is

(a) $\frac{1}{2}\frac{d}{dt}[N_2O_5]$ (b) $2\frac{d}{dt}[N_2O_5]$

(c) $\frac{1}{4}\frac{d}{dt}[NO_2]$ (d) $4\frac{d}{dt}[NO_2]$

6. For the reaction $2A + B \rightarrow C + D$, $-\frac{d[A]}{dt} = k = [A]^2[B]$. The expression for $-d[B]/dt$ will be

(a) $k[A]^2[B]$ (b) $2k[A]^2[B]$
(c) $k[2A]^2[B]$ (d) $\frac{1}{2}k[A]^2[B]$

7. For the reaction $2N_2O_5(g) \rightarrow 4NO_2(g) + O_2(g)$

$$\text{Rate} = -\frac{d[N_2O_5]}{dt} = k[N_2O_5]$$

For the reaction at the same temperature

$N_2O_5(g) \rightarrow 2NO_2(g) + \frac{1}{2}O_2(g)$

$$\text{Rate} = -\frac{d[N_2O_5]}{dt} = -k'[N_2O_5]$$

Then

(a) $k = k'$ (b) $k = 2k$
(c) $k' = 2k$ (d) no comparison is possible

8. Consider the reaction: $2NO_2(g) \rightarrow 2NO(g) + O_2(g)$. In the figure below, identify the curves, X, Y and Z associated with the three species in the reaction.

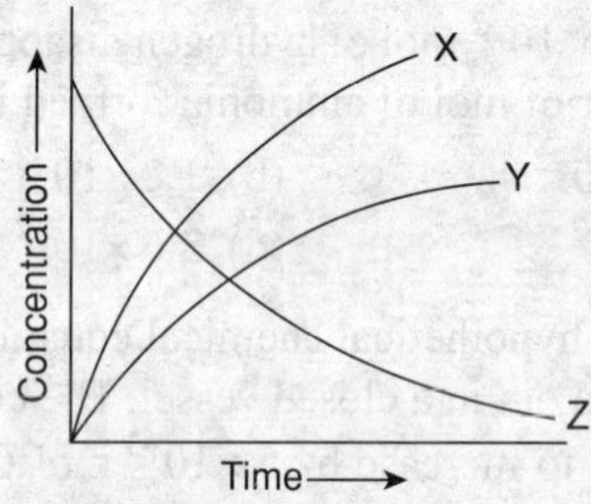

(a) $X = NO, Y = O_2, Z = NO_2$
(b) $X = O_2, Y = NO, Z = NO_2$
(c) $X = NO_2, Y = NO, Z = O_2$
(d) $X = O_2, Y = NO_2, Z = NO$

9. During the decomposition of H_2O_2 to give oxygen, 48 g of O_2 is formed per minute at a certain point of time. The rate of formation of water at this point is

(a) $0.75\ mol\ min^{-1}$ (b) $1.5\ mol\ min^{-1}$
(c) $2.25\ mol\ min^{-1}$ (d) $3.0\ mol\ min^{-1}$

10. For the reaction, $Cl_2 + 2I^- \rightarrow 2Cl^-$, the initial concentration of I^- was $0.20\ mol\ L^{-1}$ and the concentration after 20 min was $0.18\ mol\ L^{-1}$. Then, the rate of formation of I_2 in $mol\ L^{-1}\ min^{-1}$ would be

(a) 1×10^{-3} (b) 5×10^{-4} (c) 1×10^{-4} (d) 5×10^{-3}

11. In the reaction,

$BrO_3^-(aq) + 5Br^-(aq) + 6H^+ \rightarrow 3Br_2(l) + 3H_2O(l)$,

the rate of appearance of bromine (Br_2) is related to the rate of disappearance of bromide ions as follows:

(a) $\frac{d[Br_2]}{dt} = -\frac{5}{3}\frac{-[Br^-]}{dt}$ (b) $\frac{d[Br_2]}{dt} = \frac{5}{3}\frac{-[Br^-]}{dt}$

(c) $\frac{d[Br_2]}{dt} = \frac{3}{5}\frac{-[Br^-]}{dt}$ (d) $\frac{d[Br_2]}{dt} = -\frac{3}{5}\frac{-[Br^-]}{dt}$

12. For the reaction $N_2O_5(g) \rightarrow 2NO_2(g) + \frac{1}{2}O_2(g)$, the value of rate of disappearance of N_2O_5 is given as 6.25×10^{-3} mol L^{-1} s^{-1}. The rate of formation of NO_2 and O_2 is given respectively as

(a) 1.25×10^{-2} mol $L^{-1}s^{-1}$ and 6.25×10^{-3} mol $L^{-1}s^{-1}$
(b) 6.25×10^{-3} mol $L^{-1}s^{-1}$ and 6.25×10^{-3} mol $L^{-1}s^{-1}$
(c) 1.25×10^{-2} mol $L^{-1}s^{-1}$ and 3.125×10^{-3} mol $L^{-1}s^{-1}$
(d) 6.25×10^{-3} mol $L^{-1}s^{-1}$ and 3.125×10^{-3} mol $L^{-1}s^{-1}$

13. The decomposition of N_2O_5 in CCl_4 at 318 K is studied by monitoring the concentration of N_2O_5 in the solution. Initially, the concentration of N_2O_5 is 2.4 mol L^{-1} and after 200 minutes, it is reduced to 2.00 mol L^{-1}. What is the rate of production of NO_2 during this period in mol L^{-1} min^{-1}?

(a) 4×10^{-3} (b) 2×10^{-3} (c) 1×10^{-3}
(d) 2×10^{-4} (e) 5×10^{-3}

14. In the synthesis of ammonia from nitrogen and hydrogen gases, if 6×10^{-2} mol of hydrogen disappears in 10 min, the number of mol of ammonia formed in 0.3 min is

(a) 1.8×10^{-2} (b) 1.2×10^{-3}
(c) 4×10^{-2} (d) 3.6×10^{-2}

15. A gaseous hypothetical chemical equation $2A \rightleftharpoons 4B + C$ is carried out in a closed vessel. The concentration of B is found to increase by 5×10^{-3} mol L^{-1} in 10 s. The rate of appearance of B is

(a) 5×10^{-4} mol $L^{-1}s^{-1}$ (b) 5×10^{-5} mol $L^{-1}s^{-1}$
(c) 6×10^{-5} mol $L^{-1}s^{-1}$ (d) 4×10^{-4} mol $L^{-1}s^{-1}$

16. The rate law for the reaction
$RCl + NaOH(aq) \rightarrow ROH + NaCl$ is given by Rate = k[RCl]. The rate of the reaction will be

(a) doubled on doubling the concentration of sodium hydroxide
(b) halved on reducing the concentration of alkyl halide to one half
(c) decreased on increasing the temperature of the reaction
(d) unaffected by increasing the temperature of the reaction

17. Hydrogenation of vegetable ghee at 25°C reduces the pressure of H_2 from 3 atm to 1.2 atm in 50 min. The rate of the reaction in terms of molarity per second is

(a) 1.09×10^{-6} (b) 1.09×10^{-5}
(c) 1.09×10^{-7} (d) 1.09×10^{-9}

18. For the reaction A + B → C + D, the variation of the concentration of the product with time is given by the curve

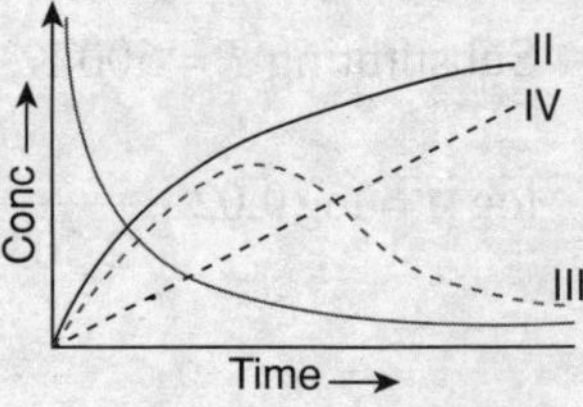

(a) I (b) II
(c) III (d) IV

19. The half-life for N_2O_5 decomposition ______ temperature.

(a) is independent of
(b) increases with an increase in
(c) decreases with an increase in
(d) is dependent on

20. For the reaction $N_2 + 3H_2 \rightarrow 2NH_3$,
if $\frac{d[NH_3]}{dt} = 2.4 \times 10^{-4}$ mol $L^{-1}s^{-1}$
the value of $\frac{d[H_2]}{dt}$ would be

(a) 4×10^{-4} mol L^{-1} s^{-1} (b) 6×10^{-4} mol L^{-1} s^{-1}
(c) 1×10^{-4} mol L^{-1} s^{-1} (d) 3×10^{-4} mol L^{-1} s^{-1}

21. The rate of a reaction is expressed in different ways as follows:

$$+\frac{1}{2}\frac{d[C]}{dt} = -\frac{1}{3}\frac{d[D]}{dt} = +\frac{1}{4}\frac{d[A]}{dt} = -\frac{d[B]}{dt}$$

The reaction is

(a) $4A + B \rightarrow 2C + 3D$ (b) $B + 3D \rightarrow 4A + 2C$
(c) $A + B \rightarrow C + D$ (d) $B + D \rightarrow A + C$

Factors Influencing Rate of a Reaction, Rate Law and Order of a Reaction

22. Which of the following is true for the order of a reaction?

(a) It is equal to the sum of exponents of the molar concentrations of the reactants in the rate equation.
(b) It is always a whole number.
(c) It is never zero.
(d) It can be determined theoretically.

23. Which one of the following statements is incorrect?

(a) The rate law expression cannot be written from the stoichiometric equation.
(b) Law of mass action expression can be written from the balanced equation.
(c) Specific reaction rate of a reaction is constant at constant temperature.
(d) The rate of reaction and rate constant have the same units.

24. If the rate equation for a reaction is: rate $k[A][B]^{1/2}$, the order of the reaction is

(a) 0.5 (b) 1 (c) 1.5 (d) 2

25. The given reaction
$2FeCl_3 + SnCl_2 \rightarrow 2FeCl_2 + SnCl_4$
is an example of
(a) first order reaction (b) second order reaction
(c) third order reaction (d) none of these

26. Which of the following is a first order reaction?
(a) $2H_2O_2(aq) \xrightarrow{Pt} 2H_2O + O_2(g)$
(b) $2HI \rightarrow H_2 + I_2$
(c) $2NO_2 \rightarrow 2NO + O_2$
(d) $2NO + O_2 \rightarrow 2NO_2$

27. An example of a zero order reaction is
(a) acid hydrolysis of methyl acetate
(b) saponification of an ester
(c) decomposition of HI on the surface of gold at high temperature
(d) decomposition of H_2O_2

28. The rate law of the reaction $2N_2O_5 \rightarrow 4NO_2 + O_2$ is
(a) $r = k[N_2O_5]$ (b) $r = k[N_2O_5]^2$
(c) $r = [N_2O_5]^5$ (d) $r = k[NO_2]^4[O_2]$

29. For the reaction $H_2 + Cl_2 \xrightarrow{Sunlight} 2HCl$ taking place on water, the order of the reaction is
(a) 1 (b) 2 (c) 3 (d) 0

30. The given reaction $2NO + O_2 \rightarrow 2NO_2$ is an example of
(a) first order reaction (b) second order reaction
(c) third order reaction (d) none of these

31. Which of the following is a reaction of second order?
(a) $CH_3COOC_2H_5 + H_2O \xrightarrow{OH^-} CH_3COH + C_2H_5OH$
(b) $CH_3COOC_2H_5 + H_2O \xrightarrow{H^+} CH_3COOH + C_2H_5OH$
(c) $C_{12}H_{22}O_{11} + H_2O \xrightarrow{H^+} C_6H_{12}O_6 + C_6H_{12}O_6$
(d) $2H_2O_2 \rightarrow 2H_2O + O_2$

32. The rate constant of a reaction is 2.3×10^{-5} L mol^{-1} s^{-1}. The order of the reaction is
(a) zero (b) one (c) two (d) three

33. The decomposition of dimethyl ether leads to the formation of CH_4, H_2 and CO and the reaction rate is given by Rate $= k[P_{CH_3OCH_3}]^{3/2}$. If the pressure is measured in bar and time in minutes, the units of thc rate constant will be
(a) bar$^{1/2}$ min^{-1} (b) bar$^{-1/2}$ min^{-1}
(c) bar min^{-1} (d) bar$^{3/2}$ min^{-1}

34. The rate of the reaction
$Cl_3CCHO + NO \rightarrow CHCl_3 + NO + CO$
is given by the equation,
Rate $= k[Cl_3.CCHO][NO]$
If the concentration is expressed in mol/L, the units of k are
(a) L^2 mol^{-2} s^{-1} (b) mol L^{-1}s^{-1}
(c) L mol^{-1} s^{-1} (d) s^{-1}

35. Decomposition of NH_3 on the surface of platinum has a rate constant of 2.5×10^{-4} mol dm^{-1}s^{-1} at 350 K. The order of the reaction is
(a) 0 (b) 1 (c) 2 (d) 3

36. The unit of the rate constant depends upon
(a) rate of reaction (b) order of reaction
(c) molecularity of reaction
(d) all of the above

37. Find the unit of the rate constant of a reaction represented with a rate equation, rate $= k[A]^{1/2}[B]^{3/2}$
(a) mol^{-1} L s^{-1} (b) s^{-1} (c) mol L^{-1} s^{-1}
(d) mol^{-1} L^{-1} s^{-1} (e) mol^{-1} L^{-1} s^{-1}

38. The rate constant of nth order has units
(a) time^{1-n} mol^{1-n} s^{-1} (b) mol^{1-n} time^{1-n} s
(c) mol$^{1-n^2}$ L$^{n^2}$ s^{-1} (d) mol^{1-n} L^{n-1} s^{-1}

39. The rate of the reaction $2NO + Cl_2 \rightarrow 2NOCl$ is given by the rate equation, rate $= k[NO]^2[Cl_2]$. The value of the rate constant can be increased by
(a) increasing the temperature
(b) increasing the concentration of NO
(c) increasing the concentration of Cl_2
(d) doing all of these

40. The rate constant of a reaction changes when
(a) a catalyst is added
(b) concentrations of the reactants are changed
(c) temperature is changed
(d) both (a) and (c)

41. Rate constant for a reaction $H_2 + I_2 \rightarrow 2HI$ is 49, then rate constant for reaction $2HI \rightarrow H_2 + I_2$ is
(a) 7 (b) 1/49 (c) 49
(d) 21 (e) 63

42. For a reaction involving solid, decreasing which of the parametres given below will increase the rate of reaction?
(a) particle size (b) concentration
(c) temperature (d) pressure

43. Which of the following does not affect the rate of reaction?
(a) amounts of reactants taken
(b) physical state of the reactants
(c) ΔH of the reaction
(d) size of the vessel

44. The reaction A + B → Products, is first order with respect to A and second order with respect to B. When 1.0 mol each of A and B were taken in a one litre flask, the initial rate of the reaction is 1.0×10^{-2} mol L^{-1} s^{-1}. The rate of the reaction when 50% of the reactants have been converted into products is

(a) 1.0×10^{-3} mol L^{-1} s^{-1}
(b) 0.05×10^{-2} mol L^{-1} s^{-1}
(c) 1.25×10^{-3} mol L^{-1} s^{-1}
(d) 4.0×10^{-2} mol L^{-1} s^{-1}
(e) 2.0×10^{-3} mol L^{-1} s^{-1}

45. In the reaction 2A + B → A_2, if the concentration of A is double and that of B is halved, then the rate of reaction will

(a) increase by 4 times (b) decrease by 2 times
(c) increase by 2 times (d) remain the same

46. The experimental rate law for the reaction 2A + 2B → Product, is $V \propto C_A C_B^{1/2}$. If the concentrations of both A and B are doubled, the rate of reaction increases by a factor of

(a) $\sqrt{2}$ (b) 2 (c) $2\sqrt{2}$ (d) 4

47. For the reaction 2A + B → A_2B, rate $= k[A][B]^2$, $k = 2.0 \times 10^{-6}$ mol^{-2}L^{2}s^{-1} . The reaction was started with [A] = 0.1 mol L^{-1} and [B] = 0.2 mol L^{-1}. The rate of reaction when [A] is reduced to 0.06 mol L^{-1} will be

(a) 3.89×10^{-9} mol L^{-1} s^{-1}
(b) 4.8×10^{-9} mol L^{-1} s^{-1}
(c) 2.59×10^{-9} mol L^{-1} s^{-1}
(d) 3.07×10^{-9} mol L^{-1} s^{-1}

48. In a second order reaction, first order in each reactant A and B, which one of the following reactant mixtures will provide the highest initial rate?

(a) 0.1 mol of A and 0.1 mol of B in 0.1 litre solvent
(b) 0.2 mol of A and 0.2 mol of B in 0.1 litre solvent
(c) 1.0 mol of A and 1.0 mol of B in 1 litre solvent
(d) 0.1 mol of A and 0.1 mol of B in 0.2 litre solvent

49. One dm^3 of 2 M ethanoic acid is mixed with one dm^3 of 3 M ethanol to form an ester

$CH_3COOH + C_2H_5OH \rightarrow CH_3COOC_2H_5 + H_2O$

The decrease in the initial rate if each solution is diluted with an equal volume of water would be

(a) 0.25 times (b) 0.5 times
(c) 2 times (d) 4 times

50. The reaction $2NO(g) + O_2(g) \rightleftharpoons 2NO_2(g)$ is of first order. If the volume of the reaction vessel is reduced to 1/3, the rate of the reaction would be

(a) $\frac{1}{2}$ times (b) $\frac{2}{3}$ times
(c) 3 times (d) 6 times

51. On increasing the pressure three fold, the rate of the reaction of $2H_2S + O_2 \rightarrow$ Products, would increase

(a) 3 times (b) 9 times
(c) 12 times (d) 27 times

52. In the reaction 2A + B → Products, the order with respect to A is found to be 1 and with respect to B equal to 2. If the concentration of A is doubled and that of B is halved, the rate of reaction will be

(a) doubled (b) halved
(c) remain unaffected (d) four times

53. $3\,BrO^- \rightarrow BrO_3^- + 2\,Br^-$

If $-\frac{d[BrO^-]}{dt} = k_1[BrO^-]^2$

$\frac{d[BrO_3^-]}{dt} = k_2[BrO^-]^2, \frac{d[BrO^-]}{dt} = k_3[BrO^-]^2$

the correct relation between them is

(a) $3k_1 = k_2 = 2k_3$ (b) $k_1 = 3k_2 = 1.5k_3$
(c) $k_1 = k_2 = k_3$ (d) $2k_1 = 3k_2 = k_3$

54. A substance undergoes first order decomposition. The decomposition follows two parallel first order reactions as

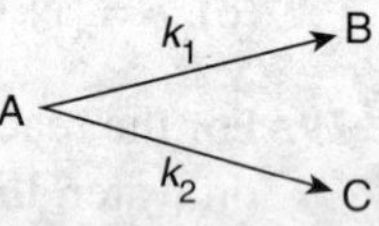

$k_1 = 1.26 \times 10^{-4}\,s^{-1}$ $k_2 = 3.8 \times 10^{-5}\,s^{-1}$

The percentage distribution of B and C are

(a) 75% B and 25% C (b) 80% B and 20% C
(c) 60% B and 40% C (d) 76.83% B and 23.17% C

Molecularity and Mechanism of a Reaction

55. A reaction involving two different reactants can never be a/an

(a) bimolecular reaction (b) second order reaction
(c) first order reaction (d) unimolecular reaction

56. The reaction of hydrogen and iodine monochloride is given as

$H_2(g) + 2ICl(g) \rightarrow 2HCl(g) + I_2(g)$

This reaction is of first order with respect to $H_2(g)$ and ICl(g). The following mechanisms were proposed:

Mechanism A: $H_2(g) + 2ICl(g) \rightarrow 2HCl(g) + I_2(g)$

Mechanism B: $H_2(g) + ICl(g) \rightarrow HCl(g) + HI(g)$; slow
$HI(g) + ICl(g) \rightarrow HCl(g) + I_2(g)$; fast

Which of the above mechanism(s) can be consistent with the given information about the reaction?

(a) A only (b) B only
(c) A and B both (d) neither A nor B

57. Consider the reaction:

$Cl_2(aq) + H_2S(aq) \rightarrow S(s) + 2H^+(aq) + 2\,Cl^-(aq)$

The rate equation for this reaction is rate = $k\,[Cl_2]\,[H_2S]$

Which of these mechanisms is/are consistent with this rate equation?

A. $Cl_2 + H_2S \rightarrow H^+ + Cl^- + Cl^+ + HS^-$ (slow)
$Cl^+ + HS^- \rightarrow H^+ + Cl^- + S$ (fast)

B. $H_2S \rightleftharpoons H^+ + HS^-$ (fast equilibrium)
$Cl_2 + HS^- \rightarrow 2\ Cl^- + H^+ + S$ (slow)

(a) neither A nor B (b) A only
(c) B only (d) both A and B

58. Which one of the following statements is incorrect about the molecularity of a reaction?

(a) The molecularity of a reaction is the number of molecules of the reactants present in the balanced equation.
(b) The molecularity of a reaction is the number of molecules in the slowest step.
(c) The molecularity is always a whole number.
(d) There is no difference between the order and molecularity of a reaction.

59. Which of the following statements is false?

(a) For a first order reaction, the rate of reaction doubles as the concentration of reactant(s) is doubled.
(b) The active mass of 64 g HI present in a two-litre flask is 0.25.
(c) For a zero order reaction, the rate does not change with temperature.
(d) Order and molecularity of even elementary reactions may not be the same.

60. For the reaction 2A + B → D + E, the following mechanism has been proposed:

$A + B \rightarrow C + D$ (slow)
$A + C \rightarrow E$ (fast)
The rate law expression for the reaction is

(a) Rate = $k[A]^2[B]$ (b) Rate = $k[A][B]$
(c) Rate = $k[A][C]$ (d) Rate = $k[A]^2[B][C]$

61. Ethyl acetate is hydrolysed in alkaline medium. Its order of reaction and molecularity are respectively

(a) 1 and 1 (b) 1 and 2 (c) 2 and 1 (d) 2 and 2

62. For a chemical reaction, the ______ can never be a fraction.

(a) order (b) half-life
(c) molccularity (d) rate constant

63. For the reaction: $H_2(g) + Br_2(g) \rightarrow 2HBr(g)$, the experimental data suggest,

Rate = $k\ [H_2]\ [Br_2]^{1/2}$
The molecularity and order of reaction for the reaction are

(a) 2 and 2 respectively (b) 2 and $1\frac{1}{2}$ respectively
(c) $1\frac{1}{2}$ and 2 respectively (d) $1\frac{1}{2}$ and $1\frac{1}{2}$ respectively

64. In a reaction involving the hydrolysis of an organic chloride

$RCl + H_2O \rightarrow ROH + HCl$

(a) molecularity is 2, order of reaction is also 2
(b) molecularity is 2, order of reaction is 1
(c) molecularity is 1, order of reaction is 2
(d) molecularity is 1, order of reaction is also 1

65. A reaction $A_2 + B_2 \rightarrow 2AB$ occurs by the following mechanism

$A_2 \rightarrow A + A$ (slow)
$A + B_2 \rightarrow AB + B$ (fast)
$A + B \rightarrow AB$ (fast)
Its order would be

(a) 3/2 (b) 1 (c) zero (d) 2

66. Mechanism of a hypothetical reaction

$X_2 + Y_2 \rightleftharpoons 2XY$ is given below.
(i) $X_2 \rightarrow X + X$ (fast)
(ii) $X + Y_2 \rightleftharpoons XY + Y$ (slow)
(iii) $X + Y \rightarrow XY$ (fast)
The overall order of the reaction will be

(a) 1 (b) 2 (c) 0 (d) 1.5

67. The reaction follows the mechanism

$A + B \underset{k_{-1}}{\overset{k_1}{\rightleftharpoons}} AB$ (fast)

$AB + B \xrightarrow{k_2} A + B_2$ (slow)

then the rate law is

(a) $r = k\ [A]\ [B]$ (b) $r = k\ [AB]\ [B]$
(c) $r = k\ [A][B]^2$ (d) $r = k[A]^2\ [B]$

68. When a reaction proceeds in a sequence of steps, the overall order of the reaction is determined by the

(a) slowest step
(b) fastest step
(c) sum of rate of all steps
(d) molecularity of all steps

69. The reactions of higher order are rare because

(a) many body collisions involve very high activation energy
(b) many body collisions have a low probability energy
(c) many body collisions are not energetically favoured
(d) many body collisions can take place only in the gaseous phase

70. According to the collision theory of chemical reactions,

(a) a chemical reaction occurs with every molecular collision

(b) the rate is directly proportional to the number of collisions per second
(c) reactions in the gas phase are always of zero order
(d) reaction rates are of the order of molecular speeds

71. The reaction $2N_2O_5 \rightarrow 2N_2O_4 + O_2$ is
(a) bimolecular and second order
(b) unimolecular and first order
(c) bimolecular and first order
(d) bimolecular and zero order

72. The following homogeneous gaseous reactions were experimentally found to be second order overall.
(i) $2NO \rightarrow N_2 + O_2$ (ii) $3O_2 \rightarrow 2O_3$
(iii) $N_2O_3 \rightarrow NO + NO_2$ (iv) $H_2 + I_2 \rightarrow 2HI$
Which of these are most likely to be elementary reactions that occur in one step?
(a) (iii) only (b) (i) and (iii)
(c) (i) and (iv) (d) (iii) and (iv)

Integrated Rate Equations

73. The $t_{1/2}$ for a zero order reaction at the initial concentration of 6×10^{-3} M is 1 min at 27°C. The rate constant at 27°C in mol dm^{-3} s^{-1} is
(a) 3×10^{-4} (b) 6×10^{-4} (c) 5×10^{-5}
(d) 5×10^{-4} (e) 3×10^{-5}

74. The decomposition of NH_3 on a platinum surface, $2NH_3(g) \xrightarrow{Pt} N_2(g) + 3H_2(g)$, is zero order with $k = 2.5\times10^{-4}$ mol L^{-1} s^{-1}. The rate of production of H_2 will be
(a) 2.5×10^{-4} mol L^{-1}s^{-1} (b) 5.0×10^{-4} mol L^{-1}s^{-1}
(c) 7.5×10^{-4} mol L^{-1}s^{-1} (d) 3.75×10^{-4} mol L^{-1}s^{-1}

75. The rate constant of the reaction $A \rightarrow B$ is 0.6×10^3 mol per litre per second. If the concentration of A is 5 M, then concentration of B after 20 minutes
(a) 0.36 M (b) 0.72 M
(c) 1.08 M (d) 3.60 M

76. During the decomposition of a gas on the surface of a solid catalyst, $A \rightarrow$ Products, which is a zero order reaction, the initial pressure of 200 atm of A is reduced to 100 atm in 100 seconds. The rate constant of the reaction is
(a) 1 atm s^{-1} (b) 2 atm s^{-1}
(c) 4 atm s^{-1} (d) 8 atm s^{-1}

77. $2A \rightarrow B + C$ would be a zero order reaction when
(a) the rate of the reaction is proportional to the square of the concentration of A
(b) the rate of the reaction remains the same at any concentration of A
(c) the rate of the reaction remains unchanged at any concentration of B and C
(d) the rate of the reaction is doubled if the concentration of B is doubled

78. If the initial concentration is reduced to 1/4th in a zero order reaction, the time taken for half the reaction to complete
(a) remains the same (b) becomes 4 times
(c) becomes one-fourth (d) doubles

79. In a zero order reaction, if the initial concentration of the reactant is doubled, the time required for half of the reactant to be consumed
(a) increases two-fold (b) increases four-fold
(c) decreases by half (d) does not change

80. A zero order reaction, $A \rightarrow$ Product, with an initial concentration $[A]_0$ has a half-life of 0.2 s. If one starts with the concentration $2\,[A]_0$, then the half-life is
(a) 0.1 s (b) 0.4 s (c) 0.2 s (d) 0.8 s

81. For a zero order reaction with a rate constant k, the slope of the plot of reactant concentration against time is
(a) $k/2.303$ (b) k (c) $-k/2.303$ (d) $-k$

82. The time required for 100% completion of a zero order reaction is
(a) $\frac{a}{k}$ (b) $\frac{a}{2k}$ (c) $\frac{2a}{k}$ (d) $\frac{k}{a}$

83. For a zero order reaction, the plot of concentration of reactant vs time is (intercept refers to concentration axis)
(a) linear with +ve slope and zero intercept
(b) linear with –ve slope and zero intercept
(c) linear with –ve slope and non-zero intercept
(d) linear with +ve slope and non-zero intercept
(e) a curve asymptotic to the concentration axis

84. For the first order reaction, A→ Products, which one of the following is the correct plot of log [A] versus time?

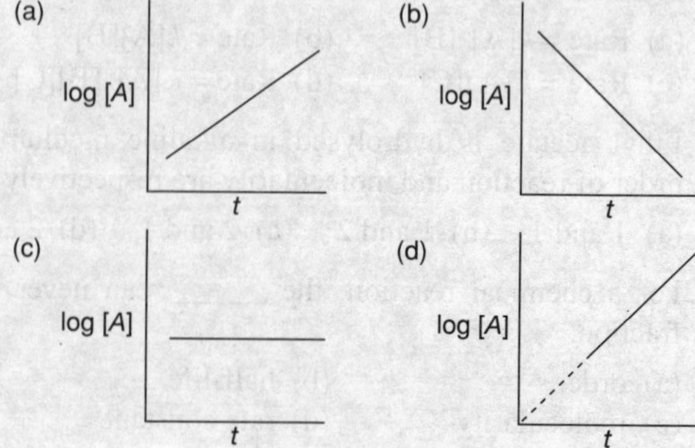

85. The half-life for the reaction $N_2O_5 \rightarrow 2NO_2 + \frac{1}{2}O_2$ is 24 h at 30°C. Starting with 10 g of N_2O_5, how many grams of N_2O_5 will remain after a period of 96 hours?
(a) 1.25 g (b) 0.63 g (c) 1.77 g (d) 0.5 g

86. For a first order reaction, the time required for 99.9% of the reaction to take place is nearly

(a) 10 times that required for half of the reaction
(b) 100 times that required for two-thirds of the reaction
(c) 10 times that required for one-fourth of the reaction
(d) 20 times that require for half of the reaction

87. DDT on exposure to water decomposes. Half-life = 10 years. How much time will it take for its decomposition to 99%?

(a) 50 years (b) 70 years
(c) 500 years (d) 700 years

88. In a first order reaction A → B, if k is rate constant and initial concentration of the reactant A is 0.5 M then the half-life is:

(a) $\frac{\ln 2}{k}$ (b) $\frac{0.693}{0.5\,k}$ (c) $\frac{\log 2}{k}$ (d) $\frac{\log 2}{k\sqrt{0.5}}$

89. In a first order reaction, 80% of the reactant at an instant was reduced to 8% in 4606 s. The rate constant of the reaction is

(a) $2.303 \times 10^{-4}\ s^{-1}$ (b) $4.606 \times 10^{-3}\ s^{-1}$
(c) $5.000 \times 10^{-3}\ s^{-1}$ (d) $5.000 \times 10^{-4}\ s^{-1}$
(e) $4.606 \times 10^{-4}\ s^{-1}$

90. The decomposition of a substance follows first order kinetics. Its concentration is reduced to 1/8th of its initial value in 24 min. The rate constant of the decomposition process is

(a) 1/24 min^{-1} (b) 0.692/24 min^{-1}
(c) $\frac{2.303}{3}\log\left(\frac{1}{8}\right) min^{-1}$ (d) $\frac{2.303}{3}\log\left(\frac{8}{1}\right) min^{-1}$
(e) $\frac{1}{24}\log\left(\frac{8}{1}\right) min^{-1}$

91. Which of the following is not correct for a first order reaction?

(a) $t_{1/2} = \frac{0.693}{k}$ (b) $N = N_0 e^{-kt}$
(c) $\frac{1}{N} - \frac{1}{N_0} = \ln t_{1/2}$ (d) none of these

92. In the first order thermal decomposition of N_2O_5 $[2N_2O_5(g) \rightarrow 2N_2O_4(g) + O_2(g)]$ at constant volume, initial pressure was 0.5 atm and after 100 s, it was 0.512 atm. The rate constant of the reaction is close to (log 1.05 = 0.0216)

(a) $2.5 \times 10^{-4}\ s^{-1}$ (b) $5.0 \times 10^{-4}\ s^{-1}$
(c) $10^{-3}\ s^{-1}$ (d) $10^{-5}\ s^{-1}$

93. The rate constant of a first order reaction is 60 s^{-1}. The time taken for the initial concentration to reduce to 1/16th of its value will be

(a) 0.0462 s (b) 0.462 s (c) 4.62 s (d) 46.2 s

94. For a first order reaction, the time required for 99% completion of a reaction is _____ times the time required for completion of 90%

(a) 2 (b) 3 (c) 4 (d) 10

95. For a first order reaction with half-life of 150 seconds, the time taken for the concentration of the reactant to fall from M/10 to M/100 will be approximately

(a) 1500 s (b) 500 s (c) 900 s (d) 600 s

96. For a first order, t_{av} (average life time), $t_{50\%}$ and $t_{75\%}$ are in the order:

(a) $t_{50} < t_{av} < t_{75}$ (b) $t_{50} < t_{75} < t_{av}$
(c) $t_{av} < t_{50} < t_{75}$ (d) $t_{av} = t_{50} < t_{75}$

97. Sucrose decomposes in acid solution into glucose and fructose according to first order rate law with $t_{1/2}$ = 3.00 hours. The fraction of sucrose that remains after 8 hours is

(a) 0.375 (b) 0.158 (c) 0.425 (d) 0.242

98. For the reaction $2N_2O_5(g) \rightarrow 4NO_2(g) + O_2(g)$, which of the following graphs would yield a straight line?

(a) log $p_{N_2O_5}$ vs time with –ve slope
(b) log $p_{N_2O_5}$ vs time with +ve slope
(c) $(p_{N_2O_5}) - 1$ vs time
(d) $p_{N_2O_5}$ vs time

99. While studying the decomposition of gaseous N_2O_5, it is observed that a plot of logarithm of its partial pressure versus time is linear. The kinetic parameter obtained from this observation is

(a) specific reaction rate (b) reaction rate
(c) energy of activation (d) molecularity

100. The rate of a first order reaction is 1.5×10^{-2} mol $L^{-1}\ min^{-1}$ at 0.5 M concentration of the reactant. The half-life of the reaction is

(a) 0.383 min (b) 23.1 min
(c) 8.73 min (d) 7.53 min

101. A first order reaction has a half-life of 100 seconds. What fraction of the reaction will be completed in 25 seconds?

(a) 25 % (b) 33% (c) 16% (d) 12%

102. A first order reaction is half-completed in 45 minutes. How long does it need for 99.9% of the reaction to be completed?

(a) 20 hours (b) 10 hours
(c) $7\frac{1}{2}$ hours (d) 5 hours

103. A reaction which is first order with respect to reactant A, has a rate constant of 6 min^{-1}. If we start with [A] = 0.5 mol L^{-1}, when would [A] reach the value of 0.05 mol L^{-1}

(a) 0.384 min (b) 0.15 min
(c) 3 min (d) 3.84 min

104. For a first order reaction R $\rightarrow$ P, the rate constant is k. If the initial concentration of R is $[R_0]$, the concentration of R at any time t is given by the equation

(a) $[R_0]e^{kt}$ (b) $(1-e^{-kt})$
(c) $[R_0]e^{-kt}$ (d) $[R_0](1+e^{kt})$

105. In a first order reaction, the molar concentration of a reactant decreases from 0.1 to 0.01 in 100 seconds. The rate constant of the reaction is

(a) 2.303 (b) 0.02303
(c) 0.2303 (d) 0.002303

106. The rate of a first order reaction is 0.04 mol L^{-1} s^{-1} at 10 seconds and 0.03 mol L^{-1} s^{-1} at 20 seconds after initiation of the reaction. The half-life period of the reaction is

(a) 44.1 s (b) 54.1 s (c) 24.1 s (d) 34.1 s

107. The decomposition of PH_3 on tungsten at low pressure is a first order reaction. It is because the

(a) rate is independent of surface coverage
(b) rate of decomposition is very low
(c) rate is proportional to the surface coverage
(d) rate is inversely proportional to the surface coverage

108. A first order reaction has a specific reaction rate of 10^{-2} s^{-1}. How much time will it take for 20 g of the reactant to reduce to 5 g?

(a) 238.6 second (b) 138.6 second
(c) 346.5 second (d) 693.0 second

109. The rate constant for a first order reaction is 60 s^{-1}. How much time will it take to reduce the concentration of the reactant to $1/10^{th}$ of its initial value?

(a) 3.8×10^{-2} (b) 1.26×10^{13} s
(c) 2.01×10^{13} s (d) 1.097×10^{3} s

110. $t_{1/2}$ for a first order reaction is 10 min. Starting with 10 M, the rate after 20 min is

(a) 0.0693 M min^{-1}
(b) 0.0693×5 M min^{-1}
(c) 0.0693×2.5 M min^{-1}
(d) 0.0693×10 M min^{-1}

111. In a first order reaction A $\rightarrow$ B, if k is the rate constant and the initial concentration of the reactant A is 0.5 M then the half-life is

(a) $\dfrac{0.693}{0.5\,k}$ (b) $\dfrac{\log 2}{k}$ (c) $\dfrac{\log 2}{k\sqrt{0.5}}$ (d) $\dfrac{\ln 2}{k}$

112. For a first order reaction, the plot of t against log C gives a straight line with a slope equal to

(a) $\dfrac{-2.303}{k}$ (b) $\dfrac{-k}{2.303}$ (c) $\dfrac{\ln k}{2.303}$ (d) $-k$

113. Mathematical representation for $t_{1/4}$ life of a first order reaction, that is, when $\frac{1}{4}$th of a reaction is over is given by

(a) $t_{1/4} = \dfrac{2.303}{k}\log 4$ (b) $t_{1/4} = \dfrac{2.303}{k}\log 3$

(c) $t_{1/4} = \dfrac{2.303}{k}\log \dfrac{4}{3}$ (d) $t_{1/4} = \dfrac{2.303}{k}\log \dfrac{3}{4}$

114. For a first order reaction A $\rightarrow$ B, the reaction rate at reactant concentration of 0.01 M is found to be 2.0×10^{-5} mol $L^{-1}s^{-1}$. The half-life of the reaction is

(a) 300 s (b) 30 s (c) 220 s (d) 347 s

115. The reaction A $\rightarrow$ B follows first order kinetics. The time taken for 0.8 mol of A to produce 0.6 mol of B is 1 hour. What is the time taken for conversion of 0.9 mol of A to produce 0.675 mol of B?

(a) 1 hour (b) 0.5 hour (c) 0.25 hour (d) 2 hour

116. If 60% of a first order reaction was completed in 60 minutes, 50% of the same reaction would be complete in approximately:

(a) 40 min (b) 50 min (c) 45 min (d) 60 min
[log 4 = 0.60, log 5 = 0.69]

117. The figure below depicts the change in the concentration of species A and B for the reaction A $\rightarrow$ B, as a function of time. The point of intersection of the two curves represents

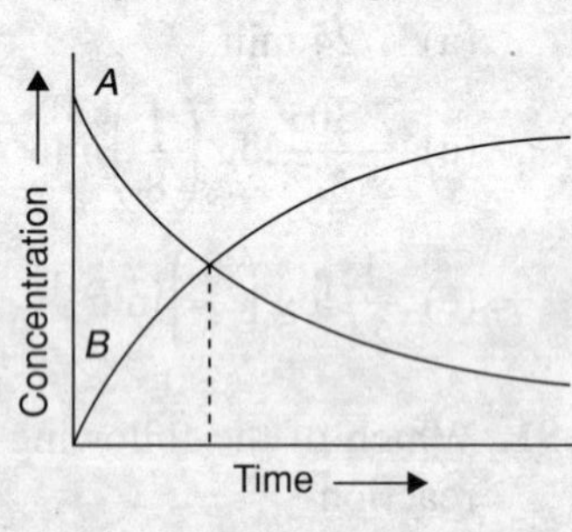

(a) $t_{1/4}$ (b) $t_{1/3}$ (c) $t_{1/2}$
(d) the method cannot be used to predict the fractional life time

118. When the initial concentration of a reactant is doubled in a reaction, its half-life period is not affected. The order of the reaction is

(a) zero (b) first (c) second
(d) more than zero but less than first

119. In the presence of acid, the initial concentration of cane sugar was reduced from 0.2 M to 0.1 M in 5 h and to 0.05 M in 10 h. The reaction must be

(a) zero order (b) first order
(c) second order (d) fractional order

120. Which of the following expressions is correct for second order reactions (C_0 refers to initial concentration of reactant)?
(a) $t_{1/2} \propto C_0$ (b) $t_{1/2} \propto C_0^{-1}$
(c) $t_{1/2} \propto C_0^{-2}$ (d) $t_{1/2} \propto C_0^0$

121. In an attempt to compare the half-lives of two radioactive elements A and B, a scientist set aside 400 g of each. After 3 months, the scientist found 25 g of A and 200 g of B. Which one of the following statements is correct?
(a) The half-life of B is twice that of A
(b) The half-life of B is four times that of A
(c) The half-life of A is twice that of B
(d) The half-life of A is four times that of B
(e) The half-life of B is eight times that of A

122. If a substance with a half-life of 3 days is checked after 12 days, what amount of substance is left?
(a) 1/4 (b) 1/8 (c) 1/16 (d) 1/32

123. A first order reaction is carried out with an initial concentration of 10 mol per litre and 80% of the reactant changes into the product. Now if the same reaction is carried out with an initial concentration of 5 mol per litre, the percentage of the reactant changing to the product is
(a) 40 (b) 80
(c) 75 (d) cannot be calculated

124. For the reaction A + B → C, it is found that doubling the concentration of A increases the rate by 4 times and doubling the concentration of A doubled the reaction rate. What is the overall order of reaction?
(a) 4 (b) 3/2 (c) 3 (d) 1

125. At 500 K, the half-life period of a gaseous reaction at the initial pressure of 80 kPa, is 350 s. When the pressure is 40 kPa, the half-life period is 175 s. The order of the reaction is
(a) zero (b) one (c) two
(d) three (e) half

126. In the reaction $2NO + Cl_2 \rightarrow 2NOCl$, it has been found that doubling the concentration of both the reactants increases the rate by a factor of eight but doubling the chlorine concentration alone only doubles that rate. Which of the following statements is incorrect?
(a) The reaction is first order in Cl_2.
(b) The reaction is second order in NO.
(c) The overall order of reaction is 2.
(d) The overall order of reaction is 3.

127. The rate of a reaction at different times $\left(-\frac{dx}{dt}\right)$ is found as follows:

Time (in minutes)	Rate (in mol L^{-1} s^{-1})
0	2.80×10^{-2}
10	2.78×10^{-2}
20	2.81×10^{-2}
30	2.79×10^{-2}

The order of the reaction is
(a) zero (b) one
(c) two (d) three

128. A plot of 1/[Z] vs time is a straight line. The order of the reaction is
(a) 1 (b) 2
(c) 3 (d) 0

129. During the kinetic study of the reaction 2A + B → C + D, the following results were obtained

Run	[A] (mol L^{-1})	[B] (mol L^{-1})	Initial rate of formation of D (mol L^{-1} min^{-1})
I	0.1	0.1	6.0×10^{-3}
II	0.3	0.2	7.2×10^{-2}
III	0.3	0.4	2.88×10^{-1}
IV	0.4	0.1	2.40×10^{-2}

Based on the above data, which one of the following is correct?
(a) rate = $k[A][B]^2$ (b) rate = $k[A]^2[B]$
(c) rate = $k[A][B]$ (d) rate = $k[A]^2[B]^2$

130. The rate of a gaseous reaction is halved when the volume of the vessel is doubled. The order of the reaction is
(a) 0 (b) 1 (c) 2 (d) 3

131. The half-life of a reaction is found to be inversely proportional to the cube of the initial concentration. The order of reaction is
(a) 4 (b) 3 (c) 5 (d) 2

132. The initial rates of reaction 3A + 2B + C → Products, at different initial concentrations are given below:

Initial rate, (M s^{-1})	$[A]_0$ (M)	$[B]_0$ (M)	$[C]_0$ (M)
5.0×10^{-3}	0.010	0.005	0.010
5.0×10^{-3}	0.010	0.005	0.015
1.0×10^{-2}	0.010	0.010	0.010
1.25×10^{-3}	0.005	0.005	0.010

The order with respect to the reactants A, B and C are respectively
(a) 3, 2, 0 (b) 3, 2, 1 (c) 2, 1, 0 (d) 2, 2, 1

133. The decomposition of H_2O_2 was studied by titration against $KMnO_4$ solution. It was found that 0.4 mol of

H_2O_2 was reduced to 0.2 mol in 20 minutes, to 0.1 mol in 40 minutes and to 0.05 mol after one hour. The order of the reaction must be

(a) 0 (b) 1 (c) 2 (d) 3

134. For the reaction $aA \rightarrow xP$, when [A] = 2.2 mM, the rate was found to be 2.4 mM s^{-1}. On reducing the concentration of A to half, the rate changes to 0.6 mM s^{-1}. The order of the reaction with respect to A is

(a) 1.5 (b) 2.0 (c) 2.5 (d) 3.0

135. The rate of reaction between two reactants A and B decreases by a factor of 4 if the concentration of reactant B is doubled. The order of this reaction with respect to the reactant B is

(a) 2 (b) –1 (c) 1 (d) –2

136. The rate of the reaction $A + 2B \rightarrow 3C$ gets increased by 72 times when the concentration of A is tripled and that of B is doubled. The orders of the reaction with respect to A and B are ______ and ______ respectively

(a) 1, 2 (b) 2, 3 (c) 3, 2
(d) 2, 2 (e) 2, 1

137. In a reaction between A and B, the initial rate of reaction was measured for different initial concentrations of A and B as given below.:

A (mol L^{-1})	0.20	0.20	0.4
B (mol L^{-1})	0.30	0.10	0.05
r_0 (mol $L^{-1}s^{-1}$)	5.07×10^{-5}	5.07×10^{-5}	7.16×10^{-5}

The overall order of the reaction is

(a) 0.5 (b) 1.0 (c) 1.5 (d) 2.0

138. For the reaction A + B → Products, it is observed that (i) on doubling the initial concentration of A only, the rate of the reaction is doubled and (ii) on doubling the initial concentration of both A and B, there is a change by a factor of 8 in the rate of the reaction.

The rate of this reaction is given by

(a) rate = $k[A][B]^2$ (b) rate = $k[A]^2[B]^2$
(c) rate = $k[A][B]$ (d) rate = $k[A]^2[B]$

139. In the reaction of $aA + bB + cC \rightarrow$ Products,

(i) if the concentration of A is doubled, keeping the concentration of B and C constant, the rate of the reaction becomes double
(ii) if the concentration of B is halved keeping the concentration of A and C constant, the rate of the reaction remains unaffected
(iii) if the concentration of C is made 1.5 times, the rate of the reaction becomes 2.25 times

The order of reaction is

(a) 1 (b) 2.5 (c) 3 (d) 3.5

140. The rate of the reaction between A and B increases by a factor of 100, when the concentration of A is changed from 0.1 mol L^{-1} to 1 mol L^{-1}. The order of reaction with respect to A is

(a) 10 (b) 1 (c) 3 (d) 2

141. For the reaction A → B, the rate of the reaction is quadrupled when the concentration of A is doubled, the rate expression of the reaction is $r = k[A]^n$, when the value of n is

(a) 1 (b) zero (c) 3 (d) 2

142. Diazonium salt decomposes as

$$C_6H_5N_2^+Cl^- \rightarrow C_6H_5Cl + N_2$$

At 0°C, the evolution of N_2 becomes two times faster when the initial concentration of the salt is doubled. Therefore, it is

(a) a first order reaction (b) a second order reaction
(c) independent of the initial concentration of the salt
(d) a zero order reaction

143. The plot of concentration of the reactant versus time for a reaction is a straight line with a negative slope. The reaction follows a

(a) first order the equation
(b) zero order rate equation
(c) second order rate equation
(d) third order rate equation

144. From the data given below for the reaction, A + B → Products

[A]	[B]	Rate
0.35 M	1.28 M	0.032 M s^{-1}
0.35 M	0.64 M	0.008 M s^{-1}
0.70 M	0.64 M	0.016 M s^{-1}

the expression for the rate law is

(a) rate = $k[A]^0[B]$ (b) rate = $k[A][B]$
(c) rate = $k[A]^2[B]$ (d) rate = $k[A][B]^2$

145. In a particular reaction, the time required to complete half the reaction was found to increase 9 times when the initial concentration of the reactants was reduced to one third. What is order of the reaction?

(a) zero (b) first (c) second (d) third

146. The concentrations of the reactant A in the reaction A → B at different times are given below.

Concentration (M)	Time (min)
0.069	0
0.052	17
0.035	34
0.018	51

The rate constant of the reaction according to the correct order of reaction is

(a) 0.001 M min^{-1} (b) 0.001 min^{-1}
(c) 0.001 min M^{-1} (d) 0.001 M^{-1} min^{-1}

147. At 518°C, the rate of decomposition of a sample of gaseous acetaldehyde, initially at a pressure of 363 torr, was 1.00 torr s^{-1} when 5% had reacted and 0.5 torr s^{-1} when 33% had reacted. The order of the reaction is

(a) 2 (b) 3 (c) 1 (d) 0

148. For the reaction $2A + 2B \rightarrow$ Products, the following initial rates were obtained at various initial concentrations.

[A]	[B]	Rate (mol L^{-1} s^{-1})
0.1 M	0.2 M	0.46
0.2 M	0.2 M	1.84
0.2 M	0.1 M	0.92

The order of reaction with respect to A and B respectively are

(a) 1, 1 (b) 1, 2 (c) 2, 1 (d) 2, 2

149. The bromination of acetone that occurs in acid solution is represented by this equation

$CH_3COCH_3(aq) + Br_2(aq) \rightarrow CH_3COCH_2Br(aq) + H^+(aq) + Br^-(aq)$

These kinetic data were obtained for the given reaction concentration. Initial concentrations, M

$[CH_3COCH_3]$	$[Br_2]$	$[H^+]$	Initial rate, disappearance of Br_2 (Ms^{-1})
0.30	0.05	0.05	5.7×10^{-5}
0.30	0.10	0.05	5.7×10^{-5}
0.30	0.10	0.10	1.2×10^{-4}
0.40	0.05	0.20	3.1×10^{-4}

Based on these data, the rate equation is

(a) Rate = k $[CH_3COCH_3]$ $[H^+]$
(b) Rate = k $[CH_3COCH_3]$ $[Br_2]$
(c) Rate = k $[CH_3COCH_3]$ $[Br_2]$ $[H^+]^2$
(d) Rate = k $[CH_3COCH_3]$ $[Br_2]$ $[H^+]$

150. Which among the following plots are linear?

I. $(a-x)$ vs t, for a first order reaction
II. $(a-x)$ vs t, for a zero order reaction
III. $(a-x)$ vs t, for a second order reaction
IV. $\frac{1}{(a-x)}$ vs t, for a second order reaction

Here, $(a-x)$ is the concentration of the reactant remaining after a time t.

(a) I and II (b) I and III
(c) II and III (d) II and IV
(e) I and IV

151. For the reaction $A \rightarrow B$, the rate increases by a factor of 2.25 when the concentration of A is increased by 1.5. What is the order of the reaction?

(a) 3 (b) 0 (c) 2 (d) 1

152. The rate constant (k) for the reaction, $2A + B \rightarrow$ Product, was found to be 2.5×10^{-5} L mol^{-1} s^{-1} after 15 s, 2.60×10^{-5} L mol^{-1} s^{-1} after 30 s and 2.55×10^{-5} L mol^{-1} s^{-1} after 50 s. The order of the reaction is

(a) 2 (b) 3 (c) 0 (d) 1

153. Which of the following reactions ends in finite time?

(a) 0 order (b) 1st order
(c) 2nd order (d) 3rd order

154. For the second order reaction A + B → Products, when a mol of A react with b mol of B, the rate equation is given by

$$k_2 t = \frac{1}{(a-b)} \ln \frac{b(a-x)}{a(b-x)}$$

When $a \gg b$, the rate expression becomes that of

(a) first order (b) zero order
(c) unchanged, second order
(d) third order

155. For a second order reaction, 2A → Products, a plot of log $t_{1/2}$ vs log a (where a is the initial concentration) will give an intercept equal to which of the following?

(a) $1/k$ (b) log (1/2 k)
(c) log (1/k) (d) log k

156. The rate law for the reaction

RCl + NaOH → ROH + NaCl

is given by Rate = k [RCl]. The rate of this reaction

A. is doubled by doubling the concentration of NaOH
B. is halved by reducing the concentration of RCl by one half
C. is increased by increasing the temperature of the reaction
D. is unaffected by a change in temperature

Which is correct?

(a) A and B (b) B and C
(c) C and D (d) B and D

157. Which of the following is not correct?

(a) $t_{1/2} = \frac{0.693}{k}$ (b) $N = N_0 e^{-kt}$

(c) $\frac{1}{N} - \frac{1}{N_0} = \ln t_{1/2}$ (d) none of these

158. The hydrolysis of methyl acetate in alkaline medium

$(CH_3COOCH_3 + OH^- \rightarrow CH_3COO^- + CH_3OH)$

follows the rate law Rate = k [CH_3COOCH_3] [OH^-] The value of k at 298 K is found to be 0.137 L mol^{-1} s^{-1}. Starting with an initial concentration of each reactant as 0.05 M, the time taken for 5% methyl acetate to be hydrolysed (assuming the rate will remain constant during this interval) will be

(a) 7.4 s (b) 74 s
(c) 740 s (d) none of these is correct

159. Which of the following statements is not correct?

(a) In zero order reaction the rate of the reaction remains constant throughout
(b) A second order reaction would become a pseudo first order reaction when one of the reactants is taken in large excess
(c) The value of first order rate constant depends on the units of the concentration terms used
(d) In a first order reaction the plot of log $(a-x)$ *vs* time gives a straight line

160. A graph plotted between log $t_{50\%}$ vs log concentration is a straight line. What conclusion can you draw from this graph?

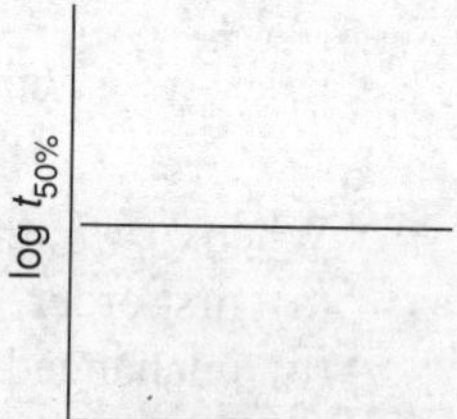

(a) $n = 1; t_{1/2} = \frac{1}{x \times a}$

(b) $n = 2; t_{1/2} = \frac{1}{a}$

(c) $n = 1; t_{1/2} = \frac{0.693}{k}$ (d) none of these.

161. The correct difference between a first and second order reaction is,

(a) the rate of a first order reaction does not depend on reactant concentrations; the rate of a second order reaction does depend on reactant concentrations
(b) the half-life of a first order reaction does not depend on $[A]_0$; the half-life of a second order reaction does depend on $[A]_0$
(c) a first order reaction can be catalysed; a second order reaction cannot be catalysed
(d) the rate of a first order reaction does depend on reactant concentrations; the rate of a second order reaction does not depend on reactant concentrations

162. Under what conditions, is the order of the following reaction, zero?

$2HI(g) \xrightarrow{\Delta,\ \text{catalyst}} H_2(g) + I_2(g)$

(a) at high temperature
(b) at high partial pressure of HI
(c) at low partial pressure of HI
(d) at high partial pressure of H_2
(e) at high partial pressure of I_2

163. The decomposition of ammonia on a tungsten surface at 500 K follows zero order kinetics. The half-life period of this reaction is 45 minutes when the initial pressure is 4 bar. The half-life period (minutes) of the reaction when the initial pressure is 16 bar at the same temperature is

(a) 120 (b) 60 (c) 240
(d) 180 (e) 300

Pseudo-First Order Reaction

164. The reaction $CH_3COOCH_3 + H_2O \rightarrow CH_3COOH + CH_3OH$ is a

(a) bimolecular reaction
(b) first order reaction
(c) pseudounimolecular reaction
(d) zero order reaction

165. Which one of the following is an example of a pseudo first order reaction?

(a) alkali hydrolysis of an ester
(b) acid hydrolysis of sucrose
(c) decomposition of PCl_5
(d) dissociation of HI

166. In the presence of HCl, sucrose gets hydrolysed into glucose and fructose. The concentration of sucrose was found to reduce form 0.4 M to 0.2 M in 1 hour and to 0.1 M in 2 hours. The order of the reaction is

(a) zero (b) one
(c) two (d) none of these

167. The value of the rate constant of a pseudo fist order reaction

(a) depends only on temperature
(b) depends on the concentration of reactants present in small amounts
(c) depends on the concentration of reactants present in excess
(d) is independent of the concentration of the reactants

168. The hydrolysis of ethyl acetate was carried out separately with 0.05 M HCl and 0.05 M H_2SO_4. The rate constants were found to be k_1 and k_2 respectively. Then

(a) $k_1 = k_2$ (b) $k_1 > k_2$ (c) $k_1 < k_2$ (c) $k_2 = 2k_1$

169. In the reaction, $CH_3COOC_2H_5 + H_2O \xrightarrow{OH^-} CH_3COOH + C_2H_5OH$ and $(CH_3)_3CBr + OH^- \rightarrow (CH_3)_3COH + Br^-$, the overall orders of reactions respectively are

(a) 2, 2 (b) 1, 1 (c) 2, 1 (d) 1, 2

170. Acid catalysed hydrolysis of ethyl acetate follows pseudo first order kinetics with respect to the ester. If the reaction is carried out with a large excess of the ester, the order with respect to the ester will be

(a) 1.5 (b) 0 (c) 2 (d) 1

Temperature Dependence of the Rate of a Reaction

171. For an endothermic reaction, where ΔH represents the enthalpy of the reaction in kJ/mol, the minimum value for the energy of activation will be

(a) less than ΔH (b) zero
(c) more than ΔH (d) equal to ΔH

172. The activation energy for a simple chemical reaction $A \rightarrow B$ is E_a in the forward direction. The activation energy for the reverse reaction

(a) is negative of E_a
(b) is always less than E_a
(c) can be less than or more than E_a
(d) is always double E_a

173. If the activation energy for the forward reaction is 150 kJ mol^{-1} and that of the reverse reaction is 260 kJ mol^{-1}, what is the enthalpy change for the reaction?

(a) 410 kJ mol^{-1} (b) –110 kJ mol^{-1}
(c) 110 kJ mol^{-1} (d) –410 kJ mol^{-1}

174. For the decomposition of N_2O_5 at a particular temperature, according to the equations

$$2N_2O_5 \rightarrow 4NO_2 + O_2;\ N_2O_5 \rightarrow 2NO_2 + \frac{1}{2}O_2$$

the activation energies are E_1 and E_2 respectively. Then

(a) $E_1 > E_2$ (b) $E_1 < E_2$ (c) $E_1 = 2E_2$ (d) $E_1 = E_2$

175. An exothermic chemical reaction occurs in two steps as follows:

(i) $A + B \rightarrow X$ (fast); (ii) $X \rightarrow AB$ (slow);

The progress of the reaction can be best represented by

(a)
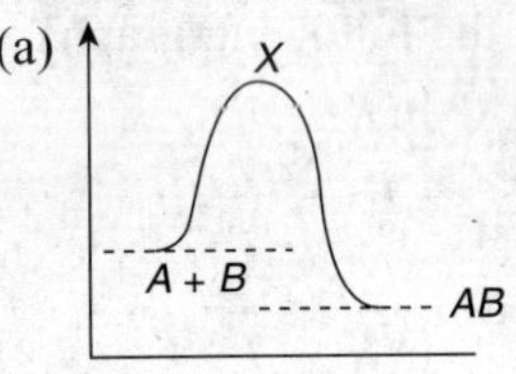

(b)
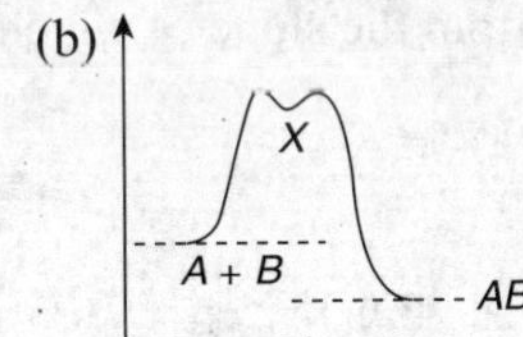

(c)
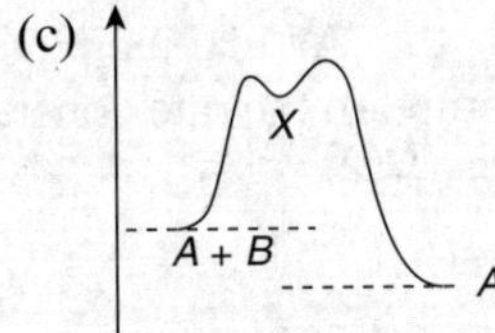

(d) all are correct

176. An endothermic reaction with a high activation energy for the forward reaction is given by

(a)
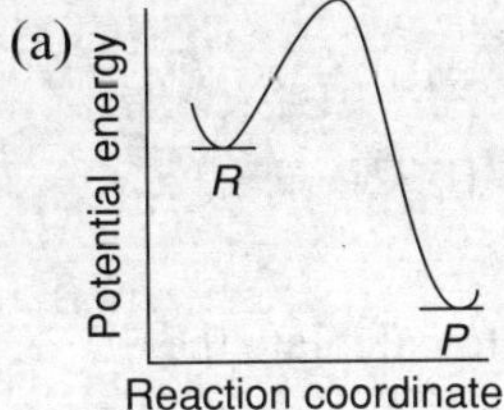

(b)
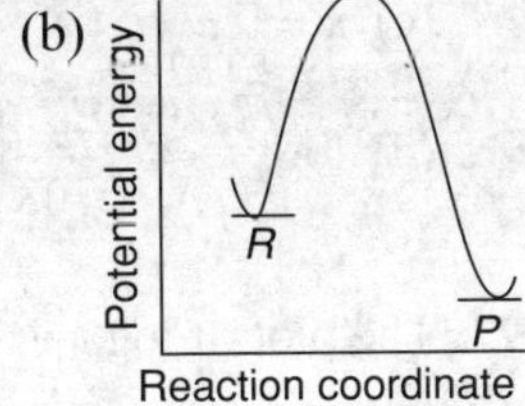

(c)
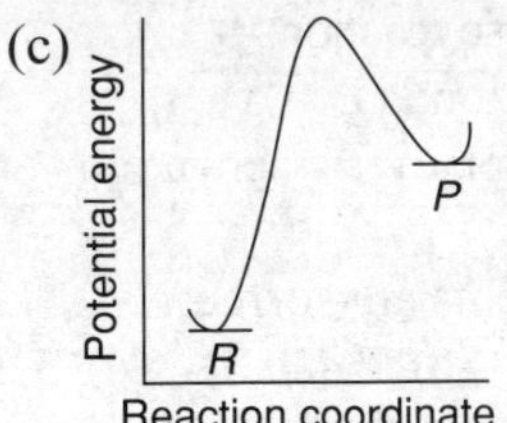

(d)
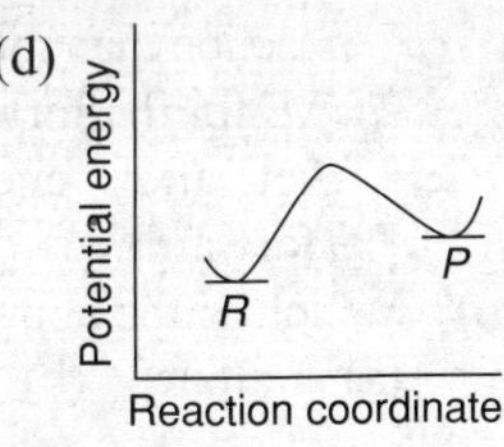

177. The energies of activation for the forward and reverse reactions for $A_2 + B_2 \rightleftharpoons 2AB$ are 180 kJ mol^{-1} and 200 kJ mol^{-1} respectively. The presence of a catalyst lowers the activation energy of both (forward and reverse) reactions by 100 kJ mol^{-1}. The enthalpy change of the reaction ($A_2 + B_2 \rightleftharpoons 2AB$) in the presence of catalyst will be (in kJ mol^{-1})

(a) 20 (b) 300 (c) 120 (d) 280

178. From the given figure, the activation energy for the reverse reaction would be

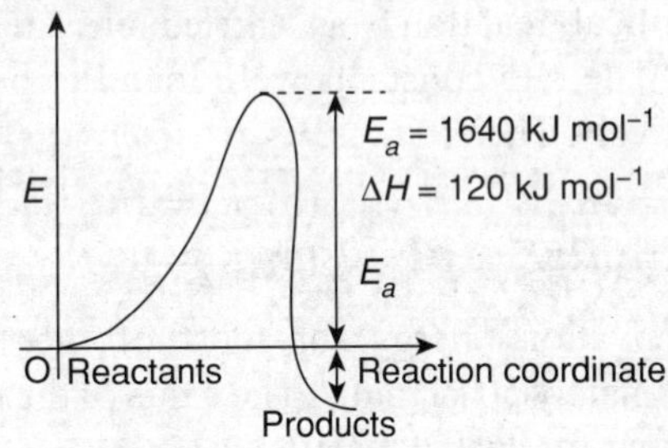

(a) –120 kJ mol^{-1} (b) +152 kJ mol^{-1}
(c) +120 kJ mol^{-1} (d) +1760 kJ mol^{-1}

179. The energy of activation of an exothermic reaction is

(a) zero (b) negative
(c) positive (d) can't be predicted

180. The chemical reactions in which reactants require high amount of activation energy are generally

(a) slow (b) fast
(c) instantaneous (d) spontaneous

181. The potential energy diagram for a reaction $R \rightarrow P$ is given below.

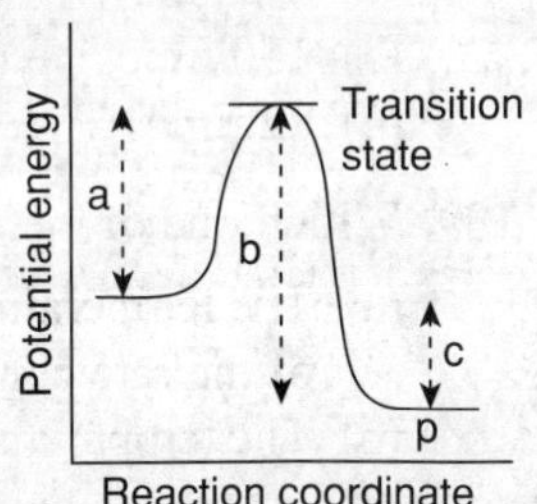

$\Delta H°$ of the reaction corresponds to the energy

(a) a (b) b
(c) c (d) $a + b$

182. Consider the following statements regarding the potential energy diagram for the reaction $A \rightarrow B$ shown below.

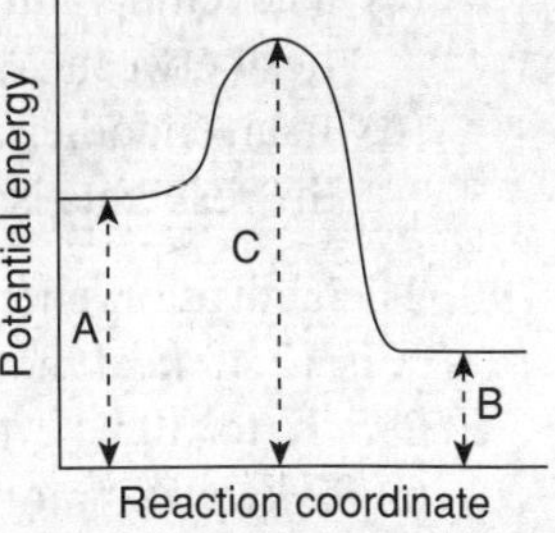

1. The potential energy for the activated complex is greater for the forward

reaction than for the reverse reaction.
2. ΔE for the forward reaction is B – A.
3. Activation energy (reverse) > activation energy (forward).

Which of the above statements are correct?

(a) 1 alone (b) 1 and 2 (c) 2 and 3 (d) 3 alone

183. An endothermic reaction A → B has an activation energy as x kJ/mol. If the energy change of the reaction is y kJ, the activation energy of the reverse reaction is

(a) $-x$ (b) $x-y$ (c) $x+y$ (d) $y-x$

184. A large increase in the rate constant with small rise in temperature for a gaseous reaction is indicative of

(a) a large number of collisions at a higher temperature
(b) a high value of activation energy of the reaction
(c) a high value of the pre-exponential factor
(d) an increase in the average speed of the molecules

185. A chemical reaction was carried out at 300 K and 280 K. The rate constants were found to be K_1 and K_2 respectively. Then

(a) $K_2 = 4K_1$ (b) $K_2 = 2K_1$
(c) $K_2 = 0.25K_1$ (d) $K_2 = 0.5K_1$

186. The activation energy for most of the reactions is approximately 50 kJ mol^{-1}. The value of the temperature coefficient for such a reaction is

(a) approx. 2 (b) approx. 3
(c) < 1 (d) > 4

187. In a zero order reaction, for every 10° rise in temperature, the rate is doubled. If the temperature is increased from 10°C to 100°C, the rate of the reaction will become

(a) 256 times (b) 512 times
(c) 64 times (d) 128 times

188. The temperature coefficient of a reaction is 2. When the temperature is increased from 30°C to 90°C, the rate of reaction is increased by

(a) 150 times (b) 410 times
(c) 72 times (d) 64 times

189. Which one of the following statements is incorrect?

(a) The temperature coefficient of a reaction is the ratio of the rate constants at any two temperatures.
(b) The temperature coefficient of a reaction is the ratio of the rate constants at 298 K and 308 K.
(c) The temperature coefficient of most of the reactions lies between 2 and 3.
(d) In an endothermic reaction, the activation energy of the reactants is more than that of the products.

190. The activation energy for a hypothetical reaction A → X is 12.49 kcal mol^{-1}. If the temperature is raised from 295 K to 305 K, the reaction rate increases by (R = 0.002 kcal K^{-1} mol^{-1})

(a) ≈ 60% (b) ≈ 50%
(c) ≈ 100% (d) unpredictable

191. The rate constant of a chemical reaction at a very high temperature will approach

(a) the Arrhenius frequency factor divided by the ideal gas constant
(b) the activation energy
(c) the Arrhenius frequency factor
(d) the activation energy divided by the ideal gas constant

192. Increasing the temperature increases the rate of reaction but does not increase the

(a) number of collisions
(b) activation energy
(c) average energy of collisions
(d) average velocity of the reactant molecules

193. The rate constant of a first order reaction at 27°C is 10^{-3} min^{-1}. The temperature coefficient of this reaction is 2. What is the rate constant (in min^{-1}) at 17°C for this reaction?

(a) 10^{-3} (b) 5×10^{-4} (c) 2×10^{-3} (d) 10^{-2}

194. For a first order reaction, the plot of log k against $1/T$ is a straight line. The slope of the line is equal to

(a) $-\dfrac{E_a}{R}$ (b) $-\dfrac{2.303}{E_a R}$
(c) $-\dfrac{E_a}{2.303}$ (d) $-\dfrac{E_a}{2.303\,R}$

195. The activation energy of a reaction can be determined from the slope of which of the following graphs?

(a) $\ln K$ vs T (b) $\dfrac{\ln K}{T}$ vs T
(c) $\ln K$ vs $\dfrac{1}{T}$ (d) $\dfrac{T}{\ln K}$ vs $\dfrac{1}{T}$

196. The correct expression for the Arrhenius equation showing the effect of temperature on the rate constant is

(a) $\dfrac{k_2}{k_1} = \dfrac{E_a}{2.303\,R}\left(\dfrac{T_2 - T_1}{T_1 T_2}\right)$
(b) $\ln \dfrac{k_2}{k_1} = \dfrac{E_a}{R}\left(\dfrac{1}{T_1} - \dfrac{1}{T_2}\right)$
(c) $k = Ae^{E_a/RT}$
(d) $\log \dfrac{k_2}{k_1} = \dfrac{E_a}{2.303}\left(\dfrac{T_2 T_1}{T_2 - T_1}\right)$

197. The plot of log k vs $\dfrac{1}{T}$ helps to calculate the

(a) energy of activation
(b) rate constant of the reaction

(c) order of reaction
(d) energy of activation as well as the frequency factor

198. The rate constant of a reaction follows
(a) an exponential increase with increase in temperature
(b) an exponential decrease with increase in temperature
(c) linear increase with increase in temperature
(d) linear decrease with increase in temperature

199. Among the following graphs showing various of rate constants (k) with temperature (T) for a reaction, the one that exhibits Arrhenius behaviour over the entire temperature range is

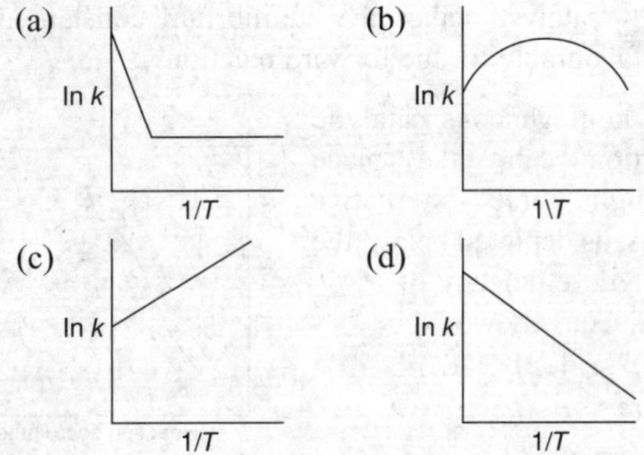

200. In the respect of the equation, $k = Ae^{-E_a/RT}$ in chemical kinetics, which one of the following statements is correct?
(a) k is the equilibrium constant
(b) A is the adsorption factor
(c) E_a is the energy of activation
(d) R is the Rydberg constant

201. In the Arrhenius plot, intercept is equal to
(a) $\frac{-E_a}{R}$ (b) $\ln A$ (c) $\ln K$ (d) $\log_{10} A$

202. Rate of a reaction can be expressed by the Arrhenius equation as:

$$k = Ae^{-E/RT}$$

In this equation, E represents
(a) the energy above which all the colliding molecules will react
(b) the energy below which all the colliding molecules will react
(c) the total energy of the reacting molecules at a temperature, T
(d) the fraction of molecules with an energy greater than the activation energy of the reaction

203. In the Arrhenius equation $K = Ae^{-E_a/RT}$, the quantity $\frac{-E_a}{RT}$ is referred to as
(a) Boltzmann factor (b) frequency factor
(c) activation factor (d) none of these

204. The following equation is the Arrhenius equation, $k = Ae^{-E_a/RT}$, where E_a is the minimum energy the molecules must possess in order to react to form a product, k is the rate constant, A is the frequency factor, R is the gas constant and T is the temperature in kelvin. Under normal circumstances, the Arrhenius plot is obtained by plotting
(a) the logarithm of the inverse of rate constant $1/k$, versus the inverse temperature $1/T$
(b) the logarithm of the rate constant k, versus the temperature T
(c) the logarithm of the rate constant k, versus the inverse temperature $1/T$
(d) the logarithm of the inverse rate constant $1/k$, versus the temperature T

205. What is the activation energy for a reaction if its rate doubles when the temperature is raised from 20°C to 35°C? ($R = 8.314$ J mol^{-1} K^{-1})
(a) 342 kJ mol^{-1} (b) 269 kJ mol^{-1}
(c) 34.7 kJ mol^{-1} (d) 15.1 kJ mol^{-1}

206. The rate constant k of a reaction varies with temperature according to the equation $\log k = \text{constant} - \frac{E_a}{2.303\,R} \times \frac{1}{T}$ where E_a is the energy of activation for the reaction. When a graph is plotted for $\log k$ vs $\frac{1}{T}$, a straight line with a slope –6670 K is obtained. The activation energy for this reaction will be ($R = 8.314$ J K^{-1} mol^{-1})
(a) 122.65 kJ mol^{-1} (b) 127.71 kJ mol^{-1}
(c) 142.34 kJ mol^{-1} (d) 150.00 kJ mol^{-1}

207. The rate constant of a first order reaction becomes six times when the temperature is raised from 350 K to 400 K. Calculate the activation energy of the reaction (R = 8.314 J K^{-1} mol^{-1})
(a) 4.17 k J K^{-1} mol^{-1} (b) 41.7 k J K^{-1} mol^{-1}
(c) 417 k J K^{-1} mol^{-1} (d) 4170 k J K^{-1} mol^{-1}

208. The decomposition of a hydrocarbon follows the equation $k = \left(4.5 \times 10^{11}\ \text{s}^{-1}\right) e^{-28000\,K/T}$. The activation energy of the reaction is approximately
(a) 28 kJ mol^{-1} (b) 56 kJ mol^{-1}
(c) 112 kJ mol^{-1} (d) 232 kJ mol^{-1}

209. The rate constant of a reaction at temperature 200 K is 10 times less than the rate constant at 400 K. What is the activation energy (E_a) of the reaction?
(a) 1842.4 R (b) 921.2 R
(c) 460.6 R (d) 2303.3 R

210. The decomposition of H_2O_2 follows first order kinetics, given by $K = \dfrac{3200}{e^{32/RT}}$. The activation energy of the reaction will be
(a) 2700 cal/mol (b) 2700 kJ/mol
(c) 2800 kJ/mol (c) 32 cal/mol

211. The activation energy of a reaction is zero. The rate constant of the reaction
(a) increases with an increase in temperature
(b) decreases with an increase in temperature
(c) decreases with a decrease in temperature
(d) is nearly independent of temperature

212. The activation energy of a reaction is 58.3 kJ mol^{-1}. The ratio of the rate constant at 305 K and 300 K is about ($R = 8.3$ JK^{-1} mol^{-1})
(a) 1.25 (b) 1.50 (c) 1.75 (d) 2.0

213. The activation energy of a reaction at a given temperature is found to be 2.303 RT J mol^{-1}. The ratio of the rate constant to the Arrhenius factor is
(a) 0.01 (b) 0.1 (c) 0.02 (d) 0.001

214. The Arrhenius plots of two reactions I and II are shown graphically. The graph suggests that

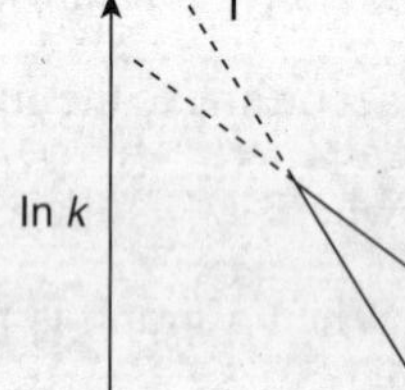

(a) $E_I > E_{II}$ and $A_I > A_{II}$
(b) $E_{II} > E_I$ and $A_{II} > A_I$
(c) $E_I > E_{II}$ and $A_{II} > A_I$
(d) $E_{II} > E_I$ and $A_I > A_{II}$

215. The rate constant of a first order decomposition reaction is described by the Arrhenius equation

$$\log k = 14.34 \times \frac{1.25 \times 10^4}{T}$$

At what temperature will the half-life period be 256 minutes?
(a) 338 K (b) 570 K (c) 490 K (d) 669 K

216. The reactions $2NO + O_2 \rightarrow 2NO_2$

$$2CO + O_2 \rightarrow CO_2$$

look to be identical, yet the first is faster than the second. The reason is that
(a) the first reaction has a lower enthalpy change than the second
(b) the first reaction has a lower internal energy change than the second
(c) the first reaction has a lower activation energy than the second
(d) the first reaction has a higher activation energy than the second

217. A reaction having equal energies of activation for forward and reverse reaction has:
(a) $\Delta S = 0$ (b) $\Delta G = 0$
(c) $\Delta H = 0$ (d) $\Delta H = \Delta G = \Delta S = 0$

Effect of Catalyst on the Rate of Reaction

218. Which of the following statements about a catalyst is true?
(a) A catalyst accelerates the rate of reaction by bringing down the energy of activation.
(b) A catalyst does not participate in the reaction mechanism.
(c) A catalyst makes the reaction more feasible by making ΔG more negative.
(d) A catalyst makes the equilibrium constant more favourable for the forward reaction.

219. If a homogeneous catalytic reaction can take place through three alternative paths, as depicted below, the catalytic efficiency of P, Q, R respectively would be

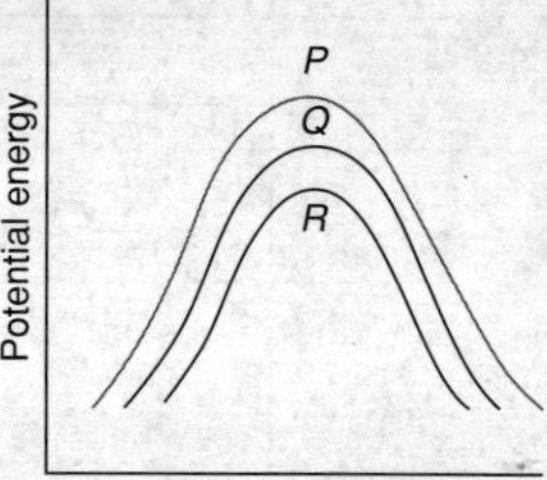

(a) $P > Q > R$\
(b) $Q > P > R$
(c) $P > R > Q$
(d) $R > Q > P$
(e) $P = Q = R$ as the initial and final states are the same

220. Which of the following explains the increases of reaction rate by a catalyst?
(a) A catalyst provides the necessary energy to the colliding molecules to cross the barrier.
(b) A catalyst decreases the rate of the backward reaction so that the rate of the forward reaction increases.
(c) A catalyst decreases the enthalpy change of the reaction.
(d) A catalyst provides an alternative path of lower activation energy.

221. An enzyme-catalysed reaction is faster than a metal-catalysed reaction because
(a) its activation energy is greater
(b) its activation energy is lower
(c) enzymes are present in large amounts
(d) none of the above

Collision Theory of Chemical Reactions; Theory of Absolute Reaction Rates (Transition State Theory)

222. The salient feature of the theory of absolute reaction rates is the
(a) formation of the activated complex
(b) collision of the reactant molecules
(c) matching potential energy of the reactant molecules
(d) decrease of entropy of the reactant molecules

223. Collision theory is most satisfactory for a

(a) first order reaction (b) second order reaction
(c) bimolecular reaction (d) any order reaction

224. Pick the appropriate choice about the collision theory of reaction rates.

I. It explains the effect of temperature on the rate of reaction.
II. It assumes that the reactants must be in the correct orientation to react.
III. It says the rate depends upon the frequency at which reactants collide.
IV. The collisions having energy higher than the threshold value give successful reactions.

The correct points are

(a) I, III, IV (b) II, IV
(c) I, IV (d) I, II, III, IV

Photochemical reactions

225. Which of the following statements is correct about photochemical reactions?

(a) They can take place even in the dark.
(b) They get speeded up at higher temperature.
(c) Their free energy change (ΔG) is positive.
(d) The quantum yield of similar photochemical reactions like photosynthesis of HCl and HBr is the same.

226. An example of a photochemical reaction is

(a) darkening of silver chloride in light
(b) blackening of white lead upon prolonged exposure to air
(c) rusting of iron in moist air
(d) glowing of charcoal

227. H_2 dissociates in the presence of light only when Hg vapours are present. This is an example of

(a) autocatalysis (b) fluorescence
(c) photosensitisation (d) chemiluminescence

Miscellaneous

228. When ethyl acetate was hydrolysed in the presence of 0.1 N HCl, the rate constant was found to be 5.40×10^{-5} s^{-1}. But when 0.1 N H_2SO_4 was used for the hydrolysis, the rate constant was found to be 6.20×10^{-5} s^{-1}. From these values we can say that

(a) H_2SO_4 is stronger than HCl
(b) H_2SO_4 is weaker than HCl
(c) both the acids have equal strength
(d) the data is insufficient to compare the strengths of HCl and H_2SO_4

229. Which of the following is a fast reaction?

(a) $H_2 + Cl_2 \xrightarrow{hv} 2HCl$
(b) $NO_2 + CO \rightarrow NO + CO_2$
(c) $CH_3CHO \rightarrow CH_4 + CO$
(d) $6CO_2 + 6H_2O \xrightarrow{hv} C_6H_{12}O_6 + 6O_2$

230. The hydrolysis of methyl formate in acid solution has the rate expression:

rate = k [$HCOOCH_3$] [H^+]

The raw law contains [H^+] though the balanced equation does not contain [H^+] because

(a) more for convenience to express the rate law
(b) H^+ ion is a catalyst
(c) H^+ is an important constituent of any reaction
(d) all acids contain H^+ ions

231. The following is the correct statement:

(a) Order of a reaction has always an integral value.
(b) Mechanism of a reaction proposed is always final.
(c) Zero order reactions are multi-step reactions.
(d) Order of a reaction can predicted even without knowing the rate law.

232. Consider the following statements:

(i) An increase in the concentration of the reactant increases the rate of a zero order reaction.
(ii) The rate constant k is equal to the collision frequency A if $E_a = 0$.
(iii) The rate constant k is equal to the collision frequency A if $E_a = \infty$.
(iv) ln k vs T is a straight line
(v) ln k vs $1/T$ is a straight line.

The correct statements are:

(a) (i) and (iv) (b) (ii) and (v)
(c) (iii) and (iv) (d) (ii) and (iii)
(e) (i) and (v)

233. Which of the following statements is incorrect?

(a) The catalyst does not affect the equilibrium of a reaction.
(b) The reaction with a higher activation energy has a higher rate constant.
(c) In an exothermic reaction, the activation energy of the reverse reaction is higher than that of the forward reaction.
(d) The half-life period of a first order reaction is independent of the initial concentration.

Final Preparation

234. $SO_2Cl_2 \rightarrow SO_2 + Cl_2$ is a first order gas reaction with $k = 2.2 \times 10^{-5}$ s^{-1} at 320°C. The percentage of SO_2Cl_2 decomposed on heating for 90 minutes is

(a) 1.118 (b) 0.1118 (c) 18.11 (d) 11.18

235. The rate of a first order reaction is 1.5×10^{-2} mol L^{-1} min^{-1} at 0.5 M concentration of the reaction. The half-life of the reaction is

(a) 0.383 min (b) 23.1 min
(c) 8.73 min (d) 7.53 min

236. The reaction X $\rightarrow$ Product follows first order kinetics. In 40 minutes, the concentration of X changes from 0.1 M to 0.025 M, then the rate of the reaction when the concentration of X is 0.01 M is

(a) 1.73×10^{-4} M/min (b) 3.47×10^{-5} M/min
(c) 3.47×10^{-4} M/min (d) 1.73×10^{-5} M/min

237. A substance A decomposes in solution following first order kinetics. Flask I contains 1 L of 1 M solution of A and flask II contains 100 mL of 0.6 M solution. After 8 h, the concentration of A in flask I becomes 0.25 M. What will be the time taken for the concentration of A in flask II to become 0.3 M?

(a) 0.4 h (b) 2.4 h (c) 4.0 h
(d) unpredictable as rate constant is not given

238. For a first order reaction, to obtain a positive slope, we need to plot (where [A] is the concentration of reactant A)

(a) $-\log_{10}[A]$ vs $\log t$ (b) $-\log_e[A]$ vs t
(c) $\log_{10}[A]$ vs $\log t$ (d) $[A]$ vs t

239. T_{50} for a first-order reaction is 10 min. Starting with 10 mol, the rate after 20 min is

(a) 0.0693 mol L^{-1} min^{-1}
(b) 0.0693×2.5 mol L^{-1} min^{-1}
(c) 0.0693×5 mol L^{-1} min^{-1}
(d) 0.0693×10 mol L^{-1} min^{-1}

240. The inactivation of a viral preparation in a chemical bath is found to be a first order reaction. If in the beginning 2.5% of the virus is inactivated per minute, the rate constant of the viral inactivation is

(a) 4.16×10^{-2} s^{-1} (b) 4.16×10^{-3} s^{-1}
(c) 4.16×10^{-4} s^{-1} (d) 4.16×10^{-5} s^{-1}

241. The decomposition of Cl_2O_7 at 400 K in the gas phase is a first order reaction. After 50 seconds at 400 K, the pressure of Cl_2O_7 falls from 0.062 to 0.044 atm. Calculate the pressure of Cl_2O_7 after 100 s of decomposition at this temperature

(a) 0.0112 atm (b) 0.0212 atm
(c) 0.0312 atm (d) 0.0412 atm

242. The rate constant of an isomerisation reaction, A $\rightarrow$ B is 4.5×10^{-3} min^{-1}. If the initial concentration of A is 1 M, the rate of reaction after 1 hour will be

(a) 1.44×10^{-3} M min^{-1} (b) 2.44×10^{-3} M min^{-1}
(c) 3.44×10^{-3} M min^{-1} (d) 4.44×10^{-3} M min^{-1}

243. $A(g) \xrightarrow{\Delta} P(g) + Q(g) + R(g)$, follows first order kinetics with a half-life of 69.3 s at 500°C. Starting from gas A enclosed in container at 500°C and at a pressure of 0.4 atm, the total pressure of the system after 230 s will be

(a) 1.15 atm (b) 1.32 atm
(c) 1.22 atm (d) 1.12 atm

244. For a first order reaction, the time taken to reduce the initial concentration by a factor of $\frac{1}{4}$ is 20 minutes. The time required to reduce initial concentration by a factor of 1/16 is

(a) 20 min (b) 10 min (c) 80 min (d) 40 min

245. The rate constant of a second order reaction, 2A $\rightarrow$ Products, is 10^{-4} lit mol^{-1} min^{-1}. The initial concentration of the reactant is 10^{-2} mol lit^{-1}. What is the half-life (in min)?

(a) 10 (b) 1000 (c) 100 (d) 10^6

246. The half-lives of a first order and zero order reaction are the same. Then, the ratio of the initial rates of the first order reaction that of zero order reaction is

(a) $\frac{1}{0.693}$ (b) 2×0.693 (c) 0.693 (d) $\frac{2}{0.693}$

247. The half-life for the reaction $N_2O_5 \rightarrow 2NO_2 + \frac{1}{2}O_2$ is 24 h at STP. Starting with 10.8 g of N_2O_5, how much oxygen will be obtained after a period of 9.6 h?

(a) 1.5 L (b) 3.36 L (c) 1.05 L (d) 0.07 L

248. A reaction P $\rightarrow$ Q is 25% complete in 25 min, 50% complete in 25 min if [P] is halved, 25% complete in 50 min if [P] is doubled. The order of reaction is

(a) 1 (b) 2 (c) 0 (d) 3

249. A reacts to form P. A plot of the reciprocal of the concentration of A vs time is a straight line. When the initial concentration of A is 1.0×10^{-2} M, its half-life is found to be 20 min. When initial concentration of A is 3.0×10^{-3} M, the half-life will e

(a) 20 min (b) 40 min
(c) 56 min (d) 67 min

250. The rate of reaction between two reactants A and B decreases by a factor of 4, if the concentration of reactant B is doubled. The order of this reaction with respect to reactant B is

(a) –1 (b) –2 (c) 1 (d) 2

251. The following data is obtained during the first order thermal decomposition of

$$2A(g) \rightarrow B(g) + C(s)$$

at constant volume and temperature.

S. no	Time	Total pressure in pascals
1.	At the end of 10 minutes	300
2.	After completion	200

The rate constant in min^{-1} is
(a) 0.0693 (b) 6.93 (c) 0.00693 (d) 69.3

252. For the reaction $N_2O_5(g) \rightarrow 2NO_2(g) + \frac{1}{2}O_2(g)$, a plot of $\ln[N_2O_5]$ versus time is shown in the Fig. The value of the specific rate constant of the reaction is

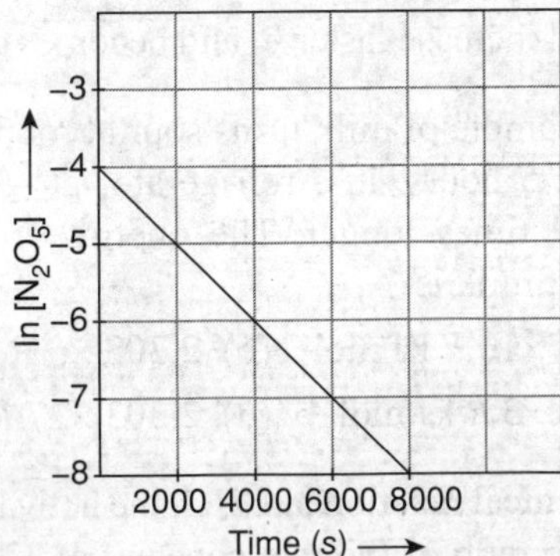

(a) 2×10^{-4} (b) 10^{-5} (c) 5×10^{-4} (d) 10^{-3}

253. In the reversible reaction, $2NO_2 \rightleftharpoons N_2O_4$, the rate of disappearance of NO_2 is equal to

(a) $\frac{2k_1}{k_2}[NO_2]^2$ (b) $2k_1[NO_2]^2 - 2k_2[N_2O_4]$
(c) $2k_1[NO_2]^2 - k_2[N_2O_4]$
(d) $(2k_1 - k_2)[NO_2]$

254. The chemical reaction $2O_3 \rightarrow 3O_2$ proceeds as follows:
$O_3 \rightleftharpoons O_2 + O$ (fast)
$O + O_3 \rightarrow 2O_2$ (slow)
The rate law expression should be
(a) $r = k[O_3]^2$ (b) $r = k[O_3]^2[O_2]^{-1}$
(c) $r = k[O_3][O_2]$ (d) unpredictable

255. For a consecutive reaction $R_1 \xrightarrow{k_1} R_2 \xrightarrow{k_1} R_3$, if the initial concentration of R_1 is 100 M and $k_1 : k_2 = 1 : 0.15$, then value of t_{max} is (Given $k_1 = 4.0\times10^{-2}\ min^{-1}$)
(a) 27.8 min (b) 8.34 min
(c) 55.6 min (d) none of these is correct

256. The correct rate law equation for the reaction
$OCl^- + I^- \xrightarrow{OH^-} OI^- + Cl^-$ is
(a) Rate = $k[OCl^-][I^-]$
(b) Rate = $k[OCl^-][I^-][OH^-]^{-1}$
(c) Rate = $k[OCl^-][I^-][OI^-]^{-1}$
(d) Rate = $k[OCl^-][I^-][Cl^-]^{-1}$

257. The value of the concentration of C after 5 h of reaction (parallel) if the initial concentration of A is 0.25 (M) will be, the parallel path is given as:

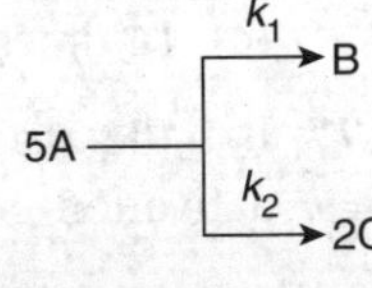

where $k_1 = 1.5\times10^{-5}\ s^{-1}$ and $k_2 = 5 \times10^{-6}\ s^{-1}$
(a) 7.56×10^{-2} M (b) 7.56×10^{-3} M
(c) 0.756 M (d) 7.56×10^{-4} M

258. A first order reaction has $k = 1.5\times10^{-6}$| per second at 200°C. If the reaction in allowed to take place for 10 hours, what percentage of the initial concentration would have changed into the product?
(a) 5.26% (b) 6.26%
(c) 7.26% (d) 8.26%

259. The half-life (T_1) of the first order reaction and half-life (T_2) of the second order reaction are equal. Hence the ratio of the rate at the start of the reaction
(a) 1 (b) 2 (c) 0.693 (d) 1.44

260. What will be the order of the reaction and rate constant for a chemical change having $t_{50\%}$ vs concentration curves as

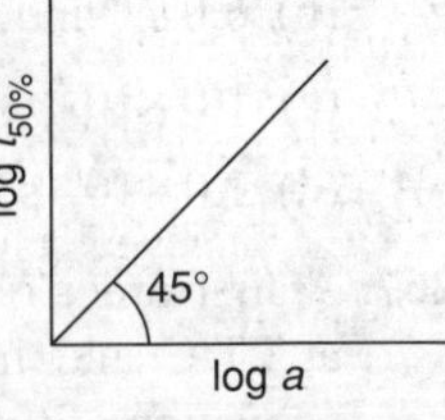

(a) 0, 1 (b) 1, 1
(c) 0, 0.5 (d) 1, 0.5

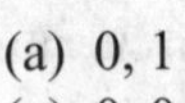

261. Hydrogenation of vegetable ghee at 25°C reduces pressure of H_2 from 3 atm to 1.2 atm in 50 minutes. The rate of reaction in terms of molarity per second as
(a) 1.09×10^{-6} (b) 1.09×10^{-5}
(c) 1.09×10^{-7} (d) 1.09×10^{-9}

262. Ethylene is produced by

$$\underset{\text{Cyclobutane}}{C_4H_8} \xrightarrow{\Delta} 2C_2H_4$$

The rate constant is $2.48\times10^{-4}\ s^{-1}$. In what time will the molar ratio of ethylene to cyclobutane in reaction mixture attain the value 1?
(a) 27.25 min (b) 28.25 min
(c) 25 min (d) 20 min

263. When inversion of sucrose is studied at pH = 5, the half-life period is always found to be 500 minutes irrespective of any initial concentration but when it is studied at pH = 6, the half-life period is found to be 50 minutes. The rate law expression for the inversion of sucrose is
(a) Rate = $k\,[\text{Sucrose}]\,[H^+]^0$
(b) Rate = $k\,[\text{Sucrose}]\,[H^+]^1$
(c) Rate = $k\,[\text{Sucrose}]^0[H^+]$
(d) Rate = $k\,[\text{Sucrose}]\,[H^+]^2$

264. The rate of a certain reaction is given by, rate = $k[H^+]^n$. The rate increases 100 times when the pH changes from 3 to 1. The order (n) of the reaction is
(a) 2 (b) 0 (c) 1 (d) 1.5

265. The rate constant k_1 and k_2 for two different reactions are $10^{16}.\ e^{-2000/T}$ and $10^{15}.\ e^{-1000/T}$ respectively. The temperature at which $k_1 = k_2$ is

(a) 1000 K (b) $\frac{2000}{2.303}K$
(c) 2000 K (d) $\frac{1000}{2.303}K$

266. For a first order reaction A → P, the temperature (T) dependent rate constant (k) was found to follow the equation $\log k = -(2000)\frac{1}{T}+6.0$. The pre-exponential factor A and the activation energy E_a, respectively, are

(a) $1.0\times10^6\ s^{-1}$ and 9.2 kJ mol^{-1}
(b) 6.0 s^{-1} and 16.6 kJ mol^{-1}
(c) $1.0\times10^{-1}\ s^{-1}$ and 16.6 kJ mol^{-1}
(d) $1.0\times10^6\ s^{-1}$ and 38.3 kJ mol^{-1}

267. A first order reaction is 50% complete in 30 minutes at 27°C and in 10 minutes at 47°C. The energy of activation of the reaction is

(a) 43.84 kJ mol^{-1} (b) 34.84 kJ mol^{-1}
(c) 84.00 kJ mol^{-1} (d) 30.00 kJ mol^{-1}

268. The rate of a certain reaction increases by 2.5 times when the temperature is raised from 300 K at 310 K. If k is the rate constant at 300 K then the rate constant at 310 K will be equal to

(a) k (b) 2 k
(c) 2.5 k (d) 3 k

269. Plots showing the variation of the rate constant (k) with temperature (T) are given below. The plot that follows Arrhenius equation is

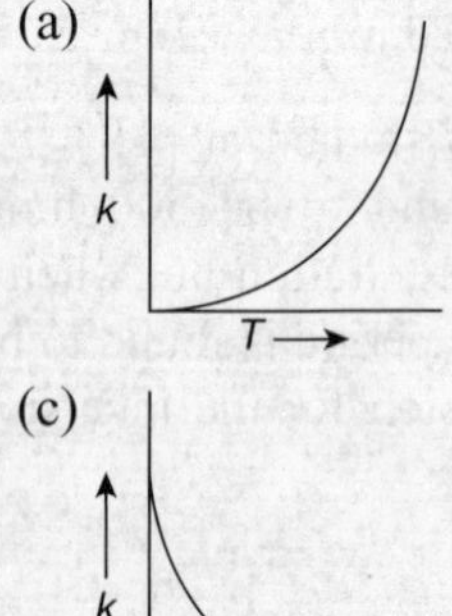

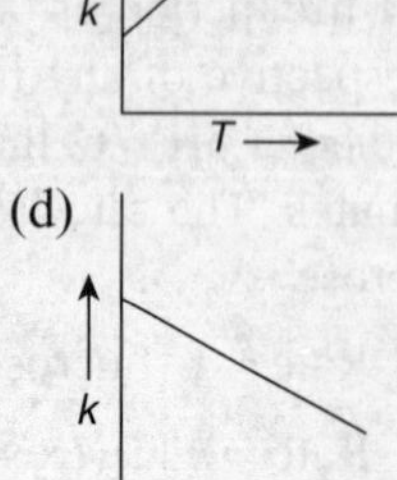

270. At a certain temperature, the first order rate constant k_1 is found to be smaller than the second order rate constant k_2. If the energy of activation E_1 of the first order reaction is greater than energy of activation E_2 of the second order reaction then with increase in temperature

(a) k_1 will increase faster than k_2, but always will remain less than k_2
(b) k_2 will increase faster than k_1
(c) k_1 will increase faster than k_2 and becomes equal to k_2
(d) k_1 will increase faster k_2 and becomes greater than k_2

271. A given sample of milk turns sour at room temperature (27°C) in 5 hours. In a refrigerator at –3°C, it can be stored 10 times longer. The energy of activation of souring of milk is

(a) $2.303\times10\ R$ kJ mol^{-1} (b) $2.303\times5\ R$ kJ mol^{-1}
(c) $2.303\times3\ R$ kJ mol^{-1} (d) $2.303\times27\ R$ kJ mol^{-1}

272. For a chemical reaction at 27°C, the activation energy is 600R. The ratio of the rate constant at 327°C to that at 27°C will be

(a) 2 (b) 40 (c) e (d) e^2

273. A plot of $\ln k$ versus the inverse of absolute temperature for a reaction is shown below:

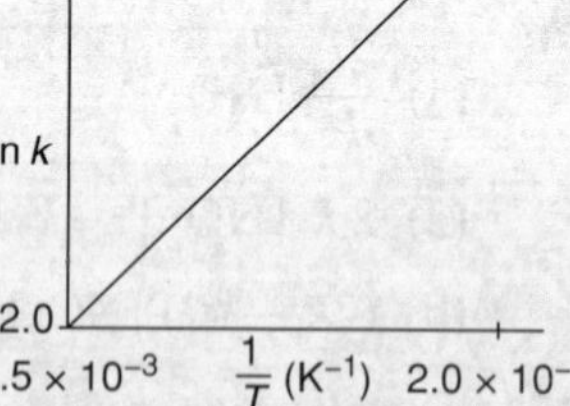

The reaction must be

(a) exothermic
(b) endothermic
(c) one with a negligible enthalpy change
(d) highly spontaneous at ordinary temperature

274. If for a first order reaction, the values of A and E_a are $4\times10^{13}\ s^{-1}$ and 98.6 kJ/mol respectively, then at what temperature will its half-life period be 10 minutes?

(a) 330 K (b) 300 K
(c) 330.95 K (d) 311.15 K

275. Graph between $\log k$ and $1/T$ (k is constant in s^{-1} and T is in K) is a straight line with OX = 5, $\theta = \tan^{-1}(1/2.303)$ Hence, E_a is

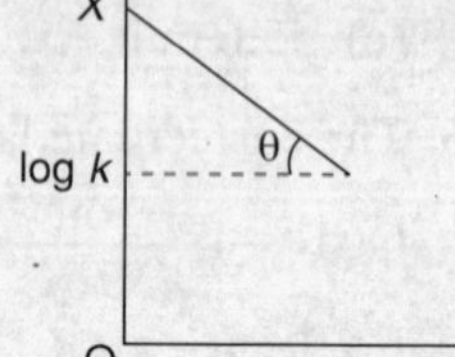

(a) 2.303 × 2 cal
(b) $\frac{2}{2.303}$ cal
(c) 2 cal
(d) none of these

276. In the presence of a catalyst, the activation energy of a reaction is forward by 2 kcal at 27°C. Hence, the rate will be

(a) 20 times (b) 28 times
(c) 14 times (d) remains the same

277. For the reaction A → B, carried out at 300 K, the activation energy is lowered by 8.314 kJ mol^{-1} when carried out in the presence of a catalyst. The rate of the catalysed reaction as compared to uncatalysed reaction is

(a) 15 times (b) 22 times
(c) 28 times (d) 38 times

278. Organic catalysts differ from inorganic catalysts
(a) by acting at very high temperature
(b) by acting at low temperature
(c) by being used up
(d) by being proteinaceous in nature

279. The enzyme activity of the human enzymes is maximum at
(a) 298 K (b) 310 K (c) 320 K (d) 330 K

280. The rate of reaction between A and B increases by a factor of 100 when the concentration of A is increased 10 fold; the order of reaction with respect to A is
(a) 10 (b) 1 (c) 4 (d) 2

281. In the reaction A + B → Products, if B is taken in excess, then it is an example of a
(a) second order reaction
(b) zero order reaction
(c) pseudounimolecular reaction
(d) can never be a bimolecular reaction

282. A gaseous reaction, $A_2(g) \rightarrow B(g) + \frac{1}{2} C(g)$ shows an increase in pressure from 100 to 120 mm in 5 minutes. The rate of disappearance of A_2 is
(a) 4 mm min^{-1} (b) 8 mm min^{-1}
(c) 16 mm min^{-1} (d) 2 mm min^{-1}

283. In the synthesis of ammonia from nitrogen and hydrogen gases, if 6×10^{-2} mol of hydrogen disappears in 10 minutes, the number of mol of ammonia formed in 0.3 minutes is
(a) 1.8×10^{-2} (b) 1.2×10^{-3}
(c) 4×10^{-2} (d) 3.6×10^{-2}

284. For a chemical reaction $Y_2 + 2Z \rightarrow$ Products, the rate controlling step is

$$Y + \frac{1}{2} Z \rightarrow Q$$

If the concentration of Z is doubled, the rate of reaction will
(a) remain the same (b) become four times
(c) become 1.414 times (d) become double

285. For the reaction A + 3B → 2C + 2D, the concentration of A changes from 0.0150 M to 0.0135 M in 1 minute. What is the rate of formation of C in M s^{-1}?
(a) 5.0×10^{-5} (b) 2.5×10^{-5}
(c) 3.0×10^{-5} (d) 5.0×10^{-4}

286. Consider the decomposition of N_2O_5 as

$$N_2O_5 \rightarrow 2NO_2 + \frac{1}{2} O_2$$

The rate of reaction is given by

$$-\frac{d[N_2O_5]}{dt} = \frac{1}{2}\frac{d[NO_2]}{dt} = 2\frac{d[O_2]}{dt} = k_1 [N_2O_5]$$

Therefore, $-\frac{d[N_2O_5]}{dt} = k_1 [N_2O_5]$

$$+\frac{d[NO_2]}{dt} = 2k_1 [N_2O_5] = k'_1 [N_2O_5]$$

$$+\frac{d[NO_2]}{dt} = \frac{1}{2} k_1 [N_2O_5] = k''_1 [N_2O_5]$$

Choose the correct option
(a) $k_1 = k'_1 = k''_1$ (b) $k_1 = 2k'_1 = k''_1$
(c) $2k_1 = k'_1 = 4k''_1$ (d) $4k_1 = k'_1 = k''_1$

287. The reaction $2SO_2(g) + O_2(g) \rightleftharpoons 2SO_3(g)$ is carried out in a 1 dm^3 vessel and a 2 dm^3 vessel separately. The ratio of the reaction velocities will be
(a) 1 : 8 (b) 1 : 4
(c) 4 : 1 (d) 8 : 1

288. Which is the correct relation among $\frac{dC}{dt}, \frac{dn}{dt}$ and $\frac{dP}{dt}$ where C, n, P, represents concentration, mole and pressure terms for the gaseous phase reaction, A(g) → Product?
(a) $-\frac{dC}{dt} = -\frac{1}{V}\frac{dn}{dt} = -\frac{1}{RT}\frac{dP}{dt}$
(b) $\frac{dC}{dt} = \frac{dn}{dt} = -\frac{dP}{dt}$
(c) $\frac{dC}{dt} = \frac{RT}{V}\frac{dn}{dt} = -\frac{dP}{dt}$
(d) all of these

289. A hypothetical reaction $A_2 + B_2 \rightarrow 2AB$ follows the mechanism as given below:
$A_2 \rightleftharpoons A + A$ (fast); $A + B_2 \rightarrow AB + B$ (slow)
$A + B \rightarrow AB$ (fast)
The order of the overall reaction is:
(a) 2 (b) 1 (c) $1\frac{1}{2}$ (d) 0

290. The following mechanism has been proposed for the reaction of NO with Br_2 to form NOBr

$$NO(g) + Br(g) \rightleftharpoons NOBr_2(g)$$
$$NOBr(g) + NO(g) \rightarrow 2NOBr(g)$$

If the second step is the rate determining step, the order of the reaction with respect to NO(g) is
(a) 3 (b) 2 (c) 1 (d) 0

291. The time for the half-life period of a certain reaction A → Products is 1 hour when the initial concentration of the reactant A, is 2.0 mol L^{-1}. How much time does it take for its concentration to come from 0.50 to 0.25 mol L^{-1} if it is a zero order reaction?

(a) 0.25 h (b) 1 h
(c) 4 h (d) 0.5 h

292. Consider the following in respect of a zero order reaction.

1. $t_{1/2}$ is directly proportional to the initial concentration.
2. Time taken for the completion of the reaction is twice its $t_{1/2}$.
3. Concentration of the reactant decreases linearly with time.

Which of the statements given above are correct?

(a) 1 and 2 only (b) 1 and 3 only
(c) 2 and 3 only (d) 1, 2 and 3

293. The rate constant of a zero order reaction is 0.2 mol dm^{-3} h^{-1}. If the concentration of the reactant after 30 minutes is 0.05 mol dm^{-3}, then its initial concentration would be

(a) 0.01 mol dm^{-3} (b) 0.15 mol dm^{-3}
(c) 0.25 mol dm^{-3} (d) 4.00 mol dm^{-3}

MATCH THE FOLLOWING

294.

Column I	Column II
(A) Half-life of zero order reaction	(p) $[A]_0 / 2k$
(B) Total life of zero order reaction	(q) 1/k
(C) Half-life of 2nd order reaction	(r) $\frac{[A]_0}{k}$
(D) Average life of a 1st order reaction	(s) $1/(k[A]_0)$

(a) (A)—(p), (B)—(r), (C)—(q), (D)—(s)
(b) (A)—(s), (B)—(r), (C)—(q), (D)—(p)
(c) (A)—(p), (B)—(r), (C)—(s), (D)—(q)
(d) (A)—(p), (B)—(r), (C)—(s), (D)—(q)

295.

Column I	Column II
(A) Concentration vs time for zero order reaction	(p) k
(B) Half-life period vs initial concentration for zero order reaction	(q) $-k$
(C) Reciprocal of concentration vs time for 2nd order reaction	(r) $\frac{1}{2k}$
(D) Half -life period vs initial concentration for 1st order reaction	(s) zero

(a) (A)—(r), (B)—(q), (C)—(q), (D)—(s)
(b) (A)—(q), (B)—(r), (C)—(p), (D)—(s)
(c) (A)—(s), (B)—(r), (C)—(p), (D)—(q)
(d) (A)—(p), (B)—(q), (C)—(r), (D)—(s)

296.

Column I	Column II
(A) $2HI \xrightarrow{Au} H_2 + I_2$	(p) 1
(B) $2N_2O_5 \rightarrow 4NO_2 + O_2$	(q) 2
(C) $CH_3COOC_2H_5 \xrightarrow{OH^-}$	(r) 1.5
(D) $H_2 + Br_2 \rightarrow 2HBr$	(s) 0

(a) (A)—(p), (B)—(s), (C)—(q), (D)—(r)
(b) (A)—(s), (B)—(p), (C)—(q), (D)—(r)
(c) (A)—(r), (B)—(p), (C)—(q), (D)—(s)
(d) (A)—(s), (B)—(p), (C)—(r), (D)—(q)

ASSERTION REASON

Directions: In each of the following questions, a statement of Assertion (A) is given followed by a corresponding statement of Reason (R) just below it. Of the statements, mark the correct answer as

(a) if both the assertion and reason are true and the reason is the correct explanation of the assertion.
(b) if both the assertion and reason are true but the reason is not the correct explanation of the assertion.
(c) if the assertion is true but the reason is false.
(d) if both the assertion and reason are false.

297. Assertion: Molecularity has no meaning for a complex reaction.

Reason: The overall molecularity of a complex reaction is equal to the molecularity of the slowest step.

298. Assertion: Hydrolysis of ethyl acetate in the presence of an acid is a reaction of the first order whereas in the presence of an alkali, it is a reaction of the second order.

Reason: The acid only acts as a catalyst whereas the alkali acts as one of the reactants.

299. Assertion: 50% of a zero order reaction is completed in 100 s, therefore, 75% reaction will be complete in 150 s.

Reason: The rate constant of a zero order reaction depends upon time.

300. Assertion: In a zero order reaction, if the concentration of the reactant is doubled, the half-life period is also doubled.

Reason: For a zero order reaction, the time taken for 100% of the reaction to be complete is directly proportional to its initial concentration.

301. Assertion: According to the steady state principle, in a multi-step reaction, the change in concentration with time for reactive intermediates is zero.

Reason: The intermediates are so reactive that after a brief period, their concentrations rise from zero to a small value and then remains constant during the reaction.

302. Assertion: The average life of a radioactive substance is that period in which 63% of it is decayed.

Reason: Average life $T = 1.44\ t_{1/2}$.

303. Assertion: The hydrolysis of methyl acetate by dilute HCl is a pseudo first order reaction

Reason: HCl acts as a catalyst for the hydrolysis.

304. Assertion: The reaction $2NO + O_2 \rightarrow 2NO_2$ and $2CO + O_2 \rightarrow 2CO_2$ proceed at the same rate because they are similar.

Reason: Both the reactions have the same activation energy.

305. Assertion: According to transition state theory, for the formation of an activated complex, one of the vibrational degrees of freedom is converted into a translational degree of freedom.

Reason: The energy of the activated complex is higher than the energy of the reactant molecules.

306. Assertion: The rate of reaction is accelerated by the presence of a catalyst.

Reason: The presence of a catalyst makes the value of $\Delta G°$ more negative.

307. Assertion: The rate of a reaction normally increases by a factor of 2 or 3 for every 10^0 rise in temperature.

Reason: Increase in temperature increases the number of collisions.

308. Assertion: If the activation energy of a reaction is zero, the temperature will have no effect on the rate constant.

Reason: Lower the activation energy, faster is the reaction.

309. Assertion: A catalyst increases the rate of a reaction.

Reason: In the presence of a catalyst, the activation energy of the reaction decreases.

310. Assertion: Arrhenius equation, $k = Ae^{-E_a/RT}$ shows that rate of a reaction increases exponentially with a rise in temperature.

Reason: Energy-wise distribution of molecules in a gas is an exponential function of temperature.

311. Assertion: The photochemical reactions $H_2 + Cl_2 \rightarrow 2HCl$ and $H_2 + Br_2 \rightarrow 2HBr$ have equal quantum efficiencies.

Reason: Both the reactions proceed by a similar mechanism.

312. Assertion: Chlorophyll in photosynthesis acts as a photosensitiser.

Reason: Chlorophyll helps to start the photochemical reaction of photosynthesis.

313. Assertion: 0A photochemical reaction that can take place in the presence of red light can also take place in the presence of violet light but the reverse is not true.

Reason: Red light has a lower wavelength than violet light.

Answer Key

1. (b)	2. (b)	3. (c)	4. (d)	5. (c)	6. (d)	7. (a)	8. (a)	9. (d)	10. (b)
11. (d)	12. (c)	13. (a)	14. (b)	15. (d)	16. (b)	17. (b)	18. (b)	19. (c)	20. (d)
21. (c)	22. (a)	23. (d)	24. (c)	25. (c)	26. (a)	27. (c)	28. (a)	29. (d)	30. (c)
31. (a)	32. (c)	33. (b)	34. (c)	35. (a)	36. (b)	37. (a)	38. (d)	39. (a)	40. (d)
41. (b)	42. (a)	43. (c)	44. (c)	45. (c)	46. (c)	47. (a)	48. (b)	49. (a)	50. (c)
51. (d)	52. (b)	53. (b)	54. (d)	55. (d)	56. (b)	57. (b)	58. (d)	59. (c)	60. (b)
61. (d)	62. (c)	63. (b)	64. (a)	65. (b)	66. (d)	67. (c)	68. (a)	69. (b)	70. (b)
71. (c)	72. (c)	73. (c)	74. (c)	75. (b)	76. (a)	77. (b)	78. (c)	79. (a)	80. (b)
81. (d)	82. (a)	83. (c)	84. (b)	85. (b)	86. (a)	87. (b)	88. (a)	89. (d)	90. (d)
91. (c)	92. (b)	93. (a)	94. (a)	95. (b)	96. (a)	97. (b)	98. (a)	99. (a)	100. (b)
101. (c)	102. (c)	103. (a)	104. (c)	105. (b)	106. (c)	107. (c)	108. (b)	109. (a)	110. (c)
111. (d)	112. (a)	113. (c)	114. (d)	115. (a)	116. (c)	117. (c)	118. (b)	119. (b)	120. (b)
121. (b)	122. (c)	123. (b)	124. (c)	125. (a)	126. (c)	127. (a)	128. (b)	129. (a)	130. (b)

131. (a) 132. (c) 133. (b) 134. (b) 135. (d) 136. (b) 137. (a) 138. (a) 139. (c) 140. (d)
141. (d) 142. (a) 143. (b) 144. (d) 145. (d) 146. (a) 147. (a) 148. (c) 149. (a) 150. (d)
151. (c) 152. (a) 153. (a) 154. (a) 155. (c) 156. (b) 157. (c) 158. (a) 159. (c) 160. (c)
161. (b) 162. (b) 163. (d) 164. (c) 165. (b) 166. (b) 167. (a) 168. (c) 169. (c) 170. (b)
171. (c) 172. (c) 173. (b) 174. (d) 175. (c) 176. (c) 177. (a) 178. (d) 179. (c) 180. (a)
181. (c) 182. (c) 183. (b) 184. (c) 185. (c) 186. (a) 187. (b) 188. (d) 189. (a) 190. (c)
191. (c) 192. (b) 193. (b) 194. (d) 195. (c) 196. (b) 197. (d) 198. (a) 199. (d) 200. (c)
201. (b) 202. (b) 203. (a) 204. (c) 205. (c) 206. (b) 207. (b) 208. (d) 209. (b) 210. (d)
211. (d) 212. (b) 213. (b) 214. (a) 215. (d) 216. (c) 217. (c) 218. (a) 219. (d) 220. (d)
221. (b) 222. (a) 223. (c) 224. (d) 225. (c) 226. (a) 227. (c) 228. (a) 229. (d) 230. (b)
231. (c) 232. (b) 233. (b) 234. (d) 235. (b) 236. (c) 237. (c) 238. (b) 239. (b) 240. (c)
241. (c) 242. (c) 243. (d) 244. (d) 245. (d) 246. (b) 247. (c) 248. (c) 249. (d) 250. (b)
251. (a) 252. (c) 253. (b) 254. (b) 255. (c) 256. (b) 257. (b) 258. (a) 259. (c) 260. (c)
261. (b) 262. (a) 263. (a) 264. (c) 265. (d) 266. (d) 267. (a) 268. (c) 269. (a) 270. (a)
271. (d) 272. (c) 273. (a) 274. (d) 275. (c) 276. (b) 277. (c) 278. (d) 279. (b) 280. (d)
281. (c) 282. (b) 283. (b) 284. (c) 285. (a) 286. (c) 287. (d) 288. (a) 289. (c) 290. (b)
291. (a) 292. (d) 293. (b) 294. (c) 295. (b) 296. (b) 297. (b) 298. (a) 299. (c) 300. (b)
301. (a) 302. (b) 303. (b) 304. (a) 305. (a) 306. (c) 307. (b) 308. (b) 309. (d) 310. (a)
311. (d) 312. (a) 313. (c)

Hints and Solutions

OBJECTIVE QUESTIONS

Rate of a Chemical Reaction

1. (b): $-\frac{d[\mathrm{A}]}{dt} = -\frac{1}{2}\frac{d[\mathrm{B}]}{dt}$

Hence $-\frac{d[\mathrm{B}]}{dt} = 2\times\frac{-d[\mathrm{A}]}{dt} = 2\times 2.6\times 10^{-2}\,\mathrm{Ms^{-1}}$

$= 5.2\times 10^{-2}\ \mathrm{Ms^{-1}}$

2. (b): $3\mathrm{A}\rightarrow 2\mathrm{B}$

Rate $= -\frac{1}{3}\frac{d[\mathrm{A}]}{dt} = +\frac{1}{2}\frac{d[\mathrm{B}]}{dt}$

Hence, $+\frac{1}{2}\frac{d[\mathrm{B}]}{dt} = -\frac{2}{3}\frac{d[\mathrm{A}]}{dt}$

3. (c): For the given reaction,

Rate $= -\frac{1}{2}\frac{d[\mathrm{A}]}{dt} = -\frac{d[\mathrm{B}]}{dt} = \frac{1}{3}\frac{d[\mathrm{C}]}{dt} = \frac{d[\mathrm{D}]}{dt}$

4. (d): For the given reaction,

Rate $= -\frac{d[\mathrm{N_2}]}{dt} = -\frac{1}{3}\frac{d[\mathrm{H_2}]}{dt} = +\frac{1}{2}\frac{d[\mathrm{NH_3}]}{dt}$

Thus, $\frac{d[\mathrm{NH_3}]}{dt} = -\frac{2}{3}\frac{d[\mathrm{H_2}]}{dt}$

5. (c): For the given reaction

Rate $= -\frac{1}{2}\frac{d}{dt}[\mathrm{N_2O_5}] = \frac{1}{4}\frac{d}{dt}[\mathrm{NO_2}] = \frac{d}{dt}[\mathrm{O_2}]$

6. (d): Rate $\frac{1}{2}\frac{d[\mathrm{A}]}{dt} = -\frac{d[\mathrm{B}]}{dt}$

Hence $-\frac{d[\mathrm{B}]}{dt} = -\frac{1}{2}\frac{d[\mathrm{A}]}{dt} = \frac{1}{2}k[\mathrm{A}]^2[\mathrm{B}]$

7. (a): The rate constant of a reaction is a constant at constant temperature irrespective of the way it is written.

8. (a): Concentration of NO_2 decreases with time. Hence, Z = NO_2. Concentration of NO and O_2 increase with time but NO increases by double the amount of O_2. Hence, X = NO, Y = O_2.

9. (d): $\mathrm{H_2O_2}\rightarrow \mathrm{H_2O} + \frac{1}{2}\mathrm{O_2}$

Rate of formation of O_2 = 48 g $\mathrm{min^{-1}}$

$= \frac{48}{32}$ mol $\mathrm{min^{-1}}$ = 1.5 mol $\mathrm{min^{-1}}$

Rate of formation of H_2O is double the rate of formation of O_2.

Hence, rate of formation of H_2O = 2×1.5 mol $\mathrm{min^{-1}}$ = 3 mol $\mathrm{min^{-1}}$.

10. (b): Rate of disappearance of I^-

$\frac{d[\mathrm{I^-}]}{dt} = \frac{(0.20-0.18)\,\mathrm{mol\,L^{-1}}}{20\ \mathrm{min}} = 10^{-3}\,\mathrm{mol\,L^{-1}\,min^{-1}}$

Rate of reaction $= -\frac{1}{2}\frac{d[\mathrm{I^-}]}{dt} = +\frac{d[\mathrm{I_2}]}{dt}$

∴ Rate of formation of I_2,

$$\frac{d[I_2]}{dt}=-\frac{1}{2}\frac{d[I^-]}{dt}=\frac{10^{-3}}{2}=5\times10^{-4}\ \text{L}^{-1}\ \text{min}^{-1}$$

11. (d): Rate $=\frac{1}{3}\frac{d[Br_2]}{dt}=-\frac{1}{5}\frac{d[Br^-]}{dt}$

or $\frac{d[Br_2]}{dt}=-\frac{3}{5}\frac{d[Br^-]}{dt}$

12. (c): Rate $=-\frac{d[N_2O_5]}{dt}=+\frac{1}{2}\frac{d[NO_2]}{dt}=2\frac{d[O_2]}{dt}$

Given $\frac{-d[N_2O_5]}{dt}=6.25\times10^{-3}\ \text{mol L}^{-1}\ \text{s}^{-1}$

Rate of formation of $NO_2=\frac{d[NO_2]}{dt}=-2\frac{-d[N_2O_5]}{dt}$

$=2\times6.25\times10^{-3}\ \text{mol L}^{-1}\ \text{s}^{-1}=12.50\times10^{-3}\ \text{mol L}^{-1}\ \text{s}^{-1}$

$=1.25\times10^{-2}\ \text{mol L}^{-1}\ \text{s}^{-1}$

Rate of formation of O_2, that is,

$\frac{d[O_2]}{dt}=-\frac{1}{2}\frac{d[N_2O_5]}{dt}=\frac{1}{2}\times6.25\times10^{-3}\ \text{mol L}^{-1}\text{s}^{-1}$

$=3.125\times10^{-3}\ \text{mol L}^{-1}\text{s}^{-1}$

13. (a): $2N_2O_5\rightarrow4NO_2+O_2$

Rate of reaction $-\frac{1}{2}\frac{d[N_2O_5]}{dt}=+\frac{1}{4}\frac{d[NO_2]}{dt}$ ...(i)

Rate of disappearance of N_2O_5

$=\frac{(2.4-2.0)}{200\ \text{min}}\ \text{mol L}^{-1}=\frac{0.4}{200}=2\times10^{-3}\ \text{mol}^{-1}\text{min}^{-1}$

From Eq. (i),

Rate of production of $NO_2\left(+\frac{d(NO_2)}{dt}\right)=-4\times\frac{1}{2}\frac{(N_2O_5)}{dt}$

$=-2\times(-2\times10^{-3})\ \text{mol L}^{-1}\ \text{min}^{-1}$

$=4\times10^{-3}\ \text{mol L}^{-1}\ \text{min}^{-1}$

14. (b): $N_2+3H_2\rightarrow2NH_3$

Rate $=-\frac{d[N_2]}{dt}=-\frac{1}{3}\frac{d[H_2]}{dt}=\frac{1}{3}\frac{d[NH_3]}{dt}$

$\frac{d[NH_3]}{dt}=\frac{-2}{3}\frac{d[H_2]}{dt}=\frac{2}{3}\times\frac{6\times10^{-2}}{10}=4\times10^{-2}\ \text{mol min}^{-1}$

$\therefore$ NH_3 formed in 0.3 min $=(4\times10^{-2})\times(0.3)$

$=1.2\times10^{-3}$ mol

15. (d): $\therefore\ aA+bB\rightarrow cC+dD$

$\frac{-1}{a}\frac{d[A]}{dt}=\frac{1}{C}\frac{d[C]}{dt}$

$\therefore\ \frac{-d[A]/dt}{d[C]/dt}=\frac{a}{c}$

16. (b): When the volume of the vessel is reduced to half, the concentrations are doubled. Hence,
new rate $=k\ 2\,[A]\times2\,[B]=4\,[A]\,[B]$

17. (b): Change in molarity $=\frac{n}{V}=\frac{\Delta P}{RT}$

$=\frac{2-1.2}{0.0821\times298}=0.0327$

$\therefore$ Rate of reaction $=\frac{0.0327\ \text{mol L}^{-1}}{50\times60\ \text{s}}$

$=1.09\times10^{-5}\ \text{mol L}^{-1}\ \text{s}^{-1}$

18. (b): Rate concentration of products increases with time (note that it is an irreversible reaction).

19. (c): Decrease with an increase in temperature.

20. (d): Rate $=-\frac{1}{3}\frac{d[H_2]}{dt}=\frac{1}{2}\frac{d[NH_3]}{dt}$

$\therefore\ -\frac{d[H_2]}{dt}=\frac{3}{2}\frac{d[NH_3]}{dt}=\frac{3}{2}\times2\times10^{-4}$

$=3\times10^{-4}\ \text{mol L}^{-1}\ \text{s}^{-1}$

21. (c): The rate of reaction is the same as expressed in terms of any reactant or product.

Factors Influencing Rate of a Reaction, Rate Law and Order of a Reaction

22. (a): By definition of order of reaction.

23. (d): The units of rate constant depend upon the order of reaction.

24. (c): Order of reaction $=1+\frac{1}{2}=1.5$

25. (c): The given reaction is of 3rd order.

26. (a): Only (a) is a reaction of the 1st order.

27. (c): Decomposition of HI on the surface of gold at high temperature is a reaction of zero order.

28. (a): Reaction $2N_2O_5\rightarrow2NO_2+O_2$ is a reaction of 1st order.
Rate $=k\ [N_2O_5]$

29. (d): The rate of the given photochemical reaction is independent of the concentration of the reactants. Hence, it is a zero order reaction

30. (c): For the reaction $2NO+O_2\rightarrow2NO_2$, rate $=k\ [NO]^2$, rate $=k\ [NO]^2\,[O_2]$, that is, it is a third order reaction.

31. (a): Hydrolysis of ethyl acetate in the presence of alkali is a reaction of the 2nd order.

32. (c): Based on the units of rate constant, order of reaction = 2

33. (b): Rate $=k\ [P_{CH_3OCH_3}]^{3/2}$

$\therefore\ k=\frac{\text{Rate}}{[P_{CH_3OCH_3}]^{3/2}}=\frac{\text{bar min}^{-1}}{(\text{bar})^{3/2}}=\text{bar}^{-1/2}\text{min}^{-1}$

34. (c): $\frac{dx}{dt} = k\ (\text{Conc.})^2$

or $k = \frac{\text{Conc.}}{\text{Time}} \times \frac{1}{(\text{Conc.})^2} = \text{Conc.}^{-1}\ \text{time}^{-1} = \text{L mol}^{-1}\ \text{s}^{-1}$

35. (a): The units of the rate constant show that it is a reaction of zero order.

36. (b): For a reaction of n th order, rate = $k[\text{conc}]^n$

or $k = \frac{\text{Rate}}{[\text{conc}]^n} = \frac{\text{mol L}^{-1}\ \text{s}^{-1}}{(\text{mol L}^{-1})^n} = (\text{mol L}^{-1})^{1-n}\ \text{s}^{-1}$

Thus, units of rate constant depend upon order n of the reaction.

37. (a): Rate = $k\ [\text{A}]^{1/2}\ [\text{B}]^{3/2}$ or $k = \frac{\text{Rate}}{[\text{A}]^{1/2}\ [\text{B}]^{3/2}}$

$= \frac{\text{mol L}^{-1}\ \text{s}^{-1}}{(\text{mol L}^{-1})^{1/2}(\text{mol L}^{-1})^{3/2}} = \text{mol}^{-1}\ \text{L s}^{-1}$

38. (d): $\frac{dx}{dt} = k(\text{Conc.})^n$ or $k = \frac{\text{Conc.}}{\text{Time}} \times \frac{1}{(\text{Conc.})^n}$

$= (\text{Conc.})^{1-n}\ \text{time}^{-1} = (\text{mol L}^{-1})^{1-n}\ \text{s}^{-1}$

$= \text{mol}^{1-n}\text{L}^{n-1}\ \text{s}^{-1}$

39. (a): The rate constant of a reaction depends only on temperature and does not depend upon concentrations of the reactants.

40. (d): The rate constant of a reaction changes when either the temperature is changed or a catalyst is added.

41. (b): When the reaction is reversed, the rate constant is inversed (higher the rate constant for the forward reaction, lower is the rate constant for the reverse reaction).

42. (a): Decreasing particle size increases the surface area and hence increases the rate of the reaction.

43. (c): ΔH of a reaction has no effect on the rate of reaction.

44. (c): Rate = $k[\text{A}][\text{B}]^2$

$1.0 \times 10^{-3} = k(1)(1)^2 = k$

New rate = $k\left(\frac{1}{2}\right)\left(\frac{1}{2}\right)^2 = 1.0 \times 10^{-2} \times \frac{1}{8}$

$= 1.25 \times 10^{-3}\ \text{mol L}^{-1}\text{s}^{-1}$

45. (c): Initially rate $= k\ [\text{A}]^2[\text{B}] = ka^2b$

New rate = $k(2a)^2\left(\frac{b}{2}\right) = 2ka^2b$.

That is, increased by 2 times.

46. (c): $\text{V}_t \propto ab^{1/2}$, $\text{V}_f \propto (2a)(2b)^{1/2} = 2\sqrt{2}\ ab^{1/2}$

That is, the rate will become $2\sqrt{2}$ times.

47. (a): When [A] is reduced from 0.1 mol L^{-1} to 0.06 mol L^{-1},

[A] reacted = $0.1 - 0.06\ \text{mol L}^{-1}$

$= 0.04\ \text{mol L}^{-1} = 0.04\ \text{mol L}^{-1}$

[B] reacted = $\frac{1}{2}$ [A] reacted

$= \frac{1}{2} \times 0.04\ \text{mol L}^{-1} = 0.02\ \text{mol L}^{-1}$

[B] now present = $0.2 - 0.02 = 0.18\ \text{mol L}^{-1}$

[A] now present = $0.06\ \text{mol L}^{-1}$ (Given)

Rate = $k\ [\text{A}][\text{B}]^2 = (2.0 \times 10^{-6})(0.06)(0.18)^2$

$= 3.89 \times 10^{-9}\ \text{mol L}^{-1}\ \text{s}^{-1}$

48. (b): Concentration in mol L^{-1} are highest in (b).

49. (a): Rate = $k\ [\text{CH}_3\text{COOH}]\ [\text{C}_2\text{H}_5\text{OH}]$

$= k\ C_1 . C_2$

On dilution with an equal volume, the concentrations are halved.

Hence,

now rate = $k\frac{C_1}{2} \times \frac{C_2}{2} = \frac{1}{4}k\ C_1C_2 = 0.25\ k\,C_1C_2$

Thus, now the rate would be 0.25 times.

50. (c): As the given reaction is of 1st order, rate $= k$ [conc]

When volume is reduced to $\frac{1}{3}$, concentration will become 3 times.

Hence, now rate of reaction = 3 times

51. (d): Rate $= k\ p_{\text{H}_2\text{S}}^2 \times p_{\text{O}_2}$

on increasing the pressure three-fold,

New rate = $k(3 \times p_{\text{H}_2\text{S}})^2\ (3 \times p_{\text{O}_2})$

$= 27k\ p_{\text{H}_2\text{S}}^2 \times\ p_{\text{O}}^2$, that is, 27 times.

52. (b): Rate = $k\,a\,b^2$

New rate = $k\ (2a)\left(\frac{b}{2}\right)^2 = \frac{1}{2}k\,a\,b^2$

53. (b): For the given reaction,

Rate $= -\frac{1}{3}\frac{d[\text{BrO}^-]}{dt} = +\frac{d[\text{BrO}_3^-]}{dt} = +\frac{1}{2}\frac{d[\text{Br}^-]}{dt}$

Substituting the given values,

$\frac{1}{3}k_1[\text{BrO}^-]^2 = k_2[\text{BrO}^-]^2 = \frac{1}{2}k_3\ [\text{BrO}^-]^2$

or $\frac{k_1}{3} = k_2 = \frac{k_3}{2}$ or $k_1 = 3k_2 = 1.5k_3$

54. (d): % of B = $\frac{k_1}{k_1 + k_2} = \frac{1.26 \times 10^{-4}}{1.26 \times 10^{-4} + 3.8 \times 10^{-5}} \times 100$

$= \frac{1.26 \times 10^{-4}}{10^{-4}(1.26 + 0.38)} \times 100 = 76.83\%$

Molecularity and Mechanism of a Reaction

55. (d): A reaction involving two different reactants is at least bimolecular (for example, A + B → Products). It cannot be unimolecular though it can be of 1st order.

56. (b): As the given reaction is first order with respect to H_2 and ICl, the slow step should involve 1 molecule of H_2 and 1 molecule of ICl. Hence, B is the correct mechanism.

57. (b): Rate depends upon the slow step. Thus, slow step should involve 1 molecule of Cl_2 and 1 molecule of H_2S. Hence, A is the correct mechanism.

58. (d): Order may or may not be equal to molecularity.

59. (c): The rate of even zero order reactions changes with temperature.

60. (b): Rate of reaction depends upon the slowest step.

61. (d): $CH_3COOC_2H_5 + NaOH \rightarrow CH_3COONa + C_2H_5OH$, Order = 2, molecularity = 2.

62. (c): Molecularity of a chemical reaction is never fractional.

63. (b): Moleculaity = 2, order = $1\frac{1}{2}$

64. (a): Hydrolysis of the primary alkyl halide is bimolecular and of second order.

65. (b): Order of reaction = Molecularity of slowest step = 1.

66. (d): As rate depends upon the slowest step.

Rate $= k\,[X][X_2]$ ...(i)

Taking step (i) to be reversible (not given),

$K_{eq} = \frac{[X]^2}{[X_2]}$ or $[X] = K_{eq}^{1/2}\,[X_2]^{1/2}$

Substituting in (i),

Rate $= k\,K_{eq}^{1/2}\,[X_2]^{1/2}\,[X_2] = k'[X_2]^{1/2}\,[Y_2]$

Overall order $= \frac{1}{2} + 1 = \frac{3}{2} = 1.5$

67. (c): As rate depends upon the slow step,

Rate, $r = r_2\,[AB]\,[B]$ ...(i)

When the fast reaction reaches equilibrium

$k_1\,[A]\,[B] = k_{-1}\,[AB]$

$\therefore [AB] = \frac{k_1[A][B]}{k_{-1}}$ ...(ii)

Substituting in Eq. (i),

$r = \frac{k_2k_1[A][B]}{k_{-1}} \times [B] = \frac{k_1k_2}{k_{-1}} \times [A]\,[B]^2 = k[A]\,[B]^2$

68. (a): Overall order of reaction is determined by the slowest step.

69. (b): Many-body collisions have low probability.

70. (b): Rate is directly proportional to the number of collisions per second.

71. (c): $2N_2O_5 \rightarrow 2N_2O_4 + O_2$

72. (c): According to the data given, (c) is the correct option.

Integrated Rate Equations

73. (c): For a zero reaction

$$t_{1/2} = \frac{[A_0]}{2k} \text{ or } k = \frac{[A_0]}{2 \times t_{1/2}} = \frac{6\times10^{-3}}{2\times60} = 5\times10^{-5}\text{ mol dm}^{-3}\text{ s}^{-1}$$

74. (c): Rate $= -\frac{1}{2}\frac{d[NH_3]}{dt} = \frac{d[N_{23}]}{dt} = \frac{1}{3}\frac{d[H_2]}{dt}$

For a zero order reaction, rate = k

$= 2.5\times10^{-4}$ mol L^{-1} s^{-1} (Given)

$\therefore \frac{1}{3}\frac{d[H_2]}{dt} = 2.5\times10^{-4}$ mol L^{-1} s^{-1}

or $= \frac{d[H_2]}{dt} = 7.5\times10^{-4}$ mol L^{-1} s^{-1}

75. (b): The unit mol L^{-1} s^{-1} of the constant shows that it is a reaction of zero order. For a zero order reaction, $x = kt$.

$\therefore$ Amount of A reacted (x) = (0.6 10^{-3} mol L^{-1} s^{-1}) ($20 \times 60\,s$) = 0.72 mol L^{-1}. [B] formed = [A] reacted = 0.72 mol L^{-1}

76. (a): $t_{1/2} = 100$ s. For a zero order reaction,

$$t_{1/2} = \frac{[A_0]}{2k} \text{ or } k = \frac{2t_{\frac{1}{2}}}{[A_0]} = \frac{2\times100\,s}{220\,\text{atm}} = 1\,\text{atm s}^{-1}$$

77. (b): The rate of a zero order reaction is independent of the concentration of the reactant.

78. (c): For zero order reactions,

$t_{1/2} = \frac{[A_0]}{2k}$

When $[A_0]$ is reduced to $\frac{1}{4}$ th, $t_{1/2}$ will become $\frac{1}{4}$ th.

79. (a): For a zero order reaction,

$t_{1/2} = \frac{[A_0]}{2k}$

If $[A_0]$ is doubled, $t_{1/2}$ will also be doubled.

80. (b): For a zero order reaction, $t_{1/2} \propto [A_0]$

81. (d): For a zero order reaction,

$k = \frac{1}{t}\,\{[A_0]-[A]\}$ or $kt = [A_0]-[A]$ or $[A] = [A_0]-kt$

Hence, plot of [A] vs t will be linear with slope = $-k$.

82. (a): Time required for 100% completion of a zero order reaction

$(t_{100}) = \frac{a}{k}$

83. (c): For a zero order reaction

$k = \frac{1}{t}\,\{[A_0]-[A]\}$ or $kt = [A_0]-[A]$ or $[A] = -kt + [A_0]$

Hence, plot of [A] vs t will be linear with negative slope ($-k$) and intercept = $[A_0]$, that is, non-zero intercept.

84. (b): Plot of log [A] vs time is linear with a –ve slope.

85. (b): $k = \frac{0.693}{24}\,h^{-1} = \frac{2.303}{96}\log\frac{10}{a-x}$ or $\log\frac{10}{a-x} = 1.2036$

or $1 - \log(a-x) = 1.2036$

or $\log(a-x) = -0.2036 = \bar{1}.7964$

or $(a-x)$ = antilog $\bar{1}.7964 = 0.6258 = 0.63$ g

Alternatively 96 hours = 4 half lives

86. (a): $t_{1/2} = \frac{2.303}{k}\log 2 = \frac{2.303}{k}(0.301)$

$t_{99.9\%} = \frac{2.303}{k}\log\frac{a}{a-0.999a} = \frac{2.303}{k}\log 10^3 = \frac{2.303}{k}\times 3$

$\therefore \frac{t_{99.9\%}}{t_{1/2}} = \frac{3}{0.301} = 10$ times

87. (b): $k = \frac{0.693}{10}\ \text{yr}^{-1} = \frac{2.303}{t}\log\frac{a}{a-0.99a} = \frac{2.303}{t}\log 10^2$

or $t = \frac{10}{0.693}\times 2.303\times 2 = 66.5$ years

$\simeq 70$ years

88. (a): Half-life of a first order reaction does not depend upon the initial concentration. It is equal to $\ln 2/k$.

89. (d): $k = \frac{2.303}{t}\log\frac{[A_0]}{[A]} = \frac{2.303}{4606\,s}\log\frac{80}{8} = 5\times 10^{-4}\,s^{-1}$

90. (d): $k = \frac{2.303}{t}\log\frac{a}{a-x}$

$= \frac{2.303}{24}\log\frac{1}{a/8} = \frac{2.303}{24}\log 8\ \text{min}^{-1}$

91. (c): (a) and (b) are correct

$k = \frac{1}{t}\ln\frac{N_0}{N}$ or $\frac{N_0}{N} = kt$ or

$\ln\frac{N}{N_0} = -kt$ or $\frac{N}{N_0} = e^{-kt}$

Thus, no relation exists corresponding to (c).

92. (b):

	$2N_2O_5(g)$	$\rightarrow$	$2N_2O_5(g)$ + $O_2(g)$	
At $t = 0$	0.5 atm		0	0
At $t = 100$ s	$(0.5-2x)$ atm		$2x$ atm	x atm

$P_t = (0.5-2x)+2x+x = 0.5+x = 0.512$ atm (Given)

or $x = 0.012$ atm

$\therefore$ At $t = 100$ s,

$p_{N_2O_5} = 0.5 - 2(0.012)$

$= 0.5 - 0.024 = 0.476$ atm

$k = \frac{2.303}{t}\log\frac{p^{\circ}_{N_2O_5}}{p_{N_2O_5}} = \frac{2.303}{100}\log\frac{0.5}{0.476} = \frac{2.303}{100}\log(1.05)$

$= \frac{2.303}{100}\times 0.0216 = 4.98\times 10^{-4}\,s^{-1} \simeq 5.0\times 10^{-4}\,s^{-1}$

93. (a): $t = \frac{2.303}{k}\log\frac{a}{a/16} = \frac{2.303}{60\,s^{-1}}\log 16$

$= \frac{2.303}{60}\times\log 2^4 = \frac{2.303}{60}\times 4\times 0.301\ s = 0.0462$ s

94. (a): $t_{99\%} = \frac{2.303}{k}\log\frac{a}{a-0.99a} = \frac{2.303}{k}\log 10^2 = 2\times\frac{2.303}{k}$

$t_{90\%} = \frac{2.303}{k}\log\frac{a}{a-0.90a}$

$= \frac{2.303}{k}\log 10 = \frac{2.303}{k}$

$\frac{t_{99\%}}{t_{90\%}} = 2$ or $t_{99\%} = 2\times t_{90\%}$

95. (b): $k = \frac{0.693}{150}\,s^{-1} = \frac{2.303}{t}\log\frac{1/10}{1/100}$

or $t = \frac{2.303\times 150}{0.693}\log 10 = 498\,s \simeq 500$ s

96. (a): $t_{av} = \frac{1}{k} = \frac{1}{0.693\,t_{1/2}} = \frac{t_{1/2}}{0.693} = 1.44\ t_{50\%}$

Also, we know that $t_{75\%} = 2\times t_{50\%}$

Hence, $t_{50\%} < t_{av} < t_{75\%}$.

97. (b): As sucrose decomposes according to the first order rate law,

$k = \frac{2.303}{t}\log\frac{[A]_0}{[A]}$

The aim is to find $[A]/[A]_0$

$k = \frac{2.303}{t_{1/2}} = \frac{0.693}{3.0\text{ hour}} = 0.231\ \text{hr}^{-1}$

Hence, $0.231\ h^{-1} = \frac{2.303}{8\text{ hr}}\log\frac{[A]_0}{[A]}$

Or, $\log\frac{[A]_0}{[A]} = 0.8024$ or $\frac{[A]_0}{[A]}$

= Antilog (0.8024) = 6.345

$\frac{[A]}{[A]_0} = \frac{1}{6.345} = 0.158$

98. (a): As it is a reaction of 1st order, $\log[N_2O_5]$ vs time gives a straight line graph with a –ve slope.

99. (a): As it is a reaction of 1st order,

$k = \frac{2.303}{t}\log\frac{[A]_0}{[A]}$, that is,

$k = \frac{2.303}{t}\log\frac{p^{\circ}_{N_2O_5}}{p_{N_2O_5}}$

or $\frac{kt}{2.303} = \log p^{\circ}_{N_2O_5} - \log p_{N_2O_5}$

or $\log p_{N_2O_5} = -\frac{k}{2.303}t = p^{\circ}_{N_2O_5}$

From slope, k can be calculated.

100. (b): Rate $\left(\frac{dx}{dt}\right) = k\ [A]$

$\therefore 1.5\times 10^{-2}$ mol L^{-1} min^{-1} = $k\times 0.5$ mol L^{-1}

or $k = \frac{1.5\times 10^{-2}}{0.5}$ min^{-1}

For 1st order reaction, $t_{1/2}$

$$= \frac{0.693}{k} = \frac{0.693}{1.5\times10^{-2}} \times 0.5 \text{ min} = 23.1 \text{ min}$$

101. (c): $k = \frac{0.693}{t_{1/2}} = \frac{0.693}{100} \text{s}^{-1} = 6.93\times10^{-3} \text{ s}^{-1}$

Again, $k = \frac{2.303}{t}\log\frac{a}{a-x}$

or $6.93\times10^{-3} = \frac{2.303}{25}\log\frac{a}{a-x}$

or $\log\frac{a}{a-x} = 0.075$

or $\frac{a}{a-x}$ = Antilog (0.075) = 1.189

or $\frac{a}{a-x} = \frac{1}{1.189}$ or $1 - \frac{x}{a} = \frac{1}{1.189}$

or $\frac{x}{a} = 1 - \frac{1}{1.189} = \frac{0.189}{1.189} = 0.16 = 16\%$

102. (c): $k = \frac{0.693}{45} \text{ min}^{-1} = \frac{2.303}{t_{99.9\%}} \log\frac{a}{a-0.999\,a}$

or $t_{99.9\%} = \frac{2.303\times45}{0.693}\log10^3 = 448 \text{ min} \approx 7\frac{1}{2}$ hours

103. (a): $t = \frac{2.303}{k}\log\frac{a}{a-x} = \frac{2.303}{6}\log\frac{0.5}{0.05}$

$$= \frac{2.303}{k}\log10 = 0.384 \text{ min}$$

104. (c): For a first order reaction, $k = \frac{1}{5}\ \ln\frac{a}{a-x}$

or $kt = \ln\frac{[R_0]}{[R]}$ or $\frac{[R_0]}{[R]} = e^{kt}$

or $\frac{[R]}{[R_0]}\ e^{kt}$ or $[R] = [R_0]e^{kt}$

105. (b): $k = \frac{2.303}{t}\log\frac{a}{a-x} = \frac{2.303}{100}\log\frac{0.1}{0.001}$

$$= 0.02303\log10 = 0.02303 \text{ s}^{-1}$$

106. (c): For a first order reaction,
A → Products, and for concentration of the reactant at two different times,

$$k = \frac{2.303}{(t_2 - t_1)}\log\frac{[A]_1}{[A]_2}$$

Also, for a first order reaction, rate ∝ [A]
Hence,

$$k = \frac{2.303}{t_2 - t_1}\log\frac{(\text{Rate})_1}{(\text{Rate})_2} = \frac{2.303}{(20-10)}\log\left(\frac{0.04}{0.03}\right) = 0.0287 \text{ s}^{-1}$$

$$t_{1/2} = \frac{0.693}{k} = \frac{0.693}{0.0287 \text{ s}^{-1}} = 24.14 \text{ s}$$

107. (c): The decomposition of PH_3 on tungsten at low pressure is a first order reaction because rate is proportional to the surface coverage.

108. (b): Given, $k = 10^{-2}\text{ s}^{-1}$

Hence, $t_{1/2} = \frac{0.693}{k} = \frac{0.693}{10^{-2}}$ second

20 g → 5 g takes two half lives
(20 g → 10 g → 5 g)

Hence, $t = \frac{2\times0.693}{10^{-2}} = 138.6$ second

109. (a): $t = \frac{2.303}{k}\log\frac{a}{a-x}$

$$= \frac{2.303}{60 \text{ s}^{-1}}\ \log\frac{1}{1/10} = \frac{2.303}{60}\log10$$

$$= 0.038 \text{ s} = 3.8\times10^{-2} \text{ s}$$

110. (c): $[A]_0$ = 10 M. After 20 min, that is, 2 half-lives,

$$[A] = \frac{1}{4}\ [A]_0 = \frac{1}{4}\times10 = 2.5 \text{ M}$$

Rate = k [A] = 0.0693 min^{-1} × 2.5 M = 0.0693 × M min^{-1}

111. (d): For a first order reaction,

$$k = \frac{1}{t}\ln\frac{a}{a-x} \text{ or } t = \frac{1}{k}\ln\frac{a}{a-x}$$

For half-life, $x = \frac{a}{2}$. Hence, $t_{1/2} = \frac{1}{k}\ln\frac{a}{a-\frac{a}{2}} = \frac{\ln2}{k}$

112. (a): For a 1st order reaction

$$k = \frac{2.303}{k}\log\frac{[A]_0}{[A]} \text{ or } t = \frac{2.303}{k}\{\log[A]_0 - \log[A]\}$$

or $t = -\frac{2.303}{k}\log[A] + \frac{2.303}{k}\log[A]_0$

It is like $y = mx + c$

Plot of t vs log [A] will be linear with slope = $\frac{-2.303}{k}$

113. (c): For a 1st order reaction,

$$k = \frac{2.303}{k}\log\frac{a}{a-x}$$

When $\frac{1}{4}$ th of the reaction is complete, $x = a/4$. Hence,

$$t_{1/4} = \frac{2.303}{k}\log\frac{a}{a-a/4} = \frac{2.303}{k}\log\frac{4}{3}$$

114. (d): Rate = k[A], that is, 2.0×10^{-5}
$= k(0.01)$ or $k = 2.0\times10^{-3}$

$$t_{1/2} = \frac{0.693}{2.0\times10^{-3}} = 347 \text{ s}$$

115. (a): In case I, fraction of A reacted = $\frac{0.6}{0.8} = \frac{3}{4}$

In case II, fraction of A reacted = $\frac{0.675}{0.9} = \frac{3}{4}$

For a first order reaction, time taken for the same faction of reaction is independent of initial concentration.

116. (c): $k = \frac{2.303}{60 \text{ min}} \log \frac{a}{a - 0.6a} = \frac{2.303}{60} \log \frac{1}{0.4}$

$= \frac{2.303}{60} \times 0.398 = 0.0153 \text{ min}^{-1}$

For 50% completion

$t_{1/2} = \frac{0.693}{k} \quad \frac{0.693}{0.0153 \text{ min}^{-1}} = 45.3 \text{ min} \doteq 45 \text{ min}$

117. (c): At the point of intersection, [A] = [B], that is, half of the reactant has reacted. Hence, it represents $t_{1/2}$.

118. (b): Half-life period of a first order reaction is independent of the initial concentration of the reactant.

119. (b): As the half-life period is independent of initial concentration, the reaction must be of first order.

120. (b): $t_{1/2} \propto C_0^{1-n}$

For 2nd order, $n = 2$

Hence, $t_{1/2} \propto C_0^{-1}$.

121. (b): For A, 400 g $\xrightarrow{t_{1/2}}$ 200 g $\xrightarrow{t_{1/2}}$ 100 g

$\xrightarrow{t_{1/2}}$ 50 g $\xrightarrow{t_{1/2}}$ 25 g

Thus, it takes 4 half-lives. Hence, $4 \times (t_{1/2})_4 = 3$ months

or $(t_{1/2})_A = \frac{3}{4}$ month

For B 400 g $\xrightarrow{t_{1/2}}$ 200 g

Thus, it takes one half-life. Hence $(t_{1/2})_B = 3$ months

$\therefore (t_{1/2})_B$ is four times $(t_{1/2})_A$.

122. (c): $t_{1/2} = 3$ days,

$\therefore$ 12 days = 4 half-lives. After 4 half lives amount left

$= \frac{1}{2^n} [A_0] = \frac{1}{16}$th of $[A_0]$

123. (b): For a first order reaction, the time taken for a definite fraction of the reaction to complete is independent of the initial concentration. Hence, % of reactant changing into product will be the same, that is, 80%.

124. (c): From the given data, rate $\propto [A]^2$ and also rate $\propto [B]$. Hence,
rate $= k[A]^2 [B]$. Thus, overall order is 3.

125. (a): When the initial pressure is halved, the half-life period is also halved. This shown that $t_{1/2} \propto$ initial pressure. This is so for reaction of zero order.

126. (c):
(i) $r = k\ [NO]^\alpha [Cl_2]^\beta = ka^\alpha b^\beta$

(ii) $8r = k(2a)^\alpha\ (2b)^\beta$

(iii) $2r = ka^\alpha\ (2b)^\beta$.

Dividing (ii) by (iii), $4 = 2^\alpha$ or $\alpha = 2$
Dividing (iii) by (i), $2 = 2^\beta$ or $\beta = 1$
Overall order = 2 + 1 = 3

127. (a): As rate is not changing with time, it is independent of concentration, order = 0.

128. (b): log [A] vs time is linear for 1st order reactions.

$\frac{1}{[A]}$ vs time is linear for 2nd order reactions.

$\frac{1}{[A]^2}$ vs time is linear for 3rd order reactions.

129. (a): From runs I and IV, keeping [B] constant, [A] is made 4 times, the rate becomes 4 times. Hence, Rate $\propto$ [A]. From runs II and III, keeping [A] constant, [B] is doubled, rate becomes 4 times. Hence, Rate $\propto [B]^2$. Thus,
Rate $\propto [A][B]^2$ or Rate $= k[A][B]^2$

130. (b): (i) $r = ka^n$ (ii) $\frac{r}{2} = k\left(\frac{a}{2}\right)^n$

(because when volume is doubled, concentration is halved)
Dividing (i) by (ii), $2 = 2^n$. Hence, $n = 1$.

131. (a): $t_{1/2} \propto a^{1-n}$. Hence, $t_{1/2} \propto 1/a^3$ only when $n = 4$.

132. (c): Suppose order with respect to A, B and C are α, β and γ respectively, then,

$5.0 \times 10^{-3} = (0.010)^\alpha (0.005)^\beta (0.010)^\gamma$ ...(i)

$5.0 \times 10^{-3} = (0.010)^\alpha (0.005)^\beta (0.015)^\gamma$ ...(ii)

$1.0 \times 10^{-2} = (0.010)^\alpha (0.010)^\beta (0.010)^\gamma$ ...(iii)

$1.25 \times 10^{-3} = (0.005)^\alpha (0.005)^\beta (0.010)^\gamma$ ...(iv)

Dividing (i) by (ii),

$1 = \left(\frac{0.010}{0.015}\right)^\gamma$ or $\left(\frac{2}{3}\right)^\gamma = 1 = \left(\frac{2}{3}\right)^0$

$\therefore \gamma = 0$

Dividing (iii) by (ii),

$\frac{1.0 \times 10^{-2}}{5.0 \times 10^{-3}} = (2)^\beta \left(\frac{2}{3}\right)^\gamma = (2)^\beta \left(\frac{2}{3}\right)^0 \beta$

or $2^\beta = 2$ or $\beta = 1$

Dividing (i) by (iv), $4 = (2)^\alpha$ or $\alpha = 2$

$\therefore$ Orders with respect to A, B and C are 2, 1, 0

133. (b): As $t_{1/2}$ is independent of initial conc, it is a reaction of 1st order.

134. (b): Rate $= k\ [\text{conc.}]^n$

$2.4 = k(2.2)^n$

$0.6 = k(1.1)^n \therefore \frac{2.4}{0.6} = \left(\frac{2.2}{1.1}\right)^n$

or $4 = (2)^n$ or $n = 2$

135. (d): $r = k[A]^\alpha [B]^\beta = ka^\alpha b^\beta$ ...(i)

If concentration of B is doubled

$\frac{r}{4} = k\ (a)^\alpha (2b)^\beta$ ...(i)

Dividing Eq. (ii) by Eq. (i),

$\frac{1}{4} = 2^\beta$ or $2^\beta = 2^{-2}$

$\therefore \beta = -2$

136. (b): $r = k\ [A]^\alpha [B]^\beta$ ...(i)

$72\,r = k\ [3A]^\alpha [2B]^\beta$ ...(ii)

Dividing Eq. (ii) by Eq. (i), $72 = 3^\alpha 2^\beta$

Test by substituting the given value of α and β.

When $\alpha = 2, \beta = 3$, we have

$3^\alpha 2^\beta = 3^2 \times 2^3 = 9 \times 8 = 72$

137. (a): Substituting the given data in the equation $r_0 = [A]^\alpha [B]^\beta$

$5.07 \times 10^{-5} = (0.20)^\alpha (0.30)^\beta$ ...(i)

$5.07 \times 10^{-5} = (0.20)^\alpha (0.10)^\beta$ ...(ii)

$7.16 \times 10^{-5} = (0.40)^\alpha (0.05)^\beta$ ...(iii)

Eq. (i)/Eq. (ii) gives $\left(\frac{0.30}{0.10}\right)^\beta = 1$ or $3^\beta = 3^\circ \therefore \beta = 0$

Eq. (iii)/Eq. (ii) gives $\frac{7.16}{5.07} = \left(\frac{0.40}{0.20}\right)^\alpha \left(\frac{0.05}{0.10}\right)^\beta$

or $1.412 = 2^\alpha \left(\frac{1}{2}\right)^\beta = 2^\alpha$ $(\because \beta = 0)$

or $\sqrt{2} = 2^\alpha$ or $2^\alpha = 2^{1/2}$ or $\alpha = \frac{1}{2} = 0.5$

Overall order = 0.5 + 0 = 0.5

138. (a): $r = ka^\alpha b^\beta$. Then $2r = k$ $(2a)^\alpha b^\beta$ and $8r = k\ (2a)^\alpha (2b)^\beta$

$\therefore \frac{2r}{r} = \frac{(2a)^\alpha}{(a)^\alpha}$

or $2^\alpha = 2$ or $\alpha = 1$

$\frac{8r}{2r} = \frac{(2a)^\alpha}{(a)^\alpha}$ or $2^\alpha = 2$ or $\alpha = 1$

$\frac{8r}{2r} = \frac{(2b)^\beta}{b^\beta}$ or $2^\beta = 4 = 2^2$ or $\beta = 2$

139. (c): Rate $\propto$ $[A][B]^0[C]^2$

Hence, order = 3.

140. (d): If the order with respect to A is n, then as the initial conc. is 0.1 M,

Rate $(r) = k\ (1)^n$ ...(i)

When the concentration is increased to 1 M,

$100\ r = k(1)^n$ ...(ii)

Dividing Eq. (ii) by Eq. (i),

$100 = \left(\frac{1}{0.1}\right)^n = 10^n$

Hence, $n = 2$, that is, order with respect to A = 2

Or directly, as concentration is increased 10 times (from 0.1 M to 1 M) and eate becomes 100 times, order = 2.

141. (d): (i) $r = k(A)^n$ (ii) $4r = k(2A)^n$. Dividing (iii) by (i), $4 = 2^n$ or $n = 2$.

142. (a): As doubling the initial conc. doubles the rate of reaction, order = 1.

143. (b): For zero order reaction,

$k = \frac{1}{t}\,[[A]_0 - [A]]$ or $[A] = [A]_0 - kt$

Thus, plot of [A] vs t is a straight line with a negative slope.

144. (d): Keeping [B] constant when [A] is doubled, the rate is also doubled, that is, Rate $\propto$ [A]. Keeping [A] constant, when [B] is doubled, the rate becomes 4 times, that is, Rate $\propto [B]^2$. Hence, rate law is, Rate = $[A][B]^2$.

145. (d): $t_{1/2} \propto \frac{1}{a^2}$. Hence, order = 3

146. (a):

Interval	Change in conc.	Rate
0–17 min	0.069 – 0.052 = 0.017 M	$\frac{0.017}{17} = 0.001$
17–34 min	0.052 – 0.035 = 0.017 M	$\frac{0.017}{17} = 0.001$
34–51 min	0.035 – 0.018 = 0.017 M	$\frac{0.017}{17} = 0.001$

As the rate remains constant independent of concentration, the reaction is of zero order. Rate law is

Rate = $k(\text{conc.})^0 = k = 0.001\ M\ \text{min}^{-1}$

147. (a): Suppose order of reaction = x. Then

1st case: Rate $= k\ [CH_3CHO]^x$

$1 = k(363 \times 0.95)^x$

or $1 = k(344.85)^x$ ...(i)

2nd case: $0.5 = k(363 \times 0.67)^x$

or $0.5 = k\,(243.21)^x$ ...(ii)

Dividing Eq. (i) by Eq. (ii),

$\frac{1}{0.5} = \left(\frac{344.85}{243.21}\right)^x$ or $2 = (1.414)^x$ or $x = 2$

148. (c): Keeping [B] constant, if [A] is doubled, rate becomes 4 times

$\therefore$ Order with respect to A = 2

When [A] is kept constant at 0.2, and the concentration of B is doubled from 0.1 to 0.2, the rate of reaction is doubled.

$\therefore$ Order with respect to [B] = 1

149. (a): Suppose Rate = $k\ [CH_3COCH_3]^\alpha [Br_2]^\beta [H^+]^\gamma$

Then

$5.7 \times 10^{-5} = k(0.30)^\alpha (0.05)^\beta (0.05)^\gamma$ ...(i)

$5.7 \times 10^{-5} = k(0.30)^\alpha (0.10)^\beta (0.05)^\gamma$ ...(ii)

$1.2 \times 10^{-4} = k(0.30)^\alpha (0.10)^\beta (0.10)^\gamma$ ...(iii)

$3.1 \times 10^{-4} = k(0.40)^\alpha (0.05)^\beta (0.20)^\gamma$ ...(iv)

$\frac{(i)}{(ii)}$ gives $1 = \left(\frac{1}{2}\right)^\beta$ or $2^\beta = 1$

or $2^{\beta} = 2^{\circ}$ or $\beta = 0$

$\frac{\text{(iii)}}{\text{(ii)}}$ gives $\frac{3.1\times10^{-4}}{5.7\times10^{-4}} = \left(\frac{4}{3}\right)^{\alpha} (4)^{\gamma}$

or $5.4 = \left(\frac{4}{3}\right)^{\alpha} (4)^{1}$

or $\left(\frac{4}{3}\right)^{\alpha} = \frac{5.4}{4}$ or $(1.33)^{\alpha} = 1.35$ or $\alpha = 1$

Hence, rate = k $[CH_3COOCH_3][H^+]$

150. (d):

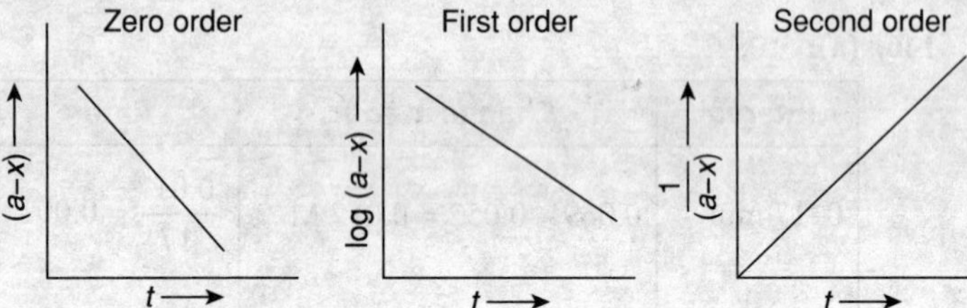

Hence, for zero order, plot of $(a-x)$ vs t is linear and for second order, plot of $\frac{a}{a-x}$ vs t is linear.

151. (c): Rate $= k[A]^n$ ...(i)

$r = ka^n$

When concentration of A is increased by 1.5,

$2.25\, r = k(1.5\, s)^n$ ...(ii)

$\frac{\text{(ii)}}{\text{(i)}}$ gives $2.25 = (1.5)^n$ or $n = 2$

152. (a): Rate constant $[k]$ does not change with time. Also, the units of k suggest that it is a reaction of 2nd order.

153. (a): The rate of a zero order reaction is independent of the concentration of the reactants. Hence, its concentration decreases linearly with time and therefore, ends in a finite time.

154. (a): When $a \gg b, a-b \simeq a, b(a-b) \simeq ba$,

$\therefore k_2 t = \frac{1}{a}\ln\frac{ba}{a(b-x)} = \frac{1}{a}\ln\frac{b}{b-x}$

That is, it becomes a reaction of first order.

155. (c): For a second order reaction,

$2A \rightarrow$ Products.

$k = \frac{1}{t}\left[\frac{1}{[A]} - \frac{1}{[A]_0}\right]$

When $t = t_{1/2}$

$[A] = \frac{[A]_0}{2}$

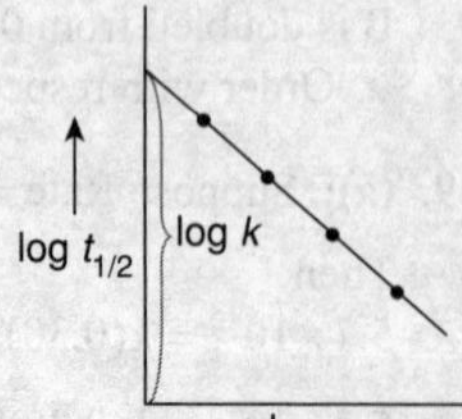

Hence, $t_{1/2} = \frac{1}{k}\left[\frac{2}{[A]_0} - \frac{1}{[A]_0}\right] = \frac{1}{k[A]_0}$

$\therefore \log t_{1/2} = -\log k - \log[A]_0 = -\log k - \log a$

Plot of $\log t_{1/2}$ vs $\log a$ will be linear with an intercept $= -\log k = \log(1/k)$.

156. (b): As rate = k [RCl], the rate is halved when [RCl] is halved. Also, the rate increases with an increase of temperature.

157. (c): (a) and (b) are correct.

$k = \frac{1}{t}\ln\frac{N_0}{N}$ or $\ln\frac{N_0}{N} = kt$

or $\ln\frac{N_0}{N} = -kt$ or $\frac{N_0}{N} = e^{-kt}$

Thus, no relation exists corresponding to (c).

158. (a): Initial rate $= k[CH_3COOCH_3][OH^-]$

$= (0.137\ M^{-1}s^{-1})(0.05\ M)^2 = 3.4\times10^{-4}\ M\ s^{-1}$

Amount hydrolysed = 5% of 0.05 M

$= \frac{5}{100}\times 0.05 = 2.5\times10^{-3}\ M$

$\therefore$ Time taken $= \frac{2.5\times10^{-3}}{3.4\times10^{-4}} = 7.4\ s$

159. (c): The value of the 1st order rate constant for a particular reaction at a particular temperature does not depend upon the units of concentration terms (because k has the units of time^{-1}).

160. (c): The given plot shows that $t_{1/2}$ $(t_{50\%})$ is independent of initial concentration (a). Hence, it is a reaction of 1st order for which $t_{1/2} = \frac{0.693}{k}$.

161. (b): The half-life of a first-order reaction is independent of $[A]_0$ whereas the half-life of a second order reaction is inversely proportional to $[A]_0$.

162. (b): $2HI(g) \xrightarrow{\Delta,\ \text{catalyst}} H_2(g) + I_2(g)$

For such a decomposition reaction on the surface of catalyst, the exact expression for rate is,

Rate $= \frac{k_1[HI]}{1 + k_2[HI]}$

When [HI] is high, 1 can be neglected in comparison to [HI] in the denominator so that,

Rate $= \frac{k_1}{k_2}$ = constant

That is, rate becomes constant, it becomes a reaction of zero order.

163. (d): For a zero order reaction $t_{1/2} \propto a_0$ (initial concentration or pressure)

$(t_{1/2})_1 \propto P_1$, $(t_{1/2})_2 \propto P_2$

$\frac{(t_{1/2})_2}{(t_{1/2})_1} = \frac{P_2}{P_1}$ or $\frac{(t_{1/2})_2}{45} = \frac{16}{4}$

or $(t_{1/2})_2 = \frac{16}{4}\times 45 = 180$ min

Pseudo-First Order Reactions

164. (c): The given reaction is a pseudo-unimolecular reaction.

165. (b): Acid hydrolysis of sucrose ($C_{12}H_{22}O_{11} + H_2O \xrightarrow{H^+} C_6H_{12}O_6 + C_6H_{12}O_6$) is an example of a pseudo first order reaction.

166. (b): 0.4 M to 0.2 M takes half-lives (= 1 hour)
0.2 M to 0.1 M takes again 1 hour, that is, $t_{1/2} = 1$ hour again. This shows that the half-life is independent of the initial concentration. Hence, it is a reaction of the 1st order.

167. (a): The value of the rate constant of a particular reaction including a pseudo-first order reaction depends only on temperature.

168. (c): In the presence of an acid, hydrolysis of ethyl acetate is a pseudo-unimolecular reaction but the actual value of k depends upon the concentration of the H^+ ion. As H_2SO_4 is a stronger acid than HCl and moreover H^+ ions produced from 0.05 M H_2SO_4 is double that produced from 0.05 M HCl, $k_2 \gg k_1$ or $k_1 < k_2$.

169. (c): For $CH_3COOC_2H_5 + H_2O \xrightarrow{OH^-} CH_3COOH + C_2H_5OH$,
Rate $= k\,[CH_3COOC_2H_5]\,[OH^-]$
For $(CH_3)_3\,CBr + OH^- \rightarrow (CH_3)_3COH + Br^-$,
Rate $= k\,[(CH_3)_3CBr]$

170. (b): The rate of reaction is independent of the concentration of the reactant present in large excess.

Temperature Dependence of the Rate of a Reaction

171. (c):

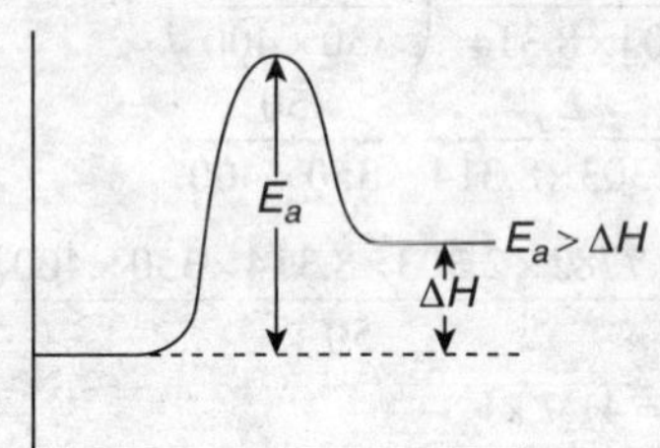

172. (c): The activation energy for the reverse reaction can be less than or more than E_a depending upon whether the reaction is endothermic or exothermic.

173. (b): $\Delta H = E_f - E_b = 150 - 260$ kJ $= -110$ kJ

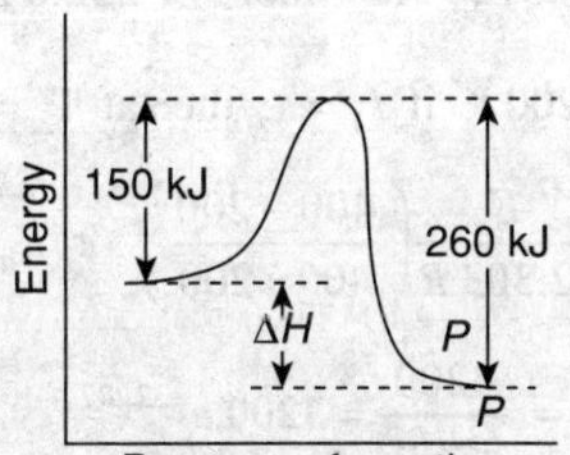

174. (d): Activation energy of a particular reaction is constant at constant temperature.

175. (c): The reaction occurring in two steps has two activation energy peaks. The first step, being fast, needs less activation energy. The second step, being slow, needs more activation energy. Therefore, the second peak will be higher than the first.

176. (c): Plot (c) represents an endothermic reaction with high activation energy.

177. (a): The presence of a catalyst does not affect the enthalpy change of the reaction. Hence, $\Delta H = 200 - 180 = 20$ kJ mol^{-1}

178. (d): From the given figure,
$\Delta H = -200$ kJ mol^{-1}
$E_a = 1640$ kJ mol^{-1}
For the reverse reaction,
$\Delta H = +\,120$ kJ mol^{-1}
Activation energy for the reverse reaction
$= 1640 + 120 = +1760$ kJ mol^{-1}

179. (c): Activation energy is always positive.

180. (a): Higher the activation energy for reactants, slower is the reaction.

181. (c): $\Delta H° = c$

182. (c): Potential energy for the activated complex is the same for the forward as well as the reverse reaction. Hence, statement 1 is wrong.

183. (b):

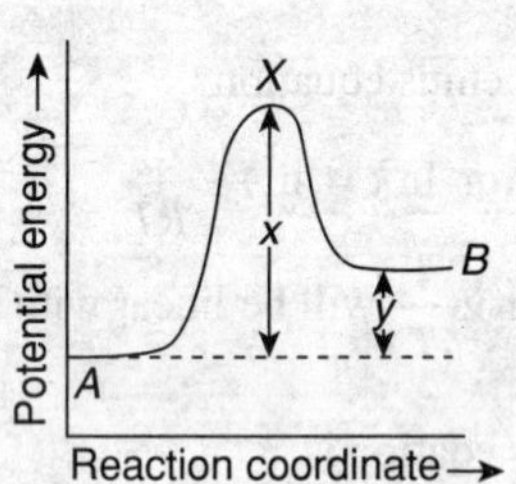

Activation energy for reverse reaction = B to X = $x - y$.

184. (c): A small increase in $e^{-E/RT}$ resulting in a large increase in k is due to the high value of A.

185. (c): For every 10° rise, the rate constant is doubled. Hence, for a 20°C rise, the rate constant will become 4 times, that is, $K_1 = 4\,K_2$ or $K_2 = 0.25\,K_1$.

186. (a): When activation energy is nearly 50 kJ mol^{-1}, the temperature coefficient of the reaction is,
$k_{t+10} / k_t = 2$

187. (b):
$10° \xrightarrow{2r} 20° \xrightarrow{4r} 30° \xrightarrow{8r} 40° \xrightarrow{16r} 50° \xrightarrow{32r}$
$60° \xrightarrow{64r} 70° \xrightarrow{128r} 80° \xrightarrow{256r} 90° \xrightarrow{512r} 100°$ or from 10° to 100°, a 10° rise has been done 9 times.
Final rate = Rate at $10° \times 2^9 = 512r$

188. (d): Temperature coefficient of 2 means, the rate of reaction doubles for every 10° rise in temperature. Rise from 30°C means temperature has been increased 6 times by 10° each time. Hence, increase in rate = $2^6 = 64$ times.

189. (a): Temperature coefficient is not the ratio of the rate constant at any two temperatures but at 308 K and 298 K.

190. (c): $\log \frac{k_2}{k_1} = \frac{12.49}{2.303 \times 0.002} \times \left(\frac{10}{2.95 \times 305}\right) = 0.301$

$\therefore \frac{k_2}{k_1} = 2$ or $k_2 = 2k_1$

That is, reaction rate increases by 100%.

Remember. For $E_a = 12.5$ kcal or 50 kJ, temperature coeff. = 2.

191. (c): $\ln k = \ln A - \frac{E_a}{RT}$

At very high temperature, $T \frac{E_a}{RT} = 0$

Hence, $\ln k \to \ln A$ or $k \to A$

192. (b): Activation energy of a reaction has a fixed value and does not change with a change in temperature.

193. (b): Temperature coefficient of the reaction = $2\left(\frac{k_t + 10}{k_t}\right)$

$\therefore \frac{k_{27°}}{k_{17°}} = 2$ or $k_{17°} = \frac{k_{27°}}{2} = \frac{10^{-3}}{2} \times 10^{-4}$

194. (d): According to the Arrhenius equation

$k = Ae^{-E_a/RT}$

$\therefore \log k = \log A - \frac{E_a}{2.303R}$

Hence, plot of $\log k$ vs $\frac{1}{T}$ will be linear with a slope of $\frac{-E_a}{2.303R}$.

195. (c): From Arrhenius equation

$k = Ae^{-E_a/RT}$ or $\ln k = \ln A - \frac{E_a}{RT}$

Thus, plot of $\ln$ vs $\frac{1}{T}$ will be linear with slope = $-\frac{E_a}{RT}$.

196. (b): Arrhenius eqation is:

$$\frac{k_2}{k_1} = \frac{E_a}{RT}\left(\frac{1}{T_1} - \frac{1}{T_2}\right)$$

197. (d): Plot of $\log k$ vs $1/T$ helps to calculate E_a and A.

198. (a): According to Arrhenius equation,

$k = Ae^{-E/RT}$

Thus, k increases exponentially with an increase in temperature.

199. (d): $k = Ae^{-E/RT}$

$\therefore \ln k = \ln A - \frac{E_a}{RT}$

Hence, plot of $\ln k$ vs $1/T$ is linear with a –ve slope ($-E_a/R$) and intercept = $\ln A$.

200. (c): k = rate constant, A = frequency factor, E_a = activation energy and R = gas constant.

201. (b): $\ln k = \ln A - \frac{E_a}{RT}$

The plot of $\ln k$ vs $\frac{1}{T}$ is linear with intercept = $\ln A$.

202. (b): In the Arrhenius equation, E represents the energy below which colliding molecules will not react or above which the colliding molecules will react.

203. (a): In Arrhenius equation, $k = Ae^{-E_a/RT}$, the factor $-E_a/RT$ is called the Boltzmann factor having an energy equal to or greater than E_a.

204. (c): $k = Ae^{-E_a/RT}$

Taking the logarithm of both sides, we get

$\ln k = \ln A - \frac{E_a}{RT}$

or $\log k = \log A - \frac{E_a}{2.303R}\left(\frac{1}{T}\right)$

Thus, $\log k$ is plotted against $1/T$ to get the Arrhenius plot.

205. (c): $\log\frac{k_2}{k_1} = \frac{E_a}{2.303R} = \left(\frac{1}{T_1} - \frac{1}{T_2}\right) = \frac{E_a}{2.303R}\left(\frac{T_2 - T_1}{T_1T_2}\right)$

$\therefore \log 2 = \frac{E_a}{2.303 \times 8.314}\left(\frac{308 - 293}{293 \times 308}\right)$

or $E_a = \frac{0.3010 \times 2.303 \times 8.314 \times 293 \times 308}{15}$

$= 34.67 \text{ kJ mol}^{-1} \simeq 34.7 \text{ kJ mol}^{-1}$

206. (b): Slope of the line = $-\frac{E_a}{2.303R} = -6670$ K

$\therefore E_a = 2.303 \times 8.314 \text{ JK}^{-1} \text{ mol}^{-1} \times 6670$ K

$= 127711.4 \text{ J mol}^{-1} = 127.7 \text{ kJ mol}^{-1}$

207. (b): $\log\frac{k_2}{k_1} = \frac{E_a}{2.303R} = \left(\frac{T_2 - T_1}{T_1T_2}\right)$

$\log\frac{6}{1} = \frac{E_a}{2.303 \times 8.314}\left(\frac{400 - 350}{350 \times 400}\right)$

$0.7782 = \frac{E_a}{2.303 \times 8.314} \times \frac{50}{350 \times 400}$

or $E_a = \frac{0.7782 \times 2.303 \times 8.314 \times 350 \times 400}{50}$ J

$= 41720 \text{ J} = 41.7 \text{ kJ}$

208. (d): According to Arrhenius equation,

$k = Ae^{-E_a/RT}$ $\therefore \frac{E_a}{RT} = -\frac{2800 K}{T}$

or $E_a = 28000 K \times R$

$= 28000 K \times 8.314 \text{ JK}^{-1} \text{ mol}^{-1} = 232.8 \text{ kJ mol}^{-1}$

209. (b): At $T_1 = 200 K$ if $k_1 = k$, then at $T_2 = 400$ K, $k_2 = 10k$

$\therefore \log\frac{10k}{k} = \frac{E_a}{2.303R}\left(\frac{400 - 200}{400 \times 200}\right)$ or $E_a = 921.2R$

210. (d): Given $K = \frac{3200}{e^{32/RT}} = 3200e^{-32/RT}$

Comparing with Arrhenius equation,

$k = Ae^{-E_a/RT}$ $E_a = 32$ cal/mol

211. (d): If $E_a = 0, k = Ae^{-E_a/RT}$

$= Ae^0 = A$. Hence, k becomes independent of T.

212. (b): $\log\frac{k_2}{k_1} = \frac{E_a}{2.303\,R} = \left(\frac{T_2 - T_1}{T_1 T_2}\right)$

$= \frac{58300}{2.303 \times 8.3}\left(\frac{5}{300 \times 305}\right) = 0.1667$

$\therefore\ \frac{k_2}{k_2} = \text{antilog } 0.1667 = 1.468 \approx 1.5$

213. (b): $\log k - \log A = \frac{-E_a}{2.303\,R}$

or $\log\left(\frac{k}{A}\right) = -\frac{E_a}{2.303\,R} = -\frac{2.303\,RT}{2.303\,RT} = -1$

or $\frac{k}{A} = \text{Antilog}\,(-1) = 10^{-1} = 0.1$

214. (a): $\ln k = \ln A - \frac{E_a}{R}.\frac{1}{T}$

Plot I is more steep, k increases faster with $\frac{1}{T}$ or k increases less faster with T. Hence, reaction I has a higher activation energy. That is, $E_I > E_{II}$. The intercept on $\ln k$ axis by plot I is greater.

Hence, $[\ln A]_I > \ln A]_{II} >$ or A_I or $A_I > A_{II}$.

215. (d): $k = \frac{0.693}{t_{1/2}} = \frac{0.693}{256 \times 60}\text{s}^{-1} = 4.51 \times 10^{-5}\,\text{s}^{-1}$

Substituting this value in the given expression,

$\log(4.51 \times 10^{-5}) = 14.34 - \frac{1.25 \times 10^4}{T}$

or $-4.346 = 14.34 - \frac{1.25 \times 10^4}{T}$

or $\frac{1.25 \times 10^4}{T} = 14.34 + 4.346 = 18.686$

or $T = \frac{1.25 \times 10^4}{18.686} = 669\ \text{K}$

216. (c): Lower the activation energy, faster is the reaction.

217. (c): If activation energies for forward and backward reaction are equal, $\Delta H = 0$.

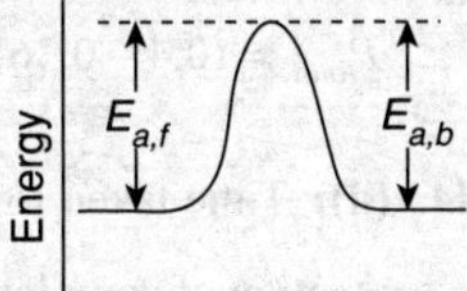

Effect of Catalyst on the Rate of Reaction

218. (a): A catalyst brings down the energy of activation.

219. (d): Lower the activation energy, faster is the reaction. Hence, the relative ease of P, Q and R will be $R > Q > P$.

220. (d): The catalyst provides an alternative path of lower activation energy.

221. (b): Enzyme catalysed reactions have lower activation energy.

Collision Theory of Chemical Reactions, Theory of Absolute Reaction Rates (Transition State Theory)

222. (a): According to the theory of absolute reaction rates (also called transition state theory), the reactants first combine to form an activated complex.

223. (c): Collision theory is satisfactory for bimolecular reactions.

224. (d): All the given statements are correct according to collision theory.

Photochemical Reactions

225. (c): The free energy change (ΔG) of a photochemical reaction is positive because a part of the light energy absorbed is converted into free energy.

226. (a): Darkening of AgCl in light is a photochemical reaction.

227. (c): Hg vapour acts as a photosensitiser.

Miscellaneous

228. (a): For equinormal solutions of the two acids,

$\frac{\text{Strength of Acid}_1}{\text{Strength of Acid}_2} = \frac{k_2}{k_1}$

229. (d): Photosynthesis in plants is a fast reaction.

230. (b): H^+ ions act as catalyst for the given reaction.

231. (c): Zero order reactions are multi-step reactions. For example, in the decomposition of NH_3 on the surface of platinum, the first step is the adsorption of reactants on the surface, followed by chemical reaction with the surface and finally desorption of products from the surface.

232. (b): The rate of a zero order reaction is independent of concentration. Hence, (i) is wrong.

$k = A\,e^{-E_a/RT}$

When $E_a = 0 = k = A$.

When $E_a = \infty, k \neq A$.

Plot of $\ln k$ vs $1/T$ is a straight line.

Hence, only (ii) and (v) are correct.

233. (b): Higher the activation energy, lower is the rate constant. Hence, (b) is incorrect.

Final Preparation

234. (d): $k = \frac{2.303}{t}\log\frac{a}{a-x}$

or $\log\frac{a}{a-x} = \frac{kt}{2.303} = \frac{2.2 \times 10^{-5} \times 60 \times 90}{2.303} = 0.0516$

Hence, $\frac{a}{a-x} = \text{Antiog } (0.0516) = 1.127$

or $\frac{a-x}{a} = \frac{1}{1.127} = 0.887$

or $1 - \frac{x}{a} = 0.887$ or $\frac{x}{a} = 0.113 = 11.3\,\%$

235. (b): Rate $\left(\frac{dt}{dt}\right) = k[A]$

$\therefore$ 1.5 $\times 10^{-2}$ mol L^{-1} $min^{-1} = k \times 0.5$ mol L^{-1}

or $k = \frac{1.5\times10^{-2}}{0.5} min^{-1}$

For 1st order reaction, $t_{1/2} = \frac{0.693}{k}$

$= \frac{0.693}{1.5\times10^{-2}} \times 0.5$ min = 23.1 min

236. (c): $k = \frac{2.303}{t}\log\frac{C_0}{C_t} = \frac{2.303}{40 \text{ min}}\log\frac{0.1 \text{ M}}{0.025 \text{ M}}$

$= \frac{2.303}{40}\log 4 = \frac{2.303\times0.6021}{40} min^{-1}$

Rate $= k[X] = \frac{2.303\times0.6021}{40} min^{-1} \times 0.01$ M

$= 3.47 \times 10^{-4}$ M/min

237. (c): From data of flask I,

$k = \frac{2.303}{8}\log\frac{1}{0.25} = \frac{2.303}{8}\log 4 = \frac{2.303}{4}\log 2$

From data of flask II,

$t = \frac{2.303}{k}\log\frac{0.6}{0.3} = \frac{2.303}{k}\log 2 = 4$ hours

(Substituting the value of k from first equation)

238. (b): For a first order reaction,

$k = \frac{1}{t}\log_e\frac{[A]_0}{[A]}$ or $kt = \log_e\frac{[A]_0}{[A]}$

or $kt = \log_e[A]_0 - \log_e[A]$

or $-\log_e [A] = kt - \log_0 [A]$

Thus, slope (k) will be +ve when we plot $-\log_e$ [A] vs t .

239. (b): $k = \frac{0.693}{T_{50}} = \frac{0.693}{10} min^{-1} = 0.0693 min^{-1}$

Concentration after 20 minutes, that is, after two half-lives,

$= \frac{1}{2}\left(\frac{1}{2}\times 10\right)$ mol L^{-1} = 2.5 mol L^{-1}

Rate, $\frac{dx}{dt} = k[A] = 0.0693 \times 2.5$ mol $L^{-1}min^{-1}$

240. (c): $\frac{-d[A]}{dt} = k$ or $k = \frac{-1\, d[A]}{dt}$

It is gives that $\frac{d[A]}{dt} = \frac{25}{100}$ in $dt = 60s$

$\therefore k = \frac{25}{100}\times\frac{1}{60}s^{-1} = 4.16\times10^{-4}\ s^{-1}$

241. (c): $a \propto P_0$ and $(a-x) \propto P_t$.

Hence, $k = \frac{2.303}{t}\log\frac{P_0}{P_t}$ (P_t = pressure of Cl_2O_7 at time t)

(i) $t = 50$ s, $P_0 = 0.062$ atm, $P_t = 0.044$ atm.

$k = \frac{2.303}{50\ s}\log\frac{0.062 \text{ atm}}{0.044 \text{ atm}} = 6.86\times10^{-3}\ s^{-1}$

(ii) $t = 100$ sec, $P_t = ?, k = 6.86 \times 10^{-3} s^{-1}$

$6.86 \times 10^{-3} s^{-1} = \frac{2.303}{100\ s}\log\frac{0.062 \text{ atm}}{P_t}$

$\log\frac{0.062}{P_t} = 0.2979$ or $\frac{0.062}{P_t}$ = Antilog 0.2979 = 1.986

or $P_t = 0.0312$ atm

242. (c): Rate constant in min^{-1} shows that it is a reaction of 1st order.

Hence,

$k = \frac{2.303}{t}\log\frac{[A]_0}{[A]}$

or $4.5\times10^{-3}\ min^{-1} = \frac{2.303}{60 \text{ min}}\log\frac{1}{[A]}$

or $\log[A] = -0.1172 = \bar{1}.8828$

or [A] = Antilog ($\bar{1}.8828$)

$\therefore$ [A] = 0.7635 mol L^{-1}

This is the concentration after 1 h .

Rate after 1 h = $k[A] 4.5\times10^{-3} \times 0.7635$ mol L^{-1} min^{-1}

$= 3.44 \times 10^{-3}$ mol L^{-1} min^{-1}

243. (d): $k = \frac{0.693}{69.3s} = 0.01\,s^{-1}$

$k = \frac{2.303}{t}\log\frac{a}{a-x}$

$\therefore 0.01 = \frac{2.303}{230s}\log\frac{0.4}{0.4-x}$. On calculation,

$x = 0.36$

Now,	A(g)	$\rightarrow$ P(g) +	Q(g) +	R(g)
Initial	0.4 atm	0	0	0
Final	0.4 $-x$	x	x	x
	0.4 – 0.36	0.36	0.36	0.36

$P_{total} = (0.4 - 0.36) + 0.36 + 0.36 + 0.36 = 1.12$ atm

244. (d): Time taken to reduce by a factor of $\frac{1}{4}$ (that is, 75% of reaction of complete) = 20 min. (= two half lives)

$\therefore$ Time take to reduce by factor of $\frac{1}{2}$ (that is, 50% of reaction of complete)

That is, $t_{1/2} = 10$ min

$a \xrightarrow{t_{1/2}} \frac{a}{2} \xrightarrow{t_{1/2}} \frac{a}{4} \xrightarrow{t_{1/2}} \frac{a}{8} \xrightarrow{t_{1/2}} \frac{a}{16}$

Total time required = $4 \times t_{1/2} = 4 \times 10$ min = 40 min

245. (d): Half-life period of a second order reaction

$t_{1/2} = \frac{1}{\text{Rate constant} \times \text{Intial conc.}} = \frac{1}{ka}$

$$= \frac{1}{10^{-4}\ \text{L mol}^{-1}\ \text{min}^{-1} \times 10^{-2}\ \text{mol L}^{-1}} = 10^6\ \text{min}$$

246. (b): $t_{1/2}$ for 1st order reaction $= \frac{0.693}{k}$

$t_{1/2}$ for zero order reaction $\frac{[A]_0}{2k'}$

Initial rate for 1st order reaction

$(r_1) = k[A]_0$

Initial rate for zero order reaction

$(r_0) = k'$

$\therefore \frac{r_1}{r_0} = \frac{k[A]_0}{k'}$

But $\frac{0.693}{k} = \frac{[A]_0}{2\,k'}$ (Given)

$\therefore \frac{k\,[A]_0}{k'} = 2 \times 0.693$, that is, $\frac{r_1}{r_0} = 2 \times 0.693$

247. (c): 10.8 g of $N_2O_5 = \frac{10.8}{108}$ mol = 0.1 mol

No. of half-lives in 9.6 h $= \frac{9.6}{2.4} = 4$

Amount left after 4 half-lives $= \frac{1}{2^4} \times 0.1 = \frac{0.1}{16}$ mol

Mol of N_2O_5 decomposed $= 0.1 - \frac{0.1}{16} = \frac{1.5}{16}$ mol

Mol of O_2 formed $= \frac{1}{2} \times \frac{1.5}{16} \times \frac{1.5}{32}$

Volume of O_2 at STP $= \frac{1.5}{32} \times 22.4$ L = 1.05 L

248. (c): By hit and trial method, if reaction is of zero order,

$k = \frac{1}{t}\{[A]_0 - [A]\}$

Case I. $k = \frac{1}{25} \times \frac{25}{100} = 10^{-2}$

Case II. $k = \frac{1}{25} \times \frac{1}{2}\{[A]_0 - [A]\} = \frac{1}{25} \times \frac{1}{2} \times \frac{25}{100} = 10^{-2}$

Case III. $k = \frac{1}{50} \times 2\,\{[A]_0 - [A]\} = \frac{1}{50} \times 2 \times \frac{25}{100} = 10^{-2}$

As k comes out to be constant, the given reaction is of zero order.

249. (d): A → P. A plot of 1/[A] vs time is a straight line. Hence, it is a reaction of second order. For a second order reaction,

$t_{1/2} \propto \frac{1}{[A]_0}$

$\therefore \frac{(t_{1/2})_1}{(t_{1/2})_2} = \frac{[A_0]_2}{[A_0]_1}$

$\therefore \frac{20}{(t_{1/2})_2} = \frac{3.0 \times 10^{-3}}{1.0 \times 10^{-2}}$ or $(t_{1/2})_2 = \frac{2.0 \times 10^{-2}}{3 \times 10^{-3}} = 67$ min.

250. (b): A + B → Products

Rate, $r = k[A]^\alpha [B]^\beta = ka^\alpha b^\beta$ ...(i)

When [B] is doubled, $\frac{r}{4} = ka^\alpha (2b)^\beta$ ...(ii)

Dividing Eq. (ii) by Eq. (i),

$2^\beta = \frac{1}{4} = 2^{-2}$ or $\beta = -2$

251. (a):

	2A(g)	→	B(g) + C(s)	
Initial	P_0		0	0
After time t	$P_0 - 2p$		p	0

∴ Pressure after time, t $P_t = P_0 - 2p + p = P_0 - p$

After completion Total pressure $= P_0/2$

Thus, $P_0 - p = 300$ pascals, $\frac{P_0}{2} = 200$ pascals

∴ $P_0 = 400$ pascals, $p = 100$ pascals

$a \propto P_0, x \propto 2p$

$k = \frac{2.303}{t}\log\frac{a}{a-x} = \frac{2.303}{t}\log\frac{P_0}{P_0 - 2p}$

$= \frac{2.303}{10}\log\frac{400}{400-20} = \frac{2.303}{10} \times 0.3010\ \text{min}^{-1}$

$= 0.0693\ \text{min}^{-1}$

252. (c): Rate constant (k) = Slope of the line

$= \frac{-5-(-6)}{4000-2000} = \frac{1}{2000} = 5 \times 10^{-4}\,\text{s}^{-1}$

253. (b): $2NO_2 \underset{k_2}{\overset{k_1}{\rightleftharpoons}} N_2O_4$

Rate $= -\frac{1}{2}\frac{d[NO_2]}{dt} = k_1[NO_2]^2 - k_2[N_2O_4]$

∴ Rate of disappearance of NO_2

That is, $-\frac{d[NO_2]}{dt} = 2k_1[NO_2]^2 - 2k_2[N_2O_4]$

254. (b): Rate depends upon slowest step.

Hence, from Eq. (ii), $r = k\,[O_3][O]$.

From Eq. (i),

$K_{eq} = \frac{[O_2][O]}{[O_3]}$ or $[O] = \frac{K_{eq}[O_3]}{[O_2]}$

Hence, $r = k[O_3]\frac{K_{eq}[O_3]}{[O_2]} = k'[O_3]^2[O_2]^{-1}$

255. (c): t_{max} represents the time corresponding to the maximum concentration of the intermediate R_2.

The value of t_{max} is given by the reaction

$t_{max} = \frac{2.303}{(k_1 - k_2)}\log\frac{k_1}{k_2}$

$k_1 - 4.0 \times 10^{-2}$

$\therefore k_2 = 4.0 \times 10^{-2} \times 0.5 = 6 \times 10^{-3}$

$\therefore t_{max} = \frac{2.303}{(4-0.6)10^{-2}}\log\frac{4 \times 10^{-2}}{6 \times 10^{-3}}$

$= \frac{2.303}{3.4 \times 10^{-2}} \times 0.82 = 55.6$ min

256. (b): For $OCl^- + I^- \xrightarrow{OH^-} OI^- + Cl^-$

Rate = $k[OCl^-][I^-][OH^-]^{-1}$

257. (b): $k_{av} = k_1 + k_2 = 2\times10^{-6}\ s^{-1}$

Also, $2.303 \log \frac{[A_0]}{[A_t]} = kt$

$\log\frac{0.25}{[A_t]} = \frac{20\times10^{-6}\times5\times60\times60}{2.303}$ or $\frac{0.25}{[A_t]} = 1.43$

$\therefore [A_t] = \frac{0.25}{1.433} = 0.1744$

$\therefore$ [A] decomposed $[A_0]-[A_t] = 0.25 - 0.1744 = 0.0756$ M

Fraction of C formed $= \frac{k_2}{k_1+k_2}\times[A^0]_{decomposed}\times\frac{2}{5}$

$= 0.0756\times\frac{5\times10^{-6}}{20\times10^{-6}}\times\frac{2}{5} = 7.56\times10^{-3}$ M

258. (a): For a first order reaction

$k = \frac{2.303}{t}\log\frac{a}{a-x}$

$\therefore 1.5\times10^{-6} = \frac{2.303}{10\times60\times60}\log\frac{a}{a-x}$

or $\log\frac{a}{a-x} = \frac{1.5\times10^{-6}\times10\times60\times60}{2.303} = 0.02344$

or $\log\frac{a}{a-x} = -0.02344 = \bar{1}.9756$ or $\frac{a-x}{a} = 0.9474$

$\therefore$ % of the reaction remaining $= 0.9474\times100 = 94.74\%$

$\therefore$ % of initial concentration changed into products
= 100 − 94.74 = 5.26%

259. (c): For 1st order reaction, $t_{1/2} = \frac{0.693}{k_1}$

For 2nd order reaction, $t_{1/2} = \frac{1}{k_2 a}$

As $t_{1/2}$ values are equal, $\frac{0.693}{k_1} = \frac{1}{k_2 a}$

or $\frac{k_1}{k_2} = 0.693\,a$

Initially, rate of 1st order reaction,
$r_1 = k_1 a$

Rate of 2nd order reaction, $r_2 = k_2 a^2$

$\therefore \frac{r_1}{r_2} = \frac{k_1 a}{k_2 a^2} = \frac{k_1}{k_2 a} = \frac{k_1}{k_2}\frac{1}{a} = 0.693\,a\times\frac{1}{a} = 0.693$

260. (c): For a zero order reaction, $t_{1/2}$ or $t_{50\%} = \frac{a}{2k}$

Hence, plot of $t_{50\%}$ vs a will be linear passing through the origin with slope $= \frac{1}{2k}$. As slope = tan 45° = 1.

$= \frac{1}{2k} = 1$ or $k = 0.5$

261. (b): Change in molarity

$= \frac{n}{V} = \frac{\Delta P}{RT} = \frac{2-1.2}{0.0821\times298} = 0.0327$

$\therefore$ Rate of reaction $= \frac{0.0327\ \text{mol L}^{-1}}{50\times60\ \text{s}}$

$= 1.09\times10^{-5}\ \text{mol L}^{-1}\ \text{s}^{-1}$

262. (a):

	$C_4H_8 \xrightarrow{\Delta} 2C_2H_4$	
Moles at $t=0$	a	0
Moles after time t	$(a-x)$	$2x$

When $\frac{2x}{a-x} = 1$, then $2x = a - x$ or $3x = a$, that is, $x = \frac{a}{3}$

As rate constant is in s^{-1}, it is a reaction of 1st order. Hence,

$t = \frac{2.303}{k}\log\frac{a}{a-x}$

$= \frac{2.303}{2.48\times10^{-4}\ s^{-1}}\log\frac{a}{a-a/3} = \frac{2.303}{2.48\times10^{-4}}\log\frac{3}{2}$

$= 16355.2$ s $= 27.25$ min

263. (a): At pH = 5, as half-life period is found to be independent of initial concentration of sucrose, this means with respect to sucrose, it is a reaction of first order, that is, Rate = k [Sucrose].

In n is the order with respect to H⁺ ion,

$t_{1/2} \propto [H^+]^{1-n}$, that is, $500 \propto (10^{-5})^{1-n}$ ...(i)

[pH = 5 means $[H^+] = 10^{-5}$ M]

and $50 \propto (10^{-6})^{1-n}$ ...(ii)

[pH = 6 means $[H^+] = 10^{-6}$ M]

Dividing (i) by (ii), $10 = (10)^{1-n}$

$1 - n = 1$ or = 0, that is, the order with respect to H⁺ ion = 0.

Hence, overall rate law is

Rate = k [Sucrose]$[H^+]^0$

264. (c): Rate $(r) = k[H^+]^n$

When $pH = 3$, $[H^+] = 10^{-3}$ M.

When $pH = 1$, $[H^+] = 10^{-1}$ M

$\frac{r_1}{r_2} = \frac{k(10^{-3})^n}{k(10^{-1})^n}$

$\therefore \frac{1}{100} = \left(\frac{10^{-3}}{10^{-1}}\right)^n$ ($\because r_2 = 100$ M)

$\therefore (10^{-2})^1 = (10^{-2})^n$

$\therefore n = 1$

265. (d): $k_1 = 10^{16}e^{-2000/T}$

$k_2 = 10^{15}e^{-1000/T}$

When $k_1 = k_2$, $10^{16}e^{-2000/T} = 10^{15}e^{-1000/T}$

or $10\,e^{-2000/T} = e^{-1000/T}$

Taking natural logarithm of both sides, we get,

$\ln\frac{2000}{T} = \frac{-1000}{T}$ or $2.303 - \frac{2000}{T} = \frac{-1000}{T}$

or $\frac{1000}{T} = 2.303$ or $T = \frac{2000}{2.303}$

266. (d): Given $\log k = 6 - \frac{2000}{T}$

Comparing with $\log k = \log A - \frac{E_a}{2.303\,RT}$

log A = 6, that is,

$A = 10^6$ and $\frac{E_a}{2.303} = 2000$

or $E_a = 2000 \times 2.303 \times 8.314 \text{ J mol}^{-1}$

$= 38294 \text{ J mol}^{-1} \approx 38.3 \text{ kJ mol}^{-1}$

267. (a): $k_{27°C} = \frac{0.693}{30} \text{min}^{-1}$

$k_{47°C} = \frac{0.693}{10} \text{min}^{-1}$

$\therefore \frac{k_{47°C}}{k_{27°C}} = 3$

$\log\frac{k_{47°C}}{k_{27°C}} = \log 3 \; \frac{E_a}{2.303 \times 8.314}\left(\frac{20}{300 \times 320}\right)$

which gives

$E_a = \frac{0.4771 \times 2.303 \times 8.314 \times 300 \times 320}{20} = 43.84 \text{ kJ}$

268. (c): Rate of reaction $\propto$ Rate constant. As rate of reaction increases 2.5 times the rate constant will become 2.5 times. (Alternatively, temperature coefficient = 2.5.)

269. (a): $k = Ae^{-E_a/RT} = \frac{A}{e^{-E_a/RT}}$

Thus, as T increases, the exponential factor in the denominator decreases or $Ae^{-E_a/RT}$ increases. Hence, k increases exponentially as T increases.

270. (a): According to Arrhenius equation,

$\ln k = \ln A - \frac{E_a}{RT}$

Differentiating with respect to T, $\frac{d\ln k}{dT} = \frac{E_a}{RT^2}$

Given k_1 for 1st order > k_2 for 2nd order and E_1 for 1st order > E_2 for 2nd order

Now, as E_a increases, $\ln k$ will also increase but k_1 will increase faster than k_2 but will always remain less than k_2.

271. (d): $T_1 = 27 + 273 = 300$ K

$T_2 - 273 - 3 = 270$ K

$k_2 = k, k_1 = 10\,k$ (higher the temperature, greater is the value of k)

$\log\frac{k_2}{k_1} = \frac{E_a}{2.303\,R}\left(\frac{1}{T_1} - \frac{1}{T_2}\right)$

or $\log\frac{1}{10} = \frac{E_a}{2.303\,R}\left(\frac{1}{300} - \frac{1}{270}\right)$

$-1 = \frac{E_a}{2.303\,R}\left(\frac{-30}{300 \times 270}\right)$

or $E_a = 2.303\,R \times 2700 \text{ J mol}^{-1}$

$= 2.303 \times 2.7 \text{ kJ mol}^{-1}$

272. (c): $\ln\frac{k_2}{k_1} = \frac{E_a}{R}\left(\frac{1}{T_1} - \frac{1}{T_2}\right)$ or $\ln\frac{k_2}{k_1} = \frac{E_a}{R}\left(\frac{1}{300} - \frac{1}{600}\right)$

or $\ln\frac{k_2}{k_1} = \frac{600\,R}{R}\left(\frac{1}{300} - \frac{1}{600}\right)$

$= \frac{600R}{R}\left(\frac{2-1}{600}\right) = 1 = \ln e$

$\therefore \frac{k_2}{k_1} = e$

273. (a): From the given plot, when $\frac{1}{T_1}$

$= 1.5 \times 10^{-3}, \ln k_1 = 2.0$ and when $\frac{1}{T_2}$

$= 2.0 \times 10^{-3}, \ln k_2 = 6.0$

$\ln\frac{k_2}{k_1} = \frac{\Delta H}{R}\left[\frac{1}{T_1} - \frac{1}{T_2}\right]$

$\therefore \ln\frac{6}{2} = \frac{\Delta H}{R}[1.5 \times 10^{-3} - 2.0 \times 10^{-3}]$

or $1.0987 = \frac{\Delta H}{R}(-0.5 \times 10^{-3})$

or ΔH is – ve, the reaction is exothermic.

274. (d): According to Arrhenius equation,

$\log k = \log A - \frac{E_a}{2.303\,RT}$ ...(i)

For a 1st order reaction,

$k = \frac{0.693}{t_{1/2}} = \frac{0.693}{600\text{s}} = 1.1 \times 10^{-3}\text{s}^{-1}$

Substituting the values, of k, A and E_a in Eq. (i), we get

$\log(1.1 \times 10^{-3}) = \log(4 \times 10^{13})$

$-\frac{98.6 \times 10^3}{2.303 \times 8.314 \times T}$

On solving, we get $T = 311.15$ K.

275. (c): $\log k = \log A - \frac{E_a}{2.303\,RT}$

Slope $= \frac{E_a}{2.303\,RT} = \tan\theta = \frac{1}{2.303}$ (Given)

$E_a = 2.303\,R \times$ Slope

$= 2.303R \times \frac{1}{2.303} = R = 2$ cal

276. (b): In absence of a catalyst, suppose rate constant = k , then

$$\log k = \log A - \frac{E_a}{2.303\ RT}$$

In presence of catalyst, suppose rate constant = k'
Now activation energy
$= E_a - 2$ (if E_a is in kcal mol^{-1})

$$\log k' = \log A - \frac{E_a - 2}{2.303\ RT}$$

Eq. (ii) – Eq. (i) gives

$$\log k' = \log k - \frac{2 \text{ kcal mol}^{-1}}{2.303\ RT}$$

$$\log \frac{k'}{k} = \frac{2 \text{ kcal mol}^{-1}}{2.303(2\times10^{-3} \text{kcal K}^{-1}\text{mol}^{-1})(300 \text{ K})} = 1.4474$$

$$\frac{k'}{k} = \text{Antilog } 1.4474 = 28 \text{ or } k' = 28k$$

277. (c): $k_{uc} = Ae^{E_{uc}/RT}$

$k_c = Ae^{E_c/RT}$

$$\frac{k_c}{k_{uc}} = \frac{e^{-E_{uc}/RT}}{e^{-E_c/RT}} = e^{(E_c - E_{uc})/RT}$$

$$= e^{8.314\times10^3/8.314\times300} = e^{3.33}$$

$$\ln\frac{k_c}{k_{uc}} = 3.33 \quad \text{or} \quad \log\frac{k_c}{k_{uc}} = \frac{3.33}{2.303} = 1.4459$$

$$\therefore \frac{k_c}{k_{uc}} = \text{Antilog } 1.4459 = 27.92 = 28 \text{ times}$$

278. (d): Being proteinaceous in nature.

279. (b): 310 K.

280. (d): 2.

281. (c): Pseudo unimolecular reaction.

282. (b): $A_2(g) \rightarrow B(g) + \frac{1}{2}\ C(g)$

100	0	0
$100 - p$	p	$\frac{1}{2}p$

$$100 - p + p + \frac{1}{2}p = 120 \quad \text{or} \quad p = 40 \text{mm}$$

$$\therefore -\frac{dp_{A_2}}{dt} = \frac{40}{5} = 8 \text{mm min}^{-1}$$

283. (b): $N_2 + 3H_2 \rightarrow 2NH_3$

$$\text{Rate} = -\frac{d[N_2]}{dt} = -\frac{1}{3}\frac{d[H_2]}{dt} = +\frac{1}{2}\frac{d[NH_3]}{dt}$$

Rate of disappearance of H_2,

$$\frac{d[NH_3]}{dt} = \frac{2}{3}\left(-\frac{d[H_2]}{dt}\right)$$

$$= \frac{2}{3} \times 6 \times 10^{-3} \text{ mol min}^{-1}$$

$= 4 \times 10^{-3}$ mol min^{-1}
Now, if $dt = 0.3$ min
NH_3 formed = (4×10^{-3} mol min^{-1})
(0.3 min) = 1.2×10^{-3} mol

284. (c): Initially Rate = $k[Y][Z]^{1/2}$
New rate = $k[Y][2Z]^{1/2}$

$$= \sqrt{2}k[Y][Z]^{\frac{1}{2}} = 1.414k\ [Y][Z]^{1/2}$$

285. (a): Rate of reaction = $-\frac{\Delta[A]}{\Delta t}$

$$= -\left(\frac{0.0135 - 0.0150}{60\ s}\right) = 2.5 \times 10^{-5} \text{ M s}^{-1}$$

But, rate of reaction = $\frac{1}{2}\frac{d[C]}{dt}$

$= 2.5\times10^{-5}$ M s^{-1}

$\therefore$ Rate of formation of C

$$\left(\frac{d[C]}{dt}\right) = 5\times10^{-5} \text{Ms}^{-1}$$

286. (c): $-\frac{d[N_2O_5]}{dt} = \frac{1}{2}\frac{d[NO_2]}{dt} = 2\frac{d[O_2]}{dt}$

$$k_1\ [N_2O_5] = \frac{1}{2}\ k_1'\ [N_2O_5] = 2k_1''\ [N_2O_5]$$

or $k_1 = \frac{1}{2}\ k_1' = 2k_1''$

or $2k_1 = k_1' = 4k_1''$

287. (d): Rate $(r_1) = k\ [SO_2]^2[O_2] = k\ x^2y$ (in one dm^3)

If volume is doubled (= 2 dm^3), concentrations will be halved.

$$\text{Hence, rate } (r_2) = k\left(\frac{x}{2}\right)^2\left(\frac{y}{2}\right) = k\frac{x^2y}{8}$$

$$\therefore r_1 : r_2 = 1 : \frac{1}{8} = 8:1$$

288. (a): Rate $= -\frac{d[C]}{dt}$

As $C = \frac{n}{V}$ $\therefore$ Rate $= -\left[\frac{dn}{dt}\right]\frac{1}{V}$

Also, $PV = n\ RT$ or $P = \frac{n}{V}\ RT = CRT$

or $C = \frac{P}{RT}$

$$\therefore \text{Rate} = -\frac{d[C]}{dt} = -\frac{1}{RT}\left[\frac{dP}{dt}\right]$$

289. (c): From slow step, rate $= k\ [B_2]\ [A]$.

From 1st Eq., $K_{eq} = \frac{[A]^2}{[A_2]}$

or $[A] = \sqrt{K_{eq}[A_2]} = K_{eq}^{1/2}[A_2]^{1/2}$

Hence, rate $k\ [B_2]\ K_{eq}^{\frac{1}{2}}[A_2]^{\frac{1}{2}} = k'[A_2]^{1/2}[B_2]$

Hence, order $= 1\frac{1}{2}$

290. (b): Rate $= k\ [NOBr_2]\ [NO]$ ...(i)

From step I, $K_{eq} = \dfrac{[NOBr_2]}{[NO][Br_2]}$

or $[NOBr_2] = K_{eq}\ [NO][Br_2]$

Substituting in Eq. (i), we get

Rate $= k\ K_{eq}\ [NO]^2[Br_2]$

$= k'[NO]^2[Br_2]$

Hence, order with respect to NO is 2.

291. (a): For a zero order reaction,

$$k = \frac{[A]_0}{2t_{1/2}} = \frac{2.0 \text{ mol L}^{-1}}{2\times 1 \text{ hr}} = 1.0 \text{ mol L}^{-1} \text{ hr}^{-1}$$

$$t = \frac{1}{k}\{[A_0]-[A]\} = \frac{1}{1.0}(0.50-0.25) = 0.25 \text{ h}$$

292. (d): $t_{1/2} = \dfrac{[A]_0}{2\,k}$

Thus, $t_{1/2} \propto [A]_0$

$t_{100\%} = \dfrac{[A]_0}{2k}$. Hence, $t_{100\%} = 2\times t_{1/2}$

Rate, $-\dfrac{d[A]}{dt} = k[A]^\circ = k$

$\therefore\ d[A] = -k\,dt$ or $[A] = -kt + I$

Thus, the concentration of the reactant decreases linearly with time. Hence, all the three statements are correct.

293. (b): For zero order reaction

$$x = kt = 0.2 \text{ mol dm}^{-3} \text{ hr}^{-1} \times \frac{30}{60}\text{h} = 0.1 \text{ mol dm}^{-3}$$

Conc. now $= 0.05$ mol dm^{-3}

Hence, initial conc. $= 0.1 + 0.05 = 0.15$ mol dm^{-3}.

MATCH THE FOLLOWING

294. (c): $t_{1/2}$ for zero order reaction $= [A]_0 / 2k$

Hence, (A) $\rightarrow$ (p)

Total life of a zero order reaction $= [A]_0 / k$

Hence, (B) $\rightarrow$ (r)

Half-life of a 2nd order reaction $= 1/(k[A]_0)$

Hence, (C) $\rightarrow$ (s)

Average life of a 1st order reaction $= 1/k$

Hence, (D) $\rightarrow$ (q)

295. (b): For zero order reaction,

$[A] = -kt + [A]_0$

Hence, plot of [A] vs t is linear with slope $= -k$ (A) $\rightarrow$ (q)

For a zero order reaction $t_{1/2} = \dfrac{[A]_0}{2k}$.

Hence, plot of $t_{1/2}$ *vs* $[A]_0$ is linear with slope $= 1/2\ k$

$\therefore$ (B) $\rightarrow$ (r)

For a 2nd order reaction,

$$k = \frac{1}{t}\left[\frac{1}{[A]} - \frac{1}{[A]_0}\right] \text{ or } \frac{1}{[A]} = kt + \frac{1}{[A]_0}$$

Hence, plot of 1/[A] vs t is linear with slope $= k$

$\therefore$ (C) $\rightarrow$ (p)

For a 1st order reaction, $t_{1/2}$ is independent of initial concentration. Hence, plot of $t_{1/2}$ vs $[A]_0$ is a horizontal line, that is, slope = zero.

$\therefore$ (D) $\rightarrow$ (s)

296. (b): (A) is a reaction of zero order

(B) is a reaction of the 1st order

(C) is a reaction of the 2nd order

(D) is a reaction of order 1.5

[Rate $= k\ [H_2]\ [Br_2]^{1/2}$]

ASSERTION REASON

297. (b): Correct explanation. In a complex reaction all the reactant molecules cannot collide simultaneously with each other.

298. (a): R is the correct explanation of A.

299. (c): Correct R. Rate constant of any reaction is constant at constant temperature and does not change with time or concentration. However, A is correct because

$$t = \frac{1}{k}\{[A]_0 - [A]\}$$

For 50%, $t_{50\%} = \dfrac{1}{k}\left\{[A]_0 - \dfrac{[A]_0}{2}\right\} = \dfrac{[A]_0}{2k} = 50$ s

For 75% $t_{75\%} = \dfrac{1}{k}\left\{[A]_0 - \dfrac{[A]_0}{4}\right\} = \dfrac{[A]_0}{k}\times\dfrac{3}{4}$

$= \dfrac{[A]_0}{2k}\times\dfrac{3}{2} = 50\times\dfrac{3}{2} = 75$ s

300. (b): Correct explanation. For a zero order reaction,

$t_{1/2} = \dfrac{[A]_0}{2k}$, that is,

$t_{1/2} \propto \left(t_{100\%}\ \dfrac{[A]_0}{k}\right)$

301. (a): R is the correct explanation of A.

302. (b): Correct explanation. Average life of a first order reaction is the time in which the concentration of the reactant is reduced to $1/e$ of its original concentration $[A] = [A]_0 / e$ $= [A]_0 / 2.71828\ \ldots = 0.37\ [A]_0$

$\therefore$ Amount rcacted 63% of $[A]_0$

303. (b): Correct explanation. In the hydrolysis of methyl acetate with dilutc IICl, water is taken in excess so that its concentration does not change during hydrolysis

304. (a): Correct A. The given reactions proceed at different rates.

Correct R. The given reactions have different activation energies.

305. (a): $A + B \rightarrow X^* \rightarrow$ Products
The activated complex X^* has a higher energy than the reactants. It is a special molecule which decomposes such that one vibrational degree of freedom is converted into a translational degree of freedom along the reaction coordinate. Hence, R is the correct explanation of A.

306. (c): Correct R. The presence of a catalyst lowers the activation energy barrier.

307. (b): Correct explanation. With an increase in temperature by 10°, the fraction of molecules possessing energy equal to or greater than the threshold value becomes 2 or 3 times.

308. (b): Correct explanation. According to Arrhenius equation, $k = Ae^{-E_a/RT}$. When $E_a = 0, k = A$.

309. (d): Correct A. A catalyst may increase or decrease the rate of a reaction.
Correct R. A negative catalyst does not decrease the activation energy of a reaction.

310. (a): R is the correct explanation of A.

311. (d): Correct A. $H_2 + Cl_2 \rightarrow 2HCl$ has a much higher quantum efficiency than $H_2 + Br_2 \rightarrow 2HBr$.
Correct R. The first step of the secondary process of $H_2 + Cl_2 \rightarrow 2HCl$ is exothermic while the same for $H_2 + Br_2 \rightarrow 2HBr$ is endothermic.

312. (a): R is the correct explanation of A.

313. (c): Correct R. Red light has a lower frequency or energy than violet light.

Surface Chemistry

5.1 General Introduction

Certain solids like charcoal and silica which when added into a closed vessel containing some gas or to an aqueous solution of a solute (such as acetic acid solution), attract the molecules of the gas or the solute from the solution towards the surface of the solid and then retained on the surface. As a result, the concentration of the gas or the solute on the surface of the solid increases. These molecules, however, remain only at the surface of the solid and do not penetrate into the bulk. This is known as *adsorption* (Fig. 5.1).

The substance thus adsorbed on the surface is called the *adsorbate* and the substance on which it is adsorbed is called the *adsorbent*. The reverse process, that is, the removal of the adsorbed substance from the surface is called *desorption* (which can be brought about by heating or reducing the pressure). The adsorption of gases on the surface of metals is called *occlusion*.

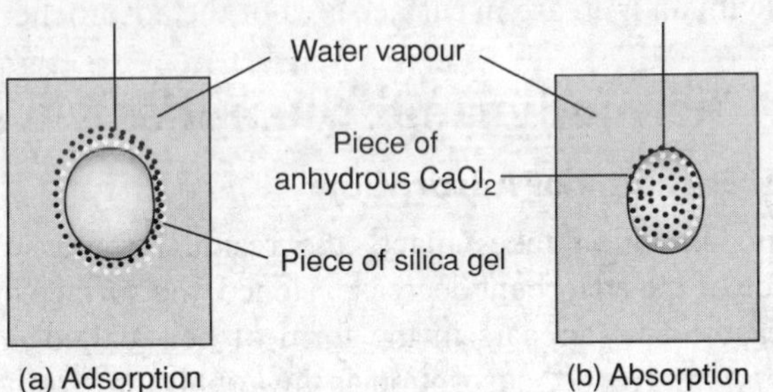

Fig. 5.1 Phenomena of adsorption and absorption

5.1.1 Positive and Negative Adsorption

When the concentration of the adsorbate is more on the surface of the adsorbent than in the bulk, it is called *positive adsorption*. In the case of positive adsorption by solids from the solutions, mostly the solute is adsorbed on the surface of the solid adsorbent so that the concentration of solute on the surface of the adsorbent is greater than in the bulk.

If the concentration of the adsorbate increases in the bulk after adsorption, it is called *negative adsorption.* In the case of negative adsorption, the solvent from the solution may be adsorbed by the adsorbent so that the concentration of the solution increases as compared with the initial concentration. For example, when a concentrated solution of KCl is shaken with activated charcoal, it shows positive adsorption but with a dilute solution of KCl, it shows negative adsorption.

5.1.2 Examples of Adsorption

The following experiments and results show that adsorption occurs.

(i) To the solution of an organic dye such as methylene blue, add animal charcoal and stir. The intensity of the colour in the solution decreases due to *adsorption.*

(ii) If a gas like ammonia, sulfur dioxide, chlorine, oxygen, hydrogen, carbon monoxide or phosgene is taken in a closed vessel containing powdered charcoal, it is observed that the pressure of the gas decreases; the gases are adsorbed at the surface.

(iii) If silica gel is placed in a closed vessel containing moist air, the air becomes dry after some time. This is because the water molecules are adsorbed on the surface of silica gel.

5.1.3 Mechanism of Adsorption

A molecule at the surface of a liquid is surrounded by a larger number of molecules in the liquid phase and fewer molecules in the vapour phase (in the space above the liquid surface). As a result, these molecules lying at the surface experience some net inward force of attraction which causes surface tension. Similar inward forces of attraction exist at the surface of a solid [Fig. 5.2(b)]. Alternatively, in the case of certain solids such as transition metals (like Ni), there are unutilised free valencies at the surface [Fig. 5.2(c)].

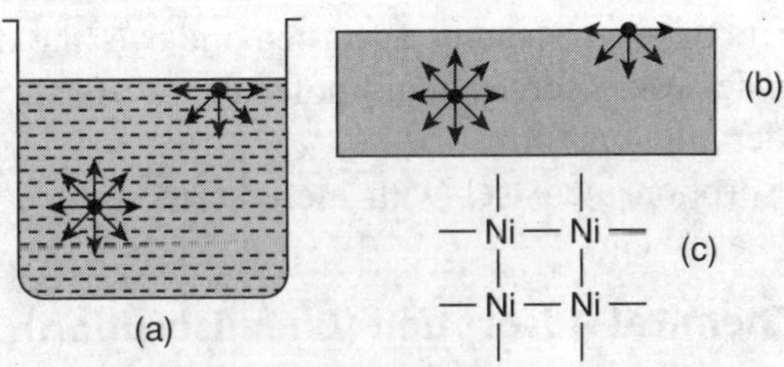

Fig. 5.2 Molecules at the surface experiencing a net inward force of attraction in case of **(a)** liquid **(b)** solid **(c)** metal with free valencies

Because of the unbalanced (or residual) inward forces of attraction or free valencies at the surface, liquids and solids have the property to attract and retain the molecules of a gas or a dissolved substance with which they come in contact on to their surface. The extent of adsorption increases with the increase in surface area per unit mass of the adsorbent at a given temperature and pressure.

5.2 Types of Adsorption

There are two main types of adsorption.

5.2.1 Physical Adsorption (Physisorption)

When particles of a gas are held (adsorbed) on the surface of a solid by van der Waals forces without resulting in the formation of any chemical bond between the adsorbate and the adsorbent, it is called *physical adsorption* or *physisorption*. The attractive forces are weak and can be easily overcome either by increasing the temperature or by decreasing the pressure. Therefore, physical adsorption can be easily reversed or decreased.

Characteristics of Physisorption

(i) No chemical bond is formed.

(ii) The surface of the solid adsorbent does not have any preference for a particular gas (non-specific in nature).

(iii) The extent of physical adsorption depends upon the ease of liquefaction of the gas. Those having high critical temperature are adsorbed more strongly. For example, 1 g of activated charcoal adsorbs more SO_2 (critical temperature 630 K) than methane (critical temperature 190 K). Physisorption is a reversible process represented as follows:

$$\underset{\text{(Adsorbate)}}{\text{Gas}} + \underset{\text{(Adsorbent)}}{\text{Solid}} \rightleftharpoons \text{Gas/Solid} + \text{Heat}$$

Applying Le Chatelier's principle, when we increase or decrease the temperature, the equilibrium shifts forward, that is, the adsorption increases. On reversing the conditions, the adsorption will decrease.

(iv) The process is exothermic but the enthalpy of adsorption is quite low and is of the order of 20–40 kJ mol^{-1}.

(v) This type of adsorption involves no chemical reaction, no activation energy or very low activation energy. As layers of the gas can be adsorbed one over the other by van der Waals forces, multimolecular layers are formed under *high pressure.*

(vi) Adsorption increases with increase in surface area of the adsorbent.

5.2.2 Chemical Adsorption (Chemisorption)

When a gas is held on to the surface of a solid by forces similar to those of a chemical bond (which may be covalent or ionic in nature), the type of adsorption is called *chemical adsorption* or *chemisorption.*

Characteristics of Chemisorption

(i) This type of adsorption is highly specific in nature because it occurs only if there is a chance of a chemical bond formation between the adsorbate and the adsorbent. For example, oxygen will be chemisorbed only on those solid adsorbents (such as carbon or metals) with which it can form oxides.

(ii) As it involves the formation of a compound, the adsorbed gas will be released as a compound instead of free gas. For example, oxygen adsorbed on tungsten or carbon is liberated as tungsten oxide, carbon monoxide or carbon dioxide. Hence, it is irreversible in nature.

(iii) Chemisorption requires high energy of activation. Hence, chemisorption increases with an increase in temperature. Thus, a gas may be physically adsorbed at low temperature but chemisorbed at a higher temperature. For example, it happens in the case of adsorption of hydrogen on nickel. When chemisorption takes place by raising the temperature, that is, by supplying activation energy, the process is called *activated adsorption*.

(iv) Chemisorption is exothermic and is accompanied by the evolution of a large amount of heat (200–400 kJ mol^{-1}) which is of the same magnitude as those involved in chemical reactions.

(v) As chemical bonds can be formed only with the layer of molecules coming in direct contact with the surface of the adsorbent, this type of adsorption is unimolecular.

(vi) Like physical adsorption, chemisorption also increases with an increase in surface area of the adsorbent.

5.3 Thermodynamic Quantities

5.3.1 Enthalpy of Adsorption

When adsorption takes place, the residual forces on the surface of the adsorbent decrease. Hence, the surface energy decreases. This appears in the form of heat called *heat of adsorption*. Hence, adsorption is invariably an exothermic process, that is, $\Delta H_{\text{adsorption}}$ is always negative. The enthalpy of adsorption for chemisorption is larger than that for physisorption.

5.3.2 Entropy Change During Adsorption, Adsorption Equilibrium

As the molecules of the adsorbate are held on the surface of the solid adsorbent, the entropy decreases, that is, ΔS is also negative. As $\Delta G = \Delta H - T\Delta S$, for the process of adsorption to occur, ΔG must be negative. As ΔS is negative, ΔG can be negative only if ΔH is negative and $\Delta H > T\Delta S$ in magnitude. This is true in the beginning. However, as the adsorption proceeds, ΔH keeps on decreasing and $T\Delta S$ keeps on increasing till ultimately ΔH becomes equal to $T\Delta S$ so that $\Delta G = 0$. This state is called *adsorption equilibrium*.

5.4 Factors Affecting Adsorption of Gases on Solids

Almost all solids adsorb gases to some extent. However, the exact amount of a gas adsorbed depends upon a number of factors.

(i) *Nature and surface area of the adsorbent*: The greater the surface area of the adsorbent, greater is the volume of the gas adsorbed. Substances such as charcoal and silica gel are excellent adsorbents because they have highly porous structures and hence large surface areas. Gases such as H_2, N_2 and O_2 are generally adsorbed on finely divided transition metals such as Ni and CO.

(ii) *Nature of the gas (adsorbate)*: Different gases are adsorbed to different extents by the same adsorbent at the same temperature. The critical temperatures of the gases determine this.

Critical temperature increases → Ease of liquefaction increases → Adsorption increases

(iii) *Effect of temperature*: Adsorption is a process involving a true equilibrium. The two opposing processes involved are *condensation* (adsorption) of the gas molecules on the surface of the solid and *evaporation* (desorption) of the molecules from the surface of the solid into the gaseous phase.

$$\text{Gas (Adsorbate)} + \text{Solid (Adsorbent)} \underset{\text{Evaporation}}{\overset{\text{Condensation}}{\rightleftharpoons}} \text{Gas adsorbed on solid} + \text{Heat}$$

According to Le-Chatelier's principle, the increase in temperature will favour the reverse process of desorption.

(iv) *Effect of pressure*: At constant temperature, the adsorption of a gas increases with an increase in pressure. Adsorption of a gas leads to a decrease in pressure and therefore, according to Le Chatelier's principle, the magnitude of adsorption increases with an increase in pressure (Fig. 5.3).

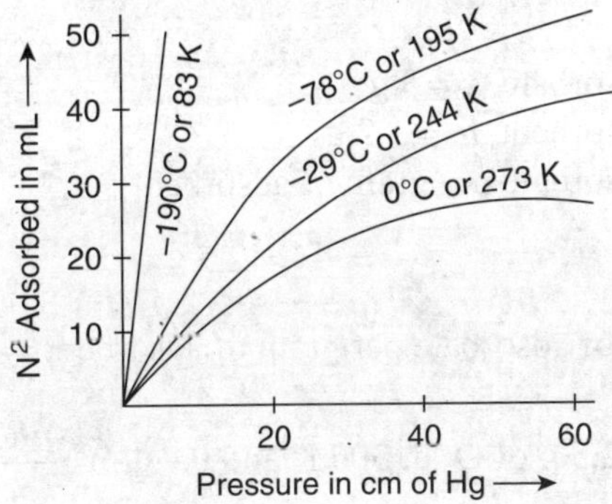

Fig. 5.3 Variation of adsorption of N_2 on charcoal with pressure at different constant temperatures

(v) *Activation of the solid adsorbent* involves increasing the adsorbing power of an adsorbent by increasing the surface area of the adsorbent which can be achieved:

- by mechanical rubbing or by chemical action or by depositing finely dispersed metals on the surface of the adsorbent by electroplating.
- if the adsorbent is broken into fine particles that it becomes almost powder, then the penetration of the gas becomes difficult and this will obstruct adsorption.
- by *removing the gases already adsorbed*. For example, charcoal is activated by heating in superheated steam or in vacuum at a temperature between 623 K and 1273 K.

5.5 Freundlich Adsorption Isotherm

The relation between the amount of substance adsorbed by the adsorbent and the equilibrium gas pressure (or concentration for solutions) at constant temperature is called an *adsorption isotherm*. The extent of adsorption is usually expressed as x/m, where m is the mass of the adsorbent and x is the mass of the adsorbate when adsorption equilibrium is reached. Thus, x/m is the mass adsorbed per gram of the adsorbent.

The simplest type of adsorption isotherm is shown in Fig. 5.4. At a value of P_s of equilibrium pressure, x/m reaches its maximum value and then it remains constant even though the pressure P is increased. This is the *saturation state* and P_s is the *saturation pressure*. At low values of P, the graph is nearly straight and sloping (shown by OA in Fig. 5.4). This is represented by the following equation.

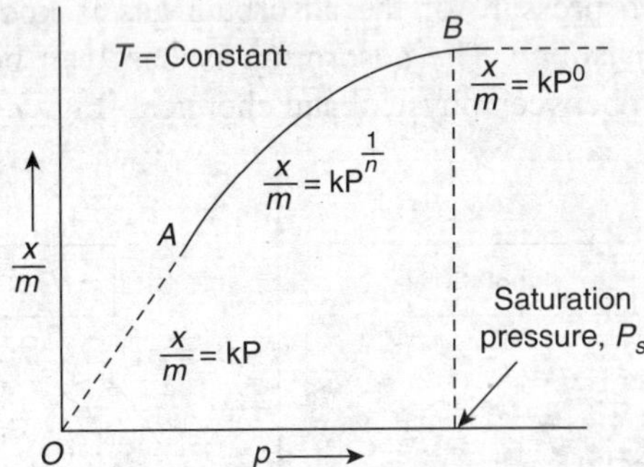

Fig. 5.4 Variation of x/m with increase in pressure at constant temperature (Freundlich adsorption isotherm)

$$\frac{x}{m} \propto P \text{ or } \frac{x}{m} = \text{constant} \times P^1 \tag{5.1}$$

At high pressure, x/m becomes independent of the values of P (beyond point B in Fig. 5.4). In this range of pressure,

$$\frac{x}{m} \propto P^0 \text{ or } \frac{x}{m} = \text{constant} \times P^0 \tag{5.2}$$

In the intermediate range of pressure (shown by AB in Fig. 5.4), x/m will depend on P raised to powers between 1 and 0, that is, fractions. For a small range of pressure values, we can write,

$$\frac{x}{m} \propto P^{1/n} \text{ or } \frac{x}{m} = kP^{1/n} \tag{5.3}$$

where n is a positive integer and n and k are constants depending upon the nature of the adsorbate and adsorbent at a particular temperature. The factor $1/n$ has values between 0 and 1 (probable range is 0.1 to 0.5). This is known as the *Freundlich adsorption isotherm.*

$$\log\frac{x}{m} = \log k + \frac{1}{n}\log P \tag{5.4}$$

If we plot a graph between $\log \frac{x}{m}$ on the y axis against log P on the x axis, it gives a straight line with a slope equal to $1/n$ and an ordinate intercept equal to log k (Fig. 5.5).

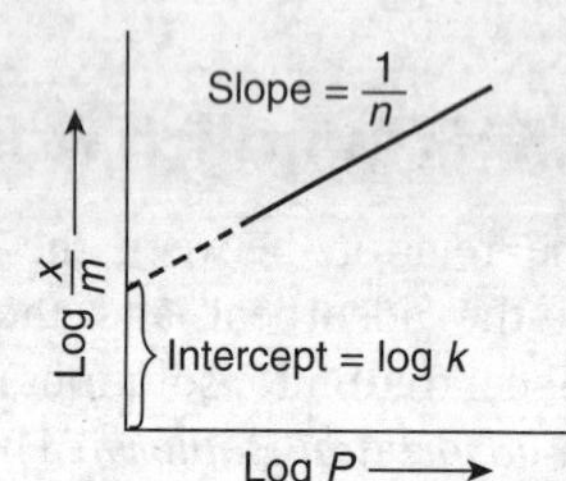

Fig. 5.5 Linear graph between $\log x/m$ and $\log P$

5.5.1 Limitation of Freundlich Isotherm

The Freundlich adsorption isotherm fails at high pressure of the gas. Therefore, this relation is considered as approximate and is applicable only at low pressure.

5.5.2 Adsorption Isobars

A graph drawn between the amount of the gas adsorbed per gram of the adsorbent (x / m) and temperature t at a constant equilibrium pressure of the adsorbate gas is known as an *adsorption isobar*. The adsorption isobars can be used to distinguish between physical and chemical [Fig. 5.6(b)].

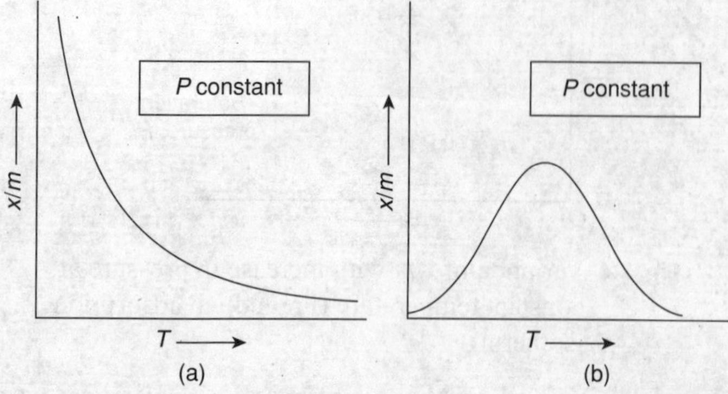

Fig. 5.6 Adsorption isobars for **(a)** physical adsorption and **(b)** chemical adsorption

5.6 Adsorption from Solutions

Solid surfaces can also adsorb solutes from the solutions. For example, when a solution of acetic acid is shaken with charcoal, some amount of acetic acid from the solution is adsorbed on the charcoal and hence the concentration of the acid in the solution decreases. If litmus solution is shaken with charcoal, it becomes colourless because the dye of the litmus solution is adsorbed by charcoal.

Solid adsorbents adsorb certain solutes from solution in preference to other solutes and solvents. For example, animal charcoal decolourises impure sugar solution by adsorbing the colouring dye in preference to sugar molecules.

5.6.1 Factors Affecting Adsorption from Solutions

The adsorption from solutions by solid adsorbents is found to depend upon the following factors.

- *Nature* of the adsorbate and the adsorbent.
- The adsorption decreases with an increase in *temperature*.
- Greater the *surface area* of the adsorbent, greater is the adsorption.
- *Concentration* of the solute in the solution.

The isotherm for the adsorption of solutes from solutions (by the solid adsorbents) is found to be similar to that shown in Fig. 5.6. Hence, the relationship between $\frac{x}{m}$ (mass of the solute adsorbed per gram of the adsorbent) and the equilibrium concentration C of the solute in the solution is also similar. That is,

$$\frac{x}{m} = kC^{1/n} \tag{5.5}$$

Taking logarithms of both sides of the equation, we get, $\log k + \frac{1}{n}\log C$. Equation 5.5 implies that a plot of $\log\frac{x}{m}$ against log C should be a straight line with slope $\frac{1}{n}$ and intercept $\log k$ (similar to that shown in Fig. 5.6).

Worked Out Problem 5.1

Three grams of oxygen are adsorbed on 1.2 g of charcoal powder at 300 K and 0.7 atm. Express the mass, number of moles and volume of oxygen at 300 K, 0.7 atm and at STP adsorbed per gram of the adsorbent.

Solution

Mass of adsorbate, $x = 3$ g

Mass of adsorbent, $m = 1.2$ g

Mass of adsorbate per gram of adsorbent

$$= \frac{x}{m} = \frac{3}{1.2} = 2.5 \text{ g}$$

No. of mol of adsorbate per gram of adsorbent $= \frac{2.5}{32} = 0.078$

Volume of 2.5 g of O_2 at 300 K and 0.7 atm $= \frac{nRT}{P}$

$$= \frac{0.078 \times 82.0 \times 300}{0.7} \text{ (where } R = 82.0 \text{ cm}^3 \text{ atm K}^{-1})$$

$$= 2741.1 \text{ cm}^3$$

Volume of 2.5 g of O_2 at 273 K and 1 atm = $\frac{0.078 \times 82.0 \times 273}{1} = 1746.1\ cm^3$

Amount of oxalic acid adsorbed per gram of charcoal = 6.30 g

Worked Out Problem 5.2

Applying Freundlich adsorption isotherm, calculate the amount of acetic acid adsorbed by 1 kg of blood charcoal at 25°C from a 5% vinegar solution (mass/volume). Given that if the concentration is expressed in molarity (mol dm^{-3}), x/m is the mass of the solute adsorbed per gram of adsorbent, then $k = 0.160$ and $n = 2.32$.

Solution

According to Freundlich adsorption isotherm, $\frac{x}{m} = kC^{1/n}$ (i)

5% vinegar (acetic acid solution) means 5 g of acetic acid is present in 100 mL of the solution

Molar mass of acetic acid (CH_3COOH) = 60 g mol^{-1} ∴ 5 g of acetic acid = $\frac{5}{60}$ mol

∴ 1000 mL of the solution will contain acetic acid

$$= \frac{5}{60} \times \frac{1}{100} \times 1000 = 0.837 \text{ mol}$$

That is, concentration of the solution (C) = 0.837 mol L^{-1}

Substituting the values in Eq. (i), we get

$$\frac{x}{m} = 0.160 \times (0.837)^{1/2.32}$$

$$\therefore \quad \log\frac{x}{m} = \log(0.160) + \frac{1}{2.32}\log(0.837)$$

$$= -0.7959 + 0.435(-0.0773)$$

$$= -0.8295 = \bar{1}.1705$$

$$\therefore \frac{x}{m} = \text{Antilog}\ (\bar{1}.1705) = 0.1481 \text{ g (charcoal)}^{-1}$$

∴ Amount adsorbed by 1 kg (1000 g) of charcoal = 148.1 g

5.7 Applications of Adsorption

(i) *In gas masks*: Activated charcoal or a mixture of adsorbents is generally used in gas masks to adsorb poisonous and toxic gases from air. These masks are commonly used by the miners because there are poisonous gases like CO and CH_4 in the atmosphere in the coal mines.

(ii) *Removal of colouring matter from solutions*: Many substances such as sugar, juice and vegetable oils which are coloured due to the presence of impurities, can be decolourised by placing in them contact with adsorbents such as activated charcoal or Fuller's earth.

(iii) *In chromatographic analysis:* The selective adsorption of certain substances from a solution by a particular solid adsorbent has helped to develop a technique for the separation of the components of the mixture.

(iv) *Heterogeneous catalysis*: Adsorption of reactants on the solid surface of catalysts increases the rate of reaction. Metals such as Fe, Ni, Pt and Pd are used in manufacturing processes.

(v) Many adsorption indicators are being used in volumetric analysis. For example, dyes such as eosin and fluorescein are used as adsorption indicators.

(vi) The use of ion exchangers for softening of hard water is based upon the principle of adsorption.

(vii) *Separation of inert gases*: Due to the difference in the degree of adsorption of gases by charcoal, a mixture of noble gases can be separated. Silica and aluminium gels are commonly used to adsorb humidity or moisture from air. This is necessary for storage of delicate instruments which might otherwise be damaged by moisture.

(viii) A number of drugs are used to kill the germs by getting adsorbed on them.

5.8 Catalysis

The phenomenon of increasing the rate of reaction by the use of a catalyst is called *catalysis*.

5.8.1 Positive and Negative Catalysis

If a catalyst increases the speed of a reaction, it is called a *positive catalyst* and the phenomenon is called *positive catalysis*. On the other hand, if a catalyst decreases the speed of a reaction, it is called a *negative catalyst* and the phenomenon is called *negative catalysis*. For example, oxidation of SO_2 to SO_3 in the presence of NO (lead chamber process) or in the presence of V_2O_5 (contact process) are examples of positive catalysis. However, the decomposition of H_2O_2 in the presence of glycerol or acetanilide or phosphoric acid and the oxidation of chloroform in the presence of alcohol are examples of negative catalysis.

5.8.2 Function of a Catalyst

A chemical reaction takes place by a reaction path, is first converted to the activated state and then finally to the products. A catalyst forms a new activated complex of lower potential energy. This means that the catalyst provides a new pathway of lower activation energy. Consequently, the fraction of the total number of collisions possessing lower activation energy is increased and hence, the rate of reaction also increases (Fig. 5.7).

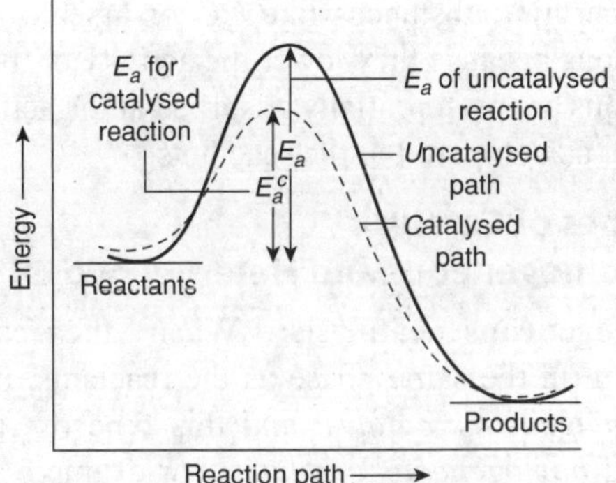

Fig. 5.7 Comparison of activation energies of a catalysed and an uncatalysed reaction

Note that while a positive catalyst lowers the activation energy of the reaction, a negative catalyst increases the activation energy (Fig. 5.8).

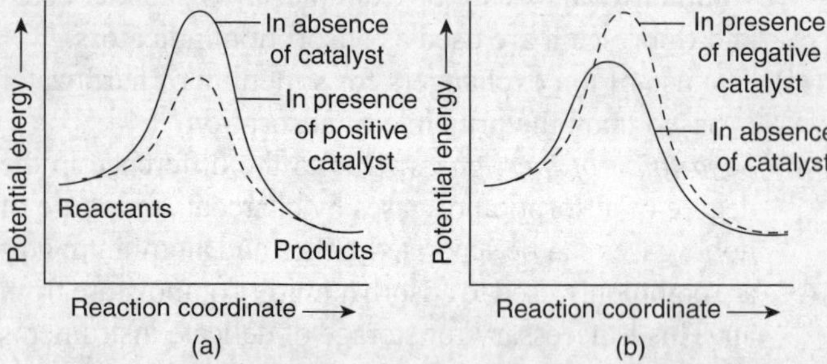

Fig. 5.8 **(a)** Positive catalyst lowers the potential energy barrier, **(b)** Negative catalyst raises the potential energy barrier

Functions of a catalyst:

- A catalyst forms temporary chemical bonds with the reactants but it is recovered unchanged in the original form at the end of the reaction.
- Although a catalyst speeds up the reaction, it does not shift the position of equilibrium.
- Catalysts are highly specific in nature.
- The catalyst does not change ΔE of the reaction. It is clear that the addition of a catalyst does not change the energies of reactants (E_r) and products (E_p); therefore, $\Delta E(E_p - E_r)$ remains the same.
- The catalyst does not change thermodynamic parameters such as change in internal energy (ΔU), enthalpy (ΔH), entropy (ΔS) or Gibbs free energy (ΔG) for a reaction.

5.8.3 Promoters and Poisons

If a substance when present along with the catalyst, enhances the activity of the catalyst, it is called a *catalytic promoter*. For example, molybdenum acts as a promoter for iron catalyst in the manufacture of ammonia by Haber's process.

$$N_2(g) + 3\,H_2(g) \xrightleftharpoons[\text{Mo (promoter)}]{\text{Fe (catalyst)}} 2NH_3(g)$$

The promoter increases the roughness of the catalyst surface. As a result, free valences increase. Hence, adsorption increases and so does the rate. The substances which decrease the activity of the catalyst are called *catalytic poisons*. For example, certain substances like CO or arsenic if present, act as poisons because they lower the activity of the catalyst. these poisons are preferentially adsorbed at the active sites of the catalyst as compared to the reactants.

5.8.4 Types of Catalysis (Homogeneous and Heterogeneous)

(i) Homogeneous catalysis: When the catalyst is present in the same phase as the reactants, it is called a *homogeneous catalyst* and this type of catalysis is called *homogeneous catalysis*. For example, oxidation of sulfur dioxide to sulfur trioxide in the presence of nitric oxide as catalyst (in the lead chamber process for the manufacture of H_2SO_4).

$$2SO_2(g) + O_2(g) \xrightarrow{NO(g)} 2SO_3(g)$$

Mechanism of Homogeneous Catalysis

According to modern views, a catalyst first enters into chemical combination with one or more of the reactants forming an intermediate compound. It then decomposes or combines with one of the reactants to produce the product and the catalyst is regenerated. A new more efficient path is followed. Example, oxidation of SO_2 to SO_3 in the presence of NO.

$$2SO_2(g) + O_2(g) \xrightarrow{NO(g)} 2SO_3(g)$$

In this reaction, nitric oxide combines with one of the reactants to form an intermediate compound (NO_2). This intermediate (NO_2) combines readily with SO_2 to form SO_3 and the catalyst NO is regenerated in the last step.

$$\underset{\text{Reactant}}{O_2(g)} + \underset{\text{Catalyst}}{2NO(g)} \rightarrow \underset{\text{Intermediate}}{2NO_2(g)}$$

$$\underset{\text{Reactant}}{SO_2(g)} + \underset{\text{Intermediate}}{NO_2(g)} \rightarrow \underset{\text{Product}}{SO_3(g)} + \underset{\text{Regenerated catalyst}}{NO(g)}$$

(ii) Heterogeneous catalysis: If the catalyst is present in a different phase than that of the reactants, it is called a *heterogeneous catalyst* and this type of catalysis is called *heterogeneous catalysis*. Here, the catalyst is generally a solid and the reactants are mostly gases and sometimes liquids; the reaction starts at the surface of the solid catalyst. That is why it is also known as *surface catalysis*. Example, manufacture of NH_3 from N_2 and H_2 by Haber's process using iron as catalyst.

$$N_2(g) + 3\,H_2(g) \xrightarrow{Fe(s)} 2\,NH_3(g)$$

Here, the reactants are gaseous whereas the catalyst is solid.

Synthesis of methyl alcohol (CH_3OH) from CO and H_2 using a mixture of Cu, ZnO and Cr_2O_3 as catalyst.

$$CO(g) + 2\,H_2(g) \xrightarrow[\substack{ZnO(s)+\\ Cr_2O_3(s)}]{Cu(s)+} CH_3OH$$

Old Theory of Heterogeneous Catalysis (Adsorption Theory)

According to the *old adsorption theory* of heterogeneous catalysis, it was believed that the reactants in the gaseous state or from the solutions are adsorbed on the surface of the catalyst. As a result, the concentration of the reactant molecules on the surface increases and hence the rate of reaction increases. As adsorption is always exothermic, the heat released further helps to speed up the reaction.

Another theory of heterogeneous catalysis, is the *intermediate compound formation theory*. This theory suggests that the reactants (A and B) first combine with the catalyst (C) to form an intermediate complex which decomposes to form the products and regenerates the catalyst.

The *modern adsorption theory* is a combination of both the above theories. According to this theory, there are free valencies on the surface of solid catalyst (generally metals) and the mechanism of catalysis involves the following five steps.

(i) Diffusion of reactant molecules towards the surface of the catalyst [Fig. 5.9(a)].

(ii) Adsorption of the reactant molecules on the surface of the catalyst by forming loose bonds with the catalyst due to the presence of free valencies [Fig. 5.9(b)].

(iii) Occurrence of a chemical reaction between the reactants and the catalyst forming an intermediate.

(iv) Desorption of the product molecule from the surface due to the lack of affinity towards the catalyst surface, thereby making the surface free for fresh adsorption of reactant molecules.

(v) Diffusion of product molecules away from the surface of the catalyst.

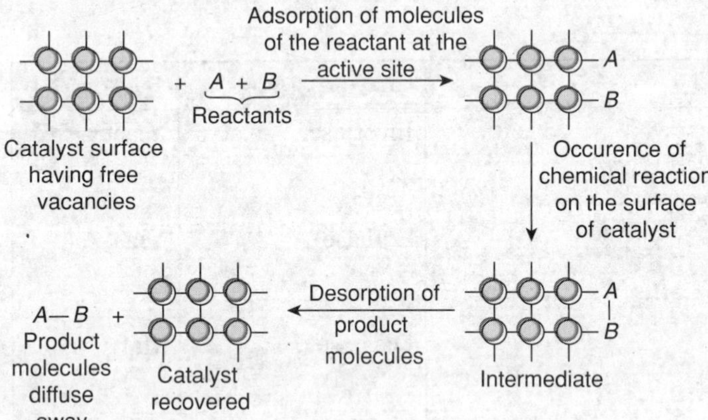

Fig. 5.9 Adsorption theory for mechanism of heterogenous catalysis

This theory can explain the following. Also, adsorption helps the reaction in the following ways.

- Adsorption increases the concentration of reactants on the surface of the catalyst. Due to increased concentration of the reactants, the reactions proceed rapidly.
- Adsorbed molecules get dissociated to form active species such as free radicals which react faster than molecules.
- The adsorbed molecules are not free to move about and, therefore, they collide with other molecules on the surfacc.
- The heat of adsorption evolved acts as energy of activation for the reaction (chemisorption).

Advantages of Modern Adsorption Theory

A small quantity of the catalyst is sufficient because the catalyst is regenerated again and again.

- The catalyst takes part in the reaction but is produced back unchanged in mass and chemical composition at the end of the reaction.
- Catalytic poisons, if present, are preferentially adsorbed on the catalyst surface, thereby hindering the adsorption of the reactant molecules. Hence, they slow down the activity of the catalyst.

5.8.5 Some Important Features of Solid Catalysts (Heterogeneous Catalysis)

(i) *Activity of a catalyst* is the capacity of the catalyst to increase the speed of the chemical reaction. The reactant must be adsorbed reasonably strongly for the catalyst to be active but must not get adsorbed so strongly that they become immobile and the other reactants do not get space on the catalyst surface for adsorption. In certain cases, the extent to which speed of the reaction is increased is as high as 10^{10} times. Combination of H_2 and O_2 in the presence of platinum (catalyst) to form water with explosive violence is an example of catalytic activity. In the absence of the catalyst platinum, H_2 and O_2 do not combine and can be stored as such for an indefinite period.

(ii) *Selectivity of a catalyst* is the ability of the catalyst to direct a reaction to give a particular product. Some examples are:

- CO and H_2 react to form different products in the presence of different catalysts.

$$CO(g) + H_2(g) \xrightarrow{Cu} HCHO(g)$$

$$CO(g) + 2\,H_2(g) \xrightarrow{Cu/ZnO-Cr_2O_3} CH_3OH(g)$$

$$CO(g) + 3\,H_2(g) \xrightarrow{Ni} CH_4(g) + H_2O(g)$$

Similarly, *n*-heptane in the presence of Pt as catalyst selectively gives toluene.

- Acetylene on reaction with H_2 in presence of platinum as catalyst gives ethane while in the presence of Lindlar's catalyst (palladium + $BaSO_4$ poisoned with quinoline or sulfur), it gives ethylene.

(iii) *Specificity of the catalyst* means, a given substance can act as a catalyst only in a particular reaction and may fail to catalyse other reactions.

$$H-C\equiv C-H + H_2 \xrightarrow{Pt} H_3C-CH_3 \text{ (Ethane)}$$

$$H-C\equiv C-H + H_2 \xrightarrow{\text{Lindlar's Catalyst } (Pd + BaSO_4 + \text{quinoline})} H_2C=CH_2 \text{ (Ethylene (Ethene))}$$

Acetylene (Ethyne)

5.9 Zeolites as Shape-selective Catalysts

Zeolites are aluminosilicates with the general formula, $M_{x/n}[(AlO_2)_x(SiO_2)_y].zH_2O$, where *n* is the charge on the metal cation M^{n+}, which is usually Na^+, K^+ or Ca^{2+} and *z* is the number of water molecules of hydration which is highly variable. They are microporous three dimensional network silicates in which some silicon atoms are replaced by aluminium atoms giving an Al–O–Si frame work. Zeolites are heated in vacuum, lose the water of hydration and become porous. The size of the pores generally varies between 260 pm and 740 pm and thus zeolites act as selective adsorbents and hence as *molecular sieves*. For example, the zeolite, sodium alumina silicate, can adsorb straight chain hydrocarbons and not branched chain or aromatic ones.

Zeolites are widely used as catalysts in petrochemical industries for cracking of hydrocarbons and isomerisation. An important zeolite catalyst used in the petroleum industry is ZSM-5 (Zeolite Sieve of Molecular Porosity 5). It converts alcohols directly into gasoline (petrol) by first dehydrating them so that a mixture of hydrocarbons is formed.

$$\text{Alcohols} \xrightarrow[\text{Dehydration}]{\text{ZSM-5}} \text{Hydrocarbons}$$

Hydrated zeolites are used as ion exchangers in softening of hard water.

5.10 Enzymes as Catalysts

Enzymes are defined as biochemical catalysts. Enzymes are produced by living plants and animals. Many of them have been obtained in the pure crystalline state from living cells. Chemically, all enzymes are globular proteins (which are complex nitrogenous compounds) with a high molar mass ranging from 15,000 to 1,000,000 g mol^{-1} and form colloidal solutions in water. Every biological reaction requires a different kind of enzyme. A typical cell, on the average, contains about 3000 different kinds of enzymes, each catalysing a different reaction. Examples of a few enzyme-catalysed reactions are given in Table 5.1.

Table 5.1 Enzyme-catalysed reactions

S. No.	Reaction	Enzyme	Source
(i)	Inversion of cane sugar $\underset{\text{Sucrose}}{C_{12}H_{22}O_{11}(aq)} + H_2O(l) \xrightarrow{\text{Invertase}} \underset{\text{Glucose}}{C_6H_{12}O_6(aq)} + \underset{\text{Fructose}}{C_6H_{12}O_6(aq)}$	Invertase	Yeast
(ii)	Conversion of glucose into ethyl alcohol $\underset{\text{Glucose}}{C_6H_{12}O_6(aq)} \xrightarrow{\text{Zymase}} 2\,C_2H_5OH(aq) + 2\,CO_2(g)$	Zymase	Yeast
(iii)	Conversion of starch into maltose $\underset{\text{Starch}}{2(C_6H_{10}O_5)n(aq)} + n\,H_2O(l) \xrightarrow{\text{Diastase}} n\,\underset{\text{Maltose}}{C_{12}H_{22}O_{11}(aq)}$	Diastase	Malt
(iv)	Conversion of maltose into glucose $\underset{\text{Maltose}}{C_{12}H_{22}O_{11}(aq)} + H_2O(l) \xrightarrow{\text{Maltase}} 2\,\underset{\text{Glucose}}{C_6H_{12}O_6(aq)}$	Maltase	Yeast
(v)	Manufacture of acetic acid from ethyl alcohol $CH_3CH_2OH(l) + O_2(g) \rightarrow CH_3COOH(l) + H_2O(l)$	Mycoderma aceti	Old vinegar
(vi)	Decomposition of urea into NH_3 and CO_2 $\underset{\text{Urea}}{NH_2CONH_2(aq)} + H_2O(l) \xrightarrow{\text{Urease}} 2\,NH_3(g) + CO_2(g)$	Urease	Soyabean
(vii)	Conversion of proteins into peptides in the stomach	Pepsin	Stomach
(viii)	Conversion of proteins into amino acids by hydrolysis in intestines	Trypsin	Intestines
(ix)	Conversion of milk into curd	Lactic bacilli	Curd

5.10.1 Characteristics of Enzymes

(i) *Efficiency*: Enzymes are very efficient catalysts. They speed up the rate of a reaction by factors of up to 10^{20}. Consider the hydrolysis of amides. Amide bonds are chemically very stable. That is why, hydrolysis of amides requires the heating of the amide with an alkali for a few hours. In contrast, proteins present in our food which also contain amide (peptide) bonds, are easily hydrolysed in our body by different enzymes to individual α-amino acids.

(ii) *Specificity*: Each enzyme catalyses only one chemical reaction. For example, the enzyme *urease* hydrolyses urea to NH_3 and CO_2 but it does not catalyse the hydrolysis of N-methylurea which is similar in constitution to urea. Similarly, invertase hydrolyses sucrose to glucose and fructose but does not hydrolyse maltose to glucose though both are hydrolytic reactions.

For the hydrolysis of maltose, the enzyme *maltase* is used.

(iii) *Optimum temperature and pH*: Enzyme catalysed reactions have a maximum rate at the physiological pH of around 7.4 and human body temperature of 37°C (310 K) under one atmospheric pressure.

(iv) *Small quantity*: Very small amounts of enzymes can be highly efficient. This is because, just like chemical catalysts, enzymes are also regenerated after their catalytic activity. For example, the enzyme *renin* which is used for coagulation of milk to make cheese coagulates over a million times its own weight of milk protein.

(v) *Enzyme activators (coenzymes)*: The activity of certain enzymes is increased in the presence of certain substances, called *coenzymes*. If a protein contains a small amount of vitamin as the non-protein part, its activity is enhanced considerably. The activators are generally metal ions such as Na^+, Mn^{2+}, Cu^{2+}, Co^{2+}, and so on.

(vi) *Enzyme inhibitors and poisons*: the activity of an enzyme is slowed down in the presence of certain substances called inhibitors or poisons. They act by combining with the active functional group thereby reducing or completely destroying the catalytic activity of the enzymes.

5.10.2 Mechanism of Enzyme Catalysis

The most accepted mechanism of enzyme catalysed reaction is known as the *Lock and Key mechanism.* The specificity of the enzymes is due to the presence of some specific regions, called the *active sites*, on their surface. These active sites are associated with some functional groups such as $-NH_2$, –COOH, –OH, –SH, and so on, which form weak bonds such as H-bonds or van der Waals attraction, with the substrate (reactant) molecules. The shape of the active site of any given enzyme is like a cavity such that only a specific substrate can fit into it, in the same way as *one key can fit into a particular lock.* This specific binding leads to the formation of an *enzyme–substrate complex* which accounts for the high specificity of enzyme-cataysed reactions (Fig. 5.10).

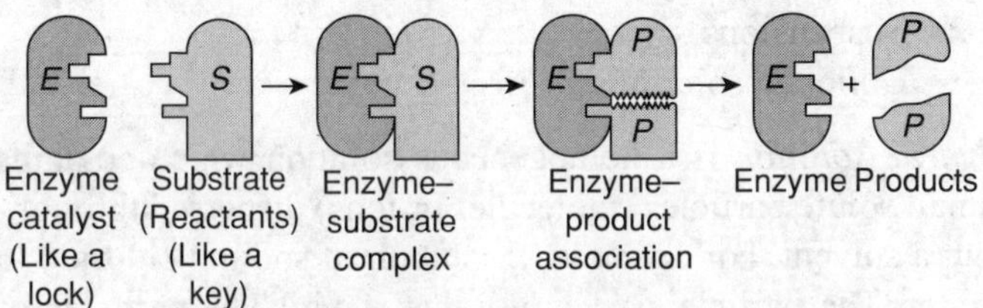

Fig. 5.10 Lock and key mechanism of enzyme action

5.10.3 Catalysts used in Industries

A few common examples are given in Table 5.2.

Table 5.2 Industrial processes and catalysts used

Process	Reactions with catalyst and other conditions
1. Haber's process for the manufacture of ammonia	$N_2(g) + H_2(g) \xrightarrow[\text{200 bar pressure, 723–773 K temp.}]{\text{Finely divided iron (catalyst)}} 2\,NH_3(g)$ Molybdenum (Promoter)
2. Oswald's process for the manufacture of nitric acid	$4\,NH_3(g) + 5\,O_2(g) \xrightarrow[\text{Asbestos (catalyst)}]{\text{Platinised}} 4\,NO(g) + 6\,H_2O(g)$ $2\,NO(g) + O_2(g) \xrightarrow{573\text{ K}} 2\,NO_2(g)$ $4\,NO_2(g) + 2\,H_2O(l) + O_2(g) \rightarrow 4\,HNO_3(l)$
3. Contact process for the manufacture of sulfuric acid	$2\,SO_2(g) + O_2(g) \underset{\text{Or } V_2O_5 \text{ (catalyst)}}{\overset{\text{Plantinised asbestos}}{\rightleftharpoons}} 2\,SO_3(g)$ $SO_3(g) + H_2SO_4(l) \xrightarrow{673–723\text{ K}} \underset{\text{Oleum}}{H_2S_2O_7(l)} \xrightarrow{+H_2O(l)} 2\,H_2SO_4(aq)$
4 Bosch's process for the manufacture of hydrogen	$\underbrace{CO + H_2}_{\text{Water gas}} + H_2O(g) \xrightarrow[\text{+ } Cr_2O_3 \text{ (promoter), 673–873 K}]{Fe_2O_3 \text{ (Catalyst)}} CO_2(g) + 2\,H_2(g)$
5. Deacon's process for the manufacture of chlorine	$4\,HCl(g) + O_2(g) \xrightarrow[773\text{ K}]{CuCl_2} 2\,H_2O(l) + 2\,Cl_2(g)$
6. Synthesis of methanol	$CO(g) + 2\,H_2(g) \xrightarrow[\text{200 bar 432 K}]{ZnO + Cr_2O_3} CH_3OH(l)$
7. Hydrogenation of vegetable oils	$Oil(l) + H_2(g) \xrightarrow[\text{427–473 K High pressure}]{\text{Finely divided Ni}} \text{Vanaspati ghee}(s)$
8. Wacker process for preparation of aldehydes and ketones from alkenes	$CH_2{=}CH_2 + H_2O \xrightarrow[(+CuCl_2)]{PdCl_2} \underset{\text{Acetaldehyde}}{CH_3CHO} + Pd + 2\,HCl$ $CH_3{-}CH{=}CH_2 + H_2O \xrightarrow[(CuCl_2)]{PdCl_2} \underset{\text{Acetone}}{CH_3COCH_3} + Pd + 2\,HCl$

5.11 Colloidal State of Matter

The substances such as common salt, sugar and urea, which can be obtained in the crystalline form and in the dissolved state diffused readily through parchment membrane were termed as *crystalloids*, and the substances such as starch, gum glue, gelatine, albumin and silicic acid which are non-crystalline in nature and in the dissolved state do not diffuse (or diffuse at a very slow rate) through the parchment membrane were called *colloids*.

5.11.1 Three Types of Solutions

On the basis of the particle size of the substance, solutions may be divided into three types.

- True solutions
- Suspensions
- Colloidal solutions

A *true solution* is a homogeneous solution which contains small solute particles (molecules or ions) dispersed throughout a solvent. For example, a solution of sodium chloride in water. The particle size is less than 1 nm. The particles of a solute in a true solution are invisible even under a microscope and its particles can pass through ordinary filter paper as well as through an animal membrane.

A *suspension* is a heterogeneous mixture which contains small insoluble particles. The particle size is more than 1000 nm. For example, dirt particles in water. The particles of a suspension may not be visible to the naked eye but are visible under a microscope. The particles of a suspension can neither pass through an ordinary filter paper nor through an animal membrane.

A *colloidal solution* is a heterogeneous solution which contains particles of intermediate size. For example, milk. The particles of a colloidal solution have diameters between 1 and 1000 nm. Such particles cannot be normally seen with the naked eye..However, light reflected by them can be seen under an ultramicroscope. The particles of a colloidal solution can pass through ordinary filter paper but not through an animal membrane. In a colloid, the dispersed phase may consist of particles of a single macromolecule (such as a synthetic polymer or protein) or an aggregate of many atoms, molecules or ions.

Thus, colloidal solutions are intermediate between true solutions and suspensions. Solutions formed by crystalloids are called true solutions while those formed by colloids are called colloidal solutions.

5.11.2 Dispersed Phase and Dispersion Medium

In a colloidal system, the terms solute and solvent are replaced by the terms *dispersed phase* and *dispersion medium* respectively. Thus, *dispersed phase* means, the substance distributed in the dispersion medium is in the form of colloidal particles and *dispersion medium* means, the medium in which the substance that is dispersed, is in the form of colloidal particles.

5.12 Classification of Colloids

Colloids are classified in three different ways.

5.12.1 Based on Physical State

Depending upon whether the dispersed phase and the dispersion medium are solids, liquids or gases, eight types of colloidal systems are possible. A gas mixed with another gas forms a homogeneous mixture and not a colloidal system. The examples of the various types along with their typical names are listed in Table 5.3. Out of the various types of colloidal systems listed, the most common are *sols* (solids in liquids), *gels* (liquids in solids) and *emulsions* (liquids in liquids).

Table 5.3 Types of colloidal systems (or colloidal dispersions)

S. No.	Dispersed phase	Dispersion medium	Name	Examples
1.	Solid	Solid	Solid sol	Some coloured glasses, gem stones
2.	Solid	Liquid	Sol	Some paints, cell fluids, muddy water
3.	Solid	Gas	Aerosol	Smoke, dust
4.	Liquid	Solid	Gel	Cheese, butter, jellies
5.	Liquid	Liquid	Emulsion	Milk, hair cream
6.	Liquid	Gas	Aerosol	Fog, mist, cloud, insecticide sprays
7.	Gas	Solid	Solid foam	Pumice stone, foam rubber
8.	Gas	Liquid	Foam	Froth, whipped cream, soap lather

Further, it may be mentioned that depending upon the dispersion medium, sols are given special names.

Dispersion medium	Name of the sol
Water	Aquasol or hydrosol
Alcohol	Alcosol
Benzene	Benzosol
Gases	Aerosol

5.12.2 Based on Nature of Interaction

Based on the nature of interaction between dispersed phase and dispersion medium, colloidal sols are divided into two categories—*lyophilic* and *lyophobic*. If *water* is the dispersion medium, the terms used are *hydrophilic* and *hydrophobic*.

(i) *Lyophilic colloids*: The colloidal solutions in which the particles of the dispersed phase have a great affinity (or love) for the dispersion medium, are called *lyophilic colloids* meaning, *liquid-loving.* For example, substances like gum, gelatine, starch and rubber when mixed with a suitable liquid as the dispersion medium, directly form the colloidal sol. These are called lyophilic and the sols thus obtained are called lyophilic sols. As they form the colloidal sol directly, they are also called *intrinsic colloids*. An important characteristic of these sols is that if the dispersed phase is separated from the dispersion medium (say, by evaporation), the sol can be made again by simply remixing with the dispersion medium and shaking. That is why these sols are also called *reversible sols.* Further, these sols are quite stable and cannot be easily precipitated.

(ii) *Lyophobic colloids*: The colloidal solutions in which there is no affinity between particles of the dispersed phase and the dispersion medium are called *lyophobic colloids*. For example, substances like metal sulfides when simply mixed with the dispersion medium do not form the colloidal sol. The sols formed by them are called lyophobic sols. As their colloidal sols have to be prepared by indirect methods, they are also called *extrinsic colloids.* The greater stability of the lyophilic colloidal sols than the lyophobic colloidal sols is due to the fact that the former are highly *hydrated* in the solution. These sols need some stabilising agents for their preservation. In case the dispersion medium is water, the lyophobic sol is called a hydrophobic colloid. For example, the solutions of metals like Ag and Au, hydroxides like $Al(OH)_3$, $Fe(OH)_3$ and metal sulfides like As_2S_3.

5.12.3 Based on Type of Particles of Dispersed Phase

Colloidal dispersions may be divided into three categories.

(i) **Multimolecular colloids:** When a substance is dispersed in the dispersion medium, a large number of atoms or smaller molecules of the substance aggregate together to form species with size in the colloidal range; the species thus formed are called *multimolecular colloids*. In these sols, the dispersed phase consists of aggregates of atoms or molecules with a molecular size less than 1 nm. For example, sols of gold atoms and sulfur (S_8) molecules.

(ii) **Macromolecular colloids:** These are the substances having big sized molecules (called macromolecules) which on dissolution form a solution in which the dispersed phase particles have a size in the colloidal range. Such substances are called *macromolecular colloids*. These macromolecular substances are generally polymers with very high molecular masses, mainly naturally occurring macromolecules such as starch, cellulose, proteins, enzymes and gelatine and synthesised macromolecules like polyethylene, nylon, polystyrene and synthetic rubber.

(iii) **Associated colloids—Micelles:** Substances which when dissolved in a medium at low concentrations behave as normal, strong electrolytes but at higher concentrations exhibit colloidal state properties due to the formation of aggregated particles are called *associated colloids*. The aggregate particles thus formed are called *micelles.* For example, in aqueous solution, soap (sodium stearate) ionises as:

$$\underset{\text{Sod. stearate (soap)}}{C_{17}H_{35}COONa} \rightleftharpoons \underset{\text{Stearate ion}}{C_{17}H_{35}COO^-} + Na^+$$

The formation of *micelles* takes place only above a particular temperature called *Kraft temperature* (T_k) and above a particular concentration called the *Critical Micelle Concentration (CMC).*

Mechanism of micelle formation: Micelles are generally formed by the aggregation of several ions or molecules with lyophobic as well as lyophilic parts. Soap is the sodium salt of a higher fatty acid and may be represented as RCOONa. For example, sodium stearate $[CH_3(CH_2)_{16}COO^-Na^+]$ or sodium palmitate $[CH_3(CH_2)_{14}COO^-Na^+]$. When dissolved in water, it dissociates into $RCOO^-$ and Na^+ ions. The $RCOO^-$ ions, however, consist of two parts—non-polar long hydrocarbon chain R called the *tail*, which is hydrophobic (water repelling) and the polar group COO^- called the *head*, which is hydrophilic (*water* loving) (Fig.5.11).

The stearate ions are present on the surface with their COO^- groups in water and the hydrocarbon tail staying away from it and remaining at the surface. At critical micelle concentration, the anions are pulled into the bulk of the solution and form a cluster of molecules in which the hydrocarbon tails are in the interior of the cluster and ionic ends are at the surface of the cluster. This formation is called micelle formation and the aggregate thus formed is known as an ionic micelle (Fig. 5.12). These micelles may contain as many as up to 100 ions. When the concentration of the solution is below its CMC (10^{-3} mol L^{-1}), it behaves as a normal electrolyte. But above this concentration, it is aggregated to behave as micelles. Some other examples of micelles are:

- Sodium palmitate ($C_{15}H_{31}COONa$)
- Cetyltrimethylammonium bromide $CH_3(CH_2)_{15}(CH_3)_3NH_4^{|}Br^-$
- Sodium laurylsulfate $[CH_3(CH_2)_{11}SO_3O^-]Na^+$

Similarly, in the case of detergents such as sodium lauryl sulfate, $CH_3(CH_2)_{11}OSO_3^-Na^+$, the polar group is SO_4^{2-} along with the long hydrocarbon chain. Therefore, the mechanism of micelle formation is the same as that of soaps.

Sodium stearate ($C_{17}H_{35}COO^{-}Na^{+}$)

Hydrophobic tail

Hydrophobic head

Stearate ion

2 4 6 8 10 12 14 16 ⊖ Hydrophilic head

1 3 5 7 9 11 13 15 17

Hydrophobic tail

Fig. 5.11 Hydrobobic tail and hydrophilic head of stearate ion

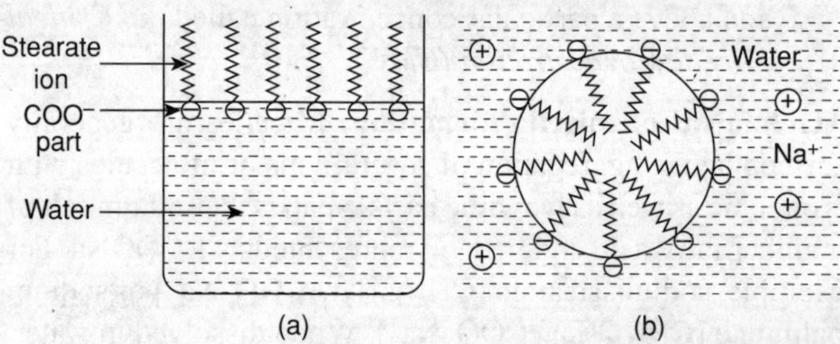

Fig. 5.12 **(a)** Stearate ions present on the surface of water at low concentration of soap solution, **(b)** stearate ions pulled together to form a spherical ionic micelle inside the bulk of water at high concentrate (CMC)

5.12.4 The Cleansing Action of Soap

The cleansing action of soap is due to its tendency to act as micelles and form emulsions. A soap, for example sodium stearate, is composed of a long alkyl group called the tail and the polar part of COO^{-} ion called the head (Fig. 5.13).

$CH_3(CH_2)_{15}CH_2 — COO^{-} Na^{+}$

Tail Head

Hydrocarbon (Tail) Electrically charged (Head)

Fig. 5.13

When grease or oil sticking on the surface of a cloth [Fig. 5.14(a)] comes in contact with soap solution, the stearate ions arrange themselves around it in such a way that the hydrophobic parts of the stearate ions are in the oil (or grease) and the hydrophilic parts project outside the grease droplet [Fig. 5.14(b)]. In this manner, each oil droplet is surrounded by a number of negatively charged carboxylate ions [Fig. 5.14(c)]. Since similar charges repel each other, the oil droplets break up and form small droplets or globules. The negatively charged sheath around the globules prevents them from coming together and forming aggregates. These small droplets get dispersed in water forming an emulsion. These are washed away with water along with dust particles.

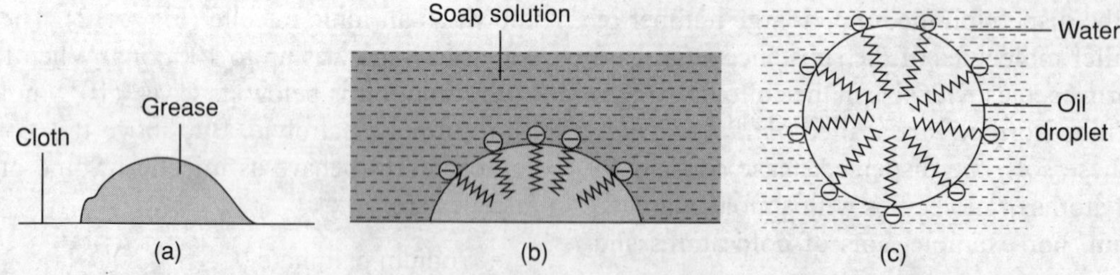

Fig. 5.14 **(a)** Grease or oil on surface of cloth **(b)** stearate ions arranged around the oil droplet **(c)** ionic micelle formed surrounded by sheath of negative charge

Similarly, in case of detergents such as sodium lauryl sulfate [$CH_3(CH_2)_{11}OSO_3^{-}$ Na^{+}], the polar group is OSO_3^{-} along with the long hydrocarbon chain. This is an example of an *anionic detergent* as anions associate together to form an ionic micelle, similar to that of soap. A well-known example of a cationic detergent forming an associated colloid is cetyl trimethyl ammonium bromide [$CH_3(CH_2)_{15}(CH_3)_3N^{+}Br^{-}$]. The mechanism of micelle formation in these cases is similar to that of soap.

5.13 Preparation of Colloidal Sols

Some of the common methods for preparing lyophilic and lyophobic colloids are discussed below.

5.13.1 Preparation of Lyophilic Colloids

Colloidal sols of starch, gelatine, gum Arabic and soaps are prepared by simply dissolving these substances in warm water. Similarly, a colloidal sol of cellulose nitrate is obtained by dissolving it in a mixture of ethyl alcohol and ether. The product (4% solution) obtained is called *collodion.*

Preparation of Lyophobic Colloids: The lyophobic sols cannot be prepared directly. These can be prepared as follows.

(i) Dispersion or disintegration methods

- *Mechanical dispersion*: Mechanical disintegration is carried out in a *colloid mill* or *ball mill* or *ultrasonic disintegrator* (Fig. 5.15). The size of suspension particles is reduced to that of colloidal size.

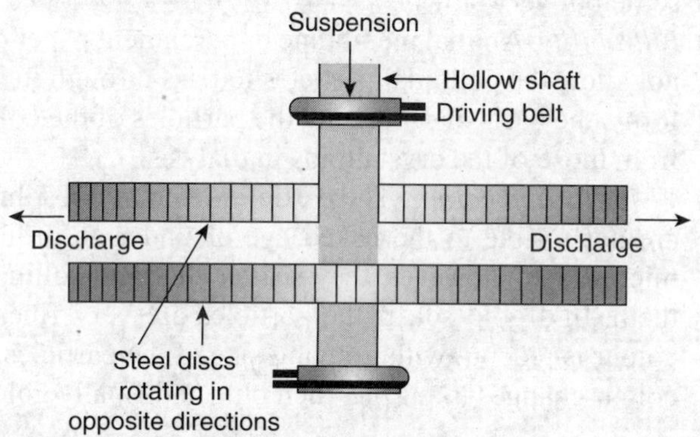

Fig. 5.15 Colloid mill

- *By electrical dispersion or electro-disintegration (Bredig's method)*: This method is basically used for obtaining colloidal solutions of metals like gold, silver and platinum stabilised by adding a small amount of KOH.
- *Peptisation*: The process of converting a fresh precipitate into colloidal particles by shaking it with the dispersion medium in the presence of a small amount of a suitable electrolyte is called *peptisation.* The electrolyte added is called a *peptising agent.*

Cause of peptisation: When an electrolyte is added to a freshly precipitated substance, the particles of the precipitate preferentially adsorb one particular type of ions of the electrolyte (ions common with the precipitated substance) getting dispersed due to electrostatic repulsions. This gives particles of colloidal size. An example is peptisation of freshly precipitated ferric hydroxide with ferric chloride solution (Fig. 5.16). A reddish brown coloured colloidal solution is obtained by adding a small quantity of ferric chloride solution to the freshly precipitated ferric hydroxide. Freshly prepared precipitates are preferred as they are easily peptised.

$$\underset{\text{Precipitate}}{Fe(OH)_3} + \underset{\text{Electrolyte}}{Fe^{3+}} \rightarrow \underset{\text{Colloidal sol}}{Fe(OH)_3, Fe^{3+}}$$

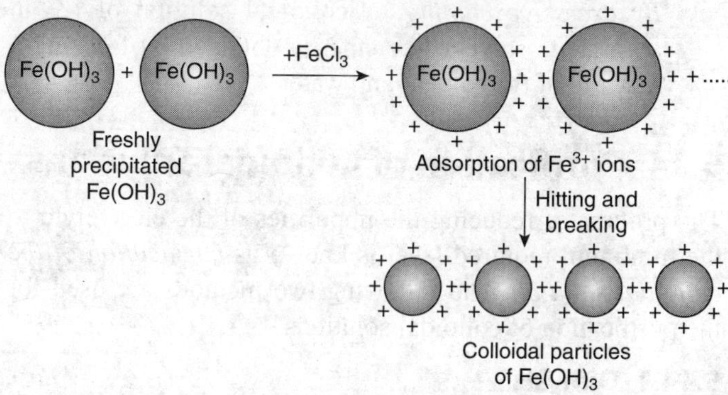

Fig. 5.16

(ii) Condensation (aggregation) methods: In these methods, smaller particles of the dispersed phase are condensed suitably to be of colloidal size. This is done as follows.

- *By reduction:* Gold, silver, platinum, and so on, are obtained in colloidal form by the reduction of very dilute solutions of their salts with suitable reducing agents. For example,

$$2AuCl_3 + 3SnCl_2 \rightarrow \underset{\text{Gold sol}}{2Au} + 3SnCl_4$$

Gold sol can also be obtained by the reduction of $AuCl_3$ solution with formaldehyde and tannic acid or with hydrazine.

$$2AuCl_3 + \underset{\text{Formaldehyde}}{3HCHO} + 3H_2O \rightarrow \underset{\text{Gold sol}}{2Au} + \underset{\text{Formic acid}}{3HCOOH} + 6HCl$$

or

$$4AuCl_3 + \underset{\text{Hydrazine}}{3NH_2NH_2} \rightarrow \underset{\text{Gold sol}}{4Au} + 3N_2 + 12HCl$$

- *By hydrolysis:* Fe $(OH)_3$ and $Al(OH)_3$ sols are obtained by boiling solutions of their corresponding chlorides.

$$FeCl_3 + 3H_2O \rightarrow \underset{\text{(Colloidal sol)}}{Fe(OH)_3} + 3HCl$$

- *By double decomposition:* When H_2S is passed through a dilute solution of arsenious oxide in water, a colloidal solution of arsenious sulfide is obtained.

$$As_2O_3 + 3H_2S \rightarrow \underset{\text{(Colloidal solution)}}{As_2S_3} + 3H_2O$$

- *By oxidation:* Sulfur is obtained in the colloidal form when H_2S is bubbled through a solution of an oxidising agent such as nitric acid or bromine water.

$$H_2S + Br_2 \rightarrow S + 2HBr;$$
$$H_2S + 2HNO_3 \rightarrow 2H_2O + 2NO_2 + S$$

- *By condensing vapours of a substance into the solvent*: Sols of substances like mercury and sulfur are prepared by passing their vapours through cold water containing a suitable stabiliser such as an ammonium salt or citrate.

- *By excessive cooling*: A colloidal solution of ice in an organic solvent like ether is obtained by freezing a mixture of the solvent and water.

5.14 Purification of Colloidal Solutions

The process of reducing the impurities of the electrolyte to the minimum required level is known as *purification of the colloidal solution*. The following two methods are used for the purification of colloidal solutions.

5.14.1 Dialysis

The process of separating the particles of colloids from those of crystalloids by diffusion of the mixture through a parchment or an animal membrane is known as *dialysis*. The separation of crystalloids from the colloids is based upon the *principle* that the particles of the crystalloids pass through an animal membrane (bladder) or parchment paper or cellophane sheet whereas those of the colloids do not. The *apparatus* used is called a *dialyser*.

Electrodialysis: To increase the rate of purification, the dialysis is carried out by applying an electric field. This process is called *electrodialysis*. The most important application of dialysis is in the purification of blood in an artificial kidney machine (Fig. 5.17). The dialysis membrane permits small particles of the excess ions and waste products to pass through whereas colloid-sized particles such as hemoglobin do not pass through the membrane.

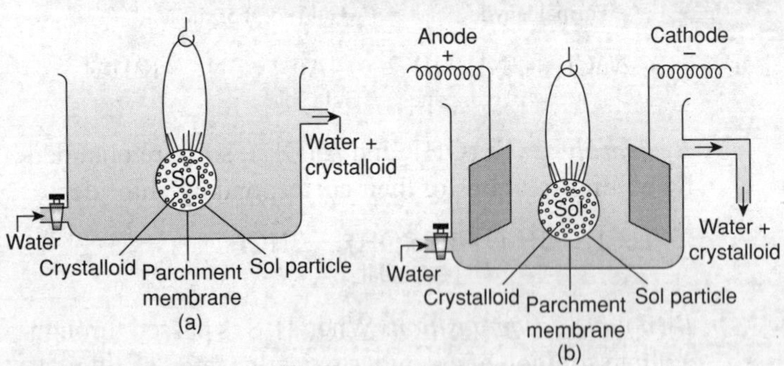

Fig. 5.17 (a) Dialysis (b) Electrodialysis

5.14.2 Ultrafiltration

Ultrafiltration is the process of removing the impurities from the colloidal solution by passing it through graded filter papers called ultrafilter papers. An ultrafilter paper may be prepared by soaking the filter paper in a colloidion solution, hardening by dipping in formaldehyde solution and then finally drying it.

Ultracentrifugation: In this method, the impure sol is taken in a tube which is placed in an ultracentrifuge. In this machine, the tube is rotated at a very high speed. As a result, the colloidal particles settle down at the bottom of the tube whereas the crystalloids and other soluble impurities remain in solution. This solution is decanted off and the colloid particles are remixed with the dispersion medium to give the pure colloidal sol.

5.15 Properties of Colloidal Solutions

5.15.1 Physical Properties

(i) *Heterogeneous character*: Colloidal sols form a heterogeneous mixture consisting of particles of the dispersed phase and the dispersion medium. The phenomena of Tyndall effect, electrophoresis and electrosmosis confirm the heterogeneity of colloidal systems.

(ii) *Stability*: Colloidal sols are quite stable. Only a few colloidal particles of comparatively larger size may settle but very slowly.

(iii) *Filtrability*: Animal membrane or parchment paper does not allow the colloidal particles to pass through it. This forms the basis of separating the particles of the colloid from those of the crystalloids in dialysis.

(iv) *Visibility and colour*: The particles in colloidal solution are not visible to the naked eye or under an ordinary microscope. However, they scatter the light falling on them. In a gold sol, if the particles are very fine, the colour is red, but with growing size of the particles, the colour changes to purple, then blue and finally golden.

5.15.2 Colligative Properties

Osmotic pressure: Colloidal particles have very high average molecular masses, and hence the number of moles present in solution will be extremely small. Thus, the value for any of the colligative properties for a particular substance will be smaller as compared to its value when it is a part of a true solution. However, some colloids have measurable osmotic pressures which have been determined with a reasonable degree of accuracy. Hence, measurement of osmotic pressure has been used to determine the average molecular masses of colloidal particles.

5.15.3 Mechanical Properties

Brownian movement: When colloidal solutions are viewed through an ultramicroscope, colloidal particles are seen continuously moving in a zig–zig manner. It is called *Brownian movement* (Fig. 5.18).

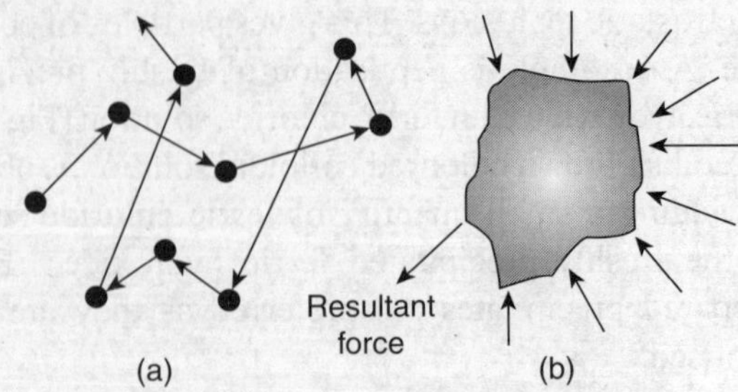

Fig. 5.18 Brownian movement

Thus, Brownian movement does not depend upon the nature of the colloid but depends upon the size of the colloidal particles and viscosity of the sol. Smaller the size, lesser the viscosity, faster is the movement of the particles.

Cause of Brownian movement: When a molecule of the dispersion medium collides with a colloidal particle, it is then displaced in one direction. Then another molecule strikes it, displacing it to another direction and so on. This process gives rise to a zig–zag motion. Thus, Brownian movement has a stirring effect which does not allow the particles to settle down and hence is responsible for the stability of the sols. The resultant force causes them to move [Fig. 5.18(b)]. However, colloidal particles being comparatively heavier, move with a slower speed.

Importance of Brownian Movement

- Brownian movement opposes the force of gravity and does not allow the colloidal particles to settle down. Thus, it is responsible for the stability of the colloidal solution. It has also helped in the determination of Avogadro's number.
- Brownian movement provides a direct demonstration of the ceaseless motion of molecules as postulated by kinetic theory.

Diffusion: The sol particles diffuse from a higher concentration to a lower concentration region. However, due to bigger size, they diffuse at a lesser speed.

Sedimentation: The colloidal particles settle down under the influence of gravity at a very slow rate. This phenomenon is called *sedimentation* and is used to determine the molecular mass of macromolecules.

5.15.4 Optical Properties

Tyndall Effect

When a strong converging beam of light is passed through a colloidal solution placed in a dark room, the path of the beam gets illuminated with a bluish light when viewed at right angles to the direction of the passage of light. The path of the light becomes visible due to scattering of light by the colloidal particles (Fig. 5.19). The phenomenon is called the Tyndall effect. The Tyndall effect confirms the heterogeneous nature of the colloidal solutions. It can be observed due to scattering of dust particles when a beam of sunlight enters a dark room through a slit. For example, when a beam of light is projected in a cinema hall.

The diameter of the dispersed particles is not much smaller compared to the wavelength of the light used. There is a large difference in the refractive indices of the dispersed phase and the dispersion medium.

Importance of Tyndall effect: The Tyndall effect has been used to devise an instrument called the ultramicroscope. An intense beam of light (from an arc lamp) is focused on the colloidal solution taken in a glass vessel and then observed using the microscope at right angles to the beam. The light scattered by each individual colloidal particle appears as a bright star against a dark background. Thus, the number of colloidal particles can be counted; knowing the volume of the solution, the number of particles per unit volume can be determined.

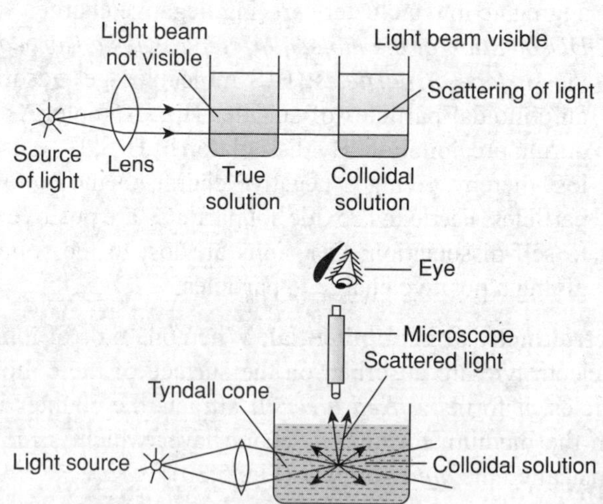

Fig. 5.19 Tyndall effect

5.15.5 Electrical Properties

The particles of colloidal solutions possess electrical charge—positive or negative. The stability of a colloidal solution is due to electrical charges. The particles therefore repel one another and do not coalesce. Colloidal particles carry either positive or negative charge. All the dispersed particles in a colloidal solution carry the same charge while the dispersion medium has an equal and opposite charge. For example, the colloidal solutions of gold, arsenious sulfide (As_2S_3) are negatively charged while those of $Fe(OH)_3$ and $Al(OH)_3$ have a positive charge.

Origin of electrical charge on colloidal particles: The various theories for the origin of electrical charge on the colloidal particles are discussed.

(i) *Frictional electrification*: It is caused by the mutual rubbing of the colloidal particles with molecules of the dispersion medium due to the movement of the colloidal particles in the dispersion medium.

(ii) Electrons are captured by particles from the air and during electrodispersion in Bredig's arc method.

(iii) *Due to selective adsorption of ions from solutions*: The particles constituting the dispersed phase adsorb only those ions preferentially which are common with their own lattice ions. For example, if a colloidal sol of AgI is prepared by adding KI solution to $AgNO_3$ solution till KI is in slight excess, iodide ions (I^-) will be adsorbed on the surface of AgI particles thereby giving them a negative charge:

$$\underset{(\text{from } AgNO_3)}{AgI} + \underset{\text{Positive sol}}{I^-} \rightarrow AgI \vdots Ag^+$$

In this case, the let out ions (K^+) will remain in the dispersion medium thereby giving equal and opposite charge (positive) to the dispersion medium.

(iv) *Dissociation of molecules followed by aggregation of ions*: In the case of soap, the $RCOO^-$ groups get dissociated from the Na^+ ions and have a tendency to aggregate into a cluster carrying negative charge.

(v) *Dissociation of the molecular electrolytes adsorbed on the surface of particles*: H_2S molecules get adsorbed on colloidal particles of sulfides (for example, As_2S_3) during precipitation. By dissociaton of H_2S, H^+ ions are lost thereby giving a negative charge to the colloidal particles. Ferric hydroxide sol particles are positive due to self-dissociation; OH^- ions are lost to the solution giving a positive charge to particles.

Electrokinetic or zeta potential: When one type of ions of the electrolyte are adsorbed on the surface of the colloidal particles, it forms a *fixed layer*. It attracts the counter ions from the medium forming a second layer which is mobile and is called the *diffused layer* (Fig. 5.20).

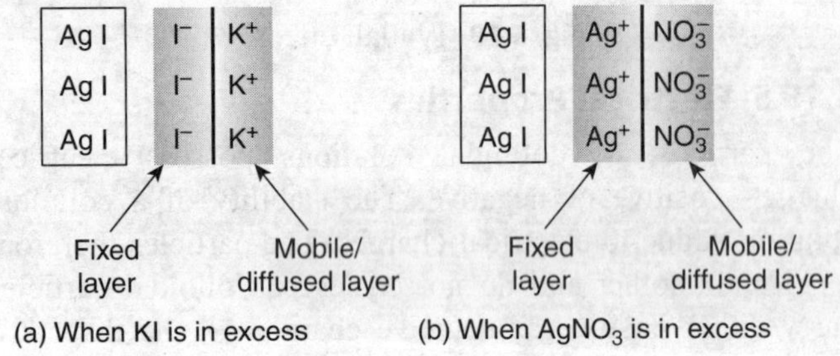

Fig. 5.20 Formation of electrical double layer

The double layer of opposite charges is called the *Helmholtz electrical double layer*. As a result, a difference of potential exists between the fixed layer and the diffused layer. This potential difference is known as the *electrokinetic potential* or *zeta (ξ) potential.*

Electrophoresis or cataphoresis: The presence of a charge on the sol particles and its nature, whether positive or negative, can be determined with the help particles moving towards the positive or negative electrodes depending upon their charge under the influence of an electrical field (Fig. 5.21).

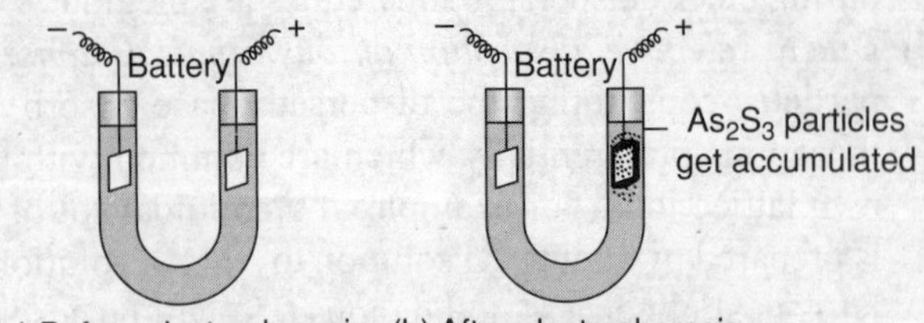

Fig. 5.21 Process of electrophoresis

The phenomenon of the movement of colloidal particles under the influence of an electric field is called *electrophoresis* or *cataphoresis*. As soon as the colloidal particles reach the oppositely charged electrode, they get neutralised and hence coagulated.

Electroosmosis: *Electroosmosis* is the phenomenon of the movement of the molecules of the dispersion medium under the influence of an electric field whereas colloidal particles are not allowed to move (Fig. 5.22).

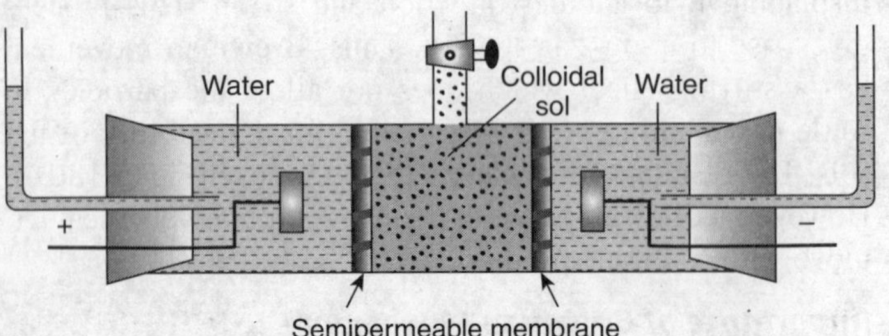

Fig. 5.22 Electroosmosis

Coagulation/ flocculation/ precipitation of colloidal solutions: A small amount of an electrolyte is necessary for the stability of the colloidal sol. The ions of the electrolytes are adsorbed on the sol particles and impart them some charge—positive or negative. The charged colloidal particles repel one another and are prevented from coming close together to unite into bigger particles (Fig. 5.22). If, somehow, the charge is removed, the particles will come nearer to each other to form aggregates (or coagulate) and settle down under the force of gravity. This is known as coagulation or precipitation.

Mechanism of coagulation: Coagulation is generally brought about by the *addition of electrolytes*. When an electrolyte is added to a colloidal solution, the particles of the sol take up the ions which are oppositely charged and thus get neutralised. The ion responsible for the neutralisation of charge on the colloidal particles is called the *coagulating ion* or *flocculating ion*. The neutral particles then start accumulating to form particles of larger size which settle down. When the concentration of the electrolyte added is low, the process is called *flocculation*.

The minimum amount of an electrolyte (millimoles) that must be added to one litre of a colloidal solution to bring about complete coagulation is called the *coagulation* or *flocculation* or *precipitation value* of the electrolyte. Thus, smaller the coagulation value of an electrolyte, greater is its coagulating or precipitating power.

Hardy–Schulze Law

The coagulation capacity of different electrolytes depends upon the valency of the active ion called flocculating ion, which is the ion carrying charge opposite to the charge on the colloidal particles. This is known as **Hardy–Schulze law**, the main points of which may be stated as follows.

- The ions carrying the charge opposite to that of sol particles are effective in causing coagulation of the sol.
- The coagulating power of an electrolyte is directly proportional to the fourth power of the valency of the active ions (ions causing coagulation). Greater the valency of the oppositely charged ion of the electrolyte being added, the faster is the coagulation.

Thus, for the coagulation of negatively charged arsenious sulfide sol, trivalent cations (Al^{3+}) are far more effective than divalent (Ba^{2+}) cations which in turn are more effective than monovalent (Na^+) cations. As coagulating power is inversely proportional to coagulation/flocculation value, to compare the relative coagulation powers of two electrolytes for the same colloidal sol, we have

$$\frac{\text{Coagulating power of electrolyte 1}}{\text{Coagulating power of electrolyte 2}} = \frac{\text{Coagulation value of electrolyte 2}}{\text{Coagulation value of electrolyte 1}}$$

For example, for coagulation of negative As_2S_3 sol,

$$\frac{\text{Coagulating power of } AlCl_3}{\text{Coagulating power of NaCl}} = \frac{\text{Coagulation value of NaCl}}{\text{Coagulation value of } AlCl_3}$$

$$= \frac{52}{0.093} = 559$$

Thus, $AlCl_3$ has 559 times more coagulating power than NaCl.

For a negatively charged sol such as that of As_2S_3, the coagulating powers of the *cations* are in the order:

$$Al^{3+} > Ba^{2+} > Na^+$$

For a positively charged sol such as that of $Fe(OH)_3$, the coagulating powers of the anions are in the order:

$$[Fe(CN)_6]^{4-} > PO_4^{3-} > SO_4^{2-} > Cl^-$$

Other Methods of Coagulation

Apart from the addition of the electrolyte, coagulation of a colloidal sol can be carried out by the following methods.

(i) *By prolonged dialysis*: The stability of a colloidal sol is due to the presence of a small amount of the electrolyte. On prolonged dialysis, the electrolyte is completely removed. As a result, the colloidal sol becomes unstable and gets coagulated.

(ii) *By mutual precipitation*: Mutual precipitation is a process in which oppositely charged sols get remixed in proper proportions to neutralise the charges of each other causing coagulation of both the sols. For example, if positively charged ferric hydroxide and negatively charged arsenious sulfide sols are mixed, both the sols get coagulated.

(iii) *By heating (boiling) or cooling*: In some cases, heating the sol results in coagulation. For example, coagulation of butter. Similarly, in some cases, cooling the sol results in coagulation. For example, coagulation of milk; on cooling milk, fat starts floating on the surface.

(iv) *By electrophoresis*: In electrophoresis, the particles of the dispersed phase move towards the oppositely charged electrode and get neutralised.

Comparison of Stability or Coagulation of Lyophobic and Lyophilic Colloids

Lyophilic sols are more stable than lyophobic sols. The stability of lyophilic sols is due to two factors—same charge on all the colloidal particles and solvation of the colloidal particles. When these two factors are removed, a lyophilic sol can be coagulated. This can be done by adding an electrolyte, and adding a suitable solvent.

When a solvent like alcohol or acetone is added to a hydrophilic sol, the dehydration of the colloidal particles occurs. A small amount of the electrolyte can bring about coagulation. The stability of lyophobic sol is only due to charge. This factor can be removed by adding only electrolyte. Hence, they can be easily coagulated.

∴ By definition, flocculation value of NaCl = 50

5.16 Protection of Lyophilic Colloids and Gold Number

Lyophobic sols like those of metals (Au, Ag) are unstable and are easily precipitated by the addition of electrolytes. The addition of certain lyophilic colloids like gums, soaps and gelatine to lyophobic colloids (like a metal sol) render them, making it difficult to coagulate them by the addition of electrolytes. The process is known as *protection* and the lyophilic colloids are termed as *protective colloids.* It is believed that the protective action of the lyophilic colloids is due to the covering up of the particles of the lyophobic colloids by those of the lyophilic colloid (Fig. 5.23).

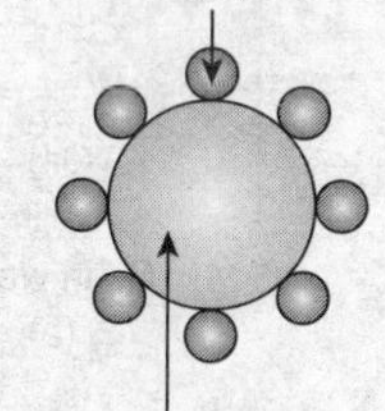

Fig. 5.23 Protection of colloids

To compare the protective action of different lyophilic colloids, Zsigmondy (in 1901) introduced a term called the *gold number*. Gold number is defined as the minimum amount of the protective colloid in milligrams required to just prevent the coagulation of 10 mL of a given gold sol when 1 mL of a 10% solution of sodium chloride is added to it. Smaller the gold number of a protective colloid, the greater is its protective action.

By definition, gold number of starch = 25.

5.17 Emulsions

An emulsion is a colloidal dispersion in which both the dispersed phase and the dispersion medium are liquids. For example, milk is a naturally occurring emulsion in which the particles (or globules) of liquid fat are dispersed in water.

5.17.1 Method of Preparation

An emulsion is prepared by vigorously shaking the mixture of the two liquids or by passing the mixture through a colloid mill, called a homogeniser. The emulsions thus prepared from the pure liquids are usually not stable and the two liquids separate out on standing. To get a stable emulsion, small quantities of certain *emulsifiers* or *emulsifying agents* are added. The substances commonly used as emulsifying agents are soaps of various kinds, long chain sulfonic acid or lyophilic colloids (proteins, gum, agar).

Role of Emulsifier

The main function of the emulsifier is to reduce the interfacial tension between the two liquids forming the emulsion. Some commonly used stabilising agents are soaps, proteins, gums and agar.

5.17.2 Types of Emulsions

If the term *oil* is used for any liquid which is immiscible with water and is capable of forming and emulsion with water, then the various types of emulsions may be classified into two types (Fig. 5.24).

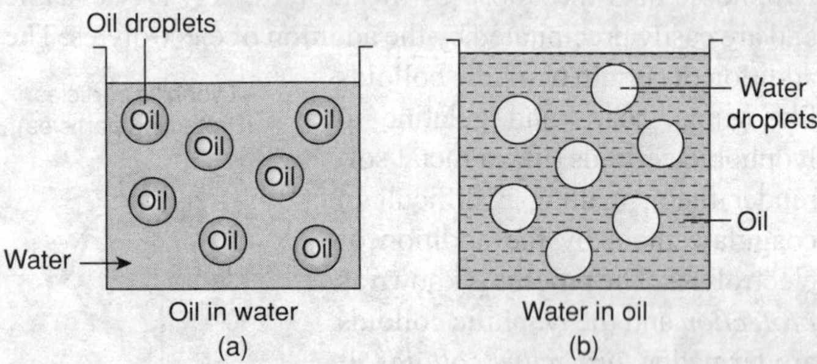

Fig. 5.24 Types of emulsions

(i) *Oil-in-water (o/w) emulsion*: In this case, oil is the dispersed phase and water is the dispersion medium. For example, milk is an emulsion of liquid fat dispersed in water. Another example is vanishing cream.

(ii) *Water-in-oil (w/o) emulsion*: In this case, water is the dispersed phase and oil is the dispersion medium. For example, cod liver oil is an emulsion of water in oil, that is, water is the dispersed phase and oil is the dispersion medium. Two other common examples of this type are butter and cold cream.

If water is in excess, it is an oil-in-water emulsion. If oil is excess, it is a water-in-oil emulsion. Some very commonly used emulsifying agents for o/w emulsions are proteins, gums, natural and synthetic soaps whereas for those for w/o emulsions are heavy metal salts of fatty acids, long chain alcohols and lamp black.

To Test the Type of Emulsion

The type to which the given emulsion belongs can be tested experimentally by any of the following methods.

- *Dilution test*: To a small amount of the given emulsion, a few drops of water are added. The water will mix completely if the emulsion is oil-in-water type.
- *Dye method: A* small amount of an oil-soluble dye is added to the emulsion. If it is water-in-oil type, it becomes deeply coloured, otherwise it remains colourless.
- *Conductance method*: This method is based upon adding a small amount of an electrolyte to the emulsion. If the conductance increases, the emulsion is an oil-in-water type and if there is no significant change, it is a water-in-oil type.

5.17.3 Properties of Emulsions

- Emulsions exhibit all the characteristic properties of colloidal solutions such as Tyndall effect, Brownian movement, electrophoresis, coagulation on addition of electrolyte (containing multivalent positive ions, as the dispersed particles, that is, globules are usually negatively charged) as shown by colloidal sols.
- These can also be separated into their constituent liquids by boiling, freezing, centrifuging, electrostatic precipitation by adding large amounts of the electrolytes to precipitate out the dispersed phase or by chemical destruction of the emulsifying agent. The separation of cream from milk is a well-known example of centrifuging.

This process of separation of the constituent liquids of an emulsion is called *demulsification*.

- Emulsions can be diluted by adding any amount of the dispersion medium, that is, water for o/w emulsions and oils for w/o emulsions. However, if the dispersed phase is added into the emulsion, it forms a separate layer.

5.17.4 Applications of Emulsions

Emulsions are useful in a number of ways. A few of the applications are given below.

(i) *Concentration of ores in metallurgy*: In metallurgical processes, the concentration of ore by the froth floatation process is based upon the treatment of the powdered ore with an oil emulsion. The valuable particles of the ore form foam which comes to the surface and is skimmed off.

(ii) Asphalt emulsified in water is used for building roads without the necessity of melting the asphalt.

(iii) Milk which is an important constituent of our diet is an emulsion of liquid fats in water.

(iv) Several oily drugs are prepared in the form of emulsions.

(v) Certain disinfectants such as *dettol* and *lysol* give emulsions of oil-in-water type on mixing with water.

(vi) The cleansing action of ordinary soap for washing clothes and utensils is based upon the formation of oil-in-water emulsion.

(vii) The digestion of fats in the intestines takes place by the process of emulsification. A small amount of the fat reacts with the alkaline solution present in the intestines to form a sodium soap. This soap causes the emulsification of the rest of the fat thereby making the function of the digestive enzymes easier in carrying out the metabolic processes.

(viii) The various pharmaceuticals and cosmetics available in liquid form such as cod-liver oil, B-complex, ointments, and so on, are emulsions of water-in-oil type. These are readily adsorbed in the intestines.

Harmful Effect of Emulsions

The formation of emulsions is sometimes harmful. For example, petroleum forms an emulsion with water. Thus, in the petroleum wells, we sometimes get the emulsion instead of petroleum alone. Likewise, in the areas where small amounts of petroleum are present, the well water becomes unfit for domestic use.

5.18 Gels

A gel is a colloidal system in which a liquid is dispersed in a solid. Under certain conditions, lyophilic sols may be coagulated to give a semi-solid jelly-like mass which encloses all the liquid present in the sol. The process of gel formation is called *gelation* and the colloidal system formed is called a *gel*. The common examples of gels are gum arabic, gelatine, processed cheese, silicic acid and ferric hydroxide. Gels may be classified into two types—elastic gels and non-elastic gels.

5.18.1 Elastic Gels

These are gels that possess the property of elasticity. They readily change their shape on applying force and return to their original shape when the applied force is removed. They change to a solid mass on dehydration which can again be converted into the gel by the addition of water followed by heating and cooling. When these gels are placed in contact with water, they absorb water and swell. This property is called *imbibition*. Common examples are gelatine, agar and starch.

5.18.2 Non-elastic Gels

These are gels that are rigid and do not have the property of elasticity. They change into a solid mass on dehydration which becomes rigid and cannot be converted into the original form by heating with water. Unlike elastic gels, they do not show the phenomenon of imbibition. For example, silica gel.

5.19 Common Examples of Colloids

(i) *Blue colour of the sky*: This is due to the scattering of light by colloidal dust particles present in air (Tyndall effect). These dust particles along with water suspended in air scatter blue light which reaches our eyes and therefore, the sky looks blue to us. Similarly, the sea water looks blue due to scattering of light by the colloidal impurities present in sea water.

(ii) *Fog, mist and cloud*: In winters, at night, when a large mass of air containing dust particles is cooled below its dew point, the moisture present in the air condenses on the surface of these particles and forms fine droplets. These droplets are colloidal in size and hence continue to float in the air in the form of fog or mist. Clouds are aerosols consisting of small droplets of water suspended in the air. In the upper atmosphere where the temperature is low, they condense together to form bigger drops which come down in the form of rain. Rain is also caused when two oppositely charged clouds meet each other.

(iii) *Food articles*: A large number of food articles that we eat are colloidal in nature—milk, butter, ice creams, fruit juices, halwa.

(iv) *Formation of deltas*: River water contains charged colloidal particles of clay, sand and many other materials. As soon as river water comes in contact with sea water, the electrolytes present in sea water coagulate the suspended colloidal particles which ultimately settle down at the point of contact. Thus, the level of the river bed rises. As a result, a delta is formed (Fig. 5.25).

(v) *Tail of comets*: It is seen as a Tyndall cone due to the scattering of light by the tiny solid particles left by the comet in its path.

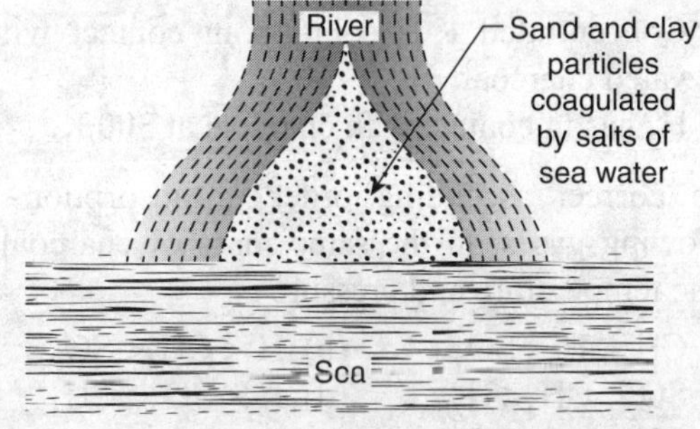

Fig. 5.25 Formation of delta

(vi) *Blood*: It is a colloidal solution of an albuminoid and the bleeding stops on applying ferric chloride solution due to coagulation of blood to form a clot.

5.20 Applications of Colloids

5.20.1 Applications of Colloids in Everyday Life

(i) *Medicines*: Most of the medicines used are in the colloidal form since they can be more easily assimilated due to the large surface area and hence are more effective. For example,
- Argyrol is a silver sol used as an eye lotion,
- colloidal antimony is used for curing kala-azar,
- colloidal gold is used as an intramuscular injection, and,
- milk of magnesia, which is an emulsion, is used as an antacid.

(ii) *Cleansing action of soap*: Soap solution is colloidal in nature. It removes the dirt particles either by adsorption or by emulsifying the greasy matter sticking to the cloth.

(iii) *Smoke screen:* In warfare, smoke screens are used which are nothing but colloidal dispersions of certain substances (such as titanium oxide or $SiCl_4$) in the air.

5.20.2 Industrial Applications of Colloids

(i) *Sewage disposal*: Colloidal particles of dirt, mud, and so on, carry electric charge. Hence, when sewage water is passed through the plates kept at a high potential, the colloidal particles are coagulated due to electrophoresis and the suspended matter gets removed.

(ii) *Purification of water*: The precipitation of colloidal impurities present in water can be done by adding certain electrolytes like alum. The negatively charged colloidal particles of impurities get coagulated by the Al^{3+} ions and settle down; pure water can be decanted off.

(iii) *Smoke precipitation*: Smoke particles are actually electrically charged colloidal particles of carbon in the air. Precipitation of smoke particles is carried out using the Cottrell precipitator which is based on the principle of electrophoresis.

(iv) *Photography*: A colloidal solution of silver bromide in gelatine is applied on glass plates or celluloid films or paper to form sensitive plates in photography.

(v) *Rubber industry*: Latex is a colloidal solution of negatively charged rubber particles. From latex, rubber can be obtained by coagulation.

(vi) *Tanning/leather industry*: The process of hardening of leather is known as *tanning*. Tannin is a mixture of derivatives of polyhydroxy benzoic acids. It contains negatively charged colloidal particles. Animal hides contain positively charged particles. When they are soaked in tannin, their mutual coagulation takes place and leather becomes hard.

(vii) *Colloidal industrial products*: A number of industrial products which we use in our everyday life are colloidal in nature. For example, ink, paints, lubricants, synthetic plastics, rubber and cement.

Exercises

OBJECTIVE QUESTIONS

Introduction to Adsorption

1. Which one of the following is a case of negative adsorption?
(a) Acetic acid solution in contact with animal charcoal.
(b) Dilute KCl solution in contact with activated charcoal.
(c) Concentrated KCl solution in contact with activated charcoal.
(d) H_2 gas in contact with charcoal at 300 K.

2. The correct ascending order of adsorption of the following gases on the same mass of charcoal at the same temperature and pressure is
(a) $CH_4 < H_2 < SO_2$ (b) $H_2 < CH_4 < SO_2$
(c) $SO_2 < CH_4 < H_2$ (d) $H_2 < SO_2 < CH_4$
(e) $CH_4 < CO_2 < H_2$

3. Which one of the following substances adsorbs hydrogen gas most strongly?
(a) activated carbon (b) silica gel
(c) platinum black (d) iron powder

4. Adsorption is an exothermic process. The amount of substance adsorbed should
(a) increase with a decrease in temperature
(b) increase with an increase in temperature
(c) decrease with a decrease in temperature
(d) decrease with an increase in temperature

5. The volumes of gases H_2, CH_4, CO_2 and NH_3 adsorbed by 1 g of charcoal at 288 K are in the order:
(a) $H_2 > CH_4 > CO_2 > NH_3$
(b) $CH_4 > CO_2 > NH_3 > H_2$
(c) $CO_2 > NH_3 > H_2 > CH_4$
(d) $NH_3 > CO_2 > CH_4 > H_2$

6. Which one of the following is a cause of adsorption?
(a) Anhydrous $CaCl_2$ in contact with water vapour.
(b) Silica gel in contact with water vapour.
(c) Ammonia gas in contact with water.
(d) Cotton clothes dipped in a dye solution.

7. Which of the following statements is correct for the spontaneous adsorption of a gas?
(a) ΔS is negative and, therefore, ΔH should be highly positive.

(b) ΔS is negative and, therefore, ΔH should be highly negative.
(c) ΔS is positive and, therefore, ΔH should be negative.
(d) ΔS is positive and, therefore, ΔH also should be highly positive.

8. Which one of the following is not explained by adsorption?
(a) When acetic acid solution is shaken with charcoal, the concentration of the acid decreases.
(b) The white precipitate of $Mg(OH)_2$ attains a blue colour when precipitated in the presence of magneson reagent.
(c) The air becomes dry in the presence of silica gel.
(d) An aqueous solution of NaOH turns pink with a drop of phenolphthalein.
(e) When animal charcoal is shaken with coloured methylene blue solution, the solution turns colourless.

9. Which of the following is adsorbed in maximum amount by activated charcoal?
(a) N_2 (b) CO_2 (c) Cl_2 (d) O_2

10. The critical temperature of O_2, N_2, H_2 and CO_2 are 154.3 K, 126 K, 33.2 K and 304 K respectively. The extent of adsorption on tungsten may be highest in the case of
(a) H_2 (b) N_2 (c) O_2 (d) CO_2

11. The adsorption of inert gases on the surface of activated charcoal increases with
(a) a decrease in both atomic mass and temperature
(b) an increase in both atomic mass and temperature
(c) an increase in atomic mass and decrease in temperature
(d) a decrease in atomic mass and increase in temperature

12. Which of the following statements is true about absorption?
(a) $\Delta H < 0$ and $\Delta S < 0$ (b) $\Delta H > 0$ and $\Delta S < 0$
(c) $\Delta H < 0$ and $\Delta S > 0$ (d) $\Delta H = 0$ and $\Delta S < 0$
(e) $\Delta H = 0$ and $\Delta S > 0$

13. Which of the following is not true for the adsorption of a gas on a solid?
(a) Increase in temperature favours adsorption.
(b) Enthalpy change is negative.
(c) Adsorption is more specific.
(d) Entropy change is negative.

14. Which one of the following characteristics is associated with adsorption?
(a) ΔG and ΔH are negative but ΔS is positive.
(b) ΔG and ΔS are negative but ΔH is positive.
(c) ΔG is negative but ΔH and ΔS are positive.
(d) ΔG, ΔH and ΔS all are negative.

15. 0.2 g of fine animal charcoal is mixed with half a litre of acetic acid solution and shaken for 30 minutes.
(a) the concentration remains the same
(b) the concentration increases
(c) the concentration of the solution decreases
(d) none of these

16. The variation of the amount of gas absorbed per gram of adsorbent with pressure at different temperatures is given in the figure below.

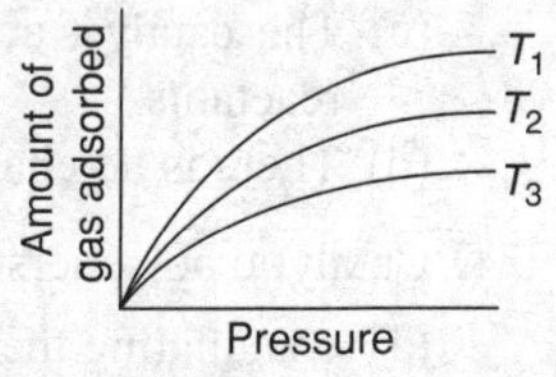

Which of the following is a correct relation?
(a) $T_1 > T_2 > T_3$ (b) $T_2 > T_1 > T_3$
(c) $T_3 > T_2 > T_1$ (d) $T_1 = T_2 = T_3$

17. Which among the following statements is false?
(a) Adsorption may be monolayered or multi-layered.
(b) The particle size of the adsorbent will not affect the amount of adsorption.
(c) Increase in pressure increases the amount of adsorption.
(d) All of the above.

18. The gas that is adsorbed to a larger extent on charcoal is
(a) H_2 (b) CO_2 (c) CO (d) NH_3

19. The gas which is least adsorbed on charcoal (under identical conditions) is
(a) HCl (b) O_2 (c) CO_2 (d) NH_3
(e) SO_2

20. Identify the correct statement for the adsorption of a real gas on charcoal at 1 atm and 15°C.
(a) Gases which are small in molecular size are adsorbed more.
(b) A decrease in pressure increases the extent of adsorption.
(c) Gases which are easily liquefiable are adsorbed more in quantity.
(d) A gas which has a behaviour similar to an inert gas is adsorbed more.

21. 50 mL of 1 M oxalic acid is shaken with 0.5 g of wood charcoal. The final concentration of the solution after adsorption is 0.5 M. The amount of oxalic acid absorbed per gram of charcoal is
(a) 3.45 g (b) 3.15
(c) 6.30 g (d) none of the above

22. Noble gases are adsorbed by
(a) anhydrous calcium chloride
(b) ferric hydroxide
(c) conc. H_2SO_4
(d) activated coconut charcoal

Types of Adsorption

23. Which of the statements is not correct for heterogeneous catalysis?
(a) The catalyst decreases the energy of activation.
(b) The surface of the catalyst plays an important role.
(c) The catalyst actually forms a compound with the reactants.
(d) There is no change in the energy of activation.

24. Catalytic poisoners act by:
(a) coagulating the catalyst
(b) getting adsorbed on the active centres on the surface of the catalyst
(c) chemical combination with any one of the reactants
(d) none of the above

25. Which one of the following statements is wrong?
(a) Physical adsorption of a gas is directly related to its critical temperature.
(b) Chemical adsorption decreases regularly as the temperature is increased.
(c) Adsorption is an exothermic process.
(d) A solid with a rough surface is a better adsorbent than the same solid with a smooth surface.

26. Which one of the following is wrong about chemisorption?
(a) It involves the formation of a compound on the surface of the solid adsorbent.
(b) It is specific in nature.
(c) It first increases with an increase in temperature and then decreases.
(d) It is reversible in nature.

27. Chemical adsorption
(a) decreases with an increase in temperature
(b) increases with an increase in temperature
(c) first increases and then decreases with an increase in temperature
(d) first decreases and then increases with an increase in temperature

28. The heats of adsorption in physisorption lie in the range (in kJ/mole)
(a) 40–400 (b) 40–100 (c) 10–40 (d) 1–10

29. In which one of the following properties, do physisorption and chemisorption resemble each other?
(a) force of attraction
(b) enthalpy of adsorption
(c) temperature effect
(d) effect of surface area
(e) number of adsorption layers

30. Which of the following is not a favourable condition for physical adsorption?
(a) high pressure
(b) low temperature
(c) high temperature
(d) higher critical temperature of adsorbate

31. Physisorption decreases with an increase in temperature because
(a) ΔG is –ve (b) ΔS is –ve
(c) ΔH is –ve (d) all the three are –ve

32. Choose the incorrect statement with respect to physisorption.
(a) It is not specific in nature.
(b) It arises because of van der Waals forces.
(c) It is reversible in nature.
(d) No appreciable activation energy is needed.
(e) Enthalpy of adsorption is in the range 80–240 kJ mol^{-1}.

33. Select the incorrect statement.
(a) Physical adsorption is reversible while chemical is irreversible.
(b) High pressure favours physical adsorption while low pressure favours chemical adsorption.
(c) Physical adsorption is not specific while chemical is highly specific.
(d) High activation energy is involved in chemical adsorption.

34. Which of the following curve(s) represents chemical adsorption?

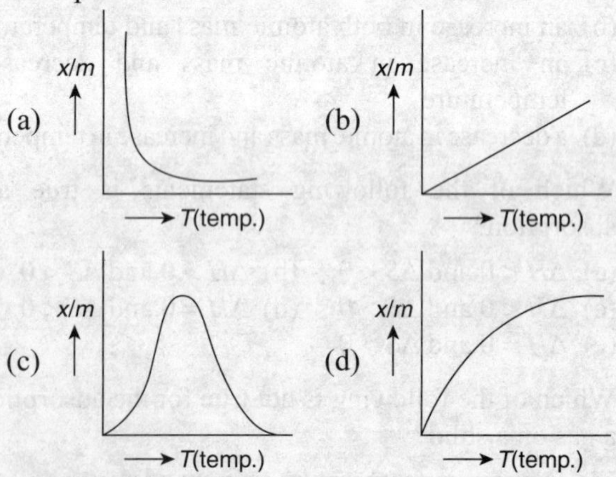

35. Which of the statements is true regarding chemisorption of a gas on a solid surface?
(a) This type of adsorption first increases with an increase in temperature.
(b) No compound formation takes place in this case.
(c) The forces operating in this are weak van der Waals' forces.
(d) It forms multimolecular layers of gas molecules on the surface.

Adsorption Isotherms, Isobars and Isosteres

36. Which statement about enzymes in not correct?
(a) Enzymes are in the colloidal state.
(b) Enzymes are catalysts.
(c) Enzymes can catalyse any reaction.
(d) Urease is an enzyme.

37. In Langmuir's model of adsorption of gas on a solid surface,
(a) the mass of gas striking a given area of surface is proportional to the pressure of the gas.
(b) the mass of the gas striking a given area of surface is independent of the pressure of the gas
(c) the rate of dissociation of the adsorbed molecules on the surface does not depend on the surface covered
(d) the adsorption at a single site on the surface may involve multiple molecules at the same time

38. The correct expression for the Langmuir adsorption isotherm is
(a) $\frac{x}{m}=\frac{1+aP}{b}$ (b) $\frac{x}{m}=\frac{aP}{1+bP}$
(c) $\frac{x}{m}=\frac{1+aP}{1+bP}$ (d) $\frac{x}{m}=\frac{1}{a}+\frac{bP}{a}$

39. What is the equation form of the Langmuir isotherm under high pressure?
(a) $\frac{x}{m}=\frac{a}{b}$ (b) $\frac{x}{m}=aP$
(c) $\frac{x}{m}=\frac{1}{a.P}$ (d) $\frac{x}{m}=\frac{b}{a}$

40. Langmuir adsorption isotherm is deduced using the assumption,
(a) the adsorbed molecules interact with each other
(b) the adsorption takes place in multi-layers
(c) the adsorption sites are equivalent in their ability to adsorb the particles
(d) the heat of adsorption varies with the coverage

41. According to the Langmuir adsorption isotherm, the amount of gas adsorption at very high pressure
(a) reaches a constant limiting value
(b) goes on increasing with pressure
(c) goes on decreasing with pressure
(d) first increases and then decreases with pressure

42. Freundlich adsorption isotherm gives a straight line on plotting
(a) $\frac{x}{m}$ vs P (b) $\log\frac{x}{m}$ vs P
(c) $\log\frac{x}{m}$ vs $\log P$ (d) $\frac{x}{m}$ vs $\frac{1}{P}$

43. A straight line will be obtained according to the Langmuir adsorption isotherm if we plot
(a) $\log x/m$ vs $\log P$ (b) x/m vs P
(c) m/x vs a/P (d) x/m vs $1/P$

44. The adsorption coefficient of a gas is given by the relation $x = ap/(1+bp)$ where x is moles of the gas adsorbed per gram of the adsorbent, p is the pressure of the gas and a and b are constants. Then x
(a) increases with p
(b) remains unchanged with p
(c) decreases with p
(d) increases with p at low pressure and then remains the same at high pressure

45. For a linear plot of $\log(x/m)$ versus $\log p$ in a Freundlich adsorption isotherm, which of the following statements is correct? (k and n are constants)
(a) Both k and $1/n$ appear in the slope term.
(b) $1/n$ appears in the intercept.
(c) Only $1/n$ appears in the slope.
(d) $\log(1/n)$ appears in the intercept.

46. In the Freundlich adsorption isotherm equation $\log\frac{x}{m}=\log k+\frac{1}{n}\log P$, the value of n is
(a) any value from 0 to 1
(b) a negative integer
(c) a positive integer
(d) a positive or a negative fractional number

47. The adsorption of a gas on a solid surface varies with pressure as follows:
(a) fast → slow → independent of the pressure
(b) slow → fast → independent of the pressure
(c) independent of the pressure → fast → slow
(d) independent of the pressure → slow → fast

48. For adsorption of a gas on a solid, the plot of $\log x/m$ log P is linear with a slope equal to (n being whole number)
(a) k (b) $\log k$ (c) n (d) $1/n$

49. If x is the amount of adsorption and m is the amount of adsorbent, which of the following relations is not related to the adsorption process?
(a) $\frac{x}{m}=p\times T$
(b) $\frac{x}{m}=f(p)$ at constant T
(c) $\frac{x}{m}=f(T)$ at constant p
(d) $p=f(T)$ at constant $\left(\frac{x}{m}\right)$

50. In the adsorption of a gas on solid, the Freundlich isotherm is obeyed. The slope of the plot is zero. Then the extent of adsorption is
(a) directly proportional to the pressure of the gas
(b) directly proportional to the square root of the pressure of the gas
(c) inversely proportional to the square root of the pressure of the gas
(d) inversely proportional to the pressure of the gas
(e) independent of the pressure of the gas

Applications of Adsorption

51. Which is correct in the case of van der Waals adsorption?
(a) high temperature, low pressure
(b) low temperature, high pressure
(c) low temperature, low pressure
(d) high temperature, high pressure

52. Which of the following is not an application of adsorption?
(a) ion exchange process in softening of hard water
(b) chromatographic analysis
(c) clarification of sugar
(d) theory of homogeneous catalysis

53. In the Dewar flask used in a thermos flask, charcoal powder is placed in the annular space between the two walls of the flask. This is done
(a) to increase the strength of the flask
(b) to provide insulation to the inner wall
(c) to create a vacuum in the annular space
(d) all the three above

54. In the sugar industry, activated charcoal is used for the decolourisation of cane juice as
(a) an adsorbent (b) an adsorbate
(c) an oxidising agent (d) a reducing agent

Introduction to Catalysis

55. Which of the following statements about a catalyst is/are true?
(a) A catalyst accelerates the reaction by bringing down the free energy of activation.
(b) A catalyst does not take part in the reaction mechanism.
(c) A catalyst makes the reaction more feasible by making the $\Delta G°$ more negative.
(d) A catalyst makes the equilibrium constant of the reaction more favourable for the forward reaction.

56. In the case of a reversible gaseous reaction, a positive catalyst
(a) increases the rate of both the forward and backward reaction by increasing the activation energy
(b) increases the rate of the forward and backward reactions by decreasing the activation energy
(c) increases the rate of only the forward reaction
(d) does not influence the rate of a reversible reaction

57. Decomposition of hydrogen peroxide can be prevented by adding
(a) NaOH (b) MnO_2
(c) urea (d) oxalic acid

58. Which of the following is not true about a catalyst?
(a) Mechanism of the reaction in the presence and absence of the catalyst could be different.
(b) Enthalpy of the reaction does not change with the catalyst.
(c) A catalyst enhances both the forward and backward reaction at an equal rate.
(d) A catalyst participates in the reaction but is not consumed in the process.
(e) The use of a catalyst cannot change the order of the reaction.

59. Which one of the following statements regarding catalysts is not true?
(a) A catalyst remains unchanged in composition and quantity at the end of the reaction.
(b) A catalyst cannot initiate a reaction.
(c) A catalyst does not take part in a reaction.
(d) A catalyst does not alter the equilibrium in a reversible reaction.

60. A catalytic poison renders the catalyst ineffective because
(a) it adsorbs the molecules of the reactants
(b) it is preferentially adsorbed on the catalyst
(c) it combines chemically with the catalyst
(d) it combines with one of the reactants

61. The addition of a catalyst during a chemical reaction alters which of the following quantities?
(a) enthalpy (b) activation energy
(c) entropy (d) internal energy

62. For the following reaction,

$$C_6H_{12}O_6(aq) + H_2(g) \rightleftharpoons C_6H_{14}O_6(aq)$$

which one of the following is not affected by the addition of catalyst?
(a) rate of the forward reaction
(b) rate of the backward reaction
(c) time required to reach equilibrium
(d) spontaneity

63. Catalytic poisons act by
(a) making the products chemically inactive
(b) increasing the rate of the backward reaction

(c) chemical combination with any one of the reactants
(d) preferential adsorption on the catalyst surface

64. Which types of metals form effective catalysts?
(a) alkali metals (b) transition metals
(c) alkaline earth metals (d) radioactive metals

65. The addition of 1% alcohol to chloroform acts as a/an
(a) auto-catalyst (b) bio-catalyst
(c) positive catalyst (d) negative catalyst

66. A catalyst
(a) increases the free energy change in a reaction
(b) decreases the free energy change in the reaction
(c) does not increase or decrease the free energy change in a reaction
(d) can either increase or decrease the free energy change depending on what catalyst we use

67. A catalyst remains unchanged at the end of the reaction regarding
(a) mass
(b) physical state
(c) physical state and chemical composition
(d) mass and chemical composition

68. Pick out the correct statement.
(a) A catalyst speeds up the reaction by increasing the activation energy.
(b) A catalyst speeds up the reaction by decreasing the activation energy keeping the reaction mechanism the same.
(c) A catalyst speeds up the reaction by providing an alternate path of lower activation energy.
(d) A catalyst alters the position of equilibrium.

Homogeneous and Heterogeneous Catalysis

69. The minimum energy level necessary to permit a reaction to occur is:
(a) internal energy (b) threshold energy
(c) activation energy (d) free energy

70. Which process does not involve a catalyst?
(a) Haber's process (b) Thermite process
(c) Ostwald's process (d) Contact process

71. Which one of the following is an example of heterogeneous catalysis?
(a) Oxidation of SO_2 and SO_3 by NO.
(b) Hydrolysis of ethyl acetate by dilute H_2SO_4.
(c) Inversion of cane sugar in the presence of H^+.
(d) Cracking of hydrocarbons in the presence of hydrogen by zeolite catalysts.

72. Intermediate compound formation theory is the mechanism of
(a) homogeneous catalysis
(b) heterogeneous catalysis
(c) auto-catalysis
(d) negative catalysis

73. Which one of the following is an example of homogeneous catalysis?
(a) Haber's process of synthesis of ammonia.
(b) Catalytic conversion of SO_2 to SO_3 in the contact process.
(c) Catalytic hydrogenation of oils.
(d) Catalytic conversion of water gas to methanol.
(e) Acid hydrolysis of methyl acetate.

74. Which of the following kind of catalysis can be explained by the adsorption theory?
(a) homogeneous catalysis
(b) acid–base catalysis
(c) heterogeneous catalysis
(d) enzyme catalysis

75. Which one of the following is an example for heterogeneous catalysis?
(a) $2\,SO_2 + O_2 \xrightarrow{NO} 2\,SO_3$
(b) $C_{12}H_{22}O_{11} + H_2O \xrightarrow[H_2SO_4]{Dilute} C_6H_{12}O_6 + C_6H_{12}O_6$
(c) $N_2 + O_2 \xrightarrow{Pt} 2\,NO$
(d) $CH_3COOCH_3 + NaOH \rightarrow CH_3COONa + CH_3OH$

76. Which one of the following is an example for homogeneous catalysis?
(a) hydrogenation of oils
(b) synthesis of ammonia by Haber's process
(c) manufacture of sulfuric acid by the lead chamber process
(d) manufacture of sulfuric acid by the contact process

77. The following reaction is catalysed by Br^- (*aq*).
$2\,H_2O_2(aq) \rightarrow 2\,H_2O(l) + O_2(g)$
This is an example of
(a) homogeneous catalysis
(b) heterogeneous catalysis
(c) autocatalysis
(d) enzyme catalysis

78. Hydrolysis of ethyl acetate is catalysed by aqueous
(a) Na_2SO_4 (b) K_2SO_4 (c) H_2SO_4 (d) $BaSO_4$

79. Which one is false in the following statements?
(a) A catalyst is specific in its action.
(b) A very small amount of the catalyst alters the rate of a reaction.
(c) The number of free valencies on the surface of the catalyst increases on subdivision.
(d) Ni is used as catalyst in the manufacture of ammonia.

80. Which one of the following is not an example of heterogeneous catalysis?

(a) Manufacture of NH_3 by Haber's process.
(b) Oxidation of NH_3 to nitric oxide (NO) in the manufacture of nitric acid by Ostwald's process.
(c) Oxidation of SO_2 to SO_3 in the manufacture of sulfuric acid by the lead chamber process.
(d) Conversion of vegetable oil into margarine by hydrogenation.

81. According to adsorption theory of catalysis, the speed of the reaction increases because

(a) the concentration of the reactant molecules at the active centres of the catalyst becomes high due to adsorption
(b) in the process of adsorption, the activation energy of the molecules becomes large
(c) adsorption produces heat which increases the speed of the reaction
(d) adsorption lowers the activation energy of the reaction

82. Homogeneous catalysis implies that

(a) all reactants and products must be in the same phase
(b) the reactants and the catalyst must be in the same phase
(c) the products and the catalyst must be in the same phase
(d) the composition of the reaction mixture must be homogeneous throughout

83. Which one of the following is an example of homogenous catalysis?

(a) oxidation of SO_2 to SO_3 in the lead chamber process
(b) oxidation of SO_2 to SO_3 in the contact process
(c) manufacture of NH_3 by the Haber's process
(d) oxidation of NH_3 to NO in Ostwald's process

Autocatalysis and Induced Catalysis

84. In the case of auto catalysis, the

(a) reactant catalyses
(b) heat produced in the reaction catalyses
(c) product catalyses
(d) solvent catalyses

85. Which one of the following reactions is an example of autocatalysis?

(a) $2\,AsH_3(s) \rightarrow 2\,As(s) + 3\,H_2(g)$
(b) $N_2(g) + 3\,H_2 \xrightarrow{Fe(s)} 2\,NH_3(g)$
(c) $2\,SO_2(g) + O_2(g) \xrightarrow{NO(g)} 2\,SO_3(g)$
(d) $C_{12}H_{22}O_{11}(l) + H_2O(l) \xrightarrow{H^+(l)} C_6H_{12}O_6(l) + C_6H_{12}O_6(l)$

86. An example of autocatalysis is

(a) oxidation of NO to NO_2
(b) oxidation of SO_2 to SO_3
(c) decomposition of $KClO_3$ to KCl and O_2
(d) oxidation of oxalic acid by acidified $KMnO_4$

87. Hydrolysis of ester ($RCOOR' + H_2O \rightleftharpoons RCOOH + R'OH$)

(a) is fast in the beginning and then slows down with time
(b) is slow in the beginning and then speeds up
(c) takes place at a uniform speed throughout
(d) needs a catalyst to speed up the reaction

88. Air can oxidise sodium sulfite in aqueous solution but not sodium arsenite. However, if air is passed through a solution containing both, then both are oxidised. This is an example of

(a) autocatalysis (b) positive catalysis
(c) negative catalysis (d) induced catalysis

89. Which acts as an auto catalyst during the titration of $KMnO_4$ and oxalic acid in the presence of H_2SO_4?

(a) H_2SO_4 (b) $KMnO_4$
(c) oxalic acid (d) $MnSO_4$

90. Whichis an example of an autocatalysis reaction?

(a) decomposition of $KClO_3 + MnO_2$ mixture
(b) decomposition of nitroglycerine
(c) breakdown of $_6C^{14}$
(d) hydrogenation of vegetable oils using Ni catalyst

Shape Selective Catalysis by Zeolites

91. Which one of the following is not correct about zeolites?

(a) Zeolites are hydration aluminosilicates.
(b) The size of pores in them varies from 260 to 740 pm.
(c) They do not require any treatment before being used as catalysts.
(d) They act as molecular sieves.

92. Zeolites have shape selective structures because of

(a) high adsorption capacity
(b) three dimensional network of atoms
(c) presence of aluminosilicates
(d) honeycomb-like structures

93. In the petrochemical industry, alcohols are directly converted to gasoline by passing over heated

(a) platinum (b) ZSM-5 (c) iron (d) nickel

94. Shape selective catalysts are so called because of

(a) the shape of the catalysts
(b) the specificity of the catalysts
(c) the size of the pores of the catalysts which can trap only selective molecules
(d) their use for only some selected reactions

95. Which one of the following is a shape selective catalyst?

(a) V_2O_5 (b) Cr_2O_3
(c) hydrated zeolites (d) ZSM-5

Enzyme Catalysis

96. The optimum pH range for enzyme activity is

(a) 4–5 (b) 5–7
(c) 7–9 (d) < 4

97. The enzyme used in the conversion of starch into maltose is

(a) diastase (b) maltase
(c) zymase (d) invertase

98. Which one of the following statements is not correct?

(a) A catalyst does not initiate any reaction.
(b) The value of the equilibrium constant is changed in the presence of a catalyst in the reaction at equilibrium.
(c) Enzymes catalyse many biochemical reactions.
(d) Coenzymes increase the catalytic activity of an enzyme.

99. Which enzyme converts sucrose into ethanol?

(a) diastase (b) invertase
(c) zymase (d) both (b) and (c)

100. A biological catalyst is

(a) the N_2 molecule (b) an enzyme
(c) an amino acid (d) a carbohydrate

101. The conversion of maltose to glucose is possible by the enzyme

(a) zymase (b) lactase
(c) maltase (d) diastase

102. Which one of the following statements is wrong in the case of enzyme catalysis?

(a) Enzymes work best at an optimum temperature.
(b) Enzymes work at an optimum pH.
(c) Enzymes are highly specific for substances.
(d) An enzyme raises the activation energy.

103. The efficiency of an enzyme in catalysing a reaction is due to its capacity

(a) to form a strong enzyme–substrate complex
(b) to decrease the bond energies of the substrate molecule
(c) to change the shape of the substrate molecule
(d) to lower the activation energy of the reaction

104. The figure given below shows three velocity–substrate concentration curves for an enzyme reaction. What do the curves a, b and c depict respectively?

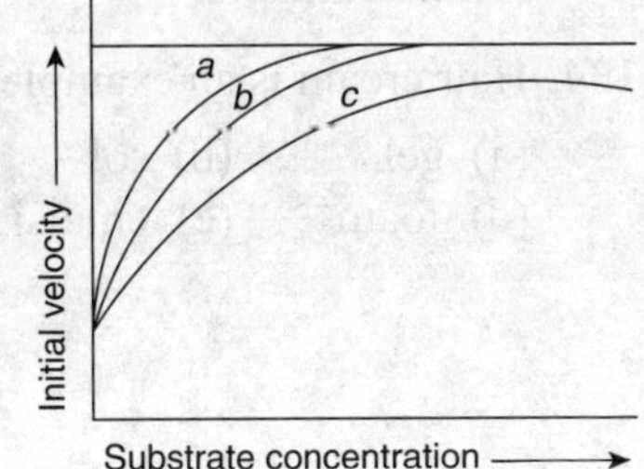

(a) a: normal enzyme reaction, b: competitive inhibition, c:non-competitive inhibition
(b) a: enzyme with an allosteric modulator added, b: normal enzyme activity, c:competitive inhibition
(c) a: enzyme with an allosteric stimulator, b: competitive inhibitor added, c: normal enzyme reaction
(d) a: normal enzyme reaction, b: non-competitive inhibitor added, c: allosteric inhibitor added

105. The optimum temperature range for the enzyme activity is

(a) 278–288 K (b) 288–298 K
(c) 298–310 K (d) 310–318 K

106. Which one of the following statements is incorrect about enzyme catalysis?

(a) Enzymes are mostly proteinaceous in nature.
(b) Enzyme action is specific.
(c) Enzymes are denatured by ultraviolet rays and at high temperature.
(d) Enzymes are least reactive at optimum temperature.

107. Which one of the following is not correct about enzymes?

(a) Enzymes form colloidal solutions in water.
(b) Enzymes act as catalysts only in biological processes.
(c) The activity of enzymes depends upon temperature as well as pH.
(d) Each enzyme catalysed reaction requires a different enzyme.

108. Glucose or fructose can be converted into ethanol in the presence of

(a) invertase (b) zymase
(c) maltase (d) diastase

Catalysis in Industry

109. Vanaspati ghee is prepared from oils by

(a) hydrolysis (b) distillation
(c) oxidation (d) reduction

110. The catalyst used in the manufacture of H_2SO_4 by the contact process is

(a) V_2O_3 (b) V_2O_5 (c) FeO (d) Cu

111. In the Ostwald process of manufacturing of HNO_3, the catalyst used is

(a) Mo (b) Fe (c) Mn (d) Pt

112. The catalyst used in the hydrogenation of oils is

(a) Pt (b) Mo (c) Fe (d) Ni

113. Adam's catalyst is

(a) platinum (b) iron
(c) molybdenum (d) nickel

114. In which of the following processes is platinum used as a catalyst?

(a) oxidation of ammonia to form nitric acid
(b) hardening of oil
(c) production of synthetic rubber
(d) synthesis of methanol

115. The catalyst used for olefin polymerisation is
(a) Zeigler–Natta catalyst
(b) Wilkinson catalyst
(c) Raney nickel catalyst
(d) Merrifield resin

116. Zeigler–Natta catalyst is
(a) $ZnCl_2$ (b) $Et_3Al + TiCl_4$
(c) $Cu/ZnO–Cr_2O_3$ (d) Pt (e) PF_3

117. The catalyst used in the manufacture of NH_3 by Haber's process is
(a) finely divided iron
(b) finely divided molybdenum
(c) finely divided nickel
(d) finely divided platinum

118. Consider the following reactions
(A) $2\ SO_2 + O_2 \rightleftharpoons 2\ SO_3$ (B) $N_2 + 3\ H_2 \rightleftharpoons 2\ NH_3$
(C) $N_2 + O_2 \rightleftharpoons 2\ NO$ (D) $H_2 + I_2 \rightleftharpoons 2\ HI$
The reactions which require a catalyst are
(a) (A) and (C) (b) (B) and (D)
(c) (A) and (B) (d) all of these

Introduction to Colloids

119. Colloidal particles have a size in the range
(a) 1–100 nm (b) 10–1000 nm
(c) 1–1000 nm (d) 10–1000 nm

120. Which one of the following is true about colloids and crystalloids?
(a) Only particular substances act as colloids.
(b) Only particular substances act as crystalloids.
(c) The same substance may act as a colloid as well as a crystalloid.
(d) Colloidal solutions are homogeneous.

121. Which of the following is not a colloid?
(a) latex (b) blood (c) butter (d) ghee

122. The size of colloidal particles is
(a) $10^{-6} - 10^{9}$ m (b) $10^{-9} - 10^{-12}$ m
(c) $10^{-3} - 10^{-9}$ m (d) $10^{-6} - 10^{-19}$ m

123. Which one of the following is not a colloid?
(a) ink (b) glycerol (c) blood (d) paint

Classification of Colloids

124. Which one of the following is a false statement?
(a) Cell fluid is an example of a sol.
(b) Butter is an example of a gel.
(c) Hair cream is an example of an emulsion.
(d) Whipped cream is an example of foam.
(e) Cheese is an example of an emulsion.

125. Which one of the following is correctly matched?
(a) emulsion—smoke (b) gel—butter
(c) aerosol—hair cream (d) sol—whipped cream
(e) foam—mist

126. Which one of the following is called an aerosol?
(a) a solid dispersed in a gas
(b) a liquid dispersed in a gas
(c) both (a) and (b)
(d) a gas dispersed in a solid or liquid

127. Smoke is a colloidal dispersion of
(a) a gas in a solid (b) a solid in a gas
(c) a gas in a gas (d) a liquid in a gas

128. An emulsion is a colloidal dispersion of
(a) a liquid in a gas (b) a liquid in a liquid
(c) a solid in a liquid (d) a gas in a solid

129. Mist is an example of colloidal system of
(a) a liquid dispersed in a gas
(b) a gas dispersed in a gas
(c) a solid dispersed in agas
(d) a solid dispersed in a liquid

130. Butter is an example of a/an
(a) gel (b) emulsion (c) sol (d) foam

131. Fog is a colloid consisting of
(a) a gas dispersed in a liquid
(b) a liquid dispersed in a gas
(c) a gas dispersed in a gas
(d) a solid dispersed in a gas

132. Milk is a colloid in which
(a) a liquid is dispersed in a liquid
(b) a solid is dispersed in a liquid
(c) a gas is dispersed in a liquid
(d) some sugar is dispersed in water

133. The colloidal system in which the dispersed phase and dispersion medium are both liquids is known as
(a) a gel (b) an aerosol
(c) an emulsion (d) a foam

134. Hair cream is an example of a/an
(a) gel (b) sol (c) aerosol
(d) foam (e) emulsion

135. Which of the following is an incorrect match?

Name of colloidal solution	Examples	Dispersed phase	Dispersion medium
(a) Foam	Soap leather, soda water	Gas	Liquid
(b) Solid foam	Rubber, bread	Gas	Solid
(c) Aerosol	Mist, fog, cloud	Liquid	Solid
(d) Emulsion	Milk, cod liver oil	Liquid	Liquid

136. Which one is an example of a gel?
(a) soap (b) cheese (c) milk (d) fog

137. If the dispersed phase is a liquid and the dispersion medium is a solid, the colloid is known as
(a) a sol (b) an emulsion (c) a gel (d) a foam

138. Which one of the following is not a colloidal solution?
(a) smoke (b) ink (c) air (d) blood

139. The continuous phase contains the dispersed phase throughout, an example is
(a) water in milk (b) fat in milk
(c) water droplets in mist (d) oil in water

140. In shaving cream, the dispersion medium is
(a) liquid (b) gas
(c) solid (d) none of these

141. Whipped cream is an example of

	Dispersion medium	Dispersed phase
(a)	gas	liquid
(b)	liquid	gas
(c)	liquid	liquid
(d)	liquid	solid

142. Milk, blood and blood clot are the colloidal state particles, respectively
(a) gel, sol and emulsion (b) emulsion, gel and sol
(c) aerosol, sol and gel (d) emulsion, sol and gel

143. Lyophilic sols are more stable than lyophobic sols because
(a) the colloidal particles have a positive charge
(b) the colloidal particles have no charge
(c) the colloidal particles are solvated
(d) there are strong electrostatic repulsions between the negatively charged colloidal particles

144. Which one of the following is a hydrophobic sol?
(a) starch solution (b) gum solution
(c) protein solution (d) arsenious sulfide sol

145. Surface tension of lyophilic sols is
(a) lower than that of H_2O
(b) more than that of H_2O
(c) equal to that of H_2O
(d) none of the above

146. Which one of the following is not a property of hydrophilic sols?
(a) high concentration of dispersed phase can be easily attained
(b) coagulation is reversible
(c) viscosity and surface tension are about the same as for water
(d) the charge of the particle depends upon the pH value of the medium, it may be positive, negative or even zero.

147. Which of the following constitutes an irreversible colloidal system in water as the dispersion medium?
(a) clay (b) platinum
(c) $Fe(OH)_3$ (d) all of these

148. Which of the following is correct for lyophilic sols?
(a) they are irreversible
(b) they are formed by inorganic substances
(c) they are readily coagulated by the addition of electrolytes
(d) they are self-stabilised

149. Choose the correct statement out of the following.
(a) Hydrophilic sols are more easily coagulated than hydrophobic sols.
(b) Hydrophobic sols are more easily coagulated than hydrophilic sols.
(c) Both are coagulated with equal ease depending upon the electrolyte used for coagulation.
(d) Hydrophobic sols undergo solvation whereas hydrophilic sols do not.

150. Which one of the following is a hydrophilic colloidal sol?
(a) barium sulfate sol (b) arsenic sulfide sol
(c) starch solution (d) silver chloride sol

151. Which substance is not used for preparing lyophilic sols?
(a) starch (b) gum
(c) gelatine (d) metal sulfide

152. The dispersed phase, dispersion medium and nature of colloidal solution (lyophilic or lyophobic) of gold sol respectively, are
(a) solid, solid, lyophobic
(b) liquid, liquid, lyophobic
(c) solid, liquid, lyophobic
(d) solid, liquid, lyophilic

153. An example of an intrinsic colloid is

(a) glue (b) sulfur
(c) Fe (d) As_2S_3

154. When a sulfur sol is evaporated, sulfur is obtained. On mixing with water, sulfur sol is not formed. The sol is

(a) lyophilic (b) reversible
(c) hydrophobic (d) hydrophilic

155. The stability of lyophilic colloids is due to

(a) the charge on their particles
(b) a layer of dispersion medium on their particles
(c) the smaller size of their particles
(d) the large size of their particles

156. Which of the following makes a lyophilic solution unstable?

(a) dialysis
(b) addition of electrolyte
(c) addition of alcohol
(d) addition of alcohol and electrolyte both

157. Which of the following does not contain a hydrophobic structure?

(a) linseed oil (b) lanolin
(c) glycogen (d) rubber

158. Which one of the following forms micelles in an aqueous solution above a certain concentration?

(a) glucose
(b) urea
(c) dodecyltrimethylammonium chloride
(d) pyridinium chloride

159. The formation of micelles which occurs only beyond a certain temperature is called

(a) critical temperature
(b) critical sol temperature
(c) consulate temperature
(d) Kraft temperature

160. Sulfur sol contains

(a) discrete sulfur atoms
(b) discrete sulfur molecules
(c) large aggregates of sulfur molecules
(d) water dispersed in solid sulfur

161. Which one of the following is correctly matched?

(a) S_8 = macromolecular colloid, starch = multimolecular colloid, soap solution = associated colloid
(b) S_8 = multimolecular colloid, starch = macromolecular colloid, soap solution = associated colloid
(c) S_8 = associated colloid, starch = multimolecular colloid, soap solution = multimolecular colloid
(d) S_8 = multimolecular colloid, starch = associated colloid, soap solution = macro molecular colloid

162. Which of the following forms cationic micelles above a certain concentration?

(a) sodium dodecylsulfate
(b) sodium acetate
(c) urea
(d) cetyltrimethylammonium bromide

163. Gold sol is not a

(a) macromolecular colloid
(b) lyophobic colloid
(c) multimolecular colloid
(d) negatively charged colloid

164. Sodium stearate in water forms a/an

(a) true solution (b) suspension
(c) emulsion (d) colloidal solution

165. Some substances behave as electrolytes in dilute solutions and as colloids in their concentrated solutions. Their colloidal forms are said to form

(a) emulsions (b) gels
(c) micelles (d) sols

166. Which of the following represents a surfactant molecule?

(a) $C_{17}H_{36}$ (b) $C_{17}H_{35}COO^-Na^+$
(c) H_2O (d) none of these

167. Which one is an example of a micellar system?

(a) soap + water (b) protein + water
(c) rubber + benzene (d) As_2O_3 +$Fe(OH)_3$

168. The example of a heteropolar sol is

(a) starch sol in water (b) rubber sol in water
(c) protein sol in water (d) sulfur sol

169. At the critical micellar concentration, the surfactant molecules

(a) decompose (b) dissociate
(c) associate
(d) become completely soluble

170. An example of an associated colloid is

(a) milk (b) soap solution
(c) rubber latex (d) vegetable oil

171. Which one of the following is not a surfactant?

(a) $CH_3-(CH_2)_{15}-\overset{\overset{CH_3}{|}}{\underset{\underset{CH_3}{|}}{N}}-CH_3Br^-$
(b) $CH_3-(CH_2)_{14}-CH_2-NH_2$
(c) $CH_3-(CH_2)_{16}-CH_2OSO_2^-\ Na^+$
(d) $OHC-(CH_2)_{14}-CH_2-COO^-Na^+$

172. Position of the non-polar and polar parts in a micelle:

(a) polar at the outer surface and non-polar at the inner surface

(b) polar at the inner surface and non-polar at the outer surface
(c) distributed over all the surface
(d) are present at the surface only

173. Which of the following shows the maximum hydrophobic behaviour?
(a) glycerine (b) stearic acid
(c) glucose (d) adenine

174. The difference between a lyophilic and lyophobic colloid is in their
(a) particle size
(b) behaviour towards the dispersion medium
(c) filterability
(d) none of these

175. Which of the following is a lyophobic colloid solution?
(a) aqueous starch solution
(b) aqueous protein solution
(c) gold sol
(d) polymer solvent in some organic solvents

176. Lyophilic sols are
(a) irreversible sols
(b) prepared from inorganic compounds
(c) coagulated by adding electrolytes
(d) self-stabilising

177. Which of the following molecules is most suitable to disperse in benzene?

(a) O, O^-Na^+

(b) Na^+O^-, O, O, O^-Na^+

(c) CH_3

(d) Cl

Preparation of Colloidal Sols

178. When dilute aqueous solution of $AgNO_3$ (excess) is added to KI solution, a positively charged sol of AgI is formed due to the adsorption of
(a) NO_3^- (b) O_2^- (c) Ag^+ (d) K^+

179. On adding a few drops of dil. HCl to freshly precipitated ferric hydroxide, a red coloured colloidal solution is obtained. This phenomenon is known as
(a) peptisation (b) dialysis
(c) protective action (d) dissolution

180. Colloidal gold is prepared by
(a) mechanical dispersion
(b) peptisation
(c) Bredig's arc method
(d) hydrolysis

181. The formation of colloid from a suspension is
(a) peptisation (b) condensation
(c) sedimentation (d) fragmentation

182. Peptisation is the process in which
(a) a suspension is converted into a true solution
(b) a precipitate dissolves to give a true solution
(c) colloid particles get settled as precipitates
(d) precipitates are converted into colloids

183. Which of the following metal sols cannot by prepared by Bredig's arc method?
(a) copper (b) potassium
(c) gold (d) platinum

184. Peptisation denotes
(a) digestion of food
(b) hydrolysis of proteins
(c) breaking and dispersion into the colloidal state
(d) precipitation of solid from the colloidal dispersion

185. A colloidal solution of mercury in water can be easily obtained by
(a) mechanical precipitation
(b) Bredig's arc method
(c) repeated washing
(d) ultrasonic dispersion

186. The white of an egg is partly coagulated by heating which can be again obtained back by some pepsin and little HCl. This process is called
(a) peptisation (b) coagulation
(c) precipitation (d) none of these

187. Colloidal solutions of metals like gold, silver and platinum are generally prepared by using
(a) peptisation (b) Bredig's arc method
(c) exchange of solvent (d) oxidation method

188. In Bredig's arc method, some alkali is added
(a) because it increases electrical conductance
(b) to obtain a molecular colloid
(c) to obtain colloidal particles of the same size
(d) to stabilise the sol

189. The charge on $Fe(OH)_3$ sol is due to the
(a) adsorption of hydroxyl ion
(b) adsorption of hydrogen ion
(c) adsorption of ferric acid
(d) adsorption of ferric ion

190. Collodion is a 4% solution of which one of the following in an alcohol–ether mixture?

(a) nitroglycerine (b) cellulose acetate
(c) glycoldinitrate (d) nitrocellulose
(e) methyl cellulose

191. When H_2S gas is passed through nitric acid, the product is

(a) plastic S (b) prismatic S
(c) amorphous S (d) monoclinic S

192. To the solution of sulfur in alcohol, a small amount of water is added. Which of the following will happen?

(a) it will become a suspension
(b) it will become a colloidal sol
(c) it will remain a true solution
(d) it will be something between a true solution and a colloidal sol

193. A colloid of which one of the following can be prepared by electrical dispersion method as well as reduction method?

(a) sulfur (b) ferric hydroxide
(c) arsenious sulfide (d) gold

194. $SO_2 + 2\ H_2S \rightarrow 3\ S + 2\ H_2O$. This equation represents the preparation of sulfur sol by

(a) hydrolysis (b) oxidation
(c) reduction (d) double decomposition

195. Sulfur colloid is prepared by

(a) mechanical dispersion (b) oxidation
(c) electrical dispersion (d) reduction

196. Which of the following reactions leads to the formation of a substance in the colloidal state?

(a) $Cu + HgCl_2 \rightarrow CuCl_2 + Hg$
(b) $2\ HNO_3 + 3\ H_2S \rightarrow 3\ S + 4\ H_2O + 2\ NO$
(c) $2\ Mg + CO_2 \rightarrow 2\ MgO + C$
(d) $Cu + CuCl_2 \rightarrow Cu_2Cl_2$ (in the presence of excess of HCl)

197. The process of preparation of a colloidal sol from a precipitate is called

(a) coagulation (b) dissolution
(c) dispersion (d) peptisation

198. Bredig's arc method cannot be used to prepare a colloidal solution of which of the following?

(a) Pt (b) Fe (c) Ag (d) Au

Purification of Colloidal Solutions

199. Purification of colloids is done by the process of

(a) electrophoresis (b) electrodispersion
(c) peptisation (d) ultrafiltration

200. Dialysis can be used to separate

(a) glucose and fructose
(b) protein and starch
(c) glucose and protein
(d) glucose and NaCl

201. In gravimetric analysis, the precipitate is washed with water before estimation

(a) to bring about hydration of the precipitate
(b) to increase the stability of the precipitate
(c) to remove the impurities adsorbed on the surface of the precipitate
(d) all the three above

202. The process of separation of colloids by passing through a semi-permeable membrane is called

(a) filtration (b) electrophoresis
(c) dialysis (d) ultrafiltration

Properties of Colloidal Solutions

203. The colour of the colloidal particles of gold obtained by different methods differ because of the

(a) variable valency of gold
(b) different concentrations of gold particles
(c) different types of impurities
(d) different diameters of colloidal particles

204. When a colloidal solution is observed under an ultramicroscope, we can see

(a) light scattered by colloidal particles
(b) the size of the colloidal particles
(c) the shape of the colloidal particles
(d) the relative size of the colloidal particles

205. The Tyndall effect is observed only when the following conditions are satisfied.

(i) The diameter of the dispersed particles is much smaller than the wavelength of the light used.
(ii) The diameter of the dispersed particles is not much smaller than the wavelength of the light used.
(iii) The refractive indices of the dispersed phase and dispersion medium are almost similar in magnitude.
(iv) The refractive indices of the dispersed phase and dispersion medium differ greatly in magnitude.

(a) (i) and (iii) (b) (ii) and (iii)
(c) (i) and (iv) (d) (ii) and (iv)

206. The simplest way to check whether a system is colloidal is

(a) electrodialysis
(b) finding out particle size
(c) Tyndall effect
(d) Brownian movement

207. Tyndall effect is observed

(a) in the solution (b) in the precipitate
(c) in sols (d) in vapour

208. The Brownian motion is due to
(a) temperature fluctuation within the liquid phase
(b) attraction and repulsion between charges on the colloidal particles
(c) impact of molecules of the dispersion medium on the colloidal particles
(d) convectional currents

209. The reason for the stability of a lyophobic sol is
(a) Brownian movement
(b) Tyndall effect
(c) electric charge
(d) Brownian movement and electric charge

210. Arsenic sulfide sol is prepared by passing H_2S through arsenic oxide solution. The charge developed on the particles is due to the adsorption of
(a) H^+ (b) S^{2-} (c) OH^- (d) O^{2-}

211. The colour of colloids depends on which of the following factors?
(a) size (b) mass (c) charge (d) nature

212. Which one of the following colloidal solutions is a positive sol?
(a) blood (b) clay soil (c) smoke
(d) gelatine in strongly acidic solution

213. When an excess of a very dilute aqueous solution of KI is added to a very dilute aqueous solution of silver nitrate, the colloidal particles of silver iodide are associated with which of the following Helmholtz double layers?
(a) $AgI \vdots Ag^+ \vdots I^-$ (b) $AgI \vdots K^+ \vdots NO_3^-$
(c) $AgI \vdots NO_3^- \vdots Ag^+$ (d) $AgI \vdots I^- \vdots K^+$

214. At the isoelectric point
(a) colloidal particles become uncharged
(b) a colloidal sol becomes highly stable
(c) peptisation can be carried out
(d) none of these

215. Which of the following sols is positively charged in terms of its colloidal particles?
(a) gold sol (b) silicic acid
(c) starch sol (d) Prussian blue

216. Which of the following processes is not responsible for the presence of electric charge on the sol particles?
(a) electron capture by sol particles
(b) adsorption of ionic species from solution
(c) formation of Helmholtz electrical double layer
(d) absorption of ionic species from solution

217. Identify the positively charged sol
(a) hemoglobin (blood) (b) gold sol
(c) As_2O_3 (d) clay

218. Which one of the following substances gives a positively charged sol?
(a) gold (b) a metal sulfide
(c) ferric hydroxide (d) an acidic dye

219. Point out the false statement.
(a) The size range of colloidal particles is 10–2000Å.
(b) Colloidal solutions are homogeneous systems.
(c) Colloids carry charge.
(d) Colloids show Tyndall effect.

220. When a dilute aqueous solution of $AgNO_3$ (excess) is added to KI solution, a positively charged sol of AgI is formed due to the adsorption of
(a) NO_3^- (b) O_2^- (c) Ag^+ (d) K^+

221. The impurities present in rain water possess ______ charge.
(a) positive (b) negative
(c) zero (d) positive and negative

222. Which property of colloids is not dependent on the charge of the colloidal particles?
(a) coagulation (b) electrophoresis
(c) electro-osmosis (d) Tyndall effect

223. When an electric current is passed through a colloidal sol,
(a) all colloidal particles move towards one particular electrode
(b) colloidal particles lose their charge and become neutral
(c) the colloidal particles get coagulated
(d) all the three above take place

224. Movement of colloidal particles under the influence of an electric field is called
(a) electrophoresis (b) electrolysis
(c) electrodialysis (d) electro-osmosis

225. Which of the following ions has the minimum flocculation value?
(a) Cl^- (b) SO_4^{2-}
(c) PO_4^{3-} (d) $[Fe(CN)_6]^{4-}$

226. The best electrolyte for coagulation of an As_2S_3 sol is
(a) NaCl (b) $CuSO_4$ (c) $Al(NO_3)_3$ (d) $Th(SO_4)_2$

227. The coagulation values of $AlCl_3$ and NaCl are 0.093 and 52 respectively. Then, the coagulating power of $AlCl_3$ as compared to that of NaCl is
(a) (52 × 0.093) times (b) (52/0.093) times
(c) (0.093/52) times (d) (52 – 0.093) times

228. Which one of the following acts as the best coagulating agent of ferric hydroxide sol?
(a) magnesium chloride (b) aluminium chloride
(c) potassium oxalate (d) potassium ferricyanide

229. The method which does not result in sol destruction is
(a) electrophoresis
(b) addition of electrolyte
(c) diffusion through animal membrane
(d) mixing two oppositely charged sols

230. The flocculation value of an electrolyte is
(a) the amount of electrolyte in grams required to bring about coagulation of one litre of colloidal sol
(b) the amount of electrolyte in milligrams to bring about coagulation of 10 mL of the colloidal sol
(c) the amount of the electrolyte in millimoles required to bring about the coagulation of 1 litre of the colloidal sol
(d) the reciprocal of coagulating power

231. Which of the following electrolytes will have maximum coagulating value for the AgI/Ag^+ sol?
(a) Na_2S (b) Na_3PO_4 (c) Na_2SO_4 (d) NaCl

232. The electrolyte which has the least effect in the coagulation of $Fe(OH)_3$ sol is
(a) potassium carbonate (b) sodium sulfate
(c) potassium ferrocyanide (d) potassium iodide

233. The coagulation values in millimoles per litre of the electrolytes used for the coagulation of As_2O_3 are given below:
I. (NaCl) = 52 II ($BaCl_2$) = 0.69
III ($MgSO_4$) = 0.22
(a) III > II > I (b) III > I > II
(c) I > II > III (d) II > I > III

234. Which of the following ions can cause coagulation of proteins?
(a) Ag^+ (b) Na^+ (c) Mg^{2+} (d) Ca^{2+}

235. Which of the following has the maximum coagulation power with ferric hydroxide sol?
(a) cryolite (b) $K_2C_2O_4$
(c) $K_3[Fe(CN)_6]$ (d) $K_4[Fe(CN)_6]$

236. 100 mL of a colloidal solution is completely precipitated by the addition of 5 mL of 1 M NaCl solution. What is the coagulation value of NaCl?
(a) 50 (b) 40
(c) 30 (d) none of these

237. Which one of the following is the most effective in causing the coagulation of an As_2S_3 sol?
(a) KCl (b) $AlCl_3$
(c) $MgSO_4$ (d) $K_3Fe(CN)_6$

238. In an electrical field, the particles of a colloidal system move towards the cathode. The coagulation of the same sol is studied using K_2SO_4 (I), $NaPO_4$ (II), $K_4[Fe(CN)_6]$ (III) and NaCl (IV). Their coagulating power should be
(a) I > II > III > IV (b) III > II > I > IV
(c) III > I > II > IV (d) IV > III > I > II
(e) IV > I > II > III

239. A negatively charged suspension of clay in water for precipitating will need a minimum/amount of
(a) aluminium chloride (b) potassium sulfate
(c) sodium hydroxide (d) hydrochloric acid

240. Flocculation value is expressed in terms of
(a) mmol per litre (b) mol per litre
(c) gram per litre (d) mol per mL

241. Which of the following has the minimum value of flocculating power?
(a) Pb^{+2} (b) Pb^{+4} (c) Sr^{+2} (d) Na^+

242. The minimum quantity of sodium chloride which is necessary to precipitate 10 litres of sol in two hours is 0.585 g. The flocculation value of sodium chloride is
(a) 0.585 (b) 0.0585
(c) 0.1 (d) one

243. Which of the following is used for the destruction of colloids?
(a) dialysis (b) condensation
(c) ultrafiltration (d) addition of electrolyte

244. On which of the following properties does the coagulating power of an ion depend?
(a) the magnitude of the charge on the ion
(b) size of the ion alone
(c) both magnitude and sign of the charge on the ion
(d) the sign of charge on the ion alone

245. The coagulating power of an electrolyte for arsenious sulfide decreases in the order
(a) $Na^+ > Al^{3+} > Ba^{2+}$ (b) $PO_4^{3-} > SO_4^{2-} > Cl^-$
(c) $Cl^- > SO_4^{2-} > PO_4^{3-}$ (d) $Al^{3+} > Ba^{2+} > Na^+$

246. Which of the following is the correct increasing order of coagulating power of electrolytes required to precipitate a negatively charged As_2S_3 colloid?
(a) $NaCl < BaCl_2 < AlCl_3$ (b) $BaCl_2 < AlCl_3 < NaCl$
(c) $AlCl_3 < NaCl < BaCl_2$ (d) $AlCl_3 < BaCl_2 < NaCl$

Protection of Colloids and Gold Number

247. Gold number is associated with
(a) electrophoresis (b) purple of Casius
(c) protective colloids (d) amount of pure gold

248. Which of the following is not correct?

(a) Every solid substance can be brought into the colloidal state.
(b) Every solid substance can be made to behave like a lyophobic colloid.
(c) The term gold number is only for lyophilic colloids.
(d) Latex is a colloidal dispersion.

249. Amount of protective colloid in milligrams is called

(a) coagulation value (b) Congo Rubin number
(c) coagulating power (d) none of the above

250. Gold number is

(a) the number of mg of the lyopohilic colloid which should be added to 10 mL of ferric hydroxide sol so as to prevent its coagulation by the addition of 1 mL of 10% sodium chloride solution
(b) the number of mg of lyophilic colloid which should be added to 10 mL of standard gold sol so as to prevent its coagulation by the addition of 1 mL of 10% NaCl
(c) the mg of gold salt to be added to lyophilic colloid to coagulate it
(d) the mg of an electrolyte required to coagulate a colloid

251. Gold number is a measure of the

(a) protective action by a lyophilic colloid on a lyophobic colloid
(b) protective action by a lyophobic colloid on a lyophilic colloid
(c) number of mg of gold in a standard red gold sol
(d) stability of gold sol

252. Which one of the sols acts as protective colloid?

(a) As_2S_3 (b) gelatine (c) Au (d) $Fe(OH)_3$

253. Gold number is minimum in the case of

(a) gelatine (b) egg albumin
(c) gum Arabic (d) starch

254. Which one of the following statements is wrong?

(a) Greater the gold number of a protective colloid, less is its protective power.
(b) The Hardy–Schulze rule is applicable only to the coagulation of lyophilic sols.
(c) Greater flocculation value of an electrolyte means its poor coagulating power.
(d) For coagulation of a positive sol, positive ions of the electrolyte have no significance.

255. Gold number that is maximum for a lyophilic sol is for

(a) gelatine (b) hemoglobin
(c) sodium oleate (d) potato starch

256. The correct order of gold number is

(a) gelatine> albumin > gum Arabic > starch
(b) albumin > gelatine > gum Arabic > starch
(c) gum Arabic > gelatine > albumin > starch
(d) starch > gum Arabic > albumin >gelatine

257. On addition of one mL solution of 10% NaCl to 10 mL gold sol in the presence of 0.025 g starch, the coagulation is just prevented. Then starch has the following gold number,

(a) 25 (b) 0.025 (c) 0.25 (d) 2.5

Emulsions and Gels

258. Cod liver oil is an example

(a) oil in water emulsion
(b) water in oil emulsion
(c) both (a) and (b)
(d) none of these

259. Which one of the following emulsifying agents helps in the formation of w/o emulsion?

(a) proteins (b) gums
(c) insoluble soaps (d) soluble soaps

260. The spontaneous outflow of internal liquid from gels is called

(a) syneresis (b) swelling
(c) thixotropy (d) imbibition

261. Addition of alcohol to a saturated aqueous solution of calcium acetate first forms a sol and then sets to a gelatinous mass called solid alcohol which is a

(a) gel (b) solid foam
(c) solid sol (d) aerosol

262. Cow milk is an example of a natural emulsion stabilised by

(a) fat (b) water (c) casein (d) Mg^{++} ions

263. In which of the following properties do emulsions differ from colloidal sols?

(a) Tyndall effect
(b) Brownian movement
(c) electrophoresis
(d) size of the particles of the dispersed phase

264. Demulsification can be done by

(a) freezing (b) boiling
(c) centrifugation (d) all the three

265. The cementation process is the formation of

(a) solid sol (b) solid form
(c) gel (d) any one of these

266. The cleaning action of soap is due to

(a) its dissociation into ions in water
(b) the presence of Na^+ ions in soap
(c) the formation of associated colloids
(d) its action as an emulsifying agent

267. An emulsifier is a substance which

(a) stabilises the emulsion
(b) homogenises the emulsion
(c) coagulates the emulsion
(d) accelerates the dispersion of liquid in liquid

268. Milk can be preserved by adding a few drops of

(a) formic acid solution
(b) formaldehyde solution
(c) acetic acid solution
(d) acetaldehyde solution

269. Emulsifiers are generally

(a) soaps (b) synthetic detergents
(c) lyophilic sols (d) all of these

Colloids Around Us

270. Gelatine is mostly used in making ice cream in order to

(a) prevent making of a colloid
(b) stabilise the colloid and prevent crystallisation
(c) stabilise the mixture
(d) enrich the aroma

271. The colloidal sol that is found effective in treating eye disease is

(a) colloidal sulfur (b) colloidal antimony
(c) colloidal gold (d) colloidal silver

272. The substance used as a smoke screen in warfare is

(a) $SiCl_4$ (b) PH_3
(c) PCl_5 (d) acetylene

273. Colloidal solution commonly used in the treatment of skin diseases is

(a) colloidal gold (b) colloidal silver
(c) colloidal antimony (d) colloidal sulfur

274. The name aquadag stands for

(a) copper in water sol (b) silver in water sol
(c) platinum in water sol (d) graphite in water sol

275. Purple of Cassius is a/an

(a) colloidal sol of gold
(b) colloidal sol of silver
(c) colloidal sol of platinum
(d) oxyacid of gold

276. The basic principle of Cottrell's precipitator is

(a) neutralisation of charge on colloidal particles
(b) scattering of light
(c) Le Chatelier's principle
(d) peptisation

277. The process which is responsible for the formation of a delta at a place where a river meets the sea is

(a) peptisation (b) colloidal formation
(c) emulsification (d) coagulation

278. **Statement:** 'To stop bleeding from an injury, ferric chloride can be applied.' Which comment about the statement is justified?

(a) It is not true, ferric chloride is a poison.
(b) It is true; Fe^{3+} ions coagulate blood which is a negatively charged sol.
(c) It is not true, Cl^- ions form a positively charged sol; profuse bleeding takes place.
(d) It is true, coagulation takes place because of the formation of a negatively charged sol with Cl^-.
(e) It is not true, ferric chloride is ionic and gets into the blood stream.

279. Which of the following is a use of alum?

(a) making explosives (b) bleaching clothes
(c) water softening (d) all of these

280. Muddy water can be purified through coagulation using

(a) common salt (b) alums
(c) sand (d) lime

281. Pick out the statement which is not relevant in the discussion of colloids.

(a) Sodium aluminium silicate is used in the softening of hard water.
(b) Potash alum is used in shaving rounds and as an antiseptic in medicine.
(c) Artificial rain is caused by throwing electrified sand on the clouds from an aeroplane.
(d) Deltas are formed at a place where the river pours its water into the sea.

282. The function of gum Arabic in the preparation of Indian ink is

(a) coagulation (b) peptisation
(c) protective active (d) absorption

Final Preparation

283. In an adsorption experiment, a graph of log (x/m) versus log p is found to be linear with a slope of 45°. The intercept on the log (x/m) axis was found to be 0.3010. The amount of the gas adsorbed per gram of charcoal under a pressure of 0.5 atm will be

(a) 1.0 (b) 2.0 (c) 0.5 (d) 0.25

284. In the given Freundlich adsorption isotherm plot, a, b and c are respectively

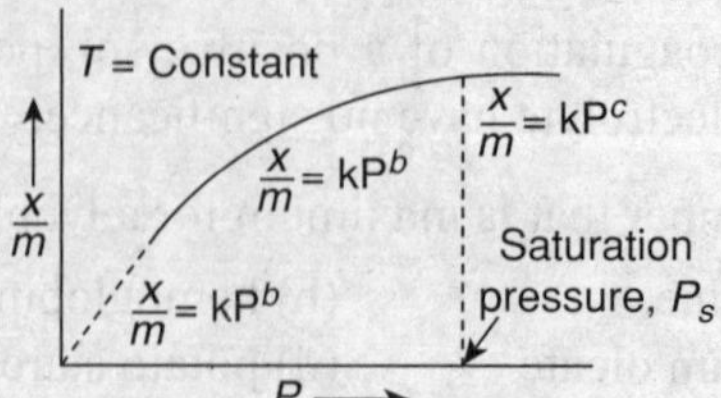

(a) $1, \frac{1}{n}, 0$ (b) $\frac{1}{n}, 1, 0$ (c) $0, 1, \frac{1}{n}$ (d) $0, \frac{1}{n}, 1$

285. Which among the following statements are correct with respect to adsorption of gases on a solid?

1. The extent of adsorption is equal to $k\,p^n$ according to the Freundlich isotherm.
2. The extent of adsorption is equal to $k\,p^{1/n}$ according to the Freundlich isotherm.
3. The extent of adsorption is equal to $(1 + bP)a/P$ according to the Langmuir isotherm.
4. The extent of adsorption is equal to $a\ P/(1+bP)$ according to the Langmuir isotherm.
5. Freundlich adsorption isotherm fails at low pressure.

(a) 1 and 3 (b) 1 and 4 (c) 2 and 3 (d) 2 and 4

286. 50 mL of 1 M oxalic acid is shaken with 0.5 g wood charcoal. The final concentration of the solution after adsorption is 0.5 M. What is the amount of oxalic acid absorbed per gram of carbon?

(a) 3.15 g (b) 3.45 g (c) 6.30 g (d) none

287. 1 g charcoal adsorbs 100 mL of 0.5 M CH_3COOH to form a monolayer. As a result, the molarity of acetic acid reduces to 0.49 M. What will be the surface area covered by each molecule of acetic acid given that surface area of charcoal = $3.01 \times 10^2\ m^2/g$.

(a) $2.5\times10^{-19}\ m^2$ (b) $5.0\times10^{-19}\ m^2$
(c) $4.0\times10^{-18}\ m^2$ (d) $2.0\times10^{-18}\ m^2$

288. The volume of nitrogen gas required at STP to cover a sample of silica gel with a mono-molecular layer is $112\ cm^2 g^{-1}$. If each molecule of N_2 gas occupies $16 \times 10^{-20}\ m^2$, then the specific surface area of the gel is ($N_A = 6.0\times10^{23}\ mol^{-1}$)

(a) 240 m^2 (b) 480 m^2
(c) 720 m^2 (d) 960 m^2

289. Given below, the catalyst and the corresponding process/reaction are matched. The mismatch is

(a) $[RhCl(PPH_3)_3]$: hydrogenation
(b) $TiCl_4 + Al(C_2H_5)_3$: polymerisation
(c) V_2O_5: Haber–Bosch process
(d) nickel: hydrogenation

290. Which of the following gas molecules will have the maximum enthalpy of physisorption in a gas mask?

(a) CH_4 (b) N_2 (c) SO_2 (d) H_2

291. Although nitrogen does not adsorb on iron surface at room temperature, it adsorbs on the same surface at 83 K. Which one of the following statements is correct?

(a) At 83 K, there is the formation of a monomolecular layer.
(b) At 83 K, there is the formation of a multimolecular layer
(c) At 83 K, nitrogen molecules are held by chemical bonds.
(d) At 83 K, nitrogen is adsorbed as atoms.

292. Select the incorrect statement.

(a) Physical absorption is reversible while chemical adsorption is irreversible.
(b) High pressure favours physical adsorption while low pressure favours chemical adsorption.
(c) Physical adsorption is not specific while chemical adsorption is highly specific.
(d) High activation energy is involved in chemical adsorption.

293. Which of the following are the characteristics of chemisorption?

1. high heat of adsorption
2. irreversibility
3. low activation energy

(a) 1 and 2 only (b) 1 and 3 only
(c) 2 and 3 only (d) 1, 2 and 3

294. An example of an auto-catalytic reaction is

(a) the decomposition of nitroglycerine
(b) thermal reaction between $KClO_3$ and MnO_2
(c) break down of ^{14}C
(d) hydrogenation of vegetable oil using nickel catalyst

295. Which one of the following statements about the zeolites is false?

(a) They are used as cation exchangers.
(b) They have an open structure which enables them to take up small molecules.
(c) Zeolites are aluminosilicates having a three dimensional network.
(d) Some of the SiO_4^{4-} units are replaced by AlO_4^{5-} and AlO_6^{9-} ions in zeolites.

296. Enzyme-catalysed reactions have the order

(a) one at low concentration of substrate and two at high concentration of the substrate.
(b) one at high concentration of the substrate and two at low concentration of the substrate.
(c) one at low as well as high concentrations.
(d) two at low as well as high concentrations.

297. The range of a certain biochemical reaction catalysed by an enzyme in the human body is 10^4 times faster than when it is carried out in the laboratory. The activation energy of the enzyme catalysed reaction as compared to that in the laboratory is

(a) same (b) higher
(c) lower (d) may be higher or lower

298. When the size of a spherical nanoparticle decreases from 30 nm to 10 nm, the ratio of surface area/volume becomes

(a) 1/3 of the original (b) 3 times the original
(c) 1/9 of the original (d) 9 times the original

299. The volume of a colloidal particle V_c as compared to the volume of solute particle in a true solution V_S could be

(a) $V_C / V_S = 1$ (b) $V_C / V_S = 10^{23}$
(c) $V_C / V_S = 10^{-3}$ (d) $V_C / V_S = 10^{3}$

300. Potassium stearate is obtained by saponification of an oil or fat. It has the formula $CH_3–(CH_2)_{16}–COO^-K^+$. The molecule has a lyophobic end (CH_3) and a lyophilic end (COO^-K^+). Potassium stearate is an example of a/an

(a) lyophobic colloid
(b) multimolecular colloid
(c) macromolecular colloid
(d) associated colloid or micelle

301. Among the following surfactants that will form micelles in an aqueous solution at the lowest molar concentration at ambient conditions is

(a) $(CH_3)(CH_2)_{15}N^+(CH_3)_3Br^-$
(b) $CH_3(CH_2)_{11}OSO_3^-N^+$
(c) $CH_3(CH_2)_6COO^-Na^+$
(d) $CH_3(CH_2)_{11}N^+(CH_3)_3Br^-$

302. Which of the following forms cationic micelles above a certain temperature?

(a) urea (b) sodium acetate
(c) cetyltrimethylammonium bromide
(d) sodium dodecylsulfate

303. Consider the following statements about micelles.

(i) At the critical micelle concentration, several properties of the solutions of surfactants such as molar conductivity, surface tension and osmotic pressure exhibit a dramatic change.
(ii) No micelles from ionic surfactants are formed below a particular temperature.
(iii) The enthalpy of micelle formation in an aqueous solution is slightly negative.

Which of these are correct?

(a) (i) only (b) (i) and (ii)
(c) (i), (ii) and (iii) (d) (i) and (iii)

304. Which of the following plots correctly represents the variation of the concentration of a surfactant (for example, sodium dodecylsulfate) versus molar conductivity with regard to its behaviour at the CMC?

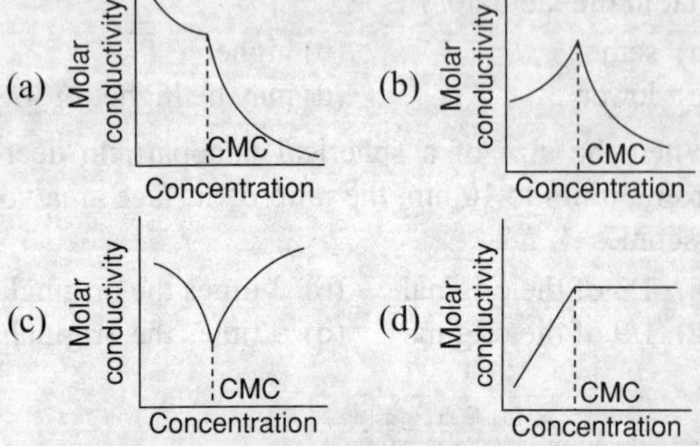

305. A freshly obtained precipitate of SnO_2 is peptised using a small amount of KOH solution to form a sol. The sol particles formed may be represented as

(a) $SnO_2 \vdots Sn^{4+}$ (b) $SnO_2 \vdots K^+$
(c) $SnO_2 \vdots OH^-$ (d) $SnO_2 \vdots SnO_3^{2-}$

306. The pK_{a_1} and pK_{a_2} of an amino acid are 2.3 and 9.7 respectively. The isoelectric point of the amino acid is

(a) 12.0 (b) 7.4 (c) 6.0 (d) 3.7

307. Zeta potential (or electrokinetic potential) is the

(a) potential required to bring about coagulation of a colloidal sol
(b) potential required to give the particles a speed of 1 cm/s in the sol
(c) potential difference between fixed charged layer and the diffused layer having opposite charge
(d) potential energy of the colloidal particles

308. A colloidal solution is subjected to an electrical field. The particles move towards the anode. The coagulation of the same sol is studied using NaCl, $BaCl_2$ and $AlCl_3$ solutions. Their coagulating power should be

(a) NaCl > $BaCl_2$ > $AlCl_3$ (b) $BaCl_2$ > $AlCl_3$ > NaCl
(c) $AlCl_3$ > $BaCl_2$ > NaCl (d) $BaCl_2$ > NaCl > $AlCl_3$

309. The dispersed phase in colloidal iron (II) hydroxide and colloidal gold is positively and negatively charged respectively. Which of the following statements of NOT correct?

(a) Magnesium chloride solution coagulates the gold sol more readily than iron (III) hydroxide sol.
(b) Sodium sulfate solution causes coagulation in both sols.
(c) Mixing the sols has no effect.
(d) Coagulation in both sols can be brought about by electrophoresis.

310. The coagulation of 200 mL of a positive colloid took place when 0.73 g HCl was added to it without changing the volume much.

The flocculation value of HCl for the colloid is

(a) 0.365 (b) 36.5 (c) 100 (d) 150

311. The number of moles of lead nitrate needed to coagulate 2 mol of colloidal $[AgI]\,I^-$ is

(a) 2 (b) 1 (c) 1/2 (d) 2/3

312. In a coagulation experiment, 5 mL of As_2S_3 is mixed with 0.1 M solution of an electrolyte AB so that the total volume is 10 mL. It was found that all of the solution coagulates leaving AB equivalent to 0.4 mL of 0.1 M in the solution. What is the flocculation value of AB for As_2S_3 sol?

(a) 4.6 (b) 46 (c) 460 (d) 4600

313. To coagulate gelatine sol, which of the following is most effective?

(a) NaCl (b) Na_2PO_4 (c) $AlCl_3$ (d) alcohol

314. The coagulation values in mmol per litre of electrolytes used for the coagulation of Ag_2O_3 sol are given below:

I. NaCl = 52 II. KCl = 5
III. $BaCl_2$ = 0.69 IV. $MgSO_4$ = 0.22
The correct order of their flocculating power is
(a) I > II > III > IV (b) I > II > III = IV
(c) IV > III > II > I (d) IV = III > II > I

315. 10^{-4} g of gelatine is required to be added to 100 cm^3 of a standard gold solution to just prevent its precipitation by the addition of 1 cm^3 of 10% NaCl solution to it. Hence the gold number of gelatine is

(a) 10 (b) 1.0 (c) 0.1 (d) 0.01

316. Which one of the following emulsifying agents helps in the formation of o/w emulsion?

(a) fatty acids (b) long chain alcohols
(c) lamp black (d) proteins

317. Which one of the following statements is not correct?

(a) Shrinking of a gel on losing the liquid held by it is called syneresis.
(b) The swelling of a gel on absorbing water is called imbibition.
(c) The reversible phenomenon involving gel–sol transformation is called thixotropy.
(d) The gels which can be stretched like an elastic are called elastic gels.

318. Elastic gels when placed in contact with water absorb water and swell. This property is called

(a) thixotropy (b) weeping
(c) syneresis (d) imbibition

319. The cementation process is the formation of

(a) solid sol (b) solid foam
(c) gel (d) any one of these

320. Bleeding due to a cut can be stopped by applying ferric chloride solution in the laboratory. The is due to

(a) coagulation of negatively charged blood particles by Fe^{3+} ions
(b) coagulation of positively charged blood particles by Cl^- ions
(c) reaction taking place between ferric ions and the hemoglobin forming a complex
(d) the common element, iron, in both $FeCl_3$ and hemoglobin

321. A person is suffering from poisoning due to arsenic, then which one of the following is helpful in removing arsenic?

(a) colloidal sulfur (b) colloidal antimony
(c) colloidal $Fe(OH)_3$ (d) colloidal sol of gold

322. Silver iodide is used in bringing about artificial rain because silver iodide

(a) is easily decomposed in the presence of sunlight
(b) contains iodide ions which are large in size
(c) has a crystal structure similar to ice and leads to coagulation
(d) being heavy, its spray brings the water droplets down

323. Select the wrong statement.

(a) If a very small amount of $AlCl_3$ is added to gold sol, coagulation occurs but if a large quantity of $AlCl_3$ is added, there is no coagulation.
(b) Organic ions are more strongly adsorbed on a charged surface in comparison to inorganic ions.
(c) Both emulsifiers and peptising agents stabilise colloids but their actions are different.
(d) Colloidal solutions are thermodynamically stable.

MATCH THE FOLLOWING

324.

Column I (Gas)	Column II (Volume adsorbed per g of charcoal at 288 K
(A) CO	(p) 48 cc
(B) CO_2	(q) 181 cc
(C) SO_2	(r) 9.3 cc
(D) NH_3	(s) 380 cc

(a) (A)—(p); (B)—(q); (C)—(r); (D)—(s)
(b) (A)—(r); (B)—(s); (C)—(p); (D)—(q)
(c) (A)—(r); (B)—(p); (C)—(s); (D)—(q)
(d) (A)—(q); (B)—(p); (C)—(s); (D)—(r)

325.

Column I	Column II
(A) Smoke	(p) Foam
(B) Butter	(q) Emulsion
(C) Hair cream	(r) Aerosol
(D) Whipped cream	(s) Gel

(a) (A)—(r); (B)—(s); (C)—(q); (D)—(p)
(b) (A)—(r); (B)—(q); (C)—(s); (D)—(p)
(c) (A)—(p); (B)—(s); (C)—(q); (D)—(r)
(d) (A)—(s); (B)—(p); (C)—(r); (D)—(q)

326.

Column I	Column II
(A) White of egg shaken with water	(p) Multi-molecular colloid
(B) Mercury vapour passed through cold water	(q) Macromolecular colloid

Column I	Column II
(C) Cellulose nitrate shaken with ethanol	(r) Associated colloid
(D) Detergent dissolved in water	(s) Collodion

(a) (A)—(p); (B)—(q); (C)—(r); (D)—(s)
(b) (A)—(r); (B)—(p); (C)—(s); (D)—(q)
(c) (A)—(s); (B)—(p); (C)—(r); (D)—(q)
(d) (A)—(q); (B)—(p); (C)—(s); (D)—(r)

327.

Column I	Column II
(A) Positive catalysis	(p) Hydrolysis of esters in the presence of H^+ ion
(B) Negative catalysis	(q) Oxidation of SO_2 to SO_3 in the presence of NO
(C) Induced catalysis	(r) Decomposition of H_2O_2 in the presence of phosphoric acid
(D) Autocatalysis	(s) Oxidation Na_3AsO_3 in the presence of Na_2SO_3

(a) (A)—(r); (B)—(q); (C)—(s); (D)—(p)
(b) (A)—(p); (B)—(r); (C)—(s); (D)—(q)
(c) (A)—(s); (B)—(r); (C)—(q); (D)—(p)
(d) (A)—(q); (B)—(r); (C)—(s); (D)—(p)

328.

Column I (Process)	Column II (Catalysis)
(A) Ostwald process	(p) Pt
(B) Bosch process	(q) Fe
(C) Deacon's process	(r) Fe_2O_3
(D) Haber's process	(s) $CuCl_2$

(a) (A)—(q); (B)—(r); (C)—(s); (D)—(p)
(b) (A)—(r); (B)—(p); (C)—(s); (D)—(q)
(c) (A)—(p); (B)—(r); (C)—(s); (D)—(q)
(d) (A)—(s); (B)—(r); (C)—(p); (D)—(q)

ASSERTION REASON

Directions: In each of the following questions, a statement of Assertion (A) is given followed by a corresponding statement of Reason (R) just below it. Of the statements, mark the correct answer as

(a) if both the assertion and reason are true and the reason is the correct explanation of the assertion.
(b) if both assertion and reason are true but reason is not the correct explanation of assertion
(c) If assertion is true but reason is false
(d) If both assertion and reason are false

329. Assertion: Gases are easily adsorbed on the surface of metals; especially transition metals.

Reason: Transition metals have free valencies.

330. Assertion: A gas with a higher critical temperature is adsorbed more than a gas with lower critical temperature on the same adsorbent.

Reason: A higher critical temperature implies that the gas is more easily liquefiable.

331. Assertion: For adsorption ΔG, ΔS and ΔH all have negative values.

Reason: Adsorption is a spontaneous process accompanied by a decrease in randomness.

332. Assertion: NH_3 absorbs more readily than CO_2 on activated charcoal.

Reason: NH_3 is more polar.

333. Assertion: In chemisorption, adsorption goes on increasing with temperature.

Reason: Heat keeps on providing more and more activation energy.

334. Assertion: Physical absorption of molecules takes place on the surface only.

Reason: In the process, the bonds of the adsorbed molecules are broken.

335. Assertion: According to the Freundich equation, $\frac{x}{m} = kp^{1/n}$.

Reason: As the Freundlich equation does not involve temperature, the adsorption isotherm is the same at any temperature for a particular gas on a particular adsorbent.

336. Assertion: The Langmuir adsorption isotherm is $\frac{x}{m} = \frac{aP}{1+bP}$.

Reason: Plot of $\frac{x}{m}$ vs P at constant temperature will be linear.

337. Assertion: While dyeing, clothes are first dipped in a mordant and then in the solution of the dye.

Reason: The mordant is first adsorbed on the clothes and then the dye is adsorbed on the mordant.

338. Assertion: The micelles formed by sodium stearate in water have–COO^- groups at the surface.

Reason: The surface tension of water is reduced by the addition of sodium stearate.

339. Assertion: Lyophilic sols are reversible.

Reason: Lyophilic sols are liquid-loving.

340. Assertion: Colloidal silver iodide is prepared by adding silver nitrate in slight excess to potassium iodide solution. When subjected to an electric field, the colloidal particles migrate to the anode.

Reason: Colloidal particles of a particular substance always carry the same charge irrespective of the method of preparation.

341. Assertion: A colloidal sol of $Fe(OH)_3$ formed by peptisation carries a positive charge.

Reason: During the formation of $Fe(OH)_3$ sol, electrons are lost by the particles.

342. Assertion: Aqueous gold colloidal sol is red in colour.

Reason: The colour arises due to scattering of light by colloidal gold particles.

343. Assertion: Fe^{3+} can be used for coagulation of As_2S_3 sol.

Reason: Fe^{3+} reacts with As_2S_3 to give Fe_2S_3.

344. Assertion: On prolonged dialysis, a colloidal sol becomes unstable and starts coagulating.

Reason: Colloidal particles start losing their charge on prolonged dialysis.

345. Assertion: A colloidal sol of As_2S_3 is coagulated faster by 0.1 M $BaCl_2$ than by 0.1 M NaCl.

Reason: $BaCl_2$ gives double the number of Cl^- ions than NaCl.

346. Assertion: Colloidal solutions are stable but colloidal particles do not settle down.

Reason: Brownian movement counters the force of gravity actively on colloidal particles.

347. Assertion: Isoelectric point is the pH at which colloidal particles can move towards either of the electrodes.

Reason: At the isoelectric point, colloidal particles may carry positive or negative charge.

348. Assertion: Electric shock causes the death of an animal.

Reason: Electric shock coagulates the blood.

349. Assertion: Potato starch has greater protecting power than gelatine in protecting lyophobic colloids from coagulation.

Reason: Higher the gold number of a protective colloid, greater is its protective power.

350. Assertion: An emulsion becomes stable if soap is added to it.

Reason: Soap contains hydrophilic and hydrophobic parts.

351. Assertion: A small quantity of soap is used to prepare a stable emulsion.

Reason: Soap lowers the interfacial tension between oil and water.

352. Assertion: Most of the emulsions are negatively charged.

Reason: The emulsifier is adsorbed at the interface between oil and water.

353. Assertion: The reaction of oxalic acid with acidified $KMnO_4$ is first slow and then speeds up by itself.

Reason: Acidified $KMnO_4$ is a strong oxidising agent.

354. Assertion: The catalytic convertor in a car's exhaust system converts polluting exhaust gases into non-toxic gases.

Reason: A catalytic convertor contains a mixture of transition metals and their oxides embedded in the inner support.

355. Assertion: The activity of a catalyst depends upon the strength of physisorption.

Reason: The reactant must adsorb very strongly for the catalyst to be active.

356. Assertion: Alcohols are dehydrated to hydrocarbons in the presence of acidic zeolites.

Reason: Zeolites are porous catalysts.

357. Assertion: The activity of an enzyme is pH-dependent.

Reason: A change in pH affects the solubility of the enzyme in water.

358. Assertion: ZSM-5 is used as a catalyst in petrochemical industries.

Reason: Zeolites are three dimensional network silicates in which some silicon atoms are replaced by aluminium atoms.

Answer Key

1. (b)	2. (b)	3. (c)	4. (d)	5. (d)	6. (b)	7. (b)	8. (d)	9. (b)	10. (d)
11. (c)	12. (a)	13. (c)	14. (d)	15. (c)	16. (c)	17. (b)	18. (d)	19. (b)	20. (c)
21. (c)	22. (d)	23. (d)	24. (b)	25. (b)	26. (d)	27. (c)	28. (c)	29. (d)	30. (c)
31. (c)	32. (e)	33. (b)	34. (c)	35. (a)	36. (c)	37. (a)	38. (b)	39. (a)	40. (c)
41. (a)	42. (c)	43. (b)	44. (d)	45. (c)	46. (c)	47. (a)	48. (d)	49. (a)	50. (e)
51. (b)	52. (d)	53. (c)	54. (a)	55. (a)	56. (b)	57. (c)	58. (e)	59. (c)	60. (b)

61. (b)	62. (d)	63. (d)	64. (b)	65. (d)	66. (c)	67. (d)	68. (c)	69. (b)	70. (b)
71. (d)	72. (a)	73. (e)	74. (c)	75. (c)	76. (c)	77. (a)	78. (c)	79. (d)	80. (c)
81. (a)	82. (b)	83. (a)	84. (c)	85. (a)	86. (d)	87. (b)	88. (d)	89. (d)	90. (b)
91. (c)	92. (d)	93. (b)	94. (c)	95. (d)	96. (b)	97. (a)	98. (b)	99. (d)	100. (b)
101. (c)	102. (d)	103. (a)	104. (a)	105. (c)	106. (d)	107. (b)	108. (b)	109. (d)	110. (b)
111. (d)	112. (d)	113. (a)	114. (a)	115. (a)	116. (b)	117. (a)	118. (c)	119. (c)	120. (c)
121. (d)	122. (a)	123. (b)	124. (e)	125. (b)	126. (c)	127. (b)	128. (b)	129. (a)	130. (a)
131. (b)	132. (a)	133. (c)	134. (e)	135. (c)	136. (b)	137. (c)	138. (c)	139. (b)	140. (a)
141. (b)	142. (d)	143. (c)	144. (d)	145. (a)	146. (c)	147. (d)	148. (d)	149. (b)	150. (c)
151. (d)	152. (c)	153. (a)	154. (c)	155. (b)	156. (d)	157. (d)	158. (c)	159. (d)	160. (c)
161. (b)	162. (d)	163. (a)	164. (d)	165. (c)	166. (b)	167. (a)	168. (c)	169. (c)	170. (b)
171. (b)	172. (a)	173. (d)	174. (b)	175. (c)	176. (d)	177. (c)	178. (c)	179. (a)	180. (c)
181. (d)	182. (d)	183. (b)	184. (c)	185. (d)	186. (a)	187. (b)	188. (d)	189. (d)	190. (d)
191. (c)	192. (b)	193. (d)	194. (b)	195. (b)	196. (b)	197. (d)	198. (b)	199. (d)	200. (c)
201. (c)	202. (c)	203. (d)	204. (a)	205. (d)	206. (c)	207. (c)	208. (c)	209. (d)	210. (b)
211. (a)	212. (d)	213. (d)	214. (a)	215. (d)	216. (d)	217. (a)	218. (c)	219. (b)	220. (c)
221. (b)	222. (d)	223. (d)	224. (a)	225. (d)	226. (c)	227. (b)	228. (d)	229. (c)	230. (c)
231. (d)	232. (d)	233. (a)	234. (d)	235. (d)	236. (a)	237. (b)	238. (b)	239. (a)	240. (a)
241. (d)	242. (d)	243. (d)	244. (a)	245. (d)	246. (a)	247. (c)	248. (b)	249. (b)	250. (b)
251. (a)	252. (b)	253. (a)	254. (b)	255. (d)	256. (d)	257. (a)	258. (b)	259. (b)	260. (a)
261. (a)	262. (c)	263. (d)	264. (d)	265. (c)	266. (d)	267. (a)	268. (b)	269. (d)	270. (b)
271. (d)	272. (a)	273. (d)	274. (d)	275. (a)	276. (a)	277. (d)	278. (b)	279. (c)	280. (b)
281. (a)	282. (c)	283. (a)	284. (a)	285. (d)	286. (c)	287. (b)	288. (b)	289. (c)	290. (c)
291. (b)	292. (b)	293. (a)	294. (a)	295. (d)	296. (b)	297. (c)	298. (b)	299. (d)	300. (d)
301. (a)	302. (c)	303. (b)	304. (a)	305. (d)	306. (c)	307. (c)	308. (c)	309. (c)	310. (c)
311. (b)	312. (b)	313. (d)	314. (c)	315. (d)	316. (d)	317. (d)	318. (d)	319. (c)	320. (a)
321. (c)	322. (c)	323. (a)	324. (a)	325. (a)	326. (d)	327. (d)	328. (c)	329. (a)	330. (b)
331. (a)	332. (b)	333. (d)	334. (d)	335. (b)	336. (c)	337. (a)	338. (a)	339. (b)	340. (d)
341. (b)	342. (a)	343. (c)	344. (c)	345. (b)	346. (a)	347. (d)	348. (a)	349. (d)	350. (a)
351. (a)	352. (b)	353. (b)	354. (a)	355. (d)	356. (b)	357. (b)	358. (b)		

Hints and Solutions

HINTS AND SOLUTIONS

Introduction to Adsorption

1. **(b):** The concentration of the adsorbate is less on the surface of the solid adsorbent; thus, the concentration of the adsorbate is higher in solution.

2. **(b):** Greater the critical temperature of a gas, greater is the adsorption. The critical temperatures (K) are $\underset{33.2}{H_2} < \underset{190.6}{CH_4} < \underset{430.3}{SO_2}$.
Thus, the adsorption increases from H_2 to SO_2 in this order.

3. **(c):** Platinum black adsorbs H_2 gas most strongly.

4. **(d):** As adsorption is exothermic, applying Le Chatelier's principle, adsorption should decrease with an increase in temperature.

5. **(d):** Greater the critical temperature of a gas, greater is the adsorption. The critical temperatures (K) are, NH_3 (406), CO_2 (304), CH_4 (190), H_2 (33). Thus, adsorption decreases from NH_3 to H_2 in this order.

6. **(b):** Silica gel adsorbs water vapour.

7. **(b):** According to the Gibbs–Helmholtz equation, $\Delta G - T\Delta S$. During adsorption of a gas, the entropy decreases, that is, ΔS is –ve. As adsorption is a spontaneous process, ΔG should be –ve. ΔG can be negative only if ΔH is highly negative ($\Delta H > T\Delta S$).

8. **(d):** Phenolphthalein indicator turns pink due to a change in the pH of the solution and not due to adsorption.

9. **(b):** The critical temperature is maximum for CO_2. Hence, it will be adsorbed to a maximum extent.

10. **(d):** Higher the critical temperature, the more easily is the gas liquefied and greater is the adsorption on a solid.

11. **(c):** Adsorption of inert gases on the surface of activated charcoal is physical adsorption. The van der Waals' forces increase with an increase in mass. Physical adsorption increases with a decrease in temperature.

12. **(a):** When a gas is adsorbed on the surface of a solid, the freedom of movement of the gas molecules decreases and hence the entropy decreases. That is, ΔS is –ve or $\Delta S< 0$. Further, when adsorption takes place, the residual forces on the surface of the adsorbent decreases. In other words,

surface energy decreases. This appears in the form of heat (called heat of adsorption). Hence, ΔH of adsorption is –ve, that is, $\Delta H < 0$. Alternatively, $\Delta G = \Delta H - T\Delta S$. For the process to be spontaneous, ΔG is –ve. As ΔS is –ve, that is $T\Delta S$ is +ve, ΔG can be –ve only if ΔH is –ve and $> T\Delta S$ in magnitude.

13. (c): Increase in temperature results in the desorption of the gas adsorbed on a solid.

14. (d): As the molecules of the adsorbate are held on the surface of the solid adsorbent, entropy decreases, that is, ΔS is = –ve.

15. (c): As some acetic acid is adsorbed by charcoal, the concentration of the solution decreases.

16. (c): Rate of adsorption decreases with an increase in temperature.

17. (b): Particle size of the adsorbent affects the amount of adsorption because the greater the surface area of the adsorbent, the greater is the adsorption.

18. (d): Greater the critical temperature of a gas, that is, the more easily the gas is liquefiable, the greater are the van der Waals' forces and hence greater is the adsorption. Out of the given gases, NH_3 has the highest critical temperature and hence will be adsorbed to the largest extent.

19. (b): Permanent gases like H_2 and O_2 have very low critical temperature and are adsorbed very little as compared to easily liquefiable gases like NH_3, CO_2, SO_2 and HCl.

20. (c): Easily liquefiable gases are those that have a high critical temperature and hence greater van der Waals' forces. This results in a greater adsorption of such gases.

21. (c): 50 mL of 1 M oxalic acid contains oxalic acid

$$= \frac{126}{1000} \times 50 = 60 \text{ g}$$

50 mL of 0.5 oxalic acid contains oxalic acid $= \frac{6.3}{2} = 3.15$ g

∴ Oxalic acid adsorbed by 0.5 g charcoal

$= 6.3 - 3.15 = 3.15$ g

∴ Oxalic acid adsorbed by 1 g charcoal

$= 2 \times 3.15 = 6.30$ g

22. (d): Noble gases are adsorbed by activated coconut charcoal to different extents. Hence, this method is used for separation of noble gases. Helium is not adsorbed because it has a very low critical temperature and is very difficult to liquefy.

Types of Adsorption

23. (d): Follow the theories of catalysis—the modern theory.

24. (b): Follow poisoning of catalyst.

25. (b): Chemical adsorption first increases and then decreases with temperature.

26. (d): Chemisorption is irreversible.

27. (c): Chemical adsorption first increases and then decreases with an increase in temperature.

28. (c): Heats of adsorption in physisorption lie the range 10–40 kJ mol^{-1}.

29. (d): Both physisorption and chemisorption increase with an increase in surface area.

30. (c): Physical adsorption is favourable at low temperature and not favourable at high temperature.

31. (c): Physisorption decreases with an increase in temperature because it is exothermic (ΔH = –ve and by Le Chatelier's principle, equilibrium,
Solid + Gas $\rightleftharpoons$ Gas/Solid + Heat shifts backward).

32. (e): Enthalpy of adsorption in the case of physisorption is low (20–40 kJ mol^{-1}).

33. (b): High pressure favours both physical adsorption as well as chemical adsorption.

34. (c): Chemical adsorption first increases with an increase in temperature and then decreases. Hence, (c) represents the correct curve.

35. (a): Chemisorption involves a chemical reaction which, therefore, first increases with an increase in temperature as the heat supplied provides activation energy.

Adsorption Isotherms, Isobars and Isosteres

36. (c): Enzyme catalysed reactions are highly specific, that is, one enzyme catalyses one reaction.

37. (a): The mass of the gas adsorbed depends upon the pressure of the gas.

38. (b): Langmuir adsorption isotherm is $\frac{x}{m} = \frac{aP}{1+bP}$.

39. (a): According to the Langmuir isotherm, $\frac{x}{m} = \frac{aP}{1+bP}$.

At high pressure, $bP >> 1$; so, 1 can be neglected in comparison to bP.

Hence, $\frac{x}{m} = \frac{aP}{bP} = \frac{a}{b}$.

40. (c): Langmuir adsorption isotherm is based on the assumption that every adsorption site is equivalent and that the ability of a particle to bind there is independent of whether nearby sites are occupied or not.

41. (a): At high pressure, the amount of the gas adsorbed reaches a limiting value.

42. (c): $\frac{x}{m} = KP^{1/n}$, that is,

$$\log \frac{x}{m} = \log K + \frac{1}{n} P$$

Freundlich adsorption isotherm gives a straight line on plotting $\log \frac{x}{m}$ vs $\log P$.

43. (b): According to Langmuir adsorption isotherm,

$$\frac{x}{m} = \frac{1+bP}{aP} = \frac{b}{a} + \frac{1}{aP}$$

Hence, a plot of m/x vs $1/P$ is a straight line.

44. (d): According to the given expression (Langmuir adsorption isotherm)

$$x = \frac{ap}{1+bp} \quad \text{(i)}$$

At low pressure, $bp << 1$ so that Eq. (i) becomes

$x = ap$ or $x \propto p$

At high pressure, $bp >> 1$ so that Eq. (i) becomes

$x = \frac{ap}{bp} = \frac{a}{b} = \text{constant}$

45. (c): For the Freundlich adsorption isotherm, the equation is:

$\frac{x}{m} = kp^{1/n}$

$\therefore \log\left(\frac{x}{m}\right) = \log k + \frac{1}{n}\log p$

Comparing this equation with $y = mx + c$

slope $(m) = \frac{1}{n}$, intercept (c) = log k

46. (c): In the Freundlich adsorption isotherm, n is a +ve integer so that $\frac{1}{n}$ lies between 0 and 1.

47. (a): According to the Freundlich adsorption isotherm,

$\frac{x}{m} = kp^{1/n}$

When $n = 1$, $\frac{x}{m} \propto P$

Hence, adsorption is fast (part OA)

When P increases, adsorption follows the path AB, that is, slow.

After point B, n is so high that $\frac{1}{n} \to 0$,

$\frac{x}{m} = kP^0 = k$, that is, it becomes constant, independent of pressure.

48. (d): $\frac{x}{m} = kp^{1/n}$

or $\log\frac{x}{m} = \log k + \frac{1}{n}\log P$

Plot of $\log\frac{x}{m}$ vs $\log P$ is linear with a slope $= 1/n$.

49. (a): $\frac{x}{m} = p \times T$ is not a correct relation.

50. (e): $\frac{x}{m} = kp^{1/n}$ $\therefore \ln\frac{x}{m} = \ln k + \frac{1}{n}\ln p$. Slope of the plot $= \frac{1}{n} = 0$

$\therefore \frac{x}{m} = k$, that is, it is independent of pressure.

Applications of Adsorption

51. (b): Physisorption or van der Waals' adsorption is more pronounced at low T and high P.

52. (d): Homogeneous catalysis is not explained on the basis of adsorption.

53. (c): Charcoal placed in the annular space adsorbs the gases present if any so as to create a vacuum.

54. (a): Activated charcoal is used as an adsorbent to adsorb the unwanted colours.

Introduction to Catalysis

55. (a): (a) is a true statement.

56. (b): A positive catalyst increases the rate of the forward and backward reactions by decreasing the activation energy.

57. (c): Urea acts as a negative catalyst in the decomposition of H_2O_2.

58. (e): The use of a catalyst may change the order of the reaction as the reaction mechanism in the presence of the catalyst could be different than that in its absence.

59. (c): A catalyst forms an intermediate with one of the reactants and hence takes part in the reaction.

60. (b): A catalytic poison is preferentially adsorbed on the catalyst and blocks the active centres of the catalyst.

61. (b): When a catalyst is added, the reaction follows a new path with lower activation energy.

62. (d): A catalyst cannot initiate a reaction. If only affects the speed of the reaction. Thus, it does not affect the spontaneity of a reaction.

63. (d): Catalytic poisons decrease the activity of the catalyst due to strong preferential adsorption of the poison on the surface of the catalyst.

64. (b): Transition metals, due to their variable valency, are able to form unstable intermediate compounds very readily. Also, due to a number of free valencies on their surface, they show greater adsorption for the reactants. Due to both these reasons, they are the most effective catalysts.

65. (d): Addition of 1% alcohol to chloroform slows down the oxidation of chloroform. Hence, it acts as a negative catalyst.

66. (c): A catalyst does not increase or decrease the free energy (or enthalpy change) of a reaction.

67. (d): The mass or chemical composition of a catalyst remains unchanged at the end of the reaction.

68. (c): A catalyst speeds up the reaction by providing an alternate path of lower activation energy.

Homogeneous and Heterogeneous Catalysis

69. (b): The minimum energy barrier required to be crossed to bring in a chemical change is called the threshold energy level.

70. (b): $4\,Al + 2\,Cr_2O_3 \rightarrow 2Al_2O_3 + 4\,Cr$ (Thermite reaction) is itself very fast reaction.

71. (d): The reactants are in the gas phase while the catalyst (zeolite) is in the solid phase.

72. (a): Intermediate compound formation theory is the mechanism of homogeneous catalysis.

73. (e): In the acid hydrolysis of methyl acetate, the reactants, products and the catalyst are all in the liquid phase.

74. (c): Adsorption theory is applicable to heterogeneous catalysis.

75. (c): Reactants (N_2, O_2) are gaseous and the catalyst (Pt) is a solid. Hence, it is an example of heterogeneous catalysis.

76. (c): In the lead chamber process, SO_2 is oxidised to SO_3 in the presence of NO as catalyst. Reactants and catalyst all are gaseous.

77. (a): As the reactants (H_2O_2) and the catalyst (Br^-) both are both in the liquid phase (aqueous solutions), it is an example of homogenous catalysis.

78. (c): Hydrolysis of ethyl acetate is catalysed by aqueous H_2SO_4.

$$CH_3COOC_2H_5 + H_2O \xrightarrow{H^+(aq)} CH_3COOH + C_2H_5OH$$

79. (d): Fe and not Ni is used as a catalyst in the manufacture of ammonia.

80. (c): In the lead chamber process, SO_2 is oxidised to SO_3 using NO as catalyst. That is, the reactants as well as the catalyst are all gaseous. Hence, it is a case of homogeneous catalysis.

81. (a): Due to adsorption, the concentration of the reactant molecules on the surface of the adsorbent increases and hence the speed of the reaction increases.

82. (b): By definition.

83. (a): Oxidation of SO_2 gas to SO_3 gas by O_2 gas in the presence of NO gas as a catalyst. All are in the same (gaseous) phase.

Autocatalysis and Induced Catalysis

84. (c): In autocatalysis, a product catalyses the reaction.

85. (a): In the reaction,

$$2\,AsH_3(s) \rightarrow 2\,As(s) + 3\,H_2(g)$$

As(*s*) produced, acts as a catalyst. Hence, it is an example of autocatalysis.

86. (d): In (d) Mn^{2+} ions produced in the reaction act as the autocatalyst.

87. (b): The acid produced acts as an autocatalyst which speeds up the reaction after some time.

88. (d): It is an example of induced catalysis.

89. (d): The reaction is,

$$2\,KMnO_4 + 3\,H_2SO_4 + 5\,H_2C_2O_4 \rightarrow K_2SO_4 + 2\,MnSO_4 + 10\,CO_2 + 8\,H_2O$$

90. (b): The gaseous products obtained during decomposition of nitroglycerine act as autocatalysts.

Shape Selective Catalysis by Zeolites

91. (c): To use them as catalysts, they have to be heated so that the water of hydration in the pores is lost and the pores become vacant.

92. (d): Zeolites have shape selective structures because of the honey comb like structure which have cavities for selective adsorption.

93. (b): Alcohols are directly converted into gasoline by passing over heated ZSM-5.

94. (c): Shape selective catalysts are so called because the size of the pores of the catalyst is such that it can trap only selective molecules of the same size as that of the pores.

95. (d): ZSM-5 (that is, Zeolite Sieve of Molecular porosity 5) is a shape selective catalyst.

Enzyme Catalysis

96. (b): The optimum pH range for enzyme activity is 5–7.

97. (a): The enzyme diastase converts starch into maltose.

98. (b): A catalyst decreases the activation energy of the forward as well the backward reaction by the same amount, therefore, it increases the speed of the forward as well as the backward reaction to the same extent. As $K = k_f / k_b$, the value of the equilibrium constant(K) remains unaffected by the presence of the catalyst at a particular temperature.

99. (d):

$$\underset{\text{(Sucrose)}}{C_{12}H_{22}O_{11}} \xrightarrow{\text{Invertase}} \underset{\text{(Glucose)}}{C_6H_{12}O_6} + \underset{\text{(Fructose)}}{C_6H_{12}O_6}$$

$$\underset{\text{Glucose}}{C_6H_{12}O_{12}} \xrightarrow{\text{Zymase}} \underset{\text{Ethanol}}{2\,C_2H_5OH} + 2\,CO_2$$

100. (b): An enzyme is a biological catalyst.

101. (c): In the presence of the enzyme maltase, maltose is hydrolysed to produce two molecules of aD-glucose.

$$\underset{\text{Maltose}}{C_{12}H_{22}O_{11}(aq)} + H_2O \xrightarrow{\text{Maltase}} \underset{\text{Glucose}}{2\,C_6H_{12}O_6(aq)}$$

102. (d): Enzymes to not raise the activation energy.

103. (a): The efficiency of an enzyme in catalysing a reaction is due to its capacity to form a strong enzyme–substrate complex.

104. (a): Curve *a* represents a normal enzyme reaction, *b* represents a competitive inhibition (because upto a certain concentration, it has a lower velocity than *a* and then after a certain concentration, it becomes equal to that of *a* and *c* represents a non-competitive inhibition (because it is slower but never becomes equal to that of *a*).

105. (c): The optimum temperature range for enzyme activity is 298–310 K.

106. (d): (d) is incorrect because enzymes are most reactive at optimum temperature.

107. (b): There are many industrial processes such as fermentation of sucrose which use enzymes as catalysts.

108. (b): In the presence of zymase (catalyst), glucose or fructose can be converted into ethanol.

Catalysts in Industry

109. (d): Oils are esters of unsaturated fatty acids whereas vanaspati ghee is an ester of saturated fatty acids. The former are converted into the latter by catalytic hydrogenation, that is, reduction.

110. (b): V_2O_5 is used as catalyst in the manufacture of H_2SO_4 by the contact process.

111. (d): In the Ostwald's process, in the manufacture of HNO_3, the first step is oxidation of NH_3 to NO in the presence of Pt as catalyst.

112. (d): The catalyst used in the hydrogenation of oils is finely divided nickel.

113. (a): Adam's catalyst is another name of platinum catalyst.

114. (a): Oxidation of NH_3 to NO and then to form HNO_3 by Ostwald process uses Pt as a catalyst.

115. (a): Zeigler–Natta catalyst $[(C_2H_5)_3Al + TiCl_4]$ is used for linear polymerisation to prepare high density polyethylene (HDPE).

116. (b): Zeigler–Natta catalyst is $(C_2H_5)_3Al + TiCl_4$ used for polymerisation of alkenes.

117. (a): Finely divided iron is a catalyst used in Haber's process for the manufacture of NH_3.

118. (c): Reactions (A) and (B) require V_2O_5 and Fe as catalysts respectively.

Introduction to Colloids

119. (c): The size of colloidal particles is in the range 1–11000 nm.

120. (c):A colloid is not a substance but is the state of a substance depending only on particle size. For example, NaCl in water solution acts as a crystalloid but when dispersed in benzene acts as a colloid.

121. (d): Ghee is not a colloid.

122. (a): Size of colloidal particles is 10^{-6} m to 10^{-9} m.

123. (b): Glycerol is a compound and not a colloid.

Classification of Colloids

124. (e): Cheese is a gel and not an emulsion.

125. (b): Butter is a gel. Hence, only (b) is correctly matched.

126. (c): A colloidal dispersion is called aerosol when the dispersion medium is a gas.

127. (b): Smoke is a colloidal dispersion of a solid (carbon particles) in a gas (air) called aerosol.

128. (b): An emulsion is a colloidal dispersion of a liquid in a liquid.

129. (a): Mist is a colloidal system of a liquid dispersed in a gas.

130. (a): Butter is an example of a colloidal dispersion of a liquid in a solid (that is, gel).

131. (b): Fog is liquid dispersed in gas.

132. (a): Milk is a colloid of a liquid dispersed in a liquid.

133. (c): The colloidal system in which both the dispersed phase and dispersion medium are liquids is known as an emulsion. For example, milk and hair cream.

134. (e): Hair cream is a colloidal sol of a liquid dispersed in another liquid. Hence, it is an emulsion.

135. (c): An aerosol is a gas in a liquid.

136. (b): Soap = colloidal sol (above CMC)
Cheese = gel (liquid in solid)
Milk = emulsion (liquid in liquid)
Fog = aerosol (liquid in gas)

137. (c): Liquid in solid is called a gel. For example, cheese, butter and jellies.

138. (c): Air is a homogeneous mixture of gases and not a colloidal solution.

139. (b): Milk is an emulsion of liquid fats in liquid water. In this case, the dispersed phase (liquid fact) is dispersed throughout in the continuous phase (milk).

140. (a): In shaving cream, the dispersion medium is mainly water (liquid).

141. (b): Whipped cream is an example of gas dispersed in liquid.

142. (d): Milk is emulsion, blood is sol and blood clot is gel.

143. (c): Lyophilic sols are more stable than lyophobic sols because in this case, colloidal particles are solvated.

144. (d): As_2S_3 is a hydrophobic sol

145. (a): The surface tension of a lyophilic sol is lower than that of the dispersion medium.

146. (c): The viscosity of hydrophilic sols is higher and surface tension is lower than water (dispersion medium).

147. (d): All these form irreversible colloidal systems.

148. (d): Lyophilic sols are self-stabilised because they undergo hydration.

149. (b): Hydrophobic sols are more easily coagulated because their stability is only due to charge whereas the stability of hydrophilic sols is due to charge as well as solvation.

150. (c): Starch solution is a hydrophilic sol.

151. (d): Lyophilic sols are obtained by directly shaking the substance with water. Examples are starch, gum and gelatine. Metal sulfides to not form lyophilic sols.

152. (c): Gold sol is gold (solid) particles dispersed in water (liquid). Gold sol cannot be prepared directly by shaking with water. Hence, it is a lyophobic sol.

153. (a): Glue on shaking with water directly forms a colloidal sol. Hence, it is an intrinsic colloid.

154. (c): Hydrophobic sols are irreversible. Once precipitated, they cannot be made again by simply shaking with the dispersion medium.

155. (b): The stability of a lyophilic colloid is due to its property of solvation. That is, a layer of dispersion medium is formed on their particles.

156. (d): Addition of alcohol is replacement of the dispersion medium. Addition of electrolyte may cause coagulation. Hence, both these factors make the lyophilic solution unstable.

157. (d): Linseed oil, lanolin and glycogen interact with water showing that they contain a hydrophilic structure. Rubber does not interact with water showing that it does not contain a hydrophilic structure but has a hydrophobic structure.

158. (c): Dodecyltrimethylammonium cations aggregate to form cationic micelles.

159. (d): Micelles are formed above a certain temperature called the Kraft temperature.

160. (c): Sulfur sol contains large aggregates of S_8 molecules.

161. (b): S_8 = multi-molecular, starch = macromolecular, soap solution = associated.

162. (d): Cetyltrimethylammonium cations aggregate to form cationic micelles.

163. (a): Gold sol contains aggregates of atoms of gold. Hence, it is a multi-molecular and not a macromolecular colloid.

164. (d): Sodium stearate (soap) solution is a colloidal sol (consisting of associated colloids).

165. (c): Soaps act as electrolytes in dilute solutions but form colloids in concentrated solutions due to the formation of micelles.

166. (b): Soaps such as sodium stearate ($C_{17}H_{35}COO^-Na^+$) are called surfactant molecules because at low concentration, stearate ions have high concentration on the surface of the solution.

167. (a): Soap solutions above critical micellar concentration (CMC) constitute a micellar system.

168. (c): A protein sol in water is an example of a heteropolar sol.

169. (c): At critical micellar concentration (CMC), surfactant molecules associate to form micelles. For soap, CMC is 10^{-3} mol L^{-1}.

170. (b): Soap solution is an associated colloid.

171. (b): Surfactants are long chain molecules which dissociate to produce long chain ions which can associate tighter. (b) is non-ionic and cannot dissociate. Hence, it is not a surfactant.

172. (a): In a micelle, the polar group is at the outer surface and the non-polar group at the inner surface.

173. (d): Adenine is an aromatic compound. It has least interaction with water. Hence, it is most hydrophobic.

174. (b): Lyophilic sols are obtained by direct shaking of the substance with the dispersion medium whereas it is not so in the case of lyophobic sols.

175. (c): Gold sol is a lyophobic sol.

176. (d): Lyophilic sols are self-stabilising because they are highly hydrated in the solution.

177. (c): The compound (c) is non-polar while all others are polar. As benzene is non-polar, compound (c) will be the most suitable to disperse in benzene.

Preparation of Colloidal Sols

178. (c): When excess of $AgNO_3$ is added, the precipitate of AgI formed changes into a positively charged precipitate due to the adsorption of Ag^+ ions (AgI : Ag^+).

179. (a): $\underset{\text{Freshly ppted}}{Fe(OH)_3} + \underset{\text{Dil.}}{HCl} \xrightarrow{\text{Peptisation}} \underset{\text{(positively charged colloidal sol)}}{Fe(OH)_3}$

180. (c): Colloidal gold is prepared by Bredig's arc method.

181. (d): Breaking down of a suspension into colloidal particles is called fragmentation.

182. (d): Peptisation is a process of converting a precipitate into a colloidal sol on shaking with a suitable electrolyte.

183. (b): Potassium reacts vigorously with water. Hence, its sol cannot be prepared by Bredig's arc method.

184. (c): Breaking down of a fresh precipitate into colloidal particles on shaking with a suitable electrolyte is called peptisation.

185. (d): A colloidal solution of mercury in water in easily obtained by ultrasonic dispersion.

186. (a): The white of an egg is a colloidal sol. Converting a precipitate (coagulated egg) back into colloidal sol with a suitable substance is equivalent to peptisation.

187. (b): Colloidal sols of metals are in general obtained by Bredig's arc method.

188. (d): In Bredig's arc method, some alkali is added to stabilise the sol.

189. (d): The charge on the $Fe(OH)_3$ sol is +ve due to the adsorption of Fe^{3+} from $FeCl_3$ as a sol is formed by adding $FeCl_3$ to hot water [$Fe(OH)_3 + Fe^{3+}$].

190. (d): Colloidion is a 4% solution of nitrocellulose (or cellulose nitrate) in an alcohol–ether mixture.

191. (c): Colloidal particles of amorphous S are obtained.

192. (b): Sulfur is less soluble in water and thus forms a colloidal solution.

193. (d): Gold sol is obtained by Bredig's arc method as well as by reduction of $AuCl_3$ with $SnCl_2$ or HCHO or NH_2NH_2.

194. (b): In the given reaction, H_2S has been oxidised to given colloidal sulfur.

195. (b): Sulfur sol is prepared by oxidation of H_2S by Br_2

$$H_2S + Br_2 \rightarrow 2\,HBr + \underset{(sol)}{S}$$

196. (b): Reaction (b) forms a colloidal sol of sulfur.

197. (d): Freshly precipitated substance is converted into a colloidal sol by peptisation.

198. (b): Bredig's arc method cannot be used for Fe because it is oxidised. All others are noble metals.

Purification of Colloidal Solutions

199. (d): One of the processes for the purification of colloidal sols, that is, separation of colloids from crystalloids is called ultrafiltration.

200. (c): Protein forms a colloidal sol while glucose is crystalloid.

201. (c): Washing of the precipitate is done to remove the impurities adsorbed on the surface of the precipitate.

202. (c): The process of separation of colloids from crystalloids by passing through a semi-permeable membrane is called dialysis.

Properties of Colloidal Solutions

203. (d): The colour of gold sol prepared by different methods is different because of different particle sizes.

204. (a): When a colloidal solution is observed under an ultramicroscope, we can see light scattered by colloidal particles.

205. (d): For Tyndall effect, the refractive indices of the dispersed phase and dispersion medium must differ significantly. Secondly, the size of the dispersed particles should not differ much from the wavelength of light used.

206. (c): The simplest way to check a colloidal system is to throw light on it. A colloidal sol scatters light (Tyndall effect) and the path becomes visible whereas a true solution does not scatter light.

207. (c): The Tyndall effect is observed only in sols.

208. (c): Brownian motion is due to the impact of molecules of the dispersion medium on the colloidal particles.

209. (d): The stability of lyophobic sols is due to the same electric charge on all colloidal particles in a sol (so that they keep repelling and cannot coagulate) and Brownian movement (which does not allow them to settle down).

210. (b):

$$As_2O_3(aq) + 3\,H_2S(aq) \rightarrow \underset{\text{Colloidal sol}}{As_2S_3} + 3\,H_2O$$

As_2S_3 then adsorbs S^{2-} ions from H_2S solution containing H^+ and S^{2-} ions and becomes negatively charged.

211. (a): The colour of a colloidal sol depends upon the size of the colloidal particles. For example, in a gold sol, as the size of colloidal gold particles increases, the colour of the sol changes from red to blue and finally to golden.

212. (d): Gelatine in a strongly acidic solution is a positively charged sol.

213. (d): As an excess of KI has been added, I^- ions are adsorbed on AgI forming a fixed layer (and giving it a negative charge). It then attracts the counter ions (K^+) from the medium forming a second layer (diffused layer).

214. (a): At the isoelectric point, colloidal particles become neutral.

215. (d): Prussian blue, $Fe_4^{III}[Fe^{II}(CN)_6]_3$ (ferri-ferrocyanide) adsorbs Fe^{3+} ions from $FeCl_3$ solution and is thus positively charged colloid (it is a basic dye).

216. (d): The charge on sol particles is not due to absorption but due to adsorption of ionic species from the solution.

217. (a): Hemoglobin forms a positively charged sol.

218. (c): $Fe(OH)_3$ gives a positively charged sol as it adsorbs Fe^{3+} ions from $FeCl_3$ solution.

219. (b): Colloidal solutions are heterogeneous systems.

220. (c): When excess of $AgNO_3$ solution is added to KI solution, first AgI precipitate is formed. It undergoes peptisation due to the presence of excess of $AgNO_3$. The colloidal particles formed get a +ve charge due to the preferential adsorption of Ag^+ ions.

221. (b): The impurities present in rain water are dust particles which are colloidal in nature and a carry negative charge.

222. (d): Tyndall effect, that is, scattering of light by colloidal particles is due to the size of the particles and not due to the charge on the particles.

223. (d): On passing electric current through a colloidal sol, all colloidal particles move towards the oppositely charged electrode. Here, they lose their charge and become neutral and then get coagulated.

224. (a): Movement of (charged) colloidal particles under the influence of an electric field is called electrophoresis.

225. (d): $[Fe(CN)_6]^{4-}$ ion has the highest magnitude of charge. Hence, it has the minimum flocculation value.

226. (c): Though Th^{4+} ions have maximum charge, the solubility of $Th(SO_4)_2$ is very less. Hence, $Al(NO_3)_3$ is the best.

227. (b): $\dfrac{\text{Coagulation power of } AlCl_3}{\text{Coagulation power of NaCl}} = \dfrac{\text{Coagulation value of NaCl}}{\text{Coagulation value of } AlCl_3}$

228. (d): $Fe(OH)_3$ sol is positively charged. Hence, the anion with highest valency will be the best coagulating agent. That is, $[Fe(CN)_6]^{3-}$.

229. (c): Diffusion through an animal membrane does not result in sol destruction.

230. (c): By definition.

231. (d): Less the charge on the oppositely charged ion of the electrolyte, greater is the amount of the electrolyte required for coagulation and hence greater is the coagulation value (remember that greater the charge on the oppositely charged ion of the electrolyte, greater is the coagulating power. Thus, coagulating power $\propto \dfrac{1}{\text{Coagulation value}}$)

232. (d): $Fe(OH)_3$ sol is positively charged. It can be coagulated by the –ve ions of the electrolyte added. Lesser the charge on the –ve ions, the less effective they are. In KI, I^- ions have the least charge.

233. (a): Coagulating power $\propto \dfrac{1}{\text{Coagulation value}}$

Hence, the order is III > II > I.

234. (d): Coagulation of proteins takes place by Ca^{2+} ions.

235. (d):$Fe(OH)_3$ is a +vely charged sol. Greater the charge on the –ve ions of the electrolyte added, greater is the coagulation power. $[Fe(CN)_6]^{4-}$ ions have the maximum negative charge.

236. (a): Coagulation value of an electrolyte is its amount in mmol that must be added to 1 L of a colloidal solution for its complete coagulation.

5 mL of 1 M NaCl $= \frac{1}{1000} \times 5$ mol = 5 mmol

Thus, 100 mL of colloidal sol requires NaCl for complete coagulation = 5 mmol

∴ 1 L (1000 mL) of colloidal sol will require NaCl for complete coagulation = 50 mmol

∴ Coagulation value of NaCl = 50

237. (b): As_2S_3 is a –ve sol. Greater the +ve charge on the ion of the electrolyte added, the more effective is the coagulation. Here, Al^{3+} ions have the maximum +ve charge and hence $AlCl_3$ will be the most effective.

238. (b): As the colloidal particles move towards cathode (–ve electrode), they carry +ve charge. Greater the charge on the –ve ions of the electrolyte added, greater is the coagulating power. Hence, the coagulating power will be in the order:

$$\underset{III}{[Fe(CN)_6]^{4-}} > \underset{II}{PO_4^{3-}} > \underset{I}{SO_4^{2-}} > \underset{IV}{Cl^-}$$

239. (a): Negatively charged particles will require for coagulation, a minimum amount of that electrolyte in which +ve ions have maximum charge, that is, Al^{3+}.

240. (a): Flocculation value is the minimum amount of the electrolyte in mmol that must be added to one litre of the colloidal sol to bring about its complete coagulation. Hence, it is expressed in terms of mmol per litre.

241. (d): Flocculating power is directly proportional to the charge on the ion. As Na^+ has minimum charge, it has minimum flocculating power.

242. (d): Flocculation value is mmol of electrolyte required to bring about coagulation of 1 L of the colloidal sol.

10 L of colloidal sol require NaCl = 0.585 g

$\frac{0.585}{58.5}$ mol = 0.01 mol = 10 mmol

∴ 1 L of colloidal sol will require NaCl = 1 mmol

Hence, flocculation value of NaCl = 1.

243. (d): Addition of an electrolyte results in coagulation of the colloidal sol which means, there is destruction of the colloidal sol.

244. (a): The coagulating power of an ion depends upon the magnitude of the charge on the ion.

245. (d): Arsenious sulfide is a negatively charged sol. Hence, the coagulating powers are in the order $Al^{3+} > Ba^{2+} > Na^+$.

246. (a): For a negatively charged sol, greater the charge on the +ve ion (cation) of the electrolyte, greater is the coagulating power. Hence,

$$\overset{3+}{AlCl_3} > \overset{2+}{BaCl_2} > \overset{1+}{NaCl}$$

or $NaCl < BaCl_2 < AlCl_3$

Protection of Colloids and Gold Number

247. (c): Gold number is associated with protective colloids.

248. (b): Every solid substance cannot be made to behave like a lyophobic colloid.

249. (b): Congo Rubin number is the minimum amount of the protective colloid in milligrams that prevents the colour change of 100 mL of 0.01 of Congo Rubin dye to which 0.16 g equivalent of KCl is added.

250. (b): The statement (b) is the correct definition of gold number.

251. (a): Gold number is a measure of the protective action of a lyophilic colloid on a lyophobic colloid.

252. (b): Gelatine acts as a protective colloid.

253. (a): Gelatine has the lowest value of gold number (0.005–0.01).

254. (b): The Hardy–Schulze rule is applicable only to the coagulation of lyophobic sols.

255. (d): Gold number is maximum for potato starch (20–25).

256. (d): Gold numbers are:

starch > gum Arabic > albumin > gelatine
(20–25) (0.15–0.25) (0.1–0.2) (0.005–0.01)

257. (a): Gold number is the mass of the protective colloid in mg to be added to 10 mL of gold sol. Here, 0.025 g = 25 mg.

Emulsions and Gels

258. (b): Cod liver oil is an example of water in oil emulsion.

259. (b): Insoluble soaps favour water in oil (w/o) emulsion.

260. (a): Shrinking of the gel due to the loss of internal liquid is called syneresis.

261. (a): The solid in liquid system which sets to form a gelatinous mass forms a liquid in solid system called gel.

262. (c): Cow milk is an emulsion stabilised by casein.

263. (d): Size of colloidal particles is 10–1000 Å whereas that of particles of an emulsion is 1000–10,000 Å.

264. (d): Demulsification (separation of the constituent liquids of an emulsion) takes place on freezing, boiling or centrifugation of the emulsion.

265. (c): A small quantity of liquid water is held in the solid cement. Hence, it is a gel formation.

266. (d): The cleaning action of soap is due to its action as an emulsifying agent.

267. (a): An emulsifier is a substance which stabilises the emulsion.

268. (b): Milk can be easily preserved by adding a few drops of formaldehyde (HCHO). Formaldehyde is an emulsifier.

269. (d): Soaps, synthetic detergents and lyophilic sols act as emulsifiers.

Colloids Around Us

270. (b): Gelatine stabilises the colloid and prevents crystallisation.

271. (d): Colloidal silver is used in treating eye disease.

272. (a): $SiCl_4$ gets hydrolysed in moist air to produce white fumes which act as a smoke screen in warfare.

273. (d): Colloidal sulfur is used in the treatment of skin diseases.

274. (d): Sol of graphite in water is called aquadag.

275. (a): Purple of Cassius is a colloidal sol of gold.

276. (a): In Cottrell's precipitator, the charged plates neutralise the charge on the smoke particles which get precipitated.

277. (d): The formation of a delta is due to the coagulation of the mud particles (colloidal in nature) by the electrolytes (salts) present in sea water.

278. (b): Blood is a negatively charged sol. Hence, it is easily coagulated by Fe^{3+} ions provided by $FeCl_3$ solution and as a result bleeding stops.

279. (c): Alum coagulates the mud particles present in water. Hence, it is used for water softening. It is also used in tanning of leather, as mordant in dyeing and to stop bleeding.

280. (b): Mud particles present in muddy water, being –vely charged, are coagulated by the Al^{3+} ions of the alum.

281. (a): Softening of hard water using sodium aluminium silicate is only by exchanging Ca^{2+} and Mg^{2+} ions of hard water by Na^+ ions of the silicate. It has nothing to do with colloids.

282. (c): Gum Arabic is a protective colloid. Hence, it is added to Indian ink during its preparation to give a protective action.

Final Preparation

283. (a): $\frac{x}{m} = kp^{1/n}$ or $\log k + \frac{1}{n}\log p$

$\therefore$ Plot of $\log \frac{x}{m}$ versus $\log p$ is linear with slope $= \frac{1}{n}$ and intercept $= \log k$

Thus, $\frac{1}{n} = \tan\theta = \tan 45° = 1$, that is, $n = 1$

$\log k = 0.3010$ or $k = \text{Antilog } 0.3010 = 2$

At $p = 0.5$ atm, $\frac{x}{m} = kp^{1/n} = 2\times(0.5)^1 = 1.0$

284. (a): According to the Freundlich adsorption isotherm plot,

At low pressure, $\frac{x}{m} \propto p^1$

At high pressure, $\frac{x}{m} \propto p^0$

At intermediate pressure, $\frac{x}{m} \propto p^{1/2}$ where n is an integer

285. (d): According to the Freundlich isotherm, $\frac{x}{m} = kP^{1/n}$

According to Langmuir, $\frac{x}{m} = \frac{aP}{1+bP}$

286. (c): Amount of oxalic acid initially present in 50 mL of 1 M oxalic acid solution

$= \frac{1\times 50}{1000}\times 126 = 6.30$ g

Amount of oxalic acid after adsorption present in 50 mL of 0.5 M oxalic acid solution

$= \frac{0.5}{1000}\times 50\times 126 = 3.15$ g

Amount adsorbed $= 6.30 - 3.15 = 3.15$ g

Amount adsorbed per gram of charcoal

$= 3.15/0.5\times 2 = 6.30$g

287. (b): 100 mL of 0.5 M CH_3COOH contains $CH_3COOH = 0.05$ mol

100 mL of 0.49 M CH_3COOH contains

$CH_3COOH = 0.049$ mol

Acetic acid adsorbed by 1 g of charcoal

$= 0.05 - 0.049$ mol

$= 0.001$ mol $= 6.02\times 10^{20}$ molecules

Surface area of 1 g of charcoal $= 3.01\times 10^2$ m^2

$\therefore (3.01\times 10^2\,\text{m}^2)/(6.02\times 10^{20})$

$= 5\times 10^{-19}$ m^2

288. (b): 22400 cc of N_2 gas at STP contains $= 6.0\times 10^{23}$ molecules

$\therefore$ 112 cc of N_2 at STP will contain

$= \frac{6.0\times 10^{23}}{22400}\times 112 = 3.0\times 10^{21}$ molecules

Area occupied by one molecule

$= 16\times 10^{-20}$ m^2

$\therefore (3.0\times 10^{21})\times(16\times 10^{-20}\,\text{m}^2) = 480$ m^2

289. (c): The Haber–Bosch process is used for the synthesis of ammonia. The best catalyst is finely divided iron along with molybdenum or oxides of K and Al as promoters.

290. (c): A gas mask contains an adsorbent. Higher the critical temperature of the gas being adsorbed, greater is the adsorption and hence greater is the enthalpy of physisorption. The order is $SO_2 > CH_4 > N_2 > H_2$.

291. (b): At 83 K, there is physisorption and hence it is multimolecular.

292. (b): High pressure favours physical as well as chemical adsorption. However, the difference is that a decrease in pressure results in desorption of the physical adsorption but not that of chemical adsorption.

293. (a): Chemisorption has a high heat of adsorption and is irreversible.

294. (a): Decomposition of nitroglycerine gives oxides of nitrogen which then catalyse the reaction.

295. (d): AlO_4^{5-} ion has nearly the same size as the SiO_4^{4-} ion and can replace the latter from silicates provided electrical neutrality is maintained.

296. (b): Enzyme catalysed reactions are of the first order at high concentration of the substrate.

297. (c): Faster the reaction, lower is its activation energy.

298. (b): $\frac{\text{Surface area}}{\text{Volume}} = \frac{4\pi r^2}{\frac{4}{3}\pi r^3} = \frac{3}{r} = \frac{3}{d/2} = \frac{6}{d}$

$\frac{(\text{Surface area / volume})_i}{\text{Surface area / volume})_f}$

$= 3\ (\text{Surface area/ volume})_i$

299. (d): The diameter of colloidal particles is about 10 times larger than solute particles in a true solution. Hence, the volume is about 1000 times greater.

That is, $\frac{V_c}{V_s} = \frac{(4/3)\pi r_c^3}{(4/3)\pi r_s^3} = \frac{r_c^3}{r_s^3} = \left(\frac{r_c}{r_s}\right)^3 = \left(\frac{d_c}{d_s}\right)^3$

300. (d): Potassium stearate, being a soap molecule, forms an associated colloid or micelles.

301. (a): Longer the carbon chain, that is, greater the size of the hydrophobic chain (tail), less is the solubility in water and greater is the tendency of the surfactant molecules to associate to form micelles, that is, lower is the CMC. Hence, (a) with the longest carbon chain has the lowest CMC.

302. (c): Long chain fatty acids form micelles. Cetyltrimethylammonium bromide forms cationic micelles while sodium dodecylsulfate forms anionic micelles.

303. (b): Enthalpy of formation of micelles in aqueous solutions is +ve, that is, it is endothermic with $\Delta H = 1 - 2$ kJ mol^{-1} of the surfactant. Hence, (iii) is not correct. Only (i) and (ii) are correct.

304. (a): The molar conductivity varies as shown in plot (a). With an increase in concentration below CMC, the molar conductivity keeps on decreasing. After CMC, the decrease becomes steeper and a discontinuity is observed at the CMC.

305. (d): $SnO_2(s) + 2\,KOH(aq) \rightarrow K_2SnO_3(aq) + H_2O$
SnO_3^{2-} ions will be preferentially adsorbed by SnO_2 particles.

306. (c): Isoelectric point $= \frac{2.3 + 9.7}{2} = 6$

307. (c): Zeta potential is the potential difference between the fixed charged layer and the diffused layer having opposite charge.

308. (c): As the particles move towards the anode, they are –vely charged and are coagulated by given salts in the order, $AlCl_3 > BaCl_2 > NaCl$

309. (c): On mixing two oppositely charged sols, their charged are neutralised. Hence, coagulation occurs.

310. (c): 200 mL of the sol requires = 0.73 g HCl

$= \frac{0.73}{36.5}$ mol = 0.02 mol = 20 mmol

$\therefore$ 1000 mL (1 L) of the sol will require

$= \frac{20}{200} \times 1000 = 100$ mmol

311. (b): $2\,[AgI]\,I^- + Pb^{2+} \rightarrow PbI_2 + 2\,AgI$
Thus, 2 mol of $[AgI]\,I^-$ are coagulated by 1 mol of Pb^{2+}, that is, 1 mol of $Pb\,(NO_3)_2$.

312. (b): Amount of 0.1 M AB solution added = 10 – 5 mL = 5 mL
0.1 M AB left behind in the solution = 0.4 mL
$\therefore$ 0.1 M AB used up for coagulation = 5 – 0.4 = 4.6 mL
4.6 mL of 0.1 M AB contains AB

$= \frac{4.6}{1000} \times 0.1$ mole = 0.46 mmol

As total volume of the sol after mixing with electrolyte solution is 10 mL, the amount of AB required for coagulation of 1 L, that is, 1000 mL of the sol = 46 mmol.
$\therefore$ Flocculation value = 46

313. (d): Gelatine is lyophilic which is most easily coagulated by alcohol.

314. (c): Smaller the coagulation value, higher is its flocculating power. Hence, the order of flocculating power is IV > III > II > I.

315. (d): 10^{-4} g = 0.1 mg
100 cm^3 of gold sol requires 0.1 mg
$\therefore$ 10 cm^3 of gold sol will require 0.01 mg
Hence, gold number = 0.01.

316. (d): Proteins favour oil in water (o/w) emulsion.

317. (d): Elastic gels are those which change to solid on dehydration which can be converted back into the gel by the addition of water followed by heating and cooling.

318. (d): By definition.

319. (c): A small quantity of liquid water is held in the solid cement. Hence, it is a gel formation.

320. (a): Bleeding due to a cut can be stopped by applying $FeCl_3$ or alum solution. This is due to coagulation of negatively charged colloidal blood particles (albuminoid substance) by the positively charged Fe^{3+} ions. These substances are used as styptic (which check the flow of blood).

321. (c): Colloidal $Fe(OH)_3$ is given because it adsorbs arsenic which then can be vomitted out.

322. (c): Ag^+I^- brings about coagulation of water droplets easily.

323. (a): Coagulation occurs even when a large quantity of $AlCl_3$ is added.

MATCH THE FOLLOWING

324. (a): The critical temperatures of the given gases are, CO = 134 K, CO_2 = 304 K, SO_2 = 430 K, N_3 = 4063 K. Thus, the ease of liquefaction is in the order, $SO_2 > NH_3 > CO_2 > CO$. Greater the ease of liquefaction, greater are the van der Waals forces and hence greater is the adsorption.

325. (a): (A) Smoke is carbon particles dispersed in air (gas). Hence, it is an aerosol.
(B) Butter is liquid water dispersed in solid fats. Hence, it is a gel.
(C) Hair cream is liquid dispersed in liquid. Hence, it is an emulsion.
(D) Whipped cream is gas dispersed in liquid. Hence, it is foam.

326. (d): (A) White of egg contains protein. Hence, it forms a macromolecular colloid.
(B) Mercury vapours contain atoms which aggregate together to form a multimolecular colloid.

(C) Cellulose nitrate shaken with ethanol forms a lyophilic sol called collodion.
(D) Detergents (or soaps) form associated colloids.

327. (d): NO acts as a positive catalyst for the oxidation of SO_2 to SO_3.
Hence, (A) → (q)
Phosphoric acid slows down the decomposition of H_2O, that is, it acts as a negative catalyst. Hence, (B) → (r).
Na_2SO_3 induces oxidation of Na_3AsO_4, that is, it is a case of induced catalysis. Hence, (C) → (s).
Hydrolysis of esters is slow in the beginning but automatically becomes faster as the acid produced (RCOOH) acts as an autocatalyst. Hence, (D) → (p).

328. (c): Ostwald process:
$$4\,NH_3 + 5\,O_2 \xrightarrow{Pt} 4\,NO + 6\,H_2O$$
Bosch process:
$$\underbrace{CO + H_2}_{\text{Water gas}} + H_2O(g) \xrightarrow{Fe_2O_3} CO + 2\,H_2$$
Deacon's process:
$$4\,HCl + O_2 \xrightarrow{CuCl_2} 2\,H_2O + 2\,Cl_2$$
Haber's process:
$$N_2 + 3\,H_2 \xrightarrow{Fe} 2\,NH_3$$

ASSERTION REASON

329. (a): R is the correct explanation of A

330. (b): Correct explanation. Higher critical temperature implies that the intermolecular forces of attraction are strong and hence the adsorption is more.

331. (a): R is the correct explanation of A.

332. (b): Correct explanation. NH_3 has greater intermolecular forces of attraction than CO_2 or has higher critical temperature than CO_2 or is more easily liquefiable than CO_2.

333. (d): Correct A. In chemisorption, adsorption first increases with temperature and then decreases.
Correct R. Heat absorbed initially provides activation energy for the reaction between adsorbate and adsorbent.

334. (d): Correct A. Physical absorption takes place not only on the surface but within the body also.
Correct R. Physical absorption is not due to breaking of bond but due to van der Waals forces.

335. (b): Correct R. As adsorption varies with temperature, different adsorption isotherms are obtained at different constant temperatures.

336. (c): Correct R. A plot of $\frac{x}{m}$ vs $\frac{1}{P}$ will be linear $\left(as\ \frac{m}{x} = \frac{1}{aP} + \frac{b}{a}\right)$.

337. (a): R is the correct explanation of A.

338. (a): R is the correct explanation of A.

339. (b): Correct explanation. If the dispersed phase is separated out from the dispersion medium, it can be converted into the colloidal sol again by simply shaking with the dispersion medium.

340. (d): Correct A. As $AgNO_3$ is in excess, the AgI particles will adsorb Ag^+ ions and hence will be +ve and move towards the cathode.
Correct R. Colloidal particles of AgI may be positively or negatively charged depending upon whether $AgNO_3$ is in excess or KI is in excess.

341. (b) Correct R. During the formation of $Fe(OH)_3$ sol, Fe^{3+} ions are adsorbed on the particles.

342. (a):R is the correct explanation of A.

343. (c): Correct R. Fe^{3+} neutralises the charge on the negatively charged As_2S_3 particles.

344. (c): Correct R. All the electrolytes are completely removed on prolonged dialysis and hence the sol becomes unstable.

345. (b): Correct explanation. As_2S_3 being negatively charged, is coagulated faster by Ba^{2+} ions than by Na^+ ions.

346. (a): R is the correct explanation of A.

347. (d): Correct A. Isoelectric point is the pH at which the colloidal particles do not move towards the cathode or anode.
Correct R. At the isoelectric point, colloidal particles do not carry any charge.

348. (a): R is the correct explanation of A.

349. (d): Correct A. Gelatine has greater protective power than starch.
Correct R. Smaller the gold number, greater is its protective power.

350. (a): R is the correct explanation of A.

351. (a): R is the correct explanation of A.

352. (b): Correct explanation. The negative charge is due to R COO^- ions of the emulsifier.

353. (b): Correct explanation. The $MnSO_4$ formed as a product acts as an autocatalyst.

354. (a): R is the correct explanation of A.

355. (d): Correct A. The activity of a catalyst depends largely on the extent of chemisorption.
Correct R. The catalyst must adsorb reasonably strongly but not so strongly that they are immobilised and further adsorption stops.

356. (b): Correct explanation. Dehydration is not due to the porous nature but is due to the acidic group present in zeolites.

357. (b): Correct explanation. Activity of the enzyme is maximum at pH = 7.4 (physiological pH). [In fact, as the pH is increased, the rate rises to a maximum and then falls off.]

358. (b): Correct explanation. ZSM-5 converts alcohols directly into gasoline (petrol) by dehydrating them so that a mixture of hydrocarbons is formed.

General Principles and Processes of Isolation of Elements

6.1 Introduction

Most metals occur in the combined state in the form of oxides, carbonates, sulfides, silicates, halides, sulfates, arsenides and phosphates. The naturally occurring chemical substances in the form of which the metals occur in the earth along with impurities are called *minerals*. The mineral from which a metal is conveniently and economically extracted is called an *ore*. Some important minerals of aluminium, iron, copper and zinc are given in Table 6.1.

Table 6.1 Principal minerals of some important metals

Metal	Minerals	
Aluminium	Bauxite	$AlO_x(OH)_{3-2x}$ where $0 < x < 1$
	Kaolinite (a form of clay)	$[Al_2(OH)_4Si_2O_5]$ or $Al_2O_3.2SiO_2.2H_2O$
Iron	Haematite	Fe_2O_3
	Magnetite	Fe_3O_4
	Siderite	$FeCO_3$
	Iron pyrites or Fool's gold	FeS_2
Copper	Copper pyrites	$CuFeS_2$
	Malachite	$CuCO_3.Cu(OH)_2$
	Cuprite	Cu_2O
	Copper glance or Chalcocite	Cu_2S
Zinc	Zinc blende or Sphalerite	ZnS
	Calamine	$ZnCO_3$
	Zincite	ZnO

A metal may be found in form of a number of minerals. But every mineral is not suitable for the extraction of that metal. This is because it may contain either low concentration of the metal, or may contain impurities which may be difficult to remove or the process of extraction from that mineral may not be chemically feasible or commercially viable. Thus, all ores are minerals but all minerals are not ores.

6.2 Metallurgical Processes

The ores mined from the earth's crust are generally contaminated with earthy or undesired materials (impurities) called *gangue* or *matrix*. The process of metallurgy depends upon the nature of the ore and the impurities present in it. Some important metallurgical operations are discussed below.

6.2.1 Crushing and Grinding of the Ore

The lumps are broken into small pieces with the help of *crushers* or *grinders* and are then reduced to a fine powder This process is called *pulverisation*.

6.2.2 Concentration or Benefaction of the Ore (Ore Dressing)

The process of removal of unwanted impurities (gangue or matrix) from the ore is called *ore concentration* or *ore dressing* or *ore benefaction*. The finely ground ore is concentrated by the following methods.

(i) Hand picking: In case the impurities can be differentiated by the naked eye, they may be separated by hand picking.

(ii) Gravity separation or levigation: This method is frequently used when the ore particles are heavier than the earthy or rocky gangue particles. The process by which lighter earthy particles are removed from heavier ore particles by washing with water is called *hydraulic washing* or *gravity separation* or *levigation*.

(iii) Electromagnetic separation: If either the ore or the gangue (one of these two) is attracted by a magnet then the ore can be separated from the impurities with the help of the magnetic separation method.

(iv) Electrostatic separation: The method is based upon the principle that when an electrostatic field is applied, the ore particles which are good conductors of electricity get electrically charged and hence are repelled by the electrode having the same charge and thus are thrown away.

(v) Froth floatation: It is used for the extraction of those metals in which the ore particles are preferentially wetted by oil and gangue by water. This method has been used for the concentration of sulfide ores such as galena (PbS), zinc blende (ZnS) and copper pyrites ($CuFeS_2$). The suspension is violently agitated by the rotating paddle which draws in air, causing frothing. During this process, the ore particles which are preferentially wetted by the oil become lighter and thus rise to the surface along with the froth. The gangue particles which are preferentially wetted by water, collapse and are finally dried to get the concentrated ore.

Separation of two sulfide ores: The froth floatation method can also be used for separating one sulfide ore from another by adjusting the proportion of oil to water. Sometimes, depressants are used to prevent certain types of particles from forming the froth with air bubbles. For example, sodium cyanide can be used as a depressant in the separation of zinc sulfide ore (ZnS) and lead sulfide ore (PbS).

(vi) Leaching: This process consists of treating the powdered ore with a suitable reagent (such as acids, bases or other chemicals) which can selectively dissolve the ore but not the impurities. The impurities left undissolved are removed by filtration. The leaching method is used for concentrating the ores of aluminium, silver, gold, and so on.

6.2.3 Extraction of Crude Metals from Concentrated Ores

The process of working the concentrated ore to extract the metal depends upon the nature of the ore as well as the nature of the impurities present in the ore. Therefore, the extraction of metals actually involves the following two chemical processes:

- conversion of the ore into metal oxide,
- reduction of the metal oxide to the free metal.

Conversion of the Ore into Metal Oxide

The concentrated ore is either a hydrated oxide, a carbonate or a sulfide. It can be converted into its oxide form by:

(i) Calcination: Calcination is the process of converting an ore into its oxide by heating it strongly below its melting point either in the absence or in a limited supply of air. For example, hydrated oxide and carbonate ores are generally calcined to give oxides.

(ii) Roasting: Roasting is the process of heating the ore strongly in the presence of excess of air at a temperature below the melting point of the metal. This method is mainly employed in the case of sulfide ores.

Flux

If the calcined or the roasted ore still contains non-fusible impurities of earthy matter, then during reduction, an additional substance called the flux is also added to the ore. It combines with the impurities to form an easily fusible product known as slag.

$$\underset{\text{(present in the ore)}}{\text{Impurities}} + \text{Flux} \rightarrow \text{Fusible product (slag)}$$

Slag is not soluble in the molten metal. Being lighter, it can be easily skimmed off from the surface of the molten metal. Therefore, removal of gangue becomes easier.

Conversion of the Oxide of the Metal to the Metallic Form:

The metal oxides are usually reduced to free metals by using a suitable reducing agent such as carbon, carbon monoxide or even another metal. Heating the metal oxide with a suitable reducing agent is called *thermal reduction* or *pyrometallurgy*.

(i) Reduction with carbon and carbon monoxide: The process of extraction of a metal by reduction of its oxide with carbon (in the form of charcoal, coke or carbon monoxide) is called *smelting*.

$$\underset{\text{Metal oxide}}{M_xO_y} + \underset{\text{carbon}}{yC} \rightarrow \underset{\text{Metal}}{xM} + \underset{\text{Carbon monoxide}}{yCO}$$

(ii) Reduction by hydrogen: For example, molybdenum and tungsten oxides are reduced by a current of hydrogen at higher temperature (1270–1470 K).

$$\underset{\text{Tungsten trioxide}}{WO_3} + 3H_2 \xrightarrow{\text{Heat}} \underset{\text{Tungsten}}{W} + 3H_2O$$

$$\underset{\text{Molybdenum trioxide}}{MoO_3} + 3H_2 \rightarrow \underset{\text{Molybdenum}}{Mo} + 3H_2O$$

(iii) Reduction by aluminium (aluminothermy): Many oxides such as CrO_3 and Mn_3O_4 are not reduced easily by carbon or CO. These metal oxides are reduced by strongly electropositive metals such as aluminium. This process is called *aluminothermy*. For example,

$$Cr_2O_3 + 2Al \rightarrow 2Cr + Al_2O_3$$

(iv) Reduction by sodium, magnesium or calcium: Certain metal halides are reduced to the pure metal state by reduction with Na, Mg or Ca, in a closed vessel on heating. For example, titanium, zirconium or vanadium metals are obtained by the reduction of their halides.

$$TiCl_4 + 4Na \rightarrow Ti + 4NaCl$$

(v) Reduction with water gas: Nickel oxide (NiO) is reduced to nickel by heating carefully with water gas ($CO + H_2$) which act as a reducing agent.

$$NiO + CO \rightarrow Ni + CO_2$$

$$NiO + H_2 \rightarrow Ni + H_2O$$

(vi) Self-reduction or auto-reduction: This is used for the reduction of sulfide ores of Pb, Hg and Cu. No reducing agent is required. For example, mercury is directly obtained by the roasting of its ore cinnabar (HgS) in air.

$$\underset{\text{Cinnabar}}{HgS} + O_2 \rightarrow Hg + SO_2$$

or $$HgS + 3O_2 \rightarrow 2HgO + 2SO_2$$

$$2HgO \rightarrow 2Hg + O_2$$

and $$2HgO + HgS \rightarrow 3Hg + SO_2$$

6.3 Thermodynamic Principles of Metallurgy

Thermodynamic considerations help in deciding the temperature and the choice of reducing agents in the reduction processes. The feasibility of extraction of metals from their oxides by using a particular reducing agent can be predicted in terms of Gibbs energy change (ΔG) at any specified temperature. This is related to the enthalpy change (ΔH) and entropy change (ΔS) as:

$$\Delta G = \Delta H - T\Delta S \qquad (6.1)$$

The free energy change is also related to the equilibrium constant K of the reactant–product system at a temperature T by the following equation,

$$\Delta G° = -RT \ln K \qquad (6.2)$$

If $\Delta G°$ is –ve, then K will be positive. This means that the reaction will proceed towards the products.

(i) For any reaction to occur, the value of ΔG must be negative. This will be possible if ΔH is negative and ΔS is positive. On increasing the temperature (T), the value of $T\Delta S$ would increase and then ΔG will become more negative and the reaction will be feasible.

(ii) A reaction with ΔG positive can still be made to occur by coupling it with another reaction having large negative ΔG so that the net ΔG of the two reactions is negative.

6.3.1 Ellingham Diagrams

The Ellingham diagrams helps in predicting the feasibility of thermal reduction of an ore. The Gibbs energy change of the reaction must be negative. The Ellingham diagram for the oxidation of metals to metal oxides per mole of O_2 is given in Fig. 6.1.

$$2x\, M(s) + O_2(g) \rightarrow 2\, M_xO(s)$$

(i) In this reaction, dioxygen (a gas) has been used up and metal oxide (a solid) is formed. Gases have higher entropy than liquids and solids, therefore, during this reaction, ΔS becomes negative. Thus, if the temperature is increased, $T\Delta S$ becomes more and more negative. $T\Delta S$ is subtracted in Eq. 6.1, therefore, ΔG becomes less and less negative. In other words, *ΔG increases with an increase in temperature* (normally, ΔG decreases with an increase in temperature). In other words, $\Delta_f G°$ vs T lines have +ve slopes for most of the reactions involving the formation of metals oxides, $M_xO(s)$ (Fig. 6.1).

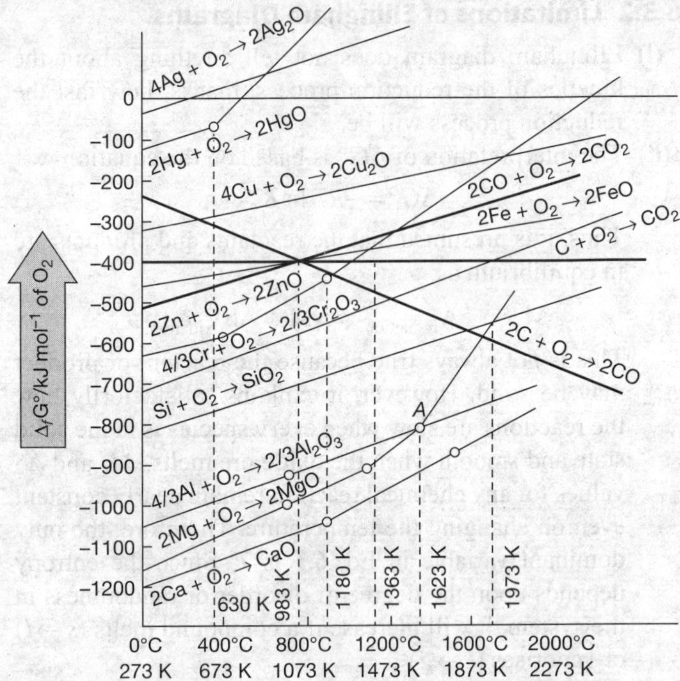

Fig. 6.1 Ellingham diagram $-\Delta_f G°$ vs T plots for formation of oxides of some metals. The small circles on the curves indicate melting and boiling points of metals

(ii) The ΔG vs T plot is a straight line except when some change in phase (solid → liquid or liquid → gas) takes place. The temperature at which such a change occurs, is indicated by an increase in the slope on the +ve side. For example, in the Zn–ZnO plot, at the boiling point of zinc (1180 K), there is an abrupt increase in the +ve slope of the curve. Similarly, the +ve slope of the Mg–MgO curve increases abruptly at the boiling point of Mg at 1363 K. The small circles on the curve indicate melting points (circle on the left) and boiling points (circle on the right) of the metals.

(iii) When the temperature is raised, a point would be reached where the $\Delta_f G°$ vs T graphs cross the $\Delta G = 0$ line. Below this temperature, ΔG is negative and hence the oxide is stable. Above this temperature, the Gibbs energy change is positive and the oxides formed would, therefore, be unstable and would decompose to give metals and oxygen.

(iv) In the Ellingham diagram, the plots of some reducing agents such as carbon and carbon monoxide are also given. The coupling or combination of oxidation and reduction reactions helps in interpreting whether the given reducing agent will be useful or not.

(v) Similar diagrams are also constructed for sulfides and halides. These diagrams show why reduction of M_xS is difficult for the reactions in which $\Delta_f G$ of M_xS is not compensated.

6.3.2 Limitations of Ellingham Diagrams

(i) Ellingham diagram does not tell anything about the kinetics of the reduction process, that is, how fast the reduction process will be.

(ii) The interpretation of $\Delta G°$ is based on the equation

$$\Delta G° = -RT \ln K$$

Thus, it is presumed that the reactants and products are in equilibrium as:

$$M_xS + A_{\text{reduction}} \rightleftharpoons xM + AS_{\text{oxidation}}$$

This is not always true because the reactant or product may be solid. However, it explains satisfactorily how the reactions are slow when every species is in the solid state and smooth when the oxide ore melts. ΔH and ΔS values for any chemical reaction remain nearly constant even on changing the temperature. Therefore, the only dominant variable in Eq. 6.1 is T. Since the entropy depends upon the degree of disorder or randomness in the system, it will increase if a compound melts ($s \rightarrow l$) or vaporises ($l \rightarrow g$)

6.4 Theory of Pyrometallurgy

During reduction, the oxide of the metal decomposes

Reduction: $M_xO(s) \rightarrow xM(s \text{ or } l) + 1/2\ O_2(g)$ (6.3)

and the reducing agent takes away the oxygen given by the metal oxide.

Oxidation: $C(s) + 1/2\ O_2(g) \rightarrow CO(g)$ (6.4)

The role of the reducing agent here is to provide a large negative $\Delta G°$ to make the sum of the $\Delta G°$ of the above two reactions (that is, reduction of the metal oxide and oxidation of the reducing agent) negative.

$$x\,M(s \text{ or } l) + \frac{1}{2}O_2(g) \rightarrow M_xO(s);\ \Delta G°_{(M,M_xO)} \quad (6.5)$$

However, if instead of partial oxidation of C to CO, complete oxidation of C to CO_2 occurs, the oxidation of the reducing agent may be represented as follows.

$$\frac{1}{2}C(s) + \frac{1}{2}O_2(g) \rightarrow \frac{1}{2}CO_2(g);\ \frac{1}{2}\Delta G°_{(C,CO_2)} \quad (6.6)$$

If instead of C, CO is used as the reducing agent, the oxidation of the reducing agent may be represented as follows.

$$CO(g) + \frac{1}{2}O_2(g) \rightarrow CO_2(g);\ \Delta G°_{(CO,CO_2)} \quad (6.7)$$

On subtracting Eq. 6.5 from each of the three equations, 6.4, 6.6 and 6.7, we have

$$M_xO(s) + C(s) \rightarrow x\,M\,(s \text{ or } l) + CO(g) \quad (6.8)$$

$$M_xO(s) + \frac{1}{2}C(s) \rightarrow xM(s \text{ or } l) + \frac{1}{2}CO_2(g) \quad (6.9)$$

$$MxO(s) + CO(g) \rightarrow x\,M(s \text{ or } l) + CO_2(g) \quad (6.10)$$

These three equations 6.8, 6.9 and 6.10 describe the actual reduction of the metal oxide, M_xO to the free metal, M. The $\Delta_rG°$ values for these reactions, in general, can be obtained by the subtraction of the corresponding $\Delta_fG°$ values from the Ellingham diagram. If these values are –ve, the reduction is feasible; otherwise not.

At any given temperature, any element (metal) will reduce the oxides of other metals which lie above it in the Ellingham diagram because the free energy change ($\Delta_rG°$) for the combined redox reaction will be negative by an amount equal to the difference between the free energy of formation ($\Delta_fG°$) of the two oxides at that temperature. Further, greater the difference, easier is the reduction.

For example, Mg can reduce Al_2O_3, ZnO, FeO and Cu_2O more readily than Al can reduce ZnO, FeO and Cu_2O. Similarly, Al can reduce ZnO, FeO and Cu_2O more readily than Zn reduces FeO and Cu_2O. Thus, the relative tendency of these metals to act as reducing agents is Mg > Al > Zn > Fe > Cu. However, in the case of less reactive metals like silver and mercury, $\Delta_fG°$ becomes positive at higher temperatures. This suggests that both silver oxide (Ag_2O) and mercury oxide (HgO) are unstable and hence decompose at high temperature to liberate the corresponding metal.

$$2\,Ag_2O(s) \xrightarrow{\text{Heat}} 4\,Ag(s) + O_2(g);$$

$$2\,HgO(s) \xrightarrow{630\text{ K}} 2\,Hg(l) + O_2(g)$$

Effect of Temperature on the Free Energy Change ($\Delta_rG°$) of the Overall Reduction Process

If a particular reduction process does not occur at a lower temperature, it may occur at a higher temperature. The only thing we have to do is to select the temperature in such a way that the $\Delta_rG°$ of the overall redox reaction becomes –ve. In the Ellingham diagram (Fig. 6.1), this temperature is indicated by the intersection of the two curves (that is, the curve for the formation of M_xO and the curve for the oxidation of the reducing agent). At the point of intersection of the two curves, $\Delta G° = 0$. Below this temperature, the $\Delta G°$ is –ve and hence the oxide is stable. Above this temperature, $\Delta G°$ is +ve and hence the oxide is unstable, that is, it will give the metal and oxygen.

6.5 Metallurgy of Iron

6.5.1 Ores

- **Oxide ores:** Magnetite (Fe_3O_4), hematite (Fe_2O_3) and limonite or hydrated ferric oxide ($Fe_2O_3.3H_2O$).
- **Carbonate ores:** Siderite or sepathic iron ($FeCO_3$).
- **Sulfide ores:** Iron pyrites (FeS_2), chalcopyrites ($CuFeS_2$).

6.5.2 Processes Involved

(i) Concentration of ore: The concentration of the ore is done by the gravity process. The ore is washed with water to remove silicious impurities and then subjected to electromagnetic separation.

(ii) Calcination: The concentrated ore is then calcined; the following changes occur.

- Moisture is removed.
- Sulfur, phosphorus, arsenic and so on, are oxidised to their oxides and are, thus, removed as volatile gases.

$$S_8 + 8\,O_2 \rightarrow 8\,SO_2\uparrow;\ P_4 + 5\,O_2 \rightarrow P_4O_{10}\uparrow;$$
$$2\,As + 5\,O_2 \rightarrow As_2O_5\uparrow$$

Ferrous oxide is oxidised to ferric oxide thereby preventing the loss of iron as slag during smelting.

$$4\,FeO(s) + O_2(g) \rightarrow 2\,Fe_2O_3(s)$$

- The ore becomes porous and hence is more suitable for reduction to the metallic state.

In the case of carbonate ore (siderite), during calcinations, it is converted into ferric oxide.

$$FeCO_3(s) \rightarrow FeO(s) + CO_2(g);$$
$$4\,FeO(s) + O_2(g) \rightarrow 2\,Fe_2O_3(s)$$

However, in the case of the sulfide or (iron pyrites), conversion to the oxide is carried out by roasting.

$$4\,FeS_2(s) + 11\,O_2(g) \rightarrow 2\,Fe_2O_3(s) + 8\,SO_2(s)$$

(iii) Smelting: The calcined ore is reduced with carbon, that is, smelted in a blast furnace

6.5.3 Theory of the Reduction Process

In the Ellingham diagram (Fig. 6.2), there are three curves which illustrate the formation of ferric oxide from iron, formation of CO from carbon and formation of CO_2 from CO. The curves cross each other at 1073 K. Above 1073 K, $\Delta G°$ for the formation of Fe_2O_3 is less negative than $\Delta G°$ for the formation of carbon monoxide from carbon. Thus, above 1073 K, carbon (coke) can reduce Fe_2O_3, that is, $\Delta_r G°$ for the reaction

$$FeO(s) + C(s) \rightarrow Fe(s/l) + CO(g) \quad (6.11)$$

This redox reaction can be divided into the following two half reactions—one involving reduction and the other oxidation.

Reduction: $FeO(s) \rightarrow Fe(s) + \frac{1}{2}O_2(g);\ \Delta G°_{(FeO,\,Fe)}$ (6.12)

Oxidation: $C(s) + \frac{1}{2}O_2(g) \rightarrow CO(g);\ \Delta G°_{(C,\,CO)}$ (6.13)

The net free energy change of these two combined reactions is

$$\Delta G°_{(C,CO)} + \Delta G°_{(FeO,\,Fe)} = \Delta_r G°$$

or $$\Delta G°_{(C,CO)} - \Delta G°_{(Fe,\,FeO)} = \Delta_r G° \quad (6.14)$$

Obviously, the resultant reaction, Eq. 6.11, will take place only when $\Delta_r G°$ is –ve.

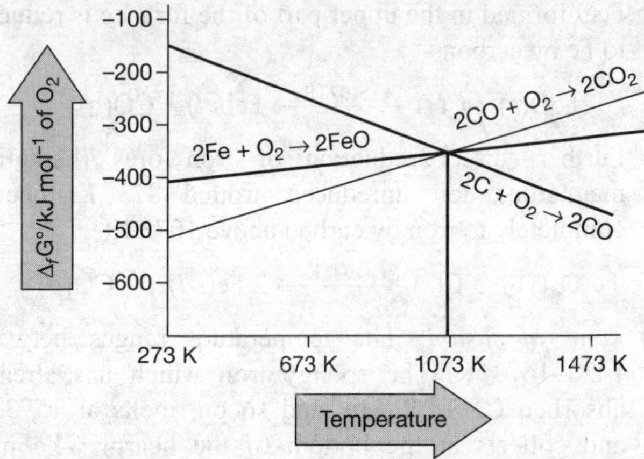

Fig. 6.2 Ellingham diagram for formation of FeO from Fe, CO from C and CO_2 from CO

6.5.4 Reactions Taking Place in the Furnace

The following reactions occurs in the blast furnace.

(i) *Zone of combustion*: Near the tuyeres, coke burns to form carbon dioxide.

$$C(s) + O_2(g) \rightarrow CO_2(g);\ \Delta H = -393.3\ kJ$$

The temperature here is around 2170 K.

(ii) *Zone of heat absorption*: This is the lower part of the furnace and the temperature here is between 1423–1673 K. The coke present in the charge reduces CO_2 to CO.

$$CO_2(g) + C(s) \rightarrow 2\,CO(g);\ \Delta H = +163.2\ kJ$$

Since this reaction is endothermic, the temperature gradually falls to 1423 K.

(iii) *Slag formation zone*: The limestone present in the charge decomposes into calcium oxide and carbon dioxide.

$$CaCO_3(s) \xrightarrow{1123\ K} CaO(s) + CO_2(g);\ \Delta H = +179.9\ kJ$$

Silica is present as an impurity.

$$CaO(s) + SiO_2(s) \xrightarrow{1123\ K} \underset{\text{Calcium silicate (slag)}}{CaSiO_3(s)}$$

(iv) *Reduction zone*: The temperature varies from 523 to 973 K. The oxide ore is reduced to iron in this zone. The reduction takes place through the following stages.

$$3\,Fe_2O_3(s) + CO(g) \xrightarrow{573\text{–}673\ K} 2\,Fe_3O_4(s) + CO_2(g)$$

$$Fe_3O_4(s) + 4\,CO(g) \xrightarrow{773\text{–}873\ K} 3\,Fe(s) + 4\,CO_2(g)$$

$$Fe_2O_3(s) + CO(g) \xrightarrow{773\text{–}873\ K} 2\,FeO(s) + CO_2(g)$$

In the middle part of the furnace, the temperature is between 900–1500 K. At a temperature above 1073 K,

FeO formed in the upper part of the furnace is reduced to Fe by carbon.

$$FeO(s) + C(s) \xrightarrow{>1073\text{ K}} Fe(s/l) + CO(g)$$

Further, direct reduction of iron ores (hematite, magnetite), left unreduced around 873 K, occurs completely to iron by carbon above 1073 K.

$$Fe_2O_3(s) + 3\ C(s) \xrightarrow{>1073\text{ K}} 2\ Fe(s/l) + 3\ CO(g)$$

(v) *Zone of fusion*: The temperature ranges between 1423–1673 K. The spongy iron which has already absorbed C, Si, P, Mn, and so on, melts at 1573 K and collects at the bottom of the hearth. The iron obtained from the blast furnace is called pig iron. It contains about 4% carbon and many impurities such as Mn, P and Si in minor amounts. The pig iron is remelted with scrap iron and cast or poured into moulds. This is known as *cast iron*.

6.5.5 Preparation of Wrought Iron

The cast iron is melted on the hearth of the furnace by the hot gases. The impurities of cast iron are rapidly oxidised by the oxygen of hematite. Oxides of carbon and sulfur, being volatile, escape while those of Mn, P and Si form slag. The pure form of cast iron is wrought iron.

6.6 Extraction of Copper from Cuprous Oxide [Copper(i) Oxide]

The principal ores of copper are sulfides, oxide and basic carbonates.

(i) Chalcopyrites of copper pyrites	$CuFeS_2$
(ii) Calcocite or copper glance	Cu_2S
(iii) Bornite	Cu_3FeS_3
(iv) Cuprite (red)	Cu_2O
(v) Malachite (green)	$CuCO_3.Cu(OH)_2$
(vi) Azurite (blue)	$2CuCO_3.Cu(OH)_2$

6.6.1 Extraction

In the Ellingham diagram (Fig. 6.3), the (Cu, Cu_2O) curve is almost at the top while (C, CO) and (CO, CO_2) lines lie much below it particularly in the temperature range 500–600 K. Therefore, it is quite easy to reduce the oxides of copper directly to copper by heating with coke. However, most of the ores of copper are sulfide ores. These (after concentration by the froth floatation process) are first converted to oxides.

$$2\ Cu_2S + 3\ O_2 \rightarrow 2\ Cu_2O + 2\ SO_2$$

The oxides can then be reduced to metallic copper using coke as the reducing agent.

$$Cu_2O + C \rightarrow 2\ Cu + CO$$

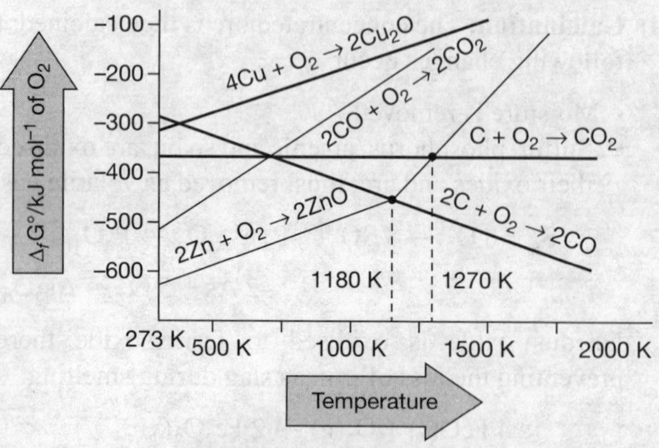

Fig. 6.3 Ellingham diagram showing the function of Cu_2O from Cu, ZnO from Zn, CO from C and CO_2 from C and CO

Dry Process for the Extraction of Copper from Copper Pyrites

The extraction of copper from copper pyrites involves the following steps.

(i) Concentration of the ore: The concentration of the ores is done by the froth floatation process.

(ii) Roasting: The concentrated ore is heated strongly in a current of air on the hearth of a reverberatory furnace. During roasting the following changes occur.

- Free sulfur is oxidised and removed as sulfur dioxide.

$$S + O_2 \rightarrow SO_2$$

- The arsenic and antimony present in the ore are removed as volatile oxides.

$$4As + 3\ O_2 \rightarrow 2As_2O_3$$
$$4Sb + 3O_2 \rightarrow 2Sb_2O_3$$

- The pyrites is converted into cuprous sulfide and ferrous sulfide with the evolution of sulfur dioxides.

$$2\ CuFeS_2 + O_2 \rightarrow Cu_2S + 2FeS + SO_2$$

- The sulfides of copper and iron are partially oxidised.

$$2FeS + 3O_2 \rightarrow 2FeO + 2SO_2$$
$$2Cu_2S + 3O_2 \rightarrow 2Cu_2O + 2SO_2$$

(iii) Smelting: The roasted ore is mixed with coke and silica and transferred to a small blast furnace (Fig. 6.4). The mixture is heated in the presence of excess of air. The following changes occur in the blast furnace.

- The cuprous oxide reacts with ferrous sulfide.

$$FeS + Cu_2O \rightarrow FeO + Cu_2S$$

- Most of the iron sulfide is oxidised to ferrous oxide.

$$2FeS + 3O_2 \rightarrow 2FeO + 2SO_2$$

- Ferrous oxide combines with silica and forms ferrous silicate. By this reaction most of the iron is removed as slag.

$$FeO + SiO_2 \rightarrow \underset{\text{Ferrous silicate(slag)}}{FeSiO_3}$$

Fig. 6.4 Blast furnace

(iv) **Bessemerisation:** The molten matte from the blast furnace is transferred into a Bessemer converter (Fig. 6.5). During this process, the following reactions take place.

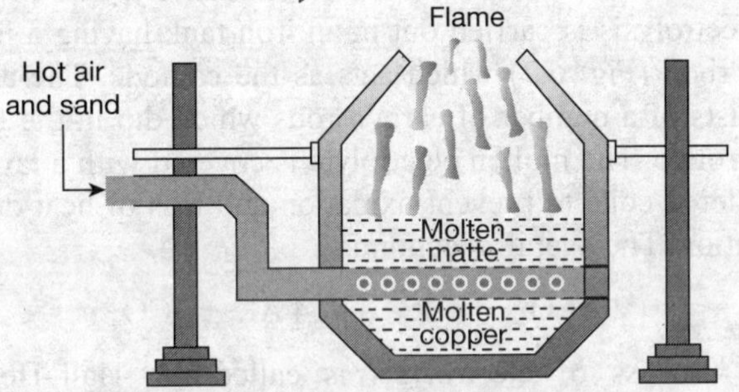

Fig. 6.5 Bessemer converter for copper

- Traces of ferrous sulfide present in the matte is oxidised to FeO which combines with silica to form slag.

$$2FeS + 3O_2 \rightarrow 2FeO + 2SO_2$$

$$FeO + SiO_2 \rightarrow FeSiO_3 \text{ (Slag)}$$

- Copper sulfide is partially oxidised to cuprous oxide which further reacts with remaining copper sulfide to form copper and sulfur dioxide.

$$2Cu_2S + 3O_2 \rightarrow 2Cu_2O + 2SO_2$$

$$Cu_2S + 2\,Cu_2O \rightarrow 6Cu + SO_2$$

Extraction of Copper from Non-sulfide Ores

The carbonate decomposes to form the oxide and the impurities either volatilise or are oxidised.

$$CuCO_3.Cu(OH)_2 \rightarrow 2CuO + CO_2 + H_2O$$

The oxide so formed is either reduced with carbon in a reverberatory furnace or leached with dilute H_2SO_4.

$$CuO + C \rightarrow Cu + CO$$

$$Cu_2O + C \rightarrow 2Cu + CO$$

$$\text{or } CuO + H_2SO_4 \rightarrow CuSO_4 + H_2O$$

(v) **Electrolytic refining:** The crude copper is further purified by the electrolytic method. In this method, a thin sheet of metal is made the cathode and the block of crude metal is made the anode. Both the electrodes are placed in an acidified copper sulfate solution (Fig. 6.5). When electric current is passed through the solution, impure copper from the anode goes into the solution and pure copper from the solution gets deposited on the cathode.

6.7 Extraction of Zinc from Zinc Oxide

Zinc is usually found in the combined state. Its chief ores are:

(i) Zinc blende	ZnS
(ii) Calamine	$ZnCO_3$
(iii) Zincite	ZnO
(iv) Willemite	Zn_2SiO_4

Extraction: Zinc is extracted from its ores by two methods—reduction process and electrolytic process.

6.7.1 Reduction Process

It involves the following steps.

(i) **Concentration:** When zinc blende is used, the powdered ore is concentrated by the froth floatation process. In the case of calamine ore, the concentration is done by the gravity process. If the ore contains iron oxide, it is removed by magnetic separation.

(ii) **Roasting:** The concentrated ore is roasted in the presence of excess of air at about 1200 K.

$$2ZnS + 3O_2 \rightarrow 2ZnO + 2SO_2$$

$$ZnS + 2O_2 \rightarrow ZnSO_4$$

$$2ZnSO_4 \rightarrow 2ZnO + 2SO_2 + O_2$$

$$ZnCO_3 \rightarrow ZnO + CO_2$$

The roasting is done in a reverberatory furnace.

(iii) **Reduction:** Zinc oxide is reduced to zinc by heating with crushed coke at 1673 K in vertical fire clay retorts.

$$ZnO + \underset{\text{(Coke)}}{C} \xrightarrow{1673\text{ K}} Zn + CO$$

The vapours of zinc formed are collected and condensed. It is evident from Fig. 6.6 that the intersection of (Zn, ZnO) and (C, CO) curves lies at a higher temperature than that of (Cu, Cu_2O) and (C and CO) curves. Therefore, the reduction of ZnO with coke is carried out at a higher temperature than that of Cu_2O.

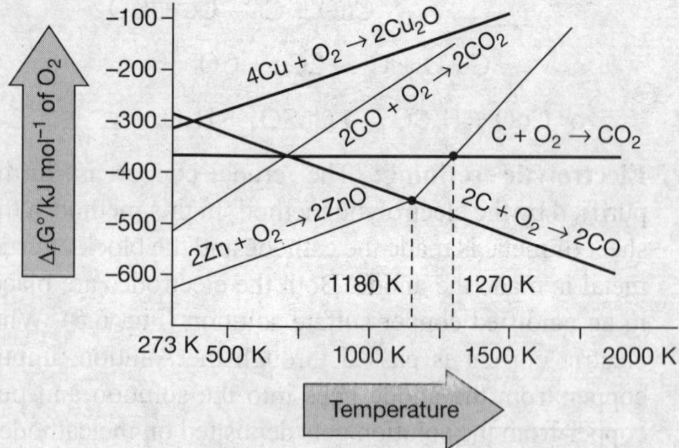

Fig. 6.6 Ellingham diagram showing the formation of Cu_2O from Cu, ZnO from Zn, CO from C and CO_2 from C and CO

(iv) **Refining:** The impure metal is refined by fractional distillation or by the electrolytic method.

- *Fractional distillation*: Impure zinc contains impurities of cadmium (BP = 1073 K), lead (BP = 2024 K) and iron (BP = 3273 K). The boiling point of zinc is 1183 K. The impure metal is distilled when zinc and cadmium with low boiling points distil over leaving behind lead and iron.
- *Electrolytic refining*: In this process, impure zinc is made the anode while a plate of pure zinc is made the cathode. The electrolyte is zinc sulfate containing a small amount of dilute sulfuric acid. On passing current, zinc from the electrolyte is deposited at the cathode while an equivalent amount of zinc from the anode goes into the electrolyte. Therefore, pure zinc is obtained on the cathode.

6.8 Electrochemical Principles of Metallurgy

The electrochemical principles of this method (electrolysis) can be understood in terms of the following equation,

$$\Delta G° = -nFE° \qquad (6.15)$$

where n is the number of electrons involved in the reduction process, $E°$ is the standard electrode potential of the redox couple (M/M^{n+}) present in the system. More reactive metals have large negative values of electrode potentials and hence are difficult to reduce. If the difference in the $E°$ values of two redox couples is positive, and consequently the $\Delta G°$ in Eq. 6.15 is negative, then the more reactive metal will displace the less reactive metal from the solution. The electrolytic method is used for the extraction of active metals like Na, Mg, Ca and Al.

6.9 Applications of Electrolysis to Metallurgy

The process of extraction of metals by electrolysis of their fused salts is called *electrometallurgy*. In this process, the electrons serve as the reducing agent.

6.9.1 Extraction of Aluminium from Alumina

The main ores of aluminium are:

(i) Bauxite	$Al_2O_3.2H_2O$
(ii) Cryolite	Na_3AlF_6
(iii) Feldspar	$KAlSi_3O_8$
(iv) Mica	$KAlSi_2O_{10}(OH)_2$

Extraction of Aluminium

Aluminium is generally extracted from bauxite ore, $Al_2O_3.2H_2O$.

Electrolysis of fused alumina

In this method, purified alumina is mixed with molten cryolite (Na_3AlF_6) or fluorspar (CaF_2) and is electrolysed in an iron tank lined inside with carbon. The molten cryolite (Na_3AlF_6) decreases the melting point to about 1173 K and also increases the electrical conductivity. The process of electrolysis is carried out in an iron tank having a lining of carbon (Fig. 6.7) which acts as the cathode. The anode consists of a number of carbon rods which dip in the fused electrolyte. The molten electrolyte is covered with a layer of powdered coke to prevent oxidation and loss of heat due to radiation. The overall reaction is

$$2\,Al_2O_3 \;+\; 3C \;\rightarrow\; 4\,Al \;+ 3CO_2$$

This process of electrolysis is called the Hall–Heroult process. During electrolysis, the following reactions occur:

- *Cathode*: $Al^{3+}(melt) + 3\,e^- \rightarrow Al(l)$
- *Anode*: $C(s) + O^{2-}(melt) \rightarrow CO(g) + 2\,e^-$
  $C(s) + 2\,O^{2-}(melt) \rightarrow CO_2(g) + 4e^-$

Therefore, aluminium is liberated at the cathode.

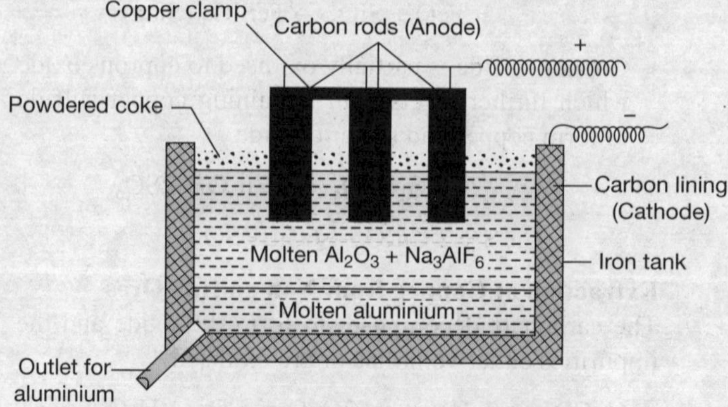

Fig. 6.7 Electrolysis of fused alumina

6.9.2 Extraction of Copper from Low Grade Ores and Scrap

The process of electrometallurgy can be applied to the isolation of copper from low grade ores. The ore is leached by a suitable acid. The solution containing Cu^{2+} ions is treated by either scrap iron or by hydrogen. The Cu^{2+} ions are reduced to the metallic form.

$$Cu^{2+}(aq) + Fe(s) \rightarrow Cu(s) + Fe^{2+}(aq);\ Cu^{2+}(aq) + H_2(g) \rightarrow Cu(s) + 2\,H^+(aq)$$

$E°$ for the above two reactions are positive.

$$\text{(i)}\ Cu^{2+}(aq) + 2e \rightarrow Cu(s);\ E^\circ_{red} = 0.34\text{ V}$$
$$Fe(s) \rightarrow Fe^{2+}(aq) + 2e;\ E^\circ_{ox} = 0.44\text{ V}$$
$$Cu^{2+}(aq) + Fe(s) \rightarrow Cu(s) + Fe^{2+}(aq);\ E^\circ = 0.78\text{ V}$$

$$\text{(ii)}\ Cu^{2+}(aq) + 2e \rightarrow Cu(s);\ E^\circ_{red} = 0.34\text{ V}$$
$$H_2(g) \rightarrow 2\,H^+(aq) + 2e;\ E^\circ_{ox} = 0.0\text{ V}$$
$$Cu^{2+}(aq) + H_2(g) \rightarrow Cu(s) + 2H^+(aq);\ E^\circ = 0.34\text{ V}$$

Thus, the $\Delta G°$ for these reactions have negative values and therefore, the reduction of Cu^{2+} ions occurs in solution.

6.9.3 Extraction of Non-Metals by Oxidation

Chemical oxidation of a mineral is sometimes used to obtain a non-metal. In such cases, a stronger oxidising agent is used to remove electrons from the non-metal anion to give the free non-metal.

$$2I^-(aq) + Cl_2(g) \rightarrow 2Cl^-(aq) + I_2(s)$$
$$2\,Br^-(aq) + Cl_2(g) \rightarrow 2Cl^-(aq) + Br_2(s)$$

6.9.4 Extraction of Metals both by Oxidation and Reduction

Gold and silver

Extraction of gold and silver involves leaching of the metals present in the ore with CN^- ions. This is also an *oxidation reaction* because during the leaching process, Ag is oxidised to Ag^+ and Au to Au^+ which then combine with the CN^- ions to form their respective soluble complexes.

$$\underset{\text{Silver}}{4\,Ag(s)} + 8\,CN^-(aq) + 2\,H_2O(l) + O_2(g) \rightarrow \underset{\text{Soluble complex}}{4\,[Ag(CN)_2]^-(aq)} + 4\,OH^-(aq)$$

$$\underset{\text{Gold}}{4\,Au(s)} + 8\,CN^-(aq) + 2\,H_2O(l) + O_2(g) \rightarrow \underset{\text{Soluble complex}}{4\,[Au(CN)_2]^-(aq)} + 4\,OH^-(aq)$$

The metals are then recovered from these complexes by *reduction* or displacement method using a more electropositive metal (zinc). In these displacement reactions, zinc acts as the reducing agent.

6.10 Refining

Metals obtained by the application of various methods from the concentrated ores are usually impure. They may be associated with small amounts of

- unchanged ore,
- other metals produced by the simultaneous reduction of their compounds originally present in the ore,
- non-metals like silicon, carbon, phosphorus,
- residual slag, and
- residual flux.

The following refining processes may be applied depending upon the nature of the metal under treatment and the nature of the impurities.

6.10.1 Liquation

This method is used for the purification of such metals that contain impurities which are less fusible than the metals themselves. That is, the melting points of the metals are lower than those of the impurities. The crude metal is heated in an inert atmosphere of carbon monoxide on the slopping hearth of a reverberatory furnace (Fig. 6.8). The metal melts and flows down into the receiver leaving the infusible impurities on the heath. Metals like *tin* and *lead* are purified by this method.

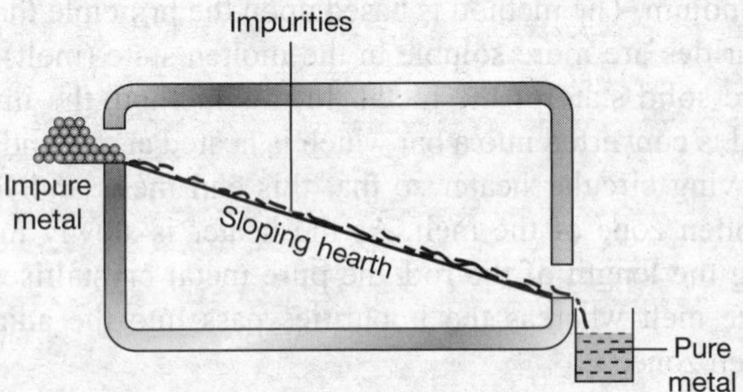

Fig. 6.8 Liquation process

6.10.2 Distillation

This process is useful for those metals which are highly volatile and have low boiling points. Metals like zinc and mercury can be purified by such distillation processes. The impure metal is heated in a retort and its vapours are separately condensed in a receiver.

6.10.3 Electrolytic Refining

In this method, the impure metal is made the anode. A strip of the same metal in pure form is used as the cathode (Fig. 6.9). They are put in a suitable electrolytic bath containing a soluble salt of the same metal. The more basic metal remains in the solution and the less basic ones go to the anode mud. This process is also explained using the concept of electrode potential, over potential, and Gibbs energy. The reactions are:

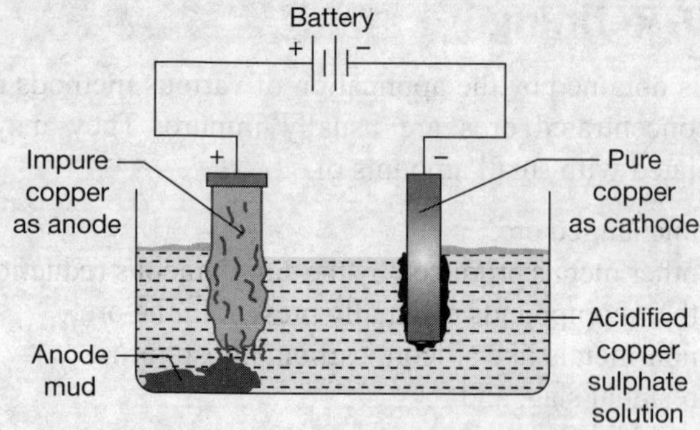

Fig. 6.9 Electrolytic-refining of copper

- Anode: $M(s) \rightarrow M^{n+}(aq) + ne^-$
- Cathode: $M^{n+}(aq) + ne^- \rightarrow M(s)$

Copper is refined using this electrolytic method.

Electrolytic Refining of Silver

The anode is made of impure silver, the cathode is pure silver and the electrolyte is an aqueous solution of $AgNO_3$ + 1% HNO_3. Silver from the anode (impure silver) dissolves and pure silver deposits at the cathode.

6.10.4 Zone Refining (Fractional Crystallisation)

This method is extremely useful for producing metals of very high purity such as germanium, silicon, boron, gallium and indium. The method is based upon the principle that the impurities are more soluble in the molten state (melt) than in the solid state of the metal. In this method, the impure metal is converted into a bar which is heated at one end with a moving circular heater so that this end melts and forms a molten zone of the melt. As the heater is slowly moved along the length of the rod, the pure metal crystallises out of the melt whereas the impurities pass into the adjacent molten zone.

6.10.5 Vapour Phase Refining

In this refining method, the metal is firstly converted into its volatile compound and collected elsewhere. After that it is decomposed to pure metal.

(i) Mond's process: In this process, nickel is heated in a stream of carbon monoxide forming a volatile complex—nickel tetracarbonyl.

$$\underset{\text{Impure nickel}}{Ni(s)} + 4\,CO(g) \xrightarrow{330\text{–}350\text{ K}}$$

$$\underset{\text{Nickel tetracarbonyl}}{Ni(CO)_4(g)} \xrightarrow{450\text{–}470\text{ K}} \underset{\text{Pure nickel}}{Ni(s)} + 4\,CO(g)$$

The carbonyl is subjected to higher temperature so that it is decomposed giving the pure metal.

(ii) Van Arkel method: This method is very useful for removing all the oxygen and nitrogen present in the form of impurities in certain metals such as Zr and Ti.

$$\underset{\text{Impure zirconium}}{Zr(s)} + 2\,I_2(g) \xrightarrow{870\text{ K}}$$

$$ZrI_4(g) \xrightarrow[\text{Tungsten filament}]{2075\text{ K}} \underset{\text{Pure zirconium}}{Zr(s)} + 2\,I_2(g)$$

6.10.6 Chromatographic Methods

Chromatography is essentially a physical technique. The method is based upon the principle that the different components of a mixture are adsorbed to different extents on an adsorbent. It consists of two phases, the stationary phase and the mobile phase. The stationary phase can be either a *solid* (such as alumina, silica gel) or tightly bound *liquid* on a solid support (such as paper in which the liquid water is held by the solid cellulose). The mobile phase, on the other hand, can be a liquid, gas or a super critical fluid such as CO_2. Depending upon the physical state of the stationary phase and the moving phase and also on the process of passage of the moving phase, chromatography can be of several types such as column chromatography, partition chromatography, gas chromatography, and so on.

Column Chromatography

This is based on the adsorption phenomenon. The extent of adsorption of various constituents present in a mixture liquid (moving phase) varies with a given adsorbent (stationary phase). The common adsorbents used are alumina, silica gel, magnesium oxide, cellulose powder or active animal charcoal.

6.11 Common Alloys of Aluminium, Copper, Zinc and Iron

Table 6.2 Alloys of aluminium

Alloy	Composition	Important properties	Uses
1. Aluminium bronze	Al 95%, Cu 5%	Light strong alloy with golden lustre, resistant to corrosion	Coins, utensils, jewellery, picture frames
2. Magnalium	Al 95%, Mg 5%	Light, tough and strong	Light instruments, balance beams, pressure cookers
3. Duralumin	Al 95%, Cu 4%, Mg 0.5%, Mn 0.5%	Light, tough, ductile, resistant to corrosive action	Making aeroplanes, automobile parts, pressure cookers
4. Alnico	Al 12%, Fe 60% Ni 20%, Co 8%	Strongly magnetic	Permanent magnets

Table 6.3 Alloys of copper

Alloy	Composition	Uses
1. Brass	Cu 60%, Zn 40%	For making utensils, condenser tubes, wires, parts of machinery
2. Bronze	Cu 80%, Zn 10%, Sn 10%	For making cooking utensils, statues, coins
3. German silver	Cu 25%–30%, Zn 25%–30%, Ni 40%–50%	For making silver wires, resistance wires
4. Aluminium bronze	Cu 90%, Al 10%	Coins, picture frames, golden powder for paints, cheap jewellery
5. Bell metal	Cu 80%, Sn 20%	Bells, gongs
6. Gun metal	Cu 88%, Sn 10%, Zn 2%	Gears, bearings, castings
7. Phosphor bronze	Cu 95%, Sn 4.8%, P 0.2%	Springs, electrical equipment
8. Monel metal	C 30%, Ni 67%, Fe and Mn 3%	Acid pumps and acid containers
9. Gold copper alloy	Au 90%, Cu 10%	Gold coins, jewellery, watch cases, spectacle rims
10. Constantan	Cu 60%, Ni 40%	Electrical apparatus

Table 6.4 Alloys of steel

Alloy steel	Composition	Properties	Uses
1. Stainless steel	Fe73%, Cr 18%, Ni 8% and carbon 1%	Resists corrosion	For making utensils, cutlery, cycles, automobiles, pens
2. Nickel steel	Fe 96%–98%, Ni 2%–4%	Resistant to corrosion, hard and elastic	For making cables, automobiles, aeroplane parts
3. Chrome steel	F 96%–98%, Cr 2%–4%	High tensile strength	For making axles, ball bearings, cutting tools, crushing machines
4. Invar	Fe 64%, Ni 36%	Practically no coefficient of expansion	For making watches, meter scales, pendulum rods
5. Alnico	Fe 60%, Al 12%, Ni 20%, Co 8%	Highly magnetic	For making permanent magnets
6. Tungsten steel	Fe 94%, W 5%, C 1%	Hard, resistant to corrosion	High-speed cutting tools, springs
7. Silicon steel	Fe 85%, Si 15%	Hard and resistant to acids	Pumps and pipes for carrying acids
8. Manganese	Fe 86%, Mn 14%	Extremely hard	Rock crushers, burglar proof safes
9. Steel	Mn 13%, C 87%	Resistant to wear and tear	Rail road trucks

Exercises

OBJECTIVE QUESTIONS

Occurrence of Elements

1. The most abundant transition metal in human body is
(a) copper (b) iron
(c) zinc (d) manganese

2. The metal which is found in the native state is
(a) Au (b) Na (c) Ca (d) Al

3. Which of the following metals is not found in the free state?
(a) Na (b) Au (c) Ag (d) Pb

4. Which metal is found in the free state?
(a) iron (b) gold
(c) aluminium (d) sodium

5. Silicon is the main constituent of
(a) alloys (b) rocks
(c) animals (d) vegetables

6. What is believed to be the second most common element in the universe?

(a) helium (b) hydrogen
(c) nitrogen (d) silicon

7. Which one of the following is the most abundant element in the universe?

(a) nitrogen (b) hydrogen
(c) oxygen (d) silicon

8. The region in which the main metals are found on earth is called the

(a) atomophile (b) lithophile
(c) chalcophile (d) siderophile

9. The most abundant metal ion present in the human body is

(a) Zn^{2+} (b) Ca^{2+} (c) Na^+ (d) Fe^{2+}

10. Iron is found in the earth's crust as oxides, carbonates and sulfates. Out of these, oxides of iron are employed for extraction of the metal. Which of the following are the ores of iron?

(a) carbonates (b) oxides
(c) sulfides (d) all

11. The ore of aluminium is

(a) carnallite (b) malachite
(c) galena (d) bauxite

12. Which of the following is an oxide ore?

(a) malachite (b) haematite
(c) copper glance (d) zinc blende

13. Which of the following does not contain silicon?

(a) kaolin (b) agate (c) ruby (d) quartz

14. The chief impurity present in red bauxite is

(a) SiO_2 (b) Fe_2O_3 (c) K_2SO_4 (d) NaF

15. The most important ore of tin is

(a) cassiterite (b) cryolite
(c) cerussite (d) none of these

16. The formula for agate is

(a) Na_2SiO_3 (b) $K_2O.SiO_2.Al_2O_3$
(c) SiO_2 (d) CaF_2

17. Match the following columns

Column I (Metal)	Column II (Ore)
A. Aluminium	Bauxite
B. Copper	Dolomite
C. Potassium	Pyrites
D. Magnesium	Pitchblende
E. Radium	Sylvine

Codes:

	A	B	C	D	E
(a)	1	3	4	5	2
(b)	1	3	4	2	5
(c)	4	5	2	1	3
(d)	4	2	1	5	3
(e)	1	3	5	2	4

18. A titanium-containing mineral found in our country is

(a) bauxite (b) dolomite
(c) chalcopyrites (d) ilmenite

19. The ore pitchblende, is the main source of

(a) Ra (b) Ce
(c) Th (d) both (a) and (c)

20. Which of the following does not contain Mg?

(a) magnetite (b) asbestos
(c) magnesite (d) carnallite

21. Which of the following ores is used for industrial extraction of aluminium in India?

(a) corundum (b) kaolin
(c) cryolite (d) bauxite

22. Bauxite is an oxide ore of

(a) barium (b) boron
(c) bismuth (d) aluminium

23. An important oxide ore of iron is

(a) hematite (b) siderite
(c) pyrites (d) malachite

24. Aluminium is the most abundant metal in the earth's crust; yet it is obtained from bauxite because

(a) bauxite is available in large quantities
(b) of easy extraction of aluminium from it
(c) bauxite contains maximum aluminium
(d) bauxite is less impure

25. Sapphire is mineral of

(a) Cu (b) Zn (c) Al (d) Mg

26. Which of the following is a carbonate ore?

(a) pyrolusite (b) malachite
(c) diaspore (d) cassiterite

27. Cerussite is an ore of

(a) Na (b) Cu (c) Pb (d) Fe

28. Composition of azurite mineral is

(a) $CuCO_3CuO$ (b) $Cu(HCO_3)_2.Cu(OH)_2$
(c) $2\ CuCO_3.Cu(OH)_2$ (d) $CuCO_3.2Cu(OH)_2$

29. Metal which can be extracted from all the three—dolomite, magnesite and carnallite is

(a) Na (b) K (b) Mg (d) Ca

30. Which of the following is not an ore of lead?
(a) galena (a) anglesite
(c) calamine (d) cerussite

31. The salt which is least likely to be found in minerals is
(a) chloride (b) sulfate (c) sulfide (d) nitrate

32. Which of the following is not present in minerals?
(a) KNO_3 (b) $CaCO_3$ (c) NaCl (d) CaO

33. The most abundant metal in the earth's crust is
(a) calcium (b) aluminium
(c) iron (d) magnesium

34. The metal that occurs in the native state as well as in the combined form is
(a) silver (b) magnesium
(c) aluminium (d) manganese

35. Sea weeds are an important source of
(a) chlorine (b) bromine (c) iodine (d) zinc

36. The element vanadium is present in
(a) sea weeds (b) hemoglobin
(c) eyes of animals (d) none of these

37. Living organisms contain iron in
(a) chlorophyll (b) hemoglobin
(c) eyes of animals (d) none of these

38. Most abundant element in the earth's crust by weight is
(a) oxygen (b) silicon
(c) aluminium (d) iron

39. Most abundant element in the earth's crust in terms of number of atoms per 100 atoms is
(a) oxygen (b) silicon
(c) aluminium (d) hydrogen

40. Which is correct?
(a) galena: Mg_2CO_3
(b) cassiterite: $CaCO_3.MgCO_3$
(c) dolomite: SnO_2
(d) magnesite: $MgCO_3$

41. Which is correct?
(a) aluminium: calamine (b) copper: malachite
(c) magnesium: calamine (d) zinc: carnallite

42. Which one of the following does not occur as sulfide ore?
(a) Zn (b) Cr (c) Ag
(d) Fe (e) Hg

43. Cinnabar is
(a) HgS (b) PbS (c) SnO_2 (d) $PbCO_3$

44. Indicate the mineral from which copper is manufactured
(a) galena (b) cuprite
(c) sphalerite (d) chalcopyrites

45. Among the following statements, the incorrect one is
(a) calamine and siderite are carbonated
(b) argentite and cuprite are oxide
(c) zinc blende and pyrites are sulfides
(d) malachite and azurite are ores of copper

46. Black jack is an ore of
(a) Cr (b) Sn (c) Zn (d) Ni

47. Identify the ore not containing iron
(a) limonite (b) siderite
(c) carnallite (d) chalcopyrites

48. What are the metal ions present in carnallite?
(a) Mg, K (b) Al, Na (c) Na, Mg (d) Zn, Mg

49. Apatite is an ore of
(a) fluorine (b) chlorine (c) bromine (d) iodine

50. Important ore of Mg is
(a) gypsum (b) carnallite
(c) magnetite (d) carnotite

51. An example of a halide ore is
(a) galena (b) bauxite (c) cinnabar (d) cryolite

52. Which of the following minerals does not contain Al?
(a) cryolite (b) mica (c) feldspar (d) fluorspar

53. Cryolite is an ore of
(a) iron (b) silver (c) zinc (d) aluminium

54. Which one of the following ores is a chloride?
(a) horn silver (b) zincite
(c) bauxite (d) feldspar

55. The ore carnallite is represented by the formula
(a) $Na_2Al_2O_3$ (b) Na_3AlF_6
(c) $KCl.MgCl_2.6H_2O$ (d) Fe_3O_4

56. Of the following substances, the one that does not contain oxygen is
(a) bauxite (b) epsom salt
(c) cryolite (d) dolomite

57. Which of the following ore is not an ore of Al?
(a) mica (b) anglesite
(c) orthoclase (d) beryl

58. Which of the following minerals is not an ore of aluminium?
(a) bauxite (b) gypsum
(c) cryolite (d) corundum

59. Which of the following is not an ore of magnesium?
(a) magnesite (b) dolomite
(c) gypsum (d) carnallite

60. Asbestos is
(a) sodium aluminium silicate
(b) calcium aluminium silicate
(c) calcium magnesium silicate
(d) sodium borosilicate

61. Match the following columns

Column I	Column II
A. Feldspar	$2\,AgSbS_2$
B. Asbestos	$Al_2O_3.H_2O$
C. Pyrargyrite	$MgSO_4.H_2O$
D. Diaspore	$KAlSi_3O_8$
	$CaMg_3(SiO_3)_4$

Codes:

	A	B	C	D
(a)	4	5	2	1
(b)	4	5	1	2
(c)	4	1	3	2
(d)	2	5	4	1

62. Lapis lazuli is a blue coloured precious stone. It is mineral of the class
(a) sodiumalumino silicate (b) zinc cobaltate
(c) basic copper carbonate (d) Prussian blue

63. Most of the metals which occur in the native state
(a) are very reactive
(b) do not form ionic compounds
(c) are not reactive
(d) have low density

64. An ore of aluminium is
(a) Na_3AF_6 (b) $Al_2O_3.2H_2O$
(c) Al_2O_3 (d) $Al_2O_3.H_2O$

65. Which of the following elements occur free in nature?
(a) iodine (b) sulfur
(c) phosphorus (d) magnesium

Concentration of Ores

66. The common impurity present in bauxite is
(a) CuO (b) ZnO (c) Fe_2O_3 (d) Cr_2O_3

67. Bauxite ore is made up of $Al_2O_3 + SiO_2 + TiO_2 + Fe_2O_3$. This ore is treated with conc. NaOH solution at 500 K and 35 bar pressure for few hours and filtered hot. In the filtrate the species present, are
(a) $NaAl(OH)_4$ only (b) $Na_2Ti(OH)_6$ only
(c) $NaAl(OH)_4$ and Na_2SiO_3 both
(d) Na_2SiO_3 only

68. The process of ore dressing is carried out to
(a) remove the siliceous materials
(b) add flux to the mineral
(c) covert the ore to oxide
(d) remove the poisonous impurities

69. Gravity separation method is based upon
(a) preferential washing of ores and gangue particles
(b) difference in densities of ore particles and impurities
(c) difference in chemical properties of ore particles and impurities
(c) none of the above

70. Copper pyrites is concentrated by
(a) froth floatation process
(b) gravity separation
(c) distillation (d) fractionation

71. The substance used as an activator in the froth floatation process is
(a) potassium ethyl xanthate
(b) sodium cyanide
(c) copper sulfate (d) copper sulfate

72. Choose the incorrect statement.
(a) Hydraulic washing is a method of ore dressing.
(b) Hydraulic washing is also known as levigation.
(c) Gravity separation is generally not carried out by using a hydraulic classifier.
(d) Gravity separation is generally carried out by using a Wilfley table.

73. Gravity separation process is used for the concentration of
(a) calamine (b) hematite
(c) chalcopyrites (d) bauxite

74. Rutile is separated from chlorapatite by
(a) froth floatation method
(b) levigation
(c) magnetic separation method
(d) electrostatic separation method

75. Which of the following ores when associated with silica and other impurities cannot be separated by the magnetic separation method?
(a) hematite (Fe_2O_3) (b) magnetite (Fe_3O_4)
(c) siderite ($FeCO_3$) (d) cuprite (Cu_2O)

76. Cassiterite is concentrated by
(a) levigation
(b) electromagnetic separation
(c) floatation (d) liquefaction

77. An ore of tin containing $FeCrO_4$ is concentrated by
(a) magnetic separation (b) froth floatation
(c) electrostatic method (d) gravity separation

78. Ores like magnetite or ferrous tungstates in tin ores are concentrated by

(a) froth floatation (b) magnetic separation
(c) gravity separation (d) electrostatic separation

79. Wolframite ore is separated from tinstone ore by the process of

(a) roasting
(b) electromagnetic separation
(c) smelting (d) calcination

80. Select the ore that is not concentrated by the froth floatation process?

(a) cinnabar (b) pyrolusite
(c) zinc blende (d) copper pyrites

81. Sodium cyanide is added as a depressant in the froth floatation process when the ore contains a mixture of ZnS and PbS. This is because

(a) $Pb(CN)_2$ gets precipitated without any effect on ZnS
(b) ZnS forms a soluble complex $Na_2[Zn(CN)_4]$, while PbS forms froth
(c) PbS forms a soluble complex $Na_2[Pb(CN)_4]$, while ZnS forms froth
(d) $Zn(CN)_2$ gets precipitated without any effect on PbS

82. Which one of the following ores is best concentrated by the froth floatation method?

(a) magnetite (b) siderite
(c) galena (d) malachite

83. Which of the following statements is incorrect?

(a) A furnace lined with hematite is used to convert cast iron to wrought iron.
(b) Collectors enhance the wettability of mineral particles during froth floatation.
(c) In vapour phase refining, the metal should from a volatile compound.
(d) Copper is extracted by hydrometallurgy from its lower grade ores.

84. The ore that is concentrated by froth floatation process is

(a) cinnabar (b) bauxite
(c) malachite (d) zincite

85. Copper pyrites is concentrated by

(a) electromagnetic method
(b) gravity method
(c) froth floatation process
(d) all of these

86. Froth floatation process is used for the concentration of

(a) oxide ores (b) sulfide ores
(c) chloride ores (d) amalgams

87. A process used for the concentration of ore is

(a) froth floatation (b) roasting
(c) electrolysis (d) bessemerisation

88. The froth floatation process for the concentration of ores is an illustration of the practical application of

(a) adsorption (b) absorption
(c) coagulation (d) sedimentation

89. The froth floatation method is successful in separating impurities from ores because

(a) the pure ore is lighter than water containing additives likes pine oil and cresylic acid
(b) the pure ore is soluble in water containing additives like pine oil and cresylic acid
(c) the impurities are soluble in water containing additives like pine oil and cresylic acid
(d) the pure ore is not as easily wetted by water as by pine oil and cresylic acid

90. Froth floatation process is used for the concentration of

(a) chalcopyrites (b) bauxite
(c) haematite (d) calamine

91. Which one of the following benefaction processes is used for the mineral, $Al_2O_3.2H_2O$?

(a) froth floatation (b) leaching
(c) liquation (d) magnetic separation

92. Leaching process in the extraction of aluminium has a great significance because (select the wrong statement)

(a) the impurities of silica (SiO_2), iron oxide (Fe_2O_3) and titanium oxide (TiO_2)are removed from alumina (Al_2O_3)
(b) the regent used for leaching is 40% NaOH at 473–523 K which is simple and common
(c) alumina dissolves as sodium meta aluminate leaving SiO_2, Fe_2O_3, TiO_2 and other impurities behind
(d) pure alumina is obtained from the bauxite ore

93. Which one of the following ores is concentrated by a chemical leaching method?

(a) galena (b) copper pyrites (c) cinnabar
(d) argentite (e) copper glance

94. In aluminium extraction by the Baeyer's process, alumina is extracted from bauxite by sodium hydroxide at high temperature and pressure.

$$Al_2O_3(s) + 2\,OH^-(aq) \rightarrow 2\,AlO_2^-(aq) + H_2O(l)$$

Solid impurities such as Fe_2O_3 and SiO_2 are removed and then $Al(OH)_4^-$.

$$2\,Al(OH)_4^- \rightarrow Al_2O_3.3\,H_2O(s) + 2\,OH^-(aq)$$

In the industrial world,

(a) carbon dioxide is added to precipitate the alumina
(b) temperature and pressure are dropped and the supersaturated solution seeded

(c) both (a) and (b) are practised
(d) the water is evaporated

95. Wolframite is separated from cassiterite by
(a) froth floatation method
(b) levigation
(c) electromagnetic separation method
(d) electrostatic separation method

96. Cyanide process is used in the leaching extraction of
(a) Au (b) Ag
(c) both (a) and (b) (d) Cu

Extraction of Crude Metal from Concentrated Ore

97. Heating of ore in the presence of air to remove sulfur impurities is called
(a) calcination (b) roasting
(c) smelting (d) none of these

98. Roasting is generally done in the case of the following:
(a) oxide ores (b) silicate ores
(c) sulfide ores (d) carbonate ores

99. Heating of pyrites in air for oxidation of sulfur is called
(a) roasting (b) calcination
(c) smelting (d) slagging

100. When copper pyrites is roasted in excess of air, a mixture of CuO + FeO is formed. FeO is present as impurities. This can be removed as slag during the reduction of CuO. The flux added to form slag is
(a) SiO_2 which is an acidic flux
(b) limestone, which is a basic flux
(c) SiO_2, which is a basic flux
(d) CaO, which is a basic flux

101. Matte contains mainly
(a) Cu_2S and FeS (b) CuS and Fe_2S_3
(c) Fe (d) Cu_2S

102. The process of heating the ore strongly in excess of air so that the volatile impurities are removed and the ore is changed to an oxide is known as
(a) calcination (b) roasting
(c) froth floatation (d) leaching

103. Roasting of copper pyrites ore is for the following purposes
(a) to burn off sulfur, arsenic and antimony as oxides and convert all the iron and copper to their oxides
(b) to burn off arsenic and antimony as oxides and burn off sulfur so that enough of it remains to combine with all the copper
(c) to burn off As and Sb as oxides and burn off sulfur partially to leave enough to combine with Cu and Fe and Cu_2S and FeS and to convert partially the iron and copper to oxides
(d) to melt arsenic and antimony sulfidesand remove them by liquation and to burn off sulfur partially to leave enough to combine with copper and iron

104. Which of the following ores is subjected to roasting during metallurgical operations for getting the metal oxide?
(a) horn silver (b) zinc blende
(c) malachite (d) limonite

105. The metallurgical process in which a metal is obtained in a fused state is called
(a) smelting (b) roasting
(c) calcinations (d) froth floatation

106. In the metallurgy of zinc, flux is not used because
(a) zinc ore has no impurities
(b) zinc is volatile hence easily separated
(c) zinc reacts with flux
(d) flux is volatile

107. Extraction of zinc from zinc blende is achieved by
(a) electrolytic reduction
(b) roasting followed by reduction with carbon
(c) roasting followed by reduction with another metal
(d) roasting followed by self-reduction

108. Which is not a basic flux?
(a) $CaCO_3$ (b) lime (c) SiO_2 (d) CaO

109. The cheap compound having a high melting point used in furnaces is
(a) PbO (b) CaO (c) HgO (d) ZnO

110. Smelting is the term for the process in which
(a) the ore is heated in the absence of air
(b) the ore is cold
(c) the ore is heated in the presence of air
(d) the ore is melted

111. Which of the following process involves smelting?
(a) $ZnCO_3 \rightarrow ZnO + CO_2$
(b) $Fe_2O_3 + 3\,C \rightarrow 2\,Fe + 3\,CO$
(c) $2\,PbS + 3\,O_2 \rightarrow 2\,PbO + SO_2$
(d) $Al_2O_3.2H_2O \rightarrow Al_2O_3 + 2\,H_2O$

112. A reverberatory furnace is employed in the metallurgical process mainly for
(a) reduction of oxide ores
(b) smelting of sulfide ores
(c) conversion of chloride to sulfate
(d) getting magnetic materials

113. Calcination is used in metallurgy for the removal of
(a) water and sulfide (b) water and CO_2
(c) CO_2 and H_2S (d) H_2O and H_2S

114. The process of converting hydrated alumina into anhydrous alumina is called

(a) roasting (b) smelting
(c) dressing (d) calcination

115. When limestone is heated strongly, it gives off CO_2. In metallurgy this process is known as
(a) calcination (b) roasting
(c) smelting (d) ore dressing

116. The role of calcination in metallurgical operations is
(a) to remove moisture
(b) to decompose carbonate
(c) to drive off organic matter
(d) to achieve all the above

117. The highest temperature is achieved in which type of furnace?
(a) blast (b) reverberatoy
(c) electric (d) muffle

118. Which one of the following statements is false?
(a) During roasting, moisture is removed from the ore.
(b) The ore is freed from almost all non-metallic impurities
(c) Calcination of the ore is carried out in the absence of any blast of air.
(d) The concentrated zinc blende is subjected to calcination during its extraction by pyrometallurgy.

119. Roasted tinstone ore after washing with water is known as
(a) block tin (b) white tin
(c) black tin (d) granulated tin

120. Which statement is correct?
(a) Gangue is carefully chosen to combine with the slag present in the ore to produce easily fusible flux to carry away the impurities.
(b) Slag is carefully chosen to combine with the flux present in the ore to produce easily fusible gangue to carry away the impurities.
(c) Gangue is carefully chosen to combine with the flux present in the ore to produce easily fusible slag to carry away the impurities.
(d) Flux is carefully chosen to combine with the gangue present in the ore to produce easily fusible slag to carry away the impurities.

121. Flux is used to remove
(a) silica (b) metal oxide
(c) all impurities from ores
(d) silica and undesirable metal oxide

122. Which of the following fluxes is used to remove acidic impurities in metallurgical processes?
(a) silica (b) limestone
(c) sodium chloride (d) sodium carbonate

123. Refractory materials are used in the construction of furnaces because
(a) they can withstand high temperature
(b) they are chemically inert
(c) their melting point is high
(d) none of these

124. How is limestone used in Fe extraction?
(a) for oxidation of Fe ore
(b) for reduction of Fe ore
(c) for formation of slag
(d) for purification of Fe formed

125. In a lime kiln, to get higher yield of CO_2, the measure that can be taken is
(a) to remove CaO
(b) to add more $CaCO_3$
(c) to maintain high temperature
(d) to pump out CO_2

126. Which out of the following is used as a reducing agent in smelting?
(a) C (b) Al
(c) Zn (d) none of these

127. Blast furnace is employed in the smelting of oxide ore with coke and flux in the metallurgy of
(a) iron (b) copper (c) lead (d) all the above

128. Furnaces are lined with calcium oxide because
(a) it gives off oxygen on heating
(b) it gives strong light on heating
(c) it is refractory and basic
(d) it is not affected by acids

129. Carbon reduction process is used for the extraction of
(a) Hg (b) Al (c) Cr (d) Fe

130. Which one of the following metals is extracted by thermal reduction process?
(a) copper (b) iron
(c) aluminium (d) magnesium

131. Chemical reduction is not suitable for converting
(a) bauxite into aluminium
(b) cuprite into copper
(c) hematite into iron
(d) zinc oxide into zinc

132. Choose the temperature range (condition) in the following under which magnesium could reduce alumina.
(a) at 1623 K (b) above 1623 K
(c) below 1623 K (d) at 1673 K

133. In practice, magnesium metal is not used for the reduction of aluminium in the metallurgy of aluminium. This is because

(a) the reaction between Mg and Al_2O_3 is thermodynamically not feasible
(b) magnesium is a much costlier metal than aluminium
(c) the process will be more economical
(d) Mg is less electropositive than Al

134. Which of the following factors is of no significance for roasting sulfide ores to the oxides and not subjecting the sulfide ores to carbon reduction directly?
(a) CO_2 is more volatile than CS_2
(b) metal sulfides are thermodynamically more stable than CS_2
(c) CO_2 is thermodynamically more stable than CS_2
(d) metal sulfides are less stable than the corresponding oxides

135. The reduction of a metal oxide is easier if the metal formed is in the liquid state at the temperature of reduction because (select the wrong statement in the following)
(a) the entropy is lower if the metal is in the liquid state than when it is in the solid state
(b) ΔS of the reduction process is more on +ve side when the metal formed is in the liquid state and the metal oxide being reduced is in the solid state
(c) the value of $\Delta G°$ becomes more on the negative side and the reduction becomes easier
(d) the value of $T\Delta S$ increases and that of ΔH remains constant

136. Under certain conditions, Mg can reduce SiO_2 and Si can reduce MgO. The correct conditions are:
(a) below 1973 K, Si can reduce MgO to Mg
(b) above 1973 K, Mg can reduce SiO_2 to Si
(c) below 1973 K, Mg can reduce SiO_2 but above 1973 K, Si being less electropositive cannot reduce MgO
(d) below 1973 K, Mg can reduce SiO_2 but above 1973 K, Si can reduce MgO

137. From the Ellingham diagram, select which out of C and CO is a better reducing agent under the conditions given below:
(a) CO below 983 K (b) C below 983 K
(c) CO above 983 K
(d) both C and CO below 983 K

138. Among the metals Cr, Mn, Fe, Ba and Mg, the one that cannot be obtained by the reduction of its metal oxide by aluminium is
(a) Cr (b) Fe (c) Mn
(d) Ba (e) Mg

139. The reaction $Cr_2O_3 + 2Al \rightarrow Al_2O_3 + 2Cr$ ($\Delta G° = -421$ kJ) is thermodynamically feasible as is apparent from the Gibbs energy value. But it does not take place at room temperature because.
(a) Al is less electropositive than Cr
(b) Cr has more affinity for O_2 than Al
(c) in the given redox reaction, all the reactants and products are solids at room temperature, therefore, there does not exist any equilibrium between them and hence the reaction does not occur at room temperature. However, at high temperature, when Cr metals, the value of $T\Delta S$ increases. As a result, the value of $\Delta_r G°$ becomes more negative and hence the reaction proceeds rapidly
(d) an oxide layer is formed at the surface of Al metal which makes it passive

140. Carbon can reduce ferric oxide to iron at a temperature above 983 K because
(a) carbon monoxide formed is thermodynamically less stable than ferric oxide
(b) carbon has a higher affinity towards oxygen than iron
(c) free energy change for the formation of carbon dioxide is less negative than that for ferric oxide
(d) iron has a higher affinity towards oxygen than carbon

141. Considering the Ellingham diagram, which of the following metals can be used to reduce alumina?
(a) Mg (b) Zn (c) Fe (d) Cu

142. Chromium is obtained by reducing purified chromite ore with
(a) red hot coke (b) gaseous hydrogen
(c) aluminium powder (d) carbon monoxide

143. In the alumino-thermic process, Al acts as a/an
(a) flux (b) reducing agent
(c) oxidising agent (d) solder

144. The alumino-thermic process is used for the extraction of metals, whose oxides are
(a) fusible
(b) not easily reduced by carbon
(c) not easily reduced by hydrogen
(d) strongly basic

145. The alumino-thermic process is used for the metallurgy of
(a) Pb (b) Ag
(c) Al (d) none of these

146. Which of the following statements is incorrect?
(a) Pure aluminium oxide is obtained by heating aluminium hydroxide.
(b) Cryolite lowers the melting temperature of bauxite in the electrolytic cell for the extraction of aluminium.
(c) Carbonate ores are converted into oxides by roasting the ore in air.

(d) Mercury cannot be produced by roasting the ore cinnabar in air.

147. The mass of the carbon anode consumed (giving only carbon dioxide) in the production of 270 g of aluminium metal from bauxite by the Hall process is

(a) 180 g (b) 270 g (c) 540 g (d) 90 g

148. The electrolytic method of reduction is employed for the preparation of metals that

(a) are weakly electropositive
(b) are moderately electropositive
(c) are strongly electropositive
(d) from oxides

149. Which of the following metals cannot be extracted by the carbon reduction process?

(a) Pb (b) Al (c) Fe (d) Zn

150. Among the following groups of oxides, the group containing oxides that cannot be reduced by carbon to give the respective metals is

(a) Cu_2O, K_2O (b) Fe_2O_3, ZnO
(c) CaO, K_2O (d) PbO, Fe_3O_4

151. Aluminium is prepared in large quantities by

(a) heating cryolite in a limited quantity of air
(b) reducing aluminium oxide with coke
(c) reducing aluminium oxide with sodium
(d) electrolysing aluminium oxide dissolved in fused electrolyte

152. Aluminium is extracted from alumina (Al_2O_3) by the electrolysis of a molten mixture of

(a) $Al_2O_3 + HF + NaAlF_4$
(b) $Al_2O_3 + CaF_2 + NaAlF_4$
(c) $Al_2O_3 + Na_3AlF_6 + CaF_2$
(d) $Al_2O_3 + KF + Na_3AlF_6$

153. The metal extracted by the electrolysis of its fused salt is

(a) iron (b) lead (c) sodium (d) copper

154. Which metal can't be obtained from electrolysis?

(a) Cu (b) Mg (c) Cr (d) Na

155. To obtain chromium from chromic oxide (Cr_2O_3), the method used is

(a) alumino-thermic process
(b) electrolytic reduction
(c) carbon reduction
(d) carbon monoxide reduction

156. The process of bringing the metal or its ore into solution by the action of a suitable chemical reagent followed by extraction of the metal either by electrolysis or by a suitable precipitating agent is called

(a) electrometallurgy (b) electrorefining
(c) hydrometallurgy (d) zone refining

157. The precipitating agent used in the hydrometallurgy of silver and gold is

(a) aluminium (b) magnesium
(c) mercury (d) zinc

158. Hydrometallurgical process of extraction of metals is based on

(a) complex formation (b) hydrolysis
(c) dehydration (d) dehydrogenation

159. Which process of reduction of mineral to the metal is suited for the extraction of copper from its ores with low copper content?

(a) metal displacement (b) auto reduction
(c) chemical reduction (d) electrolytic reduction

160. Extraction of gold and silver involves leaching with CN^- ions. Silver is later recovered by

(a) distillation (b) zone refining
(c) displacement with Zn (d) liquation

161. Which of the following sulfides when heated strongly in air gives the corresponding metal?

(a) Cu_2S (b) CuS (c) Fe_2S_3
(d) FeS (e) HgS

162. Auto-reduction process is used in the extraction of

(a) Cu and Hg (b) Zn and Hg
(c) Cu and Al (d) Fe and Pb

163. Heating a mixture of Cu_2O and Cu_2S will give

(a) $Cu + SO_2$ (b) $Cu + SO_3$
(c) $CuO + CuS$ (d) Cu_2SO_3

164. The auto-reduction process is not used in the metallurgy of

(a) Hg (b) Cu (c) Pb (d) Fe

165. Pb and Sn are extracted from their chief ores by

(a) carbon reduction and self-reduction
(b) self-reduction and carbon reduction
(c) electrolysis and self-reduction
(d) self-reduction and electrolysis

166. The most electropositive metals are obtained from their ores by

(a) high temperature reduction with carbon
(b) electrolysis of fused ionic salts
(c) self-reduction
(d) thermal decomposition

167. Which of the following metals is extracted by the electrometallurgical method?

(a) Cu (b) Fe (c) Na (d) Ag

168. Which of the following methods is used for obtaining aluminium metal?

(a) by electrolysing fused Al_2O_3 and cryolite
(b) by heating alumina with carbon
(c) by heating alumina in Muffle furnace
(d) by a process called pyrometallurgy

169. The role of graphite in the electrometallurgy of aluminium is

(a) to reduce Al_2O_3 to Al metal
(b) to make the electrolyte more conducting
(c) to lower the fusion temperature of the electrolyte
(d) to prevent the liberation of O_2 at the anode which may otherwise oxidise some of the liberated Al back to Al_2O_3

170. In the Hall's process, the main reagent is mixed with

(a) NaF (b) Na_3AlF_6
(c) AlF_3 (d) none of these

171. The most active metals are extracted from their ores by the reduction with

(a) hydrogen (b) aluminium
(c) electrolysis (d) carbon

172. Which of the following metals is not manufactured by electrolysis?

(a) Na (b) Mg (c) Al
(d) Fe (e) Li

173. Cupellation is used in the metallurgy of

(a) Cu (b) Ag (c) Al (d) Fe

174. The phenomenon of removing layers of basic oxides from metals before electroplating is called

(a) galvanising (b) anodising
(c) poling (d) pickling

Refining of Crude Metals

175. The purest zinc is made by

(a) electrolytic refining (b) zone refining
(c) van Arkel method (d) Mond's process

176. Zone refining is used for the purification of

(a) Cu (b) Au (c) Ge (d) Ag

177. The main function of roasting is

(a) to remove the volatile matter
(b) to convert the ore into oxide
(c) both (a) and (b)
(d) to make slag

178. Which of the following metals is obtained by leaching its ore with dilute cyanide solution?

(a) silver (b) titanium (c) vanadium (d) zinc

179. Electrolytic reduction method is used in the extraction of

(a) highly electronegative elements
(b) highly electronegative elements
(c) transition metals
(d) noble metals

180. In the electrorefining of a metal, the impure metal is made the anode and a strip of pure metal the cathode, during the electrolysis of an aqueous solution of a complex metal salt. This method cannot be used for refining of

(a) silver (b) copper
(c) aluminium (d) gold

181. Which of the following is not employed for refining of a metal?

(a) poling (b) leaching
(c) electrolysis (d) liquation

182. van Arkel method of purification of metals involves converting the metal into a

(a) volatile stable compound
(b) volatile unstable compound
(c) non-volatile stable compound
(d) none of the above

183. The thermal decomposition method is used to purify

(a) Ni (b) Cr (c) Sn (d) Pb

184. The following set of reactions are used in refining zirconium

$$\text{Zr (impure)} + 2\,I_2 \xrightarrow{523\text{K}} ZrI_4 \xrightarrow{1800\text{K}} \text{Zr (pure)} + 2\,I_2$$

The method is known as

(a) distillation (b) liquation
(c) Hall–Heroult method (d) van Arkel method

185. Consider the following reactions and identify M

$$\underset{\text{Impure metal}}{M + 4\,CO} \xrightarrow{330\text{–}350\text{K}} \underset{\substack{\text{Volatile metal}\\ \text{tetracarbonyl}}}{M(CO)_4} \xrightarrow{450\text{–}470\text{K}} \underset{\text{Pure metal}}{M + 4\,CO}$$

(a) Fe (b) Ni (c) Mn (d) Co

186. The van Arkel method of refining zirconium involves

(a) removing all oxygen and nitrogen impurities
(b) removing CO impurity
(c) removing hydrogen impurity
(d) removing silica impurity

187. One of the following metals forms a volatile compound and this property is taken advantage of, for its extraction/purification. This metal is

(a) iron (b) nickel (c) cobalt (d) tungsten

188. What criterion is followed for the selection of the stationary phase in chromatography?

(a) Stationary phase is selected in such a way that the impurities are more strongly adsorbed on the stationary phase than the element to be purified.
(b) Stationary phase is selected in such a way that the element to be purified is more strongly adsorbed on the stationary phase than the impurities.
(c) When the column is extracted, the element will be retained by the stationary phase while the impurities are easily eluted.
(d) Stationary phase should stick to the surface of the column in which it is packed.

189. Which among the following metals is refined by the electrolytic method?

(a) aluminium (b) bismuth (c) tin (d) lead

190. In the electrolytic refining of zinc

(a) graphite is the anode
(b) the impure metal is the cathode
(c) the metal ion gets reduced at the anode
(d) acidified zinc sulfate is the electrolyte

191. Which of the following metals can be obtained by the electrolysis of the aqueous solution of its salts?

(a) Cu (b) Na (c) Mg (d) K

192. In the electrolytic refining of metals, electrolysis of an aqueous solution of a metal complex salt is done with the impure metals as the anode and a strip of the pure metal as the cathode. This method cannot be used for the refining of the metal

(a) silver (b) copper (c) aluminium (d) zinc

193. Which one of the following is manufactured by the electrolysis of fused sodium chloride?

(a) $NaOH$ (b) $NaClO$ (c) Na (d) $NaClO_3$

194. Electric refining is used for refining of

(a) lead (b) copper (c) iron (d) sodium

195. Electrolytic refining is used to purify which of the following metals?

(a) Cu and Zn (b) Ge and Si
(c) Zr and Ti (d) Zn and Hg

196. The method not used in metallurgy to refine the impure metal is

(a) Mond's process (b) van-Arkel process
(c) amalgamation process (d) liquation
(e) zone refining

197. In which process, is fused sodium hydroxide electrolysed for the extraction of sodium?

(a) Castner's process (b) cyanide process
(c) Down's process (d) both (b) and (c)

198. Mark the wrong statement.

(a) K boils at the melting point of KCl.
(b) K is insoluble in molten KCl.
(c) K is extracted by the electrolysis of fused KOH.
(d) K is extracted by the reduction of molten KCl by metallic Na.

199. Gold is extracted by a hydrometallurgical process based on its property

(a) of being electropositive
(b) of being less reactive
(c) to form complexes that are water soluble
(d) to form salts that are water soluble

200. Which of the following elements is extracted commercially by the electrolysis of an aqueous solution of its compounds?

(a) chlorine (b) bromine
(c) sodium (d) aluminium

201. Tin and lead can be refined by

(a) cupellation (b) liquation
(c) poling (d) bessemerisation

202. A metal which is refined by poling is

(a) sodium (b) blister copper
(c) zinc (d) silver

203. In order to refine blister copper it is melted in a furnace and is stirred with green logs of wood. The purpose is

(a) to expel the dissolved gases in blister copper
(b) to bring the impurities to the surface and oxidise them
(c) to increase the carbon content of copper
(d) to reduce the metallic oxide impurities with hydrocarbon gases liberated from the wood

204. Cupellation process is used in the metallurgy of

(a) copper (b) silver
(c) aluminium (d) iron

205. Gallium arsenide is purified by the

(a) froth flotation process
(b) van Arkel method
(c) zone refining method
(d) electrolytic method

Iron and Its Compounds

206. Which of the following statements is correct?

(a) The iron obtained from the blast furnace is called cast iron. It contains about 4% carbon and many other impurities in smaller amounts.
(b) Pig iron is made by melting cast iron with scrap iron and coke using a hot air blast.
(c) Pig iron has a slightly lower carbon content (about 3%) and is extremely hard and brittle.

(d) The iron obtained directly from the blast furnace is called pig iron. It contains about 4% carbon and many other impurities such as, S, P, Si, Mn in smaller amounts.

207. Which of the following statements is incorrect?

(a) Hydrogen is used to reduce NiO.
(b) Zirconium is refined by the van Arkel method.
(c) The sulfide ore galena is concentrated by froth floatation.
(d) In the metallurgy of iron, the flux used is SiO_2.

208. The temperature of the slag zone in the metallurgy of iron using a blast furnace is

(a) 1500–1600°C (b) 400–700°C
(c) 800–1000°C (d) 1200–1500°C

209. Which one of the following metals is extracted by a carbon reduction process?

(a) copper (b) iron
(c) aluminium (d) magnesium

210. Which one of the following metals is extracted on smelting of its ore in a blast furnace?

(a) iron (b) sodium
(c) potassium (d) magnesium

211. Which of the following taking place in the blast furnace is endothermic?

(a) $CaCO_3 \rightarrow CaO + CO_2$
(b) $2\,C + O_2 \rightarrow 2\,CO$
(c) $C + O_2 \rightarrow CO_2$
(d) $Fe_2O_3 + 3\,CO \rightarrow 2\,Fe + 3\,CO_2$

212. In a blast furnace, iron oxide is reduced by

(a) hot blast of air (b) carbon monoxide
(c) carbon (d) silica

213. In the manufacture of iron, limestone is added to the blast furnace, the calcium ion ends up in the form of

(a) slag (b) gangue
(c) calcium metal (d) $CaCO_3$

214. The smelting of iron in the blast furnace involves all the following processes except

(a) oxidation (b) reduction
(c) decomposition (d) sublimation

215. In the manufacture of iron from hematite, the function of limestone is as

(a) reducing agent (b) flux
(c) slag (d) gangue

216. In the modern blast furnaces, the charge consists of a mixture of

(a) calcined iron oxides + lime + anthracite coal
(b) calcined iron oxides + limestone + coke
(c) hydrated iron oxides + dolomite + coke
(c) iron pyrites + lime + bituminous coal
(d) The impurities present in cast iron are oxidised by air.

217. During the extraction of Fe, the slag obtained is

(a) FeO (b) $FeSiO_3$ (c) $MgSiO_3$ (d) $CaSiO_3$

218. Iron is obtained on a large scale from Fe_2O_3 by

(a) reduction with Al (b) reduction with CO
(c) reduction with H_2 (d) reduction with sodium

219. Identify the reaction that does not take place in a blast furnace

(a) $2\,Fe_2O_3 + 3\,C \rightarrow 4\,Fe + 3\,CO_2$
(b) $CO_2 + C \rightarrow 2\,CO$
(c) $CaCO_3 \rightarrow CaO + CO_2$
(d) $FeO + SiO_2 \rightarrow FeSiO_3$

220. Which of the following has the highest melting point?

(a) pig iron (b) cast iron
(c) steel (d) wrought iron

221. Wrought iron is resistant to rusting and corrosion due to the presence of

(a) cementite (Fe_3C)
(b) low percentage of carbon
(c) $CaSiO_3$ and $FePO_4$ slags
(d) $MnSiO_3$ and $FePO_4$ slags

222. The cores of electromagnets are prepared from

(a) pig iron (b) steel
(c) stainless steel (d) wrought iron

223. If steel is heated to a temperature well below red heat and is then cooled slowly, the process is called

(a) tempering (b) hardening
(c) softening (d) annealing

224. The protection of steel by chrome plating is due to

(a) cathodic protection
(b) anodic protection
(c) covering of steel surface
(d) formation of alloy with iron

225. The percentage of carbon in cast iron is

(a) 5–10 (b) 0.250–2.5
(c) 2.5–4.5 (d) 0.12–0.2

226. Mark the wrong statement.

(a) Wrought iron is prepared by heating cast iron in a reverberatory furnace.
(b) The impurities are oxidised by Fe_2O_3.
(c) CO burns with a blue flame and the Si, Mn and other impurities form slag with silica.
(d) The impurities present in cast iron are oxidised by air.

227. Iron is rendered passive by treatment with concentrated
(a) HCl (b) H_2SO_4 (c) H_3PO_4 (d) HNO_3

228. Finely divided iron combines with CO to give
(a) $Fe(CO)_5$ (b) $Fe_2(CO)_9$
(c) $Fe_3(CO)_{12}$ (d) $Fe(CO)_6$

229. The most stable oxidation state of iron is
(a) +2 (b) –2 (c) +3 (d) –3

230. The approximate percentage of iron in misch metal is
(a) 10 (b) 20 (c) 50
(d) 95 (e) 5

231. Railway wagon axles are made by heating iron rods embedded in charcoal powder. This process is known as
(a) tempering (b) annealing
(c) sherardising (d) case hardening

232. Which among the following metals is employed to provide cathodic protection to iron?
(a) zinc (b) nickel (c) tin (d) lead

233. Which among FeO and Fe_2O_3 is more basic?
(a) FeO (b) Fe_2O_3
(c) both have the same basic strength
(c) none of them is basic

234. Which of the following iron salts exists as a dimer?
(a) ferric chloride (b) ferrous chloride
(c) ferrous sulfate (d) Mohr's salt

235. The nature of an aqueous solution of $FeCl_3$ is
(a) acidic (b) basic
(c) amphoteric (d) neutral

236. Mohr's salt on oxidation with concentrated HNO_3 gives
(a) potash alum (b) chrome alum
(c) ferric alum (d) none of these

237. Ferric ion forms a Prussian blue precipitate due to the formation of
(a) $K_4[Fe(CN)_6]$ (b) $K_3[Fe(CN)_6]$
(c) $Fe(CNS)_3$ (d) $Fe_4[Fe(CN)_6]_3$

238. Which metal cannot be obtained by electrolysis?
(a) Ca (b) Mg (c) Cr (d) Al

239. Purification of silicon used in semiconductors is done by
(a) zone refining (b) heating
(c) froth floatation (d) heating in vacuum

240. Which of the following is not a mineral of iron?
(a) magnetite (b) siderite (c) smithsonite
(d) limonite (e) hematite

241. Formula of magnetite is
(a) Fe_2O_3 (b) FeS_2 (c) $FeCO_3$ (d) Fe_3O_4

242. In a blast furnace, the maximum temperature is in the
(a) zone of fusion (b) zone of combustion
(c) zone of slag combustion (d) zone of reduction

Copper and its Compounds

243. When $CuSO_4$ is electrolysed using platinum electrodes,
(a) copper is liberated at the cathode, sulfur at the anode
(b) copper is liberated at the cathode, oxygen at the anode
(c) sulfur is liberated at the cathode, oxygen at the anode
(d) oxygen is liberated at the cathode, copper at the anode

244. The extraction of which of the following metals involves bessemerisation?
(a) Fe (b) Ag (c) Al (d) Cu

245. Copper is extracted from copper pyrites ore by heating in a blast furnace. The method is based on the principle that
(a) copper has more affinity for oxygen than sulfur at high temperature
(b) iron has less affinity for oxygen than sulfur at the temperature
(c) sulfur has less affinity for oxygen at high temperature
(d) copper has less affinity for oxygen than sulfur at high temperature

246. In the electrolysis of aqueous solution of copper sulfate using copper strips as anode and cathode, the anode reaction is
(a) $Cu^{2+} + 2e^- \rightarrow Cu$
(b) $Cu \rightarrow Cu^{2+} + 2\,e^-$
(c) $2\,OH^- \rightarrow + \frac{1}{2}\,O_2 + 2\,e^-$
(d) $SO_4^{2-} \rightarrow SO_4 + 2e^-$
(e) $2\,HSO_4^- \rightarrow H_2S_2O_8 + 2\,e^-$

247. Which of the following elements is not present in the anode mud during the electrolytic refining of copper?
(a) Sb (b) Se (c) Te (d) Co

248. The extraction of copper from pyrites is more difficult than that from its oxide ore though reduction. This is because

I. $\Delta_f G^\circ$ of Cu_2S is more +ve than that of CS_2 and H_2S. Therefore, neither carbon not hydrogen can reduce Cu_2S to Cu metal.

II. $\Delta_f G°$ of CuS is more –ve than those of CS_2 and H_2S and H_2S. Therefore, neither carbon not hydrogen can reduce Cu_2S to Cu metal.
III. $\Delta_f G°$ of Cu_2O is less +ve than that of CO and hence carbon can easily reduce Cu_2O to Cu metal.
IV. $\Delta_f G°$ of Cu_2O is less –ve than that of CO and hence carbon can easily reduce Cu_2O to Cu metal.

Which of the following pairs show the correct statements?
(a) I, III (b) II, IV (c) I, IV (d) II, III

249. At a site, low grade copper ores are available and zinc and iron scraps are also available. Which of the two scraps would be more suitable for reducing the leaching copper ore? (Select the incorrect statement in the following.)
(a) The $E°$ value for the redox couple Zn^{2+}/Zn is –0.76 V.
(b) The $E°$ value for the redox couple Fe^{2+}/Fe is –0.44 V.
(c) Zinc is less reactive than iron and hence reduction will be slower in case zinc scraps are used.
(d) Zinc is a costlier metal than iron so using iron scraps would be more advisable and economical.

250. The composition of copper matte is
(a) $Cu_2S + FeS$ (b) $Cu_2S + Cu_2O$
(c) $Cu_2S + FeO$ (d) $Cu_2O + FeS$

251. Extraction of copper from copper pyrites ($CuFeS_2$) involves
(a) crushing followed by concentration of the ore by froth floatation
(b) removal of iron as slag
(c) self-reduction step to produce blister copper following the evolution of SO_2
(d) all the three above

252. The metal which can be used to obtain metallic Cu from aqueous $CuSO_4$ solution is
(a) Na (b) Ag (c) Hg (d) Fe

253. Roasted copper pyrites on smelting with sand produces
(a) $FeSiO_3$ as fusible slag and Cu_2S as matte
(b) $CaSiO_3$ as infusible slag and Cu_2O as matte
(c) $Ca_3(PO_4)_2$ as fusible slag and Cu_2S as matte
(d) $Fe_2(PO_4)_2$ as infusible slag and Cu_2S as matte

254. Which is the strongest reducing agent?
(a) Rb (b) Na (c) K (d) Mg

255. An important ore of copper is
(a) bauxite (b) galena
(c) siderite (d) chalcopyrites

256. The formula of malachite ore is
(a) Fe_3O_4 (b) Mn_3O_4
(c) NiAs (d) $Cu(OH)_2.CuCO_3$

257. Azurite is an ore of
(a) gold (b) silver (c) copper (d) zinc

258. Which of the following ores is an ore of copper?
(a) argentite (b) hematite
(c) malachite (d) calamine

259. Which of the following is the chief ore of copper?
(a) Cu_2S (b) Cu_2O
(c) $CuFeS_2$ (d) $CuCO_3.Cu(OH)_2$

260. The slag formed in the extraction of copper is
(a) $CuFeS_2$ (b) $Cu_2O + FeS$
(c) $Cu_2S + FeO$ (d) $FeSiO_3$

261. In the extraction of copper from its sulfide ore, the metal is formed by the reduction of Cu_2O with
(a) FeS (b) CO (c) Cu_2S (d) SO_2

262. Blister copper is
(a) impure Cu (b) Cu alloy
(c) Pure Cu (d) Cu having 1% impurity

263. The final step for the extraction of copper from copper pyrites in the Bessemer converter involves the reaction
(a) $4\ Cu_2O + FeS \rightarrow 8\ Cu + FeSO_4$
(b) $Cu_2S + 2\ Cu_2O \rightarrow 6\ Cu + SO_2$
(c) $2\ Cu_2O + FeS \rightarrow 4Cu + Fe + SO_2$
(d) $Cu_2S + 2\ FeO \rightarrow 2\ Cu + 2\ Fe + SO_2$

264. After partial roasting, the sulfide of copper is reduced by
(a) reduction by carbon (b) electrolysis
(c) self-reduction (d) cyanide process

265. High purity copper metal is obtained by
(a) carbon reduction (b) hydrogen reduction
(c) electrolytic reduction (d) thermite reduction

266. Among K, Mg, Au and Cu, the one which is extracted by heating its ore in air is
(a) K (b) Mg (c) Au (d) Cu

267. Copper displaces which of the metals from their salt solution?
(a) $AgNO_3$ (b) $ZnSO_4$
(c) $FeSO_4$ (d) all of the above

268. Which of the following properties would you not expect copper (Cu) to exhibit?
(a) high thermal conductivity
(b) low electrical conductivity
(d) ductility
(d) malleability

269. Which of the following ions will liberate iodine when treated with KI?
(a) Cu^{2+} (b) Fe^{2+} (c) Pb^{2+} (d) Sn^{2+}

270. Bordeaux used as a fungicide is a mixture of
(a) $CuSO_4 + Ca(OH)_2$ (b) $CaSO_4 + Cu(OH)_2$
(c) $CuCO_3 + Cu(OH)_2$ (d) $CuO + CaO$

271. Malachite and azurite are used respectively as
(a) blue and green pigments
(b) green and blue pigments
(c) red and green pigments
(d) green and red pigments

272. German silver does not contain
(a) Cu (b) Zn (c) Ni (d) Mn

273. Bronze used for making status, coins and utensils is an alloy of
(a) Cu, Zn (b) Cu, Zn, Sn
(c) Cu, Sn (d) Cu, Ni

274. A solution of copper sulfate is
(a) acidic (b) basic
(c) neutral (d) amphoteric

275. The enthalpies of solution for copper sulfate pentahydrate and anhydrous copper sulfate are respectively –117.7 and 65.5 kJ mol^{-1}. The hydration enthalpy of anhydrous copper sulfate is
(a) 53.8 kJ mol^{-1} (b) –9.8 kJ mol^{-1}
(c) –77.2 kJ mol^{-1} (d) –53.8 kJ mol^{-1}
(e) 77.2 kJ mol^{-1}

276. When heated in air, brown copper powder turns black. This black powder would turn brown again when heated with
(a) CO (b) O_2 (c) H_2 (d) NH_3

277. The chief source of iodine, in which it is present as sodium iodate, is
(a) carnallite (b) sea weed (c) caliche
(d) iodine never exists as sodium iodate

278. The composition of bell metal is
(a) Cu (80%), Zn (20%) (b) Cu (60%), Ni (40%)
(c) Cu (90%), Sn (10%) (d) Cu (80%), Sn (20%)

279. Copper sulfate is commercially made from copper scraps by
(a) dissolving in hot conc. H_2SO_4
(b) the action dil. H_2SO_4 and air
(c) heating with sodium sulfate
(d) heating with sulfur

280. Which of the following is ionic in nature?
(a) CuF_2 (b) $CuCl_2$ (c) $CuBr_2$ (d) none of these

281. Copper can be extracted from
(a) kupfernickel (b) dolomite
(c) galena (d) malachite

282. The slag obtained during the extraction of copper from copper pyrites is composed mainly of
(a) Cu_2S (b) $FeSiO_3$ (c) $CuSiO_3$ (d) SiO_2

283. The role of silica in the metallurgy of copper is
(a) to expedite the oxidation of Cu_2S to Cu_2O
(b) to expedite the oxidation of FeS to FeO
(c) to isolate copper as copper silicate
(d) to remove FeO as $FeSiO_3$ slag

284. Impure copper containing 1% impurity obtained from bessemerisation of molten matte is called
(a) blister copper (b) bronze
(c) brass (d) none of the above

Silver, Its Compounds and Photography

285. In the cyanide extraction process of silver from argentite ore, the oxidising and reducing agents used are
(a) O_2 and CO respectively
(b) O_2 and Zn dust respectively
(c) HNO_3 and Zn dust respectively
(d) HNO_3 and CO respectively

286. '925 fine silver' means
(a) 9.5% Ag + 90.75%
(b) 95.5 % Ag + 7.5% Cu
(c) 9.25% Cu + 90.75% Ag
(d) 7.5% Ag + 92.5% Cu

287. Coinage alloy has the following composition
(a) Ag + Cu + Ni (b) Cu + Ag + Au
(c) Au + Zn + Ag (d) Ag + Fe + Cu

288. Silver plating is carried out from which of the following?
(a) silver nitrate (b) silver chloride
(c) potassium argento cyanide
(d) none of these

289. White AgCl dissolves in a solution of NH_3 but not in water because
(a) NH_3 is a better solvent than H_2O
(b) Ag^+ forms a complex ion with NH_3
(c) NH_3 is a stronger base than H_2O
(d) the dipole moment of water is higher than that of NH_3

290. When $AgNO_3$ comes in contact with the skin, it leaves a black stain. This is because of
(a) HNO_3 produced by hydrolysis of $AgNO_3$
(b) AgOH produced by hydrolysis of $AgNO_3$
(c) its reduction to silver
(d) its oxidation to silver oxide

291. Addition of sodium thiosulfate solution to a solution silver nitrate gives X as a white precipitate insoluble in water but soluble in excess of thiosulfate solution to give Y. On boiling in water, Y gives Z. X, Y and Z respectively, are

(a) $Ag_2S_2O_3$, $Na_3[Ag(S_2O_3)_2]$, Ag_2S
(b) Ag_2SO_4, $Na[Ag(S_2O_3)_2]$, Ag_2S_2
(c) $Ag_2S_2O_3$, $Na_5[Ag(S_2O_3)_3]$, AgS
(d) Ag_2SO_3, $Na_3[Ag(S_2O_3)_2]$, Ag_2O

292. When AgCl is treated with KCN

(a) Ag is precipitated
(b) a complex ion is formed
(c) double decomposition takes place
(d) no reaction takes place

293. Metallic silver may be obtained from AgCl by

(a) heating it in the current of H_2
(b) fusing it with sand
(c) treating it with carbon monoxide
(d) fusing it with Na_2CO_3

294. Silver chloride dissolves in excess of ammonium hydroxide solution. The cation present in the resulting solution is

(a) $[Ag(NH_3)_6]^+$ (b) $[Ag(NH_3)_4]^+$
(c) Ag^+ (d) $[Ag(NH_3)_2]^+$

295. The black image on an exposed and developed photographic film is composed of

(a) Ag (b) AgBr
(c) $Na_3[Ag(S_2O_3)_2]$ (d) Ag_2O

296. Photographic films and plates have an essential ingredient of

(a) silver nitrate (b) silver bromide
(c) sodium chloride (d) oleic acid

297. Development of a photographic plate involves the use of

(a) an oxidising agent (b) a complexing agent
(c) a neutralising agent (d) a precipitating agent
(e) a reducing agent

298. Argentite is a mineral of

(a) copper (b) silver
(c) platinum (d) aluminium

299. The principal ores of silver are argentite, horn silver and pyrargyrite. Their formulae respectively are

(a) Ag_2S, AgCl and 2 $AgSbS_2$
(b) AgCl, $AgSbS_2$ and Ag_2S
(c) 2 $AgSbS_2$, Ag_2S and AgCl
(d) AgCl, Ag_2S and $AgSbS_2$

300. Parke's process is used in the extraction of

(a) iron (b) zinc (c) silver (d) sodium

301. Horn silver ore dissolves in excess of sodium cyanide solution forming

(a) AgCN (b) $Na[Ag(CN)_2]$
(c) $Na_2[Ag(CN)_3]$ (d) $Na_4[Ag(CN)_5]$

302. Extraction of silver is achieved by initial complexation of the ore (argentite) with X followed by reduction with Y. X and Y respectively, are

(a) CN^- and Zn (b) CN^- and Cu
(c) Cl^- and Zn (d) Br^- and Zn

303. These are the extraction processes of silver except

(a) as a side product in electrolytic refining of copper
(b) Parke's process in which Zn is used to extract silver by solvent extraction from molten lead
(c) by reaction of silver sulfide with KCN and then reaction of soluble complex with Zn
(d) by heating $Na[Ag(CN)_2]$

304. The reagent used to extract silver from Ag_2S is

(a) NaCN (b) NaCN in the presence of O_2
(c) NaCl (d) $AgNO_3$

305. In the Mac-Arthur Forrest method, silver is extracted from a solution of $Na[Ag(CN)_2]$ by the use of

(a) Fe (b) Mg (c) Cu (d) Zn

306. A complex is formed in the extraction of

(a) Na (b) Cu (c) Ag (d) Fe

307. Silver obtained from argentiferous lead containing lead as impurity is purified by

(a) distillation (b) froth floatation
(c) cupellation (d) treatment with KCN

Gold and its Compounds

308. Which of the following is not an element?

(a) graphite (b) diamond
(c) 22 carat gold (d) rhombic sulfur

309. Gold and silver are extracted from their respective ores by

(a) leaching (b) smelting
(c) roasting (d) hydrometallurgy

310. The Mac-Arthur process is used for the extraction of

(a) Au (b) Ag
(c) Cu (b) both for Au and Ag

311. In the process of extraction of gold,

Roasted gold ore + CN^- + $H_2O \xrightarrow{O_2}$ [X] + OH^-
[X] + Zn → [Y] + Au
The complexes [X] and [Y] are

(a) $X = [Au(CN)_2]^-$, $Y = [Zn(CN)_4]^{2-}$
(b) $X = [Au(CN)_4]^{3-}$, $Y = [Zn(CN)_4]^{2-}$
(c) $X = [Au(CN)_2]^-$, $Y = [Zn(CN)_6]^{4-}$
(d) $X = [Au(CN)_4]^-$, $Y = [Zn(CN)_4]^{2-}$

312. Impurities of Cu and Ag from gold are removed by
(a) boiling impure gold with dil. H_2SO_4
(b) boiling impure gold with conc. H_2SO_4
(c) electrolytically
(d) both (b) and(c)

313. Noble metals are soluble in
(a) NH_4OH (b) aqua regia
(c) H_2SO_4 (d) water gas

314. In the case of gold
(a) +1 state is more stable
(b) +3 state is more stable
(c) both +2 and +3 states have equal stability
(d) none of these

315. The metal extracted by the cyanide process is
(a) silver (b) copper
(c) iron (d) sodium/aluminium

Zinc and its Compounds

316. The reaction $2ZnS + 3O_2 \rightarrow 2ZnO + 2SO_2$ in the metallurgical process of zinc is called
(a) calcination (b) cupellation
(c) smelting (d) roasting

317. Zinc metal dissolves in cold concentrated solution of
(a) NaCl (b) $NaHCO_3$
(c) NaOH (d) NH_4OH

318. $MSO_4 \xrightarrow{NH_4OH} X\downarrow \xrightarrow{NH_4OH} Y \xrightarrow{H_2S} Z\downarrow$
White ppt. excess

Here M and Z are
(a) Zn, ZnS (b) Al, Al_2S_3
(c) Cu, ZnS (d) Fe, FeS

319. The reaction of zinc with dilute and concentrated nitric acid, respectively, produces
(a) N_2O and NO_2 (b) NO_2 and NO
(c) NO and N_2O (d) NO_2 and N_2O

320. 'Electron' is an alloy of
(a) Mg and Zn (b) Fe and Mg
(c) Ni and Zn (d) Al and Zn

321. Which of the following is a constituent of lithopone?
(a) $ZnSO_4$ (b) ZnS (c) $ZnCl_2$ (d) ZnO

322. Willemite is
(a) Zn_2SiO_4 (b) H_2PtCl_6
(c) ZnO (d) $ZnO.Fe_2O_3$

323. The trace metal present in insulin is
(a) Fe (b) Co (c) Zn (d) Mn

324. Calamine is
(a) $CaCO_3$ (b) $MgCO_3$
(c) $ZnCO_3$ (d) $CaCO_3 + CaO$

325. Which of the following statements is incorrect?
(a) Silver glance mainly contains silver sulfide.
(b) Gold is found in the native state.
(c) Zinc blende mainly contains zinc chloride.
(d) Copper pyrites also contains Fe_2S_3.

326. Spelter is
(a) impure Cu (b) impure Zn
(c) ZnO (d) CuO

327. From the Ellingham graphs on carbon, show that ZnO is better reduced by
(a) C above 1180 K (b) C above 1270 K
(c) CO above 1523 K (d) C around 1673 K

328. In the conversion of zinc ore to zinc metal, the process of roasting involves
(a) $ZnCO_3 \rightarrow ZnO$ (b) $ZnO \rightarrow ZnSO_4$
(c) $ZnS \rightarrow ZnO$ (d) $ZnS \rightarrow ZnSO_4$

329. The major products of the following reaction are
$ZnS(s) + O_2(g) \xrightarrow{Heat}$
(a) ZnO and SO_2 (b) $ZnSO_4$ and SO_3
(c) $ZnSO_4$ and SO_2 (d) Zn and SO_2

Final Preparation

330. Which of the following reactions is an example of the calcination process?
(a) $2Ag + 2HCl + |O| \rightarrow 2AgCl + H_2O$
(b) $2Zn + O_2 \rightarrow 2ZnO$
(c) $2ZnS + 3O_2 \rightarrow 2ZnO + SO_2$
(d) $MgCO_3 \rightarrow MgO + CO_2$

331. Which of the following statements about the advantage of roasting of sulfide ore before reduction is not true?
(a) Roasting of the sulfide to the oxide is thermodynamically feasible.
(b) Carbon and hydrogen are suitable reducing agents for metal sulfides.
(c) The $\Delta_f G°$ of the sulfide is greater than those for CS_2 and H_2S.
(d) The $\Delta_f G°$ is negative for roasting of sulfide ore to oxide.

332. Roasting of sulfides gives the gas X as a byproduct. This is a colourless gas with a choking smell of burnt sulfur and causes greater damage to respiratory organs as a result of acid rain. Its aqueous solution is acidic, acts as a reducing agent and its acid has never been isolated. The gas X is
(a) H_2S (b) SO_2 (c) CO_2 (d) SO_3

333. When a metal is to be extracted from its ore and if the gangue associated with the ore is silica, then

(a) an acidic flux is needed
(b) a basic flux is needed
(c) both acidic and basic fluxes are needed
(d) neither of them is needed

334. Thomas slag is prepared by the reaction between

(a) MnO and SiO_2 (b) CaO and SiO_2
(c) CaO and P_4O_{10} (d) FeO and SiO_2

335. Carbon monoxide is a more effective reducing agent than carbon below T°C but above this temperature, the reverse is true. The value of T is

(a) 983 (b) 710 (c) 596 (d) 1133

336. $\Delta G°$ versus T plot in the Ellingham diagram slopes downward for

(a) $C + \frac{1}{2}O_2 \rightarrow CO$ (b) $CO + \frac{1}{2}O_2 \rightarrow CO_2$

(c) $2\,Ag + \frac{1}{2}O_2 \rightarrow Ag_2O$ (d) $Mg + \frac{1}{2}O_2 \rightarrow MgO$

337. According to the Ellingham diagram, the oxidation reaction of carbon to carbonmonoxide may be used to reduce which one of the following oxides at the lowest temperature?

(a) Al_2O_3 (b) Cu_2O (c) MgO (d) ZnO

338. Reduction of a metal oxide by excess carbon at a high temperature is a method for the commercial preparation of some metals. This method can be successfully applied in the case of

(a) BeO and Al_2O_3 (b) ZnO and Fe_2O_3
(c) CaO and Cr_2O_3 (e) BaO and U_3O_8

339. Carbon cannot reduce Fe_2O_3 to Fe at a temperature below 983 K because

(a) free energy change for the formation of CO is more negative than that for Fe_2O_3
(b) CO is thermodynamically more stable than Fe_2O_3
(c) carbon has a higher affinity towards oxygen than iron
(d) iron has higher affinity towards oxygen than carbon

340. If an impurity in a metal has a greater affinity for oxygen and is more easily oxidised than the metal, then the purification of metal may be carried out by

(a) poling (b) zone refining
(c) electrolytic refining (d) cupellation

341. The method of zone refining of metals is based on the principle of

(a) greater mobility of the pure metal than that of the impurity
(b) higher melting point of the impurity than that of the pure metal
(c) greater noble character of the solid metal than that of the impurity
(d) greater solubility of the impurity in the molten state than in the solid state of metal.

342. In the zone refining method, the molten zone

(a) contains impurities
(b) contains purified metal only
(c) contains more impurity than the original metal
(d) moves on either side

343. Four metals and their methods of refinement are given

(i) Ni, Cu, Zr, Ga
(ii) electrolysis, van Arkel process, zone refining, Mond's process

Choose the right method for each.

(a) Ni: electrolysis, Cu: van Arkel process, Zr: zone refining, Ga: Mond's process
(b) Ni: Mond's process, Cu: electrolysis, Zr: van Arkel process, Ga: zone refining
(c) Ni: Mond's process, Cu: van Arkel process, Zr: zone refining, Ga: electrolysis
(d) Ni: electrolysis, Cu = zone refining, Zr: van Arkel process, Ga: Mond's process

344. Match items of **column I** with the items of **column II** and assign the correct code.

Column I	Column II
(A) Cyanide process	(i) Ultra-pure Ge
(B) Froth floatation process	(ii) Dressing of ZnS
(C) Electrolytic reduction	(iii) Extraction of Al
(D) Zone refining	(iv) Extraction of Au
	(v) Purification of Ni

	A	B	C	D
(a)	(i)	(ii)	(iii)	(iv)
(b)	(iii)	(iv)	(v)	(i)
(c)	(iv)	(ii)	(iii)	(i)
(d)	(ii)	(iii)	(i)	(v)

345. The following reactions take place in the blast furnace in the preparation of impure iron. Identify the reaction pertaining to the formation of slag.

(a) $Fe_2O_3(s) + 3\,CO(g) \rightarrow 2\,Fe(l) + 3\,CO_2(g)$
(b) $CaCO_3(s) \rightarrow CaO(s) \rightarrow CO_2(g)$
(c) $CaO(s) + SiO_2(s) \rightarrow CaSiO_3(s)$
(d) $2\,C(s) + O_2(g) \rightarrow 2\,CO(g)$

346. Carbon in wrought iron is present as

(a) silicon carbide
(b) iron carbide
(c) graphite
(d) partly as iron carbide and partly as graphite

347. Steel contains

(a) Fe + C + Mn (b) Fe + C + Al
(c) Fe + Mn (d) Fe + Mn + Cr

348. Which of the following elements is present as the impurity to the maximum extent in the pig iron?

(a) manganese (b) carbon
(c) silicon (d) phosphorus

349. Which of the following is a ferrous alloy?

(a) invar (b) solder
(c) magnalium (d) type metal

350. Invar, an alloy of Fe and Ni is used in watches and meter scales. Its characteristic property is

(a) small coefficient of expansion
(b) resistance to corrosion
(c) hardness and elasticity
(d) resistance to water
(e) magnetic nature

351. Identify the alloy containing a non-metal as a constituent in it

(a) invar (b) steel (c) bell metal (d) bronze

352. Iron, once dipped in concentrated H_2SO_4, does not displace copper from copper sulfate solution, because

(a) it is less reactive than copper
(b) a layer of sulfate is deposited on it
(c) an inert layer of iron oxide is deposited on it
(d) all valence electrons of iron are consumed.

353. Iron exhibits +2 and +3 oxidation states. Which of the following statements about iron is incorrect?

(a) Ferrous compounds are relatively more ionic than the corresponding ferric compounds.
(b) Ferrous compounds are less volatile than the corresponding ferric compounds.
(c) Ferrous compounds are more easily hydrolysed than the corresponding ferric compounds.
(d) Ferrous oxide is more basic in nature than the ferric oxide.

354. Ferric chloride is used for etching copper and silver metals. This is due to

(a) oxidation action of Fe^{3+} ions
(b) reducing action of Fe^{3+} ions
(c) both oxidising and reducing actions of Fe^{3+} ions
(d) reducing action of Fe^{2+} ions

355. Which of the following gives a blood red colour with KCNS?

(a) Cu^{2+} (b) Fe^{3+} (c) Al^{3+} (d) Zn^{2+}

356. Which of the following process does not involve the oxidation of iron?

(a) formation of $Fe(CO)_5$ from Fe
(b) liberation of H_2 from steam by iron at high temperature
(c) rusting of iron sheets
(d) decolourisation of blue $CuSO_4$ solution by iron

357. Anhydrous ferric chloride is prepared by

(a) dissolving $Fe(OH)_3$ in conc. HCl
(b) dissolving $Fe(OH)_3$ in dil. HCl
(c) passing dry HCl over heated iron scrap
(d) passing dry Cl_2 gas over heated iron scrap

358. Corrosion of iron can be prevented by coating the surface with

(a) Zn (b) Sn
(c) Ni (d) any of the above

359. Copper ore is heated in a reverberatory furnace after mixing with silica. Iron oxide slags off as iron silicate and copper is produced in the forms of

(a) copper sulfate (b) copper silicate
(c) copper matte (d) copper hydroxide

360. In the extraction of copper from its sulfide ore, the metal is finally obtained by the reduction of cuprous oxide with

(a) copper (I) sulfide (Cu_2S)
(b) sulfur dioxide (SO_2)
(c) iron sulfide (FeS)
(d) carbon monoxide (CO)

361. Heating a mixture of Cu_2O and Cu_2S will give

(a) Cu_2SO_3 (b) $CuO + CuS$
(c) $Cu + SO_3$ (d) $Cu + SO_2$

362. Zinc can be coated on iron to produce galvanised iron but the reverse is not possible. This is because

(a) zinc has a higher negative electrode potential than iron
(b) zinc is lighter than iron
(c) zinc has a lower melting point than iron
(d) zinc has lower negative electrode potential than iron

363. Which of the following metal oxides is white in colour but becomes yellow on heating?

(a) Ag_2O (b) ZnO (c) FeO (d) MgO

364. Philosopher's wool on heating with BaO at 1100°C produces

(a) $Ba + ZnCl_2$ (b) $BaCdO_2$
(c) $BaZnO_2$ (d) $BaO_2 + Zn$

365. For which ore of the metal, is froth floatation method used for concentration?

(a) horn silver (b) bauxite
(c) cinnabar (d) hematite

366. Which of the following metals is leached by the cyanide process?

(a) Ag (b) Na (c) Al (d) Cu

367. During the process of electrolytic refining of copper, some metals present as impurities settle as anode mud. These are

(a) Fe and Ni (b) Ag and Au
(c) Pb and Zn (d) Se and Ag

368. The most suitable method for extraction of copper from low grade sulfide ore is the

(a) smelting process (b) leaching process
(c) electrolytic process
(d) hydrometallurgical process

369. Addition of iron filings to $CuSO_4$ solution causes precipitation of Cu owing to the

(a) reduction of Cu^{2+} (b) oxidation of Cu^{2+}
(c) reduction of Fe (d) reduction of Fe^{3+}

370. Both copper carbonate and copper hydroxide are present in

(i) malachite (ii) azurite
(iii) chalcocite (iv) verdigris
(a) (i), (ii) and (iii) (b) (i) and (ii)
(c) (ii) and (iv) (d) (ii), (iii), and (iv)

371. Cu^{2+} is more stable than Cu^{+}. This is due to

(a) extensive hydration of the Cu^{2+} ion
(b) higher charge and smaller size of the Cu^{2+} ion as compared to the Cu^{+} ion
(c) both (a) and (b)
(d) none of these

372. The products of reaction of copper with dilute nitric acid are

(a) $Cu(NO_3)_2 + H_2$
(b) $Cu(NO_3)_2 + NO + H_2O$
(c) $Cu(NO_3)_2 + H_2O + NO_2$
(d) $CuNO_3 + H_2$

373. When copper is heated with conc. HNO_3, it produces

(a) $Cu(NO_3)_2$, NO and NO_2
(b) $Cu(NO_3)_2$ and N_2O
(c) $Cu(NO_3)_2$ and NO_2
(d) $Cu(NO_3)_2$ and NO

374. Which one of the following metals has no action with dil. H_2SO_4?

(a) Mg (b) Fe (c) Zn (d) Cu

375. Boiling $CuCl_2$ with excess of copper turnings and conc. HCl gives

(a) $CuCl(s)$ (b) $Cu_2O(s)$
(c) $[CuCl_3]^-$ (d) $[CuCl_2]^-$

376. In solid $CuSO_4.5H_2O$, copper is coordination to

(a) five water molecules (b) four water molecules
(c) one sulfate ion (d) one water molecule

377. What is the effect of shaking dil. H_2SO_4 with a small quantity of anhydrous $CuSO_4$?

(a) The white solid dissolves to form a colourless solution.
(b) The white solid dissolves to form a blue solution.
(c) The white solid dissolves to form a green solution.
(d) The white solid turns blue but does not dissolve.

378. Copper sulfate dissolves in excess of KCN to give

(a) $[Cu(CN)_4]^{2-}$ (b) $Cu(CN)_2$
(c) CuCN (d) $[Cu(CN)_4]^{3-}$

379. A blue colouration is not obtained when

(a) ammonium hydroxide dissolves in copper sulfate
(b) copper sulfate solution reacts with $K_4[Fe(CN)_6]$
(c) ferric chloride reacts with sodium ferrocyanide
(d) anhydrous $CuSO_4$ is dissolved in water

380. Verdigris is

(a) basic copper acetate (b) basic lead acetate
(c) basic lead (d) none

381. The compound used for gravimetric estimation of Cu(II) is

(a) $Cu_2(SCN)_2$ (b) Cu_2O
(c) Cu_2I_2 (d) Cu_2CO_3

382. From argentite, Ag_2S ore, the method used in obtaining metallic silver is

(a) fused mixture of Ag_2S and KCl is electrolysed
(b) Ag_2S is reduced with CO
(c) Ag_2S is roasted to Ag_2O which is reduced with carbon
(d) treating argentite with NaCN solution followed by metal displacement with zinc

383. $(Ag + Pb)\text{ Alloy} \xrightarrow[\text{zinc is added}]{\text{Melt and}} (Ag + Pb + Zn)\text{ melt} \xrightarrow{\text{Cool}} \begin{matrix}\text{Layer X}\\ \text{Layer Y}\end{matrix}$

Select the correct statement based on the above scheme.

(a) Layer X contains Zn and Ag.
(b) Layer Y contains Pb and Ag but amount of Ag in this layer is smaller than in layer X.
(c) X and Y are immiscible layers.
(d) All are correct statements.

384. Which of the following oxides is least stable at room temperature?

(a) CuO (b) Ag_2O (c) ZnO (d) Hg_2O

385. The black compound formed during the reaction between sodium thiosulfate and silver nitrate is

(a) silver thiosulfate ($Ag_2S_2O_3$)
(b) silver sulfide (Ag_2S)
(c) silver sulfate (Ag_2SO_4)
(d) silver sulfite (Ag_2SO_3)

386. $AgNO_3$ solution is kept in coloured bottles in the laboratory. This is done
(a) because the colours in the glass act as negative catalysts
(b) to cut off the entry of light
(c) simply to give it a distinction from other reagent bottles as it is costly
(d) as ordinary white glass reacts with $AgNO_3$

387. Which one of the following nitrates will leave behind a metal on strong heating?
(a) copper nitrate (b) manganese nitrate
(c) silver nitrate (d) ferric nitrate

388. Which of the following is used in medicine?
(a) $AgNO_3$ (b) AgCl (c) AgBr (d) AgF

389. Sodium thiosulfate is used in photography as fixer to
(a) reduce silver bromide to silver
(b) convert metallic silver to silver salt
(c) remove and decompose unchanged AgBr as a soluble silver thiosulfate complex
(d) remove reduced silver

390. Which one of the following reactions represents 'developing' in photography?
(a) $AgNO_3 + NaBr \rightarrow AgBr + NaNO_3$
(b) $AgBr + 2\ Na_2\ S_2O_3 \rightarrow Na_3[Ag\ (S_2O_3)_2] + NaBr$
(c) $AgBr + h\nu \rightarrow AgBr^*$
(d) $C_6H_4(OH)_2 + 2\ AgBr^* \rightarrow C_6H_4O_2 + 2HBr + 2\ Ag$
(e) $AgBr + 2\ NH_3 \rightarrow [Ag\ (NH_3)_2]\ Br$

391. In the equation, $4\ M + 8\ CN^- + 2\ HO \xrightarrow{X}$ $4\ [M(CN)_2]^- + 4\ OH^-$, the metal M and reactant X are respectively
(a) copper, air (b) iron, air
(c) gold, oxygen (d) zinc, oxygen

392. Consider the following reactions at 1000°C.

A. $Zn(s) + \frac{1}{2}\ O_2(g) \rightarrow ZnO(s);\ \Delta G° = -360\ kJ\ mol^{-1}$

B. $C(gr) + \frac{1}{2}\ O_2(g) \rightarrow CO(g);\ \Delta G° = -460\ kJ\ mol^{-1}$

Choose the correct statement at 1000°C.
(a) Zinc can be oxidised by CO.
(b) Zinc oxide can be reduced by graphite.
(c) Both statements (A) and (B) are true.
(d) CO can be reduced by zinc.

393. Zinc is resistant to atmospheric corrosion because its surface is covered with a thin layer of
(a) ZnO (b) $Zn\ (OH)_2$
(c) $ZnCO_3$ (d) $ZnCO_3.3Zn(OH)_2$

394. In the reaction $Zn + NaOH \xrightarrow{\Delta} X$, the product X is
(a) Na_2ZnO_2 (b) $2\ NaZnO_2$
(c) $Zn\ (OH)_2$ (d) none of these

395. Zn gives H_2 gas with H_2SO_4 and HCl but not with HNO_3 because
(a) Zn acts as an oxidising agent when it reacts with HNO_3
(b) HNO_3 is a weaker acid than H_2SO_4 and HCl
(c) in the electrochemical series, Zn is above hydrogen
(d) NO_3^- ion is reduced in preference to the hydronium ion

396. The sulfide ore which is red in colour is
(a) zinc blende (b) iron pyrites
(c) cinnabar (d) galena

397. The ore having two different metal atoms is
(a) hematite (b) galena
(c) magnetite (d) copper pyrites

398. Pick up the incorrect statement.
(a) Asbestos and willemite are silicate minerals.
(b) Anglesite and barites are sulfate minerals.
(c) Sylvine and fluorspar are halide minerals.
(d) Calamine and sphalerite are the minerals of calcium.

399. 'Metals are usually not found as nitrates in their ores'. Out of the statements below,
(1) Metal nitrates are highly unstable.
(2) Metal nitrates are highly soluble in water.
(a) 1 and 2 are false
(b) 1 is false but 2 is true
(c) 1 is true but 2 is false
(d) 1 and 2 are true

400. Which of the following is correct?
(a) Tinstone is magnetic in nature.
(b) Wolframite is non-magnetic in nature.
(c) Wolframite is $FeWO_4$.
(d) Cassiterite and rutile are sulfides of the metals.

401. Heating pyrites to remove sulfur is called
(a) smelting (b) calcination
(c) liquation (d) roasting

402. The most electropositive metals are isolated from their ores by
(a) high temperature reduction with carbon
(b) thermal decomposition
(c) electrolysis of fused ionic salts
(d) displacement method

403. Magnetic separation is used for increasing the concentration of the following:
(a) horn silver (b) calcite
(c) haematite (d) magnesite

404. Which of the following acts as an activator in the froth floatation process?

(a) amyl xanthate (b) sodium cyanide
(c) copper sulfate (d) pine oil

405. Frothers (used in froth floatation process) are
(a) molecules with a hydrophilic head and a hydrophobic tail
(b) molecules with a hydrophobic head and a hydrophilic tail
(c) both of the above
(d) none of these

406. Aniline or cresol when added in a froth floatation process acts as a
(a) stabiliser (b) depressant
(c) wetting agent (d) all of these

407. Sphalerite is concentrated by
(a) gravity separation (b) froth floatation
(c) magnetic separation (d) hydraulic washing
(e) leaching

MATCH THE FOLLOWING

408.

Column I	Column II
(A) Silver	(p) Zincite
(B) Calamine	(q) Carbonate ore
(C) Cerussite	(r) Amalgamation
(D) Zinc oxide	(s) Cupellation

(a) (A)—(r,s); (B)—(q); (C)—(q); (D)—(p)
(b) (A)—(q); (B)—(q); (C)—(p); (D)—(r,s)
(c)(A)—(p); (B)—(q); (C)—(r,s); (D)—(q)
(d) (A)—(s); (B)—(p); (C)—(q); (D)—(r)

409.

Column I	Column II
(A) $PbS \rightarrow PbO$	(p) Calcination
(B) $CaCO_3 \rightarrow CaO$	(q) Roasting
(C) $ZnS \rightarrow Zn$	(r) Self reduction
(D) $Cu_2S \rightarrow Cu$	(s) Carbon reduction

(a) (A)—(p); (B)—(q); (C)—(r); (D)—(s)
(b) (A)—(q); (B)—(p); (C)—(q,s); (D)—(q,r)
(c) (A)—(r); (B)—(r); (C)—(q); (D)—(s)
(d) (A)—(q); (B)—(s); (C)—(r); (D)—(p)

410.

Column I	Column II
(A) Decomposition of iodide	(p) Silver
(B) Complex formation and displacement by metal	(q) Bismuth
(C) liquation	(r) Ultrapure gallium
(D) Zone refining	(s) Zirconium

(a) (A)—(r); (B)—(s); (C)—(p); (D)—(q)
(b) (A)—(s); (B)—(q); (C)—(p); (D)—(r)
(c) (A)—(p); (B)—(q); (C)—(r); (D)—(s)
(d) (A)—(s); (B)—(p); (C)—(q); (D)—(r)

ASSERTION REASON

Directions: In each of the following questions, a statement of Assertion (A) is given followed by a corresponding statement of Reason (R) just below it. Of the statements, mark the correct answer as

(a) if both the assertion and the reason are true and the reason is the correct explanation of the assertion.
(b) if both the assertion and the reason are true but the reason is not the correct explanation of the assertion.
(c) if the assertion is true but the reason is false.
(d) if both the assertion and the reason are false.

411. Assertion: In the smelting process, the roasted ore is heated with powdered coke in the presence of a flux.
Reason: Oxides are reduced to metal by carbon or carbon monoxide and impurities are removed as slag.

412. Assertion: Al is used as a reducing agent in aluminothermy.
Reason: Al has a lower melting point than Fe, Cr and Mn.

413. Assertion: Noble metals like Au, Ag are obtained using cyanide by amalgamation process.
Reason: Reverberatory furnace is used for roasting and smelting.

414. Assertion: Highly electropositive metals are extracted by the electrolysis of their fused salts.
Reason: Highly electropositive metals cannot be reduced by chemical reduction methods.

415. Assertion: Lead, tin and bismuth are purified by the liquation method.
Reason: Lead, tin and bismuth have low MP as compared to the impurities.

416. Assertion: Iron is found in the free state in nature.
Reason: Iron is the least reactive element.

417. Assertion: Extraction of iron metal from iron oxide ore is carried out by heating with coke.
Reason: The reaction $Fe_2O_3(s) \rightarrow Fe(s) + 3/2\ O_2(g)$ is a spontaneous process.

418. Assertion: The non-fusible impurities present in iron ore are removed by $CaCO_3$.

Reason: $CaCO_3$ decomposes to CaO which reacts with SiO_2 to form $CaSiO_3$ slag.

419. Assertion: Galvanised iron does not rust.

Reason: Zinc has a more negative electrode potential than iron.

420. Assertion: Nitriding is a process of heating steel in an atmosphere of nitrogen.

Reason: Steel becomes brittle after nitriding.

421. Assertion: A solution of $FeCl_3$ in water produces a brown precipitate on standing.

Reason: Hydrolysis of $FeCl_3$ takes place in water.

422. Assertion: Copper reacts with HCl and liberates hydrogen.

Reason: Hydrogen is present below copper in the reactivity series.

423. Assertion: Zn replaces Ag from the complex $[Ag(CN)_2]^-$ to give $[Zn(CN)_4]^{2-}$.

Reason: Zn is more electropositive than Ag.

424. Assertion: $AgNO_3$ is called lunar caustic.

Reason: When it comes in contact with organic substances (such as skin, clothes) it produces a burning sensation (like caustic) and is reduced to metallic silver which is white (like the moon, luna).

425. Assertion: Gold is recovered from its solution containing aurocyanide complex by adding zinc dust.

Reason: Zinc is more electropositive than gold.

426. Assertion: Zinc oxide (ZnO) is commonly known as philosopher's wool.

Reason: It is a white powder, insoluble in water and is very light.

427. Assertion: Levigation is used for the separation of oxide ores from impurities.

Reason: Ore particles are removed by washing in a current of water.

428. Assertion: Wolframite impurities are separated from cassiterite by electromagnetic separation.

Reason: Cassiterite being magnetic, is attracted by the magnet and forms a separate heap.

429. Assertion: Carbonate and hydroxide ores are concentrated by the froth floatation process.

Reason: In the froth floatation process, mineral oil is used since it preferentially wets the gangue particles.

430. Assertion: Froth floatation process is based on the different wetting nature of the ore and gangue particles.

Reason: Mustard oil is used as a frother in the froth floatation process.

431. Assertion: Ethyl xanthate is used as a collector in the froth floatation process.

Reason: Collectors depress the floatation property of one of the components of the ore.

432. Assertion: Leaching involves treatment of the ore with a suitable reagent in order to make it soluble while impurities remain insoluble.

Reason: Leaching is a process of reduction.

433. Assertion: In calcination, the ore is heated below its melting point usually in the absence of air.

Reason: Calcination is carried out in a reverberatory furnace.

434. Assertion: Roasting is a process in which the ore is heated in the presence of air.

Reason: Concentration of the sulfide ore is done by calcination.

Answer Key

1. (b)	2. (a)	3. (a)	4. (b)	5. (b)	6. (d)	7. (b)	8. (d)	9. (b)	10. (b)
11. (d)	12. (b)	13. (c)	14. (b)	15. (a)	16. (c)	17. (e)	18. (d)	19. (d)	20. (a)
21. (d)	22. (d)	23. (a)	24. (a)	25. (c)	26. (b)	27. (c)	28. (c)	29. (c)	30. (c)
31. (d)	32. (a)	33. (b)	34. (a)	35. (c)	36. (d)	37. (b)	38. (a)	39. (a)	40. (d)
41. (b)	42. (b)	43. (a)	44. (d)	45. (b)	46. (c)	47. (c)	48. (a)	49. (a)	50. (b)
51. (d)	52. (d)	53. (d)	54. (a)	55. (c)	56. (c)	57. (b)	58. (b)	59. (c)	60. (c)
61. (b)	62. (a)	63. (c)	64. (b)	65. (b)	66. (c)	67. (c)	68. (a)	69. (b)	70. (a)
71. (c)	72. (c)	73. (b)	74. (c)	75. (d)	76. (b)	77. (a)	78. (b)	79. (b)	80. (b)
81. (b)	82. (c)	83. (b)	84. (a)	85. (c)	86. (b)	87. (a)	88. (a)	89. (d)	90. (a)
91. (b)	92. (c)	93. (d)	94. (c)	95. (d)	96. (c)	97. (b)	98. (c)	99. (a)	100. (a)
101. (a)	102. (b)	103. (c)	104. (b)	105. (a)	106. (b)	107. (b)	108. (c)	109. (b)	110. (d)
111. (b)	112. (a)	113. (b)	114. (d)	115. (a)	116. (d)	117. (c)	118. (d)	119. (c)	120. (d)

121. (d) 122. (b) 123. (a) 124. (c) 125. (a) 126. (a) 127. (d) 128. (c) 129. (b) 130. (b)
131. (a) 132. (c) 133. (b) 134. (a) 135. (d) 136. (d) 137. (a) 138. (e) 139. (c) 140. (b)
141. (a) 142. (c) 143. (b) 144. (b) 145. (d) 146. (c) 147. (d) 148. (c) 149. (b) 150. (c)
151. (d) 152. (c) 153. (c) 154. (c) 155. (a) 156. (c) 157. (d) 158. (a) 159. (a) 160. (c)
161. (e) 162. (a) 163. (d) 164. (d) 165. (b) 166. (b) 167. (c) 168. (a) 169. (d) 170. (b)
171. (c) 172. (d) 173. (b) 174. (d) 175. (b) 176. (c) 177. (c) 178. (a) 179. (b) 180. (c)
181. (b) 182. (a) 183. (a) 184. (d) 185. (b) 186. (a) 187. (b) 188. (a) 189. (a) 190. (d)
191. (a) 192. (c) 193. (c) 194. (b) 195. (a) 196. (c) 197. (a) 198. (b) 199. (c) 200. (a)
201. (b) 202. (b) 203. (d) 204. (b) 205. (c) 206. (d) 207. (d) 208. (c) 209. (b) 210. (a)
211. (b) 212. (b) 213. (a) 214. (d) 215. (b) 216. (b) 217. (d) 218. (b) 219. (d) 220. (d)
221. (d) 222. (d) 223. (d) 224. (c) 225. (c) 226. (b) 227. (d) 228. (a) 229. (c) 230. (a)
231. (d) 232. (a) 233. (a) 234. (a) 235. (a) 236. (c) 237. (d) 238. (c) 239. (b) 240. (c)
241. (d) 242. (b) 243. (b) 244. (d) 245. (d) 246. (b) 247. (d) 248. (b) 249. (c) 250. (a)
251. (d) 252. (a) 253. (a) 254. (a) 255. (d) 256. (d) 257. (c) 258. (c) 259. (b) 260. (d)
261. (c) 262. (d) 263. (b) 264. (c) 265. (c) 266. (d) 267. (a) 268. (b) 269. (a) 270. (a)
271. (b) 272. (d) 273. (b) 274. (a) 275. (d) 276. (c) 277. (c) 278. (d) 279. (b) 280. (a)
281. (d) 282. (b) 283. (d) 284. (a) 285. (d) 286. (b) 287. (a) 288. (c) 289. (b) 290. (c)
291. (a) 292. (b) 293. (d) 294. (d) 295. (a) 296. (b) 297. (e) 298. (b) 299. (a) 300. (c)
301. (b) 302. (a) 303. (d) 304. (b) 305. (d) 306. (c) 307. (c) 308. (a) 309. (d) 310. (d)
311. (a) 312. (d) 313. (b) 314. (a) 315. (a) 316. (d) 317. (c) 318. (a) 319. (a) 320. (a)
321. (b) 322. (a) 323. (c) 324. (c) 325. (c) 326. (b) 327. (a) 328. (c) 329. (a) 330. (d)
331. (b) 332. (b) 333. (b) 334. (c) 335. (b) 336. (a) 337. (b) 338. (b) 339. (d) 340. (d)
341. (d) 342. (c) 343. (b) 344. (c) 345. (b) 346. (d) 347. (a) 348. (b) 349. (a) 350. (a)
351. (b) 352. (c) 353. (c) 354. (a) 355. (b) 356. (a) 357. (d) 358. (d) 359. (c) 360. (a)
361. (d) 362. (a) 363. (b) 364. (c) 365. (c) 366. (a) 367. (b) 368. (d) 369. (a) 370. (b)
371. (c) 372. (b) 373. (c) 374. (d) 375. (a) 376. (b) 377. (b) 378. (d) 379. (b) 380. (a)
381. (a) 382. (d) 383. (d) 384. (b) 385. (b) 386. (b) 387. (c) 388. (a) 389. (c) 390. (d)
391. (c) 392. (b) 393. (d) 394. (a) 395. (d) 396. (c) 397. (d) 398. (d) 399. (b) 400. (c)
401. (d) 402. (d) 403. (c) 404. (c) 405. (a) 406. (a) 407. (b) 408. (a) 409. (b) 410. (d)
411. (a) 412. (b) 413. (b) 414. (a) 415. (a) 416. (d) 417. (c) 418. (a) 419. (a) 420. (d)
421. (a) 422. (d) 423. (a) 424. (a) 425. (a) 426. (a) 427. (c) 428. (c) 429. (d) 430. (c)
431. (c) 432. (c) 433. (b) 434. (c)

Hints and Solutions

Occurrence of Elements

1. **(b):** Most abundant transition metal in the human body is iron (Fe).

2. **(a):** Au metal is found in the native state in nature.

3. **(a):** Na is an alkali metal, highly reactive. Hence it is present in the combined state.

4. **(b):** Gold, Ag and Pt are called noble metals. They are unreactive and found in the free state.

5. **(b):** Silicon is the main constituent of rocks.

6. **(d):** The second most common element in the universe after hydrogen is silicon.

7. **(b):** Hydrogen is the most abundant element in the universe.

8. **(d):** Siderophile contains metals.

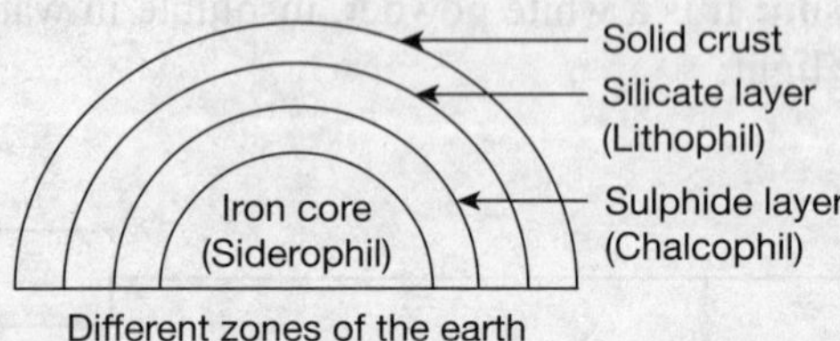

Different zones of the earth

9. **(b):** Cu^{2+} ion is mainly present in the bones of the human body and is most abundant. All other ions are required in lower amounts in the body.

10. **(b):** Iron is found in the earth's crust as oxides, carbonates and sulfides. These are the minerals of iron. Out of these minerals, the oxides of iron are employed for extraction of the metal. Therefore, the oxides of iron are the ores of iron.

11. **(d):** (a) Carnallite $KCl.MgCl_2.6H_2O$
(b) Malachite $CuCO_3.Cu(OH)_2$

(c) Galena PbS
(d) Bauxite $Al_2O_3.2H_2O$
∴ Ore of aluminium is bauxite.

12. (b):

Ore	Formula	Nature
(a) Malachite	$CuCO_3.Cu(OH)_2$	Carbonate ore
(b) Hematite	Fe_2O_3	Oxide ore
(c) Copper glance	Cu_2S	Sulfide ore
(d) Zinc blende	ZnS	Sulfide ore

13. (c): Ruby is a mineral of aluminium, that is, Al_2O_3 containing Cr. It does not contain silicon.

14. (b): The main impurity found in red bauxite is ferrite (Fe_2O_3) while silica is the chief impurity in white bauxite.

15. (a): The chief ore of tin is cassiterite or tinstone, SnO_2.

16. (c): Quartz is found in many varieties which have different colours due to impurities. For example, amethyst (purple), opal (white), carnelian and agate. Hence, agate is SiO_2.

17. (e):

Metal	Ore
Aluminium	Bauxite ($Al_2O_3.2H_2O$)
Copper	Pyrites ($CuFeS_2$)
Potassium	Sylvine (KCl)
Magnesium	Dolomite ($MgCO_3.CaCO_3$)
Radium	Pitchblende

18. (d): Titanium containing mineral found in our country is ilmenite ($FeTiO_3$ or $FeO.TiO_2$).

19. (d): The ore pitchblende is the main source of Ra and Th metals.

20. (a): All the ores contain magnesium except magnetite (Fe_3O_4) which is an iron ore.

21. (d): Bauxite ($Al_2O_3.2H_2O$) ore is used for industrial extraction of aluminium in India.

22. (d): Bauxite ($Al_2O_3.2H_2O$) is an oxide ore of aluminium.

23. (a): Hematite Fe_2O_3.

24. (a): Aluminium is obtained from bauxite ($Al_2O_3.2H_2O$) ore because bauxite is available in large quantities.

25. (c): Sapphire (Al_2O_3 containing traces of Ti and Fe acquires a blue colour) is a mineral of Al.

26. (b): Malachite (basic copper carbonate) $CuCO_3.Cu(OH)_2$ is a carbonate ore. Pyrolusite (MnO_2), diaspore ($Al_2O_3.H_2O$) and cassiterite or tinstone (SnO_2) are oxide ores.

27. (c): Cerussite is an ore of lead (Pb). Its chemical formula is $PbCO_3$.

28. (c): Azurite is a basic carbonate ore of copper $2CuCO_3.Cu(OH)_2$.

29. (c):
Dolomite.: $MgCO_3.CaCO_3$
Magnesite : $MgCO_3$
Carnallite : $KCl.MgCl_2.6H_2O$
Mg can be extracted from all the three ores mentioned above.

30. (c): Galena (PbS), anglesite ($PbSO_4$), calamine ($ZnCO_3$) is not an ore of Pb, cerussite ($PbCO_3$).

31. (d): Nitrate salt being highly soluble in water, is the least likely to be found in minerals.

32. (a): KNO_3 salt being highly soluble in water is not present in minerals.

33. (b): Aluminium is the most abundant metal in the earth's crust.

34. (a): Silver occurs in the native state as well as in the combined state.

35. (c): Sea weed contains iodine.

36. (d): Vanadium is found in sea weed.

37. (b): Iron is present in hemoglobin (blood).

38. (a): Oxygen is the most abundant in the earth's crust by weight.

39. (a): Oxygen is the most abundant in the earth's crust in terms of number of atoms per 100 atoms.

40. (d): $MgCO_3$ is the formula of magnesite.

41. (b): Malachite $[CuCO_3.Cu(OH)_2]$ is an ore of copper.

42. (b): Cr does not exist as a sulfide ore. It occurs as the chromite ore, $FeO.Cr_2O_3$ or $FeCr_2O_4$.

43. (a): Cinnabar is HgS

44. (d): Chalcopyrites ($CuFeS_2$).

45. (b): Cuprite (Cu_2O) and argentite (Ag_2S). Thus, argentite is a sulfide ore.

46. (c): Black jack (ZnS), also called zinc blende, is an ore of zinc.

47. (c):
Limonite : $Fe_2O_3.3H_2O$ (ore of iron)
Siderite : $FeCO_3$ (ore of iron)
Carnallite :$KCl.MgCl_2.6H_2O$ (does not contain iron)
Chalcopyrites : $CuFeS_2$ (ore of iron)
Hence, carnallite is not an iron containing ore.

48. (a): Formula of carnallite is $KCl.MgCl_2.6H_2O$. So, carnallite contains K and Mg.

49. (a): Apatite is $[CaF_2.3Ca_3(PO_4)_2]$. It is an ore of fluorine with calcium. It is also called fluorapatite.

50. (b): Carnallite is $KCl.MgCl_2.6H_2O$. It is an ore of Mg, gypsum is $CaSO_4.2H_2O$, magnetite is Fe_3O_4, carnotite is $K_2(UO_2)_2(VO_4)_2.3H_2O$.

51. (d): Cryolite (Na_3AlF_6) → Halide ore

$$\left.\begin{array}{l}\text{Galena (PbS)}\\ \text{Cinnabar (HgS)}\end{array}\right\}\text{Sulfide ore}$$

Bauxite $Al_2O_3.2H_2O \rightarrow$ Oxide ore

52. **(d):** Fluorspar (CaF_2) does not contain Al, cryolite (Na_3AlF_6), feldspar ($KAlSi_3O_8$), mica($K_2O.3Al_2O_3.6SiO_2.2H_2O$).

53. **(d):** Cryolite (Na_3AlF_6) is an (halide) ore of aluminium.

54. **(a):** Horn silver (AgCl) is a chloride ore.

55. **(c):** Carnallite is an important ore of magnesium. It is KCl. $MgCl_2.6H_2O$.

56. **(c):** Cryolite (Na_3AlF_6) does not contain oxygen.

57. **(b):** Anglesite ($PbSO_4$) is not an ore of aluminium. It is an ore of lead.

58. **(b):** $\left.\begin{array}{l}\text{Bauxite}\,(Al_2O_3).2H_2O \\ \text{Cryolite}\,(Na_3AlF_6) \\ \text{Corundum}\,(Al_2O_3)\end{array}\right\}$ Minerals of Al

Gypsum ($CaSO_4.2H_2O$), is not an ore of aluminium.

59. **(c):** Gypsum ($CaSO_4.2H_2O$) is an ore of calcium, dolomite ($CaCO_3.MgCO_3$), magnesite ($MgCO_3$) and carnallite (KCl. $MgCl_2.6H_2O$) are ores of magnesium.

60. **(c):** Asbestos is a sheet silicate having the formula $CaMg_3(SiO_3)_4$.

61. **(b):** Feldspar (orthoclase) is $KAlSi_3O_8$.
It is used in the manufacture of porcelain.
Asbestos is $CaMg_3(SiO_3)_4$. It is used for fireproof sheets, cloth, and so on. Pyrargyrite (ruby silver) is $2AgSbS_2$ or $Ag_2S.Sb_2S_3$. It is an ore of silver.
Diaspore is $Al_2O_3.H_2O$. It is an ore of aluminium.

62. **(a):** Lapis lazuli is the sodium aluminosilicate present in earth rocks as blue stone.

63. **(c):** Metals which are not reactive (noble metals) occur in the native state in nature.

64. **(b):** Bauxite, $Al_2O_3.2H_2O$ is an ore of Al.

65. **(b):** Sulfur occurs free in nature.

Concentration of Ores

66. **(c):** The common impurity present in bauxite is Fe_2O_3, SiO_2 and to some extent TiO_2.

67. **(c):** In bauxite ore, Al_2O_3 reacts with conc. NaOH and forms sodium metaaluminate. This, further dissolves in water.

$$Al_2O_3 + 2\,H_2O + 2\,NaOH \xrightarrow[35\text{ bar}]{500\text{ K}} 2\,NaAlO_2 + 3\,H_2O$$

$$NaAlO_2 + 2\,H_2O \rightarrow NaAl(OH)_4$$

SiO_2 also dissolves in NaOH to give sodium silicate.

$$SiO_2 + 2\,NaOH \xrightarrow[35\text{ bar}]{500\text{ K}} Na_2SiO_3 + H_2O$$

68. **(a):** Removal of siliceous matter from ores is known as dressing or concentration of ore.

69. **(b):** Gravity separation method is based on the difference in densities of ore particles and impurities.

70. **(a):** Copper pyrites, a sulfide ore of copper, is concentrated by froth floatation.

71. **(c):** Copper sulfate acts as an activator in the froth floatation process.

72. **(c):** Hydraulic classifier is generally used to carry out gravity separation.

73. **(b):** Gravity separation is used when there is a large difference between the densities of the gangue and the ore particles. Hence, heavy metal oxide ores like hematite are concentrated by this process.

74. **(c):** Rutile (magnetic) is separated from chlorapatite (non-magnetic) by the magnetic separation method.

75. **(d):** As cuprite (Cu_2O) is non-magnetic in nature, it cannot be separated from silica and other impurities by the magnetic separation method.

76. **(b):** Cassiterite SnO_2 or tinstone, an ore of tin, being non-magnetic can be separated from magnetic impurities like Fe and Mn by this method.

77. **(a):** An ore of tin (being non-magnetic in nature) containing $FeCrO_4$ (being magnetic in nature) is concentrated by magnetic separation.

78. **(b):** Ores like magnetite (Fe_3O_4) or ferrous tungstates ($FeWO_4$) (magnetic in nature) in tin ores (non-magnetic in nature) are concentrated by magnetic separation.

79. **(b):** Wolframite ore [$FeWO_4$] is present in tinstone as an impurity and it has the same mass per unit volume as that of tinstone. So, it is separated by an electromagnetic separator as wolframite is magnetic and hence gets attracted by the magnet while tinstone doesn't.

80. **(b):** Pyrolusite (MnO_2) is an oxide ore which is not concentrated by the froth floatation process.

81. **(b):** Floatation property of ZnS is depressed by forming a soluble complex with CN^- and PbS forms froth.

$$ZnS + 4\,NaCN \rightarrow \underset{\text{Soluble complex}}{Na_2[Zn(CN)_4]} + Na_2S$$

82. **(c):** Galena (PbS) is best concentrated by the froth floatation process.

83. **(b):** In froth floatation, the substances like pine oil, xanthates and fatty acids are added as collectors. These substances attach themselves by their polar groups to the minerals which then become water repellent and thus pass on into the froth. Thus, in other words, collectors enhance the non-wettability of mineral particles.

84. **(a):** Froth floatation is used for the concentration of sulfide ores only. Thus, cinnabar (HgS) is concentrated by this method. Bauxite ($Al_2O_3.2H_2O$), malachite [$CuCO_3.Cu(OH)_2$] and incite (ZnO) cannot be concentrated by this method.

85. **(c):** Sulfide ores are concentrated by froth floatation. Thus, copper pyrites ($CuFeS_2$) is concentrated by forth floatation.

86. **(b):** Froth floatation process is used for the concentration of sulfide ores.

87. **(a):** Out of the given methods, froth floatation is used for the concentration of ores.

88. (a): Froth floatation process for the concentration of sulfide ores is an illustration of the practical application of adsorption of the oil at the surface of the ore particles and water at the surface of the gangue particles.

89. (d): Froth floatation is successful in separating impurities from the ores because the pure ore is not as easily wetted by water as by pine oil, cresylic acid.

90. (a): Chalcopyrites is a sulfide ore; that is why it is concentrated by froth floatation.

91. (b): $Al_2O_3.2H_2O$ (bauxite) is concentrated by leaching with NaOH.Al_2O_3 dissolves leaving other impurities undissolved.
$Al_2O_3.2H_2O + 2\ NaOH \rightarrow 2\ NaAlO_2 + 3\ H_2O$

92. (c): The correct statement is: Alumina dissolves as sodium meta-aluminate and silica (SiO_2) as sodium silicate leaving Fe_2O_3, TiO_2 and other impurities behind.

$$\underset{\text{Alumina}}{Al_2O_3} + 2\ NaOH + 3\ H_2O \xrightarrow{475-523K} \underset{\text{Sodium meta-aluminate}}{2\ Na[Al(OH)_4]}$$

$$\underset{\text{Silica}}{SiO_2} + 2\ NaOH \xrightarrow{475-523K} \underset{\text{Sodium silicate}}{Na_2SiO_3 + H_2O}$$

The impurities are filtered off and the solution of sodium meta-aluminate is neutralised by passing CO_2 when hydrated alumina separates out. Sodium silicate remains in the solution.

$$2\ Na[Al(OH)_4] + 2CO_2 \rightarrow Al_2O_3.x\ H_2O + 2\ NaHCO_3$$

Hydrated alumina is filtered, dried and heated to give back pure alumina.

$$Al_2O_3.x\ H_2O \xrightarrow{1473K} Al_2O_3 + x\ H_2O$$

93. (d): Gold and silver ores are concentrated by leaching. In this method, the ore is treated with a suitable reagent in which the ore is soluble but impurities are not. Thus, impurities are removed by filtration.
Among galena (PbS), copper pyrites ($CuFeS_2$), cinnabar (HgS), argentite (Ag_2S) and copper glance (Cu_2S), argentite being the silver ore is concentrated by the chemical leaching method.

$$\underset{\text{Argentite}}{Ag_2S + 4\ NaCN} \rightarrow \underset{\text{Soluble complex}}{2Na[Ag(CN)_2]} + Na_2S$$

94. (c): Both (a) and (b) are practised. For example,

$$2AlO_2^- + 4\ H_2O \rightarrow 2\ [Al(OH)_4]^-$$
$$2\ [Al(OH)_4]^- + 2\ CO_2 \rightarrow Al_2O_3.xH_2O + 2\ HCO_3^-$$
$$Al_2O_3.xH_2O \xrightarrow{1473K} Al_2O_3 + x\ H_2O$$

95. (d): Wolframite (ferromagnetic) is separated from cassiterite (non-magnetic) by magnetic separation.

96. (c): The cyanide process is used in the leaching/extraction of both silver and gold because these from complex salts with CN^- ions due to the presence of a lone pair of electrons on the nitrogen atom.

Extraction of Crude Metal from Concentrated ore

97. (b): Roasting is the process of heating the ore in an excess supply of air below its melting point. This process is employed when oxidation of the ore is required. During roasting, moisture is drawn away, volatile impurities are removed, impurities like sulfur, phosphorus, arsenic are removed as oxides, the ore undergoes oxidation to form the metal oxide or sulfate.

$$2\ PbS + 3\ O_2 \rightarrow PbO + 2\ SO_2\uparrow$$

98. (c): In this process,sulfide ores are converted into oxide ores.
$2\ ZnS + 3\ O_2 \rightarrow 2\ ZnO + 2\ SO_2\uparrow$

99. (a): Heating of pyrites in air for the oxidation of sulfur is called roasting.

100. (a): The compounds which combine with impurities present in the ore (at high temperature) and remove them as a fusible substance (slag), are known as fluxes. When basic impurities are present, an acid flux is used.

$$\underset{\text{Basic impurity}}{FeO} + \underset{\text{Acidic flux}}{SiO_2} \rightarrow \underset{\text{Slag}}{FeSiO_3}$$

101. (a): Matte contains mainly Cu_2S and FeS.

102. (b): The process of heating the ore strongly in an excess of air so that the volatile impurities are removed and the ore is changed to oxide is known as roasting.

103. (c): Roasting of copper pyrites ore is for the following purposes. To burn off As, Sb as oxides and sulfur partially to leave enough to combine with Cu and Fe as Cu_2S and FeS and to convert the iron and copper partially to oxides.

$$2\ CuFeS_2 + O_2 \xrightarrow{\Delta} Cu_2S + 2\ FeS + SO_2$$
$$2\ FeS + 3\ O_2 \rightarrow 2FeO + 2\ SO_2$$
$$2\ Cu_2S + 3\ O_2 \rightarrow 2Cu_2O + 2\ SO_2$$
$$Cu_2O + FeS \rightarrow Cu_2S + FeO$$

104. (b): Zinc blende (ZnS)
$2\ ZnS + 3\ O_2 \xrightarrow{\Delta} 2\ ZnO + 2\ SO_2$

105. (a): The process in which metal is obtained in the fused state is called smelting. During roasting and calcination, metal oxides are formed while floatation is used to concentrate the ore.

106. (b): In the metallurgy of zinc, flux is not used because zinc is volatile and hence easily separated.

107. (b): Extraction of Zn from ZnS is achieved by roasting followed by reduction with carbon.
$2\ ZnS + 3\ O_2 \rightarrow 2\ ZnO + 2\ SO_2$
$ZnO + C \rightarrow Zn + CO$

108. (c): $\underset{\text{Acidic flux}}{SiO_2}, \underbrace{CaCO_3, Lime, CaO}_{\text{Basic flux}}$

109. (b): The cheap compound having a high melting point used in furnaces is CaO.

110. (d): The term 'smelting' is used to describe the process in which ore is melted.

111. (b): Reduction with carbon is called smelting.
$Fe_2O_3 + 3\ C \rightarrow 2\ Fe + 3\ CO$

112. (a): It is used for smelting (reduction) of oxide ores and for roasting of sulfide ores.

113. (b): Calcination is used to remove organic matter, water from hydrated oxides and CO_2 from carbonates.

114. (d): Calcination is a process in which the ore is heated generally in the absence of air to expel water from a hydrated oxide or carbon dioxide from a carbonate.

115. (a): $CaCO_3 \rightarrow CaO + CO_2$
Heating the ore in the absence of air is calcination.

116. (d): The role of calcination in metallurgical operations is to remove moisture, decompose carbonate and to drive off organic matter.

117. (c): Electric furnace gives the highest temperature.

118. (d): Zinc blende is heated in a regular supply of air in a furnace at a temperature below the melting point of the metal (roasting).
$2\,ZnS + 3\,O_2 \rightarrow 2\,ZnO + SO_2$

119. (c): Tinstone (SnO_2) after roasting and washing is called black tin.

120. (d): The correct statement is: Fluxes are carefully chosen to combine with the gangue present in the ore to produce easily fusible slag to carry away the impurities.

121. (d): Flux is used to remove silica and undesirable metal oxides.

122. (b): Limestone which is a basic flux, is used to remove acidic impurities in metallurgical processes.

123. (a): Refractory materials such as SiO_2, CaO, MgO and SiC are used in construction of furnaces because they can withstand high temperatures.

124. (c): Limestone ($CaCO_3$) is used for the formation of slag in Fe extraction.

$$\underset{\text{Limestone}}{CaCO_3} \xrightarrow{\Delta} \underset{\text{Basic flux}}{CaO} + CO_2\uparrow$$

$$CaO + \underset{\text{Gangue or impurity}}{SiO_2} \rightarrow \underset{\text{Slag}}{CaSiO_3}$$

125. (a): In a lime kiln, to get higher yield of CO_2, the measure that can be taken is to remove CaO formed as a product so that the reaction will proceed in the forward direction.

$$CaCO_3 \underset{}{\overset{\Delta}{\rightleftharpoons}} CaO + CO_2$$

126. (a): Carbon is used as a reducing agent in smelting. For example,

$$Fe_2O_3 + 3\,C \xrightarrow{\Delta} 2\,Fe + 3\,CO$$

127. (d): A blast furnace is employed in the metallurgy of iron, copper and lead for the smelting of oxide ore with coke and flux.

128. (c): Furnaces are lined with CaO because it is refractory and basic in nature.

129. (b): Heating with carbon in the absence of air is known as carbon reduction. This is used in iron metallurgy.

$$Fe_2O_3 + 3\,C \xrightarrow{\text{(Blast furnace)}} 2\,Fe + 3\,CO$$

130. (b): Iron is extracted by the thermal reduction process in the blast furnace.

$$Fe_2O_3 + 3\,C \xrightarrow{>1123\text{K}} 2\,Fe + 3\,CO$$

131. (a): Chemical reduction is not suitable for converting bauxite into aluminium because Al is a strong reducing agent and it has a strong affinity for oxygen other than carbon.

132. (c): In the Ellingham diagram, the (Mg, MgO) and (Al, Al_2O_3) curves intersect at point A (1623 K). The $\Delta_f G°$ value of Al_2O_3 at a temperature below 1623 K is less –ve than that of MgO. Therefore, below 1623 K, Mg can reduce Al_2O_3 to Al. However, above 1623 K, the $\Delta_f G°$ value for Al_2O_3 is more negative than that of MgO. Therefore, above 1623 K, Al can reduce MgO to Mg.

133. (b): Below 1623 K, Mg can reduce Al_2O_3. But Mg is a much costlier metal than Al and hence, the process will be uneconomical.

134. (a): The reduction process is based on the thermodynamic stability of the products formed and not on their volatility.

135. (d): Correct statement is: The reduction of a metal oxide is easier if the metal formed is in the liquid state at the temperature of reduction because the entropy is higher if the metal is in the liquid state than when it is in the solid state.

136. (d): Refer to the Ellingham diagram. Below 1973 K, the $\Delta_f G°$ curve for the formation of SiO_2 lies above the $\Delta_f G°$ curve for the formation of MgO. Therefore, below 1973 K, Mg can reduce SiO_2 to Si.

$$SiO_2 + 2\,Mg \xrightarrow{<1973\text{K}} 2\,MgO + Si;$$

$\Delta_r G° = -\text{ve}$

Above 1973 K, the $\Delta_f G°$ curve for the formation of SiO_2 lies below the corresponding curve for the formation of MgO. Therefore, above 1973 K, silicon can reduce MgO to Mg.

$$2MgO + Si \xrightarrow{>1973\text{K}} SiO_2 + 2\,Mg$$

137. (a): In the Ellingham diagram, the three lines, (C, CO_2), (C, CO) and of CO_2 from C as well as from CO is energetically more favourable and above this temperature, the formation of CO from C is energetically more favourable. In other words, below 983 K, both C and CO can act as reduction agents but since CO can be more easily oxidised to CO_2 than C to CO_2, below 983 K, CO is a more effective reducing agent than C. Thus, option (a) is correct.

138. (e): Mg is more electropositive than Al and hence cannot be obtained by reduction of MgO with Al.

139. (c): The interpretation of ($\Delta G° = -RT\ln K$), the equilibrium constant. In the given redox reaction, all the species are solids at room temperature, therefore, there does not exist any equilibrium between them and hence the reaction does not occur at room temperature. However, at high temperature, when Cr melts, the value of $T\Delta S$ increases. As a result, the value of $\Delta_r G°$ becomes more –ve and hence the reaction proceeds rapidly.

140. (b): Above 983 K, free energy change for the formation of CO_2 is more negative than that for ferric oxide. Thus, above this temperature, carbon has a higher affinity towards oxygen than iron.

141. (a): The metal which is more reactive than Al can reduce alumina (Al_2O_3). Considering the Ellingham diagram, the metals for which the free energy of formation ($\Delta_f G°$) of their oxides is more negative can reduce those metal oxides for which $\Delta_f G^\circ$ of formation of their respective oxides is less negative. Hence, Mg can be used to reduce Al_2O_3.

142. (c): Chromite ore ($FeO.Cr_2O_3$) is first converted into free Cr_2O_3 which is then reduced by Al to pure Cr metal.

$Cr_2O_3 + 2\,Al \rightarrow Al_2O_3 + 2\,Cr$

143. (b): In the thermite reaction, Al acts as a reducing agent. In this process, a mixture of 3 parts (by weight) Fe_2O_3 and 1 part (by weight) Al powder is used.

$Fe_2O_3 + 2\,Al \rightarrow Al_2O_3 + 2\,Fe$

144. (b): The alumino-thermite process involves the reduction of oxides such as Fe_2O_3, Mn_3O_4 and Cr_2O_3 to metals with aluminium.

$Cr_2O_3 + 2\,Al \rightarrow Al_2O_3 + 2\,Cr;\ \Delta H = -ve$

These oxides are not reduced by C easily.

145. (d): The alumino-thermic process is used for the metallurgy of Fe, Cr and Mn where their oxides are reduced by Al powder to the respective metals. It is not used for Pb, Ag and Al.

146. (c): The roasting process is commonly used for sulfide ores.

147. (d): In the Hall–Heroult process,

$2\,Al_2O_3 \rightarrow 4\,Al + 3\,O_2$

$4\,C + 3\,O_2 \rightarrow 2\,CO_2 + 2\,CO\uparrow$

$2\,Al_2O_3 + 4\,C \rightarrow 4\,Al + 2\,CO_2 + 2\,CO$

Only for the removal of CO_2, the following equation is possible.

$2\,Al_2O_3 + 3C \rightarrow 4\,Al + 3\,CO_2$

$3 \times 12 = 364 \times 27 = 108$

$\because$ For 108 g of Al, 36 g of C is required in the above reaction.

$\therefore$ For 270 g of Al, the required amount of

$C = \frac{36}{108} \times 270 = 90$ g

148. (c): Strongly electropositive metals are prepared by electrolytic reduction.

149. (b): Al is highly electropositive. It can be obtained by electrolytic reduction and not by carbon reduction.

150. (c): CaO and K_2O cannot be reduced by carbon to give the respective metals because C is less electropositive than Ca and K.

151. (d): Aluminium is prepared in large quantities by electrolysing Al_2O_3 dissolved in a fused electrolyte ($Na_3AlF_3 + CaF_2$).

152. (c): Na_3AlF_6 and CaF_2 increase the conductance and decrease the MP of Al_2O_3.

153. (c): Sodium is a highly reactive metal. It is extracted by the electrolysis of its fused salt

154. (c): The reduction potential of Cr ($Cr^{3+}/Cr = -0.74$ V) is less negative than that of H_2O ($H_2O/H_2 = -0.83$ V). Therefore, Cr cannot be obtained by electrolysis.

155. (a): $Cr_2O_3 + 2\,Al \rightarrow Al_2O_3 + 2\,Cr$

156. (c): This process is called hydrometallurgy.

157. (d): $Zn + 2\,K[Ag(CN)_2] \rightarrow K_2[Zn(CN)_4] + 2\,Ag\downarrow$

$Zn + 2K[Au(CN)_2] \rightarrow K_2[Zn(CN)_4] + 2\,Au\downarrow$

158. (a): Hydrometallurgical process of extraction of metals is based on complex formation. For example, Ag_2S is converted into $Na[Ag(CN)_2]$. When Zn is added, Ag is displaced.

159. (a): Metal displacement is used for the extraction of copper from its ore with low copper content. Solution of Cu^{2+} ions is treated with scrap iron to get Cu metal.

$Cu^{2+}(aq) + Fe(s) \rightarrow Cu(s) + Fe^{2+}(aq)$

160. (c): Extraction and recovery of Ag and Au.

Leaching:

$\underset{\text{(Argentite)}}{2\,Ag_2S} + 8\,NaCN + O_2 + 2\,H_2O \rightarrow$

$\underset{\text{(Soluble complex)}}{4\,Na\,[Ag(CN)_2]} + 4\,NaOH + 2\,S$

Recovery:

$2\,Na[Ag(CN)_2] + Zn \xrightarrow{\text{Displacement}} Na_2[Zn(CN)_4] + 2\,Ag\downarrow$

Similarly, gold ore is leached and recovery of Au is done by displacement with Zn.

$4\,Au + 8KCN + O_2 + 2\,H_2O \rightarrow \underset{\text{(Soluble complex)}}{4\,K\,[Au(CN)_2]} + 4\,KOH$

$2\,K\,[Au(CN)_2] + Zn \rightarrow K_2\,[Zn(CN)_4] + 2\,Au\downarrow$

161. (e): $HgS + O_2 \xrightarrow{\Delta} Hg + SO_2$

162. (a): Auto-reduction process is used in the extraction Cu and Hg.

$2\,Cu_2S + 3\,O_2 \rightarrow 2\,Cu_2O + 2\,SO_2$

$2\,Cu_2O + Cu_2S \rightarrow 6\,Cu + SO_2$

$2\,HgS + 3\,O_2 \rightarrow 2\,HgO + 2\,SO_2$

$2\,HgO \xrightarrow{\Delta} 2\,Hg + O_2$.

163. (d): $Cu_2S + 2\,Cu_2O \rightarrow \underset{\text{(Auto-reduction)}}{6\,Cu + SO_2}$

This reaction occurs in the reverberatory furnace to get metallic copper.

164. (d): $2\,HgS + 3\,O_2 \rightarrow 2\,HgO + 2\,SO_2$

$2\,HgO + HgS \rightarrow 3\,Hg + SO_2$

$2\,Cu_2S + 3\,O_2 \rightarrow 2\,Cu_2O + 2\,SO_2$

$Cu_2S + 2\,Cu_2O \rightarrow 6\,Cu + SO_2$

$PbS + 3\,O_2 \rightarrow 2\,PbO + 2\,SO_2$

$2\,PbO + PbS \rightarrow 3\,Pb + SO_2$

This method is used for less electropositive metals.

165. (b): PbO and $PbSO_4$ get reduced by PbS itself which is already present in the mixture. Because the reduction takes place by the mixture itself, it is known as self-reduction.

$2\,PbO + PbO \xrightarrow{\Delta} 3\,Pb + SO_2\uparrow$

$PbSO_4 + PbS \xrightarrow{\Delta} 2\,Pb + 2\,SO_2\uparrow$

166. (b): The most electropositive metals are obtained from their ores by electrolysis of their fused ionic salts because these metals have large negative values of electrode potentials and hence are difficult to reduce.

167. (c): Na is extracted by the electrometallurgical method.

168. (a): Aluminium metal is obtained by the electrolysis of fused Al_2O_3 and cryolite (Na_3lF_6).

169. (d): In the electrometallurgy of Al, a fused mixture of alumina (Al_2O_3), cryolite (Na_3AlF_6) and fluorspar (CaF_2) is electrolysed using graphite as the anode and graphite lined iron as the cathode. During electrolysis, Al is liberated at the cathode while CO and CO_2 are liberated at the anode.

At cathode: $Al^{3+}(melt) + 3e^- \rightarrow Al(l)$

At anode: $C(s) + O^{2-}(melt) \rightarrow CO(g) + 2e^-$

$C(s) + 2\,O^{2-}(melt) \rightarrow CO_2(g) + 24e^-$

If instead of graphite, some other metal is used as the anode, then the O_2 liberated will not only oxidise the metal of the electrode but would also convert some of the Al liberated at the cathode back to Al_2O_3. Since graphite is much cheaper than any other metal, it is used as the anode.

170. (b): Pure alumina is a bad conductor of electricity and the fusion temperature of pure alumina is about 2000°C.At this temperature, when the electrolysis is carried out, thefused mass of the metal vaporises as the boiling point of Al is 1800°C. To overcome this difficulty, Na_3AlF_6 and CaF_2 are mixed with alumina.

171. (c): The most active metals are extracted from their ores by electrolytic reduction.

172. (d): The reduction potential of Fe is less negative than that of H_2O, so it not manufactured by electrolysis.

173. (b): Impurities of Pb present in silver can be removed as the volatile oxide PbO in the process of cupellation.

174. (d): Pickling is done by dipping the impure metal in dilute acid to remove the basic layer on it.

Refining of Crude Metals

175. (b): The purest zinc is made by zone refining.

176. (c): Zone refining is employed for preparing extremely pure metals. It is based on the principle that when a molten solution of the impure metal is allowed to cool, the pure metal crystallises out while the impurities remain in the melt. Semiconductors like Si, Ge and Ga are purified by this method.

177. (c): The main function of roasting is to remove volatile impurities and to convert the ore into the oxide.

178. (a): Silver is obtained by leaching its ore with dilute cyanide solution.

179. (b): Electrolytic reduction method is used in the extraction of highly electropositive elements.

180. (c): Aluminium cannot be electro-refined by using an aqueous solution of its salt.

181. (b): Leaching is not employed for refining of metals.

182. (a): The van Arkel method involves converting the metal to a volatile stable compound.

$\underset{\text{Impure}}{Ti + 2\,I_2} \xrightarrow{500\,K} TiI_4$ (volatile stable)

$TiI_4 \xrightarrow{1700\,K} \underset{\text{Pure}}{Ti} + 2\,I_2$

183. (a): Ni combines with CO at 323 K to form $Ni(CO)_4$ which decomposes thermally at 423 K to give pure Ni metal.

$Ni\,(CO)_4 \xrightarrow{423\,K} Ni + 4\,CO\uparrow$

184. (d): In the van Arkel method, the impure metal is first converted into a volatile compound, generally iodide, at a lower temperature which is then decomposed at a higher temperature to give the pure metal.

185. (b): Here, M is Ni metal and this process used for the refining of nickel is called the Mond's process or vapour phase refining. When impure Ni is heated in a current of CO at 330–350 K, it forms the volatile nickel tetracarbonyl complex leaving behind impurities. The complex is then heated to a higher temperature (450–470 K), when it undergoes thermal decomposition to give pure Ni.

186. (a): The van Arkel method of refining zirconium removes all oxygen and nitrogen impurities.

187. (b): Ni combines with CO to form volatile $Ni(CO)_4$ which decomposes to give pure Ni metal and CO on heating.

188. (a): The stationary phase is selected in such a way that the impurities are more strongly adsorbed on the stationary phase than the element to be purified. Under these conditions, when the column is extracted, the impurities will be retained by the stationary phase while the pure component (element) is easily eluted.

189. (a): Metals like Na, K, Mg, Ca and Al are reduced by the electrolytic method.

190. (d): In the electrolytic refining of zinc, the anode is made up of impure zinc while a strip of pure zinc acts as the cathode. An acidified solution of zinc sulfate acts as the electrolyte. When electricity is passed, the following reactions occur.

At cathode: $Zn^{2+} + 2\,e^- \rightarrow \underset{\text{Pure}}{Zn}$

At anode: $\underset{\text{Impure}}{Zn} \rightarrow Zn^{2+} + 2e^-$

191. (a): Copper metal (Cu) is obtained by the electrolysis of the aqueous solution of its salts.

192. (c): Refining of Al is done by Hoope's electrolytic method. The cell consists of three layers which differ in specific gravity, The uppermost layer is of pure Al which acts as the cathode, the middle layer contains a mixture of AlF_3, BaF_2 and NaF which acts as the electrolyte whereas the lowest layer is of impure Al (Cu + Al + Si alloy) which acts as the anode.

193. (c): $\underset{\text{(Fused)}}{2\,NaCl} \rightarrow 2\,Na^+ + 2\,Cl^-$(Down's cell)

Anode: $2\,Cl^- \rightarrow 2\,e^- + Cl_2$ (oxidation)

Cathode: $2\,Na^+ + 2\,e^- \rightarrow 2\,Na$ (reduction)

194. (b): Electrolytic refining is used for Cu.

195. (a): Less reactive metals such as Cu, Zn, Au, Cr and Ni are purified by the electrolytic refining method.

196. (c): Amalgamation method is used for the extraction of noble metals like Au, Ag from native ores.

197. (a): In Castner's process, fused caustic soda (or sodium hydroxide) is electrolysed to get Na. The reactions of the process are as follows:

$NaOH \rightleftharpoons Na^+ + OH^-$

$Na^+ + e^- \rightarrow Na$ (At cathode)

$4\,OH^- \rightarrow O_2 + 2\,H_2O + 4\,e^-$ (At anode)

198. (b): Potassium is highly soluble in molten KCl, thus it is not prepared by the electrolysis of molten KCl. All other statements are correct.

199. (c): Hydrometallurgy is the process of dissolving the metal or its ore by the action of a suitable chemical reagent (complexing agent to form soluble complexes) followed by recovery of the metal either by electrolysis or by the use of a suitable precipitating agent.

$$\underset{\text{Complexing agent}}{4\,Au + 8\,KCN} + 2\,H_2O + O_2 \rightarrow \underset{\text{Soluble}}{4\,K[Au(CN)_2]} + 4\,KOH$$

$$2\,K[Au(CN)_2] + \underset{\text{Precipitating agent}}{Zn} \rightarrow 2\,Au + K_2[Zn(CN)_4]$$

200. (a): Electrolysis of NaCl(*aq*) gives Cl_2 at the anode.

201. (b): Tin and lead are both readily fusible. Hence these metals are purified by the liquation method.

202. (b): Poling is used for the purification of metals which contain their own oxide as impurity. For example, Cu_2O in Cu, SnO_2 in Sn.

203. (d): $2\,Cu_2S + 3\,O_2 \rightarrow 2Cu_2O + 2\,SO_2$

$$3\,Cu_2O + \underset{\text{(From green wood)}}{CH_4} \rightarrow 6\,Cu + 2\,H_2O + CO$$

204. (b): Cupellation method is used when the impure metals contain an impurity of another metal which forms a volatile oxide.

205. (c): Gallium arsenide is purified by the zone refining method.

Iron and its Compounds

206. (d): The iron obtained directly from the blast furnace is called pig iron. It contains about 4% carbon and many other impurities such as S, P, Si, Mn in smaller amounts.

207. (d): CaO acts as a flux as it combines with the silica present as an impurity (gangue) to form a fusible slag, $CaSiO_3$.

208. (c): Slag formation zone is the central zone in the blast furnace where the temperature varies from 800 to 1000°C. Here, limestone decomposes into CaO and CO_2.

$$CaCO_3 \xrightarrow{1000°C} CaO + CO_2$$

CaO acts as a flux as it combines with silica present as an impurity (gangue) to form a fusible stag of $CaSiO_3$.

$$CaO + SiO \xrightarrow{1000°C} \underset{\text{Slag}}{CaSiO_3}$$

209. (b): The less electropositive metals such as Fe, Zn and Sn are extracted from their oxides by reduction with carbon or coal.

$Fe_2O_3 + 3\,C \rightarrow 2\,Fe + 3\,CO$

$$Fe_2O_3 + CO \rightarrow \underset{\text{Iron}}{2\,Fe} + 3\,CO_2$$

210. (a): The process of extraction of a metal by heating the roasted ore with coke in the presence of a flux is called smelting. It is done in a blast furnace. Iron is extracted by this process.

$$Fe_2O_3 + 3\,C \xrightarrow{>1123\,K} 2\,Fe + 3\,CO$$

$$Fe_2O_3 + 3\,CO \xrightarrow{1123K} 2\,Fe + 3\,CO_2$$

211. (b): Bond breaking process or decomposition process are endothermic processes. Thus,

$2\,C + O_2 \rightarrow 2\,CO;\ \Delta H = +ve$

is an endothermic reaction.

212. (b): In the blast furnace, iron oxide is reduced as:

$$3\,FeO_3 + CO \xrightarrow{300-400°C} 2\,Fe_3O_4 + CO_2$$

$$Fe_3O_4 + CO \xrightarrow{500-600°C} 3\,FeO + CO_2$$

$$FeO + CO \xrightarrow{700°C} Fe + CO_2$$

213. (a): $\underset{\text{Limestone}}{CaCO_3} \xrightarrow{\Delta} CaO + CO_2\uparrow$

$$\underset{\text{Impurity}}{SiO_2} + \underset{\text{Flux}}{CaO} \rightarrow \underset{\text{Slag}}{CaSiO_3}$$

214. (d): Smelting of iron in a blast furnace involves oxidation, reduction and decomposition reactions but not sublimation.

215. (b): $CaCO_3 \rightarrow \underset{\text{Flux}}{CaO} + CO_2$

$$CaO + \underset{\text{Impurity of hematite}}{SiO_2} \rightarrow \underset{\text{Slag}}{CaSiO_3}$$

Thus, limestone acts as a basic flux.

216. (b): $CaCO_3$ + Coke + Calcined ore of iron

1 : 4 : 8

217. (d): During extraction of Fe, calcium silicate ($CaSiO_3$) slag is obtained.

218. (b): $Fe_2O_3 + 3\,CO \rightarrow 3\,CO_2 + 2\,Fe$

219. (d): Reaction (d) does not take place in the blast furnace.

220. (d): Wrought iron melts at the highest temperature, 1673 K.

221. (d): Due to the presence of $MnSiO_3$ and $FePO_4$ as impurities (slag), wrought iron is resistant to rusting and corrosion.

222. (d): Wrought iron is used to make cores of electromagnets.

223. (d): It is called annealing.

224. (c): In chrome plating, the steel surface is covered with chromium.

225. (c): Cast iron has 2.5–4.5 per cent of carbon.

226. (b): The wrong statement is: The impurities present in cast iron are oxidised by air. The correct statement is: The impurities such as C, S, Si, P and Mn present in cast iron are oxidised by hematite (Fe_2O_3) to CO, SO_2, P_4O_{10} and MnO respectively. For example

$$Fe_2O_3 + 3\,C \xrightarrow{\Delta} 2\,Fe + 3\,CO$$

227. (d): Conc. HNO_3 renders iron passive by forming a thin protective film of Fe_3O_4 on its surface.

228. (a): $Fe + 5\,CO \rightarrow Fe\,(CO)_5$

229. (c): +3 is the most stable oxidation state of iron.

230. (a): Misch metal is a pyrophoric alloy which contains 95% lanthanide elements such as La, Nd and Ce and 5% Fe.

231. (d): In the case-hardening technique, iron rods embedded in charcoal powder are heated repeatedly and this technique is used in making axles of railway wagons.

232. (a): Cathodic protection of iron involves using another more reactive metal or a sacrificial anode. In the electrochemical series, Zn is placed above Fe, so it is used for such action.

233. (a): FeO is basic, Fe_2O_3 is amphoteric.

234. (a): Fe_2Cl_6 is a covalent compound in which Fe has only 6 electrons and hence completes its octet by forming a coordinate bond with the chlorine atom of the other molecule. Hence it exists as a dimer.

235. (a): $FeCl_3 + 3\,H_2O \rightarrow Fe(OH)_3 + 3\,HCl$

236. (c): $FeSO_4$ of Mohr's salt is oxidised to $Fe_2(SO_4)_3$ by HNO_3 in the presence of an acid. The new compound is known as ferric alum.

$2\,HNO_3 \rightarrow 2\,NO_2 + H_2O + O$

$2\,FeSO_4 + H_2SO_4 + O \rightarrow Fe_2(SO_4)_3 + H_2O$

Thus, the compound

$(NH_4)_2SO_4.Fe_2(SO_4)_3.24H_2O$ is known as ferric alum.

237. (d): $\underset{\text{Ferrocyanide ion}}{4\,Fe^{3+} + 3[Fe(CN)_6]^{4-}} \rightarrow \underset{\text{Prussian blue ppt.}}{Fe_4\,[Fe(CN)_6]_3}$

238. (c): Chromium cannot be obtained by electrolysis.

239. (b): Purification of Si, used in semiconductors, is carried out by zone refining.

240. (c): Smithsonite or calamine ($ZnCO_3$) is not a mineral of iron.

241. (d): The formula of magnetite ore is Fe_3O_4.

242. (b): In a blast furnace, the zone of combustion has a temperature of 2170 K, the zone of fusion 1423–1673 K, the zone of heat absorption, the middle zone (1423 K) and the zone of reduction (823 K) are other zones of the furnace.

Copper and its Compounds

243. (b): $CuSO_4 \rightleftharpoons Cu^{2+} + SO_4^{2-}$; $H_2O \rightleftharpoons H^+ + OH^-$

At the cathode: $Cu^{2+} + 2\,e^- \rightarrow Cu$

At the anode: $4\,OH^- \rightarrow 2\,H_2O + O_2 + 4\,e^-$

244. (d): In a Bessemer converter, copper pyrites is oxidised to FeO and Cu_2O. Cu_2O reacts with Cu_2S left unoxidised, to give Cu.

$2\,Cu_2S + 3\,O_2 \rightarrow 2\,Cu_2O + 2\,SO_2\uparrow$

$2\,Cu_2O + CuS \rightarrow 6\,Cu + SO_2\uparrow$

245. (d): The reaction at high temperature in the blast furnace shows that Cu has less affinity for O_2.

$2\,CuFeS_2 + O_2 \rightarrow Cu_2S + 2\,FeS + SO_2$

246. (b): Electrolysis of $CuSO_4$ solution using copper electrodes: $CuSO_4$ ionises as:

$CuSO_4 \rightleftharpoons Cu^{2+} + SO_4^{2-}$

At anode: $Cu(s) \rightarrow Cu^{2+}(aq) + 2\,e^-$ (Oxidation)

At cathode: $Cu^{2+}(aq) + 2e^- \rightarrow Cu(s)$ (Reduction)

The copper dissolves at the anode and is deposited at the cathode.

247. (d): Co along with Fe, Ni and Zn, being more electropositive, pass into the electrolytic solution and are not present in the anode mud during the electrolytic refining of copper.

248. (b): The $\Delta_f G^\circ$ of Cu_2S is more –ve than those of CS_2 and H_2S. Therefore, neither carbon nor hydrogen can reduce Cu_2S to Cu metal. On the other hand, $\Delta_f G^\circ$ of Cu_2O is less –ve than that of CO and hence carbon can easily reduce Cu_2O to Cu metal.

$$Cu_2O + C \rightarrow 2\,Cu + CO$$

It is because of this reason that the extraction of Cu from pyrites is more difficult than from its oxide ore through reduction.

249. (c): The correct statement is: zinc is more reactive than iron and hence reduction will be faster in case zinc scrap is used. But zinc is a costlier metal than iron; so, using iron scrap would be more economical.

250. (a): 'Copper matte' contains Cu_2S and small amounts of FeS.

251. (d): Extraction of copper from copper pyrites ($CuFeS_2$) involves crushing followed by concentration of the ore by froth floatation process. The ore is then roasted. Iron is removed as $FeSiO_3$ slag. Cu_2O thus obtained reacts with Cu_2S to give copper metal (self-reduction) in molten stage. On solidification, SO_2 escapes and blister copper is obtained.

252. (a): Iron displaces Cu from $CuSO_4$ solution.

$Fe(s) + CuSO_4(aq) \rightarrow FeSO_4(aq) + Cu(s)$

253. (a): The roasted ore which is a mixture of Cu_2S and FeS is mixed with sand and heated strongly (smelting) when most of the iron is converted into iron oxide. It then combines with silica (sand SiO_2) and is removed as $FeSiO_3$ slag.

$2\,FeS + 3\,O_2 \rightarrow 2\,FeO + 2\,SO_2$

$FeO + SiO_2 \rightarrow FeSiO_3$(slag)

Thus, the above process produces $FeSiO_3$ (fusible slag) and Cu_2S as matte.

254. (a): The strongest reducing agent is Rb.

255. (d): Chalcopyrites is $CuFeS_2$.

256. (d): Malachite is an ore of copper. The molecular formula of malachite ore is $Cu(OH)_2.CuCO_3$.

257. (c): The composition of an azurite is $Cu(OH)_2.2CuCO_3$. Hence, it is an ore of copper.

258. (c): Argentite: Ag_2S

Haematite: Fe_2O_3

Malachite: $Cu(OH)_2.CuCO_3$, an ore of copper

Calamine: $ZnCO_3$

259. (b): Copper pyrites ($CuFeS_2$) is the chief ore of copper.

260. (d): In the extraction of copper, the impurities of iron oxide combine with silica (flux) and form an insoluble slag.
$FeO + SiO_2 \rightarrow \underset{\text{Slag}}{FeSiO_3}$

261. (c): Copper metal is mainly extracted from its sulfite ore, copper pyrites ($CuFeS_2$). The Cu_2O obtained can be reduced to copper by treating with Cu_2S.
$2\,Cu_2S \xrightarrow{3O_2} 2\,Cu_2O + 2\,SO_2$
$2\,Cu_2O + Cu_2S \rightarrow 6\,Cu + SO_2$

262. (d): Blister copper is obtained by the process of bessemerisation from the copper matte in the metallurgy of Cu. It is impure. Blister copper contains about 98% to 99% pure copper and 1% to 2% impurities such as Ag, Au and Ni.

263. (b): In the Bessemer converter, copper sulfide is partially oxidised to cuprous oxide which further reacts with the remaining copper sulfide to from copper and sulfur dioxide.
$Cu_2S + 2\,Cu_2O \rightarrow 6\,Cu + SO_2$

264. (c): Self-reduction: Reduction of oxide ore of a metal by its own sulfide.
$2\,Cu_2O + Cu_2S \rightarrow 6\,Cu + SO_2$

265. (c): High purity copper metal is obtained by electrolytic reduction.

266. (d): $\underset{\text{Ore}}{2\,CuFeS_2} + O_2 \xrightarrow{\text{Roasting}} Cu_2S + 2\,FeS + SO_2$
$2\,FeS + 3\,O_2 \rightarrow 2\,FeO + 2\,SO_2$
$\underset{\text{(Impurity)}}{2\,FeO} + \underset{\text{(Flux)}}{SiO_2} \rightarrow \underset{\text{(Slag)}}{FeSiO_3}$
$2\,Cu_2S + 3\,O_2 \rightarrow 2\,Cu_2O + 2\,SO_2$
$2\,Cu_2O + Cu_2S \rightarrow 6\,Cu + SO_2$
Hence, copper is extracted by heating its ore in air.

267. (a): Cu is more electropositive than Ag.
$Cu + 2\,AgNO_3 \rightarrow Cu\,(NO_3)_2 + 2\,Ag$

268. (b): Cu has a high electrical conductivity and not low.

269. (a): $2\,Cr^{2+} + 4\,I^- \rightarrow 2\,CuI + I_2$

270. (a): Bordeaux mixture is $CuSO_4 + Ca(OH)_2$.

271. (b): Malachite and azurite are used respectively as green and blue pigments.

272. (d): German silver contains Cu, Zn, Ni and not Mn.

273. (b): Bronze contains Cu = 80%, Zn = 10% and Sn = 10%.

274. (a): $CuSO_4 + 2\,H_2O \rightarrow Cu\,(OH)_2 + H_2SO_4$; due to hydrolysis the solution is rendered acidic.

275. (d): Given
(i) $CuSO_4(s) + aq \rightarrow CuSO_4(aq);\ \Delta_{sol}H = -65.5$ kJ mol^{-1}
(ii) $CuSO_4.5H_2O(s) + aq \rightarrow CuSO_4(aq)$
$\Delta_{sol}H = -11.7$ kJ mol^{-1}
To find $CuSO_4(s) + 5\,H_2O(l) \rightarrow CuSO_4.5H_2O(s)$,
$\Delta_{hyd}.H = ?$
Equation (i) can be written in two steps as:
(iii) $CuSO_4(s) + 5\,H_2O(l) \rightarrow CuSO_4.5H_2O(s)$;
$\Delta H = \Delta H_1$ kJ mol^{-1}
(iv) $CuSO_4.5H_2O(s) + aq \rightarrow CuSO_4(aq)$;
$\Delta H = \Delta H_2$kJ mol^{-1}
According to Hess's law,
(v) $\Delta H_1 + \Delta H_2 = -65.5$ kJ mol^{-1}
As equations (ii) and (iv) are the same,
$\therefore \Delta H_2 = -11.7$kJ mol^{-1}
Putting this value in equation (v) above,
$\Delta H_1 - 11.7 = -65.5$
or $\Delta H_1 = -65.5 + 11.7 = -53.8$kJ mol^{-1}

276. (c): $\underset{\substack{\text{Brown powder}\\\text{(Cuprous oxide)}}}{2\,Cu_2O} + O_2 \xrightarrow[\text{Oxidation}]{\Delta} \underset{\substack{\text{Black powder}\\\text{(Cupric oxide)}}}{4\,CuO}$
$\underset{\substack{\text{Black}\\\text{(Cupric oxide)}}}{2\,CuO} + H_2 \xrightarrow[\text{Redution}]{\Delta} \underset{\substack{\text{Brown}\\\text{(Cuprous oxide)}}}{Cu_2O} + H_2O$

277. (c): Caliche (chile saltpetre) contains 0.5% sodium iodate.

278. (d): The composition of bell metal is Cu 80% and Sn 20%.

279. (b): $\underset{\text{Scrap}}{Cu} + \underset{\text{Dil.}}{H_2SO_4} + \frac{1}{2}O_2\ (\text{air}) \rightarrow$
$CuSO_4 + H_2O$

280. (a): CuF_2 is ionic because of the high electronegativity of F.

281. (d): Malachite $Cu(OH)_2.CuCO_3$.

282. (b): $\underset{\text{(Impurities)}}{FeO} + \underset{\text{(Flux)}}{SiO_2} \rightarrow \underset{\text{(Slag)}}{FeSiO_3}$

283. (d): Copper pyrites is converted into a mixture of FeO and Cu_2O during roasting.
$\underset{\text{Copper pyrites}}{2\,CuFeS_2} + O_2 \xrightarrow{\Delta} Cu_2S + 2\,FeS + SO_2$
$2\,CuS + 3\,O_2 \xrightarrow{\Delta} 2\,Cu_2O + 2\,SO_2$
and $2\,FeS + 3\,O_2 \rightarrow 2\,FeO + 2\,SO_2$

To remove FeO (basic), an acidic flux silica (SiO_2) is added during smelting. It forms ferrous silicate slag which floats over molten matte and hence can be easily removed.
$FeO + SiO_2 \rightarrow FeSiO_3$

284. (a): On cooling bessemerised copper, the metal solidifies and the dissolved SO_2 escapes, leaving large blisters on the surface.

Silver, Its Compounds, Photography

285. (d): In the extraction of silver, Ag_2S is leached with KCN in the presence of air.
$2\,Ag_2S + 8\,NaCN + 2\,O_2 + H_2O \rightarrow$
$4\,Na[Ag(CN)_2] + Na_2S_2O_3 + 2\,NaOH$
Thus, O_2 is the oxidant.
$2[Ag(CN)_2]^- + Zn \rightarrow [Zn(CN)_4]^{2-} + 2\,Ag\downarrow$

286. (b): 925 fine silver means, 925 parts by weight of pure Ag present in an Ag–Cu alloy of 1000 parts by weight.

287. (a): Earlier, coins contained Ag, Cu and Ni as their constituents.

288. (c): Generally, in electroplating, the complex salt of the metal is taken as the electrolyte.

289. (b): $AgCl + 2\,NH_4OH \rightarrow [Ag(NH_3)_2]\,Cl + 2\,H_2O$

290. (c): In contact with organic matter (skin, cloth) $AgNO_3$ is reduced to metallic silver (which has a black colour).

$2\,AgNO_3 + H_2O \rightarrow 2\,Ag + 2\,HNO_3 + O$

291. (a): $2\,AgNO_3 + Na_2S_2O_3 \longrightarrow \underset{\text{(x) White ppt.}}{Ag_2S_2O_3} + 2NaNO_3$

$\downarrow$ 3 $Na_2S_2O_3$ Excess

$\underset{\text{(Z) Black ppt.}}{3\,Na_2S_2O_3 + H_2SO_4 + Ag_2S} \xleftarrow[\text{Boil}]{H_2O} \underset{\text{(Y) Soluble complex sod. argentothiosulphate}}{2Na_3[Ag(S_2O_3)_2]}$

292. (b): $AgCl + 2\,KCN \rightarrow K[Ag(CN)_2] + KCl$

293. (d): On fusing AgCl with Na_2CO_3, metallic silver is obtained.

$2\,AgCl + Na_2CO_3 \xrightarrow{\text{Fuse}} \underset{\text{Metallic silver}}{2\,Ag\downarrow} + 2\,NaCl + CO_2 + \frac{1}{2}\,O_2$

294. (d): $AgCl + 2\,NH_4OH \xrightarrow{\text{Excess}} \underset{\text{Soluble complex}}{[Ag(NH_3)_2]Cl} + 2\,H_2O$

$[Ag(NH_3)_2]Cl \rightleftharpoons [Ag(NH)_3)_2]^+ + Cl^-$

295. (a): Alkaline solution of hydroquinone is used as a developer in photography which reduces some of the exposed AgBr to black silver.

$\underset{\text{Hydroquinone}}{C_6H_5(OH)_2} + 2\,AgBr \rightarrow \underset{\text{Black}}{2Ag} + \underset{\text{Quinone}}{C_6H_4O_2} + 2HBr$

296. (b): AgBr is highly photosensitive and is used in photographic films and plates.

297. (e): A reducing agent (quinol) is used as the developer of a photographic plate.

298. (b): The chemical formula of argentite or silver glance is Ag_2S.
Hence, argentite is a mineral of silver.

299. (a): Argentite: Ag_2S, horn silver: AgCl, pyrargyrite: $2\,AgSbS_2$ or $Ag_2S.\,Sb_2S_3$.

300. (c): Parke's process is used for the extraction of Ag from argentiferous lead.

301. (b): Horn silver ore is AgCl.

$AgCl + 2\,NaCN \rightarrow \underset{\text{Soluble}}{Na[Ag(CN)_2]} + NaCl$

302. (a): $\underset{\text{Argentite (X)}}{2\,Ag_2S} + 8\,NaCN + O_2 + 2H_2O \rightarrow$

$\underset{\text{Soluble complex}}{Na[Ag(CN)_2]} + NaCl + 4\,NaOH + 2\,S$

$2\,Na[Ag(CN)_2] + \underset{\text{(Y)}}{Zn} \xrightarrow{\text{Reduction}} Na_2[Zn(CN_4)] + 2Ag\downarrow$

Thus, X = CN^- and Y = Zn

303. (d): Silver is not obtained by heating $Na[Ag(CN)_2]$. It is obtained by treating $Na[Ag(CN)_2]$ with a more electropositive metal Zn, which replaces Ag from it.

$2Na\,[Ag(CN)_2] + Zn \rightarrow Na_2\,[Zn(CN)_4] + 2\,Ag\downarrow$

304. (b): The reaction is based on the fact that silver and its compounds form a soluble complex with NaCN. This reaction is reversible and accumulation of Na_2S must be prevented. A free excess of air (O_2) is continuously passed through the solution which oxidises Na_2S to Na_2SO_4 and $Na_2S_2O_3$.

$Ag_2S + 4\,NaCN \rightleftharpoons 2\,Na[Ag(CN)_2] + Na_2S$

$2Na_2S + 2\,O_2 + H_2O \rightarrow Na_2S_2O_3 + 2\,NaOH$

Silver is recovered from solution by precipitating with zinc.

$2Na[Ag(CN)_2] + 4\,NaOH + Zn \rightarrow Na_2ZnO_2 + 4\,NaCN + 2\,H_2O + 2\,Ag$

305. (d): In the MacArthur–Forrest method, silver is extracted from a solution of sodium argentocyanide by using zinc.

$2\,Na[Ag(CN)_2] + Zn \rightarrow Na_2[Zn(CN)_4] + 2\,Ag\downarrow$

306. (c): Hydrometallurgy is used for the extraction of Ag from Ag_2S by forming a complex.

$Ag_2S + 4NaCN \rightarrow \underset{\text{Soluble Complex}}{2Na[Ag(CN)_2]} + Na_2S$

$2Na[Ag(CN)_2] + Zn \rightarrow Na_2[Zn(CN)_4] + 2Ag.$

307. (c): Cupellation: If a metal possess an impurity of another metal which forms a volatile oxide, then cupellation method is used.

Gold and its Compounds

308. (a): Gold jewellery is made from 22 carat gold, that is, $\frac{22}{24} \times 100 = 91.66\%$ pure gold. 22 Carat gold is an aloy of Au and Cu.

309. (d): Hydrometallurgy involves both leaching and precipitation of the metal from its solution by adding a precipitating agent.

310. (d): MacArthur or cyanide pocess is applicable for the extraction of both Au and Ag.

311. (a): $4\,Au + 8\,CN^- + 2\,H_2O \xrightarrow{O_2} \underset{\text{X}}{4[Au(CN)_2]^-} + 4\,OH^-$

$4[Au(CN)_2]^- + 2\,Zn \rightarrow \underset{\text{Y}}{2[Zn(CN)_4]^{2-}} + 4\,Au$

312. (d): Impurities of Cu and Ag from gold are removed by boiling impure gold with conc. H_2SO_4 and also by the electrolytic method.

313. (b): Noble metals are soluble in aqua regia (3 HCl + 1 HNO_3).

314. (a): +1 state of gold is more stable than the +3 state.

315. (a): The metal obtained by the cyanide process is Ag.

Zinc and its Compounds

316. (d): Roasting (sulfide ore is heated in excess of air).

317. (c): $Zn + 2\,NaOH + 2\,H_2O \rightarrow \underset{\text{Soluble}}{Na_2[Zn(OH)_4]} + H_2$

318. (a):

$\underset{\text{(X)}}{ZnSO_4} + 2\,NH_4OH \rightarrow \underset{\text{White ppt.}}{Zn(OH_2)\downarrow} + (NH_4)_2SO_4$

Excess $\downarrow$ 2 NH_4OH

$2\ H_2O + 2\ NH_4OH + ZnS \xrightleftharpoons{\downarrow H_2S} (NH_4)_2\ [Zn(OH)_4]$
(Z) Dirty (Y) Soluble complex white ppt.

319. (a):
$4\ Zn + 10\ HNO_3 \rightarrow 4\ Zn(NO_3)_2 + N_2O + 5\ H_2O$
(Dil.)

$Zn + 4\ HNO_3 \rightarrow Zn(NO_3)_2 + 2\ NO_2 + 2\ H_2O$
(Conc.)

320. (a): Electron alloy (Mg = 95%, Zn = 5%) is used in the construction of aircrafts.

321. (b): Lithopone, a white pigment, is a mixture of ZnS and $BaSO_4$.

322. (a): Willemite, a rare zinc silicate mineral, is Zn_2SiO_4. It has trigonal symmetry and is strongly fluorescent green.

323. (c): Zinc metal in traces is present in insulin.

324. (c): Calamine ($ZnCO_3$) is the carbonate ore of zinc.

325. (c): Zinc blende is ZnS not $ZnCl_2$.

326. (b): Impure zinc containing Cd, Pb and Fe as impurities is called spelter.

327. (a): From the Ellingham diagram, it is clear that the reduction of Cu_2O with coke occurs at a temperature less than 473 K but the reduction of ZnO with coke occurs at about 1180 K.

328. (c): $2\ ZnS + 3\ O_2 \xrightarrow{950°C} 2\ ZnO + 2\ SO_2$;
$ZnS + 2\ O_2 \xrightarrow{950°C} ZnSO_4$
$2\ ZnSO_4 \xrightarrow{950°C} 2ZnO + 2\ SO_2 + O_2$

329. (a): $2\ ZnS(s) + 3\ O_2(g) \xrightarrow{Heat} 2\ ZnO(s) + 2\ SO_2(g)$

Final Preparation

330. (d): Calcination is usually done for the hydroxide and carbonate ores to convert them to oxides.
$MgCO_3 \xrightarrow[\text{(Calcination)}]{\Delta} MgO + CO_2$

331. (b): Metal sulfides are not reduced by C and hydrogen as conveniently as metal oxides.

332. (b): In roasting, sulfide ores are heated in the presence of air to remove sulfur as SO_2 gas.

$MS \xrightarrow[\text{(X)}]{\text{Excess air}} MO + SO_2\uparrow$
Sulfide ore roasting

$SO_2 + H_2O \rightarrow H_2SO_3$
Colourless, smell; Sulfurous acid in of burnt sulfur solution reduction agent

So, the gas X is SO_2.

333. (b): Silica is acidic (as impurity, gangue). To remove it as slag, basic flux such as CaO is added.

$SiO_2 + CaO \rightarrow CaSiO_3$
Acidic gangue; Basic flux; Slag

334. (c): $6\ CaO + P_4O_{10} \rightarrow 2\ Ca_4(PO_4)_2$
Thomas slag

It contains 14%–18% P_2O_5 and when mixed with $CaSiO_3$ is used as a fertiliser.

335. (b): Ellingham diagram shows that below 710°C (983 K) (point of intersection of the plots for three reactions $C \rightarrow Co$; $C \rightarrow CO_2$ and $CO \rightarrow CO_2$), the oxidation of CO to CO_2 is easier than C to CO_2. Thus, Co is a more effective reducing agent than carbon below 710°C. Above this temperature, CO lines come below the carbon andCO_2 lines. Thus, above 710°C (983 K), carbon is a better reducing agent.

336. (a): In the reaction $C + \frac{1}{2}O_2 \rightarrow CO$, the ΔS increases. Therefore, as the temperature increases, $T\Delta S$ increases and thus ΔG (ΔH–$T\Delta S$) decreases. In other words, the slope of the curve for the formation of CO decreases whereas for all other oxides, it increases.

337. (b): The graph of $\Delta_f G°$ vs T in the Ellingham diagram shows that the Cu–Cu_2O line is almost at the top (that is, much higher than those of Al–Al_2O_3, Mg–MgO, Zn–ZnO and Fe–FeO lines). Therefore, Cu_2O can be reduced to Cu at the lowest temperature by carbon.

338. (b): Ellingham diagram shows that ZnO and Fe_2O_3 can be reduced by carbon at high temperatures (more than 983 K) to the respective metals.

$ZnO + C \xrightarrow{1083K} Zn + CO$

$Fe_2O_3 + 3\ C \xrightarrow{\text{above 983 K}} 2\ Fe + 3\ CO$

339. (d): Below 983 K, the conversion of iron to Fe_2O_3 (ferric oxide) is more favourable because $\Delta_f G°$ for this reaction is more negative than the C–CO reaction. Hence, C cannot reduce Fe_2O_3 to Fe below 983 K.

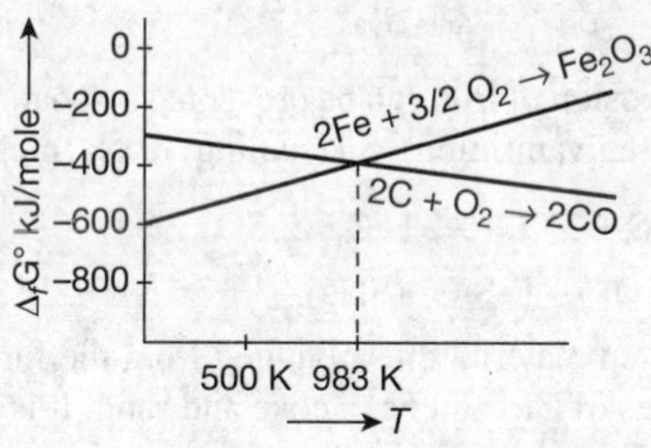

340. (d): In this case, purification of the metal can be carried out by cupellation.

341. (d): Greater solubility of the impurity in the molten state than in the solid state of metal.

342. (c): In the zone refining method, the molten zone contains more impurities than the original metal.

343. (b): Ni is purified by the Mond's process, Cu by electrolysis, Zr by the Van Arkel process and Ga is purified by zone refining.

344. (c): Cyanide process (A) is used for the extraction of Au (iv). Froth floatation process (B) is used for the concentration (dressing) of ZnS (ii). Electrolytic reduction (C) is used for the extraction of highly electropositive metals like Al (iii). Zone refining (D) is used for producing ultra-pure Ge (i).

345. (b): Near the top of the blast furnace, only CO is present which reduces Fe_2O_3 to spongy iron.

346. (d): In wrought iron, the carbon in present as Fe_3C (cementite), that is, iron carbide and graphite.

347. (a): Steel contains Fe, Mn, C (manganese steel).

348. (b): Pig iron contains about 4% carbon and many impurities such as Mn, P, Si and S in minor amounts.

349. (a): Invar is an alloy of iron and nickel. So, it is a ferrous alloy. Duralumin is an alloy of Mg, Cu, Al and Mn.

350. (a): Invar (Fe = 64%, Ni = 36%) has practically no coefficient of expansion.

351. (b): Steel is an alloy of 0.1%–1.4% C (non-metal) and Fe (metal).

352. (c): Iron becomes passive due to the formation of Fe_3O_4, an inert layer at the surface of the metal.

353. (c): Ferrous compounds are less easily hydrolysed than the corresponding ferric compounds. In fact, higher the charge on the metal cation, the more easily its compounds will be hydrolysed.

354. (a): Cu and Ag metals are etched by $FeCl_3$ solution due to the oxidising nature of Fe^{3+}.

$Cu + 2\,Fe^{3+} \rightarrow 2\,Fe^{2+} + Cu^{2+}$

355. (b): $Fe^{3+} + 3\,SCN^- \rightarrow \underset{\text{(Blood red colour)}}{Fe(SCN)_3}$

356. (a): $Fe + 5\,CO \rightarrow Fe(CO)_5$
Here, the oxidation number of Fe in $Fe(CO)_5$ is zero.

357. (d): $\underset{\text{Hot}}{2\,Fe} + \underset{\text{Dry}}{3Cl_2} \rightarrow \underset{\text{Anhydrous}}{2\,FeCl_3}$

358. (d): Corrosion of iron can be prevented by coating the surface with Zn (galvanisation), Sn (tinning) or Ni (nickel plating).

359. (c): $2\,FeS + 3\,O_2 \rightarrow 2\,FeO + 2\,SO_2$

$FeO + SiO_2 \rightarrow FeSiO_3$ (Slag)

The molten material thus obtained from the furnace consists of sulfides of Cu^+ and Fe^{2+}, coke and sand. It is called matte.

360. (a): $2\,Cu_2O + Cu_2S \rightarrow 6\,Cu + SO_2$
The reaction is known as self-reduction or self-electronation or auto-reduction.

361. (d): $2\,Cu_2O + Cu_2S \xrightarrow{\Delta} 6\,Cu + SO_2$

362. (a): $E^\circ_{Zn^{2+}/Zn} = -0.76$ V and $E^\circ_{Fe^{2+}/Fe} = -0.44$ V

Thus, Zn has a higher negative standard reduction potential than Fe. Therefore, when coated on iron (galvanisation), Zn works as the anode and makes Fe as the cathode and protects it from rusting.

363. (b): ZnO on heating develops a metal excess defect due to interstitial cations and electrons. It loses oxygen reversibly. The colour is due to the excitation of interstitial electrons.

$$\underset{\text{(White)}}{ZnO} \underset{\text{cool}}{\overset{\text{heat}}{\rightleftharpoons}} \underset{\text{(yellow)}}{Zn^{2+}} + \frac{1}{2}O_2 + 2e^-$$

364. (c): Philosopher's wool is ZnO (amphoteric oxide).

$$BaO + ZnO \xrightarrow{1000°C} \underset{\text{(Barium zincate)}}{BaZnO_2}$$

365. (c): Cinnabar (HgS) is concentrated by the froth floatation process.

366. (a): Ag is leached by the cyanide process.

367. (b): Impure copper usually contains Ag, Au, Ni, Zn, Fe, Pb, Sn, and so on, as impurities. In the electrolytic refining of Cu, impure metal is made the anode, acidified solution of copper sulfate is taken as the electrolyte. During electrolysis, the impurities of Ni, Fe and Zn pass into solution as sulfates while impurities of Ag, Au and Sn are thrown down as anode mud below the anode.

368. (d): Low grade sulfide ore of copper is Cu_2S (copper glance). Copper is extracted from this ore by hydrometallurgy.

$2\,Cu_2S + 5\,O_2 \rightarrow 2\,CuSO_4 + 2\,CuO$

$CuSO_4 + Fe \rightarrow FeSO_4 + Cu\downarrow$

369. (a): $\underset{\text{Solution}}{CuSO_4} + \underset{\text{Metal}}{Fe} \xrightarrow[\text{(Reduction of } Cu^{2+})]{} FeSO_4 + Cu\downarrow$

370. (b): Both basic copper carbonate or malachite $[CuCO_3.Cu(OH)_2]$ and azurite $[2CuSO_3.Cu(OH)_2]$ contain copper carbonate and copper hydroxide.

371. (c): Cu^{2+} because of its higher charge and smaller size is extensively hydrated which makes it more stable than Cu^+.

372. (b): $3\,Cu + 8\,HNO_3\,(dil.) \rightarrow 3\,Cu\,(NO_3)_2 + 2\,NO + 4\,H_2O$

373. (c): $Cu + \underset{\text{(conc.)}}{4\,HNO_3} \rightarrow Cu(NO_3)_2 + 2\,NO_2 + 2\,H_2O$

374. (d): Cu does not react with dil. H_2SO_4.

375. (a): $CuCl_2 + Cu \xrightarrow{HCl} 2\,CuCl$ (white precipitate)

376. (b): In solid $CuSO_4.5H_2O$, copper (lying at the centre of a square) is coordinated to four water molecules as $[Cu(H_2O)_4]SO_4.H_2O$ and the fifth water molecule is held between SO_4^{2-} and two of the coordinated water molecules though hydrogen bonding as shown.

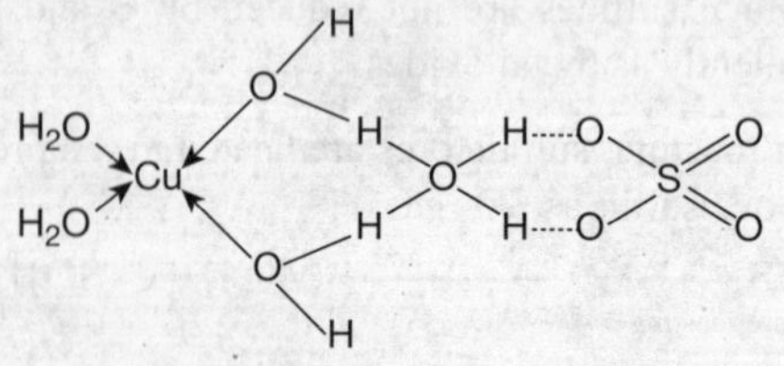

377. (b): Dil. H_2SO_4 contains water. Anhydrous $CuSO_4$ (white) is converted into blue $CuSO_4.5H_2O$ which dissolves in dil. H_2SO_4 to give a blue solution.

378. (d): $2\,Cu^{2+} + 4\,CN^- \rightarrow 2\,Cu^+CN^- + (CN)_2$

$CuCN + 3\,CN^- \rightarrow [Cu(CN)_4]^{3-}$

379. (b): $2\,CuSO_4 + K_4[Fe(CN)_6] \rightarrow \underset{\text{Chocolate ppt.}}{Cu_2[Fe(CN)_6]} + 2\,K_2SO_4$.

380. (a): Basic copper acetate, Cu $(CH_3COO)_2.Cu(OH)_2$ is called Veridigris which is used as a green pigment in paints.

381. (a): $Cu_2(SCN)_2$ is a white precipitate and is used for the gravimetric estimation of Cu (II) by first reducing it with H_2SO_3 and then precipitating Cu (I) thus obtained with SCN^-.

382. (d): The cyanide process is used in the metallurgy of Ag.
$2\,Ag_2S + 8\,NaCN + O_2 + 2\,H_2O \rightarrow 4\,Na[Ag(CN)_2] + 4\,NaOH + 2\,S$
$2\,Na[Ag(CN)_2] + Zn \rightarrow Na_2[Ag(CN)_4] + 2\,Ag\downarrow$

383. (d): Ag is extracted from argentiferous lead by Parke's process where Zn and Pb in molten state are immiscible and form separate layers, zinc being lighter forms the upper layer. Ag is soluble in both but more soluble in the upper layer. So, all the statements are correct.

384. (b): Hg_2O decomposes only on heating white Ag_2O decomposes at room temperature. CuO and ZnO are, however, quite stable.

385. (b): $2\,AgNO_3 + Na_2S_2O_3 \rightarrow Ag_2S_2O_3 + 2\,NaNO_3$
$Ag_2S_2O_3 + H_2O \rightarrow H_2SO_4 + Ag_2S$ (Black)

386. (b): To cut off the entry of light, $AgNO_3$ solution is kept in coloured bottles.

387. (c): $2\,AgNO_3 \xrightarrow{\Delta} 2\,Ag + 2\,NO_2 + O_2$

388. (a): A very dilute solution of $AgNO_3$ is used in cauterisation of the eyes and as a dental antiseptic.

389. (c): $\underset{\text{Undecomposed}}{AgBr} + \underset{\text{Hypo}}{2\,Na_2S_2O_3} \longrightarrow Na_3[Ag(S_2O_3)_2] + NaBr$

390. (d): The developer, quinol, reduces exposed AgBr to black Ag.

391. (c): M is gold (Au) and the reaction represents the extraction of Au by the MacArthur or cyanide process.
$4\,Au + 8\,CN^- + 2\,H_2O + O_2 \rightarrow 4\,[Au(CN)_2]^- + 4\,OH^-$

392. (b): $\Delta G°$ is more negative for the reaction B, therefore, C(*gr*) will reduce ZnO to zinc metal.

393. (d): A thin layer of basic zinc carbonate $ZnCO_3.3Zn(OH)_2$ is formed at the surface of the zinc metal.

394. (a): $Zn + 2\,NaOH \rightarrow Na_2ZnO_2 + H_2$

395. (d): $4\,Zn + 10\,HNO_3 \rightarrow 4\,Zn(NO_3)_2 + NH_4NO_3 + 3\,H_2O$

396. (c): Cinnabar, HgS is red in colour.

397. (d): Copper pyrites or chalcopyrites is $CuFeS_2$.

398. (d): Calamine ($ZnCO_3$) and sphalerite (ZnS) both are minerals of zinc.

399. (b): All the nitrates are soluble in water and are quite stable as they do not decompose easily on heating. Thus, metals are usually not found as nitrates in their ores.

400. (c): Wolframite is ferrous tungstate $FeWO_4$ which is magnetic in nature.

401. (d): Heating pyrites to remove sulfur is called roasting.

402. (d): The most electropositive metals are isolated from their ores by the electrolysis of their fused ionic salts.

403. (c): Hematite (Fe_2O_3) mineral (magnetic) can be separated by the magnetic separation method.

404. (c): $CuSO_4$ acts as an activator in the froth floatation process.

405. (a): The type of molecules having a hydrophilic head and hydrophobic tail are used as frothers in the froth floatation process.

406. (a): Aniline and cresols act as froth stabilisers when added in the froth floatation process.

407. (b): Sphalerite is zinc sulfide (ZnS). Therefore, it is concentrated by the froth floatation process.

MATCH THE FOLLOWING

408. (a): (A) Silver is extracted by the amalgamation method where Ag dissolves in Hg to form an amalgam (alloy with Hg) leaving behind impurities and can be separated from Hg by distillation under reduced pressure. It can be purified by the cupellation method.
(B) Calamine is $ZnCO_3$ ore.
(C) Cerussite is also a carbonate ($PbCO_3$) ore.
(D) Zinc oxide is zincite (ZnO) ore.

409. (b): (A) Conversion of PbS to PbO by roasting.
$2\,PbS + 2\,O_2 \xrightarrow{\Delta} 2\,PbO + 2\,SO_2$
(B) Calcination of $CaCO_3$ ore.
$CaCO_3 \xrightarrow{\Delta} CaO + CO_2$
(C) Roasting of ZnS to get ZnO and then reduction of ZnO by carbon to get Zn metal.
$2\,ZnS + 3\,O_2 \xrightarrow{\Delta} 2\,ZnO + 2\,SO_2$
$ZnO + C \xrightarrow{\Delta} Zn + CO$
(D) Roasting of Cu_2S to get Cu_2O and then self-reduction to get Cu metal.
$2\,Cu_2S + 3\,O_2 \xrightarrow{\Delta} 2\,Cu_2O + 2\,SO_2$
$2\,Cu_2O + Cu_2S \xrightarrow{\Delta} 6\,Cu + SO_2$

410. (d): (A) The van Arkel method (vapour phase method) involves decomposition of ZrI_4 at a higher temperature to get pure Zr and I_2.
(B) It involves extraction of Ag first by complex formation as $[Ag(CN)_2]^-$ and then displacement by Zn metal to get Ag metal (MacArthur cyanide process).
(C) Liquation method is used for the purification of Bi which is readily fusible as compared to impurities.
(D) Ultra-pure gallium is obtained by the zone refining method.

ASSERTION REASON

411. (a): R is the correct explanation of A.

412. (b): **Correct explanation**. Al is more electropositive than Fe, Cr and Mn.

413. (b): **Correct explanation**. Noble metals form soluble cyanide complexes which on displacement give a precipitate of the metal. Noble metals also form alloys (amalgams) with mercury which can be used for their recovery.

414. (a): R is the correct explanation of A.

415. (a): R is the correct explanation of A.

416. (d): Correct A. Iron does not occur in the free state in nature.
Correct R. Iron is a highly reactive element.

417. (c): Correct R. The reaction
$Fe_2O_3(s) \rightarrow Fe(s) + 3/2O_2(g)$ is not spontaneous as, for this reaction both ΔH and ΔS are negative, so ΔG will be positive.

418. (a): R is the correct explanation of A.

419. (a): R is the correct explanation of A.

420. (d): Correct A. Nitriding is a process of heating steel in an atmosphere of ammonia.
Correct R. Nitriding imparts a hard coating of iron nitride on the surface of steel.

421. (a): R is the correct explanation of A.

422. (d): Correct A. Copper does not react with HCl.
Correct R. Hydrogen is present above copper in the reactivity series.

423. (a): R is the correct explanation of A.

424. (a): R is the correct explanation of A.

425. (a): R is the correct explanation of A.

426. (a): R is the correct explanation of A.

427. (c): Correct R. Oxide ores being heavier than the earthy or rocky gangue particles, settle down while the lighter impurities are washed away.

428. (c): Correct R. Wolframite ($FeWO_4$) being magnetic in nature, is attracted by the magnetic roller and forms a heap under it.

429. (d): Correct A. Sulfide ores are concentrated by the froth floatation process.
Correct R. In the froth floatation process, pine oil is used because it preferentially wets the ore particles.

430. (c): Correct R. Pine oil is used as a frother which wets the ore particles whereas the gangue particles are wetted by water.

431. (c): Correct R. Collectors attach themselves by polar groups to grains of ores which then become water repellent and pass on into the froth.

432. (c): Correct R. Leaching is a process of concentration.

433. (b): Correct explanation. On heating strongly, carbonates and hydrated oxide ores are converted into metal oxides and volatile impurities are also removed.

434. (c): Correct R. concentration of sulfate ore is done by the froth floatation process.

CHAPTER 7

p-Block Elements

7.1 Indroduction to Group 15

The general electronic configuration of this group may be expressed as ns^2np^3 where $n = 2$ to 6 (Table 7.1).

Table 7.1 Electronic configuration of elements of Group 15

Element	Atomic number	Electronic configuration	
		Complete	With noble gas core
Nitrogen (N)	7	$1s^2 2s^2 2p^3$	$[He] 2s^2 2p^3$
Phosphorus (P)	15	$1s^2 2s^2 2p^6 3s^2 3p^3$	
Arsenic (As)	33	$1s^2 2s^2 2p^6 3s^2 3p^6 3d^{10} 4s^2 4p^3$	$[Ar] 3d^{10} 4s^2 4p^3$
Antimony (Sb)	51	$1s^2 2s^2 2p^6 3s^2 3p^6 3d^{10} 4s^2 4p^6 4d^{10} 5s^2 5p^3$	$[Kr] 4d^{10} 5s^2 5p^3$
Bismuth (Bi)	83	$1s^2 2s^2 2p^6 3s^2 3p^6 3d^{10} 4s^2 4p^6 4d^{10} 4f^{14} 5s^2 5p^6 5d^{10} 6s^2 6p^3$	$[Xe] 4f^{14} 5d^{10} 6s^2 6p^3$

7.1.1 Atomic and Physical Properties

Table 7.2 Some atomic and physical properties of group 15 elements

Property		Elements				
		N	P	As	Sb	Bi
Atomic Number		7	15	33	51	83
Atomic mass/g mol^{-1}		14·01	30·97	74·92	121·76	208·98
Ionisation enthalpy ($\Delta_i H$)/kJ mol^{-1}	$\Delta_i H_1$ $\Delta_i H_2$ $\Delta_i H_3$	1402 2856 4577	1012 1903 2910	947 1798 2736	834 1595 2443	703 1610 2466
Electronegativity		3·0	2·1	2·0	1·9	1·9
Covalent radius/pm		70	110	121	141	148
Ionic radius/pm		171 (N^{3-})	212 (P^{3-})	222 (As^{3-})	76 (Sb^{3+})	103 (Bi^{3+})
Melting point/K		63	317·1 (white P)	1089 (grey α-form at 38·6 atm)	904	544
Boiling point/K		77·2	554 (white P)	888 (sublimation temperature)	1860	1837
Density/g cm^{-3} at 298 K		0·879 at 63 K	1·823	5·778 (grey α-form)	6·697	9·808

7.2 Atomic Properties

Some atomic properties of the elements of group 15 are discussed below.

7.2.1 Atomic and Ionic Radii

The atomic and ionic radii of group 15 elements are smaller than the atomic radii of the corresponding group 14 elements. On going down the group, the atomic radii increase with an increase in atomic number.

Explanation: On moving from left to right, in a given period, the electrons screen each other. Therefore, the effective nuclear charge increases and hence the electrons are more strongly attracted towards the nucleus. This results in a decrease in the covalent radii. The same is true for ionic radii. On moving down the group, the atomic radii increase due to the addition of a new principal shell in each succeeding element. However, from As to Bi, only a small increase in the covalent radius is observed. This is due to the presence of completely filled *d*- and/or *f* orbitals in the heavier members.

7.2.2 Ionisation Enthalpy

The first ionisation enthalpies of the group 15 elements are higher than the corresponding members of the group 14 elements. On going down the group, the ionisation enthalpies decrease.

Explanation: Due to increased nuclear charge, reduced atomic radii and stable half-filled electronic configurations, the valence electrons of the group 15 elements are strongly attracted by the nucleus and hence they have less tendency to lose electrons. The decrease in the values of ionisation energies as we move down the group is due to a gradual increase in the atomic size which reduces the forces of attraction of the electrons by the nucleus. As expected, successive ionisation enthalpies of these elements increase in the order, $\Delta_i H_1 < \Delta_i H_2 < \Delta_i H_3$.

7.2.3 Electronegativity

The electronegativity values of the elements of group 15 are higher than the corresponding elements of group 14. On going down the group, the electronegativity value decreases.

Explanation: The elements of group 15 have a smaller size and a greater nuclear charge and therefore, they have higher electronegativity values. The decrease in electronegativity on going down the group is due to an increase in the size of the atoms and the shielding effect of inner electron shells on going down the group.

7.2.4 Metallic Character

The metallic character increases from N to Bi. For example, N and P are non-metallic, As and Sb are partly non-metallic while Bi is a metal.

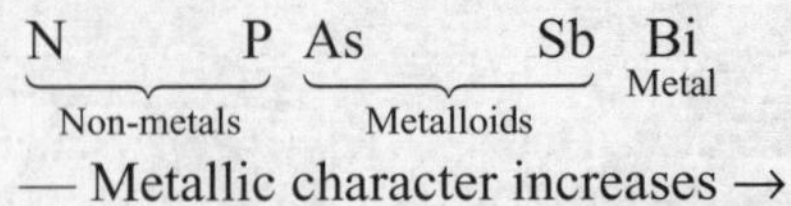

Explanation: Due to increased nuclear charge and higher electronegativity, the elements of group 15 are less metallic than the corresponding elements of group 14. On moving down the group, the electronegativity decreases. As a result, valence electrons are lost more readily and hence the metallic character increases.

7.2.5 Melting and Boiling Points

The melting points of the group 15 elements first increase from nitrogen to arsenic and then decrease to antimony and bismuth. The boiling points, however, increase regularly as we move from N to Bi.

Explanation: The unexpected decrease in the melting points of Sb and Bi is because of their tendency to form three covalent bonds instead of five covalent bonds, due to the inert pair effect. As a result, the attraction among their atoms is weak and hence their melting points are low. Because, of the large size of the atom, Bi has still weaker interatomic forces than Sb and therefore, has a still lower melting point. The boiling points increase down the group from N to Bi because of the increase in their atomic size.

7.2.6 Density

The density of the elements of group 15 increases regularly from the top to bottom, that is, from N to Bi.

7.2.7 Allotropy

Except nitrogen and bismuth, all other elements of this group show allotropy. For example,

Phosphorus exists as: white, black or red phosphorus
Arsenic exists as: yellow or grey arsenic
Antimony exists as: yellow or silvery grey allotropic forms

7.3 Chemical Properties

7.3.1 Oxidation States

The elements of group 15 exhibit various oxidation states from –3 to +5.

(i) *Negative oxidation states:* Nitrogen being the smallest and most electronegative element of the group forms the N^{3-} (nitride) ion and shows an oxidation state of –3 in the nitrides of some highly electropositive metals such as Mg_3N_2, Ca_3N_2, and so on. Other elements of this group form covalent compounds even with metals and show a formal oxidation state of –3. For example, calcium phosphide (Ca_3P_2), sodium arsenide (Na_3As), zinc stibide (Zn_3Sb_2) and magnesium bismuthide (Mg_3Bi_2). However, the tendency of these elements to show the –3 oxidation state decreases as we move down the group from N to Bi due to a gradual decrease in their electronegativity and ionisation enthalpy. In addition to the –3 oxidation state, N and P show oxidation states of –2 in hydrazine (NH_2NH_2) and diphosphine (P_2H_4) respectively. Nitrogen also shows an oxidation state of –1 in hydroxyl amine (NH_2OH) but P does not.

(ii) *Positive oxidation states:* On moving down the group, the stability of the +5 oxidation state decreases while that of the +3 oxidation state increases due to the inert pair effect. All the compounds of group 15 elements having the +5 oxidation state (PF_5, PCl_5, SbF_5, BiF_5) are essentially covalent compounds. The covalent character decreases in the order, N > P > As > Sb > Bi.

(iii) *Maximum covalency:* Nitrogen does not have vacant d orbitals in its outermost valence shell ($n = 2$). Therefore, it cannot extend its valency beyond four [for example, NH_4^+, $(CH_3)_4N^+$]. That is why nitrogen does not form pentahalides such as NF_5 or NCl_5. On the other hand, phosphorus and all other elements exhibit covalency of five or six. For example, PF_5, PCl_5, AsF_5, PF_6^-, $[SbF_6]^-$.

(iv) *Disproportionation:* In the case of nitrogen, all oxidation states from +1 to +4 tend to disproportionate in acid solution. For example,

$$\overset{+3}{3\,HNO_2} \rightarrow \overset{+5}{HNO_3} + \overset{+2}{2\,NO} + H_2O$$

Nitrous acid → Nitric acid + Nitric oxide

7.4 Trends in Chemical Reactivity

Nitrogen differs from the rest of members of the group due to its (i) smaller size, (ii) high electronegativity, (iii) high ionisation enthalpy and (iv) non-availability of dorbitals in the valence shell. Nitrogen forms $p\pi$–$p\pi$ multiple bonds with itself and with other elements that have small size and high electronegativity (C and O). However, the heavier elements of this group do not form $p\pi$–$p\pi$ bonds because of their large atomic orbitals. Two nitrogen atoms are held together by a triple bond (one σ and two $\neq$) and have very high bond enthalpy (941.4 kJmol^{-1}).

$$:N::N: \quad \text{or} \quad :N\equiv N:$$

Due to this, the nitrogen molecule is inert and has very low reactivity.

7.4.1 Reactivity Towards Hydrogen (Formation of Hydrides)

All the elements of group 15 form gaseous trihydrides of the formula EH_3 (where E = N, P, As, Sb and Bi).

NH_3	PH_3	AsH_3	SbH_3	BiH_3
Ammonia	Phosphine	Arsine	Stibine	Bismuthine

The lighter elements also form hydrides of the formula M_2H_4 such as N_2H_4 (hydrazine), P_2H_4 (diphosphine) and As_2H_4 (diarsine) (Table 7.3). Nitrogen also forms a special hydride of the formula HN_3 known as hydrogen azide or hydrazoic acid.

Preparation

(i) *Hydrolysis of binary metal compounds:* The trihydrides of can be easily obtained by the hydrolysis of their binary metal compounds with water of dilute acids.

$$\underset{\text{Magnesium nitride}}{Mg_3N_2} + 6H_2O \rightarrow 3Mg(OH)_2 + \underset{\text{Ammonia}}{2NH_3}$$

$$\underset{\text{Calcium phophide}}{Ca_3P_2} + 6H_2O \rightarrow 3Ca(OH)_2 + \underset{\text{Phosphine}}{2PH_3}$$

(ii) *Reduction of trichlorides:* The trichlorides of these elements except that of bismuth upon reduction with Zn/acid or $LiAlH_4$ give the corresponding hydrides.

$$ECl_3 + 3\,LiAlH_4 \rightarrow EH_3 + 3\,LiCl + 3\,AlH_3$$
$$(E = N, P, As, Sb)$$

Structure: All these hydrides are covalent in nature and have a pyramidal structure (Fig. 7.1). These involve sp^3 hybridisation of the central atom. As we go down the group the bond angle decreases.

NH_3	PH_3	AsH_3	SbH_3	BiH_3
107.8°	93.6°	91.8°	91.3°	90°

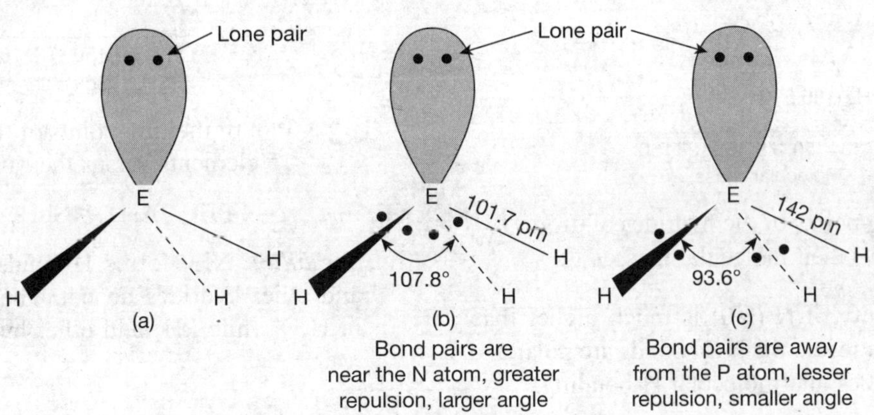

Fig. 7.1 Pyramidal structure of (a) EH_3 molecules; bond angle and bond length in (b) NH_3 molecule and (c) PH_3 molecule

Lone pair–bond pair repulsion is larger than bond pair–bond pair repulsion. As a result, the tetrahedral shape of the molecule gets distorted and the bond angle becomes less than 109°28’ (tetrahedral angle).

Characteristics of Hydrides

(i) *Basic nature:* All these hydrides have one lone pair of electrons on their central atom. Therefore, they act as Lewis bases. NH_3 is distinctly basic; PH_3 is weakly basic; AsH_3, SbH_3 and BiH_3 are very weakly basic. As the size of the central atom increases, the lone pair of electrons occupies a larger volume, the electron density on the central atom decreases and consequently its tendency to donate a pair of electrons decreases and hence the basic strength decreases as we move from NH_3 to BiH_3.

(ii) *Thermal stability:* NH_3 is most stable, the stability of PH_3, AsH_3 and SbH_3 decreases progressively while BiH_3 is the least stable. On going down the group, the size of the central atom increases and therefore, its tendency to form a stable covalent bond with the small hydrogen atom decreases. As a result, the M–H bond strength decreases and therefore the thermal stability decreases.

(iii) *Reducing character:* Ascending order of reducing character is as follows:

$$NH_3 < PH_3 < AsH_3 < SbH_3 < BiH_3$$

Explanation: As we move from NH_3 to BiH_3, the thermal stability of the hydrides decreases. In order words, their tendency to liberate hydrogen increases and hence their reducing character increases from NH_3 to BiH_3.

(iv) *Boiling points:* The boiling points increase regularly as we move from PH_3 to BiH_3. However, the boiling point of NH_3 is higher than those of PH_3 and AsH_3 (Fig. 7.2).

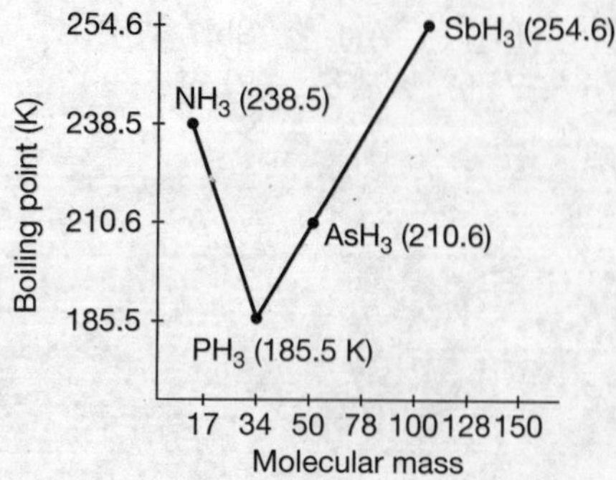

Fig. 7.2 Plot of boiling points of the hydrides of group 15 elements versus their molecular masses

The electronegativity of N (3.0) is much higher than that of H (2.1) As a result, the N–H bonds are polar and hence NH_3 undergoes intermolecular H-bonding.

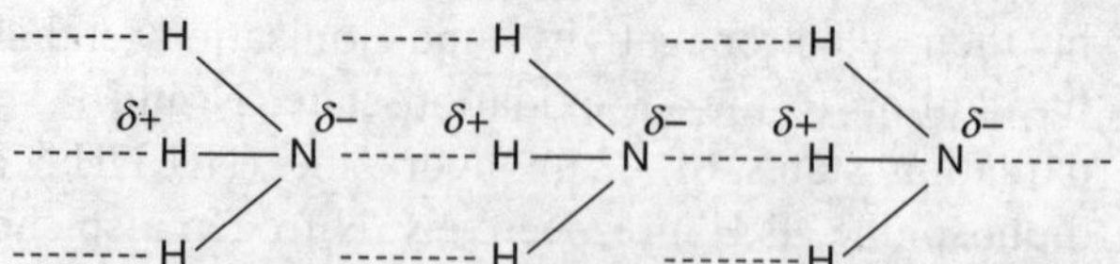

In contrast, the electronegativity of P (2.1), As (2.0), Sb (1.9) and Bi (1.9) are close to H (2.1) and hence PH_3, AsH_3, SbH_3 and BiH_3 do not form H-bonds. Thus, the abnormally high BP of NH_3 is due to intermolecular H-bonding. Further, as we move from PH_3 to BiH_3, the molecular mass increases. As a result, the van der Waals forces of attraction increase and the boiling points increase regularly from PH_3 to BiH_3. However, the BP of NH_3 is higher than those of PH_3 and AsH_3 but lower than those of SbH_3 and BiH_3. This is probably due to the reason that the increase in the boiling points of SbH_3 and BiH_3 because of higher van der Waals forces of attraction more than compensates for the increase in bp of NH_3 because of H-bonding.

$$PH_3 < AsH_3 < NH_3 < SbH_3 < BiH_3$$

(v) *Melting points:* Because of intermolecular H-bonding, NH_3 has the highest melting point. The other hydrides of this group do not form H-bonds and hence their melting points are lower than that of NH_3. However, as we move down the group from PH_3 to SbH_3, the molecular size increases and hence the melting points increase regularly due to a corresponding increase in their van der Waals forces of attraction (Fig. 7.3). Thus, the melting points of the hydrides of group 15 elements follow the sequence:

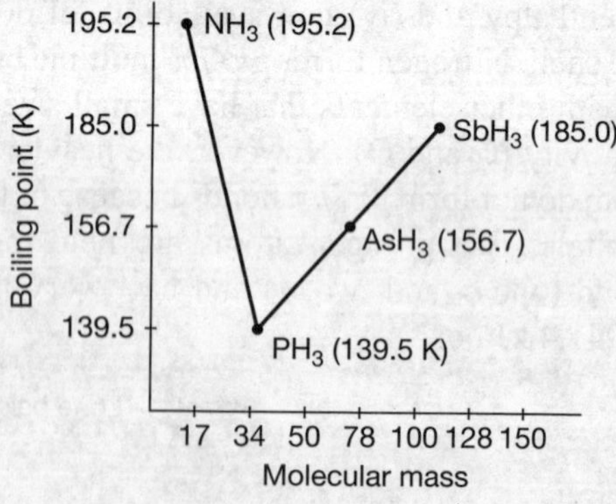

Fig. 7.3 Plot of melting points of the hydrides of group 15 elements versus their molecular masses

$$PH_3 < AsH_3 < SbH_3 < NH_3$$

(iv) *Solubility:* NH_3 forms H-bonds with H_2O while PH_3 and other hydrides do not. Therefore, NH_3 is soluble in H_2O while PH_3 and other hydrides are insoluble in water.

7.4.2 Reactivity Towards Oxygen (Formation of Oxides)

The elements of group 15 combine with oxygen directly or indirectly to form two types of oxides—E_2O_3 (trioxides) and E_2O_5 (pentaoxides) (Table 7.3). However, nitrogen forms a number of oxides with oxidation states ranging from +1 to +5 This is mainly because of the strong tendency of nitrogen to form $p\pi - p\pi$ multiple bonds with oxygen.

Table 7.3 Oxides of group 15 elements

Oxidation state of elements	Oxides of nitrogen	Oxides of phosphorus	Oxides of arsenic	Oxides of antimony	Oxides of bismuth
+1	N_2O Nitrous oxide	—	—	—	—
+2	NO Nitric oxide	—	—	—	—
+3	N_2O_3 Dinitrogen trioxide	P_4O_6 Phosphorus trioxide	As_4O_6 Arsenic trioxide	Sb_4O_6 Antimony trioxide	Bi_2O_3 Bismuth trioxide
+4	N_2O_4 Dinitrogen tetroxide or NO_2 nitrogen dioxide	P_4O_8 Phosphorus tetroxide	—	—	—
+5	N_2O_5 Dinitrogen pentoxide	P_4O_{10} Phosphorus pentoxide	As_4O_{10} Arsenic pentoxide	Sb_4O_{10} Antimony pentoxide	—

The oxides in the higher oxidation states of the elements are more acidic than the oxides in the lower oxidation state. The acidic character of the oxides of the group 15 elements decreases down the group.

7.4.3 Reactivity Towards Halogens (Formation of Halides)

The trihalides are formed by all the elements while the pentahalides are formed by all the elements except nitrogen (Table 7.4). Nitrogen cannot form pentahalides due to the absence of vacant d orbitals in its outermost shell. Similarly, the last element, Bi has little tendency to form pentahalides

Table 7.4(a) Trihalides (EX_3) of group 15 elements

E	Flourine	Chlorine	Bromine	Iodine
N	NF_3	NCl_3	$NBr_3.NH_3$	$NI_3.NH_3$
P	PF_3	PCl_3	PBr_3	PI_3
As	AsF_3	$AsCl_3$	$AsBr_3$	AsI_3
Sb	SbF_3	$SbCl_3$	$SbBr_3$	SbI_3
Bi	BiF_3	$BiCl_3$	$BiBr_3$	BiI_3

Table 7.4(b) Pentahalides (EX_5) of group 15 elements

E	Fluorine	Chlorine	Bromine	Iodine
N	–	–	–	–
P	PF_5	PCl_5	PBr_5	–
As	AsF_5	$AsCl_5$	–	–
Sb	SbF_5	$SbCl_5$	–	–
Bi	BiF_5	–	–	–

Structure

All the trihalides have a pyramidal structure, that is, the central element is sp^3 hybridised (Fig. 7.4).

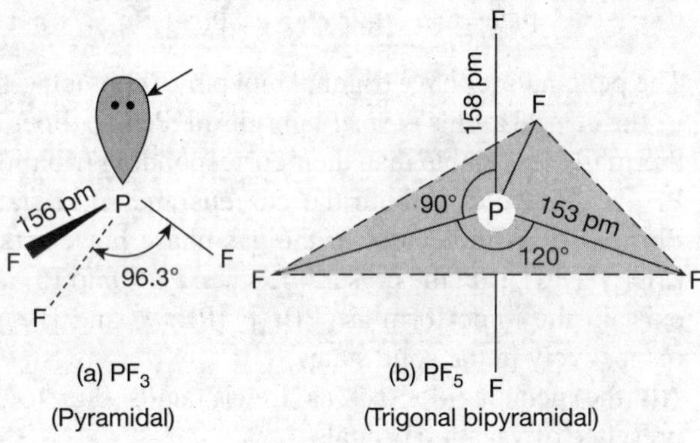

Fig. 7.4 Structures of (a) PF_3 and (b) PH_5

$$\underset{(96.3^\circ)}{PF_3} < \underset{(100.4^\circ)}{PCl_3} < \underset{(101^\circ)}{PBr_3} < \underset{(102^\circ)}{PI_3}$$

As the electronegativity of halogen increases, the bond pairs move away from the central P atom. As a result, bond pair–bond pair repulsions decrease and hence the bond angles also decrease. These trihalides are mainly covalent with the ionic character increasing down the group. For example, BiF_3 is ionic while the other halides of Bi ($BiCl_3$, $BiBr_3$) and SbF_5 are partly covalent and partly ionic.

- Out of all the trihalides, the trihalides of nitrogen are the least stable. Though NF_3 is stable, NCl_3 is explosive. NBr_3 and NI_3 are known only as their unstable ammoniates, Pure NBr_3 also explodes.

- The trihalides are easily hydrolysed by water. Antimony and bismuth trichlorides are only partially hydrolysed to form oxychlorides.

$$SbCl_3 + H_2O \rightleftharpoons \underset{\text{Antimony oxychloride}}{SbOCl\ (\text{or } SbO^+Cl^-)} + 2\ HCl$$
$$BiCl_3 + H_2O \rightleftharpoons \underset{\text{Bismuth oxychloride}}{BiOCl\ (\text{or } BiO^+Cl^-)} + 2\ HCl$$

- The trihalides of P, As and Sb (especially the fluorides and chlorides) act as Lewis acids The Lewis acid strength, however, decreases, in the order:

  $PCl_3 > AsCl_3 > SbCl_3$ and $PF_3 > PCl_3 > PBr_3 > PI_3$.

  The trihalides of nitrogen, due to the absence of d orbitals and the presence of a lone pair of electrons, behave as Lewis bases. The Lewis base strength of the other trihalides increases as the electronegativity of halogen decreases, that is, $NF_3 < NCl_3 < NBr_3 < NI_3$.

P, As and Sb form pentahalides due to the presence of vacant d orbitals in their respective valence shells. The pentahalides of group 15 elements are thermally less stable than the trihalides.

Preparation

The pentahalides are prepared as:

$$3\ PCl_5 + 5\ AsF_3 \rightarrow 3\ PF_5 + 5\ AsCl_3$$
$$PCl_3 + Cl_2\ (\text{in } CCl_4) \rightarrow PCl_5$$

- The pentahalides have trigonal bipyramid geometry, that is, the central atoms is sp^3d hybridised. Pentahalides are thermally less stable than their corresponding trihalides. PF_5 is molecular in both the gaseous and solid states. PbI_5 exists as molecules in the gas phase but exists as $[PCl_4]^+ [PCl_6]^-$ in the crystalline state. PBr_5 and PI_5 also exist in the ionic form as $[PBr_4]^+ [PBr_6]^-$ and $[PI_4]^+ I^-$ respectively in the solid state.

  All the pentahalides act as Lewis acids due to the presence of vacant d orbitals.

  PF_5 does not undergo hydrolysis since the P–F bond is stronger than the P–O bond. All other pentahalides of P, however, undergo hydrolysis to yield H_3PO_4.

7.4.4 Reactivity Towards Metals

Nitrogen forms nitrides (Mg_3N_2 magnesium nitride, Ca_3N_2 calcium nitride), arsenic forms arsenides (Na_3As sodium arsenide), antimony forms antimonides (Zn_2Sb_3 zinc antimonide) and bismuth forms bismuthides (Mg_3Bi_2 magnesium bismuthides).

7.4.5 Anomalous Behaviour of Nitrogen

Some of the characteristics in which nitrogen differs from other family members are given below.

(i) ***pπ–pπ*** **multiple bonds:** Nitrogen because of its small size and high electronegativity, forms *pπ–pπ* multiple bonds with itself and with other elements having small size and high electronegativity (as with C, O). Thus, nitrogen exists as a diatomic molecule with a triple bond (N≡N, one σ- and two ≠-bonds) between the two atoms. These N_2 molecules are held together by weak van der Waals forces of attraction which can be easily broken by the collisions of the molecules at room temperature. Therefore, N_2 is a gas at room temperature.

The other elements of this group do not form *pπ–pπ* multiple bonds because their atomic orbitals are so large and diffused that they cannot have effective overlapping. Instead, they prefer to form single bonds as P–P, As–As and Sb–Sb, while bismuth forms metallic bonds in the elemental state. They exist as discrete tetraatomic tetrahedral molecules such as P_4, As_4, Sb_4, and so on, containing E–E single bonds. Due to the larger size, the forces of attraction holding the tetraatomic molecules are quite strong. Therefore, P_4, As_4 and Sb_4 are all solids at room temperature.

(ii) Catenation: Among the elements of group 15, phosphorus has the maximum tendency for catenation forming cyclic as well open chain compounds consisting of many phosphorus atoms. Nitrogen can form chains containing up to three N atoms as in hydrazoic acid N_3H, or azide ions N_3^-.

Hydrazoic acid: $H-\ddot{N}=\overset{+}{N}=\ddot{N}-$

Azide ion: $-:\ddot{N}=N=\ddot{N}:-$

(iii) Reactivity: Due to the presence of a triple bond between the two N atoms, the bond length is very small (109 pm) and hence the bond dissociation energy is very large (941.4 kJ mol^{-1}). As a result, N_2 is inert and underactive in its elemental state. Since the P–P single bond is much weaker (213 kJ mol^{-1}) than the N≡N triple bond, phosphorus is much more reactive than nitrogen. The reactivity of other elements decreases down the group from As to Bi.

(v) ***dπ–dπ*** **Multiple bonds:** Due to the absence of *d* orbitals in the valence shell, nitrogen cannot form *dπ–dπ* multiple bonds. That is why nitrogen does not form compounds of the type, $R_3N=O$ and $R_3N=CH_2$ while phosphorus and the heavier elements of group 15 readily from *dπ–pπ* multiple bonds. Phosphorus forms compounds of the type $R_3P=O$, $R_3P=CH_2$ (R may be any alkyl group), $O=PX_3$ and $RN=PX_3$ (X =F, Cl or Br). Phosphorus and arsenic can also form *dπ–pπ* bonds with transition elements when their compounds such as $P(C_2H_5)_3$ (triethylphosphine) and $As(C_6H_5)_3$ (triphenylarsine) act as ligands.

7.5 Dinitrogen, N_2

It is a typical non-metal with high electronegativity next only to fluorine and oxygen.

7.5.1 Preparation of Dinitrogen

(i) **In the laboratory:** Dinitrogen can be prepared in the laboratory by the following three methods.

- *By thermal decomposition of ammonium nitrite:*

$$NH_4Cl(aq) + NaNO_2(aq) \rightarrow \underset{\text{Ammonium nitrite}}{NH_4NO_2(aq)} + NaCl(aq)$$

$$NH_4NO_2(aq) \xrightarrow{\text{Heat}} N_2(g) + 2\ H_2O(l)$$

- *From ammonium dichromate:*

$$\underset{\text{Ammoniumdichromate}}{(NH_4)_2Cr_2O_7} \xrightarrow{\text{Heat}} N_2 + 4\ H_2O + \underset{\text{Chromic oxide}}{CrO_3}$$

Ammonium dichromate may be prepared in situ by following method:

$$K_2Cr_2O_7 + 2\ NH_4Cl \xrightarrow{\text{Heat}} (NH_4)_2Cr_2O_7 + 2\ KCl$$

- By thermal decomposition of sodium or barium azide:

$$\underset{\text{Sodium azide}}{2\ NaN_3} \xrightarrow{573\ K} 2\ Na + 3\ N_2$$

$$\underset{\text{Barium azide}}{Ba(N_3)_2} \xrightarrow{\text{Heat}} Ba + 3\ N_2$$

(ii) Commercial preparation of dinitrogen from air: When the liquid air is allowed to boil, dinitrogen with a lesser boiling point gets distilled first leaving behind dioxygen. The dinitrogen obtained from air contains traces of oxygen and some other gases as impurities.

7.5.2 Properties of Dinitrogen

Physical Properties

- Dinitrogen is a colourless, odourless and tasteless gas.
- It has two stable isotopes—$_{14}N$ and $_{15}N$.
- It is very slightly soluble in water (23.2 cm^3 per litre of water at 273 K and 1 bar pressure).
- Its melting and boiling points are low—63.2 K and 77.2 K respectively.
- It is adsorbed by activated charcoal.
- It is a non-toxic gas.
- It is slightly lighter than air and its vapour density is 14.

Chemical Properties

Dinitrogen is chemically unreactive at room temperature. However, the reactivity increases rapidly with a rise in temperature. At higher temperatures dinitrogen combines with some metals to form predominantly ionic nitrides and with non-metals to form covalent nitrides.

(i) **Action of litmus:** Dinitrogen is neutral towards litmus because it has no action on blue or red litmus.

(ii) **Action of active metals:** It combines with a number of active metals on strong heating to form their respective nitrides. For example,

$$6\ Li + N_2 \xrightarrow{\text{Heat}} \underset{\text{Lithium nitride}}{2\ Li_3N}$$

$$3\ Mg + N_2 \xrightarrow{\text{Heat}} \underset{\text{Magnesium nitride}}{Mg_3N_2}$$

(iii) **Combination with non-metals:**

- *Combination with dihydrogen:*

$$N_2 + 3H_2 \xrightarrow{\text{Fe, Mo}} \underset{\text{Ammonia}}{2\ NH_3} \quad \Delta_f H^\circ = -46.1\ \text{kJ mol–1}$$

- *Combination with dioxygen:*

$$N_2 + O_2 \xrightarrow{>2000\ K} \underset{\text{Nitric oxide}}{2\ NO} \quad \Delta_r H^\circ = -135\ \text{kJ mol–1}$$

Nitric oxide is a colourless gas and is very unstable. It immediately reacts with more of oxygen to form nitrogen dioxide.

$$2\ NO + O_2 \rightarrow 2\ NO_2$$

(iv) **Combination with compounds:** With calcium carbide.

$$\underset{\text{Calcium carbide}}{CaC_2} + N_2 \xrightarrow{1300\ K} \underset{\text{Calcium cyanamide}}{CaCN_2} + \underset{\text{Carbon}}{C}$$

With alumina in the presence of carbon.

$$\underset{\text{Aluminium oxide}}{Al_2O_3} + 3\ C + N_2 \xrightarrow{1273\ K} \underset{\text{Aluminium nitride}}{2\ AlN} + 3\ CO$$

Both these compounds are hydrolysed on boiling with water to give ammonia.

$$CaCN_2 + 3\ H_2O \rightarrow CaCO_3 + 2\ NH_3$$
$$AlN + 3\ H_2O \rightarrow Al(OH)_3 + NH_3$$

(v) Active nitrogen: It can be made by passing an electric spark through N_2 gas at low pressure (of about 2 mm). Active nitrogen is very reactive and reacts with a number of elements and breaks many stable molecules.

$$\underset{\text{Acetylene}}{HC{\equiv}CH} + \underset{\text{Active nitrogen}}{2N} \rightarrow \underset{\text{Cyanogen}}{N{\equiv}C{-}C{\equiv}N} + H_2$$

7.6 Ammonia

Ammonia is formed by the decay of nitrogenous organic matter such as urea.

$$\underset{\text{Urea}}{NH_2CONH_2} + 2\ H_2O \rightarrow \underset{\text{Ammonium carbonate}}{(NH_4)_2CO_3} \rightleftharpoons \underset{\text{Ammonia}}{2\ NH_3} + H_2O + CO_2 + H_2O$$

7.6.1 Preparation of Ammonia

(i) **By heating ammonium salts with a strong base:**

$$\underset{\text{Ammonium sulfate}}{(NH_4)_2SO_4} + 2\ NaOH \xrightarrow{\text{Heat}} \underset{\text{Ammonia}}{2\ NH_3} + 2\ H_2O + Na_2SO_4$$

$$NH_4Cl + KOH \xrightarrow{\text{Heat}} NH_3 + H_2O + KCl$$

Ammonia is also prepared by heating a mixture of slaked lime and ammonium chloride.

$$2\ NH_4Cl + \underset{\text{Slaked lime}}{Ca(OH)_2} \xrightarrow{\text{Heat}} 2\ NH_3 + 2\ H_2O + CaCl_2$$

(ii) By the action of water on metal nitrides: It can be prepared by the hydrolysis of magnesium nitride.

$$\underset{\text{Magnesium nitride}}{Mg_3N_2} + 6H_2O \rightarrow 3\ Mg(OH)_2 + 2\ NH_3;$$

$$\underset{\text{Aluminium nitride}}{AlN} + 3\ H_2O \rightarrow Al(OH)_3 + NH_3$$

Conc. H_2SO_4 reacts with it forming ammonium sulfate.

$$2\ NH_3 + H_2SO_4 \rightarrow (NH_4)_2SO_4$$

$$P_2O_5 + 3\ H_2O \rightarrow 2\ H_3PO_4;\ 3\ NH_3 + H_3PO_4 \rightarrow (NH_4)_3PO_4$$

(iii) Manufacture of ammonia: On a commercial scale, ammonia is manufactured by the Haber's process.

$$N_2(g) + 3\ H_2(g) \rightleftharpoons 2\ NH_3(g);\ \Delta_f H° = -92.4\ \text{kJ mol}^{-1}$$

This reaction is reversible, exothermic and occurs with a decrease in volume. Therefore, according to the Le Chatelier's principle, the favourable conditions for the manufacture of ammonia are the following.

- *Low temperature:* Since the forward reaction is exothermic, low temperature will favour the formation of ammonia.
- *High pressure:* High pressure of the order of 200 atmospheres or 200×10^5 Pa is required for the forward reaction to be favoured.
- *Presence of catalyst:* The use of a catalyst such as iron oxide containing a small amount of molybdenum or potassium oxide (K_2O) and aluminium oxide (Al_2O_3) as promoter, increases the rate of attainment of equilibrium of ammonia. The flow chart for the production of ammonia is shown in Fig. 7.5.

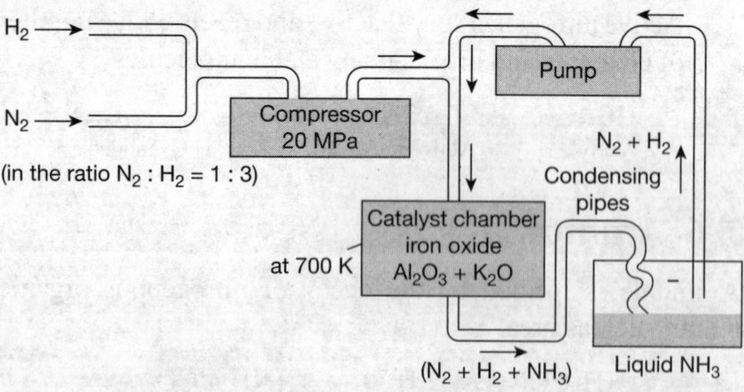

Fig. 7.5 Flow chart for Haber's process for the manufacture of ammonia

7.6.2 Physical Properties of Ammonia

- Ammonia is a colourless, pungent, lachrymatory gas.
- It is lighter than air (density = 0.68 g/cm^3).
- The high solubility of ammonia in water is due to its tendency to form intermolecular hydrogen bonding.
- Ammonia can be easily liquefied under pressure.

7.6.3 Structure of Ammonia

The NH_3 molecule has a pyramidal geometry with the N–H bond length being 101.7 pm and the bond angle 107.8° (Fig. 7.6).

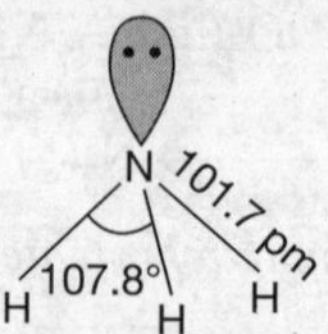

Fig. 7.6 Structure of ammonia

7.6.4 Chemical Properties of Ammonia

(i) Basic nature: Ammonia gas is highly soluble in water. Its aqueous solution turns red litmus blue indicating its weakly basic character.

$$NH_3(aq) + H_2O(aq) \rightleftharpoons NH_4^+(aq) + OH^-(aq)$$

Being basic, ammonia forms salts with both weak and strong acids such as NH_4Cl, $(NH_4)_2SO_4$, $(NH_4)_2CO_3$, and so on.

$$NH_3(aq) + HCl(aq) \rightarrow NH_4Cl(s)$$

$$2\ NH_4OH(aq) + H_2SO_4 \rightarrow (NH_4)SO_4(s)$$

(ii) Reaction with heavy metal salts: Ammonium hydroxide reacts with many metallic salts and precipitates them as hydroxides.

$$\underset{\text{Ferric chloride}}{FeCl_3(aq)} + 3\ NH_4OH(aq) \rightarrow \underset{\text{Brown ppt}}{Fe(OH)_3(s)\downarrow} + 3\ NH_4Cl(aq)$$

$$\underset{\text{Aluminium chloride}}{AlCl_3(aq)} + 3\ NH_4OH(aq) \rightarrow \underset{\text{Gelatinous white ppt}}{Al(OH)_3(s)\downarrow} + 3\ NH_4Cl(aq)$$

(iii) As a Lewis base: It can form coordinate bonds with electron deficient molecules (such as BF_3) or a number of transition metal cations forming complex compounds. For example,

$$BF_3 + NH_3 \rightarrow BF_3 \leftarrow NH_3$$

$$Ag^+(aq) + 2\ NH_3(aq) \rightarrow \underset{\text{Colourless}}{[Ag(NH_3)_2]^+(aq)}$$

$$Cu^{2+}(aq) + 4\ NH_3(aq) \rightarrow \underset{\text{Deep blue}}{[Cu(NH_3)_2]^{2+}(aq)}$$

(iv) Action of halogens:

Excess NH_3: $8\ NH_3 + 3\ Cl_2 \rightarrow 6\ NH_4Cl + N_2$

Excess Cl_2: $NH_3 + 3\ Cl_2 \rightarrow NCl_3 + 3\ HCl$

(v) Oxidation: $3\ CuO + 2\ NH_3 \rightarrow 3\ Cu + N_2 + 3\ H_2O$

Similarly, $4\ NH_3 + 3\ Ca(OCl)_2 \rightarrow 2\ N_2 + 3\ CaCl_2 + 6H_2O$

When vapours of NH_3 and O_2 are passed over red hot platinum gauze at 1075 K, it is oxidised to nitric oxide.

$$4\ NH_3 + 5\ O_2 \xrightarrow[1075\ K]{Pt/Rh\ gauze} \underset{\text{Nitric oxide}}{4\ NO} + 6\ H_2O$$

(vi) Formation of amides (Action of metals):

$$2\,Na + 2\,NH_3 \xrightarrow{575\,K} \underset{\text{Sodamide}}{2\,NaNH_2} + H_2$$

$$2K + 2\,NH_3 \xrightarrow{575\,K} \underset{\text{Potassium amide}}{2KNH_2} + H_2$$

(vii) Reaction with carbon dioxide:

$$2\,NH_3 + CO_2 \xrightarrow[220\,atm]{453\text{–}473\,K} \underset{\text{Ammonium carbamate}}{[NH_2COONH_4]} \xrightarrow{\Delta}$$

$$\underset{\text{Urea}}{NH_2CONH_2} + H_2O$$

Urea has a very high nitrogen content (46.66%). It is widely used as a fertiliser since it slowly decomposes in soil to give NH_3 and CO_2.

$$NH_2CONH_2 + H_2O \rightarrow 2\,NH_3 + CO_2$$

(viii) Reaction with Nessler's reagent: With Nessler's (an alkaline solution of K_2HgI_4) reagent, ammonia or ammonium salts give a brown precipitate.

$$\underset{\text{Nessler's reagent}}{2\,K_2HgI_4} + NH_3 + 3\,KOH \rightarrow \underset{\text{Iodide of Millon's base (brown ppt)}}{H_2N\text{–}O\text{–}Hg\text{–}I} + 7\,KI + 2\,H_2O$$

(ix) Reaction with sodium hypochlorite: When a large excess of aqueous ammonia is treated with sodium hypochlorite in the presence of glue or gelatine, it gets oxidised to hydrazine.

$$2\,NH_3 + NaOCl \rightarrow \underset{\text{Hydrazine}}{NH_2.NH_2} + NaCl + H_2O$$

(x) Liquid ammonia as a solvent: Ammonia also undergoes self-ionisation in the liquid state.

$$2\,NH_3 \rightleftharpoons NH_4^+ + NH_2^-;\ (2\,H_2O \rightleftharpoons H_3O^+ + OH^-)$$

Therefore, liquid ammonia is used for dissolving many polar compounds and also for carrying out many reactions in the *non-aqueous medium.*

7.6.5 Tests for Ammonia

- It turns moist red litmus paper blue and moist turmeric paper brown.
- It gives a brown precipitate with Nessler's reagent.
- With a drop of HCl, it produces dense white fumes of ammonium chloride.
- With copper sulfate solution, it gives a deep blue solution.
- It gives a yellow precipitate with chloroplatinic acid.

$$\underset{\text{Chloroplatinic acid}}{H_2PtCl_6} + 2\,NH_3 \rightarrow \underset{\text{Ammoniumchloroplatinate (yellow ppt)}}{(NH_4)_2PtCl_6}$$

7.7 Oxides of Nitrogen

7.7.1 Nitrous Oxide (N_2O)

It is prepared by heating ammonium nitrate.

$$NH_4NO_3 \xrightarrow{475\text{–}533\,K} N_2O + 2\,H_2O$$

It can also be prepared by the following methods.

$$HNO_2 + \underset{\text{Hydroxylamine}}{NH_2OH} \xrightarrow{Aq} N_2O + 2\,H_2O$$

$$HNO_2 + \underset{\text{Hydrazoic acid}}{HN_3} \xrightarrow{Aq} N_2O + N_2 + H_2O$$

Physical appearance and chemical nature: It is a colourless neutral gas with a sweet odour.

(i) It is a neutral oxide and reacts with sodamide to form sodium azide.

$$N_2O + NaNH_2 \xrightarrow{473\,K} \underset{\text{Sodium azide}}{NaN_3} + H_2O$$

(ii) It decomposes into nitrogen and oxygen at 873 K.

$$2\,N_2O(g) \xrightarrow{873\,K} 2\,N_2(g) + O_2(g)$$

7.7.2 Nitric Oxide (NO)

It is prepared by the catalytic oxidation of ammonia at 1100 K in the presence of platinum.

$$4\,NH_3 + 5\,O_2 \xrightarrow[1100\,K]{Pt} 4\,NO + 6\,H_2O$$

It can also be prepared by the reaction of nitric acid on copper.

$$3\,Cu + 8\,HNO_3(dil) \rightarrow 3\,Cu(NO_3)_2 + 2\,NO + 4\,H_2O$$

It can also be prepared by the reduction of sodium nitrite with ferrous sulfate in the presence of sulfuric acid.

$$2\,NaNO_2 + 2\,FeSO_4 + 3\,H_2SO_4 \rightarrow Fe_2(SO_4)_3 + 2\,NaHSO_4 + 2\,H_2O + 2\,NO$$

Physical appearance and chemical nature: It is a colourless neutral gas.

(i) $2\,NO(g) \xrightarrow{1373\text{–}1473\,K} N_2(g) + O_2(g)$

(ii) Due to the presence of an odd electron (paramagnetic), it instantly reacts with O_2 to form NO_2 and with Cl_2 to form nitrosyl chloride (NOCl).

$$2\,NO + O_2 \rightarrow 2\,NO_2$$
$$2\,NO + Cl_2 \rightarrow 2\,NOCl$$

7.7.3 Dinitrogen Trioxide (N_2O_3)

It can be prepared by reacting nitric oxide and dinitrogen tetraoxide at 250 K.

$$2\,NO + N_2O_4 \xrightarrow{<250\,K} 2\,N_2O_3$$

Physical appearance and chemical nature: It is a blue liquid/solid, acidic in nature.

$$N_2O_3 + H_2O \rightarrow 2\,HNO_2$$
$$N_2O_3 \xrightarrow{<250\,K} NO + NO_2$$

7.7.4 Nitrogen Dioxide (NO_2)

It is prepared by heating dried lead nitrate in a steel reaction vessel.

$$2\ Pb(NO_3)_2 \rightarrow 2\ PbO + 4\ NO_2 + O_2$$

Above 415 K, it contains mainly NO_2 and at 250 K, it consists of mainly N_2O_4.

$$\underset{\text{(Brown)}}{2NO_2} \underset{\text{Heat}}{\overset{\text{Cold}}{\rightleftharpoons}} \underset{\text{(Colourless)}}{N_2O_4}$$

Physical appearance and chemical nature: NO_2 is a brown gas, acidic in nature while N_2O_4 is a colourless solid/liquid, acidic in nature.

(i) Being paramagnetic, NO_2 reacts with F_2 and Cl_2 forming nitryl fluoride (NO_2F) and nitryl chloride (NO_2Cl) respectively.

$$2\ NO_2 + F_2 \rightarrow 2\ NO_2F$$

$$2\ NO_2 + Cl_2 \rightarrow 2\ NO_2Cl$$

7.7.5 Dinitrogen Pentoxide (N_2O_5)

It is prepared by dehydrating the concentrated nitric acid with phosphorus pentoxide.

$$4\ HNO_3 + P_4O_{10} \rightarrow 4\ HPO_3 + 2\ N_2O_5$$

Physical appearance and chemical nature: It exists as a colourless solid below 273 K. Above this temperature, it starts decomposing.

$$N_2O_5 \rightarrow NO_2 + NO + O_2$$

(i) It is acidic in nature.

$$N_2O_5 + H_2O \rightarrow 2\ HNO_3$$

Table 7.5 Structures of oxides of nitrogen

Formula	Resonance structure	Bond parameters	Other characteristic properties
N_2O		113 pm 119 pm N≡N—O	Linear molecule, has low dipole moment(0.17D).
NO		:N═O: 115 pm (Linear) Dim of nitric oxide O═N—N═O or N- - - O 238 pm 115 pm O- - - N	Odd electron molecule, paramagnetic in the gaseous state, diamagnetic in the liquid and solid states due to dimerisation.
N_2O_3 or $O_2N—O—NO_2$ Symmetric form	Asymmetric form	114 pm, 186 pm, 105°, 114 pm, 130°, 117°, 121 pm (Planar)	It exists in two different forms, symmetric and asymmetric. These may be interconverted by irradiation with light of appropriate wavelength. The N–N bond in asymmetric forms is very weak as compared with the N–N bond in hydrazine.
NO_2		120 pm 134° Resonance hybrid (*Angular*)	Odd electron molecule, paramagnetic, dimerises on cooling to form N_2O_4.
N_2O_4		121 pm 175 pm 135° Resonance hybrid (*Planar*)	(i) NO_2–N_2O_4 system is a strong oxidising agent. It oxidises HCl to Cl_2 and CO to CO_2. $2NO_2 + 4HCl \rightarrow 2NOCl + Cl_2 + 2H_2O$ $NO_2 + CO \rightarrow NO + CO$ (ii) Diamagnetic, dissociates on heating to form NO_2.
N_2O_5		151 pm 119 pm 112° 134° Resonance hybrid (*Planar*)	Solid N_2O_5 exists as NO_3^- and hence is called nitrogen nitrate. It acts as a strong oxidising agent. $N_2O_5 + Na \rightarrow NaNO_3 + NO_2$ $N_2O_5 + I_2 \rightarrow I_2O_5 + N_2$

7.8 Nitric Acid, HNO_3

The common oxoacids of nitrogen are given below.

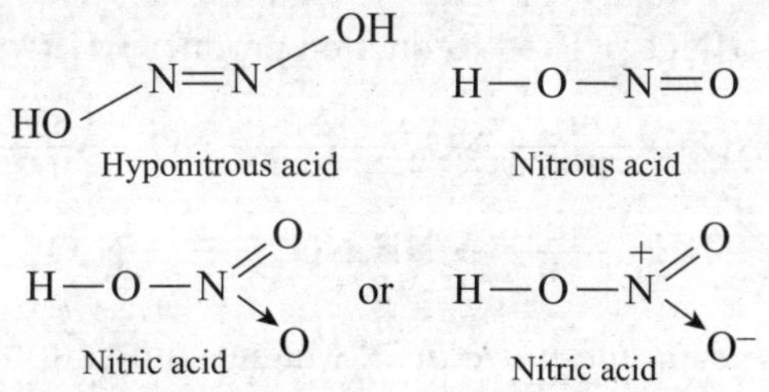

HO–N=N–OH (Hyponitrous acid) H–O–N=O (Nitrous acid)

$H-O-N(=O)\rightarrow O$ (Nitric acid) or $H-O-\overset{+}{N}(=O)-O^-$ (Nitric acid)

Laboratory preparation: In the laboratory, nitric acid can be prepared by heating sodium or potassium nitrate with concentrated sulfuric acid to about 423–475 K.

$$NaNO_3 + H_2SO_4 \xrightarrow{\text{Heat}} NaHSO_4 + HNO_3$$

On a commercial scale, it is mainly prepared by *Ostwald's process*. This method is based upon the catalytic oxidation of ammonia by atmospheric oxygen.

$$4\,NH_3(g) + 5\,O_2(g) \xrightarrow{\text{Pt/Rh gauze catalyst}} 4NO(g) + 6\,H_2O(g)$$

Nitric oxide thus formed combines with oxygen to form nitrogen dioxide.

$$2\,NO(g) + O_2(g) \rightarrow 2\,NO_2(g)$$

Nitrogen dioxide so formed dissolves in water to give nitric acid.

$$3\,NO_2(g) + H_2O(l) \rightarrow 2\,HNO_3(aq) + NO(g)$$

7.8.1 Structure of Nitric Acid

HNO_3 exists as a planar molecule with the bond angle and bond length as shown.

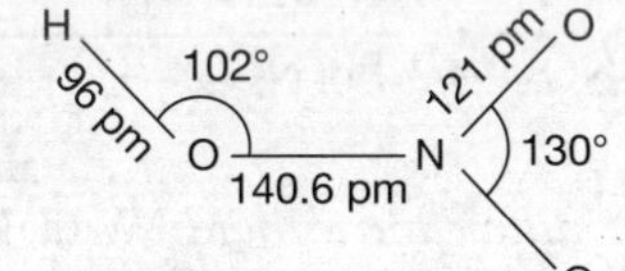

H 96 pm 102° O 140.6 pm N 121 pm O 130° O

Gaseous nitric acid

Actually, nitric acid is a resonance hybrid of the following two structures:

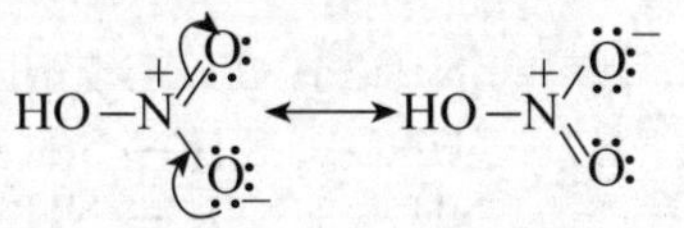

$HO-\overset{+}{N}(=O)-O^- \longleftrightarrow HO-\overset{+}{N}(-O^-)=O$

Resonance structures of HNO_3

Like nitric acid, the nitrate (NO_3^-) ion is a resonance hybrid of the following three resonance structures:

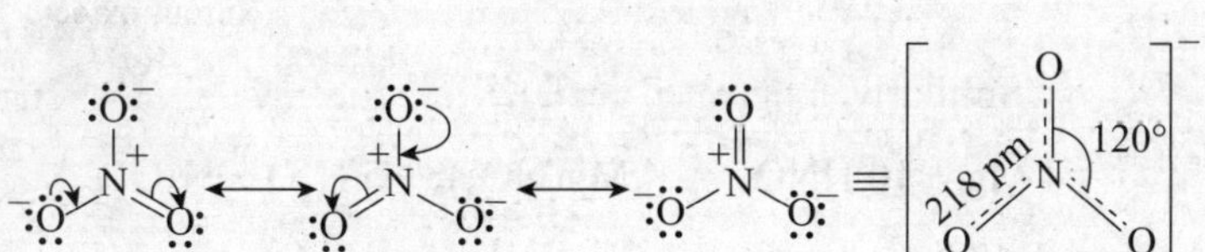

Resonating structures of NO_3^- ion

120° 218 pm

Resonance hybrid

As a result of resonance, all the three N–O bond lengths in NO_3^- ion are equal and are 218 pm long.

7.8.2 Physical Properties of Nitric Acid

- Pure nitric acid is a colourless, *fuming liquid* with a pungent odour.
- It has a boiling point of 355.6 K and a freezing point of 231.4 K.
- It has a specific gravity of 1.504.
- Fuming nitric acid is pure nitric acid containing oxides of nitrogen dissolved in it.

7.8.3 Chemical Properties of Nitric Acid

(i) Acidic character: It is one of the strongest acids because it is highly ionised in aqueous solution

$$HNO_3(aq) + H_2O(l) \rightarrow H_3O^+(aq) + NO_3^-(aq)$$

It turns blue litmus red. Being a monobasic acid, it reacts with metallic oxides, hydroxides, carbonates and bicarbonates giving only one series of salts called *nitrates*.

$$CaO + 2\,HNO_3 \rightarrow Ca(NO_3)_2 + H_2O$$
$$NaHCO_3 + HNO_3 \rightarrow NaNO_3 + CO_2 + H_2O$$
$$Na_2CO_3 + 2\,HNO_3 \rightarrow 2\,NaNO_3 + CO_2 + H_2O$$

(ii) Decomposition: Nitric acid decomposes on heating giving nitrogen dioxide, water and oxygen.

$$4\,HNO_3(aq) \xrightarrow{\text{Heat}} 4\,NO_2(g) + O_2(g) + 2\,H_2O(l)$$

(iii) Oxidising agent: Nitric acid is a very strong oxidising agent since it readily gives nasent oxygen, both in the concentrated as well as in the dilute form.

$$2\,HNO_3(conc.) \rightarrow H_2O + 2\,NO_2 + [O]$$
$$2\,HNO_3(dil.) \rightarrow H_2O + 2\,NO + 3\,[O]$$

Oxidation of non-metals: Dilute nitric acid has no action on non-metals.. However, concentrated nitric acid oxidises many non-metals as given below.

- Nitric acid oxidises sulfur to sulfuric acid.

$$2\,HNO_3 \rightarrow H_2O + 2\,NO_2 + [O] \times 2$$
$$C + 2\,[O] \rightarrow CO_2$$
$$\overline{C + 4\,HNO_3 \rightarrow CO_2 + 2H_2O + 4\,NO_2}$$

- Nitric acid oxidises carbon to carbonic acid.

$$2\,HNO_3 \rightarrow H_2O + NO_2 + [O] \times 24$$
$$S_8 + 24\,[O] + 8\,H_2O \rightarrow 8\,H_2SO_4$$
$$\overline{S_8 + 48HNO_3 \rightarrow 8H_2SO_4 + 48NO_2 \,|\, + 16H_2O}$$

- Nitric acid oxidises phosphorus to phosphoric acid.

$$2\,HNO_3 \rightarrow H_2O + 2\,NO_2 + [O] \times 5$$
$$I_2 + 5\,[O] \rightarrow I_2O_5$$
$$I_2O_5 + H_2O \rightarrow 2\,HIO_3$$
$$\overline{I_2 + 10HNO_3 \rightarrow 2HIO_3 + 10NO_2 + 4H_2O}$$

- Phosphorus is oxidised to orthophosphoric acid (H_3PO_4).

$$2\,HNO_3 \rightarrow H_2O + 2\,NO_2 + [O] \times 10$$
$$P_4 + 10\,[O] \rightarrow P_4O_{10}$$
$$P_4O_{10} + 6\,H_2O \rightarrow 4\,H_3PO_4$$
$$\overline{P_4 + 20HNO_3 \rightarrow 4H_3PO_4 + 20NO_2 + 4H_2O}$$

- Nitric acid oxidises arsenic to arsenic acid.

$$2\,HNO_3 \rightarrow H_2O + 2\,NO_2 + [O] \times 5$$
$$2\,As + 5\,[O] \rightarrow As_2O_5$$
$$As_2O_5 + 3\,H_2O \rightarrow 2\,H_3AsO_4$$
$$\overline{2\,As + 10\,HNO_3 \rightarrow 2\,H_3AsO_4 + 2H_2O + 10\,NO_2}$$

or $$As + 5\,HNO_3 \rightarrow \underset{\text{Arsenic acid}}{H_3AsO_4} + H_2O + 5\,NO_2$$

Similarly, $$Sb + 5\,HNO_3 \rightarrow \underset{\text{Antimonic acid}}{H_3SbO_4} + H_2O + 5\,NO_2$$

Oxidation of compounds:
With conc. HNO_3

$$2\,HNO_3 \rightarrow H_2O + 2\,NO_2 + [O]$$
$$H_2S + [O] \rightarrow H_2O + S$$
$$\overline{H_2S + 2\,HNO_3 \rightarrow 2H_2O + 2NO_2 + S\downarrow}$$

With dil. HNO_3

$$2\,HNO_3 \rightarrow H_2O + 2\,NO + 3\,[O]$$
$$H_2S + [O] \rightarrow H_2O + S] \times 3$$
$$\overline{3H_2S + 2HNO_3 \rightarrow 4H_2O + 2NO_2 + 3S\downarrow}$$

- Sulfur dioxide is oxidised to sulfuric acid
  With conc. HNO_3

$$2\,HNO_3 \rightarrow H_2O + 2\,NO_2 + [O]$$
$$SO_2 + H_2O + [O] \rightarrow H_2SO_4$$
$$\overline{SO_2 + 2HNO_3 \rightarrow H_2SO_4 + 2NO_2}$$

With dil. HNO_3

$$2\,HNO_3 \rightarrow H_2O + 2\,NO + 3\,[O]$$
$$SO_2 + H_2O + [O] \rightarrow H_2SO_4] \times 3$$
$$\overline{3SO_2 + 2HNO_3 + 2H_2O \rightarrow 3H_2SO_4 + 2NO}$$

- Ferrous sulfate is oxidised to ferric sulfate
  With conc. HNO_3

$$2\,HNO_3 \rightarrow H_2O + 2\,NO_2 + [O]$$
$$2\,FeSO_4 + H_2SO_4 + [O] \rightarrow Fe_2(SO_4)_3 + H_2O$$
$$\overline{2FeSO_4 + 2HNO_3 + H_2SO_4 \rightarrow Fe_2(SO_4)_3 + 2H_2O + 2NO_2}$$

With dil. HNO_3

$$2\,HNO_3 \rightarrow H_2O + 2\,NO + 3\,[O]$$
$$2\,FeSO_4 + H_2SO_4 + [O] \rightarrow Fe_2(SO_4)_3 + H_2O] \times 3$$
$$\overline{6FeSO_4 + 2HNO_3 + 3H_2SO_4 \rightarrow 3Fe_2(SO_4)_3 + 4H_3O + 2NO}$$

This reaction forms the basis of the *brown-ring test* for nitrates.

(iv) Action on metals: Reaction with metals which are more electropositive than hydrogen (Mg, Al, Mn, Zn, Fe, Pb).

In this case, nascent hydrogen is liberated which further reduces nitric acid.

$$\text{Metal} + HNO_3 \rightarrow \text{Metal nitrate} + H$$
$$HNO_3 + H \rightarrow \text{Reduction product} + H_2O$$

$$HNO_3 \xrightarrow[-H_2O]{+H} NO_2 \xrightarrow[-H_2O]{+2\,H} NO \xrightarrow[-H_2O]{+5\,H}$$
$$NH_3 \xrightarrow[-H_2O]{HNO_3} NH_4NO_3 \xrightarrow{\Delta} N_2O$$

(a) *Very dilute nitric acid*: Magnesium and manganese are the only metals which produce hydrogen with very dilute (1%–2%) nitric acid.

$$Mg + 2HNO_3 \rightarrow Mg(NO_3)_2 + H_2$$
$$Mn + 2HNO_3 \rightarrow Mn(NO_3)_2 + H_2$$

(b) *Cold dilute nitric acid*: More active metals like magnesium, zinc, tin and iron react with cold dil. HNO_3 to form ammonium nitrate.

$$Zn + 2HNO_3 \rightarrow Zn(NO_3)_2 + 2H] \times 4$$
$$HNO_3 + 8H \rightarrow NH_3 + 3H_2O$$
$$NH_3 + HNO_3 \rightarrow NH_4NO_3$$
$$\overline{4Zn + 10HNO_3 \rightarrow 4Zn(NO_3)_2 + 3H_2O + \underset{\text{Ammonium nitrate}}{NH_4NO_3}}$$

Similarly,

$$4\,Sn + 10\,HNO_3 \rightarrow 4\,Sn(NO_3)_2 + 3\,H_2O + NH_4NO_3$$
$$4\,Fe + 10\,HNO_3 \rightarrow 4\,Fe(NO_3)_2 + 3\,H_2O + NH_4NO_3$$

Lead, under similar conditions, gives nitric oxide instead of ammonium nitrate.

$$Pb + 2\,HNO_3 \rightarrow Pb(NO_3)_2 + 2H] \times 3$$
$$HNO_3 + 3H \rightarrow NO + 2H_2O] \times 2$$
$$\overline{3\,Pb + 8\,HNO_3 \rightarrow 3\,Pb(NO_3)_2 + 4\,H_2O + \underset{\text{Nitric oxide}}{2\,NO}}$$

(c) *With hot dilute nitric acid*: With hot dilute nitric acid, ammonium nitrate formed, . undergoes decomposition to form nitrous oxide (N_2O).

$$N + 2\,HNO_3 \rightarrow Zn(NO_3)_2 + 2\,H] \times 4$$
$$HNO_3 + 8\,H \rightarrow 3\,H_2O + NH_3$$
$$NH_3 + HNO_3 \rightarrow NH_4NO_3$$
$$NH_4NO_3 \rightarrow N_2O + 2\,H_2O$$
$$\overline{4\,Zn + 10\,HNO_3 \rightarrow 4\,Zn(NO_3)_2 + 5\,H_2O + \underset{\text{Nitrous oxide}}{2\,NO}}$$

Similarly,

$$4\,Mg + 10\,HNO_3 \rightarrow 4\,Mg(NO_3)_2 + 5\,H_2O + N_2O$$

(d) *With conc. nitric acid:* With conc. HNO_3, metals like zinc, magnesium, bismuth and lead, form nitrogen dioxide (NO_2).

$$Zn + 2\,HNO_3 \rightarrow Zn(NO_3)_2 + 2\,H$$
$$HNO_3 + H \rightarrow H_2O + NO_2] \times 2$$

$$Zn + 4\,HNO_3 \rightarrow Zn(NO_3)_2 + 2\,H_2O + \underset{\text{Nitrogen dioxide}}{2\,NO_2}$$

Similarly,

$$Mg + 4\,HNO_3 \rightarrow Mg(NO_3)_2 + 2\,H_2O + 2\,NO_2$$
$$Bi + 6\,HNO_3 \rightarrow Bi(NO_3)_3 + 3\,H_2O + 3\,NO_2$$
$$Pb + 4\,HNO_3 \rightarrow Pb(NO_3)_2 + 2\,H_2O + 2\,NO_2$$

Exception: Tin, however, reacts with conc. HNO_3 to form metastannic acid (H_2SnO_3) and nitrogen dioxide.

$$[2\,HNO_3 \rightarrow H_2O + 2\,NO_2 + O] \times 2$$
$$Sn + 2\,[O] + H_2O \rightarrow H_2SnO_3$$
$$Sn + 4HNO_3 \rightarrow \underset{\text{Metastannic acid}}{H_2SnO_3} \text{ or } SnO_2.H_2O + 4\,NO_2 + H_2O$$

Passivity: The passivity of the metals is due to the formation of a thin protective layer of the metal oxide on the surface of the metal which prevents further action. For example, in the case of iron, a protective layer of ferrosoferric oxide, $FeO.Fe_2O_3$ or Fe_3O_4 is formed on the surface of iron

$$3\,Fe + 8\,HNO_3 \rightarrow FeO.Fe_2O_3 + 8\,NO_2 + 4\,H_2O$$

Reaction with metals which are less electropositive than Cu, Bi, Hg, Ag: In this case, nascent hydrogen is not liberated. Instead, nitric acid oxidises these metals to their corresponding oxides while it is itself reduced to form either brown fumes of NO_2 or colourless vapours of NO. The metal oxide thus formed reacts further with excess of nitric acid to form the corresponding metal nitrate and water. For example,

$$\text{Metal} + HNO_3 \rightarrow \text{Metal oxide} + NO_2 \text{ or } NO + H_2O$$
$$\text{Metal oxide} + HNO_3 \rightarrow \text{Metal nitrate} + H_2O$$

(a) *With conc. HNO_3*: Nitrogen dioxide (NO_2) is formed.

$$2\,HNO_3 \rightarrow H_2O + 2\,NO_2 + [O]$$
$$Cu + [O] \rightarrow CuO$$
$$CuO + 2HNO_3 \rightarrow Cu(NO_3)_2 + H_2O$$
$$Cu + 4HNO_3 \rightarrow Cu(NO_3)_2 + 2H_2O + 2NO_2$$

Similarly, $Ag + 2\,HNO_3 \rightarrow AgNO_3 + H_2O + NO_2$

$$Hg + 4\,HNO_3 \rightarrow Hg(NO_3)_2 + 2\,H_2O + 2\,NO_2$$

(b) *With dil HNO_3*: Nitric oxide is evolved.

$$[2\,HNO_3 \rightarrow H_2O + 2\,NO + 3\,[O]$$
$$Cu + [O] \rightarrow CuO] \times 3$$
$$CuO + 2\,HNO_3 \rightarrow Cu(NO_3)_2 + H_2O] \times 3$$
$$3\,Cu + 8\,HNO_3 \rightarrow 3\,Cu(NO_3)_2 + 4\,H_2O + 2NO$$

Similarly, $3\,Ag + 4\,HNO_3 \rightarrow 3\,AgNO_3 + 2\,H_2O + NO$

$$6\,Hg + 8\,HNO_3 \rightarrow 3\,Hg_2(NO_3)_2 + 4\,H_2O + 2\,NO$$

- *Reaction with noble metals*: Noble metals like gold and platinum are not attacked by nitric acid. However, these metals are attacked by aqua regia (3 parts conc. HCl and 1 part conc. HNO_3), forming their chlorides.

$$\underbrace{3\,HCl + HNO_3}_{\text{Aqua regia}} \rightarrow \underset{\text{Nitrosyl chloride}}{NOCl} + 2\,H_2O + \underset{\text{Nascent chlorine}}{2\,Cl}$$

$$Au + 3\,Cl \rightarrow \underset{\text{Auric chloride}}{AuCl_3}; \quad Pt + 4\,Cl \rightarrow \underset{\text{Platinic chloride}}{PtCl_4}$$

These chlorides subsequently dissolve in excess of HCl forming their corresponding soluble complexes. Thus,

$$\underset{\text{Auric chloride}}{AuCl_3} + HCl \rightarrow \underset{\text{Aurochloric acid}}{H[AuCl_4]}; \quad \underset{\text{Platinic chloride}}{PtCl_4} + 2\,HCl \rightarrow \underset{\text{Chloroplatinic acid}}{H_2[PtCl_6]}$$

(v) Action of organic compounds

(a) Oxidation: Many organic compounds are oxidised by conc. HNO_3. For example, cane sugar (sucrose) on oxidation gives oxalic acid.

$$\underset{\text{Sucrose}}{C_{12}H_{22}O_{11}} + 36\,HNO_3 \rightarrow 6 \underset{\text{Oxalic acid}}{\begin{array}{c} COOH \\ | \\ COOH \end{array}} + 36\,NO_2 + 23\,H_2O$$

(b) Nitration: A mixture of conc. HNO_3 and conc. H_2SO_4 (*also called nitrating mixture*) is used for introducing one or more $-NO_2$ (nitro) groups into the benzene ring. This process is called *nitration*. For example,

$$\underset{\text{Benzene}}{C_6H_6} + \underset{(Conc.)}{HNO_3} \xrightarrow[330\,K]{\text{Conc. } H_2SO_4} \underset{\text{Nitrobenzene}}{C_6H_5NO_2} + H_2O$$

$$\underset{\text{Toluene}}{C_6H_5CH_3} + \underset{(Conc.)}{3HNO_3} \xrightarrow[\Delta]{\text{Conc. } H_2SO_4} \underset{\text{2, 4, 6-Trinitrotoluene (TNT)}}{C_6H_2(CH_3)(NO_2)_3} + 3H_2O$$

$$\underset{\text{Glycerol}}{\begin{array}{l} CH_2-OH \\ | \\ CH-OH \\ | \\ CH_2-OH \end{array}} + \underset{(Conc.)}{3\,HNO_3} \xrightarrow{\text{Conc. } H_2SO_4} \underset{\text{Trinitroglycerol}}{\begin{array}{l} CH_2-O-NO_2 \\ | \\ CH-O-NO_2 \\ | \\ CH_2-O-NO_2 \end{array}} + 3\,H_2O$$

Nitric acid also reacts with proteins giving a yellow compound called *xanthoprotein*.

7.8.4 Brown Ring Test for NO_3^- Ion

Nitrates give the brown ring test with Fe^{2+} ions in the presence of conc. H_2SO_4. This is based on the tendency of Fe^{2+} to reduce nitrates to nitric oxide which reacts with Fe^{2+}

to form a brown coloured complex during the qualitative test for nitrates. A brown ring at the interface between the solution and sulfuric acid indicates the presence of NO_3^- ion.

$$NO_3^-(aq) + 3\,Fe^{2+}(aq) + 4\,H^+(aq) \rightarrow NO(g) + 3\,Fe^{3+}(aq) + 2\,H_2O(l)$$

Nitric oxide

$$[Fe(H_2O)_6]^{2+} + NO(g) \rightarrow [Fe^+(H_2O)_5NO^+](aq) + H_2O(l)$$

Pentaaquanitrosoniumiron (I) (Brown complex)

7.9 Phosphorus and Its Compounds

It occurs mainly in the form of phosphate minerals in the crust of earth. Phosphorus is produced by heating bond ash (containing about 58% of calcium phosphate) or phosphate rock [phosphorite, $Ca_3(PO_4)_2$] with silica (SiO_2) and coke in an electric furnace at 1775 K. The reactions taking place are:

$$2\,Ca_3(PO_4)_2 + 6\,SiO_2 \xrightarrow{1773\text{ K}} 6\,CaSiO_3 + P_4O_{10}$$

$$P_4O_{10} + 10C \xrightarrow{1773\text{ K}} P_4 + 10\,CO$$

7.9.1 Allotropic Forms of Phosphorus

(i) White phosphorus: It is obtained when phosphate rock is heated with coke and sand in an electric furnace at 1773 K. On exposure to light, white phosphorus turns yellow, therefore, it is also called *yellow phosphorus.* It is very poisonous. Persons working with white phosphorus develop a disease known as *phossy jaw* in which jaw bones decay.

- The P_4 molecules of white phosphorus are held together by weak van der Waals forces; hence the melting point (317 K) and boiling point (553 K) are quite low.
- It is insoluble in water but soluble in organic solvents such as CS_2, alcohol and ether.
- It is a soft, translucent waxy white solid with a garlic odour. Being soft, it can be cut with a knife.
- At temperatures higher than 1070 K, P_4 molecules dissociate to give P_2 molecules.

$$P_4 \xrightleftharpoons{>1070\text{ K}} 2P_2$$

- White phosphorus is very reactive. It readily catches fire in air
- *Reaction with metals*: Phosphorus combines with a number of metals such as Na, Mg, Ca, Ag and Cu, forming their respective phosphides.

$$12\,Na + P_4 \rightarrow 4\,Na_3P; \qquad 6\,Mg + P_4 \rightarrow 2\,Mg_3P_2$$

Sodium phosphide; Magnesium phosphide

$$12\,Ag + P_4 \rightarrow 4\,Ag_3P; \qquad 6\,Ca + P_4 \rightarrow 2\,Ca_3P_2$$

Silver phosphide; Calcium phosphide

- *Reaction with halogens*: It readily combines with halogens to form trihalides (PX_3) and on prolonged treatment, forms pentahalides (PX_5). $P_4 + 6\,Cl_2 \rightarrow 4\,PCl_3$; $P_4 + 10\,Cl_2 \rightarrow 4\,PCl_5$
- *Reaction with aqueous alkalies*: On heating with caustic soda solution, it forms phosphine.

$$P_4 + 3\,NaOH + 3\,H_2O \xrightarrow{\Delta,\,CO_2} PH_3 + 3\,NaH_2PO_2$$

Phosphine; Sodium hypophosphite

- White phosphorus acts as a strong reducing agent; it reduces HNO_3 to NO_2 and H_2SO_4 to SO_2.

$$P_4 + 20\,HNO_3 \rightarrow 20\,NO_2 + 4\,H_3PO_4 + 4\,H_2O$$

$$P_4 + H_2SO_4 \rightarrow 10\,SO_2 + 4\,H_3PO_4 + 4\,H_2O$$

It also reduces solutions of copper, silver and gold salts to their corresponding metals.

$$P_4 + 3\,CuSO_4 + 6\,H_2O \rightarrow Cu_3P_2\downarrow + 2\,H_3PO_3 + 3\,H_2SO_4$$

$$Cu_3O_2 + 5\,CuSO_4 + 8\,H_2O \rightarrow 8\,Cu\downarrow + 5\,H_2SO_4 + 2\,H_3PO_4$$

(ii) Red phosphorus: It is obtained by heating white phosphorus in an inert atmosphere (out of contact of air) at 573 K for several days.

$$P_4(s) \xrightarrow[CO_2\text{ or coal gas}]{573\text{ K}} P_4(s)$$

White phosphorus; Red phosphorus

P_4 tetrahedra are joined together through covalent bonds to give a polymeric structure. Because of its polymeric structure, the melting point (883 K) is much higher than that of white phosphorus (317 K).

- It is a hard, crystalline, odourless solid with an iron-grey lustre.
- It is non-poisonous in nature.
- It is insoluble in water as well in organic solvents such as CS_2, alcohol and ether.
- It is a relatively stable allotrope of phosphorus at room temperature. It sublimes on heating giving vapours It is denser (2.16 g cm^{-3}) than white phosphorus (1.84 gcm^{-3}) and is a bad conductor of electricity.
- Being polymeric in nature, it is less reactive than white phosphorus.
- It burns in oxygen at 565 K to yield phosphorus pentoxide.

$$P_4(s) + 5\,O_2(g) \xrightarrow{565\text{ K}} P_4O_{10}(s)$$

- Being less reactive than white phosphorus, it reacts with halogens, sulfur and alkali metals only when heated forming their corresponding salts.

$$P_4 + 6\,Cl_2 \xrightarrow{\Delta} 4\,PCl_3$$

$$P_4 + 10\,Cl_2 \xrightarrow{\Delta} 4\,PCl_5$$

$$8\,P_4 + 3\,S_8 \xrightarrow[\text{Inert atmosphere}]{453\text{ K}} 8\,P_4S_3$$

$$P_4 + 12\,Na \xrightarrow{\Delta} 4\,Na_3P$$

(iii) Black phosphorus:

$$\text{Red phosphorus} \xrightarrow[\text{Sealed tube}]{803\text{ K}} \alpha\text{-Black phosphorus}$$

β-Black phosphorus (orthorhombic) is prepared by heating white phosphorus at 473 K under a very high pressure (4000–12000 atm) in an inert atmosphere.

$$\text{White phosphorus} \xrightarrow[4000\text{–}12000\text{ atm pressure}]{473} \beta\text{-black phosphorus}$$

β-black phosphorus a graphite-like structure. The important characteristics of black phosphorus are given below.

- It has a black metallic lustre.
- It has a sharp melting point of 860 K. Its specific gravity is 2.69.
- It has a highly polymeric layered structure and exists in three crystalline and one amorphous form. Therefore, it has high density.
- It is a moderate conductor of heat and electricity.
- It is thermodynamically the most stable and inactive form of phosphorus. It does not burn in air up to 673 K.

7.10 Phosphine, PH_3

Phosphine (PH_3) is also known as *hydrogen phosphide* or *phosphoretted hydrogen*.

7.10.1 Preparation

Phosphine may be prepared by the following methods.

(i) From metal phosphides: By the action of water or dilute mineral acid on metallic phosphides (Ca_3P_2, AlP).

$$\underset{\text{Calcium phosphide}}{Ca_3P_2} + 6\,H_2O \rightarrow 3\,Ca(OH)_2 + \underset{\text{Phosphine}}{2\,PH_3\uparrow}$$

$$Ca_3P_2 + 6\,HCl \rightarrow 3\,CaCl_2 + 2\,PH_3\uparrow$$

$$\underset{\text{Aluminium phosphide}}{AlP} + 3\,H_2O \rightarrow Al(OH)_3 + PH_3\uparrow$$

(ii) From phosphorus acid: Pure phosphine can be prepared by heating phosphorus acid at 478–483 K.

$$\underset{\text{Phosphorus acid}}{4\,H_3PO_3} \xrightarrow{473\text{ K}} \underset{\text{Phosphoric acid}}{3\,H_3PO_4} + \underset{\text{Phosphine}}{PH_3\uparrow}$$

(iii) From phosphorus trichloride by reaction with lithium aluminium hydride or lithium hydride

$$4\,PCl_3 + 3\,LiAlH_4 \xrightarrow[\text{Ether}]{<273\text{ K}} 4\,PH_3 + 3\,LiCl + 3\,AlCl_3$$

$$PCl_3 + 3\,LiH \xrightarrow{\text{Warm}} PH_3 + 3\,LiCl$$

(iv) From phosphonium iodide: Pure phosphine can also be obtained by heating phosphonium iodide with caustic soda solution.

$$\underset{\text{Phosphonium iodide}}{PH_4I} + NaOH \rightarrow NaI + H_2O + \underset{\text{Phosphine}}{PH_3\uparrow}$$

(v) Laboratory method of preparation: Phosphine is prepared in the laboratory by heating white phosphorus with concentrated sodium hydroxide solution in an inert atmosphere of carbon dioxide or coal gas.

$$P_4(s) + 3\,NaOH(aq) + 3\,H_2O(l) \rightarrow \underset{\text{Sodiumhypophosphite}}{3\,NaH_2PO_2(aq)} + \underset{\text{Phosphine}}{PH_3(g)\uparrow}$$

The gas produced usually catches fire in air due to the presence of impurity of diphosphine (P_2H_4) which is highly inflammable. The vapours of PH_3 thus produced are passed into water through a delivery tube. Each bubble of gas when it comes in contact with air, undergoes combustion and forms a ring of smoke. These rings are called *vortex rings* or *philospher's rings*. These are due to the formation of phosphorus pentoxide (P_4O_{10}).

7.10.2 Structure of Phosphine

Like NH_3, phosphine is also pyramidal. The HPH bond angle in PH_3 is however, much lower (93.6°) than that in NH_3 (107.8°) due to less repulsions between the bond pairs. Further, due to the bigger size of P than N, the P–H bond length is longer (142 pm) than the N–H bond length (101.7 pm).

7.10.3 Physical Properties of Phosphine

- Phosphine is a colourless gas possessing unpleasant odour similar to that of garlic or rotten fish and is highly poisonous.
- It is slightly soluble in water; However, more soluble in CS_2 and other organic solvents.
- Its vapour density is 17, a little heavier than air.
- On cooling to 185.5 K, phosphine condenses to a liquid and on cooling to 139.5K, it solidifies.

7.10.4 Chemical Properties of Phosphine

(i) Basic nature: It is feebly basic and reacts with halogen acids to form a phosphonium salt (basic nature).

$$\underset{\text{Phosphine}}{PH_3} + HX \rightarrow \underset{\text{Phosphonium halide}}{PH_4^+X^-} \quad (X = Cl, Br, I)$$

(ii) Combustibility: When heated to 423 K in air or oxygen, it burns forming phosphoric acid.

$$PH_3 + 2\,O_2 \xrightarrow{423\text{ K}} H_3PO_4$$

It explodes in contact with traces of oxidising agents like HNO_3, Cl_2 or Br_2 vapours.

(iii) Decomposition: By heating in the absence of air at 713 K or by passing an electric spark through it, phosphine breaks into its elements.

$$4\,PH_3 \xrightarrow{713\text{ K}} P_4 + 6\,H_2$$

The solution of phosphine in water decomposes in the presence of light giving red phosphorus and H_2.

$$4\,PH_3(aq) \xrightarrow{h\nu} \underset{\text{Red phosphorus}}{P_4(s)} + 6\,H_2(g)$$

(iv) Action of chlorine:

$$PH_3 + 3\,Cl_2 \rightarrow \underset{\text{Phosphorus trichloride}}{PCl_3} + 3\,HCl;\; PH_3 + 4\,Cl_2 \rightarrow \underset{\text{Phosphorus pentachloride}}{PCl_5} + 3\,HCl$$

(v) Action of nitrous and nitric oxides: When sparked with nitrous oxide, it reduces the latter to nitrogen.

$$PH_3 + 4\,N_2O \rightarrow H_3PO_4 + 4\,N_2;\; PH_3 + 4\,NO \rightarrow H_3PO_4 + 2\,H_2$$

(vi) Reaction with metallic salt solutions: When bubbled through certain metallic salt solutions, phosphides of the metals get precipitated.

$$\underset{\text{Copper sulfate}}{3\,CuSO_4} + 2\,PH_3 \rightarrow \underset{\text{Copper phosphide}}{Cu_3P_2\downarrow} + 3\,H_2SO_4$$

$$\underset{\text{Mercuric chloride}}{3\,HgCl_2} + 2\,PH_3 \rightarrow \underset{\text{Mercuric phosphide}}{Hg_3P_2\downarrow} + 6\,HCl$$

(vii) Reaction with silver nitrate:

$$PH_3 + 6\,AgNO_3 \rightarrow \underset{\text{Intermediate complex}}{Ag_3P.3AgNO_3} + 3HNO_3$$

$$Ag_3P.3AgNO_3 + 3\,H_2O \rightarrow \underset{\text{Black ppt}}{6\,Ag\downarrow} + 3\,HNO_3 + H_3PO_3$$

7.11 Phosphorus Halides

7.11.1 Phosphorus Trichloride, PCl_3

Preparation: It is prepared in the laboratory by passing dry chlorine gas over heated white phosphorus.

$$P_4(s) + 3\,Cl_2(g) \rightarrow 4\,PCl_3(l)$$

It can also be obtained by the reaction of thionyl chloride with white phosphorus.

$$P_4 + \underset{\text{Thionyl chloride}}{8\,SOCl_2} \rightarrow \underset{\text{Phosphorus trichloride}}{4\,PCl_3} + 4\,SO_2 + \underset{\text{Sulfur monochloride}}{2\,S_2Cl_2}$$

Structure: Like in PH_3, P in PCl_3 is sp^3 hybridised. like PH_3, PCl_3 is also pyramidal. The ClPCl bond angle in PCl_3 is, however, greater (100.4°) than in PH_3 (93.6°) due to steric crowding of the two Cl atoms. As expected, the P–Cl bond is much longer (204 pm) than the P–H bond (142 pm) due to the bigger size of the Cl atom.

Physical Properties

- It is a colourless oily liquid fuming constantly in moist air.
- Its specific gravity is 1.6.
- Its boiling point and freezing point values are 347 K and 161 K respectively.
- It has a highly pungent smell.

Chemical Properties

(i) *Action with water*: It fumes in moist air and reacts with water violently to form phosphorus acid.

$$PCl_3 + 3\,H_2O \rightarrow H_3PO_3 + 3\,HCl$$

(ii) *Action of conc. H_2SO_4*: It reacts with conc. H_2SO_4 forming chlorosulfonic acid.

$$\underset{\text{Sulfuric acid}}{2\,HO\text{–}SO_2\text{–}OH} + PCl_3 \rightarrow$$

$$\underset{\text{Chlorosulfonic acid}}{HO\text{–}SO_2\text{–}Cl} + HPO_3 + SO_2 + 2\,HCl$$

(iii) *Action of Cl_2, O_2 and S*: It combines with chlorine or sulfur to form phosphorus pentachloride or thiophosphorus oxychloride.

$$PCl_3 + Cl_2 \rightarrow PCl_5$$

$$2\,PCl_3 + O_2 \rightarrow \underset{\text{Phosphorus oxychloride}}{2\,POCl_3};\quad PCl_3 + S \rightarrow \underset{\text{Thiophosphorus oxychloride}}{PSCl_3}$$

(iv) *Action with sulfur monochloride, thionyl chloride and sulfuryl chloride*: It is readily oxidised to phosphorus (V) derivatives, PCl_5, $POCl_3$ and $PSCl_3$.

$$PCl_3 + SO_3 \rightarrow POCl_3 + SO_2;\quad PCl_3 + \underset{\text{Sulfuryl chloride}}{SO_2Cl_2} \rightarrow PCl_5 + SO_2$$

$$3\,PCl_3 + SOCl_2 \rightarrow POCl_3 + PSCl_3 + PCl_5;$$

$$3\,PCl_3 + S_2Cl_2 \rightarrow PCl_5 + 2\,PSCl_3$$

(v) *Reaction with Grignard reagents*: PCl_3 reacts with Grignard reagents to form substituted phosphines. For example,

$$PCl_3 + \underset{\text{Phenylmagnesiumchloride}}{3\,C_6H_5MgCl} \rightarrow \underset{\text{Triphenyl phosphine}}{P(C_6H_5)_3} + 3\,MgCl_2$$

(vi) *Action of finely divided metals*: Finely divided metals react on heating to form metal chlorides.

$$12\,Ag + 4\,PCl_3 \xrightarrow{\Delta} 12\,AgCl + P_4$$

$$6\,Na + PCl_3 \xrightarrow{\Delta} 3\,NaCl + Na_3P$$

Uses: Phosphorus trichloride is widely used as an important reagent in organic chemistry for replacing hydroxyl groups by chlorine atoms in organic reactions.

(i) $\underset{\text{Ethanol}}{3\,CH_3CH_2OH} + PCl_3 \rightarrow \underset{\text{Chloroethane}}{3\,CH_3CH_2Cl} + H_3PO_3$

(ii) $\underset{\text{Acetic acid}}{3\,CH_3COOH} + PCl_3 \rightarrow \underset{\text{Acetyl chloride}}{3\,CH_3COCl} + H_3PO_3$

(iii) $\underset{\text{Benzenesulfonic acid}}{3\,C_6H_5SO_2OH} + PCl_3 \rightarrow \underset{\text{Benzenesulfonyl chloride}}{3\,C_6H_5SO_2Cl} + H_3PO_3$

7.11.2 Phosphorus Pentachloride, PCl_5

Preparation: Phosphorus pentachloride is prepared by the reaction of white phosphorus with excess of dry chlorine.

$$P_4(s) + 10\,Cl_2(g) \rightarrow 4\,PCl_5(s)$$

It can also be obtained by the reaction of dry chlorine on phosphorus trichloride.

$$PCl_3(l) + Cl_2(g) \rightarrow PCl_5(s)$$

Phosphorus pentachloride can also be prepared by the action of SO_2Cl_2 on phosphorus.

$$P_4(s) + 10\ SO_2Cl_2(l) \rightarrow 4\ PCl_5(s) + 10\ SO_2(g)$$

Structure: In PCl_5, phosphorus undergoes sp^3d hybridisation and has trigonal bipyramidal geometry (Fig. 7.7) in the gaseous and liquid states. It has two axial (*a*) bonds and three equatorial (*e*) P–Cl bonds. The axial bonds are repelled by the three equatorial bond pairs while the three equatorial bonds are repelled by the two axial bond pairs; therefore, the axial bonds are longer (240 pm) than the equatorial bonds (202 pm).

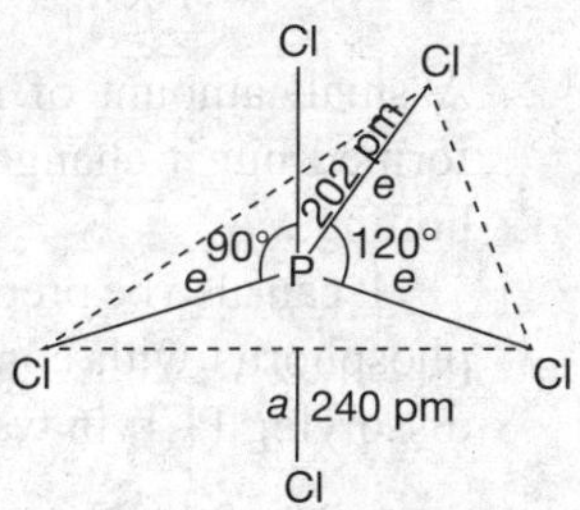

Fig. 7.7 Structure of phosphorus pentachloride

Physical Properties

- It is a yellowish white powder having a pungent smell.
- It fumes in moist air due to its strong affinity for water.
- On heating, it sublimes at 433 K and can be melted (mp 318 K) only by heating it under pressure.

Chemical Properties

(i) *Dissociation*: PCl_5 is thermally less stable than PCl_3. On heating it sublimes, but decomposes on stronger heating into the trichloride and chlorine.

$$PCl_5 \rightleftharpoons PCl_3 + Cl_2$$

(ii) *Action of moisture, air and water*: In moist air, it hydrolyses to $POCl_3$ and finally gets converted to phosphoric acid.

$$PCl_5 + H_2O \rightarrow POCl_3 + 2\ HCl;$$
$$POCl_3 + 3\ H_2O \rightarrow H_3PO_4 + 3\ HCl$$

However, with excess of water it reacts violently to form H_3PO_4 and HCl.

$$PCl_5 + 4\ H_2O\ (excess) \rightarrow H_3PO_4 + 5\ HCl$$

(iii) *Reaction with compounds containing hydroxyl groups*:

$$\underset{\text{Acetic acid}}{CH_3COOH} + PCl_5 \rightarrow \underset{\text{Acetyl chloride}}{CH_3COCl} + POCl_3 + HCl$$

$$\underset{\text{Ethyl alcohol}}{CH_3CH_2OH} + PCl_5 \rightarrow \underset{\text{Ethyl chloride}}{CH_3CH_2Cl} + POCl_3 + HCl$$

$$\underset{\text{Sulfuric acid}}{HO–SO_2–OH} + 2\ PCl_5 \rightarrow \underset{\text{Sulfuryl chloride}}{Cl\ SO_2–Cl} + 2\ POCl_3 + 2\ HCl$$

(iv) *Reaction with metals*:

$$Zn + PCl_5 \rightarrow ZnCl_2 + PCl_3;\ 2\ Ag + PCl_5 \rightarrow 2\ AgCl + PCl_3$$
$$Sn + 2\ PCl_5 \rightarrow SnCl_4 + 2\ PCl_3$$

(v) *Reaction with phosphorus pentoxide, phosphorus pentasulfide and sulfur dioxide*:

$$6\ PCl_5 + P_4O_{10} \rightarrow \underset{\text{Phosphorus oxychloride}}{10\ POCl_3};\ 6\ PCl_5 + \underset{\text{Phosphorus pentasulfide}}{P_4S_{10}} \rightarrow \underset{\text{Phosphorus thiochloride}}{10\ PSCl_3}$$

$$PCl_5 + SO_2 \rightarrow POCl_3 + \underset{\text{Thionyl chloride}}{SOCl_2}$$

(vi) *Reaction with chloride ion acceptors*:

$$PCl_5 + BCl_3 \rightarrow [PCl_4]^+\ [BCl_4]^-;\ PCl_5 + NbCl_4 \rightarrow [PCl_4]^+\ [NbCl_5]^-$$

(vii) *Reaction with potassium fluoride*:

$$PCl_5 + 6\ KF \rightarrow K^+\ [PF_6]^- + 5\ KCl$$

(viii) *Reaction with H_2*:

$$PCl_5 + H_2 \rightarrow PCl_3 + 2\ HCl$$

In this reaction, PCl_5 acts as an oxidising agent and thus oxidises H_2 to HCl.

7.12 Oxides and Oxoacids of Phosphorus

7.12.1 Oxides of Phosphorus

Phosphorus forms two oxides—phosphorus (III) oxide, P_4O_6 and phosphorus (V) oxide, P_4O_{10}. Due to its large size and lower electronegativity, phosphorus does not form $p\pi–p\pi$ multiple bonds. As a result, oxides of phosphorus have cage structures and exist as dimers.

Preparation: Phosphorus trioxide is formed when phosphorus is burnt in a limited supply of air.

$$P_4 + 3\ O_2\ (limited) \rightarrow P_4O_6;\quad P_4 + 5\ O_2\ (excess) \rightarrow P_4O_{10}$$

Structure: Figure 7.8.

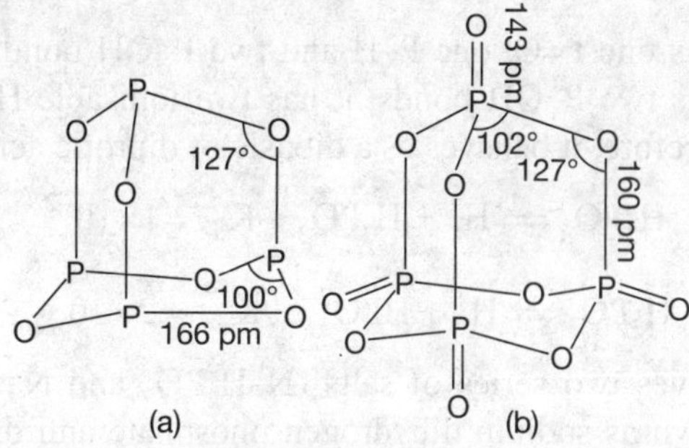

Fig. 7.8 Sturctrues of **(a)** phosphorus trioxide (P_4O_6) and **(b)** phosphorus pentaxide (P_4O_{10})

Properties: Both P_4O_6 and P_4O_{10} are *acidic* oxides which dissolve in water to form *phosphonic acid* (orthophosphorus acid, H_3PO_3) and *phosphoric acid* (orthophophoric acid, H_3PO_4) respectively.

$$P_4O_6 + 6\ H_2O \rightarrow 4\ H_3PO_3;\quad P_4O_{10} + 6\ H_2O \rightarrow 4\ H_3PO_4$$

P_4O_{10} acts as a *powerful dehydrating agent*. It is able to extract water from many inorganic and organic compounds.

$$2\,H_2SO_4 + P_4O_{10} \rightarrow 2\,SO_3 + 4\,HPO_3$$
$$4\,HNO_3 + P_4O_{10} \rightarrow 2\,N_2O_5 + 4\,HPO_3$$

$$\underset{\text{Perchloric acid}}{4\,HClO_4} + P_4O_{10} \rightarrow 2\,Cl_2O_7 + 4\,HPO_3$$

$$\underset{\text{Acetamide}}{2CH_3CONH_2} + P_4O_{10} \rightarrow \underset{\text{Acetonitrile}}{2\,CH_3CN} + 4HPO_3$$

7.12.2 Oxoacids of Phosphorus

(i) Phosphinic acid or Hypophosphorus acid, H_3PO_2

Preparation: It is prepared by heating phosphorus with alkalies like barium hydroxide when a precipitate of barium phosphate is formed.

$$3\,Ba(OH)_2 + 2\,P_4 + 6\,H_2O \xrightarrow{\text{Heat}} 2PH_3 + \underset{\text{ppt}}{3Ba(H_2PO_2)_2}$$

$$Ba(H_2PO_2)_2 + H_2SO_4 \rightarrow BaSO_4 + 2H_3PO_2$$

It behaves as a monobasic acid, ionising as:

$$H_3PO_2 \rightleftharpoons H^+ + H_2PO_2^-$$

On heating to 313 K, it decomposes to phosphine.

$$3\,H_3PO_2 \xrightarrow{315\text{ K}} \underset{\text{Phosphine}}{PH_3} + \underset{\text{Phosphorus acid}}{2H_3PO_3}$$

However, on heating above 333K, it decomposes to phosphoric acid and phosphine.

$$2\,H_3PO_2 \xrightarrow{>333\text{ K}} \underset{\text{Phosphoric acid}}{H_3PO_4} + \underset{\text{Phosphine}}{PH_3}$$

(ii) Orthophosphorus acid or phosphonic acid, H_3PO_3

Preparation: It is prepared by the hydrolysis of phosphorus trichloride or trioxide.

$$PCl_3 + 3\,H_2O \rightarrow H_3PO_3 + 3\,HCl$$
$$P_4O_6 + 6H_2O \rightarrow 4H_3PO_3$$

It has one P=O, one P–H and two P–OH bonds. Since it has two P–OH bonds, it has two ionisable H atoms. Therefore, it behaves as a dibasic or diprotic acid.

$$H_3PO_3 \rightleftharpoons H^+ + H_2PO_3 \quad K_{a_1} = 1\times10^{-2}$$

$$H_2PO_3^- \rightleftharpoons H^+ + HPO_3^{2-} \quad K_{a_2} = 2\times10^{-7}$$

It gives two series of salts (NaH_2PO_3 and Na_2HPO_3), known as sodium dihydrogen phosphate and disodium hydrogen phosphate respectively.

On heating it decomposes into phosphoric acid and phosphine.

$$4H_3PO_3 \xrightarrow{457\text{ K}} 3H_3PO_4 + PH_3$$

It is readily oxidised by air in the presence of a catalyst (iodine) into phosphoric acid.

$$2H_3PO_3 + O_2 \xrightarrow{\text{Iodine}} 2H_3PO_4$$

It is a strong reducing agent.

(iii) Orthophosphoric acid, H_3PO_4

Preparation: It is prepared by adding phosphorus pentoxide to water and boiling the solution.

$$P_4O_{10} + 6H_2O \rightarrow 4H_3PO_4$$

A small amount of metaphosphoric acid may also be formed but it changes readily into phosphoric acid on boiling.

It can also be prepared by heating phosphorus with conc. HNO_3 or by dissolving PCl_5 in water.

O=P(OH)(OH)(OH)
Orthophosphoric acid
Basicity = 3

$$\therefore\ P_4 + 20\,HNO_3 \xrightarrow{\text{Heat}} 4H_3PO_4 + 20\,NO_2 + 4H_2O$$

$$PCl_5 + 4H_2O \xrightarrow{\text{Heat}} H_3PO_4 + 5HCl$$

It has one P=O and three P–OH bonds. Since it has three P–OH bonds, it has three ionisable H atoms. Therefore, it behaves as a tribasic or triprotic acid and ionises in three stages.

$$H_3PO_4 \rightleftharpoons H^+ + H_2PO_4^- \quad K_{a_1} = 7.5\times10^{-3}$$

$$H_2PO_4^- \rightleftharpoons H^+ + HPO_4^{2-} \quad K_{a_2} = 6.2\times10^{-8}$$

$$HPO_4^{2-} \rightleftharpoons H^+ + PO_4^{3-} \quad K_{a_3} = 1.0\times10^{-13}$$

Therefore, it forms three series of salts; for example, NaH_2PO_4 (sodium dihydrogen phosphate), Na_2HPO_4 (disodium hydrogen phosphate) and Na_3PO_4 (sodium phosphate).

(iv) Pyrophosphoric acid, $H_4P_2O_7$

It contains phosphorus in the +5 oxidation state.

Preparation: It is prepared by heating orthophosphoric acid to 523 K.

$$2H_3PO_4 \xrightarrow{523\text{ K}} \underset{\text{Pyrophosphoric acid}}{H_4P_2O_7} + H_2O$$

The acid is formed by the loss of a molecule of water from two molecules of phosphoric acid and has the following structure.

(HO)(HO)P(=O)–O–P(=O)(OH)(OH)

Since it contains four OH groups, it is tetrabasic. It dissolves in water to form orthophosphoric acid.

$$H_4P_2O_7 + H_2O \xrightarrow{\text{Heat}} \underset{\text{Orthophosphoric acid}}{2H_3PO_4}$$

Upon strong heating, it decomposes to form meta phosphoric acid

$$H_4P_2O_7 \xrightarrow{873\text{ K}} \underset{\text{Metaphosphoric acid}}{2HPO_3} + H_2O$$

(v) Metaphosphoric acid, HPO_3

It has one P–OH bond and therefore, exists as a monobasic acid.

Preparation: It is prepared by heating orthophosphoric acid to 525 K.

$$\underset{\text{Orthophosphoric acid}}{H_3PO_4} \xrightarrow{523\text{ K}} \underset{\text{Metaphosphoric acid}}{HPO_3} + H_2O$$

However, it may be noted that metaphosphoric acid does not exist as a simple monomer; rather, it exists as cyclometaphosphoric acid or polymetaphosphoric acid.

Trimetaphosphoric acid $(HPO_3)_3$

The structures of these oxoacids are given below.

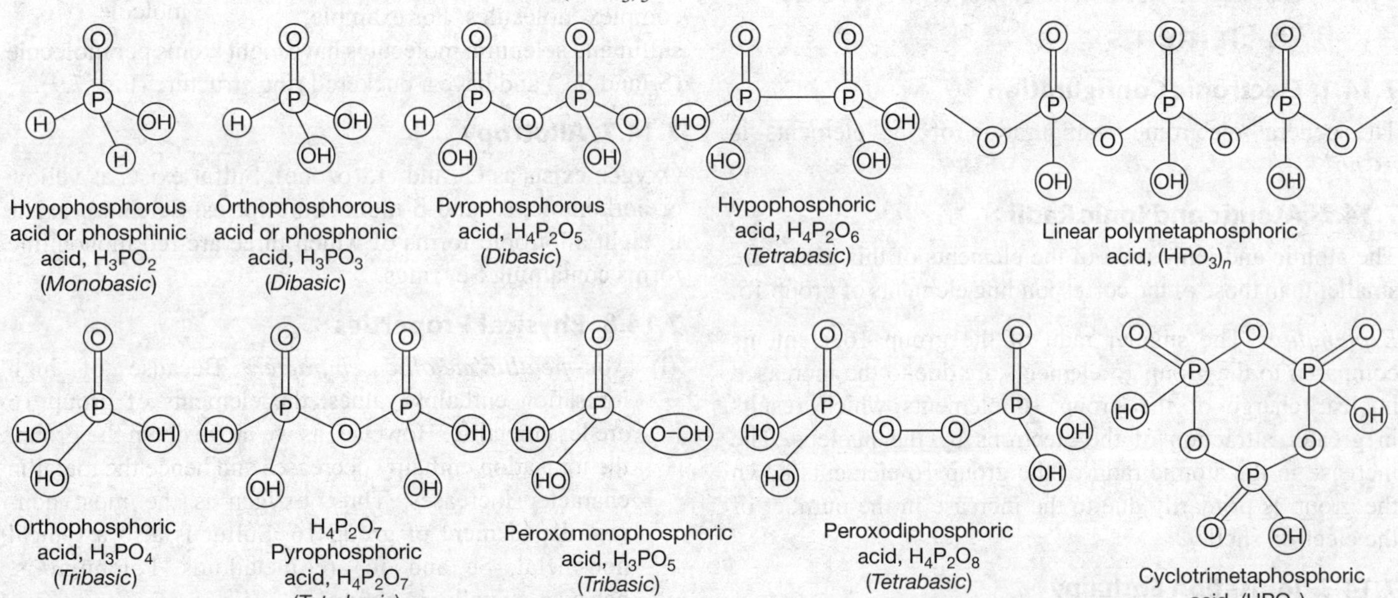

7.12.3 Important Characteristics of Oxoacids

- In all oxoacids, phosphorus is tetrahedrally surrounded by four other atoms or groups.
- All these acids contain one P=O and at least one P–OH bond.
- The oxoacids in which phosphorus has an oxidation state less than +5, contain in addition to P=O and P–OH bonds, either a P–H (as in H_3PO_2, H_3PO_3) or a P–P (as in $H_4P_2O_6$) bonds, but not both.
- The oxoacids in the +3 oxidation state undergo disproportionation reaction to yield compounds in higher and lower oxidation states. For example,

$$\underset{\text{Orthophosphorus acid}}{4\overset{+3}{H_3PO_3}} \xrightarrow{\text{Heat}} \underset{\text{Phosphine}}{\overset{-3}{PH_3}} + \underset{\text{Orthophosphoric acid}}{3\overset{+5}{H_3PO_4}}$$

- Hypophosphorus acid (H_3PO_2) is a good reducing agent as it contains two P–H bonds and thus reduces $AgNO_3$ to metallic silver and $HgCl_2$ to Hg.

$$4\,AgNO_3 + H_3PO_2 + 2\,H_2O \rightarrow 4\,Ag\downarrow + H_3PO_4 + 4\,HNO_3$$
$$2\,HgCl_2 + H_3PO_2 + 2\,H_2O \rightarrow 2\,Hg + H_3PO_4 + 4\,HCl$$

It is used in organic chemistry to reduce arenediazonium salts to arenes.

$$\underset{\text{Benzenediazonium chloride}}{2\,C_6H_5N_2Cl} + H_3PO_2 + 2\,H_2O \rightarrow \underset{\text{Benzene}}{2\,C_6H_6} + H_3PO_4 + 2\,N_2 + 2\,HCl$$

H_3PO_3 also acts as a reducing agent though weaker than H_3PO_2 because it contains only one P–H bond as compared to two in H_3PO_2. It reduces acidified $KMnO_4$, I_2 and salts of copper, silver mercury, and so on.

$$2\,KMnO_4 + 3\,H_2SO_4 + 5\,H_3PO_3 \rightarrow K_2SO_4 + 2\,MnSO_4 + 5\,H_3PO_4 + 3\,H_2O$$
$$I_2 + H_3PO_3 + H_2O \rightarrow H_3PO_4 + 2\,HI$$
$$CuSO_4 + H_3PO_3 + H_2O \rightarrow Cu\downarrow + H_3PO_4 + H_2SO_4$$
$$2\,AgNO_3 + H_3PO_3 + H_2O \rightarrow 2\,Ag\downarrow + H_3PO_4 + 2\,HNO_3$$
$$2\,HgCl_2 + H_3PO_3 + H_2O \rightarrow Hg_2Cl_2\downarrow + h_3PO_4 + 2\,HCl$$

- *The number of OH groups present decides the basicity of the acid.* For example, H_3PO_2 is *monobasic* because, it has one –OH group, and hence forms only one series of salts called hypophosphites, namely, NaH_2PO_2 or $Ba(H_2PO_2)_2$. H_3PO_3 is dibasic since it contains two OH groups and hence forms two series of salts, namely, NaH_2PO_3 (sodium dihydrogen phosphate) and Na_2HPO_3 (disodium hydrogen phosphate).

7.13 Introduction to Group 16

The elements oxygen (O), sulfur (S), selenium (Se), tellurium (Te) and polonium (Po) constitute the group 16 elements of the periodic table. The first four elements of this group are collectively known as chalcogens.

7.14 General Characteristics of Group 16 Elements

7.14.1 Electronic Configuration

The general electronic configuration of the elements is ns^2np^4.

7.14.2 Atomic and Ionic Radii

The atomic and ionic radii of the elements of this group are smaller than those of the corresponding elements of group 15.

Explanation: The smaller radii of the group 16 elements compared to the group 15 elements are due to the increased nuclear charge of the group 16 elements which results in greater attraction of the electrons by the nucleus. The increase in the atomic radii of the group 16 elements down the group is primarily due to the increase in the number of the electron shell.

7.14.3 Ionisation Enthalpy

The first ionisation enthalpy ($\Delta_i H_1$) of the group 16 elements is lower than those of the group 15 elements due to the relatively symmetrical and more stable electronic configuration of the elements of group 15 as compared to those of the elements of group 16 (oxygen family). The $\Delta_i H_2$ values are higher than those of the nitrogen family because, after the removal of the first electron, the second electron has to be removed from a more symmetrical exactly half-filled stable electronic configuration of the unipositive ion. The first and second ionisation enthalpy values of the elements decreases down the group due to increasing atomic size and increasing shielding effect of the inner electrons.

7.14.4 Electron Gain Enthalpy

The elements of this family have high negative electron gain enthalpies. The values decrease down the group. Oxygen is small, so its electron cloud is distributed over a small region of space and therefore, it repels the incoming electron. Thus, the electron gain enthalpy of oxygen is unexpectedly less negative in the family.

7.14.5 Electronegativity

The elements of group 16 have higher values of electronegativity than the corresponding elements of group 15. The electronegativity decreases on going down the group. The decrease in electronegativity down the group is due to the increase in the size of the atom.

7.14.6 Elemental State

There is $p\pi$–$p\pi$ overlap between two oxygen atoms forming a double bond, O=O. Due to weak van der Waals forces, oxygen exists as a gas. The other elements of the family do not form stable $p\pi$–$p\pi$ bonds, atoms are linked by single bonds and form polyatomic complex molecules. For example, sulfur and selenium molecules have eight atoms per molecule (S_8 and Se_8) and have a puckered ring structure (Fig. 7.9).

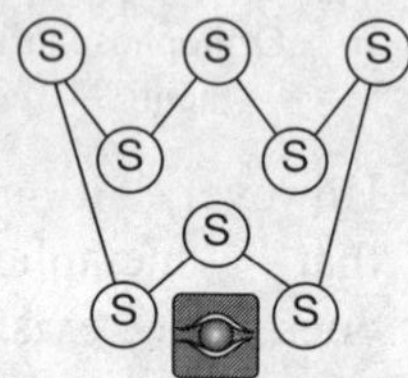

Fig. 7.9 Puckered ring structure of S_8 molcule

7.14.7 Allotropy

Oxygen exists as O_2 and O_3 (ozone). Sulfur exists as yellow orthorhombic, α- and β-monoclinic forms. Selenium exists in eight allotropic forms of which three are red monoclinic forms containing Se_8 rings.

7.14.8 Physical Properties

(i) *Non-metallic/metallic character*: Because of high ionisation enthalpy values, the elements of group 16 are less metallic. However, as we move down the group, the ionisation enthalpy decreases and hence the metallic character increases. Thus, oxygen is the most non-metallic element of group 16. Sulfur is also a typical non-metal, Se and Te are metalloids. Polonium is, however, metallic in nature.

(ii) *Melting and boiling points*: As we move down the group, the atomic size increases. As a result, the van der Waals forces of attraction among their atoms also increase and hence the melting and boiling points regularly increase from O to Te. However, the inert pair effect is maximum in polonium. Consequently, the *s*-valence electrons in polonium are less available as compared to those in tellurium. As a result, the van der Waals forces of attraction will be weaker in Po than in Te and therefore, the MP and BP of Po will be lower than that of Te.

(iii) *Multiple bonding*: The tendency of the elements to form $p\pi$–$d\pi$ multiple bonds decreases from S to Se. For example, S=C=S is moderately stable, Se=C=Se undergoes decomposition readily while Te=C=Te is unstable.

7.14.9 Catenation

Due to its small size, the lone pairs of electrons on the oxygen atoms repel the bond pair of the O–O bond to a greater extent than the lone pairs of electrons on the sulfur atoms in the S–S bond. As a result, the S–S bond is much stronger (213 kJ mol^{-1}) than the O–O bond (138 kJ mol^{-1}) and hence sulfur has a much stronger tendency for catenation than oxygen. As the size of the atom increases down the group from S to Po, the strength of the element–element bond decreases and hence tendency for catenation decreases.

7.14.10 Chemical Properties

Oxidation states: The atoms of these elements gain or share two electrons to achieve the noble gas configuration. Therefore, these elements show two types of oxidation states.

(i) *Negative oxidation states*: Oxygen, due to high electronegativity, completes its octet by gaining electrons. As a result, all metal oxides are ionic and contain O^{2-} ions in which oxygen shows an oxidation state of –2. In addition, oxygen shows an oxidation state of –1 in peroxides such as H_2O_2, –½ in superoxides such as KO_2, zero in O_2 and O_3, +1 in O_2F_2 and +2 in OF_2. Since the electronegativities decrease down the group, the tendency of these elements to show the –2 oxidation state decreases from sulfur to polonium.

(ii) *Positive oxidation states*: Oxygen does not show positive oxidation states except in O_2F_2 and OF_2. The other elements of this group show positive oxidation states of +2, +4 and +6 due to promotion of electrons to the vacant *d* orbitals

7.15 Trends in Chemical Reactivity

Due to small size, high electronegativity, high ionisation enthalpy and the absence of *d* orbitals in its valence shell, the covalency of oxygen is limited to four. However, in the case of other elements the covalency exceeds four. The reactivity decreases as O > S > Se >Te. Oxygen in very reactive and reacts with almost all the elements.

7.15.1 Reactivity Towards Hydrogen (Formation of Hydrides)

Group 16 elements form hydrides, H_2E where E = O, S, Se, Te, Po, that is, H_2O, H_2S, H_2Se, H_2Te and H_2Po.

Preparation: The hydrides of S, Se and Te are prepared by the action of acids on metal sulfides, selenides and tellurides respectively.

$$FeS(s) + 2\,H_3O^+(aq) \rightarrow Fe^{2+}(aq) + H_2S(g) + 2\,H_2O(l)$$

Structure: All these hydrides have an angular shape (Fig. 7.10) involving the sp^3 hybridisation of the central atom. The bond angles, however, decrease from H_2O to H_2Te.

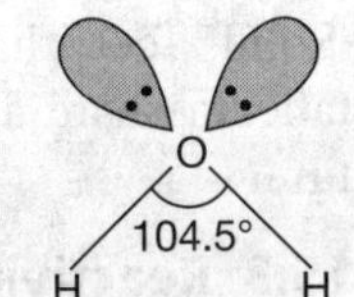

Fig. 7.10 Structure of water

H_2O	H_2S	H_2Se	H_2Te
104.5°	92.1°	91°	90°

Explanation: Due to stronger lone pair–lone pair than bond pair–bond pair repulsions, the bond angle in water decreases from the tetrahedral value of 109°28′ to 104.5°. As we move down the group, the size of the central atom goes on increasing and its electronegativity goes on decreasing. As a result, the position of the two bond pairs shifts further away from the central atom as we move from H_2O to H_2Te. Consequently, the repulsions between the bond pairs decreases as we move from H_2O to H_2Te and, therefore the bond angle decreases in the same order. Oxygen forms another important hydride, H_2O_2.

Trends in characteristics: These properties are briefly discussed below.

Boiling point: The boiling point first decreases and then increases (Fig. 7.11).

H_2O	H_2S	H_2Se	H_2Te
373 K	213 K	232 K	269 K

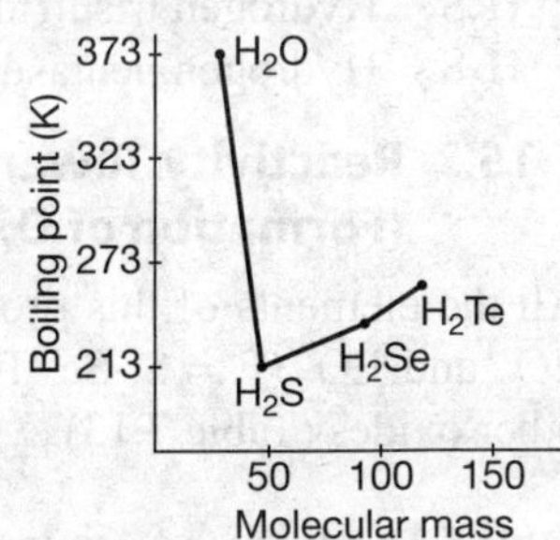

Fig. 7.11 Plots of boiling points of hydrides of group 16 elements versus their molecular masses

Explanation: The abnormally high boiling point of H_2O is due to strong *intermolecular H-bonding*. Since all other elements have much lower electronegativity than O, they do not undergo H-bonding. However, since the size of the atom increases regularly from O to Te, therefore, van der Waals forces of attraction increase with increase in the molecular size and hence the boiling point increases gradually from H_2S to H_2Se. Thus, the overall trend in volatility is $H_2S > H_2Se > H_2Te > H_2O$.

(iii) *Acidic character*: The hydrides of this group are weakly acidic in character. For example, H_2O behaves as a weak diprotic acid ionising as shown.

$$H_2S + aq \rightleftharpoons H^+(aq) + HE^-(aq)$$
$$HE^- + aq \rightleftharpoons H^+(aq) + E^{2-}(aq)$$

Their acidic strength increases down the group $H_2O < H_2S < H_2Se < H_2Te$. As the atomic size increases down the group, the bond length increases and hence the bond strength decreases. As a result, the tendency to release hydrogen as proton increases.

(iv) *Thermal stability*: The thermal stability of the hydrides decreases from H_2O to H_2Te. $H_2O > H_2S > H_2Se > H_2Te$ On going down the group, the size of the central atom increases. As a result, the M–H bond becomes weak and therefore, thermal stability decreases.

(v) *Reducing character*: The reducing power of these hydrides increases from H_2O to H_2Te.

$$H_2O < H_2S < H_2Se < H_2Te$$

This is due to the decrease in the thermal stability of the hydrides. Greater the instability of the hydride, the greater is its reducing character.

Other hydrides: H_2O_2 is fairly stable whereas H_2S_2 is unstable and decomposes readily to give sulfur and hydrogen sulfide. H_2O_2 is a strong oxidising agent but H_2S_2 is not. H_2O_2 forms highly associated molecules because of hydrogen bonding while H_2S_2 forms discrete molecules.

Sulfur forms a few hydrogen polysulfides called sulfanes. Some of these are:

H_2S_2	Hydrogen disulfide	H–S–S–H
H_2S_3	Hydrogen trisulfide	H–S–S–S–H
H_2S_5	Hydrogen pentasulfide	H–S–S–S–S–S–H

7.15.2 Reactivity Towards Oxygen (Formation of Oxides)

All the elements of this group forms two types of oxides—EO_2 and EO_3 (E = S, Se, Te or Po). In addition, they form other oxides (Table 7.13).

Table 7.13 Oxides of group 16 elements

Oxide	S	Se	Te	Po
Monoxides	SO		TeO	PoO
Dioxides	SO_2	SeO_2	TeO_2	PoO_2
Trioxides	SO_3	SeO_3	TeO_3	
Heptoxides	S_2O_7	-	-	-
Other oxides	S_2O, S_2O_3, SO_4	-	-	-

Monoxides: Sulfur monoxide is formed by heating a mixture of sulfur dioxide and sulfur under reduced pressure at 425–475 K.

$$SO_2 + S \xrightarrow{425\text{–}475\ K} 2SO$$

It can also be prepared by the action of silver on thionyl chloride.

$$\underset{\text{Thionyl chloride}}{SOCl_2} + 2\,Ag \rightarrow SO + 2\,AgCl$$

Tellurium monoxide and polonium monoxides are formed by heating their corresponding trioxides. Monoxides are assigned the structure E=O (E = S, Te, Po).

Dioxides: All the members of oxygen family (S, Se, Te and Po) form dioxides of the formula EO_2 (SO_2, SeO_2, TeO_2, PoO_2). The dioxides are obtained by direct union of the elements.

$$E(s) + O_2(g) \rightarrow EO_2(g)$$
$$S_8(s) + 8\,O_2(g) \rightarrow 8\,SO_2(g)$$

Sulfur dioxide exists as discrete molecules even in the solid state. These molecules are held together by weak van der Waals forces of attraction. Therefore, SO_2 is a gas at room temperature. In SO_2, S is sp^2 hybridised. Two of the three sp^2 orbitals form two σ-bonds with oxygen atoms while the third contains the lone pair of electrons,

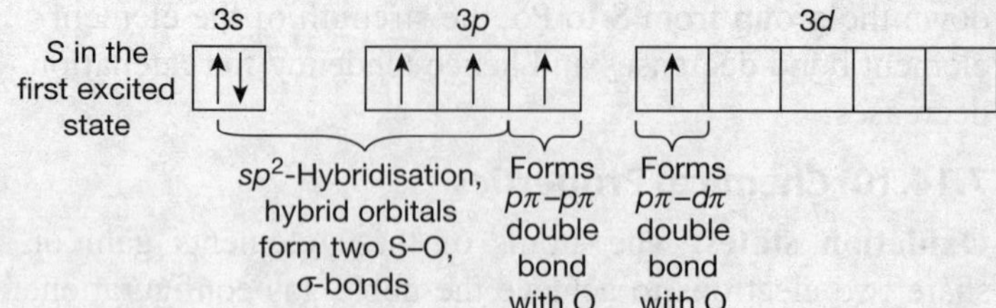

Sulfur is now left with one half-filled p orbital and one half-filled d orbital. These form one $p\pi$–$p\pi$ double bond and one $p\pi$–$d\pi$ double bond with the oxygen atoms. Thus, SO_2 has a bent (angular) structure. Because of its bent structure, the SO_2 molecule has a dipole moment of 1.63 D. The actual bond angle is 119.5°.

Selenium dioxide is a white crystalline solid. In the gaseous state, it exists as discrete monomeric molecules having a structure similar to that of SO_2. However, in the solid state, it has a non-planar polymeric structure consisting of infinite chains. TeO_2 and PoO_2 are non-volatile crystalline ionic solids and each one of these exists in two crystalline forms. TeO_2 in the solid state has a layered structure consisting of TeO_4 units.

The acidic character of the dioxides of group 16 elements decreases as we move down the group from S to Po.

Since the +6 oxidation state of S is more stable than +4, SO_2 acts as a reducing agent. the stability of the +6 oxidation state decreases from S to Te, the reducing character of the dioxides decreases while their oxidising character increases. Thus, TeO_2 acts as an oxidising agent.

Trioxides: All the elements of this group form trioxides with the formula EO_3. Sulfur trioxide is prepared by direct combination of sulfur dioxide and oxygen in the presence of finely divided platinum or divanadium pentoxide at 2 atmospheric pressure and 450°C.

$$SO_2(g) + O_2(g) \xrightarrow[450°C]{Pt\ or\ V_2O_5} 2SO_3(g)$$

Sulfur trioxide can also be prepared by heating ferric sulfate, which decomposes to give sulfur trioxide.

$$Fe_2(SO_4)_3 \xrightarrow{Heat} Fe_2O_3 + 3SO_3$$

SO_3 has a trigonal planar structure in the gaseous state in which the S atom is sp^2 hybridised. The bond angles are exactly 120° each, the net dipole moment is zero.

Solid TeO_3 has a network structure in which TeO_6 octahedra share all vertices. All the trioxides are acidic in nature.

7.15.3 Reactivity Towards Halogens (Formation of Halides)

The elements of group 16 form a large number of halides of the type EX_6, EX_4 and EX_2 (X = halogen) (Table 7.14). The stability of the halides decreases in the order $F^- > Cl^- > Br^- > I^-$.

Table 7.14 Some important halides of elements of group 16

Type of halide	Oxygen	Sulphur	Selenium	Tellurium	Polonium
1. Monohalides	O_2F_2	S_2F_2, S_2Cl_2, S_2Br_2	Se_2Cl_2, Se_2Br_2	—	—
2. Dihalides	OF_2, Cl_2O, Br_2O	SF_2, SCl_2	—	$TeCl_2$, $TeBr_2$	$PoCl_2$, $PoBr_2$
3. Tetrahalides	—	SF_4, SCl_4	SeF_4, $SeCl_4$, $SeBr_4$,	$TeBr_4$, TeI_4	PoI_4
4. Hexahalides	—	SF_6	SeF_6	TeF_6	—

In addition to the above compounds, some other halides of group 16 are S_2F_{10}, Te_2F_{10}, Cl_2O_6, I_2O_4 and I_2O_5.

Monohalides: The monohalides are dimeric in nature. Examples, are S_2F_2, S_2Cl_2, S_2Br_2, Se_2Cl_2 and Se_2Br_2.

Dihalides: All elements except selenium form stable dihalides and dibromides. These dihalides are formed by sp^3 hybridisation. they have bent structures.

Tetrahalides: SF_4 is a gas, SeF_4 is a liquid while TeF_4 is a solid. These fluorides have sp^3d hybridisation and, thus, have trigonal bipyramidal structures. The tetrahalides can act both as *Lewis bases* due to the presence of a lone pair of electrons and *Lewis acids* because the central atom can extend its coordination number to six. SF_6 does not undergo hydrolysis as the six F atoms protect the sulfur atom from attack by water due to *steric hindrance,* SF_4 readily undergoes hydrolysis since the four F atoms cannot protect the S atom from attack by water.

$$SF_4 + 2\,H_2O \rightarrow 4\,HF + SO_2;\ SF_6 + H_2O \rightarrow \text{No action}$$

Hexahalides: These are all gaseous in nature. SF_6 is extremely stable and chemically inert.

The S in SF_6 is sp^3d^2 hybridised and hence it has an octahedral structure.

7.15.4 Anomalous Behaviour of Oxygen

Like all other first elements of the groups, oxygen also differs from its family members. The anomalous behaviour of oxygen is due to its

- small size,
- high value of ionisation enthalpy and electronegativity, and
- absence of *d* orbitals in the valence shell.

7.16 Dioxygen

7.16.1 Preparation of Dioxygen

(i) By decomposition of oxygen-rich compounds:

$$\underset{\text{Potassium permanganate}}{2\,KMnO_4} \xrightarrow{\text{Heat}} \underset{\text{Potassium manganate}}{K_2MnO_4} + MnO_2 + O_2;$$

$$\underset{\text{Potassium chlorate}}{2\,KClO_3} \xrightarrow{\text{Heat}} \underset{\text{Potassium chloride}}{2\,KCl} + 3O_2$$

$$\underset{\text{Potassium nitrate}}{2\,KNO_3} \xrightarrow{\text{Heat}} \underset{\text{Potassium nitrite}}{2\,KNO_2} + O_2;$$

$$\underset{\text{Barium peroxide}}{2BaO_2} \xrightarrow{\text{Heat}} \underset{\text{Barium oxide}}{2\,BaO} + O_2$$

$$2\,KClO_3(s) \xrightarrow{MnO_2} 2\,KCl(s) + 3\,O_2(g)$$

(ii) By heating dioxides, peroxides and higher oxides:

$$\underset{\text{Mercuric oxide}}{2\,HgO} \xrightarrow{\text{Heat}} \underset{\text{Mercury}}{2\,Hg} + O_2;\ \underset{\text{Red lead}}{2Pb_3O_4} \xrightarrow{\text{Heat}} \underset{\text{Litharge}}{6PbO} + O_2$$

$$\underset{\text{Silver oxide}}{2\,Ag_2O} \xrightarrow{\text{Heat}} \underset{\text{Silver}}{4\,Ag} + O_2;\ \underset{\text{Manganese dioxide}}{3\,MnO_2} \xrightarrow{\text{Heat}} \underset{\text{Trimanganic tetroxide}}{Mn_3O_4} + O_2$$

(iii) From hydrogen peroxide: Hydrogen peroxide is readily decomposed into water and dioxygen by catalysts such as finely divided metals and manganese dioxide.

$$2\,H_2O_2(aq) \rightarrow 2H_2O(l) + O_2(g)$$

(iv) Laboratory method: In the laboratory, dioxygen is prepared by the following methods.

- *Thermal decomposition of potassium chlorate*: The manganese dioxide acts as a catalyst.

$$2\,KClO_3 \xrightarrow{420\text{ K}} 2KCl + 3O_2$$

- *By the action of water on sodium peroxide*:

$$2\,NaO_2(s) + 2\,H_2O(l) \rightarrow 4\,NaOH(aq) + O_2(g)$$

$$2\,KMnO_4 + 3\,H_2SO_4 \rightarrow K_2SO_4 + 2\,MnSO_4 + 3\,H_2O + 5[O]$$
$$Na_2O_2 + H_2SO_4 \rightarrow Na_2SO_4 + H_2O_2] \times 5$$
$$H_2O_2 + [O] \rightarrow H_2O + O_2] \times 5$$

$$2KMnO_4 + 5Na_2O_2 + 8H_2SO_4 \rightarrow$$
$$K_2SO_4 + 2MnSO_4 + 5Na_2SO_4 + H_2O + 5O_2$$

In this case, acidified $KMnO_4$ solution is added from the thistle funnel.

- *From barium hydroxide*: Pure dioxygen can be prepared by the electrolysis of a solution of $Ba(OH)_2$ using nickel or platinum electrodes.
- *Industrial preparation*: The main sources for the large scale preparation of dioxygen are (i) air and (ii) water.

From liquid air: Oxygen is prepared from air by first removing carbon dioxide and water vapour and then by the fractional distillation of air.

From water: Dioxygen can also be prepared by the electrolysis of water containing a small amount of a mineral acid or an alkali.

$$2H_2O(l) \xrightarrow{\text{Electrolysis}} 2H_2(g) + O_2(g)$$

Dioxygen is collected at the anode while dihydrogen is liberated at the cathode.

7.16.2 Chemical Properties

Dioxygen is quite stable and its bond dissociation enthalpy is very high. Therefore, it is not very reactive.

$O_2 \rightarrow O + O$ Bond dissociation enthalpy = 493.4 kJ mol^{-1}

(i) *Action of litmus*: Like dihydrogen, it is also neutral and has no action on blue or red litmus

(ii) *Supporter of combustion*: Dioxygen is a supporter of combustion but is itself not combustible.

(iii) *Oxidation*: Dioxygen is a powerful oxidising agent and hence can oxidise metals, non-metals and other compounds to their respective oxides.

Reaction with metals: Dioxygen directly combines with most of the metals (except noble metals such as gold and platinum) to form their respective oxides.

$$4Na(s) + O_2(g) \rightarrow 2\,Na_2O(s);\; 2\,Ca(s) + O_2(g) \rightarrow 2\,CaO(s)$$

$$2\,Na(s) + O_2(g) \xrightarrow{575\,K} Na_2O_2(s)$$

$$2\,Mg(s) + O_2(g) \xrightarrow{Heat} 2\,MgO(s)$$

$$4\,Al(s) + 3\,O_2(g) \xrightarrow{Heat} 2\,Al_2O_3(s);$$

$$4\,Fe(s) + 3\,O_2(g) \xrightarrow{Heat} 2\,Fe_2O_3(s)$$

- Less active metals like gold and platinum (noble metals) do not combine with dioxygen.

Reaction with non-metals: Dioxygen combines with many non-metals except noble gases. For example,

- With dihydrogen:

$$2\,H_2(g) + O_2(g) \xrightarrow[\text{or Electric discharge}]{1073\,K} 2\,H_2O(g)$$

- With dinitrogen: $N_2(g) + O_2(g) \xrightarrow[\text{Nitric oxide}]{3300\,K} 2\,NO(g)$

This reaction occurs in the atmosphere, when lightning occurs in the sky.

- With carbon:

$$\underset{\text{(Limited)}}{2\,C(s) + O_2(g)} \xrightarrow{Heat} \underset{\text{(Excess)}}{2\,CO(g)}$$

$$C(s) + O_2(g) \xrightarrow{Heat} CO_2(g)$$

(iv) *Reaction with compounds*: Dioxygen is an oxidising agent and it oxidises many compounds under specific conditions.

With ammonia:

$$4\,NH_3(g) + 5O_2(g) \xrightarrow{1100\,K,\,Pt} 4\,NO(g) + 6\,H_2O(g)$$

With hydrogen chloride:

$$4\,HCl(g) + O_2(g) \xrightarrow{700\,K,\,CuCl_2} 2\,H_2O(g) + Cl_2(g)$$

With carbon disulfide:

$$CS_2(g) + 3\,O_2(g) \xrightarrow{Heat} CO_2(g) + 2\,SO_2(g)$$

With metal sulfides:

$$2\,ZnS(s) + 3\,O_2(g) \xrightarrow{Heat} 2\,ZnO(s) + 2\,SO_2(g)$$

$$2\,HgS(s) + 3\,O_2(g) \xrightarrow{Heat} 2\,HgO(s) + 2\,SO_2(g)$$

With hydrocarbons: These reactions are called combustion reactions The hydrocarbons are used as fuels.

$$\underset{\text{Methane}}{CH_4(g)} + 2O_2(g) \rightarrow CO_2(g) + 2\,H_2O(g)$$

$$\Delta_c H^\circ = -890\text{ kJ mol}^{-1}$$

$$\underset{\text{Ethylene}}{CH_2{=}CH_2(g)} + 3O_2(g) \rightarrow 2CO_2(g) + 2H_2O(g)$$

$$\Delta_c H^\circ = -1411\text{ kJ mol}^{-1}$$

(v) *Action of silent electric discharge*: Under the action of silent electric discharge, dry dioxygen gets converted into trioxygen (ozone) which is an allotropic form of oxygen.

$$\underset{\text{Dioxygen}}{3O_2} \xrightarrow{\text{Silent electric discharge}} \underset{\text{Ozone}}{2O_3}$$

7.17 Oxides

7.17.1 Classification of Oxides

(i) Simple oxides: These may be classified into four types.

- *Basic oxides*: The oxides that combine with water to give a basic solution are called basic oxides. These are mostly the oxides of metals. For example,

$$Na_2O(s) + H_2O(l) \rightarrow 2NaOH(aq)$$

$$MgO(s) + H_2O(l) \rightarrow Mg\,(OH)_2(aq)$$

$$Fe_2O_3(s) + 3H_2O(l) \rightarrow 2Fe(OH)_3(aq)$$

The basic oxides react with acids to form salts and water.

$$Na_2O(s) + 2\,HCl(aq) \rightarrow 2NaCl(aq) + H_2O(l)$$

$$Fe_2O_3(s) + 3\,H_2SO_4(aq) \rightarrow Fe_2(SO_4)_3(aq) + 3\,H_2O(l)$$

- *Acidic oxides*: The oxides that combine with water to give acids are called acidic oxides. These are generally the oxides of non-metals. For example,

$$CO_2(g) + H_2O(l) \rightarrow \underset{\text{Carbonic acid}}{H_2CO_3(aq)}$$

$$SO_2(g) + H_2O(l) \rightarrow \underset{\text{Sulfurous acid}}{H_2SO_3(aq)}$$

$$P_4O_{10}(s) + 6H_2O(l) \rightarrow \underset{\text{Phosphoric acid}}{4H_3PO_4(aq)}$$

$$N_2O_5(l) + H_2O(l) \rightarrow \underset{\text{Nitric acid}}{2\,HNO_3(aq)}$$

These acidic oxides react with bases to form salts and water. For example,

$$SO_2(g) + 2NaOH(aq) \rightarrow Na_2SO_3(aq) + H_2O(l)$$

$$P_4O_{10}(s) + 12\,NaOH(aq) \rightarrow 4Na_3PO_4(aq) + 6H_2O(l)$$

Amphoteric oxides: The oxides that show acidic as well as basic character are called amphoteric oxides. For example, aluminium oxide (Al_2O_3) reacts with both acids (hydrochloric acid) and alkalies (sodium hydroxide).

$$\underset{\text{(Basic)}}{Al_2O_3(s)} + 6HCl(aq) + 9\,H_2O(l) \rightarrow 2\,\underset{\text{Hexaaquaaluminium (III) ion}}{[Al(H_2O)_6]^{3+}(aq)} + 6\,Cl^-(aq)$$

$$\underset{\text{(Acidic)}}{Al_2O_3(s)} + 6NaOH(aq) + 3H_2O(l) \rightarrow \underset{\text{Sodium hexahydroxoaluminate (III)}}{2Na_3(Al(OH)_6](aq)}$$

- *Neutral oxides*: The oxides that neither react with acids nor with bases are called neutral oxides. These are neutral to litmus solution. For example, N_2O, CO, NO.

(ii) Mixed oxides: Metal oxides that consist of two simple oxides with the metal in different oxidation states are called *mixed oxides*. These mixed oxides show the properties of both the metal oxides simultaneously. For example, red lead (Pb_3O_4) is a mixture of lead oxide (PbO) and lead dioxide (PbO_2) as $PbO_2.2PbO$. Mixed oxide of manganese Mn_3O_4 (trimanganese tetroxide), is considered to be a mixed oxide of manganese oxide (MnO) and manganese dioxide (MnO_2) having the formula $2MnO.MnO_2$.

7.17.2 Trends in Acid–Base Behaviour of Oxides in the Periodic Table

(i) On moving from left to right in a given period in the periodic table, the nature of the oxides shows a gradual variation from strongly basic through amphoteric to strongly acidic. For example,

Na_2O	MgO	Al_2O_3	SiO_2
Strongly basic	Basic	Amphoteric	Weakly acidic

P_4O_{10}	SO_2	Cl_2O_7
Moderately acidic	Strongly acidic	Very strongly acidic

(ii) Amongst the *s*-block elements, on moving down the group, the basic character of the oxides increases.

(iii) Among the *p*-block elements, on moving down the group, the acidic character of the oxides decreases while the basic character increases. For example, in group 13, the acidic character of the oxides decreases and the basic character increases.

(iv) Among the non-metallic oxides, the acidic character increases as the oxidation state of the non-metal increases. For example,

+1	+2	+3	+4	+5
N_2O	NO	N_2O_3	N_2O_4	N_2O_5
Neutral	Neutral	Acidic	Strongly acidic	Very strongly acidic

(v) Among the *d*-block elements, the basic character decreases and the acidic character increases with an increase in the oxidation state of the element. For example,

+2	+8/3	+3	+4	+7
MnO	Mn_3O_4	Mn_2O_3	MnO_2	Mn_2O_7
Basic	Amphoteric	Amphoteric	Amphoteric	Acidic

7.18 Ozone

Ozone is an allotropic form of oxygen. It is present about 20 km above the surface of the earth. It is believed to be formed by the action of ultraviolet rays on oxygen.

$$3\,O_2\text{ (Ultraviolet rays)} \rightarrow 2O_3\ \Delta H_{298\,K} = 142.7\text{ kJ mol}^{-1}$$

The layer of ozone thus formed also prevents the remaining ultraviolet rays from reaching the earth's surface. The ozone layer in the stratosphere is depleted by (a) nitric oxide, (b) atomic oxygen and (c) reactive hydroxyl radicals which are also present in the atmosphere due to biomass burning. Flights of supersonic aeroplanes, nuclear explosions and lighting release NO into the atmosphere.

7.18.1 Preparation of Ozone (Trioxygen)

Ozone is prepared when a silent electric discharge is passed through pure, cold and dry dioxygen.

$$3O_2(g) \xrightleftharpoons{\text{Silent electric discharge}} 2O_3(g);$$
$$\Delta H°(298\text{ K}) = +142\text{ kJ mol}^{-1}$$

7.18.2 Structure of Ozone

The central oxygen atom in ozone is sp^2 hybridised and contains a lone pair of electrons. As a result, ozone has an angular structure with a bond angle of 117° (Fig. 7.12, 7.13).

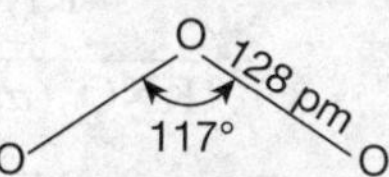

Fig. 7.12 Structure of ozone

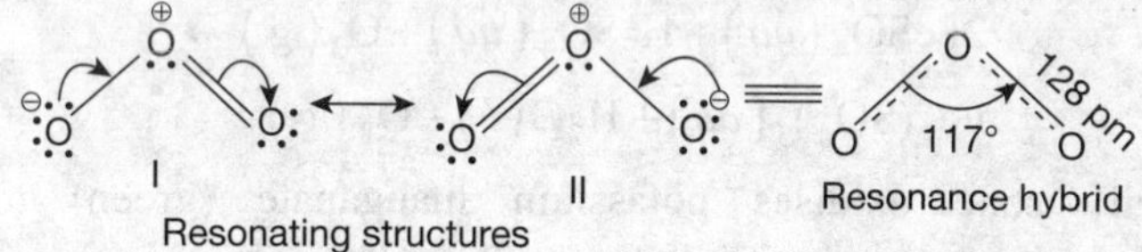

Fig. 7.13 Resonance structures of ozone

7.18.3 Chemical Properties of Ozone

(i) Action with litmus: Ozone is neutral towards litmus because it does not give any colour change with blue or red litmus.

(ii) Decomposition: Ozone is thermodynamically unstable with respect to oxygen. A high concentration of ozone can be dangerously explosive. Pure ozone decomposes even at room temperature. However, on heating above 475 K, it decomposes readily to form oxygen gas.

$$\underset{\text{Ozone}}{2O_3(g)} \xrightarrow{473\text{ K}} \underset{\text{Dioxygen}}{3O_2(g)}$$

(iii) Oxidising agent: Ozone is one of the most powerful oxidising agents.

$$\underset{\text{Ozone}}{O_3(g)} \rightarrow \underset{\text{Dioxygen}}{O_2(g)} + \underset{\text{Atomic oxygen}}{O(g)}$$

The atomic oxygen thus liberated brings about the oxidation while molecular oxygen is set free.

Oxidation of Compounds

(i) Ozone oxidises black lead sulfide to white lead sulfate.

$$O_3(g) \rightarrow O_2(g) + O(g)\ ] \times 4$$
$$PbS(s) + 4\,O(g) \rightarrow PbSO_4(s)$$
$$\overline{PbS(s) + 4O_3(g) \rightarrow PbSO_4(s) + 4O_2(g)}$$

Similarly, ozone oxidises the sulfides of Cu, Zn and Cd to their respective sulfates.

$$CuS(s) + 4\,O_3(g) \rightarrow CuSO_4(s) + 4\,O_2(g)$$
$$ZnS(s) + 4\,O_3(g) \rightarrow ZnSO_4(s) + 4\,O_2(g)$$
$$CdS(s) + 4\,O_3(g) \rightarrow CdSO_4(s) + O_2(g)$$

(ii) Ozone oxidises halogen acids to the corresponding halogens.

$$O_3(g) \rightarrow O_2(g) + O(g)$$
$$2HCl(aq) + O(g) \rightarrow Cl_2(g) + H_2O(l)$$
$$\overline{2HCl(aq) + O_3(g) \rightarrow Cl_2(g) + H_2O(l) + O_2(g)}$$

Similarly, HBr is oxidised to Br_2 and HI to I_2.

(iii) Ozone oxidises nitrites to nitrates.

$$O_3(g) \rightarrow O_2(g) + O(g)$$
$$KNO_2(aq) + O(g) \rightarrow KNO_3(aq)$$
$$\overline{KNO_2(aq) + O_3(g) \rightarrow KNO_3(aq) + O_2(g)}$$

(v) Ozone oxidises acidified ferrous salts to ferric salts.

$$O_3(g) \rightarrow O_2(g) + O(g)$$
$$2FeSO_4(aq) + H_2SO_4(aq) + O(g) \rightarrow Fe_2(SO_4)_3(aq) + H_2O(l)$$
$$\overline{2FeSO_4(aq) + H_2SO_4(aq) + O_3(g) \rightarrow}$$
$$Fe_2(SO_4)_3(aq) + H_2O(l) + O_2(g)$$

(vii) Ozone oxidises potassium manganate (green) to potassium permanganate (pink–violet).

$$O_3(g) \rightarrow O_2(g) + O(g)$$
$$2K_2MnO_4(aq) + H_2O(l) + O(g) \rightarrow$$
$$2KMnO_4(aq) + 2\,KOH(aq)$$
$$\overline{2K_2MnO_4(aq) + H_2O(l) + O_3(g) \rightarrow}$$
$$2KMnO_4(aq) + 2KOH(aq) + O_2(g)$$

Oxidation of Non-metals

(i) Ozone oxidises moist iodine to iodic acid (HIO_3).

$$O_3(g) \rightarrow O_2(g) + O(g)] \times 5$$
$$I_2(s) + 5O(g) \rightarrow I_2O_5(s)$$
$$I_2O_5(s) + H_2O(l) \rightarrow 2HIO_3(aq)$$
$$\overline{I_2(s) + 5O_3(g) + H_2O(l) \rightarrow 2HIO_3(aq) + 5O_2(g)}$$

(ii) Ozone oxidises moist phosphorus to phosphoric acid (H_3PO_4).

$$O_3(g) \rightarrow O_2(g) + O(g)] \times 10$$
$$P_4(s) + 10\,(O)(g) \rightarrow P_4O_{10}(s)$$
$$P_4O_{10}(s) + 6H_2O(l) \rightarrow 4H_3PO_4(aq)$$
$$\overline{P_4(s) + 10O_3(s) + 6H_2O(l) \rightarrow 4H_3PO_4(aq) + 10O_2(g)}$$

Oxidation of Metalloids

(i) Ozone oxidises moist arsenic to arsenic acid (H_3AsO_4).

$$O_3(g) \rightarrow O_2(g) + O(g)] \times 5$$
$$2\,As(s) + 5O(g) \rightarrow As_2O_5(s)$$
$$As_2O_5(s) + 3H_2O(l) \rightarrow 2H_3AsO_4(aq)$$
$$\overline{2\,As(s) + 5O_3(g) + 3H_2O(l) \rightarrow 2H_3AsO_4(aq) + 5O_2(g)}$$

(ii) Ozone oxidises moist antimony to antimonic acid (H_3SbO_4).

$$O_3(g) \rightarrow O_2(g) + O(g)] \times 5$$
$$2Sb(s) + 5O(g) \rightarrow Sb_2O_5(s)$$
$$Sb_2O_5(s) + 3H_2O(l) \rightarrow 2H_3SbO_4(aq)$$
$$\overline{2Sb(s) + 5O_3(g) + 3H_2O(l) \rightarrow 2H_3SbO_4(aq) + 5O_2(g)}$$

Oxidation of Metals

(i) Silver is oxidised to silver oxide (Ag_2O).

$$O_3(g) \rightarrow O_2(g) + O(g)$$
$$2Ag(s) + O(g) \rightarrow Ag_2O(s)$$
$$\overline{2Ag(s) + O_3(g) \rightarrow Ag_2O(s) + O_2(g)}$$

(ii) Mercury is oxidised to mercurous oxide (Hg_2O).

$$O_3(g) \rightarrow O_2(g) + O(g)$$
$$2Hg(l) + O(g) \rightarrow Hg_2O(s)$$
$$\overline{2Hg(l) + O_3(g) \rightarrow Hg_2O(s) + O_2(g)}$$

Bleaching Action

Due to the oxidising action of ozone, it acts as a sterilising agent. It also acts as a bleaching agent for vegetable colouring matter. Ozone bleaches indigo, ivory, litmus, delicate fabrics like silk and wool.

Vegetable colouring matter + $O_3 \rightarrow$ Colourless oxidised matter + O_2

Action of Peroxides

$$H_2O_2(aq) + O_3(g) \rightarrow H_2O(l) + 2O_2(g)$$
$$BaO_2(s) + O_3(g) \rightarrow BaO(s) + 2\,O_2(g)$$

Formation of Ozonides

$CH_2{=}CH_2$ (Ethylene) + O_3 $\xrightarrow[CCl_4]{196\ K}$ Ethylene ozonide

$CH{\equiv}CH$ (Acetylene) + O_3 $\xrightarrow[CCl_4]{196\ K}$ Acetylene ozonide

$$CH_3-CH=CH_2 + O_3 \xrightarrow[CCl_4]{196\text{ K}} CH_3-CH(-O-O-)(-O-)CH_2$$

Propylene → Propylene ozonide

7.19 Chemistry of Sulfur and Its Compounds

Two important allotropes of sulfur are *yellow rhombic* (α-sulfur) and *monoclinic* (β-sulfur).

Rhombic Sulfur (Orthorhombic, Octahedral, α-Sulfur)

- It is the most stable form of sulfur at room temperature while all other varieties of sulfur gradually change into this form on standing.
- It is insoluble in water but dissolves to some extent in benzene, alcohol and ether. However, it is readily soluble in CS_2.

$$Na_2SO_3 + S \xrightarrow{\text{Boil}} Na_2S_2O_3$$

Monoclinic Sulfur (β-Sulfur)

- This form of sulfur is prepared by melting rhombic sulfur in a dish and cooling till a crust is formed. Two holes are made in the crust and the remaining liquid poured out. On removing the crust, colourless needle-shaped crystals of β-sulfur are formed.
- It is dull yellow in colour and is soluble in CS_2 but insoluble in H_2O.
- It is stable only above 369 K. Below this temperature, it slowly changes into rhombic sulfur.

$$\text{Rhombic sulfur} \underset{<369\text{ K}}{\overset{>369\text{ K}}{\rightleftharpoons}} \text{Monoclinic sulfur}$$

Structure

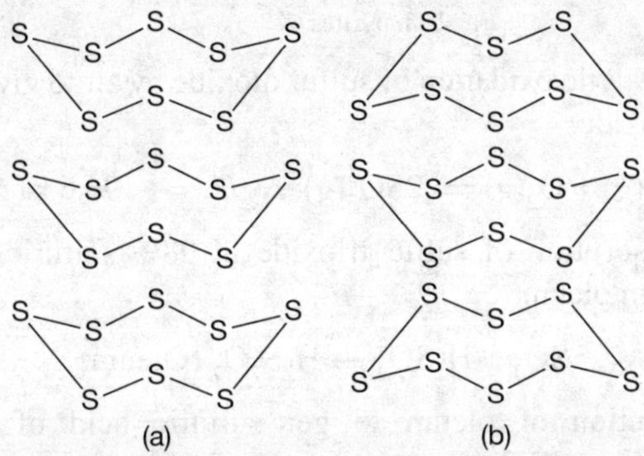

Fig. 7.14 Packing of 8-membered ring structrure of **(a)** orthothombic sulphur **(b)** monoclinic sulphur in the crystal in the crystal lattice

Plastic Sulfur (δ-Sulfur)

- Plastic sulfur is obtained by pouring molten sulfur into cold water when a soft rubber like mass called plastic sulfur is formed.
- It is an amorphous form of sulfur. It has no sharp melting point.
- It is soft and elastic in the beginning but hardens on standing and gradually changes to rhombic sulfur.
- It is insoluble in carbon disulfide. Plastic sulfur is regarded as a super cooled liquid, that is, a liquid which due to rapid cooling below its freezing point had no time to settle in a crystalline form.

Cyclo-S_6 Form

Structure: Plastic sulfur consists of zig–zig chains (Fig. 7.16) and sometimes S_8 and other rings.

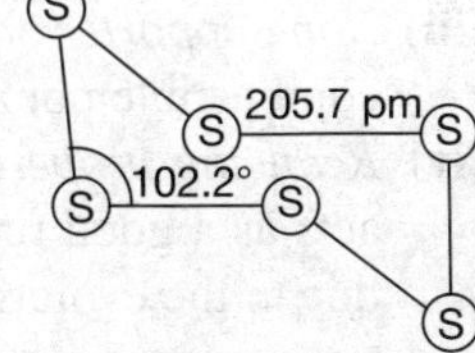

Fig. 7.15 Structure of cyclo-S_6 allotropic form of sulfur

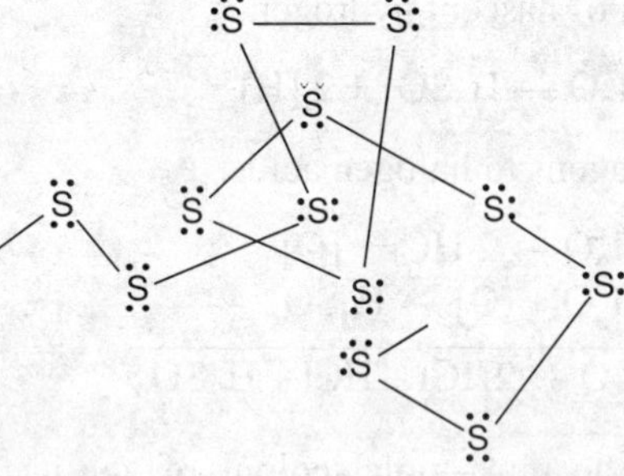

Fig. 7.16 Zig.zag chains of sulphur atoms in plastic sulphur

7.20 Sulfur Dioxide

Preparation

Sulfurdioxide is formed together with a little (6%–8%) sulfur trioxide when sulfur is burnt in air or oxygen.

$$S_8(s) + 8\,O_2(g) \rightarrow 8\,SO_2(g)$$

In the laboratory, sulfur dioxide is prepared by treating a sulfite with dilute sulfuric acid.

$$Na_2SO_3(s) + H_2SO_4(aq) \rightarrow SO_2(g) + Na_2SO_4(aq) + H_2O(l)$$

Properties

(i) Sulfur dioxide dissolves in water to form sulfurous acid.

$$SO_2(g) + H_2O(l) \rightarrow H_2SO_3(aq)$$

Therefore, SO_2 is regarded as the *anhydride of sulfurous acid*. Its aqueous solution is acidic and turns blue litmus red.

- Being acidic, it reacts readily with sodium hydroxide solution, forming sodium sulfite, which then reacts with more sulfur dioxide to form sodium bisulfite (sodium hydrogen sulfite).

$$2\,NaOH(aq) + SO_2(g) \rightarrow \underset{\text{Sodium sulfite}}{Na_2SO_3(aq)} + H_2O(l)$$

$$Na_2SO_3(aq) + SO_2(g) + H_2O(l) \rightarrow \underset{\text{Sodium bisulfite}}{2\,NaHSO_3(aq)}$$

- Being acidic, it also decomposes carbonates and bicarbonates evolving CO_2 gas.

$$Na_2CO_3(aq) + 2\,SO_2(aq) + H_2O(l) \rightarrow 2\,NaHSO_3(aq) + CO_2(g)$$

- Like CO_2, it turns lime water milky due to the formation of insoluble calcium sulfide. However, if SO_2 is passed for a longer time, milkiness disappears due to the formation of soluble sodium bisulfite.

$$\underset{\text{(Milkyness)}}{Ca(OH)_2 + SO_2 \rightarrow CaSO_3 + H_2O}$$

$$CaSO_3 + SO_2 + H_2O \rightarrow \underset{\text{Calcium bisulfite (soluble)}}{Ca(HSO_3)_2} + H_2O$$

(iii) *Non-supporter of combustion*: SO_2 gas is neither combustible nor a supporter of combustion.

(iv) *Reducing properties*: In the presence of moisture, SO_2 acts as a good reducing agent. Its reducing character is due to the evolution of nascent hydrogen.

$$SO_2 + 2\,H_2O \rightarrow H_2SO_4 + 2\,[H]$$

- SO_2 reduces halogens to halogen acids.

$$Cl_2 + H_2O \rightarrow 2\,HCl + [O]$$
$$SO_2 + H_2O + [O] \rightarrow H_2SO_4$$
$$\overline{Cl_2 + SO_2 + 2H_2O \rightarrow 2HCl + HCl + H_2SO_4}$$

- It decolourises the pink–violet colour of acidified $KMnO_4$ solution.

$$2\,KMnO_4 + 3\,H_2SO_4 \rightarrow K_2SO_4 + 2\,MnSO_4 + 3\,H_2O + 5\,[O]$$
$$SO_2 + H_2O + [O] \rightarrow H_2SO_4] \times 5$$
$$\overline{\underset{\text{(Pink–violet)}}{2KMnO_4} + 5SO_2 + 2H_2O \rightarrow K_2SO_4 + \underset{\text{(Colourless)}}{2MnSO_4} + 2H_2SO_4}$$

(v) *Bleaching action*: In the presence of moisture, sulfur dioxide acts as a bleaching agent.

$$SO_2 + 2\,H_2O \rightarrow H_2SO_4 + 2\,[H]$$

Colouring matter + [H] → Colourless vegetable matter

(vi) *Oxidising properties*: It oxidises H_2S to S: $2\,H_2S + SO_2 \rightarrow 2\,H_2O + 3\,S$

- Active metals are oxidised: $3\,Mg + SO_2 \rightarrow 2\,MgO + MgS$

$$4\,K + 3\,SO_2 \rightarrow K_2SO_3 + K_2S_2O_3$$

CO is oxidised to CO_2: $2\,CO + SO_2 \rightarrow 2\,CO_2 + S$

- In the presence of HCl, stannous and mercurous salts are oxidised.

$$2\,SnCl_2 + SO_2 + 4\,HCl \rightarrow 2\,SnCl_4 + 2\,H_2O + S$$
$$2\,Hg_2Cl_2 + SO_2 + 4\,HCl \rightarrow 4\,HgCl_2 + 2\,H_2O + S$$

- It reacts with Cl_2 in the presence of charcoal as catalyst to form sulfuryl chloride.

$$SO_2 + Cl_2 \xrightarrow{\text{Charcoal}} \underset{\text{Sulfuryl chloride}}{SO_2Cl_2}$$

- It combines with sodium peroxide to form sodium sulfate.

$$Na_2O_2 + SO_2 \rightarrow Na_2SO_4$$

7.21 Oxoacids of Sulfur

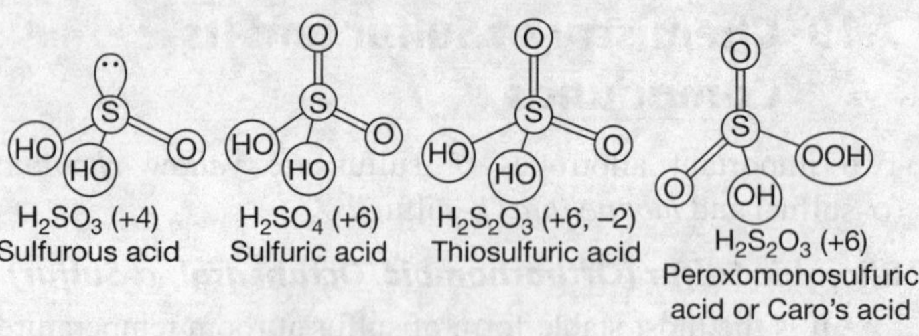

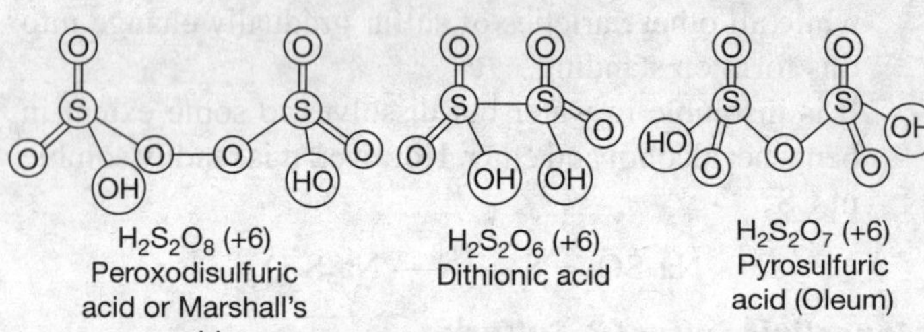

Fig. 7.17 Structure of some important oxoacids of sulphur

7.22 Sulfuric Acid

Sulfuric acid is called the *king of chemicals*.

7.22.1 Manufacture of Sulfuric Acid (H_2SO_4) by the Contact Process

It involves the following steps.

- Production of SO_2 by burning sulfur or roasting iron pyrites.

$$S_8 + 8O_2 \rightarrow 8SO_2\,;\ \underset{\text{Iron pyrites}}{4FeS_2} + 11O_2 \rightarrow 2\,Fe_2O_3 + 8SO_2$$

- Catalytic oxidation of sulfur dioxide by air to give sulfur trioxide.

$$2SO_2(g) + O_2(g) \rightleftharpoons 2SO_3(g);\ \Delta_f H^\circ = -196.6\ \text{kJ mol}^{-1}$$

- Absorption of sulfur trioxide in 98% sulfuric acid to form oleum.

$$SO_3 + H_2SO_4 \rightarrow H_2S_2O_7\ \text{(Oleum)}$$

- Dilution of oleum to get sulfuric acid of desired concentration.

$$H_2S_2O_7 \rightarrow 2H_2SO_4$$

A flowchart of the Contact process is given in Fig. 7.18.

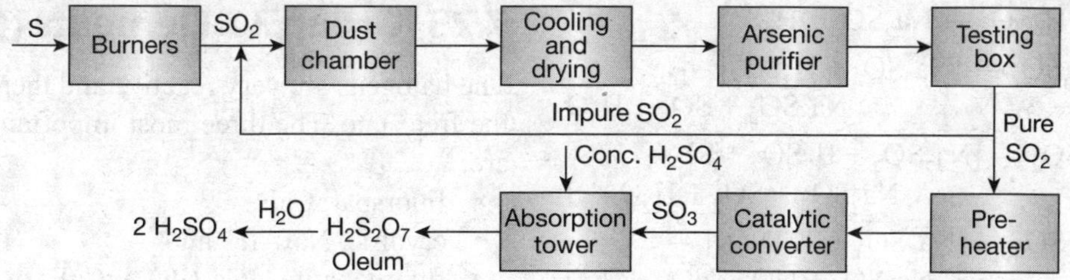

Fig. 7.18 Flow-sheet diagram of contact process

7.22.2 Physical Properties of Sulfuric Acid

- Sulfuric acid has a high boiling point (590 K) and a high viscosity because its molecules are associated due to intermolecular hydrogen bonding.

(Structure: H_2SO_4 molecules linked through hydrogen bonds: ···HO, HO–S(=O)(=O)···HO, labelled "Hydrogen bonds")

7.22.3 Chemical Properties of Sulfuric Acid

(i) *Dissociation*: Sulfuric acid is quite stable but on strong heating, it dissociates into SO_3 and H_2O.

$$H_2SO_4 \rightleftharpoons H_2O + SO_3$$

(ii) *Acidic character*: It is a strong dibasic acid and ionises in aqueous solution.

$$H_2SO_4(aq) \rightarrow H^+(aq) + HSO_4^-(aq); \quad K_1 = 1 \times 10^3$$

$$HSO_4^-(aq) \rightarrow H^+(aq) + SO_4^{2-}(aq); \quad K_2 = 1.2 \times 10^{-2}$$

- Being an acid, it neutralises alkalies to form salts and water and decomposes carbonates and bicarbonates with the evolution of carbon dioxide gas.

$$NaOH + H_2SO_4 \rightarrow \underset{\text{Sodium hydrogen sulfate}}{NaHSO_4} + H_2O$$

$$2\,NaOH + H_2SO_4 \rightarrow \underset{\text{Sodium sulfate}}{Na_2SO_4} + 2\,H_2O$$

$$2\,NaHCO_3 + H_2SO_4 \rightarrow Na_2SO_4 + 2\,CO_2 + 2\,H_2O$$

$$Na_2CO_3 + H_2SO_4 \rightarrow Na_2SO_4 + CO_2 + H_2O$$

- Being an acid, it reacts with active metals like Zn and Mg to evolve H_2 gas.
- Charring of sugar.

$$\underset{\text{Sugar}}{C_{12}H_{22}O_{11}} \xrightarrow{\text{Conc. } H_2SO_4} \underset{\text{Sugar charcoal}}{12C} + 11H_2O$$

- Dehydration of formic acid and oxalic acid.

$$\underset{\text{Formic acid}}{HCOOH} \xrightarrow{\text{Conc. } H_2SO_4} H_2O + CO$$

$$\underset{\text{Oxalic acid}}{\begin{matrix} COOH \\ | \\ COOH \end{matrix}} \xrightarrow{\text{Conc. } H_2SO_4} H_2O + CO + CO_2$$

- It removes water of crystallisation from hydrated salts. For example,

$$\underset{\text{Hydrated copper sulfate (blue)}}{CuSO_4.5H_2O} \xrightarrow{\text{Conc. } H_2SO_4} \underset{\text{Anhydrous copper sulfate (white)}}{CuSO_4} + 5\,H_2O$$

- Action on ethyl alcohol.

$$\underset{\text{Ethyl alcohol}}{CH_3CH_2\text{–}OH} \xrightarrow[443\text{ K}]{\text{Conc. } H_2SO_4} \underset{\text{Ethylene}}{CH_2\text{=}CH_2} + H_2O$$

(Intramolecular dehydration)

$$\underset{\text{Ethyl alcohol}}{2CH_3CH_2OH} \xrightarrow{\text{Conc. } H_2SO_4} \underset{\text{Diethyl ether}}{CH_3CH_2OCH_2CH_3} + H_2O$$

(Intermolecular dehydration)

(iv) *Oxidising agent*: The oxidising character of H_2SO_4 is due to the fact that it decomposes to give nascent oxygen.

$$H_2SO_4 \xrightarrow{\text{Heat}} H_2O + SO_2 + O$$

This nascent oxygen brings about the oxidation of a number of non-metals and metals.

- It oxidises carbon to carbon dioxide.

$$H_2SO_4 \rightarrow H_2O + SO_2 + O] \times 2$$
$$C + 2\,O \rightarrow CO_2$$
$$\overline{C + 2H_2SO_4 \rightarrow 2SO_2 + CO_2 + 2H_2O}$$

- It oxidises sulfur to sulfur dioxide.

$$H_2SO_4 \rightarrow H_2O + SO_2 + O] \times 16$$
$$S_8 + 16\,O \rightarrow 8\,SO_2$$
$$\overline{S_8 + 16H_2SO_4 \rightarrow 24SO_2 + 16H_2O}$$

- It oxidises phosphorus to phosphoric acid.

$$H_2SO_4 \rightarrow H_2O + SO_2 + O] \times 10$$
$$P_4 + 10\,O \rightarrow P_4O_{10}$$
$$P_4O_{10} + 6\,H_2O \rightarrow 4\,H_3PO_4$$
$$\overline{P_4 + 10H_2SO_4 \rightarrow 4H_3PO_4 + 10SO_2 + 4H_2O}$$

(v) *Action on salts*: It is a strong non-volatile acid and decomposes the salts of the voltaic cell forming its own salts.

- With dilute acid: Carbonates, bicarbonates, sulfites, sulfides, thiosulfates and nitrites are decomposed by dil. H_2SO_4 at room temperature. For example,

$$Na_2CO_3 + \underset{\text{Strong acid}}{H_2SO_4} \rightarrow [Na_2SO_4 + \underset{\text{Weak acid}}{H_2CO_3}] \rightarrow Na_2SO_4 + CO_2 + H_2O$$

$$2\,NaHCO_3 + H_2SO_4 \rightarrow [2NaHSO_4 + 2H_2CO_3] \rightarrow 2NaHSO_4 + 2CO_2 + 2H_2O$$

$$Na_2S + H_2SO_4 \rightarrow Na_2SO_4 + H_2S$$
$$Na_2SO_3 + H_2SO_4 \rightarrow [Na_2SO_4 + H_2SO_3] \rightarrow Na_2SO_4 + SO_2 + H_2O$$
$$Na_2S_2O_3 + H_2SO_4 \rightarrow [Na_2SO_4 + H_2SO_3 + S] \rightarrow Na_2SO_4 + SO_2 + H_2O + S$$
$$2NaNO_2 + H_2SO_4 \rightarrow [Na_2SO_4 + 2\,HNO_2] \rightarrow Na_2SO_4 + NO + NO_2 + H_2O$$

- With hot concentrated acid: Fluorides, chlorides, nitrates, acetates, oxalates and tartarates are decomposed by hot conc. H_2SO_4 liberating their corresponding acids. For example,

$$CaF_2 + H_2SO_4 \rightarrow CaSO_4 + 2HF$$
$$NaCl + H_2SO_4 \rightarrow NaHSO_4 + HCl$$
$$KNO_3 + H_2SO_4 \rightarrow KHSO_4 + HNO_3$$
$$2CH_3COOK + H_2SO_4 \rightarrow K_2SO_4 + 2\,CH_3COOH$$
$$\begin{matrix} COONa \\ | \\ COONa \end{matrix} + H_2SO_4 \longrightarrow \begin{matrix} COOH \\ | \\ COOH \end{matrix} + Na_2SO_4$$

In the case of bromides and iodides, the halogen acid first liberated, being a reducing agent, reduces H_2SO_4 to SO_2 while it itself is oxidised to the corresponding free halogen. For example,

$$NaBr + H_2SO_4 \rightarrow NaHSO_4 + HBr \times 2$$
$$H_2SO_4 \rightarrow H_2O + SO_2 + O$$
$$2\,HBr + O \rightarrow H_2O + Br_2$$
$$\overline{2NaBr + 3H_2SO_4 \rightarrow 2NaHSO_4 + SO_2 + Br_2 + 2H_2O}$$

Similarly, $2\,NaI + 3\,H_2SO_4 \rightarrow 2\,NaHSO_4 + SO_2 + I_2 + 2\,H_2O$

(vi) *Precipitation reactions*: Sulfuric acid gives a white precipitate when treated with solutions of lead and barium salts.

$$BaCl_2 + H_2SO_4 \rightarrow \underset{\text{(White ppt)}}{BaSO_4} + 2HCl$$
$$CaCl_2 + H_2SO_4 \rightarrow \underset{\text{(White ppt)}}{CaSO_4} + 2\,HCl$$
$$\underset{\text{Lead acetate}}{(CH_3COO)_2Pb} + H_2SO_4 \rightarrow \underset{\text{(White ppt)}}{PbSO_4} + 2\,CH_3COOH$$

7.22.4 Structure of Sulfuric Acid and Sulfates

Both sulfuric acid and the sulfate ion have a tetrahedral structure (Fig. 7.19) in which sulfur is sp^3 hybridised with an oxidation state of +6.

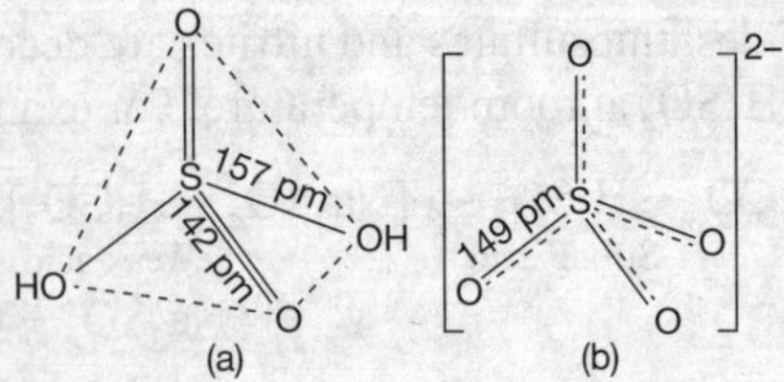

Fig. 7.19 Tetrahedral structures of **(a)** sulfuric acid and **(b)** sulfate ion

7.23 Group 17 Elements (Halogens)

The halogens are very reactive and therefore, do not occur in the free state. The three most important minerals of fluorine are:

- fluorspar, CaF_2
- cryolite, Na_3AlF_6 and
- fluoroapatite, $3Ca_3(PO_4)_2.CaF_2$ or $Ca_5(PO_4)_3F$.

The chief sources of chlorine are sea water (2.8% by mass), salt wells and salt beds. In salt beds, it mainly occurs as, (i) sodium chloride (rock salt) NaCl (ii) carnallite KCl. $MgCl_2.6H_2O$, and (iii) calcium chloride, $CaCl_2$. Bromides occur in sea water and salt lakes as bromides of alkali and alkaline earth metals—NaBr, KBr, $MgBr_2$, and so on. Iodine occurs in various sea weeds, (up to 0.2%) as sodium iodate ($NaIO_3$).

7.23.1 Electronic Configuration

Their general electronic configuration is ns^2np^5, that is, $ns^2np_x^2\,np_y^2\,np_z^1$ where $n = 2 - 6$.

7.24 Atomic and Physical Properties

(i) Atomic and ionic radii: The halogens have the smallest atomic radii in their respective periods due to maximum effective nuclear charge. *The radius of the halide ion is always greater than the corresponding halogen atom.* This is because, the effective nuclear charge per electron is reduced and the electron cloud is held less tightly by the nucleus. This causes an increase in size.

(ii) Ionisation enthalpy: They have very little tendency to lose electrons. However, on going down the group, the ionisation enthalpy decreases due to a gradual increase in atomic size.

(iii) Electron gain enthalpy: Halogens have one electron less than the nearest noble gas configuration. Therefore, they have *large negative electron gain enthalpies.* Further, as we move down the group, the electron gain enthalpies become less and less negative as the size of the halogen increases. Due to the small size of the fluorine atom strong electron–electron repulsions are present. Thus, it has less negative electron gain enthalpy.

(iv) Electronegativity: Due to the small size and higher nuclear charge, each halogen has the highest electronegativity in its period. As we move down the group, electronegativity decrease due to a corresponding increase in the size of the atom.

(v) Melting and boiling points: The melting and boiling points of the halogens increase with an increase in the atomic number as we go down the group. The forces existing between these molecules are weak van der Waals forces which increase down the group.

7.24.1 Physical Properties

- **Atomicity:** Each halogen has one electron less than the nearest inert gas. They readily share their single unpaired electron with other atoms to form covalent bonds. Thus, all halogens exist as diatomic molecules.

- **Melting and boiling points:** The different molecules of a halogen are held together by weak van der Waals forces of attraction. The strength of these van der Waals forces increases as the size of the halogen increases from fluorine to iodine. As we move down the group, the melting points and boiling points increase.
- **Non-metallic character:** Because of very high ionisation energy values, all halogens are non-metallic in character. The non-metallic character decreases as we go down the group.
- **Enthalpy of dissociation:** Enthalpy of dissociation decreases as the bond distance increases from F_2 to I_2 due to a corresponding increase in the size of the atom.
- **Colour:** All the halogens are coloured. The colours of different halogens are given below.

Halogen	Fluorine	Chlorine
Colour	Pale yellow	Greenish yellow
Halogen	Bromine	Iodine
Colour	Reddish brown	Deep violet

- **Solubility:** F_2 and Cl_2 react with water. Br_2 and I_2 are sparingly soluble in water but are soluble in various organic solvents such as chloroform, carbon tetrachloride, carbon disulfide and hydrocarbons such as hexane and benzene, to give coloured solutions. However, I_2 dissolves in an aqueous solution of KI due to the formation of the complex, KI_3.

7.24.2 Chemical Properties

Oxidation States

They can get the noble gas configuration either by gaining one electron to form an uninegative ion, X^-, or by sharing electrons with other atoms. Thus, they show an oxidation of state of –1 or +1. Fluorine being the most electronegative element, does not show any positive oxidation state. The other elements also show positive oxidation states of +1, +3, +5 and +7 due to the presence of vacant *d* orbitals in their valence shells. As a result, the outer *s* or *p* electrons can easily be promoted to the vacant *d* orbitals. Thus, the halogens exhibit the following oxidation states.

Halogen	F	Cl	Br	I
Oxidation state	–1	–1, +1, +3 +5, + 7	–1, +1, +3 +5, +7	–1, +1, +3 +5, +7

Trends in Chemical Reactivity of Elements and their Compounds

The high reactivity of halogens is due to low bond dissociation energy ($X_2 \rightarrow 2X$) and high negative electron gain enthalpies.

Reactivity and oxidising power: Halogens have a strong tendency to take up an electron and are powerful oxidising agents. The electrode potential of the F_2/F^- couple is the maximum while that of I_2/I^- is the minimum, that is, F_2 is reduced most easily but I_2 is reduced least easily, the I^- ion is the strongest reducing agent while the F^- ion is the weakest reducing agent.

The relative oxidising power of halogens can further be illustrated by their reactions with water. F_2 oxidises H_2O to O_2 and O_3 whereas Cl_2 and Br_2 react with water to form the corresponding hydrohalic and hypohalous acids.

$$2F_2(g) + 2H_2O(l) \rightarrow 4H^+(aq) + 4F^-(aq) + O_2(g)$$

$$3F_2(g) + 3H_2O(l) \rightarrow 6H^+(aq) + 6F^-(aq) + O_3(g)$$

$$Cl_2(g) + H_2O(l) \rightarrow HCl(aq) + \underset{\text{Hypochlorous acid}}{HOCl(aq)}$$

$$Br_2(g) + H_2O(l) \rightarrow HBr(aq) + \underset{\text{Hypobromous acid}}{HOBr(aq)}$$

Reactivity towards hydrogen: All the halogens combine with hydrogen to form hydrogen halides (HX).

$$H_2 + F_2 \xrightarrow{\text{Violent}} 2HF$$

$$H_2 + Cl_2 \xrightarrow[\text{sunlight}]{\text{Diffused}} 2HCl$$

The reactivity of halogens towards hydrogen decreases from fluorine to iodine.

Preparation of HF and HCl: HF and HCl are prepared by heating the fluorides and chlorides respectively with concentrated sulfuric acid.

$$CaF_2(s) + H_2SO_4(\text{Conc.}) \xrightarrow{\text{Heat}} CaSO_4(s) + 2HF(g)$$

$$2NaCl(s) + H_2SO_4(\text{Conc.}) \xrightarrow{\text{Heat}} Na_2SO_4(aq) + 2HCl(g)$$

Preparation of HBr and HI: These acids are usually prepared by heating the bromide or the iodide with a non-oxidising acid such as phosphoric acid.

$$3NaBr + H_3PO_4 \xrightarrow{\text{Heat}} Na_3PO_4 + 3HBr;$$

$$2NaI + H_3PO_4 \xrightarrow{\text{Heat}} Na_3PO_4 + 3HI$$

Commercially, HBr is prepared by the direct reaction of H_2 and Br_2 at around 570 K in the presence of Pt as catalyst.

$$H_2(g) + Br(g) \xrightarrow[\text{570 K}]{\text{Pt/asbestos}} 2HBr(g)$$

On the other hand, HI is produced by the reaction of I_2 either with H_2S or with hydrazine (N_2H_4).

$$I_2(s) + H_2S(g) \rightarrow 2HI(g) + S(s)$$

$$2I_2(s) + N_2H_4(aq) \xrightarrow{\text{573 K}} 4HI(aq) + N_2(g)$$

Properties of hydrogen halides: Some important characteristics of hydrogen halides are discussed.

(i) Hydrogen fluoride is a low boiling liquid (BP 293 K) whereas HBr, HCl and HI are gases. The anomalous behaviour of HF is due to the presence of intermolecular hydrogen bonding in its molecules. Consequently, it exists as associated molecules, $(HF)_n$. In the solid state, $(HF)_n$ has a zig–zig structure.

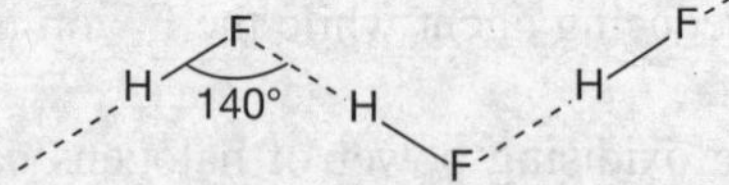

The other hydrogen halides do not show hydrogen bonding because of the lower electronegativity of the halogens in them.

(ii) *Dipole moments*: As the electronegativity of the halogen decreases, the dipole moment of the hydrogen halides decreases as HF (1.86 D) > HCl (1.1 D) > HBr (0.79 D) > HI (0.38 D).

(iii) *Nature of bonds*: All the halides are covalent compounds with some ionic character. The degree of ionic character decreases in the order:

$$HF > HCl > HBr > HI$$

(iv) *Bond length*: It increases in the order HF < HCl, HBr < HI as the size of the halogen atom increases.

(v) *Bond strength*: Shorter the bond length, higher is the bond strength. Since the bond lengths increase in the order HF < HCl < HBr < HI, the bond dissociation energies increase in the reverse order, that is, HI < HBr < HCl < HF.

(vi) *Thermal stability*: It increases in the order HI < HBr < HCl < HF. Thermal stability is directly proportional to the bond dissociation energy.

(vii) *Acid strength*: Higher the bond dissociation energy, lower is the degree of ionisation and hence weaker is the acid. The strength of the acids increases that is, HF < HCl < HBr < HI.

(viii) *Reducing power*: It increases in the order HF < HCl < HBr < HI.

Table 7.19 Oxides of halogens and their oxidation states

Oxidation state	F	Cl	Br	I
–1	OF_2, O_2F_2	–	–	–
+ 1	–	Cl_2O	Br_2O	–
+4	–	ClO_2	BrO_2	I_2O_4
+5	–	–	–	I_2O_5
+6	–	Cl_2O_6, ClO_3	–	–
+7	–	Cl_2O_7	–	–

Preparation of Oxides of Fluorine

$$\underset{(2\%)}{2\,F_2 + 2\,NaOH} \rightarrow 2\,NaF + H_2O + \underset{\text{Oxygen difluoride}}{OF_2}$$

$$F_2 + O_2 \xrightarrow[\text{Liquid air temp., low pressure}]{\text{Electric discharge}} \underset{\text{Dioxygen difluoride}}{O_2F_2}$$

OF_2 dissolves in water and gives a neutral solution, therefore, it is not an acid anhydride. It dissolves in NaOH to give sodium fluoride and dioxygen.

$$2\,NaOH + OF_2 \rightarrow 2\,NaF + H_2O + O_2$$

Structure: The structure of OF_2 is similar to that of H_2O while that of O_2F_2 is similar to that of H_2O_2 involving sp^3 hybridiation of O atoms.

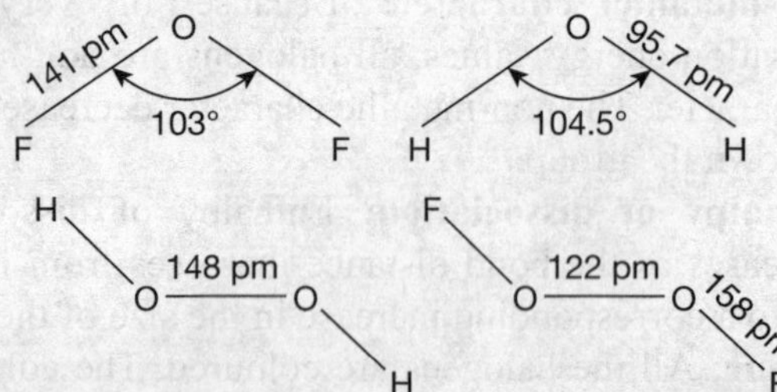

Both OF_2 and O_2F_2 are strong oxidising and fluorinating agents. O_2F_2 oxidises plutonium (Pu) to PuF_6. O_2F_2 also oxidises H_2S to SF_6.

$$H_2S + 4\,O_2F_2 \rightarrow SF_6 + 2\,HF + 4\,O_2$$

Oxides of Other Halogens

Chlorine forms the largest number of oxides while iodine forms the least. The stability of oxides of iodine is greater than those of chlorine while bromine oxides are the least stable.

Preparation of Chlorine Oxides

(i) *Dichlorine monoxide* (Cl_2O):

$$2\,Cl_2 + 2\,HgO \xrightarrow{573\,K} HgCl_2.HgO + Cl_2O(g)$$

(ii) *Chlorine dioxide* (ClO_2):

$$2\,NaClO_3 + 2\,(COOH)_2 \xrightarrow{H_2O,\,363\,K} 2\,ClO_2 + 2\,CO_2 + (COONa)_2 + 2\,H_2O$$

It can also be prepared by reduction of $NaClO_3$ with SO_2.

$$2\,NClO_3(aq) + SO_2(g) \rightarrow 2\,ClO_2(aq) + Na_2SO_4(aq)$$

(iii) *Dichlorinehexaoxide* is the anhydride of perchloric acid and is conveniently prepared by the careful dehydration of $HClO_4$ with P_4O_{10} or with H_3PO_4 at 263 K followed by distillation at 238 K under a pressure of 1 mm Hg.

$$2\,HClO_4 \xrightarrow{P_4O_{10}\text{ or }H_3PO_4} Cl_2O_7 + H_2O$$

Structure of chlorine oxides: The O atom in Cl_2O is sp^3 hybridised and its structure is similar to that OF_2. However, due to steric crowding of the two Cl atoms, the Cl–O–Cl bond angle is 111° as compared to 103° in OF_2. In ClO_2, the central Cl atom is sp^2 hybridised with an O–Cl–O angle of 118°.

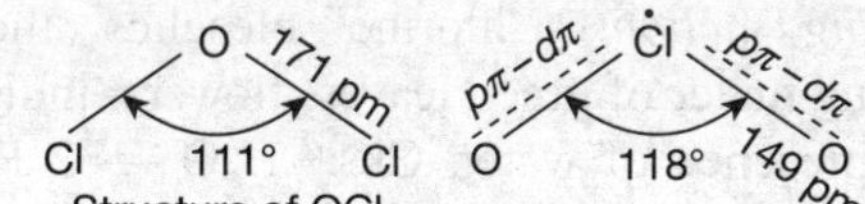

Structure of OCl_2 (Cl–O–Cl, 111°, 171 pm)

Structure of ClO_2 (O–Cl–O, 118°, 149 pm, pπ–dπ)

Cl_2O_6 is a solid. It exists in equilibrium with the monomer, ClO_3, which is a liquid. The possible structures of Cl_2O_6 are:

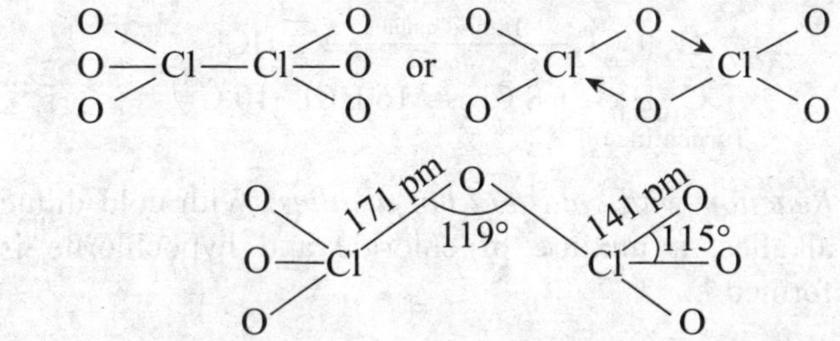

(171 pm, 119°, 141 pm, 115°)

Bromine oxide: The bromine oxides, Br_2O, BrO_2, BrO_3, are the least stable halogen oxides and exist only at low temperatures. They are very powerful oxidising agents. Their structures are similar to those of chlorine oxides having comparable molecular formulae.

Iodine oxides: Iodine forms three oxides, I_2O_4, I_2O_5 and I_4O_9. Out of these, I_2O_5 is the most stable. I_2O_4 is probably $IO^+IO_3^-$ and I_4O_9 is probably $I^{3+}(IO_3^-)^3$.

Preparation: I_2O_5 is obtained by dehydrating iodic acid at 473 K.

$$2\,HIO_3 \xrightarrow{473\,K} I_2O_5 + H_2O$$

Therefore, it is the anhydride of iodic acid. It is a strong oxidising agent and oxidises CO to CO_2

$$I_2O_5 + 5\,CO \xrightarrow{\text{Room temp.}} I_2 + 5\,CO_2$$

Structure: I_2O_5 consists of two IO_3 pyramidal units joined through a common oxygen atom. Each iodine has two I→O coordinate bonds, one I–O covalent bond and a lone pair of electrons.

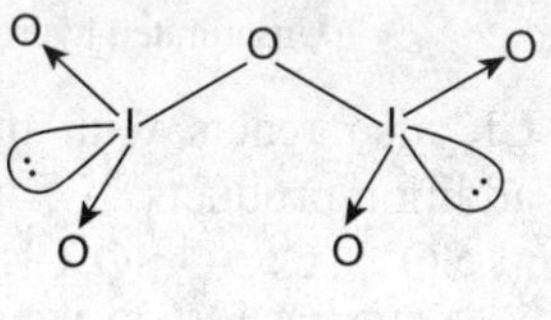

Reactivity Towards Metals

Because of high oxidising power, halogens combine directly with most metals to form their corresponding halides. For example, $Mg(s) + Br_2(l) \rightarrow MgBr_2(s)$

The ionic character of the M–X bond decreases as M–F > M–Cl > M–Br > M–I. This is due to a corresponding decrease in the electronegativity of the halogen from F to I.

Reactivity of Halogens Towards Other Halogens

Halogens react with each other to form a number of compounds called interhalogens of the type XX′, XX'_3 XX'_5 and XX'_7 where X is the larger sized halogen.

Anomalous Behaviour of Fluorine

Fluorine shows a remarkably different behaviour from rest of the halogens. For example, the ionisation enthalpy, electronegativity and electrode potential of fluorine are higher while the electron gain enthalpy and bond dissociation enthalpy are lower than the trends set by other halogens. The main reasons for the anomalous behaviour of fluorine are (i) its small atomic size, (ii) highest electronegativity, (iii) low bond dissociation enthalpy of the F_2 molecule and (iv) the absence of *d* orbitals in the valence shell.

Some points of difference between fluorine and rest of the halogens are as follows.

(i) *Reactivity*: Fluorine is the most reactive of all the halogens due to its higher electrode potential.

(ii) *Oxidation state*: Since it is the most electronegative element, it mostly shows a negative oxidation state of –1, except +1 in HOF. Further, it does not show any higher oxidation state.

(iii) *Hydrogen bonding*: Hydrogen bonding (due to the small atomic size and high electronegativity of fluorine) is a distinct phenomenon observed in some fluorine compounds.

(iv) *Nature of compounds*: Because of its highest electronegativity, fluorides have the maximum ionic character. For example, AlF_3 is ionic whereas other halides of aluminium are covalent.

(v) *Oxidising power*: Fluorine brings about the highest oxidation state of other elements with which it combines. For example, with sulfur it gives SF_6 and with osmium it gives OsF_8. Other halogens do not always bring about the highest oxidation state of the element.

(vi) *Reactivity of halogen acids*: HF is the most reactive of all halogen acids. It can attack glass because of its ability to displace oxygen from silicates to form fluorosilicates.

$$\underset{\text{(Simplified formula of glass)}}{Na_2SiO_3} + 6HF \rightarrow Na_2SiF_6 + 3H_2O$$

7.25 Halogens and Their Compounds

Preparation

- *Managanese dioxide with concentrated hydrochloric acid*: Chlorine is prepared easily by heating manganese dioxide with conc. HCl.

$$MnO_2 + 2\,HCl \rightarrow MnCl_2 + H_2O + O$$
$$2\,HCl + O \rightarrow Cl_2 + H_2O$$
$$\overline{MnO_2 + 4HCl \rightarrow MnCl_2 + 2H_2O + Cl_2}$$

In the laboratory, Cl_2 is prepared by heating a mixture of sodium chloride, manganese dioxide and conc. H_2SO_4. The HCl produced in situ is oxidised by MnO_2 as shown above.

$$NaCl + H_2SO_4 \rightarrow NaHSO_4 + HCl] \times 2$$
$$MnO_2 + H_2SO_4 \rightarrow MnSO_4 + H_2O + O$$
$$2\,HCl + O \rightarrow H_2O + Cl_2$$

$$2NaCl + 3H_2SO_4 + MnO_2 \rightarrow 2NaHSO_4 + MnSO_4 + 2H_2O + Cl_2$$

- *Action of HCl on potassium permanganate or potassium dichromate:*

$$2\,KMnO_4 + 16\,HCl \rightarrow 2\,KCl + 2\,MnCl_2 + 8\,H_2O + 5\,Cl_2$$
$$K_2Cr_2O_7 + 14\,HCl \rightarrow 2\,KCl + 2\,CrCl_3 + 7\,H_2O + 3\,Cl_2$$

Manufacture of chlorine: Chlorine is obtained by the electrolysis of a concentrated solution of NaCl (brine), when Cl_2 is liberated at the anode and the sodium metal liberated at the cathode reacts with H_2O to form NaOH and H_2.

At anode: $Cl^- \rightarrow Cl + e^-$; $2\,Cl \rightarrow Cl_2$

At cathode: $Na^+ + e^- \rightarrow Na$; $2\,Na + 2\,H_2O \rightarrow 2\,NaOH + H_2$

Chemical Properties

(i) *Reaction with metals, non-metals and metalloids*:

$2\,Na + Cl_2 \rightarrow NaCl$; $2\,Al + 3\,Cl_2 \rightarrow 2\,AlCl_3$

$2\,Fe + 3\,Cl_2 \rightarrow 2\,FeCl_3$; $P_4 + 6\,Cl_2 \rightarrow 4\,PCl_3$

$S_8 + 4\,Cl_2 \rightarrow 4\,S_2Cl_2$; $2\,As + 3\,Cl_2 \rightarrow 2\,AsCl_3$

(ii) *Oxidising properties*:

$$Cl_2 + H_2O \rightarrow [HCl + HOCl] \rightarrow 2\,HCl + \underset{\text{Nascent oxygen}}{[O]}$$

Thus, in the presence of moisture or in aqueous solution, Cl_2 acts as a powerful oxidising agent. Some of these oxidising properties are discussed below:

- It oxidises acidified ferrous to ferric salts.

$$Cl_2 + H_2O \rightarrow 2\,HCl + O$$
$$2\,FeSO_4 + H_2SO_4 + O \rightarrow Fe_2(SO_4)_3 + H_2O$$
$$2FeSO_4 + H_2SO_4 + Cl_2 \rightarrow Fe_2(SO_4)_3 + 2HCl$$

- It oxidises sulfites to sulfates: $Na_2SO_3 + Cl_2 + H_2O \rightarrow Na_2SO_4 + 2\,HCl$
- It oxidises thiosulfates to bisulfates:

$$\underset{\text{Sodium thiosulfate}}{Na_2S_2O_3} + 4\,Cl_2 + 5\,H_2O \rightarrow 2\,NaHSO_4 + 8\,HCl$$

- It oxidises sulfur dioxide to sulfuric acid in aqueous solution.

$$SO_2 + 2\,H_2O + Cl_2 \rightarrow H_2SO_4 + 2\,HCl$$

- It oxidises moist iodine to iodic acid:

$$\underset{\text{Iodine}}{I_2} + 6\,H_2O + 5\,Cl_2 \rightarrow \underset{\text{Iodic acid}}{2\,HIO_3} + 10\,HCl$$

- It oxidises H_2S to S in the presence of water:

$$H_2S + Cl_2 \xrightarrow{\text{water}} 2\,HCl + S$$

- It oxidises nitrites to nitrates:

$$NaNO_2 + Cl_2 + H_2O \rightarrow NaNO_3 + 2\,HCl$$

- It oxidises sodium arsenite to sodium arsenate.

$$\underset{\text{Sodium arsenite}}{Na_3AsO_3} + H_2O + Cl_2 \rightarrow \underset{\text{Sodium arsenate}}{Na_3AsO_4} + 2\,HCl$$

(iii) *Bleaching action*: Chlorine bleaches the natural colouring mater of green leaves, flowers, indigo, litmus in the presence of water. $Cl_2 + H_2O \rightarrow 2\,HCl + \underset{\text{(Nascent oxygen)}}{[O]}$

Coloured substance + O → Colourless substance

(iv) *Affinity for hydrogen*: It reacts with compounds containing hydrogen to form HCl.

$$H_2 + Cl_2 \xrightarrow{\text{Diffusd sunlight}} 2\,HCl;$$
$$\underset{\text{Turpentine oil}}{C_{10}H_{16}} + 8\,Cl_2 \rightarrow 16\,HCl + 10\,C$$

(v) *Reaction with cold and hot alkalies*: With cold dilute alkalies, a mixture of chloride and hypochlorite is formed.

$$\overset{0}{Cl_2} + 2\,NaOH\,(dil.) \xrightarrow{\text{Cold}} \overset{-1}{NaCl} + \underset{\text{Sodium hypochlorite}}{\overset{-1}{NaOCl}} + H_2O$$

$$2\,Cl + 2\,Ca(OH)_2(dil.) \xrightarrow{\text{Cold}} CaCl_2 + \underset{\text{Calcium hypochlorite}}{Ca(OCl)_2} + 2\,H_2O$$

(vi) *Reaction with dry slaked lime*: Chlorine reacts with dry slaked lime to form bleaching powder.

$$\underset{\text{Slaked lime}}{2\,Ca(OH)_2} + 2\,Cl_2 \rightarrow \underset{\text{Calcium hypochlorite}}{Ca(OCl)_2} + CaCl_2 + H_2O$$

(vii) *Substitution reactions*: Chlorine reacts with saturated hydrocarbons to form substitution products.

$$\underset{\text{Methane}}{CH_4} + Cl_2 \xrightarrow{h\nu} \underset{\text{Methyl chloride}}{CH_3Cl} + HCl$$

(viii) *Addition reactions*:

$$\underset{\substack{\text{Ethene} \\ \text{(Unsaturated hydrocarbon)}}}{CH_2{=}CH_2} + Cl_2 \xrightarrow{\text{Room temp.}} \underset{\substack{\text{1,2-Dichloroethane} \\ \text{(Addition product)}}}{ClCH_2{-}CH_2Cl}$$

Cl_2 also reacts with many oxides of non-metals to form addition products.

$SO_2 + Cl_2 \rightarrow SO_2Cl_2$ (Sulfuryl chloride)

$2\,NO + Cl_2 \rightarrow 2\,NOCl$ (Nitrosyl chloride)

$CO + Cl_2 \rightarrow COCl_2$ (Carbonyl chloride or phosgene)

Hydrogen Chloride, HCl

Preparation of Hydrogen Chloride

(i) In this method, conc. H_2SO_4 is added to rock salt (NaCl).

$$NaCl + H_2SO_4 \xrightarrow{420\,K} NaHSO_4 + HCl;$$
$$NaCl + NaHSO_4 \xrightarrow{823\,K} Na_2SO_4 + HCl$$

(ii) HCl is produced in the conversion of 1,2-dichloroethane to vinyl chloride and in the manufacture of chlorinated ethanes and chlorinated fluorocarbons (used as refrigerants).

$$\underset{\text{1,2-Dichloroethane}}{ClCH_2{-}CH_2Cl} \xrightarrow{\text{Heat}} \underset{\text{Vinyl chloride}}{CH_2{=}CHCl} + HCl$$

(iii) Highly pure HCl is made by the direct combination of H_2 and Cl_2.

(iv) $NaCl + H_2SO_4 \xrightarrow{420\ K} NaHSO_4 + HCl$

Chemical Properties of Hydrogen Chloride

(i) *Acidic nature*:

$$HCl(g) + H_2O(l) \rightarrow H_3O^+(aq) + Cl^-(aq);\ K_a = 10^7$$

The high value of the dissociation constant (K_a) indicates that it is a strong acid in water. It reacts with NH_3 and gives white fumes of NH_4Cl.

$$NH_3 + HCl \rightarrow NH_4Cl$$

(ii) *Reaction with metals*: Active metals such as Zn, Mg, Fe and Al, react with HCl to produce the corresponding metal chlorides with the liberation of H_2 gas.

$$Zn + 2\ HCl \rightarrow ZnCl_2 + H_2;\quad Mg + 2\ HCl \rightarrow MgCl_2 + H_2$$
$$Fe + 2\ HCl \rightarrow FeCl_2 + H_2;\quad 2\ Al + 6\ HCl \rightarrow 2\ AlCl_3 + 3\ H_2$$

(iii) *Reaction with oxidising agent*: Concentrated hydrochloric acid reacts with strong oxidising agents such as $KMnO_4$, MnO_2, $K_2Cr_2O_7$ and PbO_2, to yield chlorine gas.

(iv) *Reaction with nitric acid*: Three parts of conc. HCl and one part of conc. HNO_3 (*aqua regia*) dissolves noble metals like gold and platinum.

$$\underset{\text{Gold}}{Au} + 4H^+ + NO_3^- + 4Cl^- \rightarrow \underset{\text{Tetrachloroaurate (III)}}{[AuCl_4]^-} + NO + 2\ H_2O$$

$$\underset{\text{Platinum}}{3\ Pt} + 16H^+ + 4NO_3^- + 18Cl^- \rightarrow \underset{\text{Hexachloroplatinate (IV)}}{3[PtCl_6]^{2-}} + 4NO + 8H_2O$$

(v) *Reaction with salts of weak acids*: Hydrochloric acid decomposes salts of weaker acids such as carbonates, hydrogen carbonates, sulfides, phosphides, sulfites, thiosulfates and nitrites.

$$Na_2CO_3 + 2\ HCl \rightarrow 2\ NaCl + H_2O + CO_2$$
$$NaHCO_3 + HCl \rightarrow NaCl + H_2O + CO_2$$
$$Na_2S + 2\ HCl + \rightarrow 2\ NaCl + H_2S$$
$$Na_2SO_3 + 2\ HCl \rightarrow 2\ NaCl + H_2O + SO_2$$

(vi) *Precipitation reaction*: HCl forms insoluble chlorides with soluble salts of silver, lead and mercury(I).

$$AgNO_3 + HCl \rightarrow \underset{\text{(White ppt)}}{AgCl\downarrow} + HNO_3$$

$$Pb(NO_3)_2 + 2\ HCl \rightarrow \underset{\text{(White ppt)}}{PbCl_2\downarrow} + 2\ HNO_3$$

$$Hg_2(NO_3)_2 + 2\ HCl \rightarrow \underset{\text{(White ppt)}}{Hg_2Cl_2\downarrow} + 2\ HNO_3$$

7.26 Oxoacids of Halogens

The names of some important oxoacids along with their oxidation states are given in Table 7.20.

Table 7.20 Oxoacids of halogens

Name/Oxidation state	Fluorine	Chlorine	Bromine	Iodine
Halic (I) acid (Hypohalous acid)	HOF (Hypofluorous acid)	HOCl (Hypochlorous acid)	HOBr (Hypobromous acid)	HOI (Hypoidous acid)
Halic (III) acid (Halic acid)	—	HOClO or $HClO_2$ (Chloric acid)	—	—
Halic (V) acid (Halid acid)	—	$HOClO_2$ or $HClO_3$ (Chloric acid)	$HOBrO_2$ or $HBrO_3$ (Bromic acid)	$HOIO_2$ or HIO_3 (Iodic acid)
Halic (VII) acid (Perhalic acid)	—	$HOClO_3$ or $HClO_4$ (Perchloric acid)	$HOBrO_3$ or $HBrO_4$ (Perbromic acid)	$HOIO_3$ or HIO_4 (Periodic acid)

The structures of oxoacids of chlorine are given in Fig. 7.37.

Hypochlorous acid — Chlorous acid — Chloric acid — Perchloric acid

Fig. 7.37 Oxoacids of chlorine

In all these oxoacids, Cl is sp^3 hybridised.

(i) *Acid strength of hypohalous acids*: Acid strength of oxoacids is as given below.

$$\overset{+1}{HOCl} > \overset{+1}{HOBr} > \overset{+1}{HOI}$$

Oxygen is more electronegative than the halogen (Cl, Br or I). Now, as the electronegativity of the halogen decreases from Cl to I, the shared pair of electrons of the oxygen–halogen bond move closer and towards the oxygen atom. As result, the O–H breaks most readily in H–OCl and least easily in H–OI.

(ii) *Oxidising power of hypohalous acids*: As the size of the halogen increases, the thermal stability of the O–X bond increases and the oxidising power of the hypohalous acid or the hypohalite ion decreases.

Acid strength of perhalic acids: As the electronegativity of the halogen decreases, the tendency of the XO_3 group to withdraw the electrons of the O–H bond towards itself decreases and hence the acid strength of the perhalic acid decreases in the same order. That is, $HClO_4 > HBrO_4 > HIO_4$.

(iii) *Oxidising power of perhalates*: Perhalates are powerful oxidising agents. Their oxidising power decreases in the order $BrO_4^- > IO_4^- > ClO_4^-$. Thus, BrO_4^- is the strongest oxidising agent among the perhalates because of its very high electrode potential.

(iv) *Acid strength of oxoacids of the same halogen in different oxidation states*:

	+7		+5		+3		+1
Acid	$HClO_4$	>	$HClO_3$	>	$HClO_2$	>	$HClO$
pK_a	–10		–1.2		2.0		7.5

$$\underset{\substack{\text{Oxoacid}\\(n=1\text{–}4)}}{HClO_n} + H_2O \rightleftharpoons H_3O^+ + \underset{\substack{\text{Anion}\\\text{(Conjugate base)}}}{ClO_n^-}$$

Greater the number of oxygen atoms in the anion (conjugate base), greater will be the dispersal of the negative charge through $p\pi - d\pi$ back bonding and hence greater will be the stability of the anion.

7.27 Interhalogen Compounds

Compounds that contain two or more halogen atoms are called interhalogen compounds. They may be represented by the general formula XX'_n where X is a halogen of larger size and X′ is a halogen of smaller size, X being more electronegative than X′. For example, ClF, ICl_3, BrF_5.

Types: Depending upon the oxidation state of halogen X (+1, +3, +5 or +7), these are divided into the following four types.

XX'	XX'_3	XX'_5	XX'_7
ClF, BrF	ClF_3, BrF_3	ClF_5	–
BrCl	IF_3	BrF_5	–
ICl, IBr, IF	ICl_3 (I_2Cl_6)	IF_5	IF_7

7.27.1 Preparation of Interhalogen Compounds

$$\underset{\text{(Equal volumes)}}{Cl_2(g) + F_2(g)} \xrightarrow{473\text{ K}} \underset{\text{Chlorine monofluoride}}{2\,ClF(g)}$$

$$\underset{\text{(Excess)}}{Cl_2(g) + 3\,F_2(g)} \xrightarrow{573\text{ K}} \underset{\text{Chlorine trifluoride}}{2\,ClF_3(g)}$$

$$ClF(g) + F_2(g) \xrightarrow{475\text{–}575\text{ K}} ClF_3(g)$$

$$\underset{\text{(Equimolar)}}{I_2(s) + Cl_2(l)} \rightarrow \underset{\text{Iodine monochloride}}{2\,ICl(s)}$$

$$\underset{\text{(Diluted with }N_2)}{Br_2(l) + 3\,F_2(g)} \rightarrow \underset{\text{Bromine trifluoride}}{2BrF_3(l)}$$

$$\underset{\text{(Excess)}}{Br_2(l) + 5\,F_2(g)} \rightarrow \underset{\text{Bromine pentafluoride}}{2BrF_5(l)}$$

$$\underset{\text{(In }CCl_3F\text{ soln)}}{I_2(g) + F_2(g)} \xrightarrow{228\text{ K}} \underset{\substack{\text{Iodine monofluoride}\\\text{(Unstable)}}}{2\,IF(g)}$$

$$I_2(s) + 5F_2(g) \xrightarrow{293\text{ K}} \underset{\text{Iodine pentafluoride}}{2IF_5(g)}$$

$$I_2(g) + 7\,F_2(g) \xrightarrow{523\text{–}573\text{ K}} \underset{\text{Iodine heptafluoride}}{2IF_7(g)}$$

7.27.2 Properties of Interhalogen Compounds

Table 7.21 Properties of interhalogen compounds

Type	Formula	Physical state and colour	Structure
XX'	ClF	Colourless gas	Linear
	BrF	Pale brown gas	Linear
	IF (very unstable)	Detected spectroscopically	Linear
	BrCl	Gas	Linear
	ICl	Ruby red solid (α-form) Brown red solid (β-form)	Linear
	IBr	Black solid	Linear
XX'_3	ClF_3	Colourless gas	Bent T-shaped
	BrF_3	Yellow green liquid	Bent T-shaped
	IF_3	Yellow powder	Bent T-shaped
	ICl_3 (dimerises as Cl-bridged dimer, I_2Cl_6)	Orange solid	Bent T-shaped
XX'_5	IF_5	Colourless gas but solid below 77 K	Square pyramidal
	BrF_5	Colourless liquid	Square pyramidal
	ClF_5	Colourless liquid	Square pyramidal
XX'_7	IF_7	Colourless gas	Pentagonal bipyramidal

due to a corresponding increase in the magnitude of their van der Waals forces of attraction as the size of the atom increases.

(v) Ease of liquefaction: Due to an increase in the atomic size and therefore an increase in van der Waals forces, the ease of liquefication increases down the group from He to Rn.

(vi) Solubility in water: Water, a polar molecule, when it comes close to a noble gas, it induces a dipole in the noble gas by distorting its symmetrical electron cloud. As a result of this dipole–dipole interaction, the noble gas dissolves in water. As the size of the noble gas increases, the extent of polarisation increases. Consequently, the magnitude of the dipole–induced dipole interaction increases and hence the solubility of the noble gas in water increases from He to Rn.

(vii) Enthalpy of fusion and enthalpy of vaporisation: The enthalpy of fusion and enthalpy of vaporisation of noble gases are very low due to weak interatomic forces of attraction in the liquefied state. The values of these properties are found to increase from He to Rn due to an increase in the magnitude of the interatomic forces as the atomic size of the noble gas increases.

(viii) Adsorption over charcoal: Except He, all the other noble gases are adsorbed by coconut charcoal at low temperatures. The extent of adsorption increases as the atomic size of the noble gas increases.

7.31 Xenon Fluorides

7.31.1 Xenon Difluoride, XeF_2

It is prepared by heating a mixture of xenon and fluorine in a molecular ratio of 2 : 1.

$$\underset{(2:1 \text{ ratio})}{Xe + F_2} \xrightarrow[\substack{673\text{ K} \\ 1\text{ bar}}]{\text{Ni vessel}} XeF_2$$

Structure: XeF_2 has a linear structure. It involves sp^3d hybridisation of xenon which adopts a trigonal bipyramidal geometry

Reaction with water: XeF_2 hydrolyses slowly but completely in acidic, neutral or alkaline solutions.

$$2XeF_2 + 2H_2O \rightarrow 2Xe + 4HF + O_2$$

$$2\,XeF_2 + 2\,NaOH \rightarrow 2\,Xe + 4NaF + O_2 + 2\,H_2O$$

7.31.2 Xenon Tetrafluoride, XeF_4

It is prepared in good yield by heating a mixture of xenon and fluorine, in a molar ratio of 1:5, in a nickel vessel, at 873 K under a pressure of 6–7 bar pressure.

$$\underset{(1:5 \text{ ratio})}{Xe(g) + 2\,F_2(g)} \xrightarrow[6\text{–}7\text{ bar}]{873\text{ K}} XeF_4(s)$$

Structure: XeF_4 has a square planar structure (Fig. 7.43). It involves sp^3d^2 hybridisation of xenon which adopts an octahedral geometry.

Reaction with water: XeF_4 undergoes slow hydrolysis with moisture and forms XeO_3 which is highly explosive.

$$6XeF_4 + 12H_2O \xrightarrow{-80°C} \underset{\text{Xenon oxyfluoride}}{XeOF_2} + 2HF$$

7.31.3 Xenon Hexafluoride, XeF_6

It is prepared by heating xenon with excess of fluorine (in a molar ratio of 20) in a nickel vessel at 573 K under 60–70 bar pressure.

$$\underset{(1:20 \text{ ratio})}{Xe + 3\,F_2} \xrightarrow[60\text{–}70\text{ bar}]{573\text{ K}} XeF_6$$

Structure: XeF_6 has a distorted octahedral structure. It involves sp^3d^3 hybridisation of xenon.

Reaction with water: It undergoes slow hydrolysis with atmospheric moisture and forms XeO_3 which is highly explosive.

$$XeF_6(s) + 3\,H_2O(l) \rightarrow XeO_3(s) + 6\,HF(aq)$$

With two equivalents of H_2O, XeO_2F_2 is obtained.

$$XeF_6 + 2\,H_2O \rightarrow XeO_2F_2 + 4\,HF$$

Xenon fluorides react with fluoride ion acceptors to form cationic species and with fluoride ion donors to form fluoroanions.

$$XeF_2 + PF_5 \rightarrow [XeF]^+\,[PF_6]^-$$

$$XeF_4 + SbF_5 \rightarrow [XeF_3]^+\,[SbF_6]^-$$

$$XeF_6 + MF \rightarrow M^+\,[XeF_7]^- \text{ where M = Na, K, Rb or Cs}$$

7.32 Xenon Oxides

7.32.1 Xenon Trioxide, XeO_3

Xenon trioxide is prepared by the hydrolysis of XeF_6 or XeF_4.

$$6\,XeF_4 + 12H_2O \rightarrow 2XeO_3 + 4Xe + 6HF + 3O_2$$

$$XeF_6 + 3H_2O \rightarrow XeO_3 + 6HF$$

However, the last reaction proceeds through the following stages.

$$XeF_6 + H_2O \rightarrow XeOF_4 + 2\,HF$$

$$XeOF_4 + H_2O \rightarrow XeO_2F_2 + 2\,HF$$

$$XeO_2F_2 + H_2O \rightarrow XeO_3 + 2\,HF$$

Structure: It has pyramidal structure and It involves sp^3 hybridisation of xenon.

Reaction with water: It is soluble in water and quite stable in the aqueous solution. However, it explodes violently when dry. XeO_3 reacts with aqueous alkali to form the hydrogen xenate ion $HXeO_4^-$ which slowly disproportionates to give xenon and perxenate ion, XeO_6^{4-}, in which xenon has an oxidation state of +8.

$$XeO_3 + OH^- \rightarrow HXeO_4^-$$

$$2HXeO_4^- + 2OH^- \rightarrow XeO_6^{4-} + Xe\,O_2 + 2H_2O$$

7.32.2 Xenon Tetraoxide, XeO_4

It is prepared by the action of conc. H_2SO_4 on sodium or barium xenate (Na_4XeO_6 or Ba_2XeO_6) at room temperature.

$$Na_4XeO_6 + 2\,H_2SO_4 \rightarrow XeO_4 + 2\,Na_2SO_4 + 2H_2O$$

Structure: It has tetrahedral structure and sp^3 hybridisation

Reaction with water:

$$XeO_4 + 2\,H_2O \rightarrow H_4XeO$$

7.33 Xenon Oxyfluorides

7.33.1 Xenon Oxydifluoride, $XeOF_2$

$$XeF_4 + H_2O \rightarrow XeOF_2 + 2\,HF$$

Structure: It has a T-shaped structure with Xe undergoing sp^3d hybridisation giving a trigonal bipyramidal geometry.

7.33.2 Xenon Oxytetrafluoride, $XeOF_4$

It is prepared by the partial hydrolysis of xenon hexafluoride.

$$XeF_6 + H_2O \rightarrow XeOF_4 + 2\,HF$$

It can also be prepared by the action of XeF_6 on silicon dioxide.

$$2\,XeF_6 + SiO_2 \xrightarrow{50°C} 2\,XeOF_4 + SiF_4$$

The contents are immediately quenched with solid CO_2 as soon as the yellow colour of XeF_6 disappears. It is done to avoid the formation of XeO (explosive).

$$XeOF_4 + SiO_2 \rightarrow XeO_3 + SiF_4$$

Structure: It has square pyramidal structure in which Xe undergoes sp^3d^2 hybridisation.

Reaction with water: It reacts with water giving xenon dioxyfluoride (XeO_2F_2) which further reacts with water to give an explosive compound, XeO_3.

$$XeOF_4 + H_2O \rightarrow XeO_2F_2 + 2HF$$
$$XeO_2F_2 + H_2O \rightarrow XeO_3 + 2\,HF$$

7.33.3 Xenon Dioxydifluoride, XeO_2F_2

It is prepared by mixing XeO_3 and $XeOF_4$ at a low temperature of –78°C.

$$XeO_3 + XeOF_4 \xrightarrow{-78°C} 2\,XeO_2F_2$$

The compound is purified by fractional distillation.

It is also formed when $XeOF_4$ is hydrolysed or reacts with silica.

$$2XeOF_4 + SiO_2 \rightarrow 2XeO_2F_2 + SiF_4$$
$$XeOF_4 + H_2O \rightarrow XeO_2F_2 + 2HF$$

Structure: XeO_2F_2 has a distorted trigonal bipyramidal geometry in which Xe undergoes sp^3d hybridisation.

Reaction with water: It is easily hydrolysed to give xenon trioxide.

$$XeO_2F_2 + H_2O \rightarrow XeO_3 + 2\,HF$$

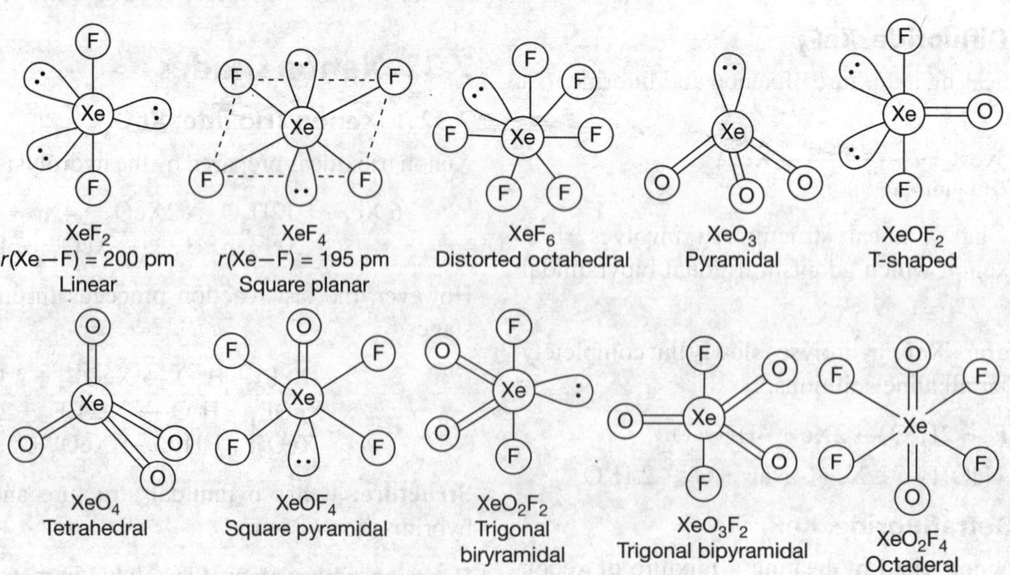

Fig. 7.43 Shapes of compounds of xenon

Exercises

OBJECTIVE QUESTIONS

GROUP 15

Atomic and Physical Properties

1. Phosphine on reaction with hydrobromic acid gives
(a) PBr_3 (b) PH_4Br (c) PBr_5 (d) P_2H_4

2. Glacial phosphoric acid is
(a) H_3PO_4 (b) HPO_3 (c) $H_4P_2O_7$ (d) H_3PO_2

3. Which coagulates the white of an egg?
(a) orthophosphoric acid
(b) metaphosphoric adic
(c) hypophosphoric acid
(d) pyrophosphoric acid

4. Which metal liberates H_2 with dil. nitric acid?
(a) Zn (b) Cu (c) Mn (d) Hg

5. The electronegativity of the following elements increases in the order
(a) C, N, Si, P (b) N, Si, C, P
(c) Si, P, C, N (d) P, Si, N, C

6. Which of the following is an excellent conductor of heat and electricity
(a) Bi (b) Sb (c) P (d) As

7. Which of the following elements does not form stable diatomic molecules?
(a) iodine (b) phosphorus
(c) nitrogen (d) oxygen

8. The electronic configuration of an element is $1s^2 2s^2 2p^6 3s^2 3p^3$. The atomic number of the element which is just below the above element in the vertical column of the periodic table is
(a) 33 (b) 37 (c) 49 (d) 34

9. In the P^{3-}, S^{2-} and Cl^- ions the increasing order of size is
(a) $Cl^- < S^{2-} < P^{3-}$ (b) $P^{3-} < S^{2-} < Cl^-$
(c) $S^{2-} < Cl^- < P^{3-}$ (d) $S^{2-} < P^{3-} < Cl^-$

Chemical Properties

10. Which halide of nitrogen is least basic?
(a) NF_3 (b) NCl_3 (c) NI_3 (d) NBr_3

11. Conc. HNO_3 reacts with iron to:
(a) render iron passive
(b) give ferrous nitrate and nitric oxide
(c) give ferric nitrate and ammonium nitrate
(d) give ferric nitrate and nitrogen dioxide

12. The three important oxidation states of phosphorus are
(a) –3, +3 and +5 (b) –3, +3 and –5
(c) –3, +4 and –4 (d) –3, +3 and +4
(e) –3, +3 and +2

13. The covalence of nitrogen in N_2O_5 is
(a) 5 (b) 4 (c) 3 (d) 2

14. The compound $R_3P{=}O$ exists but $R_3N{=}O$ does not (R = alkyl group). This is because
(a) N due to the absence of *d*orbitals, cannot form $p\pi - p\pi$ multiple bonds
(b) N cannot expand its covalency beyond four but in $R_3N{=}O$, N has a covalency of five. Therefore, the compound $R_3N{=}O$ does not exist
(c) P due to the presence of *d*orbitals, forms $p\pi - p\pi$ multiple bonds and hence can expand its covalency beyond four. Therefore, P forms $R_3P{=}O$ compound in which the covalency of P is five
(d) all (a), (b) and (c) above

15. Which of the following tendencies remains unchanged on going down in the nitrogen family (group 15)?
(a) highest oxidation state
(b) non-metallic character
(c) stability of hydrides
(d) physical state

16. Oxidation number of As in $H_2AsO_4^-$ is
(a) 6 (b) 7 (c) 5 (d) 9

17. Which of the following is a non-combustible hydride?
(a) PH_3 (b) NH_3 (c) AsH_3 (d) SbH_3

18. Which of the following has the weakest E–H bond?
(a) NH_3 (b) PH_3 (c) SbH_3 (d) BiH_3

19. Amongst the elements of group 15, the property which increases down the group is
(a) stability of –3 oxidation state
(b) electronegativity
(c) reducing character of hydrides
(d) acidic nature of oxides

20. Which of the following is the strongest reducing agent?
(a) NH_3 (b) PH_3 (c) AsH_3 (d) SbH_3

21. The basic character of hydrides of the 15 group elements decreases in the order
(a) $SbH_3 > PH_3 > AsH_3 > NH_3$
(b) $NH_3 > SbH_3 > PH_3 > AsH_3$
(c) $NH_3 > PH_3 > AsH_3 > SbH_3$
(d) $SbH_3 > AsH_3 > PH_3 > NH_3$

22. NH_3 forms hydrogen bonds but PH_3 does not. This is because

(a) the electronegativity of N (3.0) is much higher than that of H (2.1)
(b) the N–H bond in NH_3 is quite polar and hence NH_3 undergoes intermolecular H-bonding
(c) both P and H have an electronegativity of 2.1. Therefore, the P–H bond is not polar and hence PH_3 does not undergo H-bonding
(d) all (a), (b) and (c) above

23. The decreasing order of the boiling points of the following hydrides is

(i) NH_3 (ii) PH_3 (iii) AsH_3 (iv) SbH_3 (v) H_2O
(a) (v) > (iv) > (i) > (iii) > (ii)
(b) (v) > (i) > (ii) > (iii) > (iv)
(c) (ii) > (iv) > (iii) > (i) > (v)
(d) (iv) > (iii) > (i) > (ii) > (v)
(e) (v) > (iv) > (iii) > (ii) > (i)

24. Which of the following is the correct sequence of increasing boiling point of the hydrides of group 15 elements?

(a) $NH_3 < PH_3 < AsH_3 < SbH_3 < BiH_3$
(b) $PH_3 < AsH_3 < SbH_3 < BiH_3 < NH_3$
(c) $AsH_3 < PH_3 < NH_3 < SbH_3 < BiH_3$
(d) $PH_3 < AsH_3 < NH_3 < SbH_3 < BiH_3$

25. In which of the following arrangements, is the sequence not strictly according to the property written against it?

(a) $CO_2 < SiO_2 < SnO_2 < PbO_2$: increasing oxidising power
(b) HF < HCl < HBr < HI: increasing acid strength
(c) $NH_3 < PH_3 < AsH_3 < SbH_3$: increasing basic strength
(d) B < C < O < N: increasing first ionisation enthalpy

26. The most stable hydride is

(a) NH_3 (b) PH_3 (c) AsH_3 (d) SbH_3

27. Which of the following statements is wrong?

(a) The stability of the hydrides increases from NH_3 to BiH_3 in group 15 of the periodic table.
(b) Nitrogen cannot form a $d\pi - p\pi$ bond.
(c) A single N–N bond is weaker than a single P–P bond.
(d) N_2O_4 has two resonance structures.

28. The correct order of decreasing thermal stability is,

(a) $NH_3 > PH_3 > AsH_3 > SbH_3$
(b) $PH_3 > NH_3 > AsH_3 > SbH_3$
(c) $AsH_3 > PH_3 > NH_3 > SbH_3$
(d) $SbH_3 > AsH_3 > PH_3 > NH_3$

29. Which of the following exhibits the highest solubility in water?

(a) NH_3 (b) PH_3 (c) AsH_3 (d) SbH_3

30. Which of the following is amphoteric?

(a) CO_2 (b) Sb_2O_3 (c) MgO (d) Mn_2O_3

31. Which of the following oxides of nitrogen is thermally most stable?

(a) N_2O_5 (b) N_2O (c) NO (d) N_2O_3

32. The *p*-block element that forms predominantly a basic oxide is

(a) N (b) P (c) As
(d) Sb (e) Bi

33. Which of the following oxides is least acidic?

(a) P_4O_6 (b) P_4O_{10} (c) As_4O_6 (d) As_4O_{10}

34. The correct order of the acidic nature of oxides is in the order

(a) $NO < N_2O < N_2O_3 < NO_2 < N_2O_5$
(b) $N_2O < NO < N_2O_3 < NO_2 < N_2O$
(c) $N_2O_5 < NO_2 < N_2O_3 < NO < N_2O$
(d) $N_2O_5 < N_2O_3 < NO_2 < NO < N_2O$

35. Which nitrogen trihalide is least basic?

(a) NF_3 (b) NCl_3 (c) NBr_3 (d) NI_3

36. Which of the following is not hydrolysed?

(a) $AsCl_3$ (b) PF_3 (c) $SbCl_3$ (d) NF_3

37. Which of the following compounds does not exist?

(a) $SbCl_3$ (b) $BiCl_5$ (c) $SbCl_5$ (d) $AsCl_5$

38. In compound of type ECl_3, where E = B, P, As or Bi, the angles Cl – E – Cl for different E are in the order

(a) B > P = As = Bi (b) B > P > As > Bi
(c) Bi < P = As = Bi (d) B < P < As < Bi

39. Which of the following halides is most acidic?

(a) PCl_3 (b) $BiCl_3$ (c) $SbCl_3$ (d) CCl_4

40. What will be the resultant products formed when the phosphorus halide PBr_5 splits up?

(a) $[PBr_4]^+$ and Br^- (b) $[PBr_6]^-$ and $[PBr_4]^+$
(c) $[PBr_4]^+$ (d) $[PBr_6]^-$

41. Which element of the nitrogen family produces the maximum number of oxyacids?

(a) N (b) P (c) As (d) Sb

42. Which of the following oxides is the most acidic?

(a) N_2O_5 (b) P_2O_5 (c) Sb_2O_3 (d) Sb_2O_5

43. BCl_3 is a planar molecule whereas NCl_3 is pyramidal because

(a) BCl_3 has no lone pair of electrons but NCl_3 has a lone pair of electrons
(b) B–Cl bond is more polar than N–Cl bond
(c) nitrogen atom is smaller than boron atom
(d) N–Cl bond is more covalent than B–Cl bond

44. Hydrolysis of NCl_3 by H_2O produces
(a) NH_4OH and HOCl (b) NH_2NH_2 and HCl
(c) NH_2OH and HOCl (d) NH_2Cl and HOCl

Dinitrogen, N_2 and its Compounds

45. The dipole moment of NHF_3 is less than NH_3 because:
(a) F is more reactive than H
(b) NH_3 forms associated molecules
(c) the resultant of the bond polarity is less
(d) the resultant of the individual polarities is opposed by the polarity of lone pair

46. The skin turns yellow in contact with conc. HNO_3, because:
(a) proteins are converted into xanthoproteins
(b) water is removed by the acid
(c) skin gets burnt
(d) nitrocellulose is formed

47. By which of the following processes, is pure nitrogen gas is prepared?
(a) $(NH_4)_2Cr_2O_7 \xrightarrow{\Delta}$
(b) $NH_4Cl + NaNO_2 \xrightarrow{\Delta}$
(c) $NH_3 + NaNO_2 \xrightarrow{\Delta}$
(d) $N_2O + Cu \xrightarrow{\Delta}$

48. The compound that does not produce nitrogen gas by thermal decomposition is
(a) $Ba(N_3)_2$ (b) $(NH_4)_2Cr_2O_7$
(c) NH_4NO_2 (d) $(NH_4)_2SO_4$

49. Light blue colour of nitrous acid is due to dissolved
(a) O_2 (b) N_2 (c) N_2O (d) N_2O_3

50. Very pure N_2 can be obtained by
(a) the thermal decomposition of ammonium dichromate
(b) treating the aqueous solution of NH_4Cl with $NaNO_2$
(c) the liquefaction and fractional distillation of liquid air
(d)the thermal decomposition of sodium azide

51. Consider the following compounds
(1) $(NH_4)_2Cr_2O_7$ (2) NH_4NO_2 (3) NH_4VO_3 (4) NH_4NO_2
Which compound(s) yields(s) nitrogen gas upon heating?
(a) 1 and 2 (b) 2 and 3 (c) 3 and 4
(d) 1 and 4 (e) all

52. The compound(s) which generate(s) N_2 gas upon thermal decomposition below 300°C is(are)
(a) NH_4NO_3 (b) $(NH_4)_2Cr_2O_7$
(c) $Ba(N_3)_2$ (d) Mg_3N_2

53. The cyanide ion, CN^- and N_2 are isoelectronic. But in contrast to CN^-, N_2 is chemically inert because of
(a) low bond energy
(b) absence of bond polarity
(c) unsymmetrical electron distribution
(d) presence of more number of electrons in bonding orbitals

54. Nitrogen is a relatively inactive element because
(a) its atom has a stable electronic configuration
(b) it has a low atomic radius
(c) its electronegativity is fairly high
(d) the dissociation energy of its molecule is fairly high

55. Which one of the following can form a chain of three atoms?
(a) N (b) P (c) As (d) Sb

56. The oxidation state of nitrogen is highest in
(a) N_3H (b) NH_2OH (c) N_2H_4 (d) NH_3

57. In NH_4NO_2, the oxidation number of nitrogen will be
(a) +3 (b) +5
(c) –3 and +3 (d) +3 and +5

58. N_2 combines with metals to form
(a) nitride (b) nitrate
(c) nitrite (d) nitrosyl chloride

59. What type of structure does $(NPCl_2)_4$ have?
(a) linear (b) hexagonal
(c) cyclic (d) polymeric

60. The statement true for N_3^- is:
(a) It has a non-linear structure.
(b) It is called a pseudohalogen.
(c) The formal oxidation state of nitrogen in this anion is –1.
(d) It is isoelectronic with NO_2.

61. Which of the following is manufactured from molecular nitrogen by bacteria?
(a) NO_3^- (b) NO_2^-
(c) amino acids (d) ammonia

62. The element which is essential in nitrogen fixation is
(a) zinc (b) copper
(c) molybdenum (d) boron

63. On heating a mixture of NH_4Cl and KNO_2, we get
(a) NH_4NO_3 (b) $KNH_4(NO_3)_2$
(c) N_2 (d) NO

64. Sodium azide on thermal decomposition gives
(a) $Na_3N + N_2$ (b) $Na + N_2$
(c) $NaNO_2 + N_2$ (d) $Na + NH_3$

65. One mol of magnesium nitride on reaction with an excess of water gives
(a) 1 mol of ammonia (b) 1 mol of nitric acid
(c) 2 mol of nitric acid (d) 2 mol of ammonia

66. Ammonia is a Lewis base. It forms complexes with cations. Which one of the following cations does not form complex with ammonia?
(a) Ag^+ (b) Cu^{2+} (c) Cd^{2+} (d) Pb^{2+}

67. Ammonia on reaction with excess of chlorine gives
(a) NCl_3 and HCl (b) N_2 and NH_4Cl
(c) NCl_3 and NH_4Cl (d) N_2 and HCl

68. The hybridised state of N in R_2NH is
(a) sp^3 (b) sp^2 (c) sp (d) dsp^2

69. Blasting of TNT is done by mixing
(a) NH_4Cl (b) NH_4NO_3
(c) NH_4NO_2 (d) $(NH_4)_2SO_4$

70. When plants and animals decay, the organic nitrogen is converted into inorganic nitrogen. The inorganic nitrogen is in the form of
(a) ammonia (b) elements of nitrogen
(c) nitrates (d) nitrides

71. When heated NH_3 is passed over CuO, gas evolved is
(a) N_2 (b) N_2O (c) HNO_3 (d) NO_2

72. Which of the following is the most suitable drying agent for ammonia gas?
(a) calcium oxide (quicklime)
(b) anhydrous calcium chloride
(c) phosphorus pentoxide
(d) conc. sulfuric acid

73. Ammonium dichromate on heating gives
(a) chromium oxide and ammonia
(b) chromium oxide and nitrogen
(c) chromium oxide and nitrogen
(d) chromic acid and ammonia

74. A solution of ammonia in water contains
(a) H^+
(b) OH^-
(c) only NH_4^+
(d) OH^-, NH_4^+ and NH_4OH molecules

75. A mixture of ammonia and air at about 800°C in the presence of Pt gauze (catalytic oxidation of NH_3) forms
(a) N_2O (b) NO (c) NH_2OH (d) N_2O_3

76. Calcium cyanamide on treatment with steam under pressure (cyanide process) gives ammonia and
(a) calcium carbonate (b) calcium hydroxide
(c) calcium oxide (d) calcium bicarbonate

77. When ammonia reacts with sodium hypochlorite, the product containing nitrogen is
(a) N_2 (b) N_2O
(c) NH_2OH (d) $H_2N.NH_2$

78. Which of the following compounds is sparingly soluble in ammonia solution?
(a) AgI (b) AgBr (c) AgCl (d) $CuCl_2$

79. Liquor ammonia bottles are opened only after cooling. This is because
(a) it is a mild explosive
(b) it is a corrosive liquid
(c) it is a lachrymatory
(d) it generates high vapour pressure

80. Consider the following statements concerning N_2H_4.
1. It is an exothermic compound.
2. It burns in air with the evolution of heat.
3. It has kinetic stability.
4. It reduces Fe^{3+} to Fe^{2+} in acidic medium.

Which of the following combinations is correct?
(a) 2 and 3 are correct (b) 1 and 2 are correct
(c) all are correct (d) 3 and 4 are correct
(e) 2, 3 and 4 correct

81. Which one of the following nitrogen oxides is an anhydride of nitric acid?
(a) N_2O_5 (b) N_2O_4 (c) N_2O_3 (d) N_2O

82. Which oxide does not act as a reducing agent?
(a) NO (b) NO_2 (c) N_2O (d) N_2O_5

83. Which of the following oxides of nitrogen is the anhydride of nitrous acid?
(a) NO (b) N_2O_3 (c) N_2O_4 (d) N_2O_5

84. When concentrated H_2SO_4 is added to dry KNO_3, brown fumes evolve. These fumes are due to
(a) SO_2 (b) SO_3 (c) NO_2 (d) NO

85. NO_2 dimerises because
(select the incorrect statement out of the following)
(a) NO_2 is an odd electron molecule. Even electron molecules are more stable. So, NO_2 dimerises to achieve even electron configuration
(b) in NO_2, N has seven electrons in the valence shell and hence is less stable
(c) to achieve more stability, N has the tendency to acquire aqninert gas configuration of eight electrons in the valence shell
(d) to achieve inert gas configuration, NO_2 undergoes dimerisation to form N_2O_4

86. One of the oxidants used with liquid propellants is
(a) ammonium perchlorate
(b) nitrocellulose

(c) sulfuric acid
(d) nitrogen tetroxide (N_2O_4)
(e) phosphorus pentoxide

87. An example of a neutral oxide is
(a) NO (b) CO_2 (c) CaO
(d) ZnO (e) SO_2

88. Which of the following oxides of nitrogen is solid?
(a) NO_2 (b) N_2O (c) N_2O_3 (d) N_2O_5

89. Which statement is wrong for NO?
(a) It is the anhydride of nitrous acid.
(b) Its dipole moment is 0.22 D.
(c) It forms a dimer.
(d) It is paramagnetic.

90. Which of the following oxides of nitrogen contains the N–O–N bond?
(a) dinitrogen oxide (b) nitrogen monoxide
(c) dinitrogen pentoxide (d) dinitrogen trioxide
(e) dinitrogen tetroxide

91. Products formed on heating $Pb(NO_3)_2$ are
(a) PbO, N_2, O_3 (b) $Pb(NO_2)_2$, O_2
(c) PbO, NO_2, O_2 (d) Pb, N_2, O_2

92. NO_2 is a mixed oxide which is proved by the fact that with NaOH, it forms
(a) a nitrite salt
(b) a nitrate salt
(c) a mixture of nitrate and nitrite
(d) ammonia

93. Which of the following metals produces nitrous oxide with dil. HNO_3?
(a) Fe (b) Zn (c) Cu (d) Ag

94. Which oxide does not act as a reducing agent?
(a) NO (b) NO_2 (c) N_2O (d) N_2O_5

95. Which of the following is not correct for N_2O?
(a) It is called laughing gas. Its chemical name is nitrous oxide.
(b) It supports combustion of sulfur.
(c) It is not a linear molecule.
(d) It is the least reactive of all oxides of nitrogen.

96. Nitrogen dioxide is released by heating
(a) $Pb(NO_3)_2$ (b) KNO_3
(c) $NaNO_2$ (d) $NaNO_3$

97. Of the following, which has a three-electron bond in its structure?
(a) nitrous oxide (b) nitric oxide
(c) dinitrogen trioxide (d) nitrogen pentoxide

98. Which one of the following oxides does not form acidic aqueous solution?
(a) N_2O_3 (b) NO_2 (c) N_2O_5 (d) NO

99. Which blue liquid is obtained on reacting equimolar amounts of two gases at −30°C?
(a) N_2O (b) N_2O_3 (c) N_2O_4 (d) N_2O_5

100. The incorrect statements among the following is/are
I. NCl_5 does not exist while PCl_5 does.
II. Lead prefers to form tetravalent compounds.
III. The three C–O bonds are not equal in the carbonate ion.
IV. Both O_2^+ and NO are paramagnetic.
(a) I, III and IV (b) I and IV (c) II and III
(d) I and III (e) IV only

101. Which of the following oxides is diamagnetic?
(a) NO (b) N_2O_4 (c) NO_2 (d) N_2O_5

102. Which of the following is the correct electron dot structure of the N_2O molecule?
(a) $\ddot{\underset{\cdot\cdot}{N}}=N=\ddot{\underset{\cdot\cdot}{O}}$ (b) $:\ddot{N}-N=\ddot{O}:$
(c) $:\ddot{N}=N=\ddot{O}:$ (d) $:N\equiv \overset{+}{N}-\ddot{\underset{\cdot\cdot}{O}}:^-$

103. Action of concentrated nitric acid on metallic tin produces
(a) passive metal (b) stannous nitrate
(c) stannic nitrate
(d) hydrated stannic oxide or metastannic acid

104. Ostwald's process for the manufacture of nitric acid involves
(a) oxidation of N_2 to NO
(b) oxidation of NH_3 to NO by oxygen at 1075 K in the presence of Pt gauze as catalyst
(c) combination of N_2 and H_2
(d) passage of steam over red hot coke

105. Which of the following metal(s) is/are rendered passive on treatment with conc. HNO_3?
(a) iron (b) aluminium
(c) chromium (d) all

106. When copper is heated with dilute nitric acid, the gas formed is
(a) H_2 (b) NO_2 (c) N_2O_3 (d) NO

107. Zinc reacts with cold dil. HNO_3 to give zinc nitrate and
(a) NO_2 (b) NH_4NO_3 (c) NO (d) O_2

108. Which of the following metals, Fe, Zn Pb, Ag and Pt, do not give a metal nitrate on treatment with conc. HNO_3?
(a) Fe and Zn (b) Fe and Pt
(c) Pb, Ag and Pt (d) Fe, Ag and Pt
(e) Fe, Zn and Pt

109. The bond order of the N–O bonds in

(a) 0.33 (b) 1.00 (c) 1.33 (d) 1.50

110. The nitrogen containing compound produced in the reaction of HNO_3 with P_4O_{10}

(a) can also be prepared by the reaction of P_4 and HNO_3
(b) is diamagnetic and reacts with Na metal producing a brown gas
(c) contains one N–N bond
(d) is a colourless gas

111. When PbO_2 reacts with conc.HNO_3 the gas evolved is

(a) NO_2 (b) O_2 (c) N_2 (d) N_2O

112. When tin is treated with concentrated nitric acid

(a) it is converted into stannous nitrate
(b) it is converted into stannic nitrate
(c) it is converted into metastannic acid
(d) it becomes passive

113. Concentrated nitric acid oxidises cane sugar to

(a) CO_2 and H_2O (b) CO and H_2O
(c) CO, CO_2 and H_2O
(d) oxalic acid and water

114. What would happen when a solution of potassium chromate is treated with an excess of dilute nitric acid?

(a) Cr^{3+} and $Cr_2O_7^{2-}$ are formed
(b) $Cr_2O_7^{2-}$ and H_2O are formed
(c) $Cr_2O_7^{2-}$ is reduced to the +3 state of Cr
(d) $Cr_2O_7^{2-}$ is oxidised to the +7 state of Cr

115. Conc. HNO_3 can be stored in a container of

(a) Al (b) Sn (c) Cu (d) Zn

116. Which gas is obtained when urea is heated with HNO_2?

(a) N_2 (b) H_2 (c) O_2 (d) NH_3

117. An aqueous solution of nitrous acid (HNO_2) free of salts, can be obtained from the reaction

(a) $Ba(NO_2)_2 + H_2SO_4 \rightarrow$
(b) $NaNO_2 + H_2SO_4 \xrightarrow{\text{cold}}$
(c) $NH_4NO_2 + H_2SO_4 \rightarrow$
(d) $KNO_3 + HNO_3 \rightarrow$

118. The metal which does not form ammonium nitrate by reaction with dilute nitric acid is

(a) Al (b) Fe (c) Pb (d) Mg

119. Which of the following statements is true?

(a) H_3PO_3 is a stronger acid than H_2SO_3.
(b) In the aqueous medium, HF is a stronger acid than HCl.
(c) $HClO_4$ is a weaker acid than $HClO_3$.
(d) HNO_3 is a stronger acid than HNO_2.

120. A filter paper soaked in salt X turns brown when exposed to HNO_3 vapour. The salt X is

(a) KCl (b) KBr (c) KI (d) K_2SO_4

Phosphorus and its Compounds

121. On heating NH_4NO_3 strongly, which of the following is obtained?

(a) NO_2 (b) NH_3 (c) N_2 (d) N_2O

122. One of the products of the following reaction is

$KCNO + (NH_4)_2 SO_4 \xrightarrow{\Delta}$

(a) NH_4NO_3 (b) NH_2CONH_2
(c) N_2 (d) NO_2

123. Ammonia forms the complex ion $[Cu(NH_3)_4]^{2+}$ with copper ions in the alkaline solution but not in acidic solution. What is the reason?

(a) In acidic solutions, hydration protects the copper ions.
(b) In acidic solutions, protons coordinate with ammonia molecules forming MH_4^+ ions and NH_3 molecules are not available
(c) In alkaline solutions, insoluble $Cu(OH)_2$ is precipitated which is soluble in excess of any alkali.
(d) Copper hydroxide is an amphoteric substance.

124. Which hydride possesses the maximum complex forming nature?

(a) NH_3 (b) PH_3 (c) BiH_3 (d) SbH_3

125. The most common minerals of phosphorus are

(a) hydroxyapatite and kernite
(b) colemanite and fluorapatite
(c) borax and fluorapatite
(d) hydroxyapatite and colemanite
(e) hydroxyapatite and fluorapatite

126. The reduction of calcined phosphate rock (bone ash) with coke and sand in an electric arc furnace at 1773 K gives a number of products including

(a) phosphorus (b) silicon
(c) calcium hydride (d) calcium oxide

127. The total number of lone pairs of electrons present, the total number of single bonds formed and the number of bonds formed by each P atom in a P_4 molecule respectively are

(a) 2, 4, 4 (b) 6, 3, 6 (c) 4, 6, 3 (d) 8, 5, 5

128. Red P can be obtained from white P by

(a) heating it with a catalyst in an inert atmosphere
(b) distilling it in an inert atmosphere
(c) dissolving it in CS_2 and crystallising
(d) melting it and pouring the liquid into water

129. Which of the following is not correct? White phosphorus (P_4) has

(a) six P–P single bonds
(b) four P–P single bonds
(c) four lone pairs of electrons
(d) PPP angle is 60°

130. Which phosphorus reacts with KOH solution to produce phosphine gas?
(a) white phosphorus (b) red phosphorus
(c) both (a) and (b) (d) none of the above

131. Each of the following is true for white and red phosphorus except that they
(a) are both soluble in CS_2
(b) can be oxidised by heating in air
(c) consists of the same kind of atoms
(d) can be converted into one another

132. Of the different allotropes of phosphorus, the one which is most reactive is
(a) violet phosphorus (b) scarlet phosphorus
(c) red phosphorus (d) white phosphorus

133. The percentage of *p*-character in the orbitals forming P–P bonds on P_4 is
(a) 25 (b) 33 (c) 50 (d) 75

134. Which of the following properties of white phosphorus are shared by red phosphorus?
(a) it shows phosphorescence in air
(b) it reacts with hot aqueous naoh to give phosphine
(c) it dissolves in carbon disulfide
(d) it burns when heated in air

135. Bone black is a polymorphic form of
(a) phosphorus (b) sulfur
(c) carbon (d) nitrogen

136. Which element exists as a solid at 25°C and 1 atmospheric pressure among the following
(a) Br (b) Cl (c) Hg (d) P

137. In the reaction $P_4 + 3\ KOH + 3\ H_2O \rightarrow PH_3 + 3\ KH_2PO_2$ phosphorus is
(a) reduced only (b) oxidised only
(c) both oxidised and reduced
(d) neither oxidised nor reduced

138. The oxidation state of phosphorus in $Ba(H_2PO_2)_2$ is
(a) +3 (b) +2 (c) +1 (d) –1

139. The pair in which phosphorus atoms have a formal oxidation state of +3 is
(a)orthophosphorous and pyrophosphorous acids
(b)pyrophosphorous and hypophosphoric acids
(c) orthophosphorous and hypophosphoric acids
(d) pyrophosphorous and pyrophosphoric acids

140. The reaction of elemental P_4 in aqueous NaOH gives
(a) PH_3, NaH_2PO_2 (b) PH_3, Na_2PO_4
(c) $NaHPO_4$, Na_2PO_4 (d) Na_3P, Na_3PO_4

141. Atoms in a P_4 molecule of white phosphorus are arranged regularly in the following way
(a) at the corners of a cube
(b) at the corners of an octahedron
(c) at the corners of a tetrahedron
(d) at the centre and corners of a tetrahedron

142. An element forms a solid oxide which when dissolved in water forms an acidic solution. The element is
(a) neon (b) sodium
(c) phosphorus (d) sulfur

143. Nitric acid oxidises phosphorus to
(a) $H_2P_2O_7$ (b) H_3PO_3 (c) P_2O_5 (d) H_3PO_4

144. Ordinary phosphine is spontaneously inflammable due to the presence of
(a) vapours of P_4 (b) vapours of P_2H_6
(c) vapours of P_2H_4 (d) moisture

145. PH_4I + NaOH forms
(a) PH_3 (b) NH_3 (c) P_4O_6 (d) P_4O_{10}

146. One mol of calcium phosphide on reaction with excess of water gives
(a) one mol of phosphine
(b) two mol of phosphoric acid
(c) two mol of phosphine
(d) one mol of phosphorus oxide

147. Phosphine is prepared by the action of
(a) P and H_2SO_4 (b) P and NaOH
(c) P and H_2S (d) P and HNO_3

148. The substance used in smoke screens is
(a) sodium chloride (b) zinc phosphate
(c) calcium phosphide (d) calcium fluoride
(e) calcium phosphate

149. P in both PH_4^+ and PH_3 is sp^3-hybridised but
(a) the bond angle in PH_4^+ is higher than in PH_3
(b) the bond angle in PH_4^+ is lower than in PH_3
(c) the bond angle in both PH_4^+ and PH_3 is equal
(d) the shape of PH_4^+ is square planar whereas the shape of PH_3 is tetrahedral

150. Which statementis not correct?
(a) Hypophosphorous acid reduces silver nitrate to silver.
(b) In the solid state, PCl_5 exists as $[PCl_4]^+ [PCl_6]^-$.
(c) Pure phosphine is non-inflammable.
(d) Phosphorus acid on heating disproportionates to give metaphosphoric acid and phosphine.

151. When aluminium phosphide is treated with dil. sulfuric acid

(a) SO_2 is liberated (b) PH_3 is evolved
(c) H_3S is evolved (d) H_2 is evolved

152. Which is true with regard to the properties of PH_3?

(a) PH_3 is not very stable.
(b) PH_3 is neutral towards litmus.
(c) PH_3 has a fishy smell.
(d) PH_3 is insoluble in water.

153. What may be expected to happen when phosphine gas is mixed with chlorine gas?

(a)the mixture only cools down
(b) PCl_3 and HCl are formed and the mixture warms up
(c) PCl_5 and HCl are formed and the mixture cools down
(d) $PH_3.Cl_2$ is formed with warming up

154. Which of the following has the least covalent P–H bond?

(a) PH_3 (b) P_2H_6 (c) P_2H_5 (d) PH_6^+

155. The correct order of decreasing Lewis acid strength of the trichlorides of the group 15 elements is

(a) $AsCl_3 > PCl_3 > BiCl_3 > SbCl_3$
(b) $PCl_3 > AsCl_3 > SbCl_3 > BiCl_3$
(c) $NCl_3 > PCl_3 > AsCl_3 > SbCl_3$
(d) $SbCl_3 > BiCl_3 > PCl_3 > AsCl_3$

156. When PCl_5 is heated, the products obtained are

(a) $P + Cl_2$ (b) $PCl_3 + Cl_2$
(c) $PCl_4^- + PCl_2^+$ (d) No change

157. Sulfuric acid reacts with PCl_5 to give

(a) thionyl chloride (b) sulfuric monochloride
(c) sulfuryl chloride (d) sulfur tetrachloride

158. Hydrolysis of PCl_5 gives

(a) H_3PO_3 (b) HPO_3
(c) H_3PO_2 (d) H_3PO_4

159. Reaction of PCl_3 and PhMgBr would give

(a) bromobenzene (b) chlorobenzene
(c) triphenylphosphine (d) dichlorobenzene

160. PCl_3 reacts with water to form

(a) PH_3 (b) H_3PO_3, HCl
(c) $POCl_3$ (d) H_3PO_4

161. Which of the following sets of properties belongs to PCl_5?

(a) sp^3, tetrahedral, 4 valence shell pairs of electrons
(b) sp^3d, trigonal bipyramidal, 5 valence shell pairs of electrons
(c) sp^3d^2, octahedral, 6 valence shell pairs of electrons
(d) sp^3d, square planar, 4 valence shell pairs of electrons

162. Phosphorus reacts with chlorine gas to give a colourless liquid, which fumes in moist air to produce HCl and

(a) $POCl_3$ (b) H_3PO_3 (c) PH_3 (d) H_3PO_4

163. The acid obtained when P_4O_6 reacts with water is

(a) H_3PO_2 (b) H_3PO_3 (c) H_3PO_4 (d) $H_4P_2O_7$

164. The number of P–O bonds in P_4O_{10} is

(a) 16 (b) 12 (c) 8 (d) 4

165. Of the following compounds, the most acidic is

(a) As_2O_3 (b) P_2O_5 (c) Sb_2O_3 (d) Bi_2O_3

166. $HNO_3 + P_2O_5 \rightarrow A + B$

A is an oxyacid of phosphorus and B is an oxide of nitrogen. A and B respectively are

(a) H_3PO_4, N_2O_3 (b) HPO_3, N_2O_3
(c) HPO_3, N_2O_5 (d) H_3PO_3, N_2O_5

167. In which compound is the oxidation state of phosphorus +4?

(a) P_4O_{11} (b) P_4O_8 (c) P_4O_6 (d) H_3PO_4

168. In the reaction, P_2O_5 + 3 CaO $\rightarrow$ $Ca_3(PO_4)_2$;P_2O_5 acts as

(a) acidic flux (b) basic flux
(c) basic impurity (d) acidic impurity

169. In the reaction HNO_3 + $P_4O_{10} \rightarrow$ $4HPO_3$ + X, the product X is

(a) N_2O_3 (b) N_2O_5 (c) NO_2 (d) H_2O

170. In the electrothermal process, the compound displaced by silica from calcium phosphate is

(a) calcium (b) phosphine
(c) phosphorus (d) phosphorus pentoxide

171. P_4O_{10} is the anhydride of

(a) H_3PO_2 (b) H_3PO_3
(c) H_3PO_4 (d) $H_4P_2O_7$

172. The number of P–OH, P–H and P=O bonds present in H_3PO_4 are respectively

(a) 3, 0, 1 (b) 2, 1, 1 (c) 2, 0, 2 (d) 3, 1, 0

173. The acid which forms two series of salts is

(a) H_3PO_4 (b) H_3PO_3 (c) H_3BO_3 (d) H_3PO_2

174. The equivalent weight of phosphoric acid (H_3PO_4) in the reaction $NaOH + H_3PO_4 \rightarrow NaH_2PO_4 + H_2O$ is

(a) 25 (b) 49 (c) 59 (d) 98

175. The monobasic acid which exists in polymeric form is

(a) H_3PO_4 (b) H_3PO_3 (c) H_3PO_2 (d) HPO_3

176. Pick out the stronger reducing agent among the following oxyacids of phosphorus

(a) hypophosphorous acid (b) phosphorous acid
(c) hypophosphoric acid (d) pyrophosphorous acid
(e) phosphoric acid

177. Arrange the following oxoacids of phosphorus in increasing order of their reducing behaviour H_3PO_2, H_3PO_3, H_3PO_4

(a) $H_3PO_4 < H_3PO_3 < H_3PO_2$
(b) $H_3PO_3 < H_3PO_2 < H_3PO_4$
(c) $H_3PO_2 < H_3PO_3 < H_3PO_4$
(d) $H_3PO_4 < H_3PO_2 < H_3PO_3$

178. The oxoacid of phosphorus that reduces silver nitrate into metallic silver is

(a) H_3PO_2 (b) $H_4P_2O_6$ (c) H_3PO_4
(d) $H_4P_2O_7$ (e) $(HPO_3)_n$

179. The maximum number of P–H bonds are contained in which of the following molecules?

(a) H_3PO_2 (b) H_3PO_3 (c) H_3PO_4 (d) $H_4P_2O_7$

180. The basicity of pyrophosphorous acid is

(a) 2 (b) 4 (c) 1 (d) 5 (e) 3

181. The oxidation state of P in cyclotrimetaphosphoric acid is

(a) +3 (b) +5 (c) –3 (d) +2 (e) –2

182. The correct arrangement of the following acids of phosphorus in the increasing order of oxidation state of phosphorus is

(a) hypophosphorus acid < orthophosphorous acid < pyrophosphoric acid
(b) hypophosphorous acid < pyrophosphoric acid = orthophosphorous acid
(c) pyrophosphoric acid < hypophosphorous acid < orthophosphorous acid
(d) pyrophosphoric acid < orthophosphorous acid < hypophosphorous acid

183. Given are H_3PO_2, H_3PO_3, H_3PO_4 and $H_4P_2O_7$.
Which of the above oxoacids results into two series of salts?

(a) H_3PO_2 (b) H_3PO_3
(c) H_3PO_4 (d) $H_4P_2O_7$

184. The correct formula of salt formed by the neutralisation of hypophosphorous acid with NaOH is

(a) Na_3PO_3 (b) Na_3PO_2
(c) Na_2HPO_2 (d) NaH_2PO_2

185. As the number of –OH groups increases in hypophosporous acid, phosphorous acid and phosphoric acid, the acidic strength

(a) increase (b) decreases
(c) remains nearly same
(d) remains appropriately same

186. If phosphoric acid is allowed to react with sufficient quantity of NaOH, the product obtained is

(a) $NaHPO_3$ (b) Na_2HPO_4
(c) NaH_2PO_4 (d) Na_3PO_4

187. Which is not an acid salt?

(a) NaH_2PO_3 (b) NaH_2PO_2
(c) $Na_3HP_2O_6$ (d) $Na_4P_2O_7$

188. Which one is correct statement?

(a) Basicity of H_3PO_4 and H_3PO_4 is 3 and 3 respectively
(b) Acidity of H_3PO_4 and H_3PO_4 is 3 and 3 respectively
(c) Acidity of H_3PO_4 and H_3PO_3 is 3 and 2 respectively
(d) Basicity of H_3PO_4 and H_3PO_4 is 3 and 2 respectively

189. The oxyacid of phosphorus, in which phosphorus has the lowest oxidation state is

(a) hypophosphorous acid (b) orthophosphoric acid
(c) pyrophosphoric acid (d) metaphosphoric acid

190. Which of the following is a cyclic metaphosphoric acid?

(a) $H_5P_3O_{10}$ (b) $H_6P_4O_{13}$
(c) $H_5P_5O_{15}$ (d) $H_7P_5O_{16}$

191. The number of P–O–P bonds in cyclic metaphosphoric acid is

(a) zero (b) two (c) three (d) four

192. The structural formula of hypophosphorous acid is

(a) P with =O, H, H, OH
(b) P with –O, H, OH, OH
(c) P with →O, HO, OH, OH
(d) P with =O, HO, OOH, OH

193. Which salt can be classified as an acid salt?

(a) Na_2SO_4 (b) BiOCl
(c) Pb(OH)Cl (d) Na_2HPO_4

194. When orthophosphoric acid is heated to 600°C, the product formed is

(a) phosphine, PH_3
(b) phosphorus pentoxide, P_2O_5
(c) phosphorous acid, H_3PO_3
(d) metaphosphoric acid, HPO_3

195. The order of the oxidation state of the phosphorus atom in H_3PO_2, H_3PO_4, H_3PO_3 and $H_4P_2O_6$ is

(a) $H_3PO_4 > H_3PO_2 > H_3PO_3 > H_4P_2O_6$
(b) $H_3PO_2 > H_3PO_3 > H_4P_2O_6 > H_3PO_4$
(c) $H_3PO_3 > H_3PO_2 > H_3PO_4 > H_4P_2O_6$
(d) $H_3PO_4 > H_4P_2O_6 > H_3PO_3 > H_3PO_3$

196. The total number of compounds having at least one bridging oxo group among the molecules given below is ______

N_2O_3, N_2O_5, P_4O_6, P_4O_7, $H_4P_2O_5$, $H_5P_3O_{10}$, $H_2S_2O_3$, $H_2S_2O_5$

(a) 6 (b) 4 (c) 5 (d) 7

197. Phosphide ion has an electronic structure similar to that of the

(a) nitride ion (b) fluoride ion
(c) sodium ion (d) chloride ion

198. The role of phosphate in detergent powder is to

(a) control the pH level of the detergent water mixture
(b) remove Ca^{2+} and Mg^{2+} ions from the water that cause the hardnessof water
(c) provide whiteness to the fabrics
(d) form solid detergent as phosphate-less detergents are liquid in nature

199. The pentavalency in phosphorus is more stable as compared to that of nitrogen even though they belong to the same group. It is due to

(a) inert nature of nitrogen
(b) reactivity of phosphorus
(c) larger size of phosphorus atom
(d) dissimilar electronic configuration

200. In an organic compound, phosphorus is estimated as

(a) $Mg_2P_2O_7$ (b) $Mg_3(PO_4)_2$
(c) H_3PO_4 (d) P_2O_5

201. Ammonia and phosphine resemble each other in:

(a) solubility in water (b) forming salt with acid
(c) stability (d) reducing character

202. The oxide which is the anhydride of orthophosphoric acid is

(a) P_4O_{10} (b) P_2O_5 (c) P_4O_6 (d) P_2O_3

203. Phosphorus pentoxide finds use as

(a) an oxidising agent (b) a reducing agent
(c) a bleaching agent (d) a dehydrating agent

204. Number of sigma bonds in P_4O_{10}

(a) 14 (b) 16 (c) 17 (d) 10

205. The species that is not hydrolysed in water is

(a) P_4O_{10} (b) BaO_2 (c) Mg_3N_2 (d) CaC_2

206. When conc. H_2SO_4 is heated with P_2O_5, the acid is converted to

(a) sulfur trioxide (b) sulfur dioxide
(c) sulfur
(d) a mixture of sulfur dioxide and sulfur trioxide

Fertilisers

207. The oxidising property of nitric acid is due to:

(a) its concentration
(b) the positive valency of N
(c) its dilution
(d) the unstability of its molecule and the presence of nitrogen in its highest state of oxidation

208. Which is the best phosphatic fertiliser?

(a) superphosphate (b) triple superphosphate
(c) phosphatic slag (d) none of the above

209. Superphosphate of lime is a mixture of

(a) $Ca(H_2PO_4)_2.H_2O + CaCl_2.2H_2O$
(b) $Ca_3(PO_4)_2.H_2O + CaCl_2.2H_2O$
(c) $Ca_3(PO_4)_2.H_2O + 2\ CaSO_4.2H_2O$
(d) $Ca(H_2PO_4)_2.H_2O + 2\ CaSO_4.2H_2O$

210. Which of the following potash fertilisers provides maximum potassium (in terms of K_2O) to soil?

(a) muriate of potash (b) sulfate of potash
(c) nitrate of potash (d) carbonate of potash

211. When equal weights of the two fertilisers urea and ammonium, it has

(a) less nitrogen than ammonium sulfate
(b) as much nitrogen as ammonium sulfate
(c) twice the amount of nitrogen present in ammonium sulfate
(d) more than twice the amount of nitrogen present in ammonium sulfate

212. A neutral fertiliser among the following is

(a) CAN (b) ammonium sulfate
(c) ammonium nitrate (d) urea

213. Urea is preferred to ammonium sulfate as a nitrogenous fertiliser because

(a) it is more soluble in water
(b) it is cheaper than ammonium sulfate
(c) it is quite stable
(d) it does not cause acidity in the soil

214. Which of the following is a nitrogenous fertiliser?

(a) bone meal (b) Thomas meal
(c) nitrophosphate (d) ammonium sulfate

Final Preparation

215. Which of the following is the most basic oxide?

(a) SeO_2 (b) Al_2O_3 (c) Sb_2O_3 (d) Bi_2O_3

216. Which of the following trihalides of P is least acidic?

(a) PF_3 (b) PCl_3 (c) PI_3 (d) PBr_3

217. Among the following species, identify the isostructural pairs.

NF_3, NO_3^-, BF_3, H_3O^+, HN_3
(a) [NF_3, NO_3^-] and [BF_3, H_3O^+]
(b) [NF_3 HN_3] and [NO_3^-, BF_3]
(c) [NF_3, H_3O^+] and [NO_3^-, BF_3]
(d) [NF_3, H_3O^+] and [HN_3, BF_3]

218. The bond angle in $PH_3$is less than the bond angle in PF_3. This is attributed to
(a) enhanced repulsion due to the presence ofa double bond in PF_3
(b) increased bond pair–bond pair repulsion due to the multiple bond
(c) both (a) and (b)
(d) displacement of electron cloud in P–F bond towards the F in PF_3

219. When excess of water is added to $BiCl_3$ solution in HCl,
(a) ionisation of $BiCl_3$ is increased
(b) a white precipitate of $Bi(OH)_3$ is obtained
(c) $BiCl_3$ is hydrolysed to give a white precipitate of BiOCl
(d) $BiCl_3$ is precipitated

220. Pure nitrogen is prepared in the laboratory by heating a mixture of
(a) $NH_4OH + NaCl$ (b) $NH_4NO_3 + NaCl$
(c) $NH_4Cl + NaOH$ (d) $NH_4Cl + NaNO_2$

221. The gas obtained when bleaching powder is treated with a warm concentrated solution of NH_3 is
(a) Cl_2 (b) N_2 (c) NO (d) H_2

222. On heating ammonium dichromate and barium azide separately we get
(a) N_2in both cases
(b) N_2 with ammonium dichromate and NO with barium azide
(c) N_2O with ammonium dichromate and N_2 with barium azide
(d) N_2O with ammonium dichromate and NO_2 with barium azide

223. Which of the following substances can be used to remove nitrogen from air?
(a) phosphorus (b) magnesium
(c) calcium chloride (d) conc. H_2SO_4

224. An element (X) forms compounds of the formula XCl_3. X_2O_5 and Ca_3X_2 but does not form XCl_5. Which of the following is the element X?
(a) B (b) Al (c) N (d) P

225. The product obtained as a result of a reaction of nitrogen with CaC_2 is
(a) $CaCN_3$ (b) Ca_2CN (c) $CaCN_2$ (d) CaCN

226. The reaction $3\ CuO + 2\ NH_3 \rightarrow 3\ Cu + 3\ H_2O + N_2$ suggests that NH_3
(a) behaves as a base
(b) acts as an acid
(c) acts as an oxidising agent
(d) acts as a reducing agent

227. A substance soluble in ammonia is
(a) $Al(OH)_3$ (b) $Fe(OH)_3$
(c) $Cr(OH)_3$ (d) $Cu(OH)_2$

228. Liquid ammonia and liquor ammonia are respectively
(a) ammonium hydroxide and a solution of NH_3 in alcohol
(b) liquefied ammonia gas and concentrated solution of NH_3 in water
(c) a solution of NH_3 in alcohol, and ammonium hydroxide
(d) concentrated solution of NH_3 in water and liquefied ammonia gas

229. In which of the following is the bond angle maximum?
(a) NH_3 (b) NH_4^+ (c) PCl_3 (d) SCl_2

230. Which of the following order about their basic strength is correct?
(a) $NH_3 < NH_2OH < HN_3 < NH_2NH_2$
(b) $NH_2OH < HN_3 < NH_2NH_2 < NH_3$
(c) $HN_3 < NH_3 < NH_2OH < NH_2NH_2$
(d) $HN_3 < NH_2OH < NH_2NH_2 < NH_3$

231. The hydride of nitrogen which is acidic is
(a) NH_3 (b) N_2H_4 (c) N_2H_2 (d) N_3H

232. Which of the following does not give NO_2 on heating?
(a) KNO_3 (b) $Pb(NO_3)_2$
(c) $Cu(NO_3)_2$ (d) $AgNO_3$

233. The bonds present in N_2O_5 are
(a) only ionic (b) covalent and coordinate
(c) only covalent (d) covalent, ionic

234. The correct order of Ncompounds in its decreasing order of oxidation states is
(a) HNO_3, NO, N_2, NH_4Cl
(b) HNO_3, NO, NH_4Cl, N_2
(c) NH_4Cl, N_2, NO, HNO_3
(d) NHO_3, NH_4Cl, NO, N_2

235. $[Fe(H_2O)_5NO]^{2+}$ is a complex formed during the brown ring test for NO_3^- ion. In this complex,
(a) there are three unpaired electrons so that its magnetic moment is 3.89 B.M.
(b) NO transfers its electron to Fe^{2+} so that iron is as Fe(I) and NO as NO^+
(c) the colour is because of charge transfer
(d) all of the above statements are correct

236. A compound (A) forms an unstable pale blue coloured solution in water which rapidly decomposes even in the cold. The solution acts as a reducing agent and decolourises bromine water. It also oxidises $SnCl_2$ in dil. HCl solution. It also shows complex forming ability. The compound (A) is

(a) HNO_3 (b) HNO_2 (c) $CuSO_4$ (d) N_2O_3

237. The O–N–O bond angle is maximum in

(a) NO_3^- (b) NO_2^- (c) NO_2 (d) NO_2^+

238. In which of the following molecules/ions BF_3, NO_2^-, NH_2^- and H_2O, isthe central atom sp^2 hybridised?

(a) BF_3 and NO_2^- (b) NO_2^- and NH_2^-
(c) NH_2^- and H_2O (d) NO_2^- and H_2O

239. Which of the two ions from the list given below have the geometry that is explained by the same hybridisation of orbitals—NO_2^-, NO_3^-, NH_2^-, NH_4^+, SCN^-?

(a) NO_2^- and NH_2^- (b) NO_2^- and NO_3^-
(c) NH_4^+ and NO_3^- (d) SCN^- and NH_2^-

240. The oxidising property of nitric acid is due to

(a) its concentration
(b) the positive valency of N
(c) its dilution
(d) presence of nitrogen in its highest oxidation state

241. Nitrogen forms N_2 but phosphorus is converted into P_4 from P_2 because the

(a) triple bond is present between phosphorus atoms
(b) $p\pi - p\pi$ bonding is weak
(c) $p\pi - p\pi$ bonding is strong
(d) multiple bond is formed easily

242. In the nitrogen family, the H–M–H bond angle in the hydrides gradually becomes closer to 90° on going from N to Sb. This shows that gradually

(a) the basic strength of the hydrides increases
(b) almost pure *p*orbitals are used for M–H bonding
(c) the bond energies of M–H bonds increases
(d) the bond pairs of electrons become nearer to the central atom

243. The following are some statements related to group 15 hydrides.

I. Reducing property increases from NH_3 to BiH_3.
II. Tendency to donate a lone pair decreases from NH_3 to BiH_3.
III. The thermal stability of the hydrides decreases from NH_3 to BiH_3.
IV. The bond angle of the hydrides decreases from NH_3 to BiH_3.

The correct statements are

(a) I, II, III and IV (b) I, III and IV
(c) I, II and IV (d) I and IV

244. Amongst the following, the most stable pentoxide is

(a) As_2O_5 (b) N_2O_5 (c) P_2O_5 (d) Sb_2O_5

245. Concentrated nitric acid on long standing develops a brownish yellow colour which is due to the presence of

(a) NO (b) N_2O (c) NO_2 (d) N_2O_4

246. In the NO_3^- ion, the number of bond pairs and lone pairs of electrons on the nitrogen atom are

(a) 2, 2 (b) 3,1 (c) 1, 3 (d) 4, 0

247. The mixture of conc. HCl and HNO_3 made in 3 : 1 ratio (aqua regia) contains

(a) ClO_2 (b) NOCl (c) NCl_3 (d) N_2O_4

248. When nitric acid reacts with nitric oxide, a gas is released which converts H_2S into

(a) SO_4^{2-} (b) S^{2-} (c) S (d) $S_2O_3^{2-}$

249. Some of the properties of the two species, NO_3^- and H_3O^+ are described below. Which one of these is correct?

(a) Dissimilar in hybridisation for the central atom with different structure.
(b) Isostructural with same hybridisation for the central atom.
(c) Isostructural with different hybridisation for the central atom.
(d) Similar in hybridisation for the central atom with different structures.

250. Ammonium salts are oxidised in the soil to nitrites by:

(a) denitritying bacteria (b) nitrifying bacteria
(c) ammonifying bacteria (d) nitrosifying bacteria

251. In the preparation of HNO_3 we get NO gas by catalytic oxidation of ammonia. The moles of NO produced by the oxidation of two moles of NH_3 will be

(a) 2 (b) 3 (c) 4 (d) 6

252. Which of the following leaves no residue on heating?

(a) $Pb(NO_3)_2$ (b) NH_4NO_3
(c) $Cu(NO_3)_2$ (d) $NaNO_3$

253. The brown ring test for NO_2^- and NO_3^- is due to the formation of complex ion with a formula

(a) $[Fe(H_2O)_6]^{2+}$ (b) $[Fe(NO)(CN)_5]^{2+}$
(c) $[Fe(H_2O)_5NO]^{2+}$ (d) $[Fe(H_2O)(NO)_5]^{2+}$

254. Which of the nitrates on strong heating leaves the metal as the residue?

(a) $AgNO_3$ (b) $Pb(NO_3)_2$
(c) $Cu(NO_3)_2$ (d) $Al(NO_3)_3$

255. By the action of hot conc. H_2SO_4, phosphorus changes to

(a) phosphorous acid (b) orthophosphoric acid
(c) metaphosphoric acid (d) pyrophosphoric acid

256. Cold fire and phossy jaw are both related to
(a) white P (b) red P (c) PH_3 (d) P_2O_5

257. The sides of the match box have a coating of
(a) potassium chlorate and red lead
(b) potassium chlorate and antimony sulfide
(c) antimony sulfide and red phosphorus + sand powder
(d) antimony sulfide and red lead

258. The mixture used for the tips of the matchsticks is
(a) S + K (b) Sb_2S_3
(c) $K_2Cr_2O_7$ + S + red P (d) $K_2Cr_2O_7$ + K + S

259. Phosphine is not obtained by the reaction when
(a) white P is heated with NaOH
(b) red P is heated with NaOH
(c) Ca_3P_2 reacts with water
(d) P_4O_6 is boiled with water

260. The compound which has a molecular nature in the gas phase but is ionic in the solid state is
(a) PCl_5 (b) CCl_4 (c) PCl_3 (d) $POCl_3$

261. In the compounds of the type POX_3, P atoms show multiple bonding of the type
(a) $p\pi$–$p\pi$ (b) $d\pi$–$d\pi$
(c) $p\pi$–$d\pi$ (d) none of these

262. The number of P–O–P bonds/bridges in the structure of phosphorus pentoxide and phosphorus trioxide are respectively
(a) 6, 6 (b) 5, 5 (c) 5, 6 (d) 6, 5

263. Consider the sequence of oxides: Na_2O, SiO_2, P_4O_{10}. Which factor decreases from Na_2O to SiO_2 and also from SiO_2 to P_4O_{10}?
(a) covalent character
(b) melting point
(c) pH when mixed with water
(d) solubility in aqueous alkali

264. In the PO_4^{3-} ion, the formal charge on each oxygen atom and the P–O bond order respectively are
(a) –0.75, 1.25 (b) –3, 1,25
(c) –0.75, 1.0 (d) –0.75, 0.6

265. There is very little difference in acid strength in the series H_3PO_4, H_3PO_3 and H_3PO_2 because
(a) phosphorus in these acids exists in different oxidation states
(b) the number of unprotonated oxygen atoms responsible for an increase of acidity due to inductive effect remains the same
(c) phosphorus is not a highly electronegative element
(d) phosphorus oxides are less basic

266. In the given reaction,

$$H_3PO_2 + CuSO_4 \rightarrow \underset{\text{(Red ppt.)}}{X} + H_3PO_4 + H_2SO_4$$

the red precipitate (X) is
(a) Cu (b) Cu_2O (c) CuO (d) Cu_2H_2

267. The oxidation states of P in $H_4P_2O_5$, $H_4P_2O_6$ and $H_4P_2O_7$ are respectively
(a) +3, +4, +5 (b) +3, +5, +4
(c) +5, +3, +4 (d) +5, +4, +3

268. Which of the following statements is not valid for the oxoacids of phosphorus?
(a) Orthophosphoric acid is used in the manufacture of triple phosphate.
(b) Hypophosphorous acid is a diprotic acid.
(c) All oxoacids contain tetrahedral four coordinated phosphorus.
(d) All oxoacids contain at least one P=O unit and one P–OH group.

269. Which is the correct statement for the given acids?
(a) Phosphinic acid is a monoprotic acid while phosphonic acid is a diprotic acid.
(b) Phosphinic acid is a diprotic acid while phosphonic acid is a monoprotic acid.
(c) Both are diprotic.
(d) Both are triprotic.

270. Which of the following statements is correct?
(a) Zeolites have a more closed structure than feldspar.
(b) $H_4As_2O_7$ is an ortho acid.
(c) Pseudo-alum does not have Na^+ and K^+.
(d) Superphospahte of lime is $4Ca(H_2PO_4)_2$.

271. The strength of potash fertilisers is determined on the basis of the percentage of
(a) K_2O (b) K (c) K_2CO_3 (d) KNO_3

MATCH THE FOLLOWING

272.

Column I	Column II
(A) Laughing gas	(p) SbF_3
(B) Swart's reagent	(q) P_4S_3
(C) Vortex ring	(r) N_2O
(D) Chemical used in strike anywhere matches	(s) P_2O_5

(a) (A)—(p); (B)—(q); (C)—(r); (D)—(s)
(b) (A)—(q); (B)—(R); (C)—(s);(D)—(p)
(c) (A)—(r); (B)—(q); (C)—(p); (D)—(s)
(d) (A)—(r); (B)—(p); (C)—(s); (D)—(q)

273.

Column I	Column II
(A) N_2O	(p) Brown coloured gas
(B) NO_2	(q) Blue coloured liquid at 243 K
(C) N_2O_3	(r) White crystalline solid
(D) N_2O_5	(s) Colourless gas, produces hysterical laughter when inhaled

(a) (A)—(s); (B)—(p); (C)—(q); (D)—(r)
(b) (A)—(p); (B)—(q); (C)—(r); (D)—(s)
(c) (A)—(q); (B)—(r); (C)—(s); (D)—(p)
(d) (A)—(r); (B)—(s); (C)—(p); (D)—(q)

274.

Column I	Column II
(A) H_3PO_3	(p) —3
(B) Ca_3P_2	(q) +5
(C) $POCl_3$	(r) +3
(D) NaH_2PO_2	(s) +1

(a) (A)—(p); (B)—(q); (C)—(r); (D)—(s)
(b) (A)—(q); (B)—(r); (C)—(s); (D)—(p)
(c) (A)—(r); (B)—(p); (C)—(q); (D)—(s)
(d) (A)—(s); (B)—(q); (C)—(r); (D)—(r)

ASSERTION REASON

Directions: In each of the following questions, a statement of Assertion (A) is given followed by a corresponding statement of Reason (R) just below it. Of the statements, mark the correct answer as

(a) if both the assertion and reason are true and the reason is the correct explanation of the assertion.
(b) if both the assertion and reason are true but the reason is not the correct explanation of assertion
(c) if the assertion is true but the reason is false
(d) if both the assertion and the reason are false

275. Assertion: Nitrogen is unreactive at room temperature but becomes reactive at elevated temperature or in the presence of a catalyst.

Reason: In the nitrogen molecule, there is extensive delocalisation of electrons.

276. Assertion: The BP of hydrides of the nitrogen family are in the order $NH_3 > BiH_3 > SbH_3 > AsH_3 > PH_3$.

Reason: The abnormality in bp is due to the decomposition of NH_3.

277. Assertion: Among nitrogen halides NX_3, the dipole moment is highest for NI_3 and lowest for NF_3.

Reason: Nitrogen halides, NX_3, have trigonal pyramidal structure.

278. Assertion: The bond angle to PBr_3 is greater than that of PH_3 but the bond angle of NBr_3 is less than that of NH_3.

Reason: The size of bromine is less than that of hydrogen.

279. Assertion: NF_3 is a weaker ligand than $N(CH_3)_3$.

Reason: NF_3 ionises to give F^- ions in aqueous solution.

280. Assertion: Ammonia is adsorbed more readily over activated charcoal than CO_2.

Reason: Ammonia is non-polar.

281. Assertion: NO_3^- is pyramidal while NH_3 is planar.

Reason: N in NO_3^- is sp^3-hybridrised but in NH_3, it is sp^2-hybridised.

282. Assertion: White phosphorus is more reactive than red phosphorus.

Reason: Red phosphorus consists of P_4 tetrahedral units linked to one another to form linear chains.

283. Assertion: Elementary phosphorus exists in three principal allotropic forms—white (or yellow), red (or violet) and black.

Reason: Of the three forms, white phosphorus is the most important and most reactive.

284. Assertion: Like PH_3, PCl_3 has a pyramidal structure but the P–Cl bond is much longer than the P–H bond.

Reason: Due to the bigger size of the chlorine atom in PCl_3, the P–Cl bond length is much larger (204 pm) when compared to the P–H bond length (142 pm) in PH_3.

285. Assertion: Both hypophosphoric acid and isohypophosphoric acid have same composition $H_4P_2O_6$ but their properties are different.

Reason: Due to different structural arrangements, their basicities, oxidation numbers of the P atoms their reducing properties are different.

GROUP 16

Atomic and Physical Properties

286. Which of the following oxides are acidic?

(a) Mn_2O_7 (b) CrO_3
(c) both (a) and (b) (d) none of these

287. Which statement is false for ozone?

(a) It is obtained by silent electric discharge on oxygen.
(b) It is an endothermic compound.
(c) It can be obtained by the action of ultraviolet rays on oxygen.
(d) It cannot be regarded as an allotrope of oxygen.

288. Ozone reacts with dry iodine to give:
(a) IO_2 (b) I_2O_3 (c) I_2O_4 (d) I_2O_9

289. Which does not liberate O_2 on heating?
(a) MgO (b) $NaNO_3$ (c) Pb_3O_4 (d) $KClO_3$

290. Which burns to form an oxide which is a gas at room temperature?
(a) hydrogen (b) phosphorus
(c) sodium (d) sulfur

291. Consider the following transformations

$$M(g) \xrightarrow{\Delta_i H_1} M^+(g) \xrightarrow{\Delta_i H_2} M^{2+}$$
$$O(g) \xrightarrow{\Delta_{eg} H_1} O^-(g) \xrightarrow{\Delta_{eg} H_2} O^{2-}(g)$$
$$M^{2+}(g) + 2\,O^-(g) \xrightarrow{\text{Lattice energy}_1} M^{2+}(O^-)_2(s)$$
$$M^{2+}(g) + O^{2-}(g) \xrightarrow{\text{Lattice energy}_2} M^{2+}O^{2-}(s)$$

Which of the following observations is wrong?
(a) $\Delta_i H_1 < \Delta_i H_2$
(b) $\Delta_{eg} H_1$ is –ve, $\Delta_{eg} H_2$ is +ve
(c) Lattice energy$_1$ < Lattice energy$_2$
(d) Lattice energy$_1$ > Lattice energy$_2$

292. In the S_8 molecule, the type of hybridisation exhibited by sulfur is
(a) sp^2 (b) sp^3 (c) sp (d) sp^3d

293. Which among the following group 16 elements exists in more than two allotropic states?
(a) polonium (b) telluriun
(c) selenium (d) oxygen

294. Which shows polymorphism?
(a) O (b) S
(c) Se (d) all the above

295. Polyanion formation is maximum in
(a) nitrogen (b) oxygen (c) sulfur (d) boron

296. Which of the following bonds has the highest energy?
(a) Se–Se (b) Te–Te (c) S–S (d) O–O

297. Which element is found in the free state?
(a) iodine (b) sulfur
(c) phosphorus (d) magnesium

298. Electron gain enthalpy is positive when
(a) O^- is formed from O (b) O^{2-} is formed from O^-
(c) O^+ is formed from O (d) O^{3-} is formed from O^-

Chemical Properties

299. Which one can be used to test for H_2S gas?
(a) a smell of rotten eggs
(b) a violet colouration with sodium intropruside
(c) turning lead acetate paper black
(d) all of the above

300. The increasing order of the volatility of the hydrides of the group 16 elements is
(a) $H_2S < H_2S < H_2S < H_2Te$
(b) $H_2O < H_2Te < H_2Se < H_2S$
(c) $H_2O < H_2S < H_2Se < H_2Te$
(d) $H_2Te < H_2Se < H_2S < H_2O$

301. Which of the following has the least bond angle?
(a) BeF_2 (b) H_2O (c) NH_3 (d) CH_4

302. The least covalent hydride out of the following is
(a) H_2O (b) H_2S (c) H_2Se (d) H_2Te

303. The decreasing order of BP is
(a) $H_2O > H_2S > H_2Se > H_2Te$
(b) $H_2O > H_2Te > H_2Se > H_2S$
(c) $H_2O > H_2Se > H_2Te > H_2S$
(d) $H_2O > H_2S > H_2Te > H_2Se$

304. H_2S is less acidic than H_2Te. This is because
(a) as the size of the element E increases down the group, the E–H bond length increases and hence the E–H bond dissociation energy decreases
(b) the H–S bond dissociation energy is higher than the H–Te bond dissociation energy
(c) the H–S bond breaks less easily than the H–Te bond; therefore, H_2S is a weaker acid than H_2Te
(d) all the three (a), (b) and (c) above

305. Bond angle is minimum for
(a) H_2O (b) H_2S (c) H_2Se (d) H_2Te

306. Among the hydrides formed by the group 16 elements, only H_2O has an abnormally low volatility (high boiling point). This is so because
(a) H_2O molecules are associated due to intermolecular hydrogen bonds
(b) H_2O is covalent in nature
(c) the O–H bond in H_2O is very strong
(d) the electronegativity difference between H and O is very large

307. Which of the following dissociates to give H^+ most easily?
(a) H_2O (b) H_2S (c) H_2Te (d) H_2Se

308. Which one of the following is non-reducing?
(a) H_2S (b) H_2Te (c) H_2Se (d) H_2O

309. Which of the following is used as an oxidising agent in organic chemistry?
(a) SO_2 (b) SeO_2 (c) TeO_2 (d) PoO_2

310. Which of the following is not hydrolysed?
(a) F_2O (b) Cl_2O (c) Br_2O (d) none

311. Which of the following trioxides can exist as a monomeric molecule?

(a) SO_3 in the gaseous state (b) TeO_3
(c) SeO_3 in all states (d) SO_3 in the solid state

312. The increasing order of acid character of the oxides, CO_2, N_2O_5, SiO_2 and SO_3 follows the sequence

(a) $CO_2 > N_2O_5 > SiO_2 > SO_3$
(b) $SiO_2 < CO_2 < N_2O_5 < SO_3$
(c) $SO_3 > N_2O > CO_2 > SiO_2$
(d) $N_2O_5 > SO_3 < SiO_2 < CO_2$

313. Which of the following molecules can act as an oxidising as well as a reducing agent?

(a) H_2S (b) SO_3 (c) H_2O_2 (d) F_2

314. Which of the following statements about the nature of the two S–O bonds formed in the SO_2 molecule is incorrect?

(a) S in SO_2 is sp^2-hybridised. Two of the three sp^2-hybrid orbitals from two σ-bonds with oxygen atoms while the third contains the lone pair of electrons.
(b) S is now left with one half-filled *p*orbital and one half-filled *d*orbital. These form one $p\pi - p\pi$ and one $p\pi - p\pi$ double bond with the oxygen atoms.
(c) The two S–O bonds are different.
(d) The two S–O bonds appear to be different but actually they are equal (bond length = 143 pm) due to resonance.

315. The type of bonds present in sulfuric anhydride

(a) 3σ and three $p\pi - d\pi$
(b) 3σ, one $p\pi - p\pi$ and two $p\pi - d\pi$
(c) 2σ and three $p\pi - d\pi$
(d) 2σ and two $p\pi - d\pi$

316. The type of hybridisation and possible geometry of the tetrafluorides of the members of the oxygen family are

(a) sp^3d, trigonal bipyramidal
(b) sp^3, tetrahedral
(c) dsp^2, square planar
(d) d^2sp^3, octahedral

317. In the OF_2 molecule, the total number of bond pairs and lone pairs of electrons present respectively are

(a) 2, 6 (b) 2, 8 (c) 2, 10 (d) 2, 9

318. The shape of the molecule SF_3Cl_3 is

(a) trigonal bipyramidal (b) cubic
(c) tetrahedral (d) square pyramidal

319. In SCl_2 the central atom involves ______ hybridisation

(a) sp^3 (b) sp^3d (c) sp^3d^2 (d) dsp^2

320. Which of the following characteristics about SF_4 are correct?

(a) gas, sp^3-hybridisation, tetrahedral
(b) liquid, sp^3d-hybridisation, trigonal planar
(c) solid, dsp^2-hybridisation, square planar
(d) gas, sp^3d-hybridisation, trigonal bipyramidal

321. Which of the following statements is correct?

(a) SF_6 does not react with water.
(b) SF_6 is sp^3d-hybridised.
(c) $S_2O_3^{2-}$ is a linear ion.
(d) There is no π-bonding in SO_4^{2-}.

322. Which of the following is not tetrahedral?

(a) SCl_4 (b) SO_4^{2-} (c) $Ni(CO)_4$ (d) $NiCl_4^{2-}$

323. The molecule which is not hydrolysed by water at 25°C is

(a) $AlCl_3$ (b) $SiCl_4$ (c) BF_3 (d) SF_6

324. Point out in which of the following properties, does oxygen differ from the rest of the members of its family (group16)?

(a) high value of ionisation enthalpy
(b) oxidation states (2, 4, 6)
(c) polymorphism
(d) formation of hydrides

325. The most common oxidation state for selenium in its compounds with oxygen is

(a) +4 (b) +2 (c) –2 (d) +6

326. Oxygen is always divalent whereas sulfur can form 2, 4 and 6 bonds. This is because

(a) oxygen is more electronegative than sulfur
(b) sulfur contains *d*-orbitals whereas oxygen does not
(c) sulfur has a larger atomic radius than oxygen
(d) sulfur is more electronegative than oxygen

Dioxygen and Oxides

327. Concentrated H_2SO_4 is not used to prepare HBr from KBr because it

(a) oxidises HBr
(b) reduces HBr
(c) causes disproportionation of HBr
(d) reacts too slowly with KBr

328. The oxide that is not reduced by hydrogen is:

(a) Ag_2O (b) Fe_2O_3 (c) CuO (d) K_2O

329. There is an ozone layer at a height of about 29 kilometres above the surface of the earth. Which of the following statements is true?

(a) It is harmful because ozone is dangerous to living organisms.
(b) It is beneficial because oxidation reactions can proceed faster in the presence of ozone.
(c) It is beneficial because ozone cuts out the ultraviolet radiation of the sun.

(d) It is harmful because ozone cuts out the important radiations of the sun which are vital for photosynthesis.

330. Oxygen will directly react with each of the following elements except

(a) P (b) Cl (c) Na (d) S

331. Which of the following is the dioxygenyl ion?

(a) O_2 (b) O_2^+ (c) O_2^- (d) O_2^{2-}

332. When oxygen is passed through a solution of Na_2SO_3 we get

(a) Na_2SO_4 (b) Na_2S (c) $NaHSO_4$ (d) NaH

333. Upon heating $KClO_3$ in the presence of catalytic amount of MnO_2, a gas W is formed. Excess amount of W reacts with white phosphorus to give X. The reaction of X with pure HNO_3 gives Y and Z, W, X, Y and Z are, respectively

(a) O_2, P_4O_{10}, N_2O_5 and HPO_3
(b) O_2, P_4O_6, N_2O_3 and H_3PO_4
(c) O_2, P_4O_6, N_2O_4 and H_3PO_3
(d) O_3, P_4O_{10}, N_2O_4 and HPO_3

334. Carbogen is a mixture of

(a) $CO_2 + N_2$ (b) $CO + O_2$
(c) $CO_2 + O_2$ (d) $C + H_2 + N_2$

335. An oxide of a non-metal has the following properties:

(i) it acts both as a proton donor as well as a proton acceptor
(ii) it reacts readily with basic and acidic oxides
(iii) it oxidises Fe at its boiling point
(iv) it is a poor conductor of electricity. The oxide is

(a) H_2O (b) SO_2 (c) NO_2 (d) CO_2

336. The acidic character of dioxides of members of oxygen family decreases in the order

(a) $SeO_2 > SO_2 > TeO_2 > PoO_2$
(b) $SO_2 > SeO_2 > TeO_2 > PoO_2$
(c) $PoO_2 > TeO_2 > SeO_2 > SO_2$
(d) $TeO_2 > PoO_2 > SeO_2 > SO_2$

337. Among the following, the most basic oxide is

(a) Al_2O_3 (b) P_2O_5 (c) SiO_2 (d) Na_2O

338. The element that combines with oxygen to give an amphoteric oxide is

(a) N (b) P (c) Al (d) Na

339. Which one of the following metals forms a superoxide?

(a) Ca (b) Zn (c) Al (d) Ti
(e) K

340. When PbO_2 reacts with conc. HNO_3, the gas evolved is

(a) NO_2 (b) O_2 (c) N_2 (d) N_2O

341. The order of stability of metal oxide is

(a) $Cr_2O_3 < MgO < Al_2O_3 < Fe_2O_3$
(b) $Fe_2O_3 < Cr_2O_3 < Al_2O_3 < MgO$
(c) $Fe_2O_3 < Al_2O_3 < Cr_2O_3 < MgO$
(d) $Al_2O_3 < MgO < Fe_2O_3 < Cr_2O_3$

342. Which of the following metal oxides is most basic?

(a) ZnO (b) Al_2O_3 (c) As_2O_3 (d) K_2O

343. Which of the following is the best scientific method to test the presence of water in a liquid?

(a) taste (b) smell
(c) use of litmus paper
(d) use of anhydrous copper sulfate

344. Among KO_2, NO_2^-, BaO_2 and NO_2^+ unpaired electron is present in

(a) NO_2^+ and BaO_2 (b) KO_2 and BaO_2
(c) KO_2 only (d) BaO_2 only

345. Which of the following is a suboxide?

(a) Ba_2O (b) Pb_2O (c) C_3O_2 (d) ZnO

346. $KO_2 + CO_2 \rightarrow ?$ (gas)

(a) H_2 (b) N_2 (c) O_2 (d) CO

347. Which of the following is formed by the action of water on sodium peroxide?

(a) H_2 (b) N_2 (c) O_2 (d) CO_2

348. The species that does not contain the peroxide ion is

(a) PbO_2 (b) H_2O_2 (c) SrO_2 (d) BaO_2

349. Which one of the following metallic oxides exhibit amphoteric nature?

(a) BaO (b) Al_2O_3 (c) Na_2O (d) CaO

350. The option(s) with only amphoteric oxide(s) is(are)

(a) Cr_2O_3, BeO, SnO, SnO_2
(b) ZnO, Al_2O_3, PbO, PbO_2
(c) NO, B_2O_3, PbO, SnO_2
(d) Cr_2O_3, CrO, SnO, PbO

351. On heating $KClO_3$, we get

(a) $KClO_2 + O_2$ (b) $KCl + O_2$
(c) $KCl + O_3$ (d) $KCl + O_2 + O_3$

352. It is possible to obtain oxygen from air by fractional distillation because

(a) oxygen is in a different group of the periodic table from nitrogen
(b) oxygen is more reactive than nitrogen
(c) oxygen has a higher BP than nitrogen
(d) oxygen has a lower density than nitrogen

353. Oxygen is not evolved when conc. H_2SO_4 reacts with

(a) $KMnO_4$ (b) MnO_2
(c) $K_2Cr_2O_7$ (d) $CuSO_4$

354. Oxygen can be obtained from bleaching powder by

(a) adding dilute acid (b) adding alkalies
(c) heating with lime (d) heating with a cobalt salt

355. The compound which gives off oxygen on moderate heating is

(a) cupric oxide (b) mercuric oxide
(c) zinc oxide (d) aluminium oxide

Ozone (Trioxygen)

356. Ozone turns moist starch iodide paper

(a) green (b) blue (c) red (d) black

357. Moist iodine reacts with ozone to give

(a) HI (b) HIO_3 (c) I_2O_4 (d) I_2O_5

358. The substance which does not liberate oxygen on treatment with ozone is

(a) PbS (b) H_2S (c) SO_2 (d) Hg

359. BaO_2 and ozone react to produce

(a) Ba (b) Ba_2O_3
(c) BaO (d) $Ba(OH)_2$

360. Ozone with KI solution produces

(a) Cl_2 (b) I_2 (c) HI (d) IO_3

361. The gases respectively absorbed by alkaline pyrogallol and oil of cinnamon are

(a) O_3, CH_4 (b) O_2, O_3
(c) SO_2, CH_4 (d) N_2O, O_3

362. Ozone depletion is due to the formation of following compound in Antarctica:

(a) acrolein (b) peroxy acetyl nitrate
(c) SO_2 and SO_3 (d) chlorine nitrate
(e) formaldehyde

363. Ozone with dry iodine gives

(a) I_4O_4 (b) I_2O_3 (c) IO_2 (d) I_2O_4

364. Which of the following statements regarding ozone is not correct?

(a) The ozone molecule is angular is shape.
(b) Ozone is a resonance hybrid of two structures.
(c) The oxygen–oxygen bond length in ozone is identical with that of molecular oxygen.
(d) Ozone is used as a germicide acid disinfectant for the purification of air.

365. Which of the following is used to purify air in crowded places?

(a) SO_2 (b) Cl_2 (c) O_2 (d) O_3

366. Ozone is determined quantitatively by first reacting it with excess of KI at a particular pH and then titrating the I_2 thus liberated with a suitable titrant. The pH of the reaction and the titrant used in the titration are respectively

(a) 6, $K_2Cr_2O_7$ (b) 9.2, $Na_2S_2O_3$
(c) 6, $Na_2S_2O_3$ (d) 9.2, $KMnO_4$

367. Six volumes of oxygen is obtained on complete ozonisation, from_____volumes of ozone

(a) 4 (b) 3 (c) 2 (d) 6

368. Which of the following is incorrect?

(a) O_2 is weaker oxidant than O_3.
(b) O_2 has smaller bond length than O_3.
(c) Both O_2 and O_3 are paramagnetic.
(d) O_2 is linear and O_3 is angular in shape.

369. Ozone is not readily soluble in

(a) turpentine oil (b) CCl_4
(c) cinnamon oil (d) water

Sulfur and its Compounds

370. H_2SO_4 and H_2SO_3 can be distinguished by the addition of:

(a) litmus solution (b) $FeCl_3$ solution
(c) $NaHSO_4$ solution (d) magnesium powder

371. A compound of sulfur used in the electrical transformer is:

(a) SO_2 (b) H_2S (c) SO_3 (d) SF_6

372. A colourless gas on passing through bromine water decolourises it. The gas is:

(a) HCl (b) HBr (c) CO_2 (d) SO_2

373. Which of the following sulfides is yellow in colour ?

(a) $(NH_4)_2S_4$ (b) $(NH_4)_2S_6$
(c) $(NH_4)_2S_8$ (d) $(NH_4)_2S$

374. Which of the following statements regarding sulfur is incorrect?

(a) The S_2 molecule is paramagnetic.
(b) The vapour at 200°C consists mostly of S_8 rings.
(c) At 600°C the gas mainly consists of S_2 molecules.
(d) The oxidation state of sulfur is never less than +4 in its compounds.

375. Sulfur on boiling with NaOH solution gives

(a) $Na_2S_2O_3 + NaHSO_3$ (b) $Na_2S_2O_3 + Na_2S$
(c) $Na_2SO_3 + H_2O$ (d) $Na_2SO_3 + SO_2$

376. The gas liberated when an aqueous solution of thioacetamide is heated is

(a) SO_2 (b) SO_3 (c) NH_3 (d) H_2S

377. Which statement about H_2S is false?

(a) It is a covalent compound.
(b) It is a gas with bad smell.
(c) It is a weak base in water.

(d) It is a stronger reducing agent than H_2O.

378. H_2S does not produce a metallic sulfide with

(a) $CdCl_2$ (b) $ZnCl_2$ (c) $COCl_2$ (d) $CuCl_2$

379. If the supply of oxygen is limited, H_2S reacts with O_2 to form

(a) $H_2O + SO_3$ (b) $H_2O + S$
(c) $H_2SO_4 + S$ (d) $H_2O + SO_2$

380. The reagent(s) that can selectively precipitate S^{2-} from a mixture of S^{2-} and SO_4^{2-} in aqueous solution is(are)

(a) $CuCl_2$, $Pb(OOCH_3)_2$
(b) $BaCl_2$, $CuCl_2$
(c) $Pb(OOCCH_3)_2$, $BaCl_2$
(d) $Na_2[Fe(CN)_5NO]$, $AgNO_3$

381. When H_2S gas is passed through a hot acidic aqueous solution containing Al^{3+}, Cu^{2+}, Pb^{2+} and Ni^{2+}, a precipitate is formed which consists of

(a) CuS and Al_2S_3 (b) PbS and NiS
(c) CuS and NiS (d) PbS and CuS

382. Aqueous solution of hydrogen sulfide and sulfurdioxide when mixed together, yield

(a) sulfur trioxide and water
(b) hydro and sulfurous acid
(c) sulfur and water
(d) hydrogen peroxide and sulfur

383. When H_2S is passed through acidified $KMnO_4$, we get

(a) K_2SO_3 (b) MnO_2
(c) $KHSO_3$ (d) sulfur

384. The geometry of H_2S and its dipole moment are

(a) angular and non-zero (b) angular and zero
(c) linear and non-zero (d) linear and zero

385. Which of the following salts would give SO_2 with hot and dil. H_2SO_4 and also decolourises Br_2 water?

(a) Na_2SO_3 (b) $NaHSO_4$
(c) Na_2SO_4 (d) Na_2S

386. Which of the following is oxidised by SO_2?

(a) Mg (b) $K_2Cr_2O_7$
(c) $KMnO_4$ (d) all

387. Which of the following statements is wrong?

When sulfur dioxide is passed through an aqueous solution of Fe (III) salt

(a) the yellow colour of the solution is changed into light green
(b) SO_2 acts as a reducing agent and reduces an aqueous solution of Fe (III) salt to Fe (II) salt
(c) SO_2 acts as an oxidising agent and oxidises aqueous Fe (III) ion to aqueous Fe (IV) ion
(d) SO_2 acts as a reducing agent in the presence of moisture

388. A gas which cannot be collected over water is

(a) N_2 (b) O_2 (c) SO_2 (d) PH_3

389. $SO_2 + Cl_2 \xrightarrow{\text{Sunlight}}$ Product

The product is

(a) sulfuryl chloride (b) sulfuric acid
(c) chloroform (d) none of these

390. Bromine water reacts with SO_2 to form

(a) HBr and S (b) H_2S and HBr
(c) S and H_2S (d) H_2SO_4 and HBr

391. Which of the following cannot be used in the detection SO_2?

(a) $KMnO_4$ solutions (b) $K_2Cr_2O_7$ Solution
(c) moist $K_2Cr_2O_7$ paper (d) starch iodide paper

392. Which of the following pairs has bleaching property?

(a) O_3 and NO_2 (b) O_3 and H_2S
(c) SO_3 and Cl_2 (d) Cl_2 and NO_2

393. When SO_2 is passed into aqueous Na_2CO_3, the product(s) formed is(are)

(a) $NaHSO_4$ (b) Na_2SO_4
(c) $NaHSO_3$ (d) Na_2SO_3 and $NaHSO_3$

394. [X] + dil. $H_2SO_4 \rightarrow$ [Y] colourless suffocating gas

[Y] + $K_2Cr_2O_7$ + H_2SO_4 $\rightarrow$ green colouration of solution

(a) SO_3^{2-}, SO_2 (b) Cl^-, HCl
(c) S^{2-}, H_2S (d) CO_3^{2-}, CO_2

395. Which of the following statements is false regarding the SO_3 molecule?

(a) Sulfur can expand its octet to reduce formal charges.
(b) The S–O bond is polar.
(c) The O–S–O bond angle is 104°.
(d) It is a non-polar molecule.

396. Which is not a correct statement?

(a) The S_8 ring is not planar.
(b) Oxygen is more electronegative than sulfur.
(c) SF_4 exists but OF_4 does not exist.
(d) SO_3 and SO_3^{2-} both have trigonal planar geometry.

397. The acid containing an S–O–O–S bond is

(a) H_2SO_5 (b) $H_2S_2O_7$
(c) $H_2S_2O_6$ (d) $H_2S_2O_8$

398. The acid which has a peroxy linkage is

(a) sulfurous acid (b) pyrosulfuric acid
(c) dithionic acid (d) Caro's acid

399. Hydrolysis of one mole of peroxodisulfuric acid produces

(a) two moles of sulfuric acid
(b) two moles of peroxomonosulfuric acid

(c) one mole of sulfuric acid and one mole of peroxomonosulfuric acid
(d) one mole each of sulfuric acid, peroxo-monulphuric acid and hydrogen peroxide

400. Sulfur heptoxide is an anhydride of
(a) $H_2S_2O_8$ (b) $H_2S_2O_7$ (c) H_2SO_4 (d) H_2SO_5

401. Which of the following has a maximum number of oxo groups?
(a) H_2SO_4 (b) H_2SO_3 (c) H_3PO_3 (d) H_3PO_4

402. In the laboratory, manganese (II) salt is oxidised to permanganate ion in aqueous solution by
(a) hydrogen peroxide (b) conc. HNO_3
(c) peroxy disulfate (d) dichromate
(e) ozone

403. The oxyacid of sulfur that contains a lone pair of electrons on sulfur is
(a) sulfurous acid (b) sulfuric acid
(c) peroxodisulfuric acid (d) pyrosulfuric acid

404. There is no S–S bond in
(a) $S_2O_4^{2-}$ (b) $S_2O_5^{2-}$ (c) $S_2O_3^{2-}$ (d) $S_2O_7^{2-}$

405. Sulfur in +3 oxidation state is present in
(a) sulfurous acid (b) pyrosulfuric acid
(c) dithionous acid (d) thiosulfuric acid

406. In the manufacture of sulfuric acid by the contact process, a Tyndall box is used to
(a) filter dust particles
(b) remove impurities
(c) convert SO_2 to SO_3
(d) test the presence of dust particles

407. Sulfuric acid is a dibasic acid. It ionises in two stages and hence has two dissociation constants K_{a_1} and K_{a_2}. Which of the following is the correct observation regarding K_{a_1} and K_{a_2}?
(a) $K_{a_1} > K_{a_2}$ (b) $K_{a_1} < K_{a_2}$
(c) $K_{a_1} = K_{a_2}$ (d) $K_{a_1} = 1.2 \times 10^{-2}, K_{a_2} > 10$

408. When potassium ferrocyanide crystals are heated with conc. H_2SO_4, the gas evolved is
(a) SO_2 (b) NH_3 (c) CO_2 (d) CO

409. Oxalic acid on heating with conc. H_2SO_4 gives
(a) CO only (b) CO_2 only
(c) $CO_2 + H_2O$ (d) $CO + CO_2 + H_2O$

410. When conc. H_2SO_4 is heated with P_2O_5, then the acid is converted to
(a) sulfur trioxide (b) sulfur dioxide
(c) sulfur
(d) a mixture of sulfur dioxide and sulfur trioxide

411. Copper turnings when heated with concentrated sulfuric acid will give
(a) SO_2 (b) SO_3 (c) H_2S (d) O_2

412. In the action $2\,Ag + 2\,H_2SO_4 \rightarrow Ag_2SO_4 + 2\,H_2O + SO_2$, H_2SO_4 acts as a/an
(a) reducing agent (b) oxidising agent
(c) catalytic agent (d) dehydrating agent

413. Sulfuric acid reacts with PCl_5 to give
(a) thionyl chloride (b) sulfur monochloride
(c) sulfuryl chloride (d) sulfur tetrachloride

414. Conc. H_2SO_4 is diluted
(a) by adding water in H_2SO_4
(b) by adding H_2SO_4 in water
(c) by adding glacial acetic acid in H_2SO_4
(d) none of the above

415. $KMnO_4$ is a strong oxidising agent in acid medium. To provide an acid medium, H_2SO_4 is used instead of HCl. This is because
(a) H_2SO_4 is a stronger acid than HCl
(b) HCl is oxidised by $KMnO_4$ to Cl_2
(c) H_2SO_4 is a dibasic acid
(d) only H_2SO_4 is completely ionised

416. Which of the following acts as a pickling agent?
(a) HNO_3 (b) HCl (c) H_2SO_4 (d) HNO_2

417. Superphosphate is the mixture of
(a) calcium phosphate and dil. H_2SO_4
(b) sodium phosphate and dil. H_2SO_4
(c) potassium phosphate and dil. H_2SO_4
(d) none of these

418. Which of the following is not suitable for use in a desiccator to dry substances?
(a) Conc. H_2SO_4 (b) Na_2SO_4
(c) $CaCl_2$ (d) P_4O_{10}

419. Among C, S and P, the element(s) that produce(s) SO_2 on reaction with hot conc. H_2SO_4 is(are)
(a) only S (b) only C and S
(c) only S and P (d) C, S and P

420. When sulfur is boiled with Na_2SO_3 solution, the compound formed is
(a) sodium sulfide (b) sodium sulfate
(c) sodium persulpahte (d) sodium thiosulfate

421. The chemical reaction between $Na_2S_2O_3$ and I_2 in an aqueous medium produces
(a) $Na_2S + NaI + H_2S$ (b) $Na_2SO_4 + NaI + H_2O$
(c) $Na_2SO_3 + NaI + H_2O$ (d) $Na_2S_4O_6 + NaI + H_2O$

422. Aqueous solution of sodium thiosulfate turns milky white on acidification because of
(a) the formation of sulfurous acid
(b) the formation of colloidal sulfur
(c) precipitation of sodium sulfate
(d) precipitation of sodium sulfite

423. In the following reaction sequence in aqueous solution, the species X, Y and Z, respectively are

$$\underset{\text{Clear solution}}{S_2O_3^{2-}} \xrightarrow[\text{White precipitate}]{Ag^+} X \xrightarrow[\text{Black precipitate}]{Ag^+} Y \xrightarrow{\text{with time}} Z$$

(a) $[Ag(S_2O_3)_2]^{3-}$, $Ag_2S_2O_3$, Ag_2S
(b) $[Ag(SO_3)_2]^{3-}$, Ag_2SO_3, Ag_2S
(c) $[Ag(SO_3)_2]^{3-}$, $Ag_2S_2O_3$, Ag
(d) $[Ag(SO_3)_3]^{3-}$, Ag_2SO_4, Ag

424. The products of the chemical reaction between $Na_2S_2O_3$, Cl_2 and H_2O are
(a) S + HCl + Na_2S (b) S + HCl + Na_2SO_4
(c) S + HCl + Na_2SO_3 (d) S + $NaClO_3$ + H_2O

425. The two sulfur atoms in $Na_2S_2O_3$ have
(a) +2 and +4 oxidation states
(b) –2 and +6 oxidation states
(c) +4 and +6 oxidation states
(d) same oxidations states

426. As a fixing agent, hypo is used in photography to
(a) reduce AgBr grains to metallic silver
(b) convert metallic silver to silver salt
(c) remove undercomposed silver bromide as a soluble complex
(d) remove reduced silver

427. Which of the following sulfatesis insoluble in water?
(a) $CuSO_4$ (b) $CdSO_4$
(c) $PbSO_4$ (d) $Bi(SO_4)_3$

428. Which of the elements of the oxygen family is most poisonous to human race?
(a) O (b) S (c) Se (d) none

429. Which form of sulfur shows paramagnetic behaviour?
(a) monoclinic S_8 molecules in solid state
(b) S_2 molecules in the vapour state
(c) cyclo-S_6 chair form
(d) rhombic sulfur

430. K_2CS_3 can be called potassium
(a) sulfocyanide (b) thiocarbide
(c) thiocarbonate (d) thiocyanate

Final Preparation

431. When fluoride is heated with conc. H_2SO_4 and MnO_2, the gas evolved is
(a) HF (b) MnF_2
(c) F_2 (d) none of these

432. Oxygen is more electronegative than sulfur, yet H_2S is acidic while H_2O is neutral. This is because:
(a) water is a highly associated compound
(b) H–S bond is weaker than the H–O bond
(c) H_2S is a gas while H_2O is a liquid
(d) the molecular weight of H_2S is more than that of H_2O

433. Which of the following statements is incorrect?
(a) SO_3 is a stronger oxidising agent and more acidic than SO_2.
(b) Selenium forms only two oxoacids—selenous acid (H_2SeO_3) and selenic acid (H_2SeO_4).
(c) The acidic strength and oxidising power of the oxoacids is greater in the +6 oxidation state than in the +4 oxidation state.
(d) The thermal stability of the oxides of the group 16 elements decreases in the order $SO_2 > SeO_2 > TeO_2 > PoO_2$.

434. The most stable tetrachloride formed by the group 16 elements is
(a) SCl_4 (b) $SeCl_4$ (c) $TeCl_4$ (d) OCl_4

435. The shape of O_2F_2 is similar to that of
(a) C_2F_2 (b) H_2O_2 (c) H_2F_2 (d) C_2H_2

436. Which of the statements given below is incorrect?
(a) O_3 molecule is bent.
(b) ONF is isoelectronic with O_2N^-.
(c) OF_2 is an oxide of fluorine.
(d) Cl_2O_7 is an anhydride of perchloric acid.

437. Which of the following oxides is expected to exhibit paramagnetic behaviour?
(a) CO_2 (b) SO_2 (c) ClO_2 (d) SiO_2

438. The bond angles of the SF_4 molecule are
(a) 102°, 173° (b) 89°, 117°
(c) 120°, 180° (d) 45°, 118°

439. Among the following, the pair in which the two species are not isostructural is
(a) SiF and SF_4 (b) IO_3^- and XeO_3
(c) BH_4^- and NH_4^+ (d) PF_6^- and SF_6

440. Which of the following would have a permanent dipole moment?
(a) BF_3 (b) SF_4 (c) SiF_4 (d) XeF_4

441. Sulfur reacts with chlorine in a 1 : 2 ratio and forms X. Hydrolysis of X gives a sulfur compound Y. What is the structure and hybridisation of anion of Y?

(a) tetrahedral, sp^3 (b) linear, sp
(c) pyramidal, sp^3 (d) trigonal planar, sp^2

442. Which one of the following halogens liberates oxygen when passed through hot concentrated KOH solution?
(a) I_2 (b) Cl_2 (c) Br_2 (d) F_2

443. Which of the following oxides is not expected to react with sodium hydroxide?
(a) BeO (b) B_2O_3 (c) CaO (d) SiO_2

444. Consider the sequence of oxides: Na_2O, SiO_2, P_4O_{10}. Which factor decreases from Na_2O to SiO_2 and also from SiO_2 to P_4O_{10}?
(a) covalent character
(b) melting point
(c) pH when mixed with water
(d) solubility in aqueous alkali

445. The name and composition of the product x in the following reaction are
$2\ KOH + 5\ O_3 \rightarrow x + 5\ O_2 + H_2O$
(a) potassium oxide, K_2O
(b) potassium peroxide, K_2O_2
(c) potassium superoxide, KO_2
(d) potassium ozonide, KO_3

446. In the following reaction,
$H_2O_2 + O_3 \rightarrow H_2O + 2\ O_2$
O_3 behaves as a/an
(a) oxidant (b) reductant
(c) bleaching agent (d) acid

447. The correct order in which the O–O bond length increases in the following is:
(a) $O_3 < H_2O_2 < O_2$ (b) $O_2 < O_3 < H_2O_2$
(c) $O_2 < H_2O_2 < O_3$ (d) $H_2O_2 < O_2 < O_3$

448. The angular shape of the ozone molecule (O_3) consists of
(a) 1 sigma and 1 pi bond
(b) 2 sigma and 1 pi bond
(c) 1 sigma and 2 pi bonds
(d) 2 sigma and 2 pi bonds

449. Which of the following should have the greatest enthalpy of combustion at 25°C?
(a) rhombic sulfur (b) monoclinic sulfur
(c) plastic sulfur (d) colloidal sulfur

450. Passing H_2S gas through nitric acid produces
(a) rhombic sulfur (b) colloidal sulfur
(c) amorphous sulfur (d) plastic sulfur

451. When H_2S gas is passed through a HCl-containing aqueous solution of $CuCl_2$, $HgCl_2$, $BiCl_3$ and $CoCl_2$, it does not precipitate out
(a) CuS (b) HgS (c) Bi_2S_3 (d) CoS

452. Identify the correct order of solubility in aqueous medium?
(a) CuS> ZnS > Na_2S (b) ZnS > Na2S >CuS
(c) Na_2S >CuS> ZnS (d) Na_2S > ZnS >CuS

453. The reaction of the nitroprusside anion with sulfide ion gives a purple colouration due to the formation of
(a) the tetranionic complex of iron (II) coordinating to one NOS^- ion
(b) the dianiomic complex of iron (II) coordinating to one NCS^- ion
(c) the tranionic complex of iron (III) coordinating to one NOS^- ion
(d) the tetranionic complex of iron (III) coordinating to one NCS^- ion

454. S^{2-} and SO_3^{2-} can be distinguished by using
(a) $(CH_3COO)_2Pb$ (b) $Na_2[Fe(CN)_5NO]$
(c) both (a) and (b) (d) none of these

455. A solution of sulfur dioxide in water reacts with H_2S, precipitating sulfur. Here,sulfur dioxide acts as
(a) an oxidising agent (b) a reducing agent
(c) an acid (d) a catalyst

456. Which of the following is used to absorb sulfur dioxide?
(a) conc. H_2SO_4 (b) KOH solution
(c) water (d) anhydrous $CaCl_2$

457. The oxide which acts as a reducing, oxidising, bleaching agent and a Lewis base is base is
(a) SO_3 (b) SO_2 (c) MnO_2 (d) CO_2

458. When SO_2 is passed through a solution of potassium iodate, the oxidation state of iodine changes from
(a) +5 to 0 (b) +5 to –1
(c) –5 to 0 (d) –7 to –1

459. When an inorganic compound (X) reacts with SO_2 in an aqueous medium, it produces a compound (A). Compound (A) on reaction with Na_2CO_3 gives the compound (B) which with sulfur gives another compound (C) used in photography. The compounds (X), (A) and (C) are respectively
(a) Na_2CO_3, $NaHSO_3$, $Na_2S_2O_3$
(b) $NaHSO_3$, Na_2SO_3, $Na_2S_2O_3$
(c) $NaHSO_3$, Na_2SO_3, $Na_2S_2O_3$
(d) Na_2CO_3, Na_2SO_3, $NaHSO_3$

460. Na_2CO_3 reacts with SO_2 in the alkaline medium to give
(a) Na_2SO_3 (b) $NaHSO_3$
(c) Na_2SO_4 (d) $NaHSO_4$

461. When SO_2 is passed through cupric chloride solution
(a) a white precipitate is obtained

(b) the solution becomes colourless
(c) the solution becomes colourless and a white precipitate of Cu_2Cl_2 is obtained
(d) no visible change takes place

462. Which one of the following statements is correct? When SO_2 is passed through acidified $K_2Cr_2O_7$ solution
(a) the solution turns blue
(b) the solution is decolourised
(c) SO_2 is reduced
(d) green $Cr_2(SO_4)_3$ is formed

463. Name the gas that can readily decolourise acidified $KMnO_4$ solution
(a) CO_2 (b) SO_2 (c) NO_2 (d) P_2O_5

464. Nitrogen dioxide and sulfur dioxide have some properties in common. Which property is shown by one of these compounds, but not by the other?
(a) is soluble in water
(b) is used as a food preservative
(c) forms 'acid rain'
(d) is a reducing agent

465. In $SOCl_2$, the Cl–S–Cl and Cl–S–O bond angles are
(a) 130° and 115° (b) 106° and 96°
(c) 107° and 108° (d) 96° and 106°

466. SO_3 can be obtained by which of the following reactions?
(a) $S + H_2SO_4 \xrightarrow{\Delta}$
(b) $H_2SO_4 + PCl_5 \xrightarrow{\Delta}$
(c) $CaSO_4 + C \xrightarrow{\Delta}$
(d) heating ferric sulfate $[Fe_2(SO_4)_2]$

467. In which pair of ions do both the species contain the S–S bond?
(a) $S_2O_7^{2-}, S_2O_3^{2-}$ (b) $S_4O_6^{2-}, S_2O_3^{2-}$
(c) $S_2O_7^{2-}, S_2O_8^{2-}$ (d) $S_4O_6^{2-}, S_2O_7^{2-}$

468. Which of the following structures is the most preferred and hence of lowest energy for SO_3?

(a) 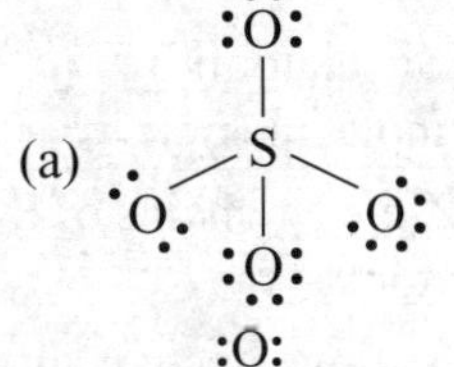

(b) 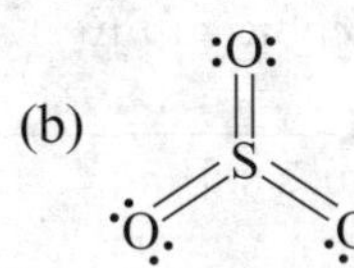

(c) 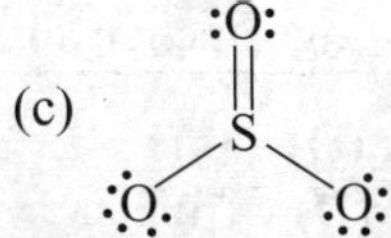

(d)

469. Which of the following species has the same number of X–O–X linkages, where X = S or P?
I. $S_2O_6^{2-}$ II. $S_3O_6^{2-}$ III. $S_2O_5^{2-}$ IV. $P_3O_9^{2-}$
(a) II and IV (b) II and III
(c) I and III (d) I and IV

470. The oxidation states of sulfur in the anions SO_3^{2-}, $S_2O_4^{2-}$ and $S_2O_6^{2-}$ follow the order
(a) $S_2O_4^{2-} < SO_3^{2-} < S_2O_6^{2-}$
(b) $SO_3^{2-} < S_2O_4^{2-} < S_2O_6^{2-}$
(c) $S_2O_4^{2-} < S_2O_6^{2-} < SO_3^{2-}$
(d) $S_2O_6^{2-} < S_2O_4^{2-} < SO_3^{2-}$

471. Perdisulfuric acid has the following bond
(a) O←O=O (b) ←O=O→
(c) >O→O< (d) –O–O–

472. In tetrathionic acid, what is the number of S–S bonds?
(a) two (b) three (c) four (d) one

473. What is X in the following reaction?
$KHSO_4 + F_2 \rightarrow HF + X$
(a) K_2SO_4 (b) $K_2S_2O_4$
(c) $K_2S_2O_3$ (d) $K_2S_2O_8$

474. Which of the following species is basic and reducing?
(a) SO_3^{2-} (b) SO_4^{2-} (c) HSO_4^{2-} (d) $S_2O_3^{2-}$

475. When PCl_5 reacts with sulfuric acid, sulfuryl chloride (SO_2Cl_2) is formed as the final product. This shows that sulfuric acid
(a) has two hydroxyl groups in its structure
(b) is a derivative of sulfur dioxide
(c) is a dibasic acid
(d) has great affinity for water

476. Which of the following has $p\pi$–$d\pi$ bonding?
(a) NO_3^- (b) SO_3^{2-} (c) BO_3^{3-} (d) CO_3^{2-}

477. The oxidation states of the most electronegative element in the products of the reaction of BaO_2 with dil. H_2SO_4 are
(a) 0 and 1 (b) –1 and –2
(c) –2 and 0 (d) –2 and +1

478. If cold barium nitrite is mixed with H_2SO_4, which of the following is formed?
(a) $HNO_2 + BaSO_4$ (b) $HNO_3 + BaSO_4$
(c) $BaSO_4 + NO_2$ (d) $BaSO_4 + N_2O$

479. Hot concentrated sulfuric acid is a moderately strong oxidising agent. Which of the following reactions does not show oxidising behaviour?
(a) $Cu + 2\,H_2SO_4 \rightarrow CuSO_4 + SO_2 + 2\,H_2O$
(b) $S + 2\,H_2SO_4 \rightarrow 3\,SO_2 + 2\,H_2O$
(c) $C + 2\,H_2SO_4 \rightarrow CO_2 + 2\,SO_2 + 2\,H_2O$
(d) $CaF_2 + H_2SO_4 \rightarrow CaSO_4 + 2\,HF$

480. An inorganic halide (A) reacts with water to form two acids (B) and (C). (A) also reacts with NaOH to form two salts (D) and (E) which remain in solution. The solution gives a white precipitate with both $AgNO_3$and $BaCl_2$ solution respectively. (A) is a useful organic reagent. The compound (A) is

(a) $SOCl_2$ (b) SO_2Cl_2 (c) S_2Cl_2 (d) SF_4

481. A crystalline solid X reacts with dil. HCl to liberate a gas Y. Y decolourises acidified $KMnO_4$ solution. When a gas Z is slowly passed into an aqueous solution of Y, colloidal sulfur is obtained. X and Z could be, respectively

(a) Na_2S, SO_3 (b) Na_2SO_4, H_2S
(c) Na_2SO_3, H_2S (d) Na_2SO_4, SO_2

482. Which of the following is used as a reagent in iodometric titrations?

(a) Na_2SO_3 (b) $Na_2S_2O_3.5H_2O$
(c) $Na_2SO_4.10H_2O$ (d) $NaHSO_3$

483. A pale yellow precipitate and a gas with a pungent odour are formed on warming dilute hydrochloric acid with an aqueous solution containing the

(a) sulfate ion (b) sulfide ion
(c) thiosulfate ion (d) sulfite ion

484. Which is a wrong statement?

(a) Rhombic sulfurdisproportionates in aqueous alkali.
(b) In $Na_2S_2O_3$, the two sulfur atoms are in different oxidation states.
(c) Thiosulfate ion.
(d) $2\ Na_2S_2O_3 + Cl_2 \rightarrow Na_2S_4O_6 + 2\ NaCl$

485. A while crystalline salt P reacts with dilute HCl to liberate a suffocating gas Q and also forms a yellow precipitate. The gas Q turns potassium dichromate acidified with dilute H_2SO_4 to a green coloured solution R. The salt P, gas Q and solution R are respectively

(a) $Na_2S_2O_3$, SO_2, $Cr_2(SO_4)_3$
(b) Na_2SO_3, SO_2, $Cr_2(SO_4)_3$
(c) Na_2SO_4, SO_2, $Cr_2(SO_4)_3$
(d) Na_2S, H_2S, Cr_2S_3

486. Which of the following does not react with AgCl?

(a) $Na_2S_2O_3$ (b) NH_4OH
(c) $NaNO_3$ (d) Na_2CO_3

487. α and β forms of sulfurare at equilibrium at what temperature and what is it called?

(a) 369 K, critical temperature
(b) 369 K, transition temperature
(c) 300 K, Boyle's temperature
(d) 269 K, inversion temperature

488. Identify the correct order of stability of oxidation states of the group 16 elements.

(a) $Se^{4+} < Te^{4+} < Po^{4+}$ (b) $Se^{6+} > Te^{6+} > Po^{6+}$
(c) $Se^{6+} = Te^{6+} < Po^{6+}$ (d) both (a) and (b)

489. What is the correct relationship between the pHs of isomolar solutions of sodium oxide (pH_3), sodium sulfide (pH_2), sodium selenide (pH_3) and sodium telluride (pH_4)?

(a) $pH_1 < pH_2 < pH_3 < pH_4$
(b) $pH_1 > pH_2 > pH_3 > pH_4$
(c) $pH_1 < pH_2 < pH_3 \approx pH_4$
(d) $pH_1 > pH_2 \approx pH_3 > pH_4$

490. Acidity of diprotic acids in aqueous solution increases in the order

(a) $H_2S < H_2Se < H_2Te$ (b) $H_2Se < H_2S < H_2Te$
(c) $H_2Te < H_2S < H_2Se$ (d) $H_2Se < H_2Te < H_2S$

491. H_2O is dipolar whereas BeF_2 is not. This is because

(a) the electronegativity of F is greater than that of O
(b) H_2O involves hydrogen bonding whereas BeF_2 is a discrete molecule
(c) H_2O is angular and BeF_2 is smaller
(d) H_2O is angular and BeF_2 is linear

MATCH THE FOLLOWING

492.

Column I (Substances)	Column II (Processes)
(A) Sulfuric acid	(p) Siemen's and Brodies
(B) Sulfur	(q) Frasch process
(C) Sodium thiosulfate	(r) Spring's reaction
(D) Ozone	(s) Lead chamber process

(a) (A)—(p); (B)—(s); (C)—(q); (D)—(r)
(b) (A)—(p); (B)—(q); (C)—(r); (D)—(s)
(c) (A)—(s); (B)—(r); (C)—(q); (D)—(p)
(d) (A)—(s); (B)—(q); (C)—(r); (D)—(p)

493.

Column I (Allotropic form)	Column II
(A) Plastic sulfur	(p) S_8 puckered rings in crown form
(B) Rhombic sulfur	(q) S_2 (diatomic) molecules
(C) Engel's sulfur	(r) Zig–zag chains of S atoms
(D) Monoclinic sulphur	(s) S_6 rings in chair form

(a) (A)—(p); (B)—(q); (C)—(r); (D)—(s)
(b) (A)—(r); (B)—(p); (C)—(s); (D)—(p)
(c) (A)—(s); (B)—(q); (C)—(p); (D)—(q)
(d) (A)—(p); (B)—(r); (C)—(q); (D)—(r)

494.

Column I (Hydride)	Column II (Melting point, K)
(A) H_2O	(p) 222
(B) H_2S	(q) 273
(C) H_2Se	(r) 188
(D) H_2Te	(s) 208

(a) (A)—(q); (B)—(r); (C)—(s); (D)—(p)
(b) (A)—(r); (B)—(s); (C)—(p); (D)—(q)
(c) (A)—(s); (B)—(p); (C)—(q); (D)—(r)
(d) (A)—(p); (B)—(q); (C)—(r); (D)—(s)

495.

Column I	Column I
(A) $H_2S_2O_4$	(p) +5
(B) $H_2S_2O_6$	(q) +4
(C) H_2SO_5	(r) +3
(D) H SO_3	(s) +6

(a) (A)—(p); (B)—(q); (C)—(r); (D)—(s)
(b) (A)—(q); (B)—(r); (C)—(s); (D)—(p)
(c) (A)—(r); (B)—(p); (C)—(s); (D)—(q)
(d) (A)—(s); (B)—(q); (C)—(p); (D)—(r)

ASSERTION REASON

Directions: In each of the following questions, a statement of Assertion (A) is given followed by a corresponding statement of Reason (R) just below it. Of the statements, mark the correct answer as

(a) if both the assertion and reason are true and the reason is the correct explanation of the assertion.
(b) if both the assertion and the reason are true but reason is not the correct explanation of assertion
(c) if the assertion is true but the reason is false
(d) if both the assertion and reason are false

496. Assertion: Hydrides of group 16 elements show volatility in the order $H_2O > H_2S > H_2Se > H_2Te$.
Reason: The electronegativity of the group 16 elements increases down the group from oxygen to tellurium.

497. Assertion: SeO_3 exists as a cyclic trimer (Se_3O_9) in the solid state and in the dimeric state in the vapour phase.
Reason: Se does not conduct electricity even on exposure to light.

498. Assertion: In SO_2, the bond angle is 119° whereas in SO_3, the bond angle is 120°.
Reason: The S atom in both SO_2 and SO_3 is sp^2-hybridised.

499. Assertion: $SeCl_4$ does not have a tetrahedral structure.
Reason: Se in $SeCl_4$ has two lone pairs.

500. Assertion: The O–O bond length in H_2O_2 is shorter than that of O_2F_2.
Reason: H_2O_2 is an ionic compound.

501. Assertion: All F–S–F angles in SF_4 are greater than 90° but less than 180°.
Reason: The lone pair–bond pair repulsion is weaker than the bond pair–bond pair repulsion.

502. Assertion: Hemoglobin is an oxygen carrier.
Reason: Oxygen binds as O_2^- to Fe of hemoglobin.

503. Assertion: Sb(III) is not precipitated as a sulfide when H_2S is passed in its alkaline solution.
Reason: The concentration of S^{2-} ion in the alkaline medium is inadequate for precipitation.

504. Assertion: Sb_2S_3 is not soluble in yellow ammonium sulfide.
Reason: The common ion effect due to S^{2-} ions reduces the solubility of Sb_2S_3.

505. Assertion: Both SO_2 and SO_3 are reducing agents.
Reason: Both SO_2 and SO_3 bleach the articles by reduction.

GROUP 17

Atomic and Physical Properties

506. Fluorine absorbs _____ portion of light and appears yellow
(a) yellow (b) green (c) violet (d) red

507. Which radical can bring about the highest oxidation state of a transition metal?
(a) F^- (b) Cl^- (c) Br^- (d) I^-

508. The tendency to form the anion X^- (in the gaseous state) is greatest with
(a) fluorine (b) bromine
(c) iodine (d) chlorine

509. The correct order of electron gain enthalpy with negative sign of F, Cl, Br and I having atomic number 9, 17, 35 and 53 respectively is
(a) F > Cl > Br > I (b) Cl > F > Br > I
(c) Br > Cl > I > F (d) I > Br > Cl > F

510. Which of the following bonds will be most polar?
(a) N–Cl (b) O–F (c) I–F (d) N–N

511. At ordinary temperature and pressure, chlorine is a gas, bromine is a liquid and iodine is a solid. This is because
(a) of these three, chlorine is the lightest and iodine is the heaviest
(b) chlorine has the lowest specific heat
(c) chlorine molecule is the least stable

(d) intermolecular forces are the weakest in chlorine and strongest in iodine

512. Which statement is correct about the halogens?

(a) They are all diatomic and form univalent ions.
(b) They are all capable of exhibiting several oxidation states.
(c) They are all diatomic and form divalent ions.
(d) They can mutually displace each other from the solution of their compounds with metals.

513. The colour of the X_2 molecules of group 17 elements changes gradually from yellow to violet down the group. This is due to

(a) a decrease in the $\sigma - \pi$ gap or HOMO–LUMO gap down the group
(b) a decrease in the ionisation energy down the group
(c) the change of physical state of X_2 at room temperature from gas to solid as we go down the group
(d) decrease in electronegativity down the group

514. Iodine dissolves readily in

(a) water (b) potassium iodide
(c) carbon tetrachloride (d) alcohol

515. Which of the following exhibits clear electropositive properties?

(a) F (b) Cl (c) Br (d) I

516. Fluorine molecule is formed by

(a) the axial *p–p* orbital overlap
(b) the sideways *p–p* orbital overlap
(c) the *s–s* orbital overlap
(d) the *s–p* orbital overlap
(e) the overlap of two sp^2-hybrid orbitals

517. Which of the following statements is wrong? Halogens have maximum negative electron gain enthalpy. This is because

(a) they have the smallest size in their respective periods
(b)they have high effective nuclear charge
(c)they readily accept one electron to acquire the stable electronic configuration of the nearest noble gas
(d) large amount of energy is absorbed when a halogen atom accepts an electron to form the corresponding halide ion

Chemical Properties

518. Which halogen does not react with water?

(a) F_2 (b) Cl_2 (c) Br_2 (d) I_2

519. When fluoride is heated with conc. H_2SO_4 and MnO_2, the gas evolved is:

(a) HF (b) F_2
(c) SF (d) none of these

520. F_2 on treatment with methane gives:

(a) CH_2F_2 (b) CH_3F
(c) I_2 (d) all of these

521. Which of the following has no action with starch solution?

(a) F_2 and Cl_2 (b) Br_2
(c) I_2 (d) none of these

522. Which of the following statements is not true for halogens?

(a) All form monobasic oxyacids.
(b) All are oxidising agents.
(c) All but fluorine show positive oxidation states.
(d) Chlorine has the highest electron gain enthalpy.

523. Greater reactivity of fluorine is due to

(i) low energy of the F–F bond
(ii) small size
(iii) high heat of hydration
(iv) high energy of the F–F bond

(a) (i), (ii) and (iii) (b) (i), (iii) and (iv)
(c) (i) and (ii) (d) (i), (ii), (iii) and (iv)

524. Which of the following is the most active halogen?

(a) Cl_2 (b) Br_2 (c) I_2 (d) F_2

525. The lowest value of 0.53 for the electrode potential ($E°$) for the reaction X_2 (solution) + 2 e^- = 2 $X^-(aq)$ may be assigned to

(a) F_2 (b) Cl_2 (c) Br_2 (d) I_2

526. Iodine is liberated when chlorine is passed through an acidified solution of potassium iodide because

(a) chlorine is a more powerful reducing agent than iodine
(b) chlorine is a more powerful reducing agent than iodine
(c) chlorine is more electronegative than iodine
(d) chlorine is less electronegative than iodine

527. Which one of the following parameters does not contribute much in making halogens strong oxidising agents?

(a) low bond dissociation enthalpy
(b) high electronegativity
(c) large electron gain enthalpy
(d) high ionisation enthalpy

528. When Br_2 is treated with aqueous solutions NaF, NaCl and NaI separately

(a) F_2, Cl_2 and I_2 are liberated
(b) only F_2 and Cl_2 are liberated
(c) only I_2 is liberated
(d) only Cl_2 is liberated
(e) only Cl_2 and I_2 are liberated

529. Which one of the following reactions does not take place?

(a) $2F_2 + 2H_2O \rightarrow 4H^+ + 4F^- + O_2$
(b) $Cl_2 + H_2O \rightarrow HCl + HOCl$
(c) $3F_2 + 3H_2O \rightarrow 6H^+ + 6F^- + O_3$
(d) $I_2 + H_2O \rightarrow HI + HOI$

530. Br^- is converted into Br_2 by using

(a) Cl_2 (b) conc. HCl
(c) HBr (d) H_2S

531. A one litre flask is full of brown bromine vapours. The intensity of brown colour of vapours will not decrease appreciably on adding to the flask some

(a) pieces of marble
(b) carbon disulfide
(c) carbon tetrachloride
(d) animal charcoal powder

532. When iodine reacts with NaF, NaBr and NaCl

(a) it gives mixture of F_2, Cl_2 and Br_2
(b) it gives chlorine
(c) it gives bromine
(d) none of these

533. Chlorine cannot displace

(a) fluorine from NaF (b) iodine from NaI
(c) bromine from NaBr (d) none of these

534. Among Cl^-, Br^-, I^-, the correct order for being oxidised to the dihalogen is

(a) $I^- > Cl^- > Br^-$ (b) $Cl^- > Br^- > I^-$
(c) $I^- > Br^- > Cl^-$ (d) $Br^- > I^- > Cl^-$

535. The element which water never acts as reducing agent in a chemical reaction is

(a) O (b) Li (c) F (d) C

536. Which of the following compounds has the lowest boiling point (maximum vapour pressure, most volatile)?

(a) HF (b) HCl (c) HBr (d) HI

537. Which of the following has the highest percentage of ionic character?

(a) HCl (b) HF (c) HBr (d) HI

538. The correct order of increasing conjugate base strength is

(a) $I^- < Br^- < Cl^- < F^-$ (b) $F^- < Cl^- < Br^- < I^-$
(c) $Cl^- < Br^- < I^- < F^-$ (d) $Br^- < I^- < F^- < Cl^-$

539. Which of the following sets gives the correct arrangement of the compounds involved based on their bond strengths?

(a) HF > HCl > HBr > HI (b) HI > HBr > HCl > HF
(c) HF > HBr > HCl > HI (d) HF < HCl > HBr > HI
(e) HCl > HF > HBr > HI

540. At room temperature, HCl is a gas while HF is a low boiling liquid. This is because

(a) H–F bond is covalent (b) H–F bond is ionic
(c) HF has metallic bond (d) HF has hydrogen bonds

541. The correct order of the thermal stability of hydrogen halides (H–X) is

(a) HI > HBr > HCl > HF (b) HF > HCl > HBr > HI
(c) HCl > HF > HBr < HI (d) HI > HCl > HF > HBr

542. HI cannot be prepared by the action of conc. H_2SO_4 on KI because

(a) HI is stronger than H_2SO_4
(b) HI is more volatile than H_2SO_4
(c) H_2SO_4 is an oxidising agent
(d) H_2SO_4 forms a complex

543. The comparatively high bp of HF is due to

(a) high reactivity of fluorine
(b) small size of hydrogen atom
(c) formation of hydrogen
(d) small size of fluorine atom
(e) high IE of fluorine

544. Which of the hydrogen halides forms salts KHX_2 (where X is a halogen atom)?

(a) HF (b) HCl (c) HI
(d) HBr (e) all of these

545. The boiling points of HF, HCl, HBr and HI follow the order

(a) HF > HCl > HBr > HI (b) HF > HI > HBr > HCl
(c) HI > HBr > HCl > HF (d) HCl > HF > HBr > HI

546. The increasing order of reducing power of the halogen acids is

(a) HCl < HBr < HF < HI (b) HF < HCl < HBr < HI
(c) HI < HBr < HCl < HF (d) HBr < HCl < HF < HI

547. In the dark, which of the following reacts with hydrogen?

(a) Br_2 (b) F_2 (c) I_2 (d) Cl_2

548. Aqueous solution of which of the following acids cannot be kept in a bottle of glass?

(a) HF (b) HCl (c) HBr (d) HI

549. The least active halogen with hydrogen is

(a) Cl (b) I (c) Br (d) F

550. The correct order of acidic strength is

(a) HF > HCl > HBr > HI
(b) HCl < HBr < HF < HI
(c) HBr < HCl < HI < HF
(d) HI < HBr <HCl< HF

551. Which of the following statements is incorrect?

(a) ICl is a good conductor of electricity in the fused state.
(b) Cl_2O_7 is the anhydride of perchlorid acid.
(c) Melting and boiling points of HBr are less than that of HCl.
(d) F_2 forms only one oxoacid.

552. A bad conductor of electricity is
(a) H_2F_2 (b) HCl (c) HBr (d) HI

553. Which reaction cannot be used for the production of halogen acid?
(a) $2\,KBr + H_2SO_4 \rightarrow K_2SO_4 + 2\,HBr$
(b) $NaHSO_4 + NaCl \rightarrow Na_2SO_4 + HCl$
(c) $NaCl + H_2SO_4 \rightarrow NaHSO_4 + HCl$
(d) $CaF_2 + H_2SO_4 \rightarrow CaSO_4 + 2\,HF$

554. Which can do glass etching?
(a) HIO_4 (b) SiF_4 (c) HF (d) HNO_3

555. When fluoride is heated with conc. H_2SO_4 and MnO_2, the gas evolved is
(a) F_2 (b) SF_4 (c) HF (d) none

556. Of the following, which species is primarily obtained in a solution containing KHF_2?
(a) K^+, H^+ and F^- (b) H^+ and KF_2^-
(c) KF and H^- (d) K^+ and HF_2^-

557. Which of the following is the correct reason for HI solution turning brown on exposure to air?
(a) HI reacts with H_2O to form I_2
(b) HI dissolves NO_2
(c) HI reacts with O_2 to form I_2
(d) HI reacts with N_2 and O_2 to form NO_2

558. The correct order of the X–O–X bond angles is
(a) $F_2O > Cl_2O > Br_2O$ (b) $F_2O < Cl_2O < Br_2O$
(c) $Br_2O > Cl_2O < F_2O$ (d) $Cl_2O > F_2O > Br_2O$

559. Which one of the following oxides of halogens has a linear structure?
(a) OF_2 (b) ClO_2 (c) Br_2O (d) none

560. Which of the following halogen oxides is ionic?
(a) ClO_2 (b) BrO_2 (c) I_2O_5 (d) I_4O_9

561. The oxide containing the highest oxidation state of halogen is
(a) Br_2O (b) O_2F_2 (c) Cl_2O_7 (d) I_2O_5

562. Cl_2O_7 can be regarded as an anhydride of
(a) hypochlorous acid (b) chlorous acid
(c) chloric acid (d) perchloric acid

563. Chlorine dioxide is best prepared by passing dry
(a) chlorine gas over hot HgO
(b) Cl_2 and O_2 gas over hot Pt catalyst
(c) HCl and O_2 over hot Ag_2O
(d) HCl over P_2O_5
(e) Cl_2 over hot silver chlorate

564. Which of the following properties is not shown by ClO_2?
(a) powerful oxidising agent
(b) chlorinating agent
(c) excellent bleaching agent
(d) diamagnetic character

565. The correct order of acidic strength is
(a) $Cl_2O_7 > SO_2 > P_4O_{10}$
(b) $K_2O > CaO > MgO$
(c) $CO_2 > N_2O_5 > SO_3$
(d) $Na_2O > MgO > Al_2O_3$

566. Which of the following molecules is theoretically not possible?
(a) OF_4 (b) OF_2 (c) SF_4 (d) O_2F_2

567. The hybridisation of the central atom and the shape of $[IO_2F_5]^{2-}$ ion, respectively, are

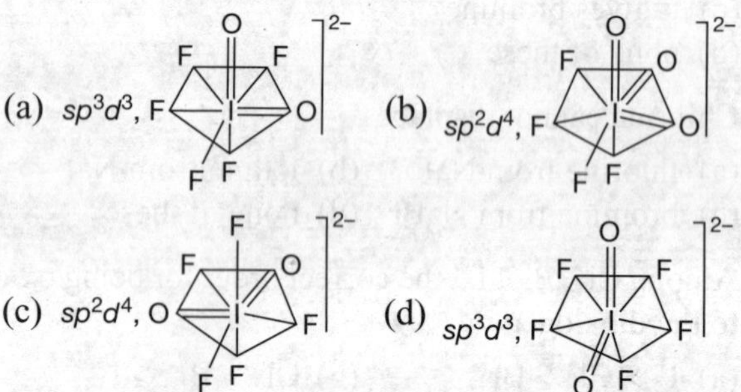

568. Which of the following dissolves in water but does not give any oxyacid solution?
(a) SO_2 (b) OF_2 (c) SCl_4 (d) SO_3

569. The least stable oxide of chlorine is
(a) Cl_2O (b) ClO_2 (c) Cl_2O_7 (d) ClO_3

570. On heating $NaClO_3$ with SO_2 and conc. H_2SO_4, we get
(a) Cl_2O (b) ClO_2 (c) ClO_3 (d) Cl_2O_7

571. ClO_2 reacts with O_3 to give
(a) Cl_2O_4 (b) Cl_2O (c) Cl_2O_6 (d) ClO_4

572. The reactivity of the following compounds towards water is in the order
(a) $Cl_2O_7 < P_2O_5 < B_2O_3$ (b) $B_2O_3 < P_2O_5 < Cl_2O_7$
(c) $P_2O_5 < B_2O_3 < Cl_2O_7$ (d) $B_2O_3 < Cl_2O_7 < P_2O_5$

573. Which of the following fluorides will combine further with fluorine?
(a) IF_5 (b) NaF (c) CaF_2 (d) SF_6

574. The T-Shaped interhalogen compound is
(a) ClF_3 (b) ICl (c) ClF_5 (d) IF_5

575. BrF_3 molecule contains
(a) three lone pairs and two bond pairs
(b) two lone pairs and three bond pairs
(c) lone pairs that occupy axial positions
(d) all the bonds equal

576. The compound used for the preparation of UF_6 in the enrichment of $_{92}U^{235}$ is
(a) AlF_3 (b) CaF_2 (c) HF (d) ClF_3

577. The interhalogen ICl is more reactive than I_2. This is because
(a) the I–Cl bond is weaker than the I–I bond. consequently, the I–Cl bond breaks easily to form the halogen atoms which readily bring about the reaction
(b) the I–Cl bond is polar and thus is more reactive than the non-polar I–I bond
(c) there is a large difference in the sizes of the atoms which provides instability to the molecule and consequently, it is more reactive than I_2
(d) none of the above

578. The stability of interhalogen compounds follows the order
(a) $IF_3 > BrF_3 > ClF_3$ (b) $BrF_3 > IF_3 > ClF_3$
(c) $ClF_3 > BrF_3 > IF_3$ (d) $ClF_3 > IF_3 > BrF_3$

579. In the structure of ClF_3, the number of lone pairs of electrons on the central atom Cl is
(a) one (b) two (c) four (d) three

580. Which of the following oxoacids of chlorine is the best oxidising agent?
(a) HOCl (b) $HClO_2$ (c) $HClO_3$ (d) $HClO_4$

581. The type of hybrid orbitals used by ClO_2^- is
(a) sp^3 (b) sp^2
(c) sp (d) none of these

582. The correct order of increasing hydration energy of the following conjugate bases of the oxoacids of chlorine is
(a) $ClO^- < ClO_2^- < ClO_3^- < ClO_4^-$
(b) $ClO_4^- < ClO_3^- < ClO_2^- < ClO^-$
(c) $ClO_4^- < ClO_3^- < ClO^- < ClO_2^-$
(d) $ClO_3^- < ClO_4^- < ClO_2^- < ClO^-$

583. All the four sigma bonds in perchlorate ion are
(a) $sp^3 - sp^3$ bonds (b) $sp^3 - p$ bonds
(c) $sp^2 - sp^2$ bonds (d) $sp^2 - p$ bonds

584. What is the equivalent mass of IO_4^- when it is converted into I_2 in the acid medium?
(a) M/6 (b) M/7 (c) M/5 (d) M/4
(e) none of these

585. Which of the following statements is correct?
(a) Only chlorine and bromine form oxyacids.
(b) All halogens form oxyacids.
(c) All halogens form more than one oxyacid, except fluorine which forms only one oxyacid.
(d) Only iodine forms oxyacids.

586. The incorrect statement about the oxoacids, $HClO_4$ and HClO is
(a) the central atom in both $HClO_4$ and HClO is sp^3-hybridised
(b) $HClO_4$ is formed in the reaction between Cl_2 and H_2O
(c) the conjugate base of $HClO_4$ is a weaker base than H_2O
(d) $HClO_4$ is more acidic than HClO because of the resonance stabilisation of its anion

587. The pK_a of oxoacids of chlorine in water follow the order
(a) $HClO < HClO_3 < HClO_2 < HClO_4$
(b) $HClO_4 < HClO_3 < HClO_2 < HClO$
(c) $HClO_4 < HClO_2 < HClO_3 < HClO$
(d) $HClO_2 < HClO < HClO_3 < HClO_4$

588. $3\,ClO^-(aq) \rightarrow ClO_3^- + 2\,Cl^-$ is an example of a(an)
(a) oxidation reaction (b) reduction reaction
(c) disproportionation reaction
(d) decomposition reaction

589. The gaseous product formed when HOCl reacts with H_2O_2 in the acidic medium is
(a) H_2 (b) Cl_2 (c) O_2
(d) $HClO_2$ (e) $HClO_3$

590. Which of the following compounds gives chlorine dioxide when it reacts with SO_2 in the presence of an acid?
(a) sodium chlorine (b) sodium chlorate
(c) sodium perchlorate (d) sodium chlorite

591. In which caseisthe order of acidic strength not correct?
(a) HI > HBr > HCl
(b) $HIO_4 > HBrO_4 > HClO_4$
(c) $HClO_4 > HClO_3 > HClO_2$
(d) $HF > H_2O > NH_3$

592. Which of the following is isolated in pure form?
(a) $HClO_4$ (b) $HClO_3$ (c) $HClO_2$ (d) HClO

593. NaOCl is used as a bleaching agent and sterilising agent. It can be synthesised by the action of
(a) NaCl with H_2O
(b) NH_4Cl and NaOH
(c) Cl_2 with cold and dilute NaOH
(d) Cl_2 with hot and concentrated NaOH

594. Which one of the following compounds in aqueous solution gives a white precipitate with perchloric acid?

(a) NaCl (b) KCl (c) $MgCl_2$ (d) $FeCl_3$

595. Of the following acids, the one that is strongest is

(a) $HBrO_4$ (b) HOCl (c) HNO_2 (d) H_3PO_3

596. Select the correct option(s) for the following statements.

1. Cl_2O and ClO_2 are used as bleaching agents.
2. OCl^- salts are used as detergents.
3. OCl^- disproportionates in the alkaline medium.
4. BrO_3^- is oxidised in an acidic medium.

(a) 1, 2, 3 correct (b) 2, 3, 4 correct
(c) 1, 2, 4 correct (d) 1, 3, 4 correct
(e) all are correct

597. If I_2 is dissolved in aqueous KI, the intense yellow species I_3^- is formed. The structure of I_3^- ion is

(a) square pyramidal (b) trigonal bipyramidal
(c) octahedral (d) pentagonal bipyramidal

598. What is the hybridisation and geometry of the given species? The species are XeF_2 and ICl_2^-.

(a) sp^3d and trigonal bipyramidal
(b) sp^3d^2 and square planar
(c) sp^3d and linear
(d) sp^3 and irregular tetrahedron

599. The lattice energy of the lithuium halides is in the following order

(a) LiF > LiCl > LiBr > LiI
(b) LiCl > LiF > LiBr > LiI
(c) LiBr > LiCl > LiF > LiI
(d) LiI > LiBr > LiCl > LiF

600. The alkali metal halides are soluble in water but LiF is insoluble because

(a) it is amphoteric
(b) the Li–F bond is highly ionic
(c) its lattice energy is high
(d) Li^+ ion is least hydrated

601. Reaction of NaCl with conc. H_2SO_4 liberates a gas X, that turns moist blue litmus paper red. When gas X is passed into a test tube containing egg shell powder suspended in water another gas Y is generated which when passed through lime water makes it milky. The gases X and Y respectively are

(a) HCl and CO_2 (b) SO_2 and CO_2
(c) Cl_2 and CO_2 (d) SO_2 and HCl

602. Amongst LiCl, RbCl, $BeCl_2$ and $MgCl_2$, the maximum and minimum ionic character will be shown by the compounds

(a) LiCl, $MgCl_2$ (b) RbCl, $BeCl_2$
(c) RbCl, $MgCl_2$ (d) $MgCl_2$, $BeCl_2$

603. Which of the following chlorides is water insoluble?

(a) HCl (b) AgCl
(c) both (a) and (b) (d) none of these

604. A metal M forms chlorides in its +2 and +4 oxidation states.Which of the following statements about these chlorides is correct?

(a) MCl_2 is more volatile than MCl_4.
(b) MCl_2 is more volatile in anhydrous ethanol than MCl_4.
(c) MCl_2 is more ionic than MCl_4.
(d) MCl_2 is more easily hydrolysed than MCl_4.

Halogens and their Compounds

605. Which of the following oxidises H_2O to oxygen?

(a) chlorine (b) fluorine
(c) bromine (d) iodine

606. With cold and dilute sodium hydroxide, fluorine reacts to give

(a) NaF and OF_2 (b) NaF + O_3
(c) O_2 and O_3 (d) NaF + O_2

607. Which of the following has the lowest solubility?

(a) CaF_2 (b) $CaCl_2$ (c) $CaBr_2$ (d) CaI_2

608. The reaction of the type 2 X_2 + S $\rightarrow$ SX_4 is shown by sulfur when X is

(a) fluorine or chlorine (b) chlorine only
(c) chlorine and bromine only
(d) F, Cl, Br, all

609. At room temperature, the reaction between water and fluorine produces

(a) HF and H_2O_2 (b) HF, O_2 and F_2O_2
(c) F^-, O_2 and H^+ (d) HOF and HF

610. The compounds used as gaseous insulations in high voltage generators is

(a) SeF_4 (b) SiF_4 (c) SF_4 (d) SF_6

611. In the preparation of chlorine from HCl, MnO_2 acts as an(a)

(a) oxidising agent (b) catalytic agent
(c) reducing agent (d) dehydrating agent

612. Which of the following conditions is used to find atomic chlorine from molecular Cl_2?

(a) high temperature, high pressure
(b) low temperature, high pressure
(c) high temperature, low pressure
(d) low temperature, low pressure

613. One gas bleaches the colours of flowers by reduction and the other by oxidation. The two gases are respectively

(a) Cl_2 and SO_2 (b) Br_2 and H_2S
(c) SO_2 and Cl_2 (d) NH_3 and SO_3

614. Chlorine acts as a bleaching agent only in the presence of
(a) dry air (b) moisture
(c) sunlight (d) pure oxygen

615. When chlorine is passed through hot concentrated alkali solution, which one of the following is formed?
(a) tetraoxochlorate (b) trioxochlorate (V)
(c) chloric (III) acid (d) monooxochlorate (I)

616. Select the wrong statement in the following:
The balanced chemical equation
$3\,Cl_2 + 6\,NaOH\,(conc.) \xrightarrow{Hot} 5\,NaCl + NaClO_3 + 3\,H_2O$
(a) represents disproportionation reaction
(b) represents acid-base reaction
(c) has chlorine in three different oxidation states
(d) has chlorine in the +5 oxidation state in sodium chlorate (one of the products)

617. Phosgene and mustard gas are the two poisonous gases which can be prepared from chlorine gas. To prepare mustard gas, the reagent which does not play any role is
(a) S_8 (b) Cl_2 (c) S_2Cl_2 (d) CH_4

618. Chlorine reacts with excess of ammonia to form
(a) NH_4Cl (b) $Na_2 + HCl$
(c) $NCl_3 + HCl$ (d) $N_2 + NCl_3$

619. The products obtained when chlorine gas reacts with cold and dilute aqueous NaOH are
(a) Cl^- and ClO^- (b) Cl^- and ClO_2^-
(c) ClO^- and ClO_3^- (d) ClO_2^- and ClO_3^-

620. When chlorine gas is passed through an aqueous solution of KBr, the solution turns orange brown due to the formation of
(a) KCl (b) HCl (c) HBr (d) Br_2

621. S_2Cl_2 hydrolyses slowly to form HCl, SO_2 and X. Which of the following is X?
(a) SO_3 (b) H_2 (c) O_2 (d) S

622. Bromine is liberated when an aqueous solution of potassium bromide is treated with
(a) Cl_2 (b) I_2 (c) dilute H_2SO_4 (d) SO_2

623. When Cl_2 gas is passed through a hot and conc. solution of KOH, the following compound is not formed
(a) KCl (b) $KClO_3$ (c) $KClO_2$ (d) H_2O

624. Chlorine gas is dried over
(a) CaO (b) NaOH (c) KOH (d) conc. H_2SO_4

625. When chlorine water is exposed to sunlight, O_2 is liberated. Hence,
(a) hydrogen has little affinity to O_2
(b) hydrogen has more affinity to O_2
(c) hydrogen has more affinity to Cl_2
(d) it is a reducing agent

626. A gas reacts with CaO, but not with $NaHCO_3$. The gas is
(a) CO_2 (b) Cl_2 (c) N_2 (d) O_2

627. Chlorine cannot be used
(a) as bleaching agent
(b) in sterilisation
(c) in preparation of antiseptic
(d) for extraction of silver and copper

628. Euchlorine is a mixture of
(a) Fischer's salt (b) epsom salt
(c) Ferming's salt (d) spirit of salt

629. A solution of potassium bromide is treated with each of the following. Which one would liberate bromine?
(a) hydrogen iodide (b) sulfur dioxide
(c) chlorine (d) iodine

630. Bromine vapours will turn moist starch iodide paper
(a) brown (b) red
(c) blue (d) colourless

631. Bromine water reacts with SO_2 to form
(a) HBr and S (b) H_2O and HBr
(c) S and H_2O (d) H_2SO_4 and HBr

632. In the reaction,
$3\,Br_2 + 6\,CO_3^{2-} + 3\,H_2O \rightarrow 5\,Br^- + BrO_3^- + 6\,HCO_3^-$
Choose the correct statement.
(a) Bromine is oxidised and carbonate is reduced.
(b) Bromine is reduced and carbonate is oxidised.
(c) Bromine is neither oxidised nor reduced.
(d) Bromine is both oxidised and reduced.

633. When a colourless gas is passed through bromine water, only decolourisation taken place. The gas is
(a) SO_2 (b) HBr (c) HCl (d) H_2S

634. Colour of the solution when KI reacts with Br_2 is
(a) blue (b) black (c) red (d) no change

635. To obtain iodine, seaweeds are dried, burnt and extracted with
(a) chloride (b) conc. H_2SO_4
(c) conc. NaOH (d) MnO_2 + conc. H_2SO_4
(e) MnO_2 alone

636. Which of the following solutions will turn violet when a drop of lime juice is added to it?
(a) a solution of NaI
(b) a solution mixture of KI and $NaIO_3$

(c) a solution mixture of NaI and KI
(d) a solution mixture of KIO_3 and $NaIO_3$

637. A NaCl, NaBr and NaI mixture on heating with conc. H_2SO_4 gives the gases, respectively
(a) HCl, HBr, HI (b) HCl, Br_2, I_2
(c) Cl_2, Br_2, I_2 (d) Cl_2, HBr, HI

638. A salt, which on heating with conc. H_2SO_4 gives violet vapours, is
(a) iodide (b) nitrate (c) sulfate (d) bromide

639. Which of the following halogens can be purified by sublimation?
(a) F_2 (b) Cl_2 (c) Br_2 (d) I_2

640. Iodine is released when potassium iodide reacts with
(a) $ZnSO_4$ (b) $CuSO_4$
(c) $FeSO_4$ (d) $(NH_4)_2SO_4$

641. The colour of iodine solution is discharged by shaking it with an aqueous solution of
(a) Fe^{2+} (b) Cu^{2+} (c) Pb^{2+} (d) Ag^{+}

642. Which reaction is not feasible?
(a) $2\ KI + Br \rightarrow 2\ KBr + I_2$
(b) $2\ KBr + I_2 \rightarrow 2\ KI + Br_2$
(c) $2\ KBr + Cl_2 \rightarrow 2\ KCl + Br_2$
(d) $2\ H_2O + 2\ F_2 \rightarrow 4\ HF + O_2$

643. Solubility of iodine in water may be increased by adding
(a) chloroform (b) potassium iodide
(c) carbon disulfide (d) sodium thiosulfate

644. When thiosulfate ion is oxidised by iodine, which one of the following ions is produced?
(a) SO_3^{2-} (b) SO_4^{2-}
(c) $S_4O_6^{2-}$ (tetrathionate) (d) $S_2O_6^{2-}$

645. When I_2 is dissolved in CCl_4, the colour that results is
(a) brown (b) violet
(c) colourless (d) bluish green

646. Concentrated HNO_3 reacts with I_2 to give
(a) HI (b) HOI (c) $HOIO_2$ (d) $HOIO_3$

647. Which of the following sequences is correct with reference to the oxidation number of iodine?
(a) I_2>ICl> HI > HIO_4 (b) HIO_4<ICl< I_2< HI
(c) I_2< HI <ICl< HIO_4 (d) HI < I_2<ICl< HIO_4

648. When I_2 is passed through KCl, KF and KBr solutions
(a) Cl_2 and Br_2 are evolved
(b) Cl_2 is evolved
(c) Cl_2, Br_2 and F_2 are evolved
(d) none of the above

649. Which of the following halides is least stable and has doubtful existence?
(a) CCl_4 (b) GeI_4 (c) SnI_4 (d) PbI_4

650. Among the halogens, the one that is oxidised by nitric acid is
(a) fluorine (b) iodine
(c) chlorine (d) bromine

651. I-131 is used for the treatment of
(a) thyroid disorders (b) skin disorders
(c) brain tumour (d) kidney stones

652. The compound which is added to table salt for maintaining proper health is
(a) KCl (b) KBr (c) NaI (d) $MgBr_2$

653. Finely powdered iron reacts with HCl to give
(a) $FeCl_3$ (b) $FeCl_2$
(c) $HFeCl_4$ (d) no reaction takes place

654. Of the following compounds, which one is the strongest Brönsted acid in aqueous solution?
(a) $HClO_3$ (b) HOBr (c) HOCl (d) HOBr

655. Fluorine is obtained by the reaction of K_2MnF_6 with a Lewis acid SbF_5 because of the
(a) acidolysis of MnF_4 (b) decomposition of MnF_4
(c) ionisation of MnF_4 (d) decomposition of SbF_6

656. Which of the following is used during the preparation of fluorine by Whytlaw–Gray method?
(a) aqueous KF (b) aqueous HF
(c) molten KHF_2 (d) NH_4F

657. Which of the following is prepared by the electrolytic method?
(a) Ca (b) Sn (c) S (d) F_2

658. To purify fluorine gas, fumes of HF are removed by
(a) solid NaF (b) H_2 gas
(c) solid KHF_2 (d) none of these

659. High concentrations of fluoride are poisonous and harmful to bones and teeth at levels over
(a) 1 ppm (b) 3 ppm (c) 5 ppm (d) 10 ppm

660. To make a painting over glass, we use
(a) fluorine (b) chlorine
(c) bromine (d) hydrogen chloride

661. Fluorine reacts with dilute NaOH and forms a gaseous product A. The bond angle in the molecule of A is
(a) 104 °40′ (b) 103°
(c) 107° (d) 109°28′

Bleaching Powder, $CaOCl_2$ (Calcium Clorohypochlorite, Chloride of Lime)

662. Which is soluble in water?
(a) AgCl (b) AgBr (c) AgI (d) AgF

663. Which are hydrolysed by water?

(a) XeF_2 (b) XeF_4
(c) XeF_6 (d) all of these

664. Oxygen is obtained from bleaching powder by

(a) the action of dilute acids
(b) the action of alkalies
(c) heating with lime
(d) heating with a cobalt sale

665. Aqueous solution of bleaching powder gives a test for

(a) only Cl^- ions (b) only OCl^- ions
(c) only Ca^{2+} (d) all Cl^-, OCl^- and Ca^{2+} ions

666. Bleaching powder reacts with a few drops of conc. HCl to give

(a) chlorine (b) hypochlorous acid
(c) calcium oxide (d) oxygen

667. Auto-oxidation of bleaching powder gives

(a) only calcium chlorate
(b) only calcium chloride
(c) only calcium hypochlorite
(d) both (a) and (b)

668. When CO_2 is passed through an aqueous solution of bleaching powder, the gas evolved is

(a) oxygen (b) chlorine
(c) ozone (d) chlorine dioxide

669. Bleaching powder loses its power on keeping for a long time because

(a) it changes into calcium hypochlorate
(b) it changes into calcium chloride and calcium hydroxide
(c) it absorbs moisture
(d) it changes into calcium chloride and calcium chlorate

670. The reaction of Cl_2 with X gives bleaching powder. X is

(a) CaO (b) $Ca(OH)_2$
(c) $Ca(OCl)_2$ (d) $Ca(ClO_3)_2$

671. The estimation of available chlorine in bleaching powder is done by

(a) acid–base titration
(b) permanganometric titration
(c) iodimetric titration
(d) iodometric titration

Pseudohalogens and Pseudohalides (Halogenoid Ions)

672. Which of the following is a pseudohalogen?

(a) N_3^- (b) ONC^- (c) $(SCN)_2$ (d) SCN^-

673. The correct order of pseudohalide, polyhalide and interhalogen is

(a) BrI_2^-, OCN^-, IF_5 (b) IF_5, BrI_2^-, OCN^-
(c) OCN^-, IF_5, BrI_2^- (d) OCN^-, BrI_2^-, IF_5

Final Preparation

674. HBr and HI reduce sulfuric acid; HCl can reduce $KMnO_4$ and HF reduces:

(a) H_2SO_4 (b) $KMnO_4$
(c) $K_2Cr_2O_7$ (d) none of these

675. Which of the following statements is not true?

(a) Among the halide ions, iodide is the most powerful reducing agent.
(b) Fluorine is the only halogen that does not show a variable oxidation state.
(c) HOCl is a stronger acid than HOBr.
(d) HF is a stronger acid than HCl.

676. In which of the following arrangements is the given sequence not strictly according to the property indicated against it?

(a) $NH_3 < PH_3 < AsH_3 < SbH_3$: increasing acidic character
(b) $CO_2 < SiO_2 < SnO_2 < PbO_2$: increasing acidic character
(c) HF < HCl < HBr < HI: increasing acidic strength
(d) $H_2O < H_2S < H_2Se < H_2Te$: increasing pK_a values

677. The variation of the boiling points of the hydrogen halides is in the order HF > HI > HBr > HCl because

(a) There is strong hydrogen bonding between the HF molecules.
(b) The bond energy of HF molecules is greater than in other hydrogen halides.
(c) The effect of nuclear shielding is much reduced in fluorine which polarises the HF molecule.
(d) The electronegativity of fluorine is much higher than for other elements in the group.

678. HF is corrosive and causes painful skin wounds which are slow to heal. Choose the incorrect statement among the following.

(a) HF dehydrates the tissue.
(b) HF is acidic in nature and causes skin wounds.
(c) Healing of tissue requires Ca^{2+} ions which are removed from the tissue by F^- forming insoluble CaF_2, so the healing is slow.
(d) HF oxidises the tissue material which cannot restore its original state easily.

679. Which one of the following sequences represents the correct increasing order of bond angles in the given molecule?

(a) $H_2O < OF_2 < OCl_2 < ClO_2$
(b) $OCl_2 < ClO_2 < H_2O < OF_2$
(c) $OF_2 < H_2O < OCl_2 < OClO_2$

(d) $ClO_2 < OF_2 < OCl_2 < H_2O$

680. The correct order of increasing bond angles in the following species is
(a) $ClO_2^- < Cl_2O < ClO_2$ (b) $Cl_2O < ClO_2 < ClO_2^-$
(c) $ClO_2 < Cl_2O < ClO_2^-$ (d) $Cl_2O < ClO_2^- < CO_2$

681. Which one of the following oxides is expected to exhibit paramagnetic behaviour?
(a) CO_2 (b) ClO_2 (c) SO_2 (d) SiO_2

682. Which one of the following oxides of chlorine is obtained by passing dry chlorine over silver chlorate at 90°C?
(a) Cl_2O (b) ClO_3 (c) ClO_2 (d) ClO_4

683. Cl_2O_6 is diamagnetic in the solid state but in the vapour state, it exhibits paramagnetism. Choose the incorrect statement among the following.
(a) In the vapour state, Cl_2O_6 exists as ClO_3 monomer having one unpaired electron and is paramagnetic in nature.
(b) In the solid state, it is diamagnetic and dimeric having all the electrons paired.
(c) In Cl_2O_6, Cl is d^2sp^3 hybridised.
(d) In Cl_2O_6, Cl is sp^3-hybridised.

684. Which one of the following is the true covalent oxide of iodine?
(a) I_2O_4 (b) I_2O_5 (c) I_2O_7 (d) I_2O_9

685. A 500 gtoothpaste sample has 0.2 g fluoride concentration. What is the concentration of F^- ions in terms of ppm?
(a) 250 (b) 200 (c) 400 (d) 1000

686. Which of the following is soluble in water?
(a) AgF (b) AgCl (c) AgBr (d) AgI

687. In which of the following molecules are all the bonds not equal?
(a) NF_3 (b) ClF_3 (c) BF_3 (d) AlF_3

688. Which of the following is not paramagnetic?
(a) ClF_3 (b) ClO_2 (c) ClO_3 (d) BrO_3

689. Which of the following interhalogens of the type XX'_3 exhibits a dimeric planar structure?
(a) ClF_3 (b) ICl_3 (c) BrF_3 (d) IF_3

690. In the BrF_3 molecule, the lone pairs occupy equatorial positions to minimise
(a) lone pair–bond pair repulsion only
(b) bond pair–bond pair repulsion only
(c) lone pair–lone pair repulsion and lone pair–bond pair repulsion
(d) lone pair–lone pair repulsion only

691. Which of the following does not form polyhalide ions while acting as a central atom?
(a) F (b) Cl (c) Br (d) I

692. Which products are expected from the disproportionation reaction of hypochlorous acid?
(a) $HClO_3$ and Cl_2O (b) $HClO_2$ and $HClO_4$
(c) HCl and Cl_2O (d) HCl and $HClO_3$

693. Which of the following species will not exhibit disproportionation reaction?
(a) ClO^- (b) ClO_2^- (c) ClO_3^- (d) ClO_4^-

694. The oxidation states of iodine in HIO_4, H_3IO_5 and H_5IO_6 are, respectively
(a) +1, +3, +7 (b) +7, +7, +3
(c) +7, +7, +7 (d) +7, +5, +3

695. Which of the following is not a peroxy acid?
(a) perphosphoric acid (b) pernitric acid
(c) perdisulfuric acid (d) perchloric acid

696. The correct other of acid strength is
(a) $HClO < HClO_2 < HClO_3 < HClO_4$
(b) $HClO_4 < HClO < HClO_2 < HClO_3$
(c) $HClO_2 < HClO_3 < HClO_4 < HClO$
(d) $HClO_4 < HClO_3 < HClO_2 < HClO$

697. Which is the strongest acid in the following?
(a) H_2SO_4 (b) $HClO_3$ (c) $HClO_4$ (d) H_2SO_3

698. Which of the following is the correct order of decreasing oxidising power of perhalates?
(a) $ClO_4^- > BrO_4^- > IO_4^-$ (b) $BrO_4^- > ClO_4^- > IO_4^-$
(c) $IO_4^- > BrO_4^- > ClO_4^-$ (d) $BrO_4^- > IO_4^- > ClO_4^-$

699. The type of hybrid orbitals used by the iodine atom in the hypoiodous acid molecule are
(a) sp^3 (b) sp^2 (c) sp (d) sp^3d

700. When I^- is oxidised by $KMnO_4$ in the alkaline medium, I^- converts into
(a) IO_3^- (b) I_2 (c) IO_4^- (d) IO^-

701. In the balanced chemical equation
$IO_3^- + pI^- + +H^+ \rightarrow r\,H_2O + s\,I_2$
p, *q*, *r* and *s* respectively correspond to
(a) 5, 6, 3, 3 (b) 5, 3, 6, 3
(c) 3, 5, 3, 6 (d) 5, 6, 5, 5

702. Which two of the following salts are used for preparing iodised salt?
(i) KIO_3, (ii) KI, (iii) I_2, (iv) HI
(a) (i) and (ii) (b) (i) and (iii)
(c) (ii) and (iv) (d) (iii) and (iv)

703. Fluorine reacts with water to give
(a) HF and O_2 (b) HF and OF_2

(c) HF and O_3 (d) HF, O_2 and O_3

704. F_2 is formed by reacting K_2MnF_6 with

(a) SbF_5 (b) MnF_3
(c) $KSbF_6$ (d) MnF_4

705. A gas (X) is passed through water to form a saturated solution. The aqueous solution on treatment with silver nitrate gives a white precipitate. The saturated aqueous solution also dissolves magnesium ribbon with the evolution of a colourless gas (Y). The gases (X) and (Y) are respectively

(a) SO_2, Cl_2 (b) Cl_2, CO_2
(c) Cl_2, H_2 (d) NO_2, Cl_2

706. A black powder (A) when heated with NaCl and conc. H_2SO_4 gives off a greenish yellow gas (B). The gas (B) on passing through liquor ammonia liberates N_2 gas. The black powder (A) and the gas (B) are respectively

(a) charcoal, Cl_2 (b) CuS, H_2S
(c) MnO_2, Cl_2 (d) C, SO_2

707. Which of the following is used to prepare Cl_2 gas at room temperature from concentrated HCl?

(a) MnO_2 (b) H_2S (c) $KMnO_4$ (d) Cr_2O_3

708. Aqueous solution of $Na_2S_2O_3$ on reaction with Cl_2 gives

(a) $Na_2S_4O_6$ (b) $NaHSO_4$ (c) NaCl (d) NaOH

709. When Cl_2 gas reacts with hot and concentrated sodium hydroxide solution, the oxidation number of chlorine changes from

(a) zero to –1 and zero to –5
(b) zero to –1 and zero to +5
(c) zero to –1 and zero to +3
(d) zero to –1 and zero to –3

710. Iodine displaces chlorine from the aqueous solution of ________ on boiling

(a) KCl (b) HCl (c) $BaCl_2$ (d) $KClO_3$

711. When KI and $CuSO_4$ solution are mixed, it gives

(a) $K_2SO_4 + I_2$ (b) $Cu_2I_2 + K_2SO_4$
(c) $CuI_2 + K_2SO_4$ (d) $Na_2SO_4 + I_2$

712. Cl_2, Br_2 and I_2 react with $Na_2S_2O_3$. Pick out the correct statement from the following.

(a) All the halogens react in a similar way.
(b) Cl_2 and Br_2 react in a similar way but I_2 reacts differently.
(c) Br_2 and I_2 react in a similar way.
(d) Cl_2 reacts differently.

713. Which of the following statements is wrong?

In the reaction $2\ KClO_3 + I_2 \rightarrow 2\ KIO_3 + Cl_2$

(a) Cl_2 is more reactive than I_2.
(b) When $KClO_3$ reacts with I_2, Cl_2 is liberated.
(c) $KClO_3 + I_2$ is a redox reaction and I_2 is oxidised.
(d) In the above reaction, I_2 is reduced.

714. Which of the following will not occur?

(a) $Fe + H_2SO_4 \rightarrow FeSO_4 + H_2$
(b) $Cu + 2\ AgNO_3 \rightarrow Cu(NO_3)_2 + 2\ Ag$
(c) $2\ KBr + I_2 \rightarrow 2\ KI + Br_2$
(d) $CuO + H_2 \rightarrow Cu + H_2O$

715. Match the interhalogen compound of column I with the geometry in column II and assign the correct code:

Column I	**Column II**
(A) XX′	(i) T-shaped
(B) XX'_3	(ii) Pentagonal bipyramidal
(C) XX'_5	(iii) Linear
(D) XX'_7	(iv) Square pyramidal
	(v) Tetrahedral

Code:

	(A)	(B)	(C)	(D)
(a)	(iii)	(iv)	(i)	(ii)
(b)	(iii)	(i)	(iv)	(ii)
(c)	(v)	(iv)	(iii)	(ii)
(d)	(iv)	(iii)	(ii)	(i)

716. $HgCl_2$ and I_2 both, when dissolved in water containing I^- ions, the pair of species formed is

(a) HgI_2, I_3^- (b) HgI_2, I^-
(c) HgI_4^{2-}, I_3^- (d) Hg_2I_2, I^-

717. Sodium chloride when heated with conc. H_2SO_4 and solid potassium dichromate gives

(a) chromic chloride (b) chromyl chloride gas
(c) chromous chloride (d) none of the above

718. Dilute hydrochloric acid solution cannot be concentrated by boiling beyond

(a) 11% (b) 33% (c) 44% (d) 20.4%

719. A mixture of conc. HCl and HNO_3 made in a 3:1 ratio contains

(a) ClO_2 (b) NOCl (c) NCl_3 (d) N_2O_4

720. Which of the following is not a pseudohalide?

(a) $RCOO^-$ (b) CN^- (c) CNO^- (d) N_3^-

721. The statement true for N_3^- is,

(a) it has a non-linear structure
(b) it is called pseudohalogen
(c) the formal oxidation state of nitrogen in this anion is –1
(d) it is isoelectronic with NO_2

722. Ozonised oxygen can be obtained from H_2O by the action of

(a) conc. H_2SO_4 (b) $KMnO_4$

(c) MnO_4^{2-} (d) F_2

723. HBr and HI can reduce sulfuric acid; HCl can reduce $KMnO_4$ and HF can reduce

(a) H_2SO_4 (b) $KMnO_4$
(c) $K_2Cr_2O_7$ (d) none of the above

724. In the reaction $HNO_3 + HF \rightarrow H_2NO_3^+ + F^-$, the base is

(a) HF (b) HNO_3
(c) HF and HNO_3 (d) aqua regia

MATCH THE FOLLOWING

725.

Column (I) (Reactants)	Column II (Products)
(A) $NaOH + Cl_2 \rightarrow$	(p) $ClO_2 + CO_2 + Na_2C_2O_4 + H_2O$
(B) $NaClO_3 + H_2C_2O_4 \rightarrow$	(q) $NaClO_3 + NaClO_4 + H_2O$
(C) $ClO_2 + NaOH \rightarrow$	(r) $NaCl + NaClO_3 + H_2O$
(D) $Cl_2O_6 + NaOH \rightarrow$	(s) $NaClO_2 + NaClO_3 + H_2O$

(a) (A)—(s); (B)—(r); (C)—(q); (D)—(p)
(b) (A)—(r); (B)—(p); (C)—(s); (D)—(q)
(c) (A)—(p); (B)—(q); (C)—(s); (D)—(r)
(d) (A)—(q); (B)—(r); (C)—(p); (D)—(s)

726.

Column (I) (Compounds)	Column II (No. of lone pairs)
(A) BrF_5	(p) 2 occupying axial positions
(B) ICl_4^-	(q) 1 occupying equatorial position
(C) ClF_3	(r) 1 occupying axial position
(D) SF_4	(s) 2 occupying equatorial positions

(a) (A)—(r); (B)—(p); (C)—(s); (D)—(q)
(b) (A)—(s); (B)—(q); (C)—(p); (D)—(r)
(c) (A)—(p); (B)—(r); (C)—(q); (D)—(s)
(d) (A)—(q); (B)—(s); (C)—(r); (D)—(p)

727.

Column (I) (Halogen acids)	Column II (Property)
(A) HCl	(p) Strong reducing agent
(B) HF	(q) Strongest acid
(C) HBr	(r)Etches glass
(D) HI	(s) Monobasic

(a) (A)—(p); (B)—(r); (C)—(q); (D)—(s)
(b) (A)—(q); (B)—(s); (C)—(r); (D)—(p)
(c) (A)—(r); (B)—(p); (C)—(s); (D)—(q)
(d) (A)—(s); (B)—(r); (C)—(s); (D)—(p,q,s)

ASSERTION REASON

Directions: In each of the following questions, a statement of Assertion (A) is given followed by a corresponding statement of Reason (R) just below it. Of the statements, mark the correct answer as

(a) if both the assertion and reason are true and the reason is the correct explanation of the assertion.
(b) if both the assertion and reason are true but the reason is not the correct explanation of the assertion
(c) if the assertion is true but the reason is false
(d) if both the assertion and reason are false

728. Assertion: The F atom has less negative electron gain enthalpy than the Cl atom.

Reason: Additional electrons are repelled more effectively by the *sp*-electrons in Cl than by the 2*p*-electrons in the F atom.

729. Assertion: Chlorine has a higher electron gain enthalpy than fluorine.

Reason: Chlorine is a poorer oxidising agent a than fluorine.

730. Assertion: Fluorine molecule has a bond order of one.

Reason: The number of electrons in the antibonding molecular orbitals is two less than that in the bonding molecular orbitals.

731. Assertion: Heat of hydration of the halide ion (X^-) increases down the group from F to I.

Reason: Size of the halogens decreases from F to I.

732. Assertion: Iodine forms a positive iodinium ion I^+, and thus shows electropositive or metallic character.

Reason: Iodine has a comparatively low value of ionisation enthalpy and thus has a tendency to lose an electron to form the positive iodinium ion, I^+.

733. Assertion: F_2 does not show disproportionation reaction.

Reason: F_2 is the strongest oxidising agent and it is always reduced.

734. Assertion: All the halogens are chemically very reactive elements.

Reason: This is due to their low dissociation energies (as compared to common molecules like H_2, O_2, N_2) and high negative electron gain enthalpy values.

735. Assertion:F_2 has high reactivity.

Reason: F–F bond has a low bond dissociation enthalpy.

736. Assertion: Amongst the halogens, fluorine can oxidise the elements to their highest oxidation state.

Reason: Due to the small size of the fluoride ion, it is difficult to oxidise the fluoride ion to fluorine. Hence, the reverse reaction takes place more easily.

737. Assertion: Concentrated sulfuric acid cannot be used for the preparation of HBr from NaBr.

Reason: HBr being strong reducing agent, reduces H_2SO_4 to SO_2 and is itself oxidised to Br_2.

738. Assertion: O_2F_2 is a strong fluorinating agent. It oxidises Pu to PuF_6.

Reason: Pu is removed from spent nuclear fuel as PuF_6 by treating it with O_2F_2.

739. Assertion: The acid strength of oxoacids of the same halogen increases with an increase in the oxidation number of the halogen. For example,

$\overset{+7}{HClO_4} > \overset{+5}{HClO_3} > \overset{+3}{HClO_2} > \overset{+1}{HClO}$

Reason: The acid strength in these cases can be explained by the relative stability of the anion left after the removal of a proton.

740. Assertion: $HClO_4$ is a stronger acid than $HClO_3$.

Reason: The oxidation state of Cl in $HClO_4$ is VII and in $HClO_3$ is V.

741. Assertion: The HOF bond angle is higher than HOCl bond angle in HOX.

Reason: Oxygen is more electronegative than the halogens.

GROUP 18

General Introduction

742. Which noble gas does not form clathrates?

(a) Xe (b) Kr (c) He (d) Ar

743. Noble gases are adsorbed by:

(a) finely divided Pd and Pt
(b) colloidal Pd
(c) coconut charcoal
(d) all of the above

744. What is the correct order of occurrence (1% by weight) in air of Ne, Ar and Kr?

(a) Ne >Ar> Kr (b) Ar> Ne > Kr
(c) Ar> Kr > Ne (d) Ne >Kr >Ar

745. The spectrum of helium is similar to that of

(a) H (b) Li^+ (c) Na (d) He^+

746. The noble gas which is obtained by radioactive disintegration is

(a) He (b) Ne (c) Ar (d) Rn

747. In the separation of a noble gas mixture from air by Ramsay–Rayleigh's first method, the substances used for the removal of N_2 and O_2 respectively, are

(a) Cu and Mg (b) Mg and Cu
(c) C and CaC_2 (d) KOH solution

748. The noble gas mixture is cooled in a coconut bulb at 173 K. The gases that are not adsorbed are

(a) Ne and Xe (b) He and Xe
(c) Ar and Kr (d) He and Ne

749. Which element was used in the isolation of radon?

(a) plutonium (b) radium
(c) uranium (d) thorium

750. Which of the following statements is not correct for a noble gas?

(a) Ar is used in electric bulbs.
(b) Kr is obtained during radioactive disintegration.
(c) Half life of Rn is only 3.8 days.
(d) He is used in producing very low temperature.

751. The atomic weight of noble gases is determined with the help of the following relationship:

(a) Atomic weight = Equivalent weight × valency
(b) Atomic weight = Equivalent weight/valency
(c) Atomic weight = 2 × Vapour density = Molecular weight
(d) Atomic weight = Valency/Equivalent weight

752. Which radioactive element is an inert gas?

(a) Ra (b) Rn (c) Pu (d) Po

753. When the mineral cleveite is heated, it gives off an inert gas

(a) helium (b) xenon (c) radon (d) argon

754. Which one of the following noble gases is not found in the atmosphere?

(a) Rn (b) Kr (c) Ne (d) Ar

Atomic and Physical Properties

755. In colour discharge tubes, which is used?

(a) Ne (b) Ar (c) Kr (d) He

756. The gas used for inflating the tyres of aeroplanes is:

(a) H_2 (b) He (c) N_2 (d) Ar

757. Which of the following exhibits the weakest intermolecular forces?

(a) He (b) HCl (c) NH_3 (d) H_2O

758. Noble gases exist only in the monoatomic state. This is due to

(a) non availability of unpaired electrons
(b) their high ionisation enthalpy
(c) their very large sizes
(d) their almost zero electron gain enthalpy

759. In the solid state, argon atoms are held by

(a) ionic bonds (b) covalent bonds

(c) hydrogen bonds (d) van der Waals forces

760. Argon possesses

(a) translational motion only
(b) translational + rotational motion
(c) translational + vibrational motion
(d) translation + rotational + vibration motion

761. The atomic radii of fluorine and neon in angstrom units are respectively given by

(a) 0.72, 1.60 (b) 1.60, 1.60
(c) 0.72, 0.72 (d) none of these values

762. Noble gases have comparatively large atomic sizes. This is because the atomic sizes of noble gases are usually expressed in terms of their

(a) atomic radii (b) covalent radii
(c) van der Waals radii (d) metallic radii

763. The noble gas whose ionisation enthalpy is closest to that of oxygen gas is

(a) He (b) Ar (c) Kr (d) Xe

764. The elements which occupy the peaks of the ionisation enthalpy curve are

(a) Na, K, Rb, Cs (b) Na, Mg, Cl, I
(c) Cl, Br, I, F (d) He, Ne, Ar, Kr

765. Which of the following statements about noble gases are correct?

I. XeO_3 is an explosive tetrahedral molecule.
II. In the Fisher–Ringe's method, a mixture of $CaCl_2$ and CaC_2 is used to remove N_2 and O_2.
III. He and Ne are chemically inert due to the lack of *d*-orbitals and high ionisation potential.
IV. At 173 K, He and Ne are absorbed on activated charcoal.

(a) I and II (b) II and III
(c) II, III and IV (d) I, II, III and IV

766. Gradual addition of an electronic shell in the noble gases causes a decrease in their

(a) ionisation energy (b) atomic radius
(c) boiling point (d) density

767. The increase in boiling points of the noble gases from He to Xe is due to a/an

(a) decrease in ionisation enthalpy
(b) increase in polarisation
(c) increase in atomic volume
(d) increase in electron gain enthalpy

768. Among the following, the most volatile of all liquids is

(a) Ne (b) Ar (c) Xe (d) He

769. The melting points and boiling points of the noble gases show

(a) a very little difference (b) a very large difference
(c) no difference at all (d) none of the above

770. Which inert gas has the highest boiling point?

(a) Xe b) Ar (c) Kr (d) He

771. Which of the following is more soluble in water?

(a) N_2 (b) O_2 (c) Ar (d) He

772. The correct order of solubility in water for He, Ne, Ar, Kr, Xe is

(a) He > Ne > Ar > Kr > Xe
(b) Ne > He > Kr > Ar > Xe
(c) Xe > Kr > Ar > Ne > He
(d) Ar > Ne > He > Kr > Xe

773. Which of the noble gases has the highest polarisability?

(a) He (b) Ar (c) Kr (d) Xe

774. Which one of the following noble gases is the least polarisable?

(a) Xe (b) Ar (c) Ne (d) He

775. Which of the following inert gas liquefies easily?

(a) Kr (b) He (c) Ne (d) Ar

776. The noble gas which can diffuse through rubber, glass or plastic easily is

(a) Xe (b) Ne (c) Ar (d) He

777. The noble gas showing least thermal conductivity at 273 K and atmospheric pressure is

(a) He (b) Ne (c) Ar (d) Xe

778. Nuclear fusion produces

(a) argon (b) deuterium
(c) helium (d) krypton

779. Which inert gas shows an abnormal behaviour on liquefaction?

(a) Xe (b) He (c) Ar (d) Kr

780. Noble gases are adsorbed by

(a) anhydrous calcium chloride
(b) ferric hydroxide
(c) conc. H_2SO_4
(d) activated coconut charcoal

781. The lightest gas is

(a) N_2 (b) Ar (c) Rn (d) He

782. Noble gases are a group of elements which exhibit very

(a) high chemical activity
(b) low chemical activity
(c) minimum electronegativity
(d) much paramagnetic properties

Chemical Properties (Compounds of Noble Gases)

783. The forces of cohesion in liquid helium are
(a) covalent (b) ionic
(c) van der Waals' (d) metallic

784. Which is called the 'stranger' gas?
(a) Kr (b) Xe (c) He (d) Ne

785. Among the noble gases (from He to Xe) only xenon reacts with fluorine to form stable xenon fluorides because xenon
(a) has the largest size
(b) has the lowest ionisation enthalpy
(c) has the highest heat of vaporisation
(d) is the most readily available noble gas

786. The first compound of xenon synthesised by Bartlett was
(a) $[XeF]^+ [XePtF_5]^-$ (b) $[XeO_3]$
(c) $Xe[PtF_6]$ (d) $O_2[XeF_6]$

787. Which element out of He, Ar, Kr and Xe forms the least number of compounds?
(a) He (b) Ar (c) Kr (d) Xe

788. The noble gas which forms the maximum number of compounds is
(a) Ar (b) He (c) Xe (d) Ne

789. Which of the noble gases is most reactive?
(a) He (b) Ne (c) Ar (d) Xe

790. Least chemical activity is shown by
(a) nitrogen (b) argon
(c) methane (d) ammonia

791. Fluorine forms chemical compounds with
(a) He (b) Ne (c) Ar (d) Xe

792. The inert gases producing a maximum number of compounds are
(a) He and Ne (b) Ar and Ne
(c) Kr and Ne (d) Ar and Xe

793. It has been difficult to study the chemistry of radon because
(a) it is a rare gas
(b) it does not occur in the atmosphere
(c) it is radioactive
(d) it has a short half-life period of only 3–82 days

794. The total number of electrons surrounding Kr in KrF_2 are
(a) 4 (b) 6 (c) 2 (d) 10

795. Which of the following compounds does not exist?
(a) $[KrF]^+ [SbF_6]^-$ (b) $[KrF_3]^-[SbF_4]^+$
(c) $[KrF]^+ [MoOF_5]^-$ (d) $[KrF]^+[WOF_5]^-$

796. The reaction between xenon and fluorine in excess molar ratio at 673 K gives
(a) XeF_4 (b) XeF_6 (c) XeF_2
(d) they do not react as Xe is inert

797. The geometry of the XeF_2 molecule is
(a) linear (b) triangular planar
(c) square planar (d) trigonal bipyramidal

798. Which of the following has a maximum number of lone pairs associated with Xe?
(a) XeO_3 (b) XeF_4 (c) XeF_6 (d) XeF_2

799. What is the hybridisation and geometry of the given species? The species are XeF_2 and ICl_2^-?
(a) sp^3d and trigonal bipyramidal
(b) sp^3d^2 and square planar
(c) sp^3d and linear
(d) sp^3 and irregular tetrahedron

800. Which of the following is incorrect?
(a) XeF_2 is a powerful reducing agent.
(b) XeF_2 is obtained by the direct reaction between F_2 and Xe at high pressure.
(c) XeF_2 undergoes alkaline hydrolysis to give O_2 and Xe.
(d) XeF_4 contains two bond pairs and three lone pairs.

801. By heating a mixture of xenon and fluorine in the ratio 1 : 5 in a nickel vessel at 873 K and 7 bar, the compound obtained is
(a) XeF_2 (b) XeF_6
(c) XeF_4 (d) XeO_2F_2

802. Which of the following is planar?
(a) XeF_2 (b) XeO_3F (c) XeO_2F_2 (d) XeF_4

803. XeF_4 on partial hydrolysis produces
(a) XeF_2 (b) $XeOF_2$ (c) $XeOF_4$ (d) XeO_3

804. XeF_4 reacts with water at –80°C to give
(a) $XeOF_2$ (b) $XeOF_4$
(c) XeO_3 (d) XeO_2F_2

805. Which of the following has sp^3 hybridisation?
(a) XeO_3 (b) $XeOF_4$ (c) XeF_4 (d) BBr_3

806. Hydrolysis of XeF_6 leads to a
(a) redox reaction (b) disproportion reaction
(c) acid–base reaction (d) none of these

807. The following balanced chemical equation
$XeF_6 + H_2O \rightarrow XeO_2F_2 + HF$
(a) has the stoichiometric coefficient of HF as 4
(b) represents a disproportionation reaction
(c) shows complete hydrolysis of XeF_6
(d) represents a redox reaction

808. XeO_3 is prepared by the
(a) complete hydrolysis of XeF_4
(b) partial hydrolysis of XeF_6
(c) partial hydrolysis of XeF_4.
(d) action of conc. H_2SO_4 on sodium perxenate

809. Which of the following noble gas compound is isostructural with BrO_3^-?
(a) XeO_4 (b) XeO_3 (c) XeO_2F_2 (d) $XeOF_4$

810. Which of the following is not correct?
(a) XeO_3 has four σ- and four π-bonds.
(b) The hybridisation of Xe in XeF_4 is sp^3d^2.
(c) Among the noble gases, the occurrence (percent by weight) of argon is highest in air.
(d) Liquid helium is used in cryogenic liquids.

811. Which of the following compounds of xenon has a pyramidal geometry?
(a) XeF_2 (b) XeF_4 (c) $XeOF_4$ (d) XeO_3

812. The number $p\pi$–$d\pi$ 'pi' bonds present in XeO_3 and XeO_4 molecules, respectively are
(a) 3, 4 (b) 4, 2 (c) 2, 3 (d) 3, 2

813. Which one of the following reactions of xenon compounds is not feasible?
(a) $XeO_3 + 6\,HF \rightarrow XeF_6 + 3\,H_2O$
(b) $3\,XeF_4 + 6\,H_2O \rightarrow 2\,Xe + XeO_3 + 1_2\,HF + 1.5\,O_2$
(c) $2\,XeF_2 + 2\,H_2O \rightarrow 2\,Xe + 4\,HF + O_2$
(d) $XeF_6 + RbF \rightarrow Rb[XeF_7]$

814. In the $XeOF_2$ molecule, the hybridisation of Xe orbitals is
(a) sp^3d^3 (b) sp^3d^2 (c) sp^3d (d) sp^3

815. The geometry of $XeOF_2$ is
(a) pyramidal (b) T-shaped
(c) octahedral (d) tetrahedral

816. Which of the following can be stored in glass or pyrex vessels?
(a) XeO_3 (b) $XeOF_2$ (c) XeF_4
(d) XeO_4 (e) all

817. The oxidation number of xenon in $XeOF_2$ is
(a) zero (b) 2 (c) 4 (d) 3

818. The shape number of the XeO_2F_2 molecule is
(a) trigonal bipyramidal (b) square planar
(c) tetrahedral (d) see–saw

819. Which of the following compounds does not have Xe in the +1 oxidation state?
(a) XeF radical (b) $XePtF_6$
(c) $XeRhF_6$ (d) $[XeF]^+[PF_6]^-$

820. The shape of XeF_5^- will be
(a) square pyramid (b) trigonal bipyramid
(c) planar (d) pentagonal bipyramid

821. Welding of magnesium can be done in an atmosphere of
(a) Xe (b) He (c) Kr (d) O_2

822. Helium is used in balloons instead of hydrogen because it is
(a) lighter than hydrogen
(b) incombusitile
(c) more abundant than hydrogen
(d) radioactive and easily detected

823. Which of the following is not a use of argon?
(a) To create an inert atmosphere in chemical reactions.
(b) For filling incandescent and fluorescent lamps.
(c) For filling Geiger-counter tubes.
(d) As argon lamps in botanical gardens and green houses.

824. The noble gas which is commonly used to provide an inert atmosphere in certain metallurgical processes is
(a) He (b) Ne (c) Ar (d) Kr

825. A sea-diver goes deep into the sea with a mixture of which of the following gases?
(a) O_2 and CO_2 (b) O_2 and He
(c) CO_2 and Ar (d) O_2 and Ar

826. Helium is used in the diving apparatus because
(a) it is lighter than air
(b) it is much less soluble in blood even under high pressure as compared to nitrogen
(c) it has a high lifting power
(d) it is non-inflammable

827. Which one of the following statements regarding helium is incorrect?
(a) It is used to produce and sustain powerful super-conducting magnets.
(b) It is used as a cryogenic agent for carrying out experiments at low temperatures.
(c) It is used to fill gas balloons instead of hydrogen because it is lighter and non-inflammable.
(d) It is used in gas-cooled nuclear reactors.

828. Which of the following is the life-saving mixture for an asthma patient?
(a) mixture of helium and oxygen
(b) mixture of xenon and nitrogen
(c) mixture of xenon and nitrogen
(d) mixture of argon and oxygen

829. Noble gases are used in discharge tubes to give different colours. A reddish–orange glow is due to

(a) Ar (b) Ne (c) Xe (d) Kr

830. Match the following

Column I (Substance)	Column II (Application)
A. Helium	1. Chlorinating agent
B. Argon	2. Inert atmosphere (metallurgy)
C. Neon	3. Cryogenics
D. P_4O_{10}	4. Advertising signs
E. PCl_5	5. Dehydrating agent

	A	B	C	D	E
(a)	3	2	1	4	5
(b)	3	4	1	5	2
(c)	3	2	4	5	1
(d)	5	4	1	2	3
(e)	5	2	1	3	4

831. Clathrates are

(a) non-stoichiometric compounds
(b) complex compounds
(c) interstitial compounds
(d) normal salts

832. In the clathrates of xenon with water, the nature of bonding between xenon and water molecules is

(a) covalent
(b) hydrogen bonding
(c) coordinate bonding
(d) dipole–induced dipole interaction

833. Xenon forms compounds only with

(a) oxygen and chlorine (b) oxygen and fluorine
(c) oxygen and bromine (d) oxygen and ozone

834. The idea which prompted Bartlett to prepare the first ever compound of a noble gas was the

(a) high bond energy of Xe–F
(b) low bond energy of F–F in the F_2 molecule
(c) ionisation enthalpy of molecular oxygen and xenon are almost similar
(d) none of the above

Final Preparation

835. Which noble gas is not found in the atmosphere?

(a) Rn (b) Kr (c) Ne (d) Ar

836. When a mixture of noble gases obtained from air is taken in a bulb filled with activated coconut charcoal and kept at 173 K for 30 minutes, the gases not adsorbed are

(a) Ar, Kr and Xe (b) He and Ne
(c) He and Kr (d) He and Xe

837. Molecules of a noble gas do not possess vibrational energy because a noble gas

(a) is monoatomic (b) is chemically inert
(c) has completely filled shells
(d) is diamagnetic

838. If the ionisation enthalpy for the hydrogen atom is 13.6 eV, then the ionisation enthalpy for He^+ will be

(a) 54.4 eV (b) 6.8 eV (c) 13.6 eV (d) 24.5 eV

839. Which of the following noble gases has the highest positive electron gain enthalpy value?

(a) helium (b) krypton (c) argon
(d) neon (e) xenon

840. In the case of noble gases, the following trend

Xe > Kr >Ar> Ne > He is correct for
(i) boiling point (ii) solubility in water
(iii) ionisation enthalpy (iv) ease of liquefaction
(a) (i) and (ii) only (b) (i) and (iii) only
(c) (ii), (iii) and (iv) only (d) (i), (ii) and (iv) only

841. Liquids flow from a higher to a lower level. Which of the following liquids can climb up the walls of the glass vessel in which it is placed?

(a) mercury (b) liquid N_2
(c) liquid He II (d) water

842. In xenon halides XeF_2, $XeCl_2$, $XeBr_2$, the stability decreases in the order

(a) $XeBr_2 > XeCl_2 > XeF_2$
(b) $XeF_2 > XeCl_2 > XeBr_2$
(c) $XeCl_2 > XeBr_2 > XeF_2$
(d) $XeBr_2 > XeF_2 > XeCl_2$

843. The oxidation state of oxygen in O_2PtF_6 is

(a) zero (b) $+\frac{1}{2}$ (c) –1/2 (d) +1

844. XeF_4 exists whereas $XeCl_4$ is not stable because the

(a) electron gain enthalpy of Cl is greater than that of F
(b) oxidation potential of F is greater than that of Cl
(c) the size of F is smaller than that of Cl
(d) none of the above

845. The reason that only xenon fluorides are known but the corresponding chlorides have not been reported is

(a) high bond energy of the Xe–F bond and low bond dissociation energy of the F_2 molecule
(b) smaller bond energy of the Xe–Cl bond and larger bond dissociation energy of the Cl_2 molecule
(c) both (a) and (b)
(d) none of the above

846. The formation of dioxygenyl hexafluoroplatinate (V), $O_2^+[PtF_6]^-$ is the basis for the formation of xenon fluorides. This is because

(a) O_2 and Xe have comparable sizes
(b) both O_2 and Xe are gases
(c) O_2 and Xe have comparable ionisation enthalpies
(d) O_2 and Xe have comparable electronegativities
(e) both (a) and (c)

847. In the reaction of Xe and PtF_6 acts as a/an
(a) oxidising agent (b) reducing agent
(c) acid (d) base

848. XeF_2 reacts with PF_5 to give
(a) XeF_4 (b) $[XeF]^+ [PF_6]^-$
(c) $[XeF_3]^- [PF_4]^+$ (d) $[XeF_4]^{2-} [PF_3]^{2+}$

849. In the reaction
$XeF_2 + 2\ SbF_5 \rightarrow [XeF]^+ [Sb_2F_{11}]^+$
XeF_2 behaves as a/an
(a) oxidising agent (b) reducing agent
(c) Lewis base (d) Lewis acid

850. In which of the following speciesis the bond angle expected to be more than 120°?
(a) PCl_4^+ (b) NO_2^- (c) XeO_3 (d) XeF_2

851. The compound of xenon that is isostructural with IBr_2^- is
(a) XeO_3 (b) XeF_2 (c) XeF_4 (d) $XeOF_4$

852. In the following reaction
$XeF_2 + I_2 \xrightarrow{BF_3} 2\ IF_3 + Xe$
XeF_2 acts as a/an
(a) reductant (b) oxidant
(c) Lewis acid (d) Lewis base

853. Which of the following pairs are isostructural?
(a) XeF_2, IF_2^- (b) NH_3, BF_3
(c) CO_3^{2-}, SO_3^{2-} (d) PCl_5, ICl_5

854. The molecular shapes of SF_4, CF_4 and XeF_4 are
(a) the same with 2, 0 and 1 lone pairs of electrons on the central atoms respectively
(b) the same with 1, 1 and 1 lone pairs of electrons on the central atoms respectively
(c) different with 0, 1 and 2 lone pairs of electrons on the central atoms respectively
(d) different with 1, 0 and 2 lone pairs of electrons on the central atoms respectively

855. XeF_4 reacts with SF_4 to give
(a) $XeOF_4$ and SO_2 (b) Xe and SF_6
(c) XeF_6 and SF_6 (d) SF_6 and XeO_3

856. Select the type of the following reaction.
$3\ XeF_4 + 6\ H_2O \rightarrow 2\ Xe + XeO_3 + 12\ HF + 3/2\ O_2$
(a) acid–base (b) redox
(c) disproportionation (d) none of these

857. Among the following, the species having a square planar structure are
(i) XeF_4 (ii) SF_4 (iii) $[NiCl_4]^{2-}$ (iv) $[PtCl_4]^{2-}$
(a) (i) and (iv) (b) (i) and (ii)
(c) (ii) and (iii) (d) (iii) and (iv)

858. Xeon hexafluoride reacts with strong alkalis to form a xenon compound X. The oxidation state of Xe in X is
(a) +2 (b) +4 (c) +6 (d) +8

859. Xenon hexafluoride reacts with potassium fluoride to yield
(a) $[XeF_5]^+ [KF_2]^-$ (b) $K^+[XeF_7]^-$
(c) XeF_4 (d) none of these

860. Under ambient conditions, the total number of gases released as products in the final step of the reaction scheme shown below is:

$XeF_6 \xrightarrow[\text{hydrolysis}]{\text{Complete}}$ P + other product
P $\xrightarrow{OH^-/H_2O}$ Q
Products $\xleftarrow[\text{in } OH^-/H_2O]{\text{Slow disproportionation}}$ Q

(a) 0 (b) 1 (c) 2 (d) 3

861. The structure of the XeF_5^+ ion is
(a) trigonal bipyramidal (b) square pyramidal
(c) octahedral (d) pentagonal

862. In which of the following arrangements of XeF_2, XeF_4 and XeF_6, is the decreasing order of the Xe–F bond length correct?
(a) $XeF_2 > XeF_4 > XeF_6$ (b) $XeF_6 > XeF_4 > XeF_2$
(c) $XeF_4 > XeF_6 > XeF_2$ (d) $XeF_2 > XeF_6 > XeF_4$

863. Give the final product in the reaction between XeO_3 and aqueous alkali.
(a) $HXeO_4^-$ (b) XeO_4^{2-}
(c) $XeO_4^{2-} + Xe + O_2 + H_2O$ (d) $Ze + O_2$

864. In the redox reaction $XeO_3 + 6\ I^- \rightarrow$ the gas evolved is
(a) H_2 (b) O_2 (c) I_2 (d) O_2 and I_2

865. Which of the following is an explosive compound?
(a) $XeOF_4$ (b) $XeOF_2$ (c) XeF_2 (d) XeO_3

866. Neon lights are used in warning signal illuminations because
(a) neon lights are visible from long distances
(b) neon lights are visible through fog and mist
(c) neon lights have beautiful colouration
(d) both (a) and (b)

867. Which noble gas is generally used in safety devices for protecting electrical instruments?
(a) He (b) Ne (c) Ar (d) Kr

868. Helium is added to the oxygen supply used by deep sea divers in preference to nitrogen because
(a) He is less soluble in blood than nitrogen at high pressure
(b) He is lighter than nitrogen
(c) He is readily miscible with oxygen
(d) He is less poisonous than nitrogen

869. Which of the following pairs is employed in flash tubes in photography?
(a) He, Ar (b) Ar, Ne (c) He, Ne (d) Kr, Xe

870. Which of the following is used in very low temperature thermometers?
(a) He (b) Ne (c) H_2 (d) N_2

871. Which of the following statements is correct for a noble gas?
(a) Ne is used in electric bulbs.
(b) Kr is obtained during radioactive disintegration.
(c) The half-life of Rn is only 3.8 days.
(d) Xe is used in producing very low temperatures.

872. The density of nitrogen gas prepared from air is slightly greater than that of nitrogen prepared by a chemical reaction from a compound of nitrogen due to the presence of the following in aerial nitrogen.
(a) argon (b) CO_2
(c) some nitrogen molecules analogous to O_2
(d) greater amount of nitrogen molecules derived from the N^{15} isotope

873. If one litre of air is passed repeatedly over heated copper and magnesium till no further reduction in volume takes place, the volume finally obtained would be approximately
(a) 800 mL (b) 200 mL (c) 10 mL (d) zero

874. In Fischer–Ringe's method of separation of noble gases mixture from air, the compound used is
(a) 90% $CaCO_3$ + 10% NH_2CONH_2
(b) coconut charcoal
(c) soda lime + potash solution
(d) 90% CaC_2 + 10% $CaCl_2$

MATCH THE FOLLOWING

875.

Column I	Column II
(A) XeO_3	(p) planar triangular
(B) $XeOF_4$	(q) T-shaped
(C) BO_3^{3-}	(r) Trigonal pyramidal
(D) ClF_3	(s) Linear
(E) I_3^- (aq)	(t) Square pyramidal

(a) (A)—(p); (B)—(s); (C)—(r); (D)—(q); (E)—(t)
(b) (A)—(q); (B)—(s); (C)—(p); (D)—(r); (E)—(t)
(c) (A)—(r); (B)—(s); (C)—(p); (D)—(q); (E)—(t)
(d) (A)—(r); (B)—(t); (C)—(p); (D)—(q); (E)—(s)
(e) (A)—(p); (B)—(q); (C)—(r); (D)—(s); (E)—(t)

876.

Column I	Column II
(A) $XeF_2 + H_2O \rightarrow$	(p) XeO_3 + HF
(B) $XeF_4 + H_2O \rightarrow$	(q) Xe + HF + O_2
(C) $XeF_6 + H_2O \rightarrow$	(r) Xe + HF + O_2 + XeO_3
(D) $XeO_2F_2 + H_2O \rightarrow$	(s) $XeOF_2$ + HF

(a) (A)—(q); (B)—(r,s); (C)—(p); (D)—(p)
(b) (A)—(p); (B)—(q); (C)—(r); (D)—(s)
(c) (A)—(r); (B)—(s); (C)—(p); (D)—(q)
(d) (A)—(s); (B)—(p); (C)—(q); (D)—(r)

877.

Column I	Column II
(A) XeF_2	(p) sp^3d, 0 L.P.
(B) $XeOF_2$	(q) sp^3d, 3 L.P.
(C) XeO_2F_2	(r) sp^3d, 2 L.P.
(D) XeO_3F_2	(s) sp^3d, 1 L.P.

(a) (A)—(r); (B)—(p); (C)—(q); (D)—(s)
(b) (A)—(q); (B)—(r); (C)—(s); (D)—(p)
(c) (A)—(q); (B)—(s); (C)—(p); (D)—(r)
(d) (A)—(r); (B)—(p); (C)—(q); (D)—(s)

ASSERTION REASON

Directions: In each of the following questions, a statement of Assertion (A) is given followed by a corresponding statement of Reason (R) just below it. Of the statements, mark the correct answer as
(a) if both the assertion and reason are true and the reason is the correct explanation of the assertion.
(b) if both the assertion and reason are true but the reason is not the correct explanation of the assertion
(c) if the assertion is true but the reason is false
(d) if both the assertion and reason are false

878. Assertion: A mixture of noble gases can be separated by using coconut charcoal.

Reason: Activated coconut charcoal adsorbs different noble gases at different temperatures.

879. Assertion: All the noble gases have ns^2np^6 electronic configuration in their outermost shell.

Reason: In noble gases all the energy levels which are occupied are partially filled.

880. Assertion: He and Be have similar outer electronic configuration of the type ns^2.

Reason: Both are chemically inert.

881. Assertion: Noble gases have positive electron gain enthalpy.

Reason: Noble gases have a stable closed shell electronic configuration.

882. Assertion: Helium is regarded as the most volatile of all liquids.

Reason: The boiling point of liquid helium is 4.2 K which is the lowest of all known liquids.

883. Assertion: The mp/bp of noble gases are quite high.

Reason: The interparticle forces among noble gases in their liquid state are covalent forces.

884. Assertion: Noble gases are highly soluble in water.

Reason: Solubility in water increases with decreasing size of the noble gas.

885. Assertion: FeHe is an example of an interstitial compound.

Reason: He, due to its small size which matches the size of the interstices of most of the heavy metals has a very high tendency to form such compounds.

886. Assertion: Most of the compounds of noble gases involve only fluorine and oxygen.

Reason: Fluorine and oxygen are highly electronegative.

887. Assertion: He and Ne form compounds with fluorine.

Reason: He and Ne contain *d*-orbitals in their valence shells.

888. Assertion: Noble gases form compounds with fluorine and oxygen only.

Reason: Oxygen has higher electronegativity than fluorine.

889. Assertion: Xenon forms fluorides in its +2, +4 and +6 oxidation states.

Reason: In xenon, 5*d* orbitals are available for valence shell expansion.

890. Assertion: XeF_4 is square planar in shape.

Reason: Xe atom is dsp^2-hybridised.

891. Assertion: Hydrogenxenate ion in aqueous alkali gives xenon and perxenate ion.

Reason: Hydrogen xenate ion is reduced to xenon.

892. Assertion: Perxenate (XeO_6^{4-}) solutions are powerful oxidising agents.

Reason: These are prepared by disproportionation of hydrogen xenate ion ($HXeO_6^{4-}$) in alkaline solution.

893. Assertion: The geometry of XeO_3F_2 is trigonal bipyramidal.

Reason: Xe shows sp^3d^2-hybridisation with one lone pair occupying one of the axial positions.

Answer Key

1. (b)	2. (a)	3. (b)	4. (c)	5. (c)	6. (a)	7. (b)	8. (a)	9. (a)	10. (a)
11. (a)	12. (a)	13. (b)	14. (d)	15. (a)	16. (d)	17. (b)	18. (d)	19. (c)	20. (d)
21. (c)	22. (d)	23. (a)	24. (d)	25. (c)	26. (b)	27. (a)	28. (e)	29. (a)	30. (b)
31. (c)	32. (e)	33. (c)	34. (b)	35. (a)	36. (d)	37. (b)	38. (b)	39. (a)	40. (a)
41. (b)	42. (a)	43. (a)	44. (a)	45. (d)	46. (a)	47. (b)	48. (d)	49. (d)	50. (d)
51. (a)	52. (b,c)	53. (b)	54. (d)	55. (a)	56. (a)	57. (c)	58. (a)	59. (c)	60. (c)
61. (d)	62. (c)	63. (c)	64. (b)	65. (d)	66. (d)	67. (a)	68. (a)	69. (b)	70. (a)
71. (a)	72. (a)	73. (c)	74. (d)	75. (b)	76. (a)	77. (d)	78. (b)	79. (a,d)	80. (e)
81. (a)	82. (d)	83. (b)	84. (c)	85. (a)	86. (d)	87. (a)	88. (d)	89. (a)	90. (c)
91. (c)	92. (c)	93. (b)	94. (d)	95. (c)	96. (a)	97. (b)	98. (d)	99. (b)	100. (c)
101. (b)	102. (d)	103. (d)	104. (b)	105. (d)	106. (d)	107. (b)	108. (b)	109. (c)	110. (b)
111. (b)	112. (c)	113. (d)	114. (b)	115. (a)	116. (a)	117. (a)	118. (c)	119. (d)	120. (c)
121. (d)	122. (b)	123. (b)	124. (a)	125. (e)	126. (a)	127. (c)	128. (a)	129. (b)	130. (a)
131. (a)	132. (d)	133. (d)	134. (d)	135. (a)	136. (d)	137. (c)	138. (c)	139. (a)	140. (a)
141. (c)	142. (c)	143. (d)	144. (c)	145. (a)	146. (c)	147. (b)	148. (c)	149. (a)	150. (c)
151. (b)	152. (d)	153. (b)	154. (d)	155. (b)	156. (b)	157. (c)	158. (d)	159. (c)	160. (b)
161. (b)	162. (b)	163. (b)	164. (a)	165. (b)	166. (c)	167. (b)	168. (d)	169. (b)	170. (d)
171. (c)	172. (a)	173. (b)	174. (d)	175. (d)	176. (a)	177. (a)	178. (a)	179. (a)	180. (a)
181. (b)	182. (a)	183. (b)	184. (d)	185. (c)	186. (d)	187. (d)	188. (d)	189. (b)	190. (c)
191. (c)	192. (c)	193. (d)	194. (d)	195. (d)	196. (c)	197. (d)	198. (b)	199. (c)	200. (a)

201. (b) 202. (a) 203. (d) 204. (b) 205. (a) 206. (a) 207. (d) 208. (b) 209. (b) 210. (a)
211. (d) 212. (a) 213. (d) 214. (d) 215. (d) 216. (c) 217. (c) 218. (c) 219. (c) 220. (d)
221. (b) 222. (a) 223. (b) 224. (c) 225. (c) 226. (d) 227. (d) 228. (b) 229. (b) 230. (b)
231. (d) 232. (a) 233. (b) 234. (a) 235. (d) 236. (b) 237. (d) 238. (a) 239. (b) 240. (d)
241. (b) 242. (b) 243. (a) 244. (c) 245. (c) 246. (d) 247. (b) 248. (c) 249. (a) 250. (a)
251. (a) 252. (b) 253. (c) 254. (a) 255. (b) 256. (a) 257. (c) 258. (c) 259. (b) 260. (a)
261. (c) 262. (a) 263. (c) 264. (a) 265. (b) 266. (d) 267. (a) 268. (b) 269. (a) 270. (c)
271. (a) 272. (d) 273. (a) 274. (c) 275. (c) 276. (d) 277. (b) 278. (d) 279. (c) 280. (c)
281. (d) 282. (b) 283. (a) 284. (a) 285. (a) 286. (c) 287. (d) 288. (a) 289. (a) 290. (d)
291. (d) 292. (b) 293. (c) 294. (d) 295. (c) 296. (c) 297. (b) 298. (b) 299. (d) 300. (b)
301. (b) 302. (a) 303. (d) 304. (b) 305. (d) 306. (a) 307. (c) 308. (d) 309. (b) 310. (a)
311. (b) 312. (b) 313. (c) 314. (c) 315. (b) 316. (a) 317. (b) 318. (c) 319. (a) 320. (a)
321. (a) 322. (a) 323. (d) 324. (b) 325. (a) 326. (b) 327. (a) 328. (d) 329. (c) 330. (b)
331. (b) 332. (a) 333. (a) 334. (c) 335. (a) 336. (b) 337. (d) 338. (c) 339. (e) 340. (b)
341. (b) 342. (d) 343. (d) 344. (c) 345. (c) 346. (c) 347. (c) 348. (a) 349. (b) 350. (a,b)
351. (b) 352. (c) 353. (d) 354. (d) 355. (b) 356. (b) 357. (b) 358. (c) 359. (c) 360. (b)
361. (b) 362. (d) 363. (a) 364. (c) 365. (d) 366. (b) 367. (a) 368. (c) 369. (d) 370. (b)
371. (d) 372. (d) 373. (b) 374. (d) 375. (b) 376. (d) 377. (c) 378. (c) 379. (b) 380. (a)
381. (d) 382. (a) 383. (d) 384. (a) 385. (a) 386. (a) 387. (c) 388. (c) 389. (a) 390. (d)
391. (d) 392. (c) 393. (d) 394. (a) 395. (c) 396. (d) 397. (d) 398. (d) 399. (c) 400. (a)
401. (a) 402. (c) 403. (a) 404. (d) 405. (c) 406. (d) 407. (a) 408. (d) 409. (d) 410. (a)
411. (a) 412. (b) 413. (c) 414. (b) 415. (b) 416. (c) 417. (a) 418. (a) 419. (d) 420. (d)
421. (d) 422. (b) 423. (a) 424. (b) 425. (b) 426. (c) 427. (c) 428. (c) 429. (b) 430. (c)
431. (d) 432. (b) 433. (d) 434. (c) 435. (b) 436. (c) 437. (c) 438. (a) 439. (a) 440. (b)
441. (c) 442. (d) 443. (c) 444. (c) 445. (d) 446. (b) 447. (b) 448. (b) 449. (c) 450. (b)
451. (d) 452. (d) 453. (a) 454. (c) 455. (a) 456. (b) 457. (b) 458. (b) 459. (a) 460. (a)
461. (c) 462. (d) 463. (b) 464. (b) 465. (d) 466. (d) 467. (b) 468. (b) 469. (a) 470. (a)
471. (d) 472. (b) 473. (d) 474. (a) 475. (a) 476. (b) 477. (b) 478. (a) 479. (d) 480. (b)
481. (c) 482. (b) 483. (c) 484. (d) 485. (a) 486. (c) 487. (b) 488. (d) 489. (b) 490. (a)
491. (d) 492. (d) 493. (b) 494. (a) 495. (c) 496. (d) 497. (d) 498. (b) 499. (c) 500. (d)
501. (c) 502. (c) 503. (d) 504. (d) 505. (d) 506. (c) 507. (a) 508. (d) 509. (b) 510. (c)
511. (d) 512. (a) 513. (a) 514. (b) 515. (d) 516. (a) 517. (d) 518. (d) 519. (a) 520. (d)
521. (a) 522. (c) 523. (a) 524. (d) 525. (d) 526. (b) 527. (d) 528. (c) 529. (d) 530. (a)
531. (a) 532. (d) 533. (a) 534. (c) 535. (c) 536. (b) 537. (b) 538. (a) 539. (a) 540. (d)
541. (b) 542. (c) 543. (c) 544. (a) 545. (b) 546. (b) 547. (b) 548. (a) 549. (b) 550. (a)
551. (c) 552. (a) 553. (a) 554. (c) 555. (c) 556. (d) 557. (c) 558. (b) 559. (d) 560. (d)
561. (c) 562. (d) 563. (e) 564. (d) 565. (a) 566. (a) 567. (d) 568. (b) 569. (a) 570. (b)
571. (c) 572. (b) 573. (a) 574. (a) 575. (b) 576. (d) 577. (a) 578. (a) 579. (b) 580. (a)
581. (a) 582. (a) 583. (b) 584. (b) 585. (c) 586. (b) 587. (b) 588. (c) 589. (c) 590. (b)
591. (b) 592. (a) 593. (c) 594. (b) 595. (a) 596. (a) 597. (b) 598. (c) 599. (a) 600. (c)
601. (a) 602. (b) 603. (b) 604. (c) 605. (b) 606. (a) 607. (a) 608. (a) 609. (c) 610. (d)
611. (a) 612. (c) 613. (c) 614. (b) 615. (d) 616. (b) 617. (d) 618. (c) 619. (a) 620. (d)
621. (d) 622. (a) 623. (c) 624. (d) 625. (c) 626. (b) 627. (d) 628. (d) 629. (c) 630. (c)
631. (d) 632. (d) 633. (a) 634. (b) 635. (a) 636. (b) 637. (b) 638. (a) 639. (d) 640. (b)
641. (b) 642. (b) 643. (b) 644. (c) 645. (b) 646. (c) 647. (d) 648. (d) 649. (d) 650. (b)
651. (a) 652. (c) 653. (b) 654. (a) 655. (b) 656. (c) 657. (d) 658. (a) 659. (d) 660. (a)
661. (b) 662. (d) 663. (d) 664. (d) 665. (d) 666. (a) 667. (d) 668. (a) 669. (d) 670. (b)
671. (d) 672. (c) 673. (d) 674. (d) 675. (d) 676. (d) 677. (a) 678. (d) 679. (c) 680. (a)
681. (b) 682. (c) 683. (c) 684. (b) 685. (c) 686. (a) 687. (b) 688. (a) 689. (b) 690. (d)
691. (a) 692. (d) 693. (d) 694. (c) 695. (d) 696. (a) 697. (c) 698. (d) 699. (a) 700. (a)
701. (a) 702. (a) 703. (d) 704. (a) 705. (c) 706. (c) 707. (c) 708. (b) 709. (b) 710. (d)
711. (b) 712. (b) 713. (d) 714. (c) 715. (b) 716. (c) 717. (b) 718. (d) 719. (b) 720. (a)
721. (c) 722. (d) 723. (d) 724. (b) 725. (b) 726. (a) 727. (d) 728. (c) 729. (c) 730. (a)
731. (d) 732. (a) 733. (a) 734. (a) 735. (a) 736. (b) 737. (a) 738. (a) 739. (a) 740. (b)

741. (d) 742. (c) 743. (d) 744. (b) 745. (b) 746. (d) 747. (b) 748. (d) 749. (b) 750. (b)
751. (c) 752. (b) 753. (a) 754. (a) 755. (b) 756. (b) 757. (a) 758. (a) 759. (d) 760. (a)
761. (a) 762. (c) 763. (d) 764. (d) 765. (b) 766. (a) 767. (b) 768. (d) 769. (d) 770. (a)
771. (c) 772. (c) 773. (d) 774. (d) 775. (a) 776. (d) 777. (d) 778. (c) 779. (b) 780. (d)
781. (d) 782. (b) 783. (c) 784. (b) 785. (b) 786. (c) 787. (a) 788. (c) 789. (d) 790. (b)
791. (d) 792. (a) 793. (d) 794. (d) 795. (b) 796. (c) 797. (a) 798. (d) 799. (c) 800. (a)
801. (c) 802. (d) 803. (b) 804. (a) 805. (a) 806. (d) 807. (a) 808. (a) 809. (b) 810. (a)
811. (d) 812. (a) 813. (c) 814. (c) 815. (b) 816. (e) 817. (c) 818. (d) 819. (d) 820. (c)
821. (b) 822. (b) 823. (d) 824. (c) 825. (b) 826. (b) 827. (c) 828. (a) 829. (b) 830. (c)
831. (a) 832. (d) 833. (b) 834. (c) 835. (a) 836. (b) 837. (a) 838. (a) 839. (d) 840. (d)
841. (c) 842. (b) 843. (c) 844. (c) 845. (c) 846. (c) 847. (a) 848. (b) 849. (c) 850. (d)
851. (b) 852. (b) 853. (a) 854. (d) 855. (b) 856. (c) 857. (a) 858. (d) 859. (b) 860. (c)
861. (b) 862. (a) 863. (c) 864. (c) 865. (d) 866. (d) 867. (b) 868. (a) 869. (d) 870. (a)
871. (c) 872. (a) 873. (c) 874. (d) 875. (d) 876. (a) 877. (b) 878. (a) 879. (d) 880. (c)
881. (a) 882. (a) 883. (d) 884. (d) 885. (a) 886. (b) 887. (d) 888. (c) 889. (a) 890. (c)
891. (c) 892. (b) 893. (c)

Hints and Solutions

Objective Questions

GROUP 15

Atomic and Physical Properties

1. **(b):** $PH_3 + HBr \rightarrow PH_4Br$
2. **(a):** It is a fact.
3. **(b):** It is a fact.
4. **(c):** Only Mg and Mn liberate H_2 from dil. HNO_3.
5. **(c):** EN increases from left to right across a period and from bottom to top up the group. Therefore, the order of increasing EN is Si < P < C < N.
6. **(a):** Bi is a metal amongst the group 15 elements and hence is an excellent conductor of heat and electricity.
7. **(b):** Due to its reluctance to form multiple bonds, P does not form a stable diatomic molecule. Instead, it exists as a discrete tetratomic tetrahedral (P_4) molecule.
8. **(a):** The atomic number of the element below atomic number 15 (P) in group 15 will be 15 + 18 = 33.
9. **(a):**Cl^-, S^{2-}, P^{3-} are isoelectronic species. Their sizes increase as the nuclear charge decreases from Cl to P.

Chemical Properties

10. **(a):** The basic charcter of halides of N is: $NF_3 < NCl_3 < NBr_3 < NI_3$
11. **(a):** Due to the formation of thin oxide film on iron surface.
12. **(a):** The three important oxidation states of P are –3 in PH_3, +3 in P_2O_3 and +5 in P_2O_5.
13. **(b):** Covalency depends upon the number of shared pairs of electrons. In N_2O_5, each nitrogen atom has four shared pairs of electrons as shown. Therefore, the covalency of N in N_2O_5 is 4.

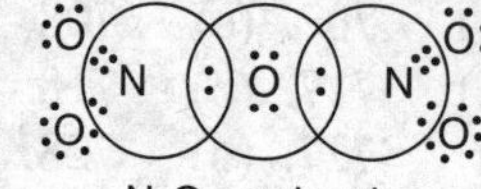

N_2O_5 molecule each N has four shared pairs of electrons

14. **(d):** Refer to all the three (a), (b) and (c) options given in the question.
15. **(a):**The highest oxidation state is +5 which remains unchanged on going down group 15.
16. **(d):** Oxidation number of As in $H_2AsO_4^-$
$$2 + x - 8 = -1$$
$$x - 6 = -1$$
$$x = 5$$
17. **(b):** NH_3 is non-combustible. It burns in dioxygen with a pale yellow flame.
$$4NH_3 + 3\,O_2 \rightarrow 2\,N_2 + 6\,H_2O$$
The same reaction occurs in air, but the heat of reaction is insufficient to maintain combustion unless heat is supplied. The other hydrides are flammable.
18. **(d):** As we move down the group, the size of the element increases and therefore, the length of the E–H bond increases and its strength decreases, that is, the E–H bond can break more easily to evolve H_2 gas which acts as the reducing agent. Thus, the Bi–H bond is the weakest amongst the hydrides of the elements of group 15.
19. **(c):** Reducing character of the hydrides increases down the group.
20. **(d):** As SbH_3 is least stable compared to the other hydrides listed, it has maximum tendency to give hydrogen and thus acts as the strongest reducing agent.
21. **(c):** As the size of the atom M increases in MH_3, the stability of the conjugate acid MH_4^+ decreases and hence the basic character decreases in the order as mentioned.
22. **(d):** Refer to all the three (a), (b) and (c) options given in the question.

23. (a): The decreasing order of the BP is $H_2O > SbH_3 > NH_3 > AsH_3 > PH_3$, that is, H_2O has the highest and PH_3 the lowest BP.

24. (d): The boiling points increase regularly as we move from PH_3 to BiH_3. However, the BP of NH_3 is higher than those of PH_3 and AsH_3. This variation in BP can be explained on the basis of (i) hydrogen bonding and (ii) van der Waals forces of attraction. The electronegativity of N (3.0) is much higher than that of H (2.1). As a result, N–H bonds are polar and hence NH_3 undergoes intermolecular H-bonding. In contrast, the EN of P, As, Sb and Bi are close to H and hence their hydrides do not form H-bonds.

Further, as we move from PH_3 to BiH_3, the molecular mass increases. As a result, the van der Waals forces of attraction increase and the BP increases regularly from PH_3 to BiH_3. However, the BP of NH_3 is higher than those of PH_3 and AsH_3 but lower than those of SbH_3 and BiH_3. The increase in BP of SbH_3 and BiH_3 is due to higher van der Waals forces of attraction.

25. (c): In the hydrides of group 15 elements, the basic strength decreases down the group and the correct order is, $NH_3 > PH_3 > AsH_3 > SbH_3$.

26. (b): Except NH_3, the boiling point smoothly increases down the group due to an increase in magnitude of the van der Waals force. Ammonia shows intermolecular H-bonding. Its boiling point is higher than that of AsH_3 but lower than that of SbH_3.

27. (a): NH_3 is the most stable hydride among the hydrides of the nitrogen family.

28. (e): As we move from NH_3 to BiH_3, the size of the central atom increases and its tendency to form covalent bonds with the comparatively small H-atom decreases, that is, the E–H bond weakens. Hence, the stability decreases down the group.

29. (a): NH_3 is highly soluble due to H-bonding.

H-bonding
$\overset{\delta+}{H}–\overset{\delta-}{N}\cdots\overset{\delta+}{H}–\overset{\delta-}{O}$ (with H below N and H below O)
Ammonia Water

30. (b): Out of C, Sb, Mg and Mn, carbon is highly electronegative and is a non-metal, Sb is metalloid, Mg is a typical metal and Mn is a transition metal. Their oxides will be CO_2 weakly (acidic), Sb_2O_3 (amphoteric), MgO (distinctly basic) and Mn_2O_3 (basic). Therefore, the only oxide which is amphoteric is Sb_2O_3.

31. (c): NO is the most stable oxide of N.

32. (e): As we go down the group, the metallic character increases. Bi being a metal forms Bi_2O_3 which is a basic oxide.

33. (c): Trioxides are less acidic than pentoxides. Therefore, As_4O_6 is the least acidic.

34. (b): The acidic character of the oxides of N increases with an increase in the oxidation number of the element. However,

$\underbrace{N_2O, NO}_{\text{Neutral}}\ \underbrace{N_2O_3, NO_2, N_2O_5}_{\text{Acidic character increases}}$

35. (a): NF_3
It is the least basic because of the high electronegativity of 3 F atoms. The lone pair present on the nitrogen atom is not easily available for donation.

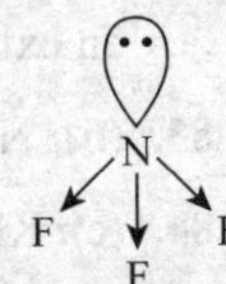

36. (d): Since the difference in the size of N (75 pm) and F (72 pm) is small, the N–F bond is quite strong. As a result, NF_3 is an exothermic compound. This accounts for stability of the compound. Therefore, NF_3 does not undergo hydrolysis with water, dilute acids or alkalies.

37. (b): $BiCl_5$ does not exist because the +3 oxidation state of Bi is more stable than the +5 due to the inert pair effect.

38. (b): B > P > As > Bi; Cl–E–Cl bond angle decreases in this order.As we go down the group, the bond angle decreases because repulsion between the bonded pairs of electrons decreases.

39. (a): The trihalides of P, Sb and Bi (especially the fluorides and chlorides) due to the presence of the *d* orbitals, accept a pair of electrons and thus behave as Lewis acids $PF_3 + F_2 \rightarrow PF_5$; $BiCL_3 + 2\,Cl^- \rightarrow [BiCl_5]^{2-}$. But carbon does not have *d* orbitals. Therefore, its halide CCl_4 does not act as a Lewis acid. The Lewis acid strength decreases in the order $PCl_3 > SbCl_3 > BiCl_3$.
Thus, PCl_3 is the most acidic.

40. (a): $NF_5 \rightleftharpoons [PBr_4]^+[Br^-]$
Thus, PBr_5 splits into a stable tetrahedral structure as $[PBr_4]^+$ and $[Br^-]$.

41. (b): Phosphorus produces a maximum number of oxyacids among the members of the nitrogen family.

42. (a): N is the most non-metallic and electronegative amongst the nitrogen family. So, its pentoxide will be most acidic.

43. (a): B is sp^2-hybridised in BCl_3 and has no lone pair of electrons whereas N is sp^3-hybridised in NCl_3 and has a lone pair of electrons due to which it has a pyramidal structure.

44. (a): $NCl_3 + 4\,H_2O \rightarrow 3\,HOCl + NH_4OH$

Dinitrogen, N_2 and its Compounds

45. (d): It is a reason for the given fact.

46. (a): It is a test for proteins.

47. (b): In the laboratory, pure N_2 gas is prepared by heating NH_4Cl with sodium nitrite.

$$NH_4Cl + NaNO_2 \xrightarrow{\Delta} NH_4NO_2 + NaCl$$
$$NH_4NO_2 \xrightarrow{\Delta} N_2 + 2\,H_2O$$

48. (d): $(NH_4)_2SO_4$ on thermal decomposition gives NH_3 and not dinitrogen as shown below. However, other given compounds produce dinitrogen gas.

$(NH_4)_2SO_4 \xrightarrow{\Delta} 2\,NH_3 + H_2SO_4$

$Ba\,(N_3)_2 \xrightarrow{\Delta} Ba + 3\,N_2$

$(NH_4)_2\,Cr_2O_7 \xrightarrow{\Delta} N_2 + Cr_2O_3 + 4\,H_2O$

$NH_4NO_2 \xrightarrow{\Delta} N_2 + 2\,H_2O$

49. (d): N_2O_3 is blue coloured.

50. (d): Very pure N_2 can be obtained by heating sodium or barium azide in vacuum.
$2\ NaN_3 \xrightarrow{\Delta} 3\ N_2 + 2\ Na$

51. (a): $(NH_4)_2Cr_2O_7 \xrightarrow{\Delta} Cr_2O_7 + N_2 + 4\ H_2O$
$NH_4NO_2 \xrightarrow{\Delta} N_2 + 2\ H_2O$
$2\ NH_4VO_3 \xrightarrow{\Delta} V_2O_5 + 2\ NH_3 + H_2O$
$NH_4NO_3 \xrightarrow{\Delta} N_2O + 2\ H_2O$

52. (b,c): $NH_4NO_3 \xrightarrow[<300\ °C]{\Delta} N_2O + 2\ H_2O$
$(NH_4)_2Cr_2O_7 \xrightarrow{\Delta} N_2 + Cr_2O_3 + 4\ H_2O$
$Ba(N_3)_2 \xrightarrow{\Delta} Ba + 3\ N_2$
$Mg_3N_2 \xrightarrow{\Delta}$ No decomposition

53. (b): N_2 is chemically inert as compared to CN^- because of the absence of bond polarity.

54. (d): The N_2 molecule contains a triple bond between the N atoms and has a very high dissociation energy (941.4 kJ mol^{-1}) due to which it is relatively inactive.

55. (a): Nitrogen in the azide ion $\left(N_3^-\right)$ can form a chain of three N atoms.

56. (a): Oxidation state of N in

$N_3H = 3x + 1 = 0$ or $x = -\frac{1}{3}$
$NH_2OH = x + 2 - 1 = 0$ or $x = -1$
$N_2H_4 = 2x + 4 = 0$ or $x = -2$
$NH_3 = x + 3 = 0$ or $x = -3$
Therefore, the highest oxidation state is –1/3 in N_3H.

57. (c): $\underset{\text{(Oxidation number of N)}}{NH_4NO_2} \rightleftharpoons \underset{\substack{x+4=+1 \\ x=1-4=1-3}}{\overset{x}{N}H_4^+} + \underset{\substack{x-4=-1 \\ x=+3}}{\overset{x}{N}O_2^+}$

58. (a): Nitrogen reacts with metals to form a nitride.
$6\ Li + N_2 \xrightarrow{450°C} 2\ Li_3N$ (Lithium nitride)

59. (c): Phosphonitrilic compounds are known as phosphazenes. Their general formula is $(NPCl_2)_n$. Their structure is cyclic as shown.

$(NPCl_2)_4 = P_4N_4Cl_8 \longrightarrow$ [cyclic ring of alternating P and N atoms, each P bearing two Cl]

Cyclic structure

60. (c): N_3^- (azide ion) derived from N_3H (hydrazoic acid) contains nitrogen in the –1 oxidation state.

61. (d): Molecular N_2 is converted into NH_3 by nitrifying bacteria which can be readily utilised by plants.

62. (c): Molybdenum is essential for nitrogen fixation.

63. (c): $NH_4Cl + KNO_2 \xrightarrow{\Delta} [NH_4NO_2] \xrightarrow{\Delta} N_2 + 2\ H_2O$

64. (b): $2\ NaN_3 \xrightarrow{\Delta} 2\ Na + 3\ N_2$

65. (d):
$\underset{\text{1 mol (excess)}}{Mg_3N_2} + 6\ H_2O \rightarrow 3\ Mg(OH)_2 + \underset{\text{2 mol}}{2\ NH_3}$

66. (d): $Cu^{2+}(aq) + 4\ NH_4OH(aq) \rightarrow$
$\underset{\text{Tetraammine copper (II) ion (Deep blue)}}{[Cu(NH_3)_4]^{2+}} + H_2O$

67. (a): $NH_3 + 3\ Cl_2 \rightarrow NCl_3 + 3\ HCl$
NCl_3 is an explosive material.

68. (a): R_2NH is a derivative of NH_3. In NH_3, N is sp^3 hybridised with one orbital occupied by a lone pair of electrons.
–hybrid

69. (b): Blasting of TNT is done by mixing it with NH_4NO_3. This mixture of 1: 5 ratio is called amatol.

70. (a): The inorganic nitrogen exists in the form of ammonia, which may be lost as gas to the atmosphere, may be acted upon by nitrifying bacteria, or may be taken up directly by plants.

71. (a): $3\ CuO + 2\ NH_3 \rightarrow 3\ Cu + N_2 \uparrow + 3\ H_2O$

72. (a): CaO (quicklime) is the most suitable drying agent for NH_3 gas as it reacts with moisture and not NH_3. Anhydrous $CaCl_2$ forms a complex with ammonia as $[Ca(NH_3)_6]Cl_2$. P_2O_5 and conc. H_2SO_4 are acidic and react with NH_3 gas.

73. (c): $(NH_4)_2Cr_2O_7 \xrightarrow{\Delta} Cr_2O_3 + N_2 + 4H_2O$

74. (d): NH_3 when dissolved in water forms
$NH_3 + H_2O \rightarrow NH_4^+ + OH^- \rightleftharpoons NH_4OH$

75. (b): $4\ NH_3 + 5\ O_2 \xrightarrow{Pt} 4\ NO + 6H_2O$

76. (a): $\underset{\text{Calcium cyanide}}{CaCN_2} + \underset{\text{Steam}}{3\ H_2O} \xrightarrow{\text{Pressure}} CaCO_3 + 2\ NH_3$

77. (d): $2\ NH_3 + NaOCl \rightarrow NH_2.NH_2 + NaCl + H_2O$

78. (b): AgBr is sparingly soluble in NH_3 solution due to complex formation.
$AgBr + 2\ NH_4OH \rightarrow Ag(NH_3)_2Br + 2\ H_2O$

79. (a,d): Liquor ammonia has high vapour pressure, so cooling of bottles is done to lower the vapour pressure before opening, otherwise the gas rushes out with a mild explosion.

80. (e): Hydrazine burns in air with the evolution of heat.
$N_2H_4 + O_2 \rightarrow N_2 + 2\ H_2O$
It is stable and reduces Fe^{3+} to Fe^{2+} in an acidic medium.
$N_2H_4 + H^+ \rightarrow N_2H_5^+$
$N_2H_5^+ \rightarrow N_2 + 5\ H^+ + 4e^-$
$Fe^{3+} + e^- \rightarrow Fe^{2+}] \times 4$
$N_2H_5^+ + 4Fe^{3+} \rightarrow N_2 + 5\ H^+ + 4\ Fe^{2+}$

81. (a): N_2O_5 is the anhydride of nitric acid as it gives HNO_3 on adding water.
$N_2O_5 + H_2O \rightarrow 2\ HNO_3$

82. (d): N_2O, where N is in the +5 oxidation state, can act only as an oxidising agent and not as a reducing agent.

83. (b): $N_2O_3 + H_2O \rightarrow 2\ HNO_2$

84. (c): $KNO_3 + \underset{\text{Conc.}}{H_2SO_4} \rightarrow KHSO_4 + HNO_3$

$4HNO_3 \xrightarrow[\text{or heat}]{\text{Sunlight}} 4NO_2 + 2H_2O + O_2$

85. (a): Refer to all the (b), (c) and (d) options given in the question.

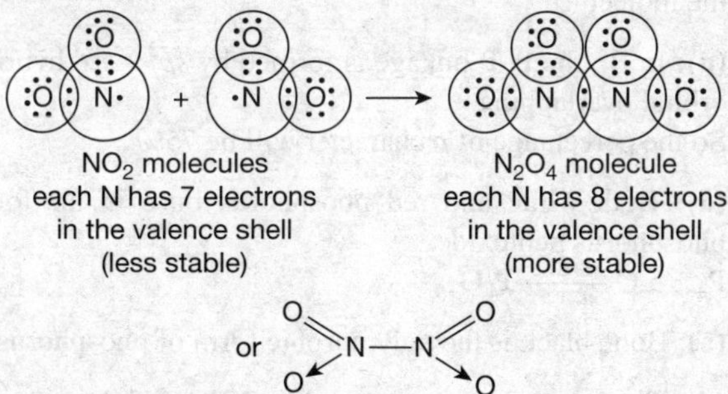

or $O_2N{-}NO_2$

86. (d): Liquid propellants used in rockets use N_2O_4 as an oxidant.

87. (a): NO is a neutral oxide.

88. (d): N_2O_5 is solid and exists as $NO_2^+NO_3^-$.

89. (a): NO is not an anhydride of nitrous acid.

90. (c): Dinitrogen pentoxide, N_2O_5, has the following resonating structures and contains an N–O–N bond.

$O_2N{-}O{-}NO_2 \longleftrightarrow O_2N{-}O{-}NO_2$

91. (c): $2Pb(NO_3)_2 \rightarrow 2PbO + 4NO_2 + O_2$

92. (c): $2NO_2 + H_2O \rightleftharpoons HNO_2 + HNO_3$

When dissolved in water, it gives a mixture of nitrous acid and nitric acid.

$N_2O_4 + H_2O \rightarrow HNO_2 + HNO_3$

$HNO_3 + HNO_2 + 2NaOH \rightarrow NaNO_2 + NaNO_3 + 2H_2O$

93. (b):

$\underset{\text{dil.}}{4Zn + 10HNO_3} \rightarrow 4Zn(NO_3)_2 + 5H_2O + \underset{\text{Nitrous oxide}}{N_2O}$

94. (d): N_2O_5 is an anhydride of HNO_3 and contains N in the highest oxidation state.

$2HNO_3 \rightarrow N_2O_5 + H_2O$

Therefore, it can act only as oxidising agent.

95. (c): N_2O is a linear molecule.

96. (a): $2Pb(NO_3)_2 \xrightarrow{\Delta} 2PbO + 4NO_2 + O_2$

97. (b): NO (11 electrons) is an odd electron molecule and hence is paramagnetic in the gaseous state. It has a three-electron-bond in its structure.

$:N \overset{\cdot\cdot}{=\!=} O:$
st. of NO

98. (d): All other oxides of nitrogen except N_2O and NO are acidic in nature. N_2O and NO are neutral oxides.

99. (b): $\underset{\text{1 mol}}{NO(g)} + \underset{\text{1 mol(Blue)}}{NO_2(g)} \xrightarrow{-30°C} N_2O_3(l)$

100. (c): Lead prefers to form divalent compounds because the +2 oxidation state of lead is the most stable due to inert pair effect.

In the carbonate ion, all the three C–O bonds are equal due to resonance.

101. (b): NO_2 contains one electron on N. It dimerises to give N_2O_4 where a single electron is paired up to form an N–N bond in N_2O_4 and the paramagnetic NO_2 changes to diamagnetic N_2O_4.

$\underset{\substack{\text{Reddish brown (gas)}\\ \text{(Paramagnetic)}}}{2\dot{N}O_2} \underset{}{\overset{\text{cooling}}{\rightleftharpoons}} \underset{\substack{\text{Colourless (l/s)}\\ \text{(Diamagnetic)}}}{N_2O_4}$

$O_2N{-}NO_2$
St. of N_2O_4

102. (d): $:\overset{-}{\underset{\cdot\cdot}{N}}{=}\overset{+}{N}{=}\underset{\cdot\cdot}{\overset{\cdot\cdot}{O}}: \longleftrightarrow :N{\equiv}\overset{+}{N}{-}\underset{\cdot\cdot}{\overset{\cdot\cdot}{O}}:^-$

103. (d): $Sn + 4HNO_3 \rightarrow H_2SnO_3 \text{ (or } SnO_2 \cdot H_2O) + 4NO_2 + H_2O$

104. (b): $4NH_3 + 5O_2 \xrightarrow{\text{Pt, 1975 K}} 4NO + 6H_2O$ (Ostwald's process)

$2NO + O_2 \rightleftharpoons 2NO_2$

$4NO_2 + 2H_2O + O_2 \rightarrow 4HNO_3$

105. (d): Fe, Al, Cr all are rendered passive on treatment with conc. HNO_3.

106. (d): $3Cu + \underset{\text{Dil.}}{4HNO_3} \xrightarrow{\Delta}$

$3Cu(NO_3)_2 + 2NO + 4H_2O$

107. (b): $4Zn + 10HNO_3 \text{ (very dil.)} \rightarrow$

$4Zn(NO_3)_2 + 3H_2O + NH_4NO_3$

108. (b): Fe becomes passive due to the formation of an oxide layer on its surface and Pt does not react with nitric acid.

109. (c): NO_3^- has sp^2-hybridisation and three resonating structures.

Therefore, bond order $= \dfrac{2+1+1}{3} = 1.33$

St. of NO_3^- ion

110. (b): $P_4O_{10} + 4HNO_3 \rightarrow 2N_2O_5 + 4HPO_3$

N_2O_5 cannot be obtained by the reaction of P_4 and HNO_3

$P_4 + 20HNO_3 \rightarrow 4H_3PO_4 + 20NO_2 + 4H_2O$

N_2O_5 is diamagnetic and does not have an N–N bond.

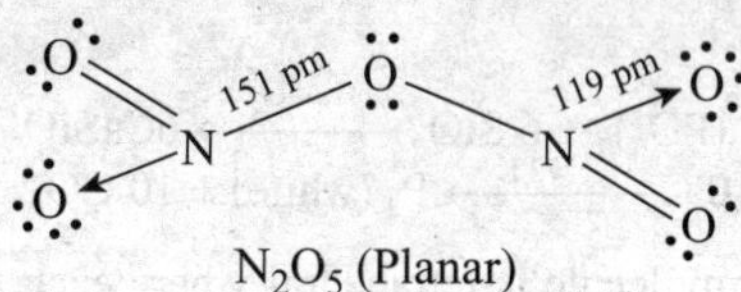

N_2O_5 (Planar)

N_2O_5 is decomposed by alkali metals to brown NO_2 gas.

$N_2O_5 + Na \rightarrow NaNO_3 + \underset{\text{(Brown gas)}}{NO_2}$

N_2O_5 is a colourless solid at room temperature.

111. (b): PbO_2 being a powerful oxidising agent, liberates O_2 when treated with conc. HNO_3.

$2PbO_2 + 4HNO_3 \rightarrow 2Pb(NO_3)_2 + 2H_2O + O_2$

112. (c):

$Sn + \underset{\text{(Conc.)}}{4HNO_3} \rightarrow \underset{\text{Metastannic acid}}{H_2SnO_3} + 4NO_2 + H_2O$

113. (d): $\underset{\text{Cane sugar}}{C_{12}H_{22}O_{11}} \xrightarrow[\text{18 [O]}]{\text{conc. } HNO_3} 6\,\underset{\text{Oxalic acid}}{\begin{matrix}COOH\\|\\COOH\end{matrix}} + 5H_2O$

114. (b): $2CrO_4^{2-} + 2H^+ \rightarrow Cr_2O_7^{2-} + H_2O$
Yellow (HNO$_3$) Orange

115. (a): As Al is rendered passive by conc. HNO_3, it can be safely stored in containers of Al.

116. (a): $NH_2-CO-NH_2 + 2HNO_2 \rightarrow CO_2 + 3H_2O + 2N_2$

117. (a): Nitrous acid can be obtained by the reaction of sulfuric acid with $Ba(NO_2)_2$.
$Ba(NO_2)_2 + H_2SO_4 \rightarrow BaSO_4\downarrow + 2HNO_2$
White ppt.

118. (c): Pb forms nitric oxide (NO) with dil. HNO_3.
$3Pb + 8HNO_3 \rightarrow 3Pb(NO_3)_2 + 2NO + 4H_2O$
Dil. Nitric oxide

119. (d): HNO_3 has a higher (+5) oxidation number of N than HNO_2 (+3). Therefore, HNO_3 is a stronger acid than HNO_2.

120. (c): $2KI + 4HNO_3 \rightarrow I_2 + 2NO_2 + 2KNO_3 + 2H_2O$
Iodide ion I^-, is a strong reducing agent and reduces HNO_3 vapour to NO_2 (brown gas). Thus, the salt X is KI.

Phosphorus and its Compounds

121. (d): On heating ammonium nitrate, nitrous oxide or nitrogen (I) oxide is formed.
$NH_4NO_3 \xrightarrow{475-430°C} N_2O + 2H_2O$
Nitrous oxide
Nitrous oxide is called laughing gas.

122. (b): $KCNO + (NH_4)_2SO_4 \rightarrow 2NH_4CNO$ or $2NH_2CONH_2 + K_2SO_4$

123. (b): In acidic solutions, the pairs of electrons present with nitrogen will not be available for donation, as H^+ of the acid will consume that one to form NH_4^+ ions. Thus, no NH_3 molecules are available for complex formation.

124. (a): Lone pair density is maximum in NH_3 due to its small size.

125. (e): Hydroxyapatite is $Ca_5(PO_4)_3OH$ and fluorapatite is $Ca_5(PO_4)_3F$.

126. (a): $2Ca_3(PO_4)_2 + 6SiO_2 \xrightarrow{1773\,K} 6CaSiO_3 + P_4O_{10}$
$P_4O_{10} + 10C \xrightarrow{1773\,K} P_4\text{(white)} + 10CO$

127. (c): A P_4 molecule is tetrahedral where each P is bonded to three other P atoms leaving one lone pair of electrons on each P atom. Hence, there are a total of four lone pairs of electrons in a P_4 molecule. The total number of single bonds formed is six and the number of bonds formed by each P atom is three.

128. (a): White P on heating in the presence of a catalyst (sunlight) in an inert atmosphere gives red P.

129. (b): Hence, white phosphorus has six P–P single bonds, four lone pairs of electrons and the PPP angle is 60°.

60°
White phosphorus

130. (a): White phosphorus on heating with an aqueous solution of KOH produces phosphine (PH_3) gas.
$P_4 + 3KOH + 3H_2O \rightarrow 3KH_2PO_2 + PH_3$
White phosphorus Potassium hypophosphite Phosphine

131. (a): White phosphorus is soluble in CS_2 whereas red phosphorus is insoluble in it.

132. (d): White phosphorus (P_4) is most reactive due to strain in the molecule.

133. (d): In P_4, the P–P linkage is formed by $sp^3 - sp^3$ hybridised orbital overlapping.
So the percentage of p character will be 75%.

134. (d): Both white and red phosphorus burn in air forming phosphorus pentoxide.
$P_4 + 5O_2 \xrightarrow{\Delta} P_4O_{10}$

135. (a): Bone black is the polymorphic form of phosphorus.

136. (d): Phosphorus exists as solid at 25°C and 1 atmospheric pressure (mp of white phosphorus = 44°C).

137. (c):
$\overset{0}{P_4} + 3KOH + 3H_2O \rightarrow \overset{-3}{PH_3} + 3KH_2\overset{+1}{P}O_2$
Here P is reduced to –3 in PH_3 and oxidised to +1 in KH_2PO_2.

138. (c): The oxidation state of P in $Ba(H_2PO_2)_2$ is +1.
$Ba^{2+}(H_2^{+1}P^xO_2^{2-})_2$
$= 2 + (+2 + x - 4)_2 = 0$
or $2 + 2(x-2) = 0$ or $2x - 4 = -2$
or $2x = -2 + 4 = +2$ or $x = +1$

139. (a): The oxidation state of P in orthophosphorous acid, H_3PO_3 is +3; pyrophosphorous acid, $H_4P_2O_5$ is +3; hypophosphoric acid, $H_4P_2O_6$ is +4; pyrophosphoric acid, $H_4P_2O_7$ is +5.

140. (a): $P_4 + 3NaOH + 3H_2O \rightarrow 3NaH_2PO_2 + PH_3$

141. (c): In a P_4 white phosphorus molecule, atoms are placed at the corners of a tetrahedron.

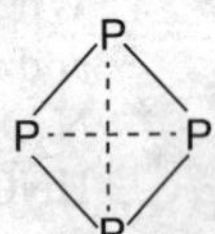

142. (c): $P_4 + 3O_2 \rightarrow P_4O_6$
Crystalline solid
In cold water it gives phosphorous acid.
$P_4O_6 + 6H_2O \rightarrow 4H_3PO_3$
With hot water it gives phosphoric acid.
$P_4O_6 + 6H_2O \xrightarrow{\text{Hot}} 3H_3PO_4 + PH_3$

143. (d): $P_4 + 20HNO_3 \rightarrow 4H_3PO_4 + 20NO_2 + 4H_2O$

144. (c): Ordinary phosphine contains P_2H_4 as an impurity which is highly inflammable.

145. (a): $PH_4I + NaOH \rightarrow NaI + PH_3 + H_2O$

146. (c): $Ca_3P_2 + 6H_2O \rightarrow 3Ca(OH)_2 + 2PH_3$
One mol Two mol

147. (b): $P_4 + 3NaOH + 3H_2O \rightarrow PH_3 + 3NaH_2PO_2$
White Caustic soda Phosphine Sodium hypophosphite

148. (c): $Ca_3P_2 + 6H_2O \rightarrow 3Ca(OH)_2 + 2PH_3$
PH_3 contains P_2H_4 (diphosphine) as an impurity which on burning gives P_2O_5 and white smoke.

149. (a): P in PH_3 is sp^3-hybridised. It has three bond pairs and one lone pair around P. Due to stronger lone pair–bond pair repulsions than bond pair–bond pair repulsions, the tetrahedral angle decreases from 109.5° to 93.6°. As a result, PH_3 is pyramidal. However, when it reacts with a proton, it forms a PH_4^+ ion which has four bond pairs and no lone pair. Due to the absence of lone pair–bond pair repulsions and the presence of four identical bond pair–bond pair interactions, PH_4^+ assumes a tetrahedral geometry with a bond angle of 109.5°. This explains why the bond angle in PH_4^+ is higher than in PH_3.

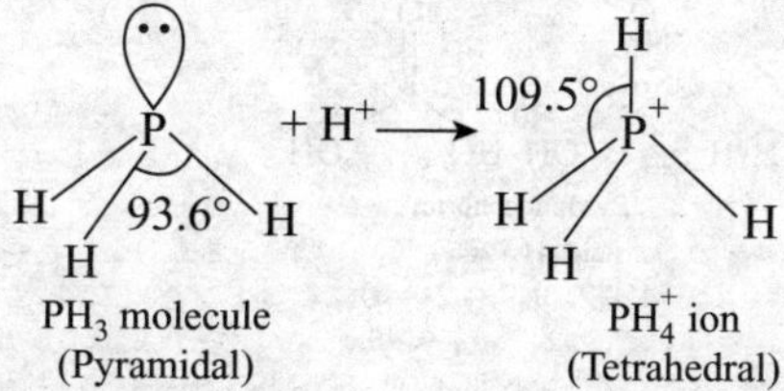

PH_3 molecule (Pyramidal) PH_4^+ ion (Tetrahedral)

150. (c): Pure phosphine gas is stable in air and not inflammable at normal temperature but on heating upto 150°C), it catches fire and produces phosphorus pentaoxide.
$2\ PH_3 + 4\ O_2 \rightarrow P_2O_5 + 3\ H_2O$

151. (b): $2\ AlP + 3\ \underset{\text{Dil.}}{H_2SO_4} \rightarrow Al_2(SO_4)_3 + 2\ \underset{\text{Phosphine}}{PH_3}$

152. (d): PH_3 is insoluble in water because it does not form hydrogen bonds.

153. (b): $PH_3 + 3\ Cl_2 \rightarrow PCl_3 + 3\ HCl$
(exothermic) makes the solution warm. Option (c) is not possible because it shows an endothermic reaction.

154. (d): The formal charge distributed on each P–H bond in PH_3, P_2H_6 and P_2H_5 is zero. The formal charge distributed on each P–H bond in $PH_6^+ = +\frac{1}{6} = +0.16$
Therefore, the least covalent P–H bond present is in PH_6^+.

155. (b): The Lewis acid strength of trichlorides of group 15 elements decreases down the group from P to Bi as the electronegativity of the central atom decreases.

156. (b): PCl_5 has three shorter (202 pm) equatorial and two longer (240 pm) axial bonds. The axial bonds are weaker than equatorial bonds, therefore, when PCl_5 is heated, the less stable axial bonds break to form PCl_3 and Cl_2 gas.
$PCl_5 \xrightarrow{\text{Heat}} PCl_3 + Cl_2$

157. (c): $H_2SO_4 + 2\ PCl_5 \rightarrow \underset{\text{Sulfuryl chloride}}{SO_2Cl_2} + 2\ POCl_3 + 2\ HCl$

158. (d): PCl_5, on hydrolysis, with insufficient quantity of water, gives $POCl_3$ while with an excess of water, gives phosphoric acid, (H_3PO_4).
$PCl_5 + 4\ H_2O \xrightarrow{\text{Excess of water}} H_3PO_4 + 5\ HCl$

159. (c): Reaction between PCl_3 and PhMgBr gives triphenyl phosphine.
$3\ C_6H_5MgBr + PCl_3 \rightarrow (C_6H_5)_3P + 3MgClBr$

160. (b): $PCl_3 + 3\ H_2O \rightarrow H_3PO_3 + 3\ HCl$

161. (b): Valence shell electronic configuration of PCl_5 is given.

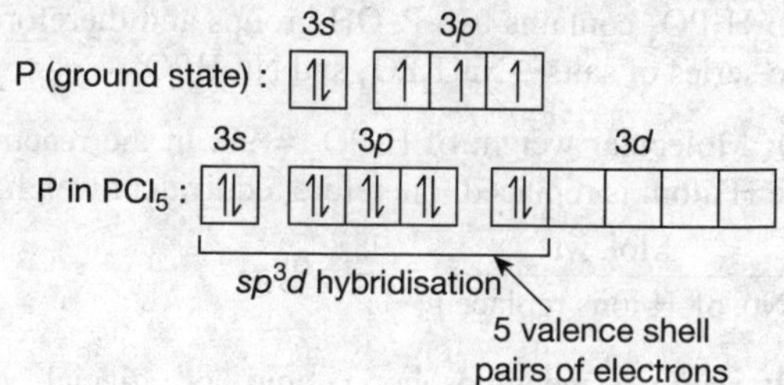

Since there is no lone pair of electrons on the P atom, PCl_5 has the expected trigonal bipyramidal shape.

162. (b): $P_4 + 6\ Cl_2(g) \rightarrow \underset{\text{Colourless fumes in moist air}}{4PCl_3(l)}$
$PCl_3 + 3\ H_2O \rightarrow H_3PO_3 + 3\ HCl$

163. (b): $P_4O_6 + 6\ H_2O \rightarrow 4\ H_3PO_3$

164. (a): The structure of P_4O_{10} is
Number of P–O single bonds = 12
Number of P=O bonds = 4
Total number of P–O bonds = 12 + 4 = 16

165. (b): Acidic strength of the oxides decreases as we move down the group from N to Bi. Thus, the order of acidic strength is $P_2O_5 > As_2O_3 > Sb_2O_3 > Bi_2O_3$.

166. (c):
$\underset{(A)}{4\ HNO_3} + \underset{(B)}{P_4O_{10}} \rightarrow 4\ HPO_3 + 2N_2O_5$

167. (b): P_4O_8
$4\,x + (-2 \times 8) = 0$
$4x - 16 = 0$
$x = \frac{16}{4} = +4$

168. (d): In the reaction
$\underset{\text{(Acidic impurity)}}{P_2O_5} + \underset{\text{(Basic flux)}}{3\ CaO} \rightarrow \underset{\text{(Slag)}}{Ca_3(PO_4)_2}$
Thus, P_2O_5 acts as an acidic impurity.

169. (b): Consider the reaction
$4\ HNO_3 + P_4O_{10} \rightarrow 4\ HPO_3 + 2\ \underset{X}{N_2O_5}$
The product X is dinitrogen pentoxoide (N_2O_5).

170. (d): $Ca_3(PO_4)_2 + 3\ SiO_2 \rightarrow 3\ CaSiO_3 + P_2O_5$

171. (c): $P_4O_{10} + 6\ H_2O \rightarrow \underset{\text{Orthophosphoric acid}}{4\ H_3PO_4}$
Therefore, P_4O_{10} is the anhydride of H_3PO_4.

172. (a): The tetrahedral structure of H_3PO_4 is shown.

Structure of H_3PO_4

It contains three ionisable P–OH bonds, no P–H bond and one P=O bond.

173. (b): H_3PO_3 contains two P–OH groups and therefore, forms two series of salts—NaH_2PO_3 and Na_2HPO_3.

174. (d): Molecular weight of H_3PO_4 = 98. In the reaction, only one H atom is replaced. Therefore, equivalent weight

$$= \frac{\text{Mol. wt}}{\text{No. of H ions replaced}} = \frac{98}{1} = 98$$

175. (d): HPO_3 (metaphosphoric acid or glacial phosphoric acid) contains one P–OH bond and thus is a monobasic acid. But it actually exists as a polymer $(HPO_3)_2$.

HO—P(=O)(=O)

176. (a): More the P–H bonds in the acid, more will be the reducing power. Hypophosphorous acid (H_3PO_2) contains two P–H bonds. Phosphorous acid (H_3PO_3) contains one P–H bond, hypophosphoric acid ($H_4P_2O_6$) contains no P–H bond, pyrophosphorous acid ($H_4P_2O_5$) contains one P–H bond for one P atom and phosphoric acid (H_3PO_4) contains no P–H bond. Thus, hypophosphorous acid is strongly reducing in nature.

177. (a): The structure of H_3PO_2 has two P–H bonds due to which it acts as a strong reducing agent. Similarly, H_3PO_4 has one P–H bond and H_3PO_4 has no P–H bond. The reducing character of these acids increases in the order as the number of P–H bonds present in them increases, that is, $H_3PO_4 < H_3PO_3 < H_3PO_2$.

178. (a): There are two P–H bonds present in H_3PO_2 due to which the acid is strongly reducing in character. It reduces $AgNO_3$ to metallic Ag.

$$4\,AgNO_3 + 2\,H_2O + H_3PO_2 \rightarrow 4\,Ag\downarrow + 4HNO_3 + H_3PO_4$$

179. (a):

Structure of H_3PO_2 is O=P(OH)(H)(H)

Structure of H_3PO_3 is O=P(OH)(H)(OH)

Structure of H_3PO_4 is O=P(OH)(OH)(OH)

Structure of $H_4P_2O_7$ is (HO)(HO)P(=O)–O–P(=O)(OH)(OH)

Thus, the maximum number of P–H bonds are present in H_3PO_2.

180. (a): Pyrophosphorous acid or diphosphorous acid, $H_4P_2O_5$ contains two P–OH bonds and thus is a dibasic acid.

H–P(=O)(OH)–O–P(=O)(OH)–H

181. (b): Cyclotrimetaphosphoric acid is $(HPO_3)_3$.

$$\overset{+1}{H}\,\overset{x}{P}\,\overset{-2}{O_3})_3 = 3\,[+1 + x + 3(-2)] = 0$$

Or, $x = +5$

182. (a):

H–P(=O)(H)–OH — Hypophosphorous acid (H_3PO_2): $+3 + x + 2(-2) = 0$, $x = +1$

H–P(=O)(OH)–OH — Orthophosphorous acid (H_3PO_3): $+3 + x + 3(-2) = 0$, $x = +3$

H–P(=O)(OH)–O–P(=O)(OH)–OH — Pyrophosphoric acid ($H_4P_2O_7$): $+4 + 2x + 7(-2) = 0$, $x = +5$

Thus, the correct order of acids of phosphorus in the increasing order of oxidation state of phosphorus is hypohosphorous acid < orthophosphorous acid < pyrophosphoric acid.

183. (b): Phosphorous acid (H_3PO_3) is a diprotic acid. It form two series of salts, such as NaH_2PO_3 and Na_2HPO_3, but none of the type Na_3PO_3 with NaOH. Its structure is as follows:

O=P(H)(OH)(OH)

184. (d): $NaOH + H_3PO_2 \rightarrow NaH_2PO_2 + H_2O$

Sodium hydroxide, Hypophorous acid, Sodium hypophosphite

185. (c): H_3PO_2 has 1 –OH group, H_3PO_3 has 2 –OH groups and H_3PO_4 has 3 –OH groups. In these acids, although the number of –OH groups (ionisable hydrogen) increases, the acidity does not increase very much. This is due to the fact that the number of unprotonated oxygen (P–0 groups) responsible for the enhancement of acidity due to inductive effect, remains the same with the result that the dissociation constants also remain nearly the same.

186. (d): $3\,NaOH + H_3PO_4 \rightarrow Na_3PO_4 + 3\,H_2O$

187. (d): $Na_4P_2O_7$ is a salt of strong acid and a strong base and is not an acid salt.

188. (d): Phosphoric acid, H_3PO_4 has three P–OH groups and phosphorous acid, H_3PO_3 has two P–OH groups. Therefore, their basicity is 3 and 2 respectively.

189. (b): H_3PO_3 has one non-ionisable P–H bond.

O=P(H)(OH)(OH)

190. (c): $H_5P_5O_{15}$ or $(HPO_3)_5$ is a cyclic pentametaphosphoric acid.

191. (c): Cyclic trimetaphosphoric acid $(HPO_3)_3$ has the following structure. It contains three P–O–P bonds.

St. of cyclotrimetaphosphoric acid containing three P – O – P bonds

192. (c): The structure of hypophosphorous acid, H_3PO_2 is on the right. It contains one replaceable H atom.

O=P(OH)(H)(H)

193. (d): $Na_2HPO_4 \rightarrow Na_2PO_4^- + H^+$

It can give H^+ ion in solution. Therefore, it is an acid salt.

194. (d): $H_3PO_4 \xrightarrow{\Delta,\,600°C} HPO_3 + H_2O$

195. (d): Oxidation number of P in
$H_3PO_4: +3+x+(-2\times4)=0$
or $x-5=0, x=+5$
$H_4P_2O_6: (+1\times4)+2x+(-2\times6)$
Or $2x-8=0, x=+3$
$H_3PO_3: (+1\times3)+x+(-2\times3)=0$
or $x-3=0, x=+3$
$H_3PO_2: (+1\times3)+x+(-2\times2)=0$
or $x-1=0, x=+1$

196. (c): The total number of compounds having at least one bridging oxo group is 5 which are,

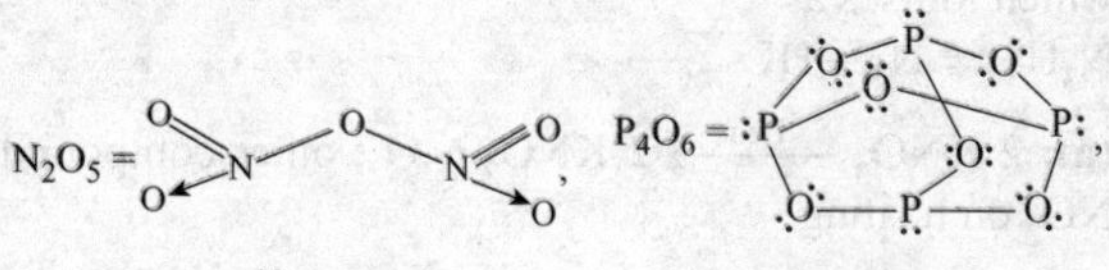

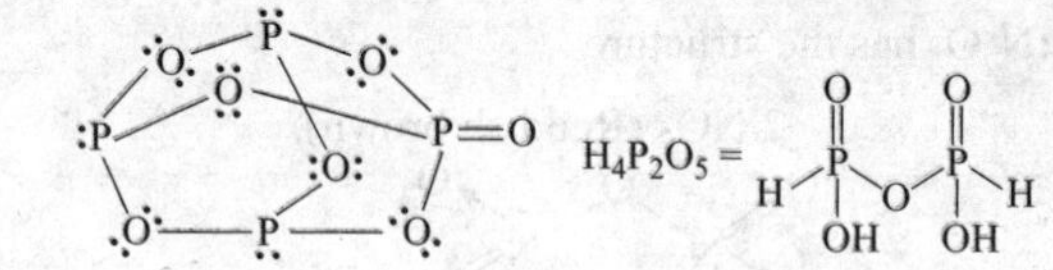

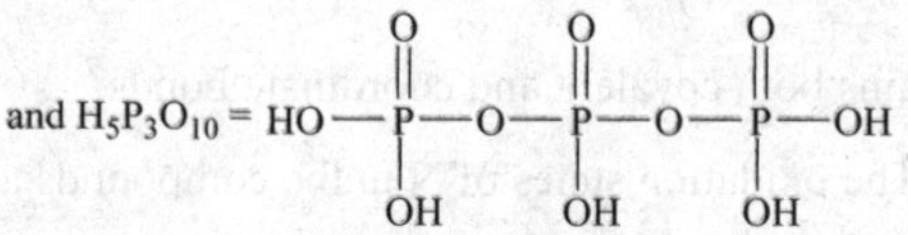

N_2O_5, P_4O_6, P_4O_{10}, $H_4P_2O_5$ and $H_5P_3O_{10}$ = HO—P(=O)(OH)—O—P(=O)(OH)—O—P(=O)(OH)—OH

Compound such as

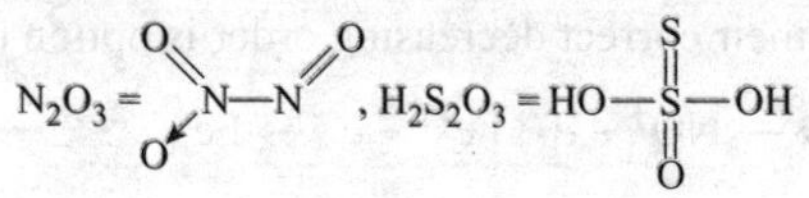

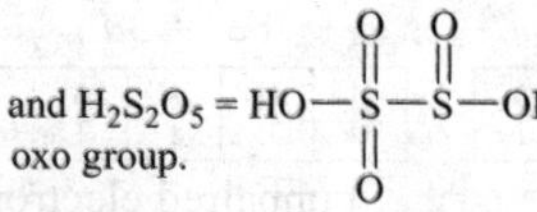

N_2O_3, $H_2S_2O_3$ = HO—S(=O)(=S)—OH

and $H_2S_2O_5$ = HO—S(=O)(=O)—S(=O)—OH do not have any bridging oxo group.

197. (d):

	Phosphide ion	Chloride ion
	(P^{3-})	(Cl^-)
Total electrons	$15+3=18$	$17+1=18$

P^{3-} and Cl^- are isoelectronic.

198. (b): The role of phosphate in detergent powder is to remove Ca^{2+} and Mg^{2+} ions from water that causes the hardness of water.

$$3\,Ca^{2+}+2\,PO_4^{3-}\rightarrow \underset{\text{White ppt.}}{Ca_3(PO_4)_2\downarrow}$$

199. (c): Pentavalency in phosphorus is more stable than that of nitrogen due to the large size of the phosphorus atom.

200. (a): A pre-weighed amount of organic compound is heated with concentrated nitric acid (HNO_3) in a tube. The phosphorus present in the compound gets converted into phosphoric acid. Now the contents of tube are heated with magnesia mixture, that is, $MgSO_4$ + NH_4Cl + NH_4OH, so that magnesium ammonium phosphate $MgNH_4PO_4$ is formed which is collected, washed, dried and ignited to get magnesium pyrophosphate $Mg_2P_2O_7$, which is then weighed.

$$\underset{\text{Phosphoric acid}}{H_3PO_4}\xrightarrow{\text{Magnesia mixtue}}\underset{\text{Magnesium ammonium phosphate (white ppt.)}}{MgNH_4PO_4}+3\,HCl$$

$$2\,MgNH_4PO_4\xrightarrow{\Delta}Mg_2P_2O_7\downarrow+2\,NH_3+H_2O$$

Knowing the weight of $Mg_2P_2O_7$, the percentage of phosphorus can be calculated.

201. (b): $NH_3+HCl\rightarrow NH_4Cl$
$PH_3+HCl\rightarrow PH_4Cl$

202. (a): Both P_4O_{10} and P_2O_5 may be regarded as anhydrides of H_3PO_4 but since P_2O_5 occurs as a dimer, the right answer is P_4O_{10} and not P_2O_5.

$$P_4O_{10}+6\,H_2O\xrightarrow{\text{Hot}}4\,H_3PO_4$$

203. (d): Phosphorus pentoxide P_4O_{10}, is used as a dehydrating agent as it absorbs moisture to give HPO_3.

$$P_4O_{10}+2\,H_2O\xrightarrow{\text{Cold}}\underset{\text{(metaphosphoric acid)}}{4\,HPO_3}$$

204. (b): Structure of P_4O_{10} is

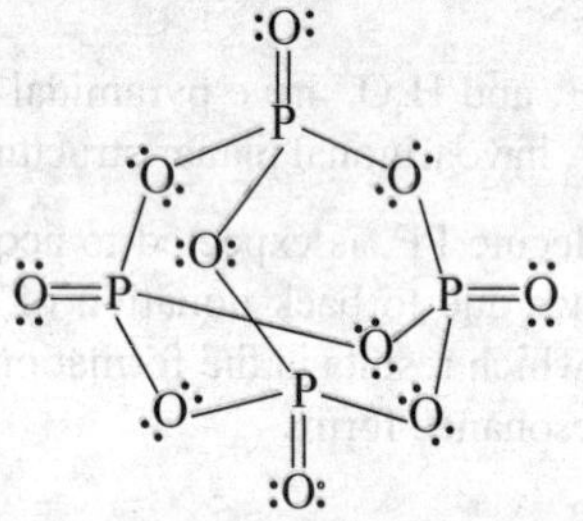

The number of sigma bonds present in P_4O_{10} is 16.

205. (a): A chemical reaction occurs when P_4O_{10}, Mg_3N_2, CaC_2 and BaO_2 react with water as shown.
$P_4O_{10}+6\,H_2O\rightarrow 4\,H_3PO_4$ (not hydrolysed)
$Mg_3N_2+6\,H_2O\rightarrow 3\,Mg(OH)_2+2\,NH_3$
$CaC_2+H_2O\rightarrow Ca(OH)_2+C_2H_2$
$BaO_2+2\,H_2O\rightarrow Ba(OH)_2+H_2O_2$

206. (a): $2\,H_2SO_4+2\,P_2O_5\rightarrow \underset{\text{Sulfur trioxide}}{2\,SO_3}+4\,HPO_3$

Fertilisers

207. (d): It is a reason for the given fact.

208. (b): Triple superphosphate $[Ca(H_2PO_4)_2.H_2O]$ is the best phosphatic fertiliser since it is free from gypsum and hence contains a higher percentage (56.35%) of phosphorus as P_2O_5.

209. (b): Superphosphate of lime is a mixture of calcium dihydrogen phosphate and gypsum and is obtained by treating phosphatic rock with conc. H_2SO_4.

$$Ca_3(PO_4)_2+2\,H_2SO_4+4\,H_2O\rightarrow \underbrace{Ca(H_2PO_4)_2.2\,H_2O+2\,CaSO_4.2H_2O}_{\text{Superphosphate of lime}}$$

210. (a): Muriate of potash (KCl) contains 63.8% K_2O. Sulfate of potash (K_2SO_4) contains 54% K_2O, nitrate of potash (KNO_3) contains 46.5% K_2O but carbonate of potash (K_2CO_3) is not a fertiliser.

211. (d): Urea contains 46.6% N and $(NH_4)_2SO_4$ contains 20% N.

212. (a): CAN or calcium ammonium nitrate is a neutral fertiliser. It gives non-acid hydrolysis products and it decreases acidity in the soil.

213. (d): Urea is preferred to ammonium sulfate as a nitrogenous fertiliser because it does not cause acidity in the soil.

$NH_2CONH_2 + H_2O \rightarrow 2\ NH_3 + CO_2$
(does not alterthe pH of the soil)

$(NH_4)_2SO_4 + 2\ H_2O \rightarrow 2\ NH_4OH + H_2SO_4$
(renders soil acidic)

214. (d): Ammonium sulfate is a nitrogenous fertiliser.

Final Preparation

215. (d): Elements with low electronegativity and low oxidation state, that is, metals form basic oxides. Thus, Bi_2O_3 is basic in nature.

216. (c): As the electronegativity of the halogen X in PX_3 decreases down the group from F to I, the Lewis acid strength also decreases.

217. (c): Both NF_3 and H_3O^+ have pyramidal structures whereas NO_3^- and BF_3 have trigonal planar structure.

218. (c): The molecule PF_3 is expected to acquire partial double bond character due to back donation of a pair of electrons from F to P which results in the formation of a $p\pi - \pi$ bond. Due to the resonance forms,

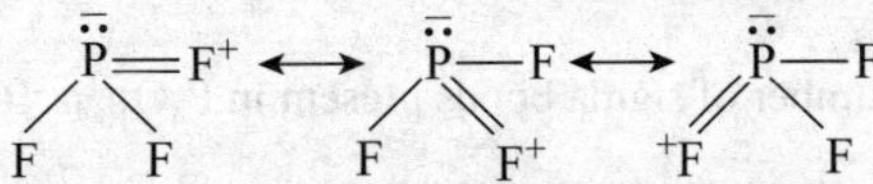

the bond pair–bond pair repulsion increases to give a higher bond angle.

219. (c): $BiCl_3 + H_2O \rightarrow BiOCl + 2\ HCl$
Bismuch oxychloride (white ppt.)

220. (d): $NH_4Cl + NaNO_2 \xrightarrow{Heat} NH_4NO_2 \xrightarrow{Heat} N_2 + 2\ H_2O$

221. (b): $3\ CaOCl_2 + 2\ NH_3 \rightarrow 3\ CaCl_2 + 3\ H_2O + N_2$

222. (a): $(NH_4)_2Cr_2O_7 \xrightarrow{\Delta} N_2 + 4\ H_2O + Cr_2O_3$
$Ba(N_3)_2 \xrightarrow{\Delta} Ba + 3\ N_2$

223. (b): Magnesium has a strong affinity for nitrogen and forms the nitride when heated in air and thus removes nitrogen completely from air.
$3\ Mg + N_2 \rightarrow Mg_3N_2$

224. (c): N can form NCl_3, N_2O_5 and Ca_3N_2 but not $NaCl_5$ due to the non-availability of *d* orbitals.

225. (c): $\underbrace{CaC_2 + N_2 \xrightarrow{1273\ K} CaCN_2 + C(\text{graphite})}_{\text{Nitrogen}}$

A mixture of calcium cyananmide ($CaCN_2$) and graphite (called nitrolim) is used as a fertiliser.

226. (d): In the reaction $3\ CuO + 2\ NH_3 \rightarrow 3\ Cu + 3\ H_2O + N_2$
NH_3 acts as a reducing agent and reduces CuO to Cu. It itself is oxidised to N_2.

227. (d): $Cu(OH)_2 + 4\ NH_3 \rightarrow [Cu(NH_3)_4](OH)_2$
(Soluble complex)

228. (b): Liquid ammonia is liquefied ammonia gas while liquor ammonia is a concentrated solution of ammonia gas (which is soluble in water) in water.

229. (b): NH_4^+ is tetrahedral in shape with a bond angle of 109.5°.

230. (b): Basicity in nitrogen compounds is attributed to the availability of a lone pair of electrons. Basicity will decrease when N is attached to more electronegative groups. Therefore, the order of basicity of these compounds is
$NH_2OH < HN_3 < NH_2NH_2 < NH_3$

231. (d): N_3H (hydrazoic acid) is the acidic hydride of nitrogen which ionises as
$N_3H \rightleftharpoons N_3^- + H^-$

232. (a): $2\ KNO_3 \xrightarrow{Heat} 2\ KNO_2 + O_2$; other compounds give NO_2 on heating.

233. (b):N_2O_5 has the structure

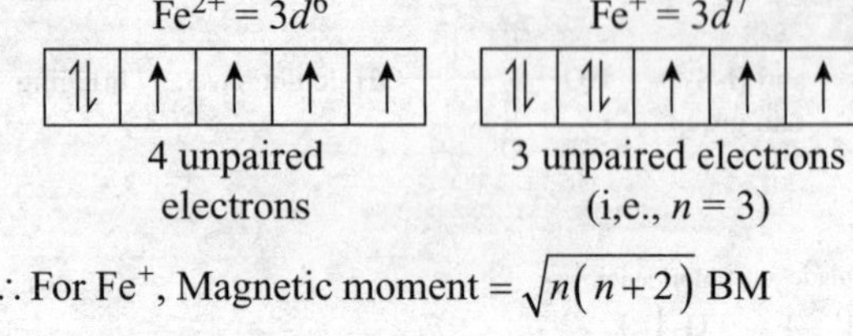

contains both covalent and coordinate bonds.

234. (a): The oxidation states of N in the compounds are
$\overset{+5}{HNO_3}$, $\overset{+2}{NO}$, $\overset{0}{N_2}$ and $\overset{-3}{NH_4Cl}$
Hence, their correct decreasing order is option (a).

235. (d): $NO \rightarrow NO^+ - e^-$; $Fe^{3+} - e^- \rightarrow Fe^+$

$Fe^{2+} = 3d^6$	$Fe^+ = 3d^7$
⇅ ↑ ↑ ↑ ↑	⇅ ⇅ ↑ ↑ ↑
4 unpaired electrons	3 unpaired electrons (i,e., $n = 3$)

$\therefore$ For Fe^+, Magnetic moment $= \sqrt{n(n+2)}$ BM

$\sqrt{3(3+2)}$ B.M. $= \sqrt{15}$ BM $= 3.87$ BM

236. (b): Compound (A) is HNO_2 which is an unstable pale blue solution of N_2O_3 in water which readily decomposes as

$\underset{\text{(A) Pale blue}}{2\ HNO_2} \rightarrow H_2O + N_2O_3 \rightleftharpoons NO + \underset{\text{(Brown)}}{NO_2}$

Also, HNO_2 acts as an oxidant as well reductant, and a ligand.

$SnCl_2 + 2HCl + \underset{\text{(Oxidant)}}{2\ HNO_2} \rightarrow SnCl_4 + 2NO + 2H_2O$

$\underset{\text{Orange}}{Br_2} + H_2O + \underset{\text{(Reductant)}}{HNO_2} \rightarrow \underset{\text{Colourless}}{2\ HBr + HNO_3}$

$HNO_2 \rightleftharpoons H^+ + NO_2^-$

$6NO_2^- + COCl_3 \rightarrow \underset{\text{(Complex forming ability)}}{[Co(NO_2)_6]^{3-}} + 3\ Cl^-$

237. (d): (180°) in NO_2^+ where N is *sp*-hybridised giving a linear structure to the nitronium ion. NO_3^- has sp^2-hybridisation, the bond angle is 120° and the structure is trigonal planar. NO_2^- has angular geometry (sp^2-hybridisation). Due to the presence of a lone pair of electrons on the N atom, the bond angle is

115°. NO_2 has an angular geometry (sp^2-hybridisation) with a bond angle of 134°.

238. (a): In BF_3 and NO_2^-, the central atoms B and N are sp^2-hybridised. In NH_2^-, N is sp^3-hybridised and in H_2O, O is sp^3-hybridised.

239. (b): N in NO_2^- and NO_3^- is sp^2-hybridised. NO_2^- is angular having a lone pair occupying one of the hybrid orbitals. NO_3^- is trigonal planar.

240. (d): HNO_3 has nitrogen in its highest oxidation state of +5; due to this, it reduces itself by oxidising other substances. Hence, it is a very strong oxidising agent.

241. (b): In the case of phosphorus, $p\pi-p\pi$ bonding is weak and thus the P_2 molecule is unstable.

242. (b): As we go down from N to Sb, the electronegativity decreases, the bond pairs of electrons in MH_3get much farther apart from the central atom and decreases the H–M–H bond angle. The bond angle becomes closer to 90° in SbH_3 which suggests that the orbitals used for bonding are closer to pure *p* orbitals.

243. (a): All I, II, III and IV statements are correct.

244. (c): P_2O_5 is the most stable pentoxide (decomposition temperature 420°C) and N_2O_5 is the least stable (decomposition temperature 30°C).

245. (c): Conc. HNO_3 decomposes in the presence of sunlight to NO_2 which imparts a brownish yellow colour to the acid.

$$4\,HNO_3 \xrightarrow{\text{Sunlight}} 4NO_2 + 2\,H_2O + O_2$$

Decomposition (Brownish colour)

246. (d): In the NO_3^- ion, N uses its sp^2-hybrid orbital which contains a lone pair to form a dative bond with one of the oxygen atoms, the other two singly occupied sp^2-hybrid orbitals form two σ-bonds with each of the other two oxygen atoms and the unhybridised singly occupied p_z orbital of N forms a π-bond with one of the oxygen atoms to give four bond pairs and zero lone pairs of electrons on the N atom.

247. (b): $3\,HCl + HNO_3 \rightarrow NOCl + 2\,H_2O + 2\,[Cl]$

248. (c): $2\,HNO_3 + NO \xrightarrow{\text{Oxidation}} H_2O + 3\,NO_2$

$NO_2 + H_2S \xrightarrow{\text{Oxidation}} H_2O + S + NO$

249. (a): In NO_3^-, N is sp^2 hybridised giving a trigonal planar structure. In H_3O^+, O is sp^3-hybridised giving a tetrahedral geometry but one of the hybrid orbitals is occupied by a lone pair of electrons giving a trigonal pyramid structure.

250. (a): It is a fact.

251. (a): $4\,NH_3 + 5\,O_2 \xrightarrow[1075\text{ K}]{\text{Pt. gauze}} 4\,NO + 6\,H_2O$

or $2\,NH_3 + 5/2\,O_2 \rightarrow 2\,NO + 3\,H_2O$

Hence, two moles of NO are produced by the catalytic oxidation of two moles of NH_3.

252. (b): On heating, NH_4NO_3 gives N_2O gas and water vapour which escape leaving no residue.

$NH_4NO_3 \xrightarrow{\text{Heat}} N_2O\uparrow + 2\,H_2O\uparrow$

253. (c): Brown ring test for NO_2^- and NO_3^- is due to the formation of $[Fe^{I}(H_2O_5)NO]^{2+}$ ion.

254. (a): $AgNO_3$ on heating strongly gives Ag metal,

$2\,AgNO_3 \xrightarrow{\text{Red heat}} 2\,Ag + 2\,NO_2 + O_2$

while others give oxides of the metal.

$2\,Pb(NO_3)_2 \xrightarrow{\Delta} 2\,PbO + 4\,NO_2 + O_2$

$2\,Cu(NO_3)_2 \xrightarrow{\Delta} 2\,CuO + 4\,NO_2 + O_2$

$4\,Al(NO_3)_3 \xrightarrow{\Delta} 2\,Al_2O_3 + 12\,NO_2 + 3\,O_2$

255. (b): $P_4 + 10\,H_2SO_4 \rightarrow 4\,H_3PO_4 + 10\,SO_2 + 4\,H_2O$

256. (a): The phenomenon of phosphorescence shown by whitephosphorus is called 'cold fire' also the disease caused by the constant touch with white phosphorus is called 'phossy jaw'.

257. (c): Sides of match boxes have a coating of Sb_2S_3 and red phosphorus.

258. (c): Tips of matchsticks contain a mixture of $K_2Cr_2O_7$ + S + red phosphorus.

259. (b): Red P does not react with NaOH. Only white P reacts with NaOH or KOH to form PH_3.

260. (a): PCl_5 is a covalent molecule in the gas phase but exists as $[PCl_4]^+[PCl_6]^-$ in the solid state.

261. (c): In the formation of POX_3, P is sp^3-hybridised. Further, the vacant *d* orbital of phosphorus will overlap with the filled *p*orbital of oxygen thereby resulting in the formation of a $p\pi-p\pi$ bond.

O ‖ $p\pi-d\pi$ bond; X—P—X; X

262. (a):

Structure of P_4O_{10}
No. of P–O–P bonds = 6

Structure of P_4O_6
No. of P–O–P bonds = 6

263. (c): The pH decreases from Na_2O to SiO_2 and then from SiO_2 to P_4O_{10} when these oxides are mixed with water. This is because Na_2O is a basic oxide which reacts with water to give a strong base NaOH so that the pH of the solution is higher than both SiO_2 and P_4O_{10}. Both SiO_2 and P_4O_{10} are acidic oxides but SiO_2 is insoluble while P_4O_{10} reacts with water to give acid the H_3PO_4 and the pH of the solution is lower than that of SiO_2.

264. (a): Four oxygens have a total formal charge = –3

Therefore, one oxygen has formal charge = –3/4 = –0.75

Total P–O bond order = PO_4^{3-} ion = 5

Therefore, P–O bond order = $\frac{5}{4} = 1.25$

Structure of PO_4^{3-} ion

265. (b): All the acids H_3PO_4, H_3PO_3 and H_3PO_2 contain only one P=O group which is responsible for an increase of acidity due to inductive effect. Therefore, there is very little difference in the acid strength of
H_3PO_4 ($Ka_1 = 7.5\times10^{-2}$)
H_3PO_3 ($Ka_1 = 1.6\times10^{-2}$) and H_3PO_2 ($Ka_1 = 1\times10^{-2}$)

266. (d): When copper sulfate reacts with hypophosphorous acid, it gets reduced to cuprous hydride (Cu_2H_2).
$4\,CuSO_4 + 3\,H_3PO_2 + 6\,H_2O \rightarrow$
$2\,Cu_2H_2 + 3\,H_3PO_4 + 4\,H_2SO_4$
Red ppt.

267. (a): $H_4P_2O_5$ (pyrophosphorus or diphosphorus acid)
$\overset{+1}{H_4}\overset{x}{P_2}\overset{-2}{O_5} = 4\,(+1) + 2\,(x) + 5\,(-2) = 0$
or $x = +3$
$\overset{+1}{H_4}\overset{x}{P_2}\overset{-2}{O_6}$ (Hypophosphoric acid)
$= 4\,(+1) + 2\,(x) + 6\,(-2) = 0$ or $x = +4$
$\overset{+1}{H_4}\overset{x}{P_2}\overset{-2}{O_7}$ (Pyrophosphoric or diphosphoric acid)
$= 4\,(+1) + 2\,(x) + 7\,(-2) = 0$ or $x = +5$

268. (b): Hypophosphorous acid

H_3PO_2 [structure: P with =O, H, H, OH] is a monoprotic acid

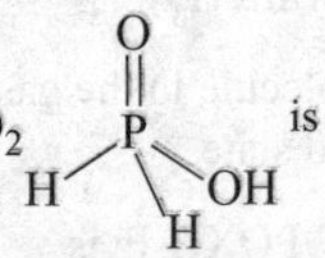

269. (a):

H_3PO_2 [structure: P with =O, H, H, OH]
Hypophosphorous acid or phosphinic acid (Monobasic)

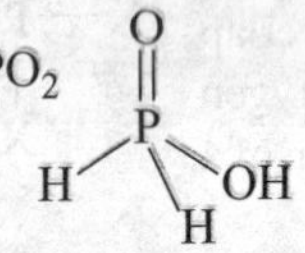

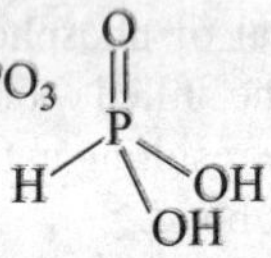

H_3PO_3 [structure: P with =O, H, OH, OH]
Orthophosphorous acid or phosphinic acid (Dibasic)

270. (c): Pseudo alums constitute a class of compounds in which the monovalent cation of true alum is replaced by a divalent cation. Hence, Na^+ and K^+ are not present in pseudo alums. Further, feldspar has a more closed structure, $H_4As_2O_7$ is a pyro acid and superphosphate of lime is $Ca(H_2)PO_4)_2$ + 2 $CaSO_4$.

271. (a): The strength of potash fertilisers is determined on the basis of K_2O%.

MATCH THE FOLLOWING

272. (d): (A) Laughing gas is N_2O (nitrous oxide); (B) Swart's reagent is SbF_3; (C) Vortex ring is formed by P_2O_5; (D) Chemical used in strike anywhere matches is P_4S_3

273. (a): (A) N_2O is a colourless gas, it produces hysterical laughter when inhaled. (B) NO_2 is a reddish brown gas at room temperature. (C) N_2O_3 is blue coloured liquid at 243 K. (D) N_2O_5 is a white crystalline solid.

274. (c):(A) H_3PO_3 has P in the +3 oxidation state; (B) Ca_3P_2 has P inthe –3 oxidation state; (C) $POCl_3$ has P in the +5 oxidation state; (D) NaH_2PO_2 has P in the +1 oxidation state.

ASSERTION REASON

275. (c): Correct R. Due to the small size and high dissociation energy (946 kJ mol^{-1}) of nitrogen, it is unreactive.

276. (d): Correct A. The bp of the hydrides of the nitrogen family decrease in the order $BiH_3 > SbH_3 > NH_3 > AsH_3 > PH_3$.
Correct R. The bp of hydrides should decrease with the molecular size from BiH_3 to PH_3. The abnormality in the bp trend due to the presence of hydrogen bonding in NH_3.

277. (b): Correct explanation. In the case of NI_3, N is more electronegative than I, the lone pair moment adds on the resultant of the N–I moments. But in the case of NF_3, F is more electronegative than N, the lone pair moment partly cancels the resultant N–F moments. Thus, the dipole moment is highest for NI_3 and lowest for NF_3.

278. (d): Correct A. The bond angles of PBr_3 and NBr_3 are greater than those of PH_3 and NH_3 respectively.
Correct R. The size of bromine is greater than that of hydrogen.

279. (c): Correct R. Because of the highly electronegative nature of F, it withdraws electrons from the N atom and thus, the lone pair of N cannot be ligated easily. On the other hand, CH_3 is an electron releasing group which increases the electron density on the N atom and $N(CH_3)_3$ behaves as a strong ligand.

280. (c): Correct R. Ammonia is polar in nature.

281. (d): Correct A.NO_3^- is planar while NH_3 is pyramidal.
Correct R. N in NO_3^- is sp^2-hybridised but in NH_3, it is sp^3-hybridised.

282. (b): Correct explanation. White phosphorus exists as a P_4 tetrahedral molecule having a P–P–P bond angle of 60°. Hence the molecule is under strain and more reactive. On the other hand red phosphorus exists as P_4 tetrahedra which are joined together though covalent bonds giving a polymeric structure.

283. (a): R is the correct explanation of A.

284. (a): R is the correct explanation of A.

285. (a): R is the correct explanation of A.

GROUP 16

Atomic and Physical Properties

286. (c): Mn_2O_7 gives $HMnO_4$ and CrO_3 gives H_2CrO_4 with H_2O.

287. (d): O_3 is an allotrope of O_2.

288. (a): $9O_3 + 2I_2 \rightarrow I_4O_9 + 9O_2$

289. (a): All the rest give O_2 on heating.

290. (d): SO_2 is a gas.

291. (d): Due to higher charge on O^{2-} and on O^- ions, the lattice energy$_2$ released during the formation of oxides having O^{2-}

species is more than that released during the formation of O^- ion.

292. (b): In the S_8 molecule, each S is sp^3-hybridised with two lone pairs of electrons occupying two of the hybrid orbitals and reducing the S–S–S bond angle to 107°.

293. (c):

Element	Allotropes
(a) Polonium	α- and β-polonium
(b) Tellurium	None
(c) Selenium	Trigonal, rhombohedral, three deep red monoclinic forms (α, β and γ-amorphous red, black vitrous selenium)
(d) Oxygen	Dioxygen and ozone

294. (d): O, S, Se, all show polymorphism.

295. (c): Due to a greater tendency for catenation, sulfur shows the property of polyanion formation to a greater extent. For example, in polysulfides, such as $S_3^{2-}, S_4^{2-}, S_5^{2-}$.

296. (c): The S–S bond has the highest bond energy (226 kJ mol^{-1}).

297. (b): Sulfur is found in the free state.

298. (b):$O^-_{(g)} + e^- \rightarrow O^{2-}_{(g)}$ + E, (ΔH = +ve; endoergic)

Chemical Properties

299. (d): All these tests are used to detect the presence of H_2S.

300. (b): As H_2O has the highest bp and H_2S the lowest, and the bp further increase from H_2Se to H_2Te, the volatility increases in the order given.

301. (b): H_2O has a bond angle of 104.5° which is the least compared to the bond angles in BaF_2 (180°), NH_3 (107.8°) and CH_4 (109.5°).

302. (a): According to Fajan's rules, the smaller the size of the anion (O^{2-}), the lesser is the polarisation and the more is the ionic character. Thus H_2O has the least covalent character.

303. (d): (a), (b) and (c) options given in the question.

304. (b): The acidic nature increases from H_2O to H_2Te. The increase in acidic character of the hydrides on moving down the group may be explained in terms of the bond length of the E–H bond; larger the bond length, lesser is the bond energy and thus easier is the ionisation of the E–H bond or better is the proton donor nature. Hence,
$H_2O < H_2S < H_2Se < H_2Te$.

305. (d):

H_2O	H_2S	H_2Se	H_2Te
104.5°	92.1°	91°	90°

As we go down the group,the electronegativity decreases due to which repulsion between the bonded pairs of electron also decreases. Hence, the bond angle decreases.

306. (a): Among the group 16 hydrides, only H_2O has an abnormally low volatility (high boiling point). This is because H_2O molecules are extensively associated due to intermolecular hydrogen bonds.

307. (c): The bond in H_2Te is weakest due to larger bond length hence it gives the H^+ ion easily.

308. (d): All hydrides except H_2O act as reducing agents. The reducing nature increases as the atomic number of the central atom increases. This is due to the weakening of the E–H bond as the bond length increases with an increase in the size of the E atom.

309. (b): SeO_2 is used as an oxidising agent in organic chemistry.

310. (a): Due to stronger O–F bonds in F_2O, it is not hydrolysed.

311. (b): SO_3 in the gaseous state exists as a monomer.

312. (b): Acidity of the oxides of non-metals increases with the electronegativity and oxidation number of the element. The electronegativity increases in the order Si < C < N. In the case of SO_3, the oxidation number of S is maximum (+6). Therefore, the increasing order of acid character of the oxides is $SiO_2 < CO_2 < N_2O_5 < SO_3$.

313. (c): H_2O_2 can act as an oxidising as well as a reducing agent.
H_2O_2 is an oxidising agent.
$PbS + 4\,H_2O_2 \rightarrow PbSO_4 + H_2O$
H_2O_2 as a reducing agent
$Ag_2O + H_2O_2 \rightarrow 2\,Ag + H_2O + O_2$

314. (c): The two S–O bonds in SO_2 are not different. They are equal (bond length = 143 pm) due to resonance.

315. (b): Sulfuric anhydride is SO_3 and its structure is
Thus, the type of bonds present are 3σ, one $p\pi - p\pi$ and two $p\pi - d\pi$.

(Structure labels: O, S, O, O; σ, σ, σ; $p\pi - d\pi$, $p\pi - p\pi$, $p\pi - d\pi$)

316. (a): MF_4 (M = S, Se, Te) has M sp^3d-hybridised with a trigonal bipyramidal geometry. There is a lone pair of electrons on M (occupying one equatorial position in the structure) due to which the bond angles decrease from 180° to 173° and from 120° to 102° and the actual shape of the compound is see–saw.

317. (b): In the OF_2 molecule, there are two bond pairs of electrons and eight lone pairs (two from O and three from each of the F atoms) of electrons.

318. (c): SF_3Cl_3 like SF_6, is an octahedral molecule with S being sp^3d^2 hybridised.

319. (a): Like Cl_2O, SCl_2 also has a bent (V-shape) structure where S undergoes sp^3-hybridisation and contains two lone pairs of electrons in two of the sp^3-hybrid orbitals.

320. (a): SF_4 is a gas, S is sp^3d-hybridised having trigonal bipyramical geometry with one lone pair occupying one of the equatorial positions thus, giving a see–saw shape.

321. (a): SF_6 is inert and most stable. It does not react with water.

322. (a): In SCl_4, S is sp^3d hybridised and one equatorial position in occupied by a lone pair of electrons giving a see–saw shape to the molecule.

323. (d): SF_6 is inert and most stable. It does not react with water and thus, is not hydrolysed.

324. (b): Except oxygen, the rest of the members show 2, 4 and 6 oxidation states

325. (a): Selenium shows the +4 oxidation state in SeO_2.

326. (b): Sulfur contains *d* orbitals and therefore, can expand its octet forming 2, 4 and 6 bonds whereas oxygen does not contain *d* orbitals and is always divalent.

Dioxygen and Oxides

327. (a): HBr is a reducing agent, H_2SO_4 is an oxidising agent.

328. (d): K has more affinity for oxygen than H; K is strongly electropositive element.

329. (c): It is a fact.

330. (b): Chlorine does not react directly with oxygen.

331. (b): O_2^+ is dioxygenyl ion.

332. (a): $2\ Na_2SO_3 + O_2 \rightarrow 2\ Na_2SO_4$

333. (a): $2\ KClO_3 \xrightarrow{\Delta} 2\ KCl + 2\ O_2$

$\underset{\text{(White)}}{P_4} + \underset{\text{(W)}}{5\ O_2} \rightarrow \underset{\text{(X)}}{P_4O_{10}}$

$P_4O_{10} + 4\ HNO_3 \rightarrow \underset{\text{(Y)}}{2N_2O_5} + \underset{\text{(Z)}}{4\ HPO_3}$

Therefore, (W), (X), (Y) and (Z) are respectively, O_2, P_4O_{10}, N_2O_5 and HPO_3.

334. (c): Carbogen is a mixture of 90% oxygen and 10% carbon dioxide.

335. (a): H_2O has all the properties mentioned.

336. (b): As the electrnegativity of the elements decreases from S to Po, the acidic character of their dioxides decreases in that order.

337. (d): Na_2O is the oxide of the most metallic element (Na), therefore, it is most basic oxide. It will give a strong base, NaOH, on reaction with water.

$Na_2O + H_2O \rightarrow 2\ NaOH$ (Strong base)

338. (c): Al combines with oxygen to give Al_2O_3 which is amphoteric in nature. It reacts with acids as well alkalies to form salts.

$4\ Al + 3\ O_2 \rightarrow 2\ Al_2O_3$ (Amphoteric)

$Al_2O_3 + 2\ NaOH \rightarrow 2\ NaAlO_2 + H_2O$

$Al_2O_3 + 3\ H_2SO_4 \rightarrow Al_2(SO_4)_3 + 3\ H_2O$

339. (e): Larger alkali metals such as K, Rb, Cs when heated with oxygen or with excess of air, form stable superoxides. This is because of stabilisation of the larger anions by larger cations through lattice energy.

$K + O_2 \rightarrow \underset{\text{Potassium superoxide}}{KO_2}$

340. (b): PbO_2 being a powerful oxidising agent, liberates O_2 when treated with conc. HNO_3.

$2\ PbO_2 + \underset{\text{conc.}}{4\ HNO_3} \rightarrow 2\ Pb(NO_3)_2 + H_2O + O_2$

341. (b): As stability is directly related to lattice energy and lattice energy depends on the charge and size of ions, theorder of stability is, $Fe_2O_3 > Cr_2O_3 < Al_2O_3 < MgO$.

342. (d): The basic character of metal oxides decreases from left to right in a period due to a decrease in the electropositive character which in turn decreases the polarity of bond as well as the internuclear distance between the oxygen and metal atom. Therefore, alkali metal oxides are the most basic and halogen oxides (oxygen halides) are the most acidic. Hence, K_2O is the most basic metal oxide.

343. (d): Add anhydrous copper sulfate (white) to a liquid. If it is turns blue, it shows the presence of water in the liquid.

$\underset{\text{Anhydrous (White)}}{CuSO_4} + \text{Water} \rightarrow \underset{\text{Blue}}{CuSO_4.5H_2O}$

344. (c):KO_2, because it contains O_2^- (superoxide ion) in which one unpaired electron is present in the antibonding molecular orbital.

345. (c): C_3O_2 is a suboxide of carbon.

346. (c): $2\ KO_2 + CO_2 \rightarrow K_2CO_3 + \frac{3}{2}O_2$

347. (c): $2\ Na_2O_2 + 2\ H_2O \rightarrow 4\ NaOH + O_2$
In this reaction, oxygen (O_2) is formed.

348. (a): PbO_2 is lead dioxide O=Pb=O and not peroxide.

349. (b): BaO, Na_2O and CaO are basic whereas Al_2O_3 is amphoteric. It reacts with acids as well as bases to give the corresponding salts.

$Al_2O_3 + 6\ HCl \rightarrow 2\ AlCl_3 + 3\ H_2O$

$Al_2O_3 + 6\ NaOH + 3\ H_2O \rightarrow 2\ Na_3[Al(OH)_6]$

350. (a,b): Cr_2O_3, BeO, SnO, SnO_2, ZnO, Al_2O_3, PbO and PbO_2 are amphoteric oxides. They react with acids as well as bases to give their corresponding salts. Among other oxides,NO is neutral, B_2O_3 is acidic and CrO is basic.

351. (b): $2\ KClO_3 \xrightarrow{\text{Heat}} 2\ KCl + 3\ O_2$

352. (c): Liquid oxygen (bp 90 K) is left behind while liquid nitrogen (bp 77 K) is distilled first.

353. (d): $CuSO_4$ does not react with H_2SO_4. All other compounds give O_2 on reacting with conc. H_2SO_4.

354. (d): $2\ CaOCl_2 \xrightarrow{Co^{2+}} 2\ CaCl_2 + O_2$

355. (b): $2\ HgO \xrightarrow{\Delta} 2\ Hg + O_2$

Ozone (Trioxygen)

356. (b): Moist starch iodide paper is turned blue by ozone.

357. (b): $I_2 + 5\ O_3 + H_2O \rightarrow 2\ HIO_3 + 5\ O_2$

358. (c): $3\ SO_2 + O_3 \rightarrow 3\ SO_3$

359. (c): $BaO_2 + O_3 \rightarrow BaO + O_2$

360. (b): $O_3 \rightarrow O_2 + [O]$

$2\ KI + H_2O + [O] \rightarrow 2\ KOH + I_2$

$2\ KI + H_2O + O_3 \rightarrow 2\ KOH + I_2 + O_2$

361. (b): O_2 is absorbed by alkaline pyrogallol while O_3 is absorbed by oil of cinnamon.

362. (d): Formation of chlorine nitrate is the main cause of ozone depletion in Antarctica.

363. (a): $4\ O_3 + 6\ I_2\ (Dry) \rightarrow 3\ I_2O_4$

364. (c): The bond length is intermediate between that for a single bond (148 pm as in H_2O_2) and for a double bond (121 pm as in O_2).

128 pm, 128 pm, 116.8°

365. (d): O_3 acts as a germicide and disinfectant and purifies air.

366. (b): When ozone is treated with excess of KI solution buffered with borate buffer (pH 9.2), I_2 is liberated quantitatively which is titrated against a standard solution of $Na_2S_2O_3$ using starch as an indicator and the amount of O_3 can thus be calculated.

$2I^- + H_2O + O_3 \xrightarrow{pH\ 9.2} 2\ OH^- + I_2 + O_2$

$\underset{\text{Sodium thiosulfate}}{2\ Na_2S_2O_3} + I_2 \rightarrow \underset{\text{Sodium tetrathionate}}{Na_2S_4O_6} + 2\ NaI$

367. (a): $6\ O_2 \xrightarrow{\text{Ozonolysis}} 4\ O_3$

Thus, complete ozonolysis of six volumes of oxygen gives four volumes of ozone.

368. (c): O_2 is paramagnetic whereas O_3 is diamagnetic.

369. (d): O_3 is not readily soluble in water.

Sulfur and its Compounds

370. (b): $FeCl_3$ acts as an oxidant whereas H_2SO_3 acts as a reductant.

371. (d): Due to its chemically inert nature.

372. (d): $SO_2 + Br_2 + H_2O \rightarrow SO_3 + 2\ HBr$

373. (b): Yellow ammonium sulfide $(NH_4)_2S_x$, is obtained by passing H_2S gas through concentrated ammonia solution till it is saturated and then flowers of sulfurare dissolved to give a 1% solution.

$2\ NH_4OH + H_2S \rightarrow (NH_4)_2S + 2\ H_2O$

$(NH_4)_2S + x\ S \rightarrow \underset{\text{Yellow amm. sulfate}}{(NH_4)_2S_{x+1}}$

374. (d): Sulfur exhibits +2, +4, +6 oxidation states but +4 and +6 are more common.

375. (b): $3\ S + 4\ NaOH \xrightarrow{\text{boiling}} Na_2S_2O_3 + Na_2S$

376. (d):

$$CH_3-\overset{S}{\overset{\|}{C}}-NH_2 + 2H_2O \xrightarrow{\text{Heat}} CH_3-\overset{O}{\overset{\|}{C}}-ONH_4 + H_2S$$

377. (c): H_2S is a weak acid in water and not a weak base.

378. (c): $COCl_2$ (phosgene) does not contain any metal in it. Therefore, it will not produce metal sulfide with H_2S. All others give corresponding metal sulfides such as CdS (yellow), ZnS (dirty white) and CuS (black).

379. (b): Sulfur is formed due to incomplete combustion when H_2S reacts with a limited supply of oxygen.

$2\ H_2S + O_2 \rightarrow 2\ H_2O + 2\ S$

380. (a): $Cu^{2+} + S^{2-} \rightarrow CuS$

(From $CuCl_2$) Black ppt.

$Cu^{2+} + SO_4^{2-} \rightarrow$ No ppt.

$Pb^{2+} + S^{2-} \rightarrow PbS$

[From $Pb(OOCCH_3)_2$] Black ppt.

$K_{sp} = (PbS) = 1.6 \times 10^{-28}$

$Pb^{2+}SO_4^{2-} \rightarrow PbSO_4$

White ppt.

$K_{sp} = (PbSO_4) = 1.6 \times 10^{-8}$

As the difference in K_{sp} of PbS and $PbSO_4$ is large, therefore, only PbS is selectively precipitated and not $PbSO_4$. Hence, both $CuCl_2$ and $Pb(OOCCH_3)_2$ reagents can be used for selective precipitation of S^{2-} from a mixture of S^{2-} and SO_4^{2-} in an aqueous solution.

381. (d): Hot acidic aqueous solution containing Al^{3+}, Cu^{2+}, Pb^{2+} and Ni^{2+} ions $\xrightarrow{H_2O}$ PbS + CuS

(Black ppt.)

Both Pb^{2+} and Cu^{2+} ions are precipitated as sulfides in acidic solution in group II of the qualitative analysis when H_2S gas is passed leaving Al^{3+} and Ni^{2+} ions as such in the solution due to the low solubility products of CuS and PbS.

382. (a): On mixing an aqueous solution of H_2S and SO_2, colloidal sulfur is obtained.

$2\ H_2S + SO_2 \rightarrow 3\ S + 2\ H_2O$

383. (d): $2\ KMnO_4 + 3\ H_2SO_4 + 5\ H_2S \rightarrow K_2SO_4 + 2\ MnSO_4 + 8\ H_2O + S$

384. (a): Geometry of H_2S is angular like the H_2O molecule and it has a particular value of dipole moment.

385. (a): Na_2SO_3 reacts with hot and diluted H_2SO_4 to give SO_2 gas which decolourises bromine water.

$Na_2SO_3 + H_2SO_4 \rightarrow Na_2SO_4 + SO_2 + H_2O$

Decolourisation of bromine water

$Br_2 + H_2O \rightarrow 2\ HBr + [O]$

$SO_2 + [O] \rightarrow SO_3$

386. (a): $2\ Mg + SO_2 \rightarrow 2\ MgO + S$, here Mg^0 is oxidised to Mg^{2+}.

387. (c): SO_2 acts as a reducing agent and hence reduces an aqueous solution (yellow) of Fe (III) salt to Fe (II) salt (light green) (in the presence of water).

$2\ Fe^{2+} + SO_2 + 2\ H_2O \rightarrow 2\ Fe^{2+} + SO_4^{2-} + 4\ H^+$

388. (c): SO_2 is highly soluble in water and therefore, cannot be collected over water.

389. (a): $SO_2 + Cl_2 \xrightarrow{\text{sunlight}} SO_2Cl_2$ (Sulfuryl chloride)

390. (d): $SO_2 + Br_2 + H_2O \rightarrow H_2SO_4 + 2\ HBr$

391. (d): SO_2 cannot oxidise iodide to iodine which would give a blue colour with starch. Therefore, starch iodide paper cannot be used for the detection of SO_2.

392. (c): Both SO_2 and Cl_2 behave as bleaching agents. SO_2 bleaches by reduction while Cl_2 bleaches by oxidation.

393. (d): $Na_2CO_3(aq) + 2\ SO_2(g) + H_2O(l) \rightarrow 2\ NaHSO_3(aq) + CO_2(g)$

$2\ NaHSO_3(aq) + Na_2CO_3(aq) \rightarrow Na_2SO_3(aq) + H_2O(l) + CO_2(g)$

Thus, both products $NaHSO_3$ and Na_2SO_3 are formed when SO_2 gas is passed through aqueous Na_2CO_3 solution.

394. (a):

$$\underset{(X)}{SO_3^{2-}} + \text{dil. } H_2SO_4 \rightarrow \underset{(Y)\text{ Colourless}}{SO_2} + H_2O + SO_3^{2-}$$

395. (c): In SO_3, the S is sp^2-hybridised giving a trigonal planar shape and having an O–S–O bond angle of 120° (no lone pair on S). S can expand its octet to reduce formal charges. Since S and O have different electronegativities, the S–O bond is polar but the overall molecule is non-polar.

396. (d): SO_3 is trigonal planar due to the sp^2 hybridised sulfur. SO_3^{2-} is sp^3 hybridised, but pyramidal due to the presence of a lone pair of electrons.

397. (d): Peroxodisulfuric acid or perdisulfuric acid, also called Marshall's acid ($H_2S_2O_8$), contains four S=O, two S–OH and one S–O–O–S bonds.

398. (d): Caro's acid is H_2SO_5 which contains one S–O–OH peroxy linkage.

399. (c): $\underset{1\text{ mol}}{H_2S_2O_8} + H_2O \xrightarrow{\text{Hydrolysis}} \underset{1\text{ mol}}{H_2SO_4} + \underset{1\text{mol}}{H_2SO_5}$

400. (a): $S_2O_7 + H_2O \rightarrow H_2S_2O_8$ (Peroxodisulfuric acid)

401. (a): Oxo group means E=O group (E = element)

HO–S(=O)(=O)–OH	HO–S(=O)–OH (lone pair on S)	HO–P(=O)(H)–OH	HO–P(=O)(OH)–OH
(H_2SO_4)	(H_2SO_3)	(H_3PO_3)	(H_3PO_4)
2-oxo groups	1-oxo group	1-oxo group	1-oxo group

402. (c): In the laboratory, potassium permanganate is prepared by oxidising manganese (II) salt by peroxodisulfate ion in aqueous solution on heating.

$$2\,Mn^{2+} + 5\,S_2O_8^{2-} + 8\,H_2O \xrightarrow{\Delta} 2\,MnO_4^- + 10\,SO_4^{2-} + 16\,H^+$$

403. (a): Sulfurous acid, HO—S(=O)—OH contains a lone pair of electrons on the sulfur atom.

$H_2S_2O_3$ = HO—P(=O)(H)—OH $H_2S_2O_8$ = HO—S(=O)(=O)—O—O—S(=O)(=O)—OH

$H_2S_2O_6$ = HO—S(=O)(H)—S(=O)(H)—OH $H_2S_4O_6$ = HO—S(=O)(=O)—S—S—S(=O)(=O)—OH

404. (d): $S_2O_7^{2-}$ contains no S–S bond. $^-$O—S(=O)(=O)—O—S(=O)(=O)—O$^-$

405. (c): Dithionous acid ($H_2S_2O_4$) has sulfur in the +3 oxidation state.

406. (d): In the manufacture of H_2SO_4 by the contact process, a Tyndall box is used to test the presence of dust particles.

407. (a): $H_2SO_4(aq) \rightarrow H^+(aq) + HSO_4^-(aq);\ K_{a_1} = 1\times10^3$

$HSO_4^-(aq) \rightarrow H^+(aq) + SO_4^{2-}(aq);\ K_{a_2} = 1.2\times10^{-2}$

Here, $K_{a_2} < K_{a_1}$ because the negatively charged HSO_4^- ion has a much less tendency to donate a proton to H_2O when compared to neutral H_2SO_4.

408. (d): $K_4[Fe(CN)_6] + 6\,H_2SO_4 + 6\,H_2O \rightarrow 2\,K_2SO_4 + FeSO_4 + 6\,CO + 3\,(NH_4)_2SO_4$

409. (d):

$$\underset{COOH}{\overset{COOH}{|}} + \underset{(\text{conc.})}{H_2SO_4} \xrightarrow{\Delta} CO + CO_2 + H_2O$$

410. (a): $2\,H_2SO_4 + 2\,P_2O_5 \rightarrow \underset{\text{Sulfur trioxide}}{2\,SO_3} + 4\,HPO_3$

411. (a): $Cu + 2\,H_2SO_4 \rightarrow CuSO_4 + 2\,H_2O + SO_2$

412. (b): $\underset{\substack{\text{Reducing}\\\text{agent}}}{2\,Ag} + \underset{\substack{\text{Oxidising}\\\text{agent}}}{2\,H_2SO_4} \rightarrow Ag_2SO_4 + H_2O + SO_2$

413. (c): $HO\text{–}SO_2\text{–}OH + PCl_5 \rightarrow Cl\text{–}SO_2\text{–}OH + POCl_3 + HCl$

$HO\text{–}SO_2\text{–}OH + 2\,PCl_5 \rightarrow \underset{\text{Sulfuryl chloride}}{Cl\text{–}SO_2\text{–}Cl} + 2\,HCl$

414. (b): Concentrated H_2SO_4 is diluted by adding the conc. H_2SO_4 into the water drop by drop with constant stirring because it is an exothermic reaction. By doing so, the heat is generated slowly and dissipated into the atmosphere.

415. (b): $KMnO_4$ is a strong oxidising agent in the acidic medium. H_2SO_4 is used instead of HCl to provide an acidic medium because HCl is oxidised by $KMnO_4$ into Cl_2.

$$2\,KMnO_4 + 3\,H_2SO_4 + 10\,HCl \rightarrow K_2SO_4 + 2\,MnSO_4 + 8\,H_2O + 5\,Cl_2$$

416. (c): H_2SO_4 acts as a pickling agent. Pickling is an industrial process for removing layers of basic oxides from metals like Fe and Cu before electroplating, enamelling, galvanising and soldering.

417. (a): Superphosphate is a mixture of calcium dihydrogen phosphate and gypsum which is obtained as follows.

$$\underset{\text{Phosphate rock}}{Ca_3(PO_4)_2} + 2\,H_2SO_4 + 2H_2O \rightarrow \underset{\text{Gypsum}}{2\,CaSO_4.2\,H_2O} + Ca(H_2PO_4)_2$$

418. (a): Conc. H_2SO_4 reacts with many substances and hence is not suitable for use in a desiccator as a dehydrating agent.

419. (d): $C + 2\,H_2SO_4 \rightarrow 2\,SO_2 + CO_2 + 2\,H_2O$

$S + 2\,H_2SO_4 \rightarrow 3\,SO_2 + 2\,H_2O$

$P_4 + 10\,H_2SO_4 \rightarrow 4\,H_3PO_4 + 10\,SO_2 + 4\,H_2O$

420. (d): $Na_2SO_3 + S \xrightarrow{\text{Boil}} Na_2S_2O_3$

421. (d): $2\,Na_2S_2O_3 + I_2 \rightarrow \underset{\text{Sodium tetrathionate (colourless)}}{Na_2S_4O_6} + 2\,NaI$

422. (b): $Na_2S_2O_3 + 2\,HCl \rightarrow 2\,NaCl + H_2O + SO_2 + \underset{\substack{\text{(Colloidal sulfur,}\\\text{milky white)}}}{S}$

423. (a): $Ag^+ + 2\,S_2O_3^{2-} \rightarrow \underset{(X)\text{ Clear solution}}{[Ag(S_2O_3)_2]^{3-}} \xrightarrow{Ag^+}$

$$Ag_2S_2O_3 \xrightarrow{\text{with time}} Ag_2S + H_2SO_4$$

White ppt. (Y) H_2O Black ppt. (Z)

424. (b): $Na_2S_2O_3 + Cl_2 + H_2O \rightarrow Na_2SO_4 + 2\ HCl + S$

425. (b):

S^{-2}, S^{+6}, O, O, O^-

Structure of $S_2O_3^{2-}$ ion

426. (c): Undecomposed AgBr forms a soluble complex with hypo.

$AgBr + 2\ Na_2S_2O_3 \rightarrow Na_3[Ag(S_2O_3)_2] + NaBr$

It is washed with water and the image is fixed.

427. (c): $PbSO_4$ is insoluble in water due to its high lattice energy.

428. (c): Se and its compounds such as H_2Se, are most poisonous to humans. Even in traces they cause headache, nausea and irritation of the mucous membrane.

429. (b): At 1000 K, sulfur mainly exists as S_2 molecules in the vapour state which are paramagnetic like dioxyen (O_2) because they have two unpaired electrons in the antibonding pi molecular orbitals.

430. (c): In K_2CO_3, replacement of O by S gives K_2CS_3 which is called potassium thiocarbonate.

Final Preparation

431. (d): HF is formed which is liquid.

432. (b): It is a reason for the given fact.

433. (d): Thermal stability of the oxides of the group 16 elements decreases in the order $SO_2 > TeO_2 > SeO_2 > PoO_2$ and not in the order mentioned. TeO_2 decomposes at > 733°C while SeO_2 has ~600°C as the decomposition temperature. PoO_2 decomposes at 500°C.

434. (c): SCl_4 exists as a monomer (liquid) whereas $SeCl_4$ and $TeCl_4$ exist as tetramers (solids). As the size of the element increases from S to Te, the van der Waals forces of attraction between the molecules increase and the stability increases. Hence, $TeCl_4$ is most stable. OCl_4 is not formed.

435. (b): Shape of O_2F_2 is similar that of H_2O_2.

436. (c): OF_2 (oxygen difluoride) is a fluoride of oxygen because fluorine is more electropositive than oxygen.

437. (c): The ClO_2 molecule is paramagnetic since it has one odd electron in a *p*orbital. CO_2, SO_2 and SiO_2 are diamagnetic in behaviour.

438. (a): In SF_4, S is sp^3d-hybridised (trigonal bipyramid geometry); one equatorial position is occupied by a lone pair which repels the axial and equatorial bond pairs thereby decreasing the bond angles from 180° to 173° and 120° to 102° giving a see–saw shape to the molecule.

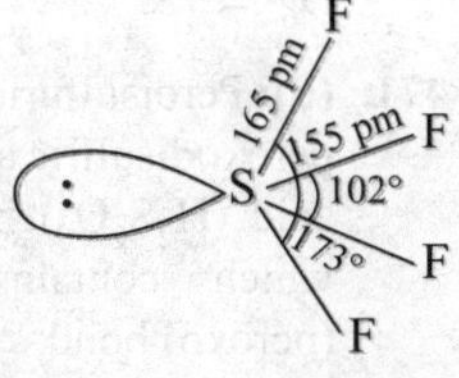

439. (a): SiF_4 is tetrahedral with sp^3-hybridisation but SF_4 has a see–saw structure with sp^3d hybridisation and one of equatorial hybrid orbital is occupied by a lone pair of electrons.

440. (b): SF_4 being unsymmetrial (see–saw shape with sp^3d hybridisation and one lone pair of electrons on one of the equatorial hybrid orbitals) has a permanent dipole moment.

441. (c): $\underbrace{S + 2Cl_2}_{1:2} \longrightarrow \underset{(X)}{SCl_4}$

$\underset{(X)}{SCl_4} + 4H_2O \xrightarrow{\text{Hydrolysis}} \underset{\text{Unstable}}{S(OH)_4} + 4HCl$

$\underset{\text{Anion of }(Y)}{SO_3^{2-} + 2H^+} \rightleftharpoons \underset{\substack{\text{Sulfurous acid}\\(Y)}}{H_2SO_3}$

Structure and hybridisation of SO_3^{2-} are pyramidal and sp^3 respectively.

Pyramidal st. of SO_3^{2-}

442. (d): $2\ F_2 + 4\ KOH \rightarrow 4\ KF + 2\ H_2O + O_2$

443. (c): CaO being basic in nature is not expected to react with NaOH.

444. (c): Na_2O is a basic oxide and reacts with water to give NaOH so that the pH of the solution is higher than both SiO_2 and P_4O_{10}. Both SiO_2 and P_4O_{10} are acidic oxides but SiO_2 is insoluble while P_4O_{10} reacts with water to give acid, H_3PO_4. Thus, for P_4O_{10}, pH when mixed with water is lower than that of SiO_2.

$[^-O—O^-]\ Ba^{2+}$ — Peroxide linkage

445. (d): $2\ KOH + 5\ O_3 \rightarrow \underset{(x)}{2\ KO_3} + 5\ O_2 + H_2O$

The product x is KO_3 (potassium ozonide).

446. (b): Ozone reduces H_2O_2 to H_2O and thus behaves as a reductant.

447. (b): The increasing order of O–O bond length in O_3, H_2O_2 and O_2 is O_2 (121 pm) < O_3 (128 pm) < H_2O_2 (148 pm) as the bond length is inversely proportional to the BO.In H_2O_2, there is a single bond between O–O (BO = 1), in O_3 there is resonance between a single and a double bond (BO = 1.5) and in O_2 there is a double bond (BO = 2).

448. (b): The angular shape of ozone molecule is shown.

O σ O σ O ⟷ O σ O σ O (π)

449. (c): Plastic sulfur possesses maximum energy and thus releases more energy during the combustion to form SO_2.

450. (b): Nitric acid being a strong oxidising agent, oxidises H_2S to colloidal sulfur.

$3\ H_2S + 2\ HNO_3 \rightarrow \underset{\text{Colloidal (Yellow ppt.)}}{3\ S} + 2\ NO + 4\ H_2O$

451. (d): Cu^{2+}, Hg^{2+} and Bi^{3+} are the basic radicals of group IIA of qualitative analysis and are precipitated as sulfides in the presence of dil. HCl by H_2S. Co^{2+} is the basic radical of group IV which is precipitated as the sulfide in the presence of NH_4OH by H_2S. As the solubility product of sulfides of the II group radicals is lesser than the solubility product of sulfides of the IV group, CoS will not be precipitated under acidic conditions.

452. (d): The correct order of solubility in the aqueous medium is $Na_2S > ZnS > CuS$
because Na_2S is ionic and soluble but the K_{sp} of sparingly soluble ZnS (1×10^{-23}) is higher than that of CuS (1×10^{-44}).

453. (a):

$$\overset{+2\ \ -5}{[Fe(CN)_5(NO)^{+1}]^{-2}} + \overset{2-}{S} \quad \overset{+2\ \ -5}{[Fe(CN)_5(NO)^{-1}]^{-4}}$$

Nitroprusside ion; Sulphuric iron; Violet colour (Thinonitroprusside ion)

So, the violet coloured complex is the tetra-anionic complex iron (II) coordinated to five CN^- ions and one $(NOS)^-$ ion.

454. (c): Only S^{2-} out of the two (S^{2-} and SO_3^{2-}) will give tests with $(CH_3COO)_2Pb$ (black ppt. of PbS) and $Na_2[Fe(CN)_5NO]$ (violet colour). SO_3^{2-} will not give any test with these reagents.

$S^{2-} + (CH_3COO)_2Pb \rightarrow \underset{\text{Black ppt.}}{PbS} + 2\,CH_3COO^-$

$S^{2-} + Na_2[Fe(CN)_5NO] \rightarrow \underset{\text{Violet colour}}{[Fe(CN)_5NOS]^{4-}} + 2\,Na^+$

455. (a): $2\,H_2S + \underset{\text{Oxidising agent}}{SO_2} \rightarrow 2\,H_2O + 3S$

456. (b): KOH absorbs SO_2 to form a salt.

$\underset{\text{Basic}}{2\,KOH} + \underset{\text{acidic}}{SO_2} \rightarrow K_2SO_3 + H_2O$

457. (b): Only SO_2 shows reducing, oxidising, bleaching and Lewis base character.

458. (b): $3\,K\overset{+5}{I}O_3 + 3\,SO_2 \rightarrow 3\,K\overset{-1}{I} + 3\,SO_3$

In this reaction, the oxidation number of iodine changes from +5 in KIO_3 to –1 in KI.

459. (a):

$\underset{(X)}{Na_2CO_3} + 2\,SO_2 + H_2O \rightarrow \underset{(A)}{2\,NaHSO_3} + CO_2$

$\underset{(A)}{2\,NaHSO_3} + Na_2CO_3 \rightarrow \underset{(B)}{2\,Na_2SO_3} + H_2O + CO_2$

$\underset{(B)}{Na_2SO_3} + S \rightarrow \underset{(C)}{Na_2S_2O_3}$

used as a fixer in photography.

460. (a): $Na_2CO_3 + SO_2 \rightarrow Na_2SO_3 + CO_2$

461. (c): Bluish green cupric chloride solution is reduced to colourless cuprous chloride (Cu_2Cl_2) precipitated by SO_2.

$\underset{\text{Blush green solution}}{2\,CuCl_2} + SO_2 + 2\,H_2O \rightarrow \underset{\text{White precipitate}}{Cu_2Cl_2} + H_2SO_4 + 2\,HCl$

462. (d): $\underset{\text{Orange}}{K_2Cr_2O_7} + H_2SO_4 + 3\,SO_2 \rightarrow K_2SO_4 + \underset{\text{Green}}{Cr_2(SO_4)_3} + H_2O$

463. (b): $\underset{\text{Purple colour}}{2\,KMnO_4} + \underset{\text{Sulfur dioxide}}{5\,SO_2} + H_2O \rightarrow$

$\underset{\text{Colourless}}{K_2SO_4 + 2\,MnSO_4 + 2\,H_2SO_4}$

464. (b): SO_2 is used as a food preservative but NO_2 is not. All other properties are common to both.

465. (d): $SOCl_2$ has one S=O double bond and two S–Cl single bonds.
S is sp^3-hybridised and the shape is pyramidal due to the presence of a lone pair of electrons on S. Since the π-electrons of the S=O bond are more polarised, they repel the bond pair of the S–Cl bond thus making the Cl–S–O bond angle larger (106°) than the Cl–S–Cl bond angle (96°). Hence, option (d) is correct.

[Structure: S with lone pair, bonded to O, Cl, Cl; angles 106°, 96°]

466. (d): Ferric sulfate on heating gives SO_3,

$Fe_2(SO_4)_3 \xrightarrow{\Delta} Fe_2O_3 + 3\,SO_3$

whereas all others give different products and not SO_3.

$S_8 + 16\,H_2SO_4 \xrightarrow{\Delta} 24\,SO_2 + 16\,H_2O$

$2\,PCl_5 + H_2SO_4 \rightarrow \underset{\text{Sulfuryl chloride}}{SO_2Cl_2} + 2\,POCl_3 + 2\,HCl$

$CaSO_4 + 4\,C \xrightarrow{\Delta} CaS + 4\,CO$

467. (b): The structure of $S_4O_6^{2-}$, tetrathionate ion. $S_4O_3^{2-}$, thiosulfate ion.

$^-O-S(=O)_2-S-S-S(=O)_2-O^-$ — Contains S-S bond

$^-O-S(=S)(=O)-O^-$ — Contains S-S bond

468. (b): Formal charges help in the selection of the lowest energy structure from a number of possible Lewis structures for a given species. Generally, the lowest energy structure is the one with the smallest formal changes on the atoms.

469. (a):

(I) $^-O-S(=O)_2-S-S-S(=O)_2-O^-$ Tetrathionate ion, $(S_4O_6)^{2-}$

(II) Cyclic trimer of SO_3, (S_3O_9)

(III) $^-O-S(=O)_2-S(=O)-O^-$ Pyrosulphite ion, $(S_2O_5)^{2-}$

(IV) Trimetaphosphate ion, $(P_3O_9)^{3-}$

470. (a): Oxidation states of S in $S_2O_4^{2-}$ = +3, SO_3^{2-} = 4 and in $S_2O_6^{2-}$ = +5.

471. (d): Perdisulfuric acid or peroxodisulfric acid or Marshall's acid ($H_2S_2O_8$) has the structure which contains one –O–O– (peroxo) bond.

$HO-S(=O)_2-O-O-S(=O)_2-OH$ Perdisulphuric acid

472. (b): As in polythionic acid $H_2S_nO_6$, the number of S–S bonds

$HO-S(=O)_2-S-S-S(=O)_2-OH$

= (n – 1), therefore, in tetrathionic acid $H_2S_4O_6$ (n = 4), the number of S–S bonds = 4 – 1 = 3 and the formula of the acid will be

473. (d): $2\ KHSO_4 + F_2 \rightarrow 2\ HF + K_2S_2O_8$ (X)
Though the oxidation number of sulfur in potassium hydrogen sulfate($KHSO_4$) and potassium perdisulfate($K_2S_2O_8$) remains the same 9+6), yet F_2 oxidises one oxide ion (O^{2-}) of each $KHSO_4$ to give one peroxo group $(O–O)^{2-}$ in $K_2S_2O_8$.

474. (a): SO_3^{2-} acts both as a reducing agent and a Lewis base since it contains a lone pair of electrons.

$$^{-}O-\ddot{S}(=O)-O^{-}$$

475. (a):

$$PCl_5 + HO-S(=O)_2-OH \longrightarrow Cl-S(=O)_2-Cl + POCl_3 + H_2O$$

476. (b): SO_3^{2-} has three σ-bonds and one $p\pi - d\pi$ bond. S is sp^3-hybridised and one of the sp^3-hybrid orbitals is occupied by a lone pair of electrons.

477. (b): $BaO_2 + H_2SO_4 \rightarrow BaSO_4 + H_2O_2$
In the products, the most electronegative element is oxygen. In $BaSO_4$, O has an oxidation state of –2 while in H_2O_2 it is –1.

478. (a): $Ba(NO_2)_2$ (cold) $+ H_2SO_4 \rightarrow BaSO_4 + 2\ HNO_2$

479. (d): $CaF_2 + H_2SO_4 \rightarrow\ + 2\ HF$
Here, the oxidation state of every atom remains the same and hence, it is not a redox reaction. H_2SO_4 does not act as an oxidising agent here.

480. (b): The inorganic halide (A) is SO_2Cl_2.

$$\underset{(A)}{SO_2Cl_2} + 2\ H_2O \rightarrow \underset{(B)}{H_2SO_4} + \underset{(C)}{2\ HCl}$$

$$\underset{(A)}{SO_2Cl_2} + 4\ NaOH \rightarrow \underset{(D)}{Na_2SO_4} + 2\ Nacl + 2\ H_2O$$

$$\underset{(D)}{Na_2SO_4} + BaCl_2 \rightarrow \underset{\text{White ppt.}}{BaSO_4} + 2\ NaCl$$

$$\underset{(E)}{NaCl} + AgNO_3 \rightarrow \underset{\text{White ppt.}}{AgCl} + NaNO_3$$

481. (c):

$$\underset{X}{Na_2SO_3(s)} + 2\ HCl(dil.) \rightarrow 2\ NaCl + \underset{Y}{SO_2(g)} + H_2O$$

$$\underset{\text{Violet colour}}{2\ KMnO_4} + 5SO_2 + 2\ H_2O \rightarrow K_2SO_4 + \underset{\text{Colourless}}{2\ MnSO_4} + 2\ H_2SO_4$$

$$H_2O + SO_2(g) \rightarrow \underset{\text{Aq. soln. of Y}}{H_2SO_3} \text{ (Sulfurous acid)}$$

$$H_2SO_3 + 2\ H_2S(g) \rightarrow \underset{\text{Colloidal}}{3S} + 3H_2O$$

482. (b): Hypo ($Na_2S_2O_3.5H_2O$) is used as a reagent for the titration of I_2 obtained from KI and $CuSO_4$ reaction.

483. (c): Sulfide and sulfite ions both react with dil. HCl on warming their aqueous solutions giving H_2S and SO_2 gases respectively but no yellow precipitate isformed. Sulfate ion does not react. The only ion left is thiosulfate which gives SO_2 gas with a pungent odour and also a pale yellow precipitate of colloidal sulfur is formed.

$$S_2O_3^{2-} + 2H^+ \xrightarrow{\Delta} \underset{\text{Gas pungent odour}}{SO_2\uparrow} + \underset{\text{Pale yellow precipitate}}{S\downarrow} + H_2O$$

484. (d):

$$Na_2S_2O_3 + Cl_2 + H_2O \rightarrow Na_2SO_4 + 2\ HCl + S$$

or

$$Na_2S_2O_3 + \underset{\text{(Excess)}}{4\ Cl_2} + 5\ H_2O \rightarrow 2NaHSO_4 + 8\ HCl$$

485. (a):

$$\underset{(P)}{Na_2S_2O_3} + 2\ HCl \rightarrow 2\ NaCl + H_2O + \underset{\text{Suffocating gas (Q)}}{SO_2} + \underset{\text{Yellow ppt.}}{S}$$

$$K_2Cr_2O_7 + \underset{(Q)}{SO_2} + H_2SO_4 \rightarrow K_2SO_4 + \underset{\text{Green solution (R)}}{Cr_2(SO_4)_3} + H_2O$$

486. (c): All the rest react with AgCl.

487. (b): β-sulfur (monoclinic from) is stable only above 369 K. Below this temperature, it changes into the α-sulfur (orthorhombic form). Thus at 369 K, both these varieties coexist. This temperature is called the transition temperature and the two sulfurs are called enantiotropic substances.

488. (d): Stability of the +6 oxidation state decreases and that of the +4 oxidation state increases going down the group due to the inert pair effect.

489. (b): $Na_2O + H_2O \rightarrow 2\ NaOH$ (pH very high)
$Na_2S + 2\ H_2O \rightarrow 2\ NaOH + H_2S$
(pH decreases due to the slight acidic nature of H_2S.)
$Na_2Se + 2\ H_2O \rightarrow 2\ NaOH + H_2Se$
(pH further decreases as H_2Se is more acidic than H_2S.)
$Na_2Te + 2\ H_2O \rightarrow 2\ NaOH + H_2Te$
(pH decreases as H_2Te is more acidic than H_2Se.)

490. (a): As the size of the element increases down the group, the element–H bond length increases and the E–H bond strength decreases. Tus, the cleavage of the E–H bond becomes easier. This will provide more acidity to the solution. Hence, the correct order of acidity is H_2S, $H_2Se < H_2Te$.

491. (d): H_2O is a dipole because it is angular.

MATCH THE FOLLOWING

492. (d): (A) Sulfuric acid is manufactured by the lead chamber process. (B) Sulfur is extracted by the Frasch process. (C) Sodium thiosulfate is prepared by Spring's reaction. (D) Ozone is manufactured by Siemen's and Brodie's ozonisers.

493. (b): (A) Structure of plastic sulfur is zig–zag chains of sulfur atoms (B) Rhombic sulfur contains S_8 puckered rings in crown conformation (C) Engel's sulfur contains S_6 rings in chain conformation (D) Monoclinic sulfur contains S_8 puckered rings in crown form.

494. (a): (A) Water (H_2O) has an MP of 273 K, (B) H_2S has an MP of 188 K, (C) H_2Se has an MP of 208 K and (D) H_2Te has an MP of 222 K.

495. (c): (A) $H_2S_2O_4$ has an ON of S = +3, (B) $H_2S_2O_6$ has an ON of S = +5, (C) H_2SO_5 has an ON of S = +6, (D) H_2SO_3 has an ON of S = +4.

ASSERTION REASON

496. (d): Correct A. Hydrides of group 16 elements show volatility in the order:
$H_2S > H_2Se > H_2Te > H_2O$
Correct R. Electronegativity of group 16 elements decreases down the group from oxygen to tellurium. Oxygen being most electronegative, undergoes H-bonding in water which shows the lowest volatility. As the size of the element increases from S to Te, van der Waals forces of attraction increase and hence, the volatility decreases from H_2S to H_2Te.

497. (d): Correct A. SeO_3 exists as a cyclic tetramer (Se_4O_{12}) in the solid state and in the monomeric state in the vapour phase.
Correct R. electrical conductivity of Se is negligible in the dark but increases on exposure to light.

498. (b): Correct explanation. S atom in both SO_2 and OS_3 is sp^2-hybridised but it contains a lone pair of electrons in SO_2.

499. (c): Correct R. Se in $SeCl_4$ has one lone pair of electrons, the hybridisation involved is sp^3d giving a see–saw structure, that is, a distorted trigonal bipyramid geometry.

500. (d): Correct A. The O–O bond length in H_2O_2 is larger than that in O_2F_2.
Correct R. H_2O_2 is a covalent compound.

501. (c): Correct R. The lone pair–bond pair repulsion is stronger than the bond pair–bond pair repulsion.

502. (c): Correct R. Oxygen binds as O_2 to Fe of the heme part of hemoglobin to form oxyhemoglobin.

503. (d): Correct A. Sb (III) is precipitated as sulfide when H_2S is passedinto its alkaline solution. But generally it is precipitated as the sulfide from HCl medium so that radicals of higher groups may not get precipitated.
Correct R. The concentration of S^{2-} ions in the alkaline medium is adequate for the precipitation of Sb (III) ions.

504. (d): Correct A. Sb_2S_3 is soluble in yellow ammonium sulfide forming ammonium thioantimonate.

$$\underset{\text{Yellow amm. sulfide}}{Sb_2S_3 + 3\,(NH_4)_2S} + 2S \rightarrow \underset{\text{Amm. thioantimonate}}{2\,(NH_4)_3SbS_4}$$

Correct R. The common ion effect due to the S^{2-} ions does not reduce the solubility of Sb_2S_3.

505. (d):Correct A. SO_2 is a reducing agent while SO_3 is an oxidising agent.
Correct R. Only SO_2 bleaches the articles by reduction.

GROUP 17

Atomic and Physical Properties

506. (c): Yellow is the complementary colour of violet.

507. (a): F^- possesses the smallest size.

508. (d): Chlorine because of its higher electron gain enthalpy has the maximum tendency to form X^- anions in the gaseous state.

509. (b): Electron gain enthalpies become less negative as the size of the atom increases. The value of fluorine is, however, less negative than that of chlorine because of its small size as a result of which interelectronic repulsions present in its $2p$- subshell are comparatively large. The decreasing order of negative electron gain enthalpy is $Cl > F > Br > I$.

510. (c): Polarity of the bond depends upon the electronegativity difference of the two atoms forming the bond. Greater the electronegativity difference, more is the polarity of the bond.

Bond	N–Cl	O–F	N–F	N–N
EN	3.0 3.0	3.5 4.0	3.0 4.0	3.0 3.0

511. (d): Chlorine is a gas and iodine is a solid at ordinary temperature and pressure because the intermolecular forces are weaker in Cl_2 and the strongest in iodine due to its larger size.

512. (a): The halogens are all diatomic (X_2) and form univalent (X^-) ions.

513. (a): The MO configuration of the X_2 molecules of the group 17 elements is $X_2 = KK\,\sigma(2s)^2, \sigma^*(2s)^2, \sigma(2p_z)^2, \pi(2p_x)^2$

$$= \pi(2p_y)^2, \underbrace{\pi^*(2p_x)^2 = \pi^*(2p_y)^2}_{\text{HOMO}}, \underbrace{\sigma^*(2p_z)^0}_{\text{LUMO}}$$

(HOMO = highest occupied molecular orbital, LUMO = lowest unoccupied molecular orbital.)The colour of the halogens is due to the fact that they absorb light in the visible region as a result of which their electrons are excited to higher energy levels while the remaining light is transmitted which is responsible for their colour.
The excitation energy decreases progressively from F to I as the size of the atom increases down the group. In other words, there is a decrease in the $\pi^* - \sigma^*$ gas or HOMO LUMO gas and excitation becomes easy (lower excitation energy) down the group. Conversely, the energy of the transmitted light increases progressively and hence there is a gradual change in colour from yellow (F_2) to violet (I_2) down the group.

514. (b): $KI + I_2 \rightarrow KI_3$ (Soluble complex)

515. (d): Iodine has a comparatively low value of ionisation enthalpy and therefore, has a tendency to lose an electron to form a positive iodinium ion I^+ and shows electropositive or metallic character.

516. (a): In the F_2 molecule, p–p orbitals overlap head on.

517. (d): A large amount of energy is released when a halogen atom accepts an electron to form the corresponding halide ion.

Chemical Properties

518. (d): All the rest react with water.

519. (a): In the case of fluorides and chlorides, HF and HCl gases are given out on heating with conc. H_2SO_4 and MnO_2. In bromides and iodides, Br_2 and I_2 are given out.

520. (d): F_2 reacts with CH_4 even in the dark to show substitution reactions giving all possible products.

521. (a): F_2 and Cl_2 have no action on starch solution, Br_2 turns it brown, I_2 turns it blue.

522. (c): Iodine (I) shows positive (+1, +3, +5 and +7) oxidation states by sharing of its unpaired electrons with more electronegative elements such as F in interhalogen compounds and also due to the availability of *d*-orbitals. It also shows a negative oxidation state by accepting an electron from highly electropositive element such as Na and K.

523. (a): Greater reactivity of fluorine is due to its small size, low bond dissociation energy and high heat of hydration.

524. (d): F_2 is the most active of all the halogens due to the lower value of F–F bond dissociation energy. It has the highest positive electrode potential, that is, it is most easily reduced and hence, acts as the strongest oxidising agent.

525. (d): The lowest $E°$ value 0.53 V may be assigned to I_2 which is the weakest oxidising agent.

526. (b): As chlorine is a more powerful oxidising agent than iodine, it will liberate iodine when passed through an acidified solution of KI.
$Cl_2 + 2\,KI \rightarrow 2\,KCl + I_2$

527. (d): High ionisation enthalpy implies that halogens cannot lose electrons easily and thus, cannot behave as reducing agents.

528. (c): $2\,NaI + Br_2 \rightarrow 2\,NaBr + I_2$

529. (d): The reaction of I_2 with water is non-spontaneous. In fact, I^- ions can be oxidised by O_2 in an acidic medium which is just the reverse of the reaction observed with F_2.
$4\,I^-(aq) + O_2(g) + 4\,H^+(aq) \rightarrow 2\,I_2(s) + 2H_2O(l)$

530. (a): $Cl_2 + 2\,Br^- \rightarrow 2\,Cl^- + Br_2$

531. (a): Pieces of marble ($CaCO_3$) do not react with brown bromine vapours. Therefore, the intensity of the brown colour of vapours will not decrease on adding some pieces of marble to the flask.

532. (d): $\left.\begin{array}{l} I_2 + NaF \rightarrow \\ I_2 + NaBr \rightarrow \\ I_2 + NaCl \rightarrow \end{array}\right\}$ No reaction

Because I_2 has the lowest reducing potential among halogens.

533. (a): $Cl_2 + NaF \rightarrow$ No reaction
Since Cl_2 has lower reduction potential than F_2. Therefore, it is unable to displace fluorine from its salt.

534. (c): As the reducing power of halide ions decreases in the order $I^- > Br^- > Cl^-$, their correct order for being oxidised to dihalogens also decreases as $I^- > Br^- > Cl^-$.

535. (c): F cannot act as a reducing agent because it has highest the reduction potential.
$F_2 + 2\,e^- \rightarrow 2\,F^-;\ E° = +2.87\,V$

536. (b): HCl has the lowest boiling point and HF has the highest due to the presence of H-bonding.

537. (b): As the electronegativity difference between H and F atoms is (4.0 – 2.1 = 1.9) maximum as compared to those of other H and X atoms, H–F will have the highest percentage of ionic character.

538. (a): Because HI is the strongest and HF the weakest acids, their conjugate bases I^- and F^- are the weakest and strongest respectively. The base strength increases from I^- to F^-.

539. (a): Bond strength decreases as the size of the halogen increases from F to I.

540. (d): Due to hydrogen bonding, association or HF molecules occurs resulting in the formation of a low boiling liquid.

541. (b): As the size of the halogen atom increases from F to I, the H–X bond length in the hydrogen halide (HX) molecules also increases from H–F to H–I. This will decrease the bond dissociation energy in the same order, that is, from HF to HI and thus, the thermal stability of the HF molecules also decreases form HF to HI.

542. (c): Conc. H_2SO_4 oxidises HI to I_2 and therefore, the reaction of KI with conc. H_2SO_4 cannot give HI.
$KI + H_2SO_4 \rightarrow KHSO_4 + HI$
$H_2SO_4 + 2\,HI \rightarrow SO_2 + I_2 + 2\,H_2O$

543. (c): In HF, the molecules are associated through hydrogen bonding resulting in an increase of the bp of the liquid.

544. (a): $KF + HF \rightarrow KHF_2$

545. (b): Strong H-bonding (in case of HF) increases the boiling point to the highest value. Increase in van der Waals forces and molecular weight,lead to an increase in the boiling point from HCl to HI. Thus, the correct decreasing order of boiling point is
HF> HI > HBr > HCl.

546. (b): The increasing order of reducing power of halogen acids is HF > HI > HBr < HCl.By increasing the size of halogen atom, the bond strength of the H–X bond decreases. Thus, the ease of hydrogen donation increases and hence, reducing power increases.

547. (b): $H_2 + F_2 \xrightarrow{\text{Dark}} 2\,HF$

548. (a): HF reacts with glass to form sodium and calcium fluorosilicates—Na_2SiF_6 and $CaSiF_6$. So, it cannot be kept in a bottle of glass (which is a mixture of sodium and calcium silicates).
$Ni_2SiO_3 + 6\,HF \rightarrow Na_2SiF_6 + 3\,H_2O$
$CaSiO_3 + 6\,HF \rightarrow CaSiF_6 + 3\,H_2O$

549. (b): As the electronegativity of the halogen decreases, the reactivity also decreases.

550. (a): HF < HCl < HBr < HI
As we go down the group, the bond dissociation energy decreases; hence, the acidic nature increases.

551. (c): The melting and boiling points of HCl are the lowest amongst the HX due to weak intermolecular H-bonding in HCl.

552. (a): Due to H-bonding, free ions are not present in the aqueous solution. Hence, H_2F_2 is bad conductor of electricity.

553. (a): $2\,KBr + H_2SO_4 \xrightarrow{\Delta} K_2SO_4 + 2\,HBr$. It further reacts with H_2SO_4 to give Br_2.
$2\,HBr + H_2SO_4 \xrightarrow{\Delta} Br_2 + 2\,H_2O + SO_2$

554. (c): Glass is a mixture of sodium and calcium silicates. It reacts with HF forming sodium and calcium fluorosilicates respectively.
$Na_2SiO_3 + 6\,HF \rightarrow Na_2SiF_6 + 3\,H_2O$
$CaSiO_3 + 6\,HF \rightarrow CaSiF_6 + 2\,H_2O$
The etching of glass is based on these reactions.

555. (c):
$$2\,NaF + 2\,H_2SO_4 + MnO_2 \xrightarrow{\Delta} 2\,HF + MnSO_4 + Na_2SO_4 + H_2O + \frac{1}{2}O_2$$
(conc.)

556. (d): $KHF_2 \rightleftharpoons K^+ + HF_2^-$

557. (c): HI is a strong reducing agent. Its aqueous solution gets oxidised even by atmospheric oxygen.
$4\,HI + O_2 \rightarrow 2\,H_2O + 2\,I_2$

558. (b): As the electronegativity of X in X_2O decreases from F to Br, the bond pairs of electrons move closer to the central atom (O) and thus bond pair repulsion increases which increases the X–O–X bond angle from F_2O to Br_2O.

559. (d): All have bent structures. OF_2 has a bond angle of 103°, ClO_2 has 118° and Br_2O has more than 111°.

560. (d): I_4O_9 is ionic as it is the iodate of the I^{3+} cation written as iodine triiodate $[I]^{+3}[IO_3]_3^-$.

561. (c): Cl_2O_7 contains Cl in its highest +7 oxidation state.

562. (d): $Cl_2O_7 + H_2O \rightarrow 2\,HClO_4$; thus, Cl_2O_7 is an anhydride of perchloric acid.

563. (e): $2\,AgClO_3 + Cl_2 \xrightarrow{365\,K} 2\,AgCl + 2\,ClO_2 + O_2$

564. (d): Due to the presence of one odd electron in a *p* orbital of Cl, the ClO_2 molecule is paramagnetic.

565. (a): Acidic nature of oxide ∝ Non metallic nature of element forming the oxide.Asthe non metallic nature decreases in the order Cl > S > P, the acidic nature of the oxide also decreases in the same order.

566. (a): OF_4 (oxygen tetrafluoride) is theoretically not possible because oxygen does not have *d*-orbitals. It has only two half-filled *p* orbitals in the ground state which can form only two bonds with two F atoms.

567. (d): Prediction of the hybridisation in the $[IO_2F_5]^{2-}$ ion:
$$Q = \frac{1}{2}[Ve \mid SA - (\pm q)] = \frac{1}{2}[7 + 5 — 2 = 1/2\,(14)] = 7$$
Then, hybridisation of the central atom = sp^3d^3 and the shape is pentagonal bipyramidal where the two oxygen atoms occupy the axial positions.

568. (b): OF_2 dissolves in water but does not give any oxyacid solution, while,
$SO_2 + H_2O \rightarrow \underset{\text{Sulfurous acid}}{H_2SO_3} + 4\,HCl$
$SCl_4 + 3\,H_2O \rightarrow \underset{\text{Sulfurous acid}}{H_2SO_3} + 4\,HCl$
$SO_3 + H_2O \rightarrow \underset{\text{Sulfuric acid}}{H_2SO_4}$

569. (a): The stability of the oxides increases with an increase in the oxidation state of the halogen.

Oxide	Oxidation state of halogen
Cl_2O	+1
ClO_2	+4
ClO_3	+6
Cl_2O_7	+7

Hence, Cl_2O is the least stable oxide of chlorine.

570. (b):
$$2\,NaClO_3 + SO_2 + H_2SO_4 \xrightarrow{heat} 2\,ClO_2 + 2\,NaHSO_4$$
Trace of NaCl

571. (c): Cl_2O_6 is formed by the reaction of ClO_2 and O_3 at 0°C.
$2\,ClO_2 + 2\,O_3 \xrightarrow{0°C} Cl_2O_6 + 2\,O_2$

572. (b): The reactivity of these oxides with water increases as the electronegativity of the central atom increases. In other words, the stronger acidic oxide reacts faster with water to form the hydroxyl acid.
$B_2O_3 + 3\,H_2O \xrightarrow{Slow} 2\,H_3BO_3$
$P_2O_5 + 3\,H_2O \rightarrow 2\,H_3PO_4$
$Cl_2O_7 + H_2O \xrightarrow{Fast} 2\,HClO_4$
Thus, the reactivity towards water increases as $B_2O_3 > P_2O_5 < Cl_2O_7$.

573. (a): Fluorine, being the strongest oxidising agent, can oxidise iodine further to its maximum +7 oxidation state in IF_5 to give IF_7.

574. (a): ClF_3 where Cl is sp^3d hybridised has a T-shaped structure with two lone pairs of electrons on the Cl atom at the equatorial positions.

575. (b): There are 7 + 3 = 10 electrons around the central Br atom in BrF_3. Therefore, the total no. of electron pairs = 10/2 = 5. There are three Br–F bonds, therefore, the number of bond pairs = 3.
Thus, there are two lone pairs and three bond pairs in BrF_3 which has a T-shaped (distorted trigonal bipyramidal) structure where two lone pairs occupy the equatorial positions. All the three bonds are not equal.

576. (d): $U + 3\,ClF_3 \rightarrow UF_6 + 3\,ClF$

577. (a): The I–Cl bond is weaker than the I–I bond. Consequently, the I–Cl bond breaks easily to form halogen atoms which readily bring about the reactions.

St. of $[IO_2F_5]^{2-}$ ion

578. (a): Due to a decrease in the electronegativity difference, the stability of the interhalogen compounds follows the following order (decreases) $IF_3 > BrF_3 > ClF_3$.

579. (b): In ClF_3, Cl is sp^3d-hybridised giving a distorted trigonal bipyramidal or T-shaped molecule due to two lone pairs occupying two equatorial positions.

580. (a): As the oxidation number of the halogen increases, the halogen–oxygen bond becomes more covalent. As a result, thermal stability of the acid increases and the oxidising power decreases. Thus, HOCl in which Cl is present in the +1 oxidation state, is a stronger oxidising agent than $HClO_2$, $HClO_3$ and $HClO_4$ in which Cl is present in the +3, +5 and +7 oxidation states respectively.

581. (a):

Outer electronic configuration of Cl atom in ground state = $3s^2 3p^5$

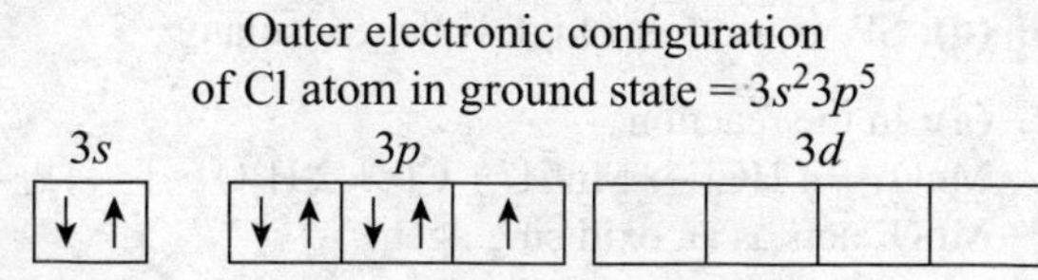

Electronic configuration in excited state

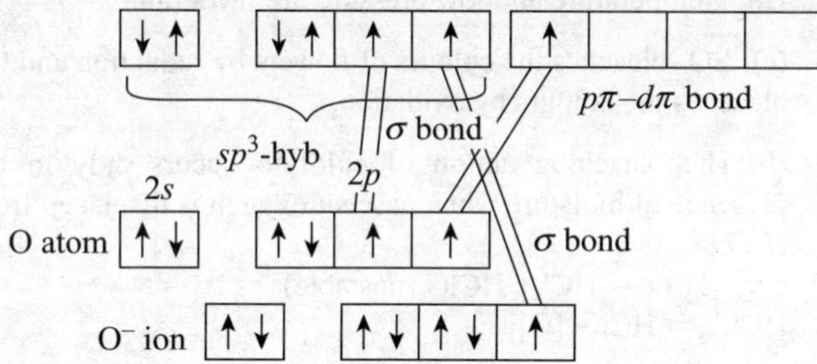

Therefore, ClO_2^- has the following structure.

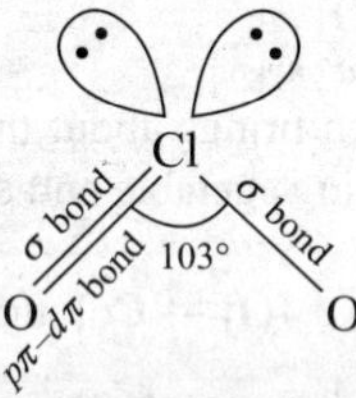

582. (a): The smallest cation is heavily hydrated. ClO_4^- has the smallest central atom Cl as it has +7 charge on it, followed by ClO_3^- (+5), ClO_2^- (+3) and ClO^- (+1). So, the correct order of increasing hydration energy is $ClO^- < ClO_2^- < ClO_3^- < ClO_4^-$.

583. (b): In perchlorate (ClO_4^-) ion, Cl is sp^3-hybridised and each hybrid orbital overlaps with a p orbital of an O to give σ-bonds.

584. (b): $2\,IO_4^- + 16\,H^+ + 14\,e^- \rightarrow I_2 + 8\,H_2O$

As one mole of IO_4^- requires seven electrons for its conversion to I_2, therefore, the equivalent mass of IO_4^- is M/7.

585. (c): All halogens except fluorine form three or more oxyacids. Fluorine however, forms only one oxyacid, that is, HOF.

586. (b):

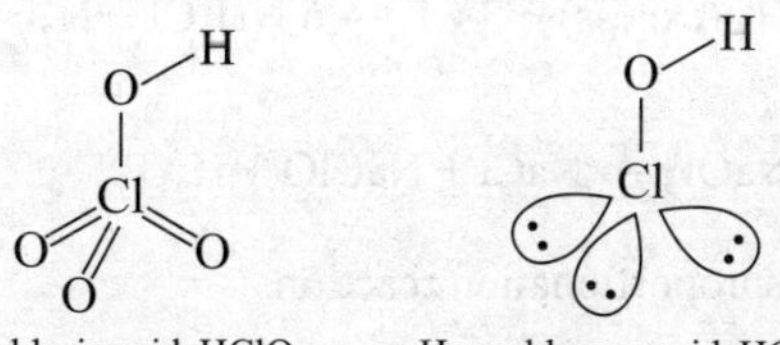

Perchloric acid, $HClO_4$ Hypochlorous acid, HClO

The central atom in both the acids is sp^3-hybridised. In the reaction between Cl_2 and H_2O, hypochlorous acid HClO is formed and not HClO.

Acid nature: $HClO_4 > H_3O^+$; Basic nature: $ClO_4^- < H_2O$

Stability of the anion (CB) increases from ICl^- to ClO_4^- due to resonance.

587. (b): Greater the pK_a ($-\log K_a$) value, weaker the acid. As the acid character decreases in the order $HClO_4 > HClO_3 > HClO_2 > HClO$, the pK_a values will increase in thereverse order.

$\underset{-10}{HClO_4} < \underset{-1.2}{HClO_3} < \underset{2.0}{HClO_2} < \underset{7.5}{HClO}$

588. (c):

$3\,\overset{+1}{ClO^-} \rightarrow \overset{+5}{ClO_3^-} + \overset{-1}{Cl^-}$

Cl in $\overset{+1}{ClO^-}$ undergoes oxidation to Cl in $\overset{+5}{ClO_3^-}$ and reduction to $\overset{-1}{Cl}$ in Cl^-. Therefore, this change is a disproportionation reaction.

589. (c): When HOCl is treated with H_2O_2 in an acidic medium, it gets reduced to Cl^- with the evolution of oxygen gas.

$HOCl(aq) + H_2O_2(aq) \rightarrow HCl(aq) + H_2O(l) + O_2(g)$

So, the correct answer is (c), that is, O_2 gas.

590. (b): Commercially, chlorine dioxide is prepared by passing SO_2 gas into a mixture of sodium chlorate and H_2SO_4 having NaCl in traces.

$\underset{\text{Sodium chlorate}}{2\,NaClO_3} + SO_2 + H_2SO_4 \xrightarrow{\text{Trace}} \underset{\text{Chlorine dioxide}}{2\,ClO_2} + 2\,NaHSO_4$

591. (b): The acidic strength of the oxyacids decreases downwards in a group as the electronegativity of the halogen decreases. The correct order of acidic strength of the oxyacids of halogens is $HClO_4 > HBrO_4 > HIO_4$.

592. (a): HClO decomposes to give Cl_2 and water. $HClO_2$ undergoes auto-oxidation to give HClO and $HClO_3$. $HClO_3$ is stable only in the dark. In the presence of light, it releases chlorine and thereby acts as an oxidising agent. $HClO_4$ is very stable and hence is obtained in the pure form.

593. (c):

$\underset{\text{Cold, dil.}}{Cl_2 + 2\,NaOH} \rightarrow NaCl + NaOCl + H_2O$

594. (b): $KCl + HClO_4 \rightarrow \underset{\text{White ppt.}}{KClO_4} + HCl$

$KClO_4$ being less soluble in water gets precipitated.

595. (a): Oxidation number of Br (+7) in $HBrO_4$ is more than that of Cl (+1) in HOCl, N (+3) in HNO_2 and P (+3) in H_3PO_3; so it is the strongest acid among these.

596. (a): Cl_2O and ClO_2 are highly reactive oxidising agents and are used as bleaching agents for paper pulp and textiles. OCl^- salts such as NaClO are used as detergents.

OCl^- disproportionates in the alkaline medium as follows:

$$3OCl^- \xrightleftharpoons{300\text{ K}} 2\,Cl^- + ClO_3^-$$

BrO_3^- is oxidised in the basic medium (and not in the acidic medium) as follows:

$$BrO_3^- + F_2 + 2\,OH^- \rightarrow BrO_4^- + 2\,F^- + H_2O$$

597. (b): $KI + I_2 \rightarrow KI_3$ (intense yellow colour)
In I_3^-, I undergoes sp^3d hybridisation where all (three) equatorial positions are occupied by lone pairs of electrons giving a linear structure to I_3^-.

598. (c): Number of hybrid orbitals (X) $= \frac{1}{2}[VE + SA - (\pm q)]$

For XeF_2: (X) $= \frac{1}{2}[8 + 2 - 0] = 5$, that is, sp^3d-hybridisation.

For ICl_2^-: (X) $= \frac{1}{2}[7 + 2 - (-1)] = 5$, that is, sp^3d-hybridisation.

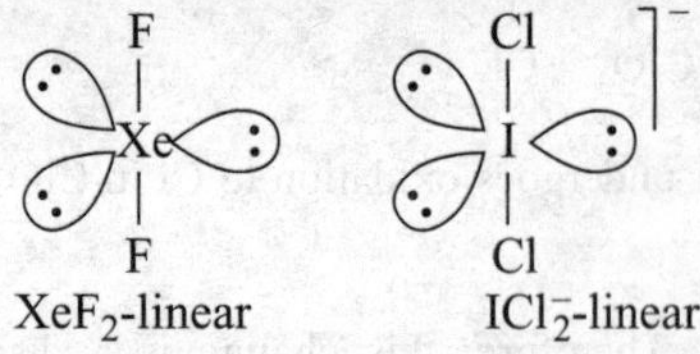

XeF_2-linear ICl_2^--linear

599. (a): Lattice energy decreases in the order LiF>LiCL>LiBr>LiI. Lattice energy depends on the size and charge of the ion. Smaller size and higher charge favour higher lattice energy.

600. (c): Due to the small atomic size of Li and F, the lattice energy of LiF is higher than its hydration energy.

601. (a):

$$\underset{\text{conc.}}{NaCl + H_2SO_4} \xrightarrow{\Delta} NaHSO_4 + \underset{X}{HCl}\uparrow$$

$$\text{Moist blue litmus paper} + HCl \xrightarrow[\text{(Acidic)}]{} \underset{\text{Red litmus paper}}{X}$$

$$\underset{\text{Egg shell powder}}{CaCO_3} + 2\,HCl \rightarrow CaCl_2 + \underset{Y}{CO_2}\uparrow + H_2O$$

$$\underset{\text{Lime water}}{Ca(OH)_2} + \underset{Y}{CO_2} \rightarrow \underset{\text{Milkyness}}{CaCO_3} + H_2O$$

Thus, gas X is HCl and gas Y is CO_2.

602. (b): According to Fajan's rules, the largest cation and smallest anion form ionic compounds whereas the smallest cation and largest anion form covalent compounds.

603. (b): AgCl is a water insoluble chloride.

604. (c): According to Fajan's rules, MCl_2 is more ionic than MCl_4.

Halogens and their Compounds

605. (b): $2\,F_2 + H_2O \rightarrow 4\,HF + O_2$

606. (a): Fluorine is the most electronegative element. It does not form oxyfluorides like other halogens. It reacts with cold and dil. NaOH to form sodium fluoride and oxygen fluoride.
$2\,NaOH + 2\,F_2 \rightarrow 2\,NaF + OF_2 + H_2O$

607. (a): Lattice energy of CaF_2 is more than that of its hydration energy and therefore, it has the lowest solubility.

608. (a): Fluorine and chlorine are more electronegative than sulfur. Therefore, the reaction $2\,X_2 + S \rightarrow SX_4$ is shown when X = F or Cl.

609. (c):

$$2\,H_2O(l) + 2\,F_2(g) \rightarrow 4\,HF(aq) + O_2$$
$$\downarrow$$
$$4\,H^+(aq) + 4\,F^-(aq)$$

Therefore, the correct option is (c).

610. (d): SF_6 is used as a high voltage insulator.

611. (a): In the reaction,
$MnO_2 + 4\,HCl \rightarrow MnCl_2 + Cl_2 + 2\,H_2O$
MnO_2 acts as an oxidising agent.

612. (c): $\underbrace{Cl_2}_{1\text{ mol}} \rightarrow \underbrace{2Cl}_{2\text{ mol}}\ \Delta H = +ve$

High temperature and low pressure are favourable.

613. (c): SO_2 bleaches the colours of flowers by reduction and Cl_2 bleaches the colours by oxidation.

614. (b): The bleaching action of chlorine occurs only in the presence of moisture when nascent oxygen is displaced from H_2O.
$Cl_2 + H_2O \rightarrow HCl + HClO$ (unstable)
$HClO \rightarrow HCl + [O]$

615. (d):
$Cl_2 + H_2O \rightarrow HCl + HClO$ (unstable)
$HOCl \rightarrow HCl + \underset{\text{Nascent oxygen}}{[O]}$

This nascent oxygen brings about the oxidation of coloured substances present in vegetable and organic matter to colourless substances.
Coloured substance + [O] → Colourless substance

616. (b): With hot and concentrated alkalies, Cl forms the trioxochlorate (V).
$6\,NaOH + 3\,Cl_2 \rightarrow 5\,NaCl + NaClO_3 + 3H_2O$
$NaClO_3 \rightleftharpoons Na^+ + ClO_3^-$

617. (d): In the preparation of mustard gas from chlorine gas, the reagents required are S_8, S_2Cl_2 and ethane (and not CH_4).
The reactions taking place are:

$$\underset{\text{(Boiling)}}{S_8 + 4Cl_2} \longrightarrow \underset{\text{(Sulfur monochloride)}}{4S_2Cl_2}$$

$$\underset{\text{Ethene}}{CH_2{=}CH_2} + Cl{-}S{-}S{-}Cl + \underset{\text{Ethene}}{CH_2{=}CH_2} \longrightarrow \underset{\text{Mustard gas}}{ClCH_2{-}CH_2{-}S{-}CH_2{-}CH_2Cl} + S$$

618. (c): $8\,NH_3$ (excess) $+ 3\,Cl_2 \rightarrow 6\,NH_4Cl + N_2$

619. (a):
$Cl_2 + \underset{\text{cold, dil.}}{2\,NaOH} \rightarrow NaCl + NaClO + H_2O$
It is a disproportionation reaction.

620. (d): $2\,KBr + Cl_2 \rightarrow 2\,KCl + \underset{\text{(Orange brown)}}{Br_2}$

621. (d):
$2\,S_2Cl_2 + 2\,H_2O \rightarrow 3S + SO_2 + 4\,HCl$
X

622. (a): $Cl_2 + 2\,KBr \rightarrow 2\,KCl + Br_2$
A more electronegative halogen can displace a less electronegative halogen.

623. (c): $6\,KOH + 3\,Cl_2 \rightarrow 5\,KCl + KClO_3 + 3\,H_2O$
Thus, $KClO_2$ is not formed.

624. (d): Cl_2 gas is dried over conc. H_2SO_4.

625. (c): $\underset{\text{Chlorine water}}{H_2O + Cl_2} \xrightarrow{hv} HCl + HClO$
$HClO \xrightarrow{hv} HCl + [O]$ or $2\,HClO \xrightarrow{hv} 2HCl + O_2$
This shows that H_2 has more affinity for Cl_2.

626. (b): $\underset{\text{Basic}}{CaO} + Cl_2 \rightarrow CaOCl_2$
$\underset{\text{Acidic}}{NaHCO_3} + Cl_2 \rightarrow$ No reaction

627. (d): Chlorine cannot be used for extraction of silver and copper.

628. (d): Spirit of salt is muriatic acid, that is, a solution of hydrochloric acid. Fischer's salt is $K_3[Co(NO_2)]_6$, Epsom salt is epsomite, $MgSO_4.7H_2O$ and Ferming's salt is KHF_2. Thus, spirit of salt contains chlorine.

629. (c): A stronger oxidising agent (Cl_2) displaces a weaker oxidising agent (Br_2) from its salt solution.
$2\,KBr + Cl_2 \rightarrow 2\,KCl + Br_2$

630. (c): Br_2 displaces I_2 from iodide (I^-) on the starch paper which gives a bue complex of starch–iodine.

631. (d): $SO_2 + Br_2 + 2\,H_2O \rightarrow H_2SO_4 + 2HBr$

632. (d):
$3\,\overset{0}{Br_2} + 6\,CO_3^{2-} + 3\,H_2O \rightarrow 5\,\overset{-1}{Br^-} + \overset{+5}{BrO_3^-} + 6\,HCO_3^-$
The oxidation number of Br_2 changes from 0 to –1 and it is reduced. Also the ON changes from 0 to +5 and it is oxidised.

633. (a): Bromine water is an oxidising agent. It oxidises SO_2 to SO_3 and itself gets reduced to colourless HBr.
$\underset{\text{Orange red}}{Br_2} + H_2O \rightarrow \underset{\text{Colourless}}{2\,HBr} + [O]$
$\underset{\text{Colourless}}{SO_2} + [O] \rightarrow SO_3$
$H_2O + SO_3 \rightarrow H_2SO_4$
H_2S is also oxidised by bromine water but in this case, decolourisation is also accompanied by the formation ofsulfur.
$H_2S + [O] \rightarrow H_2O + S$

634. (b): Bromine liberates iodine from KI solution because of its more powerful oxidising property. The colour of iodine is grey black so, black colour is obtained.
$2\,KI + Br_2 \rightarrow 2\,KBr + \underset{\text{Black or grey}}{I_2}$

635. (a): Seaweed contains iodine in the form of iodides.

636. (b): $5\,I^- + IO_3^- + 6\,H^+ \rightarrow \underset{\text{Violet}}{2\,I_2} + \underset{\text{From lime juice}}{3\,H_2O}$

637. (b): $NaCl + \underset{\text{conc.}}{H_2SO_4} \xrightarrow{\Delta} NaSO_4 + HCl\uparrow$
$HCl + \underset{\text{conc.}}{H_2SO_4} \xrightarrow{\Delta}$ No reaction
$NaBr + \underset{\text{conc.}}{H_2SO_4} \xrightarrow{\Delta} NaHSO_4 + HBr$
$2\,HBr + \underset{\text{conc.}}{H_2SO_4} \xrightarrow{\Delta} Br_2\uparrow + SO_2 + 2\,H_2O$
$NaI + \underset{\text{conc.}}{H_2SO_4} \xrightarrow{\Delta} NaHSO_4 + HI$
$2\,HI + \underset{\text{conc.}}{H_2SO_4} \xrightarrow{\Delta} I_2\uparrow + SO_2 + 2\,H_2O$
Hence, the gases released are HCl, Br_2 and I_2.

638. (a): $KI + \underset{\text{Conc.}}{H_2SO_4} \xrightarrow{\Delta} KHSO_4 + HI$
$\underset{\text{Conc.}}{H_2SO_4} + 2\,HI \rightarrow 2\,H_2O + \underset{\text{Violet}}{I_2} + SO_2\uparrow$

639. (d): Iodine sublimes on heating and therefore, can be purified by sublimation.

640. (b): $4\,KI + 2\,CuSO_4 \rightarrow Cu_2I_2 + 2\,K_2SO_4 + I_2$

641. (b):Cu^{2+} gives iodometeric titration as it gives I_2 on reacting with KI.
$Cu^{2+} + 4\,I^- \rightarrow 2CuI + I_2$

642. (b): $2\,KBr + I_2 \rightarrow 2KI + Br_2$
The reaction is not feasible because the Br^- ion is not oxidised to Br_2 with I_2 due to the higher electrode potential of Br_2compared to that of iodine.

643. (b): The solubility of I_2 in water increases by the addition of KI due to the formation of polyhalide ion, that is, I_3^- complex.
$KI + I_2 \rightarrow KI_3$

644. (c): $2\,Na_2S_2O_3 + I_2 \rightarrow 2\,NaI + Na_2S_4O_6$ (Sodium tetrathionate)

645. (b): $2\,NaI + Cl_2 \rightarrow 2\,NaCl + I_2$ (violet colour)
$CCl_4 + I_2 \rightarrow$ Violet colour in CCl_4 layer

646. (c):
$I_2 + \underset{\text{Conc.}}{10\,HNO_3} \rightarrow 2\,HIO_3 + 10\,NO_2 + 4\,H_2O$

647. (d): $\underset{-1}{HI} < \underset{0}{I_2} < \underset{+1}{ICl} < \underset{+7}{HIO_4}$

648. (d): None of the above reactions is observed as I_2 has the lowest reduction potential among the halogens.

649. (d): PbI_4 is least stable because of two reasons.
(i) Size of iodine is biggest and I^- ion acts as a reducing agent.
(ii) The +2 oxidation state of Pb is more stable than the +4 state because of inert pair effect. Therefore, PbI_4 does not exist.

650. (b): Reducing properties increase from F to I so I is oxidised by nitric acid to HIO_3
$I_2 + 10\,HNO_3 \rightarrow 2\,HIO_3 + 10\,NO_2 + 4\,H_2O$

651. (a): I-131 is used for the treatment of thyroid disorders.

652. (c): NaI is added to table salt (NaCl) to provide the iodine required for maintaining proper health.

653. (b): Fe reacts with HCl to form $FeCl_2$ and H_2.
$Fe + 2\,HCl \rightarrow FeCl_2 + H_2$
H_2 thus liberated prevents the oxidation of $FeCl_2$ to $FeCl_3$.

654. (a): Higher the oxidation state of the central atom, higher will be its electronegativity and hence higher will be its acidic strength.
$\overset{+5}{HClO_3} > \overset{+3}{HClO_2} > \overset{+1}{HClO} > HOBr$
Thus, $HClO_3$ is the strongest Brönsted acid in aqueous solution.
HOBr is least acidic due to lesser electronegativity of Br compared to Cl.

655. (b): $2\,K_2MnF_6 + 4\,SbF_5 \rightarrow 4\,KSbF_6 + 2\,MnF_4$
$2\,MnF_4 \rightarrow 2\,MnF_3 + F_2$
$2\,K_2MnF_6 + 4\,SbF_5 \rightarrow 4\,KSbF_6 + 2\,MnF_3 + F_2$
Here, the stronger Lewis acid SbF_5 displaces the weaker acid MnF_4 from K_2MnF_6. Initially, the formed MnF_4 being unstable, decomposes to MnF_3 and F_2.

656. (c): Molten KHF_2 is used as an electrolyte in the Whytlaw–Gray method for the preparation of F_2.

657. (d): F_2 is prepared by the electrolysis of a solution of KHF_2 (1 part) in anhydrous HF (5 parts) in a vessel made of Monel metal using carbon electrodes.

658. (a): Solid NaF is used to purify fluorine by removing HF fumes.
$NaF + HF \rightarrow NaHF_2$

659. (d): More than 10 ppm level of F^- is harmful to bones and teeth.

660. (a): Fluorine attacks glass but very slowly. Thus, it is used to make painting over glass.

661. (b):
$\underset{(Dil.)}{2\,F_2 + 2\,NaOH} \rightarrow NaF + OF_2\uparrow + H_2O$
The structure of A (OF_2) is F–Ö–F (σ bonds, 103.2°)
σ-bond made by O = 2
Lone pairs of electrons on O = 2
Number of orbitals used by O for hybridisation = 2 + 2 = 4
Hybridisation in OF_2 is sp^3.

Bleaching Powder, $CaOCl_2$ (Calcium Chlorohypochlorite, Chloride of Lime)

662. (d): AgF is soluble in water and all the rest of the halides of Ag are insoluble.

663. (d): All these are hydrolysed in the presence of water.

664. (d): $2\,CaOCl_2 \xrightarrow[\text{Heat}]{CoCl_2} 2\,CaCl_2 + O_2$

665. (d): $Ca(OCl)Cl \xrightarrow{H_2O} Ca^{2+}(aq) + OCl^-(aq) + Cl^-(aq)$

666. (a): $CaOCl_2 + 2\,HCl \rightarrow CaCl_2 + Cl_2 + H_2O$

667. (d): $6\,CaOCl_2 \xrightarrow{\text{Auto oxidation}} Ca(ClO_3)_2 + 5\,CaCl_2$

668. (a): $CaOCl_2 + CO_2 \rightarrow CaCO_3 + Cl_2$

669. (d): Bleaching powder loses its power on keeping for a long time because it changes into calcium chloride and calcium chlorate.
$6\,CaOCl_2 \xrightarrow{\text{On long}} Ca(ClO_3)_2 + 5\,CaCl_2$

670. (b):
$\underset{X}{Ca(OH)_2} + Cl_2 \rightarrow \underset{\text{Bleaching powder}}{Ca(OCl)Cl} + H_2O$

671. (d): Bleaching powder consists of a mixture of calcium hypochlorite, $Ca(OCl)_2.4H_2O$ and basic calcium chloride, $CaCl_2.Ca(OH)_2.H_2O$. The active ingredient in bleaching powder for bleaching action is calcium hypochlorite, $Ca(OCl)_2$. The available chlorine refers to the chlorine liberated by the action of dilute acids. The commercially available sample of bleaching powder contains 36%–38% of available chlorine. For the determination of available chlorine, the bleaching powder solution/suspension is treated with an excess of a solution of KI in the presence of conc. acetic acid.
$OCl^- + 2\,I^- + 2\,H^+ \rightleftharpoons Cl^- + I_2 + H_2O$
The liberated I_2 is titrated with standard $Na_2S_2O_3$ solution using starch as indicator (iodometric titration).

Pseudohalogens and Pseudohalides (Halogenoid Ions)

672. (c): $(SCN)_2$ (thiocyanogen) is a pseudohalogen.

673. (d): Some complex ions of nitrogen show similarities with halide ions. These are called pseudohalide ions. For example, OCN^-, NCO^-, CN^-etc.Halogens, among themselves form complex ions which are called polyhalide ions such as I_3^-, BrI_2^-. Similarly, interhalogens are the compounds of halogens in which one halogen is a cation and other halogen is an anion, as in, IF_7, ICl_5, BrF_3, IF_5.

Final Preparation

674. (d): HF does not act as reducing agent.

675. (d): HF is a weaker acid than HCl.

676. (d): Sequence (d) corresponds to increasing dissociation constant (K_a) values and not pK_a values. For example, dissociation constant are: H_2O (1.8×10^{-16}) < H_2S (1.3×10^{-7}) < H_2Se (1.3×10^{-4}) < H_2Te (3×10^{-3}). For increasing pK_a values, the correct sequence is H_2Te <HeSe< $H_2S < H_2O$.

677. (a): HF forms strong intermolecular H-bonds due to the high electronegativity of F. Hence, the boiling point of HF is abnormally high. Boiling points of other hydrogen halides gradually increase from HCl to HI due to an increase in the size of the halogen atoms from Cl to I which further increase the magnitude of the van der Waals forces.

678. (d): HF dehydrates and does not oxidise the tissues.

679. (c): Compound $OF_2 < OH_2 < OCl_2 < ClO_2$.
Bond angle 103° < 105° < 111° < 118°
In all these compounds (except ClO_2), the central atom is O.

680. (a): In ClO_2, Cl is sp^2-hybridised and the bond angle is 118°. In Cl_2O, O is sp^3-hybridised. However, due to repulsion from lone pairs, the bond angle increases from 109.5° to

111°. In ClO_2^-, Cl is sp^3-hybridised but due to $lp-bp$ repulsions, the angle decreases from 109.5° to 103°. Thus, the increasing order of bond angles is $ClO_2^- < Cl_2O < ClO_2$.

681. (b): ClO_2 has a three-electron-bond and thus is paramagnetic in nature.

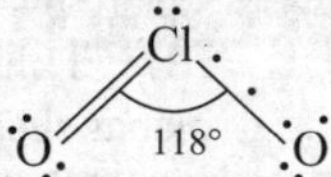

682. (c): $2\ AgClO_3 + Cl_2\ (dry) \xrightarrow{90°C} 2\ AgCl + 2\ ClO_2 + O_2$

683. (c): In Cl_2O_6, Cl is sp^3-hybridised

684. (b): I_2O_5 is the true covalent oxide of iodine whereas I_2O_7 and I_2O_9 are not formed. I_2O_4 is an iodyl iodate $[IO]^+[IO_3]^-$ which is ionic in nature.

685. (c): A 500 g toothpaste sample contains fluoride = 0.2 g. 10^6 g (one million) sample contains fluoride

$$= \frac{0.2}{500} \times 10^6 = 400 \text{ ppm}$$

That is, the concentration of fluoride is 400 ppm.

686. (a): AgF is soluble in water.

687. (b): ClF_3 is sp^3d hybridised, two lone pairs occupy equatorial positions, giving a distorted trigonal bipyramidal structure. There are two longer axial bonds and one shorter equatorial bond.

688. (a): The total number of valence electrons present are 28 in ClF_3, 19 in ClO_2 and 25 each in ClO_3 and BrO_3. Therefore, ClF_3 is not paramagnetic as it contains an even number of electrons.

689. (b): ICl_3 exhibits a dimeric planar structure with Cl bridges.

Cl   Cl   Cl
  I   I
Cl   Cl   Cl

690. (d): BrF_3 has a T-shaped structure in which two lone pairs occupy equatorial positions to minimise lone pair–lone pair repulsions.

691. (a): F does not form polyhalide ions being a central atom, due to its smaller size and higher electronegativity.

692. (d):

$$\overset{+1}{3\ HOCl} \xrightarrow{\text{Disproportionation}} 2\ \overset{-1}{HCl} + \overset{+5}{HClO_3}$$

693. (d): In a disproportionation reaction, one element of a compound will simultaneously get reduced and oxidised. In ClO_4^-, Cl will not get oxidised and thus will not undergo disproportionation reaction.

694. (c): Oxidation state of I in HIO_4
$1 + x + 4(-2) = 0$ or $x = +7$
Oxidations state of I in H_3IO_5
$3 + x + 5(-2) = 0$ or $x = +7$
Oxidation state of I in H_5IO_6
$5 + x + 6(-2) = 0$ or $x = +7$

695. (d): Perchloric acid ($HClO_4$) is not a peroxy acid while perphosphoric and (H_3PO_5), pernitric acid (HNO_4) and perdisulfuric acid ($H_2S_2O_8$) are peroxy acids.

696. (a): Acid strength increases as the oxidation number of the halogen increases. Thus, the correct order of acid strength is:

$$\overset{+1}{HClO} < \overset{+3}{HClO_2} < \overset{+5}{HClO_3} < \overset{+7}{HClO_4}$$

697. (c): The more the electronegativity and oxidation number of the central atom (here Cl), the higher is the acidic character. Thus, $HClO_4$ is the strongest acid.

698. (d): The oxidising power of perhalates can be explained on the basis of electrode potential data for the reaction,
$XO_4^- + 2\ H^+ + 2\ e^- \rightarrow XO_3^- + H_2O$
$E°$ for $ClO_4^- = 1.23$ V, $E°$ for $IO_4^- = 1.64$ V and $E°$ for $BrO_4^- = 1 + 8$ V
More the reduction potential, the more easily the ion gets reduced and greater is the oxidising power. Thus, the oxidising power decreases in the order $BrO_4^- > IO_4^- > ClO_4^-$.

699. (a): In hypoiodous acid HOI, the iodine atom uses an sp^3 hybrid orbital;iodine has three lone pairs and one bond pair of electrons.

700. (a): I^- is oxidised by $KMnO_4$ in alkaline medium to form IO_3^- (iodate ion).
$2\ KMnO_4 + KI + H_2O \rightarrow 2\ KOH + 2\ MnO_2 + KIO_3$

701. (a): $IO_3^- + 5\ I^- + 6\ H^+ \rightarrow 3\ H_2O + 3\ I_2$

702. (a): KIO_3 and KI are used for preparing iodised salt.

703. (d): $2\ H_2O + 2\ F_2 \xrightarrow{\text{Cold}} 4\ HF + O_2$
$3\ H_2O + 3\ F_2 \xrightarrow{\text{Hot}} 6\ HF + O_3$

704. (a): K_2MnF_6 reacts with SbF_5 to form F_2. In this reaction, the stronger Lewis acid SbF_5 displaces the weaker one (MnF_4) from its salt. MnF_4 being unstable, readily decomposes to give MnF_3 and fluorine.
$K_2MnF_6 + 2\ SbF_5 \rightarrow 2\ KSbF_6 + MnF_6$ (unstable)
$2\ MnF_4 \rightarrow 2\ MnF_3 + F_2$
The overall reaction becomes
$2\ K_2MnF_6 + 4\ SbF_5 \rightarrow 4\ KSbF_6 + 2\ MnF_3 + F_2$

705. (c): Since the saturated solution gives a white precipitate with $AgNO_3$, the solution must contain Cl^- ions and the gas (X) is Cl_2.

$\underset{(X)}{Cl_2} + H_2O \rightarrow \underset{\text{Saturated solution}}{2\ HCl + [O]}$

$AgNO_3 + HCl \rightarrow \underset{\text{White ppt.}}{AgCl} + HNO_3$

$\underset{\text{Saturated soln.}}{2\ HCl} + Mg \rightarrow MgCl_2 + \underset{\text{Colourless gas (Y)}}{H_2}$

706. (c): The black powder is MnO_2.
$\underset{(A)}{MnO_2} + 2\ NaCl + 3\ H_2SO_4 \rightarrow 2\ NaHSO_4 + MnSO_4 + \underset{\text{Greenish yellow gas (B)}}{Cl_2} + 2\ H_2O$

$\underset{(B)}{3\ Cl_2} + 8\ NH_3 \rightarrow N_2 + 6\ NH_4Cl$

707. (c): $2\ KMnO_4 + 16\ HCl \xrightarrow{\text{Room temp.}} 2\ KCl + 2\ MnCl_2 + 8\ H_2O + 5\ Cl_2$

708. (b): $Na_2S_2O_3 + 4\ Cl_2 + 5\ H_2O \rightarrow 2\ NaHSO_4 + 8\ HCl$

709. (b)

$$\overset{0}{6\,NaOH + 3Cl_2} \rightarrow \overset{-1}{5NaCl} + \overset{+5}{NaClO_3} + 3\,H_2O$$

710. **(d):** $2\,KClO_3 + I_2 \rightarrow 2\,KIO_2 + Cl_2$

711. **(b):** $2\,CuSO_4 + 4\,KI \rightarrow Cu_2I_2 + 2\,K_2SO_4 + I_2$

712. **(b):** $Na_2S_2O_3 + Cl_2 + H_2O \rightarrow$

$Na_2SO_4 + HCl + S$
$Na_2S_2O_3 + Br_2 + H_2O \rightarrow$ | Similar reaction
$Na_2SO_4 + 2HBr + S$

$2\,Na_2S_2O_3 + I_2 \rightarrow Na_2S_4O_6 + NaI]$ Different reaction

713. **(d):** I_2 is oxidised from 0 (I_2) to the +5 oxidation state.

714. **(c):** Oxidising power of I_2 is less than that of Br_2. Therefore, it is unable to oxidise bromide.

715. **(b):** Interhalogen compound of the type XX′ (A) is linear (iii), XX'_3 (B) is T-shaped (i) with sp^3d-hybridisation having two lone pairs of electrons in equatorial positions, XX'_5 (C) is square pyramidal (iv) due to sp^3d^2-hybridisation and a lone pair in one of the axial positions and XX'_7 (D) is pentagonal bipyramidal (ii) having sp^3-hybridisation.

716. **(c):**
$HgCl_2 + 4I^- \rightarrow [HgI_4]^{2-} + 2Cl^-$
Soluble complex
I_2 is soluble in an aqueous solution of iodide ions due to the formation of I_3^- complex ion
$I_2 + I^- \rightarrow I_3^-$

717. **(b):** $NaCl + H_2SO_4\text{ (conc.)} \rightarrow NaHSO_4 + HCl$
$K_2Cr_2O_7 + 2\,H_2SO_4\text{ (conc.)} \rightarrow 2\,KHSO_4 + 2\,CrO_3 + H_2O$
$CrO_3 + 2\,HCl \rightarrow CrO_2Cl_2 + H_2O$
Chromyl chloride gas

718. **(d):** Hydrochloric acid forms a constant boiling mixture of 20.4%.

719. **(b):** HCl + HNO_3 (concentrated acids in the ratio of 3 : 1) mixture is called aqua regia and contains NOCl.
$HNO_3 + 3\,HCl \rightarrow 2\,H_2O + NOCl + 2\,|\,Cl\,|$

720. **(a):** $RCOO^-$ is not a pseudohalide.

721. **(c):** In N_3^-, the formal oxidation state of N is –1.

722. **(d):** Fluorine reacts vigorously with water giving O_2 and O_3, the mixture is known as ozonised oxygen.
$2\,F_2 + 2\,H_2O \rightarrow 4\,HF + O_2$
$3\,F_2 + 3\,H_2O \rightarrow 6\,HF + O_3$

723. **(d):** Since HF is the weakest reducing agent of al hydracids (hydrides) of the halogens, it cannot reduce H_2SO_4, $KMnO_4$ and $K_2Cr_2O_7$.

724. **(b):** HNO_3 here acts as a base as it accepts a proton from HF to give $H_2NO_3^+$ species.

MATCH THE FOLLOWING

725. **(b):** (A) $6\,NaOH + 3\,Cl_2 \rightarrow 5\,NaCl + NaClO_3 + H_2O$
(B) $2\,NaClO_3 + 2\,H_2C_2O_4 \rightarrow Na_2C_2O_4$
$+2\,CO_2 + 2\,ClO_2 + 2\,H_2O$ (B→ p)
(C) $2\,ClO_2 + 2\,NaOH \rightarrow NaClO_2 + NaClO_3 + H_2O$ (C →s)
(D) $Cl_2O_6 + 2\,NaOH \rightarrow NaClO_3 + NaClO_4 + H_2O$ (D → q)

726. **(a):** (A) BrF_5 has 1 *lp* occupying axial positions (A → r), square pyramidal shape;
(B) ICl_4^- has 2 *lp* occupying axial positions (B → p), square planar shape;
(C) ClF_3 has 2 *lp* occupying equatorial positions (C → s), T-shape;
(D) SF_4 has 1 *lp* occupying equatorial position (D → q), see–saw shape.

727. **(d):** (A) HCl is a monobasic acid (A → s);
(B) HF is used for etching glass (B → r);
(C) HBr is a monobasic acid (C → s);
(D) HI is strong reducing agent, it is the strongest acid among the halogen acids and is monobasic (D → p, q, s).

ASSERTION REASON

728. **(c): Correct R.** Additional electrons are repelled more effectively by the 2*p* electrons in F than by the 3*p* electrons in the Cl atom.

729. **(c): Correct R.** Chlorine is a better oxidising agent than fluorine, because of its greater electron gain enthalpy.

730. **(a):** R is the correct explanation of A.

731. **(d): Correct A.** Heat of hydration of the halide ion (X^-) decreases down the group from F to I.
Correct R. Size of the halogens increases from F to I.

732. **(a):** R is the correct explanation of A.

733. **(a):** R is the correct explanation of A.

734. **(a):** R is the correct explanation of A.

735. **(a):** Fluorine is the most reactive among all the halogens due to its low bond dissociation enthalpy.Hence, R is the correct explanation of A.

736. **(b): Correct explanation.** Due to small size and highest electronegativity of fluorine, it is more easy to reduce it to the fluoride ion and hence it acts as a strong oxidising agent compared to the other halogens.

737. **(a):** R is the correct explanation of A.

738. **(a):** R is the correct explanation of A.

739. **(a):** R is the correct explanation of A.

740. **(b): Correct explanation.** Acidic strength increases as oxidation number of the halogen in the acid increases.

741. **(d): Correct A.**The HOF bond angle is lower than the HOCl bond angle in HOX.
Correct R. Oxygen is more electronegative than the halogens except fluorine.

GROUP 18

General Introduction

742. **(c):** He, Ne. Due to its very small size and low molecular weight, these possess weak forces of attraction.

743. (d): All these adsorb inert gases.

744. (b): The correct order of occurrence in air (% by weight) is

Ar > Ne > Kr

1.285 1×10^{-3} 2.8×10^{-5}

745. (b): Both He $\left(1s^2\right)$ and $Li^+\left(1s^2\right)$ have two electrons (dielectron species) and thus their spectrum would be similar.

746. (d): Radon is radioactive and is prepared by a disintegration reaction.

$^{226}_{88}Ra \rightarrow {}^{222}_{86}Rn + {}^{4}_{2}He$

747. (b): In the separation of a noble gas mixture from air by Ramsay–Rayleigh's first method, magnesium and copper are used for the removal of N_2 and O_2 respectively.

$3\,Mg + N_2 \rightarrow Mg_3N_2$

$2\,Cu + O_2 \rightarrow 2\,CuO$

748. (d): When the mixture of noble gases is cooled in a coconut bulb at 173 K then Ar, Kr and Xe are adsorbed on charcoal which He and Ne are not adsorbed.

749. (b): Radon is prepared by the disintegration of radium.

$^{226}_{88}Ra \rightarrow {}^{222}_{86}Rn + {}^{4}_{2}He$

750. (b): Rn is obtained (not Kr) during radioactive disintegration.

751. (c): Atomic weight of the noble gases = Molecular weight = 2 × Vapour Density

752. (b): Radon is an inert gas. Its atomic number is 86. It has a stable electronic configuration. It is an element of the zero group. It is a radioactive element.

753. (a): Cleveite (a uranium mineral) on heating gives He gas because it remains entrapped within it and is formed by the disintegration of U-238.

754. (a): Radon is radioactive and is prepared by the disintegration reaction of radium. It does not occur in air.

Atomic and Physical Properties

755. (b): It is an use of Ar.

756. (b): He is the lightest (after H_2), non-inflammable gas.

757. (a): He, because of its non-reactive nature and smaller size, exhibits the weakest intermolecular forces.

758. (a): No unpaired electrons are available.

759. (d): Since noble gases do not have unpaired electrons, their atoms are held together by weak van der Waals forces.

760. (a): Argon is a monoatomic gas, thus its molecules can move in any direction in space. Hence, it can have three independent motions (all translational). Therefore, argon possesses only translational motion.

761. (a): The atomic radius of fluorine is less than that of the next element, noble gas (neon), in which case only van der Waals radius is considered which is larger than the covalent radius.

762. (c): The atomic radii of noble gases are by far the largest in their respective periods. This is due to the reason that noble gases (because they do not form molecules) have only van der Waals radii while other elements have covalent radii. As van der Waals radii, by definition, are larger than covalent radii, therefore, noble gases have comparatively larger atomic sizes.

763. (d): The ionisation enthalpy of O_2 gas (1175 kJ mol^{-1} is closest to that of Xe (1170 kJ mol^{-1}).

764. (d): Peaks represent the highest values. Since noble gases have highest ionisation enthalpy values in their respective periods, these occupy peak positions in the ionisation enthalpy curve.

765. (b): XeO_3 is an explosive pyramidal molecule due to presence of one lone pair of electrons. In Fisher Ringe's method, the oxygen and nitrogen of air are removed by passing it over a mixture of calcium carbide and calcium chloride.

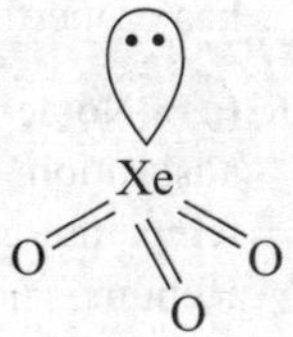

Pyramidal structure

He and Ne both have high ionisation enthalpy and lack of *d*-orbitals, so they are chemically inert. Except He, all inert gases are adsorbed on activated charcoal and the extent of adsorption increases on moving down the group.

766. (a): As the number of shells increase, size increases and the effective nuclear charge on the outermost electron decrease. Thus, IE decreases.

767. (b): As the polarisation increases with increasing size from He to Xe, induced dipole interactions, that is, van der Waals forces of attraction increase and hence the bp goes up.

768. (d): Since the heat of vaporisation of He is the lowest, it is the most difficult to liquefy. Hence He is the most volatile of all liquids.

769. (d): The MP and BP of noble gases show very little difference in their values which shows that solids change to vapours easily.

770. (a): The boiling points of noble gases show a regular increase from He to Rn due to an increase in the magnitude of the van der Waals forces of attraction as the size of the atom increases.

771. (c): Ar is more soluble in water than O_2 and N_2 and also He.

772. (c): Xe > Kr >Ar> Ne > He

Solubility in decreasing order of noble gases.

773. (d): Xe, because of its largest size, shows highest polarisability.

774. (d): He is least polarisable because of its small atomic size.

775. (a): Since the van der Waals forces of attraction increase from He to Xe, as the size of their atoms increases, the ease of liquefaction increases from He to Xe. Thus, Kr is liquefied most easily in this case.

776. (d): He, because of its very small size can diffuse through rubber, glass and PVC easily.

777. (d): Thermal conductivity of noble gases at 273 K and atmospheric pressure decreases with increasing atomic size of the gas from He to Xe.

778. (c): $_1H^2 + {}_1H^2 \xrightarrow{\text{Heat}} {}_2He^4$
Nuclear fusion

779. (b): Gaseous He on cooling below 2.2 K, at one atmosphere pressure gives a new form of helium, He (II) which is an extraordinary conductor of heat (about 600 times more than that of copper). It is frictionless and behaves like a super liquid with nearly zero viscosity. This liquid flows uphill and has properties of a degenerate gas.

780. (d): Noble gases are adsorbed by coconut charcoal. The adsorption of different noble gases occurs at different temperatures. Hence, charcoal is used to separate these gases. Helium is not adsorbed by charcoal as it is a very difficult gas to liquefy.

781. (d): The lightest gas in the periodic table is hydrogen (H_2). Its atomic weight is 1.008. But among the mentioned gases, lightest one is helium (He). Its atomic weight is 4.003.

782. (b): Zero group (group 18) elements show less chemical activity because theelements of this group have 8 electrons in the valence shell.

Chemical Properties (Compounds of Noble Gases)

783. (c): A gas is liquefied by increasing van der Waals' forces.

784. (b): In Greek language, xenon represents strange.

785. (b): Only Xe reacts with F_2 because it has the lowest ionisation enthalpy (energy).

786. (c): $Xe[PtF_6]$ was the first real compound of any of the noble gases which was synthesised in 1962 by N Bartlett.

787. (a): He, due to its very high ionisation enthalpy, forms the least number of compounds.

788. (c): Xe because of its lower ionisation enthalpy, forms the maximum number of compounds.

789. (d): As we go down the group, the reactivity of noble gases increases due to a decrease in the ionisation enthalpy.

790. (b): Out of the given options, Ar is a noble gas. Therefore, due to its completely filled electronic configuration, it shows least chemical activity.

791. (d): Fluorine, the most electronegative and oxidising halogen, forms chemical compounds (fluorides) with the noble gas xenon which has acomparatively low ionisation enthalpy.

792. (a): Among the noble gases, Ar and Xe form the maximum number of compounds due to their comparatively lower ionisation enthalpies.

793. (d): Radon is a radioactive element with a short half life period of 3.82 days which makes the study of the chemistry of radon difficult.

794. (d): In KrF_2, Kr involves sp^3d hybridisation with three lone pairs and two bond pairs surrounding Kr giving a total number of 10 electrons.

795. (b): KrF_2 is a F^- donor and forms complexes with F^- acceptors where only cationic species of Kr will be present.

796. (c): XeF_2 is obtained by the reaction of Xe and F_2 in excess molar ratio (2 : 1) at 673 K.

797. (a): The type of hybridisation of the central atom (sp^3d) here includes both the positions of the atoms as well as lone pairs of electrons whereas the shape/geometry or structure of a molecule implies only the position of atoms (linear).

798. (d): XeF_2 has trigonal bipyramid sp^3d-hybridisation of Xe. The three equatorial positions are occupied by lone pairs giving a linear shape. Thus, it has three lone pairs, XeO_3 has one, XeF_4 has two and XeF_6 has one lone pair.

799. (c): Number of hybrid orbitals (X) $= \frac{1}{2}$ (VE + MA$-c+a$)

For XeF_2: (X) $= \frac{1}{2}(8+2-0+0) = 5$, that is, sp^3d -hybridisation.

For ICl_2^-: (X) $= \frac{1}{2}(7+2-0+1) = 5$, that is, sp^3d-hybridisation.

In both the cases, sp^3d -hybridisation will give trigonal bipyramidal hybrid orbitals with the three equatorial positions occupied by lone pairs of electrons giving a linear shape/geometry to the species.

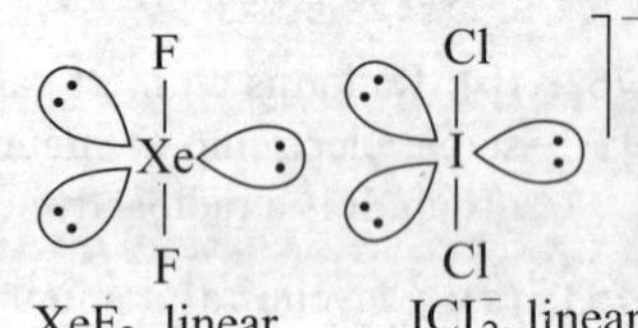

XeF_2, linear structure ICl_2^-, linear structure

800. (a): XeF_2 is a strong oxidising agent. For example, it oxidises iodine (I_2) (zero oxidation state) to I^+ cation in the following reaction.

$$\overset{0}{XeF_2 + I_2} \xrightarrow{BF_3} 2\,\overset{+1}{I}F + Xe$$

801. (c): $Xe + 2\,F_2 \xrightarrow{873\text{ K, bar}} XeF_4$
(1:5 ratio) Ni vessel

802. (d): XeF_4 has octahedral sp^3d^2-hybridisation. The xenon and four fluorine atoms are coplanar while the two axial positions are occupied by the two lone pairs of electrons giving a square planar shape to the molecule.

803. (b): XeF_4 on partial hydrolysis produces $XeOF_2$ as shown below.

$XeF_4 + H_2O \rightarrow XeOF_2 + 2\,HF$

804. (a):

$XeF_4 + H_2O \xrightarrow{-80°C} \underset{\text{Xenon oxyfluoride}}{XeOF_2} + 2\,HeOF_2 + 2\,HF$

805. (a): XeO_3 shows sp^3 hybridisation.

806. (d): Complete and partial hydrolysis of XeF_6 lead to different products as shown below:

$$\overset{+6}{XeF_6} + 3H_2O \xrightarrow[\text{hydrolysis}]{\text{Complete}} \overset{+6}{XeO_3} + 6HF$$

$$\overset{+6\;-1}{XeF_6} + \overset{+1\;-2}{H_2O} \xrightarrow[\text{hydrolysis}]{\text{Partial}} \overset{+6\;-2\;-1}{Xe\,O\,F_4} + \overset{+1\;-1}{2H\,F}$$

$$\overset{+6\;-1}{XeF_6} + \overset{+1\;-2}{2H_2O} \xrightarrow[\text{hydrolysis}]{\text{Partial}} \overset{+6\;-2\;-1}{Xe\,O\,F_2} + \overset{+1\;-1}{4H\,F}$$

Since the oxidation states of all the elements in the products of hydrolysis and reactants remain the same, it is not a redox reaction. It is also not a disproportionation reaction and acid–base reaction.

807. (a): The balanced equation is,
$XeF_6 + H_2O \rightarrow XeO_2F_2 + 4\,HF$
Here, the stoichiometric coefficient of HF is 4. The equation does not represent a redox and disproportionation reaction. It shows partial hydrolysis of XeF_6.

808. (a): Complete hydrolysis of XeF_4 and XeF_6 gives XeO_3.
$6\,XeF_4 + 12\,H_2O \rightarrow 4\,Xe + 2\,XeO_3 + 24\,HF + 3\,O_2$
$XeF_6 + 3\,H_2O \rightarrow XeO_3 + 6\,HF$

809. (b): In BrO_3^-, since O is more electronegative than Br, the –ve charge stays on the O atom. Thus, in BrO_3^-, there are two Br=O and one $Br-O^-$ bonds. According to VSEPR theory, the double bond does not contribute any electron while a single bond contributes one electron towards the total number of electrons in the valence shell of the central atom. Therefore, the total number of electrons in the valence shell of the central Br atom $= 7 + 2\times 0 + 1\times 1 = 8$.

Pyramidal

Number of electron pairs around the Br atom = 8/2 = 4
But total number of bond pairs = 2 × 1 (Br = O) + 1 ×1 $(Br-O^-)$ = 3 and lone pairs = 4 – 3 = 1.
Thus, BrO_3^- has 3 bond pairs and one lone pair. Therefore, according to VSEPR theory, it should be pyramidal.
A noble gas compound having 8 electrons in the valence shell of the central atom is XeO_3 ($8\times1+3\times0=8$). Like BrO_3^-, it also has 3 bond pairs and one lone pair. Therefore, like BrO_3^-, XeO_3 is also pyramidal.

810. (a): XeO_3 has three σ and three π-bonds.

811. (d): In XeO_3, Xe undergoes sp^3-hybridisation with one of the hybrid orbitals occupied by a lone pair of electrons giving a trigonal pyramidal shape.

St. of XeO_3

812. (a): Structure of XeO_3.
Hence, 3 $p\pi–d\pi$ bonds are present. The structure of XeO_4 is:
Hence, 4 $p\pi–d\pi$ bonds are present.

813. (c): This reaction is not feasible because XeF_6 formed will get hydrolysed according to the following reaction.
$XeF_6 + 3\,H_2O \rightarrow XeO_3 + 6\,HF$

814. (c): In $XeOF_2$, Xe undergoes sp^3d hybridisation with the two equatorial positions occupied by the lone pairs of electrons giving a T-shape to the molecule.

815. (b): The geometry is T-shaped.

St. of $XeOF_2$

816. (e): All the compounds such as XeO_3, $XeOF_2$, XeF_4 and XeO_4 can be stored in glass or pyrex vessels except XeF_6 which reacts with SiO_2 of the glass giving XeO_3, an explosive compound.

817. (c): Let us suppose the oxidation state of Xe is x in $XeOF_2$.
$x + (-2) + 2(-1) = 0 \Rightarrow x = 4$

818. (d): XeO_2F_2 has trigonal bipyramid hybrid orbitals due to sp^3d hybridisation of Xe. One equatorial position is occupied by a lone pair of electrons giving a see–saw structure to the molecule.

819. (d): In $[XeF]^+[PtF_6]^-$, the oxidation state of Xe is +2.

820. (c): In XeF_5^-, Xe has 9 electrons in the valence shell.

	5s	5p			5d				
Elec. config. of Xe = (Ground state)	↓↑	↓↑	↓↑	↓↑	↑				
Elect.config. of Xe (Second excited state) and formation of XeF_5^-	↓↑	↓↑	↑	↑	↑	↑	↑		

Xe is sp^3d^2-hybridised with two lone pairs of electrons giving pentagonal bipyramid hybrid orbitals having a pentagonal planar shape.

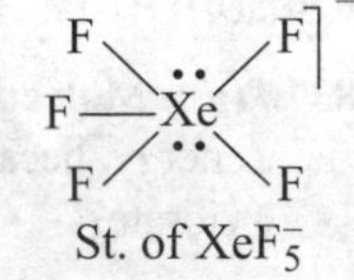

St. of XeF_5^-

821. (b): Welding of Mg is done in an atmosphere of He due to its inert and non-inflammable nature.

822. (b): He is incombustible and also has a high lifting power (92.26%) compared to that of hydrogen.

823. (d): Neon lamps (and not argon lamps) are used in botanical gardens and green houses as it (neon light) stimulates growth and is effective in the formation of chlorophyll.

824. (c): Argon is used in providing an inert atmosphere in the extraction of Ti, Mg.

825. (b): Unlike nitrogen, helium is not soluble in blood even under high pressure. Therefore, a mixture of 80% helium and 20% oxygen is used instead of ordinary air, by deep seadivers for respiration.

826. (b): Helium is much less soluble in blood even under high pressure as compared to nitrogen. Therefore, a mixture of oxygen and helium is used in the diving apparatus used by deep sea divers.

827. (c): Helium is not lighter than hydrogen. It is twice as heavy as hydrogen and also its lifting power is 92% of that of hydrogen.

828. (a):A mixture of helium and oxygen (4 : 1 ratio) is used for the treatment of asthma.

829. (b): Noble gases are used in discharge tubes to give different colours. Reddish orange flow is due to Ne.

830. (c): Helium is used as a cryogenic agent for carrying out various experiments at low temperatures.Argon provides an inert atmosphere in the welding of metals or alloys that are easily oxidised.Neon is used in electric signs (advertising signs).

P_4O_{10} is used as a valuable drying and dehydrating agent.PCl_5 is used in organic reactions for the replacement of hydroxyl group by the chlorine atom, that is, as a chlorinating agent.

831. (a): Clathrates are non-stoichiometric compounds where the ratio of the guest and host molecules does not correspond to the ideal chemical formulae.

832. (d): In the clathrate of Xe with water, the nature of bonding between Xe and H_2O is dipole–induced dipole interaction.

833. (b): Only oxygen and fluorine, due to their larger electronegativity values 3.5 and 4.0 respectively, can oxidise xenon and form compounds with it.

834. (c): The idea that ionisation enthalpies of molecular oxygen (1175 kJ mol^{-1}) and xenon (1170 kJ mol^{-1}) are almost similar prompted Bartlett to prepare the first ever compound of a noble gas.

Final Preparation

835. (a): Rn is radioactive.

836. (b): At 173 K, He and Ne are not adsorbed.

837. (a): Molecules of a noble gas do not possess vibrational energy because a noble gas is monoatomic and does not vibrate.

838. (a): The ionisation enthalpy of any hydrogen-like species (having one electron only) is given by the equation,

$$IE = \frac{2\pi^2 Z^2 me^4}{h^2} \text{ or } IE \propto Z^2$$

Since the atomic number of H is 1 and that of He is 2, the IE of He^+ is four times (2^2) the IE of H, that is, $13.6 \times 4 = 54.4$ eV.

839. (d): Neon has the highest positive (+116 kJ mol^{-1}) electron gain enthalpy.

840. (d): Boiling points, solubility in water and ease of liquefaction decrease from Xe to He as the size of atoms of noble gases decreases in that order. However, ionisation enthalpy increases in the order Xe < Kr <Ar< Ne < He.

841. (c): He II is the liquid form of helium which is obtained on cooling gaseous He to 2.2 K at 1 atm. pressure. It is able to flow uphill like a gas and thus has properties of a degenerate gas.

842. (b): As the size of the halogen increases from F to Br, the electronegativity also decreases, consequently the bond length of Xe–X will increase and thus stability decreases from XeF_2 to $XeBr_2$.

843. (c): $O_2[PtF_6]$ can be written as $O_2^+[Pt^VF_6]^-$.Therefore, the oxidation state of oxygen in $O_2[PtF_6]$ is $+\frac{1}{2}$.

844. (c): Due to the smaller size of F when compared to Cl, the Xe–F bond energy is higher than that of Xe–Cl and thus, xenon fluorides are more stable than xenon chlorides.

845. (c): The stability of new compounds formed depends upon the high bond energy of the bond formed in the new compound and low dissociation energy of the compound from which new compound is formed. Both these conditions are met in the Xe fluorides formed from the F_2 molecule and not in Xe chlorides to be formed from the Cl_2 molecule.

846. (c): If $O_2^+[PtF_6]^-$ is formed,because O_2 and Xe have comparable ionisation enthalpies(1175 and 1170 kJ mol^{-1}, respectively) and molecule diameters ($O_2 = 400$ pm; Xe = 400 pm), therefore, $Xe^+[PtF_6]^-$ can also be formed. Formation of this compound is the basis for the formation of Xe fluorides.

847. (a): 0

$$Xe + Pt^{VI}F_6 \rightarrow [Xe]^+[Pt^VF_6]^-$$

Oxidant

848. (b): $XeF_2 + PF_5 \rightarrow [Xe]^+[PF_6]^-$ (Addition compound)

849. (c):

$$\underset{\text{Lewis base}}{XeF_2} + \underset{\text{Lewis acid}}{2SbF_5} \rightarrow \underset{\text{Adduct}}{XeF_2 . 2SbF_5}$$

or

$[XeF]^+ [Sb_2F_{11}]^-$

850. (d): XeF_2 is linear and the bond angle is 180°. PCl_4^+ is tetrahedral with a bond angle of 109.5°. NO_2^- is angular with a bond angle of 115° and $XeO_3$is trigonal pyramidal with a bond angle less than 109.5°.

851. (b): IBr_2^- has trigonal bipyramidal sp^3d-hybrisation with three lone pairs at equatorial positions giving a linear shape to the anion. XeF_2 is also linear with sp^3d-hybridisation and three lone pairs at equatorial positions.

852. (b):

$$\overset{+2}{Xe}F_2 + \overset{0}{I_2} \xrightarrow{BF_3} 2\overset{+1}{I}F + \overset{0}{Xe}$$

Oxidation state of Xe decreases from +2 in XeF_2 to 0 in Xe and I_2 increases from 0 in I_2 to +1 in IF and thus, XeF_2 acts as an oxidant.

853. (a): Both XeF_2 and IF_2^- are linear species but the central atoms Xe and I undergo sp^3d hybridisation with all the three equatorial positions occupied by lone pairs of electrons.

854. (d): SF_4 has sp^3d hybridisation, a see–saw shape with one lone pair at the equatorial position. CF_4 has sp^3-hybridisation, a tetrahedral shape and no lone pair. XeF_4 has sp^3d^2-hybridisation, a square planar shape with two lone pairs at the axial positions.

855. (b): $XeF_4 + 2 SF_4 \rightarrow Xe + 2 SF_6$

856. (c):

$$3\overset{+4}{Xe}F_4 + 6 H_2O \rightarrow 2 \overset{0}{Xe} + \overset{+6}{Xe}O_3 + 12 HF + 3/2 O_2$$

The oxidation state of Xe changes from +4 in XeF_4 to 0 in Xe and +6 in XeO_3. Thus, it shows disproportionation of Xe.

857. (a): In XeF_4, Xe is sp^3d^2 hybridised with two lone pairs occupying trans positions thus giving a square planar structure. In $[PtCl_4]^{2-}$, Pt^{2+} is dsp^2 hybridised giving a square planar geometry to the complexion.

858. (d):
$2\,XeF_6 + 16OH^- \rightarrow XeO_6^{4-} + Xe$
(Strong solution) (X)
$+ O_2 + 12\,F^- + 8\,H_2O$
$XeO_6^{4-} = x + 6(-2) = -4$
or $x - 12 = -4$
$x = +8$

859. (b): KF is a fluoride ion donor, hence is reacts with XeF_6 to give a fluoroanion.
$XeF_6 + KF \rightarrow K^+[XeF_7]^-$

860. (c):

$$XeF_4 + 3\,H_2O \xrightarrow[\text{hydrolysis}]{\text{Complete}} \underset{(P)}{XeO_3} + 6HF \xrightarrow{OH^-/H_2O} \underset{\text{(Q) (Hydrogen xenate ion)}}{HXeO^-_4}$$

$$\underset{(Q)}{2\,HXeO^-_4} \xrightarrow[\text{Slow disproportionation}]{2OH^-/H_2O} \underset{\text{Perxenate ion}}{XeO_6^{4-}} + Xe(g) + 2H_2O + O_2(g)$$

Thus, the total number of gases released as products is two.

861. (b): XeF_5^+ has octahedral sp^3d^2-hybridisation with one lone pair in the trans position, giving a square pyramid structure. In XeF_5^+, the Xe atom has only seven electrons, that is, $5s^2 5p^5$. In the second excited state, five orbitals are singly occupied which form sigma bonds with five F atoms whereas the sixth hybrid orbital has a lone pair in the trans position.

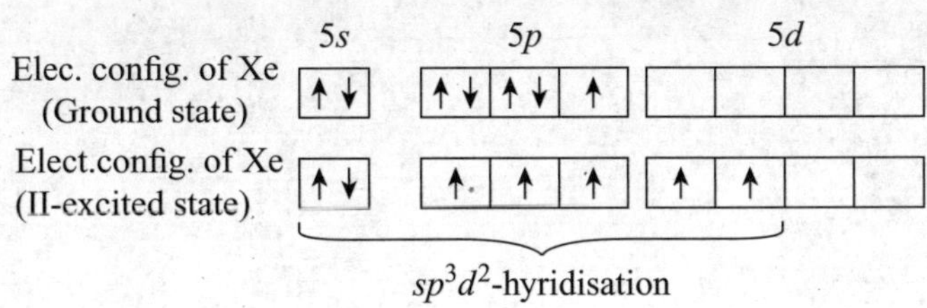

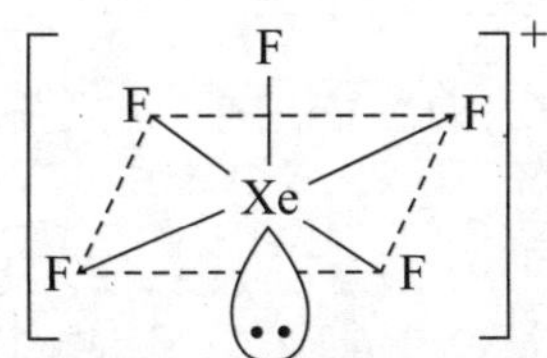

Square pyramid structure

862. (a): The correct decreasing order of the Xe–F bond length is
$XeF_2 > XeF_4 > XeF_6$
200 pm 195 pm 189 pm
Bond shortening with an increase in highly electronegative F atoms attached to Xe can be explained in terms of the increase in the charge on the Xe atom

863. (c): $XeO_3 + 2OH^- \rightarrow HXeO_4^-$
$2H\,XeO_4^- + OH^- \rightarrow XeO_6^{4-} + Xe + O_2 + 2\,H_2O$
Hydrogen xenate ion Perxenate ion

864. (c): $XeO_3 + 6\,H^+ + 6\,I^- \rightarrow Xe + 3\,H_2O + 3\,I_2$

865. (d): XeO_3 is an explosive compound when dry and its explosion power is 22 times more than that of TNT.

866. (d): Both (a) and (b) choices are correct.

867. (b): Neon has a property of carrying exceedingly high current under high voltage.

868. (a): He–O_2 (80% + 20%) mixture is used by deep sea divers for artificial respiration. Because of low intermolecular forces in He, it is much less soluble in aqueous solutions (as compared to N_2) such as blood and does not cause *caissonsickness* or *bends* by bubbling out of blood when the diver moves from high pressure (while in deep sea) to atmospheric pressure.

869. (d): A mixture of Kr and Xe has been used in flash tubes for high speed photography.

870. (a): Liquid helium is used in very low temperature thermometers.

871. (c): The half-life of Rn is only 3.8 days. Ar is used in electric bulbs. Rn is obtained during radioactive disintegration. He is used in producing very low temperatures.

872. (a): Nitrogen gas prepared from air contains Ar as an impurity which is present in the atmosphere most abundantly.

873. (c): Noble gases constitute about 1% of the total volume of air. The remaining 99% volume is mainly due to oxygen and nitrogen. When 1 litre (1000 mL) of air is passed over heated copper, oxygen is consumed and further,onpassing over magnesium, nitrogen is consumed according to the equations:
$2\,Cu + O_2 \rightarrow 2\,CuO$; $3\,Mg + N_2 \rightarrow Mg_3N_2$
In this way about 990 mL of air is consumed. The remaining volume of about 10 mL is due to mainly Ar and other noble gases.

874. (d): In this method, dry air is passed over a mixture of 90% CaC_2 and 10% $CaCl_2$ at 1073 K to remove O_2 and N_2. Now the mixture of gases containing CO_2, CO and the noble gases is passed over heated CuO to convert CO to CO_2 which is absorbed in KOH solution and the left over noble gases are dried over P_2O_5 and separated by Dewar's charcoal adsorption method.

MATCH THE FOLLOWING

875. (d): (A) XeO_3 is trigonal pyramid
(B) $XeOF_4$ is square pyramid
(C) BO_3^{3-} is planar triangular
(D) ClF_3 is T-shaped and
(E) I_3^- is linear

876. (a): (A) $2\,XeF_2 + 2\,H_2O \rightarrow 2\,Xe + 4\,HF + O_2$
(B) $6\,XeF_4 + 12\,H_2O \rightarrow 2\,XeO_3 + 4\,Xe + 24\,HF + 3\,O_2$
(Complete hydrolysis)
$XeF_4 + H_2O \rightarrow XeOF_2 + 2\,HF$ (Partial hydrolysis)

(C) $XeF_6 + 3\ H_2O \rightarrow XeO_3 + 6\ HF$
(D) $XeO_2F_2 + H_2O \rightarrow XeO_3 + 2\ HF$

877. (b): (A) XeF_2 has sp^3d hybridisation with three lone pairs at the equatorial positions giving a linear shape.
(B) In $XeOF_2$, Xe is sp^3d hybridised with two lone pairs of electrons at the equatorial positions giving a T-shape.
(C) In XeO_2F_2, Xe is sp^3d hybridised with one lone pair at the equatorial position giving a see–saw shape.
(D) In XeO_3F_2, Xe is sp^3d hybridised with no lone pair giving trigonal bipyramidal structure.

ASSERTION REASON

878. (a): R is the correct explanation of A.

879. (d): Correct A. All the noble gases except He have the ns^2np^6 electronic configuration in their outermost shell.
Correct R. In the noble gases, all the energy levels which are occupied are completely filled.

880. (c): Correct R. Electronic configuration of He (X = 2) is $1s^2$ which is a noble gas whereas the electronic configuration of Be (Z = 4) is $1s^2\ 2s^2$ which is a chemically reactive element.

881. (a): R is the correct explanation of A.

882. (a):R is the correct explanation of A.

883. (d): Correct A. The melting points/boiling points of noble gases are quite low.
Correct R. The interparticle forces among noble gases are weak van der Waals forces.

884. (d):Correct A. Noble gases are sparingly soluble in water.
Correct R. Solubility in water increases with an increase in size of the noble gas due to increase in dipole induced dipole interaction.

885. (a): R is the correct explanation of A.

886. (b): Correct explanation. Fluorine and oxygen are highly electronegative and they increase the tendency of noble gases to lose electrons and form strong bonds.

887. (d): Correct A. He and Ne do not form compounds with fluorine.
Correct R. He and Ne do not contain *d*orbitals in their valence shells

888. (c): Correct R. Fluorine has a higher electronegativity (4.0) than oxygen (3.5). Thus, both oxygen and fluorine have high electronegativity.

889. (a): R is the correct explanation of A.

890. (c): Correct R. Xe atom is sp^3d^2 hybridised with four bond pairs and two lone pairs of electrons around it.

891. (c): Correct R. Hydrogenxenate ion slowly disproportionates to give Xe and the perxenate ion, XeO_6^{4-}.

892. (b): Correct explanation. Perxenate ion $(XeO_6)^{4-}$ contains Xe in the +8 oxidation state which can be reduced to give the xenate ion $(XeO_4)^{2-}$ containing Xe in the +6 oxidation state. Thus, perxenate solutions are powerful oxidising agents.

893. (c): Correct R. Xe shows sp^3d-hybridisation with no lone pair.

d- and f-Block Elements

8.1 Transition Elements (d-Block Elements)

Transition elements are those elements which have incompletely filled (partly filled) d-subshells in their ground state or in any one of their oxidation states. In the periodic table, there are four main transition series of elements corresponding to filling of the 3*d*, 4*d*, 5*d* and 6*d* sublevels in the 4th, 5th, 6th and 7th periods (Tables 8.1–8.4). Their general electronic configuration is $(n-1)d^{1-10}\,ns^{0-2}$ here *n* is the outermost shell.

8.1.1 Transition Series

We know that half-filled and completely-filled electronic configurations (d^5 and d^{10}) have extra stability associated with them. Therefore, the electronic configuration of Cr is [Ar] $3d^5\,4s^1$ rather than [Ar] $3d^4\,4s^2$ while that of Cu is [Ar] $3d^{10}\,4s^1$ instead of [Ar] $3d^9\,4s^2$.

8.1.2 Exceptional Behaviour of Zinc, Cadmium and Mercury

Due to the presence of a completely filled d^{10} configuration, Zn, Cd and Hg show exceptional behaviour as compared to the other members of their respective series. Zinc differs from the other members in the following characteristics.

- It has a much higher atomic radius and ionisation enthalpy.
- Its compounds are white while those of the other members are coloured.

Table 8.1 First (3*d*) transition series

At. no.	21	22	23	24	25	26	27	28	29	30
Element	Sc	Ti	V	Cr	Mn	Fe	Co	Ni	Cu	Zn
EC	$3d^14s^2$	$3d^24s^2$	$3d^34s^2$	$3d^44s^1$	$3d^54s^2$	$3d^64s^2$	$3d^74s^2$	$3d^84s^2$	$3d^{10}4s^1$	$3d^{10}4s^2$

Table 8.2 Second (4*d*) transition series

At. no.	39	40	41	42	43	44	45	46	47	48
Element	Y	Zr	Nb	Mo	Tc	Co	Rh	Pd	Ag	Cd
EC	$4d^15s^2$	$4d^25s^2$	$4d^45s^1$	$4d^55s^1$	$4d^65s^1$	$4d^75s^1$	$4d^85s^1$	$4d^{10}5s^0$	$4d^{10}5s^1$	$4d^{10}5s^2$

Table 8.3 Third (5*d*) transition series

At. no.	57	72	73	74	75	76	77	78	79	80
Element	La	Hf	Ta	W	Re	Os	Ir	Pt	Au	Hg
EC	$5d^16s^2$	$5d^26s^2$	$5d^36s^2$	$5d^46s^2$	$5d^56s^2$	$5d^66s^2$	$5d^76s^2$	$5d^76s^1$	$5d^{10}6s^1$	$5d^{10}6s^2$

Table 8.4 Fourth (6*d*) transition series

At. no.	89	104	105	106	107	108	109	110	111	112
Element	Ac	Ku	Ha	Sg	Bh	Hs	Mt	Uun	Uuu	Uub
EC	$6d^17s^2$	$6d^27s^2$	$6d^37s^2$	$6d^47s^2$	$6d^57s^2$	$6d^67s^2$	$6d^77s^2$	$6d^87s^2$	$6d^{10}7s^1$	$6d^{10}7s^2$

- It does not show variable oxidation states unlike other members.
- Its compounds (containing Zn^{2+} ions) are diamagnetic while those of the other members are paramagnetic.

8.2 General Properties of Transition Elements

8.2.1 Atomic Radii

The atomic radii of the transition elements are intermediate between those of the *s*- and *p*-block elements.

(i) The atomic radii of elements of a particular series decrease with an increase in atomic number but this decrease in atomic radii becomes small after the midway point. After the midway point, as the electrons enter the penultimate shell, the added *d* electron shields (screens) the outermost electron. Hence, the screening effect increases.

(ii) In the second and third transition series, towards the end of the series, the increased electron–electron repulsions between added electrons in the same orbitals are greater than the attractive forces due to the increased nuclear charge. This results in the expansion of the electron cloud and thus the atomic radius increases.

(iii) The atomic radii increase while going down the group. But, the atomic radii of the second and third transition series are almost the same due to *lanthanide contraction*.

8.2.2 Ionic Radii

(i) The trend followed by the ionic radii is the same as that followed by the atomic radii.

(ii) Ionic radii of the transition metals are different in different oxidation states.

8.2.3 Metallic Character

All the transition elements have a typical metallic structure (hcp, ccp or bcc) except for mercury which is a liquid. The metallic character of transition elements is due to their relatively low ionisation enthalpies. The unpaired *d*-electrons also result in the formation of metallic bonds. Thus, in the formation of metallic bonds, both *ns* and $(n-1)$ *d* electrons participate. The hardness of these metals is due to overlap of unpaired electrons between different metal atoms. Therefore, these elements exhibit high enthalpies of atomisation. The greater the number of unpaired *d* electrons, the greater is the number of bonds and therefore, the greater is the strength of these bonds.

8.2.4 Melting and Boiling Points

The high melting and boiling points of these metals are due to strong metallic bonds between the atoms of these elements. The strength of bonding is roughly related to the number of unpaired electrons. In a particular series, the metallic strength increases up to the middle with the increasing number of unpaired electrons, that is, up to d^5 configuration. After Cr, the number of unpaired electrons goes on decreasing (for example, Fe has 4, Co has 3 unpaired electrons and so on). Accordingly, the melting points decrease after the middle (Cr) because of increasing pairing of electrons. There are no unpaired electrons in Zn, Cd and Hg, they are soft and have low melting points. Hg is a liquid at ordinary temperature.

8.2.5 Ionisation Enthalpies

(i) The first ionisation enthalpies of the *d*-block elements are higher than those of the *s*-block elements but are less than those of the *p*-block elements. The ionisation enthalpies increase as we move across each series, though not quite regularly.

(ii) The first ionisation enthalpies of Zn, Cd and Hg are, however, very high because of the fully filled $(n-1)d^{10}ns^2$ configuration.

(iii) The value of the second ionisation enthalpy for zinc is correspondingly low because the ionisation involves the removal of an electron, resulting in a stable $3d^{10}$ configuration.

8.2.6 Density

As we move along a transition series from the left to right, the atomic volume decreases. At the same time, the atomic mass increases. Hence, the *density increases*.

8.2.7 Standard Electrode Potentials ($E°$) and Chemical Reactivity

Smaller the ionisation enthalpy of the metal, the more stable are its compounds. For example, nickel (II) compounds are more stable than platinum (II) whereas platinum (IV) compounds are more stable than nickel (IV).

In solution, the stability of the compounds depends upon electrode potentials rather than the ionisation enthalpies. Electrode potential values depend upon factors such as enthalpy of sublimation (or atomisation) of the metal, the ionisation enthalpy and the hydration enthalpy.

$$\mathrm{M}(s) \xrightarrow{\Delta_{\text{sub}}H} \mathrm{M}(g)$$

($\Delta_{\text{sub}}H$ is enthalpy of sublimation/atomisation)

$$\mathrm{M}(g) \xrightarrow{\Delta_i H} \mathrm{M}^+(g) + e^-, \ (\Delta_i H \text{ is ionisation enthalpy})$$

$$\mathrm{M}^+(g) + aq \xrightarrow{\Delta_{\text{hyd}}H} \mathrm{M}^+(aq)$$

($\Delta_{\text{hyd}}H$ is enthalpy of hydration)

$$\Delta_{\text{T}}H = \Delta_{\text{sub}}H + \Delta_{\text{i}}H + \Delta_{\text{hyd}}H$$

Trends in the M^{2+}/M Standard Electrode Potentials

- There is no regular trend in these values. The electron potentials of transition metals are low in comparison to the elements of group 2.
- Zinc has a low enthalpy of atomisation and fairly large hydration energy. But it also has low electrode potential

(–0.76 V) because of its very high ionisation enthalpy ($IE_1 + IE_2$).

- Copper has a positive reduction potential, E° (0.34 V) and copper is the least reactive metal out of the first transition series. In general, the value becomes less negative across the series. This is related to the general increase in the sum of the first and second ionisation enthalpies.

Chemical Reactivity and E° Values

- The metals of the first transition series (except copper) are relatively more reactive than the other series. Less negative E° value for M^{2+}/M along the series indicates a decreasing tendency to form divalent cations.
- The more negative E° values than expected for Mn, Ni and Zn show greater stability for Mn^{2+}, Ni^{2+} and Zn^{2+}.
- E° values for the redox couple M^{3+}/M^{2+} indicate that Mn^{3+} and Co^{3+} ions are the strongest oxidising agents in aqueous solution whereas Ti^{2+}, V^{2+} and Cr^{2+} are the strongest reduction agents and can liberate hydrogen from a dilute acid. For example,

$$2\,Cr^{2+}(aq) + 2\,H^+(aq) \rightarrow 2\,Cr^{3+}(aq) + H_2(g)$$

8.2.8 Oxidation States

All transition elements, except the first and last member of the series, exhibit a number of oxidation states (Table 8.5).

Table 8.5 Commonly shown oxidation states of transition metals (very rare oxidation states are given in parentheses and most common ones are enclosed in boxes for first transition series)

1st Series:	Sc	Ti	V	Cr	Mn	Fe	Co	Ni	Cu	Zn
									+1	
		(+2)	+2	+2	**+2**	**+2**	**+2**	**+2**	**+2**	**+2**
	+3	+3	+3	**+3**	+3	**+3**	**+3**	+3		
		+4	+4	+4	+4	+4	+4	+4		
			+5	+5	+5					
				+6	+6	+6				
					+7					

2nd Series:	Y	Zr	Nb	Mo	Tc	Ru	Rh	Pd	Ag	Cd
									+1	
			(+2)	+2	+2	+2	+2	+2	(+2)	+2
	+3	(+3)	(+3)	+3		+3	+3	(+3)	(+3)	
		+4	(+4)	+4	(+4)	+4	+4	+4		
			+5	+5	(+5)	(+5)				
				+6		(+6)	(+6)			
					+7	(+7)				
						(+8)				

3rd Series:	La	Hf	Ta	W	Re	Os	Ir	Pt	Au	Hg	
						(+1)				+1	+1
				(+2)	+2	(+2)	+2	+2	+2		+2
		+3	(+3)	(+3)	+3)	+3	+3	+3	(+3)	+3	
			+4	(+4)	+4	+4	+4	+4	+4		
				+5	+5	+5			(+5)		
					+6	(+6)	+6	(+6)	(+6)		
						+7					
							+8				

The transition elements have their valence electrons in two different sets of orbitals, that is, $(n-1)d$ and ns. Since there is very little difference in the energies of these orbitals, both energy levels can be used for bond formation. The higher oxidation states such as +3, +4, +5, +6 and +7 correspond to the use of all 4s and 3d electrons in the transition series of elements.

Trends in the Stability of Higher Oxidation States of Transition Metal Halides

The stable halides of the transition metals of the first transition series in different oxidation states such as given in Table 8.6.

Trends in the Stability of Higher Oxidation States of Transition Metal Oxides

Some results observed from Table 8.7 are given below.

- Besides the oxides, higher oxidation states are also found in the oxocations and oxoanions. For example, V (V) in VO_2^+, V (IV) in VO^{2+} and Ti (IV) in TiO^{2+} and Mn (VII) in MnO_4^-, Cr (VI) in CrO_4^- and $Cr_2O_7^{2-}$ and V (V) in VO_4^{3-} (vanadate ion).
- The highest fluoride of Mn is MnF_4 whereas the highest oxide is Mn_2O_7. The reason for this is the ability of oxygen to form multiple bonds with the metal atoms. For example, the structure of Mn_2O_7 is shown below.

(Mn_2O_7)

- Each Mn is tetrahedrally surrounded by four O atoms including a Mn–O–Mn bridge. Similarly, $[MO_4]^{n-}$ ions in a tetrahedral structure where M = V (V), Cr (VI), Mn (V), Mn (VI) and Mn (VII).

8.2.9 Catalytic Properties

Many of the transition metals and their compounds are used as catalysts. Some examples are listed.

Table 8.6 Stable halides of the 3d series in different oxidation states ($X = F \rightarrow I$; exceptions are given in brackets)

Oxidation No.	Ti	V	Cr	Mn	Fe	Co	Ni	Cu	Zn
+6	—	—	CrF_6	—	—	—	—	—	
+5	—	VF_5	CrF_5	—	—	—	—	—	
+4	TiX_4	VX_4 (F^-, Cl^-, Br^-)	CrX_4	MnF_4	—	—	—	—	
+3	TiX_3	VX_3	CrX_3	MnF_3	FeX_3 (F^-, Cl^-, Br^-)	CoF_3	—	—	
+2	TiX_2 (Cl^-, Br^-, I^-)	VX_2 (Cl^-, Br^-, I^-)	CrX_2	MnF_2	FeX_3	CoX_2	NiX_2	CuX_2 (F^-, Cl^-)	
+1	—	—	—	—	—	—	—	CuX (Cl^-, Br^-, I^-)	

Table 8.7 Oxides of metals of first transition series in different oxidation states (mixed oxides)

Oxidation No.	Sc (Gr3)	Ti (Gr4)	V (Gr5)	Cr (Gr6)	Mn (Gr7)	Fe (Gr8)	Co (Gr9)	Ni (Gr10)	Cu (Gr11)	Zn (Gr12)
+7					Mn_2O_7	—				
+6				CrO_3	—	—				
+5			V_2O_5	—	—	—				
+4		TiO_2	V_2O_4	CrO_3	MnO_2	—	—	—	—	—
+3	Sc_2O_3	TiO_3	V_2O_3	Cr_2O_3	Mn_2O_3 $Mn_3O_4^*$	Fe_2O_3 $Fe_3O_4^*$	— $Co_3O_4^*$	—	—	—
+2	—	TiO	VO	(CrO)	MnO	FeO	CoO	NiO	CuO	ZnO
+1	—	—	—	—	—	—	—	—	Cu_2O	—
	—	—	—	—	—	—	—	—	Cu_2O	—

- *Vanadium* as V_2O_5 in the manufacture of H_2SO_4 by the contact process.
- *Cobalt* as cobalt–thorium in the Fischer–Tropsch process in the synthesis of gasoline (petrol).
- *Nickel* in the finely divided state for the hydrogenation reaction. For example, hydrogenation of oils into fats.

The catalytic properties of the transition elements are probably due to the presence of unpaired electrons in their incomplete orbitals and hence possess the capacity to absorb and re-emit a wide range of energies. In some cases, the transition element (catalyst) with varying oxidation states may form intermediate compounds with one of the reactants which provide a new path with lower activation energy. Further, they get decomposed on reaction with the other reactants, regenerating the catalyst (transition metal).

$$\underset{\text{One reactant}}{X} + \underset{\text{Transition metal}}{\text{Catalyst}} \rightarrow \underset{\substack{\text{Intermediate unstable compound}\\\text{(Activated complex)}}}{\text{X.Catalyst}}$$

$$\text{X.Catalyst} + \underset{\text{Other reactant}}{Y} \rightarrow \underset{\text{Product}}{XY} + \text{Catalyst}$$

In a number of cases, the transition metal provides a suitable large surface area with free valencies on which the reactants are adsorbed. Hence, the rate of reaction increases (*adsorption theory*).

Coloured Ions

Most of the transition metal compounds (ionic as well as covalent) are coloured both in the solid state and in aqueous solution (Table 8.8). This is due to the presence of an incomplete $(n-1)d$-subshell. Under the influence of approaching ions towards the central metal ion, the *d* orbitals of the central metal split into different energy levels. This phenomenon is called crystal field splitting (Fig. 8.1).

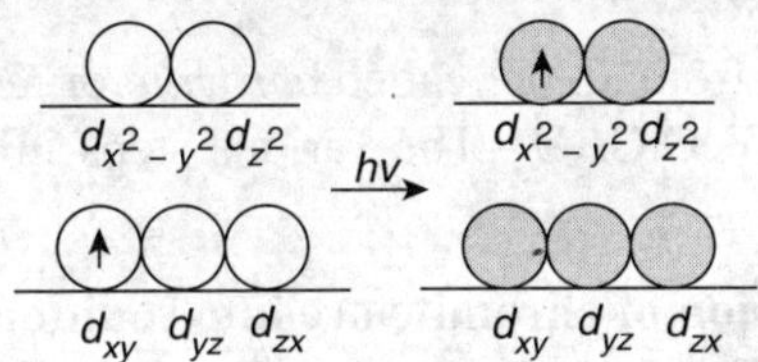

Fig. 8.1 *d–d* transition

One or more electrons are promoted from a lower to a higher level within the same *d* subshell. The energy required to promote such an electron is very small. The transition metal ions have a property to absorb such radiations from visible light and appear coloured due to emission of the remainder as coloured light. The observed colour of a substance is always the complementary colour of the colour absorbed by the substance (Fig. 8.2).

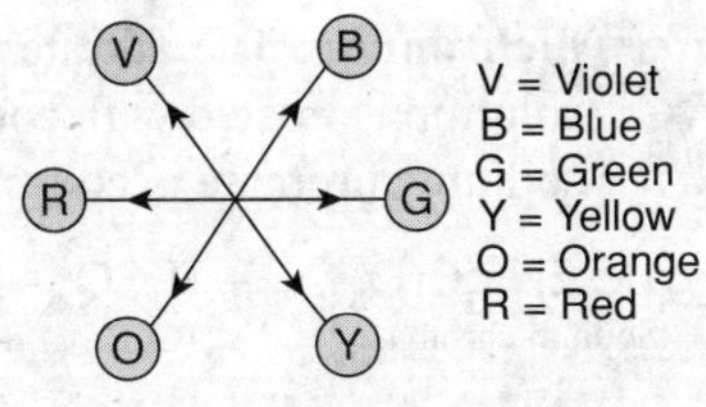

Fig. 8.2

Table 8.8 Colours of hydrated transition metal ions

Ion	Outer configuration	Colour of the ion
Sc (II), Ti (IV)	$3d^0$	Colourless
Ti (III)	$3d^1$	Purple
V (IV)	$3d^1$	Blue
V (III)	$3d^2$	Green
V (II), Cr (III)	$3d^3$	Violet
Mn (III)	$3d^4$	Violet
Cr (II)	$3d^4$	Blue
Mn (II)	$3d^5$	Pink
Fe (III)	$3d^5$	Yellow
Fe (II)	$3d^6$	Green
Co (III)	$3d^6$	Blue
Co (II)	$3d^7$	Pink
Ni (II)	$3d^8$	Green
Cu (II)	$3d^9$	Blue
Cu (I)	$3d^{10}$	Colourless
Zn (II)	$3d^{10}$	Colourless

8.2.10 Magnetic Properties

The magnetic properties of a compound are a measure of the number of unpaired electrons it has.

- *Paramagnetic substances*: The substances that are attracted by a magnetic field are called paramagnetic substances and this character arises due to the presence of unpaired electrons in the atomic orbitals.
- *Diamagnetic substances*: The substances that are repelled by a magnetic field are called diamagnetic substances and this character arises due to the presence of paired electrons in the atomic orbitals.

Substances that are very strongly attracted by the applied field are called *ferromagnetic*.

As the number of unpaired electrons increases from one to five, the magnetic moment and hence paramagnetic character also increases. Magnetic moments are calculated from the *spin only formula*,

$$\mu = \sqrt{n(n+2)}\ \text{BM}$$

where *n* is the number of unpaired electrons and BM stands for Bohr magneton.

8.2.11 Tendency to Form Complexes

Transition metal ions form a large number of complex compounds. For example, $[Fe(CN)_6]^{3-}$, $[Fe(CN)_6]^{2+}$,

$[Zn(NH_3)_4]^{2+}$, $[Ni(CN)_4]^{2-}$ and $[PtCl_4]^{2-}$. Such complex compounds are not formed by *s*- and *p*-block elements. The high tendency of transition metal ions to form complexes is due to,

- the small size of the atoms and ions of transition metals,
- high nuclear charge, and
- availability of vacant *d* orbitals of suitable energy to accept lone pairs of electrons donated by other groups (called ligands).

8.2.12 Formation of Interstitial Compounds

The small atoms of these non-metallic elements (H, B, C, N) get trapped in the vacant spaces of the lattices of the transition metal atoms (Fig. 8.3).

They are represented by formulae such as TiC, TiH_2, Mn_4N, Fe_3H, FeC. Some of their important characteristics are as follows.

- They are very hard and rigid; for example, steel which is an interstitial compound of Fe and C. They have high melting points which are higher than those of the pure metals.
- They retain metallic conductivity.
- They acquire chemical inertness.

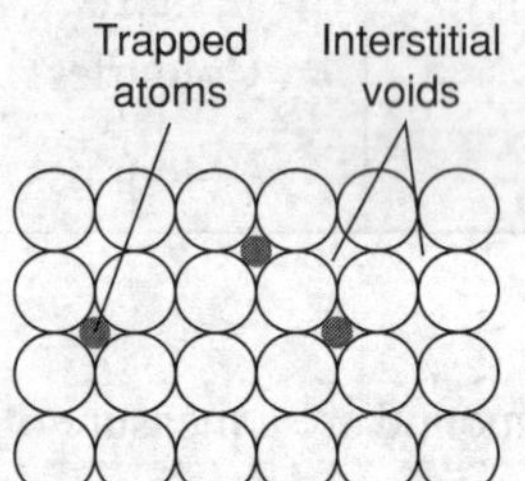

Fig. 8.3 Formation of interstitial compounds

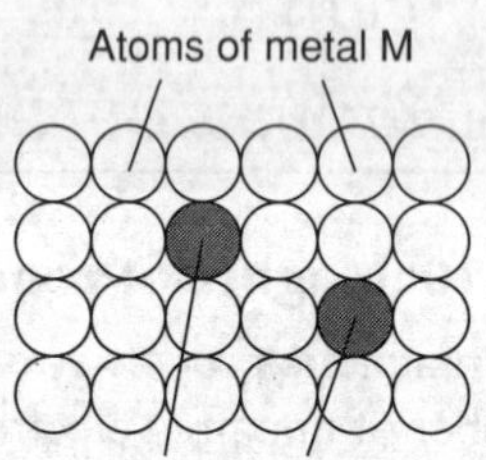

Fig. 8.4 Formation of alloys

8.2.13 Alloy Formation

Alloys are homogeneous solid solutions of two or more metals obtained by melting the components and then cooling the melt. These are formed by metals whose atomic radii differ by not more than 15% so that the atoms of one metal can easily take up the positions in the crystal lattice of the other (Fig. 8.4).

Some alloys of transition metals with non-transition metals are also very common; for example, brass (Cu + Zn) and bronze (Cu + Sn).

8.3 Important Compounds of Transition Elements

8.3.1 Oxides and Oxoanions of Metals

- The metals of the first transition series form oxides with oxygen at high temperature. The general formulae of the oxides are: MO, M_2O_3, M_3O_4, MO_2, M_2O_5 and MO_3.
- The oxides are formed in the oxidation, states +1 to +7.
- The highest oxidation state in the oxides of any transition metal is equal to its group number; for example, 7 in Mn_2O_7. All the metals except scandium form oxides with the formula MO which are ionic in nature. As the oxidation number of the metal increases, the ionic character decreases. For example, Mn_2O_7 is a covalent green oil. Even CrO_3 and V_2O_5 have low melting points.

+2	+8/3	+3	+4	+7
MnO	Mn_3O_4	Mn_2O_3	MnO_2	Mn_2O_7

Ionic character decreases →

- In general, the oxides of higher oxidation states of metal are acidic. For example, CrO is basic; Cr_2O_3 and CrO_2 are amphoteric while CrO_3 is acidic. Similarly, Mn_2O_7 is acidic.

For example, the behaviour of the oxides of manganese may be represented as follows:

+2	+8/3	+3	+4	+7
MnO	Mn_3O_4	Mn_2O_3	MnO_2	Mn_2O_7
Basic	Amphoteric	Amphoteric	Amphoteric	Acidic

Acidic character increases →

Thus, Mn_2O_7 dissolves in water to give the acid $HMnO_4$.

8.4 Potassium Dichromate ($K_2Cr_2O_7$)

8.4.1 Preparation

It is prepared from an ore called *chromite* or *ferrochrome* or *chrome* iron, $FeO.Cr_2O_3$. The various steps involved are as follows.

(i) Conversion of chromite ore into sodium chromate:

$$\underset{\text{Chromite ore}}{4\,FeCr_2O_4} + 16\,NaOH + \underset{\text{(Air)}}{7O_2} \rightarrow \underset{\text{Sodium chromate}}{8\,Na_2CrO_4} + 2\,Fe_2O_3 + 8\,H_2O$$

Or, $$4FeCr_2O_4 + 8Na_2CO_3 + 7O_2 \rightarrow 8Na_2CrO_4 + 2Fe_2O_3 + 8CO_2$$

(ii) Conversion of sodium chromate into sodium dichromate: The filtrate containing sodium chromate solution is treated with concentrated sulfuric acid when sodium chromate is converted into sodium dichromate.

$$\underset{\text{Sodium chromate}}{2Na_2CrO_4} + \underset{\text{(Conc.)}}{H_2SO_4} \rightarrow \underset{\text{Sodium dichromate}}{Na_2Cr_2O_7} + Na_2SO_4 + H_2O$$

(iii) Conversion of sodium dichromate into potassium dichromate: Hot concentrated solution of sodium dichromate is treated with a calculated amount of potassium chloride when potassium dichromate, being much less soluble than sodium salt, crystallises out on cooling as orange crystals.

$$\underset{\text{Sodium dichromate}}{Na_2Cr_2O_7} + 2KCl \rightarrow \underset{\text{Potassium dichromate}}{K_2Cr_2O_7} + 2NaCl$$

8.4.2 Properties

(i) Action of heat: It decomposes on heating to form potassium chromate, chromic oxide and oxygen.

$$4K_2Cr_2O_7 \rightarrow 4K_2CrO_4 + 2Cr_2O_3 + 3O_2$$

(ii) Action of alkalies: On heating with alkalies, the orange colour of dichromate solution changes to yellow due to the formation of chromate ions.

$$\underset{\text{Potassium dichromate}}{K_2Cr_2O_7} + 2KOH \rightarrow \underset{\text{Potassium chromate}}{2K_2CrO_4} + H_2O$$

or $Cr_2O_7^{2-} + 2\,OH^- \rightarrow 2\,CrO_4^{2-} + H_2O$

On acidifying the yellow solution, the colour again changes to orange-red due to the reversible reaction.

$$2\,K_2CrO_4 + H_2SO_4 \rightarrow K_2Cr_2O_7 + K_2SO_4 + H_2O$$

Or $2CrO_4^{2-} + 2\,H^+ \rightarrow Cr_2O_7^{2-} + H_2O$

This interconversion is explained by the fact that in dichromate solution, the $Cr_2O_7^{2-}$ ions are invariably in equilibrium with CrO_4^{2-} ions at a pH = 4.

$$\underset{\substack{\text{Orange-red}\\\text{(dichromate)}}}{Cr_2O_7^{2-}} + H_2O \xrightleftharpoons{pH=4} \underset{\substack{\text{Yellow}\\\text{(chromate)}}}{2CrO_4^{2-}} + 2H^+$$

(iii) Action of concentrated sulfuric acid

(a) In the cold, red crystals of chromic anhydride (chromium trioxide) are formed.

$$K_2Cr_2O_7 + 2H_2SO_4 \rightarrow 2CrO_3 + 2KHSO_4 + H_2O$$

(b) On heating the mixture, oxygen is evolved.

$$2K_2Cr_2O_7 + 8H_2SO_4 \rightarrow 2K_2SO_4 + 2Cr_2(SO_4)_3 + 8H_2O + 3O_2$$

(iv) Chromyl chloride test (reaction with a chloride and conc. sulfuric acid): When heated with concentrated hydrochloric acid or with a chloride and strong sulfuric acid, reddish-brown vapours of chromyl chloride are obtained.

$$K_2Cr_2O_7 + 2H_2SO_4 \rightarrow 2KHSO_4 + 2CrO_3 + H_2O$$
$$KCl + H_2SO_4 \rightarrow KHSO_4 + HCl] \times 4$$
$$2CrO_3 + 4HCl \rightarrow 2CrO_2Cl_2 + 2H_2O$$

$$K_2Cr_2O_7 + 6H_2SO_4 + 3KCl \rightarrow \underset{\substack{\text{Chromyl chloride}\\\text{(Red vapour)}}}{2CrO_2Cl_2} + 6KHSO_4 + 3H_2O$$

(v) Oxidising properties: In the presence of dilute sulfuric acid, $K_2Cr_2O_7$ liberates nascent oxygen and therefore, acts as an oxidising agent.

$$K_2Cr_2O_7 + 4H_2SO_4 \rightarrow K_2SO_4 + Cr_2(SO_4)_3 + 4H_2O + 3O$$

or $Cr_2O_7^{2-} + 14H^+ + 6e^- \rightarrow 2Cr^{3+} + 7H_2O$

In other words, $Cr_2O_7^{2-}$ ion takes up electrons and hence acts as an oxidising agent. Thus, $Cr_2O_4^{2-}$ ion gains 6 electrons. In the above reaction, Cr(+6) is reduced to Cr(+3) so that the total decrease in the oxidation state of the $Cr_2O_4^{2-}$ ion is 6.

$$\therefore \quad \text{Eq. wt of } K_2Cr_2O_7 = \frac{\text{Mol.wt.}}{6} = \frac{294}{6} = 49$$

Some of the oxidising properties of $K_2Cr_2O_7$ in presence of dilute H_2SO_4 are given below.

- It liberates I_2 from KI.

$$K_2Cr_2O_7 + 4H_2SO_4 \rightarrow K_2SO_4 + Cr_2(SO_4)_3 + 4H_2O + 3O$$
$$6KI + 3H_2SO_4 + 3O \rightarrow 3K_2SO_4 + 3I_2 + 3H_2O$$

$$K_2Cr_2O_7 + 7K_2SO_4 + 6KI \rightarrow 4K_2SO_4 + Cr_2(SO_4)_3 + 3I_2 + 7H_2O$$

or $Cr_2O_7^{2-} + 14H^+ + 6I^- \rightarrow 2Cr^{3+} + 7H_2O + 3I_2$

- It oxidises ferrous salts to ferric salts.

$$K_2Cr_2O_7 + 4H_2SO_4 \rightarrow K_2SO_4 + Cr_2(SO_4)_3 + 4H_2O + 3O$$
$$2FeSO_4 + H_2SO_4 + O \rightarrow Fe_2(SO_4)_3 + H_2O] \times 3$$

$$K_2Cr_2O_7 + 7K_2SO_4 + FeSO_4 \rightarrow K_2SO_4 + Cr_2(SO_4)_3 + 3Fe_2(SO_4)_3 + 2H_2O$$

or $Cr_2O_7^{2-} + 6Fe^{2+} + 14H^+ \rightarrow 2Cr^{3+} + 6Fe^{2+} + 7H_2O$

The above two reactions are used in the estimation of iodine and ferrous iron in volumetric analysis.

- It oxidises hydrogen sulfide to sulfur.

$$K_2Cr_2O_7 + 4H_2SO_4 \rightarrow K_2SO_4 + Cr_2(SO_4)_3 + 4H_2O + 3O$$
$$H_2S + O \rightarrow H_2O + S] \times 3$$

$$K_2Cr_2O_7 + 4H_2SO_4 + 3H_2S \rightarrow K_2SO_4 + Cr_2(SO_4)_3 + 2H_2O + 3S$$

or $Cr_2O_7^{2-} + 8H^+ + 3H_2S \rightarrow 2Cr^{3+} + 7H_2O + 3S$

- It oxidises sulfites to sulfates and thiosulfates to sulfates and sulfur.

$$K_2Cr_2O_7 + 4H_2SO_4 \rightarrow K_2SO_4 + Cr_2(SO_4)_3 + 4H_2O + 3O$$
$$Na_2SO_3 + O \rightarrow Na_2SO_4] \times 3$$

$$K_2Cr_2O_7 + 4H_2SO_4 + 3Na_2SO_3 \rightarrow K_2SO_4 + Cr_2(SO_4)_3 + 4H_2O + 3NaSO_4$$

or $$Cr_2O_7^{2-} + 8H^+ + 3SO_3^{2-} \rightarrow 2Cr^{3+} + 3SO_4^{2-} + 4H_2O$$

Similarly,

$$Cr_2O_7^{2-} + 8H^+ + 3\,\underset{\text{Thiosulfate}}{S_2O_3^{2-}} \rightarrow 2\,Cr^{3+} + 3SO_4^{2-} + 3\,S + 4\,H_2O$$

- It oxidises nitrites to nitrates.

$$K_2Cr_2O_7 + 4H_2SO_4 \rightarrow K_2SO_4 + Cr_2(SO_4)_3 + 4H_2O + 3(O)$$
$$NaNO_2 + (O) \rightarrow NaNO_3] \times 3$$
$$K_2Cr_2O_7 + 4H_2SO_4 + 3NaNO_3 \rightarrow K_2SO_4 + Cr_2(SO_4)_3 + 3NaNO_3 + 4H_2O$$

or $$Cr_2O_7^{2-} + 8H^+ + 3NO_2^- \rightarrow 2Cr^{3+} + 3SO_3^- + 4H_2O$$

- It oxidises halogen acids to halogens.

$$K_2Cr_2O_7 + 14\,HCl \rightarrow 2KCl + 2CrCl_3 + 7\,H_2O + 3Cl_2$$

- It oxidises SO_2 to sulfuric acid.

$$K_2Cr_2O_7 + 4H_2SO_4 \rightarrow K_2SO_4 + Cr_2(SO_4)_3 + 4H_2O + 3O$$
$$SO_2 + O + H_2O \rightarrow H_2SO_4] \times 3$$
$$K_2Cr_2O_7 + H_2SO_4 + 3SO_2 \rightarrow K_2SO_4 + Cr_2(SO_4)_3 + 3H_2O$$

or $$Cr_2O_7^{2-} + 2H^+ + 3SO_2 \rightarrow Cr_2(SO_4)_3 + H_2O$$

Reduction of dichromate by sulfur dioxide can be used to prepare chrome alums.

- It oxidises stannous salts to stannic salts.

$$Cr_2O_7^{2-} + 14\,H^+ + 3\,Sn^{2+} \rightarrow 2\,Cr^{3+} + 3\,Sn^{4+} + 7\,H_2O$$

- It oxidises ethyl alcohol to acetaldehyde and acetic acid.

$$K_2Cr_2O_7 + 4H_2SO_4 \rightarrow K_2SO_4 + Cr_2(SO_4)_3 + 4H_2O + 3O$$
$$\underset{\text{Ethyl alcohol}}{CH_3CH_2OH} + O \rightarrow \underset{\text{Acetaldehyde}}{CH_3CHO} + H_2O$$
$$\underset{\text{Acetaldehyde}}{CH_3CHO} + O \rightarrow \underset{\text{Acetic acid}}{CH_3COOH}$$

(vi) **Reaction with hydrogen peroxide:** Acidified $K_2Cr_2O_7$ solution reacts with H_2O_2 to give a deep blue solution due to the formation of the peroxo compound, $CrO(O_2)_2$.

$$Cr_2O_7^{2-} + 2\,H^+ + 4\,H_2O_2 \rightarrow 2\,CrO_5 + 5\,H_2O$$

The blue colour fades away gradually due to the decomposition of CrO_5 into Cr^{3+} ions and oxygen. The structure of CrO_5 is [structure: Cr bonded to two peroxo O–O groups and one double-bonded O] in which Cr is in the +6 oxidation state.

8.4.3 Structures of Chromate and Dichromate Ions

The structures of chromate and dichromate ions are given in Fig. 8.5.

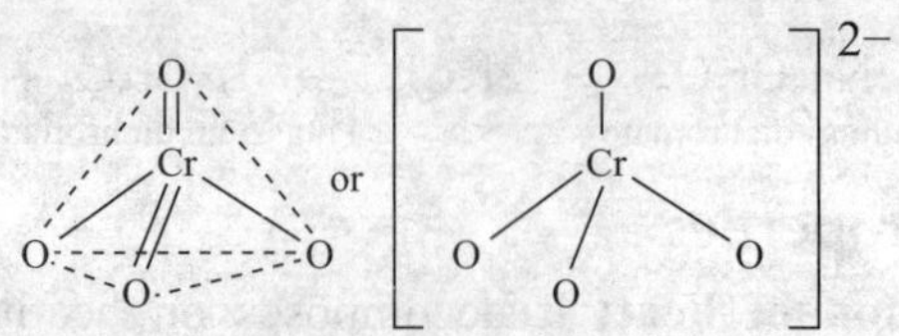

(a) Chormate ion—tetrahedral structure

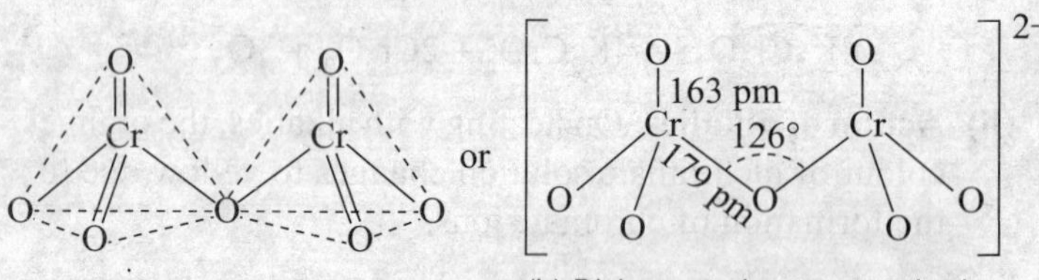

(b) Dichromate ion-two tetrahedra sharing one oxygen atom at one corner

Fig. 8.5 **(a)** Structure of chromate ion
(b) Structure of dichromate ion

8.5 Potassium Permanganate

8.5.1 Preparation

The preparation involves the following two steps:

(i) *Conversion of MnO_2 pyrolusite into potassium manganate*: The pyrolusite (MnO_2) is fused with caustic potash (KOH) or potassium carbonate in the presence of air or oxidising agent such as potassium nitrate or potassium chlorate to give a green mass due to the formation of potassium manganate.

$$2MnO_2 + 4KOH + O_2 \rightarrow \underset{\text{Potassium manganate}}{2K_2MnO_4} + 2H_2O$$
$$2MnO_2 + 2K_2CO_3 + O_2 \rightarrow 2K_2MnO_4 + 2\,CO_2$$
$$MnO_2 + 2KOH + KNO_3 \rightarrow K_2MnO_4 + KNO_2 + H_2O$$
$$3MnO_2 + 6KOH + KClO_3 \rightarrow 3K_2MnO_4 + KCl + 3H_2O$$

Potassium manganate thus formed undergoes *disproportionation* in the neutral or acidic solution.

$$\underset{\text{Manganate ion}}{\overset{\text{VI}}{3MnO_4^{2-}}} + 4\,H^+ \rightarrow \underset{\text{Permanganate ion}}{\overset{\text{VII}}{2MnO_4^-}} + \overset{\text{IV}}{MnO_2} + 2\,H_2O$$

(ii) *Oxidation of potassium manganate to potassium permanganate*: *Chemical oxidation*: The fused mass is extracted with water and the solution after filtration is converted into potassium permanganate by bubbling carbon dioxide, chlorine or ozonised oxygen through the green solution.

$$3K_2MnO_4 + 2CO_2 \rightarrow 2KMnO_4 + MnO_2 + \downarrow 2K_2CO_3$$
$$2K_2MnO_4 + Cl_2 \rightarrow 2KMnO_4 + 2KCl$$

$$2K_2MnO_4 + H_2O + O_3 \rightarrow 2KMnO_4 + 2KOH + O_2$$

Electrolytic oxidation: The reactions taking place are:

$$K_2MnO_4 \rightleftharpoons 2K^+ + MnO_4^{2-}$$

$$H_2O \rightleftharpoons H^+ + OH^-$$

At anode: $MnO_4^{2-} \rightarrow MnO_4^- + e^-$

At cathode: $H^+ + e^- \rightarrow H;$

$$2H \rightarrow H_2$$

Thus, manganate ions are oxidised to permanganate ions at the anode and hydrogen gas is liberated at the cathode. After the oxidation is complete, the solution is filtered and evaporated under controlled conditions to obtain the crystals of potassium permanganate.

Laboratory Preparation

In the laboratory, potassium permanganate is prepared by oxidation of manganese (II) ion salt by peroxodisulfate.

$$2Mn^{2+} + 5\underset{\text{Peroxodisulfate}}{S_2O_8^{2-}} + 8H_2O \rightarrow \underset{\text{Permanganate}}{2MnO_4^-} + 10SO_4^{2-} + 16H^+$$

8.5.2 Properties

(i) Action of heat: When heated to 513 K, it decomposes giving oxygen.

$$2KMnO_4 \rightarrow \underset{\text{Potassium manganate}}{K_2MnO_4} + MnO_2 + O_2$$

At red heat, potassium manganate formed decomposes into potassium manganite (K_2MnO_3) and oxygen.

$$2K_2MnO_4 \rightarrow 2K_2MnO_3 + O_2$$

(ii) Action of conc. H_2SO_4: With well cooled conc. H_2SO_4, it gives Mn_2O_7 which on warming decomposes to MnO_2.

$$2KMnO_4 + 2H_2SO_4 \rightarrow Mn_2O_7 + 2KHSO_4 + H_2O$$

$$2Mn_2O_7 \rightarrow 4MnO_2 + 3O_2$$

With warm conc. H_2SO_4, O_2 gas is given out.

$$4KMnO_4 + 6H_2SO_4 \rightarrow 2K_2SO_4 + 4MnSO_4 + 6H_2O + 5O_2$$

(iii) Action of heat in a current of hydrogen: When heated in a current of H_2, solid $KMnO_4$ gives KOH, MnO and water vapour.

$$2KMnO_4 + 5H_2 \xrightarrow{\Delta} 2KOH + 2MnO + 4H_2O$$

(iv) Oxidising property: Potassium permanganate is a *powerful oxidising agent*.

(a) *In neutral solution*: Potassium permanganate acts as a moderate oxidising agent in neutral aqueous solution because of the reaction:

$$2KMnO_4 + H_2O \rightarrow 2KOH + 2MnO_2 + 3O$$

or $MnO_4^- + 2H_2O + 3e^- \rightarrow MnO_2 + 4OH^-$

Some oxidising properties of $KMnO_4$ in the neutral medium are discussed below.

- It oxidises hot manganous sulfate to manganese dioxide.

$$2KMnO_4 + H_2O \rightarrow 2KOH + 2MnO_2 + 3O$$

$$3MnSO_4 + 3H_2O + 3O \rightarrow 3MnO_2 + 3H_2SO_4$$

$$2KOH + H_2SO_4 \rightarrow K_2SO_4 + 2H_2O$$

$$2KMnO_4 + 3MnSO_4 + 2H_2O \rightarrow K_2SO_4 + 2H_2SO_4 + 5MnO_2$$

- It oxidises sodium thiosuphate to sodium sulfate.

$$8KMnO_4 + 3Na_2S_2O_3 + H_2O \rightarrow 3K_2SO_4 + 8MnO_2 + 3Na_2SO_4 + 2KOH$$

- It oxidises hydrogen sulfide to sulfur.

$$2KMnO_4 + 2H_2S \rightarrow 2MnS + S + K_2SO_4 + 4H_2O$$

(b) *In alkaline solution*: In strongly alkaline solution, MnO_4^{2-} (manganate) ion is produced.

$$2KMnO_4 + 2KOH \rightarrow 2K_2MnO_4 + H_2O + O$$

or $MnO_4^- + e^- \rightarrow MnO_4^{2-}$

$$\therefore \text{ Eq. wt of } KMnO_4 = \frac{\text{Mol.wt.}}{1} = \frac{158}{1} = 158$$

Potassium manganate is also further reduced to MnO_2 when a reducing agent is present.

$$K_2MnO_4 + H_2O \rightarrow MnO_2 + 2KOH + O$$

or $MnO_4^{2-} + 2H_2O + 2e^- \rightarrow MnO_2 + 4OH^-$

So, the complete reaction is,

$$2KMnO_4 + H_2O \rightarrow 2MnO_2 + 2KOH + 3O$$

or $MnO_4^- + 2H_2O + 3e^- \rightarrow MnO_2 + 4OH^-$

Some oxidising properties of $KMnO_4$ in the alkaline medium are discussed below.

- It oxidises potassium iodide to potassium iodate.

$$2KMnO_4 + H_2O + KI \rightarrow 2MnO_2 + 2KOH + \underset{\text{Potassium iodate}}{KIO_3}$$

or $I^- + 6OH^- \rightarrow IO_3^- + 3H_2O + 6e^-$

In this case, iodine is not liberated unlike in the case of the acidic medium. A similar reaction takes place with KBr.

- It oxidises olefinic compounds to glycols, that is, when an olefinic compound is shaken with alkaline $KMnO_4$, the pink colour of $KMnO_4$ is discharged.

$$\underset{\text{Ethylene}}{CH_2{=}CH_2} + H_2O + (O) \xrightarrow[\text{KMnO}_4]{\text{Alkaline}} \underset{\text{Ethylene glycol}}{CH_2OH{-}CH_2OH}$$

Alkaline $KMnO_4$ used for this test is known as *Baeyer's reagent*. It is used for oxidation of a number of organic compounds.

(c) *In acidic medium*: Potassium permanganate in the presence of dil. sulfuric acid, that is, in acidic medium, acts as a strong oxidising agent because of the reaction,

$$2KMnO_4 + 3H_2SO_4 \rightarrow K_2SO_4 + 2MnSO_4 + 3H_2O + 5O$$

or $$MnO_4^- + 8H^+ + 5e^- \rightarrow Mn^{2+} + 4H_2O$$

In the above reaction, MnO_4^- ion gains 5 electrons, or, five atoms of oxygen are available from two molecules of $KMnO_4$. Hence,

$$\text{Eq. wt of } KMnO_4 = \frac{\text{Mol.wt.}}{5} = \frac{158}{5} = 31.6$$

Some oxidising properties of $KMnO_4$ in the acidic medium are discussed below.

- It oxidises H_2S to S.

$$2KMnO_4 + 3H_2SO_4 \rightarrow K_2SO_4 + 2MnSO_4 + 2H_2O + 5O$$
$$H_2S + O \rightarrow H_2O + S] \times 5$$
$$2KMnO_4 + 3H_2SO_4 + 5H_2S \rightarrow K_2SO_4 + 2MnSO_4 + 3H_2O + 5S$$

or $$2MnO_4^- + 16H^+ + 5S^{2-} \rightarrow 2Mn^{2+} + 8H_2O + 5S$$

- It oxidises sulfur dioxide to sulfuric acid.

$$2KMnO_4 + 3H_2SO_4 \rightarrow K_2SO_4 + MnSO_4 + 3H_2O + 5O$$
$$SO_2 + H_2O + O \rightarrow H_2SO_4] \times 5$$
$$KMnO_4 + 5\ SO_4 + 2H_2O \rightarrow K_2SO_4 + 2MnSO_4 + 2H_2SO_4$$

or $$2MnO_4^- + 5\ SO_4 + 2H_2O \rightarrow 5\ SO_4^{2-} + 2\ Mn^{2+} + 4H^+$$

- It oxidises nitrites (NO_2^-) to nitrates (NO_3^-), arsenates (AsO_3^{3-}) to arsentates (AsO_4^{3-}) and sulfites and thiosulfates to sulfates.

$$2KMnO_4 + 3H_2SO_4 \rightarrow K_2SO_4 + MnSO_4 + 3H_2O + 5O$$
$$KNO_2 + O \rightarrow KNO_3] \times 5$$
$$2KMnO_4 + 3H_2SO_4 + 5KNO_2 \rightarrow K_2SO_4 + 2MnSO_4 + 3H_2O + 5KNO_3$$

or $$2MnO_4^- + 6H^+ + 5NO_2^- \rightarrow 2Mn^{2+} + 3H_2O + 5NO_3^-$$

A similar equation can be written for the oxidation of arsenite to arsenate, sulfites and thiosulfates to sulfate.

$$2MnO_4^- + 6H^+ + 5AsO_3^{3-} \rightarrow 2Mn^{2+} + 3H_2O + 5AsO_4^{3-}$$
$$2MnO_4^- + 6H^+ + 5SO_3^{2-} \rightarrow Mn^{2+} + 3H_2O + 5SO_4^{2-}$$
$$2MnO_4^- + 6H^+ + 5S_2O_3^{2-} \rightarrow 2Mn^{2+} + 3H_2O + 5\ SO_4^{2-} + 5S$$

- It oxidises oxalates or oxalic acid to CO_2.

$$2KMnO_4 + 3H_2SO_4 \rightarrow K_2SO_4 + 2MnSO_4 + 3H_2O + 5O$$
$$C_2H_2O_4 + O \rightarrow H_2O + 2CO_2] \times 5$$
$$2KMnO_4 + 3H_2SO_4 + 5C_2H_2O_4 \rightarrow K_2SO_4 + 2MnSO_4 + 8H_2O + 10CO_2$$

or $$2MnO_4^- + 6H^+ + 5C_2O_4^{2-} \rightarrow 2Mn^{2+} + 8H_2O + 10CO_2$$

- It oxidises ferrous sulfate to ferric sulfate (that is, ferrous salt to ferric salt).

$$2KMnO_4 + 3H_2SO_4 \rightarrow K_2SO_4 + 2MnSO_4 + 3H_2O + 5O$$
$$2FeSO_4 + H_2SO_4 + O \rightarrow Fe_2(SO_4)_3 + H_2O] \times 5$$
$$2KMnO_4 + 8H_2SO_4 + 10FeSO_4 \rightarrow K_2SO_4 + 2MnSO_4 + 5Fe_2(SO_3)_2 + 8H_2O$$

or $$2MnO_4^- + 16H^+ + 10Fe^{2+} \rightarrow 2Mn^{2+} + 8H_2O + 10Fe^{3+}$$

- It oxidises H_2O_2 to H_2O and O_2. This is because acidified $KMnO_4$ is a stronger oxidising agent than H_2O_2.

$$2KMnO_4 + 3H_2SO_4 \rightarrow K_2SO_4 + 2MnSO_4 + 3H_2O + 5O$$
$$H_2O_2 \rightarrow H_2O + O] \times 5$$
$$O + O \rightarrow O_2] \times 5$$
$$2KMnO_4 + 3H_2SO_4 + 5H_2O_2 \rightarrow K_2SO_4 + 2MnSO_4 + 8H_2O + 5O_2$$

or $$2MnO_4^- + 6H^+ + 5H_2O_2 \rightarrow 2Mn^{2+} + 8H_2O + 5O_2$$

- It oxidises potassium iodide to iodine.

$$2KMnO_4 + 3H_2SO_4 \rightarrow K_2SO_4 + 2MnSO_4 + 3H_2O + 5\ sO$$
$$2KI + H_2SO_4 \rightarrow K_2SO_4 + 2HI] \times 5$$
$$2HI + O \rightarrow H_2O + I_2] \times 5$$
$$2KMnO_4 + 8H_2SO_4 + 10KI \rightarrow K_2SO_4 + 2MnSO_4 + 8H_2O + 5I_2$$

or $$2MnO_4^- + 16\ H^+ + 10\ I^- \rightarrow 2\ Mn^{2+} + 8H_2O + 5I_2$$

- It oxidises HX (where X = Cl, Br, I) to X_2.

$$2KMnO_4 + 3H_2SO_4 \rightarrow K_2SO_4 + 2MnSO_4 + 3H_2O + 5O$$
$$2HX + O \rightarrow H_2O + X_2] \times 5$$
$$2KMnO_4 + 3H_2SO_4 + 10HX \rightarrow K_2SO_4 + 2MnSO_4 + 8H_2O + 5X_2$$

or $$2MnO_4^- + 16H^+ + 10X^- \rightarrow 2Mn^{2+} + 8H_2O + 8X_2$$

(ix) It oxidises ethyl alcohol to acetaldehyde.

$$2KMnO_4 + 3H_2SO_4 \rightarrow K_2SO_4 + 2MnSO_4 + 3H_2O + 5O$$
$$CH_3CH_2OH + O \rightarrow CH_3CHO + H_2O] \times 5$$
$$2KMnO_4 + 3H_2SO_4 + 5CH_3CH_2OH \rightarrow K_2SO_4 + 2MnSO_4 + 5CH_3CHO + 8H_2O$$

8.5.3 Structure of Permanganate Ions

Permanganate (MnO_4^-) and manganate (MnO_4^{2-}) ions have a tetrahedral shape. The four atoms are arranged tetrahedrally around manganese.

The pi (π) bonding takes place by the overlap of the p orbitals of oxygen with the d orbitals of manganese (Fig. 8.6).

MnO_4^- (purple) ion $\quad$ MnO_4^{2-} (green) ion

Fig. 8.6 Structure of permanganate (MnO_4^-) and manganate (MnO_4^{2-}) ions

8.6 Inner Transition Elements (*f*-Block Elements)

In these elements, the last electron is added to the third to the outermost (called antepenultimate) energy level, that is, $(n-2)f$. The electronic configuration is

$$(n-2)f^{1-14}(n-1)d^{0-1}ns^2$$

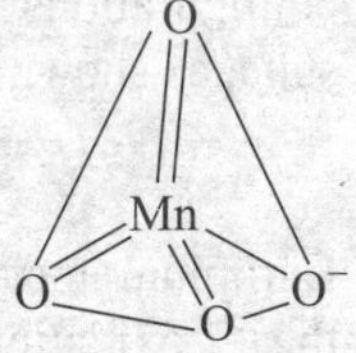

They consist of two series of elements which are generated by the filling of characteristic electrons in the 4*f* and 5*f* orbitals. Depending upon whether the last electron enters a 4*f* orbital or a 5*f* orbital, the *f*-block elements have been divided into two series (Table 8.9).

(i) Lanthanoids: The series involving the filling of 4*f* orbitals of elements that follow lanthanum La ($Z = 57$) is the called *lanthanoid series*.

(ii) Actinoids: The series involving the filling of the 5*f* orbitals of elements that follow actinium, Ac ($Z = 89$) is called the *actinoid series*.

Table 8.9 Electronic configuration of lanthanum and lanthanoids (General symbol = Ln) (General EC: [Xe] $4f^{1-14}5d^{0-1}6s^2$)

Name of the element	Symbol (Ln)	At. no (Z)	Electronic configuration	Oxidation states	EC outside [Xe] core Ln^{2+}	Ln^{3+}	Ln^{4+}
Lanthanum	La	57	[Xe] $5d^1 6s^2$	+3	$5d^1$	$4f^0$	
Cerium	Ce	58	[Xe] $4f^2 5d^0 6s^2$	+3, +4	$4f^2$	$4f^1$	$4f^0$
Praseodymium	Pr	59	[Xe] $4f^3 5d^0 6s^2$	+3, +4	$4f^3$	$4f^2$	$4f^1$
Neodymium	Nd	60	[Xe]$4f^4 5d^0 6s^2$	+2, +3, +4	$4f^4$	$4f^3$	$4f^2$
Promethium	Pm	61	[Xe]$4f^5 5d^0 6s^2$	+ 3	$4f^5$	$4f^4$	
Samarium	Sm	62	[Xe] $4f^6 5d^0 6s^2$	+2, +3	$4f^6$	$4f^5$	
Europium	Eu	63	[Xe] $4f^7 5d^0 6s^2$	+2, +3	$4f^7$	$4f^6$	
Gadolinium	Gd	64	[Xe] $4f^7 5d^1 6s^2$	+3		$4f^7 5d^1 4f^7$	
Terbium	TB	65	[Xe] $4f^9 5d^0 6s^2$	+3, +4	$4f^9$	$4f^8$	$4f^7$
Dysprosium	Dy	66	[Xe] $4f^{10} 5d^0 6s^2$	+3, +4	$4f^{10}$	$4f^9$	$4f^8$
Holmium	Ho	67	[Xe] $4f^{11} 5d^0 6s^2$	+3	$4f^{11}$	$4f^{10}$	
Erbium	Er	68	[Xe] $4f^{12} 5d^0 6s^2$	+3	$4f^{12}$	$4f^{11}$	
Thulium	Tm	69	[Xe] $4f^{13} 5d^0 6s^2$	+2, +3	$4f^{13}$	$4f^{12}$	
Ytterbium	Yb	70	[Xe] $4f^{14} 5d^0 6s^2$	+2, +3	$4f^{14}$	$4f^{13}$	
Lutetium	Lu	71	[Xe] $4f^{14} 5d^1 6s^2$	+3		$4f^{13} 5d^1 4f^{14}$	

8.7 The Lanthanoids

8.7.1 Oxidation States of Lanthanoids

The typical oxidation state of the lanthanoids is +3. The oxidation states of +2 and +4 are exhibited by some of the elements. These are shown by those elements which by losing 2 or 4 electrons acquire a stable configuration of f^0, f^7 or f^{14}. Cerium (Ce) and terbium (Tb) attain f^0 and f^7 configurations respectively when they attain the +4 oxidation state, as shown.

$$Ce^{4+} : [Xe] 4f^0; Tb^{4+} : [Xe] 4f^7$$

Europium and ytterbium attain f^7 and f^{14} configurations in the +2 oxidation state as shown.

$$Eu^{2+} : [Xe] 4f^7; Yb^{2+} : [Xe] 4f^{14}$$

La, Gd and Lu exhibit only +3 oxidation states. These elements show the +3 oxidation state only because by losing three electrons, they acquire stable configurations of empty, half-filled and completely filled 4*f* subshells. Aqueous solutions of Ce^{4+} and Tb^{4+} are good oxidising agents.

8.7.2 Atomic and Ionic Radii of Lanthanoids

In the lanthanoid series, with increasing atomic number, there is a progressive decrease in the atomic as well as ionic radii of the trivalent ions from La^{3+} to Lu^{3+}. This regular decrease (contraction) in the atomic and ionic radii of lanthanoids with increasing atomic number is known as *lanthanoid contraction.*

Cause of Lanthanoid Contraction

In the lanthanoid series, the nuclear charge increases by one unit for each successive element. The new electron is added into the same subshell (namely, the 4*f*). As a result, the attraction on the electrons by the nucleus increases and this tends to decrease the size. Further, as the new electron is added into the *f* subshell, there is imperfect shielding of one electron by another in this subshell due to the shapes of these *f* orbitals. This imperfect shielding is unable to counterbalance the effect of the increased nuclear charge. Hence, the net result is a contraction in the size though the decrease is very small. But the shielding of one 4*f* electron by another is less than one *d* electron by another with increase in nuclear charge along the series.

Consequences of Lanthanoid Contraction

- *Similarity among lanthanoids*: Since the change in ionic radii (size of the ions) in lanthanoids is very small, their chemical properties are similar.
- *Resemblance of second and third transition series:* After the lanthanoids, the increase in radii from the second to third transition series almost vanishes. The pairs of elements: Zr–Hf, Nb–Ta, Mo–W and so on, possess almost the same size. The properties of these elements are also very similar. As a result of the lanthanoid contraction, the elements of the second and third transition series resemble each other much more than the elements of the first and second transition series.
- *Effect on the basic strength of hydroxides*: As the size of the lanthanoid ions decreases from La^{3+} to Lu^{3+}, the covalent character of the hydroxides increases and hence the basic strength decreases. Thus, $La(OH)_3$ is most basic whereas $Lu(OH)_3$ is least basic.

8.7.3 Important Characteristics of Lanthanoids

- **Silvery appearance and softness:** All the lanthanoids are silvery white soft metals and tarnish rapidly in the air. Their hardness increases with increasing atomic number. Samarium (Sm) is exceptionally hard like steel.
- **Melting point:** They have high melting points in the range 1000 to 1200 K except samarium which has a very high melting point of 1623 K.
- **Magnetic behaviour:** Paramagnetism is shown by the positive ions of lanthanoids except La^{3+} (lanthanum ion, f^0) and Lu^{3+} (lutetium ion, f^{14}). This property of the lanthanoids is due to presence of unpaired electrons in the incomplete 4*f* subshell.
- **Ionisation enthalpy:** The first ionisation enthalpies of the lanthanoids are comparable with those of calcium. The loss of the first two electrons is accompanied by exchange enthalpy. Further, the loss of third electron is easier, that is, the third ionisation enthalpy is low if it leads to stable empty, half-filled or completely filled configuration, as indicated by the abnormally low third ionisation enthalpies of La, Gd and Lu.
- **Electropositive character:** They are highly electropositive because of their low ionisation enthalpies.
- **Standard electrode potential:** Their standard reduction potentials, that is, the $E°$ values for the half reaction, $M^{3+}(aq) + 3e^- \rightarrow M(s)$, lie in the range of –2.2 to –2.4 V, the only exception being europium (Eu) for which the $E°$ value is –2.0 V.
- **Reducing property:** They readily lose electrons and are thus good reducing agents.
- **Complex formation:** The tendency to form complexes and their stability increases with increasing atomic number.
- **Electrical and thermal conductivity:** All of them have a typical metallic structure and are good conductors of heat and electricity.
- **Chemical behaviour:** The first few members of the series are quite reactive, almost like calcium. However, with increasing atomic number, their behaviour becomes similar to that of aluminium. A few properties are discussed.

- They combine with H_2 on gentle heating. When heated with carbon, they form carbides. On burning in the presence of halogens, they form halides.
- They react with dilute acids to liberate H_2 gas.
- They form oxides and hydroxides of the type M_2O_3 and $M(OH)_3$ which are basic like alkaline earth metal oxides and hydroxides.

Representing the lanthanoids by the general symbol Ln, the general reactions may be represented as shown given below:

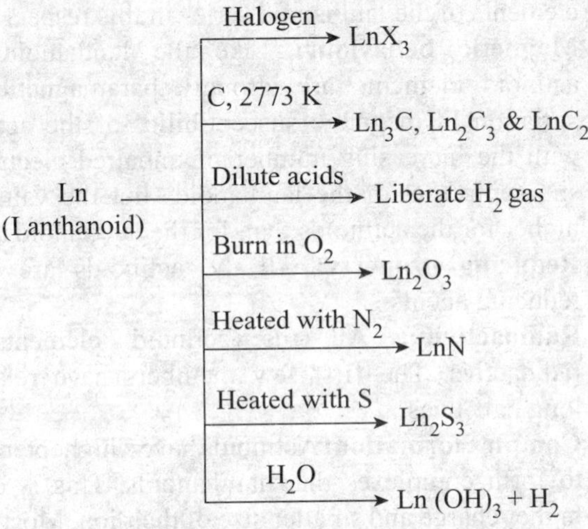

8.8 Actinoids

The fourteen elements which follow actinium, from thorium (Z = 90) to lawrencium (Z = 103), in the periodic table are called actinoids. These are analogous to lanthanoids and involve the filling of 5*f* orbitals.

8.8.1 Electronic Configurations of Actinoids

From Table 8.10, the following points may be noted.

- All the actinoids have common $7s^2$ configuration and variable occupancy of $5f$ and $6d$ subshells.
- The 14 electrons are being added into $5f$, except in thorium (Z = 90) but filling of $5f$ continues again after thorium till $5f$ orbitals are complete at Z = 103 (lawrencium).
- The irregularities in the electronic configurations of actinoids like those in the lanthanoids, are related to the stabilities of f^0, f^7 and f^{14} configurations. For example, the configurations of Am and Cm are [Rn] $5f^7 6d^0 7s^2$ and [Rn] $5f^7 6d^1 7s^2$ and [Rn] $5f^7 6d^1 7s^2$ respectively.
- Berkelium (Bk, Z = 97) also shows an exceptional configuration of [Rn] $5f^7 6d^0 7s^2$ which is neither half-filled not completely filled.

Table 8.10 Electronic configuration of actinium and actinoids (general EC = [Rn] $5f^{1-14} 6d^{0-1} 7s^2$)

Name of the element	Symbol	At. no. (Z)	Electronic configuration	Oxidation states	EC outside [Rn] core M^{3+}	M^{4+}
Actinium	Ac	89	[Rn] $6d^1 7s^2$	+3	$5f^0$	
Thorium	Th	90	[Rn] $6d^2 7s^2$	(+3), +4	$5f^1$	$5f^0$
Protactinium	Pa	91	[Rn] $5f^2 6d^1 7s^2$	+3, +4, +5	$5f^2$	$5f^1$
Uranium	U	92	[Rn] $5f^3 6d^1 7s^2$	+3, +4, +5, +6	$5f^3$	$5f^2$
Neptunium	Np	93	[Rn] $5f^4 6d^1 7s^2$	+3, +4, +5, +6, +7	$5f^4$	$5f^3$
Plutonium	Pu	94	[Rn] $5f^6 6d^0 7s^2$	+3, +4, +5, +6, +7	$5f^5$	$5f^4$
Americium	Am	95	[Rn] $5f^7 6d^0 7s^2$	+3, (+4), +5, +6	$5f^6$	$5f^5$
Curium	Cm	96	[Rn] $5f^7 6d^1 7s^2$	+3, (+4)	$5f^7$	$5f^6$
Berkelium	Bk	97	[Rn] $5f^9 6d^0 7s^2$	+3, +4	$5f^8$	$5f^7$
Californium	Cf	98	[Rn] $5f^{10} 6d^1 7s^2$	+3	$5f^9$	$5f^8$
Einsteinium	Es	99	[Rn] $5f^{11} 6d^0 7s^2$	+3	$5f^{10}$	$5f^9$
Fermium	Fm	100	[Rn] $5f^{12} 6d^0 7s^2$	+3	$5f^{11}$	$5f^{10}$
Mendelevium	Md	101	[Rn] $5f^{13} 6d^0 7s^2$	+3	$5f^{12}$	$5f^{11}$
Nobelium	No	102	[Rn] $5f^{14} 6d^0 7s^2$	+3	$5f^{13}$	$5f^{12}$
Lawrencium	Lr	103	[Rn] $5f^{14} 6d^1 7s^2$	+3	$5f^{14}$	$5f^{13}$

Note: Oxidation states given in brackets are less stable.

- Though $4f$ and $5f$ orbitals have similar shapes, $5f$ is less deeply buried than $4f$. Hence, $5f$ electrons can participate in bonding to a far greater extent.

8.8.2 Oxidation States of Actinoids

Actinoids show different oxidation states such as +2, +3, +4, +5, +6 and +7. However, the +3 oxidation state is the most common among all the actinoids. The wide range of oxidation states of the actinoids is attributed to the fact that the 5*f*, 6*d* and 7*s* energy levels are of comparable energies. Therefore, all these three subshells can participate. The actinoids form ionic species. The principle ionic species are $M^{3+}, M^{4+}, MO_2^{+}, MO_2^{2+}$. The lower oxidation state tends to be ionic while the higher ones are covalent.

8.8.3 Ionic Radii and Actinoid Contraction

The actinoids show actinoid contraction (very much like lanthanoid contraction) due to poor shielding effect of the $5f$ electrons. This is because the $5f$ orbitals extend in space beyond the 6*s* and 6*p* orbitals whereas the $4f$ orbitals are burried deep inside the atom.

8.8.4 General Characteristics of Actinoids

(i) **Silvery appearance:** Like the lanthanoids, the actinoids are metals with a silvery appearance.

(ii) **Structural variability:** As they have much greater irregularities in their metallic radii than the lanthanoids, they show great structural variability.

(iii) **Melting and boiling points:** The actinoids, like the lanthanoids, have high melting and boiling points. However, they do not show any regular trend with an increase in atomic number.

(iv) **Density:** All the actinoids except thorium and americium have high densities.

(v) **Ionisation enthalpy:** The actinoids have lower ionisation enthalpies than lanthanoids because $5f$ is less penetrating than $4f$ and hence is more effectively shielded from the nuclear charge.

(vi) **Electropositive character:** All the known actinoid metals are highly electropositive. They resemble the elements of the lanthanoid series in this respect.

(vii) **Magnetic behaviour:** Like the lanthanoids, the actinoid elements are strongly paramagnetic. The variation in magnetic susceptibility of the actinoids with the increasing number of unpaired electrons is similar to that of the lanthanoids but the values are higher for the actinoids than for the lanthanoids.

(viii) **Reducing property:** All the actinoids are strong reducing agents.

(ix) **Radioactivity:** All the actinoid elements are radioactive. The first few members have relatively long half-lives.

(x) **Complex formation:** Actinoids have a higher tendency to form complexes than lanthanoids. This is due to higher charge and smaller size of their ion. Most of the complexes are formed by the halides of actinoids with alkali metals halides.

Table 8.11 Differences between lanthanoids and actinoids

Property	Lanthanoids	Actinoids
1. Oxidation states	Lanthanoids show mainly the +3 oxidation state except in a few cases where it is +2 and +4.	In addition to the +3 oxidation state, actinoids also show higher oxidation states such as +4, +5, +6 and +7. For example, uranium exhibits oxidation states of +3, +5 and +6. The +6 oxidation state is stable in compounds such as UF_6, UO_2^{2+}.
2. Binding energies	Binding energies of 4*f* electrons are higher.	Binding energies of 5*f* electrons are lower.
3. Shielding effect	4*f* electrons have a greater shielding effect. Therefore, the contraction in their ionic radii is less.	5*f* electrons have poor shielding effect. Therefore, the contraction in their sizes in more.
4. Tendency to form complexes	The tendency to form complexes is less.	They have a greater tendency to form complexes.
5. Basic character	Lanthanoid compounds are less basic.	Actinoid compounds are more basic.
6. Tendency to form oxo ions	They do not form oxo ions.	They form oxo ions such as UO_2^{2+}, NpO_2^{+}, PuO_2^{+}, UO_2^{2+}.
7. Radioactivity	Except promethium, these are non-radioactive.	All the actinoids are radioactive.
8. Colours	Most of their ions are colourless.	Most of the actinoid ions are coloured. For example, U^{3+} (red), U^{4+} (green), UO_2^{2+} (yellow).

(xi) Chemical behaviour: They are highly reactive metals especially in the finely divided state. A few properties are discussed.

- They react with boiling water to give a mixture of oxide and hydride.
- They combine with most of the non-metals at moderate temperature.
- All these metals are attacked by hydrochloric acid but the effect of nitric acid is very small due to the formation of a protective oxide layer on their surface.
- Alkalies have no action on them.

8.8.5 Comparison of Lanthanoids and Actinoids

Similarities

- Both show mainly an oxidation state of +3.
- Both are electropositive and very reactive.
- Both exhibit magnetic and spectral properties.
- Actinoids exhibit actinoid contraction like lanthanoid contraction shown by lanthanoids.

The main differences between both series are as given in Table 8.11.

Exercises

OBJECTIVE QUESTIONS

Introduction

1. The electronic configurations of four elements are given below. Which element does not belong to the same family as the others?

(a) [Xe] $4f^{14} 5d^{10} 6s^2$ (b) [Kr] $4d^{10} 5s^2$
(c) [Ne] $3s^2 3p^5$ (d) [Ar] $3d^{10} 4s^2$

2. An atom has the electronic configuration $1s^2 2s^2 2p^6 3s^2 3p^6 3d^3 4s^2$. In which group would it be placed?

(a) fifth (b) fifteenth
(c) second (d) third

3. Which one of the following *d*-block elements has a half-filled penultimate *d* subshell as well as a half-filled valence *s* subshell?

(a) Cr (b) Pd (c) Pt (d) Cu (e) Au

4. An isoelectronic pair of ions is

(a) Sc^{2+} and V^{3+} (b) Mn^{3+} and Fe^{2+}
(c) Mn^{2+} and Fe^{3+} (d) Ni^{3+} and Fe^{2+}

5. In Cu, how many electrons have spin in one direction and in the other direction? (atomic number = 29)

(a) 13 electrons have spin in one direction and 16 electrons in the other direction
(b) 14 electrons have spin in one direction and 15 electrons in the other direction
(c) one electron can have spin only in the clockwise direction
(d) none of the above is correct

6. Among the following series of transition metal ions, the one in which all metal ions have the $3d^2, 3p^6$ electronic configuration is [atomic number Ti = 22, V = 23, Cr = 24 and Mn = 25]

(a) Ti^{3+}, V^{2+}, Cr^{3+}, Mn^{4+}
(b) Ti^{+}, V^{4+}, Cr^{6+}, Mn^{7+}
(c) Ti^{4+}, V^{3+}, Cr^{2+}, Mn^{3+}
(d) Ti^{2+}, V^{3+}, Cr^{6+}, Mn^{5+}

7. Which of the following configurations is that of a coinage metal?

(a) 2, 8, 1 (b) 2, 8, 18, 1
(c) 2, 8, 8 (d) 2, 18, 8, 3

8. Zn is related to which group?

(a) IIB (12) (b) IIA (2) (c) IA (1) (d) IB (11)

9. The electronic configuration $1s^2 2s^2 2p^6 3s^2 3p^6 3d^9$ represents a

(a) metal atom (b) non-metal atom
(c) non-metallic anion (d) metallic cation

10. $3d^{10} 4s^0$ electronic configuration exhibits

(a) Zn^{++} (b) Cu^{++} (c) Cd^{++} (d) Hg^{++}

11. Which of the following statements is not correct about the electronic configuration of the gaseous chromium atom?

(a) It has 5 electrons in the 3*d* and one electron in the 4*s* orbitals.
(b) The principal quantum numbers of its valence electrons are 3 and 4.
(c) It has 6 electrons in the 3*d* orbital.
(d) Its valence electrons have quantum number *l* as 0 and 2.

12. The outer electronic configuration of the 3*d* transition elements generally remains

(a) $(n-1)d^n$ (b) nd^2
(c) ns^2 (d) $(n-1)s^2$

13. Number of unpaired electrons in Cu^{2+} is

(a) 1 (b) 2 (c) 3 (d) 0

14. Which one of the following has the maximum number of unpaired electrons?
(a) Mg^{2+} (b) Ti^{3+} (c) V^{3+} (d) Fe^{2+}

15. Which one belongs to the 3*d* transition series?
(a) cobalt (b) gold (c) cadmium (d) silver

16. A metal M having an electronic configuration, $1s^2 2s^2 2p^6 3s^2 3p^6 3d^{10} 4s^1$ is a/an
(a) *s*-block element (b) *d*-block element
(c) *p*-block element (d) none of these

17. What is the name of element with atomic number 105?
(a) kurchatovium (b) dubnium
(c) nobelium (d) holmium

18. Which of the following does not have valence electron in the 3*d* subshell?
(a) Fe (III) (b) Mn (II) (c) Cr (I) (d) P (0)

19. An element is in the M^{3+} form. Its electronic configuration is $[Ar]3d^1$. The ion is
(a) Ti^{3+} (b) Ti^{4+} (c) Ca^{2+} (d) Sc^+

20. The general configuration of the outermost and penultimate shell is $(n-1)s^2(n-1)p^6(n-1)d^x ns^2$. If $n=4$ and $x=5$ then the number of protons in the nucleus will be
(a) > 25 (b) < 24 (c) 25 (d) 30

21. The electronic configuration of a transition element X in the +3 oxidation state is $[Ar]3d^5$. What is its atomic number?
(a) 25 (b) 26 (c) 27 (d) 24

22. Which of the following series of elements belong to the second transition series
(a) V, La, Hf, Ta (b) Nb, Mo, Tc, Ru
(c) Ir, Os, Re, Ta (d) Re, Os, Ir, Pt

23. Which one of the following is a *d*-block element?
(a) Gd (b) Hs (c) Es (d) Cm

24. Which of the following statements is correct?
(a) Iron belongs to 3rd transition series of the periodic table.
(b) Iron belongs to the *f*-block of the periodic table.
(c) Iron belongs to the second transition series of the periodic table.
(d) Iron belongs to group VIII (8) of the periodic table.

25. Choose the wrong statement among the following.
(a) TiO_2 is used in the pigment industry.
(b) MnO_2 is used in dry battery cells.
(c) V_2O_5 catalyses the oxidation of SO_2 in the manufacture of sulfuric acid.
(d) Ziegler catalyst is used in the manufacture of high density polyethylene.
(e) The 'silver' UK coins are made of Ag/Ni alloy.

26. Mercury is a liquid metal because
(a) it has a completely filled *s* orbital
(b) it has a small atomic size
(c) it has a completely filled *d* orbital that prevents *d*–*d* overlapping of orbitals
(d) it has a completely filled *d* orbital that causes *d*–*d* overlapping

27. The most malleable of all the metals is
(a) silver (b) sodium (c) gold (d) platinum

28. Which of the following is the correct sequence of atomic weights of the given elements?
(a) Fe > Co > Ni (b) Ni > Co > Fe
(c) Co > Ni > Fe (d) Fe > Ni > Co

29. Which of the following is an acidic oxide?
(a) Mn_2O_7 (b) Mn_3O_4 (c) MnO (d) Mn_2O_3

30. The silver atom has completely filled *d* orbitals $(4d^{10})$ in its ground state. Which of the following statements is not correct regarding silver?
(a) The outer electronic configuration of the Ag atom is $4d^{10}5s^1$.
(b) In addition to +1, it shows an oxidation state of +2 (as in AgO and AgF_2).
(c) In the +2 oxidation state, the configuration of silver atoms is d^9, that is, the *d* subshell is incompletely filled. Hence, it is a transition element.
(d) Silver is not a transition element as it has completely filled *d* subshells.

General Properties of Transition Elements (d-block)

31. Which of the following transition metals of the 3*d* series has the lowest melting point?
(a) Ti ($Z=22$) (b) V ($Z=23$) (c) Cr ($Z=24$)
(d) Mn ($Z=25$) (e) Fe ($Z=26$)

32. In the first transitions series, the highest BP and MP is for
(a) Cr (b) V (c) Ni (d) Fe

33. Which of the following pairs of elements has identical atomic size?
(a) Ti, Zr (b) Zr, Hf (c) Na, K (d) La, Hf

34. Which of the following has the highest ionic radius?
(a) Cr^{+3} (b) Mn^{+3} (c) Fe^{+3} (d) Co^{+3}

35. Which of the following ions has the smallest radius?
(a) Ti^{2+} (b) Ni^{2+} (c) Pt^{2+} (d) Zr^{2+}

36. The atomic radii of the elements are almost same in which series?

(a) Fe, Co, Ni (b) Na, K, Rb
(c) F, Cl, Br (d) Li, Be, B

37. The atomic radii from Cr to Cu are almost identical because of

(a) increasing nuclear charge from Cr to Cu
(b) repulsion among increased electrons
(c) increased screening effect to nullify increased charge
(d) all the above

38. In which of the following, will the ionic radius of chromium be the smallest?

(a) K_2CrO_4 (b) CrO_2 (c) $CrCl_3$ (d) CrF_2

39. Which is the heaviest among the following?

(a) iron (b) copper (c) gold (d) silver

40. The correct order of density is

(a) Cu > Ni > Zn > Sc (b) Ni > Cu > Zn > Sc
(c) Zn > Cu > Ni > SC (d) Sc > Zn > Ni > Cu

41. Which of the following pairs of transition elements exhibits the highest and lowest density?

(a) Os and Sc (b) Os and Pt
(c) Hg and Sc (d) Os and Ir

42. Among the following transition elements, pick out the element/elements with the highest second ionisation enthalpy.

(i) V (At. no. = 23) (ii) Cr (At. no. = 24)
(iii) Mn (At. no. = 25) (iv) Cu (At. no. = 29)
(v) Zn (At. no. = 30)
(a) (i) and (iii) (b) (ii) and (iv)
(c) (ii) and (v) (d) only (iv) (e) only (iii)

43. Arrange the following in the correct order of their second ionisation enthalpies

Cr, Mn, Ni, Cu, Zn
(a) Cr > Mn < Ni < Cu > Zn
(b) Cr > Mn > Ni < Cu > Zn
(c) Cr < Mn < Ni > Cu < Zn
(d) Cr < Mn < Ni < Cu > Zn

44. Cupric compounds are more stable than their cuprous counterparts in the solid state. This is because

(a) the endothermic characteristics of the 2nd IP of Cu is not so high
(b) size of Cu^{2+} is less than that of Cu^+
(c) Cu^{2+} has a stable electronic configuration compared to that of Cu^+
(d) the lattice energy released for cupric compounds is much higher than for cuprous compounds

45. In the following members of transition elements, the lowest ionisation enthalpy is of

(a) Ti (b) Sc (c) V (d) Mn

46. Which of the following has a second ionisation enthalpy less than expected?

(a) Cr (b) Zn (c) V (d) Mo

47. The ionisation potential values of the *d*-block elements compared to that of the *f*-block elements are

(a) higher (b) equal
(c) lower (d) all of these

48. Mercury is the only metal which is liquid at 0°C. This is due to its

(a) very high ionisation energy and weak metallic bonds
(b) low ionisation potential
(c) high atomic weight
(d) high vapour pressure

49. Which of the following elements has the maximum first ionisation potential?

(a) V (b) Ti (c) Cr (d) Mn

50. The atomic number of vanadium (V), chromium (Cr), manganese (Mn) and iron (Fe) are respectively 23, 24, 25 and 26. Which one of these may be expected to have the highest second ionisation enthalpy?

(a) V (b) Cr (c) Mn (d) Fe

51. Name a transition element out of the following which exhibits variable oxidation states.

(a) Sc (b) Zn (c) Y (d) Cu

52. The common oxidation states of Ti are

(a) +2, +3 (b) +3, +4
(c) –3, –4 (d) +2, +3, +4

53. The common oxidation states of scandium, a transition element, is/are (At. no. of Sc =21)

(a) +4 (b) +1
(c) +2 and +3 (d) +4 and +1

54. The stable oxidation state(s) of the transition element with $3d^5$ electronic configuration in the ground state of the atom may be

(a) +6 (b) +2, +7
(c) +3, +6 (d) +3, +6, +2, +7

55. Cu^+ ion is not stable in the aqueous solution. This is because (select the wrong statement among the following)

(a) copper (I) compounds undergo disproportionation in aqueous solution to give $Cu^{2+}(aq)$ and $Cu(s)$
(b) the $E°$ value is not favourable for this transformation

(c) the disproportionation reaction shows that $Cu^{2+}(aq)$ is much more stable than $Cu^{+}(aq)$
(d) the hydrogen enthalpy of $Cu^{2+}(aq)$ is much more negative than that for $Cu^{+}(aq)$ and hence it more than compensates for the second ionisation enthalpy of copper

56. Which of the following statements concerning transition elements is false?
(a) They are all metals.
(b) They easily form complex coordination compounds.
(c) Compounds containing their ions are mostly coloured.
(d) They show multiple oxidation states always differing by units of two.
(c) Manganese (VI) here becomes unstable relative to manganese (VII) and manganese (IV) in the acidic medium.
(d) One mol of MnO_4^{2-} is converted into two mol of MnO_4^- and 1/3 mol of MnO_2.

57. Which of the following transition metals shows variable valency?
(a) Sc (b) Y (c) Fe (d) Ac

58. Among the following pairs of ions, the lower oxidation state in aqueous solution is more stable than the other
(a) Ti^+, Ti^{3+} (b) Cu^+, Cu^{2+}
(c) Cr^{2+}, Cr^{3+} (d) V^{2+}, VO^{2+}

59. The correct order of increasing oxidising power of VO_2^+, MnO_4^- and $Cr_2O_7^{2-}$ is
(a) $MnO_4^- < Cr_2O_7^{2-} < VO_2^+$
(b) $VO_2^+ < Cr_2O_7^{2-} < MnO_4^-$
(c) $Cr_2O_7^{2-} < MnO_4^- < VO_2^+$
(d) $MnO_4^- < VO_2^+ < Cr_2O_7^{2-}$

60. The +3 oxidation state is most common in
(a) Ni (28) (b) Fe (26) (c) Zn (30) (d) Cu (29)

61. Which of the following will stabilise the highest oxidation state of a transition metal more than the others?
(a) fluorine (b) chlorine
(c) oxygen (d) sulfur

62. The titanium (At. no. 22) compound that does not exist is
(a) TiO (b) TiO_2 (c) K_2TiF_6 (d) $TiCl_3$
(e) K_2TiO_4

63. The transition metals have less tendency to form ions due to
(a) high ionisation enthalpy
(b) low heat of hydration of ions
(c) high heat of sublimation
(d) all of the above

64. Which of the following pairs of transition metal ions are the stronger oxidising agents in aqueous solutions?
(a) V^{2+} and Cr^{2+} (b) Ti^{2+} and Cr^{2+}
(c) Mn^{3+} and Co^{3+} (d) V^{2+} and Fe^{2+}
(e) Ni^{2+} and Fe^{2+}

65. Which of the M^{2+} compounds are more stable towards oxidation to their +3 state?
(a) Fe^{2+} compounds (b) Ti^{2+} compounds
(c) Cr^{2+} compounds (d) Mn^{2+} compounds

66. Mn^{2+} compounds are more stable than Fe^{2+} compounds towards oxidation to their +3 state because
(a) Mn^{2+} is more stable with a high 3rd ionisation enthalpy
(b) Mn^{2+} is bigger in size
(c) Mn^{2+} has completely filled *d* orbitals
(d) Mn^{2+} does not exist

67. Copper exhibits only the +2 oxidation state in its stable compounds. Why?
(a) Copper is a transition metal in the +2 state.
(b) The +2 state compounds of copper are formed by exothermic reactions.
(c) The electronic configuration of copper in the +2 state is [Ar] $3d^9 4s^0$.
(d) Copper gives coloured compounds in the +2 state.

68. The highest oxidation state exhibited by the transition metals is
(a) +7 (b) +8 (c) +6 (d) +5

69. Among K, Ca, Fe and Zn, the element which can form more than one binary compound with chlorine is
(a) Fe (b) Zn (c) K (d) Ca

70. A transition metal ion exists in its highest oxidation state. It is expected to behave as
(a) a chelating agent
(b) a central metal in a coordination compound
(c) an oxidising agent
(d) a reducing agent

71. In context with the transition elements, which of the following statements is incorrect?
(a) In addition to the normal oxidation states, the zero oxidation state is also shown by these elements in complexes.
(b) In the highest oxidation states, the transition metals show basic character and form cationic complexes.
(c) In the highest oxidation states of the first five transition elements (Sc to Mn), all the 4*s* and 3*d* electrons are used for bonding.

(d) Once the d^5 configuration is exceeded, the tendency to involve all the 3*d* electrons in bonding decreases.

72. In a reaction, the ferrous (Fe^{++}) ion is oxidised to the ferric (Fe^{+++}) ion. The equivalent weight of the ion in the above reaction is equal to

(a) half of the atomic weight
(b) 1/5 of the atomic weight
(c) the atomic weight
(d) twice the atomic weight

73. Transitional elements exhibit variable valencies because they release electrons from the following orbitals.

(a) *ns* orbitals (b) *ns* and *np* orbitals
(c) $(n-1)d$ and *ns* orbitals (d) $(n-1)d$ orbitals

74. The number of unpaired electrons in the gaseous species of Mn^{3+}, Cr^{3+} and V^{3+} respectively are ______ and the most stable species is ______.

(a) 4, 3 and 2 and V^{3+} is most stable
(b) 3, 3 and 2 and Cr^{3+} is most stable
(c) 4, 3 and 2 and Cr^{3+} is most stable
(d) 3, 3 and 3 and Mn^{3+} is most stable

75. All the following statements about the transition elements are true except that

(a) all of the transitional elements are predominantly metallic
(b) in aqueous solution many of their simple ions are coloured
(c) most of the transition elements show pronounced catalytic activity
(d) most of the transition elements show only one valence state

76. Which of the following transition metals can have the highest oxidation state?

(a) Cr (b) Co (c) Ni (d) Cu

77. Of the following outer electronic configuration of atoms, the highest oxidation state is achieved by which one of them?

(a) $(n-1)d^5\,ns^2$ (b) $(n-1)d^8\,ns^2$
(c) $(n-1)d^5\,ns^1$ (d) $(n-1)d^3\,ns^2$

78. The transition metal which shows an oxidation state from +2 to +7 belongs to group

(a) VIII B (7) (b) VI B (6)
(c) II B (12) (d) III B (3)

79. The 3*d* elements show variable oxidation states because the energies of the following sets of orbitals are almost similar

(a) $ns, (n-1)d$ (b) ns, nd
(c) $(n-1)s, nd$ (d) $np, (n-1)d$

80. The atomic number of an element is 22. The highest oxidation state exhibited by it in its compounds is

(a) 1 (b) 2 (c) 3 (d) 4

81. Mark the correct statement(s).

1. Manganese exhibits the +7 oxidation state.
2. Zinc forms coloured ions.
3. $[CoF_6]^{3-}$ is diamagnetic.
4. Sc forms the +4 oxidation state.
5. Zn exhibits only the +2 oxidation state.

(a) 1 and 2 (b) 1 and 5 (c) 2 and 4
(d) 3 and 4 (e) 2 and 5

82. Iron exhibits the +2 and +3 oxidation states. Which of the following statements about iron is incorrect?

(a) Ferrous oxide is more basic in nature than the ferric oxide.
(b) Ferrous compounds are relatively more ionic than the corresponding ferric compounds.
(c) Ferrous compounds are relatively less volatile than the corresponding ferric compounds.
(d) Ferrous compounds are more easily hydrolysed than the corresponding ferric compounds.

83. Which metal among following has the strongest tendency to undergo oxidation?

(a) Zn (b) Cu (c) Mg (d) Al

84. The most stable oxidation state of Mn is

(a) +2 (b) +4 (c) +5 (d) +7

85. Out of the following outer electronic configurations of atoms, the highest oxidation state is achieved by which one?

(a) $(n-1)d^8\,ns^2$ (b) $(n-1)d^5\,ns^2$
(c) $(n-1)d^3\,ns^2$ (d) $(n-1)d^5\,ns^1$

86. Which of the following is correct?

Both Cr^{2+} and Mn^{3+} have d^4 configuration but
(a) Cr^{2+} is oxidising and Mn^{3+} is reducing in character
(b) both Cr^{2+} and Mn^{3+} are oxidising in character
(c) Cr^{2+} is reducing and Mn^{3+} is oxidising in character
(d) both Cr^{2+} and Mn^{3+} are reducing in character

87. The irregularity in the E° values of the first row transition metals is due to

(a) irregular variation of ionisation enthalpies ($IE_1 + IE_2$)
(b) irregular variation of sublimation enthalpies which are relatively much lower for Mn (279 kJ mol^{-1}) and Cr (398 kJ mol^{-1})
(c) irregular variation of the sizes of the elements
(d) both (a) and (b)

88. Among the transition metals of the 3*d* series, the one that has the highest negative M^{2+}/M standard electrode potential is

(a) Ti (b) Cu (c) Mn (d) Ni (e) Zn

89. For an M^{2+}/M system, the $E°$ values for some metals are: $Cr^{2+}/Cr = -0.9$ V; $Mn^{2+}/Mn = -1.2$ V; $Fe^{2+}/Fe = -0.4$ V. On the basis of this data, the correct order of Cr, Mn and Fe metals getting oxidised will be

(a) Mn > Cr > Fe (b) Cr > Mn > Fe
(c) Fe > Mn > Cr (d) Fe > Cr > Mn

90. The $E°$ (M^{2+}/M) value for copper is positive (+0.34 V). This is because

(a) copper has a high enthalpy of atomisation
(b) copper has a low enthalpy of hydration
(c) the high energy required to transform Cu(*s*) to $Cu^{2+}(aq)$ is not balanced by its hydration enthalpy
(d) all the three above

91. The $E°$ value for Mn^{3+}/Mn^{2+} couple is much more positive than for Cr^{3+}/Cr^{2+} or Fe^{3+}/Fe^{2+} because

(a) Mn^{2+} is much more stable than Mn^{3+}
(b) Mn^{2+} has $3d^5$ configuration which is exactly half-filled and hence is very stable
(c) the third ionisation enthalpy of Mn will be very high
(d) all the three above

92. $E°$ values for the couple $Cr^{3+}/Cr^{2+} = -0.41$ V and for the couple $Fe^{3+}/Fe^{2+} = +0.77$ V. Which of the following is a stronger reducing agent?

(a) Cr^{2+} (b) Fe^{3+} (c) Fe^{2+} (d) Cr^{3+}

93. For an M^{3+}/M^{2+} system, the $E°$ values for some metals are: $Cr^{3+}/Cr^{2+} = -0.4$ V; $M^{3+}/M^{2+} = +1.5$ V; $Fe^{3+}/Fe^{2+} = +0.8$ V. On the basis of the data, the correct stability order of Cr^{3+}, Mn^{3+} and Fe^{3+} in acid solution will be

(a) $Cr^{3+} > Fe^{3+} > Mn^{3+}$ (b) $Fe^{3+} > Cr^{3+} > Mn^{3+}$
(c) $Mn^{3+} > Cr^{3+} > Fe^{3+}$ (d) $Mn^{3+} > Fe^{3+} > Cr^{3+}$

94. For which element of the first transition series is the oxidation potential value ($M \rightarrow M^{2+} + 2e^-$) the lowest?

(a) Mn (b) Fe (c) Ni (d) Cu

95. Which of the following is the weakest reducing agent?

(a) Zn (b) Cu (c) H_2 (d) Li

96. Irregular trend in the standard reduction potential value of the first row transition elements is due to

(a) regular variation of the first and second ionisation enthalpies
(b) irregular variation of sublimation enthalpies
(c) regular variation of sublimation enthalpies
(d) increase in the number of unpaired electrons

97. Which one of the following transition metal ions is paramagnetic?

(a) Ag^+ (b) Cu^{2+} (c) Zn^{2+} (d) Au^+

98. The transition metal ion with the least magnetic moment will have the configuration

(a) $3d^7$ (b) $3d^9$ (c) $3d^2$ (d) $3d^3$

99. Which of the following species is/are paramagnetic?
Fe^{2+}, Zn^0, Hg^{2+}, Ti^{4+}

(a) Fe^{2+} only (b) Zn^0 and Ti^{4+}
(c) Fe^{2+} and Hg^{2+} (d) Zn^0 and Hg^{2+}
(e) Fe^{2+} and Ti^{4+}

100. The pair in which both species have the same magnetic moment (spin only value) is

(a) $[Cr(H_2O)_6]^{2+}$, $[CoCl_4]^{2-}$
(b) $[Cr(H_2O)_6]^{2+}$, $[Fe(H_2O)_6]^{2+}$
(c) $[Mn(H_2O)_6]^{2+}$, $[Cr(H_2O)_6]^{2+}$
(d) $[CoCl_4]^{2-}$, $[Fe(H_2O)_6]^{2+}$

101. The complex $K_2[MnCl_4]$ has a magnetic moment of 5.9 BM. This shows that (select the incorrect statement)

(a) there are five unpaired electrons in the complex species
(b) as Cl^- is a weaker ligand and the coordination number of the metal ion is four, the complex will be tetrahedral
(c) the hybridisation involved will be sp^3
(d) the oxidation state of Mn in the complex will be +4

102. For which of the following pairs, is the magnetic moment the same?

(a) $MnCl_2$, $CuSO_4$ (b) $CuCl_2$, $TiCl_3$
(c) TiO_2, $CuSO_4$ (d) $TiCl_3$, $NiCl_2$

103. Which of the following pairs of transition metal ions has the same calculated values of the magnetic moment?

(a) Ti^{2+} and V^{2+} (b) Fe^{2+} and Cu^{2+}
(c) Cr^{2+} and Fe^{2+} (d) Co^{2+} and Ti^{2+}

104. The experimental value of the magnetic moment of Mn^{2+} complex is 5.96 BM. This indicates

(a) axial and orbital motion of electrons in the same direction
(b) axial and orbital motion of electrons in the opposite direction
(c) the electron does not exhibit orbital motion, it only exhibits axial motion
(d) the electron does not exhibit axial motion, it only exhibits orbital motion

105. The ion of least magnetic moment among the following is

(a) Ti^{3+} (b) Ni^{2+} (c) Co^{2+} (d) Mn^{2+}

106. Which one of the following sets correctly represents the increase in the paramagnetic property of the ions?

(a) $Cu^{2+} < V^{2+} < Cr^{2+} < Mn^{2+}$
(b) $Cu^{2+} < Cr^{2+} < V^{2+} < Mn^{2+}$
(c) $Cu^{2+} > V^{2+} > Cr^{2+} > Mn^{2+}$
(d) $V^{2+} < Cu^{2+} < Cr^{2+} < Mn^{2+}$

107. A transition metal A has a spin-only magnetic moment value of 1.8 BM. When it is reacted with dilute sulfuric acid in the presence of air, a compound B is formed. B reacts with compound C to give compound D with the liberation of iodine. Then, the metal A and compounds B, C and D are respectively,

(a) Ti, $TiSO_4$, KI and TiI_2
(b) Zn, $ZnSO_4$, KI and Zn_2I_2
(c) Cu, $CuSO_4$, KI and Cu_2I_2
(d) Cu, $CuSO_4$, Cu_2I_2 and CuI_2
(e) Cu, $CuSO_4$, KI and CuI_2

108. Which is not correct statement about the chemistry of the 3*d* and 4*f* series elements?

(a) 3*d* elements show more oxidation states than 4*f* series elements.
(b) The energy difference between 3*d* and 4*s* orbitals is very little.
(c) Europium (II) is more stable than Ce (II).
(d) The paramagnetic character in the 3*d* series elements increases from scandium to copper.

109. Which has the maximum ferromagnetic character?

(a) Fe (b) Co (c) Ni (d) Pt

110. Which of the following weighs less when weighed in a magnetic field?

(a) VCl_3 (b) $SeCl_3$ (c) $TiCl_3$ (d) $FeCl_3$

111. The atomic numbers of Cr and Fe are 24 and 26 respectively. Which of the following is paramagnetic with the spin of electron?

(a) $[Cr(NH_3)_6]^{+3}$ (b) $[Fe(CO)_5]$
(c) $[Fe(CN)_6]^{-4}$ (d) $[Cr(CO)_6]$

112. Amongst following, the lowest degree of paramagnetism per mole of the compound at 298 K will be shown by

(a) $MnSO_4.4H_2O$ (b) $CuSO_4.5H_2O$
(c) $FeSO_4.6H_2O$ (d) $FeSO_4.5H_2O$

113. In the nitroprusside ion, the iron and NO exist as Fe^{II} and NO^+ rather than Fe^{III} and NO. These forms can be differentiated by

(a) estimating the concentration of iron
(b) measuring the concentration of CN^-
(c) measuring the solid state magnetic moment
(d) thermally decomposing the compound

114. Among the species given below, the total number of diamagnetic species is ______. H atom, NO_2 monomer, O_2^- (superoxide), dimeric sulfur in the vapour phase, Mn_3O_4, $(NH_4)_2[FeCl_4]$, $(NH_4)_2[NiCl_4]$, K_2MnO_4, K_2CrO_4

(a) 2 (b) 3 (c) 1 (d) 4

115. The aqueous solution of the following salts will be coloured in the case of

(a) $Zn(NO_3)_2$ (b) $LiNO_3$
(c) $Co(NO_3)_2$ (d) potash alum

116. Which one of the transition metal ions is coloured?

(a) Cu^+ (b) Zn^{2+} (c) Sc^{3+} (d) V^{4+}

117. Of the ions Zn^{2+}, Ni^{2+} and Cr^{3+}(At nos: Zn = 30, Ni = 28, Cr = 24)

(a) only Zn^{2+} is colourless and Ni^{2+} and Cr^{3+} are coloured
(b) all three are colourless
(c) all three are coloured
(d) only Ni^{2+} is coloured and Zn^{2+} and Cr^{3+} are colourless

118. Transition metals have the electronic configuration $(n-1)d^{1-10}\ ns^{1-2}$. The *d* orbitals are degenerate. The colour of the transition metal ions is due to absorption of some wavelength. This results in

(a) *d–s* transition (b) *s–d* transition
(c) *s–s* transition (d) *d–d* transition

119. Which group contains coloured ions?

1. Cu^{2+} 2. Ti^{4+} 3. Co^{2+} 4. Fe^{2+}

(a) 1, 2, 3, 4 (b) 1, 3, 4
(c) 2, 3 (d) 1, 2

120. The dark blue colour of the solution formed when excess of ammonia is added to a solution of copper (II) sulfate is due to the presence of the ion

(a) $[Cu(OH)_4(OH)_2]^{2+}$ (b) $[Cu(H_2O)_6]^{2+}$
(c) $[Cu(NH_4)_2(H_2O)_4]^{4+}$ (d) $[Cu(NH_3)_2(H_2O)_4]^{2+}$
(e) $[Cu(NH_3)_4(H_2O)_2]^{2+}$

121. Which of the following compounds is coloured?

(a) $TiCl_3$ (b) $FeCl_3$
(c) $CoCl_2$ (d) all of these

122. Cuprous ion is colourless while cupric ion is coloured because

(a) both have half-filled *p* and *d* orbitals
(b) cuprous ion has incomplete *d* orbital and cupric ion has a complete *d* orbital
(c) both have unpaired electrons in the *d* orbitals
(d) cuprous ion has a complete *d* orbital and cupric ion has an incomplete *d* orbital

123. Which compound is expected to be coloured?

(a) CuCl (b) CuF_2 (c) Ag_2SO_4 (d) MgF_2

124. In which of the following ions are *d–d* transitions not possible?

(a) Cr^{3+} (b) Ti^{4+} (c) Cu^{2+} (d) Mn^{2+}

125. Which of the following is red in colour?

(a) Cu_2O (b) CuF (c) ZnF_2 (d) $ZnCl_2$

126. Which of the following is the green coloured powder produced when ammonium dichromate is used in fireworks?

(a) Cr (b) CrO_3 (c) Cr_2O_3 (d) $CrO(O_2)$

127. The transition metal which forms a green compound in the +3 oxidation state and a yellow-orange compound in the +6 oxidation state is

(a) Fe (b) Ni (c) Cr (d) Co

128. Which of the following will give a green hydrated ion?

(a) Fe^{+2} (b) Ni^{+2}
(c) (a) and (b) both (d) V^{+3}

129. The colour imparted by Co (II) compounds to glass is

(a) green (b) deep blue
(c) yellow (d) red

130. In which of the following ions are *d–d* transitions not possible?

(a) Ti^{4+} (b) Cr^{3+} (c) Mn^{2+} (d) Cu^{2+}

131. Which of the following pairs of ions may exhibit same colour?

(a) Cr^{+++} and Fe^{++} (b) Ti^{+++} and V^{++}
(c) Fe^{+++} and Mn^{++} (d) Cu^{+} and Ni^{++}

132. The 3*d* metal ions form coloured compounds because the energy corresponding to the following lies in the visible range of the electromagnetic spectrum.

(a) free energy change of complex formation by 3*d* metal ions
(b) *d–d* transitions of 3*d* electrons
(c) heat of hydration of 3*d* metal ions
(d) ionisation enthalpy of 3*d* metal ions
(d) They exhibit catalytic property.

133. Which of the following compounds is expected to be colourless?

(a) ScO (b) V_2O_3 (c) CuCN (d) $Cr_2(SO_4)_3$

134. Which compound has coloured aqueous solutions?

(a) $Zn(NO_3)_2$ (b) $LiNO_3$
(c) $Co\ (NO_{3)2}$ (d) $Ba(NO_3)_2$

135. Low spin complexes are generally formed by elements of

(a) 3*d* series (b) 4*d* series
(c) 5*d* series (d) both (b) and (c)

136. Which of the following octahedral hydrated transition metal ions does not have two unpaired electrons in its e_g set of orbitals?

(a) Mn^{2+} (b) Fe^{3+} (c) Cu^{2+} (d) Co^{2+}

137. On adding excess of NH_4OH to copper sulfate solution

(a) a deep blue solution is obtained
(b) a blue precipitate of $Cu(OH)_2$ is obtained
(c) a black precipitate of CuO is obtained
(d) no change takes place

138. Pt dissolves in aqua regia due to the formation of

(a) $PtCl_4$ (b) $PtCl_2$
(c) $Pt(NO_3)_2$ (d) H_2PtCl_6

139. When Co (II) chloride is dissolved in concentrated HCl, a blue solution is obtained. Upon dilution with water, the colour changes to pink because

(a) $CoCl_6^{4-}$ is converted to $CoCl_6^{3-}$
(b) $CoCl_4^{2-}$ is converted to $Co(OH_2)_6^{2+}$
(c) $Co(OH_2)_6^{2+}$ is converted to $Co(OH_2)_6^{3+}$
(d) $CoCl_4^{2-}$ is converted to $Co(OH_2)_6^{3+}$

140. Ammonia will not form a complex with

(a) Ag^{2+} (b) Pb^{2+} (c) Cu^{2+} (d) Cd^{2+}
(e) Fe^{2+}

141. When Zn is treated with excess of NaOH, the product obtained is

(a) $Zn(OH)_2$ (b) ZnOH
(c) Na_2ZnO_2 (d) none of these

142. An aqueous solution of $CoCl_2$ on addition of excess of conc. HCl turns blue due to the formation of

(a) $[Co(H_2O)]Cl_2$ (b) $[Co(H_2O)_2Cl_4]^{2-}$
(c) $[CoCl_4]^{2-}$ (d) $[Co(H_2O)_2Cl]$

143. When $CuSO_4$ reacts with KCN, it forms CuCN which is insoluble in water. It is soluble in excess of KCN, due to the formation of the following complex,

(a) $K_2[Cu(CN)_4]$ (b) $K_3[Cu(CN)_4]$
(c) $CuCN_2$ (d) $Cu[KCu(CN)_4]$

144. The formula of ammonium manganate is

(a) NH_4MnO_4 (b) $(NH_4)_2MnO_4$
(c) $NH_4(MnO_4)_2$ (d) $NH_4Mn_2O_4$

145. The coordination number in a/an _____ complex may increase to 8.

(a) cobalt (b) osmium (c) nickel (d) iron

146. Which of the following is obtained when auric chloride reacts with sodium chloride?

(a) $Na[AuCl]$ (b) $Na[AuCl_2]$
(c) $Na[AuCl_3]$ (b) $Na[AuCl_4]$

147. One of the following metals forms a volatile carbonyl compound and this property is taken advantage of for its extraction. This metal is

(a) iron (b) nickel (c) cobalt (d) tungsten

148. Pick out the correct statements from the following.

1. Cobalt (III) is more stable in octahedral complexes.
2. Zinc forms coloured complexes.
3. Most of the *d*-block elements and their compounds are ferromagnetic.
4. Osmium shows the VIII oxidation state.
5. Cobalt (II) is more stable in octahedral complexes.

(a) 1 and 2 (b) 1 and 3 (c) 2 and 4
(d) 1 and 4 (e) 2 and 5

149. The tendency of 3*d* metal ions to form stable complexes is due to their

(a) variable oxidation state
(b) strong electronegative nature
(c) high charge/size ratio and vacant *d* orbitals
(d) very low ionisation energies

150. Which of the following ions form most stable complex compounds?

(a) Cu^{++} (b) Ni^{++} (c) Fe^{++} (d) Mn^{++}

151. A hydroxide soluble in ammonia is

(a) $Ag(OH)_3$ (b) $Fe(OH)_3$
(c) $Cr(OH)_3$ (d) $Cu(OH)_2$

152. AgCl dissolves in a solution of NH_3 but not in water because

(a) NH_3 is a better solvent than H_2O
(b) Ag^+ forms a complex ion with NH_3
(c) NH_3 is a stronger base than H_2O
(d) the dipole moment of water is higher than that of NH_3

153. Given below are catalysts and the corresponding process/reaction. The mismatch is

(a) $[RhCl(Pph_3)_3]$: hydrogenation
(b) $[TiCl_4 + Al(C_2H_5)_3]$: polymerisation
(c) V_2O_5 : Haber–Bosch process
(d) nickel : hydrogenation

154. Which occludes hydrogen?

(a) Os (b) Pt
(c) Ni (d) all of these

155. Super conductors are derived from compounds of

(a) *p*-block elements (b) lanthanoids
(c) actinoids (d) transition elements
(e) scandium

156. Which of the following pairs of elements cannot form an alloy?

(a) Zn, Cu (b) Fe, Hg (c) Fe, C (d) Hg, Na

157. Which of the following metals melts in boiling water?

(a) gun metal (b) wood's metal
(c) monel metal (d) bell metal
(e) none of these

158. Which one is wrong in the following statements?

(a) Gold is considered to be the king of metals.
(b) Gold is soluble in mercury.
(c) Copper is added to gold to make it hard.
(d) None of these.

159. Super alloys are usually

(a) iron based (b) nickel based
(c) cobalt based (d) based on all of these

160. A mixture of TiO_2 and $BaSO_4$ is called

(a) titanox (b) lithopone
(c) white pigment (d) none

161. Which of the following is used as a purgative?

(a) HgS (b) Hg_2Cl_2 (c) $HgCl_2$ (d) $ZnSO_4$

162. Which of the following is known as *Bordeaux mixture*?

(a) borax and copper sulfite
(b) orthoboric acid and ferrous sulfate
(c) sodium borate and zinc sulfate
(d) copper sulfate and lime
(e) borax and manganous sulfate

163. Which of the following is used as indelible ink?

(a) aqueous $CuSO_4$ solution
(b) aqueous $AgNO_3$ solution
(c) aqueous NaCl solution
(d) aqueous NaOH solution

164. Fenton's reagent is

(a) $SnCl_2 + HCl$ (b) $AgNO_3 + NH_4OH$
(c) $CuSO_4 + NaOH$ (d) $FeSO_4 + H_2O_2$

165. A cigarette or gas lighter is made up of

(a) misch metal (b) alkali metal
(c) noble metal (d) none

166. Bullet-proof steel alloy is prepared using

(a) Sc (b) Ni (c) Zr (d) Zn

167. In making gun-barrels, the steel used is

(a) Fe–Mn (b) Fe–Cr (c) Fe–W (d) Ni–Mo

168. Niobium and tantalum metals are used in making surgical instruments because they are

(a) non-corrosive (b) hard
(c) soft (d) all

169. To support the tungsten filament in electric bulbs, the steel used is

(a) Cr (b) Ni (c) Mn (d) Mo

170. Mercury is transported in metal containers made of

(a) silver (b) lead
(c) iron (d) aluminium

171. The electroplating of chromium is undertaken because

(a) electrolysis of chromium is easier
(b) chromium can form alloys with other metals
(c) chromium gives a protective and decorative coating to the base metal
(d) of the high reactivity of metallic chromium

172. A hard and resistant metal (alloy) generally used in the tips of the nibs of fountain pens is

(a) Os. Ir (b) Pt. Cr (c) V. Fe (d) Fe. Cr

173. Out of following, which compound is used for the preservation of wood?

(a) NaCl (b) $HgCl_2$ (c) $ZnCl_2$ (d) $CaCl_2$

174. $CoO.Al_2O_3$ is called

(a) cobalt aluminate (b) Thenard's blue
(c) both (a) and (b) (d) none of these

175. Ferrosillicon is used in the steel industry as

(a) a flux (b) scavenger of hydrogen
(c) a reducing agent (d) a cutting tool
(e) alloying agent

176. Pick out the covalent halide from the following

(a) CuF_2 (b) $CuBr_2$ (c) $ZnCl_2$ (d) $CoCl_2$

177. Among the oxides, Mn_2O_7(I), V_2O_3(II), V_2O_5(III), CrO(IV) and Cr_2O_3(V), the basic oxides are

(a) I and II (b) II and III (c) III and IV
(d) II and IV (e) III and V

178. The acidic, basic or amphoteric nature of Mn_2O_7, V_2O_5 and CrO are respectively

(a) acidic, acidic and basic
(b) basic, amphoteric and acidic
(c) acidic, amphoteric and basic
(d) acidic, basic and amphoteric
(e) acidic, basic and basic

179. When a brown compound of Mn (A) is treated with HCl, it gives a gas (B). The gas (B) taken in excess reacts with NH_3 to give an explosive compound (C). The compounds A, B and C are

(a) $A = MnO_2$, $B = Cl_2$, $C = NCl_3$
(b) $A = MnO$, $B = Cl_2$, $C = NH_3Cl$
(c) $A = Mn_3O_4$, $B = Cl_2$, $C = NCl_3$
(d) $A = MnO_3$, $B = Cl_2$, $C = NCl_2$

180. The amphoteric oxide among the following is

(a) Cr_2O_3 (b) Mn_2O_7 (c) V_2O_3 (d) CrO

181. Which of the following metals forms an amphoteric oxide?

(a) Fe (b) Cu (c) Zn (d) Ca

182. Which element gives a maximum number of oxides?

(a) V (b) Cr (c) Mn (d) Fe

183. All the metals form oxides of the type MO except

(a) copper (b) barium (c) silver (d) lead

184. Though Zn and Hg belong to the same group, they differ in many of their properties. The property that is shared by both is

(a) they form oxides readily
(b) they react with steam readily
(c) they react with hot concentrated sulfuric acid
(d) they react with hot sodium hydroxide

185. Which oxide of manganese is amphoteric?

(a) MnO_2 (b) Mn_2O_3 (c) Mn_2O_7 (d) MnO

186. Which one of the following oxides is ionic?

(a) MnO (b) Mn_2O_7 (c) CrO_3 (d) P_2O_5

187. Which of the following pairs contains amphoteric oxides?

(a) V_2O_5, Cr_2O_3 (b) Mn_2O_7, Cr_2O_3
(c) CrO, V_2O_5 (d) V_2O_5, V_2O_4

188. Which of the manganese oxides is the most acidic from the given options?

(a) Mn_2O_3 (b) MnO (c) MnO_2 (d) Mn_2O_7

189. The oxidising ability of the given anions follows the order

(a) $TiO_4^{4-} < VO_4^{3-} < CrO_4^{2-} < MnO_4^{4-}$
(b) $VO_4^{3-} < CrO_4^{2-} < MnO_4^{4-} < TiO_4^{4-}$
(c) $CrO_4^{2-} < MnO_4^{4-} < VO_4^{3-} < TiO_4^{4-}$
(d) $VO_4^{3-} < TiO_4^{4-} < CrO_4^{2-} < MnO_4^{4-}$

190. Calomel (Hg_2Cl_2) on reaction with NH_4OH gives

(a) HgO (b) Hg_2O
(c) NH–Hg–Hg–Cl (d) $HgNH_2Cl$

191. Which of the following compounds on reaction with NaOH and Na_2O_2 gives yellow colour?

(a) $Zn(OH)_2$ (b) $Al(OH)_3$ (c) $Cr(OH)_3$ (d) $CaCO_3$

192. Metal ion responsible for the Minamata disease is

(a) Co^{2+} (b) Hg^{2+} (c) Cu^{2+} (d) Zn^{2+}

193. Choose the correct reaction to prepare mercurous chloride (calomel).

(a) $HgCl_2 + Hg \xrightarrow{\Delta}$ (b) $Hg + Cl \rightarrow$
(c) $HgCl_2 + SnCl_2 \rightarrow$ (d) both options (a) and (c)

194. The solid product formed on heating $AgNO_3$ strongly to 980 K is

(a) silver carbonate (b) silver nitride

(c) silver oxide (d) silver metal
(e) silver nitrite

195. Reason of passivity of iron is

(a) Fe_2O_3 (b) Fe_3O_4
(c) FeO (d) $Fe_2O_4.3H_2O$

196. Which of the following is a highly corrosive salt?

(a) $FeCl_2$ (b) $PbCl_2$ (c) Hg_2Cl_2 (d) $HgCl_2$

197. Green vitriol is formed by

(a) $FeS_2 + H_2O + O_2$ (b) $FeS_2 + H_2O + CO_2$
(c) $FeS_2 + CO + CO_2$ (d) $FeS_2 + CO$

198. Which is the most reactive metal?

(a) Fe (b) Pt (c) Ni (d) Co

199. Which metal does not give the following reaction?

M + water or steam $\rightarrow$ oxide + $H_2\uparrow$
(a) mercury (b) iron
(c) sodium (d) magnesium

200. Which one of the following organisation's iron and steel plant was built to use charcoal as a source of power, to start with, but later switched over to hydroelectricity?

(a) Tata Iron and Steel Company
(b) Indian Iron and Steel Company
(c) Mysore Iron and Steel Limited
(d) Hindustan Steel Limited

201. Mn^{2+} can be converted into Mn^{7+} by reacting with

(a) SO_2 (b) Cl_2 (c) PbO_2 (d) $SnCl_2$

202. Which transition metal reduces steam to evolve hydrogen?

(a) Mg (b) Fe (c) Sc (d) Pt

203. What is the product obtained when MnO_2 solution is boiled with PbO_2 and concentrated HNO_3?

(a) MnO_2 (b) $HMnO_4$
(c) Mn_3O_4 (d) $PbMnO_4$

204. Which of the following reactions will occur on heating $AgNO_3$ above its melting point?

(a) $2\,AgNO_3 \rightarrow 2\,Ag + 2\,NO_2 + O_2$
(b) $2\,AgNO_3 \rightarrow 2\,Ag + N_2 + 3\,O_2$
(c) $2\,AgNO_3 \rightarrow 2\,AgNO_2 + O_2$
(d) $2\,AgNO_3 \rightarrow 2\,Ag + 2\,NO + 2\,O_2$
(e) $2\,AgNO_3 \rightarrow 2\,Ag_2O + 2\,N_2O_3 + O_2$

205. Percentage of gold in 18 carat gold is:

(a) 38.67% (b) 75.0% (c) 80.0% (d) 20.0%

206. The hardness of Cr is due to _______ and metallic lustre is due to _______.

(a) covalent bond, metallic bond
(b) covalent bond, hydrogen bond
(c) metallic bond, covalent bond
(d) metallic bond, hydrogen bond

Important Compounds of Transition Elements (Salts of Oxoanions of Metals)

207. How many mol of iodine are liberated when 1 mol of potassium dichromate reacts with potassium iodide?

(a) 1 (b) 2 (c) 3 (d) 4

208. When acidified $K_2Cr_2O_7$ solution is added to Sn^{2+} salts, then Sn^{2+} changes to

(a) Sn (b) Sn^{3+} (c) Sn^{4+} (d) Sn^{+}

209. In the reaction $(NH_4)_2Cr_2O_7 \xrightarrow{\Delta} N_2 + H_2O + Cr_2O_3$ the coefficient of H_2O is

(a) 1 (b) 2 (c) 3 (d) 4

210. How many grams of potassium dichromate are required to oxidise 20.0 g of Fe^{2+} in $FeSO_4$ to Fe^{3+} if the reaction is carried out in an acidic medium? Molar masses of $K_2Cr_2O_7$ and $FeSO_4$ are 294 and 152 respectively

(a) 6.45 g (b) 7.45 g (c) 8.45 g (d) 9.45 g

211. CrO_3 dissolves in aqueous NaOH to give

(a) $Cr_2O_7^{2-}$ (b) CrO_4^{2-}
(c) $Cr(OH)_3$ (d) $Cr(OH)_2$

212. The gas produced from thermal decomposition of $(NH_4)_2Cr_2O_7$ is

(a) oxygen (b) nitric oxide
(c) ammonia (d) nitrogen

213. The number of electrons required to reduce chromium completely in $Cr_2O_7^{2-}$ to Cr^{3+} in acidic medium is

(a) 5 (b) 3 (c) 6 (d) 2

214. The oxidation state of chromium in the final product formed by the reaction between KI and acidified potassium dichromate solution is

(a) +3 (b) +2 (c) +6 (d) +4

215. When dil. H_2SO_4 is added to aqueous solution of potassium chromate, yellow colour of solution turns to orange colour. It indicates.

(a) chromate ions are reduced
(b) chromate ions are oxidised
(c) monocentric complex is converted into dicentric complex
(d) oxygen gets removed from chromate ions

216. $4\,K_2Cr_2O_7 \xrightarrow{\text{Heat}} 4\,K_2CrO_4 + 3\,O_2 + X$

In the above reaction X is

(a) CrO_3 (b) Cr_2O_7 (c) Cr_2O_3 (d) CrO_5

217. Acidified potassium dichromate is treated with hydrogen sulfide. In the reaction, the oxidation number of chromium

(a) increases from +3 to +6
(b) decreases from +6 to +3
(c) remains unchanged
(d) decreases from +6 to +2

218. When sulfur dioxide is passed into an acidified $K_2Cr_2O_7$ solution, the oxidation state of sulfur is changed from
(a) +4 to +6 (b) +6 to +4
(c) +4 to 0 (d) +4 to +2

219. The colour of $K_2Cr_2O_7$ changes from red-orange to lemon yellow on treatment with aqueous KOH because of
(a) the reduction of Cr^{VI} to Cr^{III}
(b) the formation of chromium hydroxide
(c) the conversion of dichromate to chromate
(d) the oxidation of potassium hydroxide to potassium peroxide

220. Identify the case(s) where there is a change in oxidation number.
(a)acidified solution of CrO_4^{2-}
(b) SO_2 gas bubbled through an acidic solution of $Cr_2O_7^{2-}$
(c) alkaline solution of $Cr_2O_7^{2-}$
(d) ammoniacal solution of CrO_4^{2-}
(e) aqueous solution of CrO_2Cl_2 in NaOH

221. Which is the correct statement about the structure of $Cr_2O_7^{2-}$?
(a) It has neither Cr–Cr bonds nor O–O bonds.
(b) It has one Cr–Cr bond and six O–O bonds.
(c) It has no Cr–Cr bond and has six O–O bonds.
(d) It has one Cr–Cr bond and seven Cr–O bonds.

222. Which of the following compounds is used as the starting material for the preparation of potassium dichromate?
(a) $K_2SO_4.Cr_2(SO_4)_3.24H_2O$ (chrome alum)
(b) $PbCrO_4$ (chrome yellow)
(c) $FeCr_2O_4$ (chromite)
(d) $PbCrO_4.PbO$ (chrome red)

223. The fusion of chromite ore ($FeCr_2O_7$) with Na_2CO_3 in air gives a yellow solution upon addition of water. Subsequent treatment with H_2SO_4 produces an orange solution. The yellow and orange colours, respectively, are due to the formation of
(a) Na_2CrO_4 and $Na_2Cr_2O_7$
(b) $Cr(OH)_3$ and $Na_2Cr_2O_7$
(c) $Cr_2(CO_3)_3$ and $Fe_2(SO_4)_3$
(d) $Cr(OH)_3$ and Na_2CrO_4

224. One of the products formed when $K_2Cr_2O_7$ reacts with conc. H_2SO_4 in cold is
(a) $Cr_2(SO_4)_3$ (b) Cr_2O_3
(c) CrO_3 (d) CrO_4Cl_2

225. The equivalent weight of $K_2Cr_2O_7$ in the acidic medium when it acts as an oxidant according to the equation

$Cr_2O_7^{2-} + 14\,H^+ + 6e^- \rightarrow 2\,Cr^{3+} + 7\,H_2O$ is,

(a) M (b) M/2 (c) M/6 (d) M/5

226. x mol of potassium dichromate oxidises 1 mol of ferrous oxalate in acidic medium. Here x is
(a) 3 (b) 1.5 (c) 0.5 (d) 1.0

Potassium Permanganate ($KMnO_4$)

227. Which of the following cannot reduce an acidified solution of MnO_4^- ion?
(a) $H_2C_2O_4$ (b) H_2
(c) H (nascent) (d) Fe^{2+} ions

228. One of the products formed due to the reaction between $KMnO_4$ and HCl is
(a) red liquid (b) MnO_2
(c) greenish yellow gas (d) $HClO_4$

229. Which one of the following compounds does not decolourise an acidified aqueous solution of $KMnO_4$?
(a) sulfur dioxide (b) ferric sulfate
(c) hydrogen peroxide (d) ferrous sulfate

230. $KMnO_4$ is a strong oxidising agent in acid medium. To provide an acid medium, H_2SO_4 is used instead of HCl. This is because
(a) H_2SO_4 is a stronger acid than HCl
(b) HCl is oxidised by $KMnO_4$ to Cl_2
(c) H_2SO_4 is a dibasic acid
(d) the rate is faster in the presence of H_2SO_4
(e) only H_2SO_4 is completely ionised

231. The reaction of solid $KMnO_4$ with conc. H_2SO_4 produces manganese heptoxide (Mn_2O_7) in
(a) solution state (b) solid state
(c) fine powder (d) none of these

232. Oxalic acid when treated with potassium permanganate in the presence of an acid produces
(a) O_2 (b) C (c) CO (d) CO_2

233. The number of mol of Br_2 produced when two mol of potassium permanganate is heated with excess potassium bromide in aqueous acid medium is
(a) 1 (b) 3 (c) 2 (d) 4

234. The number of mol of $KMnO_4$ required to oxidise one equivalent of KI in the presence of sulfuric acid is
(a) 5 (b) 2 (c) 1/2 (d) 1/5

235. Potassium permanganate acts as an oxidant in neutral, alkaline as well as acidic media. The final products obtained from it in the three conditions are, respectively.
(a) MnO_2, MnO_2, Mn^{2+} (b) MnO_4^{2-}, Mn^{3+}, Mn^{2+}

(c) MnO_2, MnO_4^{2-}, Mn^{3+} (d) MnO, MnO_4, Mn^{2+}

236. The purple colour of $KMnO_4$ is due to
(a) charge transfer (b) *d–d* transition
(c) *f–f* transition (d) *d–f* transition

237. The equivalent mass of $KMnO_4$ in the following reaction is (M = molecular mass)

$$MnO_4^- + 5\,Fe^{2+} + 8\,H^+ \rightarrow Mn^{2+} + 5\,Fe^{3+} + 4\,H_2O$$

(a) $\frac{M}{2}$ (b) $\frac{M}{3}$ (c) $\frac{M}{4}$ (d) $\frac{M}{5}$

238. In following reaction,

$$y\,MnO_4^- + x\,H^+ + C_2O_4^{2-} \rightarrow y\,Mn^{++} + 2\,CO_2 + \frac{x}{2}\,H_2O$$

x and *y* are
(a) 2 and 16 (b) 16 and 2
(c) 8 and 16 (d) 5 and 2

239. When an acidified solution of ferrous ammonium sulfate is treated with potassium permanganate solution, the ion which is oxidised is
(a) MnO_4^- (b) NH_4^+ (c) Fe^{++} (d) SO_4^{2-}

240. Which one of the following is reduced by hydrogen peroxide in acid medium?
(a) potassium permanganate
(b) potassium iodide
(c) ferrous sulfate
(d) potassium ferrocyanide

241. In the alkaline condition, $KMnO_4$ reacts as follows
$2\,KMnO_4 + 2\,KOH \rightarrow 2\,K_2MnO_4 + H_2O + O$
Therefore, its equivalent weight will be
(a) 31.5 (b) 52.7 (c) 72.0 (d) 158.0

242. The equivalent weight of potassium permanganate in acid solution is
(a) 158 (b) 31.6 (c) 52.16 (d) 79

243. Which statement is not correct?
(a) Potassium permanganate is a powerful oxidising substance.
(b) Potassium permanganate is a weaker oxidising substance than potassium dichromate.
(c) Potassium permanganate is a stronger oxidising substance than potassium dichromate.
(d) Potassium dichromate oxidises a secondary alcohol into a ketone.

244. $KMnO_4$ in the basic medium is reduced to
(a) K_2MnO_4 (b) MnO_2 (c) $Mn(OH)_2$ (d) Mn^{2+}

245. Acidified $KMnO_4$ is not decolourised
(a) Br_2 (b) N_2H_4 (c) HCl (d) HBr

246. $KMnO_4$ acts as an oxidising agent in the alkaline medium. When alkaline $KMnO_4$ is treated with KI, iodide ion is oxidised to
(a) I_2 (b) IO^- (c) IO_3^- (d) IO_4^-

247. How many electrons are involved during the oxidation reaction of $KMnO_4$ in the acidic medium?
(a) 1 (b) 3 (c) 5 (d) 4

248. $KMnO_4$ reacts with H_2O_2 in an acidic medium. The number of mol of oxygen produced per mol of $KMnO_4$ is
(a) 2.5 (b) 5 (c) 1.25 (d) 2

249. To measure the quantity of $MnCl_2$ dissolved in an aqueous solution, it was completely converted to $KMnO_4$ using the reaction

$$MnCl_2 + K_2S_2O_8 + H_2O \rightarrow KMnO_4 + H_2SO_4 + HCl$$

(equation not balanced)

A few drops of concentrated HCl were added to this solution and gently warmed. Further, oxalic and (225 mg) was added in portions till the colour of the permanganate ion disappeared. The quantity of $MnCl_2$ (in mg) present in the initial solution is ____.

(Atomic weights in g mol^{-1}: Mn = 55, Cl = 35.5)
(a) 252 (b) 126 (c) 63 (d) 142

250. Baeyer's reagent is
(a) $KMnO_4 + H_2SO_4$ (b) $KMnO_4 + KOH$
(c) $K_2Cr_2O_7 + H_2SO_4$ (d) $K_2Cr_2O_7 + KOH$

251. The electrolysis of potassium manganate solution gives
(a) $MnO_2 + KOH$ (b) $KOH + H_2$
(c) $KOH + O_2$ (d) $KMnO_4 + KOH$

252. In the laboratory, a manganese (II) salt is oxidised to the permanganate ion in aqueous solution by
(a) hydrogen peroxide (b) conc. HNO_3
(c) peroxydisulfate (d) dichromate
(e) ozone

253. MnO_2 when fused with KOH and oxidised in air, gives a dark green compound X. In an acidic solution, X undergoes disproportionation to give an intense purple compound X and MnO_2. The compounds X and Y respectively are
(a) K_2MnO_4 and $KMnO_4$ (b) Mn_2O_7 and $KMnO_4$
(c) K_2MnO_4 and Mn_2O_7 (d) $KMnO_4$ and K_2MnO_4

Lanthanoids and Actinoids

254. The point of dissimilarity between the lanthanides and actinides is
(a) three outermost shells are partially filled
(b) they show an oxidation state of +3 (common)
(c) they are called the inner-transition elements
(d) they are radioactive in nature

255. Lanthanum is grouped with *f*-block elements because
(a) it has partially filled *f* orbitals
(b) it is just before Ce in the periodic table
(c) it has both partially filled *f* and *d* orbitals
(d) the properties of lanthanum are very similar to the elements of the 4 *f* block

256. Lanthanoids are
(a) 14 elements in the sixth period (atomic number = 90 to 103) that are filling the 4*f* sublevel
(b) 14 elements in the seventh period (atomic number = 90 to 103) that are filling the 5*f* sublevel
(c) 14 elements in the sixth period (atomic number = 58 to 71) that are filling the 4*f* sublevel
(d) 14 elements in the seventh period (atomic number = 58 to 71) that are filling the 4*f* sublevel

257. Which of the following is the outer electronic configuration of Lu^{2+}?
(a) $[Xe]\,4f^4$ (b) $[Xe]4f^5\,5d^1$
(c) $[Xe]\,4f^{14}\,5d^1$ (d) $[Xe]4f^{12}\,5d^1\,6s^2$

258. Ce^{4+} is stable. This is because of
(a) half-filled *d* orbitals
(b) all electrons are paired in the *d* orbitals
(c) empty orbitals
(d) fully-filled *d* orbitals

259. Gd (64) has ___ unpaired electrons with sum of spin ___.
(a) 7, 3.5 (b) 8, 3 (c) 6, 3 (d) 8, 4
(e) 9, 3.5

260. The correct order of ionic radii of Y^{3+}, La^{3+}, Eu^{3+} and Lu^{3+} is
(a) $Y^{3+} < La^{3+} < Cu^{3+} < Lu^{3+}$ (b) $Lu^{3+} < Y^{3+} < Eu^{3+} < La^{3+}$
(c) $La^{3+} < Eu^{3+} < Lu^{3+} < Y^{3+}$ (d) $Y^{3+} < Lu^{3+} < Eu^{3+} < Y^{3+}$
(e) $Eu^{3+} < La^{3+} < Lu^{3+} < Y^{3+}$

261. Which one of the following is the correct increasing order of the magnitude of ionic radii of Ce^{3+}, La^{3+}, Pm^{3+} and Yb^{3+}?
(a) $Yb^{3+} < Pm^{3+} < La^{3+} < Ce^{3+}$
(b) $Yb^{3+} < Pm^{3+} < Ce^{3+} < La^{3+}$
(c) $Pm^{3+} < La^{3+} < Ce^{3+} < Yb^{3+}$
(d) $Ce^{3+} < Yb^{3+} < Pm^{3+} < L^{3+}$

262. Which of the following statements regarding lanthanoids is false?
(a) All lanthanoids are solids at room temperature.
(b) Their usual oxidation state is +3.
(c) They can be separated from one another by ion exchange method.
(d) Ionic radii of trivalent lanthanoids steadily increases with an increase in atomic number.

263. Which of the following trivalent ions has the largest ionic radius in the lanthanide series?
(a) La^{3+} (b) Ce^{3+} (c) Pm^{3+} (d) Lu^{3+}

264. The lanthanoid contraction relates to
(a) atomic radii
(b) atomic as well as M^{3+} radii
(c) valence electrons
(d) oxidation states
(e) ionisation enthalpy

265. The pair, that is referred to as 'chemical twins' is
(a) Ac, Cf (b) Hf, Ta (c) Tc, Re (d) La, Ac

266. The lanthanoid contraction is responsible for the fact that
(a) Zr and Y have about the same radius
(b) Zr and Nb have a similar oxidation state
(c) Zr and Hf have about the same radius
(d) Zr and Zn have the same oxidation state

267. Lanthanoid contraction is caused due to
(a) the appreciable shielding of the outer electrons by the 4*f* electrons from the nuclear charge
(b) the appreciable shielding of the outer electrons by the 5*d* electrons from the nuclear charge
(c) the same effective nuclear charge from Ce to Lu
(d) the imperfect shielding of the outer electrons by the 4*f* electrons from the nuclear charge

268. Which of the following is a member of the lanthanoid series which is well known to exhibit the +4 oxidation state?
(a) Pr (b) Ce (c) Nd (d) Tb

269. Cerium can show an oxidation state of +4 because
(a) it resembles the carbon family
(b) it has a very low value of IE
(c) of its tendency to attain the noble gas configuration of xenon, $4f^0\,5d^0\,6s^0$
(d) two *s* and two *f* electrons can be lost easily

270. The most common oxidation states of Ce (cerium) are
(a) +3, +4 (b) +2, +3 (c) +2, +4 (d) +3, +5

271. On which factors does the stability of any oxidation state of the lanthanoid elements depend?
(a) enthalpy (b) internal energy
(c) combined effect of hydration energy and ionisation energy
(d) electronic configuration

272. Cerium ($Z = 58$) is an important member of the lanthanoids. Which of the following statements about cerium is incorrect?
(a) The +4 oxidation state of cerium is not known in solutions.

(b) The +3 oxidation state of cerium is more stable than the +4 oxidation state.
(c) The common oxidation states of cerium are +3 and +4.
(d) Cerium (IV) acts as an oxidising agent.

273. In the context of the lanthanoids, which of the following statements is not correct?

(a) There is a gradual decrease in the radii of the memes with increasing atomic number in the series.
(b) All the members exhibit the +3oxidation state.
(c) Because of similar properties, the separation of lanthanoids is not easy.
(d) The availability of 4f electrons results in the formation of compounds in the +4 state for all the members of the series.

274. Which of the ions is colourless inspite of the presence of unpaired electrons?

(a) La^{3+} (b) Eu^{3+} (c) Gd^{3+} (d) Lu^{3+}

275. Knowing that the chemistry of the lanthanoids (Ln) is dominated by their +3 oxidation state, which of the following statements is incorrect?

(a) Because of the large size of the Ln (III) ions, the bonding in their compounds is predominantly ionic in character.
(b) The ionic sizes of Ln (III) decrease in general with increasing atomic number.
(c) Ln (III) compounds are generally colourless.
(d) Ln (III) hydroxides are mainly basic in character.

276. Which of the following statements is wrong regarding the lanthanoids?

(a) Ln (III) compounds are predominantly ionic in character.
(b) Ln (III) hydroxides are mainly basic in nature.
(c) The ionic size of the Ln (III) ions decreases with increasing atomic number.
(d) Ln (III) compounds are generally colourless.

277. Which of the following lanthanoid ions is paramagnetic?

(a) Ce^{4+} (b) Yb^{2+} (c) Lu^{3+} (c) Eu^{2+}

278. Across the lanthanide series, the basicity of the lanthanide hydroxides

(a) increases (b) decreases
(c) first increases and then decreases
(d) first decreases and then increases

279. Most basic hydroxide among the following is

(a) $Lu(OH)_3$ (b) $Eu(OH)_3$
(c) $Yb(OH)_3$ (d) $Ce(OH)_3$

280. The correct statement is

(a) the earlier members of lanthanoid series resemble calcium in their chemical properties
(b) the extent of actinoid contraction is almost the same as lanthanoid contraction
(c) in general, lanthanoids and actinoids do not show variable oxidation states
(d) Ce^{4+} in aqueous solution is not known

281. The correct basicity order of the following lanthanide ions is

(a) $La^{3+} > Lu^{3+} > Ce^{3+} > Eu^{3+}$
(b) $Ce^{3+} > Lu^{3+} > La^{3+} > Eu^{3+}$
(c) $Lu^{3+} > Ce^{3+} > Eu^{3+} > La^{3+}$
(d) $La^{3+} > Ce^{3+} > Eu^{3+} > Lu^{3+}$

282. Among Ce ($4f^1 5d^1 6s^2$), Nd ($4f^4 6s^2$), Eu ($4f^7 6s^2$) and Dy ($4f^{10} 6s^2$), the elements having the highest and lowest 3rd ionisation energies, respectively, are

(a) Nd and Ce (b) Eu and Ce
(c) Ce and Dy (d) Dy and Nd

283. The chemistry of the actinoid elements is not so smooth as that of the lanthanoids. This is because

(a) there is a large energy gap between the $4f$ and $5d$ subshells in the case of lanthanoids
(b) lanthanoids show limited number of oxidation states such as +2, +3 and +4 out of which +3 is the most common
(c) there is a small energy difference between $5f$, $6d$ and 7s subshells in the case of actinoids. Therefore, they show the +3 oxidation state and a number of other oxidation states also; for example, uranium shows +3 to +6, neptunium and plutonium show +3 to +7 oxidation states
(d) all (a), (b) and (c) above

284. Which one of the following is used for the production of UF_6 in the enrichment of U^{235}?

(a) ClF_3 (b) KF (c) KHF_2 (d) HF (e) PF_3

285. The compound used in the enrichment of uranium for the nuclear power plant is

(a) U_3O_8 (b) UF_6
(c) $UO_2(NO_3)_2$ (d) UCl_4

286. Which of the following is an artificially synthesised element?

(a) Ra (b) U (c) Np (d) C

287. Which of the following is not an actinoid?

(a) Am (b) Cm (c) Fm (d) Tm

288. Which belongs to the actinide series?

(a) Ce (b) Cf (c) Ca (d) Cs

289. The atom of which one of the following elements has the largest number of unpaired electrons?

(a) $_{25}Mn$ (b) $_{24}Cr$ (c) $_{96}Cm$ (d) $_{26}Fe$

290. The heaviest atom amongst the following is

(a) uranium (b) radium
(c) lead (d) mercury

291. The electronic configuration of the actinoids cannot be assigned with any degree of certainty because of

(a) the small energy difference between the $5f$ and $6d$ levels
(b) the overlapping of inner orbitals
(c) the free movement of electrons over all the orbitals
(d) all of the above

292. Among the following actinoid pairs, the maximum oxidation state is shown by

(a) U and Np (b) Np and Pu
(c) Pu and Am (d) U and Pa
(e) Th and Pu

293. The actinoids exhibit more number of oxidation states than the lanthanoids. This is because

(a) the $5f$ obitals are more buried than the $4f$ orbitals
(b) there is a similarity between $4f$ and $5f$ orbitals in their angular part of the wave function
(c) the actinoids are more reactive than the lanthanoids
(d) the $5f$ orbitals extend further from the nucleus than the $4f$ orbitals

294. The maximum oxidation state exhibited by actinoid ions is

(a) +5 (b) +4 (c) +7 (d) +8 (e) +6

295. Identify the incorrect statement among the following.

(a) *d*-block elements show irregular and erratic chemical properties among themselves.
(b) La and Lu have partially filled *d* orbitals.
(c) The chemistry of the various lanthanoids is very similar.
(d) $4f$ and $5f$ orbitals are equally shielded.

Final Preparation

296. E^0 values for the couples Cr^{3+}/Cr^{2+} and Mn^{3+}/Mn^{2+} are –0.41 and +1.51 volts respectively. These values suggest that

(a) Cr^{2+} acts as a reducing agent whereas Mn^{3+} acts as an oxidising agent
(b) Cr^{2+} is more stable than Cr^{3+}
(c) Mn^{3+} is more stable than Mn^{2+}
(d) Cr^{2+} acts as an oxidising agent whereas Mn^{3+} acts as a reducing agent

297. Vanadium (III) oxide is a strong

(a) drying agent (b) oxidising agent
(c) reducing agent (d) wetting agent
(e) precipitating agent

298. Which of the following ions is the most stable in aqueous solution?

(a) Mn^{3+} (b) Cr^{3+}
(c) V^{3+} (d) Ti^{3+}
(At. nos: Ti = 22, V = 23, Cr = 24, Mn = 25)

299. Which of the following does not show colour due to charge transfer transitions?

(a) CrO_4^{2-} (b) MnO_4^-
(c) $[Cu(H_2O)_4]^{2+}$ (d) $Cr_2O_7^{2-}$

300. The *d* electron configuration of Cr^{2+}, Mn^{2+}, Fe^{2+} and Ni^{2+} are $3d^4, 3d^5, 3d^6$ and $3d^8$ respectively. Which one of the following aqua complexes will exhibit the minimum paramagnetic behaviour?

(a) $[Cr(H_2O)_6]^{2+}$ (b) $[Mn(H_2O)_6]^{2+}$
(c) $[Fe(H_2O)_6]^{2+}$ (d) $[Ni(H_2O)_6]^{2+}$
(At. nos: Cr = 24, Mn = 25, Fe = 26, Ni = 28)

301. Which of the following statement(s) is/are correctly applicable to all the transition elements with atomic numbers 21–29?

1. The lowest oxidation state is +1.
2. The 4*s* orbital is completely filled in the group state.
3. The 3*d* orbital is incompletely filled in the group state.
4. The ion in the +2 oxidation state is paramagnetic.

(a) 1, 2 and 3 (b) 3 and 4 only
(c) 4 only (d) 3 only

302. A magnetic moment of 2.84 BM is shown by

(At. nos: Ni = 28, Ti = 22, Cr = 24, Co = 27)
(a) Cr^{2+} (b) Co^{2+} (c) Ni^{2+} (d) Ti^{3+}

303. Match the metal ions given in **Column I** with the spin magnetic moment of the ions given in **Column II** and assign the correct code.

Column I	Column II
A. Co^{3+}	(i) $\sqrt{8}$ BM
B. Cr^{3+}	(ii) $\sqrt{35}$ BM
C. Fe^{3+}	(iii) $\sqrt{3}$ BM
D. Ni^{2+}	(iv) $\sqrt{24}$ BM
	(v) $\sqrt{15}$ BM

	A	B	C	D
(a)	(iv)	(v)	(ii)	(i)
(b)	(i)	(ii)	(iii)	(iv)
(c)	(iv)	(i)	(ii)	(iii)
(d)	(iii)	(v)	(i)	(ii)

304. Anhydrous salts of CuF_2 and $CuSO_4$ are

(a) red (b) blue (c) white (d) none

305. The colourless species is

(a) VCl_3 (b) $VOSO_4$
(c) Na_3VO_4 (d) $[V(H_2O)_6SO_4].H_2O$

306. In which of the following pairs are both the ions coloured in the aqueous solution?

(a) Sc^{3+}, Co^{2+} (b) Ni^{2+}, Cu^{+}
(c) Ni^{2+}, Ti^{3+} (d) Sc^{3+}, Ti^{3+}
(At. Nos: Sc = 21, Ti = 22, Ni = 28, Cu = 29, Co = 27)

307. Amongst CoF_6^{2-}, CoF_6^{3-}, Cu_2Cl_2 and $NiCl_4^{2-}$ (at. Nos: Ti = 22, Co = 27, Cu = 29, Ni = 28), the colourless species are

(a) CoF_6^{2-} and $NiCl_4^{2-}$ (b) TiF_6^{2-} and CoF_6^{3-}
(c) Cu_2Cl_2 and $NiCl_4^{2-}$ (d) TiF_6^{2-} and Cu_2Cl_2

308. Which one of the following ions exhibits $d-d$ transitions and paramagnetism?

(a) CrO_4^{2-} (b) $Cr_2O_7^{2-}$ (c) MnO_4^- (d) MnO_4^{2-}

309. Which of the following statements about the interstitial compounds is incorrect?

(a) They retain metallic conductivity.
(b) They are chemically reactive.
(c) They are much harder than the pure metal.
(d) They have higher melting points than the pure metal.

310. Both an acid and a base may react with which of the following oxides?

(a) CaO (b) Na_2O_2 (c) ZnO (d) Mn_3O_4

311. Pt black is

(a) Pt metal mixed with MnO_2
(b) a velvety black powder obtained by the reduction of $PtCl_4$ with glucose or sodium formate
(c) Pt metal coated with black colour
(d) none of these

312. The percentage of gold in fool's gold is

(a) zero (b) 8 (c) 16 (d) 30

313. Sterling silver is

(a) $AgNO_3$ (b) Ag_2S
(c) alloy of 80% Ag + 20% Cu
(d) AgCl

314. Chloroplatinic acid is

(a) monobasic (b) dibasic
(c) tribasic (d) tetrabasic

315. Which is used as a fungicide?

(a) $CuSO_4$ and slaked lime
(b) CuO and quick lime
(c) $CuSO_4$ and quick lime
(d) $CuSO_4$ and calcium nitrate

316. Which among the following metals does not dissolve in aqua regia?

(a) Pt (b) Pd (c) Au (d) Ir

317. Guignet's green is

(a) $Cr_2O_3.2H_2O$ (b) $Fe_2O_3.2H_2O$
(c) Cu_2O_3 (d) $FeCO_3.Cr_2O_3$
(e) $FeO.Cr_2O_3$

318. Mercurous ion is written as

(a) Hg^+ (b) Hg^{2+} (c) Hg_2^{2+} (d) Hg_2^+

319. The compound insoluble in water is

(a) mercurous nitrate (b) mercuric nitrate
(c) mercurous chloride (d) mercurous perchlorate

320. The metals present in insulin, hemoglobin and vitamin B_{12} are respectively

(a) Zn, Hg, Cr (b) Co, Fe, Zn
(d) Mg, Fe, Co (d) Zn, Fe, Co

321. $TiCl_4$ fumes strongly in moist air and is hydrolysed to give

(a) Ti (b) $TiOCl_2$ (c) TiO_2 (d) $Ti(OH)_4$

322. The basic character of the transition metal monoxides follow the order

(a) VO > CrO > TiO > FeO (b) CrO > VO > FeO > TiO
(c) TiO > FeO > VO > CrO (d) TiO > VO > CrO > FeO

323. The deep blue colour produced on adding H_2O_2 to acidified $K_2Cr_2O_7$ solution soluble in ether is due to the formation of

(a) Cr_2O_3 (b) $Cr_2(SO_4)_3$
(c) CrO_5 (d) CrO_4^{2-}

324. The reddish-brown gas produced by heating KCl with $K_2Cr_2O_7$ (solid) and conc. H_2SO_4 is

(a) Cl_2 (b) CrO_2Cl_2
(c) CrO_3 (d) H_2CrO_4

325. Acidified K_2CrO_7 solution turns green when Na_2SO_3 is added to it. This is due to the formation of

(a) $CrSO_4$ (b) $Cr_2(SO_4)_3$
(c) CrO_4^{2-} (d) $Cr_2(SO_3)_3$

326. Which of the statements is not true?

(a) On passing H_2S through acidified $K_2Cr_2O_7$ solution, a milky colour is observed.
(b) $K_2Cr_2O_7$solution in acidic medium is orange.
(c) $Na_2Cr_2O_7$ is preferred over $K_2Cr_2O_7$ in volumetric analysis.
(d) $K_2Cr_2O_7$ solution becomes yellow on increasing the pH beyond 7.

327. Which of the following does not give oxygen on heating?

(a) $KClO_3$ (b) $Zn(ClO_3)_2$
(c) $K_2Cr_2O_7$ (d) $(NH_4)_2Cr_2O_7$

328. The colour of $CuCr_2O_7$ solution in water is green because

(a) $Cr_2O_7^{2-}$ ions are green
(b) Cu^{2+} ions are green
(b) both ions are green
(c) Cu^{2+} ions are blue and $Cr_2O_7^{2-}$ ions are yellow

329. In chromic acid anhydride (CrO_3), Cr has a d^0 configuration but is a bright orange coloured solid. The colour is due to

(a) *d–d* transition (b) CT ($L \rightarrow M$) transition
(c) CT ($M \rightarrow L$) transition (d) *p–d* transition

330. Pick out the wrong reaction from

(a) $2\ Na_2CrO_4 + H^+ \rightarrow Na_2Cr_2O_7 + 2\ Na^+ + H_2O$
(b) $2\ MnO_2 + 4\ KOH + O_2 \rightarrow 4\ KMnO_4 + 2\ H_2O$
(c) $MnO_4^- + 8H^+ + 5\ Fe^{2+} \rightarrow 5\ Fe^{3+} + Mn^{2+} + 4\ H_2O$
(d) $2MnO_4^- + 5\ C_2O_7^{2-} + 16H^+ \rightarrow 2\ Mn^{2+} + 10\ CO_2 + 8\ H_2O$

331. When CO_2 is passed through a green solution of K_2MnO_4

(a) a purple solution is obtained
(b) a brown solid is obtained
(c) a purple solution along with brown precipitate is obtained
(d) a light pink solution is obtained

332. The strength as oxidising agents of the following species in acidic solution decreases in the order

(a) $S_2O_8^{2-} > Cr_2O_7^{2-} > MnO_4^- > VO_2^+$
(b) $VO_2^+ > MnO_4^- > Cr_2O_7^{2-} > S_2O_8^{2-}$
(c) $S_2O_8^{2-} > MnO_4^- > Cr_2O_7^{2-} > VO_2^+$
(d) $Cr_2O_7^{2-} > VO_2^+ > S_2O_8^{2-} > MnO_4^-$

333. The equivalent weight of $KMnO_4$ (formula weight = M) when it is used as an oxidant in neutral medium is

(a) M (b) M/2 (c) M/3 (d) M/5

334. For decolourisation of 1 mol of $KMnO_4$, the number of mol of H_2O_2 required is

(a) 1/3 (b) 3/2 (c) 5/2 (d) 7/2

335. The number of mol of acidified $KMnO_4$ required to oxidise one mol of ferrous oxalate (FeC_2O_4) is

(a) 5 (b) 3 (c) 0.6 (d) 1.5

336. Equivalent weight of $KMnO_4$ in alkaline solution is equal to

(a) one-fifth of molar mass of $KMnO_4$
(b) one-sixth of molar mass of $KMnO_4$
(c) one-third of molar mass of $KMnO_4$
(d) one-tenth of molar mass of $KMnO_4$

337. The number of mol of $KMnO_4$ reduced by one molar of KI in alkaline medium is

(a) one (b) two
(c) five (d) one-fifth

338. The reaction of aqueous $KMnO_4$ with H_2O_2 in acidic conditions gives

(a) Mn^{4+} and O_2 (b) Mn^{2+} and O
(c) Mn^{2+} and O_2 (d) Mn^{4+} and MnO_2

339. A metallic oxide which imparts purple colour to pottery is

(a) manganese dioxide (b) sodium oxide
(c) copper oxide (d) lead oxide

340. MnO_4^- is an intense pink colour, though Mn is in the +7 oxidation state. It is due to

(a) oxygen which gives colour to it
(b) charge transfer when Mn gives its electron to oxygen
(c) charge transfer when oxygen gives its electron to Mn making it Mn (+VI)
(d) presence of unpaired electrons

341. The lanthanoid for which +2 and +3 oxidation states are common is

(a) La (b) Nd (c) Ce (d) Eu

342. Which of the following oxidation states is the most common among the lanthanoids?

(a) 4 (b) 2 (c) 5 (d) 3

343. CeI_2 has a metallic lustre. It is explained by formulating it as

(a) Ce (III), 2 I^-, e^- (b) Ce (II), 2 I^-
(c) Ce (IV), 2 I^-, e^- (d) none of the above

344. The electronic configurations of Eu (atomic no. 63), Gd (atomic no. 64) and Tb (atomic no. 65) are

(a) $[Xe]4f^6 5d^1 6s^2$, $[Xe]4f^7 5d^1 6s^2$ and $[Xe]4f^8 5d^1 6s^2$
(b) $[Xe]4f^7 6s^2$, $[Xe]4f^7 5d^1 6s^2$ and $[Xe]4f^9 6s^2$
(c) $[Xe]4f^7 6s^2$, $[Xe]4f^8 6s^2$ and $[Xe]4f^8 5d^1 6s^2$
(d) $[Xe]4f^6 5d^1 6s^2$, $[Xe]4f^7 5d^1 6s^2$ and $[Xe]4f^9 6s^2$

345. Consider the following statements.

(I) $La(OH)_3$ is the least basic among the hydroxides of lanthanoids.
(II) Zr^{4+} and Hf^{4+} possess almost the same ionic radii.
(III) Ce^{4+} can act as an oxidising agent.
Which of the above is/are true?

(a) I and III (b) II and III (c) II only
(d) I and II (e) I only

346. Identify the incorrect statement among the following.

(a) The shielding power of the $4f$ electrons is quite weak.

(b) There is a decrease in the radii of the atoms or ions as one proceeds from La to Lu.

(c) Lanthanoid contraction is the accumulation of successive shrinkages.

(d) As a result of lanthanoid contraction, the properties of the $4d$ series of the transition elements have no similarities with the $5d$ series of elements.

347. Consider the following statements with respect to lanthanoids.

1. The basic strength of the hydroxides of the lanthanoids increases from $La(OH)_3$ to $Lu(OH)_3$.
2. The lanthanoid ions Lu^{3+}, $Yb^{2+}$and Ce^{4+} are diamagnetic.

Which of the statements given above is/are correct?

(a) 1 only (b) 2 only
(c) both 1 and 2 (d) neither 1 nor 2

348. Which one of the following statements related to the lanthanoids is incorrect?

(a) Europium shows the +2 oxidation state.

(b) The basicity decreases as the ionic radius decreases from Pr to Lu.

(c) All the lanthanoids are much more reactive than aluminium.

(d) Ce (+4) solutions are widely used as oxidising agents in volumetric analysis.

349. Which lanthanoid compound is used as a most powerful liquid lasers after dissolving it in selenium oxychloride?

(a) cerium oxide (b) neodymium oxide
(c) promethium sulfate (d) ceric sulfate

350. The oxidation state of Np in the compound $Li_5[NpO_6]$ is

(a) +5 (b) +6 (c) +4 (d) +7

351. More number of oxidation states are exhibited by the actinoids than by the lanthanoids. The main reason for this is

(a) the greater metallic character of the lanthanoids compared to that of the corresponding actinoids

(b) more active nature of the actinoids

(c) more energy difference between $5f$ and $6d$ orbitals than that between $4f$ and $5d$ orbitals

(d) lower energy difference between $5f$ and $6d$ orbitals than that between $4f$ and $5d$ orbitals

352. The reason for the greater range of oxidation states in the actinoids is attributed to

(a) actinoid contraction

(b) $5f$, $6d$ and $7s$ levels having comparable energies

(c) $4f$ and $5d$ levels being close in energies

(d) the radioactive nature of actinoids

353. If M is an element of the actinoid series, the degree of complex formation decreases in the order

(a) $M^{4+} > M^{3+} > MO_2^{2+} > MO_2^{+}$

(b) $MO_2^{+} > MO_2^{2+} > M^{3+} > M^{4+}$

(c) $M^{4+} > MO_2^{2+} > M^{3+} > MO_2^{+}$

(d) $MO_2^{2+} > MO_2^{+} > M^{4+} > M^{3+}$

354. Which of the following transition metals has the highest melting point?

(a) Cr (b) Mo (c) W (d) Hg

355. Which one of the following does not correctly represent the correct order of the property indicated against it?

(a) Ti < V < Cr < Mn: increasing number of oxidation states

(b) $Ti^{3+} < V^{3+} < Cr^{3+} < Mn^{3+}$: increasing magnetic moment

(c) Ti < V < Cr < Mn: increasing melting point

(d) Ti < V < Mn < Cr: increasing 2nd ionisation enthalpy

356. Which of the following pairs has the same size?

(a) Zn^{2+}, Hf^{4+} (b) Fe^{2+}, Ni^{2+}
(c) Zr^{4+}, Ti^{4+} (d) Mo^{VI}, W^{VI}

357. Which one of the following transition metal ions has the lowest density?

(a) copper (b) nickel (c) scandium (d) zinc

358. The correct order of decreasing second ionisation enthalpy of Ti (22), V (23), Cr (24) and Mn (25) is

(a) Cr > Mn > V >Ti (b) V > Mn > Cr >Ti
(c) Mn > Cr >Ti> V (d) Ti> V > Cr > Mn

359. For the four successive transition elements (Cr, Mn, Fe and Co), the stability of the +2 oxidation state will be in which of the following orders?

(a) Mn > Fe > Cr > Co (b) Fe > Mn > Co > Cr
(c) Co > Mn > Fe > Cr (d) Cr > Mn > Co > Fe

360. Which of the following exhibits only the +3 oxidation state?

(a) U (b) Th (c) Ac (d) Pa

MATCH THE FOLLOWING

361.

Column I (Metal Ion)	Column II (Colour in aq. solution)
(A) V^{2+}	(p) Pink
(B) Ti^{3+}	(q) Green
(C) Ni^{2+}	(r) Purple
(D) Co^{2+}	(s) Blue
(E) Cr^{3+}	(t) Yellow

(a) (A)—(p); (B)—(q); (C)—(r); (D)—(s); (E)—(t)
(b) (A)—(q); (B)—(r); (C)—(q); (D)—(p); (E)—(q)
(c) (A)—(r); (B)—(s); (C)—(q); (D)—(p); (E)—(s);
(d) (A)—(s); (B)—(t); (C)—(r); (D)—(q); (E)—(p)

ASSERTION REASON

Directions: In each of the following questions, a statement of Assertion (A) is given followed by a corresponding statement of Reason (R) just below it. Of the statements, mark the correct answer as

(a) if both the assertion and reason are true and the reason is the correct explanation of the assertion.
(b) if both the assertion and reason are true but the reason is not the correct explanation of the assertion.
(c) if the assertion is true but the reason is false.
(d) if both the assertion and reason are false.

362. Assertion: Atomic size of silver is almost equal to that of gold.

Reason: *d*-subshell has low penetration power and produce poor shielding.

363. Assertion: The highest oxidation state of Os is +8.

Reason: Osmium is a 5*d*-block element.

364. Assertion: $E°$ for Mn^{3+}/Mn^{2+} is more positive than that for Cr^{3+}/Cr^{2+}.

Reason: The third ionisation enthalpy of Mn is larger than that of Cr.

365. Assertion: Hg^{2+} is diamagnetic.

Reason: The electrons are lost from the 6*s* orbital to form Hg^{2+}.

366. Assertion: $VOSO_4$ is colourless and diamagnetic.

Reason: Vanadium is in the (+V) oxidation state.

367. Assertion: In any transition series, the magnetic moment of an M^{2+} ion first increases and then decreases.

Reason: In any transition series, the number of unpaired electrons first increases, afterwards decreases.

368. Assertion: Mercury vapour is shining silvery in appearance.

Reason: Mercury is a solid metal with a shining silvery appearance at room temperature.

369. Assertion: On adding zinc pieces to aqueous $FeCl_3$ solution, the colour changes from deep yellow to light green.

Reason: Aqueous $FeCl_3$ is acidic and on adding Zn, nascent hydrogen is produced which reduces the deep yellow $FeCl_3$ solution to light green $FeCl_2$ solution.

370. Assertion: A solution of Na_2CrO_4 in water is intensely coloured.

Reason: The oxidation state of Cr in Na_2CrO_4 is +VI.

371. Assertion: AgCl is soluble in NH_4OH solution.

Reason: This is due to the formation of a soluble complex.

372. Assertion: Many transition metals and their compounds behave as good catalysts.

Reason: V_2O_5 or Pt is used as a catalyst in the manufacture of H_2SO_4 by contact process.

373. Assertion: $FeCl_3$ hydrolyses in water.
Reason: An aqueous solution of $FeCl_3$ is basic in nature.

374. Assertion: $K_2Cr_2O_7$ is used as a primary standard in volumetric analysis.

Reason: It has good solubility in hot water.

375. Assertion: The equivalent mass of $KMnO_4$ is equal to one-third of its molecular mass when it acts as an oxidising agent in an alkaline medium.

Reason: The oxidation number of Mn is +7 in $KMnO_4$.

376. Assertion: In MnO_4^-, the Mn–O bonds are ionic.

Reason: The oxidation number of Mn in MnO_4^- is –1.

377. Assertion: The purple colour of $KMnO_4$ is due to charge transfer transition.

Reason: The intense colour in most of the transition metal complexes is due to $d-d$ transitions.

378. Assertion: Ce^{4+} is used as an oxidising agent in volumetric analysis.

Reason: Ce^{4+} has the tendency to attain the +3 oxidation state.

379. Assertion: The compound $UO_2(NO_3)_2$ is called uranyl nitrate.

Reason: $UO_2(NO_3)_2$ contains uranyl, UO_2^{2+} cation.

380. Assertion: The magnetic moment values of the actinoids are less than the theoretically predicted values.
Reason: The actinoids are strongly paramagnetic.

381. Assertion: The degree of complex formation in the actinoids decreases in the order $M^{4+} > MO_2^{2+} > M^{3+} > MO_2^+$.

Reason: The acitinoids form complexes with π-bonding ligands such as alkyl phosphines and thioethers.

382. Assertion: Mn atom loses *ns* electrons first during ionisation as compared to $(n-1)d$ electrons.

Reason: The effective nuclear charge experienced by the $(n-1)d$ electrons is greater than that by the *ns* electrons.

383. Assertion: Tungsten has a very high melting point.

Reason: Tungsten is a covalent compound.

Answer Key

1. (c)	2. (a)	3. (a)	4. (c)	5. (b)	6. (d)	7. (b)	8. (a)	9. (d)	10. (a)
11. (c)	12. (c)	13. (a)	14. (d)	15. (a)	16. (b)	17. (b)	18. (d)	19. (a)	20. (c)
21. (b)	22. (b)	23. (b)	24. (d)	25. (e)	26. (c)	27. (c)	28. (c)	29. (a)	30. (d)
31. (d)	32. (a)	33. (b)	34. (a)	35. (b)	36. (a)	37. (c)	38. (a)	39. (c)	40. (a)
41. (a)	42. (d)	43. (a)	44. (a,d)	45. (b)	46. (b)	47. (a)	48. (b)	49. (d)	50. (b)
51. (d)	52. (b)	53. (c)	54. (d).	55. (b)	56. (d)	57. (c)	58. (a)	59. (b)	60. (b)
61. (c)	62. (e)	63. (d)	64. (c)	65. (d)	66. (a)	67. (b)	68. (b)	69. (a)	70. (c)
71. (b)	72. (c)	73. (c)	74. (c)	75. (d)	76. (a)	77. (a)	78. (a)	79. (a)	80. (d)
81. (b)	82. (d)	83. (c)	84. (a)	85. (b)	86. (c)	87. (d)	88. (a)	89. (a)	90. (d)
91. (d)	92. (a)	93. (a)	94. (d)	95. (b)	96. (c)	97. (b)	98. (b)	99. (a)	100. (b)
101. (d)	102. (b)	103. (c)	104. (a)	105. (a)	106. (a)	107. (c)	108. (d)	109. (a)	110. (b)
111. (a)	112. (c)	113. (c)	114. (c)	115. (c)	116. (d)	117. (a)	118. (d)	119. (b)	120. (e)
121. (d)	122. (d)	123. (b)	124. (b)	125. (a)	126. (c)	127. (c)	128. (c)	129. (b)	130. (a)
131. (a)	132. (d)	133. (c)	134. (c)	135. (d)	136. (c)	137. (a)	138. (d)	139. (b)	140. (b)
141. (c)	142. (c)	143. (b)	144. (b)	145. (b)	146. (d)	147. (b)	148. (d)	149. (c)	150. (a)
151. (d)	152. (b)	153. (c)	154. (d)	155. (d)	156. (b)	157. (b)	158. (d)	159. (d)	160. (a)
161. (b)	162. (d)	163. (b)	164. (d)	165. (a)	166. (c)	167. (d)	168. (a)	169. (d)	170. (c)
171. (c)	172. (b)	173. (c)	174. (c)	175. (e)	176. (b)	177. (d)	178. (c)	179. (a)	180. (a)
181. (c)	182. (c)	183. (c)	184. (a)	185. (a)	186. (a)	187. (a)	188. (d)	189. (a)	190. (d)
191. (c)	192. (b)	193. (d)	194. (d)	195. (b)	196. (d)	197. (a)	198. (a)	199. (a)	200. (d)
201. (c)	202. (b)	203. (b)	204. (c)	205. (b)	206. (a)	207. (c)	208. (c)	209. (d)	210. (a)
211. (b)	212. (d)	213. (c)	214. (c)	215. (c)	216. (c)	217. (b)	218. (a)	219. (c)	220. (b)
221. (a)	222. (c)	223. (a)	224. (c)	225. (c)	226. (c)	227. (b)	228. (c)	229. (b)	230. (b)
231. (a)	232. (d)	233. (None)	234. (d)	235. (a)	236. (a)	237. (d)	238. (b)	239. (c)	240. (a)
241. (d)	242. (b)	243. (b)	244. (b)	245. (a)	246. (c)	247. (c)	248. (a)	249. (b)	250. (b)
251. (d)	252. (c)	253. (a)	254. (d)	255. (d)	256. (c)	257. (c)	258. (c)	259. (d)	260. (b)
261. (b)	262. (d)	263. (a)	264. (b)	265. (c)	266. (c)	267. (d)	268. (b)	269. (c)	270. (a)
271. (c)	272. (a)	273. (d)	274. (c)	275. (c)	276. (d)	277. (d)	278. (b)	279. (d)	280. (a)
281. (d)	282. (b)	283. (d)	284. (a)	285. (a)	286. (a)	287. (d)	288. (b)	289. (c)	290. (a)
291. (a)	292. (b)	293. (d)	294. (c)	295. (d)	296. (a)	297. (c)	298. (b)	299. (c)	300. (d)
301. (c)	302. (c)	303. (a)	304. (c)	305. (c)	306. (c)	307. (d)	308. (d)	309. (b)	310. (c)
311. (b)	312. (a)	313. (c)	314. (b)	315. (a)	316. (d)	317. (a)	318. (c)	319. (c)	320. (d)
321. (d)	322. (d)	323. (c)	324. (b)	325. (b)	326. (b)	327. (d)	328. (d)	329. (b)	330. (b)
331. (c)	332. (c)	333. (c)	334. (c)	335. (c)	336. (c)	337. (b)	338. (b)	339. (a)	340. (c)
341. (d)	342. (d)	343. (c)	344. (b)	345. (b)	346. (d)	347. (b)	348. (c)	349. (b)	350. (d)
351. (d)	352. (b)	353. (c)	354. (c)	355. (c)	356. (d)	357. (c)	358. (a)	359. (a)	360. (c)
361. (b)	362. (c)	363. (b)	364. (b)	365. (b)	366. (d)	367. (a)	368. (d)	369. (a)	370. (b)
371. (a)	372. (b)	373. (c)	374. (b)	375. (b)	376. (d)	377. (b)	378. (a)	379. (a)	380. (b)
381. (b)	382. (a)	383. (c)							

Hints and Solutions

OBJECTIVE QUESTIONS

Introduction

1. **(c):** [Ne] $3s^2 3p^5$ is the electronic configuration of a *p*-block element whereas the other configurations are those of *d*-block elements.

2. **(a):** As there are 5 (3 in the *p* and 2 in the *s* orbitals) valence electrons, the atom belongs to group 5 of the periodic table.

3. **(a):** The electronic configuration of the Cr atom = $3d^5 4s^1$, that is, half-filled penultimate *d* subshell as well as half-filled valence *s* subshell.

4. **(c):** Mn^{2+} ($Z = 25$) and Fe^{3+} ($Z = 26$) have 23 electrons each and are isoelectronic.

5. **(b):** Cu (atomic number = 29): $1s^2, 2s^2, 2p^6, 3s^2, 3p^6, 3d^{10}, 4s^1$.

Since in an orbital the two electrons must have the opposite spin, in Cu, 14 electrons have spin in one direction and 15 electrons in the other direction.

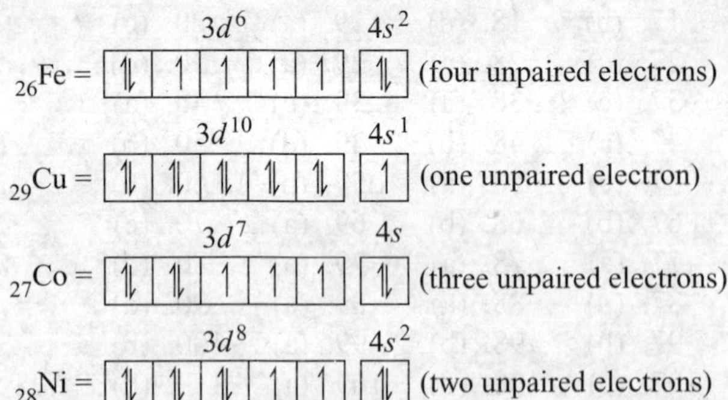

6. (d):
$Ti^{2+} = 1s^2, 2s^2, 2p^6, 3s^2, 3p^6, 3d^2, 4s^0$
$V^{3+} = 1s^2, 2s^2, 2p^6, 3s^2, 3p^6, 3d^2, 4s^0$
$Cr^{4+} = 1s^2, 2s^2, 2p^6, 3s^2, 3p^6, 3d^2, 4s^0$
$Mn^{5+} = 1s^2, 2s^2, 2p^6, 3s^2, 3p^6, 3d^2, 4s^0$
All these metal ions have $3d^2, 3p^6$.

7. (b): 2, 8, 18, 1 = Cu

8. (a): $_{30}Zn$ has been placed in the II B (12) group of the *d*-block in the long form of the periodic table.

9. (d): The electronic configuration of Cu is $1s^2 2s^2 2p^6 3s^2 3p^6 3d^{10} 4s^1$.
$Cu^{2+} \rightarrow 1s^2 2s^2 2p^6 3s^2 3p^6 3d^9$
This shows the configuration of Cu^{2+}, that is, metallic cation.

10. (a): Zn: $3d^{10} 4s^2$; Zn^{++}: $3d^{10} 4s^0$

11. (c): It has 5 electrons in the 3*d* orbital and 1 electron in the 4*s* orbital.

12. (c): The outer electronic configuration of 3*d* transition elements generally remains ns^2.

13. (a): Valence shell electronic configuration of $_{29}Cu^{2+}$ is

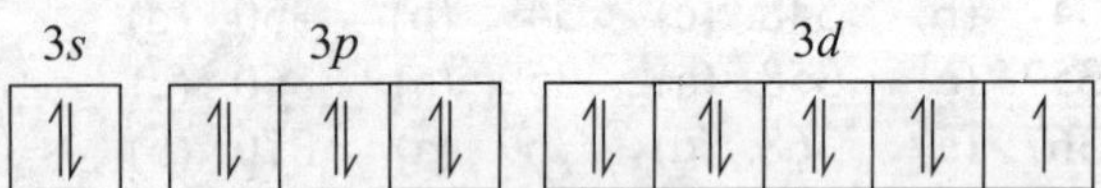

$\therefore$ Number of unpaired electrons = 1

14. (d): Mg^{2+} = 10 electrons, $1s^2 2s^2 2p^6$: no unpaired electron.
Ti^{3+} = 19 electrons, $1s^2 2s^2 p^6 3s^2 p^6 3d^1$: one unpaired electron.
V^{3+} = 20 electrons, $1s^2 2s^2 p^6 3s^2 p^6 3d^2$: two unpaired electrons.
Fe^{2+} = 24 electrons, $1s^2 2s^2 p^6 3s^2 p^6 3d^6$: four unpaired electrons.
Thus, Fe^{2+} has the maximum number of unpaired electrons.

15. (a): Cobalt 27 belongs to the 3*d* transition series as it has incomplete 3*d* orbitals, that is, $3d^7$. Sc to Zn is the 3*d* series.

16. (b): Metal M belongs to the *d*-block. Its electronic configuration can be arranged as, $1s^2 2s^2 2p^6 3s^2 3p^6 4s^1 3d^{10}$.

17. (b): The element with atomic no. 105 is dubnium. In IUPAC nomenclature, it is known as unnilpentium (unp).

18. (d): $_{15}P$ (0) = $1s^2 2s^2 2p^6 3s^2 3p^3$ does not have valence electrons in the 3*d* subshell.

19. (a): $[Ar]3d^1 + 3 = _{22}Ti$, it means the M^{3+} form will be the Ti^{3+} ion.

20. (c): Given $n = 4$ $x = 5$
So $(4-1)s^2 (4-1)p^6 (4-1)d^5 4s^2$ $3s^2 3p^6 3d^5 4s^2$
Total electrons = 2 + 6+ 5+ 2 = 15
Electrons in 1 + 2 orbitals = 2 + 8 = 10
Total electrons = 10 + 15 = 25
No. of electrons = No. of protons
So total protons = 25

21. (b): Electronic configuration of X^{3+} = [Ar] $3d^5$
$\therefore$ Electronic configuration of
X = [Ar] $3d^5 + 3e^-$ = [Ar] $3d^6\ 4s^2$
Thus, atomic number of transition element
X = 18 + 6 + 2 = 26

22. (b): Nb (Z = 41, $4d^4 5d^1$), Mo (Z = 42, $4d^5 5s^1$), Tc (Z = 43, $4d^5 5s^2$) and Ru (Z = 44, $4d^7 5s^1$) belong to the second (4*d*) transition series.

23. (b): The *d*-block elements have incompletely filled *d*-orbitals in their group state or in any of their oxidation states. The general electronic configuration of *d*-block elements is $(n-1)d^{1-10} ns^{1-2}$. Depending on the $(n-1)$ values, there are 3*d*, 4*d*, 5*d* and 6*d* series of transition elements. Hs (Z = 108) belongs to the 6*d* series with the electronic configuration [Rn] $5f^{14}, 6d^6, 7s^2$.

24. (d): Iron belongs to group VIII of the periodic table.

25. (e): The silver UK coins are made of Cu–Ni alloy and not Ag–Ni alloy.

26. (c): The electronic configuration of mercury (80) is [Xe] $4f^{14}, 5d^{10}, 6s^2$. Its *d* subshell is completely filled, thus it prevents the overlapping of *d* obitals ($d-d$ overlapping). Hence, it is a liquid at room temperature.

27. (c): The most malleable of the metals is gold.

28. (c): The atomic weights of Co, Ni and Fe are 58.90, 58.60, 55.85 respectively. Therefore, Co > Ni > Fe is the correct sequence of atomic weights.

29. (a): Acidic character increases with an increase in the oxidation state of the metal.

30. (d): Silver is a transition element because by definition, its ion (Ag^{2+}, $4d^9$) has an incompletely filled *d* subshell.

General Properties of Transition Elements (d-block)

31. (d): In the first transition series, Mn has an abnormally low MP. This can be explained on the basis that Mn has exactly half-filled *d* orbitals. As a result, the electronic configuration is stable, electrons are held tightly by the nucleus, delocalisation is less and the metallic bond is much weaker.

32. (a): Cr has the highest MP and BP due to maximum number of unpaired electrons resulting in strong metallic bonding.

33. (b): Due to the lanthanoid contraction, Zr and Hf have identical atomic sizes.

34. (a): Ionic radii $\propto \frac{1}{\text{Atomic No.}}$. The ionic radius decreases from the left to right in a period. Thus, Cr^{3+} has highest the ionic radius.

35. (b): The ionic radii of the first transition series are smaller than the second and the Mn^{2+} cations decrease with an increase in the atomic number. Thus, Ni^{2+} has the smallest radius.

36. (a): Fe, Co, Ni. With the increase in the *d* electrons, the screening effect increases, which counterbalances the increased nuclear charge due to an increase in the atomic number. As a result, atomic radii remain practically the same after chromium.

37. (c): Increased screening effect to nullify the increased nuclear charge.

38. (a): Oxidation state of Cr in K_2CrO_4 is +6, in CrO_2 is +4, in $CrCl_3$ is +3 and in CrF_2 is +2. As ionic radii decrease with an increase in the oxidation state, the ionic radius of Cr in K_2CrO_4 will be the smallest.

39. (c): Gold: [Xe] $5d^{10}\,6s^1$ is the heaviest among the given metals.

40. (a): On moving from left to right along the 3*d* transition series, the density increases but zinc is an exception having a large atomic volume and hence lower density. Thus, the correct order of decreasing density is Cu > Ni > Zn > Sc.

41. (a): Os and Sc.
Os = 22.60 gm/cm^3 (highest)
Sc = 3.01 gm/cm^3 (lowest)

42. (d): In the case of Cu (At. no. 29) = $3d^{10}\,4s^1$; the second ionisation enthalpy is the highest as the electron is to be removed from a d^{10} (fully filled) configuration which is most stable.

43. (a): After the loss of one electron, the removal of the second electron becomes difficult. Hence, the second ionisation enthalpies are much higher and in general, increase from left to right. However, Cr and Cu show much higher values because the second electron has to be removed from the stable configurations of Cr^+ ($3d^5$) and Cu^+ ($3d^{10}$). Hence, the correct order of the second ionisation enthalpies of the metals is Cr > Mn < Ni < Cu > Zn.

44. (a,d): Electronic configuration of cuprous (Cu^+) and cupric (Cu^{2+}) ions are:

Cu^+ = [Ar] $3d^{10}\,4s^0$; Cu^{2+} = [Ar] $3d^9\,4s^0$

It seems that the electronic configuration of Cu^+ is more stable but in reality, it is less stable than Cu^{2+}. Due to the small size of the Cu^{2+} ions, its nuclear charge is sufficient to hold 27 electrons but in Cu^+ such a condition is not true.
Further, the second ionisation potential of copper is large but the lattice energy released for Cu^{2+} compounds is much more negative than that for Cu^+ compounds and hence, it more than compensates for the second ionisation potential of copper. Thus, both the options (a) and (d) are correct.

45. (b): Ionisation enthalpy gradually increases with an increase in atomic number along a given transition series with some exceptions. Sc, the first member of the 3*d* series has the lowest IE.

46. (b): In the case of Zn, due to increased shielding effect, the attraction of electrons towards the nucleus decreases and thus IE_2 is lower than expected.

47. (a): Removal of an electron is easier in the *f*-block elements due to more shielding when compared to the *d*-block elements.

48. (b): Very high ionisation energy and weak metallic bond.

49. (d): The first ionisation energy of Ti, V, Cr and Mn are 656, 650, 653 and 717 kJ/mol respectively. The IE increases in a period from L $\rightarrow$ R; hence, manganese has the maximum first ionisation potential.

50. (b): $_{23}V = 1s^2\,2s^2\,2p^6\,3s^2\,3p^6\,3d^3\,4s^2$

$_{24}Cr = 1s^2\,2s^2\,2p^6\,3s^2\,3p^6\,3d^5\,4s^1$

$_{25}Mn = 1s^2\,2s^2\,2p^6\,3s^2\,3p^6\,3d^5\,4s^2$

$_{26}Fe = 1s^2\,2s^2\,2p^6\,3s^2\,3p^6\,3d^6\,4s^2$

For the second ionisation enthalpy, Cr^+ has an exactly half-filled *d* subshell and the removal of the electron will be difficult. Therefore, it will have the highest II ionisation energy (IE_2).

51. (d): Cu ($3d^{10}\,4s^1$) shows +1 and +2 oxidation states whereas Sc (+3), Zn (+2) and Y (+3) show only one oxidation state.

52. (b): Common oxidation states of Ti are +3 and +4.

53. (c): The common oxidation states of Sc ($3d^1 4s^2$) are +2 and +3 but +4 oxidation state is virtually unknown.

54. (d): The maximum oxidation states of reasonable stability correspond to the sum of the *s* and *d* electrons upto Mn (*Z* = 25). After that, there is an abrupt decrease in the stability of the higher oxidation states. For the $3d^5$ electronic configuration of the atom in the ground state, there are two possibilities for complete electronic configuration, $3d^5 4s^1$ (Cr = 24) or $3d^5 4s^2$ (Mn = 25).
For $3d^5 4s^1$, the stable oxidation states = +5, +3 and for $3d^5\,4s^2$, the stable oxidation states = +7, +2.

55. (b): Cu^+ in aqueous solution undergoes disproportionation.
$2\,Cu^+(aq) \rightarrow Cu^{2+}(aq) + Cu(s)$.
The $E°$ value for this transformation is also favourable, that is, for the Cu^+/Cu couple, $E°$ = +0.52 V whereas for the Cu^{2+}/Cu couple, $E°$ = +0.34 V.

56. (d): The false statement about transition elements is that they show multiple oxidation states always differing by units of two.

57. (c): Fe shows a variable valency of +2 and +3 whereas Sc, Y and Ac show only +3 valency.

58. (a): Ti^+ is more stable than Ti^{3+} due to inert pair effect.

59. (b): E values for the species in acidic medium are:

$VO_2^+(aq) + 2H^+ + e^- \rightarrow VO^{2+}(aq) + H_2O$; $E° = +1.77$ volts

$MnO_4^-(aq) + 8H^+ + 5e^- \rightarrow Mn^{2+}(aq) + 4H_2O$; $E° = +1.77$ volts

$Cr_2O_7^{2-}(aq) + 14H^+ + 6e^- \rightarrow 2Cr^{3+}(aq) + 7H_2O$

$E° = +1.33$ volts

Since the $E°$ values are positive and increase in the order $VO_2^+ < Cr_2O_7^{2-} < MnO_4^-$, their oxidising power also increases in the same order. Alternatively, the increasing oxidising power of these species is due to the increasing stability of the species with lower oxidation state of the metal atom to which they are reduced. For example,

$\overset{VI}{VO_2^+} \rightarrow \overset{V}{VO^{2+}}$; $\overset{VI}{Cr_2O_7^{2-}} \rightarrow \overset{III}{Cr^{3+}}$ and $\overset{VII}{MnO_4^-} \rightarrow \overset{II}{Mn^{2+}}$

their stability increases in the order $VO^{2+} < Cr^{3+} < Mn^{2+}$ and so also the oxidising power of the species.

60. (b): The +3 oxidation state is the most common in Fe as Fe (III) has a $3d^5 4s^0$ outer electronic configuration which imparts extra stability due to half-filled orbitals.

61. (c): Oxygen and fluorine have small size and high electronegativity. Hence, they can oxidise the metal to the highest oxidation state. But oxygen stabilises the highest oxidations state even more than fluorine; for example, the highest fluoride of Mn is MnF_4 whereas the highest oxide in Mn_2O_7. The reason for this is the ability of oxygen to form multiple bonds with the metal atoms.

62. (e): The outer electronic configuration of Ti = $3d^2 4s^2$.Since Ti has only four valence electrons, it can show the maximum of +4 oxidation state. In K_2TiO_4, the oxidation state of Ti is +6, therefore, this compound does not exist.

63. (d): Transition metals have less tendency to form ions due to their high IE, low heat of hydration of their ions and high heat of sublimation.

64. (c): Mn^{3+} and Co^{3+} can act as stronger oxidising agents and get reduced to the more stable +2 oxidation state.

65. (d): Electronic configuration of Mn^{2+} is $3d^5$ which is half-filled and hence stable. Therefore, the third ionisation enthalpy of Mn is very high, that is, the third electron cannot be lost easily and hence Mn^{2+} compounds are more stable towards oxidation to their +3 state. In the case of Fe^{2+}, the electronic configuration is $3d^6$. Hence, it can lose one electron easily to give the stable configuration $3d^5$ and thus, Fe^{2+} compounds are less stable towards oxidation.

66. (a): Mn^{2+} has stable half-filled ($3d^5$) electronic configuration and thus, has a high third ionisation enthalpy while Fe^{2+} after losing one more electron will acquire this stable electronic configuration. Therefore, Fe^{2+} is more prone to get oxidised to the +3 oxidation state.

67. (b): Compounds of copper in the +2 oxidation state are more stable than those in the +1 state because the lattice enthalpy released by Cu^{2+} compounds is much more negative than that of Cu^+ compounds. Thus, greater the lattice enthalpy release, the more stable is the compound. Since the release of energy is an exothermic process, more stable Cu^{2+} compounds are formed by the exothermic process.

68. (b): The maximum oxidation state of transition metals = number of electrons in $(n-1)d$ orbital + number of electrons in the *ns* orbital.

The electronic configuration of Os = [Xe] $4f^{14}, 5d^6, 6s^2$

$\therefore$ Maximum oxidation state = 6 + 2 = 8

$\therefore$ The highest oxidation state exhibited by any transition metal is +8; example, OsO_4.

69. (a): A binary compound is that compound which is formed by two different elements. Metals or elements which show variable oxidation states can form more than one binary compound. In the given elements, Fe shows +2 and +3 oxidation states. So, it can form two binary compounds with chlorine—$FeCl_2$ and $FeCl_3$.

70. (c): If a transition metal ion exists in its highest oxidation state, it is expected to behave as an oxidising agent.

71. (b): The basic character of any element changes with the oxidation state; low oxidation states are more basic and the high oxidation state are more acidic. For example, MnO and Mn_2O_3 are basic while Mn_2O_7 is acidic in nature. Also, in the highest oxidation state, transition metals form anionic complexes. For example, MnO_4^-, CrO_4^{2-}.

72. (c): $\text{Equivalent weight} = \dfrac{\text{Atomic weight}}{\text{No. of } e^- \text{ lost or gained}}$

$Fe^{2+} \rightarrow Fe^{3+} + e^-$

$\therefore$ Equivalent weight = Atomic weight/1 = Atomic weight

73. (c): $(n-1)d$ and *ns* orbitals.

74. (c): Fully filled or half-filled electronic configuration favours stability.

Mn^{3+} = [Ar] $3d^4$ = [Ar] | 1 | 1 | 1 | 1 | |

Number of unpaired electrons = 4

Cr^{3+} = [Ar] $3d^3$ = [Ar] | 1 | 1 | 1 | | |

No. of unpaired electrons = 3

V^{3+} = [Ar] $3d^2$ = [Ar] | 1 | 1 | | | |

No. of unpaired electrons = 2

Cr^{3+} is the most stable species due to half-filled t_{2g} orbitals.

75. (d): The correct statement is that all transition elements, except the first and last member of the series show a number of oxidation states.

76. (a): Cr: maximum oxidation state = +6

Co: maximum oxidation state = +4

Ni: maximum oxidation state = +4

Cu: maximum oxidation state = +2

77. (a): For the elements of the transition series in which $(n-1)d$ electrons are present. Thus, option (a) has the highest oxidation state.

For the elements where $(n-1)d$ shell is more than half-filled, the maximum oxidation state is not related to their electronic configuration.

78. (a): Group VII B (7), as the metal must contain 7 electrons in the penultimate and outermost shells in order to show a +7 oxidation state.

79. (a): The 3*d* elements show variable oxidation states because the energies of then *ns* and $(n-1)d$ orbitals are almost similar.

80. (d): Highest oxidation state → no. of *s* e^- + no. of *d* e^-
$2+2=4$

81. (b):
(1) The outer electronic configuration of Mn is $3d^5 4s^2$ and it hence exhibits the +7 oxidation state.
(2) Zinc does not form coloured ions as it has a completely filled $3d^{10} 4s^2$ configuration.
(3) In $[CoF_6]^{3-}$, Co^{3+} is a d^7 system. Fluoride is a weak field ligand and hence does not cause pairing of electrons.

Co^{3+} | ↑↓ | ↑↓ | ↑ | ↑ | ↑ |

Paramagnetic and not diamagnetic.
(4) Sc can form a maximum of +3 oxidation state as it has an outer electronic configuration of $3d^1 4s^2$.
(5) Zn exhibits only the +2 oxidation state as this is the most stable one.

82. (d): Correct statement is: Ferrous compounds are less easily hydrolysed than the corresponding ferric compounds.

83. (c): Mg, because of its hydration energy.

84. (a):

	$3d^5$					$4s^2$
Mn	1	1	1	1	1	↑↓
Mn^{2+}	1	1	1	1	1	

As half-filled orbitals are more stable than partially filled ones, +2 is the most stable oxidation state of Mn.

85. (b): $(n-1)d^5ns^2$ can give the +7 oxidation state as both the 5*d* and the 2*s* electrons can take part in bond formation.

86. (c): $Cr^{2+}(3d^4)$ can lose an electron to form Cr^{3+} which has the stable $3d^3$ (half-filled t_{2g}^3) configuration. Hence, it is reducing. On the other hand, $Mn^{3+}(3d^4)$ can gain an electron to form Mn^{2+} which has a stable $3d^5$ (exactly half-filled) configuration. Hence, it is oxidising.
Alternatively, the *E*° value for Cr^{3+}/Cr^{2+} is negative (–0.41 V) whereas the *E*° value for Mn^{3+}/M^{2+} is positive (+1.57 V). Hence, Cr^{2+} can easily undergo oxidation to give the Cr^{3+} ion and therefore, acts as a strong reducing agent whereas Mn^{3+} can easily undergo reduction to give Mn^{2+} and hence acts as an oxidising agent.

87. (d): The *E*° values for the first row transition metals are irregular. This is because the *E*° values are the sum of sublimation, ionisation and hydration enthalpies. The irregularity is due to the irregular variation of ionisation enthalpies (IE_1 + IE_2) and also the sublimation enthalpies which are relatively much lower for Mn (279 kJ mol^{-1}) and Cr (398 kJ mol^{-1}).

88. (a): $E^\circ_{Ti^{2+}/Ti} = -1.63$ V is the highest negative value among the transition metals of the 3*d* series.

89. (a): Oxidation potentials for the given redox couples will be +0.9, +1.2 and +0.4 V. Thus, the order of these getting oxidised will be Mn > Cr > Fe.

90. (d): The *E*° (M^{2+}/M) for any metal is related to the sum of the enthalpy changes taking place in the following steps:

$$M(s) + \Delta_a H \rightarrow M(g)$$
($\Delta_a H$ = enthalpy of atomisation/ sublimation)

$$M(g) + \Delta_i H \rightarrow M^{2+}(g)$$
($\Delta_i H$ = ionisation enthalpy)

$$M^{2+}(g) + aq \rightarrow M^{2+}(aq) + \Delta_{hyd} H$$
(Δ_{hyd} H = hydration enthalpy)

Copper has a high enthalpy of atomisation (energy absorbed) and low enthalpy of hydration (energy released). The high energy required to transform Cu(*s*) to $Cu^{2+}(aq)$, that is, the sum of enthalpies of sublimation and ionisation is not balanced by its hydration enthalpy. Hence, *E*°(Cu^{2+}/Cu) is positive.

91. (d): The large positive *E*° value for Mn^{3+}/M^{2+} shows that Mn^{2+} is much more stable than Mn^{3+}. This is due to the fact that Mn^{2+} has $3d^5$ configuration which is half-filled and hence, is very stable. Thus, the third ionisation enthalpy of Mn will be very high. In fact, this is the reason that the +3 state of Mn is of little importance.

92. (a): $E^\circ_{Cr^{3+}/Cr^{2+}}$ is –ve (–0.41 V) whereas $E^\circ_{Fe^{3+}/Fe^{2+}}$ is +ve (+0.77 V). Thus, Cr^{2+} is easily oxidised to Cr^{3+} but Fe^{2+} cannot be easily oxidised to Fe^{3+}. Hence, Cr^{2+} is a stronger reducing agent than Fe^{2+}.

93. (a): Cr^{3+}/Cr^{2+} has a negative reduction potential. Hence, Cr^{3+} cannot be reduced to Cr^{2+}, that is, Cr^{3+} is most stable. Mn^{3+}/Mn^{2+} has a large positive *E*° value. Hence, Mn^{3+} can be easily reduced to Mn^{2+}, that is, Mn^{3+} is least stable. The *E*° value for Fe^{3+}/Fe^{2+} is positive but small. Hence, Fe^{3+} is more stable than Mn^{3+} but less stable than Cr^{3+}. Thus, the correct stability order is $Cr^{3+} > Fe^{3+} > Mn^{3+}$.

94. (d): In the electrochemical series, the standard electrode reduction potential of Cu is higher than these three. Thus, its oxidation potential is the lowest.

95. (b): Cu, as it comes after H in electrochemical series. It has a positive standard reduction potential and thus does not provide electrons for reduction.

96. (c): There is no regular tend in the *E*° (Mn^{2+}/M) values because of irregular variation of ionisation energies and sublimation energies of the atoms of the members of the first row transition series.

97. (b): Cu^{2+} has d^9 configuration with one unpaired electron and is paramagnetic whereas Ag^+, Zn^{2+} and Au^+ have a d^{10} configuration and are diamagnetic.

98. (b): $3d^9$ configuration has only one unpaired electron and thus has the lowest value of magnetic moment.

99. (a): The outermost electronic configuration of Fe^{2+}

$= 3d^6 4s^0$ 3d: ↿⇂ ↑ ↑ ↑ ↑

Since the Fe^{2+} ion has 4 unpaired electrons, it is paramagnetic in nature.

100. (b): $[Cr(H_2O)_6]^{2+} = Cr^{2+} = 3d^4$ (4 unpaired electrons)
$[Fe(H_2O)_6]^{2+} = Fe^{2+} = 3d^6$ (4 unpaired electrons)
Thus, both the complexes have the same magnetic moment.

101. (d): Oxidation state of Mn in the complex $K_2[MnCl_4]$ will be $2\times(+1)+x+4\times(-1)=0$ or $x-2=0$ or $x=+2$

102. (b): Species having the same number of unpaired electrons have the same magnetic moment.
$MnCl_2 = Mn^{2+} = 3d^5$, 5 unpaired electrons
$CuSO_4 = Cu^{2+} = 3d^9$, 1 unpaired electron
$CuCl_2 = Cu^{2+} = 3d^9$, 1 unpaired electron
$TiCl_3 = Ti^{3+} = 3d^1$,1 unpaired electrons
Thus, $CuCl_2$ and $TiCl_3$ have the same magnetic moment.

103. (c): $Cr^{2+} = 3d^4, 4s^0$; four unpaired electrons
$Fe^{2+} = 3d^6, 4s^0$; four unpaired electrons
As Cr^{2+} and Fe^{2+} have the same number of unpaired electrons, they have the same value of magnetic moment.

104. (a): It shows axial and orbital motion of electrons in the same direction, because it has 5 unpaired electrons with the same spin.

105. (a):

Metal ion	Configuration	Number of unpaired electrons	Magnetic moment
Ti^{3+}	$3d^1$	1	1.75
Ni^{2+}	$3d^8$	2	2.76
Co^{2+}	$3d^7$	3	3.86
Mn^{2+}	$3d^5$	5	5.76

Thus, Ti^{3+}has the least magnetic moment.

106. (a): Paramagnetic property depends upon the number of unpaired electrons. Higher the number of unpaired electrons, higher will be the paramagnetic property.
$Cu^{2+} = [Ar]3d^9$, number of unpaired electrons = 1.
$V^{2+} = [Ar]3d^3$, number of unpaired electrons = 3.
$Cr^{2+} = [Ar]3d^4$, number of unpaired electrons = 4.
$Mn^{2+} = [Ar]3d^5$, number of unpaired electrons = 5.
Hence, correct order is $Cu^{2+} < V^{2+} < Cr^{2+} < Mn^{2+}$.

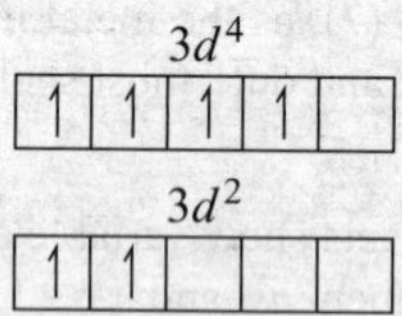

Number of unpaired electrons = 2

107. (c): The spin only magnetic moment is given by $\mu = \sqrt{n(n+2)}$ where, n = number of unpaired electrons. Thus,

Squaring both sides to get, $n(n+2) = 3.24$

$\Rightarrow n^2 + 2n = 3$ $(\because 3.24 \approx 3)$

$\therefore n^2 + 2n - 3 = 0$

$\Rightarrow n^2 + 3n - n - 3 = 0$

$\Rightarrow (n-1)(n+3) = 0$

$\Rightarrow n = 1$ but $n \neq 3$ (not possible)

Thus, $n = 1$

It means one unpaired electron is present, that is, it is copper. Thus,

$$\underset{(A)}{2Cu} + \underset{(B)}{2\,H_2SO_4} + O_2 \rightarrow 2CuSO_4 + 2\,H_2O$$

$$\underset{(B)}{2\,CuSO_4} + \underset{(C)}{4KI} \rightarrow 2K_2SO_4 + \underset{\text{Unstable}}{2\,CuI_2}$$

$$2\,CuI_2 \rightarrow \underset{(D)}{Cu_2I_2} + I_2$$

108. (d): Elements having unpaired electrons in their outermost orbit are termed as paramagnetic. In the 3d series elements, the number of unpaired electrons increases from Sc to Mn and then decreases from Fe to Zn. Therefore, the paramagnetic character increases from Sc to Mn and then decreases from Fe to Zn.

109. (a): Iron:

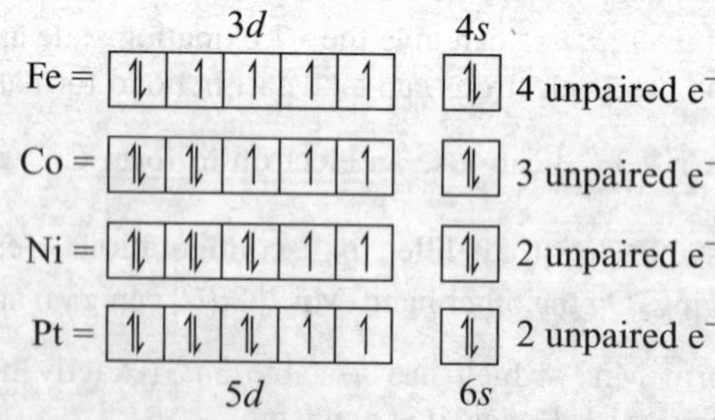

Therefore, Fe is the most ferromagnetic as it has the maximum number of unpaired electrons.

110. (b): $ScCl_3 \rightarrow Sc^{+3} + 3\,Cl^-$

Sc^{+3}: $3s^2$ ↿⇂ $3p^6$ ↿⇂ ↿⇂ ↿⇂ $3d^0$ ☐☐☐☐☐ $4s^0$ ☐

In Sc^{3+}, no unpaired electron is present so, it will show diamagnetic character and will be repelled and will weigh less.

111. (a): All metal carbonyls are diamagnetic and cyanide complexes are also diamagnetic.

112. (c): $CuSO_4.5H_2O$, because it has only one unpaired electron.

113. (c): The existence of Fe^{2+} and NO^+ in the nitroprusside ion $[Fe(CN)_5NO]^{2-}$ can be established by measuring the magnetic moment of the solid compound which should correspond to ($Fe^{2+} = 3d^6$) four unpaired electrons.

114. (c): H atom contains 1 unpaired electron, so it is paramagnetic.
NO_2 monomer contains 1 unpaired electron, so it is paramagnetic.
O_2^- (superoxide) contains 1 unpaired electron, so it is paramagnetic.
S_2 (vapour state) contains 2 unpaired electrons, so it is paramagnetic.
Mn_3O_4 contains Mn in +8/3 ON, thus, it has $\frac{13}{5}$ unpaired e^-; so it is paramagnetic.
$(NH_4)_2[FeCl_4]$ contains Fe^{2+} having 4 unpaired electrons, so it is paramagnetic.
$(NH_4)_2[NiCl_4]$ contains Ni^{2+} having 2 unpaired electrons, so it is paramagnetic.
K_2MnO_4 contains Mn^{6+} having 1 unpaired electron, so it is paramagnetic.
K_2CrO_4 contains Cr^{6+} having 0 unpaired electrons, so it is diamagnetic.

115. (c): An aqueous solution of $Co(NO_3)_2$ in which Co^{2+} (d^7) contains incompletely filled d orbitals is coloured.

116. (d): V^{4+} (d^1 configuration) ion is coloured.

117. (a): Only Zn^{2+} (d^{10} configuration) is colourless while Ni^{2+} (d^8 configuration) and Cr^{3+} (d^3 configuration) are coloured.

118. (d): When a transition metal compound is formed, the degeneracy of the d orbitals is resolved giving two sets of orbitals slightly differing in energy. Absorption of light causes the promotion of electrons from the lower energy set of orbitals to the higher energy set within the same d subshell. This is called a d–d transition.

119. (b): Cu^{2+}, Co^{2+} and Fe^{2+} ions are coloured.

120. (e): $[Cu(H_2O)_6SO_4] + 4\,NH_3 \rightarrow$

$$\underset{\text{(Dark blue colour)}}{[Cu(NH_3)_4(H_2O)_2]SO_4} + 4\,H_2O$$

121. (d): The compounds having metal ions with unpaired electrons are coloured.

$TiCl_3 = Ti^{3+} = 3d^1$, One unpaired electron

$FeCl_3 = Fe^{3+} = 3d^5$, Five unpaired electrons

$CoCl_2 = Co^{2+} = 3d^7$, Three unpaired electrons

Hence, all these compounds are coloured.

122. (d): Cuprous ion is colourless while cupric ion is coloured because cuprous ion has a complete d orbital, that is, $3d^{10}$, $4s^0$ configuration and cupric ion has an incomplete d orbitals due to $3d^9$, $4s^0$ configuration.

123. (b): In CuF_2, Cu is present as Cu^{2+}.
$Cu^{2+} = [Ar]\,3d^9, 4s^0$
Since an unpaired electron is present, it is coloured.

124. (b): The electronic configuration of Ti^{4+} is $1s^2,2s^2,2p^6,3s^2,3p^6,3d^0$. In Ti^{4+}, the d orbitals are empty, hence $d-d$ transition is not possible.

125. (a): Most of the cuprous compounds are usually colourless and diamagnetic as the $3d$ orbital is completely filled ($3d^{10}$). Cu_2O is an exception and is red in colour due to charge transfer.

126. (c): Ammonium dichromate on heating gives a green coloured powder of Cr_2O_3.

$$(NH_4)_2Cr_2O_7 \xrightarrow{\Delta} \underset{\text{Chromic oxide}}{Cr_2O_3} + 4\,H_2O + N_2$$

127. (c): Cr^{+6} in $K_2Cr_2O_7$is yellow, Cr^{+3} in $Cr_2(SO_4)_3$is green.

128. (c): Both Fe^{+2} and Ni^{+2} form hydrated ions such as $[Fe(H_2O)_6]^{2+}$ and $[Ni(H_2O)_6]^{2+}$ respectively.

129. (b): Co (II) compounds impart deep-blue colour to glass.

130. (a): Due to the absence of d electrons in Ti^{4+} ($[Ar])^{18}3d^0 4s^0$), $d-d$ transition is not possible.

131. (a): $Cr^{+++} \rightarrow$ green
$Fe^{++} \rightarrow$ Pale-green

132. (d): d–d transition of $3d$ electrons.

133. (c): CuCN contains Cu^+ ($3d^{10}4s^0$) where all the electrons are paired and it is expected to be colourless.

134. (c): $Co(NO_3)_2$ is coloured in the aqueous solution due to the formation of $[Co(H_2O)_6]^{2+}$ ion.

135. (d): As the crystal field splitting energies in the case of complexes of metal ions in the $4d$ and $5d$ transition series are much larger, the electrons of the metal ion are paired up first in the lower energy set of orbitals before going to the higher energy set within the same d subshell causing maximum pairing and thus low spin (or spin paired) complexes are formed.

136. (c): $Mn^{2+}\left(3d^5\right)$ has 5 electrons in the $3d$ subshell which they will occupy the two sets of $3d$ orbitals as $t_{2g}^2 e_g^2$. $Fe^{3+}\left(3d^5\right)$ is similar to that of Mn^{2+}. $Co^{2+}\left(3d^7\right)$ has 7 electrons in the $3d$ subshell which will get distributed in the two sets of $3d$ orbitals as $t_{2g}^2 e_g^2$. $Cu^{2+}\left(3d^9\right)$ has 9 electrons in the $3d$ subshell and they will occupy the two sets of $3d$ orbitals as $t_{2g}^6 e_g^3$. Thus, Cu^{2+} does not have two unpaired electrons in its e_g set of orbitals.

137. (a): With NH_4OH solution, $CuSO_4$ forms a stable deep blue complex. First it forms (blue) of $Cu(OH)_2$ which dissolves in excess of NH_4OH solution giving a deep blue solution of a complex.

$$CuSO_4 + 2\,NH_4OH \longrightarrow Cu(OH)_2 + (NH_4)_2SO_4$$

$$Cu(OH)_2 + 2\,NH_4OH + (NH_4)_2SO_4 \longrightarrow \underset{\text{Tetramminecopper(II) sulfate}}{[Cu(NH_3)_4]\,SO_4} + 4\,H_2O$$

138. (d): $Pt + 2\ HNO_3 + 8\ HCl \rightarrow H_2PtCl_6 + 2\ NOCl + 4\ H_2O$

139. (b): $\underset{\text{Conc.Blue solution}}{CoCl_2 + 2\ HCl} \rightarrow [CoCl_4]^{2-} + 4Cl^-$

$$\underset{\text{Blue solution}}{[CoCl_4]^{2-}} + 6\ H_2O \longrightarrow \underset{\text{Pink solution}}{[Co(H_2O)_6]^{2+}} + 4Cl^-$$

140. (b): Generally, *d*-block elements form complexes and lead is a *p*-block element. So, ammonia does not form a complex with Pb^{2+}.

141. (c): On treating zinc with excess of NaOH, sodium zincate is obtained as the major product.

$$Zn + 2\ NaOH \longrightarrow \underset{\text{Sodium zincate}}{Na_2ZnO_2} + H_2$$

142. (c): $CoCl_2$, a weak Lewis acid, reacts with chloride ion to produce a complex containing the tetrahedral $[CoCl_4]^{2-}$ ion. It is blue when anhydrous and a deep magenta colour when hydrated, for this reason it is widely used as an indicator for water.

$$CoCl_2 + 2\ Cl^- \longrightarrow [CoCl_4]^{2-}\ \text{Blue}$$

$$[CoCl_4]^{2-} + 6\ H_2O \longrightarrow \underset{\text{Deep magenta colour}}{[Co(H_2O)_6]^{2+}} + 4\ Cl^-$$

143. (b): $CuSO_4 + 2{\cdot}KCN \rightarrow K_2SO_4 + Cu(CN)_2$

$$2\ Cu(CN)_2 \longrightarrow \underset{\text{Insoluble}}{2\ CuCN} + \underset{\text{Cyanogen}}{CN{-}CN}$$

$$CuCN + 3KCN \longrightarrow \underset{\text{Soluble}}{K_3[Cu(CN)_4]}$$

144. (b): The formula of ammonium manganate is $(NH_4)_2MnO_4$.

145. (b): Os (Z = 76): $[Xe]4f^{14}, 5d^6, 6s^2$
Hence, the coordination number in an osmium complex may increase to 8.

146. (d): $AuCl_3 + NaCl \rightarrow \underset{\text{Sodium chloroaurate}}{Na[AuCl_4]}$

147. (b): Nickel; $Ni + 4\ CO \rightarrow [Ni(CO)_4]$ (volatile)

148. (d): Co (III) is more stable in octahedral complexes and osmium shows (VIII) oxidation state.

149. (c): High charge/size ratio and vacant *d* orbitals favour the formation of stable complexes.

150. (a): The magnitude of stable constants for some divalent metal ions of the first transition series with oxygen or nitrogen donor ligands increases in the order:

$Mn^{2+} < Fe^{2+} < Co^{2+} < Ni^{2+} < Cu^{2+} < Zn^{2+}$

Thus Cu^{2+} will form the most stable complex compound.

151. (d): Due to the formation of a complex, $Cu(OH)_2$ is soluble in NH_3.

$$\underset{\text{Ppt.}}{Cu(OH)_2} + 4\ NH_3 \longrightarrow \underset{\text{Soluble}}{[Cu(NH_3)_4](OH)_2}$$

152. (b): Ag^+ forms a complex ion with NH_3 which is soluble whereas in water no such complex is formed and thus, AgCl is insoluble.

$AgCl + 2\ NH_3 \rightarrow [Ag\ (NH_3)_2]$ (Soluble in NH_3)

153. (c): V_2O_5 is used not in the Haber–Bosch process for the manufacture of NH_3 but is used in the contact process for the manufacture of H_2SO_4 in the reaction,

$$2SO_2 + O_2 \rightleftharpoons 2SO_3$$

154. (d): All these metals occlude hydrogen.

155. (d): Transition metals such as Nb, Ti, Y, Cu along with many other metals such as Ba, Ca, Sr, Pb and metalloids Ge, Si form a large number of oxides of varying composition which show superconductivity at different temperatures.

156. (b): An alloy is a homogeneous mixture of two or more metals. Mercury forms amalgams (alloy) with gold, silver and tin. But it does not react with iron and platinum due to large difference in the size of these metals and Hg.

157. (b): Wood's metal (Bi = 50%, Pb = 25%, Sn = 12.5%, Cd = 12.5%) has a melting point of 344 K and thus melts in boiling water.

158. (d): None of the statements is wrong.

159. (d): Super alloys are iron-, nickel- and cobalt-based.

160. (a): Mixture of TiO_2 and $BaSO_4$ is called titanox.

161. (b):
(a) HgS is used in ayurvedic medicine as makardhwaja.
(b) Hg_2Cl_2 is used as purgative in medicines and in making the standard calomel electrode.
(c) $HgCl_2$ is poisonous and its antidote is egg white.
(d) $ZnSO_4$ is used in eye lotion.

162. (d): Bordeaux mixture consists of copper sulfate and lime. It is used as a fungicide.

163. (b): Aqueous silver nitrate solution is used as indelible ink.

164. (d): A solution of H_2O_2 with Fe^{2+} (ferrous) salt is known as Fenton's reagent ($FeSO_4 + H_2O_2$).

165. (a): Cigarette or gas lighter is made up of misch metal which is an alloy of rare earth elements (94%–95%), iron (up to 5%) and traces of S, C, Ca and Al.

166. (c): Bullet-proof steel alloy is prepared by using Zr as one of the constituents.

167. (d): In making gun barrels, the steel used is Ni–Mo steel.

168. (a): Nb and Ta metals are used in making surgical instruments because they are non-corrosive in nature.

169. (d): To support tungsten filament in electric bulbs, Mo-steel is used.

170. (c): Iron, because mercury does not from an amalgam with iron.

171. (c): Chromium gives a protective and decorative coating to the base metal.

172. (b): A hard and resistant alloy generally used in the tip of the nib of a fountain pen is Pt.Cr.

173. (c): $ZnCl_2$ is used for preservation of wood.

174. (c): $CoO.Al_2O_3$ is called cobalt aluminate or Thenard's blue.

175. (e): Ferrosilicon is used in the steel industry as an alloying agent.

176. (b): $CuBr_2$ is a covalent compound.

177. (d): In general, the oxides of transition metals in lower oxidation states are basic and those in higher oxidation states are acidic. Thus,

$\overset{III}{V_2O_3}$ and $\overset{II}{CrO}$ are basic and the others are acidic in nature.

178. (c): Mn_2O_7 is acidic, V_2O_5 is amphoteric and CrO is basic.

179. (a): $\underset{\text{Brown (A)}}{MnO_2} + 4\,HCl \rightarrow MnCl_2 + \underset{\text{(B)}}{Cl_2} + 2\,H_2O$

$\underset{\text{(B)}}{3Cl_2} + NH_3 \rightarrow \underset{\text{(C) Explosive}}{NCl_3} + 3\,HCl$

180. (a):

(i) The oxides with lower oxidation states are basic in nature.

(ii) The oxides with intermediate oxidation states are amphoteric.

(iii) The oxides with higher oxidation states are acidic in nature.

Thus, Cr_2O_3 is an amphoteric oxide.

181. (c): Zinc metal forms an amphoteric oxide.

$ZnO + H_2SO_4 \rightarrow ZnSO_4 + H_2O$

$ZnO + 2\,NaOH \rightarrow Na_2ZnO_2 + H_2O$

182. (c): Among the transition metals, Mn forms the maximum number of oxides. For example,

MnO	Mn_3O_4	Mn_2O_3	MnO_2	Mn_2O_7
basic	amphoteric	amphoteric	amphoteric	acidic

183. (c): $4\,Ag + O_2 \rightarrow 2\,Ag_2O$ (M_2O type)

184. (a): They form the oxides (MO) readily.

185. (a): MnO_2 forms an amphoteric oxide due to intermediate (+4) oxidation state.

$2\,MnO_2 + 4\,KOH + O_2 \rightarrow 2\,K_2MnO_4 + 2\,H_2O$

$MnO_2 + 4\,HCl \rightarrow MnCl_2 + 2\,H_2O + Cl_2$

186. (a): MnO is ionic due to lower (+2) oxidation state.

187. (a): Amphoteric oxides: V_2O_5, Cr_2O_7

Acidic oxide: Mn_2O_7

Basic oxides: CrO, V_2O_4

188. (d): Oxide of Mn in the highest oxidation state will be the most acidic.

Therefore, $\overset{+7}{Mn_2O_7}$ is most acidic among the given options.

189. (a): The oxidising ability of the given anions increases as the oxidation number of the metal present in the anion increases from Ti^{4+} to Mn^{7+}, that is, $TiO_4^{4-}(Ti^{4+}) < VO_4^{3-}(V^{5+}) < CrO_4^{2-}(Cr^{6+}) < MnO_4^-(Mn^{7+})$.

190. (d):

$\underset{\text{White ppt.}}{Hg_2Cl_2} + 2\,NH_3 \rightarrow \underset{\text{White ppt.}}{HgNH_2Cl} + \underset{\text{Black}}{Hg} + NH_4Cl$

191. (c): Yellow colour is obtained due to the formation of CrO_4^{2-} (chromate) ion when $Cr(OH)_3$ is oxidised by Na_2O_2 in the basic medium.

$Cr(OH)_3 + NaOH + Na_2O_2 \rightarrow Na_2CrO_4 + 2\,H_2O$

192. (b): Eating animal flesh poisoned with mercury (Hg^{2+}) cause deformities. This condition is known as Minamata disease which is characterised by diarrhoea, hemolysis, impairment of various senses, meningitis and death.

193. (d): Mercurous chloride (calomel) is prepared by heating $HgCl_2$ and Hg in an iron vessel.

$$HgCl_2 + Hg \xrightarrow{\Delta} Hg_2Cl_2$$

It can also be prepared by the reduction of mercury (II) chloride with tin (II) chloride in a limited quantity.

$$2\,HgCl_2 + SnCl_2 \rightarrow Hg_2Cl_2 + SnCl_4$$

194. (d): $AgNO_3$ when heated above its melting point (212°C), decomposes to give silver nitrite and oxygen but when heated at high temperature (980 K), it gives silver metal (Ag).

$$2\,AgNO_3 \xrightarrow[\Delta]{>212°C} 2\,AgNO_2 + O_2$$

$$2\,AgNO_3 \xrightarrow{980\text{ K}, \Delta} 2\,Ag\downarrow + 2\,NO_2 + O_2$$

195. (b): Iron is rendered passive due to the formation of a layer of ferro–ferric oxide ($FeO.Fe_2O_3$ or Fe_3O_4).

196. (d): Mercuric chloride ($HgCl_2$) is also known as corrosive sublimate as it is highly poisonous and corrosive. It is used (9% solution) for sterilisation of surgical instruments, washing hands, preservative for wood and hide. Its antidote is the white of an egg. It is commercially prepared as follows.

$$HgSO_4 + 2\,NaCl \rightarrow HgCl_2 + Na_2SO_4$$

197. (a): $\underset{\text{Pyrites}}{2FeS_2} + 2\,H_2O + 7\,O_2 \rightarrow \underset{\text{Green vitriol}}{2FeSO_4} + 2\,H_2SO_4$

198. (a): Fe, because it easily gets oxidised in most air.

$Fe \xrightarrow[H_2O/H^+]{\text{Air}} \underset{\text{Rust}}{Fe_2O_3.x\,H_2O}$

199. (a): Mercury does not give H_2 on reacting with water because its ionisation energy is so high.

200. (d): It is Tata Iron and Steel Company.

201. (c): Strong oxidising agents such as PbO_2 or sodium bismuthate ($NaBiO_3$) oxidise Mn^{2+} to MnO_4^- or Mn^{7+} in acidic medium (HNO_3).

$2\,MnSO_4 + 5\,PbO_2 + 6\,HNO_3 \rightarrow 2HMnO_4 + 3\,Pb(NO_3)_2 + 2\,PbSO_4 + 2\,H_2O$

$2\,MnSO_4 + 5\,NaBiO_3 + 16\,HNO_3 \rightarrow 2HMnO_4 + 5\,Bi(NO_3)_3 + NaNO_3 + 2\,Na_2SO_4 + 7\,H_2O$

202. (b): Iron decomposes steam into hydrogen when it is passed over red hot iron.

$$2\,Fe + 3\,H_2O \longrightarrow Fe_2O_3 + 3\,H_2\uparrow$$

203. (b): $2\,MnO_2 + 3\,PbO_2 + 6\,HNO_3 \rightarrow 3Pb(NO_3)_2 + 2\,HMnO_4 + 2\,H_2O$

204. (c): Melting point of $AgNO_3$ is 212°C.

$$2\,AgNO_3 \xrightarrow{\Delta > 212\,°C} 2\,AgNO_2 + O_2$$

When heated to red heat, it decomposes to metallic silver.

$$2AgNO_3 \xrightarrow{\text{Red hot}} 2\,Ag + 2\,NO_2 + O_2$$

205. (b): Pure gold (100%) = 24 carat

$\therefore$ 18 carat gold $= \dfrac{100}{24} \times 18 = 75\%$

206. (a): A covalent bond is constituted by the electrons of the *d* orbitals and lustre is due to the free electrons of the *s* orbital in a metallic bond.

Important Compounds of Transition Elements (Salts of Oxoanions of Metals)

207. (c):

$$K_2Cr_2O_7 + 4\,H_2SO_4 \longrightarrow K_2SO_4 + Cr_2(SO_4)_3, + 4\,H_2O + 3\,(O)$$

$$[2\,KI + H_2SO_4 + (O) \longrightarrow K_2SO_4 + I_2 + H_2O] \times 3$$

$$K_2Cr_2O_7 + 7\,H_2SO_4 + 6\,KI \longrightarrow 4\,K_2SO_4 + Cr_2(SO_4)_3 + 7\,H_2O + 3\,I_2$$

Thus, 1 mol of $K_2C_2O_7$ reacts with KI to give 3 mol of I_2.

208. (c): $Cr_2O_7^{2-} + 14H^+ + 3Sn^{2+} \rightarrow 2\,Cr^{3+} + 3\,Sn^{4+} + 7\,H_2O$

209. (d): $(NH_4)_2Cr_2O_7 \xrightarrow{\Delta} N_2 + 4\,H_2O + Cr_2O_3.$

210. (a): Number of mol of $FeSO_4 = \dfrac{20\text{ g}}{152\text{ g mol}^{-1}} = 0.132$ mol

The complete ionic reaction is

$Cr_2O_7^{2-} + 6\,Fe^{2+} + 14H^+ \rightarrow 2\,Cr^{3+} + 6\,Fe^{3+} + 7\,H_2O$

6 mol of Fe^{2+} = 1 mol of $K_2Cr_2O_7$

$\therefore$ 0.132 mol of $Fe^{2+} = \dfrac{1}{6} \times 0.132 = 0.022$ mol of $K_2Cr_2O_7$

Mass of $K_2Cr_2O_7$ in 0.022 mol

$= 0.022\text{ mole} \times 294\text{ g mol}^{-1} = 6.468\text{ g}$

211. (b): $CrO_3 + 2\,NaOH \rightarrow Na_2CrO_4 + H_2O$

212. (d): $(NH_4)_2Cr_2O_7 \xrightarrow{\Delta} N_2 + Cr_2O_3 + 4\,H_2O$. So, N_2 gas is evolved.

213. (c): $Cr_2O_7^{2-} + H^+ + 6e^- \rightarrow 2\,Cr^{3+} + 7\,H_2O$

Thus, Cr^{VI} in $Cr_2O_7^{2-}$ requires 6 e^- to undergo reduction completely to Cr^{3+} in an acidic medium.

214. (c): $Cr_2O_7^{2-} + 14H^+ + 6\,I^- \rightarrow 2\,Cr^{3+} + 7H_2O + 3\,I_2$

Thus, the final oxidation state of Cr is +3.

215. (c): On acidification of potassium chromate solution, the yellow colour changes to orange colour due to reformation of dichromate. This suggests a monocentric complex, that is, potassium monochromate is converted into a dicentric complex, that is, potassium dichromate.

$$\underset{\text{Potassium chromate}}{2\,K_2CrO_4} + H_2SO_4 \longrightarrow \underset{\text{Potassium dichromate}}{K_2Cr_2O_7} + K_2SO_4 + H_2O$$

216. (c): $4\,\underset{X}{K_2Cr_2O_7} \xrightarrow{\Delta} 4\,K_2CrO_4 + 3\,O_2 + 2\,Cr_2O_3$

217. (b): $K_2\overset{+6}{Cr_2}O_7 + 4\,H_2SO_4 + 3\,H_2S \longrightarrow K_2SO_4 + \overset{+3}{Cr_2}(SO_4)_3 + 7\,H_2O + 3\,S$

Thus, in this reaction, the oxidation number of Cr decreases from +6 to +3.

218. (a):

$$K_2Cr_2O_7 + H_2SO_4 + 3\,\overset{+4}{S}O_2 \longrightarrow K_2\overset{+6}{S}O_4 + Cr_2(SO_4)_3 + H_2O$$

In this reaction, the oxidation state of S is changed from +4 to +6.

219. (c): The colour of $K_2Cr_2O_7$ changes from red-orange to lemon-yellow on treatment with aqueous KOH because of the conversion of dichromate (red-orange) to chromate (lemon-yellow).

$$K_2Cr_2O_7 + 2\,KOH \rightarrow 2\,K_2CrO_4 + H_2O$$

220. (b): (*a*) $2\overset{+6}{Cr}O_4^{2-} + 2\,H^+ \longrightarrow \overset{+6}{Cr_2}O_4^{2-} + H_2O$

(no change in ON of Cr)

(*b*) $\overset{+6}{Cr_2}O_7^{2-} + 2H^+ + 3\,SO_2 \longrightarrow \overset{+3}{Cr_2}(SO_4)_3 + H_2O$

(ON of Cr changes from +6 to +3)

(*c*) $\overset{+6}{Cr_2}O_7^{2-} + 2\,OH^- \longrightarrow 2\,\overset{+6}{Cr}O_7^{2-} + H_2O$

(no change in ON of Cr)

(*d*) $\overset{+6}{Cr}O_7^{2-} + 2\,NH_4OH \longrightarrow (NH_4)_2\overset{+6}{Cr}O_4 + 2\,OH^-$

(no change in ON of Cr)

(*e*) $\overset{+6}{Cr}O_2Cl_2 + 4\,NaOH \longrightarrow Na_2\overset{+6}{Cr}O_4 + 2\,H_2O + 2\,NaCl$

(no change in O.N. of Cr)

$$CrO_7^{2-} + 14\,H^+ + 6\,e^- \longrightarrow 2\,Cr^{3+} + 7\,H_2O$$

$$[Fe^{2+} \longrightarrow Fe^{2+} + e^-] \times 6$$

$$CrO_7^{2-} + 6\,Fe^{2+} + 14\,H^+ \longrightarrow 2\,Cr^{3+} + 6\,Fe^{3+} + 7\,H_2O$$

221. (a): The structure of $Cr_2O_7^{2-}$ ions is

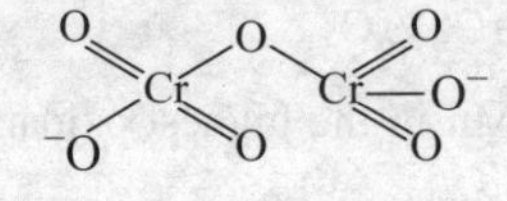

Thus, it has neither Cr–Cr bonds nor O–O bonds.

222. (c): $K_2Cr_2O_7$ is prepared from chromite, $FeCr_2O_4$.

223. (a): $4\,\underset{\text{Chromite ore}}{FeCr_2O_4} + 8\,Na_2CO_3 + 7\,O_2 \xrightarrow{\text{Fusion}} \underset{\text{Yellow solution}}{8\,Na_2CrO_4} + 2\,Fe_2O_3 + 8\,CO_2$

$$\underset{\text{Yellow}}{2\,Na_2CrO_4} + \underset{\text{Dil.}}{H_2SO_4} \rightarrow \underset{\text{Orange}}{Na_2Cr_2O_7} + Na_2SO_4 + H_2O$$

224. (c): $K_2Cr_2O_7 + 2\,H_2SO_4 \xrightarrow{\text{cold}} 2\,CrO_3 + 2\,KHSO_4 + H_2O$
CrO_3 is highly acidic and oxidising and is called chromic acid.

225. (c): $K_2Cr_2O_7 + 4\,H_2SO_4 \rightarrow K_2SO_4 + Cr(SO_4)_3 + 4\,H_2O + 3[O]$

or $Cr_2O_7^{2-} + 14H^+ + 6\,e^- \rightarrow 2Cr^{3+} + 7\,H_2O$

Eq. mass of $K_2Cr_2O_7 = \dfrac{\text{Mol. mass}}{6}$

226. (c): Potassium dichromate oxidises ferrous oxalate in the acidic medium as follows.

$2\,FeC_2O_4 + Cr_2O_7^{2-} + 14H^+ \rightarrow 2\,Fe^{3+} + 2\,Cr^{3+} + 4\,CO_2 + 7\,H_2O$

Since 2 mol of $FeC_2O_4$is oxidised by 1 mol of $Cr_2O_7^{2-}$, 1 mol of FeC_2O_4 will be oxidised by 0.5 mol of $Cr_2O_7^{2-}$.

Potassium Permanganate ($KMnO_4$)

227. (b): H_2 cannot reduce acidified solution of MnO_4^- ion.

228. (c): $2\,KMnO_4 + 3\,H_2SO_4 \rightarrow K_2SO_4 + 2\,MnSO_4 + 3\,H_2O + 5\,(O)$

$2\,HCl + (O) \rightarrow H_2O + \underset{\text{(Greenish yellow gas)}}{Cl_2\uparrow}$

229. (b): $Fe_2(SO_4)_3$ is not a reducing agent. It will not react with the oxidising agent $KMnO_4$ and no colour is discharged.

230. (b): $2\,KMnO_4 + 16\,HCl \rightarrow 2\,KCl + 2\,MnCl_2 + 8\,H_2O + 5\,Cl_2$

231. (a): Solid $KMnO_4$ on treatment with well cooled conc. H_2SO_4 forms manganese heptoxide (Mn_2O_7) which is an explosive red brown oil.

$2\,KMnO_4 + 2\,H_2SO_4\text{ (cold)} \rightarrow Mn_2O_7 + 2\,KHSO_4 + H_2O$

Mn_2O_7 on warming decomposes to MnO_2.

$2Mn_2O_7 \xrightarrow{\text{Warm}} 4\,MnO_2 + 3\,O_2$

232. (d): $2KMnO_4 + 3\,H_2SO_4 + 5\,C_2H_2O_4 \rightarrow K_2SO_4 + 2\,MnSO_4 + 10\,CO_2 + 8\,H_2O.$

233. (None):

$\underset{\text{2 mol}}{2\,KMnO_4} + 8\,H_2SO_4 + 10\,KBr \xrightarrow{\Delta} 6\,K_2SO_4 + 2\,MnSO_4 + \underset{\text{5 mol}}{5\,Br_2} + 8\,H_2O$

Thus, 2 mol of $KMnO_4$ when heated with excess KBr in acidic medium produces 5 mol of Br_2.

234. (d):

$\underset{\text{2 moles}}{2\,KMnO_4} + 8\,H_2SO_4 + \underset{\text{10 moles}}{10\,KI} \rightarrow 6\,K_2SO_4 + 2\,MnSO_4 + 8\,H_2O + \underset{\text{5 mol}}{5I_2}$

10 equivalent (or mol) of KI is oxidised by 2 mol of $KMnO_4$.
1 equivalent (or mol) of KI is oxidised by 2/10 mol of $KMnO_4$.
or $\frac{1}{5}$ mol of $KMnO_4$is required to oxidise one equivalent (or 1 mol) of KI in the presence of H_2SO_4.

$\underset{\text{Purple}}{2\,\overset{+7}{KmnO_4}} + 8\,H_2SO_4 + 10\,FeSO_4 \longrightarrow K_2SO_4 + \underset{\text{Colourless}}{2\,\overset{+2}{MnSO_4}} + 5\,Fe_2(SO_4)_3 + 8\,H_2O$

Hence, Mohr's salt decolourises $KMnO_4$ by reducing Mn^{7+} ion to Mn^{2+} ions.

235. (a): In the neutral medium:

$2\,KMnO_4 + H_2O \rightarrow 2\,MnO_2 + 2\,KOH + 3\,(O)$

In the alkaline medium:

$2\,KMnO_4 + H_2O \rightarrow 2\,MnO_2 + 2\,KOH + 3\,(O)$

In the acidic medium:

$2\,KMnO_4 + 3\,H_2SO_4 \longrightarrow K_2SO_4 + 2\,\overset{+2}{MnSO_4} + 3\,H_2O + 5\,(O)$

Thus, the final products obtained in neutral, alkaline and acidic media respectively are MnO_2, MnO_2 and Mn^{2+}.

236. (a): The purple colour of $KMnO_4$ is due to charge transfer (CT) from ligand (L) oxygen to metal (M) manganese (that is, L → M and not due to *d–d* transitions.

237. (d): Number of electrons lost/gained in the reaction = 5. Therefore, the equivalent mass of $KMnO_4$ (M = Molecular mass) $= \frac{M}{5}$.

238. (b): In the balanced equation,

$2\,MnO_4^- + 16\,H^+ + C_2O_4^{2-} \longrightarrow 2\,Mn^{+2} + 2\,CO_2 + 8\,H_2O$

$x = 16$ and $y = 2$

239. (c): $Fe^{2+} \xrightarrow[KMnO_4]{\text{oxidised}} Fe^{3+}$

$2\,\overset{+7}{KMnO_4} + 3\,H_2\,SO_4 \longrightarrow K_2SO_4 + 2\,\overset{+2}{MnSO_4} + 3\,H_2O + 5\,(O)$

$K_2SO_4 + 2\,\overset{+2}{MnSO_4} + 5\,\overset{+3}{Fe_2}\,(SO_4)_3 + 8\,H_2O$

240. (a): H_2O_2 being the weaker oxidising agent reduces acidified $KMnO_4$ solution. As a result, the pink colour of $KMnO_4$ is discharged.

$2\,KMnO_4 + 3\,H_2SO_4 + 5\,H_2O_2 \rightarrow K_2SO_4 + 2\,MnSO_4 + 8\,H_2O + 5\,O_2$

241. (d): In the alkaline medium, $KMnO_4$ reacts as follows:

$2\,KMnO_4 + 2\,KOH \rightarrow 2K_2MnO_4 + H_2O + (O)$

or $MnO_4^- + e^- \rightarrow MnO_4^{2-}$

$\therefore$ Equivalent weight of $KMnO_4 = \frac{M}{1} = \frac{158}{1} = 158$

242. (b): In the acidic medium, $KMnO_4$ reacts as follows:

$2\,KMnO_4 + 3\,H_2SO_4 \rightarrow K_2SO_4 + 2\,MnSO_4 + 3\,H_2O + 5\,(O)$

or $MnO_4^- + 8\,H^+ + 5e^- \rightarrow Mn^{2+} + 4\,H_2O$

$\therefore$ Equivalent weight of $KMnO_4 = \frac{M}{5} = \frac{158}{5} = 31.6$

243. (b): The correct statement is that potassium permanganate is a stronger oxidising agent than potassium dichromate because $KMnO_4$ accepts 5 e^- per Mn atom while $K_2Cr_2O_7$ accepts 3 e^- per Cr atom in the acidic medium.

$$MnO_4^- + 8H^+ + 5e^- \longrightarrow Mn^{2+} + 4H_2O$$

$$Cr_2O_7^{2-} + 14H^+ + 6e^- \longrightarrow 2Cr^{3+} + 7H_2O$$

244. (b): $2KMnO_4 + H_2O \rightarrow 2MnO_2 + 2KOH + 3(O)$

245. (a): Acidified $KMnO_4$ is not decolourised by Br_2.

246. (c): In the alkaline medium,

$$2KMnO_4 + KI + H_2O \rightarrow 2KOH + 2MnO_2 + KIO_3$$

247. (c): Oxidation reaction of $KMnO_4$ in the acidic medium:

$$MnO_4^- + 8H^+ + 5e^- \longrightarrow Mn^{2+} + 4H_2O$$

Thus, 5 electrons are involved in the above reaction.

248. (a): $\underset{2\text{ mol}}{2KMnO_4} + 3H_2SO_4 + 5H_2O_2 \rightarrow$

$$K_2SO_4 + 2MnSO_4 + 8H_2O + \underset{5\text{ mol}}{5O_2}$$

2 mol of $KMnO_4$ produce mol of oxygen = 5

$\therefore$ 1 mol of $KMnO_4$ produces mol of oxygen $= \frac{5}{2} = 2.5$ mol

249. (b): The balanced equations are

$$2MnCl_2 + 5K_2S_2O_8 + 8H_2O \longrightarrow 2KMnO_4 + 4K_2SO_4 + 6H_2SO_4 + 4HCl \quad ...(1)$$

$$2KMnO_4 + 5K_2C_2O_4 + 3H_2SO_4 \longrightarrow K_2SO_4 + 4MnSO_4 + 8H_2O + 10CO_2 \quad ...(2)$$

Mass of oxalic acid added = 225 mg

$\therefore$ millimol of oxalic acid added $= \frac{225}{90} = 2.5$

From the second equation,

Millimol of $KMnO_4$ used to react with oxalic acid $= \frac{2}{5} \times \frac{2.5}{1} = 1$

and millimol of $MnCl_2$ required initially = 1 (From first equation)

$\therefore$ Mass of $MnCl_2$ required initially = 1 × 126 = 126 mg

250. (b): Dilute alkaline solution of $KMnO_4$ is called Baeyer's reagent.

251. (d): The oxygen evolved at the anode converts manganate to permanganate.

$$\underset{\text{(Green)}}{2K_2MnO_4} + H_2O + O \longrightarrow \underset{\text{(Violet)}}{2KMnO_4} + 2KOH$$

252. (c): In the laboratory, $KMnO_4$ is prepared by oxidising a manganese (II) salt with peroxodisulfate $(S_2O_8)^{2-}$ ion.

$$2Mn^{2+} + 5S_2O_8^{2-} + 8H_2O \rightarrow 2MnO_4^- + 10SO_4^{2-} + 16H^+$$

253. (a): $2MnO_2 + 4KOH + O_2 \xrightarrow[\text{Air }\Delta]{\text{Fusion}} \underset{\text{Dark green (X)}}{2K_2MnO_4} + 2H_2O$

$$\underset{\text{(X)}}{3K_2MnO_4} + 4HCl \xrightarrow[\text{-rtionation}]{\text{Dispropo}} \underset{\text{Intense purple(Y)}}{2KMnO_4} + MnO_2 + 4KCl + 2H_2O$$

Lanthanoids and Actinoids

254. (d): Except promethium, all lanthanoids are non-radioactive while all actinoids are radioactive.

255. (d): Lanthanum is grouped with the *f*-block elements because the properties of lanthanum are very similar to the elements of the 4*f*-block.

256. (c): Lanthanoids are 14 elements in the 6th period (At. nos 58–71) in which the 4*f* sublevel is filled up.

257. (c): The outer electronic configuration of Lu ($Z = 71$) = [Xe] $4f^{14}5d^16s^2$. The outer electronic configuration of Lu^{2+} = [Xe] $4f^{14}5d^1$.

258. (c): The electronic configuration of Ce is

$${}_{58}Ce = [Xe]\ 4f^1, 5d^1, 6s^2 \text{ (predicted)}$$

$$= [Xe]\ 4f^2, 5d^0, 6s^2 \text{ (observed)}$$

$$Ce^{4+} = [Xe]\ 4f^0, 5d^0, 6s^0$$

In the +4 oxidation state, all (4*f*, 5*d* and 6*s*) orbitals are empty and Ce gains the stable configuration of nearest inert gas xenon, thus, Ce^{4+} is most stable.

259. (d): Electronic configuration of Gd (64) = [Xe] $4f^75d^16s^2$.

4f							5d					6s
↑	↑	↑	↑	↑	↑	↑	↑					↑↓

Therefore, total number of inpaired electrons = 7 + = 8

Sum of spin $= \frac{1}{2} + \frac{1}{2} + \frac{1}{2} + \frac{1}{2} + \frac{1}{2} + \frac{1}{2} + \frac{1}{2} + \frac{1}{2} = 4$

260. (b): Due to the lanthanoid contraction, the ionic size decreases from La^{3+} to Lu^{3+} and the size of Lu^{3+} is further reduced below that for Y^{3+}. Hence, the correct order is

Lu^{3+} (86 pm) < Y^{3+} (90 pm) < Eu^{3+} (95 pm) < La^{3+} (103 pm).

261. (b): La^{3+} > Ce^{3+} > Pm^{3+} > Yb^{3+}
106 pm 103 pm 98 pm 87 pm

Ionic size decreases from La^{3+} to Lu^{3+} due to lanthanoid contraction. Thus, the correct increasing order of ionic radii is $Yb^{3+} < Pm^{3+} < Ce^{3+} < La^{3+}$.

262. (d): Ionic radii of trivalent lanthanoids steadily decrease (and not increase) with an increase in the atomic number. This is the cause for lanthanoid contraction.

263. (a): Lanthanum is the first element of the lanthanoid series and the size decreases with an increase in atomic number, therefore, La has the largest atomic radius.

264. (b): Lanthanoid contraction is related to atomic as well as M^{3+} radii.

265. (c): Due to the presence of *f* electrons, the nucleus is not screened effectively. Thus, the atomic radii of elements of second transition series (Nb, Mo, Tc, and so on) are similar to those of the corresponding third transition series elements (Ta, W, Re). Hence, Nb–Ta, Mo–W and Tc–Re are called chemical twins.

266. (c): Zr and Hf have about the same radius and are called twins of the periodic table due to lanthanoid contraction. On going down the group, the lanthanoid contraction appears and the radius becomes nearly the same.

267. (d): Lanthanoid contraction is caused due to the imperfect shielding of the outer electrons by the $4f$ electrons from the nuclear charge.

268. (b): Ceric sulfate $\overset{IV}{Ce}(SO_4)_2$ and ceric ammonium sulphate $\overset{IV}{Ce}(SO_4)_2.2(NH_4)_2SO_4.2H_2O$ are well known analytical reagents in which cerium has its oxidation state +4. Other lanthanoids such as Pr, Nd, Tb and Dy also exhibit +4 oxidation sate but only in oxides MO_2.

269. (c): By losing all the electrons of $4f$, $5d$ and $6s$ orbitals Ce^{4+} acquires more stable noble gas configuration of Xe.

270. (a): Cerium Ce_{58} = [Xe] $4f^1$, $5d^1$, $6s^2$
Its most stable oxidation state is +3 but +4 also exists.

271. (c): Stability of the oxidation state of the lanthanoids depends upon the combined effect of ionisation energy and hydration energy. For stability, the element should have a low value of ionisation energy and ions should have a high value of hydration energy.

272. (a): The +4 oxidation state of cerium is also known in solution.

273. (d): Availability of the $4f$ electrons does not result in the formation of compounds in the +4 state for all the members of the series.

274. (c): Gadolinium does not absorb light in the visible region of the spectrum; hence, it is colourless in spite of the presence of 7 unpaired electrons.
Since it is colourless, gadolinium is sometimes used as a support for other rare earth phosphors and luminescence in the knowledge that it will not quench their intense colour.

275. (c): Most of the trivalent lanthanoid compounds except that of La^{3+} and Lu^{3+} are coloured both in the solid state and in the aqueous solution. The colour of these ions can be attributed to the presence of f electrons.

276. (d): Many of the Ln (III) compounds are coloured both in the solid state as well as in solution. This colour arises due to the absorption of light from the visible region of spectrum resulting in $f-f$ transitions as lanthanoids have partly filled f orbitals.

277. (d):

Ce $\longrightarrow$ [Xe] $4f^1\,5d^1\,6s^2$; Ce^{4+} $\longrightarrow$ [Xe], diamagnetic

Yb $\longrightarrow$ [Xe] $4f^{14}\,6s^2$; Yb^{2+} $\longrightarrow$ [Xe] $4f^{14}$, diamagnetic

Lu $\longrightarrow$ [Xe] $4f^{14}\,5d^1\,6s^2$; Lu^{3+} $\longrightarrow$ [Xe] $4f^{14}$, diamagnetic

Eu $\longrightarrow$ [Xe] $4f^7\,6s^2$; Eu^{2+} $\longrightarrow$ [Xe] $4f^7$, paramagnetic

278. (b): Across the lanthanoid series, due to lanthanoid contraction, the size of the cations decreases which results in an increase in the covalent character and decrease in the ionic character. So, the basicity of the hydroxides decreases.

279. (d): Due to lanthanoid contraction, the size of M^{3+} ions [*i.e.* Lu^{3+}, Eu^{3+}, Yb^{3+} and Ce^{3+}] decreases and thus, the basic strength of their hydroxides decreases.
The order of size of given M^{3+} ions is

$$Ce^{3+} > Eu^{3+} > Yb^{3+} > Lu^{3+}$$

$\therefore$ The order of basic strength of hydroxides is

$$\underset{\text{(Most Basic)}}{Ce(OH)_3} > Eu(OH)_3 > Yb(OH)_3 > Lu(OH)_3$$

280. (a): The earlier members of the lanthanoid series resemble calcium in some of their chemical properties. For example, the hydroxides of both are ionic and basic.

281. (d): Due to lanthanoid contraction, the size of the trivalent lanthanoids decreases as the atomic number increases which results in an increase in covalent character of the hydroxides and hence the basicity decreases from La^{3+} to Lu^{3+}. Thus, option (d) is correct.

282. (b): Eu = $4f^7 6s^2$
$Eu^{2+} = 4f^7$ (half-filled electronic configuration)
3rd IE, $Eu^{2+} = Eu^{3+} + e^-$, as the third electron is to be removed from relatively more stable half-filled f orbitals, the energy required is very high. Therefore, the 3rd IE of Eu is the highest.

$$Ce = 4f^1\,5d^1\,6s^2\,;\ Ce^{2+} = 4f^1\,5d^1$$

As the 3rd electron is to be removed from 5dorbital, the energy required is lowest. Therefore, the 3rd IE of Ce is the lowest among the given elements.

283. (d): The chemistry of the actinoids is not so smooth as that of the lanthanoids. This is because, the lanthanoids show a limited number of oxidation states whereas the actinoids show a large number of oxidation states. All the statements given in questions as (a), (b) and (c) explain this fact.

284. (a): ClF_3 is mainly used to produce uranium hexafluoride, UF_6, as a part of nuclear fuel processing and reprocessing.

$$U(s) + 3\,ClF_3(l) \rightarrow UF_6(g) + 3\,ClF(g)$$

285. (a): U_3O_8 is uranite or pitch blende, an ore of uranium. It is concentrated (enriched) by roasting and freed from impunities such as Pb, Th, Fe, Ca, Ra, Bi, Sb and Zn.

$$2\,U_3O_8 + 6\,Na_2CO_3 + O_2 \xrightarrow{\text{Roasting}} 6\,Na_2UO_4 + 6\,CO_2$$

286. (a): The elements present after uranium in the periodic table are synthesised artificially by nuclear reactions. Hence, these are called synthetic or man-made or transuranic elements. Thus, Np is an artificially synthesised element.

287. (d): Tm $\rightarrow$ Thulium $\rightarrow$ Atomic number 69
It is a lanthanoid because lanthanoids are present in the sixth period of the periodic table [atomic number 58 (cerium) to atomic number 71 (lutetium)].

288. (b): The fourteen elements which follow actinium, from thorium (Z = 90) to lawrencium (Z = 103), are called actinoids.

They involve filling of the $5f$ subshell. Californium (Cf) has the atomic number 98 and its configuration is

$$_{98}Cf = [Rn]5f^{10}, 6d^0, 7s^2$$

Hence, it is a member of the actinoid series.

289. (c):

Metal	Configuration	No. of unpaired electrons
$_{25}Mn$	[Ar] $3d^5\,4s^2$	5
$_{24}Cr$	[Ar] $3d^5\,4s^1$	6
$_{96}Cm$	[Rn] $5f^7\,6d^1\,7s^2$	8
$_{26}Fe$	[Ar] $3d^6\,4s^2$	4

Thus, Cm has the largest number of unpaired electrons.

290. (a): The heaviest atom amongst the given elements is uranium ($Z = 92$).

291. (a): Since there is a very small difference between the energies of the 5*f* and 6*d* levels, the electrons can go to the 6*d* level or can remain in the 5*f* level. Hence, the electronic configuration of the actinoids cannot be assigned with any degree of certainty.

292. (b): Both Np and Pu show a highest oxidations state of +7.

293. (d): The actinoids exhibit more number of oxidation states in general than the lanthanoids. Hence, (d) is correct.

294. (c): The maximum oxidation state exhibited by the actinoid ions is +7 (Np and Pu).

295. (d): $4f$ and $5f$ orbitals belong to different shells and thus experience different amounts of shielding.

Final Preparation

296. (a):

$$Cr^{3+}\,e^- \longrightarrow Cr^{2+},\ E° = -0.41 \text{ volts and}$$

$$Mn^{3+} + e^- \longrightarrow Mn^{2+},\ E° = +1.51 \text{ volts}$$

The $E°$ values show that Cr^{2+} is stable and has a tendency to acquire a more stable Cr^{3+} state by acting as a reducing agent. On the other hand, Mn^{3+} is unstable and is reduced to the more stable Mn^{2+} form.

297. (c): V_2O_3 is a strong reducing agent.

298. (b): $Cr^{3+} = 3\,d^3$ has all the electrons in the more stable t_{2g} orbitals which imparts more stability to the ions. Also, $Cr^{3+} + e^- \rightarrow Cr^{2+}$; $E° = -0.41$ V, which indicates that Cr^{3+} is more stable than the Cr^{2+} ion.

299. (c): $[Cu(H_2O)_4]^{2+}$ shows a blue colour due to *d–d* transition.

300. (d): In the case of $Ni^{2+} = d^8$ configuration, there are only two unpaired electrons in the *d*-orbitals whereas in the case of Cr^{2+}, Mn^{2+} and Fe^{2+}, there are 4, 5 and 4 unpaired electrons respectively.

301. (c): Ions in the +2 oxidation state of all the elements with atomic numbers 21–29 have unpaired electrons and therefore, are paramagnetic. Hence, option (c) is correct.

302. (c): Magnetic moment $\mu = \sqrt{n(n+2)}$ BM = 2.84 BM corresponding to 2 unpaired electrons.

$Cr^{2+} = 3d^4$, 4 unpaired electrons

$Co^{2+} = 3d^7$, 3 unpaired electrons

$Ni^{2+} = 3d^8$, 2 unpaired electrons

$Ti^{3+} = 3d^1$, 1 unpaired electron

Hence, Ni^{2+} gives a magnetic moment of 2.84 BM.

303. (a): $Co^{3+} = [Ar]\,3d^6$, unpaired $e^-(n) = 4$

A. $Co^{3+} = [Ar]3d^6$, unpaired $e^-(n) = 4$

Spin magnetic moment

$$(\mu) = (\mu) = \sqrt{n(n+2)} = \sqrt{4(4+2)} = \sqrt{24} \text{ BM} \quad \text{(iv)}$$

B. $Cr^{3+} = [Ar]3d^3$, unpaired $e^-(n) = 3$

Spin magnetic moment

$$(\mu) = (\mu) = \sqrt{3(3+2)} = \sqrt{15} \text{ BM} \quad \text{(v)}$$

C. $Fe^{3+} = [Ar]3d^5$, unpaired $e^-(n) = 5$

Spin magnetic moment

$$(\mu) = (\mu) = \sqrt{5(5+2)} = \sqrt{35} \text{ BM} \quad \text{(ii)}$$

D. $Ni^{2+} = [Ar]3d^8$, unpaired $e^-(n) = 2$

Spin magnetic moment $(\mu) = (\mu) = \sqrt{2(2+2)} = \sqrt{8}$ BM (ii)

304. (c): Because SO_4^{2-} and F^- ligands are very weak and do not cause the splitting of *d* orbitals for absorption of radiation.

305. (c): Na_3VO_4 contains vanadium in the +5 oxidation state which has vacant *d* orbitals and is colourless.

306. (c): $Ni^{2+} = 3d^8$ has two unpaired electrons, $Ti^{3+} = 3d^1$ has one unpaired electron in the *d* orbital. Hence, in this pair both the ions are coloured in the aqueous solution.

307. (d): Transition metal ions having outer electronic configuration as $3d^0$.

$$TiF_6^{2-} = Ti^{4+} = 3d^0,\ Cu_2Cl_2 = Cu^+ = 3d^{10}.$$

Thus, both these compounds will be colourless.

308. (d):

In CrO_4^{2-}, $Cr^{+6} = 3d°(n = 0)$, diamagnetic

In $Cr_2O_7^{2-}$, $Cr^{+6} = 3d°(n = 0)$, diamagnetic

In MnO_4^-, $Mn^{+7} = 3d°(n = 0)$, diamagnetic

In MnO_4^{2-}, $Mn^{+6} = 3d^1(n = 1)$, paramagnetic

Thus, in MnO_4^{2-}, one unpaired electron ($n = 1$) is present the *d* orbital; so, *d – d* transition is possible.

309. (b): Interstitial compounds are chemically inert and not reactive as stated.

310. (c): ZnO is amphoteric and dissolves in both acids and bases.

$$ZnO + 2HCl \rightarrow ZnCl_2 + H_2O;$$

$$ZnO + 2NaOH \rightarrow Na_2ZnO_2 + H_2O$$

311. (b): A velvety black powder which is obtained by reduction of $PtCl_4$ with glucose or sodium formate is known as Pt black.

312. (a): Fool's gold is FeS_2 and does not contain Au at all.

313. (c): Alloy of Ag (80%) and Cu (20%) is called sterling silver.

314. (b): Chloroplatinic acid is $H_2[PtCl_6]$ which is dibasic.

315. (a): $CuSO_4 + Ca(OH)_2$ mixture is called Bordeaux mixture and is used as a fungicide.

316. (d): It does not dissolve in aqua regia as it is much more noble than Au or Pt.

317. (a): Hydrated Cr_2O_3 is called Guignet's green.

318. (c): Mercurous ion $Hg^+ = 3d^{10}4s^1$ should be paramagnetic but is actually diamagnetic. Thus, it is written as Hg_2^{2+} diatomic cation with no unpaired electrons.

319. (c): All nitrates, acetate and perchlorates are water soluble. Mercurous chloride (Hg_2Cl_2) is water insoluble.

320. (d): Insulin contains zinc (Zn), hemoglobin contains iron (Fe) and vitamin B_{12} contains cobalt (Co).

321. (d): $TiCl_4 + 4\,H_2O \rightarrow Ti(OH)_4 + 4\,HCl$

322. (d): As the size of the metal atom decreases from Ti to Fe, the basic character of their monoxides decreases in that order.

323. (c): $Cr_2O_7^{2-} + 4H_2O_2 + 2H^+ \rightarrow \underset{\text{Chromic peroxide, deep blue colour}}{2CrO_5} + 5H_2O$

(Structure of CrO_5: Cr bonded to one O by a double bond and to two peroxo O–O groups.)

$$Cr_2O_7^{2-} + 4H_2O_2 + 2H^+ \rightarrow 2CrO_5 + 5H_2O$$

324. (b): $K_2Cr_2O_7 + 6\,H_2SO_4 + 4\,KCl \rightarrow$

$$\underset{\text{Reddish-brown}}{2CrO_2Cl_2\uparrow} + 6\,KHSO_4 + 3\,H_2O$$

325. (b): $K_2Cr_2O_7 + 3\,Na_2SO_3 + 4\,H_2SO_4 \rightarrow$

$$3\,NaSO_4 + K_2SO_4 + \underset{\text{(Green)}}{Cr_2(SO_4)_3}$$

On explosion, green coloured Cr_2O_3 is blown out, hence the name is 'chemical volcano'. The reaction is highly exothermic.

326. (b): $Na_2Cr_2O_7$ is hygroscopic while $K_2Cr_2O_7$ is not. Thus, $K_2Cr_2O_7$ is preferred over $Na_2Cr_2O_7$ for use in volumetric analysis as a primary standard.

327. (d): $(NH_4)_2Cr_2O_7 \xrightarrow{\text{Heat}} Cr_2O_3 + N_2 + 4\,H_2O$

328. (d): $CuCr_2O_7$ solution is green because Cu^{2+} ions are blue and $Cr_2O_7^{2-}$ ions are yellow in an aqueous medium. Both blue and yellow colours mix to give a composite green colour.

329. (b): The colour of CrO_3 (d^0 configuration) is due to CT (charge transfer) from ligand (oxygen) to metal (chromium) transition and not due to $d-d$ transition.

330. (b): The correct reaction is

$$2\,MnO_2 + 4\,KOH + O_2 \rightarrow 2\,K_2MnO_4 + 2\,H_2O$$

331. (c): $CO_2 + H_2O \rightarrow H_2CO_3 \rightleftharpoons H^+ + HCO_3^-$

In the presence of H^+ ions, K_2MnO_4 undergoes disproportionation reaction.

$$\underset{\text{Green colour}}{3\,MnO_4^{2-}} + 4H^+ \rightarrow \underset{\text{Purple colour}}{2\,MnO_4^-} + \underset{\text{Brown ppt.}}{MnO_2} + 2\,H_2O$$

332. (c): $E°$ values (standard reaction potentials) for these species in acidic medium are

$$S_2O_8^{2-}(aq) + 2e^- \rightarrow 2SO_4^{2-}(aq); E° = +2.01 \text{ Volts}$$

$$MnO_4^-(aq) + 8H^+ + 5e^- \rightarrow Mn^{2+}(aq) + 4H_2O; \quad E° = +1.77 \text{ Volts}$$

$$Cr_2O_7^{2-}(aq) + 14H^+ + 6e^- \rightarrow 2Cr^{3+} + 7H_2O; \quad E° = +1.33 \text{ Volts}$$

$$VO_2^-(aq) + 2H^+ + 5e^- \rightarrow Vo^{2+}(aq) + H_2O; \quad E° = +1.0 \text{ Volts}$$

Since the standard reducing potential values $E°$ for the above redox reactions are positive and decrease in the order $S_2O_8^{2-} > MnO_4^- > Cr_2O_7^{2-} > VO_2^-$, the strength as an oxidising agent decreases in the same order as shown in option (c).

333. (c): In neutral medium, the reaction of $KMnO_4$ is

$$MnO_4^- + 2\,H_2O + 3e^- \rightarrow MnO_2 + 4\,OH^-$$

Therefore, its equivalent weight in terms of molecular weight is M/3.

334. (c): $\underset{\text{2 mol}}{2\,KMnO_4} + 3\,H_2SO_4 + \underset{\text{5 mol}}{5H_2O_2} \rightarrow$

$$K_2SO_4 + 2\,MnSO_4 + 8\,H_2O + 5\,O_2.$$

Therefore, for 1 mol of $KMnO_4$, $\frac{5}{2}$ mol of H_2O_2 is required.

335. (c): $\underset{\text{6 M}}{6\,KMnO_4} + \underset{\text{10 M}}{10FeC_2O_4} + 24H_2SO_4 \rightarrow 3K_2SO_4 +$

$$6MnSO_4 + 5Fe_2(SO_4)_3 + 20CO_2 + 24\,H_2O$$

10 M of Fe_2CO_4 is oxidised by 6 M of $KMnO_4$

10 M of Fe_2CO_4 is oxidised by $\frac{6}{10}$ M of $KMnO_4$

336. (c): In alkaline solution

$$\overset{+7}{MnO_4^-} + 2\,H_2O + 3e^- \rightarrow \overset{+4}{MnO_2} + 4\,OH^-$$

Total number of electrons gained = 3

Total change in ox. number of Mn = 7 – 4 = 3

Thus, eq. wt. of $KMnO_4 = \dfrac{\text{molar mass of } KMnO_4}{3}$

337. (b): $2\,KMnO_4 + H_2O + KI \rightarrow 2\,MnO_2 + 2\,KOH + KIO_3$.

338. (b): Hydrogen peroxide is oxidised to H_2O and O_2.

$2\,KMnO_4 + 3\,H_2SO_4 + 5\,H_2O_2 \rightarrow$

$$K_2SO_4 + 2\,MnSO_4 + 8\,H_2O + 5\,O_2$$

or $2\,MnO_4^- + 5\,H_2O_2 + 6\,H^+ \rightarrow 2\,Mn^{2+} + 8\,H_2O + 5\,O_2$

339. (a): MnO_2 imparts purple colour to pottery.

340. (c): In MnO_4^-, $Mn^{7+} = 3d^0$ but still it is coloured. This is because ligand (oxygen) gives its one electron momentarily to the metal (Mn) and converts it to Mn (+6) which shows colour. Thus, the colour of MnO_4^- is due to charge transfer (CT) from L $\rightarrow$ M.

341. (d): Eu shows +2 and +3 oxidation states.

342. (d): The most common and stable oxidation state of the lanthanoids is +3.

343. (c): CeI_2 is supposed to have metal excess defect due to anion vacancies and the electrons associated with the anions are left behind trapped in the vacancies. Thus, CeI_2 is formulated as Ce (IV) 2 I^-, 2 e^-. Due to the presence of these trapped electrons, the compound shows a metallic lustre.

344. (b): The electronic configuration of Eu (Z = 63) is [Xe] $4f^7 6s^2$, Gd (Z = 64) is [Xe] $4f^7 5d^1 6s^2$ and Tb (Z = 65) is [Xe] $4f^9 6s^2$.

345. (b): Due to lanthanoid contraction, Zr^{4+} and Hf^{4+} possess almost the same ionic radii. Ce^{4+} acts as an oxidising agent and tends to change to stable Ce^{3+} ions (reduction).

346. (d): As a result of the lanthanoid contraction, the sizes of elements the of $4d$ transition series are almost similar to those of the $5d$ transition series. Hence, they show similarities in properties.

347. (b): Ce = [Xe] $4f^1 5d^1 6s^2$; Cu^{4+} = [Xe], Yb = [Xe] $4f^{14} 6s^2$; Yb^{2+} = [Xe] $4f^{14}$, Lu = [Xe] $4f^{14} 5d^1 6s^2$; Lu^{3+} = [Xe] $4f^{14}$. The given ions contain no unpaired electrons and therefore, are diamagnetic.

348. (c): The first few members of the lanthanoids are quite reactive like calcium. However, with increasing atomic number, their behaviour becomes similar to that of aluminium.

349. (b): Neodymium oxide, (Nd_2O_3) dissolved in selenium oxychloride is one of the most powerful liquid lasers known so far.

350. (d): Oxidation state of Np in $Li_5[NpO_6]$

$$\overset{+1}{Li_5}[\overset{x}{N}p\overset{-2}{O_6}] + 5 + x + 6\times(-2) = 0$$

$$x + 5 = 12 \quad \therefore \quad x = 12 - 5 = +7$$

351. (d): In actinoids, there is a lesser energy difference between the $5f$ and the $6d$ orbitals than that between the $4f$ and $5d$ orbitals in the lanthanoids. Hence, the actinoids show more number of oxidation states.

352. (b): Actinoids have a greater range of oxidation states due to comparable energies of $5f$, $6d$ and 7s orbitals. Hence, all their electrons can take part in bond formation.

353. (c): The higher the charge on the metal ion, smaller is the ionic size and more is the complex forming ability. Thus, the degree of complex formation decreases in the order

$$M^{4+} > MO_2^{2+} > M^{3+} > MO_2^{+}$$

The higher tendency of complex formation of MO_2^{2+} as compared to M^{3+} is due to the high concentration of charge on the metal atom M in MO_2^{2+}.

354. (c): Tungsten (W) has the highest melting point (3683 K) among the d-block elements.

355. (c):

Increasing no. of ox, states	Ti	<	V	<	Cr	<	Mn
	4		5		6		7

Increasing magnetic moment	$\sqrt{3}$	$\sqrt{8}$	$\sqrt{15}$	$\sqrt{24}$

B.M. of M^{3+} ions

Melting point order	Mn	<	Ti	<	Cr	<	Cr
m.p. in °C	1245		1668		1875		1900
IE_2 order	Ti	<	V	<	Mn	<	Cr
kJ/mol	1320		1376		1376		1513

356. (d): Mo (VI) and W (VI) have the same size due to lanthanoid contraction.

357. (c): Sc has the lowest density (3.1 g cm^{-1}) and is the lighest transition element.

358. (a): The electronic configurations of the given elements are: $_{22}Ti$ = [Ar]$3d^2$ $4s^2$, $_{23}V$ = [Ar]$3d^3$ $4s^2$, $_{24}Cr$ = [Ar]$3d^5$ $4s^1$, $_{25}Mn$ = [Ar]$3d^5$ $4s^2$
Their effective nuclear charges increase from Ti to Mn; therefore, their first ionisation enthalpies increase in the same order Mn > Cr > V >Ti. However, after the removal of the 1st electron, Cr acquires a stable $3d^5$ configuration. Hence, it shows exceptional behaviour and has a very high 2nd ionisation enthalpy. For the remaining elements, the trend remains the same. Thus, the 2nd ionisation enthalpies will be in the order Cr > Mn > V >Ti.

359. (a): Mn^{2+} (d^5) gets the highest stabilisation due to its half-filled configuration. In the case of Fe^{2+} (d^6), addition of one extra electron in the subshell destabilises it. Addition of two electrons in the case of Co^{2+} (d^7) destabilises it more. Cr^{2+} (d^4) has one vacant d subshell which also imparts destabilisation. But Fe^{2+} gets more stability as compared to Cr^{2+} though exchange energy. So, the correct order is Mn > Fe > Cr > Co.

360. (c): Ac exhibits the +3 oxidation state only, whereas U, Th and Pa exhibit variable oxidation states.

MATCH THE FOLLOWING

361. (b): $V^{2+} = 3d^3$, 3 unpaired electrons
(B) $Ti^{3+} = 3d^1$, 1 unpaired electron
(C) $Fe^{3+} = 3d^5$, 5 unpaired electrons
(D) $M^{3+} = 3d^4$, 4 unpaired electrons

ASSERTION REASON

362. (c): Correct R. The atomic size of silver is almost equal to that of gold due to lanthanoid contraction.

363. (b): Correct explanation. Osmium has an outer electronic configuration of $5d^6 6s^2$ where $5d$ and $6s$ orbitals are close in energy. Therefore, all the 8 electrons can participate in bonding.

364. (b): Correct explanation. Mn^{3+} is a stronger oxidising agent than Cr^{3+}.

365. (b): Correct explanation. Hg^{2+} has a $5d^{10}$ configuration and thus, there is no unpaired electron present in it.

366. (d): Correct A. $VOSO_4$ is coloured and paramagnetic. **Correct R.** In $VOSO_4$, V is in the (+IV) oxidation state.

367. (a): R is the correct explanation of A.

368. (d): Correct A. Mercury vapour is invisible and colourless. **Correct R.** Mercury is a liquid metal with a shining silvery appearance at room temperature.

369. (a): R is the correct explanation of A.

370. (b): Correct explanation. The intense yellow colour of Na_2CrO_4 in aqueous solution is due to charge transfer from oxygen to Cr (VI) thereby converting it to Cr (V) momentarily which is coloured.

371. (a): R is the correct explanation of A.

372. (b): Correct explanation. Due to their ability to adopt variable oxidation states, they easily absorb and re-emit a wide range of energies to provide the necessary activation energy and also, they easily combine with one of the reactants to form an intermediate which reacts with the second reactant to form the final products.

373. (c): Correct R. An aqueous solution of $FeCl_3$ is acidic in nature.

374. (b): Correct explanation. $K_2Cr_2O_7$ is pure, non-hygroscopic and appreciably soluble in hot water.

375. (b): Correct explanation. In the alkaline medium, $KMnO_4$ is reduced to MnO_2 which involves $3e^-$ reduction.

376. (d): Correct A. In MnO_4^-, Mn–O bonds are covalent. **Correct R.** The oxidation number of Mn in MnO_4^- is +7.

377. (b): Correct explanation. The intense colour in some of the transition metal complexes is due to charge transfer transitions. The intense purple colour of $KMnO_4$ arises due to charge transfer from oxygen (ligand) to Mn (metal). In this way, one of the oxygens acquires O^- and Mn changes from +VII to +VI momentarily.

378. (a): R is the correct explanation of A.

379. (a): R is the correct explanation of A.

380. (b): Correct explanation. This is due to the fact that the 5 *f* electrons of actinoids are less effectively shielded which results in quenching of the orbital contribution.

381. (b): Correct explanation. The higher the charge on the metal ion, the smaller is the ionic size and more is the complex forming ability. The degree of complex formation in the actinoids decreases in the order $M^{4+} > MO_2^{2+} > M^{3+} > MO_2^+$. The higher tendency of complex formation of MO_2^{2+} is due to the high concentration of charge on the metal atom in the MO_2^{2+} ion.

382. (a): R is the correct explanation of A.

383. (c): Correct R. Due to the presence of a greater number of unpaired *d* electrons, the metallic bonding in W is very strong.

Coordination Compounds

9.1 Coordination Compounds and Complex Ions

Coordination compounds are the compounds in which the central metal atom is linked to a number of ions or neutral molecules by coordinate bonds, that is, by the donation of lone pairs of electrons by these ions or neutral molecules to the central metal atom. For example, nickel tetracarbonyl, $[Ni(CO)_4]$, is a coordination compound. In this, the CO molecules are linked to the central nickel atom by coordinate bonds by donating lone pairs of electrons.

If the species formed by linking of a number of ions or molecules by coordinate bonds to the central metal atom (or ion) carries a positive or negative charge, it is called a *complex ion*. For example, $[Fe(CN)_6]^{4-}$, $[Cu(NH_3)_4]^{2+}$, $[Ag(CN)_2]^-$, and so on.

9.1.1 Types of Complexes

There are three types of complexes:

(i) Cationic complex: A complex in which the complex ion carries a net positive charge is called a cationic complex, as in $[Co(NH_3)_6]^{3+}$, $[Ni(NH_3)_6]^{6+}$, and so on.

(ii) Anionic complex: A complex in which the complex ion carries a net negative charge is called an anionic complex, as in $[Ag(CN)_2]^-$, $[Fe(CN)_6]^{4-}$, and so on.

(iii) Neutral complex: A complex carrying no net charge is called a neutral complex, as in $[Ni(CO)_4]$, $[Co(NH_3)_3Cl_3]$, and so on.

The common double salts are, Mohr's salt $FeSO_4.(NH_4)_2SO_4.6H_2O$, potash alum $K_2SO_4.Al_2(SO_4)_3.24H_2O$, carnallite $KCl.MgCl_2.6H_2O$. Mohr's salt dissolves in water and gives the characteristic properties of Fe^{2+}, NH_4^+ and SO_4^{2-} ions.

Table 9.1 Differences between a double salt and a complex compound

Double salt	Complex compound
1. They usually contain two simple salts in equimolar proportions.	1. The simple salts from which they are formed may or may not be in equimolar proportions.
2. They exist only in the solid state. In aqueous solution, they dissociate completely into ions.	2. They exist in the solid state as well as in aqueous solution. This is because even in solution, the complex ion does not dissociate into ions.
3. They are ionic compounds and do not contain any coordinate bond.	3. They may or may not be ionic but the complex part always contains coordinate bonds.
4. The properties of the double salt are the same as those of its constituent compounds.	4. The properties of the coordination compound are different from its constituents.
5. In a double salt, the metal ions show their normal valency.	5. In a coordination compound, the metal ion satisfies two types of valencies—primary and secondary.
6. A double salt loses its identity in the solution.	6. A coordination compound (complex) retains its identity in the solution.

The ligand may contain one or more than one donor atom for coordination with the central atom. Accordingly, the ligands are classified as follows.

- *Unidentate or monodentate ligands*: only one donor atom is present in its molecule For examples, NH_3, H_2O,Cl^-, CN^-, OH^-, O^{2-}, NO_2^-, CO.

- *Didentate or bidentate ligands*: the ligand contains two donor atoms. For example, ethane-1,2-diamine [ethylenediamine (en)] and oxalate ion (ox).

$$\begin{matrix} CH_2-\ddot{N}H_2 \\ | \\ CH_2-\ddot{N}H_2 \end{matrix} \qquad \begin{matrix} COO^- \\ | \\ COO^- \end{matrix} \text{ or } \begin{matrix} O=C-O:^- \\ | \\ O=C-O:^- \end{matrix}$$

- *Polydentate ligands*: Ligands have more than two donor atoms present in the molecule. For example, diethylene triamine (abbreviated as dien) acts as a terdentate ligand with three donor N atoms.

$$\begin{matrix} H_2C-\ddot{N}\begin{matrix} CH_2COO:^- \\ CH_2COO:^- \end{matrix} \\ | \\ H_2C-\ddot{N}\begin{matrix} CH_2COO:^- \\ CH_2COO:^- \end{matrix} \end{matrix}$$

$(EDTA^{4-})$

The number of coordinating or ligating groups present in a ligand is called the *denticity* of that ligand. For example,

- Didentate chelation, $[PtCl_2(en)]$.

$$\begin{matrix} Cl & & \overset{H_2}{N} - CH_2 \\ & \searrow Pt \swarrow & | \\ Cl & & \underset{H_2}{N} - CH_2 \end{matrix}$$

ethylenediamine (en, ethane-1,2-diamine).

- Terdentate chelation, $[PtCl(dien)]^+$.

$$\begin{matrix} & CH_2-CH_2 & \\ H_2N & & NH-CH_2 \\ & \searrow Pt \leftarrow & | \\ Cl & & \underset{H_2}{N}-CH_2 \end{matrix}$$

N-(2-aminoethyl) ethane-1,2-diamine

- Tetradentate chelation, $[Pt(trien)]^{2+}$.

$$\begin{matrix} & CH_2-CH_2 & \\ CH_2-\overset{H}{N} & & \overset{H}{N}-CH_2 \\ | & \searrow Pt \swarrow & | \\ CH_2-\underset{H_2}{N} & & \underset{H_2}{N}-CH_2 \end{matrix}$$

N,N′-bis-(2-aminoethyl)ethane-1,2-diamine.

- Greater the denticity of the ligand, the more stable is the complex (chelate) formed.
- Chelating ligands which do not contain double bonds, such as ethylenediamine, form five membered stable rings.

Ambidentate ligands: The monodentate ligands can coordinate with the central atom through more than one site. For example, NO_2 can coordinate to the metal atom through N or O as shown.

$$M \leftarrow N\begin{matrix} \nearrow O \\ \searrow O \end{matrix} \quad \text{and} \quad M \leftarrow O-N=O$$

nitrito –N   nitrito –O

Similarly –CN can coordinate through C or N as shown.

$M \leftarrow CN$ (Cyanide) $M \leftarrow NC$ (Isocyanide)

Thiocyanato (SCN) can coordinate through S or N.

$M \leftarrow SCN$ (Thiocyanato) $M \leftarrow NCS$ (Isothiocyanato)

Coordination number may be defined as the number of coordinate bonds formed with the central metal atom/ion by the ligands. For example, in the complex ions,

$[Ni(NH_3)_4]^{2+}$	CN of Ni^{2+}	= 4
$[Fe(C_2O_4)_3]^{3-}$	CN of Fe^{3+}	= 6
$[Co(en)_3]^{3+}$	CN of Co^{3+}	= 6

Charge of a complex ion: The charge carried by a complex ion is the algebraic sum of charges carried by the central metal ion and the ligands coordinated to it. For example, $[Ni(NH_3)_6]^{2+}$ carries a charge of +2 because Ni^{2+}ion carries a charge of +2 and the ammonia molecule is neutral. The complex $[CoCl_3(NH_3)_3]$ carries no charge because Co^{3+} ion carries a charge of +3, three ammonia molecules are neutral and three Cl^- ions together carry a charge of –3.

$$[CoCl_3(NH_3)_3]\text{: Charge} = 3 - 3 + 3(0) = 0$$

The *coordination polyhedron* is the spatial arrangement of the ligand atoms which are directly attached to the central atom. The coordination polyhedra are tetrahedral, square planar, octahedral, square pyramidal and trigonal bipyramidal. For example, $[PtCl_4]^{2-}$ is square planar, $Ni(CO)_4$ is tetrahedral, $[Co(NH_3)_6]^{3+}$ is octahedral while $Fe(CO)_5$ is trigonal bipyramidal (Fig. 9.1, 9.2).

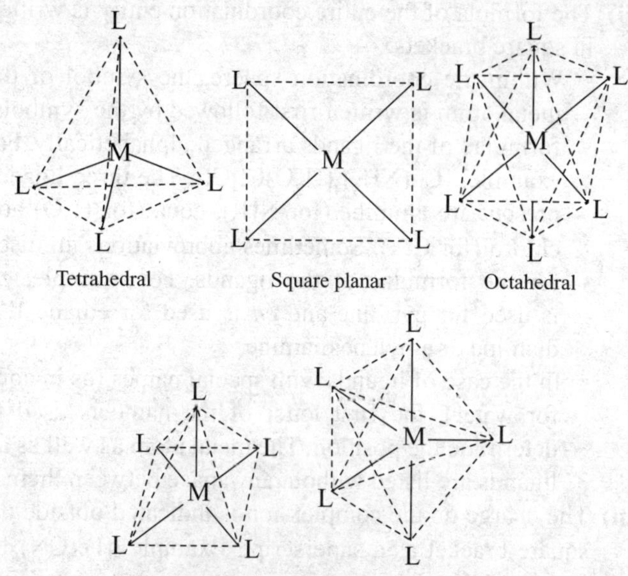

Fig. 9.1 Shapes of different coordination polyhedra (M = central metal atom/ion, L = unidentate ligand)

Calculation of Oxidation Number

The oxidation number of the central metal atom can be calculated from the charge on the complex ion. Assuming the oxidation number of metal atom to be x, the sum of the charges of all the ligands and x is put equal to the charge on the complex ion. From the equation formed, the value of x can be calculated. For example,

- in $[Co(NH_3)_5Cl]^{2+}$, $x-1+5(0)=+2 \therefore x=+3$, that is, the oxidation number of CO = +3,
- in $K_4[Fe(CN)_6]$, that is, $[Fe(CN)_6]^{4-}$, $x+6(-1)=-4 \therefore x=+2$, oxidation number of Fe = +2.

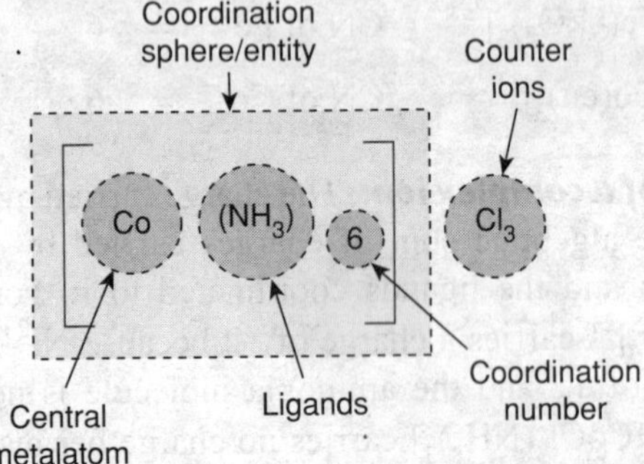

Fig. 9.2 Depicting various terms usesd in a complex

9.2 Formula Writing and Nomenclature of Coordination Compounds

9.2.1 Rules for Writing the Formula of Mononuclear Coordination Compounds

The following rules are applied while writing the formula.

(i) The formula of the cation is written first followed by that of the anion.

(ii) The formula of the entire coordination entity is written in square brackets.

- Within the coordination sphere, the symbol of the metal atom is written first followed by the symbols/formulae of the ligands arranged alphabetically. For example, $[Co(NH_3)_4(H_2O)Cl]Cl_2$. The three ligands present are ammine (for NH_3), aqua (for H_2O) and chloro (for Cl^-). Sometimes abbreviations are used for the formulae of the ligands. For example, *py* is used for pyridine and *en* is used for ethane-1,2-diamine or ethylene diamine.
- In the case of ligands with special names (as in aqua for water), the first letter of the name is used to determine the position. The metal atom as well as all ligands are listed without any space between them.

(iii) The charge on the complex ion is indicated outside the square bracket as a superscript. Example, $[Fe(CN)_6]^{3-}$ and $[Cu(NH_3)_4]^{2+}$.

(iv) *Numerical prefixes to indicate number of ligands*: When more than one ligand of a particular kind is present in the complex, the prefixes di, tri-tetra-, penta-, hexa-, and so on, are used to indicate their numbers—two, three, four, five and six respectively. The prefixes bis, tris, tetrakis are used for two, three, four ligands, respectively. Such ligands are called complex ligands. For example, to indicate two complex ligands such as ethylenediamine, we used the prefix 'bis(ethylenediamine)' or 'bis(1,2-ethanedamine)'. The name of the complex ligand is given in brackets. For example: $[NiCl_2(PPh_3)_2]$: dichloridobis(triphenylphosphine)nickel(II).

If the complex ion is a *cation* or the coordination compound is *non-ionic*, the name of the central metal ion is written as such followed by its oxidation state indicated by a Roman numeral (such as II, III, IV) in parentheses at the end of the name of the metal without any space between the two. (0) is used for an oxidation state of zero. For example,

$[Cu(NH_3)_4]SO_4$	tetramminecopper(II) sulfate
$[Ni(dmg)_2]$	bis(dimethylglyoximato)nickel(II)
$[Pt[NH_3)_2Cl_4]$	diamminetetrachloridoplatinum(IV)

(v) If the complex ion is an *anion*, the name of the central metal atom is made to end in *-ate* followed by the oxidation number in brackets without any space between them. For example, $Na_3[AlF_6]$ is named as sodiumhexafluoridoaluminate(III).

When the complex is an acid, that is, the cation is H^+, the name of the metal is made to end in -ic followed by the word 'acid'. For example, $H_4[Pt(CN)_6]$ is named as hexacyanoplatinic(II) acid.

(vi) *Naming of geometrical isomers*: Geometrical isomers are named by the use of the terms *cis*- to designate adjacent positions and *trans*- to designate opposite positions. For example,

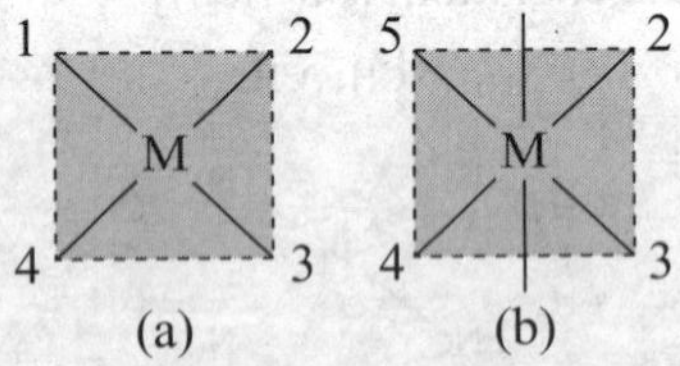

Complex	Similar Groups For	
	trans	***cis***
(a) Square planar	At 1, 3, and 2, 4	At 1, 4 and 2, 3
(b) Octahedral	At 1, 6; 2, 4 and 3, 5	or 1, 2 and 3, 4 At 1 , 2 ; 1 , 3... or 2, 3 ; 3, 4 ; 4, 5...

(vii) *Naming of optical isomers*: Dextro and laevo rotatory optically active compounds are respectively designated either by (+) and (–) or by *d*-, *l*-. For example, (+) or *d*-$K_3[Cr(C_2O_4)_3]$ is potassium (+) or *d*-trioxalatochromate(III).

(viii) If the complex contains two or more metal ions, it is termed *polynuclear*. The monodentate ligands that link the two metal atoms simultaneously are called *bridging ligands* which are separated from the rest of the complex by hyphens and denoted by the prefix μ. For example,

$$\left[(en)_2\,Co \begin{matrix} NH_2 \\ OH \end{matrix} Co\,(en)_2\right](SO_4)_2$$

is named as bis(ethane-1,2-diamine)cobalt(III)-μ-imido-μ-nitrotetrammine cobalt(III) ion.

Some complexes with their names are given in Table 9.2, Table 9.3.

Table 9.2 Some complexes and their names

Complex compound	Name
1. $[CoCl_2(en)_2]SO_4$	Dichloridobis(ethane-1,2-diamine)cobalt(IV) sulfate
2. $[Cr(H_2O)_6]Cl_3$	Hexaaquachromium(III) chloride
3. $[CoCl(en)_2(ONO)]^+$	Chloridobis(ethane-1,2-diamine)nitritocobalt(III) ion
4. $[Co(NH_3)_5(CO_3)]Cl$	Pentamminecarbonatocobalt(III) chloride
5. $[(NH_3)_5Cr\text{-}OH\text{-}Cr(NH_3)_5]Cl_5$	Pentamminechromium(III)-μ-hydroxo-pentamminechromium(II) chloride
Compounds containing anionic complex ions	
6. $K_3[Pt(CN)_5(NO)]$	Potassium pentacyanonitrosylcobaltate(II)
7. $Hg[Co(NCS)_4]$	Mercury tetraisothiocyanatocobaltate(II) or mercury tetrathiocyanato-N-cobaltate(II)
8. $Fe_4[Fe(CN)_6]_3$	Ferric hexacyanoferrate(II)
9. $Na_2[CrF_4O]$	Sodium tetrafluoridooxochromate(IV)
10. Dextro $K_3[Ir(CrO_4)_3]$	Potassium (+) or *d*-trioxaltoiridate(III)
11. $Na_3[Fe(C_2O_4)_3]$	Sodium trioxalatoferrate(III)
Compounds containing complex cationic and anionic ions	
12. $[Pt(NH_3)_4Cl_2]\,[PtCl_4]$	Tetraamminedichloridoplatinum(IV) tetrachloridoplatinate(II)
13. $[Ag(NH_3)_2]\,[Ag(CN)_2]$	Diamminesilver(I) dicyanidoargentite(I)
14. $[Cr(NH_3)_5(CNS)]\,[ZnCl_4]$	Pentammineisothiocyanatochromium(III) tetrachloridozincate(II)
Non-ionic coordination compounds	
15. $[Cr(PPh_3)(CO)_5]$	Pentacarbonyltriphenylphosphinechromium(0)
16. $[Mn_3(CO)_{12}]$	Dodecacarbonyltrimanganese(0)
17. $[Ni(dmg)_2]$	Bis(dimethylglyoximato)nickel(II)
Note that dmg is a negative ligand with a charge of –1.	
18. $[(CO)_3Fe(CO)_3Fe(CO)_3]$	Tri-μ-carbonyl-bis(tricarbonyliron(0)) or (diironenneacarbonyl)

Table 9.3 Common and IUPAC names

Complex	Commonly used name	IUPAC name
$K_4[Fe(CN)_6]$	Potassium ferrocyanide	Potassium hexacyanoferrate(II)
$K_3[Fe(CN)_6]$	Potassium ferricyanide	Potassium hexacyanoferrate(III)
$Na_3[Co(ONO)_6]$	Sodium cobaltinitrite	Sodium hexanitritocobaltate(III)
$Na_2[Fe(CN_5)NO]$ (NO is present as NO^+)	Sodium nitroprusside	Sodium nitrosodiumpentacyanoferrate(II)

9.3 Writing Formula of a Complex When Name is Given

This is done as explained in the worked out problems.

Worked Out Problem 9.1

Formulate the compound tetrammineaquachloridocobalt(III) chloride.

Solution

Anion (simple ion) = Cl^-

For the coordination entity, writing first the symbol for metal atom and then the ligands in the alphabetical order, we have

Cation (complex ion) = $[Co(NH_3)_4(H_2O)Cl]^x$ where x is the charge on the complex ion.

x = oxidation state of cobalt + charge on the ligands

$$x = +3 + 0 + 0 + (-1) = +2$$

(H_2O and NH_3 are neutral and carry no charge; only the chloride group carries a charge = −1)
Charge on one anion = −1
Charge on complex cation = +2
Clearly, two anions will neutralise the charge of the cation.
Hence, the formula of the given compound is $[Co(NH_3)_4(H_2O)Cl]Cl_2$.

Worked Out Problem 9.2

Write the formulae of the following coordination compounds.

(i) Sodium pentacyanonitrosylsulfidoferrate(III)
(ii) Potassium tetrahydroxozincate (II)

Solution

(i) Cation (simple ion) = Na^+
For the coordination entity, writing first the symbol for the metal atom and then the ligands in the alphabetical order, we have,
Anion (complex ion) = $[Fe(CN)_5(NO)S]^x$
$x = +3 + (-5) + (0) + (-2) = -4$, that is, Charge on the anion = −4
Balancing the positive and negative charges, the formula of the compound will be $Na_4[Fe(CN)_5(NO)S]$

(ii) Cation = K^+
Anion (complex ion) = $[Zn(OH)_4]^x$
$x = +2 + (-4) = -2$, that is, Charge on the anion = −2
Balancing the positive and negative charges, the formula of the compound will be $K_2[Zn(OH)_4]$.

9.4 Isomerism in Coordination Compounds

Isomers can be broadly classified into two major categories—structural isomers and stereoisomers. These are further subdivided as shown below (Fig. 9.3).

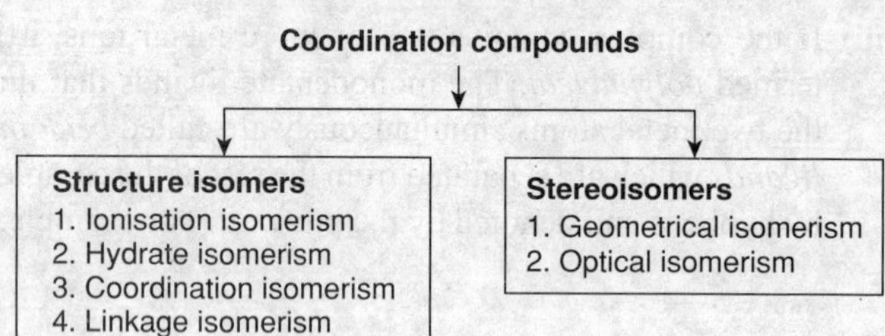

Fig. 9.3 Isomerism in coordination compounds

9.4.1 Structural Isomerism

This type of isomerism arises due to the difference in structures of coordination compounds. It may be further subdivided into different types as in Fig. 9.3.

Ionisation Isomerism

The compounds which have same the molecular formula but give different ions in solution are called *ionisation isomers*. The difference arises from the interchange of groups within or outside the coordination entity. For example, $[Co(NH_3)_5Br]^{2+}SO_4^{2-}$, that is, pentamminebromidocobalt(III) sulfate is red violet and in solution gives a precipitate with $BaCl_2$ confirming the presence of the SO_4^{2-} ion. On the other hand, $[Co(NH_3)_5(SO_4)]^+Br^-$, that is, pentaamminesulfatocobalt(III) bromide is red and does not give the test for the sulfate ion in solution, instead, it gives a precipitate of AgBr with $AgNO_3$.

Other examples of ionisation isomerism are:

- $[Pt(NH_3)_4Cl_2]Br_2$ and $[Pt(NH_3)_4Br_2]Cl_2$
- $[Pt(NH_3)_4(OH)_2]SO_4$ and $[Pt(NH_3)_4(SO_4)](OH)_2$
- $[Co(NH_3)_5NO_3]SO_4$ and $[Co(NH_3)_5(SO_4)]NO_3$

Solvate or Hydrate Isomerism

These compounds have the same molecular formula but differ in the number of solvent molecules present as ligands (in the coordination sphere) and as free solvent molecules (present outside the coordination sphere) in the crystal lattice. It is also known as *hydrate isomerism* in case water is involved as a solvent. For example,

$[Cr(H_2O)_6]Cl_3$ Violet (three ionic chlorines) $[Cr(H_2O)_5Cl]Cl_2.H_2O$ Blue green (two ionic chlorines)

$[Cr(H_2O)_4Cl_2]Cl.2H_2O$ Dark green (one ionic chlorine)

Linkage Isomerism

The compounds which have the same molecular formula but differ in the mode of attachment of a ligand to the metal atom or ion are called *linkage isomers*. This type of isomerism arises in compounds containing ambidentate ligands (when more than one atom in a unidentate ligand may act as a donor). For example, in the case of the ligand NO_2^-, either nitrogen or oxygen atom may act as a donor giving two different isomers. $[Cr(H_2O)_5(SCN)]^{2+}$ and $[Cr(H_2O)_5(NCS)]^{2+}$, $[Co(NH_3)_2(NO_2)_2(py)_2]NO_3$ and $[Co(NH_3)_2(ONO)_2(py)_2]NO_3$.

Coordination Isomerism

This type of isomerism occurs in compounds containing both cationic and anionic entities and the isomers differ in the distribution of ligands in the coordination entity of cationic and anionic parts.

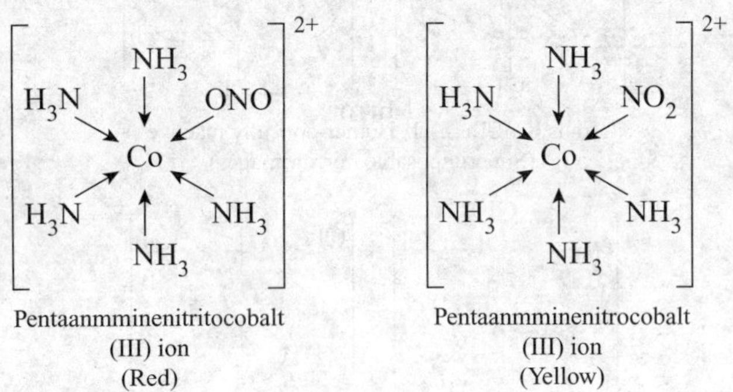

Pentaamminenitritocobalt (III) ion (Red) | Pentaamminenitrocobalt (III) ion (Yellow)

- $[Co(NH_3)_6]$ $[Cr(CN)_6]$ and $[Cr(NH_3)_6]$ $[Co(CN)_6]$
- $[Cr(NH_3)_6]$ $[Co(C_2O_4)_3]$ and $[Co(NH_3)_6]$ $[Cr(C_2O_4)_3]$
- $[Co(en)_3]$ $[Cr(CN_6)$ and $[Cr(en)_3]$ $[Co(CN)_6]$

9.4.2 Stereo Isomerism or Spatial Isomerism

In coordination compounds, the ligands are arranged in space in specific orientation around a given metal atom or ion. Some common examples are represented in Fig. 9.4. *Spatial isomerism* is of two types—geometrical isomerism and optical isomerism.

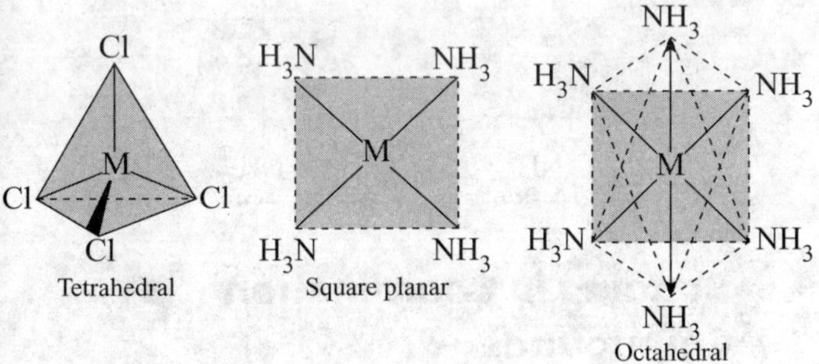

Fig. 9.4 Arrangements of ligands around the central metal

Geometrical or Cis-Trans Isomerism

Geometrical isomerism arises in heteroleptic complexes due to ligands occupying different positions around the central ion. These are referred to as the *cis*-form (ligands occupy adjacent positions) and the *trans*-form (ligands occupy opposite positions).

Square planar complexes (*Coordination number = 4*): Representing the central metal atom by M and the unidentate ligands by A, B, C, D, and so on, the square planar complexes may be classified into the following different types.

(i) MA_2B_2 type: For example, $[Pt(NH_3)_2Cl_2]$, that is, diamminedichloridoplatinum(II).

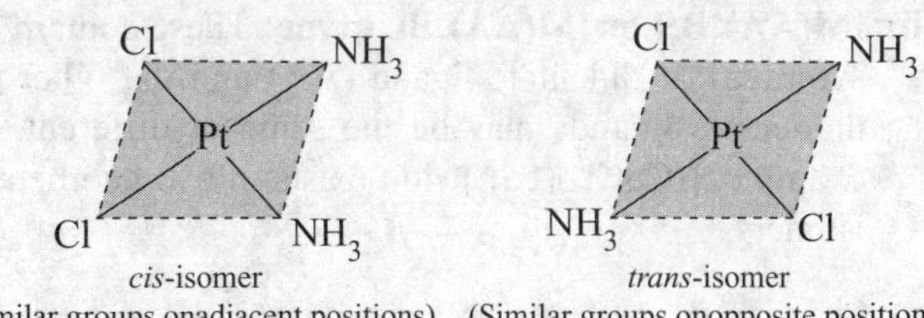

cis-isomer (Similar groups onadjacent positions) | *trans*-isomer (Similar groups onopposite positions)

A few other examples of this type include $[Pt(NH_3)_2(NO_2)_2]$, $[PtCl_2(py)_2]$. Usually X-ray diffraction methods are used to distinguish between the *cis* and *trans* isomers.

(ii) MA_2BC type: For example, $[Pt(NH_3)Cl(py)_2]$.

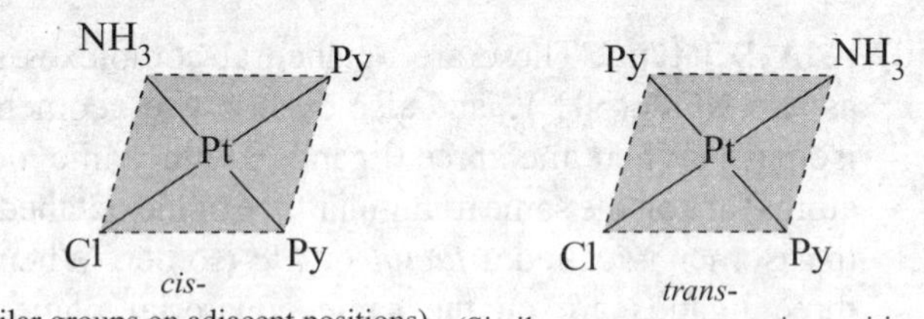

cis- (Similar groups on adjacent positions) | *trans*- (Similar groups on opposite positions)

(iii) $M(AB)_2$ type: Here, AB represents an unsymmetrical didentate ligand. For example, $[Pt(gly)_2]$ where gly = $NH_2CH_2COO^-$, called glycinato.

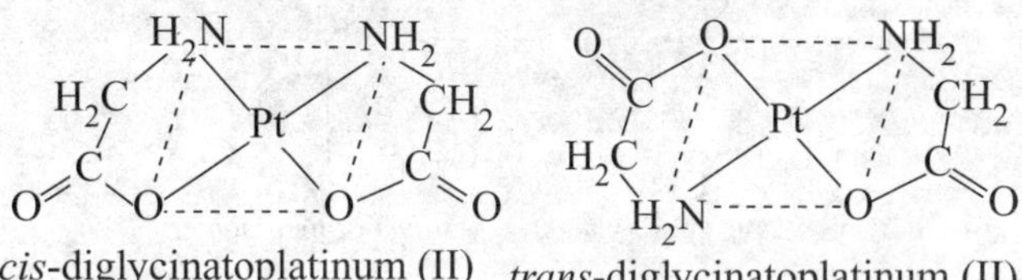

cis-diglycinatoplatinum (II) | *trans*-diglycinatoplatinum (II)

(iv) MABCD type: Square planar complexes of the type MABCD show three isomers. The structures of these isomers can be written by fixing the position of one ligand (say A) and placing the other ligands B, C and D trans to it. It may be noted that the fourth structure in which A is trans to D is identical to the third.

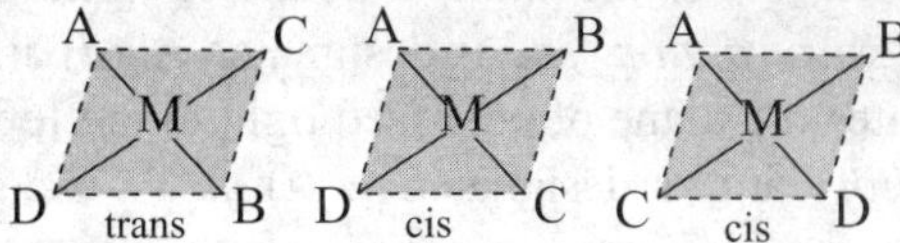

Two of these are *cis* and one is *trans*.

Octahedral complexes (*Coordination number = 6*): These may be classified into the following different types.

(i) MA_4B_2 or MA_2B_4 type: An example of this type is $[Cr(NH_3)_4Cl_2]^+$ ion or $[Co(NH_3)_4Cl_2]^+$ ion. The *cis* and *trans* isomers of the first complex are represented below.

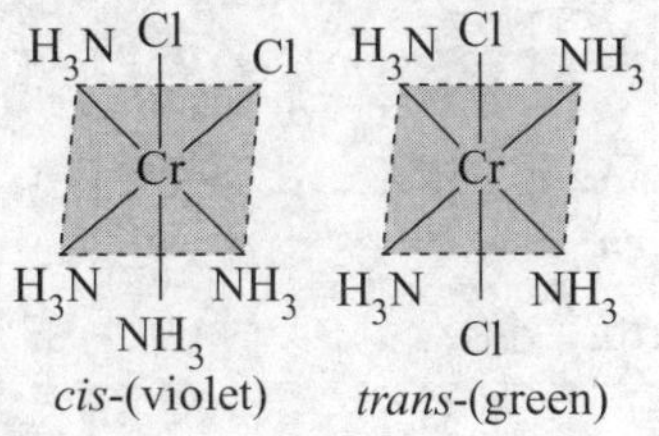

cis-(violet) | *trans*-(green)

(ii) $[M(AA)_2B_2]$ or $[M(AA)_2BC]$ type: These contain one symmetrical didentate ligand (AA) and the other two unidentate ligands may be the same or different. For example, $[(CoCl_2)(en)_2]^+$ ion exists in two geometrical isomers.

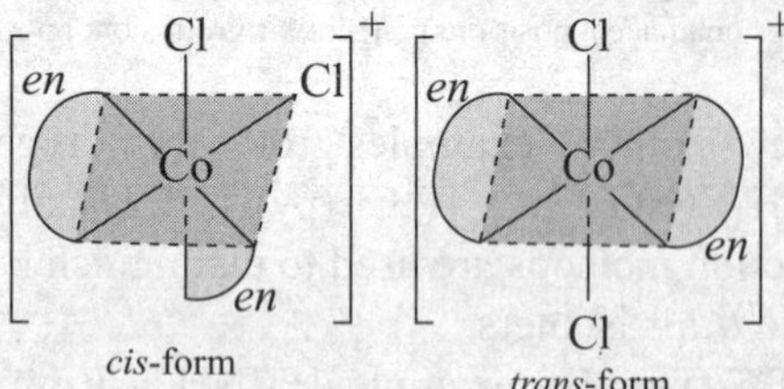

cis-form *trans*-form

(iii) $[MA_3B_3]$ type: These are octahedral complexes such as $[Co(NO_2)_3(NH_3)_3]$ and also exist in two geometrical isomers. When the three ligands (with same donor atoms) are on the same triangular face of the octahedron, the isomer is called a *facial* or *fac* isomer. When the three ligands are on the same equatorial plane, the isomer is called the *meridional* or *mer* isomer.

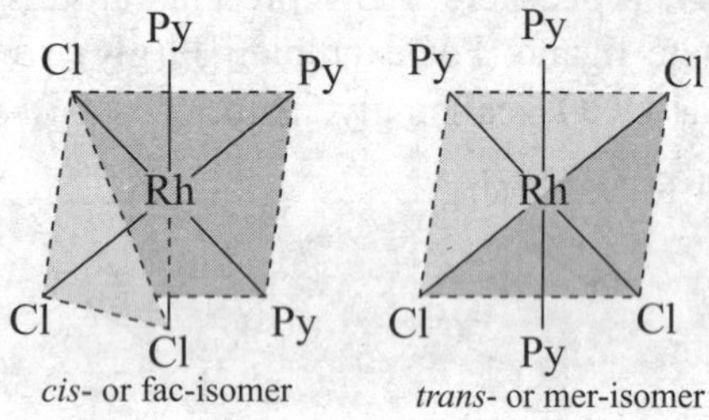

cis- or fac-isomer *trans*- or mer-isomer

Some other examples of this type are $[Co(NH_3)_3Cl_3]$ and $[Co(NH_3)_4(NO_2)_3]$.

Optical Isomerism

Isomers which rotate the plane of polarised light equally but in opposite directions are called *optically active isomers*. These are also called *enantiomers* or *enantiomorphs*. The isomer which rotates the plane of polarised light to the right is called *dextro rotatory* and is designated as (*d*) and the one which rotates the plane of polarised light to the left is called *laevo rotatory* and is designated as (*l*). A 1 : 1 equilibrium mixture of *d* and *l* isomers gives a net zero rotation and is called a *racemic mixture*. These are classified into the following different types.

(i) $[M(AA_3]$ type: These contain three symmetrical didentate ligands; for example, $[Co(en)_3]^{3+}$ and $[Cr(ox)_3]^{3-}$. Their dextro and laevo forms are represented below.

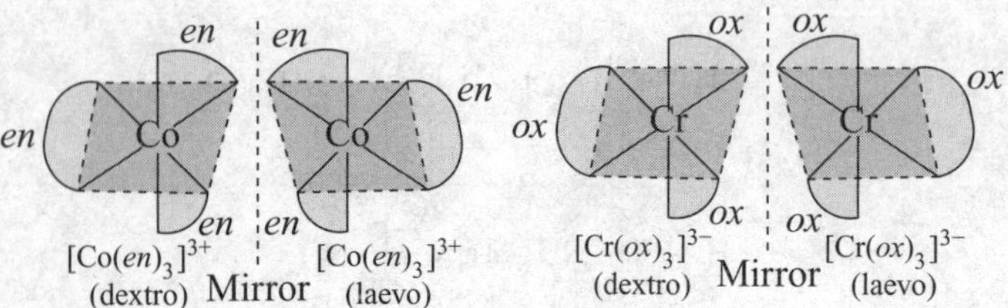

$[Co(en)_3]^{3+}$ (dextro) $[Co(en)_3]^{3+}$ (laevo) $[Cr(ox)_3]^{3-}$ (dextro) $[Cr(ox)_3]^{3-}$ (laevo)

(ii) $[M(AA)_2B_2]$ or $[M(AA)_2BC]$ type: These contain two symmetrical didentate ligands; for example $[CoCl_2(en)_2]^+$. The *trans* form does not show optical isomerism because the molecule has a plane of symmetry. On the other hand, the *cis*-isomer is unsymmetrical and can be resolved into optical isomers, as shown below.

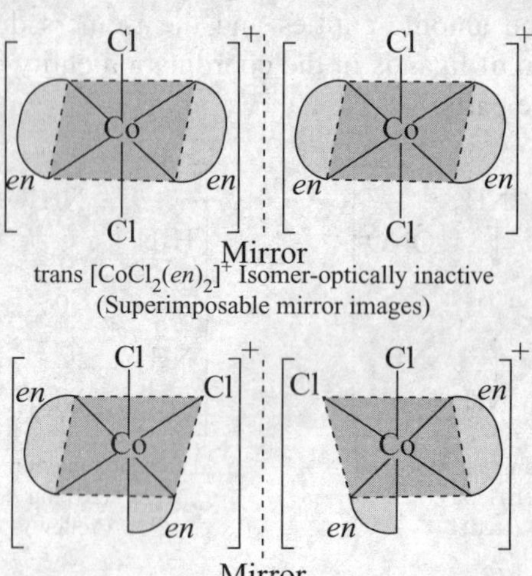

trans $[CoCl_2(en)_2]^+$ Isomer-optically inactive (Superimposable mirror images)

cis $[CoCl_2(en)_2]^+$ Isomer-optically active (Non-superimposable mirror images)

Thus, the total number of isomers shown by a complex of the above type is *three* (one *trans* form and two optical isomers of the *cis* form).

(iii) $[M(AA)B_2C_2]$ type: These contain one symmetrical didentate ligand; for example, $[Co(en)(NH_3)_2Cl_2]$. Its two optical isomers may be represented as follows.

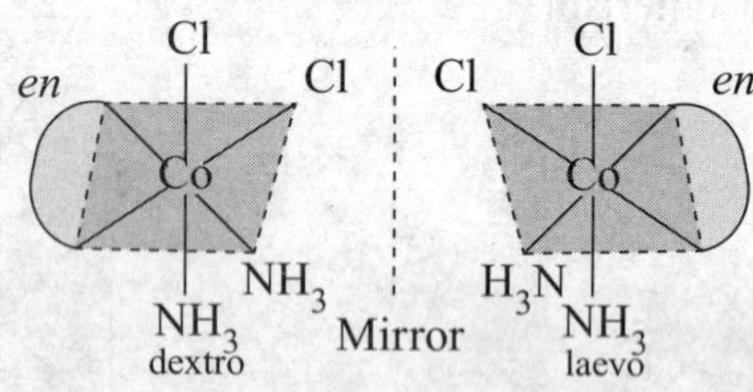

dextro laevo

9.5 Bonding in Coordination Compounds

In order to explain the nature of bonding and the structure of coordination compounds, different theories were proposed—namely valence bond theory (VBT), crystal field theory (CFT), ligand field theory (LFT) and molecular orbital theory (MOT).

9.5.1 Werner's Theory of Coordination Compounds

The main *postulates* of this theory are:

(i) Metals possess two types of valencies called *primary* or *principal* or *ionisable valency* and *secondary* or *non-ionisable valency.*

- *Primary valencies* are those which a metal exhibits in the formation of its simple salts. Thus, in the formation of $PtCl_4$, $CoCl_3$, $CuSO_4$ and AgCl, the primary valencies of Pt, Co, Cu and Ag are 4, 3, 2 and 1 respectively. Primary valency is also referred to as oxidation state.

- *Secondary valencies* are those which a metal atom or cation exercises towards neutral molecules or negative groups (ligands) in the formation of its complex ions. Every metal cation has a fixed number of secondary valencies, the secondary valency is also termed as the *coordination number* (CN) of the metal cation. In $[Pt(NH_3)_6]Cl_4$, $[Co(NH_3)_6]Cl_3$, $[Cu(NH_3)_4]SO_4$ and $[Ag\ (NH_3)_2]Cl$, the secondary valencies are 6 for Pt^{4+}, 6 for Co^{3+}, 4 for Cu^{2+} and 2 for Ag^+ cations respectively.

(ii) The metal atom tends to satisfy both its primary as well as secondary valencies. Primary valencies are satisfied by negative ions whereas secondary valencies are satisfied either by negative ions or by neutral molecules.

(iii) The secondary valencies are always directed towards fixed positions in space and this leads to definite geometry of the coordination compound. Such spatial arrangements are called coordination polyhedra. For example, if a metal ion has six secondary valencies, these are arranged octahedrally around the central metal ion. If the metal ion has four secondary valencies, these are arranged in either tetrahedral or square planar arrangement around the central metal ion. On the other hand, the primary valency is non-directional.

Thus, a metal atom exhibits primary valencies in the formation of its salt ($CoCl_2$, $AgNO_3$) while the metal atom exhibits its secondary valencies in the formation of its complex ions {$[Co(NH_3)_6]^{3+}$, $[Ag(NH_3)_2]^+$}.

Determination of the Structure of a Complex on the Basis of Werner's Theory

Taking the example of complexes formed between $CoCl_3$ and NH_3, the ionisable chloride ions are found by precipitation with $AgNO_3$. These are linked by primary valencies. The remaining Cl atoms and NH_3 molecules are present around the central metal atom in such directions that the repulsions between them are minimum thereby giving a definite shape. These atoms and groups are linked by secondary valencies. Representing the primary valencies by dotted lines and secondary valencies by solid lines, the structures of the different complexes formed between $CoCl_3$ and NH_3 are given below.

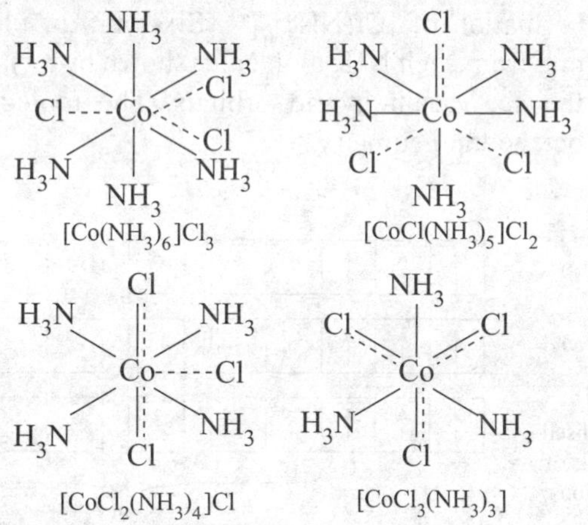

$[Co(NH_3)_6]Cl_3$ $[CoCl(NH_3)_5]Cl_2$

$[CoCl_2(NH_3)_4]Cl$ $[CoCl_3(NH_3)_3]$

Some important observations

On the basis of his studies, Werner put forward the following important observations. The complex compounds do not retain any of the properties of the central metal ion or of the ligands. The chloride ions which enter into coordination lose their ionic character. These chloride ions can no longer be precipitated on the addition of silver nitrate solution (Table 9.4).

Table 9.4 Complexes formed from platinum(IV) chloride and ammonia in aqueous solution

Composition of the complex	Formula of the complex compound	Ion formed	Total number of ions
$PtCl_4.6NH_3$	$[Pt(NH_3)_6]Cl_4$	$[Pt(NH_3)_6]^{4+} + 4Cl^-$	5
$PtCl_4.5NH_3$	$[PtCl(NH_3)_5]Cl_3$	$[PtCl(NH_3)_5]^{3+} + 3Cl^-$	4
$PtCl_4.4NH_3$	$[PtCl_2(NH_3)_4]Cl_2$	$[PtCl_2(NH_3)_4]^{2+} + 2Cl^-$	3
$PtCl_4.3NH_3$	$[PtCl_3(NH_3)_3]Cl$	$[PtCl_3(NH_3)_3] + Cl^-$	2
PtCl4.2NH3	$[PtCl_4(NH_3)_2]$	No ions are formed; the complex is neutral	0

In the first compound, all six ligands are NH_3 molecules. In the subsequent compounds, one or more of the NH_3 molecules are replaced by Cl^- ions. It will be observed that the coordination number of Pt^{4+} remains the same, that is, 6 in all cases although the net positive charge falls to 3, 2, 1 or zero, depending upon the number of Cl^- ions coordinated to the Pt^{4+} ion.

9.5.2 Valence Bond (VB) Theory

The following are the main postulates of this theory.

- The central metal in the complex makes available a number of empty orbitals for the formation of coordination bonds with suitable ligands. If the coordination number is 6, six empty orbitals are made available and if the coordination number is 4, four empty orbitals are made available in the central metal ion.

- The d orbitals involved in the hybridisation may be either inner d orbitals outer d orbitals, that is, nd.

With the approach of the ligands, metal–ligand bonds are then formed by the overlap of these orbitals with those of the ligands, by donation of electron pairs by the ligands to the empty hybridised orbitals. If after the formation of the complex, no unpaired electron is present, the complex is diamagnetic. If however, some unpaired electrons are present, the complex is paramagnetic. A few examples are given below.

(i) Octahedral Complexes (*Coordination number = 6*)

- Formation of $[Cr(NH_3)_6]^{3+}$: Six pairs of electrons, one from each NH_3 molecule (shown by xx), occupy the six vacant hybrid orbitals. The molecule has octahedral geometry.

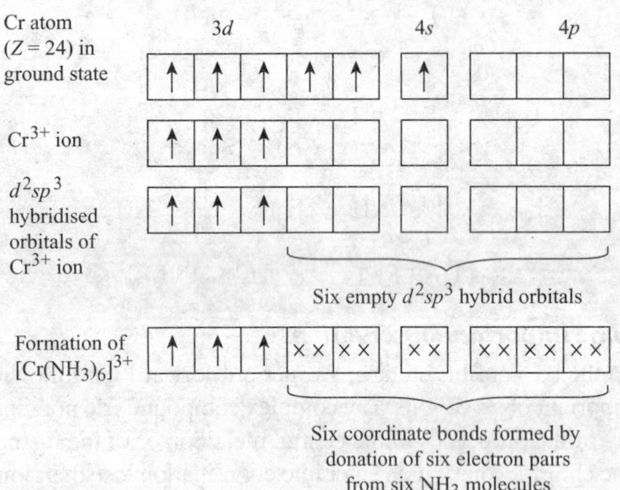

The presence of these unpaired electrons in the complex explains its paramagnetic character.

- Formation of ferricyanide ion, $[Fe(CN)_6]^{3-}$: The oxidation state of Fe in this complex ion is +3. Hence, we have,

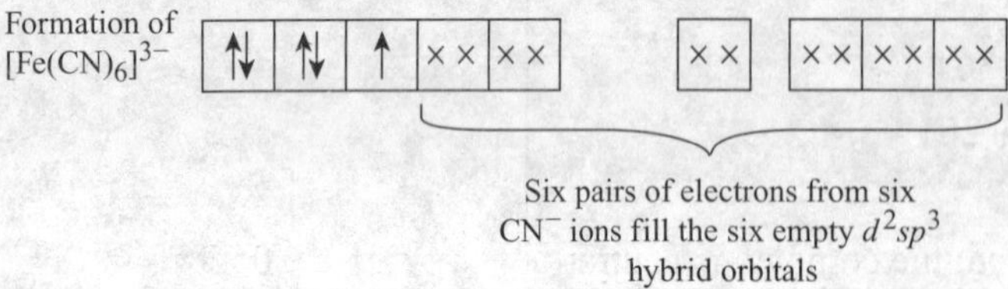

The resulting complex involves d^2sp^3 hybridisation and is thus an octahedral complex. Further, due to one unpaired electron, it should be slightly paramagnetic, which is actually so.

- Formation of ferrrocyanide ion, $[Fe(CN)_6]^{4-}$:

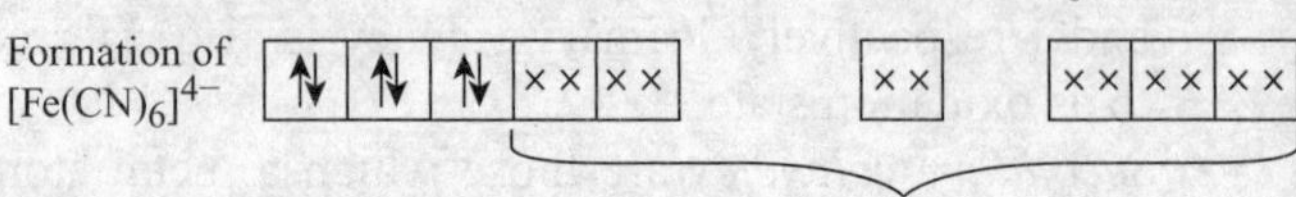

The resulting complex ion (involving d^2sp^3 hybridisation) is octahedral and diamagnetic as it does not contain any unpaired electron.

- Formation of $[CoF_6]^{3-}$ ion: In this case, cobalt is in the +3 oxidation state and has the electronic configuration $3d^6$. This complex has been found to be paramagnetic due to the presence of four unpaired electrons.

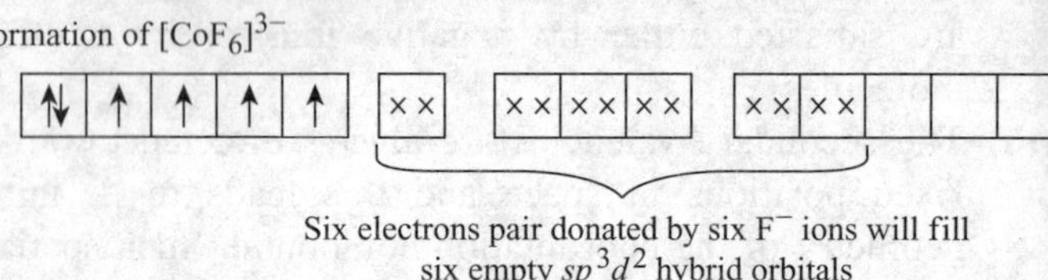

Here, the F^- ion provides a weak ligand field and is unable to pair up the unpaired electrons of the $3d$ orbitals. Hence, six equivalent hybrid orbitals are obtained by mixing up of one $4s$, three $4p$ and two $4d$ orbitals. The highly paramagnetic nature of the complex further confirms the presence of four unpaired electrons. As the d orbitals of the outermost shell take part in hybridisation, the complexes thus formed are called *outer orbital complexes*.

Inner orbital complexes: If the complex is formed by the use of the inner d orbitals for hybridisation (written as d^2sp^3), it is called an *inner orbital complex*. In the formation of an inner orbital complex, the electrons of the metal are forced to pair up and hence the complex will be either diamagnetic or will have a lesser number of unpaired electrons. Such a complex is also called a *low spin complex*. For example, $[V(H_2O)_6]^{3+}$, $[Co(NH_3)_6]^{3+}$, $[Mn(CN)_6]^{3-}$, $[Co(CN)_6]^{4-}$, $[Co(CN)_6]^{3-}$, $[Co(C_2O_4)_3]^{3-}$, $[Cr(H_2O)_6]^{3+}$, $[Cr(ox)_3]^{3-}$.

Outer orbital complex: When the complex formed involves the use of the outer nd orbitals for hybridisation (sp^3d^2), the complex is called an *outer orbital complex* or *hypoligated complex*. This type of complex is also called a *high spin complex*. One example, that is of $[CoF_6]^{3-}$, has been discussed above. Some other examples of outer orbital complexes are: $[MnCl_6]^{3-}$, $[FeF_6]^{3-}$, $[Ni(H_2O)_6]^{2+}$, $[Ni(NH_3)_6]^{2+}$, $[Fe(H_2O)_6]^{2+}$, $[Fe(H_2O)_6]^{3+}$.

Predicting the type of hybridisation from magnetic behaviour: For metal ions having up to 3 unpaired electrons in the d orbitals, like Ti^{3+} (d^1), V^{3+} (d^2) and Cr^{3+} (d^3), two vacant d orbitals are available for octahedral hybridisation with 4s and 4p orbitals. Their magnetic moments are found to be corresponding to 1, 2 and 3 unpaired electrons respectively. For metal ions containing more than 3 unpaired electrons in the d orbitals, two empty d orbitals can be made available only if the 3d electrons pair up; for example, d^4 (Cr^{2+}, Mn^{3+}), d^5 (Mn^{2+}, Fe^{3+}) and d^6 (Fe^{2+}, Co^{3+}). The magnetic moment data show that maximum spin pairing occurs in many cases, especially in compounds with d^6 ions, but there are complications with species having d^4 and d^5 ions. A few examples are given. $[Mn(CN)_6]^{3-}$ has magnetic moment of two unpaired electrons while $[MnCl_6]^{3-}$ has for four unpaired electrons.

- $[Fe(CN)_6]^{3-}$ has magnetic moment of one unpaired electron while $[FeF_6]^{3-}$ has magnetic moment of five unpaired electrons.
- $[CoF_6]^{3-}$ has magnetic moment of four unpaired electrons while $[Co(C_2O_4)_3]^{3-}$ is diamagnetic.

  The above results help us to explain whether the hybridisation involved will be d^2sp^3 or sp^3d^2. Thus, $[Mn(CN)_6]^{3-}$, $Fe(CN)_6]^{3-}$ and $[Co(C_2O_4)_3]^{3-}$ are inner orbital complexes involving d^2sp^3 hybridisation, and $[MnCl_6]^{3-}$, $[FeF_6]^{3-}$ and $[CoF_6]^{3-}$ are outer orbital complexes involving sp^3d^2 hybridisation.

(ii) Tetrahedral Complexes (*Coordination number* = 4)

- **Formation of $[Ni(CO)_4]^0$:** Nickel(0) has $3d^8 4s^2$ as its outer electronic configuration. For complexes with coordination number 4, the central atom may involve sp^3 or dsp^2 type of hybridisation. The electrons of the 4s orbitals are forced into 3d orbitals to pair up with the two unpaired d electrons. Therefore, the complex is diamagnetic. This results in sp^3 hybridisation and the complex has a tetrahedral structure.

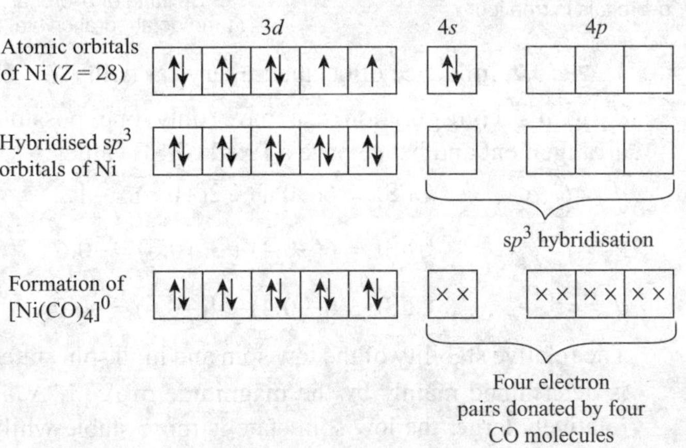

- **Formation of $[Zn(NH_3)_4]^{2+}$:** Complexes of Zn^{2+} are invariably tetrahedral because they involve sp^3 hybridisation.

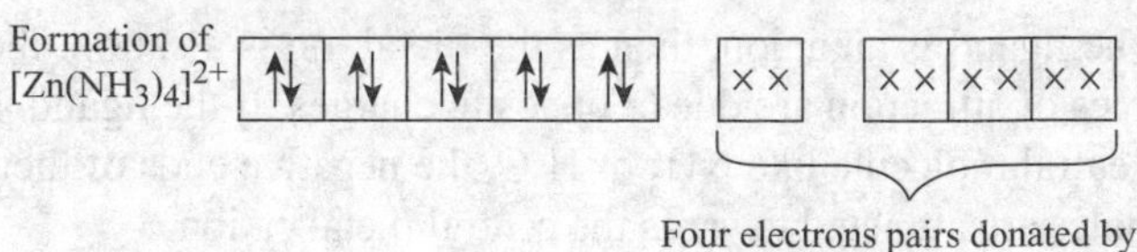

In the above case, the 3d orbitals are fully occupied; therefore, they cannot participate in hybridisation. Four sp^3 orbitals can be formed by the mixing of one 4s and three 4p orbitals. These four sp^3 hybrid orbitals accommodate four pairs of electrons from four :NH_3 molecules. The resulting $[Zn(NH_3)_4]^{2+}$ will be tetrahedral and will be diamagnetic as there are no unpaired electrons. Some other examples of tetrahedral complexes are $[NiCl_4]^{2-}$, $[FeCl_4]^{2-}$.

(iii) Square Planar Complexes (*Coordination number* = 4)

- Formation of $[Ni(CN)_4]^{2-}$: The nickel atom has the ground state electronic configuration as $3d^8 4s^2$. In this case nickel is in the +2 oxidation state and its electronic configuration is $3d^8$. The hybridisation involved in this case dsp^2, the structure of the complex would be square planar.

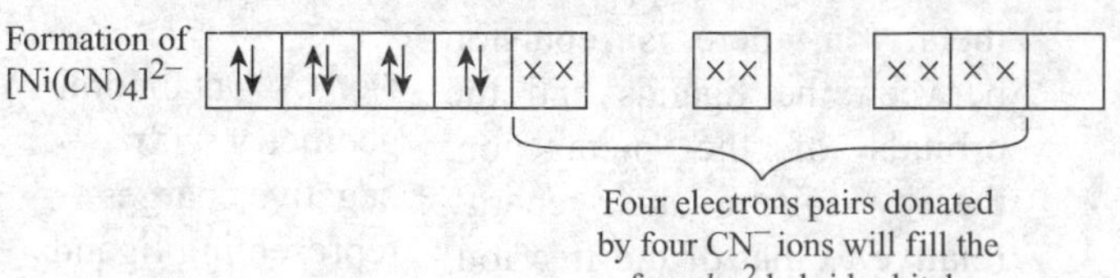

(iv) Complexes with Trigonal Bipyramidal Geometry (*Coordination number* = 5)

In $Fe(CO)_5$, iron is in the zero oxidation state.

In the presence of the ligand CO, being the strongest ligand, the 3d electrons pair up and the 4s electrons are also pushed into the 3d orbital. Thus, one 3d orbital remains empty which along with one 4s and three 4p orbitals undergoes dsp^3 hybridisation. Each hybridised orbital accepts a lone pair of electrons from the CO ligands.

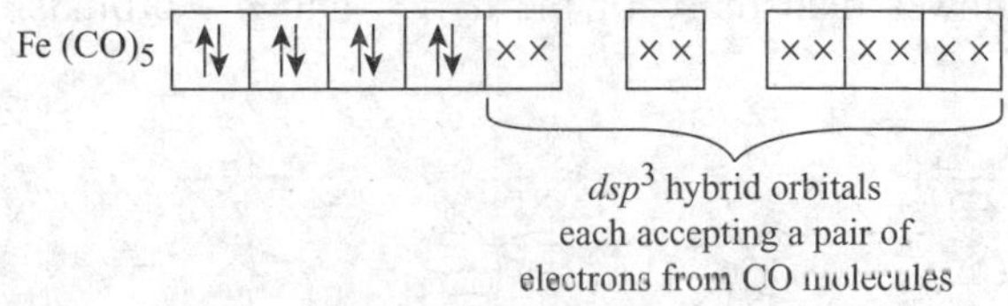

Hence, it has a *trigonal bipyramidal* geometry and is *diamagnetic*.

9.5.3 Crystal Field Theory

The main points of this theory are: Crystal Field Theory considers the metal–ligand bond to be ionic arising purely from *electrostatic interactions* between the metal ion and the ligands.

If the ligand is an anion, then as the metal ion is a cation, the forces of attraction are due to opposite charges. If the ligand is a neutral molecule like NH_3 or H_2O, the negative ends of their dipoles are attracted towards the central metal cation.

The orbitals lying in the direction of the ligands will experience a greater repulsion and their energies will be raised relative to their positions in a symmetrical field. The degeneracy of orbitals is maintained if the negative charges present around the central metal atom/ion form a spherically symmetrical field. However, if the negative field is due to ligands which may be anions or polar molecules such as H_2O or NH_3 with their negative ends towards the central metal atom/ion (the metal atom/ion involved in the complex formation), the field no longer remains symmetrical.

(i) Crystal Field Theory for Octahedral Complexes: The geometry of the octahedral complex may be represented as in Fig. 9.5. Here, the negative charges lie along the X, Y and Z-axes and the metal ion is at the origin.

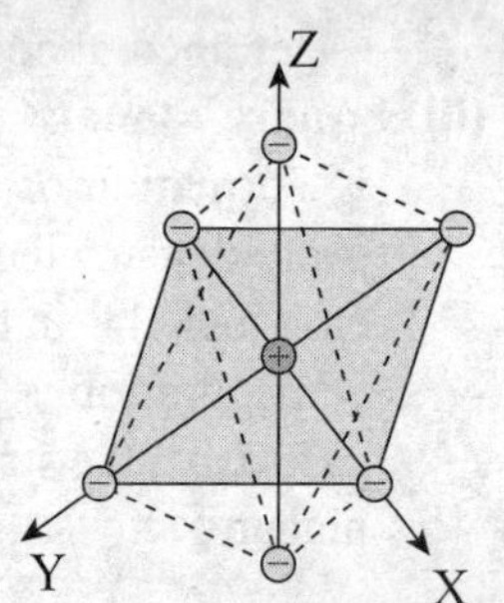

Fig. 9.5 Octahedral geometry with negative charges representing ligands and positive charge representing central metal ion

As the ligands approach the metal ion, there is repulsion between the ligands and the orbitals of the metal ion, thereby raising their energy relative to that of the free ion. The mean value of energy of these perturbed *d* orbitals is taken as zero (*barycentre*). However, as the $d_{x^2-y^2}$ and d_{z^2} orbitals have lobes along the axes, they point towards the ligands whereas the lobes of d_{xy}, d_{xz} and d_{yz} orbitals lie between the axes, hence they lie between the ligands (Fig. 9.6). As a result, the repulsions between the ligands and the $d_{x^2-y^2}$ and d_{z^2} orbitals are greater than the repulsions between the ligands and the remaining three *d* orbitals. Consequently, the energies of d_{xy}, d_{yz} and d_{xz} orbitals are lower than those of the $d_{x^2-y^2}$ and d_{z^2} orbitals. The

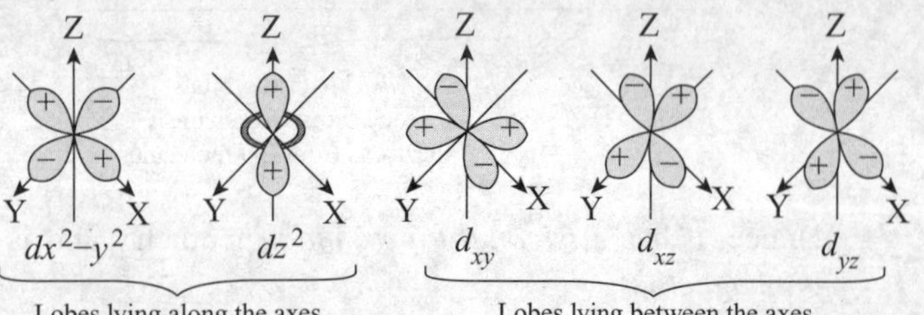

Fig. 9.6 Shapes and orientations of the five *d*-orbitals

former three orbitals of lower energy are called the t_{2g} orbitals and the latter two of higher energy are called the e_g orbitals.

The difference of energy between the two sets of *d* orbitals is called *crystal field splitting energy* or *crystal field stabilisation energy (CFSE)*. It is usually represented by the symbol Δ_o (the subscript 'o' stands for octahedral). It is found that the e_g orbitals are $+0.6\ \Delta_o$ or (3.5) Δ_o above the average energy level and the t_{2g} orbitals are $-0.4\ \Delta_o$ or $-(2/5)\ \Delta_o$ below the average (Fig. 9.7). Some ligands produce strong fields and hence the splitting is large whereas some others produce weak fields and hence they result in small splitting of the *d* orbitals. The experimentally observed values of some of the ligands in increasing order are given below.

$I^- < Br^- < S^{2-} < SCN^- < Cl^- < F^- < OH^- < C_2O_4^{2-} < O^{2-}$
$H_2O < NCS^- < NH_3 < en < NO_2^- < CN^- < CO$

Weak field ligands → Increasing order of Δ_o → Strong field ligands

The ligands with small values of Δ_o are called *weak field ligands* whereas those with large values of Δ_o are called *strong field ligands.*

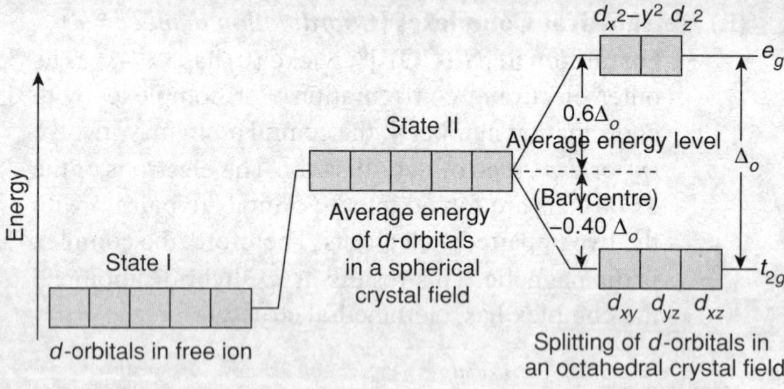

Fig. 9.7 Influence of octahedral crystal field

d^8 to d^{10} configuration can have only one possible arrangement and hence have a fixed CFSE value.

$d^8 = t_{2g}^6 e_g^2$, CFSE = 6(−0.4) + 2(+0.6) = −1.2

$d^9 = t_{2g}^6 e_g^3$, CFSE = 6(−0.4) + 3(+0.6) = −0.6

$d^{10} = t_{2g}^6 e_g^4$, CFSE = 6(−0.4) + 4(+0.6) = −0.0

The relative stability of the low spin and high spin states is determined mainly by the magnitude of Δ_o. If Δ_o is relatively large, the low spin state is more stable while if Δ_o is small, the high spin state is more stable.

Table 9.5 Calculation of CFSE (Δ_0) value for d^4 to d^7 configurations

Metal ion configuration	Low spin state (Strong ligand field)	CFSE (Δ_0)	High spin state (Weak ligand field)	CFSE (Δ_0)
d^4	e_g [	] t_{2g} [↑↓	↑	↑]	$4 \times (-0{\cdot}4) = -1{\cdot}6$	e_g [↑	] t_{2g} [↑	↑	↑]	$3 \times (-0{\cdot}4) + 0{\cdot}6 = -0{\cdot}6$
d^5	e_g [	] t_{2g} [↑↓	↑↓	↑]	$5 \times (-0{\cdot}4) = -2{\cdot}0$	e_g [↑	↑] t_{2g} [↑	↑	↑]	$3 \times (-0{\cdot}4) + 2\ (+0{\cdot}6) = 0{\cdot}0$
d^6	e_g [	] t_{2g} [↑↓	↑↓	↑↓]	$6 \times (-0{\cdot}4) = -2{\cdot}4$	e_g [↑	↑] t_{2g} [↑↓	↑	↑]	$4 \times (-0{\cdot}4) + 2\ (+0{\cdot}6) = -0{\cdot}4$
d^7	e_g [↑	] t_{2g} [↑↓	↑↓	↑↓]	$6 \times (-0{\cdot}4) + 0{\cdot}6 = -1{\cdot}8$	e_g [↑	↑] t_{2g} [↑↓	↑↓	↑]	$5 \times (-0{\cdot}4) + 2\ (0{\cdot}6) = -0{\cdot}8$

Thus, d^4 to d^7 have lower CFSE values for low spin. The value of Δ_o is usually compared with the energy required for electron pairing in a single orbital. This energy is usually represented by P and is called *pairing energy*. Thus,

- Ligands for which $\Delta_o < P$ are called *weak field ligands*.
- Ligands for which $\Delta_o > P$ are known as *strong field ligands*.

(ii) Magnetic behaviour of complexes: Let us consider the complexes of Fe(III) such as $[Fe(CN)_6]^{3-}$ and $[Fe(H_2O)_6]^{3+}$. Fe^{3+} has $3d^5$ electronic configuration with five electrons. Now, CN^- is a strong field ligand and we expect a large splitting of d orbitals. As a result, the five d electrons will try to remain in the lower set and will pair, that is, t_{2g}^5. This results in a low spin complex which will have only one unpaired electron. On the other hand, H_2O is a weak field ligand and we expect a small splitting of the d orbitals. As a result, after filling one electron each in the lower set of orbitals, the remaining two electrons will go to the higher set of orbitals, that is, $t_{2g}^3 e_g^2$. Thus, the complex will be paramagnetic due to the presence of five unpaired electrons. It is also called a high spin complex.

(iii) Colour: The transition metals have the property to absorb certain radiations from the visible region of the spectrum and as a result, the transmitted or reflected light is coloured. The visible light (while light), as we know, is a mixture of radiations of many wavelengths ranging from blue (about 400 nm) to red (about 700 nm). If red light (long wavelength) is a absorbed from white light, then it appears to us to be green (short wavelength).

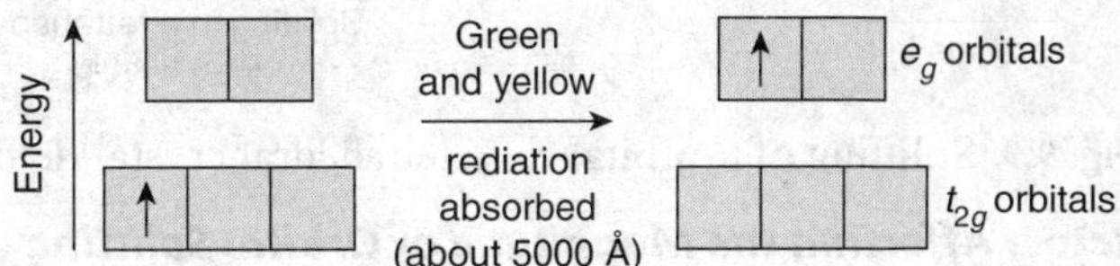

Fig. 9.8 Absorption of green and yellow radiation by $[Ti(H_2O)_6]^{3+}$ complex ion

This means that green and yellow portions of the light are absorbed (Fig. 9.8). The solution of the complex is, therefore, purple which is a complementary colour of the radiation absorbed.

When visible light falls on a complex, the electron gets raised from the lower set of orbitals to the higher set of orbitals. For example, in the case of octahedral complexes, the electron goes from the set of d_{xy}, d_{yz}, d_{zx} to the set of $d_{x^2-y^2}, d_{z^2}$ orbitlas. As a result of absorption of some selected wavelength of visible light corresponding to the energy difference between these sets of energy levels, the transmitted light gives colour to the complexes. For example, the complex $[Ti(H_2O)_6]^{3+}$ is purple.

The CFSE of the ligands is in the order $H_2O < NH_3 < CN^-$ (from the spectrochemical series). Hence, the excitation energies will be in the order $[Co(H_2O)_6]^{3+} < [Co(NH_3)_6]^{3+} < [Co(CN_6)]^{3-}$. The wavelengths absorbed will be in the opposite order $\left(\because E = \dfrac{hc}{\lambda}\right)$. The complementary colour will be transmitted or reflected. Thus, in the above case, we have,

	$[Co(H_2O)_6]^{3+}$	$[Co(NH_3)_6]^{3+}$	$[Co(CN)_6]^{3-}$
Colour absorbed	Orange	Blue	Violet
Colour transmitted	Blue	Yellow orange	Yellow

In the absence of ligands, crystal field splitting does not occur and hence the substance is colourless. For example, if $[Ti(H_2O)_6]Cl_3$ is heated so that water is lost, the product obtained is colourless.

Crystal Field Theory for Tetrahedral Complexes

The splitting pattern for tetrahedral complexes is just the reverse of the splitting pattern of the octahedral complexes, that is, the three-fold degenerate set, t_2, has higher energy than the two-fold degenerate set, e. Moreover, the splitting is much smaller than that in the case of the octahedral complexes. Hence, all tetrahedral complexes have high spin configuration. The splitting pattern of tetrahedral complexes may be represented as in Fig. 9.9.

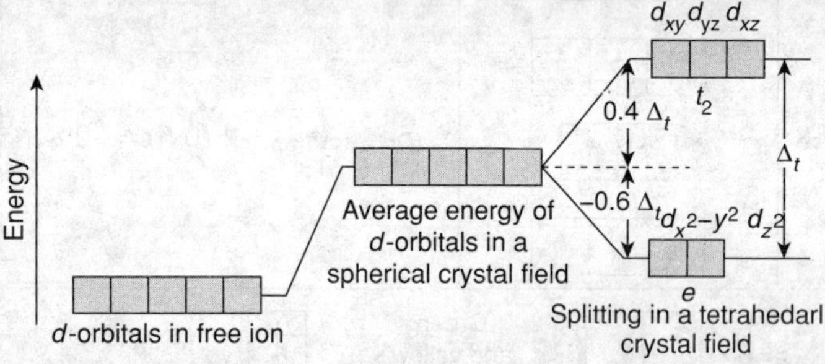

Fig. 9.9 Splitting of *d*-orbitals in a tetrahedral crystal field

Factors Affecting the Magnitude of Orbital Splitting Energy (Δ)

The important factors are as follows:

- Higher the oxidation state of the central ion, larger the value of Δ.
- As we move from 3*d* to 4*d* to 5*d* elements, the Δ_o increases and hence the tendency to form low spin complexes increases. Thus, the elements of the second and third transition series have a greater tendency to form low spin complexes than the first transition series.
- *Nature of the ligand*: For the same metal ion, different ligands result in different amounts of splitting, as already explained under the spectrochemical series.

9.6 Stability of Coordination Compounds in Solution

The stability of a complex in solution means, the *degree of association* between the metal ion and the ligands involved, in the state of equilibrium. The magnitude of the (stability or formation) equilibrium constant for the association expresses the stability quantitatively. For example, for the complex $[Cu(NH_3)_4]^{2+}$ in solution, we have

$$[Cu(NH_3)_4]^{2+} \rightleftharpoons Cu^{2+} + 4\,NH_3$$

$$\text{Instability constant, } K_i = \frac{[Cu^{2+}][NH_3]^4}{[Cu(NH_3)_4]^{2+}}$$

In the formation of a complex ion in the solution, the reaction will be the reverse of the above reaction, that is,

$$Cu^{2+} + 4NH_3 \rightleftharpoons [Cu\,(NH_3)_4]^{2+}$$

The equilibrium constant for this reaction is therefore called the *stability constant*. Representing it by β, we have

$$\text{Stability constant, } \beta = \frac{[Cu(NH_3)_4]^{2+}}{[Cu^{2+}][NH_3]^4}$$

Greater the magnitude of the stability constant, the more stable is the complex. If the reaction is believed to take place in steps with a suitable formation constant for each step, as given below.

$$[M\,(H_2O)_n] + n\,L \rightleftharpoons [ML\,(H_2O)_{n-1}] + H_2O,$$

$$K_1 = \frac{[ML(H_2O)_{n-1}]}{[M(H_2O)_n][L]}$$

$$[ML\,(H_2O)_{n-1}] + L \rightleftharpoons [ML_2\,(H_2O)_{n-2}] + H_2O,$$

$$K_2 = \frac{[ML_2(H_2O)_{n-2}]}{[M(H_2O)_n][L]}$$

and so on till finally, we have

$$[ML_{n-1}\,(H_2O)] + L \rightleftharpoons [ML_n] + H_2O$$

$$K_n = \frac{[ML_n]}{[ML_{n-1}(H_2O)][L]}$$

Adding all these steps, we get the overall reaction. The overall stability constant will be

$$\beta_n = K_1 \times K_2 \times K_3 \ldots\ldots\ldots \times K_n$$

Factors Affecting the Stability of a Complex Ion

The stability of a complex ion depends upon the following factors.

(i) Charge on the central metal ion: In general, the greater the charge and the smaller the size of an ion (the larger the charge/radius ratio of an ion), the greater is the stability of its complexes. The stability of the divalent metal ions of the first transition series is in the following order: Mn (II) < Fe (II) < Co (II) < Ni (II) < Cu (II) < Zn (II).

(ii) Greater the basic strength of the ligand, greater is the stability of the complex.

(iii) Presence of chelate rings: Formation of chelate rings increases the stability of the complex.

(iv) Effect of multidentate cyclic ligands: If the ligand happens to be multidentate and cyclic without any steric effects, the stability of the complex is further increased. The effect is called the *macrocyclic effect*. For example, Zn (II) complex with the ligand.

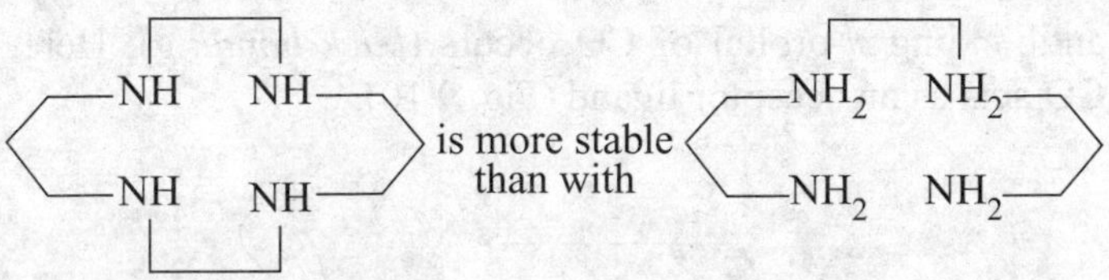

[Cyclam-type macrocycle with four NH groups] is more stable than with [open-chain tetraamine with NH_2 groups]

9.7 Organometallics/Organometallic Compounds

Organometallic compounds are those compounds that contain at least one metal–carbon bond. The carbon atom is bonded not only to the metal atom but also to metalloids like boron, silicon, arsenic and tellurium. Thus, an *organometallic compound* is one that contains at least one of the following bonds:

- metal–carbon,
- metalloid (B, Si, As, Te)–carbon.

For example, in diethyl zinc (C_2H_5–Zn–C_2H_5), two C_2H_5 groups are directly linked with zinc forming Zn–C bonds.

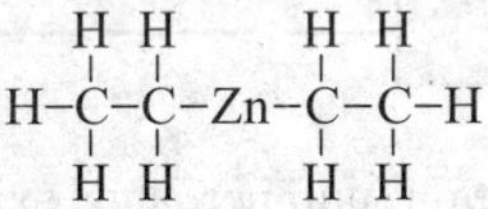

```
    H H     H H
    | |     | |
  H-C-C-Zn-C-C-H
    | |     | |
    H H     H H
```

Similarly, methyl magnesium bromide (CH_3MgBr) has one Mg–C bond and is an organometallic compound. $CH_3B(OCH_3)_2$ is another example as it has one B–C bond.

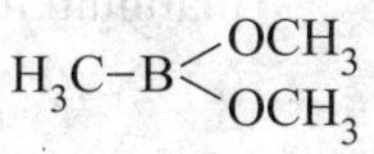

$H_3C-B(OCH_3)_2$

Note that although a compound may contain many hydrocarbon radicals, it is not classified as organometallic when its carbon atoms are linked to metal through atoms like oxygen, nitrogen or sulfur as in trimethyl orthoborate, $B(OCH_3)_3$.

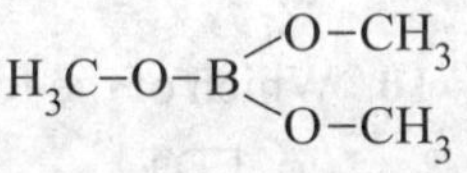

$H_3C-O-B(O-CH_3)_2$

Compounds like carbides, cyanides and carbonates which, of course, contain metal–carbon bonds are not considered as organometallic compounds. These are not included in this category as their properties are much different from those of other compounds belonging to the class of organometallic compounds. For example, $K_2[Zn(CN)_4]$ is a coordination compound but not an organometallic compound and does not show any similarity to $(C_2H_5)_2Zn$.

9.8 Metal Carbonyls

There is another important class of coordination compound known as metal carbonyls in which carbon monoxide (CO) acts as the ligand. These are also called homoleptic carbonyls (compounds containing carbonyl ligands only). These compounds contain both σ and π character. These are formed by many transition metals. These are mostly formed by transition metals (elements of the *d*-block). A few stable metal carbonyls are given below:

$[Ni(CO)_4]$, $[Fe(CO)_4]$, $[Cr(CO)_6]$, $[V(CO)_6]$, $[Mo(CO)_6]$, $[W(CO)_6]$, $[Co_2(CO)_8]$, $[Mn_2(CO)_{10}]$.

9.8.1 Structure of Metal Carbonyls

The structures of a few simple metal carbonyls along with the names of their geometries are given.

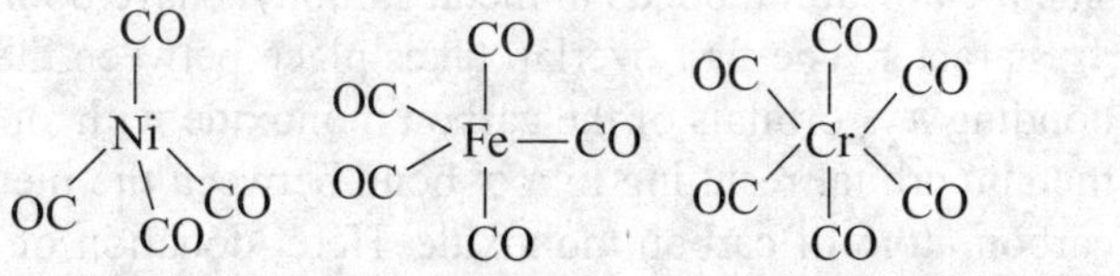

$Ni(CO)_4$ Tetrahedral $Fe(CO)_5$ Trigonal bipyramidal* $Cr(CO)_6$ Octahedral

The carbonyl, $Mn_2(CO)_{10}$ [Decacarbonyldimanganese(0)], may be considered to be formed from two square pyramidal $Mn(CO)_5$ units in which the two Mn atoms are linked together.

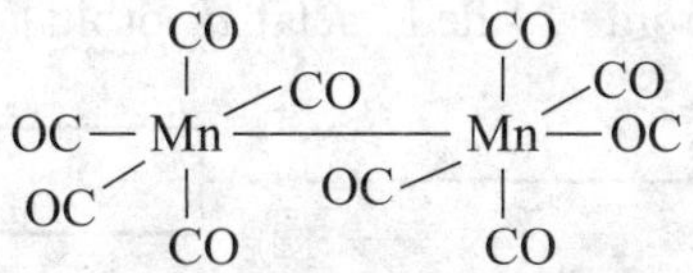

$(OC)_5Mn—Mn(CO)_5$

The carbonyl $Co_2(CO)_8$ [octacarbonyldicobalt(0)] has two cobalt atoms linked together and also by two CO bridges.

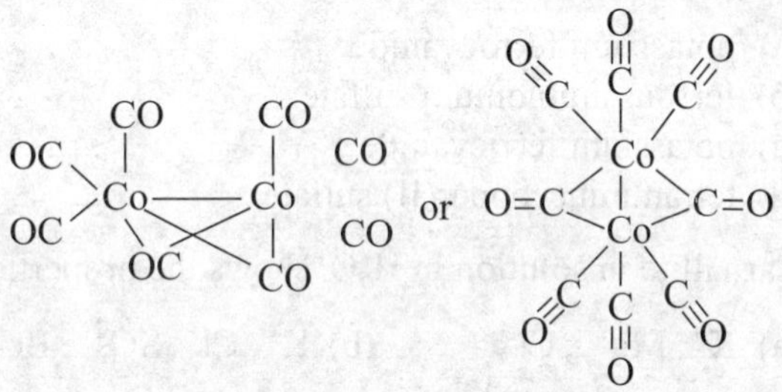

9.8.2 Properties of Metal Carbonyls

- The metal carbonyls are mostly solids at room temperature and pressure.
- The iron and nickel carbonyls are liquids.
- The mononuclear carbonyls are volatile and toxic. With the exception of $Fe_2(CO)_9$, enneacarbonyliron(0), carbonyls are soluble in hydrocarbon solvents.
- Mononuclear carbonyls are either colourless or light coloured. For example, $Fe(CO)_5$ is a light straw-coloured liquid. On the other hand, polynuclear carbonyls are more deeply coloured. For example, $Fe_3(CO)_{12}$, dodecacarbonyltriiron(0) is a deep grass green solid.
- The metal–carbon bond in metal carbonyls possesses both σ and π character.
- The reactivity of metal carbonyls is due to (i) the metal centre of the carbonyl and (ii) the CO ligands.
- Metal carbonyl are used as industrial catalysts and as precursors in organic synthesis.

9.8.3 Uses of Metal Carbonyls

- They are used as industrial catalysts.
- They are used as precursors in the synthesis of organic compounds.

9.8.4 Bonding in Metal Carbonyls

The metal–carbon bonds in metal carbonyls have both σ and π character. The first overlap takes place between the filled bonding π_{2p} orbitals of the carbon monoxide with an empty metal *d* orbital resulting in a σ-bond between the metal and carbon atom of carbon monoxide. Here, donation of a lone pair of electrons on carbon into a vacant *d* orbital of the metal takes place. As CO is a weak base/weak donor, the σ-bond formed with the metal atom is weak.

The second overlap takes place between the filled metal *d* orbital and an empty antibonding π_{2p} orbital of the carbon monoxide resulting in an additional π bond between the metal and same carbon monoxide molecule. Here, donation of electrons from a filled metal *d* orbital into a vacant antibonding π-orbital of CO occurs (*back bonding*). Here, CO acts as an acceptor ligand (Fig. 9.10).

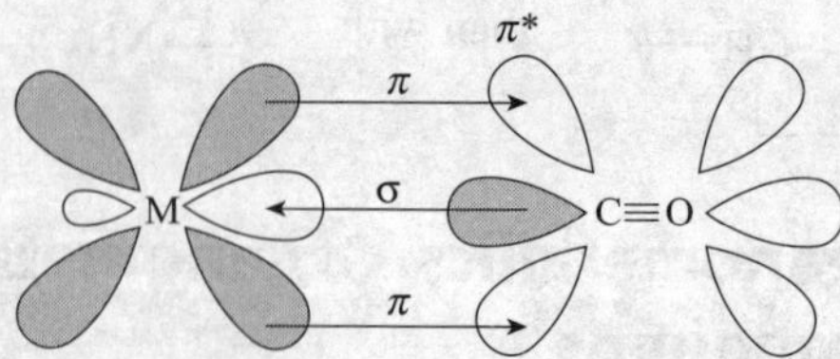

Fig. 9.10 σ-and π-overlap

σ-overlap involves the donation of the lone pair of electrons on carbon into a vacant *d*-orbital on the metal leading to the formation of a metal–carbon sigma bond. π-overlap involves the donation of electrons from a filled metal *d*-orbital into a vacant antibonding π-orbital of CO leading to the formation of a metal–carbon pi-bond. The effect of σ bond formation strengthens the π bond and vice versa. This is called *synergic effect*.

Exercises

OBJECTIVE QUESTIONS

1. Which of the following is the odd one out?
(a) potassium ferrocyanide
(b) ferrous ammonium sulfate
(c) potassium ferricyanide
(d) tetramminecopper(II) sulfate

2. Carnallite in solution in H_2O, shows the properties of
(a) K^+, Mg^{2+}, Cl^- (b) $K^+, Cl^-, SO_4^{2-}, Br^-$
(c) K^+, Mg^{2+}, CO_3^{2-} (d) K^+, Mg^{2+}, Cl^-, Br^-

3. An aqueous solution of potash alum gives
(a) two types of ions (b) only one type of ion
(c) four types of ions (d) three types of ions
(c) for N and two O (d) three N and three O

4. According to Lewis theory, the ligands are
(a) acidic in nature
(b) basic in nature (Lewis base)
(c) neither acidic nor basic
(d) some are acidic and others are basic

5. Which one of the following is a tridentate ligand?
(a) NO_2^- (b) oxalate ion
(c) glycinate ion (d) dien (e) EDTA

6. The ligand $N(CH_2CH_2NH_2)_3$ is
(a) tridentate (b) pentadentate
(c) tetradentate (d) bidentate

7. How many EDTA molecules can surround calcium?
(a) 2 (b) 1 (c) 3 (d) 8

8. The coordination number and oxidation number of platinum in the complex $[Pt(NH_3)_4Cl_2]Cl_2$ is
(a) 2, +2 (b) 4, +4 (c) 6, +4 (d) 8, +2

9. The oxidation number of Ni in $[Ni(C_2O_4)_3]^{4-}$ is
(a) 3 (b) 4 (c) 2 (d) 6

10. Which of the following ligands is not a chelating agent?
(a) EDTA (b) en
(c) oxalate (d) pyridine

11. Bidentate ligand is
(a) CN^- (b) ethylene diamine (en)
(c) SCN^- (d) EDTA

12. In the compound lithium tetrahydroaluminate, the ligand is
(a) H^+ (b) H^-
(c) H (d) none of these

13. The basic ligand is
(a) NH_3 (b) CN^- (c) F^- (d) all

14. Ammonia forms the complex ion $[Cu(NH_3)_4]^{2+}$ with copper ions in alkaline solutions but not in acidic solution. What is the reason for this?
(a) in acidic solutions, hydration protects copper ions
(b) in acidic solutions, protons coordinate with ammonia molecules forming NH_4^+ ions and NH_3 molecules are not available

(c) in alkaline solutions, insoluble $Cu(OH)_2$ is precipitated which is soluble in excess of any alkali
(d) copper hydroxide is an amphoteric substance

15. The correct structure of ethylenediaminetetraacetic acid (EDTA) is

(a) $\begin{matrix} HOOC-CH_2 \\ HOOC-CH_2 \end{matrix}\!\!>N-CH=CH-N\!\!<\!\!\begin{matrix} CH_2-COOH \\ CH_2-COOH \end{matrix}$

(b) $\begin{matrix} HOOC \\ HOOC \end{matrix}\!\!>N-CH_2-CH_2-N\!\!<\!\!\begin{matrix} COOH \\ COOH \end{matrix}$

(c) $\begin{matrix} HOOC-CH_2 \\ HOOC-CH_2 \end{matrix}\!\!>N-CH_2-CH_2-N\!\!<\!\!\begin{matrix} CH_2-COOH \\ CH_2-COOH \end{matrix}$

(d) $HOOC-CH_2 \atop H$ $>N-\underset{\underset{\underset{HOOC}{|}}{CH_2}}{\overset{\overset{COOH}{|}}{\overset{CH_2}{CH}}}-\underset{|}{CH}-N<$ $H \atop CH_2-COOH$

16. The oxidation number of Pt in $[Pt(C_2H_4)Cl_3]^-$ is
(a) +1 (b) +2 (c) +3 (d) +4

17. When EDTA solution is added to Mg^{2+} ion solution, then which of the following statements is not true?
(a) Four coordination sites of Mg^{2+} are occupied by EDTA and remaining two sites are occupied by water molecules.
(b) All six coordination sites of Mg^{2+} are occupied.
(c) The pH of the solution is decreased.
(d) Colourless $[Mg\text{–}EDTA]^{2-}$ chelate is formed.

18. Aluminium reacts with NaOH and forms compound X. If the coordination number of aluminium in X is 6, the correct formula of X is
(a) $[Al(H_2O)_4(OH)_2]^+$ (b) $[Al(H_2O)_3(OH)_3]$
(c) $[Al(H_2O)_2(OH)_4]^-$ (d) $[Al(H_2O)_6]Cl_4$

19. Which one of the following is formed with an excess of CN^- (cyanide), and is a complex having coordination number two?
(a) Cu^+ (b) Ag^+ (c) Ni^{2+} (d) Fe^{2+}

20. In the extraction of which of the following is a complex ion formed?
(a) Cu (b) Ag (c) Fe (d) Na

21. In $K_4[Fe(CN)_6]$, Fe is in the form of
(a) an atom (b) an ion
(c) cationic complex (d) anionic complex

22. Which of the following statements is not true for CoF_6^{3-}?
(a) It is paramagnetic due to the presence of 4 unpaired electrons.
(b) It has a coordination number of 6.
(c) It is an outer orbital complex.
(d) It involves d^2sp^3 hybridisation.

23. The number of ions formed on dissolving one molecule of $FeSO_4.(NH_4)_2SO_4.6H_2O$ is/are
(a) 6 (b) 3 (c) 5 (d) 4

24. Which of the following is not a double salt but is a complex salt?
(a) $KCl.MgCl_2.6H_2O$
(b) $FeSO_4.(NH_4)_2SO_4.6H_2O$
(c) $K_2SO_4.Al_2(SO_4)_3.24H_2O$
(d) $4KCN.Fe(CN)_2$

25. The complex $CoCl_2.3NH_3$ ionises to give
(a) 2 Cl^- ions (b) 1 Cl^- ion
(c) 3 Cl^- ions (d) no Cl^- ions

26. Some salts although containing two different metallic elements give a test for only one of them in solution. Such salts are
(a) complex salts (d) double salts
(c) normal salts (d) none

27. The number of ions produced from one molecule of $[Pt(NH_3)_5Cl]Cl_3$ in an aqueous solution will be
(a) 3 (b) 4 (c) 5 (d) 6

28. The solution of which compound will show maximum ionic conductivity?
(a) $K_4[Fe(CN)_6]$ (b) $Co(NH_3)_6]Cl_3$
(c) $[Cu(NH_3)_4]Cl_2$ (d) $[Ni(CO)_4]$

29. The number of ions produced in water by dissolution of the complex having the empirical formula $CoCl_3.4NH_3$ is
(a) 1 (b) 2 (c) 4 (d) 3

30. Which of the following complexes has the lowest molar conductance?
(a) $CoCl_3.3NH_3$ (b) $CoCl_3.4NH_3$
(c) $CoCl_3.5NH_3$ (d) $CoCl_3.6NH_3$

31. Excess of silver nitrate solution is added to 100 mL of 0.01 M pentaaquachlorochromium(III) chloride solution. The mass of silver chloride obtained (in grams) is [Atomic mass of silver is 108]
(a) 287×10^{-3} (b) 143.5×10^{-3}
(c) 143.5×10^{-2} (d) 287×1^{-2}

32. Which of the following 0.1 M complex compound solution will have the minimum electrical conductivity?
(a) hexaammineplatinum(IV) chloride
(b) chloropentaammineplatinum(IV) chloride

(c) dichlorotetraammineplatinum(IV) chloride
(d) triamminetrichloroplatinum (IV) chloride

Nomenclature of Coordination Compounds

33. Give the IUPAC name and magnetic moment of the complex $K[Cr(H_2O)_2(C_2O_4)_2].3H_2O$
(a) potassium diaquadioxalatochromate(III) trihydrate, 3.87 BM
(b) potassium diaquadioxalatochromium(III) hydrate, 3.87 BM
(c) potassium dioxalatodiaquachromate(VI) trihydrate, 1.73 BM
(d) potassium diaquadioxalato chromium chromium hydrate, 3.87 BM

34. As per IUPAC names, the name of the complex $[Co(en)_2(ONO)Cl]Cl$ is
(a) chloridobis(ethane-1,2-diamine)nitro-O-cobalt(III) chloride
(b) chlorobis(ethylene diamine)nitro-O-nitrocobalt(III) chloride
(c) diaminenitrocobalt(III) chloride
(d) chloroetylenediaminenitro-O-cobalt(III) chloride

35. The IUPAC name of the complex ion formed when gold dissolves in aquaregia is
(a) tetrachloridoaurate(III) (b) tetrachloridoaurated(I)
(c) tetrachloridoaurate(II) (d) dichloridoaurate(III)

36. Ammonia gas does not evolve from the complex $FeCl_3.4NH_3$ but it gives a white precipitate with an aqueous solution of $AgNO_3$. The coordination number of central metal ion in the above complex is six. Give the IUPAC name of the complex.
(a) ammoniumtrichlorotriammineferric(III)
(b) tetraammineferric(III) chloride
(c) dichlorotetraammineferrate(II) chloride
(d) tetraamminedichloroferric(III) chloride

37. The IUPAC name of the complex $[Pt(NH_3)_3 Br(NO_2)Cl]Cl$ is
(a) triamminechlorobromonitroplatinum(IV) chloride
(b) triamminebromonitrochloroplatinum(IV) chloride
(c) triamminebromochloronitroplatinum(IV) chloride
(d) triamminenitrochlorobromoplatinum(IV) chloride

38. The IUPAC name of the compound $[CuCl_2(CH_3NH_2)_2]$ is
(a) dichlorobis(dimethylamine)copper(II)
(b) dichlorobis(methylamine)copper(II)
(c) dimethylaminecopper(II) chloride
(d) bis(dimethylamine)copper(II) chloride

39. The correct IUPAC name of potassium cuprochloride is
(a) potassium copper(I) tetrachloride
(b) potassium tetrachlorocuprate(I)
(c) tetrachloropotassiumcuprate(I)
(d) tetrachlorocopper(I) potassiate

40. Which among the following will be named as dibromidobis(ethylene diamine)chloromium(III) bromide?
(a) $[Cr(en)_3]Br_3$ (b) $[Cr(en)_2Br_2]Br$
(c) $[Cr(en)Br_4]^-$ (d) $[Cr(en)Br_2]Br$

41. The hypothetical complex chlorodiaquatriamminecobalt(III) chloride can be represented as
(a) $[Co(NH_3)_3(H_2O)_2Cl]Cl_2$
(b) $[Co(NH_3)_3(H_2O)Cl_3]$
(c) $[Co(NH_3)_3(H_2O)_2Cl]$
(d) $[Co(NH_3)_3(H_2O)_3]Cl_3$

42. The formula of dichlorobis(urea) copper(II) is
(a) $[Cu\{O{=}C(NH_2)_2\}Cl_2]$
(b) $[CuCl_2\{O{=}C(NH_2)_2\}_2]$
(c) $[Cu\{O{=}C(NH_2)_2\}Cl]Cl$
(d) $[CuCl_2\{O{=}(NH_2)_2H_2]$

43. The formula of sodium nitroprusside is
(a) $Na_4[Fe(CN)_5NOS]$ (b) $Na_2[Fe(CN)_5NO]$
(c) $NaFe[Fe(CN)_6]$ (d) $Na_2[Fe(CN)_6NO_2]$

44. The formula of potassium dicyanobis(oxolato) nickelate(II) is
(a) $K_4[Ni(CN)_2(ox)_2]$ (b) $K_3[Ni_2(Ni_2(CN)_2(ox)_2]$
(c) $K[Ni(CN)(ox)_2]$ (d) $K_2[Ni(CN)_2(ox)_2]$

45. A coordination complex compound of cobalt has the molecular formula containing five ammonia molecules, one nitro group and two chlorine atoms for one cobalt atom. One mole of this compound produces three mole ions in an aqueous solution. On reacting with excess of $AgNO_3$, AgCl is precipitated. The ionic formula for this complex would be
(a) $[Co(NH_3)_5(NO_2)]Cl_2$
(b) $[Co(NH_3)_5Cl]\ [Cl(NO_2)]$
(c) $[Co(NH_3)_4(NO)_2Cl]\ [(NH_3)Cl]$
(d) $[Co(NH_3)_5]\ [(NO_2)_2Cl_2]$

46. A solution containing 2.675 g of $CoCl_3.6NH_3$ (molar mass = $267.5 mol^{-1}$) is passed through a cation exchanger. The $AgNO_3$ to give 4.78 g of AgCl (molar mass = 143.5 g mol^{-1}). The formula of the complex is(At. mass of Ag = 108 u)
(a) $[CoCl(NH_3)_5]Cl_2$ (b) $[Co(NH_3)_6]Cl_3$
(c) $[CoCl_2(NH_3)_4]Cl$ (d) $CoCl_3(NH_3)_3]$

47. An ambidentate ligand is one which
(a) is linked to a metal atom at two points
(b) has two donor atoms but only one of them has the capacity to form a coordinate bond

(c) has two donor atoms but either of the two can form a coordinate bond
(d) forms chelate rings

48. The IUPAC name of the following coordination compound is $Hg[Co(NCS)_4]$
(a) mercury tetrathicyanatocobaltate(II)
(b) mercury tetraisothicyanatocobaltate(II)
(c) mercury tetrathiocyanatocobaltate(III)
(d) mercury isothiocyanatocobaltate(III)

Geometrical Isomerism

49. Fac–Mer isomerism is associated with which of the following complexes? (M = central metal)
(a) $[M(AA)_2]$ (b) $[MA_3B_3]$ (c) $[M(AA)_3]$
(d) [MABCD] (e) $[MA_4B_2]$

50. Both geometrical and optical isomerisms are exhibited by
(a) dichlorobis(ethylenediamine)cobalt(III) ion
(b) pentaamminechlorocobalt(III) ion
(c) triamminotrichlorocobalt(III) ion
(d) tetramminedichlorocobalt(III) ion
(e) trioxalatochromate(III) ion

51. Which kind of isomerism is exhibited by octahedral $[Co(NH_3)_4Br_2]Cl$?
(a) geometrical and ionisation
(b) geometrical and optical
(c) optical and ionisation
(d) geometrical only

52. The number of geometric isomers possible for the complex $[CoL_2Cl]^-$ ($L= H_2NCH_2CH_2O^-$) is
(a) 2 (b) 3 (c) 5 (d) 6

53. The number of geometrical isomers of $[CrCl_2(en)(NH_3)_2]$ where en = ethylenediamine, is
(a) 2 (b) 3 (c) 4 (d) 1

54. The number of isomers of Co(diethylene triamine) Cl_3 is
(a) 2 (b) 3 (c) 4 (d) 5

55. Which can exist both as diastereoisomers and enantiomers?
(a) $[Pt(en)_3]^{4+}$ (b) $[Pt(en)_2ClBr]^{2+}$
(c) $[Ru(NH_3)_4Cl_2]^0$ (d) $[PtCl_2Br_2]^0$

56. Facial and meridonal isomerism will be exhibited by
(a) $[Co(NH_3)_3Cl_3]$ (b) $[Co(NH_3)_4Cl_2]Cl$
(c) $[Co(en)_3]Cl_3$ (d) $[Co(NH_3)_5Cl]Cl_2$
(e) $K_3[Co(CN)_4Cl_2]$

57. For the square planar complex [M(a)(b)(c)(d)] (where, M= central metal and a, b, c and d are monodentate ligands), the number of possible geometrical isomers is
(a) 1 (b) 2 (c) 3 (d) 4

58. Which one amongst the following, exhibits geometrical isomerism?
(a) $Co^{III}(NH_3)_5Br]SO_4$ (b) $Co^{III}[EDTA]^{1-}$
(c) $Cr^{III}(SCN)_6]^{3-}$ (d) $Pt^{II}(NH_3)_2Cl_2]$

59. Which of the following complexes does not show geometrical isomerism?
(a) $[Co[NH_3)_4Cl_2]^+$ (b) $[Fe(NH_3)_2(CN)_4]^-$
(c) $[Cr(ox)_3]^{3-}$ (d) $[Co(NH_3)_3(NO_2)_3]$

60. For the given complex $[CoCl_2(en)(NH_3)_2]^+$, the number of geometrical isomers, the number of optical isomers and total number of isomers of all types possible respectively are
(a) 2, 2 and 4 (b) 3, 2 and 4
(c) 2, 0 and 2 (d) 0, 2 and 2

61. Which one of the following has the largest number of isomers?
(a) $[Ir(PR_3)_2H(CO)]^{2+}$ (b) $[Co(NH_3)_5Cl]^{2+}$
(c) $[Ru(NH_3)_4Cl_2]^+$ (d) $[Co(en)_2Cl_2]^+$
(R = alkyl group; en = ethylenediamine)

62. Which kind of isomerism is exhibited by the octahedral complex $Co(NH_3)_4Br_2Cl$?
(a) geometrical and ionisation
(b) geometrical and optical
(c) optical and ionisation
(d) geometrical only

63. A square planar complex of the type M (AXBL) (where A, B, X and L are unidentate ligands) shows following set of isomers
(a) two *cis* and one *trans* (b) two *trans* and one *cis*
(c) two*cis*and two *trans* (d) three *cis* and one *trans*

64. Consider the following reaction and statements.
$[Co(NH_3)_4Br_2]^+ + Br^- \rightarrow [Co(NH_3)_3Br_3] + NH_3$
(I) Two isomers are produced if the reactant complex ion is a *cis*-isomer.
(II) Two isomers are produced if the reactant complex ion is a *trans*-isomer.
(III) Only one isomer is produced if the reactant complex ion is a *trans*-isomer.
(IV) Only one isomer is produced if the reactant complex ion is a *cis*-isomer.
The correct statements are
(a) (I) and (II) (b) (I) and (III)
(c) (III) and (IV) (d) (II) and (IV)

65. The incorrect option regarding the complex $[Co(en)(NH_3)_2(H_2O)^{3+}]$ (en = $H_2NCH_2CH_2NH_2$)is
(a) it has two geometrical isomers

(b) it will have three geometrical isomers if bidentate 'en' is replaced by two cyanide ligands
(c) it is paramagnetic
(d) it absorbs light at longer wavelength as compared to $[Co(en)(NH_3)_4]^{3+}$

66. The total number of geometrical isomers possible for an octahedral complex of the type $[MA_2B_2C_2]$ is (M = transition metal; A, B and C are monodentate ligands)
(a) 3 (b) 4 (c) 5 (d) 6

67. Which of the following is not optically active?
(a) $[Co(en)_3]^{3+}$ (b) $[Cr(ox)_3]^{3-}$
(c) *cis*-$[CoCl_2(en)_2]^+$ (d) *trans*-$[CoCl_2(en_2)]^+$

68. Among the following complexes, optical activity is possible in
(a) $[Co(NH_3)_6]^{3+}$ (b) $[Co(H_2O)_2(NH_3)_2Cl_2]^+$
(c) $[Cr(H_2O)_4Cl_2]^+$ (d) $Co(CN)_5NC]$

69. Which of the following coordination compounds would exhibit optical isomerism?
(a) pentaamminenitrocobalt(III) iodide
(b) diamminedichloroplatinum(II)
(c) *trans*-dicyanobis(ethylenediamine)chromium(III) chloride
(d) *tris*-(ethylenediamine)cobalt(III) bromide

70. Which of the following compounds show optical isomerism?
(i) *cis*-$[Co(NH_3)_4Cl_2]^+$ (ii) *trans*-$[Co(en)_2Cl_2]^+$
(iii) *cis*-$[Co(en)_2Cl_2]^+$ (iv) $[Co(en)_3]^{3+}$
Choose the correct answer codes given below:
(a) (i) and (ii) (b) (ii) and (iii)
(c) (iii) and (iv) (d) (i), (iii) and (iv)
(e) (i), (ii), (iii) and (iv)

71. Benzoylacetonatoberyllium exhibits ______ isomerism.
(a) structural (b) geometrical
(c) optical (d) conformational

72. The possible number of optical isomers in $[Co(en)_2Cl_2]^+$ are
(a) 2 (b) 3 (c) 4 (d) 6

73. Which of the following coordination compounds would exhibit optical isomerism?
(a) *trans*-dicyanobis-(ethylenediamine)chromium(II) chloride
(b) *tris*-(ethylenediamine)cobalt(II) bromide
(c) pentaamminenitrocobalt(III) iodide
(d) diamminedichloroplatinum(II)

74. Among (i) $[Cr(en)_3]^{3+}$ (ii) *trans*-$[Cr(en)_2Cl_2]^+$
(iii) *cis*-$[Cr(en)_2Cl_2]^+$ (iv) $[Co(NH_3)_4Cl_2]^+$
The optically active complexes are
(a) (i) and (ii) (b) (i) and (iii)
(c) (ii) and (iii) (d) (ii) and (iv)

75. The type(s) of isomerism exhibited by the following complex $[Co(NH_3)_5(NO_2)] (NO_3)_2$]is(are)
(a) ionisation isomerism only
(b) linkage isomerism only
(c) both ionisation and linkage isomerisms
(d) geometrical isomerism

76. Which of the following compounds exhibits linkage isomerism?
(a) $[Co(en)_3]Cl_3$ (b) $[Co(NH_3)_6[Cr(CN)_6]$
(c) $[Co(en)_2NO_2Cl]Br$ (d) $[Co(NH_3)_5Cl] Br_2$

77. $[Fe(NO_2)_3Cl_3]$ and $[Fe(O–NO)_3Cl_3]$ shows
(a) linkage isomerism (b) geometrical isomerism
(c) optical isomerism (d) none of the above

78. Change in composition of the coordination sphere yields which types of isomers?
(a) optical (b) geometrical
(c) ionisation (d) none of these

79. The ionisation isomer of $[Cr(H_2O)_4Cl(NO_2)]Cl$ is
(a) $[Cr(H_2O)_4(O_2N)]Cl_2$
(b) $[Cr(H_2O)_4Cl_2](NO_2)$
(c) $[Cr(H_2O)_4Cl(ONO)]Cl$
(d) $[Cr(H_2O)_4Cl_2(NO_2)]H_2O$

80. Coordination isomerism is caused by the interchange of ligands between the
(a) *cis* and *trans* structure
(b) complex cation and complex anion
(c) inner sphere and outer sphere
(d) low oxidation and higher oxidation states

81. The total number of possible isomers for the complex compound $[Cu^{II}(NH_3)_4][Pt^{II}Cl_4]$ are
(a) 3 (b) 4 (c) 5 (d) 6

82. Which among the following statements is/are true for the complex
$[Co(NH_3)_6][Cr(CN)_6]$?
1. It is a non-electrolyte.
2. The magnitude of the charge on each complex ions is 3.
3. The complex will not conduct current.
4. The complex will exhibit coordination isomerism.
5. The magnitude of the charge on each complex ion is 1.
(a) 1 and 4 (b) 1 and 2 (c) 1 and 3
(d) 3 and 5 (e) 2 and 4

83. The pair of complex compounds $[Cr(H_2O)_6Cl_3]$ and $[Cr(H_2O)_5Cl]Cl_2H_2O$ is an example of

(a) linkage isomerism (b) ionisation isomerism
(c) coordination isomerism (d) hydrate isomerism

84. Which one of the following will not show geometrical isomerism?

(a) $[Cr(NH_3)_4Cl_2]Cl$ (b) $[Co(en)_2Cl_2]Cl$
(c) $Co(NH_3)_5NO_2]Cl_2$ (d) $[Pt(NH_3)_2Cl_2]$

85. Which one of the following octahedral complexes does not show geometric isomerism? (A and B are monodentate ligands?

(a) $[MA_2B_4]$ (b) $[MA_3B_3]$
(c) $[MA_4B_2]$ (d) $[MA_5B]$

86. The number of possible isomers of an octahedral complex $[Co(C_2O_4)_2(NH_3)_2]^-$ is

(a) 1 (b) 2 (c) 3 (d) 4

Bonding in Coordination Compounds

87. According to Werner's theory

(a) primary valency can be ionised
(b) secondary valency can be ionised
(c) primary and secondary valencies both cannot be ionised
(d) only primary valency cannot be ionised

88. Given the molecular formula of the hexacoordinated complexes, (A) $CoCl_3.6NH_3$, (B) $CoCl_3.5NH_3$, (C) $CoCl_3.4NH_3$,if the number of coordinated NH_3 molecules in A, B and C respectively, are 6, 5 and 4, the primary valency in (A), (B) and (C) are

(a) 6, 5, 4 (b) 3, 2, 1 (c) 0, 1, 2 (d) 3, 3, 3

89. The primary and secondary valencies of chromium in the complex ion, dichlorodioxalatochromate(III), are respectively

(a) 3, 4 (b) 4, 3 (c) 3, 6
(d) 6, 3 (e) 4, 4

90. One mol of the complex compound $Co(NH_3)_5Cl_3$, gives 3 mol of ions on dissolution in water. One mol of the same complex reacts with two mol of $AgNO_3$ solution to yield two mol of $AgCl(s)$. the structure of the complex is

(a) $[Co(NH_3)_5Cl]Cl_2$ (b) $[Co(NH_3)_3Cl_3].2NH_3$
(c) $[Co(NH_3)_4Cl_2]Cl.NH_3$ (d) $[Co(NH_3)_4Cl]Cl_2.NH_3$

91. The bonds in $K_4[Fe(CN)_6]$ are

(a) all ionic (b) all covalent
(c) ionic and covalent
(d) ionic, covalent and coordinate covalent

92. A mixture X = 0.02 mol of $[Co(NH_3)_5SO_4]Br$ and 0.02 mol of $[Co(NH_3)_5Br]SO_4$ was prepared in 2 litre of solution.

1 litre of mixture X + excess $AgNO_3 \rightarrow Y$

1 litre of mixture X + excess $BaCl_2 \rightarrow Z$

Number of mol of Y and Z are

(a) 0.01, 0.01 (b) 0.02, 0.01
(c) 0.01, 0.02 (d) 0.02, 0.02

93. Which of the following statements is incorrect?

(a) In $K_3[Fe(CN)_6]$, the ligand has satisfied only the secondary valencies of the ferric ion.
(b) In $K_3[Fe(CN)_6]$, the ligand has satisfied both primary and secondary valencies of the ferric ion.
(c) In $K_4[Fe(CN)_6]$, the ligand has satisfied both primary and secondary valencies of the ferrous ion.
(d) In $[Cu(NH_3)_4]SO_4$, the ligand has satisfied only the secondary valencies of copper.

94. On treatment of 100 mL of 0.1 M solution of $CoCl_3.6H_2O$ with excess $AgNO_3$, 1.2×10^{22} ions are precipitated. The complex is

(a) $[Co(H_2O)_6Cl_3$ (b) $[Co(H_2O)_5Cl]Cl_2.H_2O$
(c) $[Co(H_2O)_4Cl_2]Cl.2H_2O$ (d) $[Co(H_2O)_3Cl_3].3H_2O$

95. The hybrid state of Co in the high spin K_3CoF_6 complex is

(a) sp^3d^2 (b) sp^3 (c) d^2sp^3 (d) sp^3d

96. Which of the following contains one unpaired electron in the $4p$ orbitals?

(a) $[Cu(NH_3)_2]^+$ (b) $[Cu(NH_3)_4]^{2+}$
(c) $[Cu(CN)_4]^{3-}$ (d) $[Ni(CN)_4]^{2-}$

97. Which of the following is paramagnetic?

(a) $[Fe(CN)_4]^{4-}$ (b) $[Ni(CO)_4]$
(c) $[Ni(CN)_4]^{2-}$ (d) $[CoF_6]^{3-}$
(At. no. of Co = 27)

98. The number of unpaired electrons in the square planar $[Pt(CN)_4]^{2-}$ complex ion will be

(a) 2 (b) 1 (c) zero (d) 4

99. The ion which is not tetrahedral in shape is _______.

(a) BF_4^- (b) NH_4^+
(c) $[Cu(NH_3)_4]^{2+}$ (d) $NiCl_4^{2-}$

100. The anion $[Co(C_2O_4)_3]^{3-}$ involves _______ hybridisation

(a) sp^3d^2 (b) d^2sp^3 (c) sp^2d^3 (d) d^3sp^2

101. Among the following, the species having square planar geometry for the central atom are

(i) XeF_4 (ii) SF_4
(iii) $[NiCl_4]^{2-}$ (iv) $[PdCl_4]^{2-}$
(a) (i) and (iv) (b) (i) and (ii)
(c) (ii) and (iii) (d) (iii) and (iv)

102. In $[Ag(CN)_2]^-$, the number of π-bonds is
(a) 2 (b) 3 (c) 4 (d) 6

103. The species having a tetrahedral shape is
(a) $[PdCl_4]^{2-}$ (b) $[Ni(CN)_4]^{2-}$
(c) $[Pd(CN)_4]^{3-}$ (d) $[NiCl_4]^{2-}$

104. Which statement is incorrect?
(a) $Ni(CO)_4$— Tetrahedral, paramagnetic
(b) $[Ni(CN)_4]^{2-}$— Square planar, diamagnetic
(c) $Ni(CO)_4$— Tetrahedral, diamagnetic
(d) $[NiCl_4]_2$— Tetrahedral, paramagnetic

105. Which one of the following is an inner orbital complex as well as diamagnetic in behaviour?
(Atomic number of Zn = 30, Cr = 24, Co = 27, Ni = 28)
(a) $[Zn(NH_3)_6]^{2+}$ (b) $[Cr(NH_3)_6]^{3+}$
(c) $[Co(NH_3)_6]^{3+}$ (d) $[Ni(NH_3)_6]^{2+}$

106. Amongst the following ions, which one has the highest paramagnetism?
(a) $[Cr(H_2O)_6]^{3+}$ (b) $[Fe(H_2O)_6]^{2+}$
(c) $[Cu(H_2O)_6]^{2+}$ (d) $[Zn(H_2O)_6]^{2+}$

107. The pair in which both species have the same magnetic moment (spin only value) is
(a) $[Cr(H_2O)_6]^{2+}$, $[Co(Cl_4]^{2-}$
(b) $[Cr(H_2O)_6]^{2+}$, $[Fe(H_2O)_6]^{2+}$
(c) $[Mn(H_2O)_6]^{2+}$, $[Cr(H_2O)_6]$
(d) $[CoCl_4]^{2-}$, $[Fe(H_2O)_6]^{2+}$

108. Among the following complexes, which has a magnetic moment of 5.9 B.M.?
(a) $Ni(CO)_4$ (b) $[Fe(H_2O)_6]^{2+}$
(c) $[Co(NH_3)_6]^{2+}$ (d) $[MnBr_4]^{2-}$

109. The expected spin only magnetic moments for $[Fe(CN)_6]^{4-}$ and $[FeF_6]^{3-}$
(a) 1.73 and 1.73 BM (b) 1.73 and 5.92 BM
(c) 0.0 and 1.73 BM (d) 0.0 and 5.92 BM

110. Which of the following is diamagnetic in nature?
(a) Co^{3+}, octahedral complex with weak field ligands
(b) Co^{3+}, octahedral complex with strong field ligands
(c) Co^{2+} in a tetrahedral complex
(d) Co^{2+} in a square planar complex

111. The complex showing a spin only magnetic moment of 2.82 BM is
(a) $[Ni(CO)_4]$ (b) $[NiCl_4]^{2-}$
(c) $[Ni(PPh_3)_4]$ (d) $[Ni(CN)_4]^{2-}$

112. The spin only magnetic moment of $[MnBr_4]^{2-}$ is 5.9 BM. The geometry of the complex ion is
(a) square planar (b) tetrahedral
(c) square pyramidal (d) trigonal bipyramidal

113. Consider the following two complex ions: $[CoF_6]^{3-}$ and $[Co(C_2O_4]_3]^{3-}$. Which of the following statement(s) is/are false?
I. Both are octahedral.
II. $[Co(C_2O_4]_3]^{3-}$ is diamagnetic while $[CoF_6]^{3-}$ is paramagnetic.
III. Both are outer orbital complexes.
IV. In both the complexes, the central metal is in the same oxidation state.
(a) II and III (b) II, III and IV
(c) III only (d) III and IV

114. Among $[Ni(CO)_4]$, $[NiCl_4]^{2-}$, $[Co(NH_3)_4Cl_2]Cl$, $Na_3[CoF_6]$, Na_2O_2 and CsO_2, the total number of paramagnetic compounds is
(a) 2 (b) 3 (c) 4 (d) 5

115. The geometries of the ammonia complexes of Ni^{2+}, Pt^{2+} and Zn^{2+} respectively, are
(a) octahedral, square planar and tetrahedral
(b) square planar, octahedral and tetrahedral
(c) tetrahedral, square planar and octahedral
(d) octahedral, tetrahedral and square planar

116. The spin only magnetic moment of the tetrahedral complex $[ZCl_4]^{2-}$ is 3.87 BM. The metal Z is
(a) Mn (b) Ni (c) Co (d) Cu

117. The geometry and the number of unpaired electrons(s) of $[MnBr_4]^{2-}$, respectively are
(a) tetrahedral and 1 (b) square planar and 1
(c) tetrahedral and 5 (d) square planar and 5

118. The spin only magnetic moments of $[Fe(NH_3)_6]^{3+}$ and $[FeF_6]^{3-}$ in BM are, respectively
(a) 1.73 and 1.73 (b) 5.92 and 1.73
(c) 1.73 and 5.92 (d) 5.92 and 5.92

119. Select the diamagnetic complex ion among the following complexes (Atomic number of Fe = 26, Co = 27)
(a) $K_3[Fe(CN)_6]$ (b) $[Co(NH_3)_6]Cl_3$
(c) $K_3[FeF_6]$ (d) $K_3[CoF_6]$

120. The incorrect statement is
(a) $[Co(NH_3)_6]^{2+}$ is paramagnetic
(b) $[MnBr_4]^{2-}$ is tetrahedral
(c) $[CoBr_2(en)_2]^-$ exhibits linkage isomerism
(d) $[Ni(NH_3)_6]^{2+}$ is not an inner orbital complex

121. Choose the correct statement.
(a) $[Co(NH_3)_6]^{2+}$is oxidises to diamagnetic $[Co(NH_3)_6]^{3+}$ by the oxygen in air

(b) Tetrahedral complexes are more stable than octahedral complexes
(c) $[Fe(CN)_6]^{3-}$ is stable but $[FeF_6]^{3-}$ is unstable
(d) The $[Cu(NH_3)_4]^{2+}$ ion has a tetrahedral geometry and is diamagnetic

122. Which one of the following is wrongly matched?
(a) $[Cu(NH_3)_4]^{2+}$ — Square planar
(b) $[Ni(CO)_4]$ — Neutral ligand
(c) $[Fe(CN)_6]^{3-}$ — sp^3d^2
(d) $[Co(en)_3]^{3+}$ — Follows EAN rule

123. The correct order of magnetic moments (spin only values in BM) among the following is
(a) $[MnCl_4]^{2-} > [CoCl_4]^{2-} > [Fe(CN)_6]^{4-}$
(b) $[MnCl_4]^{2-} > [Fe(CN)_6]^{4-} > [CoCl_4]^{2-}$
(c) $[Fe(CN)_6]^{4-} > [MnCl_4]^{2-} > [CoCl_4]^{2-}$
(d) $[Fe(CN)_6]^{4-} > [CoCl_4]^{2-} > [MnCl_4]^{2-}$

124. $[Sc(H_2O)_6]^{3+}$ ion is
(a) colourless and diamagnetic
(b) coloured and octahedral
(c) colourless and paramagnetic
(d) coloured and paramagnetic

125. The magnetic moment of $(NH_3)_2[MnBr_4]$ is _____ BM.
(a) 5.91 (b) 4.91 (c) 3.91 (d) 2.46

126. The species having a tetrahedral shape is
(a) $[PdCl_4]^{2-}$ (b) $[Ni(CN)_4]^{2-}$
(c) $[Pd(CN)_4]^{2-}$ (d) $[NiCl_4]^{2-}$

127. The geometry of $Ni(CO)_4$ and $Ni(PPh_3)_2Cl_2$ are
(a) both square planar
(b) tetrahedral and square planar respectively
(c) both tetrahedral
(d) square planar and tetrahedral respectively

128. Match the following

Column I (Complex)	Column II (Structure and magnetic moment)
A. $[Ag(NH_3)_2]^+$	1. Square planar and 1.73 BM
B. $[Co(NH_3)_6]^{3+}$	2. Linear and 0
C. $[Fe(CN)_6]^{3-}$	3. Octahedral and 0
D. $[Cu(NH_3)_4]^{2+}$	4. Octahedral and 0
E. $[Fe(CN)_6]^{4-}$	5. Octahedral and 1.73 BM

Codes:

	A	B	C	D	E
(a)	1	2	3	4	5
(b)	1	3	2	5	4
(c)	2	4	5	1	3
(d)	5	4	3	2	1

129. The compound which does not show paramagnetism is
(a) $[Cu(NH_3)_4]Cl_2$ (b) $[Ag(NH_3)_2]Cl$
(c) NO (d) NO_2

130. Which one has the highest paramagnetism?
(a) $Ni(CO)_4$ (b) $[Ni(NH_3)_4]Cl_2$
(c) $[Ni(NH_3)_6]Cl_2$ (d) $[Cu(NH_3)_4]Cl_2$

131. The spin only magnetic moment value (in Bohr magneton units) of $Cr(CO)_6$ is
(a) 0 (b) 2.84 (c) 4.90 (d) 5.92

132. Which one of the following complexes is not diamagnetic?
(a) $[Fe(CN)_6]^{4-}$ (b) $[Ti(H_2O)_6]^{3+}$
(c) $[Pt(CN)_4]^{2-}$ (d) $[Co(NH_3)_6]^{3+}$

133. The magnetic moment of a salt containing the Zn^{2+} ion is
(a) 0 (b) 1.87 (c) 5.92 (d) 2

134. The reaction $[Fe(CNS)_6]^{3-} \rightarrow [FeF_6]^{3-}$ takes place with a/an
(a) decrease in magnetic moment
(b) increase in magnetic moment
(c) decrease in coordination number
(d) increase in coordination number

135. The complex showing a spinonly magnetic moment of 2.82 BM is
(a) $Ni(CO)_4$ (b) $[NiCl_4]^{2-}$
(c) $Ni(PPh_3)_4$ (d) $[Ni(CN)_4]^{2-}$

136. Which one of the following has a square planar geometry?
(a) $[CoCl_4]^{2-}$ (b) $[FeCl_4]^{2-}$
(c) $[NiCl_4]^{2-}$ (d) $[PtCl_4]^{2-}$

137. Which of the following facts about the complex $[Cr(NH_3)_6]Cl_3$ is wrong?
(a) The complex involves d^2sp^3 hybridisation and is octahedral in shape.
(b) The complex is paramagnetic.
(c) The complex is an outer orbital complex.
(d) The complex gives a white precipitate with silver nitrate solution.

138. In the complex $[SbF_5]^{2-}$, sp^3d hybridisation is present. Geometry of the complex is
(a) square pyramidal (b) square bipyramidal
(c) tetrahedral (d) square planar

139. Which of the following complexes has a square planar geometry?

(a) $Ag(NH_3)_2^+$ (b) $Cu(en)_2^+$
(c) $[MnCl_4]^{2-}$ (d) $Ni(CO)_4$

140. The number of d electrons in $[Cr(H_2O)_4]^{3+}$ is

(a) 2 (b) 3 (c) 4 (d) 5

141. The complex ion which has no d electrons in the central metal atom is

(a) $[MnO_4]^-$ (b) $[Co(NH_3)_6]^{3+}$
(c) $[Fe(CN)_6]^{3-}$ (d) $[Cr(H_2O)_6]^{3+}$

142. A strong ligand gives a complex which is generally called

(a) high spin (b) high energy
(c) low spin (d) stable

143. The value of the spin only magnetic moment for one of the following configurations is 2.84 BM. The correct one is

(a) d^4 (in strong ligand filed)
(b) d^2 (in weak ligand field)
(c) d^3 (in weak as well as in strong ligand field)
(d) d^5 (in strong ligand field)

144. Which has square planar geometry?

(a) $[Pt(NH_3)_2Cl_2]$ (b) $[Ni(CN)_4]^{2-}$
(c) both (a) and (b) (d) none of these

145. Which of the following complexes are not correctly matched with the hybridisation of their central metal ions?

(i) $[Ni(CO)_4]sp^3$ (ii) $[Ni(CN)_4]^{2-}$ sp^3
(iii) $[CoF_6]^{3-}$ d^2sp^3 (iv) $[Fe(CN)_6]^{3-}$ sp^3d^2
Select the correct answer using the codes given below
(a) (i) and (ii) (b) (i) and (iii)
(c) (ii) and (iv) (d) (i), (iii) and (iv)
(e) (ii), (iii) and (iv)

146. In which of the following complex ions is the central metal ion in a state of sp^3d^2 hybridisation?

(a) $[CoF_6]^{3-}$ (b) $[Co(NH_3)_6]^{3+}$
(c) $[Fe(CN)_6]^{3-}$ (d) $[Cr(NH_3)_6]^{3+}$

147. Hybridisation, shape and magnetic moment of $K_3[Co(CO_3)_3]$ are

(a) d^2sp^3, octahedral, 4.9 BM
(b) sp^3d^2, octahedral, 4.9 BM
(c) dsp^2, square planar, 4.9 BM
(d) sp^3, tetrahedral, 4.9 BM

148. In $[Ni(CN)_4]^{2-}$, $[MnBr_4]^{2-}$ and $[FeF_6]^{3-}$, geometry, hybridisation and magnetic moment of the ions respectively are,

(a) tetrahedral, square planar, octahedral: sp^3, dsp^2, sp^3, d^2: 5.9, 0, 4.9
(b) tetrahedral, square planar, octahedral: dsp^2, sp^3, sp^3, d^2: 0, 5.9, 0, 4.9
(c) square planar, tetrahedral, octahedral: dsp^2, sp^3, d^2, sp^3: 5.9, 4.9, 0
(d) square planar, tetrahedral octahedral: dsp^2, sp^3, sp^3, d^2: 0, 5.9, 4.93

149. Geometrical shapes of the complexes formed by the reaction of Ni^{2+} with Cl^-, CN^- and H_2O, respectively, are

(a) octahedral, tetrahedral and square planar
(b) tetrahedral, square planar and octahedral
(c) square planar, tetrahedral and octahedral
(d) octahedral, square planar and tetrahedral

150. Among the following complexes (K–P), $K_3[Fe(CN)_6]$ (K), $[Co(NH_3)_6]Cl_3$ (L), $Na_3[Co(oxalate)_3]$ (M), $[Ni(H_2O)_6]Cl_2$ (N), $K_2[Pt(CN)_4]$ (O) and $[Zn(H_2O)_6](NO_3)_2$ (P), the diamagnetic complexes are

(a) K, L, M, N (b) K, M, O, P
(c) L, M, O, P (d) L, M, N, O

151. Which complex compound obeys the 18-electon rule?

(a) $[V(CO)_5]$ (b) $[Fe(NH_3)_6]^{2+}$
(c) $[Ni(CO)_6]$ (d) $[Mn(H_2O)_6]^{2+}$

152. Which one of the following is an inner orbital complex as well as diamagnetic in behaviour? (Atomic number: Zn = 30, Cr = 24, Co = 27, Ni = 28)

(a) $[Zn(NH_3)_6]^{2+}$ (b) $[Cr(NH_3)_6]^{3+}$
(c) $[Co(NH_3)_6]^{3+}$ (d) $[Ni(NH_3)_6]^{2+}$

153. Addition of excess aqueous ammonia to a pink coloured aqueous solution of $MCl_2.6H_2O$ (X) and NH_4Cl gives an octahedral complex (Y) in the presence of air. In aqueous solution, complex (Y) behaves as 1 : 3 electrolyte. The reaction of (X) with excess of HCl at room temperature results in the formation of a blue coloured complex (Z). The calculated spin only magnetic moment of (X) and (Z) is 3.87 BM whereas it is zero for complex (Y). Among the following options, which statement is incorrect?

(a) The hybridisation of the central metal ion in (Y) is d^2sp^3.
(b) When (X) and (Z) are in equilibrium at 0°C, the colour of the solution is pink.
(c) (Z) is tetrahedral complex.
(d) Addition of silver nitrate to (Y) gives only two equivalents of silver chloride.

154. What will be the geometry and magnetic moment of the complex $[NiCl_4]^{2-}$?
(a) tetrahedral and 3.87 BM
(b) tetrahedral and 2.82 BM
(c) square planar and 2.82 BM
(d) square planar and 4.89 BM

155. Match each set of hybrid orbitals from List I with complex(es) given in List II.

List I	List II
P. dsp^2	1. $[FeF_6]^{4-}$
Q. sp^3	2. $[Ti(H_2O)_3Cl_3]$
R. sp^3d^2	3. $[Cr(NH_3)_6]^{3+}$
S. d^2sp^3	4. $[FeCl_4]^{2-}$
	5. $[Ni(CO)_4]$
	6. $[Ni(CN)_4]^{2-}$

The correct option is
(a) P →5; Q→4,6; R→2,3; S→1
(b) P→5,6; Q→4; R→3; S→1,2
(c) P→6; Q→4,5 ; R→1; S→2,3
(d) P→4,6; Q→5,6; R→1,2; S→3

156. CN^- is a strong field ligand. This is because
(a) it carries negative charge
(b) it is a pseudohalide
(c) it can accept electrons from metal species
(d) it forms high spin complexes with metal species

157. The increasing order of the crystal field splitting power of some common ligands is
(a) $H_2O < OH^- < Cl^- < F^- < CN^-$
(b) $H_2O < Cl^- < OH^- < CN^- < F^-$
(c) $CN^- < H_2O < OH^- < F^- < Cl^-$
(d) $Cl^- < F^- < OH^- < H_2O < CN^-$

158. Which of the following complexes has the minimum magnitude of Δ_o ?
(a) $[Cr(CN)_6]^{3-}$ (b) $[Co(NH_3)_6]^{3+}$
(c) $[CoCl_6]]^{3-}$ (d) $[Cr(H_2O)_6]^{3+}$

159. Consider the following complexes of manganese
(i) hexaaquamanganese(II) ion
(ii) hexacyanidomanganate(II) ion
The number of electrons present in the e_g set of orbitals in each of the above complexes on the basis of crystal field theory are respectively,
(a) 2,0 (b) 3, 1 (c) 3, 5 (d) 2,1

160. Which of the following configurations of ions has zero CFSE in both strong and weak ligand fields?
(a) d^{10} (b) d^8 (c) d^0 (d) d^4

161. Blue aqueous copper sulfate solution when treated with aqueous potassium fluoride solution, gives a
(a) green solution (b) green precipitate
(c) colourless solution (d) deep blue colour

162. Which of the following coordination entities should be expected to absorb light of lowest frequency?
(a) $[Cr(en)_3]^{3+}$ (b) $[CrCl_6]^{3-}$
(c) $[Cr(NH_3)_6]^{3+}$ (d) $[Cr(CN)_6]^{3-}$

163. Both the complexes of nickel, $[Ni(H_2O)_6]^{2+}$ and $[Ni(CN)_4]^{2-}$ have Ni^{2+}, $3d^8$ configuration but the solution of $[Ni(H_2)_6]^{2+}$ is green while the solution of $[Ni(CN)_4]^{2-}$ is colourless. This is because,
(a) in $[Ni(H_2O)_6]^{2+}$, Ni^{2+} has two unpaired electrons which do not pair up in the presence of the weak H_2O ligands;hence, $d-d$ transition absorbs red light and the complementary light emitted is green
(b) in the case of $[Ni(CN)_4]^{2-}$, due to the presence of strong CN^- ligands, the two unpaired electrons pair up in the 3*d* orbitals and to unpair and excite these electrons, a large amount of energy is required which is not available in the visible region and hence, the complex appears colourless
(c) $[Ni(H_2O)_6]^{2+}$ is coloured due to charge transfer transitions whereas no such transition occurs in $[Ni(CN)_4]^{2-}$ and hence, it is colourless
(d) both (a) and (b)

164. The magnitude of crystal field stabilisation energy (CFSE or Δ_t) in tetrahedral complexes is considerably less than in the octahedral field. This is because
(a) there are only four ligands instead of six making the ligand field only 2/3 the size hence the Δ_t is only 2/3 the size
(b) the direction of the orbitals does not coincide with the direction of the ligands; this reduces the crystal field stabilisation energy (Δ_t) by a further 2/3
(c) both points (a) and (b) are correct
(d) both points (a) and (b) are wrong

165. In an aqueous solution, Cr^{2+} is a stronger reducing agent than Fe^{2+}. This is because
(a) Cr^{2+} ion is more stable than Fe^{2+}
(b) Cr^{3+} ion with a d^3 configuration has a favourable crystal field stabilisation energy
(c) Cr^{3+} has a half-filled configuration and hence is more stable
(d) Fe^{3+} in aqueous solution is more stable than Cr^{3+}
(e) Fe^{2+} ion with d^6 configuration has a favourable crystal field stabilisation energy

166. CO is a stronger ligand than Cl^- because
(a) CO is a neutral molecule
(b) CO has π bonds
(c) CO is poisonous
(d) CO is more reactive

167. Which of the following sequences is correct regarding the field strength of ligands as per the spectrochemical series?
(a) $SCN^- < F^- < CN^- < CO$
(b) $F^- < SCN^- < CN^- < CO$
(c) $CN^- < F^- < CO < SCN^-$
(d) $SCN^- < CO < F^- < CN^-$

168. The crystal field stabilisation energies (CFSE) of high spin and low spin d^6 metal complexes in terms of Δ_o, respectively, are
(a) –0.4 and –2.4 (b) –2.4 and –0.4
(c) –0.4 and 0.0 (d) –2.4 and 0.0

169. The crystal field stabilisation energy (CFSE) and the spin magnetic moment in Bohr Magneton (BM) for the complex $K_3[Fe(CN)_6]$ are, respectively
(a) 0.0 Δ_o and $\sqrt{35}$ BM (b) 2.0 Δ_o and $\sqrt{3}$ BM
(c) 0.4 Δ_o and $\sqrt{24}$ BM (d) 2.4 Δ_o and 0.0 BM

170. Crystal field theory does not explain which of the following properties of coordination compounds?
(a) the covalent character of the bond between the metal and the ligand
(b) magnetic property
(c) colour
(d) structure of coordination compounds

171. Which of the following salts is colourless?
(a) $CdCl_2$ (b) $CuSO_4.5H_2O$
(c) $MnSO_4.7H_2O$ (d) $NiSO_4.7H_2O$

172. For transition metal octahedral complexes, (the choice given below) low spin electronic configuration arises only for
(a) d^1 to d^3 complexes (b) d^4 to d^7 complexes
(c) d^7 to d^9 complexes (d) d^1, d^2 to d^8 complexes

173. The crystal field splitting energy for tetrahedral (Δ_t) and octahedral Δ_o complexes is related as
(a) $\Delta_t = -\frac{1}{2}\Delta_o$ (b) $\Delta_t = -\frac{4}{9}\Delta_o$ (c) $\Delta_t = -\frac{3}{5}\Delta_o$
(d) $\Delta_t = -\frac{2}{5}\Delta_o$ (e) $\Delta_t = -\frac{9}{4}\Delta_o$

174. Which of the following is false for tetrahedral complexes?
(a) low spin (b) high spin
(c) d–d transition (d) coloured

175. Among the following, the coloured compound is
(a) CuCl (b) $K_3[Cu(CN)_4]$
(c) CuF_2 (d) $[Co(CH_3(CN)_4BF_4]$

176. Which of the following compounds is coloured?
(a) $TiCl_3$ (b) $FeCl_3$
(c) $CoCl_2$ (d) all of these

177. Which of the following statements is correct?
(a) $[Cu(NH_3)_6]^{2+}$ is a colourless ion.
(b) $[Zn(H_2O)_6]^{2+}$ ion is blue coloured.
(c) $[Ni(CN)_4]^{2-}$ ion has a tetrahedral shape.
(d) Nickel dimethylglyoximate is red in colour.

178. Which of the following configurations can undergo distortion?
(a) $t_{2g}^6 e_g^1$ (b) $t_{2g}^6 e_g^2$ (c) $t_{2g}^6 e_g^4$ (d) $t_{2g}^6 e_g^0$

179. According to the crystal field theory, the M–L bond in a complex is
(a) purely ionic (b) purely coordinate
(c) purely covalent (d) partially covalent

180. Which of the following is the correct configuration of the complex $[RhCl_6]^{3-}$?
(a) high spin $t_{2g}^4 e_g^2$ (b) low spin $t_{2g}^6 e_g^0$
(c) low spin $t_{2g}^3 e_g^3$ (d) high spin $t_{2g}^5 e_g^1$

181. Identify the correct increasing order of the crystal field stabilisation energy values for the given complexes.
(a) $[Ir(NH_3)_6]^{3+} < [Rh(NH_3)_6]^{3+} < [Co(NH_3]^{3+}$
(b) $[Rh(NH_3)_6]^{3+} < [Co(NH_3]^{3+} < [Ir(NH_3)_6]^{3+}$
(c) $[Co(NH_3]^{3+} < [Ir(NH_3)_6]^{3+} < [Rh(NH_3)_6]^{3+}$
(d) $[Co(NH_3]^{3+} < [Rh(NH_3)_6]^{3+} < [Ir(NH_3)_6]^{3+}$

182. The effective atomic number of Cr (atomic no. 24) in $[Cr(NH_3)_6] Cl_3$ is
(a) 35 (b) 27 (c) 33 (d) 36

183. The metal ion in complex A has an EAN identical to the atomic number of krypton. A is
(atomic number of Cr = 24, Fe = 26, Pd = 46)
(a) $[Pd(NH_3)_6]Cl_4$ (b) $[Cr(NH_3)_5Cl]SO_4$
(c) $Na_4[Fe(CN)_6]$ (d) $K_3[Fe(CN)_6]$

184. Which of the following pairs is not correctly matched?
(a) Effective atomic number of Pt in $[PtCl_6]^{2-}$ = 84
(b) Absorption peak for $[Cr^{III}(NH_3)_6]^{3+}$ = 21680 cm^{-1}
(c) Crystal field stabilisation energy of d^2 in weak ligand field = (–) 0.8 Δ_o

(d) Example of weak ligand field for d^5 configuration = $[Mn^{II}F_6]^{-4}$

185. In $[Ni(NH_3)_4]SO_4$, the EAN of Ni is

(a) 34 (b) 35 (c) 36 (d) 37

186. The EAN of iron in potassium ferricyanide is

(a) 18 (b) 54 (c) 35 (d) 23

187. Pick out the complex compound in which the central metal atom obeys EAN rule strictly

(a) $K_4[Fe(CN)_6]$ (b) $K_3[Fe(CN)_6]$
(c) $[Cr(H_2O)_6]Cl_3$ (d) $[Cu(NH_3)_4]SO_4$

188. The oxidation state and effective atomic number (EAN) of cobalt in $[CoF_6]^{2-}$ are, respectively

(a) 3 and 36 (b) 4 and 35
(c) 4 and 37 (d) 2 and 35

189. If the effective atomic number (EAN) of $[A(NH_3)_6]Cl_3$ is 33, the atomic number of the element (A) will be

(a) 23 (b) 27 (c) 24 (d) 29

190. Which of the following will exhibit maximum ionic conductivity?

(a) $K_4[Fe(CN)_6]$ (b) $[Co(NH_3)_6]Cl_3$
(c) $[Cu(NH_3)_4]Cl_2$ (d) $[Ni(CO)_4]$

191. The colour of $CoCl_3.5NH_3.H_2O$ is

(a) orange yellow (b) orange
(c) pink (d) violet

192. The number of chloride ions produced by the complex tetramminechloroplatinum(IV) chloride in an aqueous solution is

(a) four (b) two (c) one
(d) three (e) none

193. The compound $PtCl_4.2HCl$ gives no precipitate with excess of $AgNO_3$ solution. The primary and secondary valencies of the metal in the compound are respectively,

(a) +4, 6 (b) +2, 4 (c) +4, 4 (d) +2, 6

Stability of Coordination Compounds

194. For the reactions and their equilibrium constants given below

$CuCl_4^{2-} + Br^- \rightleftharpoons CuCl_3Br^{2-} + Cl^- \ldots K_1$
$CuCl_3Br^{2-} + \rightleftharpoons CuCl_2Br_3^{2-} + Cl^- \ldots K_2$
$CuCl_2Br_2^{2-} + Br^- \rightleftharpoons CuClBr_3^{2-} + Cl^- \ldots K_3$
$CuClBr_3^{2-} + Br^- \rightleftharpoons CuBr_2^{2-} + Cl^- \ldots K_4$

the equilibrium constant, K, for the reaction is,

$CuCl_4^{2-} + Br^- \rightleftharpoons CuCl_3Br^{2-} + 3Cl^-$

(a) $K_1 K_2 K_3$ (b) $K_1K_2K_3K_4$
(c) $K_1 + K_2 + K_3$ (d) $1/(K_1 K_2 K_3)$

195. The most stable complex among the following is

(a) $[Pd(CN)_4]^{2-}$ (b) $[Fe(CO)_5]$
(c) $[Ni(CN)_4]^{4-}$ (d) $[Ni(CN)_4]^{3-}$

196. Which of the following complexes has the highest stability constant at 298 K?

(a) $[CdCl_4]^{2-}$ (b) $[CdBr_4]^{2-}$
(c) $[CdI_4]^{2-}$ (d) $[Cd(CN)_4]^{2-}$

197. How many EDTA (ethylenediaminetetraacetic acid) molecules are required to make an octahedral complex with a Ca^{2+} ion?

(a) six (b) three (c) one (d) two

198. Silver sulfide dissolves in a solution of sodium cyanide to form the complex

(a) $Na[Ag(CN)_2]$ (b) $Na_3[Ag(CN)_4]$
(c) $Na_5[Ag(CN)_6]$ (d) $Na[Ag(CN)_2]$

199. $Ag^+ + NH_3 \rightleftharpoons [Ag(NH_3)]^+$

$k_1 = 3.5\times10^{-3}$

$[Ag(NH_3)]^+ + NH_3 \rightleftharpoons [Ag(NH_3)_2]^+$

$k_2 = 1.7\times10^{-3}$

then the formation constant of $[Ag(NH_3)_2]^+$ is

(a) 5.95×10^{-6} (b) 6.08×10^{6}
(c) 6.08×10^{-7} (d) none of these

200. In the process of extraction of gold,

Roasted gold ore + $CN^- + H_2O \xrightarrow{O_2} [X] + OH^-$ [X] + Zn → [Y] + Au

(a) $X = [Au(CN)_2]^-, Y = [Zn(CN)_4]^{2-}$
(b) $X = [Au(CN)_4]^{3-}, Y = [Zn(CN)_4]^{2-}$
(c) $X = [Au(CN)_2]^-, Y = [Zn(CN)_6]^{4-}$
(d) $X = [Au(CN)_4]^-, Y = [Zn(CN)_4]^{2-}$

201. Which of the following factors tends to increase the stability of metal ion complexes?

(a) higher ionic radius of the metal ion
(b) higher charge/size ratio of the metal ion
(c) lower ionisation potential of the metal ion
(d) lower basicity of the ligand

202. A complex salt can be made by the combination of $[Co^{III}(NH_3)_5Cl]^x$ with

(a) PO_4^3 (b) Cl^- (c) $2\ Cl^-$ (d) $2\ K^+$

203. Aqueous $CuSO_4 \xrightarrow[\text{Aqueous KCN}]{\text{Excess}} A \xrightarrow{H_2S(g)} B$

A and B are respectively

(a) $K_3[Cu(CN)_4]$, no precipitate
(b) $K_2[Cu(CN)_4]$, no precipitate
(c) $K_4[Cu(CN)_6]$, white precipitate
(d) $K_2[Cu(CN)_4]$, black precipitate

204. Which of the following is the correct Irving–Williams order of metal ions for the stability of their complexes?
(a) $Mn^{2+} < Fe^{2+} < Co^{2+} < Ni^{2+}$
(b) $Ni^{2+} < Co^{2+} < Fe^{2+} < Mn^{2+}$
(c) $Fe^{2+} < Mn^{2+} < Ni^{2+} < Co^{2+}$
(d) $Co^{2+} < Mn^{2+} < Ni^{2+} < Fe^{2+}$

205. 'Class a' acceptors forming their most stable complexes with ligands containing N, O or F donor atoms are the metal ions belonging to
(a) groups 1 and 2
(b) inner transition elements
(c) transition elements belonging to group 3 to 6
(d) all the above (a), (b) and (c)

206. The most stable complex among the following is
(a) $K_3[Al(C_2O_4)_3]$ (b) $[Pt(en)_2]Cl_2$
(c) $[Ag(NH_3)_2]Cl$ (d) $K_2[Ni(EDTA)]$

207. In aqueous solution, $[Co(H_2O)_6]^{2-}$ (X) reacts with molecular oxygen in the presence of excess liquor NH_3 to give a new complex (Y). The number of unpaired electrons in (X) and (Y) are, respectively
(a) 3, 1 (b) 3, 0 (c) 3, 3 (d) 7, 0

Organometallic Compounds

208. Which one is an organometallic compound among the following?
(a) C_2H_5ONa (b) C_2H_5–S–S–C_2H_5
(c) $Al_2(CH_3)_6$ (d) $Al(C_6H_5S)_3$

209. Which of the following is an organometallic compound?
(a) $Ti(C_2H_5)_4$ (b) $Ti(OC_2H_5)_4$
(c) $Ti(OCOCH_3)_4$ (d) $Ti(OC_6H_5)_4$

210. CH_3MgI is an organometallic compound due to
(a) Mg–I bond (b) C–I bond
(c) C–Mg bond (d) C–H bond

211. The ligand called π-acid is
(a) CO (b) NH_3
(c) $C_2O_4^{2-}$ (d) ethylenediamine

212. Among the following which is not the api-bonded organometallic compound?
(a) $K[PtCl_3(\eta^2\text{-}C_2H_4)]$ (b) $Fe(\eta^5\text{-}C_5H_5)_2$
(c) $Cr(\eta^6\text{-}C_6H_6)_2$ (d) $(CH_3)_4Sn$

213. Among the following, the π-acid ligand is
(a) F^- (b) NH_3 (c) CN^- (d) I^-

214. The π-bonded organometallic compound which has ethane as one of its components is
(a) Zeise's salt (b) ferrocene
(c) dibenzene chromium (d) tetraethyl tin

215. Which of the following is a π-complex?
(a) trimethyl aluminium (b) ferrocene
(c) diethyl zinc (d) nickel carbonyl

216. The formula of ferrocene is
(a) $[Fe(CN)_6]^{4-}$ (b) $[Fe(CN)_6]^{3-}$
(c) $[Fe(CO)_5]$ (d) $[(C_5H_5)_2Fe]$

217. π-bonding is not present in
(a) Grignard reagent (b) dibenzene chromium
(c) Zeise's salt (d) ferrocene

218. Which of the following organometallic compounds is sigma and pi-bonded?
(a) $[Fe(\eta^5\text{-}C_5H_5)_2]$ (b) $[PtCl_3(\eta^2\text{-}C_2H_4)]$
(c) $[Co(CO)_5NH_3]^{2+}$ (d) $Al(CH_3)_3$

219. The number of sigma and pi bonds in the following compound respectively are

(NC)(NC)C=C($M(CO)_3$)(C_2H_5)

(a) 19, 11 (b) 19, 5
(c) 13, 11 (d) 7, 3

220. In the metal carbonyls of the general formula $M(CO)_x$ where M = metal : $x = 4$, the metal is bonded to?
(a) carbon and oxygen (b) carbon
(c) oxygen (d) C–O triple bond

221. Which of the following is the correct value of n in $Cr(CO)_n$?
(a) 2 (b) 4 (c) 6 (d) 0

222. The oxidation state of cobalt in the following molecule is

$(OC)_3Co(\mu\text{-}CO)_2Co(CO)_3$

(a) 3 (b) 1 (c) 2 (d) 0

223. In $Ni(CO)_4$, the nickel atom is ________ hybridised.
(a) sp^2 (b) sp^3 (c) dsp^2 (d) sp^3d

224. The non-existent metal carbonyl among the following is
(a) $Cr(CO)_6$ (b) $Mn(CO)_5$
(c) $Ni(CO)_4$ (d) $Fe(CO)_5$

225. In metal carbonyl (organometallic) complexes, the M–C bond is
(a) ionic (b) covalent with ionic character
(c) covalent (d) coordinate covalent

226. The metal which does not form a polynuclear carbonyl is

(a) Mn (b) Co (c) Cr (d) Fe

227. In which compound is synergic effect present?

(a) $[Ni(CO)_4]$ (b) $[NiCl_4]^{2-}$

(c) $[CuCl_4]^{2-}$ (d) $[Mn(H_2O)_6]^{2+}$

228. What is the EAN of nickel in $Ni(CO)_4$?

(a) 34 (b) 35 (c) 32 (d) 36

229. Which of the following statements is not true for metal carbonyls?

(a) The oxidation state of the metal in the carbonyls is zero.

(b) The secondary carbonyls are obtained from photodecomposition.

(c) Metal carbonyls are single bonded species.

(d) $d\pi - d\pi$ overlap is observed in meta carbonyls.

230. What is the shape of $Fe(CO)_5$?

(a) linear (b) tetrahedral

(c) square planar (d) trigonal bipyramidal

231. Chromium hexacarbonyl is an octahedral compound involving ______ hybridisation.

(a) sp^3d^2 (b) dsp^2 (c) d^2sp^3 (d) d^3sp^2

232. In $Fe(CO)_5$, the Fe–C bond possesses

(a) π-character only (b) both σ and π character

(c) ionic character (d) σ-character only

233. Among the following metal carbonyls, the C–O bond order is the lowest in

(a) $[Mn(CO)_6]^+$ (b) $[Fe(CO)_5]$

(c) $[Cr(CO)_6]$ (d) $[V(CO)_6]^-$

234. $Fe_2(CO)_9$ contains which of the following?

(a) only Fe–Fe bond

(b) only three bridging carbonyl groups

(c) both Fe–Fe bond and three bridging carbonyl groups

(d) two bridging carbonyl groups but no Fe–Fe bond

235. The incorrect statement(s) regarding the binary transition metal carbonyl compounds is(are),

(Atomic numbers: Fe = 26, Ni = 28)

(a) The total number of valence shell electrons at the metal centre in $[Fe(CO)_5]$ or $Ni(CO)_4$ is 16.

(b) These are predominantly low spin in nature.

(c) The metal–carbon bond strengthens when the oxidation state of the metal is lowered.

(d) the carbonyl C–O bond weakens when the oxidation state of the metal is increased.

236. Wilkinson's catalyst, used as a homogeneous catalyst in the hydrogenation of alkenes, contains

(a) iron (b) aluminium

(c) rhodium (d) cobalt

237. Which of the following is considered to be an anticancer species?

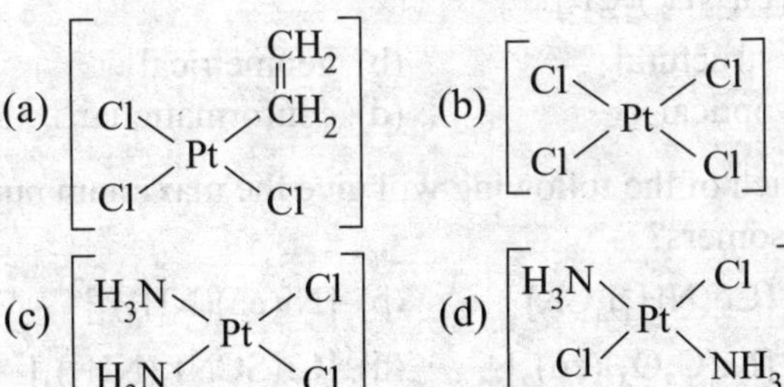

238. Which ligand is useful for the removal of the toxic effect of lead metal in the body during chelate therapy treatment?

(a) COO^-–COO^- (b) CH_3COO^-

(c) $^-OOC{\cdot}H_2C$, $^-OOC{\cdot}H_2C$ $\ddot{N}-CH_2CH_2-\ddot{N}$ $CH_2{\cdot}COO^-$, $CH_2{\cdot}COO^-$

(d) AsO_4^{3-}

239. Coordination compounds have great importance in biological systems. In this context which of the following statements is incorrect?

(a) Cyanocobalamin is vitamin B_{12} and contains cobalt.

(c) Hemoglobin is the red pigment of blood and contains iron.

(c) Chlorophyll is the green pigment in plants and contains calcium.

(d) Carboxypeptidase-A is an enzyme and contains zinc.

240. In any ferric salt, on adding potassium ferrocyanide, a Prussian blue colour is obtained which is due to the formation of

(a) $K_3[Fe(CN)_6]$ (b) $KFe^{III}[Fe^{II}(CN)_6]$

(c) $Fe_4[Fe(CN)_6]_3$ (d) both (b) and (c)

241. Dimethyl glyoxime gives a red precipitate with Ni^{2+}, which is used for its detection. To get this precipitate readily, the best pH range is

(a) < 1 (b) 2.3 (c) 3–4 (d) 9–11

242. Which of the following reagents is commonly used for the detection of sulfide ion?

(a) 1-nitroso-2-naphthol

(b) potassium ferricyanide

(c) disodium hydrogen phosphate

(d) sodium nitroprusside

Final Preparation

243. The complex $[Pt(Py)(NH_3)BrCl)]$ will have how many geometrical isomers?

(a) 3 (b) 4 (c) 0 (d) 2

244. Which one amongst the following isomerisms is shown by $[Pt(NH_3)_2Cl_2]$?

(a) structural (b) geometrical
(c) optical (d) conformational

245. Which of the following will give the maximum number of isomers?

(a) $[Co(NH_3)_4Cl_2]$ (b) $[Ni(en)(NH_3)_4]^{2+}$
(c) $[Ni(C_2O_4)(en)_2]$ (d) $[Cr(SCN)_2(NH_3)_4]^+$

246. In which of the following pairs do both the complexes show optical isomerism?

(a) *cis*-$[Cr(C_2O_4)_2Cl_2]^{3-}$, *cis*-$[Co(NH_3)_4Cl_2]$
(b) $[Co(en)_3]Cl_3$, *cis*-$[Co(en)_2Cl_2]Cl$
(c) $[PtCl(dien)Cl]$, $[NiCl_2Br_2]^{2-}$
(d) $[Co(NO_3)_3(NH_3)_3]$, *cis*-$[Pt(en)_2Cl_2]$

247. Which of the following does not show optical isomerism?

(a) $[Co(NH_3)_3Cl_3]^0$ (b) $[Co(en)Cl_2(NH_3)_2]^+$
(c) $[Co(en)_3]^{3+}$ (d) $[Co(en)_2Cl_2]^+$

248. The existence of two different coloured complexes with the composition of $[Co(NH_3)_4Cl_2]^+$ is due to

(a) ionisation isomerism
(b) linkage isomerism
(c) geometrical isomerism
(d) coordination isomerism

249. $[CoCl_2(NH_3)_4]^{3+} + Cl^- \rightarrow [CoCl_3(NH_3)_3] + NH_3$
In the reaction, only one isomer of the complex product is obtained. The initial complex is

(a) the *cis*-isomer
(b) the *trans*-isomer
(c) not having stereoisomers
(d) neither *cis*-not *trans*-

250. The number of possible isomers for the complex $[Co(en)_2Cl_2]Cl$ will be (en = ethylenediamine)

(a) 2 (b) 1 (c) 3 (d) 4

251. Which of the following will give a pair of enantiomorphs?

(a) $[Pt(NH_3)_4][PtCl_6]$ (b) $[Co(NH_3)_4Cl_2]NO_2$
(c) $[Cr(NH_3)_6][Co(CN)_6]$ (d) $[Co(en)_2Cl_2]Cl$

252. Consider the following arrangement of the octahedral complex ion $[Co(NH_3)_4Cl_2]^+$.

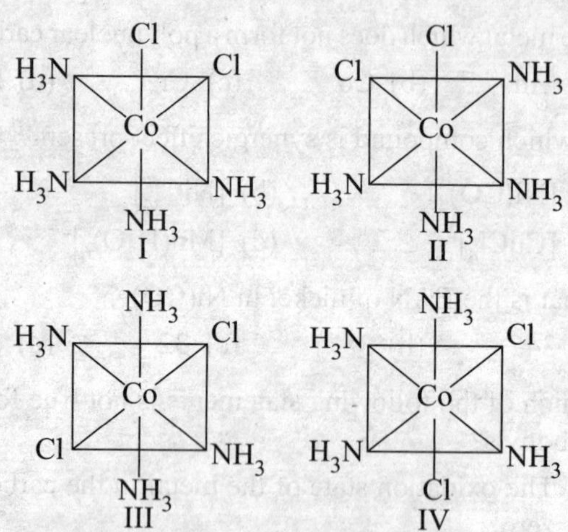

Which of the following statements is false?

(a) II and III are the *cis* and *trans*-isomers respectively.
(b) III and IV are the *trans* and *cis*-isomers respectively.
(c) I and II are enantiomers.
(d) All are identical.

253. The total number of ions produced by Tollen's reagent on ionisation are

(a) 2 (b) 3 (c) 0 (d) 4

254. When $AgNO_3$ is added to a solution of $Co(NH_3)_5Cl_3$, the precipitate of AgCl shows two ionisable chloride ions. This means:

(a) two chlorine atoms satisfy the primary valency and one secondary valency
(b) one chlorine atom satisfies the primary as well as secondary valency
(c) three chlorine atoms satisfy the primary valency
(d) three chlorine atoms satisfy the primary valency

255. An excess of $AgNO_3$ is added to 100 mL of 0.01 M solution of dichlorotetraquachromium(III) chloride. The number of mol of AgCl precipitated would be

(a) 0.001 (b) 0.002 (c) 0.003 (d) 0.01

256. The correct order of the stoichiometries of AgCl formed when $AgNO_3$ in excess is treated with the complexes: $CoCl_3.6NH_3$, $CoCl_3.5NH_3$, $CoCl_3.4NH_3$ respectively is

(a) 3 AgCl, 1 AgCl, 2 AgCl
(b) 3 AgCl, 2 AgCl, 1 AgCl
(c) 2 AgCl, 3 AgCl, 2 AgCl
(d) 1 AgCl, 3 AgCl, 2 AgCl

257. The deep blue complex of the cuprammonium ion $[Cu(NH_3)_4]^{2+}$ obtained when excess ammonia is added to $CuSO_4$ solution is

(a) tetrahedral and paramagnetic
(b) tetrahedral and diamagnetic
(c) square planar and paramagnetic
(d) square planar and diamagnetic

258. Which of the following complexes has a shape different from the others?

(a) $[Zn(NH_3)_4]^{2+}$ (b) $[Ni(CO)_4]$
(c) $[Cu(CN)_4]^{3-}$ (d) $[Cu(NH_3)_4]^{2+}$

259. Which of the these statements about $[Co(CN)_6]^{3-}$ is true?

(a) $[Co(CN)_6]^{3-}$ has four unpaired electrons and will be in a high spin configuration.
(b) $[Co(CN)_6]^{3-}$ has no unpaired electrons and will be in a high spin configuration.
(c) $[Co(CN)_6]^{3-}$ has no unpaired electrons and will be in a low spin configuration.
(d) $[Co(CN)_6]^{3-}$ has four unpaired electrons and will be in a low spin configuration.

260. Among $[Ni(CO)_4]$, $[Ni(CN)_4]^{2-}$, $[NiCl_4]^{2-}$ species, the hybridisation states at the Ni atom are, respectively

(a) sp^3, dsp^2, dsp^2 (b) sp^3, dsp^2, sp^3
(c) sp^3, sp^3, dsp^2 (d) dsp^2, sp^3, sp^3
[Atomic number of Ni = 28]
(a) A–2, B–4, C–5, D–1, E–3
(b) A–5, B–4, C–1, D–3, E–2
(c) A–1, B–3, C–4, D–2, E–5
(d) A–4, B–5, C–2, D–1, E–3
(e) A–4, B–2, C–5, D–3, E–1

261. Which one of the following is an inner orbital complex as well as diamagnetic in behaviour?

(a) $[Zn(NH_3)_6]^{2+}$ (b) $[Ni(NH_3)_6]^{2+}$
(c) $[Cr(NH_3)_6]^{3+}$ (d) $[Co(NH_3)_6]^{3+}$
(Atomic number: Zn = 30, Cr = 24, Co = 27, Ni = 28)

262. $[Fe(CN)_6]^{3-}$ ion has a magnetic moment of 1.73 BM while $[Fe(H_2O)_6]^{3+}$ has a magnetic moment of 5.92 BM. Thus, hybridisation of Fe in both the complexes are respectively

(a) d^2sp^3, sp^3d^2 (b) sp^3d^2, d^2sp^3
(c) d^2sp^3, d^2sp^3 (d) sp^3d^2, sp^3d^2

263. Which of the following complexes exhibits the highest paramagnetic behaviour?

(a) $[V(gly)_2(OH)_2(NH_3)_2]^+$
(b) $[Fe(en)(bpy)(NH_3)_2]^{3+}$
(c) $[Co(ox)_2(OH)_2]^{2-}$
(d) $[Ti(NH_3)_6]^{3+}$

where *gly* = glycine, *en* = ethylenediamine and *bpy* = bipyridyl. (At. nos: Ti = 22, V = 23, Fe = 26, Co = 27)

264. Of the following complex ions, which is diamagnetic in nature?

(a) $[NiCl_4]^{2-}$ (b) $[Ni(CN)_4]^{2-}$
(c) $[CuCl_4]^{2-}$ (d) $[CoF_6]^{3-}$

265. Which of the following complex compounds will exhibit the highest paramagnetic behaviour?

(a) $[Ti(NH_3)_6]^{3+}$ (b) $[Cr(NH_3)_6]^{3+}$
(c) $[Co(NH_3)_6]^{3+}$ (d) $[Zn(NH_3)_6]^{2+}$

266. Pick out the correct statement with respect to $[Mn(CN)_6]^{3-}$.

(a) It is sp^3d^2 hybridised and tetrahedral.
(b) It is d^2sp^3 hybridised and octahedral.
(c) It is dsp^2 hybridised and square planar.
(d) It is sp^3d^2 hybridised and octahedral.

267. The geometry and magnetic behaviour of the complex $[Ni(CO)_4]$ are

(a) square planar geometry and diamagnetic
(b) tetrahedral geometry and diamagnetic
(c) square planar geometry and paramagnetic
(d) tetrahedral geometry and paramagnetic

268. Iron carbonyl, $Fe(CO)_5$ is

(a) tetranuclear (b) mononuclear
(c) trinuclear (d) dinuclear

269. In which of the following octahedral complexes of Co (At. no 27) will the magnitude of Δ_o (CFSE in octahedral field) be the highest?

(a) $[Co(NH_3)_6]^{3+}$ (b) $[Co(CN)_6]^{3-}$
(c) $[Co(C_2O_4)_3]^{3-}$ (d) $[Co(H_2O)_6]^{3+}$

270. Which of the following pairs of *d* electron configurations exhibit both low and high spin octahedral complexes?

(a) d^2, d^3 (b) d^7, d^{10} (c) d^7, d^9 (d) d^5, d^6

271. $[Cr(H_2O)_6Cl_3]$ (At. no. of Cr = 24) has a magnetic moment of 3.83 BM. The correct distribution of 3*d* electrons in the Cr of the complex is

(a) $3d^1_{xy}, 3d^1_{yz}, 3d^1_{xz}$ (b) $3d^1_{xy}, 3d^1_{yz}, 3d^1_{z^2}$
(c) $3d^1_{x^2-y^2}, 3d^1_{z^2}, 3d^1_{xz}$ (d) $3d^1_{xy}, 3d^1_{x^2-y^2}, 3d^1_{yz}$

272. Crystal field stabilisation energy for a high spin d^4 octahedral complex is

(a) $-0.6\,\Delta_o$ (b) $-1.8\,\Delta_o$ (c) $-1.6\,\Delta_o + P$ (d) $-1.2\,\Delta_o$

273. A low spin complex of a d^6 cation in an octahedral field will have the following energy.

(a) $\frac{-2}{5}\Delta_o + 2P$ (b) $\frac{-2}{5}\Delta_o + P$
(c) $\frac{-12}{5}\Delta_o + P$ (d) $\frac{-12}{5}\Delta_o + 3P$

(Δ_0 = crystal field splitting energy in an octahedral field, P = electron pairing energy)

274. Among the following complexes, the one which shows zero crystal field stabilisation energy (CFSE) is

(a) $[Mn(H_2O)_6]^{3+}$ (b) $[Fe(H_2O)_6]^{3+}$
(c) $[Co(H_2O)_6]^{2+}$ (d) $[Co(H_2O)_6]^{3+}$

275. The correct order for the wavelength of absorption in the visible region is

(a) $[Ni(NO_2)_6]^{4-} < [Ni(NH_3)_6]^{2+} < [Ni(H_2O)_6]^{2+}$
(b) $[Ni(NO_2)_6]^{4-} < [Ni(H_2O)_6]^{2+} < [Ni(NH_3)_6]^{2+}$
(c) $[Ni(H_2O)_6]^{2+} < [Ni(NH_3)_6]^{2+} < [Ni(NO_2)_6]^{4-}$
(d) $[Ni(NH_3)_6]^{2+} < [Ni(H_2O)_6]^{2+} < [Ni(NO_2)_6]^{4-}$

276. Correct increasing order for the wavelengths of absorption in the visible region for the complexes of Co^{3+} is

(a) $[Co(H_2O)_6]^{3+}$, $[Co(en)_3]^{3+}$, $[Co(NH_3)_6]^{3+}$
(b) $[Co(H_2O)_6]^{3+}$, $[Co(NH_3)_6]^{3+}$, $[Co(en)_3]^{3+}$
(c) $[Co(NH_3)_6]^{3+}$, $[Co(en)_3]^{3+}$, $[Co(H_2O)_6]^{3+}$
(d) $[Co(en)_3]^{3+}$, $[Co(NH_3)_6]^{3+}$, $[Co(H_2O)_6]^{3+}$

277. An aqueous solution of $[Ni(CN)_4]^{2-}$ is

(a) green (b) blue
(c) yellow (d) colourless

278. Out of TiF_6^{2-}, CoF_6^{3-}, Cu_2Cl_2 and $NiCl_4^{2-}$ (Z of Ti = 22, Co = 27, Cu = 29, Ni = 28), the colourless species are

(a) Cu_2Cl_2 and TiF_6^{2-} (b) TiF_6^{2-} and Cu_2Cl_2
(c) CoF_6^{3-} and $NiCl_4^{2-}$ (d) TiF_6^{2-} and CoF_6^{3-}

279. Which of the following complex ions is expected to absorb visible light?

(a) $[Ti(en)_2(NH_3)_2]^{4+}$ (b) $[Cr(NH_3)_6]^{3-}$
(c) $[Cr(NH_3)_6]^{3+}$ (d) $[Fe(H_2O)_6]^{2+}$

280. Which of the following complex ions is not expected to absorb visible light?

(a) $[Ni(H_2O)_6]^{2+}$ (b) $[Ni(CN)_4]^{2-}$
(c) $[Cr(NH_3)_6]^{3+}$ (d) $[Fe(H_2O)_6]^{2+}$

281. The energy sequence of five d orbitals in a square planar strong ligand field is (assume that the z-axis is perpendicular to the plane of molecule)

(a) $d_{x^2-y^2} > d_{xy} > d_{z^2} > d_{xz} = d_{yz}$

(b) $d_{x^2-y^2} > d_{z^2} > d_{xy} > d_{xz} = d_{yz}$

(c) $d_{z^2} > d_{x^2-y^2} > d_{xy} > d_{xz} = d_{yz}$

(d) none of the above

282. The correct increasing order of the *trans*-effect of the following species is

(a) $NH_3 > CN^- > Br^- > C_6H_5^-$
(b) $CN^- > C_6H_5^- > Br^- NH_3$
(c) $Br^- > CN^- > NH_3 > C_6H_5^-$
(c) $CN^- > Br^- > C_6H_5^- > NH_3$

283. An aqueous solution of $CoCl_2$ on addition of excess of conc. HCl turns blue due to the formation of

(a) $[Co(H_2O)_4Cl_2]$ (b) $[Co(H_2O)_2Cl_4]^{2-}$
(c) $[CoCl_4]^{2-}$ (d) $[Co(H_2O)_2Cl_2]$

284. AgCl is dissolved in excess of each of NH_3, KCN and $Na_2S_2O_3$. The products are,

(a) $[Ag(NH_3)_2]^+$, $[Ag(CN)_2]^-$ and $[Ag(S_2O_3)_2]^{3-}$
(b) $[Ag(NH_3)_2]^{2+}$, $[Ag(CN)_2]^{3-}$ and $[Ag(S_2O_3)_2]^{2-}$
(c) $[Ag(NH_3)_4]^{2+}$, $[Ag(CN)_2]^{3-}$ and $[Ag(S_2O_3)_2]^{2-}$
(d) $[Ag(NH_3)_2]^+$, $[Ag(CN)_2]^{3-}$ and $[Ag(S_2O_3)_2]^{3-}$

285. Copper sulfate dissolves in excess of KCN to give

(a) $[Cu(CN)_4]^{2-}$ (b) $Cu(CN)_2$
(c) CuCN (d) $[Cu(CN)_4]^{3-}$

286. Which of the following is an organometallic compound?

(a) lithium methoxide (b) lithium acetate
(c) lithium dimethylamide (d) methyllithium

287. An example of a sigma bonded organometallic compound is

(a) Grignard reagent (b) ferrocene
(c) cobaltocene (d) ruthenocene

288. In $Fe(CO)_5$, the Fe←CO σ bond results by the overlap between the filled *sp* hybrid orbital of the Catom of the CO molecule and a vacant ______ hybrid orbital of Fe.

(a) d^2sp^3 (b) sp^3 (c) dsp^3 (d) dsp^2

289. Which of the following carbonyls will have the strongest C–O bonds?

(a) $[Mn(CO)_6]^+$ (b) $Cr(CO)_6$
(c) $V(CO)_6^-$ (d) $Fe(CO)_6$

290. Which one of the following metal carbonyls is prepared by the direct interaction of finely divided metal with CO?

(a) $V(CO)_6$ (b) $Fe(CO)_5$
(c) $Cr(CO)_6$ (d) $Mn_2(CO)_{10}$

291. Which of the following has a longer C–O bond length? (Free C–O bond length in CO is 1.128 Å)

(a) $[Fe(CO)_4]^{2-}$ (b) $[Mn(CO)_6]^+$
(c) $[Ni(CO)_4$ (d) $[Co(CO)_4]^-$

292. The metals present in chlorophyll, hemoglobin, vitamin B_{12} and carboxypeptidase A (enzyme) are respectively

(a) Fe, Mg, Co and Cu (b) Mg, Fe, Co and Zn
(c) Co, Mg, Fe and Cu (d) none of the above

293. Turnbull's blue is
(a) ferricyanide (b) ferrous ferricyanide
(c) ferrous cyanide (d) ferriferrocyanide

294. The hybridisation, oxidation number of the central metal ion and shape of Wikinson's catalyst are
(a) dsp^2, +1, square planar
(b) sp^3, +4, tetrahedral
(c) sp^3d, +2, trigonal bipyramidal
(d) d^2sp^3, +6, octahedral

295. A red precipitate is obtained when an ethanolic solution of dimethylglyoxime is added to ammoniacal Ni(II). Which of the following statements is not true?
(a) The red complex has a square planar geometry.
(b) The complex has symmetrical H-bonding.
(c) The red complex has a tetrahedral geometry.
(d) Dimethyglyoxime functions as a bidentate ligand.

dimethylglyoxime = $\left[\begin{array}{l} H_3C-C=N-OH \\ \quad\;\;\; | \\ H_3C-C=N-OH \end{array}\right]$

296. An organometallic compound used in the purification of metals is
(a) $Ni(CO)_4$ (b) $Pb(C_2H_5)_4$
(c) LiC_4H_9 (d) $Na_2[Ni(CN)_4]$

297. In the silver plating of copper, $K[Ag(CO)_2]$ is used instead of $AgNO_3$. The reason is
(a) a thin layer of Ag is formed on Cu
(b) more voltage is required
(c) Ag^+ ions are completely removed from solution
(d) less availability of Ag^+ ions, as Cu cannot displace Ag from the $[Ag(CN)_2]^-$ ion

298. Which one of the following complex compounds is used to treat lead poisoning?
(a) cisplatin (b) EDTA complex of calcium
(c) $Fe(CO)_5$ (d) $[(Ph_3P)_3RhCl]$

299. Which of the following acts as a ligand but does not possess any unshared pair of electrons?
(a) C_2H_4 (b) NH_3 (c) *en* (d) CN^-

300. Which of the following statements is wrong?
(a) Hydrazine possesses two electron pairs for donation.
(b) Hydrazine does not act as a chelating agent.
(c) Due to the presence of two donor N-atoms, hydrazine forms a stable chelate with metal ions.
(d) Coordination by hydrazine leads to a three membered highly unstable strained ring.

301. The sum of the coordination number and oxidation number of the metal M in the complex $[M(en)_2(C_2O_4)]Cl$ (where en is enthylene-diamine) is
(a) 9 (b) 6 (c) 7 (d) 8

302. The correct name for the complex ion $[Co(en)_2Cl(ONO)]^+$ is
(a) cobaltdiethylene diamine chloronitrate
(b) chlorodiethyldiaminenitrito cobalt (III)
(c) chloronitritodiethyldiamine cobalt (III)
(d) chloridobis(ethylenediamine)nitritocobalt(III) ion

303. The IUPAC name of $K_3[Ir(C_2O_4)_3]$ is
(a) potassium trioxalatoridium (III)
(b) potassium trioxalatoiridate(III)
(c) potassium tris(oxalate)iridium (III)
(d) potassium tris(oxalate)iridate (III)

304. According to IUPAC nomenclature, sodium nitroprusside is named as
(a) sodium nitroferricyanide
(b) sodium nitroferrocyanide
(c) sodium pentacyanonitrosylferrate (II)
(d) Sodium pentacyanonitrosoniumferrate(II)

305. A solution containing 0.319 g of $CrCl_6.6H_2O$ was passed through a cation exchange resin and acid coming out of the cation exchange resin required 28.5 mL of 0.125 M NaOH. Determine the correct formula of the complex [mol. wt. of the complex = 266.5 g]
(a) $[Cr(H_2O)_6]Cl_3$ (b) $[Cr(H_2O)_5Cl]H_2O.Cl_2$
(c) $[Cr(H_2O)_4Cl_2]Cl.H_2O$ (d) $Cr(H_2O)_3Cl_3]_3H_2O$

306. The hybridisation state of Fe in $[Fe(H_2O)_5NO]SO_4$ is (At. no. of Fe = 26]
(a) dsp^2 (b) sp^3d (c) sp^3d^2 (d) d^2sp^3

307. Which one of the following complexes is not expected to exhibit isomerism?
(a) $[Ni(NH_3)_4(H_2O)_2]^{2+}$ (b) $[Pt(NH_3)_2Cl_2]$
(c) $[Ni(NH_3)_2Cl_2]$ (d) $[Ni(en)_3]^{2+}$

MATCH THE FOLLOWING

308.

Column I (Complex)	Column II (No. of ions furnished per molecule)
(A) $PtCl_4.6NH_3$	(p) 4
(B) $K_3[Fe(CN)_6]$	(q) 0
(C) $CoCl_3.5H_2O$	(r) 5
(D) $[Cr(NH_3)_3(NO_2)_3]$	(s) 3

(a) (A)—(s); (B)—(p); (C)—(q); (D)—(r)
(b) (A)—(p); (B)—(q); (C)—(r); (D)—(s)
(c) (A)—(r); (B)—(p); (C)—(s); (D)—(q)
(d) (A)—(q); (B)—(r); (C)—(s); (D)—(p)

309.

Column I (Complex)	Column II (ON of metal)
(A) $Ni(CO)_4$	(p) +1
(B) $[Fe(H_2O)_5NO]^{2+}$	(q) Zero
(C) $[Co(CO)_5]^{2-}$	(r) –1
(D) $[Cr_2(CO)_{10}]^{2-}$	(s) –2

(a) (A)—(q); (B)—(p); (C)—(s); (D)—(r)
(b) (A)—(r); (B)—(q); (C)—(p); (D)—(s)
(c) (A)—(s); (B)—(r); (C)—(q); (D)—(p)
(d) (A)—(p); (B)—(s); (C)—(r); (D)—(q)

ASSERTION REASON

Directions: In each of the following questions, a statement of Assertion (A) is given followed by a corresponding statement of Reason (R) just below it. Of the statements, mark the correct answer as

(a) if both the assertion and reason are true and the reason is the correct explanation of the assertion.
(b) if both the assertion and reason are true but the reason is not the correct explanation of the assertion.
(c) if the assertion is true but the reason is false.
(d) if both the assertion and reason are false.

310. Assertion: $[Pt(en)_2Cl_2]^{2+}$ complex ion shows a total of three isomers.

Reason: $[Pt(en)_2Cl_2]^{2+}$ complex ion has an octahedral geometry.

311. Assertion: $[Co(NO_3)_3(NH_3)_3]$ does not show optical isomerism.

Reason: It has a plane of symmetry.

312. Assertion: F^- ion is a weak ligand and forms outer orbital complexes.

Reason: F^- ion cannot force the electrons of the orbitals of the inner shell to occupy the t_{2g} orbitals of the same shell.

313. Assertion: $K_4[Fe(CN)_6]$ is diamagnetic and $[Fe(H_2O)_6]Cl_3$ is paramagnetic.

Reason: Hybridisation of the central metal in $K_4[Fe(CN)_6]$ is d^2sp^3.

314. Assertion: $[Ti(H_2O)_6]^{3+}$ is coloured while $[Sc(H_2O)_6]^{3+}$ is colourless.

Reason: *d–d* transition is not possible in $[Sc(H_2O)_6]^{3+}$.

315. Assertion: $[Cu(NH_3)_4]^{2+}$ is coloured while $[Cu(CN)_4]^{3-}$ ion is colourless.

Reason: $[Cu(NH_3)_4]^{2+}$ has dsp^2 hybridisation.

316. Assertion: $[Ni(en)_3]Cl_2$ (en = ethylene diamine) has a lower stability than $[Ni(NH_3)_6]Cl_2$.

Reason: In $[Ni(en)_3]Cl_2$, the geometry of the complex is trigonal bipyramidal.

317. Assertion: Concentrated aqueous solution of $CuCl_2$ is green in colour.

Reason: The solution contains two complex ions $[Cu(H_2O)_4]^{2+}$and $[CuCl_4]^{2-}$in equilibrium.

318. Assertion: The oxidation state of Fe in $Fe(CO)_5$ is zero.

Reason: The EAN of Fe in the complex is 36.

319. Assertion: CO and $CN^-$are referred to as π-acid ligands.

Reason: In CO and CN^-, vacant π-type orbitals are present.

320. Assertion: Toxic metal ions are removed by the chelating agents.

Reason: Chelate complexes tend to be more stable.

321. Assertion: Glycinate ion is an example of a monodentate ligand.

Reason: It contains N as the only donor atom.

322. Assertion: NF_3 is a weaker ligand than $N(CH_3)_3$.

Reason: NF_3 ionises to give F^- ions in an aqueous solution.

323. Assertion: The oxidation number of platinum in Zeise's salt is +2.

Reason: C_2H_4 ligand carries a –2 charge.

324. Assertion: When NO reacts with $FeSO_4$, a brown-coloured complex is formed.

Reason: In the complex, the coordination number of Fe is 6.

Answer Key

1. (b)	2. (a)	3. (b)	4. (b)	5. (d)	6. (c)	7. (b)	8. (c)	9. (c)	10. (d)
11. (b)	12. (b)	13. (d)	14. (b)	15. (c)	16. (b)	17. (a)	18. (c)	19. (b)	20. (b)
21. (d)	22. (d)	23. (c)	24. (d)	25. (d)	26. (a)	27. (b)	28. (a)	29. (b)	30. (a)
31. (a)	32. (d)	33. (a)	34. (a)	35. (a)	36. (d)	37. (c)	38. (b)	39. (b)	40. (b)
41. (a)	42. (b)	43. (b)	44. (a)	45. (a)	46. (b)	47. (c)	48. (b)	49. (b)	50. (a)
51. (a)	52. (c)	53. (b)	54. (a)	55. (b)	56. (a)	57. (c)	58. (d)	59. (c)	60. (b)
61. (d)	62. (a)	63. (a)	64. (b)	65. (c)	66. (c)	67. (d)	68. (b)	69. (d)	70. (c)
71. (c)	72. (a)	73. (b)	74. (b)	75. (c)	76. (c)	77. (a)	78. (c)	79. (b)	80. (b)
81. (d)	82. (e)	83. (d)	84. (c)	85. (d)	86. (c)	87. (a)	88. (b)	89. (c)	90. (a)
91. (d)	92. (a)	93. (b)	94. (b)	95. (a)	96. (b)	97. (d)	98. (c)	99. (c)	100. (b)
101. (a)	102. (c)	103. (d)	104. (a)	105. (c)	106. (b)	107. (b)	108. (d)	109. (d)	110. (b)
111. (b)	112. (b)	113. (c)	114. (b)	115. (a)	116. (c)	117. (c)	118. (c)	119. (b)	120. (c)
121. (a)	122. (c)	123. (a)	124. (d)	125. (a)	126. (d)	127. (c)	128. (c)	129. (b)	130. (c)
131. (a)	132. (b)	133. (a)	134. (b)	135. (b)	136. (d)	137. (c)	138. (a)	139. (b)	140. (b)
141. (a)	142. (c)	143. (b)	144. (c)	145. (e)	146. (a)	147. (b)	148. (d)	149. (b)	150. (c)
151. (b)	152. (c)	153. (d)	154. (b)	155. (c)	156. (b)	157. (e)	158. (c)	159. (a)	160. (a)
161. (b)	162. (b)	163. (d)	164. (c)	165. (b)	166. (b)	167. (a)	168. (a)	169. (b)	170. (a)
171. (a)	172. (b)	173. (b)	174. (a)	175. (c)	176. (d)	177. (d)	178. (a)	179. (a)	180. (b)
181. (d)	182. (c)	183. (c)	184. (a)	185. (a)	186. (c)	187. (a)	188. (b)	189. (c)	190. (a)
191. (e)	192. (d)	193. (a)	194. (a)	195. (b)	196. (d)	197. (c)	198. (a)	199. (a)	200. (a)
201. (b)	202. (c)	203. (a)	204. (a)	205. (d)	206. (d)	207. (b)	208. (c)	209. (a)	210. (c)
211. (a)	212. (d)	213. (c)	214. (a)	215. (b)	216. (d)	217. (a)	218. (c)	219. (a)	220. (d)
221. (c)	222. (d)	223. (b)	224. (b)	225. (d)	226. (c)	227. (a)	228. (d)	229. (d)	230. (d)
231. (c)	232. (b)	233. (d)	234. (c)	235. (d)	236. (c)	237. (c)	238. (c)	239. (c)	240. (d)
241. (d)	242. (d)	243. (a)	244. (b)	245. (a)	246. (b)	247. (a)	248. (c)	249. (b)	250. (c)
251. (d)	252. (c)	253. (a)	254. (a)	255. (a)	256. (b)	257. (c)	258. (d)	259. (c)	260. (b)
261. (d)	262. (a)	263. (c)	264. (b)	265. (b)	266. (b)	267. (b)	268. (b)	269. (b)	270. (d)
271. (a)	272. (a)	273. (d)	274. (b)	275. (a)	276. (d)	277. (d)	278. (b)	279. (b)	280. (b)
281. (a)	282. (b)	283. (c)	284. (d)	285. (d)	286. (d)	287. (a)	288. (c)	289. (a)	290. (b)
291. (a)	292. (b)	293. (b)	294. (a)	295. (c)	296. (a)	297. (d)	298. (b)	299. (a)	300. (c)
301. (a)	302. (d)	303. (b)	304. (d)	305. (a)	306. (c)	307. (c)	308. (c)	309. (a)	310. (b)
311. (a)	312. (a)	313. (c)	314. (a)	315. (b)	316. (d)	317. (a)	318. (b)	319. (a)	320. (a)
321. (d)	322. (c)	323. (c)	324. (b)						

Hints and Solutions

1. (b): Ferrous ammonium sulfate is a double salt. Other compounds are complexes.

2. (a): Carnallite is a double salt with a molecular formula KCl. $MgCl_2.6H_2O$. It gives K^+, Mg^{2+} and Cl^-

3. (b): $Al_2(SO_4)_3$ and on dissolving, it gives all three ions Al^{3+}, K^+ and SO_4^{2-} of which it is made.

4. (b): According to the Lewis theory of acids and bases, ligands donate electron pairs and thus are bases.

5. (d): Dien is (diethylenetriamine),
$H_2N–CH_2–CH_2–NH–CH_2–CH_2–NH_2$
which is a tridentate ligand.

6. (c): As there are four donor N atoms, $\ddot{N}(CH_2CH_2\ddot{N}H_2)_3$ behaves as a tetradentate ligand.

7. (b): The coordination number of Ca is 6. EDTA is a hexadentate ligand. Hence, Ca can be surrounded by only a single molecule of EDTA.

8. (c): CN of Pt in $[Pt(NH_3)_4Cl_2]Cl_2$ is $4 + 2 = 6$
ON of Pt is $x + (0)\times 4 + (-1)\times 2 + (-1)\times 2 = 0$ or $x = +4$

9. (c): Oxidation number of Ni in $[Ni(C_2O_4)_3]^{4-}$ is,

$x + 3\times(-2) = -4$

$x - 6 = -4$

$x = +2$

10. (d): Pyridine is a monodentate ligand. Pyridine coordinates with a metal only from the N site, that is, the lone pair is on N. Thus, it is a monodentate ligand, while the other three are chelating ligands, that is, these are attached to a central metal ion by bonds from two or more donor atoms.

11. (b): Ethylene diamine (en), $H_2N–CH_2–CH_2–NH_2$ is a bidentate ligand.

12. (b): Lithium tetrahydroaluminate is $LiAl(H)_4$ where the ligand is H^-.

13. (d): Ligands are Lewis bases.

14. (b): $NH_3 + H^+ \rightarrow NH_4^+$ which contains no electron pairs to act as a ligand. Therefore, in acidic medium, ammonia will not form a complex with Cu^{2+}.

15. (c): The structure of EDTA is

$$\begin{matrix} HOOC–CH_2 & & CH_2–COOH \\ & N–CH_2–CH_2–N & \\ HOOC–CH_2 & & CH_2–COOH \end{matrix}$$

16. (b): $x + 0 + (-3) = -1$ or $x = +2$

+6 +7

17. (a): $[H_2EDTA]^{2-} + Mg^{2+} \rightarrow [Mg–EDTA]^{2-} + 2H^+$

(i) In this complex, four donor sites are occupied by oxygen and two donor sites are occupied by nitrogen.

(ii) This complex is six coordinated.

(iii) The complex $[Mg–EDTA]^{2-}$ is colourless.

(iv) Increase in $[H^+]$ decreases the pH of the solution.

18. (c): $2Al + 2NaOH + H_2O \rightarrow \underset{\text{Sodium meta aluminate}}{2NaAlO_2} + 3H_2$

$NaAlO_2 + 4H_2O \rightarrow Na[Al(OH)_4(H_2O)_2]$

Sodium metaaluminate, thus formed, is soluble in water and changes into complex $[Al(H_2O)(OH)_4]^-$, in whichthe coordination number of Al is 6.

19. (b): Ag^+ has a coordination number of two and forms a complex with excess of CN^- as $[Ag(CN)_2]^-$.

20. (b): $Ag_2S + 4NaCN \rightleftharpoons \underset{\text{Sodium dicyanoargentate}}{2Na[Ag(CN)_2]} + Na_2S$

$2Na[Ag(CN_2)] + Zn \rightarrow \underset{\text{Sodium tetracyanozincate (ppt)}}{Na_2[Zn(CN)_4] + 2Ag \downarrow}$

21. (d): $K_4[Fe(CN)_6] \rightarrow 4K^+ + [Fe(CN)_6]^{4-}$

The complex has a negative charge; so, it is an anionic complex.

22. (d): It involves sp^3d^2 hybridisation and not d^2sp^3.

23. (c): $FeSO_4.(NH_4)_2SO_4.6H_2O \rightarrow Fe^{2+} + 2SO_4^{2-} + 2NH_4^+$

24. (d): $4KCN.Fe(CN)_2$ or $K_4[Fe(CN)_6]$ is a complex salt.

25. (d): $CoCl_3.3NH_3$ is $[Co(NH_3)_3Cl_3]$ which gives no Cl^- ions on ionisation.

26. (a): A metal atom in the complex part does not give its test.

27. (b): $[Pt(NH_3)_5Cl]Cl_3$ ionises to $[Pt(NH_3)_5Cl]^{3+}$ and $3Cl^-$ ions giving a total of 4 ions.

28. (a): $K_4[Fe(CN)_6] \rightleftharpoons 4K^+ + [Fe(CN)_6]^{4-}$

On ionisation, a total of five ions are produced which is the maximum. Thus, the solution will show maximum ionic conductivity.

29. (b): The compound $CoCl_3.4NH_3$ is written in the complex form as $[Co(NH_3)_4Cl_2]Cl$ with a coordination number of Co = 6.

In water, the complex ionises as $[Co(NH_3)_4Cl_2]^+ + Cl^-$ thus, giving two ions.

30. (a): Molar conductance is the conducting power of all the ions produced by dissolving 1 g-mol of an electrolyte. Therefore, the molar conductance ∝ number of ions produced.

Werner complex	Modern notation	Ionisation
(a) $CoCl_3 \cdot 3NH_3$	$[Co(NH_3)_3]Cl_3]$	$[Co(NH_3)_3]Cl_3]$ (No ionisation)
(b) $CoCl_3 \cdot 4NH_3$	$[Co(NH_3)_4]Cl_2]Cl$	$[Co(NH_3)_4Cl_2]^+ + Cl^-$ (2 ions)
(c) $CoCl_3 \cdot 5NH_3$	$[Co(NH_3)_5]Cl]Cl_2$	$[Co(NH_3)_5Cl]^{2+} + 2Cl^-$ (3 ions)
(d) $CoCl_3 \cdot 6NH_3$	$[Co(NH_3)_6]Cl_3$	$[Co(NH_3)_6]^{3+} + 3Cl^-$ (4 ions)

From the above table, it is clear that the molar conductance of the complexes will be in the following order $a < b < c < d$.

31. (a): $[CrCl(H_2O)_5]Cl_2 \rightarrow [CrCl(H_2O)_5]^{2+} + 2Cl^-$

$\frac{100 \times 0.01}{1000} = 0.001\text{ mol} = 0.001 \times \text{mol of } Cl^-$

$Ag^+ + Cl^- \rightarrow AgCl$

0.002 mol 0.002 mol

0.001 mol of $[CrCl(H_2O)_5]Cl_2$ gives 0.002 mol of AgCl

∴ Mass of silver chloride = $143.5 \times 0.002 = 0.287$ g

$= 287 \times 10^{-3}$ g

32. (d): The formulae of the given complexes are as follows.

(a) Hexaammineplatinum(IV) chloride $[Pt(NH_3)_6]Cl_4$

(b) Chloropentaammineplatinum(IV) chloride $[Pt(NH_3)_5Cl]Cl_3$

(c) Dichlorotetraammineplatinum(IV) chloride $[Pt(NH_3)_4Cl_2]Cl_2$

(d) Trichlorotriammineplatinum(IV) chloride $[Pt(NH_3)_4Cl_3]Cl$

In aqueous solution, the complexes ionise as

$$[Pt(NH_3)_6]Cl_4 \rightleftharpoons \underbrace{[Pt(NH_3)_6]^{4+} + 4Cl^-}_{\text{5 ions}}$$

$$[Pt(NH_3)_5Cl]Cl_3 \rightleftharpoons \underbrace{[Pt(NH_3)_5Cl]^{3+} + 3Cl^-}_{\text{4 ions}}$$

$$[Pt(NH_3)_4Cl_2]Cl_2 \rightleftharpoons \underbrace{[Pt(NH_3)_4Cl_2]^{2+} + 2Cl^-}_{\text{3 ions}}$$

$$[Pt(NH_3)_3Cl_3]Cl \rightleftharpoons \underbrace{[Pt(NH_3)_3Cl_3]^+ + Cl^-}_{\text{2 ions}}$$

Trichlorotriammineplatinum(IV) chloride gives the minimum number of ions in the solution. Hence, it has the minimum electrical conductivity.

Nomenclature of Coordination Compounds

33. (a): In the complex, Cr is in the +3 oxidation state.

$Cr\ (Z = 24) = 3d^5\,4s^1$

$Cr^{3+} = 3d^3$, there are thus, three unpaired electrons.

$\mu = \sqrt{n(n+2)} = \sqrt{3(3+2)} = \sqrt{15}$

$= 3.87$ BM

The IUPAC name of the complex is potassium diaquadioxalatochromate(III) trihydrate and the magnetic moment is 3.87 BM.

34. (a): The IUPAC name of the complex is chloridobis(ethane-1,2-diamine)nitro-O-cobalt(III) chloride.

35. (a): Aqua regia is a solution containing conc. HCl and conc. HNO_3 in the ratio 3 : 1. It dissolves noble metals like Au and Pt.

$HNO_3 + 3\,HCl \rightarrow 2\,H_2O + 2\,Cl + NOCl$

$Au + 3\,Cl \rightarrow AuCl_3$

$AuCl_3 + HCl \rightarrow \underset{\text{Tetrachloridoauric acid}}{HAuCl_4}$

36. (d): Tetraamminedichloroferric(III) chloride; $[Fe(NH_3)_4Cl_2]$ Cl.

37. (c): The IUPAC name of the complex $[Pt(NH_3)_3Br(NO_2)Cl]Cl$ is triamminebromochloronitroplatinum(IV) chloride. The names of the different ligands are arranged alphabetically.

38. (b): The correct IUPAC name of $[CuCl_2(CH_3NH_2)_2]$ is dichlorobis(methyl amine)copper(II).

39. (b): Potassium tetrachlorocuperate(I).

40. (b): $[Cr(en)_2Br_2]Br$ is named as dibromidobis(ethylenediamine)chromium(III) bromide.

41. (a): $[Co(NH_3)_3(H_2O)_2Cl]Cl_2$.

42. (b): $[CuCl_2\{O{=}C(NH_2)_2\}_2]$

43. (b): $Na_2[Fe(CN)_5NO]$

44. (a): $K_4[Ni(CN)_2(ox)_2]$

45. (a): The most probable complex which gives three mol of ions in aqueous solution may be $[Co(NH_3)_5NO_2]Cl_2$ because it gives two chloride ions on ionisation.

$[Co(NH_3)_5NO_2]Cl_2 \rightarrow [Co(NH_3)_5NO_2]^{2+} + 2\,Cl^-$

46. (b): Mol of $CoCl_3.6NH_3$

$= \frac{2.675}{267.5} = \frac{1}{100}$ mol $= 0.01$ mol

Mol of $AgCl = \frac{4.78}{143.5} = \frac{3}{100}$ mol $= 0.03$ mol

1 mol of compound gives mol of

$AgCl = \frac{0.03}{0.01} = 3$ mol

So, the structural formula of the compound will have 3 Cl^- ions outside the coordination sphere, $[Co(NH_3)_6]Cl_3$.

47. (c): An ambidentate ligand is monodentate but contains two donor atoms.

48. (b): The IUPAC name is mercury tetraisothiocyanatocobaltate(II).

Geometrical Isomerism

49. (b): $[MA_3B_3]$ type of complexes show *fac–mer* geometrical isomerism.

50. (a): Compound (a) is $[CoCl_2(en)_2]^+$ which shows geometrical *cis-* and *trans-* isomerism. The *cis*-isomer is also optically active.

51. (a): There is no symmetrical bidentate ligand present. Hence, it will not show optical isomerism. The geometrical isomers are:

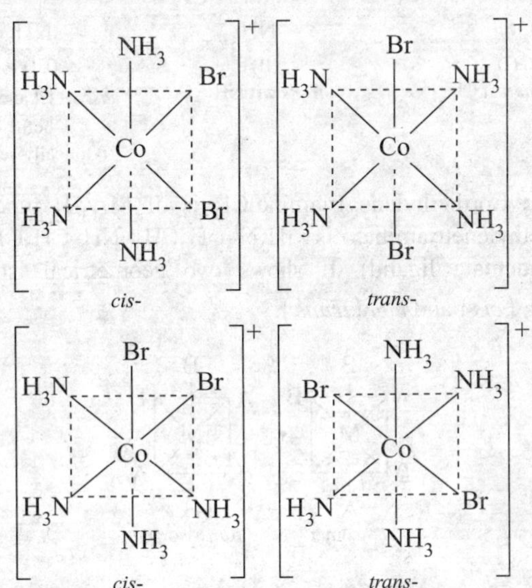

The ionisation isomers of the complex will be $[Co(NH_3)_4Br_2]Cl$ and $[Co(NH_3)_4BrCl]Cl$.

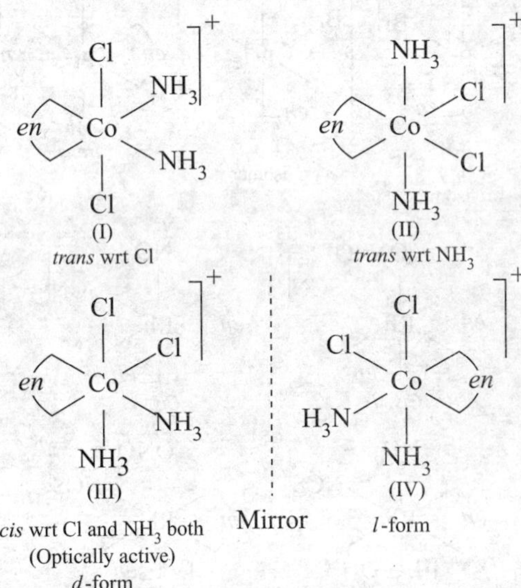

52. (c): A total five isomers are possible as shown below.

(I) (II) (III) (IV) (V)

53. (b): Three geometrical isomers are possible

(I) *trans* wrt Cl | (II) *trans* wrt NH_3 | (III) *cis* wrt Cl and NH_3 both (Optically active)

54. (a): Co(diethylene triamine)Cl_3 is of MA_3B_3 type where diethylenetriamine is $H_2N–CH_2CH_2–NH–CH_2CH_2–NH_2$ (tridentate ligand). It shows two geometrical isomers—*fac* (*cis*) and *mer* (*trans*).

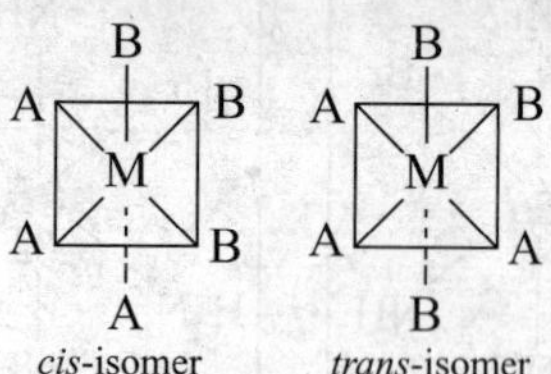

cis-isomer *trans*-isomer

55. (b): $[Pt(en)_2ClBr]^{2+}$ can exist both as diastereoisomers (geometrical) and enantiomers (optical).

Cis (+) *d*-isomer | (–) *l*-isomer | *trans*

I *Cis, d–* | II *Cis, d–* | III *Cis, d–* | IV *Cis, d–*

I to IV each will have further two more isomers—*cis* and *trans* (shown below).

trans– | *trans–* | *trans–* | *trans–*

thus, giving total isomeric forms = 12

56. (a): Facial (*fac*) and meridonal (*mer*) isomerism, a type of geometrical isomerism, is shown by octahedral complexes having a general formula Ma_3b_3, where M is the central metal and a and b are monodentate ligands. Hence, $[Co(NH_3)_3Cl_3]$ exhibits *fac–mer* isomerism.

fac-form | *mer*-form

57. (c): For a [M(a)(b)(c)(d)] square planar complex, the number of possible geometrical isomers is three which is obtained by fixing the position of one of the ligands, say a, while the other ligands b, c and d are placed *trans* to it.

58. (d): $[Pt^{II}(NH_3)_2Cl_2]$ shows geometrical isomerism.

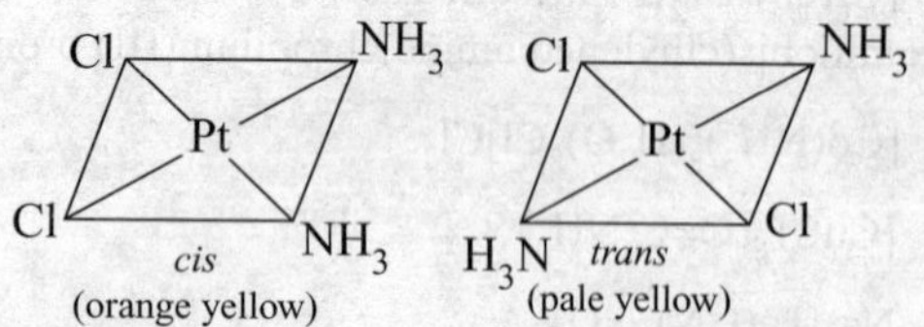

cis (orange yellow) | *trans* (pale yellow)

59. (c): Octahedral complexes of the type MA_4X_2, MA_3X_3, MA_2X_4, $M(AA)_2X_2$, $M(AA)_2XY$ exist as *cis* and *trans* isomers (show geometrical isomerism). Therefore, $M(AA)_3$ cannot exhibit geometrical isomerism.

60. (b):

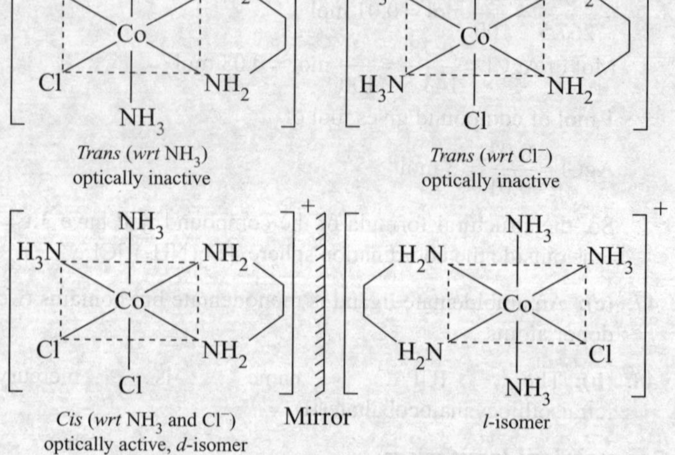

Trans (*wrt* NH_3) optically inactive | *Trans* (*wrt* Cl^-) optically inactive

Cis (*wrt* NH_3 and Cl^-) optically active, *d*-isomer | *l*-isomer

Therefore, the number of geometrical isomers, optical isomers and total number of isomers are 3, 2 and 4 respectively. In this complex, the three ligands are on the same triangular face of the octahedron.

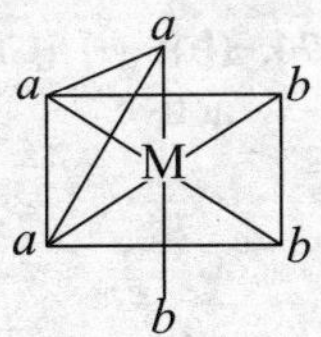

61. (d): $[Co(en)_2Cl_2]^+$ shows geometrical as well as optical isomerism. It has a total of three isomers.

62. (a): The complex shows geometrical as well as ionisation isomerism.

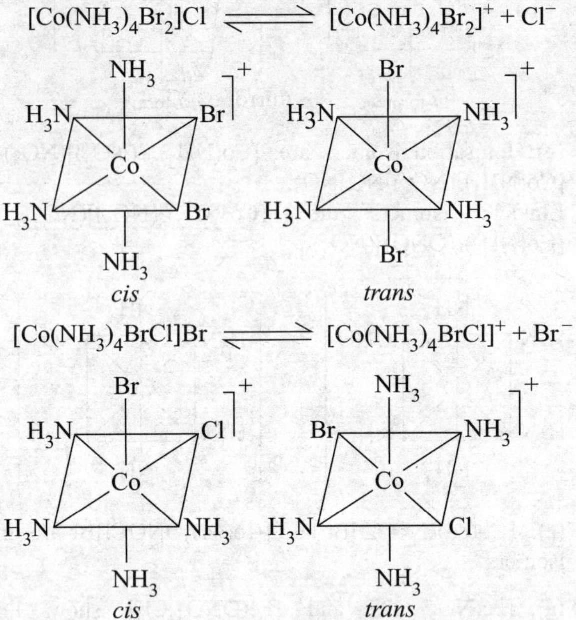

63. (a): Square planar complex of the type M(AXBL) will show two *cis* and one *trans* isomers.

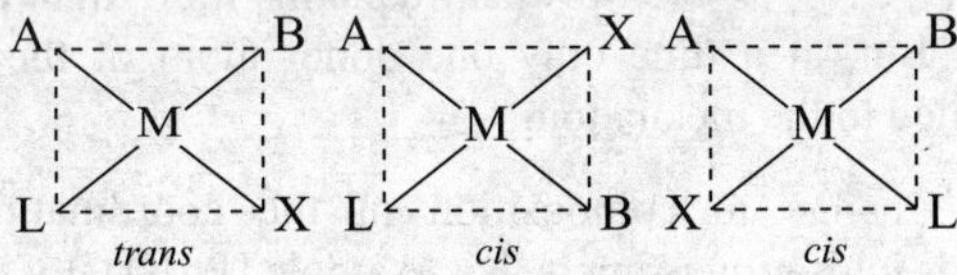

These isomers are formed by fixing the position of one ligand say A while the other ligands are placed trans to it.

64. (b): Case (i): If the reactant complex ion is *cis*, it will give two isomers – *fac* and *mer*– as shown below.

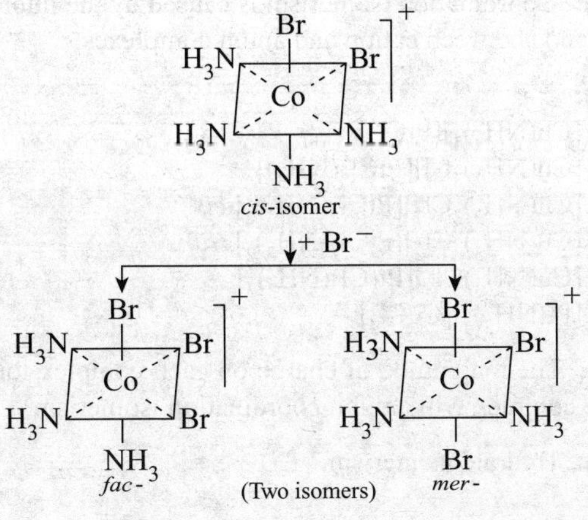

Case (ii): If the reaction complex ion is trans, it will give only one isomer, *mer*, as shown below.

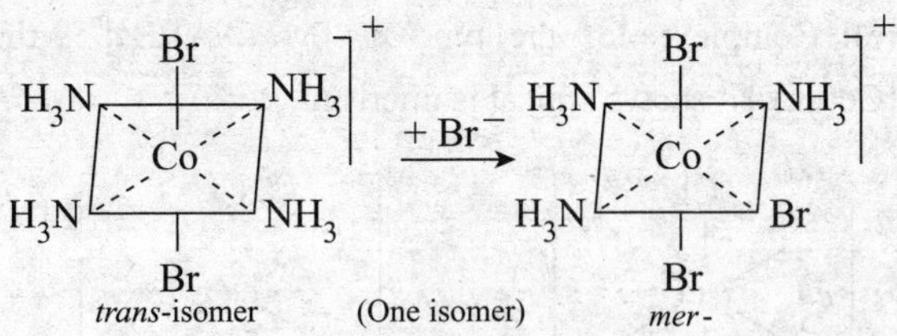

65. (c): $[Co(en)(NH_3)_3(H_2O)]^{3+}$ has two geometrical isomers.

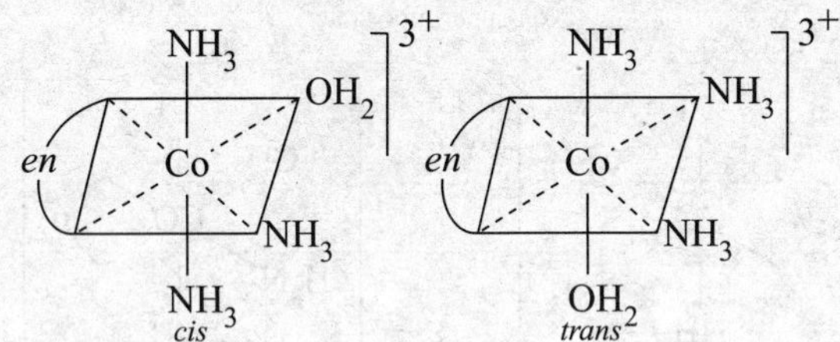

(b) $[Co(CN)_2(NH_3)_3(H_2O)]^+$ will have three geometrical isomers.

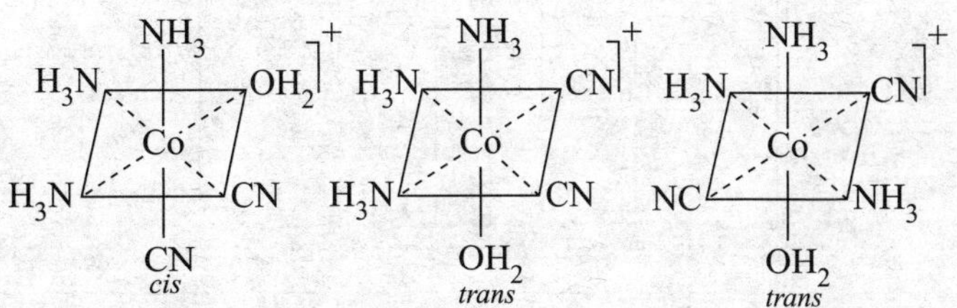

(c) $[Co(en)(NH_3)_3(H_2O)]^{3+}$ contains Co^{3+} = [Ar] $3d^6\,4s^0$ where all the electrons are paired up giving a diamagnetic nature and not paramagnetic.

(d) $[Co(en)(NH_3)_3(H_2O)]^{3+}$ absorbs light at longer wavelengths as compared to $[Co(en)(NH_3)_4]^{3+}$ as H_2O is a weaker ligand than NH_3.

66. (c): The complex of the type $[MA_2B_2C_2]$ shows a total of five geometrical isomers when two A, B and C groups each are in the *cis* and *trans* positions respectively.

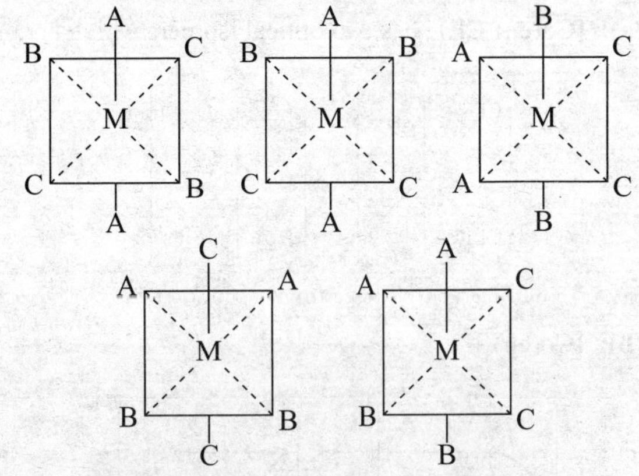

67. (d): The *trans* complex is optically inactive.

68. (b): It is optically active when two Cl atoms are in the *cis* position.

69. (d): Tris(ethylenediamine)cobalt(III) bromide will show optical isomerism.

70. (c): Complexes of the type *cis*-$[M\ (AA)_2B_2]^{n\pm}$, that is, $[Co(en)_3]^{3+}$ shows optical isomerism.

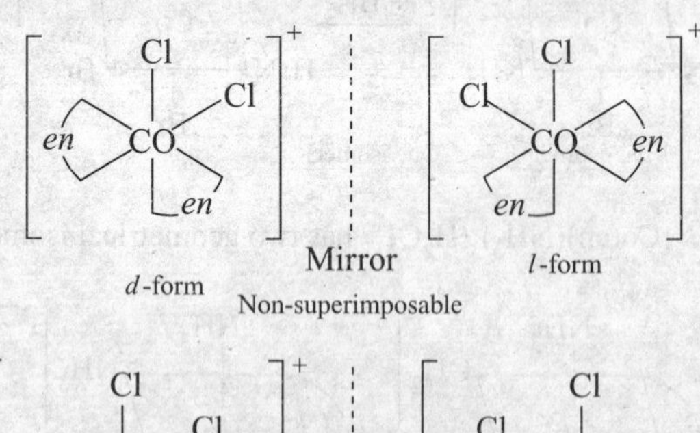

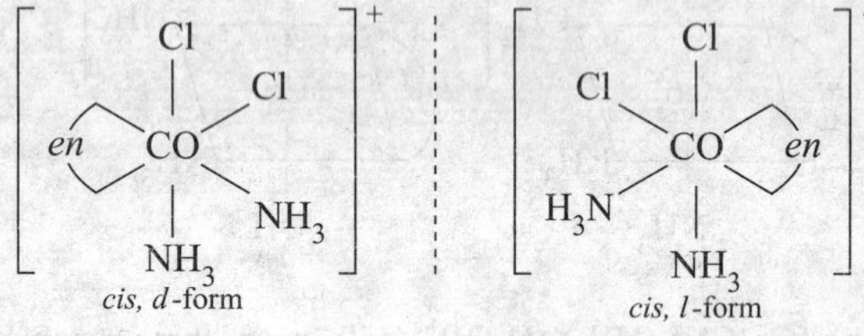

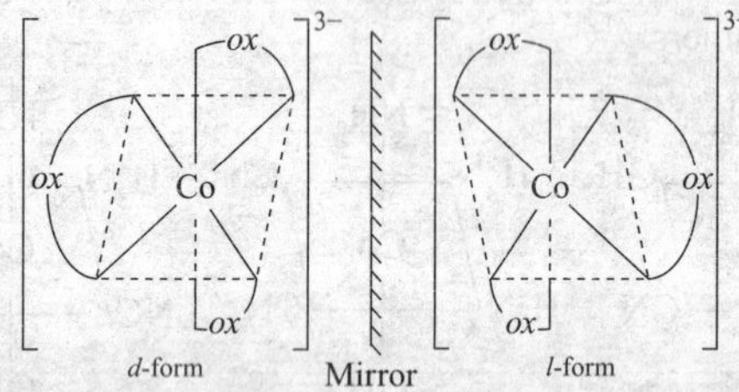

71. (c): Benzoylacetonatoberyllium exhibits optically isomerism as follows. It contains unsymmetrical bidentate ligand and is tetrahedral.

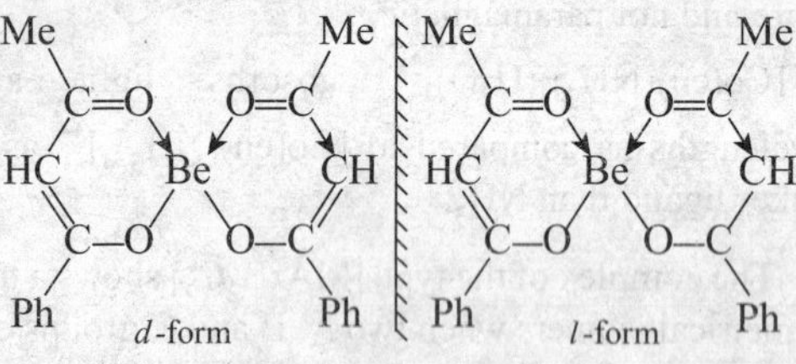

72. (a): $[Co(en)_2Cl_2]^+$ has two optical isomers which are,

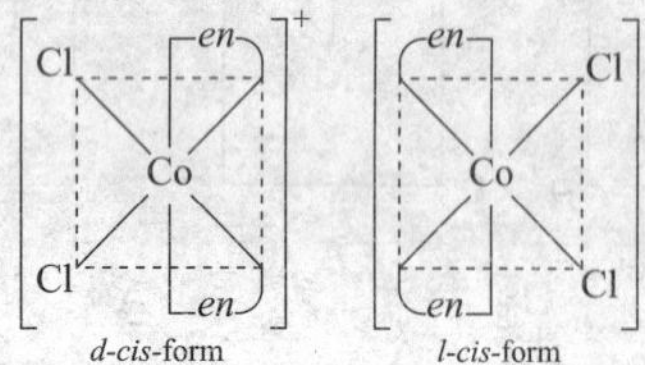

73. (b): $[Co(en)_3]^{3+}$

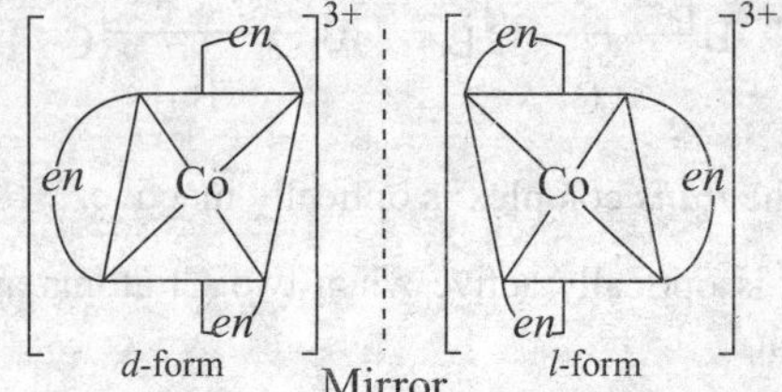

74. (b): (i) $(Cr(en)_3]^{3+}$ and (iii) *cis*-$[Cr(en)_2Cl_2]^+$ are optically active.

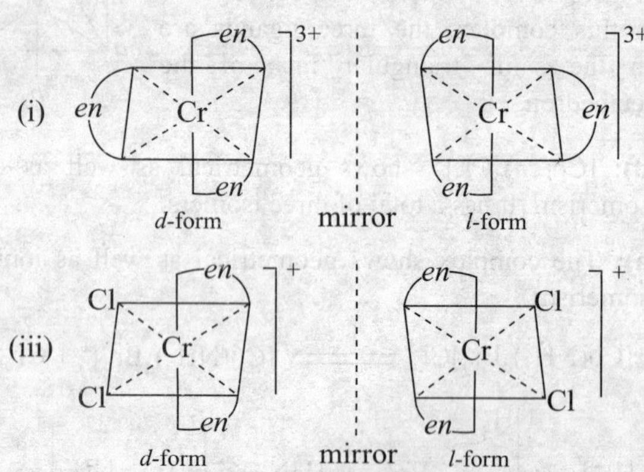

75. (c): Ionisation isomers are: $[Co(NH_3)_5\ (NO_2)](NO_3)_2$ and $[Co(NH_3)_5(NO_3)]NO_2NO_3$.
Linkage isomers are: $[Co(NH_3)_5(NO_2)](NO_3)_2$ and $[Co(NH_3)_5(ONO)](NO_3)_2$.

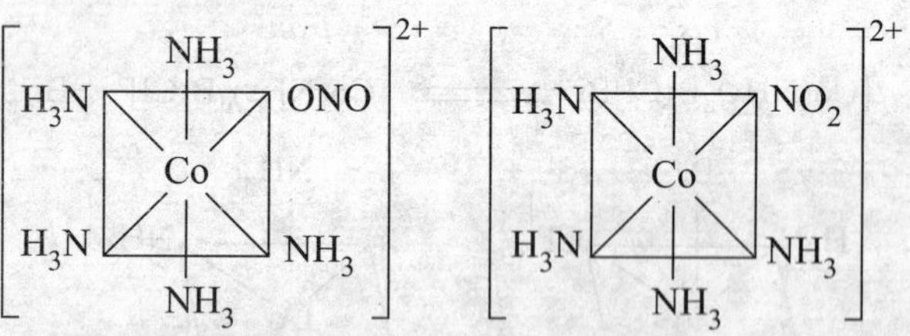

76. (c): $[Co(en)_2NO_2Cl]Br$ and $[Co(en)_2ONOCl]Br$ are linkage isomers.

77. (a): $[Fe(NO_2)_3Cl_3]$ and $[Fe(ONO)_3Cl_3]$ show linkage isomerism. This type of isomerism is shown by the complexes in which an ambidentate ligand is present, such as NO_2^-, SCN^-, CN^-, as each of them contains more than one donor site. But, at a time only one donor atom of the ligand is bonded to the metal atom.

78. (c): Change in composition of the coordination sphere yields ionisation isomers. For example, $[Pt(NH_3)_4Cl_2]\ Br_2$ and $[Pt(NH_3)_4Br_2]\ Cl_2$.

79. (b): The ionisation isomer for the given compound will be obtained by exchanging a ligand with the counter ion as in $[Cr(H_2O)_4Cl_2](NO_2)$.

80. (b): Coordination isomerism is caused by the interchange of ligands between cation and anion complexes.

81. (d):
1. $[Cu(NH_3)_4][PtCl_4]$
2. $[Cu(NH_3)_3Cl][PtCl_3(NH_3)]$
3. $[Cu(NH_3)_2Cl_2][PtCl_2(NH_3)_2]$ *cis*
4. $[Cu(NH_3)_2Cl_2][PtCl_2(NH_3)_2]$ *trans*
5. $[Cu(NH_3)Cl_3][Pt(Cl)(NH_3)_3]$
6. $[Pt(NH_3)_4][CuCl_4]$

82. (e): The magnitude of charge on each complex ion is 3 and the complex will exhibit coordination isomerism.

83. (d): Hydrate isomerism.

84. (c): $[Co(NH_3)_5NO_2]Cl_2$ will not show geometrical isomerism.

85. (d): $[MA_5B]$ is not a disubstituted complex and does not show geometric isomerism.

86. (c): As the complex is disubstituted octahedral, it will show *cis–trans* geometrical isomerism, out of which the *cis*-isomer will again show optical isomerism. The total number of isomers will be three.

Bonding in Coordination Compounds

87. (a): According to Werner's theory, primary valencies are ionisable.

88. (b): The complexes can be written as follows:

$[Co(NH_3)_6]Cl_3$, $[Co(NH_3)_5Cl]Cl_2$, $[Co(NH_3)_4Cl_2]Cl$
(A) (B) (C)

Hence, number of primary valencies are 3, 2 and 1 respectively.

89. (c): Primary valency corresponds to the oxidation number and secondary valency represents the coordination number of the metal in a coordination compound. Therefore, in the complex dichlorodioxalatochromate(III), the primary valency is 3 and secondary valency is 6.

90. (a): 2 Cl^- ions are ionisable from 1 mol of the complex.

$$\therefore \underset{\text{1 mole}}{[Co(NH_3)_5Cl]Cl_2} \rightleftharpoons \underbrace{[Co(NH_3)_5Cl]^{2+} + 2Cl^-}_{\text{3 ions (3 moles)}}$$

$$\underset{\text{2 moles}}{2Cl^-} + 2AgNO_3 \rightarrow \underset{\text{2 moles}}{2AgCl} + 2NO_3^0$$

91. (d):

Covalent
Ionic

$$4K^+\left[\begin{array}{ccc} N\equiv C & & C\equiv N \\ N\equiv C & \rightarrow Fe \leftarrow & C\equiv N \\ N\equiv C & & C\equiv N \end{array}\right]^{4-}$$

Coordinate covalent

92. (a):

$$\underset{\substack{\text{0.02 mole}\\ \text{(X)}}}{[Co(NH_3)_5SO_4]Br} + AgNO_3 \rightarrow \underset{\text{0.02 mole (Y)}}{[Co(NH_3)_5SO_4]NO_3} + \underset{\text{Ppt.}}{AgBr};$$

$$\underset{\substack{\text{0.02 mole}\\ \text{(X)}}}{[Co(NH_3)_5Br]SO_4} + BaCl_2 \rightarrow \underset{\text{0.02 mole (Z)}}{[Co(NH_3)_5Br]Cl_2} + \underset{\text{Ppt.}}{BaSO_4}$$

On using 1 L of solution, we will get 0.01 mol Y and 0.01 mol Z.

93. (b): In $K_3[Fe(CN)_6]$, the ligands are negatively charged which are present in the coordination sphere showing a dual behaviour. These may satisfy both the primary and secondary valencies of the metal while the neutral ligand satisfies only secondary valencies.

94. (b): Number of mol of the complex

$$= \frac{M \times V(mL)}{1000} = \frac{0.1 \times 100}{1000} = 0.01$$

Mol of ions precipitated with excess of $AgNO_3$

$$= \frac{1.2 \times 10^{22}}{6.022 \times 10^{23}} = 0.02$$

Or, 1 mol of the complex produces ions to be precipitated with excess of $AgNO_3 = 2$ mol

Therefore, the complex is $[Co(H_2O)_5Cl]Cl_2.H_2O$ which ionises to give $[Co(H_2O)_5Cl]^{2+} + 2\,Cl^-$ ions.

$2\,Cl^- + 2\,AgNO_3 \rightarrow 2\,AgCl$ (precipitate)

95. (a): In K_3CoF_6, the hybrid state of Co is sp^3d^2 giving a high spin complex.

96. (b): $[Cu(NH_3)_4]^{2+}$ involves dsp^2 hybridisation with one electron occupying the 4*p* orbital.

97. (d): $[CoF_6]^{3-}$ contains four unpaired electrons whereas all other complexes have zero unpaired electrons each.

98. (c): Pt (*Z* = 78) lies in group 10 with the configuration $5d^9 6s^1$.

	5d					6s	6p		
Pt^{2+} =	↑↓	↑↓	↑↓	↑	↑				

For a square planar shape, the hybridisation is dsp^2. Hence, in the presence of strong CN^- ligands, the unpaired electrons in the 5*d* orbitals pair up to make one *d*-orbital empty for dsp^2 hybridisation. Thus, there is no unpaired electron.

99. (c): $[Cu(NH_3)_4]^{2+}$ is square in shape.

100. (b): The complex ion $[Co(C_2O_4)_3]^{3-}$ involves d^2sp^3 hybridisation to form an inner orbital diamagnetic complex.

101. (a): XeF_4 is square planar, and $[PdCl_4]^{2-}$ is also square planar with dsp^2 hybridisation.

102. (c): In the $[Ag(CN)_2]^-$ complex, the ligand CN^- has two π-bonds. So, the number of π-bonds in- the complex is $2 \times 2 = 4$.

103. (d): $[NiCl_4]^{2-}$, $Ni^{2+}, = 3d^8$, $Cl^- \rightarrow$ weak field ligand, structure will be tetrahedral with sp^3 hybridisation.

	3d					4s	4p		
$[NiCl_4]^{2-}$ =	↑↓	↑↓	↑↓	↑	↑	××	××	××	××

sp^3 -hybridisation

No. of unpaired electrons = 2, complex is paramagnetic.

104. (a): $Ni(CO)_4$ is tetrahedral, diamagnetic.

105. (c): $[Co(NH_3)_6]^{3+}$, $Co^{3+} = 3d^6$

As NH_3 is a strong field ligand, it will cause pairing of all the electrons in three 3*d* orbitals making two 3*d* orbitals vacant, required for d^2sp^3 hybridisation, to give an inner orbital octahedral complex which is diamagnetic due to the absence of unpaired electrons.

(a) $[Zn(NH_3)_6]^{2+}$, sp^3d^2 hybridisation, outer orbital octahedral, diamagnetic complex.

(b) $[Cr(NH_3)_6]^{3+}$, d^2sp^3 hybridisation, inner orbital octahedral complex, paramagnetic due to the presence of three unpaired electrons.

(d) $[Ni(NH_3)_6]^{2+}$, sp^3d^2 hybridisation, outer orbital octahedral complex, paramagnetic due to the presence of two unpaired electrons.

106. (b): In $[Fe(H_2O)_6]^{2+}$, Fe^{2+} with $3d^6$ configuration (sp^3d^2-hybridisation having 4 unpaired electrons) shows maximum paramagnetism.

107. (b): In $[Cr(H_2O)_6]^{2+}$, Cr is in the +2 oxidation state with d^4 configuration. In $[Fe(H_2O)_6]^{2+}$, Fe is in the +2 oxidation state with d^6 configuration. As H_2O is a weak ligand, no forcible pairing will take place in both the complexes. Hence, the complexes will be outer orbital with 4 unpaired electrons each and the magnetic moment value will also be the same.

108. (d): $[MnBr_4]^{2-}$ complex ion has Mn^{2+} (d^5 configuration) with 5 unpaired electrons and $\mu = 5.9$ BM for $n = 5$.

109. (d): In the inner orbital octahedral $[Fe(CN)_6]^{4-}$ complex, $Fe^{2+} = 3d^6$. Here, all the six electrons are paired up within three 3*d* level thus giving a magnetic moment of zero. On the other hand, in the outer orbital octahedral $[FeF_6]^{3-}$ complex, $Fe^{3+} = 3d^5$. Here, all the five electrons are unpaired and the magnetic moment corresponds to $n = 5$.

$\sqrt{n(n+2)} = \sqrt{5(5+2)} = \sqrt{35} = 5.92$ BM

110. (b): ${}_{27}Co = 3d^7\,4s^2$, $Co^{3+} = 3d^6$

3*d* 4*s*

Co^{3+} = [↑↓ | ↑ | ↑ | ↑ | ↑] [ ]

In a strong field ligand, electrons pair up. Hence, the complex containing the Co^{3+} ion will be diamagnetic in nature.

111. (b): $\mu = 2.82$ BM

$2.82 = \sqrt{n(n+2)}$ BM

$\therefore n$ = number of unpaired electrons = 2

$[NiCl_4]^{2-}$, $Ni^{2+} = 3d^8$, CN = 4, sp^3 hybridisation, tetrahedral structure. As Cl^- is a weak field ligand, it will not cause pairing of electrons and the number of unpaired electrons will be two.

3*d* 4*s* 4*p*

$[NiCl_4]^{2-}$ = [↑↓ | ↑↓ | ↑↓ | ↑ | ↑] [× ×] [× × | × × | × ×]

sp^3-hybridisation

(a) $[Ni(CO)_4]$, $Ni^0 = 3d^8 4s^2$

As CO is a strong field ligand, two 4*s* electrons jump to 3*d* orbitals and pair up giving sp^3 hybridisation and a diamagnetic complex.

(c) $[Ni(PPh_3)_4$, $Ni^0 = 3d^8 4s^2$, the structure is similar to $[Ni(CO)_4]$ and the complex is diamagnetic with no unpaired electrons.

(d) $[Ni(CN)_4]^{2-}$, $Ni^{2+} = 3d^8$, dsp^2 hybridisation, square planar complex CN^- is a strong field ligand, all the electrons will be paired up giving a diamagnetic complex. Thus, the complex having L = 2.82 BM corresponding to two unpaired electrons is $[NiCl_4]^{2-}$.

112. (b): As the coordination number of Mn^{2+} in the given complex is 4, the geometry can be either tetrahedral (sp^3 hybridisation) or square planar (dsp^2 hybridisation). In $[MnBr_4]^{2-}$, Mn is in the +2 oxidation state with $3d^5 4s^0$ configuration having $\mu = 5.9$ BM. It means that the number of unpaired electrons in the complex is 5 ($\mu = \sqrt{n(n+2} = 5.9$ BM, $n = 5$); as Br^- is a weak ligand, no pairing of electrons occurs in the 3*d* orbitals. Hence, the hybridisation will be sp^3 with tetrahedral geometry.

113. (c): In $[CoF_6]^{3-}$, cobalt is in the +3 oxidation state.

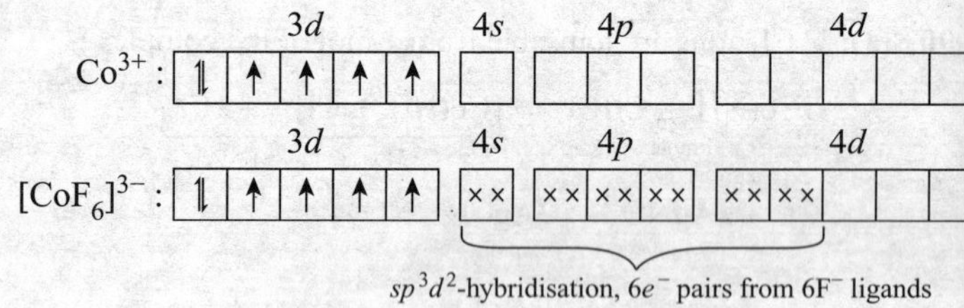

Hence, due to the presence of 4 unpaired electrons $[CoF_6]^{3-}$ is paramagnetic and F^- being a weak field ligand forms an outer orbital complex.

In $[Co(C_2O_4)_3]^{3-}$, cobalt is in the +3 oxidation state.

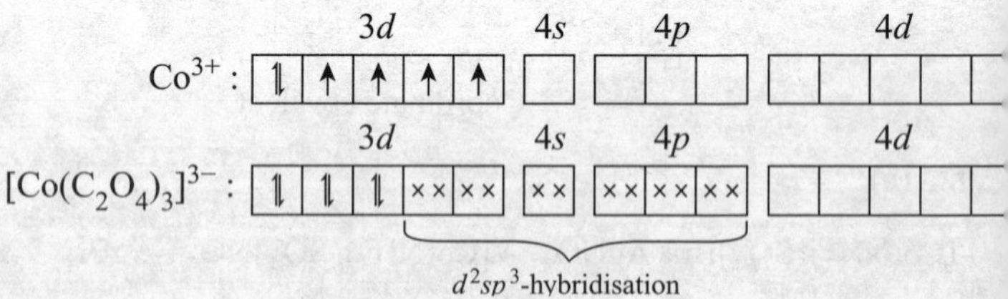

Hence, $[Co(C_2O_4)_3]^{3-}$ is diamagentic due to absence of unpaired electrons and $C_2O_4^{2-}$ being a strong field ligand causes pairing of electrons and forms an inner orbital complex.

114. (b): $[NiCl_4]^{2-}$ contains $Ni^{2+} = 3d^8\,4s^0$. The complex is tetrahedral with sp^3hybridisation, has two unpaired electrons and is paramagnetic.

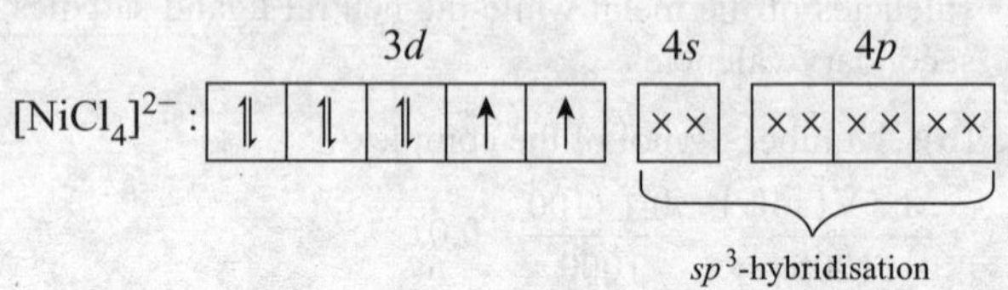

$Na_3[CoF_6]$ ionises to $3 Na^+ + [CoF_6]^{3-}$ which contains $Co^{3+} = 3d^6 4s^0$. $[CoF_6]^{3-}$ is an outer orbital octahedral complex with sp^3d^2 hybridisation, has four unpaired electrons and is paramagnetic.

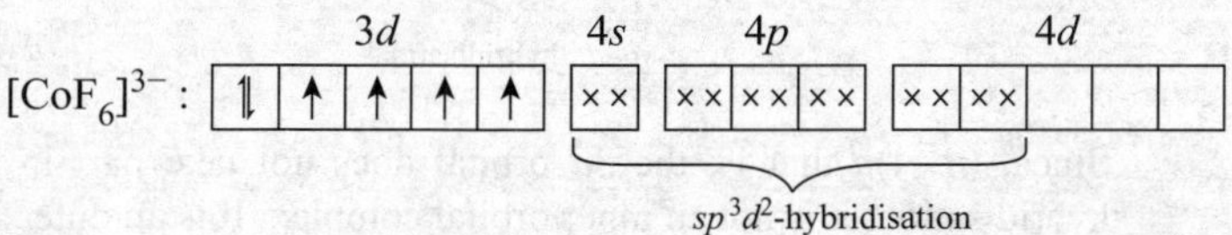

CsO_2 contains the O_2^- anion which has one unpaired electron in the antibonding π molecular orbital and is paramagnetic. All other compounds are diamagnetic in character.

115. (a): The ammonia complex of Ni^{2+} is $[Ni(NH_3)_6]^{2+}$ with sp^3d^2 hybridisation and has octahedral geometry. The ammonia complex of Pt^{2+} is $[Pt(NH_3)_4]^{2+}$ which has a square planar geometry with dsp^2 hybridisation. The ammonia complex of Zn^{2+} is $[Zn(NH_3)_4]^{2+}$ which has a tetrahedral geometry with sp^3 hybridisation.

116. (c): $[ZCl_4]^{2-}$; oxidation state of Z = +2, μ_{eff} = 3.87 BM; therefore, the number of unpaired electrons = 3. Hence $Z^{2+} = d^7$. The complex is tetrahedral with sp^3 hybridisation and Z is cobalt.

117. (c): In $[MnBr_4]^{2-}$, oxidation state of Mn = +2. Thus, $Mn^{2+} = 3d^5$. As Br^- is a weak field ligand, it cannot cause pairing of electrons and the geometry of the complex will be tetrahedral with 5 unpaired electrons.

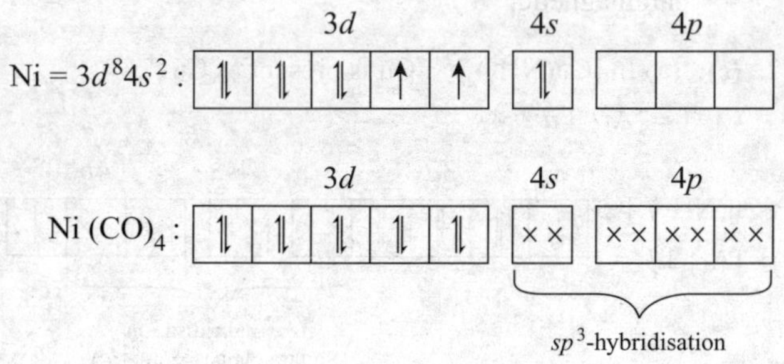

118. (c): In both the complexes, iron is in the +3 oxidation state.

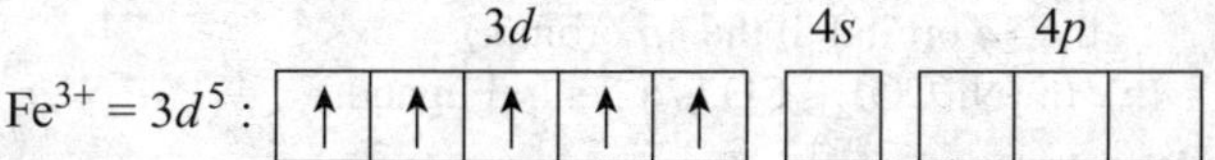

In $[Fe(NH_3)_6]^{3+}$, NH_3 is a strong field ligand. Therefore, pairing of electrons takes place leaving one electron unpaired. So, μ = 1.73 BM.

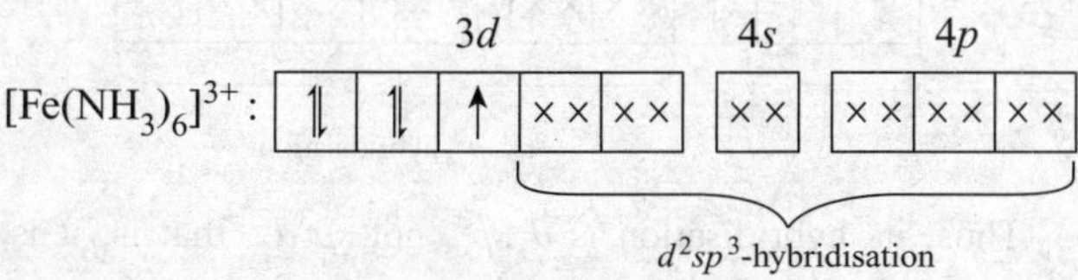

In $[FeF_6]^{3-}$, F^- is a weak field ligand, therefore, it cannot cause pairing of electrons. So, μ = 5.92 BM corresponding to five unpaired electrons.

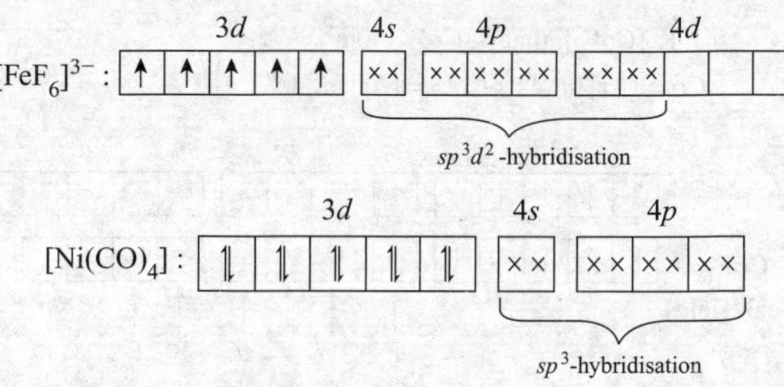

$[Cr(H_2O)_6]^{2+}$ contains $Cr^{2+} = 3d^4$. One of the electrons pairs up giving two unpaired electrons and two vacant 3d orbitals required for d^2sp^3 hybridisation.

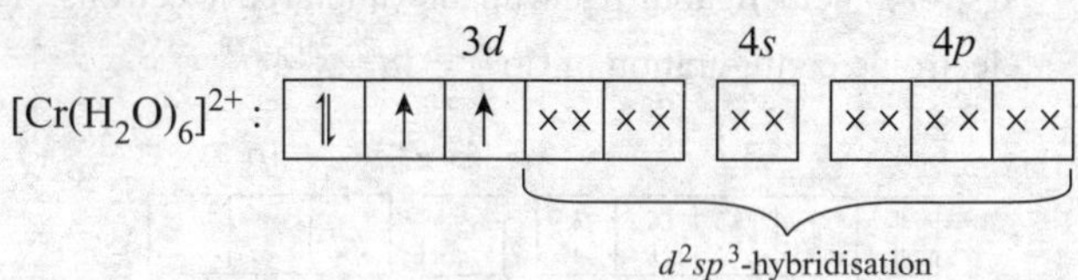

119. (b): A coordination compound/ion having unpaired electrons is paramagnetic in nature while if it has all the electrons paired, it is diamagnetic.

(a) $K_3[Fe(CN)_6]$, that is, $K_3[Fe(CN)_6]^{3-}$ ion.
$_{26}Fe = [Ar]3d^6 4s^2$, $Fe^{3+} = [Ar]\ 3d^5, 4s^0$

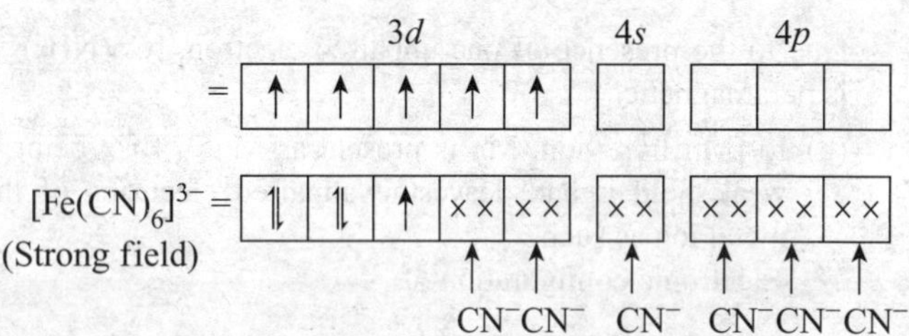

(b) $[Co(NH_3)_6]Cl_3$, that is, $[Co(NH_3)_6]^{3+}$ ion
$_{27}Co = [Ar]3d^7 4s^2$; $Co^{3+} = [Ar]3d^6 4s^0$

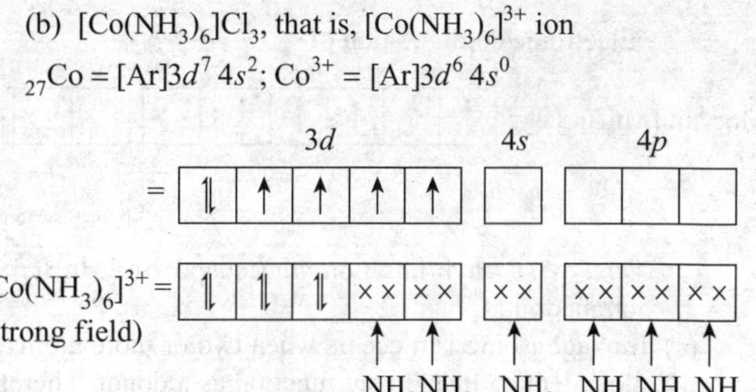

(c) $K_3[FeF_6]$, that is, FeF_6^{3-} ion
$_{26}Fe = [Ar]3d^6 4s^2$; $Fe^{3+} = [Ar]3d^5 4s^0$

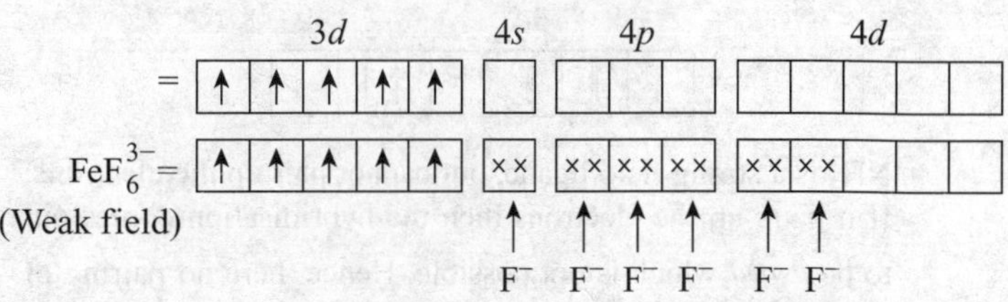

(d) $K_3[CoF_6]$, that is, CoF_6^{3-} ion

${}_{27}Co = [Ar]3d^7 4s^2$; $Co^{3+} = [Ar]3d^6 4s^0$

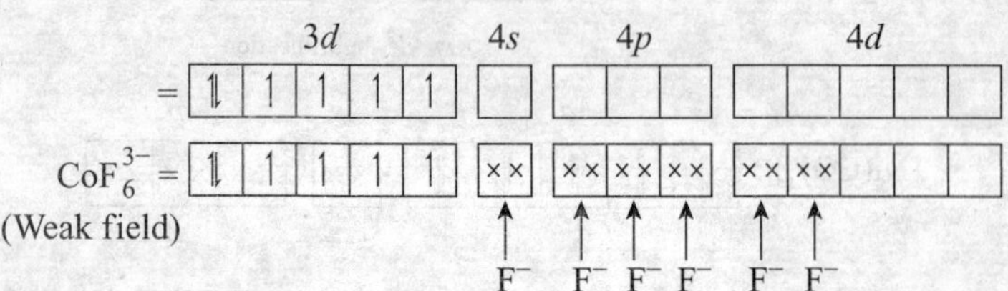

Therefore, $[Co(NH_3)_6]Cl_3$ is diamagnetic in nature.

120. (c): In $[Co(NH_3)_6]^{2+}$, Co is present as Co^{2+}; NH_3 being a strong field ligand, pairs up the unpaired electrons. The electronic configuration of $Co^{2+} = 3d^7 4s^0 4p^0$.

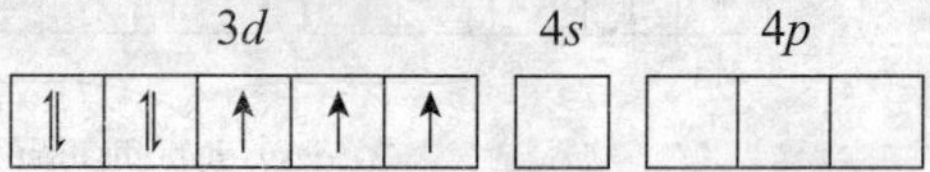

The electronic configuration of Co^{2+} in $[Co(NH_3)_6]^{2+}$ =

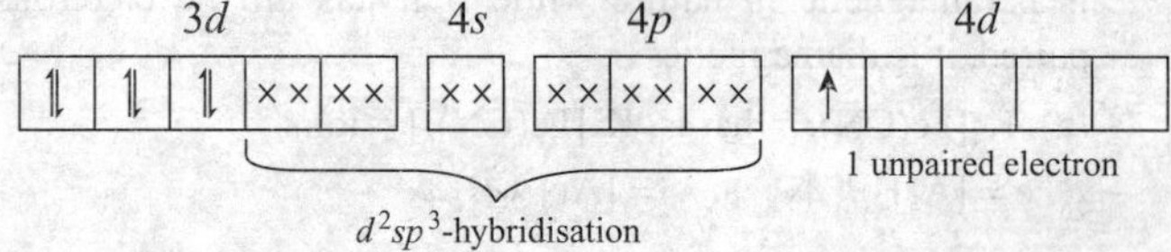

Due to the presence of one unpaired electron, $[Co(NH_3)_6]^{2+}$ is paramagnetic.

(b) In $[MnBr_4]^{2-}$ ion, Mn is present as Mn^{2+}. Br^-, being a weak field ligand, leavesthe unpaired electrons of the metal ion as such.

Electronic configuration of

$Mn^{2+} = 3d^5, 4s^0, 4p^0$ = [3d: ↑ ↑ ↑ ↑ ↑] [4s:] [4p:]

Electronic configuration of

Mn^{2+} in $[MnBr_4]^{2-}$ = [3d: ↑ ↑ ↑ ↑ ↑] [4s: ××] [4p: ×× ×× ××]

sp^3-hybridisation

Due to sp^3 hybridisation, the shape of $[MnBr_4]^{2-}$ is tetrahedral.

(c) Linkage isomerism occurs when two or more atoms in a monodentate ligand may function as a donor. Therefore, $[CoBr_2(en)_2]^-$ does not exhibit linkage isomerism.

(d) In $[Ni(NH_3)_6]^{3+}$ ion, Ni is present as Ni^{2+}. The electronic configuration of $Ni^{2+} = [Ar]\ 3d^8 4s^0$.

= [3d: ⥮ ⥮ ⥮ ↑ ↑] [4s:]

NH_3 is a strong field ligand, but cannot pair up the electrons. If it pairs up the electrons then the hybridisation comes out to be dsp^3d which is not possible. Hence, here no pairing of e^- takes place.

The electronic configuration of Ni in $[Ni(NH_3)_6]^{2+}$ is

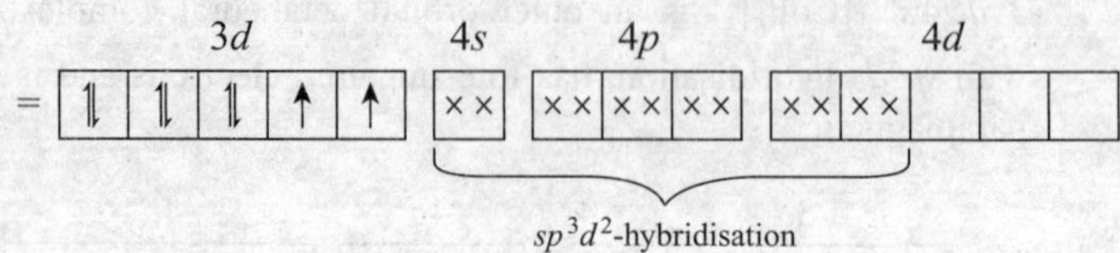

Since, $(n-1)d$, that is, the 3d orbital does not take part in hybridisation, it is not an inner orbital complex. It is an outer orbital complex.

121. (a): $[Co(NH_3)_6]^{2+}$ contains $Co^{2+} = [Ar]\ 3d^7$.

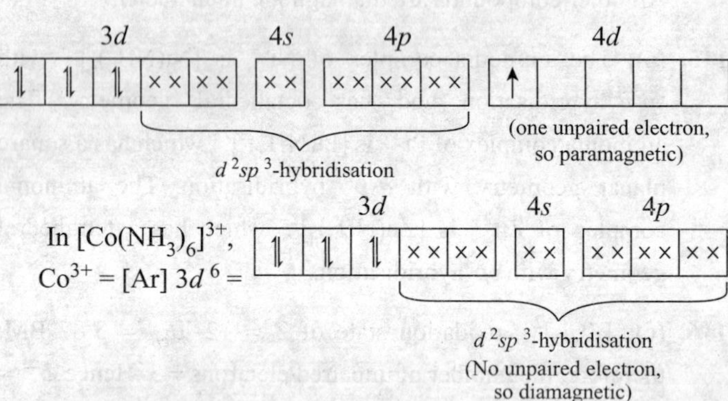

(b) Tetrahedral complexes are less stable than octahedral complexes.

(c) $[Fe(CN)_6]^{3-}$ and $[FeF_6]^{3-}$ are both stable but the former is more stable.

(d) $[Cu(NH_3)_4]^{2+}$ has a square planar geometry and is paramagnetic.

122. (c): (a) In $[Cu(NH_3)_4]^{2+}$, Cu is present as Cu^{2+}.

$Cu^{2+} = [Ar]\ 3d^9\ 4s^0$

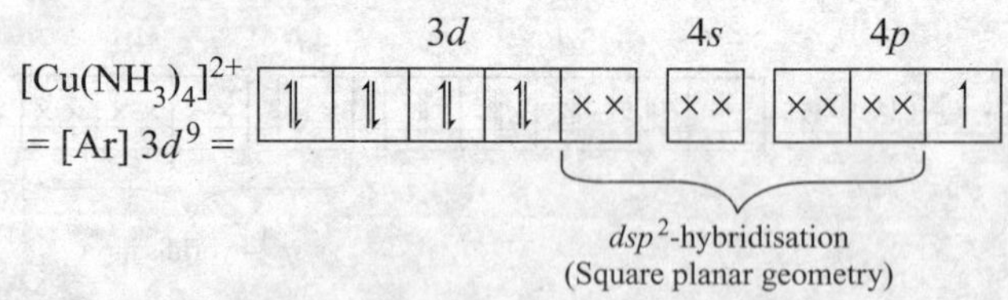

(NH_3 being a strong field ligand shifts one electron from the 3d orbital to the 4p orbital.)

(b) In $[Ni(CO)_4]$, CO is a neutral ligand.

(c) In $[Fe(CN)_6]^{3-}$, Fe is present as Fe^{3+}.

$Fe^{3+} = [Ar]3d^5, 4s^0 \Rightarrow [Fe(CN)_6]^{3-} = [Ar]3d^5$

= [3d: ⥮ ⥮ ↿ ×× ××] [4s: ××] [4p: ×× ×× ××]

d^2sp^3-hybridisation

Thus, its hybridisation is d^2sp^3, not sp^3d^2, that is, it is an inner orbital complex.

(d) $[Co(en)_2]^{3+}$ contains a total of 36 electrons, that is, it follows the EAN rule.

123. (a): As the number of unpaired electrons in the central metal atom increases, the magnetic moment of the complex increases.

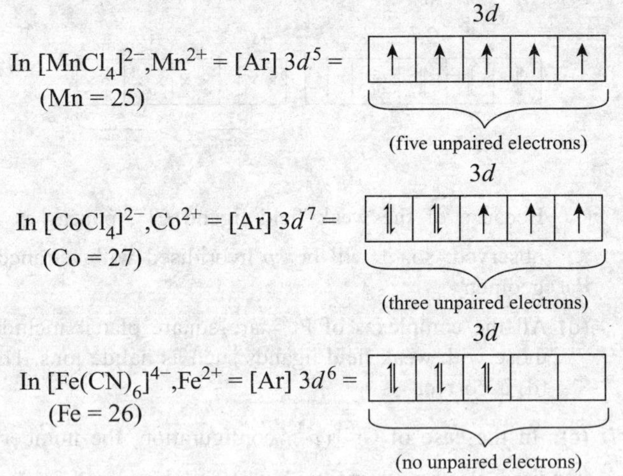

∴ The order of magnetic moments is
$[MnCl_4]^{2-} > [CoCl_4]^{2-} > [Fe(CN)_6]^{4-}$.

124. (d): In $[Sc(H_2O)_6]^{3+}$, Sc (21) = $3d^1\ 4s^2$. The oxidation state of Sc is +3.

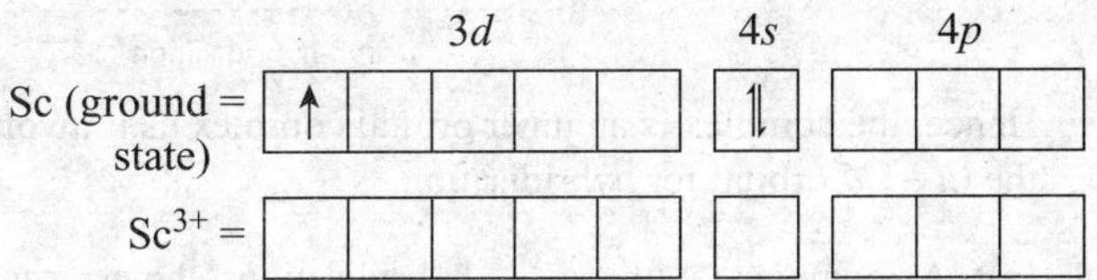

Since Sc^{3+} has no unpaired electrons, $[Sc(H_2O)_6]^{3+}$ is diamagnetic and colourless.

125. (a): $[MnBr_4]^{2-}$ has Mn in the +2 state (d^5 ion) and in the sp^3 hybridised form.

$Mn^{2+} = 3d^5$ 3d   4s   4p

$[MnBr_4]^{2-}$ = ↑ ↑ ↑ ↑ ↑ | ×× | ×× ×× ××

Unpaired electrons = 5 sp^3-hybridisation

$\mu_{eff} = \sqrt{5(5+2} = 5.91$ BM

126. (d): The complex in which the size of the transition metal is small and the ligand is weak field, has a tetrahedral shape and sp^3 hybridisation.

Ni^{2+} = [Ar] $3d^8 4s^0$

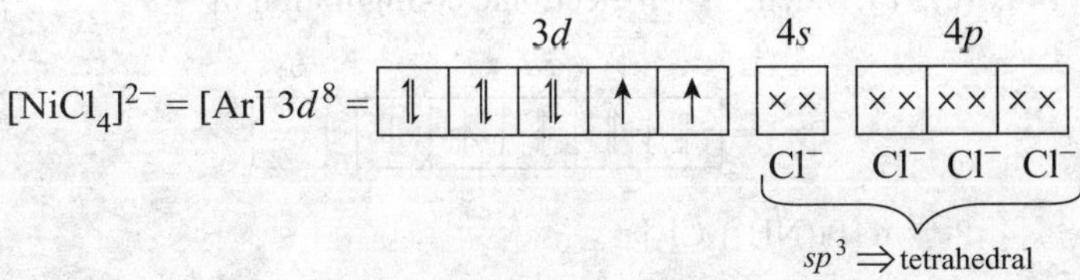

127. (c): $Ni(CO)_4$ and $Ni(PPh_3)_2Cl_2$ are tetrahedral in geometry with sp^3hybridisation. The coordination number of Ni is 4 in both cases.

In $Ni(CO)_4$, $Ni^0 = 3d^8 4s^2$; CO is a strong field ligand. It causes shifting and pairing of 4s electrons in the 3d orbitals ($3d^{10}$ configuration) resulting in sp^3hybridisation.

In Ni $(PPh_3)_2Cl_2$ or $[Ni(PPh_3)_2Cl_2]$, $Ni^{2+} = 3d^8$. As PPh_3 and Cl^- are weak field ligands, no pairing of electrons occurs and sp^3 hybridisation (two unpaired electrons) gives a tetrahedral structure.

128. (c):

(a) $[Ag(NH_3)_2]^+$ has a coordination number 2. It has a linear structure and because of no unpaired electrons, its dipole moment is zero.

(b) $[Co(NH_3)_6]^{3+}$ has d^2sp^3 hybridisation and octahedral structure. Because of no unpaired electrons, it is diamagnetic, that is, magnetic moment = zero.

(c) $[Fe(CN)_6]^{3-}$ has d^2sp^3 hybridisation and octahedral structure. It has one unpaired electron. So, it is paramagnetic and has magnetic moment.

(d) $[Cu(NH_3)_4]^{2+}$ has dsp^2 hybridisation, is square planar in structure and has unpaired electrons. So, it paramagnetic and has magnetic moment.

(e) $[Fe(CN)_6]^{4-}$ has d^2sp^3 hybridisation and octahedral structure. It has no unpaired electron, hence the magnetic moment is zero.

129. (b): In $[Ag(NH_3)_2]Cl$, Ag^+ contains d^{10} configuration and is diamagnetic. All others contain unpaired electrons and are paramagnetic.

130. (c): $[Ni(NH_3)_6]Cl_2$ has a maximum of two unpaired electrons where as other complexes have one or zero unpaired electrons.

131. (a): Chromium is in the zero oxidation state in $Cr(CO)_6$ with configuration $[Ar]3d^5 4s^1$. CO is a strong field ligand so it causes the pairing of electrons. Thus, the complex has d^2sp^3 hybridisation and is diamagnetic.

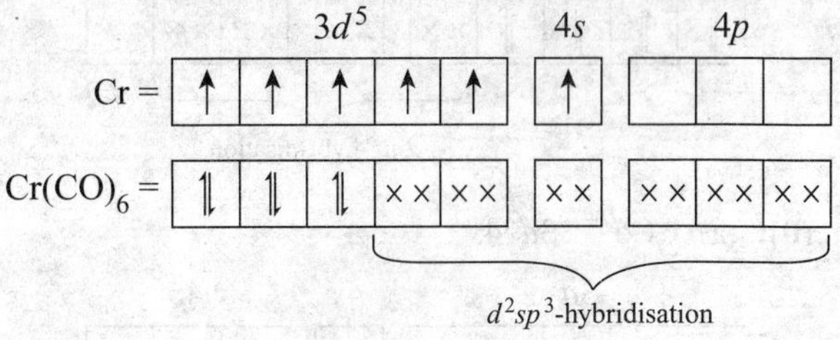

$\mu = \sqrt{n(n+2} = 0$ as there are no unpaired electrons.

$Co^{2+} \longrightarrow 3d^7\ 4s^0$ = ⇅ ⇅ ↑ ↑ ↑ | (3d, 4s)

132. (b): $[Ti(H_2O)_6]^{3+}$, due to the presence of one unpaired electron is paramagnetic.

133. (a): Magnetic moment $= \sqrt{n(n+2)}$ where n = number of unpaired electrons. In $Zn^{2+} \rightarrow 1s^2 2s^2 2p^6 3s^2 3d^6 4s^0 3d^{10}$, that is, the number of unpaired electrons in the d orbital is zero, so the magnetic moment will also be zero.

134. (b): F^- is a weakfield ligand and $[FeF_6]^{3-}$ is an outer orbital complex.

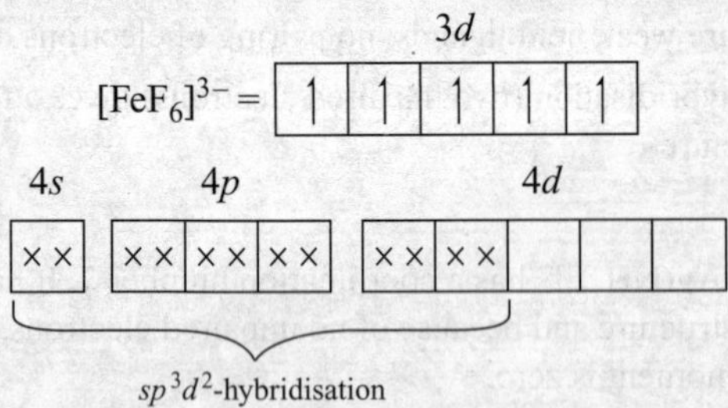

CNS^- is a strongfield ligand, so, $[Fe(CNS)_6]^{3-}$ is an innerorbital complex.

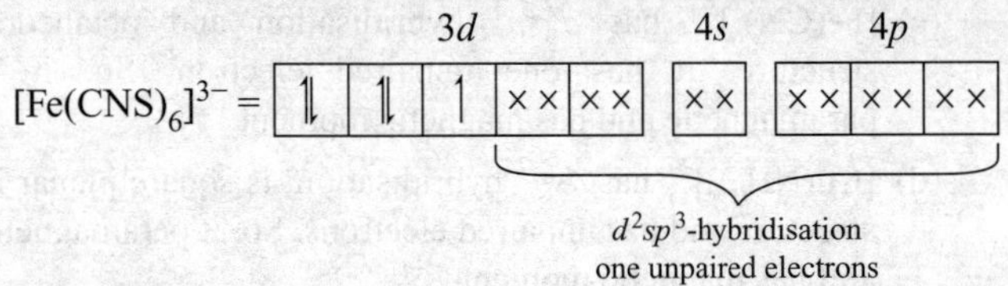

Thus, conversion takes place with an increase in magnetic moment.

135. (b): Ni: $3d^8 4s^2$

$Ni^{2+} : 3d^8$

Since Cl^- is a weak field ligand, it will not cause pairing of electrons.

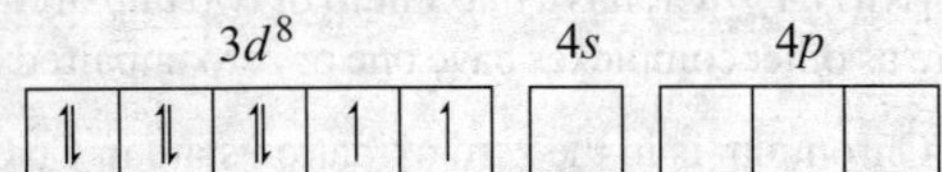

Hence, $n = 2$.

$\mu = \sqrt{n(n+2} = \sqrt{2(2+2}$ BM= 2.82 BM

3d 4s 4p

dsp^2-hybridisation

136. (d): (a) $_{27}Co^{2+} : 3d^7 4s^0$

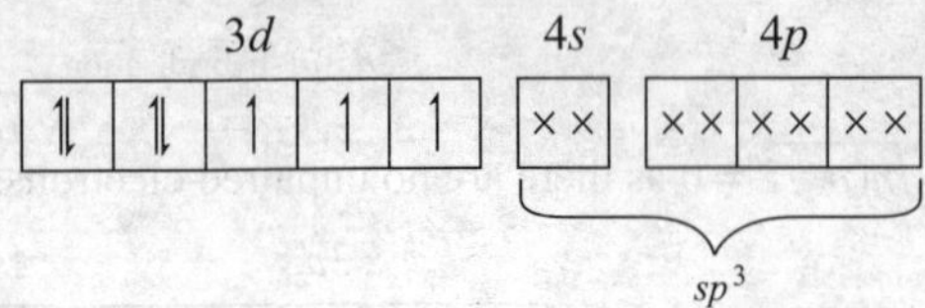

As Cl^- is a weak field ligand, no pairing takes place. Hence, it is sp^3 hybridised with tetrahedral geometry.

(b) $Fe^{2+} : 3d^6 4s^0$

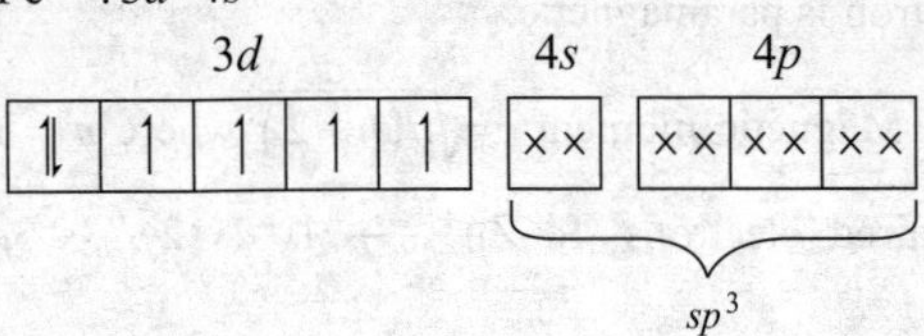

Due to the weak field ligand Cl^-, pairing is not observed so it will be sp^3 hybridised with tetrahedral geometry.

(c) $Ni^{2+} : 3d^8 4s^0$

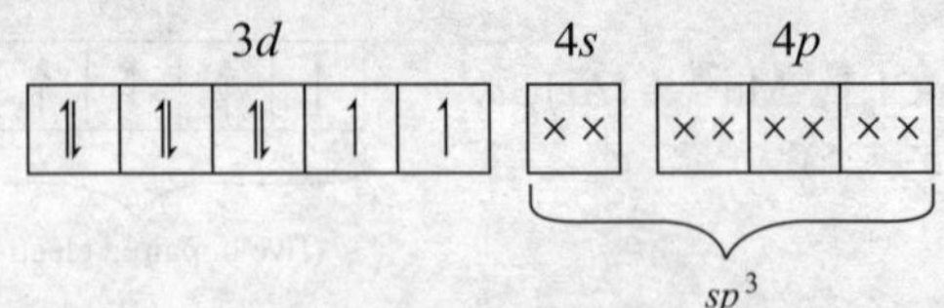

Because of the weak field ligand Cl^-, pairing is not observed; so, it will be sp^3hybridised with tetrahedral geometry.

(d) All the complexes of Pt^{2+} are square planar including those with weak field ligands such as halide ions. Thus, (d) is correct.

137. (c): In the case of $Cr^{3+}(d^3)$ configuration, the number of unpaired electrons remains 3 whether the ligand is strong field or weak field. The hybridisation scheme can be shown as follows.

3d 4s 4p

$[Cr(NH_3)_6]^{3+}$ =

d^2sp^3-hybridisation

Hence, the complex is an inner orbital complex as it involves the $(n-1)d$ orbital for hybridisation.

138. (a): A complex with sp^3d hybridisation shows square pyramidal geometry.

139. (b): Copper complexes usually involve a coordination number of four and are thus square planar in shape.

140. (b): Cr^{3+} (24): [Ar] $4s^0 3d^3$

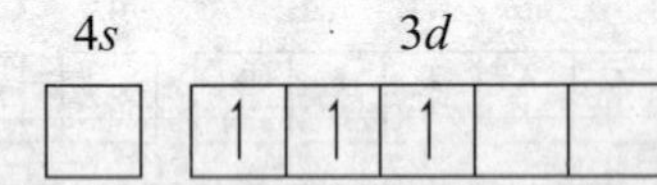

The number of d electrons in $[Cr(H_2O)_6]^{3+}$ is 3.

141. (a): $[MnO_4]^-$ contains $Mn^{7+} = 3d^0 4s^0$, that is, no d electrons in the central metal, Mn.

142. (c): A strong field ligand produces low spin complexes.

143. (b): d^2 (in a weak ligand field) gives $\mu = 2.84$ BM.

144. (c): (a) Valence shell electronic configuration of

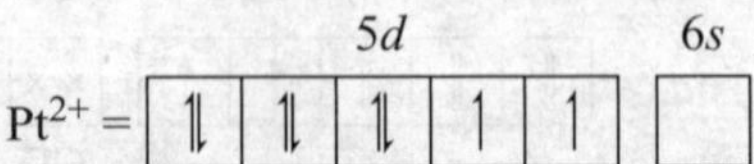

Pt^{2+} in $[Pt(NH_3)_2Cl_2]$ =

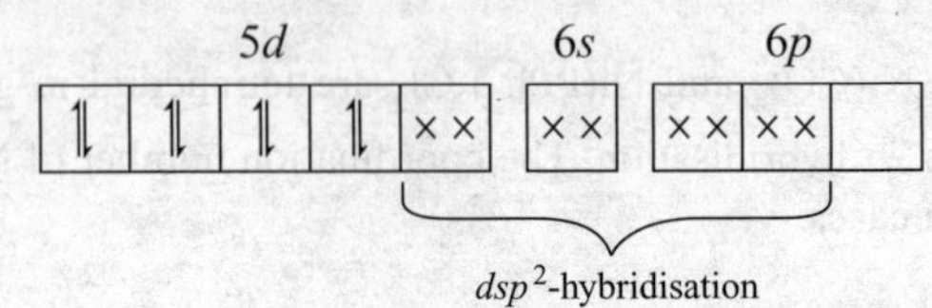

The resulting complex is square planar.
(b) Valence shell electronic configuration of

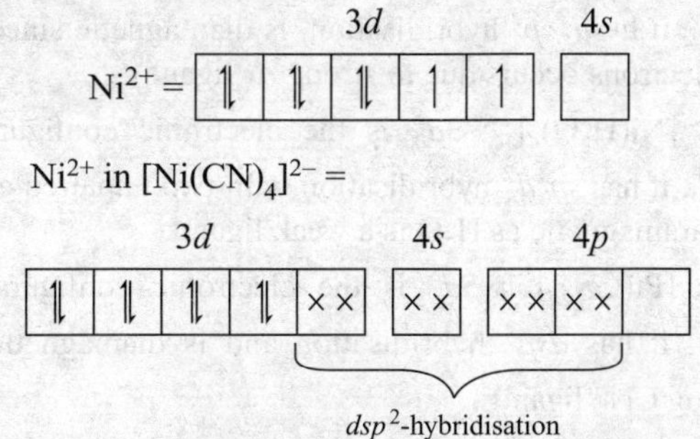

The resulting complex is square planar.

145. (e): Valence shell electronic configuration of

(i)

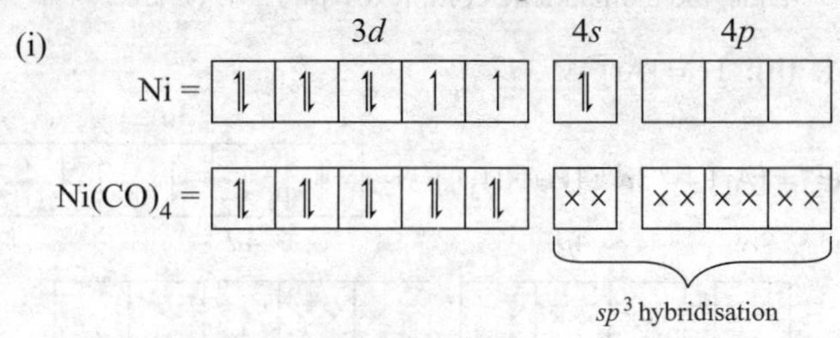

(ii)

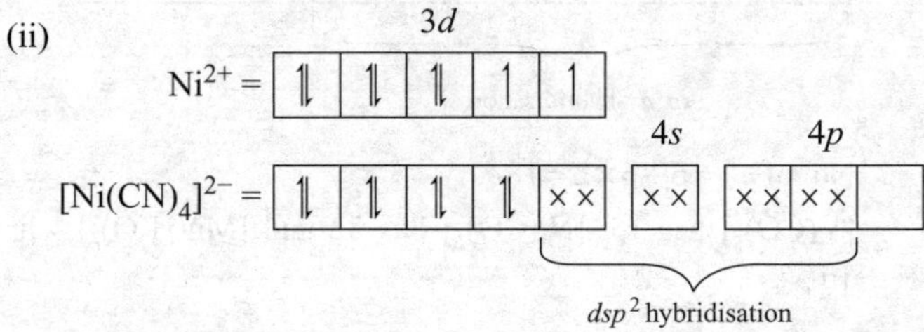

(iii)

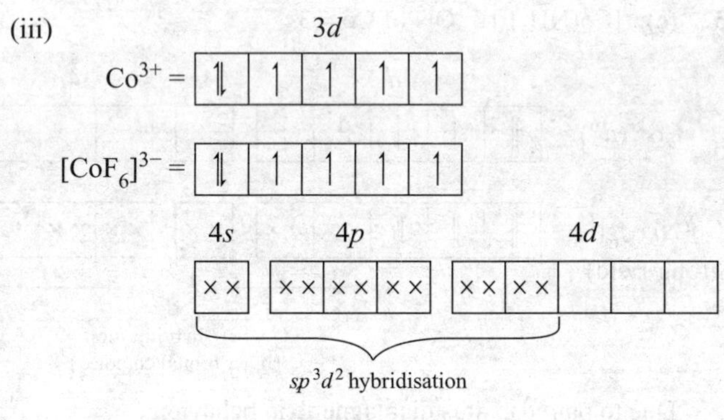

(iv)

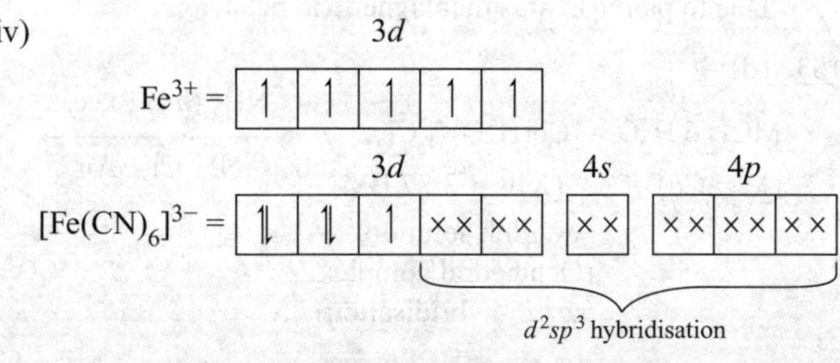

F^- is a weak field ligand, it cannot cause forcible pairing of electrons within the 3*d* subshell and thus forms outer orbital octahedral complexes. CO and CN^- are strong field ligands, so they can form inner orbital octahedral complexes after forcible pairing of electrons within the 3*d* subshell. Thus, the complexes (ii), (iii) and (iv) are not correctly matched with the hybridisation of their central metal ion.

146. (a): (a) Electronic configuration of

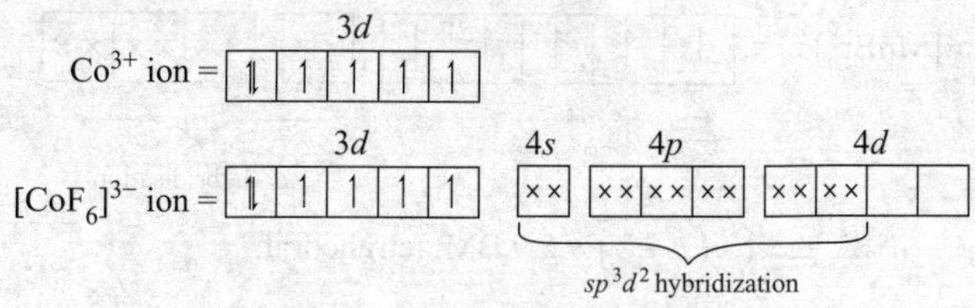

F^-, being a weak field ligand canot cause forcible pairing of electrons within the 3*d* subshell and forms an outer orbital octahedral complex.

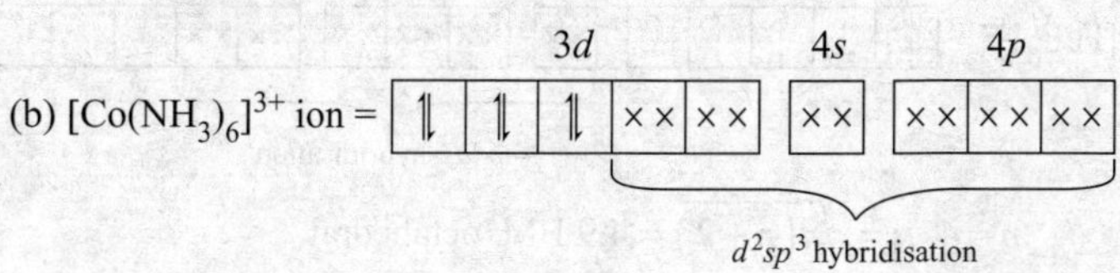

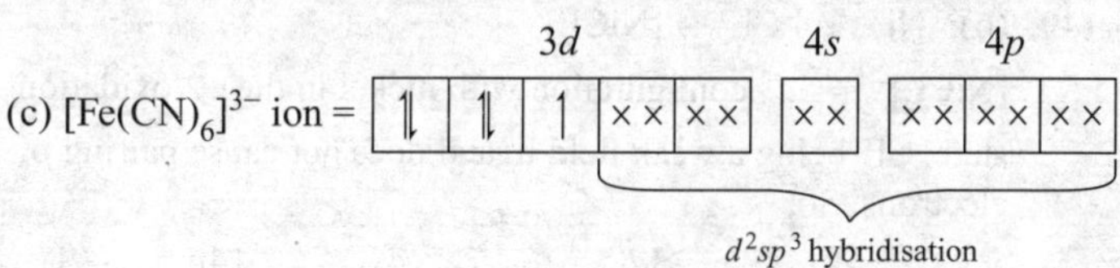

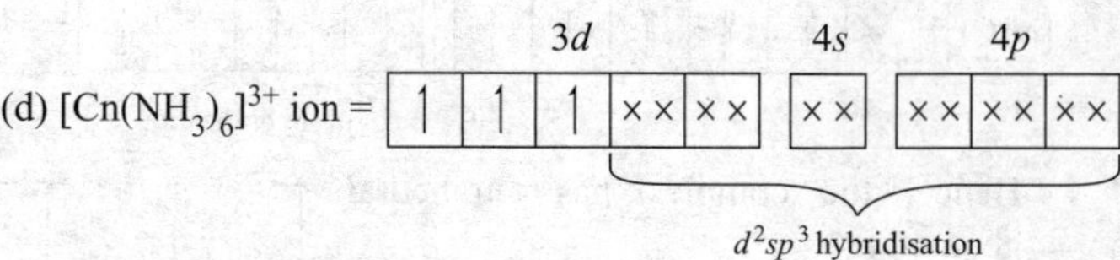

NH_3 and CN^- are strong ligands, so they form inner orbital octahedral complexes (d^2sp^3 hybridisation) whereas F^- being a weak field ligand forms an outer orbital octahedral complex (sp^3d^2hybridisation)

147. (b): μ = 4.9 BM in all the choices is an excellent clue. It shows that the complex has 4 unpaired electrons. Cobalt is in the +3 oxidation state (d^6 ion). A d^6 ion having 4 unpaired electrons and a CN of 6 indicates that it is in the sp^3d^2 hybridised state.

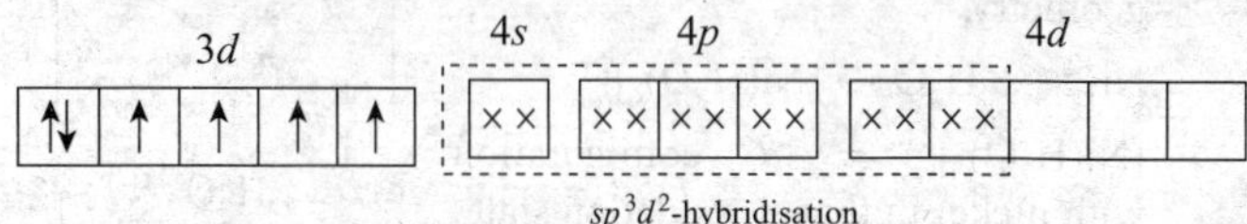

If it were d^2sp^3, the complex would have been diamagnetic. Though CO_3^{2-} can act as a monodentate ligand in some cases, here it is a bidentate ligand with a weak field.

148. (d): A majority of the four coordinated complexes of nickel are square planar.

Ni^{2+} (d^8) : 3*d* 4*s* 4*p*

$[Ni(CN)_4]^{2-}$ = ⥮ ⥮ ⥮ ⥮ ×× ×× ×× ××

*dsp*²-hybridisation

No unpaired electrons: $\mu = 0$, diamagnetic, square planar. MnX_4^{2-} complexes are tetrahedral.

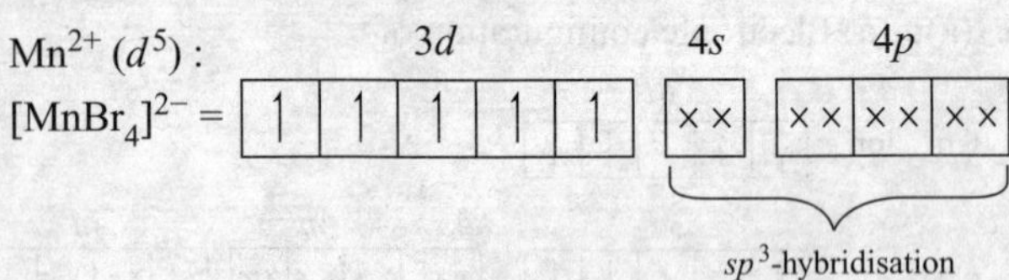

$n = 5, \mu = \sqrt{n(n+2)} = 5.9$ BM, tetrahedral.

F^- is a weak field ligand. $[FeF_6]^{3-}$ is thus a high spin complex with sp^3d^2 hybridisation.

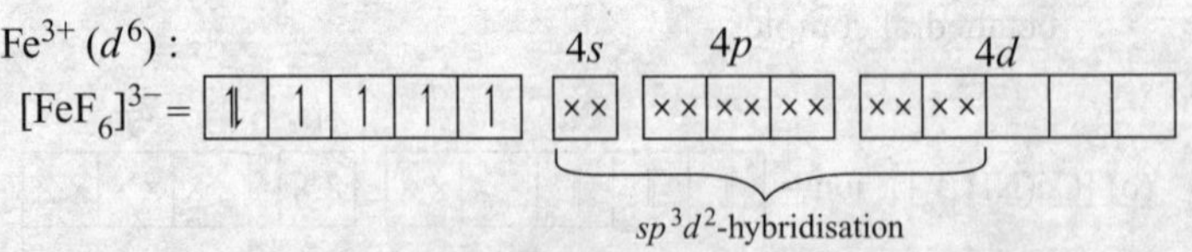

$n = 4, \mu = \sqrt{n(n+2)} = 4.9$ BM, octahedral.

149. (b): $Ni^{+2} + 4\,Cl^- \rightarrow [NiCl_4]^{2-}$

$[NiCl_4]^{2-} = 3d^8$ configuration with nickel in the +2 oxidation state. Cl^- being a weak field ligand does not cause pairing of electrons. So,

$[NiCl_4]^{2-}$ = 3d: ⇅ ⇅ ⇅ ↑ ↑ | 4s: ⇅ | 4p: ⇅ ⇅ ⇅

sp^3-hybridisation

Hence, the complex has tetrahedral geometry.

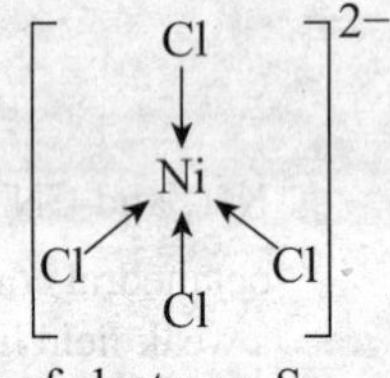

$Ni^{+2} + 4\,Cl^- \rightarrow [Ni(CN)_4]^{2-}$

$[Ni(CN)_4]^{2-} = 3d^8$ configuration with nickel in the +2 oxidation state. CN^- being a strong field ligand, causes pairing of electrons. So,

$[NiCN_4]^{2-}$ = 3d: ⇅ ⇅ ⇅ ⇅ ⇅ | 4s: ⇅ | 4p: ⇅ ⇅ □

dsp^2-hybridisation

Hence, the complex has square planar geometry.

$\begin{bmatrix} NC & & CN \\ & Ni & \\ NC & & CN \end{bmatrix}^{2-}$

$Ni^{+2} + 6\,H_2O \rightarrow [Ni(H_2O)_6]^{2+}$

$[Ni(H_2O)_6]^{2+} = 3d^8$ configuration with nickel in the +2 oxidation state. H_2O is a weak field ligand, it cannot cause pairing of electrons. As with $3d^8$ configuration, two $d$orbitals are not available for d^2sp^3 hybridisation.

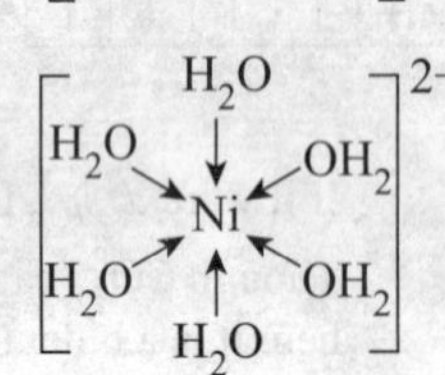

So, hybridisation of Ni(II) is sp^3d^2 and Ni(II) with six coordination will have octahedral geometry.

150. (c): (K): $Fe(CN)_6]^{3-}$: $3d^5$is the electronic configuration of Fe^{3+}, after pairing of electrons for d^2sp^3 hybridisation it contains one unpaired electron due to strong CN^- ligand, so it is paramagnetic.

(L): $[Co(NH_3)_6]^{3+}$: $3d^6$is the electronic configuration for Co^{3+}, it has d^2sp^3 hybridisation, is diamagnetic since pairing of electrons occurs due to strong NH_3 ligands.

(M): $[Co(ox)_3]^{3-}$: $3d^6$ is the electronic configuration for Co^{3+}, it hasd^2sp^3 hybridisation, is diamagnetic since pairing of electrons occurs due to strong *ox* ligands.

(N): $[Ni(H_2O)_6]^{2+}$: $3d^8$ is the electronic configuration of Ni^{2+}, it has sp^3d^2 hybridisation with two unpaired electrons, is paramagnetic as H_2O is a weak ligand.

(O): $[Pt(CN)_4]^{2-}$: $5d^8$ is the electronic configuration for Pt^{2+}, it has dsp^2 hybridisation and is diamagnetic due to strong CN^- ligands.

(P): $[Zn(H_2O)_6]^{2+}$: $3d^{10}$ is the electronic configuration, it has sp^3d^2 hybridisation and is diamagnetic.

Thus, the diamagnetic complexes are L,M, O, P.

151. (b): $Fe = [Ar]\,4s^2\,3d^6$

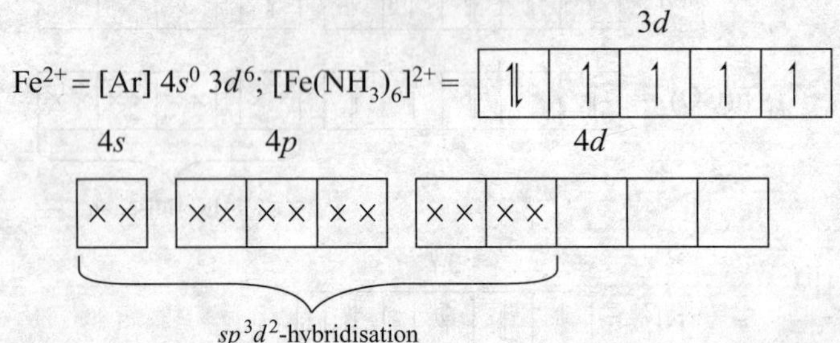

No. of $e^- = 6 + 6 \times 2 = 18e^-$

$[V(CO)_5]$ has 15, $[Ni(CO)_6]$ has 22 and $[Mn(H_2O)_6]^{2+}$ has 17 e^-.

152. (c): $[Co(NH_3)_6]^{3+}$, ON of Co = 3

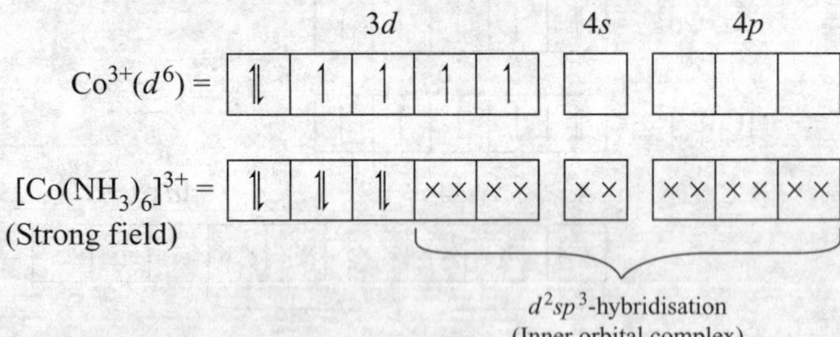

Due to paired e^- it is diamagnetic in behaviour.

153. (d):

$MCl_2.6\,H_2O = [Co(H_2O)_6]\,Cl_2 \xrightarrow[NH_4Cl\,+\,Air]{NH_3\,(aq)\text{ Excess}}$

(M = Co) (X)$\mu = 3{\cdot}87$ BM

Pink solution

(Octahedral complex. sp^3d^2-hybridisation)

↓ HCl (excess), Room temperature

$[CoCl_4]^{2-}$

(Z)$\mu = 3{\cdot}87$ BM

Blue solution

(Tetrahedral complex. sp^3-hybridisation)

$$[Co(NH_3)_6]Cl_3 \rightleftharpoons \underbrace{[Co(NH_3)_6]^{3+} + 3Cl^-}_{\text{1:3 electrolyte}}$$

(Y) $\mu = 0$ BM
(Octahedral d^2sp^3-hybridisation)

$\downarrow 3AgNO_3$

3AgCl ppt.

Complexes (X) (Z) contain

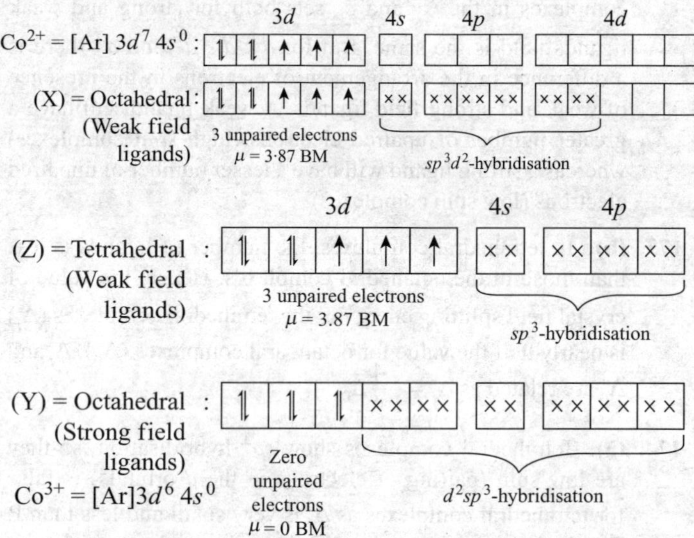

Complexes (X) and (Z) are in equilibrium at 0°C, then the equilibrium is shifted towards (X), making the colour of the solution pink.

154. (b): In $[NiCl_4]^{2-}$, Ni^{2+} = [Ar] $3d^8 4s^0$

3d 4s

= ⇅ ⇅ ⇅ ↑ ↑ | ☐

As Cl^- is a weak field ligand, pairing does not take place. Therefore,

3d 4s 4p

$[NiCl_4]^{2-}$: ⇅ ⇅ ⇅ ↑ ↑ | ×× | ×× ×× ××

sp^3-hybridisation

Geometry of the complex is tetrahedral with two unpaired electrons.

Magnetic moment $\mu = \sqrt{n(n+2)} = \sqrt{2(2+2)} = \sqrt{8} = 2.82$ BM.

155. (c): P → 6; Q → 4, 5 ; R → 1, S → 2, 3

dsp^2 hybridisation (P) is shown by $[Ni(CN)_4]^{2-}$ complex (6) which contains $Ni^{2+} = 3d^8$, strong field ligands, square planar geometry and zero unpaired electrons.

sp^3 hybridisation (Q) is shown by $[FeCl_4]^{2-}$ (4) and $[Ni(CO)_4]$ (5) complexes. $[FeCl_4]^{2-}$ contains $Fe^{2+} = 3d^6$, weak field ligands, tetrahedral geometry and four unpaired electrons.

$[Ni(CO)_4]$ contains $Ni^0 = 3d^8 4s^2 = 3d^{10}$, strong field ligands, tetrahedral geometry and zero unpaired electrons.

sp^3d^2 hybridisation (R) is shown by $[FeF_6]^{3-}$ complex (1) which contains $Fe^{2+} = 3d^6$, weak field ligands, outer orbital octahedral geometry and four unpaired electrons.

d^2sp^3 hybridisation (S) is shown by $[Ti(H_2O)_3Cl_3]$ (2) and $[Cr(NH_3)_6]^{3+}$ (3) complexes.

$[Ti(NH_3)_6]^{3+}$ contains $Cr^{3+} = 3d^3$, strong field ligands, octahedral geometry and three unpaired electrons.

156. (b): CN^- is a pseudohalide and can donate a pair of electrons like halides and behaves as a strong field ligand.

157. (e): In the spectrochemical series, the correct order of increasing crystal field splitting power is $Cl^- < F^- < OH^- < H_2O < CN^-$.

158. (c): The magnitude of Δ_0 depends upon the strength of the ligand to cause crystal field splitting. The strength can be compared from the position on the ligand in the spectrochemical series. The order of increasing strength is $Cl^- < H_2O < NH_3 < CN^-$.

As Cl^- is the weakest ligand, the complex $[CoCl_6]^{3-}$ has minimum magnitude of Δ_0.

159. (a): Mn is in the +2 oxidation state with $3d^5 4s^0$ configuration in both complexes $[Mn(H_2O)_6]^{2+}$ and $[Mn(CN)_6]^{4-}$. As H_2O is a weak field ligand, the magnitude of the crystal field spitting (Δ_0) will be very small, the distribution of five electrons in the two sets of t_{2g} and e_g orbitals will be $t_{2g}^3 e_g^2$, that is, all the electrons remain unpaired and thus, the complex ion (i) contains 2 electrons (unpaired) in the e_g set of orbitals. On the other hand, CN^- is a strong field ligand, the Δ_0 will be very large in this case, all the five electrons will prefer to occupy the lower energy t_{2g} set of orbitals keeping e_g set vacant and the distribution of electrons will be $t_{2g}^5 e_g^0$. Thus, the complex ion (ii) contains zero electrons in the e_g set of orbitals.

160. (a): d^8 to d^{10} configurations have only one possible arrangement in weak and strong ligand fields and hence have a fixed CFSE value.

$d^{10} = t_{2g}^6 e_g^4 \therefore$ CFSE = $(-0.4 \times 6 + 0.6 \times 4)\ \Delta_0 = 0.0$.

161. (b): Aqueous $CuSO_4$ solution exists as $[Cu(H_2O)_4]SO_4$ which has a blue colour due to $[Cu(H_2O)_4]^{2+}$ ions. When KF solution is added, a green precipitate of potassium tetrafluoridocuprate(II) complex compound is formed.

$$CuSO_4(aq) + 4\,KF(aq) \rightarrow \underset{\substack{\text{Potassiumtetrafluoridocuprate(II)} \\ \text{(Green ppt.)}}}{K_2[CuF_4]} + K_2SO_4$$

162. (b): The coordination entity for which the crystal field splitting is smaller, absorbs light of lowest frequency. Weaker the ligand field strength, smaller will be the crystal field splitting. The order of the field strength of various ligands is $CN^- >$ en $> NH_3 > Cl^-$

Hence, $[CrCl_6]^{3-}$ due to the presence of weak ligands (Cl^-), absorbs light of the lowest frequency.

163. (d): The complementary colour of the absorbed colour is transmitted.

164. (c): CFSE in the case of tetrahedral complexes is less than the octahedral field due to the points (a) and (b).

165. (b): Cr^{3+} ion with a $d^3\left(t_{2g}^3\right)$ configuration has a favourable crystal field stabilisation energy $(-0.4 \times 3+0=-1.2\ \Delta_0)$ as compared to the Fe^{3+} ion with a $d^5\left(t_{2g}^3 e_g^2\right)$ configuration having unfavourable crystal field stabilisation energy $(-0.4 \times + 0.6 \times 2 = 0\,\Delta_0)$.

166. (b): CO is a π-donor ligand which acts as a stronger ligand than Cl^-.

167. (a): As per the spectrochemical series, the correct increasing order of field strength of ligands is $SCN^- < F^- < CN^- < CO$.

168. (a):

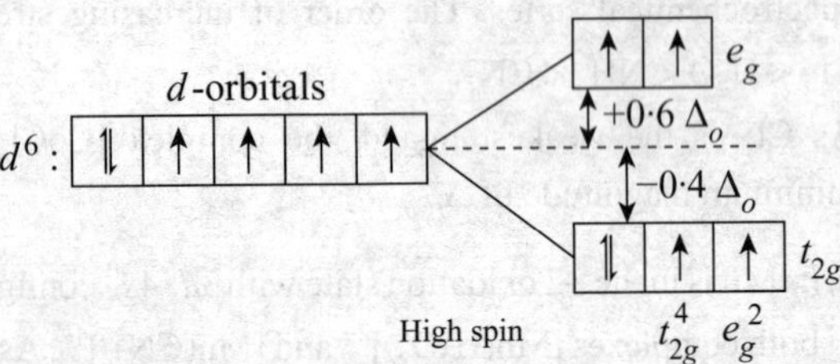

$$\text{CFSE} = (-0.4x + 0.6y)\Delta_o$$
$$= (-0.4 \times 4 + 0.6 \times 2)\Delta_o = -0.40\ \Delta_o$$

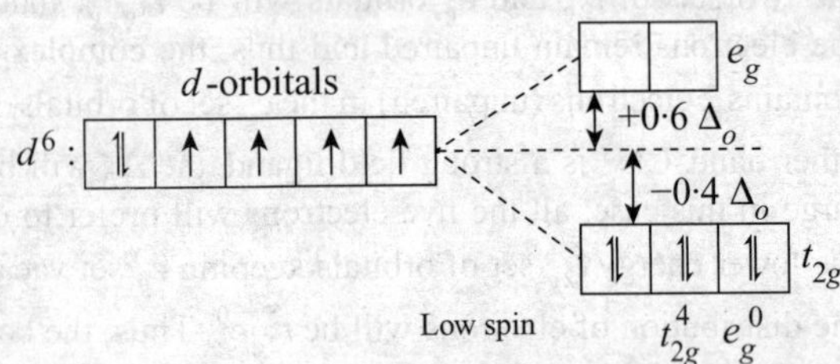

$$\text{CFSE} = (-0.4x + 0.6y)\Delta_o$$
$$= (-0.4 \times 6 + 0.6 \times 0)\Delta_o = -2.4\ \Delta_o$$

169. (b): $K_3[Fe(CN)_6]$ contains $Fe^{3+} = 3d^5$. As CN^- is a strong field ligand, it will split the d orbitals to a greater extent resulting in a low spin complex with one unpaired electron.

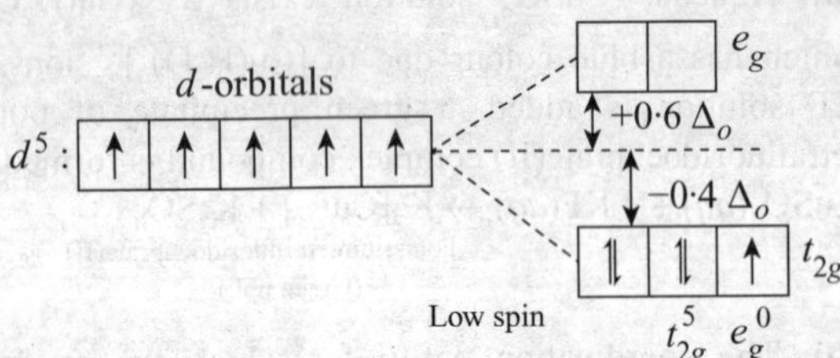

$$\text{CFSE} = (-0.4 \times x + 0.6 \times y)\Delta_o$$
$$= (-0.4 \times 5 + 0.6 \times 0)\Delta_o = -2.0\ \Delta_o$$
$$n = 1,\ \mu = \sqrt{n(n+2)}\ \text{BM} = \sqrt{1(1+2)} = \sqrt{3} = 1.73\ \text{BM}$$

170. (a): The crystal field theory can explain the spectra, that is, colour, magnetic property and structure of coordination compounds. However, the position of intensities of spectral bands (or covalent character of covalent bonds) cannot be explained on the basis of this theory.

171. (a): $CdCl_2$ has the Cd^{2+} ion $\left(4d^{10}\right)$ which is colourless.
Here, the d^{10} configuration suggests that it has completely filled d-orbitals. Thus, there will be no d–d transition. Hence, it is colourless.

172. (b): The distribution of electrons of d^1, d^2, d^3, d^8, d^9 complexes in the t_{2g} and e_g sets both for strong and weak ligands field is the same. But for d^4, d^5, d^6 and d^7 there is a difference in the arrangement of electrons in the presence of weak and strong field ligands. A weak ligand will have a greater number of upaired electrons (high spin complexes) whereas a strong ligand will have a lesser number of unpaired electrons (low spin complexes).

173. (b): In tetrahedral complexes, the number of ligands is less than those in the octahedral complexes. Hence, the value of crystal field splitting energy of the tetrahedral complexes (Δ_t) is nearly half the value for octahedral complexes (Δ_0). Δ_t and Δ_0 are related as $\Delta_t = -\frac{4}{9}\Delta_0$.

174. (a): Tetrahedral complexes show sp^3 hybridisation, so they are low spin (pairing of electrons in the d orbitals) is false for tetrahedral complexes as Δ_t is very small and less than P. Tetrahedral complexes show d–d transitions due to high spin of the d orbitals. Tetrahedral complexes are coloured due to the absence of symmetry and presence of unpaired electrons in the d orbitals.

175. (c): CuF_2 contains $Cu^{2+} = 3d^9$, one unpaired electron due to which it will be coloured. All other compounds contain $Cu^+ = 3d^{10}$ and are colourless.

176. (d): The compounds having metal ions with unpaired electrons are coloured. Thus, (a) in $TiCl_3$, the ion $Ti^{3+} = [\text{Ar}]3d^1$ (one unpaired electron)

(b) in $FeCl_3$, the ion $Fe^{3+} = [\text{Ar}]\ 3d^5$ (five unpaired electrons)

(c) in $CoCl_2$, the ion $Co^{2+} = [\text{Ar}]\ 3d^7$ (three unpaired electrons)

Hence, all compounds are coloured.

177. (d): $[Cu(NH_3)_6]^{2+}$ is blue, $[Zn(H_2O)_6]^{2+}$is colourless, $[Ni(CN)_4]^{2-}$ ion has a square planar shape and nickel dimethylglyoximate is red in colour.

178. (a): Repulsion by six ligands in an octahedral complex splits the d orbitals on the central atom into t_{2g} and e_g levels.
It follows that there is a corresponding repulsion between the symmetrically arranged ligands, they will repel all six ligands equally. Thus the structure will be a regular octahedron.
If the d electrons are asymmetrically arranged, they will repel some ligands in the complex more than others. Thus, the structure is distorted. Out of the given options, symmetrical arrangements are:
(b) $t_2^6 e_g^2$ (c) $t_2^6 e_g^4$ and (d) $t_2^6 e_g^0$.The unsymmetrical arrangement is: (a) $t_2^6 e_g^1$ which will undergo distortion.

179. (a): According to the crystal field theory, the bonding in a complex is purely electrostatic or ionic. This is based on the assumption that the metal ion and the ligands act as point charges.

180. (b): The complex $[RhCl_6]^{3-}$ contains Rh^{3+} which belongs to the 4*d* transition series. The magnitude of Δ_o increases by about 30% between adjacent members down a group of transition elements, that is, from 3*d* to 4*d* and 4*d* to 5*d* series. Therefore, the elements of the 4*d* and 5*d* series are more prone to spin pairing and thus, form low spin complexes.

181. (d): The elements of the 4*d* and 5*d* transition series have a larger crystal field splitting, Δ, than those of the 3*d* transition series. Therefore, the correct increasing order of CFSE values is

$[Co(NH_3)_6]^{3+} < [Rh(NH_3)_6]^{3+} < [Ir(NH_3)_6]^{3+}$

182. (c): Effective atomic number, EAN = number of electrons in Cr (that is, AN) + 2 × number of ligands (that is, CN) – charge $= 24 + 2 \times 6 - 3 = 33$

183. (c): EAN = *Z*– (ON) + 2 (CN)
where, ON = oxidation number, CN = coordination number and *Z* = atomic number.
$[Fe(CN)_6]^{4-}$: EAN = 26 – (2) + 2 (6) = 26 – 2 + 12 = 36
$\therefore$ A is $Na_4[Fe(CN)_6]$.

184. (a): EAN = $(78 - 4) + 6 \times 2 = 86$

185. (a): EAN = (atomic no) – (oxidation state + 2 × number of ligands) = 27 - 3 + 2 × 4 = 34

186. (c): EAN of the central metal ion = (atomic no. of central atom) – oxidation state + no. of ligands ×2 $= 26 - 3 + (6 \times 2)$ = 23 + 12 = 35.

187. (a): In the complex $K_4[Fe(CN)_6]$, Fe obeys the EAN rule strictly. [EAN = 36 (Kr)], that is, $26 - 2 + 2 \times 6 = 36$.

188. (b): In $CoF_6]^{2-}$, the oxidation state of Co = *x*. $\therefore x + (-6) = -2$ or $x = +4$
EAN of Co = At. no. – ON + 2 × CN = $27 - 4 + 2 \times 6 = 35$

189. (c): $Z - 3 + 12 = 33 \Rightarrow Z = 24$

190. (a): $K_4[Fe(CN)_6]$ ionises to give five ions giving maximum conductivity.

191. (e): The complex gives a pink colour.

192. (d): $[Pt(NH_3)_4Cl]Cl_3 \rightleftharpoons [Pt(NH_3)_4Cl]^{3+} + 3\,Cl^-$; the complex produces three Cl^- ions in aqueous solution on dissociation.

193. (a): The compound $PtCl_4.2HCl$ is written in the complex form as $H_2[PtCl_6]$. It does not give a precipitate of AgCl with excess of $AgNO_3$ because it does not ionise to give Cl^- ions. The primary valency of Pt is its oxidation number which can be calculated as
$2 \times (+1) + x + 6 \times (-1) = 0$
$2 + x - 6 = 0$ or $x = +4$
The secondary valency of Pt is its coordination number in the complex = 6.

Stability of Coordination Compounds

194. (a): The equilibrium constant, *K* for the reaction $CuCl_4^{2-} + 3\,Br^- \rightleftharpoons CuClBr_3^{2-} + 3\,Cl^-$ is equal to the multiplication of the step-wise formation constant of each step, that is, $K = K_1 \times K_2 \times K_3$

195. (b): The stability of a complex depends upon the strength of the ligand and the charge of the central metal ion.
Stability of a complex $\propto$ strength of ligand $\propto$ charge of central metal ion
Among the given complexes, in $Fe(CO)_5$, the charge of central metal ion is zero while CO is the strongest field ligand. Also, it obeys the EAN rule. Hence, $[Fe(CO)_5]$ is the most stable complex among the given complexes.

196. (d): The cyano and ammine complexes are far more stable than those formed by the halide ions. This is due to the fact that NH_3 and CN^- are strong Lewis bases.

197. (c): Ca^{2+} forms an octahedral complex with just one molecule of EDTA as it has four donor oxygen atoms and two donor nitrogen atoms in each molecule.

198. (a): $Ag_3S + NaCN \rightleftharpoons Na[Ag(CN)_2] + Na_2S$

199. (a): $Ag^+ + NH_3 \rightleftharpoons [Ag(NH_3]^+$; $k_1 = 3.5 \times 10^{-3}$
$[Ag(NH_3)]^+ + NH_3 \rightleftharpoons Na\,[Ag(NH_3)_2]^+$; $k_2 = 1.7 \times 10^{-3}$
The overall stability constant β_2 or formation constant of $[Ag(NH_3)_2]^+ = k_1 \times k_2 = 3.5 \times 10^{-3} = 5.95 \times 10^{-6}$

200. (a): Roasted gold ore + $CN^- + H_2O \xrightarrow[(X)]{O_2} [Au(CN_2)]^{2-}$ + OH^- gold ore
$2[Au(CN)_2]^- + Zn \rightarrow [Zn(CN)_4]^{2-} + 2\,Au$
(X) (Y)

201. (b): Greater the charge on the central metal ion, greater is the stability of complex.

202. (c): $[Co(NH_3)_5Cl]^x + 2\,Cl^- \rightarrow [Co(NH_3)_5Cl]Cl_2$
Complex ion — Complex salt

203. (a):
$2\,CuSO_4 + 10\,KCN \rightarrow 2\,K_3[Cu(CN)_4] + 2\,K_2SO_4 + (CN)_2$
(A)
$H_2S \downarrow$
No precipitate
(B)
As CN^- is a strong ligand, the complex formed is highly stable and does not dissociate to give Cu^{2+} ions. Hence, no precipitate of CuS is formed when H_2S gas is passed through the solution.

204. (a): The correct Irving–Willams order is $Mn^{2+} < Fe^{2+} < Co^{2+} < Ni^{2+}$.

205. (d): Metal ions of groups, 1, 2, 3, 4, 5, 6 and inner transition elements are classified as 'class a' acceptors.

206. (d): In $K_2[Ni(EDTA)]$, there are five rings in the structure and thus it is the most stable complex.

207. (b):

$$\underset{(X)}{[Co(H_2O)_6]^{2+}} + 6NH_3 \rightarrow \underset{\text{Liquor} + 6\,H_2O}{[Co(NH_3)_6]^{2+}}$$

$$\xrightarrow[-e^-\,(\text{oxidation})]{O_2} \underset{(Y)}{[Co(NH_3)_6]^{3+}}$$

$[Co(H_2O)_6]^{2+}$ (X) contains $Co^{2+} = 3\,d^7$, H_2O is a weak field ligand (so, no pairing of electrons takes place. Hence, the number of unpaired electrons is three.

$[Co(NH_3)_6]^{3+}$ (Y) contains $Co^{2+} = 3\,d^6$; NH_3 is a strong field ligand so, pairing of electrons occurs. Hence, the number of unpaired electrons is zero.

Organometallic Compounds

208. (c): In $Al_2(CH_3)_6$, there is an Al–C bond and thus it is an organometallic compound.

209. (a): Because there is direct bonding of the metal ion with carbon in $Ti(C_2H_5)_4$.

210. (c): Due to C–Mg bond, it is organometallic.

211. (a): The ligands which have vacant π-type orbitals and that can receive back donated π-electrons from metals are called π-acid ligands or π-acceptor ligands. For example, CO, NO have lone pairs as well as π or π^* orbitals which take part in the formation of π-bonds with the central metal atom as is observed in the carbonyls.

212. (d): $(CH_3)_4Sn$ is a σ-bonded organometallic compound.

213. (c): CN^- accepts electrons from the metal ion into its vacant π^* antibonding molecular orbital and thus is regarded as a π-acid ligand.

214. (a): Zeise's salt $K[PtCl_3(C_2H_4)]$ is a π-bonded organometallic compound. Its structure is as follows:

215. (b): The complexes in which the metal and ligand form a bond that involves the π-electrons of the ligand are known as π-complexes. For example, ferrocene $Fe(\eta^5\text{-}C_5H_5)_2$, Zeise's salt $K[PtCl_3(\eta^2\text{-}C_2H_4)]$.

216. (d): The formula of ferrocene is $[(C_5H_5)_2Fe]$.

217. (a): Grignard's reagent is, R–Mg–X. There is no π-bonding present.

218. (c): The CO ligand is bonded to the metal through sigma and pi bonding.

219. (a): No. of sigma bonds is 19 and pi bonds is 11. Each CN contains 1 sigma and two pi bonds, so also each CO group.

220. (d): In $M(CO)_4$, M is bonded as M–C≡O.

221. (c): EAN = Z– (ON) + 2 × (CN)

$36 = 24 - 0 + 2\,x$ (x = CN (n) of metal)

$\therefore n = 6$, the formula is $Cr(CO)_6$

222. (d): In cobalt carbonyl, the oxidation state of Co is zero.

223. (b): In $Ni(CO)_4$, nickel is present in the 0 oxidation state. Here, the ligand (CO) is a strong ligand, so it can cause the unpaired electrons to pair up. Hence, the 4s electrons go to the 3d orbital and make it completely filled, but the 4s and 4p are still available for sp^3 hybridisation.

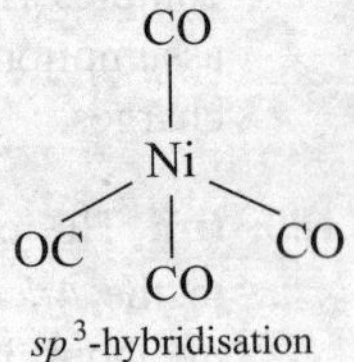

sp^3-hybridisation (tetrahedral)

Ni = [Ar] $4s^2, 3d^8$ (3d: ⇅ ⇅ ⇅ ↑ ↑; 4s: ⇅; 4p: empty)

CO ligands pull the 4s electrons 3d orbital

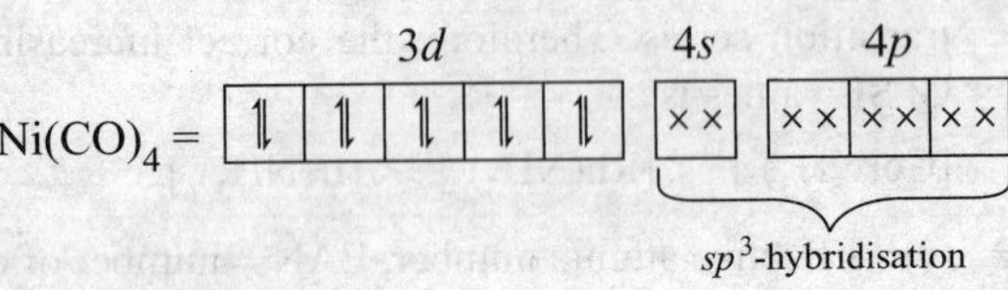

224. (b): By applying the EAN rule, the stability of the metal carbonyls can be predicted. All the given metal carbonyls except $Mn(CO)_5$ follow the EAN rule and thus are stable. But $Mn(CO)_5$ exists as the dimer $Mn_2(CO)_{10}$.

225. (d): Metal carbonyl complexes are regarded as coordination compounds formed by the donation of the lone pairs of electrons of CO into suitable empty orbitals of zerovalent transition metals such as Ni, Fe, and so on. Therefore, the M–C bond is coordinate covalent.

226. (c): Cr does not form a polynuclear carbonyl as $Cr(CO)_6$ itself follows the EAN rule ($24 - 0 + 2 \times 6 = 36$).

227. (a): In a π-acid ligand, back bonding also takes place between the filled orbitals of the metal (donor) and vacant orbitals of the ligand (acceptor) which stabilises the metal–ligand interaction. This is called synergic effect.

228. (d): EAN = (At. number – OS + 2 × CN)

Hence, EAN of Ni in $Ni(CO)_4$ is $= 28 - 0 + 2 \times 4 = 36$.

229. (d): Metal carbonyls do not show $d\pi - p\pi$ overlapping.

230. (d): $Fe(CO)_5$ has dsp^3 hybridisation so, it shows trigonal bipyramidal geometry.

231. (c): $Cr(CO)_6$ contains $Cr^0 = 3d^5\,4s^1$. As CO is a strong field ligand, it causes pairing of all the electrons within the 3$d$orbitals leading to d^2sp^3 hybridisation and an inner orbital octahedral complex.

232. (b): There is $d\pi - p\pi$ metal to ligand back bonding in the Fe–C bond of the organometallic compound $Fe(CO)_5$. So it possesses both σ and π characteristics.

233. (d): An anionic carbonyl complex can delocalise more electron density to antibonding pi orbital of CO and hence lowers the bond order

234. (c): $Fe_2(CO)_9$ contains both Fe–Fe and three bridging carbonyl groups.

Structure of $Fe_2(CO)_9$

235. (d):

(a) In $Fe(CO)_5$, the total number of valence electrons is 8 + 10 = 18, CO being a strong field ligand, causes pairing of electrons and gives a low spin complex.

In $Ni(CO)_4$, the total number of valence electrons is 10 + 8 = 18 and it is also a low spin complex.

(b) Both the complexes are low spin in nature.

(c) The metal–carbon bond strengthens when the oxidation state of the metal is lowered due to synergic effect.

(d) The carbonyl C–O bond is stronger in the case of an increased oxidation state of the metal.

236. (c): Wikinson's catalyst is $[Rh(PPh_3)_3Cl]$ in which Rh^{I} is dsp^2 hybridised giving a square planar geometry. It is used in homogeneous catalysis for the hydrogenation of alkenes.

237. (c): Cisplatin, that is, *cis*-$[Pt(NH_3)_2Cl_2]$ is an anticancer species.

238. (c): (Ethyleneiaminetetraacetate) EDTA ion in used for the removal of the toxic effect of lead metal in the body using chelate therapy treatment because it forms a complex with lead.

239. (c): Chlorophyl is the green pigment in plants and contains magnesium instead of calcium.

240. (d): $4Fe^{3+} + 3[Fe(CN)_6]^{4-} \rightarrow \underset{\text{Prussian blue}}{\overset{\text{III}}{Fe_4}[\overset{\text{II}}{Fe}(CN)_6]_3}$

or $Fe^{3+} + K_4[Fe(CN)_6] \rightarrow \underset{\text{Prussian blue}}{K\overset{\text{III}}{Fe}[\overset{\text{II}}{Fe}(CN)_6]}$

241. (d): This reaction is carried out in alkaline pH, that is, 9–11.

242. (d): The sulfide ion S^{2-} reacts with sodium nitroprusside to give a dark purple complex.

$$S^{2-} + \underset{\text{Sod. nitroprusside}}{Na_2[Fe(CN)_5 NO]} \rightarrow \underset{\text{dark purple complex}}{Na_2[Fe(CN)_5 NOS]^{--}}$$

Final Preparation

243. (a): The given complex is square planar and has three geometrical isomers, two *cis* and one *trans*. It is of [M(ABCD)] type.

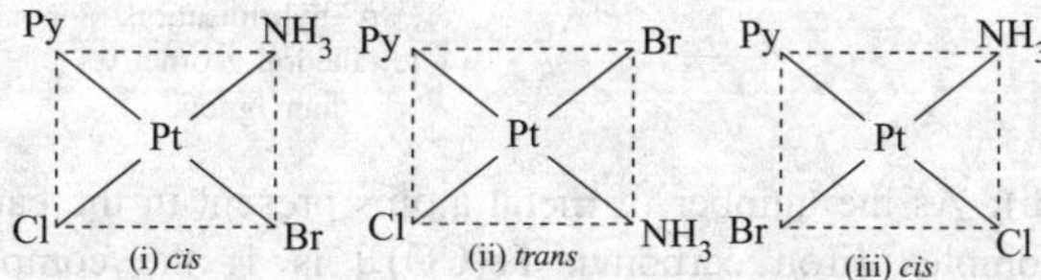

(i) *cis* (ii) *trans* (iii) *cis*

244. (b): $[Pt(NH_3)_2Cl_2]$ is a square planar complex and shows geometrical isomerism—*cis* and *trans*.

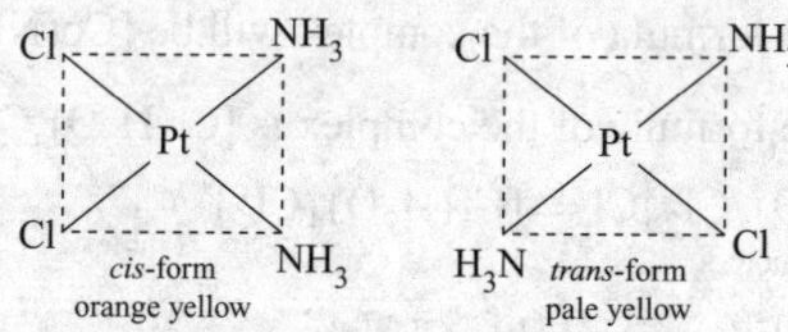

cis-form orange yellow; *trans*-form pale yellow

245. (a): The complex $[CoCl_2(en)_2]$ is a disubstituted octahedral complex with CN = 6. It is of $[M(AA)_2X_2]$ type and shows geometrical isomerism having *cis* and *trans* isomers.

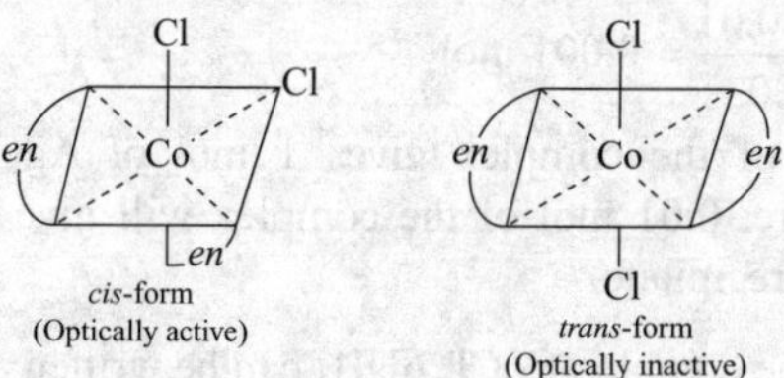

cis-form (Optically active); *trans*-form (Optically inactive)

246. (b): $[Co(en)_3Cl_3$ and *cis*-$[Co(en)_2Cl_2]$ Cl will both show optical isomerism.

247. (a): Complexes of the type $[MA_3B_3]$ show geometrical isomerism known as *fac–mer* geometrical isomerism and not optical isomerism

248. (c): *Cis* and *trans* geometrical isomers of the given complex have different colours.

249. (b): The original complex must have Cl^- ions in the *trans*-position. Only then, all other four NH_3 positions which could be replaced are equivalent and only one isomer would be expected. If the original complex is *cis*, the third Cl^- ion could replace an ammonia *cis* to both or *trans* to one and thus, two isomers would be expected.

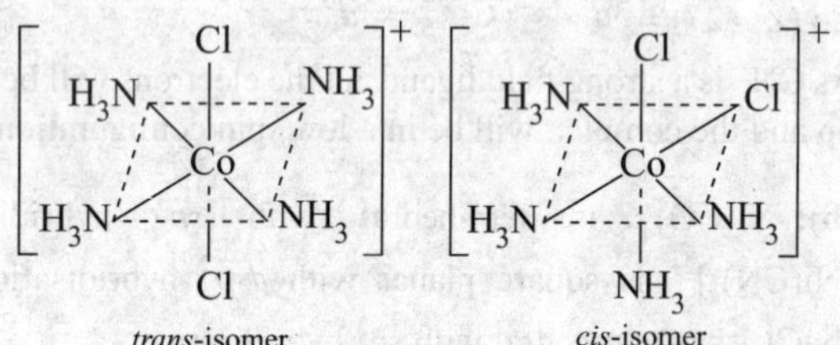

trans-isomer; *cis*-isomer

250. (c): The complex $[Co(en)_2Cl_2]Cl$ is of the $[M(AA)_2X_2]$ type, disubstituted octahedral and shows geometrical *cis* and *trans*isomerism. The *cis* form will be optically active and shows the *d* and *l* forms. Thus, the total number of isomers will be three.

251. (d):

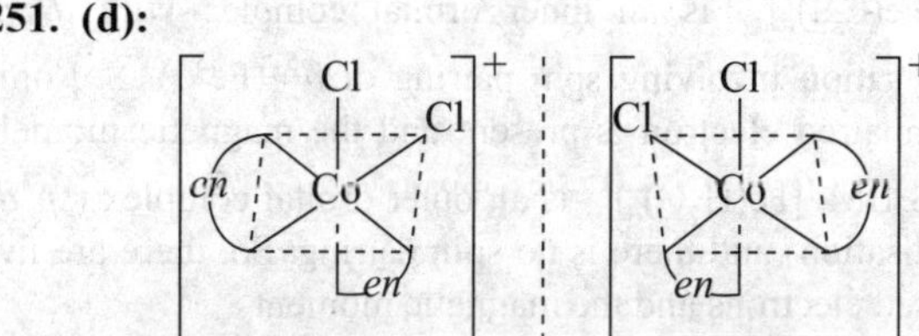

d-isomer; mirror; *l*-isomer

252. (c): Complex ions I and II do not show optical activity and hence are not enantiomers.

253. (a): Tollen's reagent is $[Ag(NH_3)_2]OH \rightleftharpoons [Ag(NH_3)_2]^+ + OH^-$ giving a total of two ions.

254. (a): The formula of the complex will be $[Co(NH_3)_5Cl]Cl_2$.

255. (a): The formula of the complex is $[Cr(H_2O)_4Cl_2]Cl$.

$$\underset{1\text{ mole}}{[Cr(H_2O)_4Cl_2]Cl} \rightleftharpoons [Cr(H_2O)_4Cl^2]^+ \underset{1\text{ mole}}{Cl^-}$$

It has only one ionizable Cl^- ion

$$AgNO_3 + \underset{1\text{ mole}}{Cl^-} \rightarrow \underset{1\text{ mole}}{AgCl\downarrow}$$

Number of mol of the complex

$$= \frac{100 \times 0.01}{1000} = 0.001 \text{ mol}$$

1 mol of the complex gives 1 mol of AgCl precipitate, therefore, 0.01 mol of the complex will give 0.001 mol of AgCl precipitate.

256. (b): The complex $CoCl_3.6NH_3$ can be written as $[Co(NH_3)_6]Cl_3$and it provides 3 Cl^- ions that can be precipitated with an excess of $AgNO_3$ solution giving 3 mol of AgCl precipitate. Similarly, $CoCl_3.5NH_3$ is $[Co(NH_3)_5Cl]Cl_2$and it gives 2 mol of AgCl precipitate. $CoCl_3.4NH_3$ is $[Co(NH_3)_4Cl_2]Cl$ and it gives 1 mol of AgCl precipitate with $AgNO_3$ solution. Thus, the correct order of stoichiometric amount of AgCl formed is 3 AgCl, 2 AgCl and 1 AgCl.

257. (c): $[Cu(NH_3)_4]^{2+}$, deep blue in colour, is square planar with one unpaired electron present in the 3*d*orbital promoted to one of the 4*p* orbitals of Cu and is paramagnetic in behaviour.

258. (d): $[Cu\ (NH_3)_4]^{2+}$ is square planar but the others are tetrahedral in shape.

259. (c): In $[Co(CN)_6]^{3-}$, the oxidation number of Co = +3.

$Co\ (Z = 27) = 3d^7 4s^2; Co^{3+} = 3d^6$

As CN^- is a strong field ligand, all the electrons will be paired up and the complex will be in a low spin configuration.

260. (b): $Ni(CO)_4$ is tetrahedral with sp^3 hybridisation, $[Ni(CN)_4]^{2-}$ is square planar with dsp^2 hybridisation and $[NiCl_4]^{2-}$ is tetrahedral with sp^3 hybridisation

261. (d): $[Co(NH_3)_6]^{3+}$is an inner orbital octahedral complex with Co^{2+} possessing the d^6 configuration where all the electrons are paired up within the 3*d* level making it a diamagnetic complex..

262. (a): $[Fe(CN)_6]^{3-}$ is an inner orbital complex with d^2sp^3 hybridisation involving spin pairing of d^5 (Fe^{3+}). So, only one unpaired electron is present and the magnetic moment is 1.73 BM. $[Fe(H_2O)_6]^{3+}$ is an outer orbital complex (sp^3d^2 hybridisation) and there is no spin pairing. So, there are five unpaired electrons and the magnetic moment

$$\mu = \sqrt{n(n+2)} = \sqrt{35} = 5.92 \text{ BM}$$

263. (c): In complex (a), OS of V = +5

$= 3d^0$

In complex (b), OS of Fe = +2 = $3d^6$, *en* is a strong ligand, d^2sp^3 hybridisation gives zero unpaired electrons.

In complex (c), OS of Co = +4 = $3d^5$ (5 unpaired electrons as *ox* is a weaker ligand).

In complex (d), OS of Ti = +$3d^1$ (1 unpaired electron). Hence, complex (c) exhibits maximum paramagnetism.

264. (b): $[NiCl_4]^{2-}$, $Ni^{2+} = 3d^8$,

$Cl^- \rightarrow$ weak field ligand, structure will be tetrahedral with sp^3 hybridisation. Number of unpaired electrons = 2, complex is paramagnetic.

$[Ni(CN)_4]^{2-}$, $Ni^{2+} = d^8$, $CN^- \rightarrow$ strong field ligand, structure will be square planar with dsp^2 hybridisation. Number of unpaired electrons = 0, complex is diamagnetic.

$[CuCl_4]^{2-}$, $Cu^{2+} = 3d^9$, $Cl^- \rightarrow$ weak field ligand, structure will be tetrahedral with sp^3 hybridisation. Number of unpaired electrons = 1, complex is paramagnetic.

$[CoF_6]^{3-}$, $Co^{3+} = 3d^6$,$F^- \rightarrow$ weak field ligand, structure will be octahedral with sp^3d^2 hybridisation. Number of unpaired electrons = 4, complex is paramagnetic.

265. (b): $[Ti(NH_3)_6]^{3+}$, $Ti^{3+} = 3d^1$, 1 unpaired electron.

$[Cr(NH_3)_6]^{3+}$, $Cr^{3+} = 3d^6$, 0 unpaired electron because of pairing.

$[Zn(NH_3)_6]^{2+}$, $Zn^{2+} = 3d^{10}$, no unpaired electrons.

Hence, $[Cr(NH_3]^{3+}$ exhibits the highest paramagnetic behaviour due to the presence of 3 unpaired electrons.

266. (b): In $[Mn(CN)_6]^{3-}$, $Mn^{3+} = 3d^4$

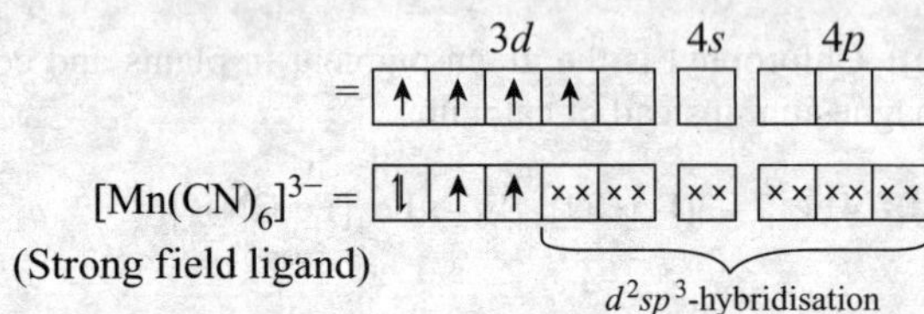

Thus, the complex shows d^2sp^3 hybridisation with an octahedral shape.

267. (b): In $Ni(CO)_4$, Ni^0 = [Ar] $3d^8 4s^2$

3*d* 4*s*

= ⥮ ⥮ ⥮ ↑ ↑ | ⥮

As CO is a strong field ligand, it causes pairing of the 4*s*electrons with the 3*d*electrons giving a $3d^{10}$ configuration with no unpaired electrons.

3*d* 4*s* 4*p*

$Ni(CO)_4$: ⥮ ⥮ ⥮ ⥮ ⥮ | ×× | ×× ×× ××

sp^3-hybridisation, tetrahedral geometry, diamagnetic

268. (b): As the number of metal atoms present in the carbonyl complex [iron carbonyl, $Fe(CO)_5$] is 1, the complex is mononuclear.

269. (b): The increasing order of the strength of the given ligands in the spectrochemical series in $C_2O_4^{2-} < H_2O < NH_3 < CN^-$.

As CN^- is the strongest field ligand, the magnitude of Δ_0 will be maximum in this case, that is, $[Co(CN)_6]^{3-}$, Δ_0 is the highest.

270. (d): d^5 and d^6 systems can have either $t_{2g}^3\, e_g^2$ or $t_{2g}^4\, e_g^2$ (high spin state) configurations respectively in weak ligand fields or, $t_{2g}^5\, e_g^0$ or $t_{2g}^6\, e_g^0$ (low spin state) configurations respectively in strong ligand fields.

271. (a): In $[Cr(H_2O)_6]Cl_3$, $Cr^{3+} = d^3$ configuration is present. These electrons are distributed one each in the more stable (having lower energy) $3d_{xy}$, $3d_{yz}$ and $3d_{xz}$ (t_{2g}) orbitals.

272. (a): A high spin d^4 octahedral complex has the electronic configuration $t_{2g}^3\, e_g^1$.

$\therefore$ CFSE $= (-0.4x + 0.6y)\Delta_o + zP$

where x = no. of electrons in t_{2g}, y = no. of electrons in e_g, z = no. of electron pairs.

$\therefore$ CFSE $= (-0.4\times3 + 0.6\times1)\Delta_o + 0$

$= (-1.2 + 0.6)\Delta_o = -0.6\Delta_o$

273. (d): Electronic configuration of d^6 cations in low spin octahedral complexes $= t_{2g}^6\, e_g^0$.

CFSE $= (-0.4x + 0.6y)\Delta_o$

or $\left(-\frac{2}{5}\times + \frac{3}{5}y\right)\Delta_o$

where x = number of electrons in $t_{2g} = 6$ and y = number of electrons in $e_g = 0$.

$\therefore$ CFSE $= (-2/5\times6 + 0)\,\Delta_o = -\frac{12}{5}\Delta_o$

Number of electron pairs = 3 (as all the six electrons are paired up in t_{2g} orbitals)

$\therefore$ Pairing energy = 3P

Hence, energy (CFSE) of low spin d^6 cations in octahedral complexes,

$= -\frac{12}{5}\Delta_o + 3P$

274. (b): H_2O is a weak field ligand, hence $\Delta_0 <$ pairing energy.

CFSE $= (-0.4x + 0.6y)\Delta_o$ where x and y are the number of electrons occupying t_{2g} and e_g orbitals respectively.

For $[Fe(H_2O)_6]^{3+}$ ion, $Fe^{3+} = 3d^5 = t_{2g}^3 e_g^2$

$\therefore$ CFSE $= -0.4\times3 + 0.6\times2 = 0.0\Delta_o$

275. (a): As the strength of the ligand decreases in the order $NO_2^- > NH_3 > H_2O$, the frequency of light absorbed also decreases in the same order but the wavelength of radiation absorbed increases in the order $NO_2^- < NH_3 < H_2O$.

276. (d): As per the spectrochemical series, the ability to cause crystal field splitting decreases in the order *en* > $NH_3 > H_2O$. As the CFSE is inversely proportional to the wavelength of absorption in the visible region, the correct increasing order for the wavelength of absorption for Co^{3+} complexes is $[Co(en)_3]^{3+} < [Co(NH_3)_6]^{3+} < [Co(H_2O)_6]^{3+}$.

277. (d): CN^- is a strong filed ligand. The value of energy difference between the d level $s(\Delta)$ for the $[Ni(CN)_4]^{2-}$ complex is in the UV region and hence, the complex appears colourless.

278. (b): d^0 and d^{10} species will be colourless where no $d-d$ transition is possible. Hence, TiF_6^{2-}, $Ti^{4+} = 3d^0$ and $Cu_2Cl_2 = 3d^{10}$ are colourless.

279. (b): $d^0\,(Ti^{4+}, Sc^{3+})$ and $d^{10}(Zn^{2+})$ species will not absorb visible light and are colourless whereas $d^3(Cr^{3+})$ can undergo $d-d$ transition on absorption of visible light of a particular wavelength and will be coloured.

280. (b): $[Ni(CN)_4]^{2-}$ contains CN^-, which is a strong field ligand and causes pairing of all the electrons within the $3d$ level thus making one of the d orbitals vacant which is required for dsp^2 hybridisation (square planar structure). Therefore, the complex does not contain any unpaired electron. Hence, it cannot absorb visible light. In other words, the value of Δsp for the complex is in the UV region and hence, the complex appears colourless.

281. (a): The energy sequence of the five d-orbitals in a square planar strong ligand field is $d_{x^2-y^2} > d_{xy} > d_{z^2} > d_{xz} = d_{yz}$.

282. (b): The trans effect of the ligands decreases in the order $CN^- > C_6H_5^- > Br^- > NH_3$. It is the effect of a coordinated ligand already present, on the rate of substitution of the second ligand at the position trans to itself in a square planar or octahedral complex.

283. (c): $CoCl_2 + 2\,HCl \rightarrow [CoCl_4]^{2-} + 2\,H^+$

284. (d): AgCl dissolves in NH_3, KCN and $Na_2S_2O_3$ solutions to give following complexes:

$AgCl + 2\,NH_4OH \rightarrow [Ag(NH_3)_2]Cl + 2H_2O$

$AgCl + 2\,KCN \rightarrow K\,[Ag(CN)_2] + KCl$

$AgCl + Na_2S_2O_3 \rightarrow Na_3[Ag(S_2O_3)_2] + NaCl$

285. (d): $2\,CuSO_4 + 10\,KCN \rightarrow 2\,K_3[Cu(CN)_4] + (CN)_2 + 2\,K_2SO_4$

286. (d): $Li(CH_3)$ is an organometallic compound while $Li(OCH_3)$, $LiCH_3COO$, $Li(CH_3)_2NH$ are not.

287. (a): Grignard's reagent, R–Mg–X, is formed through a normal 2 electron covalent bond (σ bond) between the R group and Mg atom.

288. (c): $Fe(CO)_5$, $Fe = 3d^6\,4s^2$

CO is a strong field ligand.

	3d					4s	4p		
$Fe(CO)_5 =$	⥮	⥮	⥮	⥮	××	××	××	××	××

dsp^3 (3d, 4s, 4p ××)

Hence, the Fe $\leftarrow$ CO σ bond is formed by the overlap of filled sp hybrid orbitals of the C atom of CO and the vacant dsp^3 hybrid orbital of Fe.

289. (a): The presence of a positive charge on the metal carbonyl would resist the flow of the metal electron charge to the π-orbitals of CO. This would increase the CO bond order and hence CO in a metal carbonyl cation would absorb at a higher frequency as compared to its absorption in a neutral metal carbonyl.

290. (b): $Fe + 5\,CO \xrightarrow{\Delta} Fe(CO)_5$

291. (a): Greater the negative charge on the carbonyl complex, the more easy it would be for the metal to permit its electrons to participate in the back bonding, the higher would be the M–C bond order and simultaneously there would be a larger reduction in the C–O bond order. Thus, $[Fe(CO)_4]^{2-}$ has the lowest C–O bond order which means the longest bond length.

292. (b): Chlorophyll contains Mg^{2+}, hemoglobin contains Fe^{2+}, vitamin B12 contains Co^{3+} and carboxypeptidase A contains Zn^{2+} metal ions.

293. (b): Ferrous ferricyanide

$\overset{II}{Fe_3}[\overset{III}{Fe}(CN)_6]_2$ is called Turnbull's blue

294. (a): In Wikinson's catalyst, a homogeneous catalyst $(Ph_3P)_3RhCl$, Rh is dsp^2 hybridised giving a square planar shape to the compound and Rh is in the +1 oxidation state.

Rh ($Z = 45$), $4d^8\,5s^1$ configuration

$Rh^+ = 4d^8$, all the electrons pair up within the $4d$ orbitals leaving one $4d$ orbital vacant for dsp^2 hybridisation.

295. (c): The red complex of Ni–DMG has a square planar geometry with dsp^2 hybridisation and not tetrahedral geometry.

```
            H
          ·'  \
         O     O
         ↑     |
CH3—C=N     N=C—CH3
        Ni
CH3—C=N     N=C—CH3
         |     ↓
         O     O
          \   ·'
            H
```

Ni^{II}–DMG red complex

296. (a): $Ni(CO)_4$ is formed at low temperature and gets decomposed at higher temperature to give pure Ni metal.

297. (d): From the complex ion $[Ag(CN)_2]^-$, Ag is not displaced by Cu.

298. (b): Ca–EDTA complex replaces Ca by Pb, leading to a soluble complex (Pb–EDTA) which is excreted out through urine.

299. (a): C_2H_4 does not possess any unshared pair of electrons but still can act as a ligand; for example, in Zeise's salt $K[PtCl_3(\eta^2\text{-}C_2H_4)]$.

300. (c): Hydrazine forms a highly unstable chelate with metal ions.

301. (a): Coordination number of the metal M in the complex = 6
Oxidation number of the metal M in the complex = +3
Sum of CN and ON of the metal M = 9

302. (d): The correct name is chloridobis(ethylenediamine) nitritocobalt(III).

303. (b): The IUPAC name is potassium trioxalatoiridate(III).

304. (d): Sodium nitroprusside is $Na_2[Fe(CN)_5NO]$. In this compound, NO is present as NO^+ and Fe has +2 charge. On the basis of this, the actual name should be sodium pentacyanonitrosoniumferrate(II).

305. (a): When the solution of the complex is passed through a cation exchanger, Cl^- ions will combine with H^+ ions of the cation exchanger to form HCl.

$Cl^- + H^+ \rightarrow HCl$

$\therefore$ 1 mol of complex $\equiv n$ mol HCl

$\equiv n$ mol NaOH

mol of the complex $= \dfrac{0.319}{266.5} = 0.0012$ mol

mol of NaOH used $= \dfrac{28.5 \times 0.125}{1000}$

$= 0.0036$ mol

0.0012 mol of complex = 0.0036 mol NaOH

= 0.0036 mol HCl

$\therefore$ 1 mol of complex $= \dfrac{0.0036}{0.0012} = 3$ mol HCl

3 mol of HCl = 3 mol of Cl^- ions

Thus, all the Cl^- ions in the complex are outside the coordination sphere (that is, ionisable). Hence, the correct formula of the complex is $[Cr(H_2O)_6]Cl_3$.

306. (c): Fe is sp^3d^2 hybridised in $[Fe(H_2O)_5NO]^{2+}$ complex.

307. (c): $[Ni(NH_3)_2Cl_2]$ being a tetrahedral complex with monodentate ligands, does not exhibit isomerism.

MATCH THE FOLLOWING

308. (c): (A) $PtCl_4.6NH_3$ can be written as $[Pt(NH_3)_6]Cl_4$ which on ionisation will give a total of 5 ions (1 + 4).
(B) $K_3[Fe(CN)_6]$ gives 4 ions (3 + 1).
(C) $CoCl_3.5H_2O$ can be written as $[Co(H_2O)_5Cl]Cl_2$ which on ionisation will give 3 ions (1 + 2).
(D) $[Cr(NH_3)_3(NO_2)_3]$ gives zero ions on ionisation, that is, it does not get ionised.

309. (a): (A) ON of Ni in $Ni(CO)_4$ is zero. (B) ON of Fe in $[Fe(H_2O)_5NO]^{2+}$ is +1.
(C) ON of Co in $[Co(CO)_5]^{2-}$ is −2.
(D) ON of Cr in $[Cr_2(CO)_{10}]^{2-}$ is −1.

ASSERTION REASON

310. (b): Correct explanation. $[Pt(en)_2Cl_2]^{2+}$ is an octahedral disubstituted complex containing two symmetrical bidentate ligands. It shows geometrical isomerism. The *cis*-isomer will show optical isomerism. Hence, there are a total of three isomers.

311. (a): R is the correct explanation of **A.**

312. (a): R is the correct explanation of **A.**

313. (c): Correct R. Hybridisation of the central metal Fe^{2+} in $K_4[Fe(CN)_6]$ is d^2sp^3 with no unpaired electrons and the complex (inner orbital octahedral) is diamagnetic. The hybridisation of Fe^{3+} in $[Fe(H_2O)_6]Cl_3$ is sp^3d^2 with five unpaired electrons and the complex (outer orbital octahedral) is paramagnetic.

314. (a): R is the correct explanation of **A.**

315. (b): Correct explanation. $[Cu(NH_3)_4]^{2+}$ is coloured due to the presence of an unpaired electron whereas $[Cu(NH_4]^{3-}$ has no unpaired electrons and hence is colourless.

316. (d): Correct A. $[Ni(en)_3]Cl_2$ has a higher stability than $[Ni(NH_3)_6]Cl_2$.
Correct R. In $[Ni(en)_3]Cl_2$, the geometry of the complex is octahedral.

317. (a): R is the correct explanation of **A.**

318. (b): Correct explanation. CO is a neutral ligand and thus, Fe in $Fe(CO)_5$ has zero oxidation state.

319. (a): R is the correct explanation of **A.**

320. (a): R is the correct explanation of **A.**

321. (d): Correct A. Glycinate ion is an example of a didentate ligand.
Correct R. It contains N and O as donor atoms.

322. (c): Correct R. As F is more electronegative, it attracts the electrons on N towards itself and thus NF_3 is a poor donor and a weak ligand.

323. (c): Correct R. In Zeise's salt, $K[PtCl_3(\eta^2\text{-}C_2H_4)]$, C_2H_4 is a neutral ligand.

324. (b): Correct explanation. The colour of the complex $[Fe(H_2O)_5NO]^{2+}$ formed is due to charge transfer from NO to Fe^{2+} (transfer of odd electron on N of NO to Fe) changing NO to NO^+ and Fe^{2+} to Fe^+.

Haloalkanes and Haloarenes

10.1 Introduction

Haloalkane: RX where R is an alkyl group.

Haloarene: ArX where Ar is an arene. X is a halogen atom (F, Cl, Br, I). Thus, haloalkanes and haloarenes are halogen derivatives of aliphatic and aromatic hydrocarbons. Halogen derivatives may be broadly classified into two types—aliphatic halogen compounds and aromatic halogen compounds.

10.1.1 Aliphatic Halogen Compounds

These are considered to be derived from the corresponding aliphatic hydrocarbons by the replacement of one or more hydrogen atoms by an equal number of halogen atoms. Monohalogen derivatives can be further classified as primary (1°), secondary (2°) and tertiary (3°) alkyl halides depending upon whether the halogen atom is attached to a primary, secondary or tertiary carbon atom, respectively. For example,

CH_3-CH_2-Cl — Chloroethane (Ethyl chloride; 1°)

$CH_3-CH(Cl)-CH_3$ — 2-Chloropropane (Isopropyl chloride; 2°)

$CH_3-C(Cl)(CH_3)-CH_3$ — 2-Chloro-2-methylpropane (tert-butyl chloride; 3°)

10.1.2 Aromatic Halogen Derivatives (Haloarenes)

These can be considered to be derived from the corresponding arenes (aromatic hydrocarbons) by the replacement of one or more hydrogen atoms by an equal number of halogen atoms. These are further classified into the following two major classes.

(i) Nuclear halogen derivatives (aryl halides): The halogen atom is directly linked to the aromatic ring. These are also called aryl halides. Some examples of aryl halides are:

o-Bromotoluene *p*-Iodotoluene *m*-Chloronitrobenzene

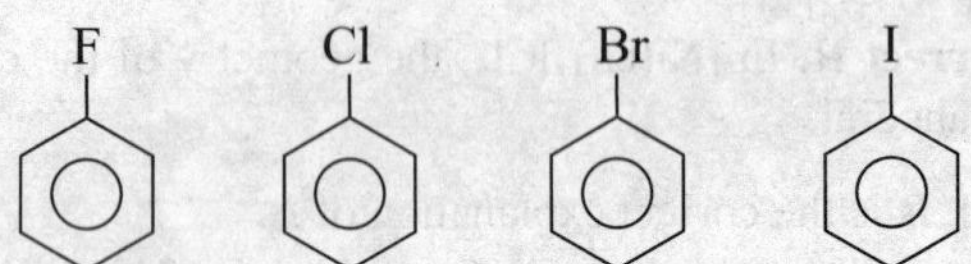

Fluorobenzene Chlorobenzene Bromobenzene Iodobenzene

In all aryl halides, the halogen is attached to a sp^2-hybridised carbon.

(ii) Side chain halogen derivatives (aralkyl halides): The halogen atom is linked to the carbon of the side chain carrying the aryl group. These are also called aralkyl halides. Some common examples are:

$C_6H_5-CH_2Cl$ — Chlorophenylmethane (Benzyl chloride)

$C_6H_5-CHCl_2$ — Dichlorophenylmethane (Benzal chloride)

$C_6H_5-CCl_3$ — Phenyltrichloromethane (Benzotrichloride)

$C_6H_5-CH_2-CH_2-Br$ — 2-Phenyl-1-bromoethane (β-Phenylethylbromide)

10.1.3 Classification on the Basis of Number of Halogen Atoms

(i) Monohalogen derivatives of alkanes are termed as alkyl halides (R–X) where R is any alkyl group having the general formula, $C_nH_{2n+1}X$.

(ii) Dihalogen derivatives of alkanes

- **Vicinal dihalides:** Vicinal dihalides have the two halogen atoms present on adjacent (vicinal) carbon atoms. These are also called *alkylene dihalides*.

  $CH_2(Cl)-CH_2(Cl)$ — Ethylene dichloride (1,2-Dichloroethane)

  $CH_3-CH(Br)-CH(Br)-CH_3$ — Propylene dibromide (1,2-Dibromopropane)

- **Germinal dihalides:** Germinal dihalides have both the halogen atoms attached on the same carbon atom. These are also called *alkylidene dihalides*.

  CH_3-CHCl_2 — Ethylidene dichloride (1,1-Dichloroethane)

  $CH_3-CBr_2-CH_3$ — Propylidene dibromide (2,2-Dibromopropane)

- α, ω **dihalides:** The halides in which the two halogens are present on the terminal carbon atoms are *α, ω dihalides* or *polymethylene dihalides.*

$ClCH_2-CH_2CH_2CH_2Cl$ — Tetramethylene dichloride (1,4-Dichlorobutane)

$Br-CH_2-(CH_2)_3-CH_2Br$ — Pentamethylene dibromide (1,5-Dibromopentane)

(iii) Trihalogen derivatives of alkane: Examples are $CHCl_3$ (chloroform, trichloromethane), $CHBr_3$ (bromoform, tribromomethane) and CHI_3 (iodoform, triiodomethane).

(iv) Tetrahalogen derivatives: An example is CCl_4 (carbon tetrachloride).

Note: Fully halogenated hydrocarbons are called perhalohydrocarbons as in $CF_3–CF_2–CF_3$ (perfluoropropane).

Halogen Derivatives of Alkenes and Alkynes

Monohalogen derivatives of unsaturated hydrocarbons are called *haloalkenes* and *haloalkynes.* The halogen is attached to an *sp*^{2} hybridised carbon. Those in which the halogen atom is present on one of the carbon atoms of the double bond are called *vinylic halides*. When the halogen is attached to the carbon atom next to the C=C bond, they are called *allylic halides*.

$CH_3–CH=CH–Cl$
1-Chloropropene

$\overset{1}{C}H_2=\overset{2}{C}H–\overset{3}{C}HCl–\overset{4}{C}H_2–\overset{5}{C}H_3$
3-Chloropent-1-ene

10.2 Preparation of Haloalkanes

10.2.1 From Alcohols

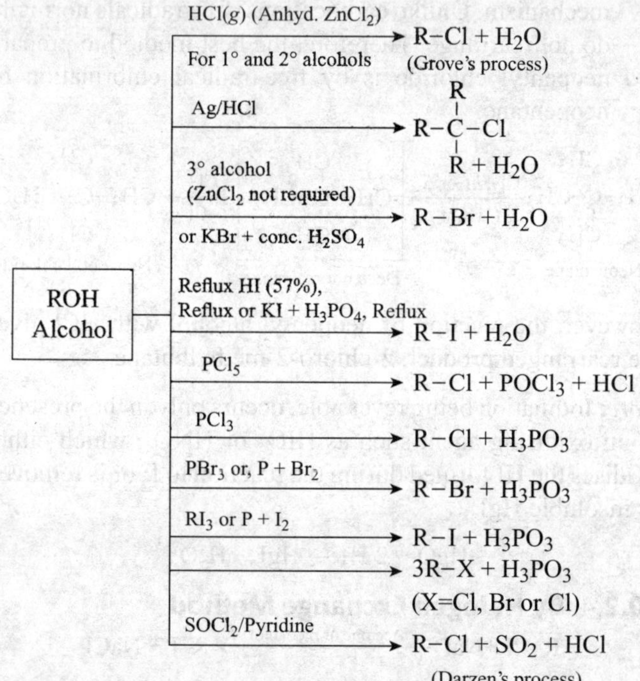

- 1° and 2° alcohols react with HCl(*g*) in the presence of anhyd. $ZnCl_2$ as catalyst while in the case of 3° alcohols, $ZnCl_2$ is not required.
- The function of anhydrous $ZnCl_2$ is to help in the cleavage of the C–O bond by coordinating with the oxygen atom of the alcohol.
- The reaction is believed to occur either by nucleophilic attack by the halide ion on the protonated alcohol (S_N2) or through the carbocation formed by the loss of H_2O from the protonated alcohol (S_N1).

$$R-\ddot{O}H + H^+ \rightleftharpoons R-\overset{+}{O}H_2 \longrightarrow R^+ + H_2O$$

$$S_N2.\ X^- + R-\overset{+}{O}H_2 \xrightarrow{Slow} R-X + H_2O$$

(b) $R–X \rightarrow R^+ + :X^-$

$$S_N1.\ X^- + R^+ \xrightarrow{Fast} R-X$$

- The stability of the carbocation or the incipient (developing) carbocation decreases in the order 3° > 2° > 1°, therefore, the reactivity of alcohols follows the order, 3° > 2° > 1°.
- The nucleophilicity (tendency to donate a pair of electrons to carbon) decreases in the order I^- > Br^- > Cl^-, therefore, the reactivity of the halogen acids decreases in the same order, HI > HBr > HCl.
- The reaction of alcohol with $SOCl_2$ to form alkyl chlorides is called S_Ni (substitution, nucleophilic, internal) reaction. This reaction may be carried out in the presence or absence of pyridine. If the starting alcohol is chiral, the presence or absence of pyridine gives the product with different stereochemistry. For example, (S)-2-butanol in the absence of pyridine (C_5H_5N) gives (S)-2-chlorobutane with retention of configuration. In the presence of pyridine, it gives 2-chlorobutane with inversion of configuration (S_N2 mechanism).

$CH_3CH_2(H)(CH_3)C–OH \xrightarrow[-Cl^-]{SOCl_2}$ $CH_3CH_2(H)(CH_3)C–O–S(=O)Cl$ $\xrightarrow[-SO_2]{S_Ni}$ $CH_3CH_2(H)(CH_3)C–Cl$

S_Ni reaction (Substitution nucleophilic internal) — (S)-2-Chlorobutane (Retention of configuration)

S_Ni reaction without pyridine

$CH_3CH_2(H)(CH_3)C–OH \xrightarrow[C_5H_5N]{SOCl_2}$ $CH_3CH_2(H)(CH_3)C–O–\overset{O}{\overset{\|}{S}}–Cl$ + $C_5H_5\overset{+}{N}HCl^-$

Pyridine hydrochloride

$S_N2$mechanism with pyridine

$$C_5H_5\overset{+}{N}HCl^- + (CH_3CH_2)(H)(CH_3)C{-}O{-}S(=O){-}Cl \xrightarrow[-C_5H_5\overset{+}{N}HCl^- - SO_2]{S_N2} Cl{-}C(CH_2CH_3)(H)(CH_3)$$

(R)-2-Chlorobutane (Inversion of configuration)

10.2.2 From Alkenes

(i) **Addition of halogen acids** to alkenes gives alkyl halides. In the absence of peroxides, addition to unsymmetrical alkenes occurs according to Markownikoff's rule while in the presence of peroxides (ROOR), that is, $(C_6H_5COO)_2$, H_2O_2, and so on, the addition of only HBr (and not of HF, HCl of HI) occurs according to anti Markownikoff's rule. This is also called *peroxide effect* or *Kharasch effect*.

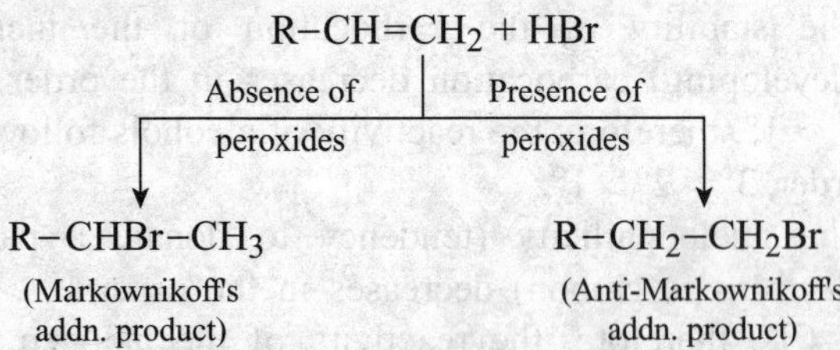

Note that the peroxide effect is observed only with HBr. Therefore, addition of HCl or HI to alkenes always gives Markownikoff's products both in the presence or absence of peroxides and the reaction occurs through a carbocation intermediate.

$$\underset{\text{Propene}}{CH_3{-}CH{=}CH_2} + HCl \xrightarrow[\text{of peroxides}]{\text{Presence or absence}} \underset{\text{2-Chloropropane}}{CH_3{-}CHCl{-}CH_3}$$

(ii) **Allylic halogenation:** The hydrogens attached to the allylic carbon are called allylic hydrogens. These hydrogens can be replaced by halogens (Cl or Br) by heating at 775 K.

$$\underset{\text{Propene}}{CH_3{-}CH{=}CH_2} + Cl_2 \xrightarrow{775\text{ K}} \underset{\substack{\text{3-Chloro-1-propene}\\ \text{(Allyl chloride)}}}{ClCH_2{-}CH{=}CH_2} + HCl$$

$$\underset{\text{Propene}}{CH_3{-}CH{=}CH_2} + Br_2 \xrightarrow{775\text{ K}} \underset{\text{3-Bromo-1-propene}}{Br{-}CH_2{-}CH{=}CH_2} + HBr$$

Allylic chlorination can also be carried out by treating an alkene with sulfuryl chloride (SO_2Cl_2) at 475 K in the presence of light and traces of organic peroxides.

$$\underset{\text{Propene}}{CH_3{-}CH{=}CH_2} + SO_2Cl_2 \xrightarrow[\text{Traces of peroxides}]{475\text{ K}, h\nu} \underset{\text{Allyl chloride}}{Cl{-}CH_2{-}CH{=}CH_2} + SO_2 + HCl$$

Allylic bromination is more easily carried out with NBS (N-bromosuccinimide) in the presence of light and traces of peroxides.

$$\underset{\text{Propene}}{CH_3{-}CH{=}CH_2} + \underset{\text{NBS}}{(CH_2{-}CO)_2NBr} \xrightarrow[\substack{\text{Benzoyl}\\ \text{peroxide}}]{h\nu} \underset{\text{Allyl bromide}}{Br{-}CH_2{-}CH{=}CH_2} + \underset{\text{Succinimide}}{(CH_2{-}CO)_2NH}$$

- At high temperature (775 K), the addition of halogens to alkenes becomes reversible and hence does not occur. Instead substitution occurs at the allylic position.
- Allylic halogenations such as side chain halogenations in arenes, occurs by a free radical mechanism.

10.2.3 From Alkanes

Direct halogenations can be carried out.

$$R{-}H + X_2 \xrightarrow{\Delta \text{ or } h\nu} R{-}X + HX\ (X = Cl, Br \text{ or } I)$$

- During direct halogenations as in the above reaction, the formation of di- tri- and polyhalogen compounds also takes place. For example,

$$CH_4 + Cl_2 \xrightarrow[\text{or } 520\text{–}670\text{ K}]{h\nu} CH_3Cl + CH_2Cl_2 + CHCl_3 + CCl_4$$

- Direct fluorination of alkanes occurs explosively with the rupture of C–C bonds. Therefore, alkyl fluorides are prepared indirectly by heating alkyl chlorides with inorganic fluorides such as AsF_3, SbF_3, AgF, Hg_2F_2.

$$2\ CH_3CH_2Cl + Hg_2F_2 \rightarrow 2\ CH_3CH_2F + Hg_2Cl_2$$

This reaction is called *Swarts reaction*.

- Direct halogenation of alkanes occurs by a free radical mechanism. Unlike carbocations, free radicals normally do not rearrange. Therefore, the best method to prepare neopentyl chloride is by free radical chlorination of neopentane.

$$\underset{\text{Neopentane}}{CH_3{-}C(CH_3)_2{-}CH_3} \xrightarrow[(-HCl)]{Cl_2,\ h\nu \text{ or } \Delta} \underset{\text{Does not rearrange}}{\left[CH_3{-}C(CH_3)_2{-}\dot{C}H_2\right]} \xrightarrow[-\dot{C}l]{Cl_2} \underset{\text{Neopentyl chloride}}{CH_3{-}C(CH_3)_2{-}CH_2Cl}$$

However, the reaction of neopentyl alcohol with HCl gives the rearranged product, 2-chloro-2-methylbutane.

Note: Iodination being reversible, occurs only in the presence of an oxidising agent such as HIO_3 or HNO_3, which either oxidises the HI formed during the reaction to I_2 or is removed as insoluble HgI_2.

$$HgO + 2\ HI \rightarrow HgI_2 + H_2O$$

10.2.4 By Halogen Exchange Method

$$R{-}Cl + NaI \xrightarrow{\text{Acetone or methanol}} R{-}I + NaCl$$

This reaction is called Finkelstein reaction.

- Only iodoalkanes can be obtained by this method by displacing Cl or Br.

- NaI is soluble but NaCl and NaBr are insoluble in methanol or acetone, therefore, these (NaCl or NaBr) can be removed from the reaction mixture simply by filtration.

10.2.5 Borodine–Hunsdiecker Reaction

The silver salts of carboxylic acids on reaction with Br_2 in refluxing CCl_4 undergo decarboxylation to form alkyl and aryl bromides with one carbon atom less than the original acid used.

$$\underset{\text{Silver acetate}}{CH_3COOAg} + Br_2 \xrightarrow{CCl_4/\text{Reflux}} \underset{\text{Methyl bromide}}{CH_3\text{–}Br} + AgBr + CO_2$$

$$\underset{\text{Silver benzoate}}{C_6H_5COOAg} + Br_2 \xrightarrow{CCl_4/\text{Reflux}} \underset{\text{Bromobenzene}}{C_6H_5Br} + AgBr + CO_2$$

Note:
- *Hunsdiecker reaction* occurs by a free radical mechanism.
- It is used to reduce the length of the carbon chain (descent of series) by one carbon atom.
- The yield of alkyl or aryl halide decreases in the order, 1° > 2° > 3°.
- Only bromides are obtained in good yield by this reaction. The yield of chlorides is usually poor while iodides cannot be prepared by this method since they form esters with silver salts.

$$2\,RCOOAg + I_2 \rightarrow RCOOR + CO_2 + 2\,AgI$$

This reaction is called *Birnbaum–Simonini* reaction.

10.3 Preparation of Haloarenes

10.3.1 From Aromatic Hydrocarbons

(i) Nuclear halogenations: The halogenation occurs in the ring. For example,

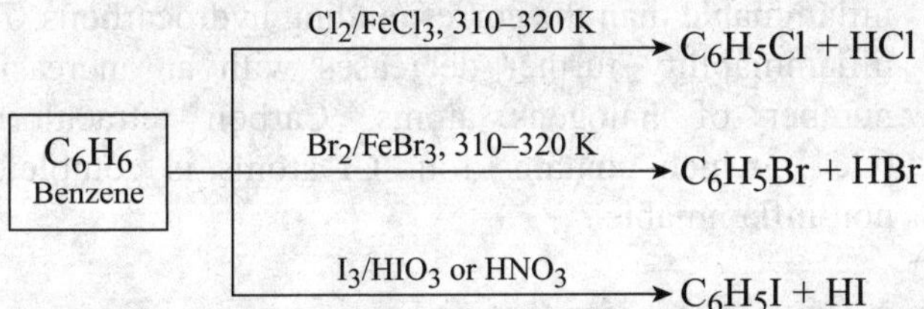

With iodine, the reaction is reversible. Therefore, to push the reaction in the forward direction, HI formed during the reaction is removed by oxidation with an oxidising agent such as HNO_3, or HIO_3.

$$5\,HI + HIO_3 \rightarrow 3\,I_2 + 3\,H_2O$$

Note: Due to resonance, the C–O bond in phenols is much stronger than the C–O bond in alcohols, and hence cannot be easily broken. Therefore, aryl halides cannot be prepared by the action of halogen acids, phosphorus halides or $SOCl_2$ on phenols.

(ii) Side chain halogenations: On the other hand, if halogenation is carried out in the presence of heat or light and in the absence of a halogen carrier, the halogenation occurs in the side chain. For example,

$$\underset{\text{Toluene}}{C_6H_5CH_3} \xrightarrow[\text{sunlight}]{Cl_2,\ 383\ K,} \underset{\text{Benzyl chloride}}{C_6H_5CH_2Cl} \xrightarrow[383\ K]{+\,Cl_2,\ h\nu,} \underset{\text{Benzyl dichloride}}{C_6H_5CHCl_2} \xrightarrow[383\ K]{+\,Cl_2,\ h\nu,} \underset{\text{Benzotrichloride}}{C_6H_5CCl_3}$$

Chlorination of toluene can also be carried out by treating it either with SO_2Cl_2 or *tert*-butyl hypochlorite in the presence of ultraviolet light or in the presence of a trace of *tert*-butyl peroxide.

- With $Cl_2/FeCl_3$, toluene undergoes nuclear halogenations to give a mixture of *o*- and *p*-chlorotoluene.

$$\underset{\text{Toluene}}{C_6H_5CH_3} \xrightarrow{Cl_2/FeCl_3} \underset{\substack{o\text{-Chlorotoluene}\\ \text{(minor)}}}{o\text{-}ClC_6H_4CH_3} + \underset{\substack{p\text{-Chlorotoluene}\\ \text{(major)}}}{p\text{-}ClC_6H_4CH_3}$$

Due to steric hindrance at the *o*-position, it is always the *p*-isomer which predominates.
- Nuclear halogenations occur by the electrophilic substitution mechanism while side chain halogenations occur by the free radical mechanism.
- If the side chain is larger than a methyl group, the halogenations always occur at the benzylic carbon, that is, the carbon atom next to the benzene ring because the benzylic free radical is always more stable than alternate non-benzylic free-radicals due to resonance. Thus,

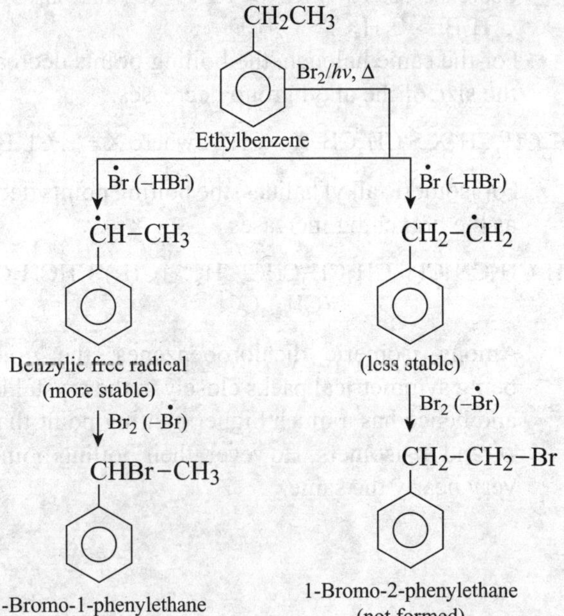

***Note*:** Benzylic bromination can also be carried out with NBS in the presence of light and a trace of peroxides such as benzoyl peroxide ($(C_6H_5COO)_2$).

10.3.2 From Diazonium Salts

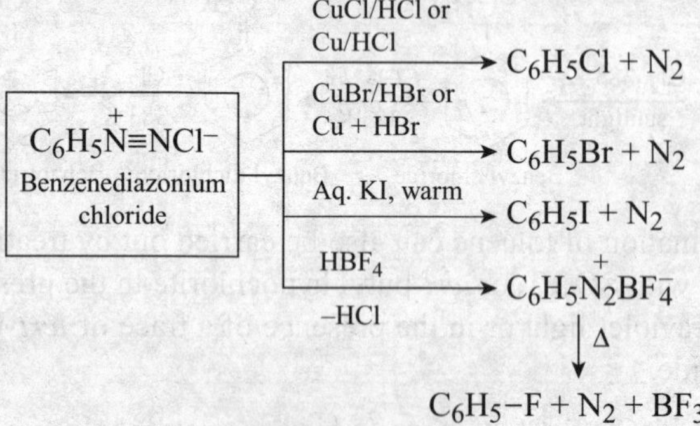

- When benzenediazonium chloride is treated with CuCl/HCl or Cu/HBr, the reaction is called the *Sandmeyer reaction*. It is the halogen attached to cuprous halide which enters the ring.
- With Cu/HCl or Cu/HBr, the reaction is called the *Gattermann reaction*.
- Thermal decomposition of benzenediazonium tetrafluoroborate to give fluorobenzene is called *Balz–Schiemann reaction*.

10.4 Physical Properties of Haloalkanes and Haloarenes (Alkyl and Aryl Halides)

(i) Melting and boiling points: Greater the molecular mass, stronger the van der Waals forces of attraction and hence higher is the melting point/boiling point.

- For the same alkyl or aryl group, boiling points decrease as: RI > RBr > RCl > RF, that is, $C_6H_5I > C_6H_5Br > C_6H_5Cl > C_6H_5F$
- For the same halogen, the boiling points decrease as the size of the alkyl group decreases.

$$CH_3CH_2CH_2X > CH_3CH_2X > CH_3X \text{ where } X = F, Cl, Br, I.$$

- For isomeric alkyl halides, the boiling points decrease as the branching increases.

$$CH_3CH_2CH_2Cl > CH_3CH_2CHClCH_3 > (CH_3)_2CHCH_2Cl > (CH_3)_3CCl$$

- Among isomeric dichlorobenzenes, the *p*-isomer being symmetrical packs closely in the crystal lattice and hence has a much higher melting point than the *o*- and *m*-isomers. However, their boiling points are very nearly the same.

(ii) Density

- RI > RBr > RCl > RF (for the same alkyl or aryl group)
- $CH_3I > C_2H_5I > C_3H_7I$ (for the same halogen)
- The density increases with increasing number of halogen atoms. $CH_3Cl < CH_2Cl_2 < CHCl_3 < CCl_4$

(iii) Bond strength: It decreases as the size of the halogen increases. $CH_3F < CH_3Cl < CH_3Br > CH_3I$

(iv) Dipole moment

Dipole moment decreases as the electronegativity of the halogen decreases from Cl to Br to I. Fluorides, however, have a lower dipole moment than chlorides due to the very small size of fluorine which outweighs the effect of greater electronegativity. The actual order is:

$$CH_3Cl\ (1.860\ D) > CH_3F\ (1.847\ D) > CH_3Br\ (1.830\ D) > CH_3I\ (1.636\ D)$$

Amongst isomeric dichlorobenzenes, the *p*-isomer being most symmetrical has zero dipole moment. Thus, the *o*-isomer with a bond angle of 60° between the two Cl atoms has the highest dipole moment (2.54 D) while the *m*-isomer with a bond angle of 120° between the two Cl atoms has dipole moment of 1.72 D which is approximately equal to that chlorobenzene (1.69 D).

(v) Stability: It decreases as the strength of the C–X bond decreases, that is, RF > RBr > RCl > RI. Thus, iodides on standing become violet or brown due to their decomposition in the presence of sunlight.

$$2\ R\text{–}I \xrightarrow{\text{Sunlight}} R\text{–}R + I_2$$

The I_2 thus liberated dissolves in the alkyl iodide to impart a dark brown colour to it.

(vi) Solubility: Alkyl and aryl halides are insoluble in water because they do not form H-bonds with water.

(vii) Inflammability: Organic halogen compounds are less inflammable than the corresponding hydrocarbons. The inflammability further decreases with an increasing number of halogens atoms. Carbon tetrachloride (CCl_4) which contains four Cl atoms is completely non-inflammable.

10.5 Chemical Reactions of Haloalkanes (Alkyl Halides)

Because of the presence of a polar C–X bond, alkyl halides are highly reactive compounds. They are known to undergo nucleophilic substitution and elimination reactions.

10.5.1 Nucleophilic Substitution Reactions

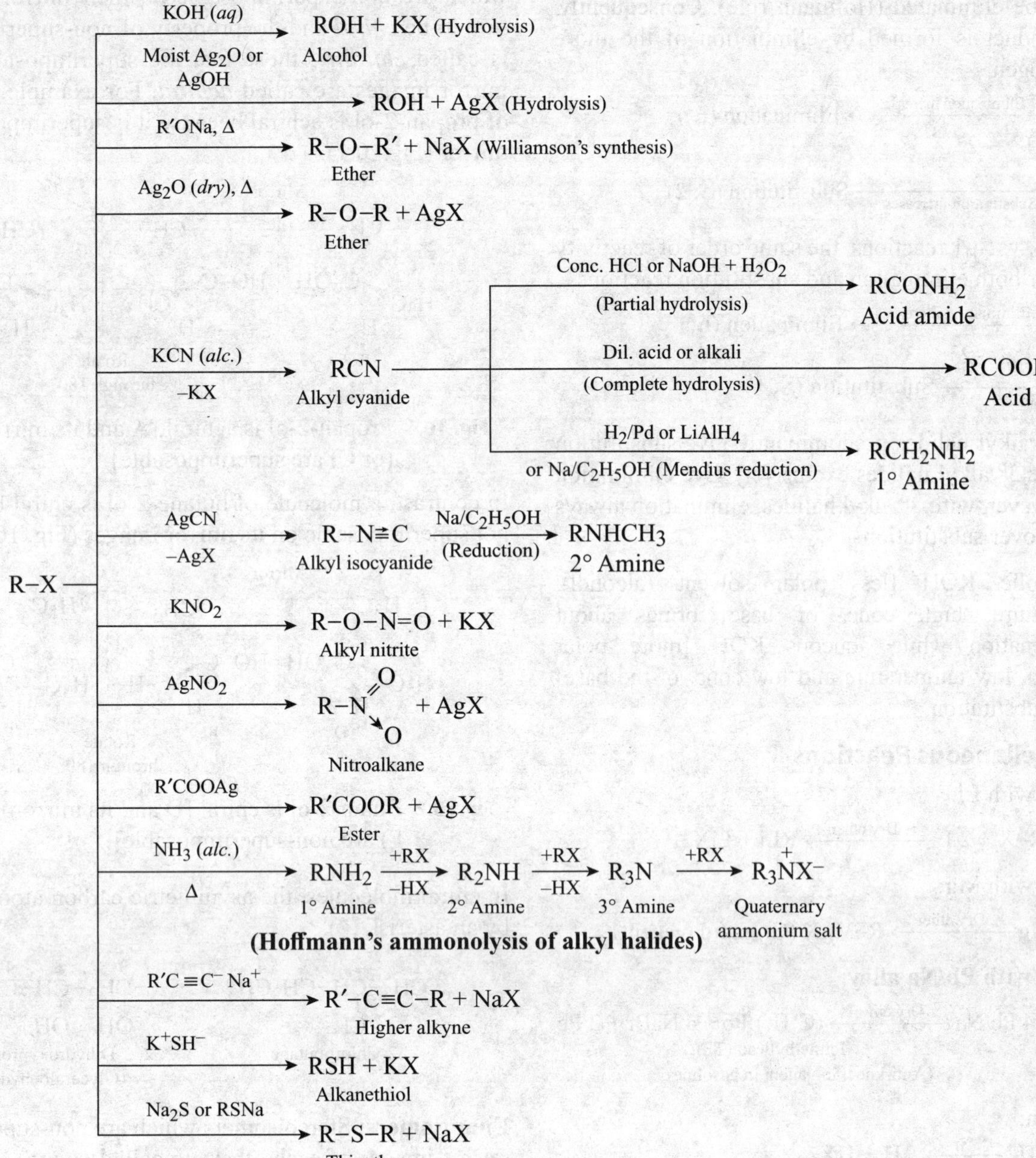

All the nucleophilic substitution reactions discussed above occur either by the S_N1 or S_N2 mechanism.

10.5.2 Dehydrohalogenation

Alkyl halides when heated with alcoholic KOH undergo dehydrohalogenation to form alkenes. The halogen is lost from the α-carbon atom and the hydrogen from the β-carbon. For example,

$$\overset{\beta}{H-CH_2}-\overset{\alpha}{CH_2}-Br + KOH\,(alc.) \xrightarrow{\Delta} CH_2{=}CH_2 + KBr + H_2O$$

$$\underset{\text{1-Bromopropane}}{CH_3CH_2CH_2-Br} \text{ or } \underset{\text{2-Bromopropane}}{CH_3-CHBr-CH_3} \xrightarrow[\Delta]{\text{Alc.KOH}} \underset{\text{Propene}}{CH_3-CH{=}CH_2} + HBr$$

(i) **Saytzeff rule:** It states that dehydrohalogenation occurs in such a way that the more highly substituted alkene is obtained as the major product. For example,

$$\underset{\text{2-Bromobutane}}{CH_3-CH_2-\overset{Br}{\overset{|}{C}H}-CH_3} \xrightarrow[-KBr,\,-H_2O]{\text{Alc. KOH. }\Delta} \underset{\text{2-Butene (major)}}{CH_3-CH{=}CH-CH_3} + \underset{\text{1-Butene (minor)}}{CH_3CH_2CH{=}CH_2}$$

The ease of dehydrohalogenation of alkyl halides follows the order 3° > 2° > 1°.

$$(CH_3)_3CCl > (CH_3)_2CHCl > CH_3CH_2Cl$$

In the case of alkyl fluorides, the orientation of elimination is not governed by the stability of the alkene being formed

(Saytzeff rule) but is governed by the acidity of the β -hydrogen to be eliminated (Hofmann rule). Consequently, the major product is formed by elimination of the more acidic β-hydrogen.

$$\xrightarrow{\text{Elimination increases}} \text{Elimination } (E_2)$$
$$1° \quad 2° \quad 3°$$
$$\xleftarrow[\text{Substitution increases}]{} \text{Substitution } (S_N2)$$

However, in E_1 vs S_N1 reactions, the same order of reactivity is observed for both elimination and substitution reactions.

$$\xrightarrow{\text{Elimination increases}} \text{Elimination } (E_1)$$
$$1° \quad 2° \quad 3°$$
$$\xrightarrow[\text{Substitution increases}]{} \text{Substitution } (S_N1)$$

In general, 1° alkyl halides predominantly give substitution products while 3° alkyl halides exclusively give elimination products. However, with 2° alkyl halides, elimination always predominates over substitution.

Note: Alcoholic KOH [less polar solvent (alcohol), high temperature, high conc. of base] brings about dehydrohalogenation while aqueous KOH [more polar solvent (water), low temperature and low conc. of the base] brings about substitution.

10.5.3 Miscellaneous Reactions

(i) Reaction with Li:

$$R\text{–}X + 2\,Li \xrightarrow{\text{Dry ether}} RLi + LiX$$

(ii) Reaction with Mg:

$$R\text{–}X + Mg \xrightarrow{\text{Dry ether}} R\text{–}MgX \text{ (Grignard reagent)}$$

(iii) Reaction with Pb/Na alloy:

$$4CH_3CH_2Br + 4\,Pb/Na \xrightarrow{\text{Dry ether}} \underset{\substack{\text{Tetraethyllead (TEL)}\\ \text{(Anti-knocking agent in gasoline)}}}{(C_2H_5)_4Pb} + 4\,NaBr + 3\,Pb$$

(iv) Reduction:

- $RX + H_2 \xrightarrow{Ni} RH + HX$
- $RI + HI \xrightarrow{\text{Red P, 423 K}} RH + I_2$
- $R\text{–}Cl \xrightarrow[\text{or Zn/Cu couple + alcohol}]{Zn+HCl} RH + HCl$

10.6 Optical Isomerism

Substances which rotate the plane of polarised light are called *optically active substances* and the property of a substance to rotate the plane of polarised light is called *optical activity*. Isomers which have the same physical and chemical properties except for their behaviour towards plane polarised light are called *optical isomers*. A carbon atom which is attached to four different atoms or groups is called an *asymmetric carbon* or *chiral carbon* or *stereocentre.* It lacks all elements of symmetry and hence is called an asymmetric molecule which is responsible for optical activity in such organic compounds. The molecules which are non-superimposable on their mirror images are said to be *chiral* and the property of non-superimposability is called *chirality*; those that are superimposable on their mirror images are called *achiral*. For example, a molecule of propan-2-ol is achiral because it is superimposable on its mirror (Fig.10.1).

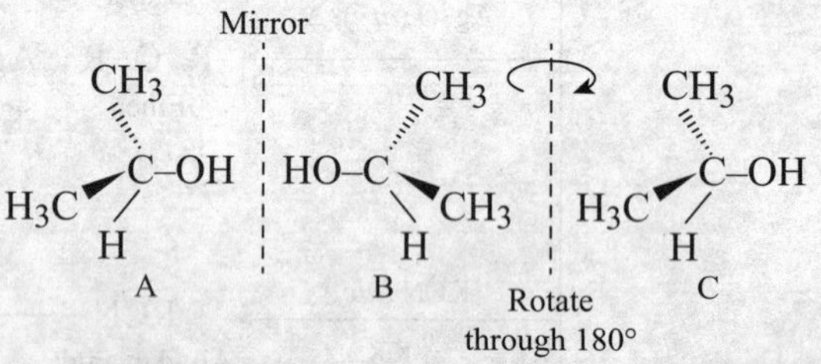

Mirror

A: CH_3, H_3C, H on C–OH | B: HO–C with CH_3, CH_3, H | C: CH_3, H_3C, H on C–OH (Rotate through 180°)

Fig. 10.1 Propan-2-ol is achiral [A and its mirror image B (or C) are superimposable]

In contrast, a molecule of butane-2-ol is chiral because it is not superimposable on its mirror images (Fig. 10.2).

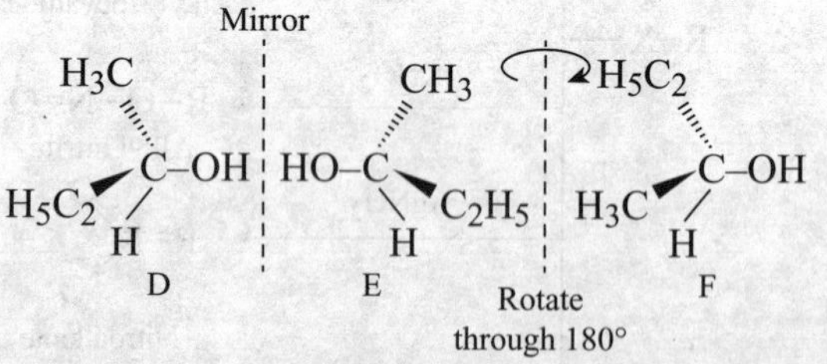

Mirror

D: H_3C, H_5C_2, H on C–OH | E: HO–C with CH_3, C_2H_5, H | F: H_5C_2, H_3C, H on C–OH (Rotate through 180°)

Fig.10.2 Butan-2-ol is chiral [D and its mirror image E (or F) are non-superimposable]

In chiral molecules, the asymmetric carbon atom is denoted by an asterisk (*).

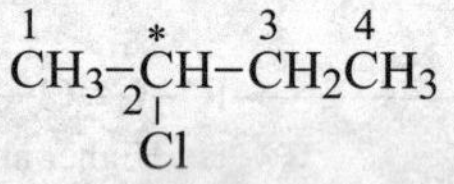

$$\overset{1}{C}H_3\text{–}\overset{*}{\underset{2}{C}}H(Cl)\text{–}\overset{3}{C}H_2\overset{4}{C}H_3 \qquad \overset{3}{C}H_2(OH)\text{–}\overset{*}{\underset{2}{C}}H(OH)\text{–}\overset{1}{C}HO$$

2-Chlorobutane 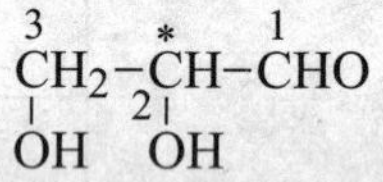 — 2, 3-Dihydroxypropanal (Glyceraldehyde)

Enantiomers: Stereoisomers which are non-superimposable mirror images of each other are called *enantiomers* and the phenomenon is called *enantiomerism*. Enantiomers have identical physical and chemical properties (except towards chiral reagents) but rotate the plane of polarised light in the opposite direction but to the same extent. The enantiomer which rotates the plane of polarised light towards the right is called *dextrorotatory*, that is, the *d* or (+)-isomer while the other which rotates the plane of polarised light towards the left is called *laevorotatory*, that is, the *l* or (–)-isomer. For example, lactic acid has two optical isomers which are enantiomers of each other.

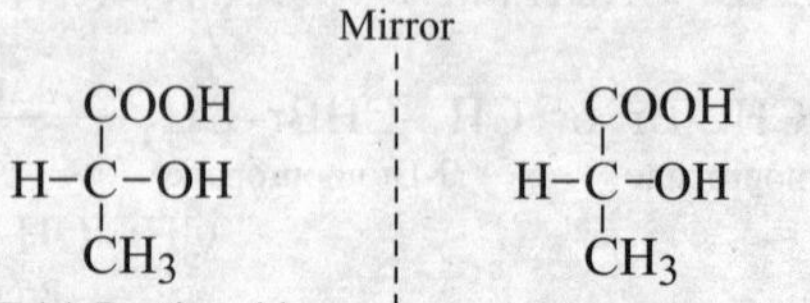

Mirror

COOH	COOH
H–C–OH	H–C–OH
CH_3	CH_3
D(–)-Lactic acid	L(+)-Lactic acid

Diastereomers: Stereoisomers which are not mirror images of each other are called diastereomers and the phenomenon is called *diastereoisomerism*. For example, 2,3-dichloropentane exists in four stereoisomeric forms—I, II, III and IV.

```
         Mirror                 Mirror
  CH3      |     CH3       CH3     |     CH3
H–C–Cl     |   Cl–C–H    H–C–Cl    |   Cl–C–H
Cl–C–H     |    H–C–Cl  Cl–C–Cl    |   Cl–C–H
  CH2CH3   |     CH2CH3    CH2CH3  |     CH2CH3
   I              II        III            IV
```

I and II are non-superimposable mirror images of each other and hence are enantiomers. Similarly, III and IV are enantiomers. On the other hand, I and III, I and IV, II and III and II and IV are not mirror images of each other and hence are diastereomers.

In contrast, tartaric acid exists in three stereoisomers forms—I, II and III.

```
              Mirror
   COOH          |       COOH
 H–C–OH          |    HO–C–H
HO–C–H           |     H–C–OH
   COOH          |       COOH
    I                     II
(+)-Tartaric acid    (–)-Tartaric acid
```

```
            Mirror
   COOH                COOH
 H–C–OH             HO–C–H
- - - - - - - - - - - - - - - - Plane of
HO–C–H               H–C–OH     symmetry
   COOH                COOH
   III                 IV
        meso-tartaric acid
```

Hence, I and II are enantiomers while I and III or II and III are diastereomers.

Meso compounds: Compounds which do not show optical activity in spite of the presence of chiral carbon atoms are called mesocompounds. The absence of optical activity in these compounds is due to the presence of a plane of symmetry in their molecules. For example, meso-tartaric acid. The structures III and IV represent the same molecule (meso-tartaric acid) since they have a plane of symmetry and hence rotation of IV through 180° gives III.

Number of stereoisomers, optical isomers and meso forms: The total number of stereoisomers, optical isomers and meso-forms of any given formula may be derived as follows.

(i) When the molecule is unsymmetrical and contains n chiral carbon atoms.
Number of optical isomers $(o) = 2^n$
Number of meso isomers $(m) = 0$
$\therefore$ Total number of stereoisomers
$(o + m) = 2^n + 0 = 2^n$

(ii) When the molecule is symmetrical and has an even number of chiral carbon atoms.
Number of optical isomers $(o) = 2^{n-1}$
Number of meso-forms $(m) = 2\left(\frac{n}{2} - 1\right)$
Total number of stereoisomers
$(o + m) = 2^{n-1} + 2\frac{n}{2} - 2$

(iii) When the molecule is symmetrical and has an odd number of chiral carbon atoms.

Number of optical isomers $(o) = 2^{n-1} - 2\left(\frac{n-1}{2}\right)$

Number of meso isomers $(m) = 2\left(\frac{n-1}{2}\right)$

$\therefore$ Total number of stereoisomers $(o + m)$
$= 2^{n-1} - 2^{(n-1)/2} + 2^{(n-1)/2} = 2^{n-1}$

Racemic mixture: An equimolar mixture of (+) and (–)-enantiomers is called a *racemic mixture* or a *racemic modification*. It is denoted by the prefix *dl* or (±) before the name of the compound. A racemic mixture is optically inactive.

Retention: Retention of configuration refers to the preservation of the spatial arrangement of bonds at an asymmetric centre during a chemical reaction. For example, consider the following general reaction.

```
   a                     a
   |  c     –Y           |  c
   C      ------->       C
 b   X      –X         b   Y
```

In this reaction, retention of configuration occurs because the relative configurations of the atoms b, a and c is the same (clockwise from b to c) both in the reactant and the product.

Inversion, retention and racemisation: Consider the replacement of a group X by Y in the following reaction.

```
     C2H5              C2H5              C2H5
H····C     <--+Y--   C····H   --+Y-->  C····H
       Y     –X     X            –X   Y
     CH3               CH3               CH3
      II            +Y ↓ –X               I
                     I + II
```

If I is the only product of the reaction, the reaction proceeds with retention of configuration. If II is the only product obtained, the reaction is said to proceed with inversion of configuration. If, on the other hand, a 50 : 50 mixture of I and II is obtained, the process is called racemisation and the product is optically inactive.

The process by which a racemic mixture can be separated into (+) and (-) enantiomers is called *resolution*.

10.7 Different Methods of Representing Chiral Molecules

In addition to the flying wedge formulae, sawhorse formulae and Newman projection formulae, chiral molecules can also be represented by the Fischer projection formulae. The main points of Fischer projection formulae are the following.

- The two of the groups (or bonds) attached to this chiral centre are horizontal and point towards the observer while the other two are vertical and point away from the observer.
  To test the identity of different Fischer projections for the same compound, the following rules must be observed.
- A Fischer projection must not be lifted from the plane of the paper and turned over. Such an operation gives the enantiomer of the original molecule. For example, structures, I and II, represent the enantiomers of bromochlorofluoromethane.

F; Br–C–Cl; H (I) —Turn over forbidden→ F; Cl–C–Br; H (II)

- A Fisher projection may be turned through 180° in the plane of the paper. Such an operation gives the same stereoisomer. For example, structures III and IV represent the same stereoisomer of lactic acid.

COOH; H–C–OH; CH_3 (III) —180° turn over allowed→ CH_3; HO–C–H; COOH (IV)

- A Fischer projection should not be turned over through 90° or 270° in the plane of the paper. Such an operation gives the enantiomer of the original molecule. For example, structures, V and VI, represent the enantiomers of 2-butanol.

H_3C; H–C–OH; CH_2CH_3 (V) —90° turn over forbidden→ H; CH_3H_2C–C–CH_3; OH (VI)

- Two interchanges of atoms/groups at the chiral centre does not change the configuration of the molecule. For example, structures VII and VIII represent the same stereoisomer of lactic acid.

COOH; H–C–OH; CH_3 (VII) —Interchange H and OH, First interchange→ COOH; HO–C–H; CH_3 —Interchange CH_3 and COOH, Second interchange→ CH_3; HO–C–H; COOH —Rotate through 180° in the plane of the paper→ COOH; H–C–OH; CH_3 (VIII)

- Let us convert the flying wedge formula (I) into the Fischer projection formula (II). Since the CH_3 group is below the plane of the paper, it is placed at the bottom of the Fischer projection formula (II) and the remaining three groups, OH → H → COOH are in the anticlockwise sequence and hence they are arranged in the same sequence in the Fisher projection formula (II).

COOH; CH_3, H, OH (Anticlockwise) (I) ≡ H; HOOC–C–OH; CH_3 (Anti-clockwise) (II)

To convert the Fischer projection formula (III) to the flying wedge formula (IV,) reverse the procedure discussed above. For example,

COOH; H–C–OH; CH_3 (Clockwise) (III) ≡ COOH; H, OH; CH_3 (Clockwise) (IV)

- **Erythro and threo isomers:** The stereoisomer in which the two identical groups are on the same side of the Fischer projection formula is called the erythro isomer while the isomer in which the two identical groups are on the opposite sides of the Fischer projection formula is called the threo isomer. For example,

CH_3; H–2–OH; H–3–Br; CH_3 — *Erythro*-3-bromo-2-butanol

CH_3; HO–2–H; H–3–Br; CH_3 — *Threo*-3-bromo-2-butanol

- The Fischer projection formulae of the erytho and thero isomers are directly converted into the sawhorse and the Newman formulae which represent the less stable eclipsed conformation of the molecule. Therefore, to get the more stable, staggered conformation, the substituents on one of the carbons is rotated through 180°. For example,

III Eclipsed (sawhorse: OH, H, CH_3 on C2; Br, H, CH_3 on C3) —Rotate C_3 clockwise→ Staggered (OH, H, CH_3 on C2; CH_3, H, Br on C3)

Erythro-3-bromo-2-butanol (CH_3; H–2–OH; H–3–Br; CH_3) ≡ Eclipsed (Newman: HO, H, CH_3; Br, H, CH_3) —Rotate C_3 clockwise→ Staggered (Newman: CH_3, H, OH; Br, H, CH_3)

Similarly, the Fischer projection formula of threo-3-bromo-2-butanol can be converted into their corresponding sawhorse and Newman formulae.

10.7.1 Optical Activity in Molecules Without Chiral Carbon Atoms

Some classes of organic compounds which show optical activity without the presence of chiral carbon atoms are discussed below.

(i) Allene derivatives: Substituted allenes of the general formula, *ab*C=C=C*ab* or *ab*C=C=C*de* are chiral molecules. The central carbon atom in allenes is *sp*-hybridised and the two π-bonds are in planes perpendicular to each other as shown below.

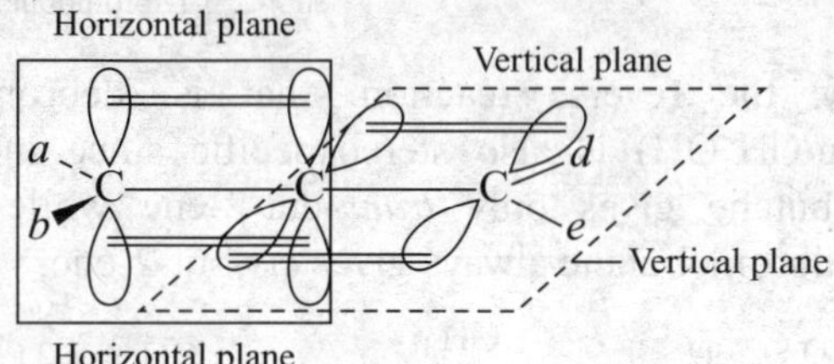

As a result, groups *d* and *e* lie in the plane of the paper while group *a* and *b* lie in a plane perpendicular to the plane of the paper. Consequently, the molecule does not a have plane or a centre of symmetry and hence is chiral, that is, its mirror image is non-superimposable, and thus shows enantiomerism. For example, penta-2,3-diene is optically active since its mirror image is non-superimposable.

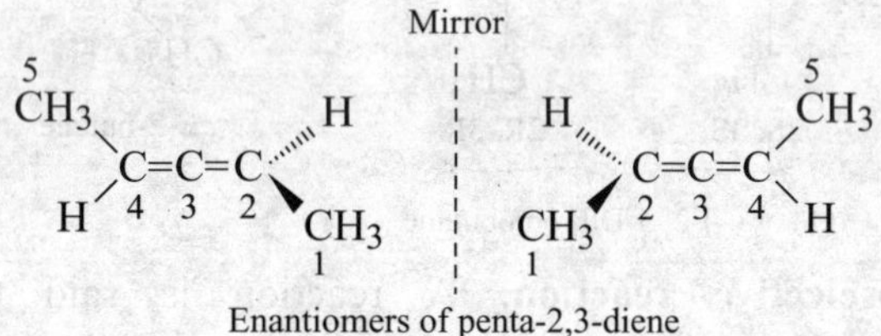

Enantiomers of penta-2,3-diene

When one or both the double bonds of the allene molecule are replaced by cycloalkane rings, the resulting molecules also become chiral and thus show optical isomerism. For example,

Mirror

CH_3, H, H, COOH | HOOC, H, CH_3, H

Enantiomers of 4-methylcyclohexylidene -1-acetic acid

Mirror

CH_3, H, NH_2, H | H_2N, H, NH_2, H

Enantiomers of a spiran

(ii) Biphenyl derivatives: Due to steric hindrance caused by the presence of bulky substituents at the *o*-positions, the two benzene rings become perpendicular to each other. As a result, substituents at the *o*-position in one ring lie in a plane which is perpendicular to that of the substituents in the other ring. Consequently, the molecule and its mirror image are non-superimposable, become chiral and hence exhibit optical isomerism.

Mirror

COOH NO_2, NO_2 COOH | O_2N COOH, HOOC NO_2

Enantiomers of 6, 6′-dinitrodiphetic acid

Similarly, 2,2′-diphenyldisulfonic acid and 2,2′-di-*tert*-butylbiphenyl are also chiral molecules and hence show optical activity.

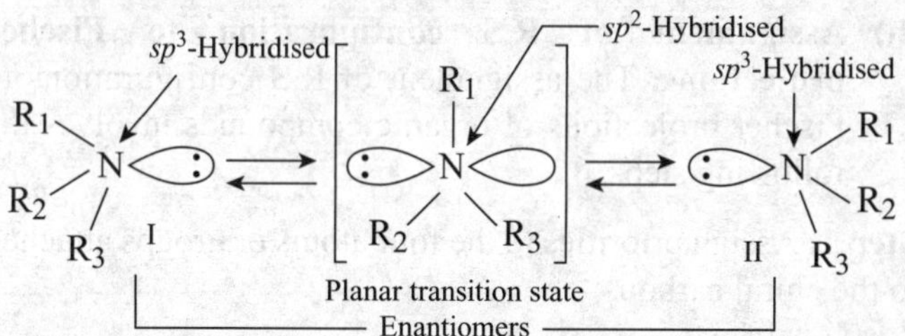

(v) Stereochemistry of cumulenes: In general, cumulenes containing an even number of double bonds show optical isomerism. While the cumulenes containing odd number of double bonds (3, 5 ...) do not show optical isomerism; instead, they show geometrical isomerism as the atoms/groups present on the terminal carbon atoms lie in the same plane. Thus, these cumulenes show geometrical isomerism depending upon whether the two similar groups lie on the same or opposite sides of the plane. For example,

$CH_3(H)C=C=C=C(CH_3)H$ — *cis*-Hexa-2,3,4-triene

$CH_3(H)C=C=C=C(H)CH_3$ — *trans*-Hexa-2,3,4-triene

As the terminal atoms/groups lie in the same plane, these molecules possess one or more symmetry elements. Their respective mirror images are superimposable and hence do not show optical isomerism.

10.7.2 Absolute Configuration–R,S System

Step 1: The four atoms or groups attached to the chiral carbon atom are assigned priority numbers such as (1), (2), (3) and (5) in accordance with a set of rules called sequence rules.

Step 2: After having assigned priorities to the four atoms or groups attached to the chiral carbon, the molecule is then oriented in space in such a way that the atom or group of the lowest priority is directed away from us. The arrangement of the remaining three atoms or groups is then viewed in the order of decreasing priorities. If in going from groups of highest priority to group of second priority and then to the group of third priority, that is, (1) → (2) → (3), the eye moves in a clockwise direction, the configuration is specified as R (Latin: rectus = right) and if the eye moves in the anticlockwise direction, the configuration is specified as S (Latin: sinister = left).

(i) Assignment of R,S configuration to 3-D structures

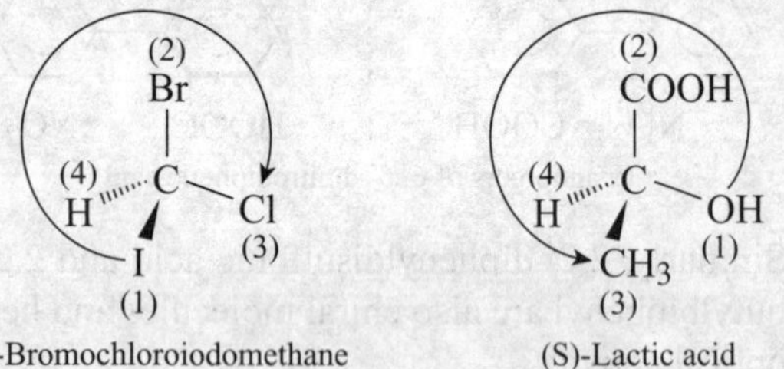

(R)-Bromochloroiodomethane (S)-Lactic acid

(ii) Assignment of R,S configuration to Fischer projections: The assignment of R,S configurations to Fischer projections of organic compounds involves the following steps.

Step 1: Assign priorities to the four atoms or groups attached to the chiral carbon.

Step 2: If the atom or group of lowest priority occupies a horizontal position (left or right) in the Fischer projection formula of the organic compound, then make two interchanges of atoms or groups in such a way that the atom or the group of lowest priority is placed either vertically upward or downward.

Step 3: Determine the direction of movement of eye in going from the group of highest priority to the group of second priority and then to the group of third priority, that is, (1) → (2) → (3) and assign the R or S configuration accordingly. The following examples illustrate the above procedure.

Glyceraldehyde

(2) CHO, (4) H, (1) OH, (3) CH_2OH —Interchange H and CH_2OH, 1st interchange→ (2) CHO, (3) HOH_2C, (1) OH, (4) H —Interchange OH and CHO, 2nd interchange→ (1) CHO, (3) HOH_2C, (2) CHO, (4) H

(R)-Glyceraldehyde

Butan-2-ol

(2) CHO, (4) H, (1) OH, (3) CH_2OH —Interchange H and CH_3, 1st interchange→ (4) H, (3) CH_3, (1) OH, (2) CH_2CH_3 —Interchange OH and CH_3CH_2, 2nd interchange→ (4) H, (3) CH_3, (2) CH_2CH_3, (1) OH

(S)-Butan-2-ol

Stereospecific reaction: A reaction is said to be stereospecific if a particular stereoisomer of the reactant produces a specific stereoisomer of the product. For example, bromination of *trans*-2-butene produces only meso-2,3-dibromobutane while that of the *cis*-isomer gives (±)2,3-dibromobutane.

trans-2-butene —Br_2 / CCl_4→ 2S, 3R *meso*-2, 3-Dibromobutane

cis-2-butene —Br_2 / CCl_4→ 2S, 3S + 2R, 3R (±)-2, 3-Dibromobutane

Similarly, the reverse reaction, that is, debromination (with Zn/CH_3OH) is also stereospecific since meso-2,3-dibromobutane gives only *trans*-but-2-ene while (+) or (–)-2,3-dibromobutane always gives *cis*-but-2-ene.

cis-2-butene; 2S, 3S *meso*-2, 3-Dibromobutane —Zn/CH_3OH, Δ→ *trans*-2-butene

2S, 3S + 2R, 3R (+) or (–)-2, 3-Dibromobutane —Zn/CH_3OH, Δ→ *cis*-2-butene

Stereoselective reaction: A reaction is said to be stereoselective if a particular stereoisomer of the reaction gives two or more stereoisomeric products but gives one of them in a greater amount than the other or even to the exclusion of the other. For example, addition of Br_2 to trans-but-2-ene is stereoselective since it can, in principle, give either *meso* or (±) 2,3-dibromobutane. Similarly, addition of Br_2 to *cis*-but-2-ene is stereoselective since it gives only (±)2,3-dibromobutane and not the *meso*isomer. Similarly, debromination reactions of mesoand (±)2,3-dibromobutane are also stereoselective.

In general, S_N2 reactions are stereospecific as well as stereoselective but S_N1 reactions are neither stereospecific nor stereoselective.

10.8 Mechanism and Stereochemistry of S_N1 and S_N2 Reactions

Nucleophilic substitution reactions occur either by S_N1 or by S_N2 mechanism.

10.8.1 S_N1 (Substitution, Nucleophilic, Unimolecular)

The reaction occurs in two steps. In the first step, the alkyl halide undergoes ionisation to produce a carbocation. This step is slow and hence is the rate determining step of the reaction.

$$(CH_3)_3C{-}X \xrightarrow[\text{slow } (-X)^-]{\text{Step 1, Ionisation}} (CH_3)_3C^+ \xrightarrow[\text{Fast}]{\text{Step 2, Nu:}^-} (CH_3)_3C{-}Nu$$

tert-Butyl halide → *tert*-Butyl carbocation → Substitution product

In the second step, the carbocation being a reactive chemical species, immediately reacts with the nucleophile to give the substitution product. This step is fast and hence does not affect the rate of the reaction. All tertiary alkyl halides undergo substitution reactions by the S_N1 mechanism.

(i) Stereochemistry of S_N1 reactions: In S_N1 reactions, if the alkyl halide is optically active, then the product is a racemic mixture, that is, S_N1 reactions are accompanied by racemisation giving a 50 : 50 mixture of the two enantiomers (Fig. 10.4).

(+) or (–)-2-Bromobutane ⇌ Carbocation + Br^-

(+)-Butan-2-ol 50% (one enantiomer) ← HO^- Rear attack (Inversion) — Carbocation (Planar) — $\bar{O}H$ Frontal attack (Retention) → (–)-Butan-2-ol 50% (other enantiomer)

Racemic mixture

Fig. 10.4 Racemisation during S_N1 reaction

(ii) Rearrangements during S_N1 reactions: Carbocations are the intermediates in S_N1 reactions, therefore, S_N1 reactions of some alkyl halides usually give unexpected rearrangement products. For example,

$$CH_3{-}C(CH_3)_2{-}CH_2Br \xrightarrow[S_N1]{OH^- \text{ (low conc.)}} CH_3{-}C(CH_3)_2{-}CH_2OH$$

Neopentyl bromide → Neopentyl alcohol (Expected, minor product)

Neopentyl bromide $\xrightarrow{-Br^-}$ $CH_3{-}C(CH_3)_2{-}\overset{+}{C}H_2$ (1° Carbocation, less stable) $\xrightarrow{\text{1, 2-Methyl shift}}$ $CH_3{-}\overset{+}{C}(CH_3){-}CH_2CH_3$ (3° Carbocation, more stable) $\xrightarrow{^-OH}$ $CH_3{-}C(CH_3)(OH){-}CH_2CH_3$

2-Methyl-2-butanol (Unexpected, major product)

10.8.2 S_N2 (Substitution, Nucleophilic, Bimolecular)

The rate of an S_N2 reaction depends upon the concentration of both the alkyl halide as well as the nucleophile. S_N2 reactions occur in one step. Such reactions occur through a transition state in which both the reactant molecules are partially bonded to each other as shown below.

$$HO^- + H_3C{-}X \longrightarrow [HO^{\delta-}\cdots CH_3 \cdots X^{\delta-}] \longrightarrow HO{-}CH_3 + X^-$$

Methyl halide → Transition state → Methanol

(i) Stereochemistry: It is interesting to note that in S_N2 reactions, the attack of the nucleophilic (OH^- ion) occurs from the back side and the halide ion leaves from the front. As a result, S_N2 reactions are always accompanied by inversion of configuration This implies that if the alkyl halide is optically active, the product is also optically active. For example, when (–)-2-bromooctane is heated with sodium hydroxide, (+)-2-octanol is formed in which the –OH group occupies a position opposite to the one bromine had occupied.

$$HO^-Na^+ + H(n\text{-}C_6H_{13})(CH_3)C{-}X \xrightarrow{\text{Heat}} HO{-}C(CH_3)(H)(n\text{-}C_6H_{13}) + Na^+Br^-$$

(–)-2-Bromooctane → (+)-2-Octanol

In S_N1 reactions, the departing halide shields the carbocation from the nucleophilic attack. As a result, in S_N1 reactions, racemisation with some inversion occurs.

(ii) Relative reactivity of haloalkanes towards S_N1 and S_N2 reactions: In S_N2 reactions, the presence of bulky substituents on or near the α-carbon atom tends to hinder (or block) the approach of the nucleophile to the α-carbon due to steric hindrance and thus make the reaction difficult to occur. Thus, the reactivity of different alkyl halides towards S_N2 reactions decreases in the order:

Methyl halide > 1° halide > 2° halide > 3° halide

In contrast, in S_N1 reactions, carbocations are the intermediates. Therefore, greater the stability of the carbocation, the more easily it is formed and faster is the rate of the reaction. The stability of the carbocations decreases in the order 3° > 2° > 1° CH_3, therefore, the reactivity of the alkyl halides towards S_N1 reactions decreases in the same order,

(iii) The protic solvents greatly decrease the reactivity of most nucleophiles by H-bonding. Polar aprotic solvents can dissolve many salts because of their high dielectric constants but they cannot solvate nucleophiles strongly. Therefore, free anions have far greater nucleophilicity in these solvents and hence S_N2 reactions take place at faster rates.

(iv) All primary alkyl halides undergo substitution by S_N2 mechanism and all tertiary alkyl halides undergo substitution by S_N1 mechanism while secondary alkyl halides may undergo substitution either by S_N1 or S_N2 mechanism depending upon the reaction conditions.

(v) $\mathbf{S_N1}$: $(CH_3)_3CX > C_6H_5CH_2X > CH_2=CHCH_2X > (CH_3)_2CHX > CH_3CH_2X > CH_3X$

$\mathbf{S_N2}$: $C_6H_5CH_2X > CH_2=CHCH_2X > CH_3X > CH_3CH_2X > (CH_3)_2CHX > (CH_3)_3CX$

- Polar solvents promote ionisation and hence favour S_N1 reactions while non-polar or weakly polar solvents favour S_N2 reactions.
- The rate of any nucleophilic substitution (S_N1 or S_N2) reaction depends upon the nature of the leaving group. In general, weaker the base, better the leaving group. The leaving group ability decreases in the order:
  $p\text{-}CF_3C_6H_4SO_3^-$ (triflate, abbreviated as Tf) > $p\text{-}CH_3C_6H_4SO_3^-$ (tosylate, abbreviated as Ts) $I^- > Br^- > Cl^- > H_2O > F^- > OAc^- > NR_3$ (or NH_3) $> RO^- > R_2N^- > NH_2^-$.
- Low concentration of nucleophiles favours S_N1 reactions while high concentration of nucleophiles favours S_N2 reactions. Likewise, strong nucleophiles favour S_N2 while weak nucleophiles favour S_N1 reactions. The relative nucleophilicity decreases in the following order:

$$RS^- > Cl^- > I^- > RO^- > OH^- > Br^- > Cl^- > C_6H_5O^- > Cl^- > Me_3N.$$

10.9 Chemical Reaction of Haloarenes (Aryl Halides)

10.9.1 Low Reactivity of Aryl Halides

Aryl halides are far less reactive than alkyl halides towards nucleophilic substitution reactions. This is due to resonance effect, sp^2 hybridisation of the carbon atom holding the halogen atom and the lower polarity of the C–X bond.

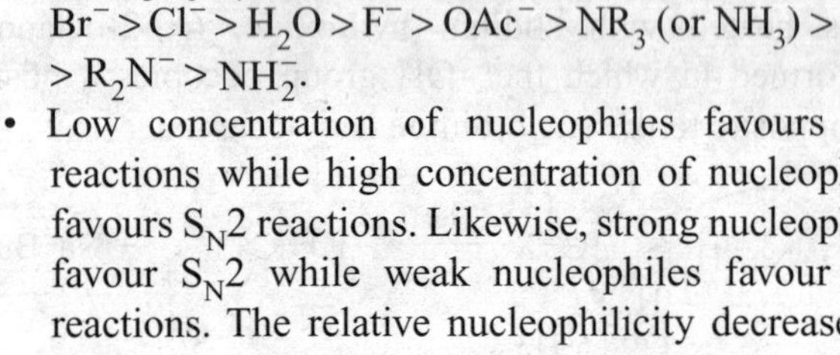

I II III IV V

The C–Cl bond in chlorobenzene acquires some double bond character and hence it is difficult to break it as compared to the C–Cl bond in alkyl halides. Similarly, due to resonance, vinyl halides are less reactive towards nucleophilic substitution reactions.

$$CH_2=CH-\ddot{C}l: \longleftrightarrow {}^-:CH_2-CH=\overset{+}{C}l:$$

Vinyl chloride

In contrast, benzyl halides are far more reactive than aryl halides, even more reactive than alkyl halides, towards nucleophilic substitution reaction. This is because the carbocation formed after the removal of halide ion is stabilised by resonance.

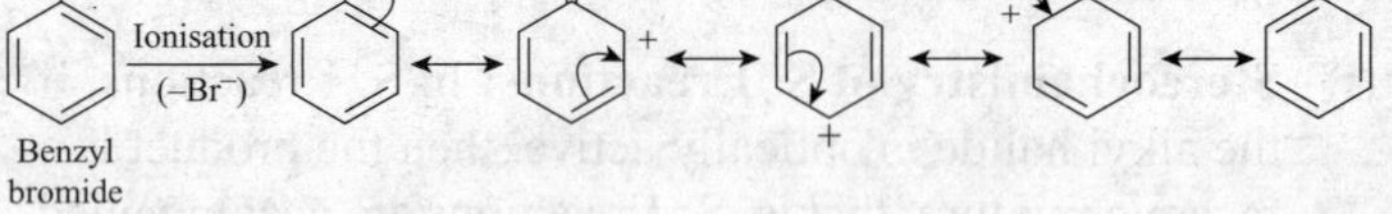

Benzyl bromide $\xrightarrow[(-Br^-)]{\text{Ionisation}}$ (resonance structures of benzyl carbocation)

In a similar way, allyl carbocations are stabilised by resonance and hence allyl halides are also more reactive than alkyl halides towards nucleophilic substitution reactions.

$$CH_2=CH-CH_2Br \xrightarrow[(-Br^-)]{\text{Ionisation}}$$

Allylbromide

$$CH_2=CH-\overset{+}{C}H_2 \longleftrightarrow \overset{+}{C}H_2-CH=CH_2$$

10.9.2 Nucleophilic Substitution Reactions

(i) Chlorobenzene $\xrightarrow[623\text{ K, 300 atm.}]{6\%\text{–}8\%\text{ NaOH}}$ Sod. phenoxide $\xrightarrow{\text{Dil. HCl}}$ Phenol

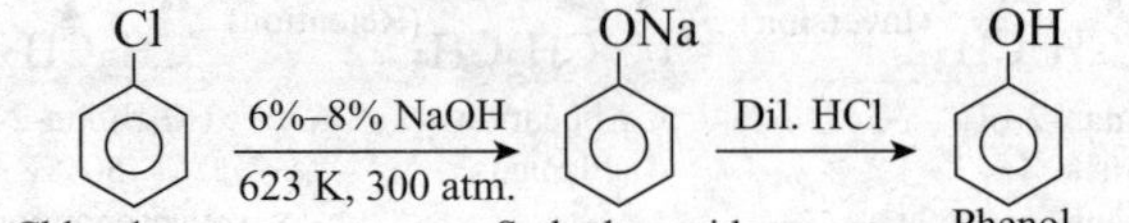

Dow's process

(ii) $2C_6H_5Cl + 2NH_3 + Cu_2O \xrightarrow{475,\ 60\text{ atm.}} 2C_6H_5NH_2 + 2CuCl + H_2O$

Aniline

(iii) $C_6H_5Br + CuCN \xrightarrow{475\text{ K, Pyridine}} C_6H_5CN + CuBr$

Benzonitrile

Mechanism

(i) Bimolecular mechanism (Addition–elimination mechanism): In the first step, the nucleophile attacks the carbon carrying the halogen to form a carbanion intermediate which is stabilised by resonance.

$+ OH^- \xrightarrow{\text{Slow}}$ [I ↔ II ↔ III] ≡

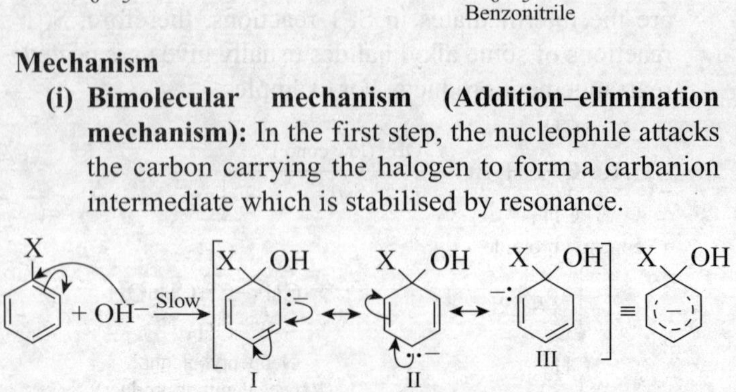

This step is slow and hence is the rate determining step of the reactions. In the second step, the intermediate carbanion loses the halide ion to give the substitution product.

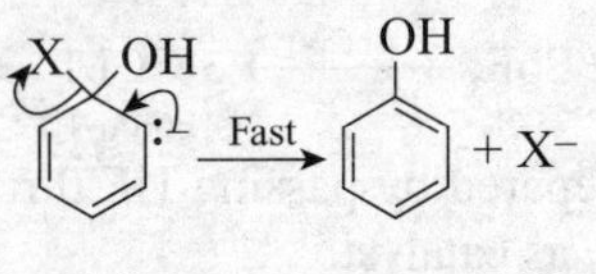

This step is fast and hence does not affect the rate of the reaction. Greater the stability of the carbanion, greater is the ease of its formation and hence more reactive is the aryl halide.

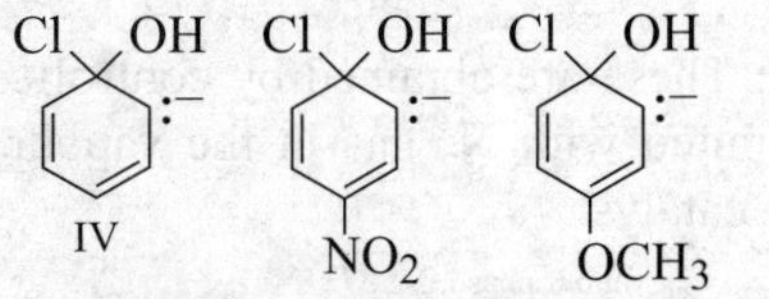

The electron withdrawing NO_2 group in carbanion (V) tends to disperse the negative charge both by –R and –I effect and hence makes it more stable than carbanion (IV). In contrast, the electron donating $-OCH_3$ group in carbanion (VI) tends to intensify the negative charge relative to carbanion (IV). As a result, carbanion (VI) is less stable than carbanion (IV). Thus, the relative stabilities of these three carbanions follows the sequence, V > IV > VI. The effect of the electron withdrawing or electron donating group is more pronounced at *o*- and *p*-positions than at the *m*-positions. The reactivity decreases in the order: 2,4,6-trinitrochlorobenzene (picryl chloride) > 2,4-dinitrochlorobenzene > 4-nitrochlorobenzene > 3-nitrochlorobenzene > chlorobenzene.

10.9.3 Electrophilic Substitution Reactions

Halogens are somewhat deactivating due to –I-effect but are *o*, *p*-directing due to the +R-effect. As a result, aryl halides undergo the usual electrophilic substitution reactions little less readily than benzene and give a mixture of *o*- and *p*-products in which the *p*-isomer usually predominates due to steric hindrance at the *o*-position.

10.9.4 Miscellaneous Reactions

Grignard reaction: Bromobenzene and iodobenzene react with Mg turnings in dry ether to form the corresponding Grignard reagents.

$$C_6H_5Cl + Mg \xrightarrow{\text{Dry THF}} \underset{\text{Grignard reagent}}{C_6H_5MgCl}$$

Fittig reaction:

$$C_6H_5Cl + 2\,Na + ClC_6H_5 \xrightarrow{\text{Dry ether, }\Delta} \underset{\text{Diphenyl}}{C_6H_5-C_6H_5} + 2\,NaCl$$

Wurtz–Fittig reaction:

$$C_6H_5Cl + 2\,Na + Cl-CH_3 \xrightarrow{\text{Dry ether, }\Delta} \underset{\text{Toluene}}{C_6H_5-CH_3} + 2\,NaCl$$

Ullmann biaryl synthesis:

$$C_6H_5-I + 2\,Cu + I-C_6H_5 \xrightarrow[\text{Sealed tube}]{\Delta} \underset{\text{Diphenyl}}{C_6H_5-C_6H_5} + 2\,CuI$$

10.10 Polyhalogen Compounds

Carbon compounds containing more than one halogen atom are called polyhalogen compounds.

10.10.1 Trichloromethane (Chloroform, $CHCl_3$)

Preparation: Chloroform is prepared in the laboratory by distilling ethyl alcohol or acetone with a suspension of bleaching powder.

$$\underset{\text{Bleaching powder}}{CaOCl_2} + H_2O \rightarrow Cl_2 + Ca(OH)_2$$

(i) Oxidation:

$$\underset{\text{Ethyl alcohol}}{CH_3CH_2OH} + Cl_2 \rightarrow CH_3CHO + 2\,HCl$$

(ii) Chlorination:

$$\underset{\text{Acetaldehyde}}{CH_3CHO} + 3\,Cl_2 \xrightarrow{Ca(OH)_2} \underset{\text{Chloral}}{CCl_3.\,CHO} + 3\,HCl$$

(iii) Hydrolysis:

$$2\,CCl_3.CHO + Ca(OH)_2 \rightarrow \underset{\text{Chloroform}}{2CHCl_3} + \underset{\text{Calcium formate}}{(HCOO)_2Ca}$$

A pure sample of $CHCl_3$ is obtained by the action of NaOH on chloral hydrate ($CCl_3.CHO$).

$$CCl_3.CHO.H_2O + NaOH \rightarrow CHCl_3 + HCOONa + H_2O$$

In case acetone is used, the reactions are given below.

(i) Chlorination:

$$\underset{\text{Acetone}}{CH_3COCH_3} + 3\,Cl_2 \xrightarrow{Ca(OH)_2} \underset{\alpha,\alpha,\alpha\text{-Trichloroacetone}}{CCl_3.COCH_3} + 3\,HCl$$

(ii) Hydrolysis:

$$2\,CCl_3.COCH_3 + Ca(OH)_2 \rightarrow 2\,CHCl_3 + \underset{\text{Cal. acetate}}{(CH_3COO)_2Ca}$$

Properties

(i) **Oxidation:** Chloroform is slowly oxidised by air in the presence of light to form an extremely poisonous gas known as phosgene (carbonyl chloride).

$$\underset{\text{Chloroform}}{2CHCl_3} + O_2 \xrightarrow{\text{Light}} 2\underset{\text{Phosgene}}{O=CCl_2} + 2HCl$$

It is therefore stored in closed dark coloured bottles. Phosgene thus formed combines with ethyl alcohol to form non toxic diethylcarbonate.

$$2\,C_2H_5OH + \underset{\text{Phosgene}}{COCl_2} \rightarrow \underset{\text{Diethyl carbonate}}{O=C(OC_2H_5)_2} + 2\,HCl$$

(ii) **Carbylamine reaction:** When warmed with any aliphatic or aromatic primary amine and alcoholic KOH, an isocyanide or carbylamine, having extremely bad smell is obtained.

$$C_6H_5NH_2 + CHCl_3 + 3\ KOH\ (alc) \xrightarrow{\Delta} C_6H_5N \equiv C + 3\ KCl + 3\ H_2O$$

The reaction occurs through a dichlorocarbene ($:CCl_2$) intermediate. This reaction is used as a test for both aromatic and aliphatic primary amines.

(iii) Dehalogenation:

$$CHCl_3 + 2\ Ag + CHCl_3 \xrightarrow{\Delta} CH{\equiv}CH + 6\ AgCl$$

(iv) Nitration:

$$CHCl_3 + HNO_3 \rightarrow Cl_3CNO_2 + H_2O$$

Chloropicrin is used as an insecticide and is a constituent of tear gas.

10.10.2 Triiodomethane (Iodoform, CHI_3)

Preparation: It is prepared by heating ethyl alcohol or acetone with iodine and NaOH or Na_2CO_3.

$$\underset{\text{Ethyl alcohol}}{CH_3CH_2OH} + 4\ I_2 + 6\ NaOH \rightarrow \underset{\text{Iodoform}}{CHI_3} + HCOONa + 5\ NaI + 5\ H_2O$$

$$\underset{\text{Acetone}}{CH_3COCH_3} + 3\ I_2 + 4\ NaOH \rightarrow CHI_3 + CH_3COONa + 3\ NaI + 3\ H_2O$$

Iodoform test: Any compound containing the CH_3CO or $CH_3CH(OH)$ group linked to a carbon or hydrogen atom, when heated with I_2 and NaOH or NaOI gives a yellow precipitate of iodoform. This reaction is called the *iodoform reaction*.

$$\underset{\text{Methylcarbinol}}{R{-}CHOH{-}CH_3} \xrightarrow[\text{or NaOH}]{I_2/NaOH} \underset{\text{Methyl ketone}}{R{-}\overset{O}{\overset{\|}{C}}{-}CH_3}$$

$$\xrightarrow{NaOI} R{-}\overset{O}{\overset{\|}{C}}{-}CI_3 \xrightarrow{NaOH} \underset{\text{Iodoform}}{CHI_3} + RCOONa$$

10.10.3 Tetrachloromethane (Carbon Tetrachloride, CCl_4)

It is prepared by the chlorination of methane in the presence of sunlight or carbon disulfide in the presence of anhydrous $AlCl_3$.

$$CH_4 + 4\ Cl_2 \xrightarrow{hv} CCl_4 + 4\ HCl$$

$$CS_2 + 3\ Cl_2 \xrightarrow{AlCl_3} CCl_4 + S_2Cl_2$$

10.10.4 Freons

Chlorofluoro compounds of methane and ethane are collective called freons. They are further classified on the basis of the number of fluorine atoms present in them. For example, CF_4 (freon-14), CF_3Cl (freon-13), CF_2Cl_2 (freon-12), $CFCl_3$ (freon-11). Out of all these, freon-12 is the most widely used refrigerant. It is manufactured from CCl_4 by Swarts reaction.

$$3\ CCl_4 + 2\ SbF_3 \xrightarrow{SbCl_5} \underset{\text{Freon-12}}{3\ CCl_2F_2} + 2\ SbCl_3$$

It may also be prepared by passing HF through CCl_4 in the presence of $SbCl_3$ as catalyst.

$$CCl_4 + 2\ HF \xrightarrow{SbCl_3} CCl_2F_2 + HCl$$

10.10.5 Perfluorocarbons (PFCs)

Their general formula is C_nF_{2n+2}.

Preparation: These are obtained by controlled fluorination of alkanes diluted with N_2 gas in the vapour phase in the presence of a catalyst.

$$\underset{\text{Heptane}}{C_7H_{16}} + 16\ F_2 \xrightarrow[\text{CoF}_2\text{ (catalyst)}]{\text{vapour phase, N}_2\text{ 573 K}} \underset{\text{Perfluoroheptane}}{C_7F_{16}} + 16\ HF$$

10.10.6 DDT [2,2-bis(*p*-chlorophenyl)-1,1,1-trichloroethane]

DDT stands for *p*, *p*-dichlorodiphenyltrichloroethane and is prepared by heating chlorobenzene with chloral in the presence of conc. H_2SO_4.

$$\underset{\text{Chlorobenzene}}{2\ Cl{-}C_6H_4{-}H} + \underset{\text{Chloral}}{O{=}CH{-}CCl_3} \xrightarrow[H_2SO_4]{\text{Conc.}} \underset{\text{DDT}}{(Cl{-}C_6H_4)_2CH{-}CCl_3} + H_2O$$

10.10.7 Benzene Hexachloride (BHC, $C_6H_6Cl_6$)

It is prepared commercially by the addition of chlorine to benzene in the presence of sunlight. It is extensively used as a pesticide in agriculture for killing termites (white ants) in the soil.

$$C_6H_5 + 3\ Cl_2 \xrightarrow{hv} \underset{\text{BHC}}{C_6H_6Cl_6}$$

10.11 Analysis of Haloalkanes and Haloarenes (Alkyl and Aryl Halides)

The presence of halogen inorganic compounds can be tested by Beilstein test and Lassaigne's test. Depending upon the type of linkage, halogens are of the following three types.

(i) Ionic halogen as in benzenediazonium halides and quaternary ammonium halides, that is,

$$C_6H_5\overset{+}{N_2}X^- \text{ and } R_4\overset{+}{N}X^- \text{ (where X = Cl, Br and I).}$$

(ii) Labile halogen as in alkyl, allyl and benzyl halides, that is, R–X, $CH_2{=}CHCH_2{-}X$, $C_6H_5CH_2{-}X$ (where X = Cl, Br or I).

(iii) Inert halogens as in aryl halides, that is, chlorobenzene, bromobenzene, iodobenzene and so on, and vinyl halides such as vinyl chloride, vinyl bromide, and so on.

A distinction between these types of halogens is carried out on the basis of the $AgNO_3$ test.

- $AgNO_3$ test in the cold. An aqueous solution of the organic halide is acidified with dil. HNO_3 and then treated with $AgNO_3$ solution in the cold. The appearance of a white or yellow precipitate indicates the presence of an ionic halogen.
- $AgNO_3$ test in the hot. The organic halide is boiled with aqueous KOH solution. The reaction mixture is cooled, acidified with dil. HNO_3 and then treated with $AgNO_3$ solution. The appearance of a white or yellow precipitate indicates a labile halogen. If both the above tests are negative, the presence of an inert halogen is indicated.

Exercises

OBJECTIVE QUESTIONS

1. The IUPAC name of the following is

(a) 4-bromo-2-phenylpent-2-ene
(b) 2-bromo-4-methylpent-2-ene
(c) 4-bromo-2-phenylpent-4-ene
(d) 2-bromo-4-phenylpent-3-ene

2. The IUPAC name of the following compound

Cl CH2CH3 / CH3 is

(a) *trans*-2-chloro-3-iodo-2-pentene
(b) *cis*-3-iodo-4-chloro-2-pentene
(c) *trans*-2-chloro-3-iodo-2-pentene
(d) *cis*-2-chloro-3-iodo-2-pentene

3. The IUPAC name of the following compound

H3C CH3 / H is / H Br / H3C

(a) *cis*-4-bromo-3-methylpent-2-ene
(b) *trans*-4-bromo-3-methylpent-2-ene
(c) *cis*-2-bromo-3-methylpent -3-ene
(d) *trans*-2-bromo-3-methylpent -3-ene

4. The IUPAC name of the following compound

$(Cl-C_6H_4)_2CH-CCl_3$ is

(a) DDT
(b) *p,p′*-dichlorodiphenyltrichloroethane
(c) 2,2-bis(4-chlorophenyl)trichloroethane
(d) 2,2-bis(4-chlorophenyl)-1,1,1-trichloroethane

5. How many structural isomers are possible for the alkyl halide having the molecular formula, $C_5H_{11}Br$?

(a) 5 (b) 6 (c) 7 (d) 8

6. Which of the following is a vinyl halide?

(a) chloroethene
(b) 1-chloro-3-phenylpropene
(c) 1-bromocyclohexene
(d) all the above

7. An α, ω-dihalide is

(a) $ClCH_2CH_2CH_2CH_2Cl$
(b) $ClCH_2CHClCH_2CH_3$
(c) $Cl_2CHCH_2CH_2CH_3$
(d) $CH_3CHClCHClCH_3$

Preparation of Haloalkanes and Haloarenes

8. For the preparation of *n*-propyl bromide from *n*-propyl alcohol, which of the following reagents is most preferred?

(a) P_4/Br_2 (b) Br_2/CH_3COOH
(c) HBr/H_2SO_4 (d) NaBr

9. In the following reaction, the major product is

Methylcyclopentane $\xrightarrow[hv]{Br_2}$

(a) CH_2Br on cyclopentane (b) CH_3 and Br (c) H_3C Br (d) CH_3 ... Br

10. The best method to prepare neopentyl chloride is

(a) $(CH_3)_2CCH_2OH \xrightarrow{PCl_5,\ \Delta}$
(b) $(CH_3)_3CCH_2OH \xrightarrow{HCl,\ \Delta}$
(c) $(CH_3)_3CCH_2OH \xrightarrow{SOCl_2/pyr.}$
(d) $(CH_3)_3CCH_3 \xrightarrow{Cl_2, hv, \Delta}$

11. The reaction of toluene with Cl_2 in the presence of $FeCl_3$ gives X and reaction in the presence of light gives Y. Thus, X and Y are

(a) X = benzyl chloride, Y = *m*-chlorotoluene
(b) X = benzal chloride, Y = *o*-chlorotoluene
(c) X = *m*-chlorotoluene, Y = *p*-chlorotoluene
(d) X = *o*- and *p*-chlorotoluene, Y = trichloromethylbenzene

12. $Ph-NH_2 \xrightarrow{HNO_2} A \xrightarrow{HF} B \xrightarrow{\Delta} C$, C is 0°C BF_3

(a) $Ph-\overset{+}{N}\equiv NBF_4^-$ (b) biphenyl–F
(c) F–biphenyl–F (d) Ph–F

13. In the reaction with HCl, an alkene reacts in accordance with the Markownikoff's rule to give a product 1-chloro-1methylcyclohexane. The possible alkene is

(a) CH_2 (methylenecyclohexane) I (b) CH_3 (1-methylcyclohexene) II (c) I + II (d) CH_3 (3-methylcyclohexene)

14. The major product of the following reaction is

HO–CH_2–CH=CH_2 $\xrightarrow{\text{Conc. HBr}}$

(a) HO–CH_2–CH(Br)–CH_3 (b) Br–CH_2–CH=CH_2

(c) HO–CH_2–CH=CH–Br (d) H_3C–CH(Br)–CH_2–Br

15. The major product obtained by the addition reaction of HBr to 4-methylpent-1-ene in the presence of peroxide is

(a) 1-bromo-4-methylpentane
(b) 4-bromo-2-methylpentane
(c) 2-bromo-4-methylpentane
(d) 3-bromo-2-methylpentane

16. H_2C=C(CH_3)–CH=CH_2 $\xrightarrow{\text{HBr (1 } eq.)}$

The major product of the above reaction is

(a) $BrCH_2$–CH(CH_3)–CH_2–CH_3 (b) H_3C–C(H_3C)=CH–CH_2–Br

(c) H_3C–C(CH_3)(Br)–CH=CH_2 (d) CH_3–CH(CH_3)–CH_2–CH_2–Br

17. The product of the following reaction

cyclohexene + Br_2 $\xrightarrow[\text{UV light}]{\text{heat}}$ is

(a) 4-bromocyclohexene (b) 3-bromocyclohexene (c) bromocyclohexane (d) 1,2-dibromocyclohexane

18. Toluene on reaction with NBS gives

(a) *p*-bromomethylbenzene
(b) *o*-bromomethylbenzene
(c) phenylbromomethane
(d) *m*-bromethylbenzene

19. Which of the following is the correct method of preparation of methyl fluoride?

(a) $CH_4 + HF \rightarrow$ (b) $CH_3OH + HF \rightarrow$
(c) $CH_4 + F_2 \rightarrow$ (d) $CH_3Br + AgF \rightarrow$

20. The best method to prepare fluoroethane is

(a) $C_2H_5OH \xrightarrow{HF/H_2SO_4,\ \Delta}$
(b) $C_2H_5OH \xrightarrow{HF/SbF_5,\ \Delta}$
(c) $C_2H_5Cl \xrightarrow{Hg_2F_2,\ \Delta}$
(d) $C_2H_6 \xrightarrow{F_2,\ h\nu}$

21. Alkyl halide can be prepared by all the following methods except

(a) $CH_3CH_2OH + HCl(g) \xrightarrow{ZnCl_2}$
(b) $CH_3\text{–}CH\text{=}CH_2 \xrightarrow{SO_2Cl_2,\ 475\ K}$
(c) $C_2H_5OH + NaCl \rightarrow$
(d) $CH_3COOAg + Br_2 \xrightarrow{CCl_4\ \text{reflux}}$

22. Which of the following is not chiral?

(a) 3-methylhexane
(b) 2,3-dihydroxypropanoic acid
(c) 2,3-dibromobutane
(d) butan-2-ol

23. Which of the following reactions(s) can be used for the preparation of alkyl halides?

(I) $CH_3CH_2OH + HCl \xrightarrow{\text{anhyd. } ZnCl_2}$
(II) $CH_3CH_2OH + HCl \rightarrow$
(III) $(CH_3)_3COH + HCl \rightarrow$
(IV) $(CH_3)_2COH + HCl \xrightarrow{ZnCl_2}$

(a) I and (II) only (b) (II) only
(c) (III) and (IV) only (d) (I), (III) and (IV) only

24. Consider the following reaction,

$C_2H_5OH + HX \xrightarrow{\Delta} C_2H_5X + H_2O$

Under similar conditions, the reaction will be fastest when HX is

(a) HF (b) HCl (c) HBr (d) HI

25. Which of the following methods cannot be used to prepare *n*-propyl iodide from *n*-propyl alcohol?

(a) $CH_3CH_2CH_2OH + HI \xrightarrow{\Delta}$
(b) $CH_3CH_2CH_2OH + KI + H_2SO_4 \xrightarrow{\Delta}$
(c) $CH_3CH_2CH_2OH \xrightarrow{P_4/I_2,\ \Delta}$
(d) $CH_3CH_2CH_2OH + KI + H_3PO_4 \xrightarrow{\Delta}$

26. Thionyl chloride method is preferred over phosphorus pentachloride method for the preparation of alkyl chlorides because

(a) the reaction goes to completion
(b) the byproducts being gases, escape into the atmosphere leaving behind almost pure alkyl chloride
(c) thionyl chloride is cheap while phosphorus pentachloride is costly
(d) none of the above

Physical Properties of Haloalkanes and Haloarenes

27. Arrange the following compounds in the increasing order of their densities.

I. benzene II. chlorobenzene
III. *m*-dichlorobenzene IV. *p*-dichlorobenzene

(a) I < II< III < IV (b) I < III < IV < II
(c) IV < III < II < I (d) II< IV < III < I

28. Which of the following has the highest dipole moment?

(a) CH_3Cl (b) CH_2Cl_2 (c) $CHCl_3$ (d) CCl_4

29. Which of the following has no dipole moment?

(a) CH_3Cl (b) $CHCl_3$ (c) CH_2Cl_2 (d) CCl_4

30. Which of the following are arranged in the decreasing order of dipole moment?

(a) CH_3Cl, CH_3Br, CH_3F (b) CH_3Cl, CH_3F, CH_3Br
(c) CH_3Br, CH_3Cl, CH_3F (d) CH_3Br, CH_3F, CH_3Cl

31. Consider the following halogen containing compounds

(i) $CHCl_3$ (ii) CCl_4 (iii) CH_2Cl_2 (iv) CH_3Cl

(v) Cl–C_6H_4–Cl

The compounds with a net zero dipole moment are

(a) (ii) and (v) only (b) (ii) only
(c) (iii) and (iv) only (d) (i) and (iv) only

32. Arrange the following compounds in the order of increasing dipole moment: toluene (I), *m*-dichlorobenzene (II), *o*-dichlorobenzene (III), *p*-dichlorobenzene (IV)

(a) I < IV < II < III (b) IV < I < II < III
(c) IV < I < III < II (d) IV < II < I < III

33. Which of the following will have maximum dipole moment?

(a) 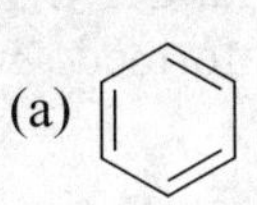 (b) 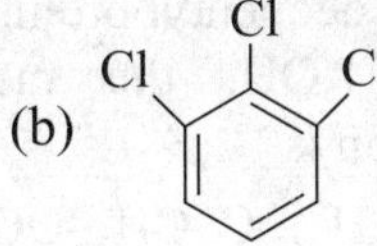

(c) 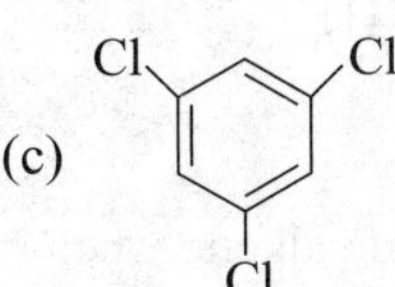

(d) 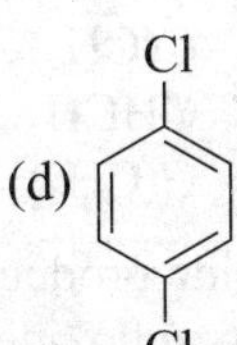

34. In the addition of HBr to propene in the absence of peroxides, the first step involves the addition of

(a) $H^•$ (b) $Br^•$ (c) H^+ (d) Br^-

35. Arrange the following setoff compounds in order of increasing boiling points.

I. I-chloropropane II. Isopropyl chloride
III. I-chloropropane

(a) II < III < I (b) I < II < III
(c) II < I <III (d) III < I < II

36. The arrange of the following compounds:

(i) bromomethane (ii) bromoform
(iii) chloromethane
(iv) dibromomethane

in increasing order of their boiling point is

(a) (iv) < (iii) < (i) < (ii) (b) (i) < (ii) < (iii) < (iv)
(c) (iii) < (i) < (iv) (ii) (d) (ii) < (iii) < (i) < (iv)

37. Which of the following is not the correct order of boiling points of the alkyl/aryl halides?

(a) $CHCl_3 > CH_2Cl_2$
(b) $CH_3(CH_2)_3Cl > CH_3(CH_2)_2Cl$
(c) $(CH_3)_3CCl > (CH_3)_2CHCH_2Cl$
(d) $CH_3(CH_2)_3Cl > CH_3CH_2CHClCH_3$
(e) $C_6H_5Br > C_6H_5Cl$

38. Which of the following has the highest melting point but least solubility in a given solvent?

(a) *o*-dichlorobenzene (b) *p*-dichlorobenzene
(c) *m*-dichlorobenzene (d) chlorobenzene

Chemical Reactions of Haloalkanes (Alkylhalides)

39. In the following groups,–OAc (I), –OMe (II), $-OSO_2Me$ (III), $-OSO_2CF_3$ (IV), the order of leaving group ability is

(a) I > II > III > IV (b) IV > III> I > II
(c) III > II > I > IV (d) II > III > IV > I

40. Consider the following nucleophiles.

I. $CF_3-SO_3^-$ II. $C_6H_5SO_3^-$
III. $C_6H_5O^-$ IV. $CH_3CO_2^-$

When attached to an sp^3 hybridised carbon, their leaving group ability in nucleophilic substitution reaction decreases in the order:

(a) II > I > III > IV (b) I > II > IV > III
(c) IV < I > II > III (d) III > I > IV > II

41. Reactivity of alkyl halides towards nucleophilic substitution reactions decreases in the order

(a) $C_2H_5F > C_2H_5Cl > C_2H_5Br > C_2H_5Cl$
(b) $C_2H_5Cl > C_2H_5Br > C_2H_5I > C_2H_5F$
(c) $C_2H_5Br > C_2H_5I > C_2H_5F > C_2H_5Cl$
(d) $C_2H_5I > C_2H_5Br > C_2H_5Cl > C_2H_5F$

42. The major product formed in the following reaction is

$$CH_3CH(Cl)CH_2CH_2OH \xrightarrow{aq.KOH}$$

(a) $CH_3CH{=}CHCH_2OH$ (b) $CH_2{=}CH{-}CH_2CH_2OH$
(c) $CH_3{-}CH{-}CH_2$ with O – CH_2 bridging (ring: CH and CH_2 joined through O – CH_2) (d) $CH_3{-}CH(OH){-}CH_2CH_2OH$

43. Identify the product in the following reaction.

$$Ph{-}C(Ph)_2{-}F \xrightarrow{Aq.\ KOH}$$

(a) 3PhOH (b) $Ph_2C(F)Ph$ (Ph, Ph, Ph, F on C)

(c) $Ph-\underset{Ph}{\overset{Ph}{C}}-OH$ (d) none of these

44. Alkyl iodide reacts with NaCN to give alkyl cyanide and a small amount of alkyl isocyanide. The formation of these two products is due to the

(a) ionic character of NaCN
(b) nucleophilic character of CN^-
(c) ambident character of CN^-
(d) electrophilic character of CN^-

45. Isopropyl cyanide can be obtained by the reaction between

(a) $CH_3CH_2CH_2I$ and AgCN
(b) $CH_3CHBrCH_3$ and KCN
(c) $(CH_3)_2CHI$ and AgCN
(d) $(CH_3)_2CHCl$ and HCN

46. The major product formed when methyl iodide reacts with sodium nitrite is

(a) methyl nitrite (b) nitromethane
(c) nitrous acid (d) nitroethane

47. $C_2H_5I \xrightarrow{AgNO_2} \underset{\text{(major product)}}{X}$

Here X is

(a) $C_2H_5–O–N=O$ (b) $C_2H_5-N(=O)\rightarrow O$

(c) $C_2H_5–N=O$ (d) $C_2H_5–N=N–C_2H_5$

48. Which of the following can be used to convert ethyl bromide to ethanethiol?

(a) sodium sulfide (b) sodium bisulfide
(c) sodium sulfite (d) sodium thiosulfate

49. For the preparation of ethyl propionate from ethyl bromide, the other reactant can be

(a) silver propionate (b) silver acetate
(c) propanoyl chloride (d) propionic anhydride

50. The reactivity order of halides for dehydrohalogenation is

(a) R–F > R–Cl > R–Br > R–I
(b) R–I > R–Br > R–Cl > R–F
(c) R–I > R–Cl > R–Br > R–F
(d) R–F > R–I > R–Br > R–Cl

51. The major product of the reaction between CH_3CH_2ONa and $(CH_3)_3CCl$ in ethanol is

(a) $CH_3CH_2OC(CH_3)_3$ (b) $CH_2=C(CH_3)_2$
(c) $CH_3CH_2C(CH_3)_3$ (d) $CH_3CH=CHCH_3$

52. Which of the following alkyl halides when subjected to dehydrohalogenation by the action of ethanolic KOH yields $CH_3CH=C(CH_3)_2$ as the major product?

(a) $CH_3–CHBr–CH(CH_3)_2$
(b) $CH_3CH_2CHBrCH_2CH_3$
(c) $BrCH_2CH_2CH(CH_3)_2$
(d) $CH_3CHBrCH_2CH_2CH_3$

53. What is the correct order of reactivity of the following alkyl halides: CH_3CH_2Cl, $CH_3CHClCH_3$ and $(CH_3)_3CCl$ towards dehydrohalogenation?

(a) $CH_3CH_2Cl > CH_3CHClCH_3 > (CH_3)_3CCl$
(b) $CH_3CHClCH_3 > (CH_3)_3CCl > CH_3CH_2Cl$
(c) $(CH_3)_3CCl > CH_3CH_2Cl > CH_3CHClCH_3$
(d) $(CH_3)_3CCl > CH_3CHClCH_3 > CH_3CH_2Cl$

54. 2-chloro-2-methylpentane on treatment with sodium methoxide in methanol yields

I. $C_2H_5CH_2-\underset{CH_3}{\overset{CH_3}{C}}-OCH_3$ II. $C_2H_5CH_2\underset{CH_3}{C}=CH_2$

III. $C_2H_5CH=\underset{CH_3}{C}-CH_3$

(a) all the three (b) I and III
(c) II only (d) I and II

55. The major product formed in the following reaction is

$$CH_3-\underset{H}{\overset{CH_3}{C}}-CH_2Br \xrightarrow[CH_3OH]{CH_3O^-}$$

(a) $CH_3-\underset{H}{\overset{CH_3}{C}}-CH_2OCH_3$ (b) $CH_3-\underset{OCH_3}{CH}-CH_2CH_3$

(c) $CH_3-\overset{CH_3}{C}=CH_2$ (d) $CH_3-\underset{OCH_3}{\overset{CH_3}{C}}-CH_3$

56. When neopentyl bromide is treated with CH_3CH_2ONa/CH_3CH_2OH, the major product formed in the reaction is

(a) $(CH_3)_3\,C–CH_2–OCH_2CH_3$
(b) $CH_3CH_2–C(CH_3)_2–OCH_2CH_3$
(c) $(CH_3)_2C=CHCH_3$
(d) $CH_3CH_2–C(CH_3)=CH_2$

57. An alkyl halide produces a single alkene when it reacts with sodium ethoxide and ethanol. This alkene on hydrogenation produces 2-methylbutane. What is the identity of the alkyl halide?

(a) 1-bromo-2, 2-dimethylpropane
(b) 1-bromobutane
(c) 1-bromo-2-methylbutane
(d) 2-bromo-2-methylbutane

58. Which of the following is obtained as the major product when 2-bromobutane is heated with alcoholic KOH?

(a) 1-butene (b) *cis*-2-butene
(c) *trans*-2-butene (d) 2-methylpropene

59. *Trans*-2-phenyl-1-bromocyclopentane on reaction with alcoholic KOH produces

(a) 4-phenylcyclopentene
(b) 2-phenylcyclopentene
(c) 1-phenylcyclopentene
(d) 3-phenylcyclopentene

60. The major product of the following reaction is

Br
$\xrightarrow[\text{MeOH}]{\text{NaOMe}}$

(a) OMe (b) (c) (d) OMe

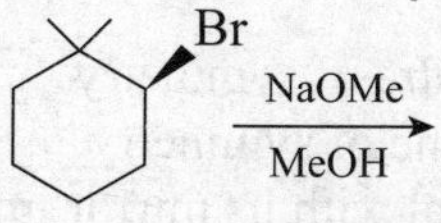

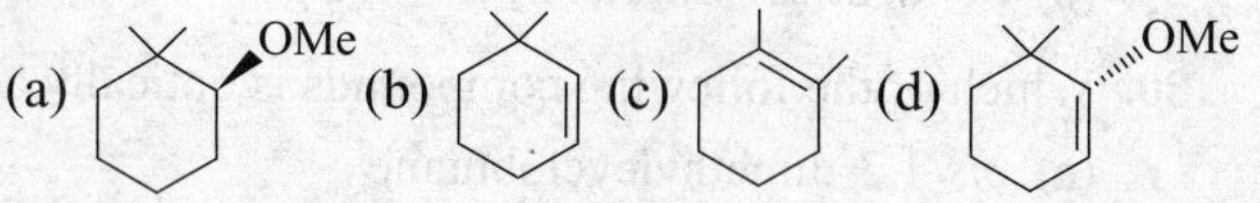

61. The major product obtained in the following reaction is

(a) (+)-$C_6H_5CH(O^tBu)CH_2C_6H_5$
(b) (–)-$C_6H_5CH(O^tBu)CH_2C_6H_5$
(c) (±) $C_6H_5CH(O^tBu)CH_2C_6H_5$
(d) $C_6H_5CH{=}CHC_6H_5$

62. The major product of the following reaction is

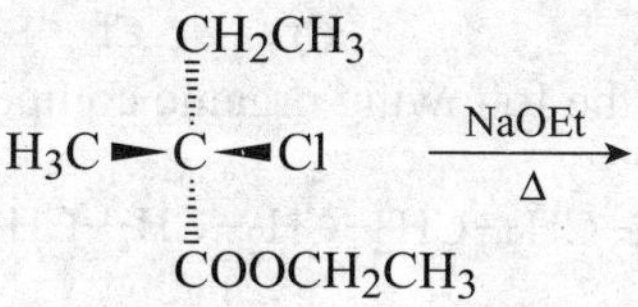

H_3C–C(CH_2CH_3)($COOCH_2CH_3$)–Cl $\xrightarrow[\Delta]{\text{NaOEt}}$

(a) 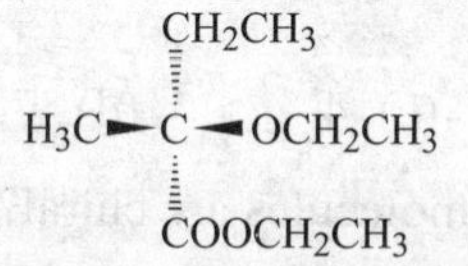 H_3C–C(CH_2CH_3)($COOCH_2CH_3$)–OCH_2CH_3 (b) $CH_3{-}\underset{}{C}(CO_2CH_2CH_3){=}CHCH_3$

(c) H_3CH_2C–C(OCH_2CH_3)(CH_3)–$CO_2CH_2CH_3$

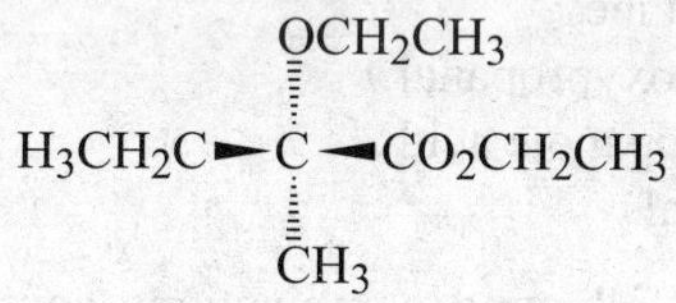

(d) $CH_3CH_2C(CO_2CH_2CH_3){=}CH_2$

63. The major product obtained on treatment of $CH_3CH_2CH(F)CH_3$ with CH_3O^-/CH_3OH is

(a) $CH_3CH_2CH(OCH_3)CH_3$
(b) $CH_3CH{=}CHCH_3$
(c) $CH_3CH_2CH{=}CH_2$
(d) $CH_3CH_2CH_2CH_2OCH_3$

64. When ethyl bromide and bromocyclohexane are treated separately with ammonia, the products formed respectively are

(a) ethylamine, cyclohexylamine
(b) ethylene, cyclohexene
(c) ethylamine, cyclohexene
(d) ethylene, cyclohexylamine

65. In the following reaction, $C_6H_5CH_2Br \xrightarrow[\text{(ii) } H_3O^+]{\text{(i) Mg–Ether}}$ X, the product X is,

(a) $C_6H_5CH_2OCH_2C_6H_5$ (b) $C_6H_5CH_2OH$
(c) $C_6H_5CH_3$ (d) $C_6H_5CH_2CH_2C_6H_5$

66. An alkyl chloride (A) on reaction with magnesium in dry ether followed by treatment with ethanol gave 2-methylbutane. Give the possible structure of A.

(a) $(CH_3)_2C(Cl)CH_2CH_3$
(b) $(CH_3)_2CHCH_2CH_2Cl$
(c) $CH_3CH_2CH_2CH_2CH_2X$
(d) both (a) and (b)

67. In the given sequence of reactions, the product S is

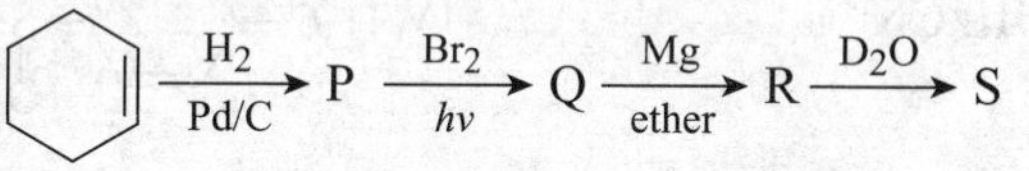

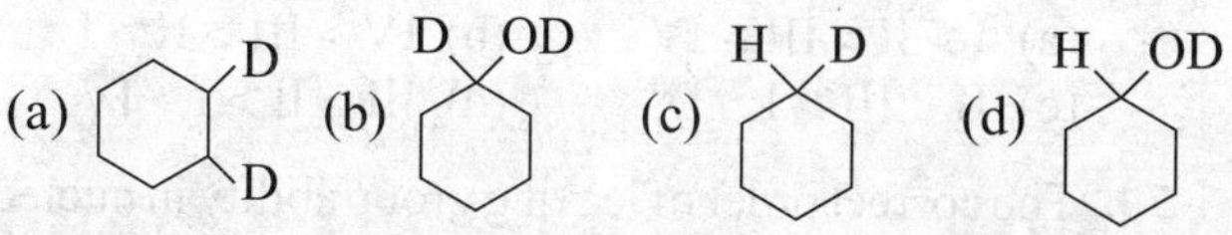

$\xrightarrow[\text{Pd/C}]{H_2}$ P $\xrightarrow[hv]{Br_2}$ Q $\xrightarrow[\text{ether}]{\text{Mg}}$ R $\xrightarrow{D_2O}$ S

(a) D, D (b) D OD (c) H D (d) H OD

68. When neopentyl bromide is subjected to the Wurtz reaction, the product formed is

(a) 2,2,4,4-tetramethylhexane
(b) 2,2,4,4-tetramethylpentane
(c) 2,2,5,5-tetramethylhexane
(d) 2,2,3,3-tetramethylhexane

69. A primary alkyl halide C_4H_9Br (A) is reacted with alcoholic KOH to give compound (B). Compound (B) is reacted with HBr to give (C) which is an isomer of (A). When (A) is treated with Na metal, it gives compound (D), C_6H_{18} which is different from the compound formed when *n*-butyl bromide is reacted with Na. Which of the following statements is correct?

(a) (C) is *n*-butyl bromide.
(b) (B) is *tert*-butyl bromide.
(c) (A) is isobutyl bromide.
(d) (A) is *n*-octane.

70. The most characteristic reactions of alkyl halides are

(a) nucleophilic substitution reactions
(b) electrophilic substitution reactions
(c) electrophilic addition reactions
(d) none of the above

71. Which of the following reactions is an example of a nucleophilic substitution reaction?

(a) 2 RX + 2 Na → R – R + 2 NaX
(b) $RX + H_2 \rightarrow RH + HX$
(c) RX + Mg → RMgX
(d) RX + KOH(*aq*) → ROH + KX

72. Which one is a nucleophilic substitution reaction?

(a) $CH_3CHO + HCN \rightarrow CH_3CH(OH)CN$

(b) $CH_3{-}CH{=}CH_2 + H_2O \xrightarrow{H^+} CH_3{-}\underset{OH}{CH}{-}CH_3$

(c) $RCHO + R'MgX \longrightarrow R{-}\underset{OH}{CH}{-}R'$

(d) $CH_3{-}CH_2{-}\overset{CH_3}{CH}{-}CH{-}CH_2Br + NH_3 \longrightarrow CH_3{-}CH_2{-}\overset{CH_3}{CH}{-}CH_2NH_2$

73. The decreasing order of nucleophilicity among the following is

I. $CH_3{-}\underset{O}{\overset{\|}{C}}{-}O^-$ II. CH_3O^-

III. CN^- IV. $H_3C{-}C_6H_4{-}SO_3^-$ (H_3C–⟨benzene⟩–$\overset{O}{\underset{O}{S}}$–$O^-$)

(a) I > II > III > IV (b) IV > III > II > I
(c) II < III > I > IV (d) III > II > I > IV

74. The correct order of leaving group ability in nucleophilic substitution reaction is

(a) $Br^- > Cl^- > CH_3COO^- > HO^- > H^-$
(b) $H^- > OH^- > CH_3COO^- > Cl^- > Br^-$
(c) $Br^- > CH_3COO^- > Cl^- > OH^- > H^-$
(d) $CH_3COO^- > Br^- > Cl^- > OH^- > H^-$

Optical Isomerism

75. Which of the following contains a chiral centre?

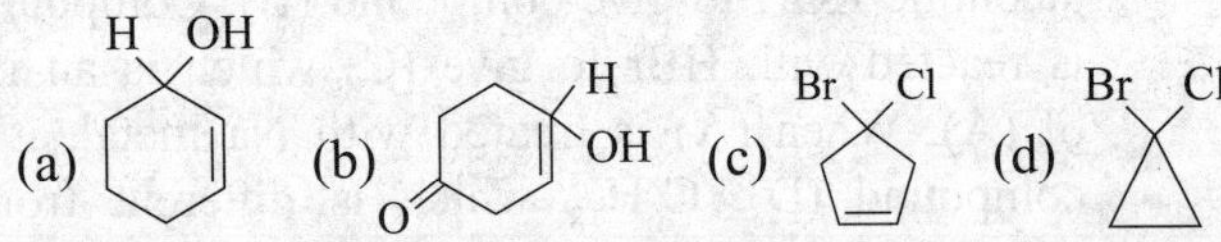

76. Which of the following carbon atoms present in the given molecule are asymmetric?

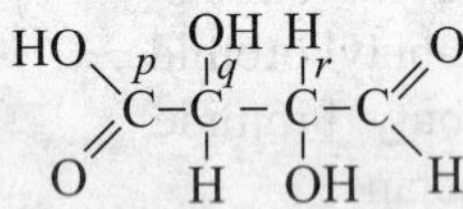

(a) *p*, *q*, *r*, *s* (b) *q*, *r*
(c) *p*, *s* (d) *p*, *q*, *r*

77. Which of the following molecules are chiral?

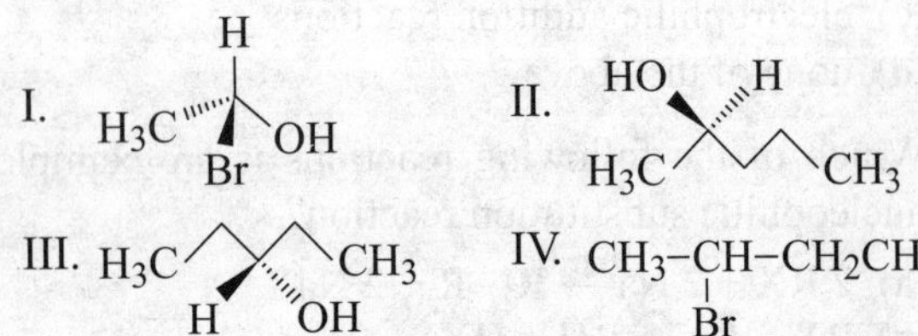

Choose the correct option

(a) I, II, IV (b) I, II, III
(c) II, III, IV (d) only III

78. Which of the following compounds is achiral?

(a) HO H (b) HO H (c) HO H (d) HO H

79. An optically active molecule must

(a) be chiral
(b) have a centre of symmetry
(c) have a plane of symmetry
(d) be identical with its mirror image

80. Which of the following compounds is optically active?

(a) *cis*-1,3-dimethylcyclobutane
(b) *trans*-1,3-dimethylcyclobutane
(c) *cis*-1,2-dimethylcyclobutane
(d) trans-1,2-dimethylcyclobutane

81. Which of the following structures is chiral?

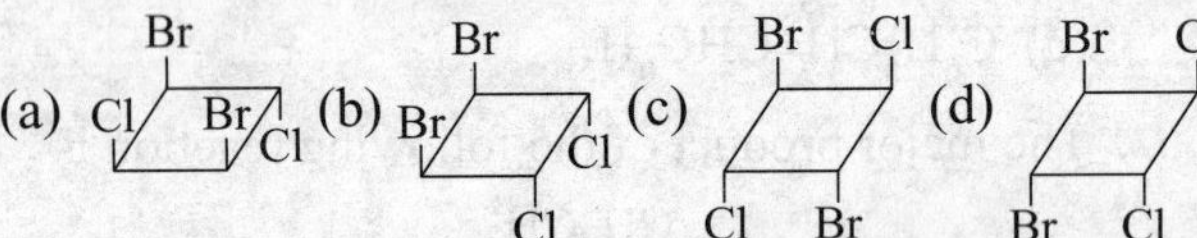

82. Consider the following organic compound.

$\overset{1}{C}H_3{-}\overset{2}{C}H_2{-}\overset{3}{C}H_2{-}\overset{4}{C}H_2{-}\overset{5}{C}H_2{-}\overset{6}{C}H_2{-}\overset{7}{C}H_3$

To make it a chiral compound, the attack should be on carbon

(a) 1 (b) 3 (c) 4 (d) 7

83. Which of the following molecules are chiral?

(a) 2-chlorobutane
(b) 2, 3-dihydroxypropanal
(c) 2-bromopropanoic acid
(d) all are chiral

84. Which of the following combinations contain chiral molecules?

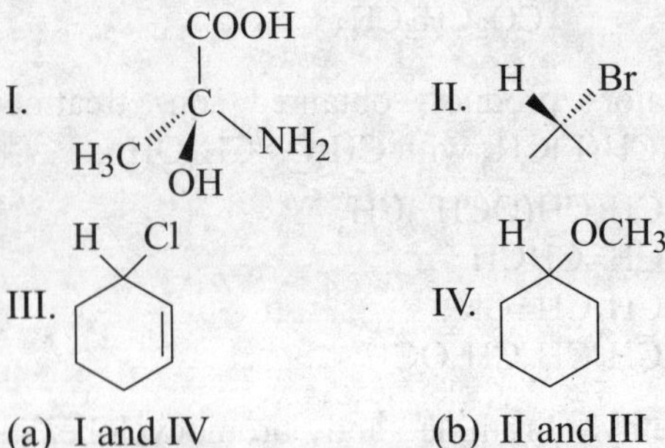

(a) I and IV (b) II and III
(c) I and III (d) II and IV

85. Which of the following acids does not exhibit optical isomerism?

(a) maleic acid (b) α-amino acids
(c) lactic acid (d) tartaric acid

86. Which of the following is chiral?

(a) 1,3-dibromo-2-chloropropane
(b) 1,1-dibromo-3-chloropropane
(c) 2,2-dibromo-1-chloropropane
(d) 1,3-dibromo-1-chloropropane

87. Out of the following, the alkene that exhibits optical isomerism is

(a) 3-methyl-1-pentene (b) 2-methyl-2-pentene
(c) 3-methyl-2-pentene (d) 4-methyl-1-pentene

88. A compound with a molecular formula C_7H_{16}, shows optical isomerism. The compound will be

(a) 2,3-dimethylpentane (b) 2,2-dimethylpentane
(c) 2-methylhexane (d) none of these

89. An optically active alkene with the MF C_6H_{12} which upon hydrogenation gives an optically inactive alkane is

(a) 2-hexene (b) 3-methyl-2-pentene
(c) 2-methyl-2-pentene (d) 3-methyl-1-pentene

90. The number of optical isomers formed by hydrogenation of the compound $(CH_3)_2C{=}CHCH_3$ is/are

(a) 1 (b) 2 (c) 3 (d) zero

91. Which of the following molecules is expected to rotate the plane of polarised light?

(a) COOH / H_2N—C—H / H (Fischer projection)
(b) CHO / HO—C—H / CH_2OH (Fischer projection)
(c) SH (d) H_2N, NH_2, H, H, Ph, Ph

92. C_8H_{16} that can form *cis – trans* geometrical isomers and also has a chiral centre, is

(a) 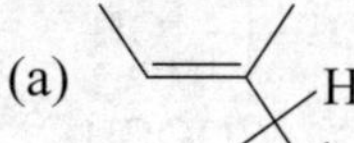 (b) 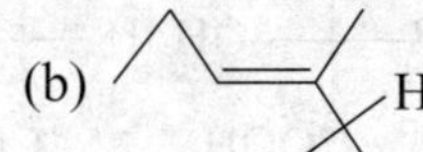

(c) both of these (d) none of these

93. Which of the following is optically inactive?

(a) 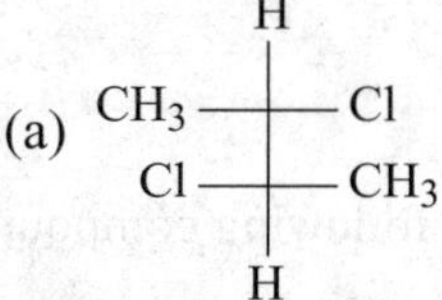 (b) 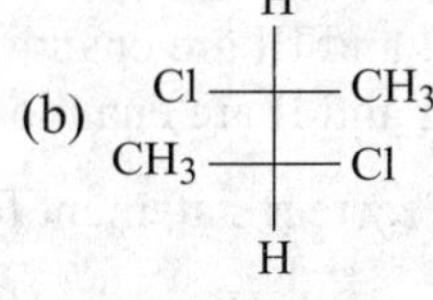

(c) H / CH_3—C—Cl / CH_3—C—Cl / H (d) none of these

94. Which of the following is a chiral molecule?

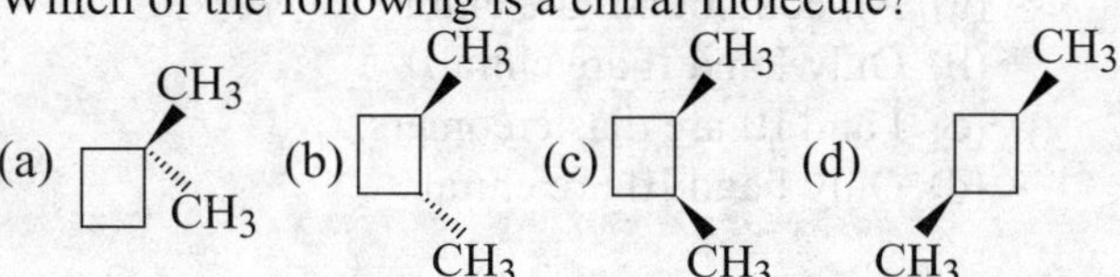

95. The optically active molecule is

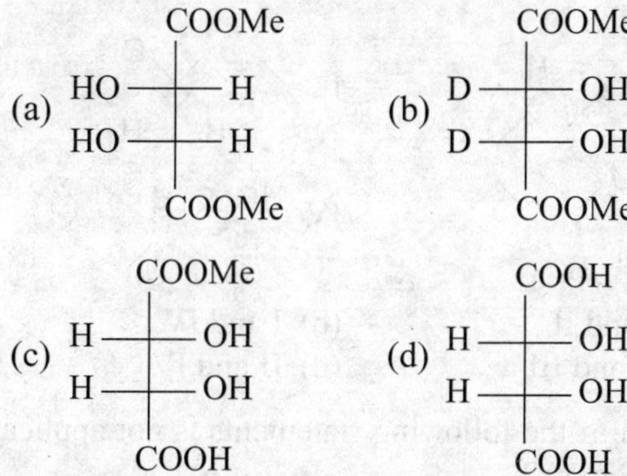

96. Consider the structures given below

H, CH_3, H, C, H, CH_3, CH_3 and H_3C, H, CH_3, H, CH_3, C, H, CH_3

They are

(a) enantiomers (b) diastereomers
(c) geometrical isomers (d) homomers
(e) meso isomers

97. The following two compounds are

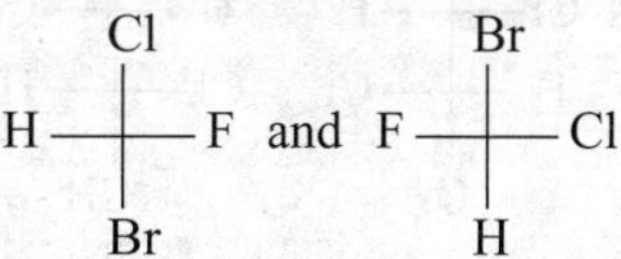

(a) enantiomers (b) diastereomers
(c) identical molecules (d) constitution isomers

98. Which of the following pairs of compounds are enantiomers?

(a) Br, Br, H, H and H, H, Br, Br
(b) CH_3, OH and OH, CH_3
(c) H, OH, Br and Br, H, OH
(d) HO, H and H, OH

99. Pairs of enantiomers from the following compounds is/are

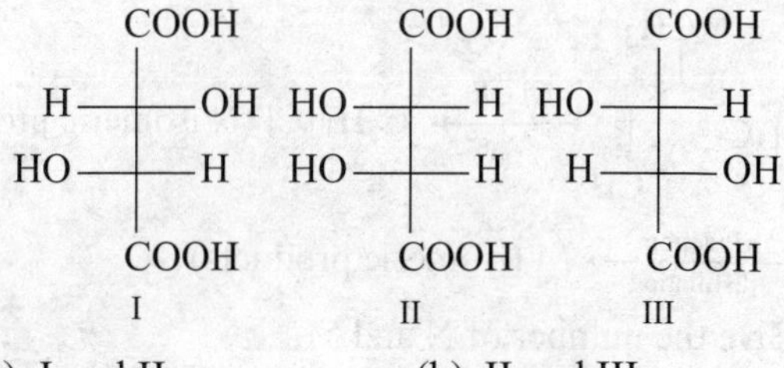

(a) I and II (b) II and III
(c) I and III (d) both (a) and (b)

100. The enantiomeric pair among the following four structures is

I. HO H   II. OH, H H

III. HO, H H   IV. HO H

(a) I and II (b) I and IV
(c) II and III (d) II and IV

101. Which of the following statements is not applicable to enantiomers?

(a) They have identical melting and boiling points.
(b) They have identical chemical properties except towards plane polarised light.
(c) They can be separated by fractional crystallisation.
(d) They rotate plane polarised light in opposite directions but to the same extent.

102. If optical rotation produced by compound (i) is +52° then that produced by compound (ii) is

I	II
CH_3	CH_3
Cl—C—H	H—C—Cl
H—C—Cl	Cl—C—H
CH_3	CH_3

(a) –52° (b) +52°
(c) 0° (d) unpredictable

103. How many chiral compounds are possible on monochlorination of 2-methylbutane?

(a) 6 (b) 8 (c) 2 (d) 4

104. How many enantiomeric pairs are obtained by monochlorination of 2,3-dimethylbutane?

(a) four (b) two (c) three (d) one

105. The number of possible enantiomeric pair(s) produced from the bromination of I and II, respectively, are

I: $(H_3C)_2C{=}C(CH_3)_2$ II: H_3C, H_3C, $=CH_3$

(a) 0,1 (b) 1,0 (c) 0, 2 (d) 1, 1

106. H_3C–$CH(CH_3)$–CH_2–CH_3 $\xrightarrow{Cl_2,\ h\nu}$ $C_5H_{11}Cl$ (N isomeric products) $\xrightarrow[\text{distillation}]{\text{Fraction}}$ M (isomeric products)

Give the number of N and M

(a) 6, 6 (b) 6, 4 (c) 4, 4 (d) 7, 3

107. The pair of structures given below represent

H, H, HO, C, CH_2CH_3 CH_2CH_3, HO, C, CH_3, H

(a) enantiomers (b) diastereomers
(c) same molecule (d) regiomers

108.

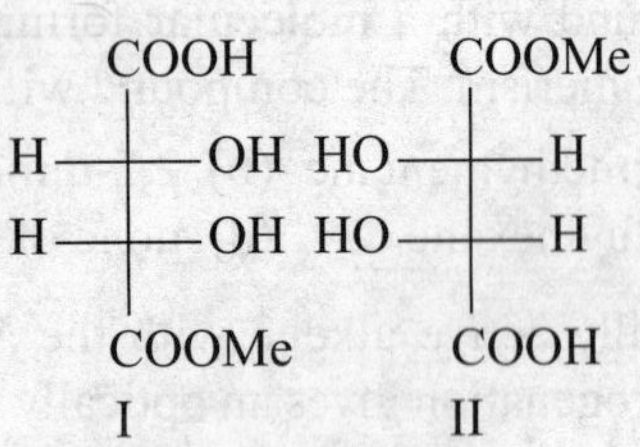

I and II are

(a) enantiomers (b) diastereomers
(c) meso compound (d) identical

109. The structures I and II represent

I		II
COOH		COOH
H—C—OH	and	H—C—OH
HO—C—H		H—C—OH
COOH		COOH

(a) enantiomers (b) diastereomers
(c) identical molecules (d) constitutional isomers

110. The correct statement about compounds I, II and III is

I	II	III
$COOCH_3$	COOH	COOH
H—C—OH	H—C—OH	H—C—OH
H—C—OH	H—C—OH	HO—C—OH
COOH	$COOCH_3$	$COOCH_3$

(a) I and II are identical.
(b) I and II are diastereomers.
(c) I and III are enantiomers.
(d) I and II are enantiomers.

111. The correct statement for the following compounds is

I: HO, OH   II: HO, OH   III: HO, OH

(a) All compounds are chiral.
(b) Only I and II are chiral.
(c) I and III are diastereomers.
(d) Only I and III are chiral.

112. The maximum number of possible optical isomers for 1-bromo-2-methylcyclobutane is

(a) 4 (b) 2 (c) 8 (d) 6

113. The number of optical isomers possible for 2,3-dichloropentane is

(a) 0 (b) 2 (c) 3 (d) 4

114. Consider the following four stereoisomers.

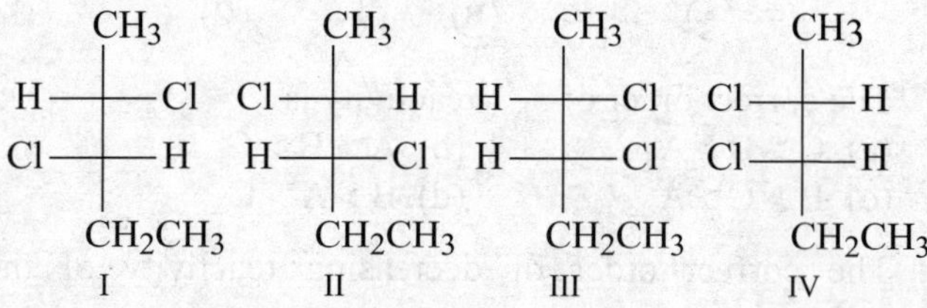

Which of the following statements are correct?

(a) I and II, and III and IV are two pairs of enantiomers.

(b) I and III, I and IV, II and III and II and IV are four pairs of diastereomers.

(c) III and IV are meso isomers.

(d) Both (a) and (b) are correct.

115. Tartaric acid has the following three stereoisomers.

COOH	COOH	COOH
H—OH	HO—H	H—OH
HO—H	H—OH	H—OH
COOH	COOH	COOH
I	II	III

Which of the following statements is/are correct?

(a) I and II are enantiomers.

(b) Both I and III, and II and III pairs are diastereomers.

(c) III is a mesoisomers.

(d) All statements are correct.

116. Meso-tartaric acid is optically inactive due to the presence of

(a) plane of asymmetry

(b) molecular asymmetry

(c) external compensation

(d) two asymmetric carbon atoms

117. The number of stereoisomers and optical isomers possible for the compound, *abd*C–C*abd* respectively

(a) 3, 3 (b) 3, 2 (c) 2, 3 (d) 2, 2

118. Catalytic reduction of both the double bonds in the following compound gives ____ stereoisomers.

$=CH_2$

H_2C

(a) 1 (b) 2 (c) 3 (d) 4

119. A compound whose molecules are superimposable on their mirror images even though they contain an asymmetric carbon atom is called

(a) a meso compound (b) an erythro isomer

(c) a threo isomer (d) a glycol

120. How many optically active stereoisomers are possible for butane-2,3-diol?

(a) 1 (b) 2 (c) 3 (d) 4

121. Among the following, which one can have a meso form?

(a) $CH_3CH(OH)CH(Cl)\,C_2H_5$

(b) $CH_3CH(OH)CH(OH)CH_3$

(c) $C_2H_5CH(OH)CH(OH)CH_3$

(d) $HOCH_2CH(Cl)CH_3$

122. Which of the following will have a meso-isomer also?

(a) 2,3-dichloropentane (b) 2,3-dichloropentane

(c) 2-chlorobutane (d) 2-hydroxypropanoic acid

123. Which of the following compounds does not have a diastereoisomer?

(a) 2,3-butanediol (b) 2-butene

(c) 2,3-dichloropentane (d) 2-butanol

124. X and Y are

H; H, Cl; Cl; H_3C, CH_3

Cl; CH_3, H; H, CH_3; Cl

(a) enantiomers (b) diastereomers

(c) constitutional isomers (d) conformers

125. Which of the following statements is not applicable to diastereomers?

(a) They are conformational isomers.

(b) They have different melting points, boiling points and solubilities.

(c) They may have same or different signs of rotation or may even be optically inactive.

(d) They can be separated by fractional crystallisation.

126. Which of the following compounds can exhibit both geometrical isomerism and enantiomerism?

(a) $CH_3–CH=CH–CH_3$

(b) $CH_3CH_2–CH(CH_3)–CH=CH–CH_3$

(c) $CH_3CH_2–C(CH_3)=CH–COOH$ (d) $CH_3–CHOH–COOH$

127. The total number of stereoisomers possible for the following compound $CH_3–CH=CH–CH_2–CHBr–CH_3$ is

(a) 6 (b) 2 (c) 3 (d) 4

128. The maximum number of isomers that can result from monobromination of 2-methyl-2-pentene bromosuccinimide in boiling CCl_4 is

(a) 1 (b) 2 (c) 3 (d) 4

129. The number of stereoisomers for the following compound is

CH_3–CH=CH–CH(Br)–CH_2CH_3

(a) 2 (b) 3 (c) 4 (d) 8

130. Total number of isomers including structural, geometrical and optical isomers possible for the compound with molecular formula C_4H_7Cl is

(a) 12 (b) 10 (c) 11 (d) 9

131. sec-Butyl chloride obtained by free radical chlorination of *n*-butane is always

(a) dextrorotatory (b) laevorotatory
(c) racemic mixture (d) none of these

132. The concentration of an organic compound in chloroform is 6.15 g/100 mL of solution. A portion of this solution in a 5 cm polarimeter tube causes an observed rotation of –1.2°. What is the specific rotation of the compound?

(a) +12° (b) –3.9° (c) –12° (d) –39°

133. Pure (+)-2-butanol has a specific rotation of +13.52°. A sample of 2-butanol prepared in the laboratory and purified by distillation has a specific rotation of – 6.76°. What is the composition of the mixture?

(a) 20% (+)-2-butanol + 80% (–)-2- butanol
(b) 50% (+)-2-butanol + 50% (–)-2-butanol
(c) 60% (+)-2-butanol + 20% racemic mixture
(d) 50% (–)-2-butanol + 25% racemic mixture

134. If in a mixture, two enantiomers are found to be present in 85% and 15% respectively, the enantiomeric excess (*ee*) is

(a) 85% (b) 15% (c) 70% (d) 60%

135. The optical rotation of an optically active compound is

(a) directly proportional to the molar concentration of the compound
(b) directly proportional to the length of the polarimeter tube only
(c) independent of the length of the polarimeter tube
(d) directly proportional to both the length of the polarimeter tube and molar concentration of the compound

136. Stereoisomers which have identical physical and chemical properties but differ only in their behaviour towards plane polarised light are called

(a) optical isomers (b) geometrical isomers
(c) conformation isomers (d) tautomers

Mechanism and Stereochemistry of S_N1 and S_N2 Reactions

137. Consider the following bromides:

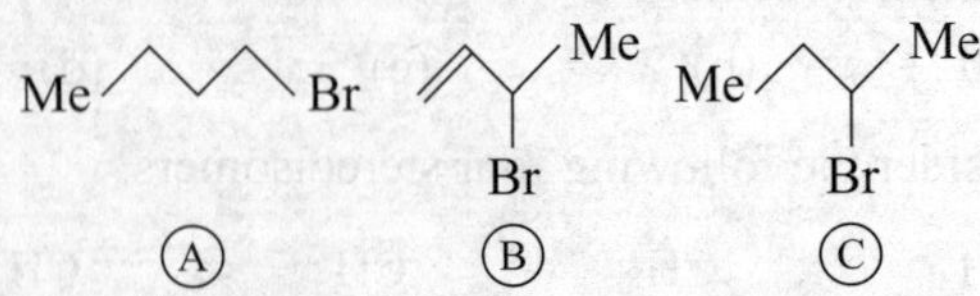

The correct order of S_N1 reactivity is

(a) C > B > A (b) A > B > C
(c) B > C > A (d) B > A > C

138. The correct order of decreasing reactivity of the following compounds:

I. $C_6H_5CH_2Br$ II. $C_6H_5CH(C_6H_5)Br$
III. $C_6H_5CH(CH_3)Br$ IV. $C_6H_5C(CH_3)(C_6H_5)Br$

towards S_N1 reactions is

(a) III > II > I > IV (b) I > II > III > IV
(c) II > IV > I > III (d) IV > II > III > I

139. Which one is the most reactive towards S_N1 reactions?

(a) $C_6H_5CH_2Br$ (b) $C_6H_5CH(Br)C_6H_5$
(c) $C_6H_5CH(CH_3)Br$ (d) $C_6H_5C(CH_3)(C_6H_5)Br$

140. In S_N1 reaction on chiral centres, there is

(a) inversion more than retention leading to partial racemisation
(b) 100% retention
(c) 100% inversion (d) 100% racemisation

141. An optically active halide when allowed to react with CN^- gives a racemic mixture. The halide is most likely to be

(a) primary (b) secondary
(c) tertiary (d) none of the above

142. Which of the following statements about S_N1 reactions is/are not correct?

(i) Rearrangement may occur.
(ii) Rate is affected by polarity of solvent.
(iii) Strength of the nucleophile is important in determining the rate.
(iv) The order of reactivity of alkyl halides is 3° > 2° > 1°.
(v) Proceeds with complete inversion of configuration.

(a) (iii), (v) (b) (ii), (iii), (v)
(c) (v) only (d) (iii) only

143. In the solvolysis of 3-methyl-3-bromohexane, which of the following statements is not correct?

(a) It involves carbocation intermediate.
(b) Polar solvents accelerate the reaction.
(c) The rate of the reaction depends upon the 3-methyl-3-bromohexane concentration.

(d) It involves inversion of configuration.

144. The following alkyl halides on heating with water undergo hydrolysis by S_N1 mechanism to form the corresponding alcohols.

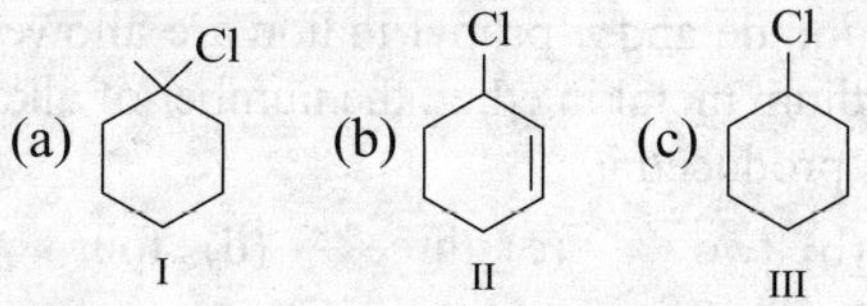

(a) I (1-chloro-1-methylcyclohexane) (b) II (chlorocyclohexene) (c) III (chlorocyclohexane) (d) CH_3Cl IV

Their order of reactivity is

(a) I > II > III > IV (b) II > I > III > IV
(c) III > II > I > IV (d) IV > I > III > II

145. Arrange the following in order of increasing reactivity towards hydrolysis by the S_N1 mechanism.

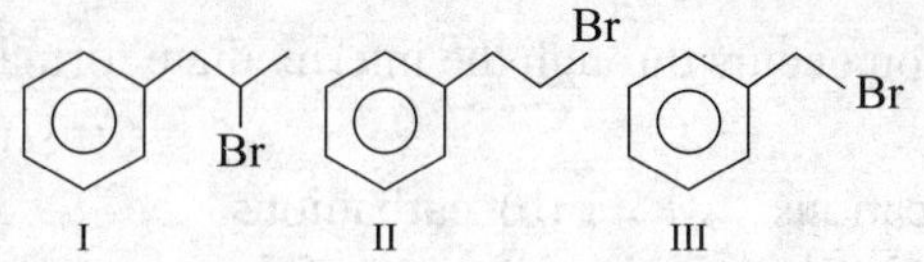

I (Ph–CH₂–CH(Br)–CH₃) II (Ph–CH(Br)–CH₂–CH₃) III (Ph–CH₂–CH₂–Br) IV $CH_3–Br$

(a) I > II > III > IV (b) I > III > II > IV
(c) III > I > II > IV (d) IV > III > II > I

146. The major product of the following S_N1 reaction is

$$CH_3-\underset{Br}{CH}-\underset{CH_3}{CH}-CH + C_2H_5O^- \longrightarrow$$

(a) $CH_3-\underset{OC_2H_5}{CH}-CH(CH_3)_2$ (b) $(CH_3)_2CH-CH_2CH_2OC_2H_5$

(c) $CH_3CH_2-\underset{OC_2H_5}{\overset{CH_3}{C}}-CH_3$ (d) none is correct

147. Which of the following is an example of an S_N2 reaction?

(a) $CH_3Br + OH^- \rightarrow CH_3OH + Br^-$
(b) $CH_3-\underset{Br}{CH}-CH + OH^- \longrightarrow CH_3-\underset{OH}{CH}-CH_3 + Br^-$
(c) $CH_3CH_2OH \xrightarrow{-H_2O} CH_2{=}CH_2$
(d) $(CH_3)_3C{-}Br + OH^- \rightarrow (CH_3)_3COH + Br^-$

148. The reaction described is

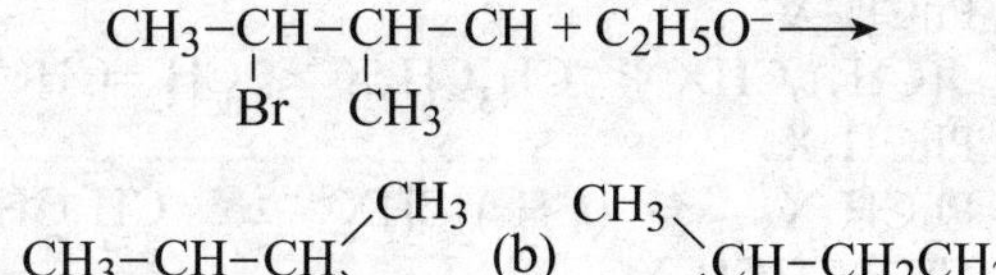

$$CH_3(CH_2)_5(H)(CH_3)C{-}Br \xrightarrow{OH^-} HO{-}C(H)(CH_3)(CH_2)_5CH_3$$

(a) E_2 (b) S_N1 (c) S_N2 (d) E_1

149. The organic chloro-compound which shows complete stereochemical inversion during an S_N2 reaction, is

(a) CH_3Cl (b) $(C_2H_5)_2CHCl$
(c) $(CH_3)_3CCl$ (d) $(CH_3)_2CHCl$

150. The product of the following reaction is,

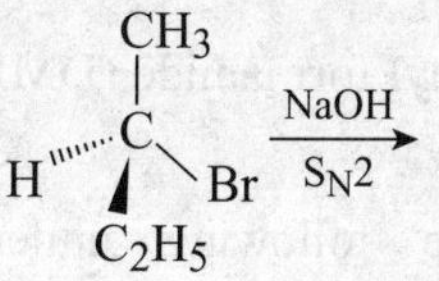

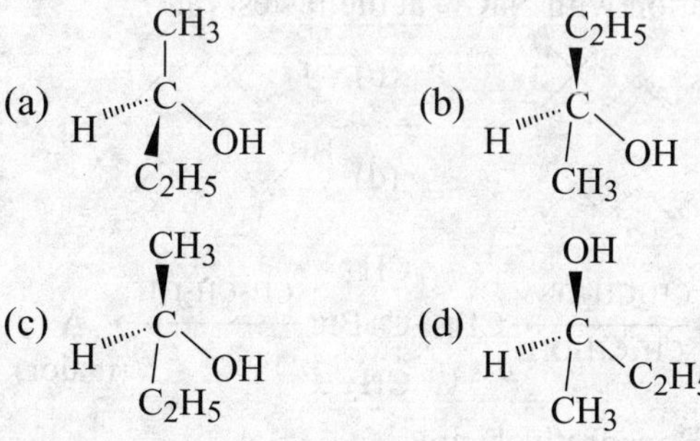

$$C(CH_3)(H)(Br)(C_2H_5) \xrightarrow[S_N2]{NaOH}$$

(a) C with CH_3 (top), H, OH, C_2H_5 (wedge, bottom)
(b) C with C_2H_5 (wedge, top), H, OH, CH_3 (bottom)
(c) C with CH_3 (wedge, top), H, OH, C_2H_5 (bottom)
(d) C with OH (wedge, top), H, C_2H_5, CH_3 (bottom)

151. Write in decreasing order of reactivity by the S_N2 pathway.

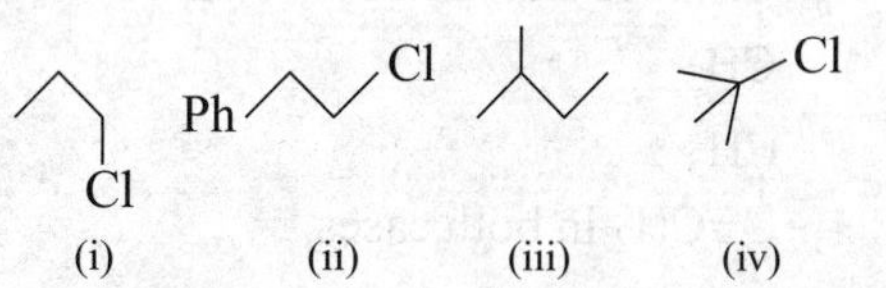

(i) (ii) Ph–CH₂CH₂CH₂–Cl (iii) (iv) (tertiary chloride)

(a) I > II > III > IV (b) II > I > III > IV
(c) IV > III > II > I (d) IV > III > I > II

152. In S_N2 reactions, the correct order of reactivity for the following compounds:

CH_3Cl, CH_3CH_2Cl, $(CH_3)_2CHCl$ and $(CH_3)_3CCl$ is
(a) $(CH_3)_2CHCl > CH_3CH_2Cl > CH_3Cl > (CH_3)_3CCl$
(b) $CH_3Cl > (CH_3)_2CHCl > CH_3CH_2Cl > (CH_3)_3CCl$
(c) $CH_3Cl > CH_3CH_2Cl > (CH_3)_2CHCl > (CH_3)_3CCl$
(d) $CH_3CH_2Cl > CH_3Cl > (CH_3)_2CHCl > (CH_3)_3CCl$

153. Arrange the following alkyl halides,

I. 1-bromobutane
II. 1-bromo-2,2-dimethylpropane
III. 1-bromo-2-methylbutane
IV. 1-bromo-3-methylbutane

in order of decreasing reactivity towards S_N2 displacement.

(a) I > III > II > IV (b) I > IV > III > II
(c) II > IV > III > I (d) III > II > I > IV

154. In an S_N2 substitution reaction of the type

$$R{-}Br + Cl^- \xrightarrow{DMF} R{-}Cl + Br^-,$$

which one of the following has the highest relative rate?

(a) $CH_3-\underset{CH_3}{CH}-CH_2Br$ (b) $CH_3-\underset{CH_3}{\overset{CH_3}{C}}-CH_2Br$

(c) CH_3CH_2Br (d) $CH_3CH_2CH_2Br$

155. Consider the reaction,

$CH_3CH_2CH_2Br + NaCN \rightarrow CH_3CH_2CH_2CN + NaBr$

This reaction will be fastest in

(a) ethanol
(b) methanol
(c) N,N-dimethyl formamide (DMF)
(d) water

156. Which of the following undergoes nucleophilic substitution with NaCN at the fastest rate?

(a)  Br (b)  Br

(c)  Br (d) 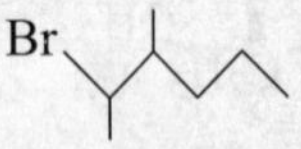 Br

157. $\underset{\text{(major)}}{B} \xleftarrow[CH_3CH_2OH]{CH_3CH_2ONa} CH_3-\underset{CH_3}{\overset{CH_3}{C}}-Br \xrightarrow{CH_3CH_2OH} \underset{\text{(major)}}{A}$

A and B respectively are

(a) $CH_3-\underset{CH_3}{\overset{CH_3}{C}}-OCH_2CH_3$ in both cases

(b) $CH_3-\overset{CH_3}{C}=CH_2$ in both cases

(c) $CH_3-\underset{CH_3}{\overset{CH_3}{C}}-OCH_2CH_3$ and $(CH_3)_2C=CH_2$

(d) $(CH_3)_2C=CH_2$ and $CH_3-\underset{CH_3}{\overset{CH_3}{C}}-OCH_2CH_3$

158. Which of the following undergoes nucleophilic substation exclusively by the S_N1 mechanism?

(a) ethyl chloride (b) isopropyl chloride
(c) benzyl chloride (d) chlorobenzene

159. Which is the least reactive towards nucleophilic substitution (S_N2)?

(a) $CH_2=CH-CH_2Cl$ (b) $(CH_3)_3C-Cl$
(c) 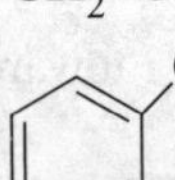 Cl (chlorobenzene) (d) $CH_3-CH(Cl)CH_3$

160. The order of reactivity of the following halides towards hydrolysis by aqueous KOH is

(a) $CH_3CH_2CH_2Cl < CH_2=CHCl < CH_2=CHCH_2Cl$
(b) $CH_2=CHCH_2Cl < CH_2=CHCl < CH_3CH_2CH_2Cl$
(c) $CH_2=CHCl < CH_3CH_2CH_2Cl < CH_2=CHCH_2Cl$
(d) $CH_2=CHCl < CH_2=CHCH_2Cl < CH_3CH_2CH_2Cl$

161. The order of decreasing reactivity of the following compounds in reaction with alcoholic $AgNO_3$ is

(a) $PhCH=CHBr > PhCHBrCH_3 > PhCH_2CH_2Br$
(b) $PhCHBrCH_3 > PhCH_2CH_2Br > PhCH=CHBr$
(c) $PhCHBrCH_3 > PhCH=CHBr > PhCH_2CH_2Br$
(d) $PhCH_2CH_2Br > PhCHBrCH > PhCH=CHBr$

162. Which of the following is the least reactive in a nucleophilic substitution reaction?

(a) $(CH_3)_3C-Cl$ (b) $CH_2=CHCl$
(c) CH_3CH_2Cl (d) $CH_2=CHCH_2Cl$

163. When ethyl iodide and *n*-propyl iodide are allowed to react with sodium metal in ether, the number of alkanes that could be produced is

(a) one (b) two (c) three (d) four

164. Which of the following is an example of an S_N1 reaction?

(a) $(CH_3)_3CBr + KOH(aq) \rightarrow (CH_3)_3COH + KBr$
(b) $CH_3Br + KCN \rightarrow CH_3CN + KBr$
(c) $C_6H_5Br + NaNH_2 \rightarrow C_6H_5NH_2 + NaBr$
(d) $2\ CH_3I + 2\ Na \rightarrow CH_3-CH_3 + 2\ NaI$

165. S_N1 reaction occurs through the intermediate formation of

(a) carbocations (b) carbanions
(c) free radicals (d) none of these

166. The correct increasing order of reactivity of halides for the S_N1 reaction is

(a) $CH_3CH_2X < (CH_3)_2CHX < CH_2=CHCH_2X < PhCH_2X$
(b) $(CH_3)_2CHX < CH_3CH_2X < CH_2=CHCH_2X < PhCH_2X$
(c) $PhCH_2X < (CH_3)_2CHX < CH_3CH_2X < CH_2=CHCH_2X$
(d) $CH_2=CHCH_2X < PhCH_2X < (CH_3)_2CHX < CH_3CH_2X$

167. The S_N1 reactivity of the following halides will be in the order

(i) $(CH_3)_3CBr$ (ii) $(C_6H_5)_2CHBr$
(iii) $(C_6H_5)_2C(CH_3)Br$ (iv) $(CH_3)_2CHBr$
(v) C_2H_5Br

(a) (v) > (iv) > (i) > (ii) > (iii)
(b) (ii) > (i) > (iii) > (v) > (iv)
(c) (i) > (iii) > (v) > (ii) > (iv)
(d) (iii) > (ii) > (i) > (iv) > (iv)

Chemical Reactions of Haloalkenes (Aryl halides)

168. The major product formed in the reaction, is

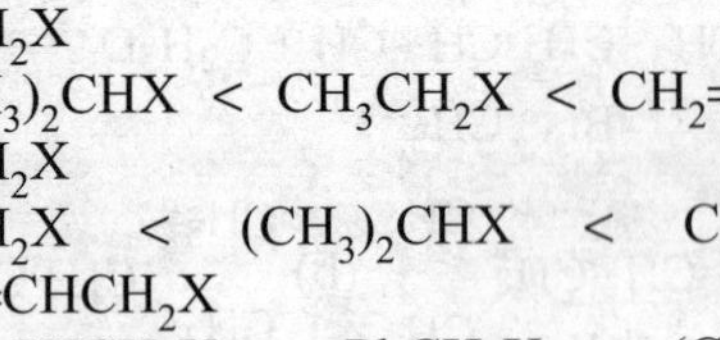

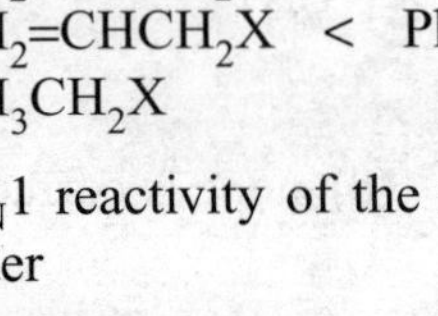

Br, Cl, I $\xrightarrow[\text{DMSO, heat}]{\text{NaCN}}$

Br, Cl, CN — I

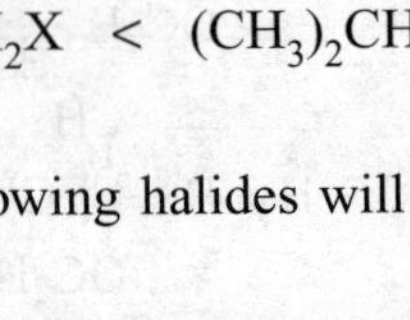

CN, Cl, CN — II

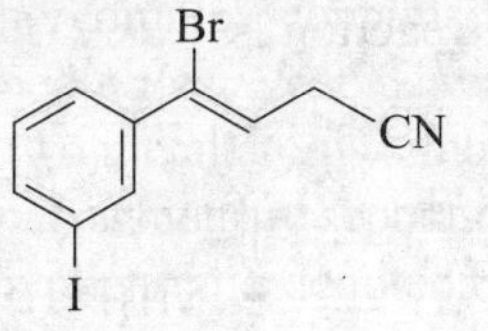

III 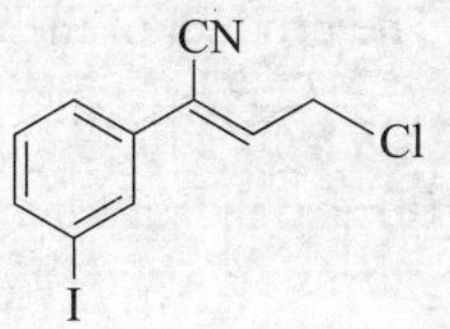 IV

(a) I (b) II (c) III (d) IV

169. 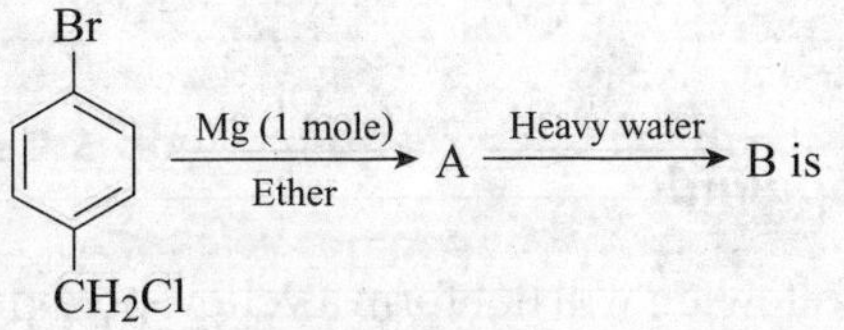 Br–C$_6$H$_4$–CH$_2$Cl $\xrightarrow[\text{Ether}]{\text{Mg (1 mole)}}$ A $\xrightarrow{\text{Heavy water}}$ B is

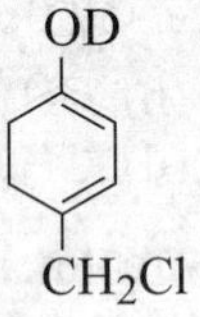

(a) 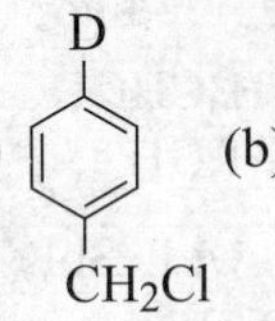 D–C$_6$H$_4$–CH$_2$Cl (b) OD–C$_6$H$_4$–CH$_2$Cl (c) Br–C$_6$H$_4$–CH$_2$D (d) Br–C$_6$H$_4$–CH$_2$OD

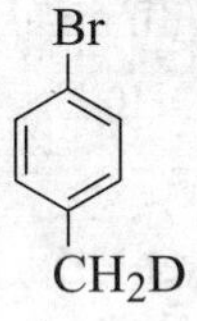

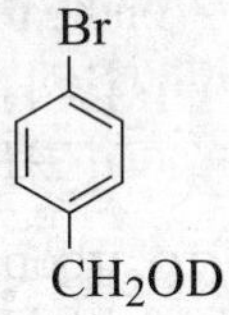

170. The increasing order of ease of hydrolysis of the following compounds is

(i) (ii) (iii) (iv) $(CH_3)_3Br$

(a) (i) < (iii) < (ii) < (iv) (b) (i) < (iv) < (iii) < (ii)
(c) (iv) < (ii) < (iii) < (i) (d) (i) < (iii) < (iv) < (ii)

171. Which of the following compounds undergoes nucleophilic substitution reactions most easily?

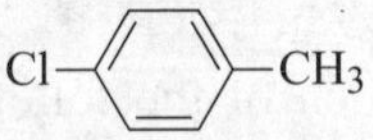

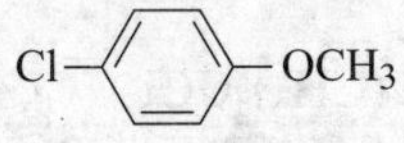

(a) 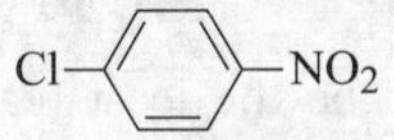 Cl–C$_6$H$_4$–NO$_2$ (b) Cl–C$_6$H$_4$–CH$_3$
(c) Cl–C$_6$H$_4$–OCH$_3$ (d) 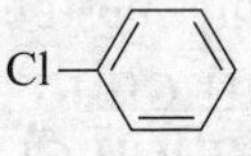 Cl–C$_6$H$_5$

172. The reactivity of the compounds decreases as

(i) MeBr (ii) $PhCH_2Br$
(iii) MeCl (iv) p-$MeOC_6H_4Br$
(a) (i) > (ii) > (iii) > (iv) (b) (iv) > (ii) > (i) > (iii)
(c) (iv) > (iii) > (i) > (ii) (d) (ii) > (i) > (iii) > (iv)

173. Which chloro derivative of benzene among the following, would undergo hydrolysis most readily with aqueous sodium hydroxide to furnish the corresponding hydroxyl derivative?

(a) 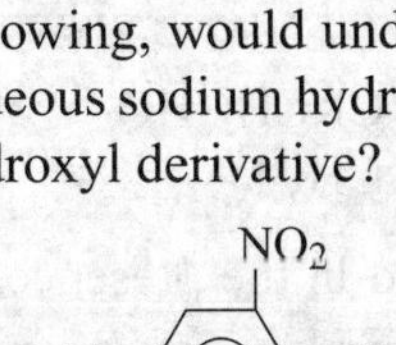 2,4,6-(NO$_2$)$_3$C$_6$H$_2$–Cl (b) O$_2$N–C$_6$H$_4$–Cl
(c) Me$_2$N–C$_6$H$_4$–Cl (d) C_6H_5Cl

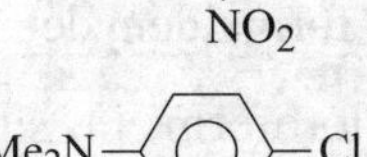

174. The order of reactivity towards nucleophilic substitution reaction of the given compounds is,

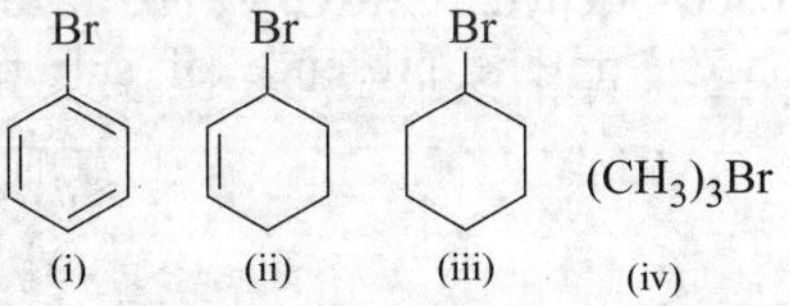

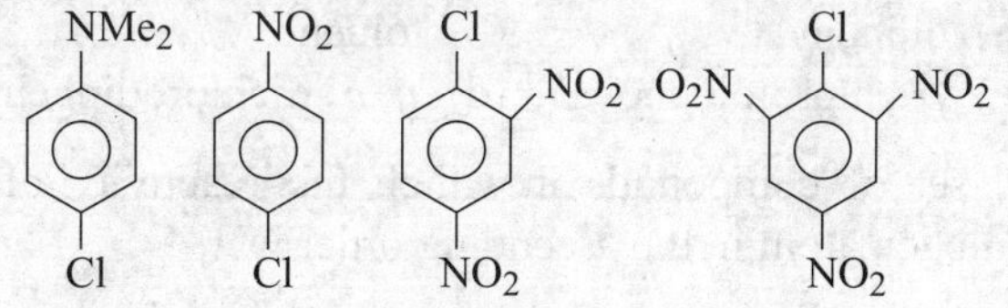

(i) (ii) (iii) (iv)

(a) (i) > (ii) > (iii) > (iv) (b) (ii) > (i) > (iii) > (iv)
(c) (iv) > (iii) > (ii) > (i) (d) (iii) > (iv) > (ii) > (i)

175. Which of the following is the least reactive towards nucleophilic displacement reaction when treated with aqueous KOH?

(a) 2,4,6-trinitrochlorobenzene
(b) 2,4-dinitrochlorobenzene
(c) 4-nitrochlorobenzene
(d) 3-nitrochlorobenzene

176. The correct order of increasing reactivity of the C–X bond towards nucleophilic substitution in the following compounds is

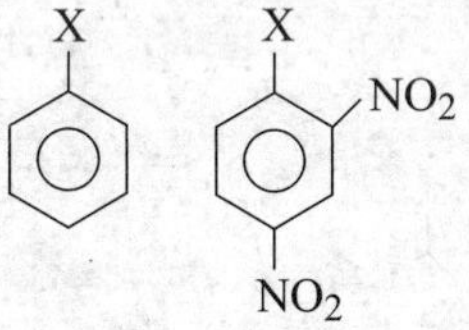

(I) (II) $(CH_3)C–X$ (III) $(CH_3)_2CH–X$ (III)

(a) III < II < I < IV (b) I < II < IV < III
(c) II < III < I < IV (d) IV < III < I < II

177. Chlorobenzene on treatment with acetyl chloride and anhyd. $AlCl_3$ gives

(a) *o*-chloroacetophenone
(b) *p*-chloroacetophenone
(c) *o*- and *p*-chloroacetophenone
(d) *m*-chloroacetophenone

178. Find the major product in the following reaction.

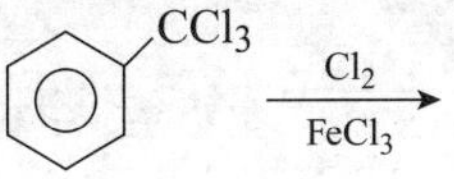

$C_6H_5CCl_3 \xrightarrow[\text{FeCl}_3]{\text{Cl}_2}$

(a) 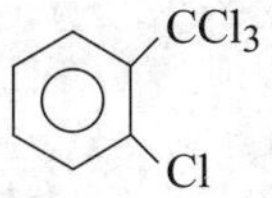 (b) 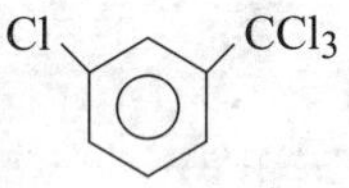 (c) 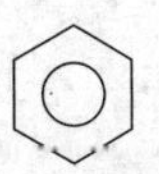 (d)

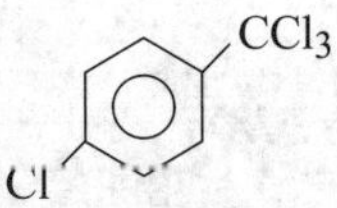

179. Chlorobenzene reacts with Mg in dry ether to give a compound (A) which further reacts with ethanol to yield

(a) phenol (b) benzene
(c) ethylbenzene (d) ethyl phenyl ether

180. Chlorobenzene and methyl chloride are treated with sodium metal in dry ether, the major product formed is

(a) diphenyl (b) toluene
(c) *p*-chlorotoluene (d) *p, p*'-dichlorodiphenyl

181. A set of compounds in which the reactivity of the halogen atom in the ascending order is
(a) chlorobenzene, vinyl chloride, chloroethane
(b) chloroethane, chlorobenzene, vinyl chloride
(c) vinyl chloride, chlorobenzene, chloroethane
(d) vinyl chloride, chloroethane, chlorobenzene

182. The reactivities of CH_3Cl, $CH_3CH_2CH_2Cl$ and C_6H_5Cl are in the order
(a) $CH_3Cl > CH_3CH_2CH_2Cl > C_6H_5Cl$
(b) $CH_3CH_2CH_2Cl > CH_3Cl > C_6H_5Cl$
(c) $C_6H_5Cl > CH_3CH_2CH_2Cl > CH_3Cl$
(d) $CH_3Cl > C_6H_5Cl > CH_3CH_2CH_2Cl$

183. The structure of the major product formed in the following reaction is,

Cl, I $\xrightarrow[\text{DMF}]{\text{NaCN}}$

(a) CN, CN (b) Cl, NC, I
(c) Cl, CN (d) CN, I

184. The major product of the following reaction is,

Me, Br, F, NO_2 $\xrightarrow[\text{Dimethylformamide}]{\text{PhS}^- \text{Na}^+}$

(a) Me, SPh, F, NO_2 (b) Me, SPh, F, NO_2
(c) Me, Br, SPh, NO_2 (d) Me, SPh, SPh, NO_2

185. Cl, Br $\xrightarrow[\text{EtOH}]{NH_3}$

The product of the above reaction is
(a) NH_2, NH_2 (b) Cl, NH_2
(c) NH_2, Br (d) NH_2, OEt

Polyhalogen Compounds

186. Which of the following will not form a yellow precipitate on heating with an alkaline solution of iodine?
(a) $CH_3CHOHCH_3$ (b) $CH_3CH_2CHOHCH_3$
(c) CH_3OH (d) CH_3CH_2OH

187. Carbon tetrachloride on treatment with SbF_3 in the presence of $SbCl_5$ as catalyst gives
(a) CCl_3F (b) CF_3Cl (c) CF_4 (d) CCl_2F_2

188. Trichloroacetaldehyde, CCl_3CHO, reacts with chlorobenzene in the presence of sulfuric acid and produces:

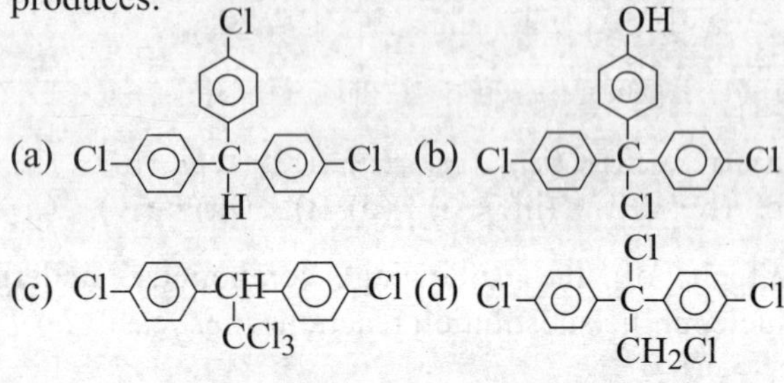

189. Which of the following will be the least reactive in nucleophilic substitution?
(a) $CH_3CH_2CH_2Cl$ (b) $(CH_3)_3CCl$
(c) $CH_2{=}CHCH_2Cl$ (d) $CH_2{=}CHCl$

190. What is the product formed when chlorine reacts with ethyl alcohol in the presence of NaOH?
(a) CH_3Cl (b) C_2H_5Cl
(c) CCl_3CHO (d) $CHCl_3$

191. Ethyl alcohol is heated with bleaching powder and water. The final product is
(a) $ClCH_2CHO$ (b) Cl_2CHCHO
(c) Cl_3CCHO (d) $CHCl_3$

192. Chloroform is slowly oxidised in the presence of light and air to form
(a) formyl chloride (b) phosgene
(c) trichloroethanol (d) formaldehyde

193. The aerial oxidation of chloroform in sunlight to phosgene can be checked by
(a) keeping chloroform in coloured bottles
(b) adding a few drops of 1% C_2H_5OH

(c) adding a few drops of dil. HCl or NaOH
(d) both (a) and (b)

194. Hydrolysis of trichloromethane with aqueous KOH gives

(a) methanol (b) acetic acid
(c) ethanol (d) formic acid

Analysis of Haloalkanes and Haloarenes

195. A compound X on treatment with NaOH at room temperature followed by acidification with dil. HNO_3 and addition of $AgNO_3$ gives a white precipitate soluble in NH_4OH solution. The compound X is

(a) chlorobenzene (b) benzyl chloride
(c) ethyl bromide (d) vinyl chloride

196. The halide which does not give a precipitate when warmed with alcoholic $AgNO_3$ solution is

(a) chlorobenzene (b) benzyl chloride
(c) allyl chloride (d) tert-butyl chloride

197. An organic compound which produces a bluish-green flame on heating in the presence of copper is

(a) chlorobenzene (b) benzaldehyde
(c) aniline (d) benzoic acid

198. A sample of chloroform before being used as an anaesthetic agent is tested by

(a) Fehling's solution
(b) ammoniacal cuprous chloride
(c) silver nitrate solution in the cold
(d) silver nitrate solution after boiling with alcoholic KOH

Final Preparation

199. Which of the following biphenyls is optically active?

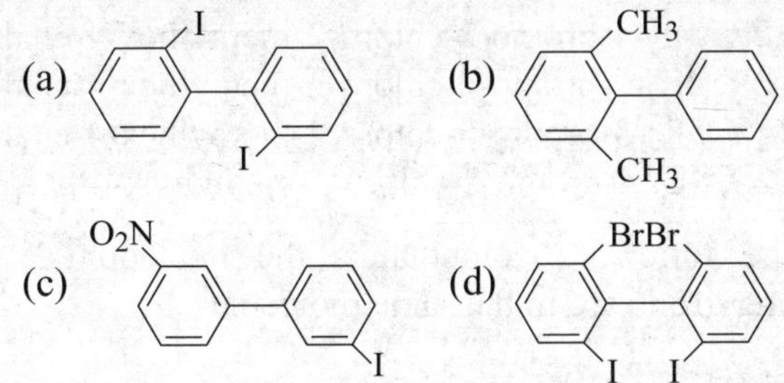

200. Which of the following are atropisomers?

(a) [structures: NO_2, COOH / COOH NO_2] and [structures: COOH NO_2 / NO_2 COOH]
(b) staggered and eclipsed conformations of ethane
(c) gauche and anti conformations of *n*-butane
(d) chair and boat conformations of cyclohexane

201. Two possible stereostructures of $CH_3CHOHCOOH$ which are optically active, are called

(a) atropisomes (b) enantiomers
(c) mesomers (d) diastereomers

202. Which of the following does not show optical activity?

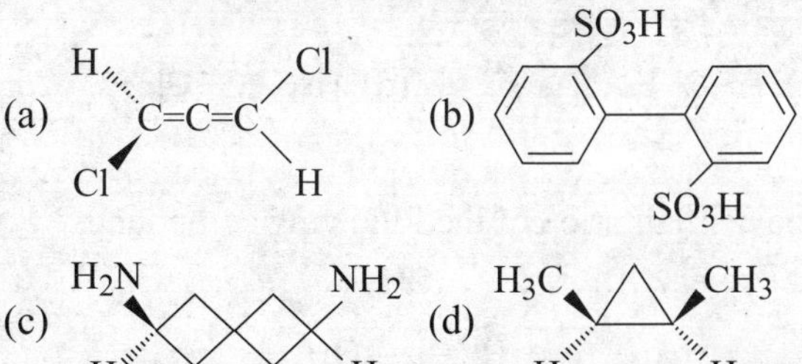

203. The possible isomers for [structure: H, HO, COOH, H] are

(a) enantiomers (b) diastereomers
(c) conformers (d) rotamers

204. When (–)-2-methylbutan-1-ol is heated with concentrated hydrochloric acid, (+)-1-chloro-2-methylbutane is obtained. This reaction is an example of

(a) retention (b) inversion (c) racemisation
(d) resolution (e) mutarotation

205. If there is no rotation of plane polarised light by a compound (thought to be chiral), in a specific solvent, it may mean that

(a) the compound is certainly meso
(b) there is no compound in the solvent
(c) the compound may be a racemic mixture
(d) the compound is certainly chiral

206. Which of the following Fischer projection formulae is identical with D-glyceraldehyde?

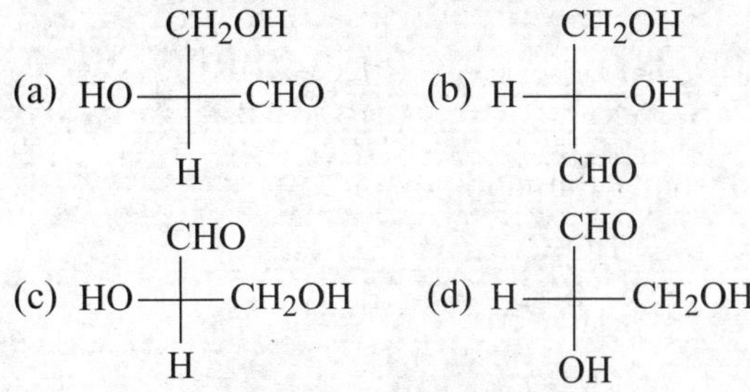

207. The chirality of the compound

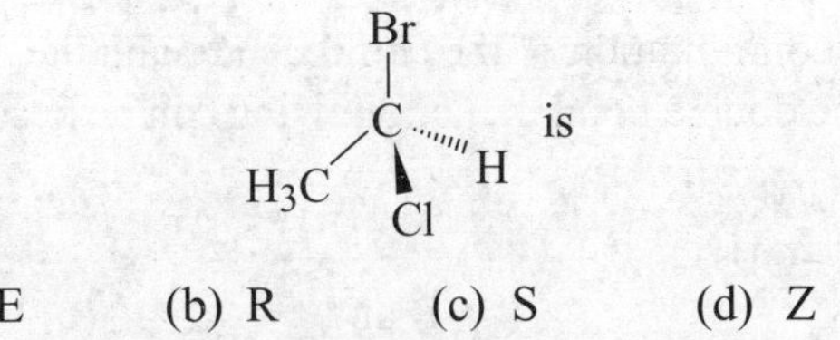

(a) E (b) R (c) S (d) Z

208. CH_3–CHCl–CH_2–CH_3 has a chiral centre. Which one of the following represents its R-configuration?

(a) $H-C(C_2H_5)(Cl)-CH_3$ (b) $Cl-C(C_2H_5)(H)-CH_3$

(c) $H-C(CH_3)(C_2H_5)-Cl$ (d) $H_3C-C(C_2H_5)(H)-Cl$

209. The configuration of the following compound,

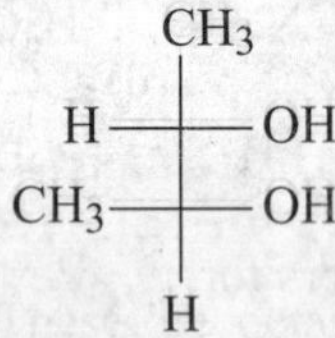

(a) 1 S, 2 S (b) 1 S, 2 R
(c) 1 R, 2 S (d) 1 R, 2 R

210. The structure of 2R,3S-dibromocinnamic acid is

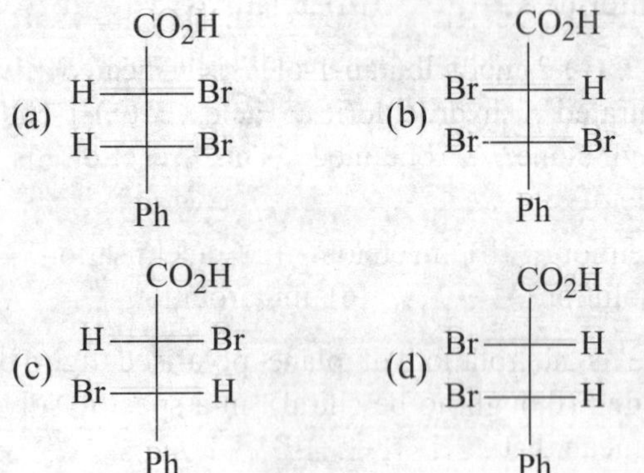

211. The absolute configuration of

CO_2H
H — OH
H — Cl
CH_3

is

(a) (2R, 3S) (b) (2 S, 3R)
(c) (2 S, 3S) (d) (2 R, 3 R)

212. The absolute configuration of

HO_2C CO_2H
HO OH
H H

is

(a) R, S (b) S, R (c) S, S (d) R, R

213. The configuration of the chiral centre and the geometry of the double bond in the following can be described by

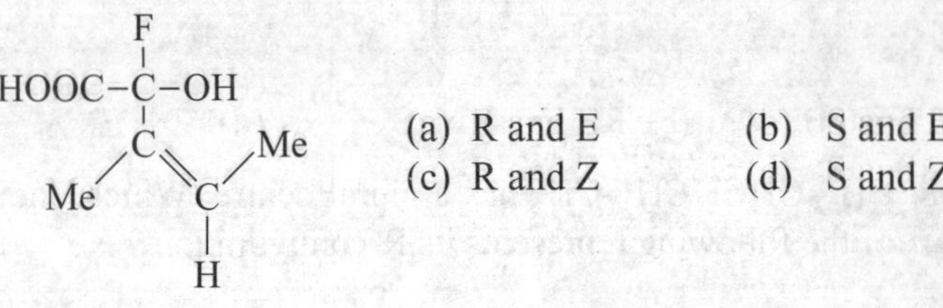

(a) R and E (b) S and E
(c) R and Z (d) S and Z

214. The number of stereoisomers obtained by bromination of *trans*-2-butene is

(a) 1 (b) 2 (c) 3 (d) 4

215. Addition of Br_2 to Z-2-butene gives

(a) (R, R)-2,3-dibromobutane only
(b) (S, S)-2,3-dibromobutane only
(c) (R,S)-2,3-dibromobutane only
(d) a mixture of (R, R) and (S, S)-2,3-dibromobutane (50% : 50%)
(e) (R, S)-1,2-dibromobutane

216. Addition of Br_2 to E-2-butane gives

(a) (R, R)-2,3-dibromobutane only
(b) (S, S)-2,3-dibromobutane only
(c) (R, S)-2,3-dibromobutane only
(d) a (1 : 1) mixture of (R, R) and (S, S)-2,3-dibromobutane

217. Optically active and meso-2,3-dibromobutane on debromination respectively give

(a) *cis*-2-butene, *trans*-2-butene
(b) *trans*-2-butene, *cis*-2-butene
(c) both give *cis*-2-butene
(d) both give *trans*-2-butene

218. The correct IUPAC name of the compound is

H Br
OH

(a) (2R, 3S)-2-bromo-3-butanol
(b) (2R, 3R)-3-bromo-2-butanol
(c) (2R, 3S)-3-bromo-2-butanol
(d) (2R, 3S)-3-bromo-2-butanol

219. The correct IUPAC name of

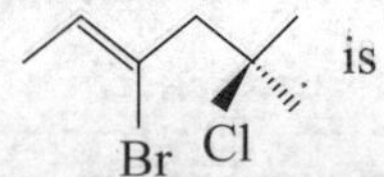

is

(a) (2R, 4E)-4-bromo-2-chloro-2-methylhex-4-enal
(b) (2R, 4Z)-4-bromo-2-chloro-2-methylhex-4-enal
(c) (2Z, 5R)-3-bromo-5-chloro-2-methylhex-4-enal
(d) (2S, 4E)-4-bromo-2-chloro-2-methylhex-4-enal

220. In the following compounds, the nucleophile and leaving group are in the same molecule

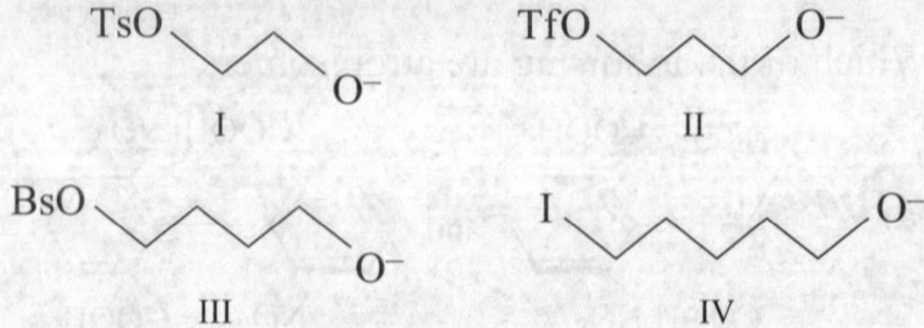

In principle, all these species can undergo both inter and intramolecular substitution reactions. For which of the given speciesis intramolecular substitutions most feasible?

(a) I, II (b) II, III (c) III, IV (d) IV

221. The product of the following reaction is

$ClCH_2CH_2CH_2–CHCl–CH_2CH_3$ (1mol) + NaI (1 mol)

(a) $Cl–CH_2CH_2–CHI–CH_2CH_2CH_3$
(b) $ClCH_2CH_2CH_2–CHI–CH_2CH_3$
(c) $ICH_2CH_2CH_2–CHCl–CH_2CH_3$
(d) $ICH_2CH_2–CHCl–CH_2CH_2CH_3$

222. The correct decreasing order of relative reactivity of the following chlorides towards KOH solution is

Cl (P) Cl (Q) HO Cl (R) Cl (S)

(a) P > Q > R > S (b) R > P > Q > S
(c) S > R > Q > P (d) R > S > Q > P

223. KI in acetone undergoes S_N2 reaction with each of P, Q, R and S. The rates of the reaction vary as

$H_3C–Cl$ (P) Cl (Q) Cl (R) O Cl (S)

(a) P > Q > R > S (b) S > P > R > Q
(c) P > R > Q > S (d) R > P > S > Q

224. The correct product of the solvolysis of the following compound

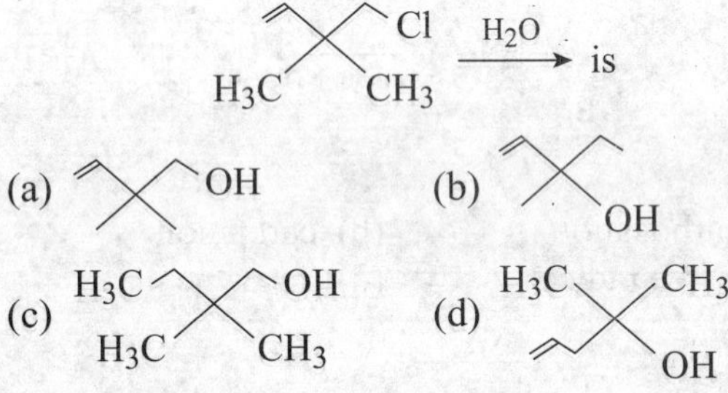

225. Predict the product (X) of the following reaction

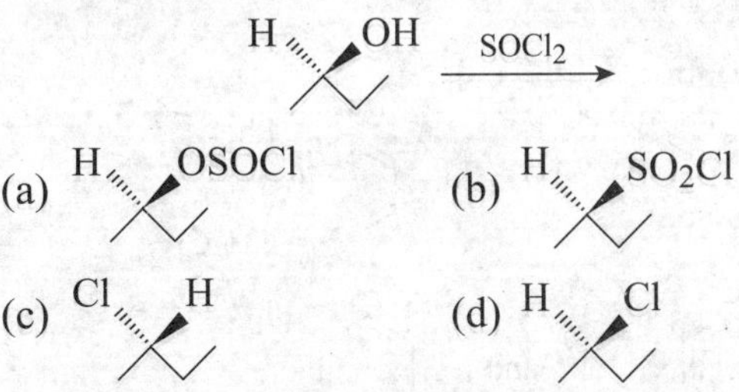

226. The reaction of (R)-1-chloro-3-methylpentane with sodium iodide in acetone will yield iodomethylpentane, that is,

(a) R (b) S (c) (±) RS (d) meso

227. R-2 Pentanol is treated separately with the following reagents. Which of them will exclusively give S-2-chloropentane?

(a) HCl + $ZnCl_2$ (b) $SOCl_2$
(c) $SOCl_2$/pyridine (d) any of the three above

228. The product in the following reaction is

CH_3 / Br–C–H / H–C–CH_3 / CH_2CH_3 + NaI $\xrightarrow{S_N2}$

(a) CH_3 / H–C–I / H–C–CH_3 / CH_2CH_3
(b) CH_3 / I–C–H / H–C–CH_3 / CH_2CH_3

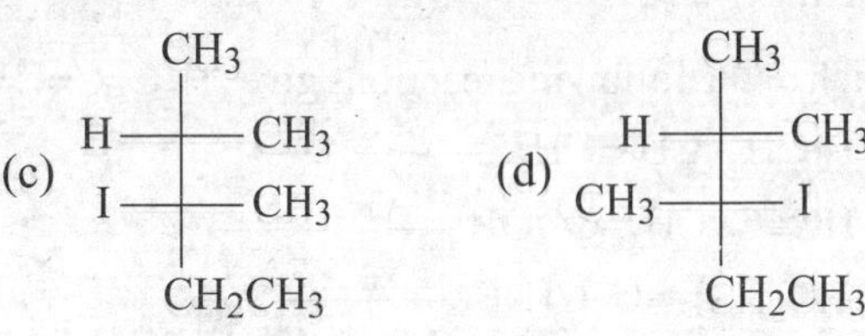

229. Identify the product.

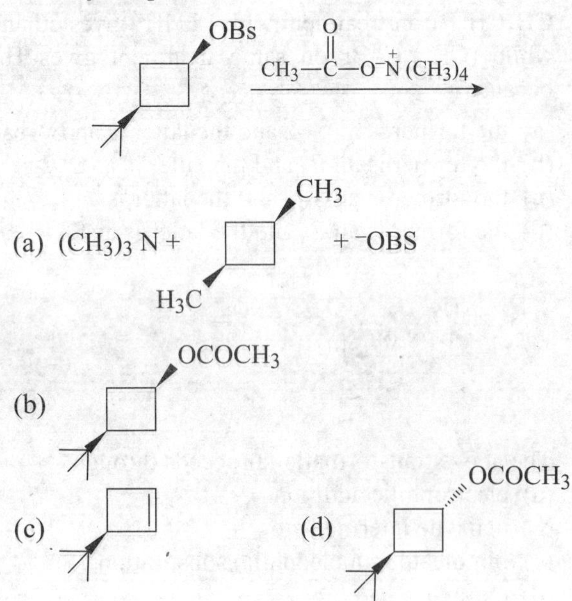

230. An S_N2 reaction at an asymmetric carbon of a compound always gives

(a) an enantiomer of the substrate
(b) a product with opposite rotation
(c) a mixture of diastereomers
(d) a single isomer

231. In the following reaction sequence, the correct structure of X is

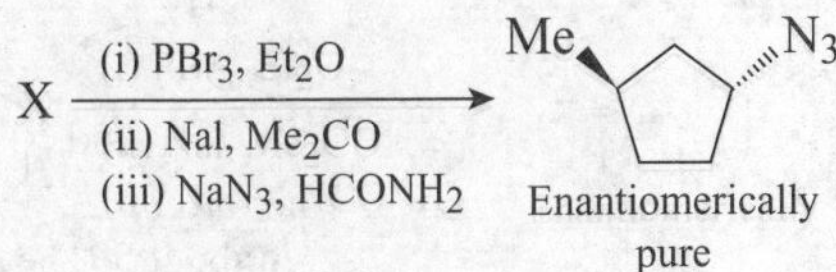

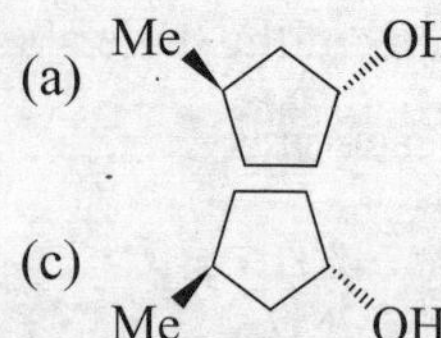

(a) (b) (c) (d)

232. Which of the following alkyl halides gives the same product in both S_N1 and S_N2 reactions?

I. (R)-$CH_3CHBrCH_2CH_3$ II. $C_6H_5CH_2Br$

III. (S)–C_6H_5–CH(CH_3)Br IV. (Cl-substituted cyclohexane)

(a) I, III (b) II, IV
(c) III, IV (d) I, IV

233. Which of the following reactions gives $H_2C{=}C{=}C{=}CH_2$?

(a) $BrCH_2{-}CBr{=}CH_2 \xrightarrow{Zn/CH_3OH}$

(b) $HC{\equiv}C{-}CH_2{-}COOH \xrightarrow{Aq.K_2CO_3}$

(c) $BrCH_2{-}C{\equiv}C{-}CH_2Br \xrightarrow{Zn,\ \Delta}$

(d) $2\ CH_2{=}CH{-}CH_2I \xrightarrow{Na}$

234. CH_3CH_2Br on treatment with $LiAlH_4$ gives ethane gas while $(CH_3)_3C{-}Br$ on same treatment gives H_2 gas because

(a) the former is an S_N2 and the latter is an E_2 reaction
(b) the former is an E_2 and the latter is an S_N2 reaction
(c) the former is an S_N1 and the latter is an E_2 reaction
(d) the former is an E_2 and the latter is an S_N1 reaction

235. 2,4-Dinitrochlorobenzene (Cl, NO_2, NO_2) $\xrightarrow{\text{Dil. NaOH}}$ sodium 2,4-dinitrophenoxide (O^-Na^+, NO_2, NO_2)

The above transformation proceeds through
(a) electrophilic addition
(b) benzyne intermediate
(c) bimolecular nucleophilic substitution
(d) oxirane

236. C-14 labelled chlorobenzene is treated with $NaNH_2$ in liq. NH_3,

Chlorobenzene (Cl on C*) $\xrightarrow[-33°C]{NaNH_2/liq.\ NH_3}$

Which of the following depicts C-14 labelled in the products correctly?

(a) NH_2 on C*
(b) NH_2 on C* and NH_2 with * on ortho carbon (about 50% each)
(c) NH_2 with * on ortho carbon
(d) NH_2 with * on ortho carbon and unlabelled aniline (about 50% each)

237. Identify A and predict the type of reaction.

m-Bromoanisole (OCH_3, Br) $\xrightarrow{NaNH_2}$ A

(a) o-Anisidine (OCH_3, NH_2 ortho) and elimination–addition reaction
(b) o-Bromoanisole (OCH_3, Br ortho) and substitution reaction
(c) Anisole (OCH_3) and substitution reaction
(d) m-Anisidine (OCH_3, NH_2 meta) and substitution reaction

238. The reactive intermediate involved in the reaction is,

2-Bromophenyl–$CH_2CH_2CH_2$–NH–Me $\xrightarrow[\text{in liq. } NH_3]{NaNH_2}$ N-methyltetrahydroquinoline (N–Me)

(a) carbocation (b) carbanion
(c) a free radical (d) an aryne

239. 2-Methylbiphenyl (Ph, CH_3) $\xrightarrow{Cl_2/hv}$ X ; $\xrightarrow{Cl_2/AlCl_3}$ Y

Compounds X and Y are

(a) Cl-substituted (Ph, CH_3) ring and (Ph, CH_2Cl) ring
(b) (Ph, CH_2Cl) ring and Cl-substituted (Ph, CH_2Cl) ring
(c) (Ph, CH_2Cl) ring and Cl-substituted (Ph, CH_3) ring
(d) Cl-substituted (Ph, CH_3) ring and 4'-chloro-2-methylbiphenyl (Cl, CH_3)

240. Predict the product (X) in the following reaction.

$$\text{(2-phenylbenzyl chloride)} \xrightarrow{\text{Anhyd. AlCl}_3} X$$

(a) fluorene (b) 9,10-dihydroanthracene
(c) 9-methylfluorene (d) 2-methyl-9,10-dihydroanthracene

241. $\xrightarrow[\text{CH}_3\text{NO}_2,\ 0°\text{C}]{\text{Anhyd. AlCl}_3}$ P

The product (P) is

(a) (b) (c) (d)

242. An alkyl halide with a molecular formula, $C_6H_{13}Br$, on treatment with alcoholic KOH gave two isomeric alkenes, A and B. Reductive ozonolysis of the mixture gave the following compounds: CH_3COCH_3, CH_3CHO, CH_3CH_2CHO and $(CH_3)_2CHCHO$. The alkyl halide is

(a) $CH_3(CH_2)_2Br$ (b) $CH_3CH(Br)CH(Br)CH_3$
(c) $CH_3CH_2CH(Br)CH_3$ (d) $Br(CH_2)_4Br$

243. Identify Y in the following reaction sequence.

$CH_2{=}CHCl \xrightarrow{Cl_2} X \xrightarrow{Ca(OH)_2} Y$

(a) 1,1,2-trichloroethane (b) 1,1-dichloroethene
(c) 1,2-dichloroethene (d) chloroethylene

244. An aromatic compound (A) is heated with another compound (B) in the presence of alcoholic KOH to give a bad smelling compound with a MF C_6H_5NC. The compound (B) can be prepared by heating another compound (C) with Cl_2 and slaked lime. The compound (C) is

(a) $C_6H_5NH_2$ (b) C_2H_5OH
(c) $CHCl_3$ (d) CH_3OCH_3

245. A compound (X), $C_4H_8Cl_2$, on hydrolysis with aqueous NaOH gives a compound (Y) which on heating with I_2 and NaOH gives a yellow precipitate of iodoform. The compound (X) is

(a) $CH_3CH_2CHClCH_2Cl$ (b) $ClCH_2CH_2CH_2CH_2Cl$
(c) $CH_3CH_2CH_2CHCl_2$ (d) $CH_3CH_2CCl_2CH_3$

246. Which of the following will give a yellow precipitate of iodoform on heating with I_2 and dil. NaOH solution?

(a) $ICH_2COCH_2CH_3$ (b) CH_3COOCH_3
(c) $PhCH_2CH_2OH$ (d) $(CH_3)_2C(OH)CH_2CH_3$

247. Which of the following will give a yellow precipitate on shaking with an aqueous solution of NaOH followed by acidification with dil. HNO_3 and addition of $AgNO_3$?

(a) p-bromochlorobenzene (b) benzyl chloride
(c) p-bromobenzyl iodide (d) o-chlorotoluene

248. The bottles containing C_6H_5I and $C_6H_5CH_2I$ lost their original labels. They were labelled A and B for testing. A and B were separately taken in test-tubes and boiled with NaOH solution. The end solution in each tube was made acidic with dilute HNO_3 and some $AgNO_3$ solution added. Solution B gave a yellow precipitate. Which one of the following statements is true for the experiment?

(a) Addition of HNO_3 was unnecessary.
(b) A was C_6H_5I.
(c) A was $C_6H_5CH_2I$.
(d) B was C_6H_5I.

249. Which of the following is the most reactive towards nucleophilic substitution reaction?

(a) C_6H_5Cl (b) $CH_2{=}CHCl$
(c) $ClCH_2CH{=}CH_2$ (d) $CH_3CH{=}CHCl$

250. $H_3C{-}CH(CH_3){-}CH{=}CH_2 + HBr \longrightarrow A$

A (predominantly) is

(a) $CH_3CH_2{-}CH(CH_3){-}CH_2Br$ (b) $CH_3{-}CH(CH_3){-}CH(Br){-}CH_3$
(c) $CH_3{-}CH(CH_3){-}CH_2{-}CH_2Br$ (d) $CH_3{-}C(Br)(CH_3){-}CH_2CH_3$

251. What is A in the following reactions?

$C_6H_5{-}CH_2{-}CH{=}CH_2 + HCl \longrightarrow A$

(a) 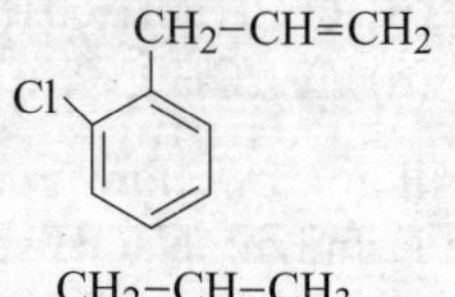 $CH_2–CH=CH_2$, Cl (b) 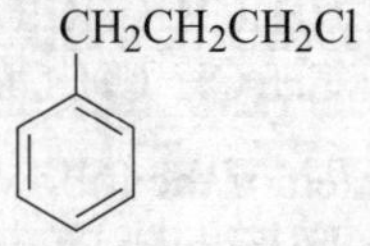 $CH_2CH_2CH_2Cl$

(c) 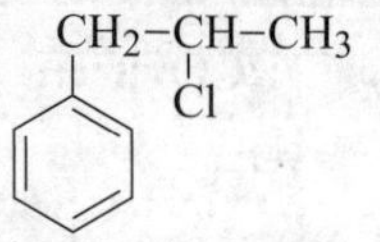 $CH_2–CH–CH_3$, Cl (d) 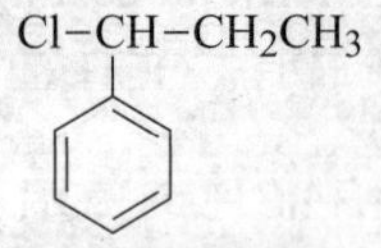 $Cl–CH–CH_2CH_3$

252. The major product of the following reaction

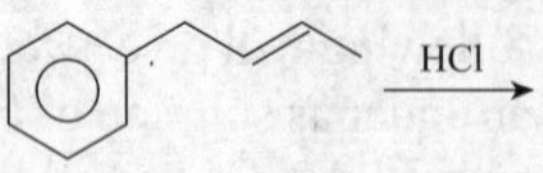

$\xrightarrow{HCl}$ is

(a) 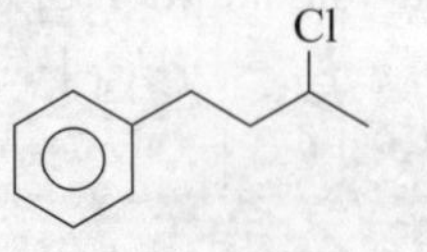 Cl (b) 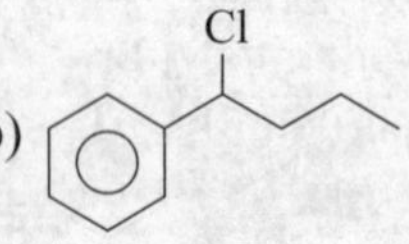 Cl

(c) 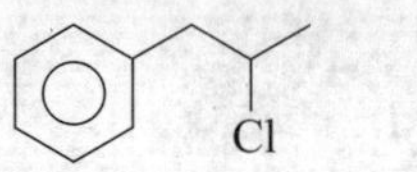 Cl (d) 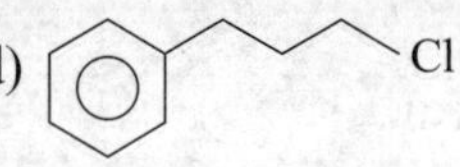 Cl

253. $(CH_3)_3C–Cl \xrightarrow[\Delta]{\text{KOH alc.}} A \xrightarrow[475\ K]{SO_2Cl_2} B$

The compound B in the above sequence is

(a) 3-chloro-2-methylpropene
(b) 1-chloro-2-methylpropene
(c) 1,2-dichloro-2-methylpropene
(d) 1,2-dichloro-2-methylpropene

254. Which of the following sequence of reactions (reagents) can be used for the conversion of $C_6H_5CH_2CH_3$ into $C_6H_5CH=CH_2$?

(a) $SOCl_2$; H_2O (b) SO_2Cl_2; alc. KOH
(c) Cl_2/hv; H_2O (d) $SOCl_2$; alc. KOH

255. Which will be the product in the following reaction?

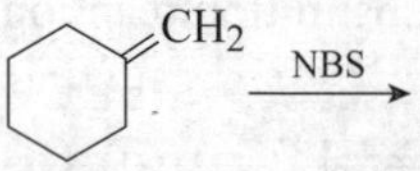

CH_2 $\xrightarrow{NBS}$

(a) 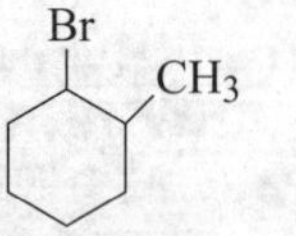 Br, CH_3 (b) 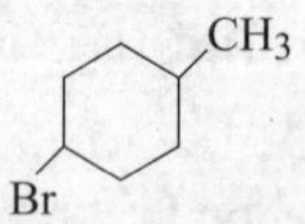 CH_3, Br

(c) 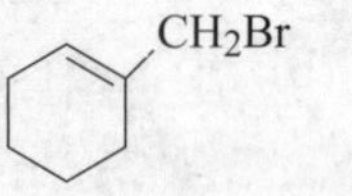 CH_2Br (d) 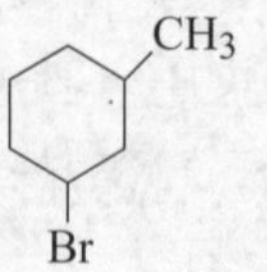 CH_3, Br

256. The product of the reaction given below is

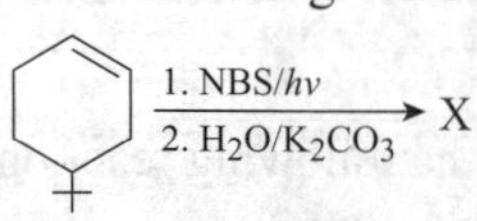

$\xrightarrow[2.\ H_2O/K_2CO_3]{1.\ NBS/hv}$ X

(a) 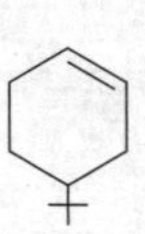 (b) 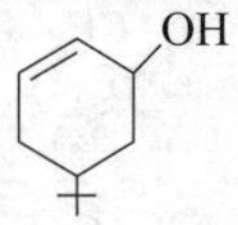 OH

(c) 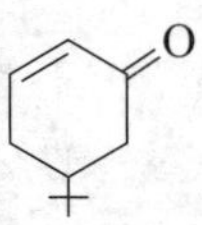 O (d) 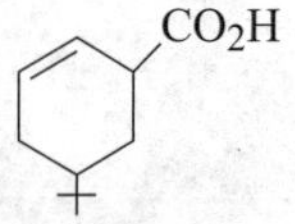 CO_2H

257. $CH_3CH=CH_2 \xrightarrow{NBS} \xrightarrow{AgCN} X$ (major)

The major product (X) is

(a) $CH_3CH=CHCN$ (b) $CH_3CH=CHNC$
(c) $CH_2=CHCH_2CN$ (d) $CH_2=CHCH_2NC$

258. The reagents required to convert 1-iodobutane from 1-butene is/are

(a) I_2/red P (b) KI
(c) HI/H_2O_2 (d) HBr/H_2O_2 and KI/acetone

259. When silver propanoate is treated with I_2 in CCl_4, the major product formed is

(a) iodoethane (b) *n*-propyl propanoate
(c) ethyl propanoate (d) 1-iodoethane

260. The best method to prepare neopentyl chloride is

(a) $(CH_3)_3CCH_2OH \xrightarrow{PCl_5,\ \Delta}$
(b) $(CH_3)_3CCH_2OH \xrightarrow{HCl,\ \Delta}$
(c) $(CH_3)_3CCH_2OH \xrightarrow{SOCl_2\ \text{pyridine}}$
(d) $(CH_3)_3CCH_3 \xrightarrow{Cl_2,\ hv,\ \Delta}$

261. $C_7H_8 \xrightarrow{3Cl_2/\Delta} A \xrightarrow{Br_2/Fe} B \xrightarrow{Zn/HCl} C$

The compound C is

(a) *o*-bromotoluene
(b) *m*-bromotoluene
(c) *p*-bromotoluene
(d) 3-bromo-2,4,6-trichlorotoluene

262. Toluene on reaction with N-bromosuccinimide gives

(a) *p*-bromomethylbenzene
(b) *o*-bromomethylbenzene
(c) phenylbromomethane
(d) *m*-bromomethylbenzene

263. 1,4-Dibromobutane (0.1 mol) is treated with Na_2S (0.1 mol) in aqueous ethanol, the product formed is

(a) $BrCH_2CH_2CH_2CH_2SH$
(b) $HSCH_2CH_2CH_2CH_2SH$
(c) $BrCH_2CH_2CH_2CH_2S^-Na^+$
(d)  S

264. 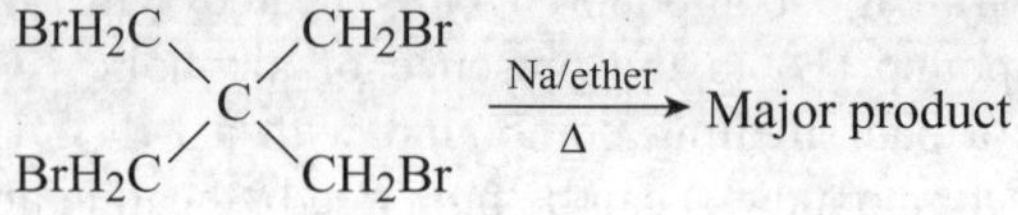 $C(CH_2Br)_4$ (BrH_2C, CH_2Br, BrH_2C, CH_2Br) $\xrightarrow[\Delta]{Na/ether}$ Major product

(a) 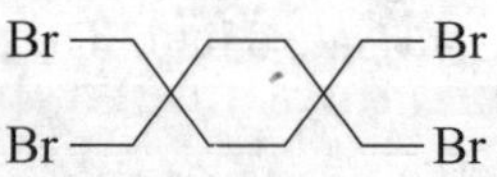 Br, Br, Br, Br (b)

(c) 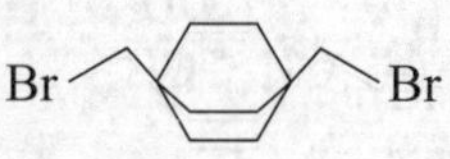 Br, Br (d) 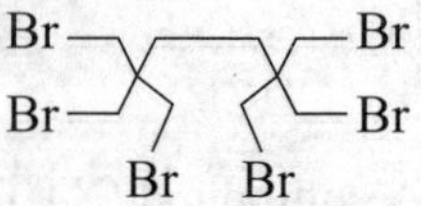 Br, Br, Br, Br, Br, Br

265. Pick out the correct statement.

(i) If a compound has no asymmetric carbon atom, it is always achiral.

(ii) If a compound has just one asymmetric carbon atom, it is chiral.
(iii) If a compound has more than one asymmetric carbon, it may or may not be chiral
(a) (i), (ii) and (iii) are correct
(b) (i) and (ii) only are correct
(c) (ii) and (iii) only are correct
(d) (ii) is only correct
(e) (i) is only correct

266. Which of the following molecules will not show optical activity?

(a) HOOC, COOH; H, H; HO, H

(b) 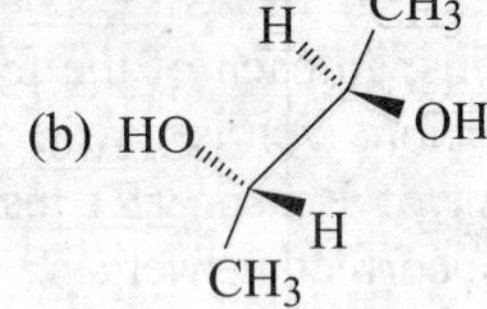

(c) $CH_3-\underset{OH}{CH}-CD_3$

(d) Br, H, H, Br (cyclopropane)

(e) $CH_3CH_2-\underset{OH}{CH}-CH_3$

267. Which of the following is a meso compound?

(a) CH_3, Cl; H, H; Cl, CH_3

(b) H, CH_3; Cl, H; CH_3, Cl

(c) Cl, CH_2CH_3; H, H; CH_3, Cl

(d) H, H; CH_3, CH_2Cl; Cl, H

268. Among the following, the Newman projections of meso-2,3-butanediol are

P: Me; H, OH; HO, H; Me

Q: Me; H, OH; H, OH; Me

R: Me; HO, Me; HO, H; H

S: Me; Me, H; H, OH; OH

(a) P, Q (b) P, R (c) R, S (d) Q, S

269. Which of the following would show enantiomorphism?

(a) NH_3

(b) $(CH_3CH_2)_2NH$

(c) $CH_3-N(CH_2CH_3)(CH_2CH_2CH_3)$

(d) $\left[CH_3-\overset{+}{N}(C_2H_5)(C_6H_5)-H\right] Br^-$

270. Which is optically inactive?

(a) a, a C=C=C=C a, a

(b) a, b C=C=C=C a, b

(c) benzene ring with a, b and N(d)(c)

(d) none of the above

271. Which of the following is optically inactive?

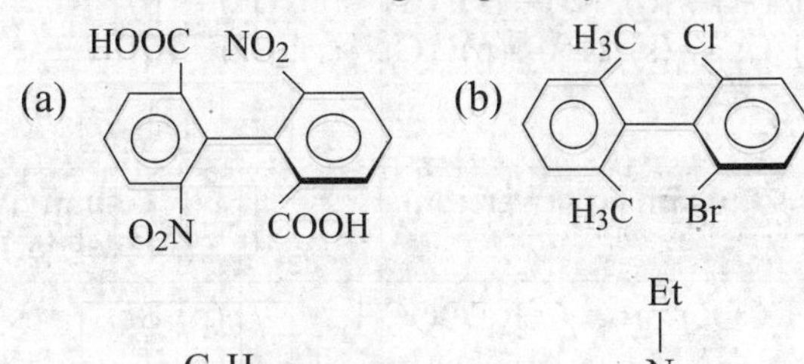

(c) 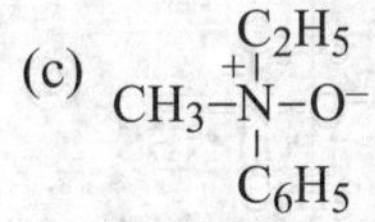

(d) 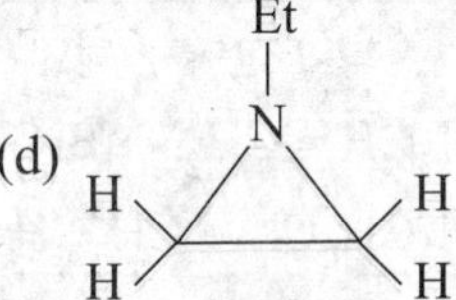

MATCH THE FOLLOWING

272.

Column I (E_2 reaction)	Column II (No. of possible products including stereoisomers)
(A) 2-bromobutane (Br) $\xrightarrow[\Delta]{\text{Alc. KOH}}$	(p) 3
(B) 3-bromopentane (Br) $\xrightarrow[\Delta]{\text{Alc. KOH}}$	(q) 0
(C) 1-bromobutane (Br) $\xrightarrow[\Delta]{\text{Alc. KOH}}$	(r) 1
(D) CH=CHBr $\xrightarrow[\Delta]{\text{Alc. KOH}}$	(s) 2

(a) (A)—(q); (B)—(r); (C)—(s); (D)—(p)
(b) (A)—(r); (B)—(p); (C)—(r); (D)—(q)
(c) (A)—(p); (B)—(r); (C)—(q); (D)—(s)
(d) (A)—(p); (B)—(s); (C)—(r); (D)—(q)

273.

Column I (Reaction)	Column II (Name of the reaction)
(A) $CH_3CH_2CH_2Cl \xrightarrow[\Delta]{\text{NaI, Acetone}} CH_3CH_2CH_2I$	(p) Hunsdieker reaction
(B) $CH_3CH_2Cl \xrightarrow[\Delta]{Hg_2F_2} CH_3CH_2F$	(q) Fitting reaction

Column I (Reaction)	Column II (Name of the reaction)
(C) $RCOOAg \xrightarrow[\Delta]{Br_2/CCl_4} RBr$	(r) Finkelstein reaction
(D) $C_6H_5Br \xrightarrow{Na, \Delta} C_6H_5{-}C_6H_5$	(s) Swarts reaction

(a) (A)—(r); (B)—(s); (C)—(p); (D)—(q)
(b) (A)—(s); (B)—(r); (C)—(q); (D)—(p)
(c) (A)—(q); (B)—(s); (C)—(r); (D)—(p)
(d) (A)—(s); (B)—(p); (C)—(r); (D)—(q)

274.

Column I (Conversion)	Column II (Reagent)
(A) $CH_3COOAg \rightarrow CH_3COOCH_3$	(p) Br_2
(B) $CH_3CH = CH_2 \rightarrow BrCHCH = CH_2$	(q) I_2
(C) $CH_3CH_2Cl \rightarrow CH_3CH_2F$	(r) NBS
(D) $C_6H_5COOAg \rightarrow C_6H_5Br$	(s) Hg_2F_2

(a) (A)—(r); (B)—(s); (C)—(p); (D)—(q)
(b) (A)—(q); (B)—(s); (C)—(r); (D)—(p)
(c) (A)—(p); (B)—(r); (C)—(s); (D)—(q)
(d) (A)—(q); (B)—(r); (C)—(s); (D)—(p)

275.

Column I (Reaction)	Column II (Product)
(A) RX + AgCN	(p) $R{-}C{\equiv}N$
(B) RX + KCN	(q) $R\,N{\equiv}C$
(C) $RX + KNO_2$	(r) $R{-}NO_2$
(D) $RX + AgNO_2$	(s) R–O–N=O

(a) (A)—(q); (B)—(p); (C)—(r); (D)—(s)
(b) (A)—(q); (B)—(p); (C)—(s); (D)—(r)
(c) (A)—(p); (B)—(q); (C)—(r); (D)—(s).
(d) (A)—(p); (B)—(q); (C)—(s); (D)—(r)

276.

Column I (Reaction)	Column II (Mechanism)
(A) Chlorobenzene $\xrightarrow[\text{in liq. } NH_3]{NaNH_2}$ Aniline	(p) S_N2
(B) Fischer projection: C with I (top), Me–C–H, Et–C–D, H (bottom) $\xrightarrow{KSH}$ SH (top), H–C–Me, Et–C–D, H (bottom)	(q) S_N1
(C) $(CH_3)_3CBr \xrightarrow{C_2H_5OH} (CH_3)_3C-OC_2H_5$	(r) Aromatic bimolecular mechanism
(D) *p*-Chloronitrobenzene $\xrightarrow[\Delta]{\text{Aq. KOH}}$ *p*-Nitrophenol	(s) Benzyne mechanism

(a) (A)—(p); (B)—(r); (C)—(q); (D)—(s)
(b) (A)—(s); (B)—(p); (C)—(q); (D)—(r)
(c) (A)—(q); (B)—(s); (C)—(p); (D)—(r)
(d) (A)—(s); (B)—(q); (C)—(r); (D)—(p)

ASSERTION REASON

Directions: In each of the following questions, a statement of Assertion (A) is given followed by a corresponding statement of Reason (R) just below it. Of the statements, mark the correct answer as

(a) if both the assertion and reason are true and the reason is the correct explanation of the assertion.
(b) if both assertion and reason are true but reason is not the correct explanation of assertion
(c) If assertion is true but reason is false
(d) If both assertion and reason are false

277. Assertion: The rate of hydrolysis of methyl chloride to methanol is higher in DMF than in water.

Reason: Hydrolysis of methyl chloride follows second order kinetics.

278. Assertion: Nucleophilic substitution reaction on an optically active alkyl halide gives a mixture of enantiomers.

Reason: The reaction occurs by S_N1 mechanism.

279. Assertion: Benzyl bromide when kept in acetone–water produces benzyl alcohol.

Reason: The reaction follows S_N2 mechanism.

280. Assertion: 2-Bromobutane on reaction with sodium ethoxide in ethanol gives 1-butene as the major product.

Reason: 1-Butene is more stable than 2-butene.

281. Assertion: In E_2 elimination, the β-H and the leaving group should be antiperiplanar.

Reason: In E_2 elimination, the base always abstracts an unhindered β-H.

282. Assertion: Aryl halides do not undergo nucleophilic substitution with ease.

Reason: The carbon–halogen bond in aryl halides has a partial double bond character.

283. Assertion: The presence of nitro groups facilitates nucleophilic substitution reactions in aryl halides.

Reason: The intermediate carbanion is stabilised due to the presence of the nitro group.

284. Assertion: Neopentyl alcohol on treatment with conc. HCl gives neopentyl chloride.

Reason: Neopentyl cation does not rearrange to the 2-methylbutyl cation.

285. Assertion: The reaction of alcohols with $SOCl_2$ is catalysed by the presence of a tertiary amine (R_3N).

Reason: The tertiary amine promotes the reaction by reacting with the byproduct, HCl.

286. Assertion: Alkyl iodides can be prepared by treating alkyl chloride/bromide with NaI in acetone.

Reason: NaCl/NaBr are soluble in acetone while NaI is not.

287. Assertion: Chlorination of ethylbenzene with Cl_2 in the presence of heat and light mainly yields 1-chloro-2-phenylethane.

Reason: The reaction occurs through intermediate formation of the $C_6H_5CH_2CH_2$ radical.

288. Assertion: Benzene reacts with iodine monochloride in the presence of anhydrous $AlCl_3$ to form iodobenzene.

Reason: Iodine monochloride reacts with anhydrous $AlCl_3$ to produce I^+ which attacks the benzene ring.

289. Assertion: *p*-Dichlorobenzene is less soluble in organic solvents than the corresponding *o*-isomer.

Reason: *o*-Dichlorobenzene is polar while *p*-dichlorobenzene is not.

290. Assertion: S_N1 reaction is basically a solvolysis reaction.

Reason: Polar protic solvents help the substrate to ionise and thus get involved in the S_N1 reaction.

291. Assertion: In comparison to ethyl chloride it is more difficult to carry out nucleophilic substitution on vinyl chloride.

Reason: The vinyl group is electron donating.

292. Assertion: Tertiary haloalkanes are more reactive than primary haloalkanes towards elimination reactions.

Reason: The +I effect of the alkyl groups weakens the C–X bond.

293. Assertion: $CH_3CH_2OCH_2Cl$ reacts faster when treated with water then $CH_3CH_2OCH_2CH_2CH_2Cl$.

Reason: Carbonium ion formed by the ionisation of $CH_3CH_2OCH_2Cl$ is stabilised by resonance.

Answer Key

1. (a)	2. (a)	3. (b)	4. (d)	5. (d)	6. (d)	7. (a)	8. (a)	9. (c)	10. (d)
11. (d)	12. (d)	13. (c)	14. (b)	15. (a)	16. (b)	17. (b)	18. (c)	19. (d)	20. (c)
21. (c)	22. (c)	23. (d)	24. (d)	25. (b)	26. (b)	27. (d)	28. (a)	29. (d)	30. (b)
31. (a)	32. (b)	33. (b)	34. (c)	35. (c)	36. (c)	37. (c)	38. (b)	39. (b)	40. (b)
41. (d)	42. (d)	43. (c)	44. (c)	45. (b)	46. (a)	47. (b)	48. (b)	49. (a)	50. (b)
51. (b)	52. (a)	53. (d)	54. (a)	55. (c)	56. (c)	57. (c)	58. (c)	59. (d)	60. (b)
61. (d)	62. (b)	63. (c)	64. (c)	65. (c)	66. (d)	67. (c)	68. (c)	69. (c)	70. (a)
71. (d)	72. (d)	73. (d)	74. (a)	75. (a)	76. (b)	77. (a)	78. (d)	79. (a)	80. (d)
81. (d)	82. (b)	83. (d)	84. (c)	85. (a)	86. (d)	87. (a)	88. (a)	89. (d)	90. (d)
91. (b)	92. (a)	93. (c)	94. (b)	95. (c)	96. (a)	97. (a)	98. (d)	99. (c)	100. (b)
101. (c)	102. (a)	103. (d)	104. (d)	105. (a)	106. (b)	107. (c)	108. (d)	109. (b)	110. (d)
111. (d)	112. (a)	113. (d)	114. (d)	115. (d)	116. (a)	117. (b)	118. (c)	119. (a)	120. (b)
121. (b)	122. (b)	123. (d)	124. (d)	125. (a)	126. (b)	127. (d)	128. (d)	129. (c)	130. (a)
131. (c)	132. (d)	133. (d)	134. (c)	135. (d)	136. (a)	137. (c)	138. (d)	139. (d)	140. (a)
141. (c)	142. (a)	143. (d)	144. (b)	145. (c)	146. (c)	147. (a)	148. (c)	149. (a)	150. (b)
151. (b)	152. (c)	153. (b)	154. (c)	155. (c)	156. (c)	157. (c)	158. (c)	159. (c)	160. (c)
161. (b)	162. (b)	163. (c)	164. (a)	165. (a)	166. (a)	167. (d)	168. (c)	169. (c)	170. (a)
171. (a)	172. (d)	173. (a)	174. (c)	175. (d)	176. (b)	177. (c)	178. (b)	179. (b)	180. (b)
181. (a)	182. (a)	183. (d)	184. (a)	185. (c)	186. (c)	187. (d)	188. (c)	189. (d)	190. (d)
191. (d)	192. (b)	193. (d)	194. (d)	195. (b)	196. (a)	197. (a)	198. (c)	199. (d)	200. (a)
201. (b)	202. (d)	203. (a)	204. (a)	205. (c)	206. (c)	207. (b)	208. (b)	209. (a)	210. (d)
211. (b)	212. (d)	213. (c)	214. (a)	215. (d)	216. (c)	217. (a)	218. (c)	219. (a)	220. (c)
221. (c)	222. (b)	223. (b)	224. (d)	225. (d)	226. (a)	227. (c)	228. (a)	229. (d)	230. (d)
231. (b)	232. (b)	233. (c)	234. (a)	235. (c)	236. (b)	237. (d)	238. (d)	239. (b)	240. (a)
241. (b)	242. (a)	243. (b)	244. (b)	245. (d)	246. (a)	247. (c)	248. (b)	249. (c)	250. (d)\
251. (d)	252. (b)	253. (a)	254. (b)	255. (c)	256. (b)	257. (d)	258. (d)	259. (c)	260. (d)
261. (b)	262. (c)	263. (d)	264. (b)	265. (c)	266. (b)	267. (a)	268. (b)	269. (d)	270. (a)\
271. (b)	272. (d)	273. (a)	274. (d)	275. (b)	276. (b)	277. (b)	278. (a)	279. (c)	280. (d)
281. (c)	282. (a)	283. (a)	284. (d)	285. (a)	286. (c)	287. (d)	288. (a)	289. (b)	290. (a)
291. (c)	292. (b)	293. (a)							

Hints and Solutions

1. (a):

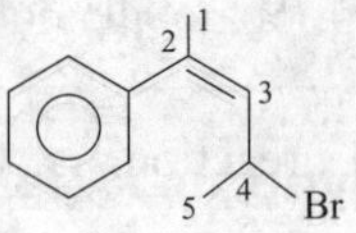

4-Bromo-2-phenylpent-2-ene

2. (a): *trans*-2-chloro-3-iodo-2-pentene

3. (b): *trans*-4-bromo-3-methylpent-2-ene

4. (d):

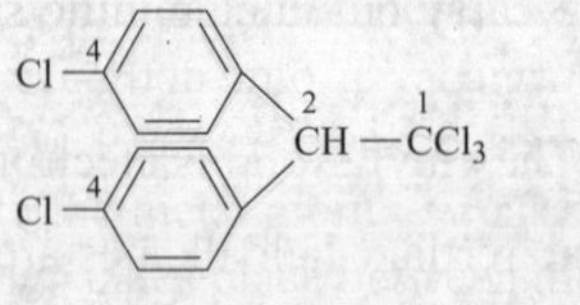

2, 2-Bis (4-chlorophenyl 1, 1, 1-trichloroethane)

5. (d): Eight isomers are possible. These are:
(i) $CH_3CH_2CH_2CC_2CH_2Br$ (ii) $CH_3CH_2CH_2CH(Br)CH_3$
(iii) $CH_3CH_2CH(Br)CH_2CH_3$ (iv) $(CH_3)_2CHCH_2CH_2Br$
(v) $(CH_3)_2CHCH(Br)CH_3$ (vi) $(CH_3)_2CBrCH_2CH_3$
(vii) $CH_3CH_2CH(CH_3)CH_2Br$ (viii) $(CH_3)_3CCH_2Br$

6. (d): $CH_2=CHCl$, $C_6H_5CH_2-CH=CHCl$

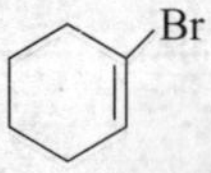

are all vinylic halides

7. (a): An α, ω dihalide has two halogens on the terminal carbon atoms, that is, $ClCH_2CH_2CH_2CH_2Cl$.

Preparation of Haloalkanes and Haloarenes

8. (a): Both P_4/Br_2 and HBr/H_2SO_4 can convert *n*-propyl alcohol to *n*-propyl bromide but due to the possibility of dehydration of *n*-propyl alcohol to propylene with HBr/H_2SO_4, the P_4/Br_2 method is preferred.

$$CH_3CH_2CH_2OH \xrightarrow{P_4/Br_2} CH_3CH_2CH_2Br$$

9. (c): Ease of abstraction of hydrogen is: 3° > 2° > 1°. Therefore, option (c) is correct.

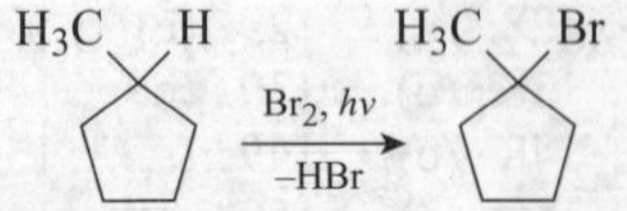

$$\text{(1-methylcyclopentane)} \xrightarrow[-HBr]{Br_2,\ h\nu} \text{(1-bromo-1-methylcyclopentane)}$$

10. (d):

$$CH_3-\underset{CH_3}{\overset{CH_3}{C}}-CH_2OH \xrightarrow[\text{or } HCl,\ \Delta \text{ or } SOCl_2/\text{pyridine}]{PCl_5,\ \Delta}$$

Neopentyl alcohol

$$\left[CH_3-\underset{CH_3}{\overset{CH_3}{C}}-\overset{+}{C}H_2 \longrightarrow CH_3-\underset{+}{\overset{CH_3}{C}}-CH_2CH_3 \xrightarrow{Cl^-}\right]$$

$$CH_3-\underset{Cl}{\overset{CH_3}{C}}-CH_2CH_3$$

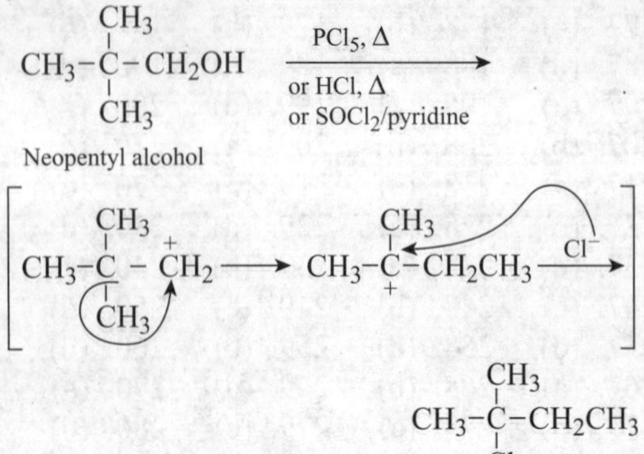

2-Chloro-2-methylbutane

Free radicals, on the other hand, do not undergo rearrangement and hence the best method of preparation is through free radical chlorination.

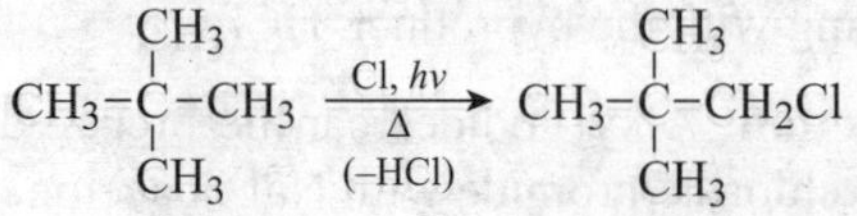

$$CH_3-\underset{CH_3}{\overset{CH_3}{C}}-CH_3 \xrightarrow[\Delta\ (-HCl)]{Cl,\ h\nu} CH_3-\underset{CH_3}{\overset{CH_3}{C}}-CH_2Cl$$

Neopentane → Neopentyl chloride

11. (d):

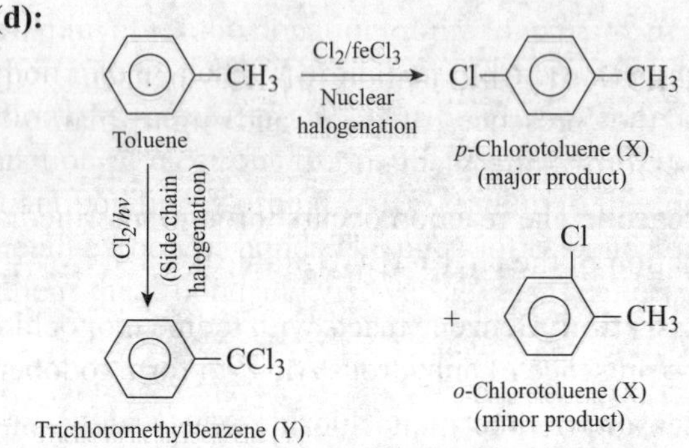

Toluene $\xrightarrow[\text{Nuclear halogenation}]{Cl_2/FeCl_3}$ *p*-Chlorotoluene (X) (major product) + *o*-Chlorotoluene (X) (minor product)

Toluene $\xrightarrow[\text{(Side chain halogenation)}]{Cl_2/h\nu}$ Trichloromethylbenzene (Y)

12. (d):

$$Ph-NH_2 \xrightarrow[0°C]{HNO_2} \underset{(A)}{Ph-\overset{+}{N}\equiv N} \xrightarrow[BF_3]{HF} \underset{(B)}{Ph-\overset{+}{N}\equiv NBF_4^-} \xrightarrow[-BF_3,\ -N_2]{\Delta} Ph-F$$

13. (c): Two alkenes are possible. These are

Methylene-cyclohexane (I) or 1-Methyl-cyclohex-1-ene (II) $\xrightarrow[\text{Mark, addn.}]{HCl}$ 1-Methyl-1-chloro-cyclohexane

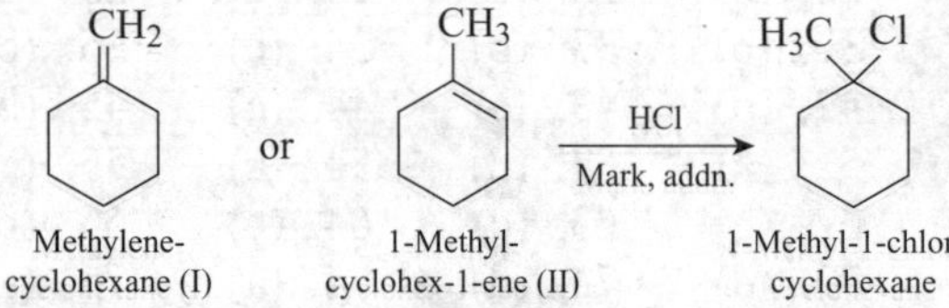

Thus, option (c) is correct.

14. (b):

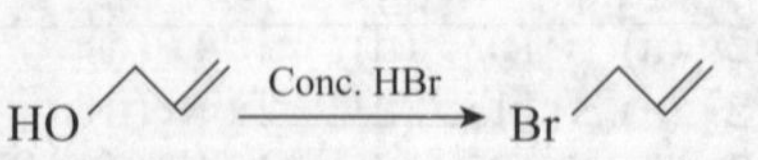

Allyl alcohol $\xrightarrow{\text{Conc. HBr}}$ Allyl brominde

15. (a):

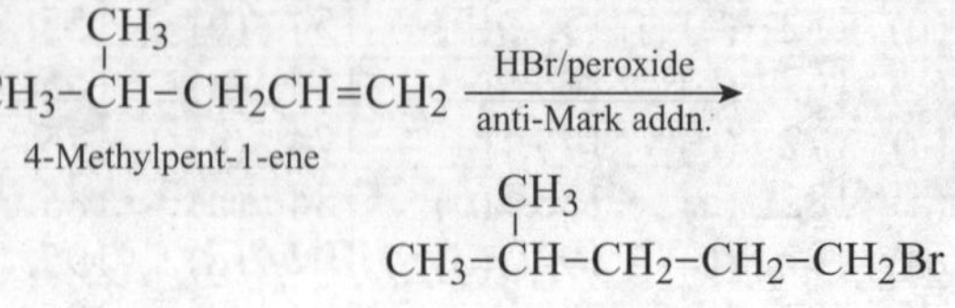

$$CH_3-\underset{}{\overset{CH_3}{C}H}-CH_2CH=CH_2 \xrightarrow[\text{anti-Mark addn.}]{HBr/\text{peroxide}}$$

4-Methylpent-1-ene

$$CH_3-\overset{CH_3}{C}H-CH_2-CH_2-CH_2Br$$

1-Bromo-4-methylpentane

16. (b):

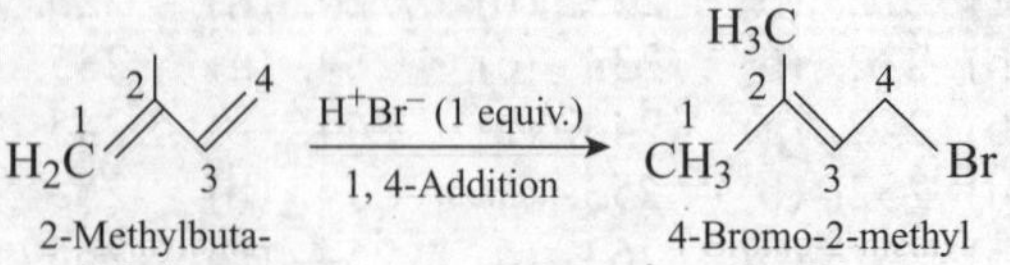

2-Methylbuta-1, 3-diene $\xrightarrow[\text{1, 4-Addition}]{H^+Br^-\text{ (1 equiv.)}}$ 4-Bromo-2-methyl but-2-ene

17. (b): Cyclohexene when treated with Br_2 in the presence of heat and light undergoes allylic bromination.

18. (c): $\underset{\text{Toluene}}{C_6H_5{-}CH_3} \xrightarrow[\text{Allylic bromination}]{\text{NBS}} \underset{\text{Phenylbromomethane}}{C_6H_5{-}CH_2Br}$

19. (d): $\underset{\text{Bromomethane}}{CH_3Br} + AgF \xrightarrow[\text{reaction}]{\text{Swartz}} \underset{\text{Fluoromethane}}{CH_3F} + AgBr$

20. (c): Fluoroethane is prepared by the halogen exchange method.
$2C_2H_5Cl + Hg_2F_2 \xrightarrow{\Delta} 2\,C_2H_5F + Hg_2Cl_2$
(Swartz reaction)

21. (c): Cl^- ion being a weak nucleophile cannot displace OH^- ion which is a stronger nuclephile.
$Na^+Cl^- + C_2H_5OH \rightarrow$ No reaction

22. (c):

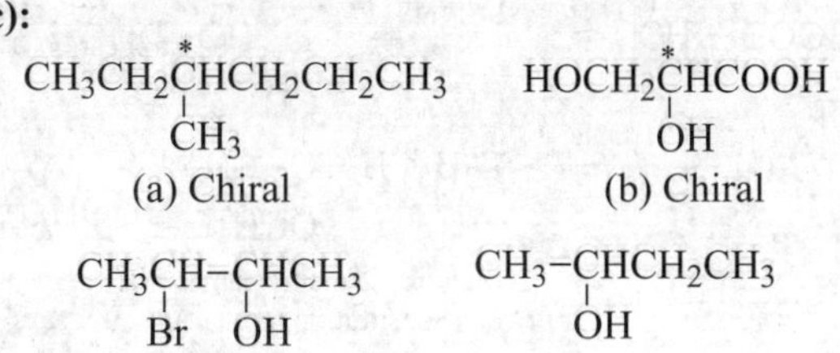

$CH_3CH_2\overset{*}{C}HCH_2CH_2CH_3$ (with CH_3 on the starred carbon) — (a) Chiral

$HOCH_2\overset{*}{C}HCOOH$ (with OH on the starred carbon) — (b) Chiral

$CH_3CH{-}CHCH_3$ (with Br and OH on the two CH carbons) — (c) Not chiral

$CH_3{-}CHCH_2CH_3$ (with OH on CH) — (d) Chiral

23. (d): 1° and 2° alcohols react only in the presence of anhydrous $ZnCl_2$ as catalyst while in the case of 3° alcohols, $ZnCl_2$ is not required. Thus, reaction (II) cannot be used to prepare alkyl halides while all other reactions can be used. In other words, option (d) is correct.

24. (d): HI is the strongest acid and hence it protonates the alcohol most readily. Further, I^- is the strongest nucleophile, therefore, it attacks the protonated alcohol molecule most easily forming the corresponding alkyl iodide.

$$C_2H_5OH \xrightarrow[-I^-]{HI} C_2H_5-\overset{+}{O}H_2 \xrightarrow[\text{Fast}]{+I^-} C_2H_5I + H_2O$$

25. (b): Both H_2SO_4 and H_3PO_4 initially react with KI to liberate HI but H_2SO_4 being an oxidising agent, oxidises the initially liberated HI to I_2. Therefore, *n*-propyl alcohol does not react with KI + H_2SO_4 to form *n*-propyl iodide.
$3KI + H_3PO_4 \rightarrow K_3PO_4 + 3\,HI$
$2\,KI + H_2SO_4 \rightarrow K_2SO_4 + 2\,HI$
$2\,HI + H_2SO_4 \rightarrow I_2 + SO_2 + 2\,H_2O$

26. (b): The byproducts being gases (SO_2 + HCl) escape into the atmosphere leaving behind almost pure alkyl chloride.

Physical Properties of Haloalkanes and Haloarenes

27. (d): The density increases as the molecular mass increases, that is, densities increase in the order I < II < III. However, due to symmetry, the molecules of *p*-dichlorobenzene pack closely in the crystal lattice and hence it has the highest density. Thus, densities increase in the order I < II < III < IV, that is, option (a) is correct.

28. (a): CCl_4 being the most symmetrical has zero dipole moment. As the number of C–Cl dipoles opposing each other decreases, the resultant dipole moment of the molecule increases. Thus, CH_3Cl has the highest dipole moment.

29. (d): CCl_4 being symmetrical has zero dipole moment.

30. (b): CH_3Cl, CH_3F, CH_3Br.

31. (a): CCl_4 and *p*-dichlorobenzene have zero dipole moment.

32. (b): *p*-Dichlorobenzene being symmetrical has zero dipole moment. Toluene, due to the +I effect of the CH_3 group, has a small but finite dipole moment. The two dipoles are 60° apart in *o*-dichlorobenzene, while they are 120° apart in *m*-dichlorobenzene, therefore, according to the parallelogram law of forces, *o*-dichlorobenzene has the highest dipolemoment followed by *m*-dichlorobenzene. Thus, option (b), that is, IV < I < II < III is correct.

33. (b): If x is the dipole moment of an individual C–Cl bond, then accoring to the parallelogram law of forces, the resultant dipole moment of the C_1–Cl and C_2–Cl bonds inclined at an angle of 120° is also x acting along the C_2–Cl bond. Thus, the total dipole moment at $C_2 = x + x = 2x$. The dipole moment of (c) is zero as shown below. The dipole moment of benzene is also zero. Thus option (b) is correct.

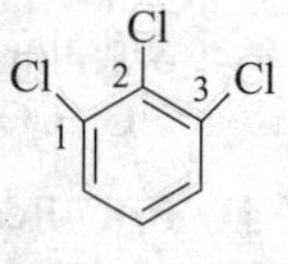

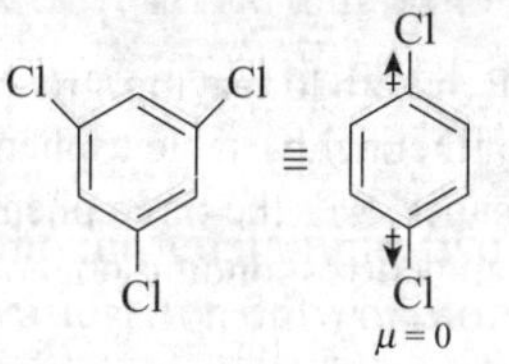

(1,2,3-trichlorobenzene: Cl at positions 1, 2, 3)

(1,3,5-trichlorobenzene: Cl, Cl, Cl) ≡ (Cl above and Cl below with opposing arrows), $\mu = 0$

34. (c): In the absence of peroxides, the first step is the electrophilic addition, that is of H^+, to form the carbocation.

35. (c): For the same halogen, the BP increases as the size of the alkyl group increases. Therefore, the BP of 1-chlorobutane (III) is higher than those of 1-chloropropane (I) and isopropyl chloride (I). Further, the BP decreases as the branching increases, therefore, the BP of isopropyl chloride (II) is lower than that of 1-chloropropane (III). Thus, the BPs increase in the order II < I < III, that is, option (c) is correct.

36. (c): For the same alkyl group, the BP increases with the size of the halogen atom. Therefore, the BP of bromomethane (i) is higher than that of chloromethane (iii).
Further, the BP increases as the number of halogen atoms increases. Therefore, the BP of bromoform (ii) with three Br atoms is the highest, followed by dibromomethane (iv) with two Br atoms while bromomethane (ii) with one Br atom is the lowest. Combining all the arguments discussed above, the BPs of the four compounds increase in the order: chloromethane (iii) < bromomethane (i) < dibromomethane (iv) < bromoform (ii). Thus, option (c) is correct.

37. (c): For the same number of carbon atoms, the BP increases as the number of halogen atoms increases, therefore, option (a) is correct. Further, for the same number of carbon atoms, the BP increases as the atomic mass of the halogen increases, therefore, option (e) is correct.
For the same halogen, the BP increases as the number of carbon atoms increases, therefore, option (b) is correct. Further, for the same halogen and same number of carbon atoms, the BP decreases with branching, therefore, option (d) is correct but option (c) is wrong.

38. (b): Due to symmetry, the molecules of *p*-dichlorobenzene fit closely in the lattice. As a result, intermolecular forces are the strongest in *p*-dichlorobenzene and hence it has the highest MP and lowest solubility.

Chemical Reactions of Haloalkanes (Alkylhalides)

39. (b): The weaker the base, the better the leaving group. Since the basicities decrease in the order OMe (II) >OAc (I) > OSO_2Me (III) > OSO_2CF_3 (IV), the order of leaving group ability decreases in the reverse order, that is, IV > III > I > II.

40. (b): Stronger the acid, weaker is its conjugate base and hence higher is its leaving group ability. Now the basicities increase in the order $CF_3\text{-}SO_3^- < C_6H_5SO_3^- < CH_3COO^- < C_6H_5O^-$ and hence their leaving group ability decreases in the reverse order, that is, $CF_3\text{-}SO_3^-$ (I) > $C_6H_5SO_3^-$ (II) > CH_3COO^- (IV) > $C_6H_5O^-$ (III), that is, option (b) is correct.

41. (d): Reactivity of the alkyl halides decreases as the nucleophilicity of the halide ion decreases in the order $I^- > Br^- > Cl^- > F^-$. Of the options, (d) is correct.

42. (d): With aq. KOH, only hydrolysis occurs, that is, option (d) is correct.

43. (c): Although F^- is a bad leaving group,in this case, due to the formation of the highly stable triphenymethyl carbocation (I) due to resonance over the three phenyl rings, substitution occurs to form the corresponding phenol (II).

$$Ph_3C\text{-}F \xrightarrow[-F^-]{\text{Ionisation}} Ph_3C^+ \text{ (I)} \xrightarrow[\text{(Hydrolysis)}]{\text{Aq. KOH}} Ph_3C\text{-}OH \text{ (II)}$$

Triphenylmethyl carbocation (highly stable)

44. (c): Due to the ambident character of CN^-, alkyl cyanide and alkyl isocyanides are formed.

45. (b): $(CH_3)_2CHBr \xrightarrow[\text{Isopropyl cyanide}]{KCN} (CH_3)_2CH\text{–}CN$

46. (a): $CH_3I + NaNO_2 \rightarrow CH_3\text{–}ONO + NaI$

47. (b): $C_2H_5I \xrightarrow[-AgI]{AgNO_2} C_2H_5\text{–}NO_2$ ($C_2H_5\text{–}N(=O)\rightarrow O$)

48. (b): $CH_3CH_2\text{–}Br + \overset{+-}{NaSH} \xrightarrow[-NaBr]{\Delta} CH_3CH_2\text{–}SH$

Ethylamine, Sodium bisulphide, Ethanethiol

49. (a):

$CH_3CH_2COOAg + C_2H_5Br \xrightarrow{-AgBr} CH_3CH_2COOC_2H_5$

Silver propionate, Ethyl propionate

50. (b): For alkyl halides with the same R group but different halogen atoms, the order of reactivity towards substitution/ dehydrohalogenation, decreases as the leaving group ability of the halide ion decreases, that is, $I^- > Br^- > Cl^- > F^-$. Thus, option (b) is correct.

51. (b): Tertiary alkyl halides readily undergo dehydrohalogenation to form alkenes.

$$(CH_3)_3C\text{–}Cl \xrightarrow[(-C_2H_5OH,\ -HCl)]{NaOC_2H_5} (CH_3)_2C{=}CH_2$$

tert-Butyl chloride, Isobutylene

52. (a): $CH_3\text{–}CHBr\text{–}CH(CH_3)_2 \xrightarrow{-HBr} CH_3\text{–}CH{=}C(CH_3)_2$

2-Methylbut-2-ene (Saytzeff product)

53. (d): The order of reactivity in dehydrohalogenation is 3° > 2° > 1°, that is, option (d) is correct.

54. (a): 2-Chloro-2-methylpentane being a 3° alkylhalide can undergo either S_N1 or E_1 reaction. Further, the intermediate carbocation can undergo elimination in different ways to give 2-methyl-2-pentene (major) and 2-methyl-1-pentene (minor) as shown below.

$$CH_3CH_2CH_2\text{–}C(CH_3)(Cl)\text{–}CH_3 \xrightarrow[-Cl^-]{\text{Ionisation}} C_2H_5CH_2\text{–}\overset{+}{C}(CH_3)\text{–}CH_3$$

3° carbocation (I)

$$\text{(I)} \xrightarrow[S_N1]{CH_3ONa} C_2H_5CH_2\text{–}C(CH_3)(OCH_3)\text{–}CH_3$$

2-Methoxy-2-methylpentene (II) (Substitution product)

$$\text{(I)} \xrightarrow[E_1]{CH_3ONa} C_2H_5CH{=}C(CH_3)\text{–}CH_3 + C_2H_5CH_2{=}C(CH_3)\text{–}CH_2\text{(IV)}$$

2-Methyl-2-pentene (major product), 2-Methyl-1-pentene (minor product)

Thus, all the products are formed, that is, option (a) is correct.

55. (c): Although the given alkyl halide is 1°, the carbocation which it generates on ionisation rearranges to form a more stable 3° carbocation which in presence of a strong base (CH_3O^-) prefers to undergo elimination rather than substitution to afford 2-methylpropene.

$$CH_3\text{–}CH(CH_3)\text{–}CH_2\text{–}Br \xrightarrow[-Br^-]{\text{Ionisation}} CH_3\text{–}CH(CH_3)\text{–}\overset{+}{C}H_2$$

1° carbocation (less stable)

$$\xrightarrow[\text{shift}]{\text{1, 2-Hydride}} CH_3\text{–}\overset{+}{C}(CH_3)\text{–}CH_3 \xrightarrow{-H^+} CH_3\text{–}C(CH_3){=}CH_2$$

3° carbocation (more stable), 2-Methylpropene

56. (c): The initially formed less stable 1° carbocation rearranges to the more stable 3° carbocation which prefers to undergo elimination in accordance with the Saytzeff rule to give the more stable alkene, that is, 2-methyl-2-butene.

$$CH_3\text{–}CH(CH_3)\text{–}CH_2\text{–}Br \xrightarrow[-Br^-]{\text{Ionisation}} CH_3\text{–}CH(CH_3)\text{–}\overset{+}{C}H_2$$

Neopentyl bromide; 1° carbocation (less stable)

$$\xrightarrow[\text{shift}]{\text{1, 2-Methyl}} CH_3\text{–}\overset{+}{C}(CH_3)\text{–}CH(H)\text{–}CH_3 \xrightarrow{-H^+} (CH_3)_2C{=}CHCH_3$$

3° carbocation (more stable), 2-Methyl-2-butene

57. (c):

$$CH_3CH_2-\underset{\displaystyle |}{\overset{CH_3}{CH}}-CH_2Br \xrightarrow[-C_2H_5OH]{C_2H_5ONa} CH_3CH_2-\overset{CH_3}{C}=CH_2$$

1-Bromo-2-methylbutane

$$\xrightarrow[Catalyst]{H_2} CH_3CH_2-\overset{CH_3}{CH}-CH_3$$

2-Methylbutane

Thus, option (c) is correct.

58. (c): 2-Bromobutane can undergo elimination in two different ways giving 1-butene and 2-butene. Further, 2-butene can show geometrical isomerism. Therefore, out of *cis*-and *trans* -2-butenes, *trans*-2-butene being more stable, is the major product.

$$\underset{Br}{CH_3-CH-CH_2CH_3} \xrightarrow[-HBr]{KOH} CH_3CH_2CH=CH_2 +$$

2-Bromobutane; 1-Butene

trans-2-Butene (major product) + cis-2-Butene (minor product)

59. (d):

trans-2-Phenyl-1-bromocyclopentene $\xrightarrow[\text{(trans-elimination of HBr)}]{\text{KOH (alc.)}}$ 3-Phenylcyclopentene

C_1–Br and C_2–H are *cis* to each other, therefore, *trans*-elimination of HBr cannot occur to form a double bond between C_2–C_3. Instead C_1–Br and C_5–H are *trans* to each other, therefore, a double bond is formed between $C_1$and C_5 to give 3-phenylcyclopentene.

60. (b): $\xrightarrow[\text{E}_2\text{ (trans-elimination of HBr)}]{\text{NaOMe/MeOH}}$

61. (d): 2° Alkyl halides exclusively undergo bimolecular elimination (E_2) particularly when the base used is bulky and the double bond being formed is stabilised by conjugation with the benzene rings as shown.

$\xrightarrow[\text{(E}_2\text{ elimination of HBr)}]{tert\text{-BuOK, }\Delta}$ $C_6H_5CH=CHC_6H_5$ + *tert*-BuOH + Br^-

62. (b): 3° Alkyl halides preferably undergo elimination rather than substitution. Further, the elimination occurs in accordance with the Saytzeff rule giving the more highly substituted alkene as the major product.

$$H_3CH_2CO_2C-C(CH_3)(Cl)-CH_2-CH_3 \xrightarrow[-EtOH,\ -HCl]{NaOEt} CH_3-\underset{CO_2CH_2CH_3}{C}=CHCH_3$$

trans-2-Butene (major product)

Thus, option (b) is correct.

63. (c): In Hofmann elimination reactions, the orientation of the product is governed by the acidity of the β-H with respect to the leaving group. In 2-fluorobutane, due to the +I effect of the CH_3 group, the β-H on C_3 is less acidic than the β-H on C_1. In other words, β-H on C_1 being more acidic is lost more easily to afford but-1-ene as the major product.

$$CH_3-\underset{F}{CH}-CH_2 \text{(2-Fluorobutane)} \xrightarrow[-HF]{CH_3O^-/CH_3OH} CH_3-CH_2-CH=CH_2$$

2-Fluorobutane; But-1-ene

64. (c): 1° alkyl halides preferably undergo substitution while 2° alkyl halides undergo elimination.

$$CH_3CH_2Br \xrightarrow[-HBr]{NH_3} CH_3CH_2NH_2$$

Ethyl bromide (1°) (Substitution product); Ethylamine

Bromocyclohexane (2°) $\xrightarrow[-NH_4Br]{NH_3}$ Cyclohexene (Elimination product)

65. (c):

$$C_6H_5CH_2Br \xrightarrow{Mg,\ Ether} C_6H_5CH_2MgBr \xrightarrow{H_3O^+} C_6H_5CH_3 + Mg(OH)Br$$

66. (d):

$$(CH_3)_2C(Cl)CH_2CH_3 \xrightarrow{Mg,\ ether} (CH_3)_2C(MgCl)CH_2CH_3$$

2-Chloro-2-methylbutane

$$\xrightarrow[-Mg(OC_2H_5)Cl]{C_2H_5OH} CH_3-\overset{CH_3}{CH}-CH_2CH_3$$

2-Methylbutane

$$(CH_3)_2CHCH_2CH_2Cl \xrightarrow{Mg,\ ether} (CH_3)_2CHCH_2CH_2MgCl$$

1-Chloro-3-methylbutane

$$\xrightarrow[-Mg(OC_2H_5)Cl]{C_2H_5OH} CH_3-\overset{CH_3}{CH}-CH_2CH_3$$

2-Methylbutane

67. (c):

Cyclohexene $\xrightarrow[\text{(Reduction)}]{H_2/Pd-C}$ Cyclohexane (P) $\xrightarrow[\text{(Bromination)}]{Br_2/h\nu}$

Bromocyclohexane (Q) $\xrightarrow[ether]{Mg}$ Grignard reagent (R) $\xrightarrow{D_2O}$ Deuteriocyclohexane (S)

68. (c):

$$2CH_3-\underset{CH_3}{\overset{CH_3}{\overset{|}{\underset{|}{C}}}}-CH_2Br + 2\,Na \xrightarrow[(-2\,NaBr)]{\text{Wurtz reaction}} CH_3-\underset{CH_3}{\overset{CH_3}{\overset{|}{\underset{|}{C}}}}-CH_2-CH_2-\underset{CH_3}{\overset{CH_3}{\overset{|}{\underset{|}{C}}}}-CH_3$$

Neopentyl bromide — 2, 2, 5, 5-Tetramethylhexane

69. (c): Two 1° alkyl halides with MF C_4H_9Br are *n*-butyl bromide and isobutyl bromide. These, when reacted with Na metal, undergo the Wurtz reaction to give *n*-octane and 2,5-dimethylhexane.

$$2CH_3CH_2CH_2CH_2Br + 2\,Na \xrightarrow[\text{(Wurtz reaction)}]{\Delta(-2HBr)} CH_3(CH_2)_6CH_3$$

n-Butyl bromide — *n*-Octane

$$2CH_3-\overset{CH_3}{\overset{|}{C}H}-CH_2Br + 2\,Na \xrightarrow[\text{(Wurtz reaction)}]{\Delta\,(-2\,HBr)} CH_3-\overset{CH_3}{\overset{|}{C}H}-CH_2-CH_2-\overset{CH_3}{\overset{|}{C}H}-CH_3$$

Isobutyl bromide (A) — 2, 5-Dimethylhexane (D) MF C_8H_{18}

Since *n*-butyl bromide on treatment with Na metal gives *n*-octane but compound (A) on treatment with Na metal gives a compound different from *n*-octane, having the same MF C_8H_{18}. Therefore, compound (A) must be isobutyl bromide and compound (D) must be 2,5-dimethylhexane. If 1° alkyl halide (A) with MF C_4H_9Br is isobutyl bromide, then compound (B) must be 2-methyl-1-propene and compound (C) which it gives on treatment with HBr must be tert-butyl bromide.

$$CH_3-\overset{CH_3}{\overset{|}{C}H}-CH_2Br \xrightarrow[-HBr]{KOH\,(alc.)} CH_3-\overset{CH_3}{\overset{|}{C}}=CH_2 \xrightarrow[\text{(Mark addn.)}]{HBr} CH_3-\underset{CH_3}{\overset{CH_3}{\overset{|}{\underset{|}{C}}}}-Br$$

Isobutyl bromide (A) MF C_4H_4Br — 2-Methyl-1-propene (B) — *tert*-Butyl bromide (C)

70. (a): Nucleophilic substitution reactions.

71. (d): $RX + KOH \rightarrow ROH + KX$ is an example of nucleophilic substitution reaction.

72. (d): Nucleophilic substitution reaction involves the displacement of a weaker nucleophile (Br^-) by a stronger nucleophilie (NH_3). Thus, option (d) is correct.

73. (d): Due to lower electronegativity of N over O, CN^- is more willing to donate electrons than CH_3O^-. Therefore, nucleophilicity of CN^- is higher than that of CH_3O^-.
Among CH_3COO^- (I) and *p*-toluenesulfonate (IV) ion, the –ve charge on O is more extensively delocalised in sulfonate ion (IV) than in the acetate ion (I). Therefore, the acetate ion (I) is more willing to donate electrons than thesulfonate ion (IV) and hence nucleophilicity of the acetate ion (I) is higher than that of the sulfonate ion (IV). Combining both the arguments discussed above, the overall nucleophilicity decreases in the order III > II > I > IV, that is, option (d) is correct.

74. (a): The leaving group ability decreases as the basicity of the nucleophile increases. Since the basicity increases in the order $Br^- < Cl^- < CH_3COO^- < OH^- < H^-$. Therefore, their leaving group ability decreases in the reverse order, that is, $Br^- > Cl^- < CH_3COO^- < OH^- < H^-$. Thus, option (a) is correct.

Optical Isomerism

75. (a): The asterisked carbon is attached to four different atoms/groups and hence is called a chiral centre.

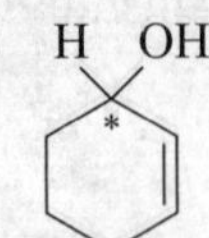

76. (b): Carbon atoms marked q and r are attached to four different atoms/groups and hence are asymmetric.

77. (a):

I: H_3C–C*(H)(OH)(Br) II: HO, H, CH_3 IV: $CH_3-\overset{*}{C}H(Br)-CH_2CH_3$

I, II and IV contain asymmetric carbons and hence are chiral. Compound (III) is not chiral since its central carbon (CHOH) is attached to two identical groups.

78. (d): The molecule (d) does not have an asymmetric carbon (because the central carbon is attached to two identical groups) and hence it is achiral.

79. (a): To be optically active, the molecule must be chiral.

80. (d):

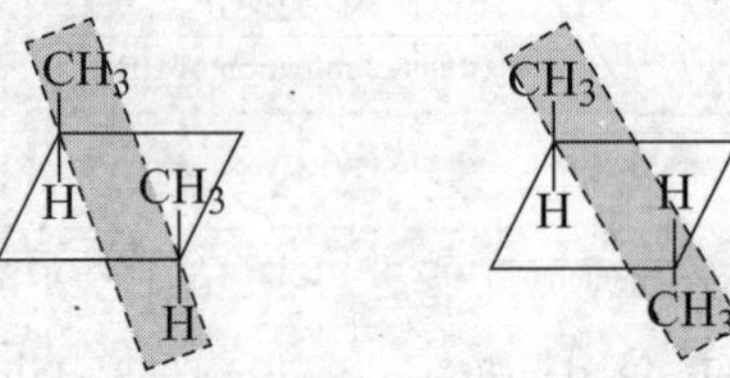

Both *cis*-and *trans*-1,3-dimethylcyclobutane have a vertical plane of symmetry and hence are optically inactive.

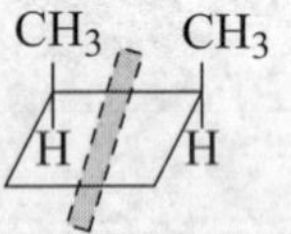

cis-1, 2-Dimethylecyclobutane has a vertical plane of symmetry and hence is optically inactive

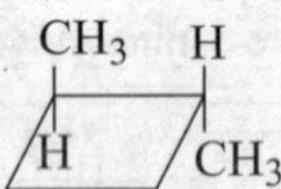

trans-1, 2-Dimethylecyclobutane neither has a plane or a centre of symmetry and hence is optically active

81. (d):

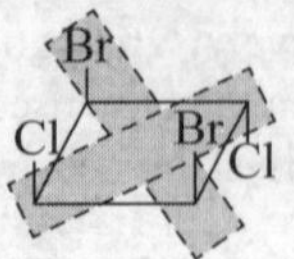

It has two diagonal planes of symmetry, *optically inactive*

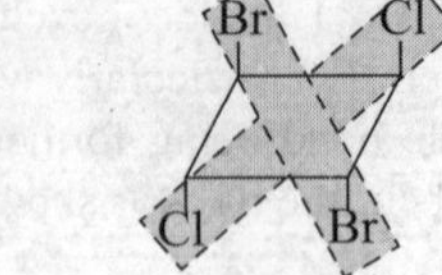

Two diagonal planes of symmetry, *optically inactive*

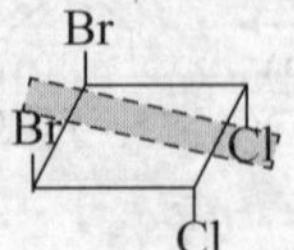

Horizontal plane of symmetry, *optically inactive*

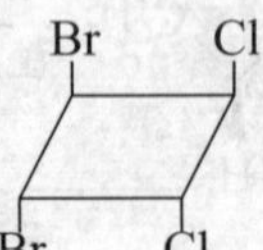

Neither a plane or a centre of symmetry, *optically inactive*

82. (b): Putting a substituent at position 3 will make the molecule chiral.

$$CH_3CH_2-\overset{*}{C}H(X)-CH_2CH_2CH_2CH_3$$

83. (d):

$CH_3-\overset{*}{C}H(Cl)-CH_2CH_3$ 2-Chlorobutane; $CH_2(OH)-\overset{*}{C}H(OH)-CHO$ 2, 3-Dihydroxypropanal (Glyceraldehyde); $CH_3-\overset{*}{C}HBr-COOH$ 2-Bromopropanoic acid

All the molecules have one chiral centre or asymmetric carbon atom and hence are chiral.

84. (c):

I: $H_3C-\overset{*}{C}(COOH)(NH_2)(OH)$; II: H, Br substituted carbon; III: cyclohexene with H and Cl at C* ; IV: cyclohexane with H and OCH_3

Molecules (I and III) have one asymmetric carbon and hence are chiral.

85. (a):

Maleic acid (H)(COOH)C=C(H)(COOH) (Optically inactive)

$R-\overset{*}{C}H(NH_2)-COOH$ α-Amino acid (Optically active)

$CH_3-\overset{*}{C}H(OH)-COOH$ Lactic acid (Optically active)

$$HOOC-\overset{*}{C}HOH-\overset{*}{C}HOH-COOH$$
Tartaric acid (Optically active)

Only maleic acid does not have a chiral centre and hence does not exhibit optical isomerism while all others do.

86. (d):

$Br-CH_2-CHCl-CH_2Br$ 1, 3-Dibromo-2-chloropropane (Optically inactive)

$Br-CH(Br)-CH_2-CH_2Cl$ 1, 1-Dibromo-3-chloropropane (Optically inactive)

$ClCH_2-CBr_2-CH_3$ 2, 2-Dibromo-1-chloropropane (Optically inactive)

$Br\overset{*}{C}H(Cl)-CH_2-CH_2Br$ 1, 3-Dibromo-1-chloropropane (Optically active)

87. (a):

$CH_2=CH-\overset{*}{C}H(CH_3)-CH_2CH_3$ 3-Methyl-1-pentene (Optically active)

$CH_2-C(CH_3)=CHCH_2CH_3$ 2-Methyl-2-pentene

$CH_3-CH=C(CH_3)-CH_2CH_3$ 3-Methyl-1-pentene

$CH_2=CH-CH_2-CH(CH_3)-CH_3$ 4-Methyl-1-pentene

Only 3-methyl-1-pentene contains an asymmetric carbon and hence exhibits optical isomerism.

88. (a): 2,3-Dimethylpentane with a MF C_7H_{16} has a chiral centre and hence shows optical isomerism.

89. (d):

$$\underset{\text{3-Methyl-1-pentene (Optically active)}}{CH_3CH_2-\overset{*}{C}H(CH_3)-CH=CH_2} \xrightarrow[\text{Hydrogenation}]{H_2/Ni} \underset{\text{3-Methylpentane (Optically inactive)}}{CH_3CH_2-CH(CH_3)-CH_2CH_3}$$

3-Methylpentane has no chiral centre and is optically inactive.

90. (d): $(CH_2)_2CCHCH_3 \xrightarrow{H_2/Ni} (CH_3)_2CH-CH_2CH_3$ (2-Methylbutane)

2-Methylbutane has no chiral centre and hence is optically inactive. The number of optical isomers is zero.

91. (b): HO–C(CHO)(CH₂OH)–H has a chiral centre and thus rotates the plane of polarised light.

Although it contains two asymmetric carbon atoms, the molecule is not chiral since it has a plane of symmetry. Therefore, it does not rotate the plane of polarised light.

(H_2N, H, Ph substituted two C* centres; Plane of symmetry)

$H_2N-C(COOH)(H)-H$ and 2-butanethiol skeleton (SH)

The remaining two molecules do not contain asymmetric carbon atoms and hence do not rotate the plane of polarised light.

92. (a): Compound (a) shows *cis–trans* isomerism and has a chiral centre.

93. (c):

$CH_3-C(H)(Cl)-C(H)(Cl)-CH_3$ (Fischer projection, plane of symmetry between)

Compound (c) has a plane of symmetry and hence is not optically active

94. (b): Compound (a) has no asymmetric carbon and hence is not chiral. Compound (c) has a horizontal while compound (d) has a diagonal plane of symmetry and hence both are not chiral. Compound (b) has neither a plane nor a centre of symmetry and hence is chiral.

95. (c):

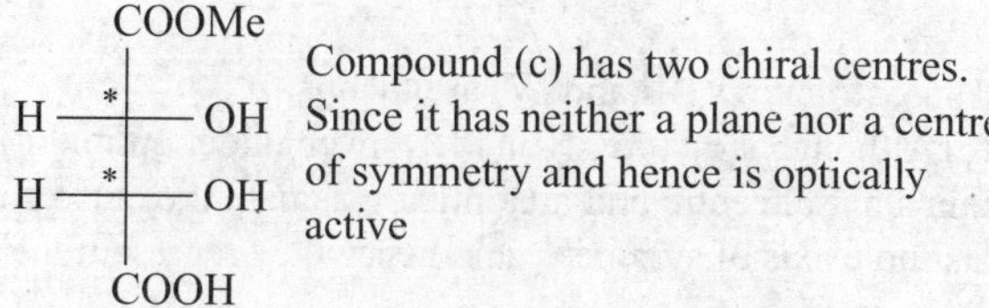

Compound (c) has two chiral centres. Since it has neither a plane nor a centre of symmetry and hence is optically active

96. (a):

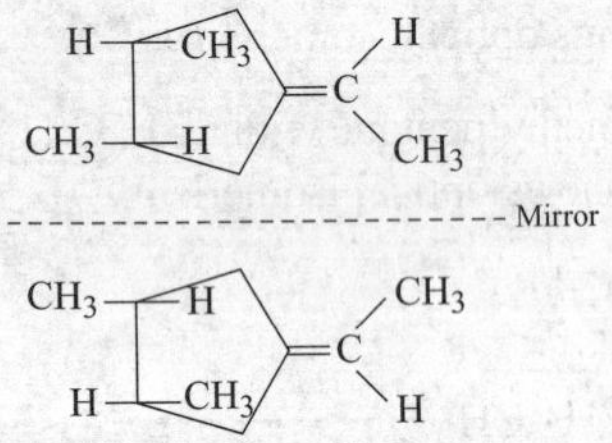

The two structures are non-superimposable mirror images of each other and hence are enantiomers.

97. (a): To determine the relationship between structures (I and II), do the following two interchanges of atoms in structure (II).

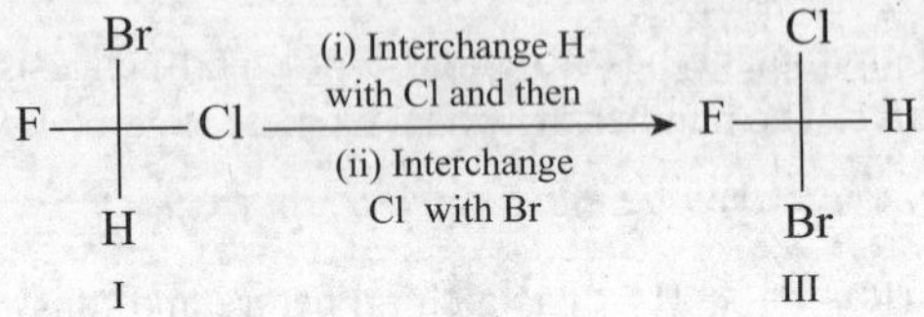

(i) Interchange H with Cl and then (ii) Interchange Cl with Br

Now structures (I and III) are non-superimposable mirror images of each other.

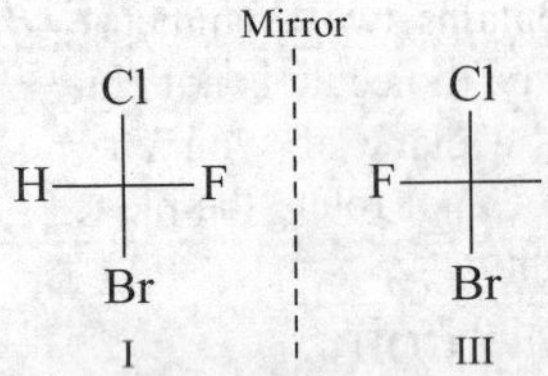

Therefore, structures (I and III) or infact structures (I and II) are enantiomers.

98. (d): The pair of structures given under options (a) and (b) do not contain a chiral centre and also contain a simple axis of symmetry and hence are identical.

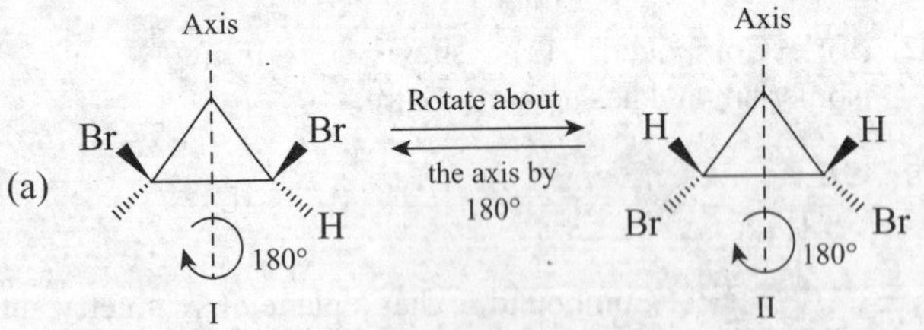

(a) Rotate about the axis by 180°

Thus, structures (I and II) are identical.

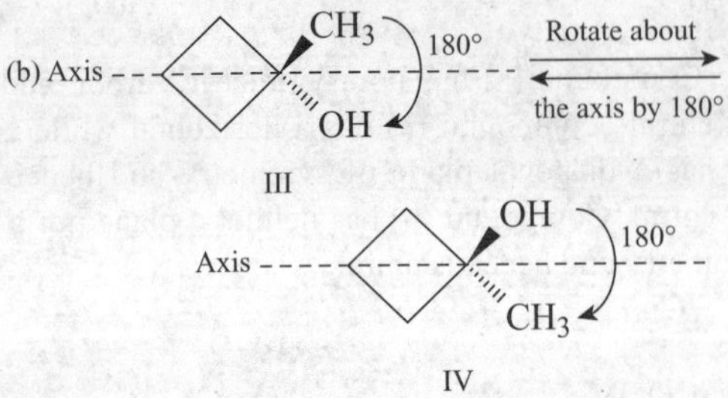

(b) Rotate about the axis by 180°

Thus, structures (III and IV) are identical.

(c) Although structure (II and III) given under option (c) contain a chiral centre and are optically active, they also contain a simple axis of symmetry and hence they represent the same stereoisomer.

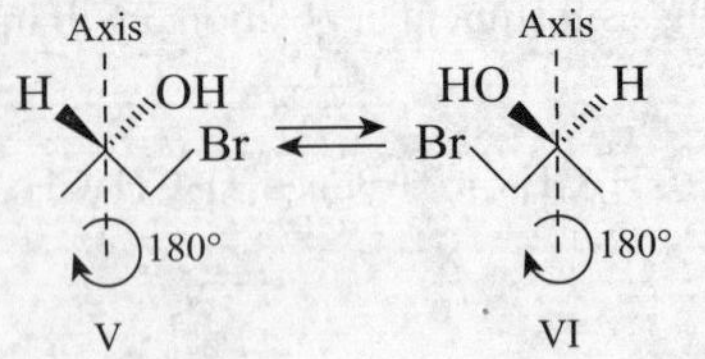

(d) Structures (VII and VIII) given under option (d) represent non-superimposable mirror images of each other and hence are enantiomers.

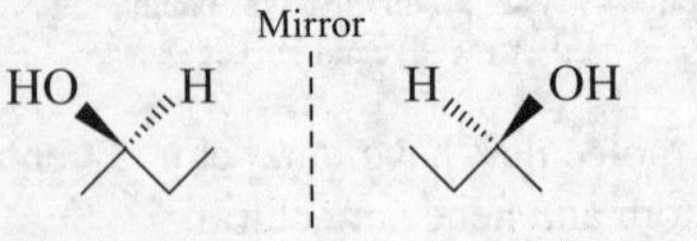

99. (c):

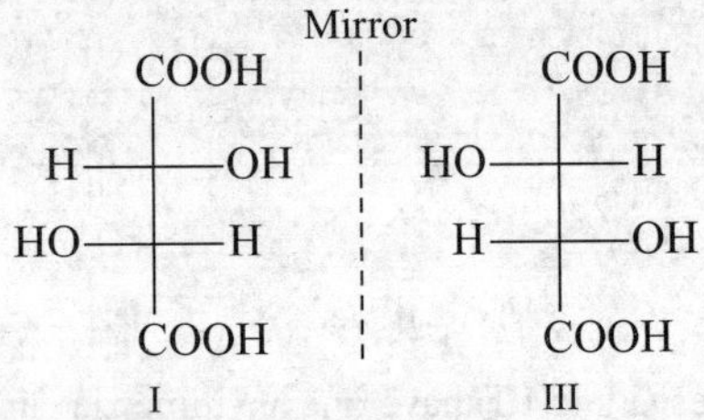

I and III represent non-superimposable mirror images and hence are enantiomers. Compound (II) is, however, a meso compound.

100. (b): Chiral molecules in which the configuration of two substituents is interchanged while that of the other two substituents remains the same are enantiomers. Thus, I and IV represent a pair of enantiomers.

101. (c): They cannot be separated by fractional crystallisation.

102. (a):

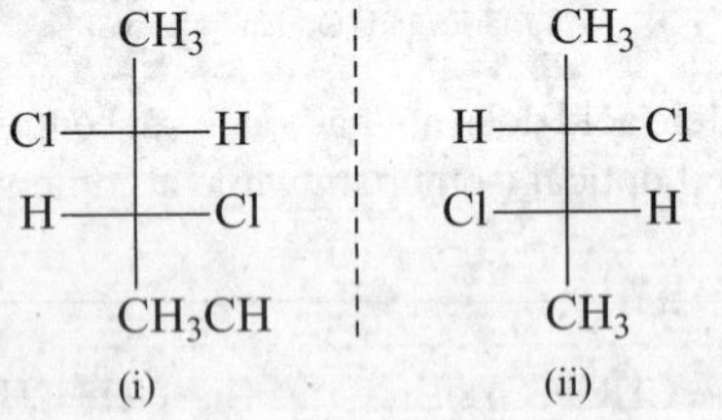

(i) and (ii) being non-superimposable mirror images of each other are enantiomers. Since enantiomers have equal but opposite sign of rotation, the optical rotation of compound (ii) is –52°.

103. (d):

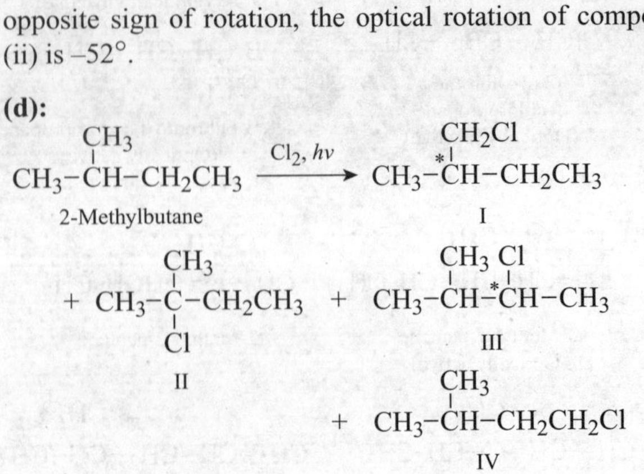

$$\underset{\text{2-Methylbutane}}{CH_3-CH(CH_3)-CH_2CH_3} \xrightarrow{Cl_2,\ h\nu} \underset{\text{I}}{CH_3-\overset{*}{C}H(CH_2Cl)-CH_2CH_3} + \underset{\text{II}}{CH_3-C(CH_3)(Cl)-CH_2CH_3} + \underset{\text{III}}{CH_3-CH(CH_3)-\overset{*}{C}H(Cl)-CH_3} + \underset{\text{IV}}{CH_3-CH(CH_3)-CH_2CH_2Cl}$$

Monochlorination of 2-methylbutane in all gives four products (I–IV) out of which products (I and III) are chiral. Since each chiral centre has two enantiomers, in all, $2 \times 2 = 4$ chiral compounds are possible.

104. (d):

$$CH_3-\underset{CH_3}{CH}-\underset{CH_3}{CH}-CH_3 \xrightarrow{Cl_2,\ hv} \underset{I}{ClCH_2-\overset{*}{C}H(CH_3)-CH(CH_3)-CH_3} + \underset{II}{CH_3-C(Cl)(CH_3)-CH(CH_3)-CH_3}$$

Monochlorination of 2,3-dimethylbutane, in all, gives two products (I and II) out of which only one product (I) is chiral. Since it has only one chiral centre, if forms only one enantiomeric pair.

105. (a):

$$\underset{I}{(H_3C)_2C=C(CH_3)_2} \xrightarrow{Br_2} \underset{III}{(H_3C)_2C(Br)-C(Br)(CH_3)_2}$$

$$\underset{II}{(H_3C)_2C=CH_2} \xrightarrow{Br_2} \underset{IV}{(H_3C)_2\overset{*}{C}(Br)-CH_2Br}$$

The product of bromination of alkene (I), that is, compound (III) has no chiral centre and hence zero enantiomeric pairs. The product of bromination of alkene (II), that is, compound (IV) has one chiral centre and hence it has only one enantiomeric pair.

106. (b):

$$\xrightarrow{Cl_2,\ hv}$$

(i) and (ii) ; (+)-and (–)-isomers (iii)

+ (iv) and (v) ; (+)-and (–)-isomers + (vi)

A total of 6 isomers will be formed. Since enantiomers have the same BP, they cannot be separated by fractional distillation, that is, (ii) and (iii) will distil together and similarly (iv) and (v) will distil together. Thus, out of 6 isomers formed, 4 can be separated by fractional distillation. Thus, option (b) is correct.

107. (c):

1st structure $\xrightarrow[\text{(ii) H and OH}]{\text{(i) Interchange } CH_3 \text{ and } CH_2CH_3}$ 2nd structure

Making two interchanges on the 1st structure, we get the 2nd structure. Thus, the two structures are identical.

108. (d):

II $\xrightarrow[\text{within the plane of the paper}]{\text{Rotate by } 180°}$ I

By rotating structure (II) by 180° within the plane of the paper, we get, structure (I). Thus, the two structures are identical.

109. (b):

(COOH / H–OH / HO–H / COOH) and (COOH / H–OH / H–OH / COOH)

Since the two stereoisomers are not mirror images of each other, they are diastereomers.

110. (d):

I $\xrightarrow[\text{within the plane of the paper}]{\text{Rotate by } 180°}$ IA | II

Thus, I and II are enantiomers.

111. (d): I and III do not have a plane or a centre of symmetry and hence are chiral.

Mirror

I II III

Rotate through 180°

Thus, I and III are enantiomers. Structure (II) has a centre of symmetry and hence is achiral.

Thus, the only option which is correct is that I and III are chiral.

112. (a):

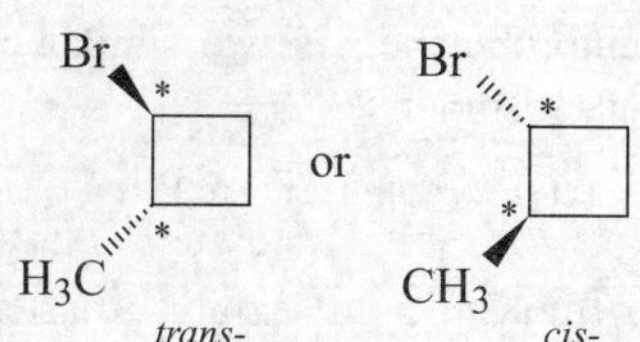

Both *cis*- or *trans*-1-bromo-2-methyclobutane have two dissimilar chiral centres and thus have $2^2 = 4$ optical isomers.

113. (d): 2,3-Dichloropentane has two dissimilar chiral centres and

$$CH_3-\overset{*}{C}H(Cl)-\overset{*}{C}H(Cl)-CH_2CH_3$$

hence has $2^2 = 4$ optical isomers.

114. (d): III and IV do not have a plane of symmetry and hence are not meso-isomers. Statements (a) and (b) are, however, correct.

115. (d): All statements are correct.

116. (a):

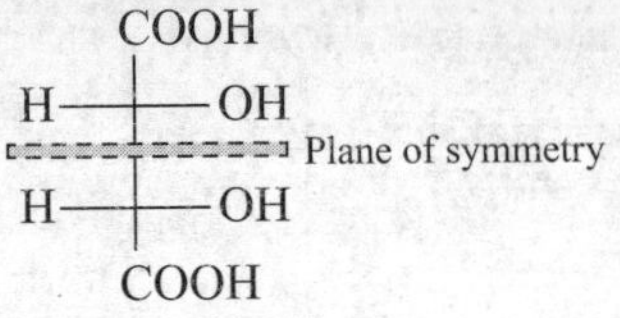

COOH
H—C—OH
- - - - - Plane of symmetry
H—C—OH
COOH
Meso-Tartaric acid

Meso-tartaric acid is optically inactive due to the presence of a plane of symmetry.

117. (b): Three stereoisomers (I–III) are possible out of which two (I and II) are optically active as shown below.

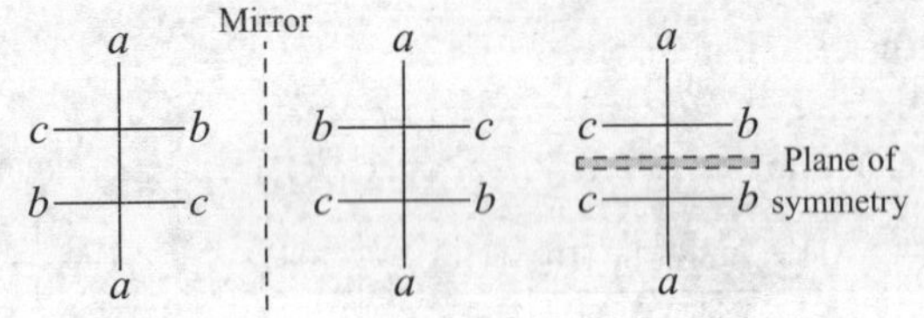

Mirror

I, II: Enantiomers (Optically active)

meso-isomer (Optically inactive) — Plane of symmetry

118. (c): Catalytic reduction gives three (I to III) stereoisomers as shown below.

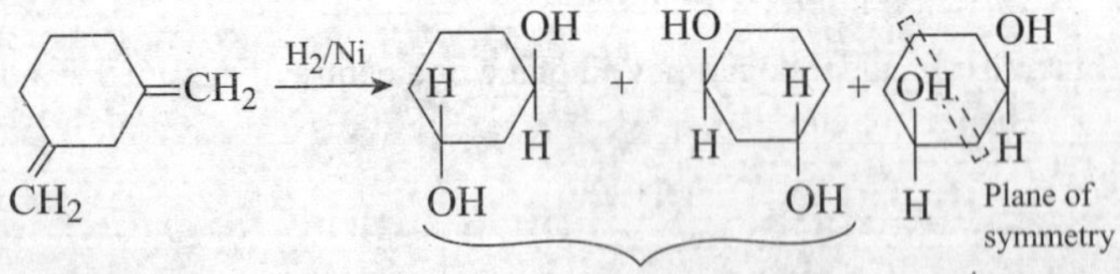

H_2/Ni

Enantiomers — *meso*-isomer (Plane of symmetry)

119. (a): A meso-isomer.

120. (b): Butane-2,3-diol has two similar chiral centres and hence exists as three stereoisomers (I–III), out of which two (I–III) are optically active while the third is an optically inactive meso-isomer.

121. (b): For a molecule to have a meso-isomer, it must have two identical chiral centres, that is,

$$CH_3-\overset{*}{C}HOH-\overset{*}{C}HOH-CH_3$$

122. (b): 2,3-Dichlorobutane has two similar chiral centres and thus has a meso-isomer.

$$CH_3-\overset{*}{C}HCl-\overset{*}{C}HCl-CH_3$$

123. (d): For a molecule to exhibit diastereoisomerism, it must have two chiral centres which may be similar or dissimilar. 2-Butanol has only one chiral centre and shows only enantiomerism. Please note that 2-butene also shows diastereoisomerism since it exists in two stereoisomers, that is, *cis*-and *trans*- which are not mirror images of each other and hence are diastereoisomers.

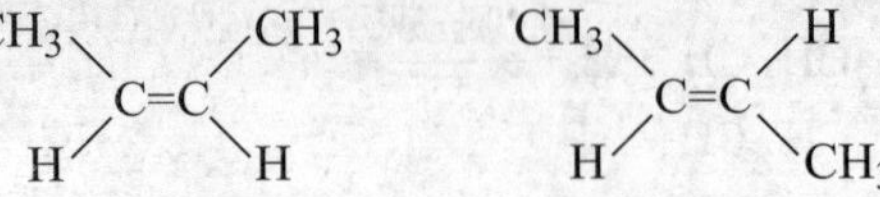

cis-2-Butene — *trans*-2-Butene

Diastereomers

124. (d):

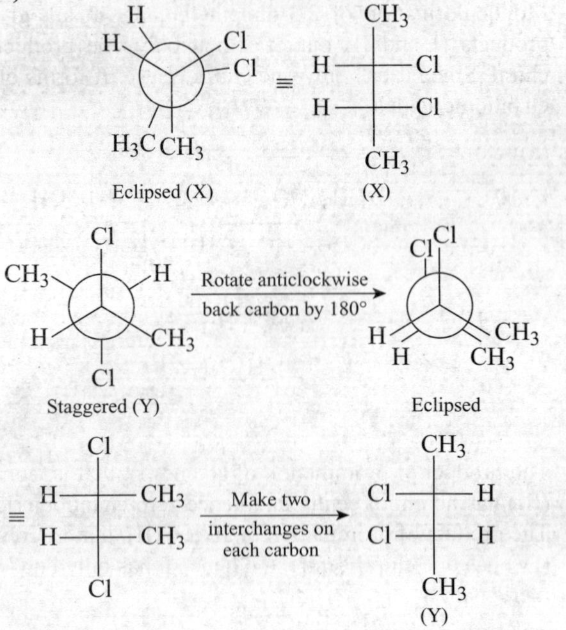

Eclipsed (X) ≡ (X)

Staggered (Y) — Rotate anticlockwise back carbon by 180° — Eclipsed

≡ — Make two interchanges on each carbon — (Y)

X and Y represent the same compound, that is, meso-2,3-dichlorobutane. Thus, X and Y are conformers.

125. (a): Conformational isomers.

126. (b):

$$CH_3CH_2-\overset{*}{C}H(CH_3)-CH=CH-CH_3$$

It has a double bond each carbon of which has two different substituents and hence shows geometrical isomerism. Since it has a chiral centre also, it shows enantiomerism also.

127. (d): $CH_3-CH=CH-CH_2-\overset{*}{C}HBr-CH_3$
Due to the presence of a double bond it exists as *cis*-and *trans*-isomers. Due to the presence of a chiral centre, each geometrical isomer has a pair of enantiomers. Hence, in all, there are $2\times2 = 4$ stereoisomers.

128. (d): Monobromination of 2-methyl-2-pentene with NBS gives two structural isomers (I and II).

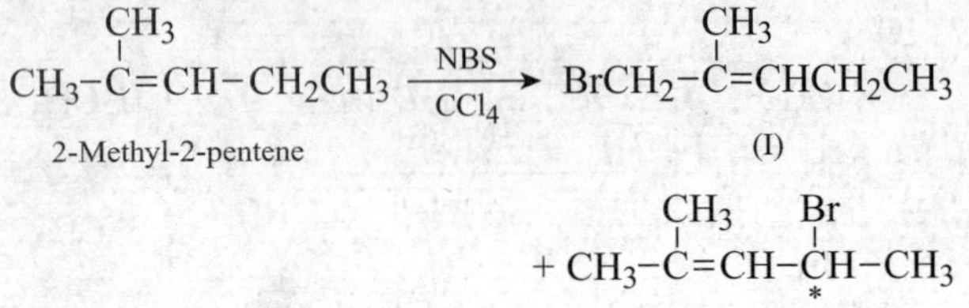

$$\underset{\text{2-Methyl-2-pentene}}{CH_3-C(CH_3)=CH-CH_2CH_3} \xrightarrow[CCl_4]{NBS} \underset{(I)}{BrCH_2-C(CH_3)=CHCH_2CH_3}$$

$$+\ CH_3-C(CH_3)=CH-\overset{*}{C}H(Br)-CH_3$$

The structural isomer (I) has a double bond and hence it has two geometrical isomers (*cis* and *trans*). The structural isomer (II) has a chiral carbon and thus exists as a pair of enantiomers. Thus, in all, there are four stereoisomers. Please note that the double bond in structural isomer (II) has two identical CH_3 groups on one of the carbon atoms of the double bond and hence does not show geometrical isomerism.

129. (c): $CH_3-CH=CH-\overset{*}{C}HBr-CH_2CH_3$
The given compound has a double bond possessing different substituents on each carbon; therefore, it has two geometrical isomers—*cis* and *trans*. Since the given compound also contains a chiral carbon, each geometrical isomer has two enantiomers. The given compound has in all, four stereoisomers.

130. (a): (a) Twelve in all. Therefore are (a) six geometrical isomers, (b) two optical isomers and (c) four structural isomers.

(a) Geometrical isomers

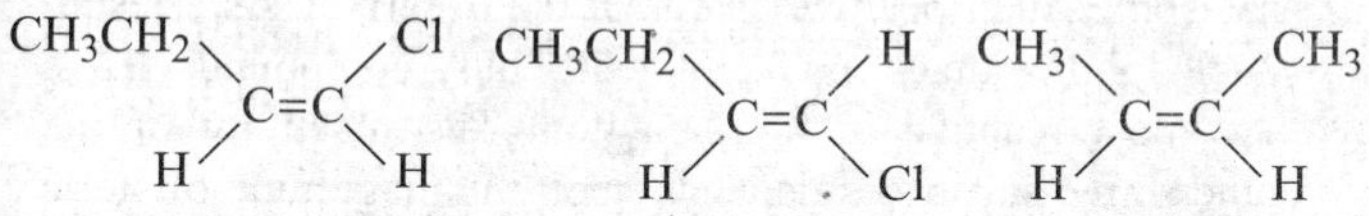

(i) (ii) (iii)

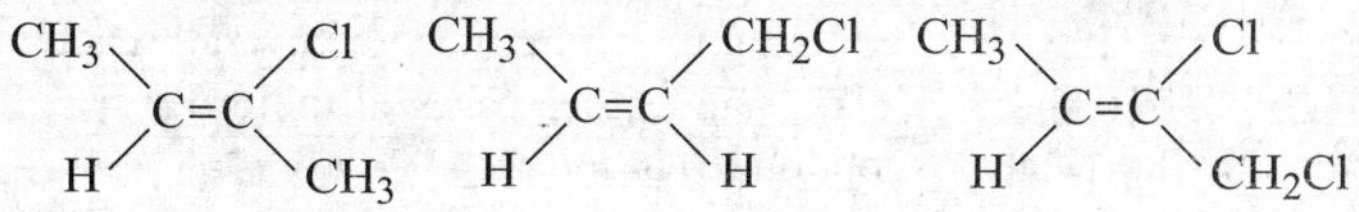

(iv) (v) (vi)

(b) Geometrical isomers

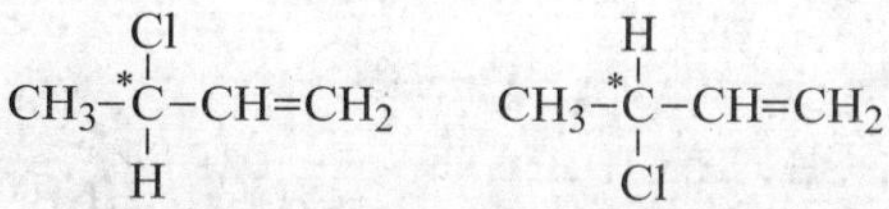

(vii) (viii)

(c) Four structural isomers

(ix) (x)

(xi) (xiii)

131. (c): Sec-butyl chloride obtained by free radical chlorination is a racemic mixture. Free radicals are a planar species. Therefore, attack by the Cl_2 molecule on the sec-butyl free radical can occur from the top or the bottom face with equal ease giving a 50 : 50 mixture of the two enantiomers, that is, racemic mixture.

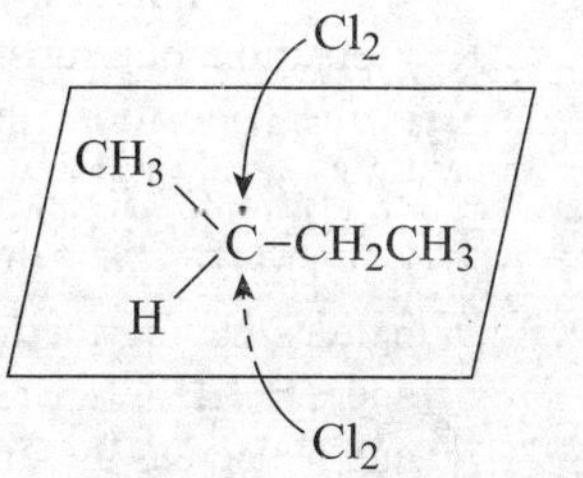

132. (d): Length of the polarimeter tube (l) = 5 cm = 5/10 = 0.5 dm. Conc. (c) is g/cm^3 = 6.15/100

$\therefore$ Specific rotation, $[\alpha]=\dfrac{\alpha}{l\times c}$ where α is the angle of rotation

$=\dfrac{-1.2°\times 100}{0.5\times 6.15}=-39°$

133. (d): Let the % of (+)-2-butanol = σ

$\therefore$ % of (–)-2-butane = 1 – σ

$[\alpha]_D$ of (+)-2-butanol = +13.52°

$\therefore$ $[\alpha]_D$ of (–)-2-butanol = –13.52°

$\therefore$ $13.52\times\sigma+(-13.52)(1-\sigma)=-6.76°$

$\therefore$ $13.52\,\sigma-13.52°+13.52\sigma=-6.76°$

or $27.04\,\sigma=+13.52-6.76=+6.76$

$\therefore\ \sigma=\dfrac{+6.76}{27.04}=0.25$

Thus, % of (+)-2-butanol =25

$\therefore$ % of (–)-2-butanol = 100 – 25 = 75

Now 25% (+)-2-butanol + 25% (–)-2-butanol = 25% racemic mixture

$\therefore$ % of (–)butanol = 75 – 25 = 50%

Thus, the mixture consists of 50% of (–)-2-butanol + 25% racemic mixture, that is, option (d) is correct.

134. (c): The two enantiomers are present in 85% and 15% respectively, therefore, 15% out of 85% will form a racemic mixture with 15% of the other isomer. Therefore, enantiomeric excess (*ee*) = 85 – 15 = 70%).

135. (d): Directly proportional to both the lengths of the polarimeter tube and molar concentration of the compound.

136. (a): Optical isomers.

Mechanism and Stereochemistry of S_N1 and S_N2 Reactions

137. (c): The reactivity in S_N1 reactions depends upon the stability of the intermediate carbocations. Since the stability of the carbocations derived from (A), (B) and (C) follows the order:

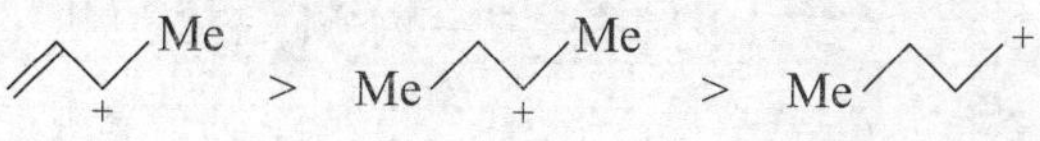

Allylic carbocation > 2° carbocation > 1° carbocation

therefore, S_N1 reactivity of these three bromides follows the order: B > C > A, that is, option (c) is correct.

138. (d): Since the reactivity in S_N1 reactions increases as the stability of the intermediate carbocation increases, therefore, $C_6H_5(CH_3)(C_6H_5)CBr$ (IV) which gives a 3° carbocation, $(C_6H_5)_2\overset{+}{C}(CH_3)$ is the most reactive. Of the two 2° bromides, the carbocation intermediate derived from $C_6H_5CH(C_6H_5)CBr$ (II), $C_6H_5\overset{+}{C}HC_6H_5$, is more stable as compared to the carbocation $C_6H_5\overset{+}{C}HCH_3$ obtained from $C_6H_5CH(CH_3)$Br (III) because it is stabilised by two phenyl groups due to resonance. The fourth bromide, $C_6H_5CH_2Br$ (I) which gives the 1° carbocation $C_6H_5\overset{+}{C}H_2$ is, however the least reactive. Therefore, the overall reactivity of these bromides towards

S_N1 reaction follows the order IV > II > III > I, that is, option (d) is correct.

139. (d): Reactivity in S_N1 reactions depends upon the stability of the carbocation intermediate. The stability of the carbocations increases in the order,

$$C_6H_5\overset{+}{C}H_2 < C_6H_5\overset{+}{C}HCH_3 < C_6H_5\overset{+}{C}HC_6H_5 < C_6H_5-\overset{+}{C}(CH_3)(C_6H_5)$$

Therefore, the alkyl halide $C_6H_5C(CH_3)(C_6H_5)Br$ is the most reactive. Thus, option (d) is correct.

140. (a): The inversion product exceeds the retention product, therefore, only partial racemisation is observed, that is, option (a) is correct.

141. (c): S_N1 reactions cause recemisation, therefore, the halide is most likely to be tertiary.

142. (a): Statements (iii) and (v) are not correct.

143. (d): 3-Methyl-3-bromohexane is a 3° alkyl halide and hence undergoes solvolysis (nucleophilic substitution reaction with the solvent) by S_N1 mechanism. S_N1 reactions do not involve inversion, therefore, option (d) is incorrect while all other options are correct.

144. (b): The stability of the cations decreases in the order:

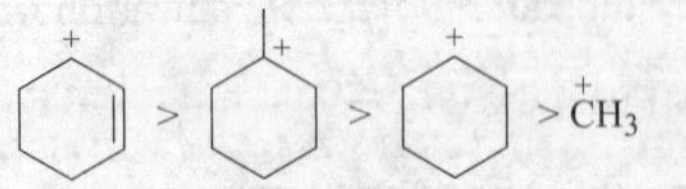

> > > $\overset{+}{C}H_3$

Therefore, the reactivity of the corresponding alkyl chlorides decreases in the same order: II> I > III > IV, that is, option (b) is correct.

145. (c): The stability of the cations decreases in the order:

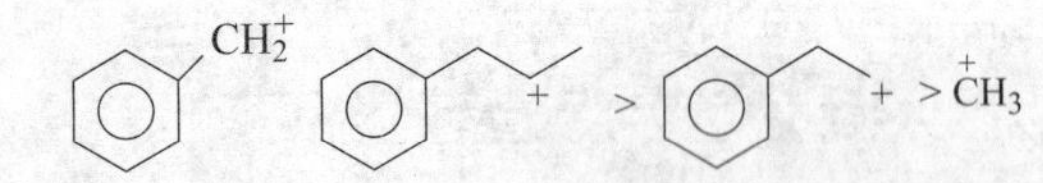

CH_2^+ > > $+ > \overset{+}{C}H_3$

Therefore, the reactivity of the corresponding halides decreases in the same order: III > I > II > IV, that is, option (c) is correct.

146. (c):

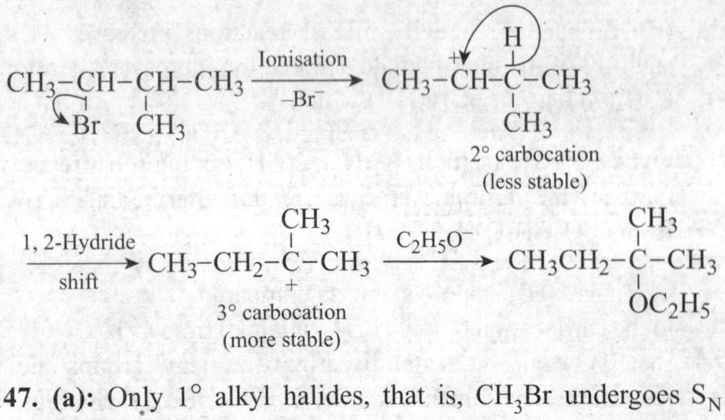

$$CH_3-CH(Br)-CH(CH_3)-CH_3 \xrightarrow[-Br^-]{\text{Ionisation}} CH_3-\overset{+}{C}H-C(H)(CH_3)-CH_3$$

2° carbocation (less stable)

$$\xrightarrow[\text{shift}]{\text{1, 2-Hydride}} CH_3-CH_2-\overset{+}{C}(CH_3)-CH_3 \xrightarrow{C_2H_5O^-} CH_3CH_2-C(CH_3)(OC_2H_5)-CH_3$$

3° carbocation (more stable)

147. (a): Only 1° alkyl halides, that is, CH_3Br undergoes S_N2 reactions.

148. (c): S_N2 reactions proceed through inversion of configuration.

149. (a): Methyl and 1° alkyl halides show complete stereochemical inversion in S_N2 reactions, that is, option (a) is correct.

150. (b):

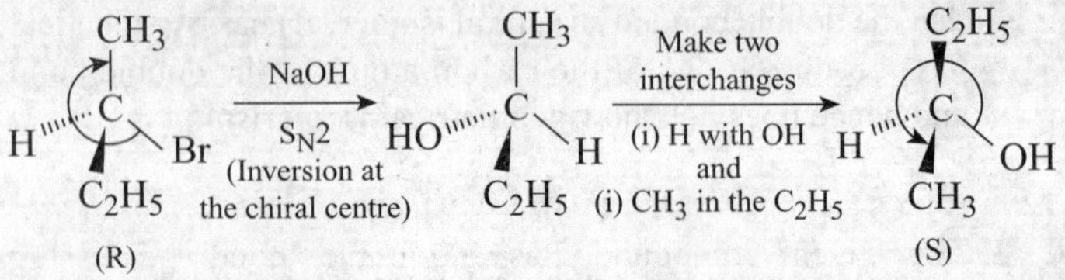

(R) [C with CH_3, H, Br, C_2H_5] $\xrightarrow[\text{(Inversion at the chiral centre)}]{\text{NaOH}, S_N2}$ [C with CH_3, HO, H, C_2H_5] $\xrightarrow[\text{(i) H with OH and (i) } CH_3 \text{ in the } C_2H_5]{\text{Make two interchanges}}$ [C with C_2H_5, H, OH, CH_3] (S)

Thus, option (b) is correct.

Alternatively, find the R and S notation for the starting material and the four products. That product which has opposite sign of stereochemical notation as compared to the starting material, is the correct product with inversion of configuration. Now the starting material and products (a), (c) and (d) have the same stereochemical notation, that is, R, while the product (b) has stereochemical notation S.

151. (b): Due to –I effect on the Ph group, the compound (II) has some small positive charge at the α-carbon. As a result, nucleophilic attack is facilitated. Thus, compound (II) is the most reactive in S_N2 reaction. The reactivity of the other three substrates depends upon the magnitude of steric hindrance. Steric hindrance increases in the order I, III < IV and hence the reactivity decreases in the opposite order I > III > IV. Combining the two trends, the overall reactivity of all the four alkyl halides decreases in the order II > I > III > IV, that is, option (b) is correct.

152. (c): Reactivity in S_N2 reactions decreases as steric hindrance increases, that is, option (c) is correct.

153. (b):

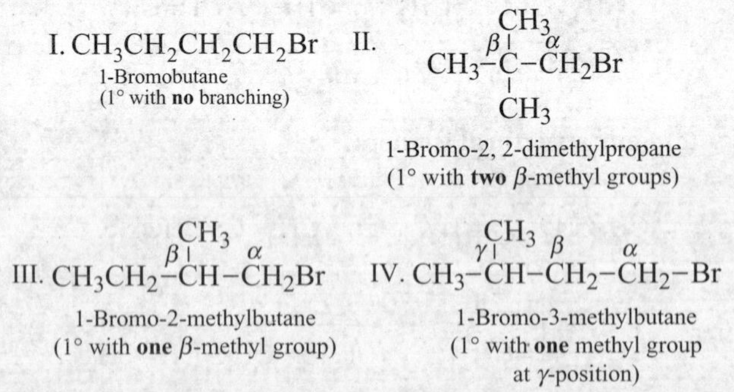

I. $CH_3CH_2CH_2CH_2Br$
1-Bromobutane (1° with **no** branching)

II. $CH_3-\overset{\beta}{C}(CH_3)_2-\overset{\alpha}{C}H_2Br$
1-Bromo-2, 2-dimethylpropane (1° with **two** β-methyl groups)

III. $CH_3CH_2-\overset{\beta}{C}H(CH_3)-\overset{\alpha}{C}H_2Br$
1-Bromo-2-methylbutane (1° with **one** β-methyl group)

IV. $CH_3-\overset{\gamma}{C}H(CH_3)-\overset{\beta}{C}H_2-\overset{\alpha}{C}H_2-Br$
1-Bromo-3-methylbutane (1° with **one** methyl group at γ-position)

In 1° alkyl halides, steric hindrance increases in the order *n*-alkyl halides, alkyl halides with one substituent at the γ-position, one substituent at the β-position, two substituents at the β-position; therefore, the reactivity decreases in the same order, that is, I > IV > III > II.

154. (c): The rate of S_N2 reaction is the maximum with 1° alkyl halides having the least steric hindrance. Out of CH_3CH_2Br and $CH_3CH_2CH_2Br$, CH_3CH_2Br has the least steric hindrance and hence has the highest relative rate.

155. (c): $CH_3CH_2CH_2Br$ being a 1° alkyl halide reacts with NaCN by S_N2 mechanism which is favoured by polar aprotic solvents, that is, DMF. Thus, option (c) is correct.

156. (c): 1° Alkyl halides which have negligible steric hindrance preferably undergo nucleophilic substitution at the fastest rate by S_N2 mechanism.

$$\text{Br}\text{-chain} \xrightarrow[S_N2]{\text{NaCN}} \text{HC-chain}$$

157. (c): 3° Alkyl halides undergo solvolysis by the S_N1 mechanism to give a substitution product. However, with strong nucleophiles, they prefer to undergo elimination to give alkenes.

$$CH_3-C(CH_3)_2-Br \xrightarrow[S_N1]{CH_3CH_2OH} CH_3-C(CH_3)_2-OCH_2CH_3$$

A (major product)

$$CH_3-C(CH_3)(CH_2-H)-Br \xrightarrow[-HBr]{CH_3CH_2\bar{O}Na^+} (CH_3)_2C=CH_2$$

B (major product)

Thus, option (c) is correct.

158. (c): Benzyl chloride on ionisation gives the stable benzyl cation, therefore, it undergoes substitution exclusively by the S_N1 mechanism.

159. (c): Aryl halides (chlorobenzene) are less reactive than alkyl and allyl halides.

160. (c): The stability of the carbocations increases in the order:

$$CH_2=\overset{+}{C}H < CH_3CH_2CH_2^+ < CH_2=CHCH_2^+$$

Therefore, the rate of hydrolysis of their corresponding halides increases in the same order, that is, option (c) is correct.

161. (b): The stability of the carbocations decreases in the order:

$Ph\overset{+}{C}HCH_3 > PhCH_2CH_2^+ > PhCH=\overset{+}{C}H_2$, therefore, the reactivity of their corresponding alkyl bromides decreases in the same order, that is, option (b) is correct.

162. (b): $CH_2=CH-\ddot{Cl}: \longleftrightarrow \;:\bar{C}H_2-CH=\overset{+}{Cl}:$
Due to resonance, the C – Cl bond has some double bond character and hence vinyl halides are much less reactive than alkyl and allyl halides towards nucleophilic substitution reactions.

163. (c): Forms three products pentane, butane and hexane.

164. (a): tert-Alkyl halides undergo hydrolysis by the S_N1 reaction.

165. (a): Carbocations.

166. (a): The stability of the carbocations increases in the order, 1° $(CH_3CH_2^+)$ < 2° $((CH_3)_2CH^+)$ < allyl $(CH_2 = CHCH_2^+)$ < benzyl $(C_6H_5CH_2^+)$, therefore, the reactivity in S_N1 reactions increases in the same order, that is, option (a) is correct.

167. (d): More stable the carbocation, the more reactive is the alkyl halide in S_N1 reactions. The stability of the carbocations decreases in the order,

$(C_6H_5)_2\overset{+}{C}(CH_3) > (C_6H_5)_2\overset{+}{C}H > (CH_3)_3\overset{+}{C} > (CH_3)_2\overset{+}{C}H > C_2\overset{+}{H}_5$, therefore, the reactivity of the alkyl halides decreases in the same order:
(iii) > (ii) > (i) > (iv) > (v).

Chemical Reactions of Haloalkenes (Aryl halides)

168. (c): Alkyl halides are the most reactive followed by vinyl halides while aryl halides are the least reactive towards nucleophilic substitution reactions. Therefore, in the following compound, sustitution occurs at the saturated carbon, that is, Cl is displaced to give product (III)

$$\text{Ar(I)}-C(Br)=CH-CH_2Cl \xrightarrow[\text{DMSO, heat}]{\text{NaCN}} \text{Ar(I)}-C(Br)=CH-CH_2CN \;(\text{III})$$

Thus, option (c) is correct.

169. (c): Benzyl halides are more reactive than aryl halides; therefore, the reaction occurs in the side chain.

$$p\text{-Br}C_6H_4CH_2Cl \xrightarrow{\text{Mg (1 mole)}} p\text{-Br}C_6H_4CH_2MgBr\ (A) \xrightarrow{D_2O} p\text{-Br}C_6H_4CH_2D\ (B)$$

170. (a): The stability of the carbocations increases in the order:

$$\text{phenyl}^+ < \text{cyclohexyl}^+ < \text{cyclohexyl}^+ < (CH_3)_3\overset{+}{C}$$

Therefore, the ease of hydrolysis of their corresponding bromides increases in the same order, (i) < (iii) < (ii) < (iv). Hence, option (d) is correct.

171. (a): The presence of electron withdrawing groups (NO_2, CN) at the *o*- and *p*-positions with respect to Cl activates it towards nucleophilic substitution reactions while the presence of electron-donating groups (CH_3, OCH_3) deactivates it towards nucleophilic substitution reactions. Thus, *p* -nitrochlorobenzene undergoes nucleophilic substitution reactions most easily. Thus, option (a) is correct.

172. (d): The order of reactivity follows the sequence benzyl halides > alkyl halides > aryl halides. Out of chlorides and bromides, bromides are more reactive, therefore, the correct order of reactivity is:
$PhCH_2Br$ (ii) > MeBr (i) . MeCl (iii) > p-$MeOC_6H_4Br$ (iv), that is, option (d) is correct.

173. (a): Cl in 2,4,6-trinitrochlorobenzene is activated by three NO_2 groups at the *o*- and *p*-positions and hence undergoes hydrolysis most readily.

174. (c): Electron withdrawing groups increase and electrondonating groups decrease the reactivity towards nucleophilic substitution. Thus, option (c), that is, (iv)>(iii)>(ii)>(i) is correct.

175. (d): Cl is actived towardsnucleophilic substitution reaction by the presence of NO_2 groups at the *o*- and *p*-positions and not at the *m*-position. Therefore, option (d), that is, 3-nitrochlorobenzene is the least reactive.

176. (b): Alkyl halides are more reactive than aryl halides. Among alkyl halides, 3° alkyl halides (III) are more reactive than 2° alkyl halides (IV). Among aryl halides, aryl halides having electronwithdrawing $-NO_2$ groups at the *o*- and *p*-positions (II) are more reactive than simple aryl halides (I). Thus, the overall reactivity increases in the order I < II < IV < III, that is, option (b) is correct.

177. (c): Cl is *o*, *p*-directing, therefore, a mixture of *o*-and *p*-chloroacetophenone is obtained.

178. (b): $-CCl_3$ group is *m*-directing.

179. (b): $C_6H_5Cl \xrightarrow{Mg} C_6H_5MgCl \xrightarrow{CH_3CH_2OH} \underset{\text{Benzene}}{C_6H_6} + CH_3CH_2OMgCl$

180. (b):

$$C_6H_5Cl + 2\,Na + ClCH_3 \xrightarrow[\text{Wurtz Fitting reaction}]{\text{Dry ether}} \underset{\text{Toluene}}{C_6H_5CH_3} + 2\,NaCl$$

181. (a): Chlorobenzene (least reactive), vinyl chloride (more reactive), chloroethane (most reactive).

182. (a): C_6H_5Cl being an aryl halide is the least reactive. Among the 1° alkyl halides, due to steric hindrance, $CH_3CH_2CH_2Cl$ is less reactive than CH_3Cl. Thus, the overall reactivity decreases in the order $CH_3Cl > CH_3CH_2CH_2Cl > C_6H_5Cl$, that is, option (a) is correct.

183. (d): Aralkyl halides are more reactive than aryl halides, therefore, only the halogen in the side chain is displaced.

m-Iodobenzyl chloride (CH_2Cl, I) $\xrightarrow[\text{DMF}]{\text{NaCN}}$ m-Iodobenzyl cyanide (CH_2CN, I)

184. (a): Benzyl halides are more reactive than aryl halides in S_N 2 reactions. Therefore, the reaction occurs in the side chain with inversion of configuration at the chiral centre. Thus, option (a) is correct

185. (c): Aralkyl halides are more reactive than aryl halides, therefore, only the halogen in the side chain is displaced.

o-Bromobenzyl chloride (Cl, Br) $\xrightarrow[\text{EtOH}]{NH_3}$ o-Bromobenzylamine (NH_2, Br)

Polyhalogen Compounds

186. (c): CH_3OH does not have the grouping CH_3CHOH- and hence does not give CHI_3 with I_2/NaOH (iodoform test).

187. (d): $3\,CCl_4 + 2\,SbF_3 \xrightarrow{SbCl_5} 3\,CCl_2F_2 + 2\,SbCl_3$

188. (c): DDT is formed, option (c) is correct.

189. (d): The halogen atom in vinyl chloride is the least reactive.

190. (d): $CH_3CH_2OH + 4\,Cl_2 + 6\,NaOH \xrightarrow{\Delta} \underset{\text{Chloroform}}{CHCl_3} + HCOONa + 5\,NaCl + 5\,H_2O$

191. (d):

$$\underset{\text{Bleaching powder}}{CaOCl_2} + H_2O \rightarrow Ca(OH)_2 + Cl_2$$

$$\underset{\text{Ethyl alcohol}}{CH_3CH_2OH} \xrightarrow{Cl_2} CH_3CHO \xrightarrow[\text{Halogenation}]{Cl_2}$$

$$\underset{\text{Chloral}}{CCl_3CHO} \xrightarrow[\text{(Hydrolysis)}]{Ca(OH)_2} \underset{\text{Chloroform}}{CHCl_3} + (HCOO)_2Ca$$

192. (b):

$$CHCl_3 + \frac{1}{2}O_2 \xrightarrow{hv} C(OH)Cl_3 \xrightarrow{-HCl} \underset{\text{Phosgene}}{COCl_2}$$

193. (d): C_2H_5OH reacts with poisonous $COCl_2$ gas to give diethylcarbonate which is not toxic.

$$\underset{\text{Phosgene}}{O{=}C(Cl)_2} + 2\,C_2H_5OH \longrightarrow \underset{\text{Diethyl carbonate}}{O{=}C(OC_2H_5)_2} + 2\,KCl$$

194. (d):

$$CHCl_3 \xrightarrow[-3KCl]{KOH} \underset{\text{Unstable}}{CH(OH)_3} \xrightarrow{-H_2O} \underset{\text{Formic acid}}{HCOOH}$$

Analysis of Haloalkanes and Haloarenes

195. (b): Benzyl chloride gets hydrolysed by H_2O at room temperature and hence gives a white precipitate with $AgNO_3$which is soluble in NH_4OH.

196. (a): Chlorobenzene does not undergo hydrolysis on warming with $AgNO_3$ solution and hence does not give a white precipitate of AgCl.

197. (a): Chlorobenzene.

198. (c): If $CHCl_3$ sample contains phosgene ($COCl_2$) then it will give a white precipitate when treated with $AgNO_3$ solution in the cold. However, after boiling $CHCl_3$ with alcoholic KOH, the resulting solution will always give a white precipitate with $AgNO_3$ solution whether it contains $COCl_2$ or not.

Final Preparation

199. (d): *o*-Substituted diphenyls having bulky substituents on both the *o*-positions of each benzene ring are optically active since the two benzene rings due to steric hindrance lie in perpendicular planes and their mirror images are non-superimposable as shown below.

Mirror

Br Br | Br Br

I I | I I

Enantiomers

200. (a): Conformational isomers which can be separated into rotational isomers because of large energy barriers (75–105 kJ mol^{-1}) due to steric hindrance are called atropisomers. For example, enantiomers of 6,6′-dinitrodiphenic acid.

201. (b): Enantiomers.

202. (d): Diphenyl derivative (b) is optically active since the presence of two bulky groups (SO_3H) cause enough steric hindrance; the two enantiomers can be separated. Like allenes, in spirans (c) also the substituents on each ring lie in perpendicular planes and hence they show optical activity. *Cis*-1,3-dimethylcyclopropane (d) is, however, optically inactive since it has a plane of symmetry.

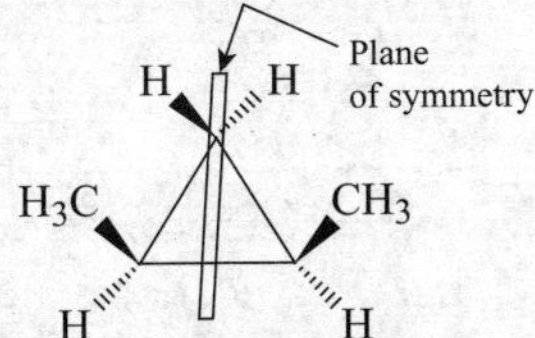

203. (a): A ring is equivalent to a double bond, therefore, substituents on the ring and the double bond lie in perpendicular planes. As a result, the molecule is optically active.

Mirror

H, HO (ring) =C(COOH)(H) | (H)(HOOC)C= (ring) H, OH

Non-superimposable mirror images—enantiomers.

204. (a): During this reaction, the bond to the chiral centre is not broken, therefore, in the product, retention of configuration of the reactant occurs.

205. (c): Since the compound thought to be optically active does not rotate the plane of polarised light, the compound must be a racemic mixture.

206. (c):

CHO / HO—C—CH_2OH / H $\xrightarrow[\text{(ii) Interchange } CH_2OH \text{ and OH}]{\text{(i) Interchange H and OH}}$ CHO / H—C—OH / CH_2OH

D-(+)-Glyceraldehyde

207. (b):

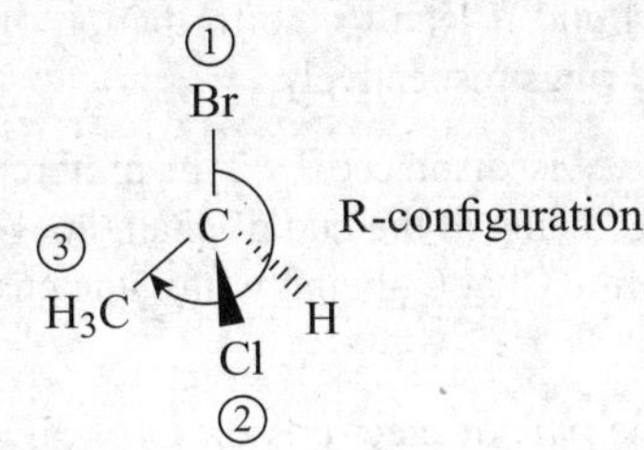

208. (b):

C_2H_5 / Cl—C—CH_3 / H

R-configuration

When atom of lowest priority lies on the vertical axis of the Fischer projection, the movement of arrow from priority ① → ② → ③ right away gives the stereochemical notation.

209. (a):

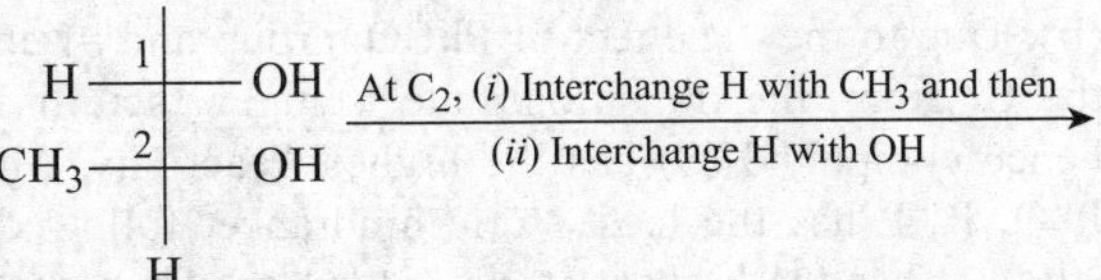

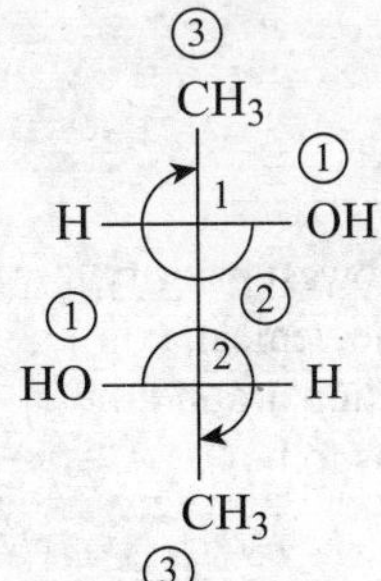

Change R to S since atom of lowest priority, that is H lies on the horizontal axis

Change R to S since atom of lowest priority, that is H lies on the horizontal axis

210. (d):

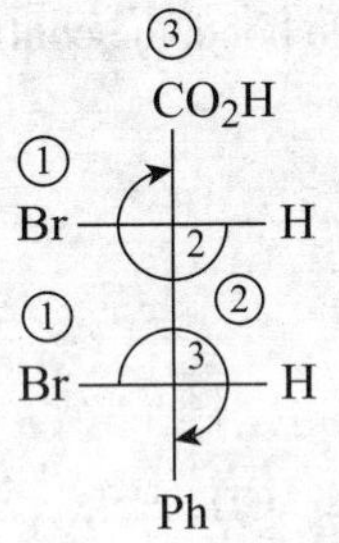

Change S to R since atom of lowest priority, that is H lies on the horizontal axis

Change R to S since atom of lowest priority, that is H lies on the horizontal axis

(2R, 3S)-configuration

211. (b):

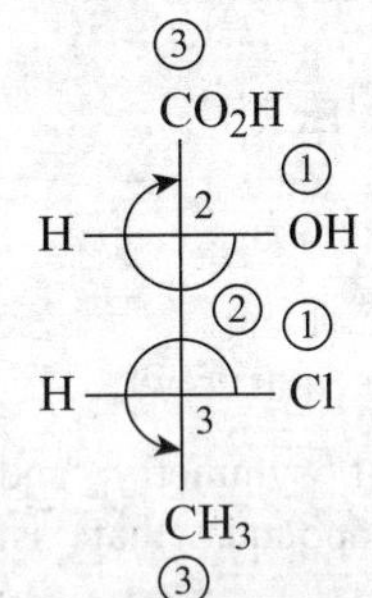

Change R to S since atom of lowest priority, that is H lies on the horizontal axis

Change S to R since atom of lowest priority, that is H lies on the horizontal axis

(2S, 3R)-Absolute configuration

212. (d):

or

Change S to R on the RHS chiral carbon since H the atom of lowest priority is above the plane of the paper.

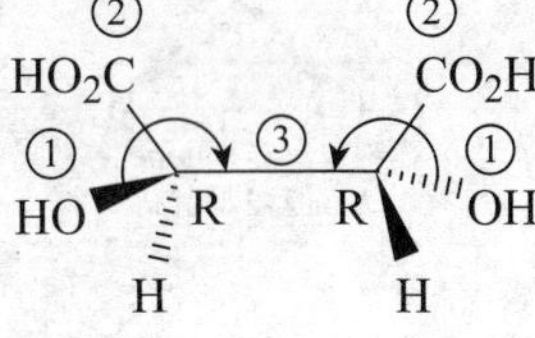

or

Change S to R on the RHS chiral carbon since the atom of lowest priority, that is, H makes two interchanges (that is, H with OH and then OH with CO_2H) on the RHS carbon. We have

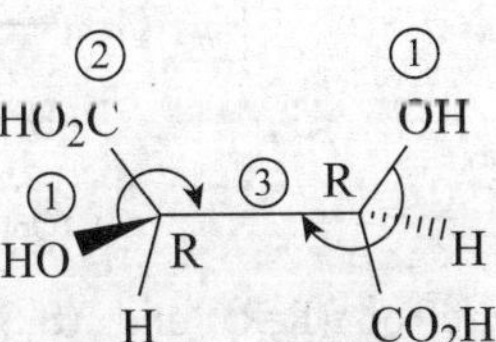

Thus, the absolute configuration of the given compound is R,R.

213. (c):

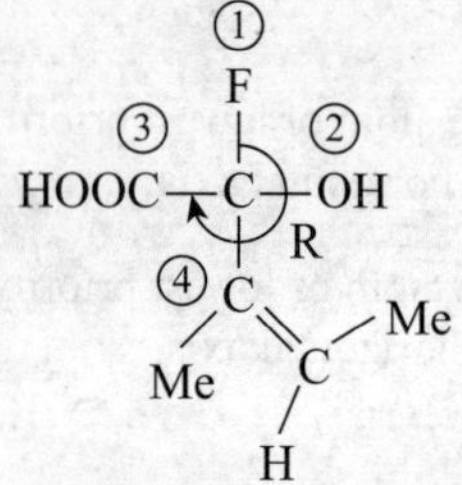

Since the group or lowest priority, that is, (4) lies on the venical axis therefore, configuration around the chiral centre remains to be R

(R, Z)-configuration

Further, since the groups of higher priority, that is, CHOH(F) COOH are on the same side of the double bond, the configuration around the double bond is Z.

214. (a):

trans-2-Butene $\xrightarrow[-Br^-]{Br-Br}$

(R, S)-2, 3-Dibromobutane (*meso*)

|||

(S, R)-2, 3-Dibromobutane (*meso*)

Both the structures have a centre of symmetry and hence they represent the same compound, that is, meso-(2R,3S)-dibromobutane.

215. (d):

cis-2-Butene or Z-2-Butene $\xrightarrow[-Br^-]{Br-Br}$

(R, S)-2, 3-Dibromobutane (Optically active)

(S, R)-2, 3-Dibromobutane (Optically active)

Thus, a mixture of (R,R) and (S,S)-2,3-dibromobutane (50% : 50%), that is, racemic mixture is obtained.

216. (c): (R,S)-2,3-Dibromobutane, that is, meso-2,3-dibromobutane is obtained.

217. (a): Elimination is the reverse of addition, that is, during elimination, trans-elimination of Br_2 occurs while during addition trans-addition of Br_2 occurs. Thus, optically active (+) or (–)-2,3-dibromobutane on elimination gives *cis*-2-butene.

218. (c):

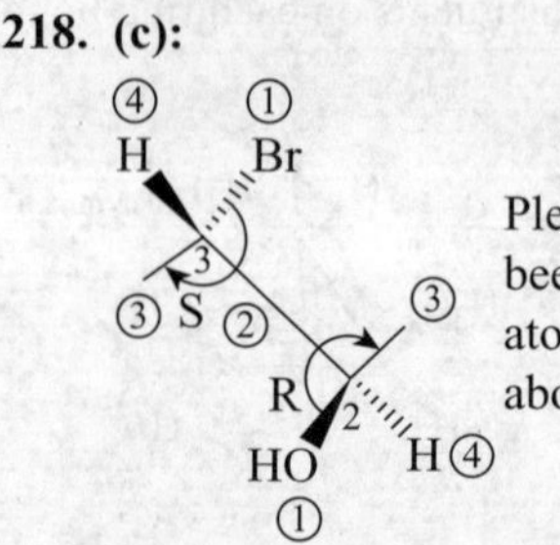

Please note that configuration at C_3 has been changed from R to S since the atom or lowest priority, that is, H lies above the plane of the paper

2R, 3S-3-Bromo-2-butanol

219. (a):

Make two interchanges CH_3 with Cl and then CH_3 with CHO

(2R, 4E)-4-Bromo-2-chloro-2-methylhex-4-enal

220. (c): Loss of BsO^- from III and I^- from VI leads to the formation of stable 5- and 6-membered rings respectively. Therefore, option (c) is correct.

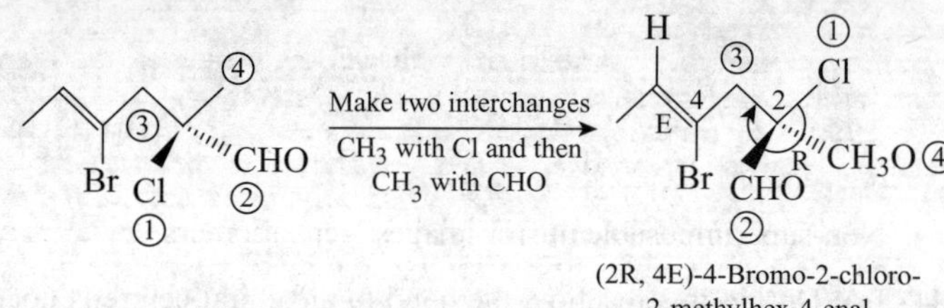

IV

In contrast, I and II lead to the formation of unstable 3-and 4-membered rings respectively.

221. (c): Cl and C_1 is displaced by I in preference to Cl at C_6 since Cl at C_1 being at the end of chain does not suffer steric hindrance while Cl at C_4 being within the chain suffers steric hindrance.

222. (b): The lone pair of electrons on O of HO compound (R) push the Cl out while no such help is available in other chlorides. Therefore, compound (R) is the most reactive. The reactivity of the remaining chlorides depends upon the magnitude of steric hindrance. The steric hindrance increases in going from P through Q to S, therefore, their reactivity decreases in the order P > Q > S. Thus, the overall reactivity of the four chlorides decreases in the order: R > P > Q > S, that is, option (b) is correct.

223. (b): Due to the –R effect of PhCO–group and –I effect of the Cl atom, the transition state is highly stabilised and hence compound (S) has the highest reactivity. Amongst P, Q, R; P has the least steric hindrance, followed by R while Q has the highest steric hindrance. Thus, reactivity decreases in the order S > P > R > Q, that is, option (b) is correct.

224. (d): Solvolysis occurs through the carbocation intermediate, that is, S_N1 mechanism.

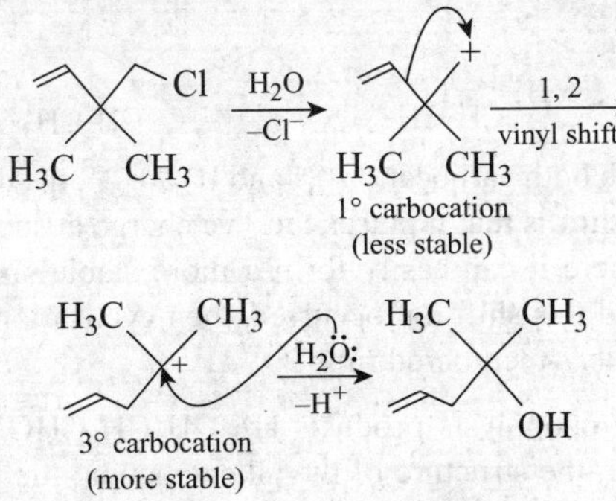

H_2O, $-Cl^-$; 1, 2 vinyl shift

H_3C CH_3 — 1° carbocation (less stable)

H_3C CH_3 — 3° carbocation (more stable); $H_2\ddot{O}$:, $-H^+$; OH

225. (d): Since the reaction with $SOCl_2$ is carried out in the absence of pyridine, S_NI reaction occurs with retention of configuration at the chiral centre, that is, option (d) is correct.

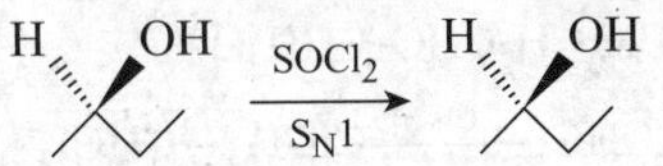

H OH $\xrightarrow[S_N1]{SOCl_2}$ H OH

226. (a):

CH_2Cl, H—C—CH_3, CH_2CH_3 $\xrightarrow[\text{acetone}, S_N2]{NaI}$ CH_2I, H—C—CH_3, CH_2Cl_3

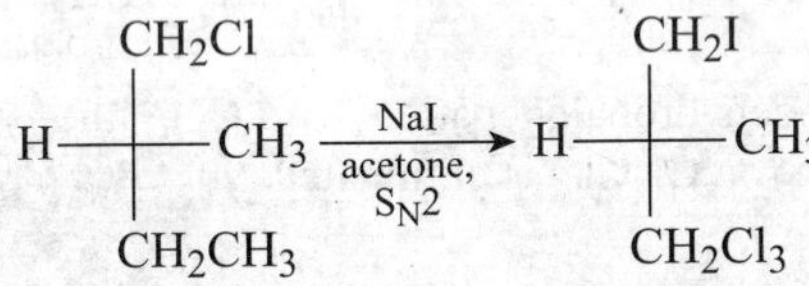

(R)-1-Chloro-3-methylpentane (R)-1-Iodo-3-methylpentane

In this reaction, the bond to the stereocentre is not broken, therefore, the original configuration, that is, R is retained.

227. (c): With $SOCl_2$, in the presence of pyridine, S_N2 reaction occurs and inversion of configuration occurs at the stereocentre, that is, option (c) is correct.

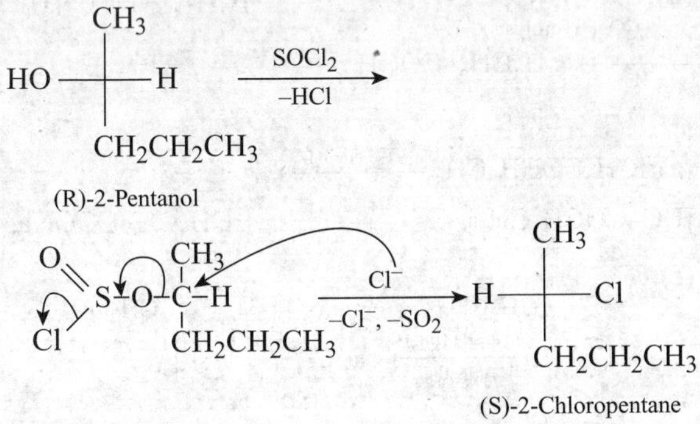

CH_3, HO—C—H, $CH_2CH_2CH_3$ $\xrightarrow[-HCl]{SOCl_2}$

(R)-2-Pentanol

O=S(Cl)—O—C(CH_3)—H, $CH_2CH_2CH_3$ $\xrightarrow[-Cl^-, -SO_2]{Cl^-}$ CH_3, H—C—Cl, $CH_2CH_2CH_3$

(S)-2-Chloropentane

228. (a):

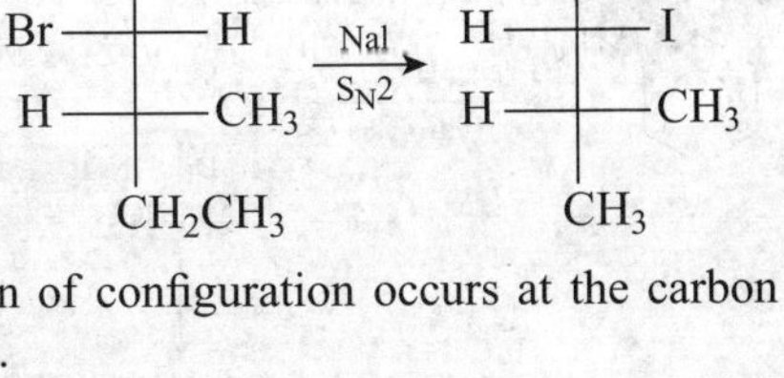

CH_3, Br—C—H, H—C—CH_3, CH_2CH_3 $\xrightarrow[S_N2]{NaI}$ CH_3, H—C—I, H—C—CH_3, CH_3

Inversion of configuration occurs at the carbon holding the Br atom.

229. (d):

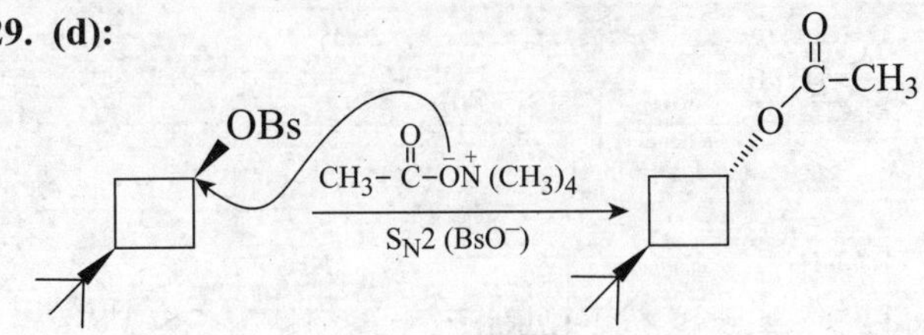

OBs $\xrightarrow[S_N2\ (BsO^-)]{CH_3-\overset{O}{\overset{\|}{C}}-\bar{O}\overset{+}{N}(CH_3)_4}$ O—C(=O)—CH_3

Inversion of configuration occurs at the chiral centre.

230. (d): In S_N2 reactions, inversion of configuration occurs, therefore, a single stereoisomer is produced. The stereoisomer is not the enantiomer of the reactant, therefore, a product with the opposite sign of rotation is not necessarily produced.

231. (b):

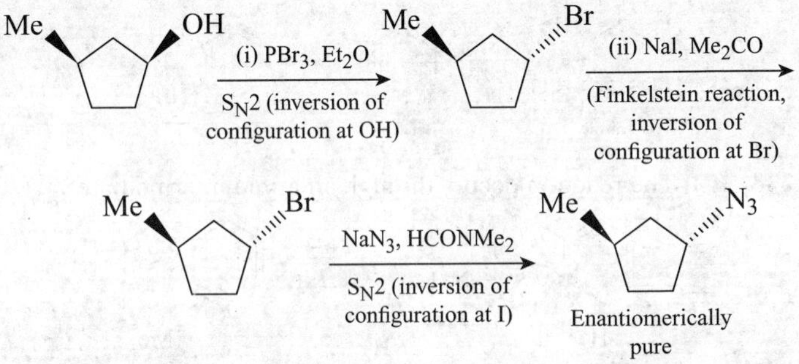

Me, OH $\xrightarrow[S_N2\ (\text{inversion of configuration at OH})]{(i)\ PBr_3, Et_2O}$ Me, Br $\xrightarrow[(\text{Finkelstein reaction, inversion of configuration at Br})]{(ii)\ NaI, Me_2CO}$

Me, Br $\xrightarrow[S_N2\ (\text{inversion of configuration at I})]{NaN_3, HCONMe_2}$ Me, N_3 — Enantiomerically pure

232. (b): II and IV are achiral molecules and their strucures do not permit rearrangement and hence they give the same product in S_N1 and S_N2 reactions. However, I and III are chiral molecules and hence give enantiomerically pure products in S_N2 reactions and racemic mixtures in S_N1 reactions.

233. (c):

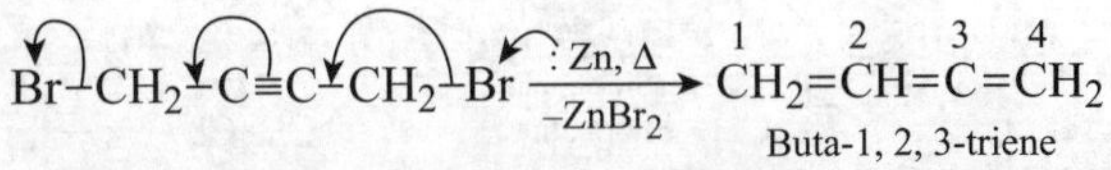

$$Br-CH_2-C\equiv C-CH_2-Br \xrightarrow[-ZnBr_2]{:Zn, \Delta} \overset{1}{C}H_2=\overset{2}{C}H=\overset{3}{C}=\overset{4}{C}H_2$$

Buta-1, 2, 3-triene

234. (a): 1° Alkyl halides undergo substitution while 3° alkyl halides undergo dehydrohalogenation.

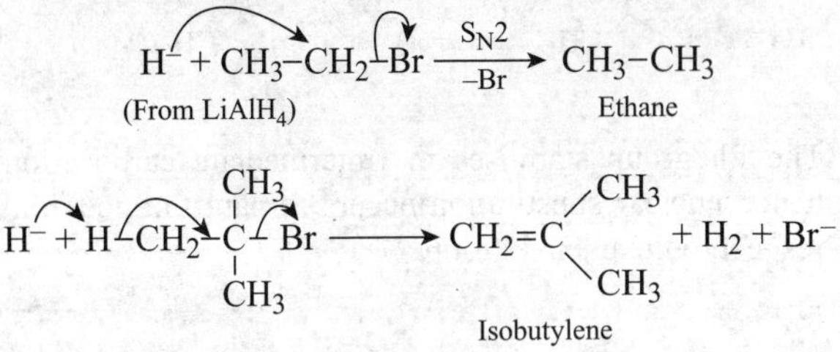

$$H^- + CH_3-CH_2-Br \xrightarrow[-Br]{S_N2} CH_3-CH_3$$

(From $LiAlH_4$) Ethane

$$H^- + H-CH_2-\underset{CH_3}{\overset{CH_3}{C}}-Br \longrightarrow CH_2=C(CH_3)_2 + H_2 + Br^-$$

Isobutylene

235. (c):

Cl, NO_2, NO_2 $\xrightarrow{^-OH}$ [Cl, OH, NO_2, NO_2 $\xrightarrow{-Cl^-}$ OH, NO_2, NO_2] $\xrightarrow[-H_2O]{NaOH}$ O^-Na^+, NO_2, NO_2

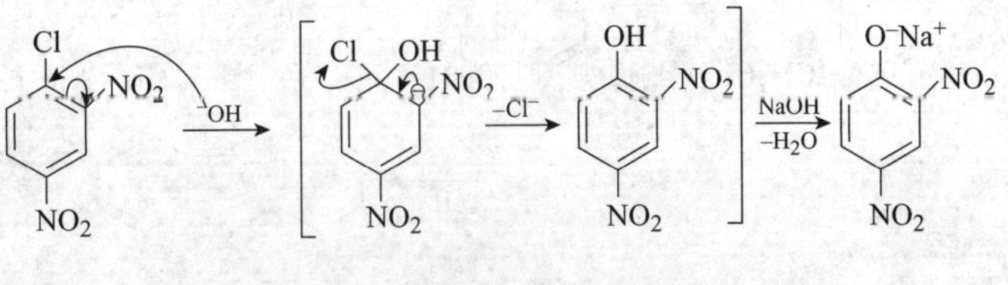

The reaction occurs by bimolecular nucleophilic substitution.

236. (b): The reaction occurs through benzyne intermediate as shown below.

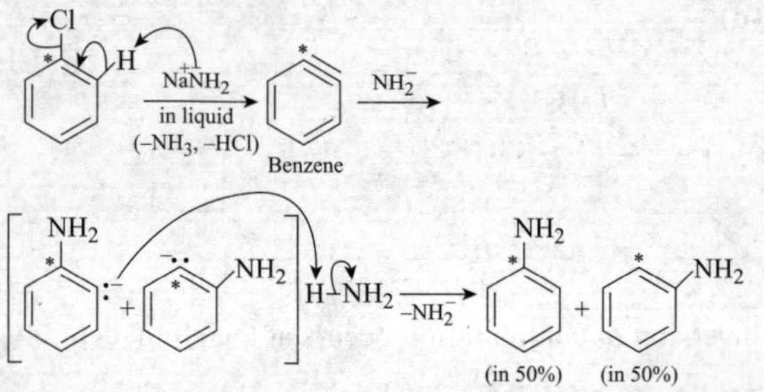

NaNH$_2$ in liquid (–NH$_3$, –HCl) Benzene; NH_2^-

(in 50%) (in 50%)

237. (d): *m*-Bromoanisole gives only the corresponding *m*-anisidine. This is a substitution reaction which occurs by elimination–addition (benzyne) mechanism as shown below.

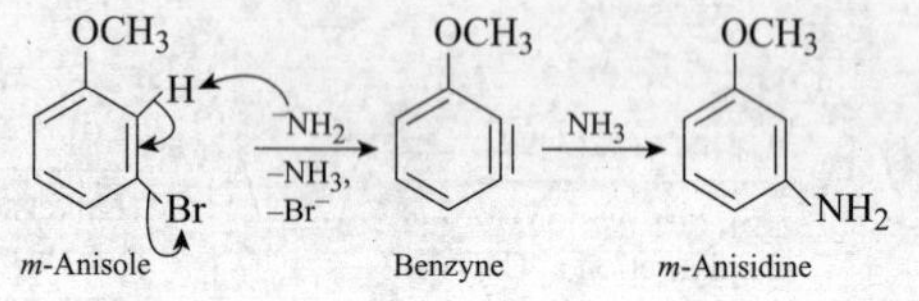

m-Anisole $\xrightarrow[-NH_3, -Br^-]{NH_2^-}$ Benzyne $\xrightarrow{NH_3}$ *m*-Anisidine

238. (d): The reaction occurs through an aryne intermediate.

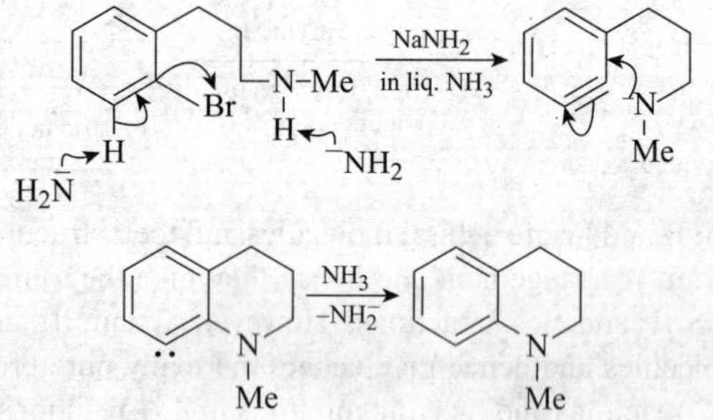

$\xrightarrow[\text{in liq. } NH_3]{NaNH_2}$ $\xrightarrow[-NH_2^-]{NH_3}$

239. (b):

$\xrightarrow[\text{(Side chain chlorination)}]{Cl_2/h\nu}$ (X)

$\xrightarrow[\text{(Nuclear chlorination)}]{Cl_2/AlCl_3}$ (Y)

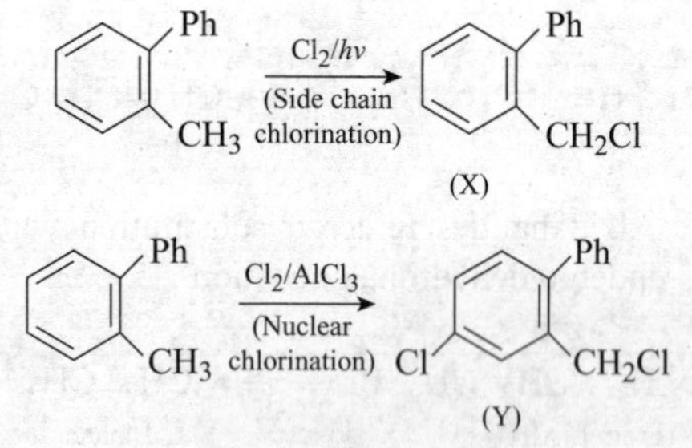

The Ph group stabilises the intermediate carbocation and hence nuclear substitution occurs at para the position with respect to the phenyl group.

240. (a):

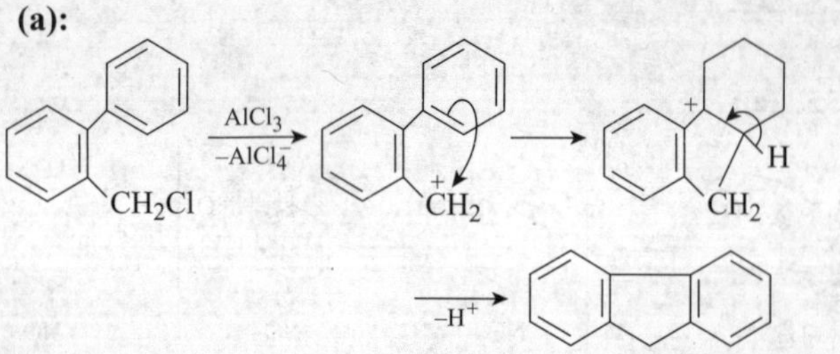

$\xrightarrow[-AlCl_4^-]{AlCl_3}$ $\longrightarrow$ $\xrightarrow{-H^+}$

241. (b):

$\xrightarrow[-AlCl_4^-]{\text{Anhyd. } AlCl_3}$ I II $\xrightarrow{-H^+}$

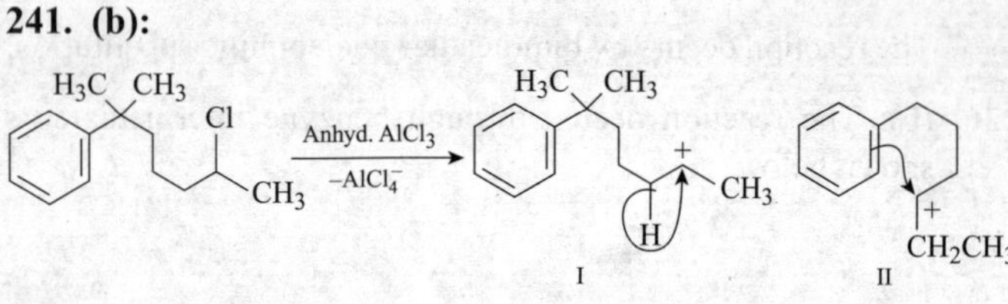

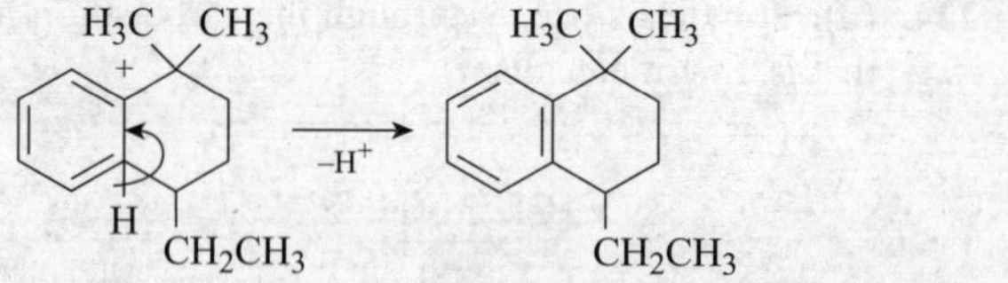

Although both carbocations (I and II) are 2°, the driving force for this shift is that it places the +ve charge at such a position from where it can easily form a more stable six-membered ring. Had this shift not occurred, then cyclisation will give a less stable 7-membered ring.

242. (a): The ozonolysis products are CH_3CH_2CHO and CH_2O, therefore, the structure of the alkene having the MF C_4H_8 is $CH_3CH_2CH{=}CH_2$. If the structure of the alkene is 1-butene, the structure of the alkyl bromide giving it on treatment with alcoholic KOH must be 1-bromobutane.

$$CH_3CH_2CH_2CH_2Br \xrightarrow{\text{KOH alc.}} CH_3CH_2CH{=}CH_2 \xrightarrow{O_3/Zn} CH_3CH_2CHO + CH_2O$$

243. (b): $CH_2 = CHCl \xrightarrow{Cl_2} \underset{(X)}{ClCH_2-CHCl_2} \xrightarrow[-HCl]{Ca(OH)_2,\ 363\ K} \underset{\text{1, 1–Dichloroethene}}{CH_2 = CCl_2}$

During dehydrohalogenation of (X), the more acidic hydrogen (on $CHCl_2$) is eliminated.

244. (b):

$$\underset{(A)}{C_6H_5NH_2} + \underset{(B)}{CHCl_3} \xrightarrow{\text{Alc.KOH}} C_6H_5NC$$

$$\underset{(C)}{CH_3CH_2OH} \xrightarrow[-2HCl]{Cl_2} [CH_3CHO] \xrightarrow[-3HCl]{3Cl_2}$$

$$\underset{\text{Chloral}}{CCl_3.CHO} \xrightarrow{Ca(OH)_2} \underset{(B)}{CHCl_3}$$

245. (d): $\underset{(X)}{CH_3CH_2CCl_2CH_3} \xrightarrow[\text{(Hydrolysis)}]{\text{Aq. NaOH}} [CH_3CH_2-C(OH)_2-CH_3] \xrightarrow{-H_2O} \underset{(Y)}{CH_3CH_2-COCH_3} \xrightarrow{I_2/NaOH} CHI_3$

246. (a): $ICH_2COCH_2CH_3 \xrightarrow[\Delta]{I_2/NaOH} [I_3C-COCH_2CH_3] \xrightarrow{NaOH} CHI_3 + CH_3CH_2COONa$

247. (c):

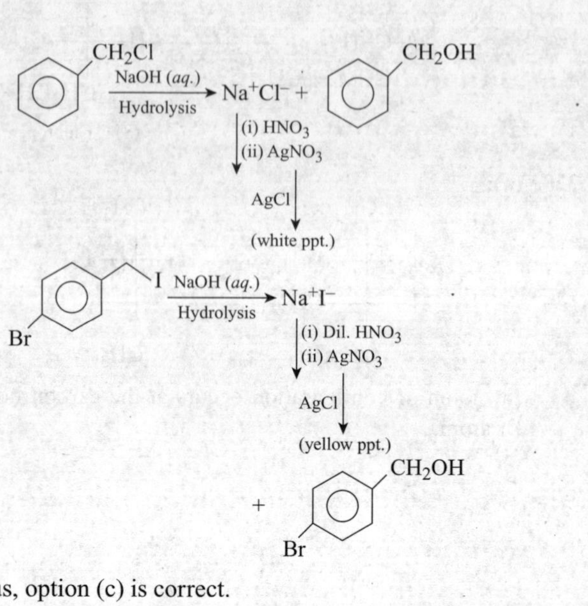

$C_6H_5CH_2Cl \xrightarrow[\text{Hydrolysis}]{NaOH\ (aq.)} Na^+Cl^- + C_6H_5CH_2OH$

Na^+Cl^- $\xrightarrow{\text{(i) } HNO_3 \text{ (ii) } AgNO_3}$ AgCl (white ppt.)

$p\text{-}BrC_6H_4CH_2I \xrightarrow[\text{Hydrolysis}]{NaOH\ (aq.)} Na^+I^-$ $\xrightarrow{\text{(i) Dil. } HNO_3 \text{ (ii) } AgNO_3}$ AgI (yellow ppt.) + $p\text{-}BrC_6H_4CH_2OH$

Thus, option (c) is correct.

248. (b): Since B gives a yellow precipitate with $AgNO_3/HNO_3$, B must be $C_6H_5CH_2I$ and hence A is C_6H_5I.

249. (c): Allylic chlorides are the most reactive.

250. (d):

$$CH_3-\underset{H}{\overset{CH_3}{C}}-CH=CH_2 \xrightarrow[-Br^-]{HBr} CH_3-\underset{H}{\overset{CH_3}{C}}-\overset{+}{C}H-CH_3 \xrightarrow[\text{shift}]{\text{1, 2-Hydride}}$$

3-Methylbut-l-ene; 2° carbocation (less stable)

$$CH_3-\overset{CH_3}{\underset{+}{C}}-CH_2-CH_3 \xrightarrow{Br^-} CH_3-\underset{Br}{\overset{CH_3}{C}}-CH_2CH_3$$

3° carbocation (more stable); 2-Bromo-2-methylbutane

251. (d):

$$C_6H_5-CH_2-CH=CH_2 \xrightarrow{H^+} C_6H_5-\underset{H}{CH}-\overset{+}{C}H-CH_3 \xrightarrow[\text{shift}]{\text{1, 2-Hydride}}$$

$$C_6H_5-\overset{+}{C}H-CH_2CH_3 \xrightarrow{Cl^-} C_6H_5-\underset{Cl}{CH}-CH_2CH_3$$

252. (b):

$$C_6H_5-CH_2-CH=CH-CH_3 \xrightarrow[Cl^-]{H^+} C_6H_5-CH_2-\overset{+}{C}H-CH_2-CH_3 \xrightarrow[\text{shift}]{\text{1, 2-Hydride}}$$

2° carbocation (less stable)

$$C_6H_5-\overset{+}{C}H-CH_2CH_2CH_3 \xrightarrow{Cl^-} C_6H_5-\underset{Cl}{CH}-CH_2CH_2CH_3$$

2° carbocation stabilised by resonance over the benzene ring

253. (a):

$$CH_3-\underset{CH_3}{\overset{CH_3}{C}}-Cl \xrightarrow[-HCl]{\text{KOH alc.}} CH_3-\overset{CH_3}{C}=CH_2 \xrightarrow[475\ K]{SO_2Cl_2} CH_3-\overset{CH_2Cl}{C}=CH_2$$

2° carbocation (less stable); 3-Chloro-2-methylpropene

254. (b): $C_6H_5CH_2CH_3 \xrightarrow[-SO_2,-HCl]{SO_2Cl_2} C_6H_5-CHCl-CH_3 \xrightarrow[-HCl]{\text{alc. KOH}} C_6H_5CH=CH_2$

255. (c): The mechanism of allylic bromination is

Methylenecyclohexane $\xrightarrow[\text{-HBr (Allylic bromination)}]{\dot{B}r}$ radical I $\leftrightarrow$ radical II (1-methylenylcyclohexene radical, $\dot{C}H_2$) $\xrightarrow[-\dot{B}r]{Br_2}$ 1-(bromomethyl)cyclohexene (CH_2Br)

Since an endocyclic (within ring) double bond is more stable than an exocyclic (outside ring) double bond, the initially formed less stable free radical (I) gets converted into the more stable free radical (II) which then reacts with Br_2 to give the product.

256. (b):

4-tert-Butylcyclohexene $\xrightarrow[\text{-HBr (Allylic bromination)}]{NBS/h\nu}$ 1a + 1b (each with its resonance structure)

Allylic bromination occurs through a free radical intermediate. Out of the two possible allylic free radicals (Ia and Ib), free radical (Ia) is stabilised by two equivalent resonance structures but free radical (Ib is stabilised by two non-equivalent resonance structures. In other words, free radical (Ia) is more stable and hence gives the allylic bromide (II) on treatement in Br_2 (obtained from NBS and HBr) which upon subsequent hydrolysis gives the allylic alcohol (III).

1b $\xrightarrow[-Br^{\bullet}]{Br-Br}$ II (Br) $\xrightarrow[\text{(Hydrolysis)}]{H_2O/Na_2CO_3}$ III (OH)

257. (d):

$$CH_3CH=CH_2 \xrightarrow[\text{(Allylic bromination)}]{NBS} BrCH_2CH=CH_2 \xrightarrow[-AgBr]{AgCN} CH_2CHCH_2NC$$

Allyl isocyanide

258. (d):

$$\underset{\text{1-Butene}}{CH_3CH_2CH=CH_2} \xrightarrow[\text{(Anti-Mark. addition)}]{HBr/H_2O_2} CH_3CH_2CH_2CH_2Br \xrightarrow[\text{(Finkelstein reaction)}]{KI/acetone} \underset{\text{1-Iodobutane}}{CH_3CH_2CH_2CH_2I}$$

259. (c):

$$\underset{\text{Silver propanoate}}{2CH_3CH_2COOAg} + I_2 \xrightarrow[\text{(Birnbaum-Silmonini reaction)}]{CCl_4} \underset{\text{Ethyl propanoate}}{CH_3CH_2COOC_2H_5} + CO_2 + 2AgI$$

This is an example of Birnbaum–Simonini reaction.

260. (d):

$$CH_3-\underset{CH_3}{\overset{CH_3}{C}}-CH_2OH \xrightarrow[\text{or HCl, }\Delta\text{ or } SOCl_2/\text{pyridine}]{PCl_5,\ \Delta} \left[CH_3-\underset{CH_3}{\overset{CH_3}{C}}-\overset{+}{C}H_2 \rightarrow CH_3-\overset{CH_3}{\underset{+}{C}}-CH_2CH_3\right] \xrightarrow{Cl^-} CH_3-\underset{Cl}{\overset{CH_3}{C}}-CH_2CH_3$$

Neopentyl alcohol

Free radicals, on the order hand, do not undergo rearrangement and hence the best method of preparation is through free radical chlorination of neopentane.

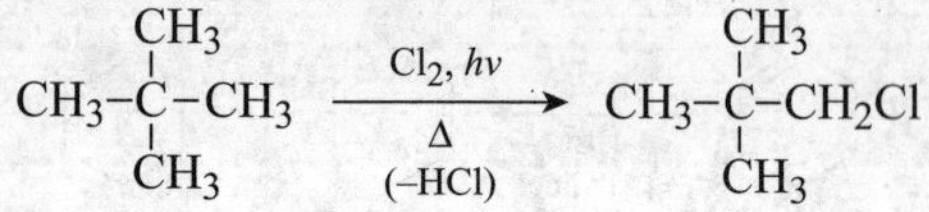

$$CH_3-C(CH_3)_2-CH_3 \xrightarrow[\Delta\ (-HCl)]{Cl_2,\ h\nu} CH_3-C(CH_3)_2-CH_2Cl$$

261. (b):

Toluene $\xrightarrow[-3\ HCl\ (\text{Side chain halogenation})]{3\ Cl_2,\ \Delta}$ $C_6H_5CCl_3$ (A) $\xrightarrow[(\text{Nuclear halogenation})]{Br_2/Fe}$ m-Br$C_6H_4CCl_3$ $\xrightarrow[(\text{Hydrogenolysis of more reactive C–Cl bonds})]{Zn/HCl}$ m-Br$C_6H_4CH_3$ (C)

m-Bromotoluene

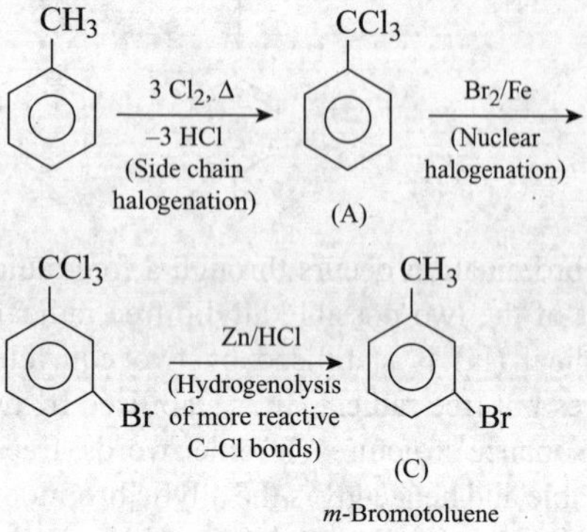

262. (c): $C_6H_5-CH_3 \xrightarrow[(\text{Benzylic bromination})]{NBS} C_6H_5CH_2Br$

Toluene → Phenylbromomethane

263. (d):

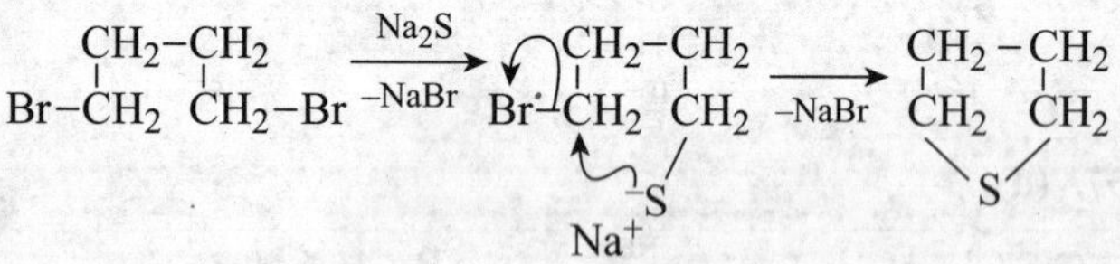

$BrCH_2-CH_2-CH_2-CH_2Br \xrightarrow[-NaBr]{Na_2S} BrCH_2CH_2CH_2CH_2S^-Na^+ \xrightarrow{-NaBr}$ tetrahydrothiophene (ring of CH_2-CH_2, CH_2, CH_2, S)

264. (b):

$C(CH_2Br)_4 \xrightarrow[(\text{Intramolecular Wurtz reaction})\ (-4\ NaBr)]{Na/ether,\ \Delta}$ Spiro [2, 2] pentane

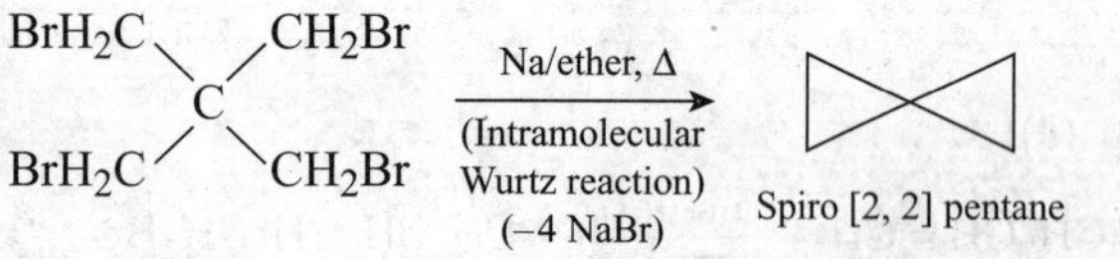

265. (c): Statement (i) is wrong since *o*-substituted biphenyls and 1,3-disubstituted alkenes which do not contain asymmetric carbons are chiral. Thus, option (c) is correct.

266. (b): Compounds (a), (c) and (e) have one chiral centre and hence are opticaly active.

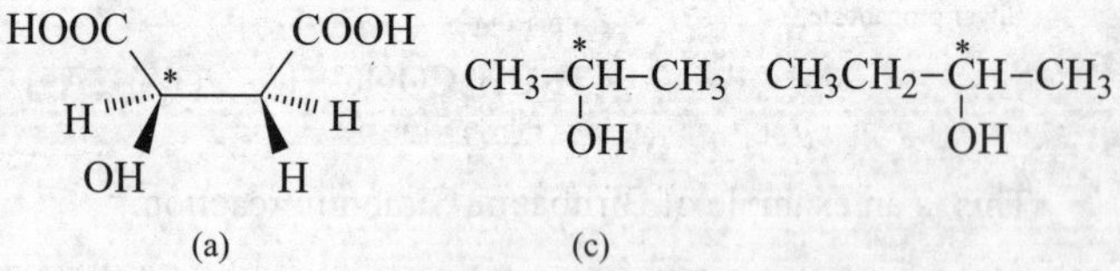

(a): HOOC–C*H(OH)–C(H)=... with COOH, H; (c): $CH_3-\overset{*}{C}H(OH)-CH_3$; $CH_3CH_2-\overset{*}{C}H(OH)-CH_3$

Compounds (d) and its miror image are non-superimposable and hence it is optically active.

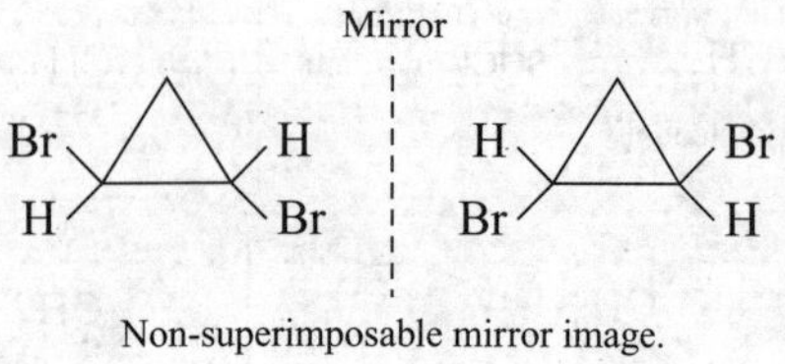

Mirror

(1,2-dibromocyclopropane: Br, H / H, Br | H, Br / Br, H)

Non-superimposable mirror image.

Compound (b) is optically inactive because it has a centre of symmetry.

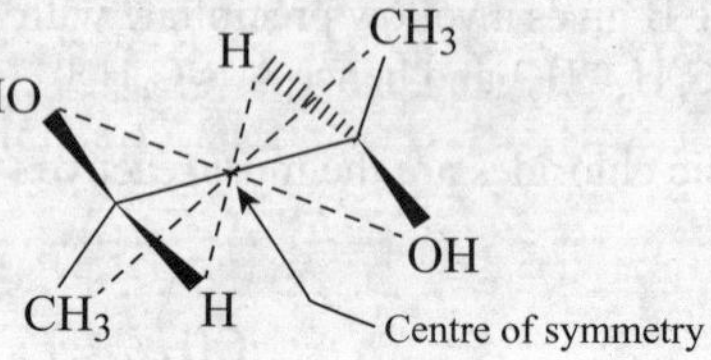

(HO, H, CH₃ / CH₃, H, OH — Centre of symmetry)

267. (a):

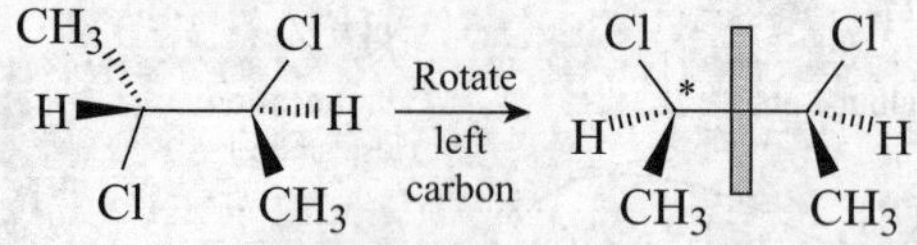

CH_3, H, Cl / Cl, H, CH_3 $\xrightarrow{\text{Rotate left carbon}}$ Cl, H, CH_3 * | Cl, H, CH_3

Rotate left the carbon compound (a), the resulting structure has a plane of symmetry and hence represents the meso-isomer. Compound (b) does not have a plane of symmetry and hence is not a meso compound.Compound (c) and (d) do not have identical chiral carbons and hence cannot represent meso isomers.

268. (b):

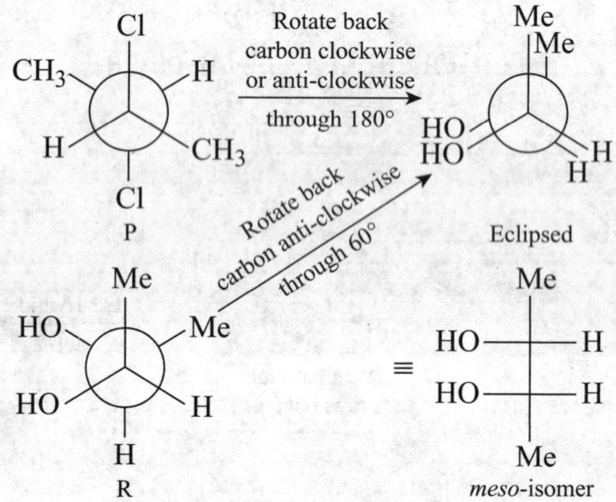

P (Newman: Cl; CH_3, H; H, CH_3; Cl) $\xrightarrow{\text{Rotate back carbon clockwise or anti-clockwise through 180°}}$ Eclipsed (Me, Me; HO, HO; H, H)

R (Newman: Me; HO, Me; HO, H; H) $\xrightarrow{\text{Rotate back carbon anti-clockwise through 60°}}$ Eclipsed

≡ Me; HO–C–H; HO–C–H; Me

meso-isomer

269. (d): Due to the presence of a lone pair of electrons on nitrogen, compounds (a), (b) and (c) undergo nitrogen inversion and hence do not show enantiomerism. In compound (d), the lone pair is involved in covalent bond formation and hence is not available for nitrogen inversion. As a result, it shows enantiomerism.

270. (a): Cumulenes containing an odd number of double bonds show *cis–trans* isomerism while those with an even number of carbons are optically inactive while (b) is optically active. Further, due to steric hindrance by the substituents (a and b) at *o*-positions (with substituents d and e present on N), the molecule (c) and its mirror image are non-superimposable and hence it shows optical isomerism.

271. (b): As a result of the presence of CH_3 groups at both the *o*-positions in one ring, compound (b) and its mirror image become superimposable and hence compound (b) is optically inactive. Please note that due to ring strain, the rate of nitrogen inversion is slowed down and hence aziridine (d) has been resolved into enantiomers at room temperature. In other words, aziridine (d) is also optically active.

MATCH THE FOLLOWING

272. (d): (A)—(p) (3); (B)—(s) (2); (C)—(r) (1); (D)—(q) (0)

273. **(a):** (A, $CH_3CH_2CH_2Cl$)—(r, Finkelstein reaction);
(B, CH_3CH_2Cl)—(s, Swarts reaction);
(C,RCOOAg)—(p,Hunsdiecker reaction);
(D, C_6H_5Br)—(q, Fitting reaction)

274. **(d):** (A, CH_3COOAg)—(q, I_2); (B, $CH_3CH=CH_2$)—(r, NBS);
(C, CH_3CH_2Cl)—(s, Hg_2F_2);
(D, C_6H_5COOAg)—(p, Br_2)

275. **(b):** (A, RX + AgCN)—(q, R–N→C);
(B, RX + KCN)—(p, R–C≡N);
(C, RX + KNO_2)—(s, R–O–N=O);
(D, RX + $AgNO_2$)—(r, R–NO_2)

276. **(b):** (A, chlorobenzene)—(s, benzyne mechanism);
(B, MeIH → HSHMe)—(p,S_N2);
(C, $(CH_3)_3CBr$)—(q,S_N1);
(D, *p*-chloronitrobenzene)—(r, aromatic bimolecular mechanism)

ASSERTION REASON

277. **(b): Correct explanation.** In CH_3OH, the nucleophiles are solvated by H-bonding while in DMF, nucleophiles exist as free anions. Free anions have a far greater nucleophilicity than solvated anions, therefore, the rate of hydrolysis of CH_3Cl is much higher in DMF than in CH_3OH.

278. **(a):** R is the correct explanation of A.

279. **(c): Correct R.** The reaction follows S_N1 mechanism.

280. **(d): Correct A.** 2-Bromobutane on reaction with sodium ethoxide in ethanol gives 2-butene as the major product.
Correct R. 2-Butene is more stable than 1-butene.

281. **(c): Correct R.** In E_2 elimination reaction, the base preferentially abstracts that β-H which gives the more stable product.

282. **(a):** R is the correct explanation of A.

283. **(a):** R is the correct explanation of A.

284. **(d): Correct A.** Neopentyl alcohol on treatment with conc. HCl gives 2-chloro-2-methylbutane.
Correct R. Neopentyl cation rearranges to form 2-methyl-butyl carbocation.

285. **(a):** R is the correct explanation of A.

286. **(c): Correct R.** NaCl/NaBr is insoluble in acetone but NaI is soluble.

287. **(d): Correct A.** Chlorination of ethylbenzene with Cl_2 in the presence of heat and light mainly yields 1-chloro-1-phenylethane.
Correct R. The reaction occurs through the intermediate formation of $PhCHCH_3$ radical.

288. **(a):** R is the correct explanation of A.

289. **(b): Correct explanation.** *p*-Dichlorobenzene being more symmetrical than the corresponding *o*-isomer fits closely in the crystal lattice. Consequently, intermolecular forces of attraction are much stronger in the *p*-isomer than in the *o*-isomer and hence the *p*-isomer is less soluble compared to the *o*-isomer,

290. **(a):** R is the correct explanation of A.

291. **(c): Correct R:** Due to resonance, the C–Cl bond in vinyl chloride has some double bond character and hence is stronger than the C–Cl bond in ethyl chloride

292. **(b): Correct explanation.** Due to steric hindrance, tertiary haloalkanes undergo elimination reactions much more readily than primary haloalkanes.

293. **(a):** R is the correct explanation of A.

Alcohols, Phenols and Ethers

11.1 Introduction

Alcohols and phenols may be regarded as monohydric, dihydric, trihydric or polyhydric according to whether they contain one, two, three or more hydroxyl groups respectively in their molecules.

CH_3CH_2OH	CH_2OH–CH_2OH	CH_2OH–$CHOH$–CH_2OH	CH_2OH–$(CHOH)_4$–CH_2OH
Ethyl alcohol (*Monohydric*)	Glycol (*Dihydric*)	Glycol (*Trihydric*)	Alditol (*Polyhydric*)

$R–CH_2OH$	R_2CHOH (2°)	$R_3C–OH$ (3°)
Primary alcohol	Secondary alcohol	Tertiary alcohol

Phenols are hydroxyl derivatives of aromatic hydrocarbons in which the hydroxyl group (–OH) is directly attached to the carbon atom of the aromatic ring.

Phenol; 2-Bromophenol (*o*-Bromophenol); 2-Methylphenol (or *o*-Methyl phenol or *o*-Cresol); 3-Methylphenol (or *m*-Methylphenol or *m*-Cresol)

Phenol (*Monohydric*); 1, 2-Benzenediol (Catechol) (*Dihydric*); 1, 3-Benzenediol (Resorcinol) (*Dihydric*); 1, 4-Benzenediol (Hydroquinone or quinol) (*Dihydric*); 1, 2, 4-Benzenetriol (Hydroxyquinol) (*Trihydric*)

11.2 Methods of Preparation of Alcohols

11.2.1 From Haloalkanes

Haloalkanes, when boiled with aqueous NaOH or KOH or moist silver oxide (AgOH), give alcohols.

$$\underset{\text{Haloalkane}}{RX} + KOH(aq) \xrightarrow{\Delta} \underset{\text{Alcohol}}{ROH} + KX$$

Example, $$\underset{\text{Bromoethane}}{C_2H_5Br} + KOH(aq) \xrightarrow{\Delta} \underset{\text{Ethanol}}{C_2H_5OH} + KBr$$

$$\underset{\text{2-Bromopropane}}{CH_3–CHBr(CH_3)} + KOH(aq) \xrightarrow{\Delta} \underset{\text{Propan-2-ol}}{CH_3–CHOH(CH_3)} + KBr$$

$$\underset{\text{Bromoethane}}{C_2H_5Br} + \underset{\text{Moist silver oxide}}{AgOH} \rightarrow \underset{\text{Ethanol}}{C_2H_5OH} + AgBr$$

$$\underset{\text{Iodoethane}}{CH_3I} + \underset{\text{Moist silver oxide}}{AgOH} \rightarrow \underset{\text{Methanol}}{CH_3OH} + AgI$$

Primary haloalkanes give a good yield of alcohols. However, tertiary haloalkanes in this reaction give mainly alkanes due to dehydrohalogenation. Secondary haloalkanes give a mixture of the alcohol and alkene.

$$\underset{\text{Primary alcohol}}{CH_3–C(CH_3)(Br)–CH_3} + KOH(aq) \longrightarrow \underset{\substack{\text{2-Methylpropene} \\ \text{(Major product)}}}{CH_3–C(CH_3)=CH_2} + KBr + H_2O$$

11.2.2 Reduction of Aldehydes and Ketones

Alcohols are easily prepared by the reduction of aldehydes and ketones. During reduction, aldehydes give primary alcohols while ketones give secondary alcohols. For example,

$$\underset{\text{Aldehyde}}{RCHO} \xrightarrow[\text{LiAlH}_4 \text{ or NaBH}_4]{H_2\text{(Ni or Pt or Pd)}\ \text{Na}/C_2H_5OH,} \underset{\text{Primary alcohol}}{RCH_2OH}$$

Example, $$\underset{\text{Ethanal}}{CH_3CHO} + H_2 \xrightarrow[\text{or LiAlH}_4]{\text{Ni or Pt}} \underset{\text{Ethanol}}{CH_3CH_2OH}$$

$$\underset{\text{Ketone}}{RCOR'} + H_2 \xrightarrow[\text{LiAlH}_4 \text{ or NaBH}_4]{H_2/\text{Ni or Pt or Na}/C_2H_5OH} \underset{\text{Secondary alcohol}}{R–CH(OH)(CH_3)}$$

Example, $$\underset{\substack{\text{Propanone} \\ \text{(Acetone)}}}{CH_3–C(CH_3)=O} + H_2 \xrightarrow[\text{or NaBH}_4]{\text{Ni or Pt}} \underset{\substack{\text{Propan-2-ol} \\ \text{(Isopropyl alcohol)}}}{CH_3–CHOH(CH_3)}$$

11.2.3 Reduction of Carboxylic Acids and Esters

$$\underset{\text{Carboxylic acid}}{RCOOH} \xrightarrow[\text{(ii) }H_2O]{\text{(i) LiAlH}_4} \underset{\text{Primary alcohol}}{RCH_2OH}$$

$$\underset{\text{Ethanoic acid}}{CH_3COOH} \xrightarrow[\text{(ii) }H_2O]{\text{(i) LiAlH}_4} \underset{\text{Ethanol}}{CH_3CH_2OH}$$

Esters are also reduced to alcohols and give a mixture of two alcohols; one from the acyl group (RCO–) and the other from the alkoxy (–OR′) group.

$$R{-}\overset{O}{\overset{\|}{C}}{=}OR' \xrightarrow[\text{or } Na/C_2H_5OH]{LiAlH_4,\ H_2O} \underset{\text{Mixture of alcohols}}{R{-}CH_2OH + R'OH}$$

$$\underset{\substack{\text{Methyl acetate}\\\text{(Ester)}}}{CH_3{-}\overset{O}{\overset{\|}{C}}{-}OCH_3} + 4[H] \xrightarrow{Na/C_2H_5OH} \underset{\text{Ethanol}}{CH_3CH_2OH} + \underset{\text{Methanol}}{CH_3OH}$$

$$\underset{\text{Ethyl acetate}}{CH_3{-}\overset{O}{\overset{\|}{C}}{-}OCH_2CH_3} + 4[H] \xrightarrow{LiAlH_4} \underset{\text{Ethanol}}{2CH_3CH_2OH}$$

11.2.4 From Grignard's Reagent

By reaction with aldehydes, ketones and esters: Due to the polar nature of the C–Mg bond, Grignard's reagent (RMgX) reacts with aldehydes, ketones and esters to form addition products which decompose with dil. HCl or dil. H_2SO_4 to give alcohols.

$$\underset{\substack{\text{Carbonyl compound}\\\text{aldehyde, ketone or}\\\text{ester)}}}{\overset{\delta+\ \delta-}{-C{=}O}} + \underset{\substack{\text{Grignard}\\\text{reagent}}}{\overset{\delta-}{R}\ \overset{\delta+}{MgX}} \xrightarrow[\text{ether}]{\text{Dry}} \underset{\text{Addition compound}}{-\underset{R}{\underset{|}{\overset{|}{C}}}{-}OMgX} \xrightarrow[\text{Hydrolysis}]{H^+,\ H_2O} \underset{\text{Alcohol}}{-\underset{R}{\underset{|}{\overset{|}{C}}}{-}OH} + \underset{\substack{\text{Hydroxy magnesium}\\\text{halide}}}{Mg(OH)\,X}$$

Comes from Grignard reagent (R)

- Formaldehyde gives primary alcohols.

$$\underset{\substack{\text{Methanal}\\\text{(Formaldehyde)}}}{H{-}\overset{O}{\overset{|}{C}}{=}O} + CH_3MgBr \xrightarrow[\text{ether}]{\text{Dry}} H{-}\underset{CH_3}{\underset{|}{\overset{H}{\overset{|}{C}}}}{-}OMgBr \xrightarrow{H+,\ H_2O} \underset{\substack{\text{Ethanol}\\(1°\text{Alcohol})}}{H{-}\underset{CH_3}{\underset{|}{\overset{H}{\overset{|}{C}}}}{-}OH} + Mg(OH)Br$$

- All aldehydes (other than formaldehyde) give secondary alcohols.

$$\underset{\substack{\text{Ethanal}\\\text{(Acetaldehyde)}}}{CH_3{-}\overset{O}{\overset{|}{C}}{=}O} + CH_3MgBr \xrightarrow[\text{ether}]{\text{Dry}} CH_3{-}\underset{CH_3}{\underset{|}{\overset{H}{\overset{|}{C}}}}{-}OMgBr \xrightarrow{H+,\ H_2O} \underset{\substack{\text{Propan-2-ol}\\(2°\text{ Alcohol})}}{CH_3{-}\underset{CH_3}{\underset{|}{\overset{H}{\overset{|}{C}}}}{-}OH}$$

- Ketones give tertiary alcohols.

$$\underset{\substack{\text{Propanone}\\\text{(Acetone)}}}{CH_3{-}\overset{O}{\overset{|}{C}}{=}O} + CH_3MgBr \xrightarrow[\text{ether}]{\text{Dry}} CH_3{-}\underset{CH_3}{\underset{|}{\overset{H}{\overset{|}{C}}}}{-}OMgBr \xrightarrow{H+,\ H_2O} \underset{\substack{\text{2-Methylpropan-2-ol}\\(3°\text{ Alcohol})}}{CH_3{-}\underset{CH_3}{\underset{|}{\overset{CH_3}{\overset{|}{C}}}}{-}OH}$$

- Esters give secondary and tertiary alcohols.

$$\underset{\substack{\text{Ethyl methanoate}\\\text{(Ethyl formate)}}}{H{-}\overset{O^{\delta-}}{\overset{\|\delta+}{C}}{-}OC_2H_5} \xrightarrow[\text{Dry ether}]{\overset{\delta-\ \delta+}{CH_3MgBr}} \left[H{-}\underset{CH_3}{\underset{|}{\overset{OMgBr}{\overset{|}{C}}}}{-}OC_2H_5\right] \xrightarrow{-Mg(OC_2H_5)Br}$$

$$\underset{\text{Acetaldehyde}}{H{-}\overset{O}{\overset{\|}{C}}{-}CH_3} \xrightarrow[\text{Dry ether}]{CH_3MgBr} H{-}\underset{CH_3}{\underset{|}{\overset{OMgBr}{\overset{|}{C}}}}{-}CH_3 \xrightarrow[-Mg(OH)Br]{H^+/H_2O} \underset{\substack{\text{Propan-3-ol}\\\text{(Isopropyl alcohol)}}}{H{-}\underset{CH_3}{\underset{|}{\overset{OH}{\overset{|}{C}}}}{-}CH_3}$$

11.2.5 Hydrolysis of Esters

Alcohols are generally prepared by hydrolysis of esters with aqueous alkalies.

$$H{-}\overset{O}{\overset{\|}{C}}{-}O\,\vdots\,R' + HO\,\vdots\,Na\,(aq) \longrightarrow \underset{\text{Sodium salt of acid}}{R{-}\overset{O}{\overset{\|}{C}}{-}ONa} + \underset{\text{Alcohol}}{R'OH}$$

$$\underset{\substack{\text{Ethyl ethanoate}\\\text{(Ethyl actate)}}}{CH_3{-}\overset{O}{\overset{\|}{C}}{-}O\,\vdots\,C_2H_5} + HO\,\vdots\,Na\,(aq) \longrightarrow \underset{\text{Sodium acetate}}{CH_3COONa} + \underset{\text{Ethyl alcohol}}{C_2H_5OH}$$

11.2.6 From Alkenes

Alkenes can be converted into alcohols by the following methods.

(i) **By acid catalysed hydration of alkenes:** The hydration of alkenes can be carried out directly or indirectly.

- In the indirect process, alkenes are passed through conc. H_2SO_4 to form alkyl hydrogen sulfates, which upon hydrolysis with boiling water give alcohols.

$$\underset{\text{Ethene}}{CH_2{=}CH_2} + \underset{\substack{\text{Sulfuric acid}\\\text{(Conc.)}}}{HOSO_2OH} \rightarrow \underset{\text{Ethyl hydrogen sulfate}}{CH_3CH_2OSO_2OH} \xrightarrow[\text{Boil}]{H_2O} \underset{\text{Ethanol}}{CH_3CH_2OH} + H_2SO_4$$

In the case of unsymmetrical alkenes, the addition of H_2SO_4 takes place in accordance with Markownikoff's rule, that is, the hydrogen goes to that carbon atom which contains the larger number of hydrogen atoms.

$$\underset{\substack{\text{Propene}\\\text{(Propylene)}}}{CH_3CH{=}CH_2} + HOSO_2OH \xrightarrow{\text{Markownikoff's rule}} CH_3{-}\underset{OSO_2OH}{\underset{|}{CH}}{-}CH_3 \xrightarrow[\text{Boil}]{H_2O} \underset{\substack{\text{Propan-2-ol}\\\text{(Isopropyl alcohol)}}}{CH_3{-}\underset{OH}{\underset{|}{CH}}{-}CH_3}$$

- Reactive alkenes directly add a molecule of water in the presence of mineral acids as catalyst to form alcohols.

$$>C{=}C< + H_2O \xrightarrow[\text{Markownikoff addition}]{H^+} \underset{\text{Alcohol}}{-\underset{OH}{\underset{|}{\overset{|}{C}}}{-}\underset{H}{\underset{|}{\overset{|}{C}}}-}$$

Example $\underset{\text{Propene}}{CH_3CH{=}CH_2} + H_2O \xrightarrow{H^+} \underset{\text{Propan-2-ol}}{CH_3{-}\underset{OH}{\underset{|}{CH}}{-}CH_3}$

$$\underset{\text{2-Methylpropene (Isobutylene)}}{CH_3-\overset{CH_3}{\overset{|}{C}}=CH_2} + H_2O \xrightarrow[\text{Markownikoff's rule}]{H^+} \underset{\text{2-Methylpropan-2-ol (tert-Butyl alcohol)}}{CH_3-\overset{CH_3}{\overset{|}{\underset{OH}{\underset{|}{C}}}}-CH_3}$$

(ii) Hydroboration, oxidation reduction: Alkenes react with diborane (B_2H_6) to form trialkylboranes which upon subsequent treatment with alkaline H_2O_2 give alcohols. This reaction involves the addition of water to a double bond using anti-Markownikoff's rule. This involves two reactions, addition of borane (BH_3) to the double bond (hydroboration, oxidation) and hydrolysis to give an alcohol.

$$>C=C< + H-B< \xrightarrow{THF} -\underset{H}{\underset{|}{C}}-\underset{B}{\underset{|}{C}}- \xrightarrow{H_2O_2,\ OH^-} -\underset{H}{\underset{|}{C}}-\underset{OH}{\underset{|}{C}}-$$

During oxidation of the trialkyl borane, boron is replaced by the –OH group.

$$(RCH_2CH_2)_3B + 3H_2O_2 \xrightarrow{OH^-,\ H_2O} \underset{\text{Alcohol}}{3RCH_2CH_2OH} + \underset{\text{Boric acid}}{B(OH)_3}$$

$$\underset{\text{Propene}}{CH_3-CH=CH_2} \xrightarrow[\text{Hydroboration}]{BH_3,\ THF} \underset{\text{Tripropyl borane}}{(CH_3CH_2CH_2)_3B} \xrightarrow[OH^-]{H_2O_2} \underset{\text{Propan-1-ol}}{3CH_3CH_2CH_2OH}$$

The reaction may also be written as:

$$CH_3-CH=CH_2 \xrightarrow[\text{(ii) } H_2O_2,\ OH^-]{\text{(i) } BH_3,\ THF} \underset{\text{Propan-1-ol}}{CH_3-CH_2-CH_2OH}$$

$$CH_3(CH_2)_2CH=CH_2 \xrightarrow[\text{(ii) } H_2O_2,\ OH^-]{\text{(i) } BH_3,\ THF} \underset{\text{Pentan-1-ol}}{CH_3(CH_2)_2-CH_2-CH_2OH}$$

$$\underset{\text{2-Methylpropene}}{CH_3-\overset{CH_3}{\overset{|}{C}}=CH_2} \xrightarrow[\text{(ii) } H_2O_2,\ OH^-]{\text{(i) } BH_3,\ THF} \underset{\text{2-Methylpropan-1-ol}}{CH_3-\overset{CH_3}{\overset{|}{C}H}-CH_2OH}$$

$$\underset{\text{2-Methylbut-2-ene}}{CH_3-CH=\overset{CH_3}{\overset{|}{C}}-CH_3} \xrightarrow[\text{(ii) } H_2O_2,\ OH^-]{\text{(i) } BH_3,\ THF} \underset{\text{3-Methylbutan-2-ol}}{CH_3-CH-\overset{CH_3}{\overset{|}{C}H}-CH_3}$$

11.3 Methods of Preparation of Phenols

In the laboratory, phenols are prepared from benzene derivatives by the following methods:

(i) From benzene sulfonic acid: Benzene is sulfonated with oleum (mixture of H_2SO_4 and SO_3, that is, $H_2S_2O_7$) and the benzene sulfonic acid so formed is converted to sodium phenoxide by heating with molten sodium hydroxide. This on acidification gives phenol.

$$\underset{\text{Benzene}}{C_6H_6} \xrightarrow[\text{Sulfonation}]{H_2SO_4 + SO_3} \underset{\text{Benzene sulfonic acid}}{C_6H_5SO_3H} \xrightarrow[-H_2O]{NaOH} \underset{\text{Sodium benzene sulfonate}}{C_6H_5SO_3Na} \xrightarrow[-Na_2SO_3,\ -H_2O]{\text{NaOH Fused, 573–623 K}} \underset{\text{Sodium phenoxide}}{C_6H_5ONa} \xrightarrow[-NaCl]{HCl} \underset{\text{Phenol}}{C_6H_5OH}$$

(ii) From diazonium salts: An aqueous solution of benzene diazonium salt on warming gives phenol.

$$\underset{\text{Benzene diazonium chloride}}{C_6H_5N_2^+Cl^-} + H_2O \xrightarrow{\text{Warm}} \underset{\text{Phenol}}{C_6H_5OH} + N_2 + HCl$$

(iii) Decarboxylation of sodium salt of salicylic acid: Phenol can be prepared by fusing sodium salicylate with soda lime (NaOH and CaO mixture) followed by acidification with dil. HCl.

$$\underset{\text{Sodium salicylate}}{C_6H_4(OH)COONa} + NaOH \xrightarrow[-Na_2CO_3]{\text{CaO, Heat}} \underset{\text{Sodium phenoxide}}{C_6H_5ONa} \xrightarrow[-NaCl]{HCl} \underset{\text{Phenol}}{C_6H_5OH}$$

(iv) From Grignard reagent: When oxygen gas is bubbled through an ethereal solution of phenyl magnesium bromide (Grignard reagent), it forms an oxy compound which upon hydrolysis with dilute mineral acid gives phenol.

$$\underset{\text{Phenyl magnesium bromide}}{C_6H_5MgBr} + \frac{1}{2}O_2 \xrightarrow{\text{Dry ether}} \underset{\text{Phenyl oxymagnesium bromide}}{C_6H_5OMgBr} \xrightarrow{H^+,\ H_2O} \underset{\text{Phenol}}{C_6H_5OH} + Mg(OH)Br$$

11.3.1 Commercial Preparation of Phenols

On a large scale, phenol is obtained by the following methods.

(i) From chlorobenzene (Dow's process): Phenol is manufactured by heating chlorobenzene with 10% aqueous sodium hydroxide solution at about 623 K under 300 atmospheres and in the presence of a copper salt acting as catalyst to form sodium phenoxide. The sodium salt when treated with dilute HCl, gives phenol. This method is called *Dow's process*.

$$\underset{\text{Chlorobenzene}}{C_6H_5Cl} + 2NaOH \xrightarrow[\text{Copper salt, } -NaCl,\ -H_2O]{\text{623 K, 300 atm,}} \underset{\text{Sodium phenoxide}}{C_6H_5ONa} \xrightarrow[-NaCl]{HCl} \underset{\text{Phenol}}{C_6H_5OH}$$

(ii) From cumene: Phenol is prepared commercially from cumene (isopropyl benzene). Cumene is prepared by Friedel Craft alkylation of benzene with propene in the presence of phosphoric acid at 523 K.

$$C_6H_6 + \underset{\text{Propane}}{CH_3CH{=}CH_2} \xrightarrow[523\ K]{H_3PO_4} \underset{\text{Cumene}}{C_6H_5{-}CH(CH_3)_2}$$

Cumene is oxidised in the presence of air to cumene hydroperoxide which upon subsequent hydrolysis with dil. H_2SO_4 gives phenol and propanone (acetone).

$$\underset{\text{Cumene}}{C_6H_5CH(CH_3)_2} \xrightarrow{O_2} \underset{\text{Cumene hydroperoxide}}{C_6H_5C(CH_3)_2{-}O{-}O{-}H} \xrightarrow{H+,\ H_2O} \underset{\text{Phenol}}{C_6H_5OH} + \underset{\text{Propanone (Acetone)}}{CH_3{-}CO{-}CH_3}$$

(iii) Addition of Grignard reagent to a ketone: A tertiary alcohol is formed.

$$\overline{R}MgX + R'_2C{=}O \rightarrow R{-}CR'_2{-}O^-(MgX)^+ \xrightarrow{H_3O^+} R{-}CR'_2{-}OH + XMg(OH)$$

$$CH_3CH_2MgBr + (CH_3CH_2)(H_3C)C{=}O \longrightarrow CH_3CH_2{-}C(CH_2CH_3)(CH_3){-}OMgBr \xrightarrow{H_3O^+} C_2H_5{-}C(CH_3)(C_2H_5){-}OH + BrMg(OH)$$

(iv) Addition of Grignard reagent to acid chlorides and esters: Acid chlorides and esters reacts with two equivalents of Grignard reagents to give tertiary alcohols.

$$2R{-}MgX + R'{-}CO{-}Cl \xrightarrow{H_3O^+} R{-}C(R)(R'){-}OH$$

$$2R{-}MgX + R'{-}CO{-}OR'' \xrightarrow{H_3O^+} R'{-}C(OH)(R){-}R''$$

11.4 Physical Properties of Alcohols

Physical state: Most of the common alcohols, up to 11 to 12 carbon atoms, are liquids at room temperature.

Boiling points: In alcohols, there are two significant intermolecular forces of attraction responsible for high boiling points compared to ethers and alkanes of comparable molecular weight. The first is H-bonding. The hydroxyl hydrogen of ethanol is strongly polarised by its bond to oxygen, and it can form a hydrogen bond with a pair of non-bonding electrons from the oxygen atom of another alcohol.

R–O–H····O(R)–H····O(R)–H

Intermolecular H-bonds

Dipole–dipole attraction also contributes to the relatively high boiling point of alcohols. Dipole moment in alcohols is much higher than any alkane due to which alkanes have very low boiling point. Among alcohols, increasing molecular weight increases the boiling point. Branching decreases boiling point.

$CH_3CH_2CH_2OH$ BP = 97°C $CH_3{-}CH(OH){-}CH_3$ BP = 82.5°C

Increasing the number of hydroxyl groups increases the boiling points greatly.

CH_3CH_2OH BP = 78°C $HO{-}CH_2{-}CH_2{-}OH$ BP = 197°C $HO{-}CH_2{-}CH(OH){-}CH_2{-}OH$ BP = 290°C

Solubility: The lower members of alcohols are highly soluble in water but the solubility decreases with an increase in molecular weight. The solubility of lower alcohols in water is due to the formation of hydrogen bonds between alcohols and water molecules. However, as the size of alcohol molecule increases, the alkyl group becomes larger and prevents the formation of hydrogen bonds with water molecules and hence the solubility goes on decreasing with an increase in the length of the carbon chain (or molecular mass of the alcohol).

Intermolecular H–bondings (denote by dotted bonds): R–O(H)····H–O(R) (With alcohol); R–O(H)····H–O(H) (With water); R–O(H)····H–O–C(=O)–R (With carboxylic acid)

Density: The density increases with an increase in the molecular mass.

11.5 Chemical Properties of Alcohols

Alcohols are versatile compounds. They behave both as nucleophiles as well as electrophiles.

- They behave as nucleophiles in the reactions in which the O–H bond is broken.

$$\underset{\substack{\text{Alcohol}\\\text{(Alcohol as nucleophile)}}}{R{-}\ddot{O}{-}H} + \underset{\substack{\text{Carbocation}\\\text{(Electrophile)}}}{{}^{+}C{<}} \longrightarrow R{-}\overset{+}{O}(H){-}C{<} \longrightarrow R{-}\ddot{O}{-}C{<} + H^+$$

- They behave as electrophiles in which the bond between C–O is broken. These reactions are carried out in the presence of acids to form protonated alcohols. Protonated alcohols react as electrophiles.

$$R{-}CH_2{-}OH \xrightarrow{H^+} \underset{\text{Protonated alcohol}}{R{-}CH_2{-}\overset{+}{O}H_2}$$

$$Br^- + \underset{\substack{|\\R}}{CH_2}-\overset{+}{O}H_2 \longrightarrow Br-\underset{\substack{|\\R}}{CH_2} + H_2O$$

(Electrophile)
(Protonated alcohols as electrophiles)

(i) Reaction with active metals: The hydroxyl proton of an alcohol is weakly acidic. A strong base can remove the hydroxyl proton to give an alkoxide ion.

$R–O–H + B^+ \rightarrow R–O^- + B–H$

The alcohols act as Brönsted acids because they donate a proton to a strong base (:B^-).

$$R-\ddot{\underset{..}{O}}:^- + H-\ddot{\underset{..}{O}}-H \longrightarrow R-O-H + OH^-$$

Base Acid Conjugate acid Conjugate base

Water is a stronger acid than alcohols. An alkoxide is a better proton acceptor than the hydroxide ion. This means alkoxides are stronger bases than the hydroxide ion. Alcohols react with active metals such as sodium, potassium, magnesium and aluminium, to liberate hydrogen gas and form the metal alkoxide. For example,

$$2ROH + 2M \rightarrow 2ROM + H_2 (M = Na, K, Mg, Al\cdots)$$

$$\underset{\text{Ethanol}}{2CH_3CH_2OH} + 2Na \rightarrow \underset{\text{Sodium ethoxide}}{2CH_3CH_2ONa} + H_2$$

$$2CH_3CH_2OH + Mg \rightarrow \underset{\text{Magnesium ethoxide}}{(CH_3CH_2O)_2Mg} + H_2$$

$$\underset{\textit{tert}\text{-Butyl alcohol}}{6CH_3-\underset{\substack{|\\CH_3}}{\overset{\substack{CH_3\\|}}{C}}-OH} + 2Al \rightarrow \underset{\text{Aluminium }\textit{tert}\text{-butoxide}}{2\left[CH_3-\underset{\substack{|\\CH_3}}{\overset{\substack{CH_3\\|}}{C}}-O\right]_3 Al} + 3H_2$$

(ii) Reaction with metal hydrides: Alcohols react with metal hydrides to form alkoxides with the evolution of hydrogen gas.

$$CH_3OH + \underset{\text{Sodium hydride}}{NaH} \rightarrow \underset{\text{Sodium methoxide}}{CH_3O^-Na^+} + H_2$$

$$CH_3CH_2OH + \underset{\text{Sodium hydride}}{NaH} \rightarrow \underset{\text{Sodium ethoxide}}{CH_3CH_2O^-Na^+} + H_2$$

(iii) Reaction with carboxylic acids (esterification): Alcohols react with monocarboxylic acids, in the presence of conc. H_2SO_4 or dry HCl gas as catalyst, to form esters. The reaction is known as *esterification*. The function of conc. H_2SO_4 is to act as a protonating agent as well as a dehydrating agent.

$$\underset{\text{Acid}}{RCO\,\boxed{OH + H}} \underset{\text{Alcohol}}{OR'} \xrightleftharpoons{\text{Conc. }H_2SO_4} \underset{\text{Ester}}{RCOOR'} + H_2O + H_2O$$

For example,

$$\underset{\substack{\text{Ethanoic acid}\\\text{(Acetic acid)}}}{CH_3CO\,\boxed{OH + H}} \underset{\substack{\text{Ethanol}\\\text{(Ethyl alcohol)}}}{OC_2H_5} \xrightleftharpoons{\text{Conc. }H_2SO_4} \underset{\substack{\text{Ethyl ethanoate}\\\text{(Ethyl acetate)}}}{CH_3COOC_2H_5} + H_2O$$

(iv) Reaction with Grignard reagents: Alcohols react with Grignard reagents (which are alkyl magnesium halides, RMgX) to form hydrocarbons.

$$\underset{\text{Alcohol}}{RO-}\underset{\text{Grignard reagent}}{\boxed{H + R'}MgX} \longrightarrow \underset{\text{Alkane}}{R'-H} + ROMgX$$

$$\underset{\substack{\text{Methyl}\\\text{alcohol}}}{CH_3O} \underset{\substack{\text{Ethyl magnesium}\\\text{bromide}}}{\boxed{H + C_2H_5}MgBr} \longrightarrow \underset{\text{Ethane}}{C_2H_6} + CH_3OMgBr$$

(v) Reaction with acyl chloride or acid anhydride (acylation): When alcohols are treated with acid chloride or acid anhydride in the presence of bases like pyridine or dimethyl aniline (as catalyst), the hydrogen atom of the –OH group is replaced by the acyl (RCO–) group forming an ester.

$$\underset{\text{Ethanoyl chloride}}{CH_3-\overset{\substack{O\\||}}{C}-\boxed{Cl + H}}\underset{\text{Ethanol}}{-O-CH_2CH_3} \xrightarrow{\text{Pyridine}} \underset{\text{Ethyl ethanoate (Ethyl acetate)}}{CH_3-\overset{\substack{O\\||}}{C}-OCH_2CH_3} + HCl$$

$$\underset{\text{Acetic anhydride}}{CH_3-\overset{\substack{O\\||}}{C}-\boxed{O-\overset{\substack{O\\||}}{C}-CH_3 + H}}OCH_2CH_3 \xrightarrow{\text{Pyridine}} \underset{\text{Ethyl ethanoate (Ethyl acetate)}}{CH_3-\overset{\substack{O\\||}}{C}-OCH_2CH_3} + CH_3COOH$$

This reaction is called *acylation reaction*.

11.5.1 Reaction Involving Cleavage of the Carbon–Oxygen Bond $-\overset{|}{\underset{|}{C}}\vdots OH$

The alkyl groups release electrons and therefore, they increase the electron density towards oxygen. As a result, the polarity of the C–O bond increases and this makes the cleavage of the bond between carbon and oxygen easier. Therefore, the greater the number of alkyl groups attached to the carbon, the easier would be the cleavage of the C–O bond and consequently the reactivity of alcohol would be greater. Thus, the reactivity follows the sequence:

$$\underset{\text{Tertiary alcohol}}{R\rightarrow\underset{\substack{\uparrow\\R}}{\overset{\substack{R\\\downarrow}}{C}}-OH} > \underset{\text{Secondary alcohol}}{R\rightarrow\underset{\substack{\uparrow\\H}}{\overset{\substack{R\\\downarrow}}{C}}-OH} > \underset{\text{Primary alcohol}}{R\rightarrow\underset{\substack{|\\H}}{\overset{\substack{H\\|}}{C}}-OH}$$

(i) Reaction with hydrogen halides: Alcohols react with hydrogen halides to form haloalkanes (alkyl halides). The order of reactivity of hydrogen halides is: HI > HBr > HCl. This is because the I^- ion is a better nucleophile than the Br^- ion, which in turn, is better than the Cl^- ion. The order of reactivity of the alcohols is: tertiary > secondary > primary. In these reactions, anhydrous $ZnCl_2$ is used as a Lewis acid catalyst. However, no such catalyst is needed for the reaction of tertiary alcohols with HCl.

$$R\text{–}OH + H\text{–}X \longrightarrow RX + H_2O$$

$$\underset{\text{Ethanol (1°)}}{CH_3CH_2OH} + HCl\,(g) \longrightarrow \underset{\text{Chloroethane}}{CH_3CH_2Cl} + H_2O$$

$$\underset{\text{Propan-2-ol (2°)}}{(CH_3)_2CHOH} + HCl\,(g) \longrightarrow \underset{\text{2-Chloropropane}}{(CH_3)_2CHCl} + H_2O$$

$$\underset{\text{2-Methylpropan-2-ol (3°)}}{(CH_3)_3C\text{–}OH} + HCl \xrightarrow{\text{Room temp.}} \underset{\text{2-Chloro-2-methylpropane}}{(CH_3)_3C\text{–}Cl} + H_2O$$

The reaction of primary and secondary alcohols with HCl gas in the presence of anhydrous $ZnCl_2$ is called *Groove's method*. In the case of HBr, a small amount of conc. H_2SO_4 is also added as a catalyst for the reaction with primary alcohols. But no catalyst is added for the reaction with secondary and tertiary alcohols which get dehydrated in the presence of conc. H_2SO_4.

$$\underset{\text{Ethanol}}{CH_3CH_2OH} + HBr \xrightarrow[\text{Reflux}]{\text{Conc. } H_2SO_4 \text{ (few drops)}} \underset{\text{Bromoethane}}{CH_3CH_2Br} + H_2O$$

In the case of HI, alkyl iodides are formed by heating the alcohol with HI. However, if the reaction between hydrogen iodide and the alcohol is carried out in the presence of red phosphorus, the alcohol gets reduced to the hydrocarbon rather than form the alkyl halide. For example,

$$CH_3CH_2OH + 2HI \xrightarrow[423\text{ K}]{\text{Red P}} C_6H_6 + I_2 + H_2O$$

(ii) Reaction with phosphorus halides: Phosphorus halides such as PCl_5, PCl_3 PBr_3 ($P + Br_2$) or PI_3 ($P + I_2$) react with alcohols to form the corresponding haloalkanes.

$$\underset{\text{Alcohol}}{R-OH} + PX_5 \rightarrow \underset{\text{Alkyl halide}}{R-X} + \underset{\text{Phosphorus oxyhalide}}{POX_3} + HX$$

$$\underset{\text{Alcohol}}{3R-OH} + PX_3 \rightarrow \underset{\text{Alkyl halide}}{3R-X} + \underset{\text{Phosphorus acid}}{H_3PO_3} \quad (X = Cl, Br \text{ or } I)$$

Example, $CH_3CH_2OH + PCl_5 \rightarrow \underset{\text{Chloroethane}}{CH_3CH_2Cl} + \underset{\text{Phosphorus oxychloride}}{POCl_3} + HCl$

$$3CH_3CH_2OH + PCl_3 \rightarrow \underset{\text{Chloroethane}}{3CH_3CH_2Cl} + \underset{\text{Phosphorus acid}}{H_3PO_3}$$

$$3CH_3CH_2OH + PBr_3 \xrightarrow{P+Br_2} \underset{\text{Bromoethane}}{3CH_3CH_2Br} + \underset{\text{Phosphorus acid}}{H_3PO_3}$$

$$3CH_3CH_2OH + PI_3 \xrightarrow{P+I_2} \underset{\text{Iodoethane}}{3CH_3CH_2I} + \underset{\text{Phosphorus acid}}{H_3PO_3}$$

(iii) Reaction with thionyl chloride: On treatment with thionyl chloride in the presence of pyridine, alcohols form chloroalkanes. For example,

$$R\text{–}OH + \underset{\text{Thionyl chloride}}{SOCl_2} \xrightarrow{\text{Pyridine}} \underset{\text{Alkyl chloride}}{R\text{–}Cl} + SO_2\uparrow + HCl\uparrow$$

$$\underset{\text{Ethyl alcohol}}{C_2H_5OH} + SOCl_2 \xrightarrow{\text{Pyridine}} \underset{\text{Ethyl chloride}}{C_2H_5Cl} + HCl\uparrow + SO_2\uparrow$$

(iv) Reaction with ammonia: When vapours of an alcohol and ammonia are passed over heated alumina (Al_2O_3) at 633 K, a mixture of primary, secondary and tertiary amines is produced.

$$ROH + NH_3 \xrightarrow[633\text{ K}]{Al_2O_3} R\text{–}NH_2 + H_2O$$

$$R\text{–}NH_2 + R\text{–}OH \xrightarrow[633\text{ K}]{Al_2O_3} R_2NH + H_2O$$

$$R_2NH + R\text{–}OH \xrightarrow[633\text{ K}]{Al_2O_3} R_3N + H_2O$$

11.5.2 Reactions Involving both the Cleavage of the Alkyl and the Hydroxyl Group

(i) Acidic dehydration: When alcohols are heated with a protonic acid such as conc. H_2SO_4 or H_3PO_4 at 443 K, they get dehydrated to form alkenes.

$$\underset{\text{Alcohol}}{\text{–}\overset{|}{\underset{H}{C}}\text{–}\overset{|}{\underset{H}{C}}\text{–}} \xrightarrow[\text{Heat}]{H^+} \underset{\text{Alkene}}{>C=C<} + H_2O$$

$$\underset{\text{Ethanol}}{H\text{–}\underset{H}{\overset{H}{C}}\text{–}\underset{H}{\overset{OH}{C}}\text{–}H} \xrightarrow{H^+,\ 443\text{ K}} \underset{\text{Ethene}}{H\text{–}\underset{H}{C}=\underset{H}{C}\text{–}H} + H_2O$$

$$\underset{\text{Propan-1-ol (2°)}}{CH_3\text{–}\underset{H}{\overset{H}{C}}\text{–}\underset{H}{\overset{OH}{C}}\text{–}H} \xrightarrow{H^+,\ 443\text{ K}} \underset{\text{Propene}}{CH_3\text{–}\underset{H}{C}=\underset{H}{C}\text{–}H} + H_2O$$

Secondary and tertiary alcohols are dehydrated under mild conditions. For example,

$$\underset{\text{Propan-2-ol (2°)}}{CH_3\underset{OH}{CH}CH_3} \xrightarrow[440\text{ K}]{85\%\ H_2SO_4} \underset{\text{Propene}}{CH_3\text{–}CH=CH_2} + H_2O$$

$$\underset{\text{2-Methylpropan-2-ol (3°)}}{CH_3\text{–}\underset{CH_3}{\overset{CH_3}{C}}\text{–}OH} \xrightarrow[358\text{ K}]{20\%\ H_2SO_4} \underset{\text{2-Methylpropene}}{CH_3\text{–}\underset{CH_3}{C}=CH_2} + H_2O$$

Thus, the relative ease of dehydration of alcohols follows the following order: tertiary alcohol > secondary alcohol > primary alcohol.

(ii) Dehydration of alcohols to ethers or alkenes can also be brought about by passing the vapour of the alcohols over heated alumina catalyst under different conditions.

- At 513–523 K, ethers are obtained.

$$2CH_3CH_2OH \xrightarrow[513\text{–}523\text{ K}]{Al_2O_3} \underset{\text{Ethoxy ethane (Diethyl ether)}}{CH_3CH_2OCH_2CH_3} + H_2O$$

- At 633 K, alkenes are obtained.

$$CH_3CH_2OH \xrightarrow[633\text{ K}]{Al_2O_3} \underset{\text{Ethene}}{CH_2=CH_2} + H_2O$$

(iii) Oxidation: The oxidation of alcohols involves the formation of a carbon–oxygen double bond with the cleavage of the O–H and C–H bonds.

$$H-\overset{|}{\underset{|}{C}}-O-H \longrightarrow \;\rangle C{=}O.$$

Bond breaking

These reactions are also called dehydrogenation reactions because these involve the loss of hydrogen from an alcohol.

- **Primary alcohols:** A primary alcohol is easily oxidised to form first an aldehyde and then a carboxylic acid. For example,

$$RCH_2OH \xrightarrow[\text{Oxidation}]{[O]} R-\underset{\underset{H}{|}}{C}{=}O \xrightarrow[\text{Oxidation}]{[O]} R-\underset{\underset{OH}{|}}{C}{=}O$$

Aldehyde — Carboxylic acid

$$CH_3-CH_2-OH \xrightarrow[\text{dil } H_2SO_4]{K_2Cr_2O_7} CH_3-\overset{\overset{H}{|}}{C}{=}O \xrightarrow[\text{(Readily)}]{[O]} CH_3COOH$$

Ethyl alcohol (*Primary*) — Acetaldehyde (Same number of carbon atoms) — Acetic acid (Same number of carbon atoms)

- **Secondary alcohols:** A secondary alcohol is easily oxidised to form a ketone with chromic anhydride (CrO_3). The ketone may be further oxidised under strong conditions to form a mixture of acids.

$$CH_3-\overset{\overset{CH_3}{|}}{\underset{\underset{H}{|}}{C}}-OH \xrightarrow{[O]} CH_3-\overset{\overset{CH_3}{|}}{C}{=}O \xrightarrow[\text{Drastic conditions}]{4[O]} CH_3COOH + CO_2 + H_2O$$

Isopropyl alcohol — Acetone (Same number of carbon atoms) — Acetic acid (Lesser number of carbon atoms)

$$CH_3-\overset{\overset{O}{|}}{C}H-CH_2CH_2CH_3 \xrightarrow{[O]} CH_3-\overset{\overset{O}{||}}{C}\vdots CH_2CH_2CH_3$$

Pentan-2-ol — Pentan-2-one

$$\xrightarrow{[O]} CH_2COOH + HOOCCH_2CH_3$$

Acetic acid — Propionic acid

- **Tertiary alcohols**: Tertiary alcohols are very difficult to oxidise in neutral or alkaline $KMnO_4$ solution because they do not have a hydrogen on the carbon bearing the –OH group. However, when treated with acidic oxidising agents ($K_2Cr_2O_7/H_2SO_4$ or $KMnO_4/H_2SO_4$) under very strong conditions at elevated temperatures, cleavage of various C–C bonds takes place. As a result, a mixture of ketones and carboxylic acids are formed. For example,

$$CH_3-\overset{\overset{CH_3}{|}}{\underset{\underset{CH_3}{|}}{C}}-OH \xrightarrow[-H_2O]{H^+,\,\Delta} \left[CH_3-\underset{\underset{CH_3}{|}}{C}{=}CH_2\right] \xrightarrow{O} CH_3-\underset{\underset{CH_3}{|}}{C}{=}O + [HCOOH]$$

tert-Butyl alcohol — 2-Methylprop-2-ene — Acetone

$$\xrightarrow{O} CO_2 + H_2O$$

Acetone can further be oxidised to acetic acid and formic acid.

$$\begin{matrix}CH_3\\ \end{matrix}\!\!\rangle C{=}O \xrightarrow[\text{Heat}]{O} CH_3COOH + HCOOH$$
$$CH_3$$

Acetic acid — Formic acid

or

$$CH_3-\overset{\overset{CH_3}{|}}{\underset{\underset{CH_3}{|}}{C}}-OH \xrightarrow[\text{(Under strong conditions)}]{4[O]} CH_3-\overset{\overset{CH_3}{|}}{C}{=}O \xrightarrow[\text{(Under strong conditions)}]{4[O]} CH_3COOH + CO_2 + H_2O$$

tert-Butyl alcohol (Tertiary) — Acetone (Lesser number of carbon atoms) — Acetic acid (Lesser number of carbon atoms)

$$CH_3-\overset{\overset{CH_3}{|}}{\underset{\underset{OH}{|}}{C}}-CH_2CH_3 \xrightarrow[\text{(Under strong conditions)}]{[O]} (CH_3)_2C{=}O + CH_3COOH$$

2-Methylbutan-2-ol — Acetone — Acetic acid

(iv) Oxidation with Jones reagent: When CrO_3 is used in aqueous acetone solution for oxidation, double bonds, if any present, are not affected.

$$R-CH=CH-CH_2OH + CrO_3/\text{aq. acetone} \rightarrow R-CH=CH-COOH$$

(v) Oxidation with PCC (pyridinium chlorochromate): Primary alcohols can be oxidised to aldehydes and then carboxylic acids.

$$R-CH_2OH + [O] \rightarrow R-CHO \xrightarrow{[O]} R-COOH$$

It is difficult to stop the oxidation of the primary alcohol at the aldehyde stage. A special oxidising agent used for this purpose called PCC.

(vi) Dehydrogenation of alcohols: When a primary or secondary alcohol is treated with copper or copper oxide (CuO) catalyst at high temperature (≈ 300°C), dehydrogenation occurs and the corresponding aldehydes or ketones are formed.

$$R-CH_2-OH + CuO/\text{heat} \rightarrow R-CHO$$
$$R_2CHOH + CuO/\text{heat} \rightarrow R_2CO$$

(vii) Dehydration: Tertiary alcohols get dehydrated on treatment with hot reduced copper to form alkenes.

$$CH_3-\overset{\overset{CH_3}{|}}{\underset{\underset{CH_3}{|}}{C}}-OH \xrightarrow{Cu,\ 573\ K} CH_3-\overset{\overset{CH_3}{|}}{C}{=}CH_2 + H_2O$$

2-Methylpropan-2-ol (*tert*-Butyl alcohol) — 2-Methylpropene (Isobutylene)

(viii) Reduction

- **Reduction of alcohol with HI/red P:** HI/red P is one of the best reducing agents used for the reduction of alcohols to alkanes.

$$ROH + HI/\text{red P} \rightarrow RH$$

- **Reduction with $LiAlH_4$ in presence of $TiCl_3$ or $AlCl_3$:** Some alcohols are directly reduced to alkanes with $LiAlH_4$ in the presence of $TiCl_3$ or $AlCl_3$ catalyst.

11.5.3 Acidic Character of Alcohols

With the exception of methanol ($K_a = 3.2\times10^{-16}$), alcohols are slightly less acidic than water ($K_a = 1.8\times10^{-16}$). Substitution by electron withdrawing groups increases the acid strength. For example, $ClCH_2CH_2OH$ (2-chloroethanol) is a stronger acid than water whereas ethanol is a weaker acid than water.

Formation of effervescence with alkali metals can be used to distinguish an alcohol from ethers, alkanes, alkenes, and so on.

$$C_2H_6O \xrightarrow{\text{Na/Heat}} \text{Effervescence} = \text{Ethanol}$$
$$C_2H_6O \xrightarrow{\text{Na/Heat}} \text{No effervescence} = CH_3\text{–}O\text{–}CH_3$$

Similar effervescence is observed when NaH reacts with alcohol.

$$C_2H_5OH \xrightarrow{\text{NaH}} CH_3CH_2ONa + H_2$$

Also, NH_3, terminal alkynes, alkanes are all weaker acids than alcohols; their conjugate bases can deprotonate alcohol.

$$C_2H_5OH + NaNH_2 \rightarrow CH_3CH_2ONa + NH_3$$
$$C_2H_5OH + R \rightarrow C \equiv \bar{C}\,Na^+ \rightarrow CH_3CH_2ONa + R\text{–}C{\equiv}CH$$
$$C_2H_5OH + CH_3MgBr \rightarrow C_2H_5OMgBr + CH_4$$

Acids stronger than alcohols, such as water, phenol, RCOOH and RSO_3H also give a similar reaction. Thus, alcohols cannot be distinguished from any of these compounds by this method. Also, since aliphatic alcohols are weaker acid than water, they do not form salts with NaOH while phenol and carboxylic acids are stronger acid than water, they do form salts with NaOH.

$$R\text{–}OH + NaOH \rightarrow \text{No salt formation}$$
$$C_6H_5OH + NaOH \rightarrow C_6H_5ONa + H_2O$$
$$RCOOH + NaOH \rightarrow RCOONa + H_2O$$

The above difference can be used to separate an aliphatic alcohol from either an alcohol–phenol mixture or an alcohol–acid (RCOOH) mixture.

11.6 Chemical Properties of Phenols

The chemical properties of phenols are of three types—reactions of the phenolic group (–OH group), reactions of the benzene ring and special reactions.

11.6.1 Reactions of the Phenolic (-OH) Group

(i) **Acidic character:** Phenols are weakly acidic in nature ($K_a = 10^{-8}$ to 10^{-10}). They turn blue litmus red and react with alkali metals and alkalies to form their salts. For example,

2 (phenol, OH) + 2 Na/NaOH ⟶ 2 (ONa) + H_2/H_2O

Sodium phenoxide

The acidic character of phenol is because of the presence of the polar O–H group. Due to the higher electronegativity of the sp^2 hybridised carbon of phenol to which –OH is attached, the electron density on oxygen decreases. This increases the polarity of the O–H bond and results in an increase in ionisation of the phenol. As a result, the H^+ ion can be easily released from an aqueous solution.

The greater acidic character of phenols as compared to alcohols can be explained on the basis of resonance. Phenol is a resonance hybrid of the following structures:

:ÖH ⟷ :ÖH ⟷ $^+$ÖH ⟷ $^+$ÖH ⟷ $^+$ÖH

I II III IV V

The +ve charge on the oxygen atom attracts the electron pair of the O–H bond strongly towards itself, weakens the O–H bond and, therefore, facilitates the release of H^+. Similarly, the phenoxide ion is resonance stabilised as follows:

:Ö:$^-$ ⟷ :Ö:$^-$ ⟷ Ö: ⟷ Ö: ⟷ Ö:

VI VII VIII IX X

The phenoxide ion is more resonance stabilised than phenol. In phenol, three contributing structures (III, IV and V) have both positive and negative charges and will require energy to separate the charge and therefore, will be unstable. On the other hand, there is no structure in the phenoxide ion that requires charge separation. Therefore, phenol is more acidic.

On the other hand, in the case of alcohols, neither the alcohol nor the alkoxide ion is stabilised by resonance. Thus, phenols are more acidic than alcohols. However, phenols are less acidic than carboxylic acids which is supported by their dissociation constant (K_a) values.

Comparison of acidic strength of nitrophenols: The nitro group ($–NO_2$) has both –R effect and –I effect. But the –R effect predominates over the –I effect. When the $–NO_2$ group is present at the *o*- and *p*-positions, it withdraws the electrons of the O–H bond towards it by a stronger –R effect whereas when the $–NO_2$ group is present at the *m*-position, it withdraws the electrons of the O–H bond only by the weaker –I effect.

:Ö–H (p-nitrophenol) ⟶ H^+ + :Ö (quinonoid, N^+ with O^-, O^-) + Other structures

p-Nitrophenol

o-Nitrophenol $\longrightarrow H^+ +$ Other structures

m-Nitrophenol $\longrightarrow H^+ +$

When the $-NO_2$ group is at the *o*- and *p*-positions, the nitrophenoxide ion is more resonance stabilised because the conjugation is extended up to the oxygen atom of the nitro group. But the *m*-nitrophenoxide ion is less stable because no such conjugation is possible in its structures. Thus, the *o*- and *p*-nitrophenols are more acidic than *m*-nitrophenol. The larger acidic character of *m*-nitrophenol is only because of the –I effect.

–I effect in *m*-Nitrophenol — Hydrogen bonding in *o*-Nitrophenol

(ii) Action with zinc dust: When heated with zinc dust, phenol is reduced to benzene.

$$\underset{\text{Phenol}}{C_6H_5OH} + Zn \xrightarrow{\text{Heat}} \underset{\text{Benzene}}{C_6H_6} + ZnO$$

(iii) Action with ammonia: Phenol reacts with ammonia in the presence of anhydrous zinc chloride to give aniline.

$$\underset{\text{Phenol}}{C_6H_5OH} + NH_3 \xrightarrow[\text{675 K}]{\text{Anhyd. } ZnCl_2} \underset{\text{Aniline}}{C_6H_5NH_2} + H_2O$$

(iv) Action with acid chlorides and acid anhydrides (acylation): When treated with acetyl chloride (in the presence of pyridine) or acetic anhydride (in the presence of a small amount of conc. H_2SO_4) esters are formed. The introduction of the acetyl group (CH_3CO–) in phenols is known as the acetylation reaction.

$$\underset{\text{Phenol}}{C_6H_5OH} + \underset{\text{Acetyl chloride}}{CH_3COCl} \xrightarrow{\text{Pyridine}} \underset{\text{Phenyl ethanoate (Phenyl acetate)}}{C_6H_5OCOCH_3} + HCl$$

$$\underset{\text{Phenol}}{C_6H_5OH} + \underset{\text{Acetyl anhydride}}{(CH_3CO)_2O} \xrightarrow{H^+} \underset{\text{Phenyl ethanoate (Phenyl acetate)}}{C_6H_5OCOCH_3} + CH_3COOH$$

Acetylation of salicylic acid produces aspirin (acetyl salicylic acid).

$$\underset{\text{Phenol}}{o\text{-}HOC_6H_4COOH} + \underset{\text{Acetic anhydride}}{(CH_3CO)_2O} \longrightarrow \underset{\text{Acetyl salicylic acid (Aspirin)}}{o\text{-}CH_3COOC_6H_4COOH}$$

(v) Action with benzoyl chloride (benozylation): Phenols react with benzoyl chloride in the presence of aqueous NaOH to form phenyl benzoate.

$$\underset{\text{Phenol}}{C_6H_5OH} + \underset{\text{Benzoyl chloride}}{C_6H_5COCl} \xrightarrow{\text{NaOH}} \underset{\text{Phenyl benzoate}}{C_6H_5OCOC_6H_5} + HCl$$

This reaction is called *Schotten Baumann reaction.*

(vi) Reaction with Grignard reagent: Like alcohols, phenols also react with Grignard reagents to form alkanes.

$$\underset{\text{Phenol}}{C_6H_5OH} + \underset{\text{Methyl magesium iodide}}{CH_3MgI} \rightarrow \underset{\text{Methane}}{CH_4} + \underset{\text{Phenoxy magnesium iodide}}{Mg(OC_6H_5)I}$$

11.6.2 Reactions of the Benzene Ring: Electrophilic Substitution Reactions

Phenols also undergo electrophilic aromatic substitution reactions. Because of the electronic effects caused by the –OH group, the ortho and para positions become electron rich. Some common examples are discussed below.

(i) Bromination: Phenol reacts with bromine water (aqueous solution) to give a precipitate of 2,4,6-tribromophenol.

$$\underset{\text{Phenol}}{C_6H_5OH} + 3Br_2\,(aq) \xrightarrow{H_2O} \underset{\text{2, 4, 6-Tribromophenol (White ppt.)}}{C_6H_2Br_3OH} + 3HBr$$

However, if the reaction is carried out in CS_2 or CCl_4, at a low temperature, a mixture of ortho and para bromophenol is obtained.

$$C_6H_5OH \xrightarrow[\text{293 K}]{Br_2 \text{ in } CS_2} \underset{\text{2-Bromophenol (ortho)}}{o\text{-}BrC_6H_4OH} + \underset{\text{4-Bromophenol (major product)}}{p\text{-}BrC_6H_4OH}$$

It may be noted that the usual halogenations are carried out in the presence of the Lewis acid $FeBr_3$, which polarises the halogen molecule. In the case of phenol, the polarisation of bromine occurs even in the absence of Lewis acid. This is because of the highly activating effect of the –OH group on the benzene ring.

OH + Br–Br ⟶ (OH, H, Br) + Br^- ⟶ (OH, Br) + H

(ii) Nitration: Phenol reacts with dilute nitric acid at low temperature (298 K) to give a mixture of ortho and *para*-nitrophenol.

Phenol + HNO_3 (dil.) $\xrightarrow{-H_2O}$ 2-Nitrophenol (*ortho*) (15%) + 4-Nitrophenol (*para*) (30–40%)

The *ortho* and *para* isomers can be separated by steam distillation. *o*-Nitrophenol is steam volatile due to intramolecular hydrogen bonding while *p*-nitrophenol is less volatile because of intermolecular hydrogen bonding.

Intramolecular hydrogen bonding in *o*-nitrophenol

Intramolecular hydrogen bonding in *p*-nitrophenol

With conc. nitric acid in the presence of sulfuric acid, phenol gives 2,4,6-trinitrophenol (picric acid). The yield of the nitro product is low because of the oxidation of the ring by conc. HNO_3.

Phenol + $3HNO_3$ (conc.) $\xrightarrow{H_2SO_4}$ 2, 4, 6-Trinitrophenol (Picric acid) + $3H_2O$

Nowadays, picric acid is prepared by treating phenols first with conc. H_2SO_4 at 373 K when a mixture of 2-phenol sulfonic acid and 4-phenolsulfonic acid is formed. This mixture is then heated with conc. HNO_3 to form 2, 4, 6-trinitrophenol (picric acid) in about 90% yield.

(iii) Sulfonation: Phenol reacts with conc. sulfuric acid to form a mixture of *o*- and *p*-phenol sulfonic acid.

Phenol $\xrightarrow[288–293\text{ K}]{H_2SO_4}$ 2-Hydroxybenzene sulfonic acid (***ortho*** product)

Phenol $\xrightarrow[373\text{ K}]{H_2SO_4}$ 4-Hydroxybenzene sulfonic acid (***para*** product)

(iv) Friedel Crafts alkylation: When phenol is heated with alkyl halides in the presence of anhydrous aluminium chloride, it forms cresols. The reaction is called *Friedel Crafts alkylation* reaction.

Phenol + CH_3Cl (Methyl chloride) $\xrightarrow[HCl]{\text{Anhy. }AlCl_3}$ 2-Methylphenol (*o*-Cresol) + 4-Methylphenol (*p*-Cresol)

11.6.3 Important Reactions of Phenol

(i) Kolbe's reaction: When sodium phenoxide is heated with carbon dioxide at about 400 K and under 4–7 atmospheric pressure, sodium salicylate is formed as the major product. This on acidification gives salicylic acid.

Sodium phenoxide + CO_2 $\xrightarrow[\text{4–7 atm pressure}]{400\text{ K}}$ Phenyl sodium carbonate $\xrightleftharpoons{\text{Rearrangement}}$ Sodium salicylate $\xrightarrow[-NaCl]{\text{dil HCl}}$ 2-Hydroxy benzoic acid (Salicylic acid)

(ii) Reimer–Tiemann reaction: When phenol is refluxed with chloroform in the presence of aqueous sodium hydroxide at 340 K followed by hydrolysis, an aldehydic group (–CHO) gets introduced in the ring at a position ortho to the phenolic group. Ortho hydroxyl benzaldehyde or salicylaldehyde is formed as the product of the reaction.

Phenol + $CHCl_3$ (Chloroform) $\xrightarrow[-NaCl,\ -H_2O]{NaOH,\ 340\text{ K}}$ (ONa, $CHCl_2$) $\xrightarrow[-2NaCl]{2NaOH}$ (ONa, CHOH) (Unstable) $\xrightarrow{-H_2O}$ (ONa, CHO) $\xrightarrow[-NaCl]{\text{dil. HCl}}$ 2-Hydroxy benzaldehyde (Salicylaldehyde)

In Reimer–Tiemann reaction, carbon tetrachloride may also be used in the place of chloroform. In this case, *o*-salicylic acid is formed as the major product.

$$\text{Phenol} + \underset{\text{Carbon tetrachloride}}{CCl_4} \xrightarrow[-NaCl,\ -H_2O]{2NaOH} \text{o-Hydroxybenzo trichloride (ONa, } CCl_3)$$

$$\xrightarrow[3NaOH]{-3NaCl} \text{(Unstable) (ONa, } C(OH)_3) \xrightarrow{-H_2O} \text{(ONa, COOH)} \xrightarrow[-NaCl]{\text{dil. HCl}} \text{2-Hydroxybenzoic acid (Salicylic acid)}$$

(iii) Coupling reaction: In the alkaline medium, an ice-cold solution of phenol combines with an ice-cold solution of benzene diazonium chloride to form coloured substances called azo dyes. This reaction is called the *coupling reaction.*

$$\underset{\text{Benzene diazonium chloride}}{C_6H_5\text{–N=NCl}} + \underset{\text{Phenol}}{H\text{–}C_6H_4\text{–OH}} \xrightarrow[\text{(pH 9–10)}]{\text{Weakly alkaline medium}} \underset{\substack{p\text{-Hydroxyazobenzene} \\ \text{Orange dye}}}{C_6H_5\text{–N=N–}C_6H_4\text{–OH}} + HCl$$

(iv) Reaction with phthalic anhydride: Phenol reacts with phthalic anhydride in the presence of conc. H_2SO_4 to give phenolphthalein.

$$\text{Phthalic anhydride} + \text{Phenol (two molecules)} \xrightarrow[\text{Heat}]{\text{Conc. } H_2SO_4} \text{Phenolphthalein}$$

(v) Hydrogenation (reduction): Phenol can be hydrogenated in the presence of finely divided nickel catalyst at 533 K to give cyclohexanol.

$$\text{Phenol} + 3H_2 \xrightarrow[533\text{ K}]{\text{Ni}} \text{Cyclohexanol}$$

(vi) Oxidation: Phenol undergoes oxidation with chromic acid and produces a conjugated diketone known as *p*-benzoquinone.

$$\text{Phenol} \xrightarrow{K_2Cr_2O_7,\ H_2SO_4} p\text{-Benzoquinone} + H_2O$$

When exposed to air, phenols are slowly oxidised to dark coloured mixtures containing quinines. Phenol can also be oxidised by potassium persulfate ($K_2S_2O_8$) in alkaline solution and gives a mixture of catechol and quinol.

$$\text{Phenol} \xrightarrow[\text{Alkaline solution}]{K_2S_2O_8} \underset{\text{(Catechol)}}{\text{1, 2-Dihydroxybenzene}} + \underset{\text{(Quinol)}}{\text{1, 4-Dihydroxybenzene}}$$

11.7 Distinction Between Primary, Secondary and Tertiary Alcohols

(i) Lucas test: In this test, an alcohol is treated with an equimolar mixture of concentrated hydrochloric acid and anhydrous $ZnCl_2$ (called Lucas reagent). The alcohols get converted into alkyl halides. Since the alkyl halides are insoluble in water, their formation is indicated by the appearance of turbidity in the reaction mixture. Since the order of reactivity of alcohols with halogen acids is tertiary > secondary > primary, the time required for the appearance of cloudiness will be different in different alcohols and this test helps to distinguish them from one another.

$$-\overset{|}{\underset{|}{C}}-OH + HCl \xrightarrow{\text{Anhyd. } ZnCl_2} \underset{\text{Alkyl chloride}}{-\overset{|}{\underset{|}{C}}-Cl} + H_2O$$

- If the turbidity appears immediately, the alcohol is tertiary.
- If the turbidity appears within five minutes, the alcohol is secondary.
- If turbidity appears only upon heating, the alcohol may be primary.

(ii) Victor Meyer's test: This test involves the following steps.

- The given alcohol is treated with red phosphorus and iodine resulting in the formation of the corresponding alkyl iodide.
- The alkyl iodide is treated with silver nitrite to form corresponding nitroalkane.
- The nitroalkane is finally reacted with nitrous acid ($NaNO_2$ + dil. H_2SO_4) and the resulting solution is made alkaline.
  - o The formation of a blood red colour indicates a primary alcohol.
  - o The formation of a blue colour shows the original alcohol to be secondary.
  - o A colourless solution means that the alcohol is a tertiary alcohol.

(iii) Iodoform test: All alcohols containing the $CH_3\overset{OH}{\overset{|}{C}H}-$ group linked to a carbon or hydrogen atom (methyl carbinols) can be distinguished from other alcohols by the iodoform test. This test is performed by heating the alcohol with aqueous NaOH or Na_2CO_3 and iodine solution. On warming the reaction mixture, a yellow precipitate of iodoform indicates a positive iodoform test. For example, ethanol gives the iodoform test.

$$\underset{\text{Ethanol}}{CH_3CH_2OH} + 4I_2 + 6NaOH \xrightarrow{\Delta} \underset{\text{Iodoform (Yellow ppt.)}}{CHI_3} + HCOONa + 5NaI + 5H_2O$$

$$\text{or } \underset{\text{Ethanol}}{CH_3CH_2OH} + 4I_2 + 3Na_2CO_3 \xrightarrow{\Delta} \underset{\text{Yellow ppt.}}{CHI_3} + HCOONa + 5NaI + 2H_2O + 3CO_2$$

11.8 Commercially Important Alcohols, Phenols

11.8.1 Methanol

Methanol or methyl alcohol was originally prepared by the destructive distillation of wood. Nowadays, it is manufactured by the catalytic hydrogenation of carbon monoxide or water gas.

$$CO + 2H_2 \xrightarrow[\substack{573\text{–}673\text{ K} \\ 200\text{–}300\text{ atm}}]{CuO\text{–}ZnO\text{–}Cr_2O_3} \underset{\text{Methanol}}{CH_3OH}$$

11.8.2 Ethanol

It can be manufactured by the following processes.

(i) **Hydration of ethene:** Ethanol is prepared by the hydration of ethene at 573 K under 200 atm pressure and in the presence of a catalyst.

$$\underset{\text{Ethene}}{CH_2{=}CH_2} + H_2O \xrightarrow[\text{Catalyst}]{573,\ 200\text{ atm}} \underset{\text{Ethanol}}{CH_3CH_2OH}$$

(ii) **Oxo process:** Ethene reacts with carbon monoxide and hydrogen in the presence of cobalt carbonyl $[CO(CO)_4]_2$ as catalyst at high temperature and pressure to give aldehydes. The catalytic hydrogenation of aldehydes gives primary alcohols.

$$\underset{\text{Ethene}}{H_2C{=}CH_2} + CO + H_2 \xrightarrow[\text{High temp. and pressure}]{[Co(CO)_4]_2} \underset{\text{Propanal}}{CH_3CH_2CHO} \xrightarrow{H_2/Ni} \underset{\text{Propan-1-ol}}{CH_3CH_2CH_2OH}$$

(iii) **Fermentation of carbohydrates:** Ethanol is manufactured by fermentation of starch or sugar.

- **Ethanol from sugar solution (molasses):** Molasses is a non-crystalline form of sugar obtained as the mother liquor after crystallisation of sugar from sugar solution. This contains about 50% sugar. Yeast supplies the enzymes invertase and zymase. The enzyme invertase hydrolyses sucrose to glucose and fructose. The enzyme zymase (found in yeast) converts glucose and fructose to ethanol.

$$\underset{\text{Sucrose}}{C_{12}H_{22}O_{11}} + H_2O \xrightarrow{\text{Invertase}} \underset{\text{Glucose}}{C_6H_{12}O_6} + \underset{\text{Fructose}}{C_6H_{12}O_6}$$

$$\underset{\text{Glucose or fructose}}{C_6H_{12}O_6} \xrightarrow{\text{Zymase}} \underset{\text{Ethanol}}{2C_2H_5OH} + 2CO_2$$

The fermented liquid which contains 8%–10% ethanol is called wash. It is fractionally distilled to rectified spirit containing 95.6% alcohol. Further dehydration with quicklime and distilling with sodium or calcium gives 99.8% ethanol.

- **Ethanol from starch:** Starchy substances are made into a paste by heating with super-heated steam at about 335 K and maltase is added. The malt contains the enzyme diastase which converts starch into maltose.

$$2\underset{\text{Starch}}{(C_6H_{10}O_5)_n} + nH_2O \xrightarrow{\text{Diastase}} n\underset{\text{Maltose}}{C_{12}H_{22}O_{11}}$$

The product is cooled to about 305 K and yeast is added. It gives the enzyme maltase which converts maltose to glucose.

$$\underset{\text{Maltose}}{C_{12}H_{22}O_{11}} + H_2O \xrightarrow{\text{Maltase}} \underset{\text{Glucose}}{2C_6H_{12}O_6}$$

The enzyme zymase, also provided by yeast, converts glucose into ethanol.

$$\underset{\text{Glucose}}{C_6H_{12}O_6} \xrightarrow{\text{Zymase}} \underset{\text{Ethanol}}{2C_2H_5OH} + 2CO_2$$

11.8.3 Industrial Alcohols

(i) **Absolute alcohol:** Fractional distillation of an aqueous solution of ethanol gives a constant boiling azeotropic mixture which contains 95% ethanol. To get 100% ethanol, a small amount of benzene is added to the azeotropic mixture and then distilled.

(ii) **Methylated spirit or denatured alcohol:** It is 95% ethyl alcohol. To some methanol, some copper sulfate (to give it a colour) and pyridine (a foul-smelling liquid), is added. The process is called denaturation of alcohol and the alcohol, thus obtained, is called *methylated spirit* or denatured alcohol. It is used for non-drinking purposes.

(iii) **Power alcohol:** It is a mixture of 20% ethanol and 50% gasoline. Since alcohol does not mix with petrol, a third solvent such as benzene, ether or (tetrahydronapthalene) is added. The use of power alcohol is as a substitute for gasoline.

(iv) **Alcoholic beverages:** There are mainly two types of beverages—distilled and undistilled. Undistilled beverages are prepared from grapes and other fruit juices and are called *wines*. The liquors obtained by distillation have higher alcoholic content and have different trade names such as whisky, rum, brandy, gin and so on.

11.9 Ethers

Ethers are compounds having two alkyl or aryl groups bonded to an oxygen atom, $R^1\text{–}O\text{–}R^2$. Ethers have –O– as the functional group. Ethers may be classified as given below.

Aliphatic ethers in which R and R′ are both alkyl groups. For example, $CH_3–O–CH_3$ (Dimethyl ether), $CH_3–O–CH_2CH_3$ (Ethyl methyl ether)

Aromatic ethers in which either one or both R and R′ groups are aryl groups. For example, $C_6H_5–O–CH_3$ (Methyl phenyl ether), $C_6H_6–O–C_6H_5$ (Diphenyl ether)

Symmetrical ethers:

CH_3OCH_3 (Dimethyl ether), $CH_3CH_2–O–CH_2CH_3$ (Diethyl ether), $C_6H_5–O–C_6H_5$ (Diphenyl ether)

Unsymmetrical ethers:

$CH_3–O–C_6H_5$ (Methyl phenyl ether), $C_6H_5–OCH_2CH_3$ Phenetole (Ethyl phenyl ether), $CH_3CH_2–O–\underset{CH_3}{CH}CH_2CH_3$ (2-Ethoxybutane)

$CH_3CH_2CH_2\underset{OCH_3}{CH}CH_3$ (2-Methoxypentane), $CH_3–\underset{CH_3}{CH}–O–\underset{CH_3}{CH}–CH_3$ (2-(2-propoxy)propane)

2-Ethoxy-1, 1-dimethylcyclohexane; $CH_3–O–CH=CH_2$ (Methoxyethene); 4-Ethoxycyclohexene

Ethers containing two or more carbon atoms are functional isomers of alcohols. For example,

$CH_3–O–CH_3$ (Methoxymethane) and CH_3CH_2OH (Ethanol); $CH_3–O–CH_2CH_3$ (Methoxyethane)

$C_6H_5OCH_3$ (Anisole); $C_6H_5CH_2OH$ (Benzyl alcohol)

11.9.1 Structure of Ethers

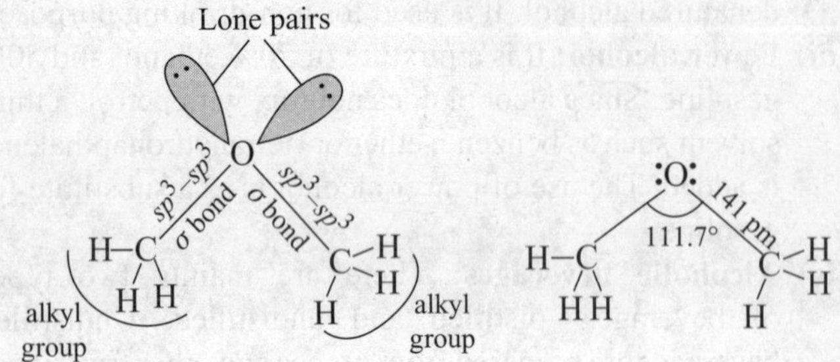

11.10 Preparation of Ethers

11.10.1 Dehydration of Alcohols

$$CH_3CH_2OH \xrightarrow[180°C]{H_2SO_4} CH_2=CH_2$$

$$CH_3CH_2OH \xrightarrow[140°C]{H_2SO_4} CH_3CH_2OCH_2CH_3$$

Ether is formed by the S_N2 mechanism with one molecule acting as the nucleophile and the other protonated molecule of the alcohol acting as the substrate. Unsymmetrical ethers can't be prepared in good yield by this method because, a mixture of products is obtained.

$$ROH + R'OH \underset{}{\overset{H^+}{\rightleftharpoons}} ROR + R'OR' + ROR'$$

11.10.2 Williamson's Synthesis

The reaction involves nucleophilic substitution (S_N2) attack by an alkoxide ion on the primary alkyl halide.

$$\underset{\text{Sodium ethoxide}}{CH_3CH_2ONa} + \underset{\text{Ethyl bromide}}{BrCH_2CH_3} \xrightarrow{330\ K} \underset{\text{Diethyl ether}}{CH_3CH_2OCH_2CH_3} + NaBr$$

$$RO^- Na^+ + R'–X \xrightarrow{S_N2} R–O–R' + NaX$$

Here, the alkoxide ion (RO^-) acts as the nucleophile and R′–X as the substrate.

The best yields of unsymmetrical ethers can be obtained when alkyl halides are primary. However, the alkoxides may be primary, secondary or tertiary. The secondary and tertiary alkyl halides if used may form alkenes as major product due to elimination.

1. $(CH_3)_2CH–O^- + C_6H_5CH_2Br \xrightarrow{S_N2} C_6H_5–CH_2–O–CH(CH_3)_2$

2. $(CH_3)_2CH–Br + C_6H_5CH_2O^- \xrightarrow{S_N2} C_6H_5–CH_2–O–CH(CH_3)_2 + CH_3CH=CH_2$ (E2 product)

However, aryl halide and sodium alkoxide cannot be used for preparing phenolic ethers because aryl halides are less reactive towards nucleophilic substitution reactions than alkyl halides.

Similarly, this method cannot be used for preparing diarylethers because aryl halides do not undergo nucleophilic substitution reactions easily.

$$\underset{\text{Sodium phenoxide}}{C_6H_5–O^-Na^+} + C_6H_5–Br \not\rightarrow \underset{\text{Diphenyl ether}}{C_6H_5–O–C_6H_5} + NaBr$$

11.10.3 From Alkyl Halides by Treating with Dry Silver Oxide

Ethers can also be prepared by heating an alkyl halide with dry silver oxide.

$$\underset{\text{Ethyl bromide (1 molecules)}}{2\,CH_3CH_2Br} + Ag_2O \xrightarrow{Heat} \underset{\text{Diethyl ether}}{CH_3CH_2OCH_2CH_3} + 2AgBr$$

11.10.4 By Alkylation of Alcohols

Tertiary ethers are conveniently prepared by dissolving an alcohol in a strong acid followed by addition of an alkene.

$$CH_2{=}C(CH_3)_2 + H^+ \longrightarrow H_3C{-}\overset{CH_3}{\underset{CH_3}{C^+}} \xrightarrow{RCH_2\ddot{O}H} H_3C{-}\overset{CH_3}{\underset{CH_3}{C}}{-}\overset{+}{O}(H)CH_2R \underset{}{\overset{-H^+}{\rightleftharpoons}} H_3C{-}\overset{CH_3}{\underset{CH_3}{C}}{-}OCH_2R$$

11.11 Physical Properties of Ethers

The important physical properties of ethers are discussed below.

(i) Physical state: Lower members (dimethyl ether, methyl ethyl ether) are gases and higher members are low boiling liquids with a pleasant smell.

(ii) Dipole moments: Due to greater electronegativity of oxygen compared to carbon, the C–O bonds are slightly polar and therefore, the ethers have a resultant dipole moment. For example, the dipole moment of dimethylether is 1.3 D and that of diethylether is 1.18 D.

(iii) Boiling points: Ethers have low polarity and as a result do not show any association by intermolecular hydrogen bonding. Therefore, ethers have low boiling points.

Net dipole moment

$CH_3CH_2OCH_2CH_3$	$CH_3CH_2CH_2CH_2OH$	$CH_3CH_2CH_2CH_2CH_3$
Diethyl ether	*n*-Butyl alcohol	*n*-Pentane
307.6 K	390 K	309.1 K

The large difference in boiling points of alcohols and ethers is due to the presence of hydrogen bonding in alcohols. Due to weak dipole–dipole forces, the boiling points of lower members such as dimethyl ether and ethyl methyl ether are only slightly higher than those of the corresponding *n*-alkanes of comparable molecular masses.

11.12 Chemical Properties of Ethers

(i) Action with concentrated acid (formation of oxonium salts): Ethers act as Lewis bases and dissolve in cold concentrated mineral acids (H_2SO_4, HCl) to form salts called oxonium salts.

$$R{-}O{-}R + H_2SO_4\ (\text{conc.}) \xrightarrow{} \left[R{-}\overset{\oplus}{\underset{H}{\ddot{O}}}{-}R\right] HSO_4^-$$

(Cold) Dialkyloxonium hydrogen sulfate

(ii) Reaction with Lewis acids (formation of coordination complexes): Being Lewis bases, ethers form coordination complexes with Lewis acids such as BF_3, $AlCl_3$, $FeCl_3$, and so on. These complexes are called etherates.

$$(CH_3CH_2)_2\ddot{O}: + BF_3 \rightarrow (CH_3CH_2)_2\ddot{O} \rightarrow BF_3$$

Boron trifluoride etherate (Complex)

$$2(CH_3CH_2)_2O + R\,MgX \rightarrow (CH_3CH_2)_2O \rightarrow Mg(R)(X) \leftarrow O(CH_2CH_3)_2$$

Grignard reagent etherate

11.12.1 Reactions Involving Cleavage of C-O Bond

(i) Cleavage by halogen acids: The carbon–oxygen bond in ethers can be cleaved by heating with hydroiodic acid (H) and hydrobromic acid (HBr) at 373 K to form an alcohol and an alkyl halide.

$$R{-}O{-}R + HX \xrightarrow{373\ K} \underset{\text{Alcohol}}{ROH} + \underset{\text{Alkyl halide}}{RX}$$

$$\underset{\text{Diethyl ether}}{CH_3CH_2OCH_2CH_3} + HI \xrightarrow{373\ K} \underset{\text{Ethyl alcohol}}{CH_3CH_2OH} + \underset{\text{Ethyl iodide}}{CH_3CH_2I}$$

However, if excess acid is used, the alcohol first formed reacts further with the halogen acid to form an alkyl halide.

$$R{-}OH + HX \xrightarrow{373\ K} RX + H_2O$$

The overall reaction may be written as:

$$R{-}O{-}R + \underset{(\text{excess})}{2HX} \xrightarrow{373\ K} 2RX + H_2O\ (HX = HI, HBr)$$

$$\underset{\text{Diethyl ether}}{CH_3CH_2{-}O{-}CH_2CH_3} + \underset{(\text{excess})}{2HI} \xrightarrow{373\ K} \underset{\text{Ethyl iodide}}{2CH_3CH_2I} + H_2O$$

Similarly, cyclic ethers are easily cleaved by HBr or HI to form dihaloalkanes.

$$\underset{\text{Tetrahydrofuran (THF)}}{\text{THF}} + \underset{(\text{excess})}{2HI} \xrightarrow{373\ K} \underset{\text{1, 4-Diiodobutane}}{ICH_2{-}CH_2{-}CH_2{-}CH_2I} + H_2O$$

(ii) Cleavage of unsymmetrical alkyl ethers (site of cleavage): If primary and secondary alkyl groups are present, then the reaction occurs by the S_N2 mechanism. Thus, in the case of unsymmetrical ethers with two different alkyl groups, the site of cleavage is such that the halide is formed from the alkyl group which is smaller in size. For example,

$$\underset{\text{Ethyl methyl ether}}{CH_3{-}O{-}CH_2CH_3} + HI \xrightarrow{373\ K} \underset{\text{Methyl iodide}}{CH_3I} + \underset{\text{Ethyl alcohol}}{CH_3CH_2OH}$$

$$\underset{\text{Isopropylmethyl ether}}{CH_3{-}O{-}CH(CH_3)_2} + HI \xrightarrow{373\ K} \underset{\text{Methyl iodide}}{CH_3I} + \underset{\text{Isopropyl alcohol}}{CH_3{-}CH(OH){-}CH_3}$$

Since the tert-butyl carbocation $[(CH_3)_3C^+]$ is more stable than the methyl carbocation (CH_3^+), the cleavage of the C–O bond gives a more stable carbocation $[(CH_3)_3C^+]$ and methanol. Then, the iodine ion I^-, attacks this tert-butyl carbocation to form tert-butyl iodide.

$$CH_3-\underset{CH_3}{\overset{CH_3}{C}}-\ddot{O}-CH_3 + H^+I^- \underset{+I^-}{\overset{-I^-}{\rightleftharpoons}} CH_3-\underset{CH_3}{\overset{CH_3}{C}}-\overset{H}{\overset{|+}{O}}-CH_3$$

tert-Butyl methyl ether — Oxonium ion

(iii) Cleavage of alkyl aryl (phenolic) ethers: With alkyl aryl ethers (phenolic ethers), the cleavage with hydrogen halide always gives the phenol and a molecule of alkyl halide and not aryl halide and alcohol.

$$C_6H_5OCH_3 + HI \longrightarrow C_6H_5OH + CH_3I$$

Anisole — Phenol

In case of anisole, methyl phenyl oxonium ion, $C_6H_5-\overset{+}{\underset{H}{O}}-CH_3$ is formed by the protonation of the ether.

The $O-CH_3$ bond is weaker than the $O-C_6H_5$ bond because the carbon of the phenyl group is sp^2 hybridised and there is partial double bond character. Therefore, the attack of the halide ion breaks the $O-CH_3$ bond to form CH_3I. It may be noted that phenols do not react further to give halides because the sp^2 hybridised carbon of phenol does not undergo nucleophilic substitution. The alkyl halide is formed by the attack of halide ion on the protonated ether. Therefore, the attack of the halide ion occurs at the smaller alkyl group which offers less hindrance.

(iv) Cleavage with phosphorus pentachloride: Ethers react with PCl_5 on heating to form the alkyl chloride as a result of the cleavage of the C–O bond.

$$CH_3CH_2-O-CH_2CH_3 + PCl_5 \xrightarrow{Heat} 2CH_3CH_2Cl + POCl_3$$

Diethyl ether — Ethyl chloride — Phosphoryl chloride

(v) Cleavage by acid chloride: Ethers react with acetyl chloride in the presence of anhydrous $ZnCl_2$ to give the alkyl halide and ester.

$$CH_3CH_2-O-CH_2CH_3 + CH_3COCl \xrightarrow[ZnCl_2]{Anhyd.} CH_3CH_2Cl + CH_3COOC_2H_5$$

Diethyl ether — Acetyl chloride — Ethyl chloride — Ethyl acetate (ester)

However, with anhydrides, only esters are formed.

$$(C_2H_5)_2O + (CH_3CO)_2O \xrightarrow[Heat]{Anhyd.\ ZnCl_2} 2CH_3COOC_2H_5$$

Diethyl ether — Acetic anhydride — Ethyl acetate

11.12.2 Reaction of Alkyl Group

Halogenation: Ethers react with chlorine or bromine in the dark to give substituted products. For example, diethyl ether reacts with chlorine in the dark to give 1,1-dichlorodiethylether in which the halogenations preferentially occur at the α-carbon atoms.

$$CH_3CH_2OCH_2CH_3 \xrightarrow[-HCl]{Cl_2\ in\ dark} CH_3\overset{Cl}{\overset{|}{C}}HOCH_2CH_3 \xrightarrow[-HCl]{Cl_2\ in\ dark} CH_3\overset{Cl}{\overset{|}{C}}H-O-\overset{Cl}{\overset{|}{C}}HCH_3$$

1-Chlorodiethyl ether — 1, 1′-Dichlorodiethyl ether

However, in the presence of light and excess of chlorine, all the hydrogen atoms are substituted by chlorine atoms.

$$CH_3CH_2-O-CH_2CH_3 + \underset{(excess)}{10Cl_2} \xrightarrow{hv} Cl_3C-CCl_2-OCCl_2-CCl_3 + 10HCl$$

Perchlorodiethtyl ether

11.12.3 Ring Substitution in Aromatic Ethers

The alkoxy group is ortho and para directing; it directs the incoming groups to the ortho and para positions in the ring. It activates the aromatic ring towards electrophilic substitution reaction in the same way as alcohols do.

[Resonance structures I ↔ II ↔ III ↔ IV ↔ V of the alkoxybenzene ($\ddot{O}R$, $^+\ddot{O}R$)]

As is clear that structures III, IV and V show high electron density at the ortho and para positions compared to the meta positions. Therefore, electrophilic substitution reactions occur mainly at the o- and p- positions.

(i) Halogenation: Phenyl alkyl ethers undergo the usual halogenations in the benzene ring. For example, bromination of anisole gives the ortho and para bromo derivatives even in the absence of iron(III) bromide catalyst. This is because of the activation of the benzene ring by the methoxy group.

$$C_6H_5OCH_3 \xrightarrow[CH_3COOH]{Br_2\ in} o\text{-}BrC_6H_4OCH_3 + p\text{-}BrC_6H_4OCH_3$$

Anisole — *o*-Bromoanisole (minor, 10%) — *p*-Bromoanisole (major, 90%)

(ii) Friedel–Crafts reaction: Anisole undergoes Friedel–Craft alkylation and acylation reaction in the presence of anhydrous aluminium halide (a Lewis acid) as catalyst in which alkyl and acyl group are introduced at the ortho and para positions.

$$C_6H_5OCH_3 + CH_3Cl \xrightarrow[CS_2]{anhyd.\ AlCl_3\ in} o\text{-}CH_3C_6H_4OCH_3 + p\text{-}CH_3C_6H_4OCH_3$$

Anisole — Methyl chloride (Alkylation) — 2-Methoxy toluene (minor) — 4-Methoxy toluene (major)

Anisole + CH_3COCl (Ethanoyl chloride (Acetyl chloride) (Acylation)) $\xrightarrow{\text{anhyd. } AlCl_3 \text{ in } CS_2}$ 2-Methoxy acetophenone (minor) + 4-Methoxy acetophenone (major)

Methyl phenyl ester (Anisole) $\xrightarrow{HNO_3 + H_2SO_4}$ Methyl-2 nitrophenyl ether (*o*-Nitroanisole) (minor) + Methyl-4 nitrophenyl ether (*p*-Nitroanisole) (major)

(iii) Nitration: When treated with a mixture of concentrated HNO_3 and H_2SO_4, anisole gives a mixture of the *o*- and *p*-nitro compounds.

It may, however, be noted that ethers are relatively less reactive than phenols towards electrophilic substitution reactions.

Exercises

OBJECTIVE QUESTIONS

Classification and Nomenclature

1. Which of the following is a neohexyl alcohol?
(a) 3,3-dimethyl-2-butanol
(b) 1,1-dimethyl-1-butanol
(c) 3,3-dimethyl-1-butanol
(d) 2,2-dimethyl-1-butanol

2. A compound with a MF of $C_6H_{12}O_2$ has two tertiary alcoholic groups. The IUPAC name of the compound is
(a) 2,3-dimethylbutane-2,3-diol
(b) 3,3-dimethyl-1,2-butanediol
(c) 2-methyl-2,3-pentanediol
(d) 2,3-dimethyl-1,2-butanediol

3. Which of the following statements about the following alcohol is/are correct? $C_6H_5-CH{=}CH-C(CH_3)_2-OH$
(a) It is a tertiary alcohol.
(b) It is an allylic alcohol.
(c) Its IUPAC name is 2-methyl-4-phenylbut-3-en-2-ol.
(d) All statements are correct.

4. Which of the following is a chiral $C_5H_{12}O$ secondary alcohol?
(a) 3-methyl-2-butanol (b) 2-methyl-2-butanol
(c) 3-methyl-1-butanol (d) 2-methyl-1-butanol

5. The IUPAC name of hydroquinol is
(a) 4-methylphenol (b) benzene-1,2-diol
(c) benzene-1,3-diol (d) benzene-1,4-diol

6. The IUPAC name of the following compound is

$CH_3CH_2-CH(CH_2Cl)-CH(CH_2OH)-CH(CH_3)-CH_3$ is

(a) 4-chloro-2,3-dimethylhexan-1-ol
(b) 3-chloromethyl-3-isopropylpentan-1-ol
(c) 3-chloromethyl-4-isopropylpentan-5-ol
(d) 3-chloromethyl-2-isopropylpentan-1-ol

7. Which of the following IUPAC names is not in accord? Isopropyl bromide on reaction with sodium isopropoxide yields a substance with IUPAC nomenclature ________.
(a) $CH_3-C(CH_3){=}C(Br)-CH_2OH$ 2-Bromo-3-methyl but-2-en-1-ol
(b) (cyclohexane with NO_2 and OC_2H_5 on adjacent carbons) 1-Nitro-2-ethoxy cyclohexane
(c) $C_6H_5-O-CH_2CH_2-CH(CH_3)-CH_3$ 3-Methylbutoxybenzene
(d) $HOCH_2CH_2-C(CH_3)(OH)-CH_2-C(CH_3)_2(OH)$ 3, 5-Dimethylhexane-1, 3, 5-triol

8. Vinyl carbinol is
(a) $HO-CH_2-CH{=}CH_2$ (b) $CH_3CH(OH){=}CH_2$
(c) $CH_3-CH{=}CH-OH$ (d) $CH_3-C(CH_2OH){=}CH_2$

Preparation of Alcohols

9. Styrene on acid-catalysed hydration gives
(a) 1-phenylethanol (b) 2-phenylethanol
(c) phenylcarbinol (d) cyclohexylmethanol

10. The major product of the reaction is

(1-methylcyclopentene) $\xrightarrow{H^+/H_2O}$ Product

I: 1-methylcyclopentanol; II: cyclopentylmethanol; III: 2-methylcyclopentanol; IV: 3-methylcyclopentanol

(a) I (b) II
(c) III (d) IV

11. The major product of the reaction is

$\xrightarrow{H^+/H_2O}$ Product

I II III IV

(a) I (b) II (c) III (d) IV

12. In the reaction, A $\xrightarrow{\text{Dil. } H_2SO_4}$ 1-Methylcyclohexanol, A is

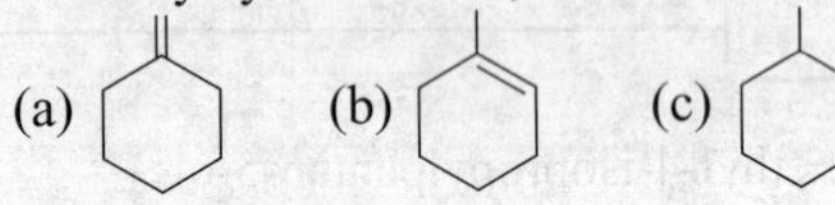

(d) both (a) and (b)

13. Hydration of 3-phenylbut-1-ene with dil. H_2SO_4 mainly gives

(a) 3-phenylbutan-1-ol (b) 3-phenylbutan-2-ol
(c) 2-phenylbutan-1-ol (d) 2-phenylbutan-2-of

14. In the following reaction,

$H_3C-C(CH_3)_2-CH=CH_2 \xrightarrow{H_2O/H^+} A + B$
(Major product) (Minor product)

The major product is

(a) $H_3C-C(CH_3)(OH)-CH(CH_3)-CH_3$ (b) $CH_2-C(CH_3)(OH)-CH_2-CH_3$ with CH_3
(c) $H_3C-C(CH_3)(H_3C)-CH(OH)-CH_3$ (d) $H_3C-C(CH_3)_2-CH_2-CH_2OH$

15. Consider the following reaction,

ethanol $\xrightarrow{PBr_3}$ X $\xrightarrow{\text{alc. KOH}}$ Y $\xrightarrow[\text{(i) } H_2O\text{, heat}]{\text{(i) } H_2SO_4\text{, room temperature}}$ Z

The product Z is

(a) $CH_3CH_2-O-CH_2CH_3$ (b) $CH_3CH_2-O-SO_3H$
(c) CH_3CH_2OH (d) $CH_2=CH_2$

16. Propene, $CH_3CH=CH_2$ can be converted into 1-propanol by oxidation. Indicate which set of reagents amongst the following is ideal to effect the above conversion?

(a) $KMnO_4$ (alkaline)
(b) osmium tetroxide (OsO_4/CH_2Cl_2)
(c) B_2H_6 and alk. H_2O_2
(d) O_3/Zn

17. $C_6H_5-CH_2-CH=CH_2$ on mercuration–demercuration produces

(a) $C_6H_5-CH_2CHOHCH_3$ (b) $C_6H_5-CH_2CH_2CH_2OH$
(c) $C_6H_5-CH_2CHOHCH_2OH$ (d) none of these

18. Oxymercuration–demercuration of 2,2-dimethyl-1-butene gives

(a) 3,3-dimethyl-1-butanol (b) 3,3-dimethyl-2-butanol
(c) 2,3-dimethyl-2-butanol (d) 2,3-dimethyl-1-butanol

19. Formation of alcohol by oxymercuration–demercuration of alkene

(a) involves carbocations and rearrangement
(b) involves carbanions and rearrangement
(c) is stereospecific
(d) does not involve carbocations and rearrangement

20. Which one of the following alkenes will give the same product by any method out of hydration, hydroboration–oxidation and oxymercuration–demercuration?

(a) $CH_3CH=CH_2$ (b) $CH_3CH=CHCH_3$
(c) $(CH_3)_2C=CH_2$ (d) cyclohexane$=CH_2$

21. Predict the product of the following reaction,

2-oxocyclohexyl$-CH_2-C(=O)-OCH_3 \xrightarrow{NaBH_4}$

(a) 2-oxocyclohexyl$-CH_2-CH_2OH$ (b) 2-oxocyclohexyl$-CH_2-C(=O)-OCH_3$
(c) 2-hydroxycyclohexyl$-CH_2CH_2OH$ (d) 2-hydroxycyclohexyl$-CH_2CH_3$

22. The most appropriate reagent to convert RCOOEt → RCH_2OH is

(a) $LiAlH_4$ (b) $NaBH_4$
(c) $H_2/Pd-C$ (d) Li/NH_3 (liq)

23. The compound, $CH_3COCH_2COOC_2H_5$ on reduction with $LiAlH_4$/ether followed by treatment with dilute acid gives

(a) $CH_3COCH_2CH_2OH + C_2H_5OH$
(b) $CH_3CHOHCH_2CH_2OH + C_2H_5OH$
(c) $CH_3CHOHCH_2COOC_2H_5$
(d) a mixture of (a) and (b)

24. Which of the esters shown, after reduction with $LiAlH_4$ and aqueous work up, will yield two molecules of only a single alcohol?

(a) $C_6H_5COOC_6H_5$ (b) $CH_3CH_2COOCH_2CH_3$
(c) $C_6H_5COOCH_2C_6H_5$ (d) CH_3COOCH_3

25. The products of the following reduction are

$CH_3CH_2CH_2COOCH_2CH_3 \xrightarrow{Na/C_2H_5OH}$

(a) $CH_3CH_2CH_2CHO + CH_3CH_2OH$
(b) $CH_3CH_2CH_2COOH + CH_3CH_2OH$
(c) $CH_3CH_2CH_2OH + CH_3CH_2OH$
(d) $CH_3CH_2CH_2OH + CH_3CH_2COOH$

26. A $\xleftarrow[CH_3OH]{NaBH_4}$ [cyclic lactone with ketone: six-membered ring containing O, C=O adjacent to ring O, and C=O at the opposite position] $\xrightarrow{LiAlH_4}$ B

The products A and B respectively are

(a) A = [lactone ring with OH in place of ketone], B = [open chain diol: HOCH₂CH₂CH(OH)CH₂CH₂OH skeleton with three OH]

(b) B, A
(c) B in both cases (d) A in both cases

27. In the following sequence of reactions,

$CH_3{-}Br \xrightarrow{KCN} A \xrightarrow{H_3O^+} B \xrightarrow[ether]{LiAlH_4} C$

the end product (C) is
(a) acetone (b) methane
(c) acetaldehyde (d) ethyl alcohol

28. Which of the following would you select to convert formaldehyde into the following alcohol? $CH_3{-}CH(CH_3){-}CH_2OH$

(a) $(CH_3)CHBr$ and anhyd. $AlCl_3$
(b) $(CH_3)_2CHMgBr$ and acid hydrolysis
(c) $CH_3CH_2CH_2MgBr$ and acid hydrolysis
(d) $(CH_3)_2CHBr$ and zinc

29. Cyclohexylmethanol can be prepared by reacting cyclohexylmagnesium bromide with which of the following reagents?
(a) formaldehyde (b) acetaldehyde
(c) cyclohexanone (d) bromocyclohexane

30. The reaction of butanal with *n*-propylmagnesium bromide gives a
(a) chiral secondary alcohol
(b) achiral secondary alcohol
(c) chiral tertiary alcohol
(d) achiral tertiary alcohol

31. $(CH_3)_2CHCHO + CH_3MgBr \xrightarrow{Ether} A \xrightarrow{H_3O^+} B$

The IUPAC name of B is
(a) 3-methylbutan-2-ol (b) 2-methylbutan-3-ol
(c) 2-methylbutan-2-ol (d) pentan-2-ol

32. $CH_3CH_2{-}C(OH)(Ph){-}CH_3$ cannot be prepared by

(a) $PhCOCH_3 + CH_3CH_2MgX$
(b) $HCHO + PhCH(CH_3)CH_2MgX$
(c) $PhCOCH_2CH_3 + CH_3MgBr$
(d) $CH_3CH_2COCH_3 + PhMgX$

33. Which among the following compounds will give a secondary alcohol on reacting with a Grignard reagent followed by acid hydrolysis?

I. HCHO II. C_2H_5CHO
III. CH_3COCH_3 IV. $RCOOC_2H_5$

Select the correct answer using the codes given below:
(a) Only I (b) Only II
(c) II and IV (d) III and IV

34. Which of the following compounds on reaction with CH_3MgBr will give a tertiary alcohol?
(a) C_6H_5CHO (b) $C_2H_5CO_2CH_3$
(c) C_2H_5COOH (d) $CH_3CH{-}CHCH_3$ (epoxide, O bridging)

35. 2-Phenylethanol may be prepared by the reaction of phenylmagnesium bromide with
(a) HCHO (b) CH_3CHO
(c) CH_3COCH_3 (d) [ethylene oxide]

36. $CH_3{-}CH(OH){-}CH_3 \xrightarrow{PBr_3} X \xrightarrow{Mg/ether} X \xrightarrow{CH_2{-}CH_2\,(O)} \xrightarrow{H_2O/H^+} \xrightarrow{\Delta}$

The final product is
(a) $CH_3{-}CH(CH_3){-}CH_2CH_2OH$ (b) $CH_3{-}O{-}CH(CH_3)CH_2CH_3$
(c) $CH_3{-}CH(CH_3){-}O{-}CH_2{-}CH_3$ (d) $CH_3CH_2{-}CH(CH_3){-}CH_2OH$

37. To prepare3-ethyl-3-pentanol, which of the following pairs of reactants should be used?
(a) $CH_3CH_2COCH_3$ and $CH_3CH_2CH_2MgBr$
(b) $CH_3CH_2COCH_2CH_3$ and CH_3CH_2MgBr
(c) $CH_3CH_2CH_2COCH_2CH_3$ and CH_3MgBr
(d) $CH_3CH_2CH_2COCH_3$ and CH_3CH_2MgBr

38. Which of the following will give 2-phenyl-2-propanol?
(a) $PhCOCH_3 \xrightarrow[(ii)\ H_3O^+]{(i)\ CH_3MgBr}$
(b) $CH_3COCH_3 \xrightarrow[(ii)\ H_3O^+]{(i)\ PhMgBr}$
(c) $PhCOOCH_3 \xrightarrow[(ii)\ H_3O^+]{(i)\ CH_3MgBr}$
(d) all these three

39. The reaction between which of the following reactants followed by acid hydrolysis would give $(CH_3)_2C(OH)CH_2CH_2CH_2OH$ as the final product?

(a) $CH_3COCH_2CH_2CH_2OH + CH_3MgBr$
(b) $CH_3O–CO–CH_2CH_2CH_2OH + CH_3MgBr$
(c) γ-butyrolactone + CH_3MgBr (1 mol)
(d) γ-butyrolactone + CH_3MgBr (excess)

40. Propanal on reaction with CH_3MgI and subsequent hydrolysis produces
(a) 1-butanol (b) (–)2-butanol
(c) (+)-2-butanol (d) (±)2-butanol

41. Benzylamine reacts with nitrous acid to form
(a) azobenzene (b) benzene
(c) benzyl alcohol (d) phenol

42. Monochlorination of toluene in the presence of sunlight followed by hydrolysis gives
(a) *o*-cresol (b) *m*-cresol
(c) 2,4-dihydroxytoluene (d) benzyl alcohol

43. 1-propanol and 2-propanol can be best distinguished by
(a) oxidation with alkaline $KMnO_4$ followed by reaction with Fehling's solution
(b) oxidation with acidic dichromate followed by reaction with Fehling's solution
(c) oxidation by heating with copper followed by reaction with Fehling's solution
(d) oxidation with conc. H_2SO_4 followed by reaction with Fehling's solution

44. Which of the following alkenes will give an optically active alcohol when treated with H_2O/H_2SO_4
(a) butene -1 (b) ethene
(c) propene (d) 2-methylpropene

Preparation of Phenols

45. Identify the major products P, Q and R in the following sequence of reactions.

$$C_6H_6 + CH_3CH_2CH_2Cl \xrightarrow{\text{Anhydrous } AlCl_3} P \xrightarrow[\text{(ii) } H_3O^+/\Delta]{\text{(i) } O_2} Q + R$$

(a) P = $C_6H_5CH_2CH_2CH_3$, Q = C_6H_5CHO, R = $CH_3CH_2–OH$
(b) P = $C_6H_5CH_2CH_2CH_3$, Q = C_6H_5CHO, R = C_6H_5COOH
(c) P = $C_6H_5CH(CH_3)_2$, Q = C_6H_5OH, R = $CH_3CH(OH)CH_3$
(d) P = $C_6H_5CH(CH_3)_2$, Q = C_6H_5OH, R = $CH_3–CO–CH_3$

46. *p*-Toluenesulfonic acid on fusion with solid KOH at 573 K followed by treatment with dilute HCl gives
(a) *p*-cresol (b) toluene
(c) benzoic acid (d) benzene-1,4-diol

47. On a commercial scale, phenol is obtained from chlorobenzene by Raschig's process. Which one of the following is Raschig's process?

(a) $C_6H_6 + Cl_2 \xrightarrow[\text{310–320 K}]{\text{Anhy. } AlCl_3} C_6H_5Cl$
(b) $C_6H_5\overset{+}{N}_2Cl^- \xrightarrow{CuCl/HCl} C_6H_5Cl$
(c) $C_6H_5\overset{+}{N}_2Cl^- \xrightarrow[\Delta]{Cu/HCl} C_6H_5Cl$
(d) $C_6H_6 + HCl + O_2(air) \xrightarrow[\text{500 K}]{CuCl_2} C_6H_5Cl$

48. The conversion of *m*-nitrophenol to resorcinol involves respectively
(a) hydrolysis, diazotisation and reduction
(b) diazotisation, reduction and hydrolysis
(c) hydrolysis, reduction and diazotisation
(d) reduction, diazotisation and hydrolysis

49. Which of the following is the strongest acid?
(a) *o*-methoxyphenol (b) *p*-methoxyphenol
(c) *m*-methoxyphenol (d) phenol

50. Phenol is more acidic than ethyl alcohol because
(a) phenoxide ion is more resonance stabilised than phenol
(b) there is more hydrogen bonding in phenol than ethyl alcohol
(c) ethoxide ion is less resonance stabilised than ethyl alcohol
(d) phenol has a higher boiling point than ethyl alcohol

51. Oxygen when passed through an ethereal solution of phenylmagnesium iodide followed by acid hydrolysis gives
(a) benzene (b) benzoic acid
(c) phenol (d) salicylic acid

52. Isopropylbenzene on aerial oxidation in the presence of dilute acid gives
(a) C_6H_5COOH (b) $C_6H_5COCH_3$
(c) C_6H_5CHO (d) C_6H_5OH

Physical Properties of Alcohols, Phenols and Ethers

53. *Ortho*-nitrophenol is less soluble in water than *p*- and *m*-nitro phenols because

(a) *o*-nitrophenol shows intramolecular H-bonding
(b) *o*-nitrophenol shows intermolecular H-bonding
(c) melting point of *o*-nitrophenol is lower than that of *m*- and *p*-nitrophenols
(d) *o*-nitrophenol is more volatile in steam than the *m*- and *p*-isomers

54. Among the compounds I–IV, the compound having the lowest boiling point is

OH (I) OH (II)

O (III) OH OH (IV)

(a) I (b) II (c) III (d) IV

55. Among (i)–(iii)

OH (i) OH OH (ii) HO OH (iii)

the boiling points follow the order

(a) (ii) < (i) < (iii) (b) (iii) < (ii) < (i)
(c) (i) < (ii) < (iii) (d) (ii) < (iii) < (i)

56. For which of the following molecules is $\mu \neq 0$?

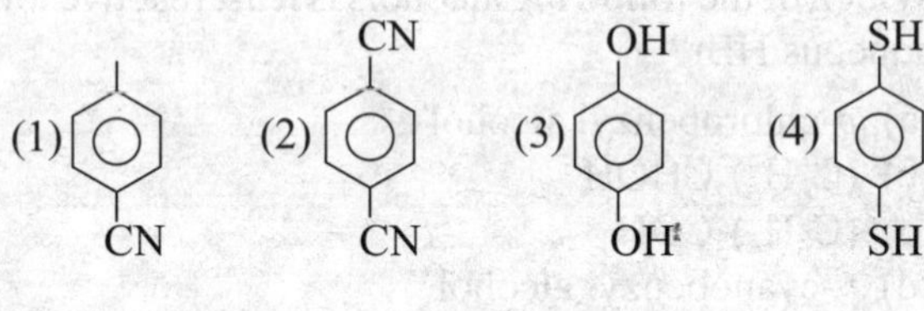

(a) 3 and 4 (b) only 1
(c) 1 and 2 (d) only 3

57. The dipole moments of CH_3OH, C_6H_5OH and CH_3OCH_3 increase in the order

(a) $CH_3OCH_3 < CH_3OH < C_6H_5OH$
(b) $CH_3OCH_3 < C_6H_5OH < CH_3OH$
(c) $C_6H_5OH < CH_3OH < CH_3OCH_3$
(d) $CH_3OH < C_6H_5OH < CH_3OCH_3$

58. CH_3OCH_3 is a gas at room temperature while its isomer CH_3CH_2OH is a liquid with a BP of 351 K. This is because

(a) CH_3OCH_3 cannot undergo molecular association as its hydrogens are all attached to carbons while the presence of the OH group in CH_3CH_2OH permits molecular association.
(b) CH_3OCH_3 forms intramolecular H-bonding while CH_3CH_2OH forms intermolecular H-bonding.
(c) CH_3 groups in CH_3OCH_3 has a weaker +I effect while CH_3CH_2 group in CH_3CH_2OH has a stronger +I effect.
(d) the lone pair of electrons on O in CH_3OCH_3 participates in resonance while in CH_3CH_2OH it does not

59. Me_2O is highly soluble in water but Et_2O is only sparingly soluble in water because

(a) the Et group has a stronger +I effect than the Me group
(b) the hyperconjugation effect of the Me group in stronger in Me_2O than that of the Et group in Et_2O
(c) Me_2O reacts with H_2O more efficiently due to the presence of the small sized Me group but Et_2O does not due to the bigger size of the Et group
(d) H-bonding between Et_2O and H_2O is less efficient due to steric crowding around the oxygen atom because of bigger size of the Et group while the H-bonding between Me_2O and H_2O is much more efficient due to the small size of the Me groups

60. The C–O–H/C–O–C bond angle in CH_3OH, C_6H_5OH and CH_3OCH_3 increase in the order

(a) $CH_3OH, CH_3OCH_3, C_6H_5OH$
(b) $C_6H_5OH, CH_3OH, CH_3OCH_3$
(c) $CH_3OH, C_6H_5OH, CH_3OCH_3$
(d) $C_6H_5OH, CH_3OCH_3, CH_3OH$

61. Which of the following is the most soluble in water?

(a) *n*-butyl alcohol (b) isobutyl alcohol
(c) *tert*-butyl alcohol (d) *sec*-butyl alcohol

62. Arrange the following compounds in increasing order of their boiling points.

(a) methanol, ethanol, propan-1-ol, butan-2-ol, butan-1-ol, pentan-1-ol
(b) ethanol, methanol, propan-1-ol, butan-1-ol, butan-2-ol, pentan-1-ol
(c) methanol, ethanol, pentan-1-ol, butan-2-ol, butan-1-ol, propan-1-ol
(d) ethanol, methanol, pentan-1-ol, butan-1-ol, butan-2-ol, propan-1-ol

Chemical Reactions of Alcohols

63. The correct order of basic strength is

(a) $H_2O < OH^- < CH_3OH < CH_3O^-$
(b) $CH_3OH < H_2O < CH_3O^- < OH^-$
(c) $H_2O < CH_3OH < OH^- < CH_3O^-$
(d) $OH^- < H_2O < CH_3O^- < CH_3OH$

64. Which of the following has the maximum pK_a value?

(a) OH (b) OH

65. The reactivities of methanol (I), 1-propanol (II), 2-butanol (III) and 2-methyl-2-propanol (IV) towards sodium metal follows the order

(a) I > II > III > IV (b) IV > III > II > I
(c) IV > II > III > I (d) I > IV > II > III

66. Which one of the following reactions suggests acidic character of ethanol?

(a) $C_2H_5OH + CH_3MgI \rightarrow$
(b) $C_2H_5OH + NaNH_2 \rightarrow$
(c) $C_2H_5OH + Mg \rightarrow$
(d) all the three

67. Among the following, the non-spontaneous reaction is

(a) $ROH + R'MgX \rightarrow R'H + Mg(OR)X$
(b) $RONa + NH_3 \rightarrow NaNH_2 + ROH$
(c) $RONa + H_2O \rightarrow NaOH + ROH$
(d) $ROH + HC{\equiv}CNa \rightarrow RONa + HC{\equiv}CH$

68. 370 mg of an alcohol reacts with the required amount of CH_3MgBr and produces 112 mL of methane at STP. The alcohol is

(a) ethanol (b) *n*-butanol
(c) *n*-propanol (d) *n*-pentanol

69. Which of the following reagents is used to determine the number of active hydrogens in a compound by Zerevitinov's method?

(a) CH_3I (b) CH_3MgI
(c) C_2H_5MgI (d) C_6H_5MgBr

70. 0.92 g of a compound with a MF $C_3H_8O_3$ on reaction with excess CH_3MgI evolves 448 mL of methane at STP. The number of active hydrogen atoms present in a molecule of the compound is

(a) one (b) two (c) three (d) four

71. A compound with a fruity smell is obtained when

(a) acetic acid is treated with ethyl alcohol in presence of a few drops of conc. H_2SO_4
(b) acetyl chloride is reacted with ethyl alcohol in presence of pyridine
(c) acetic anhydride is reacted with ethyl alcohol
(d) all the three above

72. Acetic acid reacts separately with the following alcohols. The rate of esterification is highest for

(a) CH_3OH (b) C_2H_5OH
(c) $(CH_3)_2CHOH$ (d) $(CH_3)_3COH$

73. Which of the following reacts fastest with conc. HCl?

(a) $C_6H_5-CH_2CH_2OH$ (b) $C_6H_5-CHOH-CH_3$
(c) $(CH_3)_3COH$ (d) $CH_2{=}CH{-}CH_2OH$

74. The correct product of the following reaction

$CH_3-CH(CH_3)-CH(OH)-CH_3 \xrightarrow{HBr}$ is

(a) $CH_3-CH(CH_3)-CH(Br)-CH_3$ (b) $CH_3-CH(CH_3)-CH_2-CH_2Br$
(c) $CH_3-C(Br)(CH_3)-CH_2CH_3$ (d) $BrCH_2-CH(CH_3)-CH_2CH_3$

75. HBr reacts fastest with

(a) 2-methylpropan-1-ol (b) 2-methypropan-2-ol
(c) propan-2-ol (d) propan-1-ol

76. Among the following, one which reacts most readily with ethanol is

(a) *p*-nitrobenzyl bromide
(b) *p*-chlorobenzyl chloride
(c) *p*-methoxybenzyl bromide
(d) *p*-methylbenzyl bromide

77. Consider the following alcohols

I. 1-phenyl-1-propanol II. 3-phenyl-1-propanol
III. 1-phenyl-2-propanol

The correct sequence of decreasing order of reactivity of these alcohols in their reaction with HBr is

(a) I > II > III (b) II > I > III
(c) I > III > II (d) II > III > I

78. Which of the following alcohols is least reactive towards aqueous HBr?

(a) *p*-chlorobenzyl alcohol
(b) $(C_6H_5)_2CHOH$
(c) $(C_6H_5)_3COH$
(d) *p*-cyanobenzyl alcohol

79. What will be the order of reactivity of the following alcohols towards concentrated HCl?

F, OH (I) F, OH (II) OH (III) Ph, OH (IV)

(a) I > II > III > IV (b) I > III > II > IV
(c) IV > III > II > I (d) IV > III > I > II

80. The order of reactivity of the four isomeric butyl alcohols with HBr is

(a) OH > OH > OH > OH
(b) OH > OH > OH > OH
(c) OH > OH > OH > OH

(d) 1-butanol (OH) > 2-butanol (OH) > 2-methyl-1-propanol (OH) > tert-butanol (OH)

81. In the following reactions,

The major products (A) and (C) are respectively

(i) $CH_3-CH(CH_3)-CH(OH)-CH_3 \xrightarrow{H^+/Heat} A + B$ (A: Major product; B: Minor product)

(a) $CH_2=C(CH_3)-CH_2-CH_3$ and $CH_3=C(CH_3)(Br)-CH_2-CH_3$

(b) $CH_2=C(CH_3)-CH_2-CH_3$ and $CH_3-CH(CH_3)-CH(Br)-CH_2-CH_3$

(c) $CH_2-C(CH_3)=CH-CH_3$ and $CH_3-C(CH_3)(Br)-CH_2-CH_3$

(d) $CH_2-C(CH_3)=CH-CH_3$ and $CH_3-CH(CH_3)-CH(Br)-CH_3$

82. $CH_3CH_2-C(CH_3)(CH_3OH)-CH-CH_3 \xrightarrow[heat]{H_2SO_4} P$ (Major)

What is the major product P in the above reaction?

(a) $CH_2(CH_3)-CH_2-CH(CH_3)-CH=CH_2$

(b) $CH_3-CH(CH_3)-CH(CH_3)-CH=CH_2$

(c) $CH_3CH_2-C(CH_3)(CH_3)-CH=CH_2$

(d) $CH_3CH_2-C(H_3C)=C(CH_3)-CH_3$

83. The major product formed when 3,3-dimethylbutane-2-ol is heated with conc. sulfuric acid is

(a) 2,3-dimethyl-2-butene
(b) 2,3-dimethyl-1-butene
(c) 3,3-dimethyl-1-butene
(d) *cis*- and *trans*-isomers of 2,3-dimethyl-1-butene
(e) *cis*- and *trans*- isomers of 3,3-dimethyl-2-butene

84. Which of the following is not the product of dehydration of [cyclohexyl–C(CH_3)(OH)–CH_2CH_3]

(a) [structure] (b) [structure]

(c) [structure] (d) [structure]

85. Which one of the following cannot be obtained from a mixture of ethanol and concentrated sulfuric acid if the composition of the mixture and the reaction conditions are suitably adjusted?

(a) C_2H_4 (b) CH_3CHO
(c) $CH_3CH_2OCH_2CH_3$ (d) $CH_3CH_2HSO_4$

86. The best reagent to convert pent-3-en-2-ol into pent-3-en-2-one is

(a) pyridinium chlorochromate
(b) chromic anhydride in glacial acetic acid
(c) acidic dichromate
(d) acidic permanganate

87. The most suitable reagent for the conversion of primary alcohol into aldehyde with the same number of carbon atoms is

(a) acidified $K_2Cr_2O_7$ (b) acidified $KMnO_4$
(c) alkaline $KMnO_4$
(d) pyridinium chlorochromate

88. Which of the following alcohols will not be easily oxidised by $K_2Cr_2O_7$ in dil. H_2SO_4?

(a) CH_3OH (b) CH_3CH_2OH
(c) $(CH_3)_3COH$ (d) $CH_3CHOHCH_3$

89. An alcohol on oxidation is found to give CH_3COOH and CH_3CH_2COOH. The structure of the alcohol is

(a) $CH_3CH_2CH_2OH$ (b) $(CH_3)_2C(OH)CH_2CH_3$
(c) $CH_3(CH_2)_3CH_2OH$ (d) $CH_3CHOHCH_2CH_3$

90. When the vapour of an alcohol is passed over hot reduced copper, it gives an alkene. The alcohol is

(a) primary (b) secondary
(c) tertiary (d) none of these

91. An organic compound X on treatment with pyridinium chlorochromate in dichloromethane gives a compound Y. Compound Y reacts with I_2 and alkali to form triiodomethane. The compound X is

(a) C_2H_5OH (b) CH_3CHO
(c) CH_3COCH_3 (d) CH_3COOH

92. The following compounds are given.

(i) CH_3CH_2OH (ii) CH_3COCH_3
(iii) $CH_2-CHOH(CH_3)$ (iv) $CH_3-C_2H_4OH$

Which of these, on being warmed with iodine solution and NaOH, will give iodoform?

(a) (i), (iii) and (iv) (b) only (ii)
(c) (i), (ii) and (iii) (d) (i) and (ii)

93. Ethyl alcohol can be distinguished from methyl alcohol by
(a) Lucas test (b) Victor Meyer's test
(c) passing vapour over heated Cu at 573K
(d) iodoform test

94. Identify X in the following sequence:

$$C_3H_8O \xrightarrow[(X)]{K_2Cr_2O_7} C_3H_6O \xrightarrow[H_2SO_4/I_2 + NaOH]{warm} CHI_3$$

(a) $CH_3CH_2CH_2OH$ (b) $CH_3CHOHCH_3$
(c) $CH_3OCH_2CH_3$ (d) CH_3CH_2CHO

95. There are four alcohols P, Q, R and S which have 3, 2, 1 and zero alpha hydrogen atom(s) respectively. Which one of the following will not respond to the Victor Meyer's test?
(a) P (b) Q (c) R (d) S

96. Compound A, $C_8H_{10}O$, is found to react with NaOI (produced by reacting Y with NaOH) and yields a yellow precipitate with characteristic smell. A and Y are respectively
(a) $H_3C-C_6H_4-CH_2-OH$ and I_2
(b) $C_6H_5-CH_2CH_2-OH$ and I_2
(c) $C_6H_5-CH(OH)-CH_3$ and I_2
(d) $CH_3-C_6H_3(CH_3)-OH$ and I_2

97. In CH_3CH_2OH, the bond that undergoes heterolytic cleavage most readily is
(a) C–C (b) C–O (c) C–H (d) O–H

98. Which of the following alcohols is the strongest acid?
(a) CH_3OH (b) CH_3CH_2OH
(c) $(CH_3)_2CHCH_2OH$ (d) $(CH_3)_3COH$

99. Among the following compounds, the strongest acid is
(a) HC≡CH (b) C_6H_6 (c) C_2H_6 (d) CH_3OH

100. Which of the following alcohols is expected to have the lowest pK_a?
(a) ethanol (b) isopropanol
(c) 2, 2, 2-trifluoroethanol (d) 2-chloroethanol

Ethylene Glycol

101. An organic compound with a molecular formula $C_2H_6O_2$ evolves H_2 when treated with sodium metal and gives two mol of formaldehyde on oxidation with HIO_4. The compound is
(a) acetic acid (b) methyl acetate
(c) ethylene glycol (d) ethyl alcohol

102. Ethylene glycol reacts with excess of PCl_5 or PCl_3 or $SOCl_2$ to give
(a) ethylene dichloride (b) 2-chloroethanol
(c) ethylene (d) 2,2-dichloroethanal

103. With excess of HI or PI_3, 1,2- ethanediol gives
(a) ethyl iodide (b) ethylidene diiodide
(c) ethylene diiodide (d) ethylene

104. The product, $(CH_2OCOCH_3)_2$ is obtained by the action of
(a) acetone and glycol (b) ethanal and ethanol
(c) glycol and CH_3COCl/pyridine or $(CH_3CO)_2O$
(d) glycol and ethanol

105. Ethane-1,2-diol when heated with anhydrous $ZnCl_2$ gives
(a) vinyl alcohol (b) ethanol
(c) ethanal (d) ethanoic acid

106. Ethylene glycol when distilled with conc. H_2SO_4 mainly gives
(a) 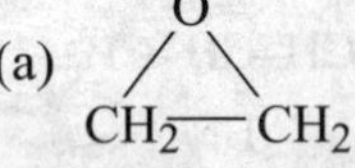
(b) OHC–CHO
(c) $HOCH_2CH_2OCH_2CH_2OH$ (d) 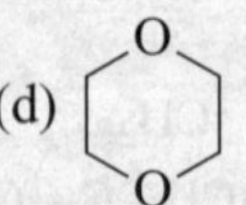

107. When heated with conc. H_3PO_4, ethylene glycol gives
(a) acrolein (b) 1,4-dioxane
(c) acetaldehyde (d) diethylene glycol

108. Oxidation of ethylene glycol with conc. HNO_3 ultimately gives
(a) glyoxal (b) glycolic acid
(c) glyoxalic acid (d) oxalic acid

109. Ethylene glycol can be prepared from ethylene by treating it with
(a) acidified $K_2Cr_2O_7$ solution
(b) dil. HNO_3
(c) cold dilute alkaline $KMnO_4$ solution
(d) hot conc. $KMnO_4$ solution

110. Identify the final product (Y) in the following reaction sequence

$$CH_2{=}CH_2 \xrightarrow[\Delta 473\,K]{O_2.Ag} X \xrightarrow{Steam} Y$$

(a) ethanol (b) ethanal
(c) epoxyethane (d) ethylene glycol

111. Which of the following, will be oxidised by HIO_4?
I. R–CO–CO–R II. R–CO–CHOH–R
III. R–CHOH–CH_2–CHOH –R
IV. R–CHOH–CHOH–R
(a) I, II and III (b) I, III and IV
(c) I, II and IV (d) II, III and IV

112. $HOCH_2–CH_2OH$ on heating with periodic acid gives
(a) 2 HCOOH (b) OCH –CHO
(c) 2 $H_2C=O$ (d) 2 CO_2

Glycerol

113. Glycerol on heating with potassium bisulfate yields
(a) acetone (b) glyceraldehyde
(c) acrolein (d) propanol

114. Which of the following reagents will convert glycerol to acrolein?
(a) P_2O_5 (b) conc. H_2SO_4
(c) $KHSO_4$ (d) all the three

115. Glycerol when treated with a mixture of conc. HNO_3 + conc. H_2SO_4 gives
(a) glyceryl mononitrate (b) glyceryl trinitrate
(c) glyceryl dinitrate (d) glyceryl sulfate

116. The shock-sensitive substance present in dynamite is
(a) CH_2ONO_2–$CHONO_2$–CH_2ONO_2 (b) CH_2NO_2–$CHNO_2$–CH_2NO_2
(c) CH_2NO_2–$CHOH$–CH_2NO_2 (d) CH_2NO_2–$CHONO_2$–CH_2OH

117. Glycerol on oxidation with HIO_4 gives
(a) HCHO (3 mol)
(b) HCHO (2 mol) + HCOOH (1 mol)
(c) HCHO (1 mol) + HCOOH (2 mol)
(d) HCOOH (3 mol)

118. Glycerol when treated with a mixture acetic acid and acetic anhydride gives
(a) glyceryl monoacetate (b) glyceryl diacetate
(c) glyceryl triacetate (d) all the three

119. Oxalic acid can be converted into formic acid in one step by heating it
(a) alone at 473 K (b) with glycerol at 383 K
(c) with glycerol at 503 K (d) with $KHSO_4$

120. When heated with oxalic at 503 K, glycerol gives
(a) formic acid (b) acrolein
(c) glycerol dioxalate (d) allyl alcohol
(d) all the three above

121. Dunston's test is used for the identification of
(a) glycerol (b) acetone
(c) glycol (d) ethanol

122. The boiling points of ethanol, ethylene glycol and glycerol increase in the order:
(a) glycerol < ethylene glycol < ethanol
(b) glycerol < ethanol < ethylene glycol
(c) ethanol < ethylene glycol < glycerol
(d) ethylene glycol < ethanol < glycerol

123. Glycerol on warming with a small amount of hydriodic acid gets converted into
(a) $CH_3–CHI–CH_3$ (b) $CH_2=CH–CH_2I$
(c) $ICH_2–CHI–CH_2I$ (d) $CH_3–CH=CH_2$

124. When glycerol is treated with excess of HI, it produces
(a) 2-iodopropane (b) allyl iodide
(c) propane (d) glycerol triiodide

125. Which of the following is not formed when glycerol reacts with HI?
(a) $CH_2=CH–CH_2I$ (b) $CH_2OH–CHI–CH_2OH$
(c) $CH_3–CH=CH_2$ (d) $CH_3–CHI–CH_3$

Chemical Reactions of Phenols

126. Correct increasing order of acidity is as follows:
(a) H_2O, C_2H_2, H_2CO_3, phenol
(b) C_2H_2, H_2O, H_2CO_3, phenol
(c) phenol, C_2H_2, H_2CO_3, H_2O
(d) C_2H_2, H_2O, phenol, H_2CO_3

127. Phenol is less acidic than
(a) ethanol (b) methanol
(c) *o*-nitrophenol (d) *p*-methylphenol

128. Which of the following compounds is most acidic?
(a) *o*-hydroxybenzaldehyde (OH, CHO on benzene ring) (b) *m*-hydroxybenzaldehyde (OH, CHO on benzene ring)
(c) HO–C_6H_4–CHO (d) $C_6H_5CH_2OH$

129. In the following compounds,
(I) C_6H_5–OH (II) CH_3–C_6H_4–OH
(III) NO_2–C_6H_4–OH (*meta*) (IV) O_2N–C_6H_4–OH
the order of acidity is
(a) III > IV > I > II (b) I > IV > III > II
(c) II > I > III > IV (d) IV > III > I > II

130. The increasing order of the pK_a values of the following compounds is

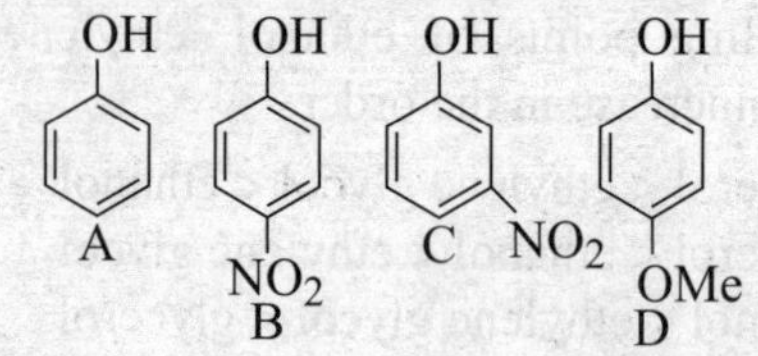

(Structures: A = phenol; B = p-nitrophenol; C = m-nitrophenol; D = p-methoxyphenol)

(a) C< B < A < D (b) B < C < D < A
(c) D < A < C < B (d) B < C< A < D

131. Strongest acid among the following is
(a) *o*-methoxyphenol (b) *p*-methoxyphenol
(c) *m*-methoxyphenol (d) phenol

132. The correct order of decreasing acidity of nitrophenols will be
(a) *m*-nitrophenol > *p*-nitrophenol > *o*-nitrophenol
(b) *o*-nitrophenol > *m*-nitrophenol > *p*-nitrophenol
(c) *p*-nitrophenol > *m*-nitrophenol > *o*-nitrophenol
(d) *p*-nitrophenol > *o*-nitrophenol > *m*-nitrophenol

133. Increasing pK_a values of *o*-, *m*- and *p*-cresols is
(a) $o < p < m$ (b) $m < p < o$
(c) $m < o < p$ (d) $p < o < m$

134. Among the following four compounds
(i) phenol (ii) methylphenol
(iii) *meta*-nitrophenol
(iii) *para*-nitrophenol, the acidity order is
(a) (iv) > (iii) > (i) > (ii) (b) (iii) > (iv) > (i) > (ii)
(c) (i) > (iv) > (iii) > (ii) (d) (ii) > (i) > (iii) > (iv)

135. The acid strength increases in the order
(a) 4-methylphenol, phenol, propan-1-ol, 3,5-dinitrophenol, 3-nitrophenol, 2,4,6-trinitrophenol
(b) phenol, 4-methylphenol, propan-1-ol, 2,4,6-trinitrophenol, 3,5-dinitrophenol, 3-nitrophenol
(c) 3-nitrophenol, propan-1-ol, 3,5-dinitrophenol, phenol,2,4,6-trinitrophenol,4-methylphenol
(d) propan-1-ol,4-methylphenol,phenol,3-nitrophenol, 3,5-dinitrophenol, 2,4,6-trinitrophenol

136. The correct order of acid strength of the following substituted phenols in water at 28°C is
(a) *p*-nitrophenol < *p*-fluorophenol < *p*-chlorophenol
(b) *p*-chlorophenol < *p*-fluorophenol < *p*-nitrophenol
(c) *p*-fluorophenol < *p*-chlorophenol < *p*- nitrophenol
(d) *p*-fluorophenol < *p*-nitrophenol < *p*-chlorophenol

137. Which of the following compounds decomposes $NaHCO_3$ solution?
(a) phenol (b) 2-nitrophenol
(c) methoxyphenol (d) 2,4,6-trinitrophenol

138. Given are cyclohexanol (I), acetic acid (II),2,4,6-trinitrophenol (III) and phenol (IV). The order of decreasing acidic character will be
(a) III > IV> II > I (b) III > II > IV > I
(c) II > III > I > IV (d) II > III > IV > I

139. Which of the following will not be soluble in sodium bicarbonate?
(a) 2,4,6-trinitrophenol (b) benzoic acid
(c) *o*-nitrophenol (d) benzenesulfonic acid

140. 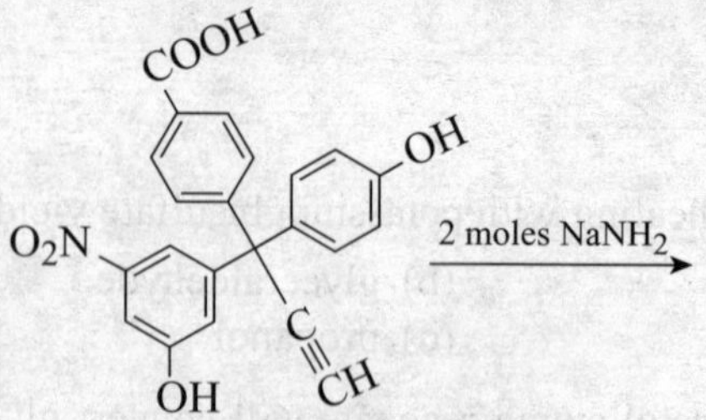 (Structure: central carbon bearing 4-COOH-phenyl, 4-OH-phenyl, C≡CH and 3-O_2N-5-OH-phenyl) $\xrightarrow{\text{2 moles } NaNH_2}$

The major product is

(a) 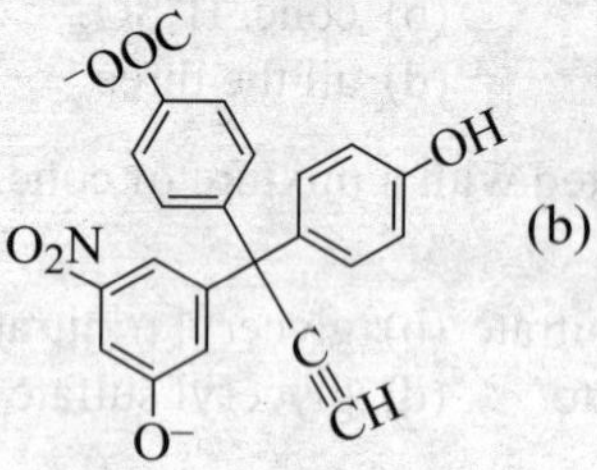 (Structure with ^-OOC, OH, O_2N, O^-, C≡CH)
(b) (Structure with ^-OOC, OH, O_2N, OH, C≡C^-)
(c) (Structure with HOOC, O^-, O_2N, O^-, C≡CH)
(d) 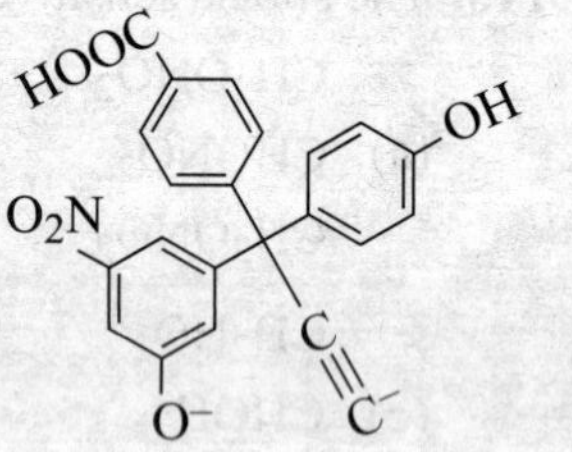 (Structure with HOOC, OH, O_2N, O^-, C≡C^-)

141. Which of the following will give purple colour with $FeCl_3$?

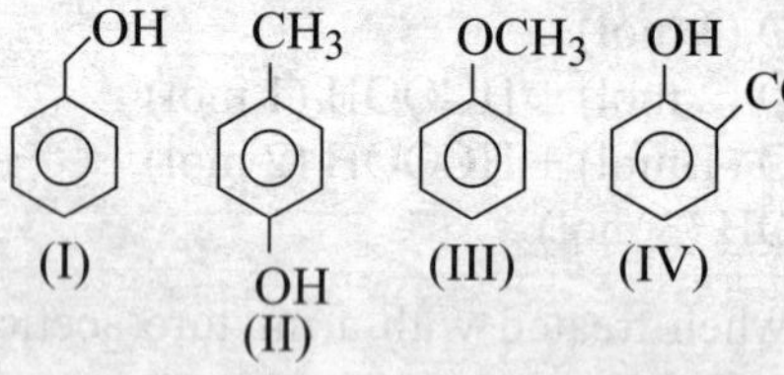

(I) benzyl alcohol ($C_6H_5CH_2OH$) (II) p-cresol (CH_3, OH) (III) anisole (OCH_3) (IV) salicylic acid (OH, COOH)

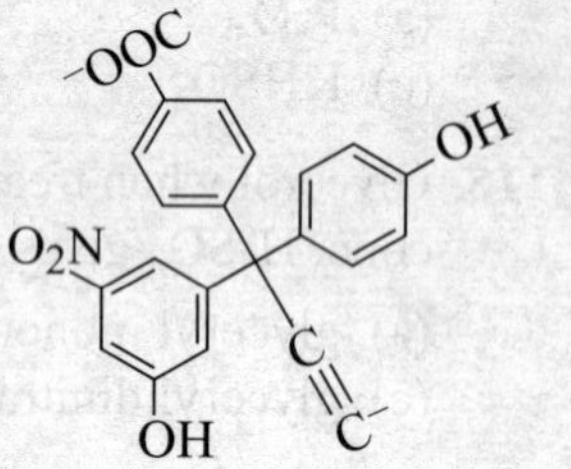

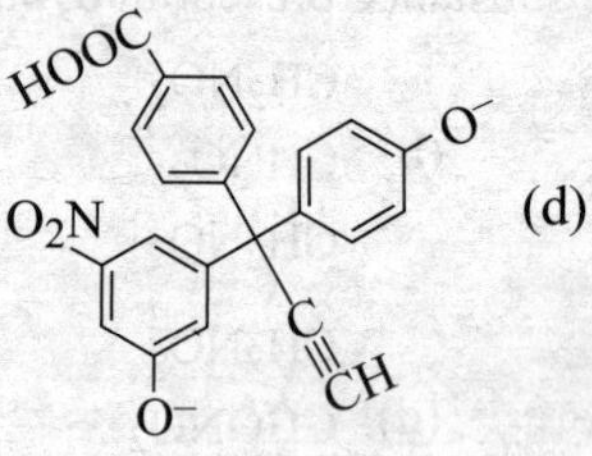

(a) II and IV (b) I and III
(c) II and III (d) III and IV

142. Which one is most reactive towards an electrophilic reagent?
(a) 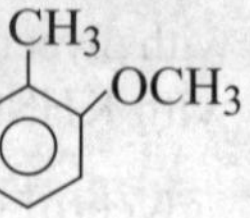 (CH_3, OCH_3 substituted benzene) (b) 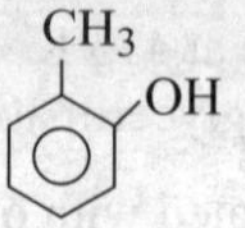 (CH_3, OH substituted benzene)
(c) 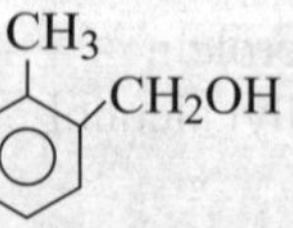 (CH_3, CH_2OH substituted benzene) (d) 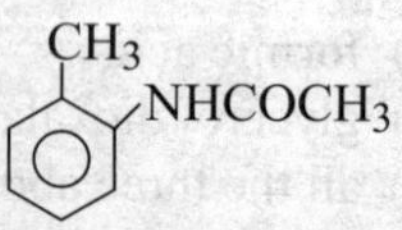 (CH_3, $NHCOCH_3$ substituted benzene)

143. The reagents used in the preparation of aspirin from salicylic acid are:
(a) $SOCl_2$, pyridine (b) $(CH_3CO)_2O$, H^+
(c) CH_3CO_2H, HCl (d) CH_3Cl, $AlCl_3$

144. The major product in the following reaction

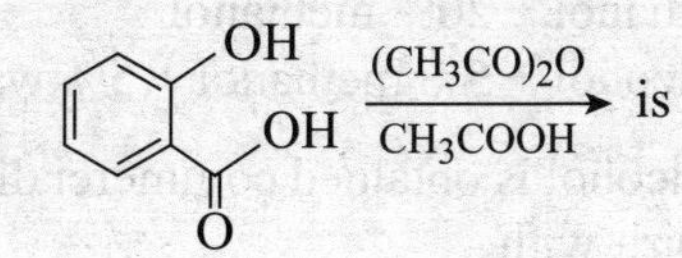

(Salicylic acid) $\xrightarrow[CH_3COOH]{(CH_3CO)_2O}$ is

(a) 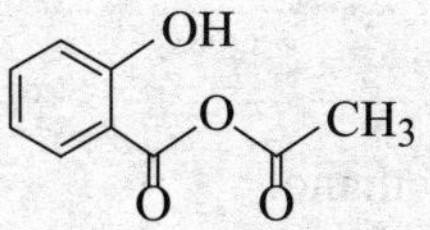 (b) 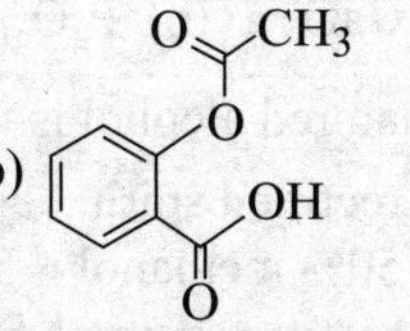 (c) 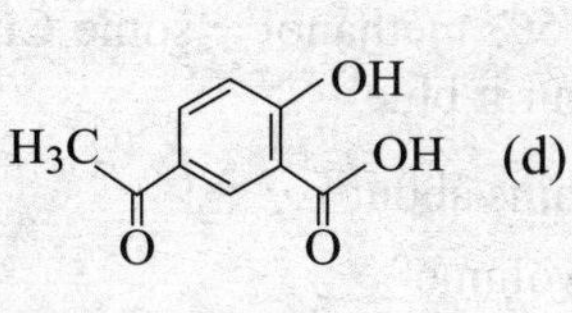 (d) 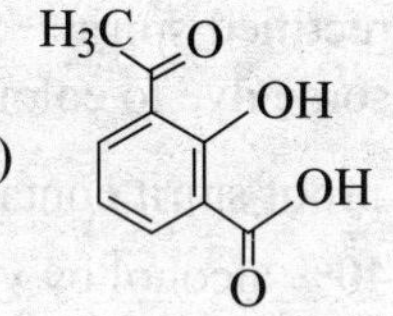 [structures]

145. Treatment of phenol with nitrous acid ($NaNO_2$ + HCl) gives mainly

(a) *p*-nitrosophenol (b) *p*-nitrophenol
(c) picric acid (d) *m*-nitrophenol

146. Phenol reacts with bromine in chloroform at low temperature to give

(a) *m*-bromophenol
(b) mixture of *ortho*- and *para* bromophenol
(c) *p*-bromophenol
(d) 2,4,6-tribromophenol

147. $C_6H_6 \xrightarrow[350\ K]{H_2SO_4} A \xrightarrow[fusion]{Alkali} B \xrightarrow[H_2O]{Br_2} C$

In the above sequence, C is

(a) *o*-bromophenol (b) *p*-bromophenol
(c) *m*- bromophenol (d) 2, 4, 6-tribromophenol

148. The structure of the compound that gives a tribromo derivative on treatment with bromine water is

(a) 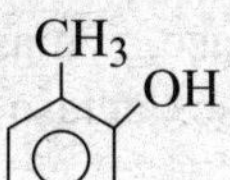 CH_3, OH (b) 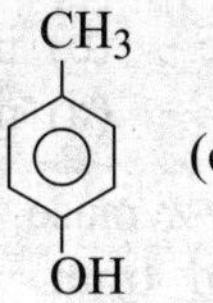 CH_3, OH (c) 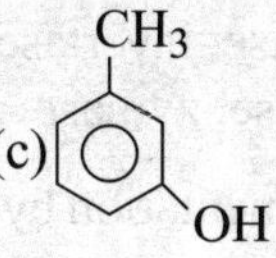 CH_3, OH (d) 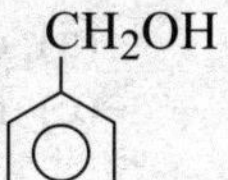 CH_2OH

149. The reaction

OH (phenol) + $CHCl_3$ $\xrightarrow[(ii)\ H^+]{(i)\ NaOH/Heat}$ OH, CHO

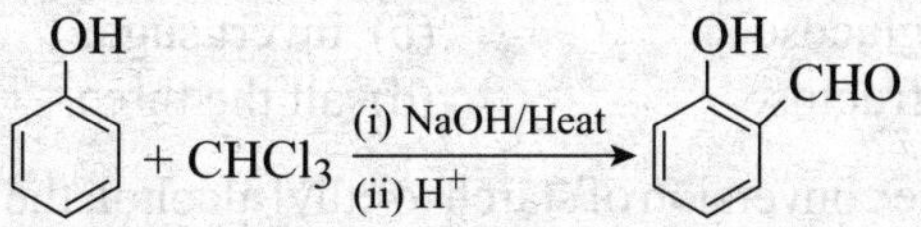

is known as

(a) Perkin reaction (b) Sandmeyer reaction
(c) Reimer–Tiemann reaction
(d) Cannizzaro reaction

150. Reaction of phenol with chloroform in the presence of dilute sodium hydroxide finally introduces which one of the following functional groups?

(a) –COOH (b) –$CHCl_2$ (c) –CHO (d) –CH_2Cl

151. Which of the following reagents can be used to prepare salicylaldehyde from phenol?

(a) CCl_4 + NaOH at 340 K
(b) CO_2 + NaOH at 410 K
(c) $CHCl_3$ + NaOH at 340 K
(d) Heat with CaO + NaOH

152. 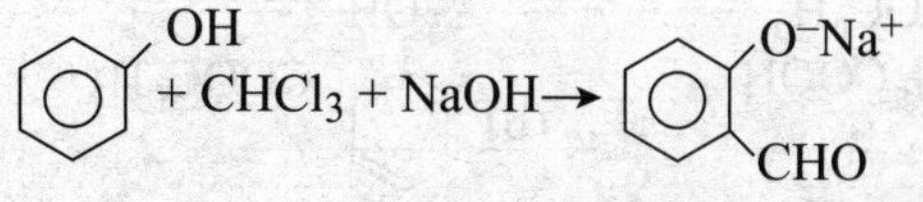 OH (phenol) + $CHCl_3$ + NaOH→ O^-Na^+, CHO

The electrophile involved in the above reaction is

(a) trichloromethyl anion ($\overset{\oplus}{C}Cl_3$)
(b) formyl cation ($\overset{\oplus}{C}HO$)
(c) dichloromethyl cation ($\overset{\oplus}{C}HCl_2$)
(d) dichlorocarbene (:CCl_2)

153. What is the compound C in the following sequence of reactions?

Phenol $\xrightarrow{NaOH}$ A $\xrightarrow{CO_2, 410\ K}$ B $\xrightarrow{HCl}$ C

(a) benzoic acid (b) salicylic acid
(c) benzaldehyde (d) salicylaldehyde

154. Phenol on treatment with CO_2 in the presence of NaOH followed by acidification produces compound X as the major product. X on treatment with $(CH_3CO)_2$ in the presence of catalytic amount of H_2SO_4 produces

(a) 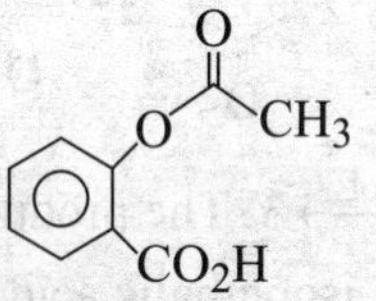 CH_3, CO_2H (b) 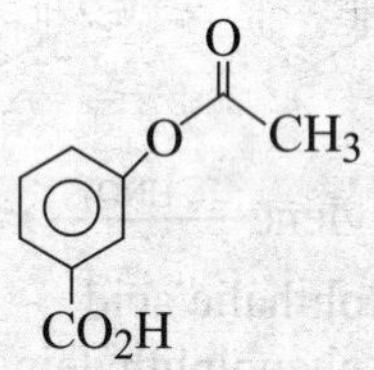 CH_3, CO_2H (c) 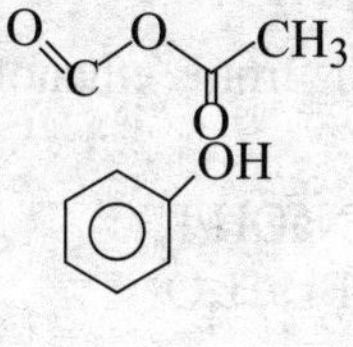 CH_3, OH (d) 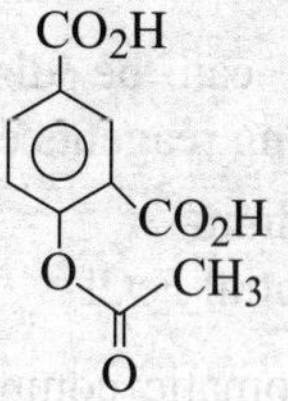 CO_2H, CO_2H, CH_3

155. Phenol reacts with methyl chloroformate in the presence of NaOH form product A. A reacts with Br_2 to form B. A and B are respectively.

(a) 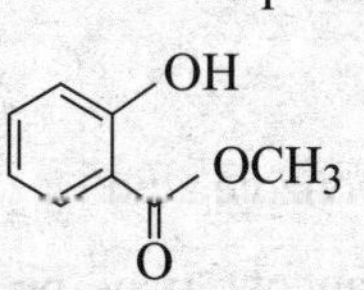 OH, OCH_3 and Br, OH, OCH_3
(b) 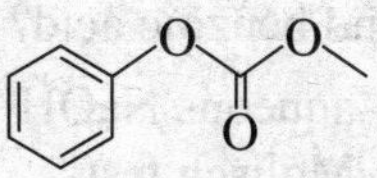 [structure] and [structure] Br
(c) 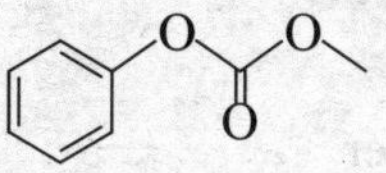 [structure] and Br [structure]

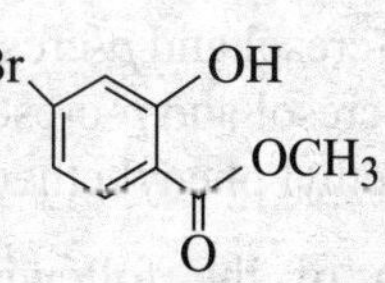

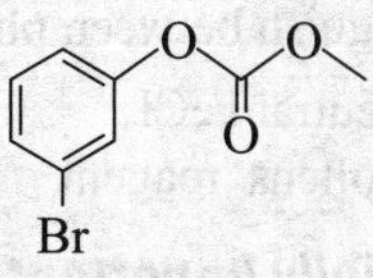

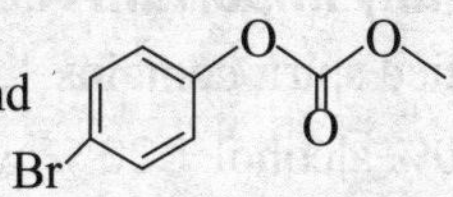

(d) OH, OCH_3, O and OH, OCH_3, Br, O

156. Phenol when heated with salicylic acid in the presence of $POCl_3$ gives salol, whose structure is

(a) $OCOC_6H_5$, COOH (b) OH, $COOC_6H_5$

(c) OC_6H_5, $COOC_6H_5$ (d) OH, $OCOC_6H_5$

157. Salicylic acid when heated with methanol in the presence of a few drops of conc. H_2SO_4 gives

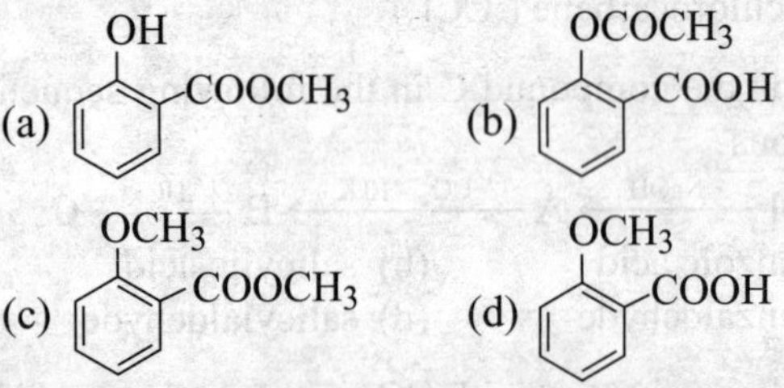

158. Oxidation of phenol with $K_2Cr_2O_7/H_2SO_4$ gives

(a) (b) (c) (d)

159. *o*-Xylene $\xrightarrow{HNO_3}$ X $\xrightarrow{Phenol}$ Y. The product Y is

(a) phthalic acid (b) isophthalic acid
(c) phenolphthalein (d) *o*-hydroxysulfonic acid

160. Phenol can be distinguished from ethanol by the following reagents except

(a) sodium (b) $NaOH/I_2$
(c) neutral $FeCl_3$ (d) Br_2/H_2O

161. The aromatic compounds having the formula C_7H_8O which are easily identifiable by the $FeCl_3$ solution test (violet colouration) are

(a) *o*-cresol and benzyl alcohol
(b) *m*-cresol and *p*-cresol
(c) *o*-cresol and *p*-cresol
(d) methyl phenyl ether and benzoic acid

162. Which of the following reagents may be used to distinguish between phenol and benzoic acid?

(a) neutral $FeCl_3$ (b) aqueous NaOH
(c) Tollens' reagent (d) Molisch test

Commercially Important Alcohols

163. Rectified spirit contains

(a) 80% alcohol + 20 % water
(b) 95.6% alcohol + 4.4% water
(c) 80% ethanol + 20% methanol
(d) 90% alcohol + 5% methanol + 5% water

164. Absolute alcohol is obtained commercially by distilling rectified spirit with

(a) CaO (b) P_4O_{10} (c) $CaCl_2$ (d) benzene

165. Denatured alcohol is

(a) rectified spirit
(b) 50% methanol + 50 % ethanol
(c) rectified spirit + 5% methanol
(d) rectified spirit + 5% methanol + some $CuSO_4$ and some dye to colour it blue

166. 100 proof spirit contains about

(a) 40% alcohol by volume
(b) 25% alcohol by volume
(c) 57.15% alcohol by volume
(d) 5% alcohol by volume

167. Commercially methanol is prepared by

(a) catalytic hydrogenation of CO under high temperature and pressure in the presence of ZnO–Cr_2O_3 as catalyst
(b) reduction of methane and water vapour at 1173 K in the presence of Ni as catalyst
(c) reduction of HCHO by $LiAlH_4$
(d) reduction of HCHO by concentrated NaOH

168. Which of the following alcohols is prepared commercially by fermentation?

(a) methanol (b) glycerol
(c) 1-propanol (d) ethanol

169. The enzymes which can bring about the fermentation of sugar present in molasses to ethyl alcohol are

(a) diastase, invertase (b) invertase, zymase
(c) maltase, zymase (d) maltase, lactase

170. In the fermentation by zymase, ethyl alcohol and carbon dioxide are produced from which of the following sugars?

(a) glucose (b) invert sugar
(c) fructose (d) all the three

171. In the conversion of starch to ethyl alcohol, the following enzymes are used

(a) invertase, zymase, emulsion
(b) maltase, zymase, emulsion
(c) diastase, maltase, zymase
(d) invertase, diastase, zymase

Preparation of Ethers

172. 2 $ClCH_2CH_2OH$ (excess) $\xrightarrow[413\text{ K}]{\text{conc. } H_2SO_4}$ X $\xrightarrow[\text{(ii) } H_3O^+]{\text{(i) KOH, fuse}}$ Y

The compound Y is

(a) ethylene glycol (b) ethanol

(c) divinyl ether (d) vinyl chloride

173. In Williamson's synthesis, ethoxyethane is prepared by

(a) heating sodium ethoxide with ethyl bromide

(b) passing ethanol over heated alumina

(c) treating ethyl alcohol over heated alumina

(d) heating alcohol with dry Ag_2O

174. The reaction,

$$CH_3-\overset{CH_3}{\underset{CH_3}{C}}-ONa + CH_3CH_2Cl \longrightarrow CH_3-\overset{CH_3}{\underset{CH_3}{C}}-O-CH_2CH_3$$

is called

(a) Etard reaction

(b) Gatterman–Koch reaction

(c) Williamson synthesis

(d) Williamson continuous etherification process

175. The compound A on treatment with Na gives B, and with PCl_5 gives C. B and C react together to give diethyl ether. A, B and C are in the order

(a) C_2H_5OH, C_2H_6, C_2H_5Cl

(b) C_2H_5OH, C_2H_5Cl, C_2H_5ONa

(c) C_2H_5Cl, C_2H_6, C_2H_5OH

(d) C_2H_5OH, C_2H_5ONa, C_2H_5Cl

176. The reaction,

$$\text{(cyclopentyl)}-OH \xrightarrow{NaH} \text{(cyclopentyl)}-O^-Na^+ \xrightarrow{Me-I} \text{(cyclopentyl)}-O-Me$$

is classified as

(a) a dehydration reaction

(b) Williamson's alcohol synthesis reaction

(c) Williamson's ether synthesis reaction

(d) alcohol formation reaction

177. The reaction that gives the following molecule as the major product is

$$(CH_3)_3C-O-CH_3$$

(a) $(CH_3)_3C-Br + CH_3ONa$ (b) $(CH_3)_3C-ONa + CH_3ONa$

(c) $(CH_3)_3C-OH$ (d) $(CH_3)_2C{=}CH_2 + CH_3ONa$

178. To prepare *tert*-butylethylether by Williamson's synthesis, the reactants needed are

(a) sodium ethoxide and sodium *tert* butoxide

(b) sodium ethoxide and *tert*-butyl bromide

(c) sodium *tert*-butoxide and ethyl bromide

(d) ethyl alcohol and *tert*-butyl alcohol

179. The major product of the reaction between CH_3CH_2ONa and $(CH_3)_3CCl$ in ethanol is

(a) $CH_3CH_2OC(CH_3)_3$ (b) $CH_2{=}C(CH_3)_2$

(c) $CH_3CH_2C(CH_3)_3$ (d) $CH_3CH{=}CHCH_3$

180. Product C in the reaction

$$C_2H_5Br \xrightarrow[\text{(aqueous)}]{NaOH} A \xrightarrow{Na} B \xrightarrow{CH_3I} C \text{ will be}$$

(a) propane (b) ethyl iodide

(c) ethane (d) ethyl methyl ether

181. Identify Z in the sequence of reactions:

$$CH_3CH_2CH{=}CH_2 \xrightarrow{HBr/H_2O_2} Y \xrightarrow{C_2H_5ONa} Z$$

(a) $CH_3-(CH_2)_3-O-CH_2CH_3$

(b) $(CH_3)_2CH-O-CH_2CH_3$

(c) $CH_3-(CH_2)_4-O-CH_3$

(d) $CH_3CH_2-CH(CH_3)-OCH_2CH_3$

182. Which of the following is an appropriate set of reactants for the preparation of 1-methoxy-4-nitrobenzene?

I. $p\text{-}BrC_6H_4NO_2 + CH_3ONa$ II. $p\text{-}NaOC_6H_4NO_2 + CH_3Br$

(a) I (b) II

(c) both I and II (d) none of these

183. Which of the following reactions will not result in the formation of anisole?

(a) phenol + dimethyl sulfate in the presence of a base

(b) sodium phenoxide is treated with methyl iodide

(c) reaction of diazomethane with phenol

(d) reaction of methylmagnesium iodide with phenol

184. Among the following sets of reactants which one produces anisole?

(a) CH_3CHO, RMgX

(b) C_6H_5OH, NaOH, CH_3I

(c) C_6H_5OH, neutral $FeCl_3$

(d) $C_6H_5CH_3$, CH_3COCl, $AlCl_3$

185. Which of the following reactions is the best choice for preparing methyl cyclohexyl ether?

(a) $C_6H_{11}OH + CH_3I \longrightarrow$ (b) $C_6H_{11}I + CH_3OH \longrightarrow$

(c) $C_6H_{11}OH + CH_3ONa$ (d) $C_6H_{11}ONa + CH_3I \longrightarrow$

186. The final product (B) formed in the above reaction is

(Toluene, CH_3 on benzene ring) $\xrightarrow[\Delta]{NBS/CCl_4}$ A $\xrightarrow{CH_3ONa}$ B

(a) $C_6H_5-CO_2CH_3$ (b) $C_6H_5-OCH_3$

(c) $CH_3O-C_6H_4-CH_3$ (d) $C_6H_5-CH_2OCH_3$

187. The final product (B) formed in the following reaction is

$CH_3CH{=}CH_2 \xrightarrow{Cl_2/773K} A \xrightarrow{CH_3CH_2ONa} B$

(a) $CH_3CH{=}CH{-}OCH_2CH_3$

(b) $CH_3{-}C(=CH_2){-}OCH_2CH_3$

(c) $CH_2{=}CHCH_2{-}O{-}CH_2CH_3$

(d) $CH_3{-}CH(CH_3){-}CH_2$ with CH_2O and OCH_2CH_3 ($CH_3-CH-CH_2$; CH_3 CH_2O OCH_2CH_3)

188. In the following reaction sequence

$CH_3CH{=}CH_2 \xrightarrow[\text{(ii) } H_2O_2/OH]{\text{(i) } B_2H_6/THF} A \xrightarrow[\text{(ii) } CH_3I]{\text{(i) NaOH}} B$

The structure of the product (B) is

(a) $CH_3CH_2CH_2OCH_3$ (b) $(CH_3)_2CH{-}OCH_3$

(c) $CH_3CHOHCH_3$ (d) $CH_3CHOHCH_2OH$

189. (Phenol, OH on benzene ring) $\xrightarrow[\Delta]{Br_2 \text{ in } CS_2}$ X $\xrightarrow[\text{(ii) Me} - I]{\text{(i) NaOH}}$ Y

In the above sequence of reactions, the major products X and Y are

(a) X = (o-bromophenol: OH, Br), Y = (o-bromoanisole: OMe, Br)

(b) X = (o-bromophenol: OH, Br), Y = (catechol: OH, OH)

(c) X = (p-bromophenol: OH, Br), Y = (p-bromophenol: OH, Br)

(d) X = (p-bromophenol: OH, Br), Y = (hydroquinone: OH, OH)

190. Decreasing order of reactivity in Williamson's ether synthesis of the following is

I. Me_3CCH_2Br II. $CH_3CH_2CH_2Br$

III. $CH_2{=}CHCH_2Cl$ IV. $CH_3CH_2CH_2Cl$

(a) III > II > IV > I (b) I > II >IV > III

(c) II > III> IV > I (d) I > III > II > IV

191. Which of the following is not expected to give an ether on reaction with sodium methoxide?

(a) $PhCH_2Cl$ (b) $CH_3CH_2CH_2Cl$

(c) $CH_2{=}CHCH_2Cl$ (d) $CH_2{=}CHCl$

192. Which of the following cannot be made by using Williamson's synthesis?

(a) methoxybenzene

(b) benzyl-*p*-nitrophenyl ether

(c) *tert*-butyl methyl ether

(d) di-*tert*-butyl ether

193. In the reaction, $CH_3CH_2ONa + (CH_3CH_2O)_2SO_2 \xrightarrow[\Delta]{THF}$ the product formed is

(a) $CH_3CH_2OSO_2OCH_2CH_3$

(b) $CH_3CH_2OSO_2OCH_3$

(c) $CH_3CH_2OCH_3$

(d) $CH_3CH_2OCH_2CH_3$

194. Which of the following reactions cannot be used to prepare methoxybenzene?

(a) $C_6H_5OH + (CH_3)_2SO_4 \xrightarrow{NaOH}$

(b) $C_6H_5OH + CH_3I \xrightarrow{NaOH}$

(c) $C_6H_5OH + CH_2N_2 \rightarrow$

(d) $C_6H_5OH + CH_3MgI \rightarrow$

195. Which of the following react with bromobenzene to form an ether?

(a) CH_3CH_2ONa (b) $CH_2{=}CHCH_2ONa$

(c) C_6H_5ONa (d) none of these

196. Isopropyl bromide on reaction with sodium isopropoxide yields

I. $CH_3CH{=}CH_2$ II. $(CH_3)_2CHOH$

III. $(CH_3)_2CH{-}O{-}CH(CH_3)_2$

(a) all of these (b) I and II

(c) III only (d) I and III

197. Acid catalysed addition of methanol to 2-methylpropenne gives

(a) *tert*-butyl alcohol (b) *tert*-butyl methyl ether

(c) di-*tert*-butyl ether (d) dimethyl ether

198. $CH_3CH{=}CH_2 \xrightarrow[\text{(ii) } NaBH_4]{\text{(i) } (CH_3COO)_2Hg,\ CH_3OH}$

The product of the above reaction is

(a) $CH_3{-}CH(CH_3){-}O{-}C(=CH_3){-}CH_3$ (b) $CH_3{-}CH(OCH_3){-}CH_3$

(c) $CH_3{-}CH(OCH_3){-}CH_2(OCOCH_3)$ (d) $CH_3{-}CH(CH_3COO){-}CH_2(OCOCH_3)$

199. Consider the following sequence of reactions

$PhOH \xrightarrow[CH_2=CH_2]{(CF_3COO)Hg} A \xrightarrow{NaBH_4} B$

The product (B) is

(a) $Ph{-}CH{-}CH_2$ (epoxide, O bridging) (b) $PhOCH_2CH_3$

(c) $PhCH_2OCH_3$ (d) $PhCH_2CH_2OH$

200. Chloromethoxymethane on reaction with sodium ethoxide yields

(a) methoxy ethane (b) 2-methoxy propane
(c) 2,4-dioxahexane (d) 1-methoxy propane

201. The major product in the following reaction is

(o-hydroxybenzyl alcohol: OH, CH_2OH) + CH_3CH_2I $\xrightarrow[\text{acetone, }\Delta]{Na_2CO_3}$

(a) OCH_2CH_3, CH_2OH (b) OH, $CH_2OCH_2CH_3$
(c) OCH_2CH_3, $CH_2OCH_2CH_3$ (d) O, CH_3, O (cyclic acetal)

202. The major product of the following reactions is

MeO, OH (benzene ring) $\xrightarrow[\text{(ii) } AlCl_3 \text{ (anhyd.)}]{\text{(i) } ClCH_2CH_2COCl}$

(a) MeO, O (b) 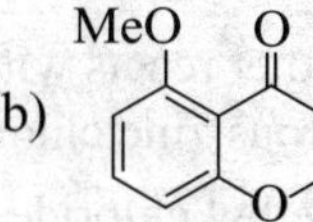

(c) O, MeO, O (d) OMe, O, O

203. An alkyl halide is heated with Ag_2O; it produces a/an

(a) ester (b) ether (c) ketone (d) alcohol

204. Chloromethoxymethane reacts with methylmagnesium iodide to form

(a) dimethyl ether (b) ethyl methyl ether
(c) dimethyl ether (d) chloromethoxyethane

205. The following compound can readily be prepared by Williamson's ether synthesis by reaction between

(a) OH (bicyclic) and benzyl Cl (b) OH (bicyclic) and benzyl I
(c) Cl (bicyclic) and benzyl OH (d) I (bicyclic) and benzyl OH

206. Ethanol is converted into ethoxyethane

(a) by heating excess of ethanol with conc. H_2SO_4 at 413 K
(b) by heating ethanol with excess of H_2SO_4 at 443 K
(c) by treating ethanol with conc. H_2SO_4 at room temperature
(d) by treating ethanol with conc. H_2SO_4 at 273 K

207. Which of the following is formed as an intermediate in the conversion of ethyl alcohol into diethyl ether by heating the former with conc. H_2SO_4?

(a) $CH_3CH_2\overset{+}{O}H_2$ (b) $CH_3CH_2OSO_3H$
(c) $CH_3CH_2-\overset{+}{\underset{H}{O}}-CH_2CH_3$ (d) all the three

208. The reaction, $2\ C_2H_5OH \xrightarrow{\text{conc. } H_2SO_4} (C_2H_5)_2O + H_2O$ is an example of a/an

(a) electrophilic substitution reaction
(b) nucleophilic substitution S_N1 reaction
(c) E_2 elimination reaction
(d) nucleophilic substitution S_N2 reaction

209. Which of the following alcohols gives the best yield of dialkyl ether on being heated with a trace of sulfuric acid?

(a) 2-pentanol (b) cyclopentanol
(c) 2-methyl-2-butanol (d) 2-propanol
(e) 1-pentanol

210. When a mixture of methanol and ethanol is heated in the presence of concentrated H_2SO_4, the resulting organic products is/are

(a) $CH_3OC_2H_5$
(b) CH_3OCH_3 and $C_2H_5OC_2H_5$
(c) $CH_3OC_2H_5$ and CH_3OCH_3
(d) $CH_3OC_2H_5$, CH_3OCH_3 and $C_2H_5OC_2H_5$

Properties of Ethers

211. $CH_3OC_2H_5$ and $(CH_3)_3COCH_3$ are treated with hydriodic acid. The products obtained after reaction are:

(a) $CH_3I + HOC_2H_5$; $(CH_3)_3C–I + HOCH_3$
(b) $CH_3OH + C_2H_5I$; $(CH_3)_3C–I + HOCH_3$
(c) $CH_3OH + C_2H_5I$; $(CH_3)_3C–OH + CH_3I$
(d) $CH_3I + HOC_2H_5$; $CH_3I + (CH_3)_3C–OH$

212. The major products formed when the following ether is heated with conc. HI are

$CH_3CH_2CH_2–O–C(CH_3)_2CH_2CH_3$

(a) $CH_3CH_2CH_2I + HO–C(CH_3)_2CH_2CH_3$
(b) $CH_3CH_2CH_2OH + I–C(CH_3)_2CH_2CH_3$
(c) $CH_3CH_2CH_2I + I–C(CH_3)_2CH_2CH_3$
(d) $CH_3CH_2CH_2OH + (CH_3)_2C=CHCH_3$

213. In the reaction,

$CH_3CH_2–CH–CH_2–O–CH_2CH_3 + HI \xrightarrow{\text{Heat}} ...$

Which of the following compounds will be formed?

(a) $CH_3CH_2–\underset{}{\overset{CH_3}{CH}}–CH_2OH + CH_3CH_2–I$

(b) $CH_3CH_2–\overset{CH_3}{CH}–CH_2I + CH_3CH_2OH$

(c) $CH_3CH_2-CH(CH_3)-CH_3 + CH_3CH_2OH$

(d) $CH_3CH_2-CH(CH_3)-CH_2OH + CH_3CH_3$

214. Among the following ethers, which one will produce methyl alcohol on treatment with hot concentrated HI?

(a) $CH_3-CH_2-CH_2-CH_2-O-CH_3$

(b) $CH_3-CH_2-CH(CH_3)-O-CH_3$

(c) $CH_3-C(CH_3)_2-O-CH_3$ (d) $CH_3-CH(CH_3)-CH_2-O-CH_3$

215. *tert*-Butyl methyl ether on heating with anhydrous hydriodic acid gives

(a) $CH_3I + (CH_3)_3COH$ (b) $CH_3OH + (CH_3)_3Cl$
(c) $CH_3OH + (CH_3)_3COH$ (d) $CH_3I + (CH_3)_3Cl$

216. In the reaction,

$C_6H_5-OCH_3 \xrightarrow[373\ K]{HBr}$ the products are

(a) $Br-C_6H_4-OCH_3 + H_2$ (b) C_6H_5-Br and CH_3Br
(c) C_6H_5-Br and CH_3OH (d) C_6H_5-OH and CH_3Br

217. Benzyl phenyl ether when heated with HI gives

(a) $C_6H_5CH_2 + C_6H_5OH$ (b) $C_6H_5CH_2I + C_6H_5OH$
(c) $C_6H_5CH_2OH + C_6H_5I$
(d) $C_6H_5CH_2OH + I-C_6H_4-OH$

218. The major product formed in the following reaction is

[Structure: benzene ring bearing $-CH(CH_3)-O-CH_3$ and ortho $-O-CH_2CH_3$] $\xrightarrow[Heat]{HI}$

(a) ring with $-CH(CH_3)OH$ and ortho $-OH$ (b) ring with $-CH(CH_3)I$ and ortho $-I$
(c) ring with $-CH(CH_3)OH$ and ortho $-I$ (d) ring with $-CH(CH_3)I$ and ortho $-OH$

219. In the following reaction,

$C_2H_5OC_2H_5 + 4\ H \xrightarrow{Red\ P+HI} 2\ X + H_2O$, X is

(a) ethane (b) ethylene
(c) butane (d) propane

220. On boiling with concentrated hydrobromic acid, ethyl phenyl ether will yield

(a) phenol and ethyl bromide
(b) bromobenzene and ethanol
(c) phenol and ethane
(d) bromobenzene and bromoethane

221. $C_6H_5OCH_2CH_2OH \xrightarrow[heat]{excess\ HBr}$

(a) $C_6H_5OH + BrCH_2CH_2Br$
(b) $C_6H_5OH + HOCH_2CH_2Br$
(c) $C_6H_5Br + HOCH_2CH_2OH$
(d) $C_6H_5Br + BrCH_2CH_2OH$

222. The following ether is subjected to hydrogenation in the presence of palladium–charcoal. The products are,

$PhCH_2OCH_2CH_2CH_2Ph \xrightarrow{H_2/Pd-C}$

(a) $PhCH_2OH + PhCH_2CH_2CH_3$
(b) $PhCH_3 + PhCH_2CH_2CH_2OH$
(c) $PhCH_2OCH_2CH_3 + PhCH_3$
(d) $PhCH_2OCH_3 + PhCH_2CH_3$

223. Which of the following ethers does not undergo cleavage on treatment with conc. HBr?

(a) $C_6H_5CH_2C_6H_5$ (b) $CH_2=CH-CH_2-O-CH_2-CH=CH_2$
(c) $(CH_3)_3C-O-C(CH_3)_3$ (d) $PhCH_2-O-CH_2Ph$

224. Diethyl ether reacts with acetyl chloride in the presence of anhydrous zinc chloride to give

(a) only ethyl chloride
(b) only ethyl acetate
(c) one mol each of ethyl chloride and ethyl acetate
(d) two mol of ethyl acetate

225. Diethyl ether on treatment with acetic anhydride in the presence of anhydrous $ZnCl_2$ gives

(a) one mol each of methyl acetate and ethyl acetate
(b) two mol of methyl acetate
(c) two mol of ethyl acetate
(d) reaction does not occur

226. Ethyl methyl ether on heating with PCl_5 produces

(a) ethyl chloride and methyl alcohol
(b) acetyl chloride and methyl chloride
(c) ethyl chloride and methyl chloride
(d) ethylidene chloride and methylene dichloride

227. Diethyl ether on prolonged exposure to air in the presence of light gives

(a) $CH_3CH_2-O-CH_2CH_2-O-O-H$ (b) $CH_3CH_2-O-CH(CH_3)-O-O-H$
(c) $CH_3CH_2-O-O-CH_2CH_2-O-CH_2CH_3$ (d) $CH_3CH_2-O-O-CH_2CH_3$

228. Which of the following is not likely to form a peroxide when exposed to light and air?

(a) $CH_3CH_2OCH_2CH_3$ (b) tetrahydrofuran
(c) $(CH_3)_2CH-OCH_3$ (d) $C_6H_5-O-C(CH_3)_3$

229. Presence of peroxides in old stocks of ethers can be tested by first treating them with Fe^{2+} ions and then adding an aqueous solution of

(a) KCNS (b) $HgCl_2$ (c) $SnCl_2$ (d) KI

230. A simple method to remove peroxides from ethers is to treat them with an aqueous solution of

(a) KI (b) KCNS (c) $Na_2S_2O_3$ (d) Br_2

231. Anisole on treatment with a mixture of conc. HNO_3 and conc. H_2SO_4, gives

(a) phenol (b) nitrobenzene
(c) *o*-and *p*-nitroanisoles (d) *o*-nitroanisole

232. Bromination of anisole with Br_2 in CS_2 gives

(a) *m*-bromoanisole (b) *o*-bromoanisole
(c) *p*-bromoanisole
(d) both *o*-and *p*-bromoanisoles

233. Anisole $\xrightarrow[AlCl_3]{(CH_3)_3CCl}$ $\xrightarrow[Heat]{Cl_2FeCl_3CCl}$ $\xrightarrow{HBr}$ X

The product X in the above series of reactions is

(a) OCH_3, Br, $C(CH_3)_3$ (b) OCH_3, Cl, $C(CH_3)_3$ (c) Br, Br, $C(CH_3)_3$ (d) OH, Cl, $C(CH_3)_3$

234. Friedel–Craft reaction of anisole with acetic anhydride mainly gives

(a) *o*-methoxyacetophenone
(b) *m*-methoxyacetophenone
(c) *p*-methoxyacetophenone
(d) 2,4-dimethoxyacetophenone

235. A compound (X) with a MF $C_6H_{14}O$ does not react with sodium. On being treated with hot conc. HI, it is converted into a mixture of two isomeric compounds having the MF C_3H_7I. The compound (X) is

(a) $CH_3CH_2CH_2OCH_3$ (b) $(CH_3)_2CH–O–CH_3$
(c) $CH_3CH_2–O–CH_2CH_3$ (d) $CH_3CH_2CH_2CH_2OH$

236. A compound (X) with a MF $C_6H_{14}O$ does not react with sodium. On being treated with hot conc. HI, it is converted into a mixture of two isomeric compounds having M.F. C_3H_7I. The compound (X) is

(a) $(CH_3CH_2CH_2)_2O$ (b) $[(CH_3)_2CH]_2O$
(c) (cyclopropyl)–$OCH_2CH_2CH_3$
(d) $(CH_3)_2CH–O–CH_2CH_2CH_3$

237. Which of the following reagents can distinguish ethylmethylether from isopropyl alcohol?

(a) Na (b) Br_2/CCl_4
(c) $I_2/NaOH$ (d) both (a) and (c)

238. Which of the following solvents cannot be used for the preparation of Grignard reagent from an alkyl halide and magnesium metal?

(a) $(C_2H_5)_2O$ (b) (tetrahydrofuran ring, O)
(c) $(C_2H_5)_3N$ (d) C_6H_6

239. Etherates are

(a) ethers
(b) solutions in ether
(c) complexes of ethers with a Lewis acid
(d) complexes of ethers with a Lewis base

240. Which of the following has the lowest dipole moment?

(a) dimethyl ether (b) methanol
(c) methyl chloride (d) phenol

241. The major organic product in the reaction,

$CH_3–O–CH(CH_3)_2 + HI \rightarrow$ Product is

(a) $CH_3OC(CH_3)_2$ with I (b) $CH_3I + (CH_3)_2CHOH$
(c) $CH_3OH + (CH_3)CHI$ (d) $ICH_2OCH(CH_3)_2$

242. Major products formed in the reaction of

(a) $CH_3–I$ and (tert-butyl)–OH (b) (isobutylene) and CH_3OH
(c) $CH_3–OH$ and (tert-butyl)–I (d) (isobutyl iodide, I) + CH_3OH

Cyclic Ethers

243. Consider the following sequence of reactions

$$CH_2 = CH_2 \xrightarrow[\Delta]{O_2/Ag} A \xrightarrow[(ii)\ H_3O^+]{(i)\ LiAlH_4} B$$

$$A + B \xrightarrow{Dil.\ H_2SO_4} C$$

The final product (X) is

(a) $CH_3CH_2OCH_2CH_3$ (b) $CH_3CH_2CHOHCH_3$
(c) $CH_3CH_2OCH_2OH$ (d) $CH_3CH_2CH_2CHO$

244. The end product in the following sequence of reactions is

(ethylene oxide) $\xrightarrow{H_3O^+}$ A $\xrightarrow[H_2SO_4]{\text{(ethylene oxide)}}$ B,

(a) HO, OH (ethylene glycol) (b) HO–O–OH (diethylene glycol)
(c) (diethyl ether, O) (d) O, OH

245. CH_3, CH_3, CH_2, O (epoxide) $\xrightarrow{LiAlH_4}$ A is

(a) $(CH_3)_2CHCH_2OH$ (b) $CH_3CH_2CH_2CH_2OH$
(c) $(CH_3)_3COH$ (d) $CH_3CHOHCH_2CH_3$

246. In the reaction, $(CH_3)_2C(-O-)CH_2$ (epoxide) $\xrightarrow[H^+]{H_2O^{18}}$ A

the product A is

(a) $CH_3-\underset{^{18}OH}{\overset{CH_3}{C}}-CH_2OH$ (b) $CH_3-\underset{OH}{\overset{CH_3}{C}}-CH_2-{}^{18}OH$

(c) $CH_3-\underset{^{18}OH}{\overset{CH_3}{C}}-CH_3$ (d) $CH_3-\overset{CH_3}{CH}-CH_2-{}^{18}OH$

247. In the following reaction sequence, X and Y respectively are,

$(CH_3)_2C=CH_2 \xrightarrow{X}$ epoxide $\xrightarrow{Y} (CH_3)_3C-OH$

(a) H_2O_2, $LiAlH_4$
(b) C_6H_5COOOH, $LiAlH_4$
(c) C_6H_5COOH, Zn/Hg–HCl
(d) Alkaline $KMnO_4$, $LiAlH_4$

248. THF is treated with excess of HBr at 373 K. The product is

(a) 1,4-dibromobutane (b) 1-bromo-2-butene
(c) 4-bromo-1-butanol (d) 4-bromo-1-butene

249. The product of the reaction,

1-methylcyclohexene oxide (CH_3, O) + HBr ⟶ is

(a) CH_3, OH, Br (b) CH_3, Br, OH
(c) CH_3 (d) CH_3, Br

250. The product (B) in the following reaction is

$CH_2=CHCH_2CH_2OH \xrightarrow{Br_2/CCl_4} A \xrightarrow[\text{Room temp.}]{\text{Dil.NaOH}} B$

(a) $BrCH_2CHBr-CH_2CH_2OH$
(b) $HOCH_2-CHOH-CH_2CH_2OH$
(c) $-CH_2Br$ (d)

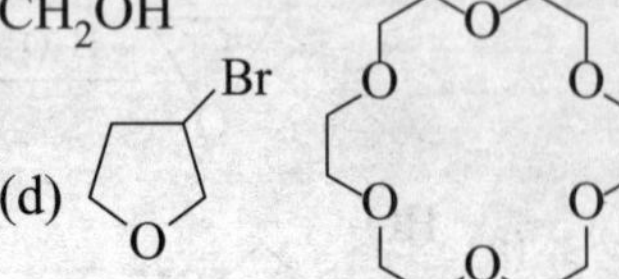

251. The product of the reaction,

tetrahydropyran + $CH_3COCl \xrightarrow{\text{Anhyd. } ZnCl_2}$ is

(a) $COCH_3$ (b) $COCH_3$
(c) $ClCH_2-(CH_2)_3-OCOCH_3$
(d) $HOCH_2-(CH_2)_3-CH_2OCH_3$

252. In the reaction, CH_3-(tetrahydrofuran) $\xrightarrow{HCl}$ A

the major product (A) is

(a) OH, Cl (b) Cl, OH
(c) Cl, Cl (d) Cl

253. In the following reaction,

(dichlorotetrahydropyran: Cl, Cl, O) $\xrightarrow{CH_3OH}$ X

the major product (X) is

(a) Cl, OCH_3 (b) OCH_3, Cl
(c) OCH_3, OCH_3 (d)

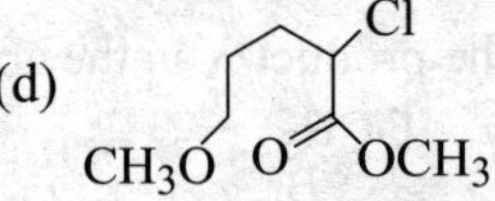

254. The product formed in the following reaction is

ROH + (dihydropyran) $\xrightarrow{PTS}$

(a) OR (b)

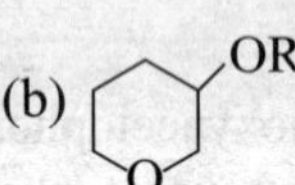

(c) OR (d) OR, OR

255. Before converting $HOCH_2CH_2CH_2Br$ into a Grignard reagent, the OH group should be protected. This can be done by the reagent

(a) PBr_3 (b) $(CH_3CO)_2O$
(c) (dihydropyran) (d) Na

256. Crown ethers are named as X-crown-Y. In the following crown ether, X and Y are respectively

(a) 6 and 12 (b) 18 and 6
(c) 24 and 6 (d) 6 and 24
(e) 6 and 18

257. In the presence of which of the following, can even non-polar solvents like benzene dissolve ionic compounds like $KMnO_4$?

(a) diethyl ether (b) chloroform
(c) dioxane (d) [18]-crown-6

258. When 2-chloroethanol (a chlorohydrin) is warmed slightly with dilute NaOH, the major product formed is

(a) $ClCH_2CH_2OCH_2CH_2Cl$
(b) $HOCH_2CH_2CH_2CH_2OH$
(c) $HOCH_2CH_2OH$
(d) 

Final Preparation

259. The reagent(s) which can be used to bring about the following transformation is(are)

(a) $LiAlH_4$ in $(C_2H_5)_2O$ (b) BH_3 in THF
(c) $NaBH_4$ in C_2H_5OH (d) Raney Ni/H_2 in THF

260. In the following diol,

(a) OH at C_2 is more basic than at C_5
(b) OH at C_2 is more acidic than at C_5
(c) both OH groups act as equally strong bases
(d) both OH groups act as equally strong acids

261. Amongst the following, the most basic but least nucleophilic alkoxide ion is

(a) CH_3O^- (b) $(CH_3)_2CHO^-$
(c) $CH_3CH_2O^-$ (d) $(CH_3)_3CO^-$

262. Consider the following sequence of reactions,

$\xrightarrow[\text{Pyridine}]{p\text{-TsCl}}$ A $\xrightarrow[\text{AcOH}]{\text{AcOK}}$ B $\xrightarrow[H_2O,\ \Delta]{\text{KOH}}$ C

The final product (C) is

(a) (b)
(c) 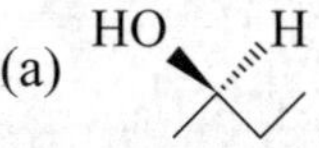 (d) (±)-2-butanol

263. The product of the following reaction is,

$\xrightarrow{H_3PO_4}$ Product

(a) (b) (c) (d)

264. The final product of the given reaction is _____ .

$\xrightarrow[\Delta]{H^+}$

(a) (b) (c) (d)

265. The major product formed in the reaction,

$\xrightarrow{\text{Dil. } H_2SO_4}$ is

(a) (b) (c) (d)

266. The final product (B) in the following reaction sequence is

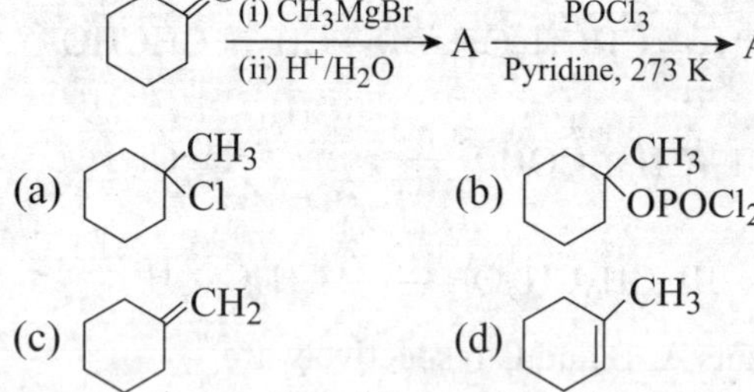

267. Cyclohexyl-CH_2OH on dehydration with conc. H_2SO_4 predominantly forms

(a) (b) (c) (d)

268. Lucas reagent can be used to distinguish
(a) methanol and ethanol
(b) allyl alcohol and 1-propanol
(c) 2-propanol and 2-butanol
(d) 1-propanol and 1-butanol

269. An unknown alcohol is treated with the Lucas reagent to determine whether the alcohol is primary, secondary or tertiary. Which alcohol reacts fastest and by which mechanism?
(a) tertiary alcohol by S_N2
(b) secondary alcohol by S_N1
(c) tertiary alcohol by S_N1
(d) secondary alcohol by S_N2

270. Identify X in the following sequence of reactions.

$$X \xrightarrow[\text{(ii) } H^+/H_2O]{\text{(i) } CH_3MgBr} C_5H_{12}O \xrightarrow[573\ K]{Cu} C_5H_{10}$$

(a) $CH_3COCH_2CH_3$ (b) $CH_3CH_2CH_2CHO$
(c) $(CH_3)_2CHCHO$ (d) $CH_3CH_2CH_2CH_2OH$

271. An alcohol on treatment with alkaline $KMnO_4$ gives a brown precipitate. The alcohol is
(a) $(CH_3)_3COH$ (b) $(C_2H_5)_3COH$
(c) $(C_2H_5)_2C(CH_3)OH$ (d) $(CH_3)_3CCH_2OH$

272. Consider the following reaction,

(2-methylcyclobut-2-enone, O and CH_3) $\xrightarrow{KMnO_4/HO^-}$ $\xrightarrow{Cu/\Delta}$ A

A formed is

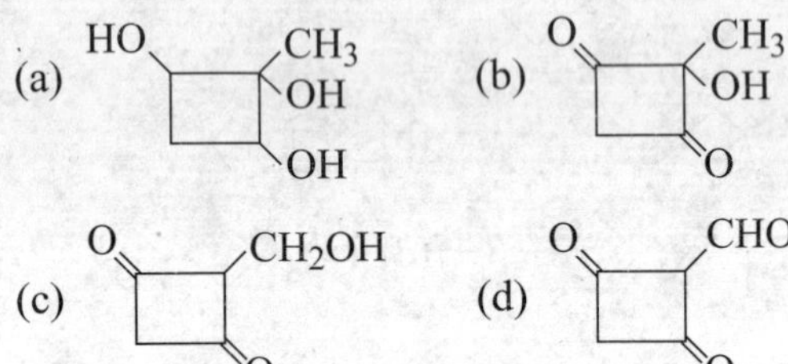

273. Consider the following reactions of alcohols.

I. $CH_2 = CHCH_2OH \xrightarrow{A} CH_2 = CHCHO$

II. $(CH_3)_3COH \xrightarrow{B}$ $(CH_3)_2C{=}CH_2$

III. $CH_3CH_2OH \xrightarrow{C} CH_3CO_2H$

Reagents A, B and C respectively are
(a) MnO_2, Cu/Δ, $K_2Cr_2O_7/H_2SO_4$
(b) Cu/Δ, MnO_2, $K_2C_{r2}O_7/ H_2SO_4$
(c) MnO_2, $K_2Cr_2O_7/H_2SO_4$, Cu/Δ
(d) $K_2Cr_2O_7/H_2SO_4$, Cu/Δ, MnO_2

274. A compound is soluble in conc. H_2SO_4. It does not decolourise bromine in carbon tetrachloride but is oxidised by chromic anhydride in aqueous sulfuric acid within two seconds, turning the orange solution to green. The original compound is
(a) a primary alcohol (b) a tertiary alcohol
(c) an alkane (d) an ether

275. The product obtained when (2-hydroxycyclohexanone: O, OH) is oxidised by HIO_4, is
(a) CHO, CHO (b) COOH, CHO
(c) COOH, COOH (d) CHO, CH_2OH

276. The following reaction can be carried out by

(1-(hydroxymethyl)cyclohexan-1-ol: HO, OH) ⟶ (cyclohexanol: OH)

(a) $H_2SO_4/\Delta, HIO_4$ (b) $NaIO_4$, H^+/Δ
(c) HIO_4, $NaBH_4$ (d) H^+/Δ, Zn/Hg–HCl

277. The correct product of the following reaction

$CH_3-C(OH)(CH_3)-C(OH)(CH_3)-CH_3 \xrightarrow{Conc.\ H_2SO_4}$ is,

(a) $CH_2{=}C(CH_3)-C(CH_3){=}CH_2$ (b) $(CH_3)_2C\overset{O}{—}C(CH_3)_2$
(c) $CH_3-C(OH)(CH_3)-C(=O)-CH_3$ (d) $CH_3-C(=O)-C(CH_3)_2-CH_3$

278. Predict the product of the following reaction,

$CH_3-C(CH_3)(OH)-CH_2OH \xrightarrow{Conc.\ H_2SO_4}$

(a) $(CH_3)_2C{=}CH_2$ (b) butan-2-one
(c) $(CH_3)_2C(OH)CHO$ (d) isobutyraldehyde

279. In the reaction,

$Ph-C(H_3O)(OH)-C(CH_3)(OH)-Ph \xrightarrow[\Delta]{H_2SO_4}$

The major product formed is
(a) $CH_3-C(=CH_2)-C(=CH_2)-Ph$ (b) $Ph-C(H_3C)(HO)-C(=CH_2)-Ph$
(c) $CH_3-C(=O)-C(CH_3)(Ph)-Ph$ (d) $Ph-C(=O)-C(CH_3)(Ph)-CH_3$

280. The major product of the following reaction is

(cyclobutane bearing HO and $C(Me)_2OH$) $\xrightarrow{H^+}$

(a) (Me, O, Me on cyclobutane) (b) (Me, cyclobutane)
(c) (O, Me, Me on cyclopentane) (d) (Me, Me on cyclopentene)

281. The major product formed in the reaction, (cyclopentyl)(OH)C–C(OH)(cyclopentyl) [1,1'-bicyclopentyl-1,1'-diol] $\xrightarrow{\text{Conc. } H_2SO_4}$ is

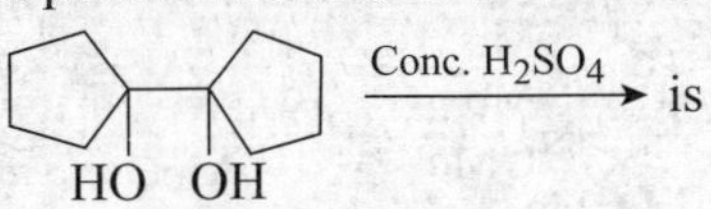

(a) 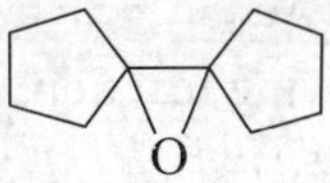 dispiro epoxide (two cyclopentane rings joined through O)
(b) 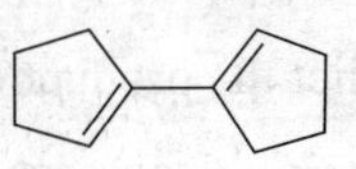 1,1'-bi(cyclopentene)
(c) 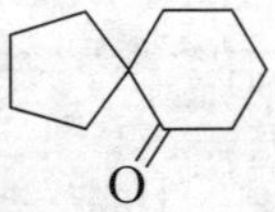 spiro[4.5]decan-6-one
(d) 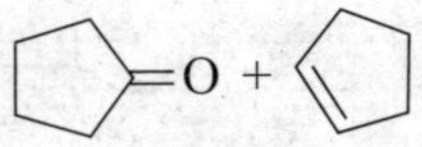 cyclopentanone + cyclopentene

282. The reaction, $(CH_3)_2C(OH)–C(NH_2)(CH_3)_2$ $\xrightarrow[\text{dil.}H_2SO_4]{NaNO_2}$ produces mainly

(a) $(CH_3)_2C(OH)–C(OH)(CH_3)_2$ (b) $(CH_3)_3C–C(=O)–CH_3$
(c) $(CH_3)_2C–C(CH_3)_2$ (bridged by H) (d) $(CH_3)_2C–C(CH_3)_2$ (bridged by NH)

283. Addition of HOCl to allyl alcohol gives
(a) 2-chloropropane-1,3-diol
(b) 3-chloropropane-1,2-diol
(c) 2,3-dichloropropanol
(d) 1,2,3-trichloropropane

284. Glycerol is obtained from propylene ($CH_3CH{=}CH_2$) by using the following reagents.
I. Cl_2 II. Na_2CO_3 III. HOCl IV. NaOH
The correct sequence in which these reagents are used is
(a) II, I, IV, III (b) II, I, III, IV
(c) I, II, IV, III (d) I, II, III, IV

285. The three products obtained in the reaction between glycerol and hydriodic acid would appear in the order
(a) propene, allyl iodide and isopropyl iodide
(b) allyl iodide, propene and isopropyl iodide
(c) allyl iodide, isopropyl iodide and propene
(d) isopropyl iodide, allyl iodide and propene

286. Glycerol is treated with excess of HI at room temperature and then with more HI at 423 K. The final product obtained is
(a) allyl iodide (b) isopropyl iodide
(c) propene (d) propane

287. The major product U in the following reaction is

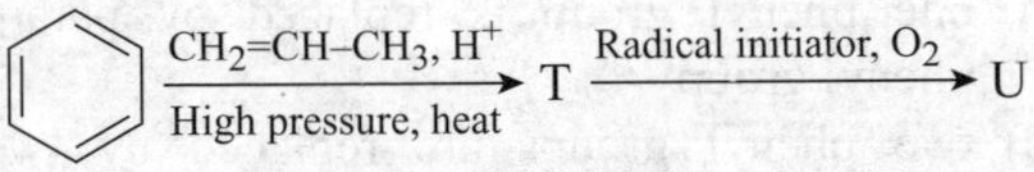

Benzene $\xrightarrow[\text{High pressure, heat}]{CH_2{=}CH–CH_3,\ H^+}$ T $\xrightarrow{\text{Radical initiator, } O_2}$ U

(a) 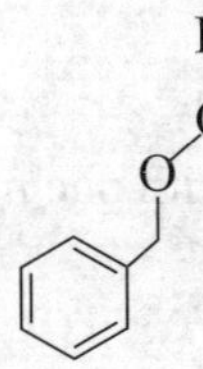 $C_6H_5CH_2–O–O–H$ (b) $C_6H_5C(CH_3)_2–O–O–H$
(c) 2-vinylbenzyl–O–O–H (d) 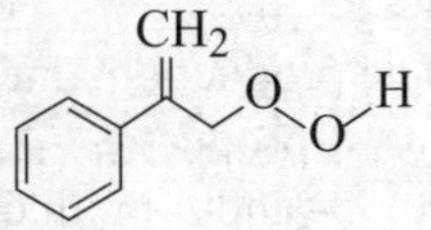 $C_6H_5C(=CH_2)CH_2–O–O–H$

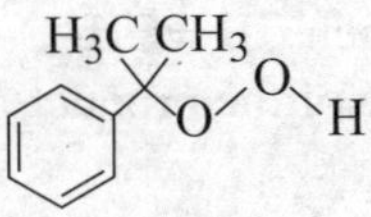

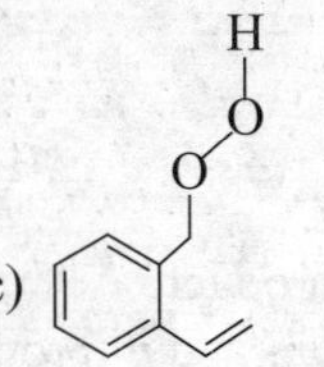

288. The stronger acid among the following is
(a) *o*-methoxyphenol (b) *p*-methoxyphenol
(c) *m*-methoxyphenol (d) phenol

289. Which of the following will not be soluble in sodium bicarbonate?
(a) 2,4,6-tribromophenol
(b) benzoic acid
(c) *o*-nitrophenol
(d) benzenesulfonic acid

290. When phenol is treated with D_2SO_4/D_2O, some of the hydrogens get exchanged. The final product in the exchange reaction is

(a) 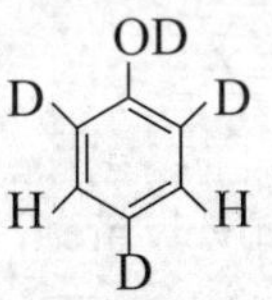 OD; 2-D, 6-D, 3-H, 5-H, 4-D
(b) OD; 2-D, 6-H, 3-H, 5-H, 4-D
(c) OD; 2-D, 6-H, 3-H, 5-D, 4-H
(d) OD; 2-H, 6-H, 3-D, 5-D, 4-H

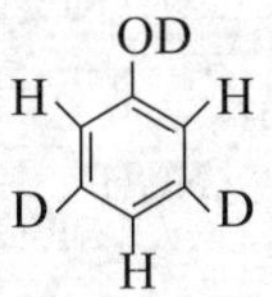

291. The major product(s) of the following reaction is(are)

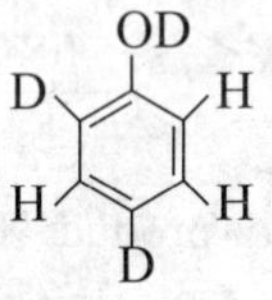

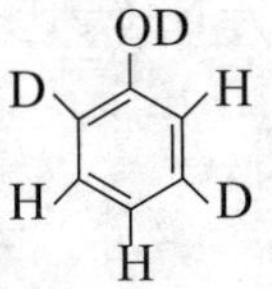

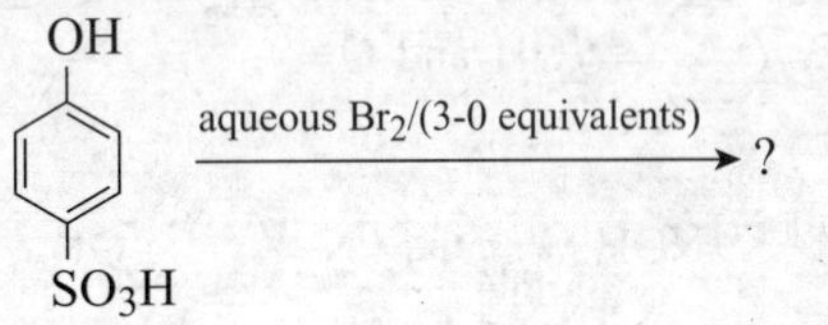

4-hydroxybenzenesulfonic acid (OH, SO_3H) $\xrightarrow{\text{aqueous } Br_2/(3\text{-}0 \text{ equivalents})}$?

(a) 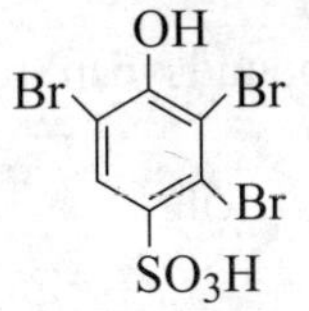 OH; 2-Br, 6-Br, 5-Br, 4-SO_3H
(b) 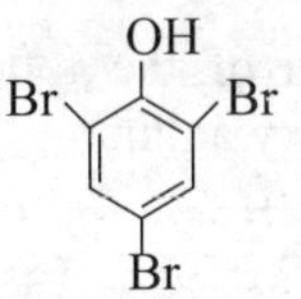 OH; 2-Br, 6-Br, 4-Br
(c) 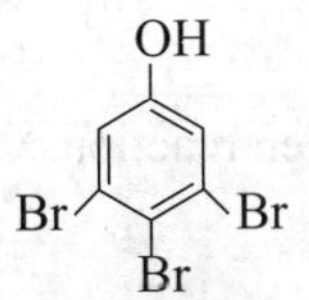 OH; 3-Br, 5-Br, 4-Br
(d) 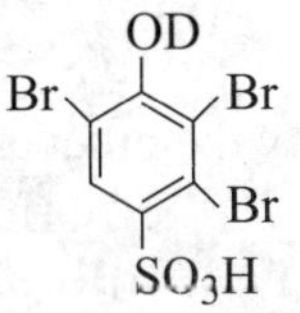 OD; 2-Br, 6-Br, 5-Br, 4-SO_3H

292. An organic compound with the molecular formula C_7H_8O dissolves in NaOH and gives a characteristic colour with $FeCl_3$. On treatment with Br_2, it gives $C_7H_5OBr_3$. The compound is
(a) benzyl alcohol (b) *o*-cresol
(c) *m*-cresol (d) *p*-cresol

293. 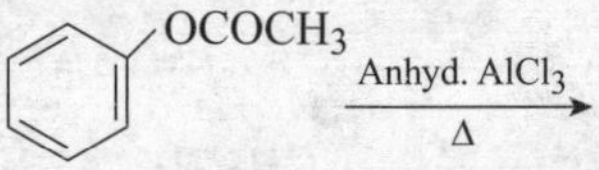 [Phenyl acetate ($C_6H_5OCOCH_3$) $\xrightarrow[\Delta]{\text{Anhyd. } AlCl_3}$]

The product obtained is/are

(a) *o*-product (b) *m*-product

(c) *o*- and *p*-products (d) *o*-, *m*- and *p*- products

294. Reactant P labelled with ^{14}C (labelled carbon marked with an asterisk) rearranged to product Q on heating.

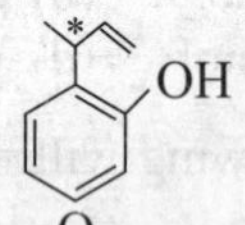

[Structure Q: OH]

Q

The structure of reactant P is

(a) 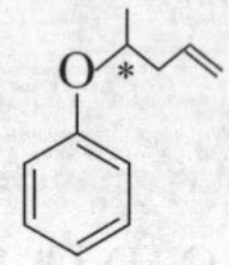 (b) 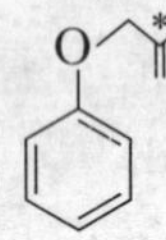 (c) 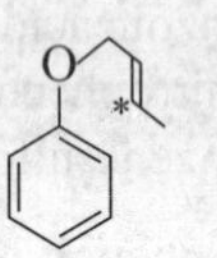 (d)

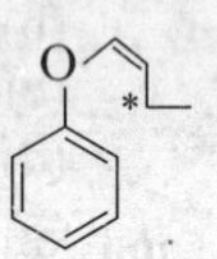

295. In the reaction sequence,

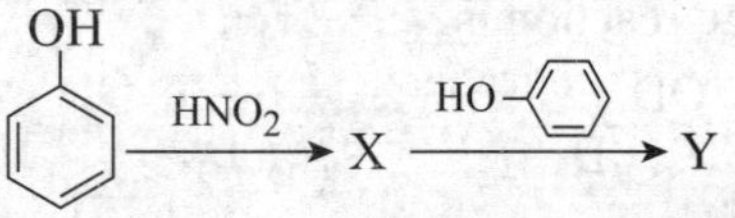

[Phenol (OH) $\xrightarrow{HNO_2}$ X $\xrightarrow{HO-C_6H_5}$ Y]

the major product X and Y respectively are

(a) 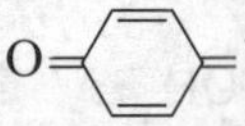 O=⟨⟩=NOH and O=⟨⟩=N–⟨⟩–OH

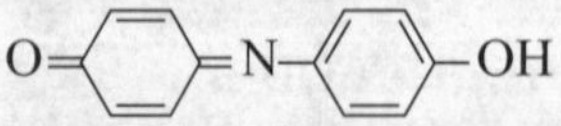

(b) 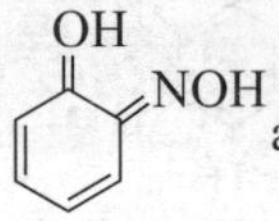 [OH, =NOH] and [O, =N–, OH]

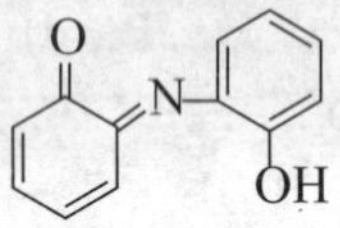

(c) 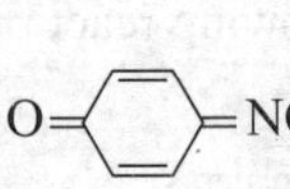 O=⟨⟩=NOH and O=⟨⟩=N–[OH]

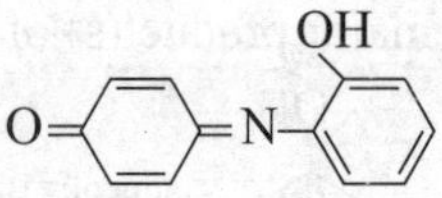

(d) 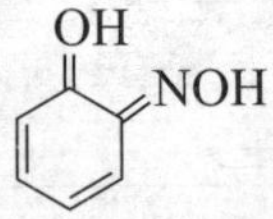 [OH, =NOH] and [O, =N–⟨⟩–OH]

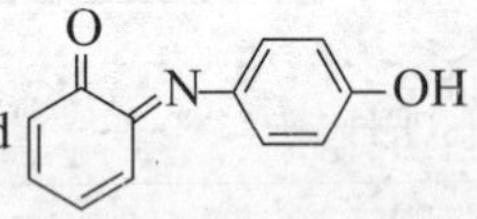

296. Which of the following compounds can react with hydroxylamine?

(a) 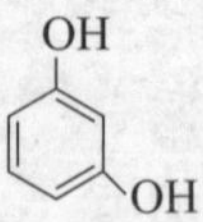 [OH, OH] (b) 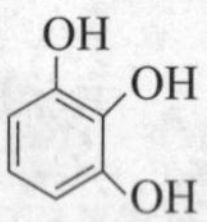 [OH, OH, OH] (c) 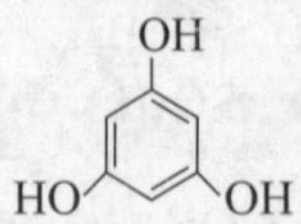 [OH, HO, OH] (d) 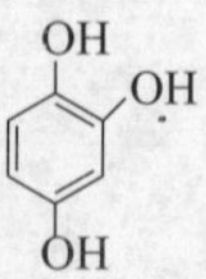 [OH, OH, OH]

297. Identify the product A in the given reaction.

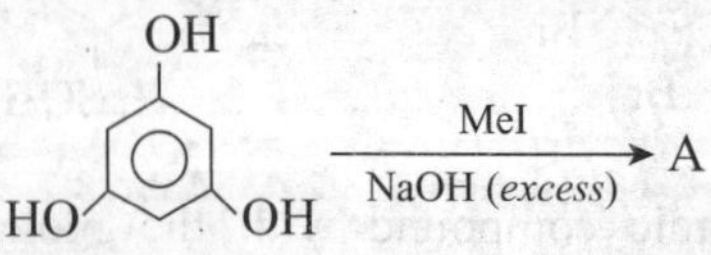

[OH, HO, OH (phloroglucinol)] $\xrightarrow[\text{NaOH } (excess)]{\text{MeI}}$ A

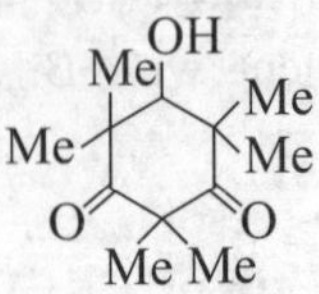

(a) [OH, Me, Me, Me, Me, O, O, Me Me] (b) 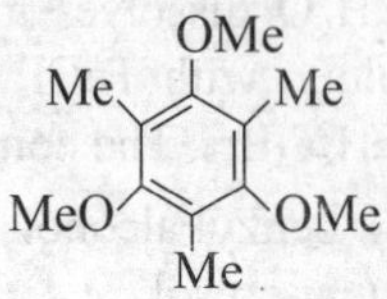 [OMe, Me, Me, MeO, OMe, Me]

(c) 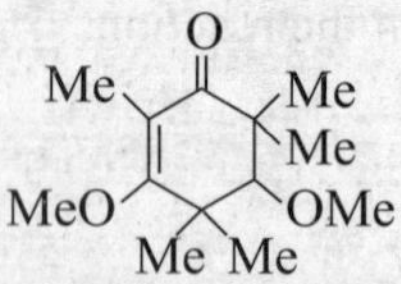 [O, Me, Me, Me, MeO, OMe, Me Me] (d) 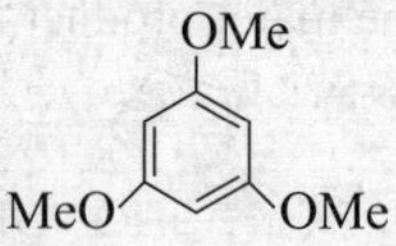 [OMe, MeO, OMe]

298. Predict the product of the following reaction.

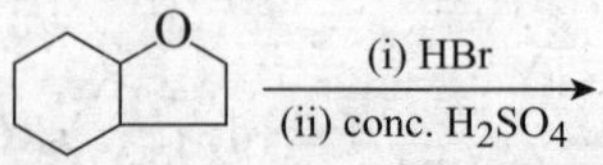

[Bicyclic ether (O)] $\xrightarrow[\text{(ii) conc. } H_2SO_4]{\text{(i) HBr}}$

(a) 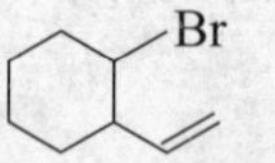 [Br] (b) 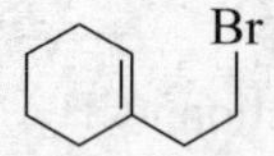 [Br] (c) 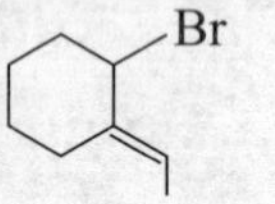 [Br] (d) 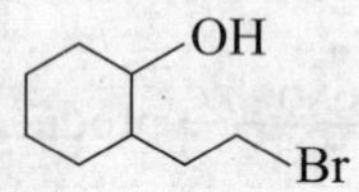 [OH, Br]

299. Consider the reactions:

(i) $(CH_3)_2CH–CH_2Br \xrightarrow{C_2H_5OH} (CH_3)_2–CH_2OCH_2H_5 + HBr$

(ii) $(CH_3)_2CH–CH_2Br \xrightarrow{C_2H_5O^-} (CH_3)_2CH–CH_2OC_2H_5 + Br^-$

The mechanisms of reactions (i) and (ii) are respectively:

(a) S_N1 and S_N2 (b) S_N1 and S_N1

(c) S_N2 and S_N2 (d) S_N2 and S_N1

300. The major product in the following reaction is

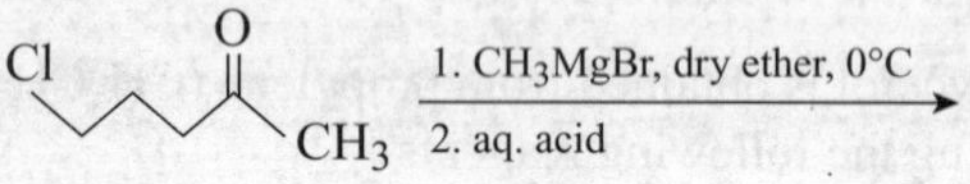

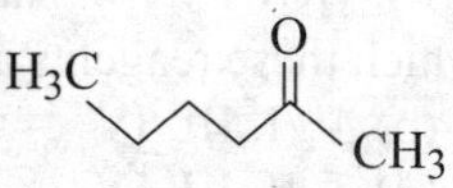

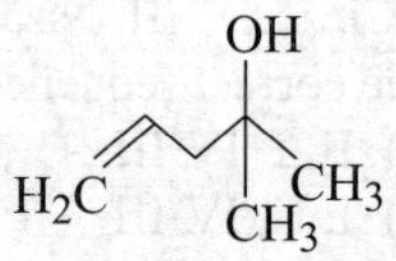

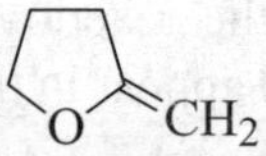

[Cl, O, CH_3] $\xrightarrow[\text{2. aq. acid}]{\text{1. } CH_3MgBr\text{, dry ether, 0°C}}$

(a) [H_3C, O, CH_3] (b) [OH, H_2C, CH_3, CH_3]

(c) [O, CH_2] (d) 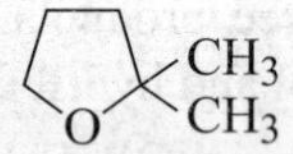 [O, CH_3, CH_3]

301. The acidic hydrolysis of ether (X) shown below is faster when

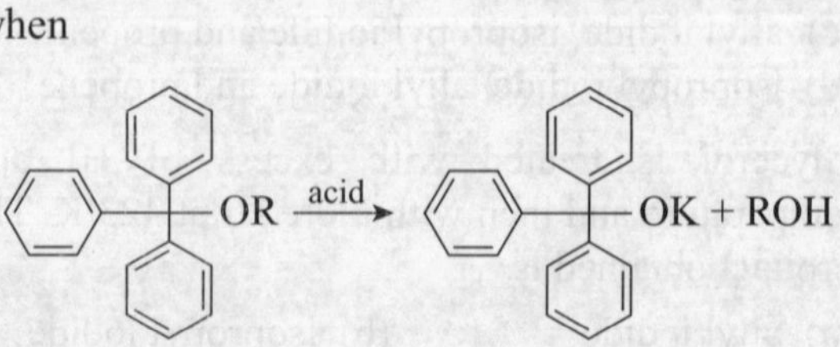

[$(C_6H_5)_3C$–OR] $\xrightarrow{\text{acid}}$ [$(C_6H_5)_3C$–OK] + ROH

[X]

(a) one phenyl group is replaced by a methyl group

(b) one phenyl group is replaced by paramethoxy phenyl group

(c) two phenyl groups are replaced by two para-methoxyphenyl groups

(d) no structural change is made to X

302. When $CH_2=CH–O–CH_2CH_3$ reacts with one mol of HI, one of the products formed is

(a) ethane (b) ethanol
(c) iodoethene (d) ethanol

303. Which of the following ethers is cleaved even by hydrogen chloride at room temperature?
(a) $C_6H_5–O–CH_2CH_3$ (b) $CH_3CH_2–O–CH_2CH_3$
(c) $(CH_3)_3C–O–CH_2CH_3$ (d) $(CH_3)_3C–O–C(CH_3)_3$

304. Which of the following compounds is resistant to nucleophilic attack by OH^- ions?
(a) methyl acetate (b) acetonitrile
(c) acetamide (d) diethyl ether

305. An unknown compound dissolves in conc. sulfuric acid, but does not decolourise bromine water and does not react with sodium. Which of the following classes of molecules would behave in this manner?
(a) alkene (b) alcohol (c) ether (d) phenol

306. Given are cyclohexanol (I), acetic acid (II), 2,4,6-trinitrophenol (III) and phenol (IV). In these, the order of decreasing acidic character will be:
(a) II > III > IV > I (b) III > IV > II > I
(c) III > II > IV > I (d) III > II > I > IV

307. Acid catalysed hydration of alkenes except ethane leads to the formation of a
(a) primary alcohol
(b) secondary or tertiary alcohol
(c) mixture of primary and secondary alcohols
(d) mixture of secondary and tertiary alcohols

308. What is Z in the following sequence of reactions?

$$Z \xrightarrow[\text{(ii) } H_2O\text{, boil}]{PCl_5} X \xrightarrow{\text{Alc.KOH}} Y \xrightarrow{\text{(i) Conc. } H_2SO_4} Z$$

(a) CH_3CH_2OH (b) $CH_3CHOHCH_3$
(c) $(CH_3)_2CHCH_2OH$ (d) $CH_3CH=CH_2$

309. 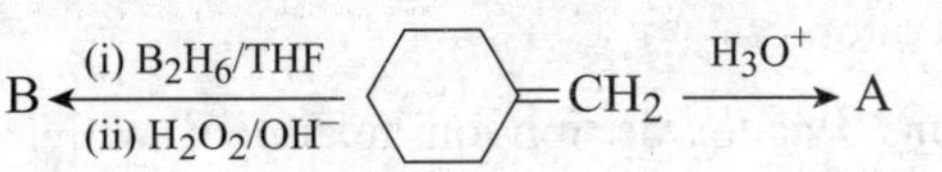 $B \xleftarrow[\text{(ii) } H_2O_2/OH^-]{\text{(i) } B_2H_6/THF}$ (cyclohexane)$=CH_2 \xrightarrow{H_3O^+} A$

A and B respectively are:
(a) both (cyclohexyl)–CH_2OH (b) both (1-methylcyclohexanol: CH_3, OH)
(c) 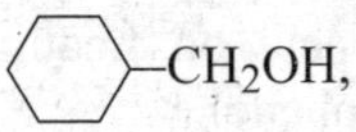 (cyclohexyl)–CH_2OH, (1-methylcyclohexanol: CH_3, OH)
(d) 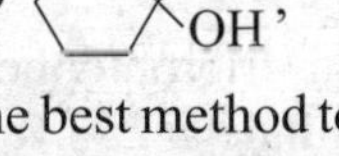 (1-methylcyclohexanol: CH_3, OH), (cyclohexyl)–CH_2OH

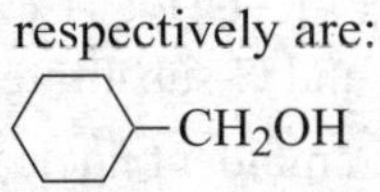

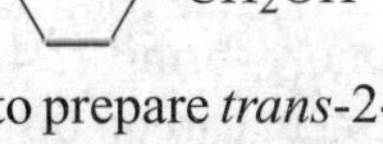

310. The best method to prepare *trans*-2-methylcyclohexanol from 1-methylcyclohexene is
(a) addition of H_2O in the presence of dil. H_2SO_4
(b) hydroboration–oxidation
(c) oxymercuration–demercuration
(d) none of the above

311. The best method to prepare 3- methylbutan-2-ol from 3-methylbut-1-ene is
(a) addition of H_2O in the presence of dil. H_2SO_4
(b) addition of HBr in the presence of peroxide followed by hydrolysis with NaOH(*aq*)
(c) hydroboration–oxidation
(d) oxymercuration–demercuration

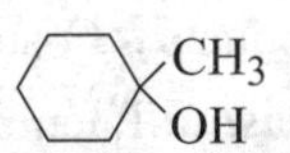

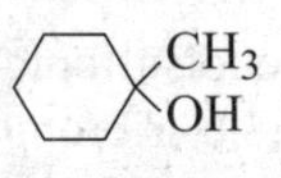

312. The major product formed during hydroboration–oxidation of 1- methylcyclopentane is
(a) 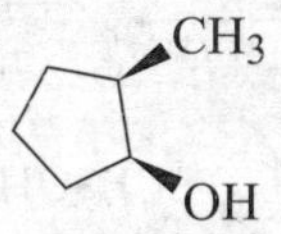 (cyclopentane with CH_3 and OH, both wedged)
(b) 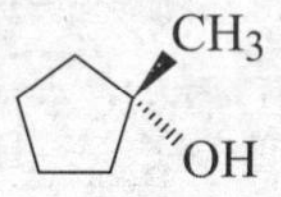 (cyclopentane with CH_3 and OH, hashed OH)
(c) 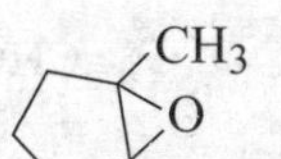 (cyclopentane epoxide with CH_3, O)
(d) 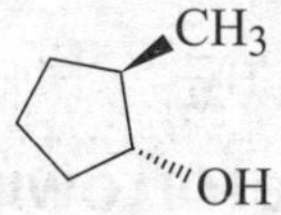 (cyclopentane with CH_3 wedged and OH hashed)

313. The compound which is obtained by treating chloropropane with alcoholic KOH, on reaction with BH_3/THF followed by acetic acid gives
(a) $CH_3CH_2CH_2OH$ (b) $CH_3CH_2CH_3$
(c) $CH_3CH(OH)CH_3$ (d) $CH_3CH_2CHOHCH_3$

314. The major product of the following reaction sequence is

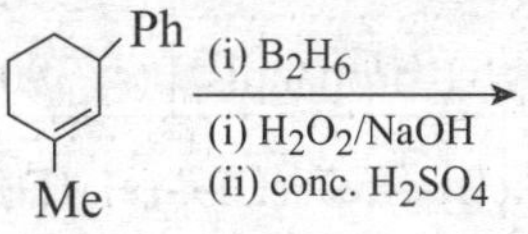

(cyclohexene with Ph and Me) $\xrightarrow[\text{(i) } H_2O_2/NaOH \text{ (ii) conc. } H_2SO_4]{\text{(i) } B_2H_6}$

(a) (Ph, Me cyclohexene) (b) (Ph, =Me exocyclic) (c) 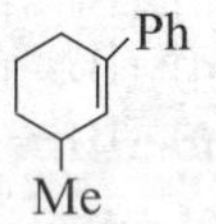 (Ph, Me cyclohexene) (d) 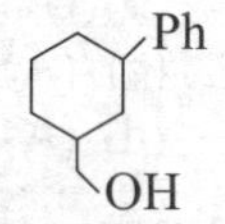 (Ph, CH_2OH cyclohexane)

315. Among the following reactions, a mixture of diastereoisomers is produced from
(a) 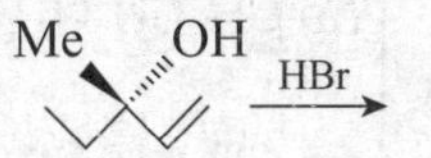 (Me, OH alkene) $\xrightarrow{HBr}$ (b) 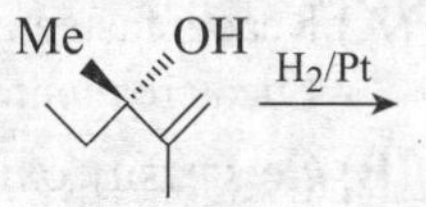 (Me, OH alkene) $\xrightarrow{H_2/Pt}$
(c) 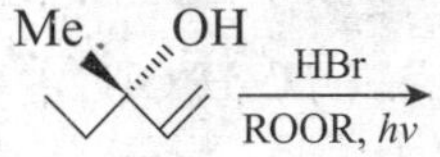 (Me, OH alkene) $\xrightarrow[\text{ROOR, } h\nu]{HBr}$ (d) 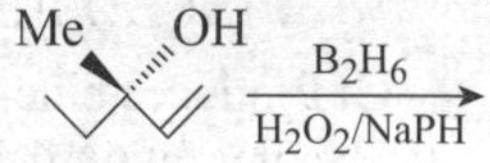 (Me, OH alkene) $\xrightarrow[H_2O_2/NaPH]{B_2H_6}$

316. Ethyl ester $\xrightarrow[\text{Excess}]{CH_3MgBr}$ P. The product P is
(a) 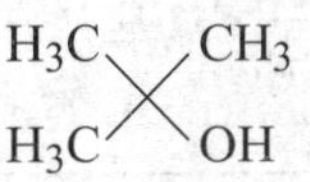 $(H_3C)(H_3C)C(CH_3)OH$ (b) $(H_3C)(H_5C_2)C(C_2H_5)OH$
(c) $(H_5C_2)(H_5C_2)C(CH_3)OH$ (d) 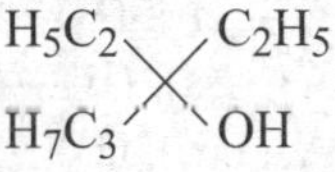 $(H_5C_2)(H_7C_3)C(C_2H_5)OH$

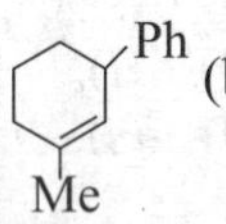

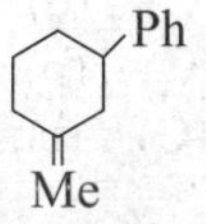

317. 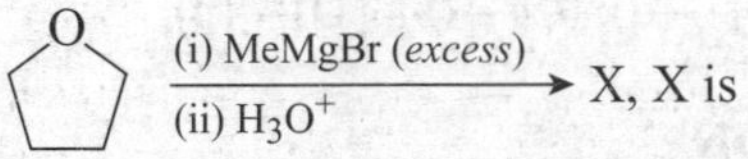 (tetrahydrofuran) $\xrightarrow[\text{(ii) } H_3O^+]{\text{(i) MeMgBr (excess)}}$ X, X is
(a) 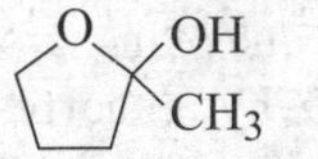 (tetrahydrofuran with OH and CH_3) (b) 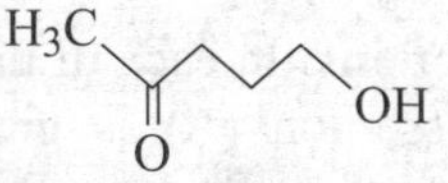 H_3C–CO–$CH_2CH_2CH_2$–OH
(c) 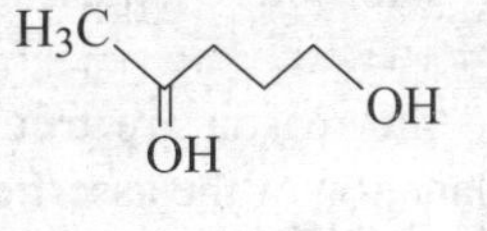 H_3C–CH(OH)–$CH_2CH_2CH_2$–OH (d) 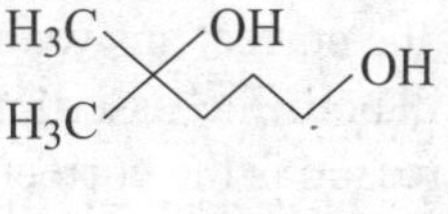 $(H_3C)_2C(OH)$–$CH_2CH_2CH_2$–OH

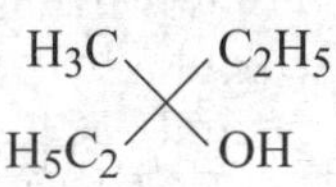

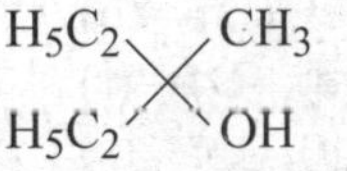

318. Acetyl bromide reacts with excess of CH_3MgI followed by treatment with a saturated solution of NH_4Cl gives

(a) acetone (b) acetamide
(c) 2-methyl-2-propanol (d) acetyl acetone

319. The final product (A) in the following reaction sequence is

$$F-\square-Br \xrightarrow{Mg/ether} \xrightarrow[(ii)\ H_3O^+]{(i)\ HCHO}$$

(a) $HOCH_2-\square-Br$ (b) $F-\square-CH_2OH$

(c) $HOCH_2-\square-CH_2OH$ (d) $OHC-\square-CHO$

MATCH THE FOLLOWING

320.

Column I (Compound)	Column II (Boiling point)
(A) 2-Methyl-2-propanol	(p) 381 K
(B) 2-Butanol	(q) 373 K
(C)1-Butanol	(r) 356 K
(D) 2-Methyl-1-propanol	(s) 390 K

(a) (A)—(r); (B)—(q); (C)—(s); (D)—(p)
(b) (A)—(p); (B)—(r); (C)—(q); (D)—(s)
(c) (A)—(q); (B)—(s); (C)—(p); (D)—(r)
(d) (A)—(p); (B)—(q); (C)—(r); (D)—(s)

321.

Column I	Column II
(A) Reacts fastest with Lucas reagent	(p) CH_3CH_2OH
(B) Gets easily oxidised by $K_2Cr_2O_7/H_2SO_4$	(q) $CH_3CH_2CHOHCH_3$
(C) Produces blue colouration in Victor Meyer's test	(r) C_6H_5OH
(D) Produces violet colouration with neutral $FeCl_3$	(s) $(CH_3)_3COH$

(a) (A)—(p); (B)—(s); (C)—(r); (D)—(q)
(b) (A)—(s); (B)—(p); (C)—(q); (D)—(r)
(c) (A)—(q); (B)—(r); (C)—(p); (D)—(s)
(d) (A)—(r); (B)—(q); (C)—(s); (D)—(p)

ASSERTION REASON

Directions: In each of the following questions, a statement of Assertion (A) is given followed by a corresponding statement of Reason (R) just below it. Of the statements, mark the correct answer as

(a) if both the assertion and the reason are true and the reason is the correct explanation of the assertion.
(b) if both the assertion and the reason are true but the reason is not the correct explanation of the assertion
(c) if the assertion is true but the reason is false
(d) if both the assertion and reason are false

322. Assertion: $F-C_6H_4-OH$ is less acidic than $Cl-C_6H_4-OH$.

Reason: F exerts better +mesomeric effect than Cl.

323. Assertion: When CO_2 is passed through an aqueous solution of sodium picrate, picric acid gets precipitated.

Reason: Carbonic acid is a stronger acid than picric acid.

324. Assertion: *o*-Nitrophenol is more acidic than *m*-nitrophenol.

Reason: *o*-Nitrophenol has more –I effect than *m*-nitrophenol.

325. Assertion:

$$p\text{-}O_2N-C_6H_4-OC_2H_5 \xrightarrow{HBr} p\text{-}O_2N-C_6H_4-Br + C_2H_5OH$$

Reason: Due to the formation of a highly stable carbocation.

326. Assertion: Addition of CH_3OH to phenyl magnesium bromide gives benzene.

Reason: CH_3OH is a stronger acid than benzene.

327. Assertion: Treatment of phenol with nitrous acid yields *p*-benzoquinone monoxime.

Reason: *p*-Nitrosophenol and *p*-benzoquinone monoxime are tautomers

328. Assertion: Phenoxide ion on treatment with active alkyl halide (such as $CH_2{=}CH{-}CH_2Cl$) gives two products—O-substituted and C-substituted.

Reason: Phenoxide is an ambident nucleophile.

329. Assertion: *p*-Phenolsulfonic acid on treatment with Br_2–H_2O gives 2,4,6-tribromophenol.

Reason: Sulfonic acid is a good leaving group.

330. Assertion: Phenol forms 2,4,6-tribromophenol on treatment with Br_2 in carbon disulfide at 273 K.

Reason: Bromine gets polarised in carbon disulphide.

331. Assertion: t-Butyl methyl ether is not prepared by the reaction of t-butyl bromide with sodium methoxide.

Reason: Sodium methoxide is a strong nucleophile.

332. Assertion: $(CH_3)_3C{-}Br$ and CH_3CH_2ONa react to form $(CH_3)_3C\ O\ CH_2CH_3$.

Reason: Good yield of the ether is obtained when tert-alkyl halides are treated with alkoxides.

333. Assertion: The major products formed by heating $C_6H_5CH_2OCH_3$ with HI are $C_6H_5CH_2I$ and CH_3OH.

Reason: Benzyl cation is more stable than methyl cation.

334. Assertion: Reaction of alcohols with $SOCl_2$ is catalysed by the presence of tertiary amines R_3N.

Reason: Tertiary amines promote the reaction by reacting with the byproduct HCl.

335. Assertion: The ease of dehydration of the following alcohols is

OH < OH < OH < OH

Reason: Alcohols leading to conjugated alkenes are dehydrated to a greater extent.

336. Assertion: The last traces of moisture in ethanol can be removed by storing it over sodium wire.

Reason: Sodium reacts with water but not with ethanol to produce H_2 gas.

337. Assertion: The change in colour of an acidic solution of potassium dichromate by breath is used to test drunk drivers.

Reason: Change is colour is due to the complexation of alcohol with potassium dichromate.

338. Assertion: Benzenediazoniumchloride on boiling with water gives phenol.

Reason: The C–N bond is polar.

Answer Key

1. (c)	2. (a)	3. (d)	4. (a)	5. (d)	6. (d)	7. (b)	8. (a)	9. (a)	10. (a)
11. (a)	12. (d)	13. (d)	14. (a)	15. (c)	16. (c)	17. (a)	18. (b)	19. (d)	20. (b)
21. (b)	22. (a)	23. (b)	24. (c)	25. (c)	26. (a)	27. (d)	28. (b)	29. (a)	30. (b)
31. (a)	32. (b)	33. (b)	34. (b)	35. (d)	36. (a)	37. (b)	38. (d)	39. (d)	40. (d)
41. (c)	42. (d)	43. (c)	44. (a)	45. (d)	46. (a)	47. (d)	48. (d)	49. (c)	50. (a)
51. (a)	52. (c)	53. (a)	54. (c)	55. (c)	56. (a)	57. (b)	58. (a)	59. (d)	60. (c)
61. (c)	62. (a)	63. (c)	64. (d)	65. (a)	66. (d)	67. (b)	68. (b)	69. (b)	70. (b)
71. (d)	72. (a)	73. (b)	74. (c)	75. (b)	76. (c)	77. (c)	78. (d)	79. (c)	80. (b)
81. (c)	82. (d)	83. (a)	84. (a)	85. (b)	86. (a)	87. (d)	88. (c)	89. (d)	90. (c)
91. (a)	92. (c)	93. (d)	94. (b)	95. (d)	96. (c)	97. (d)	98. (a)	99. (d)	100. (c)
101. (c)	102. (a)	103. (d)	104. (c)	105. (b)	106. (d)	107. (d)	108. (d)	109. (c)	110. (d)
111. (c)	112. (c)	113. (c)	114. (d)	115. (b)	116. (a)	117. (b)	118. (d)	119. (b)	120. (d)
121. (a)	122. (c)	123. (b)	124. (a)	125. (b)	126. (d)	127. (c)	128. (c)	129. (d)	130. (d)
131. (c)	132. (d)	133. (b)	134. (a)	135. (d)	136. (c)	137. (d)	138. (b)	139. (c)	140. (a)
141. (a)	142. (b)	143. (b)	144. (b)	145. (a)	146. (b)	147. (d)	148. (c)	149. (c)	150. (c)
151. (c)	152. (d)	153. (b)	154. (a)	155. (c)	156. (b)	157. (a)	158. (c)	159. (c)	160. (a)
161. (a)	162. (a)	163. (b)	164. (d)	165. (d)	166. (c)	167. (a)	168. (d)	169. (b)	170. (d)
171. (c)	172. (c)	173. (a)	174. (c)	175. (d)	176. (c)	177. (b)	178. (c)	179. (b)	180. (d)
181. (a)	182. (b)	183. (d)	184. (b)	185. (d)	186. (d)	187. (c)	188. (a)	189. (c)	190. (c)
191. (d)	192. (d)	193. (d)	194. (d)	195. (d)	196. (a)	197. (b)	198. (b)	199. (b)	200. (c)
201. (a)	202. (d)	203. (b)	204. (b)	205. (b)	206. (a)	207. (d)	208. (d)	209. (e)	210. (d)
211. (a)	212. (b)	213. (a)	214. (c)	215. (a)	216. (d)	217. (b)	218. (d)	219. (a)	220. (a)
221. (a)	222. (b)	223. (d)	224. (c)	225. (c)	226. (c)	227. (b)	228. (d)	229. (a)	230. (a)
231. (c)	232. (d)	233. (d)	234. (c)	235. (c)	236. (d)	237. (d)	238. (d)	239. (c)	240. (a)
241. (b)	242. (c)	243. (c)	244. (b)	245. (c)	246. (a)	247. (b)	248. (a)	249. (b)	250. (d)
251. (c)	252. (b)	253. (a)	254. (a)	255. (c)	256. (b)	257. (d)	258. (d)	259. (c)	260. (a)
261. (d)	262. (b)	263. (c)	264. (d)	265. (b)	266. (d)	267. (b)	268. (b)	269. (c)	270. (a)
271. (d)	272. (b)	273. (a)	274. (a)	275. (b)	276. (c)	277. (d)	278. (d)	279. (c)	280. (c)
281. (c)	282. (b)	283. (a)	284. (d)	285. (b)	286. (d)	287. (b)	288. (c)	289. (c)	290. (a)
291. (b)	292. (c)	293. (c)	294. (c)	295. (a)	296. (c)	297. (a)	298. (a)	299. (c)	300. (d)
301. (c)	302. (d)	303. (d)	304. (d)	305. (c)	306. (c)	307. (b)	308. (b)	309. (c)	310. (b)
311. (d)	312. (d)	313. (b)	314. (c)	315. (a)	316. (a)	317. (d)	318. (c)	319. (b)	320. (a)
321. (b)	322. (a)	323. (d)	324. (b)	325. (c)	326. (a)	327. (b)	328. (a)	329. (b)	330. (d)
331. (b)	332. (d)	333. (a)	334. (a)	335. (a)	336. (d)	337. (c)	338. (b)		

Hints and Solutions

Classification and Nomenclature

1. (c): $\overset{4}{C}H_3-\overset{3}{C}(CH_3)_2-\overset{2}{C}H_2\overset{1}{C}H_2OH$ 3, 3-Dimethylbutan-1-ol

2. (a): $\overset{1}{C}H_3-\overset{2}{C}(CH_3)(OH)-\overset{3}{C}(CH_3)(OH)-\overset{4}{C}H_3$ 2, 3-Dimethylbutane-2, 3-diol

3. (d): All statements are correct.

4. (a): $CH_3-\overset{3}{C}H(CH_3)-\overset{2}{C}^*HOH-\overset{1}{C}H_3$

3-Methyl-2-butanol

5. (d): The IUPAC name of hydroquinol is benzene-1,4-diol.

6. (d): $\overset{5}{C}H_3\overset{4}{C}H_2-\overset{3}{C}H(CH_2Cl)-\overset{2}{C}H(\overset{1}{C}H_2OH)-CH(CH_3)-CH_3$ 3-Chloromethyl-2-isopropylpentan-1-ol

7. (b): (cyclohexane ring with O_2N at C-2 and OC_2H_5 at C-1) '*e*' comes before '*n*' in alphabetic order therefore, correct name is: l-ethoxy-2-nitrocyclobexane

8. (a): $HO-CH_2-\boxed{CH=CH_2}$ vinyl

Methyl alcohol is called carbinol. The given compound being a vinyl derivative of carbinol is called vinyl carbinol.

Preparation of Alcohols

9. (a):

$$\underset{\text{Styrene}}{C_6H_5-CH=CH_2} \xrightarrow{H^+} \underset{2^\circ\text{ carbocation}}{C_6H_5-\overset{+}{C}H-CH_3} \xrightarrow[-H^+]{H_2O} \underset{\text{1-Phenylethanol}}{C_6H_5-CHOH-CH_3}$$

10. (a): 1-Methylcyclopentene $\xrightarrow{H^+}$ 1-methylcyclopentyl cation $\xrightarrow[-H^+]{H_2O}$ 1-methylcyclopentanol (OH)

11. (a): alkene $\xrightarrow{H^+}$ tertiary carbocation $\xrightarrow[-H^+]{H_2O}$ tertiary alcohol (OH)

12. (d): Methylenecyclohexane $\xrightarrow{H^+}$ [1-methylcyclohexyl cation $\xleftarrow{H^+}$ 1-methylcyclohexene] $\xrightarrow[-H^+]{H_2O}$ 1-Methyl-cyclohexanol

13. (d):

$$\underset{\text{3-Phenylbut-1-ene}}{C_6H_5-CH(CH_3)-CH=CH_2} \xrightarrow{H^+} \underset{\substack{2^\circ\text{ carbocation}\\ \text{(less stable)}}}{C_6H_5-C(CH_3)(H)-\overset{+}{C}H-CH_3}$$

$$\xrightarrow[\text{shift}]{\text{1, 2-Hydride}} \underset{\substack{2^\circ\text{ carbocation}\\ \text{(less stable)}}}{C_6H_5-\overset{+}{C}(CH_3)-CH_2CH_3} \xrightarrow[-H^+]{\text{(i) }H_2\ddot{O}:} \underset{\text{2-Phenylbutan-2-ol}}{C_6H_5-C(CH_3)(OH)-CH_2CH_3}$$

14. (a):

$$CH_3-C(CH_3)_2-CH=CH_2 \xrightarrow{H^+} \underset{\substack{2^\circ\text{ carbocation}\\ \text{(less stable)}}}{CH_3-C(CH_3)_2-\overset{+}{C}H-CH_3}$$

$$\xrightarrow[\text{shift}]{\text{1, 2-Methyl}} \underset{\substack{3^\circ\text{ carbocation}\\ \text{(more stable)}}}{CH_3-\overset{+}{C}(CH_3)-CH(CH_3)-CH_3} \xrightarrow[-H^+]{+H_2O} CH_3-C(CH_3)(OH)-CH(CH_3)-CH_3$$

15. (c):

$$CH_3CH_2OH \xrightarrow{PBr_3} \underset{(X)}{CH_3CHBr} \xrightarrow[-HBr]{\text{Alc. KOH}} \underset{\text{Ethene(Y)}}{CH_2=CH_2}$$

$$\xrightarrow{H_2SO_4,\text{ r.t.}} [CH_3CH_2-OSO_3H] \xrightarrow{H_2O,\text{ heat}} \underset{\text{Ethanol(Z)}}{CH_3CH_2OH}$$

16. (c): $KMnO_4$ (alkaline) and OsO_4/CH_2Cl_2 are used for hydroxylation of the double bond while O_3/Zn is used for ozonolysis. Therefore, the right option is (c), that is,

$$\underset{\text{Propene}}{6CH_3CH=CH_2} \xrightarrow{B_2H_6} 2(CH_3CH_2CH_2)_3B \xrightarrow[NaOH]{H_2O_2} \underset{\text{1-Propanol}}{6CH_3CH_2CH_2OH}$$

17. (a): Mercuration–demercuration gives alcohols (without any rearrangement) according to Markownikoff's addition of H_2O to alkenes. Thus,

$$\underset{\text{3-Phenylpropene}}{C_6H_5CH_2-CH=CH_2} \xrightarrow[\text{(ii) }NaBH_4/OH^-]{\text{(i) }(CH_3COO)_2Hg/\ THF-H_2O} \underset{\text{1-Phenyl-2-propanol}}{C_6H_5CH_2CHOHCH_3}$$

18. (b):

$$\underset{\text{3,3-Dimethyl-1-butene}}{CH_3-C(CH_3)_2-CH=CH_2} \xrightarrow[THF\text{-}H_2O]{Hg(OCOCH_3)_2}$$

$$CH_3-C(CH_3)_2-CH(OH)-CH_2HgOCOCH_3 \xrightarrow[OH^-]{NaBH_4} \underset{\text{3,3-Dimethyl-2-butanol}}{CH_3-C(CH_3)_2-CH(OH)-CH_3}$$

During oxymercuration–demercuration, Markownikoff's rule is followed.

19. (d): It does not involve either rearrangement or carbocation intermediate.

20. (b): Only symmetrical alkenes give the same product on hydration, hydroboration–oxidation or oxymercuration–demercuration, that is, option (b) is correct.

$$\underset{\text{But-2-ene}}{CH_3-CH=CH-CH_3} \xrightarrow[\substack{\text{or (i) }B_2H_6/THF,\text{ (ii) }H_2O_2/OH^-\\ \text{or }Hg(OAc)_2-THF-H_2O,\\ \text{(ii) }NaBH_4/OH^-}]{H^+/H_2O} \underset{\text{2-Butanol}}{CH_3-CHOH-CH_2CH_3}$$

21. (b): $NaBH_4$ reduces the carbonyl group but not the ester group, that is, option (b) is correct.

22. (a): $LiAlH_4$ reduces the ester group to the 1° alcoholic group.

$$R{-}COOEt \xrightarrow[\text{(ii) } H_3O^+]{\text{(i) } LiAlH_4/\text{ether}} RCH_2OH + EtOH$$

23. (b): $LiAlH_4$ reduces both the carbonyl group and the ester group, that is, $CH_3COCH_2C_6H_5 \xrightarrow{LiAlH_4} CH_3CHOHCH_2CH_2OH + C_2H_5OH$

24. (c): Acyl and the alkyl/aralkyl group contain the same number of carbon atoms, that is, option (c) is correct.

$$C_6H_5COOCH_2C_6H_5 \xrightarrow[\text{(ii) } H_3O^+]{\text{(i) } LiAlH_4/\text{ether}} \underset{\text{Benzyl alcohol}}{2C_6H_5CH_2OH}$$

25. (c): Na/C_2H_5OH (Bouveault–Blanc) reduction of unsymmetrical esters gives two alcohols—one derived from the acyl part and the other from the alkoxy part. Thus

$$CH_3CH_2CH_2CO \vdots OCH_2CH_3 \xrightarrow{Na/C_2H_5OH} \underset{\text{1-Butanol}}{CH_3CH_2CH_2CH_2OH} + \underset{\text{Ethanol}}{CH_3CH_2OH}$$

26. (a): $LiAlH_4$ reduces both ketones and esters (or lactones) to alcohols but $NaBH_4$ reduces only ketones to alcohols.

27. (d): $\underset{\text{Methyl bromide}}{CH_3{-}Br} \xrightarrow[-KBr]{KCN} \underset{\text{Acetonitrile (A)}}{CH_3{-}CN} \xrightarrow[\text{(Hydrolysis)}]{H_3O^+}$

$$\underset{\text{Acetic acid (B)}}{CH_3COOH} \xrightarrow[\text{(Reduction)}]{LiAlH_4/\text{ether}} \underset{\text{Ethyl alcohol (C)}}{CH_3CH_2OH}$$

28. (b): $\underset{\text{Formaldehyde}}{H_2C{=}O} + (CH_3)_2CHMgBr \xrightarrow[\text{reaction}]{\text{Grignard}}$

$$H_2C(OMgBr)CH(CH_3)_2 \xrightarrow{H^+/H_2O} \underset{\text{2-Methyl-1-propanol}}{(CH_3)_2CH{-}CH_2OH}$$

$$\underset{\text{Cyclohoxylmag.bromide}}{C_6H_{11}MgBr} + \underset{\text{Formaldehyde}}{H_2C{=}O} \xrightarrow[\text{(Grignard reaction)}]{\text{Dry ether}}$$

29. (a): $C_6H_{11}CH_2OMgBr \xrightarrow[-Mg(OH)Br]{H_3O^+} \underset{\text{Cyclohexylmethanol}}{C_6H_{11}CH_2OH}$

30. (b):

$$\underset{\text{Butanal}}{CH_3CH_2CH_2CHO} + \underset{n\text{-Propylmag. bromide}}{CH_3CH_2CH_2MgBr} \xrightarrow[\text{(Grignard reaction)}]{\text{Dry ether}}$$

$$CH_3CH_2CH_2{-}CH(OMgBr){-}CH_2CH_2CH_3 \xrightarrow{H^+/H_2O}$$

$$\underset{\text{4-Heptanol (Achiral 2° alcohol)}}{CH_3CH_2CH_2{-}CH(OH){-}CH_2CH_2CH_3}$$

31. (a):

$$(CH_3)_2CH{-}CHO + CH_3MgBr \xrightarrow{\text{Ether}} \underset{\text{(A)}}{(CH_3)_2CH{-}CH(OMgBr){-}CH_3} \xrightarrow{H_3O^+} \underset{\text{3-Methylbutan-2-ol}}{(CH_3)_2CH{-}CH(OH){-}CH_3}$$

32. (b): Addition of formaldehyde to any Grignard reagent after hydrolysis gives 1° alcohols.

$$Ph{-}CH(CH_3){-}CH_2{-}MgX + H{-}CO{-}H$$

$$Ph{-}CH(CH_3){-}CH_2{-}CH_2OMgX \xrightarrow{H_3O^+} Ph{-}CH(CH_3){-}CH_2{-}CH_2OH$$

Only option (b) does not yield the desired 3° alcohol while all the remaining options (a, c, d) give the required alcohol.

33. (b): Aldehydes other than formaldehyde react with Grignard reagents followed by acid hydrolysis to give 2° alcohols, that is, C_2H_5CHO.

$$\underset{\text{II}}{C_2H_5CHO} \xrightarrow{RMgX} \left[C_2H_5{-}CH(OMgX){-}R\right] \xrightarrow{H_3O^+} \underset{\text{2° Alcohol}}{C_2H_5{-}CH(OH){-}R}$$

34. (b): Esters react with a Grignard reagent to form tertiary alcohols.

$$C_2H_5{-}CO{-}OC_2H_5 \xrightarrow[-Mg(OC_2H_5)Br]{CH_3MgBr} \underset{\text{2-Butanone}}{C_2H_5{-}CO{-}CH_3} \xrightarrow[\text{(ii) } H^+/H_2O]{\text{(i) } CH_3MgBr} \underset{\text{3° Alcohol}}{C_2H_5{-}C(OH)(CH_3){-}CH_3}$$

35. (d):

$$\overset{\delta-\ \delta+}{C_6H_5MgBr} + \text{ethylene oxide} \xrightarrow{\text{Ether}} [C_6H_5CH_2CH_2OMgBr] \xrightarrow{H^+/H_2O} \underset{\text{2-Phenylethanol}}{C_6H_5CH_2CH_2OH}$$

36. (a):

$$CH_3{-}CH(OH){-}CH_3 \xrightarrow{PBr_3} CH_3{-}CH(Br){-}CH_3 \xrightarrow{\text{Mg/ether}}$$

$$CH_3{-}CH(OH){-}CH_3 \xrightarrow{PBr_3} CH_3{-}CH(Br){-}CH_3 \xrightarrow{\text{Mg/ether}}$$

$$(CH_3)_2CH{-}MgBr \xrightarrow{CH_2{-}CH_2 \text{ (epoxide)}} (CH_3)_2CH{-}CH_2CH_2OMgBr$$

$$\xrightarrow[\Delta]{H_2O/H^+} (CH_3)_2CH{-}CH_2CH_2OH$$

37. (b):

$$\underset{\text{3-Pentanone}}{(CH_3CH_2)_2C{=}O} + CH_3CH_2MgBr \xrightarrow{\text{Dry ether}}$$

$$(CH_3CH_2)_2C(OMgBr)CH_2CH_3 \xrightarrow{H_3O^+} \underset{\text{3-Ethyl-3-pentanol}}{\overset{5\ \ 4}{CH_3CH_2}\overset{3}{C}(OH)(CH_3CH_2)\overset{2\ \ 1}{CH_2CH_3}}$$

38. (d):

$$\underset{\text{Acetophenone}}{PhCOCH_3} \xrightarrow[\text{(i) } H_3O^+]{\text{(i) } CH_3MgBr} \underset{\text{2-Phenyl-2-propanol}}{Ph(OH)C(CH_3)_2}$$

$$\underset{\text{Acetone}}{(CH_3)_2C{=}O} \xrightarrow[\text{(i) } H_3O^+]{\text{(i) PhMgBr}} \underset{\text{2-Phenyl-2-propanol}}{(CH_3)_2C(OH)Ph}$$

$$\underset{\text{Methyl benzoate}}{Ph{-}\overset{O}{\overset{\|}{C}}{-}OCH_3} \xrightarrow{CH_3MgBr} Ph(OCH_3)C(CH_3)(OMgBr) \xrightarrow{-Mg(OCH_3)Br}$$

$$\underset{\text{Acetophenone}}{Ph(CH_3)C{=}O} \xrightarrow[\text{(i) } H_3O^+]{\text{(i) } CH_3MgBr} \underset{\text{2-Phenyl-2-propanol}}{Ph(OH)C(CH_3)_2}$$

39. (d):

$$\text{(cyclic lactone, } C{=}O\text{)} + CH_3{-}MgBr \longrightarrow$$

$$CH_3{-}\overset{O}{\overset{\|}{C}}{-}CH_2CH_2CH_2OMgBr \xrightarrow{CH_3MgBr}$$

$$CH_3{-}\underset{CH_3}{\overset{OMgBr}{C}}{-}CH_2CH_2CH_2OMgBr \xrightarrow{H_3O^+} (CH_3)_2C(OH)CH_2CH_2CH_2OH$$

40. (d): Whenever a chiral centre is produced during a reaction between achiral reagents, a racemic mixture of the product is always obtained.

$$CH_3CH_2{-}CHO \xrightarrow[\text{(ii) } H_3O^+]{\text{(i) } CH_3MgI} \underset{(\pm)\text{-2-Butanol}}{CH_3CH_2{-}CHOH{-}CH_3}$$

41. (c): $\underset{\text{Benzylamine}}{C_6H_5CH_2NH_2} + HONO \rightarrow \underset{\text{Benzyl alcohol}}{C_6H_5CH_2OH} + N_2 + H_2O$

42. (d):

$$\underset{\text{Toluene}}{C_6H_5CH_3} \xrightarrow[-HCl]{Cl_2/h\nu} C_6H_5CH_2Cl \xrightarrow{OH^-/H_2O} \underset{\text{Benzyl alcohol}}{C_6H_5CH_2OH}$$

43. (c): 1-Propanal and 2-Propanol in the presence of copper (heat) undergo dehydration to give CH_3CHO and CH_3CHCH_3 respectively. These can be easily distinguished by Fehling's solution.

44. (a): $\underset{\text{Butene-1}}{CH_3CH_2CH{=}CH_2} \xrightarrow[\text{Mark.addition}]{H_2O/H_2SO_4} \underset{\text{2-Butanol (optically active)}}{CH_3CH_2{-}\overset{*}{C}H(OH){-}CH_3}$

Preparation of Phenols

45. (d): $C_6H_6 + CH_3CH_2CH_2Cl \xrightarrow[\text{(FC alkylation)}]{\text{anhyd. } AlCl_3}$

$$\underset{P}{C_6H_5CH(CH_3){-}CH_3} \xrightarrow[\text{(ii) } H_3O^+, \Delta]{\text{(i) } O_2} \underset{Q}{C_6H_5OH} + \underset{R}{CH_3{-}\overset{O}{\overset{\|}{C}}{-}CH_3}$$

46. (a):

$$\underset{p\text{-Toluenesulfonic acid}}{CH_3{-}C_6H_4{-}SO_3H} + KOH \xrightarrow{-H_2O}$$

$$CH_3{-}C_6H_4{-}SO_3K \xrightarrow[-K_2SO_3]{\text{KOH fuse}} CH_3{-}C_6H_4{-}OK \xrightarrow{\text{Dil. HCl}} \underset{p\text{-Cresol}}{CH_3{-}C_6H_4{-}OH}$$

47. (d):

$$C_6H_6 + HCl + O_2\,(\text{air}) \xrightarrow[500\text{ K}]{CuCl_2} C_6H_5Cl + H_2O$$

Rashog's process

48. (d):

$$\underset{m\text{-Nitrophenol}}{m\text{-}NO_2C_6H_4OH} \xrightarrow[\text{(Reduction)}]{\text{Sn/HCl}} m\text{-}NH_2C_6H_4OH \xrightarrow[\text{273–278 K (Diazotisation)}]{NaNO_2/HCl}$$

$$m\text{-}N_2ClC_6H_4OH \xrightarrow[\text{Hydrolysis}]{H_3O+, \Delta} \underset{\text{Resorcinol}}{m\text{-}C_6H_4(OH)_2}$$

49. (c): At the *m*-position, the $-OCH_3$ group does not exert its +R effect. Instead, it exerts its –I effect and therefore, *m*-methoxyphenol is the strongest acid among phenols, *o*-, *m*- and *p*-methoxyphenol.

50. (a): The greater acidic character of phenol is due to more resonance stability of the phenoxide ion than phenol.

51. (a): Phenol.

52. (c): $C_6H_5MgBr + 1/2\ O_2 \rightarrow C_6H_5OMgBr \xrightarrow{H^+/H_2O} C_6H_5OH + Mg(OH)Br$

Physical Properties of Alcohols, Phenols and Ethers

53. (a): Due to chelation, *o*-nitrophenol cannot from H bonds with H_2O, therefore, it is less soluble in water than the *m*- and *p*-isomers.

54. (c): Due to the absence of H bonding, ethers have much lower BPs than mono- and dihydric alcohols. Thus, option (c) is correct.

55. (c): 1,2-Dihydroxybenzene (ii) undergoes chelation and hence its BP is lower than that of 1,4-dihydroxybenzene (iii) which undergoes intermolecular H bonding. Phenol (i), however, has one OH group and hence its BP is the lowest. Thus, option (c) is correct.

56. (a):

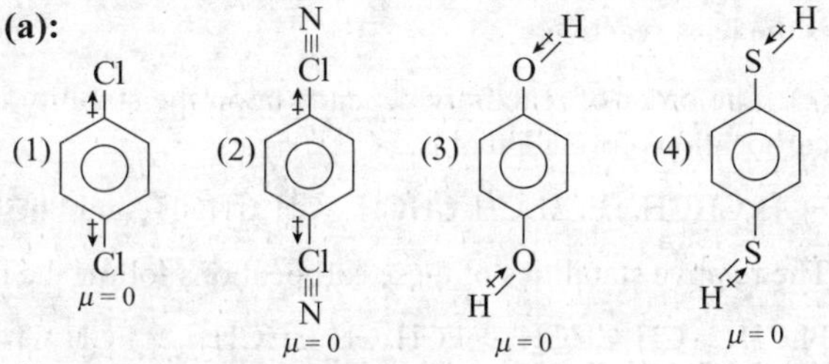

(1) Cl, Cl; $\mu = 0$ (2) $N \equiv Cl$, $Cl \equiv N$; $\mu = 0$ (3) O–H, O–H; $\mu \neq 0$ (4) S–H, S–H; $\mu \neq 0$

Due to angular shapes of C–O–H and C–S–H bonds, just as in H_2O and H_2S respectively, in compounds (3) and (4) have non-zero dipole moments.

57. (b): Phenol has a smaller dipole moment (1.54 D) than methanol (1.71 D) because the C–O bond is less polar due to the electron withdrawing effect of the benzene ring while in methanol, the C–O bond is more polar due to the electron-donating effect of the CH_3 group. Further, since the C–O bond in ethers is less polar (due to lower electronegativity difference between C and O atoms) than the O–H bond in alcohols and phenols, the dipole moment of methoxymethane (1.3 D) is much lower than those of methanol and phenol. Thus, the dipole moments of these three compounds increase in the order: methoxymethane < phenol < methanol.

58. (a): Due to intermolecular H bonding, CH_3CH_2OH undergoes molecular association and hence its BP is much higher (actually above room temperature) and it is a liquid at room temperature. Due to the absence of H bonding, CH_3OCH_3 cannot undergo molecular association. Instead its molecules are held by only weak van der Waals forces of attraction and hence its BP is much lower (actually below room temperature) and it is a gas at room temperature (actually below).

59. (d): Due to the bigger size of the C_2H_5 group in Et_2O than the size of CH_3 groups in Me_2O, H bonding in Et_2O and H_2O molecules is weaker than between Me_2O and H_2O molecules. Hence, Me_2O is highly soluble in H_2O but Et_2O is only sparingly soluble.

60. (c): Due to greater lone pair–lone repulsion than lone pair–bond pair repulsion, the COH bond angle is slightly less in methanol (108.9°) than in phenol (109°). In contrast, due to repulsion between the bulky alkyl groups, the COC bond angle is slightly greater than the tetrahedral angle in methoxymethane (111.7°). Thus, option (c) is correct.

61. (c): Solubility increases as the branching increases. Therefore, t-butyl alcohol is the most soluble in water.

62. (a): Boiling points increase as the molecular mass of the alcohol increases. Further, among isomeric alcohols, due to branching, 2° alcohols have lower boiling points than 1° alcohols. In the light of these facts, boiling points increase in the order: propan-1-ol < butan-1-ol < pentan-1-ol.

Chemical Reactions of Alcohols

63. (c): H_2O is more acidic than CH_3OH, therefore, CH_3O^- is more basic than OH^-. Further, due to the +I effect of the CH_2 group, electron density on the O atom in CH_3OH is more than on the O atom in H_2O. Therefore, CH_3OH is more basic than H_2O. Thus, the overall basicities increase in the order $H_2O < CH_3OH < OH^- < CH_3O^-$, that is, option (c) is correct.

64. (d): Tertiary alcohols are the weakest acids and hence have the highest pK_a values, that is, option (d) is correct.

65. (a): The reactivity of different alcohols towards sodium depends upon their relative acidity. Now the acidity of alcohols follows the order: 1° > 2° > 3°. Both 1-methanol (I) and propanol (II) are 1° alcohols. Since the +I effect of the $CH_3CH_2CH_2$–group is stronger than that of the CH_3– group, methanol (I) is the strongest acid followed by 1-propanol (II). Further, 2-butanol (III) being a 2° alcohol is a stronger acid than 2-methyl-2-propanol (IV) which is a 3° alcohol. Thus, the overall acidity of the four alcohols follows the order: I > II > III > IV.

66. (d): The reactions are:

(a) $C_2H_5\text{–O–H} + CH_3\text{–MgI} \rightarrow CH_4 + Mg(OC_2H_5)I$

(b) $C_2H_5O\text{–H} + Na^+NH_2^- \rightarrow C_2H_5O^-Na^+ + NH_3$

(c) $2\,C_2H_5O\text{–H} + Mg \rightarrow Mg(OC_2H_5)_2 + H_2$

In reactions (a) and (b), C_2H_5OH donates a proton to CH_3^- and NH_2^- respectively and hence it is an acid. In reaction (c), the Mg atom donates two electrons (one electron each) to two molecules of C_2H_5OH forming $Mg(OC_2H_5)_2$ and H_2. Thus, C_2H_5OH acts as an acid. Thus, all statements are correct.

67. (b): The acid strength follows the order:

ROH > HC≡CH > NH_3 > R′H

Therefore, a weaker acid (NH_3) cannot displace a stronger acid (ROH) from its salt (RONa). Thus, reaction (b) is non-spontaneous.

68. (b): 112 mL of CH_4 is produced from alcohol = 370 mg

∴ 22400 mL of CH_4 will be produced from alcohol

$$= \frac{370}{1000} \times \frac{22400}{112} = 74\text{ g mol}^{-1}$$

Thus, alcohol molecular mass = 74 g mol^{-1} is $CH_3CH_2CH_2CH_2OH$ (*n*-butanol)

69. (b): Compounds (alcohols, phenols, 1° and 2° amines, thioalcohols and terminal alkynes) react with CH_3MgI to give quantitative yield of CH_4. From the volume of CH_4 evolved at STP, the number of active hydrogens present in a molecule can be determined.

70. (b): Mol. mass of $C_3H_8O_3 = 3 \times 12 + 8 \times 16 \times 3 = 92\text{ g mol}^{-1}$

Let the number of active hydrogens present in one molecule of $C_3H_8O_3 = n$

Now 92 g of $C_3H_8O_3$ will produce $CH_4 = n \times 22400$ mL at STP

∴ 0.92 g of $C_3H_8O_3$ will produce CH_4 =

$$\frac{n \times 22400}{92} \times \frac{92}{100} = n \times 224\text{ mL}$$

But volume of CH_4 at STP actually produced = 448 mL

$\therefore n \times 224 = 448$; or, $n = 2$

71. (d): Acetic acid, acetyl chloride and acetic anhydride react with ethyl alcohol to form ethyl acetate which has a fruity smell.

$$\underset{\text{Acetic acid}}{CH_3COOH} + \underset{\text{Ethyl alcohol}}{CH_3CH_2OH} \xrightarrow[\text{(few drops)}]{\text{conc.}H_2SO_4} \underset{\substack{\text{Ethyl alcohol}\\ \text{(fruity smell)}}}{CH_3COOC_2H_5} + H_2O$$

72. (a): As the size of the hydrocarbon part (R) of the alcohol increases, the tetrahedral intermediate (I) formed during esterification becomes more and more crowded and hence the rate of esterification decreases. Thus, the smallest alcohol, that is, CH_3OH reacts at the fastest rate.

$$\underset{\text{Acetic acid}}{CH_3-\overset{\overset{O}{\|}}{C}-OH} \xrightarrow{H^+/ROH} \left[CH_3-\overset{\overset{OH}{|}}{\underset{\underset{OR}{|}}{C}}-OH \right]$$

73. (b): The rate of reaction depends upon the stability of the carbocations. Out of the following four carbocations possible,

(i) $C_6H_5CH_2\overset{+}{C}H_2$ (ii) $C_6H_5\overset{+}{C}HCH_3$

(iii) $(CH_3)_3C^+$ (iv) $CH_2=CH\overset{+}{C}H_2$

Carbocation (ii) is the most stable since it is not only a 2° carbocation but is also stabilised by resonance. Hence, alcohol (b) reacts at the fastest rate.

74. (c):

$$\underset{\substack{| \quad\ \ |\\ CH_3\ OH}}{CH_3-CH-CH-CH_3} \xrightarrow[-H_2O]{H^+} \underset{\substack{\text{2° carbocation}\\ \text{(less stable)}}}{CH_3-\overset{\overset{H}{|}}{C}-\overset{+}{C}H-CH_3 \atop \quad CH_3}$$

$$\xrightarrow[\text{shift}]{\text{1, 2-Hydride}} \underset{\substack{\text{3° carbocation}\\ \text{(more stable)}}}{CH_3-\overset{+}{\underset{\underset{CH_3}{|}}{C}}-CH_2CH_3} \xrightarrow{Br^-} CH_3-\overset{\overset{Br}{|}}{\underset{\underset{CH_3}{|}}{C}}-CH_2CH_3$$

75. (b): Greater the stability of the intermediate carbocation, the more reactive is the alcohol. Since 2-methylpropan-2-ol generates a 3° carbocation, it reacts faster with HBr.

76. (c): The carbocation resulting from *p*-methoxybenzyl bromide is stabilised by resonance and hence it is most reactive towards nucleophilic substitution reactions.

77. (c): The reactivity of alcohols towards HBr depends upon the relative stability of the intermediate carbocations. The carbocations derived from alcohols I, II, and III respectively are:

(i) $C_6H_5-\overset{+}{C}H-CH_2CH_3$ (ii) $C_6H_5CH_2CH_2\overset{+}{C}H_2$

(iii) $C_6H_5-CH_2-\overset{+}{C}H-CH_3$

Since the relative stability of these carbocations follows the order: (i) > (iii) > (ii), the reactivity of these alcohols follows the same order: I > III > II. That is, option (c) is correct.

78. (d): Out of the carbocations:

$$Cl-C_6H_4-\overset{+}{C}H_2,\ (C_6H_5)_2\overset{+}{C}H,\ (C_6H_5)_3\overset{+}{C}$$

$$\text{and } NC-C_6H_4-\overset{+}{C}H_2$$

the last carbocation is least stable due to the electron withdrawing effect of the CN group. Thus, *p*-cyanobenzyl alcohol is the least reactive.

79. (c): The order of reactivity depends upon the stability of the carbocations formed, that is,

$FCH_2\overset{+}{C}HCH_3$, $FCH_2CH_2\overset{+}{C}HCH_3$, $CH_3\overset{+}{C}HCH_3$ and $Ph\overset{+}{C}H_2$

The relative stabilities of these carbocations follow the order:

$Ph\overset{+}{C}H_2 > CH_3\overset{+}{C}HCH_3 > FCH_2CH_2\overset{+}{C}HCH_3\,_3 > FCH_2\overset{+}{C}HCH_3$

therefore, the order of reactivity of the alcohols (I, II, III and IV) follows the sequence: IV > III > II > I.

80. (b): The order of reactivity depends upon the stability of the carbocations formed, that is,

[tert-pentyl cation]+, [pentan-2-yl cation], [isobutyl-type primary cation]+ and [n-butyl primary cation]+

The relative stability of the carbocations follows the order:

[tert-pentyl cation]+ > [pentan-2-yl cation] > [isobutyl-type primary cation]+ > [n-butyl primary cation]+,

therefore, the order of reactivity of the corresponding alcohols follows the order:

[tertiary alcohol]–OH > [secondary alcohol, OH] > [branched primary alcohol] OH > [straight-chain primary alcohol] OH,

That is, option (b) is correct.

81. (c):

$$\text{(i) } CH_3-\overset{\overset{H_3C}{|}}{C}H-\overset{\overset{OH}{|}}{C}H-CH_3 \xrightarrow{H^+/\text{Heat}} CH_3-\overset{\overset{H_3C}{|}}{\underset{\underset{H}{|}}{C}}-\overset{\overset{+}{O}H_2}{\overset{|}{C}H}-CH_3 \xrightarrow{-H_2O}$$

$$\underset{\substack{\text{2° carbocation}\\ \text{(less stable)}}}{CH_3-\overset{\overset{H_3C}{|}}{\underset{\underset{H}{|}}{C}}-\overset{+}{C}H-CH_3} \xrightarrow[\text{shift}]{\text{1, 2-Hydride}} \underset{\substack{\text{3° carbocation}\\ \text{(more stable)}}}{CH_3-\overset{\overset{CH_3}{|}}{\underset{+}{C}}-CH_2-CH_3}$$

$$\xrightarrow[\text{Saytzeff rule}]{-H^+} \underset{\text{A (major)}}{CH_3-\overset{\overset{CH_3}{|}}{C}=CH-CH_3} + \underset{\text{B (minor)}}{CH_2=\overset{\overset{CH_3}{|}}{C}-CH_2CH_3}$$

$$\text{(ii) } \underset{\text{(A)}}{CH_3-\overset{\overset{CH_3}{|}}{C}=CH-CH_3} \xrightarrow[\substack{\text{in absence of peroxide}\\ \text{(Markownikoff's rule)}}]{\text{HBr, dark,}}$$

$$\underset{\text{C (major)}}{CH_3-\overset{\overset{CH_3}{|}}{\underset{\underset{Br}{|}}{C}}-CH_2CH_3} + \underset{\text{D (minor)}}{CH_3-\overset{\overset{CH_3}{|}}{C}H-\underset{\underset{Br}{|}}{C}H-CH_3}$$

82. (d):

$$CH_3CH_2-\underset{CH_3}{\overset{CH_3}{C}}-\underset{OH}{CH}-CH_3 \xrightarrow[\text{from } H_2SO_4]{-H^+} CH_3CH_2-\underset{CH_3}{\overset{CH_3}{C}}-\underset{\overset{+}{O}H_2}{CH}-CH_3$$

$$\xrightarrow{-H_2O} CH_3CH_2-\underset{CH_3}{\overset{CH_3}{C}}-\overset{+}{C}H-CH_3 \xrightarrow{\text{1, 2-Methyl shift}}$$

2° carbocation (less stable)

$$CH_3CH_2-\overset{+}{\underset{}{\overset{CH_3}{C}}}-\underset{CH_3}{\overset{H}{C}H}-CH_3 \xrightarrow{-H^+} CH_3CH_2-\overset{CH_3}{C}=\overset{CH_3}{C}-CH_3$$

3° carbocation (more stable)

83. (a):

$$CH_3-\underset{CH_3}{\overset{CH_3}{C}}-CHOH-CH_3 \xrightarrow[-H_2O]{+H^+} CH_3-\underset{CH_3}{\overset{CH_3}{C}}-\overset{+}{C}H-CH_3$$

3, 3-Dimethyl-2-butanol; 2° carbocation (less stable)

$$\xrightarrow{\text{1, 2-Methyl shift}} CH_3-\overset{+}{\overset{CH_3}{C}}-\overset{CH_3}{C}H-CH_3 \xrightarrow[\text{Saytzeff climination}]{+H^+} CH_3-\overset{CH_3}{C}=\overset{CH_3}{C}-CH_3$$

3° carbocation (more stable); 2, 3-Dimethyl-2-butene

84. (a): Dehydration is theoretically possible on all the three sides of the carbon carrying the OH group giving alkenes (b), (c) and (d).

(a) $\xrightarrow[(-H_2O)]{\text{Heat}}$ (b) + (c) + (d)

Only product (a) is formed.

85. (b): Only CH_3CHO is not formed.

(i) $CH_3CH_2OH \xrightarrow[-H_2O]{H_2SO_4} CH_3CH_2OSO_3H \xrightarrow[-H_2SO_4]{CH_3CH_2OH,\ 413\ K} CH_3CH_2OCH_2CH_3$

(ii) $CH_3CH_2OSO_3H \xrightarrow{433\ K} CH_2=CH_2 + H_2SO_4$

86. (a): Pyridinium chlorochromate (PCC) oxidises 2° alcohols to ketones without attacking the double bond.

$$CH_3-\overset{OH}{CH}-CH=CH-CH_3 \xrightarrow{PCC} CH_3-\overset{O}{\overset{\|}{C}}-CH=CH-CH_3$$

Pent-3-en-2-ol; Pent-3-en-2-one

87. (d): $\underset{1^\circ \text{ Alcohol}}{RCH_2OH} \xrightarrow[\text{chlorochromate}]{\text{Pyridinium}} \underset{\text{Aldehyde}}{RCHO}$

88. (c): Only tertiary alcohols, that is, $(CH_3)_3COH$ cannot be easily oxidised since it involves the cleavage of C–C bonds.

89. (d): $CH_3CHOHCH_2CH_3 \xrightarrow{[O]} CH_3CO-CH_2CH_3 \xrightarrow{[O]}$ $CH_3COOH + CH_3CH_2COOH$

90. (c): Tertiary alcohols when passed over heated copper undergo dehydration to give alkenes.

91. (a): Compound X on oxidation with PCC in CH_2Cl_2 gives a compound Y which gives CHI_3 on treatment with I_2/NaOH; therefore, the compound X must be a 1° alcohol containing the group CH_3CHOH–. Thus, the compound X is C_2H_5OH.

$$\underset{(X)}{CH_3CH_2OH} \xrightarrow[CH_2Cl_2]{PCC} \underset{(Y)}{CH_3CHO} \xrightarrow[\text{(Iodoform test)}]{I_2/NaOH} \underset{\text{Iodoform}}{CHI_3}$$

92. (c): Compounds containing CH_3CO^- or CH_3CHCO^- group attached to C or H, on warming with I_2 and NaOH, form iodoform. Hence, compounds (i), (ii) and (iii) will give iodoform while compound (iv), that is, CH_3OH will not give iodoform.

93. (d): Ethyl alcohol gives the iodoform test but methyl alcohol does not.

94. (b): C_3H_6O on treatment with I_2 + NaOH gives CHI_3; therefore, C_3H_6O must be a methyl ketone, that is, CH_3COCH_3. If this is so then, X must be $CH_3CHOHCH_3$

95. (d): Tertiary alcohol, that is, alcohol S does not have any α-hydrogens and hence does not respond to Victor Meyer's test.

96. (c): Compound A, $C_8H_{10}O$ on treatment with NaOI [produced by the action of I_2 (Y) on NaOH] gives a yellow precipitate (iodoform test), therefore, compound A must contain the –$CHOHCH_3$ group. The compound must be a 2° alcohol as shown below:

$$\underset{Y}{I_2} + 2\,NaOH \longrightarrow NaOI + NaI + H_2O$$

$$\underset{A(C_8H_{10}O)}{C_6H_5-\underset{OH}{CH}-CH_3} \xrightarrow{NaOI} C_6H_5-COONa + \underset{\substack{\text{Iodoform} \\ \text{(Yellow ppt.)}}}{CHI_3}$$

97. (d): The O–H bond undergoes cleavage most readily because oxygen being more electronegative can accommodate the negative charge more effectively after the cleavage.

98. (a): Of all the alcohols, methanol is the strongest acid.

99. (d): C_6H_6 and C_2H_6 being hydrocarbons, are very weak acids. Now, consider the reaction,

$$HC\equiv C^-Na^+ + \underset{\text{(Stronger acid)}}{CH_3OH} \rightarrow \underset{\text{(Weaker acid)}}{HC\equiv CH} + CH_3O^-Na^+$$

A stronger acid displaces a weaker acid from its salts, therefore, CH_3OH is a stronger acid than CH≡CH. Thus, option (d) is correct.

100. (c): Due to the strong –I effect of the three F atoms, 2,2,2-trifluoroethanol is the most acidic and hence has the lowest pK_a value.

Ethylene Glycol

101. (c): The organic compound evolves H_2 gas when treated with Na metal, therefore, it must be an alcohol. On oxidation with HIO_4, it gives two moles of formaldehyde, therefore, it must be a vic-glycol.

102. (a): $\underset{\text{Ethylene glycol}}{\begin{matrix}CH_2OH\\|\\CH_2OH\end{matrix}} \xrightarrow[\text{or } SOCl_2]{PCl_5 \text{ or } PCl_3} \underset{\text{Ethylene dichloride}}{\begin{matrix}CH_2Cl\\|\\CH_2Cl\end{matrix}}$

103. (d): $\underset{CH_2OH}{\overset{CH_2OH}{|}} \xrightarrow[\text{or } PI_3]{HI} \underset{CH_2I}{\overset{CH_2I}{|}} \xrightarrow{-I_2} \underset{CH_2}{\overset{CH_2}{\|}}$
(unstable) Ethylene

104. (c): $\underset{CH_2OH}{\overset{CH_2OH}{|}} \xrightarrow[\text{or } (CH_3CO)_2O]{CH_3COCl/\text{pyridine}} \underset{CH_2{-}OCOCH_3}{\overset{CH_2{-}OCOCH_3}{|}}$
Ethylene glycol — Ethylene glycol diacetate

105. (b): $\underset{H{-}CHO}{\overset{HO{-}CH_2}{|}} \xrightarrow[-H_2O]{\text{Anhyd. } ZnCl_2} \left[\underset{CHOH}{\overset{CH_2}{\|}}\right] \xrightarrow{\text{Tautomerises}} \underset{CHO}{\overset{CH_3}{|}}$
Vinyl alcohol (Unstable) — Ethanol

106. (d): $\underset{H{-}OCH_2{-}CH_2{-}OH}{\overset{HO{-}CH_2{-}CH_2O{-}H}{+}} \xrightarrow[-2H_2O]{\text{Conc. } H_2SO_4}$ 1, 4-Dixane

107. (d): $HOCH_2{-}CH_2{-}OH + H{-}OCH_2{-}CH_2OH \xrightarrow[-H_2O]{H_3PO_4}$
$HOCH_2{-}CH_2{-}O{-}CH_2{-}CH_2OH$
Diethylene glycol

108. (d):

$\underset{CH_2OH}{\overset{CH_2OH}{|}}$ (Ethylene glycol) $\xrightarrow{[O]}$ $\underset{CH_2OH}{\overset{CHO}{|}}$ (Glycolic aldehyde) $\xrightarrow{[O]}$ $\underset{CHO}{\overset{COOH}{|}}$ (Glyoxylic acid) $\xrightarrow{[O]}$ $\underset{COOH}{\overset{COOH}{|}}$ (Oxalic acid)

Glycolic aldehyde $\xrightarrow{[O]}$ $\underset{CHO}{\overset{CHO}{|}}$ (Glyoxal) $\rightarrow$ Glyoxylic acid

Glycolic aldehyde $\rightarrow$ $\underset{CH_2OH}{\overset{COOH}{|}}$ (Glycolic acid) $\xrightarrow{[O]}$ Glyoxylic acid

109. (c): $\underset{CH_2}{\overset{CH_2}{\|}} \xrightarrow[\text{(Baeyer's reagent)}]{\text{Cold dil. alkaline, } KMnO_4} \underset{CH_2OH}{\overset{CH_2OH}{|}}$
Ethylene — Ethylene glycol

110. (d): $CH_2{=}CH_2 \xrightarrow[\Delta]{O_2, Ag} \underset{O}{CH_2{-}CH_2} \xrightarrow[\text{(Hydrolysis)}]{\text{Steam, 473 K}} \underset{OH\quad OH}{CH_2{-}CH_2}$
(X) — Ethylene glycol

111. (c): All except III are oxidised by HIO_4.

112. (c): $\underset{CH_2OH}{\overset{CH_2OH}{|}} \xrightarrow[\text{1, 2-Glycol splitting}]{HIO_4} 2\ \underset{H}{\overset{H}{>}}C{=}O$

Glycerol

113. (c): Acrolein.

114. (d): P_2O_5, conc. H_2SO_4 and $KHSO_4$—all the three give acrolein.

115. (b): With a mixture of conc. HNO_3 + conc. H_2SO_4, glycerol forms nitroglycerine or glyceryl trinitrate or Nobel's oil.

116. (a): The shock-sensitive substance present in dynamite is nitroglycerine.

117. (b): $HOCH_2{-}CHOH{-}CH_2OH \xrightarrow{2\ HIO_4} HCHO + HCOOH + HCHO$

118. (d): Glyceryl monoacetate, glyceryl diacetate and glyceryl triacetate are all formed.

119. (b): $HOCH_2{-}CHOH{-}CH_2OH \xrightarrow[\Delta]{(COOH)_2.2H_2O}$
$HOCH_2{-}CHOH{-}CH{-}O{-}COOH \xrightarrow[-H_2O]{\Delta}$
Glycerol monoxalate
$HOCH_2{-}CHOH{-}CH{-}OOCH \xrightarrow[\text{Hydrolysis}]{+H_2O}$
$HOCH_2{-}CHOH{-}CH_2CH + HCOOH$
Glycerol — Formic acid

120. (d): $HOCH_2{-}CHOH{-}CH_2OH \xrightarrow[-2\ H_2O]{(COOH)_2\ 503\ K}$
$\left[\begin{array}{l} O{-}CH_2{-}CH{-}CH_2OH \\ OC{-}CO{-}O \end{array}\right] \xrightarrow{-2\ CO_2} CH_2{=}CH{-}CH_2OH$
Allyl alcohol

121. (a): Dunston's test is used for identification of glycerol.

122. (c): As the number of OH groups increases, the magnitude of intermolecular H bonding increases and the BPs increase accordingly.

123. (b): $HOCH_2{-}CHOH{-}CH_2OH \xrightarrow[-3H_2O]{3HI} [ICH_2{-}CHI{-}CH_2I]$
Glycerol
$\xrightarrow{-I_2} CH_2 = CH{-}CH_2I$
Allyl iodide

124. (a): 2-Iodopropane.

125. (b): $HOCH_2{-}CHOH{-}CH_2OH \xrightarrow[-3H_2O]{3HI} [ICH_2{-}CHI{-}CH_2I]$
Glycerol — (unstable)
$\xrightarrow{-I_2} CH_2 = CH{-}CH_2I \xrightarrow{HI} [CH_3{-}CHI{-}CH_2I]$
Allyl iodide
$\xrightarrow{-I_2} CH_3{-}CH{-}CH_2 \xrightarrow{+HI} CH_3{-}CHI{-}CH_3$
Propene — 2-Iodopropane

Thus, $CH_2OH{-}CHI{-}CH_2OH$ is not formed.

Chemical Reactions of Phenols

126. (d): The overall increasing order of acidity is option (d), that is, C_2H_2, H_2O, phenol, H_2CO_3.

127. (c): Phenol is more acidic than ethanol, methanol and *p*-methylphenol but is less acidic than *o*-nitrophenol.

128. (c): The phenoxide ion left from *m*-hydroxybenzaldehyde and *p*-hydroxybenzaldehyde are stabilised by the –I and –R effects of the CHO group. But in the *o*-isomer, due to chelation, it is difficult to remove the H atom. Therefore, *p*-hydroxybenzaldehyde is the strongest acid.

129. (d): Electron donating groups decrease while electron withdrawing groups increase the acidity of phenols. Therefore, the overall order of acidity is: IV > III > I > II, that is, option (d) is correct.

130. (d): We have discussed that the *p*-nitrophenol (B) is a stronger acid than *m*-nitrophenol (C). Since electron donating groups decrease the acidity of phenols with respect to phenol itself, phenol (A) is a stronger acid than *p*-methoxyphenol (B).

Thus, the overall acidity of the above four phenols decreases in the order: B > C > A > D.
Further, a stronger acid has a smaller pK_a value, therefore, the pK_a values of the above four acids increases in the reverse order, that is, B < C < A < D. Thus, option (d) is correct.

131. (c): At the *m*-position, the OCH_3 group cannot exert its +R effect Instead, it exerts its –I effect. Hence, *m*-methoxyphenol is the strongest acid among phenol, *o*-, *m*- and *p*-methoxyphenols.

132. (d): NO_2 group does not show –R effect at the *m*-position. Therefore, *m*-nitrophenol is the weakest acid. Due to intramolecular H bonding (chelation), *o*-nitrophenol is less acidic than *p*-nitrophenol. Thus, option (d) is correct.

133. (b): The acidity of cresols decreases in the order *m*>*p*>*o*.

134. (a): Since electron donating groups decrease the acidity of phenols, methylphenol (ii) is a weaker acid than phenol (i). Electron withdrawing groups increase the acidity of phenols, therefore, both *m*-and *p*-nitrophenols are more acidic than phenol and methylphenol. Further, among the *m*- and *p*-nitrophenols, the para isomer is more acidic as the presence of $-NO_2$ groups at the para-position stabilises the phenoxide ion to a greater extent than when it is present at the meta-position. Hence, the correct order of acidity is *p*-nitrophenol >*m*-nitrophenol > phenol > methylphenol, that is, (iv) (iii) > (i) > (ii).

135. (d): (i) Phenols are stronger acids than alcohols, therefore, propan-1-ol is the weakest acid.
(ii) Electron withdrawing groups increase the acidity of phenols, and the acidity increases as the number of nitro groups increases, therefore, acidity increases in the order: 3-nitrophenol, 3,5-dinitrophenol, 2,4,6-trinitrophenol.
Combining all the three arguments discussed above, the overall acidity increases in the order: propan-1-ol, 4-methylphenol, phenol, 3-nitrophenol, 3,5-dinitrophenol and 2,4,6-trinitrophenol.

136. (c): Due to almost identical sizes of the 2*p* orbitals of C and F, the +R effect and the –I effect of F almost balance each other and hence *p*-fluorophenol is almost as acidic as phenol. However, *p*-chlorophenol and *p*-nitrophenol are more acidic than phenol. Further, due to stronger –R and –I effect of the NO_2 group, *p*-nitrophenol is a much stronger acid than *p*-chlorophenol in which C has only weak +R and –I effect. Thus, option (c) is correct.

137. (d): Due to the presence of three powerful electron withdrawing $-NO_2$ groups, 2,4,6-trinitrophenol is almost as acidic as carboxylic acids and hence decomposes $NaHCO_3$ evolving CO_2 gas.

138. (b): Due to strong –I and –R effect of the three $-NO_2$ groups, 2,4,6-trinitrophenol (III) is more acidic than CH_3COOH (II). Further, due to greater resonance stabilisation of the acetate ion over the phenoxide ion, acetic acid (II) is a stronger acid than phenol (IV). Since alcohols are less acidic than phenols, cyclohexanol (I) is less acidic than phenol (IV). Thus, the overall acidic character decreases in the order: 2,4,6-trinitrophenol (III) > acetic acid (II) > phenol (IV) > cyclohexanol (I), that is, option (b) is correct.

139. (c): *o*-Nitrophenol is less acidic than carbonic acid and hence does not dissolve in Na_2CO_3 solution.

140. (a): Two moles of $NaNH_2$ will abstract two moles of the most acidic protons out of the four acidic protons. The acid strength decreases in the order COOH > nitrophenols > phenols > acetylenic H, therefore, protons are abstracted only from the COOH and OH of the nitrophenol. Thus, option (a) is correct.

141. (a): Phenols, that is, *p*-cresol (II) and salicylic acid (IV) give violet colour with $FeCl_3$.

142. (b): Electron-donating effect decreases in the order:
OH > OCH_3> $NHCOCH_3$> CH_3> CH_2OH
Therefore, OH is the most strongly electron-donating group and hence *o*-cresol (b) is the most reactive towards electrophilic reagents.

143. (b): $(CH_3CO)_2O, H^+$

144. (b): –OH group being more nucleophilic than –COOH group, gets acetylated.

Salicylic acid $\xrightarrow[CH_3COOH]{(CH_3CO)_2O}$ acetylsalicylic acid (O–CO–CH_3, COOH)

145. (a): With HNO_2, phenol gives *p*-nitrosophenol as the major product. During this reaction, the nitrosonium ion (NO^+) is the electrophile.

146. (b): As compared to H_2O, in $CHCl_3$, the degree of ionisation of phenol decreases and hence with Br_2-CHCl_3, phenol gives a mixture of *o*- and *p*-bromophenols.

147. (d): Benzene $\xrightarrow[350\ K]{H_2SO_4}$ Benzenesulphonic acid (SO_3H) (A) $\xrightarrow[(ii)\ H^+/H_2O]{(i)\ NaOH\ fusion}$ Phenol (OH) $\xrightarrow[H_2O]{Br_2}$ 2, 4, 6-Tribromophenol

148. (c): *m*-Cresol (CH_3, OH) $\xrightarrow[-3\ HBr]{3\ Br_2/H_2O}$ 2,4,6-tribromo-3-methylphenol (CH_3, Br, Br, OH, Br)

m-Cresol has two *o*- and one *p*-position free with respect to the OH group and hence gives the tribromo derivative on treatment with Br_2/H_2O.

149. (c): Reimer–Tiemann (RT) reaction.

150. (c): Phenol (OH) $\xrightarrow[(ii)\ H_3O^+\ (RT\ reaction)]{(i)\ CHCl_3/OH^-}$ Salicylaldehyde (OH, CHO)

RT reaction introduces the –CHO group in the benzene ring.

151. (c): Reaction (c), that is, Reimer–Tiemann reaction can be used to prepare salicylaldehyde.

152. (d): The electrophile involved in the Reimer–Tiemann reaction is dichlorocarbene (: CCl_2).

153. (b): Salicylic acid is formed.

154. (a):

Phenol $\xrightarrow[\text{(Kolbe's reaction)}]{\text{(i) } CO_2/NaOH \text{ (ii) Dil. } H_2SO_4}$ Salicylic acid (X) $\xrightarrow[\text{(Kolbe's reaction)}]{\text{(i) } CO_2/NaOH \text{ (ii) Dil. } H_2SO_4}$ Aspirin

155. (c): Phenol + $Cl{-}\overset{O}{\overset{\|}{C}}{-}OCH_3$ (Methyl chloroformate) $\xrightarrow[(-HCl)]{NaOH}$

Phenol $\xrightarrow[\text{(–HBr) (–O–COOCH}_3\text{ group is } o, p\text{-reacting)}]{Br_2}$ B (major isomer) *p*-Bromophenyl methyl carbonate

156. (b): Due to the presence of the electron-withdrawing–COOH group, the OH group in salicylic acid is less nucleophilic than the OH group in phenols. Hence, the nucleophilic attack of the phenolic OH group on the C=O part of the –COOH group of salicylic acid followed by the loss of H_2O occurs to give phenyl salicylate or salol.

Phenol + $HO{-}C_6H_5 \xrightarrow[-H_2O]{POCl_3}$ Phenyl salicylate or salol

157. (a): Salicylic acid $\xrightarrow[\text{Few drops of conc. } H_2SO_4 \; (-H_2O)]{CH_3OH}$ Methyl salicylate (Oil of wintergreen)

158. (c): Phenol $\xrightarrow[H_2SO_4]{K_2Cr_2O_7}$ *p*-Benzoquinone

159. (c): *o*-Xylene $\xrightarrow[\Delta]{HNO_3}$ (phthalic anhydride) $\xrightarrow[H_2SO_4]{\text{Phenol}}$ Phenolphthalein (Y)

160. (a): Only Na reacts with both ethanol and phenol. In contrast, $NaOH/I_2$ reacts only with ethanol while neutral $FeCl_3$ and Br_2/H_2O react with phenol only.

161. (a): *o*-Cresol is a phenol and hence gives a violet colour with $FeCl_3$ while benzyl alcohol being an alcohol does not.

162. (a): Neutral $FeCl_3$ gives a blue colour with phenol but not with benzoic acid.

Commercially Important Alcohols

163. (b): 95.6% alcohol + 4.4% water.

164. (d): Absolute alcohol is obtained commercially by azeotropic distillation of rectified spirit with benzene.

165. (d): Denatured alcohol is a mixture of rectified spirit + 5% methanol + some $CuSO_4$ and some dye to colour it blue.

166. (c): 100 proof spirit contains 57.15% alcohol by volume.

167. (a): Carbon monoxide (CO) and hydrogen (H_2) react to form methanol (CH_3OH) according to the following reaction:

$$CO(g) + 2H_2(g) \rightarrow CH_3OH(l)$$

168. (d): Ethanol.

169. (b): Alcoholic fermentation converts one mole of sucrose into two moles of ethyl alcohol (ethanol) and two moles of carbon dioxide, producing two moles of ATP in the process. The enzyme that is used in the conversion of glucose into ethyl alcohol is zymase.

170. (d): Zymase converts glucose, fructose and invert sugar (equimolar mixture of glucose and fructose) into ethyl alcohol.

171. (c): $\underset{\text{Starch}}{(C_6H_{10}O_5)_n} \xrightarrow[\text{Diastase}]{H_2O} \underset{\text{Maltose}}{C_{12}H_{22}O_{11}} \xrightarrow[\text{Maltase}]{H_2O} \underset{\text{Glucose}}{C_6H_{12}O_6} \xrightarrow{\text{Zymase}} 2C_2H_5OH + 2CO_2$

Preparation of Ethers

172. (c): $ClCH_2CH_2CH_2OH + HOCH_2CH_2Cl \xrightarrow[413\,K\,(-H_2O)]{\text{conc. } H_2SO_4} \underset{X}{ClCH_2CH_2{-}O{-}CH_2CH_2Cl} \xrightarrow[\text{(ii) } H_3O^+]{\text{(i) KOH, fuse}} \underset{\text{Divinyl ether}}{CH_2{=}CH{-}O{-}CH{=}CH_2}$

173. (a): $C_2H_5ONa + C_2H_5Br \xrightarrow[NaBr]{\Delta} \underset{\text{Ethoxyethane}}{C_2H_5{-}O{-}C_2H_5}$

174. (c): Williamson's synthesis.

175. (d): $\underset{\text{Ethanol (A)}}{2\,C_2H_5OH} + 2\,Na \rightarrow \underset{\text{Sodium ethoxide (B)}}{2\,C_2H_5ONa} + H_2$

$\underset{(A)}{C_2H_5OH} + PCl_5 \rightarrow \underset{\text{Ethyl chloride (C)}}{C_2H_5Cl} + POCl_3 + HCl$

$\underset{(B)}{C_2H_5ONa} + \underset{(B)}{C_2H_5Cl} \xrightarrow[\text{synthesis}]{\text{Williamson's}} \underset{\text{Diethyl ether}}{C_2H_5 - O - C_2H_5} + NaCl$

176. (c): Williamson's ether synthesis reaction.

177. (b): $(CH_3)_3C{-}ONa + CH_3Br \xrightarrow[-NaBr]{S_N2} (CH_3)_3C{-}O{-}CH_3$

tert-Butyl methyl ether

178. (c): 1° Alkyl halides on treatment with an alkoxide ion end to undergo substitution to form ethers. Thus, sodium tert-butoxide and ethyl bromide is the right choice of reagents.

$$(CH_3)_3CO^-Na^+ + CH_3CH_2Br \rightarrow (CH_3)_3C{-}O{-}CH_2CH_3 + NaBr$$

179. (b): 3° Alkyl halides on treatment with strong bases exclusively undergo elimination reaction to form alkenes.

$(CH_3)_2C(Cl){-}CH_2{-}H \xrightarrow[-CH_3CH_2OH,\ -NaBr]{Na^+O^-{-}CH_2CH_3} (CH_3)_2C{=}CH_2$

2-Methylpropene

180. (d): $C_2H_5Br \xrightarrow[\text{(aqueous)}]{NaOH} C_2H_5OH \xrightarrow{Na} C_2H_5ONa$

$\xrightarrow[\text{(Williamson's synthesis)}]{CH_3I} \underset{\text{Ethyl methyl ether}}{C_2H_5{-}O{-}CH_3} + NaI$

181. (a): $\underset{\text{But-1-ene (Anti-Mark. addn.)}}{CH_3CH_2CH{=}CH_2} \xrightarrow{HBr/H_2O_2} \underset{Y}{CH_3CH_2CH_2CH_2Br}$

$\xrightarrow[\text{(Williamson's synthesis)}]{C_2H_5ONa} \underset{\text{n-Butyl ethyl ether (Z)}}{CH_3CH_2CH_2CH_2\text{-O-}CH_2CH_3}$

182. (b): Nucleophilic attack (S_N2) on a 1° alkyl halide is more facile than on an aryl halide. Thus, option (b) is correct.

$p\text{-}NO_2C_6H_4O^-Na^+ + \underset{\text{1° Alkyl halide}}{CH_3{-}Br} \xrightarrow[(-NaBr)]{S_N2} p\text{-}NO_2C_6H_4OCH_3$ (1-Methoxy-4-nitrobenzene)

183. (d): The reaction of CH_3MgI with phenol will give only methane but no anisole.

$C_6H_5OH + CH_3MgI \rightarrow CH_4 + C_6H_5OMgI$

184. (b):

$\underset{\text{Phenol}}{C_6H_5OH} \xrightarrow[-H_2O]{NaOH} C_6H_5CO^-Na^+ \xrightarrow[\text{(Williamson synthesis)}]{CH_3I} \underset{\text{Anisole}}{C_6H_5OCH_3}$

185. (d): For good yields in Williamson's synthesis, alkyl halide should be 1° and alkoxide ion may 1°, 2° or 3°. Thus, option (d) is correct.

$C_6H_{11}O^-Na^+ + CH_3{-}I \xrightarrow[-NaI]{S_N2} C_6H_{11}OCH_3$ (Methyl cyclohexyl ether)

186. (d): $\underset{\text{Toluene}}{C_6H_5{-}CH_3} \xrightarrow[\text{(Benzylic hologenation)}]{NBS/CCl_4,\ \Delta} \underset{\text{Benzyl bromide (A)}}{C_6H_5{-}CH_2Br}$

$\xrightarrow[S_N2\ (-NaBr)]{CH_3ONa} \underset{\text{Benzyl methyl ether (B)}}{C_6H_5{-}CH_2{-}O{-}CH_3}$

187. (c): $\underset{\text{Propane}}{CH_3CH=CH_2} \xrightarrow[\text{(Allylic chlorination)}]{Cl_2/773\ K} \underset{\text{Allylchloride (A)}}{CH_2=CH{-}CH_2Cl}$

$\xrightarrow[S_N2(-NaCl)]{CH_3CH_2ONa} \underset{\text{Allylethylether}}{CH_2=CH{-}CH_2{-}O{-}CH}$

188. (a): $\underset{\text{Propane}}{CH_3CH=CH_2} \xrightarrow[\text{(ii) } H_2O_2/OH^- \text{ (Hydroboration–oxidation)}]{\text{(i) } B_2H_6/THF} \underset{\text{1-Propanol(A)}}{CH_3CH_2CH_2OH}$

$\xrightarrow[-NaI]{\text{(i) NaOH, (ii) } CH_3I} \underset{\text{Methyl } n\text{-propyl ether (B)}}{CH_3CH_2CH_2{-}O{-}CH_3}$

189. (c):

$\underset{\text{Phenol}}{C_6H_5OH} \xrightarrow[\text{(Nuclear bromination)}]{Br_2 \text{ in } CS_2} \underset{p\text{-Bromophenol (X) (major isomer)}}{p\text{-}BrC_6H_4OH} \xrightarrow[S_N2\ (-NaI)]{\text{(i) NaOH, (ii) } CH_3I} \underset{p\text{-Bromoanisole (Y)}}{p\text{-}BrC_6H_4OMe}$

190. (c): The C–Br bond is weaker than the C–Cl bond, therefore, alkyl bromide (II) reacts faster than alkyl chlorides (III) and (IV). CH_2=CH– is electron-withdrawing while CH_3CH_2– is electron-donating, therefore, CH_2 has more +ve chargeon III than on IV. In other words, nucleophilic attack occurs faster on III than on IV. Further, Williamson's synthesis occurs by S_N2 mechanism, therefore, due to steric hindrance, neopentyl bromide (I) is the least reactive. Thus, the decreasing order of reactivity is: II > III > IV > I.

$\underset{III}{CH_2{=}CH \leftarrow \overset{\delta+}{C}H_2{-}Cl} \qquad \underset{IV}{CH_3{-}CH_2 \rightarrow \overset{+\delta\delta}{C}H_2{-}Cl}$

191. (d): Vinyl halides (CH_2=CHCl) do not undergo S_N2 reactions.

192. (d): 3° alkyl halides prefer to undergo elimination S_N2 reactions than substitution, therefore, sodium tert-butoxide reacts with tert-butyl bromides or chlorides to form the elimination product isobutylene rather than the substitution product di-tert-butyl ether.

$\underset{\textit{tert}\text{-Butyl bromide}}{(CH_3)_3C{-}Br} + \underset{\text{sod. }\textit{tert}\text{-butoxide}}{Na^+\,^-O{-}C(CH_3)_3} \xrightarrow[(-NaBr)]{\text{Elimination}} \underset{\text{Isobutylene}}{(CH_3)_2C{=}CH_2} + \underset{\textit{tert}\text{-butyl alcohol}}{(CH_3)_3COH}$

193. (d): $CH_3CH_2O^-Na^+ + (CH_3CH_2O)_2SO_2 \longrightarrow \underset{\text{Diethyl ether}}{CH_3CH_2{-}O{-}CH_2CH_3} + \underset{\text{Sod. ethyl sulfate}}{Na^+O^-{-}SO_2{-}OCH_2CH_3}$

194. (d): Compounds containing active hydrogen such as C_6H_5OH and ROH, react with CH_3MgI to evolve CH_4.

$C_6H_5OH + CH_3MgI \rightarrow CH_4 + Mg(OC_6H_5)I$

195. (d): Aryl halides (C_6H_5Br) do not react with alkoxides (CH_3CH_2ONa, CH_2=$CHCH_2ONa$, C_6H_5ONa) to form ethers.

196. (a): 2° Alkyl halides react with nucleophiles to undergo substitution as well as elimination. As a result, all the three products are formed.

$\underset{\text{Isopropyl bromide}}{(CH_3)_2CH{-}Br} + \underset{\text{Sod. isoproxide}}{(CH_3)_2CH{-}O^-Na^+} \xrightarrow{-NaBr}$

$\underset{(I)}{CH_3CH{=}CH_2} + \underset{(II)}{(CH_3)_2CHOH}$ (Elimination products) $+ \underset{\text{Substitution product (III)}}{(CH_3)_2CH{-}O{-}CH(CCH_3)_2}$

197. (b): $\underset{\text{2-Methylpropene}}{CH_3{-}C(CH_3){=}CH_2} \xrightarrow[\text{Mark. addn.}]{\overset{-\delta\ \delta+}{CH_3O{-}H}} \underset{\textit{tert}\text{-Butyl methyl ether}}{CH_3{-}C(CH_3)_2{-}OCH_3}$

198. (b):

$$CH_3CH{=}CH_2 \xrightarrow[\text{(Oxymercuration)}]{Hg(OCOCH_3)_2} CH_3{-}CH{=}CH_2 \;(\text{HgOCOCH}_3)$$

Propylene

$$\xrightarrow[-H^+]{CH_3OH} CH_3{-}\underset{OCH_3}{CH}{-}\underset{HgOCOCH_3}{CH_2} \xrightarrow[\text{(Reduction)}]{NaBH_4} CH_3{-}\underset{OCH_3}{CH}{-}CH_3$$

199. (b):

$$CH_2{=}CH_2 \xrightarrow[PhOH\;(-CF_3COO^-)]{(CF_3COO)Hg} \underset{OPh}{CH}{-}\underset{HgOCOCH_3}{CH_2} \xrightarrow[-CF_3COOHg]{NaBH_4} PhOCH_2CH_3$$

Ethylene

200. (c):

$$CH_3O{-}CH_2Cl + NaOCH_2CH_3 \longrightarrow \overset{1}{C}H_3\overset{2}{O}{-}\overset{3}{C}H_2{-}\overset{4}{O}{-}\overset{5}{C}H_2\overset{6}{C}H_3$$

Chloromethoxymethane — 2, 4-Dioxahexane

201. (a): The phenolic OH group, being more acidic, forms a sodium salt with Na_2CO_3 which then reacts with CH_3CH_2I to form the corresponding ether leaving the alcoholic OH group intact.

$$o\text{-}HOC_6H_4CH_2OH \xrightarrow[Na_2CO_3,\,\Delta]{CH_3CH_2I} o\text{-}CH_3CH_2OC_6H_4CH_2OH$$

202. (d):

$$m\text{-}MeOC_6H_4OH + ClCH_2CH_2{-}\overset{O}{\overset{\|}{C}}{-}Cl \xrightarrow{-HCl} m\text{-}MeOC_6H_4{-}O{-}\overset{O}{\overset{\|}{C}}{-}CH_2CH_2Cl \xrightarrow[\text{F.C. Cyclisation }(-HCl)]{AlCl_3\text{ (anhyd.)}} \text{7-methoxy-dihydrocoumarin (MeO)}$$

203. (b): $2\,RX + Ag_2O \xrightarrow{\Delta} R{-}O{-}R + 2\,AgX$

204. (b): $CH_3OCH_2Cl + CH_3MgI \xrightarrow{-MgICl} CH_3{-}O{-}CH_2CH_3$

Chloromethoxy methane — Ethyl methyl ether

205. (b): Due to steric hindrance of the bridge, nucleophilic substitution reaction cannot occur at the bicyclic chloride (c) or the bicyclic iodide (d). Instead nucleophilic attack by the alcohol (a or b) can occur on the benzylic halide (a or b). Since iodides are more reactive than chlorides, option (b) is correct.

$$\text{HÖ–(bicyclic)} + C_6H_5CH_2{-}I \xrightarrow{-HI} C_6H_5CH_2{-}O{-}(\text{bicyclic})$$

206. (a):

$$CH_3CH_2OH + HOCH_2CH_3 \xrightarrow[413\,K(-H_2O)]{Conc.\ H_2SO_4} CH_3CH_2{-}O{-}CH_2CH_3$$

Ethanol — Ethoxythane

207. (d):

$$CH_3CH_2OH \xrightarrow{H^+} CH_3CH_2{-}\overset{+}{O}H_2 \xrightarrow[-H_3O^+]{HO{-}SO_3H} CH_3CH_2OSO_3H \xrightarrow[-OSO_3H(S_N2)]{CH_3CH_2OH} CH_3CH_2{-}\underset{H}{\overset{+}{O}}{-}CH_2CH_3 \xrightarrow{-H^+} CH_3CH_2{-}O{-}CH_2CH_3$$

Diethyl ether

208. (d): Nucleophilic substitution (S_N2) reaction.

209. (e): Only 1° alcohols undergo intermolecular S_N2 reactions involving one molecule of protonated and one molecule of unprotonated molecule to give best yields of dialkyl ethers. 2° and 3° alcohols, on the other hand, undergo intramolecular dehydration via the carbocation intermediate to form alkenes. Thus, option (e) is correct.

210. (d): Two different 1° alcohols undergo intermolecular S_N2 reaction involving protonated and unprotonated molecules to form a mixture of three different ethers.

$$CH_3OH + CH_3\overset{+}{O}H_2 \xrightarrow{Conc.\ H_2SO_4} CH_3OCH_3 + H_3O^+$$

$$CH_3OH + C_2H_5\overset{+}{O}H_2 \xrightarrow{Conc.\ H_2SO_4} CH_3OC_2H_5 + H_3O^+$$

$$C_2H_5OH + CH_3\overset{+}{O}H_2 \xrightarrow{Conc.\ H_2SO_4} CH_3OC_2H_5 + H_3O^+$$

Properties of Ethers

211. (a): In $CH_3OC_2H_5$, the attack of I^- occurs at the CH_3 group giving CH_3I and C_2H_5OH. In contrast, in $(CH_3)_3COCH_3$, the reaction occurs by S_N1 mechanism and I^- iodide attacks the more stable $(CH_3)_3C^+$ giving $(CH_3)_3Cl$ and CH_3OH. Hence, option (a) is correct.

212. (b): The high polarity of the solvent (H_2O) present in conc. HI (57%) favours S_N1 mechanism and hence I^- ion attacks the carbocation, $CH_3CH_2(CH_3)_2C^+$ giving $CH_3CH_2C(CH_3)_2I$ as the alkyl halide. Hence option (b) is correct.

213. (a): Due to steric hindrance, I^- ion attacks the smaller alkyl group giving ethyl iodide and isobutyl alcohol.

$$CH_3CH_2{-}\overset{CH_3}{\overset{|}{C}H}{-}CH_2{-}O{-}CH_2CH_3 \xrightarrow{HI} CH_3CH_2{-}\overset{CH_3}{\overset{|}{C}H}{-}CH_2OH + CH_3CH_2I$$

214. (c): Ethers can be reactive under drastic reaction conditions (high temperature, high concentration) due to the cleavage of the C–O bond. When the alkyl part of ether has a tertiary group, the reaction proceeds by the S_N2 mechanism. In the first step, protonation of the ether group occurs and then the positive charge shift to the tertiary carbocation due to its high stability. Then, the I^- will attack the carbocation to form the alkyl iodide. Option (b) has a tertiary alkyl part and a methyl part. So, the product will be tert-butyliodide and methanol.

215. (a): Conc. HI (57%) containing H_2O which due to its high polarity favours the S_N1 reaction. Hence, tert-butyl ether gives a mixture of CH_3OH and $(CH_3)Cl$. But in anhydrous ether (absence of H_2O), S_N2 reaction occurs. During the reaction, I^- attacks the smaller alkyl group, that is, CH_3 group giving CH_3I and $(CH_3)_3COH$.

$$(CH_3)_3C\text{–}\overset{+}{\underset{H}{O}}\text{–}CH_3 \xrightarrow[S_N2]{I^-} (CH_3)_3COH + CH_3I$$

Protonated *tert*-butyl methyl ether

216. (d): Protonation of anisole gives methyl phenyl oxonium ion (I). In this ion, the O–CH_3 bond is weaker than the O–C_6H_5 bond since the carbon–oxygen bond of the phenyl group is sp^2 hybridised and there is partial double bond character in the O–C_6H_5 bond due to resonance. Therefore, the attack of the Br^- ion exclusively breaks the weaker O–CH_3 bond forming CH_3Br and C_6H_5OH. Thus, option (d) is correct.

$$C_6H_5\text{–}OCH_3 \xrightarrow{H^+} C_6H_5\text{–}\overset{+}{\underset{H}{O}}\text{–}CH_3 \xrightarrow{Br^-} C_6H_5\text{–}OH + CH_3Br$$

Anisole; Phenol; Methyl bromide

217. (b): $C_6H_5CH_2\text{–}O\text{–}C_6H_5 \xrightarrow{H^+}$

$$C_6H_5CH_2\text{–}\overset{+}{\underset{H}{O}}\text{–}C_6H_5 \xrightarrow[S_N1\,cleavage]{I^-} C_6H_5CH_2I + HOC_6H_5$$

218. (d): 1° Alkyl phenyl ethers undergo the S_N2 reaction giving the corresponding phenol and the alkyl iodide corresponding to the 1° alkyl group. In contrast, ethers containing one 2° alkyl group and one 1° alkyl group undergo S_N1 reaction giving alkyl iodide corresponding to the 1° alkyl group.

HI, –I⁻ → ; I⁻, S_N2 (–CH_3CH_2I) → ; HI, –I⁻ → ; S_N1 (–CH_3OH) → ; I⁻ →

Thus, option (d) is correct.

219. (a):

$$C_2H_5OC_2H_5 \xrightarrow[\text{Cleavage of ethers}]{\text{Red P/HI}} 2C_2H_5I \xrightarrow[\text{Reduction}]{\text{Red P/HI}} \underset{\text{Ethane}}{2C_2H_6}$$

220. (a): $C_6H_5OCH_2CH_3 \xrightarrow[\Delta]{\Delta} C_6H_5OH + CH_3CH_2Br$

221. (a): $C_6H_5\text{–}O\text{–}CH_2CH_2OH \xrightarrow[\Delta]{\text{Excess HBr}}$

$$[C_6H_5OH + BrCH_2CH_2OH] \xrightarrow{HBr} C_6H_5OH + BrCH_2CH_2Br$$

222. (b): With H_2/Pd–C, hydrogenolysis of benzyl ethers occurs to form toluene and the corresponding alcohol.

$$PhCH_2\text{–}O\text{–}CH_2CH_2CH_2Ph \xrightarrow{H_2/Pd\text{-}C} \underset{\text{Toluene}}{Ph\text{–}CH_3} + \underset{\text{3-Phenylpropan-1-ol}}{HOCH_2CH_2CH_2Ph}$$

223. (d): Due to resonance (of the lone pair of electrons on O atom with the π-electrons of the benzene ring), the C–O bond in diaryl ethers is quite strong and hence cannot be cleaved by conc. HBr or HI.

224. (c):

$$\underset{\text{Diethyl ether}}{CH_3CH_2\text{–}\ddot{O}\text{–}CH_2CH_3} + \underset{\text{Acetyl chloride}}{CH_3\text{–}C(=O)Cl} \xrightarrow{\text{Anhyd } ZnCl_2}$$

$$CH_3\text{–}C(O^-)(Cl)\text{–}\overset{+}{O}(CH_2CH_3)_2 \longrightarrow \underset{\text{Ethyl acetate}}{CH_3\text{–}\overset{O}{\overset{\|}{C}}\text{–}OCH_2CH_3} + CH_3CH_2Cl$$

225. (c):

$$\underset{\text{Diethyl ether}}{(CH_3CH_2)_2\ddot{O}} + \underset{\text{Acetic anhydride}}{CH_3\text{–}C(=O)\text{–}OCOCH_3} \xrightarrow{\text{Anhyd, } ZnCl_2}$$

$$CH_3\text{–}CH_2\text{–}\overset{+}{O}(CH_2CH_3)\text{–}C(O^-)(CH_3)(OCOCH_3) \longrightarrow \underset{\text{Ethyl acetate}}{2\,CH_3\text{–}\overset{O}{\overset{\|}{C}}\text{–}OCH_2CH_3}$$

226. (c): $CH_3\text{–}O\text{–}CH_2CH_3 + PCl_5 \rightarrow CH_3Cl + CH_3CH_2Cl + POCl_3$

227. (b): Diethyl ether $\xrightarrow{O_2/h\nu}$ Diethyl ether hydroperoxide

228. (d): All ethers with hydrogen on α-carbon/s react with O_2 in the presence of light to form hydroperoxides. Since tert-butyl phenyl ether does not contain any α-hydrogens, it does not form hydroperoxides.

229. (a): Peroxides, if present in old stocks of ethers oxidise Fe^{2+} to Fe^{3+} ions which then combine with KCNS to form blood red colouration due to formation of ferric sulfocyanide.

$$Fe^{2+} \xrightarrow{\text{Peroxides}} Fe^{3+}$$

$$Fe^{3+} + 3\,KCNS \rightarrow Fe(CNS)_3 + 3\,K^+$$

230. (a): KI is added to old stocks of ethers when I^- is oxidised to I_2 by ether peroxide which itself is reduced to ether.
In actual practice, the old stock of ether is repeatedly shaken with KI solution till it ceases to impart brown colour due to the liberation of I_2.

231. (c): OCH_3 group is *o*, *p*-directing. Therefore, anisole on nitration gives a mixture of *o*- and *o*-nitroanisoles.

232. (d): OCH_3 group being *o*, *p*-directing gives a mixture of *o*- and *p*-bromoanisoles.

233. (d):

Anisole $\xrightarrow[\text{Anhyd. } AlCl_3]{(CH_3)_3CCl}$ 4-$C(CH_3)_3$-anisole $\xrightarrow{Cl_2/FeCl_3}$ (OCH_3 group is a stronger *o*, *p*-directing group than $C(CH_3)_3$) 2-chloro-4-$C(CH_3)_3$-anisole $\xrightarrow[\text{(cleavage of ethers)}]{\text{HBr, Heat}}$ 2-chloro-4-$C(CH_3)_3$-phenol

234. (c): The CH_3O group is *o*, *p*-directing. But due to steric hindrance at the *o*-position, *p*-methoxyacetophenone is the main product.

235. (c): Since compound (X) with MF $C_4H_{10}O$ does not react with Na, it may be an ether. On treatment with hot conc. HI, it gives only ethyl iodide, it must be a symmetrical ether, that is, diethyl ether.

$$\underset{\substack{\text{Diethylether}\\(\text{MF } C_4H_{10}O)}}{(CH_3CH_2)_2O} \xrightarrow{Na} \text{No reaction}$$

$$(CH_3CH_2)_2O \xrightarrow{\text{Hot conc. HI}} 2\,CH_3CH_2I$$

236. (d): Since compound (X) with MF $C_6H_{14}O$ does not react with Na, it may be an ether. On treatment with hot conc. HI, it gives a mixture of two isomeric compounds having a MF C_3H_7I, therefore, it must be an unsymmetrical ether. Now two isomeric compounds having the MF C_3H_7I must be *n*-propyl iodide and isopropyl iodide. If this is so then the compound (X) must be isopropyl *n*-propyl ether.

$$\underset{\substack{\text{Isopropyl } n\text{-propylether}\\(\text{MF } C_6H_{14}O)}}{(CH_3)_2CH{-}O{-}CH_2CH_3} \xrightarrow[-2H_2O]{2HI,\ \Delta} \underset{\text{Isopropyl iodide}}{(CH_3)_2CHI} + \underset{n\text{-Propyl iodide}}{CH_3CH_2CH_2I}$$

In the case of option (c), the cyclopropyl ring first opens up to give product (I) which then reacts with

$$I^- + \text{(cyclopropyl)}{-}OCH_2CH_2CH_3 \longrightarrow$$

$$\underset{(I)}{ICH_2CH_2CH_2{-}O{-}CH_2CH_2CH_3} \xrightarrow{HI} 2\,CH_3CH_2CH_2I$$

another molecule of HI to give two molecules of *n*-propyl iodide and not a mixture of two isomeric iodides. Therefore, option (c) is not correct.

237. (d): Na reacts with isopropyl alcohol to evolve H_2 gas but ethyl methyl ether does not. Similarly, I_2/NaOH reacts with isopropyl alcohol to give a yellow ppt. of CH_3 but ethyl methyl ether does not.

$$\underset{\text{Isoprppyl alcohol}}{2(CH_3)_2CHOH} \xrightarrow{2Na} (CH_3)_2CHONa + H_2$$

$$\underset{\text{Isoprppyl alcohol}}{CH_3{-}CHOH{-}CH_3} \xrightarrow[\text{(Idoform reaction)}]{I_2/NaOH} CH_3COONa + \underset{\text{Iodoform}}{CHI_3}$$

238. (d): RMgX dissolves in ether due to the formation of a coordinate complex.

$$RMgX + 2\,(C_2H_5)_2O \longrightarrow \text{R, X, } (C_2H_5)_2O \rightarrow Mg \leftarrow O(C_2H_5)_2$$

Similarly, $(C_2H_5)_3N$ donates a lone pair of electrons and hence can be used for the preparation of RMgX.

Benzene does not have a lone pair of electrons to form a coordinate complex with RMgX, therefore, the Grignard reagent cannot be prepared with benzene.

239. (c): Complexes of ethers with Lewis acids are called etherates.

240. (a): The dipole moment of dimethyl ether is 1.3 D, that of methanol is 1.71 D, that of methyl chloride is 1.86 D and that of phenol is 1.54 D.

241. (b): Due to steric hindrance, during the cleavage of ethers containing one primary and one secondary alkyl group, the nucleophilic attack by the I^- ion occurs on the smaller alkyl group as shown.

$$CH_3{-}O{-}CH(CH_3)_2 \xrightarrow{H^+} CH_3{-}\overset{+}{\underset{H}{O}}{-}CH(CH_3)_2 \xrightarrow{I^-} CH_3I + (CH_3)_2CHOH$$

242. (c): Due to the greater stability of tert-butyl carbocation, cleavage of protonated tert-butyl methyl ether occurs by S_N1 mechanism giving methyl alcohol and tert-butyl carbocation which upon subsequent nucleophilic attack by I^- gives tert-butyl iodide.

$$\underset{tert\text{-butyl methyl ether}}{(CH_3)_3C{-}\ddot{O}{-}CH_3} \xrightarrow{H^+} \underset{\text{Protonated } tert\text{-butyl methyl ether}}{(CH_3)_3C{-}\overset{+}{\underset{H}{O}}{-}CH_3} \xrightarrow{S_N1}$$

$$CH_3OH + (CH_3)_3C^+ \xrightarrow{I^-} \underset{\text{Methanol}}{CH_3OH} + \underset{tert\text{-butyl iodine}}{(CH_3)_3C{-}I}$$

Cyclic Ethers

243. (c): $\underset{\text{Ethene}}{CH_2{=}CH_2} \xrightarrow[\Delta]{O_2/Ag} \underset{\text{Epoxyethane (A)}}{\text{epoxyethane}} \xrightarrow{LiAlH_4} \underset{\text{Ethanol (B)}}{HOCH_2CH_3}$

$$\underset{(B)}{CH_3CH_2OH} + \text{epoxyethane} \xrightarrow[H_2SO_4]{\text{Dil.}} \left[CH_3CH_2\ddot{O}H + \text{protonated epoxyethane}\right] \longrightarrow \underset{(C)}{CH_3CH_2OCH_2CH_2OH}$$

244. (b): $\underset{\text{Epoxyethane}}{\text{epoxyethane}} \xrightarrow{H^+} \text{protonated epoxyethane} \xrightarrow[-H^+]{H_2\ddot{O}:} \underset{\text{1, 2-Ethandiol (A)}}{HOCH_2CH_2OH}$

$$\underset{\text{Epoxyethane}}{\text{epoxyethane}} \xrightarrow{H^+} \text{protonated epoxyethane} \xrightarrow[-H^+]{H_2\ddot{O}:} \underset{\text{1, 2-Ethandiol (A)}}{HOCH_2CH_2OH}$$

$$\underset{\text{Epoxyethane}}{\text{epoxyethane}} \xrightarrow{H_2SO_4} \text{protonated epoxyethane} \xrightarrow[-H^+]{HOCH_2CH_2OH} \underset{\text{Diethyleneglycol (B)}}{HOCH_2CH_2OCH_2CH_2OH}$$

245. (c):

$$(CH_3)_2C{-}CH_2\ (\text{epoxide}) \xrightarrow[\text{LiAlH}_4]{H^-\ \text{From}} (CH_3)_2C(CH_3){-}OLi \xrightarrow{H^+/H_2O} (CH_3)_2C(CH_3){-}OH$$

246. (a): $(CH_3)_2C(O)CH_2 \xrightarrow{H^+}$ protonated epoxide $\xrightarrow{H_2\ddot{O}^{18}}$ $(CH_3)_2C(^{18}OH_2^+)-CH_2OH \xrightarrow{-H^+} (CH_3)_2C(^{18}OH)CH_2OH$

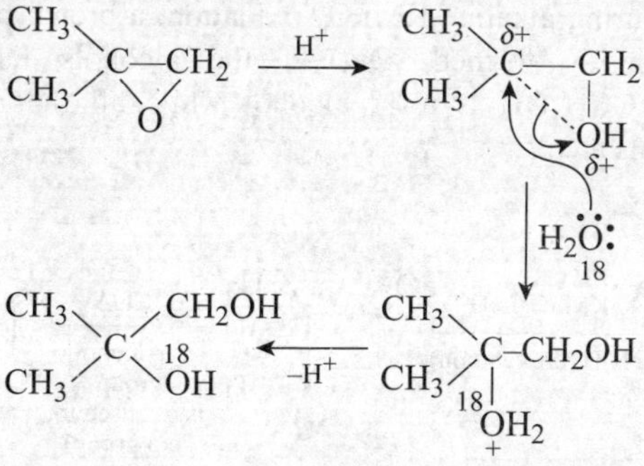

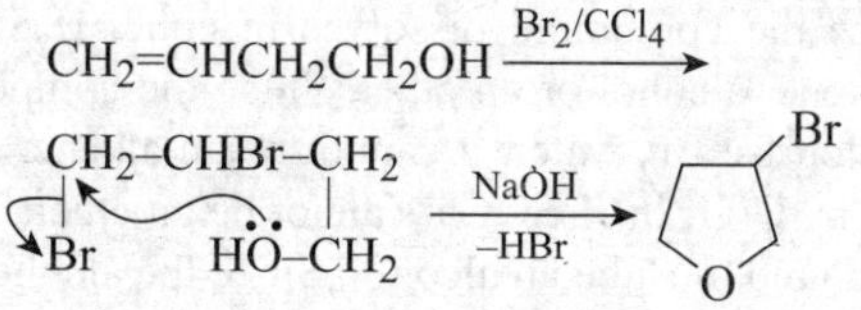

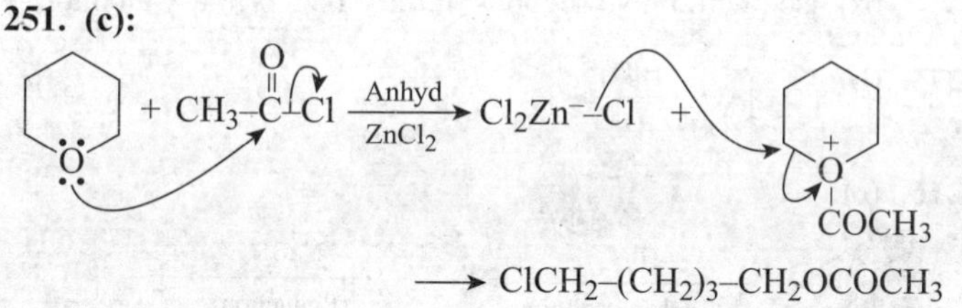

247. (b): Isobutylene $\xrightarrow{C_6H_5CO_3H(X)}$ epoxide $\xrightarrow{LiAlH_4(Y)}$ *tert*-butyl alcohol

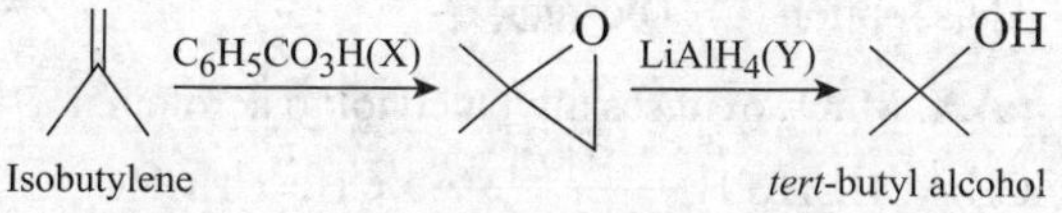

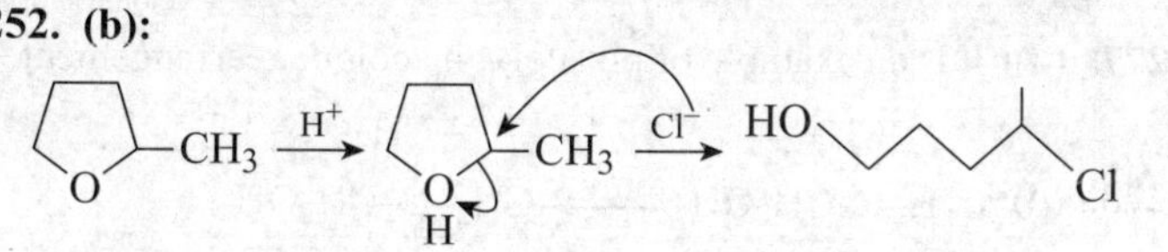

248. (a): 1,4-Dibromobutane.

249. (b): 1-methylcyclohexene oxide $\xrightarrow{H^+}$ tertiary carbocation (with OH) $\xrightarrow{Br^-}$ 2-bromo-2-methylcyclohexanol

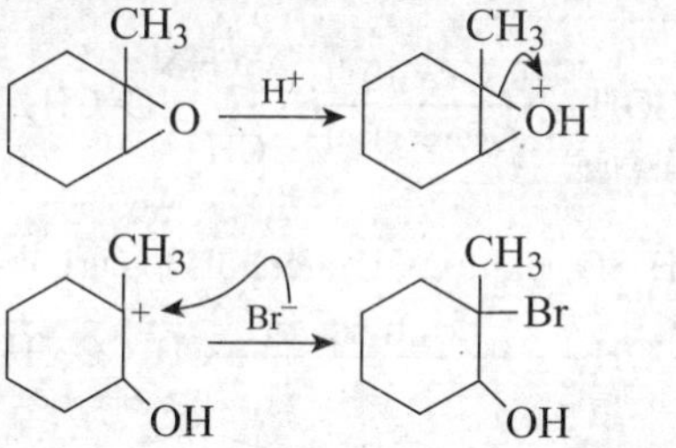

250. (d): $CH_2{=}CHCH_2CH_2OH \xrightarrow{Br_2/CCl_4}$ $CH_2Br{-}CHBr{-}CH_2{-}CH_2OH \xrightarrow[-HBr]{NaOH}$ 3-bromotetrahydrofuran

251. (c): Tetrahydropyran + $CH_3{-}\overset{O}{\overset{\|}{C}}{-}Cl \xrightarrow[ZnCl_2]{Anhyd} Cl_2Zn^-{-}Cl$ + oxonium ion ($O^+{-}COCH_3$)

$\longrightarrow ClCH_2{-}(CH_2)_3{-}CH_2OCOCH_3$

252. (b): 2-methyltetrahydrofuran $\xrightarrow{H^+}$ protonated ether $\xrightarrow{Cl^-}$ HO–CH₂CH₂CH₂–CH(Cl)–CH₃

253. (a): dichloro-tetrahydropyran $\xrightarrow{-Cl^-}$ oxocarbenium ion $\xrightarrow[-H^+]{CH_3\ddot{O}H}$ 2-methoxy-tetrahydropyran (with Cl)

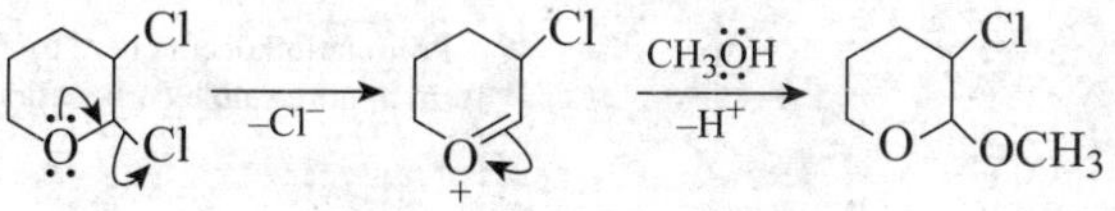

254. (a): Dihydropyran $\xrightarrow{H^+}$ oxocarbenium ion $\xrightarrow[-H^+]{R\ddot{O}H}$

$\xrightarrow{-H^+}$ 2-OR-tetrahydropyran

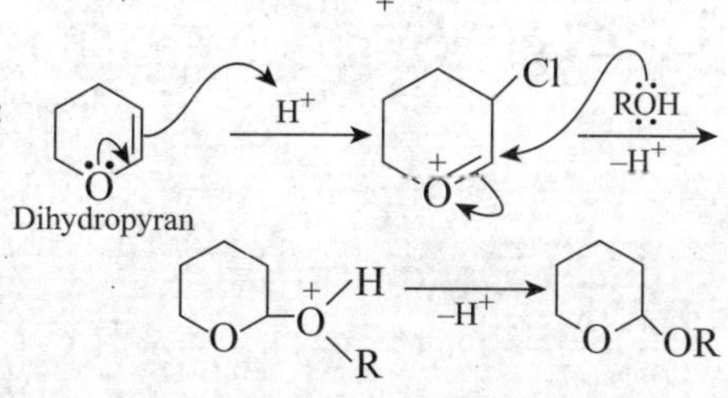

255. (c): OH reacts with the Grignard reagent, therefore, it must be protected with dihydropyran as shown.

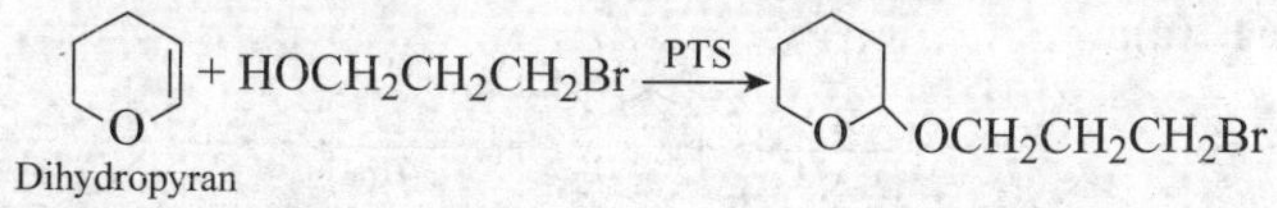

Dihydropyran + $HOCH_2CH_2CH_2Br \xrightarrow{PTS}$ THP–$OCH_2CH_2CH_2Br$

256. (b): X = 18 and Y = 6.

257. (d): Due to complex formation of metal ions, that is, K^+ with O atoms of [18]-crown-6, $KMnO_4$ dissolves in benzene in the presence of crown ethers.

258. (d): $Cl{-}CH_2{-}CH_2{-}\ddot{O}H$ (Chlorohydrin) $\xrightarrow[-HCl]{\text{Dil NaOH warm}}$ Epoxyethane

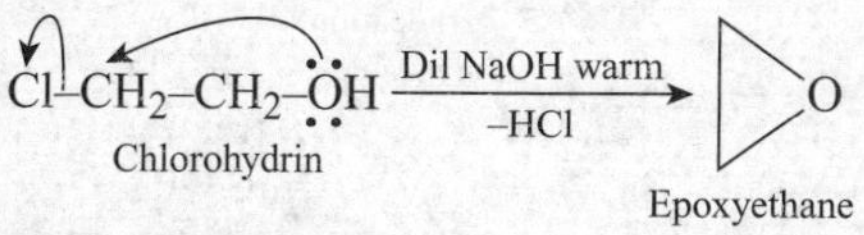

Final Preparation

259. (c): $NaBH_4$ in C_2H_5OH neither reduces the acid and esters nor opens the epoxide ring. It reduces only the –CHO group to the 1° alcoholic group.

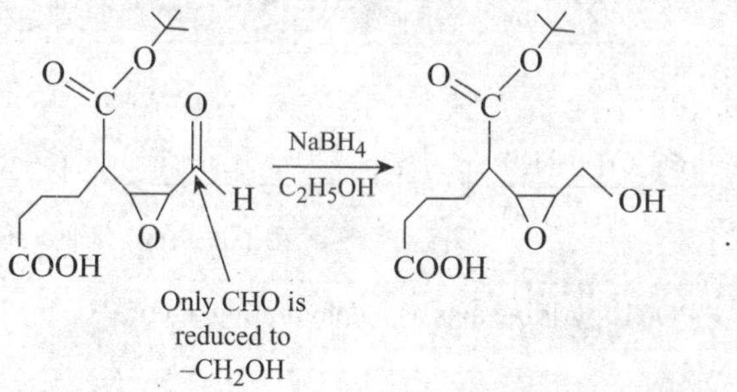

$\xrightarrow[C_2H_5OH]{NaBH_4}$ (Only CHO is reduced to $-CH_2OH$)

260. (a): C_2–OH is 3° while C_5 is 2°. 3° alcohols are weaker acids than 2° alcohols, therefore, 3° alcohols are stronger bases than 2° alcohols, that is, option (a) is correct.

261. (d): Bigger the size, stronger the base but weaker the nucleophile. Thus, $(CH_3)_3CO^-$ is the strongest base and weakest nucleophile.

262. (b): During tosylation, the bond between O and H breaks and hence the configuration at the chiral centre is retained. During the S_N2 reaction, the bond between C and O breaks and hence the configuration is inverted. Further during alkaline hydrolysis of acetate (B), the O–Ac bond breaks and hence the configuration at the chiral centre in product (C) is retained. Thus,

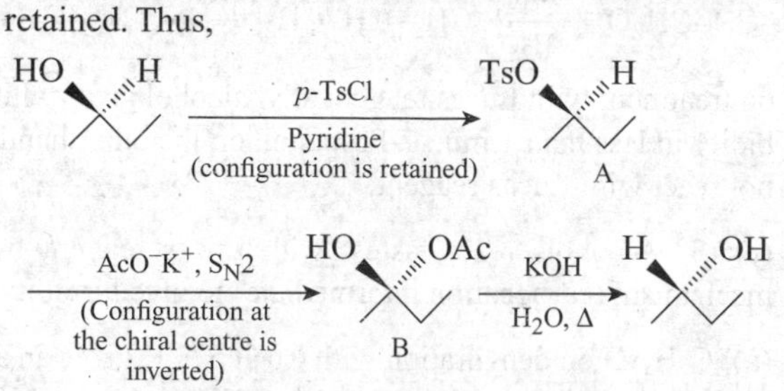

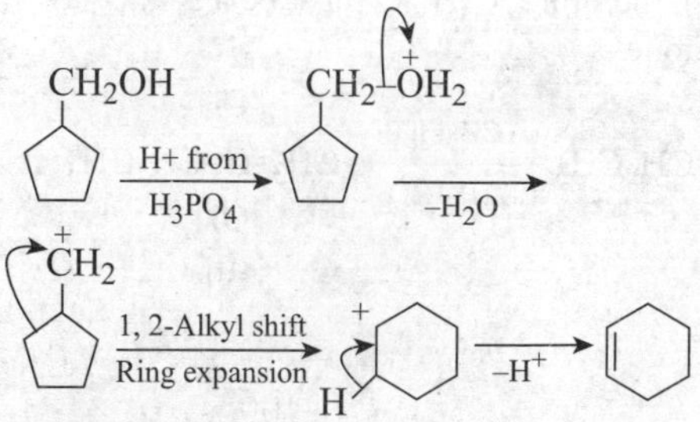

$\xrightarrow[\text{Pyridine (configuration is retained)}]{p\text{-TsCl}}$ A $\xrightarrow[\text{(Configuration at the chiral centre is inverted)}]{AcO^-K^+,\ S_N2}$ B $\xrightarrow[H_2O,\ \Delta]{KOH}$

263. (c): Cyclopentylmethanol $\xrightarrow[H_3PO_4]{H^+ \text{ from}}$ $CH_2{-}\overset{+}{O}H_2$ $\xrightarrow{-H_2O}$ $\overset{+}{C}H_2$ $\xrightarrow[\text{Ring expansion}]{\text{1, 2-Alkyl shift}}$ cyclohexyl cation $\xrightarrow{-H^+}$ cyclohexene

264. (d):

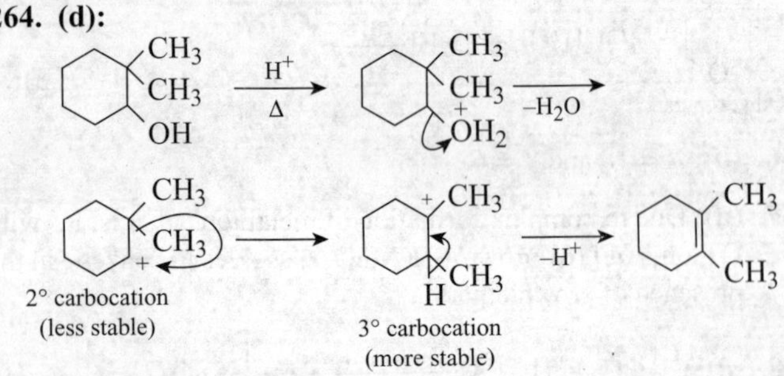

2° carbocation (less stable) → 3° carbocation (more stable)

265. (b):

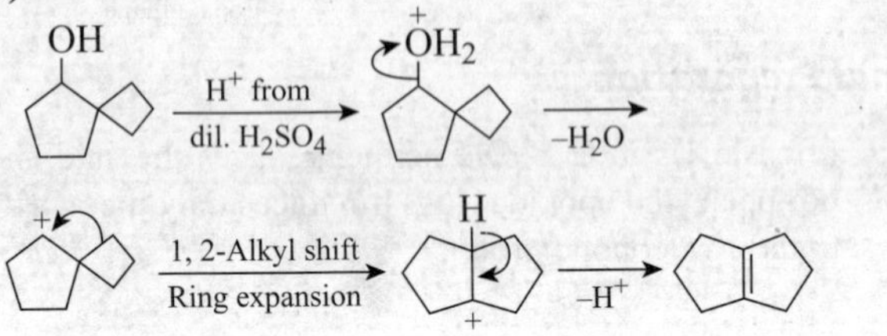

$\xrightarrow[\text{dil. } H_2SO_4]{H^+ \text{ from}}$ $\xrightarrow{-H_2O}$ $\xrightarrow[\text{Ring expansion}]{\text{1, 2-Alkyl shift}}$ $\xrightarrow{-H^+}$

266. (d):

$\xrightarrow[\text{(ii) } H^+/H_2O]{\text{(i) } CH_3MgBr}$ (A) $\xrightarrow[\text{273 K (Dehydration)}]{POCl_3, \text{ pyridine}}$ 1-Methylcylohexene (B)

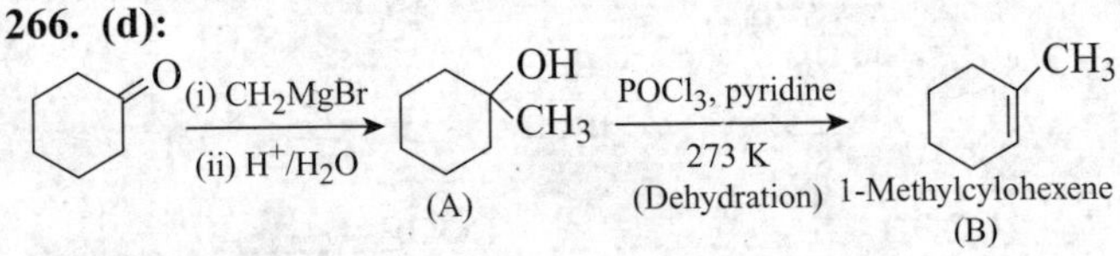

$POCl_3$/pyridine acts as a dehydrating agent.

267. (b):

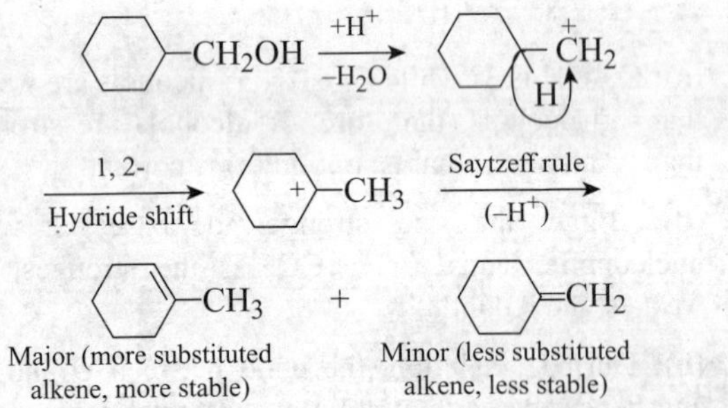

$\xrightarrow[-H_2O]{+H^+}$ $\xrightarrow[\text{Hydride shift}]{1, 2-}$ $\xrightarrow[(-H^+)]{\text{Saytzeff rule}}$

Major (more substituted alkene, more stable) + Minor (less substituted alkene, less stable)

268. (b): 1° alcohols cannot be distinguished by Lucas reagent, yet allyl alcohol gives resonance stabilised allyl carbocation which is as stable as a 3° carbocation. Therefore,

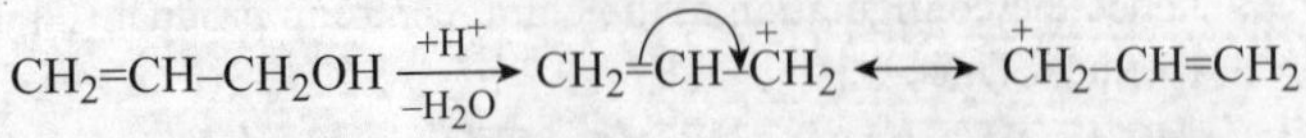

$$CH_2{=}CH{-}CH_2OH \xrightarrow[-H_2O]{+H^+} CH_2{=}CH{-}\overset{+}{C}H_2 \longleftrightarrow \overset{+}{C}H_2{-}CH{=}CH_2$$

on treatment with Lucas reagent allyl alcohol gives white turbidity in less than 1 min. 1-Propanol, on the other hand, does not react with Lucas reagent.

269. (c): 3° Alcohols react fastest with Lucas reagent by S_N1 mechanism (carbocation intermediate) to give turbidity.

270. (a): $C_5H_{12}O$ on dehydration with Cu at 573 K gives an alkene (C_5H_{10}), therefore, $C_5H_{12}O$ must be a 3° alcohol and X must be a ketone.

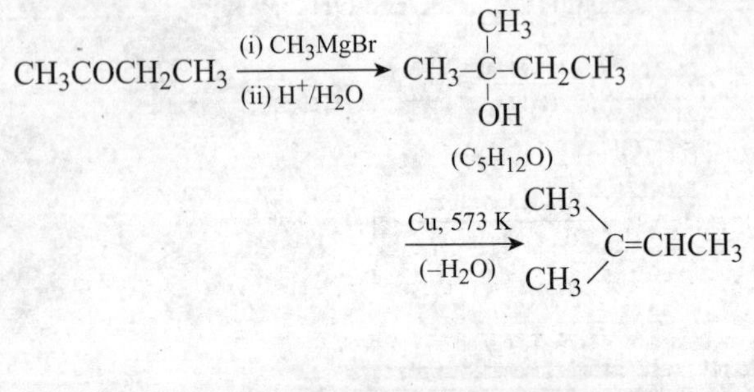

$$CH_3COCH_2CH_3 \xrightarrow[\text{(ii) } H^+/H_2O]{\text{(i) } CH_3MgBr} CH_3{-}C(CH_3)(OH){-}CH_2CH_3 \ (C_5H_{12}O)$$

$$\xrightarrow[(-H_2O)]{\text{Cu, 573 K}} (CH_3)_2C{=}CHCH_3$$

271. (d): During alkaline $KMnO_4$ oxidation, a brown precipitate of MnO_2 is formed. Out of the alcohols listed only $(CH_3)_3CCH_2OH$ is a 1° alcohol while all the remaining alcohols are 3°.

272. (b):

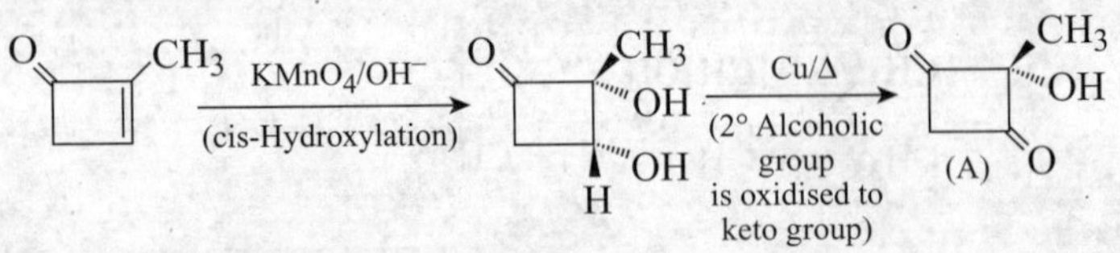

$\xrightarrow[\text{(cis-Hydroxylation)}]{KMnO_4/OH^-}$ $\xrightarrow[\text{(2° Alcoholic group is oxidised to keto group)}]{Cu/\Delta}$ (A)

Thus, option (b) is correct.

273. (a): I. MnO_2 oxidises allyl alcohol to acrolein.

$$\underset{\text{Allyl alcohol}}{CH_2{=}CHCH_2PH} \xrightarrow{MnO_2(A)} \underset{\text{Acrolein}}{CH_2{=}CHCHO}$$

II. Heated Cu converts 3° alcohols to alkenes.

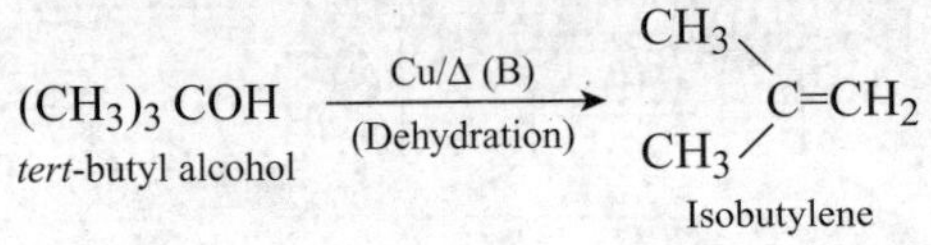

$$\underset{\textit{tert}\text{-butyl alcohol}}{(CH_3)_3COH} \xrightarrow[\text{(Dehydration)}]{Cu/\Delta\ (B)} \underset{\text{Isobutylene}}{(CH_3)_2C{=}CH_2}$$

III. $K_2Cr_2O_7/H_2SO_4$ oxidises 1° alcohols to carboxylic acids

$$\underset{\text{Ethanal}}{CH_3CH_2OH} \xrightarrow{K_2Cr_2O_7/H_2SO_4(C)} \underset{\text{Ethanoic acid}}{CH_3CO_2H}$$

274. (a): Since the compound dissolves in conc. H_2SO_4, it can be an alkene, alcohol or an ether. Since the compound does not decolourise Br_2 water, it cannot be an alkene. Since it is oxidised by CrO_3 in H_2SO_4, it cannot be an ether. Therefore, the compound must be an alcohol. Since the alcohol is easily oxidised within two seconds, it must be a primary alcohol.

275. (b): $\xrightarrow[\text{[O]}]{HIO_4}$ (COOH, CHO)

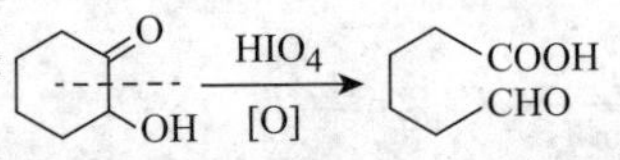

276. (c): $\xrightarrow[\text{(1, 2-Glycol splitting)}]{HIO_4}$ $\xrightarrow[\text{(Reduction)}]{NaBH_4}$ Cyclohexanol

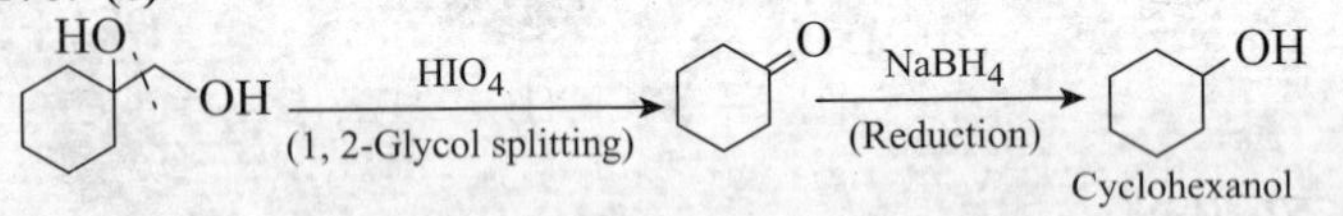

277. (d): It is an example of pinacol–pinacolone rearrangement.

278. (d): $CH_3{-}C(CH_3)(OH){-}CH_2OH \xrightarrow{H^+} CH_3{-}C(CH_3)(\overset{+}{O}H_2){-}CH_2OH$

Protonation occurs here to form a more stable carbocation

$$CH_3{-}C(CH_3)(H){-}\overset{+}{C}H{-}\ddot{O}{-}H \longleftrightarrow CH_3{-}CH(CH_3){-}CH{=}\overset{+}{O}H \xrightarrow{-H^+} \underset{\text{Isobutyraldehyde}}{(CH_3)_2CH{-}CHO}$$

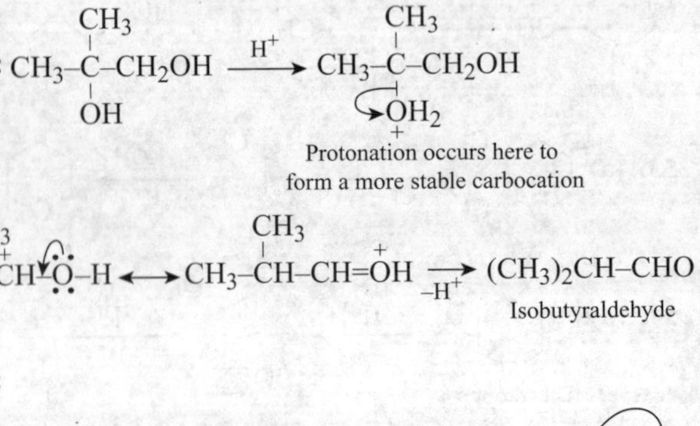

279. (c):

$$Ph{-}C(CH_3)(OH){-}C(CH_3)(OH){-}Ph \xrightarrow[\text{(Pinacol-Pinacolone rearrangement)}]{H^+, \Delta} Ph{-}C(CH_3)(\overset{+}{O}H_2){-}C(CH_3)(OH){-}Ph \xrightarrow{-H_2O} H_3C{-}\overset{+}{C}(Ph){-}C(CH_3)(Ph)(OH)$$

$$\xrightarrow[\text{than } CH_3]{\text{Ph has greater migratory power}} H_3C{-}C(Ph)(Ph){-}\overset{+}{C}(OH){-}CH_3 \xrightarrow{-H^+} H_3C{-}C(Ph)_2{-}C(=O){-}CH_3$$

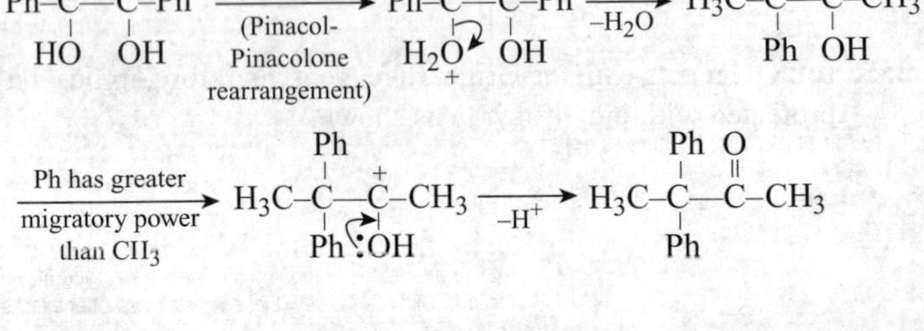

280. (c):

(Reaction scheme: cyclobutane diol → H^+ → $-H_2O$ → 1, 2-Alkyl shift (Ring expansion) → H^+ → 2,2-dimethylcyclopentanone)

281. (c):

(Reaction scheme: H^+, $-H_2O$, 1, 2-Alkyl shift (Ring expansion), $-H^+$ → spiro ketone)

282. (b):

(Reaction scheme: $NaNO_2$/dil. H_2SO_4 (Diazotisation) → $-N_2$ → 1, 2-Methyl shift → $-H^+$ → $CH_3-CO-C(CH_3)_3$)

283. (a):

$$\overset{\delta+}{CH_2}=\overset{\delta-}{CH}\rightarrow CH_2OH \xrightarrow[\text{Anti-mark. addn.}]{\overset{\delta-}{HO}-\overset{\delta+}{Cl}} HOCH_2-CHCl-CH_2OH$$

2-Chloropropane-1, 3-diol

284. (d):

$$\underset{\text{Propylene}}{CH_3CH=CH_2} \xrightarrow{Cl_2,\ 773\ K(I)} \underset{\text{Allyl chloride}}{Cl-CH_2CH=CH_2} \xrightarrow{aq.\ Na_2CO_3(II)}$$

$$\underset{\text{Allyl alcohol}}{HO-CH_2-CH=CH_2} \xrightarrow[\text{Mark addn.}]{\overset{\delta-}{HO}-\overset{\delta+}{Cl}\ (III)} HOCH_2-CHCl-CH_2OH$$

$$\xrightarrow{aq.\ NaOH(IV)} \underset{\text{Glycerol}}{HOCH_2-CHOH-CH_2OH}$$

285. (b): The mechanism is given below.

(Scheme: Glycerol + 3HI → Warm → 1, 2, 3-triiodopropane (unstable) → Allyl iodide → HI → $CH_3-CHI-CH_2I$ (unstable) → $-I_2$ → Propene → 2-iodopropane)

286. (d):

$$\underset{\text{Glycerol}}{HOCH_2-CHOH-CH_2OH} \xrightarrow[\text{r.t.}]{\text{HI, excess}} CH_3-CHI-CH_3$$

$$\xrightarrow[\text{(Reduction)}]{\text{HI, /423 K}} \underset{\text{Propane}}{CH_3-CH_2-CH_3}$$

287. (b):

(Scheme: Benzene → $CH_2=CH-CH_3$, H^+, Hight pressure, Δ (FC alkylation) → Isopropylbenzene (T) → Radical initator O_2 → (U) cumene hydroperoxide)

288. (c): At the *m*-position, the OCH_3 group cannot exert its +R effect. Instead, it exerts its –I effect, and hence *m*-methoxyphenol is the strongest acid among phenol, *o*-, *m*- and *p*-methoxy-phenols.

289. (c): *o*-Nitrophenol is less acidic than carbonic acid and hence does not dissolve in Na_2CO_3 solution.

290. (a): OH group is *o,p*-directing. Therefore, sulfonation–desulfonation introduces D atoms at two *o*- and one *p*-position. Further, due to the acidic nature of OH, H gets replaced by D. Thus, option (a) is correct.

291. (b):

(Scheme: 2,6-dibromo-4-sulfophenol + 3 Br_2 (*aq*) → intermediate → $-SO_2$, $-H^+$ → 2,4,6-tribromophenol)

SO_3H is a good leaving group and hence during bromination, the SO_3H group is knocked out and bromination occurs at both the *o*-and one *p*-positions to give tribromophenol, that is, option (b) is correct.

292. (c): Since the compound dissolves in NaOH and gives a characteristic colour with $FeCl_3$, it must be a phenol. Now three phenols having the MF C_7H_8O are *o*-, *m*- and *p*-cresol. The compound on treatment with Br_2 gives a tribromoderivative, therefore, two *o*- and one *p*-position with respect to the OH group must be free. Thus, the phenol is *m*-cresol.

(Scheme: *m*-Cresol (C_7H_8O) → Br_2–H_2O → ($C_7H_5OBr_3$))

293. (c): *o*- and *p*-products are formed in Fries rearrangement.

294. (c): This is an example of Claisen rearrangement as shown.

(Scheme: P → Δ → [Six-membered cyclic T.S.] → → Tautomerises → Q)

Thus, option (c) is correct.

295. (a):

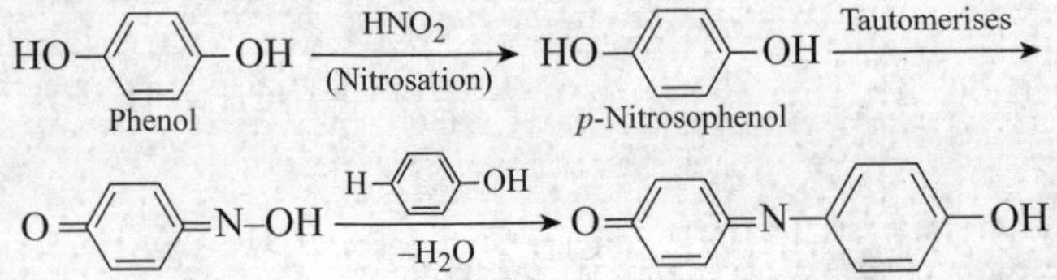

Phenol $\xrightarrow[\text{(Nitrosation)}]{HNO_2}$ p-Nitrosophenol $\xrightarrow{\text{Tautomerises}}$ $O=C_6H_4=N-OH \xrightarrow{H-C_6H_4-OH,\ -H_2O} O=C_6H_4=N-C_6H_4-OH$

296. (c): Phenols show keto–enol tautomerism and the stability of the keto form depends upon the number of keto groups, therefore, trihydric phenols should exist in the keto form provided the two keto groups are not on the adjacent carbon atoms which decreases the stability due to repulsion between the +ve charges on adjacent carbon atoms.

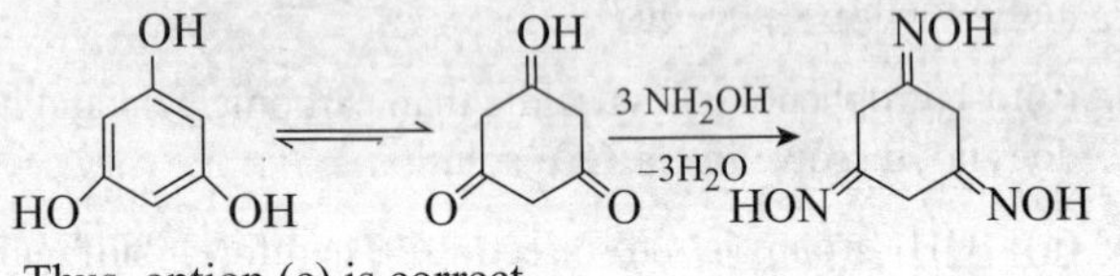

$\xrightarrow[-3H_2O]{3\ NH_2OH}$

Thus, option (c) is correct.

297. (a): Tautomerisation of trihydric phenol (I) gives triketone (II). Abstraction of a proton by the base OH^- gives a stable carbanion (III) which reacts with Me–I by the S_N2 mechanism to give product (IV). Repeated abstraction of a proton followed by S_N2 mechanism with MeI gives the final product (V).

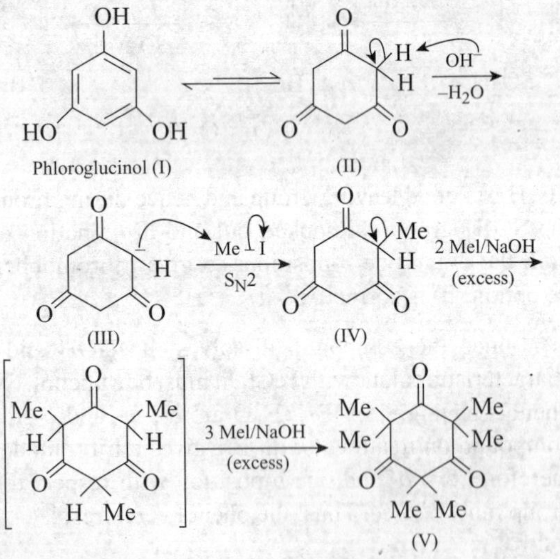

Phloroglucinol (I) ⇌ (II) $\xrightarrow[-H_2O]{OH^-}$ (III) $\xrightarrow[S_N2]{Me-I}$ (IV) $\xrightarrow[\text{(excess)}]{2\ MeI/NaOH}$ $\xrightarrow[\text{(excess)}]{3\ MeI/NaOH}$ (V)

298. (a): $\xrightarrow{H^+}$ $\xrightarrow[S_N2]{Br^-}$ $\xrightarrow[\text{(Dehydration)}]{\text{conc. }H_2SO_4}$

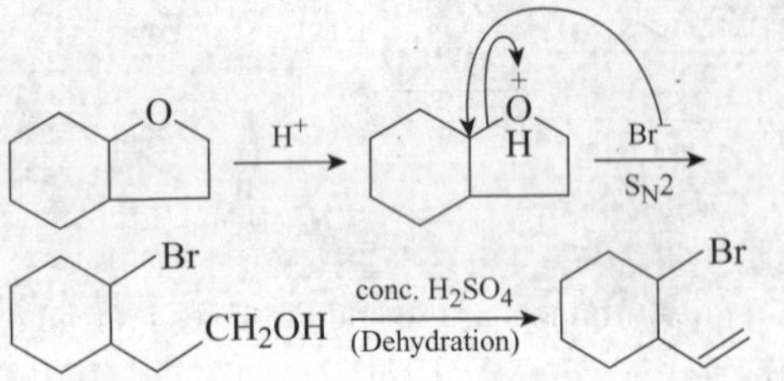

299. (c): Rearrangements do not occur in the given nucleophilic substitution reactions, therefore, carbocations are not the intermediates in these reactions. Thus, both the reactions occur by the S_N2 mechanism, that is, option (c) is correct.

300. (d): $\xrightarrow{CH_3MgBr}$ $\xrightarrow[-MgBrCl]{\text{Dil. acid}}$

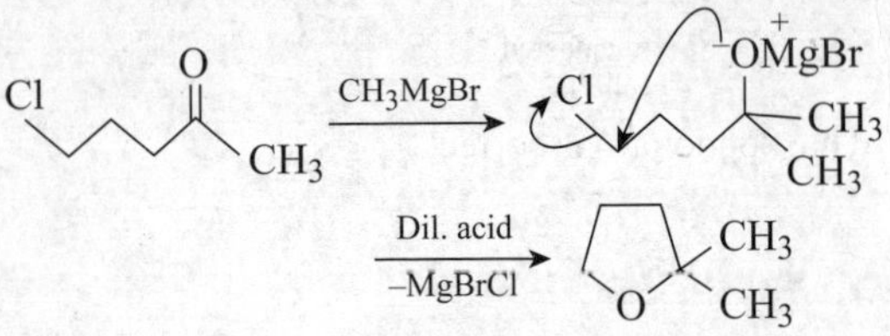

301. (c):

$\xrightarrow{H^+}$ (S_N1) $\xrightarrow{-ROH}$

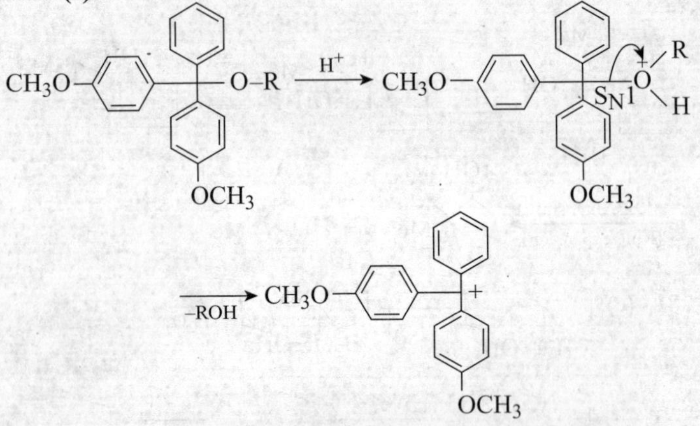

The presence of two CH_3O groups in two phenyl groups stabilises the carbocation due to their +R effect and hence the rate of the reaction is faster.

302. (d):

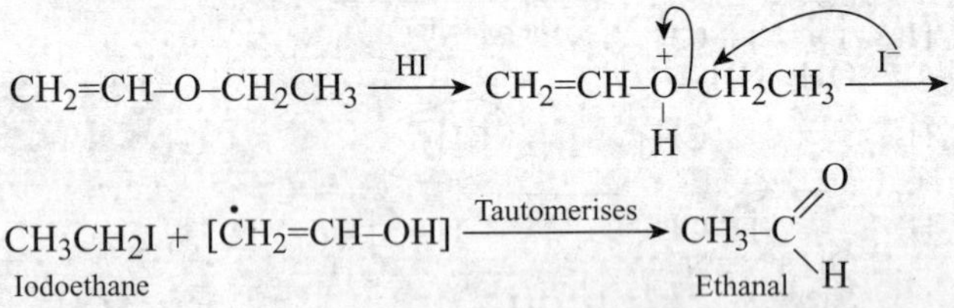

$CH_2=CH-O-CH_2CH_3 \xrightarrow{HI} CH_2=CH-\overset{+}{O}(H)-CH_2CH_3 \xrightarrow{I^-}$

$\underset{\text{Iodoethane}}{CH_3CH_2I} + [CH_2=CH-OH] \xrightarrow{\text{Tautomerises}} \underset{\text{Ethanal}}{CH_3-CHO}$

303. (d): Di-tert-butyl ether is readily cleaved by HCl due to the formation of the stable tert-butyl carbocation.

304. (d): Diethyl ether itself being a Lewis base is not attacked by nucleophiles, that is, OH^- ions. All others,

$CH_3-\overset{\delta+}{C}(=O^{\delta-})-OCH_3,\ CH_3-\overset{\delta+}{C}\equiv N^{\delta-},\ CH_3-\overset{+\delta}{C}(=O^{\delta-})-NH_2$

contain an electrophilic centre and hence are easily attacked by nucleophiles. Thus, option (d) correct.

305. (c): Ethers being basic dissolve in conc. H_2SO_4 but they neither decolorise Br_2–H_2O nor react with Na metal.

306. (c): Phenols and carboxylic acids are more acidic than aliphatic alcohols, therefore, cyclohexanol (I) is the least acidic. Out of the two phenols, III is more acidic than IV because of the presence of three electron withdrawing $-NO_2$ groups and on the benzene ring which make O–H bond highly polarised. Acetic acid (II) is more acidic than phenols and cyclohexanol but less acidic than trinitrophenol. Therefore, the correct order is:

III > II > IV > I

307. (b): Hydration of ethane gives a 1° alcohol, that is, ethanol while all other alkenes give either 2° or 3° alcohols.

$\underset{\text{Ethene}}{CH_2=CH_2} \xrightarrow[\text{(ii) }H_2O\text{, boil}]{\text{(i) conc. }H_2SO_4} \underset{1°\text{ Alcohol}}{CH_3-CH_2OH}$

$R-CH=CH_2 \xrightarrow[\text{(ii) }H_2O\text{, boil}]{\text{(i) conc. }H_2SO_4} \underset{2°\text{ Alcohol}}{R-CHOH-CH_3}$

$R_2C=CH_2 \xrightarrow[\text{(ii) }H_2O\text{, boil}]{\text{(i) Conc. }H_2SO_4} \underset{3°\text{ Alcohol}}{R_2C(OH)-CH_3}$

308. (b): The most important clue to solve this problem is the conversion of Y to Z. Addition of H_2SO_4 followed by hydrolysis, that is, hydration of alkenes follows Markownikoff's rule, therefore, Z can be only 2-propanol and not 1-propanol.

$$\underset{\text{2-Propanol (Z)}}{CH_3-CHOH-CH_3} \xrightarrow{PCl_5} \underset{X}{CH_3-\underset{Cl}{\underset{|}{C}H}-CH_3} \xrightarrow{\text{Alc. KOH}} \underset{Y}{CH_3-CH=CH_3} \xrightarrow[\text{(ii) } H_2O\text{, boil}]{\text{(i) Conc. } H_2SO_4} Z$$

309. (c): Hydroboration–oxidation gives alcohols corresponding to anti-Markownikoff addition of H_2O to alkenes while hydration gives alcohols corresponding to Markovnikov addition of H_2O to alkenes.

Methylenecyclohexane $\xrightarrow[\text{(ii) } H_2O_2/OH^-]{\text{(i) } B_2H_6/THF}$ cyclohexyl–CH_2OH (B)

Methylenecyclohexane $\xrightarrow[\text{(Markownikoff's addition)}]{H_3O^+}$ 1-methylcyclohexanol (CH_3, OH) (A)

Thus, option (c) is correct.

310. (b): Hydroboration–oxidation.

311. (d):

$$\underset{\text{3-Methylbut-1-ene}}{CH_3-\overset{CH_3}{\overset{|}{C}H}-CH=CH_2} \xrightarrow[\text{(Oxymercuration)}]{Hg(OCOCH_3)_2\text{, THF-}H_2O}$$

$$CH_3-\overset{CH_3}{\overset{|}{C}H}-\underset{OH}{\underset{|}{C}H}-\underset{HgOAc}{\underset{|}{C}H_2} \xrightarrow[\text{(Dermercuration)}]{NaBH_4/OH^-} \underset{\text{3-Methylbutan-2-ol}}{CH_3-\overset{CH_3}{\overset{|}{C}H}-\underset{OH}{\underset{|}{C}H}-CH_3}$$

312. (d):

Methylcyclopentene (CH_3) $\xrightarrow[\text{(cis-Addition of elements of H–}BH_2\text{, Hydroboration)}]{B_2H_6/THF}$ 2-methylcyclopentyl borane (CH_3, H, BH_2, H) $\xrightarrow[\text{Oxidation}]{H_2O_2/OH^-}$ *trans*-2-Methylcyclopentanol (CH_3, H, OH, H)

313. (b): $\underset{\text{Chloropropane}}{CH_3CH_2CH_2Cl} \xrightarrow[-HCl]{\text{Alc. KOH}} \underset{\text{Propene}}{CH_3CH=CH_2} \xrightarrow{BH_3/THF}$

$$(CH_3CH_2CH_2)_3B \xrightarrow[\text{(Protolysis)}]{CH_3COOH} \underset{\text{Propane}}{CH_3CH_2CH_3}$$

314. (c): 3-Phenyl-1-methylcyclohexene (Ph, Me) $\xrightarrow[\text{Hydroboration}]{B_2H_6}$ (Ph, BH_2, Me, H) $\xrightarrow[\text{Oxidation}]{H_2O_2/NaOH}$

(Ph, OH, Me, H) $\xrightarrow[\text{Dehydration } (-H_2O)]{\text{Conc. } H_2SO_4}$ (Ph, Me)

Here, dehydration occurs in accordance with Saytzeff rule to give the final product.

315. (a):

(a) (Me, H) alkene $\xrightarrow[\text{(Mark. addn.)}]{HBr}$ (Me, H, *, *, Br)

(b) (Me, H) alkene $\xrightarrow{H_2/Pd}$ (Me, H, *)

(c) (Me, H) alkene $\xrightarrow[\text{ROOR, } h\nu \text{ (Anti-Mark. addn.)}]{HBr}$ (Me, H, *, Br)

(d) (Me, H) alkene $\xrightarrow[H_2O_2/NaOH]{B_2H_6}$ (Me, H, OH)

Reaction (a) produces a product with two chiral centres and hence it gives a mixture of diastereomers while the remaining three reactions give products with only one chiral centre and hence they produce a mixture of enantiomers.

316. (a): Esters add two moles of the Grignard reagent to form 3° alcohols, therefore, two of the alkyl groups in the 3° alcohol must be identical. The Grignard reagent is CH_3MgBr, therefore, the product must contain at least two methyl groups. The only product which contains at least two methyl groups (actually three) is option (a). Thus

$$\underset{\text{Ethyl ester}}{CH_3-\overset{O}{\overset{\|}{C}}-OC_2H_5} \xrightarrow{CH_3MgBr} \left[(CH_3)(CH_3)C(OMgBr)(OC_2H_5)\right]$$

$$\xrightarrow{-Mg(OC_2H_5)Br} CH_3-\overset{O}{\overset{\|}{C}}-CH_3 \xrightarrow{CH_3MgBr}$$

$$(CH_3)_3C-OMgBr \xrightarrow[-Mg(OH)Br]{H^+/H_2O} (CH_3)_3C-OH$$

317. (d):

γ-Butyrolactone $\xrightarrow{CH_3-MgBr}$ (O⁻MgBr adduct with CH_3)

$H_3C-CO-CH_2CH_2CH_2-OMgBr \xrightarrow{CH_3MgBr} (H_3C)_2C(OMgBr)-CH_2CH_2CH_2-OMgBr$

$\xrightarrow[-2\ Mg(OH)Br]{H_3O^+} (H_3C)_2C(OH)-CH_2CH_2CH_2-OH$

318. (c):

$$\underset{\text{Acetyl bromide}}{CH_3-\overset{O}{\overset{\|}{C}}-Br} \xrightarrow{CH_3MgBr} (H_3C)_2C(OMgI)(Br)$$

$$\xrightarrow{-MgBrI} (H_3C)_2C=O \xrightarrow[\text{(ii) } H_3O^+]{\text{(i) } CH_3MgI} \underset{\text{2-Methyl-2-propanol}}{(H_3C)_2C(OH)CH_3}$$

319. (b): F being unreactive does not form a Grignard reagent.

$$F\text{-}\langle\rangle\text{-}Br \xrightarrow{Mg/ether} F\text{-}\langle\rangle\text{-}MgBr \xrightarrow{HCHO} F\text{-}\langle\rangle\text{-}CH_2OMgBr \xrightarrow[-Mg(OH)Br]{H_3O^+} F\text{-}\langle\rangle\text{-}CH_2OH$$

MATCH THE FOLLOWING

320. (a):(A, 2-methyl-2-propanol)—(r, 356 K);
(B, 2-butanol)—(q, 373 K);
(C, 1-butanol)—(s, 390 K);
(D, 2-methyl-1-propanol)—(p, 381 K)

321. (b):(A, Lucas reagent)—(s, $(CH_3)_3COH$);
(B, $K_2Cr_2O_7/H_2SO_4$)—(p, CH_3CH_2OH);
(C, blue colour in Victor Meyer's test)—(q, $CH_3CH_2CHOHCH_3$);
(D, Violet colour with $FeCl_3$)—(r, C_6H_5OH)

ASSERTION REASON

322. (a): R is the correct explanation of A.
Due to comparable size of F and C, F exerts better +mesomeric effect than Cl which has a much bigger size.

323. (d): Correct A. When CO_2 is passed through an aqueous solution of sodium picrate, picric acid is not precipitated.
Correct R. Picric acid is a much stronger acid than carbonic acid.

324. (b): Correct R. Due to –I and –R effects of the nitro group at the *o*-position, *o*-nitrophenol is a stronger acid than *m*-nitrophenol where the –R effect cannot occur but only a weak –I effect operates.

325. (c): Correct R.

$$p\text{-}O_2N\text{-}C_6H_4\text{-}OC_2H_5 \xrightarrow{HBr} p\text{-}O_2N\text{-}C_6H_4\text{-}Br + C_2H_5OH$$

Correct R. Br^- being a weak nucleophilic cannot displace a stronger nucleophile OC_2H_5.

326. (a): R is the correct explanation of A.

327. (b): Correct explanation. Nitrous acid gives the nitrosonium ion (NO^+) which attacks phenol at the less hindered *p*-position to form *p*-nitrosophenol which is a tautomer of *p*-benzoquinone monooxime.

$$HO\text{-}C_6H_4\text{-}N{=}O \rightleftharpoons O{=}C_6H_4{=}NOH$$

p-Nitrosophenol *p*-Benzoquinone monoxime

328. (a): R is the correct explanation of A.

329. (b): Correct explanation. Bromination occurs at the 2,4,6-positions with respect to the OH group with the expulsion of the SO_3H group.

330. (d): Correct assertion. Phenol forms 2,4,6-tribromophenol on treatment with Br_2 in water.
Correct reason. In H_2O, phenoxide ion is formed which highly activates it towards electrophilic substitution reaction.

331. (b): Correct explanation. In the presence of a strong base such as sodium methoxide, t-butylbromide undergoes dehydrohalogenation to form isobutylene.

332. (d): Correct A. $(CH_3)_3CCOONa$ and CH_3CH_2Br react to form $(CH_3)_3C–O–CH_2CH_3$.
Correct R. Good yields of ethers are obtained when primary alkyl halides are treated with alkoxides derived from any alcohol, 1°, 2° or 3°.

333. (a): R is the correct explanation of A.

334. (a): R is the correct explanation of A.

335. (a): R is the correct explanation of A.

336. (d): Correct A. The last traces of moisture in ethanol cannot be removed by storing it over sodium wire.
Correct R. Sodium reacts both with H_2O and ethanol.

337. (c): Correct R. Change in colour is due to the oxidation of alcohol to acetic acid by potassium dichromate in dil. H_2SO_4. The colour of $K_2Cr_2O_7$ changes from orange to green due to the formation of $Cr_2(SO_4)_3$.

338. (b): Correct explanation. Benzendiazonium chloride decomposes to form $C_6H_5^+$ which upon nucleophilic attack by H_2O followed by loss of a proton gives phenol.

Aldehydes, Ketones and Carboxylic Acids

12.1 Introduction

The organic compounds containing a carbon–oxygen double bond, >C=O, as the functional group are aldehydes, ketones, carboxylic acids and their derivatives. These are collectively called *carbonyl compounds.*

$H_2C{=}O$	$RCH{=}O$	$C_6H_5CH{=}O$	$C_6H_5CH_2CH{=}O$
Formaldehyde	Aldehyde	Benzaldehyde	Phenyl acetaldehyde

If the R and R′ groups are the same, the ketone is called a *simple* or a *symmetric ketone*; if the R and R′ groups are different, the ketone is called a *mixed* or an *unsymmetric ketone.*

$RR'C{=}O$	$(CH_3)_2C{=}O$	$C_2H_5(CH_3)C{=}O$	$C_6H_5(CH_3)C{=}O$
Ketone	Dimethyl ketone (Simple ketone)	Ethyl methyl ketone (Mixed ketone)	Methylphenyl ketone (Mixed)

In carboxylic acids, the carbonyl group is linked to a hydroxyl (–OH) group on one side.

$R{-}CO{-}OH$	$H{-}CO{-}OH$	$CH_3{-}CO{-}OH$	$C_6H_5{-}CO{-}OH$
Carboxylic acid	Formic acid	Acetic acid	Benzoic acid

In carboxylic acid derivatives, the –OH part of the –COOH group is replaced by –X (halogen atom), –OCOR′, –OR′ and $–NH_2$ groups to form acid halides, anhydrides, esters and amides respectively. These are called the *derivatives of carboxylic acids*.

$R{-}CO{-}OH$ (Carboxylic acid):

- $\xrightarrow{-OH,\ +X}$ $R{-}CO{-}X$ Acidic halide
- $\xrightarrow{-OH,\ +O{-}CO{-}R'}$ $R{-}CO{-}O{-}CO{-}R'$ Acidic anhydride
- $\xrightarrow{-OH,\ +OR'}$ $R{-}CO{-}OR'$ Ester
- $\xrightarrow{-OH,\ +NH_2}$ $R{-}CO{-}NH_2$ Acid amide

These acid derivatives contain the same acyl group, $(R{-}\overset{O}{\overset{\|}{C}}{-})$ in their molecules, hence, they are also called acyl derivatives.

12.1.1 Structure of the Carbonyl Group

The carbonyl carbon is sp^2 hybridised and forms three σ-bonds. The unhybridised *p* orbital of carbon overlaps with the *p* orbital of oxygen forming a π-bond.

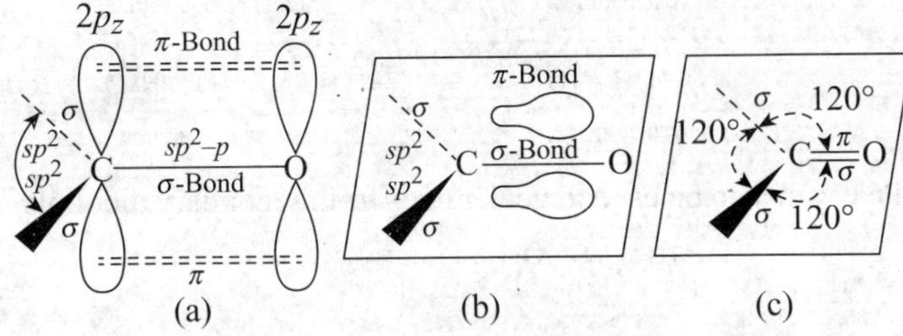

Fig. 12.1 Structure of the carbonyl group (a) orbital picture (b) π-bond lying above and below C–O σ-bond (c) planar nature

Due to the greater electronegativity of the oxygen compared to carbon, the carbon–oxygen bond is polar. It may be regarded as a resonance hybrid of the two structures (Fig. 12.2).

$$>C{=}O \longleftrightarrow >\overset{+}{C}{-}\overset{-}{O}$$

I II

Fig. 12.2 Resonance structures

Due to the polar nature of the bond, the carbon atom of the carbonyl group acts as an electrophile and the oxygen atom acts as a nucleophile. Further, being resonance hybrids, aldehydes and ketones have a much higher dipole moment (2.3–2.8 D) than the corresponding ethers (1.15–1.3 D).

Aliphatic aldehydes and ketones are the functional isomers of each other because they have the same molecular formulae but different functional groups. For example,

$CH_3{-}CH_3{-}CHO$	$CH_3{-}CO{-}CH_3$
Propanal	Propanone

12.2 Methods of Preparation of Aldehydes and Ketones

12.2.1 Oxidation of 1° and 2° Alcohols

$$\underset{\text{Primary alcohol}}{RCH_2OH} + [O] \xrightarrow{K_2Cr_2O_7/H_2SO_4} \underset{\text{Aldehyde}}{RCHO} + H_2O$$

$$\underset{\text{Ethanol (Ethyl alcohol)}}{CH_3CH_2OH} + [O] \xrightarrow{K_2Cr_2O_7/H_2SO_4} \underset{\text{Acetaldehyde}}{CH_3CHO} + H_2O$$

$$\underset{\text{Benzyl alcohol}}{C_6H_5CH_2OH} + [O] \xrightarrow{K_2Cr_2O_7/H_2SO_4} \underset{\text{Benzaldehyde}}{C_6H_5CHO}$$

Ketones can be prepared by the oxidation of secondary alcohols with similar oxidising agents.

$$\underset{\text{Isopropyl alcohol}}{(CH_3)_2CHOH} + [O] \xrightarrow{K_2Cr_2O_7/H_2SO_4} \underset{\text{Acetone}}{(CH_3)_2C{=}O} + H_2O$$

$$\underset{\text{sec-Butyl alcohol}}{(CH_3)(H_3CH_2C)CHOH} + [O] \xrightarrow{K_2Cr_2O_7/H_2SO_4} \underset{\text{Ethyl methyl ketone}}{(CH_3)(CH_3H_2C)C{=}O} + H_2O$$

$$\underset{\text{Cyclohexanol}}{C_6H_{11}OH} + [O] \xrightarrow{K_2Cr_2O_7/H_2SO_4} \underset{\text{Cyclohexanone}}{C_6H_{10}{=}O} + H_2O$$

PCC can also be used to get ketones from secondary alcohols

$$\text{Cyclohexenol (OH)} \xrightarrow[CH_2Cl_2]{\text{PCC in}} \text{Cyclohexenone (O)}$$

Ketones are not easily oxidised further and can, therefore, be obtained in high yield by this method.

- **Collin's reagent ($CrO_3.2C_5H_5N$) and pyridinium chlorochromate** (PCC, $CrO_3.C_5H_5N.$ HCl, that is, $C_5H_5NH^+CrO_3Cl^-$) in CH_2Cl_2 are better oxidising agents than $K_2Cr_2O_7/H_2SO_4$ or $KMnO_4/KOH$ for converting 1° alcohols to aldehydes since these reagents prevent the further oxidation of aldehydes to carboxylic acids.

$$\underset{1^\circ \text{ Alcohol}}{R{-}CH_2OH} \xrightarrow{PCC/CH_2Cl_2} \underset{\text{Aldehyde}}{R{-}CH{=}O}$$

$$\underset{2^\circ \text{ Alcohol}}{R_2CHOH} \xrightarrow{PCC/CH_2Cl_2} \underset{\text{Ketone}}{R_2C{=}O}$$

Another advantage of this reagent is that it does not attack the double bond present in alcohols. Thus,

$$\underset{\text{Allyl alcohol}}{H_2C{=}CHCH_2OH} \xrightarrow[CH_2Cl_2]{PCC} \underset{\text{Acrolein}}{CH_2{=}CH{-}CHO}$$

- **Oppenauer oxidation** of 2° alcohols (saturated or unsaturated) with aluminium *tert*-butoxide in the presence of excess of acetone gives ketones in good yields without the danger of being further oxidised to carboxylic acids.

12.2.2 Catalytic Dehydrogenation of 1° and 2° Alcohols

Catalytic dehydrogenation of 1° and 2° alcohols over heated copper at 573 K gives aldehydes and ketones respectively. It is carried out by passing the vapour of the alcohol over reduced copper. Primary alcohols give aldehydes while secondary alcohols give ketones.

$$\underset{1^\circ \text{ Alcohol}}{R{-}CH(H){-}O{-}H} \xrightarrow{Cu,\ 573\ K} \underset{\text{Aldehyde}}{R{-}CH{=}O} + H_2$$

Example,

$$\underset{\text{Ethyl alcohol}}{CH_3CH_2OH} \xrightarrow{Cu,\ 573\ K} \underset{\text{Acetaldehyde}}{CH_3CHO} + H_2$$

Similarily,

$$\underset{2^\circ \text{ Alcohol}}{R{-}CH(R'){-}O{-}H} \xrightarrow{Cu,\ 573\ K} \underset{\text{Ketone}}{R{-}C(R'){=}O} + H_2$$

Example,

$$\underset{\text{Propan-2-ol (Isopropyl alcohol)}}{CH_3{-}CH(OH){-}CH_3} \xrightarrow{Cu,\ 573\ K} \underset{\text{Propanone (Acetone)}}{CH_3{-}C(CH_3){=}O}$$

12.2.3 Dry Distillation of Calcium Salts of Fatty Acids

Dry distillation of calcium salts of fatty acids gives aldehydes or ketones. For example,

$$\underset{\text{Calcium acetate}}{(CH_3COO)_2Ca} + \underset{\text{Calcium formate}}{Ca(OOCH)_2} \xrightarrow{\text{Distil}} \underset{\text{Ethanal (Acetaldehyde)}}{2CH_3CHO} + 2CaCO_3$$

$$\underset{\text{Calcium propionate}}{(CH_3CH_2COO)_2Ca} \xrightarrow{\text{Distil}} \underset{\text{Pentan-2-one}}{(CH_3CH_2)_2CO} + CaCO_3$$

12.2.4 Hydration of Alkynes

Aldehydes and ketones can be prepared by the hydration of alkynes in the presence of dil. H_2SO_4 and $HgSO_4$ as catalyst. Water adds to alkynes to form unstable enol intermediates which rearrange to form aldehydes or ketones.

$$\underset{\text{Alkyne}}{R{-}C{\equiv}C{-}H} + H_2O \xrightarrow[HgSO_4]{\text{dil. }H_2SO_4} \underset{\text{enol (unstable)}}{R{-}C(OH){=}CH_2} \rightleftharpoons \underset{\text{Methyl ketone}}{R{-}C(=O){-}CH_3}$$

$$\underset{\text{Acetylene}}{HC{\equiv}CH} + H_2O \xrightarrow[HgSO_4]{\text{dil. }H_2SO_4} \underset{\text{Vinyl alcohol (Unstable intermediate)}}{H{-}C(H){=}C(OH){-}H} \xrightleftharpoons{\text{Tautomerises}} \underset{\text{Acetaldehyde}}{CH_3CHO}$$

Hydration of alkynes other than acetylene gives ketones.

$$CH_3(CH_2)_3C{\equiv}CH + H_2O \xrightarrow[HgSO_4]{H^+} \underset{\text{Hex-1-en-2-ol (Unstable)}}{CH_3(CH_2)_3C(OH){=}CH_2} \longrightarrow \underset{\text{Hexan-2-one}}{CH_3(CH_2)_3C(=O){-}CH_3}$$

Hex-1-yne

12.2.5 From Gem Dihalides

The gem dihalides, containing two halogen atoms on the same carbon atom on hydrolysis give the carbonyl group.

$$\underset{\text{1, 1-Dichloroethane (Ethylidene chloride)}}{CH_3CHCl_2} \xrightarrow[\text{or Ba (OH)}_2]{\text{aq. KOH}} \underset{\text{Unstable}}{CH_3CH(OH)_2} \longrightarrow \underset{\text{Ethanol (Acetaldehyde)}}{CH_3CHO}$$

$$\underset{\text{2, 2-Dichloropropane (Isopropylidene chloride)}}{CH_3{-}C(CH_3)(Cl){-}Cl} \xrightarrow[\text{or Ba(OH)}_2]{\text{aq. KOH}} \underset{\text{Unstable}}{CH_3{-}C(CH_3)(OH){-}OH} \longrightarrow \underset{\text{Propanone (Acetone)}}{CH_3{-}C(CH_3){=}O}$$

12.2.6 From Aromatic Hydrocarbons

(i) **By oxidation of methyl benzene:** Strong oxidising agents such as acidified or alkaline $KMnO_4$, acidified $K_2Cr_2O_7$, conc. HNO_3, and so on, oxidise toluene and its derivatives to benzoic acid through the oxidation of intermediate aldehydes.

$$\underset{\text{Toluene}}{C_6H_5CH_3} \xrightarrow[\text{Heat}]{\text{alk. KMnO}_4} \underset{\text{Benzaldehyde}}{C_6H_5CHO} \xrightarrow{[O]} \underset{\text{Benzoic acid}}{C_6H_5COOH}$$

- Aromatic aldehydes are prepared when the alkyl side chain in an aromatic ring is oxidised using chromium trioxide (CrO_3) and acetic anhydride. The aldehyde formed immediately gets acetylated with acetic anhydride forming the gem diacetate and this does not get further oxidised. Therefore, the function of acetic anhydride is to prevent further oxidation of the aldehyde to acid. The gem diacetate formed is isolated and hydrolysed with aqueous acid (dil. HCl or dil. H_2SO_4) to give the corresponding aromatic aldehyde. For example,

$$\underset{\text{Toluene}}{C_6H_5CH_3} \xrightarrow[\text{273–283 K}]{CrO_3,\ (CH_3CO)_2O} \underset{\text{Benzylidene diacetate (gem-diacetate)}}{C_6H_5CH(OCOCH_3)_2} \xrightarrow[\text{Hydrolysis}]{H_3O^+} \underset{\text{Benzaldehyde}}{C_6H_5CHO} + 2CH_3COOH$$

Similarly, *p*-nitrotoluene gives *p*-nitrobenzaldehyde (45% yield).

- **Use of chromyl chloride:** Alkyl benzenes can also be oxidised to benzaldehyde with a solution of chromyl chloride (CrO_2Cl_2) in CCl_4 or CS_2. A brown chromium complex is formed which is decomposed by water to give the corresponding benzaldehyde. This reaction is called the *Etard reaction.*

$$\underset{\text{Toluene}}{C_6H_5CH_3} \xrightarrow[CS_2]{CrO_2Cl_2} \underset{\text{Brown chromium complex}}{C_6H_5CH(OCrCl_2OH)_2} \xrightarrow[\text{Hydrolysis}]{H_3O^+} \underset{\text{Benzaldehyde}}{C_6H_5CHO}$$

In case the side chain contains a group higher than the $-CH_3$ group, the end carbon atom of the chain is oxidised by CrO_2Cl_2 to the $-CHO$ group.

$$\underset{\text{Ethyl benzene}}{C_6H_5CH_2CH_3} \xrightarrow[CCl_4]{CrO_2Cl_2} \underset{\text{Phenylethanal}}{C_6H_5CH_2CHO}$$

(ii) **By side chain chlorination followed by hydrolysis:** Side chain chlorination of toluene gives benzal chloride, which on hydrolysis gives benzaldehyde.

$$\underset{\text{Toluene}}{C_6H_5CH_3} \xrightarrow[-2HCl]{2Cl_2,\ h\nu,\ 383\ K} \underset{\text{Benzal chloride}}{C_6H_5CHCl_2} \xrightarrow[-2\ HCl]{H_2O,\ 373\ K} C_6H_5CH(OH)_2 \xrightarrow{-H_2O} \underset{\text{Benzaldehyde}}{C_6H_5CHO}$$

(iii) **By Gattermann Koch reaction:** Benzene or its derivatives are converted to benzaldehyde or substituted benzaldehyde by treatment with carbon monoxide and hydrogen chloride in the presence of anhydrous $AlCl_3$ or cuprous chloride (catalyst).

$$\underset{\text{Benzene}}{C_6H_6} + CO \xrightarrow[\text{anhyd. AlCl}_3/\text{Cu}_2\text{Cl}_2]{HCl} \underset{\text{Benzaldehyde}}{C_6H_5CHO}$$

(iv) **By Reimer–Tiemann reaction:** Phenolic aldehydes are obtained by treating the phenol with chloroform in aqueous sodium hydroxide solution at about 343 K. This reaction is called Reimer–Tiemann reaction.

$$\underset{\text{Phenol}}{C_6H_5OH} \xrightarrow[NaOH]{CHCl_3} o\text{-}NaOC_6H_4CHO \xrightarrow{H^+} \underset{\text{Salicylaldehyde}}{o\text{-}HOC_6H_4CHO}$$

12.3 Methods of Preparation of Ketones

(i) **From acyl chlorides:** Ketones can be prepared from acyl chlorides by treating with dialkyl cadmium. The dialkyl cadmium needed for this purpose is prepared by the reaction between a Grignard reagent and anhydrous cadmium chloride.

$$\underset{\text{Grignard reagent}}{2RMgX} + CdCl_2 \xrightarrow{\text{Dry ether}} \underset{\text{Dialkyl cadmium}}{R_2Cd} + 2MgXCl$$

$$2R'{-}C(=O){-}Cl + R_2Cd \xrightarrow{\text{Dry ether}} \underset{\text{Ketone}}{2R'{-}C(=O){-}R} + CdCl_2$$

$$\underset{\text{Grignard reagent}}{2CH_3CH_2MgBr} + \underset{\text{Cadmium chloride}}{CdCl_2} \xrightarrow{\text{Dry ether}} \underset{\text{Diethyl cadmium}}{(CH_3CH_2)_2Cd} + 2MgBrCl$$

$$2CH_3\overset{O}{\overset{\|}{C}}-Cl + (CH_3CH_2)_2Cd \xrightarrow[\text{ether}]{\text{Dry}} 2CH_3-\overset{O}{\overset{\|}{C}}-CH_2CH_3 + CdCl_2$$

Ethanoyl chloride (Acetyl chloride) — Diethyl cadmium — Butan-2-one

$$2\,C_6H_5COCl + (CH_3)_2Cd \xrightarrow{\text{Dry ether}} 2\,C_6H_5COCH_3 + CdCl_2$$

Benzoyl chloride — Acetophenone

(ii) From nitriles by Grignard reagent: Both aliphatic and aromatic ketones can be prepared by treating an alkyl or aryl nitrile with a suitable Grignard reagent followed by acid hydrolysis. For example:

$$\overset{\delta-}{CH_3CH_2}-\overset{\delta+}{MgBr} + CH_3-\overset{\delta+}{C}\equiv\overset{\delta-}{N} \xrightarrow{\text{Dry ether}} CH_3CH_2-\underset{CH_3}{\underset{|}{C}}=NMgBr$$

Ethyl magnesium bromide — Acetonitrile — Addition product

$$\xrightarrow[\text{Hydrolysis}]{H^+,\ H_2O} CH_3CH_2\overset{O}{\overset{\|}{C}}-CH_3 + NH_3 + Mg(OH)Br$$

Butan-2-one

1-Phenylpropanone can also be prepared by the action of ethyl magnesium bromide on benzonitrile followed by acid hydrolysis.

$$C_6H_5C\equiv N + CH_3CH_2MgBr \xrightarrow{\text{Dry ether}} C_6H_5-\overset{NMgBr}{\overset{\|}{C}}-CH_2CH_3$$

Benzonitrile — Addition product

$$\xrightarrow[\text{Hydrolysis}]{H_3O^+} C_6H_5-\overset{O}{\overset{\|}{C}}-CH_2CH_3$$

1-Phenylpropanone

(iii) From benzene or substituted benzene by Friedel–Crafts reaction: Aromatic ketones can be prepared by Friedel Crafts acylation or benzoylation by treating aromatic hydrocarbons with acid chlorides in the presence of a Lewis acid like anhydrous aluminium chloride.

$$C_6H_6 + CH_3COCl \xrightarrow{\text{Anhyd. AlCl}_3} C_6H_5COCH_3 + HCl$$

Benzene — Acetyl chloride — Acetophenone

$$C_6H_6 + C_6H_5COCl \xrightarrow{\text{Anhyd. AlCl}_3} C_6H_5COC_6H_5 + HCl$$

Benzene — Benzoyl chloride — Benzophenone

Benzophenone can also be prepared by Friedel Crafts reaction of carbonyl chloride (phosgene) with excess of benzene.

$$C_6H_6 + Cl-\overset{O}{\overset{\|}{C}}-Cl + C_6H_6 \longrightarrow C_6H_5-\overset{O}{\overset{\|}{C}}-C_6H_5$$

Benzene — Phosgene — Benzene — Benzophenone

(iv) From phenyl esters by Fries rearrangement: Phenolic esters or phenyl esters (phenyl acetate, phenyl benzoate) on heating with anhydrous $AlCl_3$ in the presence of CS_2 as solvent undergo a rearrangement in which the acyl (acetyl, benzoyl) group migrates from the phenolic oxygen atom to the *o*- and *p*-positions of the benzene ring to give a mixture of *o*-and *p*-phenolic ketones (or hydroxy ketones).

$$C_6H_5OCOCH_3 \xrightarrow[\Delta]{AlCl_3,\ CS_2} o\text{-}HOC_6H_4COCH_3 + p\text{-}HOC_6H_4COCH_3$$

Phenyl acetate — *o*-Hydroxyacetophenone — *p*-Hydroxyacetophenone

$$C_6H_5OCOC_6H_5 \xrightarrow[\Delta]{AlCl_3,\ CS_2} o\text{-}HOC_6H_4COC_6H_5 + p\text{-}HOC_6H_4COC_6H_5$$

Phenyl benzoate — *o*-Hydroxybenzophenone — *p*-Hydroxybenzophenone

12.4 Physical Properties of Aldehydes and Ketones

(i) Physical state: Formaldehyde is a pungent smelling gas. Other lower aldehydes are colourless liquids and possess an unpleasant odour. The lower ketones are colourless liquids and have a pleasant small. The higher members are colourless solids. Benzaldehyde is a colourless oily liquid and smells like bitter almonds while aromatic ketones are usually solids with a pleasant smell.

(ii) Boiling points: The boiling points of aldehydes and ketones are comparatively higher than those of hydrocarbons of similar molecular masses. This is because aldehydes and ketones contain a polar carbonyl group and therefore, they have appreciable intermolecular attraction (dipole–dipole interaction) between the opposite ends of the >C=O dipoles.

$$>\overset{\delta+}{C}=\overset{\delta-}{O}\text{-----}\overset{\delta+}{H}\quad \overset{\delta-}{O}\quad \overset{\delta+}{H}\text{-----}\overset{\delta-}{O}=C<$$

However, the boiling points of aldehydes and ketones are lower than those of the alcohols of comparable molecular masses due to the weaker intermolecular hydrogen bonding in the >C=O compounds.

Among the carbonyl compounds, ketones have slightly higher boiling points than the isomeric aldehydes. This is due to the presence of two electron repelling alkyl groups around the carbonyl carbon which makes them more polar.

$$CH_3CH_2(H)C=\ddot{O}: \qquad (CH_3)_2C=\ddot{O}:$$

Propanal ($\mu = 2.52$ D, BP = 322 K) — Propanone ($\mu = 2.88$ D, BP = 329 K)

(iii) Solubility: Lower members of the aldehyde and ketone series are soluble in water. This is due to the presence of H-bonding between the polar carbonyl group and the water molecules.

$$\overset{\delta+}{C}=\overset{\delta-}{O}\cdots\cdots\overset{\delta+}{C}=\overset{\delta-}{O}\cdots\cdots\overset{\delta+}{C}=\overset{\delta-}{O}\cdots\cdots$$

dipole-dipole interactions

However, the solubility decreases as the molecular mass increases. Similarly, the solubility of aromatic aldehydes and ketones in much lower than their corresponding aliphatic analogues because of the larger hydrocarbon part (benzene ring) present in their molecules. However, all aldehydes and ketones are freely soluble in organic solvents such as alcohols and ether.

12.5 Chemical Properties of Aldehydes and Ketones

The carbonyl carbon uses sp^2 hybrid orbitals to form three sigma bonds, one with the oxygen atom (of the CO group) and the other two with two other atoms or groups (H or R). All these three sigma bonds lie in one plane at an angle of 120°. The unhybridised $2p$ orbital of the carbonyl carbon forms a π-bond with the oxygen atom. Since both aldehydes and ketones have the carbonyl functional group, they undergo similar chemical reactions (Fig. 12.3).

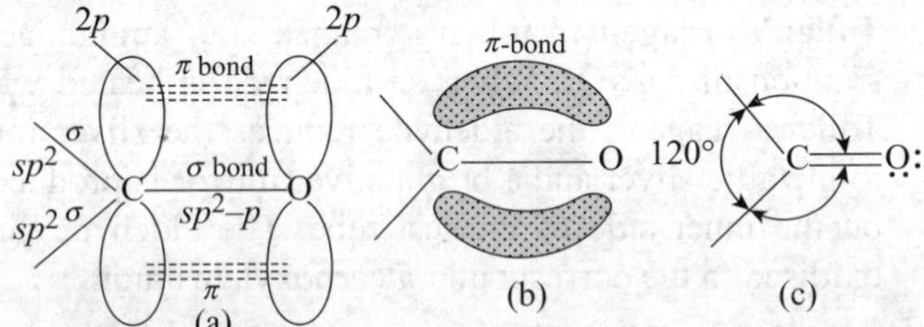

Fig. 12.3 Orbital picture of carbonyl group

12.5.1 Nucleophilic Addition Reactions

The carbonyl group is polarised due to the higher electronegativity of oxygen in comparison to carbon. The electrons between carbon and oxygen are more towards the oxygen atom.

$$>C=O \quad \text{or} \quad >\overset{\delta+}{C}\cdots\overset{\delta-}{O}$$

This gives rise to an intermediate having a negatively charged oxygen. The hybridisation of the carbonyl carbon changes from sp^2 to sp^3 and a tetrahedral alkoxide intermediate is formed. This intermediate then picks up a H^+ from the medium or another part of the reagent to give the electrically neutral addition product. The net result is the addition of the nucleophile and H^+ across the carbon–oxygen double bond (Fig. 12.4).

$$>C=O + Z^- \xrightarrow{\text{Slow}} >C(O^-)Z \xrightarrow[\text{Fast}]{H^+} >C(OH)Z$$

Aldehyde or ketone — Nucleophilic reagent — Intermediate — Addition product

Attack from the top face

Fig. 12.4 Nucleophilic attack on carbonyl carbon

If the attacking nucleophiles are weak (example, ammonia and its derivatives), the reaction of aldehydes and ketone are usually carried out in a weakly acidic medium. Such reactions are called acid catalysed nucleophilic substitutions.

$$>C=\ddot{O}: + \underset{\text{From acidic medium}}{H^+} \rightleftharpoons \left[>C=\ddot{O}H^+ \longleftrightarrow >\overset{+}{C}-\ddot{O}-H\right]$$

12.5.2 Relative Reactivity of Aldehydes and Ketones

(i) Inductive effect: A greater positive charge on the carbon atom indicates a higher reactivity. The electron releasing power of two alkyl groups in ketones is more than that of one in an aldehyde. As a result, the electron deficiency of the carbon atom (electrophilicity) in the carbonyl group is satisfied more in ketones than in aldehydes. Therefore, the reduced positive charge on the carbon in the case of ketones discourages the attack of nucleophiles. Hence, ketones are less reactive than aldehydes. Formaldehyde with no alkyl group is the most reactive of the aldehydes and ketones. Thus, the order of reactivity is:

$$\underset{\text{Formaldehyde}}{H_2C=O} > \underset{\text{Aldehyde}}{RHC=O} > \underset{\text{Ketone}}{R_2C=O}$$

(ii) Steric effect: In aldehydes, there is one alkyl group but in ketones, there are two alkyl groups attached to the carbonyl group. These cause hindrance to the attacking group. The more substituted alkyl groups on a ketone cause a larger hindrance.

Aromatic Aldehydes and Ketones

Benzaldehyde is less reactive than aliphatic aldehydes.

(I) ⟷ (II) ⟷ (III) ⟷ (IV) ⟷ (V)

Due to the electron releasing (+I) effect of the benzene ring, the magnitude of the positive charge on the carbonyl group decreases and consequently it becomes less susceptible to nucleophilic attack. Thus, aromatic aldehydes and ketones are less reactive than the corresponding aliphatic aldehydes and ketones. However, amongst aromatic aldehydes and ketones, aromatic aldehydes are more reactive than alkyl aryl ketones which in turn are more reactive than diaryl ketones. Thus, the order of reactivity of aromatic aldehydes and ketones is:

$$\underset{\text{Benzaldehyde}}{C_6H_5CHO} > \underset{\text{Acetophenone}}{C_6H_5COCH_3} > \underset{\text{Benzophenone}}{C_6H_5COC_6H_5}$$

12.5.3 Important Nucleophilic Addition Reactions

(i) **Addition of hydrogen cyanide:** Both aldehydes and ketones react with hydrogen cyanide to form addition products known as cyanohydrins.

$$\underset{\text{Aldehdye or ketone}}{>C{=}O} + HCN \longrightarrow \underset{\text{Cyanohydrin}}{>C(CN)(OH)}$$

Example,

$$\underset{\text{Acetone}}{CH_3{-}C(CH_3){=}O} + HCN \longrightarrow \underset{\text{Acetone cyanohydrin}}{CH_3{-}C(CH_3)(CN){-}OH}$$

$$\underset{\text{Benzaldehyde}}{C_6H_5\overset{O}{\overset{\|}{C}}H} + HCN \longrightarrow \underset{\text{Benzaldehyde cyanohydrin (Mandelonitrile)}}{C_6H_5\overset{OH}{\overset{|}{C}}HCN}$$

(ii) **Addition of sodium bisulphite:** Both aldehydes and ketones form crystalline addition compounds called bisulfite adducts when treated with a saturated solution of sodium bisulfite.

$$\underset{\text{Aldehdye or ketone}}{>\overset{\delta+}{C}{=}\overset{\delta-}{O}} + \underset{\text{Sodium bisulphate}}{Na\,HSO_3} \rightleftharpoons \underset{\text{Bisulphite addition product}}{>C(OH)(SO_3^-Na^+)}$$

$$\underset{\text{Aldehdye or ketone}}{(CH_3)(H)C{=}O} + NaHSO_3 \longrightarrow \underset{\text{Acetaldehyde sodium bisulphate}}{(CH_3)(H)C(OH)(SO_3Na)}$$

$$\underset{\text{Acetone}}{(CH_3)(H)C{=}O} + NaHSO_3 \longrightarrow \underset{\text{Acetone sodium bisulphate}}{(CH_3)(H)C(OH)(SO_3Na)}$$

(iii) **Reaction with Grignard reagents (RMgX):** Aldehydes and ketones react with Grignard reagents to form addition products. When the addition product is hydrolysed by water, it gives alcohols. Formaldehyde produces primary alcohols, other aldehydes give secondary alcohols, while ketones give tertiary alcohols.

$$>\overset{\delta+}{C}{=}\overset{\delta-}{O} + \overset{\delta-}{R}\overset{\delta+}{MgX} \longrightarrow >C(OMgX)(R) \xrightarrow[H_2O]{H^+} \underset{\text{Alcohol}}{>C(OH)(R)} \quad \text{(R from grignard reagent)}$$

$$\underset{\text{Formaldehyde}}{H_2C{=}O} + CH_3MgI \longrightarrow \underset{\text{Addition product}}{H_2C(OMgI)(CH_3)} \xrightarrow[H_2O]{H^+} \underset{\text{Ethyl alcohol (Primary)}}{H_2C(OH)(CH_3)} + Mg(OH)I$$

$$\underset{\text{Acetaldehyde}}{(CH_3)(H)C{=}O} \xrightarrow{CH_3MgI} \underset{\text{Addition product}}{(CH_3)(H)C(OMgI)(CH_3)} \xrightarrow[H_2O]{H^+} \underset{\text{Isopropyl alcohol (Secondary)}}{(CH_3)(H)C(OH)(CH_3)}$$

$$\underset{\text{Acetone}}{(CH_3)_2C{=}O} \xrightarrow{CH_3MgI} \underset{\text{Addition product}}{(CH_3)_2C(OMgI)(CH_3)} \xrightarrow[H_2O]{H^+} \underset{\text{Tert-butyl alcohol (Tertiary)}}{(CH_3)_2C(OH)(CH_3)}$$

12.5.4 Oxidation Reactions

Aldehydes can be easily oxidised to carboxylic acids on treatment with common oxidising agents such as nitric acid, $KMnO_4$, $K_2Cr_2O_7$, and so on.

$$\underset{\text{Aldehyde}}{RCHO} \xrightarrow{O} \underset{\text{Carbonylic acid}}{RCOOH}$$

Example, $$CH_3{-}C(=O){-}H \xrightarrow{O} \underset{\text{Ethanoic acid}}{CH_3{-}C(=O){-}OH}$$

Ketones are not easily oxidised. However, under drastic conditions, that is, with powerful oxidising agents such as conc. HNO_3, $KMnO_4/H_2SO_4$ or $K_2Cr_2SO_7/H_2SO_4$, at elevated temperatures, ketones undergo a cleavage of the carbon–carbon bond giving a mixture of carboxylic acids.

$$\underset{\text{Acetone}}{CH_3{-}\overset{O}{\overset{\|}{C}}{-}CH_3} \xrightarrow[\text{Conc. }HNO_3]{O} \underset{\text{Formic acid}}{HCOOH} + \underset{\text{Acetic acid}}{CH_3COOH}$$

In the case of unsymmetrical ketones, the cleavage occurs in such a way that the keto group stays preferentially with the smaller alkyl group.

(i) **Tollen's reagent:** Tollen's reagent is ammoniacal solution of $AgNO_3$. When an aldehyde is heated with Tollen's reagent, the aldehyde reduces the silver ions to metallic silver and a bright silver mirror is produced on the inner side of the test tube. The aldehyde gets oxidised to the corresponding carboxylate anion.

$$2AgNO_3 + 2NH_4OH \rightarrow \underset{\text{Grey ppt.}}{AgO_2} + 2NH_4NO_3 + H_2O$$

$$Ag_2O + 4NH_4OH \rightarrow \underset{\text{Tollen's reagent}}{2[Ag(NH_3)_2]^+OH^-} + 3H_2O$$

$$RCHO + \underset{\text{Tollen's reagent}}{2[Ag(NH_3)_2]^+} + 3OH^- \rightarrow RCOO^- + \underset{\text{Silver mirror}}{2Ag} + 2H_2O + 4NH_3$$

This reaction is also known as the *silver mirror test*. The silver mirror formed indicates the presence of an aldehydic group in the molecule.

(ii) **Fehling's solution:** Fehling's solution A (an aqueous solution of copper sulfate) and Fehling's solution B (an alkaline solution of sodium potassium tartarate) are mixed in equal amounts before the test. When an aldehyde is heated with Fehling's solution, a reddish-brown precipitate of cuprous oxide (Cu_2O) is formed. Aldehydes are oxidised to the corresponding carboxylate anion.

$$\underset{\text{Aldehyde}}{R{-}\overset{O}{\overset{\|}{C}}{-}H} + \underset{\text{Fehling solution}}{2Cu^{2+}} + 5OH^- \longrightarrow RCOO^- + \underset{\text{Red-brown ppt.}}{Cu_2O} + 3H_2O$$

(iii) Benedict's solution: This is an alkaline solution of cupric ion Cu(II) complexed with citrate ions. It reacts in the same way as the Fehling's solution.

(iv) Oxidation with sodium hypohalite (haloform reaction): Methyl ketones (CH_3CO–) and acetaldehyde are easily oxidised by excess of halogen in the presence of alkali (Cl_2, Br_2, I_2 in the presence of dil NaOH) or sodium hypohalite (NaOH) to give haloform (chloroform, bromoform or iodoform). For example,

$$\underset{\text{Actaldehyde}}{CH_3CHO} + 3I_2 \xrightarrow[\text{Iodination}]{\text{NaOH}} \underset{\text{Triiodoacetaldehyde}}{CI_3CHO} + 3HI$$

$$CI_3CHO + NaOH \longrightarrow \underset{\substack{\text{Iodoform}\\\text{(yellow ppt.)}}}{CHI_3} + HCOONa$$

$$\text{or } CH_3CHO + 3NaOI \rightarrow CH_3COONa + \underset{\text{(yellow ppt.)}}{CHI_3} + 2NaOH$$

12.5.5 Reduction to Alcohols

(i) Aldehydes on reduction give primary alcohols while ketones give secondary alcohols.

$$>C=O \xrightarrow[\text{LiAlH}_4,\ \text{NaBH}_4]{\text{H}_2\text{/Ni, Pt or Pd}} >CHOH$$

$$\underset{\text{Acetone}}{CH_3COCH_3} \xrightarrow{\text{LiAlH}_4} \underset{\substack{\text{Propan-2-ol}\\\text{(Isopropyl alcohol)}}}{CH_3CH(OH)CH_3}$$

$$\underset{\text{Benzaldehyde}}{C_6H_5CHO} \xrightarrow{\text{LiAlH}_4} \underset{\text{Benzyl alcohol}}{C_6H_5CH_2OH}$$

$$\underset{\text{Dicyclohexyl ketone}}{(C_6H_{11})_2C=O} \xrightarrow[\text{H}_3\text{O}^+]{\text{NaBH}_4} \underset{\text{Dicyclohexyl methanol}}{(C_6H_{11})_2CH-OH}$$

12.5.6 Reduction to Hydrocarbons

(i) **Reduction with zinc amalgam and conc. HCl:** This is called Clemmensen reduction.

$$\underset{\text{Aldehyde}}{RCHO} + 4[H] \xrightarrow[\text{HCl}]{\text{Zn/Hg}} \underset{\text{Alkane}}{R-CH_3} + H_2O$$

$$\underset{\text{Acetone}}{CH_3COCH_3} + 4[H] \xrightarrow[\text{HCl}]{\text{Zn/Hg}} \underset{\text{Pr opane}}{CH_3CH_2CH_3} + H_2O$$

$$\underset{\text{Acetophenone}}{C_6H_5COCH_3} + 4[H] \xrightarrow[\text{HCl}]{\text{Zn/Hg}} \underset{\text{Ethyl benzene}}{C_6H_5CH_2CH_3} + H_2O$$

(ii) **Reduction with HI in the presence of red phosphorus:**

$$RCHO + 4HI \xrightarrow[\text{423 K}]{\text{red P}} \underset{\text{Alkane}}{RCH_3} + H_2O + 2I_2$$

$$CH_3CHO + 4HI \xrightarrow[\text{423 K}]{\text{red P}} \underset{\text{Ethane}}{CH_3CH_3} + H_2O + 2I_2$$

$$CH_3COCH_3 + 4HI \xrightarrow[\text{423 K}]{\text{red P}} \underset{\text{Propane}}{CH_3CH_3} + H_2O + 2I_2$$

12.5.7 Miscellaneous Reactions

(i) **Aldol condensation:** Aldehydes and ketones containing at least one α-hydrogen (H atoms attached to the C atom adjacent to the carbonyl group) undergo self-condensation in the presence of dilute alkali to form a β-hydroxy aldehyde (aldol) or a β-hydroxy ketone (ketol) respectively. This reaction is called *aldol condensation*.

$$\underset{\substack{\text{2 molecules of}\\\text{acetaldehyde}}}{CH_3-CHO + H-CH_2-CHO} \xrightarrow{OH^-} \underset{\substack{\text{(Aldol)}\\\text{3-Hydroxybutanal}\\(\beta\text{-Hydroxy butyraldehyde})}}{CH_3-CH(OH)-CH_2-CHO}$$

The products of aldol condensation on heating with dilute acids undergo dehydration to form α,β-unsaturated aldehydes or ketones.

$$\underset{\text{Aldol}}{CH_3-CH(OH)-CH_2-CHO} \xrightarrow[-H_2O]{H^+,\ \text{Heat}} \underset{\text{But-2-enal (Crotonaldehyde)}}{CH_3-CH=CH-CHO}$$

Cross aldol condensation: The condensation of two different carbonyl compounds in the presence of a base is called cross aldol condensation or *mixed condensation*. Methanal (formaldehyde) and benzaldehyde have been successfully used with other aldehydes and ketones containing α-hydrogen.

$$\underset{\substack{\text{Formaldehyde}\\(\text{no }\alpha\text{-hydrogen})}}{HCHO} + \underset{\text{Acetaldehyde}}{CH_3CHO} \xrightarrow{\text{dil NaOH}} \underset{\substack{\text{3-Hydropropanal}\\(\beta\text{-Hydroxy propionaldehyde})}}{HO-CH_2-CH_2-CHO}$$

$$\underset{\substack{\text{Formaldehyde}\\(\text{no }\alpha\text{-hydrogen})}}{HCHO} + \underset{\text{Acetone}}{CH_3COCH_3} \xrightarrow{\text{dil NaOH}} \underset{\text{4-Hydroxybutan-2-one}}{HO-CH_2-CH_2-COCH_3}$$

$$\underset{\substack{\text{Benzaldehyde}\\(\text{no }\alpha\text{-hydrogen})}}{C_6H_5CHO} + \underset{\text{Acetaldehyde}}{CH_3CHO} \xrightarrow[\text{273 K}]{\text{dil NaOH}} \underset{\text{Aldol}}{C_6H_5CH(OH)CH_2CHO}$$

$$\xrightarrow[H_2O]{H^+,\ \text{Heat}} \underset{\substack{\text{3-Phenylprop-2-enal}\\\text{(Cinnamaldehyde)}}}{C_6H_5CH=CHCHO}$$

(ii) **Claisen condensation**

$$\underset{\substack{\text{Benzaldehyde}\\(\text{No }\alpha\text{-hydrogen})}}{C_6H_5CHO} + \underset{\text{Acetone}}{H-CH_2-CO-CH_3} \xrightarrow{OH^-} C_6H_5CH(OH)-CH_2-CO-CH_3$$

$$\xrightarrow[-H_2O]{H^+,\ \text{Heat}} \underset{\substack{\text{4-Phenylbut-3-en-2-one}\\\text{(Benzal acetone)}}}{C_6H_5-CH=CH-CO-CH_3}$$

Aliphatic esters containing α-hydrogen atoms also undergo Claisen–Schmidt condensation.

$$\underset{\text{Benzaldehyde}}{C_6H_5CO-H} + \underset{\text{Ethyl acetate}}{CH_3-CO-OC_2H_5} \xrightarrow{\text{dil NaOH}} C_6H_5CH(OH)-CH_2-CO-OC_2H_5$$

$$\xrightarrow[-H_2O]{H^+,\ \text{Heat}} \underset{\text{Ethyl cinnamate}}{C_6H_5CH=CHCO-OC_2H_5}$$

(iii) Cannizzaro's reaction: Aldehydes which do not contain any α-hydrogen atom such as formaldehyde (HCHO) and benzaldehyde (C_6H_5CHO) undergo self-oxidation and reduction reaction on treatment with a concentrated alkali. A mixture of an alcohol and a salt of the carboxylic acid is formed.

$$HCHO + HCHO \xrightarrow{\text{KOH (conc.)}} \underset{\text{Methyl alcohol}}{CH_3OH} + \underset{\text{Potassium formate}}{HCOO^-K^+}$$

$$C_6H_5CHO + C_6H_5CHO \xrightarrow{\text{NaOH (conc.)}} \underset{\text{Benzyl alcohol}}{C_6H_5CH_2OH} + \underset{\text{Sodium benzoate}}{C_6H_5COO^-Na^+}$$

$$\underset{\text{Two molecule of 2, 2-Dimethylpropanal}}{CH_3-C(CH_3)_2-CHO + CH_3-C(CH_3)_2-CHO} \xrightarrow[\text{Heat}]{\text{NaOH(conc.)}} \underset{\text{2, 2-Dimethyl propanal}}{CH_3-C(CH_3)_2-CH_2OH} + \underset{\text{Sodium 2, 2-dimethyl propanoate}}{CH_3-C(CH_3)_2-COO^-Na^+}$$

Cross Cannizzaro reaction: Cross Cannizzaro reaction can also take place between two different aldehydes which do not have α-hydrogen atoms.

$$\underset{\substack{p\text{-Methoxy benzaldehyde} \\ (p\text{-Anisaldehyde})}}{CH_3O-C_6H_4-CHO} + HCHO + \underset{(50\%)}{NaOH} \longrightarrow \underset{p\text{-Methoxybenzyl alcohol}}{CH_3O-C_6H_4-CH_2OH} + \underset{\text{Sodium formate}}{HCOONa}$$

(iv) Reaction with aluminium ethoxide (Tischenko reaction): All aldehydes (with or without α-hydrogen) can be made to undergo Cannizzaro reaction on treatment with aluminium ethoxide. However, under these conditions, the alcohol and the acid produced combine together to form an ester.

$$\underset{\text{Acetaldehyde}}{2CH_3CHO} \xrightarrow{Al(OC_2H_5)_3} CH_3COOH + C_2H_5OH \xrightarrow{-H_2O} \underset{\substack{\text{Ethyl acetate} \\ \text{(Ester)}}}{CH_3COOCH_2CH_3}$$

$$\underset{\text{Propionaldehyde}}{2CH_3CH_2CHO} \xrightarrow{Al(OC_2H_5)_3} CH_3CH_2COOH + CH_3CH_2CH_2OH \xrightarrow{-H_2O} \underset{n\text{-Propyl propionate}}{CH_3CH_2COOCH_2CH_2CH_3}$$

(v) Halogenation: The hydrogens are successively replaced by halogen atoms. For example, when Cl_2 is bubbled through acetaldehyde, chloral is obtained.

$$CH_3CHO + 3Cl_2 \rightarrow \underset{\text{Chloral (trichloroethanal)}}{CCl_3CHO} + 3HCl$$

Similarly, when Cl_2 is bubbled through warm acetone, a mixture of chloro-propanes is obtained.

$$CH_3COCH_3 \xrightarrow{Cl_2} CH_3COCH_2Cl + CH_3COCHCl_2...$$

(vi) Action with Schiff's reagent: When aldehydes are treated with a decolourised solution of Schiff's reagent, its pink colour is restored. This reaction is known as Schiff's test and is used as a test for aldehydes because ketones do not give this test.

$$\text{Aldehyde} + \underset{\text{(Colourless)}}{\text{Schiff's reagent}} \rightarrow \text{Pink colour}$$

12.6 Introduction to Carboxylic Acids

Aliphatic or aromatic carboxylic acids are classified as monocarboxylic acids, dicarboxylic acids, tricarboxylic acids, and so on, depending on the number of –COOH groups present in the molecule. Since the –COOH group has one replaceable hydrogen atom, its basicity is one and the acid having one carboxylic group is thus, a monobasic acid. Similarly, acids containing two or three carboxylic groups in their molecules are designated as dibasic and tribasic acids, respectively.

12.7 Methods of Preparation of Carboxylic Acids

Some of the general methods for the preparation of carboxylic acids are described below.

(i) Oxidation of primary alcohols: Primary alcohols are readily oxidised to carboxylic acids with oxidising agents such as potassium permanganate ($KMnO_4$), potassium dichromate ($K_2Cr_2O_7$) in neutral, acidic or alkaline media and chromium trioxide (CrO_3) in acidic media. The oxidation with $K_2Cr_2O_7$ or CrO_3 in acidic media generally gives some amount of esters as well. Therefore, oxidation with $KMnO_4$ in neutral or alkaline medium is preferred for the preparation of carboxylic acids. The acid is first obtained as its potassium salt, which on treatment with mineral acids gives the carboxylic acid.

$$\underset{\text{Primary alcohol}}{RCH_2OH} \xrightarrow{\text{alk. } KMnO_4} \underset{\text{Potassium carbonyl}}{RCOO^-K^+} \xrightarrow{H_2O} \underset{\text{Carboxylic acid}}{RCOOH}$$

Or, simply as,

$$\underset{\text{Primary alcohol}}{RCH_2OH} \xrightarrow[KMnO_4]{O} \underset{\text{Aldehyde}}{RCHO} \xrightarrow{O} \underset{\text{Carboxylic acid}}{RCOOH}$$

Example, $\underset{\substack{\text{Ethanol} \\ \text{(Ethyl alcohol)}}}{CH_3CH_2OH} \xrightarrow[\text{(ii) } H_3O]{\text{(i) alk. } KMnO_4} \underset{\substack{\text{Ethanoic acid} \\ \text{(Acetic acid)}}}{CH_3COOH}$

$$\underset{\text{Butan-1-ol}}{CH_3CH_2CH_2CH_2OH} \xrightarrow[\text{(ii) } H_3O]{\text{(i) alk. } KMnO_4} \underset{\text{Butanoic acid}}{CH_3CH_2CH_2COOH}$$

(ii) Oxidation of aldehydes and ketones: Aldehydes are easily oxidised to carboxylic acids even with mild oxidising agents like Tollen's reagent.

$$RCHO \xrightarrow[\text{Tollen's reagent}]{O} RCOOH$$

For example, $CH_3CHO \xrightarrow[\text{Tollen's reagent}]{O} \underset{\text{Acetic acid}}{CH_3COOH}$

(iii) Hydrolysis of nitriles (or cyanides) and amides: The nitriles are hydrolysed in dilute aqueous acidic or alkaline medium. The alkyl nitriles are first hydrolysed to amides in the presence of acid or alkali and then to acids.

$$\text{R–CN} + 2H_2O \xrightarrow[\text{Heat}]{H^+ \text{ or } OH^-} \underset{\text{Amide}}{RCONH_2} \xrightarrow[\text{Heat}]{H^+ \text{ or } OH^-} RCOOH + NH_3$$

$$\text{or R–CN} + 2H_2O \xrightarrow{H^+ \text{ or } OH^-} \text{R–COOH} + NH_3$$

$$\underset{\text{Acid amide}}{RCONH_2} \xrightarrow[\text{Heat}]{H_2O} \underset{\text{Carboxylic acid}}{RCOOH} + NH_3$$

Example, $\underset{\text{Ethane nitrile}}{CH_3\text{–}C{\equiv}N} + 2H_2O \xrightarrow[\text{Heat}]{H^+ \text{ or } OH^-} \underset{\text{Ethanamide}}{CH_3\text{–}\overset{O}{\overset{\|}{C}}\text{–}NH_2} \xrightarrow[\text{Heat}]{H^+ \text{ or } OH^-} \underset{\text{Acetic acid}}{CH_3\text{–}COOH} + NH_3$

(iv) Grignard reagents: It first forms the salt of a carboxylic acid which in turn gets decomposed with mineral acids to the corresponding carboxylic acid. For example,

$$\underset{\text{Carbon dioxide}}{O{=}C{=}O} + \underset{\text{Methyl mag. bromide}}{CH_3MgBr} \xrightarrow{\text{Dry ether}} \underset{\text{Addition product}}{CH_3\text{–}\overset{O}{\overset{\|}{C}}\text{–}OMgBr} \xrightarrow{H^+, H_2O} \underset{\text{Ethanoic acid}}{CH_3\text{–}\overset{O}{\overset{\|}{C}}\text{–}OH} + Mg(OH)Br$$

$$\underset{\text{Acid chloride}}{RCOCl} \xrightarrow{H_2O} \underset{\text{Carboxylic acid}}{RCOOH} + HCl$$

Example, $RCOCl \xrightarrow{H_2O, OH} RCOO^- \xrightarrow{H_3O^+} RCOOH$

$$\underset{\text{Benzoyl chloride}}{C_6H_5COCl} \xrightarrow{H_2O} \underset{\text{Benzoic acid}}{C_6H_5COOH} + HCl$$

(v) Hydrolysis of esters: Acidic hydrolysis of esters directly gives carboxylic acids while basic hydrolysis gives carboxylates, which on acidification give the corresponding carboxylic acids. For example,

$$RCOOR' + H_2O \xrightarrow{H^+ \text{ or } OH} \underset{\text{Carboxylic acid}}{RCOOH} + \underset{\text{Alcohol}}{R'OH}$$

$$\underset{\text{Ethyl ethanoate}}{CH_3COOC_2H_5} + H_2O \xrightarrow{H^+ \text{ or } OH} \underset{\text{Ethanoic acid}}{CH_3COOH} + \underset{\text{Ethanol}}{C_2H_5OH}$$

(vi) Carboxylation of alkanes: This reaction is called Koch reaction.

$$CH_2{=}CH_2 + CO + H_2O \xrightarrow[\text{Under pressure}]{H_3PO_4,\ 573\text{–}673\ K} \underset{\text{Propanoic acid}}{CH_3CH_2COOH}$$

$$\underset{\text{Propene}}{CH_3CH{=}CH_2} + CO + H_2O \xrightarrow[\text{Under pressure}]{H_3PO_4,\ 573\text{-}673\ K} \underset{\substack{\text{2-Methylpropanoic acid} \\ \text{(Isobutyric acid)}}}{CH_3\text{–}\underset{CH_3}{\underset{|}{C}H}\text{–}COOH}$$

(vii) Trihalogen derivatives of hydrocarbons: Carboxylic acids can be prepared by the hydrolysis of 1,1,1-trihalogen derivatives of alkanes (trihalides) with aqueous KOH. For example,

$$\underset{\substack{\text{Trichloromethane} \\ \text{(Chloroform)}}}{CHCl_3} + 3KOH \xrightarrow{-3\,KCl} \underset{\text{Unstable}}{CH(OH)_3} \longrightarrow \underset{\substack{\text{Methanoic acid} \\ \text{(Formic acid)}}}{HCOOH} + H_2O$$

$$\underset{\text{1,1,1-Trichloroethane}}{CH_3CCl_3} + 3KOH \xrightarrow{-3\,KCl} \underset{\text{Unstable}}{CH_3C(OH)_3} \longrightarrow \underset{\substack{\text{Ethanoic acid} \\ \text{(Acetic acid)}}}{H_3CCOOH} + H_2O$$

(viii) Oxidation of alkenes: Alkenes can also be cleaved by oxidising agents such as hot acidic $KMnO_4$ or $K_2Cr_2O_7$ solution. For example, substituted alkenes give only acids.

$$\underset{(cis \text{ or } trans)}{RCH{=}CHR} \xrightarrow[\text{(ii) dil } H_2SO_4]{\text{(i) } KMnO_4, OH^-, \text{Heat}} 2RCOO^-K^+ \xrightarrow{H^+} \underset{\text{Carboxylic acid}}{2RCOOH}$$

$$\underset{\text{Pent-2-ene}}{CH_3CH_2CH{=}CHCH_3} \xrightarrow[\text{(ii) dil } H_2SO_4]{\text{(i) } KMnO_4, OH^-, \text{Heat}} \underset{\text{Propanoic acid}}{CH_3CH_2COOH} + \underset{\text{Ethanoic acid}}{CH_3COOH}$$

12.8 Physical Properties of Carboxylic Acids

(i) Physical state: The first three aliphatic acids are colourless pungent smelling liquids. The next six members (C_4–C_9) are oily liquids with an odour of rancid butter. Thereafter, the higher members are colourless, odourless waxy solids. Benzoic acid and most of the other aromatic acids are colourless crystalline solids.

(ii) Solubility: The solubility decreases gradually with the rise in molecular mass. However, all are soluble in alcohol and ether. Benzoic acid is sparingly soluble in cold water but is soluble in hot water, alcohol and ether. The solubility of the lower members is due to H-bonding in which the carboxylic oxygen forms H-bonds with the H atoms of water and the hydroxylic hydrogen forms H-bonds with the oxygen atom of water as shown.

$$\cdots \overset{\delta-}{\underset{H}{\underset{|}{H\text{–}O}}} \cdots \overset{\delta+}{H}\text{–}O\text{–}\underset{R}{\underset{|}{C}}{=}\overset{\delta-}{O} \cdots \overset{\delta+}{H}\text{–}\overset{\delta-}{\underset{H}{\underset{|}{O}}} \cdots \overset{\delta+}{H}\text{–}O\text{–}\underset{R}{\underset{|}{C}}{=}\overset{\delta-}{O} \cdots$$

(iii) Boiling points: Boiling points of carboxylic acids increase regularly with an increase in molecular mass. Boiling points of carboxylic acids are higher than those of alcohols of the same molecular mass. This is due to intermolecular hydrogen bonding between two acid molecules.

Hydrogen bonding

$$CH_3\text{–}C\overset{O \cdots H\text{–}O}{\underset{O\text{–}H \cdots O}{\langle\ \ \rangle}}C\text{–}CH_3$$

Hydrogen bonding (Acetic acid dimer)

Due to the dimeric structure, the effective molecular mass of the acid becomes double the actual mass. Moreover the $\overset{\delta-}{O}\text{–}\overset{\delta+}{H}$ bond in carboxylic acids is more strongly polarised than the O–H bond in alcohols due to the adjacent electron withdrawing effect of the carbonyl group (>C=O) on the O–H bond. Therefore, carboxylic acids from stronger H-bonds.

(iv) Melting points: Carboxylic acids with an even number of carbon atoms, have the –COOH group and the terminal $-CH_3$ groups on the opposite sides of the zig–zag carbon chain. Hence, they fit closely (better) in the crystal lattice and this results in stronger intermolecular forces of attraction to cause the higher melting point. On the other hand, acids with an odd number of carbon atoms have the –COOH and the terminal $-CH_3$ groups on the same side of the zig–zag carbon chain. Therefore, they fit poorly in the crystal lattice and hence, have lower melting points.

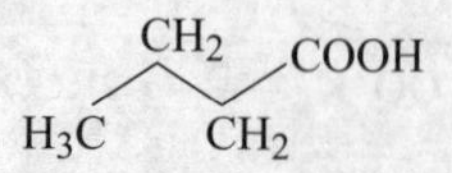

H_3C–CH_2–CH_2–CH_2–COOH (zig-zag)

Contains even no. of C-atoms fits closely, has higher MP (Terminal groups are on opposite side)

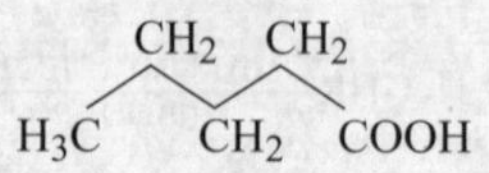

H_3C–CH_2–CH_2–CH_2–CH_2–COOH (zig-zag)

Contains odd no. of C-atoms fits poorly, has lower MP (Terminal groups are on the same side)

The melting points and boiling points of aromatic acids are usually higher than those of aliphatic acids of comparable molecular masses.

12.9 Structure of the Carboxylic Group

The two sp^2-hybridised orbitals of the carboxylic carbon atom overlap with one sp^2-hybridised orbital of each oxygen atom while the third sp^2-hybridised orbital of the carbon atom overlaps with an sp^3-hybridised orbital of the carbon atom of the alkyl group to form three σ-bonds. All the bonds to the carboxylic carbon atom lie on one plane and are separated by about 120º from each other. The molecule of carboxylic acid can be represented as a resonance hybrid of the given structure:

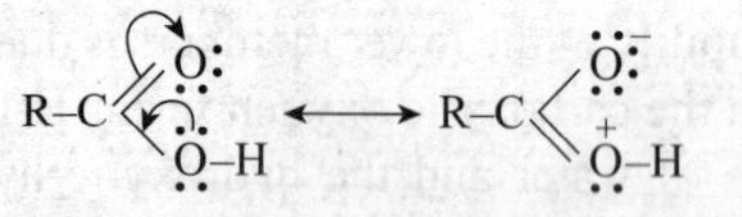

$$R-C(=\ddot{O}:)-\ddot{O}-H \;(I) \longleftrightarrow R-C(-\ddot{O}:^-)=\overset{+}{O}-H \;(II)$$

The displacement of electrons causes the release of a proton and a carboxylate ion, $RCOO^-$ is formed.

$$R-COOH \rightleftharpoons \underset{\text{Carboxylate ion}}{RCOO^-} + H^+$$

The carboxylate ion thus formed is also a resonance hybrid of structures III and IV.

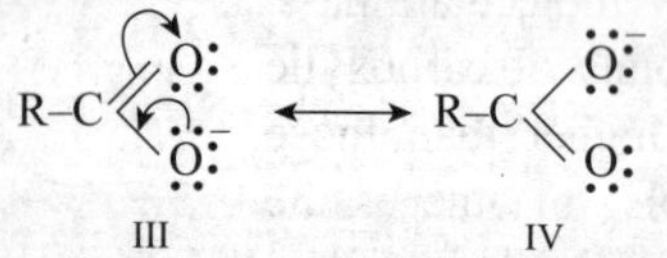

$$R-C(=\ddot{O}:)-\ddot{O}:^- \;(III) \longleftrightarrow R-C(-\ddot{O}:^-)=\ddot{O}: \;(IV)$$

12.10 Acidity of Carboxylic Acids

The strength of an acid depends on the ability of the acid to lose a proton when dissolved in water. It is expressed in terms of the dissociation constant (K_a).

$$R-\overset{O}{\overset{\|}{C}}-OH + H_2O \rightleftharpoons R-\overset{O}{\overset{\|}{C}}-\bar{O} + H_3O^+$$

$$K_a = \frac{[RCOO^-][H_3O^+]}{[RCOOH]}$$

The dissociation constant is generally called acidity constant because it measures the relative strength of an acid. The stronger the acid, the larger will be its K_a value. Carboxylic acids are by far the most acidic amongst all other organic compounds.

12.10.1 Cause of Acidic Nature of Carboxylic Acids

The carboxylic acid molecule is a resonance hybrid of the following two structures. Due to electron deficiency on the oxygen atom of the hydroxyl group (structure II) it carries a positive charge. Thus, there is a displacement of the electron pair of the O–H bond towards the oxygen atom. As a result, the O–H bond weakens and ultimately breaks to release the hydrogen as a proton. This is responsible for the acidic nature of the carboxyl group.

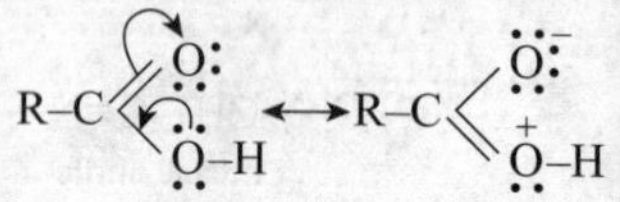

$$R-C(=\ddot{O}:)-\ddot{O}-H \;(I) \longleftrightarrow R-C(-\ddot{O}:^-)=\overset{+}{O}-H \;(II)$$

$$R-C(-\ddot{O}:^-)=\overset{+}{O}-H \longleftrightarrow R-C(-\ddot{O}:^-)=\ddot{O} + H^+$$

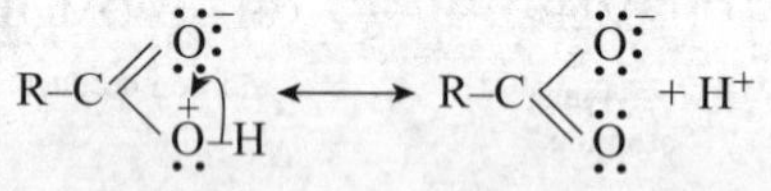

The resulting carboxylate ion is also stabilised by resonance as the resonance energy of the carboxylate ion is much higher than that of undissociated acid.

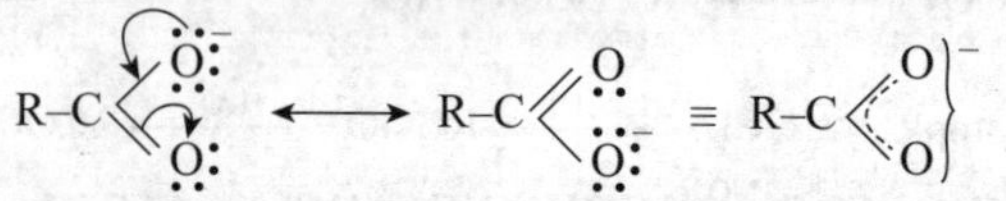

$$R-C(=\ddot{O}:)-\ddot{O}:^- \longleftrightarrow R-C(=O)-\ddot{O}:^- \equiv R-C\left\{\begin{matrix}O\\O\end{matrix}\right\}^-$$

Resonance forms of carboxylate ion | Resonance hybrid

12.11 Comparison of Acidic Character of Carboxylic Acids with Alcohols and Phenols

Carboxylic acids and alcohols: The alkoxide anion from an alcohol does not show resonance and is not stabilised since the alkyl group has an electron repelling inductive effect which is responsible for the very weak acidity of alcohols compared to carboxylic acids.

$$\underset{\text{Alcohol}}{R-OH} \rightleftharpoons \underset{\text{No resonance hybrid}}{R-O^-} + H^+$$

Both the carboxylic acid and the carboxylate ions are resonance stabilised. The carboxylic acids have a tendency to give up the H^+ ions forming the more stable carboxylate ion. However, neither the alcohols (R–OH) nor their alkoxide ions ($R-O^-$) are stabilised by resonance.

Carboxylic acids and phenols: Carboxylic acids are stronger acids than phenols. The difference in their relative acidic strengths can be explained by considering the resonating structures of the carboxylate ion and the phenoxide ion.

$$C_6H_5COOH \rightleftharpoons C_6H_5COO^- + H^+$$

Carboxylate ion

$$(R\text{–}COOH \rightleftharpoons R\text{–}COO^- + H^+)$$

$$C_6H_5OH \rightleftharpoons C_6H_5O^- + H^+$$

Phenoxide ion

The resonance hybrid structures may be represented as:

$$R\text{–}C(O^{\delta-})(O^{\delta-}) \qquad C_6H_5O^{\delta-}$$

12.12 Effect of Substituent on the Acidic Strength of Carboxylic Acid

An electron withdrawing group (EWG having –I effect), stabilises the anion by dispersing the negative charge on the carboxylate ion and therefore, increases the acidity. On the other hand, an electron donating group (EDG +I effect), intensifies the negative charge on the anion resulting in the decrease of stability and thus, decreases the acidity of the acid. The effect of the various substituents in increasing the acidity of carboxylic acids follows the order:

$$C_6H_5 < I < Br < Cl < F < CN < NO_2 < CF_3$$

(i) The alkyl group is an electron releasing group and intensifies the negative charge of the carboxylate ion, destabilises it and thus decreases the acidity. Further, with an increase in size, the +I effect of the alkyl groups increases in the order:

$$CH_3\text{–} < CH_3CH_2\text{–} < (CH_3)_2CH\text{–} < (CH_3)_3C\text{–}$$

(ii) Further, the presence of an electron withdrawing group such as the halogen atom (X), $-NO_2$ and –CN, disperses the negative charge on the carboxylate ion (decreases electron density), stabilises the carboxylate anion and thus, increases the acidity of the carboxylic acid. For example, compare the relative strengths of acetic acid and the chloro-substituted acetic acids.

$CH_3 \rightarrow C(=O) \rightarrow O \rightarrow H$ Acetic acid

$Cl \leftarrow CH_2 \leftarrow C(=O) \leftarrow O \leftarrow H$ Chloroacetic acid

$Cl \leftarrow CH(Cl) \leftarrow C(=O) \leftarrow O \leftarrow H$ Dichloroacetic acid

$Cl \leftarrow C(Cl)(Cl) \leftarrow C(=O) \leftarrow O \leftarrow H$ Trichloroacetic acid

Chlorine is an electron attracting atom (–I effect). It withdraws the electrons from the carbon to which it is attached and this effect is transmitted throughout the chain. As a result, the electrons are withdrawn more strongly towards the oxygen of the O–H bond and so chlorine makes the release of H^+ easy. The –I effect increases with an increase in the number of chlorine atoms and therefore, the acidic strength also increases. Thus, the acidic strength decreases in the order:

$$\underset{(pK_a\,0.64)}{CCl_3COOH} > \underset{(pK_a\,1.26)}{CHCl_2COOH} > \underset{(pK_a\,2.87)}{CH_2ClCOOH} > \underset{(pK_a\,4.76)}{CH_3COOH}$$

(iii) In the case of *o*-, *m*-, and *p*-nitrobenzoic acids, the $-NO_2$ group exerts a greater electron withdrawing effect when present in the *o*- and *p*-positions. So, *o*- and *p*-nitrobenzoic acids are stronger than *m*-nitrobenzoic acid which is, of course, stronger than benzoic acid.

o-Nitrobenzoic acid (pK_a 2.17) > *p*-Nitrobenzoic acid (pK_a 3.41) > *m*-Nitrobenzoic acid (pK_a 3.45) > Benzoic acid (pK_a 4.19)

12.13 Reactions

12.13.1 Reactions of the Carboxyl Group

(i) Reaction with highly electropositive metals:

$$\underset{\text{Formic acid}}{2HCOOH} + 2Na \longrightarrow \underset{\text{Sodium formate}}{2HCOONa} + H_2$$

$$\underset{\text{Acetic acid}}{2CH_3COOH} + 2K \longrightarrow \underset{\text{Potassium acetate}}{2CH_3COOK} + H_2$$

$$\underset{\text{Benzoic acid}}{2C_6H_5COOH} + 2Na \longrightarrow \underset{\text{Sodium benzoate}}{2C_6H_5COONa} + H_2$$

(ii) Reaction with alkalies:

$$CH_3COOH + NaOH \longrightarrow \underset{\text{Sodium acetate}}{CH_3COONa} + H_2O$$

$$\underset{\text{Acetic acid}}{CH_3COOH} + NH_4OH \longrightarrow \underset{\text{Ammonium acetate}}{CH_3COONH_4} + H_2O$$

$$\underset{\text{Benzoic acid}}{C_6H_5COOH} + \underset{\text{Alkali}}{NaOH} \longrightarrow \underset{\text{Sodium benzoate}}{C_6H_5COONa} + H_2O$$

Carboxylic acids can be regenerated by treating these salts with dilute mineral acids.

$$\underset{\text{Sodium acetate}}{CH_3COONa} + HCl \rightarrow \underset{\text{Acetic acid}}{CH_3COOH} + NaCl$$

(iii) Reaction with carbonates and bicarbonates: Monocarboxylic acids react with weaker bases such as carbonates and bicarbonates forming the corresponding salts with the evolution of carbon dioxide (effervescence). This is the laboratory test for the –COOH group.

$$CH_3COOH + \underset{\text{Sodium bicarbonate}}{NaHCO_3} \longrightarrow CH_3COONa + CO_2 + H_2O$$

$$2CH_3COOH + Na_2CO_3 \longrightarrow \underset{\text{Sodium acetate}}{2CH_3COONa} + CO_2 + H_2O$$

$$2CH_3COOH + CaCO_3 \longrightarrow \underset{\text{Calcium acetate}}{(CH_3COO)_2Ca} + CO_2 + H_2O$$

$$2C_6H_5COOH + \underset{\text{Sodium carbonate}}{Na_2CO_3} \longrightarrow 2C_6H_5COONa + CO_2 + H_2O$$

This reaction can be used to distinguish carboxylic acids from phenols (phenols do not give effervescence with an aqueous solution of $NaHCO_3$).

(iv) Reaction with Grignard reagents: Carboxylic acids react with Grignard reagents rapidly to give hydrocarbons along with the magnesium salt of the acid.

$$CH_3-\overset{O}{\overset{\|}{C}}-OH + C_2H_5MgBr \longrightarrow \underset{\text{Ethane}}{C_2H_6} + Mg(Br)OCOCH_3$$

12.13.2 Reactions of the Hydroxyl Group

(i) Reaction with alcohols:

$$R-COOH + HOR' \xrightleftharpoons{\text{conc. } H_2SO_4} \underset{\text{Ester}}{RCOOR'} + H_2O$$

$$\underset{\text{Acetic acid}}{CH_3COOH} + \underset{\text{Ethyl alcohol}}{HOC_2H_5} \xrightleftharpoons{\text{conc. } H_2SO_4} \underset{\text{Ethyl acetate}}{CH_3COOC_2H_5} + H_2O$$

This reaction is termed as *esterification*. It is a reversible and slow reaction, but is speeded up by the presence of small amounts of inorganic acids as a catalyst.

$$R-COOH + HOR' \xrightarrow{\text{conc. } H_2SO_4} R-COOR' + H_2O$$

(ii) Reduction to alcohols:

$$\underset{\text{Carboxylic acid}}{R-COOH} + 2H_2 \xrightarrow[\text{(ii) } H_3O^+]{\text{(i) } LiAlH_4/\text{ether}} \underset{\text{Alcohol}}{R-CH_2OH}$$

$$\underset{\text{Acetic acid}}{CH_3COOH} + 2H_2 \xrightarrow[\text{(ii) } H_3O^+]{\text{(i) } LiAlH_4/\text{ether}} \underset{\text{Ethyl alcohol}}{CH_3CH_2OH}$$

$$\underset{\text{Acid}}{R-\overset{O}{\overset{\|}{C}}-OH} + 2H_2 \xrightarrow[\text{or } B_2H_6/\text{ether}]{(CuO + Cr_2O_3)} \underset{\text{Alcohol}}{R-CH_2OH} + H_2O$$

$$\underset{\text{Benzoic acid}}{C_6H_5COOH} + 2H_2 \xrightarrow{LiAlH_4} \underset{\text{Benzyl alcohol}}{C_6H_5CH_2OH} + H_2O$$

12.13.3 Reactions of the Carboxyl Group as a Whole

(i) Decarboxylation:

$$R-\overset{O}{\overset{\|}{C}}-OH \xrightarrow{(-CO_2)} R-H$$

$$\underset{\text{Sodium salt}}{R-COONa} + NaOH \xrightarrow[\Delta,\ 630\text{ K}]{CaO} \underset{\text{Alkane}}{R-H} + Na_2CO_3$$

$$\underset{\text{Sodium acetate}}{CH_3COONa} + NaOH \xrightarrow[\Delta,\ 630\text{ K}]{CaO} \underset{\text{Methane}}{CH_4} + Na_2CO_3$$

This reaction can be employed for descending down the series, that is, decreasing one carbon atom in a chain.

$$\underset{\text{Sodium benzoate}}{C_6H_5COONa} + NaOH \xrightarrow[\Delta]{CaO} \underset{\text{Benzene}}{C_6H_6} + Na_2CO_3$$

(ii) Decarboxylation of silver salt of carboxylic acids in presence of bromine (Hunsdiecker reaction):

$$\underset{\text{Silver salt of acid}}{RCOOAg} + Br_2 \xrightarrow[\text{Reflux}]{CCl_4} \underset{\text{Alkyl bromide}}{R-Br} + CO_2\uparrow + \underset{\text{ppt.}}{AgBr}$$

$$\underset{\text{Silver acetate}}{CH_3COOAg} + Br_2 \xrightarrow[\text{Reflux}]{CCl_4} \underset{\text{Methyl bromide}}{CH_3-Br} + CO_2\uparrow + AgBr$$

$$\underset{\text{Silver benzoate}}{C_6H_5COOAg} + Br_2 \xrightarrow[\Delta]{CCl_4} \underset{\text{Bromobenzene}}{C_6H_5-Br} + CO_2\uparrow + AgBr$$

(iii) Reduction to alkanes:

$$\underset{\text{Carboxylic acid}}{R-COOH} + 6HI \xrightarrow[473-523\text{ K}]{\text{Red P}} \underset{\text{Alkane}}{R-CH_3} + 2H_2O + 3I_2$$

$$\underset{\text{Acetic acid}}{CH_3-COOH} + 6HI \xrightarrow[473-523\text{ K}]{\text{Red P}} \underset{\text{Ethane}}{CH_3-CH_3} + 2H_2O + 3I_2$$

(iv) Formation of amines (action of N_3H):

$$\underset{\text{Acid}}{R-COOH} + \underset{\text{Hydrazoic acid}}{N_3H} \xrightarrow{H_2SO_4\text{ (conc.)}} \underset{\text{Primary amine}}{R-NH_2} + CO_2 + N_2$$

$$\underset{\text{Acetic acid}}{CH_3-COOH} + N_3H \xrightarrow{H_2SO_4\text{ (conc.)}} \underset{\text{Methyl amine}}{CH_3NH_2} + CO_2 + N_2$$

Exercises

OBJECTIVE QUESTIONS

Nomenclature and Structure of Carbonyl Group

1. The IUPAC name of the compound (benzene ring with CHO, NO_2 ortho to CHO, and OCH_3 para to CHO) is
   (a) 4-methoxy-2-nitrobenzaldehyde
   (b) 4-formyl-3-nitroanisole
   (c) 2-methoxy-6-nitrobenzaldehyde
   (d) 2-formyl-5-methoxynitrobenzene

2. The structure of di-*sec* butyl ketone is
   (a) $(CH_3)_2CHCH_2-CO-CH_2(CH_3)_2$
   (b) $CH_3CH_2-\underset{CH_3}{\underset{|}{CH}}-\underset{O}{\underset{\|}{C}}-\underset{CH_3}{\underset{|}{CH}}-CH_2CH_3$
   (c) $CH_3CH_2-\underset{CH_3}{\underset{|}{CH}}-\underset{O}{\underset{\|}{C}}-CH_2-CH(CH_3)_2$
   (d) $(CH_3)_2CHCH_2-\underset{O}{\underset{\|}{C}}-CH_2CH(CH_3)_2$

3. Which of the following compounds is not named according to the IUPAC system of nomenclature?
   (a) α-methoxypropionaldehyde
   (b) 2-hydroxycyclohexanecarbaldehyde
   (c) 4-oxopentanal
   (d) 3-phenylprop-2-enal

4. The IUPAC name of the compounds (H–CO–CH(CH_3)–CO–CH=CH–CH_3) is
   (a) 5-formylhex-2-en-3-one
   (b) 5-methyl-4-oxohex-2-en-5-al
   (c) 3-keto-2-methylhex-5-enal
   (d) 3-keto-2-methylhex-4-enal

5. The IUPAC name (including the stereochemical notation for the chiral carbon atom) of the compound [structure: H, CHO] is
   (a) (S)-4-methyl-2-propylpentanal
   (b) 2-methylheptane-4-aldehyde
   (c) (R)-4-methyl-2-propylheptanal
   (d) (S)-2-(2-methylpropyl) pentanal

6. Which of the following statements is not true about the C=O group?
   (a) The carbon atom of the carbonyl group is sp^2-hybridised.
   (b) The C=O bond length is longer than the C=C bond length.
   (c) The dipole moments of aldehydes and ketones lie in the range 2.3–2.8 D.
   (d) The portion of the molecule immediately surrounding the carbonyl group is planar.

7. The molecule that can give Cannizzaro's reaction is
   (a) acetaldehyde (b) formaldehyde
   (c) butyraldehyde (d) propionaldehyde

8. Which of the following combinations of common and IUPAC names for the same compound is not correct?
   (a) phthalaldehyde, benzene-1,2-dicarbaldehyde
   (b) mesityl oxide, 4-methylpent-3-en-2-one
   (c) acrolein,prop-2-enal
   (d) 2-methoxypropionaldehyde,2-methoxylpropanal

Methods of Preparation of Aldehydes and Ketones

9. Which one of the following products is formed when the calcium salt of adipic acid is heated?
   (a) $CH_2–CH_2$ / $CH_2–CH_2$ >O
   (b) $CH_2–CH_2$ / $CH_2–CH_2$ >C=O
   (c) CH_2CH_2CO / CH_2CH_2CO >C=O
   (d) CH_2CH_2COOH / CH_2CH_2COOH

10. Which of the following alkenes is most suitable for the preparation of butanone by ozonolysis?
    (a) 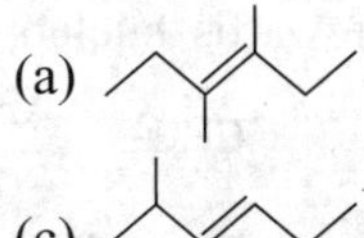 (b)
    (c) (d)

11. Predict the correct intermediate and product in the following reaction:

$$H_3C–C≡CH \xrightarrow[HgSO_4]{H_2O,\ H_2SO_4} \underset{(A)}{\text{Intermediate}} \longrightarrow \underset{(B)}{\text{Product}}$$

   (a) A : $H_3C–C(OH)=CH_2$ B : $H_3C–C(SO_4)=CH_2$
   (b) A : $H_3C–C(=O)–CH_3$ B : $H_3C–C≡CH$
   (c) A : $H_3C–C(OH)=CH_3$ B : $H_3C–C(=O)–CH_3$
   (d) A : $H_3C–C(SO_4)=CH_3$ B : $H_3C–C(=O)–CH_3$

12. The reagents to carry out the following conversion Me–≡ ⟶ Me–CH_2–C(=O)–Me are
    (a) $HgSO_4$/dil.H_2SO_4
    (b) BH_3; H_2O_2/NaOH
    (c) OsO_4, HIO_4
    (d) $NaNH_2$/CH_3I; $HgSO_4$/dil. H_2SO_4

13. Identify the reagents in the following transformations.

    [Br-substituted benzene with side chain bearing Br] $\xrightarrow{A}$ [C≡CH substituted benzene] $\xrightarrow{B}$ [benzene with C(=O)CH$_3$ side chain]

    (a) alc. KOH and H_2O, H_2SO_4, $HgSO_4$
    (b) alc. KOH and $KMnO_4/H^+$
    (c) $NaNH_2$ and H_2O, $HgSO_4$, H_2SO_4
    (d) $NaNH_2$ and $KMnO_4/H^+$

14. [C_6H_5COCl] $\xrightarrow[Pd\text{-}BaSO_4]{H_2}$ A
    The product A is
    (a) C_6H_5CHO (b) C_6H_5OH
    (c) $C_6H_5COCH_3$ (d) C_6H_5Cl

15. Which one of the following is the best method for the preparation of acetophenone?
    (a) PhCOOEt + CH_3MgBr
    (b) PhCOCl + CH_3MgBr
    (c) $PhCONH_2$ + CH_3MgBr
    (d) PhCN + CH_3MgBr

16. For the reaction, [$(CH_3)_2CH–CN$] $\xrightarrow[\text{(ii) } H_3O^+]{\text{(i) PhMgBr, THF}}$ P,
    The structure of the product P is
    (a) [$(CH_3)_2CH–CH(OH)–Ph$] (b) [$(CH_3)_2CH–C(=O)–Ph$]
    (c) [$(CH_3)_2C(CN)–Ph$] (d) [$(CH_3)_2C=C(NH_2)–Ph$]

17. $CH_3CH_2CN \xrightarrow{X} CH_3CH_2CHO$
    The compound X is
    (a) $SnCl_2$/HCl, H_2O/boil (b) H_2/Pd–$BaSO_4$
    (c) $LiAlH_4$/ether (d) $NaBH_4$/ether, H_3O^+

18. The most suitable reagent of conversion of $RCOOC_2H_5$ → RCHO is
    (a) LiAlH(O-*t*-Bu)$_3$ (b) DIBAL-H
    (c) $SnCl_2$/HCl (d) $NaBH_3CN$

19. *p*-Nitrotoluene on treatment with CrO_2Cl_2/CS_2 followed by hydrolysis gives
(a) *p*-toluidine (b) *p*-nitrobenzoic acid
(c) *p*-nitrobenzaldehyde (d) *p*-nitrobenzyl alcohol

20. Oxidation of toluene with CrO_3 in the presence of $(CH_3CO)_2O$ gives a product (A) which on treatment with aqueous NaOH produces
(a) C_6H_5CHO (b) $(C_6H_5CO)_2O$
(c) C_6H_5COONa (d) 2,4-diacetyltoluene

21. Photochemical chlorination of toluene with two equivalents of chlorine followed by hydrolysis with aqueous KOH gives
(a) $PhCH_2OH$ (b) PhCHO
(c) $PhCHCl_2$ (d) PhCOOH

22. The photochemical bromination of ethylbenzene with excess of bromine followed by hydrolysis with aqueous KOH gives
(a) PhCHO (b) $PhCH_2CHO$
(c) $PhCOCH_3$ (d) $PhCHOHCH_3$

23. A reaction by which benzaldehyde cannot be prepared is:
(a) $C_6H_5CH_3$ + CrO_2Cl_2 in CS_2 followed by H_3O^+
(b) C_6H_5COCl + H_2 in presence of Pd–$BaSO_4$
(c) C_6H_6 + CO + HCl in presence of anhydrous $AlCl_3$
(d) C_6H_5COOH + Zn/Hg and conc. HCl

24. Acetophenone will not be formed by the
(a) reaction of benzene with acetyl chloride in the presence of $AlCl_3$
(b) reaction of acetonitrile with phenylmagnesium bromide in ether followed by hydrolysis
(c) treatment of acetyl chloride with dibenzylcadmium
(d) addition of water to phenylacetylene in the presence of mercuric sulfate and dilute sulfuric acid

25. Reagents required for the conversion

(cyclohexane)$=CH_2 \longrightarrow$ (cyclohexane)–CHO

respectively are
(a) BH_3/THF, H_2O_2/OH^-, $C_5H_5NH^+CrRO_3C1^-$
(b) BH_3/THF, H_2O_2/OH^-, $K_2Cr_2O_7/H_2SO_4$
(c) $Hg(OAc)_2$, THF–H_2O,$NaBH_4/OH^-$, $C_5H_5NH^+CrO_3C1^-$
(d) H_2O/H^+, $C_5H_5NH^+CrO_3C1^-$

26. A compound X having a molecular formula $C_4H_{10}O$, gave on oxidation a ketone, C_4H_5O. Which of the following is the structure of X?
(a) $CH_3CH_2CH_2CH_2OH$ (b) $CH_3CHOHCH_2CH_3$
(c) $(CH_3)_2CHCH_2OH$ (d) $(CH_3)_3COH$

27. On heating calcium propionate, the product formed is
(a) 3-pentanone (b) 2-pentanone
(c) 3-methyl-1-butanone (d) propanone

28. Dry distillation of calcium benzoate gives
(a) benzaldehyde (b) benzophenone
(c) acetophenone (d) butyrophenone

Physical Properties of Aldehydes and Ketones

29. The dipole moment is the highest for
(a) trans-2-butene (b) 1,3-dimethylbenzene
(c) acetophenone (d) ethanol

30. Which of the following reactions will not result in the formation of a carbon–carbon bond?
(a) Wurtz reaction
(b) Friedel–Crafts acylation
(c) Reimer Tiemann reaction
(d) Cannizzaro reaction

31. The boiling points of the following compounds
I. $CH_3CH_2CH_2CHO$ II. $CH_3CH_2CH_2CH_2OH$
III. H_5C_2–O–C_2H_5 IV. $CH_3CH_2CH_2CH_2CH_3$
increase in the order
(a) IV < III < II < I (b) IV < III < I < II
(c) I < II < IV < III (d) II < III < IV < I

Chemical Reactions of Aldehydes and Ketones

32. Arrange the following carbonyl compounds in the decreasing order of their reactivity in nucleophilic addition.
benzaldehyde (A), *p*-nitrobenzaldehyde (B), acetophenone (C), *p*-tolualdehyde (D)
(a) B > C > A > D (b) B > A > D > C
(c) C > B > A > D (d) C > A > D > B

33. Which one is the most reactive towards nucleophilic addition reaction?
(a) C_6H_5CHO (b) $C_6H_5COCH_3$ (c) p-$CH_3C_6H_4CHO$ (d) p-$NO_2C_6H_4CHO$

34. Arrange the following compounds in the decreasing order of reactivity towards nucleophilic addition reaction.
Diethyl ketone (I) Benzaldehyde (II)
Propanal (III) Acetaldehyde (IV)

(a) I > II > III > IV (b) IV > III > II > I
(c) II > III > I > IV (d) IV > III > I > II

35. Which carbonyl group of the given compound is the most reactive for nucleophilic addition reaction?

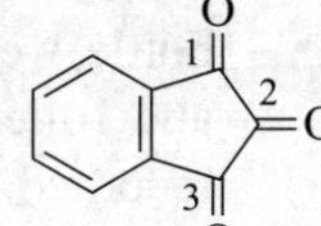

(a) 1 (b) 2
(c) 3
(d) all have equal reactivity

36. Acetaldehyde on reaction with sodium bisulfite produces

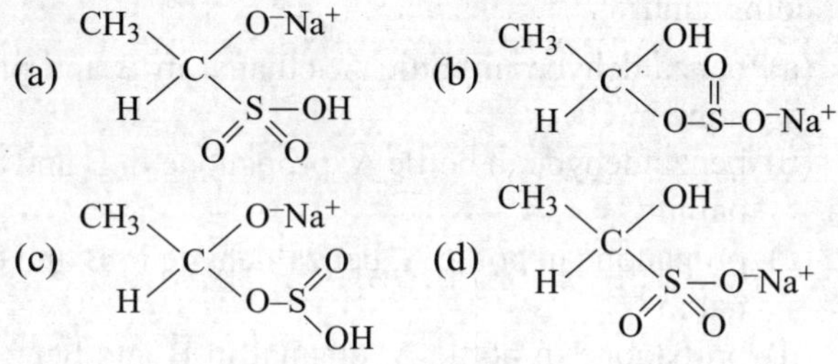

37. Which among the following compounds will give a secondary alcohol on reacting with a Grignard reagent followed by acid hydrolysis?

I. HCHO II. C_2H_5CHO
III. CH_3COCH_3 IV. $RCOOC_2H_5$

Select the correct answer using the codes given below:
(a) Only II (b) Only III
(c) II and IV (d) III and IV

38. *p*-Cresol reacts with chloroform in an alkaline medium to give a compound A which adds on hydrogen cyanide to form another compound B. This latter compound on acidic hydrolysis gives a chiral carboxylic acid. The structure of the carboxylic acid is

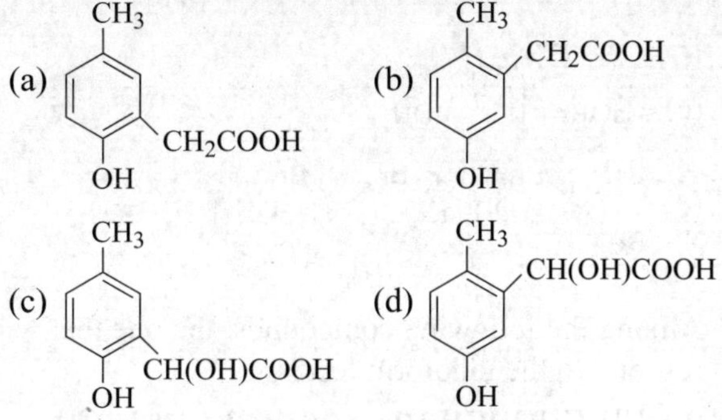

39. A and B in the following reactions are:

$$R-\underset{\underset{O}{\|}}{C}-R' \xrightarrow[KCN]{HCN} A \xrightarrow{B} RR'C(OH)(CH_2NH_2)$$

(a) $A = RR'C(OH)(COOH)$, $B = NH_3$

(b) $A = RR'C(CN)(OH)$, $B = H_3O^+$

(c) $A = RR'CH_2CN$, $B = NaOH$

(d) $A = RR'C(CN)(OH)$, $B = LiAlH_4$

40. Which of the following will react with water?
(a) $CHCl_3$ (b) Cl_3CCHO
(c) CCl_4 (d) $ClCH_2CH_2Cl$

41. Acetone is treated with an excess of ethanol in the presence of hydrochloric acid. The product obtained is

(a) $CH_3CH_2CH_2-\overset{O}{\overset{\|}{C}}-CH_3$

(b) $CH_3CH_2CH_2-\overset{O}{\overset{\|}{C}}-CH_2CH_2CH_3$

(c) $(CH_3)_2C(OH)(OC_2H_5)$

(d) $(CH_3)_2C(OC_2H_5)(OC_2H_5)$

42. During the addition of ethylene glycol to acetone in the presence of a small amount of PTS, the product formed is

(a) 2,2-dimethyl-1,3-dioxolane (cyclic, O–CH2–CH2–O ring) (b) $(CH_3)_2C(OCH_2CH_2OH)(OH)$
(c) $(CH_3)_2C(OCH_2CH_2OH)(OCH_2CH_2OH)$ (d) $(CH_3)_2C(OCH_2CH_2)(OCH_2CH_2)O$

43. The major product formed in the following reaction is

$$C_6H_5CHO \xrightarrow[\text{excess of MeOH}]{\text{HCl gas}}$$

(a) $C_6H_5CH(OMe)(OH)$ (b) $C_6H_5CH(OMe)(OMe)$
(c) $C_6H_5\overset{O}{\overset{\|}{C}}-OMe$ (d) $C_6H_5C(OMe)(OMe)(OMe)$

44. Calcium butanoate on heating followed by treatment with 1,2-ethanediol in the presence of a catalytic amount of acid produced a major product, which is

(a) cyclic ketal (1,3-dioxolane with two propyl groups) (b) HO–CH2CH2–O–C(propyl)2–O–H
(c) propyl–O–C(propyl)2–O–propyl (d) HO–CH2CH2–O–C(propyl)2–OH

45. The major product of the following reaction is

(dihydropyran) $\xrightarrow[\text{H}^+ \text{(anhydrous)}]{\text{RCH}_2\text{OH}}$

(a) hemiacetal (b) acetal
(c) an ether (d) an ester

46. Reaction of a carbonyl compound with one of the following reagents involves nucleophilic addition followed by elimination of water. The reagent is

(a) hydrazine in the presence of a feebly acidic solution
(b) hydrocyanic acid
(c) sodium hydrogen sulfide
(d) Grignard reagent

47. Brady's reagent is

(a) C_6H_5–NHNH$_2$ (b) O_2N–$C_6H_3(NO_2)$–NHNH$_2$
(c) $H_2NCONHNH_2$ (d) NH_2OH

48. The smallest ketone and its next homologue are reacted with NH_2OH to form an oxime.

(a) two different oximes are formed
(b) three different oximes are formed
(c) two oximes are optically active
(d) all oximes are optically active

49. Which of the following will give a red precipitate when reacted with complexes formed by copper sulfate and sodium tartrate?

(a) CH_3CHO (b) CH_3COCH_3
(c) CH_3COOH (d) C_2H_5COOH

50. Fehling solution will oxidise

I. C_6H_5–CHO II. C_6H_5–CH(OH)–CH$_3$
III. C_6H_5–CH$_2$CHO IV. HCHO

(a) all (b) only I and IV
(c) only II and III (d) only III and IV

51. Compound A (molecular formula C_3H_8O) is treated with acidified potassium dichromate to form a product B (molecular formula C_3H_6O). B forms a shining silver mirror on warming with ammoniacal silver nitrate. B when treated with an aqueous solution of $H_2NCONHNH_2$.HCl and sodium acetate gives a product C. Identify the structure of C.

(a) CH_3CH_2CH=NHHCINH$_2$
(b) CH_3–C(CH$_3$)=NNHCONH$_2$
(c) CH_3–C(CH$_3$)=NCONHNH$_2$
(d) CH_3CH_2CH=NCONHNH$_2$

52. Bottles containing ethanal, propanone and benzaldehyde lost their original lables. They were labelled as A, B and C for the purpose of identification. The contents of each bottle were separately treated with Fehling's solution and Tollens' reagent. The following observations were recorded. The contents of tube A neither reduced Fehling's solution nor Tollens' reagent; that of tube B reduced only Tollens' reagent but not Fehling's solution while that of tube C reduced both Tollens' reagent as well as Fehling's solution. On the basis of these observations, find out which bottle contained which compound?

(a) benzaldehyde in bottle A, ethanal in B and propanone in C
(b) benzaldehyde in bottle A, propanone in B and ethanal in C
(c) propanone in bottle A, benzaldehyde in B and ethanal in C
(d) propanone in bottle A, ethanal in B and benzaldehyde in C

53. Benzaldehyde and acetone can be best distinguished using

(a) Fehling's solution
(b) sodium hydroxide solution
(c) 2,4-DNP
(d) Tollens' reagent

54. The major products in the reaction,

$Br_3CCHO \xrightarrow{\text{NaOH}}$ are

(a) $CHBr_3$ + H–C(=O)–ONa (b) NaBr + (H)(HO)C=C(Br)(Br)

(c) NaOBr + H–C(=O)–OH

(d) Br_3C–CH_2–OH + Br_3C–C(=O)–ONa

55. Among the following compounds, the one that will not respond to the iodoform test is

(a) $CH_3CHOHCH_2CH_3$ (b) $ICH_2COCH_2CH_3$
(c) CH_3COOH (d) CH_3CHO

56. CH_3CHO and $C_6H_5CH_2CHO$ can be distinguished chemically by

(a) Benedict's test (b) iodoform test
(c) Tollens' reagent test (d) Fehling's solution test

57. The reagent used for the separation of acetaldehyde and acetophenone is

(a) $NaHSO_3$ (b) $C_6H_5NHNH_2$
(c) NH_2OH (d) NaOH–I_2

58. A carbonyl compound with a molecular weight of 86 does not reduce Fehling's solution but forms a crystalline bisulfite derivative and gives the iodoform test. The possible compounds can be

(a) 2-pentanone and 3-pentanone
(b) 2-pentanone and 3-methyl-2-butanone
(c) 2-pentanone and pentanal
(d) 3-pentanone and 3-methyl-2-butanone

59. Which of the following compounds will give a yellow precipitate with iodine and an alkali?

(a) acetamide (b) 2-hydroxypropane
(c) acetophenone (d) methyl acetate

60. The compound that does not give the iodoform test is

(a) acetaldehyde (b) acetone
(c) acetophenone (d) propiophenone

61. In the following reaction,

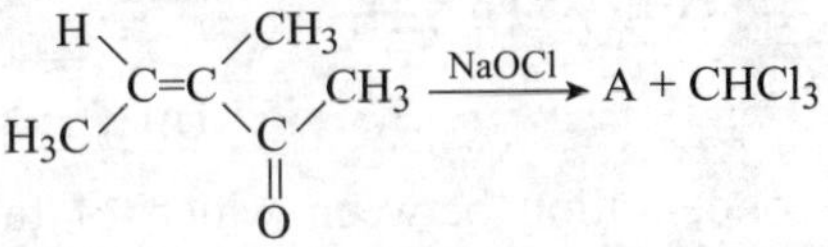

$$(H)(H_3C)C{=}C(CH_3)\text{–}C(=O)\text{–}CH_3 \xrightarrow{NaOCl} A + CHCl_3$$

The product (A) is

(a) 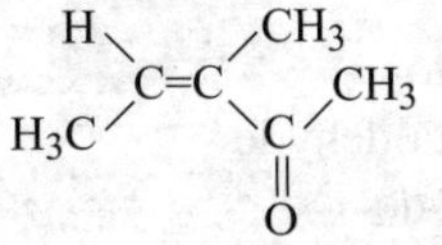 $(H)(H_3C)C{=}C(CH_3)\text{–}C(=O)\text{–}CH_3$ (b) $(H)(H_3C)C{=}C(CH_3)(CHO)$
(c) $(H)(H_3C)C{=}C(COONa)(CH_3)$ (d) 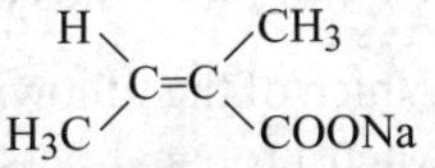 $(H)(H_3C)C{=}C(CH_3)(COONa)$

62. Compound (A) $C_5H_{10}O$ forms a phenylhydrazone and gives negative Tollens' and iodoform tests. Compound (A) on reduction gives *n*-pentane. Compound (A) is

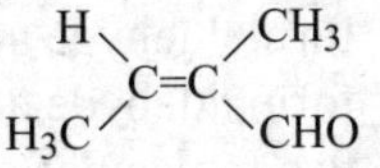

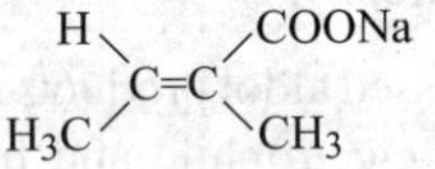

(a) pentanal (b) pentanone-2
(c) pentanone-3 (d) amyl alcohol

63. A compound A ($C_5H_{10}Cl_2$) on hydrolysis gives $C_5H_{10}O$ which reacts with NH_2OH, forms iodofom but does not give Fehling's solution test. A is

(a) $CH_3\text{–}CCl_2\text{–}CH_2CH_2CH_3$
(b) $CH_3CH_2\text{–}CCl_2\text{–}CH_2CH_3$
(c) $CH_3CH_2CH_2CH_2\text{–}CHCl_2$
(d) $CH_3\text{–}CHCl\text{–}CHCl\text{–}CH_2CH_3$

64. When acetophenone hydrazone is heated with KOH in ethylene glycol at 450–470 K, it gives

(a) 1-phenylethanol (b) 2-phenylethanol
(c) ethylbenzene (d) toluene

65. During the reduction of carbonyl compounds by hydrazine and KOH, the first intermediate formed is

(a) $RC{\equiv}N$ (b) $RCONH_2$
(c) $RCH{=}NH$ (d) $RCH{=}NH_2$

66. In the given transformation, which of the following is the most appropriate reagent?

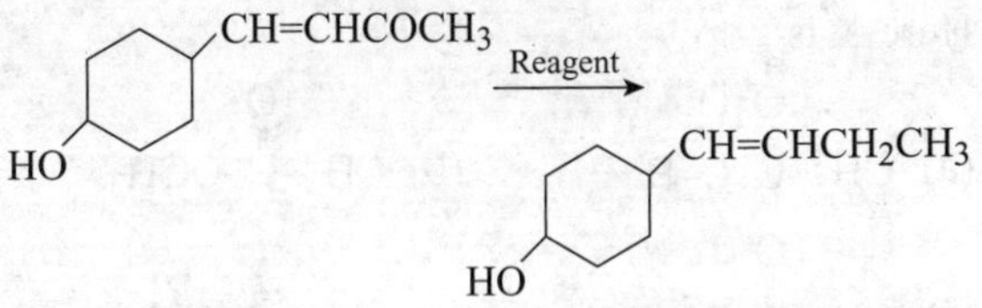

HO–(cyclohexyl)–CH=CHCOCH$_3$ $\xrightarrow{\text{Reagent}}$ HO–(cyclohexyl)–CH=CHCH$_2$CH$_3$

(a) Zn–Hg/HCl (b) Na in liq. NH_3
(c) $NaBH_4$ (d) $NH_2\text{–}NH_2$, OH^-

67. $CH_3CHO + NH_2NH_2 \rightarrow A \xrightarrow{B} CH_3CH_3 + N_2$.
Identify A and B.

(a) $CH_3CH{=}NNH_2$ and C_2H_5ONa
(b) $CH_3CH_2\text{–}NH_2$ and C_2H_5ONa
(c) $CH_3\text{–}NH\text{–}NH\text{–}CH_3$ and C_2H_5OH
(c) $CH_3CH_2NH_2$ and C_2H_5OH

68. If 3-hexanone is reacted with $NaBH_4$ followed by hydrolysis with D_2O, the product will be

(a) $CH_3CH_2CH(OH)CH_2CH_2CH_3$
(b) $CH_3CH_2CD(OH)CH_2CH_2CH_3$
(c) $CH_3CH(OD)CH_2CH_2CH_3$
(d) $CH_{3C}H_2CD(OD)CH_2CH_2CH_3$

69. In the following reactions,

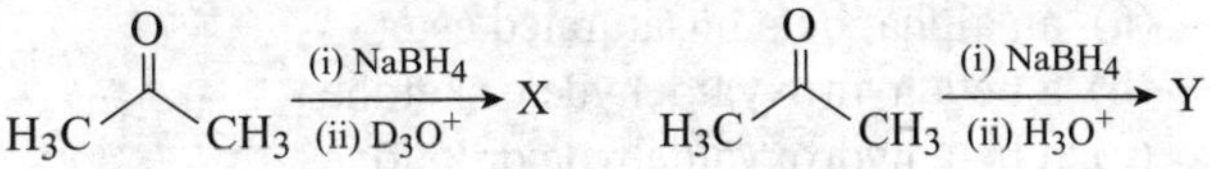

$$H_3C\text{–}C(=O)\text{–}CH_3 \xrightarrow[\text{(ii) } D_3O^+]{\text{(i) NaBH}_4} X \qquad H_3C\text{–}C(=O)\text{–}CH_3 \xrightarrow[\text{(ii) } H_3O^+]{\text{(i) NaBH}_4} Y$$

X and Y are

(a) X = $H_3C\text{–}C(H)(OD)\text{–}CH_3$, Y = $H_3C\text{–}C(D)(OH)\text{–}CH_3$
(b) X = $H_3C\text{–}C(D)(OH)\text{–}CH_3$, Y = $H_3C\text{–}C(H)(OD)\text{–}CH_3$
(c) X = Y = $H_3C\text{–}C(D)(OD)\text{–}CH_3$ (d) X = Y = $H_3C\text{–}C(H)(OH)\text{–}CH_3$

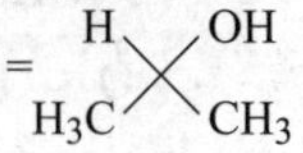

70. The correct structure of the product A formed in the reaction

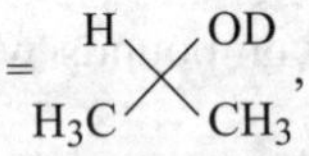

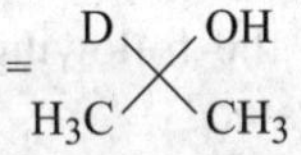

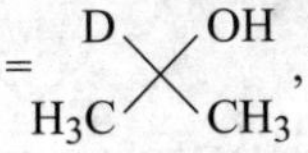

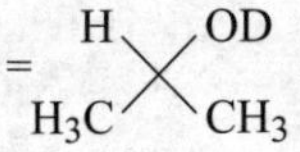

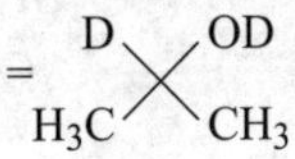

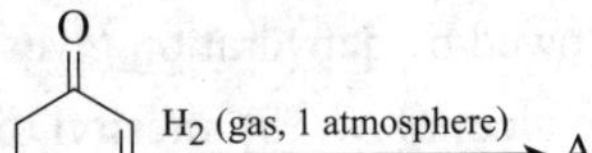

(cyclohexenone, O) $\xrightarrow[\text{Pd/carbon ethanol}]{H_2\text{ (gas, 1 atmosphere)}}$ A is

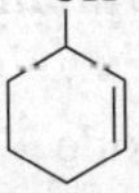

(a) OH (b)  O (c) 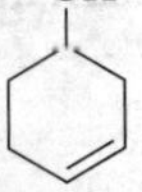 OH (d) 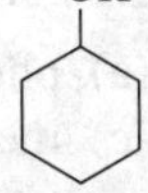 OH

71. Methyl *n*-propyl ketone on oxidation with $K_2Cr_2O_7$ and H_2SO_4 gives mainly

(a) $CH_3CH_2COOH + CH_3COOH$
(b) $CH_3CH_2CH_2COOH + HCOOH$
(c) $CH_3COOH + HCOOH$
(d) $CH_3CH_2COOH + CO_2 + H_2O$

72. $CH_3-\overset{O}{\overset{\|}{C}}-CH_3 \xrightarrow{SeO_2} X + Se + H_2O$

Here X is

(a) $CH_3-\overset{O}{\overset{\|}{C}}-\overset{O}{\overset{\|}{C}}-H$ (b) $CH_3-\overset{O}{\overset{\|}{C}}-OCH_3$

(c) $CH_3-\overset{O}{\overset{\|}{C}}-CH_2OH$ (d) none of the above

73. Treatment of cyclopentanone (cyclopentane ring =O) with methyllithium gives which of the following species?

(a) cyclopentanonyl radical
(b) cyclopentanonyl biradical
(c) cyclopentanonyl anion
(d) cyclopentanonyl cation

74. 3-Hydroxybutanal is formed when X reacts with Y in dilute Z solution What are X, Y and Z?

	X	Y	Z
(a)	CH_3CHO,	$(CH_3)_2CO$,	NAOH
(b)	CH_3CHO,	CH_3CHO,	NaCl
(c)	$(CH_3)_2CO$,	$(CH_3)_2CO$,	HCl
(d)	CH_3CHO,	CH_3CHO,	NaOH

75. The product formed in aldol condensation is

(a) an alpha, beta unsaturated ester
(b) a beta hydroxyaldehyde or ketone
(c) a beta hydroxyaldehyde or ketone
(d) an alpha hydroxyaldehyde or ketone

76. Which one of the following compounds will be most readily dehydrated?

(a) CH_3–C(=O)–CH(OH)–CH₂CH₂CH₃ (b) H_3C–C(=O)–CH(OH)–CH₂CH₂CH₃

(c) CH_3–C(=O)–CH₂–CH(OH)–CH₂CH₂CH₃ (d) CH_3–C(=O)–CH(OH)–CH₂CH₂CH₃

77. Acetone on treatment with a dilute aqueous solution of $Ba(OH)_2$ followed by dehydration gives

(a) diacetone alcohol (b) mesityl oxide
(c) crotonaldehyde (d) phorone

78. Acetone on distillation with conc. H_2SO_4 forms

(a) phorone (b) acrolein
(c) mesitylene (d) mesityl oxide

79. Consider the reactions

$\underset{(C_2H_6O)}{X} \xrightarrow[573\text{ K}]{Cu} A \xrightarrow[^-OH,\ \Delta]{[Ag(NH_3)_2]^+}$ Silver mirror observed

$A \xrightarrow{^-OH,\ \Delta} Y$

$A \xrightarrow{NH_2NHCONH_2} Z$

Identify A, X Y and Z.

(a) A-methoxymethane, X-ethanol, Y-ethanoic acid, Z-semicarbazide
(b) A-ethanal, X-ethanol, Y-but-2-enal, Z-semicarbazone
(c) A-ethanol, X-acetaldehyde, Y-butanone, Z-hydrazone
(d) A-methoxymethane, X-ethanoic acid, Y-acetate ion, Z-hydrazine

80. Of the following, which is the product formed when cyclohexanone undergoes aldol condensation followed by heating?

(a) cyclohexylidene–cyclohexanone (C=C between rings, C=O) (b) two cyclohexane rings joined, OH

(c) two cyclohexanone rings joined, O, O (d) cyclohexanone ring joined to cyclohexanol ring, O, OH

81. Aldol condensation between which of the following two compounds followed by dehydration gives methyl vinyl ketone?

(a) formaldehyde and acetone
(b) formaldehyde and acetaldehyde
(c) two molecules of acetone
(d) two molecules of acetaldehyde

82. Which of the following crossed aldol products is formed when propanal acts as an electrophile and butanal as nucleophile?

(a) 3-hydroxy-2-methylpentanal
(b) 2-ethyl-3-hydroxypentanal
(c) 3-hydroxy-2-methylbutanal
(d) 2-ethyl-3-hydroxyhexanal

83. When a mixture of benzaldehyde and acetophenone is treated with dilute NaOH at 293 K, it forms

(a) 2,3-diphenylpropanal
(b) 1,1-diphenylpropan-1-ol-2-one
(c) 1,3-diphenylprop-2-en-1-one
(d) 1,2-diphenylprop-2-en-1-one
(e) 1,3-diphenyl-2-en-1-al

84. Acetophenone when reacted with a base, C_2H_5ONa, yields a stable compound which has the structure,

(a) $C_6H_5-\underset{CH_3}{\underset{|}{C}}=CH-\overset{}{\underset{O}{\underset{\|}{C}}}-C_6H_5$ (b) $C_6H_5-\underset{CH_3}{\underset{|}{CH}}-CH_2-\underset{O}{\underset{\|}{C}}-C_6H_5$

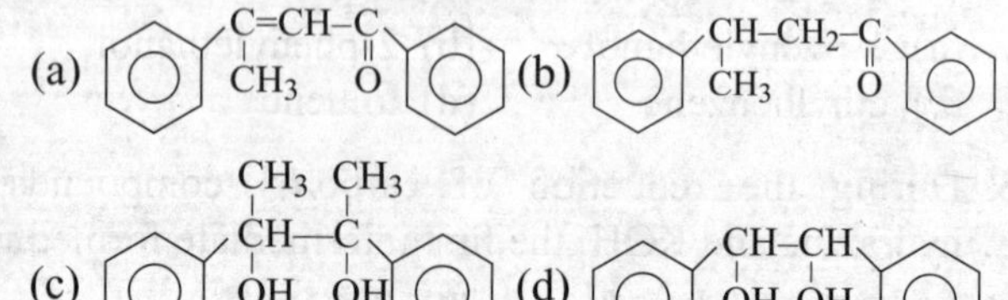

85. $C_6H_5CN \xrightarrow[\text{(ii) } H_3O^+]{\text{(i) } SnCl_2/HCl} X \xrightarrow[H_3C-C_6H_4-C(=O)CH_3]{\text{dil. NaOH}} Y$

X and Y are,

(a) X = $C_6H_5CH_2Cl$, Y = H_3C ... (structure with $C_6H_4CH_2CH_2C(=O)C_6H_5$)

(b) X = $C_6H_5CH_2Cl$, Y = $C_6H_5CH=CHC(=O)C_6H_4CH_3$

(c) X = C_6H_5CHO, Y = $H_3C-C_6H_4-CH=CHC(=O)C_6H_5$

(d) X = C_6H_5CHO, Y = $C_6H_5CH=CHC(=O)C_6H_4-CH_3$

86. The main product formed when benzaldehyde is treated with one mole of acetone in the presence of aqueous alkali is

(a) $C_6H_5CH{=}CHCHO$ (b) $(CH_3)_2C{=}CHCOCH_3$
(c) $C_6H_5CH{=}CHCOCH_3$ (d) $C_6H_5CH(OH)CH_2CHO$

87. With excess of benzaldehyde, acetone condenses in the presence of dil. NaOH to give

(a) $C_6H_5CH{=}CHCOCH_3$
(b) $C_6H_5CH{=}CHCOCH{=}CHC_6H_5$
(c) $C_6H_5CH{=}CHCOC_6H_5$
(d) $(C_6H_5)_2C{=}CHCOCH_3$

88. Which of the following aldehydes/ketones reacts with benzaldehyde in the presence of dil. NaOH to form cinnamaldehyde?

(a) acetaldehyde (b) acetophenone
(c) acetone (d) formaldehyde

89. To prepare ethyl cinnamate, benzaldehyde is reacted with which of the following in the presence of dil. NaOH?

(a) $CH_3COC_6H_5$ (b) $CH_3CO_2C_2H_5$
(c) $C_6H_5CO_2C_2H_5$ (d) $HCO_2C_2H_5$

90. In the presence of HCl, two and three molecules of acetone combine respectively to form,

(a) mesityl acetone, but-2-enal
(b) but-2-enal and mesityl oxide
(c) mesityl oxide and phorone
(d) phorone and mesityl oxide

91. Which of the following on treatment with 50% aqueous sodium hydroxide yields the corresponding alcohol and acids?

(a) $CH_3-\overset{O}{\overset{\|}{C}}-CH_3$ (b) $C_6H_5CH_2CHO$
(c) C_6H_5CHO (d) $CH_3CH_2CH_2CHO$

92. Predict the products in the given reaction.

3-chlorobenzaldehyde (CHO, Cl) $\xrightarrow{\text{50\% NaOH}}$

(a) CH_2OH (with Cl) + CH_2COO^- (with Cl)

(b) CH_2OH (with OH) + OH (with OH)

(c) CH_2OH (with Cl) + COO^- (with Cl)

(d) CH_2OH (with OH) + COO^- (with OH)

93. Crossed Cannizzaro reaction is given by

(a) CH_3CHO, HCHO (b) C_6H_5CHO, CH_3CHO
(c) C_6H_5CHO, HCHO (d) all of these

94. A mixture of benzaldehyde and formaldehyde on heating with aqueous NaOH solution gives

(a) benzyl alcohol and sodium formate
(b) sodium benzoate and methyl alcohol
(c) sodium benzoate and sodium formate
(d) benzyl alcohol and methyl alcohol

95. A compound A undergoes Cannizzaro reaction and B exhibits a positive iodoform test. Therefore,

(a) A = acetaldehyde B = 1-pentanal
(b) A = $C_6H_5CH_2CHO$ B = 3-pentanone
(c) A = formaldehyde B = 2-pentanone
(d) A = propionaldehyde B = 1-pentanol

96. Amongst the following compounds, the one that will not respond to Cannizzaro reaction upon treatment with alkali is

(a) Cl_3CCHO (b) Me_3CCHO
(c) C_6H_5CHO (d) HCHO

97. In which of the following reactions is a new carbon–carbon bond not formed?

(a) Cannizzaro reaction (b) Wurtz reaction
(c) Aldol condensation (d) Friedel–Craft reaction

98. Acetaldehyde on treatment with aluminium ethoxide gives

(a) methyl acetate (b) ethyl formate
(c) ethyl acetate (d) 3-hydroxybutanal

99. Acrolein on treatment with aluminium ethoxide gives

(a) allyl alcohol (b) acrylic acid
(c) allyl acrylate (d) none of the above

100. Examine the given sequence of reactions.

$$C_6H_5CH_3 \xrightarrow[(ii)\ H^+/H_2O]{(i)\ CrO_2O_2} X \xrightarrow{(C_2H_5O)_3Al} Y \text{ (major product)}$$

Here, Y is

(a) benzene ring with two CHO groups (ortho) (b) $C_6H_5-\overset{O}{\overset{||}{C}}-CH_2-C_6H_5$
(c) $C_6H_5CH(OC_2H_5)_2$ (d) benzene ring with CHO and OC_6H_5 (ortho)

101. $X \xrightarrow[\text{(Reductive)}]{\text{Ozonolysis}} Y + Z$

Y can be obtained by Etard's reaction. Z undergoes disproportionation reaction with concentrated alkali. X could be

(a) $C_6H_5C{\equiv}CH$ (b) $C_6H_5CH{=}CH_2$
(c) $C_6H_5CH{=}CHCH_3$ (d) $C_6H_5CH{=}C(CH_3)_2$

102. Identify Q in the following sequence of reactions.

$$\text{Cyclohexyl-}COCH_3 \xrightarrow{PCl_5} P \xrightarrow[\text{excess}]{NaNH_2} Q$$

(a) (b) (c) (d) [structures]

103. The main product (B) in the following sequence of reactions is,

$$\text{Cyclohexanone} \xrightarrow[\text{heat}]{PCl_5} A \xrightarrow[\text{heat}]{\text{alc. KOH}} B$$

(a) cyclohexane with Cl and OH on the same carbon (b) cyclohexane with HO and OC_2H_5 on the same carbon
(c) [structure] (d) 1-chlorocyclohexene (Cl)

104. Benzaldehyde reacts with ammonia to form

(a) $C_6H_5CH(OH)(NH_2)$ (b) $C_6H_5CH{=}N{-}N{=}CHC_6H_5$
(c) $(C_6H_5CH)_3N$ (d) $(C_6H_5CH{=}N)_2CHC_6H_5$

105. Acetone reacts with ammonia to form

(a) $(CH_3)_2C(OH)(NH_2)$ (b) $(CH_3)_2C{=}NH$
(c) $(CH_3)_2C(NH_2)(CH_2COCH_3)$ (d) $[(CH_3)_2]_3N$

106. Which of the following reagents reacts differently with HCHO, CH_3CHO and CH_3COCH_3?

(a) HCN (b) NH_2NH_2
(c) NH_2OH (d) NH_3

107. Which of the following on nitration gives RDX?

(a) urea (b) benzamide
(c) urotropine (d) benzanilide

108. Structure of RDX is

(a) $O_2N{-}CH$ ring with NH–CH(NO_2), NH, NH–CH(NO_2) (b) $C(CH_2ONO_2)_4$
(c) H_2C ring with N(NO_2)–CH_2, N–NO_2, N(NO_2)–CH_2 (d) $CH_2(ONO_2){-}CH(ONO_2){-}CH(ONO_2)$

109. Acetaldehyde on treatment with a few drops of conc. H_2SO_4 at room temperature gives

(a) $CH_3CHOHCH_2CHO$ (b) $CH_3CH{=}CHCHO$
(c) $CH_3{-}$(1,3-dioxolane ring)${-}CH_3$ (d) 1,3,5-trioxane ring with three CH_3 groups

110. Trioxane is a polymer of

(a) formaldehyde (b) acetaldehyde
(c) acetone (d) benzaldehyde

111. Bromination of acetophenone in acetic acid medium produces mainly

(a) benzene ring with $COCH_3$ and Br (ortho) (b) benzene ring with $COCH_3$ and Br (para)
(c) benzene ring with $COCH_3$ and Br (meta) (d) $C_6H_5COCH_2Br$

112. Acetophenone on bromination in the presence of anhydrous $AlCl_3$ gives

(a) *o*-bromoacetophenone

(b) *p*-bromoacetophenone
(c) *m*-bromoacetophenone
(d) phenacyl bromide

113. The formation of cyanohydrins from acetone is which type of reaction?
(a) electrophilic substitution
(b) electrophilic addition
(c) nucleophilic addition
(d) nucleophilic substitution

114. The general order of reactivity of carbonyl compounds towards nucleophilic addition reactions is
(a) $H_2C{=}O > RCHO > ArCHO > R_2C{=}O > Ar_2C{=}O$
(b) $ArCHO > Ar_2C{=}O > RCH{=}O > R_2C{=}O > H_2C{=}O$
(c) $Ar_2C{=}O > R_2C{=}O > ArCHO > RCHO > H_2C{=}O$
(d) $H_2C{=}O > R_2C{=}O > Ar_2C{=}O > RCHO > ARCHO$

115. The order of reactivity of phenylmagnesium bromide (PhMgBr) with the following compounds is:

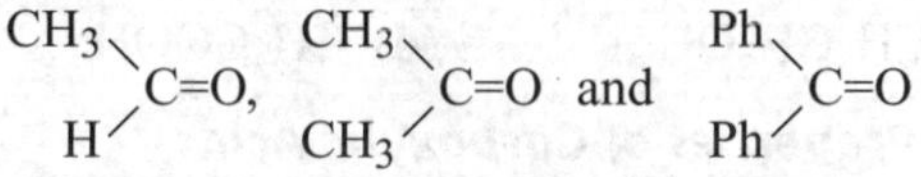

$CH_3(H)C{=}O$ (I), $(CH_3)_2C{=}O$ (II) and $Ph_2C{=}O$ (III)

(a) III > II > I (b) II > I > III
(c) I > III > II (d) I > II > III

116. Arrange the following compounds in increasing order of their reactivity towards HCN.
I. acetaldehyde II. Acetone
III. di-tert-butyl ketone IV. methyl tert-butyl ketone
(a) III < IV < II < I (b) IV < III < I < II
(c) II < III < I < IV (d) II < I < IV < III

117. Arrange the following compounds in increasing order of their reactivity in nucleophilic addition reactions:
I. ethanal II. propanal
III. propanone IV. butanone
(a) I < II < III < IV (b) IV < III < II < I
(c) II < I < III < IV (d) III < IV < II < I

Nomenclature and Structure of the Carboxyl Group

118. The names of some compounds are given. Which one is not the correct IUPAC name?
(a) $PhCH_2CH_2COOH$, 3-Phenylopanoic acid
(b) 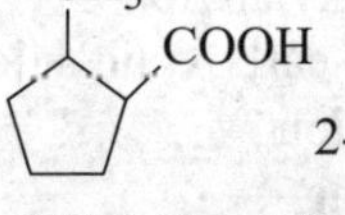 [cyclopentane ring bearing CH_3 and COOH on adjacent carbons] 2-Methylcylopentanecarboxylic acid
(c) $(CH_3)_2C{=}CHCOOH$, 3, 3-Dimethylprop-2-enoic acid
(d) 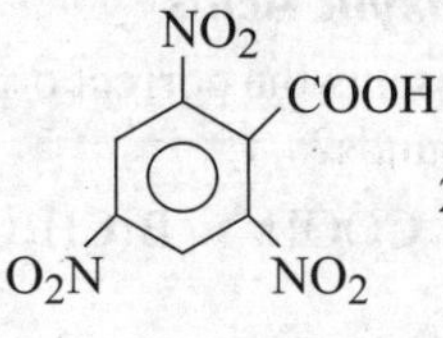 [benzene ring bearing COOH, with NO_2, O_2N and NO_2 substituents] 2, 4, 6-Trinitro-benzoic acid

119. Both aldehydes/ketones and carboxylic acids contain the C=O group. Aldehydes/ketones form oximes but carboxylic acids do not. This is because
(a) the carbonyl carbon in aldehydes/ketones is sp^2-hybridised while in carboxylic acids it is sp^3-hybridised
(b) the carbonyl carbon in both aldehydes/ketones and carboxylic acids is sp^2-hybridised
(c) the carbonyl carbon of aldehydes/ketones is less electrophilic than that of carboxylic acids
(d) the carbonyl carbon of carboxylic acids is less electrophilic than that of aldehydes/ketones

120. In the IUPAC system, $PhCH_2CH_2COOH$ is named as
(a) 3-phenylpropanoic acid
(b) 2-phenylpropanoic acid
(c) carboxyethylbenzene
(d) 2-phenylpropionic acid

121. What is the IUPAC name of the following compound?

$CH_3COCH_2CH_2CH_2COOH$ (skeletal structure shown)

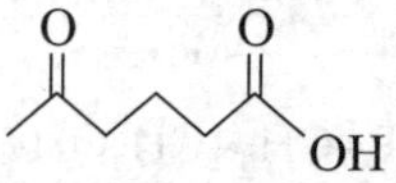

(a) hexa-2,6-dienone-6-ol
(b) 2-ketohexanoic acid
(c) 5-oxohexanoic acid
(d) 2-oxohexanoic acid
(e) 5-oxohexanoic acid

122. Glutaric acid is
(a) butane-1,4-dioic acid (b) propane-1,3-dioic acid
(c) pentane-1,5-dioic acid (d) hexane-1,6-dioic acid
(e) ethanedioic acid

Methods of Preparation of Carboxylic Acids

123. The major product formed in the oxidation of acetylene by alkaline $KMnO_4$ is
(a) ethanol (b) acetic acid
(c) formic acid (d) oxalic acid

124. The acid D obtained through the following sequence of reactions is

$$C_2H_5Br \xrightarrow[\Delta]{\text{Alc KOH}} A \xrightarrow[CCl_4]{Br_2} B \xrightarrow[\text{(excess)}]{KCN} C \xrightarrow{H_3O^+} D$$

(a) succinic acid (b) malonic acid
(c) maleic acid (d) oxalic acid

125. Chlorination of toluene in presence of light and heat followed by treatment with aqueous NaOH gives
(a) o-cresol (b) *p*-cresol
(c) 2,4-dihydroxytoluene (d) benzoic acid

126. Consider the following sequence of reactions:

$$C_6H_5NO_2 \xrightarrow[\Delta]{Br_2/FeBr_3} A \xrightarrow{\text{Mg/ether}} B \xrightarrow[H_3O^+]{\text{(i) Dry ice}} C$$

Which of the following statements is correct?
(a) A is 3-bromonitrobenzene.

(b) B is 3-nitrophenyl magnesium bromide.
(c) C is 3-nitrobenzoic acid.
(d) All statements are correct.

127. The structure of the product P of the following reaction is:

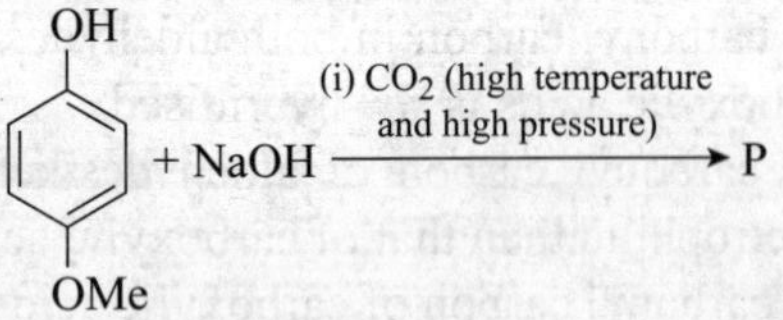

4-Methoxyphenol + NaOH $\xrightarrow[\text{and high pressure})]{\text{(i) } CO_2 \text{ (high temperature}}$ P

(a) 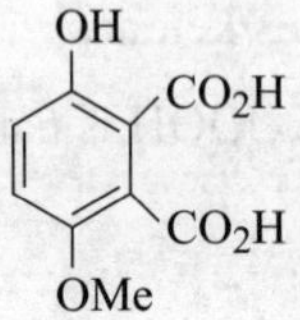 4-methoxyphenol with CO_2H at positions 2 and 3 (OH, CO_2H, CO_2H, OMe)
(b) 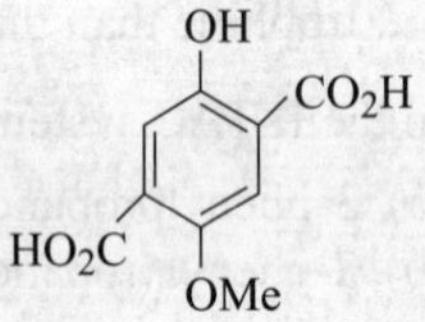 4-methoxyphenol with CO_2H at positions 2 and 5 (CO_2H, HO_2C, OMe)
(c) 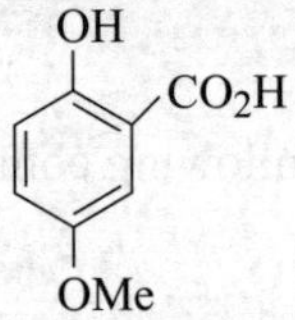 2-hydroxy-5-methoxybenzoic acid (OH, CO_2H, OMe)
(d) 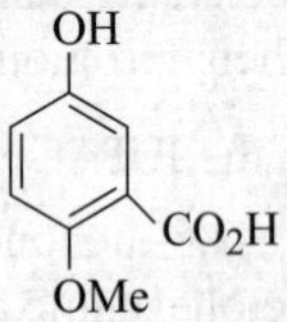 4-hydroxy-... with CO_2H ortho to OMe (OH, CO_2H, OMe)

128. $R–CH_2–CH_2OH$ can be converted into RCH_2CH_2COOH. The correct sequence of reagents is
(a) PBr_3, KCN, H^+
(b) PBr_3, KCN, H_2
(c) KCN, H^+
(d) HCN, PBr_3, H^+

129. $CH_3CHO + HCHO \xrightarrow[\text{heat}]{\text{dil NAOH}} A \xrightarrow[H_3O^+]{HCN} B$
The structure of compound B is
(a) $CH_2{=}CH–CH(OH)–COOH$
(b) $CH_2{=}CH–CH(CN)–OH$
(c) $CH_3CH_2–CH(CN)–OH$
(d) $CH_3–CH(OH)–COOH$

130. Pyruvic acid is obtained by
(a) oxidation of acetaldehyde cyanohydrin
(b) oxidation of formaldehyde cyanohydrin
(c) oxidation of acetone cyanohydrin
(d) none of the above

131. 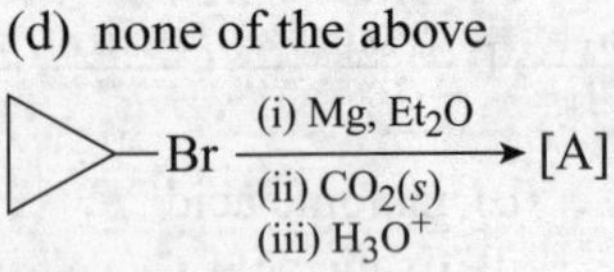 Cyclopropyl–Br $\xrightarrow[\text{(ii) } CO_2(s) \text{ (iii) } H_3O^+]{\text{(i) Mg, } Et_2O}$ [A]
Product [A] is
(a) 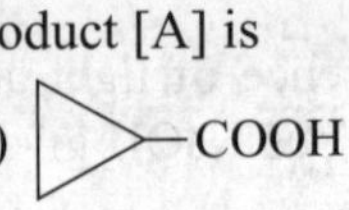 Cyclopropyl–COOH
(b) 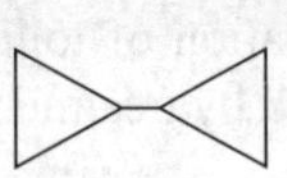 Cyclopropyl–cyclopropyl
(c) 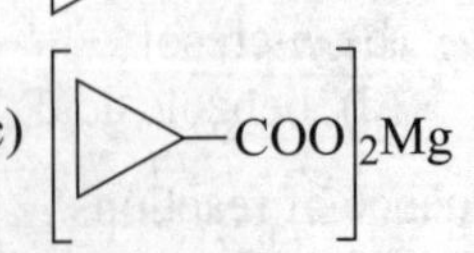 $[\text{Cyclopropyl–COO}]_2Mg$
(d)  Cyclopropane

132. The reaction sequence given below gives product R.

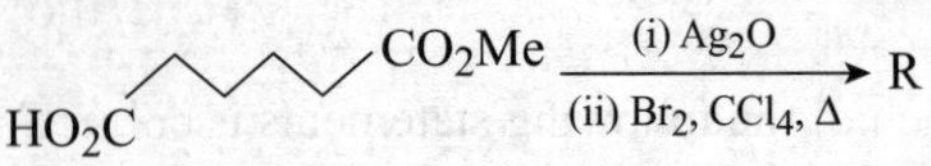

HO_2C–(chain)–CO_2Me $\xrightarrow[\text{(ii) } Br_2, CCl_4, \Delta]{\text{(i) } Ag_2O}$ R

The structure of the product R is,
(a)  Br–(chain)–CO_2Me
(b) 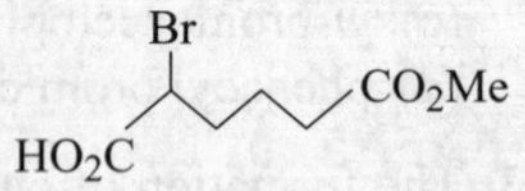 HO_2C–CH(Br)–(chain)–CO_2Me
(c) 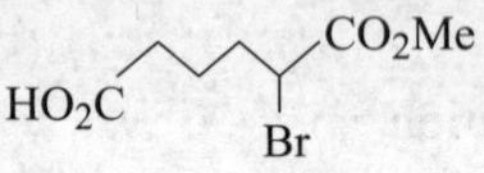 HO_2C–(chain)–CH(Br)–CO_2Me
(d) 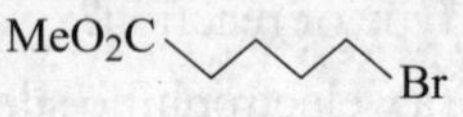 MeO_2C–(chain)–Br

133. Phenol $\xrightarrow[\text{dust}]{\text{Zn}}$ X $\xrightarrow[\text{Anhyd. } AlCl_3]{CH_3Cl}$ Y $\xrightarrow[KMnO_4]{\text{Alk.}}$ Z
The product Z is
(a) benzaldehyde
(b) benzoic acid
(c) benzene
(d) toluene

134. 4-Methylacetophenone on heating with alkaline $KMnO_4$ followed by hydrolysis with dil. H_2SO_4 gives
(a) toluene
(b) acetophenone
(c) terephthalic acid
(d) phthalic acid

135. Reaction of 2-butene with acidic $KMnO_4$ gives
(a) CH_3CHO
(b) HCOOH
(c) CH_3CH_2OH
(d) CH_3COOH

Physical Properties of Carboxylic Acids

136. Identify the correct order of boiling points of the following compounds:
$\underset{1}{CH_3CH_2CH_2CH_2OH}$ $\underset{2}{CH_3CH_2CH_2CHO}$
$\underset{3}{CH_3CH_2CH_2COOH}$
(a) 1 > 2 > 3
(b) 3 > 1 > 2
(c) 1 > 3 > 2
(d) 3 > 2 > 1

137. Which of the following statements is not correct?
(a) *n*-Valeric acid has a higher melting point than *n*-butyric acid.
(b) Anthranilic acid has a lower melting point than salicylic acid.
(c) *o*-Toluic acid has a lower melting point than benzoic acid.
(d) Oxalic acid has a higher melting point than malonic acid.

138. Carboxylic acids have higher boiling points than aldehydes, ketones and even alcohols of comparable molecular mass. This is because
(a) of intramolecular H-bonding
(b) of the formation of a carboxylate ion
(c) of extensive association of carboxylic acid via van der Waals' forces of attraction
(d) of intermolecular H-bonding

Chemical Properties of Carboxylic Acids

139. Which of the following presents the correct order of the acidity in the given compounds?
(a) $FCH_2COOH > ClCH_2COOH > BrCH_2COOH > CH_3COOH$

(b) CH_3COOH > $BrCH_2COOH$ > $ClCH_2COOH$ > FCH_2COOH
(c) FCH_2COOH > CH2COOH > $BrCH_2COOH$ > $ClCH_2COOH$
(d) $BrCH_2COOH$ > $ClCH_2COOH$ > FCH_2COOH > CH_3COOH

140. The correct order of acidity of the following compounds is

(1) benzoic acid (COOH); (2) p-OCH_3 benzoic acid (COOH); (3) p-NO_2 benzoic acid (COOH)

(a) 1 > 2 > 3 (b) 1 > 3 > 2
(c) 3 > 1 > 2 (d) 3 > 2 > 1

141. The relative acidic strength of benzoic acid, *o*-toluic acid and *p*-toluic acid in the decreasing order is:
(a) *p*-toluic acid > *o*-toluic acid > benzoic acid
(b) *o*-toluic acid > *p*-toluic acid > benzoic acid
(c) *p*-toluic acid > benzoic acid > *o*-toluic acid
(d) *o*-toluic acid > benzoic acid > *p*-toluic acid

142. The correct order of increasing acid strength of the compounds
(A) CH_3CO_2H (B) $MeOCH_2CO_2H$
(C) CF_3CO_2H (D) $(Me)_2CH$–CO_2H is
(a) B < D < A < C (b) D < A < C < B
(c) D < A < B < C (d) A < D < C < B

143. The correct order of decreasing acid strength of trichloroacetic acid (A), trifluoroacetic acid (B), acetic acid (C) and formic acid (D) is
(a) B > A > D > C (b) B > D > C > A
(c) A > B > C > D (d) A > C > B > D

144. Which of the following compounds would have the smallest value of pK_a?
(a) $CHF_2CH_2CH_2COOH$ (b) $CH_3CH_2CF_2COOH$
(c) $CH_2FCHFCH_2COOH$ (d) $CH_3CF_2CH_2COOH$

145. Arrange the following compounds in the order of decreasing acidity.
I. $CH_3CH_2CH(Br)COOH$ II. $CH_3CH(Br)CH_2COOH$
III. $(CH_3)_2CHCOOH$ IV. $CH_3CH_2CH_2COOH$
(a) I > II > III > IV (b) III < IV < II < I
(c) II > I > IV > III (d) II < I < IV < III

146. In each of following pairs of carboxylic acids which of the first acids is more acidic than the second?
(i) CH_3CO_2H or CH_2FCO_2H
(ii) CH_2FCO_2H or CH_2ClCO_2H
(iii) $CH_2FCH_2CH_2CO_2H$ or $CH_3CHFCH_2CO_2H$
(iv) F_3C–C_6H_4–COOH or H_3C–C_6H_4–COOH
(a) (i), (iii) (b) (ii), (iv)
(c) (ii), (iii) (d) (i), (iv)

147. The order of acidity of compounds I–IV, is

(I) C_6H_5–CH_2OH (II) C_6H_5–CO_2H
(III) H_3C–C_6H_4–OH (IV) C_6H_5–SO_3H

(a) I < III < II < IV (b) IV < I < II < III
(c) III < I < II < IV (d) II < IV < III < I

148. The correct order of strengths of carboxylic acids is,

I: cyclohexane-COOH; II: tetrahydropyran-COOH (O para to COOH carbon); III: tetrahydropyran-COOH (O adjacent)

(a) I > II > III (b) II > III >I
(c) III > II > I (d) II > I > III

149. What will be the correct decreasing order of acid strength of the hydroxybenzoic acids?
(a) *p*-hydroxybenzoic acid > benzoic acid > *m*-hydroxybenzoic acid > *o*-hydroxybenzoic acid
(b) *o*-hydroxybenzoic acid > *m*-hydroxybenzoic acid > benzoic acid > *p*-hydroxybenzoic acid
(c) *o*-hydroxybenzoic acid > benzoic acid > *m*-hydroxybenzoic acid > *p*-hydroxybenzoic acid
(d) *m*-hydroxybenzoic acid > benzoic acid > *o*-hydroxybenzoic acid > *p*-hydroxybenzoic acid

150. Propionic acid with Br_2/P yields a dibromo product. Its structure would be
(a) $CHBr_2$–CH_2COOH (b) CH_2Br–CH_2–COBr
(c) CH_3–CBr_2–COOH (d) CH_2Br–CHBr–COOH

151. $CH_3CH_2COOH \xrightarrow[\text{red P}]{Cl_2} A \xrightarrow{\text{alc.KOH}} B$
What is B?
(a) CH_3–CH_2–COCl (b) CH_3–CH_2–CHO
(c) CH_2=CHCOOH (d) $ClCH_2CH_2COOH$

152. When benzoic acid is treated with $LiAlH_4$, it forms:
(a) benzaldehyde (b) benzyl alcohol
(c) benzene (d) toluene

153. When CH_2=CH–COOH is reduced with $LiAlH_4$, the compound obtained will be
(a) CH_3–CH_2–CHO (b) CH_3–CH_2–COOH
(c) CH_2=CH–CH_2OH (d) CH_3–CH_2–COOH

154. Which of the following carboxylic acids undergoes decarboxylation easily?

(a) C_6H_5–CO–CH_2–COOH
(b) C_6H_5–CO–COOH
(c) C_6H_5–CH(OH)–COOH (d) C_6H_5–CH(NH_2)–COOH

155. The compound that undergoes decarboxylation most readily under mild conditions is

(a) 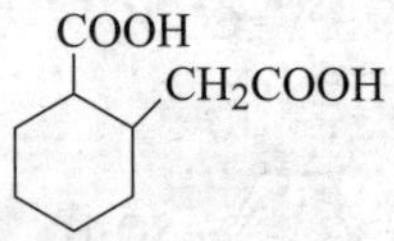 cyclohexane with COOH and CH_2COOH on adjacent carbons
(b) 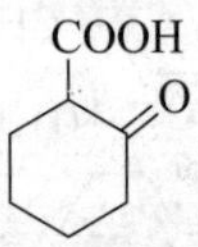 cyclohexanone with COOH (2-oxocyclohexanecarboxylic acid)
(c) 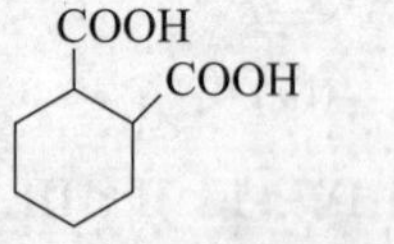 cyclohexane with COOH and COOH on adjacent carbons
(d) 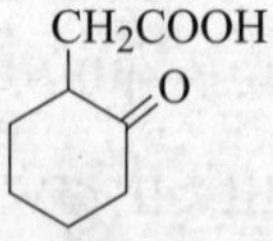 cyclohexanone with CH_2COOH

156. 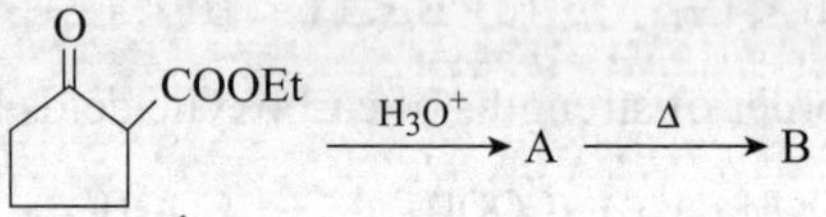 2-oxocyclopentane with COOEt $\xrightarrow{H_3O^+}$ A $\xrightarrow{\Delta}$ B

The compound B is

(a) 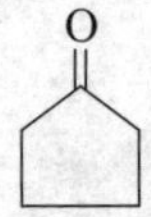 cyclopentanone (b) 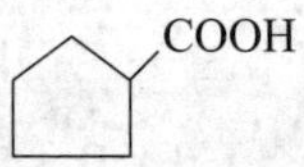 cyclopentane–COOH (c) 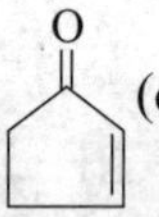 cyclohexenone (d) 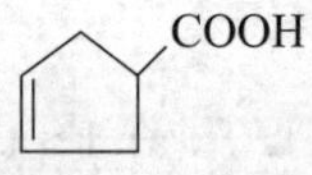 cyclopentene–COOH

157. Which of the following acids on heating loses a molecule of H_2O to form an α,β-unsaturated acid?
(a) $CH_3CHOHCOOH$
(b) $HOCH_2COOH$
(c) $CH_3CHOHCH_2COOH$
(d) $HOCH_2CH_2CH_2COO$ H

158. 4-Formylbenzoic acid on treatment with one equivalent of hydrazine by heating with alcoholic KOH gives the major product,

(a) 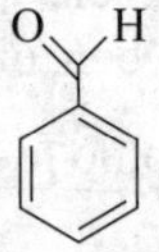 benzaldehyde (C6H5–CHO) (b) 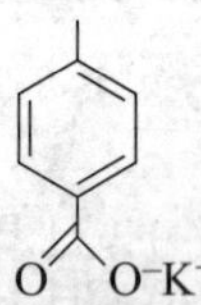 4-methylbenzoate, O^-K^+ (c) 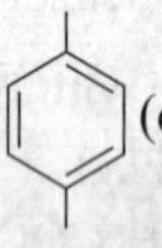 p-xylene (d) 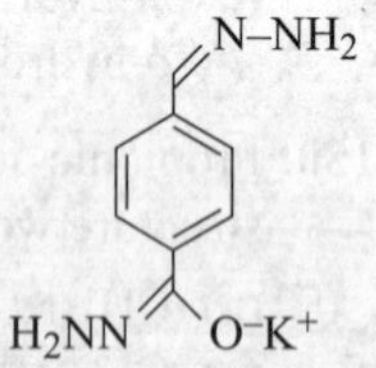 4-(CH=N–NH_2)–C6H4–C(=O)O^-K^+ with H_2NN

159. *o*-Toluic acid on reaction with $Br_2$and Fe gives

(a) 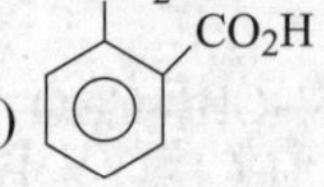 CH_2Br, CO_2H on benzene (b) 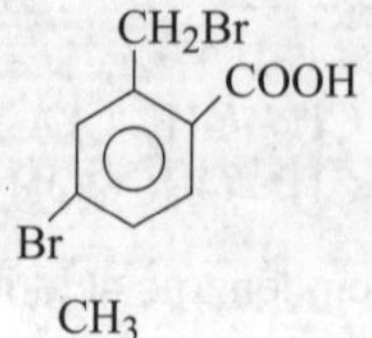 CH_2Br, COOH, Br on benzene
(c) 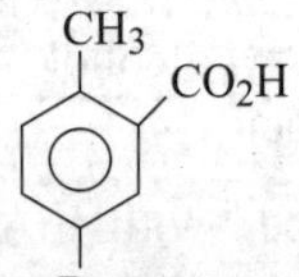 CH_3, CO_2H, Br on benzene (d) 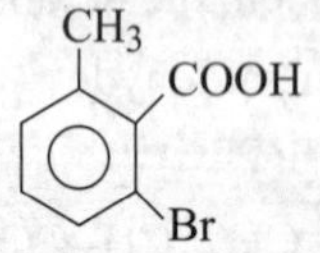 CH_3, COOH, Br on benzene

160. Consider the following reaction sequence:
$C_6H_5COOH \xrightarrow{SOCl_2} (A) \xrightarrow{NH_3\ (excess)} (B)$
The final product (B) is

(a) $C_6H_5COONH_4$ (b) $C_6H_5CONH_2$
(c) $C_6H_5NH_2$ (d) C_6H_5CN

161. Which of the following compounds when heated with conc. NaOH evolves NH_3 gas?
(a) CH_3CONH_2 (b) CH_3CN
(c) NH_2CONH_2 (d) all the three

162. $CH_3CH_2CH_2CONH_2$ is boiled with aqueous NaOH, then the reaction mixture is acidified with HCl. The products obtained are
(a) $CH_3CH_2CH_2COO^- + NH_3$
(b) $CH_3CH_2CH_2COONa + NH_3$
(c) $CH_3CH_2CH_2COOH + NH_4Cl$
(d) $CH_3CH_2CH_2COO^- + NH_4Cl$

163. The major product in the reaction of N-phenylbenzamide with Br_2/Fe is

(a) 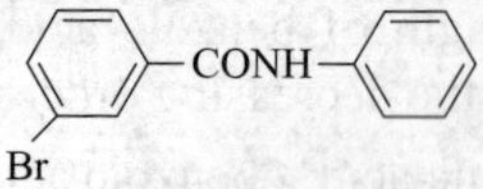 C6H4(Br)–CONH–C6H5 (b) 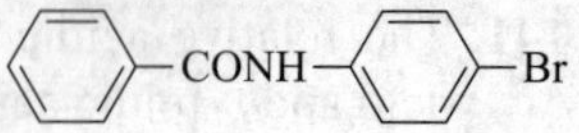 C6H5–CONH–C6H4–Br
(c) 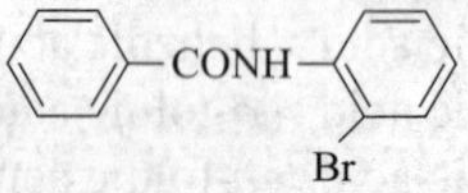 C6H5–CONH–C6H4(Br) (d) 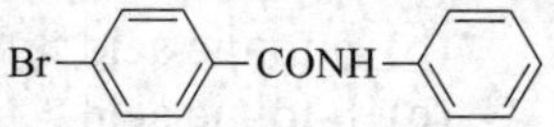 Br–C6H4–CONH–C6H5

164. Ethanol on reaction with alkaline KMnO4 gives X which when reacted with methanol in the presence of an acid gives a sweet-smelling compound Y. X and Y respectively are
(a) acetaldehyde and acetone
(b) acetic acid and methyl acetate
(c) formic acid and methyl formate
(d) ethylene and ethyl methyl ether

165. $CH_3COOH \xrightarrow{LiAlH_4} A$
$A + CH_3COOH \xrightarrow{H^+} B + H_2O$
In the above reaction, A and B respectively are,
(a) $CH_3COOC_2H_5$, C_2H_5OH
(b) CH_3CHO, C_2H_5OH
(c) C_2H_5OH, CH_3CHO (d) C_2H_5OH, $CH_3COOC_2H_5$

166. Methyl acetate and ethyl acetate can be distinguished by
(a) hot $KMnO_4$ solution (b) neutral $FeCl_3$
(c) iodoform test (d) none of the above

167. When acetyl chloride reacts with sodium propionate, the product formed is
(a) acetic anhydride
(b) acetic propionic anhydride
(c) *n*-propyl acetate
(d) pentane-2,4-diene

168. Which one of the following pairs gives effervescence with aq. $NaHCO_3$?
I. CH_3COCl II. CH_3COCH_3
III. CH_3COOCH_3 IV. $CH_3CO.O.COCH_3$
(a) I and II (b) I and IV (c) II and III (d) I and III

169. Rate of the reaction

$$R-C(=O)-Z + Nu^- \longrightarrow R-C(=O)-Nu + Z^-$$

is fastest when Z is
(a) Cl (b) NH_2 (c) OC_2H_5 (d) $OCOCH_3$

170. The relative reactivities of acyl compounds towards nucleophilic substitution are in the order of
(a) acid anhydride > amide > ester > acyl chloride
(b) acyl chloride > ester > acid anhydride > amide
(c) acyl chloride > acid anhydride > ester > amide
(d) ester > acyl chloride > amide > acid anhydride

171. Consider the following compounds.
(i) C_6H_5COCl (ii) $O_2N-C_6H_4-COCl$
(iii) $H_3C-C_6H_4-COCl$ (iv) $OHC-C_6H_4-COCl$

The correct decreasing order of their reactivity towards hydrolysis is:
(a) (ii) > (iv) > (i) > (iii) (b) (ii) > (iv) > (iii) > (i)
(c) (i) > (ii) > (iii) > (iv) (d) (iv) > (ii) > (i) > (iii)

172. Which one of the following esters gets hydrolysed most easily under alkaline conditions.
(a) $CH_3O-C_6H_4-COCOCH_3$ (b) $C_6H_5-OCOCH_3$
(c) $Cl-C_6H_4-OCOCH_3$ (d) $O_2N-C_6H_4-OCOCH_3$

173. Ethyl acetate reacts with $H_2NNHCONH_2$ to form
(a) $CH_3CONHNH_2$
(b) $CH_3CONH(NH_2)CONH_2$
(c) $CH_3CONHNHCONH_2$
(d) $CH_3CH_2NHNHCONH_2$

174. Which one of the following orders of acids strength is correct?
(a) RCOOH > ROH > HOH > HC≡CH
(b) RCOOH > HOH > ROH > HC≡CH
(c) RCOOH > HC≡CH >HOH > ROH
(d) RCOOH > HC≡CH > HOH > ROH

175. The correct acidity order of the following is

(I) phenol (OH) (II) p-chlorophenol (OH, Cl) (III) benzoic acid (COOH) (IV) p-toluic acid (COOH, CH_3)

(a) (III) > (IV) > (II) > (I) (b) (IV) > (III) > (I) > (II)
(c) (III) > (II) > (I) > (IV) (d) (II) > (III) > (IV) > (I)

Final Preparation

176. The main product of the following reaction is

[benzo-fused lactone bearing CN] $\xrightarrow[\text{(ii) } H_3O^+]{\text{DIBAL-H}}$

(a) CHO, OH, CH_2CHO (b) CHO, O (c) CH=NH, OH, OH (d) CHO, O, O

177. In a set of reactions, acetic acid yielded product D.

$$CH_3COOH \xrightarrow{SOCl_2} A \xrightarrow[\text{Anhyd. AlCl}_3]{\text{Benzene}} B \xrightarrow{HCN} C \xrightarrow{HOH} D$$

The structure of D would be
(a) $C_6H_5-C(OH)(CH_3)-COOH$ (b) $C_6H_5-CH_2-C(COOH)(OH)-CH_3$
(c) $C_6H_5-C(CN)(OH)-CH_3$ (d) $C_6H_5-CH_2-C(OH)(CN)-CH_3$

178. Arrange the following in the increasing order of their equilibrium constants for hydration.

I. $CH_3-C(=O)-CH_3$ II. $CH_3-C(=O)-H$
III. $CH_3-C(=O)-CH_2Cl$ IV. $H-C(=O)-H$
V. $Cl-CH_2-C(=O)-H$

(a) I < II < III < IV < V (b) I < III < II < V < IV
(c) I < III < IV < II < V (d) III < I < II < V < IV

179. Arrange the following gem-diols in the decreasing order of their stability.

I. cyclopropane-1,1-diol (OH, OH) II. cyclobutane-1,1-diol (OH, OH) III. cyclopentane-1,1-diol (OH, OH)

(a) I > II > III (b) III > II > I
(c) I > III > II (d) III > I > II

180. Which of the following compounds may be classified as a hemiacetal?

(a) [structure: tetrahydrofuran-2-ol] (b) [structure: 1-methoxycyclohexan-1-ol, HO OMe]

(c) [structure: epoxide with HO, H] (d) all the three

181. Which of the following reagents will distinguish *cis*-cyclopentane-1,2-diol from the *trans*-isomer?

(a) MnO_2 (b) aluminium isopropoxide
(c) acetone (d) O_3

182. [p-cresol] + $CH_2(OC_2H_5)_2$ $\xrightarrow{H^+}$ Z ; Z is

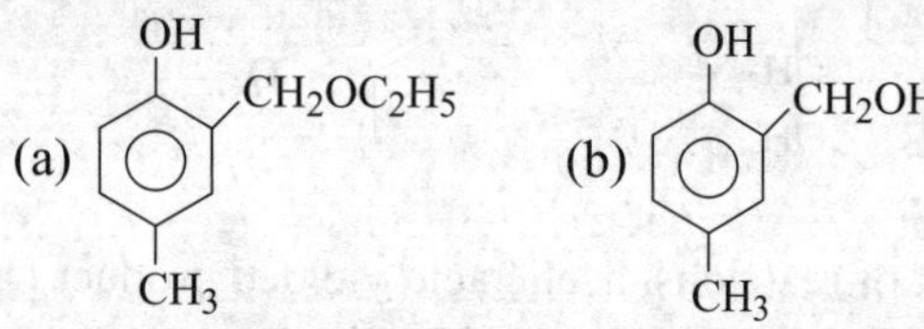

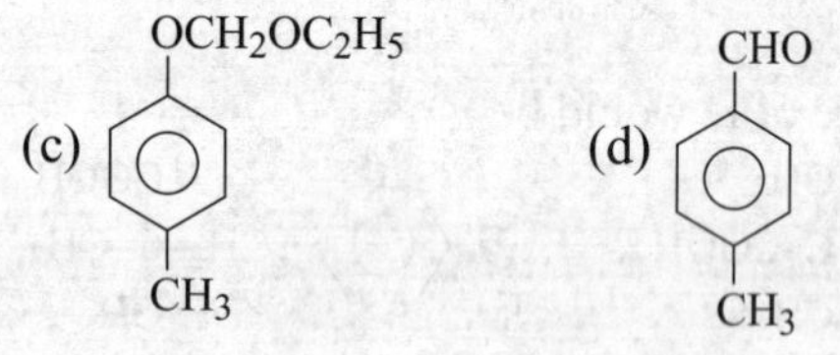

183. Reduction of the following lactol with sodium borohydride gives [structure: tetrahydrofuran-2-ol]

(a) [tetrahydrofuran] (b) [γ-butyrolactone]
(c) HO⁀⁀OH (butane-1,4-diol) (d) [butanol, ⁀⁀OH]

184. The correct sequence of reagents to carry out the following conversion, is

$CH_3COCH_2COOC_2H_5 \rightarrow CH_3COCH_2CH_2OH$

(a) (i) $LiAlH_4$/ether, (ii) $(CH_3OH)_2$/PTS, (iii) H_3O^+
(b) (i) H_3O^+, (ii) $(CH_2OH)_2$/PTS, (iii) $NaBH_4/CH_3OH$
(c) (i) $(CH_2OH)_2$/PTS, (ii) $NaBH_4/CH_3OH$, (iii) H_3O^+
(d) (i) $(CH_2OH)_2$/PTS, (ii) $LiAlH_4$/ether, (iii) H_3O^+

185. The correct sequence of reagents for the following conversion will be

[4-formylcyclohexanone → 1-methyl-4-(1-hydroxy-1-methylethyl)cyclohexan-1-ol; labels: O, CHO, HO CH₃, HO–C–CH₃, CH₃]

(a) CH_3MgBr, $[Ag(NH_3)_2]^+OH^-$, H^+/CH_3OH
(b) $[Ag(NH_3)_2]^+OH^-$, CH_3MgBr, H^+/CH_3OH
(c) $[Ag(NH_3)_2]^+OH^-$, H^+/CH_3OH, CH_3MgBr
(d) CH_3MgBr, H^+/CH_3OH, $[Ag(NH_3)_2]^+OH^-$

186. Positive Tollens' test is not given by

(a) [acrolein, H₂C=CH–CHO] (b) [benzaldehyde, CHO]
(c) [PhCH(OH)COPh] (d) [PhCH=CHCOPh]

187. The product of acid hydrolysis of P and Q can be distinguished by

(P) $H_2C=C(CH_3)OCOCH_3$ (Q) $H_3C–CH=CH–OCOCH_3$

(a) Lucas reagent (b) 2,4-DNP
(c) Fehling's solution (d) $NaHSO_3$

188. The reagent that can be used to bring about the following transformation is

[structure: epoxy aldehyde with tert-butyl ester and COOH → epoxy alcohol with tert-butyl ester and COOH]

(a) $LiAlH_4$ is $(C_2H_5)_2O$ (b) BH_3 in THF
(c) $NaBH_4$ in C_2H_5OH (d) Raney Ni/H_2 in THF

189. The reagent(s) required for all the following conversions are

[structure: cyclohexane with Et_2OC, CO_2H, CN → cyclohexane with OH, HO_2C, CHO]

(a) (i) $LiAlH_4$, (ii) H_3O^+
(b) (i) B_2H_6, (ii) DIBAL-H, (iii) H_3O^+
(c) (i) B_2H_6, (ii) $SnCl_2/HCl$, (iii) H_3O^+
(d) (i) $NaBH_4$, (ii) Raney Ni/H_2, (iii) H_3O^+

190. In which of the following compounds, are the methylene (CH_2) hydrogens the most acidic?

(a) $CH_3COCH_2COCH_3$ (b) $CH_3COCH_2COOC_2H_5$
(c) $CH_2(COOC_2H_5)_2$ (d) $CH_3CH_2COCH_3$

191. Which of the following compounds will undergo self-aldol condensation in the presence of cold dilute alkali?

(a) $CH_2{=}CH{-}CHO$ (b) $CH{\equiv}C{-}CHO$
(c) C_6H_5CHO (d) CH_3CH_2CHO

192. Base catalysed aldol condensation occurs with

(a) benzaldehyde (b) 2-methylpropanal
(c) 2,2-dimethylpropanal (d) none of the above

193. Cyclohexene on ozonolysis followed by reaction with zinc dust and water gives compound E. Compound E on further treatment with aqueous KOH yields compound F. Compound F is

(a) –CHO (b) –CHO

(c) –COOH (d) CO_2H, CO_2H

194. The diketone $CH_3–\overset{O}{\overset{\|}{C}}–(CH_2)_2–\overset{O}{\overset{\|}{C}}–CH_3$ on intramolecular aldol condensation gives the final product

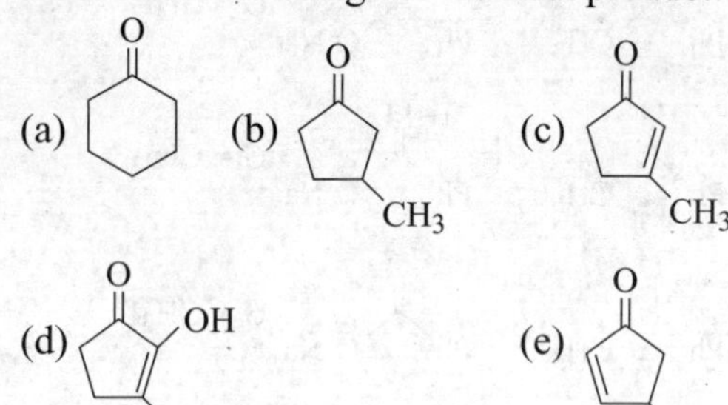

195. The major product of the following reaction is

(i) KOH, H_2O; (ii) H^+, Heat

(a) CH_3 (b) CH_3

(c) CH_3 (d) CH_3

196. Predict the product of the following reaction.

$$CH_3–\underset{COOCH_3}{\overset{COOCH_3}{CH–CH}}–CH_2–CH_2–\overset{O}{\overset{\|}{C}}–CH_3 \xrightarrow[\text{(ii) KOH, }\Delta]{\text{(i) DIBAL-H}}$$

(a) $CH_3–\underset{CHO}{CH}–$ ⟨ring⟩ $=O$ (b) $CH_3–CO–$ ⟨ring with CHO, CH_3⟩

(c) CH_3 ⟨ring with $–\overset{O}{\overset{\|}{C}}–CH_3$, CHO⟩ (d) $O=$ ⟨ring⟩ $–CHO$

197. If the enolate ion combines with the carbonyl group of an ester, we get a/an

(a) aldol (b) α, β-unsaturated ester

(c) β-ketoaldehyde (d) acid

198. An organic compound A has the molecular formula C_3H_6O. It undergoes the iodoform test. When saturated with HCl, it gives B of molecular formula $C_9H_{14}O$. A and B respectively are

(a) propanal and mesitylene

(b) propanone and mesityl oxide

(c) propanone and 2,6-dimethyl-2,5-heptadien-4-one

(d) propanone and mesitylene oxide

199. The major products X and Y, respectively, are

(a) CH_2OH, COOH and ⟨lactone⟩

(b) CO_2H, CO_2H and ⟨anhydride⟩

(c) CH_2OH, CH_2OH and ⟨cyclic ether⟩

(d) CHO, CH_2OH and ⟨lactone⟩

200. In the following reaction, the product (A) is

$$\underset{CHO}{\overset{CHO}{|}} \xrightarrow[\text{(ii) }H_3O^+]{\text{(i) Conc. NaOH}} A$$

(a) $\underset{CHO}{\overset{CH_2OH}{|}}$ (b) $\underset{CO_2H}{\overset{CHO}{|}}$ (c) $\underset{CO_2H}{\overset{CH_2OH}{|}}$ (d) $\underset{CO_2H}{\overset{CO_2H}{|}}$

201. If heavy water is taken as the solvent instead of normal water while performing the Cannizzaro reaction, the products of the reaction are

(a) $RCOO^- + RCH_2OH$ (b) $RCOO^- + RCH_2OD$

(c) $RCOOD + RCD_2OD$ (d) $RCOO^- + RCD_2OD$

202. $D–\overset{D}{\overset{|}{C}}=O + OH^- \longrightarrow X + Y$

Products X and Y are

(a) $D–\overset{D}{\overset{\|}{C}}–O^-$, $D–\underset{D}{\overset{D}{C}}–OH$ (b) $D–\overset{D}{\overset{\|}{C}}–O^-$, $D–\underset{H}{\overset{D}{C}}–OH$

(c) $H–\overset{D}{\overset{\|}{C}}–O^-$, $D–\underset{D}{\overset{D}{C}}–OH$ (d) none of these are correct

203. What will be the products when benzaldehyde is treated with NaOD in D_2O?

(a) $C_6H_5CH_2OD$ and C_6H_5COONa

(b) $C_6H_5CH_2OD$ andC_6H_5COOD

(c) C_6H_5CHDOD and C_6H_5COONa

(d) $C_6H_5COOCHDC_6H_5$

204. In the Cannizzaro reaction given below,
$2\text{ Ph–CHO} \xrightarrow{\text{OH}^-} \text{Ph–CH}_2\text{OH} + \text{PhCO}_2^-$, the slowest step is
(a) the attack of $^-$OH at the carbonyl group
(b) the transfer of the hydride ion to the carbonyl group
(c) the abstraction of a proton from the carboxylic acid
(d) the deprotonation of Ph–CH_2OH

205. In a Cannizzaro reaction, the intermediate that will be the best hydride donor is

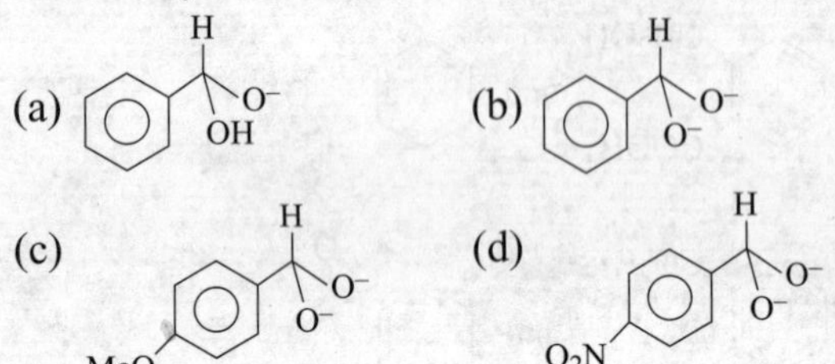

206. The product of the following reaction

$CH_3O–C_6H_4–CHO \xrightarrow{\text{Alc. KCN}}$ is

(a) $CH_3O–C_6H_4–CH_2OH$
(b) $CH_3O–C_6H_4–CH(OH)–CH(OH)–C_6H_4–OCH_3$
(c) $CH_3O–C_6H_4–C(=O)–C(=O)–C_6H_4–OCH_3$
(d) $CH_3O–C_6H_4–C(=O)–CH(OH)–C_6H_4–OCH_3$

207. Which one of the following species is likely to be the intermediate during benzoin condensation of benzaldehyde?
(a) $\text{Ph–C}\equiv\overset{+}{\text{O}}$
(b) $\text{Ph–}\overset{+}{\text{C}}\text{(OH)(CN)}$
(c) Ph–C(OH)(CN)
(d) Ph–C=O

208. The number of aldol reactions that occur in the given transformation, is

$CH_3CHO + 4HCHO \xrightarrow{\text{Conc. aq. NaOH}} C(CH_2OH)_4$

(a) 1 (b) 2 (c) 3 (d) 4

209. What is X in the following reaction?

$4\text{-MeO–C}_6H_4\text{–CHO} + X \xrightarrow{CH_3COONa} 4\text{-MeO–C}_6H_4\text{–CH=CH–COOH}$

(a) CH_3COOH
(b) $BrCH_2COOH$
(c) $(CH_3CO)_2O$
(d) OHC–COOH

210. In the following reaction sequence, the correct structures of E, F and G are

$\text{Ph–CO–}\overset{*}{C}H_2\text{–CO–OH} \xrightarrow{\text{Heat}} [E] \xrightarrow[\text{NaOH}]{I_2} [F] + [G]$

(*implies ^{18}C labelled carbon)

(a) $E = \text{Ph–}\overset{*}{C}\text{O–CH}_3$ $F = \text{Ph–}\overset{*}{C}\text{O–}\overset{\ominus}{O}\overset{\oplus}{Na}$ $G = CHI_3$
(b) $E = \text{Ph–CO–}\overset{*}{C}H_3$ $F = \text{Ph–}\overset{*}{C}\text{O–}\overset{\ominus}{O}\overset{\oplus}{Na}$ $G = CHI_3$
(c) $E = \text{Ph–CO–}\overset{*}{C}H_3$ $F = \text{Ph–CO–}\overset{\ominus}{O}\overset{\oplus}{Na}$ $G = \overset{*}{C}HI_3$
(d) $E = \text{Ph–CO–}\overset{*}{C}H_3$ $F = \text{Ph–}\overset{*}{C}\text{O–}\overset{\ominus}{O}\overset{\oplus}{Na}$ $G = CH_3I$

211. After completion of reactions (I and II), the organic compound(s) in the reaction mixture is (are)

Reaction I: $H_3C–CO–CH_3$ (1.0 mole) $\xrightarrow[\text{aqueous NaOH}]{Br_2\text{ (1.0 mole)}}$

Reaction II: $H_3C–CO–CH_3$ (1.0 mole) $\xrightarrow[CH_3COOH]{Br_2\text{ (1.0 mole)}}$

P: $H_3C–CO–CH_2Br$
Q: $H_3C–CO–CBr_3$
R: $Br_3C–CO–CBr_3$
S: $BrH_2C–CO–CH_2Br$
T: $H_3C–CO–ONa$
Y: $CHBr_3$

(a) Reaction I: P and Reaction II: P
(b) Reaction I: U, acetone and Reaction II: Q, acetone
(c) Reaction I: T, U, acetone and Reaction II: P
(d) Reaction I: R, acetone and Reaction II: S, acetone

212. Among the given compounds, the most susceptible to nucleophilic attack at the carbonyl group is
(a) MeCOCl
(b) MeCHO
(c) MeCOOMe
(d) MeCOOCOMe

213. Self-condensation of two moles of ethyl acetate in the presence of sodium ethoxide yields
(a) ethyl propionate
(b) ethyl butyrate
(c) acetoacetic ester
(d) methyl acetoacetate

214. $CH_3CO_2C_2H_5$ on reaction with sodium ethoxide in ethanol gives A, which on heating in the presence of acid gives B. The compound B is

(a) CH_3COCH_2COOH (b) CH_3COCH_3

(c) $CH_2=$ (four-membered lactone ring with =O) (d) $CH_2=C(OC_2H_5)_2$

215. A keto ester (A) with a MF $C_6H_{10}O_3$ on treatment with NaOH + I_2 does not give iodoform but on boiling with dilute KOH gives a compound (B) with MF $C_4H_5O_3K$ which upon acidification followed by heating undergoes decarboxylation to give acetone. The keto ester (A) is

(a) $CH_3COCH_2CH_2COOCH_3$
(b) $CH_3COCH_2COOC_2H_5$
(c) $CH_3CH_2OCH_2COOCH_3$
(d) $CH_3–COCH(CH_3)COOCH_3$

216. An acid reacts with an isotopically labelled methanol to produce

(a) methyl acetate having all the labelled oxygen
(b) water having all the labelled oxygen
(c) both methyl acetate and water contain isotopic oxygen
(d) no esterification

217. $(CH_3)_2C=O + HCN \xrightarrow{H^+} \xrightarrow{H_3O^+} \xrightarrow[(ii)\ PCl_5]{(i)\ H_2SO_4} \xrightarrow[(ii)\ H_2O_2,\ OH^-]{(i)\ BH_3-THF}$ Product

The final predominant product is

(a) $HOCH_2–CH(CH_3)–COOH$ (b) $CH_3–C(OH)(CH_3)–COOH$

(c) $CH_3–CH(OH)–CH_3$ (d) $CH_3CH_2–CO–COOH$

218. In a set of reactions, ethylbenzene yielded a product D.

$C_6H_5CH_2CH_3 \xrightarrow[KOH]{KMnO_4} B \xrightarrow[FeCl_3]{Br_2} C \xrightarrow[H^+]{C_2H_5OH} D$

D would be

(a) benzene ring with $COOC_2H_5$ and Br (meta) (b) $C_6H_5–CH_2–CH(Br)–COOC_2H_5$

(c) benzene ring with Br, Br and $CH_2COOC_2H_5$ (d) benzene ring with COOH and OC_2H_5 (meta)

219. An aromatic compound X with a molecular formula $C_9H_{10}O$ gives the following chemical tests.

(i) forms the 2,4-DNP derivative
(ii) reduces Tollens' reagent
(iii) undergoes Cannizzaro reaction
(iv) on vigorous oxidation, 1,2-benzenedicarboxylic acid is obtained

X is

(a) benzene ring with CHO and C_2H_5 (ortho) (b) benzene ring with CHO and C_2H_5 (para) (c) benzene ring with $COCH_3$ and CH_3 (d) benzene ring with CHO and C_2H_5 (meta)

220. Benzene + succinic anhydride $\xrightarrow[AlCl_3]{Anhyd} X \xrightarrow[\Delta]{Phosphoric\ acid} Y$

X and Y, respectively are

(a) $C_6H_5COCH_2CH_2CO_2H$ and naphthalene-1,4-dione (tetrahydro)
(b) 1-tetralone and 4-hydroxy-1-tetralone
(c) dioxo-tetrahydronaphthalene with CH_2CO_2H groups and dioxo compound with two CO_2H groups
(d) $C_6H_5COCH_2CH_2CO_2H$ and 1-tetralone

221. The major product of the following reaction is

γ-butyrolactone + o-cresol (OH, CH_3) $\xrightarrow{AlCl_3,\ \Delta}$

(a) indanone with OH, CH_3 and methyl substituent (b) tetralone with OH and CH_3
(c) tetralone with CH_3 and OH (d) indanone with OH, CH_3

222. The product of the reaction of propyne with di-isoamylborane was oxidised with alkaline H_2O_2. The final product is

(a) propan-1-ol (b) propan-2-ol
(c) propanal (d) propanone

223. Predict the product of the following reaction

$C_6H_5CH(OH)C\equiv CH \xrightarrow{Hg^{2+}/H_3O^+}$

(a) $C_6H_5CH=CHCH_2OH$ (b) $C_6H_5C\equiv CCH_2OH$
(c) $C_6H_5CH=CHCHO$ (d) $C_6H_5CH=CHCOOH$

224. 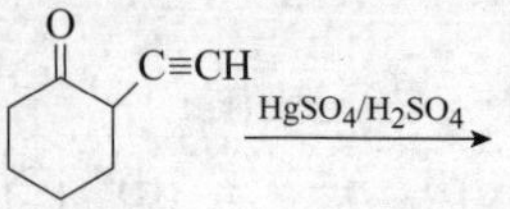 (2-ethynylcyclohexanone: cyclohexanone with C≡CH) $\xrightarrow{HgSO_4/H_2SO_4}$

Product (A) in the above reaction is

(a) 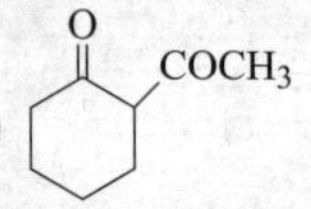 2-($COCH_3$)cyclohexanone (b) 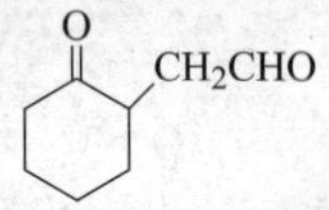 2-(CH_2CHO)cyclohexanone

(c) 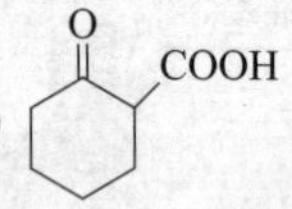 2-(COOH)cyclohexanone (d) 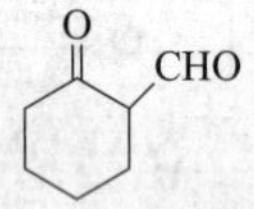 2-(CHO)cyclohexanone

225. Consider the following sequence of reactions.

$CH_3I \xrightarrow[\text{(ii) CuI}]{\text{(i)Li/dry ether}} A; (CH_3)_3CCOCl + A \rightarrow B$

The product B is

(a) $(CH_3)_3CCOCHO$ (b) $(CH_3)_3C(OH)(CH_3)_2$
(c) $(CH_3)_3CCOOCH_3$ (d) $(CH_3)_3CCOCH_3$

226. The products (A) and (B) in the following reactions respectively are

$PhCH{=}CH_2 \xrightarrow[\text{(ii) NaNH}_2\text{/liq.NH}_3]{\text{(i) Br}_2\text{/CCl}_4} (A) \xrightarrow[\text{HgSO}_4]{\text{Dil. H}_2\text{SO}_4} (B)$

(a) $PhCH_2CHO, PhCH_2CH_2OH$
(b) $PhC{\equiv}CNa, PhCOCH_3$
(c) $PhC{\equiv}CH, PhCH_2CHO$
(d) $PhCHCHCH_3, PhCOCHO$

227. The product of the reaction

$CH_2{=}CH_2 \xrightarrow[\text{High temp., high pressure}]{\text{CO,H}_2\text{,[Co(CO)}_4]_2} \text{is}$

(a) $CH_2{=}CHCHO$ (b) CH_3CH_2CHO
(c) $CH_3CH_2CH_2OH$ (d) $CH_3CHOHCH_3$

228. Which of the following is the industrial method of preparation of acetaldehyde?

(a) $CH_3CN \xrightarrow[\text{HCl}]{\text{SnCl}_2} CH_3CH{=}NH \xrightarrow{H_3O^+} CH_3CHO$

(b) $CH_3COCl + H_2 \xrightarrow[\text{BaSO}_4]{\text{Pd}} CH_3CHO + HCl$

(c) $CH_2 = CH_2 + H_2O \xrightarrow{Pd^{2+}} CH_3CHO$

(d) All of the above

229. $HC{\equiv}N + HCl \xrightarrow[\text{AlCl}_3]{\text{Anhyd.}} A \xrightarrow[\text{Anhyd.AlCl}_3]{C_6H_6} B \xrightarrow{H_2O} C$

In the above sequence of reactions, A, B and C respectively are

(a) $CHCl{=}NH, C_6H_5Cl, C_6H_5OH$
(b) $CHCl{=}NH, C_6H_5CH{=}NH, C_6H_5CHO$
(c) $CHCl{=}NH, C_6H_5Cl, C_6H_5OH$
(d) $CH_2O, C_6H_5CH_2Cl, C_6H_5CH_2OH$

230. Among the following reactions, the one that would give a good yield of acetaldehyde is

(a) $HCOOC_2H_5 \xrightarrow[\text{(ii) H}_3\text{O}^+]{\text{(i) CH}_3\text{ MgBr}}$

(b) $HC(OC_2H_5)_3 \xrightarrow[\text{(ii) H}_3\text{O}^+]{\text{(i) CH}_3\text{ MgBr}}$

(c) $HCHO \xrightarrow[\text{(ii) H}_3\text{O}^+]{\text{(i) CH}_3\text{ MgBr}}$ (d) $CH_3COCl + NaH \rightarrow$

231. Grignard reagents and organolithium compounds on addition to dry ice separately, followed by hydrolysis give

(a) ketones and carboxylic acids respectively
(b) carboxylic acids and ketones respectively
(c) only carboxylic acids (d) only ketones

232. In the following reactions:

(i) $CH_3CH_2ONa \xrightarrow[\text{under pressure}]{\text{CO, }\Delta} A$

(ii) $CH_2 = CH_2 + CO + H_2O \xrightarrow[\text{under pressure}]{H_3PO_4} B$

A and B respectively are:

(a) CH_3CH_2COOH in both cases
(b) CH_3CH_2CHO in both cases
(c) CH_3CH_2COOH, CH_3CHO
(d) CH_3CHO, CH_3COOH

233. The major product obtained in the following reaction is

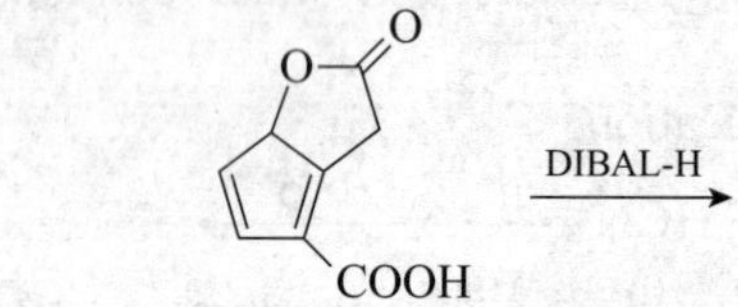

(bicyclic lactone fused to cyclopentadiene ring bearing COOH) $\xrightarrow{\text{DIBAL-H}}$

(a) 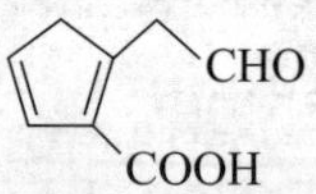 cyclopentadiene with CH_2CHO and COOH (b) 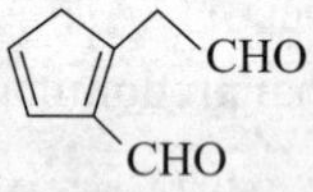 cyclopentadiene with CH_2CHO and CHO

(c) 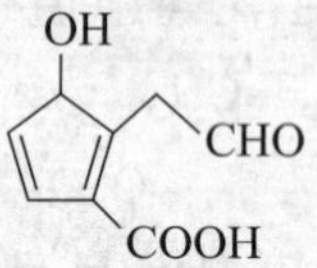 cyclopentadiene with OH, CH_2CHO and COOH (d) 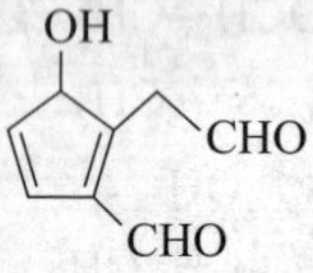 cyclopentadiene with OH, CH_2CHO and CHO

MATCH THE FOLLOWING

234.

Column I	Column II
(A) $CH_3CH_2CH_2CH_2OH \xrightarrow{PCC}$	(p) $(CH_3CH_2)_2C{=}O$
(B) $C_6H_5CH_3 \xrightarrow{CrO_2Cl_2}$	(q) CH_3COCH_3
(C) $CH_3COCl + (CH_3)_2Cd \rightarrow$	(r) $CH_3CH_2CH_2CHO$
(D) $(CH_3CH_2COO)_2Ca \xrightarrow{\Delta}$	(s) C_6H_5CHO

(a) (A)—(r); (B)—(s); (C)—(q); (D)—(p)
(b) (A)—(s); (B)—(r); (C)—(q); (D)—(p)
(c) (A)—(r); (B)—(s); (C)—(p); (D)—(q)
(d) (A)—(p); (B)—(q); (C)—(r); (D)—(s)

235.

Column I	Column II
(A) $C_6H_5COCH_3$	(p) HVZ reaction
(B) C_6H_5CHO	(q) Fehling's solution
(C) CH_3CH_2COOH	(r) Sodium bisulfite solution
(D) HCOOH	(s) Sodium hypoiodite

(a) (A)—(q); (B)—(p); (C)—(r); (D)—(s)
(b) (A)—(r); (B)—(q); (C)—(s); (D)—(p)
(c) (A)—(s); (B)—(r); (C)—(p); (D)—(q)
(d) (A)—(p); (B)—(s); (C)—(q); (D)—(r)

236.

Column I	Column II
(A) CH_3COCl	(p) Claisen ester condensation
(B) $(CH_3CO)_2O$	(q) Evolves NH_3 on heating with NaOH
(C) $CH_3COOC_2H_5$	(r) Most reactive acid derivative
(D) CH_3CONH_2	(s) Perkin condensation

(a) (A)—(p); (B)—(q); (C)—(s); (D)—(r)
(b) (A)—(r); (B)—(s); (C)—(p); (D)—(q)
(c) (A)—(q); (B)—(p); (C)—(r); (D)—(s)
(d) (A)—(s); (B)—(r); (C)—(q); (D)—(p)

237.

Column I	Column II
(A) $C_6H_5CH_3 \xrightarrow{CrO_2Cl_2}$	(p) Claisen ester condensation
(B) $CH_3CO_2C_2H_5 \xrightarrow{NaOC_2H_5} CH_3COCH_2COOC_2H_5$	(q) Tischenko reaction
(C) $CH_3CHO \xrightarrow{(Al(OC_2H_5)_3} CH_3COOC_2H_5$	(r) Rosenmund reduction
(D) $RCOCl \xrightarrow{H_2} BaSO_4 + S$	(s) Etard reaction

(a) (A)—(p); (B)—(s); (C)—(q); (D)—(r)
(b) (A)—(s); (B)—(r); (C)—(p); (D)—(s)
(c) (A)—(q); (B)—(p); (C)—(r); (D)—(s)
(d) (A)—(s); (B)—(p); (C)—(q); (D)—(r)

ASSERTION REASON

Directions: In each of the following questions, a statement of Assertion (A) is given followed by a corresponding statement of Reason (R) just below it. Of the statements, mark the correct answer as

(a) if both the assertion and reason are true and the reason is the correct explanation of the assertion.
(b) if both assertion and reason are true but reason is not the correct explanation of assertion
(c) If assertion is true but reason is false
(d) If both assertion and reason are false

238. Assertion: Isobutanal does not give the iodoform test.

Reason: It does not have α-hydrogens.

239. Assertion: Acetophenone and benzophenone can be distinguished by the iodoform test.

Reason: Acetophenone and benzophenone are both carbonyl compounds.

240. Assertion: During reaction of carboxylic acids with $NaHCO_3$, the CO_2 evolved comes from the carboxyl group and not from $NaHCO_3$.

Reason: Carbonic acid is a stronger acid than a carboxylic acid.

241. Assertion: Formic acid reacts with 2,4-dinitrophenylhydrazine to give a yellowish-brown crystalline derivative.

Reason: Formic acid contains an aldehydic group.

242. Assertion: The pK_a of acetic acid is lower than that of phenol.

Reason: Phenoxide ion is more resonance stabilised than the acetate ion.

243. Assertion: *p*-Chlorobenzoic acid is a stronger acid than benzoic acid.

Reason: Chlorine has an electron donating resonance (+R) effect.

244. Assertion: Esters which contain α-hydrogens undergo Claisen ester condensation.

Reason: $LiAlH_4$ reduction of esters gives acids.

245. Assertion: Acetamide has a more polar C=O group than ethyl acetoacetate.

Reason: The NH_2 group is more electron donating than OC_2H_5.

246. Assertion: Malonic acid ($HOOC–CH_2–COOH$) does not form a cyclic anhydride on heating.

Reason: It is like a β-keto acid; on heating, it prefers to decarboxylate.

247. Assertion: Both Grignard and dialkylcadmium reagents react with acid chlorides to form tert-alcohols.

Reason: Grignard reagents are as reactive as dialkylcadmium.

248. Assertion: Ketones react with ethylene glycol in the presence of *p*-toluenesulfonic acid to form ketals.

Reason: Ketals are hydrolysed back to ketones by aqueous alkalies.

249. Assertion: Aldol condensation can be catalysed both acids and bases.

Reason: β-Hydroxyaldehydes or ketones readily undergo acid-catalysed dehydration.

250. Assertion: Aldol condensation is usually carried out in a dilute solution of a strong base.

Reason: Concentrated solution of a strong base involves Cannizzaro reaction.

251. Assertion: Crossed Cannizzaro reaction between formaldehyde and benzaldehyde gives benzyl alcohol and formate ion.

Reason: Formaldehyde is a better hydride donor than benzaldehyde.

252. Assertion: 2,2-Dimethylpropanal gives Cannizzaro reaction with concentrated NaOH.

Reason: The Cannizzaro reaction is a disproportionation reaction.

253. Assertion: The oxidation of ketones by perbenzoic acid gives esters.

Reason: Perbenzoic acid oxidises because of the release of nascent oxygen on dissociation.

Answer Key

1. (a)	2. (b)	3. (a)	4. (d)	5. (a)	6. (b)	7. (b)	8. (d)	9. (b)	10. (a)
11. (c)	12. (d)	13. (c)	14. (a)	15. (d)	16. (b)	17. (a)	18. (b)	19. (c)	20. (a)
21. (b)	22. (c)	23. (d)	24. (c)	25. (a)	26. (b)	27. (a)	28. (b)	29. (c)	30. (d)
31. (b)	32. (b)	33. (d)	34. (d)	35. (b)	36. (d)	37. (a)	38. (c)	39. (d)	40. (b)
41. (d)	42. (a)	43. (b)	44. (a)	45. (b)	46. (a)	47. (b)	48. (b)	49. (a)	50. (d)
51. (a)	52. (c)	53. (d)	54. (a)	55. (c)	56. (b)	57. (a)	58. (b)	59. (b,c)	60. (d)
61. (d)	62. (c)	63. (a)	64. (c)	65. (d)	66. (d)	67. (a)	68. (c)	69. (a)	70. (b)
71. (a)	72. (a)	73. (c)	74. (d)	75. (c)	76. (c)	77. (b)	78. (c)	79. (b)	80. (a)
81. (a)	82. (b)	83. (c)	84. (a)	85. (d)	86. (c)	87. (b)	88. (a)	89. (b)	90. (c)
91. (c)	92. (c)	93. (c)	94. (a)	95. (c)	96. (a)	97. (a)	98. (c)	99. (c)	100. (b)
101. (b)	102. (d)	103. (d)	104. (d)	105. (c)	106. (d)	107. (c)	108. (c)	109. (d)	110. (a)
111. (d)	112. (c)	113. (c)	114. (a)	115. (d)	116. (a)	117. (b)	118. (c)	119. (b)	120. (a)
121. (e)	122. (c)	123. (d)	124. (d)	125. (d)	126. (d)	127. (c)	128. (a)	129. (a)	130. (a)
131. (a)	132. (d)	133. (b)	134. (c)	135. (d)	136. (d)	137. (a)	138. (d)	139. (a)	140. (c)
141. (d)	142. (c)	143. (a)	144. (b)	145. (b)	146. (b)	147. (a)	148. (b)	149. (b)	150. (c)
151. (c)	152. (b)	153. (c)	154. (a)	155. (b)	156. (a)	157. (c)	158. (b)	159. (c)	160. (b)
161. (d)	162. (c)	163. (b)	164. (b)	165. (d)	166. (c)	167. (b)	168. (b)	169. (a)	170. (c)
171. (a)	172. (d)	173. (c)	174. (b)	175. (a)	176. (a)	177. (a)	178. (b)	179. (a)	180. (d)
181. (c)	182. (b)	183. (c)	184. (d)	185. (c)	186. (d)	187. (c)	188. (d)	189. (c)	190. (a)
191. (d)	192. (d)	193. (a)	194. (c)	195. (a)	196. (a)	197. (c)	198. (c)	199. (a)	200. (c)
201. (b)	202. (a)	203. (a)	204. (b)	205. (d)	206. (d)	207. (c)	208. (c)	209. (c)	210. (c)
211. (a)	212. (a)	213. (c)	214. (b)	215. (b)	216. (a)	217. (a)	218. (a)	219. (a)	220. (a)
221. (b)	222. (c)	223. (c)	224. (b)	225. (d)	226. (b)	227. (b)	228. (c)	229. (b)	230. (b)
231. (b)	232. (a)	233. (d)	234. (a)	235. (c)	236. (b)	237. (d)	238. (c)	239. (b)	240. (d)
241. (d)	242. (c)	243. (b)	244. (c)	245. (a)	246. (a)	247. (d)	248. (c)	249. (b)	250. (c)
251. (a)	252. (a)	253. (c)							

Hints and Solutions

Nomenclature and Structure of Carbonyl Group

1. **(a):** 4-Methoxy-2-nitrobenzaldehyde.

2. **(b):** $CH_3CH_2-\underset{CH_3}{\underset{|}{CH}}-\overset{O}{\overset{||}{C}}-\underset{CH_3}{\underset{|}{CH}}-CH_2CH_3$ Di-*sec*-butyl ketone

3. **(a):** $CH_3-\overset{OCH_3}{\overset{|}{CH}}-CHO$ 2-Methoxypropanal

4. **(d):** 3-Keto-2-methyl-hex-4-enal

5. **(a):** H, CHO → Making two interchanges at the chiral centre → OHC, H (S)-4-Methyl-2-propylpentanal

6. **(b):** Due to the smaller size of oxygen compared to carbon, the C=O double bond is shorter (1.23 Å) than the C=C double bond (1.34 Å).

7. **(b):** Cannizzaro reaction is given by aldehydes which do not contain an α-hydrogen. Therefore, HCHO does not give this reaction.

8. (d): In the common system, substituents are designated by Greek letters α, β, γ.. and not by Arabic numerals. Therefore, the correct common name of

$$\overset{3}{CH_3}-\underset{\alpha}{\overset{\overset{OCH_3}{|}}{CH}}-\overset{1}{CHO}$$

is α-methoxypropionaldehyde.

Methods of Preparation of Aldehydes and Ketones

9. (b): $\begin{matrix} CH_2CH_2COO \\ | \\ CH_2CH_2COO \end{matrix} Ca \xrightarrow[-CaCO_3]{\Delta} \begin{matrix} CH_2CH_2 \\ | \\ CH_2CH_2 \end{matrix} C{=}O$

Cal.adipate → Cyclopentanone

10. (a): Alkene (a and c) being symmetric, on ozonolysis give,

(a) $\xrightarrow[\text{(ii) Zn/}H_2O]{\text{(i) }O_3/CH_2Cl_2}$ Butanone

(c) $\xrightarrow[\text{(ii) Zn/}H_2O]{\text{(i) }O_3/CH_2Cl_2}$ $-CHO + OHC-$ Isobutyraldehyde

11. (c): In the case of unsymmetrical alkynes, the addition of H_2O occurs in accordance with Markownikoff's rule.

$$CH_3 \rightarrow \overset{\delta+}{C} \equiv \overset{\delta-}{C}H + \overset{\delta+}{H}-\overset{\delta-}{OH} \xrightarrow[333\text{ K}]{H_2SO_4,\ HgSO_4}$$

$$\left[CH_3-\overset{\overset{OH}{|}}{C}=CH_2\right] \xrightarrow{\text{Tautomerises}} CH_3-\overset{\overset{O}{||}}{C}-CH_3$$

Intermediate (A) → Propanone (B)

12. (d): $Me-\equiv \xrightarrow[\text{(ii) }CH_3I]{\text{(i) }NaNH_2} Me-\equiv-CH_3$

$\xrightarrow[HgSO_4]{\text{Dil. }H_2SO_4} \longrightarrow Me-CH_2-\overset{\overset{O}{||}}{C}-Me$

Although alc. KOH and $NaNH_2$ can both be used for dehydrohalogenation, $NaNH_2$ gives better yields. Therefore, option (c) is correct.

13. (c):

$\xrightarrow[\text{-2 NaBr, -2 }NH_3]{NaNH_2\text{ (A)}}$ Phenylacetylene ($C{\equiv}CH$) $\xrightarrow[H_2SO_4\text{ (B)}]{H_2O,\ H_2SO_4,}$ Acetophenone

14. (a): $C_6H_5COCl \xrightarrow[\text{(Rosenmund's reduction)}]{H_2,\text{ Pd-}BaSO_4} C_6H_5CHO$

Benzaldehyde (A)

15. (d):

$$PhC\equiv N \xrightarrow{CH_3MgBr} Ph-\overset{\overset{CH_3}{|}}{C}=NMgBr \xrightarrow[-NH_3,\ -Mg(OH)Br]{H^+/H_2O} PhCOCH_3$$

Acetophenone

16. (b): $(CH_3)_2CH-C\equiv N \xrightarrow[\text{(ii) }H_3O^+]{\text{(i) PhMgBr}} (CH_3)_2CH-\overset{\overset{O}{||}}{C}-Ph$

17. (a): $CH_3CH_2CN \xrightarrow[\text{Stephen reduction}]{SnCl_2/HCl\text{-dry ether}} CH_3CH_2CH=NH.HCl$

Propanenitrile

$\xrightarrow{H_2O,\text{ boil}} CH_3CH_2CHO + NH_4Cl$

Propanal

18. (b): Reduction of esters with DIBAL-H followed by hydrolysis directly gives aldehydes.

$$RCOOC_2H_5 \xrightarrow[\text{(ii) }H_2O\text{, Aldehyde}]{\text{(i) DIBAL-H}} R-CH{=}O + C_2H_5OH$$

19. (c): p-Nitrotoluene $\xrightarrow[\text{(ii) }H_2O\text{, boil (Etard reaction)}]{\text{(i) }CrO_2Cl_2/CS_2}$ p-Nitrobenzaldehyde

20. (a): $C_6H_5CH_3 \xrightarrow[(CH_3CO)_2O]{CrO_3} \underset{A}{C_6H_5CH(OCOCH_3)_2}$

$\xrightarrow{OH^-/H_2O} C_6H_5CHO + 2\ CH_3COOH$

21. (b): Toluene (CH_3) $\xrightarrow[(-2\ HCl)]{2Cl_2,\ h\nu,\ \Delta}$ Benzal dichloride ($CHCl_2$) $\xrightarrow[-2\ KCl]{KOH\ (aq)}$ $CH(OH)_2$ $\xrightarrow{-H_2O}$ Benzaldehyde (CHO)

22. (c):

$$PhCH_2CH_3 \xrightarrow[\text{(Benzylic bromination)}]{Br_2\text{ (excess), }h\nu} Ph-CBr_2-CH_3 = \xrightarrow[Ph-COCH_3]{KOH\ (aq),\ \Delta}$$

Ethylbenzene

23. (d): Zn/Hg and conc. HCl, that is, Clemmensen reduction, cannot be used to convert benzoic acid to benzaldehyde.

24. (c): Acetyl chloride reacts with dibenzylcadmium to give benzyl methyl ketone while all other reactions give acetophenone.

$$2CH_3COCl + (C_6H_5CH_2)_2Cd \xrightarrow{(C_2H_5)_2O} 2CH_3-\overset{\overset{O}{||}}{C}-CH_2C_6H_5 + CdCl_2$$

Acetyl chloride, Dibenzyl cadmium → Benzyl methyl ketone

25. (a): $3\ C_6H_{10}{=}CH_2 \xrightarrow[THF]{BH_3} (C_6H_{11}-CH_2)_3B \xrightarrow[OH^-]{H_2O_2}$

$3\ C_6H_{11}-CH_2OH \xrightarrow[CH_2Cl_2]{C_5H_5NH^+CrO_3Cl^-} 3\ C_6H_{11}-CHO$

26. (b): $CH_3CHOHCH_2CH_3 \xrightarrow{[O]} CH_3COCH_2CH_3$

27. (a): $\begin{matrix} CH_3CH_2COO \\ CH_3CH_2COO \end{matrix} O \xrightarrow[-CaCO_3]{\Delta} \begin{matrix} CH_3CH_2 \\ CH_3CH_2 \end{matrix} CO$

Calcium propionate → 3-Pentanone

28. (b): $\begin{matrix} C_6H_5COO \\ C_6H_5COO \end{matrix} Ca \xrightarrow[-CaCO_3]{\Delta} \begin{matrix} C_6H_5 \\ C_6H_5 \end{matrix} CO$

Calcium benzoate → Benzophenon

Physical Properties of Aldehydes and Ketones

29. (c): Due to the more easily polarisable π-electrons of the C=O bond, the dipole moments of aldehydes and ketones (2.3–2.8 D) are much higher than those of alcohols (1.6–1.7 D), alkenes and arenes.

30. (d): $2HCHO \xrightarrow{\text{Conc. NaOH}} HCOONa + CH_3OH$

There is no formation of C–C bond.

31. (b): Due to intermolecular H-bonding. $CH_3CH_2CH_2CH_2OH$ (II) has the highest BP. Aldehydes are more polar than ethers, therefore, due to stronger dipole–dipole interactions, $CH_3CH_2CH_2CHO$ (I) has a higher BP than that of C_2H_5-O-C_2H_5 (III). However, due to weak van der Waals interactions, $CH_3CH_2CH_2CH_2CH_3$ (IV) has the lowest BP. Thus, the BPs of these four compounds increase in the order: IV < III < I < II. Option (b) is correct.

Chemical Reactions of Aldehydes and Ketones

32. (b): Aldehydes are more reactive that ketones, therefore, acetophenone (C) is the least reactive. Further, the presence of electron withdrawing groups increase the +ve charge on the carbonyl carbon and thus facilitate nucleophilic addition reactions while electron donating groups increase the electron density on the carbonyl carbon and thus retard the nucleophilic addition reactions.
As a result, *p*-nitrobenzaldehyde (B) is more reactive than benzaldehyde (A) which, in turn, is more reactive than *p*-tolualdehyde (D). Thus, the decreasing order of reactivity is: B > A > D > C.

33. (d): *p*-nitrobenzaldehyde (B) is more reactive than benzaldehyde (A) which in turn, is more reactive than *p*-tolualdehyde (D). Thus, the decreasing order of reactivity is: B > A > D > C.

34. (d): Aromatic aldehydes are less reactive than aliphatic aldehydes and ketones. Thus, benzaldehyde (II) is the least reactive. Among aliphatic aldehydes and ketones, the reactivity decreases as the size and number of alkyl groups increases around the C=O group. Therefore, the reactivity decreases in the order: IV (acetaldehyde) > III (propanal) > I (diethyl ketone). Thus, the overall reactivity decreases in the order: IV > III > I > II.

35. (b): Due to the strong electron withdrawing effect of the two C=O groups at C_1 and C_3, the C=O group at C_2 is the most reactive towards nucleophilic addition reactions.

36. (d):

$$CH_3(H)C{=}O + :\ddot{S}(=O)(OH)O^-Na^+ \longrightarrow CH_3(H)C(O^-Na^+)(SO_2OH) \xrightarrow{\text{Proton transfer}} CH_3(H)C(OH)(SO_2O^-Na^+)$$

Due to greater stabilisation of SO_3^- by resonance, the proton transfer occurs.

37. (à): Aldehydes other the formaldehyde react with Grignard reagents to give 2° alcohols. Thus, option (a) is correct.

$$\underset{\text{Propanal}}{C_2H_5-CH=O} \xrightarrow[\text{(ii) } H_3O^+]{\text{(i) RMgX}} \underset{2°\text{ Alcohol}}{C_2H_5-CHOH=R}$$

38. (c): The OH group is *o,p*-directing, therefore, the CHO group enters at the *o*-position with respect to the OH during the Reimer–Tiemann reaction. Addition of HCN followed by acid hydrolysis gives a chiral carboxylic acid (c).

39. (d):

$$RR'C{=}O \xrightarrow[\text{KCN}]{\text{HCN}} RR'C(CN)(OH) \xrightarrow{LiAlH_4(B)} RR'C(CH_2NH_2)(OH)$$

40. (b): Due to the –I effect of the three Cl atoms, the +ve charge on the carbonyl carbon in chloral (CCl_3CHO) increases. As a result, weak nucleophiles like H_2O readily add to the carbonyl group giving chloral hydrate, $CCl_3CH(OH)_2$.

41. (d): Aldehydes/ketones react with alcohols in the presence of dry HCl to form acetals.

$$\underset{\text{Acetone}}{(CH_3)_2C{=}O} + \underset{\text{Alcohol}}{2\,HOC_2H_5} \xrightarrow[-H_2O]{\text{HCl}} \underset{\text{Diethyl acetone acetal}}{(CH_3)_2C(OC_2H_5)_2}$$

42. (a):

$$\underset{\text{Acetone}}{(CH_3)_2C{=}O} + \begin{matrix}HOCH_2\\|\\HOCH_2\end{matrix} \xrightarrow[-H_2O]{\text{PTS}} \text{Acetone ethylene glycol acetal}$$

43. (b):

$$C_6H_5CH{=}O \xrightarrow[\text{excess of MeOH}]{\text{HCl gas}} C_6H_5CH(OMe)_2$$

In fact, two moles of MeOH add with the elimination of H_2O to form benzaldehyde methanol acetal.

44. (a):

$$\underset{\text{Cal. butanoate}}{(CH_3CH_2CH_2COO)_2Ca} \xrightarrow[-CaCO_3]{\Delta} \text{3-Heptanone} \xrightarrow[-H_2O]{\text{HO}\quad\text{OH/PTS}} \text{3-Heptanone ethylene glycol acetal}$$

45. (b): Dihydropyran reacts with alcohols in the presence of anhydrous H^+ to form acetals.

$$\text{Dihydropyran} \xrightarrow{H^+} \text{oxocarbenium ion} \xrightarrow{H\ddot{O}CH_2R} \text{(}^+O(H)CH_2R\text{ adduct)} \xrightarrow{-H^+} \underset{\text{Acetal}}{\text{2-}OCH_2R\text{-tetrahydropyran}}$$

46. (a):

$$RCHO + NH_2NH_2 \xrightarrow[\text{addition}]{\text{Nucleophilic}} \left[\begin{matrix}OH\\|\\R-CH-NHNH_2\end{matrix}\right] \xrightarrow[\text{Elimination}]{-H_2O} R-CH=NNH_2$$

47. (b): 2,4-Dinitrophenylhydrazone is called Brady's reagent.

48. (b): The smallest ketone is acetone. Being a symmetrical ketone, it forms only one oxime. The next homologue of acetone is butanone. Being unsymmetrical, it forms two oximes—*cis*-and *trans*-butanone oxime. Thus, in all, three oximes are formed.

49. (a): The complex formed by the addition of sodium tartrate to $CuSO_4$ solution is called Fehling's solution. It will give a red precipitate with aldehydes, that is, CH_3CHO.

50. (d): Fehling's solution oxidises only aliphatic aldehydes, that is, option (d) is correct.

51. (a):

$$\underset{\text{A (MF } C_3H_8O)}{CH_3CH_2CH_2OH} \xrightarrow[-H_2O]{[O]} \underset{\text{B (MF } C_3H_6O)}{CH_3CH_2CHO} \xrightarrow[-H_2O]{NH_2CONHNH_2} CH_3CH_2CH{=}NNHCONH_2$$

52. (c): Propanone, being a ketone, does not reduce Fehling's solution or Tollens' reagent. Benzaldehyde being an aromatic aldehyde reduces only Tollens' reagent but not Fehling's solution. However, ethanal being an aliphatic aldehyde, reduces both Tollens' reagent as well as Fehling's solution. Thus, option (c) is correct.

53. (d): Acetone neither reduces Fehling's solution nor Tollens' reagent. Benzaldehyde, however, reduces Tollens' reagent but not Fehling's solution.

54. (a): Although Br_3CCHO does not contain an α-hydrogen, in the presence of NaOH, it does not undergo Cannizzaro reaction. Instead it undergoes the iodoform reaction. The reason is that the carbon atom of the CH=O group is electron deficient due to the strong –I effect of the Br_3C group. Subsequent cleavage of the Br_3C–C bond gives $CHBr_3$ and HCOONa.

$$Br_3CCHO \xrightarrow{NaOH} CHBr_3 + HCOONa$$

55. (c): Although CH_3COOH contains the grouping CH_3CO, it is not attached to either C or H and hence it does not undergo the iodoform reaction. However, $CH_3CHOHCH_2CH_3$ contains the grouping CH_3CHOH attached to C and hence undergoes the iodoform reaction. Similarly, CH_3CHO contains the grouping CH_3CO attached to H and hence undergoes the iodoform reaction. $ICH_2COCH_2CH_3$ is the first iodination product of $CH_3COCH_2CH_3$ and hence undergoes the iodoform reaction as shown.

$$CH_3COOH_2CH_3 \xrightarrow{I_2/NaOH} ICH_2COCH_2CH_3 \xrightarrow{I_2/NaOH}$$

$$I_2CHCOCH_2CH_3 \xrightarrow{I_2/NaOH} I_3CCOCH_2CH_3 \xrightarrow{NaOH} \underset{\text{Iodoform}}{CHI_3} + \underset{\text{Sod. propanoate}}{CH_3CH_2COONa}$$

56. (b): Since CH_3CHO and $C_6H_5CH_2CHO$ are aldehydes, they give Benedict's test, Tollens' reagent test and Fehling's solution test. However, CH_3CHO contains the CH_3CO group (attached to C or H) and hence gives the iodoform test while $C_6H_5CH_2CHO$ does not contain the CH_3CO group and hence does not give the iodoform test.

57. (a): $NaHSO_3$ forms a crystalline addition compound with acetaldehyde but not with acetophenone.

58. (b): Both 2-pentanone and 3-methyl-2-butanone being methyl ketones form the crystalline bisulfite derivative and give the iodoform test.

59. (b,c): 2-Hydroxypropane ($CH_3CHOHCH_3$) contains the grouping CH_3CHOH and acetophenone ($C_6H_5COCH_3$) contains the grouping (CH_3CO^-) attached to carbon. Therefore, both these react with I_2 and alkali to give a yellow precipitate of CHI_3.

60. (d): Propiophenone ($C_6H_5COCH_2CH_3$) does not contain the grouping CH_3CO attached to C and hence does not give the iodoform test. All others give the iodoform test.

61. (d):

$$(H)(H_3C)C{=}C(CH_3)(COCH_3) \xrightarrow[\text{(Haloform reaction)}]{NaOCl} \underset{(A)}{(H)(H_3C)C{=}C(CH_3)(COONa)} + CHCl_3$$

62. (c): The compound ($C_5H_{10}O$) forms a phenylhydrazone but gives a negative Tollens' test; it must be a ketone. Since it does not give the iodoform test, it cannot be a methyl ketone, that is, pentanone-2. In other words, the ketone is pentanone-3.

63. (a):

$$\underset{A\ (C_5H_{10}Cl_2)}{CH_3{-}CCl_2{-}CH_2CH_3} \xrightarrow{\text{Hydrolysis}} \underset{B\ (C_5H_{10}O)}{CH_3{-}\overset{O}{\overset{\|}{C}}{-}CH_2CH_2CH_3}$$

Since B ($C_5H_{10}O$) reacts with NH_2OH, it forms iodoform but does not give Fehling's solution test. Therefore, it must be a ketone and A ($C_5H_{10}Cl_2$) must be 2,2-dichloropropane, that is, option (a) is correct.

64. (c): $C_6H_5COCH_3 \xrightarrow[\text{Ethylene glycol 450–470 K}]{NH_2NH_2.H_2O/KOH} \underset{\text{Ethylbenzene}}{C_6H_5CH_2CH_3}$

65. (d): The first intermediate formed is a hydrazine.

$$>C{=}O \xrightarrow[-H_2O]{NH_2NH_2} \underset{\text{Hydrazone}}{>C{=}NNH_2} \xrightarrow[\Delta]{KOH} >CH_2 + N_2$$

66. (d): Both Zn–Hg/HCl and NH_2NH_2, OH^- can reduce $CH{=}CHCOCH_3$ to $CH{=}CHCH_2CH_3$ but HCl will also bring about substitution of OH by Cl. Therefore, the most effective reagent is NH_2NH_2, OH^-, that is, option (d) is correct.

67. (a): $\underset{\text{Acetaldehyde}}{CH_3CHO} + \underset{\text{Hydrazine}}{NH_2NH_2} \longrightarrow \underset{\text{Acetaldehyde hydrazone (A)}}{CH_3CH = NNH_2} \xrightarrow[\text{WK reduction}]{C_2H_5ONa} CH_3CH_3 + N_2$

68. (c): $\underset{\text{3-Hexanone}}{CH_3CH_2{-}\overset{O}{\overset{\|}{C}}{-}CH_2CH_2CH_3} \xrightarrow{NaBH_4}$

$$CH_3CH_2{-}\overset{O^-}{\overset{|}{C}H}{-}CH_2CH_2CH_3 \xrightarrow[-OD^-]{D_2O} CH_3CH_2{-}\overset{OD}{\overset{|}{C}H}{-}CH_2CH_2CH_3$$

69. (a):

$$(H_3C)(CH_3)C{=}O \xrightarrow{\text{(i) }^-\text{H from }NaBH_4} (H)(H_3C)C(O^-)(OH) \xrightarrow[-D_2O]{D_3O^+} \underset{X}{(H)(H_3C)C(OD)(CH_3)}$$

$$(H_3C)(CH_3)C{=}O \xrightarrow{D^-\text{ from }NaBH_4} (D)(H_3C)C(O^-)(CH_3) \xrightarrow[-H_2O]{H_3O^+} \underset{Y}{(D)(H_3C)C(OH)(CH_3)}$$

70. (b): The C=C bond is reduced faster than the C=O bond.

$$\text{2-Cyclohexenone} \xrightarrow[Pd{-}C/C_2H_5OH]{H_2(g),\ 1\ atm} \text{Cyclohexanone}$$

71. (a): During oxidation of an unsymmetrical ketone (methyl n-propyl ketone), the keto group stays with the smaller alkyl group (Popoff's rule), that is, CH_3CH_2COOH and CH_3COOH are formed.

$$CH_3COCH_2CH_2CH_3 \xrightarrow{[O]} CH_3COOH + CH_3CH_2COOH$$

72. (a): SeO_2 oxidises compounds containing the active methylene group (CH_2 next to the C=O group) to another CO group, that is, option (a) is correct.

$$CH_3-\overset{O}{\overset{\|}{C}}-CH_3 \xrightarrow{SeO_2} \underset{X}{CH_3-\overset{O}{\overset{\|}{C}}-CHO} + Se + H_2O$$

73. (c): Methyllithium being a strong base, abstracts the weakly acidic α-hydrogen to form a carbanion.

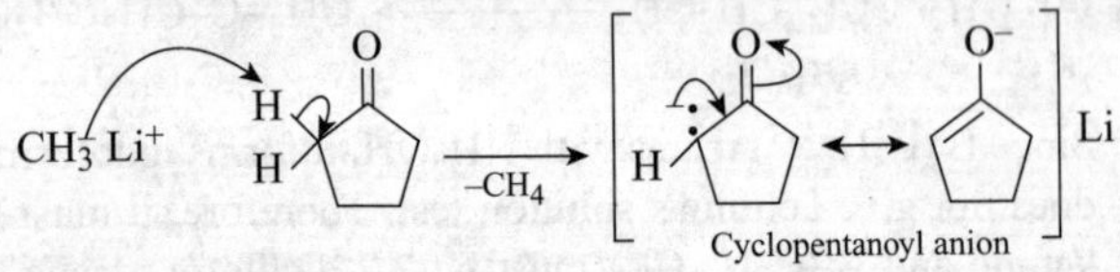

$CH_3^-Li^+$ + cyclopentanone $\xrightarrow{-CH_4}$ [Cyclopentanoyl anion] Li

Cyclopentanoyl anion

74. (d): Two molecules of CH_3CHO undergo aldol condensation to form 3-hydroxybutanal.

$$CH_3CHO + CH_3CHO \xrightarrow[\text{(Aldol condensation)}]{\text{Dil. NaOH}} \underset{\text{3-Hydroxybutanal}}{CH_3-\overset{OH}{\overset{|}{CH}}-CH_2-CHO}$$

75. (c): A β-hydroxyaldehyde/ketone is called an aldol.

76. (c): β-Hydroxy ketones readily undergo dehydration to give α,β-unsaturated ketones.

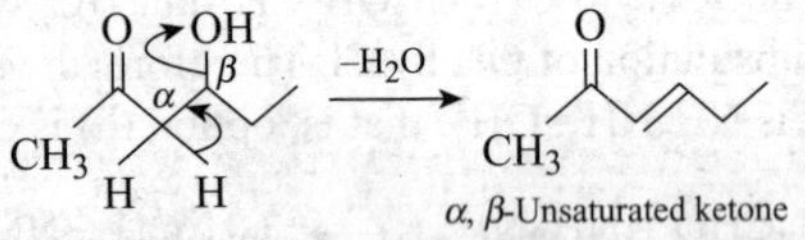

β-hydroxy ketone $\xrightarrow{-H_2O}$ α,β-Unsaturated ketone

77. (b):

$$\underset{\text{Acetone}}{(CH_3)_2C{=}O} + H-CH_2COCH_3 \xrightarrow{\text{Dil. } Ba(OH)_2}$$

$$\underset{\text{Diacetone alcohol}}{CH_3-\overset{OH}{\overset{|}{\underset{CH_3}{\underset{|}{C}}}}-\underset{H}{CH}-COCH_3} \xrightarrow[-H_2O]{\text{Dehydration}} \underset{\text{Mesityl oxide}}{CH_3-\underset{CH_3}{\underset{|}{C}}=CH-COCH_3}$$

78. (c): Mesitylene, that is, 1,3,5-trimethylbenzene is formed.

79. (b): (i) A gives the silver mirror test, so, it must be an aldehyde. Further, aldehydes are formed by the oxidation of 1° alcohols, therefore, X (MF C_2H_6O) must a 1° alcohol, that is, CH_3CH_2OH (ethanol) and A must an aldehyde, that is, CH_3CHO (ethanal).

$$\underset{\substack{\text{Ethanol (X)}\\ \text{MF } C_2H_6O}}{CH_3CH_2OH} \xrightarrow{\text{Cu, 573 K}} \underset{\text{Ethanal (A)}}{CH_3CHO} \xrightarrow[OH^-]{[Ag(NH_3)_2]^+} \text{Silver mirror}$$

(ii) Ethanal (CH_3CHO) on treatment with OH^- undergoes aldol condensation to give 3-hydroxybutanal which upon heating undergoes dehydration to give an α, β- unsaturated aldehyde (Y), that is, $CH_3CH{=}CHCHO$ (but-2-enal).

$$\underset{\text{Ethanal (A)}}{2CH_3CHO} \xrightarrow[\text{(Aldol condensation)}]{OH^-} \underset{\text{3-Hydroxybutanal}}{H_3CHOHCH_2CHO}$$

$$\xrightarrow[\text{(Dehydration)}]{\Delta(-H_2O)} \underset{\text{But-2-enal (Y)}}{CH_3CH{=}CHCHO}$$

(iii) Ethanal (A) on treatment with semicarbazide gives acetaldehyde semicarbazone (Z), that is,

$$\underset{\text{Acetaldehyde}}{CH_3CHO} + \underset{\text{Semicarbazide}}{H_2NNHCONH_2} \xrightarrow{-H_2O} \underset{\text{Acetaldehydesemicarbazone (Z)}}{CH_3CH{=}NNHCONH_2}$$

Thus, option (b) is correct.

80. (a):

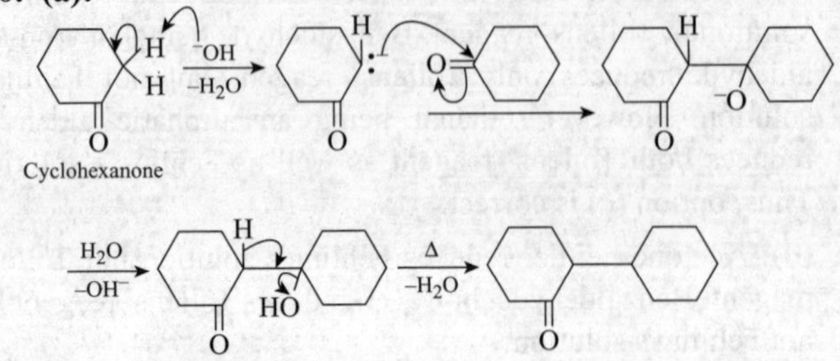

Cyclohexanone $\xrightarrow[-H_2O]{^-OH}$ enolate; enolate + cyclohexanone $\rightarrow$ alkoxide adduct $\xrightarrow[-OH^-]{H_2O}$ aldol $\xrightarrow[-H_2O]{\Delta}$ 2-cyclohexylidenecyclohexanone

Cyclohexanone

Thus, option (a) is correct.

81. (a):

$$\underset{\text{Formaldehyde}}{CH_2{=}O} + \underset{\text{Acetone}}{CH_3COCH_3} \xrightarrow[\text{(Aldol condensation)}]{\text{Dil NaOH}} HOCH_2-CH_2COCH_3$$

$$\xrightarrow[(-H_2O)]{\text{Dehydration}} \underset{\text{Methyl vinyl ketone}}{CH_2=CH-COCH_3}$$

82. (b):

$$\underset{\substack{\text{Propanal}\\ \text{(Electrophile)}}}{CH_3CH_2-CH{=}O} + \underset{\substack{\text{Butanal}\\ \text{(Nucleophile)}}}{CH_3CH_2-\overset{\alpha}{\underset{H}{\underset{|}{CH}}}-CHO}$$

$$\longrightarrow \underset{\text{2-Ethyl-3-hydroxypentanal}}{\overset{5}{C}H_3\overset{4}{C}H_2-\overset{OH}{\overset{|}{\overset{3}{C}H}}-\overset{CH_2CH_3}{\overset{|}{\overset{2}{C}H}}-\overset{1}{C}HO}$$

83. (c):

$$\underset{\text{Benzaldehyde}}{C_6H_5CH{=}O} + \underset{\text{Acetophenone}}{H_2CHCOC_6H_5} \xrightarrow[\substack{\text{(Crossed aldol}\\ \text{condensation)}}]{\text{Dil. NaOH, 293 K}}$$

$$\underset{\text{1, 3-Diphenyl-2-en-1-one}}{C_6H_5\overset{3}{C}H{=}\overset{2}{C}H\overset{1}{C}OC_6H_5} + H_2O$$

84. (a): In the presence of C_2H_5ONa, acetophenone undergoes an aldol type condensation followed by the loss of H_2O to form an α,β-unsaturated ketone called dypnone.

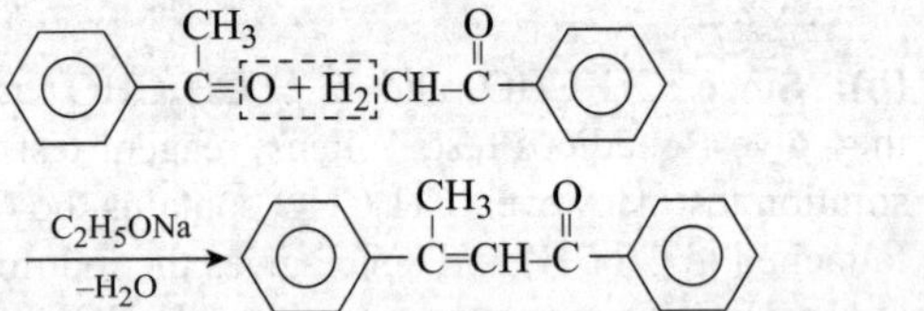

$$C_6H_5-\overset{CH_3}{\overset{|}{C}}{=}O + H_2CH-\overset{O}{\overset{\|}{C}}-C_6H_5 \xrightarrow[-H_2O]{C_2H_5ONa} \underset{\text{Dypnone}}{C_6H_5-\overset{CH_3}{\overset{|}{C}}{=}CH-\overset{O}{\overset{\|}{C}}-C_6H_5}$$

85. (d):

$$C_6H_5CN \xrightarrow[\substack{\text{(ii) } H_3O^+\\ \text{(Stephen reaction)}}]{\text{(i) } SnCl_2/HCl} \underset{(X)}{C_6H_5CH{=}O} + H_2CH-\overset{O}{\overset{\|}{C}}-C_6H_4CH_3$$

$$\xrightarrow[(-H_2O)]{\text{dil. NaOH}} \underset{(Y)}{C_6H_5CH{=}CH-\overset{O}{\overset{\|}{C}}-C_6H_4CH_3}$$

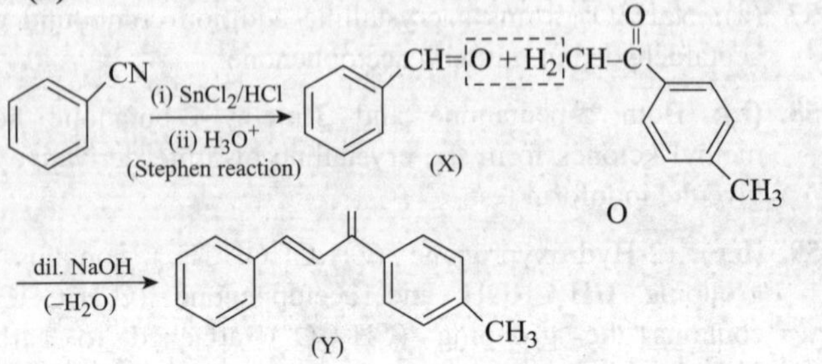

86. (c):

$$\underset{\text{Benzaldehyde}}{C_6H_5CH{=}O} + \underset{\text{Acetone}}{H_2CHCOC_6H_5} \xrightarrow[\substack{\text{(Claisen-Schmidt}\\ \text{reaction)}}]{\text{Aq NaOH}}$$

$$\underset{\text{Benzalacetone}}{C_6H_5CH{=}CHCOCH_3} + H_2O$$

87. (b):

$$\underset{\text{Benzaldehyde}}{C_6H_5CHO} + CH_3COCH_3 + O{=}CHC_6H_5 \xrightarrow[-2H_2O]{\text{Dil. NaOH}}$$

$$\underset{\text{Dibenzalacetone}}{C_6H_5CH{=}CHCOCH{=}CHC_6H_5}$$

88. (a): $C_6H_5CH=O + H_2CH-CHO \xrightarrow[\text{(Claisen-Schmidt condensation)}]{\text{Dil. NaOH}, -H_2O} C_6H_5CH=CHCHO$

Benzaldehyde Acetaldehyde Cinnamaldehyde

89. (b):

$C_6H_5CHO + CH_3COOC_2H_5 \xrightarrow[(-H_2O)]{\text{Dil NaOH}} C_6H_5CH=CHOOC_2H_5$

Benzaldehyde Ethyl acetate Ethyl cinnamate

90. (c):

$(CH_3)_2C=O + H_2CHCOCH_3 \xrightarrow{HCl} (CH_3)_2C=CHCOCH_3$

Acetone Acetone Mesityl oxide

$(CH_3)_2C=O + H_2CHCOCH H_2 + O=C(CH_3)_2 \xrightarrow[-2H_2O]{HCl} (CH_3)_2C=CHCOCH=C(CH_3)_2$

Acetone Mesityl oxide Acetone Phorone

91. (c): Cannizzaro reaction with C_6H_5CHO gives the coresponding alcohol and the acid.

92. (c): m-Chlorobenzaldehyde (CHO, Cl) $\xrightarrow[\text{(Cannizzaro reaction)}]{\text{50\% NaOH}}$ m-Chlorobenzyl alcohol (CH_2OH, Cl) + m-Chlorobenzoate (COO^-, Cl)

93. (c): Both the aldehydes should not contain α-hydrogens.

$C_6H_5CHO + HCHO \xrightarrow{NaOH} C_6H_5CH_2OH + HCO_2Na$

94. (a): A mixture of benzaldehyde and formaldehyde undergo crossed Cannizzaro reaction.

$C_6H_5CHO + HCHO \xrightarrow{NaOH} C_6H_5CH_2OH + HCOONa$

95. (c): Since compound A undergoes Cannizzaro reaction, it must be formaldehyde. Since compound B undergoes the iodoform test, it must be a methyl ketone, that is, 2-pentanone.

96. (a): Cl_3CCHO prefers to undergo haloform reaction to form $CHCl_3$.

$Cl_3CCHO + NaOH \rightarrow \underset{\text{Chloroform}}{CHCl_3} + \underset{\text{Sodium formate}}{HCOONa}$

97. (a): In Cannizzaro reaction, no new C–C bond is formed.

98. (c): $CH_3CHO + CH_3CHO \xrightarrow[\text{Tischenko reaction}]{Al(OC_2H_5)_3}$

$[CH_3COOH + CH_3CH_2OH] \xrightarrow{-H_2O} \underset{\text{Ethyl acetate}}{CH_3COOCH_2CH_3}$

99. (c): Acrolein undergoes Tischenko reaction to give allyl acrylate.

$\underset{\text{Acrolein}}{2CH_2=CHCHO} \xrightarrow{Al(OC_2H_5)_3} \underset{\text{Allyl acrylate}}{CH_2=CHCOOCH_2CH=CH_2}$

100. (b):

Toluene ($C_6H_5CH_3$) $\xrightarrow[\text{(Etard reaction)}]{\text{(i) } CrO_2Cl_2 \text{ (ii) } H^+/H_2O}$ Benzaldehyde (C_6H_5CHO) $\xrightarrow[\text{Tischenko reaction}]{(C_2H_5O)_3Al}$

$[C_6H_5COOH + C_6H_5CH_2OH] \xrightarrow{-H_2O} C_6H_5C(=O)-CH_2-C_6H_5$

Benzyl benzoate

101. (b): Since Y can be obtained by Etard reaction, it may be C_6H_5CHO. Further since Z undergoes disproportionation (Cannizzaro reaction), it may be HCHO. Since both Y (C_6H_5CHO) and Z (HCHO) are obtained by the ozonolysis of X, X may be strene.

$\underset{\text{Styrene (X)}}{C_6H_5CH=CH_2} \xrightarrow[\text{(Reduction)}]{\text{Ozonolysis}} \underset{\text{Benzaldehyde (Y)}}{C_6H_5CHO} + \underset{\text{Formaldehyde}}{HCHO}$

102. (d): Cyclohexyl–$COCH_3$ $\xrightarrow[-POCl_3]{PCl_5}$ Cyclohexyl–CCl_2-CH_3 $\xrightarrow[(-2\,HCl)]{NaNH_2 \text{ (excess)}}$ Cyclohexyl–$C\equiv CH$

Cyclohexyl acetylene

103. (d): Cyclohexanone $\xrightarrow[-POCl_3]{PCl_5}$ 1,1-Dichlorocyclohexane $\xrightarrow[(-HCl)]{\text{Alc. KOH, }\Delta}$ 1-Chlorocyclohexene

Please note that cyclohexyne, cannot be formed since a triple bond is not stable in a small ring like urotropine.

104. (d): $2C_6H_5CH=O + 2H_2N-H$ (i.e. $3NH_3$) $+ O=CHC_6H_5 \xrightarrow{-3H_2O} (C_6H_5CH=N)_2CH-C_6H_5$

Benzaldehyde Hydrobenzamide

105. (c): $(CH_3)_2C=O \xrightarrow{NH_3} (CH_3)_2C(NH_2)OH + HCH_2COCH_3 \xrightarrow{-H_2O} (CH_3)_2C(NH_2)CH_2COCH_3$

Diacetonamine

106. (d): With NH_3, HCHO gives hexamethylenetetramine, CH_3CHO gives first acetaldehyde–ammonia and then acetaldimine while acetone gives diacetoneamine.

107. (c): Nitration of urotropine gives RDX.

108. (c): RDX has structure (c). Due to the presence of three unstable N–NO_2 bonds, it acts as a powerful explosive.

109. (d): $\underset{\text{Acetaldehyde}}{3\,CH_3CHO} \xrightarrow[\text{r.t.}]{\text{conc. } H_2SO_4}$ Paraldehyde (cyclic trimer, 2,4,6-trimethyl-1,3,5-trioxane)

110. (a): Txioxane is a polymer of formaldehyde (Trioxane)

111. (d): In the acidic medium, side chain nitration occurs.

$$C_6H_5-\overset{O}{\overset{\|}{C}}-CH_3 \xrightleftharpoons{\text{Tautomerises}} C_6H_5-\overset{:\ddot{O}:}{\overset{|}{C}}=CH_2 \xrightarrow{Br-Br} C_6H_5-\overset{O}{\overset{\|}{C}}-CH_2Br + HBr$$

Phenacyl bromide

112. (c): In the presence of anhydrous $AlCl_3$, nuclear nitration occurs at the *m*-position to give *m*-bromoacetophenone.

113. (c): Nucleophilic addition reaction.

114. (a): Reactivity decreases as the magnitude of the +ve charge on the carbonyl carbon decreases or the steric hindrance in the intermediate increases, that is, $H_2C=O > RCHO > ArCHO > R_2C=O > Ar_2C=O$.

115. (d): Due to the +I effect of the two CH_3 groups in acetone (II) as compared to one CH_3 group in acetaldehyde (I), the magnitude of the +ve charge on the carbon atom of the C=O group of acetone is less than in acetaldehyde. Further, the +R effect of the Ph group is much stronger than the +I effect of the CH_3 groups, therefore, the magnitude of the +ve charge is least on the carbon atom of the C=O group in benzophenone (III). In other words, the magnitude of the +ve charge decreases in the order: I > II > III. Therefore, the reactivity towards nucleophilic addition decreases in the same order, I > II > III.

Further, the steric hindrance increases in the order: I < II < III, therefore, the reactivity decreases in the reverse order, I > II > III. Thus, option (d) is correct.

116. (a): The reactivity towards HCN addition increases as the +I effect of the alkyl groups decreases and/or steric hindrance to the nucleophilic attack by CN^- on the carbonyl group decreases. Now the +Ieffect and the steric hindrance increase in the order: I < II < IV < III. Therefore, reactivity increases in the reverse order:

III < IV < II < I, that is, option (a) is correct.

117. (b): Reactivity decreases as the steric hindrance increases. Now steric hindrance increases in the order: ethanal (I) < propanal (II) < propanone (III) < butanone (IV). Therefore, the reactivity increases in the reverse order:

IV < III < II < I, that is, option (b) is correct.

Nomenclature and Structure of the Carboxyl Group

118. (c): $\overset{4}{C}H_3-\overset{3}{\underset{}{\overset{CH_3}{\overset{|}{C}}}}=\overset{2}{C}H-\overset{1}{C}OOH$ 3-Methylbut-2-enoic acid

119. (b): $R-C(=O)-\ddot{O}H \longleftrightarrow R-C(-\ddot{O}:^-)=\overset{+}{O}-H$

I   II

Due to contribution of resonance structure (II), the carbonyl carbon atom in carboxylic acids is less electrophilic than in aldehydes/ketones.

120. (a): $Ph\overset{3}{C}H_2\overset{2}{C}H_2\overset{1}{C}OOH$ 3-Phenyl propanoic acid

121. (e): $\overset{6}{C}H_3-\overset{5}{C}(=O)-\overset{4}{C}H_2-\overset{3}{C}H_2-\overset{2}{C}H_2-\overset{1}{C}(=O)-OH$ 5-Oxohexanoic acid

122. (c): $HO_2C-CH_2CH_2CH_2-CO_2H$ Pentane-1, 5-dioic acid

Methods of Preparation of Carboxylic Acids

123. (d): $CH\equiv CH \xrightarrow{KMnO_4\text{-}KOH} COOH-COOH$

Acetylene   Oxalic acid

124. (d): $C_2H_5Br \xrightarrow[\Delta(-HBr)]{\text{Alc. KOH}} CH_2=CH_2 \xrightarrow[CCl_4]{Br_2} CH_2Br-CH_2Br$

Ethyl bromide   Ethylene (A)   1, 2-Dibromoethane

$\xrightarrow[\text{(excess)}]{KCN} CH_2CN-CH_2CN \xrightarrow[\text{(Hydrolysis)}]{H_3O^+} COOH-COOH$

1, 4-Butane-dinitrile (C)   Oxalic acid (D)

125. (d): $C_6H_5-CH_3 \xrightarrow[-3HCl]{3\,Cl_2/h\nu,\,\Delta} C_6H_5-CCl_3 \xrightarrow[-3NaCl]{\text{Aq.NaOH}} [C_6H_5C(OH)_3] \xrightarrow{-H_2O} C_6H_5COOH$

Toluene   Benzotrichloride   Benzoic acid

126. (d): Nitrobenzene $\xrightarrow[\Delta]{Br_2/FeBr_3}$ *m*-Bromo-nitrobenzene (A) $\xrightarrow[\text{ether}]{Mg}$ 3-Nitrophenyl-magnesium bromide (B) $\xrightarrow[\text{(ii) } H_3O^+]{\text{(i) Dry ice}}$ 3-Nitrobenzoic acid (C)

127. (c): OH is a stronger electron donation group than OMe, therefore, CO_2H group is ortho to the OH group.

4-Methoxyphenol $\xrightarrow[\text{(ii) } H_3O^+]{\text{(i) } CO_2 \text{ (high temperature, high pressure)}}$ 2-Hydroxy-5-methoxybenzoic acid (OH, CO_2H ortho; OMe para to OH)

128. (a): $RCH_2CH_2OH \xrightarrow{PBr_3} RCH_2CH_2Br \xrightarrow{KCN} RCH_2CH_2CN \xrightarrow{H^+} RCH_2CH_2COOH$

129. (a): $CH_3CHO + HCHO \xrightarrow[\text{(Cross aldol condensation)}]{\text{Dil. NaOH}} HOCH_2-CH_2CHO \xrightarrow[(-H_2O)]{\text{heat}} CH_2=CH-CH=O$

3-Hydroxypropanal   Prop-2-enal (A)

$\xrightarrow[\text{1, 2-Addition}]{HCN} CH_2=CH-CH(CN)(OH) \xrightarrow{H_3O^+} CH_2=CH-\underset{OH}{\underset{|}{CH}}-COOH$

2-Hydroxybut-3-enoic acid (B)

130. (a): $CH_3-CHOH-CN \xrightarrow[\text{presence of aqueous}]{\text{Oxidation in}} [CH_3-CHOH-COOH] \xrightarrow{[O]} CH_3-CO-COOH$

Acetaldehyde cyanohydrin   Pyruvic acid

131. (a): Cyclopropyl–Br $\xrightarrow{Mg,\ Et_2O}$ Cyclopropyl–MgBr $\xrightarrow{CO_2(s)}$ Cyclopropyl–COOMgBr $\xrightarrow[-Mg(OH)Br]{H_2O^+}$ Cyclopropyl–COOH

132. (d): $HO_2C\sim\sim CO_2Me \xrightarrow[\text{reaction } (-H_2O)]{Ag_2O \text{ Acid-base}} AgO_2C\sim\sim CO_2Me$ (Silver salt) $\xrightarrow[\text{Hunsdiecker reaction } (-AgBr, -CO_2)]{Br_2/CCl_4, \Delta} Br\sim\sim CO_2Me$

Methyl 5-bromopentanoate

133. (b): Phenol (OH) $\xrightarrow[-ZnO]{\text{Zn dust}}$ Benzene (X) $\xrightarrow[\text{F.C. alkylation}]{CH_3Cl + \text{Anhyd. } AlCl_3}$ Toluene (CH_3) $\xrightarrow[KMnO_4]{\text{Alkaline}}$ Benzoic acid (Z) (COOH)

134. (c):

$CH_3-C_6H_4-\overset{O}{\overset{\|}{C}}-CH_3 \xrightarrow[\text{(ii) Dil. } H_2SO_4]{\text{(i) Alc. } KMnO_4} HOOC-C_6H_4-COOH$

4-Methylacetophenone → Terephthalic acid

135. (d): $CH_3CH{=}CHCH_3 \xrightarrow{KMnO_4/H_2SO_4} 2\ CH_3COOH$

2-Butene → Acetic acid

Physical Properties of Carboxylic Acids

136. (d): Due to the –I effect of the CO group, intermolecular H-bonds in acids are much stronger than in alcohols. Aldehydes, however, do not undergo H-bonding.

137. (a): Due to alternation effect,*n*-butyric acid has a higher melting point (267 K) than *n*-valeric acid (239 K).
The rest of the statements are correct as explained below.

(i) Salicylic acid has a higher MP (432 K) than anthranilic acid (419 K) due to stronger intramolecular H-bonding between OH and C=O in salicylic acid than weaker H-bonding between N–H and C=O and C=O in anthranilic acid.

(ii) Due to steric hindrance between CH_3 and COOH groups at the *o*-position, the molecules of *o*-toluic acid do not fit closely in the crystal lattice and hence have a lower MP (379 K) than benzoic acid (395 K).

(iii) Being linear, oxalic acid (462 K) (packs closely in the crystal lattice) has a higher MP than malonic acid (409 K) which has a bent structure and hence does not pack closely in the crystal lattice.

138. (d): Due to the –I effect of the C=O intermolecular H-bonding in carboxylic acids is much stronger than in alcohols. However, aldehydes do not form H-bonds.

Chemical Properties of Carboxylic Acids

139. (a): Acid strength of haloacetic acids with respect to acetic acid decreases as the electronegativity of the halogen decreases, that is, option (a) is correct.

140. (c): Electron donating groups (OCH_3) decreases while electron withdrawing groups (NO_2) increase the acidity with respect to the parent acid, that is, benzoic acid. Thus, the correct option is 3 > 1 > 2.

141. (d): Due to ortho effect, *o*-toluic acid is the strongest acid. Further, due to the +I effect of the CH_3 group, *p*-toluic acid is a weaker acid than benzoic acid. Thus, the overall acid strength decreases in the order, *o*-toluic acid > benzoic acid >*p*-toluic acid, that is, option (d) is correct.

142. (c): CF_3 is a strong electron withdrawing group but MeO is a weak electron withdrawing group. Therefore, CF_3COOH (C) is a stronger acid than $MeOCH_2COOH$ (B). Further, $(Me)_2CH$ is a stronger electron donating group than CH_3, therefore, CH_3COOH (A) is a stronger acid than Me_2CHCO_2H (D). Thus, the overall acid character increases in the order: D < A < B < C, that is, option (c) is correct.

143. (a): Electron withdrawing groups increase the acidity. Since F has a stronger –I effect than Cl, trifluoroacetic (B) is a stronger acid than trichloroacetic acid (A).
In contrast, electron donating groups decrease the acidity. As compared to H, CH_3 is electron donating, therefore, formic acid (D) is a stronger acid than acetic acid (D). Combining these two trends, the overall acidity decreases in the order: B > A > D > C.

144. (b): The smallest value of pK_a denotes the strongest acid. Since the –I effect of F is the maximum and it decreases with distance, $CH_3CH_2CF_2COOH$ with two F atom at the α-position with respect to the COOH group, is the strongest acid.

145. (b): The +I effect decreases while the –I effect increases the acid strength of carboxylic acids. Since the +I effect of the isopropyl group is higher than that of the*n*-propyl group, $(CH_3)_2CHCOOH$ (III) is a weaker acid than $CH_3CH_2CH_2COOH$ (IV).
Further, since the –I effect decreases with distance, $CH_3CH_2CH(Br)COOH$ (I) is a stronger acid than $CH_3CH(Br)CH_2COOH$ (II). Thus, the overall acid strength increases in the order: III < IV < II < I, that is, option (b) is correct.

146. (b): (i) Due to the –I effect of F, the second acid is more acidic than the first.
(ii) Due to the greater –I effect of F over Cl, the first acid is more acidic than the second.
(iii) Since the –I effect decreases with distance, the second acid is more acidic than the first.
(iv) Due to the –I effect of the CF_3 group as compared to the +I effect of the CH_3 group, the first acid is more acidic than the second. Thus option (b), that is, (ii) and (iv) is correct.

147. (a): Alcohols (I) are the weakest acids followed by phenols (III). Sulfonic acid (IV) is the strongest acid followed carboxylic acid (II). Thus, the overall acidity increases in the order: I < III < II < IV, that is, option (a) is correct.

148. (b): The presence of electron withdrawing groups increase the acidity of substituted acids with respect to the parent acid. Thus, the parent acid (I) is the least acidic. Further, as the distance of the electron withdrawing O atom increases with respect to the COOH group, the acidity decreases. That is, the carboxylic acid (II) is more acidic than the carboxylic acid (III). Thus, the overall acidity decreases in the order: II > III > I, that is, option (b) is correct.

149. (b): Due to the ortho effect, *o*-hydroxybenzoic acid is the strongest acid. At the *m*-position, the OH group cannot exert its +R effect but instead exerts a weak –I effect. As a result, *m*-hydroxybenzoic acid is a stronger acid than benzoic acid. However, due to the +R effect of the OH group, *p*-hydroxybenzoic acid is the weakest. Thus, the overall acid strength decreases in the order: *o*-hydroxybenzoic acid >*m*-hydroxybenzoic acid > benzoic acid >*p*-hydroxybenzoic acid, that is, option (b) is correct.

150. (c): $CH_3CH_2COOH \xrightarrow[\text{HVZ reaction}]{Br_2/P} CH_3-CBr_2-COOH$

151. (c): $CH_3CH_2COOH \xrightarrow[\text{HVZ reaction}]{Cl_2,\ \text{red P}} CH_3-\underset{\underset{Cl}{|}}{CH}-COOH \xrightarrow[\text{(dehydrochlorination)}]{\text{alc. KOH}} CH_2=CH-COOH$

152. (b): $\underset{\text{Benzoic acid}}{C_6H_5COOH} \xrightarrow{LiAlH_4} \underset{\text{Benzyl alcohol}}{C_6H_5CH_2OH}$

153. (c): Only –COOH is reduced.

$CH_2=CH-COOH \xrightarrow[\text{(ii) } H_3O^+]{\text{(i) } LiAlH_4} CH_2=CH-CH_2OH$

154. (a): β-Keto acids on heating easily undergo decarboxylation via a six-membered cyclic transition state.

155. (b): β-Ketoacids on heating readily undergo decaboxylation.

$\underset{\beta\text{-Ketoacid}}{\text{(cyclic }\beta\text{-keto acid)}} \xrightarrow[-CO_2]{\Delta} [\text{enol (OH)}] \underset{}{\xrightarrow{\text{Tautomarises}}} \underset{\text{Cyclohexanone}}{\text{cyclohexanone}}$

156. (a): 2-(COOEt)cyclopentanone $\xrightarrow[\text{(Hydrolysis)}]{H_3O^+}$ $\underset{(\alpha,\ \beta\text{-keto acid})}{\text{2-(COOH)cyclopentanone}}$ $\xrightarrow[\text{(Decarboxylation)}]{\Delta\,(-CO_2)}$ cyclopentanone

157. (c): β-Hydroxy acids on heating lose a molecule of H_2O to form α, β-unsaturated acids, that is, option (c) is correct.

$\overset{\beta\quad\alpha}{CH_3CHOHCH_2COOH} \xrightarrow{\text{heat}} CH_3CH=CHCOOH + H_2O$

158. (b):

p-OHC–C$_6$H$_4$–COOH $\xrightarrow[-H_2O]{NH_2NH_2\text{ (1 mole)}}$ *p*-(H)(NNH$_2$)C=–C$_6$H$_4$–COOH $\xrightarrow[-N_2]{\text{Alc. KOH, }\Delta}$ *p*-CH$_3$–C$_6$H$_4$–COO$^-$K$^+$

Pot. *p*-toluate

159. (c): CH_3 is *o,p*-directing while COOH is *m*-directing. Both these effects reinforce at the *p*-position with respect to CH_3. Therefore, option (c) is correct.

(*o*-COOH)C$_6$H$_4$–CH$_3$ $\xrightarrow{Br_2 + Fe}$ Br–C$_6$H$_3$(COOH)–CH$_3$

160. (b):

$C_6H_5COOH \xrightarrow{SOCl_2} C_6H_5COCl \xrightarrow[-NH_4Cl]{2\,NH_3} C_6H_5CONH_2$

161. (d): $\underset{\text{Acetamide}}{CH_3CONH_2} + 2NaOH \xrightarrow{\Delta} CH_3COONa + NH_3$

$\underset{\text{Acetonitrile}}{CH_3CN} + NaOH + H_2O \xrightarrow{\Delta} CH_3COONa + NH_3$

$\underset{\text{Urea}}{NH_2CONH_2} + 2NaOH \longrightarrow NH_3 + Na_2CO_3$

162. (c): $\underset{\text{Butanamide}}{CH_3CH_2CH_2CONH_2} + NaOH \xrightarrow{\Delta}$

$[CH_3CH_2CH_2COONa + NH_3] \xrightarrow{\text{Dil.HCl}} CH_3CH_2CH_2COOH + NH_4Cl$

163. (b): Due to the electron donating effect of the NH group, bromination occurs at the less hindered *p*-position in the ring attached to it (NH group).

$C_6H_5-\overset{O}{\overset{\|}{C}}-NH-C_6H_5 \xrightarrow{Br_2/Fe} C_6H_5-\overset{O}{\overset{\|}{C}}-NH-C_6H_4-Br$

164. (b):

$\underset{\text{Ethanol}}{CH_3CH_2OH} \xrightarrow{\text{Alk. }KMnO_4} \underset{\text{Acetic acid (X)}}{CH_3-\overset{O}{\overset{\|}{C}}-OH} \xrightarrow[H^+]{CH_3OH} \underset{\substack{\text{Methylacetate}\\\text{(Fruity smell)}}}{CH_3-\overset{O}{\overset{\|}{C}}-OCH_3} + H_2O$

165. (d): $CH_3COOH \xrightarrow{LiAlH_4} \underset{(A)}{C_2H_5OH}$

$A + CH_3COOH \xrightarrow{H^+} \underset{(B)}{CH_3COOC_2H_5} + H_2O$

166. (c): The iodoform test is carried out in a hot alkaline medium. Under these conditions, the esters get hydrolysed to give the corresponding alcohols. Now ethyl acetate gives ethyl alcohol which responds to the iodoform test to give a yellow precipitate of CHI_3 while methyl acetate will give methanol which does not give the iodoform test.

$CH_3COOC_2H_5 \xrightarrow[\Delta]{I_2/NaOH} [CH_3COONa + C_2H_5OH] \xrightarrow{I_2/NaOH} CHI_3$

$CH_3COOCH_3 \xrightarrow[\Delta]{I_2/NaOH} [CH_3COONa + CH_3OH] \xrightarrow{I_2/NaOH} \text{No precipitates}$

167. (b):

$\underset{\text{Sod. propionate}}{CH_3CH_2COO^-Na^+} + \underset{\text{Acetyl chloride}}{CH_3COCl} \xrightarrow{-NaCl} \underset{\text{Acetic propionic anhydride}}{CH_3CH_2CO.O.COCH_3}$

168. (b): Both CH_3COCl and $CH_3CO.O.\ COCH_3$ react with H_2O to produce acid/s and hence give effervescence with aq. $NaHCO_3$.

169. (a): Out of the four bases listed (Cl^-, NH_2^-, $C_2H_5O^-$ and CH_3COO^-),the Cl^- ion is the weakest base and hence is the best leaving group. Thus, when Z = Cl, nucleophilic substitution is the fastest.

170. (c): Acid chloride > acid anhydride > ester > amide.

171. (a): Electron withdrawing groups increase the +ve charge on the carbonyl carbon and hence favour nucleophilic attack. Since the NO_2 group is a stronger electron withdrawing group than the CHO group, the acid chloride (ii) is more reactive than (iv) and both are more reactive than the acid chloride (i). Since electron donating groups decrease the reactivity, the acid chloride (iii) is the least reactive. Thus, the overall reactivity towards hydrolysis decreases in the order: (ii) > (iv) > (i) > (iii), that is, option (a) is correct.

172. (d): Due to the powerful –I and –R effect of the $-NO_2$ group, the +ve charge on the C=O group of the ester increases. As a result, nucleophilic attack by the OH^- ion occurs readily and hence the ester gets hydrolysed readily.

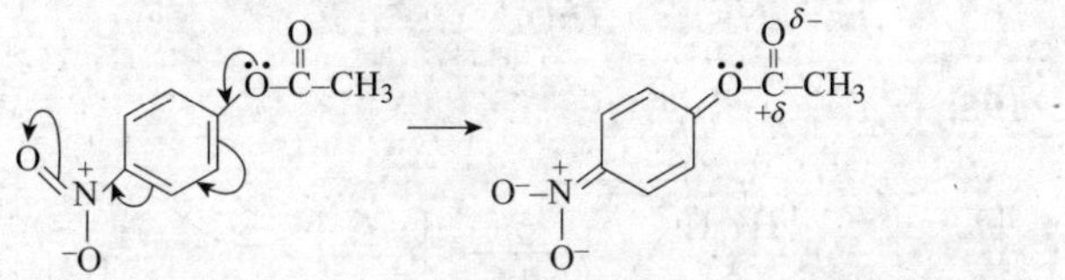

173. (c): $CH_3CO\vdots OC_2H_5 + H\vdots NHNHCONH_2 \xrightarrow{-C_2H_5OH} CH_3CONHNHCONH_2$

174. (b): RCOOH > HOH > ROH > HC≡CH

175. (a): Carboxylic acids are more acidic than phenols. Further, electron donating groups decrease while electron withdrawing groups increase the acidity of phenols/carboxylic acids. Thus, the overall acidity decreases in the order: III > IV > II > I.

Final Preparation

176. (a): $\xrightarrow{\text{DIBAL-H}}$ $\xrightarrow{H_3O^+}$

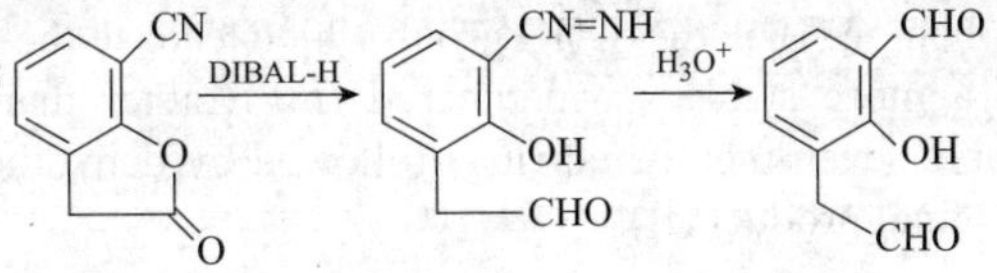

Thus, option (a) is correct.

177. (a): $CH_3COOH \xrightarrow{SOCl_2} \underset{(A)}{CH_3COCl} \xrightarrow[\text{Anhyd. AlCl}_3]{\text{Benzene}}$

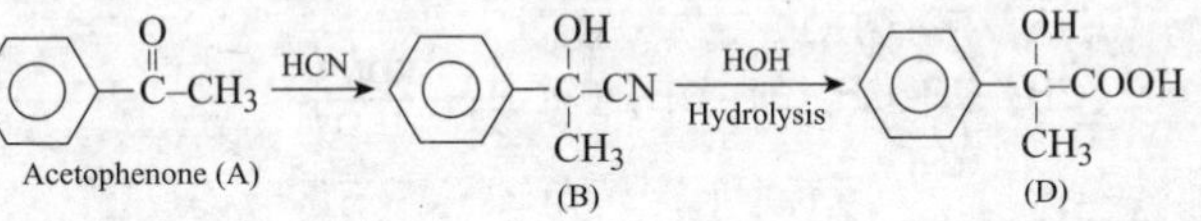

Acetophenone (A) $\xrightarrow{HCN}$ (B) $\xrightarrow[\text{Hydrolysis}]{HOH}$ (D)

178. (b): Ketones have less tendency towards hydration than aldehydes. Further, the presence of electron withdrawing groups increase the tendency towards hydration. Thus, acetone (I) has the least while formaldehyde (D) has the highest tendency towards hydrate formation.
Due to the –I effect of Cl, chloroacetone (III) has little higher tendency than acetone (I) and chloroacetaldehyde (V) has a little higher tendency than acetaldehyde (II) towards hydrate formation. Thus, the overall tendency increases in the order: I < III < II < V < IV.

179. (a): As the internal angle increases, steric hindrance increases and hence the stability of the gem-diol decreases. Thus, option (a) is correct.

180. (d): α-Alkoxy alcohols are called hemiacetals. Therefore, all are hemiacetals.

181. (c): A cyclic ketal contains a five-membered ring. Since two fused five-membered rings are more stable if the fusion is cis-, *cis*-cyclopentane-1,2-diol forms a stable ketal with acetone but the *trans*-isomer does not.

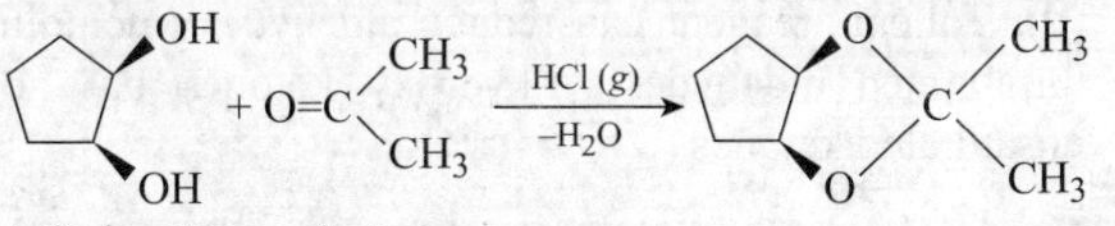

cis-Cyclopentane-1, 2-diol + $O=C(CH_3)_2$ (Acetone) $\xrightarrow[-H_2O]{HCl(g)}$

Thus, *cis*- and *trans*-cyclopentane-1,2-diol can be distinguished by reacting them with acetone/HCl(*g*).

182. (b): Acetals are decomposed in the presence of aqueous acids to give the original aldehydes. Thus,

$$\underset{\text{Acetal}}{CH_2(OC_2H_5)_2} + H_2O \xrightarrow{H^+} \underset{\text{Formaldehyde}}{CH_2O} + 2C_2H_5OH$$

The acetaldehyde thus liberated reacts with *p*-cresol in the presence of H^+ to give the electrophilic substitution product (d).

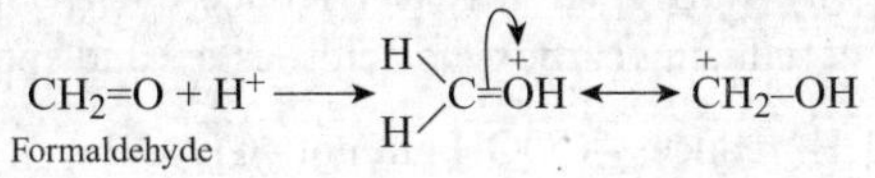

$$\underset{\text{Formaldehyde}}{CH_2=O} + H^+ \longrightarrow H_2C=\overset{+}{O}H \longleftrightarrow \overset{+}{C}H_2-OH$$

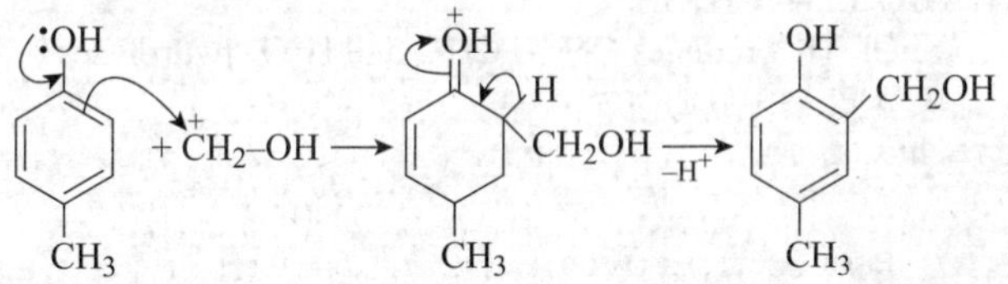

p-Cresol $+ \overset{+}{C}H_2-OH \longrightarrow \xrightarrow{-H^+}$ *o*-Hydroxymethyl *p*-Cresol

183. (c): $\xrightarrow{-H^- \text{ from } NaBH_4}$ $\xrightarrow[\text{from } H_2O]{H^+}$ $\xrightarrow[\text{Reduction of CHO group}]{NaBH_4}$ ≡ HO–CH₂CH₂CH₂CH₂–OH

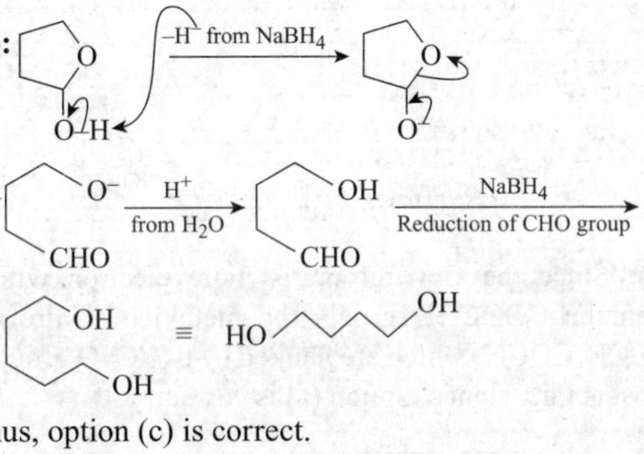

Thus, option (c) is correct.

184. (d): $CH_3-\overset{O}{\overset{\|}{C}}-CH_2-COOC_2H_5 \xrightarrow{(CH_2OH)_2/PTS.}$ (ketal) $CH_3-C-CH_2-COOC_2H_5 \xrightarrow[\text{Ether}]{LiAlH_4}$ (ketal) $CH_3-C-CH_2-CH_2OH \xrightarrow[\text{Hydrolysis}]{H_3O^+} CH_3-\overset{O}{\overset{\|}{C}}-CH_2-CH_2OH$

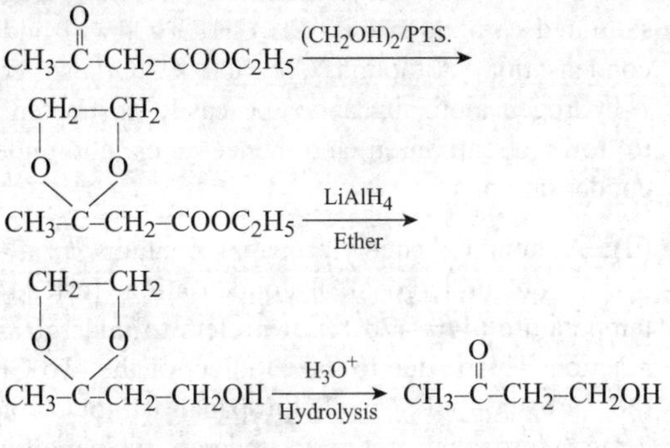

185. (c): $\xrightarrow[\text{Tollen's reagent (Oxidation of CHO to } CO_2H)]{[Ag(NH_3)_2]^+OH^-}$ $\xrightarrow[\text{(Esterification)}]{H^+/CH_3OH}$

$\xrightarrow[\text{(Addition of Grignard reagent to ketone gives 2° alcohols whie to esters it gives 3° alcohols)}]{3\,CH_3MgBr}$

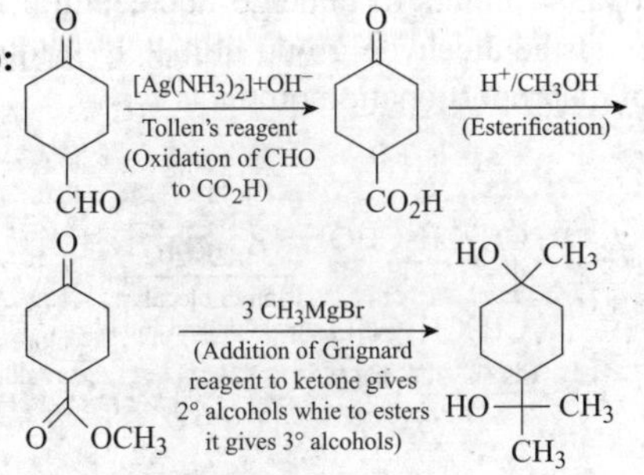

186. (d): Tollens' reagent can reduce aldehydes (including α,β-unsaturated aldehydes, α-hydroxy ketones but not α,β-unsaturated ketones.

187. (c):

$$\underset{\mathbf{P}}{H_2C{=}C(OCOCH_3)CH_3} \xrightarrow[\text{(Hydrolysis)}]{H^+/H_2O} H_2C{=}C(OH)CH_3 \xrightleftharpoons{\text{Tautomerises}} \underset{\text{(Does not reduce Fehling solution)}}{H_3C{-}\overset{O}{\overset{\|}{C}}{-}CH_3}$$

$$\underset{\mathbf{Q}}{H_3C{-}CH{=}CH{-}OCOCH_3} \xrightarrow[\text{(Hydrolysis)}]{H^+/H_2O} H_3C{-}CH{=}CH{-}OH \xrightleftharpoons{\text{Tautomerises}} \underset{\text{(Reduces Fehling's solution)}}{H_3C{-}CH_2{-}CHO}$$

188. (d): Only $NaBH_4$ in C_2H_5OH reduces $-CHO$ to $-CH_2OH$ without reducing carboxylic acids, esters and epoxides.

189. (c): B_2H_6 reduces $-COOH$ but not $-CH_2OH$

$-CO_2Et \rightarrow CH_2OH$

$SnCl_2/HCl$ reduces $CN \rightarrow CHO$ and H_3O^+ hydrolyses

$-CO_2Et \rightarrow CO_2H$

Thus,

Cyclohexane with Et_2OC, CO_2H, CN $\xrightarrow{B_2H_6}$ cyclohexane with CH_2OH, EtO_2C, CN $\xrightarrow{SnCl_2/HCl}$ cyclohexane with CH_2OH, EtO_2C, $CH{=}NH.HCl$ $\xrightarrow[\substack{\text{Hydrolysis} \\ (-CO_2Et \rightarrow -CO_2H) \\ -CH=NH-HCl \rightarrow CHO}]{H_3O^+}$ cyclohexane with CH_2OH, HO_2C, CHO

190. (a): Since the C=O group is more electron withdrawing than the $COOC_2H_5$ group, the methylene hydrogens in $-COCH_2COCH_3$ which are flanked by two C=O groups are the most acidic. Hence; option (a) is correct.

191. (d): Aldehydes which contain an α-hydrogen on a saturated carbon, that is, CH_3CH_2CHO, will undergo aldol condensation. Although $CH_2{=}CH{-}CHO$ also contains an α-hydrogen atom, it cannot be easily abstracted by a base to form a carbanion and hence does not undergo aldol condensation.

192. (d): Although 2-methylpropanal contains an α-hydrogen, it does not undergo aldol condensation. Instead, at higher temperature (440–470 K), it prefers to undergo Cannizzaro reaction. This is due to the +I effect of the two CH_3 groups, the carbanion of 2-methylpropanal is not stable. Instead 2-methylpropanal prefers to undergo nucleophilic attack by the OH^- ion at the aldehyde group utimately leading to the formation of disproportionation products.

193. (a):

Cyclohexene $\xrightarrow[\text{(ii) } Zn/H_2O]{\text{(i) Ozonolysis}}$ $\underset{\text{Hexane-1, 6-dial (E)}}{CH_2CH_2CHO{-}CH_2CH_2CHO}$ $\xrightarrow[\text{(Intramolecular aldol condensation)}]{\text{Aq. KOH}}$ Cyclopent-1-ene-1-carbaldehyde (F)

194. (c): Aldols are β-hydroxyaldehydes which upon dehydration give α,β-unsaturated aldehydes/ketones.

$$CH_3{-}\overset{O}{\overset{\|}{C}}{-}(CH_2)_2{-}\overset{O}{\overset{\|}{C}}{-}CH_3 \xrightarrow[-H_2O]{OH^-} CH_3{-}\overset{O}{\overset{\|}{C}}{-}(CH_2)_2{-}\overset{O}{\overset{\|}{C}}{-}\overset{-}{C}H_2$$

$\xrightarrow[-H_2O]{OH^-}$ cyclic β-hydroxy ketone (OH, CH_3, H) $\xrightarrow{-H_2O}$ 3-methylcyclopent-2-enone (H, CH_3)

195. (a):

2-substituted cyclohexanone with side chain ketone (H, H, CH_3) $\xrightarrow[-H_2O]{OH^-}$ enolate ($\overset{-}{C}H{-}CH_3$) $\longrightarrow$

Alkoxide (O^-, CH_3) $\xrightarrow[-OH^-]{H-OH}$ β-hydroxy ketone (HO, CH_3, H) $\xrightarrow[(-H_2O)]{H^+,\text{ heat}}$ bicyclic α,β-unsaturated ketone (CH_3, O)

196. (a): Although there are three α-hydrogens; two next to the CHO groups and one next to the CH_3CO group, the α-hydrogen next to the CH_3CO group is the least hindered and hence is preferentially abstracted by the base to give the carbanion (I). Subsequent aldol condensation initiated by carbanion (I) on the–CHO group which leads to the formation of a more stable six-membered ring (rather than the less stable seven-membered ring) followed by dehydration gives the final product (II).

$$CH_3{-}\underset{COOCH_3}{CH}{-}\overset{COOCH_3}{CH}{-}CH_2{-}CH_2{-}\overset{O}{\overset{\|}{C}}{-}CH_3 \xrightarrow[\substack{\text{(Reduction of} \\ -COOCH_3\text{ groups} \\ \text{to } -CHO)}]{\text{DIBAL-H}}$$

$$CH_3{-}\underset{CHO}{CH}{-}\overset{CHO}{CH}{-}CH_2{-}CH_2{-}\overset{O}{\overset{\|}{C}}{-}CH_3 \xrightarrow[-H_2O]{KOH}$$

$$\underset{\text{I}}{CH_3{-}\underset{CHO}{CH}{-}\overset{HC=O}{CH}{-}CH_2{-}CH_2{-}\overset{O}{\overset{\|}{C}}{-}\overset{-}{C}H_2} \xrightarrow{\text{Aldol condensation}}$$

$CH_3{-}CH(CHO){-}$(cyclohexanone with O^-) $\xrightarrow[-OH^-]{H_2O}$ $CH_3{-}CH(CHO){-}$(cyclohexanone with HO, H; β, α) — β-Hydroxyketone

$\xrightarrow[(-H_2O)]{\Delta}$ $CH_3{-}CH(CHO){-}$(cyclohexenone) — II

Thus, option (a) is correct.

197. (c):

$$\underset{\text{Carbonyl group of an ester}}{R{-}\overset{O}{\overset{\|}{C}}{-}OR'} + \underset{\text{Enolate of acetaldehyde}}{\overset{-}{C}H_2{-}\overset{O}{CH}} \longrightarrow R{-}\overset{O^-}{\underset{CH_2CHO}{C}}{-}OR'$$

$$\longrightarrow \underset{\beta\text{-Ketoaldehyde}}{R{-}\overset{O}{\overset{\|}{C}}{-}CH_2{-}CHO} + R'O^-$$

If instead of an enolate of an aldehyde, the enolate of a ketone is used, then a β-diketone is formed. Since a β-diketone is not included in the option, a β-ketoaldehyde is the right option.

198. (c): Since compound A with a MF of C_3H_6O gives the iodoform test, it must be propanone. Propanone on saturation with HCl gives a compound B which has three times the number of carbon atoms in propanone. B must be phorone, that is, 2,6-dimethyl-2,5-heptadien-4-one.

199. (a): γ-Hydroxy acids readily undergo dehydration to form lactones.

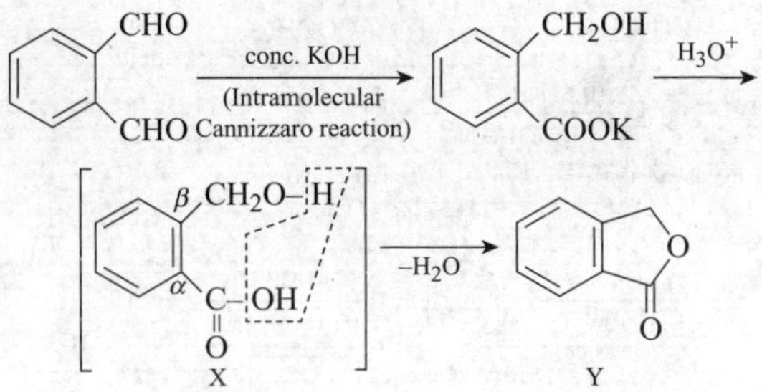

$C_6H_4(CHO)_2$ —conc. KOH (Intramolecular Cannizzaro reaction)→ $C_6H_4(CH_2OH)(COOK)$ —H_3O^+→

X (γ-Hydroxy acid) —$-H_2O$→ Y Phthalide (A lactone)

200. (c): CHO–CHO (Ethane-1, 2-dial) —NaOH (Intramolecular Cannizzaro reaction)→ CH_2OH–CO_2Na —H^+→ CH_2OH–CO_2H (A)

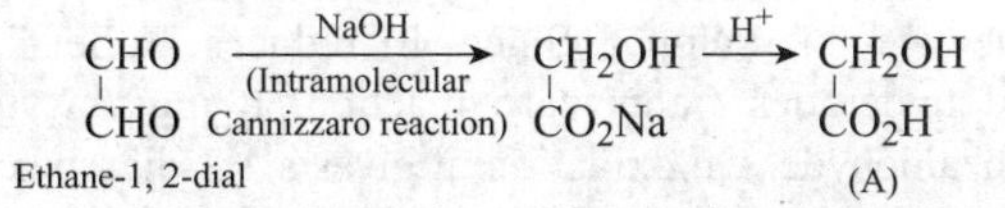

201. (b): R–CHO + $^-$OH ⟶ R–CH(O$^-$)(OH) + R–CHO ⟶

R–C(=O)–O$^-$ + RCH_2OD ←D_2O— R–C(=O)–OH + R–CH$_2$–O$^-$

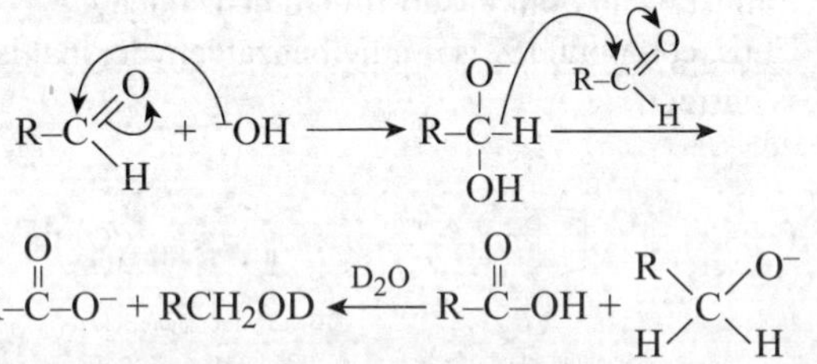

202. (a):

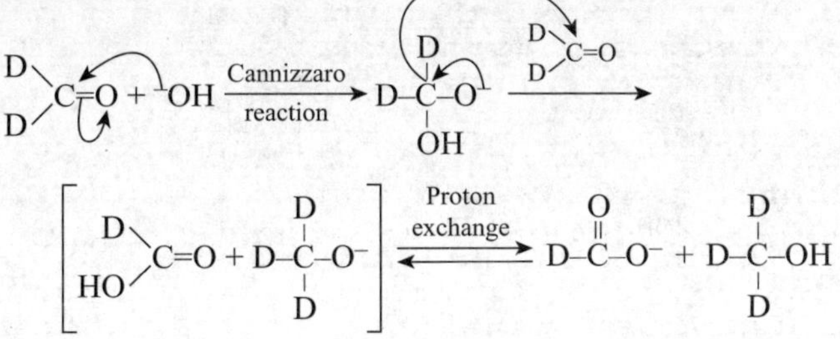

$D_2C{=}O$ + $^-$OH —Cannizzaro reaction→ D–C(D)(OH)–O$^-$ + $D_2C{=}O$ ⟶

[D(HO)C=O + D–C(D)(D)–O$^-$] —Proton exchange⇌ D–C(=O)–O$^-$ + D–C(D)(D)–OH

203. (a): C_6H_5–C(=O)–H —Na^+ $^-$OD→ C_6H_5C(DO)(H)–O$^-$ + C_6H_5C(=O)–H

C_6H_5–C(=O)–OD + $C_6H_5CH_2O^-$ —NaOD/D_2O→

C_6H_5–C(=O)–ONa + $C_6H_5CH_2OD$

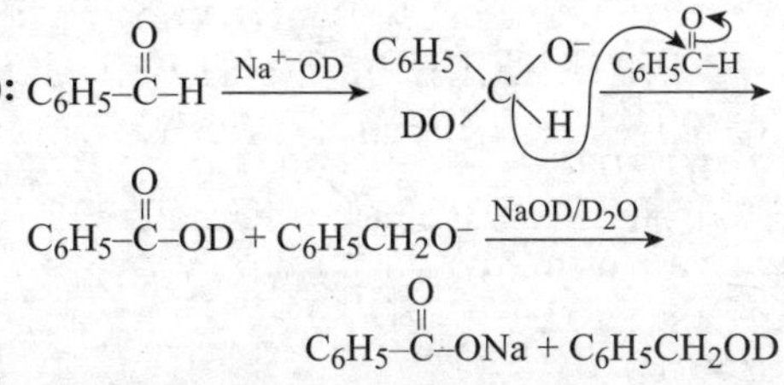

204. (b): Transfer of a hydride ion to the carbonyl group is the slowest or the rate determining step. Hence, option (b) is correct.

205. (d): The electron withdrawing nitro group facilitates the release of the hydride ion. Hence option (d) is correct.

206. (d): Aromatic aldehydes in the presence of alcoholic KCN undergo benzoin condensation to give α-hydroxy ketones usually called benzoins.

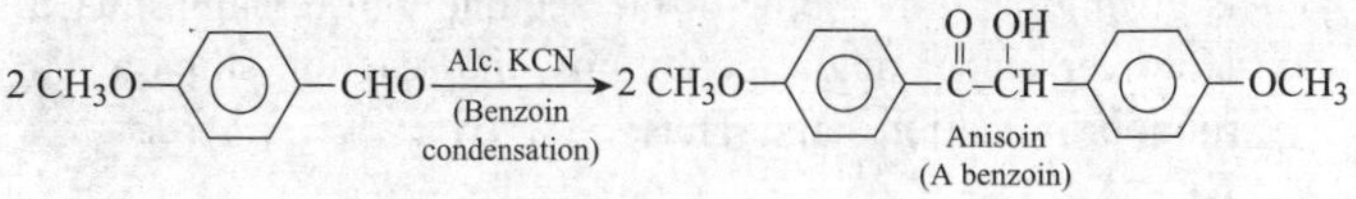

2 CH_3O–C_6H_4–CHO —Alc. KCN (Benzoin condensation)→ CH_3O–C_6H_4–C(=O)–CH(OH)–C_6H_4–OCH_3 Anisoin (A benzoin)

207. (c): Ph–CH=O + $^-$CN ⟶ Ph–C(O$^-$)(H)–CN —Hydrogen transfer→ Ph–C$^-$(OH)(CN)

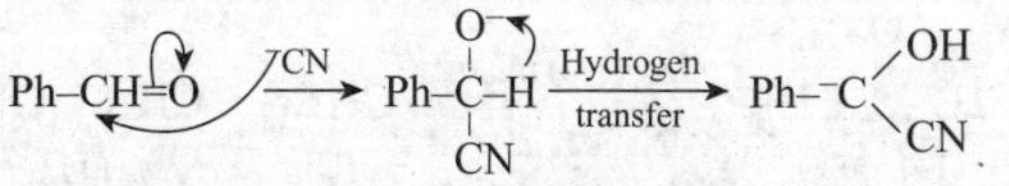

The hydrogen transfer is due to stabilisation of the resulting carbanion through resonance over the benzene ring as well as the CN group.

208. (c): CH_3CHO contains three α-H atoms but HCHO does not; therefore, in the presence of conc. alkali, three crossed aldol condensation reactions occur to yield (I).

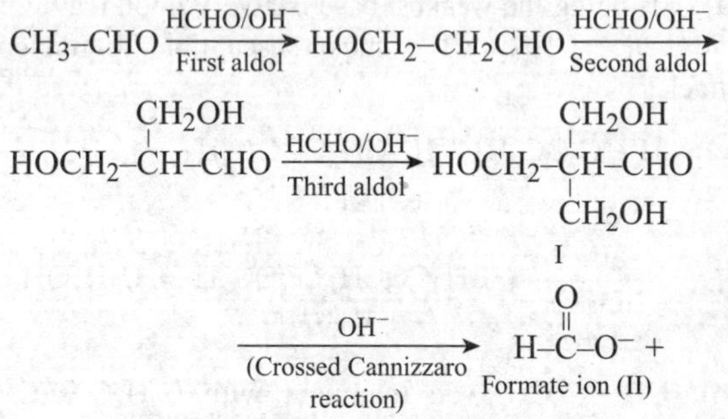

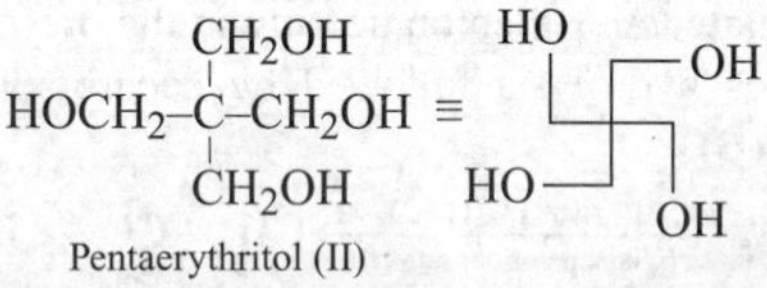

CH_3–CHO —HCHO/OH^- (First aldol)→ $HOCH_2$–CH_2CHO —HCHO/OH^- (Second aldol)→

$HOCH_2$–CH(CH_2OH)–CHO —HCHO/OH^- (Third aldol)→ $HOCH_2$–C(CH_2OH)$_2$–CHO (I)

—OH^- (Crossed Cannizzaro reaction)→ H–C(=O)–O$^-$ + Formate ion (II)

$HOCH_2$–C(CH_2OH)$_2$–CH_2OH ≡ C(CH_2OH)$_4$ Pentaerythritol (II)

Further, (I) and HCHO both do not contain any α-H, therefore, in the presence of conc. OH^-, both these aldehydes undergo crossed Cannizzaro reaction to give pentaerythritol (II) and formate ion.

209. (c): Aromatic aldehydes condense with acetic anhydride in the presence of sodium acetate to give an intermediate which upon hydrolysis give α,β-unsaturated acids. This reaction is called Perkin condensation.

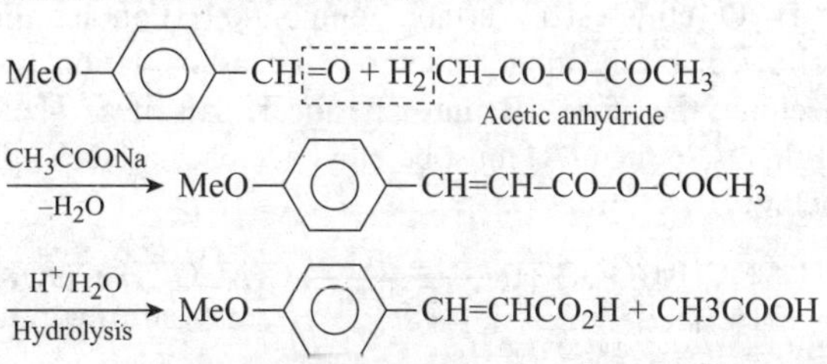

MeO–C_6H_4–CH=O + H_2CH–CO–O–$COCH_3$ (Acetic anhydride)

—CH_3COONa, $-H_2O$→ MeO–C_6H_4–CH=CH–CO–O–$COCH_3$

—H^+/H_2O Hydrolysis→ MeO–C_6H_4–CH=$CHCO_2H$ + CH3COOH

α,β-Unsaturated acid

210. (c): Ph–C(=O)–$\overset{*}{C}H_2$–C(=O)–OH (α,β-Keto acid) —Heat ($-CO_2$) (Decarboxylation)→ Ph–C(=O)–$\overset{*}{C}H_3$ Acetophenone (E)

—I_2/NaOH (Iodoform reaction)→ Ph–C(=O)–O$^-$$Na^+$ + $\overset{*}{C}HI_3$ (G)

Acetophenone (E)

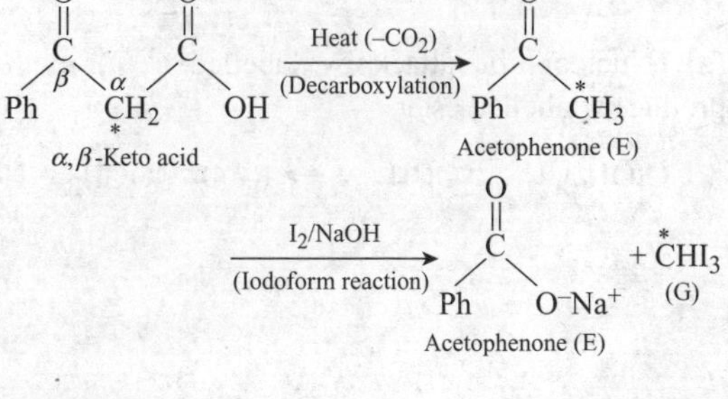

211. (a): Under basic conditions, the haloform reaction occurs to give $CHBr_3$ (U) and CH_3COONa (T). For the haloform reaction we need 3 moles of Br_2. But, only one mole of Br_2 is given, therefore, some of the acetone will remain unused. However, under acidic conditions, the reaction stops at the monobromination stage. Thus,

Reaction I:

$$\underset{(1\text{-}0\text{ mole})}{CH_3-\overset{O}{\overset{\|}{C}}-CH_3} \xrightarrow[\substack{NaOH\,(aq)\\(\text{Haloform reaction})}]{Br_2\,(1\text{-}0)\text{ mole}} \underset{(U)}{CHBr_3} + \underset{(T)}{CH_3COONa}$$

Reaction II:

$$CH_3-\overset{O}{\overset{\|}{C}}-CH_3 \xrightarrow[CH_3COOH]{Br_2\,(1\text{-}0)\text{ mole}} \underset{(P)}{CH_3-\overset{O}{\overset{\|}{C}}-CH_2Br} + HBr$$

So, option (c) is correct.

212. (a): Cl^- being the weakest base is a very good leaving group and hence CH_3COCl is most susceptible to nucleophilic attack.

213. (c): $CH_3CO\boxed{OC_2H_5 + H}-CH_2COOC_2H_5$

Ethyl acetate (two molecules)

$$\xrightarrow[\text{(Claisen condensation)}]{C_2H_5ONa} \underset{\text{Acetoacetic ester}}{CH_3COCH_2COOC_2H_5} + C_2H_5OH$$

214. (b): $CH_3CO_2C_2H_5$ on treatment with C_2H_5ONa/C_2H_5OH undergoes Claisen ester condensation to give ethyl acetoacetate (A) which on heating in the presence of an acid undergoes hydrolysis followed by decarboxylation to give acetone (B).

$$2CH_3CO_2C_2H_5 \xrightarrow[\text{(Claisen condensation)}]{NaCO_2H_5} \underset{\text{Ethyl acetoacetate (A)}}{CH_3-CO-CH_2-CO_2C_2H_5}$$

$$\xrightarrow[\text{(Hydroysis)}]{H_3O^+,\,\Delta} \underset{\beta\text{-Keto acid}}{[CH_3-CO-CH_2-COOH]} \xrightarrow[\substack{\text{Decarboxylation}\\(-CO_2)}]{\Delta} \underset{\text{Acetone (B)}}{CH_3-\overset{O}{\overset{\|}{C}}-CH_3}$$

215. (b): Compound (B) with a MF of $C_4H_5O_3$ containing four C atoms is obtained from the ketoester (A) with a MF of $C_6H_{10}O_3$ ethyl ester. Further, compound (B) on acidification followed by heating undergoes decarboxylation to give acetone, therefore, (B) must be the K salt of a β-ketoacid. If this is so then (A) must be ethyl acetoacetate as explained below.

$$\underset{\substack{\text{M.F. }C_6H_{10}O_3\text{ (A)}\\\text{Ethyl acetoacetate}}}{CH_3COCH_2COOC_2H_5} \xrightarrow[-C_2H_5OH]{KOH} \underset{\text{M.F. }C_4H_5O_3K\text{ (B)}}{CH_3COCH_2COOK}$$

$$\xrightarrow{HCl} \underset{\beta\text{-Keto acid}}{[CH_3COCH_2COOH]} \xrightarrow{\Delta} \underset{\text{Acetone}}{CH_3COCH_3} + CO_2$$

216. (a): Nucleophilic attack by labelled (^{18}O) methanol will produce a labelled ester.

$$RCO\boxed{OH + H-}{}^{18}OCH_3 \longrightarrow RCO-{}^{18}OCH_3 + H_2O$$

217. (a):

$$(CH_3)_2C{=}O + HCN \xrightarrow{H^+} (CH_3)_2C(OH)CN \xrightarrow[\text{Hydrolysis}]{H_3O^+}$$

$$(CH_3)_2C(OH)COOH \xrightarrow[\Delta\,(-H_2O)]{H_2SO_4} CH_2{=}\underset{CH_3}{\underset{|}{C}}-COOH \xrightarrow{PCl_5}$$

$$CH_2{=}\underset{CH_3}{\underset{|}{C}}-COCl \xrightarrow[\text{(ii) }H_2O_2,\,OH^-]{\text{(i) }BH_3-THF} HOCH_2-\underset{CH_3}{\underset{|}{CH}}-COOH$$

218. (a):

Ethylbenzene ($C_6H_5CH_2CH_3$) $\xrightarrow[\text{(ii) }H_3O^+]{\text{(i) }KMnO_4/KOH,\,\Delta}$ Benzoic acid (B) (C_6H_5COOH)

$\xrightarrow[\text{(Nuclear bromination)}]{Br_2/FeCl_3}$ *m*-Bromobenzoic acid (C) $\xrightarrow[\text{(Fischer-Speier esterification)}]{C_2H_5OH/H^+}$ Ethyl *m*-Bromobenzoate (D) ($COOC_2H_5$, Br)

219. (a): Since compound X forms a 2,4-DNP, it must be an aldehyde or ketone. Since it reduces Tollens' reagent and undergoes Cannizzaro reaction, it must a substituted benzaldehyde. On oxidation, it gives a 1,2-dicarboxylic acid, it must be an *o*-alkyl substituted benzaldehyde.

Thus, compound X is *o*-ethylbenzaldehyde, that is, option (a) is correct.

220. (a): Benzene + Succinic anhydride $\xrightarrow[AlCl_3]{\text{Anhyd}}$ 3-Benzoylpropanoic acid (X) ($C_6H_5CO-CH_2-CH_2-CO_2H$)

$\xrightarrow[\text{Cyclisation }(-H_2O)]{H_2SO_4}$ 5, 6-Benzocyclohexane-1, 4-dione (Y)

221. (b):

γ-Butyrolactone + *o*-cresol $\xrightarrow[\text{acylation}]{FC}$ (intermediate) $\longrightarrow$ HO–$CH_2CH_2CH_2$–CO–(4-hydroxy-3-methylphenyl)

$\xrightarrow[-HCl]{AlCl_3}$ $\xrightarrow{-AlOCl_2^-}$ $\xrightarrow{-H^+}$ (cyclised tetralone product with OH and CH_3)

222. (c):

$$CH_3C{\equiv}CH \xrightarrow{\text{Disiamylborane}} CH_3CH{=}CH{-}B\langle \xrightarrow{H_2O_2/OH^-}$$

$$[CH_3CH{=}CHOH] \xrightarrow{\text{Tautomerises}} \underset{\text{Propanal}}{CH_3CH_2CHO}$$

223. (c): Due to the –I effect of the OH group, the terminal acetylenic carbon of the complex (I) becomes electron deficient and hence carbon ultimately gives cinnamaldehyde.

$$C_6H_5-\underset{OH}{CH}-C\equiv CH \xrightarrow{Hg^{2+}} C_6H_5-\underset{OH}{CH}-\overset{\delta-}{CH}=\overset{\delta+}{CH}\cdots Hg^{2+}\ (I) \xrightarrow[-H^+]{H_2\ddot{O}}$$

$$C_6H_5-\underset{OH}{CH}-\underset{^+Hg}{C}=CHOH \xrightarrow[-Hg^{2+}]{+Hg^+} C_6H_5-\underset{OH}{CH}-\underset{H}{C}=CHOH$$

$$\xrightarrow{\text{Tautomerises}} C_6H_5-\underset{OH}{CH}-\underset{H}{CH}-CHO \xrightarrow{-H_2O} \underset{\text{Cinnamaldehyde}}{C_6H_5-CH=CH-CHO}$$

224. (b): Due to the –I effect of the C=O group, the terminal acetylenic carbon atom of the complex (I) becomes electron deficient and hence nucleophilic attack by H_2O on this electron deficient carbon occurs, ultimately giving aldehyde (II).

2-ethynylcyclohexanone ($\overset{\delta-}{C}\equiv\overset{\delta+}{CH}$) $\xrightarrow{Hg^{2+}}$ complex with Hg^{2+} (I) $\xrightarrow[-H^+]{H_2\ddot{O}}$ 2-($C(Hg^+)=CHOH$)cyclohexanone $\xrightarrow[-Hg^{2+}]{+H^+}$ 2-(CH=CHOH)cyclohexanone $\xrightarrow{\text{Tautomerises}}$ 2-(CH_2CHO)cyclohexanone (II)

225. (d): $CH_3I + 2Li \xrightarrow{\text{Dry ether}} CH_3Li + LiI$

$$2CH_3I + CuI \longrightarrow \underset{(A)}{[(CH_3)_2Cu]^-Li^+} + LiI$$

$$2(CH_3)_3C-\overset{O}{\overset{\|}{C}}-Cl + \underset{(A)}{(CH_3)_2CuLi} \longrightarrow \underset{(B)}{2(CH_3)_3C-\overset{O}{\overset{\|}{C}}-CH_3} + CuCl + LiCl$$

226. (b):

$$PhCH=CH_2 \xrightarrow{Br_2/CCl_4} PhCHBr-CH_2Br$$

$$\xrightarrow{NaNH_2/\text{liq. }NH_3} \underset{(A)}{PhC\equiv C^-Na^+} \xrightarrow[H_2SO_4]{\text{Dil } H_2SO_4} \underset{(B)}{Ph-COCH_3}$$

227. (b): $CH_2=CH_2 \xrightarrow[\text{High temp., high pressure}]{CO, H_2 . [Co(CO)_4]_2} CH_2CH_2CHO$

This reaction is called oxo process.

228. (c): $CH_2=CH_2 + H_2O \xrightarrow{Pd^{2+}} CH_3CHO$

This industrial process is called Wacker's process.

229. (b): $H-C\equiv N + HCl \longrightarrow \underset{(A)}{ClCH=NH} \xrightarrow[\text{Anhyd. } AlCl_3]{C_6H_6}$

$$\underset{(B)}{C_6H_5CH=NH} \xrightarrow[-NH_4^+]{H^+/H_2O} \underset{\text{Benzaldehyde}}{C_6H_5CH=O}$$

230. (b): HCHO reacts with a Grignard reagent to give a 1° alcohol, $HCOOC_2H_5$ gives a 2° alcohol while $HC(OC_2H_5)_3$ gives an aldehyde.

$$CH_3-MgBr + HC(OC_2H_5)_3 \xrightarrow{-C_2H_5OMgBr}$$

$$CH_3-CH(OC_2H_5)_2 \xrightarrow[-2\,C_2H_5OH]{H_3O^+} \underset{\text{Acetaldehyde}}{CH_3CH=O}$$

However, NaH being a strong base reacts with CH_3COCl to form a ketene.

$$Na^+H^- + H-CH_2-CO-Cl \longrightarrow \underset{\text{Ketene}}{CH_2=C=O} + H_2 + NaCl$$

231. (b): Lithium (EN = 1.0) is less electronegative than Mg (EN = 1.2), therefore, organolithium compounds are more nucleophilic than Grignard reagents. As a result, Grignard reagents add to CO_2 to give the addition product which upon acidification gives the corresponding carboxylic acid.

$$\overset{\delta-}{R}-\overset{\delta+}{MgX} + O=C=O \xrightarrow{\text{Dry ether}} \underset{\text{Addition product}}{R-\overset{O}{\overset{\|}{C}}-OMgX} \xrightarrow{H_3O^+} \underset{\text{Carboxylic acid}}{R-\overset{O}{\overset{\|}{C}}-OH}$$

In contrast, organolithium compounds being more nucleophilic add to the resonance stabilised lithium salt of the carboxylic acid first formed to produce ketones.

$$\overset{\delta-}{R}-\overset{\delta+}{Li} + O=C=O \xrightarrow{\text{Dry ether}} \left[R-\overset{O}{\overset{\|}{C}}-O^-Li^+ \xrightarrow{\overset{\delta-}{R}-\overset{\delta+}{Li}} R-\underset{R}{\overset{O^-Li^+}{\overset{|}{C}}}-O^-Li^+\right]$$

$$\xrightarrow{H_3O^+} \left[R-\underset{R}{\overset{OH}{\overset{|}{C}}}-OH\right] \xrightarrow{-H_2O} \underset{\text{Ketone}}{R_2C=O}$$

232. (a):

(i) $CH_3CH_2ONa \xrightarrow[\text{under pressure}]{CO,\ \Delta} CH_3CH_2COONa$

$$\xrightarrow{\text{Dil. HCl}} \underset{(A)}{CH_3CH_2COOH}$$

(ii) $CH_2=CH_2 + CO + H_2O \xrightarrow[\text{under pressure}]{H_3PO_4} \underset{(B)}{CH_3-CH_2COOH}$

233. (d): DIBAL-H is an excellent selective reducing agent which reduces cyanides, esters, lactones, amides, acid chlorides and carboxylic acids into their corresponding aldehydes.

Bicyclic lactone with COOH $\xrightarrow{\text{DIBAL–H}}$ cyclopentene bearing OH, CH_2CHO and COOH

MATCH THE FOLLOWING

234. (a): A ($CH_3CH_2CH_2CH_2OH$) — r ($CH_3CH_2CH_2CHO$);
B ($C_6H_5CH_3$) — s (C_6H_5CHO);
C (CH_3COCl) — q (CH_3COCH_3);
D [$(CH_3CH_2CO)_2Ca$] — p [$(CH_3CH_2)_2CO$]

235. (c): A ($C_6H_5COCH_3$) — s (Sodium hypoiodite);
B (C_6H_5CHO) — r (Sodium bisulfite);

C (CH_3CH_2COOH) — p (HVZ reaction);
D (HCOOH) — q (Fehling's solution)

236. (b): A (CH_3COCl) — r (most reactive);
B [$(CH_3CO)_2O$] — s (Perkin condensation);
C ($CH_3COOC_2H_5$] — p (Claisen ester condensation);
D (CH_3CONH_2) — q (Evolves NH_3 on heating with NaOH)

237. (d): A ($C_6H_5CH_3$) — s (Etard reaction);
B ($CH_3CO_2C_2H_5$) — p (Claisen ester condensation);
C (CH_3CHO) — q (Tischenko reaction);
D (RCOCl) — r (Rosenmund reduction)

ASSERTION REASON

238. (c): Correct R. Isobutanal does not contain the grouping CH_3CHOH or CH_3CO (attached to C or H) and hence does not give the iodoform test.

239. (b): Correct explanation. Acetophenone contains the grouping CH_3CO (attached to C) and hence gives the iodoform test while benzophenone does not contain this grouping and hence does not give the iodoform test.

240. (d): Correct A. During the reaction of carboxylic acids with $NaHCO_3$, the CO_2 evolved comes from $NaHCO_3$.
Correct R. Carboxylic acid is a stronger acid than carbonic acid.

241. (d): Correct A. Formic acid does not react with 2,4-DNP to form a yellowish-brown crystalline derivative.
Correct R. Due to resonance, the carbonyl carbon is less electrophilic and hence does not undergo nucleophilic addition reactions.

242. (c): Correct R. Acetate ion is more resonance stabilised than phenoxide ion.

243. (b): Correct explanation. Chlorine has both +R effect and –I effect but the –I effect outweighs the +R effect. As a result, *p*-chlorobenzoic acid is a stronger acid than benzoic acid.

244. (c): Correct R. Esters containing α-hydrogens on treatment with a base form a carbanion which brings about nucleophilic acyl substitution at the carbonyl group of the other molecule of the ester to form β-keto esters.

245. (a): R is the correct explanation of A.

246. (a): R is the correct explanation of A since malonic acid is like a β-keto acid and hence on heating, it undergoes decarboxylation.

$$(HOOC\text{–}\overset{\alpha}{C}H_2\text{–}\overset{\beta}{\boxed{COO}}H \longrightarrow CH_3COOH + CO_2)$$

Note that only 1,4 and 1,5-dicarboxylic acids on heating form anhydrides but malonic acid is a 1,3-dicarboxylic acid.

247. (d): Correct A. Grignard reagents but not dialkylcadmium react with acid chlorides to form tert-alcohols.
Correct R. Due to greater electronegativity of Cd (1.8) compared to Mg (1.2), dialkylcadmium reagents are less reactive than Grignard reagents and thus react with acid chlorides to give only ketones.

248. (c): Correct R. Ketals are hydrolysed back to ketones by aqueous acids but not by aqueous alkalis.

249. (b): Correct explanation. Both the carbanion (formed in the presence of a base) and the enol form (formed in the presence of an acid) act as nucleophiles and hence add on the carbonyl group of aldehydes and ketones to give aldols.

250. (c): Correct R. Only aldehydes which do not contain α-hydrogens on treatment with a concentrated solution of a strong base undergo Cannizzaro reaction.

251. (a): R is the correct explanation of A.

252. (a): R is the correct explanation of A.

253. (c): Correct R. Nucleophilic attack by the peroxyacid on the carbonyl group gives an intermediate which rearranges with the expulsion of the anion of the acid.

Organic Compounds Containing Nitrogen

Nitrogen is an important constituent of many organic compounds. The important classes of organic compounds containing nitrogen as a part of functional group are given in Table 13.1.

Table 13.1 Organic compounds containing nitrogen

Functional group	Class of compounds	General formula
$-NH_2$	(i) Primary amines	RNH_2
$-NH-$	(ii) Secondary amines	R_2NH
$-\overset{\vert}{\underset{\vert}{N}}-$	(iii) Tertiary amines	R_3N
$-C\equiv N$	Cyanides	RCN
$-N\equiv C$	Isocyanides	RNC
$-N\langle^{O}_{O}$	Nitro compounds	RNO_2
$-O-N=O$	Nitrites	RONO
$-N_2^+X^-$	Diazonium salts	$ArN_2^+X^-$

13.1 Amines

Amines are regarded as derivatives of ammonia in which one, two or all three hydrogen atoms are replaced by alkyl or aryl groups.

$$NH_3 \xrightarrow[-H]{+R} RNH_2 \xrightarrow[-H]{+R} R_2NH \xrightarrow[-H]{+R} R_3N$$

13.1.1 Classification of Amines

The amines are classified as primary (1°), secondary (2°) or tertiary (3°) according to whether one, two or three hydrogen atoms of the ammonia molecule are replaced by alkyl or aryl group.

$$\underset{\text{Ammonia}}{H-\overset{H}{\overset{|}{N}}-H} \quad \underset{\substack{\text{Primary amine}\\(1°)}}{R-\overset{H}{\overset{|}{N}}-H} \quad \underset{\substack{\text{Secondary amine}\\(2°)}}{R-\overset{R'}{\overset{|}{N}}-H} \quad \underset{\substack{\text{Tertiary amine}\\(3°)}}{R-\overset{R'}{\overset{|}{N}}-R''}$$

(where R, R′ and R″ are alkyl groups).

$$\underset{\text{(amino)}}{-NH_2} \quad \underset{\text{(imino)}}{-\overset{|}{N}H} \quad \underset{\text{(tert-nitrogen)}}{-\overset{|}{\underset{|}{N}}-}$$

Quaternary ammonium compounds may be regarded as derivatives of ammonium salts in which in which all the four H-atoms are replaced by alkyl or aryl groups. For example,

$[(CH_3)_4N]^+I^-$ Tetramethyl ammonium iodide,
$[(C_2H_5)_4N]^+ Cl^-$ Tetraethyl ammonium chloride,
$[(C_2H_5)_4N]^+ OH^-$ Tetraethyl ammonium hydroxide and
$[(C_6H_5)_4N]^+Br^-$ Tetraphenyl ammonium bromide.

Amines may further be classified into two categories.

13.1.2 Aliphatic Amines

Amines in which the nitrogen atom is directly bonded to one or more alkyl groups are called aliphatic amines. For example,

$$\underset{\substack{\text{Methylamine}\\(1°)}}{CH_3-NH_2} \quad \underset{\substack{\text{Dimethylamine}\\(2°)}}{CH_3-\overset{CH_3}{\overset{|}{N}H}} \quad \underset{\substack{\text{Trimethylamine}\\(3°)}}{CH_3-\overset{CH_3}{\overset{|}{N}}-CH_3}$$

13.1.3 Aromatic Amines

These are of two types:

(i) Aryl amines: Amines in which the nitrogen atom is directly bonded to one or more (same or different) aromatic rings or aryl groups are called aromatic amines. For example,

$C_6H_5-NH_2$ Aniline (1°) $\quad C_6H_5-NH-C_6H_5$ Diphenyl amine (2°) $\quad (C_6H_5)_3N$ Triphenyl amine (3°)

(ii) Aralkyl amines or side chain substituted amines: Amines in which the nitrogen atom is bonded to the side chain of the aromatic ring are called aralkyl amines. For example,

$C_6H_5-CH_2NH_2$ Benzylamine (1°) $\quad C_6H_5-CH_2-\overset{H}{\overset{|}{N}}-CH_2-C_6H_5$ Dibenzylamine (2°)

Simple and mixed amines: Secondary and tertiary amines may be classified as simple or mixed amines according to whether all the alkyl groups attached to the nitrogen atom are same or different. For example,

Simple amines: $(CH_3)_2NH$ Dimethylamine; $(CH_3CH_2)_3N$ Triethylamine; $(C_6H_5)_2NH$ Diphenylamine

Mixed amines: $C_2H_5–NH–CH_3$ Ethylmethylamine; $C_6H_5–NH–CH_3$ Methylaniline; $C_3H_7–N(CH_3)–C_2H_5$ Ethylmethyl-*n*-propylamine

13.2 IUPAC Nomenclature

13.2.1 Aromatic Amines

Benzenamine (Aniline) — $C_6H_5NH_2$

N-Methylbenzenamine (N-Methylaniline) — $C_6H_5NHCH_3$

N, N-Dimethylbenzenamine (N, N-Dimethylaniline) — $C_6H_5N(CH_3)_2$

N-Ethyl-N-methylbenzenamine (N-Ethyl-N-methylaniline) — $H_3C–N(C_6H_5)–CH_2CH_3$

2-Methylbenzenamine (2-Methylaniline or *o*-Toluidine)

4-Methylbenzenamine (4-Methylaniline or *p*-Toluidine)

In the IUPAC system, benzenamine may also be written as aminobenzene.

4-Bromobenzenamine (4-Bromoaniline)

2, 4-Dimethylbenzenamine (2, 4-Dimethylaniline)

2, 4, 6-Tribromobenzenamine (2, 4, 6-Tribromoaniline)

N, N-Diethylbenzenamine (N, N-Diethylaniline) — $C_6H_5N(C_2H_5)_2$

4-Methylbenzenamine or 4-Methylaniline (*p*-Toluidine)

4-Methoxybenzenamine or 4-Methoxyaniline (*p*-Anisidine)

N-Phenylbenzenamine or N-Phenylaniline (Diphenylamine) — $C_6H_5–NH–C_6H_5$

$\overset{3}{C}H_3\overset{2}{C}H(NH_2)\overset{1}{C}H_2COOH$ 2-Aminopropanoic acid

$H_2N\overset{2}{C}H_2\overset{1}{C}H_2OH$ 2-Aminoethanol

$\overset{3}{N}H_2–\overset{2}{C}H_2–CH_2–\overset{1}{C}N$ 3-Aminopropanenitrile

$\overset{4}{C}H_3\overset{3}{C}H(NH_2)\overset{2}{C}H_2\overset{1}{C}OOH$ 3-Aminobutanoic acid

$NH_2\overset{4}{C}H_2\overset{3}{C}H_2\overset{2}{C}(=O)\overset{1}{C}H_3$ 4-Aminobutan-2-one

If, however, all the functional groups are substituent functional groups, the compound is named as a derivative of the compound containing the functional group which comes first in the alphabetical order.

$CH_3–NH–\overset{1}{C}H_2–\overset{2}{C}H(NO_2)–\overset{3}{C}H_3$

N-Methyl-2-nitropropanamine

In the case of unsaturated amines, the amino group is given preference. For example,

$\overset{3}{C}H_3\overset{2}{C}H=\overset{1}{C}HNH_2$ Prop-1-en-1-amine

$\overset{3}{C}H_2=\overset{2}{C}H–\overset{1}{C}H_2NH_2$ Prop-2-en-1-amine (allylamine)

13.2.2 IUPAC Names of Complicated Amines

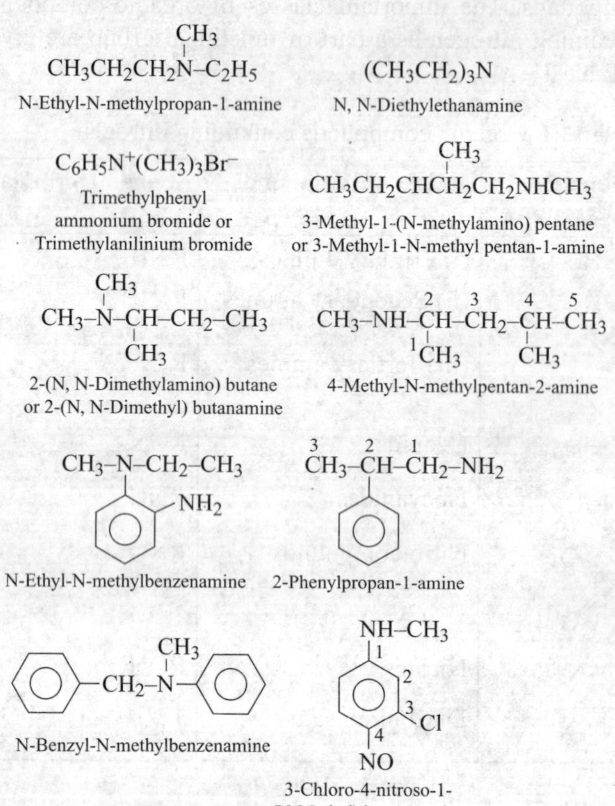

13.3 Isomerism in Amines

Amines exhibit the following types of isomerism.

(i) Chain isomerism: Aliphatic amines containing four or more carbon atoms show chain isomerism due to the difference in the nature of carbon chain of alkyl groups attached to the amino group. For example,

$CH_3CH_2CH_2CH_2NH_2$ Butan-1-amine

$CH_3–CH(CH_3)CH_2NH_2$ 2-Methylpropan-1-amine

$CH_3–C(CH_3)_2–NH_2$ Methylpropan-2-amine

(ii) Metamerism: This is due to the difference in the nature of the alkyl groups attached to the same functional group. For example,

$CH_3CH_2–NH–CH_2CH_3$ (Diethylamine) $CH_3NHCH_2CH_2CH_3$ (Methyl-*n*-propylamine)

$CH_3–NH–CH(CH_3)_2$ (Isopropylmethylamine)

(iii) Position isomerism: This is due to the difference in the position of amino group. For example,

$CH_3CH_2CH_2NH_2$ (Propan-1-amine) $CH_3–CH(NH_2)–CH_3$ (Propan-2-amine)

Similarly,

$CH_3CH_2CH_2CH_2NH_2$ (Butan-1-amine) $CH_3CH_2CH(NH_2)–CH_3$ (Butan-2-amine)

Aromatic amines also show position isomerism.

o-Toluidine *m*-Toluidine *p*-Toluidine

(iv) Functional isomerism: Primary, secondary and tertiary amines having the same molecular formula show functional isomerism among themselves because of the nature of amino groups. For example,

$CH_3CH_2CH_2NH_2$ (*n*-Propylamine (1°)) $CH_3CH_2NHCH_3$ (Ethylmethylamine (2°)) $CH_3–N(CH_3)–CH_3$ (Trimethylamine (3°))

13.4 Structure of Amines

Amines are the derivatives of ammonia in which the nitrogen atom undergoes sp^3 hybridisation forming four sp^3 hybrid orbitals. Three of these sp^3 hybrid orbitals overlap with the *s* orbital of H forming three N–H bonds. The fourth sp^3 hybrid orbital contains a lone pair of electrons.

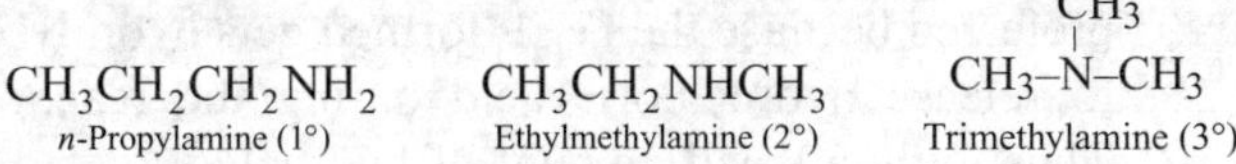

sp^3 hybridisation

The geometry of the molecule is pyramidal and the bond angle in the ammonia molecule is 107°. They are expected to have a pyramidal shape as shown below.

Ammonia Methylamine Dimethylamine Trimethylamine

In the case of 3° amines, due to the steric hindrance between three bulky alkyl groups, the bond angle increases from 107° in ammonia to 108° in trimethylamine.

13.5 Optical Activity of Amines

The amines containing different substituents on nitrogen are chiral and secondary and tertiary amines exhibit optical activity or enantiomerism. For example, methyl ethylamine $CH_3NHC_2H_5$ (a secondary amine) or methyl ethyl propylamine (a tertiary amine) are dissymmetric as shown below:

Mirror Mirror

Non-superimposable mirror image isomers Non-superimposable mirror image isomers

The two enantiomeric forms rapidly interconvert into one another by a process called nitrogen *inversion* or amines inversion. This is known as *flipping*. During nitrogen inversion, the state of hybridisation of N changes from sp^3 to sp^2 to give a planar transition state which can either revert to the starting amine or to its enantiomer (II).

sp^3 hybridised N atom — Planar transition state — sp^3 hybridised N atom (I ⇌ II, Enantiomers)

(i) Amines whose chirality is due to the presence of *asymmetric carbon atoms* can be resolved. For example, butan-2-amine can be resolved into enantiomers because the 2-butyl group is chiral.

Enantiomers of butan-2-amine

(ii) The lone pair of electrons on the nitrogen atom is involved in nitrogen inversion and therefore, it is not possible to resolve the enantiomeric forms. However, if the lone pair of electrons on nitrogen is bonded to a fourth different substituent, inversion of configuration is not possible. Therefore, quaternary ammonium salts exhibit optical activity. For example, methyl ethyl isopropyl phenyl ammonium ion salts can be resolved into enantiomers.

Enantiomers of methylethyl isopropyl phenyl ammonium ion

Similarly, N-oxides of tertiary amines having three different groups, $R_1R_2R_3N^+ - O^-$ also show optical activity because of the absence of a lone pair of electrons on N which causes nitrogen inversion.

13.6 Preparation of Amines

(i) **From alkyl halides:** When an aqueous or alcoholic solution of ammonia is heated with an alkyl halide at 373 K in a sealed tube, all the three types of amines are obtained. In this reaction, the alkyl halides undergo nucleophilic substitution reaction in which the nucleophile ammonia (or amine) displaces the halogen atom. The ammonium salt formed initially gives a primary amine on treatment with ammonia.

$$RX + NH_3 \xrightarrow{373\text{ K}} RNH_3^+X^-$$

$$RNH_3^+X^- + NH_3 \rightarrow \underset{1^\circ\text{ amine}}{RNH_2} + NH_4^+X^-$$

The primary amine also acts as a nucleophile and reacts further with the alkyl halide and this sequence of reactions can lead to the formation of secondary, tertiary and finally quaternary ammonium salts.

$$RNH_2 \xrightarrow[373\text{ K}]{RX,} \underset{2^\circ\text{ amine}}{R_2NH} \xrightarrow[373\text{ K}]{RX,} \underset{3^\circ\text{ amine}}{R_3N} \xrightarrow[373\text{ K}]{RX,} \underset{\text{Quaternary ammonium salt}}{R_4N^+X^-}$$

The process of cleavage of the C–X bond by ammonia or amines is called Hoffmann's ammonolysis.

$$CH_3I + NH_3 \xrightarrow{373\text{ K}} \underset{\text{Methylamine (Primary)}}{CH_3NH_2} + HI$$

$$CH_3 - NH_2 + CH_3I \xrightarrow{373\text{ K}} \underset{\text{Dimethylamine (Secondary)}}{CH_3 - NH - CH_3} + HI$$

$$CH_3\text{–}NH\text{–}CH_3 + CH_3I \xrightarrow{373\text{ K}} \underset{\text{Trimethylamine } (\textit{Tertiary})}{CH_3\text{–}N(CH_3)\text{–}CH_3} + HI$$

Tertiary amines also combine with methyl iodide to form quaternary ammonium salts.

$$(CH)_3N + CH_3I \rightarrow \underset{\text{Tetramethyl ammonium iodide}}{[(CH_3)_4N^+]I^-}$$

$$\underset{\text{Nucleophile Ammonia}}{H_3\ddot{N}} + \underset{\text{Alkyl halide}}{R\text{–}X} \xrightarrow{373\text{ K}} \underset{\text{Substituted ammonium salt}}{RNH_3^+X^-} \xrightleftharpoons{NH_3} \underset{1^\circ\text{ amine}}{RNH_2} + NH_4^+X^-$$

$$\underset{1^\circ\text{ Amine}}{R\ddot{N}H_2} + R\text{–}X \xrightarrow{373\text{ K}} R_2NH_2^+X^- \xrightleftharpoons{NH_3} \underset{2^\circ\text{ amine}}{R_2NH} + NH_4^+X^-$$

$$\underset{2^\circ\text{ Amine}}{R_2\ddot{N}H} + R\text{–}X \xrightarrow{373\text{ K}} R_3N^+HX^- \xrightleftharpoons{NH_3} \underset{3^\circ\text{ amine}}{R_3N} + NH_4^+X^-$$

$$\underset{3^\circ\text{ Amine}}{R_3\ddot{N}} + R\text{–}X \xrightarrow{373\text{ K}} \underset{\text{Quaternary ammonium salt}}{R_4N^+X^-}$$

The order of reactivity of the halides is, RI > RBr > RCl.

(ii) **Reduction of nitro compounds:** Aliphatic and aromatic amines can be easily prepared by the reduction of the corresponding nitro compounds. The reduction can be carried out in a number of ways.

- Nitro compounds can be catalytically reduced by passing hydrogen gas in the presence of Raney Ni, finely divided platinum or palladium as catalyst at room temperature.

$$R\text{–}NO_2 + 6\,[H] \xrightarrow[\text{Pt or Pd, room temp.}]{\text{Raney Ni}} \underset{\text{Aliphatic amine}}{R\text{–}NH_2} + 2H_2O$$

$$\text{or } Ar\text{–}NO_2 + 6\,[H] \xrightarrow[\text{Pt or Pd, room temp.}]{\text{Raney Ni}} \underset{\text{Aromatic amine}}{Ar\text{–}NH_2} + 2H_2O$$

For example,

$$\underset{\text{Nitroethane}}{CH_3CH_2NO_2} + 6[H] \xrightarrow[\text{Pt or Pd}]{\text{Raney Ni}} \underset{\text{Ethylamine}}{CH_3CH_2NH_2} + 2H_2O$$

$$\underset{\text{Nitrobenzene}}{C_6H_5NO_2} + 6\,[H] \xrightarrow{\text{Pt or Pd/C}} \underset{\text{Aniline}}{C_6H_5NH_2} + 2H_2O$$

- Nitro compounds can be reduced with active metals such as Fe, Sn, Zn and conc. hydrochloric acid. Reduction with iron scrap and hydrochloric acid is preferred because the $FeCl_3$ formed gets hydrolysed to release hydrochloric acid during the reaction. Thus, only a small amount of hydrochloric acid is needed to initiate the reaction. Nitro compounds can also be reduced to amines with lithium aluminium hydride, $LiAlH_4$.

$$\underset{\text{Nitroethane}}{CH_3CH_2NO_2} \xrightarrow{LiAlH_4\text{, dry ether}} \underset{\text{Ethylamine}}{CH_3CH_2NH_2}$$

However, the reduction of aromatic nitro compounds with $LiAlH_4$ gives azo compounds and not primary amines.

(iii) **Reduction of nitriles (cyanides) and isonitriles (isocyanides):** Nitriles can be reduced to the corresponding amines using H_2/Raney Ni or Pt, $LiAlH_4$ or Na(Hg), C_2H_5OH.

$$CH_3CN + 4[H] \xrightarrow[Na(Hg)/C_2H_5OH]{H_2/\text{Ni or } LiAlH_4} \underset{\text{Ethylamine}}{CH_3CH_2NH_2}$$

$$\underset{\text{Benzonitrile}}{C_6H_5C{\equiv}N} \xrightarrow[\text{or } H_2/\text{Raney Ni}]{LiAlH_4} \underset{\text{Benzylamine}}{C_6H_5CH_2NH_2}\;;\quad C_6H_5CH_2CN \xrightarrow[\text{or } H_2\text{, catalyst}]{LiAlH_4} \underset{\text{2-Phenylethan-1-amine}}{C_6H_5CH_2CH_2NH_2}$$

Alkyl nitriles can be readily prepared by the action of alcoholic NaCN or KCN on alkyl halides. The method can be used to prepare primary amines having one carbon more than the parent alkyl halide.

$$R\text{–}X \xrightarrow[-KX]{\text{alc.KCN}} \underset{\text{Alkyl nitrile}}{R\text{–}CN} \xrightarrow[\text{(ii) } H_2O]{\text{(i) } LiAlH_4\text{, ether}} \underset{\text{(One more carbon atom)}}{R\text{–}CH_2\text{–}NH_2}$$

The reduction of isocyanide under similar conditions gives secondary amines, that is, N-alkyl amines.

$$\underset{\text{Alkyl isocyanide}}{R{-}N{\equiv}C + 4\,[H]} \xrightarrow[\text{Raney Ni}]{LiAlH_4,\ \text{ether}} \underset{\text{N-Methyl alkylamine (2°)}}{R{-}NH{-}CH_3}$$

$$\underset{\text{Methyl isocyanide}}{CH_3NC} + 4[H] \xrightarrow[\text{Raney Ni}]{LiAlH_4,\ \text{ether}} \underset{\text{Dimethyl amine}}{CH_3-NH-CH_3}$$

$$\underset{\text{Phenyl isocyanide}}{C_6H_5N \equiv C} + 4[H] \xrightarrow[\text{or } LiAlH_4]{\text{Raney Ni}} \underset{\text{N-Methyl aniline (2°)}}{C_6H_5-NH-CH_3}$$

(iv) Reduction of amides: Amides are reduced to the corresponding amines by $LiAlH_4$ or Na/C_2H_5OH. Primary, secondary or tertiary amines can be prepared by this method by the reduction of the corresponding amides.

$$\underset{\text{Amide}}{R{-}\overset{\overset{O}{\|}}{C}{-}NH_2} \xrightarrow[\text{(ii) } H_2O]{\text{(i) } LiAlH_4,\ \text{ether}} \underset{\text{Amine}}{R{-}CH_2{-}NH_2}$$

$$\underset{\text{Acetamide}}{CH_3{-}\overset{\overset{O}{\|}}{C}{-}NH_2} + 4[H] \xrightarrow[\text{Ether}]{LiAlH_4} \underset{\text{Ethylamine}}{CH_3CH_2NH_2} + H_2O$$

$$\underset{\text{Benzamide}}{C_6H_4CONH_2} \xrightarrow[\text{Ether}]{LiAlH_4} \underset{\text{Benzylamine}}{C_6H_5CH_2NH_2}$$

Secondary and tertiary amines can be prepared by the reduction of secondary and tertiary amides respectively.

$$\underset{\text{N-Methylacetamide (2°)}}{CH_3CONHCH_3} \xrightarrow[\text{Ether}]{LiAlH_4} \underset{\text{Ethylmethylamide (2°)}}{CH_3CH_2NHCH_3}$$

$$\underset{\text{N, N-Dimethylacetamide (3°)}}{CH_3CON(CH_3)_2} \xrightarrow[\text{Ether}]{LiAlH_4} \underset{\text{Ethyldimethylamine (3°)}}{CH_3CH_2{-}N(CH_3)_2}$$

(v) Hoffmann bromamide degradation method: Primary amines can be prepared from amides by treatment with Br_2 and KOH or NaOH. The amine formed contains one carbon atom less than the parent amide.

$$\underset{\text{Amine}}{RCONH_2} + Br_2 + 4KOH \rightarrow \underset{\text{1°-Amine}}{RNH_2} + K_2CO_3 + 2KBr + 2\,H_2O$$

For example, $\underset{\text{Acetamide}}{CH_3CONH_2} + Br_2 + 4\,KOH$

$$\rightarrow \underset{\text{Methyl amine}}{CH_3NH_2} + 2HBr + K_2CO_3 + 2H_2O$$

$$\underset{\text{Benzamide}}{C_6H_5CONH_2} + Br_2 + 4KOH \rightarrow \underset{\text{Aniline}}{C_6H_5NH_2} + 2KBr + K_2CO_3 + 2H_2O$$

(vi) Gabriel's phthalimide synthesis: In this method, phthalimide is treated with alcoholic KOH to give potassium phthalimide, which is treated with alkyl halide or benzyl halide to form N-alkyl or aryl phthalimide. The hydrolysis of N-alkyl phthalimide with 20% HCl under pressure or refluxing with NaOH gives a primary amine.

$$\underset{\text{Phthalimide}}{C_6H_4(CO)_2NH} \xrightarrow[-H_2O]{\text{KOH (alc.)}} \underset{\text{Potassium phthalimide}}{C_6H_4(CO)_2\overset{-\ +}{NK}} \xrightarrow[-KBr]{C_2H_5Br}$$

$$\underset{\text{N-Ethylphthalimide}}{C_6H_4(CO)_2N{-}C_2H_5} \xrightarrow[\text{Hydrolysis}]{H^+/H_2O \text{ or } OH^-/H_2O} \underset{\text{Phthalic acid}}{C_6H_4(COOH)_2} + \underset{\text{Ethylamine}}{C_2H_5NH_2}$$

(vii) Reduction of azides: Primary amines can be prepared from alkyl halides by first converting the alkyl halide to alkyl azide. Then, the alkyl azides are reduced to alkyl amines with sodium and alcohol, or lithium aluminium hydride, or by catalytic hydrogenation with $H_2/Pd–C$.

$$RX + \underset{\text{Sodium}}{NaN_3} \rightarrow \underset{\text{Alkyl azide}}{RN_3} + NaX$$

$$RN_3 \xrightarrow[Na/C_2H_5OH]{LiAlH_4,\ \text{or}} RNH_2 + N_2$$

$$RN_3 \xrightarrow{Pd/C,\ H_2} RNH_2 + N_2$$

The reaction may also be written as:

$$\underset{\text{Sodium azide}}{Na^+\,N_3^-} + \overset{\delta+\ \delta-}{R{-}X} \longrightarrow \underset{\text{Alkyl azide}}{R{-}\ddot{N}{=}N^+{=}\ddot{N}{:}^-} \xrightarrow[\text{or } LiAlH_4]{H_2,\ Pd/C} \underset{\text{1°-Amine}}{R{-}\ddot{N}H_2} + N_2$$

For example,

$$C_6H_5CH_2CH_2X + \underset{\text{Azide ion}}{N_3^-} \xrightarrow{-X^-} \underset{\text{2-Phenyl ethyl azide}}{C_6H_5CH_2CH_2N_3}$$

$$\xrightarrow{LiAlH_4} \underset{\text{2-Phenyl ethyl amine}}{C_6H_5CH_2CH_2NH_2} + N_2$$

(viii) By reduction of oximes: Primary amines can be prepared by the reduction of oximes of aldehydes and ketones with either $LiAlH_4$ or Na/C_2H_5OH.

$$\underset{\text{Aldoxime}}{RCH{=}NOH} + 4[H] \xrightarrow[Na/C_2H_5OH]{LiAlH_4 \text{ or}} \underset{\text{1° Amine}}{RCH_2NH_2} + H_2O$$

$$\underset{\text{Acetaldoxime}}{CH_3CH{=}NOH} + 4[H] \xrightarrow[Na/C_2H_5OH]{LiAlH_4 \text{ or}} \underset{\text{Ethanamine}}{CH_3CH_2NH_2} + H_2O$$

$$\underset{\text{Ketoxime}}{R_2C{=}NOH} + 4[H] \xrightarrow[Na/C_2H_5OH]{LiAlH_4 \text{ or}} \underset{\text{1° Amine}}{R_2CHNH_2} + H_2O$$

$$\underset{\text{Acetoxime}}{(CH_3)_2C{=}NOH} + 4[H] \xrightarrow[Na/C_2H_5OH]{LiAlH_4 \text{ or}} \underset{\text{Propan-2-amine (Isopropylamine)}}{(CH_3)_2CHNH_2} + H_2O$$

(ix) Reductive amination of aldehydes and ketones: Primary amines may be prepared by reacting the aldehyde or ketone with ammonia to form intermediate imines which can be reduced with H_2, Ni.

$$R\text{-}\overset{H}{\overset{|}{C}}\text{=O} + NH_3 \xrightarrow[-H_2O]{Heat} R\text{-}\overset{H}{\overset{|}{C}}\text{=NH} \xrightarrow{H_2, Ni} R\text{-}CH_2NH_2$$

Aldehyde — Imine — 1° Amine

$$CH_3\text{-}\overset{H}{\overset{|}{C}}\text{=O} + NH_3 \xrightarrow[-H_2O]{Heat} CH_3\text{-}\overset{H}{\overset{|}{C}}\text{=NH} \xrightarrow{H_2, Ni} CH_3CH_2NH_2$$

Acetaldehyde — Acetaldimine — Ethylamine

$$R\text{-}\overset{R'}{\overset{|}{C}}\text{=O} + NH_3 \xrightarrow[-H_2O]{Heat} R\text{-}\overset{R'}{\overset{|}{C}}\text{=NH} \xrightarrow{H_2, Ni} CH_3\text{-}\overset{R'}{\overset{|}{CH}}\text{-}NH_2$$

Ketone — Dialkyl ketimine — 1° Amine

$$CH_3\text{-}\overset{CH_3}{\overset{|}{C}}\text{=O} + NH_3 \xrightarrow[-H_2O]{Heat} CH_3\text{-}\overset{CH_3}{\overset{|}{C}}\text{=NH} \xrightarrow{H_2, Ni} CH_3\text{-}\overset{CH_3}{\overset{|}{CH}}\text{-}NH_2$$

If instead of NH_3, a primary amine is used in the above reaction, a secondary amine is obtained. For example,

$$CH_3\text{-}\overset{CH_3}{\overset{|}{C}}\text{=O} + H_2NC_6H_5 \xrightarrow[-H_2O]{Heat} CH_3\text{-}\overset{CH_3}{\overset{|}{C}}\text{=NC}_6H_5$$

Acetone — Aniline — Isopropylidene aniline

$$\xrightarrow{H_2, Ni} CH_3\text{-}\overset{CH_3}{\overset{|}{CH}}\text{-}NHC_6H_5$$

N-isopropyl aniline (2° Amine)

Similarly, with secondary amines, tertiary amines are formed. For example,

$$C_6H_{10}\text{=O} + HN(CH_3)_2 \xrightarrow[-H_2O]{H^+} C_6H_{10}\text{=}\overset{+}{N}(CH_3)_2$$

Cyclohexanone — Dimethylamine — Iminum salt

$$\xrightarrow{H_2, Ni} C_6H_{11}\text{-}N(CH_3)_2$$

N, N-Dimethylcyclohexylamine (3° amine)

(x) Schmidt reaction: Carboxylic acids react with hydrazoic and (N_3H) in the presence of conc. H_2SO_4 to form primary amines with the evolution of CO_2 and N_2.

$$R\text{-}\overset{O}{\overset{||}{C}}\text{-OH} \xrightarrow[Conc.\ H_2SO_4]{N_3H} R\text{-}NH_2 + CO_2 + N_2$$

Carboxylic acid — 1°-Amine

$$e.g., C_6H_5COOH \xrightarrow[Conc.\ H_2SO_4]{N_3H} C_6H_5NH_2 + CO_2 + N_2$$

Benzoic acid — Aniline

Instead of conc. H_2SO_4 and N_3H, a mixture of NaN_3 and conc. H_2SO_4 can also be used.

13.6.1 Industrial Preparation of Amines

(i) From alcohols: On an industrial scale, aliphatic amines are prepared by passing vapours of an alcohol and ammonia over alumina at 723 K. This reaction is called *Sabatier and Mailhe method.*

$$C_2H_5OH + NH_3 \xrightarrow[Al_2O_3]{723\ K} C_2H_5NH_2 \xrightarrow[Al_2O_3]{C_2H_5OH}$$

Ethylamine

$$(C_2H_5)_2NH \xrightarrow[Al_2O_3]{C_2H_5OH} (C_2H_5)_3N$$

Diethylamine — Triethylamine

The mixture of three amines is separated by fractional distillation.

(ii) Aniline: On an industrial scale, aniline is prepared by the reduction of nitrobenzene by catalytic hydrogenation (H_2/Pt or V or CuO) or by chemical means using Fe/HCl or Sn/HCl.

$$C_6H_5NO_2 + 3H_2 \xrightarrow[680\ K]{V - Pt} C_6H_5NH_2 + 2H_2O$$

Aniline

$$C_6H_5NO_2 + 6H \xrightarrow[or\ Sn,\ HCl]{Fe,\ HCl} C_6H_5NH_2 + 2H_2O$$

Aniline

Aniline is also prepared on a large scale by treating chlorobenzene with ammonia at 473 K and 60 atm pressure using copper oxide as catalyst.

$$C_6H_5Cl \xrightarrow[473\ K,\ 60\ atm]{NH_3,\ Cu_2O} C_6H_5NH_2$$

Chlorobenzene — Aniline

13.7 Physical Properties of Amines

The important physical properties of amines are given below.

(i) Physical state and odour: The lower members of the aliphatic amines family such as methylamine, dimethyl amine and ethylamine are gases at ordinary temperatures and have ammonia-like smell. The higher members with three or more C atoms are mostly liquids with a fishy smell and still higher ones are solids.

(ii) Boiling points: Amines have higher boiling points than hydrocarbons of comparable molecular masses. Tertiary amines form associated molecules due to intermolecular hydrogen bonding between the nitrogen of one and hydrogen of another molecule as shown.

However, amines have lower boiling points than comparable alcohols or carboxylic acids. This is because the electronegativity of nitrogen (3.0) is lower than that of oxygen (3.5) and therefore the O–H bonds present in alcohols and carboxylic acids are more polar than the N–H bond in amines. As a result, the hydrogen bonds in alcohols and carboxylic acids are stronger and consequently they have higher boiling points.

In primary amines there are two hydrogen atoms available for hydrogen bond formation, while secondary amines have only one hydrogen atom for hydrogen bond formation. Tertiary amines do not have intermolecular association due to the absence of available hydrogen atoms for hydrogen bond formation. Therefore, the primary and secondary amines have higher boiling points whereas tertiary amines have the lowest boiling points. Thus, the order of boiling points of isomeric amines is: Primary > Secondary > Teritary. For example,

$CH_3CH_2CH_2NH_2$	$CH_3CH_2NHCH_3$	$(CH_3)_3N$
Propylamine (1°)	Ethylmethylamine (2°)	Trimethylamine (3°)
BP: 323 K	BP: 307 K	BP: 276 K
n-$C_4H_9NH_2$	$(C_2H_5)_2NH$	$C_2H_5N(CH_3)_2$
Butyl amine (1°)	Diethyl amine (2°)	Ethyldimethylamine
BP: 350.8 K	BP: 310.5 K	BP: 310.5 K

(iii) Solubility: The lower aliphatic amines are soluble in water because they are capable of forming hydrogen bonds with water. However, the solubility decreases with an increase in the molar mass of amines due to an increase in the size of the hydrophobic alkyl part. Therefore, the higher amines containing six or more carbon atoms are insoluble. Because of their weaker hydrogen bonds, the solubility of amines in water is less than that of alcohols. This is because the electronegativity of nitrogen is lower (3.0) than that of oxygen (3.5)

Hydrogen bond

$$\cdots\underset{H}{\overset{R}{N}}-H\cdots\underset{H}{O}-H\cdots\underset{H}{\overset{R}{N}}-H\cdots$$

Aromatic amines, on the other hand, are insoluble in water. This is due to the larger hydrocarbon part which tends to retard the formation of hydrogen bonds. For example, aniline is insoluble in water. However, it is quite soluble in organic solvents such as ether, alcohols or benzene.

13.8 Basic Character of Amines

Reaction with water (basic character of amines): Due to the presence of a lone pair on the N atom of the $-NH_2$ group, the amines are generally basic in nature (Fig. 13.1). They are more basic than water and therefore, get protonated by water to form alkyl ammonium or aryl ammonium hydroxides which ionise to furnish ^-OH ions in solution.

Lone pair

Fig. 13.1 Pyramidal shape of amine (R may be H)

$$\underset{1°\text{-Amine}}{R\ddot{N}H_2} + H_2O \rightarrow \underset{\text{Alkyl ammonium hydroxide}}{RNH_3^+OH^-} \rightleftharpoons RNH_3^+ + OH^-$$

This reaction is similar to the reaction of ammonia with water.

$$\ddot{N}H_3 + H_2O \rightarrow NH_4^+OH^- \rightleftharpoons NH_4^+ + OH^-$$

Similarly,

$$\underset{2°\text{Amine}}{R_2\ddot{N}H} + H_2O \rightarrow R_2NH_2^+OH^- \rightleftharpoons R_2NH_2^+ + OH^-$$

$$\underset{3°\text{Amine}}{R_3N} + H_2O \rightarrow R_3NH^+OH^- \rightleftharpoons R_3NH^+ + OH^-$$

Lets compare the basic strength of compounds.

13.8.1 Comparison of Aliphatic Amines and Ammonia

Aliphatic amines are stronger bases than ammonia. This is because alkyl groups are electron releasing (+I inductive effect). As a result, the electron density on the nitrogen atom increases and therefore, they can donate electron pair of electrons more easily than ammonia.

13.8.2 Comparison of Basic Strength of Primary, Secondary and Tertiary Amines

The methyl groups increase the electron density on nitrogen and therefore, the basic character increases with an increase in the number of alkyl groups. As a result, the basic character shows the order: tertiary amine > secondary amine > primary amine. This trend is followed in the gaseous phase. However, in aqueous solutions, it has been observed that tertiary amines are unexpectedly less basic than the others. For example, the correct order of methylamines and ethylamines is:

$$(CH_3)_2NH > CH_3NH_2 > (CH_3)_3N \text{ and}$$

$$(C_2H_5)_2NH > (C_2H_5)_3N > C_2H_5NH_2$$

This may be explained on the basis of the following factors.

- **Steric factor:** The size of the alkyl group is more than that of hydrogen and therefore, it hinders the attack of the acid on the amine and therefore, the basic strength decreases. Now crowding of the alkyl group increases from the primary to tertiary amines. As a result, their basic strength decreases. This is called steric hindrance. According to this effect, tertiary alkyl amines should be the least basic.
- **Solvation of ions:** When amines are dissolved in water, they undergo hydration through hydrogen bonding. The protonated amines form hydrogen bonds with water molecules and release energy called hydration energy and therefore, get stabilised. The greater the extent of hydrogen bonding in a protonated amine, more will be its stabilisation and consequently greater will be the tendency of the amine to change into a cation and greater will be the strength of the corresponding amine. As can be seen ahead, the hydration of protonated amine due to hydrogen bonding decreases as shown.

$RNH_3^+ > R_2NH_2^+ > R_3NH^+$

$RNH_2 + H_2O \longrightarrow RNH_3^+ + OH^-$ or $R{-}N^+{-}H\cdots OH_2$ (1°-Amine) — Maximum hydration

$R_2NH + H_2O \longrightarrow R_2NH_2^+ + OH^-$ or $R_2N^+H_2\cdots OH_2$ (2°-Amine)

$R_3N + H_2O \longrightarrow R_3NH^+ + OH^-$ or $R_3N^+{-}H\cdots OH_2$ (2°-Amine) — Minimum hydration

Tendency for hydration decreases

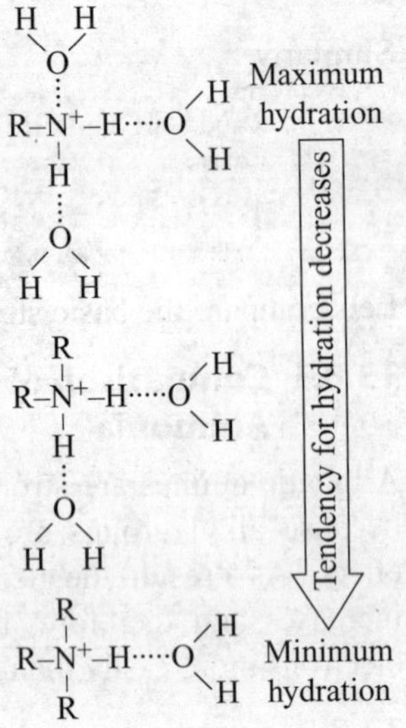

As a consequence of the combined effects of the inductive effect and solvation, the secondary amines are the strongest bases among amines. The basic strength varies as:

2°amine > 3°amine > 1°amine

Further, when the alkyl group is small, such as the $-CH_3$ group, there is no steric hindrance to hydrogen bonding. But in case the alkyl group is bigger than the $-CH_3$ group, there will be steric hindrance to hydrogen bonding. Thus, the change of nature of the alkyl group, for example from $-CH_3$ to $-C_2H_5$, results in a change in the order of basic strength. In the gas phase, where the solvent effect is missing, the basic trend is as expected, that is, 3°amine > 2°amine > 1°amine > ammonia.

13.8.3 Comparison of Basic Strength of Aniline and Ethylamine

Both aniline and ethylamine are basic in nature due to the presence of a lone pair of electrons on the N atom. But aniline is less basic than ethylamine.

In aniline or other arylamines, the $-NH_2$ group is attached directly to the benzene ring. As a result, the unshared electron pair on the nitrogen atom is present in conjugation with the benzene ring and becomes less available for protonation due to resonance. Aniline may be regarded as a resonance hybrid of the following resonating structures.

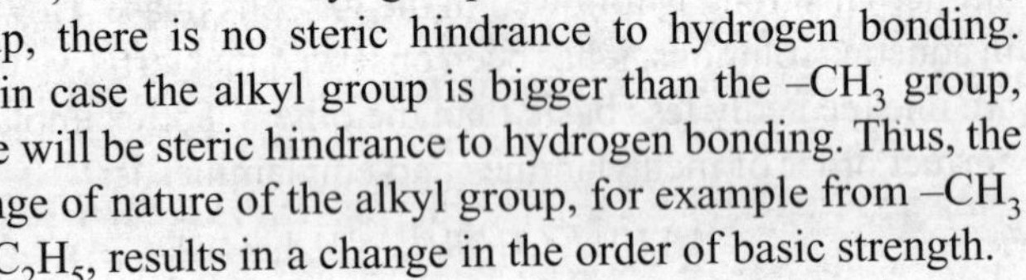

(I) ⟷ (II) ⟷ (III) ⟷ (IV) ⟷ (V)

It is clear from the above resonating structures that three of these structures (III, IV and V) acquire some positive charge on the nitrogen. As a result, the pair of electrons becomes less available for protonation. Hence, aniline is less basic than ethylamine in which there is no such resonance. The anilinium ion can have only two resonating structures:

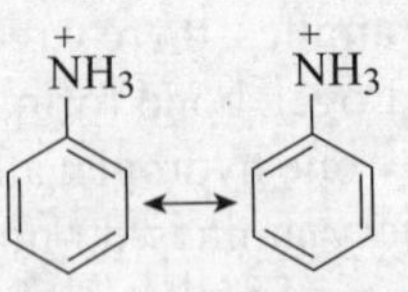

(VI) ⟷ (VII)

We know, greater the number of resonating structures, greater is the stability. Now, we have observed that aniline has five resonating structures whereas the anilinium ion has only two resonating structures. Therefore, aniline is more stable than the anilinium ion. The orbital containing the lone pair of electrons on the nitrogen atom interacts with the π-bonding of the benzene ring system. The declocalised π-cloud gets extended as shown in Fig. 13.2.

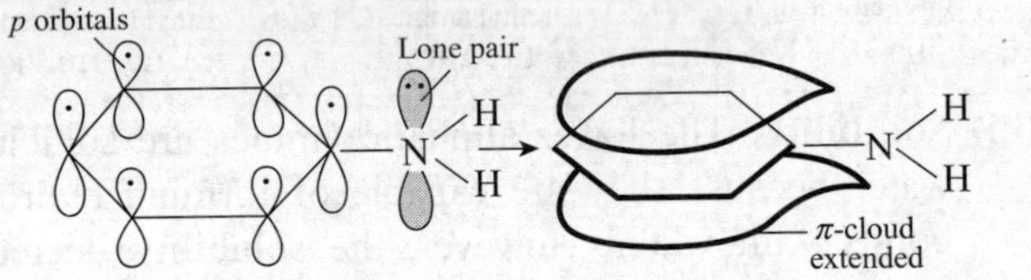

Fig. 13.2 Delocalised pi cloud on aniline

As a result, the lone pair of electrons is not readily available for protonation and therefore, aniline is less basic than ethylamine (alkyl amines).

13.8.4 Effect of Substituents on the Basic Character of Aromatic Amines

- Electron donating or releasing groups like $-OCH_3$, $-CH_3$ increase the basic strength, while electron withdrawing groups like –X (halogen), $-NO_2$, –CN, $-SO_3$, –COOH, decrease the basic strength.

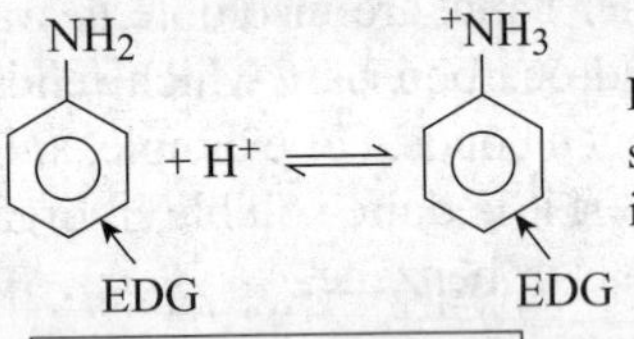

EDG-substituted aniline + H^+ ⇌ EDG-substituted anilinium ion — EDG → releases electrons, stabilises the cation and increases basic strength

EDG = $-CH_3$, $-OCH_3$, $-NH_2$

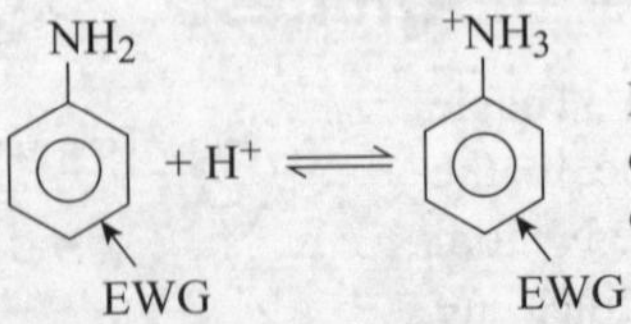

EWG-substituted aniline + H^+ ⇌ EWG-substituted anilinium ion — EWG → withdraws electrons, destabilised the cation and decreases basic strength

EWG = $-NO_2$, –CN, –X (Halogen)

For example,

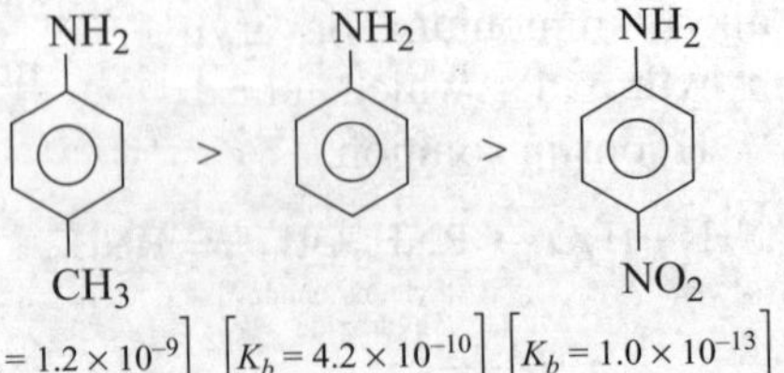

p-toluidine (CH_3) > aniline > p-nitroaniline (NO_2)

$K_b = 1.2 \times 10^{-9}$, $pK_b = 8.92$ | $K_b = 4.2 \times 10^{-10}$, $pK_b = 9.38$ | $K_b = 1.0 \times 10^{-13}$, $pK_b = 13.0$

- The base-weakening effect of the electron withdrawing group and base-strengthening effect of the electron releasing group is more marked at the *p*-position than at the *m*-position.

NH_2 NH_2 NH_2 NH_2

(*p*-toluidine, CH_3) > (aniline, CH_3 at *m*) and (*p*-nitroaniline, NO_2) > (NO_2 at *m*)

$\begin{bmatrix} K_b = 1.2 \times 10^{-9} \\ pK_b = 8.92 \end{bmatrix}$ $\begin{bmatrix} K_b = 5 \times 10^{-10} \\ pK_b = 9.30 \end{bmatrix}$ $\begin{bmatrix} K_b = 1 \times 10^{-13} \\ pK_b = 13 \end{bmatrix}$ $\begin{bmatrix} K_b = 2.9 \times 10^{-12} \\ pK_b = 11.54 \end{bmatrix}$

Electron releasing group $-CH_3$ makes *p*-isomer **more basic** than the *m*-isomer	Electron withdrawing group $-NH_2$ makes *p*-isomer **a weaker base** than the *m*-isomer

- Every *o*-substituted aniline (electron releasing or electron withdrawing) is less basic than aniline. This is due to the ortho effect which is probably due to a combination of steric and electronic factors.

NH_2 (CH_3 at *o*) > NH_2 (Aniline) and NH_2 (NO_2 at *o*) < NH_2 (Aniline)

$\begin{bmatrix} K_b = 2.6 \times 10^{-10} \\ pK_b = 9.58 \end{bmatrix}$ $\begin{bmatrix} K_b = 4.2 \times 10^{-10} \\ pK_b = 9.38 \end{bmatrix}$ $\begin{bmatrix} K_b = 6 \times 10^{-15} \\ pK_b = 14.22 \end{bmatrix}$ $\begin{bmatrix} K_b = 4.2 \times 10^{-10} \\ pK_b = 9.38 \end{bmatrix}$

Note that the base weakening effect of an electron withdrawing group is very large when present at the *o*-position than from the *m*- or *p*-position (note aniline and *o*-nitro aniline).

NH_2 (CH_3 at *p*) > NH_2 (CH_3 at *m*) > NH_2 (Aniline) < NH_2 (CH_3 at *o*)

$\begin{bmatrix} K_b = 1.2 \times 10^{-9} \\ pK_b = 8.92 \end{bmatrix}$ $\begin{bmatrix} K_b = 5 \times 10^{-10} \\ pK_b = 9.30 \end{bmatrix}$ $\begin{bmatrix} K_b = 4.2 \times 10^{-10} \\ pK_b = 9.38 \end{bmatrix}$ $\begin{bmatrix} K_b = 2.6 \times 10^{-10} \\ pK_b = 9.59 \end{bmatrix}$

13.8.5 Effect of Substituents on the Nitrogen Atom (N-substituted anilines)

When hydrogen atoms of the amino group of arylamines are replaced by electron donating alkyl groups, the basic character of the resulting arylamine increases. For example, N-methylaniline is a stronger base than aniline and N,N-dimethylaniline is even stronger than N-methylaniline. Thus,

$N(CH_3)_2$ > $NH(CH_3)$ > NH_2

N, N-Dimethylaniline ($pK_b = 8.92$) N-Methylaniline ($pK_b = 9.30$) Aniline ($pK_b = 9.38$)

On the other hand, when the hydrogen atoms of the amino groups are replaced by electron withdrawing groups (such as the phenyl group), the basic character of the resulting arylamine decreases. For example,

NH_2 > NHC_6H_5 > $N(C_6H_5)_2$

Anline ($pK_b = 9.38$) Diphenylaniline ($pK_b = 13.2$) Triphenylaniline

13.8.6 Comparison of Basic Character of Aralkyl Amines

In the case of aralkyl amines, the lone pair of electrons on the N atom is not conjugated with the benzene ring and therefore, it is not delocalised. Hence, the lone pair of electrons on the N atom in aralkyl amines is more readily available for protonation than that on the N atom of aniline. Thus, aralkyl amines are more basic than arylamines. For example, benzylamine is a stronger base than aniline.

CH_2NH_2 > NH_2

Benzylamine ($pK_b = 4.70$) Aniline ($pK_b = 9.38$)

13.9 Chemical Properties of Amines

The difference in electronegativity between the nitrogen and hydrogen atoms and the presence of the lone pair of electrons on the nitrogen atom makes the amines very reactive organic compounds. Due to the presence of a lone pair of electrons on the N atom, amines behave as nucleophiles.

13.9.1 Reaction with Acids

Amines being basic react with acids to form salts.

$RNH_2 + HX \longrightarrow RNH_3^+X^-$ (Alkylammonium halide)

$CH_3NH_2 + HCl \longrightarrow CH_3NH_2HCl$ or $CH_3NH_3^+Cl^-$
Methyl amine → Methyl ammonium chloride

$2(CH_3)_2NH + H_2SO_4 \longrightarrow [(CH_3)_2NH_2]_2 + SO_4^{2-}$
Dimethylamine → Dimethylammonium sulphate

$(CH_3)_2NH + HNO_3 \longrightarrow (CH_3)_2\overset{+}{N}H + NO_3^-$
Dimethylammonium nitrate

$(C_2H_5)_3N + HCl \longrightarrow (C_2H_5)_3N.\ HCl$
Triethylamine → Triethylamine hydrochloride

$C_6H_5-NH_2 + HCl \longrightarrow C_6H_5-NH_3^+Cl^-$
Aniline hydrochloride (Anilinium chloride)

$C_6H_5-N(CH_3)_2 + CH_3COOH \rightleftharpoons C_6H_5-\overset{+}{N}H(CH_3)_2O^-OCCH_3$
N, N-Dimethylanilium acetate

$C_6H_5-NH(CH_3) + H_2SO_4 \longrightarrow C_6H_5-NH(CH_3)_2^+HSO_4^-$
N-Methyl benzenamine → N-Methyl anilinium hydrogen sulphate

The salts of amines are ionic compounds and are soluble in water. On treatment with aqueous hydroxide, amines are regenerated.

$$RNH_3^+X^- + NaOH \rightarrow RNH_2 + H_2O + NaX$$

These amine salts are non-volatile solids and generally decompose before their melting points are reached. These are soluble in water but insoluble in non-polar solvents such as benzene, ether, chloroform, and so on. This difference in solubility behaviour of amines and their salts is often used to detect amines and separate (or purify) them from other non-basic impurities. The amines react with chloroplatinic acids (H_2PtCl_6) to form insoluble salts called chloroplatinates.

$$2RNH_2 + H_2PtCl_6 \rightarrow \underset{\text{Amine chloroplatinate}}{(R\overset{+}{N}H_3)_2PtCl_6^{2-}}$$

The salts (chloroplatinates) are used for the determination of equivalent and molecular masses of amines.

13.9.2 Reaction of Amines with Transition Metal Ions

The lone pair of electrons in NH_3 is used to form a coordinate bond between the amine and the metal ion. For example, silver chloride dissolves in methylamine to form a soluble silver amine complex.

$$AgCl + 2CH_3NH_2 \rightarrow \underset{\text{Soluble complex}}{[Ag(CH_3NH_2)_2]^+Cl^-}$$

13.9.3 Alkylation

Primary and secondary amines react with alkyl halides to form tertiary amines. The primary or secondary amine acts as a nucleophile and perform nucleophilic substitution at the alkyl halide. On removal of HX, a secondary or a tertiary amine is regenerated, respectively. The secondary amine being a more powerful nucleophile, again reacts similarly with another alkyl halide forming a tertiary amine. an equivalent amount of a strong acid so formed can protonate the amine making the lone pair on nitrogen unavailable for nucleophilic attack and therefore, stop the reaction before completion. The reaction may also be written as:

$$\underset{\text{Primary}}{RNH_2} \xrightarrow[-HI]{+RI} \underset{\text{Secondary}}{R_2NH} \xrightarrow[-HI]{+RI} \underset{\text{Tertiary}}{R_3N} \xrightarrow{+RI} \underset{\text{Tertraalkyl ammonium iodide}}{R_4NI}$$

For example,

$$\underset{\text{Methylamine}}{CH_3NH_2} \xrightarrow[-HCl]{CH_3Cl} \underset{\text{Diethylamine}}{(CH_3)_2NH} \xrightarrow{CH_3Cl} \underset{\text{Triethylamine}}{(CH_3)_3N} \xrightarrow{CH_3Cl} \underset{\text{Tetramethyl ammonium chloride}}{(CH_3)_4N^+Cl^-}$$

$$\underset{\text{Ethylamine}}{CH_3CH_2NH_2} \xrightarrow[-HBr]{CH_3CH_2Br} \underset{\text{Diethylamine}}{(CH_3CH_2)_2NH} \xrightarrow[-HBr]{CH_3CH_2Br} \underset{\text{Triethylamine}}{(CH_3CH_2)_3N} \xrightarrow[-HBr]{CH_3CH_2Br} \underset{\text{Tetraethyl ammonium bromide}}{(CH_3CH_2)_4N^+Br^-}$$

Aromatic amines also undergo similar reactions. For example, when aniline is treated with methyl iodide under pressure, quaternary ammonium salts are formed.

$$\underset{\text{Aniline}}{C_6H_5NH_2} \xrightarrow[-HI]{CH_3I} \underset{\text{N-Methylaniline}}{C_6H_5NH(CH_3)} \xrightarrow[-HI]{CH_3I} \underset{\text{N, N-Dimethyl aniline}}{C_6H_5N(CH_3)_2} \xrightarrow{CH_3I} \underset{\text{Trimethyl anilinium iodide}}{C_6H_5N^+(CH_3)_3I^-}$$

The tetramethyl ammonium salt or quaternary ammonium halide on reaction with moist silver oxide forms tetramethyl ammonium hydroxide and the silver halide gets precipitated.

$$(CH_3)_4NI \xrightarrow{\text{Moist}} (CH_3)_4N^+OH^-$$

$$(CH_3)_4N^+OH^- \xrightarrow{\text{Heat}} \underset{\text{Trimethylamine}}{(CH_3)_3N} + CH_3OH$$

If one of the alkyl groups is a group other than methyl, the quaternary ammonium hydroxide gives a tertiary amine, an alkene and water on heating. For example,

$$\left[H_3C{-}\underset{CH_3}{\overset{CH_3}{N}}{-}C_2H_5\right]^+ OH^- \xrightarrow[400\text{ K}]{\text{Heat}} \underset{\textit{tert}\text{-amine}}{H_3C{-}\underset{CH_3}{\overset{CH_3}{N}}} + \underset{\text{Ethene}}{H_2C{=}CH_2} + H_2O$$

This pyrolysis of quaternary ammonium hydroxide to give alkenes is called Hoffmann's elimination reaction.

13.9.4 Acylation

Aliphatic and aromatic primary and secondary amines (which contain replaceable hydrogen atoms) react with an acid chloride, acid anhydride or an esters to form substituted amides. For example,

$$RNH_2 + \underset{\text{Acid chloride}}{RCOCl} \xrightarrow{\text{Base}} \underset{\text{Substituted amide}}{RNHCOR} + HCl$$

$$RNH_2 + \underset{\text{Acid anhydride}}{R{-}\overset{O}{\overset{\|}{C}}{-}O{-}\overset{O}{\overset{\|}{C}}{-}R} \xrightarrow{\text{Base}} RNHCOR + RCOOH$$

$$RNHR + RCOCl \xrightarrow{\text{Base}} R_2NCOR + HCl$$

The process of introducing an acyl group ($R{-}\underset{O}{\underset{\|}{C}}{-}$) into a molecule is called acylation.

$$\underset{\text{Methanamine (1°)}}{CH_3{-}\underset{H}{N}{-}H} + \underset{\text{Acetyl chloride}}{Cl{-}\overset{O}{\overset{\|}{C}}{-}CH_3} \xrightarrow{\text{Base}} \underset{\text{N-Methyl ethanamide}}{CH_3{-}\underset{H}{N}{-}\overset{O}{\overset{\|}{C}}{-}CH_3} + HCl$$

$$\underset{\text{Ethanamine}}{C_2H_5{-}\underset{H}{N}{-}H} + Cl{-}\overset{O}{\overset{\|}{C}}{-}CH_3 \xrightarrow{\text{Base}} \underset{\text{N-Ethylethanamide}}{C_2H_5{-}\underset{H}{N}{-}\underset{H}{C}{-}CH_3} + HCl$$

$$\underset{\text{N-Methyl methanamine (2°)}}{CH_3{-}\underset{CH_3}{N}{-}H} + \underset{\text{Acetyl chloride}}{Cl{-}\overset{O}{\overset{\|}{C}}{-}CH_3} \xrightarrow{\text{Base}} \underset{\text{N, N-Dimethylethanamide}}{CH_3{-}\underset{CH_3}{N}{-}\overset{O}{\overset{\|}{C}}{-}CH_3} + HCl$$

The reaction occurs as:

$$C_2H_5-\ddot{N}H_2 + CH_3-C(=O)-Cl \xrightarrow{Base} C_2H_5-N^+H_2-C(CH_3)(O^-)-Cl$$

Ethanamine Ethanoyl chloride

$$\xrightarrow{-HCl} C_2H_5-NH-C(=O)-CH_3$$

N-Ethylethanamide (or N-Ethylacetamide)

Acylation can also take place with acid anhydrides.

$$C_2H_5-NH_2 + (CH_3CO)_2O \longrightarrow CH_3-C(=O)-NH-C_2H_5 + CH_3COOH$$

Ethanamine Acetic anhydride; N-Ethyl ethanamide

Aniline or benzenamine reacts in a similar manner.

$$C_6H_5-NH_2 + Cl-C(=O)-CH_3 \xrightarrow{Pyridine} C_6H_5-NH-C(=O)-CH_3 + HCl$$

Aniline Acetyl chloride; N-Phenylethanamide (Acetanilide)

Similarly,

$$C_6H_5-\ddot{N}H_2 + CH_3-C(=O)-O-C(=O)-CH_3 \longrightarrow C_6H_5-\ddot{N}H-C(=O)-CH_3 + CH_3COOH$$

Benzenamine Ethanoic anhydride; N-Phenyl ethanamide (or Acetanilide)

13.9.5 Benzoylation

Aliphatic and aromatic amines react with benzoyl chloride in the presence of a base such as pyridine or aqueous NaOH to form benzoyl derivatives in which the C_6H_5CO- group is introduced. This reaction is called *benzoylation*.

$$C_2H_5NH_2 + C_6H_5-C(=O)-Cl \xrightarrow{aq.\ NaOH} C_2H_5-NH-C(=O)-C_6H_5 + HCl$$

Ethylamine Benzoyl chloride; N-Ethyl benzamide

$$C_6H_5-NH_2 + C_6H_5-C(=O)-Cl \xrightarrow{aq.\ NaOH} C_6H_5-NH-C(=O)-C_6H_5 + HCl$$

Aniline Benzoyl chloride; N-Phenyl benzamide (Benzanilide)

Benzoylation of compounds containing an active hydrogen such as alcohols, phenols or amines with benzoyl chloride in the presence of dilute aqueous NaOH solution is called the *Schotten–Baumann reaction.*

13.9.6 Schiffs Base Formation

Both aliphatic and aromatic primary amines react with aldehydes and ketones to form imines, also called *Schiff's bases* or *anils*.

$$R-CH=O + H_2NR \longrightarrow R-CH=NR + H_2O$$

Schiff's base or anils

$$CH_3CHO + H_2NCH_2CH_3 \longrightarrow CH_3CH=NCH_2CH_3 + H_2O$$

Acetaldehyde Ethylamine; Ethylidine ethylamine (Schiff's base)

$$CH_3CH_2NH_2 + O=C(CH_3)_2 \xrightarrow{H^+} CH_3CH_2N=C(CH_3)_2 + H_2O$$

Ethyl amine Acetone; Isopropylidene ethylamine

Benzaldehyde reacts with aniline to give a typical Schiff's base known as benzal aniline.

$$C_6H_5-NH_2 + O=CH-C_6H_5 \longrightarrow C_6H_5-N=CH-C_6H_5 + H_2O$$

Aniline Benzaldehyde; Benzal aniline or Benzylidene aniline (Schiff's base)

A Schiff's base on reduction gives a secondary amine.

$$CH_3CH_2N=CHCH_3 \xrightarrow[or\ NaBH_4]{H_2.\ Raney\ Ni} CH_3CH_2NHCH_2CH_3$$

Ethylidene ethylamine; Diethylamine

$$C_6H_5N=CH-C_6H_5 + H_2 \xrightarrow{Raney\ Ni} C_6H_5NH-CH_2C_6H_5$$

N-Benzylaniline (Secondary amine)

Aldehydes and ketones which have an alpha hydrogen, react with secondary amines both acyclic (N,N-dimethylamine) as well as cyclic (pyrrolidene, piperidine) to form carbinolamines.

$$R-CH_2-C(=O)-R' + R_2NH \underset{PTS}{\overset{C_5H_6}{\rightleftharpoons}} \left[R-CH_2-C(OH)(NR_2)-R'\right] \overset{-H_2O}{\rightleftharpoons} R-CH=C(R')(NR_2)$$

(R′ = alkyl or H); Carbinolamine (Unstable); Enamine

Enamines can also be reduced by catalytic hydrogenation (Ni/H_2) or sodium borohydride ($NaBH_4$) to form the corresponding amines.

$$CH_2=C(CH_3)-N(CH_3)_2 \xrightarrow[or\ NaBH_4]{H_2,\ Raney\ Ni} CH_3-CH(CH_3)-N(CH_3)_2$$

N, N-Dimethylprop-1-en-2-amine; N, N-Dimethyl-2-propanamine

13.9.7 Reaction with Chloroform (Carbylamine Reaction, Isocyanide Test)

$$R-NH_2 + CHCl_3 + 3KOH\ (alc.) \xrightarrow{Warm} R-NC + 3KCl + 3H_2O$$

1°amine; Alkyl isocyanide

$$C_6H_5NH_2 + CHCl_3 + 3KOH\ (alc.) \xrightarrow{Warm} C_6H_5NC + 3KCl + 3H_2O$$

Aniline Chloroform; Phenyl isocyanide

Secondary and tertiary amines do not give this test.

13.9.8 Reaction with Nitrous Acid

$$RNH_2 + HNO_2 \xrightarrow[HCl]{NaNO_2} [R-N_2^+Cl^-] \xrightarrow{H_2O} ROH + N_2$$

Primary amino; Alcohol

For example, $C_2H_5NH_2 + HONO \longrightarrow C_2H_5OH + N_2 + H_2O$

Primary aromatic amines: The process of formation of diazonium salts by the reaction of an aromatic amino compound and nitrous acid is called diazotisation. For example,

$$\underset{\text{Aniline}}{C_6H_5NH_2} + 2HCl + NaNO_2 \xrightarrow{273\text{–}278\text{ K}} \underset{\text{Benzene diazonium chloride}}{C_6H_5N_2^+Cl^-} + NaCl + H_2O$$

However, if the temperature is more than 278 K, aromatic amines form phenols with the evolution of N_2 gas.

$$\underset{\text{Aniline}}{C_6H_5NH_2} + HONO \xrightarrow[> 278\text{ K}]{H^+} \underset{\text{Phenol}}{C_6H_5OH} + N_2 + H_2O$$

Secondary amines: Secondary aliphatic and aromatic amines react with nitrous acid slowly in the cold to form yellow oily nitroso amines.

$$\underset{\text{Secondary amine}}{R_2N\text{H} + \text{HO}NO} \xrightarrow{NaNO_2,\ HCl} \underset{\text{Nitrosoamine}}{R_2N\text{–}N{=}O} + H_2O$$

$$\underset{\text{Secondary amine}}{(C_2H_5)_2NH} + HONO \longrightarrow \underset{\text{N, N-Diethylnitrosoamine (yellow oil)}}{(C_2H_5)_2N\text{–}N{=}O} + H_2O$$

$$\underset{\text{N-Methylaniline}}{C_6H_5NHCH_3} + HONO \longrightarrow \underset{\text{N-Nitroso-N-methylaniline (yellow oil)}}{C_6H_5N(CH_3)\text{–}N{=}O} + H_2O$$

The yellow oily nitrosoamine gives a green solution when warmed with phenol and conc. sulfuric acid. On dilution with water, the colour changes to red, but it changes to greenish blue to violet on the addition of sodium hydroxide. The overall reaction is called *Libermann's nitroso reaction*. This test is used for secondary amines.

Tertiary amines: Tertiary amines dissolve in cold nitrous acid to form salts which decompose on warming to nitrosoamine and alcohol.

$$R_3N + HNO_2 \rightarrow \underset{\text{Nitrite salt}}{R_3NHNO_2} \xrightarrow{\text{Warm}} \underset{\text{Nitrosoamine}}{R_2N\text{–}N{=}O} + \underset{\text{Alcohol}}{ROH}$$

$$\underset{\text{Triethyl amine}}{(CH_3CH_2)_3N} + HNO_2 \rightarrow \underset{\text{Triethylammonium nitrite (Soluble)}}{[(CH_3CH_2)_3NH]^+NO_2^-}$$

Aromatic tertiary amines react with nitrous acid to give coloured substituted nitroso compounds.

$$C_6H_5N(CH_3)_2 + HONO \longrightarrow \underset{p\text{-Nitroso-N, N-dimethylaniline}}{p\text{-}ON\text{–}C_6H_4N(CH_3)_2} + H_2O$$

13.9.9 Reaction with Aryl Sulfonyl Chloride

Benzenesulfonyl chloride ($C_6H_5SO_2Cl$) which is also known as *Hinsberg's reagent* reacts with primary and secondary amines to form sulfonamides.

- Primary amines react with benzene sulfonyl chloride to give N-alkyl benzene sulphonamide.

$$\underset{\text{Benzenesulfonychloride}}{C_6H_5SO_2Cl} + \underset{\text{1° Amine}}{H\text{–}NH\text{–}R} \xrightarrow{-HCl} \underset{\text{N-Alkylbenzenesulfonamide (Soluble in alkali)}}{C_6H_5SO_2\text{–}NH\text{–}R}$$

$$C_6H_5SO_2\text{–}NH\text{–}R \xrightarrow[-H_2O]{KOH} \underset{\text{(Water soluble salt)}}{C_6H_5SO_2\text{–}NR^-K^+} \xrightarrow[-KCl]{+HCl} \underset{\text{(Insoluble)}}{C_6H_5SO_2\text{–}NHR}$$

$$C_6H_5SO_2Cl + H\text{–}NH\text{–}C_2H_5 \longrightarrow \underset{\text{N-Ethylbenzenesulfonamide (Soluble in alkali)}}{C_6H_5SO_2\text{–}NH\text{–}C_2H_5}$$

- Secondary amines react with benzene sulfonyl chloride to form N,N-dialkyl benzene sulfonamide. For example,

$$C_6H_5SO_2Cl + \underset{\text{2° Amine}}{H\text{–}NR\text{–}R} \xrightarrow{-HCl} \underset{\text{N, N-Dialkylbenzenesulfonamide (Insoluble in KOH)}}{C_6H_5SO_2\text{–}NR\text{–}R}$$

Since the sulfonamide does not contain any hydrogen atom attached to the nitrogen atom, it is not acidic. Hence it is not soluble in alkali (KOH).

For example

$$C_6H_5SO_2Cl + H\text{–}N(C_2H_5)\text{–}C_2H_5 \xrightarrow{-HCl} \underset{\text{N, N-Diethylbenzenesulfonamide (Insoluble in KOH)}}{C_6H_5SO_2\text{–}N(C_2H_5)\text{–}C_2H_5}$$

- Tertiary amines do not react with benzene sulfonyl chloride.

$$C_6H_5SO_2Cl + \underset{\text{3° Amine}}{R\text{–}NR\text{–}R} \xrightarrow{-HCl} \text{No reaction}$$

Since different amines react differently with benzene sulfonyl chloride, this reaction can be used for the distinction between 1°, 2° and 3° amines and also for the separation of their mixtures.

13.9.10 Reaction with Grignard Reagent

Primary and secondary amines react with Grignard reagents to form alkanes.

$$\underset{\text{1° Amine}}{RNH\text{–}H} + \underset{\text{Grignard reagent}}{R'MgX} \longrightarrow \underset{\text{Alkane}}{R'\text{–}H} + Mg(NHR)X$$

$$R_2N{:}H + R'{:}MgX \longrightarrow \underset{\text{Alkane}}{R'{-}H} + Mg\begin{matrix}NR_2\\X\end{matrix}$$
2° Amine

For example,

$$\underset{\text{Ethyl amine}}{CH_3CH_2NH{:}H} + \underset{\text{Methyl magnesium bromide}}{CH_3{:}MgBr} \longrightarrow \underset{\text{Methane}}{CH_4} + Mg\begin{matrix}NHCH_2CH_3\\Br\end{matrix}$$

$$\underset{\text{Diethyl amine}}{CH_3CH_2{-}\underset{CH_2CH_3}{N}{-}{:}H} + \underset{\text{Ethyl magnesium bromide}}{CH_3CH_2{:}MgBr} \longrightarrow \underset{\text{Ethane}}{CH_3CH_3} + Mg\begin{matrix}N(C_2H_5)_2\\Br\end{matrix}$$

Tertiary aliphatic amines to not react with Grignard reagents because they do not have a hydrogen atom attached to the nitrogen atom.

13.9.11 Reaction with Carbon Disulphide

$$\underset{\text{1°-Amine}}{R\ddot{N}H_2} + \underset{\text{Carbon disulphide}}{S{=}C{=}S} \xrightarrow{\text{Warm}} \underset{\text{Dithioalkylcarbamic acid}}{RNH{-}\overset{S}{\overset{\|}{C}}{-}SH}$$

$$\xrightarrow[\text{Heat}]{HgCl_2} \underset{\text{Alkyl isothiocyanate}}{R{-}N{=}C{=}S} + HgS + 2HCl$$

This reaction is called the *Hoffmann mustard oil reaction* and is used as a test for primary amines.

When aniline is heated with ethanolic CS_2 and solid KOH, it forms N,N′-diphenyl thiourea which on treatment with conc. HCl gives phenyl isothiocyanate.

$$\underset{\text{Aniline}}{\begin{matrix}C_6H_5NH{-}{:}H\\C_6H_5NH{-}{:}H\end{matrix}} + \underset{\text{Carbon disulphide}}{S{:}{=}C{=}S} + 2KOH$$

$$\xrightarrow{\text{Heat}} \underset{\text{N, N′-Diphenylthiourea}}{C_6H_5NH{-}\overset{S}{\overset{\|}{C}}{-}NH{-}C_6H_5} + H_2S + 2H_2O$$

$$\underset{\text{N, N′-Diphenylthiourea}}{C_6H_5NH{-}\overset{S}{\overset{\|}{C}}{-}NHC_6H_5} \xrightarrow{\text{Conc. HCl}} \underset{\text{Phenyl isothiocyanate}}{C_6H_5N{=}C{=}S} + \underset{\text{Aniline hydrochloride}}{C_6H_5NH_3^+Cl^-}$$

13.9.12 Reaction with Carbonyl Chloride (Phosgene)

Primary and secondary aliphatic amines react with carbonyl chloride to form substituted ureas.

$$\underset{\text{1° Amine}}{2R{-}NH_2} + \underset{\text{Carbonyl chlride}}{Cl{-}\overset{O}{\overset{\|}{C}}{-}Cl} \longrightarrow \underset{\text{Sym-Disubstituted urea}}{R{-}NH{-}\overset{O}{\overset{\|}{C}}{-}NH{-}R} + 2HCl$$

$$\underset{\text{2° Amine}}{2R_2NH} + \underset{\text{Carbonyl chlride}}{Cl{-}\overset{O}{\overset{\|}{C}}{-}Cl} \longrightarrow \underset{\text{Sym-Tetrasubstituted urea}}{R_2N{-}\overset{O}{\overset{\|}{C}}{-}NH_2} + 2HCl$$

Tertiary aliphatic amines form salts.

Aromatic 1° amines react with $COCl_2$ to form aryl isocyanate. For example,

$$\underset{\text{Aniline}}{C_6H_5NH_2} + COCl_2 \xrightarrow{-HCl} C_6H_5NHCOCl \xrightarrow[-HCl]{\text{Heat}} \underset{\text{Phenyl isocyanate}}{C_6H_5N{=}C{=}O}$$

13.9.13 Oxidation

Amines undergo oxidation by powerful oxidising agents such as Caro's acid (H_2SO_5), potassium permanganate ($KMnO_4$) and hydrogen peroxide (H_2O_2). The products of oxidation depend upon the nature of the amine and the oxidising agent used. For example,

(i) Oxidation with potassium permanganate

- Primary aliphatic amines on oxidation with potassium permanganate give nitro compounds through a sequence of reactions.

$$\underset{\text{1° Amine}}{RNH_2} \xrightarrow{[O]} \underset{\text{Hydroxylamine}}{RNHOH} \xrightarrow[-H_2O]{[O]} \underset{\text{Nitroso compound}}{R{-}N{=}O} \xrightarrow{[O]} \underset{\text{Nitro compound}}{R{-}NO_2}$$

Primary amines in which the $-NH_2$ group is attached to the tertiary carbon atom can be oxidised with $KMnO_4$ to the corresponding nitro compound in excellent yield (about 83%).

$$\underset{\text{2-Methyl-2-propanamine}}{CH_3{-}\overset{CH_3}{\underset{CH_3}{C}}{-}NH_2} \xrightarrow[KMnO_4]{[O]} \underset{\text{2-Methyl-2-nitropropane (excellent yield 83\%)}}{CH_3{-}\overset{CH_3}{\underset{CH_3}{C}}{-}NO_2}$$

- Secondary aliphatic amines on oxidation with potassium permanganate give tetra alkyl hydrazines.

$$\underset{\text{2° Amine}}{2R_2NH} \xrightarrow{[O]} \underset{\text{Tetraalkyl hydrazine}}{R_2N{-}NR_2}$$

- Tertiary amines are not oxidised by $KMnO_4$.

(ii) Oxidation with Caro's acid or H_2O_2

- Primary amines react with Caro's acid (H_2SO_5) or H_2O_2 in the following ways.

$$\underset{\text{1° Amine having primary alkyl group}}{RCH_2NH_2} \xrightarrow{[O]} \underset{\text{Hydroxamic acid}}{R\underset{OH}{C}{=}NOH} + \underset{\text{Aldoxime}}{RCH{=}NOH} + \underset{\text{N-Alkyl hydroxylamine}}{RCH_2NHOH}$$

$$\underset{\text{1° Amine with } sec \text{ alkyl group}}{R_2CH\ NH_2} \xrightarrow{[O]} \underset{\text{Ketoxime}}{R_2C = NOH}$$

$$\underset{\text{1° Amine with } tert \text{ alkyl group}}{R_3C - NH_2} \xrightarrow{[O]} \underset{\text{Nitroso alkane}}{R_3C = NO}$$

- Secondary amines react with Caro's acid to give the corresponding N-hydroxy amine.

$$\underset{\text{2°Amine}}{R_2NH} \xrightarrow{H_2SO_5} \underset{\text{N-Hydroxydialkylamine}}{R_2N{-}OH}$$

- Tertiary amines are not oxidised by $KMnO_4$ but are oxidised by Caro's acid, ozone or H_2O_2 to the corresponding N-oxides.

$$R_3N \xrightarrow[\text{or } H_2SO_4]{O_3 \text{ or } H_2O_2} \underset{\text{Amine N-oxide}}{R_3N{\rightarrow}O}$$

$C_6H_5NH_2 + K_2Cr_2O_7 + H_2SO_4 \rightarrow$ A black product called aniline black

However, controlled oxidation of aniline with $K_2Cr_2O_7$ and H_2SO_4, gives *p*-benzoquinone.

Aniline $\xrightarrow{K_2Cr_2O_7/H_2SO_4}$ *p*-Benzoquinone (Quinone)

13.9.14 Ring Substitution in Aromatic Amines

The presence of the amino group activates the aromatic ring and directs the incoming group preferentially to the *ortho* and *para* positions.

(I) ⟷ (II) ⟷ (III) ⟷ (IV) ⟷ (V)

Due to the strong activating effect of the $-NH_2$ group, aromatic amines undergo electrophilic substitution reactions readily. Therefore, it is difficult to stop the reaction at the monosubstitution stage. This can be done by acetylation with acetic anhydride in the presence of pyridine.

$$H-\ddot{N}-\overset{O}{\overset{\|}{C}}-CH_3 \longleftrightarrow H-\overset{+}{N}=\overset{O^-}{\overset{|}{C}}-CH_3$$

(i) Halogenation: Aniline reacts with bromine water readily to give a white precipitate of 2,4,6-tribromoaniline.

$$\text{Aniline} + 3Br_2/H_2O \longrightarrow \text{2, 4, 6-Tribromoaniline (White ppt)} + 3HBr$$

However, if the monosubstituted derivative is desired, aniline is first acetylated with acetyl chloride and then halogenation is carried out.

$$\text{Aniline} \xrightarrow[-CH_3COOH]{(CH_3CO)_2O,\ py} \text{Acetanilide} \xrightarrow{Br_2} \text{o-Bromoacetanilide (minor)} + \text{p-Bromoacetanilide (major)}$$

$$\xrightarrow[-CH_3COOH]{OH^- \text{ or } H^+} \text{o-Bromoaniline (minor)} + \text{p-Bromoaniline (major)}$$

$$\text{Aniline} \xrightarrow[288\ K]{NHO_3,\ \text{Conc. } H_2SO_4} \text{p-nitroaniline (51\%)} + \text{m-nitroaniline (47\%)} + \text{o-nitroaniline (2\%)}$$

(ii) Nitration: Under strongly acidic conditions, aniline gets protonated to the anilinium ion. This is a deactivating group and is meta directing. Therefore, to solve this problem, nitration is carried out by protecting the $-NH_2$ group by acetylation.

$$\text{Aniline} + Cl-\overset{O}{\overset{\|}{C}}-CH_3 \text{ (Acetyl chloride)} \longrightarrow \text{Acetanilide}$$

$$\text{Aceanilide} \xrightarrow[288\ K]{HNO_3,\ H_2SO_4} \text{o-Nitroacetanilide} + \text{p-Nitroacetanilide}$$

$$\xrightarrow[-CH_3COOH]{OH^- \text{ or } H^+} \text{o-Nitroaniline (minor)} + \text{p-Nitroaniline (major)}$$

(iii) Sulfonation: Sulfonation of aniline is carried out by heating aniline with sulfuric acid. The product formed is anilinium hydrogen sulfate which on heating gives sulfanilic acid.

$$\text{Aceanilide} + H_2SO_4 \longrightarrow \text{Anilinium hydrogen sulphate } (NH_3^+HSO_4^-) \xrightarrow[453-473\ K]{\text{Heat}} \text{Sulfanilic acid (I) } (SO_3H) \rightleftharpoons \text{Zwitter ion structure (II) } (NH_3^+,\ SO_3^-)$$

The sulfanilic acid exists as a dipolar ion (structure II) which has acidic and basic groups in the same molecule. Such ions are called Zwitter ions or inner salts.

13.9.15 Coupling with Diazonium Salts

Aniline couples with benzene diazonium chloride to form diazo amino benzene which ultimately changes to *p*-amino azobenzene on warming with a small quantity of hydrochloric acid.

$$C_6H_5-N\equiv NCl + H-NH-C_6H_5 \xrightarrow[\text{ice-cold}]{\text{Acid}} C_6H_5-N=N-NH-C_6H_5 \xrightarrow{\text{Rearrangement}} C_6H_5-N=N-C_6H_4-NH_2$$

Benzene diazonium chloride; Aniline; Diazoaminobenzene; *p*-Aminoazobenzene (Yellow dye)

13.10 Tests for Amines

Table 13.1 Tests to distinguish between primary, secondary and tertiary amines

Characteristic Reaction	Primary	Secondary	Tertiory
1. Action with nitrous acid ($NaNO_2 + HCl$)	N_2 is given out with the formation of alcohols : $RNH_2 + HONO \rightarrow N_2\uparrow + \text{alcohols}$	Nitrosoamines are formed which give *Libermann's Nitroso test*: $R_2NH + HONO \rightarrow R_2N{-}N{=}O + H_2O$ Nitrosoamine	They remain dissolved forming amine nitrate salt which de-composes on warming to nitrosoamines and alcohol
2. Carbylamine reaction *i.e.*, with $CHCl_3$ and alcoholic KOH	Give foul smelling carbylamine. $RNH_2 + CHCl_3 + 3KOH \rightarrow \underset{\text{Carbylamine}}{RNC} + 3KCl + 3H_2O$	No reaction	No reaction
3. Acylation *i.e.*, reaction with acetyl chloride	Form amides RCONH.R	Form amides $RCONR_2$	No reaction
4. Hinsberg's test	Give clear solution which on acidification gives insoluble material $RNH_2 + C_6H_5SO_2Cl \rightarrow RNHSO_2C_6H_5 \underset{HCl}{\overset{KOH}{\rightleftharpoons}} \underset{\text{(Insoluble)}}{RNKSO_2C_6H_5}$	Give insoluble substance which is not affected by acid $R_2NH + C_6H_3SO_2Cl \rightarrow \underset{\text{(Insoluble in alkali)}}{R_2NSO_2C_6H_5}$	Does not react
5. Azo dye test.	Primary aromatic amines give coloured dyes	No reaction	No reaction

13.10.1 Distinction Between Pairs of Compounds

(i) Ethylamine and Aniline

Azo dye test: Dissolve the compound in conc. HCl and add an ice-cold solution of HNO_2 ($NaNO_2$ + dil. HCl) at 273 K. Then treat it with an alkaline cold solution of 2-naphthol. Appearance of a brilliant orange or red dye indicates an aromatic amine (that is, aniline).

$$C_6H_5NH_2 + NaNO_2 + HCl \longrightarrow \underset{\text{Benzene diazonium chloride}}{C_6H_5N_2^+Cl^-}$$

$$C_6H_5N^+\equiv NCl^- + \underset{\text{2-Naphthol}}{C_{10}H_7OH} \xrightarrow[\text{pH 9–10}]{\text{dil. NaOH}} \underset{\text{1-Phenyl azo-2-naphthol (Orange red dye)}}{C_6H_5-N=N-C_{10}H_6OH}$$

Aliphatic amines (that is, ethylamine) does not a form dye. It givesa brisk effervescence due to the evolution of N_2 but the solution remains clear.

(ii) Ethylamine ($CH_3CH_2NH_2$) and Diethylamine

Carbylamine test: When heated with an alcoholic solution of KOH and $CHCl_3$, ethylamine gives a foul smelling ethyl isocyanide.

$$CH_3CH_2NH_2 + CHCl_3 + \underset{\text{(alc.)}}{3KOH} \rightarrow \underset{\text{Foul smell}}{CH_3CH_2NC} + 3KCl + 3H_2O$$

Diethylamine does not give this test.

$$(CH_3CH_2)_2NH \xrightarrow[\text{Heat}]{CHCl_3/KOH} \text{No reaction}$$

Hinsberg's test: When treated with Hinsberg's reagent [benzene sulfonyl chloride ($C_6H_5SO_2Cl$)], ethylamine gives N-ethyl benzene sulfonamide which is soluble in aqueous KOH solution.

$$C_6H_5SO_2Cl + CH_3CH_2NH_2 \xrightarrow{-HCl} C_6H_5SO_2NHCH_2CH_3 \xrightarrow{KOH} C_6H_5SO_2NKCH_2CH_3 + H_2O$$

Soluble in aq. KOH

Diethylamine gives N,N-diethylbenzenesulfonamide which is insoluble in aqueous KOH.

$$C_6H_5SO_2Cl + (CH_3CH_2)_2NH \xrightarrow{-HCl} C_6H_5SO_2N(CH_2CH_3)_2 + HCl$$

N,N-Diethyl benzene sulfonamide
Insoluble in aq. KOH

(iii) Aniline and N-Ethylaniline

Aniline is a primary amine. Therefore, it gives the carbylamine test. When heated with an alcoholic solution of KOH and $CHCl_3$, it gives an offensive smell of phenylisocyanide.

$$\underset{\text{Aniline}}{C_6H_5NH_2} + CHCl_3 + \underset{\text{alc.}}{3\,KOH} \rightarrow \underset{\substack{\text{Phenylisocyanide} \\ \text{(Foul smell)}}}{C_6H_5NC} + 3KCl + 3H_2O$$

But N-ethylaniline is a secondary amine and hence does not give the carbylamine test.

(iv) N-Methylpropane-2-amine and N-Ethyl-N-methylethamine

N-methypropane-2-amine is a secondary amine. On adding Hinsberg's reagent the compound formed is insoluble in aqueous NaOH.

$$\underset{\text{N-Methyl propan-2-amine}}{CH_3\underset{|}{C}HCH_3 \atop NHCH_3} + C_6H_5SO_2Cl \xrightarrow{-HCl} \underset{\text{insoluble in aq. NaOH}}{C_6H_5SO_2\text{–}\underset{|}{N}\text{–}CH(CH_3)_2 \atop CH_3}$$

But N-ethyl-N-methylethanamine does not react with Hinsberg's reagent.

(v) Aniline and Benzylamine

Azo dye test: On treatment with nitrous acid ($NaNO_2$ + dil HCl) at 273–278 K followed by reaction with an alkaline solution of β-naphthol, aniline gives an orange red coloured dye.

$$C_6H_5\text{–}NH_2 + NaNO_2 + HCl \xrightarrow{273\text{–}278\text{ K}} C_6H_5\text{–}N^+{\equiv}NCl^- + H_2O$$

$$C_6H_5\text{–}N_2^+{\equiv}NCl^- + \underset{\beta\text{-Naphthol}}{\text{(OH-naphthalene)}} \xrightarrow{\text{dil. NaOH}} \underset{\substack{\text{1-Phenyl azo-2-naphthol} \\ \text{(Orange red dye)}}}{C_6H_5\text{–N=N–}C_{10}H_6OH}$$

13.11 Diazonium Salts

They have the general formula $ArN_2^+X^-$, where X^- may be an anion like Cl^-, Br^-, HSO_4^-, BF_4^-, and the group N_2^+ ($-N \equiv N^+$) is called the diazonium group. For example,

$C_6H_5\text{–}N^+{\equiv}NCl^-$ Benzendiazonium chloride; o-$ClC_6H_4\text{–}N^+{\equiv}NCl^-$ *o*-Chlorobenzendiazonium chloride; m-$HOC_6H_4\text{–}N^+{\equiv}NBr^-$ *m*-Hydroxybenzenediazonium bromide

The diazonium salt may contain other anions also such as NO_3^-, HSO_4^-, BF_4^-, and so on.

$CH_3\text{–}C_6H_4\text{–}N^+{\equiv}NHSO_4^-$ *p*-Toluenediazonium hydrogen sulfate; $O_2N\text{–}C_6H_4\text{–}N^+{\equiv}NBF_4^-$ *p*-Nitrobenzenediazonium fluoroborate

13.11.1 Preparation of Diazonium Salts

Aromatic diazonium salts are prepared by treating an ice-cold solution of an aromatic primary amine in excess of mineral acid like HCl or H_2SO_4 with an ice-cold solution of sodium nitrite dissolved in water. The temperature is maintained between 273 and 278 K because most of the diazonium salts decompose at a higher temperature.

$$NaNO_2 + HCl \rightarrow NaCl + HONO$$

$$\underset{\text{Aromatic amine}}{ArNH_2} \xrightarrow{NaNO_2} Ar - N \equiv N^+Cl^- + NaCl + H_2O$$

For example,.

$$\underset{\text{Aniline}}{C_6H_5NH_2} + NaNO_2 + 2HCl \xrightarrow{273\text{ K}} \underset{\text{Benzene diazonium chloride}}{C_6H_5N_2^+Cl^-} + NaCl + 2H_2O$$

13.12 Chemical Properties of Diazonium Salts

13.12.1 Reactions Involving Displacement of Nitrogen

The diazo group, being a very good leaving group, is readily substituted or replaced by other groups. In these reactions, the nitrogen of the diazonium salts is lost as N_2 and different groups are introduced in its place. Some of the important replacement reactions are discussed.

(i) **Replacement by the –OH group:** When an aqueous solution of diazonium salt is boiled (up to 283 K) or steam distilled, it gives phenols; therefore, the diazonium group gets replaced by the –OH group.

$$\underset{\text{Benzene diazonium chloride}}{C_6H_5N_2^+Cl^-} + H_2O \xrightarrow{\text{Warm}} \underset{\text{Phenol}}{C_6H_5OH} + N_2 + HCl$$

(ii) Replacement by hydrogen or deamination:

$$C_6H_5N_2^+Cl^- + H_3PO_2 + H_2O \xrightarrow{Cu(I)} C_6H_6 + N_2 + H_3PO_3 + HCl$$

Benzene diazonium chloride; Benzene; Phosphorous acid

The diazo group can also be replaced by hydrogen by heating the diazonium salt with ethanol.

$$C_6H_5N_2^+Cl^- + CH_3CH_2OH \longrightarrow C_6H_6 + N_2 + CH_3CHO + HCl$$

Benzene diazonium chloride; Ethanol; Benzene; Ethanal

The complete process involving the diazotisation of an amine followed by the reduction of the diazonium salt or replacement of the diazo group by hydrogen is called deamination.

(iii) Replacement by Cl or Br group: This reaction is called *Sandmeyer reaction.*

$$C_6H_5N_2^+Cl^- \xrightarrow[HCl]{Cu_2Cl_2} C_6H_5Cl + N_2; \quad C_6H_5N_2^+Cl^- \xrightarrow[HCl]{Cu_2Br_2} C_6H_5Br + N_2$$

Chlorobenzene; Bromobenzene

When the diazonium salt solution is warmed with copper powder and the corresponding halogen acid, the respective halogen is introduced. The reaction is a modified form of the Sandmeyer reaction and is known as the *Gattermann reaction.*

$$C_6H_5N_2^+Cl^- \xrightarrow[HCl]{Cu} C_6H_5Cl + N_2; \quad C_6H_5N_2^+Cl^- \xrightarrow[HCl]{Cu,\ HBr} C_6H_5Br + N_2$$

(iv) Replacement by iodo (–I) group: When an aqueous solution of a benzene diazonium salt is warmed with an excess of potassium iodide, an aryl iodide is formed.

$$C_6H_5N_2^+Cl^- + KI \xrightarrow{Heat} C_6H_5I + N_2 + KCl$$

Iodobenzene

Iodine is not easily introduced into the benzene ring directly.

(v) Replacement by fluoro (–F) group: When a diazonium salt is treated with fluoroboric acid (HBF_4), benzene diazonium fluoroborate is precipitated, which on heating decomposes to fluorobenzene. This reaction is called Balz–Schiemann reaction.

$$C_6H_5N_2^+Cl^- + HBF_4 \longrightarrow C_6H_5N_2^+BF_4^- \xrightarrow{Heat} C_6H_5F$$

Fluoroboric acid; Benzene diazonium fluoroborate; Fluorobenzene

(vi) Replacement by cyano (–CN) group: When a benzene diazonium salt is treated with copper cyanide dissolved in aqueous KCN, cyanobenzene is formed. The nitriles can be hydrolysed to acids.

$$C_6H_5N_2^+Cl^- \xrightarrow{CuCN/KCN} C_6H_5CN + N_2 \xrightarrow{Hydrolysis} C_6H_5COOH + N_2$$

Cyanobenzene; Benzoic acid

This method of preparing carboxylic acids is more useful than carbonation of Grignard reagents.

(vii) Replacement by nitro (–NO$_2$) group: Nitrobenzene is prepared by heating diazonium fluoroborate with aqueous $NaNO_2$ in the presence of copper powder.

$$C_6H_5N_2^+Cl^- \xrightarrow{HBF_4} C_6H_5N_2^+BF_4^- \xrightarrow[Heat]{NaNO_2,\ Cu} C_6H_5NO_2 + NaBF_4 + N_2$$

Nitrobenzene

Alternatively, nitro compounds may be prepared by treating a diazonium salt with nitrous acid in the presence of cuprous oxide.

$$C_6H_5N_2^+Cl^- + HONO \xrightarrow{Cu_2O} C_6H_5NO_2 + HCl + N_2$$

Nitrobenzene

(viii) Replacement by thio (–SH) group: When a diazonium salt is treated with potassium hydrosulfide, thiophenol is produced.

$$C_6H_5N_2^+Cl^- + KSH \longrightarrow C_6H_5SH + N_2 + KCl$$

Thiophenol

13.12.2 Reactions Involving Retention of Diazo Group

(i) Coupling reactions: Benzene diazonium salts react with highly reactive (electron rich) aromatic compounds such as phenols and amines to form azo compounds, AR–N=N–Ar. The reaction is known as a coupling reaction.

Coupling with phenol occurs in the basic medium (pH ≈ 9–10) while that of the amines occurs in a faintly acidic medium (pH ≈ 4–5) at 273–278 K.

Benzenediazonium chloride + Phenol $\xrightarrow[273-275\text{ K}]{\text{Base (pH}\approx 9-10)}$ p-Hydroxyazobenzene (Orange dye)

$C_6H_5-N^+\equiv NCl^- + C_6H_5-OH \rightarrow C_6H_5-N=N-C_6H_4-OH$

Benzenediazonium chloride + Aniline $\xrightarrow[273-278\text{ K}]{H^+ \text{ (pH}\approx 4.5)}$ p-Aminoazobenzene (Yellow dye)

$C_6H_5-N^+\equiv NCl^- + C_6H_5-NH_2 \rightarrow C_6H_5-N=N-C_6H_4-NH_2$

Benzenediazonium chloride + N, N-Dimethylaniline $\xrightarrow[273-278\text{ K}]{H^+ \text{ (pH}\approx 4.5)}$ p-Dimethylamine azobenzene (Orange)

$C_6H_5-N^+\equiv NCl^- + C_6H_5-N(CH_3)_2 \rightarrow C_6H_5-N=N-C_6H_4-N(CH_3)_2$

$C_6H_5-N^+\equiv NCl^- + CH_3-C_6H_4-OH \xrightarrow[\text{(PH 9–10)}]{OH^-}$ 2-Phenylazo-4-methyl phenol

p-Cresol

2-Phenylazo-4-methyl phenol: $CH_3-C_6H_3(OH)-N=NC_6H_5$

4-Aminophenol $\xrightarrow[OH^- \text{ (pH= 9–10)}]{C_6H_5N^+\equiv NCl^-}$ 4-Amino-2-phenylazo phenol (*ortho* wrt –OH group)

4-Aminophenol $\xrightarrow[H^+ \text{ (pH= 4–5)}]{C_6H_5\overset{+}{N}\equiv NCl^-}$ 4-Amino-3-phenylazophenol (*ortho* wrt $-NH_2$ group) + HCl

All azo compounds are strongly coloured and are used as dyes. Methyl orange is an important dye obtained by coupling the diazonium salt of sulfanilic acid with N,N-dimethylaniline.

$Na^+O_3^-S-C_6H_4-NH_2 \xrightarrow[273-278\text{ K}]{NaNO_2} Na^+O_3^-S-C_6H_4-N\equiv NCl$

Sodium salt of sulfanilic acid

$Na^+O_3^-S-C_6H_4-N\equiv N\,Cl + H-C_6H_4-N(CH_3)_2$

$\xrightarrow[273-278\text{ K}]{OH^-} Na^+O_3^-S-C_6H_4-N=S-C_6H_4-N(CH_3)_2$

Methyl orange

(ii) Reduction to arylhydrazines: Arene diazonium salts are reduced to aryl hydrazines upon treatment with stannous chloride and hydrochloric acid or zinc dust and acid or sodium sulfide or even by the electrolytic method.

$$Ar-N^+\equiv NCl^- \xrightarrow[Na_2SO_3]{SnCl_2/HCl} Ar-NH-NH_2 + HCl$$

Phenylhydrazine, which is an important reagent for organic synthesis, can be easily prepared in good yield from benzene diazonium chloride.

$$C_6H_5N^+\equiv NCl^- \xrightarrow{SnCl_2/HCl} \underset{\text{Phenylhydrazine}}{C_6H_5NH-NH_2} + HCl$$

However, if a strong reducing agent such as Zn/HCl is used, the product is an aromatic amine.

$$\underset{\text{Benzene diazonium chloride}}{C_6H_5N^+\equiv NCl^-} \xrightarrow{Zn/HCl} \underset{\text{Phenylhydrazine}}{[C_6H_5NHNH_2]} \xrightarrow{Zn/HCl} \underset{\text{Aniline}}{C_6H_5NH_2} + NH_3$$

13.13 Synthesis of Important Compounds

(i) Synthesis of 1,2,3-tribromo benzene: 1,2,3-tribromo benzene is not formed in the pure state by direct bromination of benzene. However, it can be prepared by the following sequence of reactions starting from *p*-nitroaniline through the formation of the diazonium salt.

p-Nitroaniline $\xrightarrow[\text{Bromination}]{Br_2/CH_3COOH}$ 2, 6-Dibromo-4-nitroaniline $\xrightarrow[NaNO_2 + HCl,\ 273-278\text{ K}]{\text{Diazotisation}}$ (diazonium salt) $\xrightarrow[\text{Sandmeyer reaction}]{CuBr/HBr}$ 3, 4, 5-Tribromonitrobenzene $\xrightarrow{Sn,\ HCl}$ 3, 4, 5-Tribromoaniline $\xrightarrow[NaNO_2 + HCl,\ 273-278\text{ K}]{\text{Diazotisation}}$ (3,4,5-tribromobenzenediazonium chloride, $N_2^+Cl^-$) $\xrightarrow{H_3PO_2}$ 1, 2, 3-Tribromobenzene

(ii) Synthesis of 3,5-dibromotoluene: Direct bromination to toluene with $Br_2/FeBr_3$ gives, 2,4-dibromotoluene. But 3,5-dibromotoluene may by synthesised as follows.

p-Toluidine $\xrightarrow[CH_3COOH]{Br_2}$ (2,6-dibromo-4-methylaniline) $\xrightarrow[\text{Diazotisation}]{NaOH,\ HCl,\ 273-278\text{ K}}$ ($\overset{+}{N}\equiv N\bar{C}l$ diazonium salt) $\xrightarrow{H_3PO_2}$ 3, 5-Dibromotoluene

(iii) Synthesis of *o*- and *p*-dinitrobenzenes: These cannot be prepared by direct substitution. However, the diazonium salt route may be followed.

Aniline (NH_2) $\xrightarrow{(CH_3CO)_2O}$ Acetanilide ($NHCOCH_3$) $\xrightarrow{HNO_3,\ H_2SO_4}$ *o*-Nitroacetanilide ($NHCOCH_3$, NO_2) + *p*-Nitroacetanilide ($NHCOCH_3$, NO_2)

o-Nitroacetanilide $\xrightarrow{\text{Hydrolysis}}$ (NH_2, NO_2) $\xrightarrow{\text{(i) } NaNO_2 + HCl;\ \text{(ii) } HBF_4,\ NaNO_2,\ Cu}$ *o*-Dinitrobenzene (NO_2, NO_2)

p-Nitroacetanilide $\xrightarrow{\text{Hydrolysis}}$ (NH_2, NO_2) $\xrightarrow{\text{(i) } NaNO_2,\ HCl;\ \text{(ii) } HBF_4,\ NaNO_2,\ Cu}$ *p*-Dinitrobenzene (NO_2, NO_2)

(iv) Synthesis of *m*-bromotoluene: It cannot be prepared by direct bromination of toluene or Friedel–Crafts alkylation of bromobenzene because of the *o*,*p*-directing nature of the methyl group.

p-Toluidine (CH_3, NH_2) $\xrightarrow[\text{Acetylation}]{(CH_3CO)_2O,\ py}$ (CH_3, $NHCOCH_3$) $\xrightarrow{Br_2,\ CH_3COOH}$ (CH_3, Br, $NHCOCH_3$) $\xrightarrow[\text{Hydrolysis}]{H^+,\ \text{heat}}$ (CH_3, Br, NH_2) $\xrightarrow{NaNO_2,\ HCl\ 0.5°C}$ (CH_3, Br, N_2^+Cl) $\xrightarrow{H_3PO_2}$ *m*-Bromotoluene (CH_3, Br)

(v) Synthesis of *p*-toluic acid: This can be synthesised as follows.

Toluene (CH_3) $\xrightarrow[H_2SO_4]{HNO_3}$ (CH_3, NO_2) $\xrightarrow{\text{(i) Fe, HCl; (ii) NaOH}}$ (CH_3, NH_2) $\xrightarrow[0.5°C]{NaNO_2,\ HCl}$ (CH_3, N_2^+Cl) $\xrightarrow{CuCN}$ (CH_3, CN) $\xrightarrow{H^+,\ H_2O}$ *p*-Toluic acid (CH_3, COOH)

(vi) Synthesis of 1,3,5-tribromobenzene: It can be synthesised as follows.

Aniline (NH_2) $\xrightarrow[\text{Bromination}]{Br_2/H_2O}$ (NH_2, Br, Br, CH_3) $\xrightarrow[0\text{–}5°C]{NaNO_2,\ HCl}$ ($N_2^+Cl^-$, Br, Br, CH_3) $\xrightarrow{H_3PO_2}$ 1, 3, 5-Tribromobenzene (Br, Br, Br)

(vii) Synthesis of *m*-nitrophenol from benzene: It can be synthesised as follows.

Benzene $\xrightarrow[335\ K]{HNO_3/H_2SO_4}$ (NO_2) $\xrightarrow{HNO_3/H_2SO_4}$ (NO_2, NO_2) $\xrightarrow{(NH_4)_2S_x}$

m-Nitroaniline (NO_2, NO_2) $\xrightarrow[273\text{–}278\ K]{NaNO_2,\ HCl}$ ($N_2^+Cl^-$, NO_2) $\xrightarrow[\text{Boiling}]{\text{dil. } H_2SO_4}$ *m*-Nitrophenol (OH, NO_2)

(viii) Synthesis of *p*-iodonitrobenzene: It can be synthesised from *p*-nitroaniline as follows.

p-Nitroaniline (NO_2, NH_2) $\xrightarrow[273\ K\text{–}278\ K]{NaNO_2,\ HCl}$ (NO_2, $N_2^+Cl^-$) $\xrightarrow{I_2,\ KI}$ *p*-Iodonitrobenzene (NO_2, I)

Exercises

OBJECTIVE QUESTIONS

Classification and Nomenclature of Amines

1. Which of the following amines has the same common as well as IUPAC name?

(a) $C_6H_5NHCH_3$ (b) o-toluidine
(c) m-anisidine (d) phenylaminomethane

2. Which of the following combinations of names for the same amine with molecular formula $C_4H_{11}N$ is not correct?

(a) tert-butylamine, 2-methylpropan-2-amine
(b) isobutylamine, n-propylmethylamine
(c) diethylamine, n-ethylethanamine
(d) sec-butylamine, butan-2-amine

3. Parkinson's disease is linked to abnormalities in the levels of dopamine in the body. The structure of dopamine is

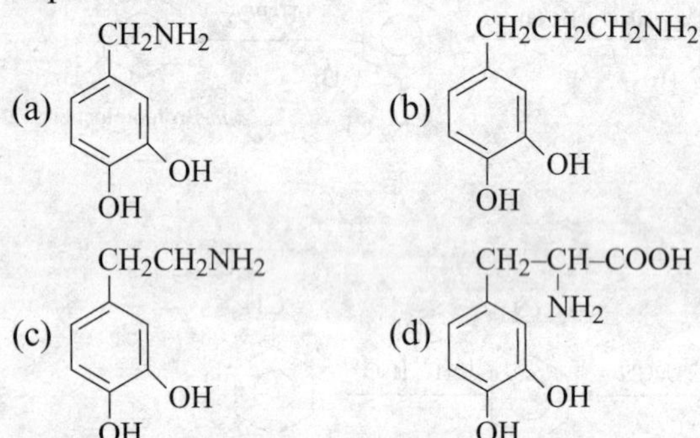

4. The IUPAC name of the following amine is

$$H_3C-\underset{CH_3}{N}-\overset{CH_3}{\underset{C_2H_5}{C}}-CH_2CH_3$$

(a) N,N-3-trimethylpentan-3-amine
(b) 3-N,N-trimethylpentan-3-amine
(c) N,N-2-trimethylpentan-2-amine
(d) 2-N,N-trimethylpentan-2-amine

5. The complete stereochemical IUPAC name of the following compound is

(structure: cyclohexane ring with H, OH and NH_2, H)

(a) *trans*-3-hydroxycyclohexanamine
(b) *cis*-3-hydroxycyclohexanamine
(c) *cis*-3-aminocyclohexanol
(d) *trans*-3-aminocyclohexanol

6. The correct IUPAC name of the following compound

$$CH_3-\underset{C_2H_5}{N}-\underset{O}{\overset{}{\underset{\|}{C}}}-CH_3$$ is

(a) N-methyl-N-ethylethanamide
(b) N-ethyl-N-methylethanamide
(c) N-methyl-N-ethylacetamide
(d) N-ethyl-N-methylacetamide

7. Which of the following amines gives the carbylamine reaction?

(a) $C_2H_5NH_2$ (b) $(C_2H_5)_2NH$
(c) $(C_2H_5)_3N$ (d) $CH_3NHC_2H_5$

8. Which of the following is a tertiary amine?

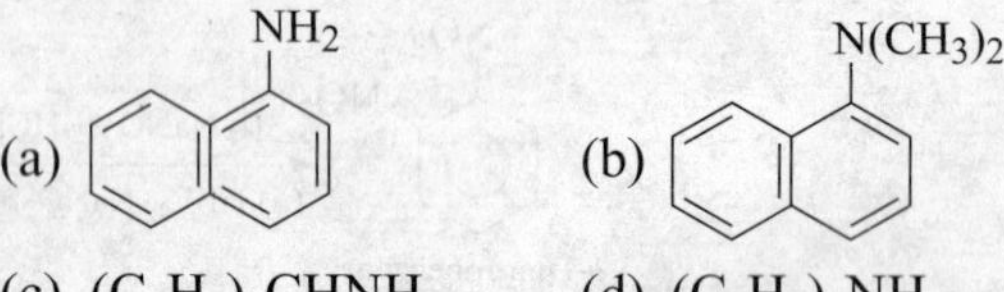

(c) $(C_2H_5)_2CHNH_2$ (d) $(C_2H_5)_2NH$

Methods of Preparation of Amines

9. The product Y in the following reaction

$$C_6H_6 \xrightarrow[\text{Conc. } H_2NO_3]{\text{Conc. } HNO_3} X \xrightarrow{LiAlH_4} Y, \text{ is}$$

(a) 2,6-dimethylaniline (ring with CH_3, NH_2, CH_3)
(b) cyclohexyl–NH_2
(c) 3,5-dimethylaniline (H_3C, H_3C, NH_2)
(d) $C_6H_5-N(CH_3)_2$

10. The major product formed in the reaction,

$$C_6H_5CH_2Br \xrightarrow{AgNO_2} \xrightarrow[\text{(ii) } H_2O]{\text{(i) } LiAlH_4}, \text{ is}$$

(a) $C_6H_5CH{=}NOH$ (b) $C_6H_5CH_2NHOH$
(c) $C_6H_5CH_2NH_2$ (d) $(C_6H_5)_2NH$

11. Which of the following reagents will not be a good choice for reducing an aryl nitro compound to an amine?

(a) H_2 (excess)/Pt (b) $LiAlH_4$ in ether
(c) Fe and HCl (d) Sn/HCl

12. The final product (B) in the following reaction sequence is

$$F-C_6H_4-NO_2 \xrightarrow[\text{DMF, } \Delta]{(CH_3)_2NH} (A) \xrightarrow{H_2/Ni} (B).$$

(a) $H_2N-C_6H_4-N(CH_3)_2$ (b) $H_2N-C_6H_4-NH_2$
(c) $H_2N-C_6H_4-N(CH_3)(CH_2NH_2)$ (d) $O_2N-C_6H_4-NH_2$

13. In the given set of reactions

$$\text{2-Bromopropane} \xrightarrow[\text{Heat}]{\text{Alc.AgCN}} X \xrightarrow{LiAlH_4} Y$$

The IUPAC name of the product Y is
(a) N-isopropylmethanamine
(b) N-methylpropan-2-amine
(c) N-methylpropanamine
(d) butan-2-amine

14. Consider the following conversion,
$CH_3CH_2-Cl \xrightarrow{A} CH_3CH_2CN \xrightarrow{B} CH_3CH_2CH_2NH_2$
The best choice of reagents A and B respectively are
(a) aq. NaCN, $LiAlH_4$
(b) alc. NaCN, Ni/H_2
(c) alc. AgCN, Na/Hg – C_2H_5OH
(d) aq. AgCN, $LiAlH_4$

15. Consider the following reactions.
$C_6H_5CONH_2 \xrightarrow{POCl_3} (A) \xrightarrow{LiAlH_4} (A)$
The products (A) and (B) respectively are
(a) $C_6H_5-C(Cl)=NH$, $C_6H_5C\equiv N$
(b) $C6H_5CCl_2-NH_2$, $C_6H_5CH_2NH_2$
(c) C_6H_5CN, $C_6H_5CH_2NH_2$
(d) C_6H_5COCl, $C_6H_5CH_2OH$

16. Which of the following on reduction with lithium aluminium hydride yields a secondary amine?
(a) methyl cyanide (b) nitroethane
(c) methyl isocyanide (d) acetamide

17. The major product of the following reaction is
$R-C\equiv N \xrightarrow[(ii)\,H_2O]{(i)\,AlH(i\,Bu)_2}$
(a) R–CHO (b) RCOOH
(c) RCH_2NH_2 (d) $RCONH_2$

18. Predict the product of the following reaction

(reactant: cyclohexane ring bearing COOH, vinyl, CH_3–C=O and NO_2 groups) $\xrightarrow{LiAlH_4\ (excess)}$

(a) (COOH, vinyl, CH_3, NO_2, OH)
(b) (OH, ethyl, CH_3, NH_2, OH)
(c) (OH, vinyl, CH_3, NH_2, OH)
(d) (vinyl, CH_3, NO_2, OH)

19. Predict the product of the following reaction
$CH_3-CH=CH-CH=NCH_3 \xrightarrow{LiAlH_4}$
(a) $CH_3-CH_2-CH_2-CH_2-NH-CH_3$
(b) $CH_3-CH=CH-CH_2-NH-CH_3$
(c) $CH_3-CH_2-CH_2-CH=N-CH_3$
(d) $CH_3-CH=CH-CH_2-NH_2$

20. $C_6H_5CONHCH_3$ can be converted into $C_6H_5CH_2NHCH_3$ by
(a) $NaBH_4$ (b) H_2–Pd/C
(c) $LiAlH_4$ (d) Zn–Hg/HCl

21. Which of the following reagents would be best for converting phenylacetamide to 2-phenylethanamine?
(a) $LiAlH_4$/ether
(b) (i) P_2O_5;heat (ii) $LiAlH_4$/ether
(c) H_2 and Pt catalyst
(d) aqueous NaOBr

22. N,N-dimethylacetamide on reduction with $LiAlH_4$ gives
(a) ethyldimethylamine (b) diethylmethylamine
(c) ethylmethylamine (d) trimethylamine

23. Predict the product of the following reaction,

(N-methylpyrrolidin-2-one) $\xrightarrow[(ii)\,H_2O]{(i)\,LiAlH_4}$

(a) 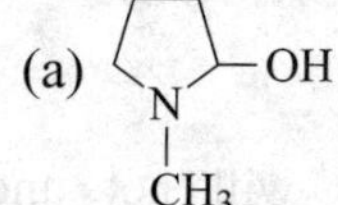
(b) 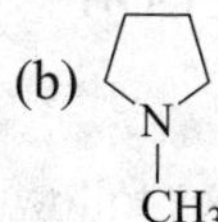
(c) 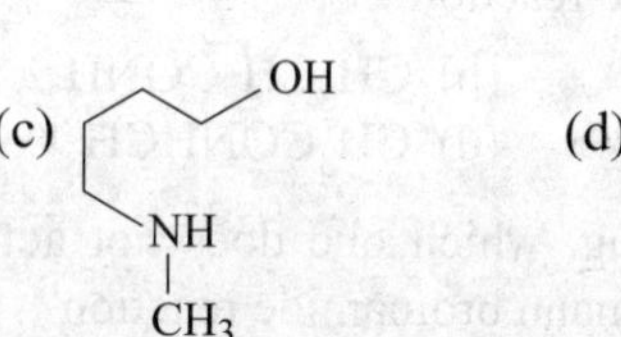
(d) (open-chain aldehyde with NH–CH_3)

24. In the following reaction sequence,
$C_6H_5C\equiv CH \xrightarrow[HgSO_4]{Aq.H_2SO_4} (A) \xrightarrow{NH_2OH} (B) \xrightarrow[(ii)\,H_2O]{(i)\,LiAlH_4} (C)$ the product (C) is
(a) $(C_6H_5)(CH_3)C=NOH$ (b) $(C_6H_5)(CH_3)CH-NH_2$
(c) $CH_3-CH(CH_3)COOH$ (d) $C_6H_5CH_2NHCH_3$

25. Which one of the following can be prepared by Gabriel's phthalimide synthesis?
(a) aniline (b) *o*-toluidine (c) benzylamine
(d) *n*-methylethanamine (e) 4-bromoaniline

26. Which of the following amines cannot be prepared by Gabriel's synthesis?
(a) butylamine (b) isopropylamine
(c) 2-phenylethylamine (d) N-methylbenzylamine

27. Acetamide is treated with the following reagents separately. Which one of these would yield methylamine?

(a) PCl_5 (b) $NaOH–Br_2$
(c) sodalime (d) hot conc. H_2SO_4

28. In the Hofmann bromamide degradation reaction, the number of moles of NaOH and Br_2 used per mole of amine produced are

(a) one mole of NaOH and one mole of Br_2
(b) four moles NaOH and two moles of Br_2
(c) two moles of NaOH and two moles of Br_2
(d) four moles of NaOH and one mole of Br_2

29. Identify X in the following sequence of reactions

$\underset{(X)}{C_4H_7OCl} \xrightarrow{NH_3} C_4H_9ON \xrightarrow{Br_2/KOH} CH_3CH_2CH_2NH_2$ is

(a) $(CH_3)_2CHCOCl$ (b) $CH_3CH_2CH(OH)CH_2Cl$
(c) $CH_3CH_2CH_2COCl$ (d) $ClCH_2CH_2CH_2CHO$

30. An organic compound A on treatment with NH_3 gives B which on heating gives C.C when treated with Br_2 in the presence of KOH produces ethylamine. Compound A is

(a) CH_3COOH (b) $CH_3CH_2CH_2COOH$
(c) $CH_3–\underset{CH_3}{\underset{|}{C}H}COOH$ (d) CH_3CH_2COOH

31. Which of the following amides will not undergo Hofmann bromamide reaction?

(a) CH_3CONH_2 (b) $CH_3CH_2CONH_2$
(c) $C_6H_5CONH_2$ (d) $CH_3CONHCH_3$

32. Among the following, which one does not act as an intermediate in Hofmann bromamide reaction?

(a) RNCO (b) $RCO\ddot{N}$: (c) $RCO\ddot{N}HBr$ (d) RNC

33. The method by which aniline cannot be prepared is

(a) degradation of benzamide with bromine in alkaline solution
(b) reduction of nitrobenzene with H_2/Pd in ethanol
(c) potassium salt of phthalimide treated with chlorobenzene following by hydrolysis with aqueous NaOH solution
(d) hydrolysis of phenyl isocyanide with acidic solution

34. Which of the following reactions is given by only primary amines?

(a) reaction with HONO
(b) reaction with chloroform and alcoholic KOH
(c) reaction with acetyl chloride
(d) reaction with Grignard reagent

35. Ammonolysis of benzyl chloride with two moles of CH_3Cl gives

(a) benzylamine
(b) N-methylphenylethanamine
(c) N,N-dimethylphenylmethanamine
(d) N,N,N-timethylphenyl ammonium chloride

36. Identify the product in the following reaction

Cyclohexyl–Br + NH_3 ⟶

(a) Cyclohexyl–NH_2 (b) Cyclohexyl–NH–Cyclohexyl
(c) Cyclohexyl–NHBr (d) Cyclohexene

37. o-Bromobenzyl chloride $\xrightarrow[EtOH]{NH_3}$

The product of the above reaction

(a) o-aminobenzylamine (NH_2CH_2 and NH_2 on ring) (b) 3-amino-5-(chloromethyl)aniline (CH_2Cl and two NH_2 on ring) (c) o-bromobenzylamine (CH_2NH_2 and Br on ring) (d) CH_2NH_2 and OEt on ring

38. What is the end product in the following sequence of reactions?

$C_6H_6 \xrightarrow[333K]{HNO_3-H_2SO_4} A \xrightarrow{Sn/HCl} B$

(a) nitrobenzene (b) aniline
(c) benzonitrile (d) phenyl carbylamines

Physical Properties of Amines

39. The boiling points of the following compounds in descending order are,

I. $CH_3(CH_2)_3OH$ II. $(C_2H_5)_2NH$
III. $C_2H_5CONH_2$ IV. CH_3CH_2COOH
(a) IV > III > I > II (b) III > IV > I > II
(c) IV > I > III > II (d) III > I > II > IV

40. The solubility in water of $C_6H_5NH_2$ (I), $(C_2H_5)_2NH$ (II) and $C_2H_5NH_2$(III) increases in the order

(a) II < III < I (b) I < II < III
(c) III < II < I (d) II < I < III

41. Which of the following should be most volatile?

(a) $CH_3CH_2CH_2CH_2$ (b) $CH_3CH_2–NH–CH_3$
(c) $(CH_3)_3N$ (d) $CH_3CH_2CH_3$

42. Which of the following compounds will dissolve in an alkali solution after it undergoes reaction with Hinsberg's reagent?

(a) CH_3NH_2 (b) $(CH_3)_2NH$
(c) $C_6H_5NHC_6H_5$ (d) $(CH_3)_3N$

Chemical Reactions of Amines

43. The most reactive amine towards dilute hydrochloric acid is ________.

(a) $CH_3–NH_2$ (b) $(H_3C)_2NH$ (c) $(H_3C)_2N–CH_3$ (d) $C_6H_5NH_2$

44. Considering the basic strength of amines in aqueous solution, which one has the smallest pK_b value?

(a) $C_6H_5NH_2$ (b) $(CH_3)_2NH$
(c) CH_3NH_2 (d) $(CH_3)_3N$

45. Arrange the following in increasing order of their basic strength

CH_3NH_2 (I), $(CH_3)_2NH$ (II), $(CH_3)_3N$ (III), $C_6H_5CH_2NH_2$ (IV)

(a) IV < III < II < I (b) IV < III < I < II
(c) I < II < III < IV (d) IV < III < I = II

46. The increasing basicity order of the following compounds is

I. $CH_3CH_2NH_2$ II. $CH_3CH_2–NH–CH_2CH_3$
III. $CH_3–N(CH_3)–CH_3$ IV. Pb–NH–CH_3

(a) IV < III < II < I (b) IV < III < I < II
(c) I < II < III < IV (d) I < II < IV < III

47. The correct decreasing order of the pK_b values of the following amines is

I. $C_2H_5NH_2$ II. $C_6H_5NHCH_3$
III. $(C_2H_5)_2NH$ IV. $C_6H_5NH_2$

(a) IV > III > I > II (b) III > IV > II > I
(c) IV > II > I > III (d) IV < I < III < II

48. Arrange the following amines, $C_6H_5NH_2$ (I), $C_6H_5N(CH_3)_2$ (II), $(C_2H_5)_2NH$ (III) and CH_3NH_2 (IV) in increasing order of their basic strength in aqueous solution.

(a) I < II < IV < III (b) II < I < IV < III
(c) IV < III < II < I (d) I < IV < II < III

49. Which of the following is the correct decreasing order of basicity of amines, $C_2H_5NH_2$ (I), $(C_2H_5)_2NH$ (II), $(C_2H_5)_3N$ (III) and NH_3 (IV) in gaseous phase or non-aqueous solvents as benzene or chlorobenzene?

(a) II > I > III > IV (b) III > II > I > IV
(c) II > III > I > IV (d) III > I > II > IV

50. Which of the following compounds is most basic?

(a) $O_2N–C_6H_4–NH_2$ (b) $C_6H_5–CH_2NH_2$
(c) $C_6H_5–NH–COCH_3$ (d) $C_6H_5–NH_2$

51. The strongest base among the following is

(a) pyridine (b) pyrrole (N–H) (c) piperidine (N–H) (d) $C_6H_5NH_2$

52. The correct order of increasing basic nature of the following bases is

1: aniline; 2: O_2N-substituted aniline (p-nitroaniline); 3: CH_3-substituted aniline (p-toluidine); 4: O_2N-substituted aniline; 5: NO_2-substituted aniline (o-nitroaniline)

(a) 2 < 5 < 1 < 3 < 4 (b) 5 < 2 < 1 < 3 < 4
(c) 2 < 5 < 1 < 4 < 3 (d) 5 < 2 < 1 < 4 < 3

53. Among the following, the weakest base is

(a) $C_6H_5CH_2NH_2$ (b) $C_6H_5CH_2NHCH_3$
(c) $O_2NCH_2NH_2$ (d) CH_3NHCHO

54. Identify the correct basicity order in the nitroanilines.

(a) *o*-nitroaniline < *p*-nitroaniline < *m*-nitroaniline
(b) *m*-nitroaniline < *p*-nitroaniline < *o*-nitroaniline
(c) *p*-Nitroaniline < *o*-nitroaniline < *m*-nitroaniline
(d) *o*-nitroaniline < *m*-nitroaniline < *p*-nitroaniline

55. Increasing pK_b values of *o*-, *m*- and *p*- toluidines is

(a) $p < m < o$ (b) $o < m < p$
(c) $p < o < m$ (d) $m < o < p$

56. Arrange the following amines in decreasing order of their basic strength

I: aniline; II: o-chloroaniline; III: m-chloroaniline; IV: p-chloroaniline

(a) I > II > III > IV (b) I > IV > II > III
(c) II > I > IV > III (d) I > IV > III > II

57. Arrange the following amines in increasing order of their basic strength.

I. aniline II. *o*-anisidine
III. *m*-anisidine IV. *p*-anisidine

(a) I < II < III < IV (b) III < II < I < IV
(c) II < III < IV < I (d) IV < I < II < III

58. The correct increasing order of basic strength for the following compounds is

(I) aniline; (II) p-nitroaniline (NO_2); (III) p-toluidine (CH_3)

(a) III < I < II (b) III < II < I
(c) II < I < III (d) II < III < I

59. The strongest base among the following is

(a) amide ion (b) hydroxide ion
(c) trimethylamine (d) ammonia
(e) aniline

60. Among the following substituted pyridines, the most basic compound is

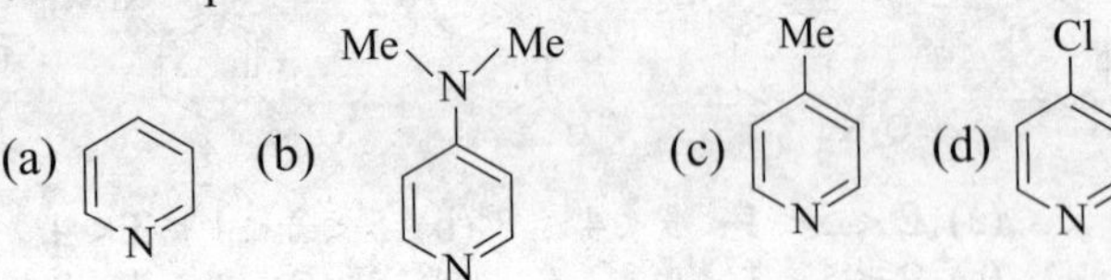

61. The order of basicity of

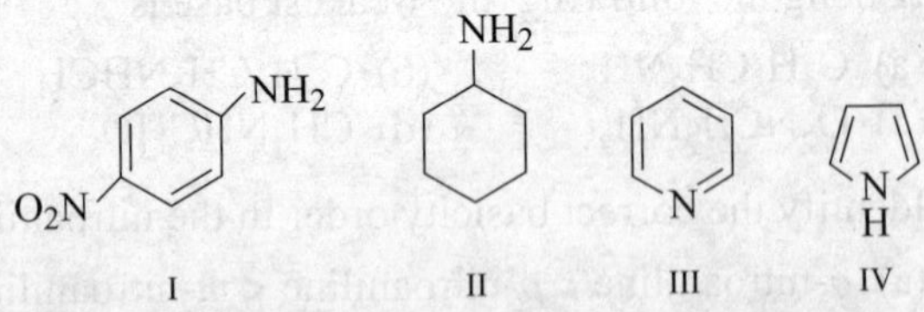

(a) IV < III < I < II (b) II < I <IV < III
(c) IV < I < III < II (d) II < III < I < IV

62. In which of the following reactions does the amine behave as an acid?

(a) $CH_3CH_2NH_2 + CH_3MgI$
(b) $[(CH_3)_2CH]_2NH + n\text{-}C_4H_9Li$
(c) $CH_3NH_2 + Br_2 \rightarrow$
(d) both (a) and (b)

63. The increasing order of basicity of the following compound is

I. NH_2 II. NH

III. NH_2 NH IV. $NHCH_3$

(a) I < II < III < IV (b) II < I < III < IV
(c) II < I < IV < III (d) IV < II < I < III

64. The correct order of basic strength of the following amines is

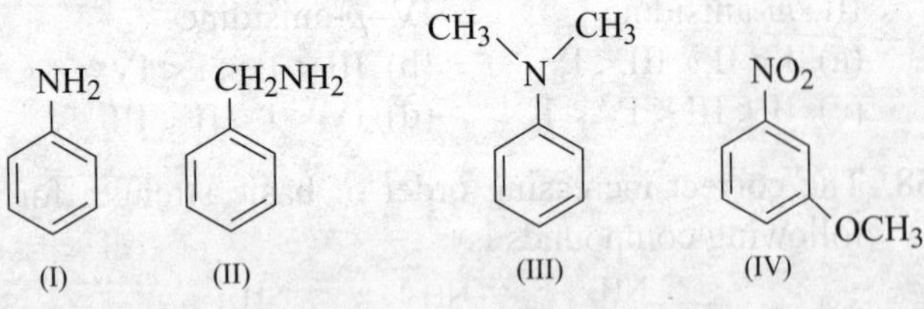

(a) I > II > III >IV (b) II > III > I > IV
(c) III > II > I > IV (d) IV > I > II > III

65. Benzylamine may be alkylated as shown in the following equation.

$C_6H_5CH_2NH_2 + RX \xrightarrow{\text{Pyridine}} C_6H_5CH_2NHR + HX$

(Pyridine is used here to remove the HX produced in the reaction).

Which of the alkyl halides is best suited for this reaction?

(a) $(CH_3)_3CCH_2Br$ (b) C_6H_5Br
(c) $C_6H_5CH_2Br$ (d) $(CH_3)_3CCl$

66. Which of the following is the major product of the following reaction?

NH + CH_3I (*excess*) $\xrightarrow{\text{Pyrine}}$

(a) N–CH_3 (b) $\overset{+}{N}$ CH_3 CH_3 I^-

(c) H_3C CH_3 N–CH_3 (d) CH_3 N–CH_3 CH_3

67. Benzylamine on treatment with two equivalents of methyl iodide in thepresence of pyridine mainly gives

(a) N-methylphenylmethanamine
(b) N,N-dimethylphenylmethanamine
(c) dibenzylamine
(d) tribenzylamine

68. Ethanamine reacts with acetyl chloride or acetic anhydride in the presence of pyridine to form

(a) N-ethylethanamide (b) N,N-diethylethanamide
(c) N-ethylacetamide (d) ethyl acetate

69. The major product obtained in the reaction of aniline with acetic anhydride is

(a) $NHCOCH_3$ (b)

(c) N $COCH_3$ $COCH_3$ (d) NH_2

70. The following reaction

NH_2 + Cl–C(=O)–Ph $\xrightarrow{\text{NaOH}}$ N(H)–C(=O)–Ph

Is known by the name

(a) Perkin's reaction
(b) acetylation reaction
(c) Schotten–Baumann reaction
(d) Friedel–Craft's reaction

71. In the reaction shown below, the major product formed is

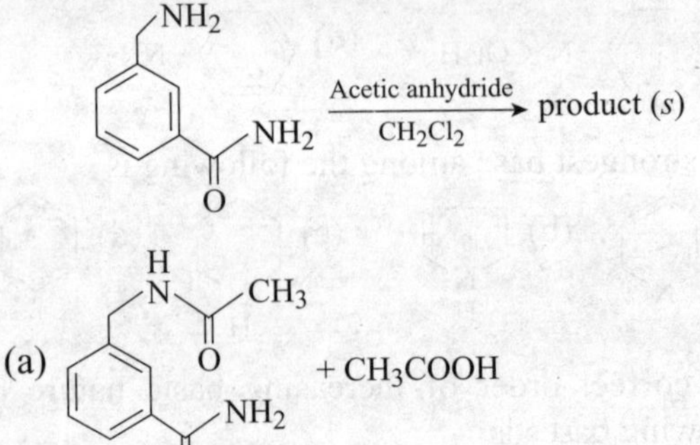

(a) H N CH_3 O NH_2 O + CH_3COOH

(b) [structure: benzene ring bearing CH_2NH– and –C(=O)–NH–C(=O)–CH_3] + CH_3COOH

(c) [structure: benzene ring bearing CH_2–NH–C(=O)–CH_3 and –C(=O)–NH–C(=O)–CH_3] + H_2O

(d) [structure: benzene ring bearing $CH_2\overset{+}{N}H_3CH_3COO^-$ and –C(=O)–NH–C(=O)–CH_3]

72. $CH_3CH_2Cl \xrightarrow{NaCN} X \xrightarrow{Ni/H_2} Y \xrightarrow{\text{acetic anhydride}} Z$

Z in the above reaction sequence is

(a) $CH_3CH_2CH_2NHCOCH_3$

(b) $CH_3CH_2CH_2NH_2$

(c) $CH3CH_2CH_2CONHCH_3$

(d) $CH_3CH_2CH_2CONHCOCH_3$

73. In the reaction,

$H_3C-C_6H_4-C(=O)NH_2 \xrightarrow[(2)\ C_6H_5COCl]{(1)\ NaOH/Br_2} T$

the structure of the product T is

(a) $H_3C-C_6H_4-C(=O)-O-C(=O)-C_6H_5$

(b) $C_6H_5-NH-C(=O)-C_6H_4-CH_3$

(c) $H_3C-C_6H_4-NH-C(=O)-C_6H_5$

(d) $H_3C-C_6H_4-C(=O)-NH-C(=O)-C_6H_5$

74. The product formed in the following reaction

$C_6H_5-NH_2 \xrightarrow{(CH_3CO)_2O} \xrightarrow[AlCl_3]{ClCH_2COCl}$, is

(a) $ClCH_2C(=O)-C_6H_4-NHCOCH_3$

(b) $H_2C(COCl)-C_6H_4-NHCOCH_3$

(c) [structure: benzene ring bearing H_3C–C(=O)–, –NH_2 and –C(=O)CH_2Cl]

(d) [structure: benzene ring bearing H_3C–C(=O)–, –NH_2 and –CH_2COCl]

(e) [structure: benzene ring bearing $ClCH_2$–C(=O)–, –NH_2 and –C(=O)CH_3]

75. The major product obtained in the following reaction is

$C_6H_5-CH(OH)-CH(NH_2)-CH_3 \xrightarrow[\text{room temp.}]{(CH_3CO)_2O/\text{pyridine (1 equiv.)}}$

(a) [structure: C_6H_5–C(=C)–... bearing $NHCOCH_3$]

(b) [structure: benzene ring bearing $COCH_3$, with side chain CH(OH)–CH(NH_2)–CH_3]

(c) $C_6H_5-CH(OCOCH_3)-CH(NH_2)-CH_3$

(d) $C_6H_5-CH(OH)-CH(NHCOCH_3)-CH_3$

76. A compound with molecular mass 180 is acylated with CH_3COCl to get a compound with molecular mass 390. The number of amino groups present per molecule of the former compound is

(a) 6 (b) 2 (c) 5 (d) 4

77. In the chemical reaction,

$CH_3CH_2NH_2 + CHCl_3 + 3\ KOH \rightarrow$ (A) + (B) + 3 H_2O. The compound (A) and (B) are respectively

(a) C_2H_5NC and 3 KCl

(b) C_2H_5CN and 3 KCl

(c) $CH_3CH_2CONH_2$ and 3 KCl

(d) C_2H_5NC and K_2CO_3

78. The reaction of $CHCl_3$ and alcoholic KOH with *p*-toluidine gives

(a) $H_3C-C_6H_4-CN$ (b) $H_3C-C_6H_4-N_2Cl$

(c) $H_3C-C_6H_4-NHCHCl_2$ (d) $H_3C-C_6H_4-NC$

79. A positive carbylamine test is shown by

(a) N,N-dimethylaniline (b) N-methylaniline

(c) dimethylamine (d) *p*-methylbenzylamine

(e) trimethylaniline

80. Which of the following reaction sequences will convert

$C_6H_{11}-C(=O)NH_2$ into $C_6H_{11}-NH-CH_3$?

(a) carbylamine reaction, Hofmann bromamide reaction reduction with Na/C_2H_5OH

(b) reduction amination, Hofmann bromamide reaction, carbylamine reaction

(c) reduction with $LiAlH_4$, carbylamine reaction, Hofmann bromamide reaction
(d) Hofmann bromamide reaction, carbylamine reaction, reduction with H_2/Pd

81. The product of reaction between chloroform and ethanamine in the presence of alcoholic KOH is allowed to react with Cl_2. The final product is
(a) ethyl chloride (b) ethylene dichloride
(c) ethyliminocarbonyl chloride
(d) ethanol

82. Isocyanides when heated with mercuric oxide and sulfur powder give products of the type R–N=C=X when X = O or S. These reactions suggest that the carbon atom of the isocyanide group is
(a) electron deficient (b) electron rich
(c) has a strong affinity for oxygen or sulfur
(d) none of the above

83. Which of the following represents the poisonous gas which caused the Bhopal tragedy in 1984?
(a) CH_3–N=C=O (b) CH_3–N=C=S
(c) CH_3–CH=N=S (d) CH_3–O–N$\underset{=}{\longrightarrow}$C

84. The product of the reaction between methyl isocyanate (MIC) and ethanol is urethane with the formula
(a) CH_3–$NHCOOC_2H_5$ (b) C_2H_5–$NHCOOCH_3$
(c) CH_3–$NHCOOCH_3$ (d) C_2H_5–NH–$COOC_2H_5$

85. An organic compound A on reduction gives compound B. B on treatment with $CHCl_3$ and alcoholic KOH gives C. C on catalytic reduction gives N-methylaniline. The compound A is
(a) methylamine (b) nitromethane
(c) aniline (d) nitrobenzene

86. An organic compound A on reduction gives compound B which on reaction with trichloromethane and caustic potash forms C. The compound C on catalytic reduction gives N-methylbenzenamine, the compound A is
(a) nitrobenzene (b) nitromethane
(c) methanamine (d) benzenamine

87. The compound that will produce a nauseating smell/odour with a hot mixture of chloroform and ethanolic potassium hydroxide is
(a) $PhCONH_2$ (b) $PhNHCH_3$ (c) $PhNH_2$ (d) PhOH

88. A compound X on treatment with Br_2/NaOH produces C_3H_9N which gives positive carbylamines test. Compound X is
(a) $CH_3COCH_2NHCH_3$ (b) $CH_3CH_2COCH_2NH_2$
(c) $CH_3CH_2CH_2CONH_2$ (d) $CH_3CON(CH_3)_2$

89. Which of the following will give N_2 gas on treatment with nitrous acid ($NaNO_2$ + HCl)?
(a) $C_2H_5NH_2$ (b) CH_3NH_2
(c) $(CH_3)_2CH$–NH_2 (d) All will give N_2

90. The amine which will not liberate nitrogen on reaction with nitrous acid is
(a) trimethylamine (b) ethylamine
(c) *sec*-butylamine (d) *t*-butylamine

91. The action of nitrous acid on ethylamine gives mainly
(a) ethyl nitrite (b) nitroethane
(c) ethane (d) ethyl alcohol

92. C_6H_5–CN $\xrightarrow[(ii)\ NaNO_2,\ HCl,\ 0–5°C]{(i)\ Sn/HCl}$ X, is
(a) C_6H_5–CH_2N_2Cl (b) C_6H_5–CH_2OH (c) C_6H_5–N_2Cl (d) C_6H_5–CHO

93. A compound which gives an oily nitorsoamine on reaction with nitrous acid at low temperature, is
(a) CH_3NH_2 (b) $(CH_3)_2CHNH_2$
(c) CH_3–NH–CH (d) $(CH_3)_3N$

94. Predict the product.

$$C_6H_5–NHCH_3 + NaNO_2 + HCl \longrightarrow \text{Product}$$

(a) C_6H_5–$N(CH_3)$–NO_2
(b) $C_6H_4(NHCH_3)$–NO + ON–C_6H_4–$NHCH_3$
(c) C_6H_5–N(OH)–CH_3 (d) C_6H_5–$N(CH_3)$–N=O

95. The product in the following reaction is

$$C_6H_5–N(CH_3)_2 + NaNO_2 + HCl \longrightarrow \text{Product}$$

(a) C_6H_5–$\overset{+}{N}$(N=O)(CH_3)–CH_3 (b) C_6H_5–$N(CH_3)$–CH=NOH
(c) ON–C_6H_4–$N(CH_3)_2$ (d) C_6H_5–$\overset{+}{N}H(CH_3)_2NO_2^-$

96. When N,N-dimethylamiline is treated with aqueous $NaNO_2$/HCl, the product formed is
(a) *p*-(N,N-dimethylamino)benzenediazonium chloride
(b) *p*-(N,N-dimethylamino)phenol
(c) *p*-nitroso-N,N-dimethylaniline
(d) *p*-nitro-N,N-dimethylaniline

97. What reagent is used in Hinsberg's test of amines?
(a) $(CH_3CO)_2O$ and pyridine
(b) $C_6H_5SO_2Cl$ in aq. NaOH
(c) $NaNO_2$ in aq. H_2SO_4
(d) CH_3I (excess) followed by AgOH

98. Which of the following compounds will dissolve in an alkali solution after it undergoes reaction with Hinsberg's reagent?

(a) CH_3NH_2 (b) $(CH_3)_3N$
(c) $(C_2H_5)_2NH$ (d) $C_6H_5NHC_6H_5$

99. Which of the following is soluble in sodium hydroxide?

(a) 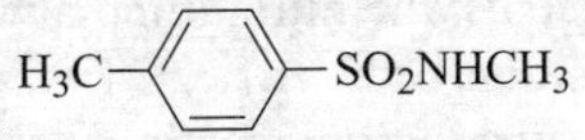 $H_3C-C_6H_4-SO_2NHCH_3$

(b)  $H_3C-C_6H_4-SO_2N(CH_3)_2$

(c) $H_3C-C_6H_4-NH_2$

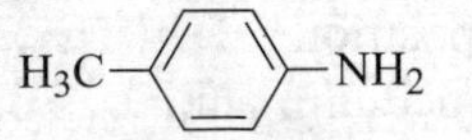

(d) 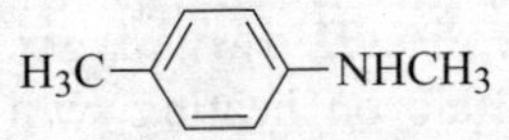 $H_3C-C_6H_4-NHCH_3$

100. An amine reacts with benzenesulfonyl chloride to form a white precipitate which is insoluble in aq. NaOH. The amine is

(a) 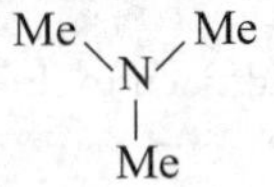 Me_3N (b) 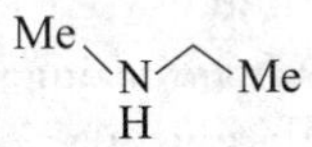 $MeNHCH_2CH_2Me$ (Me–NH–⁀Me)

(c) 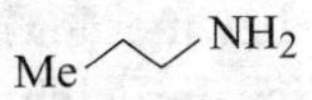 $MeCH_2CH_2NH_2$ (d) 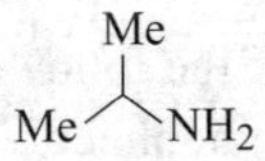 Me_2CHNH_2

101. Which one of the following methods is neither meant for the synthesis nor for the separation of amines?

(a) Hinsberg method (b) Hofmann method
(c) Wurtz reaction (d) Curtius reaction

102. The compound X (C_7H_9N) reacts with benzenesulfonyl chloride to give Y ($C_{13}H_{13}NO_2S$) which is insoluble in alkali. The compound X is

(a) 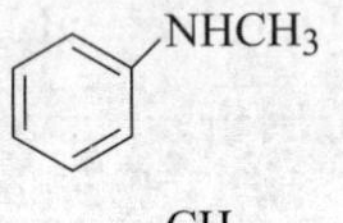 $C_6H_5NHCH_3$ (b) (methylcyclopentadienyl)CH_2NH_2 with CH_3

(c) o-toluidine (CH_3, NH_2) (d) 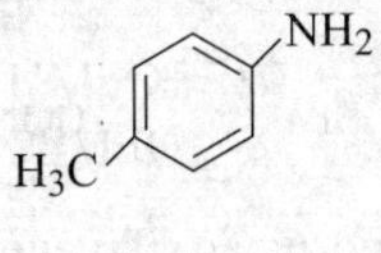 $H_3C-C_6H_4-NH_2$

103. The reaction of cyclohexanone with dimethylamine in the presence of catalytic amount of an acid forms a compound if water during the reaction is continuously removed. The compound formed is generally known as

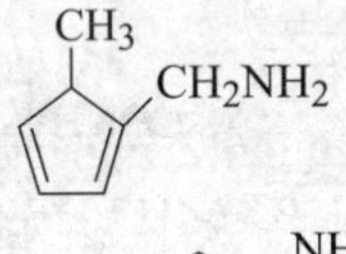

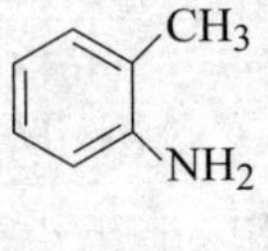

(a) an enamine (b) a Schiff's base
(c) an amine (d) an imine

104. Which of the following will be the favoured product from reaction shown below?

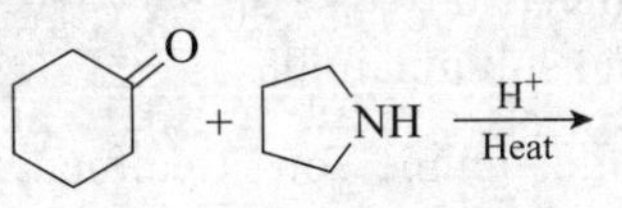

cyclohexanone + pyrrolidine (NH) $\xrightarrow[\text{Heat}]{H^+}$

(a) 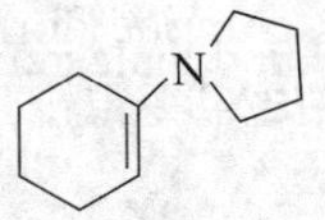 1-(cyclohex-1-enyl)pyrrolidine (N) (b) 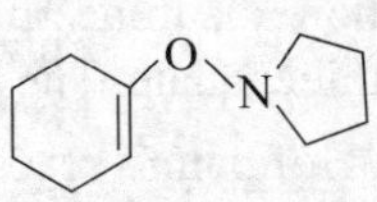 cyclohexenyl–O–N(pyrrolidine)

(c) 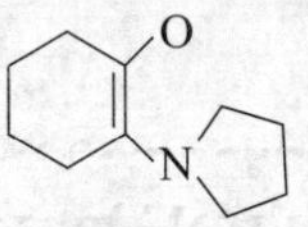 2-(pyrrolidin-1-yl)cyclohex-2-enone (O, N) (d) 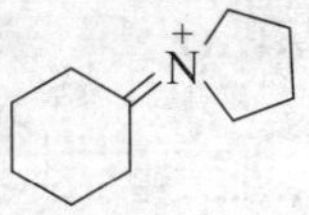 cyclohexylidene pyrrolidinium ($\overset{+}{N}$)

105. The product formed by the reaction of an aldehyde with a primary amine is a

(a) carboxylic acid (b) aromatic acid
(c) Schiff's base (d) ketone

106. Which of the following will not form a Schiff's base on reaction with p-nitrobenzaldehyde?

(a) 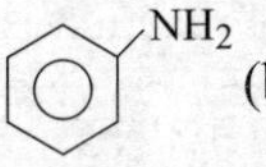 aniline (NH_2) (b) 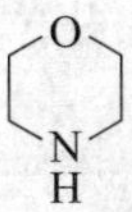 morpholine (O, N–H) (c) 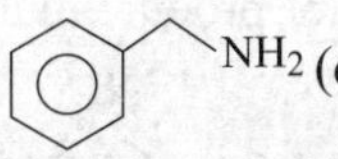 benzylamine (NH_2) (d) 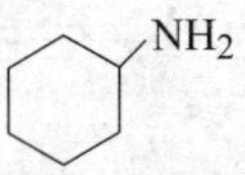 cyclohexylamine (NH_2)

107. Condensation of ethylamine with acetaldehyde gives a compound A which upon reduction with hydrogen and nickel gives

(a) diethylamine (b) ethylmethylamine
(c) triethylamine (d) dimethylamine

108. The major organic product formed from the following reaction

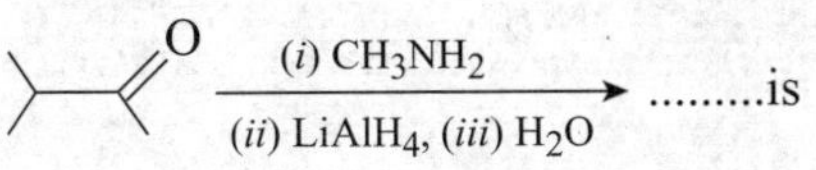

3-methylbutan-2-one (O) $\xrightarrow[(ii)\ LiAlH_4,\ (iii)\ H_2O]{(i)\ CH_3NH_2}$ ....is

(a) 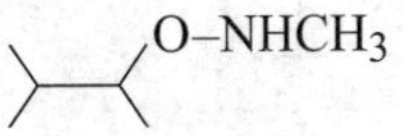 O–$NHCH_3$ derivative (b) 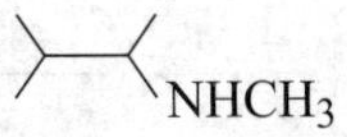 $NHCH_3$ (c) 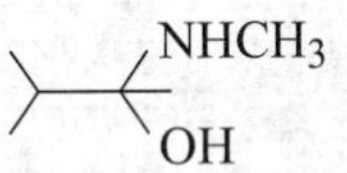 $NHCH_3$, OH (d) 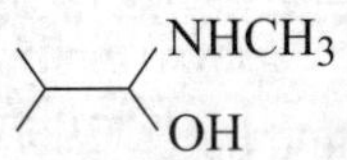 $NHCH_3$, OH

109. Aniline reacts with excess of Br_2/H_2O to give the major product

(a) 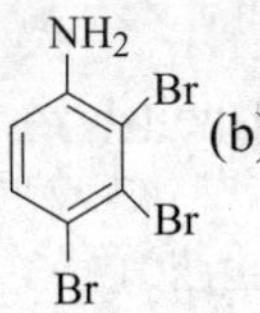 NH_2; Br, Br, Br (b) 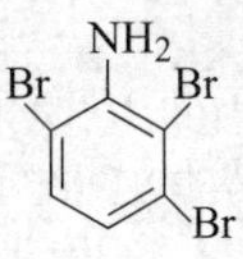 NH_2; Br, Br, Br (c) 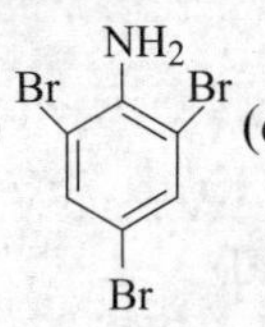 NH_2; Br, Br, Br (2,4,6-tribromoaniline) (d) 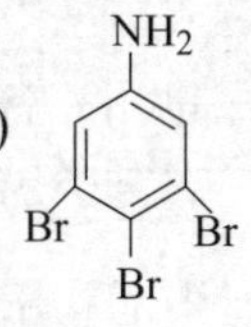 NH_2; Br, Br, Br

110. 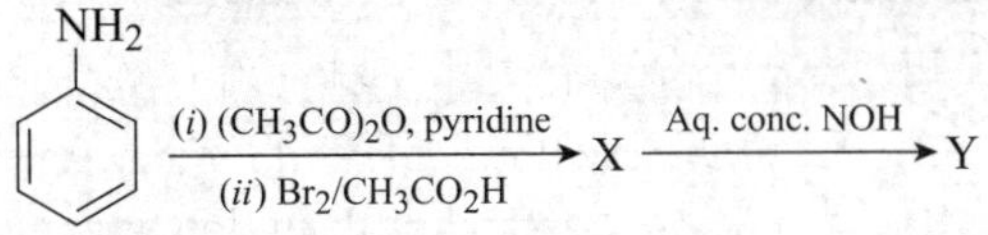 $C_6H_5NH_2$ $\xrightarrow[(ii)\ Br_2/CH_3CO_2H]{(i)\ (CH_3CO)_2O,\ \text{pyridine}}$ X $\xrightarrow{\text{Aq. conc. NOH}}$ Y

X and Y respectively are

(a) 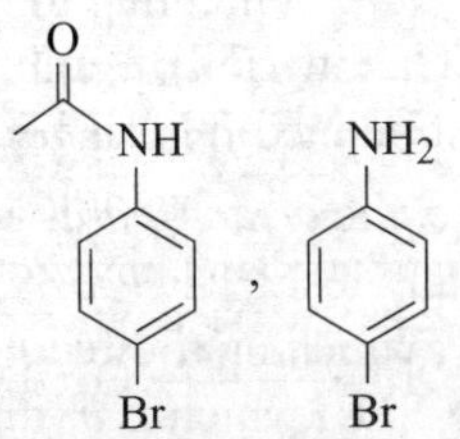 p-Br–C_6H_4–NHCOCH$_3$ (O, NH, Br), p-Br–C_6H_4–NH_2 (NH_2, Br)

(b) 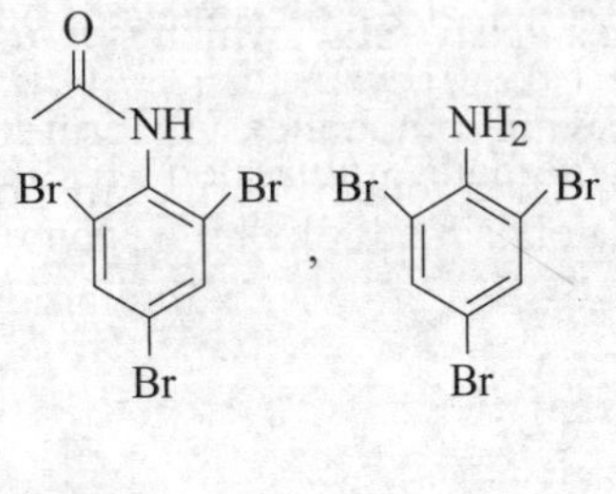 2,4,6-tribromo–C_6H_2–NHCOCH$_3$ (O, NH, Br, Br, Br), 2,4,6-tribromoaniline (NH_2, Br, Br, Br)

(c) [2-amino-5-bromoacetophenone], [2-amino-5-hydroxyacetophenone]

(d) [N-(2,6-dibromophenyl)acetamide], [N-(2,6-dihydroxyphenyl)acetamide]

111. The major product in the following reaction is

Acetanilide $\xrightarrow[\text{conc. } H_2SO_4]{\text{conc. } HNO_3}$

(a) O_2N–C_6H_4–$NHCOCH_3$ (para)
(b) $NHCOCH_3$ with NO_2 at meta position
(c) $NHCOCH_3$ with O_2N (para) and NO_2 (ortho)
(d) $NHCOCH_3$ with NO_2 at ortho position

112. p-Toluidine (NH_2, CH_3) $\xrightarrow{Ac_2O}$ A $\xrightarrow[CH_3COOH]{Br_2}$ B $\xrightarrow[H^+]{H_2O}$ C

C would be

(a) NH_2, $COCH_3$ (ortho), CH_3 (para)
(b) $COCH_3$, Br (ortho), CH_3 (para)
(c) NH_2, Br (ortho), CH_3 (para)
(d) $NHCOCH_3$, Br (ortho), CH_3 (para)

113. The amino group is *ortho, para* – directing for aromatic electrophilic substitution. On nitration of aniline, a good amount of -nitroaniline is obtained. This is because,

(a) in the nitration mixture, the *ortho-*, *para-* activity of NH_2 group is completely lost
(b) $-NH_2$ becomes $-NH_3^+$, which in *m*-directing
(c) $-NH_2$ becomes $-NH^+-SO_4^-$, which is *m*-directing
(d) $-NH_2$ becomes $-NH^--SO_2^+$, which is *m*-directing

114. Which of the following compounds will form significant amount of the meta product during mononitration reaction?

(a) $C_6H_5NH_2$ (b) $C_6H_5NHCOCH_3$ (c) C_6H_5OH (d) $C_6H_5OCOCH_3$

115. Nitration of aniline in a strong acidic medium also gives *m*-nitroaniline because

(a) inspite of substituents, the nitro group always goes to only the *m*-position
(b) in electrophilic substitution reactions, the amino group is *m*-directing
(c) in the absence of substituents, the nitro group always goes to the *m*-position
(d) in an acidic (strong) medium, aniline is present as the anilinium ion

116. Anilinium hydrogen sulfate on heating with sulfuric acid at 453–473 produces

(a) benzenesulfonic acid
(b) anthranilic acid
(c) aniline
(d) *m*-aminobenzenesulfonic acid
(e) sulfanilic acid

117. Which of the following exists as a zwitter ion?

(a) *p*-aminophenol (b) salicyalic acid
(c) sulfanilic acid (d) *p*-aminobenzoic acid

118. The major product in the reaction of N-phenylbenzamide with Br_2/Fe is

(a) Br (meta)–C_6H_4–CONH–C_6H_5
(b) C_6H_5–CONH–C_6H_4–Br (para)
(c) C_6H_5–CONH–C_6H_4–Br (ortho)
(d) Br–C_6H_4–CONH–C_6H_5 (para)
(e) Br (meta)–C_6H_4–CONH–C_6H_5

119. C_6H_5COOH $\xrightarrow[2\Delta]{1NH_3}$ P $\xrightarrow{NaOBr}$ Q $\xrightarrow[\text{2. Heat to 460 K}]{\text{1. Conc.} H_2SO_4}$ R

R is

(a) *o*-bromosulfanilic acid
(b) sulfanilamide
(c) sulfanilic acid
(d) *p*-bromo sulfanilamide

120. An aliphatic amine on treatment with alcoholic carbon disulfide and mercuric chloride forms ethyl isothiocyanate. The reaction is known as

(a) Hofmann's reaction
(b) Hofmann's rearrangement

(c) Hofmann's mustard oil reaction
(d) Hofmann's bromamide degradation reaction

121. Which gives a black precipitate on reaction with CS_2 following addition of $HgCl_2$?

(a) $(CH_3)_3CHN_2$ (b) $(C_2H_5)_2NH$
(c) $(CH_3)_3N$ (d) all the three

122. The product of the following reaction

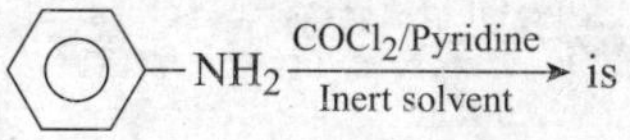

$$C_6H_5-NH_2 \xrightarrow[\text{Inert solvent}]{COCl_2/\text{Pyridine}} \text{is}$$

(a) 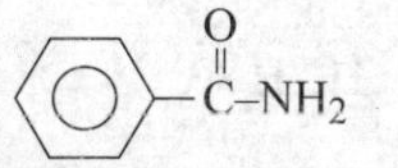 $C_6H_5-\overset{O}{\overset{\|}{C}}-NH_2$ (b) 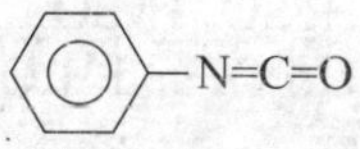 $C_6H_5-N{=}C{=}O$
(c) 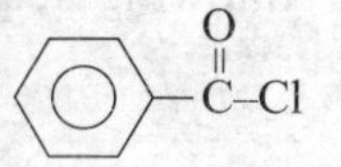 $C_6H_5-\overset{O}{\overset{\|}{C}}-Cl$ (d) 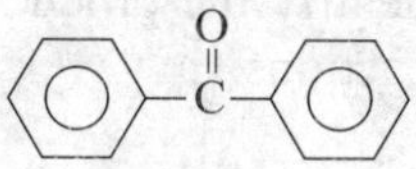 $C_6H_5-\overset{O}{\overset{\|}{C}}-C_6H_5$

123. Which among the following amines can be directly oxidised to the corresponding nitro compound by potassium permanganate?

(a) CH_3NH_2 (b) $(CH_3)_2NH$
(c) $C_6H_5NH_2$ (d) $(CH_3)_3C–NH_2$
(e) $(CH_3)_2CH–NH_2$

124. Acetamide and ethylamine can be distinguished by reacting with

(a) aqueous HCl and heating
(b) aqueous NaOH and heating
(c) acidified $KMnO_4$
(d) bromine water

125. The correct sequence of reaction to be performed to convert benzene into *m*-bromoaniline is

(a) nitration, reduction, bromination
(b) bromination, nitration, reduction
(c) nitration, bromination, reduction
(d) reduction, nitration, bromination

126. The compound shown below

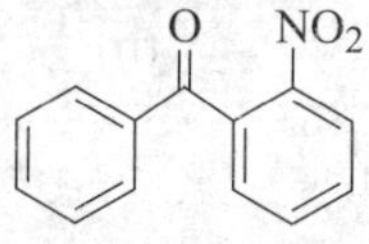

$$C_6H_5-\overset{O}{\overset{\|}{C}}-C_6H_4(NO_2)$$

can be prepared by Friedel–Crafts reaction between

(a) benzene and 2-nitrobenzoyl chloride
(b) benzyl chloride and nitrobenzene
(c) nitrobenzene and benzoyl chloride
(d) benzene and 2-nitrobenzyl chloride

127. The correct statement regarding the basicity of arylamines is

(a) arylamines are generally more basic than alkylamines because of the aryl group
(b) arylamines are generally more basic than alkylamines because the nitrogen atom in arylamines is *sp*-hybridised
(c) arylamines are generally less basic than alkylamines because the lone pair of electrons on nitrogen are delocalised by interaction with the aromatic ring π-electron system
(d) arylamines are generally more basic than alkylamines because the lone pair of electrons on nitrogen are not delocalised by interaction with the aromatic ring π-electron system.

Diazonium Salts

128. Which of the following will be the most stable diazonium salt, $RN_2^+X^-$

(a) $CH_3N_2^+X^-$ (b) $C_6H_5N_2^+X^-$
(c) $CH_3CH_2N_2^+X^-$ (d) $C_6H_5CH_2N_2^+X^-$

129. Which of the following diazonium salts is the most stable?

(a) *p*-nitrobenzenediazonium chloride
(b) 2,4-dinitrobenzenediazonium chloride
(c) 2,4,6-trinitrobenzenediazonium chloride
(d) *p*-methoxybenzenediazonium chloride

130. Aniline is treated with bromine water to give an organic compound X which when treated with $NaNO_2$ and HCl at 0°C gives a water-soluble compound Y. Compound Y on treatment with Cu_2Cl_2 and HCl gives Z. Compound Z is

(a) *o*-bromochlorobenene
(b) *p*-bromochlorobenzene
(c) 2,4,6-tribromophenol
(d) 2,4,6-tribromochlorobenzene
(e) 2,4-dibromophenol

131. The reaction of *o*-chloroaniline with a mixture of HCl and $NaNO_2$ followed by cuprous bromide dissolved in HBr will give

(a) 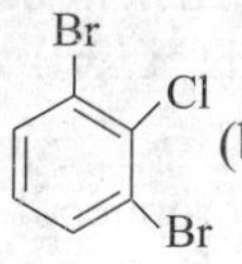 Br, Cl, Br (b) 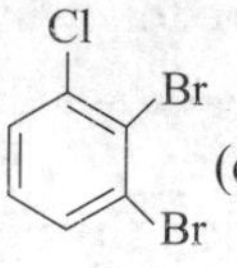 Cl, Br, Br (c) 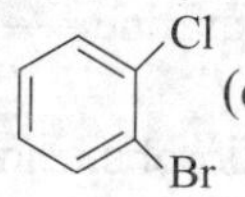 Cl, Br (d) 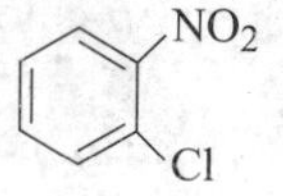 NO_2, Cl

132. Which of the following is the best method for the synthesis of 1-bromo-3-chlorobenzene?

(a) 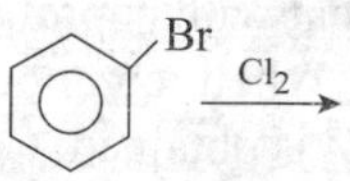 $C_6H_5Br \xrightarrow{Cl_2}$

(b) 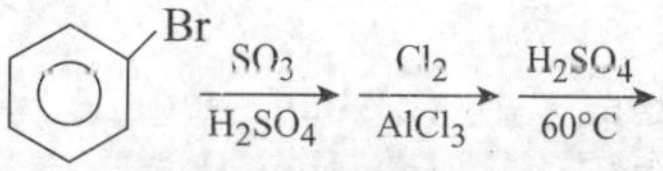 $C_6H_5Br \xrightarrow[H_2SO_4]{SO_3} \xrightarrow[AlCl_3]{Cl_2} \xrightarrow[60°C]{H_2SO_4}$

(c) $C_6H_5NO_2 \xrightarrow[AlCl_3]{Cl_2} \xrightarrow[HCl]{Zn} \xrightarrow[Cold]{HNO_2} \xrightarrow{Cu_2Br_2}$

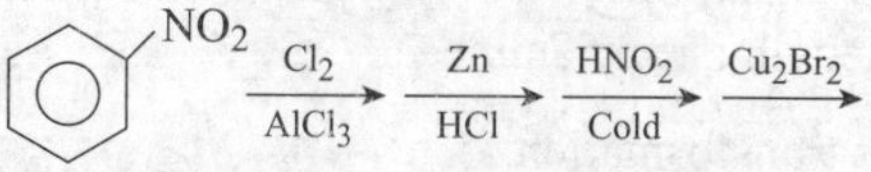

(d) 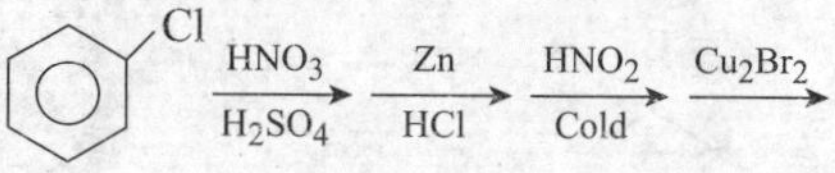 $C_6H_5Cl \xrightarrow[H_2SO_4]{HNO_3} \xrightarrow[HCl]{Zn} \xrightarrow[Cold]{HNO_2} \xrightarrow{Cu_2Br_2}$

133. The product(s) of the following reaction sequence is(are)

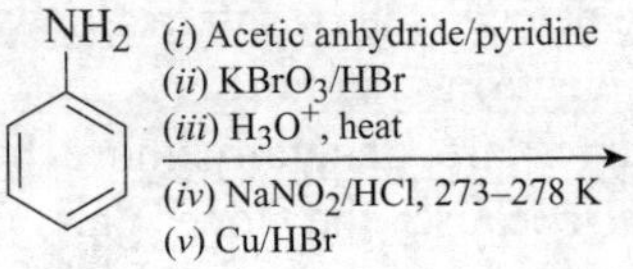

NH_2 (benzene) → (i) Acetic anhydride/pyridine (ii) $KBrO_3/HBr$ (iii) H_3O^+, heat (iv) $NaNO_2/HCl$, 273–278 K (v) Cu/HBr

(a) 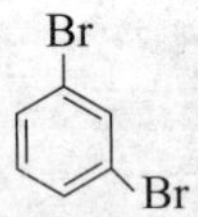 Br, Br (b) 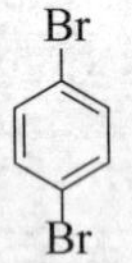 Br, Br (c) 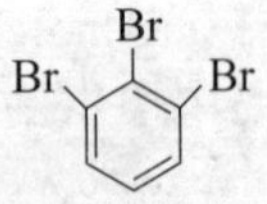 Br, Br, Br (d) 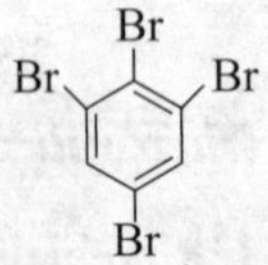 Br, Br, Br

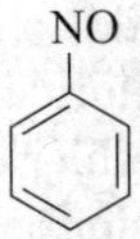

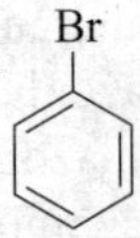

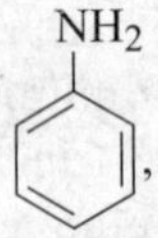

134. The products X and Y in the following reaction sequence are

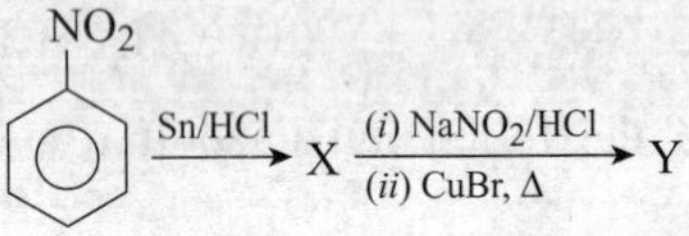

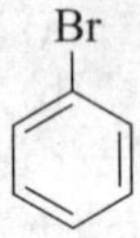

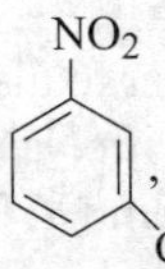

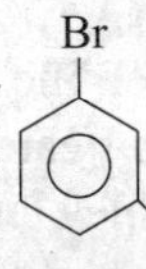

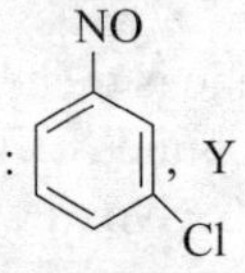

NO_2 (benzene) $\xrightarrow{Sn/HCl}$ X $\xrightarrow[(ii)\ CuBr,\ \Delta]{(i)\ NaNO_2/HCl}$ Y

(a) X: NO, Y: Br (b) X: NH_2, Y: Br

(c) X: NO_2, Cl, Y: Br, Cl (d) X: NO, Cl, Y: Cl, Cl

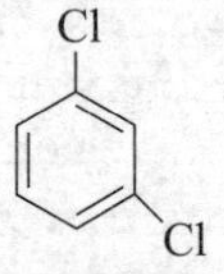

135. Aniline is reacted with bromine water and the resulting product is treated with an aqueous solution of sodium nitrite in the presence of dilute HCl. The compound so formed is converted into tetrafluoroborate which is subsequently heated dry. The final product is

(a) *p*-bromofluorobenzene
(b) *p*-bromoaniline
(c) 2,4,6-tribromofluorobenzene
(d) 1,3,5-tribromobenzene

136. The final product in the following reaction sequence is

p-chloroaniline $\xrightarrow[0°-5°C]{NaNO_2/HCl}$? $\xrightarrow{KCN}$? $\xrightarrow{LiAlH_4}$

(a) *p*-chlorobenzamide (b) p-chlorophenol
(c) *p*-chlorobenzylamine (d) *p*-chlorobenzyl alcohol

137. Aniline is treated with $NaNO_2$/HCl at 0°C to give compound X which on treatment with cuprous cyanide gives another compound Y. When compound Y is treated with H_2/Ni compound Z is obtained. Compound Z is

(a) benzyl alcohol (b) benzylamine
(c) N-ethylaniline (d) phenol
(e) phenylhydroxylamine

138. For the transformation,

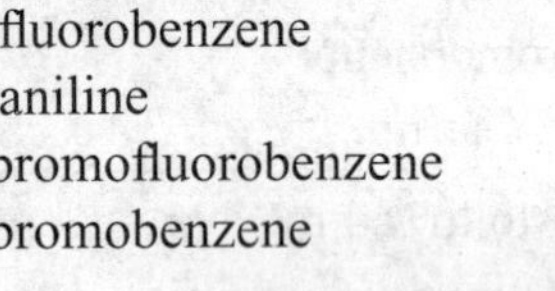

Br, N_2Cl (benzene) → Br (benzene)

The reagent used is
(a) $LiAlH_4$ (b) H_3PO_2 (c) H_3O^+ (d) H_2/Pt

139. In the reaction,

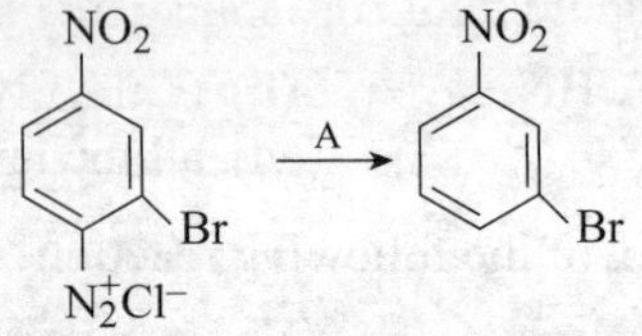

NO_2, Br, $N_2^+Cl^-$ (benzene) $\xrightarrow{A}$ NO_2, Br (benzene)

A is,
(a) $HgSO_4/H_2SO_4$ (b) Cu_2Cl_2
(c) H_3PO_2 and H_2O (d) H^+/H_2O

140. Identify the product (E) in the following sequence of reactions.

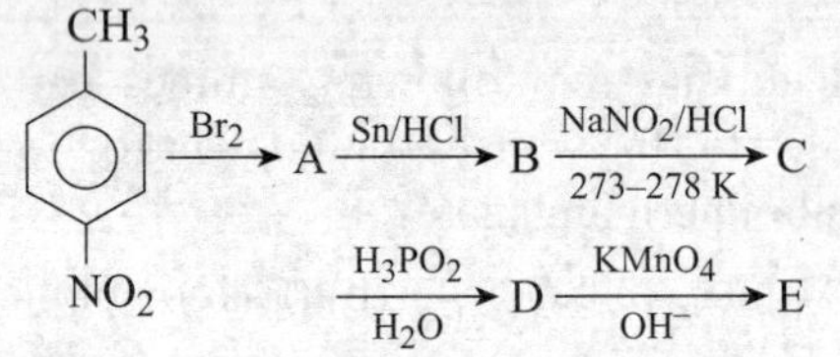

CH_3, NO_2 (benzene) $\xrightarrow{Br_2}$ A $\xrightarrow{Sn/HCl}$ B $\xrightarrow[273-278\ K]{NaNO_2/HCl}$ C $\xrightarrow[H_2O]{H_3PO_2}$ D $\xrightarrow[OH^-]{KMnO_4}$ E

(a) 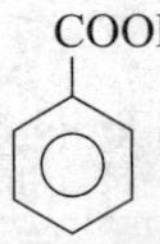 COOH (b) 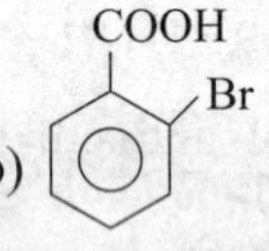 COOH, Br
(c) 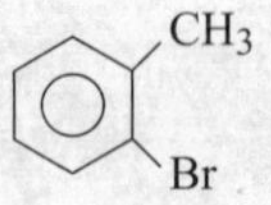 CH_3, Br (d) CH_3, O_2N, Br

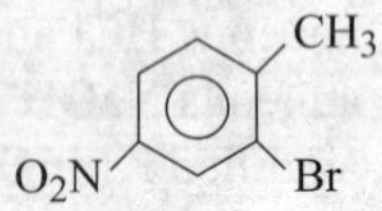

141. In the following reaction sequence, predict the compounds X and Y.

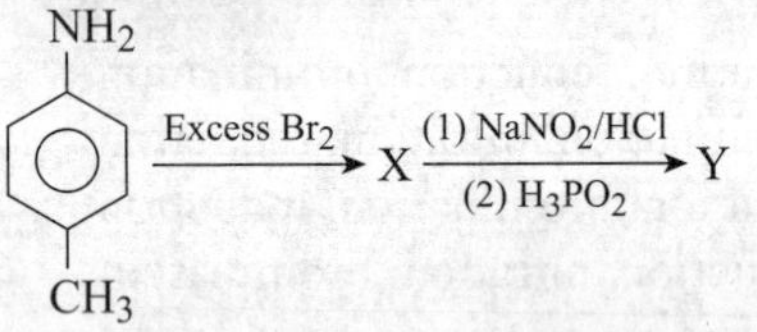

NH_2, CH_3 (benzene) $\xrightarrow{Excess\ Br_2}$ X $\xrightarrow[(2)\ H_3PO_2]{(1)\ NaNO_2/HCl}$ Y

(a) 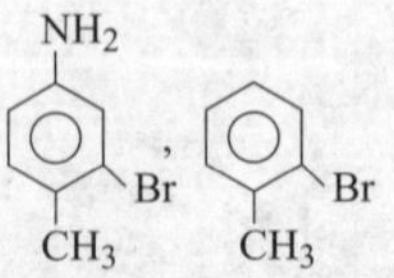 NH_2, Br, CH_3 ; Br, CH_3
(b) 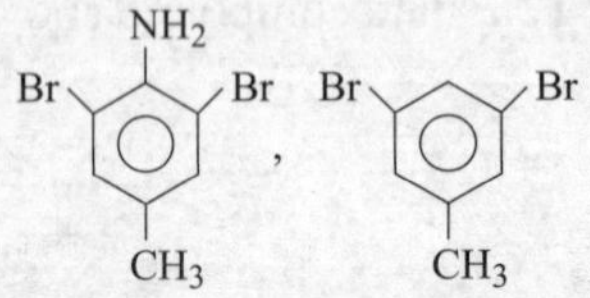 NH_2, Br, Br, CH_3 ; Br, Br, CH_3
(c) 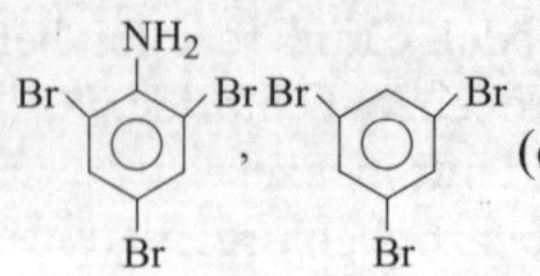 NH_2, Br, Br, Br ; Br, Br, Br
(d) 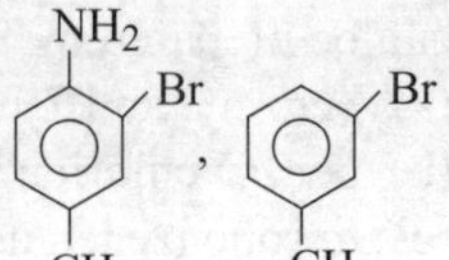 NH_2, Br, CH_3 ; Br, CH_3
(e) 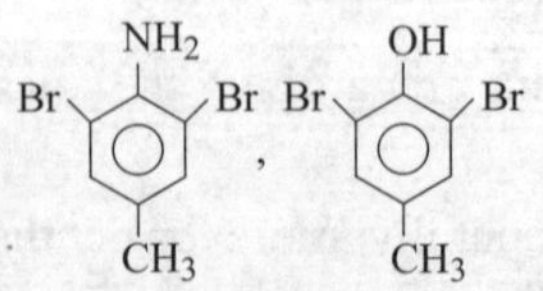 NH_2, Br, Br, CH_3 ; OH, Br, Br, CH_3

142. In the following reaction, X is

X $\xrightarrow{Bromination}$ Y $\xrightarrow{NaNO_2/HCl}$ Z $\xrightarrow{Boiling}$ sym-tribromobenzene

(a) benzoic acid (b) salicylic acid
(c) phenol (d) aniline

143. $C_6H_5NO_2 \xrightarrow[273\,K]{Fe/HCl} A \xrightarrow[283\,K]{NaNO_2/HCl} B \xrightarrow{H_2O}$

(a) C_6H_5OH (b) $C_6H_5CH_2OH$
(c) C_6H_5CHO (d) $C_6H_5NH_2$

144. The correct sequence of reactions to convert *p*-nitrophenol into quinol involves

(a) reduction, diazotisation and hydrolysis
(b) hydrolysis, diazotisation and reduction
(c) hydrolysis, reduction and diazotisation
(d) diazotisation, reduction and hydrolysis

145. Consider the following sequence of reactions

m-toluidine (CH_3, NH_2) $\xrightarrow[273\text{–}278\,K]{NaNO_3/HBF_4} A \xrightarrow[\Delta]{NaNO_2/Cu} B$

Compounds A and B are, respectively,

(a) toluene (CH_3), o-nitrotoluene (CH_3, NO_2)
(b) m-fluorotoluene (CH_3, F), (CH_3, NO_2, F)
(c) (CH_3, $N_2^+BF_4^-$), m-nitrotoluene (CH_3, NO_2)
(d) (CH_3, $N_2^+BF_4^-$), $CH_3-C_6H_4-NO_2$

146. The product formed when bromobenzene reacts with benzenediazonium chloride in the presence of NaOH is

(a) diphenyl
(b) *p*-bromodiphenyl
(c) *p,p*'-dibromodiphenyl
(d) *p*-bromoazobenzene

147. Reduction of benzenediazonium chloride with aqueous sodium sulfite gives

(a) $C_6H_5SO_3H$ (b) $H_3\overset{+}{N}-C_6H_4-SO_3^-$
(c) $C_6H_5-NHNH_2$ (d) $(C_6H_5\overset{+}{N}H_3)_2SO_3^{2-}$

148. The product of the reaction

$HO-C_6H_5 + C_6H_5-N_2Cl \xrightarrow{base}$ is

(a) $C_6H_5-N{=}N-C_6H_4-OH$
(b) $C_6H_5-O-C_6H_5$
(c) $C_6H_5-C_6H_5$ (d) $C_6H_5-C_6H_4-OH$

149. A compound A has a molecular formula C_7H_7NO. On treatment with Br_2 and KOH, A gives an amine B which gives the carbylamine test. B upon diazotisation and coupling with phenol gives an azo dye. A can be

(a) $C_6H_5CONHCOCH_3$ (b) $C_6H_5CONH_2$
(c) $C_6H_5NO_2$
(d) *o*-, *m*- or *p*-$C_6H_4(NH_2)CHO$

150. In the following reaction,

$C_6H_5-\overset{+}{N}{\equiv}NCl^- + C_6H_5-NH_2 \xrightarrow{H^+} \underset{\text{Yellow dye}}{A}$; is

(a) $C_6H_5-N{=}N-NH-C_6H_5$
(b) $C_6H_5-N{=}N-C_6H_4(NH_2)$ (o-)
(c) $C_6H_5-N{=}N-C_6H_4-NH_2$ (m-)
(d) $C_6H_5-N{=}N-C_6H_4-NH_2$ (p-)

151. In a reaction of aniline, a coloured product C was obtained.

$\underset{A}{C_6H_5NH_2} \xrightarrow[HCl]{NaNO_2} B \xrightarrow[\text{cold}]{C_6H_5-N(CH_3)_2} C$

The structure of C would be

(a) $C_6H_5-NH-NH-C_6H_4-N(CH_3)_2$
(b) $C_6H_5-N{=}N-C_6H_4-N(CH_3)_2$
(c) $C_6H_5-N{=}N-CH_2-N(CH_3)-C_6H_5$
(d) $CH_3C_6H_4-N{=}N-C_6H_4CH_3$ (o,o')

152. Coupling of diazonium salts with the following species takes place. The reactivity order is,

$C_6H_5O^-$ (I), C_6H_5OH (II), $C_6H_5NH_2$ (III), $C_6H_5\overset{+}{N}H_3$ (IV)

(a) IV < II < III < I (b) IV < III < II < I
(c) II < IV < I < III (d) I < II < III < IV

153. A given nitrogen-containing aromatic compound A reacts with Sn/HCl, followed by HNO_2 to give an unstable compound B.B on treatment with phenol, forms a beautiful coloured compound C with the molecular formula $C_{12}H_{10}N_2O$. The structure of compound A is

(a) 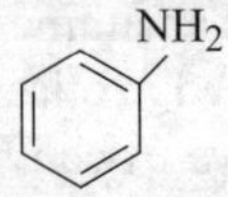 NH_2 (b) 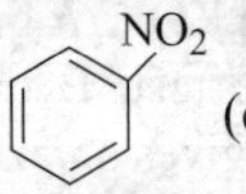 NO_2 (c) 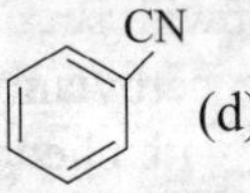 CN (d) 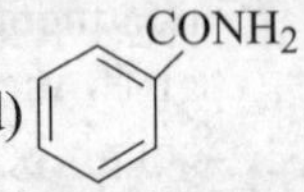 $CONH_2$

154. Amongst the compounds given, the one that would form a brilliant coloured dye on treatment with $NaNO_2$ in dil. HCl followed by addition in an alkaline solution of β-naphthol is

(a) 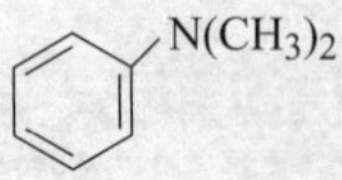 $N(CH_3)_2$ (b) 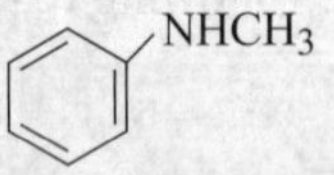 $NHCH_3$

(c) 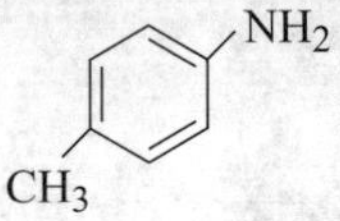 NH_2, CH_3 (d) 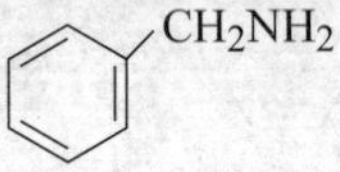 CH_2NH_2

155. In the following reactions, the major product W is

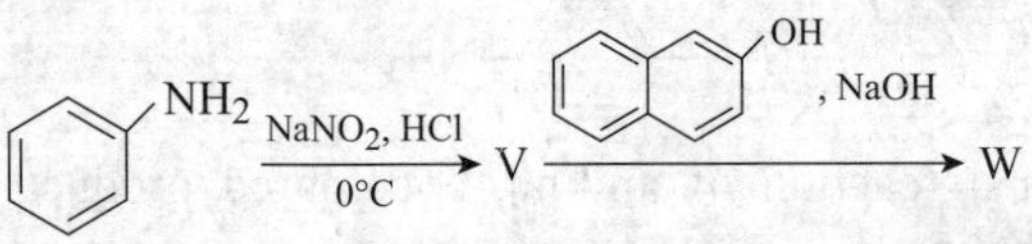

NH_2 $\xrightarrow[0°C]{NaNO_2,\ HCl}$ V $\xrightarrow{\text{OH (naphthol)},\ NaOH}$ W

(a) N=N, OH (b) N=N, OH

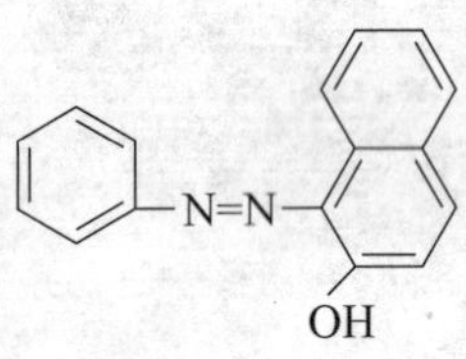

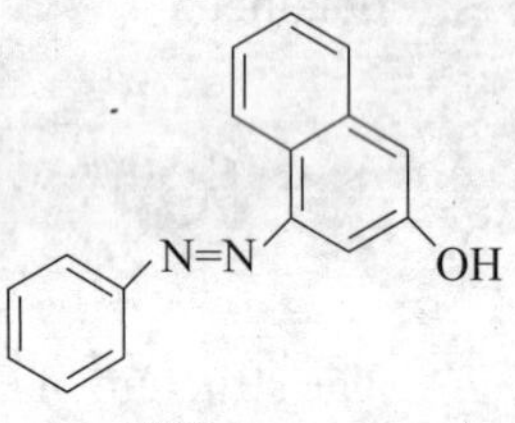

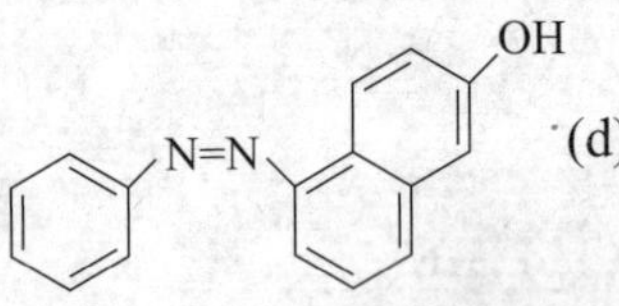

(c) N=N, OH (d) 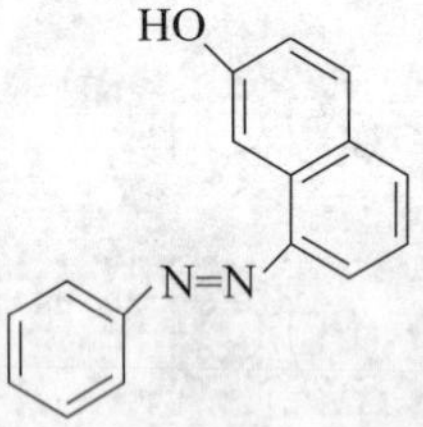 HO, N=N

156. The dye test can be used to distinguish between

(a) ethylamine and acetamide
(b) ethylamine and aniline
(c) urea and acetamide
(d) methylamine and ethylamine

157. The tests performed on compound X and their inferences are given below. Identify X.

Test	Inference
(A) 2,4-DNP test	Coloured precipitate
(B) Iodoform test	Yellow precipitate
(C) Azo dye test	No dye formation

(a) 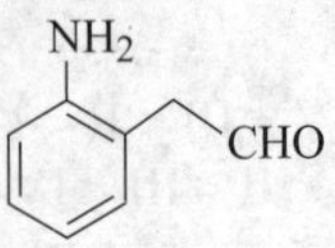 NH_2, CHO (b) 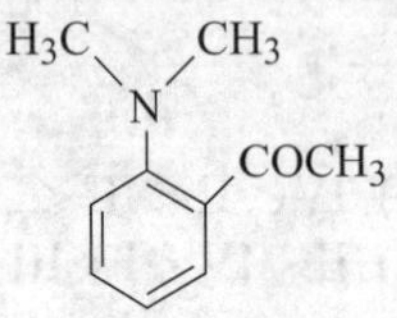 H_3C, CH_3, N, $COCH_3$

(c) 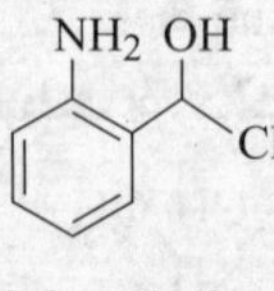 NH_2 OH, CH_3 (d) 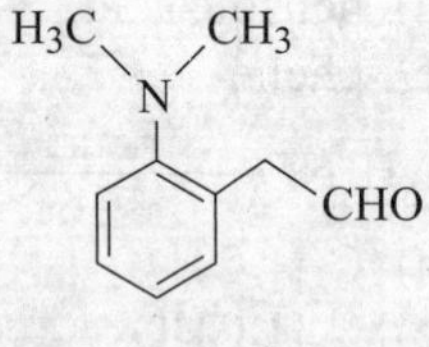 H_3C, CH_3, N, CHO

158. Which of the following statements about primary amines is 'False'?

(a) Alkylamines are stronger bases than ammonia.
(b) Alkylamines are stronger bases than aryl amines.
(c) Alkylamines react with nitrous acid to produce alcohols.
(a) Arylamines react with nitrous acid to produce phenols.

159. In the diazotisation of arylamine, the use of nitrous acid

(a) suppresses hydrolysis to give phenol
(b) acts as a source of electrophilic nitrosonium ion
(c) neutralises the base liberated
(d) does all the three above

160. During preparation of arenediazonium salts, the excess of nitrous acid, if any, is destroyed by adding

(a) aq. NaOH (b) aq. Na_2CO_3
(c) aq. NH_2CONH_2 (d) aq. KI

161. Which of the following arylamines is most difficult to diazotise?

(a) 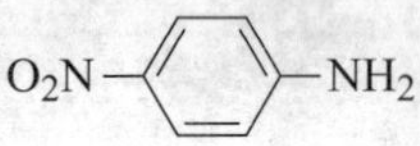 $O_2N-C_6H_4-NH_2$ (b) $Cl-C_6H_4-NH_2$

(c) $CH_3O-C_6H_4-NH_2$ (d)  $CH_3-C_6H_4-NH_2$

Final Preparation

162. The major product of the following reaction is

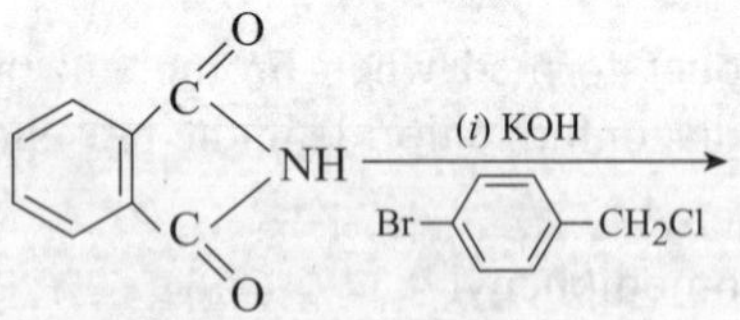

(phthalimide: C=O, NH, C=O) $\xrightarrow{(i)\ KOH,\ Br-C_6H_4-CH_2Cl}$

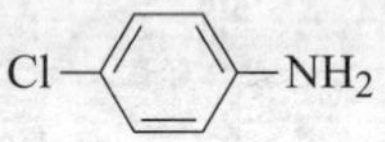

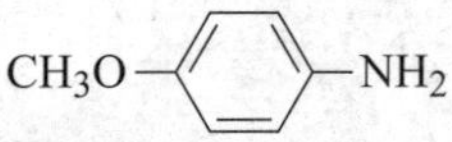

(a) 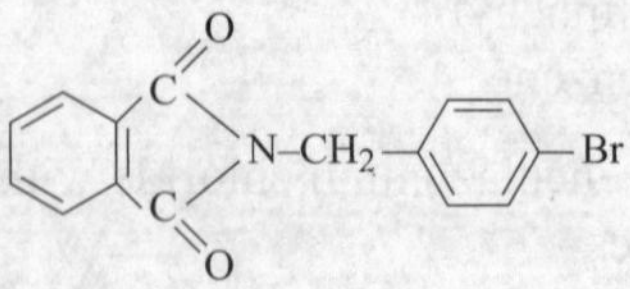 C=O, N–CH_2–C_6H_4–Br, C=O

(b) C=O, N–C_6H_4–CH_2Cl, C=O

(c) C=O, N, C–O–CH_2–C_6H_4–Br

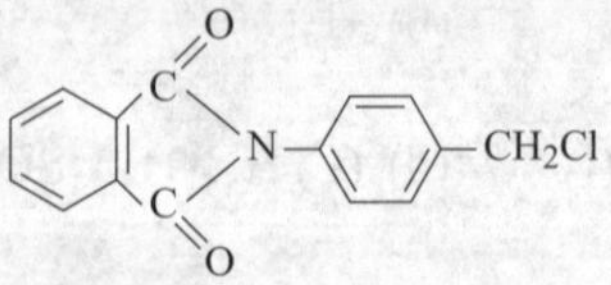

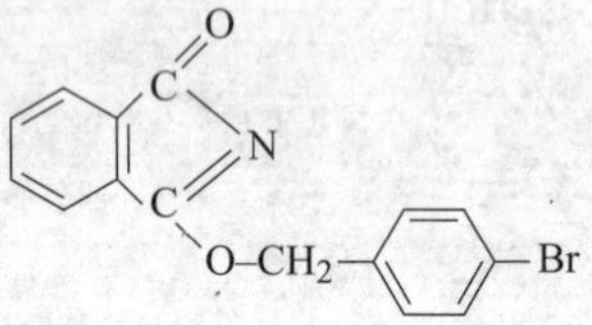

d) 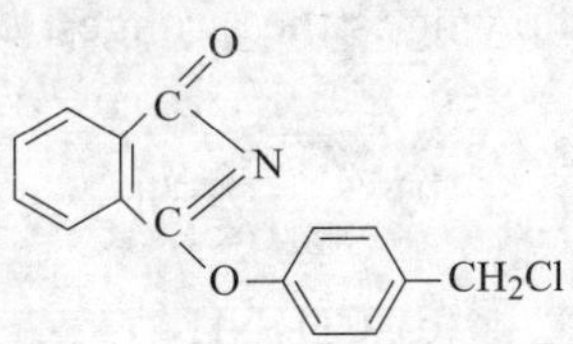 [structure: phthalimide N-linked via C(=O)–O– to a benzene ring bearing CH_2Cl]

163. To synthesise phenylalanine by Gabriel's phthalimide reaction, one needs potassium phthalimide and the ester of

(a) 3-phenylpropanoic acid
(b) 2-chloro-3-phenylpropanoic acid
(c) phenylacetic acid
(d) 2-chlorophenylacetic acid

164. In a set of reactions, *m*-bromobenzoic acid gave a product D. Identify the product D.

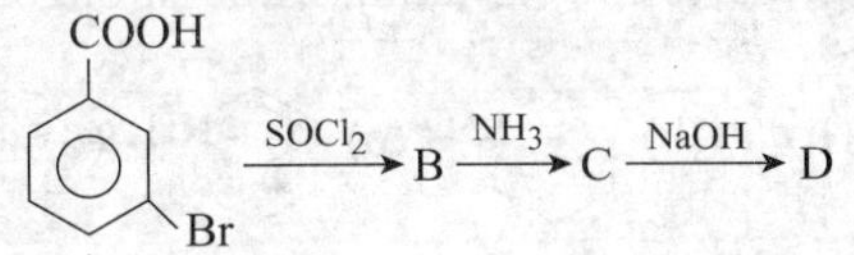

$$\underset{\text{A}}{m\text{-}BrC_6H_4COOH} \xrightarrow{SOCl_2} B \xrightarrow{NH_3} C \xrightarrow{NaOH} D$$

(a) m-Br–C6H4–CONH2 (b) m-Br–C6H4–SO2NH2
(c) m-NH2–C6H4–CONH2 (d) m-Br–C6H4–NH2

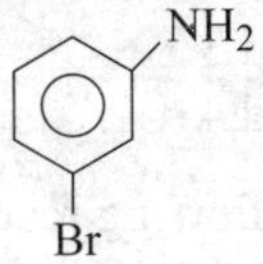

165. *m*-Bromoaniline can be prepared by

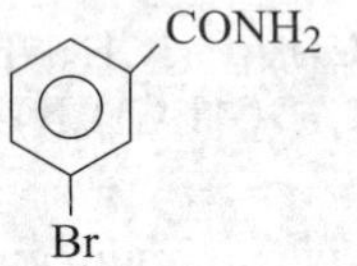

(a) $C_6H_6 \xrightarrow[H_2SO_4]{HNO_3} \xrightarrow[2.\ NaOH,\ H_2SO_4]{1.\ Sn-HCl} \xrightarrow[H_2O]{Br_2}$

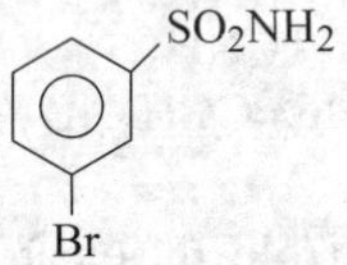

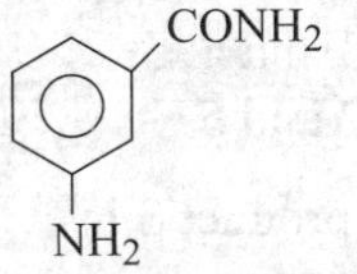

(b) $C_6H_6 \xrightarrow[FeBr_3]{Br_2} \xrightarrow[H_2SO_4]{HNO_3} \xrightarrow[Pt]{H_2}$

(c) $m\text{-}BrC_6H_4COOH \xrightarrow{SOCl_2} \xrightarrow{NH_3} \xrightarrow[H^+]{Br_2,\ NaOH}$

(d) $C_6H_5NH_2 \xrightarrow[Cu_2Br_2]{NaNO_2,\ HCl} \xrightarrow{NaNH_2}$

166. The following sequence of reactions on A gives

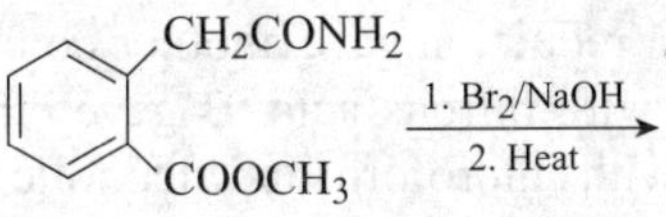

$$o\text{-}(CH_2CONH_2)C_6H_4(COOCH_3) \xrightarrow[2.\ Heat]{1.\ Br_2/NaOH}$$

(a) [isochroman-1,3-dione] (b) [isoquinoline-1,3-dione (homophthalimide, NH)]
(c) [isoindolin-1-one (NH)] (d) 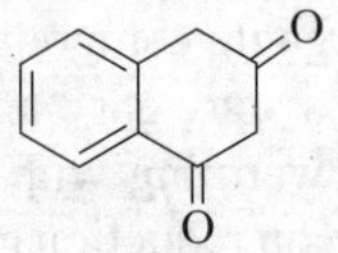 [2-tetralone-type diketone]

167. 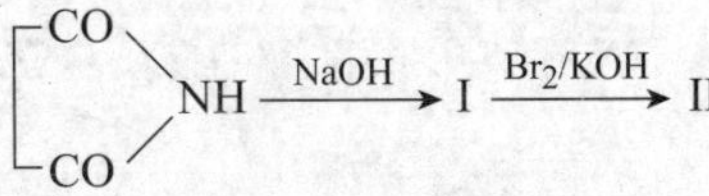 $\left[\begin{matrix}CO \\ CO\end{matrix}\right]NH \xrightarrow{NaOH} I \xrightarrow{Br_2/KOH} II$

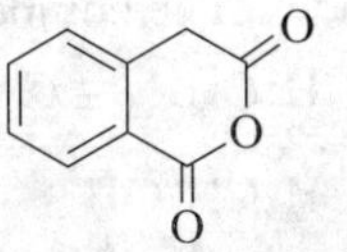

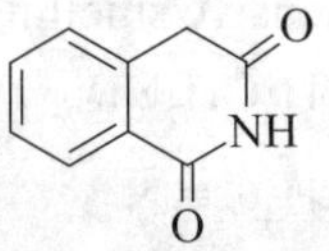

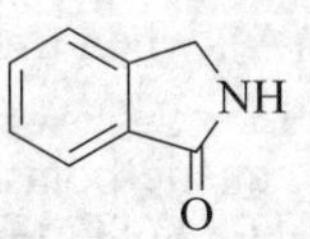

(a) β-alanine (b) α-alanine
(c) ethylenediamine (d) γ-aminobutyric acid

168. Identify M in the following sequence of reactions.

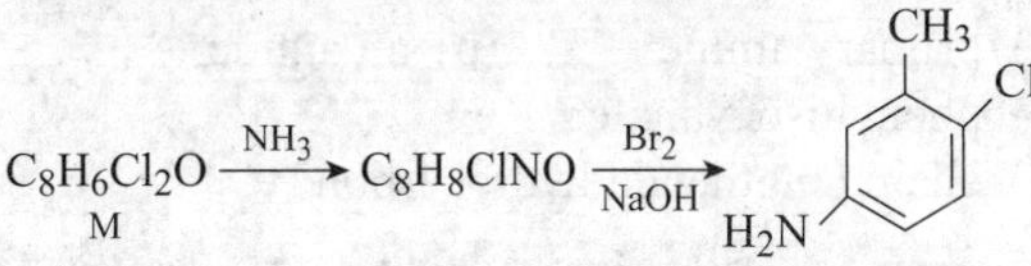

$$\underset{M}{C_8H_6Cl_2O} \xrightarrow{NH_3} C_8H_8ClNO \xrightarrow[NaOH]{Br_2} \text{4-amino-2-chlorotoluene } (CH_3, Cl, H_2N \text{ on ring})$$

(a) [benzoyl chloride with Cl and H_3N on ring] (b) [benzoyl chloride with Cl and CH_3 on ring]
(c) [benzene with CHO, Cl and CH_2Cl] (d) 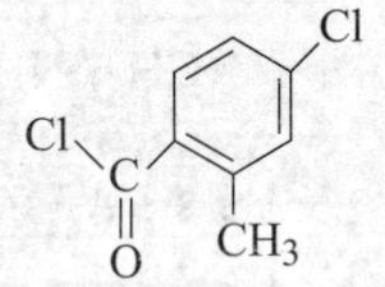 [benzoyl chloride with Cl and CH_3 on ring]

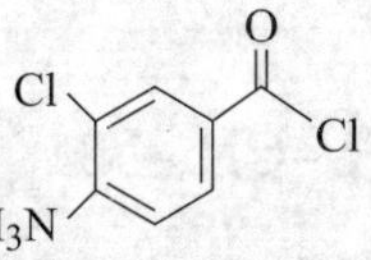

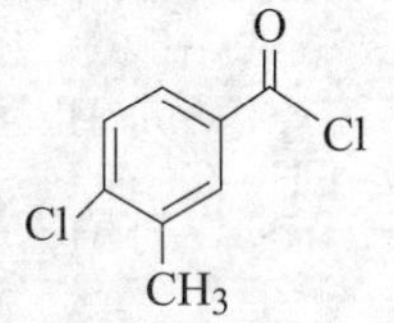

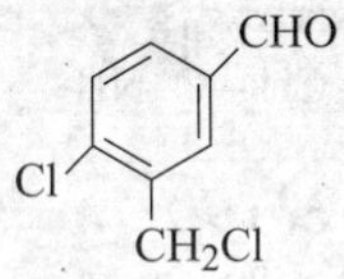

169. Amongst the given set of reactants, the most appropriate for preparing 2° amines is

(a) 2° R–Br + NH_3
(b) 2° R–Br + NaCN followed by H_2/Pt
(c) 1° R–NH_2 + RCHO followed by H_2/Pt
(d) 1° R–Br (2 mol) + potassium phthalimide followed by H_3O^+/heat

170. The product of the following reaction

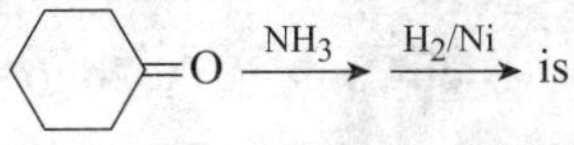

$$\text{cyclohexanone} \xrightarrow{NH_3} \xrightarrow{H_2/Ni} \text{is}$$

(a) 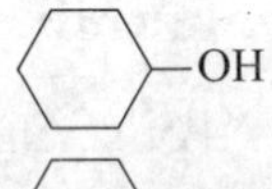 cyclohexyl–OH (b) 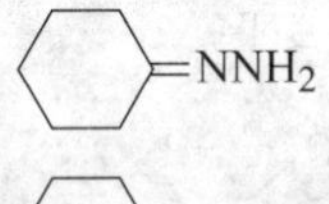 cyclohexylidene=NNH_2
(c) 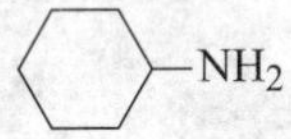 cyclohexyl–NH_2 (d) 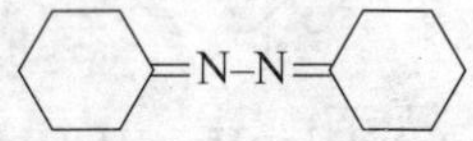 cyclohexylidene=N–N=cyclohexylidene

171. Which of the following procedures would be best for preparing N,N-dimethylcyclohexylamine, $C_6H_{11}N(CH_3)_2$?

(a) 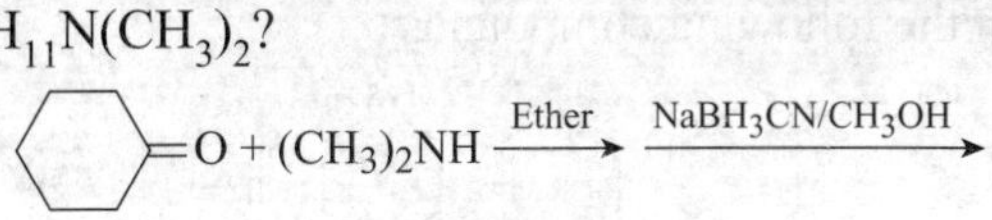 cyclohexanone + $(CH_3)_2NH \xrightarrow{Ether} \xrightarrow{NaBH_3CN/CH_3OH}$

(b) 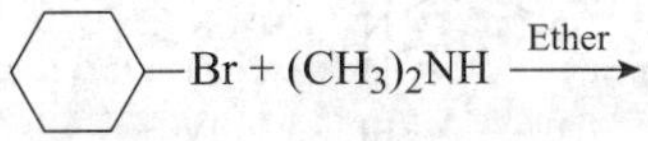 cyclohexyl–Br + $(CH_3)_2NH \xrightarrow{Ether}$

(c) 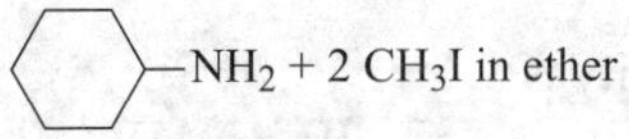 cyclohexyl–NH_2 + 2 CH_3I in ether

(d) 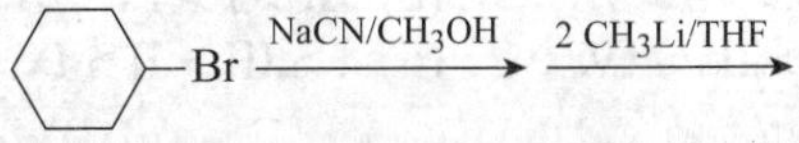 cyclohexyl–Br $\xrightarrow{NaCN/CH_3OH} \xrightarrow{2\ CH_3Li/THF}$

172. Which of the following procedures would be best for preparing isobutylisopropylamine?

(a) $(CH_3)_2CHBr + (CH_3)_2CHCH_2NH_2 \rightarrow$
(b) $(CH_3)_2CHBr + (CH_3)_2CONHNa \xrightarrow{LiAlH_4/Ether}$
(c) $(CH_3)_2CHNH_2 + (CH_3)_2CHCH \rightarrow$
(d) $(CH_3)_2CHCN + (CH_3)_2CHNH_2 \xrightarrow{H_2O}$

173. In the following sequence of reactions, what is D?

Toluene ($C_6H_5CH_3$) $\xrightarrow{[O]}$ A $\xrightarrow{SOCl_2}$ B $\xrightarrow{NaN_3}$ C $\xrightarrow{Heat}$ D

(a) primary amine (b) an amide
(c) phenyl isocyanate
(d) chain lengthened hydrocarbon

174. The correct order of basicity of the following compounds is

1. $CH_3-C(=NH)NH_2$
2. $CH_3-CH_2-NH_2$
3. $(CH_3)_2NH$
4. $CH_3-C(=O)-NH_2$

(a) 2 > 1 > 3 > 4 (b) 1 > 3 > 2 > 4
(c) 3 > 1 > 2 > 4 (d) 1 > 2 > 3 > 4

175. The correct order of basicity of the following compounds is

1. $CH_3CH_2NH_2$
2. $CH_2=CH-NH$
3. $CH_3C(=NH)NH_2$
4. $H_2N-C(=NH)NH_2$

(a) 1 < 2 < 3 < 4 (b) 1 < 2 < 4 < 3
(c) 2 < 1 < 3 < 4 (d) 4 < 3 < 2 < 1

176. The order of basicity among the following compound is

I: $H_3C-C(=NH)NH_2$; II: 2-imidazoline; III: imidazole; IV: $H_2N-C(NH_2)=NH$

(a) IV > II > III > I (b) II > I > IV > III
(c) I > IV > III > I (d) IV > I > II > III

177. In the following compounds

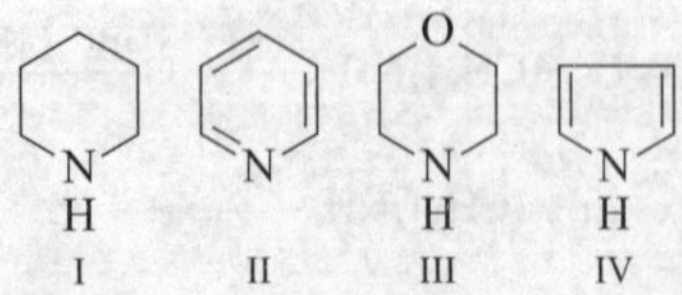

the order of basicity is

(a) IV > I > III > II (b) III > I > IV > II
(c) II > I > III > IV (d) I > III > II > IV

178. The strongest base is

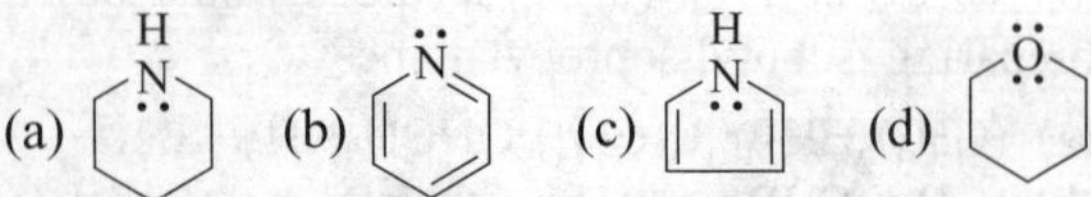

179. The basicity of $CH_3CH_2NH_2$ (I), CH_3CONH_2 (II) and $C_6H_5CONH_2$ (III) follows the order

(a) I > II > III (b) I > III > II
(c) II > III > I (d) III > II > I

180. Which among the following is the strongest conjugate acid?

(a) $C_6H_{11}-\overset{+}{N}H_3$ (cyclohexyl) (b) $C_6H_5-\overset{+}{N}H_3$
(c) $C_6H_5-CH_2\overset{+}{N}H_3$ (d) $CH_3\overset{+}{N}H_3$

181. Which of the following statements is wrong?

(a) Aniline is more acidic than ammonia.
(b) $F-C_6H_4-\overset{+}{N}H_3$ is less than $C_6H_5-\overset{+}{N}H_3$
(c) Amines are less acidic than alcohols of comparable molecular masses.
(d) $RCONH_2$ is more acidic than RCH_2NH_2.
(e) $R-C\equiv N$ is less basic than $R-CH=NH$.

182. Among the following amines, the strongest Bronsted base is

(a) NH_3 (b) piperidine (NH) (c) pyrrole-type ring (NH) (d) aniline (NH_2)

183. The strongest base is

(a) $C_6H_5NH_2$ (b) $CH_2=CHCH_2NH_2$
(c) $HC\equiv CCH_2NH_2$ (d) $CH_3CH_2CH_2NH_2$

184. In pyrrole, the electron density is maximum on (ring numbered N1, 2, 3, 4, 5; N–H)

(a) 2 and 3 (b) 3 and 4
(c) 2 and 4 (d) 2 and 5

185. In the following reactions, the product S is

Methyl-indene (H_3C-substituted) $\xrightarrow[(ii)\ Zn,\ H_2O]{(i)\ O_3}$ R $\xrightarrow{NH_3}$ S

(a) methyl-isoquinoline (H_3C, N) (b) methyl-quinoline (H_3C, N)
(c) methyl-isoquinoline (H_3C, N) (d) methyl-quinoline (H_3C, N)

186. An organic compound A with a molecular formula C_2H_3N, on reduction gave another compound B. Upon treatment with nitrous acid, B gave ethyl alcohol. On warming with chloroform and alcoholic KOH, it formed an offensive smelling compound C. The compound C is

(a) $CH_3CH_2NH_2$ (b) $CH_3CH_2N\equiv C$
(c) $CH_3C\equiv N$ (d) CH_3CH_2OH

187. An organic compound (C_3H_9N) (A), when treated with nitrous acid, gave an alcohol and N_2 gas was evolved. A on warming with $CHCl_3$ and caustic potash gave C which on reduction gave isopropylmethylamine. Predict the structure of A.

(a) $CH_3-CH(CH_3)-NH_2$ (b) $CH_3CH_2-NH-CH_3$

(c) $CH_3-N(CH_3)-CH_3$ (d) $CH_3CH_2CH_2-NH_2$

188. The optically active compound (X) $C_6H_5-\overset{*}{C}H(CH_3)-NH_2$ (X) on treatment with $NaNO_2/HCl$ gives a

(a) 1° alcohol with retention of configuration
(b) 2° alcohol with inversion of configuration
(c) racemic mixture of 2° alcohols
(d) racemic mixture of 1° alcohols

189. An optically active amine ($C_5H_{13}N$) on treatment with aq. $NaNO_2/HCl$ forms an optically inactive alcohol ($C_5H_{12}O$) with evolution of N_2 gas. The amine is

(a) 1-pentanamine (b) 2-pentanamine
(c) 3-pentanamine (d) 2-methylbutanamine

190. 1-Propanamine is treated with nitrous acid at 273 K. Which of the following products is formed besides 1-propanol?

(a) $CH_3CHOHCH_3$ (b) $CH_3CH=CH_2$
(c) $CH_3CH_2CH_2NO_2$ (d) all the three

191. Which of the following product/products is/are formed in the reaction given below``?

NH$_2$ $\xrightarrow[\text{Dil. HCl, 273 K}]{NaNO_2}$

(a) OH (b) OH, CH_3

(c) OH (d) all of these

192. Treatment of cyclobutylmethylamine with nitrous acid does not give

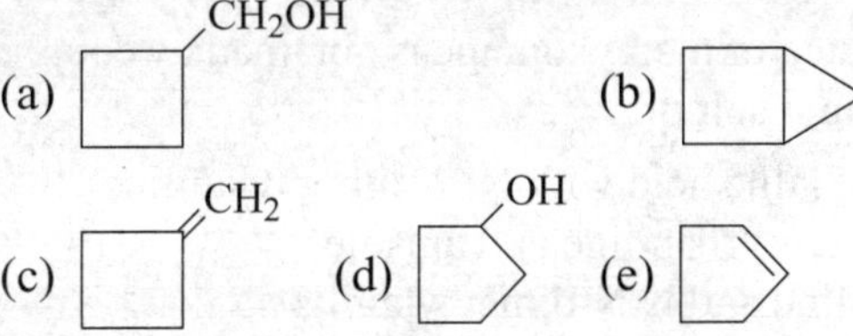

193. Which of the following compounds does not react with HNO_2?

(a) C_6H_5OH (b) $C_6H_5NH_2$
(c) $(CH_3)_3CNO_2$ (d) $(CH_3)_2CHNO_2$

194. Identify the final product,

O, NH$_2$ $\xrightarrow[(ii)\ NaBH_4]{(i)\ Heat}$

(a) O (b) OH, NH$_2$

(c) NH$_2$ (d) N H

195. Consider the following sequence of reactions.

O + N H $\xrightarrow[\Delta]{\text{Benzene}}$ (X) $\xrightarrow[(ii)\ H_3O^+,\ \Delta]{(ii)\ CH_2=CHCH_2Br}$ (Y)

The product (Y) is

(a) N (b) OH

(c) O (d)

196. A compound Z reacts with three moles of CH_3I and gives a product which on hydrolysis gives $[(CH_3)_4N]^+OH^-$. Compound Z is

(a) CH_3NH_2 (b) $(CH_3)_2NH$
(c) $(CH_3)_3N$ (d) $[(CH_3)_4\overset{+}{N}]Cl^-$

197. The compound that will react most readily with NaOH to form methanol is

(a) $(CH_3)_4N^+I^-$ (b) CH_3OCH_3
(c) $(CH_3)_3S^+I^-$ (d) $(CH_3)_3CCl$

198. Me, $\overset{+}{N}$(Me)(Et)(n-Bu) HO^- $\xrightarrow{\Delta}$

The alkene formed as a major product in the above elimination reaction is

(a) Me (b) $CH_2=CH_2$
(c) Me (d) Me

199. In the following reaction,

$\overset{+}{N}(CH_3)(CH_3)$ OH^- $\xrightarrow{\Delta}$ X

The organic product X is

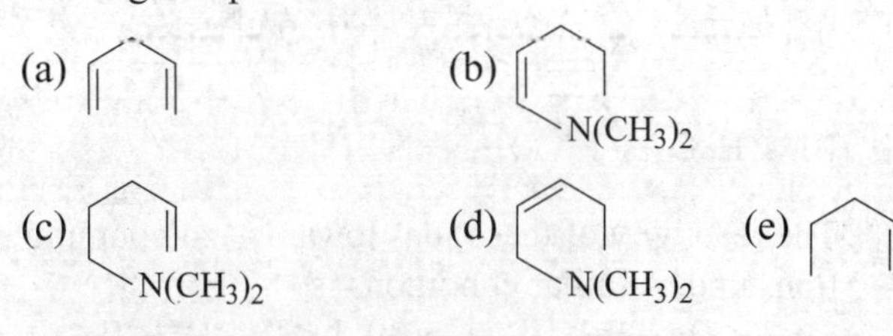

200. When $\left[CH_3CH_2CH_2-\underset{CH_3}{\overset{CH_3}{N}}-CH_2CH_3\right]OH^-$ is heated

(a) propene is the major product
(b) ethane and $C_3H_7N(CH_3)_2$ are the only products
(c) ethane and propene are obtained with ethane as the major product
(d) equimolar amounts of ethane and propene are obtained

201. What is the chief product of Hofmann elimination of 4-methyl-2-aminopentane?

(a) 4-methyl-1-pentene (b) 4-methyl-2-pentene
(c) 2-methyl-1-pentene (d) 2-methyl-2-pentene

202. Cyclohexyl–CH_2–N(O)(CH_3)(CH_3) $\xrightarrow{\Delta}$ methylenecyclohexane ($=CH_2$) + $(CH_3)_2NOH$

This reaction is called

(a) Cope reaction (b) Ritter reaction
(c) Schmidt reaction (d) Gabriel reaction

203. Pyrolysis of $Me_2\overset{+}{N}(O^-)$–CH(Me)(CD_3) would give

(a) mixture of CH_2=CH–CD_3 and CH_3–CH=CD_2
(b) CH_3–CH=CD_2 only
(c) $Me_2\overset{+}{N}$=C(CD_3)(CH_3) only
(d) CH_2=CH–CD_3 only

204. Which of the following diazonium salts when boiled with dil. H_2SO_4 gives the corresponding phenol most readily?

(a) OMe (ortho)–C_6H_4–$\overset{+}{N}\equiv N$ (b) MeO–C_6H_4–$\overset{+}{N}\equiv N$

(c) Me–C_6H_4–$\overset{+}{N}\equiv N$ (d) C_6H_5–$\overset{+}{N}\equiv N$

205. When aniline is treated with a mixture of sodium nitrite and hypophosphorous acid, the product formed is

(a) aniline diazonium hypophosphite
(b) benzene
(c) anilinium hypophosphite
(d) aniline diazonium hypophosphite

206. Consider the following ions

I. Me_2N–C_6H_4–$\overset{+}{N}\equiv N$ II. O_2N–C_6H_4–$\overset{+}{N}\equiv N$

III. CH_3O–C_6H_4–$\overset{+}{N}\equiv N$ IV. CH_3–C_6H_4–$\overset{+}{N}\equiv N$

The reactivity of these ions towards azo coupling reactions under similar conditions is

(a) I < IV < II < III (b) I < III <IV < II
(c) III < I < II < IV (d) III < I < IV < II

207. The major product of the following reaction is

Biphenyl with OH and NH_2 $\xrightarrow[(ii)\ \text{aq. NaOH}]{(i)\ NaNO_2,\ HCl,\ 0°C}$

The product (Y) is

(a) O^-Na^+ / N_2Cl biphenyl (b) OH / Cl biphenyl

(c) N=N bridged biphenyl (d) N=N, OH

208. The major product of the reaction

o-Phenylenediamine (NH_2, NH_2) $\xrightarrow[\text{Dil. HCl, 273 K}]{NaNO_2}$ is

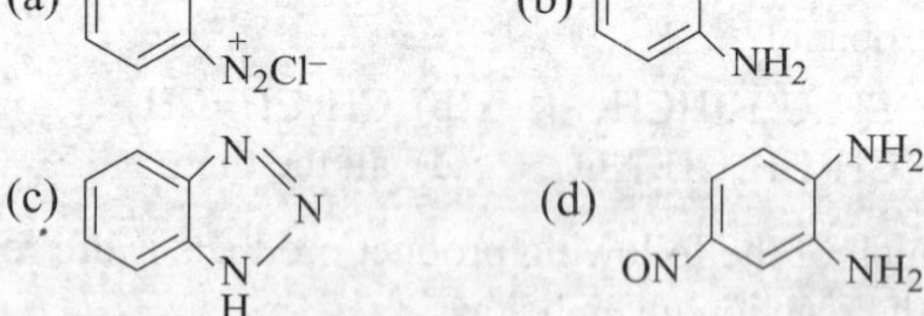

209. 2-Aminodiphenylmethane (NH_2) $\xrightarrow[\text{Dil. } H_2SO_4,\ 278\ K]{NaNO_2}$ is

The product P is

(a) (b)

(c) (d) N_2Cl

210. The indicator methyl orange is obtained by coupling the diazonium salt of

(a) sulfanilic acid with N,N-dimethylaniline
(b) 2,4-dinitroaniline and anisole
(c) aniline and N,N-dimethylaniline
(d) 2,4,6-trinitroaniline with mesitylene

211. The major product of the following reaction is

H_3C–C(=O)–O–C_6H_4–$CH_2CH_2CH_2$–NH_2 $\xrightarrow[\text{(ii) } CrO_3/H^+ \text{ (iii) } H_2SO_4\ (conc.),\ \Delta]{(i)\ NaNO_2/H^+}$

(a) HO, O (b) H_3C, O, O, O

(c) HO, O (d) H_3C, O, O, O

212. Which one of the following on reduction with lithium aluminium hydride yields a secondary amine?
(a) methyl isocyanide (b) acetamide
(c) methyl cyanide (d) nitroethane

213. A nitrogenous substance X is treated with HNO_2 and the product so formed is further treated with NaOH solution, which produces a blue colouration. X can be
(a) $CH_3CH_2NH_2$ (b) $CH_3CH_2NO_2$
(c) CH_3CH_2ONO (d) $(CH_3)_2CHNO_2$

214. Benzaldehyde reacts with methyl amine to give
(a) $C_6H_5NH_2$ (b) $C_6H_5CH_2NO_2$
(c) $C_6H_5CH{=}NCH_3$ (d) $C_6H_5CONH_2$

215. A compound which on reaction with aqueous nitrous acid gives an oily nitrosoamine is
(a) methylamine (b) ethylamine
(c) diethylamine (d) triethylamine

216. Which one of the following compounds when heated with KOH and primary amines gives the carbylamine test?
(a) $CHCl_3$ (b) CH_3Cl (c) CCl_4 (d) CH_3NC

217. The compound, N-ethyl-N-methylpropanamine forms non-superimposable mirror images but does not show optical activity. This is due to the
(a) absence of a chiral N-atom
(b) presence of a chiral N-atom
(c) presence of a lone pair on the N-atom
(d) rapid flipping of one form into its non-superimposable mirror image

218. Which of the following compounds loses optical activity due to nitrogen inversion?
(a) $CH_3CH_2{-}CH(NH_2){-}CH_3$ (b) $CH_3CH_2{-}CH(OH){-}CH_2CH_3$
(c) $CH_3CH_2CH_2{-}N(CH_3){-}CH_2CH_3$
(d) $[CH_3CH_2{-}N^+(CH_2C_6H_5)(CH_3){-}CH_2{-}CH{=}CH_2]\ I^-$

219. Which of the following compounds possesses two configurationally stable enantiomers?
(a) $CH_3CH_2NHCH_3$
(b) $CH_3CH_2CH_2{-}N(C_2H_5)CH_3$
(c) $(PhCH_2)(CH_3CH_2)N^+(CH_3)_2\ Br^-$
(d) $(PhCH_2)(CH_3)N^+(Ph)(CH_2CH_3)\ Br^-$

220. The major product (70% to 80%) of the reaction between *m*-dinitrobenzene with NH_4HS is
(a) 1,3-dinitrobenzene (NO_2, NO_2)
(b) NH_2, HS, NO_2 substituted benzene
(c) NO_2, NH_2 substituted benzene (*m*-nitroaniline)
(d) NH_2, HS, NH_2 substituted benzene

221. What is the product obtained in the following reaction,

$$C_6H_5NO_2 \xrightarrow[NH_4Cl]{Zn} \text{.............?}$$

(a) $C_6H_5NH_2$ (b) C_6H_5NHOH
(c) $C_6H_5{-}N{=}N{-}C_6H_5$ (d) $C_6H_5{-}N^+(O^-){=}N{-}C_6H_5$

222. $C_6H_5{-}NO_2 \xrightarrow[NH_4Cl]{\text{Zn dust}} A \xrightarrow[\text{conc.HCl}]{\text{cold}} B$
A and B respectively are
(a) $C_6H_5{-}NHOH$, $HO{-}C_6H_4{-}NH_2$
(b) $C_6H_5{-}NH{-}NH{-}C_6H_5$, $H_2N{-}C_6H_4{-}C_6H_4{-}NH_2$
(c) $C_6H_5{-}N(\rightarrow O){=}N{-}C_6H_5$, $C_6H_5{-}N{=}N{-}C_6H_5$
(d) none is correct

223. Electrolytic reduction of nitrobenzene in strongly acidic medium produces
(a) *p*-aminophenol (b) azoxybenzene
(c) azobenzene (d) aniline

224. In order to prepare a 1° amine from an alkyl halide with simultaneous addition of one CH_2 group in the carbon chain, the regent used as source of nitrogen is
(a) sodium amide, $NaNH_2$
(b) sodium azide, NaN_3
(c) potassium cyanide
(d) potassium phthalimide, $C_6H_4(CO)_2N^-K^+$

225. Which of the following reagents can be used to convert primary amides into primary amines containing the same number of carbon atoms?
(a) Br_2 + NaOH (b) $LiAlH_4$
(c) Sn + HCl (d) Na + C_2H_5OH

226. What reagent would be best for converting (R)-2-phenyl-propanamide into (R)-2-phenylpropanamine?

(a) excess H_2 and Pt (b) NaOBr in aqueous base
(c) $NaBH_4$ in methanol (d) $LiAlH_4$ in ether

227. The major product (X) of the reaction,

O_2N ... OCH_3, O $\xrightarrow[\Delta]{H_2/Ni}$ X, is

(a) H_2N ... OCH_3, O (b) H_2N ... OH

(c) N, H (d) N, H, O

228. Consider the following sequence of reactions.

HOOC CN $\xrightarrow{475\ K}$ [A] $\xrightarrow[(ii)\ H_3O^+]{(i)\ LiAlH_4}$ [B]

The final product (B) is

(a) HOH_2C CH_2NH_2 (b) NH_2

(c) O (d) O, O, H NH_2

MATCH THE FOLLOWING

229.

Column I (Amine)	Column II (Property)
(A) $CH_3CH_2NH_2$	(p) Undergoes Liebermann nitrosoamine reaction
(B) $C_6H_5NH_2$	(q) Undergoes Hofmann bromamine reaction
(C) $(CH_3)_2NH$	(r) Gives azo dye test
(D) CH_3CONH_2	(s) With alcohol KOH and $CHCl_3$, it produces a bad smell

(a) (A)—(s); (B)—(r); (C)—(p); (D)—(q)
(b) (A)—(r); (B)—(p); (C)—(s); (D)—(q)
(c) (A)—(s); (B)—(r); (C)—(q); (D)—(p)
(d) (A)—(r); (B)—(q); (C)—(r); (D)—(p)

230.

Column I (Reagent/Name reaction)	Column II (Replacement of diazo group by)
(A) H_3PO_2	(p) Hydroxyl group
(B) Sandmeyer reaction	(q) Aryl group
(C) Boiling with dil. H_2SO_4	(r) Hydrogen atom
(D) Gomberg reaction	(s) Chlorine atom

(a) (A)—(s); (B)—(r); (C)—(q); (D)—(p)
(b) (A)—(r); (B)—(s); (C)—(p); (D)—(q)
(c) (A)—(q); (B)—(r); (C)—(q); (D)—(s)
(d) (A)—(p); (B)—(q); (C)—(r); (D)—(s)

231.

Column I (Amine)	Column II (pK_b Value)
(A) $CH_3CH_2NH_2$	(p) 4.70
(B) $(CH_3CH_2)_2NH$	(q) 3.29
(C) $C_6H_5NH_2$	(r) 3.00
(D) $C_6H_5CH_2NH_2$	(s) 9.38

(a) (A)—(p); (B)—(q); (C)—(s); (D)—(r)
(b) (A)—(r); (B)—(s); (C)—(p); (D)—(q)
(c) (A)—(q); (B)—(r); (C)—(s); (D)—(p)
(d) (A)—(s); (B)—(p); (C)—(q); (D)—(r)

ASSERTION REASON

Directions In each of the following questions, a statement of Assertion (A) is given followed by a corresponding statement of Reason (R) just below it. Of the statements, mark the correct answer as

(a) if both the assertion and reason are true and the reason is the correct explanation of the assertion.
(b) if both assertion and reason are true but reason is not the correct explanation of assertion
(c) If assertion is true but reason is false
(d) If both assertion and reason are false

232. Assertion In benzimidiazole, both the nitrogens (N and N) are basic.

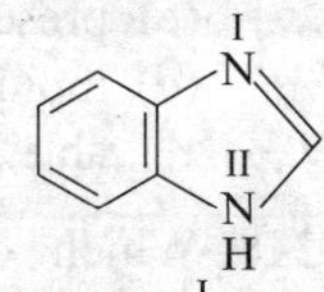

Reason The lone pair of electrons present on N is involved in delocalisation.

233. Assertion Amines are more basic than esters and ethers.

Reason Nitrogen is less electronegative than oxygen. It is in a better position to accommodate the positive charge on the proton.

234. Assertion *p*-Touidine is a stronger base than *m*-toluidine.

Reason The methyl group from the *m*-position exerts a smaller electron donating inductive +I effect than from the *p*-position.

235. Assertion N,N-Diethylethanamine is more basic than N,N- dimethylmethanamine.

Reason The +I effect of the ethyl group is more than that of the methyl group.

236. Assertion Controlled nitration of aniline at low temperature mainly gives *m*-nitroaniline.

Reason In an acidic medium, the NH_2 group gets converted into the $-\overset{+}{N}H_3$ group which is *m*-directing.

237. Assertion Nitration of aniline can be done conveniently by protecting the amino group by acetylation.

Reason Acetylation increases the electron density in the benzene ring.

238. Assertion Aniline hydrogen sulfate on heating, forms a mixture of *ortho*- and *para*-aminosulfonic acids.

Reason The sulfonic acid group is electron withdrawing.

239. Assertion Aniline does not undergo Friedel–crafts reaction.

Reason Friedel–Crafts reaction is an electrophilic substitution reaction.

240. Assertion Reduction of *m*-dinitrobenzene with ammonium sulfide gives *m*-nitroaniline.

Reason *m*-Nitroaniline formed gets precipitated and hence further reduction is prevented.

241. Assertion Deamination of diazonium salts can be carried out by boiling them with dilute mineral acids.

Reason Deamination of benzene diazonium chloride gives phenylhydrazine.

242. Assertion $C_6H_5N_2^+Cl^-$ couples with $C_6H_5N(CH_3)_2$ but not with 2,6-dimethyl-N,N-dimethylaniline.

Reason Due to steric inhibition of resonance, the *p*-position of the 2,6-dimethyl-N,N-dimethylaniline is not sufficiently activated for the coupling reaction to occur.

243. Assertion Methyl cyanide has a higher boiling point than methyl isocyanide.

Reason The dipole moment of methyl cyanide is higher than that of methyl isocyanide.

244. Assertion Alkyl isocyanides in acidified water give alkyl formamides.

Reason In isocyanides, carbon first acts as a nucleophile and then as an electrophile.

245. Assertion Ammonolysis of alkyl halides involves the reaction between alkyl halides and alcoholic ammonia.

Reason It can be used to prepare only 2° amines.

246. Assertion Gabriel's phthalimide reaction can be used to prepare both aryl and aralkylamines.

Reason Aryl halides are as reactive as aralkyl halides towards nucleophilic substitution reactions.

247. Assertion A primary amine has a higher boiling point than any tertiary amine.

Reason A tertiary amine has a greater number of N–H bonds for H bonding.

248. Assertion Anilinium chloride is more acidic than ammonium chloride.

Reason Anilinium ion is resonance stabilised.

249. Assertion Pyrrole is more basic than pyridine.

Reason In pyrrole, nitrogen is sp^3-hybridised.

Answer Key

1. (a)	2. (b)	3. (c)	4. (b)	5. (d)	6. (b)	7. (a)	8. (b)	9. (c)	10. (c)
11. (b)	12. (a)	13. (b)	14. (b)	15. (c)	16. (c)	17. (a)	18. (c)	19. (b)	20. (c)
21. (a)	22. (a)	23. (b)	24. (b)	25. (c)	26. (d)	27. (b)	28. (a)	29. (c)	30. (d)
31. (d)	32. (d)	33. (c)	34. (b)	35. (c)	36. (d)	37. (c)	38. (b)	39. (b)	40. (b)
41. (d)	42. (a)	43. (b)	44. (b)	45. (b)	46. (b)	47. (c)	48. (a)	49. (b)	50. (b)
51. (c)	52. (a)	53. (d)	54. (a)	55. (a)	56. (d)	57. (b)	58. (c)	59. (a)	60. (b)
61. (c)	62. (d)	63. (c)	64. (b)	65. (c)	66. (b)	67. (b)	68. (a)	69. (a)	70. (c)
71. (a)	72. (a)	73. (c)	74. (a)	75. (d)	76. (c)	77. (a)	78. (d)	79. (d)	80. (d)
81. (c)	82. (a)	83. (a)	84. (a)	85. (d)	86. (a)	87. (c)	88. (c)	89. (d)	90. (a)
91. (d)	92. (b)	93. (c)	94. (d)	95. (c)	96. (c)	97. (b)	98. (a)	99. (a)	100. (b)
101. (c)	102. (a)	103. (a)	104. (a)	105. (c)	106. (b)	107. (a)	108. (b)	109. (a)	110. (a)
111. (a)	112. (c)	113. (b)	114. (a)	115. (d)	116. (e)	117. (c)	118. (b)	119. (c)	120. (c)
121. (a)	122. (b)	123. (d)	124. (b)	125. (c)	126. (a)	127. (c)	128. (b)	129. (d)	130. (d)
131. (c)	132. (c)	133. (b)	134. (b)	135. (c)	136. (c)	137. (b)	138. (b)	139. (c)	140. (b)
141. (b)	142. (d)	143. (a)	144. (a)	145. (c)	146. (b)	147. (c)	148. (a)	149. (b)	150. (d)
151. (b)	152. (a)	153. (b)	154. (c)	155. (a)	156. (b)	157. (b)	158. (d)	159. (b)	160. (c)
161. (a)	162. (a)	163. (b)	164. (d)	165. (c)	166. (c)	167. (a)	168. (b)	169. (c)	170. (c)
171. (a)	172. (c)	173. (c)	174. (b)	175. (c)	176. (d)	177. (d)	178. (a)	179. (b)	180. (b)
181. (b)	182. (b)	183. (d)	184. (d)	185. (a)	186. (b)	187. (a)	188. (c)	189. (d)	190. (d)
191. (d)	192. (b)	193. (c)	194. (d)	195. (c)	196. (a)	197. (a)	198. (d)	199. (c)	200. (c)
201. (a)	202. (a)	203. (a)	204. (a)	205. (b)	206. (b)	207. (c)	208. (c)	209. (c)	210. (a)
211. (c)	212. (a)	213. (d)	214. (c)	215. (c)	216. (a)	217. (d)	218. (c)	219. (d)	220. (c)
221. (b)	222. (a)	223. (a)	224. (c)	225. (b)	226. (d)	227. (d)	228. (b)	229. (a)	230. (b)
231. (c)	232. (d)	233. (a)	234. (b)	235. (a)	236. (a)	237. (c)	238. (b)	239. (b)	240. (c)
241. (d)	242. (a)	243. (a)	244. (a)	245. (c)	246. (d)	247. (c)	248. (c)	249. (d)	

Hints and Solutions

OBJECTIVE QUESTIONS

Classification and Nomenclature of Amines

1. **(a)** N-Methylaniline is the common as well as the IUPAC name.

2. **(b)** Isobutylamine and *n*-propylmethylamine represent different compounds.

3. **(c)** $HO-C_6H_3(OH)-CH_2CH_2-NH_2$ (3,4-dihydroxyphenyl ring; ring positions 1–4, side chain carbons 2, 1)

3-(3,4-Dihydroxy)ethan-1-amine is called dopamine.

$C_6H_5-N(CH_3)_2$

N, N-Dimethylaniline

4. **(b)**

$$H_3C-\overset{3}{\underset{|}{N}}-\overset{CH_3}{\overset{|}{\underset{|}{C}}}-\overset{1}{CH_2}CH_3$$
$$CH_3 \quad CH_2CH_3$$

N, N-Trimethylpentan-3-amine
(Arabic numerals have higher priority of citation over alphabets)

5. **(d)** (cyclohexane ring: C-1 bearing H and OH, C-3 bearing NH_2 and H, trans)

trans-3-Aminocyclohexanol

6. **(b)** $CH_3-\underset{C_2H_5}{\underset{|}{N}}-\underset{O}{\underset{||}{C}}-CH_3$

N-Ethyl-N-methylethanamide

7. **(a)** Only primary amines give the carbylamine reaction.

8. **(b)** The amines in which the N atom does not carry any H atom or the amine in which N is attached to three alkyl/aryl or aralkyl groups is called a 3° amine. Thus, option (b) is correct.

Methods of Preparation of Amines

9. **(c)** Under basic conditions, bimolecular reduction of $C_6H_5NO_2$ gives azobenzene.

$$C_6H_6 \xrightarrow[\text{Conc. } H_2SO_4]{\text{Conc. } HNO_3} C_6H_5NO_2 \xrightarrow[\text{(Bimolecular reduction)}]{LiAlH_4} \underset{\text{Azobenzene}}{C_6H_5-N=N-C_6H_5}$$

10. **(c)** $C_6H_5CH_2NO_2$ is not a nitroarene but is a phenyl substituted nitromethane. Therefore, it behaves like a nitroalkane and gives an amine on $LiAlH_4$ reduction.

$$C_6H_5CH_2Br \xrightarrow{AgNO_2} C_6H_5CH_2NO_2 \xrightarrow[\text{(ii) } H_2O]{\text{(i) } LiAlH_4} \underset{\text{Benzylamine}}{C_6H_5CH_2NH_2}$$

11. **(b)** $LiAlH_4$/ether reduces aryl nitro compounds to azo compounds.

$$C_6H_6 \xrightarrow[\text{Conc. } H_2SO_4]{\text{Conc. } HNO_3} C_6H_5NO_2 \xrightarrow[\text{(Bimolecular reduction)}]{LiAlH_4} \underset{\text{Azobenzene}}{C_6H_5-N=N-C_6H_5}$$

12. **(a)** $F-C_6H_4-NO_2 \xrightarrow[\text{(Nucleophilic substituition)}]{(CH_3)_2NH,\ DMF} \underset{(A)}{(CH_3)_2N-C_6H_4-NO_2} \xrightarrow[\text{(Reduction)}]{H_2/Ni} \underset{(B)}{(CH_3)_2N-C_6H_4-NH_2}$

13. **(b)** $\underset{\text{2-Bromopropane}}{(CH_3)_2CH-Br} \xrightarrow[\text{Heat } (-AgBr)]{\text{Alc. AgCN}} \underset{\text{Isopropyl isocyanide (X)}}{(CH_3)_2CH-N\equiv C} \xrightarrow{LiAlH_4} \underset{\text{N-Methylpropan-2-amine (Y)}}{(CH_3)_2CH-NH-CH_3}$

14. **(b)** Alkyl halides are insoluble in water, therefore, for better yields an alcoholic solution of NaCN and alkyl halides is used. Thus, option (b) is correct.

15. **(c)** $\underset{\text{Benzamide}}{C_6H_5CONH_2} \xrightarrow[-H_2O]{POCl_3} \underset{\text{Benzonitrile (A)}}{C_6H_5CN} \xrightarrow{LiAlH_4} \underset{\text{Benzylamine}}{C_6H_5CH_2NH_2}$

16. **(c)** $\underset{\text{Methyl isocyanide}}{CH_3-N\equiv C} \xrightarrow{LiAlH_4} \underset{\text{2° Amine}}{CH_3-NH-CH_3}$

17. **(a)** Due to the presence of bulky isobutyl groups, $AlH(iBu)_2$ reduces cyanides only to CH=NH which upon subsequent hydrolysis with H_2O gives an aldehyde.

$$R-C\equiv N \xrightarrow[-NH_3]{AlH(iBu)_2} RCH=NH \xrightarrow{H_2O} RCH=O$$

Thus, option (a) is correct.

18. **(c)** $LiAlH_4$ reduces $-COOH \rightarrow CH_2OH$,

$$-\underset{O}{\underset{||}{C}}-CH_3 \longrightarrow -\underset{OH}{\underset{|}{CH}}-CH_3 \longrightarrow NO_2 \longrightarrow NH_2$$

but does not the reduce double bond, that is,

(cyclohexane ring bearing –COOH, –CH=CH₂, –C(=O)CH₃ and –NO₂) $\xrightarrow{LiAlH_4\ \text{(excess)}}$ (cyclohexane ring bearing –CH₂OH, –CH=CH₂, –CH(OH)CH₃ and –NH₂)

Thus, option (c) is correct.

19. **(b)** $LiAlH_4$ reduces imine into amine ($=N-CH_3 \rightarrow NH-CH_3$) but does not reduce C=C.

$$CH_3-CH=CH-CH=N-CH_3 \xrightarrow{LiAlH_4} CH_3-CH=CH-CH_2-NH-CH_3$$

Thus, option (b) is correct.

20. **(c)** $\underset{\text{2° Amide}}{C_6H_5CONHCH_3} \xrightarrow{LiAlH_4} \underset{\text{2° Amine}}{C_6H_5CH_2NHCH_3}$

21. **(a)** $LiAlH_4$/ether reduces 1° amides to 1° amines.

$$\underset{\text{Phenylacetamide}}{PhCH_2CONH_2} \xrightarrow{LiAlH_4/\text{ether}} \underset{\text{2-Phenylethanamine}}{PhCH_2\text{-}CH_2NH_2}$$

22. **(a)** $$\underset{\text{N, N-Dimethylacetamide}}{CH_3-\overset{O}{\overset{\|}{C}}-N(CH_3)_2} \xrightarrow[(ii)\ H_3O^+]{(i)\ LiAlH_4} \underset{\text{Ethyldimethylamine}}{CH_3CH_2-N(CH_3)_2}$$

23. **(b)** $$\underset{\text{N-Methylpyrrolidone}}{\text{N-Methylpyrrolidone}} \xrightarrow[(ii)\ H_2O]{(i)\ LiAlH_4} \underset{\text{N-Methylpyrrolidine}}{\text{N-Methylpyrrolidine}}$$

24. **(b)** $$\underset{\text{Phenylacetylene}}{C_6H_5C{\equiv}CH} \xrightarrow[HgSO_4]{\text{Aq. } H_2SO_4} \underset{\text{Acetophenone (A)}}{C_6H_5-\overset{O}{\overset{\|}{C}}-CH_3}$$

$$\xrightarrow[-H_2O]{NH_2OH} \underset{\text{Acetophenone oxime (B)}}{(C_6H_5)(CH_3)C{=}NOH} \xrightarrow[(ii)\ H_2O]{(i)\ LiAlH_4} \underset{\text{1-Phenylethanamine}}{(C_6H_5)(CH_3)CH{-}NH_2}$$

25. **(c)** 1° Aliphatic and 1° aralkylamines (but not 1° aromatic amines) can be prepared by Gabriel's phthalimide method. Therefore, benzylamine ($C_6H_5CH_2NH_2$) being a 1° aralkylamine, can be prepared by this method.

26. **(d)** N-Methylbenzylamine being a 2° amine cannot be synthesised by Gabriel's synthesis.

27. **(b)** $$\underset{\text{Acetamide}}{CH_3CONH_2} \xrightarrow[\text{(Hofmann bromamide reaction)}]{NaOH-Br_2} \underset{\text{Methylamine}}{CH_3NH_2}$$

28. **(a)** Hofmann's bromamide reaction can be used to prepare methanamine from acetamide.

$$\underset{\text{Acetamide}}{CH_3CONH_2} + Br_2 + 4\,NaOH \xrightarrow{\Delta} \underset{\text{Methanamine}}{CH_3NH_2} + 2\,NaBr$$

29. **(c)** $$CH_3CH_2CH_2COCl \xrightarrow{NH_3} CH_3CH_2CH_2CONH_2CH_2CH_2CONH_2 \xrightarrow{Br_2/KOH} CH_3CH_2CH_2NH_2 + C_4H_9ON$$

X=$CH_3CH_2CH_2COCl$

30. **(d)** $$\underset{\text{Propionic acid (A)}}{CH_3CH_2COOH} \xrightarrow{NH_3} \underset{\text{Ammoniumpropanoate (B)}}{CH_3CH_2COONH_4} \xrightarrow[-H_2O]{\Delta}$$

$$\underset{\text{Propanamide (C)}}{CH_3CH_2CONH_2} \xrightarrow[\text{(Hofmann bromamide Reaction)}]{Br_2/KOH} \underset{\text{Ethylamine}}{CH_3CH_2NH_2}$$

31. **(d)** Only 1° amides undergo Hofmann bromamide reaction. Since $CH_3CONHCH_3$ is a 2° amide, it does not undergo Hofmann bromamide reaction.

32. **(d)** Mechanism of Hofmann bromamide reaction. RNC is not an intermediate while all others are.

33. **(c)** Aniline cannot be prepared by Gabriel's phthalimide method because chlorobenzene (aryl halide) does not undergo nucleophilic substitution reaction with potassium phthalimide in aqueous NaOH solution. Please note that phenyl isocyanide on acid hydrolysis gives 1° amines.

34. **(b)** Only primary amines give the carbylamine reaction.

35. **(c)** $$\underset{\text{Benzyl chloride}}{C_6H_5CH_2Cl} \xrightarrow[-NH_4Cl]{2\,NH_3} \underset{\text{Benzylamine}}{C_6H_5CH_2NH_2} \xrightarrow[-2\,HCl]{2CH_3Cl} \underset{\text{N, N-Dimethylphenylmethanamine}}{C_6H_5CH_2-N(CH_3)_2}$$

36. **(d)** 2° Alkyl bromides undergo dehydrohalogenation to yield alkenes.

37. **(c)** Since benzyl halides are more reactive than aryl halides, the reaction occurs at the benzylic chloride part.

$$\underset{\text{o-Bromobenzyl chloride}}{o\text{-}BrC_6H_4CH_2Cl} \xrightarrow[-NH_4Cl]{2\,NH_3} \underset{\text{o-Bromobenzylamine}}{o\text{-}BrC_6H_4CH_2NH_2}$$

38. **(b)** $$C_6H_6 \xrightarrow[\substack{\text{(Nitration)}\\ 333\text{ K}}]{HNO_3-H_2SO_4} \underset{\text{Nitrobenzene (A)}}{C_6H_5NO_2} \xrightarrow[\text{(Reduction)}]{Sn/HCl} \underset{\text{Aniline (B)}}{C_6H_5NH_2}$$

Physical Properties of Amines

39. **(b)** Due to polymeric association, amides form stronger H bonds than carboxylic acids which mostly exist as cyclic dimers. Therefore, the BP of $C_2H_5CONH_2$ (III) is higher than that of CH_3CH_2COOH (IV). Further, due to higher electronegativity of O over N, the alcohol, that is, $CH_3(CH_2)_3OH$ (I), forms stronger H bonds than the amine, $(C_2H_5)_2NH$ (II). Thus, the BPs decrease in the order III > IV > I > II, that is, option (b) is correct.

40. **(b)** Solubility in H_2O decreases as the extent of H bonding decreases, that is, as the size of the hydrocarbon part increases. Thus, the solubility increases in the order I < II < III, that is, option (b) is correct.

41. **(d)** Among 1°, 2° and 3° amines, due to the absence of intermolecular H bonding, 3° amines have the lowest boiling point and hence are most volatile. Further, due to polar C–N bonds, 3° amines are more polar than hydrocarbons which are almost non-polar. Thus, among 3° amines and hydrocarbons of comparable molecular mass, hydrocarbons are more volatile.$CH_3CH_2CH_3$ has the lowest BP and hence is the most volatile.

42. **(a)** Primary amines form benzene sulfonamides which are soluble in alkalies.

Chemical Reactions of Amines

43. **(b)** The relative basic strength of CH_3NH_2, $(CH_3)_2NH$ and $(CH_3)_3N$ depends upon the stabilisation of their conjugate acids (formed as a result of accepting a proton from H_2O) by a number of factors such as H bonding, steric hindrance of the alkyl groups and the +I effect of the alkyl groups. All these factors are favourable for 2° amines, therefore, $(CH_3)_2NH$ is a stronger base than CH_3NH_2 and $(CH_3)_3N$. Since the CH_3 group is the smallest, it does not exert any steric hindrance. Therefore, stabilisation of the conjugate acid derived from CH_3NH_2 due to H-bonding is greater than

that of the conjugate acid derived from $(CH_3)_3N$ due to the +I effect of the three CH_3 groups, that is,

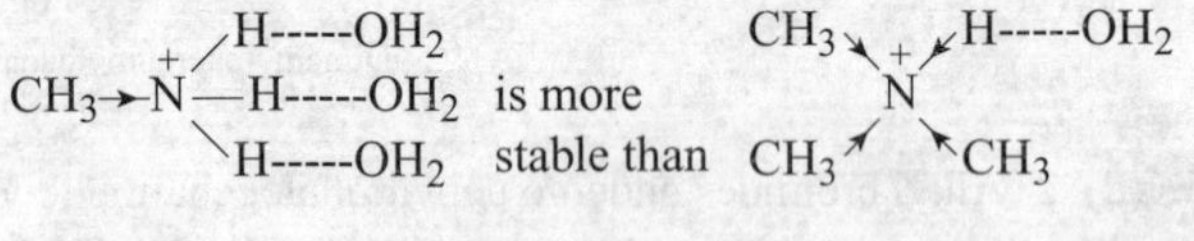

$$CH_3\rightarrow\overset{+}{N}(H\text{-----}OH_2)_3 \text{ is more stable than } (CH_3)_3\overset{+}{N}H\text{-----}OH_2$$

Therefore, CH_3NH_2 is a stronger base than $(CH_3)_3N$. Thus, the overall basic strength of these amines decreases in the order

$(CH_3)_2NH > CH_3NH_2 > (CH_3)_3N$

However, in $C_6H_5NH_2$, the lone pair of electrons on the N atom is delocalised over the benzene ring and hence is not available for protonation. As a result, $C_6H_5NH_2$ is weaker than all 1°, 2°, 3° methylamines. In other words, $(CH_3)_2NH$ is the strongest base and hence is the most reactive towards dil. HCl, that is, option (b) is correct.

44. (b) Since the strongest amine has the smallest pK_b value, option (b) is correct.

45. (b) The relative basicity of 1°, 2° and 3° methylamines increases in the order

$(CH_3)_3N$ (III) < CH_3NH_2 (I) < $(CH_3)_2NH$ (II).

However, due to the –I effect of the C_6H_5 group, the electron density on the N atom of $C_6H_5NH_2$ decreases. As a result, the overall basicity of the four amines increases in the order $C_6H_5NH_2$ (IV) < $(CH_3)_3N$ (III) < CH_3NH_2 (I) < $(CH_3)_2NH$ (II), that is, option (b) is correct.

46. (b) Due to delocalisation of the lone pair of electrons of the N atom over the benzene ring, $C_6H_5NHCH_3$ (IV) is the least basic of all the three aliphatic amines. $CH_3CH_2NHCH_2CH_3$ (II) is more basic than $CH_3CH_2NH_2$ (I). Further except CH_3NH_2, which is less basic than $(CH_3)_3N$, all other amines are more basic than their corresponding 3° amine (III). Thus, option (b) is correct, that is, IV < III < I < II.

47. (c) (i) Due to delocalisation of the lone pair of electrons of the N atom over the benzene ring, $C_6H_5NH_2$ (IV) and $C_6H_5NHCH_3$ (II) are far less basic than $C_2H_5NH_2$ (I) and $(C_2H_5)_2NH$ (III). Further, due to the +I effect of the CH_3 group, $C_6H_5NHCH_3$ (II) is a little more basic than $C_6H_5NH_2$ (IV). Among $C_2H_5NH_2$ (I) and $(C_2H_5)_2NH$ (III), $(C_2H_5)_2NH$ (II) is a more basic group than $C_2H_5NH_2$ (I) due to the greater +I effect of the two C_2H_5 groups and stabilisation of its conjugate acid by H bonding. Combining all these, the relative basic strength of these four amines decreases in the order

$(C_2H_5)_2NH$ (III) > $(C_2H_5NH_2$ (I) > $C_6H_5NHCH_3$ (II) > $C_6H_6NH_2$ (IV).

Since a stronger base has a lower pK_a value, the pK_b $C_6H_5NH_2$ (IV) > $C_6H_5NHCH_3$ (II) > $C_2H_5NH_2$ (I).

48. (a) Due to delocalisation of the lone pair of electrons of the N atom over the benzene ring, $C_6H_5NH_2$ (I) and $C_6H_5N(CH_3)_2$ (II) are far less basic than $(C_2H_5)_2NH$ (III) and CH_3NH_2 (IV), However, due to the +I effect of the CH_3 groups, $C_6H_5N(CH_3)_2$ (II) is more basic than $C_6H_5NH_2$ (I).

Among CH_3NH_2 (IV) and $(C_2H_5)_2NH$ (III), primarily due to the greater +I effect of the two C_2H_5 groups over one CH_3 group, $(C_2H_5)_2NH$ (III) is more basic than CH_3NH_2 (IV). Thus, the basic strength of the four amines increases in the order $C_6H_5NH_2$ (I) <$C_6H_5N(CH_3)_2$ (II) < CH_3NH_2 (IV) < $(C2H_5)_2NH$ (III), that is, option (a) is correct.

49. (b) In the gas phase of non-aqueous solvents such as benzene or chlorobenzene, the solvent effects are absent, that is, stabilisation of the conjugate acid obtained by the addition of a proton to the base, the basicity mainly depends on the +I effect of the alkyl groups. In other words, basicity decreases as the +I effect of the alkyl groups decreases, that is, option (b) is correct.

50. (b) In C_6H_5–$CH_2\ddot{N}H_2$, the lone pair of electrons on the N-atom is not delocalised over the benzene ring while in all other compounds, the lone pair on the N is delocalised on the benzene ring. Thus, option (b) is correct.

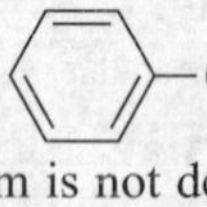

51. (c) 2° Amines are more basic than 1° and 3° amines. Among the 2° amines (b) and (c), (b) is less basic since the lone pair of electrons on the nitrogen atom contribute towards the aromatic sextet formation. Hence, piperidine, that is, option (c) is correct.

52. (a) Electron donating groups increase the basicity of amines. Further, greater the electron donating power, stronger is the base. Thus, amine (4) is the strongest followed by amine (3) followed by aniline (1). In contrast, electron withdrawing groups decrease the basicity since the $–NO_2$ group at the *p*-position can exert both its –R and –I effects but at the *m*-position, it can exert only its weaker –Ieffect. Therefore, amine (2) is the weakest while amine (5) is stronger than amine (2). Thus, the overall increasing order of basicity is 5 < 2 < 1 < 3 < 4, that is, option (a) is correct.

53. (d) Although NO_2 has a powerful –I effect, a carbonyl group has a much stronger resonance effect. Therefore, CH_3NHCHO is the weakest base.

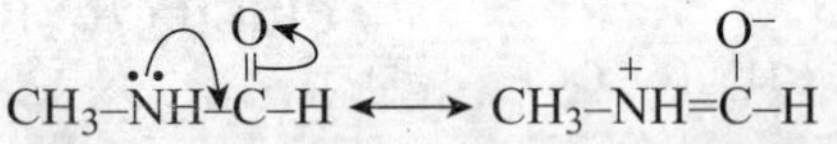

$$CH_3\text{–}\ddot{N}H\text{–}\underset{}{\overset{O}{\overset{\|}{C}}}\text{–}H \longleftrightarrow CH_3\text{–}\overset{+}{N}H{=}\overset{O^-}{\overset{|}{C}}\text{–}H$$

54. (a) *o*-Nitroaniline < *p*-nitroaniline < *m*-nitroaniline.

55. (a) The basicity of *o*-, *m*- and *p*-toluidines decreases in the order $p > m > o$. In other words, their pK_a values will increase in the reverse order, that is, option (a) is correct—$p < m < o$.

56. (d) When chlorine is present in the meta position, chlorine exerts only the electron-withdrawing inductive effect (the resonance effect does not operate at the meta position). When present at para position, the electron withdrawing inductive effect of chlorine is partly neutralised by its electron releasing resonance effect. Therefore, the electron density on nitrogen is reduced to a greater extent when chlorine is present at the meta position than when present at the para position. As a result, *m*-chloroaniline is a weaker base than *p*-chloroaniline which in turn is weaker than aniline.

57. (b) The methoxy group of anisidine is strongly electron donating from the ortho and para positions by extended π-bonding. This effect completely dominates the electron withdrawing inductive effect form these positions

Therefore we expect *o*-and *p*-anisidines to be stronger bases than anline but the correct order of basicity is *p*-anisidine > aniline > o-anisidine. *o*-Anisidine is weaker than aniline on account of the ortho effect. All *o*-substituted anilines are less basic than *p*-substituted anilines regardless of the electronic effect of the substituent. This effect is attributed to steric hindrance by the *o*-substituent to solvation of the cation. This steric effect destabilises the cation making the amine a weaker base. *m*-Anisidine is the cation making the amine a weaker base. *m*-Anisidine is the weakest base because the *m*-CH_3O group is electron withdrawing in nature on account of the –I effect. Note the there is no resonance effect at the meta position.

58. (c) Electron donating groups increase while electron withdrawing groups decrease the basicity of substituted anilines, with respect to the parent aniline. Therefore, aniline (III) is the strongest base followed by aniline (I) while nitroaniline (II) is the weakest base. Basicity increases in the order II < I < III. Thus, option (c) is correct.

59. (a) Organic bases (trimethylamine and aniline) are weaker bases than the NH_2^- and OH^- ions. Now NH_2^- is the conjugate base of the acid NH_3 and OH^- ion is the conjugate base of the acid H_2O. Since NH_3 is a weaker acid than H_2O, NH_2^- is a stronger base than the OH^- ion.

60. (b) Electron withdrawing groups (Cl, NO_2) decrease while electron donating groups (CH_3, $N(CH_3)_2$, OCH_3) increase the basicity of amines. Further, stronger the electron donating group, stronger the base. Since $N(CH_3)_2$ is a stronger electron donating group than CH_3, 4-dimethylaminopyridine is the strongest base, that is, option (b) is correct.

61. (c) In cyclohexylamine (II), the lone pair of electrons on then atom is present in an sp^3-orbital while in pyridine (III), it is present in an sp^2-orbital. Therefore, amine (II) is more basic than amine (III). In pyrrole (IV), the lone pair of electrons on N contributes towards the aromatic sextet formation hence is not at all available for protonation while in *p*-nitroaniline (I), in spite of the strong electron withdrawing NO_2 group, they are still available for protonation to some extent and hence amine (I) is more basic than pyrrole (IV). Thus, the overall basicity decreases in the order IV < I < III < II; option (c) is correct.

62. (d) In both reactions (a) and (b), the amine behaves as an acid.

(a) $\underset{\text{Acid}}{CH_3CH_2NH_2} + CH_3MgI \rightarrow CH_3CH_2NHMgI + CH_4$

(b) $\underset{\text{Acid}}{[(CH_3)_2CH]_2NH} + n\text{-}C_4H_9Li \rightarrow [(CH_3)_2CH]_2NLi + C_4H_{10}$

63. (c) The conjugate acid obtained by addition of a H^+ to amine (III) is stabilised by two equivalent resonance structures and hence is the most basic amine.

$CH_3C(=NH)NH_2 \xrightarrow{H^+} CH_3C(NH_2)=\overset{+}{N}H_2 \longleftrightarrow CH_3C(=\overset{+}{N}H_2)NH_2$

$CH_3CH_2-\overset{sp^3}{N}HCH_3$ — 2° Amine (IV); $CH_2=CHCH_2\overset{sp^3}{N}H_2$ — 1° Amine (I); $CH_3CH_2CH=\overset{sp^2}{N}H$ — Amine (II)

In amines (IV and I), the lone pair of electrons on N is present in an sp^3-orbital but in amine (II), it is present in an sp^2-orbital; therefore, amines (IV and I) are more basic than amine. Further, amine (IV) being 2° is more basic than 1° amine (I). Thus, the overall basicity increases in the order (II) < (I) < (IV) < (III), that is, option (c) is correct.

64. (b) In aniline (I), nitrogen is directly attached to the benzene ring. Because of delocalisation of the lone pair of electrons on N over the benzene ring, aniline is a weak base. In amine (IV) the OCH_3 group present at the *m*-position cannot exert its +R effect but exerts only its weak –I effect. As a result, aniline (II) is a weaker base than aniline (I).
Due to the presence of two electron donating N–CH_3 groups, aniline (III) is a stronger base than aniline (I). In benzylamine (II), N is not directly attached to the benzene ring, therefore it is the strongest base. Thus, the overall basic strength of the four amines decreases in the order II > III > I > IV, that is, option (b) is correct.

65. (c) C_6H_5Br being an aryl halide is much less reactive than alkyl halides towards nucleophilic substitution reactions. $(CH_3)_3CCl$ being a 3° alkyl halide preferably undergoes dehydrohalogenation while $(CH_3)_3CCH_2Br$ is less reactive due to steric hindrance. In other words, out of the given alkyl/aryl halides, $C_6H_5CH_2Br$ is the most reactive and hence is best suited for the above reaction.

66. (b) With excess of CH_3I, pyrrolidine forms the quaternary ammonium iodide.

$\underset{\text{Pyrrolidine}}{C_4H_8NH} + 2\,CH_3I \xrightarrow[-HI]{\text{Pyridine}} \underset{\text{Quaternary salt}}{C_4H_8\overset{+}{N}(CH_3)_2}$

67. (b) $\underset{\text{Benzylamine}}{C_6H_5CH_2NH_2} + 2\,CH_3I \xrightarrow[-HI]{\text{Pyridine}} \underset{\text{N, N-Dimethylphenyl-methanamine}}{C_6H_5CH_2-N(CH_3)_2}$

68. (a) $\underset{\text{Ethanamine}}{CH_3CH_2NH_2} + \underset{\text{Acetyl chloride}}{CH_3COCl} \xrightarrow[-HI]{\text{Pyridine}} \underset{\text{N-Ethylethanamide}}{CH_3CH_2NHCOCH_3}$

69. (a) $\underset{\text{Aniline}}{C_6H_5NH_2} + \underset{\text{Acetic anhydride}}{(CH_3CO)_2O} \longrightarrow \underset{\text{Acetanilide}}{C_6H_5NH-\overset{O}{\overset{\|}{C}}-CH_3} + \underset{\text{Acetic acid}}{CH_3-\overset{O}{\overset{\|}{C}}-OH}$

70. (c) Schotten–Baumann reaction.

71. (a) Due to resonance of the lone pair of electrons on N atom of the $CONH_2$, amides are much less nucleophilic than amines. Therefore, acetylation with acetic anhydride occurs only at the –NH_2 group, that is, option (a) is correct.

72. (a) $CH_3CH_2Cl \xrightarrow[-NaCl]{NaCN} \underset{(X)}{CH_3CH_2CN} \xrightarrow[\text{(Reduction)}]{Ni/H_2} CH_3CH_2CH_2NH_2 \xrightarrow[\text{(Acetylation)}]{\text{Acetic anhydride}}$

$$CH_3CH_2CH_2NH\text{–}COCH_3 + CH_3COOH$$
n-Propylacetamide (Z)

73. (c) $CH_3\text{–}C_6H_4\text{–}CONH_2 \xrightarrow[\text{(Hofmann bromamide reaction)}]{\text{(1) NaOH/Br}_2} CH_3\text{–}C_6H_4\text{–}NH_2$
p-Toluamide → *p*-Toluamide

$\xrightarrow[\text{(Schotten-Baumann reaction)}]{C_6H_5COCl} CH_3\text{–}C_6H_4\text{–}NH\text{–}CO\text{–}C_6H_5 + HCl$
(T)

74. (a) $C_6H_5\text{–}NH_2 \xrightarrow[\text{(Acetylation)}]{(CH_3CO)_2O} C_6H_5\text{–}NHCOCH_3$

$\xrightarrow[\text{FC Acylation}]{ClCH_2COCl} ClCH_2CO\text{–}C_6H_4\text{–}NHCOCH_3$
(I)

Since acid chlorides are more reactive than alkyl halides, the FC reaction occurs preferentially through the COCl part of $ClCH_2COCl$ and further since $NHCOCH_3$ (anilide group) is*o*,*p*-directing, the major product is the *p*-isomer.

75. (d) Since the $–NH_2$ group is more nucleophilic than the OH group, the acetylation occurs at the $–NH_2$ group.

$C_6H_5C(OH)(CH_3)\text{–}CH(NH_2)CH_3 \xrightarrow[\text{room temp.}]{(CH_3CO)_2O/\text{pyridine (1 equiv.)}} C_6H_5C(OH)(CH_3)\text{–}CH(NHCOCH_3)CH_3$

Please note that although the OH group is 3°, since the reaction is carried out at room temperature, its dehydration does not occur, that is, option (a) is incorrect.

76. (c) During acetylation one H-atom (at. mass = 1 amu) of the $–NH_2$ group is replaced by an acetyl group, that is, CH_3CO (mol. mass = 43 amu).

$–NH_2 + CH_3COCl \rightarrow –NHCOCH_3 + HCl$

In other words, acetylation of each NH_2 group increases the mass by 43 – 1 = 42 amu. Now since the molecular mass of the organic compound is 180 while that of the acetylated product is 390, the increase in mass due to acetylation = 390 – 180 = 210 amu.

∴ No. of $–NH_2$ groups

$$= \frac{\text{Total increase}}{\text{Increase due to one } NH_2 \text{ group}} = \frac{210}{42} = 5$$

77. (a) $CH_3CH_2NH_2 + CHCl_3 + 3\,KOH \rightarrow$
$\underset{A}{CH_3CH_2NC}\,(=C_2H_5NC) + \underset{B}{3KCl} + 3\,H_2O$

78. (d)
$H_3C\text{–}C_6H_4\text{–}NH_2 \xrightarrow[\text{(Carbylamine reaction)}]{CHCl_3,\ \text{alc. KOH},\ \Delta} H_3C\text{–}C_6H_4\text{–}NC$

79. (d) Only 1° amines, that is, *p*-methylbenzylamine

$H_3C\text{–}C_6H_4\text{–}CH_2NH_2$

give a positive carbylamine test.

80. (d) $C_6H_{11}\text{–}CONH_2 \xrightarrow[\text{(Hofmann bromanide reaction)}]{Br_2/KOH} C_6H_{11}\text{–}NH_2$
Cyclohexane-carboxamide → Cyclohexylamine

$\xrightarrow[\text{(Carbylamine reaction)}]{CHCl_3/\text{alc. KOH}} C_6H_{11}\text{–}\overset{+}{N}{\equiv}\overset{-}{C}\text{:} \xrightarrow[\text{(Reduction)}]{H_2/Pd} C_6H_{11}\text{–}NH\text{–}CH_3$
Cyclohexyl- → N-Methylcyclohexylamine

81. (c) $\underset{\text{Ethanamine}}{CH_3CH_2NH_2} + CHCl_3 + \underset{\text{(alc.)}}{3\,KOH}$

$\xrightarrow{\Delta} CH_3CH_2NC + 3\,KCl + 3\,H_2O$

$CH_3CH_2\text{–}\overset{+}{N}{\equiv}C^{-}Cl_2 \rightarrow \underset{\text{Ethyliminocarbonyl chloride}}{CH_3CH_2\text{–}N{=}CCl_2}$

82. (a) $\underset{I}{R\text{–}\overset{+}{N}{\equiv}C\text{:}^{-}} \longleftrightarrow \underset{II}{R\text{–}\ddot{N}{=}C\text{:}}$

In structure (II), C has only six electrons and hence is electron deficient.

83. (a) $CH_3\text{–}N{=}C{=}O$
Methylisocyanate (MIC)

84. (a) $\underset{\text{Methylisocyanate}}{CH_3 - N = \overset{+\delta}{C} = \overset{-\delta}{O}} + CH_3CH_2\,\overset{\delta-}{O} - \overset{\delta+}{H} \rightarrow$

$\left[\begin{array}{c} CH_3\text{–}N{=}C\text{–}OH \\ \quad\ |\ \\ \quad OCH_2CH_3 \end{array}\right] \xrightarrow{\text{Tautomerises}} \underset{\text{Urethane}}{CH_3\text{–}NH\text{–}\overset{O}{\overset{\|}{C}}\text{–}OC_2H_5}$

85. (d) $\underset{(A)}{C_6H_5NO_2} \xrightarrow{\text{Reduction}} \underset{(B)}{C_6H_5NH_2} \xrightarrow[\text{Alc. KOH}]{CHCl_3}$

$\underset{(C)}{C_6H_5NC} \xrightarrow{H_2/\text{Catalyst}} \underset{\text{N-Methylaniline}}{C_6H_5NHCH_3}$

86. (a) $\underset{\text{Nitrobenzene (A)}}{C_6H_5NO_2} \xrightarrow{\text{Reduction}} \underset{\text{Aniline (B)}}{C_6H_5NH_2} \xrightarrow[\text{(Carbylamine reaction)}]{CHCl_3/KOH}$

87. (c) 1° Amines react with a hot mixture of $CHCl_3$ and KOH/C_2H_5OH to produce a nauseating smell of carbylamine.

88. (c) $\underset{\text{Butanamide (X)}}{CH_3CH_2CH_2CONH_2} \xrightarrow[\text{(Hofmann bromamide reaction)}]{Br_2/NaOH}$

$\underset{\text{MF } C_3H_9N}{CH_3CH_2CH_2NH_2} \xrightarrow[\text{(Carbylamine reaction)}]{CHCl_3.KOH\,(\text{alc.})\Delta} \underset{n\text{-Propyl carbylamine}}{CH_3CH_2CH_2N{\equiv}C}$

Thus, compound (X) is butanamide, that is, option (c) is correct.

89. (d) All the amines listed in the question are aliphatic 1° amines and aliphatic 1° amines react with HNO_2 to give N_2. Therefore, option (d) is correct.

90. (a) Only 2° and 3° amines do not liberate N_2 on reaction with HNO_2. All the given amines are 1° except trimethylamine which is 3°. Thus, option (a) correct.

91. (d) $\underset{\text{Ethylamine}}{C_2H_5NH_2} + HNO_2 \rightarrow \underset{\text{Ethyl alcohol}}{C_2H_5OH} + N_2 + H_2O$

92. (b)
$\underset{\text{Benzonitrile}}{C_6H_5CN} \xrightarrow[\text{Reduction}]{Sn/HCl} \underset{\text{Benzylamine}}{C_6H_5CH_2NH_2} \xrightarrow[0\text{–}5°C]{NaNO_2,\ HCl} \underset{\text{Benzyl alcohol}}{C_6H_5CH_2OH}$

93. (c) 2° Amines, that is, dimethylamine gives yellow oily liquid called nitrosoamine, with HNO_2.

94. (d)

N-Methylaniline $\xrightarrow{NaNO_2/HCl}$ N-Nitroso-N-Methylaniline

2° Amines on treatment with HNO_2 give nitrosoamines. Thus, option (d) is correct.

95. (c) Aromatic 3° amines undergo electrophilic substitution with nitrosonium ion at the unhindered *p*-position of the phenyl ring to form green coloured *p*-nitrrosoamines. Thus,

$NaNO_2 + HCl \rightarrow NaCl + HO–NO$

$HO–NO + H^+ \longrightarrow H_2\overset{+}{O}–N{=}O \longrightarrow H_2O + \overset{+}{N}{=}O$ (Nitrosonium ion)

$C_6H_5–N(CH_3)_2 \xrightarrow[-H_2O]{+\overset{+}{N}O} O{=}N–C_6H_4–N(CH_3)_2$

p-Nitroso-N, N-dimethylaniline

96. (c) *p*-Nitroso-N,N-dimethylaniline.

97. (b) In Hinsberg's test, the reagent used is $C_6H_5SO_2Cl$ in aq. NaOH.

98. (a) 1° Amines form benzenesulfonamides which are soluble in alkali, that is, option (a) is correct.

99. (a) Sulfonamides of 1° amines have an acidic H on the N atom and hence are soluble in NaOH, that is, option (a) is correct.

100. (b) 2° Amines react with benzenesulfonyl chloride to give the corresponding benzenesulfonamides which due to the absence of acidic H on N do not dissolve in aq. NaOH, that is, option (b) is correct.

101. (c) Wurtz reaction is used for the synthesis of alkanes but not of amines.

102. (a) The benzene sulfonamides of 2° amines due to the absence of hydrogen on the N atom are insoluble in alkalis. Out of the four options given, only option (a) (N-methylaniline)is a 2° amine while all others are 1° amines.

$C_6H_5–NHCH_3 + C_6H_5–SO_2Cl \xrightarrow{NaOH}$ $C_6H_5–N(CH_3)–SO_2–C_6H_5$

N-Methylaniline (2° *Amine*); Benzenesulfonyl chloride

M.F. $C_{13}H_{13}NO_2S$ (X)

Thus, compound X is N-methylaniline.

103. (a) Cyclohexanone$=O + HN(CH_3)_2 \xrightarrow[-H_2O]{PTS}$ cyclohexene$=N(CH_3)_2$

Enamine

104. (a) Cyclohexanone + Pyrrolidine $\xrightarrow[-H_2O]{H^+, \Delta}$ Enamine

105. (c) Aldehydes react with primary amines to form Schiff's bases.

$\underset{\text{Aniline}}{C_6H_5NH_2} + \underset{\text{Benzaldehyde}}{O{=}CHC_6H_5} \xrightarrow{-H_2O} C \quad \underset{\text{Schiff's base}}{C_6H_5N{=}CHC_6H_5}$

106. (b) Only 1° amines react with aldehydes to form Schiff's bases. Only morophiline being a 2° amine does not form a Schiff's base. All others are 1° amines and hence form Schiff's bases.

107. (a) $CH_3CH_2NH_2 + O{=}CHCH_3 \xrightarrow{-H_2O}$

$CH_3CH_2N{=}CHCH_3 \xrightarrow{H_2/Ni} CH_3CH_2–NH–CH_2CH_3$

108. (b) $(CH_3)_2CH–CO–CH_3 \xrightarrow{\text{Enolisation}} (CH_3)_2C{=}C(OH)CH_3 \xrightarrow[-H_2O]{(i)\ CH_3NH_2} (CH_3)_2C{=}C(NHCH_3)CH_3 \xrightarrow[(iii)\ H_2O]{(ii)\ LiAlH_4} (CH_3)_2CH–CH(NHCH_3)CH_3$

109. (a) The–NH_2 group is *o,p*-directing, therefore, 2,4,6-tribromo aniline is formed.

110. (a) Aniline $\xrightarrow[\text{(Acetylation)}]{(CH_3CO)_2O,\ \text{Pyridine}}$ Acetanilide $\xrightarrow[\text{(Nuclear bromination)}]{Br_2/CH_3CO_2H}$ *p*-Bromoacetanilide (X) $\xrightarrow[\text{Hydrolysis}]{\text{Aq. conc. NaOH}}$ *p*-Bromoaniline (Y)

111. (a) $NHCOCH_3$ is *o,p*-directing, but due to steric hindrance at the *o*-position, the NO_2 group enters at the unhindered *p*-position to give *p*-nitroacetanilide as the major product, that is, option (a) is correct.

Acetanilide $\xrightarrow[\text{conc. } H_2SO_4]{\text{conc. } HNO_3}$ $O_2N–C_6H_4–NHCOCH_3$ p-Nitroacetanilide (major product)

112. (c)

p-Toluidine (NH_2, CH_3) $\xrightarrow{(CH_3CO)_2O}$ (A) ($NHCOCH_3$, CH_3) $\xrightarrow{Br_2/CH_3COOH}$ (B) ($NHCOCH_3$, Br, CH_3) $\xrightarrow{H^+/H_2O}$ (C) (NH_2, Br, CH_3)

113. (b) Protonation of the –NH_2 group gives –$\overset{+}{N}H_3$ which is *m*-directing. Thus, option (b) is correct.

114. (a) Protonation of the –NH_2 group gives –$\overset{+}{N}H_3$ which is *m*-directing and hence a significant amount of the *m*-product is formed during mononitration.

Aniline (NH_2) $\xrightarrow[\text{from nitrating mixture}]{H^+}$ Anilinium ion ($\overset{+}{N}H_3$) $\xrightarrow{HNO_3\text{–}H_2SO_4}$ *m*-product ($\overset{+}{N}H_3$, NO_2) $\underset{H^+}{\overset{-H^+}{\rightleftharpoons}}$ *m*-Nitroaniline (NH_2, NO_2)

115. **(d)** In a strong acidic medium, aniline is present as the anilinium ion which is *m*-directing.

116. **(e)** Sulfanilic acid, $p\text{-}H_3\overset{+}{N}\text{-}C_6H_6\text{–}SO_3^-$ is formed.

117. **(c)** Sulfanilic acid has a strongly acidic $–SO_3H$ group which transfers a proton to the weakly acidic $–NH_2$ group and hence it exists as a zwitter ion.

118. **(b)** Due to the electron donating effect of the –NH group, substitution occurs preferentially at the unhindered *p*-position, that is, option (b) is correct.

119. **(c)** $\underset{\text{Benzoic acid}}{C_6H_5COOH} \xrightarrow{NH_3} C_6H_5COONH_4 \xrightarrow[-H_2O]{\Delta}$

$\underset{\text{Benzamide (P)}}{C_6H_5CONH_2} \xrightarrow[\text{(Hofmann bromamide reaction)}]{NaOBr} \underset{\text{Aniline (Q)}}{C_6H_5NH_2}$

$\xrightarrow[\text{2. heat to 460 K}]{\text{1. conc. }H_2SO_4} {}^-O_3S\text{–}C_6H_4\text{–}\overset{+}{N}H_3$

Sulfanilic acid (R)

120. **(c)** Hofmann's mustard oil reaction.

121. **(a)** Only 1° amines undergo Hofmann's mustard oil reaction and thus give a black precipitate of HgS.

122. **(b)** $\underset{\text{Aniline}}{C_6H_5\text{–}NH_2} \xrightarrow[-HCl]{COCl_2} [C_6H_5\text{–}NHCOCl] \xrightarrow[-HCl]{\text{Pyridine}} \underset{\text{Phenyl isocyanate}}{C_6H_5\text{–}N{=}C{=}O}$

123. **(d)** Amines in which the $–NH_2$ group is attached to a *tert*-alkyl group are oxidised to the corresponding nitro compounds by $KMnO_4$. That is,

$(CH_3)_3C\text{–}NH_2 \xrightarrow{KMnO_4} (CH_3)_3C\text{–}NO_2$

$\begin{matrix} Cl & \vdots & N & \vdots & O \\ C_2H_5 & \vdots & H & \vdots & H_2 \end{matrix} \xrightarrow{NOCl} C_2H_5Cl + N_2 + H_2O$

124. **(b)** Acetamide and ethylamines can be distinguished by heating with NaOH solution when acetamide evolves NH_3 but ethylamine does not.

$CH_3CONH_2 + NaOH \xrightarrow{\Delta} CH_3COONa + NH_3$

$CH_3CH_2NH_2 + NaOH \rightarrow \text{no reaction}$

125. **(c)**

Benzene $\xrightarrow[\text{(Nitration)}]{\text{conc. }HNO_3 + \text{conc. }H_2SO_4}$ Nitrobenzene $\xrightarrow[\text{(Bromination)}]{Br_2/FeBr_3}$ *m*-Bromoaniline $\xrightarrow[\text{(Reduction)}]{Sn/HCl}$ *m*-Bromoaniline

126. **(a)** Nitrobenzene due to the strong electron withdrawing effect of the nitro group does not undergo FC reaction. Therefore, FC reaction between benzene and 2-nitrobenzoyl chloride will give the desired ketone.

Benzene + 2-Nitrobenzoyl chloride $\xrightarrow[\text{(FC reaction)}]{\text{Anhyd. }AlCl_3}$ 2-Nitrobenzophenone

127. **(c)** Arylamines are generally less basic than alkylamines because the lone pair of electrons on the nitrogen are delocalised by interaction with the π-electrons of the aromatic ring and hence are less available for protonation.

Diazonium Salts

128. **(b)** Due to delocalisation of the +ve charge on the benzene ring, aromatic diazonium salts are the most stable compared to alkyl and aralkyl diazonium salts.

129. **(d)** Electron donating groups increase the stability of diazonium cations by dispersing the +ve charge on the N atom.

130. **(d)** Aniline $\xrightarrow{Br_2/H_2O}$ 2,4,6-Tribromoaniline (X) $\xrightarrow[0°C]{NaNO_2/HCl}$ 2,4,6-Tribromobenzenediazonium chloride (Y) (Water soluble) $\xrightarrow[\text{(Sandmeyer reaction)}]{Cu_2Cl_2/HCl}$ 2,4,6-Tribromochlorobenzene (Z)

131. **(c)**

2-Chloroaniline (Cl, NH_2) $\xrightarrow[0°C]{NaNO_2/HCl}$ (Cl, N_2Cl) $\xrightarrow[\text{(Sandmeyer reaction)}]{CuBr/HBr}$ (Cl, Br)

132. **(c)**

Nitrobenzene $\xrightarrow[\text{(Chlorination)}]{Cl_2/AlCl_3}$ 3-Chloronitrobenzene $\xrightarrow[\text{(Reduction)}]{Zn/HCl}$ 3-Chloroaniline

$\xrightarrow[\text{(Diazotisation)}]{HNO_2\text{, cold}}$ ($\overset{+}{N}{\equiv}NCl^-$, Cl) $\xrightarrow[\text{(Sandmeyer reaction)}]{Cu_2Br_2}$ 1-Bromo-3-chlorobenzene

133. **(b)**

Aniline (NH_2) $\xrightarrow[\text{Acetylation}]{\text{Acetic anhydride/ pyridine}}$ Acetanilide ($NHCOCH_3$) $\xrightarrow[\text{(Bromination)}]{KBrO_3/HBr}$

p-Bromoacetanilide ($NHCOCH_3$, Br) $\xrightarrow[\text{(Hydrolysis)}]{H_3O^+/\text{heat}}$ *p*-Bromoaniline (NH_2, Br) $\xrightarrow[\text{(Diazotisation)}]{NaNO_2/HCl,\ 273\text{-}278\text{ K}}$

($\overset{+}{N}{\equiv}NCl^-$, Br) $\xrightarrow[\text{(Gattermann reaction)}]{Cu/HBr}$ p-Dibromobenzene (Br, Br)

134. (b)

$$\underset{\text{Nitrobenzene}}{C_6H_5NO_2} \xrightarrow[\text{(Reduction)}]{Sn/HCl} \underset{\text{Aniline (X)}}{C_6H_5NH_2} \xrightarrow[\text{(Diazotisation)}]{NaNO_2/HCl} \underset{\text{Benzenediazonium chloride}}{C_6H_5\overset{+}{N}\equiv NCl^-} \xrightarrow[\text{(Sandmeyer reaction)}]{CuBr, \Delta} \underset{\text{Bromobenzene (Y)}}{C_6H_5Br}$$

135. (c)

$$C_6H_5NH_2 \xrightarrow[-3\,HBr]{3\,Br_2/H_2O} \text{2,4,6-}Br_3C_6H_2NH_2 \xrightarrow[HCl]{NaNO_2} \text{2,4,6-}Br_3C_6H_2N_2Cl \xrightarrow[-HCl]{HBF_4} \text{2,4,6-}Br_3C_6H_2N_2BF_4 \xrightarrow[N_2,\,-BF_3]{\Delta} \underset{\text{2, 4, 6-Tribromofluorobenzene}}{\text{2,4,6-}Br_3C_6H_2F}$$

136. (c)

$$\underset{p\text{-Chloroaniline}}{CH_3-C_6H_4-NH_2} \xrightarrow[0°–5°C]{NaNO_2/HCl} \underset{p\text{-Chloroaniline}}{CH_3-C_6H_4-N_2^+Cl^-} \xrightarrow{KCN} CH_3-C_6H_4-CN \xrightarrow[\text{(Reduction)}]{LiAlH_4} \underset{p\text{-Chlorobenzylamine}}{CH_3-C_6H_4-CN}$$

137. (b)

$$\underset{\text{Aniline}}{C_6H_5-NH_2} \xrightarrow[0°C]{NaNO_2/HCl} \underset{(X)}{C_6H_5N_2^+Cl^-} \xrightarrow{CuCN} C_6H_5-CN \xrightarrow{H_2/Ni} \underset{\text{Benzylamine (Z)}}{C_6H_5CH_2NH_2}$$

138. (b)

$$m\text{-}BrC_6H_4N_2Cl \xrightarrow{H_3PO_2} C_6H_5Br$$

139. (c) Replacement of the diazo group by H is carried out with H_3PO_2/H_2O.

$$\text{4-nitro-2-bromobenzenediazonium chloride } (O_2N-C_6H_3(Br)-N_2^+Cl^-) \xrightarrow[-N_2,\,-HCl]{H_3PO_2/H_2O} m\text{-}O_2N-C_6H_4-Br$$

Thus, A is H_3PO_2 and H_2O, that is, option (c) is correct.

140. (b)

$$CH_3-C_6H_4-NO_2 \xrightarrow[\text{(Nuclear bromination)}]{Br_2} \underset{(A)}{CH_3-C_6H_3(Br)-NO_2} \xrightarrow[\text{(Reduction)}]{Sn//HCl} \underset{(B)}{CH_3-C_6H_3(Br)-NH_2} \xrightarrow[\substack{273–278\text{ K} \\ \text{(Diazotisation)}}]{NaNO_2/HCl} \underset{(C)}{CH_3-C_6H_3(Br)-\overset{+}{N}\equiv NCl^-}$$

$$\xrightarrow[\substack{-N_2,\,-HCl \\ \text{(Reduction)}}]{H_3PO_2} CH_3-C_6H_4-Br \xrightarrow[\text{(Oxidation)}]{KMnO_4,\ OH^-} HOOC-C_6H_4-Br$$

141. (b)

$$p\text{-}CH_3C_6H_4NH_2 \xrightarrow{Br_2\text{ (excess)}} \underset{(X)}{\text{2,6-dibromo-4-methylaniline}} \xrightarrow[(2)\ H_3PO_2]{(1)\ NaNO_2/HCl} \underset{(Y)}{\text{3,5-dibromotoluene}}$$

142. (d)

$$\underset{\text{Aniline (X)}}{C_6H_5NH_2} \xrightarrow{\text{Bromination}} \underset{(Y)}{\text{2,4,6-}Br_3C_6H_2NH_2} \xrightarrow{NaNO_2/HCl} \underset{(Z)}{\text{2,4,6-}Br_3C_6H_2N_2Cl} \xrightarrow[C_2H_5OH]{\text{Boiling}} \underset{sym\text{-Tribromobenzene}}{\text{1,3,5-}Br_3C_6H_3}$$

143. (a)

$$C_6H_5NO_2 \xrightarrow[\text{(Reduction)}]{Fe/HCl} C_6H_5NH_2 \xrightarrow[273\text{ (Diazotisation)}]{NaNO_2/HCl}$$

$$C_6H_5\overset{+}{N}\equiv NCl^- \xrightarrow[\text{Hydrolysis}]{H_2O,\ 283\text{ K}} C_6H_5OH$$

144. (a)

$$\underset{p\text{-Nitrophenol}}{HO-C_6H_4-NO_2} \xrightarrow[\text{(Reduction)}]{Sn/HCl} \underset{p\text{-Aminophenol}}{HO-C_6H_4-NH_2} \xrightarrow[\substack{278\text{ K} \\ \text{(Diazotisation)}}]{NaNO_2/HCl}$$

$$HO-C_6H_4-\overset{+}{N}\equiv NCl^- \xrightarrow[\text{(Hydrolysis)}]{Dil.\ H_2SO_4,\ \Delta} \underset{\text{Quinol}}{HO-C_6H_4-OH}$$

145. (c)

$$m\text{-}CH_3C_6H_4NH_2 \xrightarrow[273–278\text{ K}]{NaNO_2/HBF_4} \underset{(A)}{m\text{-}CH_3C_6H_4N_2^+BF_4^-} \xrightarrow[\Delta]{NaNO_2/Cu} m\text{-}CH_3C_6H_4NO_2$$

146. (b)

$$C_6H_5-N_2Cl + H-C_6H_4-Br \xrightarrow[\substack{-N_2,\,-HCl \\ \text{(Gomberg's reaction)}}]{NaOH} \underset{p\text{-Bromodiphenyl}}{C_6H_5-C_6H_4-Br}$$

147. (c)

$$C_6H_5-N_2Cl \xrightarrow{Aq.\ Na_2SO_3} C_6H_5-NHNH_2$$

148. (a) $C_6H_5-N{=}N-C_6H_4-OH$ is formed

149. (b)

$$C_6H_5NH_2CONH_2 \xrightarrow[\text{(Hofmann bromamide reaction)}]{Br_2+NaOH} A(C_7H_7NO)$$

$$\underset{(B)}{C_6H_5NH_2} \xrightarrow[\text{(Carbylamine reaction)}]{CHCl_3/KOH(alc.)} C_6H_5N\equiv C$$

B upon diazotisation gives the diazonium salt which couples with phenol to give the azo dye.

$$\underset{(B)}{C_6H_5NH_2} \xrightarrow[\text{(Diazotisation)}]{NaNO_2+HCl} C_6H_5N_2Cl \xrightarrow[NaOH]{C_6H_5OH} \underset{\text{Azo dye}}{C_6H_5-N{=}N-C_6H_4-OH}$$

Therefore, A must be benzamide.

150. (d) $\underset{\text{Yellow dye (A)}}{C_6H_5-N{=}N-C_6H_4-NH_2}$ is formed

151. (b) $C_6H_5\overset{+}{N}{\equiv}NCl^-$ (B) + $C_6H_5N(CH_3)_2$ $\xrightarrow{\text{Cold}}$ $C_6H_5{-}N{=}N{-}C_6H_4{-}N(CH_3)_2$ (C)

152. (a) Coupling is an electrophilic substitution reaction in which the diazonium cation with the positive charge on the terminal cation acts as the electrophile. Therefore, the order of reactivity increases as the nucleophilicity of the coupling species increases. Since the nucleophilicity increases in the order ammonium cation (IV) < phenol (II) < amine (III) < phenoxide ion (I), therefore, option (a) is correct.

153. (b)

$C_6H_5{-}NO_2 \xrightarrow[\text{(Reduction)}]{\text{Sn/HCl}} C_6H_5{-}NH_2 \xrightarrow[\text{(Diazotisation)}]{HNO_2}$

$C_6H_5{-}\overset{+}{N}{\equiv}NCl^-$ (Benzenediazonium chloride (B)) $\xrightarrow[\text{(Coupling reaction)}]{C_6H_5OH}$ $C_6H_5{-}N{=}N{-}C_6H_4{-}OH$

p-Hydroxyazobenzene (Beautiful coloured, MF $C_{12}H_{10}N_2O$)

154. (c) Only aromatic 1° amines form a brilliant coloured dye on treatment with $NaNO_2$ in dil. HCl followed by the addition of an alkaline solution of β-naphthol. Thus, option (c) is correct.

155. (a) $C_6H_5NH_2 \xrightarrow[0°C]{NaNO_2,\ HCl} C_6H_5\overset{+}{N}{\equiv}NCl^-$

Benzenediazonium chloride (V)

$\xrightarrow{\text{2-naphthol}}$ $C_6H_5{-}N{=}N{-}$(1-position of 2-hydroxynaphthalene; OH at 2, positions 3, 4)

(W)

Due to greater stabilisation of the carbocation resulting from the attack of the benzenediazo cation at position 1 as compared to positions 3 and 4, coupling reaction occurs at position 1 and hence option (a) is correct.

156. (b) Aromatic primary amines like aniline can be distinguished from aliphatic primary amines like ethylamine by the dye test.

157. (b) Since compound X gives 2,4-DNP and iodoform test, it must contain the $-COCH_3$ group. Further, since the compound (X) does not give the azo dye test, it does not contain a 1° aromatic amino group. Thus, option (b) is correct.

158. (d) Aryl amines react with HNO_2 to form diazonium salts. All other statements are correct.

159. (b) It is a source of electrophilic nitrosonium ion.

$H{-}O{-}N{=}O \xrightarrow{H^+} H_2\overset{+}{O}{-}N{=}O \longrightarrow H_2O + \overset{+}{N}{=}O$

Nitrosonium ion

160. (c) Urea decomposes HNO_2 to give N_2, CO_2 and H_2O.

$NH_2CONH_2 + 2\ HONO \rightarrow 2\ N_2\uparrow + CO_2\uparrow + 3\ H_2O$

161. (a) Due to the strong electron withdrawing effect of the $-NO_2$ group, the nucleophilicity of the $-NH_2$ is reduced and hence diazotisation becomes difficult.

Final Preparation

162. (a) Aralkyl halide are more reactive than aryl halides towards nucleophilic substitution reaction. Therefore, the reaction occurs at the more reactive CH_2Cl instead of at the less reactive Br atom.

Phthalimide (N–H) $\xrightarrow[-H_2O]{KOH}$ Potassium phthalimide (N^-K^+) $\xrightarrow[-KCl]{Cl{-}CH_2{-}C_6H_4{-}Br}$ Phthalimide–N–$CH_2{-}C_6H_4{-}Br$

163. (b) To prepare phenylalanine

$C_6H_5CH_2{-}CH(NH_2){-}COOH$

Phenylalanine

The ester of 2-chloro-3-phenylpropanoic acid is required.

$\overset{3}{C_6H_5CH_2}{-}\overset{2}{CH}(Cl){-}COOH$

2-Chloro-3-phenylpropanoic acid

The complete sequence of reactions is

Phthalimide (NH) $\xrightarrow[-H_2O]{KOH}$ Potassium phthalimide (N^-K^+) $\xrightarrow[-KCl]{Cl{-}CH(COOC_2H_5)(CH_2C_6H_5)}$

Phthalimide–N–$CH(COOC_2H_5)(CH_2C_6H_5)$ $\xrightarrow[\text{(Hydrolysis)}]{KOH}$

$C_6H_5CH_2{-}CH(NH_2){-}COOH$ + $C_6H_4(COOK)_2$ + C_2H_5OH

Phenylalanine

164. (d) *m*-Bromotoluic acid (A) (3-BrC_6H_4COOH) $\xrightarrow[-SO_2,\ -HCl]{SOCl_2}$ 3-BrC_6H_4COCl (B) $\xrightarrow[-NH_4Cl]{2\ NH_3}$

m-Bromobenzamide (C) (3-$BrC_6H_4CONH_2$) $\xrightarrow[\text{(Hofmann bromamide reaction)}]{NaOH/Br_2}$ 3-$BrC_6H_4NH_2$ *m*-Bromoaniline (D)

165. **(c)** The correct option is C. Benzene on reacting with HNO_3, H_2SO_4 undergoes aromatic electrophilic substitution reaction to form nitrobenzene. It reacts with Br_2 to form the meta product because NO_2 is a meta directing group. Fe, HCl is a reducing agent it will reduce the nitro group in *m*-bromo nitrobenzene to amino group. Thus, it gives *m*-bromoaniline as the final product.

Benzene $\xrightarrow{HNO_3,\ H_2SO_4}$ Nitrobenzene (NO_2) $\xrightarrow{Br_2,\ FeBr_3}$ *m*-Bromonitrobenzene (NO_2, Br) $\xrightarrow{Fe,\ HCl}$ *m*-Bromoaniline (NH_2, Br)

166. **(c)** (2-(CH_2CONH_2)-benzoate, $COOCH_3$) $\xrightarrow[\text{(Hofmann bromamide reaction)}]{Br_2/NaOH}$ (2-(CH_2NH_2)-C(=O)OCH_3) $\xrightarrow[-CH_3OH]{Heat}$ (cyclic lactam, NH, C=O)

167. **(a)** Succinimide (CO–NH–CO) $\xrightarrow[\text{(Hydrolysis)}]{NaOH}$ [$COOH$ / $CONH_2$] I $\xrightarrow[\text{(Hofmann bromamide reaction)}]{Br_2/KOH}$ $H_2N\text{–}\overset{\beta}{C}H_2\text{–}\overset{\alpha}{C}H_2\text{–}COOH$ *β*-Alanine

Phthalimide $\xrightarrow[\text{(Hydrolysis)}]{NaOH}$ [$COONa$ / $CONH_2$] $\xrightarrow[\text{(Hofmann bromamide reaction)}]{Br_2-KOH}$ [$COONa$ / NH_2] $\xrightarrow{H_3O^+}$ ($COOH$ / NH_2) Anthranilic acid

168. **(b)** Label the compound with MF C_8H_8ClNO as 'N' and the final amine as 'O'. The compound 'N' on treatment with Br_2/NaOH gives an amine 'O' (Hofmann bromamide reaction), therefore, compound 'N' must be an amide and the position of the $-CONH_2$ group is the same as that of the $-NH_2$ group in the amine 'O'. The compound 'M' on treatment with NH_3 gives the amide 'N' with one Cl less and one N and two H atoms more, therefore, compound 'M' must be an acid chloride, and the position of the COCl group must be the same as that of $CONH_2$ group in the compound 'N' and the $-NH_2$ group in compound 'O' as described below.

(3-chloro-4-methyl)–C(=O)Cl M($C_8H_6Cl_2O$) $\xrightarrow[-NH_4Cl]{2\ NH_3}$ (3-chloro-4-methyl)–C(=O)NH_2 N(C_8H_8ClNO) $\xrightarrow[\text{(Hofmann bromamide reaction)}]{Br_2/NaOH}$ (3-chloro-4-methyl)–NH_2 'O'

Thus, option (b) is correct.

169. **(c)** $R\text{–}NH_2 + RCHO \xrightarrow[\text{amination}]{\text{Reductive}}$

$(-H_2O)$

$[R\text{–}N\text{=}CHR] \xrightarrow{H_2/Pt} R\text{–}NH\text{–}CH_2R$ 2° Amine

170. **(c)** Cyclohexanone $\xrightarrow[-H_2O]{NH_3}$ [cyclohexanimine (=NH)] $\xrightarrow[\text{(Reductive amination)}]{Ni/H_2}$ Cyclohexylamine ($-NH_2$)

171. **(a)** Cyclohexanone $+ (CH_3)_2NH \xrightarrow{Ether}$ (cyclohexylidene)$=\overset{+}{N}(CH_3)_2$ $\xrightarrow[\text{(Reductive amination)}]{NaBH_3CN/CH_3OH}$ (cyclohexyl)$-N(CH_3)_2$

N, N-Dimethylcyclohexylamine

172. **(c)** $(CH_3)_2CHNH_2 + (CH_3)_2CHCHO \xrightarrow{-H_2O}$
Isopropylamine Isobutyraldehyde

$[(CH_3)_2CHCH\text{=}NCH(CH_3)_2] \xrightarrow[\text{Reductive amination}]{H_2/Pt}$

$(CH_3)_2CHCH_2\text{–}NHCH(CH_3)_2$

$C_2H_5N{\equiv}C + 2\,H_2O \xrightarrow{H^+} C_2H_5NH_2 + HCOOH$

Ethyl carbylamine — Ethylamine — reduces Fehling's solution

173. **(c)** $C_6H_5CH_3 \xrightarrow{[O]} C_6H_5COOH \xrightarrow{SOCl_2}$
Toluene (A)

$C_6H_5COCl \xrightarrow[-NaCl_3]{NaN_3} C_6H_5CON_3 \xrightarrow[\text{(Curtius rearrangement)}]{\Delta(-N_2)}$
(B)

$C_6H_5\text{–}N\text{=}C\text{=}O$ Phenyl isocyanate (D)

174. **(b)** $CH_3\text{–}\overset{\overset{\large NH}{\|}}{C}\text{–}NH_2 + H^+ \longrightarrow CH_3\text{–}\overset{\overset{\large \overset{+}{N}H_2}{\|}}{C}\text{–}NH_2$
1 (I)

$\longleftrightarrow CH_3\text{–}\overset{\overset{\large \overset{+}{N}H}{\|}}{C}\text{–}\ddot{N}H_2 \longleftrightarrow CH_3\text{–}\overset{\overset{\large NH_2}{|}}{C}\text{=}\overset{+}{N}H_2$
(i) (ii)

The conjugate acid (i) obtained by addition of a proton to (1) is stabilised by two equivalent resonance structures and hence compound (1) is the most basic. Further, 2° amines are more basic than 1° amines while amides are least basic due to delocalisation of the lone pair of electrons on N over the C=O group. Thus, the order 1 > 3 > 2 > 4, that is, option (b) is correct.

175. **(c)** The conjugate acid obtained by the addition of a proton to amine (4) is stabilised by three equivalent resonance structures (i–iii) while that obtained by addition of a proton to amine (I) is stabilised by two equivalent resonance structures (iv and v). Therefore, amine (4) is more basic than amine (3).

$H_2N-C(=NH)-NH_2$ (4) $\xrightarrow{H^+}$ (i) $\longrightarrow$ (ii) (iii)

$CH_3C(=NH)NH_2$ (3) $+ H^+ \longrightarrow$ (iv) $\longleftrightarrow$ (v)

Further, in amine (2), the lone pair of electrons is present in an sp^2-orbital while in amine (1) it is present in an sp^3-orbital. Since a lone pair of electrons in an sp^3-orbital is more easily available for protonation than in an sp^2-orbital, amine (1) is more basic than amine 2. Combining both the trends as discussed above, the basicity of the four bases increases in the order 2 < 1 < 3 < 4, that is, option (c) is correct.

176. **(d)** Compound (IV) is more basic than compound (I). Further, compound (III) is aromatic while compound (II) is not since the lone pair of electrons on the N of the NH group of compound (III) is donated towards the ring for aromatic sextet formation making it unavailable for protonation while this is not so in compound (II). Compound (II) is more basic than compound (III). Combining both the trends discussed above, the basicity of the given four compounds decreases in the order IV > I > II > III. That is, option (d) is correct.

177. **(d)** In compound II (pyridine), the lone pair of electrons on N is present in an sp^2-orbital while in compounds I (piperidine) and III (morpholine), the lone pair of electrons on N is present in an sp^3-orbital. Since an sp^2-orbital has more *s* character (33.33%) than an sp^3-orbital (25%), the lone pair of electrons on N is more easily available for protonation in I and III than in II. In other words, compound (II) is less basic I and III. Among I and III, III contains an oxygen atom which has –I effect. As a result, it will attract the lone pair of electrons on N towards itself. Consequently, the lone pair of electrons on N in III is less readily available for protonation than in I. In other words, compound I is more basic than III.
Compound IV (pyrrole) is aromatic in character. Therefore, in accordance with '*Huckel rule*', it has a cyclic cloud of six π-electrons. Out of these, four electrons are contributed by two double bonds while the remaining two are the lone pair of electrons on the N-atom which are contributed towards the aromatic sextet formation and hence are not available for protonation. Therefore, compound IV is the least basic. In fact, it is such a weak base that it is weakly acidic in character and thus reacts with K metal when heated to form the corresponding potassium salts. Thus, the overall order of basicity is I > III > II > IV, that is, option (d) is correct.

178. **(a)** Amines are more basic than ethers, therefore, (d) is least basic. Out of (a), (b), (c); (c) is the least basic due to donation of its lone pair of electrons towards the aromatic sextet formation. Out of (a) and (b), since 2° amines are more basic than 3° amines, (a) is the most basic amine.

179. **(b)** Due to delocalisation of electrons over the C=O group, amides are much less basic than amines. Thus, I is more basic than II and III. Now, due to the strong +R effect of

$CH_3-C(=O)-NH_2$ (II) $\quad C_6H_5-C(=O)-NH_2$ (III)

the C_6H_5 group, it pushes electrons into the C=O group more readily than the CH_3 group which can exert only its weak +I effect. In other words, electrons on the NH_2 group in CH_3CONH_2 (II) are more easily delocalised than on the NH_2 group of $C_6H_5CONH_2$ (III). This means that $C_6H_5CONH_2$ is a stronger base than CH_3CONH_2 (II). Thus, the overall basicity decreases in the order I > III > II.

180. **(b)** A weak base has a strong conjugate acid. Since aniline is the weakest base, its conjugate acid is the strongest acid.

181. **(b)** Due to the –I effect of F, the electron density in the N–H bond decreases and hence the release of a proton becomes easier from the *p*-fluoroanilinium ion than from the anilinium ion. Thus, option (b) is wrong. All other statements are correct.

182. **(b)** In (c), the electrons on the N atom are delocalised over two double bonds, in (d), the electrons are more strongly delocalised over the benzene ring but in (b), electrons are not delocalised at all, therefore, it is the strongest base. Further, being a 2° amine, it is more basic than even NH_3. Thus, option (b) is correct.

183. **(d)** $C_6H_5NH_2$ is the weakest base because the lone pair of electrons on the N atom is delocalised over the benzene ring. In $CH_2=CHCH_2NH_2$

$$\overset{sp^2}{CH_2=CH} \leftarrow CH_2 \leftarrow NH_2$$
$$\overset{sp}{HC\equiv C} \leftarrow CH_2 \leftarrow NH_2$$
$$\overset{sp^3}{CH_3CH_2CH_2} \rightarrow NH_2$$

and $HC\equiv CCH_2NH_2$, sp^2 and *sp* carbon atoms respectively, being more electronegative, attract the lone pair of electrons on N thereby reducing the electron density. In contrast, the +Ieffect of the $CH_3CH_2CH_2$ group increase the electron density on N. Thus, $CH_3CH_2CH_2NH_2$ is the strongest base, that is, option (d) is correct.

184. **(d)** Pyrrole has two different types of hydrogens, namely, 2(or 5) and 3(or 4).
Obviously, electron density is high where electrophilic substitution occurs predominantly. To decide this, let us compare the stabilities of carbocations resulting from attack of the electrophile at C_2 (or C_5) or at C_3 (or C_4) positions.
Attack at C_2 (or C_5)

Pyrrole $\xrightarrow{E^+}$ I $\longleftrightarrow$ II $\longleftrightarrow$ III

Attack at C_3 (or C_4)

Since the carbocation resulting from the electrophilic attack at C_2 or C_5 is stabilised by three resonance structures (I–III) while that resulting from attack at C_3 or C_4 is stabilised by only two resonance structures (IV, V), the electron density is maximum at C_2 and C_5 positions, that is, option (d) is correct.

185. (a) (i) O_3, (ii) Zn, H_2O (Reductive ozonolysis); Enolisation; NH_3, $-H_2O$ (Enamine formation); $-H_2O$, Cyclisation

186. (b) $CH_3C\equiv N$ A(MFC_2H_3N) $\xrightarrow{\text{Redn.}}$ $CH_3CH_2NH_2$ Ethylamine (B) $\xrightarrow{HNO_2}$ CH_3CH_2OH

$CH_3CH_2NH_2$ Ethylamine (B) $\xrightarrow{CHCl_3/\text{Alc.KOH}}$ CH_3CH_2NC Ethyl isocyanide (C)

187. (a) Since the organic compound (C_3H_9N) on treatment with HNO_2 gave an alcohol with the evolution of N_2 gas, (A) must be a 1° amine. Since (A) on warming with $CHCl_3$/KOH gave (C) which on reduction gave isopropylmethylamine, (A) must be isopropylamine.

$(CH_3)_2CH{-}NH_2$ Isopropylamine A (MF C_3H_9N) $\xrightarrow[-N_2]{HNO_2}$ $(CH_3)_2CH{-}OH$ Isopropyl alcohol

$CHCl_3$/KOH, Δ (Carbylamine reaction): $(CH_3)_2CH{-}NC$ Isopropyl alcohol $\xrightarrow{\text{Reduction}}$ $(CH_3)_2CH{-}NH{-}CH_3$ Isopropylmethylamine

188. (c) $CH_3{-}\overset{*}{C}H(C_6H_5){-}NH_2$ (+) or (−) $\xrightarrow{HONO}$ $CH_3{-}\overset{*}{C}H(C_6H_5){-}\overset{+}{N}\equiv N$ (unstable) $\xrightarrow{-N_2}$ $CH_3{-}\overset{*}{\overset{+}{C}}H{-}C_6H_5$ $\xrightarrow[-H^+]{H_2O}$ $CH_3{-}\overset{*}{C}H(OH){-}C_6H_5$ (+)

Since carbocations are planar species, nucleophilic attack by H_2O gives a racemic mixture of 2° alcohols.

189. (d) Since the amine ($C_5H_{13}N$) on treatment with aq. $NaNO_2$/HCl evolves N_2 gas, it must be a 1° amine. Since the amine is optically active, the $-NH_2$ group cannot be attached to a chiral centre because it will rapidly undergo racemisation due to nitrogen inversion. Therefore, the carbon skeleton must contain a chiral centre. In other words, the amine is 2-methylbutanamine.

$CH_3CH_2{-}\overset{*}{C}H(CH_3){-}CH_2NH_2$ 2-Methylbutanamine

The formation of an optically inactive alcohol from an optically active amine may be explained as follows.

$CH_3CH_2{-}CH(CH_3){-}CH_2NH_2 \xrightarrow{HONO} CH_3CH_2{-}CH(CH_3){-}CH_2{-}\overset{+}{N}{=}N$ (Unstable)

$\xrightarrow{-N_2} CH_3CH_2{-}C(H)(CH_3){-}\overset{+}{C}H_2$ 1° carbocation (less stable) $\xrightarrow{\text{1, 2-Hydride shift}}$

$CH_3CH_2{-}\overset{+}{C}(CH_3){-}CH_3 \xrightarrow[-H^+]{+H_2O} CH_3CH_2{-}C(CH_3)(OH){-}CH_3$ 2-Methyl-2-butanol (Optically inactive)

190. (d) Aliphatic 1° amines react with HNO_2 to form diazonium salts which rapidly decompose to form carbocations which can subsequently undergo rearrangement followed by substitution and elimination reactions to give a number of products depending upon the structure of the carbocation.

$CH_3CH_2CH_2{-}NH_2$ 1-Propanamine $\xrightarrow{HNO_2}$ $CH_3CH_2CH_2\overset{+}{N}{=}N$ Propane diazonium cation (unstable)

$\xrightarrow{-N_2}$ $CH_3CH_2\overset{+}{C}H_2$ 1° Carbocation (I) (less stable) $\xrightarrow{\text{1,2-Hydride Shift 2°}}$ $CH_3{-}\overset{+}{C}H{-}CH_3$ carbocation(II) (more stable)

$CH_3CH_2\overset{+}{C}H_2$ (I) $\xrightarrow[\text{Elimination}]{-H^+}$ $CH_3CH{=}CH_2$ Propene

$CH_3CH_2\overset{+}{C}H_2$ (I) $\xrightarrow[-H^+]{+H_2O}$ $CH_3CH_2CH_2OH$ 1-Propanol

$CH_2(H){-}CH_2{-}\overset{+}{C}H_2 \xrightarrow[\text{(Elimination)}]{-H^+}$ Cyclopropane

$CH_3{-}\overset{+}{C}H{-}CH_3$ (II) $\xrightarrow[-H^+]{-H_2O}$ (Substitution) $CH_3{-}CH(OH){-}CH_3$ 2-Propanol

Thus, option (d) is correct.

191. (d) Cyclopentylmethylamine $\xrightarrow{HNO_2}$ cyclopentylmethyldiazonium (unstable) $\xrightarrow{-N_2}$ I

I $\xrightarrow{\text{1, 2-Hydride shift}}$ 1-methylcyclopentyl cation $\xrightarrow[-H^+]{+H_2O}$ 1-methylcyclopentanol

I $\xrightarrow{\text{Ring expansion}}$ cyclohexyl cation $\xrightarrow[-H^+]{+H_2O}$ cyclohexanol

I $\xrightarrow[-H^+]{+H_2O}$ cyclopentylmethanol

Thus, all the three products are formed.

192. (b)

Cyclobutymethylamine $\xrightarrow{HONO}$ $CH_2-\overset{+}{N}\equiv N$ $\xrightarrow{-N_2}$ Cyclobutymethyl carbocation (CH_2^+) → ring-expanded carbocation $\xrightarrow[-H^+]{+H_2O}$ cyclopentanol; Cyclobutymethyl carbocation $\xrightarrow{-H^+}$ methylenecyclobutane ($=CH_2$); $\xrightarrow{+H_2O(-H^+)}$ cyclobutylmethanol (CH_2OH); $\xrightarrow{-H^+}$ cyclopentene

The only product which is not formed is (b).

193. (c) 3° Nitroalkanes do not have a hydrogen to which NO_2 group is attached and hence do not react with HNO_2 while all other compounds react.

Phenol $\xrightarrow{HNO_2}$ p-Nitrosophenol ($ON-C_6H_4-OH$); Aniline $\xrightarrow{HNO_2}$ Benzenediazonium chloride ($C_6H_5-\overset{+}{N}\equiv NCl^-$);

2° Nitroalkane: $(CH_3)_2C(NO_2)-H + HO-NO \longrightarrow (CH_3)_2C(NO_2)(NO)$

194. (d) $\xrightarrow[-H_2O]{Heat}$ $\xrightarrow{NaBH_4}$

195. (c)

Cyclohexanone $\underset{}{\overset{Enolisation}{\rightleftharpoons}}$ enol (OH) $\xrightarrow[\text{Benzene, }\Delta\ (-H_2O)]{\text{pyrrolidine (NH)}}$ Enamine

$\xrightarrow[(-Br^-)]{CH_2=CHCH_2Br}$ iminium salt $\xrightarrow[\text{Hydrolysis}]{H_3O^+,}$ 2-Allylcyclohexanone

196. (a) $\underset{(Z)}{CH_3NH_2} + 3\,CH_3I \longrightarrow [(CH_3)_4\overset{+}{N}]I^- \xrightarrow{\text{Hydrolysis}} [(CH_3)_4]^+OH^-$

197. (a) Due to higher electronegativity of N over S, the +ve charge on N will make the CH_3 group more electron deficient than the +ve charge on less electronegative S. Therefore, $(CH_3)_4N^+I^-$ will undergo nucleophilic substitution more readily than $(CH_3)_3S^+I^-$.

$HO^- Na^+ + CH_3-\overset{+}{N}(CH_3)_3I^- \longrightarrow CH_3OH + (CH_3)_3N + NaI$

198. (d) The more acidic β-hydrogen is lost.

Less acidic β-hydrogen; More acidic β-hydrogen

$\xrightarrow{\text{Hofmann elimination}}$ 3-methylcyclohexene (H, Me) $+ \text{Et}-N(\text{Me})(n\text{-Bu})$

199. (c) $\xrightarrow[\text{(Hofmann elimination)}]{\Delta}$ $N(CH_3)_2$ (alkene product)

200. (c) In Hofmann elimination, the more acidic β-hydrogen is preferentially abstracted and hence the least substituted alkene is the major product. Although the β-hydrogens on CH_3CH_2 are little more acidic than those on $CH_3CH_2CH_2$, their acidities are comparable. Therefore, both ethane and propene are obtained with ethane as the major product.

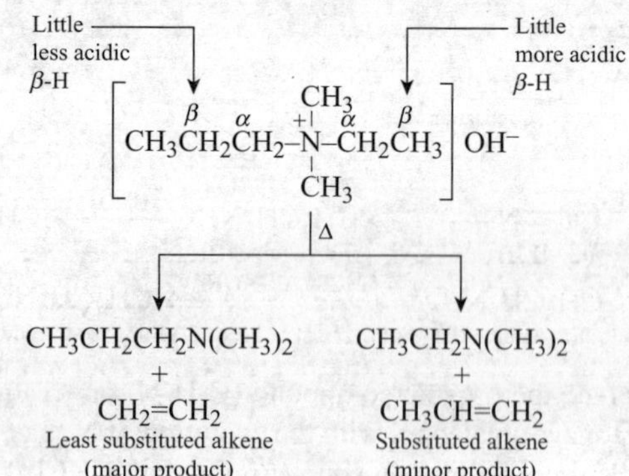

Therefore option (c) is correct.

201. (a) During Hofmann elimination reactions, the more acidic β-hydrogen is eliminated.

$CH_3-CH(NH_2)-CH_2-CH(NH_2)-CH_3 \xrightarrow{3CH_3I} CH_3-CH(\overset{+}{N}(CH_3)_3I^-)-CH_2-CH(CH_3)_2$

4-Methyl-2-aminopentane

More acidic β; Less acidic β

$CH_3-CH(\overset{+}{N}(CH_3)_3OH^-)-CH_2-CH(CH_3)-CH_3 \xrightarrow[-(CH_3)_3I]{\Delta} CH_2=CH-CH_2-CH(CH_3)_2$

4-Methyl-1-pentene

202. (a) Pyrolysis of *tert*-amine oxides to form alkenes is called Cope reaction.

203. (a) During Cope elimination, a β-hydrogen from an alkyl group with respect to N is lost to give an alkene. In the present case, with respect to N there is a β-H atom (of the Me group) or a β-D atom (of the CD_3 group), therefore, the loss of a β-H or D-atom gives a mixture of two alkenes, that is, $CH_2=CH-CD_3$ and $CH-CH=CD_2$ as shown below.

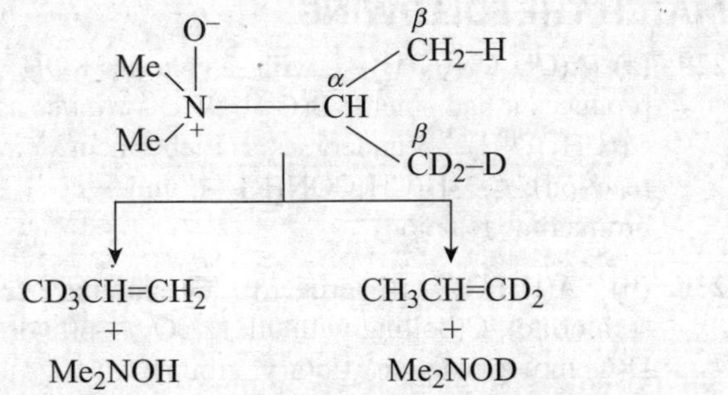

$Me_2N^+(O^-)$–CH(CH_2–H)(CD_2–D) → $CD_3CH{=}CH_2$ + Me_2NOH ; $CH_3CH{=}CD_2$ + Me_2NOD

204. (a) MeO group at the *m*-position exerts a –I effect which tends to weaken the Ar–N_2^+ bond thereby facilitating its decomposition.

205. (b) H_3PO_2 serves both as an acid as well as a reducing agent. In other words, the diazonium salt initially formed is reduced to give benzene.

$$\underset{\text{Aniline}}{C_6H_5NH_2} \xrightarrow{H_3PO_2/NaNO_2} \underset{\text{Benzenediazonium hypophosphite}}{C_6H_5\overset{+}{N_2}HPO_2^-} \xrightarrow{H_3PO_2} \underset{\text{Benzene}}{C_6H_6} + N_2$$

206. (b) Less stable the diazonium salt, the more reactive it is. Since the stability decreases in the order I > III > IV > II, the reactivity increases in the reverse order, I < III < IV < II.

207. (c) 2-amino-3'-hydroxybiphenyl $\xrightarrow{NaNO_2,\ HCl,\ 0°C}$ diazonium salt ($\overset{+}{N}{\equiv}NCl^-$) $\xrightarrow{NaOH}$ phenoxide (O^-Na^+) attacks diazonium group $\xrightarrow{-NaCl}$ cyclised product (N=N) → tautomerises to OH compound

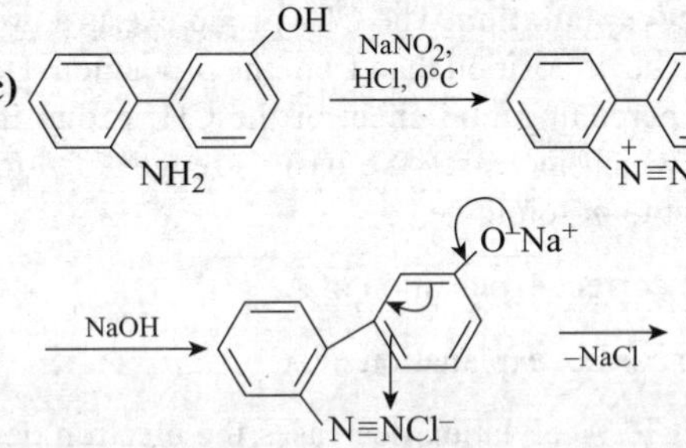

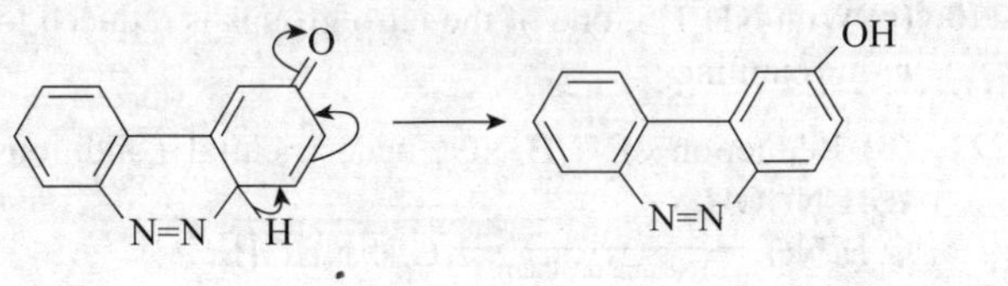

208. (c) o-Phenylenediamine $\xrightarrow[\text{Dil. NaNO}_2,\ 273\ K]{NaNO_2}$ $\overset{+}{N}{\equiv}NCl^-$ / NH_2 → cyclic intermediate $\xrightarrow{-HCl}$ benzotriazole

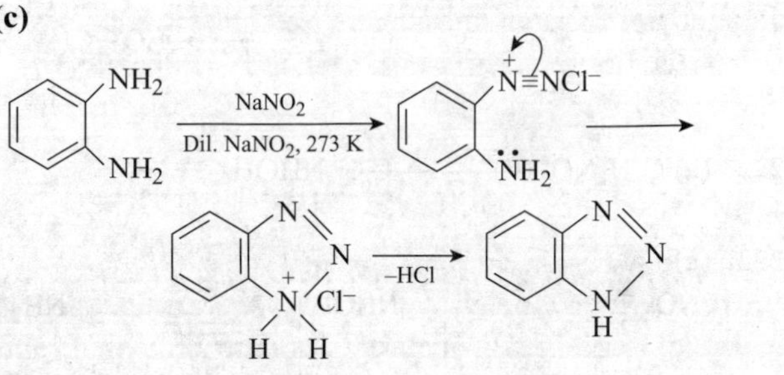

209. (c) 2-aminodiphenylmethane $\xrightarrow[\text{Dil. }H_2SO_4,\ 278\ K]{NaNO_2}$ diazonium salt ($\overset{+}{N}{\equiv}NCl^-$) $\xrightarrow{-Cl^-}$ carbocation cyclisation $\xrightarrow{-H^+}$ fluorene

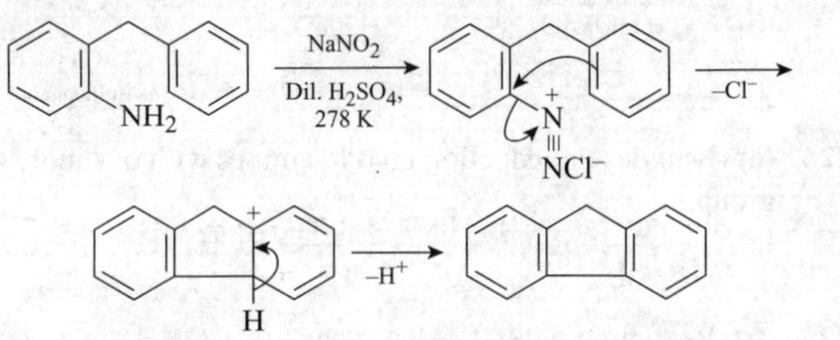

210. (a) Methyl orange is obtained by coupling the sodium salt of sulfanilic acid with N,N-dimethylaniline.

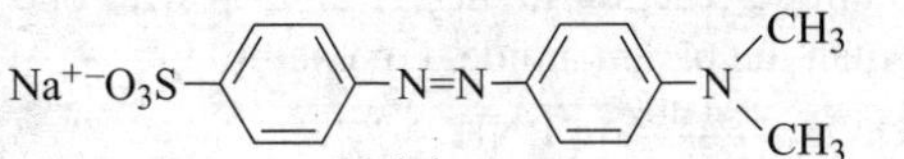

$Na^{+-}O_3S$–C_6H_4–N=N–C_6H_4–$N(CH_3)_2$

Methyl orange

211. (c) H_3C–CO–O–C_6H_4–$CH_2CH_2CH_2NH_2$ $\xrightarrow[\text{(Diazotisation)}]{HNO_2}$ H_3C–CO–O–C_6H_4–$CH_2CH_2CH_2\overset{+}{N}{\equiv}N$ $\xrightarrow[-N_2]{H_2O}$ H_3C–CO–O–C_6H_4–$CH_2CH_2CH_2OH$

$\xrightarrow[\text{(Oxidation of }CH_2OH \rightarrow \text{COOH and hydrolysis of }OCOCH_3 \rightarrow OH)]{CrO_3/H^+}$ HO–C_6H_4–CH_2CH_2–COOH $\xrightarrow[H_2SO_4]{H^+}$ HO–C_6H_4–CH_2CH_2–$\overset{+}{C}$(O)–OH_2 $\xrightarrow[-H_2O]{\text{Cyclisation}}$ intermediate $\longrightarrow$ hydroxyindanone (HO, =O)

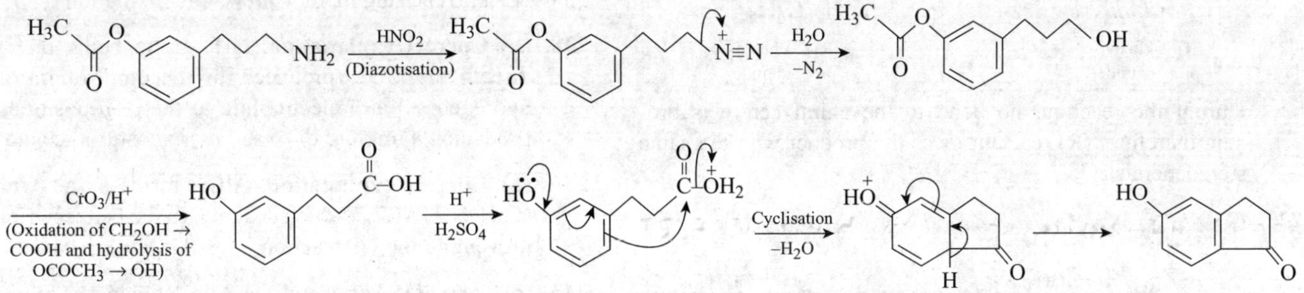

212. (a) Methylisocyanide on reduction with $LiAlH_4$ gives dimethylamine, which is a secondary amine.

213. (d) $(CH_3)_2CHNO \xrightarrow{HNO_2} (CH_3)_2C(NO_2)$–N=O

Pseudo nitrol (blue)

214. (c) $C_6H_5CH{=}O + H_2NCH_3 \rightarrow C_6H_5CH{=}NCH_3$

215. (c) Secondary amines do so,

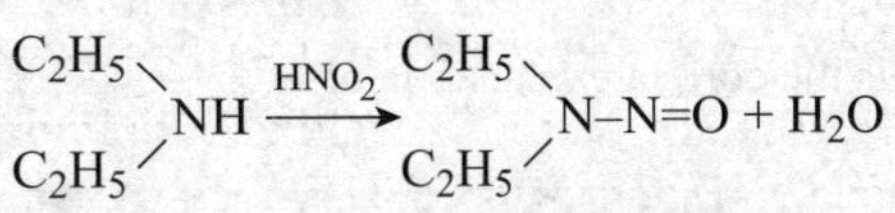

$$(C_2H_5)_2NH \xrightarrow{HNO_2} (C_2H_5)_2N{-}N{=}O + H_2O$$

Oily nitrosoamine

216. (a) $R{-}NH_2 + CHCl_3 + 3KOH \rightarrow 3KCl + H_2O + \underset{\text{Offensive smell}}{RNC}$

217. (d) 3° Amines of the type $R_1R_2R_3N$ do not show optical activity duc to rapid flipping of one form into its non-superimposable mirror image.

218. (c) Due to nitrogen inversion, 3° amines with three different alkyl groups undergo recemisation and hence lose their optical activity, that is, option (c) is correct.

219. (d) Quaternary ammonium salts having different substituents show enantiomerism, that is, option (d) is correct.

220. **(c)** With NH_4HS, one of the nitro groups is reduced to afford *m*-nitroaniline.

221. **(b)** Reduction of $C_6H_5NO_2$ under neutral conditions gives C_6H_5NHOH.

$$\underset{\text{Nitrobenzene}}{C_6H_5NO_2} \xrightarrow[\text{(Neutral medium)}]{Zn/NH_4Cl} \underset{\text{Phenylhdroxylamine}}{C_6H_5NHOH} \xrightarrow{HCl} \underset{(B)}{HO-C_6H_4-NH_2}$$

222. **(a)** $C_6H_5NO_2 \xrightarrow[NH_4Cl]{\text{Zn dust}} \underset{(A)}{C_6H_5NHOH}$

223. **(a)**

$$C_6H_5NO_2 \xrightarrow[\text{(Strongly acidic medium)}]{\text{Electrolytic reduction}} [C_6H_5NHOH] \xrightarrow[\text{(Rearrangement)}]{H^+/H_2O} \underset{p\text{-Aminophenol}}{H_2N-C_6H_4-OH}$$

224. **(c)** Cyanides on reduction give 1° amines with one more CH_2 group.

$$R\text{–}X \xrightarrow[-KX]{KCN} R\text{–}CN \xrightarrow{Na/C_2H_5OH} RCH_2NH_2$$

225. **(b)** Reduction with $LiAlH_4$ converts $CONH_2$ to CH_2NH_2 giving 1° amines with the same number of carbon atoms as the amide. In contrast, Br_2 + NaOH will bring about Hofmann bromamide reaction giving 1° amines with one cabon atom less than the parent amide. For example,

$$RCONH_2 \xrightarrow{LiAlH_4} RNH_2$$

$$RCONH_2 \xrightarrow{Br_2 + NaOH} RNH_2$$

226. **(d)**

$$\underset{\text{(R)-2-Phenyl-propanamide}}{CH_3CH(C_6H_5)CONH_2} \xrightarrow[(ii)\ H_2O]{(i)\ LiAlH_4/\text{ether}} \underset{\text{(R)-2-Phenyl-propanamine}}{CH_3CH(C_6H_5)CH_2NH_2}$$

During the reaction, no bond to the chiral centre is broken, therefore, (R) reactant gives the product with the same stereochemistry.

227. **(d)**

$$O_2N\text{–}C(CH_3)_2CH_2CH_2COOCH_3 \xrightarrow[\Delta]{H_2/Ni} H_2\ddot{N}\text{–}C(CH_3)_2CH_2CH_2COOCH_3 \longrightarrow \text{(cyclic } \overset{+}{N}H_2\text{ lactam)} \xrightarrow{-H^+} \text{(5,5-dimethylpyrrolidin-2-one, NH)}$$

228. **(b)** Acids containing an electron-withdrawing group at the *β*-position on heating undergo decarboxylation.

$$HOOC\cdot\overset{\alpha}{C}(CH_3)_2\cdot\overset{\beta}{CN} \xrightarrow[-CO_2\ (Decarboxylation)]{475\ K} (CH_3)_2CH\text{–}CN \xrightarrow[(ii)\ H_2O]{(i)\ LiAlH_4} (CH_3)_2CHCH_2NH_2$$

MATCH THE FOLLOWING

229. **(a)** A($CH_3CH_2NH_2$)—s(with alcoholic KOH and $CHCl_3$ produces a bad smell); B($C_6H_5NH_2$)—r(gives azo dye test); C($(CH_3)_2NH$)—p(undergoes Liebermann nitrosoamine reaction); D(CH_3CONH_2)—q(undergoes Hofmann bromamide reaction)

230. **(b)** A(H_3PO_2)—r(hydrogen); B(Sandmeyer reaction)—s(chlorine); C(boiling with dil. H_2SO_4)—p(hydroxyl group); D(Gomberg reaction)—q(aryl group)

231. **(c)** A($CH_3CH_2NH_2$)—q(3.29); B($(CH_3CH_2)_2NH$)—r(3.00); C($C_6H_5NH_2$)—s(9.38); D($C_6H_5CH_2NH_2$)—p(4.70)

ASSERTION REASON

232. **(d)** **Correct A.** Both the nitrogens in benzimidazole are not basic.

I II
N is basic while N is not.

Correct R. Lone pair of electrons on N is not delocalised and hence is basic while the
II
lone pair of electrons on N is delocalised and hence is not basic.

233. **(a)** R is the correct explanation of A.

234. **(b)** **Correct explanation**. The CH_3 group exerts a greater +I effect from the *m*-position than from the *p*-position. However, it is the hyperconjugation effect of the CH_3 group from the *p*-position which increases the basic strength of *p*-toluidine with respect to *m*-toluidine.

235. **(a)** R is the correct explanation of A.

236. **(a)** R is the correct explanation of A.

237. **(c)** **Correct R.** Acetylation decreases the electron density in the benzene ring thereby preventing oxidation.

238. **(b)** **Correct explanation.** NH_2 group being *o*, *p*-directing directs the SO_3 (produced by decomposition of aniline hydrogen sulfate) electrophile to the *o*, *p*-positions thereby producing a mixture of *o*- and *p*-aminosulfonic acids.

239. **(b)** **Correct explanation.** $AlCl_3$ forms a salt with aniline ($C_6H_5NH_2^+AlCl_3^-$) which deactivates the benzene ring thereby preventing the FC reaction.

240. **(c)** **Correct R.** The overall electron deficiency in *m*-nitroaniline is much less (due to the –R effect of the NO_2 group and the +R effect of the NH_2 group) than in the *m*-dinitrobenzene (–R effect of two nitro groups) and hence does not accept additional electrons from a weak reducing agent such as $(NH_4)_2S$ and thus further reduction is prevented.

241. **(d)** **Correct A.** Deamination of diazonium salts can be carried out with H_3PO_2 in the presence of Cu^+ as catalyst.
Correct R. Deamination of benzenediazonium chloride gives benzene.

242. **(a)** R is the correct explanation of A.

243. **(a)** R is the correct explanation of A.

244. **(a)** R is the correct explanation of A.

$$\left(\underset{\text{Nucleophile}}{R{-}N{\equiv}\ddot{C}^-} + E^+ \longrightarrow \underset{\text{Electrophile}}{R{-}\overset{+}{N}{\equiv}CE} \xrightarrow{Nu^-} R{-}N{=}C\begin{matrix} \diagup E \\ \diagdown Nu \end{matrix} \right)$$

245. **(c) Correct R.** It can be used to prepare, 1°, 2°, 3° amines and quaternary ammonium salts.

246. **(d) Correct A.** Gabriel's phthalimide reaction can be used to prepare only aralkylamines.
Correct R. Aryl halides are much less reactive than aralkyl halides towards nucleophilic substitution reactions.

247. **(c) Correct R.** A primary amine has a greater number of N–H bonds for H bonding.

248. **(c) Correct R.** Ammonia is a stronger base than aniline, therefore, the conjugate acid of aniline, that is, anilinium chloride is more acidic than the conjugate acid of ammonia, that is, ammonium chloride.

249. **(d) Correct A.** Pyrrole is less basic than pyridine.
Correct R. N in pyrrole is sp^2-hybridised. As a result, the lone pair of electrons on N is contributed towards the aromatic sextet formation and hence is unavailable for protonation.

Biomolecules

14.1 Carbohydrates

Carbohydrates are organic compounds of carbon, hydrogen and oxygen which are primarily produced by plants. They make up about 70% of the solid plant material.

$$x\,CO_2 + y\,H_2O \xrightarrow[\text{Chlorophyll}]{\text{Sunlight}} \underset{\text{Carbohydrate}}{C_x(H_2O)_y} + x\,O_2$$

They were considered to be *hydrates of carbon*. For example, glucose ($C_6H_{12}O_6$), fructose ($C_6H_{12}O_6$), sucrose ($C_{12}H_{22}O_{11}$). Many compounds such as formaldehyde (HCHO) and acetic acid (CH_3COOH) conform to the general formula $C_x(H_2O)_y$, but they do not show the characteristic properties of carbohydrates. Some carbohydrates like rhamnose ($C_6H_{12}O_5$), bioinonose ($C_6H_{10}O_6$) and deoxyribose ($C_5H_{10}O_4$) cannot be represented as hydrates of carbon.

Carbohydrates are also defined as *polyhydroxy aldehydes* or *polyhydroxy ketones* or *substances which give these compounds on hydrolysis* and *generally contain at least one chiral carbon atom* (except dihydroxyacetone HO–CH_2–CO–CH_2–OH). They are classified as shown in Fig. 14.1.

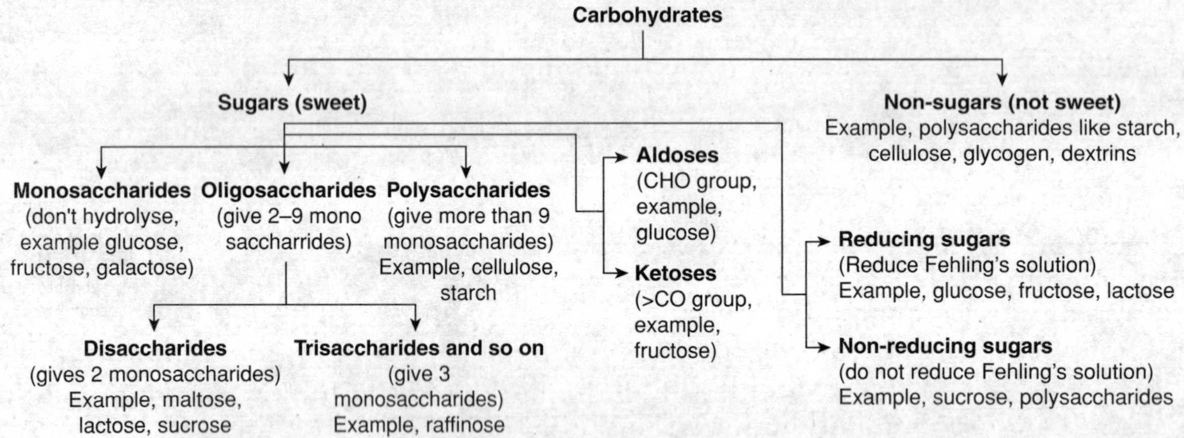

Fig. 14.1 Classification of carbohydrates

Nowadays, carbohydrates are systematically classified into three principal classes.

14.1.1 Classification Based on Reducing Properties

(i) **Reducing sugars**: Carbohydrates which reduce Tollens' reagent or Fehling's (or Benedict's) solutions are called reducing carbohydrates. Such carbohydrates usually contain a free –CHO group [as in D(+)-glucose] or contain a ketonic group at the C-2 position with an –OH group at the C-1 position. For example, D(–)-fructose is a 1-hydroxy-2-keto compound but it changes into aldehydes in alkaline solution and, therefore, responds to these tests. All monosaccharides are reducing sugars. Most disaccharides such as maltose and lactose are also reducing sugars. A typical non-reducing disaccharide is sucrose (common table sugar).

(ii) **Non-reducing sugars:** They do not reduce Tollens' reagent and Fehling's (or Benedict's) solution and do not contain free aldehydic (or ketonic group with –OH group on the C-1 carbon adjacent to the carbonyl group). For example, Starch, cellulose, glycogen and dextrins. *Sucrose* is a non-reducing sugar as the anomeric carbon of both the monosaccharides are involved in glycoside or acetal formation.

14.1.2 Classification Based on Hydrolysis Products

Depending upon the behaviour on hydrolysis, carbohydrates are classified into three main classes.

(i) **Monosaccharides:** These are the simplest carbohydrates which cannot be hydrolysed into simpler compounds. About 20 monosaccharides occur naturally. They contain up to six carbon atoms. They have the general formula $(CH_2O)_n$ where $n = 3-7$. The common examples are ribose $C_5H_{10}O_5$, glucose $C_6H_{12}O_6$, fructose $C_6H_{12}O_6$, and so on.

(ii) **Oligosaccharides:** These are the carbohydrates which give two to ten monosaccharide molecules on hydrolysis. These are further classified as disaccharides, trisaccharides, tetrasaccharides and so on, depending upon the number of monosaccharide units present in their molecules. For example, raffinose, stachyose and verbascose. The molecular formula of the oligosaccharide is $C_{37}H_{62}N_2O_{29}$.

Disaccharides: Carbohydrates which on hydrolysis give two molecules of the same or different monosaccharides. For example, sucrose, lactose, maltose. All have the molecular formula $C_{12}H_{22}O_{11}$.

Trisaccharides: Carbohydrates which on hydrolysis give three molecules of the same or different monosaccharides. For example, stachyose ($C_{24}H_{42}O_{21}$).

(iii) **Polysaccharides:** These are polymeric and can be hydrolysed to give a large number of monosaccharide units. For example, are cellulose, starch and glycogen. The general formula of starch and cellulose is $(C_6H_{10}O_5)_n$. Polysaccharides are of two types—homopolysaccharides and heteropolysaccharides.

- **Homopolysaccharides:** Those polysaccharides which on hydrolysis yield only one kind of sugar. For example, starch, cellulose and glycogen produce glucose on hydrolysis. Agar-agar produces galactose.
- **Heteropolysaccharides:** Those polysaccharides which on hydrolysis yield more than one kind of monosaccharide. For example, gums produce arabinose, galactose, rhamnose and glutaric acid. Pectins give D-galacturonic acid and its methyl ester.

14.2 Monosaccharides

The monosaccharides are classified as follows.

(i) **Aldoses:** The aldehyde group (–CHO) is always present at one end of the carbon chain, that is, at C-1.

(ii) **Ketoses:** In all naturally occurring ketoses, the keto group is present at a carbon next to the terminal carbon, that is, at C-2.

They are *water soluble* and *sweet* in taste. These are *optically active* (except dihydroxyacetone), They are colourless and crystalline solids. They exhibit the usual reactions of alcohols, aldehydes and ketones. Two molecules of monosaccharides combine with the elimination of one H_2O molecule to give a disaccharide.

14.2.1 Classification of Monosaccharides on the Basis of Number of Carbon Atoms

Monosaccharides are further classified based upon the number of carbon atoms in a molecule as trioses, tetroses, pentoses, hexoses and heptoses according to whether their molecules contain three, four, five, six or seven carbon atoms respectively (Table 14.1).

Open chain structure of some common monosaccharides: Glyceraldehyde contains one chiral carbon atom, it is optically active. Here, a positive sign before its name means that it is dextrorotatory.

Trioses $C_3H_6O_3$

$$\begin{array}{c} H-C=O \\ | \\ H-\overset{*}{C}-OH \\ | \\ CH_2OH \end{array} \qquad \begin{array}{c} CH_2-OH \\ | \\ C=O \\ | \\ CH_2OH \end{array}$$

D(+)-Glyceraldehyde (aldotriose) Optically active

Dihydroxyacetone (ketotriose) Optically inactive

Tetroses $C_4H_8O_4$

$$\begin{array}{c} H-C=O \\ | \\ H-C-OH \\ | \\ H-C-OH \\ | \\ CH_2OH \end{array} \qquad \begin{array}{c} CH_2-OH \\ | \\ C=O \\ | \\ H-C-OH \\ | \\ CH_2OH \end{array}$$

D-Erythrose (aldotetrose)

D-Erytrulose (ketotetrose)

Most of the naturally occurring monosaccharides are pentoses and hexoses. The most common aldopentoses are D(–)-ribose ($C_5H_{10}O_5$) and D(–)2-deoxyribose ($C_5H_{10}O_4$). The prefix 2-deoxy simply indicates the lack of one O atom at C-2 (a H atom instead of –OH).

Table 14.1 Classification of monosaccharides

Class	Formula	Structural formula	Name(s) of example
Aldotriose	$C_3H_6O_3$	HO–CH_2CH(OH) –CHO	Glyceraldehyde
Aldotetrose	$C_4H_8O_4$	HO–$CH_2(CHOH)_2$–CHO	Erythrose, threose
Aldopentose	$C_5H_{10}O_5$	HO–$CH_2(CHOH)_3$–CHO	Ribose, arabinose, xylose, lyxose
Aldohexose	$C_6H_{12}O_6$	HO–$CH_2(CHOH)_4$–CHO	Glucose, mannose, galactose, allose, altrose
Ketotriose	$C_3H_6O_3$	HO–CH_2–CO–CH_2OH	Dihydroxyacetone
Ketotetrose	$C_4H_8O_4$	HO–CH_2–CO–CH(OH)CH_2OH	Erythrulose
Ketopentose	$C_5H_{10}O_5$	HO–CH_2–CO–$(CHOH)_2CH_2$OH	Ribulose, xylulose
Ketohexose	$C_6H_{12}O_6$	HO–CH_2–CO–$(CHOH)_3CH_2$OH	Fructose, tagatose, sorbose, psicose

```
Pentoses  H−C=O        H−C=O          CH2−OH
C5H10O5   H−C−OH       H−C−H          C=O
          H−C−OH       H−C−OH       H−C−OH
          H−C−OH       H−C−OH       H−C−OH
            CH2OH        CH2OH        CH2OH
       D(−)-Ribose   D(−)-2-Deoxyribose   D-Ribulose
     (aldopentose)     (aldopentose)     (ketopentose)
```

The most common aldohexose is D(+)-glucose ($C_6H_{12}O_6$) and D(–)-fructose is the most commonly occurring natural ketohexose.

```
               1             1              1
Hexoses   H−C=O         H−C=O          CH2−OH
            2|            2|            2|
C6H12O6   H−C−OH        H−C−OH          C=O
            3|            3|            3|
         HO−C−H         H−C−H       HO−C−OH
            4|            4|            4|
          H−C−OH        H−C−H        H−C−OH
            5|            5|            5|
          H−C−OH        H−C−OH       H−C−OH
           6|            6|            6|
            CH2OH         CH2OH         CH2OH
      D(+)-Glucose   D(+)-Galactose   D(−)-Fructose
```

14.2.2 Relative Configuration (D and L Configurations)

Glyceraldehyde was selected as a standard of reference because it is the simplest carbohydrate (an aldotriose) capable of showing optical isomerism. (+)-Glyceraldehyde was arbitrarily assigned configuration I (with the–OH group on the right hand side) and was designated as D-glyceraldehyde; (–)-glyceraldehyde was assigned configuration II (with the –OH group on the left hand side) and was designated as L-glyceraldehyde.

```
      H−C=O                 H−C=O
        |*                    |*
      H−C−OH               HO−C−H
        |                     |
        CH2OH                 CH2OH
   Configuration-I       Configuration-II
D(+)-Glyceraldehyde    L(−)-Glyceraldehyde
```

- The optical activity of the molecule is represented by (+) and (–) which represent the direction of rotation of plane polarised light whether dextrorotatory or laevorotary.
- All the natural monosaccharides have the D-configuration.
- Monosaccharides have one or more chiral carbon atoms. Monosaccharides have 2^n optical isomers where n = number of chiral carbon atoms. For example, glucose has $2^4 = 16$ optical isomers.

14.2.3 Limitations of Open Chain Structure of Glucose

It fails to explain the following facts.

- Glucose reacts with NH_2–OH to form its oxime but its pentaacetate does not form the oxime. This suggests that glucosepentaacetate does not possess the –CHO group.
- Glucose exists in two stereoisomeric forms—α-D(+)-glucose and β-D(+)-glucose with specific rotations of +112° and +18.7° in their *fresh* aqueous solutions; however, both solutions give an equilibrium mixture with a specific rotation of +52.7° after some time. It does not undergo certain characteristic reactions of aldehydes. For example, glucose does not form an addition compound with sodium bisulfite and does not restore the pink colour of decolourised Schiff's reagent.
- Glucose, when treated with methanol in the presence of dry HCl gas, uses only one methanol molecule to form the *monomethyl glucoside*. This suggests that glucose must have a hemiacetal type of structure. It forms two isomeric monomethyl glucosides, namely, methyl-α-D-glucoside (MP 438 K, $[\alpha]_D$ = +158°) and methyl-β-D-glucoside (MP 380 K, $[\alpha]$D = –33°). They do not reduce Tollens' reagent or Fehling's solution and also do not react with hydrogen cyanide and hydroxylamine. All these facts indicate the absence of a free –CHO group.

14.2.4 Cyclic Structure of Monosaccharides

Monosaccharides contain a number of –OH groups and an aldehyde or a keto group, so any one of the –OH groups, usually at C-4 or C-5 in aldohexoses, and C-5 or C-6 in ketohexoses may combine with the carbonyl group to form an intramolecular cyclic hemiacetal or hemiketal involving 5 or 6 membered rings containing one oxygen atom. For example, consider the cyclic structure of glucose as discussed below.

```
      1                    1                        1
   H−C−OH ┐            H−C=O                    H−C−H ┐
      2|  |               2|                       2|  |
   H−C−OH |            H−C−OH                   H−C−OH |
      3|  |               3|                       3|  |
  HO−C−H  O   ⇌      HO−C−H          ⇌       HO−C−H   O
      4|  |               4|                       4|  |
   H−C−OH |            H−C−OH                   H−C−OH |
      5|  |               5|                       5|  |
   H−C────┘            H−C−O−H                  H−C────┘
     6|                  6|                       6|
      CH2OH               CH2OH                    CH2OH
α-D(+)-Glucose or     D(+)-Glucose           β-D(+)-Glucose or
α-D(+)-Glucopyranose  Two possible directions β-D(+)-Glucopyranose
                      of ring closure
```

```
                              1
                             CH2OH
        1  2                  2|                  2    1
 HOH2C−C−OH ┐                 C=O              H−C−CH2OH ┐
        3|  |                 3|                  3|     |
    HO−C−H  |             HO−C−OH             HO−C−H     |
        4|  O   ⇌             4|        ⇌         4|     O
     H−C−OH |              H−C−H               H−C−OH    |
        5|  |                 5|                  5|     |
     H−C−OH |              H−C−OH              H−C−OH    |
       6|   |                6|                  6|      |
        CH2─┘                 CH2OH               CH2────┘
  α-D-Fructose           D(−)-Fructose         β-D-Fructose or
α-D-Fructopyranose  (Open chain structure)   β-D-Fructopyranose
                    Two possible directions
                      for ring closure
```

The 5-membered rings containing one oxygen atom are called the *furanose* form; the 6-membered rings containing one oxygen atom are called the *pyranose* form.

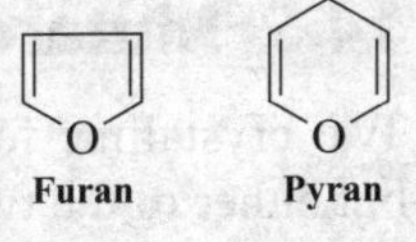

All the monosaccharides (pentoses and hexoses) in their free states always exist in the pyranose form; whereas in the combined form, some monosaccharides exist in the furanose form as in ribose and 2-deoxyribose, fructose, and so on.

14.2.5 Cyclic Structure of Glucose Anomers

Glucose forms a hemiacetal between the aldehydic –CHO group and the –OH group on C-5, becomes chiral, and thus two arrangements of the H and OH groups around C-1 are possible. As a result D(+)-glucose exists in two stereoisomeric forms, that is, α-D(+)-glucose and β-D(+)-glucose with different specific rotations and melting points. In α-D(+)-glucose, the –OH group at C-1 is towards the right, while in β-D(+)-glucose, the –OH group at C-1 is towards the left (Fig. 14.2). Such a pair of stereoisomers which differ in the configuration only around the C-1 are called *anomers* and the C-1 carbon is called the *anomeric* or *glycosidic carbon.*

α-D(+)-Glucose or α-D(+)-Glucopyranose	D(+)-Glucose (Open chain)	β-D(+)-Glucose or β-D(+)-Glucopyranose
m. pt. 419 K	0.02%	m. pt. = 423 K
36%	Two possible directions of ring closure	63.98%
$[\alpha] = +112°$		$[\alpha] = +18.7°$

Fig. 14.2 Fischer projection formulae of open chain and cyclic structures of glucose

These two forms of D(+)-glucose are also known as α-D(+)-glucopyranose and β-D(+)-glucopyranose because of their resemblance with pyran.

Haworth projection formula: The cyclic structure of monosaccharides can be better represented by the Haworth projection formulae (Fig.14.3).

Fischer projection formula — Haworth projection formula

α-D(+)-Glucose [α-D(+)-Glucopyranose]

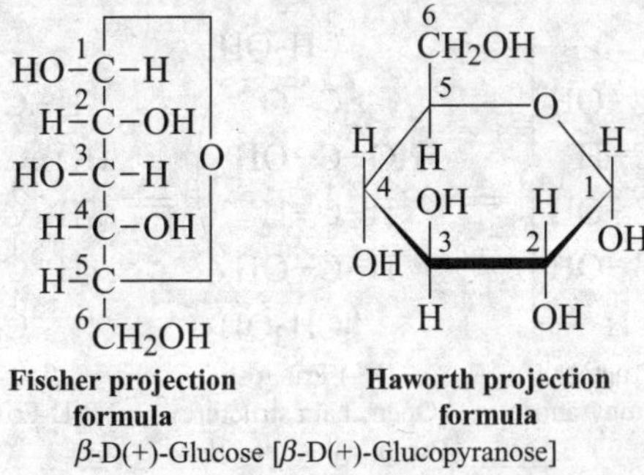

β-D(+)-Glucose [β-D(+)-Glucopyranose]

Fig. 14.3 Fischer and Haworth projection formulae of two anomeric forms of D(+)-glucose

14.3 Preparation of Glucose

(i) **From sucrose (cane sugar):** When sucrose is boiled with dilute HCl or H_2SO_4 in an alcoholic solution, glucose and fructose are obtained in equal amounts.

$$\underset{\text{Sucrose}}{C_{12}H_{22}O_{11}} + H_2O \xrightarrow{H^+} \underset{\text{Glucose}}{C_6H_{12}O_6} + \underset{\text{Fructose}}{C_6H_{12}O_6}$$

(ii) **From starch:** Glucose is produced commercially by the hydrolysis of starch by boiling it with dilute H_2SO_4 at 393 K under a pressure of 2–3 atm.

$$\underset{\text{Starch}}{(C_6H_{10}O_5)_n} + nH_2O \xrightarrow[393\text{ K, 2-3 atm}]{H^+} \underset{\text{Glucose}}{nC_6H_{12}O_6}$$

When the hydrolysis is complete, the liquid is neutralised with sodium carbonate to a pH of 4–5. The resulting solution is concentrated under reduced pressure to get the crystals of glucose.

14.4 Fructose

Fructose occurs in fruits and is called fruit sugar. It is also present in honey and sweet fruits along with glucose. In the combined state, it is also present in disaccharides (sucrose) and polysaccharides (insulin). It is obtained along with glucose by the hydrolysis of cane sugar with dilute H_2SO_4.

$$\underset{\text{Cane sugar}}{C_{12}H_{22}O_{11}} + H_2O \xrightarrow{\text{dil. }H_2SO_4} \underset{\text{D-Glucose}}{C_6H_{12}O_6} + \underset{\text{D-Fructose}}{C_6H_{12}O_6}$$

A solution having an equal number of molecules of D-glucose and D-fructose is called invert sugar.

Fructose is a ketohexose. It melts with slight decomposition at 102°C and is found to be laevorotatory. Fructose contains a keto group at C-2 and the six carbon atoms are arranged in a straight chain as in the case of glucose. It belongs to the D-series and is a laevorotatory compound. It is also called *laevulose*. In the free state D(–)-fructose exists as a six membered ring (pyranose ring). Fructose forms an internal *cyclic ketal* using the carbonyl carbon C-2 and the –OH group of C-5. Because of the ketal formation, C-2 becomes asymmetric and therefore D(–)-fructose also exists as two possible stereoisomers (anomers), α-D(–)-fructopyranose and β-D(–)-fructopyranose.

α-D-Fructose α-D-Fructopyranose

D(–)-Fructose (Open chain structure) Two possible directions for ring closure

β-D-Fructose β-D-Fructopyranose

Fischer projection formulae of the two anomeric forms of D(–)-fructose are given below.

α-D-Fructopyranose

β-D(–)-Fructopyranose

Haworth projection formulae of the two anomeric forms of D(–)-fructopyranose.

- When fructose is in the *combined state* and is a component of disaccharides, it exists in the *furanose* from, that is, a 5-membered hemiketal ring form.
- The furanose structure is obtained by internal ketal formation by the keto group of the carbon C-2 and the –OH group of C-5.
- To draw the furanose structure, draw a pentagon with the oxygen atom at the top vertex. Place all the groups (on C-2, C-3 and C-4) which are present on left hand side above the plane of the ring and all those groups which are present on the right hand side below the plane of the ring. The terminal $-CH_2OH$ group (at C-6) is always placed above the plane of the ring (in the D-series).

α-D(–)-Fructofuranose

β-D(–)-Fructofuranose

- Similarly in the combined form, *ribose* (or 2-deoxyribose) exists in the furanose form.

α-D(+)-Ribofuranose

β-D(–)-Ribofuranose

14.5 Mutarotation

Two crystalline forms of α and β-glucose are quite stable, but either of the two forms of glucose (α or β) on dissolving in water gradually changes into the other form and finally attains an equilibrium with both the α and β forms present. The specific rotation of an aqueous solution of β-D(+)-glucose gradually increases from +19° to +52.7°. At equilibrium, the solution shows the value of optical rotation as +52.7°. The transformation of one form to another and the attainment of equilibrium of the two forms takes place through the formation of the open chain structure.

$$\underset{\substack{36\% \\ [\alpha]^D = +112^\circ}}{\alpha\text{-D(+)-Glucose}} \rightleftharpoons \underset{0.02\%}{\text{Open chain}} \rightleftharpoons \underset{63.98\%}{\beta\text{-D(+)-Glucose}}$$

At equilibrium, $[\alpha]^D = 52.7^\circ$

The phenomenon involving a change in the optical rotation of an optically active compound in aqueous solution with the passage of time to an equilibrium value is called *mutarotation*. During mutarotation, the ring opens and then recloses in the inverted position or in the original position, thus giving an equilibrium mixture containing both the cyclic forms.

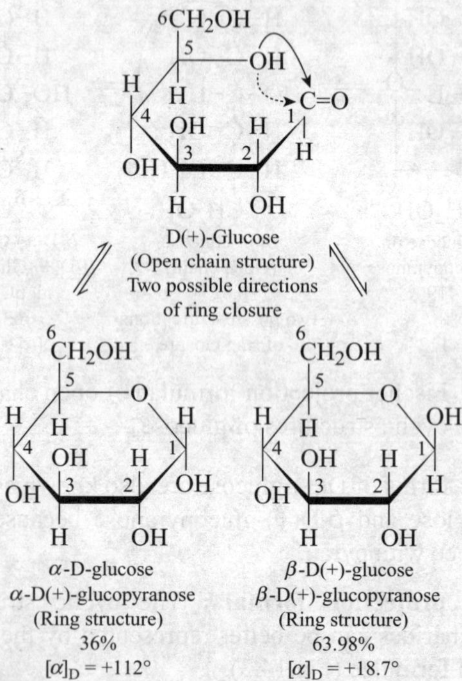

The equilibrium is reached faster if a trace amount of acid or base is present as the catalyst. All reducing sugars undergo mutarotation in aqueous solution.

Anomers: Optical isomers which differ in their configuration around the carbonyl carbon atom are called anomers and are represented as α and β anomers depending upon the direction of the –OH group on the anomeric carbon on the right and left hand side respectively.

Epimers: Isomers which differ in their configuration about a specific carbon atom other than the carbonyl carbon atom are called epimers. For example, glucose and galactose are epimers as they differ in the configuration about the C-4, that is, they are C-4 epimers. Similarly, glucose and mannose are C-2 epimers. The change in configuration around only one asymmetric carbon in a compound containing more than one asymmetric carbon is called *epimerisation*.

14.6 Chemical Properties of Glucose

In glucose, both alcoholic and aldehydic groups are present. So, glucose shows chemical reactions of both of these functional groups. The presence of the *alcoholic group* is confirmed by acylation with acetic anhydride. The presence of the aldehydic group is confirmed by the following reactions.

- Reactions with Tollens reagent and Fehling's solution where the –CHO gets oxidised to–COOH.
- By reaction with Na/Hg where the –CHO gets reduced to $-CH_2OH$.
- Condensation with reagents like NH_2-NH_2, NH_2-OH, and so on, to form the hydrazone and oxime respectively, which are typical reactions of aldehydes and ketones.
- Addition of HCN and $NaHCO_3$ wherein adducts are obtained.

14.6.1 Chemical Reactions due to –OH Group

(i) Acetylation: Glucose reacts with acetic anhydride in the presence of anhydrous zinc chloride to form glucose pentaacetate (or pentaacetyl glucose). This is known as acetylation of glucose.

$$\underset{\text{Glucose}}{CHO-[CHOH]_4-CH_2OH} \xrightarrow[-5CH_3COOH]{5(CH_3CO)_2O} \underset{\text{Pentaacetyl glucose}}{CHO-[CHOCOCH_3]_4-CH_2OCOCH_3}$$

The formation of the pentaacetyl derivative confirms the presence of five –OH groups in the glucose molecule. The five –OH groups should be attached to different carbon atoms to make it stable.

(ii) Reaction with CH_3OH in the presence of dry HCl gas: With methanol and dry HCl, glucose reacts to give (α and β) methyl glucosides. The reaction indicates the presence of a ring structure in glucose in which the free –CHO group is not present but it is changed into the –CHOH group.

CH₂OH / O / H / H / H / OH / H / HO / OH + H OCH₃ / H / OH — dry HCl → CH₂OH / O / H / H / H / OH / H / HO / OCH₃ / H / OH + H_2O

α-D-Glucose → Methyl-α-D-Glucose

CH₂OH / O / H / H / OH + H OCH₃ / OH / H / H / HO / H / OH — dry HCl → CH₂OH / O / H / H / OCH₃ / OH / H / H / HO / H / OH + H_2O + H_2O

β-D-Glucose → Methyl-β-D-Glucose

The presence of α-D-glucoside and β-D-glucoside indicates the existence of two different structures for glucose—α-D-glucose and β-D-glucose.

(iii) Reaction with metallic hydroxides: Glucose reacts with $Ca(OH)_2$ to form calcium glucosate which is water soluble.

$$\underset{\text{Glucose}}{C_6H_{11}O_5-OH} + HO-Ca-OH \rightarrow \underset{\text{Calcium glucosate}}{C_6H_{11}O_5-O-Ca-OH}$$

14.6.2 Chemical Reactions due to -CHO Group

(i) Oxidation: Oxidation can take place with mild oxidising agents such as bromine water, Tollens' reagent, Fehling's (or Benedict's) solution, or with strong oxidising agents like HNO_3.

- **With Br_2/H_2O:**

$$\underset{\text{Glucose}}{CHO-[CHOH]_4-CH_2OH} + [O] \xrightarrow[-2HBr]{Br_2/H_2O} \underset{\text{Gluconic acid}}{COOH-[CHOH]_4-CH_2OH}$$

- **With Tollens' reagent (ammonical $AgNO_3$)**

$$AgNO_3 + NH_4OH \rightarrow AgOH + NH_4 + NO_3^-$$

$$\underset{\text{Glucose}}{CHO-[CHOH]_4-CH_2OH} + Ag_2O \xrightarrow[\text{mirror}]{-2Ag\downarrow} \underset{\text{Gluconic acid}}{COOH-[CHOH]_4-CH_2OH}$$

- **With Fehling's (or Benedict's) solution (alkaline solution of $CuSO_4$)**

$$CuSO_4 + 2NaOH \rightarrow Cu(OH)_2 + Na_2SO_4$$
$$Cu(OH)_2 \rightarrow CuO + H_2O$$

$$\underset{\text{Glucose}}{CHO-[CHOH]_4-CH_2OH} + CuO \xrightarrow[\text{red ppt.}]{-Cu_2O\downarrow} \underset{\text{Gluconic acid}}{COOH-[CHOH]_4-CH_2OH}$$

- **With strong oxidising agent like HNO_3:** HNO_3 oxidises both the terminal groups –CHO and –CH_2OH to give *glucaric acid* (a dibasic acid) also known as saccharic acid.

$$\underset{\text{Glucose}}{CHO-[CHOH]_4-CH_2OH} + CuO \xrightarrow[\text{red ppt.}]{-Cu_2O\downarrow} \underset{\text{Gluconic acid}}{COOH-[CHOH]_4-CH_2OH}$$

This confirms that glucose contains one –CHO group and one primary alcoholic group.

(ii) Reduction: With Na/Hg, glucose is reduced to sorbitol and with conc. HI and red P at 373 K, glucose gives a mixture of *n*-hexane and 2-iodohexane.

$$\underset{\text{Glucose}}{CHO-[CHOH]_4-CH_2OH} + 2[H] \xrightarrow{Na(Hg)/H_2O} \underset{\text{Sorbitol}}{CH_2OH-[CHOH]_4-CH_2OH}$$

$$\underset{\text{Glucose}}{CHO-[CHOH]_4-CH_2OH} \xrightarrow[373\ K]{HI/red\ P} \underset{n\text{-Hexane}}{CH_3-[CH_2]_4-CH_3} + \underset{\text{2-Iodohexane}}{I-CH-CH_3-[CH_2]_3-CH_3}$$

This reaction confirms that six carbon atoms in glucose are arranged in a straight line.

(iii) Reaction with HCN: A cyanohydrin is obtained when glucose reacts with HCN.

$$\underset{\text{Glucose}}{CHO-[CHOH]_4-CH_2OH} \xrightarrow{HCN} \underset{\text{Glucose cynohydrin}}{HO-CH-CN-[CHOH]_4-CH_2OH}$$

The cyanohydrin on hydrolysis gives hexahydroxyheptanoic acid. On treatment with HI, it gives heptanoic acid.

(iv) Reaction with hydroxylamine: Glucose oxime is obtained when glucose reacts with NH_2OH.

$$\underset{\text{Glucose}}{CH\boxed{O\ H_2}N-OH-[CHOH]_4-CH_2OH} \xrightarrow[-H_2O]{H_2N-OH} \underset{\text{Glucoxime}}{CH=N-OH-[CHOH]_4-CH_2OH}$$

(v) Reaction with phenyl hydrazine: Glucose reacts with phenylhydrazine in different stages. If a 1:1 mixture of glucose and phenylhydrazine is taken, we get phenylhydrazone.

$$\underset{\text{Glucose}}{CH\boxed{O\ H_2}N-NH-Ph-[CHOH]_4-CH_2OH} \xrightarrow[-H_2O]{H_2N-NH-Ph} \underset{\text{Glucose phenylhydrazone}}{CH=N-NH-Ph-[CHOH]_4-CH_2OH}$$

But, on warming glucose with excess phenylhydrazine, we get glucose bis(phenylhydrazone) called glucosazone by a complicated mechanism.

$$\underset{\text{Glucose phenylhydrazone}}{CH=N-NH-Ph,\ H-C-OH,\ [CHOH]_3,\ CH_2OH} \rightleftharpoons CH-NH-NHC_6H_5,\ C-O-H,\ [CHOH]_3,\ CH_2OH \xrightarrow{-C_6H_5NH_2} \underset{\text{Product-II}}{CH=NH,\ C=O,\ [CHOH]_3,\ CH_2OH}$$

$$\xrightarrow[-H_2O]{H_2N-NH-C_6H_5} \underset{\text{Product-III}}{CH=NH,\ C=N-NH-C_6H_5,\ [CHOH]_3,\ CH_2OH} \xrightarrow[-NH_3]{H_2N-NH-C_6H_5} \underset{\text{Glucosazone}}{CH=N-NH-C_6H_5,\ C=N-NH-C_6H_5,\ [CHOH]_3,\ CH_2OH}$$

Glucose, fructose and mannose form the same osazone as these differ in their structure only at C-1 and C-2, and these are the carbons involved in osazone formation.

(vi) Miscellaneous reactions

- **Action of acids:** On being heated with conc. HCl, glucose gives *5-hydroxymethylfurfural* which is further changed by hot conc. HNO_3 to *laevulinic acid*.

$$\underset{\text{D(+)-Glucose}}{HOH_2C-CH(OH)-CHOH-CHOH-CH(OH)-CHO} \xrightarrow[-3H_2O]{HCl} \underset{\text{3-Hydroxymethylfurfural}}{HOH_2C-C=CH-CH=C(-CHO)-O}$$

$$\xrightarrow{HCl,\ \Delta} CO_2 + CO + HCOOH + \underset{\text{Laevulinic acid}}{CH_3-\overset{O}{\overset{\|}{C}}-CH_2-CH_2-COOH}$$

5-hydroxymethylfurfural formed gives a violet colouration when treated with an alcoholic solution of α-naphthol. This reaction forms the basis of the *Molisch test* for carbohydrates.

- **Fermentation:** Glucose undergoes fermentation into ethanol in the presence of the enzyme zymase present in yeast under anaerobic conditions.

$$C_6H_{12}O_6 \xrightarrow{zymase} 2C_2H_5OH + 2CO_2$$

- **Action of alkali:** In the presence of dilute solution of alkalis, it undergoes isomerisation to form an equilibrium mixture of D-glucose, D-fructose and D-mannose.

$$\underset{\text{Glucose}}{CH=O,\ H-C-OH,\ [CHOH]_3,\ CH_2OH} \rightleftharpoons \underset{\text{Enediol}}{CH-OH,\ C-O-H,\ [CHOH]_3,\ CH_2OH} \rightleftharpoons \underset{\text{Fructose}}{CH_2-OH,\ C=O,\ [CHOH]_3,\ CH_2OH} \rightleftharpoons \underset{\text{Mannose}}{CH=OH,\ H-C-OH,\ [CHOH]_3,\ CH_2OH}$$

The same equilibrium mixture is obtained even if one starts with D(+)-mannose or D(–)-fructose. Since the ketonic form of fructose gets converted to the aldehydic form of glucose and mannose, fructose shows reducing behaviour.

14.7 Disaccharides

Their general formula is $C_{12}H_{22}O_{11}$. On hydrolysis with dilute acids or enzymes these give the following two molecules of monosaccharides.

$$\underset{\text{Sucrose}}{C_{12}H_{22}O_{11}} + H_2O \xrightarrow[\text{Invertase}]{\text{H+ or}} \underset{\text{D(–)-Glucose}}{C_6H_{12}O_6} + \underset{\text{D(–)-Fructose}}{C_6H_{12}O_6}$$

$$\underset{\text{Maltose}}{C_{12}H_{22}O_{11}} + H_2O \xrightarrow[\text{or maltase}]{H^+} \underset{\text{Glucose}}{C_6H_{12}O_6} + \underset{\text{Glucose}}{C_6H_{12}O_6}$$

$$\underset{\text{Lactose}}{C_{12}H_{22}O_{11}} + H_2O \xrightarrow[\text{or lactase}]{H^+} \underset{\text{Glucose}}{C_6H_{12}O_6} + \underset{\text{Galactose}}{C_6H_{12}O_6}$$

14.7.1 Properties and Structures of Disaccharides

Except sucrose, all disaccharides are reducing sugars. All disaccharides such as maltose, lactose, sucrose, are physiologically important.

(i) Sucrose: It is a disaccharide with the molecular formula $C_{12}H_{22}O_{11}$ which is hydrolysed by the enzyme invertase to give one molecule each of D(+)-glucose and D(–)-fructose.

$$\underset{\text{Sucrose}}{C_{12}H_{22}O_{11}} + H_2O \xrightarrow[\text{Invertase}]{\text{H+ or}} \underset{\text{D(–)-Glucose}}{C_6H_{12}O_6} + \underset{\text{D(–)-Fructose}}{C_6H_{12}O_6}$$

Sucrose does not reduce Tollens' reagent or Fehling's (or Benedict's) solution. So, it is a *non-reducing* sugar and in this respect, it differs from maltose and lactose.

Structure: Sucrose is composed of α-D-glucose and β-D-fructose. These units are held together by an α,β-glycosidic linkage between the C_1 of the glucose unit (pyranose ring) and the C_2 of the fructose unit (furanose ring). Sucrose consists of α-glucose and β-fructose units. Thus, both glucose (α-C-1) and fructose (β-C-2) are connected to each other through their reducing centres (Fig. 14.4).

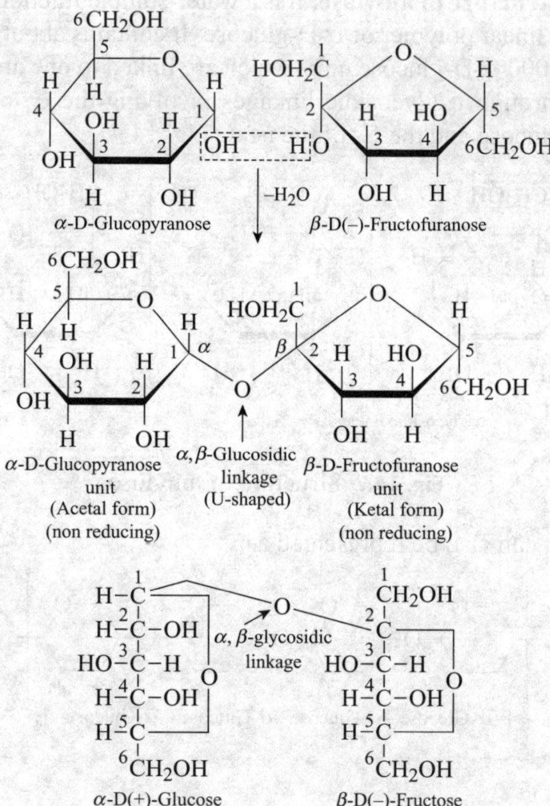

Fig. 14.4 Sucrose

The formation of sucrose may also be represented as follows:

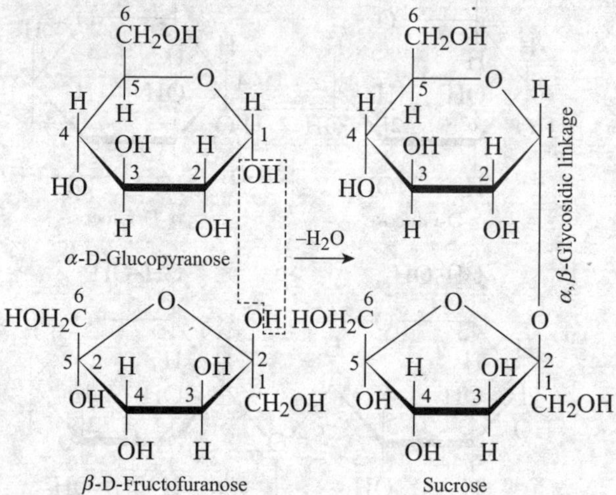

Inversion of sugar and invert sugar: Sucrose is dextrorotatory and its freshly prepared solution has specific rotation, $[\alpha]_D = +66.5°$. On hydrolysis, in the presence of HCl or an enzyme like invertase, an equimolar mixture of D(+)-glucose with a specific rotation $[\alpha]_D = +52.7°$ and D(-)-fructose with specific rotation, $[\alpha]_D = -92.4°$ which is higher than that of D(+)-glucose. It means the resulting solution becomes levorotatory with an optical rotation $\frac{52.7-92.4}{2} = -19.85°$.

Since the process of hydrolysis of sucrose to an equimolar mixture of D(+)-glucose and D(–)-fructose is accompanied by a change in sign of optical rotation from (+) to (–) (or change in the direction of rotation of plane polarised light from the right to the left), this overall process is known as *inversion of sugar* and the products of hydrolysis which is an equimolar mixture of D(+)-glucose and D(–)-fructose is called *invert sugar*.

$$\underset{\substack{\text{(+)–Sucrose} \\ [\alpha]_D = +66.5°}}{C_{12}H_{22}O_{11}} + H_2O \xrightarrow[\text{invertase}]{\text{H+ or}} \underset{\substack{\text{D(–)-Glucose} \\ +52.7°}}{C_6H_{12}O_6} + \underset{\substack{\text{D(–)-Fructose} \\ -92.4°}}{C_6H_{12}O_6}$$

(ii) Maltose: It is the principal disaccharide obtained by the partial hydrolysis of starch by diastase.

$$\underset{\text{(+)-Maltose}}{C_{12}H_{22}O_{11}} + H_2O \xrightarrow[\text{Maltase}]{\text{H+ or}} \underset{\text{D(+)-Glucose}}{C_6H_{12}O_6} + \underset{\text{D(+)-Glucose}}{C_6H_{12}O_6}$$

Structure: On hydrolysis, one mole of maltose gives two moles of α-D-glucose. It is a reducing sugar. It is composed of two α-D-glucose units which are condensed together through the C_1 of one unit and the C_4 of the other of unit. Both glucose units are in the pyranose form. This disaccharide exists in two anomeric forms, α and β (Fig. 14.5).

or 4-O-(α-D-Glucopyranosyl) α-D-glucopyranoside

(iii) Lactose: Lactose has a molecular formula $C_{12}H_{22}O_{11}$. On hydrolysis, lactose yields an equimolar mixture of D(+)-glucose and D(+)-galactose.

$$\underset{\text{(+)-Lactose}}{C_{12}H_{22}O_{11}} + H_2O \xrightarrow[\text{lactase}]{\text{H+ or}} \underset{\text{D(+)-Glucose}}{C_6H_{12}O_6} + \underset{\text{D(+)-Galactose}}{C_6H_{12}O_6}$$

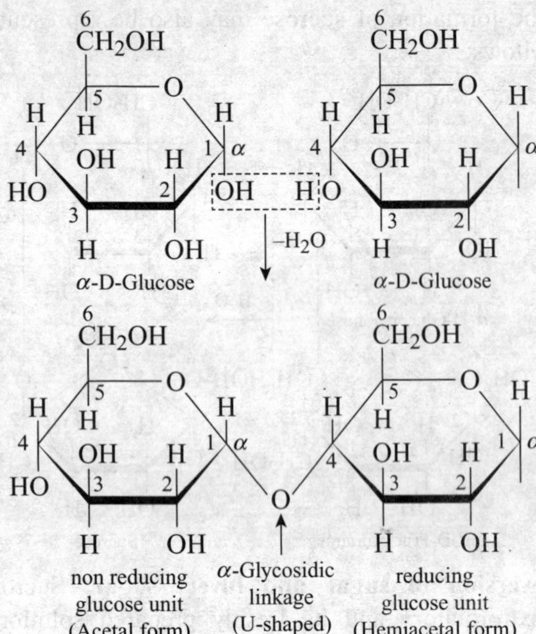

Fig. 14.5 Maltose (α-anomer)

It is obtained by the condensation of one molecule of glucose and one molecule of galactose in which the C-1 of the β-D(+)-galactose unit is connected to the non-glycosidic carbon C-4 of any of the two α or β-D(+)-glucose anomers, thus giving two possible anomers of lactose. Thus, lactose contains a hemiacetal group in the glucose unit and is, therefore, a *reducing sugar* (Fig. 14.6).

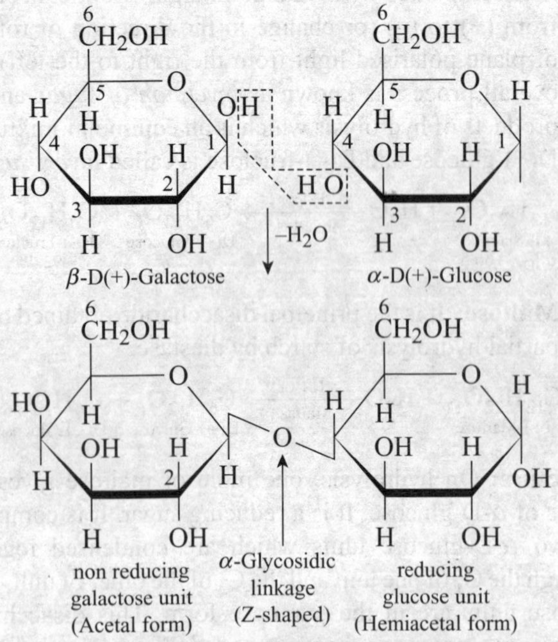

Fig. 14.6 (a) Lactose (α-anomer) or 4-O-(β-D(+)-Galactopyranoxyl) D(+)-glucopyranoside

Fischer projection formula of lactose:

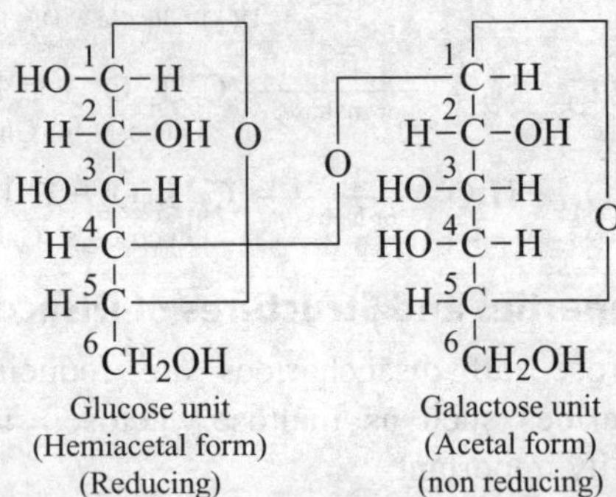

Fig. 14.6 (b) Lactose

14.8 Polysaccharides

4.8.1 Important Homopolysaccharides

Some important homopolysaccharides are discussed below.

(i) **Starch**: It is the main storage polysaccharide of plants. The molecular formula of starch is $(C_6H_{10}O_5)_n$ where the value of n is 100–3000 which varies from source to source. On hydrolysis with dilute mineral acids or enzymes, starch produces smaller units, then maltose and finally glucose molecules only because it is a polymer of α-D-glucose joined by α-glycosidic linkages. Starch is a tasteless, odourless, white amorphous material called *amylase* (10%–20%) and a water insoluble component called *amylopectin* (80%–90%).

Structure of amylase: It is a water-soluble fraction. It is a linear polymer of α-D-glucose. It contains about 200–1000 α-D-glucose units which are linked to one another through α-glycosidic linkages involving the C_1 of one glucose and the C_4 of the next (Fig. 14.7).

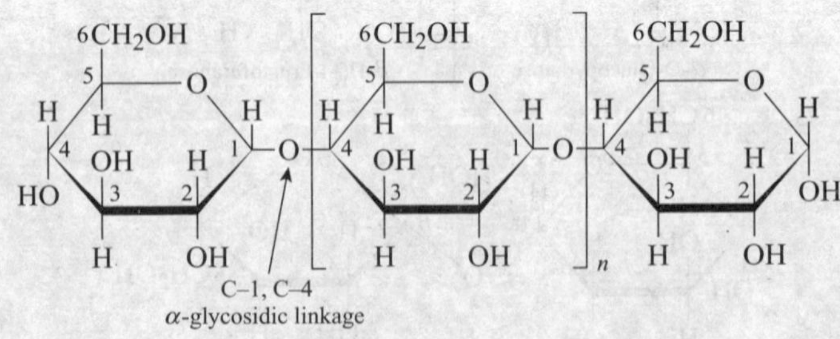

Fig. 14.7 Structure of amylose

It can also be represented as:

$[-\alpha\text{-Glucose} - \alpha\text{-Glucose} - \alpha\text{-Glucose} - \alpha\text{-Glucose} -]_n$

Structure of amylopectin: It consists of a large number (several hundreds) of short chains of 25–30 D-glucose units. In this case, the main chain involves α-linkages between the C_1 of one α-D-glucose unit and the C_4 of the other. The C_1 of the terminal glucose in each chain is further linked to a C_6 of the other glucose unit in the next chain through a C_1–C_6 α-linkage. This gives a highly branched structure (Fig. 14.8).

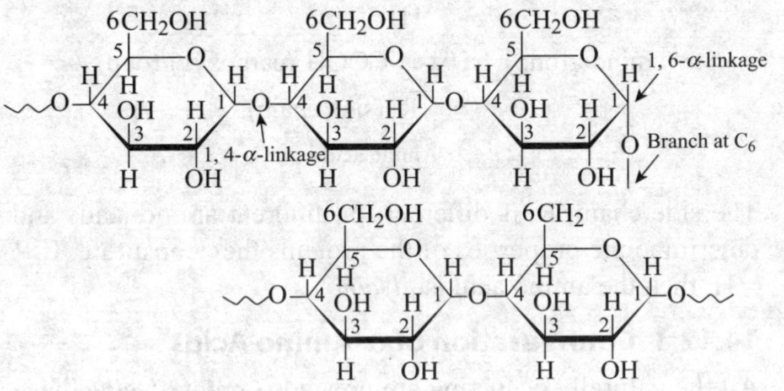

Fig. 14.8 Structure of amylopoectin

(ii) **Glycogen (animal starch):** Glycogen is a polysaccharide of α-D-glucose. It serves as a reserve carbohydrate. It is a branched polysaccharide composed entirely of α-D-glucose units which are joined to one another in a chain by glycosidic linkages involving the C-1 and C-4 carbons except at the branching point, where, like amylopectin, a 1-6 linkage is present. All the glucose units are connected by α-glycosidic linkages only.

Like amylopectin, it is also a highly branched condensation polymer of α-glucose units. The only structural difference between glycogen and amylopectin is that amylopectin chains consist of 20–25 glucose units, whereas glycogen chains consist of 10–14 glucose units. Glycogen is more highly branched than amylopectin because it has smaller linear chains of 10–14 glucose units than those of 20–25 units in amylopectin.

14.9 Cellulose

It is also a major structural polysaccharide in higher plants where it constitutes the bulk of the cell wall. Over 50% of the total organic matter in the living would is cellulose. Dry leaves contain 10%–20% cellulose, wood contains 50% and cotton contains 90% cellulose. Cellulose does not reduce Fehling's solution or Tollens' reagent. It does not form an osazone and is not fermented by yeast. It is not hydrolysed as readily as starch, but on heating with dilute sulfuric acid under pressure, it gives D-glucose. It is broken down by *cellulotytic bacteria* present in the stomach (rumen) of ruminant mammals like the cow and buffalo, with the help of the enzyme *cellulose*.

Structurally, cellulose is a straight chain polysaccharide composed of only β-D-glucose units, which are joined by β-glycosidic linkages between the C-1 of one glucose unit and the C-4 of the next glucose unit. The chains are arranged to form bundles and are held together by hydrogen bonds between glucose units of adjacent strands. Its molecular mass is in the range of 50,000–500,000 (about 300–2500 D-glucose units).

Structure: Cellulose is a linear polymer of β-glucose where the C-1 of one glucose unit is connected to the C-4 of the other through the oxygen atom. Cellulose is made up of several linear layers each containing up to 250 or more glucose units. In cellulose fibres, the linear strands lie side by side to form bundles where these strands are held together by multiple hydrogen bonds between the $–CH_2OH$ group at C-6 of one layer and the –OH group at the C-2 of another layer. Because of the linear structure, cellulose can be easily spun into fibres. Cellulose differs from starch in properties because cellulose is a linear polymer of β-D(+)-glucose by β-glycoside bonds, where as starch is a helical branched chain polymer of α-glycosidic bonds.

14.9.1 Uses of Cellulose and its Derivatives

Cellulose has also been modified chemically to get a host of useful semi-synthetic products as described below.

(i) **Cellulose diacetate:** It is used for making fabrics called *acetate rayon*. It is also obtained in the form of film and is used as a plastic wrapping film. It has also been used in shatter-proof glass. It is used in the dissolved form in the manufacture of nail polish, lacquers and varnishes.

(ii) **Cellulose nitrate**

- Crude cellulose trinitrate is known as *gun cotton*. It is used in the manufacture of *smokeless powder* and as a *binder* for solid rocket propellants.
- The plastic celluloid is obtained when *pyroxylin* (a mixture of mostly cellulose dinitrate along with a small amount of cellulose mononitrate) is mixed with a plasticiser such as camphor and alcohol. *Celluloid* is used for the manufacture of photographic films (these films are now replaced by other safer plastics as celluloid is highly inflammable), piano keys and spectacle frames.
- A large amount of cellulose nitrate is used for making high quality automotive paints called *CN* (cellulose nitrate) paints. *Collodion* which is a solution of pyroxylin in ether and alcohol is used in the manufacture of lacquers.

(iii) **Cellulose xanthate**: A colloidal sol of cellulose xanthate in alkali is called viscose and when regenerated by forcing through a spinneret into acidic solution we get *viscose rayon* fibres which give a cotton touch but a better finish than cotton fibres.

(iv) **Methyl cellulose:** It is used for sizing of fabric and in the manufacture of plastic and cosmetics.

(v) **Ethyl cellulose:** It is also used as protective plastic coats and film.

(vi) **Carboxy methyl cellulose:** It is added to ice creams, cosmetics, medicines and detergents as an emulsifying agent.

14.10 Functions of Carbohydrates

- Sugars such as ribose and 2-deoxyribose are the essential components of RNA and DNA respectively. Nucleic acids play a vital role in the transmission of hereditary characteristics and biosynthesis of proteins.
- The monosaccharide ribose is present in adenosine triphosphate (ATP) molecules, the currency of energy metabolism in a cell.
- Certain carbohydrates perform specific functions; for example, galactose in certain lipids and lactose in milk.
- Carbohydrates play a very important role in the metabolism of amino acids and fatty acids.
- **Other uses:** Carbohydrates exert a sparing action on proteins. They provide the carbon skeleton for the synthesis of some non-essential amino acids. They are essential for the oxidation of fats.

14.11 Proteins and Amino Acids

Proteins are high molecular mass, complex biomolecules of amino acids present in all living cells. The protoplasm of plant or animal cells contains 10%–20% proteins. The important proteins required for our body are the following.

- *Enzymes:* as biocatalysts to catalyse biochemical reactions.
- *Hormones:* to regulate various body functions.
- *Antibodies:* to protect the body against toxic substances and infections.
- *Transport proteins:* to carry different substances in the blood to various tissues of the body.
- *Structural proteins:* are structural elements of the cells and tissues.
- *Contractile proteins:* to help in the contraction of muscles and other cells.

All proteins contain the elements carbon, hydrogen, oxygen, nitrogen and sulfur. Some of these may also contain phosphorus, iodine and traces of metals such as iron, copper, zinc and manganese. Thus, chemically, proteins are condensation polymers (polyamides) in which the monomer units are α-amino acids. About 150–200 amino acid molecules are present in a protein molecule. There are 20 common natural amino acids present in all proteins and 6 others present in certain special tissues. These are present in proteins in different sequences, in nearly 400 different ways.

All proteins on partial hydrolysis give polypeptides which on complete hydrolysis give amino acids.

$$\text{Proteins} \rightarrow \text{Proteoses} \rightarrow \text{Peptones} \rightarrow \text{Polypeptides} \rightarrow \text{Amino acids}$$

Elemental analysis: On chemical analysis, most of the proteins have the following approximate percentage composition.

C = 50%–55%	O = 22%–24%	S ≈ 1%
H = 6.5%–7%	N = 15%–18%	P = 0.5%

Molecular weight determination: Molecular weight of the proteins is determined by the regular methods available for the determination of molecular weight of polymers except the ebullioscopic method.

14.12 Amino Acids

They are represented by the general formula:

$$\text{(amino group) } NH_2\text{–}\underset{\boxed{R}\text{ (side chain)}}{\overset{H}{\underset{|}{\overset{|}{C}}}}\text{–COOH (carboxyl group)}$$

α-Amino acids

The side chain, R, is different for different amino acids and determine the properties of the proteins they constitute. If R = H, then the amino acid is *glycine*.

14.12.1 Configuration of α-Amino Acids

All the naturally occurring amino acids *except glycine*, have at least one asymmetric (chiral) carbon atom (four different groups are attached to the α-carbon atom). As a result, these amino acids are optically active and they exist in two enantiomeric forms (Fig. 14.9).

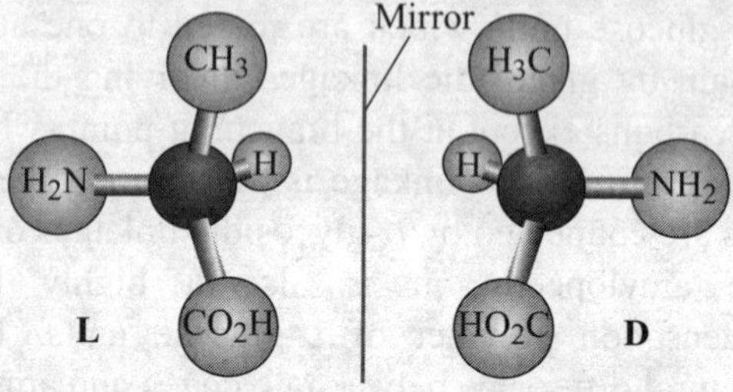

Fig. 14.9 Two enantiomers of alanine

The configuration of the α-amino acids is distinguished based upon the direction of the $-NH_2$ around the α-carbon in the Fisher projection formula.

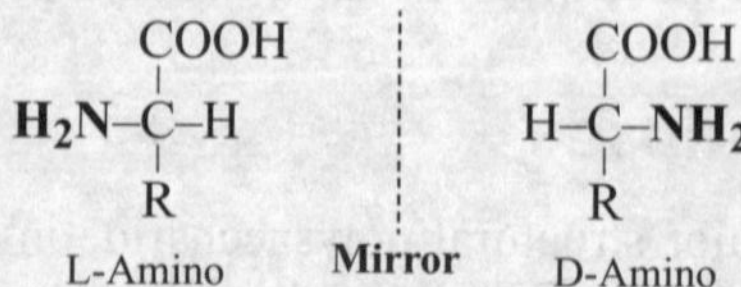

- All the naturally occurring amino acids belong to the L-series. So, the proteins consist of only L-amino acids.
- D and L configurations refer to the relative configurations around the asymmetric carbon atom and not to the direction of the optical rotation.

14.12.2 Nomenclature of Amino Acids

Although the amino acids can be named according to the IUPAC system, they are generally known by their common names or trivial names. For example, NH_2CH_2COOH is better known as glycine rather than α-aminoacetic acid or 2-aminoethanoic acid. Glycine may be abbreviated as Gly or even G. Similarly, alanine $CH_3CH(NH_2)COOH$ may be represented as Ala or A.

14.12.3 Classification of Amino Acids

(i) Classification based upon neutral, acidic or basic nature:

- **Acidic amino acids:** These contain more number of carboxyl groups than amino groups. For example, aspartic acid and glutamic acid which contain two –COOH groups and one $-NH_2$ group are acidic amino acids.

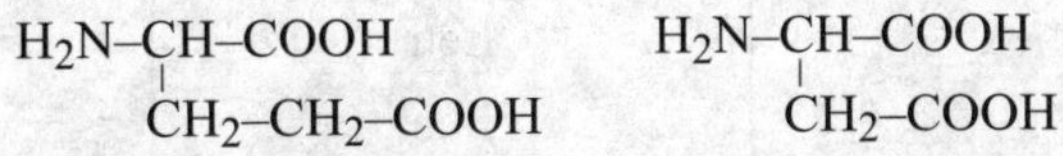

$$H_2N-CH(CH_2-CH_2-COOH)-COOH$$
Glutamic acid (Glu)

$$H_2N-CH(CH_2-COOH)-COOH$$
Aspartic acid (Asp)

- **Basic amino acids:** These contain more number of amino groups than carboxyl groups. For example, lysine, arginine and histidine, which contain two $-NH_2$ groups and one –COOH group are basic amino acids.

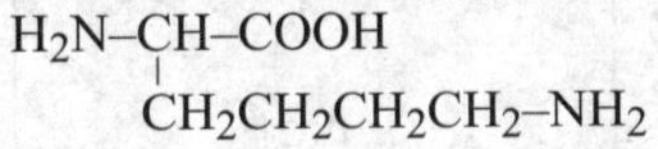

$$H_2N-CH(CH_2CH_2CH_2CH_2-NH_2)-COOH$$
Lysine (Lys)

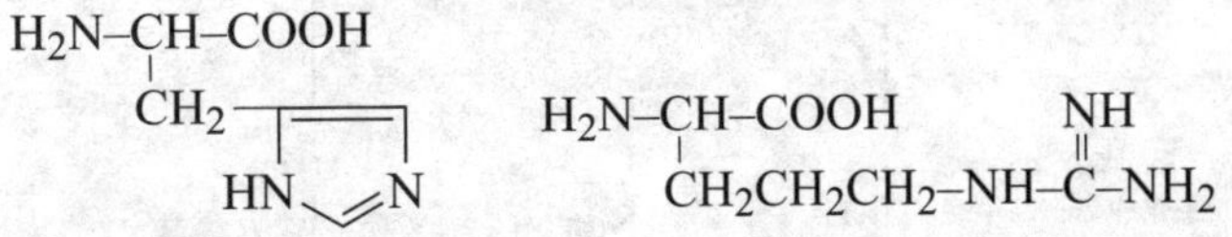

$$H_2N-CH(CH_2-\text{imidazolyl})-COOH$$
Histidine (His)

$$H_2N-CH(CH_2CH_2CH_2-NH-C(=NH)-NH_2)-COOH$$
Arginine (Arg)

- **Neutral amino acids:** These contain an equal number of amino and carboxyl groups. For example, amino acids such as glycine, alanine and valine are neutral amino acids.

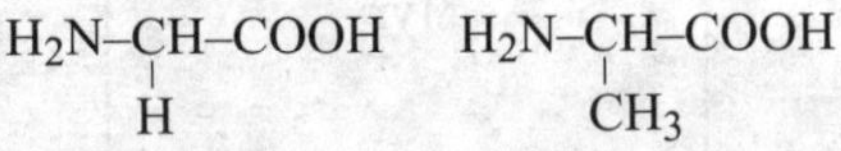

$$H_2N-CH(H)-COOH$$
Glycine (Gly)

$$H_2N-CH(CH_3)-COOH$$
Alanine (Ala)

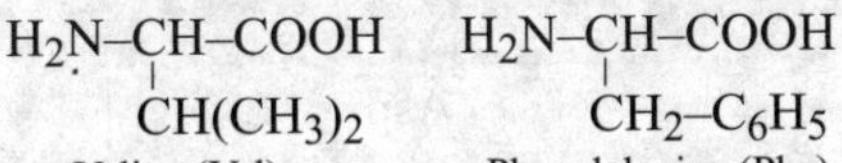

$$H_2N-CH(CH(CH_3)_2)-COOH$$
Valine (Val)

$$H_2N-CH(CH_2-C_6H_5)-COOH$$
Phenylalanine (Phe)

(ii) Essential and non-essential amino acids: So far, 26 α-amino acids have been isolated as the hydrolysis products of peptides and proteins. Out of these, 20 α-amino acids occur in all proteins and the other six are found only in special tissues. Certain amino acids can be made by our bodies and, therefore, we do not require them in our diet. These are called *non-essential amino acids*. The human body can synthesise 10 out of 20 amino acids found in proteins. Therefore, the others must be supplied through our diet and these are called *essential amino acids* (Table 14.2). The 10 essential amino acids are valine, leucine, isoleucine, arginine, lysine, threonine, methionine, phenylalanine, tryptophan and histidine. Due to the deficiency of essential α-amino acids, human beings develop a disease called *kwashiorkor*.

14.12.4 Structure of α-Amino Acids

The amino acids exist as a dipolar ion called a *zwitter ion*. It has positive as well as negative ends within the same molecule. In the formation of a zwitter ion, the proton goes from the carboxyl group to the amino group. The zwitter ion structure of an α-amino acid may be written as:

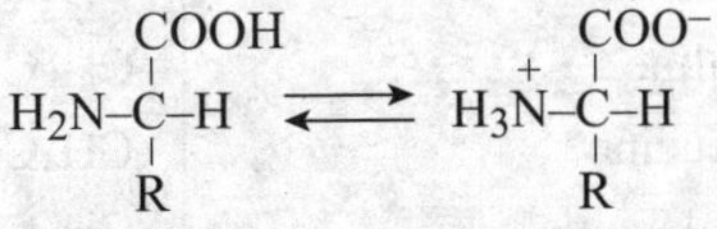

$$\underset{\text{L-Amino}}{H_2N-CH(R)-COOH} \rightleftharpoons \underset{\text{Zwitter ion}}{H_3\overset{+}{N}-CH(R)-COO^-}$$

Amino acids are quite soluble in polar solvents but are insoluble in organic or non-polar solvents. Like ionic compounds, the aqueous solutions of amino acids have *high dipole moments*.

14.12.5 Amphoteric Nature of α-Amino Acids

When the solution of an amino acid is made acidic or an acid is added to the amino acid, the COO^- accepts the proton and gets converted to the carboxyl substituent (–COOH). Therefore, the basic character is due to the $-COO^-$ group.

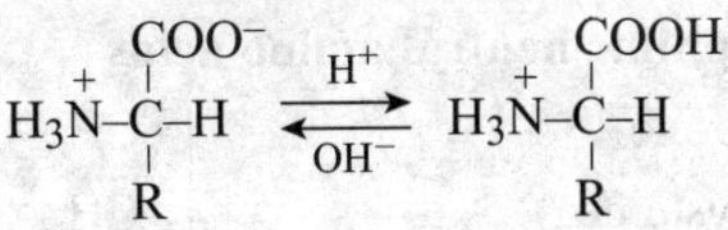

$$\underset{\text{Zwitter ion}}{H_3\overset{+}{N}-CH(R)-COO^-} \underset{OH^-}{\overset{H^+}{\rightleftharpoons}} \underset{\text{Cation}}{H_3\overset{+}{N}-CH(R)-COOH}$$

When an alkali is added to amino acid, the $-NH_3^+$ group releases the proton and changes to the amino ($-NH_2$) group. Therefore, the acidic character is due to the $-NH_3^+$ group.

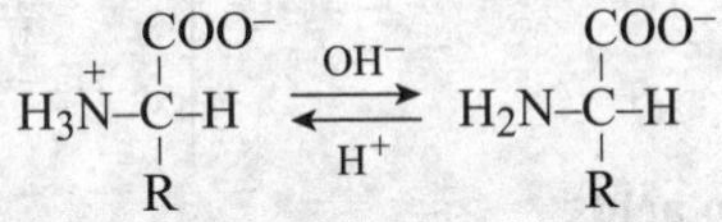

$$\underset{\text{Zwitter ion}}{H_3\overset{+}{N}-CH(R)-COO^-} \underset{H^+}{\overset{OH^-}{\rightleftharpoons}} \underset{\text{Anion}}{H_2N-CH(R)-COO^-}$$

Isoelectric point: When we place the aqueous solution of an amino acid in an electric field, its behaviour will depend upon the acidity or basicity of the solution. In an alkaline solution, an amino acid exists as a negative ion (II) and migrates towards the anode under the influence of an electric field. On the other hand, in an acidic solution, it exists as a positive ion (III) and migrates towards cathode under the influence of an electric field.

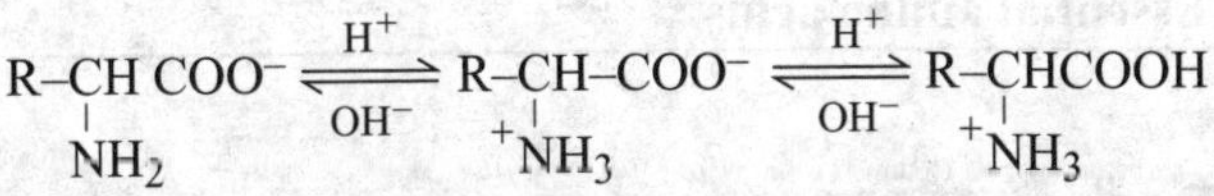

$$\underset{\text{II}}{R-CH(NH_2)\ COO^-} \underset{OH^-}{\overset{H^+}{\rightleftharpoons}} \underset{\text{II}}{R-CH(\overset{+}{N}H_3)-COO^-} \underset{OH^-}{\overset{H^+}{\rightleftharpoons}} \underset{\text{III}}{R-CH(\overset{+}{N}H_3)COOH}$$

However, at a certain hydrogen ion concentration (pH), the dipolar ion exists as a neutral ion and does not migrate to either electrode. In this solution, the structures II and III are exactly balanced. It is called the *isoelectric point* of that amino acid.

Table 14.2 Structures and names of essential α-amino acids

Sr. No.	Name of α-Amino acid	Characteristic feature of side chain, –R	Abbreviated name (Three letter code)	One letter code
Non-polar hydrophobatic neutral amino acids				
1.	Glycine	–H	Gly	G
2.	Alanine	$-CH_3$	Ala	A
3.	Valine*	$-CH(CH_3)_2$	Val	V
4.	Leucine*	$-CH_2CH(CH_3)_2$	Leu	L
5.	Isoleucine*	$-CH(CH_3)-CH_2-CH_3$	Ileu	I
6.	Phenylalanine*	$-CH_2-C_6H_5$	Phe	P
7.	Methionine*	$-CH_2-CH_2-S-CH_3$	Met	M
8.	Tryptophan*	$-CH_2-$ (indole ring, N–H)	Try	W
9.	Proline	(pyrrolidine ring, N–H, COOH)	Pro	P
Polar hydrophillic neutral amino acids				
10.	Serine	$-CH_2-OH$	Ser	S
11.	Cysteine	$-CH_2-SH$	Cys	C
12.	Aspargine	$-CH_2-CONH_2$	Asn	N
13.	Glutamine	$-CH_2-CH_2-CONH_2$	Glu	Q
14.	Threonine*	$-CH(OH)-CH_3$	Thr	T
15.	Tyrosine	$p\text{-}CH_2-C_6H_4-OH$ $-CH_2-C_6H_4-OH$	Tyr	Y
Acidic amino acids				
16.	Aspartic acid	$-CH_2-COOH$	Asp	D
17.	Glutamic acid	$-CH_2-CH_2-COOH$	Glu	E
Basic amino acids				
18.	Lysine*	$-CH_2-(CH_2)_3-NH_2$	Lys	K
19.	Arginine*	$-CH_2-(CH_2)_2-NH-C(NH_2)=NH$	Arg	R
20.	Histidine*	$-CH_2-$ (imidazole ring, N, NH)	His	H
*** Essential amino acids**				

14.13 Protiens

14.13.1 Peptides

Peptides are compounds formed by the condensation of two or more same or different α-amino acids. In this case, the carboxyl group of one amino acid and amino group of another amino acid gets condensed with the elimination of a water molecule. The resulting –CO–NH– linkage is called a peptide linkage or peptide bond.

$$\underset{\text{Glycine}}{H_2N-CH_2-CO\boxed{OH + H}}\underset{\text{Alanine}}{NH-CH(CH_3)-COOH} \xrightarrow{-H_2O} \underset{\text{Glycylalanine}}{H_2N-CH_2-\mathbf{CO-NH}-CH(CH_3)-COOH}$$

The interaction between two molecules of two different amino acids will give two different dipeptides. For example, when the –COOH group of glycine reacts with the $-NH_2$ group of alanine we get glycylalanine. But, if the $-NH_2$ group of glycine combines with the –COOH group of alanine, a different dipeptide, *alanylglycine*, is obtained.

14.13.2 Polypeptides

If a large number of α-amino acids (hundreds to thousands) are joined by peptide bonds, the resulting polyamide is called polypeptide.

$$H_2N{-}\underset{\displaystyle |}{\overset{R}{CH}}{-}CO{-}(NH{-}\overset{R}{CH}{-}CO)_n{-}NH{-}\overset{R''}{CH}{-}COOH$$

Polypeptide

(R, R′ and R″ may be H, same or different side chains.)

Like amino acids, polypeptides can also exist as zwitter ions.

$$\text{N-Terminal}\quad H_3\overset{+}{N}{-}\overset{R}{CH}{-}CO{-}(NH{-}\overset{R}{CH}{-}CO)_n{-}NH{-}\overset{R''}{CH}{-}COO^-$$

Polypeptide zwitter ion

Each polypeptide has a free amino group ($-NH_2$) at one end and a free carboxyl group (–COOH) at the other end. The amino group end is called the amino of the *N-terminal end* and the carboxyl group end having a free –COOH group is called the carboxyl or *C-terminal end.* For example, the name of a tripeptide obtained by condensation of glycine, alanine and serine in this order is *glycylalanylserine.* It is abbreviated as Gly–Ala–Ser. *All proteins are polypeptides while all polypeptides are not proteins.*

14.13.3 Classification of Proteins Based on Molecular Structure

(i) Fibrous proteins: These types of proteins consist of linear thread like molecules which tend to lie side by side to form fibres , held together at many points by hydrogen bonds or disulfide bonds. Some fibrous proteins are keratin in skin, hair, nails and wool, collagen in tendons, fibroin in silk, and myosin in muscle. The structure of fibrous proteins is shown.

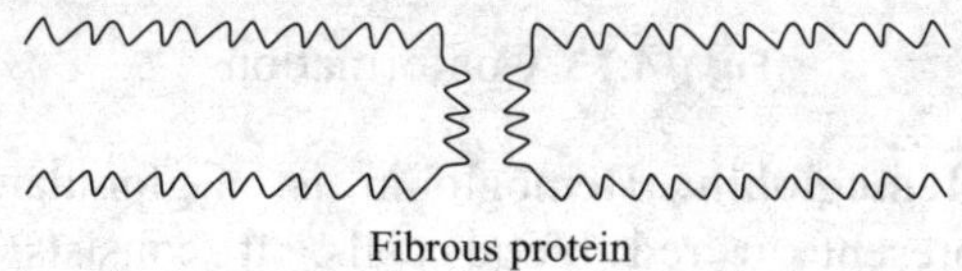

Fibrous protein

(ii) Globular proteins: In this type of proteins, the molecules are folded together into compact units forming spheroidal shapes. The peptide chains in globular proteins are also held by hydrogen bonds but these forces are comparatively weak. The common examples of globular proteins are albumin and insulin.

14.13.4 Classification of Proteins on the Basis of Hydrolysis Products or on the Basis of Chemical Composition

(i) Simple proteins: These are proteins which give amino acids only on hydrolysis with acids or enzymes. The important examples are albumins, globulins, glutalins, prolamines and keratin.

(ii) Conjugated proteins: These are proteins which on hydrolysis give a non-protein part and α-amino acids. Thus, these are formed by the combination of simple proteins with some non-proteinaceous substance. The non-proteinaceous part is called the prosthetic group and it controls the biological functions of the protein (Table 14.3).

Table 14.3 Prosthetic groups of proteins

Name of the protein	Prosthetic group
Nucleoproteins	Nucleic acids
Phospho proteins	Phosphoric acid residues
Glycoproteins or mucoproteins	Sugars
Lipoproteins	Lipids such as lecithin
Chromo proteins (hemoglobin and myoglobin)	Some colouring matter such as red coloured iron–protoporphyrin complex (heme) in hemoglobin and myoglobin

(iii) Derived Proteins: They are the products of partial hydrolysis of simple or conjugated proteins.

- **Chromoproteins:** These contain a coloured prosthetic group, usually containing a metal like Fe, Cu, Co, Mg of a group having metal and pyrrole residues. For example, haemoglobin and myoglobin contain red coloured iron-protoporphyrin complex (heme). Chlorophyll contains a coloured Mg complex.
- **Glycoproteins:** They have carbohydrates as the prosthetic group and are found in egg white and jelly fish. They are also known as mucoproteins.
- **Lipoproteins:** They have lipids as the prosthetic group and are found in phospholipids. They are found in milk, blood plasma and egg yolk.
- **Nucleoproteins:** They have nucleic acid as the prosthetic group and such type of proteins are present in the nucleus of the cell.
- **Phosphoproteins:** They have a phosphoric acid residue as the prosthetic group. Examples are casein, a major protein of milk and viteline from egg yolk.

14.13.5 Structure of Proteins

Proteins are biopolymers containing a large number of amino acids joined together through peptide bonds having three dimensional (3-D) structures.

(I) Primary structure: The sequence in which the amino acids are linked in one or more polypeptide chains of a proteins is called the primary structure of protein (Fig. 14.10).

$$\sim\!\underset{H}{N}{-}\overset{R}{\underset{H}{C}}{-}\underset{O}{\overset{}{C}}{-}\underset{}{\overset{H}{N}}{-}\underset{R'}{\overset{H}{C}}{-}\overset{O}{C}{-}\underset{H}{N}{-}\overset{R''}{\underset{H}{C}}{-}\underset{O}{C}\!\sim$$

Fig. 14.10

Normal hemoglobin:

—Val—His—Leu—Thr—Pro—Glu—**Glu**—Lys—

Sickle cell hemoglobin:

—Val—His—Leu—Thr—Pro—**Val**—Lys—

In the patients suffering from sickle cell anemia, the defective hemoglobin in red blood cells precipitates, causing the cells to sickle and sometimes even burst, leading ultimately to the death.

(ii) Secondary structure: The secondary structure gives the manner in which the polypeptide chains are folded or arranged. Proteins do not exist as straight chains of amino acids. Additional bonding such as hydrogen bonding, disulfide linkages (–S–S–) can occur between different polypeptide chains.

- *α-helix structure:* It is the most common form in which a polypeptide chain forms all possible types of hydrogen bonds by twisting into a right handed screw (helix) with the –NH group of each amino acid residue hydrogen bonded to the >C=O group of an adjacent turn of the helix (Fig. 14.11). This is called an α-helix.

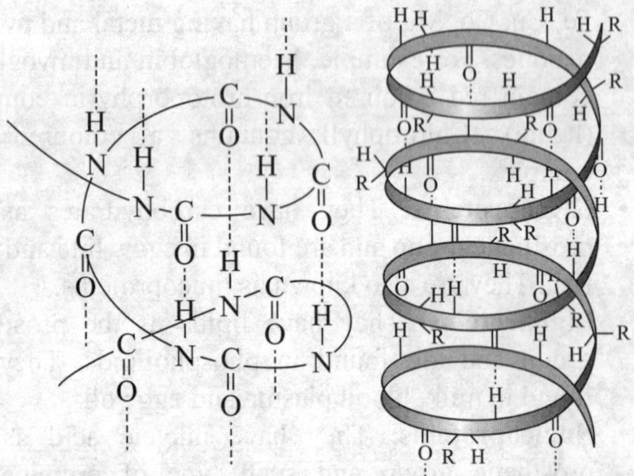

Fig. 14.11 α-helix structure of proteins (stabilised by hydrogen bonding)

This type of structure is adopted by fibrous structural proteins such as keratin found in hair and myosin found in muscles.

- **β-Pleated sheet (β-flat sheet structure):** The flat sheet structure becomes possible in proteins having amino acids with small R groups. The polypeptide chains can lie side by side in a zig–zag manner with alternate R groups on the same side situated at fixed distances apart. The two such neighbouring chains are held together by intermolecular hydrogen bonds. A number of such chains can be interbound and this results in the formation of a *flat sheet structure*. If the R group is moderate sized, these chains may contract or bend a little in order to accommodate them. This structure is known as the *β-pleated sheet structure* (Fig. 14.12).

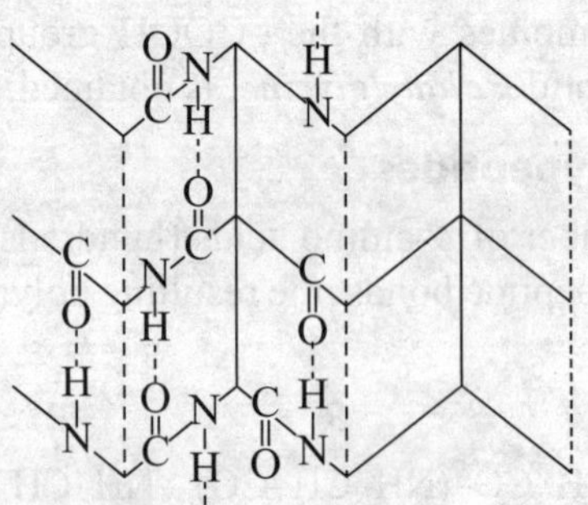

Fig. 14.12 β-pleated structure

It is due to the pleated structure that silk fibre cannot be stretched. But it can be bent or folded easily. The pleated structure may be *parallel* (N-terminus of all chains lying on the same side) or *antiparallel* (with alternate N-terminus and C-terminus lying on the same side) (Fig. 14.13).

Parallel β-conformation   Antiparallel β-conformation

Fig. 14.13 Conformations

Hemoglobin: Hemoglobin is a globular protein present in red blood cells. It consists of four polypeptide chains arranged tetrahedrally. Two α-chains have 141 amino acids and the other two β-chains contain 146 amino acids. It contains a non-protein constituent called *heme*. Heme is an iron porphyrin and is responsible for the red colour of blood. It is found that each of the polypeptide chains is associated with one heme unit (Fig. 14.14). Its molecular mass is about 65,000.

Function of hemoglobin: CO_2 and O_2 interchange between the body and the environment through the process of respiration. In the lungs where oxygen is present in a higher concentration, hemoglobin combines with oxygen to form oxyhemoglobin. Here, the oxygen gets bound to the iron of the heme. On the other hand, in tissues where the oxygen content

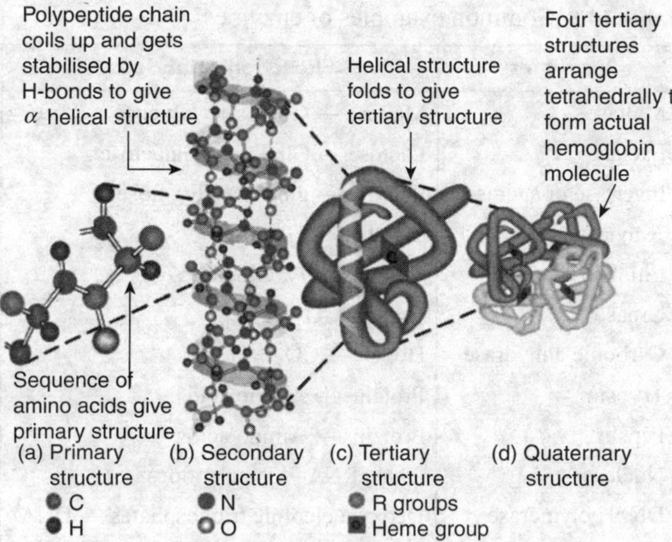

Fig. 14.14 Primary, secondary, tertiary and quaternary structure of hemoglobin

is low, oxyhemoglobin dissociates and releases oxygen for utilisation in metabolism and combines with the CO_2 to be released again in the lungs.

Myoglobin: It is a protein which stores oxygen in muscle tissues. It is made of a single polypeptide chain consisting of 153 amino acids and its molecular mass is nearly 17,000.

(iii) Tertiary structure: The tertiary structure of a protein gives the overall folding of polypeptide chains, that is, further folding of the secondary structure. Two major molecular shapes are—fibrous and globular. These have already been discussed.

(iv) Quaternary structure: There are some proteins which exist as assemblies of two or more polypeptide chains called sub-units or protomers (identical or different) which are held together by non-covalent forces such as hydrogen bonds, electrostatic interactions and van der Waals' interactions. For example, hemoglobin is an aggregate of four polypeptide chains or sub-units—two identical alpha chains (each containing 141 amino acid residues) and two identical beta chains (each containing 146 amino acid residues). The primary, secondary, tertiary and quaternary structures of haemoglobin are shown in Fig. 14.14.

14.13.6 Physical Properties of Proteins

- Proteins are generally colourless, odourless and tasteless amorphous solids. Some proteins are coloured, such as blood hemoglobin which is red in colour.
- They have very high molecular masses. The molecular masses of some proteins are given in Table 14.4.
- Proteins (globular) are hydrophylic colloids.
- They have an isoelectric point, at which its ionisation and solubility are minimum. This is used for the identification and isolation of proteins.
- They do not have sharp melting points.

Table 14.4 Molecular masses of some proteins

S. No.	Proteins	Molecular masses
1.	Insulin	6,000
2.	Casein	75,000–1,00,000
3.	Hemoglobin	65,000–70,000
4.	Milk globulin	30,000–40,000
5.	Egg albumin	34,000–44,000
6.	Pepsin	35,000
7.	Urease	4,80,000

14.13.7 Chemical Properties of Proteins

- They are hydrolysed by dil. acids, alkalies or by enzymes to give α-amino acids.
- Due to the presence of free –COOH groups and amino groups, proteins give characteristic reactions of both groups.
- They are optically active.

14.13.8 Biological Functions of Proteins

(i) Structural materials: Proteins serve as structural components of animal tissue. About 50% of the proteins present in our body are structural proteins. They are essential for growth, repair and reproduction. They are components of cell organelles, tissues and protective coverings like hair, nails and feathers. The cocoon of the silk moth is also made up of proteins. Even walls of pollen grains contain proteins.

(ii) Metabolic regulators: Some globular proteins regulate metabolic processes in the form of enzymes and hormones (insulin, parathormone). Such types of proteins are also called *functional proteins.*

(iii) Transport agents: Proteins also serve as the physical carrier of other functionally important smaller molecules. For example, the protein globulin carries the pigment heme, the two together forming hemoglobin. Heme transports oxygen in the body. Myoglobin in muscles stores oxygen. In plants, P-proteins help in the transport of organic compounds through phloem.

(iv) Defence: When any foreign organisms enter the blood, they release foreign substances called antigens. In response to these antigens, the body produces specific proteins called antibodies. These antibodies combine with the antigens, thereby protecting us. *Gamma globulins* present in blood plasma are examples of antibodies.

(v) Movement: Certain proteins like myosin and actin are responsible for mechanical movement of the muscles. They make muscle fibres contractile to bring about movements. Such proteins are called *contractile proteins.*

(vi) Storage proteins: Some proteins act simply as food reserves. For example, *ovalbumin* of egg white is meant only to be degraded for use by the growing chick. Similarly, *casein* of milk is meant to nourish the new born mammal.

Digestion of proteins: The digestion of proteins begins in the stomach (not the mouth) where the gastric juices are at a pH = 2. At this pH, the protein gets denatured and various enzymes start their coordinated work for their digestion. Various enzymes of protein digestion and their functions are as follows.

- **Proteases:** These break large protein molecules to smaller peptides.
- **Peptidases:** These convert peptides into amino acids. The pepsin in the stomach, trypsin and chymotrypsin in the pancreas and intestine help in the digestion of proteins into amino acids. These amino acids are absorbed into the blood steam either to be reassembled into newer proteins or for further break down.

14.14 Native State and Denaturation of Proteins

Native state: The most energetically stable state of a protein is called its *native state*. In other words, the native state corresponds to the proteins found in a biological system with a unique three dimensional structure (or configuration) and biological activity.

Denaturation of proteins: The denaturation that is change in the physical and biological properties of proteins, is caused by change in temperature or a change in pH, or a chemical change such as the presence of salts or certain chemical agents. Due to this, globules unfold and the helix gets uncoiled (Fig. 14.15).

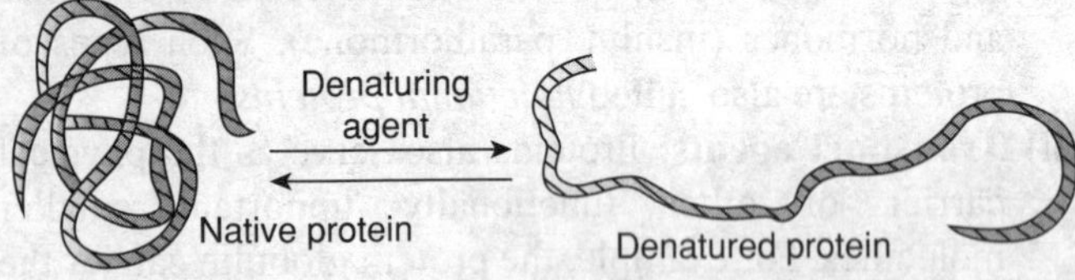

Fig. 14.15 Tertiary structure is broken

14.14.1 Examples of Denaturation of Proteins

- The coagulation of albumin present in the white of an egg. When an egg is boiled in water, the globular proteins present in it change to a rubber-like insoluble mass. This is irreversible denaturation. Curdling of milk, s caused due to the formation of lactic acid by the bacteria present in milk.
- The coagulation of milk in the presence of an acid (lemon juice) to form cheese is also an example of denaturation of proteins. During this denaturation, the globular milk protein lacto albumin becomes fibrous.

14.15 Enzymes

Enzymes are biological catalysts produced by living cells which catalyse the biochemical reactions in living organisms (Table 14.5). Almost all enzymes are globular proteins.

Table 14.5 Common examples of enzymes

Enzymes	Reaction catalysed
Maltase	Maltose $\rightarrow$ Glucose + Glucose
Lactase	Lactose $\rightarrow$ Glucose + Galactose
Invertase or sucrase	Sucrose $\rightarrow$ glucose + Fructose
Amylase	Starch $\rightarrow n$ Glucose
Emulsin or cellulase	Cellulose $\rightarrow n$ Glucose
Urease	Urea $\rightarrow CO_2 + NH_3$
Carbonic anhydrase	$H_2CO_3 \rightarrow CO_2 + H_2O$
Trypsin	Proteins $\rightarrow$ Amino acids
Pepsin	Proteins $\rightarrow$ Amino acids
Nucleases	DNA, RNA $\rightarrow$ Nucleotides
DNA polymerase	Deoxynucleotide triphosphates $\rightarrow$ DNA
RNA polymerase	Ribonucleotide triphosphates $\rightarrow$ RNA

- This is due to their *highly specific nature*, that is, each enzyme catalyses only one chemical reaction or at least a series of similar reactions such as hydrolysis of starch which requires the enzyme to act on similar bonds. Since there are a large number of biological reactions, a large number of enzymes are *required in a living* system. Without them, the living processes *would be too slow to* sustain life. For example, without the enzymes in our digestive tract, it would take us about 50 years to digest a single meal!
- Some enzymes contain some non-protein component called the *prosthetic group* which directs their activity. These prosthetic groups can either be *metal ions* called *cofactors* or some small organic molecule called *coenzymes*. Some common examples of meta*l ions which act* as cofactors are Na^+, K^+, Zn^{2+}, Mg^{2+}, Cu^{2+}, Mn^{2+}, Mo^{3+} and Co^{2+}. On the oth*er hand, coenzym*es are derived from vitamins such as thiamine, riboflavin and niacin.
- The enzymes are active at a moderate temperature (about 37°C) and a pH (around 7). For example, pepsin, a digestive enzyme for proteins in the stomach, has an optimum pH = 2 while trypsin(another digestive enzyme for proteins) has an optimum pH = 8.5.
- A number of enzymes work as a team in various metabolic processes. For example, in germinating seeds, starch is converted into glucose by two enzymes—amylase and maltase. Amylase converts starch into a disaccharide maltose and then maltase converts this maltose into two glucose molecules..
- Sometimes the activity of the enzyme is checked (inhibited) in the presence of some organic or inorganic compounds/ions. These compounds or ions are called enzyme inhibitors. For example, *cyanide poisoning* is due to the inhibition of the respiratory enzyme, cytochrome, by the cyanide ion.

14.15.1 Coenzymes

A prosthetic group which is covalently attached with the enzyme molecule is known as a *cofactor*. The prosthetic groups which get attached to the enzyme at the time of reaction are known as *coenzymes*. These are generally metal ions or small organic molecules like Zn, Mg, Mn, Fe, Cu, Co, Mo, K and Na. Several coenzymes are derived from vitamins such as thiamine, niacin and riboflavin.

14.15.2 Mechanism of Enzyme Activity

The various steps involved in an enzyme catalysed reaction are given below.

(i) Binding of the enzyme (E) to the substrate (S) to form a complex.

$$E + S \rightarrow ES$$

ES is called the enzyme–substrate complex.

(ii) Product formation in the complex.

$$ES \rightarrow EP$$

where EP is a complex of the enzyme and product.

(iii) Release of the product from the enzyme–product complex.

$$EP \rightarrow E + P$$

The catalytic property of enzymes is present at certain specific regions on their surfaces. These are called *active sites* or *catalytic sites*. The active sites have a characteristic shape; they fit only suitably shaped specific substrate molecules (Fig. 14.16).

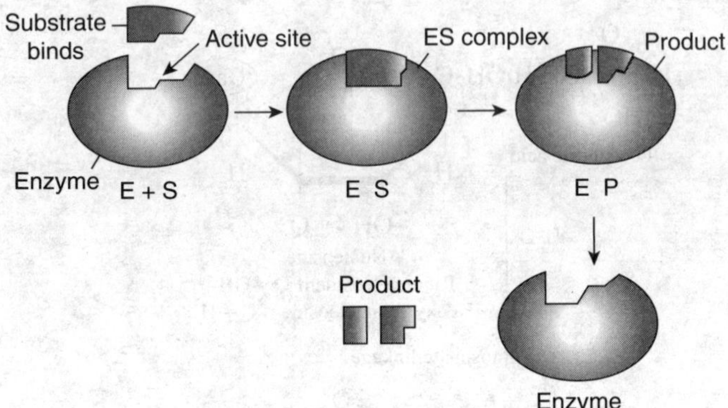

Fig. 14.16 Enzyme–substrate binding

14.15.3 Applications of Enzymes

(i) Industrial use: Enzymes are widely used for the manufacture of various useful products. Some examples are discussed below.

- Certain enzymes such as *invertase*, *zymase* and *maltase* are used in the manufacture of alcoholic drinks like wine and beer by the fermentation of carbohydrates.
- The enzyme *renin* is used for the manufacture of cheese by the coagulation of milk.
- The enzyme *maltase* is used for the manufacture of malt, which is used to manufacture health drinks such as Maltova.
- The enzyme *pepsin* is used to soften tough meats.
- The enzyme *invertase* is used for the manufacture of inert sugar used in candies and other sugar syrups.
- The enzyme *α-amylase* can be used to manufacture sweet syrup from corn starch.

(ii) For curing diseases: Certain enzymes are useful for curing certain diseases.

- *Streptokinase* is used for the treatment of heart patients and helps in dissolving blood clots.
- *Lysozyme* is used for the treatment of eye infections.
- *Asparginase* is used for the treatment of some types of leukemia.
- *Penicillinase* is used for the treatment of persons allergic to penicillin.

14.15.4 Enzyme Deficiency Diseases

Some common enzyme deficiency diseases are discussed.

(i) The congenital disease *phenylketonurea* is due to deficiency of the enzyme *phenylalanine hydroxylase* which catalyses the hydrolysis of phenylalanine. This disease causes accumulation of the amino acid phenylalanine or its compounds in the body which leads to brain damage and mental retardation of children.

(ii) *Albinism* is a disease which causes lack of the pigment melanin and leads to white skin and white hair. This is caused due to the deficiency of the enzyme *tyrosinase* (chick) enzyme.

14.16 Nucleic Acids

Nucleic acids are long chain biopolymers made up of a large number of monomeric units called *nucleotides*,that is, they are *polynucleotides.* These direct the protein synthesis and preserve the genetic information. Nucleic acids are of two types—DNA (deoxyribonucleic acid) and RNA (ribonucleic acid).

14.16.1 Composition of Nucleic Acids and Their Structure

Nucleic acids are polymers of nucleotides. A *nucleotide* is further made up of a phosphoric acid unit and a nucleoside. A *nucleoside* consists of a pentose sugar and a heterocyclic nitrogenous base. Thus, a nucleotide consists of three chemical constituents. Nucleosides of RNA and DNA are different in terms of nature of sugar and (or) the nature of base.

- A nitrogen containing heterocyclic base.
- A five-carbon (pentose) sugar.
- A phosphoric acid unit.

$$\text{Pentose sugar} + \text{Nitrogenous heterocyclic base} \xrightarrow{-H_2C} \text{Nucleoside} \xrightarrow[-H_2O]{H_3PO_4} \text{Nucleotide} \xrightarrow[\text{Polymerisation}]{\text{Enzymes}} \text{Nucleic acid}$$

(i) Nitrogen containing heterocyclic bases: Depending upon the number of rings, these are of two types.

- **Purines:** They are two ringed nitrogen containing bases derived from purine. These are adenine (A) and guanine (G) which are found in both RNA and DNA.

- **Pyrimidines:** They are single ringed nitrogen containing bases derived from pyrimidine. Cytosine (C) and thymine (T) are found in DNA but cytosine (C) and uracil (U) are found in RNA.

Purine

Adenine (A) Guanine (G)

Pyrimidine

Cytosine (C) Uracil (U) (only in RNA) Thymine (T) (only in DNA)

Adenine (A), guanine (G), cytosine (C) are present in both DNA and RNA whereas RNA contains uracil (U) instead of thymine (T) present in DNA.

(ii) Pentose sugars: In nucleic acids, two types of sugars are present. The sugar molecule *D(–)-2-deoxyribose* is associated with DNA, while *D(–)-ribose* is associated with RNA. Both these pentoses are found in the *furanose* form.

2-Deoxyribose sugar present in RNA Ribose sugar present in RNA

The suffix *2-deoxy* means that it lacks oxygen at position-2 (shown as 2′).

(iii) Phosphoric acid (phosphate) group: Phosphoric acid condenses with the hydroxyl group of sugar at the C–5′ position to form an inorganic phosphate ester linkage.

Nucleoside: It is a condensation product of a pentose sugar from the C–1′ site with the nitrogen of a heterocyclic nitrogenous base at position 1 in a pyrimidine base and position 9 in a purine base. The nucleoside in RNA is known as a *ribonucleoside*. The nucleoside in DNA is known as a *deoxyribonucleoside*.

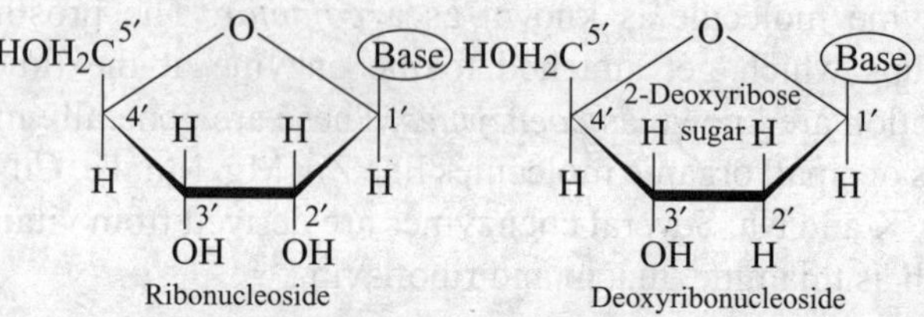

The base–sugar linkage of the ribonucleoside and deoxyribonucleoside is called the *N-glycosidic linkage*. There are eight possible types of nucleosides (Table 14.6).

Table 14.6 Types of nucleosides

Base	Abbreviation	Nucleoside
Adenine	A	Adenosine (for RNA)
Adenine	A	Deoxyadenosine (for DNA)
Guanine	G	Guanosine (for RNA)
Cytosine	C	Cytidine (for RNA)
Cytosine	C	Deoxycytidine (for DNA)
Thymine	T	Deoxythymidine (present only in DNA)
Uracil	U	Uridine (present only in RNA)

Nucleotides: Nucleotides are formed by esterification of the –OH groups at the C–5′ position of the sugar part of the nucleoside with phosphoric acid. So, the nucleotides are known as *nucleoside monophosphates*.

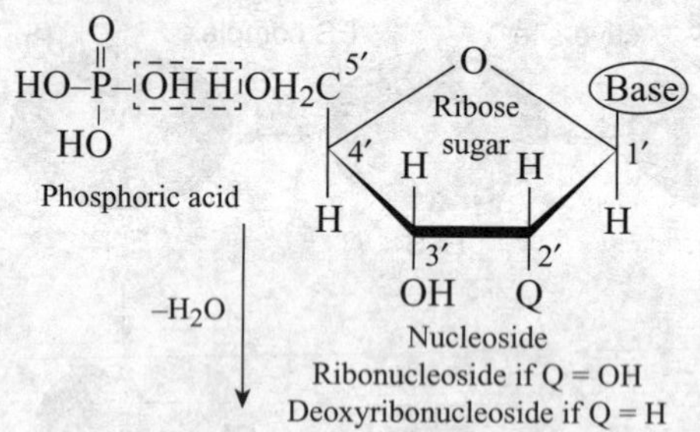

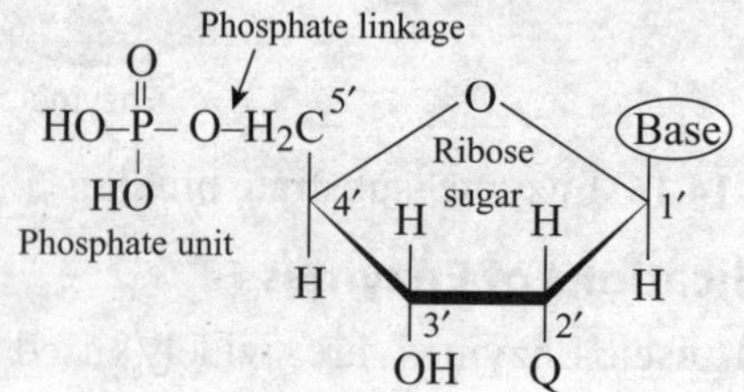

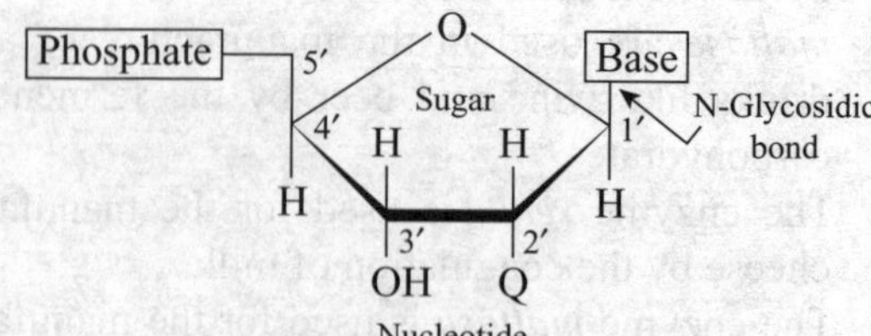

14.16.2 Primary Structure of Nucleic acids (DNA and RNA)

The double helical structure of DNA consists of two right-handed helical polynucleotide chains coiled around the same central axis. The two strands are antiparallel, that is, their 5′ → 3′ phosphodiester linkages run in opposite directions (Fig. 14.17).

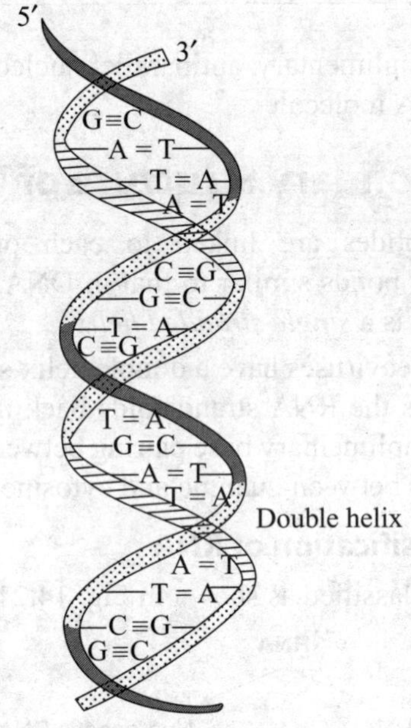

Fig. 14.17 Double helix structure of DNA

General primary structure of dinucleotide of RNA and DNA
RNA if Q = OH and base = A, G, C or U
DNA if Q = H and base = A, G, C or T

Thus, the overall formation of nucleic acids may be represented as follows:

$$(\text{Sugar} + \text{Base} + \text{Phosphate group})_n \xrightarrow[-3nH_2O]{} \text{Nucleic acid}$$

The sequence in which the four nitrogenous heterocyclic bases are attached to the sugar–phosphate backbone of the polynucleotide chain is called the *primary structure of the nucleic acids.* The 3′–5′phosphodiester bonds provide strength to the polynucleotide chain. The nitrogenous base units at the C–1′ positions of individual nucleotide projects on one side of the sugar unit. At the 5′ end, the last sugar unit has its carbon at C–5′ position with only the monophosphate linkage, that is, it is not attached to any other nucleotide. The other end of the polynucleotide chain is known as the 3′-end. At this end the last sugar unit has a free –OH group at the C-3′ position (Fig. 14.18).

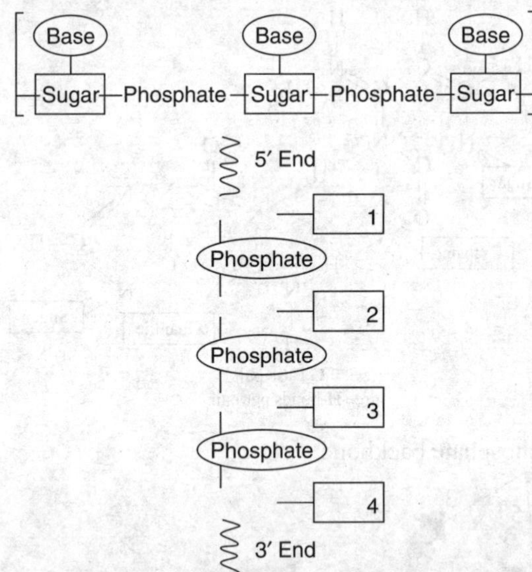

Fig. 14.18 Polunucleotide chain

Fischer Projection Formula of Oligonucleotides

The bases are represented by their respective symbols, the phosphate bond is represented by symbol 'P' and the sugar is drawn by a simple Fischer projection. Thus, the tetranucleotide ACGT can be drawn as follows:

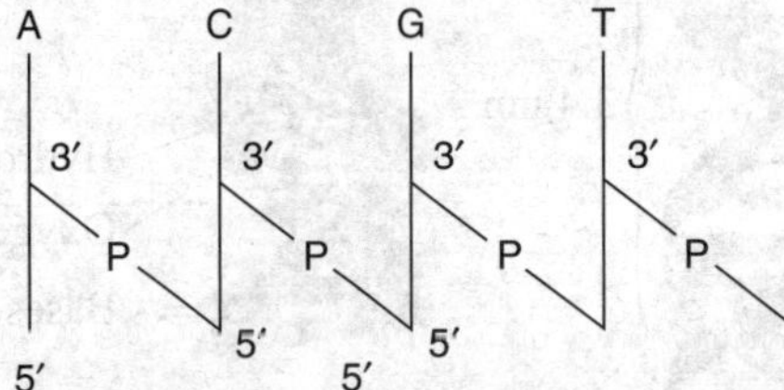

14.17 Secondary Structure of DNA

The base pairs of the two strands are linked together through hydrogen bonds. But proper hydrogen bonding can occur between specific base pairs. A purine base of one stand is always paired with a pyrimidine base of the other stand. Because of the geometries and sizes of the bases, the only possible pairings in DNA are between guanine (G) and cytosine (C) through three hydrogen bonds (G≡C) and between adenine (A) and thymine (T) though two hydrogen bonds (A=T) (Fig. 14.19). This complimentary arrangement is known as the *base pairing rule*.

A = T Base pair
two H-bonds per pair

C ≡ G Base pair
three H-bonds per pair

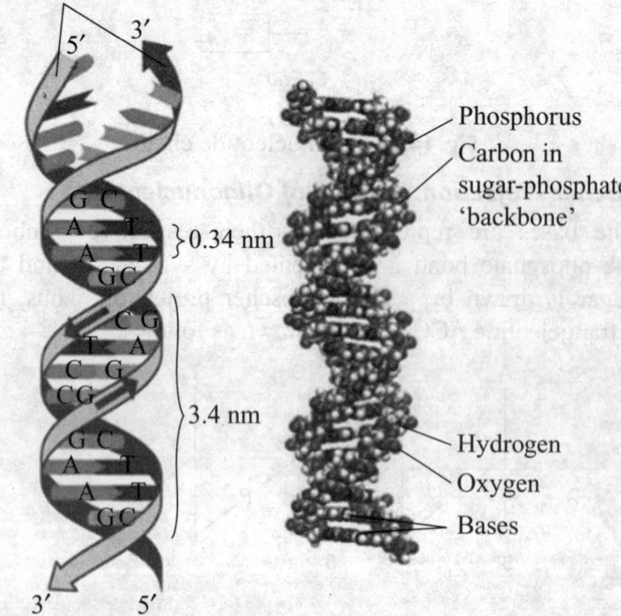

Fig. 14.19 **(a)** Space filling model of DNA
(b) Ribbon structure of DNA

The two stands of the double helix are complementary and not identical since the base sequence of one stand automatically fixes that of the other. The chains do not run in the same direction with respect to their internucleotide linkage but rather, are antiparallel (Fig. 14.20).

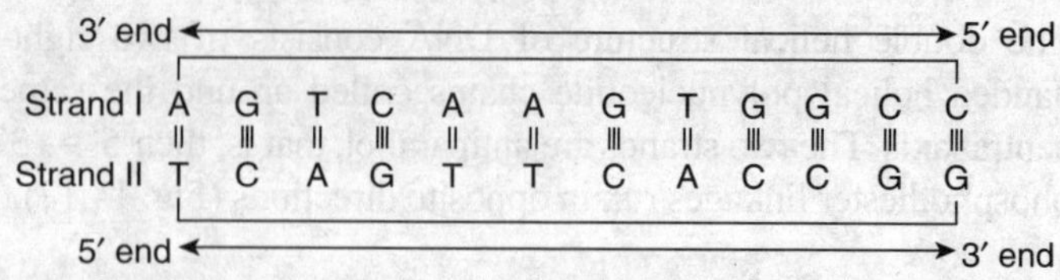

Fig. 14.20 Complimentary, antiparallel nucleotide chains in DNA molecule

14.18 Secondary Structure of RNA

The ribonuceotides are linked to each other by 3′–5′ phosphodiester bonds similar to that in DNA. However, the RNA molecule is a *single stranded helix*.

- RNAs of reoviruses have a double helix structure.
- Sometimes the RNA strand folds back upon itself and shows complimentary base pairing between adenine and uracil, and between guanine and cytosine.

14.18.1 Classification of RNA

The RNA are classified as shown in Fig. 14.21.

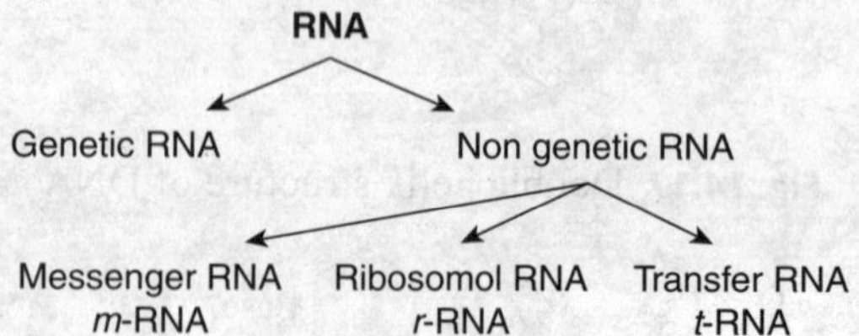

Fig. 14.21 Classification of RNA

Genetic RNA: Some organisms have only RNA as nucleic acids and they use only this RNA in their genetic mechanism. For example, the tobacco virus, foot and mouth virus, HIV, and so on.

Non-genetic RNA: Generally, organisms possess RNA along with DNA and they use their RNA in carrying out the orders of the DNA. In these cases, RNA is not used as the genetic material. Such type of RNA is called non-genetic RNA. It is further divided into three types.

(i) Messenger RNA (m-RNA): It is produced in the cell and carries genetic information from the DNA to the ribosome for the synthesis of proteins as it transmits genetic information from the DNA molecule to the cytoplasm.
- It is a complimentary copy of a segment of one stand of DNA.
- It constitutes 5% of the total RNA.
- Its life span is very short.

(ii) Ribosomal RNA (r-RNA): Ribosomal RNA (r-RNA) is an integral part of ribosomes. It is found in the ribosomes, where protein synthesis takes place.
- It constitutes 80% of the total RNA.
- The molecular weight of r-RNA varies from 40,000 to 1.5 million.

(iii) Transfer RNA (t-RNA): It is a much smaller molecule than m-RNA. It is also called *soluble RNA* (s-RNA). Its role is to collect amino acids from the cytoplasm for protein synthesis, that is, they act as carriers of amino acids.

- It constitutes about 15% of the total RNA.
- Their molecular weight varies from 23,000–25,000.
- A t-RNA molecule consists of 75–78 nucleotides only.

14.19 Biological Functions of Nucleic Acids

Two important functions of nucleic acids are—*replication* and *protein synthesis.*

14.19.1 Replication

Replication is the process by which a single DNA molecule produces two identical copies of itself. The DNA is the master molecule, storehouse of the hereditary information of the organism, the key of heredity and the secret of life. This is all because of its capacity of replicate itself. It is an enzyme catalysed process. At the time of cell division (*mitosis*), the double stranded helix of DNA partially unwinds and separates into two single strands The DNA replication follows the base pairing rules by which A pairs with T and G pairs with C. Two identical DNA molecules are then passed on to a new cell resulting from cell division (Fig. 14.22). That is how the hereditary characteristics are transmitted from parents to the children.

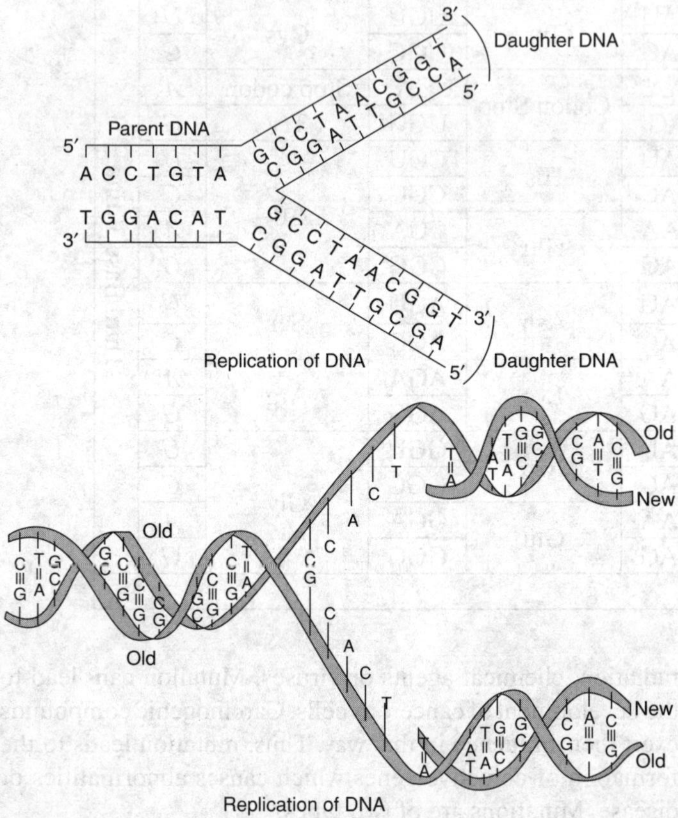

Fig. 14.22 Replication

14.20 Protein Synthesis

In this process, the genetic information coded in the DNA in the form of a specific base sequence is translated and expressed in the form of a sequence of amino acids which results in the synthesis of specific proteins which perform various functions in the cell. Actually, the proteins are synthesised by various RNA molecules in the cell but the message for the synthesis of a particular protein is coded in the DNA. This DNA directed synthesis of proteins takes place in two steps—transcription and translation.

14.20.1 Transcription

During this process, the double helix of DNA partially unwinds and one of the two DNA strands (sense chain) acts as the template (pattern) for the synthesis of an RNA chain in a manner similar to replication of DNA. According to the *base-pairing principle*, uracil (U) in RNA being formed appears opposite the adenine (A) of DNA, cytosine (C) appears opposite guanine (G), adenine (A) opposite thymine (T) and guanine (G) opposite cytosine (C) of the DNA. The RNA, thus synthesised, migrates to the cytoplasm and the DNA itself returns to its normal double helix structure. In this way, three types of RNAs are synthesised:

- messenger RNA (m-RNA),
- transfer RNA (t-RNA), and
- ribosomal RNA (r-RNA).

Each of the three different RNAs performs different functions during proteins synthesis. The process which leads to the synthesis of three types of RNAs is called *transcription.*

- During this process, ribonucleotides, rather than deoxyribonucleotides, assemble along the uncoiled template (Fig. 14.23). This process is catalysed by enzymes called *RNA polymerases*.
- The second strand of DNA which does not carry information for protein synthesis is called the *missense chain*.

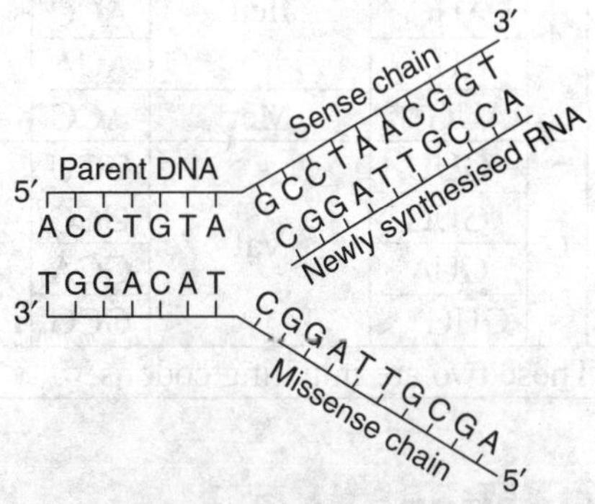

Fig. 14.23 Transcription (Synthesis of RNA)

14.20.2 Translation

m-RNA moves into the cytoplasm of the cell where it begins to attach with very small ribosome particles present in the cytoplasm. The *m*-RNA then gives the message of the DNA for a specific protein synthesis in the form of a template to the ribosome. The specific ribonucleotide sequence in *m*-RNA forms a code that determines the order in which the different amino acid residues have to be joined. A triplet out of the four bases in the *m*-RNA, that is A, C, G and U, acts as a code for a particular amino acid and is called a *codon*. Since there are four bases, there are $4^3 = 64$ *triplets* or codons possible. Out of these, 61 triplets form the code for the specific amino acids, while the remaining three triplets (UAA, UAG and UGA) constitute the code for the chain termination step. These chain termination step codons are also known as *stop codons* or *nonsense codons*.

Since there are only 20 different amino acids, so a particular amino acid is specified by more than one triplet or codon, whose first two letters are usually unchanged. This means that codons are *degenerate*. For example, CUU and CUC both code for leucine. Similarly, UUU and UUC, code for the amino acid phenylalanine.

- The m-RNA codons do not directly recognise the amino acids but do so with the help of the t-RNA. Since there are 61 triplets, there are 61 different t-RNAs, one for each triplet.
- Every t-RNA molecule has an amino acid attachment site and a site having three complementary nucleotides for recognition of the triplet in m-RNA. The codon on the m-RNA must be matched by a complimentary triplet which is on t-RNA. For example, a t-RNA molecule having an anticodon UAC carries the amino acid methionine and attaches to the codon AUG on the m-RNA. This process is repeated a number of times and leads to the formation of a polypeptide chain by stepwise addition of amino acids.
- The t-RNA after transferring its amino acid to the polypeptide chain is released to repeat its work.
- When the synthesis of a specific protein is completed, a *releasing factor* (stop codon) signals the end because there is no t-RNA with some amino acid to continue the chain growth. The protein thus synthesised is released from the ribosome (Fig. 14.24).

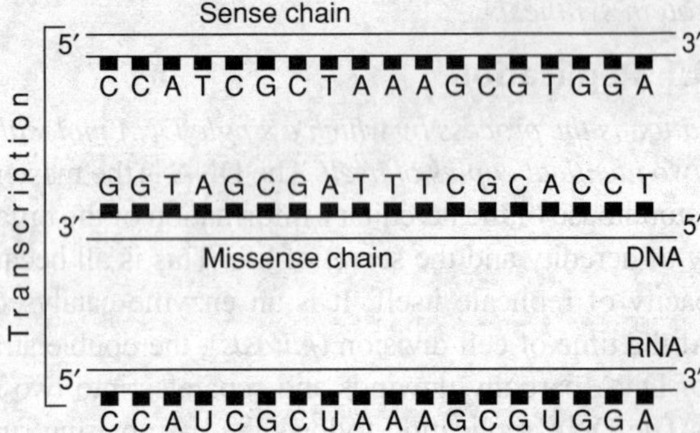

Fig. 14.24 Transcription

First Base 5′ End	Second Base: *U*	Amino acid	*C*	Amino acid	*A*	Amino acid	*G*	Amino acid	Third Base 3′ End
U	UUU	Phe	UCU	Ser	UAU	Tyr	UGU	Cys	*U*
	UUC		UCC		UAC		UGC		*C*
	UUA	Leu	UCA		UAA*	Codon Stop	UGA*	Stop codon	*A*
	UUG		UCG		UAG*		UGG	Try	*G*
C	CUU	Leu	CCU	pro	CAU	His	CGU	Arg	*U*
	CUC		CCC		CAC		CGC		*C*
	CUA		CCA		CAA	Glu	CGA		*A*
	CUG		CCG		CAG		CGG		*G*
A	AUU	Ileu	ACU	Thr	AAU	Asn	AGU	Ser	*U*
	AUC		ACC		AAC		AGC		*C*
	AUA		ACA		AAA	Lys	AGA	Arg	*A*
	AUG**	Met	ACG		AAG		AGG		*G*
G	GUU	Val	GCU	Ala	GAU	Asp	GGU	Gly	*U*
	GUC		GCC		GAC		GGC		*C*
	GUA		GCA		GAA	Glu	GGA		*A*
	GUG**		GCG		GAG		GGG		*G*

**These two are initiating codons.

14.21 Mutation

Mutation is defined as a chemical change in the DNA molecule that could lead to the synthesis of proteins with an altered sequence of amino acids. The change in the DNA molecule can occur spontaneously or may be caused by radiation, chemical agents or viruses. Mutation can lead to the development of cancerous cells. Carcinogenic compounds exert their influence in this way. Thus, mutation leads to the formation of defective genes which causes abnormalities or disease. Mutations are of two types.

(i) **Base-substitution mutation:** A base substitution mutation is the result of the substitution of one base for another without changing the total number of bases. It is also known as a *point mutation*.

(ii) **Frame-shift Mutation:** In this type of mutation, one or more bases get either inserted or deleted from the sequence. Such mutations are quite deleterious.

Mutation can occur due to any error during transcription/translation. Mutations that occur of their own without any external environmental influence are called *spontaneous mutations*. Mutation can be caused due to an exposure of cells to:

- UV rays or X-rays,
- any carcinogenic chemical which may change the base sequence of theDNA, or
- failures in the repair by enzyme systems.

Mutagen: Any external influence that causes mutation or enhances the rate of appearance of mutation is called a *mutagen*. UV light, X-rays and many chemicals are mutagenic.

Consequences of mutation: It leads to the synthesis of proteins with an altered amino acid sequence. The proteins with changed primary structure may have no biological activity leading to the death of a cell. The defective genes may cause abnormalities or can cause certain genetic diseases.

- **A gene is different from the genetic code.** Genetic code is the relationship between the amino acids and the nucleotide triplet. Whereas, a gene is a part of DNA molecule that codes for a specific protein. Every protein has the corresponding gene.
- **A codon is different from genetic code.** A codon is the nucleotide sequence in m-RNA that codes for a particular amino acid. Whereas, a genetic code is the sequence of the nitrogenous bases in m-RNA.
- Genetic code encloses the information for the linking of amino acids during protein synthesis whereas each triplet of nucleotides is called a codon for a specific amino acid which is recognised by t-RNA molecules.

14.22 Lipids

Lipids are waxy or oily substances containing esters involving long hydrocarbon chains. These are *hydrophobic* in nature and are insoluble in water. Lipids have a different chemical nature and do not possess common functional groups.

14.22.1 Classification of Lipids

Based upon their hydrolysis products, lipids can be broadly classified as in Fig. 14.25.

Simple lipids (homolipids): The simplest and the most abundant lipids produce only alcohols and carboxylic acids upon hydrolysis and are called simple lipids. These can be further subdivided into two types—oils and fats, and waxes.

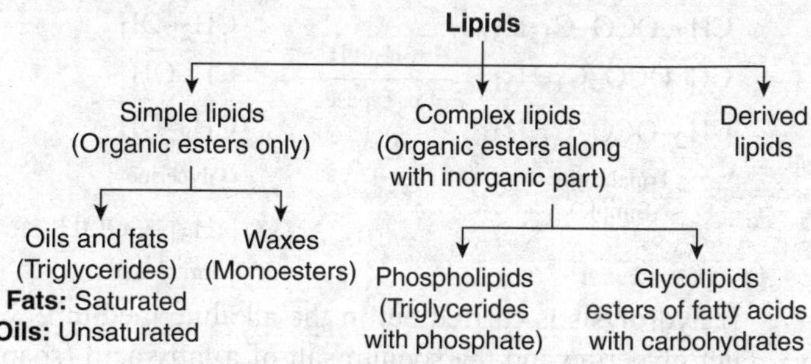

Fig. 14.25 Classification of lipids

(i) **Oils and fats:** These are *triglycerides* or *triacylglycerals*, that is, these are triesters of long chain fatty acids and glycerol and are represented by the general formula,

$$\begin{array}{l} CH_2\text{–}OCO\text{–}R_1 \\ | \\ CH\text{–}OCO\text{–}R_2 \\ | \\ CH_2\text{–}OCO\text{–}R_3 \end{array}$$

General formula of simple lipids

Here the groups R_1, R_2 and R_3 can be the same or different. If they are the same, then the glycerides are called *simple glycerides*. If the R groups are different, then the glycerides are called *mixed glycerides*. For example,

$$\begin{array}{l} CH_2\text{–}OCO\text{–}C_{15}H_{31} \\ | \\ CH\text{–}OCO\text{–}C_{15}H_{31} \\ | \\ CH_2\text{–}OCO\text{–}C_{15}H_{31} \end{array} \qquad \begin{array}{l} CH_2\text{–}OCO\text{–}C_{15}H_{31} \\ | \\ CH\text{–}OCO\text{–}C_{17}H_{33} \\ | \\ CH_2\text{–}OCO\text{–}C_{15}H_{35} \end{array}$$

Tripalmitin (Simple) Palmito-oleo-stearate (Mixed)

Types of fatty acids: The fatty acids present in oils and fats contain an even number of carbon atoms. These fatty acids may be saturated or unsaturated containing one or more double bonds per molecule. Examples of saturated fatty acids are:

- stearic acid $CH_3\text{–}[CH_2]_{16}\text{–}COOH$, MP = 69.6°C,
- palmitic acid $CH_3\text{–}[CH_2]_{14}\text{–}COOH$, MP = 63.1°C,
- myristic acid $CH_3\text{–}[CH_2]_{12}\text{–}COOH$, MP = 53.9°C,
- lauric acid $CH_3\text{–}[CH_2]_{10}\text{–}COOH$, MP = 44.2°C.

Examples of unsaturated fatty acids are:

- oleic acid, $C_{17}H_{33}COOH$ having one double bond, MP = 13.4°C,
- linoleic acid, $C_{17}H_{31}COOH$ having two double bonds, $CH_3\text{–}[CH_2]_7CH{=}CH\text{–}CH_2\text{–}CH{=}CH[CH_2]_7COOH$, MP = –5.0°C,
- linolenic acid, $C_{17}H_{29}COOH$ having three double bonds,

$CH_3CH_2CH{=}CHCH_2CH{=}CHCH_2CH{=}CH[CH_2]_7COOH$.

Unsaturated fatty acids have the *cis* configuration at the double bonds. This is of vital importance because their melting point is lower and thus these exist as liquids at body temperature and thus are easily emulsified and digested. Oils and fats that are easily hydrolysed in the presence of mineral acids or enzymes are called lipases.

$$\begin{array}{l} CH_2\text{–}OCO\text{–}C_{15}H_{31} \\ | \\ CH\text{–}OCO\text{–}C_{15}H_{31} \\ | \\ CH_2\text{–}OCO\text{–}C_{15}H_{31} \end{array} \xrightarrow[\text{or Lipase}]{+3H_2O/H^+} \begin{array}{l} CH_2\text{–}OH \\ | \\ CH\text{–}OH \\ | \\ CH_2\text{–}OH \end{array} + 3\,C_{15}H_{31}\text{–}COOH$$

Tripalmitin (Simple) — Glycerine — Palmitic acid

If hydrolysis is carried out in the alkaline medium, we get glycerine and the sodium salt of a fatty acid (soap) and the reaction is known as the *saponification reaction*.

$$\begin{array}{l} CH_2\text{–}OCO\text{–}C_{15}H_{31} \\ | \\ CH\text{–}OCO\text{–}C_{15}H_{31} \\ | \\ CH_2\text{–}OCO\text{–}C_{15}H_{31} \end{array} \xrightarrow[\text{saponification}]{+3NaOH} \begin{array}{l} CH_2\text{–}OH \\ | \\ CH\text{–}OH \\ | \\ CH_2\text{–}OH \end{array} + 3\,C_{15}H_{31}\text{–}COONa$$

Tripalmitin (Simple) — Glycerine — Sodium palmitate (Soap)

Rancidity of Fats and Oils

- Under the influence of micro-organisms or fat-splitting enzymes, certain fats get hydrolysed to give free fatty acids having a sour, rancid odour. For example, butter goes rancid on account of the production of butyric acid.
- Also, in the presence of light and moisture, the small quantities of unsaturated acids (produced by enzymatic hydrolysis) present in oils are oxidised by air to peroxides which break down into aldehydes having an unpleasant, rancid odour and taste. Saturated fatty acids are not affected under these conditions. That is why the storage life of fats is better than that of oils.
- **Oxidation of saturated fatty acids:** However, fats containing saturated fatty acids having six to twelve carbon atoms undergo ketone rancidity. Here, the acids produced as a result of enzymatic hydrolysis, undergo oxidation at the β-position to β-keto acids, which are unstable and lose carbon dioxide to give ketones having a pungent unpleasant odour. For example,

$$\underset{\text{Caprylic acid}}{CH_3[CH_2]_6COOH} \xrightarrow[-H_2O]{\beta\text{-oxidation}} \underset{\beta\text{-Ketocaprylic}}{CH_3[CH_2]_4COCH_2COOH} \xrightarrow{-CO_2} \underset{\text{Methyl n-pentyl ketone}}{CH_3[CH_2]_4COCH_3}$$

Digestion of Oils and Fats

The digestion of lipids occurs in the small intestine at a pH = 7.5. Bile juices form an emulsion with the lipid and increase their surface area. The enzyme *lipase* hydrolyses the fats into glycerol and fatty acids which pass into the blood stream where they undergo a series of enzymatic reactions to finally get oxidised to CO_2 and H_2O with the release of a large amount of energy which is stored in the form of ATP.

(ii) Waxes: They have a general formula RCOOR′ where R and R′ are long hydrocarbon chains. For example, wool wax obtained from wool grease (lanolin), beeswax and spermaceti, which is a mixture of waxes found inside the skull of the sperm whale. The chemical formulae of some waxes are given below.

Bees wax:	Myricyl palmitate	$C_{15}H_{31}\text{–}COO\text{–}C_{30}H_{61}$
Spermaceti:	Cetyl palmitate	$C_{15}H_{31}\text{–}COO\text{–}C_{16}H_{33}$
Carnauba wax:	Myricylcerotate	$C_{25}H_{51}\text{–}COO\text{–}C_{30}H_{61}$

- Waxes are more resistant to hydrolysis than oils and fats.
- All the waxes are insoluble in water but soluble in organic solvents.
- Waxes have properties of flexibility and non-reactivity. They can act as excellent coatings. They play an important role as a protective coating on fruits, leaves and animals.

Uses of Waxes

- Naturally a thin coating of wax occurs on the leaves of many plants like palms and cactus to prevent the loss of water from the surface of leaves. It also prevents them from attack by microorganisms. Waxes are widely used for the manufacture of ointments, cosmetics, floor polish and furniture polish.

14.22.2 Complex Lipids (Heterolipids)

Compound or complex lipids contain nitrogen and phosphorus. On hydrolysis they give other substances in addition to fatty acids and alcohols. They are of two types—phospholipids and glycolipids.

(i) Phospholipids: These are the esters of glycerol in which two –OH groups of glycerol are esterified by fatty acids and the third is esterified by some derivative of phosphoric acid. They can be represented by the general formula,

$$\left.\begin{array}{l} CH_2\text{–}OCO\text{–}R_1 \\ | \\ CH\text{–}OCO\text{–}R_2 \end{array}\right] \text{Hydrophobic tails}$$
$$\begin{array}{l} | \\ CH_2\text{–}O\text{–}P(=O)(O^-)\text{–}OR_3 \end{array} \quad \text{Hydrophillic head}$$

Phospholipid

- The most important class of phospholipids are *phosphoglycerides*. A molecule of phosphoglyceride contains glycerol phosphate, two fatty acids and an alcohol that may be choline, ethanolamine, serine or inositol.
- An important example of phospholipid present in egg white is *lecithin* in which two –OH groups of glycerol are esterified with palmitic acid ($C_{15}H_{31}$–COOH) while the third –OH group is esterified with phosphoric ester $[(HO)_2P(O)O\text{–}R_3]$ of an amino alcohol, *choline* $[(CH_3)_3N^+\text{–}CH_2\text{–}CH_2\text{–}OH]$.

$$\begin{array}{l} CH_2\text{–}OCO\text{–}[CH_2]_{14}\text{–}CH_3 \\ | \\ CH\text{–}OCO\text{–}[CH_2]_{14}\text{–}CH_3 \\ | \\ CH_2\text{–}O\text{–}P(=O)(O^-)\text{–}O\text{–}[CH_2]_2\text{–}N^+(CH_3)_3 \end{array}$$

Lecithin

$$\begin{array}{l} CH_2\text{–}OCO\text{–}[CH_2]_{14}\text{–}CH_3 \\ | \\ CH\text{–}OCO\text{–}[CH_2]_{14}\text{–}CH_3 \\ | \\ CH_2\text{–}O\text{–}P(=O)(O^-)\text{–}O\text{–}[CH_2]_2\text{–}NH_3^+ \end{array}$$

Cephalin

In *cephalin*, phosphoric ester is made with ethanolamine [$NH_3^+–CH_2–CH_2–OH$]. It is present in all animal and vegetable tissues.

- Phospholipids differ from simple lipids in the sense that they also contain phosphorus and nitrogen. Phospholipids are part of the materials of cell membranes.
- The phosphate group forms a polar, hydrophilic head on the molecule and two fatty acid chains constitute the non-polar hydrophobic tail. That is why phospholipids have good emulsifying properties. Phospholipids have good membrane-forming properties. This is due to their peculiar structure which has a hydrophilic (water attracting) head and a hydrophobic (water repelling) tail.

Uses of phospholipids: They act as the energy reservoir for animals. They act as heat insulators and shock absorbers for the living organisms. They serve as structural components of cell membranes.

(ii) Glycolipids: These are esters of fatty acids with carbohydrates and *may contain nitrogen but not phosphorus*. When a glycoside is bound to a primary alcohol, the product is a glycolipid. Most glycolipids are the derivatives of *sphingomyelin* in which the choline–phosphate group of the phospholipids is replaced by a glycoside. The most common glycoside is *cerebrosides* contain glucose or galactose.

$$
\begin{array}{l}
\quad\quad\ \ HO–CH–CH{=}CH–[CH_2]_{12}–CH_3 \\
\quad\quad\quad\quad\ | \\
H_2N–CH \\
\quad\quad\quad\quad\ | \\
\quad\quad\ \ CH_2–O–CH–[CHOH]_3–CH–CH_2OH \\
\quad\quad\quad\quad\quad\quad\quad\ \lfloor\_\_\_\_\_\_\_\_\_\_\_\_\ O \rfloor
\end{array}
$$

Cerebroside with glucose as carbohydrate

Substances of this class are present mainly in the brain and nervous tissue. Examples are phrenosin and kerasin but not much is known about their biochemical role.

Derived Lipids (Steroids)

Steroids are another important group of lipids which include non-fatty acid lipids.

- Steroids are compounds such as sterols, bile acids, sex hormones, vitamins and cholesterol which all occur in animal tissues (never in plants).
- Carotenoids are also a type of lipid which are polymers of isoprene. β-carotene ($C_{40}H_{50}$) is an important carotenoid that occurs in carrots and green leaves.

Functions of Lipids in Bio-systems

For all the living organisms, fats and oils are the major source of food. Their main functions are discussed.

(i) Simple lipids which are stored in the living organism can release sufficient energy, in the case of fasting or illness. Inside the living body, fats and oils are slowly hydrolysed to fatty acids and glycerol which further get oxidised to CO_2 and H_2O slowly releasing a lot of energy. Plants store their energy in the form of polysaccharides (particularly starch). Oils and fats are richer sources of energy than carbohydrates and proteins because of their higher calorific value. Fats present in the tissues of animals also act as heat insulators and shock absorbers for the organisms.

(ii) Phospholipids are structural components of nerve tissues and the chloroplasts of green leaves and cell membranes. They (phospholipids) are also used as detergents to emulsify fat for transport within the body.

(iii) Cholesterol is the principal sterol of higher animals and is the chief constituent of gallstones and nerve tissues. Cholesterol is not present in plant fats.

(iv) Some fats supply essential fatty acids.

(v) Lipids are very essential for the absorption of fat-soluble vitamins such as A, D, E and K.

14.23 Hormones

Hormones are the chemical substances which are produced in the ductless glands in the body. These are carried to different parts of the body through the blood stream and control various body functions. They are communication agents among cells, and are called *chemical messengers*. In mammals, the secretion of hormones is controlled by the anterior lobe of the pituitary gland present at the base of the brain. These hormones are transported to other glands such as adrenal cortex, thyroid and sex glands to stimulate the production of other hormones. Hormones exhibit a high degree of *specificity* in their action. They are not stored in our bodies but are produced when required. The deficiency of any hormone leads to a particular disease which can be cured by the administration of that hormone.

14.23.1 Classification of Hormones

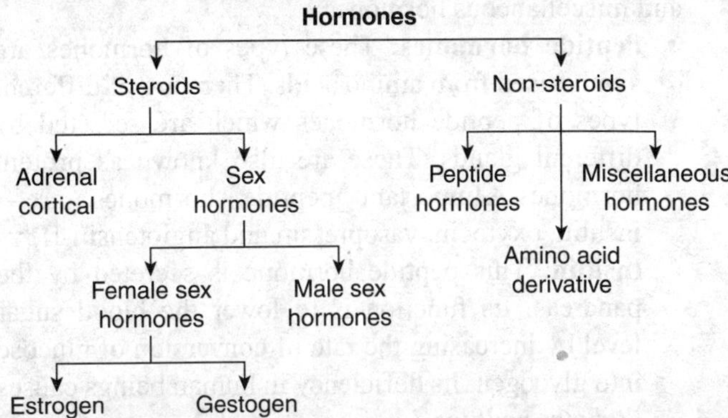

(i) Steroid hormones: These hormones have a structural resemblance to steroids. Such hormones contain a steroid nucleus which is based on a four-ring network consisting of three cyclohexane rings and one cyclopentane ring.

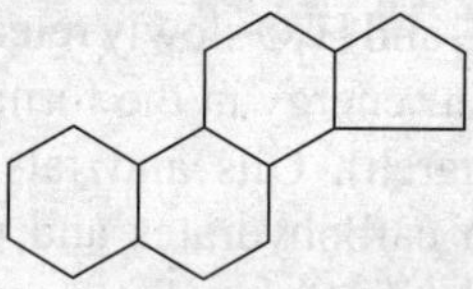

Steroid hormones are of two types—sex hormones and adrenal cortex hormones.

- **Sex hormones:** These hormones are responsible for the primary sexual process and the secondary characteristics such as growth of facial hair, change in voice and so on, which differentiate females from males. They are further classified as—androgens (male sex hormones), estrogens (female sex hormones) and gestogens (pregnancy hormones).
  - o **Male sex hormones:** Androgens are male sex hormones; for example, androsterone, testosterone and dihydrotestosterone. These are produced by the testes.
  - o **Female sex hormones:** Estrogens are female sex hormones; for example, estrone, estradiol and estriol. These are secreted by the ovaries.
  - o **Gestogens:** These are called pregnancy hormones. For example, progesterone, and pregnandiol. These are also secreted by the ovaries.
- **Adrenal cortex hormones:** Such hormones are called *corticoids* since they are produced by the cortex of the adrenal glands. They are of two types—mineralocorticoids and glucocorticoids.
  - o **Mineralocorticoids:** These regulate the NaCl content in the blood and control excretion of potassium in urine. Its deficiency leads to loss of fluids and its excess results in an increase in blood pressure.
  - o **Glucocorticoids:** They influence calcium and phosphorus metabolism and have an anti-inflammatory effect.

(ii) Non-steroid hormones: These are further classified into three types—peptide hormones, amine hormones and miscellaneous hormones.

- **Peptide hormones:** These types of hormones are synthesised from amino acids. There are of different types of peptide hormones which are secreted by different glands. These are also known as protein hormones. Important peptide hormones are—insulin, oxytocin, vasopressin and angiotensin-II.

  Insulin: This peptide hormone is secreted by the pancreas. Its function is to lower the blood sugar level by increasing the rate of conversion of glucose into glycogen. Its deficiency in human beings causes *diabetes mellitus*.

  Oxytocin: It is secreted by the posterior lobe of the pituitary gland. It contracts the uterus after child birth and produces lactation in the mammary glands.

  Vasopressin: It is also secreted by the posterior lobe of the pituitary gland. It controls the re-absorption of water in the kidneys.

  Angiotensin-II: It is present in the blood plasma of persons with high blood pressure. It contracts the blood vessels.
- **Amine hormones:** These are neither steroids nor peptides. These are water soluble amino compounds. These are structurally derived from amino acids. Thyroxine and adrenaline are two important hormones belonging to this class.

  Thyroxine is secreted by the thyroid and controls the rate of the metabolism. It controls the metabolism of carbohydrates, lipids and proteins.

  Adrenaline is secreted by the adrenal medulla. Secretion of adrenaline takes place under the conditions of stress such as fear, anger or some other emergency. It stimulates the process of breaking down of glycogen in the liver which produces glucose.

14.24 Vitamins

- Vitamins are not generally synthesised in the body and thus they must be essentially present in our diet. However, our body can synthesise vitamin D under the action of UV radiations from sunlight on ergosterol under the skin.
- Vitamins are neither structural units nor the energy suppliers. But their deficiency can cause specific diseases.
- Vitamin B_{12} is not synthesised in plants. It can be supplemented only through a non-vegetarian diet or through water supply because rain water contains some vitamin B_{12}. It is because certain bacteria which can synthesise vitamin B_{12} is sucked up by the wind.

14.24.1 Classification of Vitamins

These are classified on the basis of their solubility as fat soluble vitamins (A, D, E and K) and water soluble vitamins (B and C). *Biotin* (vitamin B_7 or vitamin H) is an exception which is insoluble in fat as well in water. Deficiency of these causes a variety of conditions (Table 14.7).

14.24.2 Avitaminosis

Multiple deficiencies caused by lack of more than one vitamin are very common in human beings. This condition of multiple vitamin deficiency is called *avitaminosis*. Its requirement for a particular person depends on the size, age and rate of metabolism of that person. Youngsters need higher amounts of vitamins than elders. The need for vitamins of growing children and of the pregnant women is more. The intestinal organisms may synthesise vitamins in significant amounts For example, vitamin K and most of the vitamins of the

Table 14.7 Vitamins, their sources and deficiency diseases

S. No.	Vitamin	Chemical name/ Common name	Source	Characteristics	Deficiency disease
1.	Vit. A	Retinol/carotenoid (Bright eye vitamin)	Meat, eggs, milk, fish oil, butter, green leafy vegetables, liver kidney, carrots sweet potatoes, rice polish	Fat soluble, stable to heat, promotes growth and improves vision and resistance to diseases	Night blindness,xeropthalmia (hardening of cornea), xerosis (drying of skin)
2.	Vit. B_1	Thiamine, aneurin (antieuritic vitamin)	Pulses, nuts, egg yolk, milk, rice polish, yeast, cabbage, tomatoes, liver	Water soluble, unstable to heat	Beri-Beri (general weakness and leg paralysis), loss of appetite
3.	Vit. B_2	Riboflavin or lactoflavin	Milk, yeast, meat, egg white, green vegetables, liver, kidney	Water soluble, stable to heat but sensitive to light;daily dose ≈ 2–3 mg	Cheilosis (cracking of lips), dermatits, inflammation of tongue (glossitis), retarded growth
4.	Vit. B_3	Niacin or nicotinic acid	Groundnuts, yeast, liver, fish, meat	Water soluble and highly stable, helps in metabolism of fats, proteins and carbohydrates	Pellagra (shrivelling of skin)
5.	Vit. B_5	Pantothinic acid	Yeast, liver, eggs, legumes	Constituent of coenzyme-A, important in cellular metabolism (synthesis of acetyl choline)	Muscular paralysis, burning feet syndrome
6.	Vit. B_6	Pyridoxine or adermin	Cereals, egg yolk, rice bran, meat, legumes, green leafy vegetables, yeast	Water soluble	Anemia, affects CNS, insomnia, irritation, pellagra (shrivelled skin)
7.	Vit. B_7 or Vit. H	Biotin/ egg white (anti-injury factor)	Yeast, liver, kidney and milk	Insoluble in water as well as in fat, it is a sulfur containing coenzyme	Dermatitis, hair loss, paralysis, muscular pain, loss of appetite, anemia
8.	Vit. B_{12}	Cyanocobalamin	Milk, liver of ox, sheep, pig;meat, eggs, rain water	Water soluble, stable to heat, it does not occur in plants	Pernicious anemia (enlargement of RBCs), inflammation of tongue
9.	Vit. C	Ascorbic acid (antiscorbutic vitamin)	Citrus fruits, green vegetables, chillies, sprouted legumes	Water soluble, lost on exposure to air and during cooking; cooking in a closed pan is suggested; daily docs ≈ 70–80 mg	Scurvy (bleeding of gums), pyorrhoea (loosening and bleeding of teeth)
10.	Vit. D	Ergocalciferol (antirachitic vitamin, sunshine vitamin)	Fish liver oil, butter, milk, meat, eggs, synthesised in skin on exposure tosun	Fat soluble, stable to heat and oxidation; controls calcium and phosphorus metabolism; daily dose ≈ 0.025 mg	Rickets, deformation of bones and teeth

S. No.	Vitamin	Chemical name/ Common name	Source	Characteristics	Deficiency disease
11.	Vit. E	Tocopherol (antisterility vitamin, beauty vitamin)	Milk, wheat germ oil, seed oils, eggs	Fat soluble, stable to heat and oxidation; it is a mixture of four vitamins named α, β, γ and δ-tocopherols	Sterility, muscular atrophy
12.	Vit. K, K_1 and K_2	Phylloquinone/ menadione (antihemorrhagic vitamin)	K_1 in alfalfa, leafy vegetables (cabbage, spinach, carrot tops) and K_2 from bacteria	Fat soluble, stable to heat but sensitive to light and alkali	Hemorrhagic conditions and impaired clotting of blood
13.	Coenzyme Q_{10}		Chloroplasts of green plants and mitochondria of animals	It is actually a coenzyme with vital significance	Low order of immunity of body against many diseases

B-complex group are synthesised by the intestinal organisms. Water soluble vitamins do not accumulate in the body even if taken in excess and get excreted through the urine. On the other hand, fat soluble vitamins tend to accumulate if consumed in excess. This may lead to *hypervitaminosis*

14.24.3 Comparison of Vitamins and Hormones

Similarities between vitamins and hormones are:

- deficiency of both of these causes some kind of disease,
- both are required in very small quantities, and
- both of these play a specific role in the functioning of the body.

Differences between vitamins and hormones are given in Table 14.8.

Table 14.8 Differences between vitamins and hormones

Property	Vitamins	Hormones
(i) Source	Vitamins (except vitamin D) are not produced in the body. Vitamins must be supplied in the diet.	Hormones are produced in the endocrine or ductless glands.
(ii) Storage	They are stored in the body up to a certain extent.	They are not stored in the body. These are produced as and when required.

Exercises

OBJECTIVE QUESTIONS

Carbohydrates

1. Which of the following is an example of a ketohexose?

(a) mannose (b) galactose
(c) maltose (d) fructose

2. Which of the following monosaccharides is a pentose?

(a) glucose (b) fructose
(c) arabinose (d) galactose

3. Which of the following are monosaccharides?

I. ribose II. deoxyribose
III. maltose IV. galactose
V. fructose VI. starch

(a) II, III, IV, VI (b) III, IV, V, VI
(c) I, II, IV, V (d) I, II, IV, VI

4. Glucose when heated with HI/red phosphorus gives

(a) *n*-hexane (b) *n*-heptane
(c) *n*-pentane (d) *n*-octane

5. Which of the following reacts with glucose?

(a) $NaHSO_3$ (b) NH_2OH
(c) 2,4-dinitrophenylhydrazine (d) NH_3

6. Glucose does not react with

(a) NH_2OH (b) NH_3
(c) $C_6H_5NHNH_2$ (d) HCN

7. Glucose does not react with

(a) hydroxylamine (b) conc. HNO_3
(c) acetic anhydride (d) sodium bisulfite
(e) Br_2/H_2O

8. Oxidation of glucose with Br_2–H_2O or Ag_2O or ammoniacal silver nitrate solution gives
(a) D-glucaric acid (b) L-glucaric acid
(c) L-gluconic acid (d) D-gluconic acid

9. Oxidation of glucose with conc. HNO_3 gives
(a) D-gluconic acid (b) D-saccharic acid
(c) L-tartaric acid (d) L-saccharic acid

10. Optical rotations of some compounds along with their structure are given below. Which of them have the D configuration?

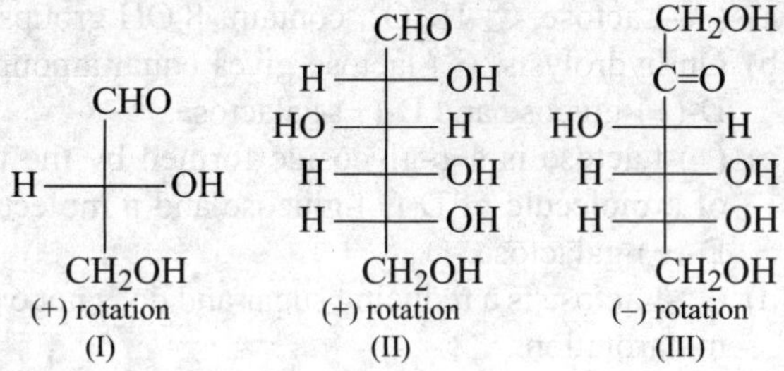

(a) I, II, III (b) II, III (c) I, II (d) III

11. Which of the following statements is not true about glucose?
(a) It is an aldohexose.
(b) On heating with HI it forms *n*-hexane.
(c) It is present in the furanose form.
(d) It does not give the 2,4-DNP test.

12. Which set of terms correctly identifies the carbohydrate shown?

1. pentose 2. hexose
3. aldose 4. ketose
5. pyranose 6. furanose
(a) 1, 3 and 6 (b) 1, 3 and 5
(c) 2, 3 and 6 (d) 2, 3 and 6
(e) 1, 4 and 6

13. Which of the following reactions of glucose can be explained only by its cyclic structure?
(a) Glucose forms a cyanohydrin with HCN.
(b) Glucose reacts with hydroxylamine to form an oxime.
(c) The pentaacetate of glucose does not react with hydroxylamine.
(d) Glucose is oxidised by nitric acid to gluconic acid.

14. α-D-glucose and β-D-(+)-glucose are
(a) enantiomers (b) conformers
(c) epimers (d) anomers

15. Methyl-α-D-glucoside and methyl-β-D-glucoside are
(a) epimers (b) anomers (c) enantiomers
(d) conformational diastereomers

16. What is the relationship between the given structures (look at the arrow)?

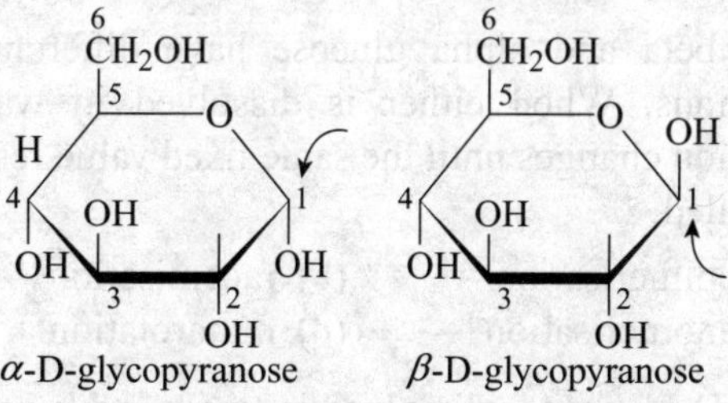

(a) enantiomers (b) anomers
(c) diastereomers (d) metamers

17. In the following structure the anomeric carbon is

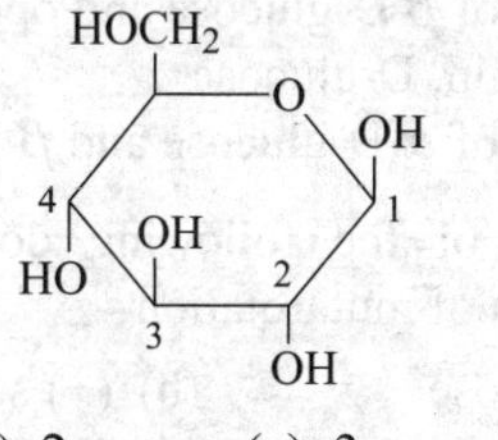

(a) 1 (b) 2 (c) 3 (d) 4

18. The number of chiral carbons in β-D (+)-glucose is
(a) five (b) six (c) three (d) four

19. How many stereoisomers does α-D-glucose have?
(a) 10 (b) 13 (c) 15 (d) 16

20. In fructose the possible optical isomers are
(a) 12 (b) 8 (d) 6 (d) 4

21. Which of the following form/s an osazone with phenylhydrazine?
(a) glucose (b) fructose
(c) maltose (d) all the three above

22. The glucose molecule reacts with X number of molecules of phenylhydrazine to yield an osazone. The value of X is
(a) three (b) two (c) one (d) four

23. Which of the following pairs forms the same osazone?
(a) glucose and fructose (b) glucose and galactose
(c) glucose and arabinose (d) lactose and maltose

24. For osazone formation, the effective structural unit necessary is
(a) CH_2OCH_3–CO– (b) CH_2OH–CO–
(c) CH_2OCH_3–CO– (d) CHO–$CHOCH_3$–

25. Which of the following hexoses will form the same osazone when treated with an excess of phenylhydrazine?

(a) D-glucose, D-fructose and D-galactose
(b) D-glucose, D-fructose and D-mannose
(c) D-glucose, D-mannose and D-galactose
(d) D-fructose, D-mannose and D-galactose

26. The beta and alpha glucose have different specific rotations. When either is dissolved in water, their rotation changes until the same fixed value results. This is called

(a) epimerisation (b) racemisation
(c) anomerisation (d) mutarotation

27. If α-D-glucose is dissolved in water and kept for a few hours, the major constituent(s) present in the solution is (are)

(a) β-D-glucose
(b) mixture of β-D-glucose and open chain D-glucose
(c) open chain, D-glucose
(d) mixture of α-D-glucose and β-D-glucose

28. Which one of the following does not exhibit the phenomenon of mutarotation?

(a) (–) fructose (b) (+) sucrose
(c) (+) lactose (d) (+) maltose

29. Raffinose on hydrolysis gives

(a) glucose (b) fructose
(c) galactose (d) all the above

30. Stachyrose is a

(a) monosaccharide (b) disaccharide
(c) trisaccharide (d) tetrasaccharide

31. Hydrolysis of sucrose is called

(a) inversion (b) esterification
(c) hydration (d) saponification

32. Acid hydrolysis of sugar gives invert sugar which contains

(a) 50% α-D-glucose + 50% β-D-glucose
(b) 36% α-D-glucose + 64% β-D-glucose
(c) 64% α-D-glucose + 36% β-D-glucose
(d) 50% D-glucose + 50% D-fructose

33. Which of the following has maximum levorotation?

(a) D-glucose (b) D-fructose
(c) sucrose (d) invert sugar

34. Which of the following sets of monosaccharides forms sucrose?

(a) α-D-galactopyranose and α-D-glucopyranose
(b) α-D-glucopyranose and β-D-fructofuranose
(c) β-D-glucopyranose and α-D-fructofuranose
(d) α-D-glucopyranose and β-D-fructopyranose

35. α-Maltose consists of

(a) one α-D-glucopyranose unit and one β-D-glucopyranose unit connected by 1,2-glycosidic linkage
(b) two α-D-glucopyranose units with 1,2-glycosidic linkage
(c) two β-D-glucopyranose units with 1,4-glycosidic linkage
(d) two α-D-glucopyranose units with 1,4-glycosidic linkage

36. Which of the following statements is not true regarding (+)-lactose?

(a) (+)-Lactose, $C_{12}H_{22}O_{11}$ contains 8 OH groups.
(b) On hydrolysis, (+)-lactose gives equal amounts of D-(+)-glucose and D-(+)-galactose.
(c) (+)-Lactose is a β-glycoside formed by the union of a molecule of D-(+)-glucose and a molecule of D-(+)-galactose.
(d) (+)-Lactose is a reducing sugar and does not exhibit mutarotation.

37. In lactose, the reducing part is

(a) galactose (b) glucose
(c) fructose (d) mannose

38. The linkage between the two monosaccharide units in lactose is

(a) C_1 of β-D-glucose and C_4 of β-D-galactose
(b) C_1 of β-D-galactose and C_4 of β-D-glucose
(c) C_1 of α-D-galactose and C_4 of β-D-glucose
(d) C_1 of α-D-glucose and C_4 of α-D-galactose

39. Which of the following statements about starch is not true?

(a) Starch is a mixture of two components, amylose (15%–20%) and amylopectin (80%–85%).
(b) Amylose is water soluble while amylopectin is water insoluble.
(c) An aqueous solution of amylose produces a blue colour with iodine.
(d) Both amylose and amylopectin contain unbranched chains of α-D-glucose units.

40. The glycosidic linkage involved in linking the glucose units in the amylose part of starch is

(a) C_1–C_4 β-linkage (b) C_1–C_6 α-linkage
(c) C_1–C_6 β-linkage (d) C_1–C_4 α-linkage

41. Which of the following statements about amylopectin is true?

(a) In the presence of the enzyme diastase, it is completely hydrolysed to give (+)-maltose.
(b) It contains only C_1–C_4 α-linkage.
(c) It contains only C_1–C_6 α-linkage.
(d) It contains both C_1–C_4 and C_1–C_6 α-linkage.

42. Glycogen is

(a) a structural polysaccharide
(b) structurally similar to amylopectin but extensively branched
(c) a polymer of β-D-glucose units
(d) structurally very similar to amylopectin

43. In which of the following aspects does amylopectin differ from glycogen?

(a) amylopectin contains α-D-glucose units while glycogen contains β-D-glucose units
(b) amylopectin contains β-D-glucose units while glycogen contains α-D-glucose units
(c) both glycogen and amylopectin are branched polymers of α-D-glycose units but glycogen is more highly branched than amylopectin
(d) both glycogen and amylopectin are branched chain polymers of α-D-glucose units but amylopectin is more highly branched than glycogen

44. Complete hydrolysis of cellulose gives

(a) L-glucose (b) D-fructose
(c) D-ribose (d) D-glucose

45. Cellulose is a straight chain polysaccharide composed of only

(a) D-glucose units joined by α-glycosidic linkage
(b) D-glucose units joined by β-glycosidic linkage
(c) D-galactose units joined by α-glycosidic linkage
(d) D-galactose units joined by β-glycosidic linkage

46. The rigidity of cellulose is due to the

(a) coiled structure of the glucose polymer
(b) β-(1,4)-glycosidic linkage
(c) hydrogen bonding with an adjacent glucose polymer
(d) cross-linking between glucose and peptides

47. Cellulose is soluble in

(a) ammoniacal cupric hydroxide solution
(b) organic solvents
(c) water
(d) none of these

48. Which substance chars when heated with conc. H_2SO_4?

(a) carbohydrate (b) hydrocarbon
(c) fat (d) protein

49. Which of the following is not true about glucose?

(a) It is an aldohexose.
(b) On heating with HI, it forms *n*-hexane.
(c) It does not give the 2,4-DNP test.
(d) It is present in the furanose form.

50. The aldehyde which is formed during photosynthesis in plants is

(a) methanal (b) acetaldehyde
(c) propanal (d) benzaldehyde

51. Which of the following is not a carbohydrate?

(a) $CH_2OHCHOHCHOHCH_2CHO$
(b) $CH_3CHHCHOHCHOHCHOHCHO$
(c) $HOCH_2$–CO–CH_2–OH
(d) $CH_2OH(CHOH)_3COCH_2OH$

52. Which of the following compounds can be detected by Molisch's test?

(a) sugars (b) amines
(c) primary alcohols (d) nitro compounds

53. Carbohydrates are treated with α-naphthol and conc. H_2SO_4. The colour developed at the junction of the two liquids is

(a) blue (b) violet (c) green (d) red

Proteins

54. The α-amino acid which does not contain the aromatic side chain is

(a) proline (b) tyrosine (c) histidine (d) tryptophan

55. Which amino acid has a phenolic OH group in its backbone?

(a) glycine (b) leucine (c) serine (d) tyrosine

56. Among the α-amino acids, threonine, tyrosine, methionine, arginine and tryptophan, those which contain an aromatic group in their side chain are

(a) threonine and arginine
(b) tyrosine and tryptophan
(c) methionine and tyrosine
(d) arginine and tryptophan

57. Which one of the pairs of amino acids contains two chiral centres?

(a) isoleucine and threonine
(b) leucine and valine
(c) valine and isoleucine
(d) threonine and leucine

58. The imino acid among these compounds is

(a) serine (b) proline
(c) tyrosine (d) lysine

59. The structural feature which distinguishes proline from other naturala-amino acids is,

(a) it is optically inactive
(b) it contains an aromatic group
(c) it is a dicarboxylic acid
(d) it is a secondary amine
(e) It contains two amino groups

60. The one letter code for the amino acid tryptophan is

(a) G (b) V (c) W (d) H (e) A

61. Which of the following is an essential amino acid?

(a) methionine (b) tyrosine (c) proline
(d) glycine (e) alanine

62. Which of the following sets consists only of essential amino acids?

(a) alanine, tyrosine, cysteine
(b) leucine, lysine, tryptophan
(c) alanine, glutamine, lysine
(d) leucine, proline, glycine

63. One of the different amino acids which cannot be synthesised in the body is

(a) lysine (b) histidine (c) valine
(d) alanine (e) phenylalanine

64. The number of amino acids found in proteins that a human body can synthesise is

(a) 20 (b) 10 (c) 5 (d) 14

65. The pH value of the solution in which a particular amino acid does not migrate under the influence of an electric field is called the

(a) eutectic point (b) flash point
(c) neutralisation point (d) isoelectric point

66. Which one of the following statements about amino acids is not true?

(a) They are constituents of all proteins.
(b) They are all high melting solids.
(c) Most naturally occurring amino acids have the D-configuration.
(d) They are characterised by isoelectric points.
(e) Glycine is the only naturally occurring amino acid which is optically inactive.

67. The relationship of isoelectric point for an amino acid to its solubility in water is

(a) the two are not related
(b) an amino acid is least soluble at its isoelectric point
(c) an amino acid has maximum solubility at the isoelectric point
(d) solubilities of some amino acids depend on it

68. Lysine has least solubility in the pH range

(a) 3 to 4 (b) 5 to 6
(c) 6 to 7 (d) 8 to 9

69. Which of the following statements is about glycine is correct?

(a) Basic group is NH_2 and acidic group is COOH.
(b) Basic groups is NH_3^+ and acidic group is COO^-.
(c) Basic group is COO^- and acidic group is NH_3^+.
(d) Basic group is NH_3 and acidic group is COO^-.

70. At the isoelectric point, amino acids are present as

(a) $H_2N-CHR-COOH$ (b) $H_3\overset{+}{N}-CHR-COOH$
(c) $H_2N-CHR-COO^-$ (d) $H_3\overset{+}{N}-CHR-COO^-$

71. At pH 4, glycine exists as

(a) $H_3\overset{+}{N}-CH_2COO^-$ (b) $H_3\overset{+}{N}-CH_2COOH$
(c) H_2NCH_2COOH (d) $H_2NCH_2COO^-$

72. Which of the following does not exist as a zwitter ion?

(a) glycine (b) glutamic acid
(c) sulfanilic acid (d) *p*-aminobenzoic acid

73. Which of the following compounds can form a zwitter ion?

(a) aniline (b) acetanilide
(c) benzoic acid (d) glycine

74. Which of the following will not exist in the zwitterionic form at a pH = 7?

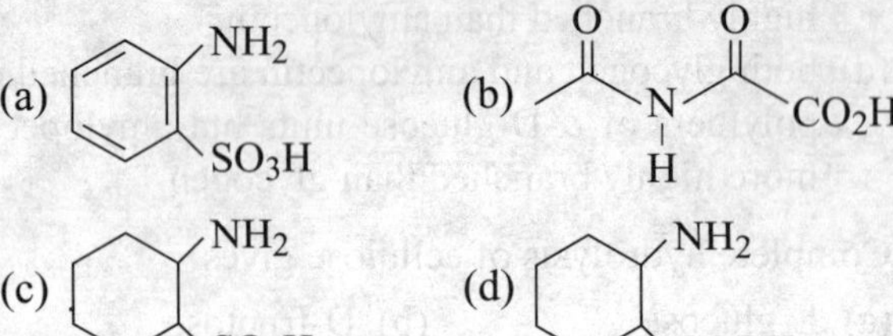

75. Which compound can exist in dipolar (zwitterion) structure?

(a) $C_6H_5-CH_2-\underset{\displaystyle N=CH_2}{\underset{|}{CH}}-COOH$
(b) $(CH_3)_2CH-CH\begin{matrix} NH_2 \\ COOH \end{matrix}$
(c) $C_6H_5CONHCH_2COOH$
(d) $HOOC-CH_2CH_2CO-COOH$

76. Which of the following acids has the highest melting point?

(a) H_2NCH_2COOH (b) $ClCH_2COOH$
(c) $BrCH_2COOH$ (d) ICH_2COOH

77. Which of the following structures represents the peptide chain?

(a)
```
 H          O
 |     |    ||
-N-C-N-C-NH-C-NH-
   || | |
   O  N
```

(b)
```
 H         H   O
 |     | | |  ||
-N-C-C-C-C-N-C-C-
   || | | |  |
   O
```

(c)
```
 H     H   O
 | |   | | ||
-N-C-C-N-C-C-
   | ||  |
     O
```

(d)
```
 H     O       H
 | | | ||  | | |   | |
-N-C-C-C-N-C-C-N-C-C-C-
   | |   | | |   || | |
         H       O
```

78. Which statement is incorrect about the peptide bond?

(a) C–N bond length in proteins is longer than the usual bond length of the C–N bond.

(b) Spectroscopic analysis shows the planar structure of the $-\overset{O}{\overset{\|}{C}}-NH-$ bond.

(c) C–N bond length in proteins is shorter than the usual bond length of the C–N bond.

(d) None of these.

79. How many different dipeptides can be made from glycine and alanine?

(a) 2 (b) 3 (c) 4 (d) 6

80. Number of tripeptides each containing three different amino acids is

(a) three (b) four (c) five (d) six

81. How many tripeptides are possible using alanine, glycine and tyrosine?

(a) 6 (b) 9 (c) 3 (d) 27

82. The number of peptide bonds in the compound,

O CH$_3$ H O
H_3C N N NHNH$_2$ is
H O CH$_3$

(a) 1 (b) 2 (c) 3 (d) 4

83. The correct structure of the dipeptide Gly–Ala is

(a) $H_2N-\overset{CH_3}{\overset{|}{CH}}-\overset{O}{\overset{\|}{C}}-NH-CH_2-COOH$

(b) $H_2N-\overset{CH_2SH}{\overset{|}{CH}}-\underset{O}{\underset{\|}{C}}-NH-CH_2-COOH$

(c) $H_2N-CH_2-\overset{O}{\overset{\|}{C}}-NH-\overset{CH_3}{\overset{|}{CH}}-COOH$

(d) $H_2N-CH_2-\overset{O}{\overset{\|}{C}}-NH-\overset{CH_2SH}{\overset{|}{CH}}-COOH$

84. The tripeptide is written as Glycine–Alanine–Glycine. The correct structure of the tripeptide is

(a) H O CH$_3$
H$_2$N N N COOH
O CH$_3$ H

(b) CH$_3$ H O CH$_3$
H$_2$N N N COOH
O H

(c) H O
H$_2$N N N COOH
O CH$_3$ H

(d) CH$_3$ H O
H$_2$N N N COOH
O CH$_3$ H

85. Which of the following is a conjugated protein?

(a) phosphoprotein (b) glycoprotein
(c) chromoprotein (d) all of these

86. The non-protein portion of a protein is called a/an

(a) functional group (b) characteristic group
(c) prosthetic group (d) enolic group

87. Each polypeptide or a protein has amino acids linked with each other in a specific sequence. This sequence of amino acids is said to be the

(a) primary structure of proteins
(b) secondary structure of proteins
(c) tertiary structure of proteins
(d) quaternary structure of proteins

88. The secondary structure of a protein refers to:

(a) fixed configuration of the polypeptide backbone
(b) α-helical backbone
(c) hydrophobic interactions
(d) sequence of α-amino acids

89. Which functional group participates in disulfide bond formation in proteins?

(a) thioether (b) thiol
(c) thioester (d) thiolactone

90. Secondary structure of proteins refers to

(a) mainly denatured proteins and the structure of the prosthetic group
(b) the three dimensional structure, especially the bonds between the amino acid residues that are distant from each other in the polypeptide chain
(c) the linear sequence of amino acid residues in the polypeptide chain
(d) the regular folding patterns of continuous portions of the polypeptide chain

91. Select the incorrect statement among the following.

(a) Hemoglobin is soluble in water.
(b) α-Keratin is soluble in water.
(c) Cellulose is a polymer of glucose.
(d) Chlorophyll is responsible for the synthesis of carbohydrates in plants.

92. Denaturation of a protein

(a) disrupts the primary or secondary or tertiary structure of the protein
(b) disrupts the secondary and tertiary structures only
(c) disrupts all the primary, secondary and tertiary and even the quaternary structure of the protein
(d) will not affect the original biological activity
(e) is always irreversible

93. Which of the following statements is not correct?

(a) Ovalbumin is a simple food reserve in egg white.
(b) Blood proteins thrombin and fibrinogen are involved in blood clotting.

(c) Denaturation makes the proteins more active.
(d) Insulin maintains sugar level in the blood of a human body.

94. Where does the water present in the egg go after boiling the egg?

(a) water gets converted to steam which escapes into the atmosphere
(b) water brings about hydrolysis of the protein present in the egg to form the constituent α-amino acids
(c) water helps in denaturation of the egg protein
(d) water gets absorbed/adsorbed in the coagulated egg protein through H-bonding

95. Sub units present in hemoglobin are

(a) 2 (b) 3 (c) 4 (d) 5

96. Violet colour is obtained when dilute $CuSO_4$ is added in an alkaline solution of protein. This test is known as

(a) biuret (b) xanthoproteic test
(c) ninhydrin test (d) Millon's test

97. What is biuret?

(a) $CH_3CONH_2CH_3$ (b) $NH_2CONHClNH_2$
(c) NH_2CONH_2 (d) NH_2OH

98. A certain compound gives a positive test with ninhydrin but a negative test with Benedict's solution. The compound is

(a) a protein (b) a monosaccharide
(c) an amino acid (d) both (a) and (c)

99. On heating with conc. HNO_3, proteins give a yellow colour. This is called

(a) biuret test (b) xanthoproteic test
(c) Million's test (d) acid–base test

100. Proteins can be denatured by

(a) carbon dioxide (b) carbon monoxide
(c) heat (d) oxygen

101. Denaturation of proteins leads to loss of its biological activity by

(a) loss of primary structure
(b) loss of primary and secondary structure
(c) loss of secondary and tertiary structure
(d) formation of amino acids

102. In which of the following pairs are both the proteins of the same type—fibrous or globular.

(a) myosin, albumin (b) insulin, collagen
(c) keratin, fibroin (d) albumin, myosin

103. Which of the following statements is correct?

(a) All amino acids are optically active.
(b) All amino acids except glycine are optically active.
(c) All amino acids except glutamic acid are optically active.
(d) All amino acids except lysine are optically active.

104. Except glycine, which is achiral, all amino acids present in proteins

(a) are chiral but racemic
(b) have the L-configuration
(c) have the R-configuration
(d) have the D-configuration

105. Among the following, L-serine is

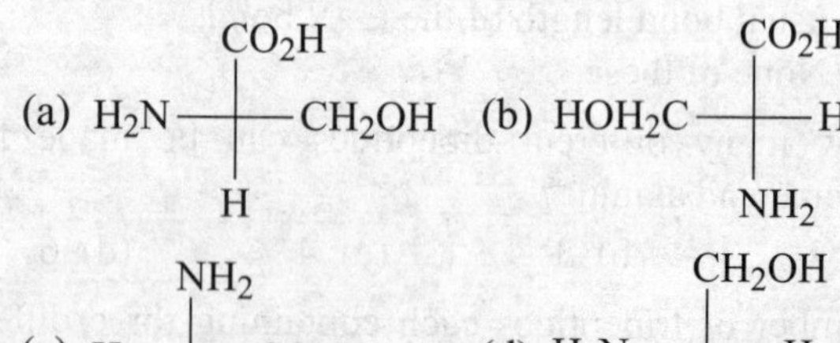

106. Among the following, the achiral amino acid is

(a) ethylalanine (b) methylglycine
(c) 2-hydroxymethylserine (d) tryptophan

107. Thiol group is present in

(a) cytosine (b) cystine
(c) cysteine (d) methionine

Enzymes

108. Mark the wrong statement about enzymes.

(a) Enzymes are biological catalysts.
(b) Each enzyme can catalyse a number of similar reactions.
(c) Enzymes are very efficient catalysts.
(d) Enzymes are needed only in very small amounts for their action.

109. Which one of the following statements is incorrect about enzyme catalysis?

(a) Enzymes are mostly proteinaceous in nature.
(b) Enzyme action is specific.
(c) Enzymes are denaturated by ultraviolet rays and at high temperature.
(d) Enzymes are least reactive at optimum temperature.

110. The efficiency of an enzyme to catalyse a reaction is due to its capacity to

(a) reduce the activation energy of the reaction
(b) form a strong enzyme–substrate complex
(c) decrease the bond energies of all the substrate molecules
(d) increase the free energy of the catalyst substrate reaction
(e) alter the substrate geometry to fit into the shape of the enzyme molecules

111. The enzyme which hydrolyses triglycerides to fatty acids and glycerol is called

(a) maltose (b) lipase (c) zymase (d) pepsin

112. Which one of the following enzymes is present in animals like cows and buffloes, to digest compounds like paper, cloth, and so on?

(a) urease (b) cellulase (c) silicones (d) sucrase

113. The enzyme which hydrolyses cellulose into glucose is

(a) invertase (b) maltase (c) emulsion (d) lactase

114. During the process of digestion, the proteins present in food materials are hydrolysed to amino acids. The two enzymes involved in the process are

$$\text{Proteins} \xrightarrow{\text{enzyme (A)}} \text{polypeptides} \xrightarrow{\text{enzyme (A)}} \text{amino acids}$$

(a) invertase and zymase (b) amylase and maltase
(c) diastase and lipase (d) pepsin and trypsin

115. The disease phenylketonurea is caused by the deficiency of

(a) phenylalanine hydroxylase
(b) vitamin A (c) lysine (d) leucine

116. The disease albinism is caused by the deficiency of

(a) phenylalanine hydroxylase
(b) tyrosinase (c) emulsion (d) lactase

117. Which of the following B-group vitamin can be stored in our body?

(a) vitamin B_1 (b) vitamin B_2
(c) vitamin B_6 (d) vitamin B_{12}

118. Which of the following statements is not correct?

(a) Cytosine and thymine are pyrimidines.
(b) DNA differs from RNA in sugar as well as nitrogenous base.
(c) In RNA, a heterocylic amine base is bonded to C-1 of the sugar and the phosphoric acid is bonded to the C-5′ sugar position.
(d) In the double helix structure of DNA, thymine can bond to cytosine by two hydrogen bonds.

119. Which of the following chemical units is certainly to be found in an enzyme?

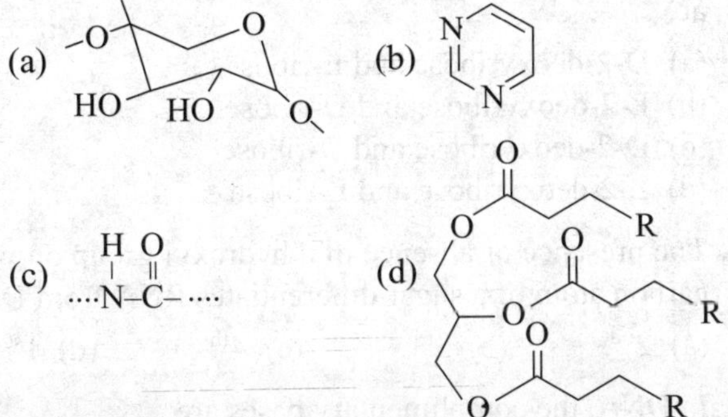

120. The non-protein component in enzymes which is necessary for its biological activity is called a

(a) nucleic acid (b) lipid
(c) phosphoric acid (d) coenzyme

121. The coenzymes are derived from

(a) hormones (b) vitamins
(c) lipids (d) carbohydrate

Vitamins

122. Pernicious anemia is caused by the deficiency of

(a) vitamin B_1 (b) vitamin B_2
(c) vitamin B_6 (d) vitamin B_{12}

123. Which of the following acids is a vitamin?

(a) aspartic adic (b) ascorbic acid
(c) adipic acid (d) saccharic acid

124. Which of the following is a water soluble vitamin?

(a) vitamin A (b) vitamin D
(c) vitamin B_1 (d) vitamin E
(e) vitamin K

125. Which of the following is not a fat soluble vitamin?

(a) vitamin B complex (b) vitamin D
(c) vitamin E (d) vitamin A

126. Biotin is an organic compound present in yeast. Its deficiency in the diet cases dermatitis and paralysis. It is also known as

(a) vitamin H (b) vitamin B_1
(c) vitamin B_{12} (d) vitamin D
(e) vitamin C

127. The vitamin which is neither soluble in water for in fat is

(a) biotin (b) phylloquinone
(c) thiamine (d) ergocalciferol
(e) pyridoxine

128. Which of the following contains cobalt?

(a) vitamin B_{12} (b) vitamin A
(c) vitamin C (d) vitamin K

129. Which of the following B group vitamins can be stored in our body?

(a) vitamin B_1 (b) vitamin B_2
(c) vitamin B_6 (d) vitamin B_{12}

130. The vitamin which is less available to vegetarians is

(a) A (b) B_{12} (c) B_2 (d) C

131. Which of the following statements about vitamin B-12 is incorrect?

(a) It has a cobalt atom.
(b) It also occurs in plants.
(c) It is also present in rain water.
(d) It is needed for the human body in small amounts.

132. Rickets and osteomalacia are due to the deficiency of

(a) vitamin A (b) vitamin D
(c) vitamin E (d) vitamin K

133. The deficiency of vitamin K causes

(a) hemorrhage
(b) lengthening of the time of blood clotting
(c) inflammation of tongue
(d) both (a) and (b)

134. Milk contains vitamins

(a) A, D, E (b) A, B_{12}, D
(c) C, D, K (d) B_1, B_6, D

135. Deficiency of which of the following vitamins causes xerophthalmia and night blindness?

(a) vitamin D (b) vitamin A
(c) vitamin C (d) vitamin B

136. Which of the following is provitamin A?

(a) β-carotene (b) calciferol
(c) chlorophyll (d) ergosterol

137. Cheilosis and digestive disorders are due to the deficiency of

(a) vitamin A (b) thiamine
(c) riboflavin (d) pyridoxine
(e) ascorbic acid

Nucleic Acids

138. Which of the following is the correct structure of adenosine?

(a) NH_2, Ribose (b) NH_2, Ribose
(c) NH_2, Ribose (d) NH_2, Ribose

139. ADP and ATP differ in the number of

(a) phosphate units (d) ribose units
(c) adenine base (d) nitrogen atom

140. Which of the following is not a pyrimidine?

(a) uracil (b) guanine (c) cytosine (d) thymine

141. Which of the following is not a purine?

(a) adenine (b) guanine (c) caffeine (d) cytosine

142. Thymine is

(a) 5-methyluracil (b) 4-methyluracil
(c) 3-methyluracil (d) 1-methyluracil

143. Which base is found only in the nucleotides of RNA?

(a) adenine (b) uracil (c) guanine (d) cytosine

144. Among the following compounds, which one is found in RNA?

(a) NH_2 (b) (c) CH_3 (d)

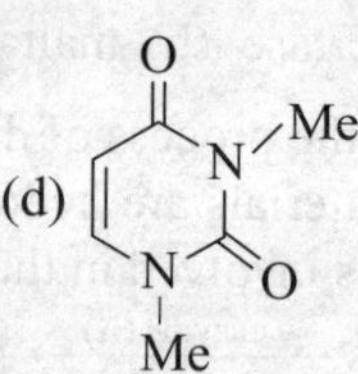

145. Which of the following sets of bases is present both in DNA and RNA?

(a) adenine, uracil, thymine
(b) adenine, guanine, cytosine
(c) adenine, guanine, uracil
(d) adenine, guanine, thymine

146. Which is the correct statement regarding RNA and DNA?

(a) The sugar component in RNA is arabinose and the sugar component in DNA is ribose.
(b) The sugar component in RNA is 2′-deoxyribose and the sugar component in DNA is arabinose.
(c) The sugar component in RNA is arabinose and the sugar component in DNA is 2′-deoxyribose.
(d) The sugar component in RNA is ribose and the sugar component in DNA is 2′-deoxyribose.

147. The sugar present in nucleotide of the DNA molecule is

(a) *β*-2-deoxyribopyranose
(b) *β*-2-deoxyribofuranone
(c) *α*-2-deoxyribofuranose
(d) *α*-2-deoxyribopyranose

148. The sugar moiety in the RNA molecule is

(a) *β*-D-2-deoxyribose (b) *β*-D-galactose
(c) *β*-D-2-fructofuranose (d) *β*-D-ribose

149. The sugar units present in DNA and RNA respectively, are

(a) D-2-deoxyribose and L-ribose
(b) L-2-deoxyribose and D-ribose
(c) D-2-deoxyribose and D-ribose
(d) L-2-deoxyribose and L-ribose

150. The presence or absence of a hydroxyl group on which carbon atom of a sugar differentiates RNA from DNA?

(a) 2nd (b) 3rd (c) 4th (d) 1st

151. In DNA, the complimentary bases are:

(a) adenine and thymine; guanine and uracil
(b) adenine and guanine; thymine and cytosine
(c) uracil and adenine; cytosine and guanine
(d) adenine and thymine; guanine and cytosine

152. Which of the following statements about RNA is not correct?
(a) It has a single strand.
(b) It does not undergo replication.
(c) It does not contain any pyridimine base.
(d) It controls the synthesis of proteins.

153. DNA and RNA are chiral molecules. Their chirality is due to
(a) D-sugar component (b) L-sugar component
(c) chiral bases (d) chiral phosphate ester unit

154. In both DNA and RNA, the heterocyclic base and phosphate ester linkages are at
(a) C_5' and C_2' respectively of the sugar moiety
(b) C_2' and C_5' respectively of the sugar moiety
(c) C_1' and C_5' respectively of the sugar moiety
(d) C_5' and C_1' respectively of the sugar moiety

155. Chargaff's rule states that in an organism, the
(a) amount of adenine (A) is equal to that of thymine (T) and the amount of guanine (G) is equal to that of cytosine (C)
(b) amount of adenine (A) is equal to that of guanine (G) and the amount of thymine (T) is equal to that of cytosine (C)
(c) amount of adenine (A) is equal to that of cytosine (C) and the amount of thymine (T) is equal to that of guanine (G)
(d) amounts of all bases are equal

156. Which of the statements about 'denaturation' (given below) are correct?
(i) Denaturation of proteins causes loss of secondary and tertiary structures of the protein.
(ii) Denaturation leads to the conversion of the double stand of DNA into a single strand.
(iii) Denaturation affects the primary structure which gets distorted.
(a) (i) and (iii) (b) (i) and (iii)
(c) (i) and (ii) (d) (i), (ii) and (iii)

157. The central dogma of molecular genetics states that the genetic information flows from
(a) Amino acid → Proteins → DNA
(b) DNA → Carbohydrates → Proteins
(c) DNA → RNA → Proteins
(d) DNA → RNA → Carbohydrates

158. The segment of DNA which acts as the instruction manual for the synthesis of protein is
(a) ribose (b) gene (c) nucleoside (d) nucleotide

159. Which of the following biomolecules is insoluble in water?
(a) α-keratin (b) hemoglobin
(c) ribonuclease (d) adenine

160. How many amino acids are present in insulin?
(a) 25 (b) 51 (c) 20 (d) 22 (e) 52

161. Which of the following enzymes helps in digestion of proteins?
(a) invertase (b) trypsin
(c) tyrosinase (d) urease

162. Which of the following compounds is responsible for the transmission of heredity characters?
(a) RNA (b) DNA
(c) glucose (d) hemoglobin

163. Which of the following statements is true?
(a) DNA are nucleotides and RNA are nucleosides.
(b) Nucleoside + phosphate ester bond = nucleotide.
(c) Nucleotide + phosphate ester bond = nucleoside.
(d) None of these.

Hormones

164. The hormone which controls the processes of burning of fats, proteins and carbohydrates to liberate energy in the body is
(a) cortisone (b) adrenaline
(c) thyroxine (d) insulin

165. Insulin production and its action in the human body are responsible for the level of diabetes. This compound belongs to which of the following categories?
(a) a coenzyme (b) a hormone
(c) an enzyme (d) an antibiotic

166. The number of disulfide linkage present in insulin are
(a) 4 (b) 3 (c) 2 (d) 1

167. Which of the following is an amine hormone?
(a) oxypurinol (b) insulin
(c) progesterone (d) thyroxine

168. Which of the following hormones contains iodine?
(a) testosterone (b) adrenaline
(c) thyroxine (d) insulin

169. Which of the following hormones is produced under the conditions of stress which stimulate glycogenolysis in the liver of human beings?
(a) thyroxin (b) insulin
(c) adrenaline (d) estradiol

170. The hormone which controls the uterine cycle in women is
(a) estrone (b) androsterone
(c) progesterone (d) testosterone

171. The sex hormone which controls the development and maintenance of pregnancy is
(a) cortisone (b) thyroxine
(c) progesterone (d) estrone

172. The hormone which controls the contraction of uterus after child birth and also causes lactation in the mammary glands is

(a) insulin (b) oxytocin (c) estrone (d) estradiol

173. The hormones used by athletes to increase the mass and strength of muscles is/are

(a) estrogens (b) gestogens
(c) androgens (d) both estrogens and androgens

Final Preparation

174. The reaction of D-glucose with ammoniacal $AgNO_3$ produces

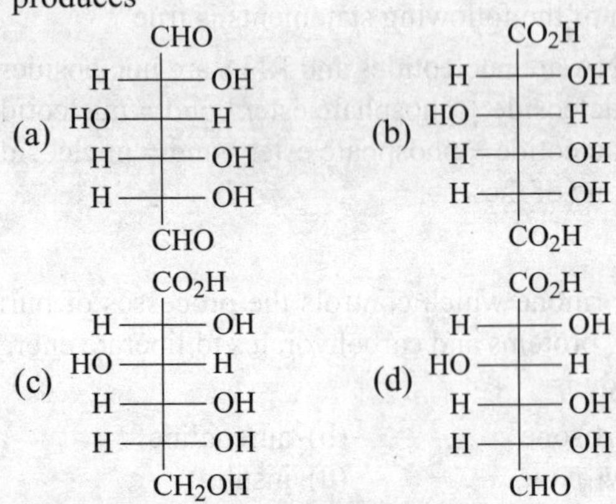

175. The structure of D-(+)-glucose is

CHO
H—OH
HO—H
H—OH
H—OH
CH_2OH

The structure of L-(−)-glucose is

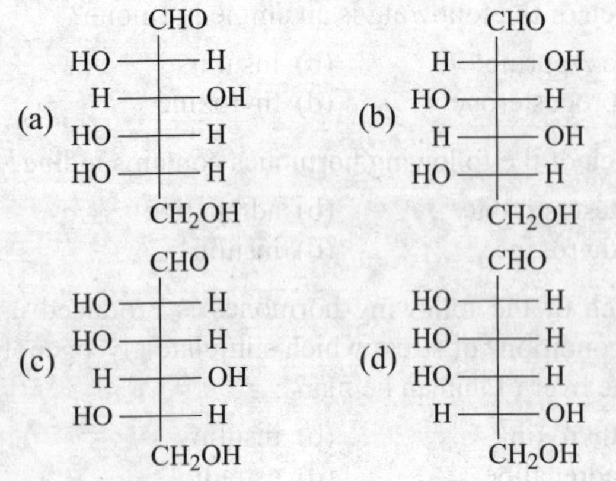

176. The Haworth projection formula of β-D-glucopyranose is

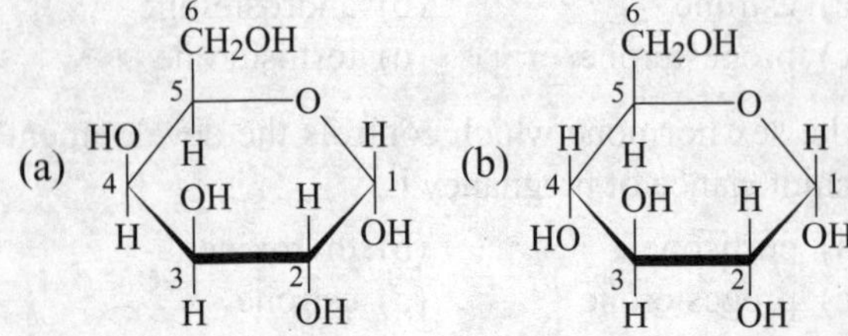

(c)
6 HOH_2C — O — 1 CH_2OH
5 H HO 2
H OH
4 3
OH H

(d)

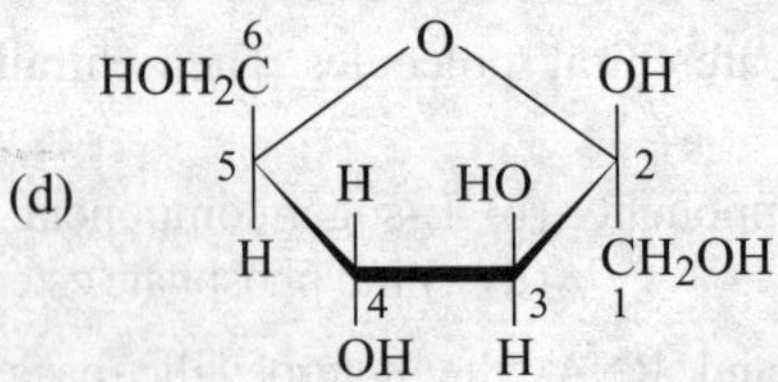

177. The following carbohydrate is

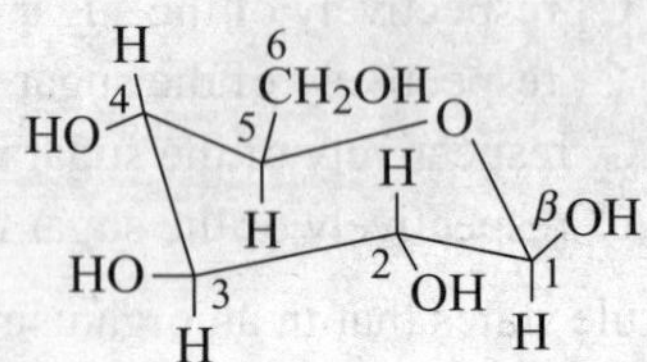

(a) a ketohexose (b) an aldohexose
(c) an α-furanose (d) an α-pyranose

178. The optical rotation of a freshly prepared solution of α-D-glucopyranose is +111° while that of β-D-glucopyranose is +19.2. In solution, an equilibrium mixture of these two anomers shows an optical rotation of 52.5°. The percentage of α-form in the equilibrium mixture is

(a) 36% (b) 64% (c) 52.5% (d) 19.2%

179. The most stable form of glucose is

(a) open chain form (b) α-D-glucose
(c) β-D-glucose
(d) all forms are equally stable

180. D-Glucose $\xrightleftharpoons{OH^-}$ A + B
(A) and (B) respectively are

(a) glucose, galactose (b) glucose, mannose
(c) glucose, fructose (d) mannose, fructose

181. Fructose reduces Tollens' reagent due to

(a) asymmetric carbons
(b) primary alcoholic group
(c) secondary alcoholic group
(d) enolisation of fructose followed by conversion to aldehyde by a base

182. Which of the following on reduction with Na–Hg and water gives a mixture of sorbitol and mannitol?

(a) D-sorbose (b) D-mannitol
(c) D-glucose (d) fructose

183. Which of the following statements is/are correct?

(a) Glucose and fructose are functional isomers.
(b) Mannose is the C_2-epimer of glucose.

(c) Galactose is the C_4-epimer of glucose.
(d) All statements are correct.

184. Starch is a mixture of two components, a water soluble amylase (15%–20%) and a water insoluble component amylopectin (80%–85%). The aqueous solution of amylase gives a blue colour with iodine solution due to the formation of

(a) amylase iodide (b) amylase iodate
(c) inclusion complex
(d) amylase tetraiodide complex

185. Ribose and 2-deoxyribose can be differentiated by

(a) Fehling's solution (b) Tollens' reagent
(c) Barfold's reagent (d) osazone formation

186. $\overset{+}{H_3N}$ (Z) – chain bearing COOH (X) – $\overset{+}{NH_3}$ (Y)

Arrange the following in the increasing order of acid strength.

(a) X > Z > Y (b) Z < X > Y
(c) X > Y > Z (d) Z > X > Y

187. In an amino acid, the carboxyl group ionises at pKa_1 = 2.34 and ammonium ion at a pKa_2 = 9.60. The isoelectric point of the amino acid is at pH

(a) 5.97 (b) 2.34 (c) 9.60 (d) 6.97

188. Find the isoelectric point of the given acid

$$CH_3\text{–}\underset{\underset{+NH_3}{|}}{CH}\text{–}COO^- \quad pK_a = 2.34, \quad pK_a = 4.32$$

(a) 3.3 (b) 6.66 (c) 6.01 (d) 3.67

189. Which of the following amino acids has the lowest isoelectric point?

(a) glycine (b) alanine
(c) aspartic acid (d) lysine

190. Lysine is least soluble in water in the pH range

(a) 3 to 4 (b) 5 to 6 (c) 6 to 7 (d) 8 to 9

191. Which of the following is Sanger's reagent?

(a) 2,4-dinitrofluorobenzene
(b) phenyl isocyanate
(c) 2,4-dinitrochlorobenzene
(d) 2,4-dinitrobromobenzene

192. Sanger's reagent is used for the identification of the

(a) N-terminal amino acid of a peptide chain
(b) C-terminal amino acid of a peptide chain
(c) molecular mass of the peptide chain
(d) number of amino acids in the peptide chain

193. Which of the following reagents is used to determine the C-terminal end of a polypeptide?

(a) hydrazine
(b) 2,4-dinitrofluorobenzene
(c) 2,4-dinitrophenylhydrazine
(d) 3,5-dinitrofluorobenzene

194. The dipeptide glycylalanine contains

(a) glycine as the C-terminal amino acid
(b) glycine as the N-terminal amino acid
(c) alanine as the N-terminal amino acid
(d) either (a) or (b)

195. The following tripeptide

H_2N–CH(CH_2Ph)–C(=O)–NH–CH(CH_3)–C(=O)–NH–CH(CH_2OH)–COOH

can be represented as

(a) Try–Val–Thr (b) Phe–Ala–Ser
(c) Phe–Leu–Cys (d) Lys–Ala–Ser

196. A tetrapeptide is made of naturally occurring alanine, serine, glycine and valine. If the C-terminal amino acid is alanine and the N-terminal amino acid is chiral, the number of possible sequences of the tetrapeptide is

(a) 12 (b) 8 (c) 6 (d) 4

197. Which of the following acids is a vitamin?

(a) aspartic acid (b) ascorbic acid
(c) adipic acid (d) saccharic acid

198. Vitamin C is a/an

(a) lactone (b) amine
(c) amide (d) alcohol

199. Which of the following if taken excessively can accumulate in the body and cause toxicity?

(a) vitamin C (b) vitamin D
(c)vitamin B_2 (b) vitamin B_{12}

200. Two vitamins absorbed from the intestine along with fats are

(a) A, D (b) A, B (c) A, C (d) D, B

201. Which of the following statements about vitamin B_{12} is incorrect?

(a) It has a cobalt atom.
(b) It also occurs in plants.
(c) It is also present in rain water.
(d) It is needed for the human body in very small amounts.

202. Which of the following structures for a nucleotide is not correct?

(a) cytosine–ribose–phosphate
(b) uracil–2-deoxyribose–phosphate
(c) uracil–ribose–phosphate
(d) thymine–2-deoxyribose–phosphate

203. RNA and DNA are chiral molecules; their chirality is due to

(a) D-sugar component (b) L-sugar component
(c) chiral bases (d) chiral phosphate ester unit

204. A dinucleotide is obtained by joining two nucleotides together by a phosphodiester linkage. Between which carbon atoms of pentose sugars of nucleotides are these linkage present?

(a) 5′ and 3′ (b) 1′ and 5′
(c) 5′ and 5′ (d) 3′ and 3′

205. If one strand of DNA has the sequence ATGCTTGA, the sequence in the complimentary strand would be

(a) TCCGAACT (b) TACGTAGT
(c) TACGAACT (d) TAGCTAGT
(e) TACGAATC

206. If the sequence of bases in DNA is TGAACCCTT then the sequence of bases in the *m*-RNA is

(a) ACUUGAA (b) TCUUGGGTT
(c) ACUUCCCAA (d) none of the above

207. The RNA(s) which take part in the synthesis of proteins is(are)

(a) *m*-RNA (b) *r*-RNA
(c) *t*-RNA (d) all the three above

208. A codon has a sequence A and specifies a particular B that is to be incorporated into C. What are A, B and C?

	A	B	C
(a)	3 bases	amino acid	carbohydrate
(b)	3 acids	carbohydrate	protein
(c)	3 bases	protein	amino acid
(d)	3 bases	amino acid	protein

209. Which of the following statements is true for protein synthesis (translation)?

(a) Amino acids are directly recognised by m-RNA.
(b) The third base of the codon is less specific.
(c) Only one codon codes for an amino acid.
(d) Every *t*-RNA has more than one amino acid attachment.

210. Which one of the following statements is correct?

(a) All amino acids are optically active.
(b) All amino acids except glycine are optically active.
(c) All amino acids except glutamic acid are optically active.
(d) All amino acids except lysine are optically active.

211. Which one of the following statements is not true regarding (+)-lactose?

(a) On hydrolysis, (+)-lactose gives an equal amount of D-(+)-glucose and D-(+)-galactose.
(b) (+)-Lactose is a β-glucoside formed by the union of a molecule of D-(+)-glucose and a molecule of D-(+)-galactose.
(c) (+)-Lactose is a reducing sugar and does not exhibit mutarotation.
(d) (+)-Lactose, $C_{12}H_{22}O_{11}$ contains 8-OH–groups.

212. Which of the following statements is not correct?

(a) Ovalbumin is a simple food reserve in egg white.
(b) The blood proteins, thrombin and fibrinogen, are involved in blood clotting.
(c) Denaturation makes the proteins more active.
(d) Insulin maintains the sugar levels in the blood of a human body.

213. The correct corresponding order of names of four aldoses with configuration given below:

CHO	CHO	CHO	CHO
H—|—OH	HO—|—H	HO—|—H	H—|—OH
H—|—OH	H—|—OH	HO—|—H	HO—|—H
CH_2OH	CH_2OH	CH_2OH	CH_2OH

respectively, is

(a) L-erythrose, L-threose, L-erythrose, D-threose
(b) D-threose, D-erythrose, L-threose, L-erythrose
(c) L-erythrose, L-threose, D-erythrose, D-threose
(d) D-erythrose, D-threose, L-erthrose, L-threose

214. Which of the following pairs represents anomers?

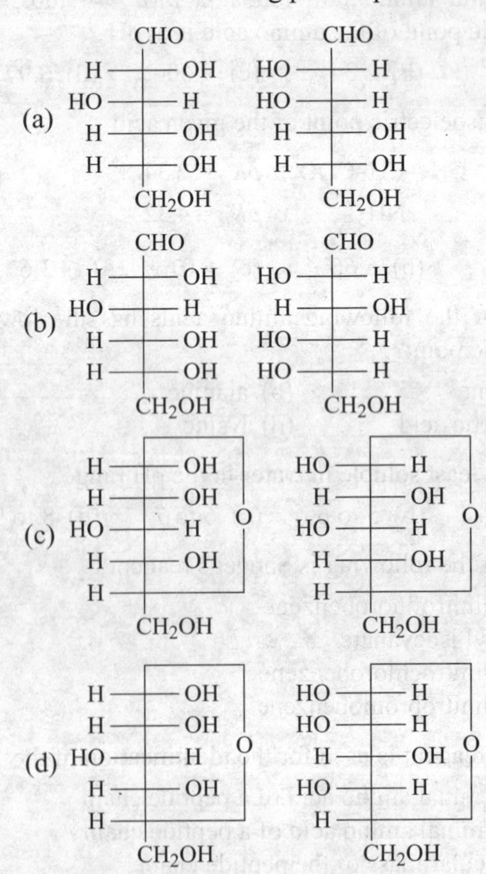

215. The cyclic structures of monosaccharides are given below. Which of these are anomers?

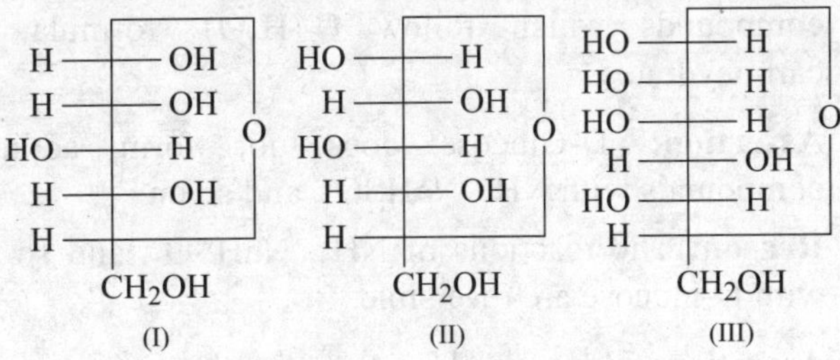

(a) I and II (b) II and III (c) I and III
(d) III is the anomer of I and II

216. D-(+)-Glucose reacts with hydroxylamine and yields an oxime. The structure of the oxime would be

(a)
CH=NOH
H–C–OH
HO–C–OH
HO–C–OH
H–C–OH
CH_2OH

(b)
CH=NOH
HO–C–H
HO–C–H
H–C–OH
H–C–OH
CH_2OH

(c)
CH=NOH
HO–C–OH
H–C–OH
HO–C–OH
H–C–OH
CH_2OH

(d)
CH=NOH
H–C–OH
HO–C–H
H–C–OH
H–C–OH
CH_2OH

217. D-Glucose upon treatment with bromine water gives

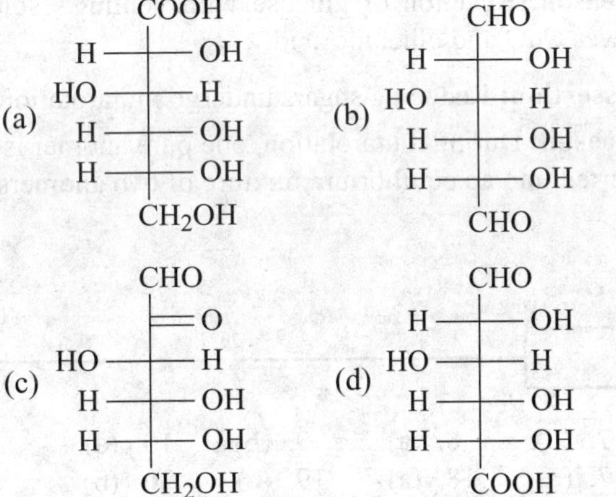

MATCH THE FOLLOWING

218.

Column I	Column II
(A) Pepsin	(p) Vitamin
(B) Nucleic acid	(q) Male sex hormone
(C) Ascorbic acid	(r) Digestive enzyme
(D) Testosterone	(s) Genetic material

(a) (A)—(p); (B)—(s); (C)—(r); (D)—(q)
(b) (A)—(q); (B)—(r); (C)—(s); (D)—(p)
(c) (A)—(s); (B)—(q); (C)—(p); (D)—(r)
(d) (A)—(r); (B)—(s); (C)—(p); (D)—(q)

219.

Column I	Column II
(A) Glycosidic linkage	(p) Globular protein
(B) Maltase	(q) Connects two monosaccharide units
(C) Peptide bond	(r) Monomeric unit of nucleic acids
(D) Nucleotide	(s) Connects two amino acid units

(a) (A)—(s); (B)—(r); (C)—(q); (D)—(p)
(b) (A)—(r); (B)—(s); (C)—(p); (D)—(q)
(c)(A)—(q); (B)—(p); (C)—(s); (D)—(r)
(d) (A)—(p); (B)—(q); (C)—(r); (D)—(s)

220.

Column I	Column II
(A) Lysine	(p) Neutral optically active amino acid
(B) Aspartic acid	(q) Basic amino acid
(C) Valine	(r) Neutral optically inactive amino acid
(D) Glycine	(s) Acidic amino acid

(a) (A)—(s); (B)—(r); (C)—(q); (D)—(p)
(b) (A)—(r); (B)—(q); (C)—(r); (D)—(p)
(c) (A)—(p); (B)—(q); (C)—(r); (D)—(s)
(d) (A)—(q); (B)—(s); (C)—(p); (D)—(r)

ASSERTION REASON

Directions In each of the following questions, a statement of Assertion (A) is given followed by a corresponding statement of Reason (R) just below it. Of the statements, mark the correct answer as

(a) if both the assertion and reason are true and the reason is the correct explanation of the assertion.
(b) if both assertion and reason are true but reason is not the correct explanation of assertion
(c) If assertion is true but reason is false
(d) If both assertion and reason are false

221. Assertion: Glycosides are hydrolysed in acidic conditions.

Reason: Glycosides are acetals.

222. Assertion: Sucrose is a non-reducing sugar.

Reason: It has a glycosidic linkage.

223. Assertion: A solution of sucrose in water is dextrorotatory but on hydrolysis in the presence of a little hydrochloric acid, it becomes levorotatory.

Reason: Sucrose on hydrolysis gives unequal amounts of glucose and fructose as a result of which a change in the sign of rotation is observed.

224. Assertion: Maltose is a reducing sugar which gives two moles of D-glucose on hydrolysis.

Reason: Maltose has a 1,4-β-glycosidic linkage.

225. Assertion: Cellulose is not digested by human beings.

Reason: Cellulose is a polymer of β-D-glucose.

226. Assertion: Alpha (a) amino acids exist as internal salts in solution as they have amino and carboxylic acid groups in close proximity.

Reason: H^+ ion given by the carboxyl group (–COOH) is captured by the amino group ($-NH_2$) having a lone pair of electrons.

227. Assertion: Insulin is a globular protein.

Reason: It transports oxygen in the blood.

228. Assertion: Carboxypeptidase is an exopeptidase.

Reason: It cleaves the N-terminal bond.

229. Assertion: Disruption of the natural structure of a protein is called denaturation.

Reason: The change in the colour and appearance of egg during cooking is due to denaturation.

230. Assertion: Activity of an enzyme is pH dependent.

Reason: Change in pH affects the solubility of an enzyme in water.

231. Assertion: Uracil occurs in DNA.

Reason: RNA undergoes replication.

232. Assertion: Deoxyribose, $C_5H_{10}O_4$, is not a carbohydrate.

Reason: Carbohydrates are hydrates of carbon so compounds which follow $C_x(H_2O)_y$ formula are carbohydrates.

233. Assertion: D-Glucose does not form addition compounds with NH_3, $NaHSO_3$, and so on.

Reason: The reactions of NH_3, $NaHSO_3$, and so on, with D-glucose are reversible.

234. Assertion: Glucose and fructose give the same osazone.

Reason: During osazone formation, the stereochemistry at C_1 and C_2 is destroyed.

235. Assertion: Fructose does not contain an aldehyde group but still reduces Tollens' reagent.

Reason: In the presence of a base, fructose undergoes a rearrangement to form glucose and mannose.

236. Assertion: The term 'anomers of glucose' refers to the isomers of glucose that differ in configuration at carbon one (C-1).

Reason: Anomers of glucose are cyclic diastereomers which differ in configuration at the C-1 existing in two forms α- and β-respectively.

237. Assertion: Galactose is the C_4-epimer of glucose.

Reason: Glucose and galactose differ in configuration at C_4.

238. Assertion: Glucose gives a reddish-brown precipitate with Fehling's solution.

Reason: Reaction of glucose with Fehling's solution gives CuO and gluconic acid.

239. Assertion: Reducing sugars undergo mutarotation.

Reason: During mutarotation, one pure anomer is converted into an equilibrium mixture of two anomers.

Answer Key

1. (d)	2. (c)	3. (c)	4. (a)	5. (b)	6. (b)	7. (d)	8. (a)	9. (b)	10. (a)
11. (c)	12. (a)	13. (c)	14. (d)	15. (b)	16. (b)	17. (a)	18. (a)	19. (c)	20. (b)
21. (d)	22. (a)	23. (a)	24. (b)	25. (b)	26. (d)	27. (d)	28. (b)	29. (d)	30. (d)
31. (a)	32. (d)	33. (b)	34. (b)	35. (d)	36. (d)	37. (b)	38. (b)	39. (d)	40. (d)
41. (d)	42. (b)	43. (c)	44. (d)	45. (b)	46. (c)	47. (a)	48. (a)	49. (d)	50. (a)
51. (c)	52. (a)	53. (b)	54. (a)	55. (d)	56. (b)	57. (b)	58. (b)	59. (d)	60. (c)
61. (a)	62. (b)	63. (d)	64. (b)	65. (d)	66. (c)	67. (b)	68. (d)	69. (c)	70. (d)
71. (b)	72. (d)	73. (d)	74. (b)	75. (b)	76. (a)	77. (c)	78. (c)	79. (c)	80. (d)
81. (d)	82. (a)	83. (c)	84. (c)	85. (d)	86. (c)	87. (a)	88. (a)	89. (b)	90. (d)
91. (b)	92. (b)	93. (c)	94. (d)	95. (c)	96. (a)	97. (b)	98. (d)	99. (d)	100. (c)
101. (c)	102. (c)	103. (b)	104. (b)	105. (c)	106. (c)	107. (c)	108. (b)	109. (d)	110. (a)
111. (b)	112. (b)	113. (c)	114. (d)	115. (a)	116. (c)	117. (d)	118. (d)	119. (c)	120. (d)
121. (b)	122. (d)	123. (b)	124. (c)	125. (a)	126. (a)	127. (a)	128. (a)	129. (d)	130. (b)
131. (b)	132. (b)	133. (d)	134. (a)	135. (b)	136. (a)	137. (c)	138. (a)	139. (a)	140. (b)

141. (d)	142. (a)	143. (b)	144. (b)	145. (b)	146. (d)	147. (b)	148. (d)	149. (c)	150. (a)
151. (d)	152. (c)	153. (a)	154. (c)	155. (a)	156. (c)	157. (c)	158. (b)	159. (a)	160. (b)
161. (b)	162. (b)	163. (b)	164. (d)	165. (b)	166. (b)	167. (d)	168. (c)	169. (c)	170. (a)
171. (c)	172. (b)	173. (d)	174. (c)	175. (a)	176. (c)	177. (b)	178. (a)	179. (c)	180. (d)
181. (d)	182. (d)	183. (d)	184. (c)	185. (d)	186. (a)	187. (a)	188. (c)	189. (c)	190. (d)
191. (a)	192. (a)	193. (a)	194. (b)	195. (b)	196. (d)	197. (b)	198. (a)	199. (b)	200. (a)
201. (b)	202. (b)	203. (a)	204. (a)	205. (c)	206. (b)	207. (d)	208. (d)	209. (b)	210. (b)
211. (c)	212. (c)	213. (d)	214. (c)	215. (a)	216. (d)	217. (a)	218. (d)	219. (c)	220. (d)
221. (a)	222. (b)	223. (c)	224. (c)	225. (b)	226. (a)	227. (c)	228. (c)	229. (b)	230. (a)
231. (d)	232. (d)	233. (a)	234. (b)	235. (a)	236. (a)	237. (a)	238. (c)	239. (a)	

Hints and Solutions

OBJECTIVE QUESTIONS

Carbohydrates

1. **(d):** Fructose is a ketohexose.

2. **(c):** Arabinose is a pentose.

3. **(c):** Ribose, deoxyribose, galactose and fructose are monosaccharides.

4. **(a):** Glucose contains six carbon atoms arranged in a straight line and hence on complete reduction with HI/red P gives *n*-hexane.

$$\underset{\text{Glucose}}{CH_2OH–(CHOH)_4–CHO} \xrightarrow{\text{HI/red P}} \underset{\text{n-Hexane}}{CH_3–(CH_2)_4–CH_3}$$

5. **(b):** The reactions of glucose with $NaHSO_3$, 2,4-DNP and NH_3 are reversible and hence no significant product is obtained. However, the reaction with NH_2OH is irreversible and it hence reacts to produce the corresponding oxime.

6. **(b):** Glucose does not react with NH_3 solution.

7. **(d):** Glucose does not react with $NaHSO_3$ solution.

8. **(a):** D-Glucose on oxidation with $Br_2–H_2O$ or Ag_2O gives D-glucaric acid in which oxidation of only the –CHO group occurs.

9. **(b):** D-Glucose on oxidation with conc. HNO_3 gives D-saccharic acid in which both the –CHO and $–CH_2OH$ groups are oxidised to –COOH groups. Note that saccharic acid is also called glycaric acid.

10. **(a):** In all the three structures (I, II and III), the configuration of OH at C_1 is towards the right and hence all have D-configuration.

11. **(c):** Glucose is never present in the furanose form.

12. **(a):** The given carbohydrate is a pentose aldose which exists in the furanose form.

13. **(c):** Due to the absence of the free OH group at C_1, the cyclic structure of glucose pentaacetate cannot revert to the open chain aldehydic form and hence cannot form an oxime.

14. **(d):** α-D-(+)-glucose and β-D-(+)-glucose differ in configuration at C_1 (that is, at the anomeric or glycosidic carbon) and hence they are called anomers.

15. **(b):** Methyl α-D-glucoside and methyl β-D-glucoside differ in configuration at C-1 and hence are anomers.

16. **(b):** Anomers.

17. **(a):** C_1 is the anomeric carbon.

18. **(a):** $HOCH_2–\overset{*}{C}H–\overset{*}{C}HOH\overset{*}{C}HOH\overset{*}{C}HOH\overset{*}{C}HOH$ (ring –O– from C-5 to C-1; carbons numbered 5, 4, 3, 2, 1)

19. **(c):** The configuration of α-D-glucopyranose is given below:

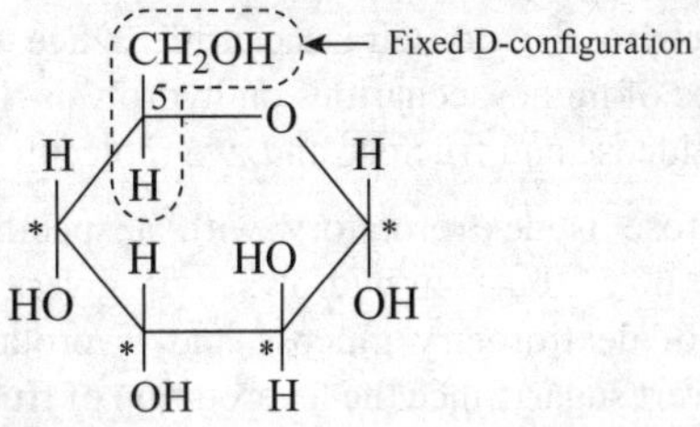

CH_2OH ← Fixed D-configuration (at C-5); ring with O; H, H, H, HO, H, HO, OH, OH, H (chiral centres marked *)

Besides the fixed D-configuration at C_5, it has four other chiral centres at C_1, C_2, C_3 and C_4 (marked by asterisks) and hence has a total of 16 stereoisomers. Out of these, one is α-D-glucose, therefore, the remaining 16 – 1 = 15 are its other stereoisomers.

20. **(b):** Fructose has three dissimilar chiral carbon atoms and hence $2^3 = 8$ optical isomers are possible.

21. **(d):** All are reducing sugars, that is, glucose, fructose and maltose, form osazones.

22. **(a):** Glucose reacts with three molecules of phenylhydrazine to form an osazone.

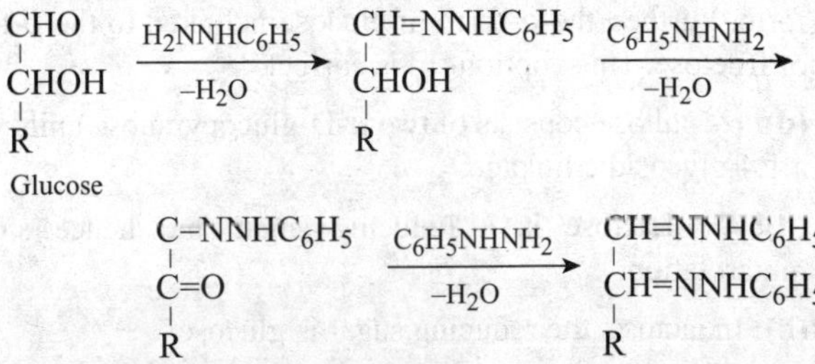

$$\underset{\text{Glucose}}{\begin{matrix}CHO\\ |\\ CHOH\\ |\\ R\end{matrix}} \xrightarrow[-H_2O]{H_2NNHC_6H_5} \begin{matrix}CH{=}NNHC_6H_5\\ |\\ CHOH\\ |\\ R\end{matrix} \xrightarrow[-H_2O]{C_6H_5NHNH_2}$$

$$\begin{matrix}C–NNHC_6H_5\\ |\\ C{=}O\\ |\\ R\end{matrix} \xrightarrow[-H_2O]{C_6H_5NHNH_2} \begin{matrix}CH{=}NNHC_6H_5\\ |\\ CH{=}NNHC_6H_5\\ |\\ R\end{matrix}$$

$R{=}HOCH_2(CHOH)_3^-$

23. **(a):** During osazone formation, the reaction occurs at C_1 and C_2 while rest of the molecule remains intact. Glucose and

fructose differ from each other only in the arrangement of atoms at C_1 and C_2, therefore, they give the same osazone.

24. (b): During osazone formation, the reaction occurs only at C_1 and C_2 while rest of the molecule remains intact, therefore, at C_1, there should be either an aldehyde or an easily oxidisable CH_2OH group and at C_2 there should be either a C=O group or an easily oxidisable CHOH group. Thus, option (b) is correct.

25. (b): Glucose, fructose and mannose differ only in the configuration at C_1 and C_2 while rest of the molecule have the same stereochemistry and hence gave the same osazone.

26. (d): The change in specific rotation of α- or β-glucose with time to a fixed value is called mutarotation.

27. (d): During mutarotation, some of the α-glucose gets converted into the more stable β-form till an equilibrium is reached. At equilibrium, the solution contains 36% of α-glucose and 64% of β-glucose.

28. (b): Only monosaccharides, that is, (–) fructose and reducing disaccharides, that is, (+)lactose and (+)maltose, show mutarotation. Since (+)sucrose is a non-reducing sugar, it does not show mutarotation. Thus, option (b) is correct.

29. (d): All the three (glucose, fructose and galactose).

30. (d): Stachyrose is a tetrasaccharide since it gives four molecules of monosaccharides on hydrolysis—one molecule each of glucose and fructose and two molecules of galactose.

31. (a): Sucrose is dextrorotatory with a specific rotation of $[\alpha]_D$ = +66.5° but on hydrolysis, it gives an equimolar mixture of dextrorotary glucose and levorotatory fructose, called invert sugar. Since the levorotation of fructose (–92.4°) is much more than the dextrorotation of glucose (+52.5°), the resulting solution of invert sugar becomes levorotatory with a specific rotation of $[\alpha]_D = -92.4 + 52.5 = -39.9°$. Since the hydrolysis of sucrose is accompanied by a change in sign of optical rotation from dextrorotation to levorotation, the overall process is called inversion of sugar.

32. (d): Invert sugar contains 50% D-glucose and 50% of D-fructose.

33. (b): Fructose (–92.4°) has maximum levorotation since invert sugar (–39.9°) has a lower levorotation.

34. (b): In sucrose, glucose exists in the pyranose (six-membered ring) form and fructose in the furanose (five-membered ring) form. Further, the α-form of glucose is linked to the β-form of fructose. Thus, option (b) is correct.

35. (d): α-Maltose consists of two α-D-glucopyranose units with a 1,4-glycosidic linkage.

36. (d): (+)-Lactose is a reducing sugar and hence shows mutarotation.

37. (b): In lactose, the reducing sugar is glucose.

38. (b): In lactose, the C_1-β of galactose is connected to the C_4-β of glucose.

39. (d): Amylose is a linear polymer of α-D-glucose units having a helical structure while amylopectin is a branched chain polymer.

40. (d): In amylase, the different glucose units are linked through the C_1 of one unit to C_4 of the other by an α-linkage.

41. (d): It is a branched polymer of α-D-glucose units in which the chains involve C_1–C_4 α-linkages while branching involves C_1–C_6 α-linkages.

42. (b): Structurally similar to amylopectin but extensively branched.

43. (c): Glycogen chains are more highly branched than amylopectin chains.

44. (d): D-glucose.

45. (b): D-glucose units joined by β-glycosidic linkages.

46. (c): Hydrogen bonding with adjacent glucose polymer.

47. (a): Cellulose is soluble in ammoniacal cupric hydroxide solution (Schweitzer's reagent).

48. (a): Carbohydrates char on heating due to dehydration and partial oxidation of carbon.

$$\underset{\text{Sugar}}{C_{12}H_{22}O_{11}} \xrightarrow[\text{Dehydration}]{H_2SO_4} \underset{\text{Sugar charcoal}}{12C} + 11\,H_2O$$

49. (d): Glucose is present in the pyranose from and it is never present in the furanose form.

50. (a): Methanal (formaldehyde).

51. (c): $HOCH_2$–CO–CH_2OH is not optically active and hence is not a carbohydrate.

52. (a): All carbohydrates give Molisch's test, that is, produce a violet colouration with an alcoholic solution of α-naphthol and conc. H_2SO_4.

53. (b): Violet.

Proteins

54. (a): Only proline does not contain an aromatic side chain.

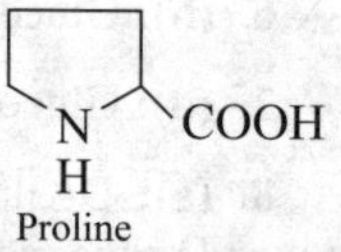

(Structure: pyrrolidine ring, N–H, with COOH) Proline

55. (d): Tyrosine has phenolic OH group.

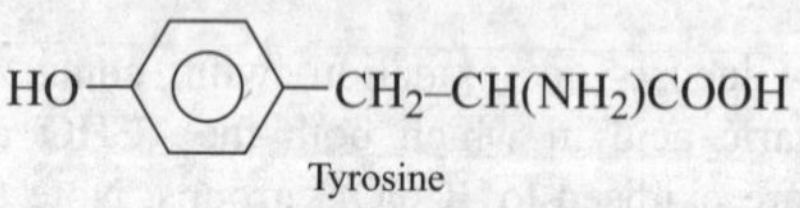

$$HO-C_6H_4-CH_2-CH(NH_2)COOH$$

Tyrosine

56. (b): Tyrosine and trypophan contain an aromatic side chain.

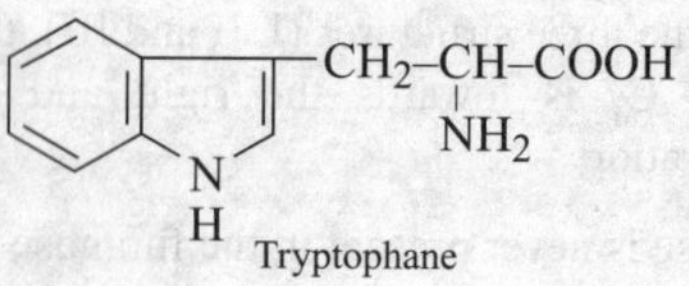

(Indole ring, N–H)–CH_2–CH(NH$_2$)–COOH

Tryptophane

57. (b): $CH_3-\overset{*}{C}H(CH_2CH_3)-\overset{*}{C}H(NH_2)-COOH$ (Isoleucine) $CH_3-\overset{*}{C}H(OH)-\overset{*}{C}H(NH_2)-COOH$ (Threonine)

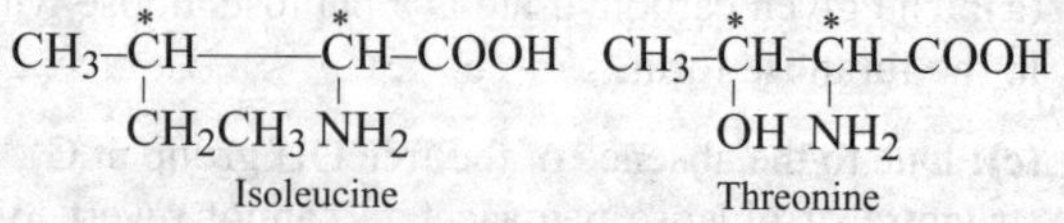

58. (b): Proline contains an imino (NH) group.

59. (d): It is a secondary amine.

60. (c): One letter code for tryptophan is 'W'.

61. (a): Methionine is an essential amino acid.

62. (b): Leucine, lysine and tryptophan are essential amino acids.

63. (d): Essential amino acids (lysine, histidine and valine) cannot be synthesised in the human body. Therefore, option (d), alanine, is correct.

64. (b): The human body can synthesise 10 out of the 20 amino acids obtained by hydrolysis of various proteins.

65. (d): Isoelectric point.

66. (c): The statement (c) is not true. The correct statement is, most naturally occurring amino acids have the L-configuration.

67. (b): Because of complete occurrence of zwitterionic structures at the isoelectric point, an amino acid has minimum solubility at the isoelectric point.

68. (d): Lysine is a basic amino acid, therefore, its isoelectric point lies in the range 8–9. At the isoelectric point, an amino acid has the lowest solubility.

69. (c): Glycine occurs as a zwitter ion. Therefore, when an acid is added, the COO^- group accepts a proton and hence acts as a base.

$$H_3\overset{+}{N}{-}CH_2{-}COO^- + H^+ \rightarrow H_3\overset{+}{N}{-}CH_2{-}COOH$$

In contrast, when a base is added, $\overset{+}{N}H_3$ donates a proton and hence acts as an acid.

$$\overset{+}{N}H_3{-}CH_2{-}COO^- + OH^+ \rightarrow H_2N{-}CH_2{-}COO^- + H_2O$$

70. (d): At the isoelectric point, there is net migration of the amino acid towards either electrode, therefore, it exists as a zwitterion.

$$\overset{a+}{H_3N}{-}CHR{-}COO^-$$

71. (b): In the acidic medium (pH = 4), the COO^- group gets protonated.

$$H_3\overset{+}{N}{-}CH_2{-}COO^- \underset{}{\overset{H^+}{\rightleftharpoons}} H_3\overset{+}{N}{-}CH_2COOH$$

72. (d): In *p*-aminobenzoic acid (PABA), the lone pair of electrons on the NH_2 group is donated towards the benzene ring. As a result, the acidic character of the COOH group and basic character of the NH_2 group decreases. Therefore, the weakly acidic COOH group cannot transfer a H^+ ion to the weakly basic NH_2 group. As a result, PABA does not exist as a zwitter ions.

$$H_2N{-}C_6H_4{-}COOH \not\rightarrow H_3\overset{+}{N}{-}C_6H_4{-}COO^-$$

73. (d): Only amino acids which contain a strong $-NH_2$ group and a strong $-COOH$ group exist in the zwitterionic form.

$$NH_2{-}CH_2{-}COOH \rightleftharpoons \overset{+}{N}H_3{-}CH_2{-}COO^-$$

74. (b): Compounds under options (a,c and d) contain both strong $-NH_2$ and $-COOH$ groups and hence form zwitterions as shown below.

(a) $C_6H_4(NH_2)(SO_3H) \rightleftharpoons C_6H_4(\overset{+}{N}H_3)(SO_3H)$

(c) $C_6H_{10}(NH_2)(SO_3H) \rightleftharpoons C_6H_4(\overset{+}{N}H_3)(SO_3^-)$

(d) $C_6H_{10}(NH_2)(COOH) \rightleftharpoons C_6H_4(\overset{+}{N}H_3)(COO^-)$

In structure (b), N atom is not basic because it is an amide nitrogen and hence does not form a zwitterion.

$$CH_3CO{-}\underset{\underset{H}{|}}{N}{-}CH(CH_3){-}CO_2H \not\leftrightarrow CH_3CO{-}\underset{H_2}{\overset{+}{N}}{-}CH(CH_3){-}COO^-$$

→ H
Weak acid

75. (b): Only α-amino acids show zwitterionic structures. Thus, option (b) is correct. In options (a) and (c), N is not basic while in option (d), there is no basic amino group at all.

76. (a): Due to salt-like (zwitterionic character, $H_3\overset{+}{N}CH_2COO^-$, H_2NCH_2COOH has strong dipole–dipole interactions and hence it has a much higher MP than the haloacids (b,c and d).

77. (c):

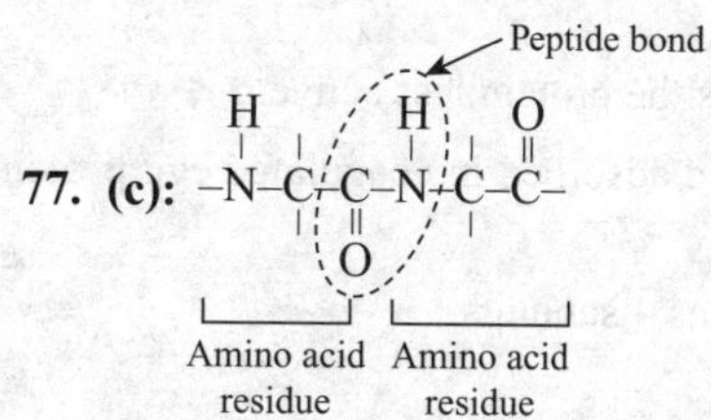

78. (c): Due to resonance, the C–N bond acquires some double bond character.

$$-\overset{:\ddot{O}:}{\overset{|}{C}}{-}\ddot{N}H \longleftrightarrow -\overset{:\ddot{O}:^-}{\overset{|}{C}}{=}\overset{+}{N}H-$$

As a result, the C–N bond in proteins is shorter than the usual bond length of the C–N bond. Thus, option (a) is incorrect.

79. (c): Four different peptides are possible. These are, Gly–Gly, Gly–Ala, Ala–Gly and Ala–Ala.

80. (d): The number of tripeptides containing each amino acid once $= 31 = 3 \times 2 \times 1 = 6$.

81. (d): Total number of possible tripeptides $= 3^3 = 3 \times 3 \times 3 = 27$.

82. (a): The given compound contains one peptide bond as shown below.

$$H_3C{-}CO{-}NH{-}CH(CH_3){-}CO{-}NH{-}CH(CH(CH_3)_2){-}CO{-}NHNH_2$$

Peptide bond

83. (c): $H_2N{-}CH_2{-}\overset{O}{\overset{||}{C}}{-}OH + H{-}NH{-}\overset{CH_3}{\overset{|}{CH}}{-}COOH$
Glycine Alanine

$$\xrightarrow[-H_2O]{} H_2N{-}CH_2{-}\overset{O}{\overset{||}{C}}{-}NH{-}\overset{CH_3}{\overset{|}{CH}}{-}COOH$$

84. (c): $H_2N-CH_2-CO-[OH + H]-NH-CH(CH_3)-CO-[OH + H]-NH-CH_2-COOH$

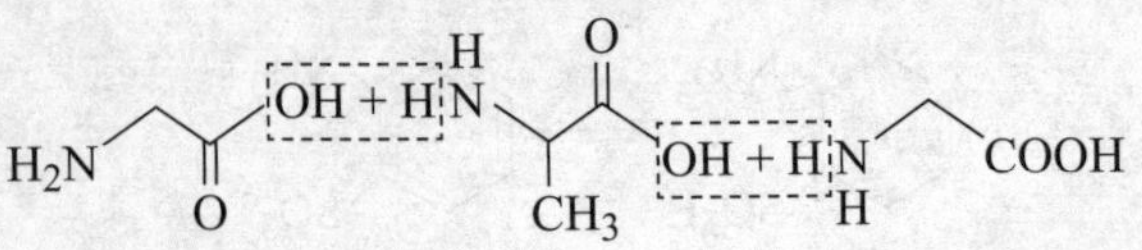

Thus, option (c) is correct.

85. (d): All are conjugated proteins.

86. (c): The non-protein portion of proteins is called a prosthetic group.

87. (a): The sequence in which various amino acids are linked in a polypeptide chain is called the primary structure of proteins.

88. (a): α-Helix and β-pleated structure have fixed configuration of the polypeptide chain.

89. (b): The thiol (SH) group gets easily oxidised to form disulfide linkages.

$$\underset{\text{Thiol}}{2-SH} \xrightarrow{[O]} \underset{\text{Disulphide}}{-S-S-} + H_2O$$

90. (d): Secondary structure refers to regular folding patterns of the continuous portion of the polypeptide chain as a result of hydrogen bonding between the >C=O and the N–H groups.

91. (b): α-Keratin, the protein of the hair, is insoluble in water.

92. (b): Denaturation disrupts the secondary and tertiary structure of proteins.

93. (c): Denaturation makes the protein less active.

94. (d): Water gets absorbed/adsorbed in coagulated egg protein through H-bonding.

95. (c): Hemoglobin contains 4 subunits.

96. (a): Biuret.

97. (b): When urea is heated, loss of one molecule of NH_3 from two molecules of urea gives biuret.

$$\underset{\text{Urea (two molecules)}}{NH_2CO[NH_2 + H]NHCONH_2} \xrightarrow[-NH_3]{\Delta} \underset{\text{Biuret}}{NH_2CONHCONH_2}$$

98. (d): Since it gives a negative test with Benedict's solution, it cannot be a monosaccharide. Since it gives a positive test with ninhydrin, it must be either an amino acid or a protein. Thus, option (d) is correct.

99. (d): Xanthoproteic test involves heating of a protein with conc. HNO_3 when yellow colour is obtained.

100. (c): Heat denatures proteins.

101. (c): During denaturation of proteins, the secondary and tertiary structures get destroyed but the primary structure remains as such.

102. (c): Keratin and fibroin are fibrous proteins.

103. (b): All amino acids except glycine are optically active.

104. (b): All amino acids have the L-configuration.

105. (c):

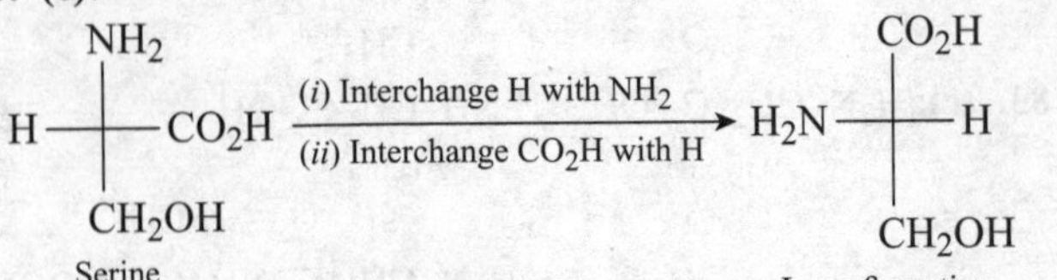

Serine (Fischer projection: NH_2 top, H left, CO_2H right, CH_2OH bottom) $\xrightarrow[\text{(ii) Interchange } CO_2H \text{ with H}]{\text{(i) Interchange H with } NH_2}$ L-configuration (CO_2H top, H_2N left, H right, CH_2OH bottom)

Since H_2N lies towards the left, it has the L-configuration.

106. (c): 2-Hydroxymethylserine does not contain a chiral carbon and hence is optically inactive.

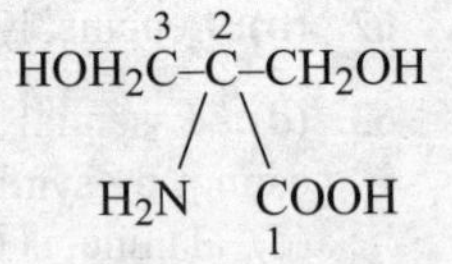

$HOH_2C-\overset{3}{C}(H_2N)-\overset{2}{C}...$: $HOH_2C-C(NH_2)(CH_2OH)-\overset{1}{COOH}$

107. (c): Cysteine ($HSCH_2-CH(NH_2)COOH$) contains the thiol (SH) group. Note that the amino acid cystine contains the disulfide group (–S–S–).

$$\underset{\text{Cystine}}{HOOC-CH(NH_2)-CH_2-S-S-CH_2-CH(NH_2)-COOH}$$

Enzymes

108. (b): Each enzyme can catalyse only one reaction. So, statement (b) is wrong.

109. (d): The enzyme activity rises with temperature and becomes maximum at optimum temperature, that is, 37°C.

110. (a): Reduce the activation energy.

111. (b): Lipase.

112. (b): The enzyme present in animals like cows and buffaloes is cellulase.

113. (c): Emulsion.

114. (d): Proteins $\xrightarrow{\text{pepsin (A)}}$ polypeptides $\xrightarrow{\text{trypsin (B)}}$

115. (a): Phenylalanine hydroxylase.

116. (c): Tyrosinase.

117. (d): Vitamin B_{12} can be stored in our body.

118. (d): Thymine can bond to adenine by 2 hydrogen bonds.

119. (c): Enzymes, being proteins, contain the grouping –NH–CO–.

120. (d): Coenzyme.

121. (b): Coenzymes are derived from vitamins.

Vitamins

122. (d): Pernicious anemia is caused by deficiency of vitamin B_{12}.

123. (b): Vitamin C is also called ascorbic acid.

124. (c): Vitamin B_1 is water soluble.

125. (a): Vitamin B complex is not fat soluble while all others (A, D, E) are fat soluble.

126. (a): Biotin is also called vitamin H.

127. (a): Biotin (vitamin H) is neither soluble in water nor in fat.

128. (a): Vitamin B_{12} contains cobalt.

129. (d): Vitamin B_{12} can be stored in our body.

130. (b): Vitamin B_{12} does not occur in plants but mostly occurs in meat items, therefore, it is less available to vegetarians.

131. (b): Vitamin B_{12} does not occur in plants.

132. (b): Deficiency of vitamin D causes rickets and osteomatalcia.

133. (d): Deficiency of vitamin K causes hemorrhage and lengthens the time of blood clotting.

134. (a): Milk contains vitamins A, D, E.

135. (b): Vitamin A.

136. (a): In the human body, β-carotene present in carrots gets converted into vitamin A, that why it is called provitamin A.

137. (c): Deficiency of riboflavin (vitamin B_2) causes cheilosis and digestive disorders.

Nucleic Acids

138. (a): Adenosine is a nucleoside in which the sugar ribose is connected to adenine through N-9 by β-linkage.

139. (a): ADP and ATP differ in the number of phosphate units, that is, ADP (adenosine diphosphate) contains two and ATP (adenosine triphosphate) contains three phosphate units.

140. (b): Guanine is a purine but the rest are all pyrimidines.

141. (d): Cytosine is a pyrimidine while all the remaining three, that is, adenine, guanine and caffeine are purines.

142. (a): 5-Methyluracil is called thymine.

143. (b): Uracil is found only in RNA but not in DNA.

144. (b): Option (b) represents the structure of uracil which is found in RNA. Structure (c) represents thymine which does not occur in RNA while structures (a) and (d) represent pyrimidines which are neither found in DNA nor in RNA.

145. (b): Adenine, guanine and cytosine are present both in DNA and RNA.

146. (d): The sugar component in RNA is ribose and the sugar component in DNA is 2′-deoxyribose.

147. (b): β-2-Deoxyribofuranose.

148. (d):β-D-ribose.

149. (c): Both deoxyribose and ribose belong to the D-series and option (c) is correct.

150. (a): Ribose contains an –OH group at C_2 but deoxyribose does not. Option (a) is correct.

151. (d): In DNA, adenine faces thymine and guanine faces cytosine.

152. (c): It contains uracil and cytosine as pyrimidine bases. Therefore, statement (c) is wrong.

153. (a): D-sugar component is chiral.

154. (c): Heterocyclic base at C_1' and phosphate ester linkage at C_5'.

155. (a): Amount of A = T and that of G =C.

156. (c): Statements (i) and (ii) are correct and hence option (c) is correct.

157. (c): DNA first codes three types of RNAs which, in turn, synthesise proteins.

158. (b): Gene.

159. (a): α-Keratin is insoluble while all others are soluble in water.

160. (b): 51 amino acids are present.

161. (b): Trypsin catalyses the hydrolysis of peptide bonds, breaking down proteins into smaller peptides.

162. (b): DNA.

163. (b): Nucleoside + phosphate ester bond = nucleotide.

Hormones

164. (d): Insulin.

165. (b): Insulin is a hormone.

166. (b): 3 (two between the chains and the one within the smaller chain).

167. (d): Thyroxine is an amine hormone.

168. (c): Thyroxine contains iodine. Its structure is

I I

HO–⟨ring⟩–O–⟨ring⟩–CH_2–CH–COOH

NH_2

I I

169. (c): Adrenaline hormone is produced under conditions of stress and stimulates conversion of liver glycogen to glucose.

170. (a): Estrone controls the uterine cycle in women.

171. (c): Progesterone.

172. (b): Oxytocin.

173. (d): Both estrogens and androgens.

Final Preparation

174. (c): Ammoniacal $AgNO_3$ or Tollens' reagent also oxidises the –CHO to COOH without oxidizing the CH_2OH group. Thus, option (c) is correct.

175. (a): The mirror image of D-(+)-glucose is L-(-)-glucose.

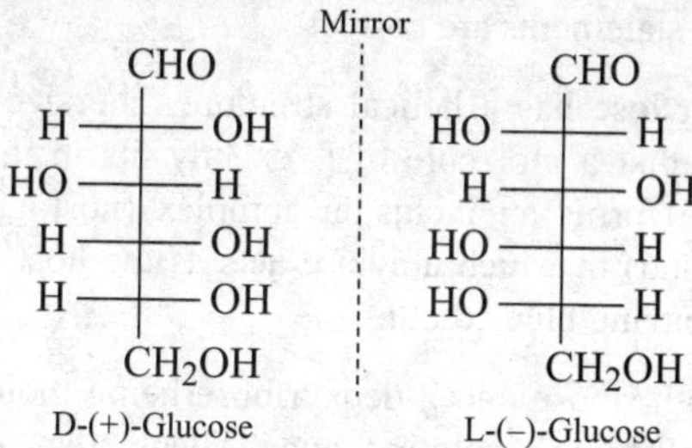

Thus, option (a) is correct.

176. (c): HOH_2C (6), O, CH_2OH; 5, 2; H, H, HO, α, OCH_3; 4, 3; OH, H

Methyl α-D-frotofuranoside

177. (b): The given carbohydrate has five carbons and one oxygen atom in the ring, therefore, it has a pyranose ring and C_1-OH is β-oriented. Further, since the carbohydrate has, in all, six carbon atoms and also has one H and one OH group at C_1, it is an aldohexose. Thus, option (b) is correct.

178. (a): α-D-Glucopyranose $\rightleftharpoons$ Equilibrium mixture $\rightleftharpoons$ β-D-Glucopyranose.

+111° +52.5 +19.2

Ratio of α: β-form $= (52.5 - 19.2) : (111 - 52.5) = 33.3 : 58.5$

$\therefore$ % of α-D-glucopyranose

$$= \frac{33.3}{(33.3 + 58.5)} \times 100 = \frac{333}{91.8} = 36.27\%$$

179. (c): The β-form of glucose is most stable since the equilibrium mixture contains 64% of the β-form, 36% of the α-form and less than 0.5% of the open chain form.

180. (d): According to Lobry de Bruyn van Eikenstein rearrangement, (A) and (B) are mannose and fructose.

$$\text{D-Glucose} \xrightleftharpoons{OH^-} \text{Mannose} + \text{Fructose}$$

181. (d): Fructose is a ketone. In the presence of a base, it is converted into a mixture of glucose and mannose, both of which contain the –CHO group and hence reduce Tollens' reagent to give the silver mirror test. Thus, option (d) is correct.

182. (d): Depending upon the orientation of –OH at C_2, fructose on reduction with Na–Hg and H_2O gives a mixture of sorbitol and mannitol.

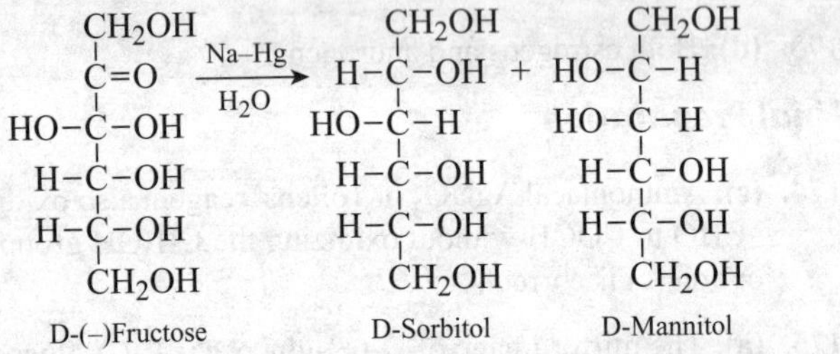

```
  CH2OH                      CH2OH            CH2OH
  C=O      --Na-Hg/H2O-->   H-C-OH    +    HO-C-H
HO-C-OH                    HO-C-H          HO-C-H
 H-C-OH                     H-C-OH          H-C-OH
 H-C-OH                     H-C-OH          H-C-OH
  CH2OH                      CH2OH           CH2OH
D-(-)Fructose              D-Sorbitol      D-Mannitol
```

183. (d): All statements are correct.

184. (c): Amylose has a helical structure. The size of the helix is such that a molecule of I_2 exactly fits in it. As a result, amylose forms an inclusion complex (host–guest addition compound) in which amylose acts as the host and I_2 as the guest) having blue colour.

185. (d): Both ribose and 2-deoxyribose being monosaccharides reduce Fehling's solution and Tollens' reagent. Barfoed's reagent is used only to distinguish monosaccharides from reducing disaccharides. For osazone formation, the presence of OHC–CHOH or CH_2OH–CO group is essential. Ribose contains the OHC–CHOH group but 2-deoxyribose contains neither of the above two groups, therefore, ribose forms the osazone but 2-deoxyribose does not.

186. (a): Carboxylic acids are stronger acids than $-\overset{+}{N}H_3$; therefore, X is the strongest acid. Since –COOH has the–Ieffect which decreases with distance, the effect is more pronounced on Z than on Y. As a result, Z is more acidic than Y. Therefore, the overall order of decreasing acid strength is X > Z > Y, that is, option (a) is correct.

187. (a): Isoelectric point (pI) $= pKa_1 + pKa_2/2$
$= (2.34 + 9.60)/2 = 5.97$

188. (c): Isoelectric point (pI) $= 1/2\ (pK_1 + pK_2)$ where pK_1 corresponds to the ionisation of the carboxyl group and pK_2 corresponds to the ionisation of the ammonium ion.

Now $pK_b + \overset{+}{N}H_3 = 4.32$

$\therefore pK_2 + \overset{+}{N}H_3 = 14 - 4.32 = 9.68$

Thus, the pI of the given amino acid $= 1/2\ (2.34 + 9.68)$
$= 1/2\ (12.02) = 6.01$

189. (c): Glycine and alanine are monoaminomonocarboxylic acids and hence their p*I*s are close to pH 6.0. Aspartic acid being a monoaminodicarboxylic acid, its p*I* lies in the acidic range. Therefore, its p*I* is the lowest (pH = 3.0). Lysine, on the other hand, is a diaminomonocarboxylic acid, therefore, its p*I* lies in the basic range. Its actual p*I* is 9.7.

190. (d): Lysine is a basic amino acid; therefore, its isoelectric point lies in the basic range 8–9. At the isoelectric point, an α-amino acid has the lowest solubility, that is, option (d) is correct.

191. (a): 2,4-Dinitrofluorobenzene is called Sanger's reagent.

192. (a): N-terminal amino acid.

193. (a): Hydrazine.

194. (b): By convention, the name of any polypeptide is written starting from the N-terminal amino acid. Thus, in glycylalanine, glycine is the N-terminal amino acid residue.

195. (b):

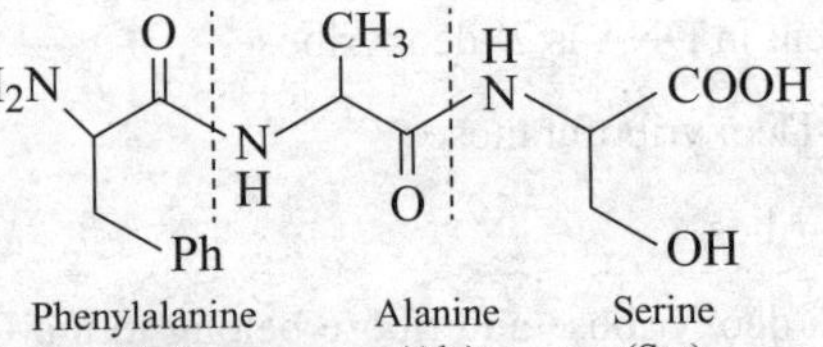

H_2N O CH_3 H COOH N H O Ph OH

Phenylalanine (Phe) Alanine (Ala) Serine (Ser)

Thus, option (b) is correct.

196. (d): Since glycine (Gly) is achiral, alanine (Ala) is the C-terminal amino acid, therefore, the N-terminal amino acid can be either valine (Val) or serine (Ser). In view of these conditions, the following four sequences for the tetrapeptide are possible:

(i) Val–Gly–Ser–Ala
(ii) Val–Ser–Gly–Ala
(iii) Ser–Gly–Val–Ala
(iv) Ser–Val–Gly–Ala

197. (b): Ascorbic acid is also called vitamin C.

198. (a): Vitamin C is a lactone.

199. (b): Vitamin D being insoluble in H_2O accumulates in the body and causes toxicity.

200. (a): Vitamin A and D are absorbed from the intestine by fats.

201. (b): Vitamin B_{12} does not occur in plants.

202. (b): Uracil is present only in RNA; it contains ribose as the sugar.

203. (a): D-sugar component is optically active due to the presence of chiral carbons.

204. (a): 5′, 3′.

205. (c): The sequence of bases in DNA is ATGCTTGA. The sequence of bases in the complimentary strand is TAGGAACT.

206. (b): The sequence of bases in DNA is TGAACCCTT. According to the base-pairing principle, T in DNA faces A in *m*-RNA, while G faces C and A faces U. Therefore, the sequence of bases in the *m*-RNA is ACUUGGGAA. Thus, option (b) is correct.

207. (d): All the three RNAs, *m*-RNA, *r*-RNA and *t*-RNA, take part in protein synthesis.

208. (d): A codon consists of three bases (A) which specifies a particular amino acid (B) which is to be incorporated into a strand of DNA or RNA.

209. (b): The third base of a codon is less specific. For example, codons CUU and CUC code for the same amino acid, leucine.

210. (b): Glycine (NH_2CH_2COO) is optically inactive while all other amino acids are optically active.

211. (c): Lactose is a reducing sugar and all reducing sugars show mutarotation.

212. (c): Denaturation of proteins causes loss of its biological activity and makes it less active.

213. (d): Refer to 'Important Information' of option (d) is correct.

214. (c): Anomers differ in configuration at the C_1 in aldoses and the C_2 in ketones, that is, option (c) is correct. Option (d), however, represents a pair of enantiomers.

215. (a): Structures (I and II) differ only in the configuration of the OH group at C_1 and hence they are anomers.

216. (d): Option (d) has the right orientation of OH groups at C_2, C_3, C_4 and C_5.

217. (a):

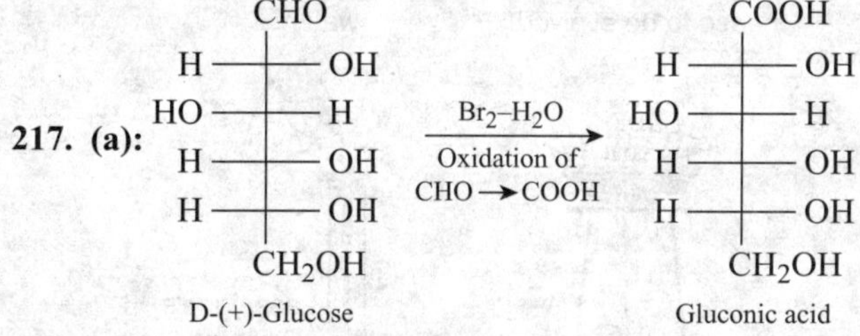

MATCH THE FOLLOWING

218. (d): A(pepsin)—r(digestive enzyme); B(nucleic acid)—s(genetic material);C(ascorbic acid)—p(vitamin);D(testosterone)—q(male sex hormone)

219. (c): A(glucosidic linkage)—q(connects two monosaccharide units);
B(maltase)—p(globular protein);
C(peptide bond)—s(connects two amino acid units);D(nucleotide)—r(monomeric unit of nucleic acids)

220. (d): A(lysine)—q(basic amino acid);
B(aspartic acid)—s(acidic amino acid);
C(valine)—p(neutral optically active amino acid;D(glycine)—r(neutral optically inactive amino acid)

ASSERTION REASON

221. (a): R is the correct explanation of A.

222. (b): Correct explanation. The glucose and the fructose units in sucrose are connected through their reducing centres.

223. (c): Correct R. Sucrose on hydrolysis gives equal amounts of glucose and fructose. Since glucose has a less +ve (+52.5°) and fructose has a more –ve (–92.4°) magnitude of optical rotation, the change in the sign of rotation is observed.

224. (c): Correct R. Maltose has 4-α-glycosidic linkage.

225. (b): Correct explanation. Enzymes which hydrolyse the β-glycosidic linkage are not present in human beings.

226. (a): R is the correct explanation of A.

227. (c): Correct R. It controls glucose level in the blood.

228. (c): Correct R. Carboxypeptidase is an exopeptidase since it cleaves the peptide chain at the C-terminal end.

229. (b): Correct explanation. Due to denaturation, a protein loses its biological activity because its folded structure uncoils and assumes a more random conformation.

230. (a): R is the correct explanation of A.

(Activity of an enzyme is pH dependent. Change of pH also affects the solubility of the enzyme in water.)

231. (d): Correct A. Uracil occurs in RNA
Correct R. RNA does not undergo replication.

232. (d): Correct A. Deoxyribose ($C_5H_{10}O_4$) is a carbohydrate.
Correct R. Optically active polyhydroxyaldehydes or ketones or substances which give these on hydrolysis are carbohydrates irrespective of the fact whether they follow the $C_x(H_2O)_y$ formula or not.

233. (a): R is the correct explanation of A.

234. (b): Correct explanation. Glucose and fructose have the same stereochemistry at C_3, C_4 and C_5 chiral carbon atoms.

235. (a): R is the correct explanation of A.

236. (a): R is the correct explanation of A.

237. (a): R is the correct explanation of A.

238. (c): Correct reason. Reaction of glucose with Fehling's solution gives a red precipitate of Cu_2O and gluconic acid.

239. (a): R is the correct explanation of A.

CHAPTER 15

Principles Related to Practical Chemistry

15.1 Qualitative Analysis of Organic Compounds

Two major steps involved in the characterisation of an organic compounds are—element detection and detection of functional group.

15.1.1 Element Detection

Detection of elements present in an organic compound constitutes an important step in its analysis. In addition to carbon and hydrogen, other elements generally present in organic compounds are oxygen, nitrogen, sulfur and the halogens. Since nearly all the organic compounds contain carbon as well as hydrogen, it is usually not necessary to carry out tests to detect them and their presence can be assumed without testing for them. Here, we shall study the tests for the detection of nitrogen, sulfur and the halogens only.

Lassaigne's Test

This is the most dependable test for the detection of nitrogen, sulfur and the halogens. This test is also known as the *sodium fusion test*. In order to perform this test, first of all, sodium extract or Lassaigne's extract is prepared as described below.

Preparation of Lassaigne's Extract: Take a small piece of dry sodium in a fusion tube. Heat the tube slightly so that it melts to a shining globule. Add a pinch of the organic compound. Heat it slowly to start with so that the compound reacts with sodium metal, then heat strongly. Plunge the red-hot tube into a china dish containing distilled water. Crush the contents with a glass rod and heat to boiling. Remove the insoluble matter by filtration. The filtrate is called Lassaigne's extract (Fig. 15.1). Nitrogen, sulfur and halogens present in an organic compound are detected by making use of Lassaigne's extract.

Detection of Nitrogen

To a small portion of Lassaigne's extract (usually alkaline), add 2 mL of freshly prepared ferrous sulfate solution and heat. Now add to it 2–3 drops of ferric chloride solution and acidify with conc. hydrochloric acid. A prussian blue colouration indicates the presence of nitrogen in the compound.

Chemistry of the test: If nitrogen is present in the compound, the sodium extract would contain sodium cyanide formed during fusion. On adding the required reagents, sodium cyanide reacts to form ferricferrocyanide which has a prussian blue colour.

$$Na + \underbrace{C + N}_{\text{(From organic compound)}} \xrightarrow{\text{Fuse}} NaCN$$

$$FeSO_4 + 2\,NaOH \longrightarrow \underset{\text{Green ppt.}}{Fe(OH)_2\downarrow} + Na_2SO_4$$

$$Fe(OH)_2 + \underset{\substack{\text{From sodium}\\\text{Extract}}}{2\,NaCN} \longrightarrow Fe(CN)_2 + 2\,NaOH$$

$$Fe(CN)_2 + 4\,NaCN \longrightarrow \underset{\text{Sodium ferrocyanide}}{Na_4[Fe(CN)_6]}$$

$$3\,Na_4[Fe(CN)_6] + 4\,FeCl_3 \longrightarrow \underset{\substack{\text{Ferric ferrocyanide}\\\text{(Prussian blue colour)}}}{Fe_4[Fe(CN)_6]_3} + 12\,NaCl$$

Sodium + compound

Test tube holder

(1) Heat sodium and substance till all fumes cease to be evolved.

(2) Plunge ignition tube in 10–15 mL distilled water.

(3) Boil the contents for five minutes.

Lassaigne's extract

(4) Filter the extract while still hot.

Fig. 15.1 Preparation of Lassaigne's extract

The purpose of acidifying the reaction mixture in the end is to dissolve any green precipitate of $Fe(OH)_2$ since it may lead to wrong inferences.

Detection of Nitrogen and Sulfur Present Together

If the organic compound contains both nitrogen and sulfur, sodium sulfocyanide reacts with ferric chloride and gives blood red colouration due to formation of ferric sulfocyanide.

$$Na + \underbrace{C + N + S}_{\text{From organic Compound}} \longrightarrow NaCNS$$

$$3\,NaCNS + FeCl_3 \longrightarrow \underset{\text{Blood red Colouration}}{Fe(CNS)_3} + 3NaCl$$

Thus, the appearance of a blood red colouration on performing Lassaigne's extract for nitrogen indicates the presence of both nitrogen and sulfur in the organic compound.

Detection of Sulfur

Sodium nitroprusside test: To a small portion of Lassaigne's extract, add a few drops of sodium nitroprusside solution.

Chemistry of the test: During preparation of Lassaigne's extract, sulfur from the organic compound combines with sodium to form sodium sulfide. Sulfides give purple colouration on reaction with sodium nitroprusside.

$$\underset{\text{(From Organic Compound)}}{2\,Na + S} \longrightarrow Na_2S$$

$$\underset{\text{(From sodium extract)}}{Na_2S} + \underset{\text{Sodium nitroprusside}}{Na_2[Fe(CN)_5NO]} \longrightarrow \underset{\text{Purple colouration}}{Na_4[Fe(CN)_5NOS]}$$

Lead acetate test: Acidify a small portion of Lassaigne's extract with acetic acid and add a few drops of lead acetate solution. The formation of a black precipitate indicates the presence of sulfur in the compound.

Chemistry of the Test

$$Na_2S + (CH_3COO)_2\,Pb \longrightarrow \underset{\text{Black ppt.}}{PbS\downarrow} + 2\,CH_3COONa$$

Detection of Halogens

Silver nitrate test: To a small portion about 2 mL of Lassaigne's extract add 1 mL of conc. nitric acid and boil for some time. Cool the contents and add to it silver nitrate solution.

- **White precipitate, soluble in ammonium hydroxide,** indicates the presence of chlorine in the organic compound.
- **Pale yellow precipitate, sparingly soluble in ammonium hydroxide,** indicates the presence of bromine in the compound.
- **Yellow precipitate, insoluble in ammonium hydroxide,** indicates the presence of iodine in the organic compound.

Chemistry of the Test

- **For chlorine**

$$Na + \underset{\text{(from organic compound)}}{Cl} \xrightarrow{\text{heat}} NaCl$$

$$NaCl + AgNO_3 \longrightarrow \underset{\text{Silver chloride (white ppt.)}}{AgCl\downarrow} + NaNO_3$$

$$AgCl + 2\,NH_4OH \longrightarrow \underset{\text{(soluble)}}{[Ag(NH_3)_2]Cl} + 2\,H_2O$$

- **For bromine**

$$Na + \underset{\text{(from organic compound)}}{Br} \xrightarrow{\text{heat}} NaBr$$

$$NaBr + AgNO_3 \longrightarrow \underset{\text{Silver bromide (pale yellow ppt.)}}{AgBr\downarrow} + NaNO_3$$

- **For iodine**

$$Na + \underset{\text{(from organic compound)}}{I} \longrightarrow NaI$$

$$NaI + AgNO_3 \longrightarrow \underset{\text{Silver iodide (yellow ppt.)}}{AgI\downarrow} + NaNO_3$$

The function of adding conc. HNO_3 and boiling is to decompose any sodium cyanide or sodium sulfide present in the extract. Otherwise these compounds will interfere with the tests of halides since NaCN gives a white precipitate with silver nitrate while Na_2S gives a black precipitate.

$$NaCN + HNO_3 \longrightarrow NaNO_3 + HCN\uparrow$$

$$Na_2S + 2\,HNO_3 \longrightarrow 2NaNO_3 + H_2S\uparrow$$

Carbon disulfide test: Acidify a small portion of Lassaigne's extract with dil. HCl and add a few drops of carbon disulfide (or CCl_4or $CHCl_3$). Then add freshly prepared chlorine water and shake vigorously.

- Appearance of **orange colour** in the carbon disulfide layer indicates the presence of **bromine**.
- Appearance of **violet colour** in the carbon disulfide layer indicates the presence of **iodine**.

Chemistry of the test: Chlorine can displace bromine and iodine from their respective halides in solution. Bromine or iodine thus liberated can turn the carbon disulfide layer orange or violet.

$$Cl_2 + \underset{\text{(from sodium extract)}}{2\,NaBr} \longrightarrow Br_2 + 2\,NaCl$$

$$Cl_2 + \underset{\text{(from sodium extract)}}{2\,NaI} \longrightarrow I_2 + 2\,NaCl$$

15.2 Detection of Functional Groups

Tests for different functional groups are given below.

15.2.1 Tests for Carboxylic (–COOH) Group

(i) **Litmus paper test:** Dip blue litmus paper in the aqueous solution or suspension of the compound. It turns red.

(ii) **Sodium bicarbonate test:** In a test tube, take a little quantity of the compound and then add a saturated solution of sodium bicarbonate. Brisk effervescence due to the formation of CO_2 shows the presence of –COOH group.

$$C_6H_5COOH + NaHCO_3 \longrightarrow C_6H_5CO\overset{-}{O}\overset{+}{Na} + H_2O + CO_2\uparrow$$

Benzoic acid — Sodium benzoate

Cool the solution and pour in a tube containing water. A fruity smell, due to the formation of an ester, indicates the presence of carboxylic group.

$$\underset{\text{Carboxylic acid}}{R\text{–}COOH} + \underset{\text{Ethanol}}{C_2H_5OH} \xrightarrow[\Delta]{\text{conc. } H_2SO_4} \underset{\substack{\text{Ester}\\ \text{(fruity smell)}}}{RCOOC_2H_5} + H_2O$$

15.2.2 Test for Alcoholic (–OH) Group

(i) **Sodium test:** In a test tube, take some organic compound and add a thin piece of sodium metal to it. A brisk effervescence due to the formation of hydrogen gas takes place.

$$2\ ROH + 2\ Na \longrightarrow 2\ R\overset{-}{O}\overset{+}{Na} + H_2\uparrow$$

(ii) **Ester test:** Heat the given compound with acetic acid in the presence of sulfuric acid. A fruity fragrance indicates the formation of ester.

$$R\text{–}OH + \underset{\text{Acetic acid}}{CH_3COOH} \xrightarrow{\text{conc. } H_2SO_4} \underset{\substack{\text{Ester}\\ \text{(fruity smell)}}}{CH_3COOR} + H_2O$$

Alcohols give crystalline esters with 3,5-dinitrobenzoyl chloride. These esters have sharp melting points and can be used for testing a given alcohol.

$$ROH + Cl\text{–}\overset{O}{\overset{\|}{C}}\text{–}C_6H_3(NO_2)_2 \longrightarrow R\text{–}O\text{–}\overset{O}{\overset{\|}{C}}\text{–}C_6H_3(NO_2)_2 + HCl$$

3, 5-dinitrobenzoyl chloride — Crystalline ester

(iii) **Ceric ammonium nitrate test:** To a small amount of the organic compound or its aqueous solution, add a few drops of ceric ammonium nitrate. A red colour indicates the presence of alcoholic hydroxyl group.

$$\underset{\text{Alcohol}}{2\ ROH} + \underset{\text{Ceric ammonium nitrate}}{(NH_4)_2Ce(NO_3)_6} \longrightarrow \underset{\text{Red colour}}{Ce(NO_3)_4.(ROH)_2} + 2\ NH_4NO_3$$

This test is useful when the compound contains less than ten C atoms.

(iv) **Lucas test:** This test is used to distinguish between primary, secondary and tertiary alcohols. In this test, treat 2 mL of organic compound with approximately 8 mL of Lucas reagent (to prepare Lucas reagent, dissolve 32 g of anhydrous $ZnCl_2$ in 20 mL of conc. HCl) and shake properly. The following observations are seen.

(a) Immediate formation of turbidity indicates the presence of **tertiary alcohol**.

(b) Formation of turbidity after 4–5 min shows the presence of **secondary alcohol**.

(c) If the solution remains clear, then **primary alcohol** is present.

15.2.3 Tests for Phenols

(i) **Ferric chloride test:** Take a few drops of ferric chloride solution and add 2–3 drops of the compound to it. Appearance of green, blue and violet colour shows the presence of phenol.

$$6\ C_6H_5OH + FeCl_3 \longrightarrow 3\ H^+ + [Fe(OC_6H_5)_6]^{3-} + 3\ HCl$$

Note: This test is also given by enols.

(ii) **Liebermann's nitroso reaction:** Take a little amount of compound and add 1 mL of conc. H_2SO_4 to it. Shake and warm the test tube. Cool and then add crystals of sodium nitrite ($NaNO_2$). A deep green to blue solution is formed which turns red on dilution. The red aqueous solution becomes again deep green or blue if made alkaline with NaOH. It shows the presence of phenol.

$$\underset{\text{Phenol}}{C_6H_5\text{–}OH} \xrightarrow{HNO_2} HO\text{–}C_6H_4\text{–}NO \xrightarrow{C_6H_5OH,\ H_2SO_4}$$

$$\underset{\text{Indophenol ion}}{HO{=}C_6H_4{=}N\text{–}C_6H_4\text{–}OH} \xrightarrow{NaOH} \underset{\text{Indophenol (blue)}}{\left[O{=}C_6H_4{=}N\text{–}C_6H_4\text{–}O^-\right]}$$

Note: Nitrophenols do not respond to $FeCl_3$ test or Liebermann's nitroso reaction.

(iii) **Phthalein test:** Phenol on heating with phthalic acid in the presence of conc. H_2SO_4 gives a colourless compound called phenolphthalein, which appears as a pink coloured compound in an alkaline medium.

$$\underset{\text{Phthalic acid}}{C_6H_4(COOH)_2} \xrightarrow{H_2SO_4,\ \Delta} \underset{\text{Phthalic anhydride}}{C_6H_4(CO)_2O} \xrightarrow{2C_6H_5OH,\ \Delta} \underset{\text{Phenolphthalein (Colourless)}}{\text{Phenolphthalein}} \xrightarrow{OH^-} \text{(Pink colour in alkaline)}$$

Phenolphthalein is used as an indicator in acid–base titrations. It is colourless in acidic medium and pink in basic medium.

15.2.4 Test for Aldehyde (–CHO) Group

(i) **Tollen's reagent test:** Take a little quantity of the compound in a test tube and add 2 mL of freshly prepared reagent. Shake, warm and allow the contents to stand for 2–3 minutes. Formation of silver mirror or a grey ppt. indicates the presence of an aldehydic group.

$$2Ag(NH_3)_2OH + R\text{–}CHO \longrightarrow 2\,Ag\downarrow + RCO\overset{-}{O}\overset{+}{N}H_4 + 3NH_3\uparrow + H_2O$$

Silver mirror or grey ppt.

(ii) Fehling's solution test: Take a mixture of equal amounts of Fehling's solution A and B, and add a few drops of organic compound and boil the contents. Formation of a red precipitate shows the presence of an aldehyde.

$$\underset{\text{Cupric oxide}}{2CuO} + \underset{\text{Aldehyde}}{RCHO} \longrightarrow \underset{\text{Red ppt.}}{Cu_2O\downarrow} + RCOOH$$

Note:

(a) Both the above tests are also given by reducing sugars.

(b) Benzaldehyde does not reduce Fehling's solution (a distinction from other aldehydes). Benzaldehyde is confirmed by malachite green test.

(iii) Schiff's reagent test: Add 5–6 drops of organic compound to 2 mL of the Schiff's reagent. Shake vigorously. After sometime, formation of a deep red or violet colour indicates the presence of an aldehydic group.

H·SO₂NH–C₆H₄, H·SO₂NH–C₆H₄ ⟩C(SO₃H)–C₆H₄–$\overset{\oplus}{N}H_2SO_2H$ $\xrightarrow[-H_2SO_4]{2R\text{-}CHO}$

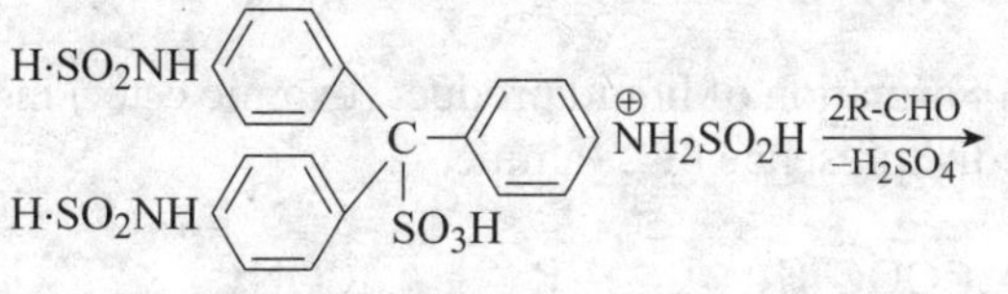

Schiff's reagent (Colourless)

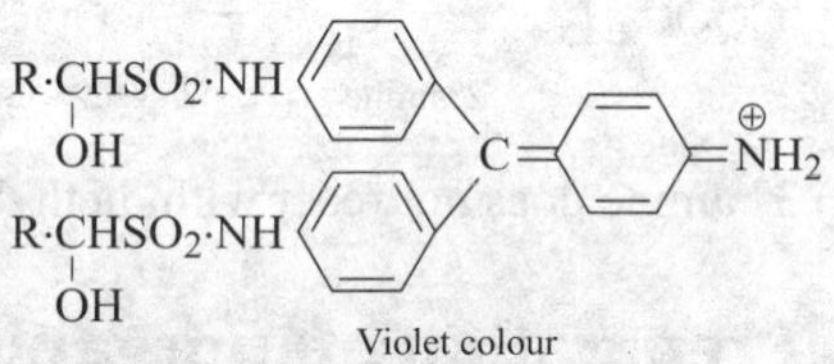

R·CH(OH)SO₂·NH–C₆H₄, R·CH(OH)SO₂·NH–C₆H₄ ⟩C=C₆H₄=$\overset{\oplus}{N}H_2$

Violet colour

(iv) Benedict's solution test: Boil the compound with 2–3 mL of Benedict's solution for few minutes. Appearance of a red–yellow precipitate confirms the presence of aliphatic aldehydes.

Note: This test is usually given by only aliphatic aldehydes, thus used to differentiate between aliphatic and aromatic aldehydes.

15.2.5 Tests for Ketone Group

(i) 2,4-dinitrophenyl hydrazine test: In a dry test tube, add few drops of the organic compound (if liquid) or its alcoholic solution (if solid) to about 2 mL of the reagent and one drop of conc. H_2SO_4. Shake vigorously, heat (if necessary) and allow to stand for about 5 minutes. A yellow or orange precipitate separates out in case of a compound containing carbonyl group due to the formation of the respective hydrazones.

$$\underset{\text{Carbonyl compound}}{>C=O} + \underset{\text{2, 4-dinitrophenyl hydrazine}}{H_2N\cdot HN\text{–}C_6H_3(NO_2)\text{–}NO_2} \longrightarrow >C=N\cdot HN\text{–}C_6H_3(NO_2)\text{–}NO_2\downarrow + H_2O$$

Yellow or orange red coloured crystalline derivative of 2, 4-dinitrophenyl hydrazine of carbonyl compound

(ii) Sodium bisulfite test: Add a very small quantity of organic compound to 1 mL of saturated solution of sodium bisulfite and shake vigorously. Formation of a white precipitate shows the presence of the carbonyl group.

$$>C=O + NaHSO_3 \xrightarrow{\text{Shake}} >C\begin{matrix}OH \\ \overset{-}{S}O_3\overset{+}{N}a\end{matrix}$$

Sodium bisulphite derivative (White crystalline ppt.)

(iii) Sodium nitroprusside test: Add 0.1 g of solid or 0.2 cc of liquid compound to 2 cc of sodium nitroprusside, $Na_2[Fe(CN)_5NO]$, solution. After that, make the solution alkaline with 2–3 drops of sodium hydroxide. A red or purple colour indicates the presence of ketone (benzophenone does not give this test).

Worked Out Problem 15.1

The organic compound that gives following qualitative analysis is

TEST	INFERENCE
(i) Dil. HCl	Insoluble
(ii) NaOH solution	Soluble
(iii) Br_2/ water	Decolourisation

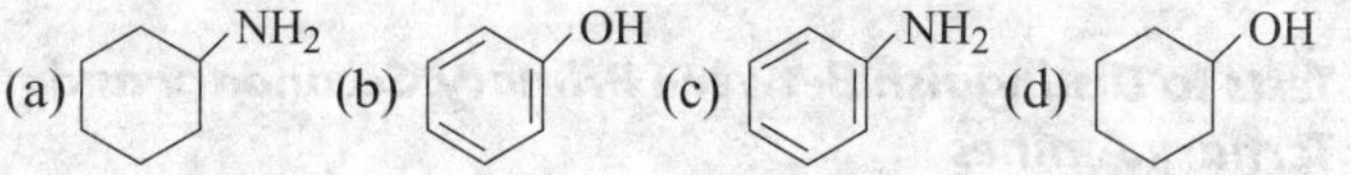

(a) cyclohexylamine ($C_6H_{11}NH_2$) (b) phenol (C_6H_5OH) (c) aniline ($C_6H_5NH_2$) (d) cyclohexanol ($C_6H_{11}OH$)

Solution (b)

Phenol (ArOH) is insoluble in dil. HCl and readily soluble in NaOH solution. It reacts with Br_2/water to give 2,4,6-tribromophenol. It readily decolourises the yellow colour of Br_2 water. Reactions involved are as follows:

(i) $\underset{\text{Phenol (Acidic in nature)}}{C_6H_5OH} \xrightarrow{\text{Dil. HCl}}$ No reaction

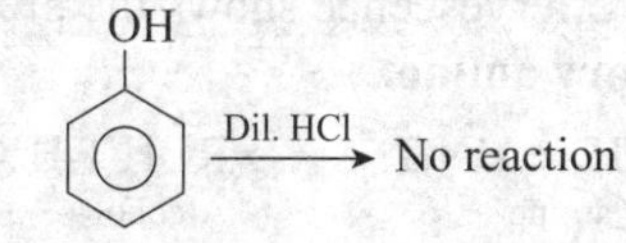

(ii) $\underset{\text{Phenol (Acidic in nature)}}{C_6H_5OH} \xrightarrow{\text{Dil. HCl}}$ No reaction

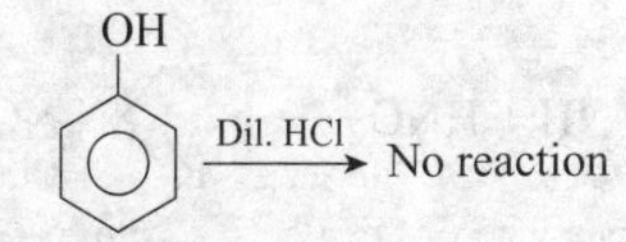

(iii) Phenol (OH on benzene) $\xrightarrow{Br_2/Water}$ 2, 4, 6-tribromophenol (OH, Br, Br, Br on benzene)

White ppt.
(2, 4, 6-tribromophenol)

15.2.6 Tests for Primary Amine ($-NH_2$) Group

(i) Carbylamine test: Boil a little quantity of the compound with 2 drops of chloroform and 2 mL of alcoholic caustic potash. An intolerable offensive odour of carbylamine indicates the presence of primary amine.

$$\underset{\text{Primary amine}}{R{-}NH_2} + CHCl_3 + KOH(alc.) \longrightarrow RNC\uparrow + 3KCl + 3H_2O$$

(ii) Dye test: Dissolve about 0.2g of the compound in dil. HCl and cool. Now, add 10% aq. $NaNO_2$ solution. Pour all this content into a beaker containing alkaline β-naphthol solution. Formation of a red and orange dye indicates the presence of aromatic amino group.

$$\underset{\text{Aniline}}{C_6H_5{-}NH_2} + NaNO_2 + 3HCl \xrightarrow{0°–10°C} \underset{\text{Benzene diazonium chloride}}{C_6H_5{-}N{=}NCl} + 2H_2O + HCl + NaCl$$

$$\underset{\text{Benzene diazonium chloride}}{C_6H_5{-}N{=}N\,\boxed{Cl + H}} + \beta\text{-naphthol} \xrightarrow{-HCl} \underset{\text{Phenyl azo-}\beta\text{-naphthol (Red dye)}}{C_6H_5{-}N{=}N{-}C_{10}H_6OH}$$

Tests to Distinguish Between Primary, Secondary and Tertiary Amines

(i) Nitrous acid test: Prepare a solution of nitrous acid by adding ice cold dil. HCl to a solution of 1% aq. $NaNO_2$. Add this solution gradually to 0.2 g of the organic compound in 10 mL dil. HCl. The observations are as follows.

(a) Brisk effervescence shows the presence of aliphatic **primary amine.**

$$\underset{\text{Primary amine}}{R{-}NH_2} + HNO_2 \longrightarrow \underset{\text{Alcohol}}{ROH} + H_2O + N_2\uparrow$$

(b) Formation of an oily dark coloured liquid indicates the presence of **secondary amine.**

$$\underset{\text{Secondary amine}}{R_2NH} + HNO_2 \longrightarrow \underset{\text{Nitroso compound (Oily)}}{R_2N{\cdot}NO} + H_2O$$

(c) No reaction indicates the presence of **aliphatic tertiary amine** while production of green or brown colour indicates the presence of **aromatic tertiary amines.**

(ii) Hinsberg's test: Take 0.2 g of the organic compound, add 1 mL of 5% NaOH and 3 mL pyridine. Shake well and add a few drops of benzene sulfonyl chloride (Hinsberg's reagent) with continuous shaking. The observations are as follows:

(a) Formation of yellow colour indicates the presence of **primary amine.**

(b) Formation of orange colour shows the presence of **secondary amine.**

(c) Formation of a red or purple colour shows the presence of **tertiary amines.**

(iii) Hofmann's method: Take some organic compound in a test tube and add diethyl oxalate solution to it, shake well. The observations are as follows:

(a) Formation of solid product (N,N′-dialkyl oxamide) indicates the presence of 1° amine.

$$\begin{matrix}COOC_2H_5\\ |\\ COOC_2H_5\end{matrix} + \underset{1°\text{amine}}{2NH_2R} \longrightarrow \underset{\text{N-N′-dialkyl oxamide (Solid)}}{\begin{matrix}CONHR\\ |\\ CONHR\end{matrix}}$$

(b) Formation of liquid product (oxamic ester) indicates the presence of 2° amine.

$$\begin{matrix}COOC_2H_5\\ |\\ COOC_2H_5\end{matrix} + \underset{2°\text{amine}}{HNR_2} \longrightarrow \underset{\text{Oxamic ester (Liquid)}}{\begin{matrix}CONR_2\\ |\\ COOC_2H_5\end{matrix}}$$

(c) 3° amine does not react with diethyl oxalate.

15.3 Preparation of Inorganic Compounds

(i) Mohr's salt or ferrous ammonium sulfate $[FeSO_4 \cdot (NH_4)_2 \cdot 6H_2O]$ is a double salt. When solutions of ferrous sulfate and ammonium sulfate are mixed together, evaporated and cooled, light green crystals of Mohr's salt are obtained.

$$(NH_4)_2SO_4 + FeSO_4{\cdot}2H_2O \longrightarrow \underset{\text{Mohr's salt (light green)}}{FeSO_4{\cdot}(NH_4)_2SO_4{\cdot}6H_2O} + H_2O$$

During the preparation of ferrous sulfate solution in boiling water, dilute H_2SO_4 (in small amount), is also added in boiling water to prevent the hydrolysis of ferrous sulfate into ferrous hydroxide.

(ii) Potash alum, $KAl(SO_4)_2{\cdot}12H_2O$ is also a double salt. Potash alum is prepared by dissolving K_2SO_4 and $Al_2(SO_4)_3$ in equimolar ratio in small amount of water containing some drops of conc. H_2SO_4. On cooling potash alum separates as colourless crystals.

$$K_2SO_4 + Al_2(SO_4)_3 + 24\,H_2O \longrightarrow K_2SO_4.Al_2(SO_4)_3.24\,H_2O$$

Worked Out Problem 15.2

Alum is found to contain the hydrated monovalent cation $[M(H_2O)_6]$, trivalent cation $[M'(H_2O)_6]^{3+}$and SO_4^{2-} in the ratio of

(a) 1:1:1 (b) 1:2:3 (c) 1:3:2 (d) 1:1:2

Solution (d)

General formula for potash alum is $KAl(SO_4)_2.12H_2O$ (1:1:2)
K^+ = monovalent cation and Al^{3+} = trivalent cation

15.4 Preparation of Organic Compounds

(i) Acetanilide: It is prepared by direct acetylation of aniline by using the mixture of equal volumes of acetic anhydride and acetic acid. Amines containing $-NH_2$ or >NH groups respectively can be directly acetylated. The reactive hydrogen atoms get replaced by the acetyl group ($-COCH_3$) to give acetyl derivatives of the type $RNH.COCH_3$which may be regarded as mono and di-alkyl substituted acetamides ($RNHCOCH_3$ and R_2NCOCH_3).

C_6H_5–NHCOCH$_3$

$$R{-}NH_2 + (CH_3CO)_2OR \longrightarrow NH.COCH_3 + CH_3COOH$$

The mechanism of this reaction is as follows:

Aniline + Acetic anhydride ⇌ intermediate ⇌ (–H⁺) ... → Acetanilide $+ \bar{O}{-}C(=O){-}CH_3$

A small amount of zinc is added to the reaction mixture to prevent the oxidation of aniline and to reduce the coloured impurities present in aniline during the reaction.

(ii) *p*-Nitroacetanilide: It is prepared by the nitration of acetanilide. It is dissolved in glacial acetic acid. Then, concentrated H_2SO_4 is added to it with vigorous stirring. The temperature of reaction mixture should be maintained below 10°C. Then, add fuming HNO_3 drop by drop with regular stirring. It gives *p*-nitro acetanilide along with a little amount of the *o*-isomer. In this process, fuming HNO_3 in the presence of conc. H_2SO_4, gives the nitronium ion (NO_2^+) which attacks acetanilide to form *p*-nitroacetanilide through the cyclopentadienyl cation (intermediate) formation.

$$HNO_3 + H_2SO_4 \longrightarrow NO_2^+ + H_2O + HSO_4^-$$

Nitronium ion

Acetanilide $+ \overset{+}{N}O_2 \xrightarrow{\text{Slow}}$ [Cyclopentadienyl cation] $\xrightarrow{\text{Fast}}$ *p*-nitroacetanilide $+ H^+$

$$H^+ + HSO_4^- \longrightarrow H_2SO_4$$

(iii) Aniline yellow or *p*-aminoazobenzene: It is an azo dye prepared from diazoamino benzene. When diazoamino benzene is heated with aniline and a little amount of hydrochloric acid at about 40°C, for a short time, it gives *p*-aminoazobenzene or aniline yellow in good yield.

C_6H_5–N=N–C_6H_4–NH

C_6H_5–N=N–NH–C_6H_5 (Diazoamino benzene) $\xrightarrow{HCl}$ C_6H_5–$\overset{+}{N}$≡N$\bar{C}l$ + C_6H_5–NH_2 $\xrightarrow{HCl}$ C_6H_5–N=N–C_6H_4–NH_2 (*p*-amino azobenzene)

The mechanism of the reaction is based on the equilibrium involving the diazoamino compound, phenyl diazonium chloride and aniline.

C_6H_5–N=N–NH–C_6H_5 (Diazoamino benzene) $+ H^+Cl^-$ ⇌ C_6H_5–$\overset{+}{N}$≡N$\bar{C}l$ (Phenyl diazonium chloride) + H_2N–C_6H_5 (Aniline)

The reaction takes place between the two latter compounds under weakly acidic conditions.

(iv) Iodoform, CHI_3: It is prepared from acetone. Acetone when treated with potassium iodide and sodium hypochloride (NaOCl), gives iodoform.

$$NaOCl + KI \longrightarrow NaOI + KCl$$

$$(H_3C)_2C{=}O + NaOH \longrightarrow (I_3C)(H_3C)C{=}O \xrightarrow{NaOH} CH_3CO\bar{O}\overset{+}{N}a + CHI_3 \downarrow$$

Iodoform

15.5 Practical Inorganic Chemistry

There are also two parts to inorganic practical chemistry—quantitative analysis (volumetric analysis) and qualitative analysis.

15.5.1 Quantitative Analysis (Volumetric Analysis)

It involves the calculations based on volume relationships for solutions. A titration is an experiment where the volume of the reactant solution (titrant) needed to react exactly with some amount of another reactant is measured. This volume is called equivalence point. A titration is performed by slowly adding a standard solution from a burette to a solution under examination until the reaction between the two is observed to be complete. The volume or mass of the reagent needed to complete the titration is determined from the difference between the initial and final readings. The solution taken in the burette during titration is known as the *titrant.* The solution being titrated is called the *titrate*.

Standard solution: A volumetric method employs one or more standard solutions which are reagents of exactly known concentrations. A standard solution used for acid–base titration is usually a solution of strong acids or bases such as HCl, H_2SO_4, NaOH, KOH and $Ba(OH)_2$. Bases, however, are not as good as acids for permanent standards because they absorb CO_2 whenever they come in contact with air. Therefore, the accuracy of a volumetric method is limited by the accuracy with which the concentration of the standard solution is known. The ideal standard solution (of known concentration) must have the following characteristics:

- It should be sufficiently stable so that it is necessary to determine its concentration only once.
- It must react rapidly with the analyte.

If the concentration of a substance can be known simply by dissolving a known amount in a given volume of solution, then the substance is called a *primary standard* and the solution formed is called a *primary standard solution.* For example, oxalic acid, potassium dichromate. In most cases, concentration can be determined by standardisation against primary standard solution. Such solutions are called *secondary standard solutions*. For example, ferrous sulfate, mineral acids (H_2SO_4, HNO_3). Their solutions are prepared by dissolving a known amount or volume but they have to be standardised using a primary standard. Thus, all these are secondary standards.

Equivalence point and end point: The equivalence point in a titration is a theoretical point where the amount of added titrant is chemically equivalent to the amount of analyte (titrate) in the sample. It cannot be determined experimentally. We can only estimate its position by observing some physical change associated with the condition so equivalence. This is called *end point* of the titration. For example, the equivalent point is reached when 1 mole of HCl is neutralised by 1 mole of NaOH. But we cannot detect this equivalent point. If one drop of suitable indicator such as phenolphthalein is added in HCl(analyte), then an additional drop of NaOH (from the burette) will give a light pink colour. This is the *end point.* Therefore, end point is the point of completion of the reaction indicated by suitable indicator. It has an additional drop of titrating reagent for the reaction.

$$NaOH + HCl \longrightarrow NaCl + H_2O$$

$$N_1V_1 = N_2V_2$$

1 equivalent of NaOH ≡ 1 equivalent of HCl
≡ 1 mol of HCl

$$2\ NaOH + H_2SO_4 \longrightarrow Na_2SO_4 + 2\ H_2O$$

1 equivalent of NaOH ≡ 1 equivalent of H_2SO_4
≡ 0.5 mol of H_2SO_4

Acid–base indicators: An indicator is a dye or substance which changes colour over a short pH range.

- Acid–base indicators are special types of substances which possess one colour in an acid solution and a different colour in an alkaline medium.
- For an acid–base titration, a weak acid or weak base is used as an indicator. Since the concentration of acid or base is controlled by pH, the colour of an indicator solution is pH dependent.
- The Henderson–Hasselbalch equation shows that that when pH = pK_a, the acid and base concentration are equal. Thus, the colour will be a mixture of both the acid and base forms. Since there is at least 20 times higher acid concentration than base, the acidic form and colour predominate at pH < pK_a–1.0. Likewise, the basic form and colour predominate at pH > pK_a + 1.0 (Table 15.1).

Table 15.1 pH transition ranges and colours of some common indicators

Indicator	pH range	Colour in acid solution	Colour in alkaline solution
Thymol blue	1.2–2.8	Red	Yellow
Bromophenol blue	3.1–4.6	Yellow	Purple
Methyl orange	3.1–4.5	Red	Yellow
Methyl red	4.2–6.3	Red	Yellow
Bromothymol blue	6.0–7.5	Orange	Blue
Phenol red	6.4–8.2	Yellow	Red
Thymol blue(base)	8.1–9.6	Yellow	Blue
Phenolphthalein	8.0–9.8	Colourless	Pink
Thymophthalein	9.3–10.5	Colourless	Blue
Alizarin yellow	10.1–12.1	Yellow	Lilac

Titration curve: By constructing a titration curve, we can easily explain how the end point of a titration can be detected. A titration curve is constructed by plotting the pH of the solution as a function of the volume of titrant added. The titrant is always a strong acid or a strong base.

Acid–Base Titration

(Neutralisation method of analysis)

The reaction between an acid and a base is called *neutralisation*. It is very fast and the equilibrium constant for a neutralisation reaction is so large that it nearly proceeds to completion. It is a simple and convenient volumetric method. The reaction is characterised by a rapid change in pH near the equivalence point, which is detected by the colour change of the indicator (Table 15.2) that occurs at the end point. There are two general classes of neutralisation reactions.

(i) Determination of acid or base or their anhydride in a sample by titrating with a standard solution of base or acid.

(ii) Determination of salts of weak acids or bases by titrating with a standard solution of a strong base or acid.

The titration of a very weak base with a strong acid, and titration of a very weak acid with a strong base cannot be performed because a sharp end point cannot be observed for them. Usually when the acid is too weak to be titrated with a standard base, a salt of acid can be titrated with a standard base solution. For example, carbonic acid cannot be titrated by sodium hydroxide quantitatively, but sodium carbonate can be titrated by hydrochloric acid or sulfuric acid.

$$CO_3^{2-} + 2H^+ \longrightarrow H_2O + CO_2$$

For example, Na_2CO_3 (strong base) vs HCl (strong acid)

The titration of Na_2CO_3 vs HCl is a neutralisation titration (acidimetry and alkalimetry) which involves the neutralisation of an acid with the base. In this, sodium carbonate is attacked by dil. HCl in the following way.

$$Na_2CO_3 + 2\,HCl \longrightarrow NaCl + H_2O + CO_2$$

Methyl orange is used as an indicator for end point detection. In this titration, sodium carbonate is estimated by titrating it with a standard solution of HCl.

Table 15.2 Indicators in acid–base titrations

Acid-base titration	Indicators
Strong acid vs strong base	Bromothymol blue, phenolphthalein, methyl orange, thymophthalein
Strong acid vs weak base	Methyl orange, methyl red, bromocresol green
Weak acid vs strong base	Phenolphthalein, thymophthalein
Weak acid vs weak base	Phenol red

Redox Titrations

Reducing agents such as Fe, Fe^{2+}, H_2O_2, $CaOCl_2$, MnO_2 can be determined by suitable oxidising agents such as $KMnO_4$, $K_2Cr_2O_7$ in acidic, basic or neutral medium. These are called redox titrations. Such reactions are accompanied by a change in the valency of ions.

(i) Oxalic acid vs $KMnO_4$ titration: This is an example of a redox titration in which a reducing agent (such as oxalic acid) is estimated by titrating it with a standard solution of an oxidising agent (such as $KMnO_4$). Such reactions are accompanied by a change in the valency of ions. In these titrations, oxidation and reduction take place simultaneously, that is, while one substance is being oxidised, the other one is being reduced.

$$\underset{\text{Oxidising agent}}{2KMnO_4} + 3H_2SO_4 \longrightarrow K_2SO_4 + 2\,MnSO_4 + 3H_2O + 5[O] \quad (E_{KMnO_4} = M/5)$$

$$\underset{\text{Reducing agent}}{\begin{array}{c}COOH\\ |\\ COOH\end{array}} + 5[O] \longrightarrow 5H_2O + 10CO_2 \; (E_{H_2C_2O_4} = M/2)$$

- $KMnO_4$ acts as a self-indicator for end point detection.
- This titration is carried out in the presence of HCl or H_2SO_4 but not in the presence of conc. HNO_3 because it is a strong oxidising agent and hence interferes with the oxidising action of $KMnO_4$.
- In $KMnO_4$ vs oxalic acid titration, the oxalic acid solution is heated with dilute H_2SO_4 upto 70–80°C.

(ii) Mohr's salt, $FeSO_4.(NH_4)_2.6H_2O$ vs $KMnO_4$ titration: In this titration, the active constituent of ferrous ammonium sulfate (Mohr's salt) is ferrous sulfate, which is oxidised to ferric sulfate by acidified potassium permanganate.

$$2KMnO_4 + 3H_2SO_4 \longrightarrow K_2SO_4 + 2MnSO_4 + 3H_2O + 5[O] \quad (E_{KMnO_4} = M/5)$$

$$[2FeSO_4 + H_2SO_4 + [O] \longrightarrow Fe_2(SO_4)_3 + H_2O] \times 5$$

$$2KMnO_4 + 8H_2SO_4 + FeSO_4 \longrightarrow K_2SO_4 + 2MnSO_4 + 5Fe_2(SO_4)_3 + 8H_2O \quad (E_{FeSO_4} = M/1)$$

- $KMnO_4$ acts as a self-indicator for end point detection.
- This titration is carried out at room temperature because Mohr's salt is oxidised by air on heating.
- Sulfuric acid should be present in excess; otherwise, a brown precipitate due to the formation of MnO_2 will be formed.

15.5.2 Salt Analysis (Qualitative Analysis) of Inorganic Mixture

Qualitative analysis of a given inorganic mixture is done in the following steps.

Dry Tests

(i) Physical observation of salt or mixture: In physical examination, colour, smell and density of a given mixture are observed.

Observation	Inference
A. If colour of the substance is	
• Blue, its aqueous solution is also blue	Cupric salt
• Green, its aqueous solution is also green	Salts of nickel
• Dark green, its aqueous solution is also dark green but becomes light on dilution	Salts of chromium
• Violet–pink, its aqueous solution is pink	Salts of cobalt
• Light pink, its aqueous solution is colourless	Salts of manganese
• Reddish brown	Fe_2O_3
• Red	HgO, HgI_2, Pb_3O_4, Cu_2O
• Orange red	Sb_2S_3
• Black	CuO, NiO, SnO, FeS, CuS, HgS, PbS, CoS, FeO, Co_3O_4, Ni_2O_3, Cu_2S, $CuBr_2$, NiS
• Yellow	As_2S_3, CdS, Bi_2O_3, As_2S_5, PbI_2, AgI, chromates
• Yellow–green, aqueous solution is light green or almost colourless	Salts of Fe^{2+}
• Yellow–brown, aqueous solution is yellow	Salts of Fe^{3+}
• Colourless	Transition metals absent except some salts of Mn^{2+}
• Purple	Some Cr^{3+} salts and permanganates
B. Odour of the substance	
• Vinegar like smell	Acetates
• Rotten egg like smell	Sulfides
• Ammoniacal smell	Ammonia salts mainly $(NH_4)_2CO_3$; some ammonium salts and sulfides do not give smell
C. Density	
Mixture of salt is light	Salts of Zn, Bi, Al, Ba, Sr, Ca and Mg
Mixture of salts is heavy	Salts of Hg

(ii) Effect of heating: Take the given substance in a clear, dry test tube and heat it first gently and then strongly. Observe the changes that takes place upon heating.

Observation	Inference
Substance melts	Salts of alkali metals, chlorides of Hg, Ag and Pb and salts having water of crystallisation
Substance cracks	$Pb(NO_3)_2$, $Ba(NO_3)_2$, NaCl and KI
Substance swells	Alums, salts of phosphate and borate
Substance sublimes on heating and the colour of the sublimate is	
• White	$HgCl_2$, As_2O_3, Hg_2Cl_2, $AlCl_3$, Sb_2O_3, halides of NH_3
• Yellow	As_2S_3 and HgI_2
• Black	Sulfides of Hg, Sb, As
• Blue, yellow or violet vapours	Iodides
• Grey (having garlic odour)	As
Colour of residue obtained after heating (Residue mainly contains metallic oxides)	
• White and non-fusible	Oxides of Ca, Ba, Sr, Mg, Zn and Al
• Red–brown	Fe_2O_3
• Yellow–brown when hot, on cooling it is brown	SnO_2
• Black and infusible	NiO, MnO_2 and CuO
• Dark orange red in heating state and sublimes	HgO
• White, infusible, becomes yellow on heating	ZnO
• Initially, it is blue or green but becomes white on heating	$CuSO_4.5H_2O$
Observation of gases evolved	
(i) Colourless, odourless gas	
• O_2, which supports combustion	Nitrates of Na and K
• CO_2, which turns lime water milky	Carbonates and oxalates

Observation	Inference
(ii) Colourless, odourless gas	
• H_2S, smell of rotten eggs	Sulfides
• HCl, pungent smell and forms white fumes with NH_3	Hydrated chloride salts
• NH_3, turns red litmus blue	Ammonium salts
• SO_2, smell of burning sulfur	Sulfites and thiosulfate
(iii) Colourless, odourless gas	
• Cl_2, yellow–green pungent smelling gas	Chloride
• I_2, violet gas	Iodides
• Br_2, red–brown gas	Bromides
• NO_2, brown gas	Nitrates or nitrites of heavy metals

(iii) Smell of compound: Smell of the compound also gives an idea about the radical present in the salt.

Smell	Inference
Ammoniacal smell	Ammonium salts
Vinegar like smell	Acetates
Chlorine like smell	Hypochlorites

(iv) Solubility of salts:

Type of the salts	Observation
Nitrates and nitrites	All metal salts are soluble in water
Acetates	All metal acetates are soluble in water
Chlorides	All common chlorides are soluble in water except AgCl, Hg_2Cl_2 and $PbCl_2$
Bromides	All common bromides are soluble in water except AgBr, Hg_2Br_2 and $PbBr_2$ and $HgBr_2$
Iodides	All common chlorides are soluble in water except AgI, Hg_2I_2, HgI_2 and PbI_2
Sulfides	All common sulfides are insoluble in water except sulfides of group I andgroup II metals and ammonium ion
Carbonates	All common carbonates are insoluble in water except carbonates of group I and $(NH_4)_2CO_3$
Sulfates	All common sulfates are soluble in water except $PbSO_4$, Hg_2SO_4, $BaSO_4$, $CaSO_4$ and Ag_2SO_4 which are sparingly soluble
Phosphates	All common phosphates are insoluble in water except phosphates of group I and $(NH_4)_3PO_4$
Hydroxides	All common metal hydroxides are insoluble in water except group I hydroxides and $Ba(OH)_2$, $Sr(OH)_2$ and $Ca(OH)_2$

(v) Flame test: This test is based upon the fact that in a state of high ionisation of chloride, some of the cations impart characteristic colour to the flame, as the cation absorbs energy from the flame and transmits the same, as light of a characteristic colour. In this method, a paste of the salt and conc. HCl is taken into the lower oxidising zone and colour imparted to the flame by the salt is observed. Salts, particularly of group V (Ba^{2+}, Ca^{2+}, Sr^{2+}), are identified by colours of the flame.

Colour in flame test

Colour	Cation
Golden yellow	Na^+
Violet	K^+
Carmine red	Li^+
Brick red	Ca^{2+}
Apple green	Ba^{2+} , Mo^{2+}
Green	Cu^{2+}, BO_3^{3-}, Tl^{3+}
Crimson red	Sr^{2+}
Blue	Cu^{2+}, As^{3+}, Sb^{3+}, Bi^{3+}

(vi) Charcoal cavity test: When a salt is fused with anhydrous Na_2CO_3 or oxidising mixture in a cavity on a charcoal block in a reducing flame, first the metal carbonate is formed followed by the metal oxide. For example,

$$M(NO_3)_2 + Na_2CO_3 \; MCO_3 + 2NaNO_3$$
$$MCO_3 \longrightarrow MO + CO_2\uparrow$$

These metallic oxides get reduced to metals by the action of carbon present in the reducing flame. On cooling, these metals form beads.

$$MO + C \longrightarrow M + CO\uparrow$$

Colours in the charcoal cavity test with different ions are shown below.

Colour in charcoal cavity test

Sample bead	Crust	Inference
Greyish white soft bead which marks paper	Brown which turns yellow on cooling	Pb^{2+}
Lustrous white bead	—	Ag^{+}
White-brown bead	Orange which turns yellow on cooling	Bi^{3+}
Garlic-like smelly fumes without bead	—	As^{3+}
—	Red-brown precipitate, easily turns into vapours	Cd^{2+}
Smell of ammonia	Red	NH_4^+
—	Black precipitate	Fe^{3+}, Co^{2+}, Mn^{2+}

(vii) Cobalt nitrate test: In this test, 1–2 drops of cobalt nitrate is added to the infusible mass obtained in the charcoal cavity and heated in the oxidising flame. The infusible mass contains metallic oxides like CaO, Al_2O_3, MgO and ZnO. The colours of some ions in the cobalt nitrate test are as follows.

Colour in cobalt nitrate test

Colour of the residue	Inference
Green	Zn^{2+}
Pink-dirty residue	Mg^{2+}
Bluish green	Sn^{2+}
Blue	Al^{3+}, PO_4^{3-}, BO_3^{3-}

Cobalt nitrate should not be used in excess, otherwise black coloured cobalt (Co_3O_4), may be formed and it is difficult to identify other colours in the presence of black colour.

(viii) Borax bead test: If borax, $Na_2B_4O_7.10H_2O$, is heated on a platinum loop, a transparent colourless glass-like bead of sodium metaborate ($NaBO_2$) and boric anhydride (B_2O_3) is formed.

$$Na_2B_4O_7 \longrightarrow 2\,NaBO_2 + B_2O_3$$

Characteristic coloured beads are produced with salts of Cu, Fe, Cr, Mn, Co and Ni. The colour of the bead depends upon the flame in which it has been heated.

$$CuO + B_2O_3 \longrightarrow \underset{\substack{\text{Copper(II) metaborate}\\ \text{(green when hot and blue}\\ \text{when cold)}}}{Cu(BO_2)_2} \text{ (Oxidising flame)}$$

$$2Cu(BO_2)_2 + C \longrightarrow 2CuBO_2 + B_2O_3 + CO\uparrow \text{ (Reducing flame)}$$

$$2\,CuBO_2 + C \longrightarrow \underset{\text{Red}}{2\,Cu\downarrow} + B_2O_3 + CO\uparrow$$

Colours of some ions shown in borax bead test are given below.

Colour in borax bead test

Oxidising flame		Reducing flame		Metal
Hot	Cold	Hot	Cold	
Green	Blue	Colourless	Opaque Red-brown	Cu
Yellowish Brown	yellow	Green	Green	Fe
Yellow	Green	Green	Green	Cr
Violet	Amethyst	Colourless	Colourless	Mn
Blue	Blue	Blue	Blue	Co
Violet	Reddish Brown	Grey	Grey	Ni
Yellow	Colourless	Brown	Brown	Mo
Rose-violet	Rose violet	Red Violet		Au
Yellow	Colourless	Yellow	Yellowish to brown	W
Yellow	pale-yellow	Green green	Bottle	U
Yellow	Greenish-yellow	Brownish	Emerald green	V
Yellow	Colourless	Grey	Pale violet	Ti
Orange-red	Colourless	Colourless	Colourless	Ce

(ix) Microcosmic salt bead test: A test similar to borax bead test is used for identification of coloured cations, if microcosmic salt $Na(NH_4)HPO_4.4H_2O$ is used.

$$Na(NH_4)HPO_4 \longrightarrow NaPO_3 + H_2O\uparrow + NH_3\uparrow$$

$$NaPO_3 + CoO \longrightarrow \underset{\text{Blue bead}}{NaCoPO_4}$$

Colours of some ions shown in microcosmic bead test are as follows.

Colour obtained in microcosmic salt bead test

Oxidising flame	Reducing flame	Metal
Green when hot, blue when cold	Colourless when hot, red when cold	Cu
Yellow or red-brown when hot, yellow when cold	Yellow when hot, colourless to green when cold	Fe
Green, hot and cold	Green, hot and cold	Cr
Violet, hot and cold	Colourless, hot and cold	Mn

Oxidising flame	Reducing flame	Metal
Blue, hot and cold	Blue, hot and cold	Co
Brown, hot and cold	Grey when cold	Ni
Yellow, hot and cold	Green when cold	V
Yellow when hot, yellow green when cold	Green, hot and cold	U
Pale yellow when hot, colourless when cold	Green when hot, blue when cold	W
Colourless, hot and cold	Yellow when hot, violet when cold	Ti

(x) Sodium carbonate bead test: The sodium carbonate bead is prepared by fusing a small quantity of sodium carbonate on a platinum wire loop in the Bunsen flame; a white opaque bead is formed. If this is moistened, dipped into a little KNO_3 and then into a small quantity of the given salt and heated in the oxidising flame, a coloured bead is formed. For example,

$$MnO+Na_2CO_3+O_2 \longrightarrow \underset{\substack{\text{Sodium manganate}\\\text{(green bead)}}}{Na_2MnO_4} + CO_2\uparrow$$

$$Cr_2O_3+4\,Na_2CO_3+3O_2 \longrightarrow 4\,Na_2CrO_4+4\,CO_2\uparrow$$

Wet tests

- In wet analysis, the substance is first dissolved in water to bring it in solution form and is analysed for acid and basic radicals.
- In the analysis of an inorganic salt mixture, first the acid radicals are analysed and then the basic radicals.

Analysis of Acid Radicals

Following sequence is adopted to analyse the acid radical

(i) Analysis of first group anions (CO_3^{2-}, S^{2-}, NO_2^-): Acidic radicals or anions of the first group, when treated with dil. H_2SO_4 (group reagent) evolve gases with characteristic colour and smell. On the basis of gases released, anions are identified.

Test for CO_3^{2-}

Experiment	Observation	Inference
Take mixture in a dry test tube and add dil. HCl or H_2SO_4, warm gently	Brisk effervescence with the evolution of colourless and odourless gas (CO_2)	May be CO_3^{2-}
Pass the evolved gas into lime water [$Ca(OH)_2$]	Lime water turns milky	CO_3^{2-} confirmed
Pass excess lime water to the evolved gas	Milkiness disappears	CO_3^{2-} confirmed

Reactions involved in the test of carbonate (CO_3^{2-})

- $Na_2CO_3+2HCl \longrightarrow 2\,NaCl+H_2O+\underset{\substack{\text{Colourless,}\\\text{Odourless Gas}}}{CO_2\uparrow}$
- $Ca(OH)_2+CO_2 \longrightarrow \underset{\substack{\text{Calcium carbonate}\\\text{(milky)}}}{CaCO_3\downarrow}+H_2O$
- $CaCO_3+H_2O+CO_2(\text{excess}) \longrightarrow \underset{\substack{\text{Calcium bicarbonate}\\\text{(colourless)}}}{Ca(HCO_3)_2}$

Tests for S^{2-}

Experiment	Observation	Inference
Take mixture in a dry test tube and add dil. HCl or H_2SO_4 and warm gently	A colourless gas (H_2S) with a smell of rotten eggs evolved	May be S^{2-}
Bring filter paper dipped in lead acetate over the mouth of test tube	Filter paper turns black due to formation of PbS	S^{2-} confirmed

Reactions involved in the test of sulfide (S^{2-})

(i) $Na_2S+H_2SO_4 \longrightarrow H_2S+Na_2SO_4$

(ii) $(CH_3COO)_2Pb+H_2S \longrightarrow \underset{\text{Black}}{PbS\downarrow}+2\,CH_3COOH$

Tests for nitrate (NO_3^-)

Experiment	Observation	Inference
Take mixture in a dry test tube and add dil. HCl or H_2SO_4 and warm gently	Brown fumes (NO_2) with pungent odour are evolved	May be NO_2^-
Take filter paper dipped in (starch + KI) solution, on the mouth of test tube	Evolved gas turns filter paper blue	NO_2^- confirmed
Add 2–3 drops of KI and starch solution in the test tube	Deep blue or violet colour appears	NO_2^- confirmed

Reactions involved in the test of nitrite (NO_2^-)

- $NaNO_2+H_2SO_4 \longrightarrow Na_2SO_4+2\,HNO_2$
  $3\,HNO_2 \longrightarrow HNO_3+2\,NO\uparrow+H_2O$
  $2\,NO+O_2 \longrightarrow \underset{\text{(brown)}}{2\,NO_2\uparrow}$
- $2\,KI+2NO_2 \longrightarrow 2\,KNO_2+I_2$
  $I_2+\text{Starch} \longrightarrow \text{Blue colour}$

(ii) Analysis of second group anions (Cl^-, Br^-, I^-, NO_3^-): Acidic radicals or anions of the second group give no response with dil. acids. However, with conc. acids (conc. H_2SO_4 is the group reagent), they evolve gases with characteristic colour and smell; thus, they can be identified by using conc. acids.

Tests for chloride (Cl^-)

Experiment	Observation	Inference
Heat the mixture with 1–2 mL conc. H_2SO_4 in a dry test tube	A colourless, pungent gas (HCl) is evolved	May be Cl^-
Bring a glass rod dipped in NH_4OH near the mouth of test tube	White dense fumes of NH_4Cl are evolved	Cl^- confirmed
Heat the mixture with conc. H_2SO_4 and MnO_2 in a dry test tube	Greenish-yellow (Cl_2) pungent gas is evolved	Cl^- confirmed
Chromyl chloride test • Heat the mixture with solid $K_2Cr_2O_7$ and conc. H_2SO_4 • Collect evolved vapours in a test tube containing NaOH. Acidify it with acetic acid and add lead acetate solution	Orange-yellow vapours of chromyl-chloride (CrO_2Cl_2) are evolved A yellow ppt. or solution of lead chromate is formed	Cl^- confirmed

Reactions involved in the test of chloride (Cl^-)

- $NaCl + H_2SO_4 \longrightarrow NaHSO_4 + \underset{\text{Pungent smelling gas}}{HCl\uparrow}$
- $HCl + NH_4OH \longrightarrow \underset{\text{White fumes}}{NH_4Cl\uparrow} + H_2O$
- $2\,NaCl + MnO_2 + 3\,H_2SO_4 \longrightarrow 2\,NaHSO_4 + MnSO_4 + 2\,H_2O + \underset{\text{Yellowish green}}{Cl_2\uparrow}$

Chromyl chloride test

- $4\,NaCl + K_2Cr_2O_7 + 3\,H_2SO_4 \longrightarrow \underset{\text{(Chromyl Chloride) (orange–yellow gas)}}{CrO_2Cl_2} + 2Na_2SO_4 + K_2SO_4 + 3\,H_2O$
- $CrO_2Cl_2 + 4NaOH \longrightarrow \underset{\text{Yellow}}{Na_2CrO_4} + 2\,NaCl + 2\,H_2O$
- $(CH_3COO)_2Pb + Na_2CrO_4 \longrightarrow \underset{\text{Yellow}}{PbCrO_4\downarrow} + 2CH_3COONa$

Note: If a mixture contains chlorate, chromyl chloride test for chloride anion should not be performed because chlorates on reaction with H_2SO_4 form chlorine dioxide gas which dissolves in H_2SO_4 and forms a highly explosive orange yellow solution.

$$3\,KClO_3 + 3\,H_2SO_4 \longrightarrow 2\,ClO_2\uparrow + ClO_4^- + 3\,SO_4^{2-} + 4\,H^+ + 3K^+ + H_2O$$

Tests for bromide (Br^-)

Experiment	Observation	Inference
Heat the mixture with 1–2 mL conc. H_2SO_4 in a dry test tube	A colourless, pungent gas (HBr) or sometimes brown fumes are evolved	May be Br^-
Heat the mixture with MnO_2 and conc. H_2SO_4	Red–brown vapour of Br_2 evolved	Br^- confirmed
To the solution of mixture in dil. HNO_3, add $AgNO_3$ solution	A pale-yellow ppt. of AgBr is formed (hardly soluble in NH_4OH)	Br^- confirmed

Reactions involved in the test of bromide (Br^-)

$$NaBr + H_2SO_4\,(Conc.) \longrightarrow NaHSO_4 + HBr\uparrow$$

$$2\,HBr + H_2SO_4\,(Conc.) \longrightarrow 2\,H_2O + SO_2\uparrow + \underset{\text{Reddish-brown}}{Br_2\uparrow}$$

$$2\,NaBr + MnO_2 + 3\,H_2SO_4 \longrightarrow 2\,NaHSO_4 + MnSO_4 + 2H_2O + \underset{\text{Reddish-brown}}{Br_2\uparrow}$$

$$NaBr + AgNO_3 \longrightarrow \underset{\text{Pale yellow}}{AgBr} + NaNO_3$$

$$AgBr + 2\,NH_4OH \longrightarrow \underset{\text{Diammine silver(I) bromide (hardly soluble)}}{[Ag(NH_3)_2]Br} + 2\,H_2O$$

Tests for iodide (I^-)

Experiment	Observation	Inference
Heat the mixture with 1–3 mL conc. H_2SO_4 in a dry test tube	Dark violet fumes (I_2) are evolved	May be I^-
Heat the mixture with MnO_2 and conc. H_2SO_4	Violet vapours in excess are evolved	May be I^-
Bring a paper dipped in starch solution on the mouth of test tube	Paper turns blue	I^- confirmed
To the solution of mixture in dil. HNO_3, add $AgNO_3$ solution	A yellow ppt. of AgI is formed (insoluble in NH_4OH)	I^- confirmed

Reactions involved in the tests of iodide (I^-)

$$NaI + H_2SO_4\ (conc.) \longrightarrow HI + NaHSO_4$$

$$H_2SO_4 + 2HI \longrightarrow \underset{\text{Violet vapours}}{I_2\uparrow} + SO_2 + 2\,H_2O$$

$$2\,NaI + MnO_2 + 3\,H_2SO_4 \longrightarrow I_2\uparrow + 2\,NaHSO_4 + MnSO_4 + 2\,H_2O$$

$$I_2 + Starch \longrightarrow \text{Blue colour}$$

$$NaI + AgNO_3 \longrightarrow AgI\downarrow + NaNO_3$$

$$AgI + NH_4OH \longrightarrow \underset{\text{Yellow ppt. (insoluble)}}{[Ag(NH_3)_2]I} + H_2O$$

Tests for nitrate (NO_3^-)

Experiment	Observation	Inference
Heat the mixture with 1–2 mL conc. H_2SO_4 in a dry test tube	Pungent light brown gas (NO_2) is evolved	May be (NO_3^-)
Heat the mixture with copper turnings and conc. H_2SO_4	Deep brown fumes (NO_2) in excess are evolved	May be (NO_3^-)
Brown ring test: To the solution of mixture in dil. HCl, add a freshly prepared solution of $FeSO_4$. Shake well and gradually add conc. H_2SO_4 along the sides of the test tube	A brown ring of $FeSO_4.NO$ is formed at the junction of two liquids	(NO_3^-) confirmed

Reactions involved in the test of nitrate (NO_3^-)

$$NaNO_3 + H_2SO_4\ (conc.) \longrightarrow NaHSO_4 + HNO_3$$

$$4\,HNO_3 \longrightarrow \underset{\text{(brown)}}{4\,NO_2\uparrow} + O_2\uparrow + 2\,H_2O$$

$$3\,Cu + 8\,HNO_3 \longrightarrow 3\,Cu(NO_3)_2 + 2\,NO\uparrow + 4H_2O$$

$$2\,NO + O_2 \longrightarrow 2\,NO_2\uparrow$$

Ring test

$$6\,FeSO_4 + 2\,HNO_3 + 3\,H_2SO_4 \longrightarrow 3Fe_2(SO_4)_3 + 4\,H_2O + 2\,NO\uparrow$$

$$FeSO_4 + NO \longrightarrow \underset{\text{Ferrous nitroso sulfate (brown ring)}}{FeSO_4.NO}$$

(iii) Analysis of third group anions (SO_4^{2-})

Third group radical is identified on the basis of the precipitate obtained.

Tests for sulfate (SO_4^{2-})

Radical or anion	Experiment	Observation	Inference
Sulfate (SO_4^{2-})	In the solution of mixture, add $BaCl_2$ solution	A curdy white ppt. ($BaSO_4$) is formed (insoluble in all conc. acids)	May be SO_4^{2-}
	In the solution of mixture, add lead acetate solution	White ppt. of $PbSO_4$ is formed	SO_4^{2-} confirmed

Reactions involved in the above test of sulfate (SO_4^{2-})

$$Na_2SO_4 + BaCl_2 \longrightarrow BaSO_4\downarrow + 2\,NaCl$$

$$CH_3COO)_2Pb + Na_2SO_4 \longrightarrow \underset{\text{White}}{PbSO_4\downarrow} + 2\,CH_3COONa$$

Analysis of Basic Radicals (Cations)

Basic radicals have been classified into six groups on the basis of the solubility products of their salts with the group reagent. The radicals have been grouped in the order of increasing solubility product (Table 15.3).

Table 15.3 Basic radicals

Group	Basic radicals	Group reagent	Precipitate as	Explanation
(I)	Ag^+, Hg_2^{2+}, Pb^{2+}	Dil. HCl	Chlorides ($AgCl$, Hg_2Cl_2, $PbCl_2$)	K_{sp} values of chlorides are low, hence precipitated. Others have higher K_{sp} values, hence not precipitated
(II)	Cu^{2+}, Cd^{2+}, Pb^{2+}, Hg^{2+}, Bi^{3+}, Sb^{3+}, Sn^{2+}, As^{3+}	H_2S gas in presence of dil. HCl	Sulfides (CuS, As_2S_3 …)	K_{sp} value of II group sulfides are low, hence precipitated by low [S^{2-}] ions. HCl (due to common H^+ ion) decreases the ionisation of weak acid H_2S which gives low [S^{2-}] ions. Hence, group II sulfides are precipitated while other with high K_{sp} values are not precipitated
(III)	Al^{3+}, Cr^{3+}, Fe^{3+}	NH_4OH in presence of NH_4Cl	Hydroxides [$Al(OH)_3$]	K_{sp} values of III group hydroxides are low. NH_4Cl decreases ionisation of weak NH_4OH due to common ion effect. Low [OH^-] is only sufficient to precipitate group III cations as their hydroxides.

Group	Basic radicals	Group reagent	Precipitate as	Explanation
(IV)	Zn^{2+}, Ni^{2+}, Mn^{2+}, Co^{2+}	H_2S in ammoniacal medium	Sulfides (ZnS, NiS)	K_{sp} values of sulfides of group IV are high. Ionisation of H_2S increases in basic medium. Hence, group IV cations are precipitated as sulfides due to increasing $[S^{2-}]$.
(V)	Ca^{2+}, Ba^{2+}, Sr^{2+}	$(NH_4)_2CO_3 + NH_4Cl$	Carbonates ($CaCO_3$, $BaCO_3$, $SrCO_3$)	K_{sp} values of carbonates are less than that of group VI (Mg^{2+}) hence, precipitated before Mg^{2+}
(VI)	Mg^{2+} (Na^+, K^+) also included	NH_4OH + Na_2HPO_4(only for Mg^{2+})	White precipitate ($MgHPO_4$)	
Zero	NH_4^+	Dilute NaOH	NH_3 gas is evolved	

Preparation of original solution: To prepare a transparent solution of salt, the following solvents are used, strictly in the order (i) cold water, (ii) hot water, (iii) dilute HCl. (iv) conc. HCl.

Note: HNO_3 and H_2SO_4 cannot be used to prepare original solution because both are oxidising agents

(i) Analysis of group I cations (basic radicals)
In cold original solution, dilute HCl is added drop by drop. Formation of white precipitate indicates the presence of group I. Cations of group I are precipitated as chlorides such as AgCl, $PbCl_2$ and Hg_2Cl_2. Among these chlorides, only $PbCl_2$ is soluble in hot water. Hence, the hot filtrate contains Pb^{2+} ions.

Tests for lead

Experiment	Observation	Inference
To the hot filtrate add $K_2Cr_2O_7$	Yellow ppt. of $PbCrO_4$ is obtained which is soluble in NaOH but insoluble in CH_3COOH	Indicates the presence of Pb^{2+}
To the hot filtrate add KI	Yellow ppt. of PbI_2 is formed	Pb^{2+} confirmed
Dilute H_2SO_4 is added to hot filtrate and the mixture is cooled	White ppt. of $PbSO_4$ is obtained which is soluble in CH_3COONH_4 solution	Pb^{2+} confirmed

Reactions involved in the above tests of Pb^{2+}

$$\underset{\text{(cold O.S)}}{Pb^{2+}} + \underset{\text{from HCl}}{2Cl^-} \longrightarrow \underset{\text{White ppt.}}{PbCl_2}$$

$PbCl_2$ is soluble in hot water, hence filtrate contains $PbCl_2$

$$\underset{\text{(Hot and soluble)}}{PbCl_2} + K_2Cr_2O_7 \longrightarrow \underset{\text{Yellow ppt.}}{PbCrO_4\downarrow} + 2\,KCl$$

$$PbCrO_4 + 4NaOH \longrightarrow \underset{\substack{\text{Sodium plumbite}\\ \text{(soluble)}}}{Na_2PbO_2} + Na_2CrO_4$$

$$PbCl_2 + 2KI \longrightarrow \underset{\text{Yellow}}{PbI_2} + 2KCl$$

$$PbCl_2 + H_2SO_4 \longrightarrow \underset{\text{White ppt.}}{PbSO_4\downarrow} + 2\,HCl$$

$$PbSO_4 + 2\,CH_3COONH_4 \longrightarrow \underset{\text{Soluble}}{(CH_3COO)_2Pb} + (NH_4)_2SO_4$$

(ii) Analysis of Group II cations
Add dilute HCl in filtrate of group I and pass H_2S gas in warm solution. Formation of a coloured precipitate indicates the presence of group II cations. Sulfides of group II B cations (As_2S_3, SnS, Sb_2S_3) are soluble in yellow ammonium sulfide while sulfides of group II A (PbS, CdS, CuS, Bi_2S_3) cations are soluble in HNO_3 (HgS is soluble in aqua regia).

Tests for copper

Experiment	Observation	Inference
To the black ppt. of CuS add HNO_3	Blue coloured solution is obtained	It indicates the presence of Cu^{2+}
Divide the blue solution obtained into three parts		
(i) Add CH_3COOH and $K_4[Fe(CN)_6]$ to the first part	Chocolate brown ppt. is formed	Cu^{2+} confirmed
(ii) Add aqueous NH_3(excess) to the second part of the blue solution	Deep blue solution is obtained	Cu^{2+} confirmed
(iii) Add KSCN in the third part of blue solution	Black ppt. is obtained	Cu^{2+} confirmed

Reactions involved in the above tests of cation (Cu^{2+})

$$\underset{\text{Black ppt.}}{3CuS} + 8\,HNO_3 \longrightarrow \underset{\text{Soluble blue}}{3\,Cu(NO_3)_2} + 2\,NO + 3S + 4\,H_2O$$

$$Cu(NO_3)_2 + 2\,CH_3COOH \longrightarrow (CH_3COO)_2Cu + 2HNO_3$$

$$2\,(CH_3COO)_2Cu + K_4[Fe(CN)_6] \longrightarrow \underset{\text{Chocolate brown ppt.}}{Cu_2[Fe(CN)_6]} + 4\,CH_3COOK$$

$$Cu^{2+} + 4\,NH_3(\text{excess}) \longrightarrow [Cu(NH_3)_4]^{2+}$$

$$Cu(NO_3)_2 + 2\,KSCN \longrightarrow \underset{\text{Black ppt.}}{Cu(SCN)_2} + 2KNO_3$$

(iii) Analysis of group III cations (Fe^{3+}, Al^{3+}, Cr^{3+})

Add few drops of conc. HNO_3 to the filtrate of group II to remove H_2S. Add NH_4Cl and NH_4OH. Group III cations (if present) are precipitated as their hydroxides—[$Fe(OH)_3$] red–brown ppt., $Cr(OH)_3$ dirty green ppt., $Al(OH)_3$ white gelatinous ppt.

Tests for aluminium (Al^{3+})

Experiment	Observation	Inference
Add NaOH solution in excess to white gelatinous ppt.	White gelatinous ppt. dissolves due to the formation of sodium metaaluminate	It indicates the presence of Al^{3+}
In soluble metaaluminate add NH_4Cl and boil	White gelatinous ppt. of $Al(OH)_3$ reappears	Al^{3+} confirmed

Reactions involved in the above tests of cation (Al^{3+})

$$\underset{\text{White ppt.}}{Al(OH)_3} + NaOH \longrightarrow \underset{\substack{\text{Sodium metaaluminate}\\ \text{(soluble)}}}{NaAlO_2} + 2H_2O$$

$$NaAlO_2 + NH_4Cl + H_2O NaCl + \longrightarrow \underset{\substack{\text{White}\\ \text{gelatinous}}}{Al(OH)_3} + NH_3$$

Tests for iron (Fe^{3+})

Experiment	Observation	Inference
Add dilute HCl to red–brown ppt. and divide it into two parts	Precipitate dissolves	Fe^{3+} confirmed
1. Add $K_4[Fe(CN)_6]$ to the first part of above solution	Dark blue colour is obtained	Fe^{3+} confirmed
2. Add KCNS to the second part of the solution	Dark (blood) red colour is obtained	Fe^{3+} confirmed

Reactions involved in the above tests of cation (Fe^{3+})

$$Fe(OH)_3 + 3\,HCl \longrightarrow \underset{\text{Reddish brown ppt.}}{FeCl_3} + 3H_2O$$

$$4\,FeCl_3 + 3K_4[Fe(CN)_6] \longrightarrow \underset{\substack{\text{Ferric ferrocyanide}\\ \text{(dark blue colour)}}}{Fe_4[Fe(CN)_6]_3} + 12KCl$$

$$FeCl_3 + \underset{\substack{\text{Potassium}\\ \text{sulfocyanide}}}{KCNS} \longrightarrow \underset{\substack{\text{Ferrithiocyanate}\\ \text{(blood red colour)}}}{[Fe(CNS)]Cl_2} + KCl$$

(iv) Analysis of group IV cations (Zn^{2+}, Ni^{2+}, Co^{2+} and Mn^{2+})

Add NH_4OH to the filtrate of group III and pass H_2S. In alkaline medium, H_2S is highly ionised so, concentration of S^{2-} is high. Due to this, group IV cations are precipitated as sulfides (ZnS, MnS, CoS and NiS).

Tests for nickel

Experiment	Observation	Inference
Dissolve the black ppt. of NiS in aqua regia (3 parts conc. HCl + 1 part conc. HNO_3) and divide it into two parts	Soluble chloride formed	It indicates the presence of Ni^{2+}
Add NH_4OH and dimethyl glyoxime to the solution	Cherry red ppt.	Ni^{2+} confirmed
Add potassium cyanide solution and heat, add $NaOH/Br_2$ water and again heat	Black ppt. is obtained	Ni^{2+} confirmed

Reactions involved in the test of cation (Ni^{2+})

$$3\,NiS + \underbrace{6\,HCl + 2HNO_3}_{\text{Aquaregia}} \longrightarrow 3\,NiCl_2 + 2NO + 3S + 4\,H_2O$$

$$NiCl_2 + \underset{\text{Dimethyl glyoxime}}{2\begin{matrix}CH_3\text{–}C\text{=NOH}\\ |\\ CH_3\text{–}C\text{=NOH}\end{matrix}} \longrightarrow \underset{\substack{\text{Cherry red ppt.}\\ \text{(Dimethyl glyoximate)}}}{\begin{matrix} & O\text{---}H\text{–}O & \\ H_3C\text{–}C\text{=}N & \searrow Ni \swarrow & N\text{=}C\text{–}CH_3 \\ H_3C\text{–}C\text{=}N & \nearrow \quad \nwarrow & N\text{=}C\text{–}CH_3 \\ & O\text{–}H\text{---}O & \end{matrix}}$$

$$NiCl_2 + 4\,KCN \longrightarrow \underset{\text{Potassium nickel cyanide}}{K_2[Ni(CN)_4]} + 2\,KCl$$

$$2\,NaOH + Br_2 \longrightarrow NaOBr + NaBr + H_2O$$

$$2\,K_2[Ni(CN)_4] + NaOBr + 4\,NaOH \longrightarrow Ni_2O_3 + 4KCN + 4NaCN + NaBr + 2H_2O$$

Tests for zinc

Experiment	Observation	Inference
Dissolve the white ppt. of ZnS in dil. HCl and divide it into two parts	Soluble chloride is formed	It indicates the presence of Zn^{2+}
Add NaOH to the solution. White ppt. is obtained which is soluble in excess of NaOH	White ppt. of ZnS reappears on passing H_2S into soluble sodium zincate solution	Zn^{2+} confirmed

Experiment	Observation	Inference
Acidify the solution with acetic acid and add $K_4[Fe(CN)_6]$	Bluish white ppt. is obtained	Zn^{2+} confirmed

Reactions involved in the test of cation (Zn^{2+})

$$ZnS + 2\,HCl \longrightarrow ZnCl_2 + H_2S$$

$$ZnCl_2 + 2\,NaOH \longrightarrow \underset{\text{White ppt.}}{Zn(OH)_2\downarrow} + 2\,NaCl$$

$$Zn(OH)_2 + 2\,NaOH \longrightarrow \underset{\text{Sodium zincate (soluble)}}{Na_2ZnO_2} + 2H_2O$$

$$Na_2ZnO_2 + H_2S \longrightarrow 2\,NaOH + \underset{\text{White ppt.}}{ZnS\downarrow}$$

$$2\,ZnCl_2 + K_4[Fe(CN)_6] \longrightarrow \underset{\text{Bluish white ppt.}}{Zn_2[Fe(CN)_6]\downarrow} + 4\,KCl$$

(v) Analysis of group V cations (Ba^{2+}, Sr^{2+}, Ca^{2+})

Boil off H_2S from the filtrate of group IV and add NH_4OH and $(NH_4)_2CO_3$. Formation of a white ppt. indicates the presence of group V cations. Group V cations are precipitated as their carbonates ($CaCO_3$, $BaCO_3$ and $SrCO_3$).

Tests for barium

Experiment	Observation	Inference
Dissolve the ppt. in acetic acid and heat it gently, add potassium chromate solution and heat again	Yellow ppt. appears	Ba^{2+} confirmed

Reactions involved in the test of cation (Ba^{2+})

$$\underset{\text{White ppt.}}{BaCO_3} + 2\,CH_3COOH \longrightarrow (CH_3COO)_2Ba + H_2O + CO_2$$

$$(CH_3COO)_2Ba + K_2CrO_4 \longrightarrow \underset{\text{Barium chromate (yellow ppt.)}}{BaCrO_4\downarrow} + 2\,CH_3COOK$$

Tests for calcium

Experiment	Observation	Inference
Dissolve the ppt. in acetic acid, add ammonium oxalate solution (excess) and heat	White ppt. appears	Ca^{2+} confirmed
Acidify the white ppt. obtained above by adding dilute CH_3COOH and add$KMnO_4$ solution drop wise and HCl	Pink colour of $KMnO_4$ disappears	Ca^{2+} confirmed

Reactions involved in the test of cation (Ca^{2+})

$$\underset{\text{White ppt.}}{CaCO_3} + 2CH_3COOH \xrightarrow{\Delta} (CH_3COO)_2Ca + H_2O + CO_2$$

$$(CH_3COO)_2Ca + (NH_4)_2C_2O_4 \longrightarrow \underset{\text{White ppt.}}{CaC_2O_4\downarrow} + 2CH_3COONH_4$$

$$5CaC_2O_4 + \underset{\text{Pink}}{2KMnO_4} + 16HCl \longrightarrow 5CaCl_2 + \underset{\text{Colourless}}{2MnCl_2} + 10CO_2 + 8H_2O + 2KCl$$

(vi) Analysis of group VI (Mg^{2+})

Experiment	Observation	Inference
Filtrate of the group V is heated with NH_4OH and Na_2HPO_4	A fine crystalline ppt. on scratching the side of the test tube	Mg^{2+} confirmed

Reactions involved in the test of cation (Mg^{2+})

$$MgCl_2 + \underset{\text{Disodium hydrogen phosphate}}{Na_2HPO_4} + NH_4OH \rightarrow \underset{\text{Magnesium ammonium phosphate (white ppt.)}}{Mg(NH_4)PO_4} + 2\,NaCl + H_2O$$

(vii) Analysis of zero group cation (NH_4^+)

Ammonium salts are decomposed by alkali and NH_3 is liberated which can be identified by a number of methods.

Tests for ammonium

Experiment	Observation	Inference
Take small amount of mixture in the test tube and heat it with NaOH solution	Smell of ammonia	NH_4^+ confirmed
Bring a glass rod moistened with conc. HCl near the mouth of the test tube	White fumes are formed	NH_4^+ confirmed
Take small amount of salt in the test tube, add NaOH and heat. Add Nessler's reagent to the solution	Brown ppt. is obtained	NH_4^+ confirmed

Reactions involved in the tests of cation NH_4^+

$$\underset{\text{From mixture}}{NH_4Cl} + NaOH \xrightarrow{\Delta} NH_3 + NaCl + H_2O$$

$$NH_3 + HCl \longrightarrow \underset{\text{Ammonium chloride (white fumes)}}{NH_4Cl}$$

$$NH_3 + 3\,NaOH + \underset{\text{Nessler's reagent}}{2K_2HgI_4} \longrightarrow \underset{\text{Iodide of Millon's base (brown ppt.)}}{O\langle{}^{Hg}_{Hg}\rangle NH_2I} + 4KI + 3NaI + 2H_2O$$

15.6 Enthalpy of Dissolution of Copper Sulfate

Molar heat of solution is the heat absorbed or released when the molecules of that substance get dissolved in water. It is denoted by ΔH. The overall heat of the solution can be either endothermic or exothermic, depending on the relative amount of energy needed to break bonds initially, as well as how much is released upon the formation of solute–solvent bonds.

During thermochemical measurement, aqueous solutions are mixed in water (medium). Change in temperature during the reaction or dissolution is measured using which molar enthalpy can be calculated. The sum of enthalpy changes occurring in the calorimeter due to either loss or gain of energy, must be zero, according to the law of conservation of energy.

Procedure:

- Take 100 mL of distilled water in the beaker with a constant calorimeter and placed it on a wooden block in a larger 500 mL beaker (Fig. 15.2).
- Pack the empty space with cotton wool between the bigger and the smaller beakers and then cover with cardboard.

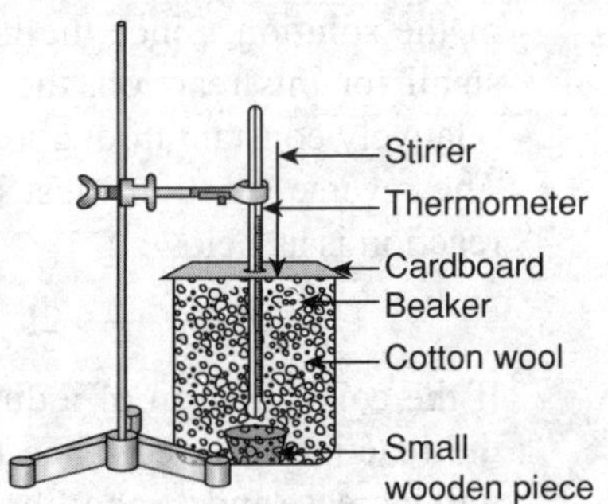

Fig. 15.2 Determination of calorimeter constant

- Record the temperature of water. Let it be T_1°C.
- Transfer copper sulfate powder which is already weighed. See that all the added solid completely dissolves.
- Keep the thermometer and stirrer intact on the foam case mouth.
- Note down the solution's maximum temperature after copper sulfate is dissolved. Let it be T_2°C.
- Total mass of the solution = Mass of the solvent + Mass of solute

$$= (100 + W_1) \text{ g}$$

(Assuming density of water to be equal to 1 gL^{-1} at the experimental temperature)

Change in temperature = $(T_2 - T_1)$°C

Enthalpy change of the calorimeter = $W(T_2 - T_1)$°C

where, W = calorimeter constant

Enthalpy change of solution = $[(100 + W_1)(T_2 - T_1)]$ 4.184J for $(T_2 - T_1)$°C rise in temperature

Total enthalpy change of the calorimeter(beaker) and solution $= [W(T_2 - T_1) + (100 + W_1)(T_2 - T_1)] \times 4.184$ J

Heat liberated on dissolution of 1 g of copper sulfate =

$$\frac{\left[W(T_2 - T_1) + (100 + W_1)(T_2 - T_1)\right] \times 4.184}{W_1} \text{ J}$$

Since 1 mol of copper sulfate weighs 249.5 g, therefore, ΔH_{sol} of $CuSO_4.5H_2O$ =

$$249.5 \times \frac{\left[W(T_2 - T_1) + (100 + W_1)(T_2 - T_1)\right] \times 4.184}{W_1} \text{ J mol}^{-1}$$

15.7 Enthalpy of Neutralisation of Strong Acid and Strong Base

Enthalpy of neutralisation is always constant for a strong acid and a strong base, that is, 57.1 kJ. This is because all strong acids and strong bases are completely ionised in dilute solution. Enthalpy changes in neutralisation are always negative—when an acid and alkali react, heat is given out. The neutralisation reaction of a strong acid with strong base is essentially the combination of one equivalent of hydrogen ions with one equivalent of hydroxyl ions. Enthalpy of neutralisation is the heat evolved when one gram equivalent of the acid is completely neutralised by a base in dilute solution.

The chemical reaction is given below:

$$H^+ + OH^- \longrightarrow H_2O + 13.7 \text{ kcal}$$

$$H^+(aq) + Cl^-(aq) + Na^+(aq) + OH^-(aq) \longrightarrow Na^+(aq) + Cl^-(aq) + H_2O + 13.7\text{kcal}$$

13.7 kcal of heat is liberated and is the heat of neutralisation for all strong acids and bases.

Procedure:

- Calculate the water equivalent of the calorimeter.
- Place 100 mL of 0.2 M hydrochloric acid solution in it.
- Now record the temperature of the acid solution.
- Take another separate vessel and place 100 mL of 0.2 M sodium hydroxide solution in it.
- Note down the initial temperature of sodium hydroxide solution taken.
- Wait till both the solutions attain the same temperature.
- Now transfer 100 mL of sodium hydroxide solution into the hydrochloric acid quickly.
- Fit the cork (which has a thermometer and a stirrer in the mouth) immediately.
- Keep noting down the temperature till the temperature becomes constant.
- Record the highest temperature reached.
- Calculate the heat evolved when the two solutions are mixed by ratio proportion method.

Let the initial temperature of the acid and base be T_1°C, the final temperature after neutralisation be T_2°C,

Therefore, the change in temperature is $(T_1 - T_2)$°C

Mass of the mixture solution after neutralisation is 200g

Water equivalent of calorimeter is W g

Enthalpy change during neutralisation of 100 mL of 0.2 M HCl

$$= (200 \times W) \times (T_1 - T_2) \times 4.2$$

Therefore, the enthalpy change during neutralisation of 1000 mL of 1M HCl

$$= \frac{(200 \times W) \times (T_1 - T_2) \times 4.2}{0.2} \times \frac{1000}{100}$$

$$\text{Enthalpy of neutralisation} = \frac{(200 \times W) \times (T_1 - T_2) \times 4.2}{0.2 \times 100} \text{ kJ}$$

15.8 The Effect of Variation in Concentration of Iodide Ions on the Reaction Rate Between Iodide Ions and Hydrogen Peroxide at Room Temperature

The reaction of iodide ions and hydrogen peroxide takes place in an acidic medium, it is represented as follows

$$2I^-(aq) + H_2O_2(l) + 2H^+(aq) \longrightarrow I_2(g) + 2H_2O(l)$$

Iodide ions are oxidised to molecular iodine by hydrogen peroxide. When sodium thiosulfate is added in the presence of starch solution to above reaction mixture, the iodine liberated reacts with thiosulfate ions immediately after it is formed and is reduced back to iodide ions as long as all the thiosulfate ions oxidise to tetrathionate ions.

$$I_2(g) + 2S_2O_3^{2-}(aq) \longrightarrow S_4O_6^{2-}(aq) + 2I^-(aq)$$

Once all the thiosulfate ions are consumed, the concentration of liberated iodine increases swiftly to a point where an intense blue complex is formed.

$$I_2 + \text{starch} \longrightarrow \text{blue complex}$$

The time for the colour to appear is recorded, therefore, the reaction is sometimes known as clock reaction. The time needed for blue colour to appear is proportional to the reaction's pace.

15.8.1 Determination of the Rate Law

The rate law for the reaction between iodide ions and hydrogen peroxide can be determined by carrying out experiments in which the concentrations of iodide and peroxide are varied. For example, consider the following reaction.

$$A + B \longrightarrow P$$

Rate = $[A]^n [B]^m$

Experiment	$[A]_0$	$[B]_0$	Initial rate $\left(\frac{M}{s}\right)$
1	0.10	0.10	0.45
2	0.20	0.10	0.90
3	0.10	0.20	1.80

For this reaction, doubling the initial concentration of reactant A doubles the initial rate of reaction (experiments 1 and 2). This relationship corresponds to $n = 1$. Likewise, doubling the initial concentration of B has the effect of quadrupling the initial rate (experiments 2 and 3). This corresponds to $m = 2$.

We can n0ow write the differential rate law for this reaction as:

$$\text{Rate} = k[A][B]^2$$

The reaction is said to be first order in A and second order in B. The overall order of the reaction is 3.

There are the following requirements to be maintained for the experiments.

- The acidity of the solution must be maintained at a constant level so that the concentration of H^+ is constant.
- The temperature of the reaction must be the same for all runs. The rate constant is dependent on the temperature of the solution. Since the heat of reaction is relatively small for this reaction, the temperature should remain relatively constant throughout the process.
- The reverse reaction must be suppressed. The reverse reaction is as below:

  $$I_2 + 2H_2O \longrightarrow 2I^- + 2H^+ + H_2O_2$$

  If the concentration of iodine is allowed to build up as the reaction proceeds then the rate of reverse reaction will increase and an equilibrium mixture will result. Any rate measured for the reaction under such conditions will not represent the rate of forward reaction but the net difference between the forward and reverse rate.
- The addition of thiosulfate ions ($S_2O_3^{2-}$) allows an accurate measurement of the rate at which the peroxide–iodide reaction is taking place. Iodine is produced slowly by the reaction between peroxide and iodide ions and the thiosulfate ions immediately react with the iodine as it is produced.

  $$I_2 + 2\,S_2O_3^{2-} \longrightarrow 2\,I^- + S_4O_6^{2-} \text{ fast reaction}$$

As long as excess thiosulfate ions are present in the solution, no free iodine can accumulate because it is immediately turned into iodide ions which are colourless.

The thiosulfate ions are the limiting reagent. So, once all the thiosulfate ions are consumed, iodine starts to form in the solution. Iodine is pale yellow. If starch is added to the solution then a more dramatic blue solution is formed by the complex of starch–iodine. The time from the addition of the peroxide solution to the appearance of blue colour is Δt for the reaction. The average rate (moles of hydrogen peroxide consumed per litre per second) of the reaction during this period can be calculated as below:

$$\text{Rate} = -\frac{\Delta[H_2O_2]}{\Delta t}$$

15.8.2 Temperature Dependence of the Rate Constant

In general, the rate of a reaction increases with increasing temperature. The relationship between the rate constant and temperature is reflected in the Arrhenius equation (Fig. 15.3).

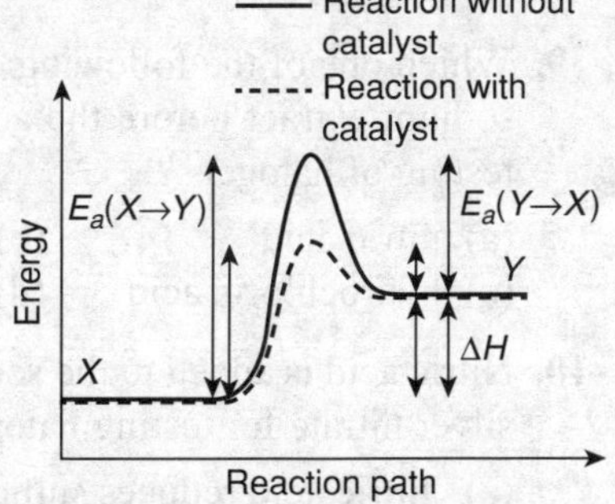

Fig. 15.3

$$k = Ae^{\frac{-E_a}{RT}}$$

where k is the rate constant, A is called the Arrhenius pre-exponential constant, E_a is the activation energy, R is the gas constant.

15.8.3 Effect of Catalyst

Some chemical species can speedup a reaction without being consumed themselves. Catalysts operate by decreasing the value of activation energy. An effective catalyst exists for the reaction of iodide with hydrogen peroxide. The catalyst is iron(II) ions dissolved in the reaction mixture.

15.9 Lyophilic and Lyophobic Sols

Lyophilic means 'solvent loving' that is there is a strong attraction between the dispersion medium and the dispersed phase which is due to the formation of a large number of hydrogen bonds between them. For example, the colloidal solutions of starch, gum, gelatine. These sols are very stable and reversible. The stability of the sol is primarily due to the solvation of colloidal particles by the solvent. The dispersed phase in lyophilic sols does not readily precipitate. They show high colligative properties. The sols can be prepared directly by mixing and shaking the substance with a suitable liquid.

Lyophobic means liquid hating that is the dispersed phase has very little affinity for the dispersion medium. For example, sols of various metals such as gold, silver, along with their insoluble compounds like sulfides and oxides (such as arsenius sulfide). These are unstable and can be easily coagulated by adding a small amount of suitable electrolyte. These can be stabilised by the charge on the colloidal particles. Due to their charges, colloidal particles remain suspended in solution and coagulation does not take place. These charges may be positive or negative.

15.9.1 Methods of Preparation of Lyophilic Sols

(i) **Egg albumin sol:** Prepare 100 mL of 5% (w/v) solution of NaCl in water in a 250 mL beaker. Break one egg in a porcelain dish and pipette out the albumin and pour it into the sodium chloride solution. Stir it well to ensure that the sol is well prepared.

(ii) **Starch/ gum sol:** Measure 100 mL of distilled water with the help of a measuring cylinder, transfer it to a 250 mL beaker and boil it. Make a paste of 500 mg starch or gum in hot water and transfer this paste to 100 mL of boiling water with constant stirring. Keep water boiling and stirring for 10 minutes after addition of paste.

15.9.2 Preparation of Lyophobic Sols

Due to the less affinity between the two phases in lyophobic colloids, the preparation requires special methods (all these methods are explained in detail in Chapter 5, Surface Chemistry).

(i) **Disintegration or dispersion method:** This method includes some physical techniques to reduce particle size to the colloidal range (1 nm to 1000 nm) such as—Electrical disintegration (Bredig's arc method), peptization, mechanical dispersion, condensation method.

(ii) **Chemical methods:** It includes a double decomposition reaction method as given below.

(a) **Preparation of ferric hydroxide / aluminium hydroxide sol:** Take 100 mL of distilled water in a 250 mL beaker and boil it. Add 2 g of ferric chloride/ aluminium chloride powder to the boiling water and stir it well. Take 100 mL of distilled water in another 250 mL beaker and boil it. Pour 10 mL of ferric chloride/ aluminium chloride solution (prepared earlier), drop by drop, into the boiling water with constant stirring. Keep the water boiling till brown/ white sol is obtained.

Chemical equations involved:

For ferric hydroxide sol:

$$FeCl_3(aq) + 3\,H_2O(l) \xrightarrow{\text{boil}} \underset{\text{Red sol}}{Fe(OH)_3(s)} + 3\,HCl(aq)$$

For Aluminium hydroxide sol:

$$AlCl_3(aq) + 3\,H_2O(l) \xrightarrow{\text{boil}} \underset{\text{White sol}}{Al(OH)_3(s)} + 3\,HCl(aq)$$

(b) **Preparation of arsenius sulfide sol:** Transfer 100 mL of distilled water to a beaker of 250 mL capacity. Add 0.2 g of arsenious oxide to it and boil the content of the beaker. Cool and filter the solution. Pass hydrogen sulfide (H_2S) gas through the filtered solution till it smells of H_2S. Expel H_2S gas from the sol by slow heating and filter it. Label the filtrate as arsenious sulfide sol.

Chemical equations involved:

$$As_2O_3(aq) + 3\,H_2O(l) \xrightarrow{\text{boil}} 2\,As(OH)_3(s)$$

$$2\,As(OH)_3(s) + 3\,H_2S \longrightarrow \underset{\text{Yellow sol}}{As_2S_3(s)} + 6\,H_2O$$

Exercises

OBJECTIVE QUESTIONS

Detection of Extra Elements (Nitrogen, Sulfur, Halogens) in Organic Compounds

1. Lassaigne's test can detect:
   (a) nitrogen, sulfur, halogens
   (b) nitrogen, cyanides, sulfur
   (c) sodium, sulfur, halogens, phosphorus
   (d) nitrogen, sulfur, halogens, phosphorus

2. During Lassaigne's test, nitrogen present in the organic compound is converted into:
   (a) sodium nitride (b) sodium azide
   (c) sodium cyanide (d) none of these

3. The formula of the compound which gives violet colour in Lassaigne's test for sulfur with sodium nitroprusside is
   (a) $Na_4[Fe(CN)_5NOS]$ (b) $Na_3[Fe(CN)_5NOS]$
   (c) $Na_2[Fe(CN)_5S]$ (d) $Na_4[Fe(CN)_4S]$

4. In Lassaigne's test, if the organic compound contains both N and S and it is fused with excess sodium metal, the sodium fusion extract will contain
   (a) NaCNS (b) NaCN
   (c) Na_2S (d) both (b) and (c)

5. Halogen in an organic compound that can be detected by:
   (a) Duma's method (b) Carius method
   (c) Kjeldahl's method (d) chromatography

6. Soda extract is prepared by:
   (a) fusing soda and mixture of hydrocarbons, and then extracted with water
   (b) dissolving $NaHCO_3$ and mixture of hydrocarbon in dil. HCl
   (c) boiling Na_2CO_3 and mixture of hydrocarbon in dil. HCl
   (d) boiling Na_2CO_3 and mixture of hydrocarbon in distilled water

7. In Kjeldahl's method of estimation of nitrogen, K_2SO_4 acts as:
   (a) an oxidising agent (b) a catalytic agent
   (c) a hydrolysing agent (d) a boiling point elevator

8. Nitrogen can be estimated by Kjeldahl's method for which of the following compound:

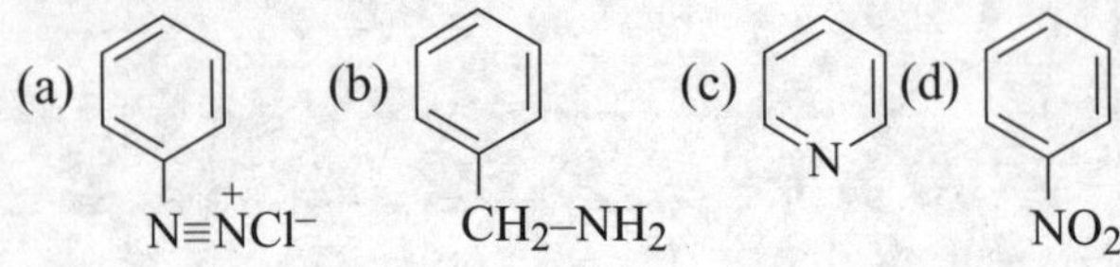

9. Which one of the following compounds is added to the sodium extract before the addition of silver nitrate for testing of halogens?
   (a) nitric acid (b) ammonia
   (c) hydrochloric acid (d) sodium hydroxide

10. Nitric acid is added to the sodium extract before adding silver nitrate for testing halogens because
   (a) nitric acid reduces sulfides
   (b) nitric acid decomposes NaCN and Na_2S
   (c) nitric acid oxidises the organic compound
   (d) nitric acid acts as a dehydrating agent

11. Metallic sodium is fused with organic compounds for testing nitrogen, sulfur and halogens. The correct reason behind this is:
   (a) to convert all compounds to their ionic form
   (b) sodium reduces the compounds
   (c) sodium converts all compounds in their covalent form
   (d) none of the above

12. Which one of the following set of elements can be detected using the sodium fusion extract?
   (a) sulfur, nitrogen, phosphorous, halogens
   (b) phosphorous, oxygen, nitrogen, halogens
   (c) nitrogen, phosphorous, carbon, sulfur
   (d) halogens, nitrogen, oxygen, sulfur

13. A gas among the following that can be absorbed by potassium hydroxide is:
   (a) carbon dioxide (b) silicon dioxide
   (c) hydrogen (d) carbon monoxide

14. The acid used for the acidification of sodium extract for testing sulfur is:
   (a) sulfuric acid (b) acetic acid
   (c) nitric acid (d) hydrochloric acid

15. 0.3780 g of an organic compound gave 0.5740 g of silver chloride in the Carius estimation. The percentage of chlorine present in the compounds is:
   (a) 25% (b) 37.59% (c) 42% (d) 5.70%

16. In the test of nitrogen, sodium fusion extract is acidified with which of the following?
   (a) dilute sulfuric acid
   (b) dilute hydrochloric acid
   (c) concentrated hydrochloric acid
   (d) concentrated sulfuric acid

17. What is the colour of the precipitate obtained in the test for sulfur?
   (a) white (b) black (c) violet (d) blue

18. A X colour precipitate, which is Y in ammonium hydroxide indicates the presence of chlorine. Identify X and Y.

(a) X = yellow Y = soluble
(b) X = yellow Y = insoluble
(c) X = white Y = insoluble
(d) X = white Y = soluble

19. The metal used to detect nitrogen in an organic compound is:

(a) Li (b) K (c) Na (d) Cs

20. Lassaigne's test for the detection of nitrogen will fail in the case of:

(a) NH_2CONH_2 (b) $NH_4CONHNH_2.HCl$
(c) $NH_2NH_2.HCl$ (d) $C_6H_6NHNH_2.2HCl$

21. Nitric acid is added to sodium extract before adding silver nitrate for testing halogens because:

(a) nitric acid reduces sulfide
(b) nitric acid decomposes NaCN and Na_2S
(c) nitric acid oxidises the organic compound
(d) nitric acid acts as a dehydrating agent

22. In case both nitrogen and sulfur are present in an organic compound, with sodium fusion extract, a blood red colour is formed because of:

(a) ammonium molybdate
(b) ferriferrocyanide
(c) ferric thiocyanate
(d) ammonium phosphomolybdate

23. When a compound is heated with copper(II) oxide, it is the test for

(a) nitrogen (b) halogens
(c) carbon (d) phosphorus

24. Laissaigne's extract is made to:

(a) convert ionic compounds to covalent compounds
(b) dissolve the compound
(c) convert covalent compounds to ionic compounds
(d) none of these

25. A compound that gives a positive Lassaigne's test for both nitrogen and halogen is:

(a) $NH_2OH.HCl$ (b) $CH_3NH_2.HCl$
(c) NH_4Cl (d) $N_2H_4.HCl$

26. The white precipitate which is formed in the detection of chloride ion is due to the formation of:

(a) ammonium chloride (b) sodium chloride
(c) aluminium sulfate (d) calcium chloride

27. A pale yellow precipitate soluble in ammonium hydroxide solution indicates the presence of:

(a) chlorine (b) iodine
(c) bromine (d) phosphorus

28. In the test for nitrogen, the Prussian blue colour is because of:

(a) nitrogen (b) sodium thiocyanate
(c) ammonium molybdate (d) ferriferrocyanide

29. In sodium extract solution, the nitrogen in an organic compound is converted into:

(a) sodalime (b) sodamide
(c) sodium nitrate (d) sodium cyanide

30. Which of the following statements is not applicable to Lassaigne's test?

(a) The extra elements (N, S and halogens) are tested as their inorganic salts.
(b) During fusion of the organic compound with sodium, Na_2S, NaCN and NaX are formed.
(c) It can even be used for the detection of hydrogen in the organic compound.
(d) It is possible to differentiate between the different halogens.

31. Detection of sulfur in the sodium extract is not done by which of the following reagents?

(a) $Pb(OAc)_2$
(b) sodium nitroprusside
(c) both $Pb(OAc)_2$ and sodium nitroprusside
(d) silver nitrate

Salt Analysis

32. Flame test is not given by:

(a) Ba^{2+} ions (b) Be^{2+} ions
(c) Ca^{2+} ions (d) Na^{+} ions

33. A brick red colour is imparted to the flame by a

(a) Ca salt (b) Sr salt (c) Na salt (d) Co salt

34. Given below are certain cations. Using inorganic qualitative analysis, arrange them in increasing group number from I to VI.

A. Al^{3+} B. Cu^{2+} C. Ba^{2+}
D. Co^{2+} E. Mg^{2+}

Choose the correct answer from the options given below

(a) B, C, A, D, E (b) E, C, D, B, A
(c) E, A, B, C, D (d) B, A, D, C, E

35. Which compound in solution produces a precipitate with aqueous ammonia that does not dissolve when an excess of ammonia is added?

(a) copper(II) sulfate (b) iron(II) chloride
(c) potassium hydroxide (d) zinc chloride

36. Refer to the scheme below to identify the unknowns.

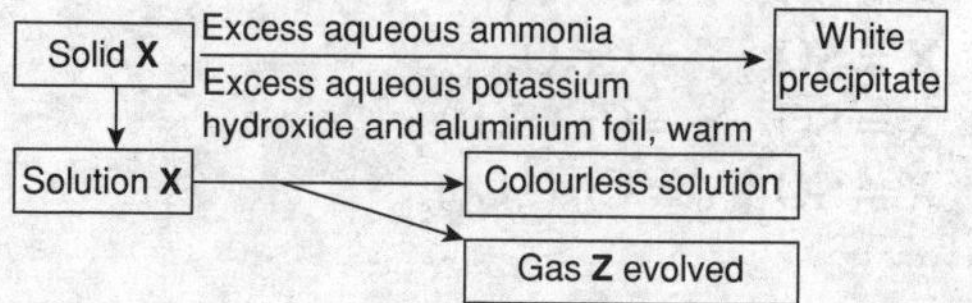

Which of the following could be solid X and gas Z?

	Solid X	Gas Z
(a)	Sodium hydroxide	Water vapour
(b)	Calcium hydroxide	Water vapour
(c)	Aluminium nitrate	Ammonia
(d)	Zinc nitrate	Ammonia

37. Solution X contains a simple salt. The table shows the results of some tests on solution X.

Test	Observation
Addition of aqueous sodium hydroxide	Green precipitate formed
Addition of acidified banium nitrate	Ammonia

What is the name of the salt in solution X?
(a) iron(II) chloride (b) iron(III) chloride
(c) iron(II) sulfate (d) iron(III) sulfate

38. When aqueous sodium hydroxide is added dropwise until in excess to an unknown salt solution, a green precipitate is formed and is insoluble in excess aqueous sodium hydroxide. The precipitate turns brown slowly. Which of the following is the unknown salt?
(a) copper(II) sulfate (b) iron(II) sulfate
(c) iron(III) sulfate (d) lead(II) sulfate

39. When heated, solid P gives off a gas which forms a white precipitate with limewater. The residue reacts with dilute acid and also with aqueous alkali. What is P?
(a) copper(II) carbonate (b) zinc carbonate
(c) zinc oxide (d) copper(II) oxide

40. 1 cm^3 of solution Q was added into two separate test tubes. To one of the test tubes, an excess of aqueous sodium hydroxide was added gradually. A white precipitate which was soluble in excess aqueous sodium hydroxide was obtained. To the other test tube, an excess of aqueous ammonia was added gradually. A white precipitate which was insoluble in excess aqueous ammonia was obtained. What could solution Q contain?
(a) lead(II) chloride (b) aluminium chloride
(c) calcium chloride (d) ammonium chloride

41. On treating a compound with warm dil. H_2SO_4, gas X is evolved which turns $K_2Cr_2O_7$ paper acidified with dil. H_2SO_4 to a green compound Y. X and Y respectively are
(a) X = SO_2, Y = Cr_2O_3
(b) X = SO_3, Y = Cr_2O_3
(c) X = SO_2, Y = $Cr_2(SO_4)_3$
(d) X = SO_3, Y = $Cr_2(SO_4)_3$

42. Reagent, 1-naphthylamine and sulfanilic acid in acetic acid, is used for the detection of
(a) N_2O (b) NO_3 (c) NO (d) NO_2

43. An inorganic compound X on treatment with concentrated H_2SO_4 produces brown fumes and gives a dark brown ring with $FeSO_4$ in the presence of concentrated H_2SO_4. Also, compound X gives precipitate Y, when its solution in dilute HCl is treated with H_2S gas. The precipitate Yon treatment with concentrated HNO_3 followed by excess of NH_4OH further gives a deep blue coloured solution. Compound X is:
(a) $Co(NO_3)_2$ (b) $Pb(NO_2)_2$
(c) $Cu(NO_3)_2$ (d) $Pb(NO_3)_2$

44. To an aqueous solution containing ions such as Al^{3+}, Zn^{2+}, Ca^{2+}, Fe^{3+}, Ni^{2+}, Ba^{2+} and Cu^{2+}, conc. HCl was added, followed by H_2S. The total number of cations precipitated during this reaction is/are:
(a) 1 (b) 3 (c) 4 (d) 2

45. What are the products formed in sequence when excess of CO_2 is passed in slaked lime?
(a) $Ca(HCO_3)_2$, $CaCO_3$ (b) $CaCO_3$, $Ca(HCO_3)_2$
(c) CaO, $Ca(HCO_3)_2$ (d) CaO, $CaCO_3$

46. Acidic ferric chloride solution on treatment with excess of potassium ferrocyanide gives a

Prussian blue coloured colloidal species. It is:
(a) $Fe_4[Fe(CN)_6]_3$ (b) $K_5Fe[Fe(CN)_6]_2$
(c) $HFe[Fe(CN)_6]$ (d) $KFe[Fe(CN)_6]$

47. The deposition of X and Y on ground surfaces is referred as wet and dry depositions, respectively. X and Y are:
(a) X = ammonium salts, Y = CO_2
(b) X = SO_2, Y = ammonium salts
(c) X = ammonium salts, Y = SO_2
(d) X = CO_2, Y = SO_2

48. The potassium ferrocyanide solution gives a Prussian blue colour, when added to:
(a) $CoCl_3$ (b) $FeCl_2$ (c) $CoCl_2$ (d) $FeCl_3$

49. In salt analysis, group V radicals (Ba^{2+}, Ca^{2+} and Sr^{2+}) are precipitated as their carbonates by adding solid NH_4Cl and excess of NH_4OH solution followed by solid $(NH_4)_2CO_3$. Choose the correct reagent used for the confirmation of Ca^{2+} ion from the following
(a) ammonium sulfate (b) potassium chromate
(c) ammonium oxalate (d) ammonium nitrate

50. In salt analysis, Cl^-, Br^- and I^- are identified by adding dilute HNO_3 followed by $AgNO_3$ solution to the salt solution. Choose the correct statements from the following.

A	Cl^- gives a pale yellow precipitate.
B	Br^- gives a pale yellow precipitate which is partially soluble in NH_4OH.
C	I^- gives a yellow precipitate which is insoluble in NH_4OH.
D	Cl^- gives a white precipitate which is insoluble in NH_4OH.
E	I^- gives a purple violet gas.

Choose the correct answer from the options given below.

(a) B and C only (b) A and B only
(c) A and E only (d) D and E only

51. Group I cations are precipitated as:

(a) sulfides (b) nitrates
(c) carbonates (d) chlorides

52. Iodine turns the carbon tetrachloride layer

(a) pink (b) violet (c) brown (d) black

53. A gas among the following that can be absorbed by potassium hydroxide is:

(a) carbon dioxide (b) silicon dioxide
(c) hydrogen (d) carbon monoxide

54. Silver sulfate solution is used to separate

(a) nitrate and bromide (b) nitrate and chlorate
(c) bromide and iodide (d) nitrate and nitrite

55. In the borax bead test, which of the following compounds is formed?

(a) metaborate (b) tetraborate
(c) double oxide (d) orthoborate

56. The metal that does not give the borax bead test is:

(a) chromium (b) nickel
(c) lead (d) manganese

57. Which of the following is a coloured compound?

(a) CuF_2 (b) CuI (c) NaCl (d) $MgCl_2$

58. When borax is heated in a platinum loop, the transparent bead formed contains:

(a) $Na_2B_4O_7$
(b) sodium metaborate + B_2O_3
(c) water (d) CaO

59. The alkaline earth metal that imparts an apple green colour to the Bunsen flame when introduced in it in the form of its chloride is

(a) barium (b) strontium
(c) calcium (d) magnesium

60. What gives a violet coloured bead in the borax bead test?

(a) Fe^{2+} (b) Ni^{2+} (c) Co^{2+} (d) Mn^{2+}

61. Which one of the following salts give a green coloured flame when the salt is tested using a Pt wire?

(a) barium salt (b) calcium salt
(c) borate (d) lead salt

62. When a salt is heated with dil. H_2SO_4 and $KMnO_4$ solution, the pink colour of $KMnO_4$ is discharged, the mixture contains

(a) sulfite (b) carbonate
(c) nitrate (d) bicarbonate

63. Sodium sulfite on heating with dilute HCl liberates a gas which

(a) turns lead acetate paper black
(b) turns acidified potassium dichromate paper green
(c) burns with a blue flame
(d) smells like vinegar

64. Starch–iodide paper is used for the test of

(a) iodine (b) iodide ion
(c) oxidising agent (d) reducing agent

65. A white salt turns yellow on heating but becomes white on cooling. It may be a salt of:

(a) Fe (b) Pb (c) Al (d) Zn

66. A blue coloured residue obtained in cobalt nitrate charcoal cavity test is due to

(a) Zn^{2+} (b) Sn^{2+} (c) Mg^{2+} (d) Al^{3+}

67. Which of the following cations can be detected by the cobalt nitrate test?

(a) Zn^{2+} (b) Na^+ (c) NH_4^+ (d) Ni^{2+}

68. A salt on reaction with dil.H_2SO_4 gives a reddish brown gas. The salt is:

(a) KNO_3 (b) $ZnBr_2$ (c) $NaNO_2$ (d) $ZnCO_3$

69. Presence of Fe^{3+} ions in $FeSO_4$ can be checked with

(a) blue litmus paper (b) red litmus paper
(c) KCNS solution (d) none of these

70. Name the compound which turns black with NH_4OH.

(a) lead chloride (b) mercurous chloride
(c) mercuric chloride (d) silver chloride

71. When chromyl chloride vapours are dissolved in water and acetic acid and lead acetate solution is added, then

(a) the solution will remain colourless
(b) the solution will become dark green
(c) a yellow solution will be obtained
(d) a yellow precipitate will be obtained

72. Which of the following solutions gives a precipitate with $Pb(NO_3)_2$, but not with $Ba(NO_3)_2$?

(a) sodium chloride (b) sodium sulfate
(c) sodium nitrate
(d) sodium hydrogen phosphate

73. To a solution of a salt, $MgSO_4$ solution is added and a white precipitate appears only on heating. The acid radical in the salt is

(a) CO_3^{2-} (b) HCO_3^{2-} (c) SO_3^{2-} (d) $C_2O_4^{2-}$

74. Formation of purple colour on the addition of sodium nitroprusside to sodium carbonate extract indicates the presence of

(a) PO_4^{3-} (b) SO_3^{2-} (c) S^{2-} (d) $S_2O_3^{2-}$

75. On heating a mixture of potassium dichromate and sodium chloride with concentrated sulfuric acid in a dry test tube, the compound formed is:

(a) chromium chloride (b) chromyl chloride
(c) chloric dioxide (d) chromic acid

76. Phosphate radical with ammonium molybdate gives precipitate of which colour?

(a) violet (b) pink
(c) canary yellow (d) green

77. Which compound is soluble in NH_4OH?

(a) $PbCl_2$ (b) $PbSO_4$ (c) AgCl (d) $CaCO_3$

78. Ammonia reacts with excess of chlorine to form:

(a) N_2 and HCl (b) NH_4Cl and NCl_3
(c) NCl_3 and HCl (d) N_2 and NH_4Cl

79. Which of the following decolourises acidified $KMnO_4$ solution?

(a) SO_4^{2-} (b) S^{2-}
(c) NO_3^- (d) CH_3COO^-

80. Which of the following does not give a precipitate with silver nitrate solution?

(a) ethyl bromide (b) sodium bromide
(c) calcium chloride (d) sodium chloride

81. When acetic acid and $K_4[Fe(CN)_6]$ are added to a copper salt, a chocolate precipitate is obtained of the compound:

(a) copper cyanide (b) copper ferrocyanide
(c) basic copper sulfate (d) basic copper cyanide

82. The compound insoluble in acetic acid is:

(a) calcium oxide (b) calcium carbonate
(c) calcium oxalate (d) calcium hydroxide

83. The reagent used in the qualitative analysis of IV group is:

(a) HCl (b) H_2S(alkaline)
(c) $(NH_4)_2S$ (d) none of these

84. The reagent used to distinguish between silver and lead salt is

(a) H_2S gas (b) hot dilute HCl solution
(c) $NH_4Cl(s) + NH_4OH(aq)$
(d) $NH_4Cl + (NH_4)_2CO_3(aq)$

85. The ion that cannot be precipitated by both HCl and H_2S is:

(a) Pb^{2+} (b) Cu^{2+} (c) Ag^+ (d) Sn^{2+}

86. $Pb(CH_3COO)_2$ gives ______ colour with H_2S.

(a) orange (b) red (c) black (d) white

87. Fe^{2+} ion can be distinguished by Fe^{3+} ion by using

(a) NH_4SCN (b) $AgNO_3$
(c) $BaCl_2$ (d) none of these

88. Which of the following changes the colour of an aqueous solution of $FeCl_3$?

(a) $K_4[Fe(CN)_6]$ (b) H_2S
(c) NH_4CNS (d) KCNS

89. [X] + H_2SO_4 → [Y], a colourless gas with irritating smell

[Y] + $K_2Cr_2O_7$ + H_2SO_4 → green solution
[X] and [Y] are

(a) SO_3^{2-}, SO_2 (b) Cl^-, HCl
(c) S^{2-}, H_2S (d) CO_3^{2-}, CO_2

90. Concentrated sodium hydroxide can separate a mixture of:

(a) Zn^{2+} and Pb^{2+} (b) Al^{3+} and Zn^{2+}
(c) Cr^{3+} and Fe^{3+} (d) Al^{3+} and Cr^{3+}

91. Al^{3+}, $Fe^{3+}$and Cr^{3+} are grouped together for qualitative analysis because their

(a) sulfides are soluble in acid
(b) hydroxides are insoluble in NH_3
(c) carbonates are insoluble in NH_3
(d) none of these

92. In qualitative analysis, Hg^{2+} can be separated from Cu^{2+} by the addition of 3 M HNO_3 because

(a) $Hg(NO_3)_2$ is less soluble than $Cu(NO_3)_2$
(b) $Cu(NO_3)_2$ is less soluble than $Hg(NO_3)_2$
(c) HgS is less soluble than CuS in 3M HNO_3
(d) CuS is less soluble than HgS in 3M HNO_3

93. Lead has been placed in qualitative analysis group 1 and 2 because:

(a) it shows the covalency one and two
(b) it forms insoluble $PbCl_2$
(c) it forms lead sulfide
(d) $PbCl_2$ is partially soluble in water

94. To avoid the precipitation of hydroxides of Ni^{2+}, Co^{2+}, Zn^{2+} and Mn^{2+} along with those of Fe^{3+}, Al^{3+} and Cr^{3+}, the third group solution should be

(a) heated with a few drops of conc. HNO_3
(b) treated with excess of NH_4Cl
(c) concentrated
(d) none of these

95. In the group III reagent, in place of NH_4Cl, which of the following can be used?

(a) NH_4NO_3 (b) $(NH_4)_2SO_4$
(c) NaCl (d) none of these

96. Which compound does not dissolve in hot dilute HNO_3?

(a) HgS (b) PbS (c) CuS (d) CdS

97. How many of the following substances are soluble in concentrated HNO_3?

$BaSO_4$, CuS, PbS, HgS

(a) 1 (b) 2 (c) 3 (d) 4

98. In qualitative analysis, in order to detect second group basic radicals, H_2S gas is passed in the presence of dilute HCl to:

(a) increase in dissociation of H_2S
(b) decrease the dissociation of salt solution
(c) decrease the dissociation of H_2S
(d) increase the dissociation of salt solution

99. The following four solutions are kept in separate beakers and copper metal is put in each of them. Which solution will become blue after some time?

(a) $AgNO_3$ solution (b) $Zn(NO_3)_2$ solution
(c) $Ba(NO_3)_2$ solution (d) $NaNO_3$ solution

100. A metal nitrate on reaction with excess sodium hydroxide solution gives a white precipitate but it rapidly turns brown on adding bromine water. An aqueous solution of a metal nitrate produces a pink precipitate with disodium hydrogen phosphate solution in the presence of ammonia. The cation is:

(a) Cu^{2+} (b) Mn^{2+} (c) Mg^{2+} (d) Zn^{2+}

101. Addition of $SnCl_2$ to $HgCl_2$ gives a precipitate that is

(a) white turning to red (b) white turning to grey
(c) black turning to white (d) none of these

102. In Nessler's reagent, for the detection of ammonia, the active species is

(a) Hg_2Cl_2 (b) Hg^{2+} (c) Hg_2I_2 (d) HgI_4^{2-}

103. Which statement is correct?

(a) Fe^{2+} gives a brown colour with ammonium thiocyanate.
(b) Fe^{2+} gives a blue precipitate with potassium ferricyanide.
(c) Fe^{3+} gives a brown colour with potassium ferricyanide.
(d) Fe^{3+} gives a red colour with potassium ferrocyanide.

104. An aqueous solution of a colourless metal sulfate M gives a white precipitate with NH_4OH. This was soluble in excess of NH_4OH. On passing H_2S through this solution a white precipitate was formed. The metal M in the salt is:

(a) Ca (b) Ba (c) Al (d) Zn

105. A white sodium salt dissolves readily in water to give a solution which is neutral to litmus. When silver nitrate solution is added to the solution, a white precipitate is obtained which does not dissolve in dil. HNO_3. The anion could be:

(a) CO_3^{2-} (b) Cl^- (c) SO_4^{2-} (d) S^{2-}

106. Nessler's reagent is used to detect

(a) CrO_4^{2-} (b) PO_4^{3-} (c) MnO_4^- (d) NH_4^+

107. $K_4[Fe(CN)_6]$ cannot be used to test

(a) Fe^{3+} (b) Zn^{2+} (c) Cd^{2+} (d) Cr^{3+}

108. A laboratory reagent imparts a green colour to the flame. On heating with solid $K_2Cr_2O_7$ and conc. H_2SO_4, it evolves an orange red gas. Identify the reagent.

(a) $CaCl_2$ (b) $BaCl_2$
(c) $CuCl_2$ (d) none of these

109. Which reagent can be used to identify nickel ion?

(a) resorcinol (b) dimethyl glyoxime
(c) diphenyl benzidine (d) potassium ferrocyanide

110. Which of the following reagents can be used to distinguish between sodium carbonate and sodium sulfite?

(a) lime water (b) baryta water
(c) acidified $K_2Cr_2O_7$ solution
(d) H_2SO_4 solution

111. The gas liberated on treating a mixture of two salts with dil. H_2SO_4 turns lime water milky and turbidity disappears with the passage of excess of gas. The aqueous solution of the mixture gives a white crystalline precipitate with NaCl solution. The filtrate gives a black precipitate when H_2S is passed into it. The aqueous solution of the mixture on heating gives a reddish brown gas and when treated with ammonium hydroxide and excess of disodium hydrogen phosphate gives a white crystalline precipitate. The mixture contains

(a) CO_3^{2-}, Pb^{2+}, NO_3^{2-}, Mg^{2+}
(b) CO_3^{2-}, Pb^{2+}, NO_3^{2-}, Ca^{2+}
(c) CO_3^{2-}, Pb^{2+}, Cl^-, Mg^{2+}
(d) CO_3^{2-}, Pb^{2+}, Cl^-, Ca^{2+}

112. For the given aqueous reaction which of the statement(s) is false?

$$KI + K_3[Fe(CN)_6] \xrightarrow{\text{Dil. } H_2SO_4} \text{brownish yellow}$$

$$\downarrow ZnSO_4$$

$$\text{Colourless solution} \longleftarrow (\text{White ppt.} + \text{brownish yellow filtrate})$$

(a) The first reaction is a redox reaction.
(b) The white precipitate is $Zn_3[Fe(CN)_6]_2$.

(c) Addition of the filtrate to starch solution gives a blue colour.
(d) The white precipitate is soluble in NaOH solution.

113. How H_2S is liberated in the laboratory?
(a) $FeSO_4 + H_2SO_4$
(b) FeS + dil. H_2SO_4
(c) FeS + conc. H_2SO_4
(d) elementary H_2 + elementary S

114. On addition of conc. H_2SO_4 to a chloride salt, colourless fumes are evolved but in the case of an iodide salt, violet fumes come out. This is because
(a) H_2SO_4 reduces HI to I_2
(b) HI is violet in colour
(c) HI gets oxidised to I_2
(d) HI changes to HIO_3

115. A brown ring is formed in the ring test of NO_3^- ion. This is due to the formation of
(a) $[Fe(H_2O)_5(NO)]^{2+}$ (b) $FeSO_4.NO_2$
(c) $[Fe(H_2O)_5(NO)]^{2+}$ (d) $FeSO_4.HNO_3$

116. In qualitative analysis, when H_2S is passed through an aqueous solution of a salt acidified with dilute HCl, a black precipitate is obtained. On boiling the precipitate with dil. HNO_3, it forms a blue solution. Addition of excess of aqueous solution of NH_3 to this solution gives a
(a) deep blue precipitate of $Cu(OH)_2$
(b) deep blue solution of $[Cu(NH_3)_4]^{2+}$
(c) deep blue solution of $Cu(NO_3)_2$
(d) deep blue solution of $Cu(OH)_2.\ Cu(NO_3)_2$

117. $CuSO_4$ decolourises on addition of KCN. The product is
(a) $[Cu(CN)_4]^{2-}$ (b) $[Cu(CN)_4]^{3-}$
(c) $Cu(CN)_2$ (d) $CuCN$

Detection of Functional Group in an Organic Compound

118. Phenol and acetic acid can be differentiated by
(a) Litmus test (b) $NaHCO_3$
(c) both (a) and (b) (d) none of these

119. Heating of oxalic acid with concentrated H_2SO_4 gives
(a) CO (b) CO_2
(c) $CO + CO_2$ (d) none of the above

120. C_6H_5OH and C_2H_5OH can be distinguished by
(a) sodium metal test (b) bromine water
(c) chlorine water (d) iron metal

121. Methyl salicylate has the smell of
(a) apple (b) bitter almonds
(c) bananas (d) none of these

122. Starch can be used as an indicator for the detection of traces of
(a) glucose in aqueous solution
(b) proteins in blood
(c) iodine in aqueous solution
(d) urea in blood

123. In organic analysis, the reagent 2,4-dinitrophenyl hydrazine is used for the detection of which of the following functional group?
(a) alcohol (b) carboxylic acid
(c) aldehyde (d) amines

124. The reagent which does not react with both acetone and benzaldehyde is
(a) sodium hydrogen sulfite
(b) phenyl hydrazine
(c) Fehling's solution (d) Grignard reagent

125. An organic compound A burns with a sooty flame. It is negative towards Tollens' reagent test and positive to Brady's reagent test. The compound A is
(a) acetophenone (b) acetone
(c) salicylic acid (d) benzaldehyde

126. An organic compound X showing the following solubility profile is

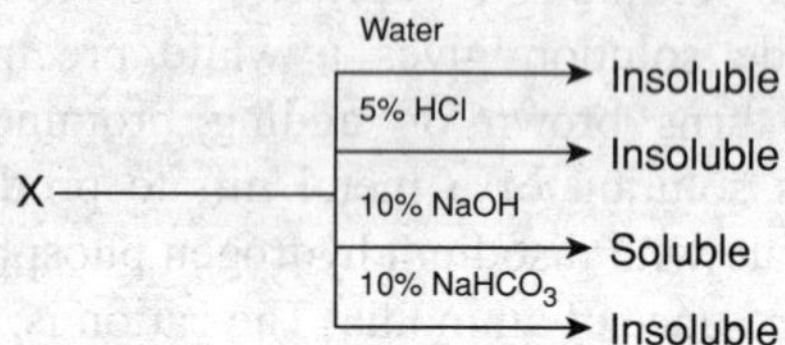

(a) *o*-toluidine (b) oleic acid
(c) *m*-cresol (d) benzamide

127. Compound A reacts with $CHCl_3$ and KOH to give an offensive smelling compound. Compound A can be a
(a) quaternary aliphatic amine
(b) primary aromatic amine
(c) secondary amine
(d) tertiary amine

128. A compound liberates CO_2 with $NaHCO_3$ and also gives colour with neutral $FeCl_3$ solution. The compound can be

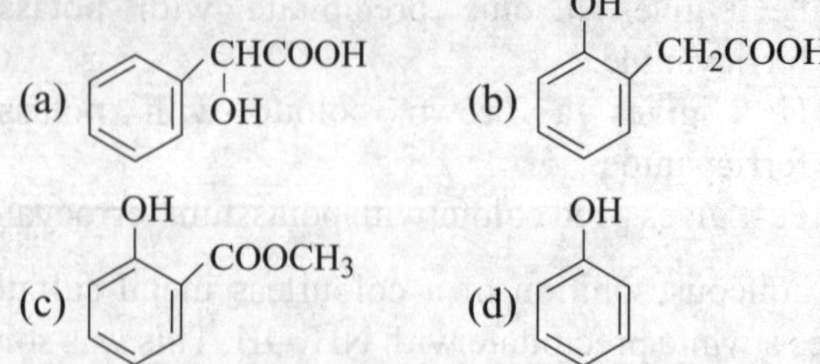

Titrations

129. What will be the pH at the equivalence point in the titration of a weak acid and a strong base?
(a) 0 (b) >7 (c) 7 (d) <7

130. The pH range of methyl orange as an indicator is
(a) 3–5 (b) 8–9 (c) 2–4 (d) 6–8

131. How many mmol of NaOH will be used in the titration with 33 mL of 3 M HCl to form NaCl and water?
(a) 10 mmol (b) 100 mmol
(c) 3 mmol (d) 33 mmol

132. The amount of NaOH used in the titration of 100 ml 0.1 N HCl is
(a) 4 g (b) 0.04 g (c) 2 g (d) 0.4 g

133. When the pH is below 8.5, the indicator ______ is colourless.
(a) EBT (b) methyl orange
(c) phenolphthalein (d) $K_2Cr_2O_7$

134. The most suitable indicator for the titration of HCOOH against NaOH is
(a) methyl orange (b) phenolphthalein
(c) thymolphthalein (d) both (b) and (c)

135. The most suitable indicator for the titration of HBr against KOH is
(a) methyl orange (b) phenolphthalein
(c) bromothymol blue (d) all are correct

136. The most suitable indicator for the titration of NH_4OH against HNO_3 is
(a) phenolphthalein (b) methyl red
(c) thymolphthalein (d) one of these

137. The most suitable indicator for the titration of $Ba(OH)_2$against HI is
(a) phenolphthalein (b) methyl orange
(c) both (a) and (b) (d) none of these

138. Phenolphthalein is the most suitable indicator for the titration of
(a) CH_3COOH and NH_4OH
(b) CH_3COOH and NaOH
(c) HCl and NH_4OH
(d) H_2CO_3 and NH_4OH

139. Phenolphthalein does not act as an indicator for the titration of
(a) HCl and NH_4OH (b) $Ca(OH)_2$ and HCl
(c) NaOH and H_2SO_4 (d)CH_3COOH and KOH

140. The end point in the conductometric titration of a strong acid vs a strong base can be determined by plotting
(a) conductance vs volume of acid
(b) conductance vs volume of base
(c) pH vs volume of acid
(d) pH vs volume of base

141. When a mixture of sodium carbonate and sodium hydroxide solution is titrated against HCl solution, the phenolphthalein end point corresponds to
(a) neutralisation of OH^- ions and CO_3^{2-}
(b) neutralisation of OH^- ions only
(c) neutralisation of CO_3^{2-} ions only
(d) neutralisation of OH^- ions and half of CO_3^{2-} ions

142. On adding a large amount of titrant, an asymptote is obtained in the titration curve. This asymptote represents
(a) K_a of the initial solution
(b) pH of the initial solution
(c) pH of the titrant
(d) none of the above

143. Phenolphthalein is an indicator for acid–base titrations; it exists as the
(a) benzenoid form in acid and the quinonoid form in basic solutions
(b) quinonoid form in acid and the benzenoid form in basic solutions
(c) quinonoid form in both
(d) benzenoid form in both

144. In the titration of oxalic acid vs potassium permanganate, potassium permanganate acts as
(a) external indicator (b) self-indicator
(c) reductant (d) both (b) and (c)

145. In the reaction of $KMnO_4$ with an oxalate in acidic medium, MnO_4^- is reduced to Mn^{2+} and $C_2O_4^{2-}$ is oxidised to CO_2. Hence, 50 mL of 0.04 M $KMnO_4$ is equivalent to
(a) 100 mL of 0.1 M $H_2C_2O_4$
(b) 50 mL of 0.2 M $H_2C_2O_4$
(c) 50 mL of 0.1 M $H_2C_2O_4$
(d) 25 mL of 0.1 M $H_2C_2O_4$

146. 0.5 g mixture of $K_2Cr_2O_7$ and $KMnO_4$ was treated with excess of KI in acidic medium. I_2 liberated required 100 cm^3 of 0.15 N $Na_2S_2O_3$ solution for titration. The amount of $K_2Cr_2O_7$ in the mixture in percentage is
(a) 85.36 (b) 14.64 (c) 58.63 (d) 26.14

147. While titrating dilute HCl solution with aqueous NaOH, which of the following will not be required?
(a) pipette and distilled water
(b) burette and distilled water
(c) Bunsen burner and measuring cylinder
(d) clamp and phenolphthalein

148. When $KMnO_4$ solution is added to oxalic acid solution, the decolourisation is slow in the beginning but becomes instantaneous after sometimes because

(a) $CO_2$is formed as the product
(b) reaction is exothermic
(c) MnO_4^- catalyses the reaction
(d) Mn^{2+} acts as an autocatalyst

149. Why is HCl not used to make the medium acidic in the oxidation reaction of $KMnO_4$ in acidic medium?

(a) both HCl and $KMnO_4$act as oxidising agents
(b) $KMnO_4$ is a weaker oxidising agent than HCl
(c) $KMnO_4$ oxidises HCl into Cl_2 which is also an oxidising agent
(d) $KMnO_4$ acts as a reducing agent in the presence of HCl

150. 100 mL of HCl + 35 mL of NaOH, colour of methyl orange in the solution will be

(a) red (b) yellow
(c) can't be predicted
(d) methyl orange is not suitable indicator

151. The equivalent weight of $KMnO_4$ in the alkaline medium will be

(a) 31.60 (b) 52.66 (c) 79.00 (d) 158.00

Preparation of Compounds

152. During the preparation of acetanilide from aniline, a small amount of zinc is added to the reaction mixture because

(a) zinc induces the precipitation
(b) zinc prevents the reduction of aniline during the reaction
(c) zinc reduces the coloured impurities in the aniline and also prevents its oxidation during the reaction
(d) zinc forms a white crystalline complex with aniline

153. During the preparation of acetanilide from aniline, excess of acetic anhydride and prolonged heating should be avoided because

(a) it is oxidised
(b) it is reduced
(c) diacetyl derivative is formed
(d) triacetyl derivative is formed

154. In the preparation of *p*-nitro acetanilide from aniline, nitration is not done using the nitrating mixture (a mixture of conc. H_2SO_4 and conc. HNO_3) because

(a) on nitration it gives *o*-nitro acetanilide
(b) it gives a mixture of *o*- and *p*-nitroaniline
(c) $-NH_2$ group gets oxidised
(d) it forms a mixture of *o*- and *p*-nitroacetanilide

155. Which of the following compounds cannot be used in the preparation of iodoform?

(a) CH_3CHO (b) CH_3COCH_3
(c) HCHO (d) 2-propanol

156. Which of the following statements is wrong about aniline yellow?

(a) It is carcinogenic.
(b) It is also called *p*-aminoazobenzene.
(c) It is an acid dye.
(d) It is also called 4-phenylazoaniline.

157. During the preparation of Mohr's salt solution (ferrous ammonium sulfate), which of the following acids is added to prevent hydrolysis of Fe^{2+} ion?

(a) concentrated sulfuric acid
(b) dilute nitric acid
(c) dilute sulfuric acid
(d) dilute hydrochloric acid

Kinetics of Iodide Ions and Hydrogen Peroxide

158. In the study of oxidation of iodide ions by hydrogen peroxide in the presence of dil. H_2SO_4, thiosulfate and starch as a clock reaction, if the concentration of iodide ions is increased

(a) less time will be taken for the blue colour to appear
(b) more time will be taken for the blue colour to appear
(c) same time will be taken for the blue colour to appear
(d) any one of the above can happen depending upon the amount of H_2SO_4 present

159. Iodine reacts with sodium thiosulfate to form sodium iodide and:

(a) sodium sulfide (b) sodium tetrathionate
(c) sodium sulfate (d) sodium sulfate + sulfur

160. In the study of oxidation of iodide ions by hydrogen peroxide in the presence of dil. H_2SO_4, thiosulfate and starch as a clock reaction, if excess of thiosulfate is added:

(a) blue colour will appear immediately
(b) blue colour will not appear at all
(c) blue colour will appear only on heating the reaction mixture
(d) blue colour will appear after a very long time

161. During the reaction between H_2O_2 and the iodide ion, the reaction involves

(a) oxidation of I^- by H_2O_2
(b) oxidation of H_2O_2 by I^- ion
(c) reduction of I^- by $H_2O_2$to I^+ ion
(d) oxidation of I^- to I^+

162. In the study of oxidation of iodide ions by hydrogen peroxide in the presence of an acid and starch as a clock reaction,

(a) thiosulfate added should be in a large amount
(b) thiosulfate added should be in a small amount
(c) the amount of thiosulfate added has no importance
(d) thiosulfate is added to speed up the reaction

163. Hydrogen peroxide oxidises thiosulfate ion to
(a) SO_3^{2-} (b) SO_4^{2-} (c) $S_4O_6^{2-}$ (d) S

164. Sodium thiosulfate reacts with iodine to give iodide and tetrathionate. In this reaction $S_2O_3^{2-}$ undergoes:
(a) oxidation (b) reduction
(c) disproportionation (d) comproportionation

165. In the kinetic study of reaction of iodide ion with hydrogen peroxide, a known volume of sodium thiosulfate solution is added to
(a) oxidise the iodide ion to iodine
(b) reduce iodine to iodide ion
(c) form a soluble blue complex
(d) induce the reaction rate

166. Levelling bulb is used during an experiment to study the kinetics of the dissociation of hydrogen peroxide to ensure
(a) uniform pressure difference between the room and the gases in the system
(b) pressure within the reaction vessel is the same as that in the room
(c) same temperature as that of the room
(d) none of the above

Neutralisation of Strong Acid and Strong Base

167. In case of a weak acid and a strong base, the heat of neutralisation is less than 13.7 kcal because some part of the heat is utilised in
(a) dissociation of base (b) association of base
(c) dissociation of acid (d) association of acid

168. 50 mL of 0.5 M oxalic acid is needed to neutralise 25 mL of sodium hydroxide solution. The amount of NaOH in 50 mL of the given sodium hydroxide solution is
(a) 4 g (b) 80 g (c) 20 g (d) 10 g

169. Enthalpy of neutralisation for strong acid and strong base forming 3 moles of water is:
(a) -57.6 kJ (b) -57.6×6 kJ
(c) $\frac{-57.6}{3}$ kJ (d) -57.6×3 kJ

Enthalpy of Dissolution of Copper Sulfate

170. An aqueous solution of copper sulfate
(a) turns blue litmus red
(b) turns red litmus blue
(c) does not affect litmus
(d) affect both red and blue litmus

171. The enthalpy of solution of anhydrous $CuSO_4$ is -15.9 kcal and that of $CuSO_4.5H_2O$ is 2.8 kcal. Calculate the enthalpy of hydration of $CuSO_4$.
(a) -28.7 kcal/mol (b) -38.7 kcal/mol
(c) -8.7 kcal/mol (d) -18.7 kcal/mol

172. In a saturated solution with endothermic dissolution, how does the concentration of the dissolved solute change with increasing and then decreasing temperature?
(a) keeps increasing (b) keeps decreasing
(c) increases and decreases
(d) decreases and increases

MATCH THE FOLLOWING

173. Match List-I with List-II

List-I Test/Reagents/Observation(s)	List-II Species detected
A. Lassaigne's test	(i) Carbon
B. Cu(II) oxide	(ii) Sulfur
C. Silver nitrate	(iii) N, S, P, and halogen
D. The sodium fusion extract Gives a black precipitate with acetic acid and lead acetate	(iv) Halogen specifically

The correct match is:
(a) (A)—(iii), (B)—(i), (C)—(ii), (D)—(iv)
(b) (A)—(i), (B)—(iv), (C)—(iii), (D)—(ii)
(c) (A)—(iii), (B)—(i), (C)—(iv), (D)—(ii)
(d) (A)—(i), (B)—(ii), (C)—(iv), (D)—(iii)

174. Match List A with List B

List A (Metal ion)	List B (Group in qualitative analysis)
(A) Mn^{2+}	(i) Group III
(B) As^{3+}	(ii) Group IIA
(C) Cu^{2+}	(iii) Group IV
(D) Al^{3+}	(iv) Group IIB

Choose the **most appropriate** answer from the options given below.
(a) (A)—(i), (B)—(ii), (C)—(iii), (D)—(iv)
(b) (A)—(iii), (B)—(iv), (C)—(ii), (D)—(i)
(c) (A)—(i), (B)—(iv), (C)—(ii), (D)—(iii)
(d) (A)—(iv), (B)—(ii), (C)—(iii), (D)—(i)

175.

I. Methyl orange	P. Yellow–orange red
II. Phenolphthalein	Q. Yellow–blue
III. Bromothymol blue	R. Orange–yellow
IV. Alizarin Yellow R	S. Colourless–pink

(a) I—R, II—P, III—S, IV—Q
(b) I—R, II—S, III—Q, IV—P
(c) I—Q, II—R, III—P, IV—S
(d) I—S, II—Q, III—R, IV—P

176. Which indicator is suitable for the titrations?

Titration	Indicator
(i) HCOOH/NaOH	(A) Bromothymol blue or methyl orange or thymolphthalein
(ii) HBr/KOH	(B) Methyl orange or methyl red or bromocresol
(iii) NH_4OH/HNO_3	(C) Phenolphthalein or thymolphthalein

(a) (i)—A, (ii)—B, (iii)—C
(b) (i)—A, (ii)—C, (iii)—B
(c) (i)—B, (ii)—C, (iii)—A
(d) (i)—C, (ii)—A, (iii)—B

177. The heat of neutralisation is the change in enthalpy that occurs when one equivalent of an acid and one equivalent of a base undergo a neutralisation reaction to form water and a salt. Heat of neutralisation of strong acid and strong base is -13.7 kcal mol^{-1}

List I (Enthalpy change in kcal)	List II (Neutralisation)
(I) < 13.7 kcal	(P) HCl + NaOH 1 mol 1 mol
(II) = 13.7 kcal	(Q) HF + NaOH 1 mol 1 mol
(III) > 13.7 kcal	(R) HCl + NH_4OH 1 mol 1 mol
(IV) = 27.4 kcal	(S) NaOH + H_2SO_4 2 mol 1 mol
	(T) NaOH + CH_3COOH 1 mol 1 mol

Which of the following options has the correct combination considering List I and Lis tII?

(a) I → Q, T II → S (b) I → Q, S II → R
(c) I → R, T II → P (d) I → R, T II → P,Q

ASSERTION REASON

Directions In each of the following questions, a statement of Assertion (A) is given followed by a corresponding statement of Reason (R) just below it. Of the statements, mark the correct answer as

(a) if both the assertion and reason are true and the reason is the correct explanation of the assertion.
(b) if both assertion and reason are true but reason is not the correct explanation of assertion
(c) If assertion is true but reason is false
(d) If both assertion and reason are false

178. Assertion: NH_2–NH_2 gives Prussian blue colour during Lassaigne test.

Reason: NaCN gives Prussian blue colour of $Fe_4[Fe(CN)_6]_3$ with $FeSO_4$ and $FeCl_3$.

179. Assertion A: A mixture contains benzoic acid and naphthalene. The pure benzoic acid can be separated out by the use of benzene.

Reason R: Benzoic acid is soluble in hot water.

Answer Key

1. (d)	2. (c)	3. (a)	4. (a)	5. (b)	6. (d)	7. (d)	8. (b)	9. (a)	10. (b)
11. (a)	12. (a)	13. (a)	14. (b)	15. (b)	16. (d)	17. (b)	18. (d)	19. (c)	20. (c)
21. (b)	22. (c)	23. (c)	24. (c)	25. (b)	26. (a)	27. (c)	28. (d)	29. (d)	30. (c)
31. (d)	32. (b)	33. (a)	34. (d)	35. (d)	36. (d)	37. (c)	38. (a)	39. (b)	40. (b)
41. (d)	42. (d)	43. (c)	44. (a)	45. (b)	46. (d)	47. (b)	48. (d)	49. (c)	50. (a)
51. (d)	52. (b)	53. (a)	54. (a)	55. (a)	56. (c)	57. (a)	58. (b)	59. (a)	60. (d)
61. (a)	62. (a)	63. (b)	64. (c)	65. (d)	66. (d)	67. (a)	68. (a)	69. (c)	70. (b)
71. (d)	72. (a)	73. (b)	74. (c)	75. (b)	76. (c)	77. (c)	78. (c)	79. (b)	80. (a)
81. (b)	82. (c)	83. (b)	84. (b)	85. (d)	86. (c)	87. (a)	88. (a)	89. (a)	90. (c)
91. (b)	92. (c)	93. (d)	94. (b)	95. (a)	96. (a)	97. (b)	98. (c)	99. (a)	100. (b)
101. (b)	102. (d)	103. (b)	104. (d)	105. (b)	106. (d)	107. (d)	108. (b)	109. (b)	110. (c)
111. (a)	112. (b)	113. (b)	114. (c)	115. (a)	116. (b)	117. (b)	118. (b)	119. (c)	120. (b)
121. (d)	122. (c)	123. (c)	124. (c)	125. (a)	126. (c)	127. (b)	128. (b)	129. (b)	130. (a)
131. (b)	132. (d)	133. (c)	134. (d)	135. (d)	136. (b)	137. (c)	138. (b)	139. (a)	140. (b)
141. (d)	142. (c)	143. (a)	144. (b)	145. (c)	146. (b)	147. (c)	148. (d)	149. (b)	150. (a)
151. (b)	152. (c)	153. (c)	154. (c)	155. (c)	156. (c)	157. (c)	158. (a)	159. (b)	160. (b)
161. (a)	162. (a)	163. (b)	164. (a)	165. (b)	166. (b)	167. (a)	168. (a)	169. (d)	170. (a)
171. (d)	172. (d)	173. (c)	174. (b)	175. (c)	176. (d)	177. (c)	178. (d)	179. (d)	

Hints and Solutions

Detection of Extra Elements (Nitrogen, Sulfur, Halogens) in Organic Compounds

1. **(d)** The organic compound is fused with sodium metal. The ionic compounds formed during fusion are extracted into aqueous solution and can be used for the detection of nitrogen, sulfur, phosphorus and halogens.

2. **(c)** $Na + \underbrace{C + N} \longrightarrow Na^+CN^-$

3. **(a)** $Na_2S + Na_2[Fe(CN)_5NO] \longrightarrow Na_4[Fe(CN)_5NOS]$

4. **(a)** $Na + \underbrace{C + N + S} \longrightarrow Na^+CNS^-$

5. **(b)** The organic compound is reacted with conc. HNO_3 in the presence of $AgNO_3$, halogens are estimated by Carius method. C and H of the organic compound get oxidised to CO_2 and H_2O while the halogen forms AgX.

6. **(d)** Soda extract is prepared by boiling Na_2CO_3 and mixture, in distilled water. Soda extract for a salt involves taking the salt and sodium carbonate together in the ratio of 1:2 and then making their solution in distilled water by completely dissolving them.

7. **(d)** Addition of K_2SO_4 increases the boiling point of H_2SO_4.

8. **(b)** Kjeldahl method is suitable for the shown compound as the nitrogen is not directly attached to the benzene ring, nor is there presence of an azo or nitro group.

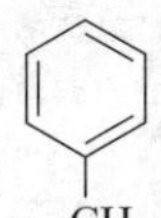

$CH_2–NH_2$

9. **(a)** If nitrogen and sulfur are together present in the compound, the sodium fusion extract is first boiled with concentrated nitric acid to decompose the cyanide of sodium formed during Lassaigne's test to the sulfide. These ions would otherwise interfere with the silver nitrate test for halogens. Hence, the sodium fusion extract is acidified with nitric acid and then treated with silver nitrate.

10. **(b)** The added nitric acid decomposes NaCN to HCN and Na_2S to H_2S.
$NaCN + HNO_3 \longrightarrow NaNO_3 + HCN$
$Na_2S + 2HNO_3 \longrightarrow HNO_3 + H_2S$
This removes all the nitrogen and sulfur present. Hence, only halogen is available for testing.

11. **(a)** The elements are covalently bonded to the organic compounds. In order to detect them, these have to be converted into their ionic form. This is done by fusing the organic compound with sodium metal. The ionic compounds formed during the fusion are extracted in aqueous solution and can be detected by simple chemical tests.

12. **(a)** By sodium fusion extract method, we can detect sulfur, nitrogen, phosphorus and the halogens because they are converted into their ionic form with sodium metal.

13. **(a)** Potassium hydroxide (KOH) absorbs $CO_2$and SO_2. When excess CO_2 is absorbed by KOH, $KHCO_3$ is formed which remains soluble in the solution.

14. **(b)** Although the addition of sulfuric acid will precipitate lead sulfate, the addition of acetic acid will ensure a complete precipitation of sulfur in the form of lead sulfate due to common ion effect. Hence, it is necessary to use acetic acid.

15. **(b)** Mass of given organic compound = 0.378 g
Mass of silver chloride formed = 0.574 g
1 mol of AgCl contains 1 mol of Cl
Thus, mass of chlorine in 0.574 g of AgCl $= \dfrac{35.5 \times 0.574}{143.32}$
$= 0.1421$ g
$\therefore$ Percentage of chlorine $= \dfrac{0.1421}{0.3780} \times 100 = 37.59\%$

16. **(d)** For the test of nitrogen, few drops of ferric chloride solution are added and then acidified with conc. hydrochloric acid. A Prussian blue colouration indicates the presence of nitrogen in the compound.

17. **(b)** In the test for sulfur, the sodium fusion extract is acidified with acetic acid and lead acetate is added to it. Once this reaction takes place, a black precipitate is formed, indicating the presence of sulfur.

18. **(d)** During the detection of chlorine, when the organic compound reacts with sodium, it forms sodium chloride. This sodium chloride gives the white precipitate of silver nitrate. This white precipitate is also soluble in ammonium hydroxide.

19. **(c)** Nitrogen is covalently bonded to the organic compound. In order to detect it, the element needs to be converted into its ionic form. This is done by fusing the organic compound with sodium metal.

20. **(c)** Lassigne's test is given by nitrogenous compounds in which carbon is also present along with nitrogen. In NH_2NH_2. HCl, carbon is absent.

21. **(b)** The sodium fusion extract is first boiled with concentrated nitric acid to decompose cyanide or sulfide formed during Lassaigne's test. Otherwise, these ions will interfere with the silver nitrate test of halogens.

22. **(c)** If both nitrogen and sulfur are present in an organic compound, sodium fusion will convert it into sodium thiocyanate which then react with Fe^{3+} to form a blood red complex $[Fe(SCN)_3]$.

23. **(c)** The compound is heated with copper oxide. Carbon is oxidised to CO_2 which is then confirmed by passing limewater that turns milky.

24. **(c)** In Lassaigne's test, a small piece of sodium metal is heated in a fusion tube, it converts all the elements into their ionic form.
$Na + C + N \longrightarrow NaCN$
$2Na + S \longrightarrow Na_2S$
$Na + X \longrightarrow NaX$ (X= Cl, Br or I)

25. **(b)** CH_3NH_2.HCl gives a positive Lassaigne's test for both nitrogen and halogen as the compound must have C, N and halogen atom in it.

26. **(a)** The white precipitate which is formed in the detection of chloride ion is due to the formation of ammonium chloride.

27. **(c)** When a solution containing bromine ions (Br^-) is added to a solution containing silver ions (Ag^+), a pale yellow precipitate of silver bromide is formed.
$Ag^+ + Br^- \longrightarrow AgBr$

28. **(d)** $Na + C + N \longrightarrow NaCN$
$6\,NaCN + FeSO_4 \longrightarrow Na_4[Fe(CN)_6] + Na_2SO_4$
$Na_4[Fe(CN)_6] + Fe^{3+} \longrightarrow \underset{\text{Prussian blue colour}}{Fe_4[Fe(CN)_6]_3}$

29. **(d)** Nitrogen containing organic compounds fuse with Na and form NaCN which is used for the detection of nitrogen.
$Na + C + N \xrightarrow{\Delta} NaCN$

30. **(c)** The correct option is (c). Method for the detection of C and H is known as Liebig's method.

31. **(d)** Detection of sulfur in sodium extract can be done both by $Pb(OAc)_2$ and sodium nitroprusside. But it cannot be done by silver nitrate. Rather, it is done by potassium nitrate and sodium carbonate.
$KNO_3 \xrightarrow{\Delta} KNO_2 + O$
$Na_2CO_3 + S + 3[O] \xrightarrow{\Delta} Na_2SO_4 + CO_2$

Salt Analysis

32. **(b)** Beryllium and magnesium cannot give flame test because they have small size and very high ionisation enthalpy.

33. **(a)** When calcium ion undergoes flame test, the electrons lost by calcium atom emit a brick red colour.

34. **(d)** The group number is as follows:

Group	Cations
II	Cu^{2+}
III	Al^{3+}
IV	Co^{2+}
V	Ba^{2+}
VI	Mg^{2+}

Hence the correct order is B, A, D, C, E.

35. **(d)** Ammonia, being a weak base, produces hydroxide ions in the water.
$Zn^{2+} + 2OH^- \longrightarrow Zn(OH)_2$
Zinc hydroxide is the white precipitate. If you continue to add the ammonia solution to the precipitate, it redissolves because of the formation of $Zn(NH_3)_4$ to give a colourless solution.

36. **(d)** When zinc nitrate is boiled with potassium hydroxide and aluminium foil, it releases fumes that have a characteristic choking smell which turns red litmus paper to blue. The gas released is ammonia. Aluminium foil acts as a powerful reducing agent.

37. **(c)** Ferrous sulfate with NaOH forms sodium sulfate along with iron hydroxide which precipitates in the form of a green coloured solid. With barium nitrate, ferrous sulfate forms a white precipitate of barium sulfate which is insoluble in water.

38. **(a)** The formation of a green precipitate that is insoluble in excess aqueous sodium hydroxide indicates the presence of a transition metal hydroxide; the slow turning of green precipitate to brown suggests the formation of a complex ion. Therefore, the unknown salt is most likely copper(II) sulfate.

39. **(b)** The salt is zinc carbonate. On heating zinc carbonate, it gives CO_2 which turns lime water milky.
$ZnCO_3 \xrightarrow{\Delta} ZnO + CO_2$
The residue is ZnO, which dissolves in dil. HCl as well as in sodium hydroxide.

40. **(b)** Al^{3+} ions form a gelatinous white precipitate of $Al(OH)_3$ with NaOH. This precipitate is insoluble in aqueous ammonia.

41. **(d)** $SO_2 + \text{dil. } H_2SO_4 \longrightarrow SO_3$
$SO_3 + K_2Cr_2O_7 \longrightarrow Cr_2(SO_4)_3$

42. **(d)** For the detection of NO_2^-, the following test is used:

$NO_2^- + CH_3COOH \longrightarrow HNO_2 + CH_3COO^-$

$$\underset{\text{(Sulphanilic acid solution)}}{\overset{\oplus}{N}H_3CH_3COO^- \text{-}C_6H_4\text{-}SO_3H} + HNO_2 \longrightarrow N{=}N\text{-}OCOCH_3\text{-}C_6H_4\text{-}SO_3H + 2H_2O$$

$$\underset{\text{Diazotised acid}}{N{=}N\text{-}OCOCH_3\text{-}C_6H_4\text{-}SO_3H} + \underset{\text{1-napthyl amine}}{C_{10}H_7NH_2} \longrightarrow$$

$$\underset{\text{(Red azo dye)}}{HO_3S\text{-}C_6H_4\text{-}N{=}N\text{-}C_{10}H_6\text{-}NH_2} + CH_3COOH$$

43. **(c)** $\underset{\substack{X \\ \text{(Anion)}}}{NO_3^-} + \underset{\text{(conc.)}}{H_2SO_4} \longrightarrow \underset{\text{Brown fumes}}{NO_2\uparrow} + H_2O$

$\underset{\text{Solution}}{FeSO_4} + \underset{\text{conc.}}{H_2SO_4} + \underset{X}{NO_3^-} \longrightarrow \underset{\text{(Dark brown ring)}}{[Fe(H_2O)_5(NO)]SO_4}$

$\underset{\substack{X \\ \text{(cation)}}}{Cu^{2+}} + \underset{\text{(Group-II reagent)}}{(\text{dil HCl} + H_2S)} \longrightarrow \underset{\substack{\text{(Black ppt)} \\ (Y)}}{CuS\downarrow}$

$\underset{\substack{X \\ \text{(Anion)}}}{CuS} \xrightarrow[HNO_3]{\text{conc}^l} \underset{\text{Soluble}}{Cu(NO_3)_2} + NO_2 + S + H_2O$

$\downarrow$ Excess NH_4OH solution

$\underset{\text{Deep blue colour solution}}{[Cu(NH_3)_4]^{2+}}$

$\therefore X \rightarrow Cu(NO_3)_2$

44. **(a)** Al^{3+} and Fe^{3+}sulfides hydrolyse in water. Ni^{2+} and Zn^{2+} require basic medium with H_2S to form a precipitate. Ca^{2+} and Ba^{2+}sulfides are soluble. Hence, we will only get a precipitate of CuS.

45. **(b)** $Ca(OH)_2 + CO_2 \longrightarrow CaCO_3\downarrow + H2O$
$CaCO_3\downarrow + CO_2 + H_2O \longrightarrow Ca(HCO_3)_2$

46. **(d)** $\underset{\text{(in excess)}}{FeCl_3 + K_4[Fe(CN)_6]} \longrightarrow \underset{\text{Colloidal species}}{KFe[Fe(CN)_6]}$

47. **(b)** Oxides of nitrogen and sulfur are acidic and settle down as dry deposit. Ammonium salts in rain drops result in wet deposit.

48. **(d)** $FeCl_3 + K_4[Fe(CN)_6] \longrightarrow \underset{\text{Prussian blue}}{Fe_4[Fe(CN)_6]_3}$

49. **(c)** If calcium is present, it is precipitated by adding oxalate ion.
$Ca^{2+}(aq) + C_2O_4^{2-}(aq) \longrightarrow \underset{\text{White ppt.}}{CaC_2O_4(s)}$

50. **(a)** (i) Formation of yellow precipitate indicates the presence of the bromide ion which is partially soluble in NH_4OH.
(ii) Formation of white precipitate indicates the presence of the chloride ion which gets completely dissolved in NH_4OH.
So, B and C are correct options.

51. **(d)** The group I reagent is dil. HCl. So, group I cations like Pb^{2+} precipitate as chlorides.

52. **(b)** Iodine dissolves easily in chloroform, carbon tetrachloride or carbon disulfide to form a violet layer.

53. **(a)** Potassium hydroxide is a basic compound that reacts with carbon dioxide released from the oxidation of the organic compound. It is used to determine the amount of carbon present in an organic compound.

54. **(a)** When silver sulfate solution is added to a solution containing both nitrate and bromide ions, a white precipitate of silver bromide forms. This is because silver bromide is insoluble in water and forms a solid precipitate. In contrast, silver nitrate is highly soluble in water and does not form a precipitate when silver sulfate is added. The nitrate ions remain in solution while the bromide ions are separated as solid.

55. **(a)** On heating, borax loses water of crystallisation and swells up to form a fluffy mass. On further heating, it melts to give a clear liquid which solidifies to a transparent glassy bead.
$Na_2B_4O_7.10\,H_2O \xrightarrow{\Delta} Na_2B_4O_7 + 10\,H_2O$
$\xrightarrow{740°C} \underset{\text{Sodium metaborate (glassy bead)}}{2NaBO_2 + B_2O_3}$

56. **(c)** Borax bead test is generally given by transition elements. Hence, Cr, Ni and Mn give the borax bead test while Pb does not give.

57. **(a)** CuF_2 is a coloured compound. The copper is in the Cu^{2+} state. It has one unpaired electron.

58. **(b)** On heating, borax loses water of crystallisation and swells up to form a fluffy mass. On further heating, it melts to give a clear liquid which solidifies to a transparent glassy bead.
$Na_2B_4O_7.10\,H_2O \xrightarrow{\Delta} Na_2B_4O_7 + 10\,H_2O$
$\xrightarrow{740°C} \underset{\text{Sodium metaborate (glassy bead)}}{2NaBO_2 + B_2O_3}$

59. **(a)** Barium gives an apple green colour in its chloride form. The electrons can be easily excited to higher energy levels. This results in characteristic colour.

60. **(d)** As Mn^{2+} has all its electrons (5) unpaired in its *d* orbital, so its extra stable configuration requires high excitation energy and so it gives a violet colour.

61. **(a)** Barium salt gives a green coloured flame as it has low ionisation enthalpy.

62. **(a)** $KMnO_4$ is an oxidising agent, the salt must contain anions that can be oxidised to the higher oxidation state. Hence, the salt must contain sulfite (SO_3^{2-}) which on oxidation with $KMnO_4$ gives sulfate(SO_4^{2-}) and $KMnO_4$ itself gets reduced to MnO_2, that is, pink colour of $KMnO_4$is discharged.
$2H^+ + 2MnO_4^- + SO_3^{2-} \longrightarrow MnO_2 + H_2O + 3\,SO_4^{2-}$

63. **(b)** $Na_2SO_3(aq) + 2\,HCl(aq) \longrightarrow 2\,NaCl(aq) + H_2O(l) + SO_2(g)$
The colourless gas of sulfur dioxide having a suffocating smell of burning sulfur, changes the colour of potassium dichromate from orange to green.

64. **(c)** Starch–iodide paper consists of potassium iodide and starch. Free chlorine and nitrite ion readily accept an electron to gain their stable configuration.
$[Cl] + e^- \longrightarrow Cl^-$
$2I^- \longrightarrow I_2 + 2e^-$
So, it is used for the detection of the oxidising agent.

65. **(d)** Zinc oxide is white in colour but turns yellow on heating because it loses oxygen reversibly at high temperature.
$ZnO \longrightarrow Zn^{2+} + \frac{1}{2}O_2 + 2e^-$

66. **(d)** $Al_2O_3.CoO$ formed in the test is blue in colour.

67. **(a)** Zinc oxide forms a green double oxide with cobalt.

68. **(a)** $2\,KNO_2 + H_2SO_4 \longrightarrow K_2SO_4 + HNO_2$
$HNO_2 \longrightarrow HNO_3 + H_2O + 2NO$
$2\,NO + \underset{\text{From air}}{O_2} \longrightarrow \underset{\text{(Reddish brown)}}{2NO_2\uparrow}$

69. **(c)** Only Fe^{3+} ions give blood red colouration with CNS^- ions
$Fe^{3+} + 3\,CNS^- \longrightarrow \underset{\text{Blood red colouration}}{Fe(CNS)_3}$

70. **(b)** Mercurous chloride (Hg_2Cl_2) turns black with NH_4OH due to the formation of finely divided mercury and $Hg(NH_2)Cl$.

71. **(d)** $\underset{\text{(Chromyl chloride)}}{Cr_2OCl_2} + 2H_2O \longrightarrow 2HCl + \underset{\text{Chromic acid (yellow solution)}}{H_2CrO_4}$
$H_2CrO_4 + (CH_3COO)_2Pb \longrightarrow CH_3COOH + \underset{\text{(yellow ppt.)}}{PbCrO_4\downarrow}$

72. **(a)** Sodium chloride gives a precipitate with $Pb(NO_3)_2$ but not with $Ba(NO_3)_2$.
$NaCl + Pb(NO_3)_2 \longrightarrow PbCl_2 + NaNO_3$
$PbCl_2$is insoluble in cold water but soluble in hot water and on cooling, white crystals are again formed.

73. **(b)** The acid radical is bicarbonate.

$$2\,NaHCO_3 + MgSO_4 \longrightarrow \underset{\text{Soluble}}{Mg(HCO_3)_2} + H_2 + CO_2$$

$$Mg(HCO_3)_2 \xrightarrow{\Delta} \underset{\text{White ppt.}}{MgCO_3\downarrow} + H_2O + CO_2$$

74. **(c)** $\underset{\text{Sodium nitroprusside}}{Na_2[(CN)_5NO]} + Na_2S \longrightarrow \underset{\text{Sodium thionitroprusside (violet purple)}}{Na_4[(CN)_5NOS]}$

75. **(b)** On heating a mixture of sodium chloride, potassium dichromate and conc. sulfuric acid, red vapour of chromyl chloride is obtained.

$$K_2Cr_2O_7 + 2\,H_2SO_4 \longrightarrow KHSO_4 + 2\,CrO_3 + H_2O$$

$$NaCl + H_2SO_4 \longrightarrow NaHSO_4 + HCl$$

$$CrO_3 + 2\,HCl \longrightarrow \underset{\text{Red vapour}}{CrO_2Cl_2}$$

76. **(c)** The phosphate compound is first treated with nitric acid and then with ammonium molybdate. A canary yellow precipitate confirms the presence of phosphate.

$$Na_3PO_4 + 3\,HNO_3 \longrightarrow H_3PO_4 + 3\,NaNO_3$$

$$H_3PO_4 + 12\,(NH_4)_2MoO_4 + 21\,HNO_3 \longrightarrow (NH_4)_3PO_4.12MoO_3 + 21\,NH_4NO_3 + 12\,H_2O$$

77. **(c)** AgCl is most soluble in NH_4OH due to formation of complex.

$$AgCl + NH_4OH \longrightarrow \underset{\text{Highly stable complex}}{Ag[NH_3]_2^+}$$

78. **(c)** Pure chlorine gas may react vigorously with ammonia gas.

$$NH_3 + 3Cl_2 \longrightarrow NCl_3 + 3\,HCl$$

79. **(b)** $KMnO_4$ reacts with sulfide to give S.

$$\underset{\text{Pink}}{2\,KMnO_4} + 5H_2S + 3\,H_2SO_4 \longrightarrow \underset{\text{Colourless}}{K_2SO_4 + 5S + 2MnSO_4 + 8H_2O}$$

80. **(a)** Ethyl bromide does not give a precipitate with silver nitrate because it does not provide free ions to react with.

81. **(b)** $[Cu(NH_3)_4](NO_3)_2 + 4\,CH_3COOH \longrightarrow Cu(NO_3)_2 + 4\,CH_3COONH_4$

$$2\,Cu(NO_3)_2 + K_4[Fe(CN)_6] \longrightarrow \underset{\text{Chocolate ppt.}}{Cu_2[Fe(CN)_6]} + 4\,KNO_3$$

82. **(c)** CaO, $CaCO_3$ and $Ca(OH)_2$ are all bases and react with acetic acid to dissolve in CH_3COOH and form salt calcium acetate $(CH_3COO)_2Ca$. But CaC_2O_4 is a salt and does not react with acetic acid. It ionises into oxalate ions.

83. **(b)** For Group IV, H_2S in the presence of NH_4Cl and NH_4OH is used as a reagent.

84. **(b)** On adding dil. HCl to silver and lead salts, white precipitates of chlorides of Ag and Pb are obtained which on heating with water are separated from each other as $PbCl_2$ is soluble in hot water but AgCl is not.

85. **(d)** The ion that cannot be precipitated by both HCl and H_2S is Sn^{2+}, while all others are precipitated by H_2S in the presence of HCl. Sn^{2+} cannot be precipitated by HCl but is precipitated by H_2S as a chocolate coloured precipitate.

86. **(c)** $H_2S(g) + Pb(CH_3COO)_2(aq) \longrightarrow \underset{\text{Black ppt.}}{PbS\downarrow} + CH_3COOH(aq)$

87. **(a)** $Fe^{2+} + NH_4SCN \longrightarrow$ No change in colour

$Fe^{3+} + NH_4SCN \longrightarrow$ Red colouration

So, NH_4SCN is used to distinguish between Fe^{2+} and Fe^{3+}.

88. **(a)** $K_4[Fe(CN)_6]$ reacts with $FeCl_3$ to form a dark blue precipitate of $Fe_4[Fe(CN)_6]_3$.

89. **(a)** [X] and [Y] are SO_3^{2-} and SO_2 respectively.

SO_3^{2-} reacts with sulfuric acid to form sulfur dioxide which is a colourless gas with an irritating smell.

$$SO_3^{2-} + H_2SO_4 \longrightarrow SO_2 + H_2O$$

Potassium dichromate oxidises sulfur dioxide to a green solution of chromium sulfate.

$$SO_2 + K_2Cr_2O_7 + H_2SO_4 \longrightarrow Cr_2(SO_4)_3 \text{ (green solution)} + K_2SO_4 + H_2O$$

90. **(c)** When the Cr^{3+} reacts with conc. NaOH, then the following reaction takes place,

$$Cr^{3+} + 3OH^- \longrightarrow Cr(OH)_3$$

which on further reaction gives $Cr(OH)_4^-$ (green coloured solution).

$$Cr(OH)_3 + OH^- \longrightarrow Cr(OH)_4^-$$

When Fe^{3+} reacts with conc. NaOH and gives $Fe(OH)_3$ precipitate.

$$Fe^{3+} + 3OH^- \longrightarrow \underset{\text{Precipitate}}{Fe(OH)_3}$$

So, as the $Cr(OH)_4^-$ is in solution and $Fe(OH)_3$ precipitates, Cr^{3+} and Fe^{3+} can be separated out from the solution.

91. **(b)** Because their hydroxides are insoluble in NH_3, III group radicals are precipitated as hydroxides.

92. **(c)** By addition of 3M HNO_3, Hg^{2+}can be separated from Cu^{2+}. This means that Hg^{2+}can be precipitated from the solution by the addition of 3M HNO_3. Hence, the solubility product of HgS and ultimately its solubility, is less than CuS in 3M HNO_3.

93. **(d)** Pb forms $PbCl_2$ in I group and PbS in II group. Lead salts are partially soluble in water.

94. **(b)** The third group solution should be treated with excess of NH_4Cl. The presence of NH_4Cl in excess reduces the degree of dissociation of NH_4OH to a considerable amount and thus $[OH^-]$ is just sufficient to cross over the ionic concentration product of hydroxides of III group elements to their K_{sp}.

95. **(a)** NH_4^+ ions are required to suppress the ionisation of NH_4OH but are sufficient to precipitate IIIrd group radicals. $(NH_4)_2SO_4$ cannot be used as SO_4^{2-} ions will precipitate Ba^{2+} as $BaSO_4$; so, NH_4NO_3 is used.

96. **(a)** HgS does not dissolve in hot dilute HNO_3.

$$3\,PbS + 8HNO_3 \longrightarrow 3\,Pb(NO_3)_2 + 2\,NO + 3S + 4\,H_2O$$

$$3\,CuS + 8HNO_3 \longrightarrow 3\,Pb(NO_3)_2 + 2\,NO + 3S + 4\,H_2O$$

$$3\,CdS + 8HNO_3 \longrightarrow 3\,Pb(NO_3)_2 + 2\,NO + 3S + 4\,H_2O$$

Thus, the sulfides of Pb, Cu and Cd dissolve in dilute HNO_3 forming the respective nitrates.

97. **(b)** $BaSO_4$ is insoluble in conc. HNO_3 because the H^+ ions of the acid cannot remove SO_4^{2-} ions from barium sulfate.

CuS is soluble in conc. HNO_3 leaving a white precipitate of sulfur.

$$CuS + 8HNO_3 \longrightarrow CuSO_4 + 8\,NO_2 + 4\,H_2O$$

PbS is also soluble in conc. HNO_3.
$3PbS + 8HNO_3 \longrightarrow 3PbSO_4 + 8\ NO + 4\ H_2O$
HgS is insoluble in conc. HNO_3.

98. (c) Its purpose is to keep the sulfide ion concentration at a minimum, so as to allow the precipitation of 2nd group cations alone. HCl decreases ionisation of H_2S due to common ion effect.

99. (a) $AgNO_3$ will turn the copper solution blue. Blue colour is due to the formation of Cu^{2+} ions. Silver is placed above copper in the electrochemical series. Thus, copper can displace silver ions from its salt solution while the others cannot.

100. (b) Manganese nitrate reacts with excess sodium hydroxide to form a white precipitate of manganese hydroxide. This precipitate is insoluble in excess NaOH.
$Mn^{2+} + 2\ OH^- \longrightarrow Mn(OH)_2\downarrow$
When bromine water is added, a brown precipitate of $MnO(OH)_2$ is obtained.
$Mn(OH)_2 + [O] \xrightarrow{Br_2\ water} MnO(OH)_2$
On reaction with disodium hydrogen phosphate solution in the presence of ammonia, manganese nitrate forms a pink precipitate of $Mn(NH_4)PO_4$.
$Mn^{2+} + NH_3 + HPO_4^{2-}\ \underset{Pink}{Mn(NH_4)PO_4\downarrow}$
Hence, the cation is Mn^{2+}.

101. (b) $SnCl_2 + HgCl_2 \longrightarrow Hg_2Cl_2 \xrightarrow{SnCl_2} Hg$

102. (d) $[HgI_4]^{2-} + NH_4Cl + 4\ OH^- \longrightarrow NH_2HgOHgI$

103. (b) The blue precipitate of Fe^{2+}ions with potassium ferricyanide is due to the formation of Turnbull's blue.
$$Fe^{2+} + K_3[Fe(CN)_6] \longrightarrow \underset{Turnbull's\ blue}{K\ \overset{II}{Fe}[\overset{III}{Fe}(CN)_6]} + 2\ K^+$$

104. (d) The metal M in the salt is zinc. An aqueous solution of colourless zinc sulfate gives a white precipitate of $Zn(OH)_2$ with NH_4OH.
$ZnSO_4 + 2\ NH_4OH \longrightarrow Zn(OH)_2\downarrow + (NH_4)_2SO_4$

105. (b) NaCl is the salt of a strong acid and a strong base, hence on dissolution, it will give a neutral solution. As a white precipitate is obtained by the addition of $AgNO_3$ to the solution of Na salt, it can be of AgCl. Further AgCl is also insoluble in HNO_3. Hence the anion is Cl^-.
$NaCl + AgNO_3 \longrightarrow AgCl\downarrow + HNO_3$

106. (d) Nessler's reagent $K_2[HgI_4]$ in alkaline medium is used to detect the NH_4^+ ion.

107. (d) For (a) $FeCl_3 + 3\ K_4[Fe(CN)_6] \longrightarrow Fe_4[Fe(CN)_6]_3 + 12\ KCl$
For (b) and (c), the reaction is
$M^{2+} + [Fe(CN)_6]^{4-} \xrightarrow{CH_3COOH} M_2[Fe(CN)_6]\downarrow$
So, it cannot be used to test Cr^{3+}.

108. (b) Ba^{2+} ion imparts green colour to the flame and Cl^- ion forms chromyl chloride (which is orange red in colour) when treated with $K_2Cr_2O_7$ and conc. H_2SO_4. Thus, the reagent is:
$Ba^{2+} + 2Cl^- \longrightarrow BaCl_2$
$$BaCl_2 + K_2Cr_2O_7 + 3\ H_2SO_4 \longrightarrow K_2SO_4 + 2\ BaSO_4 + \underset{\substack{Chromyl\ chloride \\ (orange\ red\ gas)}}{CrO_2Cl_2} + 3\ H_2O$$

109. (b) When dimethylglyoxime is added to a solution along with ammonium hydroxide, the formation of bright red precipitate indicates the presence of Ni^{2+}. This is due to the formation of dimethylglyoxime complex.

110. (c) On treatment with dil. HCl, Na_2CO_3 and Na_2SO_3 produce CO_2 and SO_2 respectively. SO_2 turns acidified $K_2Cr_2O_7$ solution green whereas CO_2 does not change the colour of the solution.

111. The correct option is (a).

112. (b)
$$K_3[\overset{+3}{Fe}(CN)_6] + \overset{-1}{KI} \xrightarrow{Dil.\ H_2SO_4} K_4[\overset{+2}{Fe}(CN)_6] + \overset{-1}{KI_3}$$
$$\underset{(excess)}{K_4[Fe(CN)_6]} + ZnSO_4 \longrightarrow \underset{White\ ppt.}{K_2Zn[Fe(CN)_6]}$$
$$\underset{\substack{Brownish \\ yellow\ filtrate}}{I_3^-} + 2\ Na_2S_2O_3 \longrightarrow \underset{\substack{Clear \\ Solution}}{Na_2S_4O_6 + 2\ NaI} + \underset{\substack{Turns\ starch \\ solution\ blue}}{I_2}$$
$K_2Zn[Fe(CN)_6]$ reacts with NaOH as follows:
$K_2Zn[Fe(CN)_6] + 4\ NaOH \longrightarrow [Zn(OH)_4]^{2-} + [Fe(CN)_6]^{4-}$

113. (b) $FeS + H_2SO_4(dilute) \longrightarrow FeSO_4(aq) + H_2S(g)$

114. (c) $NaCl + H_2SO_4 \longrightarrow NaHSO_4 + \underset{Colourless}{HCl\uparrow}$
$NaI + H_2SO_4 \longrightarrow NaHSO_4 + HI$
$HI + H_2SO_4 \longrightarrow \underset{Violet\ colour}{I_2\uparrow} + SO_2 + 2H_2O$

115. (a) $NO_3^- + 3\ Fe^{2+} + 4H^+ \longrightarrow NO + 3Fe^{3+} + 2H2O$
$[Fe(H_2O)_6]^{2+} + NO \longrightarrow \underset{Brown\ complex}{[Fe(H_2O)_5(NO)]^{2+}} + H_2O$
In the ring test of NO_3^- ion, Fe^{2+} ion reduces nitrate ion to nitric oxide, which combines with Fe^{2+}(aq) ion to form brown complex.

116. (b) On passing H_2S gas in the aqueous solution of salt in the presence of dil. HCl, a black precipitate of CuS is formed.
$3CuS + 8HNO_3 \longrightarrow 3Cu(NO_3)_2 + 2\ NO + 3\ S + 4\ H_2O$
$Cu^{2+} + 4\ NH_4OH \longrightarrow \underset{Deep\ blue\ complex}{[Cu(NH_3)_4]^{2+}} + 4\ H_2O$

117. (b) $CuSO_4$ decolourises on addition of KCN. The product is CuCN along with $(CN)_2$ but in excess of KCN, colourless potassium tetracyanocuperate(I) is obtained.
$CuSO_4 + 2\ KCN \longrightarrow Cu(CN)_2 + [K_2SO_4] \times 2$
$2\ Cu(CN)_2 \rightleftharpoons 2\ CuCN + (CN)_2$
$CuCN + 3\ KCN \longrightarrow \underset{Colourless}{K_3[Cu(CN)_4]}$

Detection of Functional Group in an Organic Compound

118. (b) Phenol and carboxylic acid can be distinguished by sodium bicarbonate $NaHCO_3$. Carboxylic acid reacts with

$NaHCO_3$ to give effervescence due to evolution of CO_2 while phenol does not give effervescence.
$RCOOH + NaHCO_3 \longrightarrow RCOONa + H_2O + CO_2$

119. (c) Oxalic acid reacts with conc. sulfuric acid to produce a mixture of carbon monoxide, carbon dioxide and water.
$(COOH)_2 + \text{conc. } H_2SO_4 \longrightarrow CO + CO_2 + H_2O$

120. (b) When phenol reacts with bromine water it results in the formation of a white precipitate of tribromophenol. Aliphatic compounds of alcohol have no reaction with bromine water.

121. (d) Methyl salicylate is known as oil of wintergreen. It smells like mint.

122. (c) Starch is colourless but changes its colour in iodine solution.
$\underset{\text{(Violet)}}{\text{Starch + Iodine}} \longrightarrow \underset{\text{(blue-black)}}{\text{Starch–Iodine}}$

123. (c) 2,4-DNP test is used for the detection of aldehydes.

124. (c) Benzaldehyde does not reduce Fehling's solution (a distinction from other aldehydes).
Acetone (ketone) also does not give any test with Fehling's solution.

125. (a) Since given compound 'A' burns with a sooty flame, it must be an aromatic compound. Again, when it reacts with Brady's reagent (acidic 2,4-dinitrophenyl hydrazine solution), it yields an orange precipitate. Therefore, it must be an aldehyde or ketone. But ketone does not give a positive Tollens' reagent; therefore, it must be a ketone. Therefore, A is acetophenone.

126. (c) *m*-cresol on reaction with 10% NaOH forms 3-methyl sodium phenoxide ion.

OH, CH_3 (m-cresol) $\xrightarrow{\text{10\% NaOH}}$ O^-Na^+, CH_3

It does not react with H_2O, 5% HCl and 10% $NaHCO_3$.
Oleic acid is soluble in 10% NaOH and 10% $NaHCO_3$ due to the presence of –COOH group.
Benzamide is insoluble in 5% HCl, 10% NaOH and 10% $NaHCO_3$ due to the presence of $–CONH_2$ group. *o*-toluidine is soluble in 5% HCl due to the presence of basic group ($–NH_2$) attached to the ring.

127. (b) $RNH_2 + CHCl_3 + 3\ KOH \longrightarrow RNC + 3\ KCl + 3\ H_2O$
(where R may be an alkyl or aryl group).

128. (b) The compound liberates CO_2 with $NaHCO_3$, so it contains the –COOH group and it also gives a colour with neutral $FeCl_3$ solution, so it also contains a –OH group directly attached to the benzene ring(phenol). Hence, (b) is the correct option.

Titrations

129. (b) For the titration of a weak acid with a strong base, the pH curve is initially acidic and has a basic equivalence point, that is, pH > 7.

130. (a) Methyl orange shows a red colour in acidic medium and a yellow colour in the basic medium. So, its pH range is 3–5.

131. (b) $HCl + NaOH \longrightarrow NaCl + H_2O$
One mole of NaOH is required for each mole of hydrochloric acid consumed.
No. of moles of HCl = 33 mL × 3 M = 100 mmol
Therefore, 100 mmol of NaOH is required.

132. (d) gram equivalent of HCl = $N \times V = 100 \times 0.1/1000 = 0.01$
Now, we calculate gram equivalent of NaOH which is also equal to 0.01.
$0.01 = w/40$
$w = 0.01 \times 40 = 0.4$ g

133. (c) Phenolphthalein is colourless below pH 8.5 and attains a pink to deep red colour above pH 9.0.

134. (d) HCOOH is a weak acid. When a weak acid is titrated with a strong base, the end point will be at a pH higher than 7 because of the weak acid's conjugate base being present. So, both phenolphthalein as well as thymolphthalein can be used as indicators since their colour changes from colourless to bright at a pH around 8.

135. (d) HBr is a strong acid and KOH is a strong base, all the three can be used as indicators in the titration.

136. (b) NH_4OH is weak base and HNO_3 is a strong acid, therefore methyl orange is the most suitable indicator.

137. (c) $Ba(OH)_2$ is a strong base and HI is a strong acid, therefore both phenolphthalein and methyl orange can be used as indicators in their titration.

138. (b) The correct option is (b). The reason is explained in the next question.

139. (a) The equivalence point of a titration is where we have mixed two substances in exactly equal proportions. We obviously need to choose an indicator which changes colour as close as possible to the equivalence point. That varies from titration to titration. Phenolphthalein can be used in the pH range between 8 to 10. Therefore, it is used for strong acid and strong base titrations or weak acid and strong base titrations. NH_4OH and HCl is a strong acid and weak base titration where phenolphthalein is useless as an indicator.

140. (b) The correct option is (b).

141. (d) The correct option is (d). When sodium carbonate is completely neutralised, it will be indicated by methyl orange.

142. (c) When an infinite amount of titrant is added, the pH should become just the pH of the titrant. The original solution gets diluted. We expect the asymptotic pH of a titration curve to approach that of the titrant.

143. (a) Phenolphthalein is colourless in acid solution (benzenoid form) and pink in alkali (basic) solution (quinoid form).

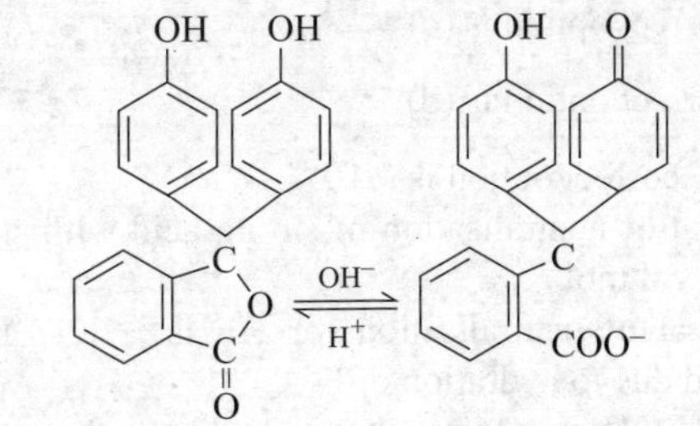

$$\text{Colourless (Acidic medium) benzenoid form} \underset{H^+}{\overset{OH^-}{\rightleftharpoons}} \text{Red (Alkaline medium) quinonoid form}$$

Colourless (Acidic medium) benzenoid form

Red (Alkaline medium) quinonoid form

144. (b) In the titration of oxalic acid vs $KMnO_4$, $KMnO_4$ acts as an oxidant as well as a self-indicator.

$2\,KMnO_4 + 3\,H_2SO_4 \longrightarrow K_2SO_4 + 2\,MnSO_4 + 3\,H_2O + 5\,[O]$

$$5\begin{array}{l}COOH\\ |\\ COOH\end{array} + 5[O] \longrightarrow 5\,H_2O + 10\,CO_2$$

145. (c) Equivalent mass of $MnO_4^- = \dfrac{\text{Molar mass}}{7-2} = \dfrac{\text{Molar mass}}{5}$

Equivalent mass of $C_2O_4^{2-} = \dfrac{\text{Molar mass}}{2(4-3)} = \dfrac{\text{Molar mass}}{2}$

Milliequivalents of $KMnO_4 = 50 \times 5 \times 0.04 = 10$ = M .eq. of $H_2C_2O_4$

which is the same for $50 \times 2 \times 0.1 = 10$

That is, 50 mL of 0.1 M $H_2C_2O_4$

146. (b) Let the amount of $K_2Cr_2O_7$ in the mixture be x g.

Then amount of $KMnO_4$ will be $(0.5 - x)$ g

$$\left(\frac{x}{49} + \frac{0.5-x}{31.6}\right) = \frac{100 \times 0.15}{1000}$$

where, 49 is the eq. wt. of $K_2Cr_2O_7$ and 31.6 is the eq. wt. of $KMnO_4$. On solving we get

$x = 0.0732$ g

Percentage of $K_2Cr_2O_7 = \dfrac{0.0732 \times 100}{0.5} = 14.64\%$

147. (c) Titration (neutralisation) of dil. HCl solution with aqueous NaOH will require the following steps and apparatus. NaOH solution made with distilled water and solid NaOH is taken in a burette and it is fitted with a clamp. The given volume of standard HCl solution is then pipetted out and taken in a conical flask for titration. Then, few drops of phenolphthalein indicator is added in this HCl solution. So, we do not require measuring cylinder and Bunsen burner as the titration takes place at room temperature.

148. (d) $5\,C_2O_4^{2-} + \underset{\text{Purple}}{2\,MnO_4^-} + 16\,H^+ \longrightarrow \underset{\text{Colourless (auto-catalyst)}}{Mn^{2+}} + 8\,H_2O + 10\,CO_2\uparrow$

149. (b) $KMnO_4$ oxidises HCl into Cl_2 which is also an oxidising agent.

$2\,Cl^- \longrightarrow Cl_2 + 2e\ ] \times 5$

$MnO_4^- + 8H^+ + 5\,e^- \longrightarrow Mn^{2+} + 4\,H_2O\ ] \times 2$

150. (a) When 100 mL HCl is added to 35 mL NaOH then 35 mL of HCl is utilised to neutralise NaOH while 65 mL HCl remains as such. Hence, the solution becomes acidic. In acidic solution, the colour of methyl orange is red due to the presence of the Me^+ ion:

$$\underset{\text{Methyl orange (yellow)}}{MeOH} \rightleftharpoons \underset{\text{Red}}{Me^+} + OH^-$$

151. (b) $MnO_4^- + 2\,H_2O + 3e^- \longrightarrow MnO_2 + 4\,OH^-$

ON of Mn = +7 ON of Mn = +4

Electrons gained = 3

Equivalent mass $= \dfrac{158.034}{3} = 52.68$ g eq^{-1}

Preparation of Compounds

152. (c) The correct option is (c).

153. (c) Excess of acetic anhydride and prolonged heating results in the formation of the diacetyl derivative.

$$\underset{\text{Aniline}}{C_6H_5\text{–}NH_2} + (CH_3CO)_2O \longrightarrow \underset{\text{Acetanilide}}{C_6H_5\text{–}NH\text{–}COCH_3} + CH_3COOH$$

$$C_6H_5NH\text{–}COCH_3 + (CH_3CO)_2O \xrightarrow[\text{heating}]{\text{prolonged}} \underset{\text{Diacetyl derivative}}{C_6H_5N(COCH_3)_2} + CH_3COOH$$

154. (c) The $-NH_2$ group gets oxidised which is not required. So, the amino group is first protected by acylation to form acetanilide which is then nitrated to give *p*-nitro acetanilide as a major product.

155. (c) Formaldehyde cannot produce iodoform, as only those compounds which contains either the $CH_3\text{–}\underset{\displaystyle OH}{\underset{|}{CH}}\text{–}$ group or $CH_3\text{–}\underset{\displaystyle O}{\underset{\|}{C}}\text{–}$ group on reaction with iodine and sodium hydroxide (alkali) yield iodoform.

156. (c) Aniline yellow is a basic dye.

157. (c) Dilute sulfuric acid prevents the Fe^{2+} ions of Mohr's salt from undergoing oxidation (Fe^{3+}).Otherwise the solution will become yellow in colour.

Kinetics of Iodide Ions and Hydrogen Peroxide

158. (a) On increasing the concentration of I^- ions, the rate of reaction will increase. After reaction with thiosulfate, less time will be taken for the blue colour to appear.

159. (b) $2\,Na_2S_2O_3 + I_2 \longrightarrow \underset{\text{Sodium tetrathionate}}{Na_2S_4O_6} + 2\,NaI$

160. (b) If thiosulfate is present in excess, all the iodine liberated will react with thiosulfate and no blue colour will appear at all.

161. (a) $2\,I^- + H_2O_2 + 2\,H_3O^+ \longrightarrow 4\,H_2O + I_2$

162. (a) Thiosulfate added should be in a small amount so that it reacts completely with iodine and the iodine further liberated can give blue colour with starch.

163. (b) Hydrogen peroxide oxidises the thiosulfate ion to water and sodium hydrogensulfate.

164. (a) $S_2O_3^{2-} \longrightarrow S_4O_6^{2-}$

165. (b) In the given experiment, the following reaction occurs.

$H_2O_2 + 2I^- + 2\,H^+ \longrightarrow 2\,H_2O + I_2$

Iodine liberated in this reaction reacts with sodium thiosulfate solution and is reduced to iodide ions.

$$\underset{\text{Thiosulfate ion}}{I_2 + 2\,S_2O_3^{2-}} \longrightarrow \underset{\text{tetrathionate ion}}{S_2O_6^{2-}} + 2\,I^-$$

166. **(b)** The correct option is (b).

167. **(a)** The bases do not ionise completely in aqueous solution. Therefore, some energy is required for their complete ionisation.

168. **(a)** $H_2C_2O_4 + 2\,NaOH \longrightarrow Na_2C_2O_4 + 2\,H_2O$
Equivalent mass of $H_2C_2O_4$ = Equivalent mass of NaOH
$50 \times 0.5 \times 2 = 25 \times N_{NaOH} \times 1$
$M_{NaOH} = N_{NaOH}$ (Since n-factor is 1)
Now, 1000 mL solution = 2×40 g NaOH
50 mL solution = 4 g NaOH

169. **(d)** The standard enthalpy of neutralisation for strong acid and base is –57.62 kJ/mol.
For 3 moles of water, it is -57.6×3 kJ

Enthalpy of Dissolution of Copper Sulfate

170. **(a)** Aqueous copper sulfate is acidic in nature. So, turns blue litmus red.

171. **(d)** $CuSO_4(s) + aq \longrightarrow CuSO_4(aq)$; $\Delta H = -16$ kcal
$CuSO_4.5H_2O + aq \longrightarrow CuSO_4(aq) + 5\,H_2O$; $\Delta H = 3$ kcal
$\Delta H = -3$ kcal (for reverse reaction)
$CuSO_4 + 5\,H_2O \longrightarrow CuSO_4.5H_2O$; $\Delta H = -16 - 3 = -19$ kcal

172. **(d)** An equilibrium exists between the undissolved solute and the dissolved solute. Since the dissolution process is endothermic, increasing and decreasing temperature will decrease and increase the concentration respectively.

MATCH THE FOLLOWING

173. The correct option is (c).

174. The correct option is (b).

175. The correct option is (c).

176. The correct option is (d).

177. **(c)** The correct option is (c).
(P) Heat of neutralisation of strong acid with strong base is –13.7 kcal mol^{-1}.
(Q) Heat of neutralisation for HF is > 13.7 kcal, heat is evolved due to hydration of F^-.
(R) NH_4OH is a weak base, so heat of neutralisation is < 13.7 kcal. Because some amount of heat will be used up in the ionisation of NH_4OH.
(S) For 2 moles of NaOH,
Heat of neutralisation = 2× 13.7 = 27.4 kcal
(T) CH_3COOH is a weak base, so heat of neutralisation is < 13.7 kcal. Because some amount of heat will be used up in the ionisation of CH_3COOH.

ASSERTION REASON

178. **(d)** The correct option is (d). The reason is a correct statement.
$Na + C + N \longrightarrow NaCN$
$6\,NaCN + FeSO_4 \longrightarrow Na_4[Fe(CN)_6] + Na_2SO_4$
$Na_4[Fe(CN)_6] + Fe^{3+} \longrightarrow \underset{\text{Prussian blue colour}}{Fe_4[Fe(CN)_6]_3}$
NH_2NH_2 does not give Prussian blue colour as there is no carbon (which is needed for Lassaigne's test for the formation of NaCN). Therefore, the assertion is incorrect.

179. **(d)** The correct option is (d). Both benzoic acid and naphthalene will dissolve in benzene. Thus, benzoic acid cannot be separated from the mixture. Hence, the assertion is wrong.
Benzoic acid is almost insoluble in cold water but soluble in hot water. Hence, the reason is true.